### SIXTH EDITION

# ECONOMETRIC ANALYSIS

D1334277

## William H. Greene

*New York University*

PEARSON
Prentice
Hall

Upper Saddle River, New Jersey 07458

**AVP/Executive Editor:** David Alexander
**Development Manager:** Ashley Santora
**Project Manager:** Mary Kate Murray
**Associate Director, Production Editorial:** Judy Leale
**Senior Managing Editor:** Cynthia Zonneveld
**Production Editor:** Melissa Feimer
**Permissions Coordinator:** Charles Morris
**Manufacturing Buyer:** Michelle Klein
**Design/Composition Manager:** Christy Mahon
**Cover Design:** Bruce Kenselaar
**Cover Illustration/Photo:** Getty Images
**Composition:** ICC Macmillan Inc.
**Full-Service Project Management:** ICC Macmillan Inc.
**Printer/Binder:** Courier/Westford
**Typeface:** 10/12 Times

Credits and acknowledgments borrowed from other sources and reproduced, with permission, in this textbook appear on appropriate page within text.

If you purchased this book within the United States or Canada you should be aware that it has been wrongfully imported without the approval of the Publisher or the Author.

Pearson Education LTD.
Pearson Education Singapore, Pte. Ltd
Pearson Education, Canada, Ltd
Pearson Education–Japan
Pearson Education Malaysia, Pte. Ltd.

Pearson Education Australia PTY, Limited
Pearson Education North Asia Ltd
Pearson Educación de Mexico, S.A. de C.V.
Pearson Education, Upper Saddle River,
   New Jersey

10 9 8 7 6 5 4
ISBN-13: 978-0-13-513740-6
ISBN-10: 0-13-513740-3

*For Margaret and Richard Greene*

# BRIEF CONTENTS

Examples and Applications        xxvi

Preface        xxxiii

**Part I        The Linear Regression Model**

Chapter 1        Introduction        1

Chapter 2        The Classical Multiple Linear Regression Model        8

Chapter 3        Least Squares        20

Chapter 4        Statistical Properties of the Least Squares Estimator        43

Chapter 5        Inference and Prediction        81

Chapter 6        Functional Form and Structural Change        106

Chapter 7        Specification Analysis and Model Selection        133

**Part II        The Generalized Regression Model**

Chapter 8        The Generalized Regression Model and Heteroscedasticity        148

Chapter 9        Models for Panel Data        180

Chapter 10        Systems of Regression Equations        252

Chapter 11        Nonlinear Regressions and Nonlinear Least Squares        285

**Part III        Instrumental Variables and Simultaneous Equation Models**

Chapter 12        Instrumental Variables Estimation        314

Chapter 13        Simultaneous Equations Models        354

**Part IV        Estimation Methodology**

Chapter 14        Estimation Frameworks in Econometrics        398

Chapter 15        Minimum Distance Estimation and the Generalized
Method of Moments        428

Chapter 16        Maximum Likelihood Estimation        482

Chapter 17        Simulation-Based Estimation and Inference        573

Chapter 18        Bayesian Estimation and Inference        600

**Part V        Time Series and Macroeconometrics**

Chapter 19        Serial Correlation        626

Chapter 20        Models with Lagged Variables        670

Chapter 21   Time-Series Models        715
Chapter 22   Nonstationary Data        739

**Part VI        Cross Sections, Panel Data, and Microeconometrics**
Chapter 23   Models for Discrete Choice        770
Chapter 24   Truncation, Censoring, and Sample Selection        863
Chapter 25   Models for Event Counts and Duration        906

**Part VII       Appendices**
Appendix A   Matrix Algebra        945
Appendix B   Probability and Distribution-Theory        987
Appendix C   Estimation and Inference        1019
Appendix D   Large-Sample Distribution Theory        1038
Appendix E   Computation and Optimization        1061
Appendix F   Data Sets Used in Applications        1081
Appendix G   Statistical Tables        1093

References        1099
Author Index        1147
Subject Index        1154

# CONTENTS

**Examples and Applications**    xxvi

**Preface**    xxxiii

## PART I    The Linear Regression Model

**CHAPTER 1    Introduction      1**
   1.1   Econometrics      1
   1.2   Econometric Modeling      2
   1.3   Methodology      5
   1.4   The Practice of Econometrics      6
   1.5   Plan of the Book      7


**CHAPTER 2    The Classical Multiple Linear Regression Model      8**
   2.1   Introduction      8
   2.2   The Linear Regression Model      8
   2.3   Assumptions of the Classical Linear Regression Model      11
          *2.3.1    Linearity of the Regression Model    12*
          *2.3.2    Full Rank    14*
          *2.3.3    Regression    15*
          *2.3.4    Spherical Disturbances    16*
          *2.3.5    Data Generating Process for the Regressors    17*
          *2.3.6    Normality    18*
   2.4   Summary and Conclusions      19


**CHAPTER 3    Least Squares      20**
   3.1   Introduction      20
   3.2   Least Squares Regression      20
          *3.2.1    The Least Squares Coefficient Vector    21*
          *3.2.2    Application: An Investment Equation    22*
          *3.2.3    Algebraic Aspects of the Least Squares
                      Solution    25*
          *3.2.4    Projection    25*
   3.3   Partitioned Regression and Partial Regression      27
   3.4   Partial Regression and Partial Correlation
          Coefficients      29

3.5     Goodness of Fit and the Analysis of Variance    32

     *3.5.1     The Adjusted R-Squared and a Measure of Fit   35*
     *3.5.2     R-Squared and the Constant Term in the Model   37*
     *3.5.3     Comparing Models   38*

3.6     Summary and Conclusions    39

**CHAPTER 4    Statistical Properties of the Least Squares Estimator     43**

4.1     Introduction    43

4.2     Motivating Least Squares    44

     *4.2.1     The Population Orthogonality Conditions   44*
     *4.2.2     Minimum Mean Squared Error Predictor   45*
     *4.2.3     Minimum Variance Linear Unbiased Estimation   46*

4.3     Unbiased Estimation    46

4.4     The Variance of the Least Squares Estimator and the Gauss–Markov Theorem    48

4.5     The Implications of Stochastic Regressors    49

4.6     Estimating the Variance of the Least Squares Estimator    51

4.7     The Normality Assumption and Basic Statistical Inference    52

     *4.7.1     Testing a Hypothesis about a Coefficient   52*
     *4.7.2     Confidence Intervals for Parameters   54*
     *4.7.3     Confidence Interval for a Linear Combination of Coefficients: The Oaxaca Decomposition   55*
     *4.7.4     Testing the Significance of the Regression   56*
     *4.7.5     Marginal Distributions of the Test Statistics   57*

4.8     Finite-Sample Properties of the Least Squares Estimator    58

     *4.8.1     Multicollinearity   59*
     *4.8.2     Missing Observations   61*

4.9     Large Sample Properties of the Least Squares Estimator    63

     *4.9.1     Consistency of the Least Squares Estimator of $\beta$   64*
     *4.9.2     Asymptotic Normality of the Least Squares Estimator   65*
     *4.9.3     Consistency of $s^2$ and the Estimator of Asy. Var[b]   67*
     *4.9.4     Asymptotic Distribution of a Function of b: The Delta Method and the Method of Krinsky and Robb   68*
     *4.9.5     Asymptotic Efficiency   71*
     *4.9.6     More General Data Generating Processes   72*

4.10   Summary and Conclusions    75

**CHAPTER 5    Inference and Prediction     81**

5.1     Introduction    81

5.2     Restrictions and Nested Models    81

5.3     Two Approaches to Testing Hypotheses    83

     *5.3.1     The F Statistic and the Least Squares Discrepancy   83*
     *5.3.2     The Restricted Least Squares Estimator   87*
     *5.3.3     The Loss of Fit from Restricted Least Squares   89*

5.4   Nonnormal Disturbances and Large Sample Tests    92

5.5   Testing Nonlinear Restrictions    96

5.6   Prediction    99

5.7   Summary and Conclusions    102

**CHAPTER 6   Functional Form and Structural Change    106**

6.1   Introduction    106

6.2   Using Binary Variables    106

    *6.2.1   Binary Variables in Regression   106*
    *6.2.2   Several Categories   107*
    *6.2.3   Several Groupings   108*
    *6.2.4   Threshold Effects and Categorical Variables   110*
    *6.2.5   Spline Regression   111*

6.3   Nonlinearity in the Variables    112

    *6.3.1   Functional Forms   112*
    *6.3.2   Identifying Nonlinearity   114*
    *6.3.3   Intrinsic Linearity and Identification   117*

6.4   Modeling and Testing for a Structural Break    120

    *6.4.1   Different Parameter Vectors   121*
    *6.4.2   Insufficient Observations   121*
    *6.4.3   Change in a Subset of Coefficients   122*
    *6.4.4   Tests of Structural Break with Unequal*
    *     Variances   123*
    *6.4.5   Predictive Test   127*

6.5   Summary and Conclusions    128

**CHAPTER 7   Specification Analysis and Model Selection    133**

7.1   Introduction    133

7.2   Specification Analysis and Model Building    133

    *7.2.1   Bias Caused by Omission of Relevant Variables   133*
    *7.2.2   Pretest Estimation   134*
    *7.2.3   Inclusion of Irrelevant Variables   136*
    *7.2.4   Model Building—A General to Simple Strategy   136*

7.3   Choosing Between Nonnested Models    137

    *7.3.1   Testing Nonnested Hypotheses   138*
    *7.3.2   An Encompassing Model   138*
    *7.3.3   Comprehensive Approach—The J Test   139*
    *7.3.4   Vuong's Test and the Kullback–Leibler Information*
    *     Criterion   140*

7.4   Model Selection Criteria    142

7.5   Model Selection    143

    *7.5.1   Classical Model Selection   144*
    *7.5.2   Bayesian Model Averaging   144*

7.6   Summary and Conclusions    146

## PART II   The Generalized Regression Model

**CHAPTER 8   The Generalized Regression Model and Heteroscedasticity      148**

8.1   Introduction      148

8.2   Least Squares Estimation      149

    8.2.1      *Finite-Sample Properties of Ordinary Least Squares    150*

    8.2.2      *Asymptotic Properties of Least Squares    151*

    8.2.3      *Robust Estimation of Asymptotic Covariance Matrices    153*

8.3   Efficient Estimation by Generalized Least Squares      154

    8.3.1      *Generalized Least Squares (GLS)    154*

    8.3.2      *Feasible Generalized Least Squares (FGLS)    156*

8.4   Heteroscedasticity      158

    8.4.1      *Ordinary Least Squares Estimation    159*

    8.4.2      *Inefficiency of Least Squares    160*

    8.4.3      *The Estimated Covariance Matrix of b    160*

    8.4.4      *Estimating the Appropriate Covariance Matrix for Ordinary Least Squares    162*

8.5   Testing for Heteroscedasticity      165

    8.5.1      *White's General Test    165*

    8.5.2      *The Breusch–Pagan/Godfrey LM Test    166*

8.6   Weighted Least Squares When $\Omega$ Is Known      167

8.7   Estimation When $\Omega$ Contains Unknown Parameters      169

8.8   Applications      170

    8.8.1      *Multiplicative Heteroscedasticity    170*

    8.8.2      *Groupwise Heteroscedasticity    172*

8.9   Summary and Conclusions      175

**CHAPTER 9   Models for Panel Data      180**

9.1   Introduction      180

9.2   Panel Data Models      180

    9.2.1      *General Modeling Framework for Analyzing Panel Data    182*

    9.2.2      *Model Structures    183*

    9.2.3      *Extensions    184*

    9.2.4      *Balanced and Unbalanced Panels    184*

9.3   The Pooled Regression Model      185

    9.3.1      *Least Squares Estimation of the Pooled Model    185*

    9.3.2      *Robust Covariance Matrix Estimation    185*

    9.3.3      *Clustering and Stratification    188*

    9.3.4      *Robust Estimation Using Group Means    188*

    9.3.5      *Estimation With First Differences    190*

    9.3.6      *The Within- and Between-Groups Estimators    191*

9.4   The Fixed Effects Model      193

    9.4.1      *Least Squares Estimation    194*

    9.4.2      *Small T Asymptotics    196*

9.4.3    *Testing the Significance of the Group Effects   197*
9.4.4    *Fixed Time and Group Effects   197*

9.5    Random Effects    200

9.5.1    *Generalized Least Squares   202*
9.5.2    *Feasible Generalized Least Squares When Σ Is Unknown   203*
9.5.3    *Testing for Random Effects   205*
9.5.4    *Hausman's Specification Test for the Random Effects Model   208*
9.5.5    *Extending the Unobserved Effects Model: Mundlak's Approach   209*

9.6    Nonspherical Disturbances and Robust Covariance Estimation    210

9.6.1    *Robust Estimation of the Fixed Effects Model   211*
9.6.2    *Heteroscedasticity in the Random Effects Model   212*
9.6.3    *Autocorrelation in Panel Data Models   213*

9.7    Extensions of the Random Effects Model    213

9.7.1    *Nested Random Effects   214*
9.7.2    *Spatial Autocorrelation   218*

9.8    Parameter Heterogeneity    222

9.8.1    *The Random Coefficients Model   223*
9.8.2    *Random Parameters and Simulation-Based Estimation   226*
9.8.3    *Two-Step Estimation of Panel Data Models   229*
9.8.4    *Hierarchical Linear Models   233*
9.8.5    *Parameter Heterogeneity and Dynamic Panel Data Models   238*
9.8.6    *Nonstationary Data and Panel Data Models   243*

9.9    Consistent Estimation of Dynamic Panel Data Models    244

9.10   Summary and Conclusions    246

**CHAPTER 10   Systems of Regression Equations    252**

10.1  Introduction    252

10.2  The Seemingly Unrelated Regressions Model    254

10.2.1    *Generalized Least Squares   256*
10.2.2    *Seemingly Unrelated Regressions with Identical Regressors   257*
10.2.3    *Feasible Generalized Least Squares   258*
10.2.4    *Testing Hypotheses   259*
10.2.5    *Heteroscedasticity   263*
10.2.6    *Autocorrelation   263*
10.2.7    *A Specification Test for the Sur Model   264*
10.2.8    *The Pooled Model   266*

10.3  Panel Data Applications    267

10.3.1    *Random Effects Sur Models   267*
10.3.2    *The Random and Fixed Effects Models   268*

10.4 Systems of Demand Equations: Singular Systems    272

    *10.4.1    Cobb–Douglas Cost Function (Example 6.3 Continued)    273*

    *10.4.2    Flexible Functional Forms: The Translog Cost Function    275*

10.5 Summary and Conclusions    280

**CHAPTER 11    Nonlinear Regressions and Nonlinear Least Squares    285**

11.1 Introduction    285

11.2 Nonlinear Regression Models    285

    *11.2.1    Assumptions of the Nonlinear Regression Model    286*

    *11.2.2    The Orthogonality Condition and The Sum of Squares    287*

    *11.2.3    The Linearized Regression    288*

    *11.2.4    Large Sample Properties of the Nonlinear Least Squares*
    *     Estimator    290*

    *11.2.5    Computing the Nonlinear Least Squares Estimator    292*

11.3 Applications    294

    *11.3.1    A Nonlinear Consumption Function    294*

    *11.3.2    The Box–Cox Transformation    296*

11.4 Hypothesis Testing and Parametric Restrictions    298

    *11.4.1    Significance Tests for Restrictions: F and Wald Statistics    298*

    *11.4.2    Tests Based on the LM Statistic    299*

11.5 Nonlinear Systems of Equations    300

11.6 Two-Step Nonlinear Least Squares Estimation    302

11.7 Panel Data Applications    307

    *11.7.1    A Robust Covariance Matrix for Nonlinear Least Squares    307*

    *11.7.2    Fixed Effects    308*

    *11.7.3    Random Effects    310*

11.8 Summary and Conclusions    311

**PART III    Instrumental Variables and Simultaneous Equations Models**

**CHAPTER 12    Instrumental Variables Estimation    314**

12.1 Introduction    314

12.2 Assumptions of the Model    315

12.3 Estimation    316

    *12.3.1    Ordinary Least Squares    316*

    *12.3.2    The Instrumental Variables Estimator    316*

    *12.3.3    Two-Stage Least Squares    318*

12.4 The Hausman and Wu Specification Tests and an Application to
    Instrumental Variable Estimation    321

12.5 Measurement Error    325

    *12.5.1    Least Squares Attenuation    325*

    *12.5.2    Instrumental Variables Estimation    327*

    *12.5.3    Proxy Variables    328*

12.6 Estimation of the Generalized Regression Model    332

12.7  Nonlinear Instrumental Variables Estimation    333

12.8  Panel Data Applications    336

    *12.8.1  Instrumental Variables Estimation of the Random Effects Model—The Hausman and Taylor Estimator  336*

    *12.8.2  Dynamic Panel Data Models—The Anderson/Hsiao and Arellano/Bond Estimators  340*

12.9  Weak Instruments    350

12.10  Summary and Conclusions    352

**CHAPTER 13  Simultaneous Equations Models    354**

13.1  Introduction    354

13.2  Fundamental Issues in Simultaneous Equations Models    354

    *13.2.1  Illustrative Systems of Equations  354*

    *13.2.2  Endogeneity and Causality  357*

    *13.2.3  A General Notation for Linear Simultaneous Equations Models  358*

13.3  The Problem of Identification    361

    *13.3.1  The Rank and Order Conditions for Identification  365*

    *13.3.2  Identification through Other Nonsample Information  370*

13.4  Methods of Estimation    370

13.5  Single Equation: Limited Information Estimation Methods    371

    *13.5.1  Ordinary Least Squares  371*

    *13.5.2  Estimation by Instrumental Variables  372*

    *13.5.3  Two-Stage Least Squares  373*

    *13.5.4  Limited Information Maximum Likelihood and the K Class of Estimators  375*

    *13.5.5  Testing in the Presence of Weak Instruments  377*

    *13.5.6  Two-Stage Least Squares in Models That Are Nonlinear in Variables  380*

13.6  System Methods of Estimation    380

    *13.6.1  Three-Stage Least Squares  381*

    *13.6.2  Full Information Maximum Likelihood  383*

13.7  Comparison of Methods—Klein's Model I    385

13.8  Specification Tests    387

13.9  Properties of Dynamic Models    389

    *13.9.1  Dynamic Models and Their Multipliers  389*

    *13.9.2  Stability  390*

    *13.9.3  Adjustment to Equilibrium  391*

13.10  Summary and Conclusions    394

**PART IV  Estimation Methodology**

**CHAPTER 14  Estimation Frameworks in Econometrics    398**

14.1  Introduction    398

14.2  Parametric Estimation and Inference     400

    *14.2.1  Classical Likelihood-Based Estimation   400*
    *14.2.2  Modeling Joint Distributions with Copula Functions   402*

14.3  Semiparametric Estimation     405

    *14.3.1  GMM Estimation in Econometrics   406*
    *14.3.2  Least Absolute Deviations Estimation   406*
    *14.3.3  Partially Linear Regression   409*
    *14.3.4  Kernel Density Methods   411*
    *14.3.5  Comparing Parametric and Semiparametric Analyses   412*

14.4  Nonparametric Estimation     413

    *14.4.1  Kernel Density Estimation   414*
    *14.4.2  Nonparametric Regression   416*

14.5  Properties of Estimators     420

    *14.5.1  Statistical Properties of Estimators   420*
    *14.5.2  Extremum Estimators   421*
    *14.5.3  Assumptions for Asymptotic Properties of Extremum Estimators   421*
    *14.5.4  Asymptotic Properties of Estimators   424*
    *14.5.5  Testing Hypotheses   425*

14.6  Summary and Conclusions     426

**CHAPTER 15  Minimum Distance Estimation and the Generalized Method of Moments     428**

15.1  Introduction     428

15.2  Consistent Estimation: The Method of Moments     429

    *15.2.1  Random Sampling and Estimating the Parameters of Distributions   430*
    *15.2.2  Asymptotic Properties of the Method of Moments Estimator   434*
    *15.2.3  Summary—The Method of Moments   436*

15.3  Minimum Distance Estimation     436

15.4  The Generalized Method of Moments (GMM) Estimator     441

    *15.4.1  Estimation Based on Orthogonality Conditions   442*
    *15.4.2  Generalizing the Method of Moments   443*
    *15.4.3  Properties of the GMM Estimator   447*

15.5  Testing Hypotheses in the GMM Framework     451

    *15.5.1  Testing the Validity of the Moment Restrictions   452*
    *15.5.2  GMM Counterparts to the WALD, LM, and LR Tests   453*

15.6  GMM Estimation of Econometric Models     455

    *15.6.1  Single-Equation Linear Models   455*
    *15.6.2  Single-Equation Nonlinear Models   461*
    *15.6.3  Seemingly Unrelated Regression Models   464*
    *15.6.4  Simultaneous Equations Models with Heteroscedasticity   466*
    *15.6.5  GMM Estimation of Dynamic Panel Data Models   469*

15.7  Summary and Conclusions     480

**CHAPTER 16  Maximum Likelihood Estimation      482**

16.1  Introduction      482

16.2  The Likelihood Function and Identification of the
           Parameters      482

16.3  Efficient Estimation: The Principle of Maximum
           Likelihood      484

16.4  Properties of Maximum Likelihood Estimators      486

    16.4.1    *Regularity Conditions  487*
    16.4.2    *Properties of Regular Densities  488*
    16.4.3    *The Likelihood Equation  490*
    16.4.4    *The Information Matrix Equality  490*
    16.4.5    *Asymptotic Properties of the Maximum Likelihood
                  Estimator  490*
        16.4.5.a  *Consistency  491*
        16.4.5.b  *Asymptotic Normality  492*
        16.4.5.c  *Asymptotic Efficiency  493*
        16.4.5.d  *Invariance  494*
        16.4.5.e  *Conclusion  494*
    16.4.6    *Estimating the Asymptotic Variance of the Maximum Likelihood
                  Estimator  494*

16.5  Conditional Likelihoods, Econometric Models, and the
           GMM Estimator      496

16.6  Hypothesis and Specification Tests and Fit Measures      498

    16.6.1    *The Likelihood Ratio Test  498*
    16.6.2    *The Wald Test  500*
    16.6.3    *The Lagrange Multiplier Test  502*
    16.6.4    *An Application of the Likelihood-Based Test
                  Procedures  504*
    16.6.5    *Comparing Models and Computing Model Fit  506*

16.7  Two-Step Maximum Likelihood Estimation      507

16.8  Pseudo-Maximum Likelihood Estimation and Robust Asymptotic
           Covariance Matrices      511

    16.8.1    *Maximum Likelihood and GMM Estimation  512*
    16.8.2    *Maximum Likelihood and M Estimation  512*
    16.8.3    *Sandwich Estimators  514*
    16.8.4    *Cluster Estimators  515*

16.9  Applications of Maximum Likelihood Estimation      517

    16.9.1    *The Normal Linear Regression Model  518*
    16.9.2    *The Generalized Regression Model  522*
        16.9.2.a  *Multiplicative Heteroscedasticity  523*
        16.9.2.b  *Autocorrelation  527*
    16.9.3    *Seemingly Unrelated Regression Models  529*
        16.9.3.a  *The Pooled Model  530*
        16.9.3.b  *The SUR Model  531*
        16.9.3.c  *Exclusion Restrictions  532*

16.9.4    *Simultaneous Equations Models   536*
16.9.5    *Maximum Likelihood Estimation of Nonlinear Regression
          Models   537*
          16.9.5.a   *Nonnormal Disturbances — The Stochastic Frontier
                     Model   538*
          16.9.5.b   *ML Estimation of a Geometric Regression Model for
                     Count Data   542*
16.9.6    *Panel Data Applications   547*
          16.9.6.a   *ML Estimation of the Linear Random Effects
                     Model   547*
          16.9.6.b   *Random Effects in Nonlinear Models: MLE using
                     Quadrature   550*
          16.9.6.c   *Fixed Effects in Nonlinear Models: Full MLE   554*
16.9.7    *Latent Class and Finite Mixture Models   558*
          16.9.7.a   *A Finite Mixture Model   559*
          16.9.7.b   *Measured and Unmeasured Heterogeneity   560*
          16.9.7.c   *Predicting Class Membership   561*
          16.9.7.d   *A Conditional Latent Class Model   561*
          16.9.7.e   *Determining the Number of Classes   564*
          16.9.7.f   *A Panel Data Application   564*
16.10  Summary and Conclusions       567

**CHAPTER 17   Simulation-Based Estimation and Inference       573**

17.1  Introduction       573
17.2  Random Number Generation       573
      17.2.1    *Generating Pseudo-Random Numbers   574*
      17.2.2    *Sampling from a Standard Uniform Population   575*
      17.2.3    *Sampling from Continuous Distributions   575*
      17.2.4    *Sampling from a Multivariate Normal Population   576*
      17.2.5    *Sampling from a Discrete Population   576*
17.3  Monte Carlo Integration       576
      17.3.1    *Halton Sequences and Random Draws for Simulation-Based
                Integration   577*
      17.3.2    *Importance Sampling   580*
      17.3.3    *Computing Multivariate Normal Probabilities Using
                the GHK Simulator   582*
17.4  Monte Carlo Studies       584
      17.4.1    *A Monte Carlo Study: Behavior of a Test Statistic   585*
      17.4.2    *A Monte Carlo Study: The Incidental Parameters
                Problem   586*
17.5  Simulation-Based Estimation       589
      17.5.1    *Maximum Simulated Likelihood Estimation of Random
                Parameters Models   590*
      17.5.2    *The Method of Simulated Moments   595*
17.6  Bootstrapping       596
17.7  Summary and Conclusions       598

**CHAPTER 18   Bayesian Estimation and Inference      600**

18.1   Introduction      600

18.2   Bayes Theorem and the Posterior Density      601

18.3   Bayesian Analysis of the Classical Regression Model      603

    18.3.1      *Analysis with a Noninformative Prior   604*

    18.3.2      *Estimation with an Informative Prior Density   606*

18.4   Bayesian Inference      609

    18.4.1      *Point Estimation   609*

    18.4.2      *Interval Estimation   610*

    18.4.3      *Hypothesis Testing   611*

    18.4.4      *Large Sample Results   613*

18.5   Posterior Distributions and the Gibbs Sampler      613

18.6   Application: Binomial Probit Model      616

18.7   Panel Data Application: Individual Effects Models      619

18.8   Hierarchical Bayes Estimation of a Random Parameters Model      621

18.9   Summary and Conclusions      623

**PART V      Time Series and Macroeconometrics**

**CHAPTER 19   Serial Correlation      626**

19.1   Introduction      626

19.2   The Analysis of Time-Series Data      629

19.3   Disturbance Processes      632

    19.3.1      *Characteristics of Disturbance Processes   632*

    19.3.2      *AR(1) Disturbances   633*

19.4   Some Asymptotic Results for Analyzing Time-Series Data      635

    19.4.1      *Convergence of Moments—The Ergodic Theorem   636*

    19.4.2      *Convergence to Normality—A Central Limit Theorem   638*

19.5   Least Squares Estimation      640

    19.5.1      *Asymptotic Properties of Least Squares   640*

    19.5.2      *Estimating the Variance of the Least Squares Estimator   642*

19.6   GMM Estimation      643

19.7   Testing for Autocorrelation      644

    19.7.1      *Lagrange Multiplier Test   644*

    19.7.2      *Box and Pierce's Test and Ljung's Refinement   645*

    19.7.3      *The Durbin–Watson Test   645*

    19.7.4      *Testing in the Presence of a Lagged Dependent Variable   646*

    19.7.5      *Summary of Testing Procedures   646*

19.8   Efficient Estimation When $\Omega$ Is Known      647

19.9   Estimation When $\Omega$ Is Unknown      648

    19.9.1      *AR(1) Disturbances   648*

    19.9.2      *Application: Estimation of a Model with Autocorrelation   649*

    19.9.3      *Estimation with a Lagged Dependent Variable   651*

19.10 Autocorrelation in Panel Data      652

19.11 Common Factors     655

19.12 Forecasting in the Presence of Autocorrelation     656

19.13 Autoregressive Conditional Heteroscedasticity     658

     19.13.1   *The ARCH(1) Model  659*

     19.13.2   *ARCH (q), ARCH-in-Mean, and Generalized ARCH*
             *Models  660*

     19.13.3   *Maximum Likelihood Estimation of the Garch Model  662*

     19.13.4   *Testing for Garch Effects  664*

     19.13.5   *Pseudo–Maximum Likelihood Estimation  666*

19.14 Summary and Conclusions     667

**CHAPTER 20  Models with Lagged Variables     670**

20.1  Introduction     670

20.2  Dynamic Regression Models     671

     20.2.1   *Lagged Effects in a Dynamic Model  672*

     20.2.2   *The Lag and Difference Operators  674*

     20.2.3   *Specification Search for the Lag Length  676*

20.3  Simple Distributed Lag Models     677

20.4  Autoregressive Distributed Lag Models     681

     20.4.1   *Estimation of the ARDL Model  682*

     20.4.2   *Computation of the Lag Weights in the ARDL Model  683*

     20.4.3   *Stability of a Dynamic Equation  684*

     20.4.4   *Forecasting  686*

20.5  Methodological Issues in the Analysis of Dynamic Models     689

     20.5.1   *An Error Correction Model  689*

     20.5.2   *Autocorrelation  691*

     20.5.3   *Specification Analysis  692*

20.6  Vector Autoregressions     693

     20.6.1   *Model Forms  695*

     20.6.2   *Estimation  696*

     20.6.3   *Testing Procedures  696*

     20.6.4   *Exogeneity  698*

     20.6.5   *Testing for Granger Causality  699*

     20.6.6   *Impulse Response Functions  701*

     20.6.7   *Structural VARs  702*

     20.6.8   *Application: Policy Analysis with a VAR  703*

          20.6.8.a   *A VAR Model for the Macroeconomic Variables  703*

          20.6.8.b   *The Sacrifice Ratio  704*

          20.6.8.c   *Identification and Estimation of a Structural*
                 *VAR Model  704*

          20.6.8.d   *Inference  707*

          20.6.8.e   *Empirical Results  707*

     20.6.9   *VARs In Microeconomics  711*

20.7  Summary and Conclusions     712

**CHAPTER 21   Time-Series Models      715**

21.1  Introduction      715

21.2  Stationary Stochastic Processes      716

21.2.1     *Autoregressive Moving-Average Processes   716*
21.2.2     *Stationarity and Invertibility   718*
21.2.3     *Autocorrelations of a Stationary Stochastic Process   721*
21.2.4     *Partial Autocorrelations of a Stationary Stochastic*
            *Process   723*
21.2.5     *Modeling Univariate Time Series   726*
21.2.6     *Estimation of the Parameters of a Univariate*
            *Time Series   728*

21.3  The Frequency Domain      731

21.3.1     *Theoretical Results   732*
21.3.2     *Empirical Counterparts   734*

21.4  Summary and Conclusions      738

**CHAPTER 22   Nonstationary Data      739**

22.1  Introduction      739

22.2  Nonstationary Processes and Unit Roots      739

22.2.1     *Integrated Processes and Differencing   739*
22.2.2     *Random Walks, Trends, and Spurious Regressions   741*
22.2.3     *Tests for Unit Roots in Economic Data   744*
22.2.4     *The Dickey–Fuller Tests   745*
22.2.5     *The KPSS Test of Stationarity   755*

22.3  Cointegration      756

22.3.1     *Common Trends   759*
22.3.2     *Error Correction and VAR Representations   760*
22.3.3     *Testing for Cointegration   761*
22.3.4     *Estimating Cointegration Relationships   764*
22.3.5     *Application: German Money Demand   764*
            *22.3.5.a   Cointegration Analysis and a Long-Run*
                        *Theoretical Model   765*
            *22.3.5.b   Testing for Model Instability   766*

22.4  Nonstationary Panel Data      767

22.5  Summary and Conclusions      768

**PART VI   Cross Sections, Panel Data, and Microeconometrics**

**CHAPTER 23   Models for Discrete Choice      770**

23.1  Introduction      770

23.2  Discrete Choice Models      770

23.3  Models for Binary Choice      772

23.3.1     *The Regression Approach   772*
23.3.2     *Latent Regression—Index Function Models   775*
23.3.3     *Random Utility Models   777*

23.4  Estimation and Inference in Binary Choice Models     777

    *23.4.1  Robust Covariance Matrix Estimation  780*
    *23.4.2  Marginal Effects and Average Partial Effects  780*
    *23.4.3  Hypothesis Tests  785*
    *23.4.4  Specification Tests for Binary Choice Models  787*
    *23.4.4.a  Omitted Variables  788*
    *23.4.4.b  Heteroscedasticity  788*
    *23.4.5  Measuring Goodness of FIT  790*
    *23.4.6  Choice-Based Sampling  793*
    *23.4.7  Dynamic Binary Choice Models  794*

23.5  Binary Choice Models for panel data     796

    *23.5.1  Random Effects Models  797*
    *23.5.2  Fixed Effects Models  800*
    *23.5.3  Modeling Heterogeneity  806*
    *23.5.4  Parameter Heterogeneity  807*

23.6  Semiparametric Analysis     809

    *23.6.1  Semiparametric Estimation  810*
    *23.6.2  A Kernel Estimator for a Nonparametric Regression Function  812*

23.7  Endogenous Right-Hand-Side Variables in Binary Choice Models     813

23.8  Bivariate Probit Models     817

    *23.8.1  Maximum Likelihood Estimation  817*
    *23.8.2  Testing for Zero Correlation  820*
    *23.8.3  Marginal Effects  821*
    *23.8.4  Recursive Bivariate Probit Models  823*

23.9  A Multivariate Probit Model     826

23.10 Analysis of Ordered Choices     831

    *23.10.1  The Ordered Probit Model  831*
    *23.10.2  Bivariate Ordered Probit Models  835*
    *23.10.3  Panel Data Applications  837*
    *23.10.3.a  Ordered Probit Models with Fixed Effects  837*
    *23.10.3.b  Ordered Probit Models with Random Effects  838*

23.11 Models for Unordered Multiple Choices     841

    *23.11.1  The Multinomial Logit Model  843*
    *23.11.2  The Conditional Logit Model  846*
    *23.11.3  The Independence from Irrelevant Alternatives Assumption  847*
    *23.11.4  Nested Logit Models  847*
    *23.11.5  The Multinomial Probit Model  850*
    *23.11.6  The Mixed Logit Model  851*
    *23.11.7  Application: Conditional Logit Model for Travel Mode Choice  852*
    *23.11.8  Panel Data and Stated Choice Experiments  858*

23.12 Summary and Conclusions     859

**CHAPTER 24   Truncation, Censoring, and Sample Selection      863**

24.1   Introduction      863

24.2   Truncation      863

    *24.2.1   Truncated Distributions   863*
    *24.2.2   Moments of Truncated Distributions   864*
    *24.2.3   The Truncated Regression Model   867*

24.3   Censored Data      869

    *24.3.1   The Censored Normal Distribution   869*
    *24.3.2   The Censored Regression (Tobit) Model   871*
    *24.3.3   Estimation   874*
    *24.3.4   Some Issues in Specification   875*
        *24.3.4.a   Heteroscedasticity   875*
        *24.3.4.b   Misspecification of Prob[y*<0]   877*
        *24.3.4.c   Corner Solutions   878*
        *24.3.4.d   Nonnormality   880*

24.4   Panel Data Applications      881

24.5   Sample Selection      882

    *24.5.1   Incidental Truncation in a Bivariate Distribution   883*
    *24.5.2   Regression in A Model of Selection   884*
    *24.5.3   Estimation   886*
    *24.5.4   Regression Analysis of Treatment Effects   889*
    *24.5.5   The Normality Assumption   891*
    *24.5.6   Estimating the Effect of Treatment on the Treated   891*
    *24.5.7   Sample Selection in Nonlinear Models   895*
    *24.5.8   Panel Data Applications of Sample Selection*
        *Models   898*
        *24.5.8.a   Common Effects in Sample Selection*
            *Models   899*
        *24.5.8.b   Attrition   901*

24.6   Summary and Conclusions      903

**CHAPTER 25   Models for Event Counts and Duration      906**

25.1   Introduction      906

25.2   Models for Counts of Events      907

    *25.2.1   Measuring Goodness of FIT   908*
    *25.2.2   Testing for Overdispersion   909*
    *25.2.3   Heterogeneity and the Negative Binomial Regression*
        *Model   911*
    *25.2.4   Functional Forms for Count Data Models   912*

25.3   Panel Data Models      915

    *25.3.1   Robust Covariance Matrices   915*
    *25.3.2   Fixed Effects   916*
    *25.3.3   Random Effects   918*

25.4   Hurdle and Zero-Altered Poisson Models      922

25.5 Censoring and Truncation in Models for Counts    924

    *25.5.1   Censoring and Truncation in the Poisson Model   925*
    *25.5.2   Application: Censoring in the Tobit and Poisson Regression*
           *Models   925*

25.6 Models for Duration Data    931

    *25.6.1   Duration Data   932*
    *25.6.2   A Regression-Like Approach: Parametric Models*
           *of Duration   933*
          *25.6.2.a   Theoretical Background   933*
          *25.6.2.b   Models of the Hazard Function   934*
          *25.6.2.c   Maximum Likelihood Estimation   936*
          *25.6.2.d   Exogenous Variables   937*
          *25.6.2.e   Heterogeneity   938*
    *25.6.3   Nonparametric and Semiparametric Approaches   939*

25.7 Summary and Conclusions    942

# PART VII   Appendices

## APPENDIX A   Matrix Algebra    945

A.1   Terminology    945

A.2   Algebraic Manipulation of Matrices    945

    *A.2.1   Equality of Matrices   945*
    *A.2.2   Transposition   946*
    *A.2.3   Matrix Addition   946*
    *A.2.4   Vector Multiplication   947*
    *A.2.5   A Notation for Rows and Columns of a Matrix   947*
    *A.2.6   Matrix Multiplication and Scalar Multiplication   947*
    *A.2.7   Sums of Values   949*
    *A.2.8   A Useful Idempotent Matrix   950*

A.3   Geometry of Matrices    951

    *A.3.1   Vector Spaces   951*
    *A.3.2   Linear Combinations of Vectors and Basis Vectors   953*
    *A.3.3   Linear Dependence   954*
    *A.3.4   Subspaces   955*
    *A.3.5   Rank of a Matrix   956*
    *A.3.6   Determinant of a Matrix   958*
    *A.3.7   A Least Squares Problem   959*

A.4   Solution of a System of Linear Equations    961

    *A.4.1   Systems of Linear Equations   961*
    *A.4.2   Inverse Matrices   962*
    *A.4.3   Nonhomogeneous Systems of Equations   964*
    *A.4.4   Solving the Least Squares Problem   964*

A.5   Partitioned Matrices    964

    *A.5.1   Addition and Multiplication of Partitioned Matrices   965*
    *A.5.2   Determinants of Partitioned Matrices   965*

A.5.3    *Inverses of Partitioned Matrices*    965
A.5.4    *Deviations from Means*    966
A.5.5    *Kronecker Products*    966

A.6    Characteristic Roots and Vectors    967

A.6.1    *The Characteristic Equation*    967
A.6.2    *Characteristic Vectors*    968
A.6.3    *General Results for Characteristic Roots and Vectors*    968
A.6.4    *Diagonalization and Spectral Decomposition of a Matrix*    969
A.6.5    *Rank of a Matrix*    969
A.6.6    *Condition Number of a Matrix*    971
A.6.7    *Trace of a Matrix*    971
A.6.8    *Determinant of a Matrix*    972
A.6.9    *Powers of a Matrix*    972
A.6.10    *Idempotent Matrices*    974
A.6.11    *Factoring a Matrix*    974
A.6.12    *The Generalized Inverse of a Matrix*    975

A.7    Quadratic Forms and Definite Matrices    976

A.7.1    *Nonnegative Definite Matrices*    977
A.7.2    *Idempotent Quadratic Forms*    978
A.7.3    *Comparing Matrices*    978

A.8    Calculus and Matrix Algebra    979

A.8.1    *Differentiation and the Taylor Series*    979
A.8.2    *Optimization*    982
A.8.3    *Constrained Optimization*    984
A.8.4    *Transformations*    986

**APPENDIX B    Probability and Distribution Theory    987**

B.1    Introduction    987

B.2    Random Variables    987

B.2.1    *Probability Distributions*    987
B.2.2    *Cumulative Distribution Function*    988

B.3    Expectations of a Random Variable    989

B.4    Some Specific Probability Distributions    991

B.4.1    *The Normal Distribution*    991
B.4.2    *The Chi-Squared, t, and F Distributions*    993
B.4.3    *Distributions With Large Degrees of Freedom*    995
B.4.4    *Size Distributions: The Lognormal Distribution*    996
B.4.5    *The Gamma and Exponential Distributions*    996
B.4.6    *The Beta Distribution*    997
B.4.7    *The Logistic Distribution*    997
B.4.8    *The Wishart Distribution*    997
B.4.9    *Discrete Random Variables*    998

B.5    The Distribution of a Function of a Random Variable    998

B.6   Representations of a Probability Distribution    1000

B.7   Joint Distributions    1002

  *B.7.1    Marginal Distributions    1002*
  *B.7.2    Expectations in a Joint Distribution    1003*
  *B.7.3    Covariance and Correlation    1003*
  *B.7.4    Distribution of a Function of Bivariate Random
             Variables    1004*

B.8   Conditioning in a Bivariate Distribution    1006

  *B.8.1    Regression: The Conditional Mean    1006*
  *B.8.2    Conditional Variance    1007*
  *B.8.3    Relationships Among Marginal and Conditional
             Moments    1007*
  *B.8.4    The Analysis of Variance    1009*

B.9   The Bivariate Normal Distribution    1009

B.10  Multivariate Distributions    1010

  *B.10.1   Moments    1010*
  *B.10.2   Sets of Linear Functions    1011*
  *B.10.3   Nonlinear Functions    1012*

B.11  The Multivariate Normal Distribution    1013

  *B.11.1   Marginal and Conditional Normal Distributions    1013*
  *B.11.2   The Classical Normal Linear Regression Model    1014*
  *B.11.3   Linear Functions of a Normal Vector    1015*
  *B.11.4   Quadratic Forms in a Standard Normal Vector    1015*
  *B.11.5   The F Distribution    1017*
  *B.11.6   A Full Rank Quadratic Form    1017*
  *B.11.7   Independence of a Linear and a Quadratic
             Form    1018*

**APPENDIX C   Estimation and Inference    1019**

C.1   Introduction    1019

C.2   Samples and Random Sampling    1020

C.3   Descriptive Statistics    1020

C.4   Statistics as Estimators—Sampling Distributions    1023

C.5   Point Estimation of Parameters    1027

  *C.5.1    Estimation in a Finite Sample    1027*
  *C.5.2    Efficient Unbiased Estimation    1030*

C.6   Interval Estimation    1032

C.7   Hypothesis Testing    1034

  *C.7.1    Classical Testing Procedures    1034*
  *C.7.2    Tests Based on Confidence Intervals    1037*
  *C.7.3    Specification Tests    1038*

**APPENDIX D   Large-Sample Distribution Theory    1038**

D.1   Introduction    1038

D.2    Large-Sample Distribution Theory    1039

     *D.2.1*    *Convergence in Probability*    *1039*

     *D.2.2*    *Other Forms of Convergence and Laws of Large*
              *Numbers*    *1042*

     *D.2.3*    *Convergence of Functions*    *1045*

     *D.2.4*    *Convergence to a Random Variable*    *1046*

     *D.2.5*    *Convergence in Distribution: Limiting Distributions*    *1048*

     *D.2.6*    *Central Limit Theorems*    *1050*

     *D.2.7*    *The Delta Method*    *1055*

D.3    Asymptotic Distributions    1056

     *D.3.1*    *Asymptotic Distribution of a Nonlinear Function*    *1058*

     *D.3.2*    *Asymptotic Expectations*    *1059*

D.4    Sequences and the Order of a Sequence    1060

**APPENDIX E    Computation and Optimization    1061**

E.1    Introduction    1061

E.2    Computation in Econometrics    1062

     *E.2.1*    *Computing Integrals*    *1062*

     *E.2.2*    *The Standard Normal Cumulative Distribution Function*    *1062*

     *E.2.3*    *The Gamma and Related Functions*    *1063*

     *E.2.4*    *Approximating Integrals by Quadrature*    *1064*

E.3    Optimization    1065

     *E.3.1*    *Algorithms*    *1067*

     *E.3.2*    *Computing Derivatives*    *1068*

     *E.3.3*    *Gradient Methods*    *1069*

     *E.3.4*    *Aspects of Maximum Likelihood Estimation*    *1072*

     *E.3.5*    *Optimization with Constraints*    *1073*

     *E.3.6*    *Some Practical Considerations*    *1074*

     *E.3.7*    *The EM Algorithm*    *1076*

E.4    Examples    1078

     *E.4.1*    *Function of One Parameter*    *1078*

     *E.4.2*    *Function of Two Parameters: The Gamma Distribution*    *1079*

     *E.4.3*    *A Concentrated Log-Likelihood Function*    *1080*

**APPENDIX F    Data Sets Used in Applications    1081**

**APPENDIX G    Statistical Tables    1093**

**References    1099**

**Author Index    1147**

**Subject Index    1154**

# EXAMPLES AND APPLICATIONS

—⌐☙☙☙⌐—

**CHAPTER 1   Introduction       1**
  Example 1.1      Behavioral Models and the Nobel Laureates   1
  Example 1.2      Keynes's Consumption Function   2

**CHAPTER 2   The Classical Multiple Linear Regression Model        8**
  Example 2.1      Keynes's Consumption Function   9
  Example 2.2      Earnings and Education   10
  Example 2.3      The U.S. Gasoline Market   13
  Example 2.4      The Translog Model   13
  Example 2.5      Short Rank   14

**CHAPTER 3   Least Squares       20**
  Example 3.1      Partial Correlations   31
  Example 3.2      Fit of a Consumption Function   34
  Example 3.3      Analysis of Variance for an Investment Equation   34

**CHAPTER 4   Statistical Properties of the Least Squares Estimator        43**
  Example 4.1      The Sampling Distribution of a Least Squares Estimator   47
  Example 4.2      Sampling Variance in the Two-Variable Regression
                       Model   48
  Example 4.3      Earnings Equation   53
  Example 4.4      Confidence Interval for the Income Elasticity of Demand for
                       Gasoline   55
  Example 4.5      $F$ Test for the Earnings Equation   57
  Example 4.6      Multicollinearity in the Longley Data   60
  Example 4.7      Nonlinear Functions of Parameters: The Delta Method   69
  Example 4.8      Nonlinear Functions of Parameters: The Krinsky and Robb
                       Method   70
  Example 4.9      The Gamma Regression Model   72

**CHAPTER 5   Inference and Prediction       81**
  Example 5.1      Restricted Investment Equation   86
  Example 5.2      Production Function   90
  Example 5.3      A Long-Run Marginal Propensity to Consume   97
  Example 5.4      Prediction for Investment   99

**CHAPTER 6   Functional Form and Structural Change       106**
  Example 6.1      Dummy Variable in an Earnings Equation   106
  Example 6.2      Analysis of Covariance   108

Example 6.3    Functional Form for a Nonlinear Cost Function    114
Example 6.4    Intrinsically Linear Regression    118
Example 6.5    CES Production Function    119
Example 6.6    The World Health Report    124
Example 6.7    Structural Break in the Gasoline Market    125

**CHAPTER 7    Specification Analysis and Model Selection    133**
Example 7.1    Omitted Variables    134
Example 7.2    *J* Test for a Consumption Function    140
Example 7.3    Vuong Test for a Consumption Function    142
Example 7.4    Bayesian Averaging of Classical Estimates    146

**CHAPTER 8    The Generalized Regression Model and Heteroscedasticity    148**
Example 8.1    Heteroscedastic Regression    159
Example 8.2    The White Estimator    164
Example 8.3    Testing for Heteroscedasticity    167
Example 8.4    Multiplicative Heteroscedasticity.    171
Example 8.5    Groupwise Heteroscedasticity    173

**CHAPTER 9    Models for Panel Data    180**
Example 9.1    Wage Equation    186
Example 9.2    Robust Estimators of the Wage Equation    190
Example 9.3    Analysis of Covariance and the World Health
                    Organization Data    192
Example 9.4    Fixed Effects Wage Equation    199
Example 9.5    Testing for Random Effects    206
Example 9.6    Estimates of the Random Effects Model    207
Example 9.7    Hausman Test for Fixed versus Random Effects    209
Example 9.8    Variable Addition Test for Fixed versus Random Effects    210
Example 9.9    Statewide Productivity    216
Example 9.10    Spatial Autocorrelation in Real Estate Sales    220
Example 9.11    Spatial Lags in Health Expenditures    221
Example 9.12    Random Coefficients Model    224
Example 9.13    Minimum Simulated Sum of Squares Estimates
                    of the Production Function    228
Example 9.14    Two-Step Estimation of Cornwell and Rupert's
                    Wage Equation    231
Example 9.15    Fannie Mae's Pass Through    232
Example 9.16    Hierarchical Linear Model of Home Prices    233
Example 9.17    Mixed Linear Model for Wages    235
Example 9.18    Dynamic Panel Data Models    238
Example 9.19    A Mixed Fixed Growth Model for Developing Countries    242

**CHAPTER 10    Systems of Regression Equations    252**
Example 10.1    Munnell's Statewide Production Data    254
Example 10.2    Estimated SUR Model for Regional Output    259
Example 10.3    Hypothesis Tests in the SUR Model    262
Example 10.4    Testing for Cross-Equation Correlation    265
Example 10.5    Demand for Electricity and Gas    268

Example 10.6    Hospital Costs   270
Example 10.7    Stone's Expenditure System   272
Example 10.8    A Cost Function for U.S. Manufacturing   278

**CHAPTER 11   Nonlinear Regressions and Nonlinear Least Squares       285**
Example 11.1    CES Production Function   285
Example 11.2    Translog Demand System   286
Example 11.3    First-Order Conditions for a Nonlinear Model   288
Example 11.4    Linearized Regression   289
Example 11.5    Analysis of a Nonlinear Consumption Function   294
Example 11.6    Multicollinearity in Nonlinear Regression   296
Example 11.7    Flexible Cost Function   296
Example 11.8    Hypothesis Tests in a Nonlinear Regression Model   300
Example 11.9    Two-Step Estimation of a Credit Scoring Model   304
Example 11.10   Health Care Utilization   307
Example 11.11   Exponential Model with Fixed Effects   309

**CHAPTER 12    Instrumental Variables Estimation       314**
Example 12.1    Models in Which Least Squares Is Inconsistent   314
Example 12.2    Streams as Instruments   320
Example 12.3    Labor Supply Model   320, 324
Example 12.4    Hausman Test for a Consumption Function   324
Example 12.5    Income and Education in a Study of Twins   329
Example 12.6    Instrumental Variables Estimates of the
                   Consumption Function   336
Example 12.7    The Returns to Schooling   339
Example 12.8    Dynamic Labor Supply Equation   348

**CHAPTER 13    Simultaneous Equations Models       354**
Example 13.1    A Small Macroeconomic Model   356
Example 13.2    Klein's Model I   357
Example 13.3    Structure and Reduced Form   360
Example 13.4    Observational Equivalence   362
Example 13.5    Identification   364
Example 13.6    Identification of Klein's Model I   369
Example 13.7    Testing Overidentifying Restrictions   388
Example 13.8    Dynamic Model   393

**CHAPTER 14    Estimation Frameworks in Econometrics       398**
Example 14.1    The Linear Regression Model   401
Example 14.2    The Stochastic Frontier Model   402
Example 14.3    Joint Modeling of a Pair of Event Counts   405
Example 14.4    LAD Estimation of a Cobb–Douglas Production
                   Function   408
Example 14.5    Partially Linear Translog Cost Function   410
Example 14.6    Semiparametric Estimator for Binary Choice Models   411
Example 14.7    A Model of Vacation Expenditures   412
Example 14.8    A Nonparametric Average Cost Function   418

**CHAPTER 15    Minimum Distance Estimation and the Generalized
                Method of Moments      428**

Example  15.1    Euler Equations and Life Cycle Consumption   428
Example  15.2    Method of Moments Estimator for $N[\mu, \sigma^2]$   430
Example  15.3    Inverse Gaussian (Wald) Distribution   431
Example  15.4    Mixtures of Normal Distributions   432
Example  15.5    Gamma Distribution   433, 435
Example  15.6    Minimum Distance Estimation of a Hospital Cost
                 Function   439
Example  15.7    GMM Estimation of the Parameters of a Gamma
                 Distribution   445
Example  15.8    Empirical Moment Equation for Instrumental Variables   447
Example  15.9    Overidentifying Restrictions   452
Example  15.10   GMM Estimation of a Dynamic Panel Data Model of Local
                 Government Expenditures   476


**CHAPTER 16    Maximum Likelihood Estimation      482**

Example  16.1    Identification of Parameters   484
Example  16.2    Log-Likelihood Function and Likelihood Equations for the
                 Normal Distribution   486
Example  16.3    Information Matrix for the Normal Distribution   493
Example  16.4    Variance Estimators for an MLE   496
Example  16.5    Two-Step ML Estimation   509
Example  16.6    Multiplicative Heteroscedasticity   526
Example  16.7    Autocorrelation in a Money Demand Equation   529
Example  16.8    ML Estimates of a Seemingly Unrelated Regressions
                 Model   534
Example  16.9    Stochastic Frontier Model   541
Example  16.10   Geometric Model for Doctor Visits   545
Example  16.11   Maximum Likelihood and FGLS Estimates of a Wage
                 Equation   549
Example  16.12   Random Effects Geometric Regression Model   553
Example  16.13   Fixed and Random Effects Geometric Regression   557
Example  16.14   Latent Class Model for Grade Point Averages   559
Example  16.15   Latent Class Regression Model for Grade
                 Point Averages   562
Example  16.16   Latent Class Model for Health Care Utilization   566


**CHAPTER 17    Simulation-Based Estimation and Inference      573**

Example  17.1    Fractional Moments of the Truncated Normal
                 Distribution   576
Example  17.2    Estimating the Lognormal Mean   579
Example  17.3    Mean of a Lognormal Distribution (Continued)   581
Example  17.4    Monte Carlo Study of the Mean Versus the Median   584
Section  17.4.1  A Monte Carlo Study: Behavior of a Test Statistic   585
Section  17.4.2  A Monte Carlo Study: The Incidental Parameters
                 Problem   586

Example 17.5    Random Effects Geometric Regression   592

Example 17.6    Maximum Simulated Likelihood Estimation of a Binary
         Choice Model   593

Example 17.7    Bootstrapping the Variance of the Median   597

**CHAPTER 18    Bayesian Estimation and Inference     600**

Example 18.1    Bayesian Estimation of a Probability   602

Example 18.2    Estimation with a Conjugate Prior   607

Example 18.3    Bayesian Estimate of the Marginal Propensity to
         Consume   609

Example 18.4    Posterior Odds for the Classical Regression Model   612

Example 18.5    Gibbs Sampling from the Normal Distribution   614

Example 18.6    Gibbs Sampler for a Probit Model   618

**CHAPTER 19    Serial Correlation     626**

Example 19.1    Money Demand Equation   626

Example 19.2    Autocorrelation Induced by Misspecification of the
         Model   626

Example 19.3    Negative Autocorrelation in the Phillips Curve   627

Example 19.4    Autocorrelation Consistent Covariance Estimation   643

Example 19.5    Panel Data Models with Autocorrelation   653

Example 19.6    Test for Common Factors   656

Example 19.7    Stochastic Volatility   658

Example 19.8    GARCH Model for Exchange Rate Volatility   665

**CHAPTER 20    Models with Lagged Variables     670**

Example 20.1    A Structural Model of the Demand for Gasoline   671

Example 20.2    Expectations-Augmented Phillips Curve   679

Example 20.3    Price and Income Elasticities of Demand for Gasoline   680

Example 20.4    A Rational Lag Model   685

Example 20.5    An Error Correction Model for Consumption   691

Example 20.6    Granger Causality   699

Section 20.6.8    Policy Analysis with a VAR   703

Example 20.7    VAR for Municipal Expenditures   711

**CHAPTER 21    Time-Series Models     715**

Example 21.1    ACF and PACF for a Series of Bond Yields   729

Example 21.2    Spectral Density Function for an AR(1) Process   733

Example 21.3    Spectral Analysis of the Growth Rate of Real GNP   735

**CHAPTER 22    Nonstationary Data     739**

Example 22.1    A Nonstationary Series   740

Example 22.2    Tests for Unit Roots   748

Example 22.3    Augmented Dickey–Fuller Test for a Unit Root in GDP   754

Section 22.3.5    German Money Demand   764

Example 22.4    Is There a Unit Root in GDP?   755

Example 22.5    Cointegration in Consumption and Output   757

Example 22.6    Several Cointegrated Series   757

Example 22.7    Multiple Cointegrating Vectors   759

Example 22.8    (Continued) Cointegration in Consumption and Output   762

**CHAPTER 23    Models for Discrete Choice    770**

Example  23.1    Labor Force Participation Model  771
Example  23.2    Structural Equations for a Probit Model  776
Example  23.3    Probability Models  781
Example  23.4    Average Partial Effects  785
Example  23.5    Specification Tests in a Labor Force Participation Model  789
Example  23.6    Prediction with a Probit Model  793
Example  23.7    An Intertemporal Labor Force Participation Equation  795
Example  23.8    Binary Choice Models for Panel Data  801
Example  23.9    Fixed Effects Logit Models: Magazine Prices Revisited  805
Example  23.10   Semiparametric Models of Heterogeneity  806
Example  23.11   Parameter Heterogeneity in a Binary Choice Model  808
Section  23.11.7  Conditional Logit Model for Travel Mode Choice  852
Example  23.12   A Comparison of Binary Choice Estimators  811
Example  23.13   Labor Supply Model  815
Example  23.14   Tetrachoric Correlation  819
Example  23.15   Bivariate Probit Model for Health Care Utilization  822
Example  23.16   A Multivariate Probit Model for Product Innovations  828
Example  23.17   Rating Assignments  834
Example  23.18   Calculus and Intermediate Economics Courses  835
Example  23.19   Health Satisfaction  838

**CHAPTER 24    Truncation, Censoring, and Sample Selection    863**

Example  24.1    Truncated Uniform Distribution  865
Example  24.2    A Truncated Lognormal Income Distribution  866
Example  24.3    Censored Random Variable  871
Example  24.4    Estimated Tobit Equations for Hours Worked  873
Example  24.5    Multiplicative Heteroscedasticity in the Tobit Model  876
Example  24.6    Incidental Truncation  883
Example  24.7    A Model of Labor Supply  884
Example  24.8    Female Labor Supply  888
Example  24.9    A Mover-Stayer Model for Migration  888
Example  24.10   Treatment Effects on Earnings  893
Example  24.11   Doctor Visits and Insurance  896

**CHAPTER 25    Models for Event Counts and Duration    906**

Example  25.1    Count Data Models for Doctor Visits  914
Example  25.2    Panel Data Models for Doctor Visits  920
Example  25.3    A Split Population Model for Major Derogatory
                 Reports  924
Example  25.4    Survival Models for Strike Duration  941
Section  25.5.2  Censoring in the Tobit and Poisson Regression Models  925

**APPENDIX C    Estimation and Inference    1019**

Example  C.1    Descriptive Statistics for a Random Sample  1022
Example  C.2    Kernel Density Estimator for the Income Data  1023
Example  C.3    Sampling Distribution of a Sample Mean  1025

Example C.4     Sampling Distribution of the Sample Minimum   1025
Example C.5     Mean Squared Error of the Sample Variance   1029
Example C.6     Likelihood Functions for Exponential and Normal
                Distributions   1030
Example C.7     Variance Bound for the Poisson Distribution   1031
Example C.8     Confidence Intervals for the Normal Mean   1033
Example C.9     Estimated Confidence Intervals for a Normal
                Mean and Variance   1034
Example C.10    Testing a Hypothesis About a Mean   1035
Example C.11    Consistent Test About a Mean   1037
Example C.12    Testing a Hypothesis About a Mean with a Confidence
                Interval   1037
Example C.13    One-Sided Test About a Mean   1038

**APPENDIX D    Large-Sample Distribution Theory        1038**
Example D.1     Mean Square Convergence of the Sample Minimum in
                Exponential Sampling   1040
Example D.2     Estimating a Function of the Mean   1042
Example D.3     Probability Limit of a Function of $\bar{x}$ and $s^2$   1046
Example D.4     Limiting Distribution of $t_{n-1}$   1048
Example D.5     The $F$ Distribution   1050
Example D.6     The Lindeberg–Levy Central Limit Theorem   1052
Example D.7     Asymptotic Distribution of the Mean of an Exponential
                Sample   1057
Example D.8     Asymptotic Inefficiency of the Median in
                Normal Sampling   1058
Example D.9     Asymptotic Distribution of a Function of Two
                Estimators   1058
Example D.10    Asymptotic Moments of the Sample Variance   1060

**APPENDIX E    Computation and Optimization        1061**
Section E4.1    Function of One Parameter   1078
Section E4.2    Function of Two Parameters: The Gamma Distribution   1079
Section E4.3    A Concentrated Log-Likelihood Function   1080

# PREFACE

## THE SIXTH EDITION OF ECONOMETRIC ANALYSIS

*Econometric Analysis* is intended for a one-year graduate course in econometrics for social scientists. The prerequisites for the course would include calculus, mathematical statistics, and an introduction to econometrics at the level of, say, Gujarati's (2002) *Basic Econometrics*, Stock and Watson's (2006) *Introduction to Econometrics,* or Wooldridge's *Introductory Econometrics: A Modern Approach* (2006). We assume, for example, that the reader has already learned about the basics of econometric methodology; the distinctions between time-series, cross section, and panel data sets; and the fundamental role of economic and statistical assumption in econometric model building. Rather than being an introduction to econometrics, this work is a bridge between an introduction to the field and the professional literature for graduate students in the social sciences.

Self-contained (for our purposes) summaries of the matrix algebra, mathematical statistics, and statistical theory used later in the book are given in Appendices A through D. This text makes heavy use of matrix algebra. This may be a bit daunting to some early on, but matrix algebra is an indispensable tool and I hope that the student will come to agree that it is a means to an end, not the end in itself. With matrices, the unity of a variety of results will emerge without being obscured by a curtain of summation signs. All the matrix algebra needed in the text is presented in Appendix A. Appendix E contains a description of numerical methods that will be useful to practicing econometricians (and to us in the latter chapters of the book).

The arrangement of this book is as follows: Our formal presentation of econometrics begins in Part I with development of its fundamental pillar, the *classical linear multiple regression model*, in Chapters 1 through 7. Estimation and inference with the linear least squares estimator is analyzed here. In Part II, Chapters 8 through 11 relax the crucial assumptions of the classical model to introduce the *generalized regression model* and *nonlinear regressions*. This provides the frameworks for the most familiar extensions of the linear model: heteroscedasticity, systems of regression equations, and fixed and random effects models for panel data sets. Part III, Chapters 12 and 13, presents the method of *instrumental variables* and its application to the estimation of simultaneous equations models. The linear model, even in its generalized form, is usually not the sole technique used in most of the current literature. In view of this, the (ever-expanding) second half of the book is devoted to topics that will extend the linear regression model in many directions. Beginning with Chapter 14, we proceed to the more involved methods of analysis that contemporary researchers use in analysis of "real-world" data. Chapters 14 to 18 present different estimation methodologies. Chapter 14 presents an overview of estimation methods by making the distinction between *parametric and nonparametric methods*. The leading application of semiparametric estimation in the current literature is the *generalized method of moments (GMM) estimator* presented in Chapter 15. This is a technique that provides the platform for much of modern econometrics. *Maximum likelihood estination* is developed in Chapter 16. Monte Carlo and simulation-based methods have become a major component of current research. Some basic results on simulation, Monte Carlo analysis, and bootstrap estimation are developed in Chapter 17. Finally, *Bayesian methods* are explored in Chapter 18. Part V, Chapters 19 to 22, and Part VI, all Chapters 23 to 25, present two (not *the* two) major subdivisions of econometric methods, macroeconometrics, which is usually associated with analysis of time-series data, and microeconometrics, which is typically based on cross-section and panel data. In Chapters 19–22, we consider models of serial correlation, lagged variables, and nonstationary data—the usual substance of macroeconomic analysis. Chapters 23 to 25 are concerned with models of discrete choice, censoring, truncation, sample selection, treatment effects, and the analysis of events (how many and when they occur).

This book has two objectives. The first is to introduce students to *applied econometrics,* including basic techniques in linear regression analysis and some of the rich variety of models that are used when the linear model proves inadequate or inappropriate. The second is to present students with sufficient *theoretical background* so that they will recognize new variants of the models learned about here as merely natural extensions that fit within a common body of principles. Thus, I have spent what might seem to be a large amount of effort explaining the mechanics of GMM estimation, nonlinear least squares, and maximum likelihood estimation, for example, of GARCH models. To meet the second objective, this book also contains a fair amount of theoretical material, such as that on maximum likelihood estimation and on asymptotic results for regression models. Modern software has made complicated modeling very easy to do, and an understanding of the underlying theory is important.

Among the changes in the order of the topics is a fairly noticeable reorientation of the maximum likelihood estimator (MLE). The development of maximum likelihood has, like its use in the literature, become somewhat more sharply focused. Where there exist robust alternatives to the MLE, such as moment-based estimators for the random effects linear model, researchers have tended to gravitate to them. By dint of its stronger distributional assumption, the MLE in that and like models is a less attractive choice. Nonetheless, the MLE is still the estimator of choice in most settings, and it is used where there is no preferable alternative. Antwiler's (2001) estimator for nested random effects is an intriguing application. In like fashion, our treatment of maximum likelihood estimation is more compartmentalized in this edition; we have moved several of the discussions of specific MLEs—for example, the multiplicative heteroscedasticity model, the random effects model, the seemingly unrelated regressions model, and a few others—to a single presentation of the ML estimator in Chapter 16, where they are developed as applications. Later in the book, in the section on microeconometrics, the MLE reemerges as the leading estimator.

I had several purposes in undertaking this revision. As in the past, readers continue to send me interesting ideas for topics in my "next edition." It is impossible to use them all, of course. Because the five received volumes of the *Handbook of Econometrics,* two volumes of the *Handbook of Applied Econometrics,* and the *Palgrave Handbook of Econometrics* already run to well over 6,000 pages, it is also unnecessary. Nonetheless, there are new and interesting developments in the field, particularly in the areas of microeconometrics (panel data and models for discrete choice) and, of course, in time series, which continues its rapid development, that students will enjoy learning about. Second, I have taken the opportunity to continue fine-tuning the text as the experience and shared wisdom of my readers accumulates. For this revision (as in the previous one), that adjustment has entailed a substantial rearrangement of the material. With this edition, I have taken the advice of some of my readers and reordered the material somewhat to make it easier to construct a course outline ("the Greene course," I have been told) with the text. Although *Econometric Analysis* has (to my great delight) become a common reference for professional analysts, at its heart, it is a textbook. It is my hope that this revision will enhance that aspect of the work. Of course, the literature in econometrics has continued to evolve, and my third objective is to grow with it. This purpose is inherently difficult to accomplish in a textbook. Most of the literature is written by professionals for other professionals, and this textbook is written for students who are in the early stages of their training. But I do hope to provide a bridge to that literature, both theoretical and applied.

This book is a broad survey of the field of econometrics. This field grows continually, and such an effort becomes increasingly difficult. (A partial list of journals devoted at least in part, if not completely, to econometrics now includes *The Journal of Applied Econometrics, Journal of Econometrics, The Econometric Journal, Econometric Theory, Econometric Reviews, Journal of Business and Economic Statistics, Empirical Economics, Foundations and Trends in Econometrics,* and *Econometrica.*) Still, my view has always been that the serious student of the field must start somewhere, and one *can* successfully seek that objective in a single textbook. This text attempts to survey, at an entry level, enough of the fields in econometrics that a student can comfortably move from here to practice or more advanced study in one or more specialized areas. At the same time, I have tried to present the material in sufficient generality so that the reader is also able to appreciate the important common foundation of all these fields and to use the tools that they all employ.

There are also quite a few recently published texts in econometrics. Several have gathered in compact, elegant treatises the increasingly advanced and advancing background theory of econometrics. Others, such as this book, focus more attention on applications of econometrics. One feature that distinguishes this work from its predecessors is its greater emphasis on nonlinear models. Computer software now in wide use has made estimation of nonlinear models as routine as estimation of linear ones, and the recent literature reflects that progression. My purpose is to provide a textbook treatment that is in line with current practice. The book includes four chapters on estimation methods used in current research and seven chapters on applications in macro- and microeconometrics. The nonlinear models used in these fields are now the staples of the applied econometrics literature. This book also contains a fair amount of material that will extend beyond many first courses in econometrics. Once again, I have included this in the hope of providing a bridge to the professional literature in these areas.

I have had one overriding purpose that has motivated all six editions of this work. For the vast majority of readers of books such as this, whose ambition is to use, not develop econometrics, I believe that it is simply not sufficient to recite the theory of estimation, hypothesis testing, and econometric analysis. Understanding the often subtle background theory is extremely important. But, at the end of the day, my purpose in writing this work, and in my continuing efforts to update it, is to show readers how to *do* econometric analysis. I unabashedly accept the unflattering assessment of a correspondent who once likened this book to a "user's guide to econometrics."

## SOFTWARE AND DATA

There are many computer programs that are widely used for the computations described in this book. All were written by econometricians or statisticians, and in general, all are regularly updated to incorporate new developments in applied econometrics. A sampling of the most widely used packages and Internet home pages where you can find information about them are:

| | | |
|---|---|---|
| *EViews* | www.eviews.com | (QMS, Irvine, CA) |
| *Gauss* | www.aptech.com | (Aptech Systems, Kent, WA) |
| *LIMDEP* | www.limdep.com | (Econometric Software, Plainview, NY) |
| *MATLAB* | www.mathworks.com | (Mathworks, Natick, MA) |
| *NLOGIT* | www.nlogit.com | (Econometric Software, Plainview, NY) |
| *RATS* | www.estima.com | (Estima, Evanston, IL) |
| *SAS* | www.sas.com | (SAS, Cary, NC) |
| *Shazam* | www.shazam.econ.ubc.ca | (Shazam, UBC, Vancouver, BC) |
| *Stata* | www.stata.com | (Stata, College Station, TX) |
| *TSP* | www.tspintl.com | (TSP International, Stanford, CA) |

Programs vary in size, complexity, cost, the amount of programming required of the user, and so on. Journals such as *The American Statistician, The Journal of Applied Econometrics,* and *The Journal of Economic Surveys* regularly publish reviews of individual packages and comparative surveys of packages, usually with reference to particular functionality such as panel data analysis or forecasting.

With a few exceptions, the computations described in this book can be carried out with any of these packages. I hesitate to link the text to any of them in particular— LIMDEP/NLOGIT was used for the computations in the chapters to follow. I will leave it to the authors of the software to show their users how to do econometrics with their programs. Many authors have produced RATS, LIMDEP, EViews, SAS, and Stata code for some of the applications as well—including, in a few cases, in the documentations for their computer programs.

Most of the data sets used in most of the examples are also on the Web site for the text. Throughout the text, these data sets are referred to "TableFn.m," for example Table F4.1. The "F" refers to Appendix F at the back of the text, which contains descriptions of the data sets. The actual data are posted in generic ASCII format on the Web site with the other supplementary materials for the text. I should also note, there are now thousands of interesting Web sites containing software, data sets, papers, and commentary on econometrics. It would be hopeless to attempt any kind of a survey here. One that is particularly agreeably structured and well targeted for readers of this book is the data archive for the *Journal of Applied Econometrics.* This journal publishes many papers that are precisely at the right level for readers of this text. They have archived all the nonconfidential data sets used in their publications since 1994. This useful site can be found at www.qed.econ.queensu.ca/jae/. Several of the examples in the text use the *JAE* data sets. Where we have done so, we direct the reader to the *JAE*'s Web site, rather than our own, for replication. (Other journals have begun to ask their authors to provide code and data to encourage replication, an effort grossly underpursued in economics. The *JAE* is far ahead of their contemporaries in this effort.) Another vast, easy to navigate site for aggregate data on the U.S. economy is www.economagic.com.

## ACKNOWLEDGMENTS

It is a pleasure to express my appreciation to those who have influenced this work. I remain grateful to Arthur Goldberger, Arnold Zellner, Dennis Aigner, Bill Becker, and Laurits Christensen for their encouragement and guidance. After six editions of this book, the number of individuals who have significantly improved it through their comments, criticisms, and encouragement has become far too large for me to thank all of them individually. Suffice to say, I hope that all of them see their contribution to this edition, and I am grateful for their help. I would like to acknowledge the many reviewers of my work whose careful reading has vastly improved the book: Badi Baltagi, Syracuse University; Neal Beck, New York University; Anil Bera, University of Illinois; John Burkett, University of Rhode Island; Leonard Carlson, Emory University; Frank Chaloupka, University of Illinois at Chicago; Chris Cornwell, University of Georgia; Craig Depken II, University of Texas at Arlington; Frank Diebold, University of Pennsylvania; Edward Dwyer, Clemson University; Michael Ellis, Wesleyan University; Martin Evans, Georgetown University; Paul Glewwe, University of Minnesota; Ed Greenberg, Washington University at St. Louis; Miguel Herce, University of North Carolina; Joseph Hilbe, Arizona State University; K. Rao Kadiyala, Purdue University; William Lott, University of Connecticut; Edward Mathis, Villanova University; Mary McGarvey, University of Nebraska-Lincoln; Ed Melnick, New York University; Thad Mirer, State University of New York at Albany; Paul Ruud, University of California at Berkeley; Sherrie Rhine, Office of the Comptroller of the Currency; Terry G. Seaks (Ret.), University of North Carolina at Greensboro; Donald Snyder, California State University at Los Angeles; Steven Stern, University of Virginia; Houston Stokes, University of Illinois at Chicago; Dmitrios Thomakos, Columbia University; Paul Wachtel, New York University; Mark Watson, Harvard University; and Kenneth West, University of Wisconsin. My numerous discussions with Bruce McCullough of Drexel University have improved Appendix E and at the same time increased my appreciation for numerical analysis. I am especially grateful to Jan Kiviet of the University of Amsterdam, who subjected my third edition to a microscopic examination and provided literally scores of suggestions, virtually all of which appear herein. I've had great support and encouragement over the years from many people close to me, especially my family, and many not so close. None has been more gratifying than the mail I've received from readers from the world over who have shared my enthusiasm for this exciting field and for this work that has taught them and me econometrics since the first edition in 1990. Finally, I would also like to thank the many people at Prentice Hall who have put this book together with me, David Alexander, Ashley Santora, Mary Kate Murray, Judy Leale, Cynthia Zonneveld, Melissa Feimer, Christy Mahon, Mohinder Singh, Maura Brown, and the composition team at ICC Macmillan Inc.

William H. Greene

# 1
# INTRODUCTION

## 1.1 ECONOMETRICS

In the first issue of *Econometrica,* the Econometric Society stated that

> its main object shall be to promote studies that aim at a unification of the theoretical-quantitative and the empirical-quantitative approach to economic problems and that are penetrated by constructive and rigorous thinking similar to that which has come to dominate the natural sciences.
>
> But there are several aspects of the quantitative approach to economics, and no single one of these aspects taken by itself, should be confounded with econometrics. Thus, econometrics is by no means the same as economic statistics. Nor is it identical with what we call general economic theory, although a considerable portion of this theory has a definitely quantitative character. Nor should econometrics be taken as synonomous [*sic*] with the application of mathematics to economics. Experience has shown that each of these three viewpoints, that of statistics, economic theory, and mathematics, is a necessary, but not by itself a sufficient, condition for a real understanding of the quantitative relations in modern economic life. It is the *unification* of all three that is powerful. And it is this unification that constitutes econometrics.

Frisch (1933) and his society responded to an unprecedented accumulation of statistical information. They saw a need to establish a body of principles that could organize what would otherwise become a bewildering mass of data. Neither the pillars nor the objectives of econometrics have changed in the years since this editorial appeared. Econometrics is the field of economics that concerns itself with the application of mathematical statistics and the tools of statistical inference to the empirical measurement of relationships postulated by economic theory.

The crucial role that econometrics plays in economics has grown over time. For example, the Nobel Prize in Economic Sciences has recognized this contribution with numerous awards to econometricians, including the first which went to (the same) Ragnar Frisch in 1969, Lawrence Klein in 1980, Trygve Haavelmo in 1989, James Heckman and Daniel McFadden in 2000, and Robert Engle and Clive Granger in 2003. The 2000 prize was noteworthy in that it celebrated the work of two scientists whose research was devoted to the marriage of behavioral theory and econometric modeling.

### Example 1.1 Behavioral Models and the Nobel Laureates

The pioneering work by both James Heckman and Dan McFadden rests firmly on a theoretical foundation of utility maximization.

For Heckman's, we begin with the standard theory of household utility maximization over consumption and leisure. The textbook model of utility maximization produces a demand for leisure time that translates into a supply function of labor. When home production (work in the home as opposed to the outside, formal labor market) is considered in the calculus, then desired "hours" of (formal) labor can be negative. An important conditioning variable is the "reservation" wage—the wage rate that will induce formal labor market participation. On the demand side of the labor market, we have firms that offer market wages that respond to such attributes as age, education, and experience. So, what can we learn about labor supply behavior based on observed market wages, these attributes and observed hours in the formal market? Less than it might seem, intuitively because our observed data omit half the market—the data on formal labor market activity are not randomly drawn from the whole population. Heckman's observations about this implicit truncation of the distribution of hours or wages revolutionized the analysis of labor markets. Parallel interpretations have since guided analyses in every area of the social sciences.

Textbook presentations of the theories of demand for goods that produce utility, since they deal in continuous variables, are consistently silent on the kinds of discrete choices that consumers make every day—what brand to choose, whether to buy a large commodity such as a car or a refrigerator, how to travel to work, whether to rent or buy a home, what candidate to vote for, and so on. Nonetheless, a model of "random utility" defined over the alternatives available to the consumer provides a theoretically sound backdrop for studying such choices. Important variables include, as always, income and relative prices. What can be learned about underlying preference structures from the discrete choices that consumers make? What must be assumed about these preferences to allow this kind of inference? What kinds of statistical models will allow us to draw inferences about preferences? McFadden's work on how commuters choose to travel to work, and on the underlying theory appropriate to this kind of modeling, has guided empirical research in discrete consumer choices for several decades.

We will examine both of these models in detail, Heckman's in Chapter 24 on sample selection and McFadden's in Chapter 23 on discrete choice models.

## 1.2 ECONOMETRIC MODELING

Econometric analysis usually begins with a statement of a theoretical proposition. Consider, for example, a classic application by one of Frisch's contemporaries:

### Example 1.2  Keynes's Consumption Function
From Keynes's (1936) *General Theory of Employment, Interest and Money*:

> We shall therefore define what we shall call the propensity to consume as the functional relationship $f$ between $X$, a given level of income, and $C$, the expenditure on consumption out of the level of income, so that $C = f(X)$.
>
> The amount that the community spends on consumption depends (i) partly on the amount of its income, (ii) partly on other objective attendant circumstances, and (iii) partly on the subjective needs and the psychological propensities and habits of the individuals composing it. The fundamental psychological law upon which we are entitled to depend with great confidence, both a priori from our knowledge of human nature and from the detailed facts of experience, is that men are disposed, as a rule and on the average, to increase their consumption as their income increases, but not by as much as the increase in their income. That is, ... $dC/dX$ is positive and less than unity.
>
> But, apart from short period changes in the level of income, it is also obvious that a higher absolute level of income will tend as a rule to widen the gap between income and consumption.... These reasons will lead, as a rule, to a greater proportion of income being saved as real income increases.

The theory asserts a relationship between consumption and income, $C = f(X)$, and claims in the second paragraph that the marginal propensity to consume (MPC), $dC/dX$, is between

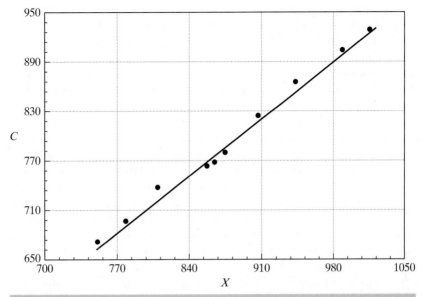

**FIGURE 1.1**   Consumption Data, 1970–1979.

zero and one.[1] The final paragraph asserts that the average propensity to consume (APC), $C/X$, falls as income rises, or $d(C/X)/dX = (\text{MPC} - \text{APC})/X < 0$. It follows that MPC < APC. The most common formulation of the consumption function is a linear relationship, $C = \alpha + X\beta$, that satisfies Keynes's "laws" if $\beta$ lies between zero and one and if $\alpha$ is greater than zero.

These theoretical propositions provide the basis for an econometric study. Given an appropriate data set, we could investigate whether the theory appears to be consistent with the observed "facts." For example, we could see whether the linear specification appears to be a satisfactory description of the relationship between consumption and income, and, if so, whether $\alpha$ is positive and $\beta$ is between zero and one. Some issues that might be studied are (1) whether this relationship is stable through time or whether the parameters of the relationship change from one generation to the next (a change in the average propensity to save, $1 - \text{APC}$, might represent a fundamental change in the behavior of consumers in the economy); (2) whether there are systematic differences in the relationship across different countries; and, if so, what explains these differences; and (3) whether there are other factors that would improve the ability of the model to explain the relationship between consumption and income. For example, Figure 1.1 presents aggregate consumption and personal income in constant dollars for the U.S. for the 10 years of 1970–1979. (See Appendix Table F1.1.) Apparently, at least superficially, the data (the facts) are consistent with the theory. The relationship appears to be linear, albeit only approximately, the intercept of a line that lies close to most of the points is positive and the slope is less than one, although not by much. (However, if the line is fit by linear least squares regression, the intercept is negative, not positive.)

Economic theories such as Keynes's are typically sharp and unambiguous. Models of demand, production, labor supply, investment, and aggregate consumption all specify precise, *deterministic* relationships. Dependent and independent variables are identified,

---

[1] Modern economists are rarely this confident about their theories. More contemporary applications generally begin from first principles and behavioral axioms, rather than simple observation.

a functional form is specified, and in most cases, at least a qualitative statement is made about the directions of effects that occur when independent variables in the model change. Of course, the model is only a simplification of reality. It will include the salient features of the relationship of interest, but will leave unaccounted for influences that might well be present but are regarded as unimportant. No model could hope to encompass the myriad essentially random aspects of economic life. It is thus also necessary to incorporate stochastic elements. As a consequence, observations on a dependent variable will display variation attributable not only to differences in variables that are explicitly accounted for, but also to the randomness of human behavior and the interaction of countless minor influences that are not. It is understood that the introduction of a random "disturbance" into a deterministic model is not intended merely to paper over its inadequacies. It is essential to examine the results of the study, in a sort of postmortem, to ensure that the allegedly random, unexplained factor is truly unexplainable. If it is not, the model is, in fact, inadequate. [In the example given earlier, the estimated constant term in the linear least squares regression is negative. Is the theory wrong, or is the finding due to random fluctuation in the data? Another possibility is that the theory is broadly correct, but the world changed between 1936 when Keynes devised his theory and the 1970s when the data (outcomes) were generated. Or, perhaps linear least squares is not the appropriate technique to use for this model, and that is responsible for the inconvenient result (the negative intercept).] The stochastic element endows the model with its statistical properties. Observations on the variable(s) under study are thus taken to be the outcomes of a random process. With a sufficiently detailed stochastic structure and adequate data, the analysis will become a matter of deducing the properties of a probability distribution. The tools and methods of mathematical statistics will provide the operating principles.

A model (or theory) can never truly be confirmed unless it is made so broad as to include every possibility. But it may be subjected to ever more rigorous scrutiny and, in the face of contradictory evidence, refuted. A deterministic theory will be invalidated by a single contradictory observation. The introduction of stochastic elements into the model changes it from an exact statement to a probabilistic description about expected outcomes and carries with it an important implication. Only a preponderance of contradictory evidence can convincingly invalidate the probabilistic model, and what constitutes a "preponderance of evidence" is a matter of interpretation. Thus, the probabilistic model is less precise but at the same time, more robust.[2]

The process of econometric analysis departs from the specification of a theoretical relationship. We initially proceed on the optimistic assumption that we can obtain precise measurements on all the variables in a correctly specified model. If the ideal conditions are met at every step, the subsequent analysis will be routine. Unfortunately, they rarely are. Some of the difficulties one can expect to encounter are the following:

- The data may be badly measured or may correspond only vaguely to the variables in the model. "The interest rate" is one example.
- Some of the variables may be inherently unmeasurable. "Expectations" is a case in point.

---

[2]See Keuzenkamp and Magnus (1995) for a lengthy symposium on testing in econometrics.

- The theory may make only a rough guess as to the correct functional form, if it makes any at all, and we may be forced to choose from an embarrassingly long menu of possibilities.
- The assumed stochastic properties of the random terms in the model may be demonstrably violated, which may call into question the methods of estimation and inference procedures we have used.
- Some relevant variables may be missing from the model.

The ensuing steps of the analysis consist of coping with these problems and attempting to cull whatever information is likely to be present in such obviously imperfect data. The methodology is that of mathematical statistics and economic theory. The product is an econometric model.

## 1.3  METHODOLOGY

The connection between underlying behavioral models and the modern practice of econometrics is increasingly strong. Practitioners rely heavily on the theoretical tools of microeconomics including utility maximization, profit maximization, and market equilibrium. Macroeconomic model builders rely on the interactions between economic agents and policy makers. The analyses are directed at subtle, difficult questions that often require intricate, complicated formulations. A few applications are as follows:

- What are the likely effects on labor supply behavior of proposed negative income taxes? [Ashenfelter and Heckman (1974).]
- Does a monetary policy regime that is strongly oriented toward controlling inflation impose a real cost in terms of lost output on the U.S. economy? [Cecchetti and Rich (2001).]
- Did 2001's largest federal tax cut in U.S. history contribute to or dampen the concurrent recession? Or was it irrelevant?
- Does attending an elite college bring an expected payoff in lifetime expected income sufficient to justify the higher tuition? [Kreuger and Dale (1999) and Kreuger (2000).]
- Does a voluntary training program produce tangible benefits? Can these benefits be accurately measured? [Angrist (2001).]
- Do smaller class sizes bring real benefits in student performance? [Hanuschek (1999), Hoxby (2000).]
- Does the presence of health insurance induce individuals to make heavier use of the health care system—is moral hazard a measurable problem? [Riphahn et al. (2003).]

Each of these analyses would depart from a formal model of the process underlying the observed data.

## 1.4 THE PRACTICE OF ECONOMETRICS

We can make a useful distinction between theoretical and applied econometrics. Theorists develop new techniques for estimation and hypothesis testing and analyze the consequences of applying particular methods when the assumptions that justify those methods are not met. Applied econometricians are the users of these techniques and the analysts of data ("real world" and simulated). Of course, the distinction is far from clean; practitioners routinely develop new analytical tools for the purposes of the study that they are involved in. This book contains a large amount of econometric theory, but it is directed toward applied econometrics. I have attempted to survey techniques, admittedly some quite elaborate and intricate, that have seen wide use "in the field."

Another useful distinction can be made between microeconometrics and macroeconometrics. The former is characterized largely by its analysis of cross section and panel data and by its focus on individual consumers, firms, and micro-level decision makers. Macroeconometrics is generally involved in the analysis of time-series data, usually of broad aggregates such as price levels, the money supply, exchange rates, output, investment, and so on. Once again, the boundaries are not sharp. The very large field of financial econometrics is concerned with long time-series data and occasionally vast panel data sets, but with a very focused orientation toward models of individual behavior. The analysis of market returns and exchange rate behavior is neither macronor microeconometric, or perhaps it is some of both. Another application that we will examine in this text concerns spending patterns of municipalities, which, again, rests somewhere between the two fields.

Applied econometric methods will be used for estimation of important quantities, analysis of economic outcomes, markets or individual behavior, testing theories, and for forecasting. The last of these is an art and science in itself, and (fortunately) the subject of a vast library of sources. Although we will briefly discuss some aspects of forecasting, our interest in this text will be on estimation and analysis of models. The presentation, where there is a distinction to be made, will contain a blend of microeconometric and macroeconometric techniques and applications. The first 18 chapters of the book are largely devoted to results that form the platform of both areas. Chapters 19 to 22 focus on time series modeling while Chapters 23 to 25 are devoted to methods more suited to cross sections and panels, and methods used more frequently in microeconometrics. We will not be spending any time on financial econometrics. For those with an interest in this field, I would recommend the celebrated work by Campbell, Lo, and Mackinlay (1997) and, for a more time-series–oriented approach, Tsay (2005). It is also necessary to distinguish between *time-series analysis* (which is not our focus) and methods that primarily use time-series data. The former is, like forecasting, a growth industry served by its own literature in many fields. While we will employ some of the techniques of time-series analysis, we will spend relatively little time developing first principles.

The techniques used in econometrics have been employed in a widening variety of fields, including political methodology, sociology [see, e.g., Long (1997) and DeMaris (2004)], health economics, medical research (how do we handle attrition from medical treatment studies?) environmental economics, transportation engineering, and numerous others. Practitioners in these fields and many more are all heavy users of the techniques described in this text.

## 1.5  PLAN OF THE BOOK

The remainder of this book is organized into seven parts:

1.  Chapters 2 through 7 present the classical linear multiple regression model. We will discuss specification, estimation, and statistical inference.
2.  Chapters 8 through 11 describe the generalized regression model, heteroscedasticity, systems of equations, panel data applications, and nonlinear regression models.
3.  Chapters 12 and 13 develop the method of instrumental variables estimation then apply this method to systems of simultaneous equations. This section allows us to extend Chapter 9 on panel data methods to a variety of models and techniques.
4.  Chapters 14 through 18 present general results on different methods of estimation including GMM, maximum likelihood, and simulation based methods. Various estimation frameworks, including non- and semiparametric and Bayesian estimation are presented in Chapters 14 and 18.
5.  Chapters 19 through 22 present topics in macroeconometrics. These chapters are devoted to topics in time-series modeling.
6.  Chapters 23 through 25 are about microeconometrics, discrete choice modeling and limited dependent variables, and the analysis of data on events—how many occur in a given setting and when they occur.
7.  Appendices A through E present background material on tools used in econometrics including matrix algebra, probability and distribution theory, estimation, and asymptotic distribution theory. Appendix E presents results on computation. Appendices A through E are chapter-length surveys of the tools used in econometrics. Because it is assumed that the reader has some previous training in each of these topics, these summaries are included primarily for those who desire a refresher or a convenient reference. We do not anticipate that these appendices can substitute for a course in any of these subjects. The intent of these chapters is to provide a reasonably concise summary of the results, nearly all of which are explicitly used elsewhere in the book.

The data sets used in the numerical examples are described in Appendix F. The actual data sets and other supplementary materials can be downloaded from the Web site for the text:

http://www.prenhall.com/greene

Useful tables related to commonly used probability distributions are given in Appendix G.

# 2

# THE CLASSICAL MULTIPLE LINEAR REGRESSION MODEL

## 2.1 INTRODUCTION

An econometric study begins with a set of propositions about some aspect of the economy. The theory specifies a set of precise, deterministic relationships among variables. Familiar examples are demand equations, production functions, and macroeconomic models. The empirical investigation provides estimates of unknown parameters in the model, such as elasticities or the effects of monetary policy, and usually attempts to measure the validity of the theory against the behavior of the observed data. Once suitably constructed, the model might then be used for prediction or analysis of behavior. This book will develop a large number of models and techniques used in this framework.

The **linear regression model** is the single most useful tool in the econometrician's kit. Although to an increasing degree in the contemporary literature, it is often only the departure point for the full analysis, it remains the device used to begin almost all empirical research. This chapter will develop the model. The next several chapters will discuss more elaborate specifications and complications that arise in the application of techniques that are based on the simple models presented here.

## 2.2 THE LINEAR REGRESSION MODEL

The **multiple linear regression model** is used to study the relationship between a **dependent variable** and one or more **independent variables.** The generic form of the linear regression model is

$$
\begin{aligned}
y &= f(x_1, x_2, \ldots, x_K) + \varepsilon \\
&= x_1\beta_1 + x_2\beta_2 + \cdots + x_K\beta_K + \varepsilon
\end{aligned}
\tag{2-1}
$$

where $y$ is the dependent or **explained** variable and $x_1, \ldots, x_K$ are the independent or **explanatory** variables. One's theory will specify $f(x_1, x_2, \ldots, x_K)$. This function is commonly called the **population regression equation** of $y$ on $x_1, \ldots, x_K$. In this setting, $y$ is the **regressand** and $x_k, k=1, \ldots,$ and $K$ are the **regressors** or **covariates.** The underlying theory will specify the dependent and independent variables in the model. It is not always obvious which is appropriately defined as each of these—for example, a demand equation, $quantity = \beta_1 + price \times \beta_2 + income \times \beta_3 + \varepsilon$, and an inverse demand equation, $price = \gamma_1 + quantity \times \gamma_2 + income \times \gamma_3 + u$ are equally valid representations of a market. For modeling purposes, it will often prove useful to think in terms of "autonomous variation." One can conceive of movement of the independent variables outside the relationships defined by the model while movement of the dependent variable is considered in response to some independent or exogenous stimulus.[1]

The term $\varepsilon$ is a random **disturbance,** so named because it "disturbs" an otherwise stable relationship. The disturbance arises for several reasons, primarily because we cannot hope to capture every influence on an economic variable in a model, no matter how elaborate. The net effect, which can be positive or negative, of these omitted factors is captured in the disturbance. There are many other contributors to the disturbance in an empirical model. Probably the most significant is errors of measurement. It is easy to theorize about the relationships among precisely defined variables; it is quite another to obtain accurate measures of these variables. For example, the difficulty of obtaining reasonable measures of profits, interest rates, capital stocks, or, worse yet, flows of services from capital stocks is a recurrent theme in the empirical literature. At the extreme, there may be no observable counterpart to the theoretical variable. The literature on the permanent income model of consumption [e.g., Friedman (1957)] provides an interesting example.

We assume that each observation in a sample $(y_i, x_{i1}, x_{i2}, \ldots, x_{iK})$, $i = 1, \ldots, n$, is generated by an underlying process described by

$$y_i = x_{i1}\beta_1 + x_{i2}\beta_2 + \cdots + x_{iK}\beta_K + \varepsilon_i.$$

The observed value of $y_i$ is the sum of two parts, a deterministic part and the random part, $\varepsilon_i$. Our objective is to estimate the unknown parameters of the model, use the data to study the validity of the theoretical propositions, and perhaps use the model to predict the variable $y$. How we proceed from here depends crucially on what we assume about the stochastic process that has led to our observations of the data in hand.

### Example 2.1    Keynes's Consumption Function

Example 1.2 discussed a model of consumption proposed by Keynes and his *General Theory* (1936). The theory that consumption, $C$, and income, $X$, are related certainly seems consistent with the observed "facts" in Figures 1.1 and 2.1. (These data are in Data Table F2.1.) Of course, the linear function is only approximate. Even ignoring the anomalous wartime years, consumption and income cannot be connected by any simple **deterministic relationship.** The linear model, $C = \alpha + \beta X$, is intended only to represent the salient features of this part of the economy. It is hopeless to attempt to capture every influence in the relationship. The next step is to incorporate the inherent randomness in its real-world counterpart. Thus, we write $C = f(X, \varepsilon)$, where $\varepsilon$ is a stochastic element. It is important not to view $\varepsilon$ as a catchall for the inadequacies of the model. The model including $\varepsilon$ appears adequate for the data not including the war years, but for 1942–1945, something systematic clearly seems to be missing. Consumption in these years could not rise to rates historically consistent with these levels of income because of wartime rationing. A model meant to describe consumption in this period would have to accommodate this influence.

It remains to establish how the stochastic element will be incorporated in the equation. The most frequent approach is to assume that it is *additive*. Thus, we recast the equation in stochastic terms: $C = \alpha + \beta X + \varepsilon$. This equation is an empirical counterpart to Keynes's theoretical model. But, what of those anomalous years of rationing? If we were to ignore our intuition and attempt to "fit" a line to all these data—the next chapter will discuss at length how we should do that—we might arrive at the dotted line in the figure as our best

---

[1]By this definition, it would seem that in our demand relationship, only income would be an independent variable while both price and quantity would be dependent. That makes sense—in a market, price and quantity *are* determined at the same time, and do change only when something outside the market changes. We will return to this specific case in Chapter 13.

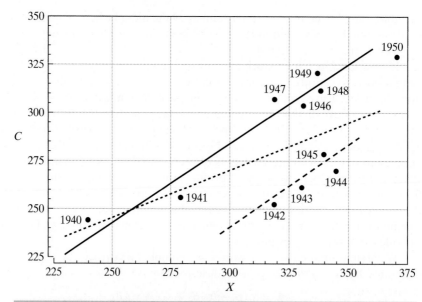

**FIGURE 2.1**    Consumption Data, 1940–1950.

guess. This line, however, is obviously being distorted by the rationing. A more appropriate specification for these data that accommodates both the stochastic nature of the data and the special circumstances of the years 1942–1945 might be one that shifts straight down in the war years, $C = \alpha + \beta X + d_{waryears}\delta_w + \varepsilon$, where the new variable, $d_{waryears}$ equals one in 1942–1945 and zero in other years and $\delta_w < 0$.

One of the most useful aspects of the multiple regression model is its ability to identify the independent effects of a set of variables on a dependent variable. Example 2.2 describes a common application.

### Example 2.2   Earnings and Education
A number of recent studies have analyzed the relationship between earnings and education. We would expect, on average, higher levels of education to be associated with higher incomes. The simple regression model

$$earnings = \beta_1 + \beta_2\ education + \varepsilon,$$

however, neglects the fact that most people have higher incomes when they are older than when they are young, regardless of their education. Thus, $\beta_2$ will overstate the marginal impact of education. If age and education are positively correlated, then the regression model will associate all the observed increases in income with increases in education. A better specification would account for the effect of age, as in

$$earnings = \beta_1 + \beta_2\ education + \beta_3\ age + \varepsilon.$$

It is often observed that income tends to rise less rapidly in the later earning years than in the early ones. To accommodate this possibility, we might extend the model to

$$earnings = \beta_1 + \beta_2\ education + \beta_3\ age + \beta_4\ age^2 + \varepsilon.$$

We would expect $\beta_3$ to be positive and $\beta_4$ to be negative.

The crucial feature of this model is that it allows us to carry out a conceptual experiment that might not be observed in the actual data. In the example, we might like to (and could) compare the earnings of two individuals of the same age with different amounts of "education" even if the data set does not actually contain two such individuals. How education should be measured in this setting is a difficult problem. The study of the earnings of twins by Ashenfelter and Krueger (1994), which uses precisely this specification of the earnings equation, presents an interesting approach. We will examine this study in some detail in Section 12.5.2.

A large literature has been devoted to an intriguing question on this subject. Education is not truly "independent" in this setting. Highly motivated individuals will choose to pursue more education (for example, by going to college or graduate school) than others. By the same token, highly motivated individuals may do things that, on average, lead them to have higher incomes. If so, does a positive $\beta_2$ that suggests an association between income and education really measure the effect of education on income, or does it reflect the result of some underlying effect on both variables that we have not included in our regression model? We will revisit the issue in Chapter 24.[2]

## 2.3   ASSUMPTIONS OF THE CLASSICAL LINEAR REGRESSION MODEL

The classical linear regression model consists of a set of assumptions about how a data set will be produced by an underlying "data-generating process." The theory will specify a deterministic relationship between the dependent variable and the independent variables. The assumptions that describe the form of the model and relationships among its parts and imply appropriate estimation and inference procedures are listed in Table 2.1.

---

**TABLE 2.1**    Assumptions of the Classical Linear Regression Model

**A1. Linearity:** $y_i = x_{i1}\beta_1 + x_{i2}\beta_2 + \cdots + x_{iK}\beta_K + \varepsilon_i$. The model specifies a linear relationship between $y$ and $x_1, \ldots, x_K$.

**A2. Full rank:** There is no exact linear relationship among any of the independent variables in the model. This assumption will be necessary for estimation of the parameters of the model.

**A3. Exogeneity of the independent variables:** $E[\varepsilon_i \mid x_{j1}, x_{j2}, \ldots, x_{jK}] = 0$. This states that the expected value of the disturbance at observation $i$ in the sample is not a function of the independent variables observed at any observation, including this one. This means that the independent variables will not carry useful information for prediction of $\varepsilon_i$.

**A4. Homoscedasticity and nonautocorrelation:** Each disturbance, $\varepsilon_i$ has the same finite variance, $\sigma^2$, and is uncorrelated with every other disturbance, $\varepsilon_j$. This assumption limits the generality of the model, and we will want to examine how to relax it in the chapters to follow.

**A5. Data generation:** The data in $(x_{j1}, x_{j2}, \ldots, x_{jK})$ may be any mixture of constants and random variables. The crucial elements for present purposes are the strict mean independence assumption A3 and the implicit variance independence assumption in A4. Analysis will be done conditionally on the observed **X**, so whether the elements in **X** are fixed constants or random draws from a stochastic process will not influence the results. In later, more advanced treatments, we will want to be more specific about the possible relationship between $\varepsilon_i$ and $x_j$.

**A6. Normal distribution:** The disturbances are normally distributed. Once again, this is a convenience that we will dispense with after some analysis of its implications.

---

[2]This model lays yet another trap for the practitioner. In a cross section, the higher incomes of the older individuals in the sample might tell an entirely different, perhaps macroeconomic story (a "cohort effect") from the lower incomes of younger individuals as time and their incomes evolve. It is not necessarily possible to deduce the characteristics of incomes of younger people in the sample *if they were older* by comparing the older individuals in the sample to the younger ones. A parallel problem arises in the analysis of treatment effects that we will examine in Chapter 24.

### 2.3.1 LINEARITY OF THE REGRESSION MODEL

Let the column vector $\mathbf{x}_k$ be the $n$ observations on variable $x_k, k = 1, \ldots, K$, and assemble these data in an $n \times K$ data matrix $\mathbf{X}$. In most contexts, the first column of $\mathbf{X}$ is assumed to be a column of 1s so that $\beta_1$ is the constant term in the model. Let $\mathbf{y}$ be the $n$ observations, $y_1, \ldots, y_n$, and let $\boldsymbol{\varepsilon}$ be the column vector containing the $n$ disturbances. The model in (2-1) as it applies to all $n$ observations can now be written

$$\mathbf{y} = \mathbf{x}_1 \beta_1 + \cdots + \mathbf{x}_K \beta_K + \boldsymbol{\varepsilon}, \tag{2-2}$$

or in the form of Assumption 1,

$$\boxed{\text{Assumption:} \quad \mathbf{y} = \mathbf{X}\boldsymbol{\beta} + \boldsymbol{\varepsilon}.} \tag{2-3}$$

**A NOTATIONAL CONVENTION.**
Henceforth, to avoid a possibly confusing and cumbersome notation, we will use a boldface $\mathbf{x}$ to denote a column *or* a row of $\mathbf{X}$. Which of these applies will be clear from the context. In (2-2), $\mathbf{x}_k$ is the $k$th column of $\mathbf{X}$. Subscripts $j$ and $k$ will be used to denote columns (variables). It will often be convenient to refer to a single observation in (2-3), which we would write

$$y_i = \mathbf{x}_i' \boldsymbol{\beta} + \varepsilon_i. \tag{2-4}$$

Subscripts $i$ and $t$ will generally be used to denote rows (observations) of $\mathbf{X}$. In (2-4), $\mathbf{x}_i$ is a column vector that is the transpose of the $i$th $1 \times K$ row of $\mathbf{X}$.

Our primary interest is in estimation and inference about the parameter vector $\boldsymbol{\beta}$. Note that the simple regression model in Example 2.1 is a special case in which $\mathbf{X}$ has only two columns, the first of which is a column of 1s. The assumption of linearity of the regression model includes the additive disturbance. For the regression to be linear in the sense described here, it must be of the form in (2-1) either in the original variables or after some suitable transformation. For example, the model

$$y = Ax^\beta e^\varepsilon$$

is linear (after taking logs on both sides of the equation), whereas

$$y = Ax^\beta + \varepsilon$$

is not. The observed dependent variable is thus the sum of two components, a deterministic element $\alpha + \beta x$ and a random variable $\varepsilon$. It is worth emphasizing that neither of the two parts is directly observed because $\alpha$ and $\beta$ are unknown.

The linearity assumption is not so narrow as it might first appear. In the regression context, *linearity* refers to the manner in which the parameters and the disturbance enter the equation, not necessarily to the relationship among the variables. For example, the equations $y = \alpha + \beta x + \varepsilon$, $y = \alpha + \beta \cos(x) + \varepsilon$, $y = \alpha + \beta/x + \varepsilon$, and $y = \alpha + \beta \ln x + \varepsilon$ are all linear in some function of $x$ by the definition we have used here. In the examples, only $x$ has been transformed, but $y$ could have been as well, as in $y = Ax^\beta e^\varepsilon$, which is a linear relationship in the logs of $x$ and $y$; $\ln y = \alpha + \beta \ln x + \varepsilon$. The variety of functions is unlimited. This aspect of the model is used in a number of commonly used functional forms. For example, the **loglinear model** is

$$\ln y = \beta_1 + \beta_2 \ln x_2 + \beta_3 \ln x_3 + \cdots + \beta_K \ln x_K + \varepsilon.$$

This equation is also known as the **constant elasticity** form as in this equation, the elasticity of $y$ with respect to changes in $x$ is $\partial \ln y / \partial \ln x_k = \beta_k$, which does not vary with $x_k$. The loglinear form is often used in models of demand and production. Different values of $\beta$ produce widely varying functions.

### Example 2.3    The U.S. Gasoline Market
Data on the U.S. gasoline market for the years 1953—2004 are given in Table F2.2 in Appendix F. We will use these data to obtain, among other things, estimates of the income, own price, and cross-price elasticities of demand in this market. These data also present an interesting question on the issue of holding "all other things constant," that was suggested in Example 2.2. In particular, consider a somewhat abbreviated model of per capita gasoline consumption:

$$\ln(G/pop) = \beta_1 + \beta_2 \ln(Income/pop) + \beta_3 \ln price_G + \beta_4 \ln P_{newcars} + \beta_5 \ln P_{usedcars} + \varepsilon.$$

This model will provide estimates of the income and price elasticities of demand for gasoline and an estimate of the elasticity of demand with respect to the prices of new and used cars. What should we expect for the sign of $\beta_4$? Cars and gasoline are complementary goods, so if the prices of new cars rise, ceteris paribus, gasoline consumption should fall. Or should it? If the prices of new cars rise, then consumers will buy fewer of them; they will keep their used cars longer and buy fewer new cars. If older cars use more gasoline than newer ones, then the rise in the prices of new cars would lead to higher gasoline consumption than otherwise, not lower. We can use the multiple regression model and the gasoline data to attempt to answer the question.

A **semilog** model is often used to model growth rates:

$$\ln y_t = \mathbf{x}_t' \boldsymbol{\beta} + \delta t + \varepsilon_t.$$

In this model, the autonomous (at least not explained by the model itself) proportional, per period growth rate is $d \ln y / dt = \delta$. Other variations of the general form

$$f(y_t) = g(\mathbf{x}_t' \boldsymbol{\beta} + \varepsilon_t)$$

will allow a tremendous variety of functional forms, all of which fit into our definition of a linear model.

The linear regression model is sometimes interpreted as an approximation to some unknown, underlying function. (See Section A.8.1 for discussion.) By this interpretation, however, the linear model, even with quadratic terms, is fairly limited in that such an approximation is likely to be useful only over a small range of variation of the independent variables. The translog model discussed in Example 2.4, in contrast, has proved far more effective as an approximating function.

### Example 2.4    The Translog Model
Modern studies of demand and production are usually done with a **flexible functional form.** Flexible functional forms are used in econometrics because they allow analysts to model **second-order effects** such as elasticities of substitution, which are functions of the second derivatives of production, cost, or utility functions. The linear model restricts these to equal zero, whereas the loglinear model (e.g., the Cobb–Douglas model) restricts the interesting elasticities to the uninteresting values of –1 or +1. The most popular flexible functional form is the **translog model,** which is often interpreted as a second-order approximation to an

unknown functional form. [See Berndt and Christensen (1973).] One way to derive it is as follows. We first write $y = g(x_1, \ldots, x_K)$. Then, $\ln y = \ln g(\ldots) = f(\ldots)$. Since by a trivial transformation $x_k = \exp(\ln x_k)$, we interpret the function as a function of the logarithms of the $x$'s. Thus, $\ln y = f(\ln x_1, \ldots, \ln x_K)$.

Now, expand this function in a second-order Taylor series around the point $\mathbf{x} = [1, 1, \ldots, 1]'$ so that at the expansion point, the log of each variable is a convenient zero. Then

$$\ln y = f(\mathbf{0}) + \sum_{k=1}^{K} [\partial f(\cdot)/\partial \ln x_k]_{|\ln \mathbf{x}=0} \ln x_k$$

$$+ \frac{1}{2} \sum_{k=1}^{K} \sum_{l=1}^{K} [\partial^2 f(\cdot)/\partial \ln x_k \partial \ln x_l]_{|\ln \mathbf{x}=0} \ln x_k \ln x_l + \varepsilon.$$

The disturbance in this model is assumed to embody the familiar factors and the error of approximation to the unknown function. Since the function and its derivatives evaluated at the fixed value $\mathbf{0}$ are constants, we interpret them as the coefficients and write

$$\ln y = \beta_0 + \sum_{k=1}^{K} \beta_k \ln x_k + \frac{1}{2} \sum_{k=1}^{K} \sum_{l=1}^{K} \gamma_{kl} \ln x_k \ln x_l + \varepsilon.$$

This model is linear by our definition but can, in fact, mimic an impressive amount of curvature when it is used to approximate another function. An interesting feature of this formulation is that the loglinear model is a special case, $\gamma_{kl} = 0$. Also, there is an interesting test of the underlying theory possible because if the underlying function were assumed to be continuous and twice continuously differentiable, then by Young's theorem it must be true that $\gamma_{kl} = \gamma_{lk}$. We will see in Chapter 10 how this feature is studied in practice.

Despite its great flexibility, the linear model does not include all the situations we encounter in practice. For a simple example, there is no transformation that will reduce $y = \alpha + 1/(\beta_1 + \beta_2 x) + \varepsilon$ to linearity. The methods we consider in this chapter are not appropriate for estimating the parameters of such a model. Relatively straightforward techniques have been developed for nonlinear models such as this, however. We shall treat them in detail in Chapter 11.

### 2.3.2 FULL RANK

Assumption 2 is that there are no exact linear relationships among the variables.

> ASSUMPTION: $\mathbf{X}$ is an $n \times K$ matrix with rank $K$.         **(2-5)**

Hence, $\mathbf{X}$ has full column rank; the columns of $\mathbf{X}$ are linearly independent and there are at least $K$ observations. [See (A-42) and the surrounding text.] This assumption is known as an **identification condition.** To see the need for this assumption, consider an example.

#### Example 2.5  Short Rank
Suppose that a cross-section model specifies

$$C = \beta_1 + \beta_2 \text{ nonlabor income} + \beta_3 \text{ salary} + \beta_4 \text{ total income} + \varepsilon,$$

where *total income* is exactly equal to *salary* plus *nonlabor income*. Clearly, there is an exact linear dependency in the model. Now let

$$\beta_2' = \beta_2 + a,$$
$$\beta_3' = \beta_3 + a,$$

and

$$\beta_4' = \beta_4 - a,$$

where *a* is any number. Then the exact same value appears on the right-hand side of *C* if we substitute $\beta_2'$, $\beta_3'$, and $\beta_4'$ for $\beta_2$, $\beta_3$, and $\beta_4$. Obviously, there is no way to estimate the parameters of this model.

If there are fewer than $K$ observations, then **X** cannot have **full rank.** Hence, we make the (redundant) assumption that $n$ is at least as large as $K$.

In a two-variable linear model with a constant term, the full rank assumption means that there must be variation in the regressor $x$. If there is no variation in $x$, then all our observations will lie on a vertical line. This situation does not invalidate the other assumptions of the model; presumably, it is a flaw in the data set. The possibility that this suggests is that we *could* have drawn a sample in which there was variation in $x$, but in this instance, we did not. Thus, the model still applies, but we cannot learn about it from the data set in hand.

### 2.3.3  REGRESSION

The disturbance is assumed to have conditional expected value zero at every observation, which we write as

$$E[\varepsilon_i \mid \mathbf{X}] = 0. \tag{2-6}$$

For the full set of observations, we write Assumption 3 as:

$$\text{ASSUMPTION:} \quad E[\boldsymbol{\varepsilon} \mid \mathbf{X}] = \begin{bmatrix} E[\varepsilon_1 \mid \mathbf{X}] \\ E[\varepsilon_2 \mid \mathbf{X}] \\ \vdots \\ E[\varepsilon_n \mid \mathbf{X}] \end{bmatrix} = \mathbf{0}. \tag{2-7}$$

There is a subtle point in this discussion that the observant reader might have noted. In (2-7), the left-hand side states, in principle, that the mean of each $\varepsilon_i$ *conditioned on all observations* $\mathbf{x}_i$ is zero. This conditional mean assumption states, in words, that no observations on **x** convey information about the expected value of the disturbance. It is conceivable—for example, in a time-series setting—that although $\mathbf{x}_i$ might provide no information about $E[\varepsilon_i|\cdot]$, $\mathbf{x}_j$ *at some other observation,* such as in the next time period, might. Our assumption at this point is that there is no information about $E[\varepsilon_i \mid \cdot]$ contained in any observation $\mathbf{x}_j$. Later, when we extend the model, we will study the implications of dropping this assumption. [See Wooldridge (1995).] We will also assume that the disturbances convey no information about each other. That is, $E[\varepsilon_i \mid \varepsilon_1, \ldots, \varepsilon_{i-1}, \varepsilon_{i+1}, \ldots, \varepsilon_n] = 0$. In sum, at this point, we have assumed that the disturbances are purely random draws from some population.

The zero conditional mean implies that the unconditional mean is also zero, since

$$E[\varepsilon_i] = E_\mathbf{x}[E[\varepsilon_i \mid \mathbf{X}]] = E_\mathbf{x}[0] = 0.$$

Since, for each $\varepsilon_i$, $\mathrm{Cov}[E[\varepsilon_i \mid \mathbf{X}], \mathbf{X}] = \mathrm{Cov}[\varepsilon_i, \mathbf{X}]$, Assumption 3 implies that $\mathrm{Cov}[\varepsilon_i, \mathbf{X}] = 0$ for all $i$. (Exercise: Is the converse true?)

In most cases, the zero mean assumption is not restrictive. Consider a two-variable model and suppose that the mean of $\varepsilon$ is $\mu \neq 0$. Then $\alpha + \beta x + \varepsilon$ is the same as $(\alpha + \mu) + \beta x + (\varepsilon - \mu)$. Letting $\alpha' = \alpha + \mu$ and $\varepsilon' = \varepsilon - \mu$ produces the original model. For an application, see the discussion of frontier production functions in Section 16.9.5.a. But, if the original model does not contain a constant term, then assuming $E[\varepsilon_i] = 0$ could be substantive. This suggests that there is a potential problem in models without constant terms. As a general rule, regression models should not be specified without constant terms unless this is specifically dictated by the underlying theory.[3] Arguably, if we have reason to specify that the mean of the disturbance is something other than zero, we should build it into the systematic part of the regression, leaving in the disturbance only the unknown part of $\varepsilon$. Assumption 3 also implies that

$$E[\mathbf{y} \mid \mathbf{X}] = \mathbf{X}\boldsymbol{\beta}. \tag{2-8}$$

Assumptions 1 and 3 comprise the *linear regression model*. The **regression** of $\mathbf{y}$ on $\mathbf{X}$ is the conditional mean, $E[\mathbf{y} \mid \mathbf{X}]$, so that without Assumption 3, $\mathbf{X}\boldsymbol{\beta}$ is *not* the conditional mean function.

The remaining assumptions will more completely specify the characteristics of the disturbances in the model and state the conditions under which the sample observations on $\mathbf{x}$ are obtained.

### 2.3.4 SPHERICAL DISTURBANCES

The fourth assumption concerns the variances and covariances of the disturbances:

$$\mathrm{Var}[\varepsilon_i \mid \mathbf{X}] = \sigma^2, \qquad \text{for all } i = 1, \ldots, n,$$

and

$$\mathrm{Cov}[\varepsilon_i, \varepsilon_j \mid \mathbf{X}] = 0, \qquad \text{for all } i \neq j.$$

Constant variance is labeled **homoscedasticity.** Consider a model that describes the profits of firms in an industry as a function of, say, size. Even accounting for size, measured in dollar terms, the profits of large firms will exhibit greater variation than those of smaller firms. The homoscedasticity assumption would be inappropriate here. Also, survey data on household expenditure patterns often display marked **heteroscedasticity,** even after accounting for income and household size.

Uncorrelatedness across observations is labeled generically **nonautocorrelation.** In Figure 2.1, there is some suggestion that the disturbances might not be truly independent across observations. Although the number of observations is limited, it does appear that, on average, each disturbance tends to be followed by one with the same sign. This

---

[3]Models that describe first differences of variables might well be specified without constants. Consider $y_t - y_{t-1}$. If there is a constant term $\alpha$ on the right-hand side of the equation, then $y_t$ is a function of $\alpha t$, which is an explosive regressor. Models with linear time trends merit special treatment in the time-series literature. We will return to this issue in Chapter 20.

"inertia" is precisely what is meant by **autocorrelation,** and it is assumed away at this point. Methods of handling autocorrelation in economic data occupy a large proportion of the literature and will be treated at length in Chapter 19. Note that nonautocorrelation does not imply that observations $y_i$ and $y_j$ are uncorrelated. The assumption is that *deviations* of observations from their expected values are uncorrelated.

The two assumptions imply that

$$E[\boldsymbol{\varepsilon}\boldsymbol{\varepsilon}' \mid \mathbf{X}] = \begin{bmatrix} E[\varepsilon_1\varepsilon_1 \mid \mathbf{X}] & E[\varepsilon_1\varepsilon_2 \mid \mathbf{X}] & \cdots & E[\varepsilon_1\varepsilon_n \mid \mathbf{X}] \\ E[\varepsilon_2\varepsilon_1 \mid \mathbf{X}] & E[\varepsilon_2\varepsilon_2 \mid \mathbf{X}] & \cdots & E[\varepsilon_2\varepsilon_n \mid \mathbf{X}] \\ \vdots & \vdots & \vdots & \vdots \\ E[\varepsilon_n\varepsilon_1 \mid \mathbf{X}] & E[\varepsilon_n\varepsilon_2 \mid \mathbf{X}] & \cdots & E[\varepsilon_n\varepsilon_n \mid \mathbf{X}] \end{bmatrix}$$

$$= \begin{bmatrix} \sigma^2 & 0 & \cdots & 0 \\ 0 & \sigma^2 & \cdots & 0 \\ & & \vdots & \\ 0 & 0 & \cdots & \sigma^2 \end{bmatrix},$$

which we summarize in Assumption 4:

$$\boxed{\text{ASSUMPTION:} \quad E[\boldsymbol{\varepsilon}\boldsymbol{\varepsilon}' \mid \mathbf{X}] = \sigma^2 \mathbf{I}.} \tag{2-9}$$

By using the variance decomposition formula in (B-69), we find

$$\text{Var}[\boldsymbol{\varepsilon}] = E[\text{Var}[\boldsymbol{\varepsilon} \mid \mathbf{X}]] + \text{Var}[E[\boldsymbol{\varepsilon} \mid \mathbf{X}]] = \sigma^2 \mathbf{I}.$$

Once again, we should emphasize that this assumption describes the information about the variances and covariances among the disturbances that is provided by the independent variables. For the present, we assume that there is none. We will also drop this assumption later when we enrich the regression model. We are also assuming that the disturbances themselves provide no information about the variances and covariances. Although a minor issue at this point, it will become crucial in our treatment of time-series applications. Models such as $\text{Var}[\varepsilon_t \mid \varepsilon_{t-1}] = \sigma^2 + \alpha\varepsilon_{t-1}^2$, a "GARCH" model (see Chapter 19), do not violate our conditional variance assumption, but do assume that $\text{Var}[\varepsilon_t \mid \varepsilon_{t-1}] \neq \text{Var}[\varepsilon_t]$.

Disturbances that meet the twin assumptions of homoscedasticity and nonautocorrelation are sometimes called **spherical disturbances.**[4]

### 2.3.5 DATA GENERATING PROCESS FOR THE REGRESSORS

It is common to assume that $\mathbf{x}_i$ is nonstochastic, as it would be in an experimental situation. Here the analyst chooses the values of the regressors and then observes $y_i$. This process might apply, for example, in an agricultural experiment in which $y_i$ is yield and $\mathbf{x}_i$ is fertilizer concentration and water applied. The assumption of **nonstochastic regressors** at this point would be a mathematical convenience. With it, we could use

---

[4]The term will describe the multivariate normal distribution; see (B-95). If $\boldsymbol{\Sigma} = \sigma^2 \mathbf{I}$ in the multivariate normal density, then the equation $f(\mathbf{x}) = c$ is the formula for a "ball" centered at $\boldsymbol{\mu}$ with radius $\sigma$ in $n$-dimensional space. The name *spherical* is used whether or not the normal distribution is assumed; sometimes the "spherical normal" distribution is assumed explicitly.

the results of elementary statistics to obtain our results by treating the vector $\mathbf{x}_i$ simply as a known constant in the probability distribution of $y_i$. With this simplification, Assumptions A3 and A4 would be made unconditional and the counterparts would now simply state that the probability distribution of $\varepsilon_i$ involves none of the constants in $\mathbf{X}$.

Social scientists are almost never able to analyze experimental data, and relatively few of their models are built around nonrandom regressors. Clearly, for example, in any model of the macroeconomy, it would be difficult to defend such an asymmetric treatment of aggregate data. Realistically, we have to allow the data on $\mathbf{x}_i$ to be random the same as $y_i$, so an alternative formulation is to assume that $\mathbf{x}_i$ is a random vector and our formal assumption concerns the nature of the random process that produces $\mathbf{x}_i$. If $\mathbf{x}_i$ is taken to be a random vector, then Assumptions 1 through 4 become a statement about the joint distribution of $y_i$ and $\mathbf{x}_i$. The precise nature of the regressor and how we view the sampling process will be a major determinant of our derivation of the statistical properties of our estimators and test statistics. In the end, the crucial assumption is Assumption 3, the uncorrelatedness of $\mathbf{X}$ and $\boldsymbol{\varepsilon}$. Now, we do note that this alternative is not completely satisfactory either, since $\mathbf{X}$ may well contain nonstochastic elements, including a constant, a time trend, and dummy variables that mark specific episodes in time. This makes for an ambiguous conclusion, but there is a straightforward and economically useful way out of it. We will assume that $\mathbf{X}$ can be a mixture of constants and random variables, and the mean and variance of $\varepsilon_i$ are both independent of all elements of $\mathbf{X}$.

$$\boxed{\text{ASSUMPTION:} \quad \mathbf{X} \text{ may be fixed or random.}} \qquad \textbf{(2-10)}$$

### 2.3.6 NORMALITY

It is convenient to assume that the disturbances are **normally distributed,** with zero mean and constant variance. That is, we add normality of the distribution to Assumptions 3 and 4.

$$\boxed{\text{ASSUMPTION:} \quad \boldsymbol{\varepsilon} \mid \mathbf{X} \sim N[\mathbf{0}, \sigma^2 \mathbf{I}].} \qquad \textbf{(2-11)}$$

In view of our description of the source of $\boldsymbol{\varepsilon}$, the conditions of the central limit theorem will generally apply, at least approximately, and the normality assumption will be reasonable in most settings. A useful implication of Assumption 6 is that it implies that observations on $\varepsilon_i$ are statistically independent as well as uncorrelated. [See the third point in Section B.9, (B-97) and (B-99).] **Normality** is often viewed as an unnecessary and possibly inappropriate addition to the regression model. Except in those cases in which some alternative distribution is explicitly assumed, as in the stochastic frontier model discussed in Section 16.9.5.a, the normality assumption is probably quite reasonable.

Normality is not necessary to obtain many of the results we use in multiple regression analysis, although it will enable us to obtain several exact statistical results. It does prove useful in constructing test statistics, as shown in Section 4.7. Later, it will be possible to relax this assumption and retain most of the statistical results we obtain here. (See Sections 4.9 and 5.4.)

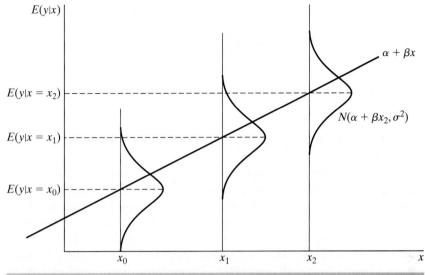

**FIGURE 2.2** The Classical Regression Model.

## 2.4 SUMMARY AND CONCLUSIONS

This chapter has framed the linear regression model, the basic platform for model building in econometrics. The assumptions of the classical regression model are summarized in Figure 2.2, which shows the two-variable case.

### Key Terms and Concepts

- Autocorrelation
- Constant elasticity
- Covariate
- Dependent variable
- Deterministic relationship
- Disturbance
- Exogeneity
- Explained variable
- Explanatory variable
- Flexible functional form
- Full rank
- Heteroscedasticity
- Homoscedasticity
- Identification condition
- Independent variable
- Linear regression model
- Loglinear model
- Multiple linear regression model
- Nonautocorrelation
- Nonstochastic regressors
- Normality
- Normally distributed
- Population regression equation
- Regressand
- Regression
- Regressor
- Second-order effects
- Semilog
- Spherical disturbances
- Translog model

# 3

# LEAST SQUARES

## 3.1 INTRODUCTION

Chapter 2 defined the linear regression model as a set of characteristics of the population that underlies an observed sample of data. There are a number of different approaches to estimation of the parameters of the model. For a variety of practical and theoretical reasons that we will explore as we progress through the next several chapters, the method of least squares has long been the most popular. Moreover, in most cases in which some other estimation method is found to be preferable, least squares remains the benchmark approach, and often, the preferred method ultimately amounts to a modification of least squares. In this chapter, we begin the analysis of this important set of results by presenting a useful set of algebraic tools.

## 3.2 LEAST SQUARES REGRESSION

The unknown parameters of the stochastic relation $y_i = \mathbf{x}_i'\boldsymbol{\beta} + \varepsilon_i$ are the objects of estimation. It is necessary to distinguish between population quantities, such as $\boldsymbol{\beta}$ and $\varepsilon_i$, and sample estimates of them, denoted $\mathbf{b}$ and $e_i$. The **population regression** is $E[y_i \mid \mathbf{x}_i] = \mathbf{x}_i'\boldsymbol{\beta}$, whereas our estimate of $E[y_i \mid \mathbf{x}_i]$ is denoted

$$\hat{y}_i = \mathbf{x}_i'\mathbf{b}.$$

The **disturbance** associated with the $i$th data point is

$$\varepsilon_i = y_i - \mathbf{x}_i'\boldsymbol{\beta}.$$

For any value of **b**, we shall estimate $\varepsilon_i$ with the **residual**

$$e_i = y_i - \mathbf{x}_i'\mathbf{b}.$$

From the definitions,

$$y_i = \mathbf{x}_i'\boldsymbol{\beta} + \varepsilon_i = \mathbf{x}_i'\mathbf{b} + e_i.$$

These equations are summarized for the two variable regression in Figure 3.1.

The **population quantity** $\boldsymbol{\beta}$ is a vector of unknown parameters of the probability distribution of $y_i$ whose values we hope to estimate with our sample data, $(y_i, \mathbf{x}_i), i = 1, \ldots, n$. This is a problem of statistical inference. It is instructive, however, to begin by considering the purely algebraic problem of choosing a vector **b** so that the fitted line $\mathbf{x}_i'\mathbf{b}$ is close to the data points. The measure of closeness constitutes a **fitting criterion.**

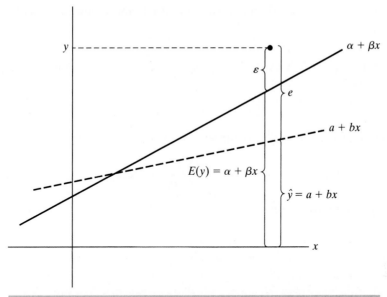

**FIGURE 3.1** Population and Sample Regression.

Although numerous candidates have been suggested, the one used most frequently is **least squares.**[1]

### 3.2.1 THE LEAST SQUARES COEFFICIENT VECTOR

The least squares coefficient vector minimizes the sum of squared residuals:

$$\sum_{i=1}^{n} e_{i0}^2 = \sum_{i=1}^{n} (y_i - \mathbf{x}_i' \mathbf{b}_0)^2, \tag{3-1}$$

where $\mathbf{b}_0$ denotes the choice for the coefficient vector. In matrix terms, minimizing the sum of squares in (3-1) requires us to choose $\mathbf{b}_0$ to

$$\text{Minimize}_{\mathbf{b}_0} \ S(\mathbf{b}_0) = \mathbf{e}_0' \mathbf{e}_0 = (\mathbf{y} - \mathbf{X}\mathbf{b}_0)'(\mathbf{y} - \mathbf{X}\mathbf{b}_0). \tag{3-2}$$

Expanding this gives

$$\mathbf{e}_0' \mathbf{e}_0 = \mathbf{y}'\mathbf{y} - \mathbf{b}_0' \mathbf{X}'\mathbf{y} - \mathbf{y}'\mathbf{X}\mathbf{b}_0 + \mathbf{b}_0' \mathbf{X}'\mathbf{X}\mathbf{b}_0 \tag{3-3}$$

or

$$S(\mathbf{b}_0) = \mathbf{y}'\mathbf{y} - 2\mathbf{y}'\mathbf{X}\mathbf{b}_0 + \mathbf{b}_0' \mathbf{X}'\mathbf{X}\mathbf{b}_0.$$

The necessary condition for a minimum is

$$\frac{\partial S(\mathbf{b}_0)}{\partial \mathbf{b}_0} = -2\mathbf{X}'\mathbf{y} + 2\mathbf{X}'\mathbf{X}\mathbf{b}_0 = \mathbf{0}. \tag{3-4}$$

---

[1]We have yet to establish that the practical approach of fitting the line as closely as possible to the data by least squares leads to estimates with good statistical properties. This makes intuitive sense and is, indeed, the case. We shall return to the statistical issues in Chapter 4.

Let **b** be the solution. Then **b** satisfies the **least squares normal equations,**

$$\mathbf{X'Xb} = \mathbf{X'y}. \tag{3-5}$$

If the inverse of **X'X** exists, which follows from the full column rank assumption (Assumption A2 in Section 2.3), then the solution is

$$\mathbf{b} = (\mathbf{X'X})^{-1}\mathbf{X'y}. \tag{3-6}$$

For this solution to minimize the sum of squares,

$$\frac{\partial^2 S(\mathbf{b}_0)}{\partial \mathbf{b}_0 \, \partial \mathbf{b}_0'} = 2\mathbf{X'X}$$

must be a positive definite matrix. Let $q = \mathbf{c'X'Xc}$ for some arbitrary nonzero vector **c.** Then

$$q = \mathbf{v'v} = \sum_{i=1}^{n} v_i^2, \quad \text{where } \mathbf{v} = \mathbf{Xc}.$$

Unless every element of **v** is zero, $q$ is positive. But if **v** could be zero, then **v** would be a linear combination of the columns of **X** that equals **0**, which contradicts the assumption that **X** has full column rank. Since **c** is arbitrary, $q$ is positive for every nonzero **c**, which establishes that $2\mathbf{X'X}$ is positive definite. Therefore, if **X** has full column rank, then the least squares solution **b** is unique and minimizes the sum of squared residuals.

### 3.2.2 APPLICATION: AN INVESTMENT EQUATION

To illustrate the computations in a multiple regression, we consider an example based on the macroeconomic data in Appendix Table F3.1. To estimate an investment equation, we first convert the investment and GNP series in Table F3.1 to real terms by dividing them by the CPI, and then scale the two series so that they are measured in trillions of dollars. The other variables in the regression are a time trend $(1, 2, \ldots)$, an interest rate, and the rate of inflation computed as the percentage change in the CPI. These produce the data matrices listed in Table 3.1. Consider first a regression of real investment on a constant, the time trend, and real GNP, which correspond to $x_1$, $x_2$, and $x_3$. (For reasons to be discussed in Chapter 22, this is probably not a well-specified equation for these macroeconomic variables. It will suffice for a simple numerical example, however.) Inserting the specific variables of the example, we have

$$
\begin{aligned}
b_1 n \quad &+ b_2 \Sigma_i T_i \quad + b_3 \Sigma_i G_i \quad = \Sigma_i Y_i, \\
b_1 \Sigma_i T_i &+ b_2 \Sigma_i T_i^2 \quad + b_3 \Sigma_i T_i G_i = \Sigma_i T_i Y_i, \\
b_1 \Sigma_i G_i &+ b_2 \Sigma_i T_i G_i + b_3 \Sigma_i G_i^2 \quad = \Sigma_i G_i Y_i.
\end{aligned}
$$

A solution can be obtained by first dividing the first equation by $n$ and rearranging it to obtain

$$
\begin{aligned}
b_1 &= \overline{Y} - b_2 \overline{T} - b_3 \overline{G} \\
&= 0.20333 - b_2 \times 8 - b_3 \times 1.2873.
\end{aligned} \tag{3-7}
$$

**TABLE 3.1**   Data Matrices

| Real Investment (Y) | Constant (1) | Trend (T) | Real GNP (G) | Interest Rate (R) | Inflation Rate (P) |
|---|---|---|---|---|---|
| 0.161 | 1 | 1 | 1.058 | 5.16 | 4.40 |
| 0.172 | 1 | 2 | 1.088 | 5.87 | 5.15 |
| 0.158 | 1 | 3 | 1.086 | 5.95 | 5.37 |
| 0.173 | 1 | 4 | 1.122 | 4.88 | 4.99 |
| 0.195 | 1 | 5 | 1.186 | 4.50 | 4.16 |
| 0.217 | 1 | 6 | 1.254 | 6.44 | 5.75 |
| 0.199 | 1 | 7 | 1.246 | 7.83 | 8.82 |
| y = 0.163 | X = 1 | 8 | 1.232 | 6.25 | 9.31 |
| 0.195 | 1 | 9 | 1.298 | 5.50 | 5.21 |
| 0.231 | 1 | 10 | 1.370 | 5.46 | 5.83 |
| 0.257 | 1 | 11 | 1.439 | 7.46 | 7.40 |
| 0.259 | 1 | 12 | 1.479 | 10.28 | 8.64 |
| 0.225 | 1 | 13 | 1.474 | 11.77 | 9.31 |
| 0.241 | 1 | 14 | 1.503 | 13.42 | 9.44 |
| 0.204 | 1 | 15 | 1.475 | 11.02 | 5.99 |

*Note:* Subsequent results are based on these values. Slightly different results are obtained if the raw data in Table F3.1 are input to the computer program and transformed internally.

Insert this solution in the second and third equations, and rearrange terms again to yield a set of two equations:

$$b_2 \Sigma_i (T_i - \overline{T})^2 \qquad + b_3 \Sigma_i (T_i - \overline{T})(G_i - \overline{G}) = \Sigma_i (T_i - \overline{T})(Y_i - \overline{Y}),$$
$$b_2 \Sigma_i (T_i - \overline{T})(G_i - \overline{G}) + b_3 \Sigma_i (G_i - \overline{G})^2 \qquad = \Sigma_i (G_i - \overline{G})(Y_i - \overline{Y}). \tag{3-8}$$

This result shows the nature of the solution for the slopes, which can be computed from the sums of squares and cross products of the deviations of the variables. Letting lowercase letters indicate variables measured as deviations from the sample means, we find that the least squares solutions for $b_2$ and $b_3$ are

$$b_2 = \frac{\Sigma_i t_i y_i \Sigma_i g_i^2 - \Sigma_i g_i y_i \Sigma_i t_i g_i}{\Sigma_i t_i^2 \Sigma_i g_i^2 - (\Sigma_i g_i t_i)^2} = \frac{1.6040(0.359609) - 0.066196(9.82)}{280(0.359609) - (9.82)^2} = -0.0171984,$$

$$b_3 = \frac{\Sigma_i g_i y_i \Sigma_i t_i^2 - \Sigma_i t_i y_i \Sigma_i t_i g_i}{\Sigma_i t_i^2 \Sigma_i g_i^2 - (\Sigma_i g_i t_i)^2} = \frac{0.066196(280) - 1.6040(9.82)}{280(0.359609) - (9.82)^2} = 0.653723.$$

With these solutions in hand, the intercept can now be computed using (3-7); $b_1 = -0.500639$.

Suppose that we just regressed investment on the constant and GNP, omitting the time trend. At least some of the correlation we observe in the data will be explainable because both investment and real GNP have an obvious time trend. Consider how this shows up in the regression computation. Denoting by "$b_{yx}$" the slope in the simple, **bivariate regression** of variable $y$ on a constant and the variable $x$, we find that the slope in this reduced regression would be

$$b_{yg} = \frac{\Sigma_i g_i y_i}{\Sigma_i g_i^2} = 0.184078. \tag{3-9}$$

Now divide both the numerator and denominator in the expression for $b_3$ by $\Sigma_i t_i^2 \Sigma_i g_i^2$. By manipulating it a bit and using the definition of the sample correlation between $G$ and $T$, $r_{gt}^2 = (\Sigma_i g_i t_i)^2 / (\Sigma_i g_i^2 \Sigma_i t_i^2)$, and defining $b_{yt}$ and $b_{tg}$ likewise, we obtain

$$b_{yg\cdot t} = \frac{b_{yg}}{1 - r_{gt}^2} - \frac{b_{yt} b_{tg}}{1 - r_{gt}^2} = 0.653723. \tag{3-10}$$

(The notation "$b_{yg\cdot t}$" used on the left-hand side is interpreted to mean the slope in the regression of $y$ on $g$ "in the presence of $t$.") The slope in the **multiple regression** differs from that in the simple regression by including a correction that accounts for the influence of the additional variable $t$ on both $Y$ and $G$. For a striking example of this effect, in the simple regression of real investment on a time trend, $b_{yt} = 1.604/280 = 0.0057286$, a positive number that reflects the upward trend apparent in the data. But, in the multiple regression, after we account for the influence of GNP on real investment, the slope on the time trend is $-0.0171984$, indicating instead a downward trend. The general result for a three-variable regression in which $x_1$ is a constant term is

$$b_{y2\cdot3} = \frac{b_{y2} - b_{y3} b_{32}}{1 - r_{23}^2}. \tag{3-11}$$

It is clear from this expression that the magnitudes of $b_{y2\cdot3}$ and $b_{y2}$ can be quite different. They need not even have the same sign.

As a final observation, note what becomes of $b_{yg\cdot t}$ in (3-10) if $r_{gt}^2$ equals zero. The first term becomes $b_{yg}$, whereas the second becomes zero. (If $G$ and $T$ are not correlated, then the slope in the regression of $T$ on $G$, $b_{tg}$, is zero.) Therefore, we conclude the following.

---

**THEOREM 3.1  Orthogonal Regression**
*If the variables in a multiple regression are not correlated (i.e., are orthogonal), then the multiple regression slopes are the same as the slopes in the individual simple regressions.*

---

In practice, you will never actually compute a multiple regression by hand or with a calculator. For a regression with more than three variables, the tools of matrix algebra are indispensable (as is a computer). Consider, for example, an enlarged model of investment that includes—in addition to the constant, time trend, and GNP—an interest rate and the rate of inflation. Least squares requires the simultaneous solution of five normal equations. Letting **X** and **y** denote the full data matrices shown previously, the normal equations in (3-5) are

$$\begin{bmatrix} 15.000 & 120.00 & 19.310 & 111.79 & 99.770 \\ 120.000 & 1240.0 & 164.30 & 1035.9 & 875.60 \\ 19.310 & 164.30 & 25.218 & 148.98 & 131.22 \\ 111.79 & 1035.9 & 148.98 & 953.86 & 799.02 \\ 99.770 & 875.60 & 131.22 & 799.02 & 716.67 \end{bmatrix} \begin{bmatrix} b_1 \\ b_2 \\ b_3 \\ b_4 \\ b_5 \end{bmatrix} = \begin{bmatrix} 3.0500 \\ 26.004 \\ 3.9926 \\ 23.521 \\ 20.732 \end{bmatrix}.$$

The solution is

$$\mathbf{b} = (\mathbf{X}'\mathbf{X})^{-1}\mathbf{X}'\mathbf{y} = (-0.50907, -0.01658, 0.67038, -0.002326, -0.00009401)'.$$

### 3.2.3   ALGEBRAIC ASPECTS OF THE LEAST SQUARES SOLUTION

The normal equations are

$$\mathbf{X}'\mathbf{X}\mathbf{b} - \mathbf{X}'\mathbf{y} = -\mathbf{X}'(\mathbf{y} - \mathbf{X}\mathbf{b}) = -\mathbf{X}'\mathbf{e} = \mathbf{0}. \qquad (3\text{-}12)$$

Hence, for every column $\mathbf{x}_k$ of $\mathbf{X}$, $\mathbf{x}'_k\mathbf{e} = 0$. If the first column of $\mathbf{X}$ is a column of 1s, then there are three implications.

1. *The least squares residuals sum to zero.* This implication follows from $\mathbf{x}'_1\mathbf{e} = \mathbf{i}'\mathbf{e} = \Sigma_i e_i = 0$.
2. *The regression hyperplane passes through the point of means of the data.* The first normal equation implies that $\bar{y} = \bar{\mathbf{x}}'\mathbf{b}$.
3. *The mean of the fitted values from the regression equals the mean of the actual values.* This implication follows from point 1 because the fitted values are just $\hat{\mathbf{y}} = \mathbf{X}\mathbf{b}$.

It is important to note that none of these results need hold if the regression does not contain a constant term.

### 3.2.4   PROJECTION

The vector of least squares residuals is

$$\mathbf{e} = \mathbf{y} - \mathbf{X}\mathbf{b}. \qquad (3\text{-}13)$$

Inserting the result in (3-6) for $\mathbf{b}$ gives

$$\mathbf{e} = \mathbf{y} - \mathbf{X}(\mathbf{X}'\mathbf{X})^{-1}\mathbf{X}'\mathbf{y} = (\mathbf{I} - \mathbf{X}(\mathbf{X}'\mathbf{X})^{-1}\mathbf{X}')\mathbf{y} = \mathbf{M}\mathbf{y}. \qquad (3\text{-}14)$$

The $n \times n$ matrix $\mathbf{M}$ defined in (3-14) is fundamental in regression analysis. You can easily show that $\mathbf{M}$ is both symmetric ($\mathbf{M} = \mathbf{M}'$) and idempotent ($\mathbf{M} = \mathbf{M}^2$). In view of (3-13), we can interpret $\mathbf{M}$ as a matrix that produces the vector of least squares residuals in the regression of $\mathbf{y}$ on $\mathbf{X}$ when it premultiplies any vector $\mathbf{y}$. (It will be convenient later on to refer to this matrix as a "**residual maker.**") It follows that

$$\mathbf{M}\mathbf{X} = \mathbf{0}. \qquad (3\text{-}15)$$

One way to interpret this result is that if $\mathbf{X}$ is regressed on $\mathbf{X}$, a perfect fit will result and the residuals will be zero.

Finally, (3-13) implies that $\mathbf{y} = \mathbf{X}\mathbf{b} + \mathbf{e}$, which is the sample analog to (2-3). (See Figure 3.1 as well.) The least squares results partition $\mathbf{y}$ into two parts, the fitted values $\hat{\mathbf{y}} = \mathbf{X}\mathbf{b}$ and the residuals $\mathbf{e}$. [See Section A.3.7, especially (A-54).] Since $\mathbf{M}\mathbf{X} = \mathbf{0}$, these two parts are orthogonal. Now, given (3-13),

$$\hat{\mathbf{y}} = \mathbf{y} - \mathbf{e} = (\mathbf{I} - \mathbf{M})\mathbf{y} = \mathbf{X}(\mathbf{X}'\mathbf{X})^{-1}\mathbf{X}'\mathbf{y} = \mathbf{P}\mathbf{y}. \qquad (3\text{-}16)$$

The matrix $\mathbf{P}$, which is also symmetric and idempotent, is a **projection matrix.** It is the matrix formed from $\mathbf{X}$ such that when a vector $\mathbf{y}$ is premultiplied by $\mathbf{P}$, the result is the fitted values in the least squares regression of $\mathbf{y}$ on $\mathbf{X}$. This is also the **projection** of the vector $\mathbf{y}$ into the column space of $\mathbf{X}$. (See Sections A3.5 and A3.7.) By multiplying it out, you will find that, like $\mathbf{M}$, $\mathbf{P}$ is symmetric and idempotent. Given the earlier results, it also follows that $\mathbf{M}$ and $\mathbf{P}$ are orthogonal;

$$\mathbf{PM} = \mathbf{MP} = \mathbf{0}.$$

Finally, as might be expected from (3-15)

$$\mathbf{PX} = \mathbf{X}.$$

As a consequence of (3-14) and (3-16), we can see that least squares partitions the vector $\mathbf{y}$ into two orthogonal parts,

$$\mathbf{y} = \mathbf{Py} + \mathbf{My} = \textbf{projection} + \textbf{residual}.$$

The result is illustrated in Figure 3.2 for the two variable case. The gray shaded plane is the column space of $\mathbf{X}$. The projection and residual are the orthogonal dotted rays. We can also see the Pythagorean theorem at work in the sums of squares,

$$\mathbf{y'y} = \mathbf{y'P'Py} + \mathbf{y'M'My}$$
$$= \mathbf{\hat{y}'\hat{y}} + \mathbf{e'e}$$

In manipulating equations involving least squares results, the following equivalent expressions for the sum of squared residuals are often useful:

$$\mathbf{e'e} = \mathbf{y'M'My} = \mathbf{y'My} = \mathbf{y'e} = \mathbf{e'y},$$
$$\mathbf{e'e} = \mathbf{y'y} - \mathbf{b'X'Xb} = \mathbf{y'y} - \mathbf{b'X'y} = \mathbf{y'y} - \mathbf{y'Xb}.$$

**FIGURE 3.2**    Projection of $\mathbf{y}$ into the Column Space of $\mathbf{X}$.

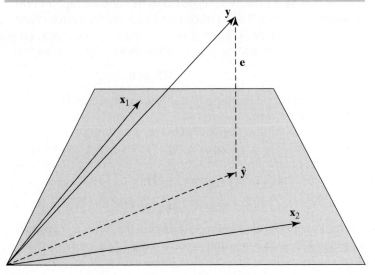

### 3.3 PARTITIONED REGRESSION AND PARTIAL REGRESSION

It is common to specify a multiple regression model when, in fact, interest centers on only one or a subset of the full set of variables. Consider the earnings equation discussed in Example 2.2. Although we are primarily interested in the association of earnings and education, age is, of necessity, included in the model. The question we consider here is what computations are involved in obtaining, in isolation, the coefficients of a subset of the variables in a multiple regression (for example, the coefficient of education in the aforementioned regression).

Suppose that the regression involves two sets of variables, $\mathbf{X}_1$ and $\mathbf{X}_2$. Thus,

$$\mathbf{y} = \mathbf{X}\boldsymbol{\beta} + \boldsymbol{\varepsilon} = \mathbf{X}_1\boldsymbol{\beta}_1 + \mathbf{X}_2\boldsymbol{\beta}_2 + \boldsymbol{\varepsilon}.$$

What is the algebraic solution for $\mathbf{b}_2$? The **normal equations** are

$$\begin{matrix} (1) \\ (2) \end{matrix} \quad \begin{bmatrix} \mathbf{X}_1'\mathbf{X}_1 & \mathbf{X}_1'\mathbf{X}_2 \\ \mathbf{X}_2'\mathbf{X}_1 & \mathbf{X}_2'\mathbf{X}_2 \end{bmatrix} \begin{bmatrix} \mathbf{b}_1 \\ \mathbf{b}_2 \end{bmatrix} = \begin{bmatrix} \mathbf{X}_1'\mathbf{y} \\ \mathbf{X}_2'\mathbf{y} \end{bmatrix}. \tag{3-17}$$

A solution can be obtained by using the partitioned inverse matrix of (A-74). Alternatively, (1) and (2) in (3-17) can be manipulated directly to solve for $\mathbf{b}_2$. We first solve (1) for $\mathbf{b}_1$:

$$\mathbf{b}_1 = (\mathbf{X}_1'\mathbf{X}_1)^{-1}\mathbf{X}_1'\mathbf{y} - (\mathbf{X}_1'\mathbf{X}_1)^{-1}\mathbf{X}_1'\mathbf{X}_2\mathbf{b}_2 = (\mathbf{X}_1'\mathbf{X}_1)^{-1}\mathbf{X}_1'(\mathbf{y} - \mathbf{X}_2\mathbf{b}_2). \tag{3-18}$$

This solution states that $\mathbf{b}_1$ is the set of coefficients in the regression of $\mathbf{y}$ on $\mathbf{X}_1$, minus a correction vector. We digress briefly to examine an important result embedded in (3-18). Suppose that $\mathbf{X}_1'\mathbf{X}_2 = \mathbf{0}$. Then, $\mathbf{b}_1 = (\mathbf{X}_1'\mathbf{X}_1)^{-1}\mathbf{X}_1'\mathbf{y}$, which is simply the coefficient vector in the regression of $\mathbf{y}$ on $\mathbf{X}_1$. The general result, which we have just proved, is the following theorem.

> ### THEOREM 3.2 Orthogonal Partitioned Regression
> *In the multiple linear least squares regression of $\mathbf{y}$ on two sets of variables $\mathbf{X}_1$ and $\mathbf{X}_2$, if the two sets of variables are orthogonal, then the separate coefficient vectors can be obtained by separate regressions of $\mathbf{y}$ on $\mathbf{X}_1$ alone and $\mathbf{y}$ on $\mathbf{X}_2$ alone.*

Note that Theorem 3.2 encompasses Theorem 3.1.

Now, inserting (3-18) in equation (2) of (3-17) produces

$$\mathbf{X}_2'\mathbf{X}_1(\mathbf{X}_1'\mathbf{X}_1)^{-1}\mathbf{X}_1'\mathbf{y} - \mathbf{X}_2'\mathbf{X}_1(\mathbf{X}_1'\mathbf{X}_1)^{-1}\mathbf{X}_1'\mathbf{X}_2\mathbf{b}_2 + \mathbf{X}_2'\mathbf{X}_2\mathbf{b}_2 = \mathbf{X}_2'\mathbf{y}.$$

After collecting terms, the solution is

$$\mathbf{b}_2 = \left[\mathbf{X}_2'(\mathbf{I} - \mathbf{X}_1(\mathbf{X}_1'\mathbf{X}_1)^{-1}\mathbf{X}_1')\mathbf{X}_2\right]^{-1}\left[\mathbf{X}_2'(\mathbf{I} - \mathbf{X}_1(\mathbf{X}_1'\mathbf{X}_1)^{-1}\mathbf{X}_1')\mathbf{y}\right]$$

$$= (\mathbf{X}_2'\mathbf{M}_1\mathbf{X}_2)^{-1}(\mathbf{X}_2'\mathbf{M}_1\mathbf{y}). \tag{3-19}$$

The matrix appearing in the parentheses inside each set of square brackets is the "residual maker" defined in (3-14), in this case defined for a regression on the columns of $\mathbf{X}_1$.

Thus, $\mathbf{M}_1\mathbf{X}_2$ is a matrix of residuals; each column of $\mathbf{M}_1\mathbf{X}_2$ is a vector of residuals in the regression of the corresponding column of $\mathbf{X}_2$ on the variables in $\mathbf{X}_1$. By exploiting the fact that $\mathbf{M}_1$, like $\mathbf{M}$, is idempotent, we can rewrite (3-19) as

$$\mathbf{b}_2 = (\mathbf{X}_2^{*\prime}\mathbf{X}_2^*)^{-1}\mathbf{X}_2^{*\prime}\mathbf{y}^*, \tag{3-20}$$

where

$$\mathbf{X}_2^* = \mathbf{M}_1\mathbf{X}_2 \quad \text{and} \quad \mathbf{y}^* = \mathbf{M}_1\mathbf{y}.$$

This result is fundamental in regression analysis.

---

**THEOREM 3.3**  Frisch–Waugh (1933)–Lovell (1963) Theorem

*In the linear least squares regression of vector $\mathbf{y}$ on two sets of variables, $\mathbf{X}_1$ and $\mathbf{X}_2$, the subvector $\mathbf{b}_2$ is the set of coefficients obtained when the residuals from a regression of $\mathbf{y}$ on $\mathbf{X}_1$ alone are regressed on the set of residuals obtained when each column of $\mathbf{X}_2$ is regressed on $\mathbf{X}_1$.*

---

This process is commonly called **partialing out** or **netting out** the effect of $\mathbf{X}_1$. For this reason, the coefficients in a multiple regression are often called the **partial regression coefficients.** The application of this theorem to the computation of a single coefficient as suggested at the beginning of this section is detailed in the following: Consider the regression of $\mathbf{y}$ on a set of variables $\mathbf{X}$ and an additional variable $\mathbf{z}$. Denote the coefficients $\mathbf{b}$ and $c$.

---

**COROLLARY 3.3.1**  Individual Regression Coefficients

*The coefficient on $\mathbf{z}$ in a multiple regression of $\mathbf{y}$ on $\mathbf{W} = [\mathbf{X}, \mathbf{z}]$ is computed as $c = (\mathbf{z}'\mathbf{Mz})^{-1}(\mathbf{z}'\mathbf{My}) = (\mathbf{z}^{*\prime}\mathbf{z}^*)^{-1}\mathbf{z}^{*\prime}\mathbf{y}^*$ where $\mathbf{z}^*$ and $\mathbf{y}^*$ are the residual vectors from least squares regressions of $\mathbf{z}$ and $\mathbf{y}$ on $\mathbf{X}$; $\mathbf{z}^* = \mathbf{Mz}$ and $\mathbf{y}^* = \mathbf{My}$ where $\mathbf{M}$ is defined in (3-14).*

---

In terms of Example 2.2, we could obtain the coefficient on education in the multiple regression by first regressing earnings and education on age (or age and age squared) and then using the residuals from these regressions in a simple regression. In a classic application of this latter observation, Frisch and Waugh (1933) (who are credited with the result) noted that in a time-series setting, the same results were obtained whether a regression was fitted with a time-trend variable or the data were first "detrended" by netting out the effect of time, as noted earlier, and using just the detrended data in a simple regression.[2]

As an application of these results, consider the case in which $\mathbf{X}_1$ is $\mathbf{i}$, a column of 1s in the first column of $\mathbf{X}$. The solution for $\mathbf{b}_2$ in this case will then be the slopes in a regression with a constant term. The coefficient in a regression of any variable $\mathbf{z}$ on $\mathbf{i}$ is

---

[2]Recall our earlier investment example.

$[\mathbf{i}'\mathbf{i}]^{-1}\mathbf{i}'\mathbf{z} = \bar{z}$, the fitted values are $\mathbf{i}\bar{z}$, and the residuals are $z_i - \bar{z}$. When we apply this to our previous results, we find the following.

---

### COROLLARY 3.3.2    Regression with a Constant Term

*The slopes in a multiple regression that contains a constant term are obtained by transforming the data to deviations from their means and then regressing the variable y in deviation form on the explanatory variables, also in deviation form.*

---

[We used this result in (3-8).] Having obtained the coefficients on $\mathbf{X}_2$, how can we recover the coefficients on $\mathbf{X}_1$ (the constant term)? One way is to repeat the exercise while reversing the roles of $\mathbf{X}_1$ and $\mathbf{X}_2$. But there is an easier way. We have already solved for $\mathbf{b}_2$. Therefore, we can use (3-18) in a solution for $\mathbf{b}_1$. If $\mathbf{X}_1$ is just a column of 1s, then the first of these produces the familiar result

$$b_1 = \bar{y} - \bar{x}_2 b_2 - \cdots - \bar{x}_K b_K \tag{3-21}$$

[which is used in (3-7)].

## 3.4    PARTIAL REGRESSION AND PARTIAL CORRELATION COEFFICIENTS

The use of multiple regression involves a conceptual experiment that we might not be able to carry out in practice, the *ceteris paribus* analysis familiar in economics. To pursue Example 2.2, a regression equation relating earnings to age and education enables us to do the conceptual experiment of comparing the earnings of two individuals of the same age with different education levels, *even if the sample contains no such pair of individuals.* It is this characteristic of the regression that is implied by the term **partial regression coefficients.** The way we obtain this result, as we have seen, is first to regress income and education on age and then to compute the residuals from this regression. By construction, age will not have any power in explaining variation in these residuals. Therefore, any correlation between income and education after this "purging" is independent of (or after removing the effect of) age.

The same principle can be applied to the correlation between two variables. To continue our example, to what extent can we assert that this correlation reflects a direct relationship rather than that both income and education tend, on average, to rise as individuals become older? To find out, we would use a **partial correlation coefficient,** which is computed along the same lines as the partial regression coefficient. In the context of our example, the partial correlation coefficient between income and education, controlling for the effect of age, is obtained as follows:

1.  $y_*$ = the residuals in a regression of income on a constant and age.
2.  $z_*$ = the residuals in a regression of education on a constant and age.
3.  The partial correlation $r_{yz}^*$ is the simple correlation between $y_*$ and $z_*$.

This calculation might seem to require a formidable amount of computation. There is, however, a convenient shortcut. Once the multiple regression is computed, the $t$ ratio in (4-13) and (4-14) for testing the hypothesis that the coefficient equals zero (e.g., the last column of Table 4.2) can be used to compute

$$r_{yz}^{*2} = \frac{t_z^2}{t_z^2 + \text{degrees of freedom}}. \tag{3-22}$$

The proof of this less than perfectly intuitive result will be useful to illustrate some results on partitioned regression and to put into context two very useful results from least squares algebra. As in Corollary 3.3.1, let $\mathbf{W}$ denote the $n \times (K+1)$ regressor matrix $[\mathbf{X}, \mathbf{z}]$ and let $\mathbf{M} = \mathbf{I} - \mathbf{X}(\mathbf{X'X})^{-1}\mathbf{X'}$. We assume that there is a constant term in $\mathbf{X}$, so that the vectors of residuals $\mathbf{y}_* = \mathbf{My}$ and $\mathbf{z}_* = \mathbf{Mz}$ will have zero sample means. The squared partial correlation is

$$r_{yz}^{*2} = \frac{(\mathbf{z}_*'\mathbf{y}_*)^2}{(\mathbf{z}_*'\mathbf{z}_*)(\mathbf{y}_*'\mathbf{y}_*)}.$$

Let $c$ and $\mathbf{u}$ denote the coefficient on $\mathbf{z}$ and the vector of residuals in the multiple regression of $\mathbf{y}$ on $\mathbf{W}$. The squared $t$ ratio in (3-22) is

$$t_z^2 = \frac{c^2}{\left[\dfrac{\mathbf{u'u}}{n - (K+1)}\right](\mathbf{W'W})_{K+1,K+1}^{-1}},$$

where $(\mathbf{W'W})_{K+1,K+1}^{-1}$ is the $(K+1)$ (last) diagonal element of $(\mathbf{W'W})^{-1}$. The partitioned inverse formula in (A-74) can be applied to the matrix $[\mathbf{X}, \mathbf{z}]'[\mathbf{X}, \mathbf{z}]$. This matrix appears in (3-17), with $\mathbf{X}_1 = \mathbf{X}$ and $\mathbf{X}_2 = \mathbf{z}$. The result is the inverse matrix that appears in (3-19) and (3-20), which implies the first important result.

---

**THEOREM 3.4  Diagonal Elements of the Inverse of a Moment Matrix**

*If* $\mathbf{W} = [\mathbf{X}, \mathbf{z}]$, *then the last diagonal element of* $(\mathbf{W'W})^{-1}$ *is* $(\mathbf{z'Mz})^{-1} = (\mathbf{z}_*'\mathbf{z}_*)^{-1}$, *where* $\mathbf{z}_* = \mathbf{Mz}$ *and* $\mathbf{M} = \mathbf{I} - \mathbf{X}(\mathbf{X'X})^{-1}\mathbf{X'}$.

---

(Note that this result generalizes the development in Section A.2.8 where $\mathbf{X}$ is only the constant term.) If we now use Corollary 3.3.1 and Theorem 3.4 for $c$, after some manipulation, we obtain

$$\frac{t_z^2}{t_z^2 + [n - (K+1)]} = \frac{(\mathbf{z}_*'\mathbf{y}_*)^2}{(\mathbf{z}_*'\mathbf{y}_*)^2 + (\mathbf{u'u})(\mathbf{z}_*'\mathbf{z}_*)} = \frac{r_{yz}^{*2}}{r_{yz}^{*2} + (\mathbf{u'u})/(\mathbf{y}_*'\mathbf{y}_*)},$$

where

$$\mathbf{u} = \mathbf{y} - \mathbf{Xd} - \mathbf{z}c$$

is the vector of residuals when $\mathbf{y}$ is regressed on $\mathbf{X}$ *and* $\mathbf{z}$. Note that unless $\mathbf{X'z} = \mathbf{0}$, $\mathbf{d}$ will not equal $\mathbf{b} = (\mathbf{X'X})^{-1}\mathbf{X'y}$. (See Section 7.2.1.) Moreover, unless $c = 0$, $\mathbf{u}$ will not equal $\mathbf{e} = \mathbf{y} - \mathbf{Xb}$. Now we have shown in Corollary 3.3.1 that $c = (\mathbf{z}'_*\mathbf{z}_*)^{-1}(\mathbf{z}'_*\mathbf{y}_*)$. We also have, from (3-18), that the coefficients on $\mathbf{X}$ in the regression of $\mathbf{y}$ on $\mathbf{W} = [\mathbf{X}, \mathbf{z}]$ are

$$\mathbf{d} = (\mathbf{X}'\mathbf{X})^{-1}\mathbf{X}'(\mathbf{y} - \mathbf{z}c) = \mathbf{b} - (\mathbf{X}'\mathbf{X})^{-1}\mathbf{X}'\mathbf{z}c.$$

So, inserting this expression for $\mathbf{d}$ in that for $\mathbf{u}$ gives

$$\mathbf{u} = \mathbf{y} - \mathbf{Xb} + \mathbf{X}(\mathbf{X}'\mathbf{X})^{-1}\mathbf{X}'\mathbf{z}c - \mathbf{z}c = \mathbf{e} - \mathbf{Mz}c = \mathbf{e} - \mathbf{z}_*c.$$

Now

$$\mathbf{u}'\mathbf{u} = \mathbf{e}'\mathbf{e} + c^2(\mathbf{z}'_*\mathbf{z}_*) - 2c\mathbf{z}'_*\mathbf{e}.$$

But $\mathbf{e} = \mathbf{My} = \mathbf{y}_*$ and $\mathbf{z}'_*\mathbf{e} = \mathbf{z}'_*\mathbf{y}_* = c(\mathbf{z}'_*\mathbf{z}_*)$. Inserting this in $\mathbf{u}'\mathbf{u}$ gives our second useful result.

---

**THEOREM 3.5** **Change in the Sum of Squares When a Variable Is Added to a Regression**
*If $\mathbf{e}'\mathbf{e}$ is the sum of squared residuals when $\mathbf{y}$ is regressed on $\mathbf{X}$ and $\mathbf{u}'\mathbf{u}$ is the sum of squared residuals when $\mathbf{y}$ is regressed on $\mathbf{X}$ and $\mathbf{z}$, then*

$$\mathbf{u}'\mathbf{u} = \mathbf{e}'\mathbf{e} - c^2(\mathbf{z}'_*\mathbf{z}_*) \le \mathbf{e}'\mathbf{e}, \tag{3-23}$$

*where $c$ is the coefficient on $\mathbf{z}$ in the long regression and $\mathbf{z}_* = [\mathbf{I} - \mathbf{X}(\mathbf{X}'\mathbf{X})^{-1}\mathbf{X}']\mathbf{z}$ is the vector of residuals when $\mathbf{z}$ is regressed on $\mathbf{X}$.*

---

Returning to our derivation, we note that $\mathbf{e}'\mathbf{e} = \mathbf{y}'_*\mathbf{y}_*$ and $c^2(\mathbf{z}'_*\mathbf{z}_*) = (\mathbf{z}'_*\mathbf{y}_*)^2/(\mathbf{z}'_*\mathbf{z}_*)$. Therefore, $(\mathbf{u}'\mathbf{u})/(\mathbf{y}'_*\mathbf{y}_*) = 1 - r^{*2}_{yz}$, and we have our result.

### Example 3.1    Partial Correlations

For the data in the application in Section 3.2.2, the simple correlations between investment and the regressors $r_{yk}$ and the partial correlations $r^*_{yk}$ between investment and the four regressors (given the other variables) are listed in Table 3.2. As is clear from the table, there is no necessary relation between the simple and partial correlation coefficients. One thing worth noting is the signs of the coefficients. The signs of the partial correlation coefficients are the same as the signs of the respective regression coefficients, three of which are negative. All the simple correlation coefficients are positive because of the latent "effect" of time.

**TABLE 3.2**    Correlations of Investment with Other Variables

|  | Simple Correlation | Partial Correlation |
|---|---|---|
| Time | 0.7496 | −0.9360 |
| GNP | 0.8632 | 0.9680 |
| Interest | 0.5871 | −0.5167 |
| Inflation | 0.4777 | −0.0221 |

## 3.5 GOODNESS OF FIT AND THE ANALYSIS OF VARIANCE

The original fitting criterion, the sum of squared residuals, suggests a measure of the fit of the regression line to the data. However, as can easily be verified, the sum of squared residuals can be scaled arbitrarily just by multiplying all the values of $y$ by the desired scale factor. Since the fitted values of the regression are based on the values of $\mathbf{x}$, we might ask instead whether *variation* in $\mathbf{x}$ is a good predictor of *variation* in $y$. Figure 3.3 shows three possible cases for a simple linear regression model. The measure of fit described here embodies both the fitting criterion and the covariation of $y$ and $\mathbf{x}$.

Variation of the dependent variable is defined in terms of deviations from its mean, $(y_i - \bar{y})$. The **total variation** in $y$ is the sum of squared deviations:

$$\text{SST} = \sum_{i=1}^{n} (y_i - \bar{y})^2.$$

In terms of the regression equation, we may write the full set of observations as

$$\mathbf{y} = \mathbf{Xb} + \mathbf{e} = \hat{\mathbf{y}} + \mathbf{e}. \tag{3-24}$$

**FIGURE 3.3**   Sample Data.

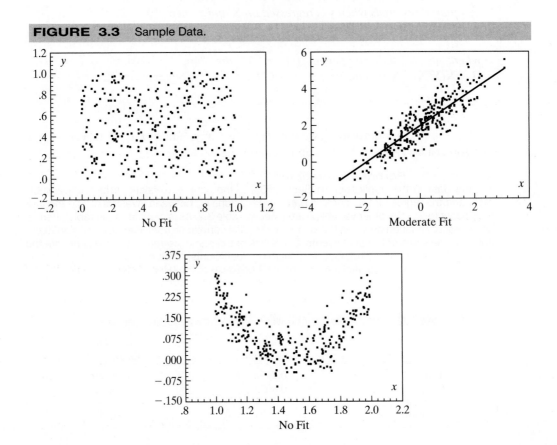

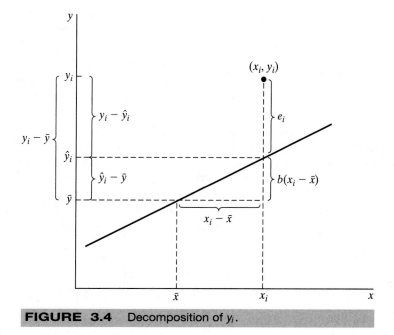

**FIGURE 3.4**    Decomposition of $y_i$.

For an individual observation, we have

$$y_i = \hat{y}_i + e_i = \mathbf{x}_i'\mathbf{b} + e_i.$$

If the regression contains a constant term, then the residuals will sum to zero and the mean of the predicted values of $y_i$ will equal the mean of the actual values. Subtracting $\bar{y}$ from both sides and using this result and result 2 in Section 3.2.3 gives

$$y_i - \bar{y} = \hat{y}_i - \bar{y} + e_i = (\mathbf{x}_i - \bar{\mathbf{x}})'\mathbf{b} + e_i.$$

Figure 3.4 illustrates the computation for the two-variable regression. Intuitively, the regression would appear to fit well if the deviations of $y$ from its mean are more largely accounted for by deviations of $x$ from its mean than by the residuals. Since both terms in this decomposition sum to zero, to quantify this fit, we use the sums of squares instead. For the full set of observations, we have

$$\mathbf{M}^0\mathbf{y} = \mathbf{M}^0\mathbf{X}\mathbf{b} + \mathbf{M}^0\mathbf{e},$$

where $\mathbf{M}^0$ is the $n \times n$ idempotent matrix that transforms observations into deviations from sample means. (See Section A.2.8.) The column of $\mathbf{M}^0\mathbf{X}$ corresponding to the constant term is zero, and, since the residuals already have mean zero, $\mathbf{M}^0\mathbf{e} = \mathbf{e}$. Then, since $\mathbf{e}'\mathbf{M}^0\mathbf{X} = \mathbf{e}'\mathbf{X} = \mathbf{0}$, the total sum of squares is

$$\mathbf{y}'\mathbf{M}^0\mathbf{y} = \mathbf{b}'\mathbf{X}'\mathbf{M}^0\mathbf{X}\mathbf{b} + \mathbf{e}'\mathbf{e}.$$

Write this as total sum of squares = regression sum of squares + error sum of squares, or

$$\text{SST} = \text{SSR} + \text{SSE}. \tag{3-25}$$

(Note that this is precisely the partitioning that appears at the end of Section 3.2.4.)

We can now obtain a measure of how well the regression line fits the data by using the

$$\text{coefficient of determination: } \frac{\text{SSR}}{\text{SST}} = \frac{\mathbf{b'X'M^0Xb}}{\mathbf{y'M^0y}} = 1 - \frac{\mathbf{e'e}}{\mathbf{y'M^0y}}. \qquad \textbf{(3-26)}$$

The coefficient of determination is denoted $R^2$. As we have shown, it must be between 0 and 1, and it measures the proportion of the total variation in $y$ that is accounted for by variation in the regressors. It equals zero if the regression is a horizontal line, that is, if all the elements of $\mathbf{b}$ except the constant term are zero. In this case, the predicted values of $y$ are always $\bar{y}$, so deviations of $\mathbf{x}$ from its mean do not translate into different predictions for $y$. As such, $\mathbf{x}$ has no explanatory power. The other extreme, $R^2 = 1$, occurs if the values of $\mathbf{x}$ and $y$ all lie in the same hyperplane (on a straight line for a two variable regression) so that the residuals are all zero. If all the values of $y_i$ lie on a vertical line, then $R^2$ has no meaning and cannot be computed.

Regression analysis is often used for forecasting. In this case, we are interested in how well the regression model predicts movements in the dependent variable. With this in mind, an equivalent way to compute $R^2$ is also useful. First

$$\mathbf{b'X'M^0Xb} = \hat{\mathbf{y}}'\mathbf{M^0}\hat{\mathbf{y}},$$

but $\hat{\mathbf{y}} = \mathbf{Xb}, \mathbf{y} = \hat{\mathbf{y}} + \mathbf{e}, \mathbf{M^0e} = \mathbf{e}$, and $\mathbf{X'e} = \mathbf{0}$, so $\hat{\mathbf{y}}'\mathbf{M^0}\hat{\mathbf{y}} = \hat{\mathbf{y}}'\mathbf{M^0y}$. Multiply $R^2 = \hat{\mathbf{y}}'\mathbf{M^0}\hat{\mathbf{y}}/\mathbf{y'M^0y} = \hat{\mathbf{y}}'\mathbf{M^0y}/\mathbf{y'M^0y}$ by $1 = \hat{\mathbf{y}}'\mathbf{M^0y}/\hat{\mathbf{y}}'\mathbf{M^0}\hat{\mathbf{y}}$ to obtain

$$R^2 = \frac{[\Sigma_i(y_i - \bar{y})(\hat{y}_i - \hat{\bar{y}})]^2}{[\Sigma_i(y_i - \bar{y})^2][\Sigma_i(\hat{y}_i - \hat{\bar{y}})^2]}, \qquad \textbf{(3-27)}$$

which is the squared correlation between the observed values of $y$ and the predictions produced by the estimated regression equation.

### Example 3.2   Fit of a Consumption Function

The data plotted in Figure 2.1 are listed in Appendix Table F2.1. For these data, where $y$ is $C$ and $x$ is $X$, we have $\bar{y} = 273.2727, \bar{x} = 323.2727, S_{yy} = 12,618.182, S_{xx} = 12,300.182, S_{xy} = 8,423.182$, so SST $= 12,618.182, b = 8,423.182/12,300.182 = 0.6848014$, SSR $= b^2 S_{xx} = 5,768.2068$, and SSE $=$ SST $-$ SSR $= 6,849.975$. Then $R^2 = b^2 S_{xx}/$SST $= 0.457135$. As can be seen in Figure 2.1, this is a moderate fit, although it is not particularly good for aggregate time-series data. On the other hand, it is clear that not accounting for the anomalous wartime data has degraded the fit of the model. This value is the $R^2$ for the model indicated by the dotted line in the figure. By simply omitting the years 1942–1945 from the sample and doing these computations with the remaining seven observations—the heavy solid line—we obtain an $R^2$ of 0.93697. Alternatively, by creating a variable *WAR* which equals 1 in the years 1942–1945 and zero otherwise and including this in the model, which produces the model shown by the two solid lines, the $R^2$ rises to 0.94639.

We can summarize the calculation of $R^2$ in an **analysis of variance** table, which might appear as shown in Table 3.3.

### Example 3.3   Analysis of Variance for an Investment Equation

The analysis of variance table for the investment equation of Section 3.2.2 is given in Table 3.4.

**TABLE 3.3**    Analysis of Variance

| | Source | Degrees of Freedom | Mean Square |
|---|---|---|---|
| Regression | $\mathbf{b'X'y} - n\bar{y}^2$ | $K - 1$ (assuming a constant term) | |
| Residual | $\mathbf{e'e}$ | $n - K$ | $s^2$ |
| Total | $\mathbf{y'y} - n\bar{y}^2$ | $n - 1$ | $S_{yy}/(n-1) = s_y^2$ |
| Coefficient of determination | $R^2 = 1 - \mathbf{e'e}/(\mathbf{y'y} - n\bar{y}^2)$ | | |

**TABLE 3.4**    Analysis of Variance for the Investment Equation

| | Source | Degrees of Freedom | Mean Square |
|---|---|---|---|
| Regression | 0.0159025 | 4 | 0.003976 |
| Residual | 0.0004508 | 10 | 0.00004508 |
| Total | 0.016353 | 14 | 0.0011681 |

$R^2 = 0.0159025/0.016353 = 0.97245$

### 3.5.1    THE ADJUSTED $R$-SQUARED AND A MEASURE OF FIT

There are some problems with the use of $R^2$ in analyzing goodness of fit. The first concerns the number of degrees of freedom used up in estimating the parameters. *$R^2$ will never decrease when another variable is added to a regression equation.* Equation (3-23) provides a convenient means for us to establish this result. Once again, we are comparing a regression of $\mathbf{y}$ on $\mathbf{X}$ with sum of squared residuals $\mathbf{e'e}$ to a regression of $\mathbf{y}$ on $\mathbf{X}$ and an additional variable $\mathbf{z}$, which produces sum of squared residuals $\mathbf{u'u}$. Recall the vectors of residuals $\mathbf{z}_* = \mathbf{Mz}$ and $\mathbf{y}_* = \mathbf{My} = \mathbf{e}$, which implies that $\mathbf{e'e} = (\mathbf{y}_*'\mathbf{y}_*)$. Let $c$ be the coefficient on $\mathbf{z}$ in the longer regression. Then $c = (\mathbf{z}_*'\mathbf{z}_*)^{-1}(\mathbf{z}_*'\mathbf{y}_*)$, and inserting this in (3-23) produces

$$\mathbf{u'u} = \mathbf{e'e} - \frac{(\mathbf{z}_*'\mathbf{y}_*)^2}{(\mathbf{z}_*'\mathbf{z}_*)} = \mathbf{e'e}\left(1 - r_{yz}^{*2}\right), \tag{3-28}$$

where $r_{yz}^*$ is the partial correlation between $\mathbf{y}$ and $\mathbf{z}$, controlling for $\mathbf{X}$. Now divide through both sides of the equality by $\mathbf{y'M^0y}$. From (3-26), $\mathbf{u'u}/\mathbf{y'M^0y}$ is $(1 - R_{\mathbf{Xz}}^2)$ for the regression on $\mathbf{X}$ and $\mathbf{z}$ and $\mathbf{e'e}/\mathbf{y'M^0y}$ is $(1 - R_{\mathbf{X}}^2)$. Rearranging the result produces the following:

---

**THEOREM 3.6**    **Change in $R^2$ When a Variable Is Added to a Regression**

*Let $R_{\mathbf{Xz}}^2$ be the coefficient of determination in the regression of $\mathbf{y}$ on $\mathbf{X}$ and an additional variable $\mathbf{z}$, let $R_{\mathbf{X}}^2$ be the same for the regression of $\mathbf{y}$ on $\mathbf{X}$ alone, and let $r_{yz}^*$ be the partial correlation between $\mathbf{y}$ and $\mathbf{z}$, controlling for $\mathbf{X}$. Then*

$$R_{\mathbf{Xz}}^2 = R_{\mathbf{X}}^2 + \left(1 - R_{\mathbf{X}}^2\right) r_{yz}^{*2}. \tag{3-29}$$

---

Thus, the $R^2$ in the longer regression cannot be smaller. It is tempting to exploit this result by just adding variables to the model; $R^2$ will continue to rise to its limit of 1.[3] The **adjusted $R^2$** (for degrees of freedom), which incorporates a penalty for these results is computed as follows[4]:

$$\overline{R}^2 = 1 - \frac{\mathbf{e}'\mathbf{e}/(n-K)}{\mathbf{y}'\mathbf{M}^0\mathbf{y}/(n-1)}.\tag{3-30}$$

For computational purposes, the connection between $R^2$ and $\overline{R}^2$ is

$$\overline{R}^2 = 1 - \frac{n-1}{n-K}(1 - R^2).$$

The adjusted $R^2$ may decline when a variable is added to the set of independent variables. Indeed, $\overline{R}^2$ may even be negative. To consider an admittedly extreme case, suppose that $\mathbf{x}$ and $\mathbf{y}$ have a sample correlation of zero. Then the adjusted $R^2$ will equal $-1/(n-2)$. (Thus, the name "adjusted $R$-squared" is a bit misleading—as can be seen in (3-30), $\overline{R}^2$ is not actually computed as the square of any quantity.) Whether $\overline{R}^2$ rises or falls depends on whether the contribution of the new variable to the fit of the regression more than offsets the correction for the loss of an additional degree of freedom. The general result (the proof of which is left as an exercise) is as follows.

---

**THEOREM 3.7  Change in $\overline{R}^2$ When a Variable Is Added to a Regression**
*In a multiple regression, $\overline{R}^2$ will fall (rise) when the variable x is deleted from the regression if the square of the t ratio associated with this variable is greater (less) than 1.*

---

We have shown that $R^2$ will never fall when a variable is added to the regression. We now consider this result more generally. The change in the residual sum of squares when a set of variables $\mathbf{X}_2$ is added to the regression is

$$\mathbf{e}'_{1,2}\mathbf{e}_{1,2} = \mathbf{e}'_1\mathbf{e}_1 - \mathbf{b}'_2\mathbf{X}'_2\mathbf{M}_1\mathbf{X}_2\mathbf{b}_2,$$

where we use subscript 1 to indicate the regression based on $\mathbf{X}_1$ alone and 1,2 to indicate the use of *both* $\mathbf{X}_1$ and $\mathbf{X}_2$. The coefficient vector $\mathbf{b}_2$ is the coefficients on $\mathbf{X}_2$ in the multiple regression of $\mathbf{y}$ on $\mathbf{X}_1$ and $\mathbf{X}_2$. [See (3-19) and (3-20) for definitions of $\mathbf{b}_2$ and $\mathbf{M}_1$.] Therefore,

$$R^2_{1,2} = 1 - \frac{\mathbf{e}'_1\mathbf{e}_1 - \mathbf{b}'_2\mathbf{X}'_2\mathbf{M}_1\mathbf{X}_2\mathbf{b}_2}{\mathbf{y}'\mathbf{M}^0\mathbf{y}} = R^2_1 + \frac{\mathbf{b}'_2\mathbf{X}'_2\mathbf{M}_1\mathbf{X}_2\mathbf{b}_2}{\mathbf{y}'\mathbf{M}^0\mathbf{y}},$$

---

[3]This result comes at a cost, however. The parameter estimates become progressively less precise as we do so. We will pursue this result in Chapter 4.

[4]This measure is sometimes advocated on the basis of the unbiasedness of the two quantities in the fraction. Since the ratio is not an unbiased estimator of any population quantity, it is difficult to justify the adjustment on this basis.

which is greater than $R_1^2$ unless $\mathbf{b}_2$ equals zero. ($\mathbf{M}_1\mathbf{X}_2$ could not be zero unless $\mathbf{X}_2$ was a linear function of $\mathbf{X}_1$, in which case the regression on $\mathbf{X}_1$ and $\mathbf{X}_2$ could not be computed.) This equation can be manipulated a bit further to obtain

$$R_{1,2}^2 = R_1^2 + \frac{\mathbf{y}'\mathbf{M}_1\mathbf{y}}{\mathbf{y}'\mathbf{M}^0\mathbf{y}} \frac{\mathbf{b}_2'\mathbf{X}_2'\mathbf{M}_1\mathbf{X}_2\mathbf{b}_2}{\mathbf{y}'\mathbf{M}_1\mathbf{y}}.$$

But $\mathbf{y}'\mathbf{M}_1\mathbf{y} = \mathbf{e}_1'\mathbf{e}_1$, so the first term in the product is $1 - R_1^2$. The second is the **multiple correlation** in the regression of $\mathbf{M}_1\mathbf{y}$ on $\mathbf{M}_1\mathbf{X}_2$, or the partial correlation (after the effect of $\mathbf{X}_1$ is removed) in the regression of $\mathbf{y}$ on $\mathbf{X}_2$. Collecting terms, we have

$$R_{1,2}^2 = R_1^2 + \left(1 - R_1^2\right)r_{y2\cdot1}^2.$$

[This is the multivariate counterpart to (3-29).]

Therefore, it is possible to push $R^2$ as high as desired just by adding regressors. This possibility motivates the use of the adjusted $R^2$ in (3-30), instead of $R^2$ as a method of choosing among alternative models. Since $\overline{R}^2$ incorporates a penalty for reducing the degrees of freedom while still revealing an improvement in fit, one possibility is to choose the specification that maximizes $\overline{R}^2$. It has been suggested that the adjusted $R^2$ does not penalize the loss of degrees of freedom heavily enough.[5] Some alternatives that have been proposed for comparing models (which we index by $j$) are

$$\tilde{R}_j^2 = 1 - \frac{n + K_j}{n - K_j}\left(1 - R_j^2\right),$$

which minimizes Amemiya's (1985) **prediction criterion,**

$$PC_j = \frac{\mathbf{e}_j'\mathbf{e}_j}{n - K_j}\left(1 + \frac{K_j}{n}\right) = s_j^2\left(1 + \frac{K_j}{n}\right)$$

and the Akaike and Bayesian information criteria which are given in (7-19) and (7-20).[6]

### 3.5.2 R-SQUARED AND THE CONSTANT TERM IN THE MODEL

A second difficulty with $R^2$ concerns the constant term in the model. The proof that $0 \le R^2 \le 1$ requires $\mathbf{X}$ to contain a column of 1s. If not, then (1) $\mathbf{M}^0\mathbf{e} \ne \mathbf{e}$ and (2) $\mathbf{e}'\mathbf{M}^0\mathbf{X} \ne \mathbf{0}$, and the term $2\mathbf{e}'\mathbf{M}^0\mathbf{X}\mathbf{b}$ in $\mathbf{y}'\mathbf{M}^0\mathbf{y} = (\mathbf{M}^0\mathbf{X}\mathbf{b} + \mathbf{M}^0\mathbf{e})'(\mathbf{M}^0\mathbf{X}\mathbf{b} + \mathbf{M}^0\mathbf{e})$ in the preceding expansion will not drop out. Consequently, when we compute

$$R^2 = 1 - \frac{\mathbf{e}'\mathbf{e}}{\mathbf{y}'\mathbf{M}^0\mathbf{y}},$$

the result is unpredictable. It will never be higher and can be far lower than the same figure computed for the regression with a constant term included. It can even be negative. Computer packages differ in their computation of $R^2$. An alternative computation,

$$R^2 = \frac{\mathbf{b}'\mathbf{X}'\mathbf{M}^0\mathbf{y}}{\mathbf{y}'\mathbf{M}^0\mathbf{y}},$$

---

[5]See, for example, Amemiya (1985, pp. 50–51).

[6]Most authors and computer programs report the logs of these prediction criteria.

is equally problematic. Again, this calculation will differ from the one obtained with the constant term included; this time, $R^2$ may be larger than 1. Some computer packages bypass these difficulties by reporting a third "$R^2$," the squared sample correlation between the actual values of $y$ and the fitted values from the regression. This approach could be deceptive. If the regression contains a constant term, then, as we have seen, all three computations give the same answer. Even if not, this last one will still produce a value between zero and one. But, it is not a proportion of variation explained. On the other hand, for the purpose of comparing models, this squared correlation might well be a useful descriptive device. It is important for users of computer packages to be aware of how the reported $R^2$ is computed. Indeed, some packages will give a warning in the results when a regression is fit without a constant or by some technique other than linear least squares.

### 3.5.3   COMPARING MODELS

The value of $R^2$ we obtained for the consumption function in Example 3.2 seems high in an absolute sense. Is it? Unfortunately, there is no absolute basis for comparison. In fact, in using aggregate time-series data, coefficients of determination this high are routine. In terms of the values one normally encounters in cross sections, an $R^2$ of 0.5 is relatively high. Coefficients of determination in cross sections of individual data as high as 0.2 are sometimes noteworthy. The point of this discussion is that whether a regression line provides a good fit to a body of data depends on the setting.

Little can be said about the relative quality of fits of regression lines in different contexts or in different data sets even if they are supposedly generated by the same data generating mechanism. One must be careful, however, even in a single context, to be sure to use the same basis for comparison for competing models. Usually, this concern is about how the dependent variable is computed. For example, a perennial question concerns whether a linear or loglinear model fits the data better. Unfortunately, the question cannot be answered with a direct comparison. An $R^2$ for the linear regression model is different from an $R^2$ for the loglinear model. Variation in $y$ is different from variation in $\ln y$. The latter $R^2$ will typically be larger, but this does not imply that the loglinear model is a better fit in some absolute sense.

It is worth emphasizing that $R^2$ is a measure of *linear* association between $x$ and $y$. For example, the third panel of Figure 3.3 shows data that might arise from the model

$$y_i = \alpha + \beta(x_i - \gamma)^2 + \varepsilon_i.$$

(The constant $\gamma$ allows $x$ to be distributed about some value other than zero.) The relationship between $y$ and $x$ in this model is nonlinear, and a linear regression would find no fit.

A final word of caution is in order. The interpretation of $R^2$ as a proportion of variation explained is dependent on the use of least squares to compute the fitted values. It is always correct to write

$$y_i - \overline{y} = (\hat{y}_i - \overline{y}) + e_i$$

regardless of how $\hat{y}_i$ is computed. Thus, one might use $\hat{y}_i = \exp(\widehat{\ln y_i})$ from a loglinear model in computing the sum of squares on the two sides, however, the cross-product term vanishes only if least squares is used to compute the fitted values and if the model contains a constant term. Thus, the cross-product term has been ignored in computing $R^2$ for the loglinear model. Only in the case of least squares applied to a linear equation with a constant term can $R^2$ be interpreted as the proportion of variation in $y$ explained by variation in **x**. An analogous computation can be done without computing deviations from means if the regression does not contain a constant term. Other purely algebraic artifacts will crop up in regressions without a constant, however. For example, the value of $R^2$ will change when the same constant is added to each observation on $y$, but it is obvious that nothing fundamental has changed in the regression relationship. One should be wary (even skeptical) in the calculation and interpretation of fit measures for regressions without constant terms.

## 3.6 SUMMARY AND CONCLUSIONS

This chapter has described the purely algebraic exercise of fitting a line (hyperplane) to a set of points using the method of least squares. We considered the primary problem first, using a data set of $n$ observations on $K$ variables. We then examined several aspects of the solution, including the nature of the projection and residual maker matrices and several useful algebraic results relating to the computation of the residuals and their sum of squares. We also examined the difference between gross or simple regression and correlation and multiple regression by defining "partial regression coefficients" and "partial correlation coefficients." The Frisch–Waugh–Lovell theorem (3.3) is a fundamentally useful tool in regression analysis which enables us to obtain in closed form the expression for a subvector of a vector of regression coefficients. We examined several aspects of the partitioned regression, including how the fit of the regression model changes when variables are added to it or removed from it. Finally, we took a closer look at the conventional measure of how well the fitted regression line predicts or "fits" the data.

### Key Terms and Concepts

- Adjusted $R^2$
- Analysis of variance
- Bivariate regression
- Coefficient of determination
- Disturbance
- Fitting criterion
- Frisch–Waugh theorem
- Goodness of fit
- Least squares
- Least squares normal equations

- Moment matrix
- Multiple correlation
- Multiple regression
- Netting out
- Normal equations
- Orthogonal regression
- Partial correlation coefficient
- Partial regression coefficient
- Partialing out
- Partitioned regression

- Prediction criterion
- Population quantity
- Population regression
- Projection
- Projection matrix
- Residual
- Residual maker
- Total variation

### Exercises

1. **The two variable regression.** For the regression model $y = \alpha + \beta x + \varepsilon$,
   a. Show that the least squares normal equations imply $\Sigma_i e_i = 0$ and $\Sigma_i x_i e_i = 0$.
   b. Show that the solution for the constant term is $a = \bar{y} - b\bar{x}$.
   c. Show that the solution for $b$ is $b = [\sum_{i=1}^{n}(x_i - \bar{x})(y_i - \bar{y})]/[\sum_{i=1}^{n}(x_i - \bar{x})^2]$.

   d. Prove that these two values uniquely minimize the sum of squares by showing that the diagonal elements of the second derivatives matrix of the sum of squares with respect to the parameters are both positive and that the determinant is $4n[(\sum_{i=1}^{n} x_i^2) - n\bar{x}^2] = 4n[\sum_{i=1}^{n}(x_i - \bar{x})^2]$, which is positive unless all values of $x$ are the same.

2. **Change in the sum of squares.** Suppose that $\mathbf{b}$ is the least squares coefficient vector in the regression of $\mathbf{y}$ on $\mathbf{X}$ and that $\mathbf{c}$ is any other $K \times 1$ vector. Prove that the difference in the two sums of squared residuals is

$$(\mathbf{y} - \mathbf{Xc})'(\mathbf{y} - \mathbf{Xc}) - (\mathbf{y} - \mathbf{Xb})'(\mathbf{y} - \mathbf{Xb}) = (\mathbf{c} - \mathbf{b})'\mathbf{X}'\mathbf{X}(\mathbf{c} - \mathbf{b}).$$

Prove that this difference is positive.

3. **Linear transformations of the data.** Consider the least squares regression of $\mathbf{y}$ on $K$ variables (with a constant) $\mathbf{X}$. Consider an alternative set of regressors $\mathbf{Z} = \mathbf{XP}$, where $\mathbf{P}$ is a nonsingular matrix. Thus, each column of $\mathbf{Z}$ is a mixture of some of the columns of $\mathbf{X}$. Prove that the residual vectors in the regressions of $\mathbf{y}$ on $\mathbf{X}$ and $\mathbf{y}$ on $\mathbf{Z}$ are identical. What relevance does this have to the question of changing the fit of a regression by changing the units of measurement of the independent variables?

4. **Partial Frisch and Waugh.** In the least squares regression of $\mathbf{y}$ on a constant and $\mathbf{X}$, to compute the regression coefficients on $\mathbf{X}$, we can first transform $\mathbf{y}$ to deviations from the mean $\bar{y}$ and, likewise, transform each column of $\mathbf{X}$ to deviations from the respective column mean; second, regress the transformed $\mathbf{y}$ on the transformed $\mathbf{X}$ without a constant. Do we get the same result if we only transform $\mathbf{y}$? What if we only transform $\mathbf{X}$?

5. **Residual makers.** What is the result of the matrix product $\mathbf{M}_1\mathbf{M}$ where $\mathbf{M}_1$ is defined in (3-19) and $\mathbf{M}$ is defined in (3-14)?

6. **Adding an observation.** A data set consists of $n$ observations on $\mathbf{X}_n$ and $\mathbf{y}_n$. The least squares estimator based on these $n$ observations is $\mathbf{b}_n = (\mathbf{X}_n'\mathbf{X}_n)^{-1}\mathbf{X}_n'\mathbf{y}_n$. Another observation, $\mathbf{x}_s$ and $y_s$, becomes available. Prove that the least squares estimator computed using this additional observation is

$$\mathbf{b}_{n,s} = \mathbf{b}_n + \frac{1}{1 + \mathbf{x}_s'(\mathbf{X}_n'\mathbf{X}_n)^{-1}\mathbf{x}_s}(\mathbf{X}_n'\mathbf{X}_n)^{-1}\mathbf{x}_s(y_s - \mathbf{x}_s'\mathbf{b}_n).$$

Note that the last term is $e_s$, the residual from the prediction of $y_s$ using the coefficients based on $\mathbf{X}_n$ and $\mathbf{b}_n$. Conclude that the new data change the results of least squares only if the new observation on $y$ cannot be perfectly predicted using the information already in hand.

7. **Deleting an observation.** A common strategy for handling a case in which an observation is missing data for one or more variables is to fill those missing variables with 0s and add a variable to the model that takes the value 1 for that one observation and 0 for all other observations. Show that this "strategy" is equivalent to discarding the observation as regards the computation of $\mathbf{b}$ but it does have an effect on $R^2$. Consider the special case in which $\mathbf{X}$ contains only a constant and one variable. Show that replacing missing values of $x$ with the mean of the complete observations has the same effect as adding the new variable.

8. **Demand system estimation.** Let $Y$ denote total expenditure on consumer durables, nondurables, and services and $E_d$, $E_n$, and $E_s$ are the expenditures on the three categories. As defined, $Y = E_d + E_n + E_s$. Now, consider the expenditure system

$$E_d = \alpha_d + \beta_d Y + \gamma_{dd} P_d + \gamma_{dn} P_n + \gamma_{ds} P_s + \varepsilon_d,$$

$$E_n = \alpha_n + \beta_n Y + \gamma_{nd} P_d + \gamma_{nn} P_n + \gamma_{ns} P_s + \varepsilon_n,$$

$$E_s = \alpha_s + \beta_s Y + \gamma_{sd} P_d + \gamma_{sn} P_n + \gamma_{ss} P_s + \varepsilon_s.$$

Prove that if all equations are estimated by ordinary least squares, then the sum of the expenditure coefficients will be 1 and the four other column sums in the preceding model will be zero.

9. **Change in adjusted $R^2$.** Prove that the adjusted $R^2$ in (3-30) rises (falls) when variable $\mathbf{x}_k$ is deleted from the regression if the square of the $t$ ratio on $\mathbf{x}_k$ in the multiple regression is less (greater) than 1.

10. **Regression without a constant.** Suppose that you estimate a multiple regression first with, then without, a constant. Whether the $R^2$ is higher in the second case than the first will depend in part on how it is computed. Using the (relatively) standard method $R^2 = 1 - (\mathbf{e}'\mathbf{e}/\mathbf{y}'\mathbf{M}^0\mathbf{y})$, which regression will have a higher $R^2$?

11. Three variables, $N$, $D$, and $Y$, all have zero means and unit variances. A fourth variable is $C = N + D$. In the regression of $C$ on $Y$, the slope is 0.8. In the regression of $C$ on $N$, the slope is 0.5. In the regression of $D$ on $Y$, the slope is 0.4. What is the sum of squared residuals in the regression of $C$ on $D$? There are 21 observations and all moments are computed using $1/(n-1)$ as the divisor.

12. Using the matrices of sums of squares and cross products immediately preceding Section 3.2.3, compute the coefficients in the multiple regression of real investment on a constant, real GNP and the interest rate. Compute $R^2$.

13. In the December, 1969, *American Economic Review* (pp. 886–896), Nathaniel Leff reports the following least squares regression results for a cross section study of the effect of age composition on savings in 74 countries in 1964:

$$\ln S/Y = 7.3439 + 0.1596 \ln Y/N + 0.0254 \ln G - 1.3520 \ln D_1 - 0.3990 \ln D_2$$

$$\ln S/N = 2.7851 + 1.1486 \ln Y/N + 0.0265 \ln G - 1.3438 \ln D_1 - 0.3966 \ln D_2$$

where $S/Y$ = domestic savings ratio, $S/N$ = per capita savings, $Y/N$ = per capita income, $D_1$ = percentage of the population under 15, $D_2$ = percentage of the population over 64, and $G$ = growth rate of per capita income. Are these results correct? Explain. [See Goldberger (1973) and Leff (1973) for discussion.]

14. **Orthogonal regression.** Prove Theorem 3.1.

## Application

The data listed in Table 3.5 are extracted from Koop and Tobias's (2004) study of the relationship between wages and education, ability, and family characteristics. (See Appendix Table F3.2.) Their data set is a panel of 2,178 individuals with a total of 17,919 observations. Those listed below are the first year and the time invariant variables for the first 15 individuals in the sample. The variables are defined in the article.

**TABLE 3.5**   Subsample from Koop and Tobias Data

| Person | Education | Wage | Experience | Ability | Mother's education | Father's education | Siblings |
|--------|-----------|------|------------|---------|--------------------|--------------------|----------|
| 1  | 13 | 1.82 | 1 | 1.00  | 12 | 12 | 1 |
| 2  | 15 | 2.14 | 4 | 1.50  | 12 | 12 | 1 |
| 3  | 10 | 1.56 | 1 | −0.36 | 12 | 12 | 1 |
| 4  | 12 | 1.85 | 1 | 0.26  | 12 | 10 | 4 |
| 5  | 15 | 2.41 | 2 | 0.30  | 12 | 12 | 1 |
| 6  | 15 | 1.83 | 2 | 0.44  | 12 | 16 | 2 |
| 7  | 15 | 1.78 | 3 | 0.91  | 12 | 12 | 1 |
| 8  | 13 | 2.12 | 4 | 0.51  | 12 | 15 | 2 |
| 9  | 13 | 1.95 | 2 | 0.86  | 12 | 12 | 2 |
| 10 | 11 | 2.19 | 5 | 0.26  | 12 | 12 | 2 |
| 11 | 12 | 2.44 | 1 | 1.82  | 16 | 17 | 2 |
| 12 | 13 | 2.41 | 4 | −1.30 | 13 | 12 | 5 |
| 13 | 12 | 2.07 | 3 | −0.63 | 12 | 12 | 4 |
| 14 | 12 | 2.20 | 6 | −0.36 | 10 | 12 | 2 |
| 15 | 12 | 2.12 | 3 | 0.28  | 10 | 12 | 3 |

Let $\mathbf{X}_1$ equal a constant, education, experience, and ability (the individual's own characteristics). Let $\mathbf{X}_2$ contain the mother's education, the father's education, and the number of siblings (the household characteristics). Let $\mathbf{y}$ be the wage.

a.  Compute the least squares regression coefficients in the regression of $\mathbf{y}$ on $\mathbf{X}_1$. Report the coefficients.

b.  Compute the least squares regression coefficients in the regression of $\mathbf{y}$ on $\mathbf{X}_1$ and $\mathbf{X}_2$. Report the coefficients.

c.  Regress each of the three variables in $\mathbf{X}_2$ on all of the variables in $\mathbf{X}_1$. These new variables are $\mathbf{X}_2^*$. What are the sample means of these three variables? Explain the finding.

d.  Using (3-26), compute the $R^2$ for the regression of $\mathbf{y}$ on $\mathbf{X}_1$ and $\mathbf{X}_2$. Repeat the computation for the case in which the constant term is omitted from $\mathbf{X}_1$. What happens to $R^2$?

e.  Compute the adjusted $R^2$ for the full regression including the constant term. Interpret your result.

f.  Referring to the result in part c, regress $\mathbf{y}$ on $\mathbf{X}_1$ and $\mathbf{X}_2^*$. How do your results compare to the results of the regression of $\mathbf{y}$ on $\mathbf{X}_1$ and $\mathbf{X}_2$? The comparison you are making is between the least squares coefficients when $\mathbf{y}$ is regressed on $\mathbf{X}_1$ and $\mathbf{M}_1\mathbf{X}_2$ and when $\mathbf{y}$ is regressed on $\mathbf{X}_1$ and $\mathbf{X}_2$. Derive the result theoretically. (Your numerical results should match the theory, of course.)

# 4

# STATISTICAL PROPERTIES OF THE LEAST SQUARES ESTIMATOR

## 4.1 INTRODUCTION

Chapter 3 treated fitting the linear regression to the data as a purely algebraic exercise. We will now examine the least squares **estimator** from a statistical viewpoint. This chapter will first consider exact, finite-sample results such as unbiased estimation and the precise distributions of certain test statistics. Some of these results require fairly strong assumptions, such as nonstochastic regressors or normally distributed disturbances. We will also examine the properties of the least squares estimator in more general cases. In these settings, we rely on approximations that do not hold as exact results but that do improve as the sample size increases.

There are other candidates for estimating $\beta$. In a two-variable case, for example, we might use the intercept, $a$, and slope, $b$, of the line between the points with the largest and smallest values of $x$. Alternatively, we might find the $a$ and $b$ that minimize the sum of absolute values of the residuals. The question of which estimator to choose is usually based on the **statistical properties** of the candidates, such as unbiasedness, efficiency, and precision. These, in turn, frequently depend on the particular distribution that we assume produced the data. However, a number of desirable properties can be obtained for the least squares estimator even without specifying a particular distribution for the disturbances in the regression.

In this chapter, we will examine in detail the least squares as an estimator of the model parameters of the classical model (defined in the following Table 4.1). We begin in Section 4.2 by returning to the question raised but not answered in Footnote 1, Chapter 3, that is, why least squares? We will then analyze the estimator in detail. We take Assumption A1, linearity of the model as given, although in Section 4.2, we will consider briefly the possibility of a different predictor for $y$. Assumption A2, the identification condition that the data matrix have full rank is considered in Section 4.8.1, where data complications that arise in practice are discussed. The near failure of this assumption is a recurrent problem in "real-world" data. Section 4.3 is concerned with unbiased estimation. Assumption A3, that the disturbances and the independent variables are uncorrelated, is a pivotal result in this discussion. Assumption A4, homoscedasticity and nonautocorrelation of the disturbances, in contrast to A3, only has relevance to whether least squares is an optimal use of the data. As noted, there are alternative estimators available, but with Assumption A4, the least squares estimator is usually going to be preferable. Sections 4.4 and 4.5 present several statistical results for the least squares estimator that depend crucially on this assumption. The assumption that the data in **X** are nonstochastic, known constants has some implications for how certain derivations proceed, but in

| TABLE 4.1 | Assumptions of the Classical Linear Regression Model |
| --- | --- |

**A1. Linearity:** $y_i = x_{i1}\beta_1 + x_{i2}\beta_2 + \cdots + \beta_K x_{iK} + \varepsilon_i$.

**A2. Full rank:** The $n \times K$ sample data matrix, **X** has full column rank.

**A3. Exogeneity of the independent variables:** $E[\varepsilon_i \mid x_{j1}, x_{j2}, \ldots, x_{jK}] = 0$, $i, j = 1, \ldots, n$. There is no correlation between the disturbances and the independent variables.

**A4. Homoscedasticity and nonautocorrelation:** Each disturbance, $\varepsilon_i$, has the same finite variance, $\sigma^2$, and is uncorrelated with every other disturbance, $\varepsilon_j$ conditioned on $x$.

**A5. Stochastic or nonstochastic data:** $(x_{i1}, x_{i2}, \ldots, x_{iK})$ $i = 1, \ldots, n$.

**A6. Normal distribution:** The disturbances are normally distributed.

practical terms, is a minor consideration. Indeed, nearly all that we do with the regression model departs from this assumption fairly quickly. It serves only as a useful departure point. The issue is considered in Section 4.5. The normality of the disturbances assumed in A6 is crucial in obtaining the **sampling distributions** of several useful statistics that are used in the analysis of the linear model. We note that in the course of our analysis of the linear model as we proceed through the text, most of these assumptions will be discarded.

The **finite-sample properties** of the least squares estimator are independent of the sample size. But the classical regression model with normally distributed disturbances and independent observations is a special case that does not include many of the most common applications, such as panel data and most time-series models. Section 4.9 will generalize the classical regression model by relaxing these two important assumptions.[1]

The linear model is one of relatively few settings in which any definite statements can be made about the exact finite sample properties of any estimator. In most cases, the only known properties of the estimators are those that apply to large samples. We can only approximate finite-sample behavior by using what we know about large-sample properties. This chapter will also examine the **asymptotic properties** of the parameter estimators in the classical regression model.

## 4.2 MOTIVATING LEAST SQUARES

Ease of computation is one reason that least squares is so popular. However, there are several other justifications for this technique. First, least squares is a natural approach to estimation, which makes explicit use of the structure of the model as laid out in the assumptions. Second, even if the true model is not a linear regression, the regression line fit by least squares is an optimal linear predictor for the dependent variable. Thus, it enjoys a sort of robustness that other estimators do not. Finally, under the very specific assumptions of the classical model, by one reasonable criterion, least squares will be the most efficient use of the data. We will consider each of these in turn.

### 4.2.1 THE POPULATION ORTHOGONALITY CONDITIONS

Let **x** denote the vector of independent variables in the population regression model and for the moment, based on assumption A5, the data may be stochastic or nonstochastic.

---

[1] Most of this discussion will use our results on asymptotic distributions. It may be helpful to review Appendix D before proceeding to this material.

Assumption A3 states that the disturbances in the population are stochastically orthogonal to the independent variables in the model; that is, $E[\varepsilon \mid \mathbf{x}] = 0$. It follows that $\text{Cov}[\mathbf{x}, \varepsilon] = \mathbf{0}$. Since (by the law of iterated expectations—Theorem B.1) $E_{\mathbf{x}}\{E[\varepsilon \mid \mathbf{x}]\} = E[\varepsilon] = 0$, we may write this as

$$E_{\mathbf{x}} E_{\varepsilon}[\mathbf{x}\varepsilon] = E_{\mathbf{x}} E_y[\mathbf{x}(y - \mathbf{x}'\boldsymbol{\beta})] = \mathbf{0}$$

or

$$E_{\mathbf{x}} E_y[\mathbf{x}y] = E_{\mathbf{x}}[\mathbf{x}\mathbf{x}']\boldsymbol{\beta}. \tag{4-1}$$

(The right-hand side is not a function of $y$ so the expectation is taken only over $\mathbf{x}$.) Now, recall the least squares normal equations, $\mathbf{X}'\mathbf{y} = \mathbf{X}'\mathbf{X}\mathbf{b}$. Divide this by $n$ and write it as a summation to obtain

$$\left(\frac{1}{n}\sum_{i=1}^{n}\mathbf{x}_i y_i\right) = \left(\frac{1}{n}\sum_{i=1}^{n}\mathbf{x}_i\mathbf{x}_i'\right)\mathbf{b}. \tag{4-2}$$

Equation (4-1) is a population relationship. Equation (4-2) is a sample analog. Assuming the conditions underlying the laws of large numbers presented in Appendix D are met, the sums on the left-hand and right-hand sides of (4-2) are estimators of their counterparts in (4-1). Thus, by using least squares, we are mimicking in the sample the relationship in the population. We'll return to this approach to estimation in Chapters 14 and 15 under the subject of GMM estimation.

### 4.2.2   MINIMUM MEAN SQUARED ERROR PREDICTOR

As an alternative approach, consider the problem of finding an **optimal linear predictor** for $y$. Once again, ignore Assumption A6 and, in addition, drop Assumption A1 that the conditional mean function, $E[y \mid \mathbf{x}]$ is linear. For the criterion, we will use the mean squared error rule, so we seek the minimum mean squared error linear predictor of $y$, which we'll denote $\mathbf{x}'\boldsymbol{\gamma}$. The expected squared error of this predictor is

$$\text{MSE} = E_y E_{\mathbf{x}}[y - \mathbf{x}'\boldsymbol{\gamma}]^2.$$

This can be written as

$$\text{MSE} = E_{y,\mathbf{x}}\{y - E[y \mid \mathbf{x}]\}^2 + E_{y,\mathbf{x}}\{E[y \mid \mathbf{x}] - \mathbf{x}'\boldsymbol{\gamma}\}^2.$$

We seek the $\boldsymbol{\gamma}$ that minimizes this expectation. The first term is not a function of $\boldsymbol{\gamma}$, so only the second term needs to be minimized. Note that this term is not a function of $y$, so the outer expectation is actually superfluous. But, we will need it shortly, so we will carry it for the present. The necessary condition is

$$\frac{\partial E_y E_{\mathbf{x}}\{[E(y \mid \mathbf{x}) - \mathbf{x}'\boldsymbol{\gamma}]^2\}}{\partial \boldsymbol{\gamma}} = E_y E_{\mathbf{x}}\left\{\frac{\partial[E(y \mid \mathbf{x}) - \mathbf{x}'\boldsymbol{\gamma}]^2}{\partial \boldsymbol{\gamma}}\right\}$$

$$= -2E_y E_{\mathbf{x}}\{\mathbf{x}[E(y \mid \mathbf{x}) - \mathbf{x}'\boldsymbol{\gamma}]\} = \mathbf{0}.$$

Note that we have interchanged the operations of expectation and differentiation in the middle step, since the range of integration is not a function of $\boldsymbol{\gamma}$. Finally, we have the equivalent condition

$$E_y E_\mathbf{x}[\mathbf{x} E(y \mid \mathbf{x})] = E_y E_\mathbf{x}[\mathbf{xx'}]\boldsymbol{\gamma}.$$

The left-hand side of this result is $E_\mathbf{x} E_y[\mathbf{x} E(y \mid \mathbf{x})] = \text{Cov}[\mathbf{x}, E(y \mid \mathbf{x})] + E[\mathbf{x}] E_\mathbf{x}[E(y \mid \mathbf{x})] = \text{Cov}[\mathbf{x}, y] + E[\mathbf{x}] E[y] = E_\mathbf{x} E_y[\mathbf{x}y]$. (We have used Theorem B.2.) Therefore, the necessary condition for finding the minimum MSE predictor is

$$E_\mathbf{x} E_y[\mathbf{x}y] = E_\mathbf{x} E_y[\mathbf{xx'}]\boldsymbol{\gamma}. \tag{4-3}$$

This is the same as (4-1), which takes us to the least squares condition once again. Assuming that these expectations exist, they would be estimated by the sums in (4-2), which means that regardless of the form of the conditional mean, least squares is an estimator of the coefficients of the minimum expected mean squared error linear predictor. We have yet to establish the conditions necessary for the if part of the theorem, but this is an opportune time to make it explicit:

---

**THEOREM 4.1**   **Minimum Mean Squared Error Predictor**
*If the data generating mechanism generating $(\mathbf{x}_i, y_i)_{i=1,\ldots,n}$ is such that the law of large numbers applies to the estimators in (4-2) of the matrices in (4-1), then the minimum expected squared error linear predictor of $y_i$ is estimated by the least squares regression line.*

---

### 4.2.3   MINIMUM VARIANCE LINEAR UNBIASED ESTIMATION

Finally, consider the problem of finding a **linear unbiased estimator.** If we seek the one that has smallest variance, we will be led once again to least squares. This proposition will be proved in Section 4.4.

The preceding does not assert that no other competing estimator would ever be preferable to least squares. We have restricted attention to linear estimators. The result immediately above precludes what might be an acceptably biased estimator. And, of course, the assumptions of the model might themselves not be valid. Although A5 and A6 are ultimately of minor consequence, the failure of any of the first four assumptions would make least squares much less attractive than we have suggested here.

## 4.3   UNBIASED ESTIMATION

The least squares estimator is unbiased in every sample. To show this, write

$$\mathbf{b} = (\mathbf{X'X})^{-1}\mathbf{X'y} = (\mathbf{X'X})^{-1}\mathbf{X'}(\mathbf{X}\boldsymbol{\beta} + \boldsymbol{\varepsilon}) = \boldsymbol{\beta} + (\mathbf{X'X})^{-1}\mathbf{X'}\boldsymbol{\varepsilon}. \tag{4-4}$$

Now, take expectations, iterating over $\mathbf{X}$;

$$E[\mathbf{b} \mid \mathbf{X}] = \boldsymbol{\beta} + E[(\mathbf{X'X})^{-1}\mathbf{X'}\boldsymbol{\varepsilon} \mid \mathbf{X}].$$

By Assumption A3, the second term is **0**, so

$$E[\mathbf{b}\,|\,\mathbf{X}] = \boldsymbol{\beta}.$$

Therefore,

$$E[\mathbf{b}] = E_{\mathbf{X}}\{E[\mathbf{b}\,|\,\mathbf{X}]\} = E_{\mathbf{X}}[\boldsymbol{\beta}] = \boldsymbol{\beta}.$$

The interpretation of this result is that for any particular set of observations, **X**, the least squares estimator has expectation $\boldsymbol{\beta}$. Therefore, when we average this over the possible values of **X** we find the unconditional mean is $\boldsymbol{\beta}$ as well.

### Example 4.1   The Sampling Distribution of a Least Squares Estimator

The following sampling experiment, which can be replicated with any regression program that provides a random number generator and a means of drawing a random sample of observations from a master data set, shows the nature of a sampling distribution and the implication of unbiasedness. We drew two samples of 10,000 random draws on $w_i$ and $x_i$ from the standard normal distribution (mean zero, variance 1). We then generated a set of $\varepsilon_i$s equal to $0.5w_i$ and $y_i = 0.5 + 0.5x_i + \varepsilon_i$. We take this to be our population. We then drew 500 random samples of 100 observations from this population, and with each one, computed the least squares slope (using at replication $r$, $b_r = [\sum_{j=1}^{100}(x_{jr} - \bar{x}_r)y_{jr}]/[\sum_{j=1}^{100}(x_{jr} - \bar{x}_r)^2])$. The histogram in Figure 4.1 shows the result of the experiment. Note that the distribution of slopes has a mean roughly equal to the "true value" of 0.5, and it has a substantial variance, reflecting the fact that the regression slope, like any other statistic computed from the sample, is a random variable. The concept of unbiasedness relates to the central tendency of this distribution of values obtained in repeated sampling from the population.

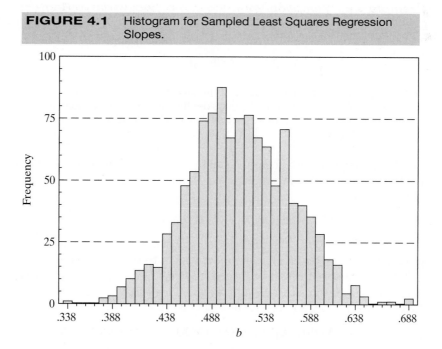

**FIGURE 4.1**   Histogram for Sampled Least Squares Regression Slopes.

## 4.4 THE VARIANCE OF THE LEAST SQUARES ESTIMATOR AND THE GAUSS–MARKOV THEOREM

If the regressors can be treated as nonstochastic, as they would be in an experimental situation in which the analyst chooses the values in $\mathbf{X}$, then the **sampling variance** of the least squares estimator can be derived by treating $\mathbf{X}$ as a matrix of constants. Alternatively, we can allow $\mathbf{X}$ to be stochastic, do the analysis conditionally on the observed $\mathbf{X}$, then consider averaging over $\mathbf{X}$ as we did in the preceding section. Using (4-4) again, we have

$$\mathbf{b} = (\mathbf{X}'\mathbf{X})^{-1}\mathbf{X}'(\mathbf{X}\boldsymbol{\beta} + \boldsymbol{\varepsilon}) = \boldsymbol{\beta} + (\mathbf{X}'\mathbf{X})^{-1}\mathbf{X}'\boldsymbol{\varepsilon}. \tag{4-5}$$

Since we can write $\mathbf{b} = \boldsymbol{\beta} + \mathbf{A}\boldsymbol{\varepsilon}$, where $\mathbf{A}$ is $(\mathbf{X}'\mathbf{X})^{-1}\mathbf{X}'$, $\mathbf{b}$ is a linear function of the disturbances, which by the definition we will use makes it a **linear estimator.** As we have seen, the expected value of the second term in (4-5) is $\mathbf{0}$. Therefore, *regardless of the distribution of $\boldsymbol{\varepsilon}$, under our other assumptions, $\mathbf{b}$ is a linear, unbiased estimator of $\boldsymbol{\beta}$.* The covariance matrix of the least squares slope estimator is

$$\begin{aligned}
\text{Var}[\mathbf{b} \,|\, \mathbf{X}] &= E[(\mathbf{b} - \boldsymbol{\beta})(\mathbf{b} - \boldsymbol{\beta})' \,|\, \mathbf{X}] \\
&= E[(\mathbf{X}'\mathbf{X})^{-1}\mathbf{X}'\boldsymbol{\varepsilon}\boldsymbol{\varepsilon}'\mathbf{X}(\mathbf{X}'\mathbf{X})^{-1} \,|\, \mathbf{X}] \\
&= (\mathbf{X}'\mathbf{X})^{-1}\mathbf{X}' E[\boldsymbol{\varepsilon}\boldsymbol{\varepsilon}' \,|\, \mathbf{X}]\mathbf{X}(\mathbf{X}'\mathbf{X})^{-1} \\
&= (\mathbf{X}'\mathbf{X})^{-1}\mathbf{X}'(\sigma^2\mathbf{I})\mathbf{X}(\mathbf{X}'\mathbf{X})^{-1} \\
&= \sigma^2(\mathbf{X}'\mathbf{X})^{-1}.
\end{aligned}$$

**Example 4.2  Sampling Variance in the Two-Variable Regression Model**
Suppose that $\mathbf{X}$ contains only a constant term (column of 1s) and a single regressor $\mathbf{x}$. The lower right element of $\sigma^2(\mathbf{X}'\mathbf{X})^{-1}$ is

$$\text{Var}[b \,|\, \mathbf{x}] = \text{Var}[b - \beta \,|\, \mathbf{x}] = \frac{\sigma^2}{\sum_{i=1}^{n}(x_i - \bar{x})^2}.$$

Note, in particular, the denominator of the variance of $b$. The greater the variation in $x$, the smaller this variance. For example, consider the problem of estimating the slopes of the two regressions in Figure 4.2. A more precise result will be obtained for the data in the right-hand panel of the figure.

We will now obtain a general result for the class of linear unbiased estimators of $\boldsymbol{\beta}$. Let $\mathbf{b}_0 = \mathbf{Cy}$ be another linear unbiased estimator of $\boldsymbol{\beta}$, where $\mathbf{C}$ is a $K \times n$ matrix. If $\mathbf{b}_0$ is unbiased, then

$$E[\mathbf{Cy} \,|\, \mathbf{X}] = E[(\mathbf{CX}\boldsymbol{\beta} + \mathbf{C}\boldsymbol{\varepsilon}) \,|\, \mathbf{X}] = \boldsymbol{\beta},$$

which implies that $\mathbf{CX} = \mathbf{I}$. There are many candidates. For example, consider using just the first $K$ (or, any $K$) linearly independent rows of $\mathbf{X}$. Then $\mathbf{C} = [\mathbf{X}_0^{-1} : \mathbf{0}]$, where $\mathbf{X}_0^{-1}$ is the inverse of the matrix formed from the $K$ rows of $\mathbf{X}$. The covariance matrix of $\mathbf{b}_0$ can be found by replacing $(\mathbf{X}'\mathbf{X})^{-1}\mathbf{X}'$ with $\mathbf{C}$ in (4-5); the result is $\text{Var}[\mathbf{b}_0 \,|\, \mathbf{X}] = \sigma^2\mathbf{CC}'$. Now let $\mathbf{D} = \mathbf{C} - (\mathbf{X}'\mathbf{X})^{-1}\mathbf{X}'$ so $\mathbf{Dy} = \mathbf{b}_0 - \mathbf{b}$. Then,

$$\text{Var}[\mathbf{b}_0 \,|\, \mathbf{X}] = \sigma^2[(\mathbf{D} + (\mathbf{X}'\mathbf{X})^{-1}\mathbf{X}')(\mathbf{D} + (\mathbf{X}'\mathbf{X})^{-1}\mathbf{X}')'].$$

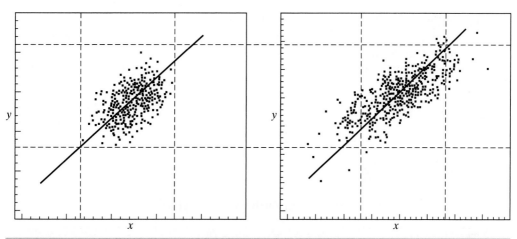

**FIGURE 4.2**    Effect of Increased Variation in x Given the Same Conditional and Overall Variation in y.

We know that $\mathbf{CX} = \mathbf{I} = \mathbf{DX} + (\mathbf{X'X})^{-1}(\mathbf{X'X})$, so $\mathbf{DX}$ must equal $\mathbf{0}$. Therefore,

$$\text{Var}[\mathbf{b}_0 \mid \mathbf{X}] = \sigma^2 (\mathbf{X'X})^{-1} + \sigma^2 \mathbf{DD'} = \text{Var}[\mathbf{b} \mid \mathbf{X}] + \sigma^2 \mathbf{DD'}.$$

Since a quadratic form in $\mathbf{DD'}$ is $\mathbf{q'DD'q} = \mathbf{z'z} \geq 0$, the conditional covariance matrix of $\mathbf{b}_0$ equals that of $\mathbf{b}$ plus a nonnegative definite matrix. Therefore, every quadratic form in $\text{Var}[\mathbf{b}_0 \mid \mathbf{X}]$ is larger than the corresponding quadratic form in $\text{Var}[\mathbf{b} \mid \mathbf{X}]$, which implies a very important property of the least squares coefficient vector.

---

**THEOREM 4.2    Gauss–Markov Theorem**

*In the classical linear regression model with regressor matrix* $\mathbf{X}$, *the least squares estimator* $\mathbf{b}$ *is the minimum variance linear unbiased estimator of* $\boldsymbol{\beta}$. *For any vector of constants* $\mathbf{w}$, *the minimum variance linear unbiased estimator of* $\mathbf{w'\beta}$ *in the classical regression model is* $\mathbf{w'b}$, *where* $\mathbf{b}$ *is the least squares estimator.*

---

The proof of the second statement follows from the previous derivation, since the variance of $\mathbf{w'b}$ is a quadratic form in $\text{Var}[\mathbf{b} \mid \mathbf{X}]$, and likewise for any $\mathbf{b}_0$, and proves that each individual slope estimator $b_k$ is the best linear unbiased estimator of $\beta_k$. (Let $\mathbf{w}$ be all zeros except for a one in the $k$th position.) The theorem is much broader than this, however, since the result also applies to every other linear combination of the elements of $\boldsymbol{\beta}$.

## 4.5    THE IMPLICATIONS OF STOCHASTIC REGRESSORS

The preceding analysis is done conditionally on the observed data. A convenient method of obtaining the unconditional statistical properties of $\mathbf{b}$ is to obtain the desired results conditioned on $\mathbf{X}$ first, then find the unconditional result by "averaging" (e.g., by integrating over) the conditional distributions. The crux of the argument is that if we can establish unbiasedness conditionally on an arbitrary $\mathbf{X}$, then we can average over $\mathbf{X}$'s to obtain an unconditional result. We have already used this approach to show the unconditional unbiasedness of $\mathbf{b}$ in Section 4.3, so we now turn to the conditional variance.

The conditional variance of $\mathbf{b}$ is

$$\text{Var}[\mathbf{b} \mid \mathbf{X}] = \sigma^2 (\mathbf{X}'\mathbf{X})^{-1}.$$

For the exact variance, we use the decomposition of variance of (B-69):

$$\text{Var}[\mathbf{b}] = E_{\mathbf{X}}[\text{Var}[\mathbf{b} \mid \mathbf{X}]] + \text{Var}_{\mathbf{X}}[E[\mathbf{b} \mid \mathbf{X}]].$$

The second term is zero since $E[\mathbf{b} \mid \mathbf{X}] = \boldsymbol{\beta}$ for all $\mathbf{X}$, so

$$\text{Var}[\mathbf{b}] = E_{\mathbf{X}}[\sigma^2 (\mathbf{X}'\mathbf{X})^{-1}] = \sigma^2 E_{\mathbf{X}}[(\mathbf{X}'\mathbf{X})^{-1}].$$

Our earlier conclusion is altered slightly. We must replace $(\mathbf{X}'\mathbf{X})^{-1}$ with its expected value to get the appropriate covariance matrix, which brings a subtle change in the interpretation of these results. The unconditional variance of $\mathbf{b}$ can only be described in terms of the average behavior of $\mathbf{X}$, so to proceed further, it would be necessary to make some assumptions about the variances and covariances of the regressors. We will return to this subject in Section 4.9.

We showed in Section 4.4 that

$$\text{Var}[\mathbf{b} \mid \mathbf{X}] \leq \text{Var}[\mathbf{b}_0 \mid \mathbf{X}]$$

for any $\mathbf{b}_0 \neq \mathbf{b}$ and for the specific $\mathbf{X}$ in our sample. But if this inequality holds for every particular $\mathbf{X}$, then it must hold for

$$\text{Var}[\mathbf{b}] = E_{\mathbf{X}}[\text{Var}[\mathbf{b} \mid \mathbf{X}]].$$

That is, if it holds for every particular $\mathbf{X}$, then it must hold over the average value(s) of $\mathbf{X}$.

The conclusion, therefore, is that the important results we have obtained thus far for the least squares estimator, unbiasedness, and the Gauss–Markov theorem hold whether or not we regard $\mathbf{X}$ as stochastic.

**THEOREM 4.3** Gauss–Markov Theorem (Concluded)
*In the classical linear regression model, the least squares estimator $\mathbf{b}$ is the minimum variance linear unbiased estimator of $\boldsymbol{\beta}$ whether $\mathbf{X}$ is stochastic or nonstochastic, so long as the other assumptions of the model continue to hold.*

## 4.6 ESTIMATING THE VARIANCE OF THE LEAST SQUARES ESTIMATOR

If we wish to test hypotheses about $\beta$ or to form confidence intervals, then we will require a sample estimate of the covariance matrix $\text{Var}[\mathbf{b} \mid \mathbf{X}] = \sigma^2(\mathbf{X}'\mathbf{X})^{-1}$. The population parameter $\sigma^2$ remains to be estimated. Since $\sigma^2$ is the expected value of $\varepsilon_i^2$ and $e_i$ is an estimate of $\varepsilon_i$, by analogy,

$$\hat{\sigma}^2 = \frac{1}{n} \sum_{i=1}^{n} e_i^2$$

would seem to be a natural estimator. But the least squares residuals are imperfect estimates of their population counterparts; $e_i = y_i - \mathbf{x}_i'\mathbf{b} = \varepsilon_i - \mathbf{x}_i'(\mathbf{b} - \beta)$. The estimator is distorted (as might be expected) because $\beta$ is not observed directly. The expected square on the right-hand side involves a second term that might not have expected value zero.

The least squares residuals are

$$\mathbf{e} = \mathbf{My} = \mathbf{M}[\mathbf{X}\beta + \varepsilon] = \mathbf{M}\varepsilon,$$

as $\mathbf{MX} = \mathbf{0}$. [See (3-15).] An estimator of $\sigma^2$ will be based on the sum of squared residuals:

$$\mathbf{e}'\mathbf{e} = \varepsilon'\mathbf{M}\varepsilon. \tag{4-6}$$

The expected value of this quadratic form is

$$E[\mathbf{e}'\mathbf{e} \mid \mathbf{X}] = E[\varepsilon'\mathbf{M}\varepsilon \mid \mathbf{X}].$$

The scalar $\varepsilon'\mathbf{M}\varepsilon$ is a $1 \times 1$ matrix, so it is equal to its trace. By using the result on cyclic permutations (A-94),

$$E[\text{tr}(\varepsilon'\mathbf{M}\varepsilon) \mid \mathbf{X}] = E[\text{tr}(\mathbf{M}\varepsilon\varepsilon') \mid \mathbf{X}].$$

Since $\mathbf{M}$ is a function of $\mathbf{X}$, the result is

$$\text{tr}(\mathbf{M}E[\varepsilon\varepsilon' \mid \mathbf{X}]) = \text{tr}(\mathbf{M}\sigma^2\mathbf{I}) = \sigma^2\text{tr}(\mathbf{M}).$$

The trace of $\mathbf{M}$ is

$$\text{tr}[\mathbf{I}_n - \mathbf{X}(\mathbf{X}'\mathbf{X})^{-1}\mathbf{X}'] = \text{tr}(\mathbf{I}_n) - \text{tr}[(\mathbf{X}'\mathbf{X})^{-1}\mathbf{X}'\mathbf{X}] = \text{tr}(\mathbf{I}_n) - \text{tr}(\mathbf{I}_K) = n - K.$$

Therefore,

$$E[\mathbf{e}'\mathbf{e} \mid \mathbf{X}] = (n - K)\sigma^2,$$

so the natural estimator is biased toward zero, although the bias becomes smaller as the sample size increases. An unbiased estimator of $\sigma^2$ is

$$s^2 = \frac{\mathbf{e}'\mathbf{e}}{n - K}. \tag{4-7}$$

The estimator is unbiased unconditionally as well, since $E[s^2] = E_{\mathbf{X}}\{E[s^2 \mid \mathbf{X}]\} = E_{\mathbf{X}}[\sigma^2] = \sigma^2$. The **standard error of the regression** is $s$, the square root of $s^2$. With $s^2$, we can then compute

$$\text{Est. Var}[\mathbf{b} \mid \mathbf{X}] = s^2(\mathbf{X}'\mathbf{X})^{-1}.$$

Henceforth, we shall use the notation Est. Var[·] to indicate a sample estimate of the sampling variance of an estimator. The square root of the $k$th diagonal element of this matrix, $\{[s^2(\mathbf{X}'\mathbf{X})^{-1}]_{kk}\}^{1/2}$, is the **standard error** of the estimator $b_k$, which is often denoted simply "the standard error of $b_k$."

## 4.7 THE NORMALITY ASSUMPTION AND BASIC STATISTICAL INFERENCE

To this point, our specification and analysis of the regression model is **semiparametric** (see Section 14.3). We have not used Assumption A6 (see Table 4.1), normality of $\boldsymbol{\varepsilon}$, in any of our results. The assumption is useful for constructing statistics for testing hypotheses. In (4-5), $\mathbf{b}$ is a linear function of the disturbance vector $\boldsymbol{\varepsilon}$. If we assume that $\boldsymbol{\varepsilon}$ has a multivariate normal distribution, then we may use the results of Section B.10.2 and the mean vector and covariance matrix derived earlier to state that

$$\mathbf{b}\,|\,\mathbf{X} \sim N[\boldsymbol{\beta}, \sigma^2(\mathbf{X}'\mathbf{X})^{-1}]. \tag{4-8}$$

This specifies a multivariate normal distribution, so each element of $\mathbf{b}\,|\,\mathbf{X}$ is normally distributed:

$$b_k\,|\,\mathbf{X} \sim N[\beta_k, \sigma^2(\mathbf{X}'\mathbf{X})^{-1}_{kk}]. \tag{4-9}$$

The distribution of $\mathbf{b}$ is conditioned on $\mathbf{X}$. The normal distribution of $\mathbf{b}$ in a finite sample is a consequence of our specific assumption of normally distributed disturbances. Without this assumption, and without some alternative specific assumption about the distribution of $\boldsymbol{\varepsilon}$, we will not be able to make any definite statement about the exact distribution of $\mathbf{b}$, conditional or otherwise. In an interesting result that we will explore at length in Section 4.8, we *will* be able to obtain an approximate normal distribution for $\mathbf{b}$, with or without assuming normally distributed disturbances and whether the regressors are stochastic or not.

### 4.7.1 TESTING A HYPOTHESIS ABOUT A COEFFICIENT

Let $S^{kk}$ be the $k$th diagonal element of $(\mathbf{X}'\mathbf{X})^{-1}$. Then, assuming normality and conditioned on $\mathbf{X}$,

$$z_k = \frac{b_k - \beta_k}{\sqrt{\sigma^2 S^{kk}}} \tag{4-10}$$

has a standard normal distribution. If $\sigma^2$ were known, then statistical inference about $\beta_k$ could be based on $z_k$. By using $s^2$ instead of $\sigma^2$, we can derive a statistic to use in place of $z_k$ in (4-10). The quantity

$$\frac{(n-K)s^2}{\sigma^2} = \frac{\mathbf{e}'\mathbf{e}}{\sigma^2} = \left(\frac{\boldsymbol{\varepsilon}}{\sigma}\right)'\mathbf{M}\left(\frac{\boldsymbol{\varepsilon}}{\sigma}\right) \tag{4-11}$$

is an idempotent quadratic form in a standard normal vector $(\boldsymbol{\varepsilon}/\sigma)$. Therefore, it has a chi-squared distribution with rank $(\mathbf{M})$ = trace$(\mathbf{M})$ = $n - K$ degrees of freedom.[2] The

---

[2]This result is proved in Section B.11.4.

chi-squared variable in (4-11) is independent of the standard normal variable in (4-10). To prove this, it suffices to show that

$$\frac{\mathbf{b} - \boldsymbol{\beta}}{\sigma} = (\mathbf{X}'\mathbf{X})^{-1}\mathbf{X}'\left(\frac{\boldsymbol{\varepsilon}}{\sigma}\right) \tag{4-12}$$

is independent of $(n - K)s^2/\sigma^2$. In Section B.11.7 (Theorem B.12), we found that a sufficient condition for the independence of a linear form $\mathbf{Lx}$ and an idempotent quadratic form $\mathbf{x}'\mathbf{Ax}$ in a standard normal vector $\mathbf{x}$ is that $\mathbf{LA} = \mathbf{0}$. Letting $\boldsymbol{\varepsilon}/\sigma$ be the $\mathbf{x}$, we find that the requirement here would be that $(\mathbf{X}'\mathbf{X})^{-1}\mathbf{X}'\mathbf{M} = \mathbf{0}$. It does, as seen in (3-15). The general result is central in the derivation of many test statistics in regression analysis.

> ### THEOREM 4.4   Independence of b and $s^2$
> *If $\boldsymbol{\varepsilon}$ is normally distributed, then the least squares coefficient estimator $\mathbf{b}$ is statistically independent of the residual vector $\mathbf{e}$ and therefore, all functions of $\mathbf{e}$, including $s^2$.*

Therefore, the ratio

$$t_k = \frac{(b_k - \beta_k)/\sqrt{\sigma^2 S^{kk}}}{\sqrt{[(n - K)s^2/\sigma^2]/(n - K)}} = \frac{b_k - \beta_k}{\sqrt{s^2 S^{kk}}} \tag{4-13}$$

has a $t$ distribution with $(n - K)$ degrees of freedom.[3] We can use $t_k$ to test hypotheses or form confidence intervals about the individual elements of $\boldsymbol{\beta}$.

A common test is whether a parameter $\beta_k$ is significantly different from zero. The appropriate test statistic

$$t = \frac{b_k}{s_{b_k}} \tag{4-14}$$

is presented as standard output with the other results by most computer programs. The test is done in the usual way. This statistic is usually labeled the *t* **ratio** for the estimator $b_k$. If $|b_k|/s_{b_k} > t_{\alpha/2}$, where $t_{\alpha/2}$ is the $100(1 - \alpha/2)$ percent critical value from the $t$ distribution with $(n - K)$ degrees of freedom, then the hypothesis is rejected and the coefficient is said to be "statistically significant." The value of 1.96, which would apply for the 95 percent significance level in a large sample, is often used as a benchmark value when a table of critical values is not immediately available. The $t$ ratio for the test of the hypothesis that a coefficient equals zero is a standard part of the regression output of most computer programs.

### Example 4.3   Earnings Equation
Appendix Table F4.1 contains 753 observations used in Mroz's (1987) study of labor supply behavior of married women. We will use these data at several points below. Of the 753 individuals in the sample, 428 were participants in the formal labor market. For these individuals,

---

[3]See (B-36) in Section B.4.2. It is the ratio of a standard normal variable to the square root of a chi-squared variable divided by its degrees of freedom.

| TABLE 4.2 | Regression Results for an Earnings Equation | | |
|---|---|---|---|

| Sum of squared residuals: | | | 599.4582 |
|---|---|---|---|
| Standard error of the regression: | | | 1.19044 |

| $R^2$ based on 428 observations | | | 0.040995 |
|---|---|---|---|

| Variable | Coefficient | Standard Error | t Ratio |
|---|---|---|---|
| Constant | 3.24009 | 1.7674 | 1.833 |
| Age | 0.20056 | 0.08386 | 2.392 |
| $Age^2$ | −0.0023147 | 0.00098688 | −2.345 |
| Education | 0.067472 | 0.025248 | 2.672 |
| Kids | −0.35119 | 0.14753 | −2.380 |

*Estimated Covariance Matrix for b* ($e - n =$ *times* $10^{-n}$)

| Constant | Age | $Age^2$ | Education | Kids |
|---|---|---|---|---|
| 3.12381 | | | | |
| −0.14409 | 0.0070325 | | | |
| 0.0016617 | −8.23237e−5 | 9.73928e−7 | | |
| −0.0092609 | 5.08549e−5 | −4.96761e−7 | 0.00063729 | |
| 0.026749 | −0.0026412 | 3.84102e−5 | −5.46193e−5 | 0.021766 |

we will fit a semilog earnings equation of the form suggested in Example 2.2;

$$\ln earnings = \beta_1 + \beta_2\, age + \beta_3\, age^2 + \beta_4\, education + \beta_5\, kids + \varepsilon,$$

where *earnings* is *hourly wage* times *hours worked*, *education* is measured in years of schooling, and *kids* is a binary variable which equals one if there are children under 18 in the household. (See the data description in Appendix F for details.) Regression results are shown in Table 4.2. There are 428 observations and 5 parameters, so the *t* statistics have 423 degrees of freedom. For 95 percent significance levels, the standard normal value of 1.96 is appropriate when the degrees of freedom are this large. By this measure, all variables are statistically significant and signs are consistent with expectations. It will be interesting to investigate whether the effect of kids is on the wage or hours, or both. We interpret the schooling variable to imply that an additional year of schooling is associated with a 6.7 percent increase in earnings. The quadratic age profile suggests that for a given education level and family size, earnings rise to the peak at $-b_2/(2b_3)$ which is about 43 years of age, at which they begin to decline. Some points to note: (1) Our selection of only those individuals who had positive hours worked is not an innocent sample selection mechanism. Since individuals chose whether or not to be in the labor force, it is likely (almost certain) that earnings potential was a significant factor, along with some other aspects we will consider in Chapter 23. (2) The earnings equation is a mixture of a labor supply equation—hours worked by the individual, and a labor demand outcome—the wage is, presumably, an accepted offer. As such, it is unclear what the precise nature of this equation is. Presumably, it is a hash of the equations of an elaborate structural equation system. (See Example 1.1 for discussion.)

### 4.7.2 CONFIDENCE INTERVALS FOR PARAMETERS

A confidence interval for $\beta_k$ would be based on (4-13). We could say that

$$\text{Prob}(b_k - t_{\alpha/2} s_{b_k} \le \beta_k \le b_k + t_{\alpha/2} s_{b_k}) = 1 - \alpha,$$

where $1 - \alpha$ is the desired level of confidence and $t_{\alpha/2}$ is the appropriate critical value from the *t* distribution with $(n - K)$ degrees of freedom.

**TABLE 4.3** Regression Results for a Demand Equation

| Sum of squared residuals: | 0.120871 |
| Standard error of the regression: | 0.050712 |
| $R^2$ based on 52 observations | 0.958443 |

| Variable | Coefficient | Standard Error | t Ratio |
| --- | --- | --- | --- |
| Constant | −21.21109 | 0.75322 | −28.160 |
| ln $P_G$ | −0.021206 | 0.04377 | −0.0485 |
| ln $Income/Pop$ | 1.095874 | 0.07771 | 14.102 |
| ln $P_{nc}$ | −0.373612 | 0.15707 | −2.379 |
| ln $P_{uc}$ | 0.02003 | 0.10330 | 0.194 |

*Example 4.4* *Confidence Interval for the Income Elasticity of Demand for Gasoline*

Using the gasoline market data discussed in Example 2.3, we estimated the following demand equation using the 52 observations:

$$\ln(G/Pop) = \beta_1 + \beta_2 \ln P_G + \beta_3 \ln(Income/Pop) + \beta_4 \ln P_{nc} + \beta_5 \ln P_{uc} + \varepsilon.$$

Least squares estimates of the model parameters with standard errors and $t$ ratios are given in Table 4.3.

To form a confidence interval for the income elasticity, we need the critical value from the $t$ distribution with $n - K = 52 - 5 = 47$ degrees of freedom. The 95 percent critical value is 2.012. Therefore a 95 percent confidence interval for $\beta_3$ is $1.095874 \pm 2.012\,(0.07771) = [0.9395, 1.2522]$.

We are interested in whether the demand for gasoline is income inelastic. The hypothesis to be tested is that $\beta_3$ is less than 1. For a one-sided test, we adjust the critical region and use the $t_\alpha$ critical point from the distribution. Values of the sample estimate that are greatly inconsistent with the hypothesis cast doubt on it. Consider testing the hypothesis

$$H_0 : \beta_3 < 1 \quad \text{versus} \quad H_1 : \beta_3 \geq 1.$$

The appropriate test statistic is

$$t = \frac{1.095874 - 1}{0.07771} = 1.234.$$

The critical value for a one-tailed test using the $t$ distribution with 47 degrees of freedom is 1.678, which is greater than 1.234. We conclude that the data are consistent with the hypothesis that the income elasticity is less than one, so we do not reject the null hypothesis.

### 4.7.3 CONFIDENCE INTERVAL FOR A LINEAR COMBINATION OF COEFFICIENTS: THE OAXACA DECOMPOSITION

With normally distributed disturbances, the least squares coefficient estimator, **b**, is normally distributed with mean **β** and covariance matrix $\sigma^2(\mathbf{X'X})^{-1}$. In Example 4.4, we showed how to use this result to form a confidence interval for one of the elements of **β**. By extending those results, we can show how to form a confidence interval for a linear function of the parameters. **Oaxaca** (1973) and **Blinder's** (1973) **decomposition** provides a frequently used application.[4]

Let **w** denote a $K \times 1$ vector of known constants. Then, the linear combination $c = \mathbf{w'b}$ is normally distributed with mean $\gamma = \mathbf{w'\beta}$ and variance $\sigma_c^2 = \mathbf{w'}[\sigma^2(\mathbf{X'X})^{-1}]\mathbf{w}$,

---

[4]See Bourgignon et al. (2002) for an extensive application.

which we estimate with $s_c^2 = \mathbf{w}'[s^2(\mathbf{X}'\mathbf{X})^{-1}]\mathbf{w}$. With these in hand, we can use the earlier results to form a confidence interval for $\gamma$:

$$\text{Prob}[c - t_{\alpha/2}s_c \le \gamma \le c + t_{\alpha/2}s_c] = 1 - \alpha.$$

This general result can be used, for example, for the sum of the coefficients or for a difference.

Consider, then, Oaxaca's application. In a study of labor supply, separate wage regressions are fit for samples of $n_m$ men and $n_f$ women. The underlying regression models are

$$\ln \text{wage}_{m,i} = \mathbf{x}'_{m,i}\boldsymbol{\beta}_m + \varepsilon_{m,i}, \quad i = 1, \ldots, n_m$$

and

$$\ln \text{wage}_{f,j} = \mathbf{x}'_{f,j}\boldsymbol{\beta}_f + \varepsilon_{f,j}, \quad j = 1, \ldots, n_f.$$

The regressor vectors include sociodemographic variables, such as age, and human capital variables, such as education and experience. We are interested in comparing these two regressions, particularly to see if they suggest wage discrimination. Oaxaca suggested a comparison of the regression functions. For any two vectors of characteristics,

$$\begin{aligned} E[\ln \text{wage}_{m,i}] - E[\ln \text{wage}_{f,j}] &= \mathbf{x}'_{m,i}\boldsymbol{\beta}_m - \mathbf{x}'_{f,j}\boldsymbol{\beta}_f \\ &= \mathbf{x}'_{m,i}\boldsymbol{\beta}_m - \mathbf{x}'_{m,i}\boldsymbol{\beta}_f + \mathbf{x}'_{m,i}\boldsymbol{\beta}_f - \mathbf{x}'_{f,j}\boldsymbol{\beta}_f \\ &= \mathbf{x}'_{m,i}(\boldsymbol{\beta}_m - \boldsymbol{\beta}_f) + (\mathbf{x}_{m,i} - \mathbf{x}_{f,j})'\boldsymbol{\beta}_f. \end{aligned}$$

The second term in this decomposition is identified with differences in human capital that would explain wage differences naturally, assuming that labor markets respond to these differences in ways that we would expect. The first term shows the differential in log wages that is attributable to differences unexplainable by human capital; holding these factors constant at $\mathbf{x}_m$ makes the first term attributable to other factors. Oaxaca suggested that this decomposition be computed at the means of the two regressor vectors, $\bar{\mathbf{x}}_m$ and $\bar{\mathbf{x}}_f$, and the least squares coefficient vectors, $\mathbf{b}_m$ and $\mathbf{b}_f$. If the regressions contain constant terms, then this process will be equivalent to analyzing $\overline{\ln y_m} - \overline{\ln y_f}$.

We are interested in forming a confidence interval for the first term, which will require two applications of our result. We will treat the two vectors of sample means as known vectors. Assuming that we have two independent sets of observations, our two estimators, $\mathbf{b}_m$ and $\mathbf{b}_f$, are independent with means $\boldsymbol{\beta}_m$ and $\boldsymbol{\beta}_f$ and covariance matrices $\sigma_m^2(\mathbf{X}'_m\mathbf{X}_m)^{-1}$ and $\sigma_f^2(\mathbf{X}'_f\mathbf{X}_f)^{-1}$. The covariance matrix of the difference is the sum of these two matrices. We are forming a confidence interval for $\bar{\mathbf{x}}'_m\mathbf{d}$ where $\mathbf{d} = \mathbf{b}_m - \mathbf{b}_f$. The estimated covariance matrix is

$$\text{Est. Var}[\mathbf{d}] = s_m^2(\mathbf{X}'_m\mathbf{X}_m)^{-1} + s_f^2(\mathbf{X}'_f\mathbf{X}_f)^{-1}. \tag{4-15}$$

Now, we can apply the result above. We can also form a confidence interval for the second term; just define $\mathbf{w} = \bar{\mathbf{x}}_m - \bar{\mathbf{x}}_f$ and apply the earlier result to $\mathbf{w}'\mathbf{b}_f$.

### 4.7.4 TESTING THE SIGNIFICANCE OF THE REGRESSION

A question that is usually of interest is whether the regression equation as a whole is significant. This test is a joint test of the hypotheses that *all* the coefficients except the constant term are zero. If all the slopes are zero, then the multiple correlation coefficient is zero as well, so we can base a test of this hypothesis on the value of $R^2$. The central result needed to carry out the test is the distribution of the statistic

$$F[K-1, n-K] = \frac{R^2/(K-1)}{(1-R^2)/(n-K)}. \tag{4-16}$$

If the hypothesis that $\beta_2 = 0$ (the part of $\beta$ not including the constant) is true and the disturbances are normally distributed, then this statistic has an $F$ distribution with $K-1$ and $n-K$ degrees of freedom.[5] Large values of $F$ give evidence against the validity of the hypothesis. Note that a large $F$ is induced by a large value of $R^2$.

The logic of the test is that the $F$ statistic is a measure of the loss of fit (namely, all of $R^2$) that results when we impose the restriction that all the slopes are zero. If $F$ is large, then the hypothesis is rejected.

### Example 4.5   F Test for the Earnings Equation
The $F$ ratio for testing the hypothesis that the four slopes in the earnings equation are all zero is

$$F[4, 423] = \frac{0.040995/4}{(1 - 0.040995)/(428 - 5)} = 4.521,$$

which is far larger than the 95 percent critical value of 2.37. We conclude that the data are inconsistent with the hypothesis that all the slopes in the earnings equation are zero.

We might have expected the preceding result, given the substantial $t$ ratios presented earlier. But this case need not always be true. Examples can be constructed in which the individual coefficients are statistically significant, while jointly they are not. This case can be regarded as pathological, but the opposite one, in which none of the coefficients is significantly different from zero while $R^2$ is highly significant, is relatively common. The problem is that the interaction among the variables may serve to obscure their individual contribution to the fit of the regression, whereas their joint effect may still be significant. We will return to this point in Section 4.8.1 in our discussion of multicollinearity.

### 4.7.5   MARGINAL DISTRIBUTIONS OF THE TEST STATISTICS

We now consider the relation between the sample test statistics and the data in $\mathbf{X}$. First, consider the conventional $t$ statistic in (4-14) for testing $H_0 : \beta_k = \beta_k^0$,

$$t \mid \mathbf{X} = \frac{(b_k - \beta_k^0)}{\left[s^2(\mathbf{X}'\mathbf{X})_{kk}^{-1}\right]^{1/2}}. \tag{4-17}$$

*Conditional on* $\mathbf{X}$, if $\beta_k = \beta_k^0$ (i.e., under $H_0$), then $t \mid \mathbf{X}$ has a $t$ distribution with $(n - K)$ degrees of freedom. What interests us, however, is the marginal, that is, the unconditional, distribution of $t$. As we saw, $\mathbf{b}$ is only normally distributed conditionally on $\mathbf{X}$; the marginal distribution may not be normal because it depends on $\mathbf{X}$ (through the conditional variance). Similarly, because of the presence of $\mathbf{X}$, the denominator of the $t$ statistic is not the square root of a chi-squared variable divided by its degrees of freedom, again, except conditional on this $\mathbf{X}$. But, because the distributions of $\{(b_k - \beta_k)/[\sigma^2(\mathbf{X}'\mathbf{X})_{kk}^{-1}]^{1/2}\} \mid \mathbf{X}$ and $[(n - K)s^2/\sigma^2] \mid \mathbf{X}$ are still independent $N[0, 1]$ and $\chi^2[n - K]$, respectively, which do not involve $\mathbf{X}$, we have the surprising result that,

---

[5]The proof of the distributional result appears in Section 5.3.1. The $F$ statistic given above is the special case in which $\mathbf{R} = [\mathbf{0} \mid \mathbf{I}_{K-1}]$.

regardless of the distribution of $\mathbf{X}$, or even of whether $\mathbf{X}$ is stochastic or nonstochastic, the marginal distributions of $t$ is still $t$, even though the marginal distribution of $b_k$ may be nonnormal. This intriguing result follows because $f(t \mid \mathbf{X})$ is not a function of $\mathbf{X}$. The same reasoning can be used to deduce that the usual $F$ ratio used for testing linear restrictions is valid whether $\mathbf{X}$ is stochastic or not. This result is very powerful. The implication is that *if the disturbances are normally distributed, then we may carry out tests and construct confidence intervals for the parameters without making any changes in our procedures, regardless of whether the regressors are stochastic, nonstochastic, or some mix of the two.*

## 4.8 FINITE-SAMPLE PROPERTIES OF THE LEAST SQUARES ESTIMATOR

A summary of the results we have obtained for the least squares estimator appears in Table 4.4. For constructing confidence intervals and testing hypotheses, we derived some additional results that depended explicitly on the normality assumption. Only FS7 depends on whether $\mathbf{X}$ is stochastic or not. If so, then the *marginal* distribution of $\mathbf{b}$ depends on that of $\mathbf{X}$. Note the distinction between the properties of $\mathbf{b}$ established using A1 through A4 and the additional inference results obtained with the further assumption of normality of the disturbances. The primary result in the first set is the Gauss–Markov theorem, which holds regardless of the distribution of the disturbances. The important additional results brought by the normality assumption are FS9 and FS10.

The behavior of the least squares estimator can be drastically affected by the characteristics of the data in a small (finite) sample. We consider two practical problems that arise in the setting of regression analysis, multicollinearity and missing observations.

**TABLE 4.4**   Finite Sample Properties of Least Squares

**General results:**

**FS1.**  $E[\mathbf{b} \mid \mathbf{X}] = E[\mathbf{b}] = \boldsymbol{\beta}$. Least squares is unbiased.

**FS2.**  $\text{Var}[\mathbf{b} \mid \mathbf{X}] = \sigma^2 (\mathbf{X'X})^{-1}$; $\text{Var}[\mathbf{b}] = \sigma^2 E[(\mathbf{X'X})^{-1}]$.

**FS3.**  **Gauss–Markov theorem:** The MVLUE of $\mathbf{w'}\boldsymbol{\beta}$ is $\mathbf{w'b}$.

**FS4.**  $E[s^2 \mid \mathbf{X}] = E[s^2] = \sigma^2$.

**FS5.**  $\text{Cov}[\mathbf{b}, \mathbf{e} \mid \mathbf{X}] = E[(\mathbf{b} - \boldsymbol{\beta})\mathbf{e'} \mid \mathbf{X}] = E[(\mathbf{X'X})^{-1}\mathbf{X'}\boldsymbol{\varepsilon}\boldsymbol{\varepsilon}'\mathbf{M} \mid \mathbf{X}] = \mathbf{0}$ as $\mathbf{X'}(\sigma^2\mathbf{I})\mathbf{M} = \mathbf{0}$.

**Results that follow from Assumption A6, normally distributed disturbances:**

**FS6.**  $\mathbf{b}$ and $\mathbf{e}$ are statistically independent. It follows that $\mathbf{b}$ and $s^2$ are uncorrelated and statistically independent.

**FS7.**  The exact distribution of $\mathbf{b} \mid \mathbf{X}$, is $N[\boldsymbol{\beta}, \sigma^2(\mathbf{X'X})^{-1}]$.

**FS8.**  $(n - K)s^2/\sigma^2 \sim \chi^2[n - K]$. $s^2$ has mean $\sigma^2$ and variance $2\sigma^4/(n - K)$.

**Test statistics based on results FS6 through FS8:**

**FS9.**  $t[n - K] = (b_k - \beta_k)/[s^2(\mathbf{X'X})_{kk}^{-1}]^{1/2} \sim t[n - K]$ independently of $\mathbf{X}$.

**FS10.**  The test statistic for testing the null hypothesis that all slopes in the model are zero, $F[K - 1, n - K] = [R^2/(K - 1)]/[(1 - R^2)/(n - K)]$ has an $F$ distribution with $K - 1$ and $n - K$ degrees of freedom when the null hypothesis is true.

### 4.8.1    MULTICOLLINEARITY

The Gauss–Markov theorem states that among all linear unbiased estimators, the least squares estimator has the smallest variance. Although this result is useful, it does not assure us that the least squares estimator has a small variance in any absolute sense. Consider, for example, a model that contains two explanatory variables and a constant. For either slope coefficient,

$$\text{Var}[b_k \mid \mathbf{X}] = \frac{\sigma^2}{\left(1 - r_{12}^2\right) \sum_{i=1}^{n}(x_{ik} - \bar{x}_k)^2} = \frac{\sigma^2}{\left(1 - r_{12}^2\right) S_{kk}}, \quad k = 1, 2. \tag{4-18}$$

If the two variables are perfectly correlated, then the variance is infinite. The case of an exact linear relationship among the regressors is a serious failure of the assumptions of the model, not of the data. The more common case is one in which the variables are highly, but not perfectly, correlated. In this instance, the regression model retains all its assumed properties, although potentially severe statistical problems arise. The problem faced by applied researchers when regressors are highly, although not perfectly, correlated include the following symptoms:

- Small changes in the data produce wide swings in the parameter estimates.
- Coefficients may have very high standard errors and low significance levels even though they are jointly significant and the $R^2$ for the regression is quite high.
- Coefficients may have the "wrong" sign or implausible magnitudes.

For convenience, define the data matrix, $\mathbf{X}$, to contain a constant and $K - 1$ other variables measured in deviations from their means. Let $\mathbf{x}_k$ denote the $k$th variable, and let $\mathbf{X}_{(k)}$ denote all the other variables (including the constant term). Then, in the inverse matrix, $(\mathbf{X'X})^{-1}$, the $k$th diagonal element is

$$
\begin{aligned}
\left(\mathbf{x}_k' \mathbf{M}_{(k)} \mathbf{x}_k\right)^{-1} &= \left[\mathbf{x}_k' \mathbf{x}_k - \mathbf{x}_k' \mathbf{X}_{(k)} \left(\mathbf{X}_{(k)}' \mathbf{X}_{(k)}\right)^{-1} \mathbf{X}_{(k)}' \mathbf{x}_k\right]^{-1} \\
&= \left[\mathbf{x}_k' \mathbf{x}_k \left(1 - \frac{\mathbf{x}_k' \mathbf{X}_{(k)} \left(\mathbf{X}_{(k)}' \mathbf{X}_{(k)}\right)^{-1} \mathbf{X}_{(k)}' \mathbf{x}_k}{\mathbf{x}_k' \mathbf{x}_k}\right)\right]^{-1} \\
&= \frac{1}{\left(1 - R_{k.}^2\right) S_{kk}},
\end{aligned}
\tag{4-19}
$$

where $R_{k.}^2$ is the $R^2$ in the regression of $x_k$ on all the other variables. In the multiple regression model, the variance of the $k$th least squares coefficient estimator is $\sigma^2$ times this ratio. It then follows that the more highly correlated a variable is with the other variables in the model (collectively), the greater its variance will be. In the most extreme case, in which $\mathbf{x}_k$ can be written as a linear combination of the other variables so that $R_{k.}^2 = 1$, the variance becomes infinite. The result

$$\text{Var}[b_k \mid \mathbf{X}] = \frac{\sigma^2}{\left(1 - R_{k.}^2\right) \sum_{i=1}^{n}(x_{ik} - \bar{x}_k)^2}, \tag{4-20}$$

shows the three ingredients of the precision of the $k$th least squares coefficient estimator:

- Other things being equal, the greater the correlation of $x_k$ with the other variables, the higher the variance will be, due to multicollinearity.

- Other things being equal, the greater the variation in $x_k$, the lower the variance will be. This result is shown in Figure 4.2.
- Other things being equal, the better the overall fit of the regression, the lower the variance will be. This result would follow from a lower value of $\sigma^2$. We have yet to develop this implication, but it can be suggested by Figure 4.2 by imagining the identical figure in the right panel but with all the points moved closer to the regression line.

Since nonexperimental data will never be orthogonal ($R_k^2 = 0$), to some extent multicollinearity will always be present. When is multicollinearity a problem? That is, when are the variances of our estimates so adversely affected by this intercorrelation that we should be "concerned"? Some computer packages report a **variance inflation factor** (VIF), $1/(1 - R_{k.}^2)$, for each coefficient in a regression as a diagnostic statistic. As can be seen, the VIF for a variable shows the increase in $\text{Var}[b_k]$ that can be attributable to the fact that this variable is not orthogonal to the other variables in the model. Another measure that is specifically directed at **X** is the **condition number** of **X′X**, which is the square root of the ratio of the largest characteristic root of **X′X** (after scaling each column so that it has unit length) to the smallest. Values in excess of 20 are suggested as indicative of a problem [Belsley, Kuh, and Welsch (1980)]. (The condition number for the Longley data of Example 4.6 is over 15,000!)

### Example 4.6   Multicollinearity in the Longley Data

The data in Appendix Table F4.2 were assembled by J. Longley (1967) for the purpose of assessing the accuracy of least squares computations by computer programs. (These data are still widely used for that purpose.) The Longley data are notorious for severe multicollinearity. Note, for example, the last year of the data set. The last observation does not appear to be unusual. But, the results in Table 4.5 show the dramatic effect of dropping this single observation from a regression of employment on a constant and the other variables. The last coefficient rises by 600 percent, and the third rises by 800 percent.

Several strategies have been proposed for finding and coping with multicollinearity.[6] Under the view that a multicollinearity "problem" arises because of a shortage of information, one suggestion is to obtain more data. One might argue that if analysts had such additional information available at the outset, they ought to have used it before reaching this juncture. More information need not mean more observations, however. The obvious practical remedy (and surely the most frequently used) is to drop variables suspected of causing the problem from the regression—that is, to impose on the regression an assumption, possibly erroneous, that the "problem" variable

| TABLE 4.5 | Longley Results: Dependent Variable is Employment | | |
|---|---|---|---|
| | *1947–1961* | *Variance Inflation* | *1947–1962* |
| Constant | 1,459,415 | | 1,169,087 |
| Year | −721.756 | 143.4638 | −576.464 |
| GNP deflator | −181.123 | 75.6716 | −19.7681 |
| GNP | 0.0910678 | 132.467 | 0.0643940 |
| Armed Forces | −0.0749370 | 1.55319 | −0.0101453 |

---

[6]See Hill and Adkins (2001) for a description of the standard set of tools for diagnosing collinearity.

does not appear in the model. In doing so, one encounters the problems of specification that we will discuss in Section 7.2. If the variable that is dropped actually belongs in the model (in the sense that its coefficient, $\beta_k$, is not zero), then estimates of the remaining coefficients will be biased, possibly severely so. On the other hand, overfitting—that is, trying to estimate a model that is too large—is a common error, and dropping variables from an excessively specified model might have some virtue. Several other practical approaches have also been suggested. An approach sometimes used [see, e.g., Gurmu, Rilstone, and Stern (1999)] is to use a small number, say $L$, of **principal components** constructed from the $K$ original variables. [See Johnson and Wichern (2005).] The problem here is that if the original model in the form $\mathbf{y} = \mathbf{X}\boldsymbol{\beta} + \boldsymbol{\varepsilon}$ were correct, then it is unclear what one is estimating when one regresses $\mathbf{y}$ on some small set of linear combinations of the columns of $\mathbf{X}$. Algebraically, it is simple; at least for the principal components case, in which we regress $\mathbf{y}$ on $\mathbf{Z} = \mathbf{X}\mathbf{C}_L$ to obtain $\mathbf{d}$, it follows that $E[\mathbf{d}] = \boldsymbol{\delta} = \mathbf{C}'_L \boldsymbol{\beta}$. In an economic context, if $\boldsymbol{\beta}$ has an interpretation, then it is unlikely that $\boldsymbol{\delta}$ will. (How do we interpret the price elasticity minus twice the income elasticity?)

Using diagnostic tools to detect multicollinearity could be viewed as an attempt to distinguish a bad model from bad data. But, in fact, the problem only stems from a prior opinion with which the data seem to be in conflict. A finding that suggests multicollinearity is adversely affecting the estimates seems to suggest that but for this effect, all the coefficients would be statistically significant and of the right sign. Of course, this situation need not be the case. If the data suggest that a variable is unimportant in a model, then, the theory notwithstanding, the researcher ultimately has to decide how strong the commitment is to that theory. Suggested "remedies" for multicollinearity might well amount to attempts to force the theory on the data.

### 4.8.2 MISSING OBSERVATIONS

It is common for data sets to have gaps, for a variety of reasons. Perhaps the most frequent occurrence of this problem is in survey data, in which respondents may simply fail to respond to the questions. In a time series, the data may be missing because they do not exist at the frequency we wish to observe them; for example, the model may specify monthly relationships, but some variables are observed only quarterly. In panel data sets, the gaps in the data may arise because of **attrition** from the study. This is particularly common in health and medical research, when individuals choose to leave the study—possibly because of the success or failure of the treatment that is being studied.

There are several possible cases to consider, depending on why the data are missing. The data may be simply unavailable, for reasons unknown to the analyst and unrelated to the completeness or the values of the other observations in the sample. This is the most benign situation. If this is the case, then the complete observations in the sample constitute a usable data set, and the only issue is what possibly helpful information could be salvaged from the incomplete observations. Griliches (1986) calls this the **ignorable case** in that, for purposes of estimation, if we are not concerned with efficiency, then we may simply delete the incomplete observations and ignore the problem. Rubin (1976, 1987) and Little and Rubin (1987) label this case **missing completely at random,** or MCAR.

A second case, which has attracted a great deal of attention in the econometrics literature, is that in which the gaps in the data set are not benign but are systematically related to the phenomenon being modeled. This case happens most often in surveys when the data are "self-selected" or "self-reported."[7] For example, if a survey were designed to study expenditure patterns and if high-income individuals tended to withhold information about their income, then the gaps in the data set would represent more than just missing information. The clinical trial case is another instance. In this (worst) case, the complete observations would be qualitatively different from a sample taken at random from the full population. The missing data in this situation are termed **not missing at random,** or NMAR. We treat this second case in Chapter 24 with the subject of **sample selection,** so we shall defer our discussion until later.

The intermediate case is that in which there is information about the missing data contained in the complete observations that can be used to improve inference about the model. The incomplete observations in this **missing at random** (MAR) case are also ignorable, in the sense that unlike the NMAR case, simply using the complete data does not induce any biases in the analysis, so long as the underlying process that produces the missingness in the data does not share parameters with the model that is being estimated, which seems likely. [See Allison (2002).] This case is unlikely, of course, if missingness is based on the values of the dependent variable in a regression. Ignoring the incomplete observations when they are MAR but not MCAR does ignore information that is in the sample and therefore sacrifices some efficiency.

Researchers have used a variety of **data imputation** methods to fill gaps in data sets. The (far) simpler case occurs when the gaps occur in the data on the regressors. For the case of missing data on the regressors, it helps to consider the simple regression and multiple regression cases separately. In the first case, **X** has two columns: the column of 1s for the constant and a column with some blanks where the missing data would be if we had them. The **zero-order method** of replacing each missing $x$ with $\bar{x}$ results in no changes and is equivalent to dropping the incomplete data. (See Exercise 7 in Chapter 3.) However, the $R^2$ will be lower. An alternative, **modified zero-order regression** fills the second column of **X** with zeros and adds a variable that takes the value 1 for missing observations and zero for complete ones.[8] We leave it as an exercise to show that this is algebraically identical to simply filling the gaps with $\bar{x}$. There also is the possibility of computing fitted values for the missing $x$'s by a regression of $x$ on $y$ in the complete data. The sampling properties of the resulting estimator are largely unknown, but what evidence there is suggests that this is not a beneficial way to proceed.[9]

These same methods can be used when there are multiple regressors. Once again, it is tempting to replace missing values of $\mathbf{x}_k$ with simple means of complete observations or with the predictions from linear regressions based on other variables in the model for which data are available when $\mathbf{x}_k$ is missing. In most cases in this setting, a general

---

[7]The vast surveys of Americans' opinions about sex by Ann Landers (1984, passim) and Shere Hite (1987) constitute two celebrated studies that were surely tainted by a heavy dose of self-selection bias. The latter was pilloried in numerous publications for purporting to represent the population at large instead of the opinions of those strongly enough inclined to respond to the survey. The former was presented with much greater modesty.

[8]See Maddala (1977a, p. 202).

[9]Afifi and Elashoff (1966, 1967) and Haitovsky (1968). Griliches (1986) considers a number of other possibilities.

characterization can be based on the principle that for any missing observation, the "true" unobserved $x_{ik}$ is being replaced by an erroneous proxy that we might view as $\hat{x}_{ik} = x_{ik} + u_{ik}$, that is, in the framework of **measurement error.** Generally, the least squares estimator is biased (and inconsistent) in the presence of measurement error such as this. (We will explore the issue in Chapter 12.) A question does remain: Is the bias likely to be reasonably small? As intuition should suggest, it depends on two features of the data: (a) how good the prediction of $x_{ik}$ is in the sense of how large the variance of the measurement error, $u_{ik}$, is compared to that of the actual data, $x_{ik}$, and (b) how large a proportion of the sample the analyst is filling.

The more manageable (and interesting) case is missing values of the dependent variable, $y_i$. Once again, it must be the case that $y_i$ is at least MAR and that the mechanism that is determining presence in the sample does not share parameters with the model itself. Assuming the data on $\mathbf{x}_i$ are complete for all observations, one might consider filling the gaps in the data on $y_i$ by a two-step procedure: (1) estimate $\beta$ with $\mathbf{b}_c$ using the complete observations, $\mathbf{X}_c$ and $\mathbf{y}_c$, then (2) fill the missing values, $\mathbf{y}_m$, with predictions, $\hat{\mathbf{y}}_m = \mathbf{X}_m\mathbf{b}_c$, and recompute the coefficients. We leave as an exercise (Exercise 17) to show that the second step estimator is exactly equal to the first. However, the variance estimator at the second step, $s^2$ must underestimate $\sigma^2$, intuitively because we are adding to the sample a set of observations that are fit perfectly. [See Cameron and Trivedi (2005, Chapter 27).] So, this is not a beneficial way to proceed. The flaw in the method comes back to the device used to impute the missing values for $y_i$. Recent suggestions that appear to provide some improvement involve using a randomized version, $\hat{\mathbf{y}}_m = \mathbf{X}_m\mathbf{b}_c + \hat{\boldsymbol{\varepsilon}}_m$, where $\hat{\boldsymbol{\varepsilon}}_m$ are random draws from the (normal) population with zero mean and estimated variance $s^2[\mathbf{I} + \mathbf{X}'_m(\mathbf{X}'_c\mathbf{X}_c)^{-1}\mathbf{X}'_m]$. (The estimated variance matrix corresponds to $\mathbf{X}_m\mathbf{b}_c + \boldsymbol{\varepsilon}_m$.) This defines an iteration. After reestimating $\beta$ with the augmented data, one can return to re-impute the augmented data with the new $\hat{\beta}$, then recompute $\mathbf{b}$, and so on. The process would continue until the estimated parameter vector stops changing. (A subtle point to be noted here: The same random draws should be used in each iteration. If not, there is no assurance that the iterations would ever converge.)

In general, not much is known about the properties of estimators based on using predicted values to fill missing values of $y$. Those results we do have are largely from simulation studies based on a particular data set or pattern of missing data. The results of these Monte Carlo studies are usually difficult to generalize. The overall conclusion seems to be that in a single-equation regression context, filling in missing values of $y$ leads to biases in the estimator which are difficult to quantify. The only reasonably clear result is that imputations are more likely to be beneficial if the proportion of observations that are being filled is small—the smaller the better.

## 4.9 LARGE SAMPLE PROPERTIES OF THE LEAST SQUARES ESTIMATOR

Using only assumptions A1 through A4 of the classical model (as listed in Table 4.1), we have established that the least squares estimators of the unknown parameters, $\beta$ and $\sigma^2$, have the **exact, finite-sample properties** listed in Table 4.4. For this basic model, it is straightforward to derive the large-sample, or **asymptotic properties** of the least squares estimator. The normality assumption, A6, becomes inessential at this point, and will be discarded save for discussions of maximum likelihood estimation in Chapter 16. This section will also consider various forms of Assumption A5, the data generating mechanism.

### 4.9.1 CONSISTENCY OF THE LEAST SQUARES ESTIMATOR OF β

To begin, we leave the data generating mechanism for **X** unspecified—**X** may be any mixture of constants and random variables generated independently of the process that generates $\boldsymbol{\varepsilon}$. We do make two crucial assumptions. The first is a modification of Assumption A5 in Table 4.1;

   **A5a.** $(\mathbf{x}_i, \varepsilon_i)$ $i = 1, \ldots, n$ is a sequence of *independent* observations.

The second concerns the behavior of the data in large samples;

$$\underset{n \to \infty}{\text{plim}} \frac{\mathbf{X}'\mathbf{X}}{n} = \mathbf{Q}, \quad \text{a positive definite matrix.} \tag{4-21}$$

[We will return to (4-21) shortly.] The least squares estimator may be written

$$\mathbf{b} = \boldsymbol{\beta} + \left(\frac{\mathbf{X}'\mathbf{X}}{n}\right)^{-1}\left(\frac{\mathbf{X}'\boldsymbol{\varepsilon}}{n}\right). \tag{4-22}$$

If $\mathbf{Q}^{-1}$ exists, then

$$\text{plim } \mathbf{b} = \boldsymbol{\beta} + \mathbf{Q}^{-1}\text{plim}\left(\frac{\mathbf{X}'\boldsymbol{\varepsilon}}{n}\right)$$

because the inverse is a continuous function of the original matrix. (We have invoked Theorem D.14.) We require the probability limit of the last term. Let

$$\frac{1}{n}\mathbf{X}'\boldsymbol{\varepsilon} = \frac{1}{n}\sum_{i=1}^{n}\mathbf{x}_i\varepsilon_i = \frac{1}{n}\sum_{i=1}^{n}\mathbf{w}_i = \overline{\mathbf{w}}. \tag{4-23}$$

Then

$$\text{plim } \mathbf{b} = \boldsymbol{\beta} + \mathbf{Q}^{-1}\text{ plim } \overline{\mathbf{w}}.$$

From the exogeneity Assumption A3, we have $E[\mathbf{w}_i] = E_{\mathbf{x}}[E[\mathbf{w}_i \mid \mathbf{x}_i]] = E_{\mathbf{x}}[\mathbf{x}_i E[\varepsilon_i \mid \mathbf{x}_i]]$ $= \mathbf{0}$, so the exact expectation is $E[\overline{\mathbf{w}}] = \mathbf{0}$. For any element in $\mathbf{x}_i$ that is nonstochastic, the zero expectations follow from the marginal distribution of $\varepsilon_i$. We now consider the variance. By (B-70), $\text{Var}[\overline{\mathbf{w}}] = E[\text{Var}[\overline{\mathbf{w}} \mid \mathbf{X}]] + \text{Var}[E[\overline{\mathbf{w}} \mid \mathbf{X}]]$. The second term is zero because $E[\varepsilon_i \mid \mathbf{x}_i] = 0$. To obtain the first, we use $E[\boldsymbol{\varepsilon\varepsilon}' \mid \mathbf{X}] = \sigma^2\mathbf{I}$, so

$$\text{Var}[\overline{\mathbf{w}} \mid \mathbf{X}] = E[\overline{\mathbf{w}}\,\overline{\mathbf{w}}' \mid \mathbf{X}] = \frac{1}{n}\mathbf{X}'E[\boldsymbol{\varepsilon\varepsilon}' \mid \mathbf{X}]\mathbf{X}\frac{1}{n} = \left(\frac{\sigma^2}{n}\right)\left(\frac{\mathbf{X}'\mathbf{X}}{n}\right).$$

Therefore,

$$\text{Var}[\overline{\mathbf{w}}] = \left(\frac{\sigma^2}{n}\right)E\left(\frac{\mathbf{X}'\mathbf{X}}{n}\right).$$

---

**TABLE 4.6**    Grenander Conditions for Well-Behaved Data

**G1.** For each column of $\mathbf{X}$, $\mathbf{x}_k$, if $d_{nk}^2 = \mathbf{x}_k'\mathbf{x}_k$, then $\lim_{n\to\infty} d_{nk}^2 = +\infty$. Hence, $\mathbf{x}_k$ does not degenerate to a sequence of zeros. Sums of squares will continue to grow as the sample size increases. No variable will degenerate to a sequence of zeros.

**G2.** $\lim_{n\to\infty} x_{ik}^2/d_{nk}^2 = 0$ for all $i = 1, \ldots, n$. This condition implies that no single observation will ever dominate $\mathbf{x}_k'\mathbf{x}_k$, and as $n \to \infty$, individual observations will become less important.

**G3.** Let $\mathbf{R}_n$ be the sample correlation matrix of the columns of $\mathbf{X}$, excluding the constant term if there is one. Then $\lim_{n\to\infty} \mathbf{R}_n = \mathbf{C}$, a positive definite matrix. This condition implies that the full rank condition will always be met. We have already assumed that $\mathbf{X}$ has full rank in a finite sample, so this assumption ensures that the condition will never be violated.

---

The variance will collapse to zero if the expectation in parentheses is (or converges to) a constant matrix, so that the leading scalar will dominate the product as $n$ increases. Assumption (4-21) should be sufficient. (Theoretically, the expectation could diverge while the probability limit does not, but this case would not be relevant for practical purposes.) It then follows that

$$\lim_{n\to\infty} \text{Var}[\overline{\mathbf{w}}] = 0 \cdot \mathbf{Q} = \mathbf{0}.$$

Since the mean of $\overline{\mathbf{w}}$ is identically zero and its variance converges to zero, $\overline{\mathbf{w}}$ **converges in mean square to zero,** so plim $\overline{\mathbf{w}} = \mathbf{0}$. Therefore,

$$\text{plim} \frac{\mathbf{X}'\boldsymbol{\varepsilon}}{n} = \mathbf{0}, \tag{4-24}$$

so

$$\text{plim } \mathbf{b} = \boldsymbol{\beta} + \mathbf{Q}^{-1} \cdot \mathbf{0} = \boldsymbol{\beta}. \tag{4-25}$$

This result establishes that under Assumptions A1–A4 and the additional assumption (4-21), $\mathbf{b}$ is a **consistent estimator** of $\boldsymbol{\beta}$ in the classical regression model.

    Time-series settings that involve time trends, polynomial time series, and trending variables often pose cases in which the preceding assumptions are too restrictive. A somewhat weaker set of assumptions about $\mathbf{X}$ that is broad enough to include most of these is the **Grenander conditions** listed in Table 4.6.[10] The conditions ensure that the data matrix is "well behaved" in large samples. The assumptions are very weak and likely to be satisfied by almost any data set encountered in practice.[11]

### 4.9.2   ASYMPTOTIC NORMALITY OF THE LEAST SQUARES ESTIMATOR

To derive the asymptotic distribution of the least squares estimator, we shall use the results of Section D.3. We will make use of some basic central limit theorems, so in addition to Assumption A3 (uncorrelatedness), we will assume that the observations

---

[10] Judge et al. (1985, p. 162).

[11] White (2001) continues this line of analysis.

are *independent*. It follows from (4-22) that

$$\sqrt{n}(\mathbf{b} - \boldsymbol{\beta}) = \left(\frac{\mathbf{X'X}}{n}\right)^{-1} \left(\frac{1}{\sqrt{n}}\right) \mathbf{X'\varepsilon}. \tag{4-26}$$

Since the inverse matrix is a continuous function of the original matrix, $\text{plim}(\mathbf{X'X}/n)^{-1} = \mathbf{Q}^{-1}$. Therefore, if the limiting distribution of the random vector in (4-26) exists, then that limiting distribution is the same as that of

$$\left[\text{plim}\left(\frac{\mathbf{X'X}}{n}\right)^{-1}\right]\left(\frac{1}{\sqrt{n}}\right)\mathbf{X'\varepsilon} = \mathbf{Q}^{-1}\left(\frac{1}{\sqrt{n}}\right)\mathbf{X'\varepsilon}. \tag{4-27}$$

Thus, we must establish the limiting distribution of

$$\left(\frac{1}{\sqrt{n}}\right)\mathbf{X'\varepsilon} = \sqrt{n}(\overline{\mathbf{w}} - E[\overline{\mathbf{w}}]), \tag{4-28}$$

where $E[\overline{\mathbf{w}}] = \mathbf{0}$. [See (4-23).] We can use the multivariate Lindeberg–Feller version of the central limit theorem (D.19.A) to obtain the limiting distribution of $\sqrt{n}\overline{\mathbf{w}}$.[12] Using that formulation, $\overline{\mathbf{w}}$ is the average of $n$ independent random vectors $\mathbf{w}_i = \mathbf{x}_i \varepsilon_i$, with means $\mathbf{0}$ and variances

$$\text{Var}[\mathbf{x}_i \varepsilon_i] = \sigma^2 E[\mathbf{x}_i \mathbf{x}_i'] = \sigma^2 \mathbf{Q}_i. \tag{4-29}$$

The variance of $\sqrt{n}\overline{\mathbf{w}}$ is

$$\sigma^2 \overline{\mathbf{Q}}_n = \sigma^2 \left(\frac{1}{n}\right)[\mathbf{Q}_1 + \mathbf{Q}_2 + \cdots + \mathbf{Q}_n]. \tag{4-30}$$

As long as the sum is not dominated by any particular term and the regressors are well behaved, which in this case means that (4-21) holds,

$$\lim_{n \to \infty} \sigma^2 \overline{\mathbf{Q}}_n = \sigma^2 \mathbf{Q}. \tag{4-31}$$

Therefore, we may apply the Lindeberg–Feller central limit theorem to the vector $\sqrt{n}\,\overline{\mathbf{w}}$, as we did in Section D.3 for the univariate case $\sqrt{n}\overline{x}$. We now have the elements we need for a formal result. If $[\mathbf{x}_i \varepsilon_i]$, $i = 1, \ldots, n$ are independent vectors distributed with mean $\mathbf{0}$ and variance $\sigma^2 \mathbf{Q}_i < \infty$, and if (4-21) holds, then

$$\left(\frac{1}{\sqrt{n}}\right)\mathbf{X'\varepsilon} \xrightarrow{d} N[\mathbf{0}, \sigma^2 \mathbf{Q}]. \tag{4-32}$$

It then follows that

$$\mathbf{Q}^{-1}\left(\frac{1}{\sqrt{n}}\right)\mathbf{X'\varepsilon} \xrightarrow{d} N[\mathbf{Q}^{-1}\mathbf{0}, \mathbf{Q}^{-1}(\sigma^2 \mathbf{Q})\mathbf{Q}^{-1}]. \tag{4-33}$$

Combining terms,

$$\sqrt{n}(\mathbf{b} - \boldsymbol{\beta}) \xrightarrow{d} N[\mathbf{0}, \sigma^2 \mathbf{Q}^{-1}]. \tag{4-34}$$

---

[12]Note that the Lindeberg–Levy version does not apply because $\text{Var}[\mathbf{w}_i]$ is not necessarily constant.

Using the technique of Section D.3, we obtain the **asymptotic distribution** of **b**:

---

**THEOREM 4.5** **Asymptotic Distribution of b with Independent Observations**

*If $\{\varepsilon_i\}$ are independently distributed with mean zero and finite variance $\sigma^2$ and $x_{ik}$ is such that the Grenander conditions are met, then*

$$\mathbf{b} \overset{a}{\sim} N\left[\boldsymbol{\beta}, \frac{\sigma^2}{n}\mathbf{Q}^{-1}\right]. \tag{4-35}$$

---

In practice, it is necessary to estimate $(1/n)\mathbf{Q}^{-1}$ with $(\mathbf{X}'\mathbf{X})^{-1}$ and $\sigma^2$ with $\mathbf{e}'\mathbf{e}/(n-K)$.

If $\boldsymbol{\varepsilon}$ is normally distributed, then Result **FS7** in (Table 4.4, Section 4.8) holds in *every* sample, so it holds asymptotically as well. The important implication of this derivation is that *if the regressors are well behaved and observations are independent,* then the **asymptotic normality** *of the least squares estimator does not depend on normality of the disturbances; it is a consequence of the central limit theorem.* We will consider other, more general cases in the sections to follow.

### 4.9.3 CONSISTENCY OF $s^2$ AND THE ESTIMATOR OF Asy. Var[b]

To complete the derivation of the asymptotic properties of **b**, we will require an estimator of Asy. Var$[\mathbf{b}] = (\sigma^2/n)\mathbf{Q}^{-1}$.[13] With (4-21), it is sufficient to restrict attention to $s^2$, so the purpose here is to assess the consistency of $s^2$ as an estimator of $\sigma^2$. Expanding

$$s^2 = \frac{1}{n-K}\boldsymbol{\varepsilon}'\mathbf{M}\boldsymbol{\varepsilon}$$

produces

$$s^2 = \frac{1}{n-K}[\boldsymbol{\varepsilon}'\boldsymbol{\varepsilon} - \boldsymbol{\varepsilon}'\mathbf{X}(\mathbf{X}'\mathbf{X})^{-1}\mathbf{X}'\boldsymbol{\varepsilon}] = \frac{n}{n-k}\left[\frac{\boldsymbol{\varepsilon}'\boldsymbol{\varepsilon}}{n} - \left(\frac{\boldsymbol{\varepsilon}'\mathbf{X}}{n}\right)\left(\frac{\mathbf{X}'\mathbf{X}}{n}\right)^{-1}\left(\frac{\mathbf{X}'\boldsymbol{\varepsilon}}{n}\right)\right].$$

The leading constant clearly converges to 1. We can apply (4-21), (4-24) (twice), and the product rule for **probability limits** (Theorem D.14) to assert that the second term in the brackets converges to 0. That leaves

$$\overline{\varepsilon^2} = \frac{1}{n}\sum_{i=1}^{n}\varepsilon_i^2.$$

This is a narrow case in which the random variables $\varepsilon_i^2$ are independent with the same finite mean $\sigma^2$, so not much is required to get the mean to converge almost surely to $\sigma^2 = E[\varepsilon_i^2]$. By the Markov theorem (D.8), what is needed is for $E[|\varepsilon_i^2|^{1+\delta}]$ to be finite, so the minimal assumption thus far is that $\varepsilon_i$ have finite moments up to slightly greater than 2. Indeed, if we further assume that every $\varepsilon_i$ has the same distribution, then by the Khinchine theorem (D.5) or the corollary to D8, finite moments (of $\varepsilon_i$) up to 2 is

---

[13] See McCallum (1973) for some useful commentary on deriving the asymptotic covariance matrix of the least squares estimator.

sufficient. **Mean square convergence** would require $E[\varepsilon_i^4] = \phi_\varepsilon < \infty$. Then the terms in the sum are independent, with mean $\sigma^2$ and variance $\phi_\varepsilon - \sigma^4$. So, under fairly weak conditions, the first term in brackets converges in probability to $\sigma^2$, which gives our result,

$$\text{plim } s^2 = \sigma^2,$$

and, by the product rule,

$$\text{plim } s^2(\mathbf{X}'\mathbf{X}/n)^{-1} = \sigma^2\mathbf{Q}^{-1}.$$

The appropriate *estimator* of the asymptotic covariance matrix of **b** is

$$\text{Est. Asy. Var}[\mathbf{b}] = s^2(\mathbf{X}'\mathbf{X})^{-1}.$$

### 4.9.4  ASYMPTOTIC DISTRIBUTION OF A FUNCTION OF b: THE DELTA METHOD AND THE METHOD OF KRINSKY AND ROBB

We can extend Theorem D.22 to functions of the least squares estimator. Let $\mathbf{f}(\mathbf{b})$ be a set of $J$ continuous, linear, or nonlinear and continuously differentiable functions of the least squares estimator, and let

$$\mathbf{C}(\mathbf{b}) = \frac{\partial \mathbf{f}(\mathbf{b})}{\partial \mathbf{b}'},$$

where **C** is the $J \times K$ matrix whose $j$th row is the vector of derivatives of the $j$th function with respect to $\mathbf{b}'$. By the Slutsky theorem (D.12),

$$\text{plim } \mathbf{f}(\mathbf{b}) = \mathbf{f}(\boldsymbol{\beta})$$

and

$$\text{plim } \mathbf{C}(\mathbf{b}) = \frac{\partial \mathbf{f}(\boldsymbol{\beta})}{\partial \boldsymbol{\beta}'} = \boldsymbol{\Gamma}.$$

Using our usual linear Taylor series approach (see Section 5.5), we expand this set of functions in the approximation

$$\mathbf{f}(\mathbf{b}) = \mathbf{f}(\boldsymbol{\beta}) + \boldsymbol{\Gamma} \times (\mathbf{b} - \boldsymbol{\beta}) + \text{higher-order terms.}$$

The higher-order terms become negligible in large samples if plim $\mathbf{b} = \boldsymbol{\beta}$. Then, the asymptotic distribution of the function on the left-hand side is the same as that on the right. Thus, the mean of the asymptotic distribution is plim $\mathbf{f}(\mathbf{b}) = \mathbf{f}(\boldsymbol{\beta})$, and the asymptotic covariance matrix is $\{\boldsymbol{\Gamma}[\text{Asy. Var}(\mathbf{b} - \boldsymbol{\beta})]\boldsymbol{\Gamma}'\}$, which gives us the following theorem:

---

**THEOREM 4.6**  **Asymptotic Distribution of a Function of b**

*If $\mathbf{f}(\mathbf{b})$ is a set of continuous and continuously differentiable functions of $\mathbf{b}$ such that $\boldsymbol{\Gamma} = \partial \mathbf{f}(\boldsymbol{\beta})/\partial \boldsymbol{\beta}'$ and if Theorem 4.5 holds, then*

$$\mathbf{f}(\mathbf{b}) \stackrel{a}{\sim} N\left[\mathbf{f}(\boldsymbol{\beta}), \boldsymbol{\Gamma}\left(\frac{\sigma^2}{n}\mathbf{Q}^{-1}\right)\boldsymbol{\Gamma}'\right]. \tag{4-36}$$

*In practice, the estimator of the asymptotic covariance matrix would be*

$$\text{Est. Asy. Var}[\mathbf{f}(\mathbf{b})] = \mathbf{C}[s^2(\mathbf{X}'\mathbf{X})^{-1}]\mathbf{C}'.$$

---

If any of the functions are nonlinear, then the property of unbiasedness that holds for **b** may not carry over to **f(b)**. Nonetheless, it follows from (4-25) that **f(b)** is a consistent estimator of **f(β)**, and the asymptotic covariance matrix is readily available.

### Example 4.7   Nonlinear Functions of Parameters: The Delta Method

A dynamic version of the demand for gasoline model in Example 4.4 would be used to separate the short and long term impacts of changes in income and prices. The model would be

$$\ln(G/Pop)_t = \beta_1 + \beta_2 \ln P_{G,t} + \beta_3 \ln(Income/Pop)_t + \beta_4 \ln P_{nc,t}$$

$$+ \beta_5 \ln P_{uc,t} + \gamma \ln(G/Pop)_{t-1} + \varepsilon_t.$$

In this model, the short run price and income elasticities are $\beta_2$ and $\beta_3$. The long run elasticities are $\phi_2 = \beta_2/(1 - \gamma)$ and $\phi_3 = \beta_3/(1 - \gamma)$, respectively. (See Section 20.3 for development of this model.) To estimate the long run elasticities, we will estimate the parameters by least squares and then compute these two nonlinear functions of the estimates. We can use the delta method to estimate the standard errors.

Least squares estimates of the model parameters with standard errors and $t$ ratios are given in Table 4.7. Note the much improved fit compared to the model in Example 4.4—this is typical when lagged values of the dependent variable are added to the regression.

The estimated short run elasticities are the estimates given in the table. The two estimated long run elasticites are $f_2 = b_2/(1 - c) = -0.069532/(1 - 0.830971) = -0.411358$ and $f_3 = 0.164047/(1 - 0.830971) = 0.970522$. (Note how close this estimate is to the estimate from the static equation in Example 4.4.). To compute the estimates of the standard errors, we need the partial derivatives of these functions with respect to the six parameters in the model:

$$\mathbf{g_2}' = \partial \phi_2 / \partial \boldsymbol{\beta}' = [0, 1/(1 - \gamma), 0, 0, 0, \beta_2/(1 - \gamma)^2] = [0, 5.91613, 0, 0, 0, -2.43365],$$

$$\mathbf{g_3}' = \partial \phi_3 / \partial \boldsymbol{\beta}' = [0, 0, 1/(1 - \gamma), 0, 0, \beta_3/(1 - \gamma)^2] = [0, 0, 5.91613, 0, 0, 5.74174].$$

### TABLE 4.7   Regression Results for a Demand Equation

| | |
|---|---|
| Sum of squared residuals: | 0.0127352 |
| Standard error of the regression: | 0.0168227 |
| $R^2$ based on 52 observations | 0.9951081 |

| Variable | Coefficient | Standard Error | t Ratio |
|---|---|---|---|
| Constant | −3.123195 | 0.99583 | −3.136 |
| ln $P_G$ | −0.069532 | 0.04377 | −4.720 |
| ln $Income/Pop$ | 0.164047 | 0.07771 | 2.981 |
| ln $P_{nc}$ | −0.178397 | 0.15707 | −3.377 |
| ln $P_{uc}$ | 0.127009 | 0.10330 | 3.551 |
| last period ln $G/Pop$ | 0.830971 | 0.04576 | 18.158 |

*Estimated Covariance Matrix for b (e − n = times 10⁻ⁿ)*

| Constant | ln $P_G$ | ln(Income/Pop) | ln $P_{nc}$ | ln $P_{uc}$ | ln(G/Pop)_{t−1} |
|---|---|---|---|---|---|
| 0.99168 | | | | | |
| −0.0012088 | 0.00021705 | | | | |
| −0.052602 | 1.62165e−5 | 0.0030279 | | | |
| 0.0051016 | −0.00021705 | −0.00024708 | 0.0030440 | | |
| 0.0091672 | −4.0551e−5 | −0.00060624 | −0.0016782 | 0.0012795 | |
| 0.043915 | −0.0001109 | −0.0021881 | 0.00068116 | 8.57001e−5 | 0.0020943 |

Using (4-36), we can now compute the estimates of the asymptotic variances for the two estimated long run elasticities by computing $\mathbf{g}_2'[s^2(\mathbf{X}'\mathbf{X})^{-1}]\mathbf{g}_2$ and $\mathbf{g}_3'[s^2(\mathbf{X}'\mathbf{X})^{-1}]\mathbf{g}_3$. The results are 0.023194 and 0.026368, respectively. The two asymptotic standard errors are the square roots, 0.152296 and 0.162386. We can also form confidence intervals in the same way that we did in Example 4.4. The 95 percent confidence interval for the long run price elasticity would be $-0.411361 \pm 2.013\,(0.152296) = [-0.717914, -0.104801]$. The interval for the income elasticity is $0.970527 \pm 2.013\,(0.162382) = [0.643656, 1.29739]$.

The recent literature contains some occasional skepticism about the accuracy of the delta method. The method of Krinsky and Robb (1986, 1990, 1991) is often suggested as an alternative. In a study of the behavior of estimated elasticities based on a translog model (see Example 2.4 and Section 10.4.2), Krinsky and Robb (1986) advocated an alternative approach based on Monte Carlo methods (see Chapter 17). The method is based on the law of large numbers. We have consistently estimated $\beta$ and $(\sigma^2/n)\mathbf{Q}^{-1}$, the mean and variance of the asymptotic distribution of the estimator $\mathbf{b}$. It follows that we could estimate the mean and variance of the distribution of a function of $\mathbf{b}$ by drawing a random sample of observations from the population generating $\mathbf{b}$, and using the empirical mean and variance of the sample of functions to estimate the parameters of the distribution of the function. The authors found some striking differences (orders of magnitude) in the resulting estimates of asymptotic standard errors. To detail their method, we continue the preceding example.

### Example 4.8 Nonlinear Functions of Parameters: The Krinsky and Robb Method

We have estimated the parameters $\beta_2$, $\beta_3$, and $\gamma$ by least squares. The estimates are shown in Table 4.7. The estimated asymptotic covariance matrix is the $3 \times 3$ submatrix of the estimated matrix shown in the example. These are

$$Est.\begin{pmatrix} \beta_2 \\ \beta_3 \\ \gamma \end{pmatrix} = \begin{pmatrix} b_2 \\ b_3 \\ c \end{pmatrix} = \begin{pmatrix} -0.069532 \\ 0.164047 \\ 0.830971 \end{pmatrix},$$

$$Est.\ Asy.\ Var\begin{pmatrix} b_2 \\ b_3 \\ c \end{pmatrix} = \begin{pmatrix} 0.00021705 & 1.61265e{-}5 & -0.0001109 \\ 1.61265e{-}5 & 0.0030279 & -0.0021881 \\ -0.0001109 & -0.0021881 & 0.0020943 \end{pmatrix}.$$

The suggested method would use a random number generator to draw a large trivariate sample, $(b_2, b_3, c)_r, r = 1, \ldots, R$, from the normal distribution with this mean vector and covariance matrix, then compute the sample of observations on $f_2$ and $f_3$ and obtain the empirical mean and variance from the sample. The method of drawing such a sample is shown in Section 17.2.4. We will require the square root of the covariance matrix—we will use the Cholesky matrix;

$$\mathbf{C} = \begin{pmatrix} 0.0147326 & 0 & 0 \\ 0.00109461 & 0.0550155 & 0 \\ -0.0075275 & -0.0396227 & 0.0216259 \end{pmatrix}.$$

The sample is drawn by drawn by obtaining vectors of three random draws from the standard normal population, $\mathbf{v}_r = (v_1, v_2, v_3)_r', r = 1, \ldots, R$. The draws needed for the estimation are obtained by computing $\mathbf{b}_r = \mathbf{b} + \mathbf{C}\mathbf{v}_r$ where $\mathbf{b}$ is the set of least squares estimates. We then compute the sample of estimated long run elasticities, $f_{2r} = b_{2r}/(1 - c_r)$ and $f_{3r} = b_{3r}/(1 - c_r)$. The mean and variance of the sample observations constitute the estimates of the functions and asymptotic standard errors. Table 4.8 shows the results of these computations based on 1,000 draws from the underlying distribution.

The two sets of estimates are in reasonable agreement.

| TABLE 4.8 | Simulation Results | | | |
|-----------|----------|------------|-------------|----------------|
| *Parameter* | *Estimate* | *Std. Error.* | *Sample Mean* | *Sample Std. Dev.* |
| $\beta_2$ | −0.069532 | 0.04377 | −0.069453 | 0.035074 |
| $\beta_3$ | 0.164047 | 0.07771 | 0.16410 | 0.053602 |
| $\gamma$ | 0.830971 | 0.04576 | 0.83083 | 0.044533 |
| $\phi_2$ | −0.41361 | 0.152296 | −0.44913 | 0.19444 |
| $\phi_3$ | 0.97527 | 0.162382 | 0.96313 | 0.18787 |

Krinsky and Robb (1986) report huge differences in the standard errors produced by the delta method compared to the simulation based estimator. In a subsequent paper (1990), they report that the entire difference can be attributed to a bug in the software they used—upon redoing the computations, their estimates are essentially the same with the two methods. It is difficult to draw a conclusion about the effectiveness of the delta method based on the received results—it does seem at this juncture that the delta method remains an effective device that can often be employed with a hand calculator as opposed to the much more computation intensive Krinsky and Robb (1986) technique. Unfortunately, the results of any comparison will depend on the data, the model, and the functions being computed. The amount of nonlinearity in the sense of the complexity of the functions seems not to be the answer. Krinsky and Robb's case was motivated by the extreme complexity of the translog elasticities. In another study, Hole (2006) examines a similarly complex problem, and finds that the delta method still appears to be the most accurate. For another (now classic) application, see Example 6.5.

### 4.9.5 ASYMPTOTIC EFFICIENCY

We have not established any large-sample counterpart to the Gauss–Markov theorem. That is, it remains to establish whether the large-sample properties of the least squares estimator are optimal by any measure. The Gauss–Markov theorem establishes finite sample conditions under which least squares is optimal. The requirements that the estimator be linear and unbiased limit the theorem's generality, however. One of the main purposes of the analysis in this chapter is to broaden the class of estimators in the classical model to those which might be biased, but which are consistent. Ultimately, we shall also be interested in nonlinear estimators. These cases extend beyond the reach of the Gauss–Markov theorem. To make any progress in this direction, we will require an alternative estimation criterion.

---

**DEFINITION 4.1**  **Asymptotic Efficiency**
*An estimator is asymptotically efficient if it is consistent, asymptotically normally distributed, and has an asymptotic covariance matrix that is not larger than the asymptotic covariance matrix of any other consistent, asymptotically normally distributed estimator.*

In Chapter 16, we will show that if the disturbances are normally distributed, then the least squares estimator is also the **maximum likelihood estimator.** Maximum likelihood estimators are asymptotically efficient among consistent and asymptotically normally distributed estimators. This gives us a partial result, albeit a somewhat narrow one since to claim it, we must assume normally distributed disturbances. If some other distribution is specified for $\varepsilon$ and it emerges that **b** is not the maximum likelihood estimator, then least squares may not be efficient.

### Example 4.9   The Gamma Regression Model
Greene (1980a) considers estimation in a regression model with an asymmetrically distributed disturbance,

$$y = (\alpha + \sigma\sqrt{P}) + \mathbf{x}'\boldsymbol{\beta} + (\varepsilon - \sigma\sqrt{P}) = \alpha^* + \mathbf{x}'\boldsymbol{\beta} + \varepsilon^*,$$

where $\varepsilon$ has the gamma distribution in Section B.4.5 [see (B-39)] and $\sigma = \sqrt{P}/\lambda$ is the standard deviation of the disturbance. In this model, the covariance matrix of the least squares estimator of the slope coefficients (not including the constant term) is,

$$\text{Asy. Var}[\mathbf{b} \mid \mathbf{X}] = \sigma^2 (\mathbf{X}'\mathbf{M}^0\mathbf{X})^{-1},$$

whereas for the maximum likelihood estimator (which is not the least squares estimator),[14]

$$\text{Asy. Var}[\hat{\boldsymbol{\beta}}_{ML}] \approx [1 - (2/P)]\sigma^2 (\mathbf{X}'\mathbf{M}^0\mathbf{X})^{-1}.$$

But for the asymmetry parameter, this result would be the same as for the least squares estimator. We conclude that the estimator that accounts for the asymmetric disturbance distribution is more efficient asymptotically.

### 4.9.6   MORE GENERAL DATA GENERATING PROCESSES

The asymptotic properties of the estimators in the classical regression model were established under the following assumptions:

**A1.** *Linearity:* $y_i = x_{i1}\beta_1 + x_{i2}\beta_2 + \cdots + x_{iK}\beta_K + \varepsilon_i$.
**A2.** *Full rank:* The $n \times K$ sample data matrix, $X$ has full column rank.
**A3.** *Exogeneity of the independent variables:* $E[\varepsilon_i \mid x_{j1}, x_{j2}, \ldots, x_{jK}] = 0$, $i, j = 1, \ldots, n$.
**A4.** *Homoscedasticity and nonautocorrelation.*
**A5.** *Data generating mechanism-independent observations.*

The following are the crucial results needed: For consistency of **b**, we need (4-21) and (4-24),

$$\text{plim}(1/n)\mathbf{X}'\mathbf{X} = \text{plim}\,\overline{\mathbf{Q}}_n = \mathbf{Q}, \quad \text{a positive definite matrix,}$$

$$\text{plim}(1/n)\mathbf{X}'\varepsilon = \text{plim}\,\overline{\mathbf{w}}_n = E[\overline{\mathbf{w}}_n] = \mathbf{0}.$$

---

[14]The matrix $\mathbf{M}^0$ produces data in the form of deviations from sample means. (See Section A.2.8.) In Greene's model, $P$ must be greater than 2.

(For consistency of $s^2$, we added a fairly weak assumption about the moments of the disturbances.) To establish asymptotic normality, we will require consistency and (4-32) which is

$$\sqrt{n}\,\overline{\mathbf{w}}_n \xrightarrow{d} N[0, \sigma^2 \mathbf{Q}].$$

With these in place, the desired characteristics are then established by the methods of Sections 4.9.1 and 4.9.2. To analyze other cases, we can merely focus on these results. It is not necessary to reestablish the consistency or asymptotic normality themselves, since they follow as a consequence.

Exceptions to the assumptions made here are likely to arise in two settings. In a **panel data** set, the sample will consist of multiple observations on each of many observational units. For example, a study might consist of a set of observations made at different points in time on a large number of families. In this case, the $\mathbf{x}$'s will surely be correlated across observations, at least within observational units. They might even be the same for all the observations on a single family. They are also likely to be a mixture of random variables, such as family income, and nonstochastic regressors, such as a fixed "family effect" represented by a dummy variable. The second case would be a time-series model in which lagged values of the dependent variable appear on the right-hand side of the model.

The panel data set could be treated as follows. Assume for the moment that the data consist of a fixed number of observations, say $T$, on a set of $N$ families, so that the total number of rows in $\mathbf{X}$ is $n = NT$. The matrix

$$\overline{\mathbf{Q}}_n = \frac{1}{n} \sum_{i=1}^{n} \mathbf{Q}_i$$

in which $n$ is all the observations in the sample, could be viewed as

$$\overline{\mathbf{Q}}_n = \frac{1}{N} \sum_{i} \frac{1}{T} \underbrace{\sum}_{\substack{\text{observations} \\ \text{for family } i}} \mathbf{Q}_{it} = \frac{1}{N} \sum_{i=1}^{N} \overline{\mathbf{Q}}_i,$$

where $\overline{\mathbf{Q}}_i$ = average $\mathbf{Q}_{it}$ for family $i$. We might then view the set of observations on the $i$th unit as if they were a single observation and apply our convergence arguments to the number of families increasing without bound. The point is that the conditions that are needed to establish convergence will apply with respect to the number of observational units. The number of observations taken for each observation unit might be fixed and could be quite small.

The second difficult case arises when there are lagged dependent variables among the variables on the right-hand side or, more generally, in time-series settings in which the observations are no longer independent or even uncorrelated. Suppose that the model may be written

$$y_t = \mathbf{z}_t' \boldsymbol{\theta} + \gamma_1 y_{t-1} + \cdots + \gamma_p y_{t-p} + \varepsilon_t. \tag{4-37}$$

(Since this model is a time-series setting, we use $t$ instead of $i$ to index the observations.) We continue to assume that the disturbances are uncorrelated across observations. Since $y_{t-1}$ is dependent on $y_{t-2}$ and so on, it is clear that although the disturbances are uncorrelated across observations, the regressor vectors, including the lagged $y$'s surely are not. Also, although $\text{Cov}[\mathbf{x}_t, \varepsilon_s] = 0$ if $s \geq t$ $(\mathbf{x}_t = [\mathbf{z}_t, y_{t-1}, \ldots, y_{t-p}])$, $\text{Cov}[\mathbf{x}_t, \varepsilon_s] \neq 0$ if $s < t$. Every observation $y_t$ is determined by the entire history of the disturbances. Therefore, we have lost the crucial assumption $E[\boldsymbol{\varepsilon} \mid \mathbf{X}] = \mathbf{0}$; $E[\varepsilon_t \mid \text{future } \mathbf{x}\text{s}]$ is not equal to 0. The conditions needed for the finite-sample results we had earlier no longer hold. Without Assumption A3, $E[\boldsymbol{\varepsilon} \mid \mathbf{X}] = \mathbf{0}$, our earlier proof of unbiasedness dissolves, and without unbiasedness, the Gauss–Markov theorem no longer applies. We are left with only asymptotic results for this case.

This case is considerably more general than the ones we have considered thus far. The theorems we invoked previously do not apply when the observations in the sums are correlated. To establish counterparts to the limiting normal distribution of $(1/\sqrt{n})\mathbf{X}'\boldsymbol{\varepsilon}$ and convergence of $(1/n)\mathbf{X}'\mathbf{X}$ to a finite positive definite matrix, it is necessary to make additional assumptions about the regressors. For the disturbances, we replace Assumption A3 following.

**AD3.** $E[\varepsilon_t \mid \mathbf{x}_{t-s}] = 0,$  for all s $\geq 0$.

This assumption states that the disturbance in the period "$t$" is an innovation; it is new information that enters the process. Thus, it is not correlated with any of the history. It is not uncorrelated with future data, however, since $\varepsilon_t$ will be a part of $x_{t+r}$ for $r > 0$. Assumptions A1, A2, and A4 are retained (at least for the present). We will also replace Assumption A5 and result (4-21) with two assumptions about the right-hand variables. First,

$$\text{plim}\frac{1}{T-s} \sum_{t=s+1}^{T} \mathbf{x}_t\mathbf{x}'_{t-s} = \mathbf{Q}(s), \quad \text{a finite matrix, } s \geq 0, \quad \textbf{(4-38)}$$

and $\mathbf{Q}(0)$ is nonsingular if $T \geq K$. [Note that $\mathbf{Q} = \mathbf{Q}(0)$.] This matrix is the sums of cross products of the elements of $\mathbf{x}_t$ with lagged values of $\mathbf{x}_t$. Second, we assume that the roots of the polynomial

$$1 - \gamma_1 z - \gamma_2 z^2 - \cdots - \gamma_P z^P = 0 \quad \textbf{(4-39)}$$

are all outside the unit circle. (See Section 21.2 for further details.) Heuristically, these assumptions imply that the dependence between values of the $\mathbf{x}$'s at different points in time varies only with how far apart in time they are, not specifically with the points in time at which observations are made, and that the correlation between observations made at different points in time fades sufficiently rapidly that sample moments such as $\mathbf{Q}(s)$ above will converge in probability to a population counterpart.[15] Formally, we obtain these results with

**AD5.**  The series on $\mathbf{x}_t$ is **stationary** and **ergodic**.

---

[15]We will examine some cases in later chapters in which this does not occur. To consider a simple example, suppose that $\mathbf{x}$ contains a constant. Then the assumption requires sample means to converge to population parameters. Suppose that all observations are correlated. Then the variance of $\bar{x}$ is $\text{Var}[(1/T)\Sigma_t x_t] = (1/T^2)\Sigma_t\Sigma_s\text{Cov}[x_t, x_s]$. Since none of the $T^2$ terms is assumed to be zero, there is no assurance that the double sum converges to zero as $T \rightarrow \infty$. But if the correlations diminish sufficiently with distance in time, then the sum may converge to zero.

This assumption also implies that $\mathbf{Q}(s)$ becomes a matrix of zeros as $s$ (the separation in time) becomes large. These conditions are sufficient to produce $(1/n)\mathbf{X}'\boldsymbol{\varepsilon} \to \mathbf{0}$ and the consistency of $\mathbf{b}$. Further results are needed to establish the asymptotic normality of the estimator, however.[16]

In sum, the important properties of consistency and asymptotic normality of the least squares estimator are preserved under the different assumptions of stochastic regressors, provided that additional assumptions are made. In most cases, these assumptions are quite benign, so we conclude that the two asymptotic properties of least squares considered here, consistency and asymptotic normality, are quite robust to different specifications of the regressors.

## 4.10   SUMMARY AND CONCLUSIONS

This chapter has examined a set of properties of the least squares estimator that will apply in all samples, including unbiasedness and efficiency among unbiased estimators. The assumption of normality of the disturbances produces the distributions of some test statistics which are useful for a statistical assessment of the validity of the regression model. The finite sample results obtained in this chapter are listed in Table 4.3. We also considered some practical problems that arise when data are less than perfect for the estimation and analysis of the regression model, including multicollinearity and missing observations.

The formal assumptions of the classical model are pivotal in the results of this chapter. All of them are likely to be violated in more general settings than the one considered here. For example, in most cases examined later in the book, the estimator has a possible bias, but that bias diminishes with increasing sample sizes. Also, we are going to be interested in hypothesis tests of the type considered here, but at the same time, the assumption of normality is narrow, so it will be necessary to extend the model to allow nonnormal disturbances. These and other "large sample" extensions of the linear model were considered in Section 4.9.

This chapter concluded by obtaining the large sample properties of the least squares estimator. The main result is that in large samples, the estimator behaves according to a normal distribution and converges in probability to the true coefficient vector. We examined several data types, with one of the end results being that consistency and asymptotic normality would persist under a variety of broad assumptions about the data.

## Key Terms and Concepts

- Assumptions
- Asymptotic covariance matrix
- Asymptotic distribution
- Asymptotic efficiency
- Asymptotic normality
- Asymptotic properties
- Attrition
- Condition number
- Confidence interval
- Consistency
- Consistent estimator
- Data imputation
- Dynamic regression
- Efficient scale

---

[16]These appear in Mann and Wald (1943), Billingsley (1995), and Dhrymes (1998).

- Ergodic
- Estimator
- Finite sample properties
- Gauss–Markov theorem
- Grenander conditions
- Identification
- Ignorable case
- Indicator
- Lindeberg–Feller central limit theorem
- Linear estimator
- Linear unbiased estimator
- Maximum likelihood estimator
- Mean square convergence
- Mean squared error
- Measurement error
- Minimum mean squared error
- Minimum variance linear unbiased estimator
- Missing at random
- Missing completely at random
- Missing observations
- Modified zero-order regression
- Multicollinearity
- Not missing at random
- Oaxaca's and Blinder's decomposition
- Optimal linear predictor
- Orthogonal random variables
- Panel data
- Principal components
- Probability limit
- Sample selection
- Sampling distribution
- Sampling variance
- Semiparametric
- Standard error
- Standard error of the regression
- Stationary process
- Statistical properties
- Stochastic regressors
- $t$ ratio
- Variance inflation factor
- Zero-order method

## Exercises

1. Suppose that you have two independent unbiased estimators of the same parameter $\theta$, say $\hat{\theta}_1$ and $\hat{\theta}_2$, with different variances $v_1$ and $v_2$. What linear combination $\hat{\theta} = c_1\hat{\theta}_1 + c_2\hat{\theta}_2$ is the minimum variance unbiased estimator of $\theta$?

2. Consider the simple regression $y_i = \beta x_i + \varepsilon_i$ where $E[\varepsilon \mid x] = 0$ and $E[\varepsilon^2 \mid x] = \sigma^2$
   a. What is the minimum mean squared error linear estimator of $\beta$? [Hint: Let the estimator be $(\hat{\beta} = \mathbf{c}'\mathbf{y})$. Choose $\mathbf{c}$ to minimize $\mathrm{Var}(\hat{\beta}) + (E(\hat{\beta} - \beta))^2$. The answer is a function of the unknown parameters.]
   b. For the estimator in part a, show that ratio of the mean squared error of $\hat{\beta}$ to that of the ordinary least squares estimator $b$ is

$$\frac{\mathrm{MSE}\,[\hat{\beta}]}{\mathrm{MSE}\,[b]} = \frac{\tau^2}{(1+\tau^2)}, \quad \text{where } \tau^2 = \frac{\beta^2}{[\sigma^2/\mathbf{x}'\mathbf{x}]}.$$

   Note that $\tau$ is the square of the population analog to the "$t$ ratio" for testing the hypothesis that $\beta = 0$, which is given in (4-14). How do you interpret the behavior of this ratio as $\tau \to \infty$?

3. Suppose that the classical regression model applies but that the true value of the constant is zero. Compare the variance of the least squares slope estimator computed without a constant term with that of the estimator computed with an unnecessary constant term.

4. Suppose that the regression model is $y_i = \alpha + \beta x_i + \varepsilon_i$, where the disturbances $\varepsilon_i$ have $f(\varepsilon_i) = (1/\lambda)\exp(-\varepsilon_i/\lambda)$, $\varepsilon_i \geq 0$. This model is rather peculiar in that all the disturbances are assumed to be nonnegative. Note that the disturbances have $E[\varepsilon_i \mid x_i] = \lambda$ and $\mathrm{Var}[\varepsilon_i \mid x_i] = \lambda^2$. Show that the least squares slope is unbiased but that the intercept is biased.

5. Prove that the least squares intercept estimator in the classical regression model is the minimum variance linear unbiased estimator.

6. As a profit-maximizing monopolist, you face the demand curve $Q = \alpha + \beta P + \varepsilon$. In the past, you have set the following prices and sold the accompanying quantities:

| $Q$ | 3 | 3 | 7 | 6 | 10 | 15 | 16 | 13 | 9 | 15 | 9 | 15 | 12 | 18 | 21 |
|---|---|---|---|---|---|---|---|---|---|---|---|---|---|---|---|
| $P$ | 18 | 16 | 17 | 12 | 15 | 15 | 4 | 13 | 11 | 6 | 8 | 10 | 7 | 7 | 7 |

Suppose that your marginal cost is 10. Based on the least squares regression, compute a 95 percent confidence interval for the expected value of the profit-maximizing output.

7. The following sample moments for $x = [1, x_1, x_2, x_3]$ were computed from 100 observations produced using a random number generator:

$$\mathbf{X'X} = \begin{bmatrix} 100 & 123 & 96 & 109 \\ 123 & 252 & 125 & 189 \\ 96 & 125 & 167 & 146 \\ 109 & 189 & 146 & 168 \end{bmatrix}, \quad \mathbf{X'y} = \begin{bmatrix} 460 \\ 810 \\ 615 \\ 712 \end{bmatrix}, \quad \mathbf{y'y} = 3924.$$

The true model underlying these data is $y = x_1 + x_2 + x_3 + \varepsilon$.
a. Compute the simple correlations among the regressors.
b. Compute the ordinary least squares coefficients in the regression of $y$ on a constant $x_1$, $x_2$, and $x_3$.
c. Compute the ordinary least squares coefficients in the regression of $y$ on a constant $x_1$ and $x_2$, on a constant $x_1$ and $x_3$, and on a constant $x_2$ and $x_3$.
d. Compute the variance inflation factor associated with each variable.
e. The regressors are obviously collinear. Which is the problem variable?

8. Consider the multiple regression of $\mathbf{y}$ on $K$ variables $\mathbf{X}$ and an additional variable $\mathbf{z}$. Prove that under the assumptions A1 through A6 of the classical regression model, the true variance of the least squares estimator of the slopes on $\mathbf{X}$ is larger when $\mathbf{z}$ is included in the regression than when it is not. Does the same hold for the sample estimate of this covariance matrix? Why or why not? Assume that $\mathbf{X}$ and $\mathbf{z}$ are nonstochastic and that the coefficient on $\mathbf{z}$ is nonzero.

9. For the classical normal regression model $\mathbf{y} = \mathbf{X}\boldsymbol{\beta} + \boldsymbol{\varepsilon}$ with no constant term and $K$ regressors, assuming that the true value of $\boldsymbol{\beta}$ is zero, what is the exact expected value of $F[K, n - K] = (R^2/K)/[(1 - R^2)/(n - K)]$?

10. Prove that $E[\mathbf{b'b}] = \boldsymbol{\beta}'\boldsymbol{\beta} + \sigma^2 \sum_{k=1}^{K}(1/\lambda_k)$ where $\mathbf{b}$ is the ordinary least squares estimator and $\lambda_k$ is a characteristic root of $\mathbf{X'X}$.

11. For the classical normal regression model $\mathbf{y} = \mathbf{X}\boldsymbol{\beta} + \boldsymbol{\varepsilon}$ with no constant term and $K$ regressors, what is plim $F[K, n - K] = $ plim $\frac{R^2/K}{(1-R^2)/(n-K)}$, assuming that the true value of $\boldsymbol{\beta}$ is zero?

12. Let $e_i$ be the $i$th residual in the ordinary least squares regression of $\mathbf{y}$ on $\mathbf{X}$ in the classical regression model, and let $\varepsilon_i$ be the corresponding true disturbance. Prove that $\text{plim}(e_i - \varepsilon_i) = 0$.

13. For the simple regression model $y_i = \mu + \varepsilon_i$, $\varepsilon_i \sim N[0, \sigma^2]$, prove that the sample mean is consistent and asymptotically normally distributed. Now consider the alternative estimator $\hat{\mu} = \sum_i w_i y_i$, $w_i = \frac{i}{(n(n+1)/2)} = \frac{i}{\sum_i i}$. Note that $\sum_i w_i = 1$. Prove that this is a consistent estimator of $\mu$ and obtain its asymptotic variance. [Hint: $\sum_i i^2 = n(n + 1)(2n + 1)/6$.]

14. In the discussion of the instrumental variables estimator, we showed that the least squares estimator **b** is biased and inconsistent. Nonetheless, **b** does estimate something: plim $\mathbf{b} = \theta = \beta + \mathbf{Q}^{-1}\gamma$. Derive the asymptotic covariance matrix of **b**, and show that **b** is asymptotically normally distributed.

15. Suppose we change the assumptions of the model to **AS5**: $(\mathbf{x}_i, \varepsilon)$ are an independent and identically distributed sequence of random vectors such that $\mathbf{x}_i$ has a finite mean vector, $\boldsymbol{\mu}_\mathbf{x}$, finite positive definite covariance matrix $\boldsymbol{\Sigma}_\mathbf{xx}$ and finite fourth moments $E[x_j x_k x_l x_m] = \phi_{jklm}$ for all variables. How does the proof of consistency and asymptotic normality of **b** change? Are these assumptions weaker or stronger than the ones made in Section 4.1?

16. Now, assume only finite second moments of **x**; $E[x_i^2]$ is finite. Is this sufficient to establish consistency of **b**? (Hint: the Cauchy–Schwarz inequality (Theorem D.13), $E[|xy|] \leq \{E[x^2]\}^{1/2}\{E[y^2]\}^{1/2}$ will be helpful.) Is this assumption sufficient to establish asymptotic normality?

17. Consider a data set consisting of $n$ observations, $n_c$ complete and $n_m$ incomplete for which the dependent variable, $y_i$, is missing. Data on the independent variables, $\mathbf{x}_i$, are complete for all $n$ observations, $\mathbf{X}_c$ and $\mathbf{X}_m$. We wish to use the data to estimate the parameters of the linear regression model $\mathbf{y} = \mathbf{X}\boldsymbol{\beta} + \boldsymbol{\varepsilon}$. Consider the following the imputation strategy: Step 1: Linearly regress $\mathbf{y}_c$ on $\mathbf{X}_c$ and compute $\mathbf{b}_c$. Step 2: Use $\mathbf{X}_m$ to predict the missing $\mathbf{y}_m$ with $\mathbf{X}_m\mathbf{b}_c$. Then regress the full sample of observations, $(\mathbf{y}_c, \mathbf{X}_m\mathbf{b}_c)$, on the full sample of regressors, $(\mathbf{X}_c, \mathbf{X}_m)$.
    a. Show that the first and second step least squares coefficient vectors are identical.
    b. Is the second step coefficient estimator unbiased?
    c. Show that the sum of squared residuals is the same at both steps.
    d. Show that the second step estimator of $\sigma^2$ is biased downward.

## Applications

1. Data on U.S. gasoline consumption for the years 1953 to 2004 are given in Table F2.2. Note, the consumption data appear as total expenditure. To obtain the per capita quantity variable, divide GASEXP by GASP times Pop. The other variables do not need transformation.
    a. Compute the multiple regression of per capita consumption of gasoline on per capita income, the price of gasoline, all the other prices and a time trend. Report all results. Do the signs of the estimates agree with your expectations?
    b. Test the hypothesis that at least in regard to demand for gasoline, consumers do not differentiate between changes in the prices of new and used cars.
    c. Estimate the own price elasticity of demand, the income elasticity, and the cross-price elasticity with respect to changes in the price of public transportation. Do the computations at the 2004 point in the data.
    d. Reestimate the regression in logarithms so that the coefficients are direct estimates of the elasticities. (Do not use the log of the time trend.) How do your estimates compare with the results in the previous question? Which specification do you prefer?
    e. Compute the simple correlations of the price variables. Would you conclude that multicollinearity is a "problem" for the regression in part a or part d?

    f. Notice that the price index for gasoline is normalized to 100 in 2000, whereas the other price indices are anchored at 1983 (roughly). If you were to renormalize the indices so that they were all 100.00 in 2004, then how would the results of the regression in part a change? How would the results of the regression in part d change?

    g. This exercise is based on the model that you estimated in part d. We are interested in investigating the change in the gasoline market that occurred in 1973. First, compute the average values of log of per capita gasoline consumption in the years 1953–1973 and 1974–2004 and report the values and the difference. If we divide the sample into these two groups of observations, then we can decompose the change in the expected value of the log of consumption into a change attributable to change in the regressors and a change attributable to a change in the model coefficients, as shown in Section 4.7.3. Using the Oaxaca–Blinder approach described there, compute the decomposition by partitioning the sample and computing separate regressions. Using your results, compute a confidence interval for the part of the change that can be attributed to structural change in the market, that is, change in the regression coefficients.

2. Christensen and Greene (1976) estimated a generalized Cobb–Douglas cost function for electricity generation of the form

$$\ln C = \alpha + \beta \ln Q + \gamma \left[ \tfrac{1}{2} (\ln Q)^2 \right] + \delta_k \ln P_k + \delta_l \ln P_l + \delta_f \ln P_f + \varepsilon.$$

$P_k$, $P_l$ and $P_f$ indicate unit prices of capital, labor, and fuel, respectively, $Q$ is output and $C$ is total cost. To conform to the underlying theory of production, it is necessary to impose the restriction that the cost function be homogeneous of degree one in the three prices. This is done with the restriction $\delta_k + \delta_l + \delta_f = 1$, or $\delta_f = 1 - \delta_k - \delta_l$. Inserting this result in the cost function and rearranging produces the estimating equation,

$$\ln(C/P_f) = \alpha + \beta \ln Q + \gamma \left[ \tfrac{1}{2} (\ln Q)^2 \right] + \delta_k \ln(P_k/P_f) + \delta_l \ln(P_l/P_f) + \varepsilon.$$

The purpose of the generalization was to produce a U-shaped average total cost curve. [See Example 6.3 for discussion of Nerlove's (1963) predecessor to this study.] We are interested in the **efficient scale,** which is the output at which the cost curve reaches its minimum. That is the point at which $(\partial \ln C / \partial \ln Q)_{|Q=Q^*} = 1$ or $Q^* = \exp[(1-\beta)/\gamma]$.

    a. Data on 158 firms extracted from Christensen and Greene's study are given in Table F4.3. Using all 158 observations, compute the estimates of the parameters in the cost function and the estimate of the asymptotic covariance matrix.

    b. Note that the cost function does not provide a direct estimate of $\delta_f$. Compute this estimate from your regression results, and estimate the asymptotic standard error.

    c. Compute an estimate of $Q^*$ using your regression results, then form a confidence interval for the estimated efficient scale.

    d. Examine the raw data and determine where in the sample the efficient scale lies. That is, determine how many firms in the sample have reached this scale, and whether, in your opinion, this scale is large in relation to the sizes of firms in the sample. Christensen and Greene approached this question by computing the proportion of total output in the sample that was produced by firms that had not yet reached efficient scale. (Note, there is some double counting in the data set— more than 20 of the largest "firms" in the sample we are using for this exercise are holding companies and power pools that are aggregates of other firms in the sample. We will ignore that complication for the purpose of our numerical exercise.)

# 5

# INFERENCE AND PREDICTION

## 5.1 INTRODUCTION

The linear regression model is used for three major functions: estimation, which was the subject of the previous two chapters (and most of the rest of this book), hypothesis testing, and prediction or forecasting. In this chapter, we will examine some applications of hypothesis tests using the classical model. The basic statistical theory was developed in Chapter 4 and Appendix C, so the methods discussed here will use tools that are already familiar. After the theory is developed in Sections 5.2–5.4, we will examine some applications in Sections 5.4 and 5.5. We will be primarily concerned with linear restrictions in this chapter, and will turn to nonlinear restrictions near the end of the chapter, in Section 5.5. Section 5.6 discusses the third major use of the regression model, prediction.

## 5.2 RESTRICTIONS AND NESTED MODELS

One common approach to testing a hypothesis is to formulate a statistical model that contains the hypothesis as a restriction on its parameters. A theory is said to have **testable implications** if it implies some testable restrictions on the model. Consider, for example, a simple model of investment, $I_t$, suggested in Section 3.2.2,

$$\ln I_t = \beta_1 + \beta_2 i_t + \beta_3 \Delta p_t + \beta_4 \ln Y_t + \beta_5 t + \varepsilon_t,$$

which states that investors are sensitive to nominal interest rates, $i_t$, the rate of inflation, $\Delta p_t$, (the log of) real output, $\ln Y_t$, and other factors that trend upward through time, embodied in the time trend, $t$. An alternative theory states that "investors care about real interest rates." The alternative model is

$$\ln I_t = \beta_1 + \beta_2 (i_t - \Delta p_t) + \beta_3 \Delta p_t + \beta_4 \ln Y_t + \beta_5 t + \varepsilon_t.$$

Although this new model does embody the theory, the equation still contains both nominal interest and inflation. The theory has no testable implication for our model. But, consider the stronger hypothesis, "investors care *only* about real interest rates." The resulting equation,

$$\ln I_t = \beta_1 + \beta_2 (i_t - \Delta p_t) + \beta_4 \ln Y_t + \beta_5 t + \varepsilon_t,$$

is now restricted; in the context of the first model, the implication is that $\beta_2 + \beta_3 = 0$. The stronger statement implies something specific about the parameters in the equation that may or may not be supported by the empirical evidence.

The description of testable implications in the preceding paragraph suggests (correctly) that testable restrictions will imply that only some of the possible models contained in the original specification will be "valid"; that is, consistent with the theory. In the example given earlier, the first equation specifies a model in which there are five unrestricted parameters $(\beta_1, \beta_2, \beta_3, \beta_4, \beta_5)$. But, the third equation shows that only some values are consistent with the theory, that is, those for which $\beta_3 = -\beta_2$. This subset of values is contained within the unrestricted set. In this way, the models are said to be **nested.** Consider a different hypothesis, "investors do not care about inflation." In this case, the smaller set of coefficients is $(\beta_1, \beta_2, 0, \beta_4, \beta_5)$. Once again, the restrictions imply a valid **parameter space** that is "smaller" (has fewer dimensions) than the unrestricted one. The general result is that the hypothesis specified by the restricted model is contained within the unrestricted model.

Now, consider an alternative pair of models: $\text{Model}_0$: "Investors care only about inflation"; $\text{Model}_1$: "Investors care only about the nominal interest rate." In this case, the two parameter vectors are $(\beta_1, 0, \beta_3, \beta_4, \beta_5)$ by $\text{Model}_0$ and $(\beta_1, \beta_2, 0, \beta_4, \beta_5)$ by $\text{Model}_1$. In this case, the two specifications are both subsets of the unrestricted model, but neither model is obtained as a restriction on the other. They have the same number of parameters; they just contain different variables. These two models are **nonnested.** We are concerned only with nested models in this chapter. Nonnested models are considered in Section 7.3.

Beginning with the linear regression model

$$\mathbf{y} = \mathbf{X}\boldsymbol{\beta} + \boldsymbol{\varepsilon}, \tag{5-1}$$

we consider a set of **linear restrictions** of the form

$$
\begin{aligned}
r_{11}\beta_1 + r_{12}\beta_2 + \cdots + r_{1K}\beta_K &= q_1 \\
r_{21}\beta_1 + r_{22}\beta_2 + \cdots + r_{2K}\beta_K &= q_2 \\
&\vdots \\
r_{J1}\beta_1 + r_{J2}\beta_2 + \cdots + r_{JK}\beta_K &= q_J.
\end{aligned}
\tag{5-2}
$$

These can be combined into the single equation

$$\mathbf{R}\boldsymbol{\beta} = \mathbf{q}. \tag{5-3}$$

Each row of $\mathbf{R}$ is the coefficients in one of the restrictions. The matrix $\mathbf{R}$ has $K$ columns to be conformable with $\boldsymbol{\beta}$, $J$ rows for a total of $J$ restrictions, and full row rank, so $J$ must be less than or equal to $K$. The rows of $\mathbf{R}$ must be linearly independent. Although it does not violate the condition, the case of $J = K$ must also be ruled out.[1] The restriction $\mathbf{R}\boldsymbol{\beta} = \mathbf{q}$ imposes $J$ restrictions on $K$ otherwise free parameters. Hence, with the restrictions imposed, there are, in principle, only $K - J$ free parameters remaining. One way to view this situation is to partition $\mathbf{R}$ into two groups of columns, one with $J$ and one with $K - J$, so that the first set are linearly independent. (There are many ways to do so; any one will do for the present.) Then, with $\boldsymbol{\beta}$ likewise partitioned and its elements

---

[1] If the $K$ slopes satisfy $J = K$ restriction, then $\mathbf{R}$ is square and nonsingular and $\boldsymbol{\beta} = \mathbf{R}^{-1}\mathbf{q}$. There is no estimation or inference problem.

reordered in whatever way is needed, we may write

$$\mathbf{R}\boldsymbol{\beta} = \mathbf{R}_1\boldsymbol{\beta}_1 + \mathbf{R}_2\boldsymbol{\beta}_2 = \mathbf{q}.$$

If the $J$ columns of $\mathbf{R}_1$ are independent, then

$$\boldsymbol{\beta}_1 = \mathbf{R}_1^{-1}[\mathbf{q} - \mathbf{R}_2\boldsymbol{\beta}_2]. \tag{5-4}$$

The implication is that although $\boldsymbol{\beta}_2$ is free to vary, once $\boldsymbol{\beta}_2$ is determined, $\boldsymbol{\beta}_1$ is determined by (5-4). Thus, only the $K - J$ elements of $\boldsymbol{\beta}_2$ are free parameters in the restricted model.

## 5.3 TWO APPROACHES TO TESTING HYPOTHESES

Hypothesis testing of the sort suggested in the preceding section can be approached from two viewpoints. First, having computed a set of parameter estimates, we can ask whether the estimates come reasonably close to satisfying the restrictions implied by the hypothesis. More formally, we can ascertain whether the failure of the estimates to satisfy the restrictions is simply the result of sampling error or is instead systematic. An alternative approach might proceed as follows. Suppose that we impose the restrictions implied by the theory. Since unrestricted least squares is, by definition, "least squares," this imposition must lead to a loss of fit. We can then ascertain whether this loss of fit results merely from sampling error or whether it is so large as to cast doubt on the validity of the restrictions. We will consider these two approaches in turn, then show that (as one might hope) within the framework of the linear regression model, the two approaches are equivalent.

### AN IMPORTANT ASSUMPTION
To develop the test statistics in this section, we will assume normally distributed disturbances. As we saw in Chapter 4, with this assumption, we will be able to obtain the exact distributions of the test statistics. In the next section, we will consider the implications of relaxing this assumption and develop an alternative set of results that allows us to proceed without it.

### 5.3.1 THE F STATISTIC AND THE LEAST SQUARES DISCREPANCY

We now consider testing a set of $J$ linear restrictions stated in the **null hypothesis**

$$H_0 : \mathbf{R}\boldsymbol{\beta} - \mathbf{q} = \mathbf{0}$$

against the **alternative hypothesis,**

$$H_1 : \mathbf{R}\boldsymbol{\beta} - \mathbf{q} \neq \mathbf{0}.$$

Each row of $\mathbf{R}$ is the coefficients in a linear restriction on the coefficient vector. Typically, $\mathbf{R}$ will have only a few rows and numerous zeros in each row. Some examples would be as follows:

1. One of the coefficients is zero, $\beta_j = 0$

$$\mathbf{R} = [0 \quad 0 \quad \cdots \quad 1 \quad 0 \quad \cdots \quad 0] \quad \text{and} \quad \mathbf{q} = 0.$$

2. Two of the coefficients are equal, $\beta_k = \beta_j$,

$$\mathbf{R} = [0 \quad 0 \quad 1 \quad \cdots \quad -1 \quad \cdots \quad 0] \quad \text{and} \quad \mathbf{q} = 0.$$

3. A set of the coefficients sum to one, $\beta_2 + \beta_3 + \beta_4 = 1$,

$$\mathbf{R} = [0 \quad 1 \quad 1 \quad 1 \quad 0 \quad \cdots] \quad \text{and} \quad \mathbf{q} = 1.$$

4. A subset of the coefficients are all zero, $\beta_1 = 0$, $\beta_2 = 0$, and $\beta_3 = 0$,

$$\mathbf{R} = \begin{bmatrix} 1 & 0 & 0 & 0 & \cdots & 0 \\ 0 & 1 & 0 & 0 & \cdots & 0 \\ 0 & 0 & 1 & 0 & \cdots & 0 \end{bmatrix} = [\mathbf{I} : \mathbf{0}] \quad \text{and} \quad \mathbf{q} = \begin{bmatrix} 0 \\ 0 \\ 0 \end{bmatrix}.$$

5. Several linear restrictions, $\beta_2 + \beta_3 = 1$, $\beta_4 + \beta_6 = 0$, and $\beta_5 + \beta_6 = 0$,

$$\mathbf{R} = \begin{bmatrix} 0 & 1 & 1 & 0 & 0 & 0 \\ 0 & 0 & 0 & 1 & 0 & 1 \\ 0 & 0 & 0 & 0 & 1 & 1 \end{bmatrix} \quad \text{and} \quad \mathbf{q} = \begin{bmatrix} 1 \\ 0 \\ 0 \end{bmatrix}.$$

6. All the coefficients in the model except the constant term are zero. [See (4-15) and Section 4.7.4.]

$$\mathbf{R} = [\mathbf{0} : \mathbf{I}_{K-1}] \quad \text{and} \quad \mathbf{q} = \mathbf{0}.$$

Given the least squares estimator $\mathbf{b}$, our interest centers on the **discrepancy vector** $\mathbf{Rb} - \mathbf{q} = \mathbf{m}$. It is unlikely that $\mathbf{m}$ will be exactly $\mathbf{0}$. The statistical question is whether the deviation of $\mathbf{m}$ from $\mathbf{0}$ can be attributed to sampling error or whether it is significant. Since $\mathbf{b}$ is normally distributed [see (4-8)] and $\mathbf{m}$ is a linear function of $\mathbf{b}$, $\mathbf{m}$ is also normally distributed. If the null hypothesis is true, then $\mathbf{R}\boldsymbol{\beta} - \mathbf{q} = \mathbf{0}$ and $\mathbf{m}$ has mean vector

$$E[\mathbf{m} \,|\, \mathbf{X}] = \mathbf{R}E[\mathbf{b} \,|\, \mathbf{X}] - \mathbf{q} = \mathbf{R}\boldsymbol{\beta} - \mathbf{q} = \mathbf{0}.$$

and covariance matrix

$$\text{Var}[\mathbf{m} \,|\, \mathbf{X}] = \text{Var}[\mathbf{Rb} - \mathbf{q} \,|\, \mathbf{X}] = \mathbf{R}\{\text{Var}[\mathbf{b} \,|\, \mathbf{X}]\}\mathbf{R}' = \sigma^2 \mathbf{R}(\mathbf{X}'\mathbf{X})^{-1}\mathbf{R}'.$$

We can base a test of $H_0$ on the **Wald criterion.** Conditioned on $\mathbf{X}$, we find:

$$W = \mathbf{m}'\{\text{Var}[\mathbf{m} \,|\, \mathbf{X}]\}^{-1}\mathbf{m}.$$

$$= (\mathbf{Rb} - \mathbf{q})'[\sigma^2 \mathbf{R}(\mathbf{X}'\mathbf{X})^{-1}\mathbf{R}']^{-1}(\mathbf{Rb} - \mathbf{q}) \tag{5-5}$$

$$= \frac{(\mathbf{Rb} - \mathbf{q})'[\mathbf{R}(\mathbf{X}'\mathbf{X})^{-1}\mathbf{R}']^{-1}(\mathbf{Rb} - \mathbf{q})}{\sigma^2}$$

$$\sim \chi^2[J].$$

The statistic $W$ has a chi-squared distribution with $J$ degrees of freedom if the hypothesis is correct.[2] Intuitively, the larger $\mathbf{m}$ is—that is, the worse the failure of least squares to satisfy the restrictions—the larger the chi-squared statistic. Therefore, a large chi-squared value will weigh against the hypothesis.

---

[2]This calculation is an application of the "full rank quadratic form" of Section B.11.6. Note that although the chi-squared distribution is conditioned on $\mathbf{X}$, it is also free of $\mathbf{X}$.

The chi-squared statistic in (5-5) is not usable because of the unknown $\sigma^2$. By using $s^2$ instead of $\sigma^2$ and dividing the result by $J$, we obtain a usable $F$ statistic with $J$ and $n - K$ degrees of freedom. Making the substitution in (5-5), dividing by $J$, and multiplying and dividing by $n - K$, we obtain

$$F = \frac{W}{J}\frac{\sigma^2}{s^2}$$

$$= \left(\frac{(\mathbf{Rb} - \mathbf{q})'[\mathbf{R}(\mathbf{X}'\mathbf{X})^{-1}\mathbf{R}']^{-1}(\mathbf{Rb} - \mathbf{q})}{\sigma^2}\right)\left(\frac{1}{J}\right)\left(\frac{\sigma^2}{s^2}\right)\left(\frac{(n - K)}{(n - K)}\right) \qquad \textbf{(5-6)}$$

$$= \frac{(\mathbf{Rb} - \mathbf{q})'[\sigma^2\mathbf{R}(\mathbf{X}'\mathbf{X})^{-1}\mathbf{R}']^{-1}(\mathbf{Rb} - \mathbf{q})/J}{[(n - K)s^2/\sigma^2]/(n - K)}.$$

If $\mathbf{R}\boldsymbol{\beta} = \mathbf{q}$, that is, if the null hypothesis is true, then $\mathbf{Rb} - \mathbf{q} = \mathbf{Rb} - \mathbf{R}\boldsymbol{\beta} = \mathbf{R}(\mathbf{b} - \boldsymbol{\beta}) = \mathbf{R}(\mathbf{X}'\mathbf{X})^{-1}\mathbf{X}'\boldsymbol{\varepsilon}$. [See (4-4).] Let $\mathbf{C} = [\mathbf{R}(\mathbf{X}'\mathbf{X})^{-1}\mathbf{R}']$ since

$$\frac{\mathbf{R}(\mathbf{b} - \boldsymbol{\beta})}{\sigma} = \mathbf{R}(\mathbf{X}'\mathbf{X})^{-1}\mathbf{X}'\left(\frac{\boldsymbol{\varepsilon}}{\sigma}\right) = \mathbf{D}\left(\frac{\boldsymbol{\varepsilon}}{\sigma}\right),$$

the numerator of $F$ equals $[(\boldsymbol{\varepsilon}/\sigma)'\mathbf{T}(\boldsymbol{\varepsilon}/\sigma)]/J$ where $\mathbf{T} = \mathbf{D}'\mathbf{C}^{-1}\mathbf{D}$. The numerator is $W/J$ from (5-5) and is distributed as $1/J$ times a chi-squared $[J]$, as we showed earlier. We found in (4-6) that $s^2 = \mathbf{e}'\mathbf{e}/(n - K) = \boldsymbol{\varepsilon}'\mathbf{M}\boldsymbol{\varepsilon}/(n - K)$ where $\mathbf{M}$ is an idempotent matrix. Therefore, the denominator of $F$ equals $[(\boldsymbol{\varepsilon}/\sigma)'\mathbf{M}(\boldsymbol{\varepsilon}/\sigma)]/(n - K)$. This statistic is distributed as $1/(n - K)$ times a chi-squared $[n - K]$. [See (4-11).] Therefore, the $F$ statistic is the ratio of two chi-squared variables each divided by its degrees of freedom. Since $\mathbf{M}(\boldsymbol{\varepsilon}/\sigma)$ and $\mathbf{T}(\boldsymbol{\varepsilon}/\sigma)$ are both normally distributed and their covariance $\mathbf{TM}$ is $\mathbf{0}$, the vectors of the quadratic forms are independent. The numerator and denominator of $F$ are functions of independent random vectors and are therefore independent. This completes the proof of the $F$ distribution. [See (B-35).] Canceling the two appearances of $\sigma^2$ in (5-6) leaves the $F$ statistic for testing a linear hypothesis:

$$F[J, n - K|\mathbf{X}] = \frac{(\mathbf{Rb} - \mathbf{q})'\left\{\mathbf{R}[s^2(\mathbf{X}'\mathbf{X})^{-1}]\mathbf{R}'\right\}^{-1}(\mathbf{Rb} - \mathbf{q})}{J}. \qquad \textbf{(5-7)}$$

For testing one linear restriction of the form

$$H_0 : r_1\beta_1 + r_2\beta_2 + \cdots + r_K\beta_K = \mathbf{r}'\boldsymbol{\beta} = q$$

(usually, some of the $r$s will be zero), the $F$ statistic is

$$F[1, n - K] = \frac{(\Sigma_j r_j b_j - q)^2}{\Sigma_j \Sigma_k r_j r_k \, \text{Est. Cov}[b_j, b_k]}.$$

If the hypothesis is that the $j$th coefficient is equal to a particular value, then $\mathbf{R}$ has a single row with a 1 in the $j$th position and 0s elsewhere, $\mathbf{R}(\mathbf{X}'\mathbf{X})^{-1}\mathbf{R}'$ is the $j$th diagonal element of the inverse matrix, and $\mathbf{Rb} - \mathbf{q}$ is $(b_j - q)$. The $F$ statistic is then

$$F[1, n - K] = \frac{(b_j - q)^2}{\text{Est. Var}[b_j]}.$$

Consider an alternative approach. The sample estimate of $\mathbf{r}'\boldsymbol{\beta}$ is

$$r_1 b_1 + r_2 b_2 + \cdots + r_K b_K = \mathbf{r}'\mathbf{b} = \hat{q}.$$

If $\hat{q}$ differs significantly from $q$, then we conclude that the sample data are not consistent with the hypothesis. It is natural to base the test on

$$t = \frac{\hat{q} - q}{\text{se}(\hat{q})}. \tag{5-8}$$

We require an estimate of the standard error of $\hat{q}$. Since $\hat{q}$ is a linear function of $\mathbf{b}$ and we have an estimate of the covariance matrix of $\mathbf{b}$, $s^2(\mathbf{X}'\mathbf{X})^{-1}$, we can estimate the variance of $\hat{q}$ with

$$\text{Est. Var}[\hat{q} \mid \mathbf{X}] = \mathbf{r}'[s^2(\mathbf{X}'\mathbf{X})^{-1}]\mathbf{r}.$$

The denominator of $t$ is the square root of this quantity. In words, $t$ is the distance in standard error units between the hypothesized function of the true coefficients and the same function of our estimates of them. If the hypothesis is true, then our estimates should reflect that, at least within the range of sampling variability. Thus, if the absolute value of the preceding $t$ ratio is larger than the appropriate critical value, then doubt is cast on the hypothesis.

There is a useful relationship between the statistics in (5-7) and (5-8). We can write the square of the $t$ statistic as

$$t^2 = \frac{(\hat{q} - q)^2}{\text{Var}(\hat{q} - q \mid \mathbf{X})} = \frac{(\mathbf{r}'\mathbf{b} - q)\{\mathbf{r}'[s^2(\mathbf{X}'\mathbf{X})^{-1}]\mathbf{r}\}^{-1}(\mathbf{r}'\mathbf{b} - q)}{1}.$$

It follows, therefore, that for testing a single restriction, the $t$ statistic is the square root of the $F$ statistic that would be used to test that hypothesis.

### Example 5.1 Restricted Investment Equation

Section 5.2 suggested a theory about the behavior of investors: that they care only about real interest rates. If investors were only interested in the real rate of interest, then equal increases in interest rates and the rate of inflation would have no independent effect on investment. The null hypothesis is

$$H_0 : \beta_2 + \beta_3 = 0.$$

Estimates of the parameters of equations (5-1) and (5-3) using 1950.1 to 2000.4 quarterly data on real investment, real GDP, an interest rate (the 90-day T-bill rate), and inflation measured by the change in the log of the CPI given in Appendix Table F5.1 are presented in Table 5.1. (One observation is lost in computing the change in the CPI.)

| TABLE 5.1 | Estimated Investment Equations (Estimated standard errors in parentheses) | | | | |
|---|---|---|---|---|---|
| | $\beta_1$ | $\beta_2$ | $\beta_3$ | $\beta_4$ | $\beta_5$ |
| **Model (5-1)** | −9.135 | −0.00860 | 0.00331 | 1.930 | −0.00566 |
| | (1.366) | (0.00319) | (0.00234) | (0.183) | (0.00149) |
| | $s = 0.08618$, $R^2 = 0.979753$, $\mathbf{e}'\mathbf{e} = 1.47052$, | | | | |
| | Est. $\text{Cov}[b_2, b_3] = -3.718e{-}6$ | | | | |
| **Model (5-3)** | −7.907 | −0.00443 | 0.00443 | 1.764 | −0.00440 |
| | (1.201) | (0.00227) | (0.00227) | (0.161) | (0.00133) |
| | $s = 0.8670$, $R^2 = 0.979405$, $\mathbf{e}'\mathbf{e} = 1.49578$ | | | | |

To form the appropriate test statistic, we require the standard error of $\hat{q} = b_2 + b_3$, which is

$$se(\hat{q}) = [0.00319^2 + 0.00234^2 + 2(-3.718 \times 10^{-6})]^{1/2} = 0.002866.$$

The $t$ ratio for the test is therefore

$$t = \frac{-0.00860 + 0.00331}{0.002866} = -1.845.$$

Using the 95 percent critical value from $t$ [203-5] = 1.96 (the standard normal value), we conclude that the sum of the two coefficients is not significantly different from zero, so the hypothesis should not be rejected.

There will usually be more than one way to formulate a restriction in a regression model. One convenient way to parameterize a constraint is to set it up in such a way that the standard test statistics produced by the regression can be used without further computation to test the hypothesis. In the preceding example, we could write the regression model as specified in (5-2). Then an equivalent way to test $H_0$ would be to fit the investment equation with both the real interest rate and the rate of inflation as regressors and to test our theory by simply testing the hypothesis that $\beta_3$ equals zero, using the standard $t$ statistic that is routinely computed. When the regression is computed this way, $b_3 = -0.00529$ and the estimated standard error is 0.00287, resulting in a $t$ ratio of −1.844(!). (Exercise: Suppose that the nominal interest rate, rather than the rate of inflation, were included as the extra regressor. What do you think the coefficient and its standard error would be?)

Finally, consider a test of the joint hypothesis

$$\beta_2 + \beta_3 = 0 \quad \text{(investors consider the real interest rate),}$$

$$\beta_4 = 1 \quad \text{(the marginal propensity to invest equals 1),}$$

$$\beta_5 = 0 \quad \text{(there is no time trend).}$$

Then,

$$\mathbf{R} = \begin{bmatrix} 0 & 1 & 1 & 0 & 0 \\ 0 & 0 & 0 & 1 & 0 \\ 0 & 0 & 0 & 0 & 1 \end{bmatrix}, \quad \mathbf{q} = \begin{bmatrix} 0 \\ 1 \\ 0 \end{bmatrix} \quad \text{and} \quad \mathbf{Rb} - \mathbf{q} = \begin{bmatrix} -0.0053 \\ 0.9302 \\ -0.0057 \end{bmatrix}.$$

Inserting these values in $F$ yields $F = 109.84$. The 5 percent critical value for $F[3, 198]$ is 2.65. We conclude, therefore, that these data are not consistent with the hypothesis. The result gives no indication as to which of the restrictions is most influential in the rejection of the hypothesis. If the three restrictions are tested one at a time, the $t$ statistics in (5-8) are −1.844, 5.076, and −3.803. Based on the individual test statistics, therefore, we would expect both the second and third hypotheses to be rejected.

## 5.3.2    THE RESTRICTED LEAST SQUARES ESTIMATOR

A different approach to hypothesis testing focuses on the fit of the regression. Recall that the least squares vector **b** was chosen to minimize the sum of squared deviations, **e′e**. Since $R^2$ equals $1 - \mathbf{e'e}/\mathbf{y'M^0y}$ and $\mathbf{y'M^0y}$ is a constant that does not involve **b**, it follows that **b** is chosen to maximize $R^2$. One might ask whether choosing some other value for the slopes of the regression leads to a significant loss of fit. For example, in the investment equation in Example 5.1, one might be interested in whether assuming the hypothesis (that investors care only about real interest rates) leads to a substantially worse fit than leaving the model unrestricted. To develop the test statistic, we first examine the computation of the least squares estimator subject to a set of restrictions.

Suppose that we explicitly impose the restrictions of the general linear hypothesis in the regression. The restricted least squares estimator is obtained as the solution to

$$\text{Minimize}_{\mathbf{b}_0} \; S(\mathbf{b}_0) = (\mathbf{y} - \mathbf{Xb}_0)'(\mathbf{y} - \mathbf{Xb}_0) \quad \text{subject to } \mathbf{Rb}_0 = \mathbf{q}. \tag{5-9}$$

A Lagrangean function for this problem can be written

$$L^*(\mathbf{b}_0, \lambda) = (\mathbf{y} - \mathbf{Xb}_0)'(\mathbf{y} - \mathbf{Xb}_0) + 2\lambda'(\mathbf{Rb}_0 - \mathbf{q}).^3 \tag{5-10}$$

The solutions $\mathbf{b}_*$ and $\lambda_*$ will satisfy the necessary conditions

$$\frac{\partial L^*}{\partial \mathbf{b}_*} = -2\mathbf{X}'(\mathbf{y} - \mathbf{Xb}_*) + 2\mathbf{R}'\lambda_* = \mathbf{0}$$

$$\frac{\partial L^*}{\partial \lambda_*} = 2(\mathbf{Rb}_* - \mathbf{q}) = \mathbf{0}. \tag{5-11}$$

Dividing through by 2 and expanding terms produces the partitioned matrix equation

$$\begin{bmatrix} \mathbf{X}'\mathbf{X} & \mathbf{R}' \\ \mathbf{R} & \mathbf{0} \end{bmatrix} \begin{bmatrix} \mathbf{b}_* \\ \lambda_* \end{bmatrix} = \begin{bmatrix} \mathbf{X}'\mathbf{y} \\ \mathbf{q} \end{bmatrix} \tag{5-12}$$

or

$$\mathbf{Ad}_* = \mathbf{v}.$$

Assuming that the partitioned matrix in brackets is nonsingular, the restricted least squares estimator is the upper part of the solution

$$\mathbf{d}_* = \mathbf{A}^{-1}\mathbf{v}. \tag{5-13}$$

If, in addition, $\mathbf{X}'\mathbf{X}$ is nonsingular, then explicit solutions for $\mathbf{b}_*$ and $\lambda_*$ may be obtained by using the formula for the partitioned inverse (A-74),[4]

$$\mathbf{b}_* = \mathbf{b} - (\mathbf{X}'\mathbf{X})^{-1}\mathbf{R}'[\mathbf{R}(\mathbf{X}'\mathbf{X})^{-1}\mathbf{R}']^{-1}(\mathbf{Rb} - \mathbf{q})$$

$$= \mathbf{b} - \mathbf{Cm}$$

and

$$\lambda_* = [\mathbf{R}(\mathbf{X}'\mathbf{X})^{-1}\mathbf{R}']^{-1}(\mathbf{Rb} - \mathbf{q}). \tag{5-14}$$

Greene and Seaks (1991) show that the covariance matrix for $\mathbf{b}_*$ is simply $\sigma^2$ times the upper left block of $\mathbf{A}^{-1}$. Once again, in the usual case in which $\mathbf{X}'\mathbf{X}$ is nonsingular, an explicit formulation may be obtained:

$$\text{Var}[\mathbf{b}_* \mid \mathbf{X}] = \sigma^2(\mathbf{X}'\mathbf{X})^{-1} - \sigma^2(\mathbf{X}'\mathbf{X})^{-1}\mathbf{R}'[\mathbf{R}(\mathbf{X}'\mathbf{X})^{-1}\mathbf{R}']^{-1}\mathbf{R}(\mathbf{X}'\mathbf{X})^{-1}. \tag{5-15}$$

Thus,

$$\text{Var}[\mathbf{b}_* \mid \mathbf{X}] = \text{Var}[\mathbf{b} \mid \mathbf{X}] - \text{a nonnegative definite matrix.}$$

---

[3] Since $\lambda$ is not restricted, we can formulate the constraints in terms of $2\lambda$. The convenience of the scaling shows up in (5-11).

[4] The general solution given for $\mathbf{d}_*$ may be usable even if $\mathbf{X}'\mathbf{X}$ is singular. Suppose, for example, that $\mathbf{X}'\mathbf{X}$ is $4 \times 4$ with rank 3. Then $\mathbf{X}'\mathbf{X}$ is singular. But if there is a parametric restriction on $\boldsymbol{\beta}$, then the $5 \times 5$ matrix in brackets may still have rank 5. This formulation and a number of related results are given in Greene and Seaks (1991).

One way to interpret this reduction in variance is as the value of the information contained in the restrictions.

Note that the explicit solution for $\lambda_*$ involves the discrepancy vector $\mathbf{Rb} - \mathbf{q}$. If the unrestricted least squares estimator satisfies the restriction, the Lagrangean multipliers will equal zero and $\mathbf{b}_*$ will equal $\mathbf{b}$. Of course, this is unlikely. The constrained solution $\mathbf{b}_*$ is equal to the unconstrained solution $\mathbf{b}$ plus a term that accounts for the failure of the unrestricted solution to satisfy the constraints.

### 5.3.3    THE LOSS OF FIT FROM RESTRICTED LEAST SQUARES

To develop a test based on the restricted least squares estimator, we consider a single coefficient first, then turn to the general case of $J$ linear restrictions. Consider the change in the fit of a multiple regression when a variable $z$ is added to a model that already contains $K - 1$ variables, $\mathbf{x}$. We showed in Section 3.5 (Theorem 3.6) (3-29) that the effect on the fit would be given by

$$R^2_{\mathbf{Xz}} = R^2_{\mathbf{X}} + \left(1 - R^2_{\mathbf{X}}\right) r^{*2}_{yz}, \tag{5-16}$$

where $R^2_{\mathbf{Xz}}$ is the new $R^2$ after $z$ is added, $R^2_{\mathbf{X}}$ is the original $R^2$ and $r^*_{yz}$ is the partial correlation between $y$ and $z$, controlling for $\mathbf{x}$. So, as we knew, the fit improves (or, at the least, does not deteriorate). In deriving the partial correlation coefficient between $y$ and $z$ in (3-22) we obtained the convenient result

$$r^{*2}_{yz} = \frac{t^2_z}{t^2_z + (n - K)}, \tag{5-17}$$

where $t^2_z$ is the square of the $t$ ratio for testing the hypothesis that the coefficient on $z$ is zero in the *multiple* regression of $\mathbf{y}$ on $\mathbf{X}$ and $\mathbf{z}$. If we solve (5-16) for $r^{*2}_{yz}$ and (5-17) for $t^2_z$ and then insert the first solution in the second, then we obtain the result

$$t^2_z = \frac{\left(R^2_{\mathbf{Xz}} - R^2_{\mathbf{X}}\right)/1}{\left(1 - R^2_{\mathbf{Xz}}\right)/(n - K)}. \tag{5-18}$$

We saw at the end of Section 5.3.1 that for a single restriction, such as $\beta_z = 0$,

$$F[1, n - K] = t^2[n - K],$$

which gives us our result. That is, in (5-18), we see that the squared $t$ statistic (i.e., the $F$ statistic) is computed using the change in the $R^2$. By interpreting the preceding as the result of *removing z* from the regression, we see that we have proved a result for the case of testing whether a single slope is zero. But the preceding result is general. The test statistic for a single linear restriction is the square of the $t$ ratio in (5-8). By this construction, we see that for a single restriction, $F$ is a measure of the loss of fit that results from imposing that restriction. To obtain this result, we will proceed to the general case of $J$ linear restrictions, which will include one restriction as a special case.

The fit of the restricted least squares coefficients cannot be better than that of the unrestricted solution. Let $\mathbf{e}_*$ equal $\mathbf{y} - \mathbf{Xb}_*$. Then, using a familiar device,

$$\mathbf{e}_* = \mathbf{y} - \mathbf{Xb} - \mathbf{X}(\mathbf{b}_* - \mathbf{b}) = \mathbf{e} - \mathbf{X}(\mathbf{b}_* - \mathbf{b}).$$

The new sum of squared deviations is

$$\mathbf{e}'_*\mathbf{e}_* = \mathbf{e}'\mathbf{e} + (\mathbf{b}_* - \mathbf{b})'\mathbf{X}'\mathbf{X}(\mathbf{b}_* - \mathbf{b}) \geq \mathbf{e}'\mathbf{e}.$$

(The middle term in the expression involves $\mathbf{X}'\mathbf{e}$, which is zero.) The loss of fit is

$$\mathbf{e}'_*\mathbf{e}_* - \mathbf{e}'\mathbf{e} = (\mathbf{Rb} - \mathbf{q})'[\mathbf{R}(\mathbf{X}'\mathbf{X})^{-1}\mathbf{R}']^{-1}(\mathbf{Rb} - \mathbf{q}). \tag{5-19}$$

This expression appears in the numerator of the $F$ statistic in (5-7). Inserting the remaining parts, we obtain

$$F[J, n - K] = \frac{(\mathbf{e}'_*\mathbf{e}_* - \mathbf{e}'\mathbf{e})/J}{\mathbf{e}'\mathbf{e}/(n - K)}. \tag{5-20}$$

Finally, by dividing both numerator and denominator of $F$ by $\Sigma_i(y_i - \bar{y})^2$, we obtain the general result:

$$F[J, n - K] = \frac{(R^2 - R_*^2)/J}{(1 - R^2)/(n - K)}. \tag{5-21}$$

This form has some intuitive appeal in that the difference in the fits of the two models is directly incorporated in the test statistic. As an example of this approach, consider the earlier joint test that all of the slopes in the model are zero. This is the overall $F$ ratio discussed in Section 4.7.4 (4-16), where $R_*^2 = 0$.

For imposing a set of **exclusion restrictions** such as $\beta_k = 0$ for one or more coefficients, the obvious approach is simply to omit the variables from the regression and base the test on the sums of squared residuals for the restricted and unrestricted regressions. The $F$ statistic for testing the hypothesis that a subset, say $\boldsymbol{\beta}_2$, of the coefficients are all zero is constructed using $\mathbf{R} = (\mathbf{0} : \mathbf{I})$, $\mathbf{q} = \mathbf{0}$, and $J = K_2 =$ the number of elements in $\boldsymbol{\beta}_2$. The matrix $\mathbf{R}(\mathbf{X}'\mathbf{X})^{-1}\mathbf{R}'$ is the $K_2 \times K_2$ lower right block of the full inverse matrix. Using our earlier results for partitioned inverses and the results of Section 3.3, we have

$$\mathbf{R}(\mathbf{X}'\mathbf{X})^{-1}\mathbf{R}' = (\mathbf{X}'_2\mathbf{M}_1\mathbf{X}_2)^{-1}$$

and

$$\mathbf{Rb} - \mathbf{q} = \mathbf{b}_2.$$

Inserting these in (5-19) gives the loss of fit that results when we drop a subset of the variables from the regression:

$$\mathbf{e}'_*\mathbf{e}_* - \mathbf{e}'\mathbf{e} = \mathbf{b}'_2\mathbf{X}'_2\mathbf{M}_1\mathbf{X}_2\mathbf{b}_2.$$

The procedure for computing the appropriate $F$ statistic amounts simply to comparing the sums of squared deviations from the "short" and "long" regressions, which we saw earlier.

### Example 5.2   Production Function
The data in Appendix Table F5.2 have been used in several studies of production functions.[5] Least squares regression of log output (value added) on a constant and the logs of labor and capital produce the estimates of a Cobb–Douglas production function shown in Table 5.2. We will construct several hypothesis tests based on these results. A generalization of the

---

[5]The data are statewide observations on SIC 33, the primary metals industry. They were originally constructed by Hildebrand and Liu (1957) and have subsequently been used by a number of authors, notably Aigner, Lovell, and Schmidt (1977). The 28th data point used in the original study is incomplete; we have used only the remaining 27.

**TABLE 5.2**    Estimated Production Functions

|  | Translog | Cobb–Douglas |
|---|---|---|
| Sum of squared residuals | 0.67993 | 0.85163 |
| Standard error of regression | 0.17994 | 0.18837 |
| R-squared | 0.95486 | 0.94346 |
| Adjusted R-squared | 0.94411 | 0.93875 |
| Number of observations | 27 | 27 |

| Variable | Coefficient | Standard Error | t Ratio | Coefficient | Standard Error | t Ratio |
|---|---|---|---|---|---|---|
| Constant | 0.944196 | 2.911 | 0.324 | 1.171 | 0.3268 | 3.582 |
| $\ln L$ | 3.61364 | 1.548 | 2.334 | 0.6030 | 0.1260 | 4.787 |
| $\ln K$ | −1.89311 | 1.016 | −1.863 | 0.3757 | 0.0853 | 4.402 |
| $\frac{1}{2}\ln^2 L$ | −0.96405 | 0.7074 | −1.363 | | | |
| $\frac{1}{2}\ln^2 K$ | 0.08529 | 0.2926 | 0.291 | | | |
| $\ln L \times \ln K$ | 0.31239 | 0.4389 | 0.712 | | | |

*Estimated Covariance Matrix for Translog (Cobb–Douglas) Coefficient Estimates*

|  | Constant | $\ln L$ | $\ln K$ | $\frac{1}{2}\ln^2 L$ | $\frac{1}{2}\ln^2 K$ | $\ln L \ln K$ |
|---|---|---|---|---|---|---|
| Constant | 8.472 (0.1068) | | | | | |
| $\ln L$ | −2.388 (−0.01984) | 2.397 (0.01586) | | | | |
| $\ln K$ | −0.3313 (0.001189) | −1.231 (−0.00961) | 1.033 (0.00728) | | | |
| $\frac{1}{2}\ln^2 L$ | −0.08760 | −0.6658 | 0.5231 | 0.5004 | | |
| $\frac{1}{2}\ln^2 K$ | −0.2332 | 0.03477 | 0.02637 | 0.1467 | 0.08562 | |
| $\ln L \ln K$ | 0.3635 | 0.1831 | −0.2255 | −0.2880 | −0.1160 | 0.1927 |

Cobb–Douglas model is the *translog* model,[6] which is

$$\ln Y = \beta_1 + \beta_2 \ln L + \beta_3 \ln K + \beta_4\left(\tfrac{1}{2}\ln^2 L\right) + \beta_5\left(\tfrac{1}{2}\ln^2 K\right) + \beta_6 \ln L \ln K + \varepsilon.$$

As we shall analyze further in Chapter 10, this model differs from the Cobb–Douglas model in that it relaxes the Cobb–Douglas's assumption of a unitary elasticity of substitution. The Cobb–Douglas model is obtained by the restriction $\beta_4 = \beta_5 = \beta_6 = 0$. The results for the two regressions are given in Table 5.2. The F statistic for the hypothesis of a Cobb–Douglas model is

$$F[3, 21] = \frac{(0.85163 - 0.67993)/3}{0.67993/21} = 1.768.$$

The critical value from the F table is 3.07, so we would not reject the hypothesis that a Cobb–Douglas model is appropriate.

The hypothesis of constant returns to scale is often tested in studies of production. This hypothesis is equivalent to a restriction that the two coefficients of the Cobb–Douglas production function sum to 1. For the preceding data,

$$F[1, 24] = \frac{(0.6030 + 0.3757 - 1)^2}{0.01586 + 0.00728 - 2(0.00961)} = 0.1157,$$

---

[6]Berndt and Christensen (1973). See Example 2.4 and Section 10.4.2 for discussion.

which is substantially less than the 95 percent critical value of 4.26. We would not reject the hypothesis; the data are consistent with the hypothesis of constant returns to scale. The equivalent test for the translog model would be $\beta_2 + \beta_3 = 1$ and $\beta_4 + \beta_5 + 2\beta_6 = 0$. The $F$ statistic with 2 and 21 degrees of freedom is 1.8991, which is less than the critical value of 3.47. Once again, the hypothesis is not rejected.

In most cases encountered in practice, it is possible to incorporate the restrictions of a hypothesis directly on the regression and estimate a restricted model.[7] For example, to impose the constraint $\beta_2 = 1$ on the Cobb–Douglas model, we would write

$$\ln Y = \beta_1 + 1.0 \ln L + \beta_3 \ln K + \varepsilon$$

or

$$\ln Y - \ln L = \beta_1 + \beta_3 \ln K + \varepsilon.$$

Thus, the restricted model is estimated by regressing $\ln Y - \ln L$ on a constant and $\ln K$. Some care is needed if this regression is to be used to compute an $F$ statistic. If the $F$ statistic is computed using the sum of squared residuals [see (5-20)], then no problem will arise. If (5-21) is used instead, however, then it may be necessary to account for the restricted regression having a different dependent variable from the unrestricted one. In the preceding regression, the dependent variable in the unrestricted regression is $\ln Y$, whereas in the restricted regression, it is $\ln Y - \ln L$. The $R^2$ from the restricted regression is only 0.26979, which would imply an $F$ statistic of 285.96, whereas the correct value is 9.935. If we compute the appropriate $R_*^2$ using the correct denominator, however, then its value is 0.92006 and the correct $F$ value results.

Note that the coefficient on $\ln K$ is negative in the translog model. We might conclude that the estimated output elasticity with respect to capital now has the wrong sign. This conclusion would be incorrect, however; in the translog model, the capital elasticity of output is

$$\frac{\partial \ln Y}{\partial \ln K} = \beta_3 + \beta_5 \ln K + \beta_6 \ln L.$$

If we insert the coefficient estimates and the mean values for $\ln K$ and $\ln L$ (not the logs of the means) of 7.44592 and 5.7637, respectively, then the result is 0.5425, which is quite in line with our expectations and is fairly close to the value of 0.3757 obtained for the Cobb–Douglas model. The estimated standard error for this linear combination of the least squares estimates is computed as the square root of

$$\text{Est. Var}[b_3 + b_5 \overline{\ln K} + b_6 \overline{\ln L}] = \mathbf{w}'(\text{Est. Var}[\mathbf{b}])\mathbf{w},$$

where

$$\mathbf{w} = (0, 0, 1, 0, \overline{\ln K}, \overline{\ln L})'$$

and **b** is the full $6 \times 1$ least squares coefficient vector. This value is 0.1122, which is reasonably close to the earlier estimate of 0.0853.

## 5.4 NONNORMAL DISTURBANCES AND LARGE SAMPLE TESTS

The distributions of the $F$, $t$, and chi-squared statistics that we used in the previous section rely on the assumption of normally distributed disturbances. Without this assumption,

---

[7]This case is not true when the restrictions are nonlinear. We consider this issue in Chapter 10.

the exact distributions of these statistics depend on the data and the parameters and are not $F$, $t$, and chi-squared. At least at first blush, it would seem that we need either a new set of critical values for the tests or perhaps a new set of test statistics. In this section, we will examine results that will generalize the familiar procedures. These large-sample results suggest that although the usual $t$ and $F$ statistics are still usable, in the more general case without the special assumption of normality, they are viewed as approximations whose quality improves as the sample size increases. By using the results of Section D.3 (on asymptotic distributions) and some large-sample results for the least squares estimator, we can construct a set of usable inference procedures based on already familiar computations.

Assuming the data are well behaved, the *asymptotic* distribution of the least squares coefficient estimator, $\mathbf{b}$, is given by

$$\mathbf{b} \overset{a}{\sim} N\left[\boldsymbol{\beta}, \frac{\sigma^2}{n}\mathbf{Q}^{-1}\right] \quad \text{where } \mathbf{Q} = \text{plim}\left(\frac{\mathbf{X'X}}{n}\right). \tag{5-22}$$

The interpretation is that, absent normality of $\boldsymbol{\varepsilon}$, as the sample size, $n$, grows, the normal distribution becomes an increasingly better approximation to the true, though at this point unknown, distribution of $\mathbf{b}$. As $n$ increases, the distribution of $\sqrt{n}(\mathbf{b} - \boldsymbol{\beta})$ *converges* exactly to a normal distribution, which is how we obtain the finite sample approximation above. This result is based on the central limit theorem and does not require normally distributed disturbances. The second result we will need concerns the estimator of $\sigma^2$:

$$\text{plim } s^2 = \sigma^2, \quad \text{where } s^2 = \mathbf{e'e}/(n - K).$$

With these in place, we can obtain some large-sample results for our test statistics that suggest how to proceed in a finite sample with nonnormal disturbances.

The sample statistic for testing the hypothesis that one of the coefficients, $\beta_k$ equals a particular value, $\beta_k^0$ is

$$t_k = \frac{\sqrt{n}(b_k - \beta_k^0)}{\sqrt{s^2(\mathbf{X'X}/n)^{-1}_{kk}}}.$$

(Note that two occurrences of $\sqrt{n}$ cancel to produce our familiar result.) Under the null hypothesis, with normally distributed disturbances, $t_k$ is exactly distributed as $t$ with $n - K$ degrees of freedom. [See Theorem 4.4, Section 4.7.5, and (4-17).] The exact distribution of this statistic is unknown, however, if $\boldsymbol{\varepsilon}$ is not normally distributed. From the results above, we find that the denominator of $t_k$ converges to $\sqrt{\sigma^2 \mathbf{Q}^{-1}_{kk}}$. Hence, if $t_k$ has a limiting distribution, then it is the same as that of the statistic that has this latter quantity in the denominator. That is, the large-sample distribution of $t_k$ is the same as that of

$$\tau_k = \frac{\sqrt{n}(b_k - \beta_k^0)}{\sqrt{\sigma^2 \mathbf{Q}^{-1}_{kk}}}.$$

But $\tau_k = (b_k - E[b_k])/(\text{Asy. Var}[b_k])^{1/2}$ from the asymptotic normal distribution (under the hypothesis $\beta_k = \beta_k^0$), so it follows that $\tau_k$ has a standard normal asymptotic distribution, and this result is the large-sample distribution of our $t$ statistic. Thus, as a large-sample approximation, we will use the standard normal distribution to approximate the true distribution of the test statistic $t_k$ and use the critical values from the standard normal distribution for testing hypotheses.

The result in the preceding paragraph is valid only in large samples. For moderately sized samples, it provides only a suggestion that the $t$ distribution may be a reasonable approximation. The appropriate critical values only *converge* to those from the standard normal, and generally *from above,* although we cannot be sure of this. In the interest of conservatism—that is, in controlling the probability of a type I error—one should generally use the critical value from the $t$ distribution even in the absence of normality. Consider, for example, using the standard normal critical value of 1.96 for a two-tailed test of a hypothesis based on 25 degrees of freedom. The nominal size of this test is 0.05. The actual size of the test, however, is the true, but unknown, probability that $|t_k| > 1.96$, which is 0.0612 if the $t[25]$ distribution is correct, and some other value if the disturbances are not normally distributed. The end result is that the standard $t$-test retains a large sample validity. Little can be said about the true size of a test based on the $t$ distribution unless one makes some other equally narrow assumption about $\varepsilon$, but the $t$ distribution is generally used as a reliable approximation.

We will use the same approach to analyze the $F$ statistic for testing a set of $J$ linear restrictions. Step 1 will be to show that with normally distributed disturbances, $JF$ converges to a chi-squared variable as the sample size increases. We will then show that this result is actually independent of the normality of the disturbances; it relies on the central limit theorem. Finally, we consider, as above, the appropriate critical values to use for this test statistic, which only has large sample validity.

The $F$ statistic for testing the validity of $J$ linear restrictions, $\mathbf{R}\boldsymbol{\beta} - \mathbf{q} = \mathbf{0}$, is given in (5-6). With normally distributed disturbances and under the null hypothesis, the exact distribution of this statistic is $F[J, n - K]$. To see how $F$ behaves more generally, divide the numerator and denominator in (5-6) by $\sigma^2$ and rearrange the fraction slightly, so

$$F = \frac{(\mathbf{Rb} - \mathbf{q})' \left\{ \mathbf{R}[\sigma^2 (\mathbf{X'X})^{-1}] \mathbf{R}' \right\}^{-1} (\mathbf{Rb} - \mathbf{q})}{J(s^2/\sigma^2)}. \tag{5-23}$$

Since plim $s^2 = \sigma^2$, and plim$(\mathbf{X'X}/n) = \mathbf{Q}$, the denominator of $F$ converges to $J$ and the bracketed term in the numerator will behave the same as $(\sigma^2/n)\mathbf{RQ}^{-1}\mathbf{R}'$. Hence, regardless of what this distribution is, if $F$ has a limiting distribution, then it is the same as the limiting distribution of

$$W^* = \frac{1}{J}(\mathbf{Rb} - \mathbf{q})'[\mathbf{R}(\sigma^2/n)\mathbf{Q}^{-1}\mathbf{R}']^{-1}(\mathbf{Rb} - \mathbf{q})$$

$$= \frac{1}{J}(\mathbf{Rb} - \mathbf{q})' \left\{ \text{Asy. Var}[\mathbf{Rb} - \mathbf{q}] \right\}^{-1} (\mathbf{Rb} - \mathbf{q}).$$

This expression is $(1/J)$ times a **Wald statistic,** based on the asymptotic distribution. The large-sample distribution of $W^*$ will be that of $(1/J)$ times a chi-squared with $J$ degrees of freedom. It follows that with normally distributed disturbances, $JF$ converges to a chi-squared variate with $J$ degrees of freedom. The proof is instructive. [See White (2001, 9.76).]

**THEOREM 5.1** **Limiting Distribution of the Wald Statistic**

*If $\sqrt{n}(\mathbf{b} - \boldsymbol{\beta}) \xrightarrow{d} N[\mathbf{0}, \sigma^2\mathbf{Q}^{-1}]$ and if $H_0 : \mathbf{R}\boldsymbol{\beta} - \mathbf{q} = \mathbf{0}$ is true, then*

$$W = (\mathbf{Rb} - \mathbf{q})'\{\mathbf{R}s^2(\mathbf{X'X})^{-1}\mathbf{R'}\}^{-1}(\mathbf{Rb} - \mathbf{q}) = JF \xrightarrow{d} \chi^2[J].$$

**Proof:** *Since $\mathbf{R}$ is a matrix of constants and $\mathbf{R}\boldsymbol{\beta} = \mathbf{q}$,*

$$\sqrt{n}\mathbf{R}(\mathbf{b} - \boldsymbol{\beta}) = \sqrt{n}(\mathbf{Rb} - \mathbf{q}) \xrightarrow{d} N[\mathbf{0}, \mathbf{R}(\sigma^2\mathbf{Q}^{-1})\mathbf{R'}]. \tag{1}$$

*For convenience, write this equation as*

$$\mathbf{z} \xrightarrow{d} N[\mathbf{0}, \mathbf{P}]. \tag{2}$$

*In Section A.6.11, we define the inverse square root of a positive definite matrix $\mathbf{P}$ as another matrix, say $\mathbf{T}$, such that $\mathbf{T}^2 = \mathbf{P}^{-1}$, and denote $\mathbf{T}$ as $\mathbf{P}^{-1/2}$. Then, by the same reasoning as in (1) and (2),*

$$\text{if } \mathbf{z} \xrightarrow{d} N[\mathbf{0}, \mathbf{P}], \quad \text{then } \mathbf{P}^{-1/2}\mathbf{z} \xrightarrow{d} N[\mathbf{0}, \mathbf{P}^{-1/2}\mathbf{PP}^{-1/2}] = N[\mathbf{0}, \mathbf{I}]. \tag{3}$$

*We now invoke Theorem D.21 for the limiting distribution of a function of a random variable. The sum of squares of uncorrelated (i.e., independent) standard normal variables is distributed as chi-squared. Thus, the limiting distribution of*

$$(\mathbf{P}^{-1/2}\mathbf{z})'(\mathbf{P}^{-1/2}\mathbf{z}) = \mathbf{z'}\mathbf{P}^{-1}\mathbf{z} \xrightarrow{d} \chi^2(J). \tag{4}$$

*Reassembling the parts from before, we have shown that the limiting distribution of*

$$n(\mathbf{Rb} - \mathbf{q})'[\mathbf{R}(\sigma^2\mathbf{Q}^{-1})\mathbf{R'}]^{-1}(\mathbf{Rb} - \mathbf{q}) \tag{5}$$

*is chi-squared, with $J$ degrees of freedom. Note the similarity of this result to the results of Section B.11.6. Finally, if*

$$\text{plim } s^2\left(\frac{1}{n}\mathbf{X'X}\right)^{-1} = \sigma^2\mathbf{Q}^{-1}, \tag{6}$$

*then the statistic obtained by replacing $\sigma^2\mathbf{Q}^{-1}$ by $s^2(\mathbf{X'X}/n)^{-1}$ in (5) has the same limiting distribution. The n's cancel, and we are left with the same Wald statistic we looked at before. This step completes the proof.*

The appropriate critical values for the $F$ test of the restrictions $\mathbf{R}\boldsymbol{\beta} - \mathbf{q} = \mathbf{0}$ converge from above to $1/J$ times those for a chi-squared test based on the Wald statistic (see the Appendix tables). For example, for testing $J = 5$ restrictions, the critical value from the chi-squared table (Appendix Table G.4) for 95 percent significance is 11.07. The critical values from the $F$ table (Appendix Table G.5) are $3.33 = 16.65/5$ for $n - K = 10$, $2.60 = 13.00/5$ for $n - K = 25$, $2.40 = 12.00/5$ for $n - K = 50$, $2.31 = 11.55/5$ for $n - K = 100$, and $2.214 = 11.07/5$ for large $n - K$. Thus, with normally distributed disturbances, as $n$ gets large, the $F$ test can be carried out by referring $JF$ to the critical values from the chi-squared table.

The crucial result for our purposes here is that the distribution of the Wald statistic is built up from the distribution of **b**, which is asymptotically normal even without normally distributed disturbances. The implication is that an appropriate large sample test statistic is chi-squared $= JF$. Once again, this implication relies on the central limit theorem, not on normally distributed disturbances. Now, what is the appropriate approach for a small or moderately sized sample? As we saw earlier, the critical values for the $F$ distribution converge from above to $(1/J)$ times those for the preceding chi-squared distribution. As before, one cannot say that this will always be true in every case for every possible configuration of the data and parameters. Without some special configuration of the data and parameters, however, one, can expect it to occur generally. The implication is that absent some additional firm characterization of the model, the $F$ statistic, with the critical values from the $F$ table, remains a conservative approach that becomes more accurate as the sample size increases.

Exercise 7 at the end of this chapter suggests another approach to testing that has validity in large samples, a **Lagrange multiplier test.** The vector of Lagrange multipliers in (5-14) is $[\mathbf{R}(\mathbf{X'X})^{-1}\mathbf{R'}]^{-1}(\mathbf{Rb} - \mathbf{q})$, that is, a multiple of the least squares discrepancy vector. In principle, a test of the hypothesis that $\boldsymbol{\lambda}_*$ equals zero should be equivalent to a test of the null hypothesis. Since the leading matrix has full rank, this can only equal zero if the discrepancy equals zero. A Wald test of the hypothesis that $\boldsymbol{\lambda}_* = \mathbf{0}$ is indeed a valid way to proceed. The large sample distribution of the Wald statistic would be chi-squared with $J$ degrees of freedom. (The procedure is considered in Exercise 7.) For a set of exclusion restrictions, $\boldsymbol{\beta}_2 = \mathbf{0}$, there is a simple way to carry out this test. The chi-squared statistic, in this case with $K_2$ degrees of freedom can be computed as $nR^2$ in the regression of $\mathbf{e}_*$ (the residuals in the short regression) on the full set of independent variables.

## 5.5 TESTING NONLINEAR RESTRICTIONS

The preceding discussion has relied heavily on the linearity of the regression model. When we analyze nonlinear functions of the parameters and nonlinear regression models, most of these exact distributional results no longer hold.

The general problem is that of testing a hypothesis that involves a nonlinear function of the regression coefficients:

$$H_0 : c(\boldsymbol{\beta}) = q.$$

We shall look first at the case of a single restriction. The more general one, in which $\mathbf{c}(\boldsymbol{\beta}) = \mathbf{q}$ is a set of restrictions, is a simple extension. The counterpart to the test statistic we used earlier would be

$$z = \frac{c(\hat{\boldsymbol{\beta}}) - q}{\text{estimated standard error}} \tag{5-24}$$

or its square, which in the preceding were distributed as $t[n - K]$ and $F[1, n - K]$, respectively. The discrepancy in the numerator presents no difficulty. Obtaining an estimate of the sampling variance of $c(\hat{\boldsymbol{\beta}}) - q$, however, involves the variance of a nonlinear function of $\hat{\boldsymbol{\beta}}$.

The results we need for this computation are presented in Sections 4.9.4, B.10.3, and D.3.1. A linear Taylor series approximation to $c(\hat{\boldsymbol{\beta}})$ around the true parameter vector $\boldsymbol{\beta}$ is

$$c(\hat{\boldsymbol{\beta}}) \approx c(\boldsymbol{\beta}) + \left(\frac{\partial c(\boldsymbol{\beta})}{\partial \boldsymbol{\beta}}\right)'(\hat{\boldsymbol{\beta}} - \boldsymbol{\beta}). \tag{5-25}$$

We must rely on consistency rather than unbiasedness here, since, in general, the expected value of a nonlinear function is not equal to the function of the expected value. If plim $\hat{\boldsymbol{\beta}} = \boldsymbol{\beta}$, then we are justified in using $c(\hat{\boldsymbol{\beta}})$ as an estimate of $c(\boldsymbol{\beta})$. (The relevant result is the Slutsky theorem.) Assuming that our use of this approximation is appropriate, the variance of the nonlinear function is approximately equal to the variance of the right-hand side, which is, then,

$$\text{Var}[c(\hat{\boldsymbol{\beta}})] \approx \left(\frac{\partial c(\boldsymbol{\beta})}{\partial \boldsymbol{\beta}}\right)' \text{Var}[\hat{\boldsymbol{\beta}}]\left(\frac{\partial c(\boldsymbol{\beta})}{\partial \boldsymbol{\beta}}\right). \tag{5-26}$$

The derivatives in the expression for the variance are functions of the unknown parameters. Since these are being estimated, we use our sample estimates in computing the derivatives. To estimate the variance of the estimator, we can use $s^2(\mathbf{X}'\mathbf{X})^{-1}$. Finally, we rely on Theorem D.22 in Section D.3.1 and use the standard normal distribution instead of the $t$ distribution for the test statistic. Using $\mathbf{g}(\hat{\boldsymbol{\beta}})$ to estimate $\mathbf{g}(\boldsymbol{\beta}) = \partial c(\boldsymbol{\beta})/\partial \boldsymbol{\beta}$, we can now test a hypothesis in the same fashion we did earlier.

### Example 5.3   A Long-Run Marginal Propensity to Consume

A consumption function that has different short- and long-run marginal propensities to consume can be written in the form

$$\ln C_t = \alpha + \beta \ln Y_t + \gamma \ln C_{t-1} + \varepsilon_t,$$

which is a **distributed lag** model. In this model, the short-run marginal propensity to consume (MPC) (elasticity, since the variables are in logs) is $\beta$, and the long-run MPC is $\delta = \beta/(1-\gamma)$. Consider testing the hypothesis that $\delta = 1$.

Quarterly data on aggregate U.S. consumption and disposable personal income for the years 1950 to 2000 are given in Appendix Table F5.1. The estimated equation based on these data is

$$\ln C_t = 0.003142 + 0.07495 \ln Y_t + 0.9246 \ln C_{t-1} + e_t, \quad R^2 = 0.999712, \quad s = 0.00874$$
$$\quad\quad (0.01055) \quad (0.02873) \quad\quad\quad (0.02859)$$

Estimated standard errors are shown in parentheses. We will also require Est. Asy. Cov[b, c] = −0.0008207. The estimate of the long-run MPC is $d = b/(1-c) = 0.07495/(1 - 0.9246) = 0.99403$. To compute the estimated variance of $d$, we will require

$$g_b = \frac{\partial d}{\partial b} = \frac{1}{1-c} = 13.2626, \quad g_c = \frac{\partial d}{\partial c} = \frac{b}{(1-c)^2} = 13.1834.$$

The estimated asymptotic variance of $d$ is

$$\text{Est. Asy. Var}[d] = g_b^2 \text{Est. Asy. Var}[b] + g_c^2 \text{Est. Asy. Var}[c] + 2g_b g_c \text{Est. Asy. Cov}[b, c]$$
$$= 13.2626^2 \times 0.02873^2 + 13.1834^2 \times 0.02859^2$$
$$+ 2(13.2626)(13.1834)(-0.0008207) = 0.0002585.$$

The square root is 0.016078. To test the hypothesis that the long-run MPC is greater than or equal to 1, we would use

$$z = \frac{0.99403 - 1}{0.41464} = -0.37131.$$

Because we are using a large sample approximation, we refer to a standard normal table instead of the $t$ distribution. The hypothesis that $\gamma = 1$ is not rejected.

You may have noticed that we could have tested this hypothesis with a linear restriction instead; if $\delta = 1$, then $\beta = 1 - \gamma$, or $\beta + \gamma = 1$. The estimate is $q = b + c - 1 = -0.00045$. The estimated standard error of this linear function is $[0.02873^2 + 0.02859^2 - 2(0.0008207)]^{1/2} = 0.00118$. The $t$ ratio for this test is $-0.38135$, which is almost the same as before. Since the sample used here is fairly large, this is to be expected. However, there is nothing in the computations that ensures this outcome. In a smaller sample, we might have obtained a different answer. For example, using the last 11 years of the data, the $t$ statistics for the two hypotheses are 7.652 and 5.681. The Wald test is not invariant to how the hypothesis is formulated. In a borderline case, we could have reached a different conclusion. This **lack of invariance** does not occur with the likelihood ratio or Lagrange multiplier tests discussed in Chapter 16. On the other hand, both of these tests require an assumption of normality, whereas the Wald statistic does not. This illustrates one of the trade-offs between a more detailed specification and the power of the test procedures that are implied.

The generalization to more than one function of the parameters proceeds along similar lines. Let $\mathbf{c}(\hat{\boldsymbol{\beta}})$ be a set of $J$ functions of the estimated parameter vector and let the $J \times K$ matrix of derivatives of $\mathbf{c}(\hat{\boldsymbol{\beta}})$ be

$$\hat{\mathbf{G}} = \frac{\partial \mathbf{c}(\hat{\boldsymbol{\beta}})}{\partial \hat{\boldsymbol{\beta}}'}. \tag{5-27}$$

The estimate of the asymptotic covariance matrix of these functions is

$$\text{Est. Asy. Var}[\hat{\mathbf{c}}] = \hat{\mathbf{G}}\{\text{Est. Asy. Var}[\hat{\boldsymbol{\beta}}]\}\hat{\mathbf{G}}'. \tag{5-28}$$

The $j$th row of $\hat{\mathbf{G}}$ is $K$ derivatives of $c_j$ with respect to the $K$ elements of $\hat{\boldsymbol{\beta}}$. For example, the covariance matrix for estimates of the short- and long-run marginal propensities to consume would be obtained using

$$\mathbf{G} = \begin{bmatrix} 0 & 1 & 0 \\ 0 & 1/(1-\gamma) & \beta/(1-\gamma)^2 \end{bmatrix}.$$

The statistic for testing the $J$ hypotheses $\mathbf{c}(\boldsymbol{\beta}) = \mathbf{q}$ is

$$W = (\hat{\mathbf{c}} - \mathbf{q})'\{\text{Est. Asy. Var}[\hat{\mathbf{c}}]\}^{-1}(\hat{\mathbf{c}} - \mathbf{q}). \tag{5-29}$$

In large samples, $W$ has a chi-squared distribution with degrees of freedom equal to the number of restrictions. Note that for a single restriction, this value is the square of the statistic in (5-24).

## 5.6 PREDICTION

After the estimation of parameters, a common use of regression is for prediction.[8] Suppose that we wish to predict the value of $y^0$ associated with a regressor vector $\mathbf{x}^0$. This value would be

$$y^0 = \mathbf{x}^{0\prime}\boldsymbol{\beta} + \varepsilon^0.$$

It follows from the Gauss–Markov theorem that

$$\hat{y}^0 = \mathbf{x}^{0\prime}\mathbf{b} \qquad\qquad (5\text{-}30)$$

is the minimum variance linear unbiased estimator of $E[y^0|\mathbf{x}^0]$. The forecast error is

$$e^0 = y^0 - \hat{y}^0 = (\boldsymbol{\beta} - \mathbf{b})'\mathbf{x}^0 + \varepsilon^0.$$

The **prediction variance** to be applied to this estimate is

$$\mathrm{Var}[e^0|\mathbf{X}, \mathbf{x}^0] = \sigma^2 + \mathrm{Var}[(\boldsymbol{\beta} - \mathbf{b})'\mathbf{x}^0|\mathbf{X}, \mathbf{x}^0] = \sigma^2 + \mathbf{x}^{0\prime}[\sigma^2(\mathbf{X}'\mathbf{X})^{-1}]\mathbf{x}^0. \qquad (5\text{-}31)$$

If the regression contains a constant term, then an equivalent expression is

$$\mathrm{Var}[e^0] = \sigma^2 \left[ 1 + \frac{1}{n} + \sum_{j=1}^{K-1}\sum_{k=1}^{K-1} \left(x_j^0 - \bar{x}_j\right)\left(x_k^0 - \bar{x}_k\right)(\mathbf{Z}'\mathbf{M}^0\mathbf{Z})^{jk} \right]$$

where $\mathbf{Z}$ is the $K-1$ columns of $\mathbf{X}$ not including the constant. This result shows that the width of the interval depends on the distance of the elements of $\mathbf{x}^0$ from the center of the data. Intuitively, this idea makes sense; the farther the forecasted point is from the center of our experience, the greater is the degree of uncertainty.

The prediction variance can be estimated by using $s^2$ in place of $\sigma^2$. A confidence interval for $y^0$ would be formed using a

$$\textbf{prediction interval} = \hat{y}^0 \pm t_{\lambda/2}\,\mathrm{se}(e^0).$$

Figure 5.1 shows the effect for the bivariate case. Note that the prediction variance is composed of three parts. The second and third become progressively smaller as we accumulate more data (i.e., as $n$ increases). But the first term $\sigma^2$ is constant, which implies that no matter how much data we have, we can never predict perfectly.

### Example 5.4   Prediction for Investment
To continue the analysis of Example 5.1, suppose that we wish to "predict" the first quarter 2001 value of real investment. The average rate (secondary market) for the 90-day T-bill was 4.48% (down from 6.03 at the end of 2000); real GDP was 9316.8; the CPI_U was 528.0 and the time trend would equal 204. (We dropped one observation to compute the rate of inflation. Data were obtained from www.economagic.com.) The rate of inflation on a yearly

---

[8]It is necessary at this point to make a largely semantic distinction between "prediction" and "forecasting." We will use the term "prediction" to mean using the regression model to compute fitted values of the dependent variable, either within the sample or for observations outside the sample. The same set of results will apply to cross sections, time series, or panels. These are the methods considered in this section. It is helpful at this point to reserve the term "forecasting" for usage of the time-series models discussed in Chapter 20. One of the distinguishing features of the models in that setting will be the explicit role of "time" and the presence of lagged variables and disturbances in the equations and correlation of variables with past values.

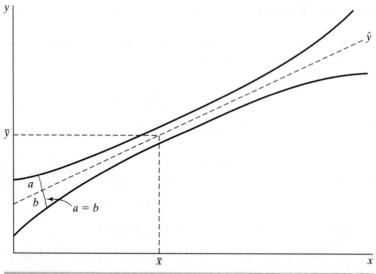

**FIGURE 5.1**   Prediction Intervals.

basis would be $100\% \times 4 \times \ln(528.0/521.1) = 5.26\%$. The data vector for predicting $\ln I_{2001.1}$ would be $\mathbf{x}^0 = [1, 4.48, 5.26, 9.1396, 204]'$. Using the regression results in Example 5.1,

$$\mathbf{x}^{0\prime}\mathbf{b} = [1, 4.48, 5.26, 9.1396, 204] \times [-9.1345, -0.008601, 0.003308, 1.9302, -0.005659]'$$

$$= 7.3312.$$

The estimated variance of this prediction is

$$s^2[1 + \mathbf{x}^{0\prime}(\mathbf{X}'\mathbf{X})^{-1}\mathbf{x}^0] = 0.0076912. \tag{5-32}$$

The square root, 0.087699, gives the prediction standard deviation. Using this value, we obtain the prediction interval:

$$7.3312 \pm 1.96(0.087699) = \langle 7.1593, 7.5031 \rangle.$$

The yearly rate of real investment in the first quarter of 2001 was 1721. The log is 7.4507, so our forecast interval contains the actual value.

We have forecasted the log of real investment with our regression model. If it is desired to forecast the level, the natural estimator would be $\hat{I} = \exp(\ln I)$. Assuming that the estimator, itself, is at least asymptotically normally distributed, this should systematically underestimate the level by a factor of $\exp(\hat{\sigma}^2/2)$ based on the mean of the lognormal distribution. [See Wooldridge (2006) and Section B.4.4.] It remains to determine what to use for $\hat{\sigma}^2$. In (5-32), the second part of the expression will vanish in large samples, leaving (as Wooldridge suggests) $s^2 = 0.007427$.[9] Using this scaling, we obtain a prediction of 1532.9, which is still 11 percent below the actual value. Evidently, this model based on an extremely long time series does not do a very good job of predicting at the end of the sample period. One might surmise various reasons, including some related to the model specification that we will address in Chapter 21, but as a first guess, it seems optimistic to apply an equation this simple to more than 50 years of data while expecting the underlying structure to be unchanging through the

---

[9]Wooldridge suggests an alternative not necessarily based on an assumption of normality. Use as the scale factor the single coefficient in a within sample regression of $y_i$ on the exponents of the fitted logs.

entire period. To investigate this possibility, we redid all the preceding calculations using only the data from 1990 to 2000 for the estimation. The prediction for the level of investment in 2001.1 is now 1885.2 (using the suggested scaling), which is an overestimate of 9.54 percent. But, this is more easily explained. The first quarter of 2001 began the first recession in the U.S. economy in nearly 10 years, and one of the early symptoms of a recession is a rapid decline in business investment.

All the preceding assumes that $\mathbf{x}^0$ is either known with certainty, ex post, or forecasted perfectly. If $\mathbf{x}^0$ must, itself, be forecasted (an ex ante forecast), then the formula for the forecast variance in (5-31) would have to be modified to include the variation in $\mathbf{x}^0$, which greatly complicates the computation. Most authors view it as simply intractable. Beginning with Feldstein (1971), derivation of firm analytical results for the correct forecast variance for this case remain to be derived except for simple special cases. The one qualitative result that seems certain is that (5-31) will understate the true variance. McCullough (1996) presents an alternative approach to computing appropriate forecast standard errors based on the method of bootstrapping. (See Chapter 17.)

Various measures have been proposed for assessing the predictive accuracy of forecasting models.[10] Most of these measures are designed to evaluate **ex post forecasts,** that is, forecasts for which the independent variables do not themselves have to be forecasted. Two measures that are based on the residuals from the forecasts are the **root mean squared error**

$$\text{RMSE} = \sqrt{\frac{1}{n^0} \sum_i (y_i - \hat{y}_i)^2}$$

and the mean absolute error

$$\text{MAE} = \frac{1}{n^0} \sum_i |y_i - \hat{y}_i|,$$

where $n^0$ is the number of periods being forecasted. (Note that both of these, as well as the measures below, are backward looking in that they are computed using the observed data on the independent variable.) These statistics have an obvious scaling problem—multiplying values of the dependent variable by any scalar multiplies the measure by that scalar as well. Several measures that are scale free are based on the **Theil $U$ statistic:**[11]

$$U = \sqrt{\frac{(1/n^0) \sum_i (y_i - \hat{y}_i)^2}{(1/n^0) \sum_i y_i^2}}.$$

This measure is related to $R^2$ but is not bounded by zero and one. Large values indicate a poor forecasting performance. An alternative is to compute the measure in terms of the changes in $y$:

$$U_\Delta = \sqrt{\frac{(1/n^0) \sum_i (\Delta y_i - \Delta \hat{y}_i)^2}{(1/n^0) \sum_i (\Delta y_i)^2}},$$

---

[10]See Theil (1961) and Fair (1984).

[11]Theil (1961).

where $\Delta y_i = y_i - y_{i-1}$ and $\Delta \hat{y}_i = \hat{y}_i - y_{i-1}$, or, in percentage changes, $\Delta y_i = (y_i - y_{i-1})/y_{i-1}$ and $\Delta \hat{y}_i = (\hat{y}_i - y_{i-1})/y_{i-1}$. These measures will reflect the model's ability to track turning points in the data.

## 5.7 SUMMARY AND CONCLUSIONS

This chapter has focused on two uses of the linear regression model, hypothesis testing and basic prediction. The central result for testing hypotheses is the $F$ statistic. The $F$ ratio can be produced in two equivalent ways; first, by measuring the extent to which the unrestricted least squares estimate differs from what a hypothesis would predict, and second, by measuring the loss of fit that results from assuming that a hypothesis is correct. We then extended the $F$ statistic to more general settings by examining its large sample properties, which allow us to discard the assumption of normally distributed disturbances and by extending it to nonlinear restrictions.

## Key Terms and Concepts

- Alternative hypothesis
- Distributed lag
- Discrepancy vector
- Exclusion restrictions
- Ex post forecast
- Lack of invariance
- Lagrange multiplier test
- Linear restrictions
- Nested models
- Nonnested models
- Nonnormality
- Null hypothesis
- Parameter space
- Prediction interval
- Prediction variance
- Restricted least squares
- Root mean squared error
- Testable implications
- Theil $U$ statistic
- Wald statistic

## Exercises

1. A multiple regression of $y$ on a constant $x_1$ and $x_2$ produces the following results: $\hat{y} = 4 + 0.4x_1 + 0.9x_2$, $R^2 = 8/60$, $\mathbf{e'e} = 520$, $n = 29$,

$$\mathbf{X'X} = \begin{bmatrix} 29 & 0 & 0 \\ 0 & 50 & 10 \\ 0 & 10 & 80 \end{bmatrix}.$$

Test the hypothesis that the two slopes sum to 1.

2. Using the results in Exercise 1, test the hypothesis that the slope on $x_1$ is 0 by running the restricted regression and comparing the two sums of squared deviations.

3. The regression model to be analyzed is $\mathbf{y} = \mathbf{X}_1\boldsymbol{\beta}_1 + \mathbf{X}_2\boldsymbol{\beta}_2 + \boldsymbol{\varepsilon}$, where $\mathbf{X}_1$ and $\mathbf{X}_2$ have $K_1$ and $K_2$ columns, respectively. The restriction is $\boldsymbol{\beta}_2 = \mathbf{0}$.

   a. Using (5-14), prove that the restricted estimator is simply $[\mathbf{b}_{1*}, \mathbf{0}]$, where $\mathbf{b}_{1*}$ is the least squares coefficient vector in the regression of $\mathbf{y}$ on $\mathbf{X}_1$.

   b. Prove that if the restriction is $\boldsymbol{\beta}_2 = \boldsymbol{\beta}_2^0$ for a nonzero $\boldsymbol{\beta}_2^0$, then the restricted estimator of $\boldsymbol{\beta}_1$ is $\mathbf{b}_{1*} = (\mathbf{X}_1'\mathbf{X}_1)^{-1}\mathbf{X}_1'(\mathbf{y} - \mathbf{X}_2\boldsymbol{\beta}_2^0)$.

4. The expression for the restricted coefficient vector in (5-14) may be written in the form $\mathbf{b}_* = [\mathbf{I} - \mathbf{CR}]\mathbf{b} + \mathbf{w}$, where $\mathbf{w}$ does not involve $\mathbf{b}$. What is $\mathbf{C}$? Show that the covariance matrix of the restricted least squares estimator is

$$\sigma^2(\mathbf{X'X})^{-1} - \sigma^2(\mathbf{X'X})^{-1}\mathbf{R'}[\mathbf{R}(\mathbf{X'X})^{-1}\mathbf{R'}]^{-1}\mathbf{R}(\mathbf{X'X})^{-1}$$

and that this matrix may be written as

$$\text{Var}[\mathbf{b} \mid \mathbf{X}]\{[\text{Var}(\mathbf{b} \mid \mathbf{X})]^{-1} - \mathbf{R}'[\text{Var}(\mathbf{Rb}) \mid \mathbf{X}]^{-1}\mathbf{R}\}\text{Var}[\mathbf{b} \mid \mathbf{X}].$$

5. Prove the result that the restricted least squares estimator never has a larger covariance matrix than the unrestricted least squares estimator.

6. Prove the result that the $R^2$ associated with a restricted least squares estimator is never larger than that associated with the unrestricted least squares estimator. Conclude that imposing restrictions never improves the fit of the regression.

7. An alternative way to test the hypothesis $\mathbf{R}\boldsymbol{\beta} - \mathbf{q} = \mathbf{0}$ is to use a Wald test of the hypothesis that $\boldsymbol{\lambda}_* = \mathbf{0}$, where $\boldsymbol{\lambda}_*$ is defined in (5-14). Prove that

$$\chi^2 = \boldsymbol{\lambda}_*'\{\text{Est. Var}[\boldsymbol{\lambda}_*]\}^{-1}\boldsymbol{\lambda}_* = (n - K)\left[\frac{\mathbf{e}_*'\mathbf{e}_*}{\mathbf{e}'\mathbf{e}} - 1\right].$$

Note that the fraction in brackets is the ratio of two estimators of $\sigma^2$. By virtue of (5-19) and the preceding discussion, we know that this ratio is greater than 1. Finally, prove that this test statistic is equivalent to $JF$, where $J$ is the number of restrictions being tested and $F$ is the conventional $F$ statistic given in (5-6). Formally, the Lagrange multiplier test requires that the variance estimator be based on the restricted sum of squares, not the unrestricted. Then, the test statistic would be $LM = nJ/[(n - K)/F + J]$. See Godfrey (1988).

8. Use the test statistic defined in Exercise 7 to test the hypothesis in Exercise 1.

9. Prove that under the hypothesis that $\mathbf{R}\boldsymbol{\beta} = \mathbf{q}$, the estimator

$$s_*^2 = \frac{(\mathbf{y} - \mathbf{Xb}_*)'(\mathbf{y} - \mathbf{Xb}_*)}{n - K + J},$$

where $J$ is the number of restrictions, is unbiased for $\sigma^2$.

10. Show that in the multiple regression of $\mathbf{y}$ on a constant, $\mathbf{x}_1$ and $\mathbf{x}_2$ while imposing the restriction $\beta_1 + \beta_2 = 1$ leads to the regression of $\mathbf{y} - \mathbf{x}_1$ on a constant and $\mathbf{x}_2 - \mathbf{x}_1$.

## Applications

1. The application in Chapter 3 used 15 of the 17,919 observations in Koop and Tobias's (2004) study of the relationship between wages and education, ability, and family characteristics. (See Appendix Table F3.2.) We will use the full data set for this exercise. The data may be downloaded from the *Journal of Applied Econometrics* data archive at http://www.econ.queensu.ca/jae/12004-vl9.7/koop-tobias/. The data file is in two parts. The first file contains the panel of 17,919 observations on variables:

   Column 1; *Person id* (ranging from 1 to 2,178),
   Column 2; *Education,*
   Column 3; *Log of hourly wage,*
   Column 4; *Potential experience,*
   Column 5; *Time trend.*

Columns 2–5 contain time varying variables. The second part of the data set contains time invariant variables for the 2,178 households. These are:

Column 1; *Ability,*
Column 2; *Mother's education,*
Column 3; *Father's education,*
Column 4; *Dummy variable for residence in a broken home,*
Column 5; *Number of siblings.*

To create the data set for this exercise, it is necessary to merge these two data files. The $i$th observation in the second file will be replicated $T_i$ times for the set of $T_i$ observations in the first file. The *person id* variable indicates which rows must contain the data from the second file. (How this preparation is carried out will vary from one computer package to another.) (Note: We are not attempting to replicate Koop and Tobias's results here—we are only employing their interesting data set.) Let $\mathbf{X}_1 = [constant, education, experience, ability]$ and let $\mathbf{X}_2 = [mother's\ education, father's\ education, broken\ home, number\ of\ siblings]$.

a. Compute the full regression of log *wage* on $\mathbf{X}_1$ and $\mathbf{X}_2$ and report all results.
b. Use an $F$ test to test the hypothesis that all coefficients except the constant term are zero.
c. Use an $F$ statistic to test the joint hypothesis that the coefficients on the four household variables in $\mathbf{X}_2$ are zero.
d. Use a Wald test to carry out the test in part c.

2. The generalized Cobb–Douglas cost function examined in Application 2 in Chapter 4 is a special case of the **translog cost function,**

$$
\begin{aligned}
\ln C =\ & \alpha + \beta \ln Q + \delta_k \ln P_k + \delta_l \ln P_l + \delta_f \ln P_f \\
& + \phi_{kk}[\tfrac{1}{2}(\ln P_k)^2] + \phi_{ll}[\tfrac{1}{2}(\ln P_l)^2] + \phi_{ff}[\tfrac{1}{2}(\ln P_f)^2] \\
& + \phi_{kl}[\ln P_k][\ln P_l] + \phi_{kf}[\ln P_k][\ln P_f] + \phi_{lf}[\ln P_l][\ln P_f] \\
& + \gamma[\tfrac{1}{2}(\ln Q)^2] \\
& + \theta_{Qk}[\ln Q][\ln P_k] + \theta_{Ql}[\ln Q][\ln P_l] + \theta_{Qf}[\ln Q][\ln P_k] + \varepsilon.
\end{aligned}
$$

The theoretical requirement of linear homogeneity in the factor prices imposes the following restrictions:

$$
\begin{array}{lll}
\delta_k + \delta_l + \delta_f = 1 & \phi_{kk} + \phi_{kl} + \phi_{kf} = 0 & \phi_{kl} + \phi_{ll} + \phi_{lf} = 0 \\
\phi_{kf} + \phi_{lf} + \phi_{ff} = 0 & \theta_{QK} + \theta_{Ql} + \theta_{Qf} = 0 &
\end{array}
$$

Note that although the underlying theory requires it, the model can be estimated (by least squares) without imposing the linear homogeneity restrictions. [Thus, one could "test" the underlying theory by testing the validity of these restrictions. See Christensen, Jorgenson, and Lau (1975).] We will repeat this exercise in part b.

A number of additional restrictions were explored in Christensen and Greene's (1976) study. The hypothesis of homotheticity of the production structure would add the additional restrictions

$$
\theta_{Qk} = 0, \quad \theta_{Ql} = 0, \quad \theta_{Qf} = 0.
$$

Homogeneity of the production structure adds the restriction $\gamma = 0$. The hypothesis that all elasticities of substitution in the production structure are equal to $-1$ is imposed by the six restrictions $\phi_{ij} = 0$ for all $i$ and $j$.

We will use the data from the earlier application to test these restrictions. For the purposes of this exercise, denote by $\beta_1, \ldots, \beta_{15}$ the 15 parameters in the cost function above in the order that they appear in the model, starting in the first line and moving left to right and downward.

a. Write out the **R** matrix and **q** vector in (5-3) that are needed to impose the restriction of linear homogeneity in prices.

b. "Test" the theory of production using all 158 observations. Use an $F$ test to test the restrictions of linear homogeneity. Note, you can use the general form of the $F$ statistic in (5-7) to carry out the test. Christensen and Greene enforced the linear homogeneity restrictions by building them into the model. You can do this by dividing cost and the prices of capital and labor by the price of fuel. Terms with $f$ subscripts fall out of the model, leaving an equation with ten parameters. Compare the sums of squares for the two models to carry out the test. Of course, the test may be carried out either way and will produce the same result.

c. Test the hypothesis homotheticity of the production structure under the assumption of linear homogeneity in prices.

d. Test the hypothesis of the generalized Cobb–Douglas cost function in Chapter 4 against the more general translog model suggested here, once again (and henceforth) assuming linear homogeneity in the prices.

e. The simple Cobb–Douglas function appears in the first line of the model above. Test the hypothesis of the Cobb–Douglas model against the alternative of the full translog model.

f. Test the hypothesis of the generalized Cobb–Douglas model against the homothetic translog model.

g. Which of the several functional forms suggested here to you conclude is the most appropriate for these data?

3. The gasoline consumption model suggested in part d of Application 1 in Chapter 4 may be written as

$$\ln(G/Pop) = \alpha + \beta_P \ln P_g + \beta_I \ln (Income/Pop) + \gamma_{nc} \ln P_{nc} + \gamma_{uc} \ln P_{uc} + \gamma_{pt} \ln P_{pt}$$
$$+ \tau \text{year} + \delta_d \ln P_d + \delta_n \ln P_n + \delta_s \ln P_s + \varepsilon.$$

a. Carry out a test of the hypothesis that the three aggregate price indices are not significant determinants of the demand for gasoline.

b. Consider the hypothesis that the microelasticities are a constant proportion of the elasticity with respect to their corresponding aggregate. Thus, for some positive $\theta$ (presumably between 0 and 1), $\gamma_{nc} = \theta \delta_d$, $\gamma_{uc} = \theta \delta_d$, $\gamma_{pt} = \theta \delta_s$. The first two imply the simple linear restriction $\gamma_{nc} = \gamma_{uc}$. By taking ratios, the first (or second) and third imply the nonlinear restriction

$$\frac{\gamma_{nc}}{\gamma_{pt}} = \frac{\delta_d}{\delta_s} \quad \text{or} \quad \gamma_{nc}\delta_s - \gamma_{pt}\delta_d = 0.$$

Describe in detail how you would test the validity of the restriction.

c. Using the gasoline market data in Table F2.2, test the two restrictions suggested here, separately and jointly.

# 6

# FUNCTIONAL FORM AND STRUCTURAL CHANGE

## 6.1 INTRODUCTION

In this chapter, we are concerned with the functional form of the regression model. Many different types of functions are "linear" by the definition considered in Section 2.3.1. By using different transformations of the dependent and independent variables, and dummy variables and different arrangements of functions of variables, a wide variety of models can be constructed that are all estimable by linear least squares. Section 6.2 considers using binary variables to accommodate nonlinearities in the model. Section 6.3 broadens the class of models that are linear in the parameters. Sections 6.4 and 6.5 then examine the issue of specifying and testing for change in the underlying model that generates the data, under the heading of **structural change.**

## 6.2 USING BINARY VARIABLES

One of the most useful devices in regression analysis is the **binary,** or **dummy variable.** A dummy variable takes the value one for some observations to indicate the presence of an effect or membership in a group and zero for the remaining observations. Binary variables are a convenient means of building discrete shifts of the function into a regression model.

### 6.2.1 BINARY VARIABLES IN REGRESSION

Dummy variables are usually used in regression equations that also contain other quantitative variables. In the earnings equation in Example 4.3, we included a variable *Kids* to indicate whether there were children in the household, under the assumption that for many married women, this fact is a significant consideration in labor supply behavior. The results shown in Example 6.1 appear to be consistent with this hypothesis.

#### Example 6.1   Dummy Variable in an Earnings Equation
Table 6.1 following reproduces the estimated earnings equation in Example 4.3. The variable Kids is a dummy variable, which equals one if there are children under 18 in the household and zero otherwise. Since this is a **semilog equation,** the value of −0.35 for the coefficient is an extremely large effect, one which suggests that all other things equal, the earnings of women with children are nearly a third less than those without. This is a large difference, but one that would certainly merit closer scrutiny. Whether this effect results from different labor market effects that influence wages and not hours, or the reverse, remains to be seen. Second, having chosen a nonrandomly selected sample of those with only positive earnings to begin with, it is unclear whether the sampling mechanism has, itself, induced a bias in this coefficient.

**TABLE 6.1**   Estimated Earnings Equation

$ln\ earnings = \beta_1 + \beta_2\ age + \beta_3\ age^2 + \beta_4\ education + \beta_5\ kids + \varepsilon$

| | |
|---|---|
| Sum of squared residuals: | 599.4582 |
| Standard error of the regression: | 1.19044 |
| $R^2$ based on 428 observations | 0.040995 |

| Variable | Coefficient | Standard Error | t Ratio |
|---|---|---|---|
| Constant | 3.24009 | 1.7674 | 1.833 |
| Age | 0.20056 | 0.08386 | 2.392 |
| Age$^2$ | −0.0023147 | 0.00098688 | −2.345 |
| Education | 0.067472 | 0.025248 | 2.672 |
| Kids | −0.35119 | 0.14753 | −2.380 |

In recent applications, researchers in many fields have studied the effects of **treatment** on some kind of **response.** Examples include the effect of college on lifetime income, sex differences in labor supply behavior as in Example 6.1 in salary structures in industries, and in pre- versus postregime shifts in macroeconomic models, to name but a few. These examples can all be formulated in regression models involving a single dummy variable:

$$y_i = \mathbf{x}'_i \boldsymbol{\beta} + \delta d_i + \varepsilon_i$$

One of the important issues in policy analysis concerns measurement of such treatment effects when the dummy variable results from an individual participation decision. For example, in studies of the effect of job training programs on post-training earnings, the "treatment dummy" might be measuring the latent motivation and initiative of the participants rather than the effect of the program itself. We will revisit this subject in Section 24.5.

It is common for researchers to include a dummy variable in a regression to account for something that applies only to a single observation. For example, in time-series analyses, an occasional study includes a dummy variable that is one only in a single unusual year, such as the year of a major strike or a major policy event. (See, for example, the application to the German money demand function in Section 22.3.5.) It is easy to show (we consider this in the exercises) the very useful implication of this:

A dummy variable that takes the value one only for one observation has the effect of deleting that observation from computation of the least squares slopes and variance estimator (but not *R*-squared).

### 6.2.2   SEVERAL CATEGORIES

When there are several categories, a set of binary variables is necessary. Correcting for seasonal factors in macroeconomic data is a common application. We could write a consumption function for quarterly data as

$$C_t = \beta_1 + \beta_2 x_t + \delta_1 D_{t1} + \delta_2 D_{t2} + \delta_3 D_{t3} + \varepsilon_t,$$

where $x_t$ is disposable income. Note that only three of the four quarterly dummy variables are included in the model. If the fourth were included, then the four dummy variables would sum to one at every observation, which would reproduce the constant term—a case of perfect multicollinearity. This is known as the **dummy variable trap.** Thus, to avoid the dummy variable trap, we drop the dummy variable for the fourth quarter. (Depending on the application, it might be preferable to have four separate dummy variables and drop the overall constant.)[1] Any of the four quarters (or 12 months) can be used as the base period.

The preceding is a means of *deseasonalizing* the data. Consider the alternative formulation:

$$C_t = \beta x_t + \delta_1 D_{t1} + \delta_2 D_{t2} + \delta_3 D_{t3} + \delta_4 D_{t4} + \varepsilon_t. \tag{6-1}$$

Using the results from Chapter 3 on partitioned regression, we know that the preceding multiple regression is equivalent to first regressing $C$ and $x$ on the four dummy variables and then using the residuals from these regressions in the subsequent regression of deseasonalized consumption on deseasonalized income. Clearly, deseasonalizing in this fashion prior to computing the simple regression of consumption on income produces the same coefficient on income (and the same vector of residuals) as including the set of dummy variables in the regression.

### 6.2.3  SEVERAL GROUPINGS

The case in which several sets of dummy variables are needed is much the same as those we have already considered, with one important exception. Consider a model of statewide per capita expenditure on education $y$ as a function of statewide per capita income $x$. Suppose that we have observations on all $n = 50$ states for $T = 10$ years. A regression model that allows the expected expenditure to change over time as well as across states would be

$$y_{it} = \alpha + \beta x_{it} + \delta_i + \theta_t + \varepsilon_{it}. \tag{6-2}$$

As before, it is necessary to drop one of the variables in each set of dummy variables to avoid the dummy variable trap. For our example, if a total of 50 state dummies and 10 time dummies is retained, a problem of "perfect multicollinearity" remains; the sums of the 50 state dummies and the 10 time dummies are the same, that is, 1. One of the variables in each of the sets (or the overall constant term and one of the variables in one of the sets) must be omitted.

#### Example 6.2   Analysis of Covariance
The data in Appendix Table F6.1 were used in a study of efficiency in production of airline services in Greene (1997b). The airline industry has been a favorite subject of study [e.g., Schmidt and Sickles (1984); Sickles, Good, and Johnson (1986)], partly because of interest in this rapidly changing market in a period of deregulation and partly because of an abundance of large, high-quality data sets collected by the (no longer existent) Civil Aeronautics Board. The original data set consisted of 25 firms observed yearly for 15 years (1970 to 1984), a "balanced panel." Several of the firms merged during this period and several others experienced strikes, which reduced the number of complete observations substantially. Omitting these and others because of missing data on some of the variables left a group of 10 full

---

[1] See Suits (1984) and Greene and Seaks (1991).

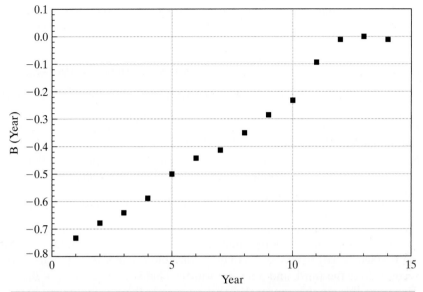

**FIGURE 6.1**    Estimated Year Dummy Variable Coefficients.

observations, from which we have selected six for the examples to follow. We will fit a cost equation of the form

$$\ln C_{i,t} = \beta_1 + \beta_2 \ln Q_{i,t} + \beta_3 \ln^2 Q_{i,t} + \beta_4 \ln P_{fuel\ i,t} + \beta_5\ Loadfactor_{i,t}$$

$$+ \sum_{t=1}^{14} \theta_t D_{i,t} + \sum_{i=1}^{5} \delta_i F_{i,t} + \varepsilon_{i,t}.$$

The dummy variables are $D_{i,t}$ which is the year variable and $F_{i,t}$ which is the firm variable. We have dropped the last one in each group. The estimated model for the full specification is

$$\ln C_{i,t} = 13.56 + 0.8866 \ln Q_{i,t} + 0.01261 \ln^2 Q_{i,t} + 0.1281 \ln P_{fi,t} - 0.8855 LF_{i,t}$$

$$+ \text{time effects} + \text{firm effects}.$$

The year effects display a revealing pattern, as shown in Figure 6.1. This was a period of rapidly rising fuel prices, so the cost effects are to be expected. Since one year dummy variable is dropped, the effect shown is relative to this base year (1984).

We are interested in whether the firm effects, the time effects, both, or neither are statistically significant. Table 6.2 presents the sums of squares from the four regressions. The $F$ statistic for the hypothesis that there are no firm-specific effects is 65.94, which is highly significant. The statistic for the time effects is only 2.61, which is larger than the critical value

**TABLE 6.2**    $F$ tests for Firm and Year Effects

| Model | Sum of Squares | Restrictions | F | Deg.Fr. |
|---|---|---|---|---|
| Full model | 0.17257 | 0 | — | |
| Time effects only | 1.03470 | 5 | 65.94 | [5, 66] |
| Firm effects only | 0.26815 | 14 | 2.61 | [14, 66] |
| No effects | 1.27492 | 19 | 22.19 | [19, 66] |

of 1.84, but perhaps less so than Figure 6.1 might have suggested. In the absence of the year-specific dummy variables, the year-specific effects are probably largely absorbed by the price of fuel.

### 6.2.4 THRESHOLD EFFECTS AND CATEGORICAL VARIABLES

In most applications, we use dummy variables to account for purely qualitative factors, such as membership in a group, or to represent a particular time period. There are cases, however, in which the dummy variable(s) represents levels of some underlying factor that might have been measured directly if this were possible. For example, education is a case in which we typically observe certain thresholds rather than, say, years of education. Suppose, for example, that our interest is in a regression of the form

$$income = \beta_1 + \beta_2\ age + effect\ of\ education + \varepsilon.$$

The data on education might consist of the highest level of education attained, such as high school ($HS$), undergraduate ($B$), master's ($M$), or Ph.D. ($P$). An obviously unsatisfactory way to proceed is to use a variable $E$ that is 0 for the first group, 1 for the second, 2 for the third, and 3 for the fourth. That is, $income = \beta_1 + \beta_2\ age + \beta_3 E + \varepsilon$. The difficulty with this approach is that it assumes that the increment in income at each threshold is the same; $\beta_3$ is the difference between income with a Ph.D. and a master's and between a master's and a bachelor's degree. This is unlikely and unduly restricts the regression. A more flexible model would use three (or four) binary variables, one for each level of education. Thus, we would write

$$income = \beta_1 + \beta_2\ age + \delta_B\ B + \delta_M\ M + \delta_P\ P + \varepsilon.$$

The correspondence between the coefficients and income for a given age is

High school: $\quad E[income\,|\,age, HS] = \beta_1 + \beta_2\ age,$

Bachelor's: $\quad E[income\,|\,age, B] \;= \beta_1 + \beta_2\ age + \delta_B,$

Master's: $\quad E[income\,|\,age, M] = \beta_1 + \beta_2\ age + \delta_M,$

Ph.D.: $\quad E[income\,|\,age, P] \;= \beta_1 + \beta_2\ age + \delta_P.$

The differences between, say, $\delta_P$ and $\delta_M$ and between $\delta_M$ and $\delta_B$ are of interest. Obviously, these are simple to compute. An alternative way to formulate the equation that reveals these differences directly is to redefine the dummy variables to be 1 if the individual has the degree, rather than whether the degree is the highest degree obtained. Thus, for someone with a Ph.D., all three binary variables are 1, and so on. By defining the variables in this fashion, the regression is now

High school: $\quad E[income\,|\,age, HS] = \beta_1 + \beta_2\ age,$

Bachelor's: $\quad E[income\,|\,age, B] \;= \beta_1 + \beta_2\ age + \delta_B,$

Master's: $\quad E[income\,|\,age, M] = \beta_1 + \beta_2\ age + \delta_B + \delta_M,$

Ph.D.: $\quad E[income\,|\,age, P] \;= \beta_1 + \beta_2\ age + \delta_B + \delta_M + \delta_P.$

Instead of the difference between a Ph.D. and the base case, in this model $\delta_P$ is the marginal value of the Ph.D. How equations with dummy variables are formulated is a matter of convenience. All the results can be obtained from a basic equation.

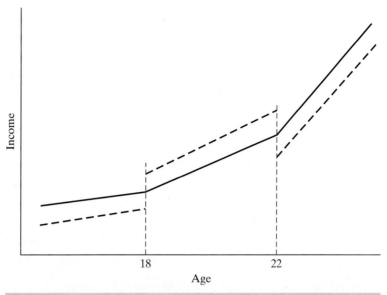

**FIGURE 6.2** Spline Function.

### 6.2.5 SPLINE REGRESSION

If one is examining income data for a large cross section of individuals of varying ages in a population, then certain patterns with regard to some age thresholds will be clearly evident. In particular, throughout the range of values of age, income will be rising, but the slope might change at some distinct milestones, for example, at age 18, when the typical individual graduates from high school, and at age 22, when he or she graduates from college. The **time profile** of income for the typical individual in this population might appear as in Figure 6.2. Based on the discussion in the preceding paragraph, we could fit such a regression model just by dividing the sample into three subsamples. However, this would neglect the continuity of the proposed function. The result would appear more like the dotted figure than the continuous function we had in mind. Restricted regression and what is known as a **spline** function can be used to achieve the desired effect.[2]

The function we wish to estimate is

$$E[income \,|\, age] = \alpha^0 + \beta^0 \, age \quad \text{if } age < 18,$$
$$\alpha^1 + \beta^1 \, age \quad \text{if } age \geq 18 \text{ and } age < 22,$$
$$\alpha^2 + \beta^2 \, age \quad \text{if } age \geq 22.$$

The threshold values, 18 and 22, are called **knots.** Let

$$d_1 = 1 \quad \text{if } age \geq t_1^*,$$
$$d_2 = 1 \quad \text{if } age \geq t_2^*,$$

---

[2]An important reference on this subject is Poirier (1974). An often-cited application appears in Garber and Poirier (1974).

where $t_1^* = 18$ and $t_2^* = 22$. To combine all three equations, we use

$$income = \beta_1 + \beta_2\, age + \gamma_1 d_1 + \delta_1 d_1\, age + \gamma_2 d_2 + \delta_2 d_2\, age + \varepsilon. \qquad \textbf{(6-3)}$$

This relationship is the dashed function in Figure 6.2. The slopes in the three segments are $\beta_2$, $\beta_2 + \delta_1$, and $\beta_2 + \delta_1 + \delta_2$. To make the function **piecewise continuous,** we require that the segments join at the knots—that is,

$$\beta_1 + \beta_2 t_1^* = (\beta_1 + \gamma_1) + (\beta_2 + \delta_1)t_1^*$$

and

$$(\beta_1 + \gamma_1) + (\beta_2 + \delta_1)t_2^* = (\beta_1 + \gamma_1 + \gamma_2) + (\beta_2 + \delta_1 + \delta_2)t_2^*.$$

These are linear restrictions on the coefficients. Collecting terms, the first one is

$$\gamma_1 + \delta_1 t_1^* = 0 \quad \text{or} \quad \gamma_1 = -\delta_1 t_1^*.$$

Doing likewise for the second and inserting these in (6-3), we obtain

$$income = \beta_1 + \beta_2\, age + \delta_1 d_1\,(age - t_1^*) + \delta_2 d_2\,(age - t_2^*) + \varepsilon.$$

Constrained least squares estimates are obtainable by multiple regression, using a constant and the variables

$$x_1 = age,$$
$$x_2 = age - 18 \quad \text{if } age \geq 18 \text{ and } 0 \text{ otherwise,}$$

and

$$x_3 = age - 22 \quad \text{if } age \geq 22 \text{ and } 0 \text{ otherwise.}$$

We can test the hypothesis that the slope of the function is constant with the joint test of the two restrictions $\delta_1 = 0$ and $\delta_2 = 0$.

## 6.3   NONLINEARITY IN THE VARIABLES

It is useful at this point to write the linear regression model in a very general form: Let $\mathbf{z} = z_1, z_2, \ldots, z_L$ be a set of $L$ independent variables; let $f_1, f_2, \ldots, f_K$ be $K$ linearly independent functions of $\mathbf{z}$; let $g(y)$ be an observable function of $y$; and retain the usual assumptions about the disturbance. The linear regression model is

$$\begin{aligned} g(y) &= \beta_1 f_1(\mathbf{z}) + \beta_2 f_2(\mathbf{z}) + \cdots + \beta_K f_K(\mathbf{z}) + \varepsilon \\ &= \beta_1 x_1 + \beta_2 x_2 + \cdots + \beta_K x_K + \varepsilon \qquad \textbf{(6-4)} \\ &= \mathbf{x}'\boldsymbol{\beta} + \varepsilon. \end{aligned}$$

By using logarithms, exponentials, reciprocals, transcendental functions, polynomials, products, ratios, and so on, this "linear" model can be tailored to any number of situations.

### 6.3.1   FUNCTIONAL FORMS

A commonly used form of regression model is the **loglinear model,**

$$\ln y = \ln \alpha + \sum_k \beta_k \ln X_k + \varepsilon = \beta_1 + \sum_k \beta_k x_k + \varepsilon.$$

In this model, the coefficients are elasticities:

$$\left(\frac{\partial y}{\partial x_k}\right)\left(\frac{x_k}{y}\right) = \frac{\partial \ln y}{\partial \ln x_k} = \beta_k. \tag{6-5}$$

In the loglinear equation, measured changes are in proportional or percentage terms; $\beta_k$ measures the percentage change in $y$ associated with a 1 percent change in $x_k$. This removes the units of measurement of the variables from consideration in using the regression model. An alternative approach sometimes taken is to measure the variables and associated changes in standard deviation units. If the data are "standardized" before estimation using $x_{ik}^* = (x_{ik} - \overline{x}_k)/s_k$ and likewise for $y$, then the least squares regression coefficients measure changes in standard deviation units rather than natural units or percentage terms. (Note that the constant term disappears from this regression.) It is not necessary actually to transform the data to produce these results; multiplying each least squares coefficient $b_k$ in the original regression by $s_k/s_y$ produces the same result.

A hybrid of the linear and loglinear models is the semilog equation

$$\ln y = \beta_1 + \beta_2 x + \varepsilon. \tag{6-6}$$

We used this form in the investment equation in Section 5.2,

$$\ln I_t = \beta_1 + \beta_2 (i_t - \Delta p_t) + \beta_3 \Delta p_t + \beta_4 \ln Y_t + \beta_5 t + \varepsilon_t,$$

where the log of investment is modeled in the levels of the real interest rate, the price level, and a time trend. In a semilog equation with a time trend such as this one, $d \ln I/dt = \beta_5$ is the average rate of growth of $I$. The estimated value of $-0.00566$ in Table 6.1 suggests that over the full estimation period, after accounting for all other factors, the average rate of growth of investment was $-0.566$ percent per year.

The coefficients in the semilog model are partial- or semi-elasticities; in (6-6), $\beta_2$ is $\partial \ln y/\partial x$. This is a natural form for models with dummy variables such as the earnings equation in Example 5.1. The coefficient on *Kids* of $-0.35$ suggests that all else equal, earnings are approximately 35 percent less when there are children in the household.

The quadratic earnings equation in Example 6.1 shows another use of nonlinearities in the variables. Using the results in Example 6.1, we find that for a woman with 12 years of schooling and children in the household, the age-earnings profile appears as in Figure 6.3. This figure suggests an important question in this framework. It is tempting to conclude that Figure 6.3 shows the earnings trajectory of a person at different ages, but that is not what the data provide. The model is based on a cross section, and what it displays is the earnings of different people of different ages. How this profile relates to the expected earnings path of one individual is a different, and complicated question.

Another useful formulation of the regression model is one with **interaction terms.** For example, a model relating braking distance $D$ to speed $S$ and road wetness $W$ might be

$$D = \beta_1 + \beta_2 S + \beta_3 W + \beta_4 SW + \varepsilon.$$

In this model,

$$\frac{\partial E[D \mid S, W]}{\partial S} = \beta_2 + \beta_4 W,$$

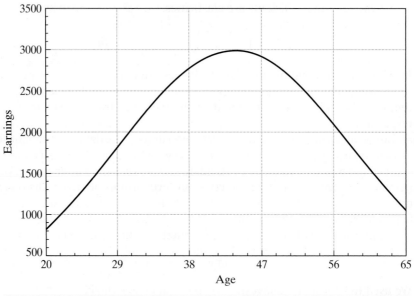

**FIGURE 6.3** Age-Earnings Profile.

which implies that the **marginal effect** of higher speed on braking distance is increased when the road is wetter (assuming that $\beta_4$ is positive). If it is desired to form confidence intervals or test hypotheses about these marginal effects, then the necessary standard error is computed from

$$\text{Var}\left(\frac{\partial \hat{E}[D \mid S, W]}{\partial S}\right) = \text{Var}[\hat{\beta}_2] + W^2 \, \text{Var}[\hat{\beta}_4] + 2W \, \text{Cov}[\hat{\beta}_2, \hat{\beta}_4],$$

and similarly for $\partial E[D \mid S, W]/\partial W$. A value must be inserted for $W$. The sample mean is a natural choice, but for some purposes, a specific value, such as an extreme value of $W$ in this example, might be preferred.

### 6.3.2 IDENTIFYING NONLINEARITY

If the functional form is not known a priori, then there are a few approaches that may help at least to identify any nonlinearity and provide some information about it from the sample. For example, if the suspected nonlinearity is with respect to a single regressor in the equation, then fitting a quadratic or cubic polynomial rather than a linear function may capture some of the nonlinearity. By choosing several ranges for the regressor in question and allowing the slope of the function to be different in each range, a piecewise linear approximation to the nonlinear function can be fit.

#### Example 6.3 Functional Form for a Nonlinear Cost Function

In a celebrated study of economies of scale in the U.S. electric power industry, Nerlove (1963) analyzed the production costs of 145 American electricity generating companies. This study produced several innovations in microeconometrics. It was among the first major applications of statistical cost analysis. The theoretical development in Nerlove's study was the first to show how the fundamental theory of duality between production and cost functions could be used to frame an econometric model. Finally, Nerlove employed several useful techniques to sharpen his basic model.

The focus of the paper was economies of scale, typically modeled as a characteristic of the production function. He chose a Cobb–Douglas function to model output as a function of capital, $K$, labor, $L$, and fuel, $F$:

$$Q = \alpha_0 K^{\alpha_K} L^{\alpha_L} F^{\alpha_F} e^{\varepsilon_i}$$

where $Q$ is output and $\varepsilon_i$ embodies the unmeasured differences across firms. The economies of scale parameter is $r = \alpha_K + \alpha_L + \alpha_F$. The value 1 indicates constant returns to scale. In this study, Nerlove investigated the widely accepted assumption that producers in this industry enjoyed substantial economies of scale. The production model is loglinear, so assuming that other conditions of the classical regression model are met, the four parameters could be estimated by least squares. However, he argued that the three factors could not be treated as exogenous variables. For a firm that optimizes by choosing its factors of production, the demand for fuel would be $F^* = F^*(Q, P_K, P_L, P_F)$ and likewise for labor and capital, so certainly the assumptions of the classical model are violated.

In the regulatory framework in place at the time, state commissions set rates and firms met the demand forthcoming at the regulated prices. Thus, it was argued that output (as well as the factor prices) could be viewed as exogenous to the firm and, based on an argument by Zellner, Kmenta, and Dreze (1966), Nerlove argued that at equilibrium, the *deviation* of costs from the long run optimum would be independent of output. (This has a testable implication which we will explore in Chapter 9.) Thus, the firm's objective was cost minimization subject to the constraint of the production function. This can be formulated as a Lagrangean problem,

$$\text{Min}_{K,L,F} \, P_K K + P_L L + P_F F + \lambda(Q - \alpha_0 K^{\alpha_K} L^{\alpha_L} F^{\alpha_F}).$$

The solution to this minimization problem is the three factor demands and the multiplier (which measures marginal cost). Inserted back into total costs, this produces an (intrinsically linear) loglinear cost function,

$$P_K K + P_L L + P_F F = C(Q, P_K, P_L, P_F) = r A Q^{1/r} P_K^{\alpha_K/r} P_L^{\alpha_L/r} P_F^{\alpha_F/r} e^{\varepsilon_i/r}$$

or

$$\ln C = \beta_1 + \beta_q \ln Q + \beta_K \ln P_K + \beta_L \ln P_L + \beta_F \ln P_F + u_i \tag{6-7}$$

where $\beta_q = 1/(\alpha_K + \alpha_L + \alpha_F)$ is now the parameter of interest and $\beta_j = \alpha_j/r$, $j = K, L, F$.[3] Thus, the duality between production and cost functions has been used to derive the estimating equation from first principles.

A complication remains. The cost parameters must sum to one; $\beta_K + \beta_L + \beta_F = 1$, so estimation must be done subject to this constraint.[4] This restriction can be imposed by regressing $\ln(C/P_F)$ on a constant, $\ln Q$, $\ln(P_K/P_F)$, and $\ln(P_L/P_F)$. This first set of results appears at the top of Table 6.3.

---

[3]Readers who attempt to replicate the original study should note that Nerlove used common (base 10) logs in his calculations, not natural logs. This change creates some numerical differences.

[4]In the context of the econometric model, the restriction has a testable implication by the definition in Chapter 5. But, the underlying economics require this restriction—it was used in deriving the cost function. Thus, it is unclear what is implied by a test of the restriction. Presumably, if the hypothesis of the restriction is rejected, the analysis should stop at that point, since without the restriction, the cost function is not a valid representation of the production function. We will encounter this conundrum again in another form in Chapter 10. Fortunately, in this instance, the hypothesis is not rejected. (It is in the application in Chapter 10.)

| | *log* Q | *log* $P_L$ − *log* $P_F$ | *log* $P_K$ − *log* $P_F$ | $R^2$ |
|---|---|---|---|---|
| All firms | 0.721 | 0.594 | −0.0085 | 0.932 |
| | (0.0174) | (0.205) | (0.191) | |
| Group 1 | 0.398 | 0.641 | −0.093 | 0.512 |
| Group 2 | 0.668 | 0.105 | 0.364 | 0.635 |
| Group 3 | 0.931 | 0.408 | 0.249 | 0.571 |
| Group 4 | 0.915 | 0.472 | 0.133 | 0.871 |
| Group 5 | 1.045 | 0.604 | −0.295 | 0.920 |

**TABLE 6.3** Cobb–Douglas Cost Functions (standard errors in parentheses)

Initial estimates of the parameters of the cost function are shown in the top row of Table 6.3. The hypothesis of constant returns to scale can be firmly rejected. The *t* ratio is $(0.721 − 1)/0.0174 = −16.03$, so we conclude that this estimate is significantly less than 1 or, by implication, *r* is significantly greater than 1. Note that the coefficient on the capital price is negative. In theory, this should equal $\alpha_K/r$, which (unless the marginal product of capital is negative) should be positive. Nerlove attributed this to measurement error in the capital price variable. This seems plausible, but it carries with it the implication that the other coefficients are mismeasured as well. [Christensen and Greene's (1976) estimator of this model with these data produced a positive estimate. See Section 10.4.2.]

The striking pattern of the residuals shown in Figure 6.4[5] and some thought about the implied form of the production function suggested that something was missing from the model.[6] In theory, the estimated model implies a continually declining average cost curve, which in turn implies persistent economies of scale at all levels of output. This conflicts with the textbook notion of a U-shaped average cost curve and appears implausible for the data. Note the three clusters of residuals in the figure. Two approaches were used to analyze the model.

By sorting the sample into five groups on the basis of output and fitting separate regressions to each group, Nerlove fit a piecewise loglinear model. The results are given in the lower rows of Table 6.3, where the firms in the successive groups are progressively larger. The results are persuasive that the (log)linear cost function is inadequate. The output coefficient that rises toward and then crosses 1.0 is consistent with a U-shaped cost curve as surmised earlier.

A second approach was to expand the cost function to include a quadratic term in log output. This approach corresponds to a much more general model and produced the result given in Table 6.4. Again, a simple *t* test strongly suggests that increased generality is called for; $t = 0.117/0.012 = 9.75$. The output elasticity in this quadratic model is $\beta_q + 2\gamma_{qq} \log Q$.[7] There are economies of scale when this value is less than 1 and constant returns to scale when it equals one. Using the two values given in the table (0.151 and 0.117, respectively), we find that this function does, indeed, produce a U-shaped average cost curve with minimum at $\log_{10} Q = (1 − 0.151)/(2 \times 0.117) = 3.628$, or $Q = 4248$, which was roughly in the middle of the range of outputs for Nerlove's sample of firms.

[5]The residuals are created as deviations of predicted total cost from actual, so they do not sum to zero.

[6]A Durbin–Watson test of correlation among the residuals (see Section 19.7) revealed to the author a substantial autocorrelation. Although normally used with time series data, the Durbin–Watson statistic and a test for "autocorrelation" can be a useful tool for determining the appropriate functional form in a cross-sectional model. To use this approach, it is necessary to sort the observations based on a variable of interest (output). Several clusters of residuals of the same sign suggested a need to reexamine the assumed functional form.

[7]Nerlove inadvertently measured economies of scale from this function as $1/(\beta_q + \delta \log Q)$, where $\beta_q$ and $\delta$ are the coefficients on log Q and $\log^2 Q$. The correct expression would have been $1/[\partial \log C/\partial \log Q] = 1/[\beta_q + 2\delta \log Q]$. This slip was periodically rediscovered in several later papers.

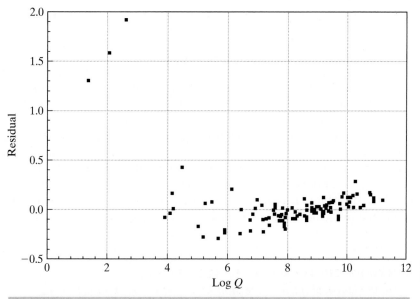

**FIGURE 6.4**    Residuals from Predicted Cost.

This study was updated by Christensen and Greene (1976). Using the same data but a more elaborate (translog) functional form and by simultaneously estimating the factor demands and the cost function, they found results broadly similar to Nerlove's. Their preferred functional form did suggest that Nerlove's generalized model in Table 6.4 did somewhat underestimate the range of outputs in which unit costs of production would continue to decline. They also redid the study using a sample of 123 firms from 1970, and found similar results. In the latter sample, however, it appeared that many firms had expanded rapidly enough to exhaust the available economies of scale. We will revisit the 1970 data set in a study of production costs in Examples 14.5 and 14.8 and efficiency in Application 16.2.

The preceding example illustrates three useful tools in identifying and dealing with unspecified nonlinearity: analysis of residuals, the use of piecewise linear regression, and the use of polynomials to approximate the unknown regression function.

### 6.3.3   INTRINSIC LINEARITY AND IDENTIFICATION

The loglinear model illustrates an intermediate case of a nonlinear regression model. The equation is **intrinsically linear** by our definition; by taking logs of $Y_i = \alpha X_i^{\beta_2} e^{\varepsilon_i}$, we obtain

$$\ln Y_i = \ln \alpha + \beta_2 \ln X_i + \varepsilon_i \tag{6-8}$$

**TABLE 6.4**    Log-Quadratic Cost Function (standard errors in parentheses)

|  | *log* **Q** | *log²* **Q** | *log*(**P$_L$/P$_F$**) | *log*(**P$_K$/P$_F$**) | **R²** |
|---|---|---|---|---|---|
| All firms | 0.151 | 0.117 | 0.498 | −0.062 | 0.95 |
|  | (0.062) | (0.012) | (0.161) | (0.151) |  |

or

$$y_i = \beta_1 + \beta_2 x_i + \varepsilon_i.$$

Although this equation is linear in most respects, something has changed in that it is no longer linear in $\alpha$. Written in terms of $\beta_1$, we obtain a fully linear model. But that may not be the form of interest. Nothing is lost, of course, since $\beta_1$ is just $\ln \alpha$. If $\beta_1$ can be estimated, then an obvious estimate of $\alpha$ is suggested.

This fact leads us to a second aspect of intrinsically linear models. Maximum likelihood estimators have an "invariance property." In the classical normal regression model, the maximum likelihood estimator of $\sigma$ is the square root of the maximum likelihood estimator of $\sigma^2$. Under some conditions, least squares estimators have the same property. By exploiting this, we can broaden the definition of linearity and include some additional cases that might otherwise be quite complex.

---

**DEFINITION 6.1  Intrinsic Linearity**
*In the classical linear regression model, if the K parameters $\beta_1, \beta_2, \ldots, \beta_K$ can be written as K one-to-one, possibly nonlinear functions of a set of K underlying parameters $\theta_1, \theta_2, \ldots, \theta_K$, then the model is intrinsically linear in $\theta$.*

---

**Example 6.4  Intrinsically Linear Regression**
In Section 16.6.4, we will estimate the parameters of the model

$$f(y \mid \beta, x) = \frac{(\beta + x)^{-\rho}}{\Gamma(\rho)} y^{\rho - 1} e^{-y/(\beta + x)}$$

by maximum likelihood. In this model, $E[y \mid x] = (\beta \rho) + \rho x$, which suggests another way that we might estimate the two parameters. This function is an intrinsically linear regression model, $E[y \mid x] = \beta_1 + \beta_2 x$, in which $\beta_1 = \beta \rho$ and $\beta_2 = \rho$. We can estimate the parameters by least squares and then retrieve the estimate of $\beta$ using $b_1 / b_2$. Because this value is a nonlinear function of the estimated parameters, we use the delta method to estimate the standard error. Using the data from that example, the least squares estimates of $\beta_1$ and $\beta_2$ (with standard errors in parentheses) are $-4.1431$ (23.734) and 2.4261 (1.5915). The estimated covariance is $-36.979$. The estimate of $\beta$ is $-4.1431/2.4261 = -1.7077$. We estimate the sampling variance of $\hat{\beta}$ with

$$\text{Est. Var}[\hat{\beta}] = \left(\frac{\partial \hat{\beta}}{\partial b_1}\right)^2 \widehat{\text{Var}}[b_1] + \left(\frac{\partial \hat{\beta}}{\partial b_2}\right)^2 \widehat{\text{Var}}[b_2] + 2\left(\frac{\partial \hat{\beta}}{\partial b_1}\right)\left(\frac{\partial \hat{\beta}}{\partial b_2}\right)\widehat{\text{Cov}}[b_1, b_2]$$

$$= 8.6889^2.$$

Table 6.5 compares the least squares and maximum likelihood estimates of the parameters. The lower standard errors for the maximum likelihood estimates result from the inefficient (equal) weighting given to the observations by the least squares procedure. The gamma distribution is highly skewed. In addition, we know from our results in Appendix C that this distribution is an exponential family. We found for the gamma distribution that the sufficient statistics for this density were $\Sigma_i y_i$ and $\Sigma_i \ln y_i$. The least squares estimator does not use the second of these, whereas an efficient estimator will.

**TABLE 6.5**   Estimates of the Regression in a Gamma Model: Least Squares versus Maximum Likelihood

| | $\beta$ | | $\rho$ | |
| --- | --- | --- | --- | --- |
| | *Estimate* | *Standard Error* | *Estimate* | *Standard Error* |
| Least squares | −1.708 | 8.689 | 2.426 | 1.592 |
| Maximum likelihood | −4.719 | 2.403 | 3.151 | 0.663 |

The emphasis in intrinsic linearity is on "one to one." If the conditions are met, then the model can be estimated in terms of the functions $\beta_1, \ldots, \beta_K$, and the underlying parameters derived after these are estimated. The one-to-one correspondence is an **identification condition.** If the condition is met, then the underlying parameters of the regression ($\theta$) are said to be **exactly identified** in terms of the parameters of the linear model $\beta$. An excellent example is provided by Kmenta (1986, p. 515, and 1967).

### Example 6.5   CES Production Function

The constant elasticity of substitution production function may be written

$$\ln y = \ln \gamma - \frac{\nu}{\rho} \ln[\delta K^{-\rho} + (1 - \delta) L^{-\rho}] + \varepsilon. \tag{6-9}$$

A Taylor series approximation to this function around the point $\rho = 0$ is

$$\ln y = \ln \gamma + \nu\delta \ln K + \nu(1 - \delta)\ln L + \rho\nu\delta(1 - \delta)\left\{-\tfrac{1}{2}[\ln K - \ln L]^2\right\} + \varepsilon'$$
$$= \beta_1 x_1 + \beta_2 x_2 + \beta_3 x_3 + \beta_4 x_4 + \varepsilon', \tag{6-10}$$

where $x_1 = 1$, $x_2 = \ln K$, $x_3 = \ln L$, $x_4 = -\tfrac{1}{2}\ln^2(K/L)$, and the transformations are

$$\beta_1 = \ln \gamma, \quad \beta_2 = \nu\delta, \quad \beta_3 = \nu(1 - \delta), \quad \beta_4 = \rho\nu\delta(1 - \delta),$$
$$\gamma = e^{\beta_1}, \quad \delta = \beta_2/(\beta_2 + \beta_3), \quad \nu = \beta_2 + \beta_3, \quad \rho = \beta_4(\beta_2 + \beta_3)/(\beta_2\beta_3). \tag{6-11}$$

Estimates of $\beta_1, \beta_2, \beta_3$, and $\beta_4$ can be computed by least squares. The estimates of $\gamma, \delta, \nu$, and $\rho$ obtained by the second row of (6-11) are the same as those we would obtain had we found the nonlinear least squares estimates of (6-10) directly. As Kmenta shows, however, they are not the same as the nonlinear least squares estimates of (6-9) due to the use of the Taylor series approximation to get to (6-10). We would use the delta method to construct the estimated asymptotic covariance matrix for the estimates of $\theta' = [\gamma, \delta, \nu, \rho]$. The derivatives matrix is

$$\mathbf{C} = \frac{\partial \theta}{\partial \beta'} = \begin{bmatrix} e^{\beta_1} & 0 & 0 & 0 \\ 0 & \beta_3/(\beta_2 + \beta_3)^2 & -\beta_2/(\beta_2 + \beta_3)^2 & 0 \\ 0 & 1 & 1 & 0 \\ 0 & -\beta_3\beta_4/(\beta_2^2\beta_3) & -\beta_2\beta_4/(\beta_2\beta_3^2) & (\beta_2 + \beta_3)/(\beta_2\beta_3) \end{bmatrix}.$$

The estimated covariance matrix for $\hat{\theta}$ is $\hat{\mathbf{C}}\, [s^2(\mathbf{X}'\mathbf{X})^{-1}]\hat{\mathbf{C}}'$.

Not all models of the form

$$y_i = \beta_1(\theta)x_{i1} + \beta_2(\theta)x_{i2} + \cdots + \beta_K(\theta)x_{ik} + \varepsilon_i \tag{6-12}$$

are intrinsically linear. Recall that the condition that the functions be one to one (i.e., that the parameters be exactly identified) was required. For example,

$$y_i = \alpha + \beta x_{i1} + \gamma x_{i2} + \beta\gamma x_{i3} + \varepsilon_i$$

is nonlinear. The reason is that if we write it in the form of (6-12), we fail to account for the condition that $\beta_4$ equals $\beta_2\beta_3$, which is a **nonlinear restriction.** In this model, the three parameters $\alpha$, $\beta$, and $\gamma$ are **overidentified** in terms of the four parameters $\beta_1, \beta_2, \beta_3,$ and $\beta_4$. Unrestricted least squares estimates of $\beta_2, \beta_3,$ and $\beta_4$ can be used to obtain two estimates of each of the underlying parameters, and there is no assurance that these will be the same.

## 6.4 MODELING AND TESTING FOR A STRUCTURAL BREAK

One of the more common applications of the $F$ test is in tests of **structural change.**[8] In specifying a regression model, we assume that its assumptions apply to all the observations in our sample. It is straightforward, however, to test the hypothesis that some or all of the regression coefficients are different in different subsets of the data. To analyze a number of examples, we will revisit the data on the U.S. gasoline market that we examined in Examples 2.3, 4.4, 4.7, and 4.8. As Figure 6.5 following suggests, this market behaved in predictable, unremarkable fashion prior to the oil shock of 1973 and was quite volatile thereafter. The large jumps in price in 1973 and 1980 are clearly visible, as is the much greater variability in consumption.[9] It seems unlikely that the same regression model would apply to both periods.

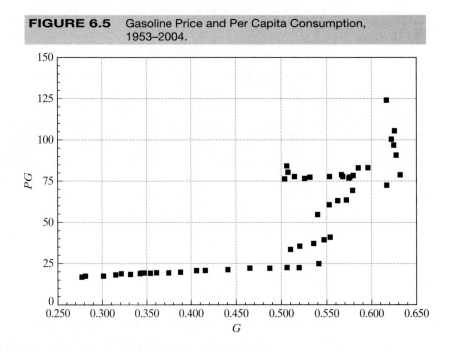

**FIGURE 6.5** Gasoline Price and Per Capita Consumption, 1953–2004.

---

[8]This test is often labeled a **Chow test,** in reference to Chow (1960).

[9]The observed data will doubtless reveal similar disruption in 2006.

### 6.4.1 DIFFERENT PARAMETER VECTORS

The gasoline consumption data span two very different periods. Up to 1973, fuel was plentiful and world prices for gasoline had been stable or falling for at least two decades. The embargo of 1973 marked a transition in this market, marked by shortages, rising prices, and intermittent turmoil. It is possible that the entire relationship described by our regression model changed in 1974. To test this as a hypothesis, we could proceed as follows: Denote the first 21 years of the data in $\mathbf{y}$ and $\mathbf{X}$ as $\mathbf{y}_1$ and $\mathbf{X}_1$ and the remaining years as $\mathbf{y}_2$ and $\mathbf{X}_2$. An unrestricted regression that allows the coefficients to be different in the two periods is

$$\begin{bmatrix} \mathbf{y}_1 \\ \mathbf{y}_2 \end{bmatrix} = \begin{bmatrix} \mathbf{X}_1 & \mathbf{0} \\ \mathbf{0} & \mathbf{X}_2 \end{bmatrix} \begin{bmatrix} \boldsymbol{\beta}_1 \\ \boldsymbol{\beta}_2 \end{bmatrix} + \begin{bmatrix} \boldsymbol{\varepsilon}_1 \\ \boldsymbol{\varepsilon}_2 \end{bmatrix}. \tag{6-13}$$

Denoting the data matrices as $\mathbf{y}$ and $\mathbf{X}$, we find that the unrestricted least squares estimator is

$$\mathbf{b} = (\mathbf{X}'\mathbf{X})^{-1}\mathbf{X}'\mathbf{y} = \begin{bmatrix} \mathbf{X}_1'\mathbf{X}_1 & \mathbf{0} \\ \mathbf{0} & \mathbf{X}_2'\mathbf{X}_2 \end{bmatrix}^{-1} \begin{bmatrix} \mathbf{X}_1'\mathbf{y}_1 \\ \mathbf{X}_2'\mathbf{y}_2 \end{bmatrix} = \begin{bmatrix} \mathbf{b}_1 \\ \mathbf{b}_2 \end{bmatrix}, \tag{6-14}$$

which is least squares applied to the two equations separately. Therefore, the total sum of squared residuals from this regression will be the sum of the two residual sums of squares from the two separate regressions:

$$\mathbf{e}'\mathbf{e} = \mathbf{e}_1'\mathbf{e}_1 + \mathbf{e}_2'\mathbf{e}_2.$$

The restricted coefficient vector can be obtained in two ways. Formally, the restriction $\boldsymbol{\beta}_1 = \boldsymbol{\beta}_2$ is $\mathbf{R}\boldsymbol{\beta} = \mathbf{q}$, where $\mathbf{R} = [\mathbf{I} : -\mathbf{I}]$ and $\mathbf{q} = \mathbf{0}$. The general result given earlier can be applied directly. An easier way to proceed is to build the restriction directly into the model. If the two coefficient vectors are the same, then (6-13) may be written

$$\begin{bmatrix} \mathbf{y}_1 \\ \mathbf{y}_2 \end{bmatrix} = \begin{bmatrix} \mathbf{X}_1 \\ \mathbf{X}_2 \end{bmatrix} \boldsymbol{\beta} + \begin{bmatrix} \boldsymbol{\varepsilon}_1 \\ \boldsymbol{\varepsilon}_2 \end{bmatrix},$$

and the restricted estimator can be obtained simply by stacking the data and estimating a single regression. The residual sum of squares from this restricted regression, $\mathbf{e}_*'\mathbf{e}_*$, then forms the basis for the test. The test statistic is then given in (5-6), where $J$, the number of restrictions, is the number of columns in $\mathbf{X}_2$ and the denominator degrees of freedom is $n_1 + n_2 - 2k$.

### 6.4.2 INSUFFICIENT OBSERVATIONS

In some circumstances, the data series are not long enough to estimate one or the other of the separate regressions for a test of structural change. For example, one might surmise that consumers took a year or two to adjust to the turmoil of the two oil price shocks in 1973 and 1979, but that the market never actually fundamentally changed or that it only changed temporarily. We might consider the same test as before, but now only single out the four years 1974, 1975, 1980, and 1981 for special treatment. Because there are six coefficients to estimate but only four observations, it is not possible to fit the two separate models. Fisher (1970) has shown that in such a circumstance, a valid way to proceed is as follows:

1. Estimate the regression, using the full data set, and compute the restricted sum of squared residuals, $\mathbf{e}'_* \mathbf{e}_*$.
2. Use the longer (adequate) subperiod ($n_1$ observations) to estimate the regression, and compute the unrestricted sum of squares, $\mathbf{e}'_1 \mathbf{e}_1$. This latter computation is done assuming that with only $n_2 < K$ observations, we could obtain a perfect fit and thus contribute zero to the sum of squares.
3. The $F$ statistic is then computed, using

$$F[n_2, n_1 - K] = \frac{(\mathbf{e}'_* \mathbf{e}_* - \mathbf{e}'_1 \mathbf{e}_1)/n_2}{\mathbf{e}'_1 \mathbf{e}_1/(n_1 - K)}. \tag{6-15}$$

Note that the numerator degrees of freedom is $n_2$, not $K$.[10] This test has been labeled the Chow **predictive test** because it is equivalent to extending the restricted model to the shorter subperiod and basing the test on the prediction errors of the model in this latter period.

### 6.4.3 CHANGE IN A SUBSET OF COEFFICIENTS

The general formulation previously suggested lends itself to many variations that allow a wide range of possible tests. Some important particular cases are suggested by our gasoline market data. One possible description of the market is that after the oil shock of 1973, Americans simply reduced their consumption of gasoline by a fixed proportion, but other relationships in the market, such as the income elasticity, remained unchanged. This case would translate to a simple shift downward of the loglinear regression model or a reduction only in the constant term. Thus, the unrestricted equation has separate coefficients in the two periods, while the restricted equation is a pooled regression with separate constant terms. The regressor matrices for these two cases would be of the form

$$(\text{unrestricted}) \ \mathbf{X}_U = \begin{bmatrix} \mathbf{i} & \mathbf{0} & \mathbf{W}_{\text{pre73}} & \mathbf{0} \\ \mathbf{0} & \mathbf{i} & \mathbf{0} & \mathbf{W}_{\text{post73}} \end{bmatrix}$$

and

$$(\text{restricted}) \ \mathbf{X}_R = \begin{bmatrix} \mathbf{i} & \mathbf{0} & \mathbf{W}_{\text{pre73}} \\ \mathbf{0} & \mathbf{i} & \mathbf{W}_{\text{post73}} \end{bmatrix}.$$

The first two columns of $\mathbf{X}_U$ are dummy variables that indicate the subperiod in which the observation falls.

Another possibility is that the constant and one or more of the slope coefficients changed, but the remaining parameters remained the same. The results in Table 6.6 suggest that the constant term and the price and income elasticities changed much more than the cross-price elasticities and the time trend. The Chow test for this type of restriction looks very much like the one for the change in the constant term alone. Let $\mathbf{Z}$ denote the variables whose coefficients are believed to have changed, and let $\mathbf{W}$

---

[10]One way to view this is that only $n_2 < K$ coefficients are needed to obtain this perfect fit.

denote the variables whose coefficients are thought to have remained constant. Then, the regressor matrix in the constrained regression would appear as

$$\mathbf{X} = \begin{bmatrix} \mathbf{i}_{\text{pre}} & \mathbf{Z}_{\text{pre}} & \mathbf{0} & \mathbf{0} & \mathbf{W}_{\text{pre}} \\ \mathbf{0} & \mathbf{0} & \mathbf{i}_{\text{post}} & \mathbf{Z}_{\text{post}} & \mathbf{W}_{\text{post}} \end{bmatrix}. \tag{6-16}$$

As before, the unrestricted coefficient vector is the combination of the two separate regressions.

### 6.4.4 TESTS OF STRUCTURAL BREAK WITH UNEQUAL VARIANCES

An important assumption made in using the Chow test is that the disturbance variance is the same in both (or all) regressions. In the restricted model, if this is not true, the first $n_1$ elements of $\boldsymbol{\varepsilon}$ have variance $\sigma_1^2$, whereas the next $n_2$ have variance $\sigma_2^2$, and so on. The restricted model is, therefore, heteroscedastic, and our results for the classical regression model no longer apply. As analyzed by Schmidt and Sickles (1977), Ohtani and Toyoda (1985), and Toyoda and Ohtani (1986), it is quite likely that the actual probability of a type I error will be larger than the significance level we have chosen. (That is, we shall regard as large an $F$ statistic that is actually less than the *appropriate* but unknown critical value.) Precisely how severe this effect is going to be will depend on the data and the extent to which the variances differ, in ways that are not likely to be obvious.

If the sample size is reasonably large, then we have a test that is valid whether or not the disturbance variances are the same. Suppose that $\hat{\boldsymbol{\theta}}_1$ and $\hat{\boldsymbol{\theta}}_2$ are two consistent and asymptotically normally distributed estimators of a parameter based on independent samples,[11] with asymptotic covariance matrices $\mathbf{V}_1$ and $\mathbf{V}_2$. Then, under the null hypothesis that the true parameters are the same,

$\hat{\boldsymbol{\theta}}_1 - \hat{\boldsymbol{\theta}}_2$ has mean $\mathbf{0}$ and asymptotic covariance matrix $\mathbf{V}_1 + \mathbf{V}_2$.

Under the null hypothesis, the Wald statistic,

$$W = (\hat{\boldsymbol{\theta}}_1 - \hat{\boldsymbol{\theta}}_2)'(\hat{\mathbf{V}}_1 + \hat{\mathbf{V}}_2)^{-1}(\hat{\boldsymbol{\theta}}_1 - \hat{\boldsymbol{\theta}}_2), \tag{6-17}$$

has a limiting chi-squared distribution with $K$ degrees of freedom. A test that the difference between the parameters is zero can be based on this statistic.[12] It is straightforward to apply this to our test of common parameter vectors in our regressions. Large values of the statistic lead us to reject the hypothesis.

In a small or moderately sized sample, the Wald test has the unfortunate property that the probability of a type I error is persistently larger than the critical level we use to carry it out. (That is, we shall too frequently reject the null hypothesis that the parameters are the same in the subsamples.) We should be using a larger critical value.

---

[11]Without the required independence, this test and several similar ones will fail completely. The problem becomes a variant of the famous Behrens–Fisher problem.

[12]See Andrews and Fair (1988). The true size of this suggested test is uncertain. It depends on the nature of the alternative. If the variances are radically different, the assumed critical values might be somewhat unreliable.

Ohtani and Kobayashi (1986) have devised a "bounds" test that gives a partial remedy for the problem.[13]

It has been observed that the size of the **Wald test** may differ from what we have assumed, and that the deviation would be a function of the alternative hypothesis. There are two general settings in which a test of this sort might be of interest. For comparing two possibly different populations—such as the labor supply equations for men versus women—not much more can be said about the suggested statistic in the absence of specific information about the alternative hypothesis. But a great deal of work on this type of statistic has been done in the time-series context. In this instance, the nature of the alternative is rather more clearly defined.

### Example 6.6    The World Health Report

The 2000 version of the World Health Organization's (WHO) *World Health Report* contained a major country-by-country inventory of the world's health care systems. [World Health Organization (2000). See also http://www.who.int/whr/en/.] The book documented years of research and thousands of pages of material. Among the most controversial and most publicly debated (and excoriated) parts of the report was a single chapter that described a comparison of the delivery of health care by 191 countries—nearly all of the world's population. [Evans et al. (2000a,b). See, e.g., Hilts (2000) for reporting in the popular press.] The study examined the efficiency of health care delivery on two measures: the standard one that is widely studied, (disability adjusted) life expectancy (DALE), and an innovative new measure created by the authors that was a composite of five outcomes (COMP) and that accounted for efficiency and fairness in delivery. The regression-style modeling, which was done in the setting of a frontier model (see Section 14.6.3), related health care attainment to two major inputs, education and (per capita) health care expenditure. The residuals were analyzed to obtain the country comparisons.

The data in Appendix Table F6.2 were used by the researchers at WHO for the study. (They used a panel of data for the years 1993 to 1997. We have extracted the 1997 data for this example.) The WHO data have been used by many researchers in subsequent analyses. [See, e.g., Hollingsworth and Wildman (2002), Gravelle et al. (2002), and Greene (2004).] The regression model used by the WHO contained DALE or COMP on the left-hand side and health care expenditure, education, and education squared on the right. Greene (2004) added a number of additional variables such as per capita GDP, a measure of the distribution of income, and World Bank measures of government effectiveness and democratization of the political structure.

Among the controversial aspects of the study was the fact that the model aggregated countries of vastly different characteristics. A second striking aspect of the results, suggested in Hilts (2000) and documented in Greene (2004), was that, in fact, the "efficient" countries in the study were the 30 relatively wealthy OECD members, while the rest of the world on average fared much more poorly. We will pursue that aspect here with respect to DALE. Analysis of COMP is left as an exercise. Table 6.6 presents estimates of the regression models for DALE for the pooled sample, the OECD countries, and the non-OECD countries, respectively. Superficially, there do not appear to be very large differences across the two subgroups. We first tested the joint significance of the additional variables, income distribution (GINI), per capita GDP, etc. For each group, the $F$ statistic is $[(\mathbf{e}'_*\mathbf{e}_* - \mathbf{e}'\mathbf{e})/7]/[\mathbf{e}'\mathbf{e}/(n - 11)]$. These $F$ statistics are shown in the last row of the table. The critical values for $F[7,184]$ (all), $F[7,23]$ (OECD), and $F[7,154]$ (non-OECD) are 2.060, 2.442, and 2.070, respectively. We conclude that the additional explanatory variables are significant contributors to the fit for the non-OECD countries (and for all countries), but not for the OECD countries. Finally, to conduct

---

[13]See also Kobayashi (1986). An alternative, somewhat more cumbersome test is proposed by Jayatissa (1977). Further discussion is given in Thursby (1982).

**TABLE 6.6**    Regression Results for Life Expectancy

| | All Countries | | OECD | | Non-OECD | |
|---|---|---|---|---|---|---|
| Constant | 25.237 | 38.734 | 42.728 | 49.328 | 26.812 | 41.408 |
| Health exp | 0.00629 | −0.00180 | 0.00268 | 0.00114 | 0.00955 | −0.00178 |
| Education | 7.931 | 7.178 | 6.177 | 5.156 | 7.0433 | 6.499 |
| Education$^2$ | −0.439 | −0.426 | −0.385 | −0.329 | −0.374 | −0.372 |
| Gini coeff | | −17.333 | | −5.762 | | −21.329 |
| Tropic | | −3.200 | | −3.298 | | −3.144 |
| Pop. Dens. | | −0.255e−4 | | 0.000167 | | −0.425e−4 |
| Public exp | | −0.0137 | | −0.00993 | | −0.00939 |
| PC GDP | | 0.000483 | | 0.000108 | | 0.000600 |
| Govt. Eff. | | 1.629 | | −0.546 | | 1.909 |
| Democracy | | 0.748 | | 1.224 | | 0.786 |
| $R^2$ | 0.6824 | 0.7299 | 0.6483 | 0.7340 | 0.6133 | 0.6651 |
| Std. Err. | 6.984 | 6.565 | 1.883 | 1.916 | 7.366 | 7.014 |
| Sum of sq. | 9121.795 | 7757.002 | 92.21064 | 69.74428 | 8518.750 | 7378.598 |
| N | | 191 | | 30 | | 161 |
| GDP/Pop | | 6609.37 | | 18199.07 | | 4449.79 |
| F test | | 4.524 | | 0.874 | | 3.311 |

the structural change test of OECD vs. non-OECD, we computed

$$F = \frac{[7757.007 - (69.74428 + 7378.598)]/11}{(69.74428 + 7378.598)/(191 - 11 - 11)} = 0.637.$$

The 95 percent critical value for $F[11,169]$ is 1.846. So, we do not reject the hypothesis that the regression model is the same for the two groups of countries. The Wald statistic in (6-17) tells a different story. The statistic is 35.221. The 95 percent critical value from the chi-squared table with 11 degrees of freedom is 19.675. On this basis, we would reject the hypothesis that the two coefficient vectors are the same.

### Example 6.7    Structural Break in the Gasoline Market
The previous Figure 6.5 shows a plot of prices and quantities in the U.S. gasoline market from 1953 to 2004. The first 21 points are the layer at the bottom of the figure and suggest an orderly market. The remainder clearly reflect the subsequent turmoil in this market.

We will use the Chow tests described to examine this market. The model we will examine is the one suggested in Example 2.3, with the addition of a time trend:

$$\ln(G/Pop)_t = \beta_1 + \beta_2 \ln(Income/Pop)_t + \beta_3 \ln PG_t + \beta_4 \ln PNC_t + \beta_5 \ln PUC_t + \beta_6 t + \varepsilon_t.$$

The three prices in the equation are for $G$, new cars, and used cars. *Income/Pop* is per capita income, and *G/Pop* is per capita gasoline consumption. Regression results for four functional forms are shown in Table 6.7. Using the data for the entire sample, 1953 to 2004, and for the two subperiods, 1953 to 1973 and 1974 to 2004, we obtain the three estimated regressions in the first and last two columns. The $F$ statistic for testing the restriction that the coefficients in the two equations are the same is

$$F[6, 40] = \frac{(0.101997 - (0.00202244 + 0.007127899))/6}{(0.00202244 + 0.007127899)/(21 + 31 - 12)} = 67.645.$$

The tabled critical value is 2.467, so, consistent with our expectations, we would reject the hypothesis that the coefficient vectors are the same in the two periods. Using the full set of 52 observations to fit the model, the sum of squares is $\mathbf{e}_*'\mathbf{e}_* = 0.101997$. When the $n_2 = 4$ observations for 1974, 1975, 1980, and 1981 are removed from the sample, the sum of squares falls to $\mathbf{e'e} = 0.0973936$. The $F$ statistic is 0.496. Because the tabled critical value for $F[4, 48 - 6]$ is 2.594, we would not reject the hypothesis of stability. The conclusion to this point would be that although something has surely changed in the market, the hypothesis of a temporary disequilibrium seems not to be an adequate explanation.

An alternative way to compute this statistic might be more convenient. Consider the original arrangement, with all 52 observations. We now add to this regression four binary variables, Y1974, Y1975, Y1980, and Y1981. Each of these takes the value one in the single year indicated and zero in all 51 remaining years. We then compute the regression with the original six variables and these four additional dummy variables. The sum of squared residuals in this regression is 0.0973936 (precisely the same as when the four observations are deleted from the sample—see Exercise 7 in Chapter 3), so the $F$ statistic for testing the joint hypothesis that the four coefficients are zero is

$$F[4, 42] = \frac{(0.101997 - 0.0973936)/4}{0.0973936/(52 - 6 - 4)} = 0.496$$

once again. (See Section 6.4.2 for discussion of this test.)

The $F$ statistic for testing the restriction that the coefficients in the two equations are the same apart from the constant term is based on the last three sets of results in the table;

$$F[5, 40] = \frac{(0.092082 - (0.00202244 + 0.007127899))/5}{(0.00202244 + 0.007127899)/(21 + 31 - 12)} = 72.506.$$

The tabled critical value is 2.449, so this hypothesis is rejected as well. The data suggest that the models for the two periods are systematically different, beyond a simple shift in the constant term.

The $F$ ratio that results from estimating the model subject to the restriction that the two automobile price elasticities and the coefficient on the time trend are unchanged is

$$F[3, 40] = \frac{(0.01441975 - (0.00202244 + 0.007127899))/3}{(0.00202244 + 0.007127899)/(52 - 6 - 6)} = 7.678.$$

(The restricted regression is not shown.) The critical value from the $F$ table is 2.839, so this hypothesis is rejected as well. Note, however, that this value is far smaller than those we obtained previously. This fact suggests that the bulk of the difference in the models across the two periods is, indeed, explained by the changes in the constant and the price and income elasticities.

The test statistic in (6-17) for the regression results in Table 6.7 gives a value of 158.753. The 5 percent critical value from the chi-squared table for 6 degrees of freedom is 12.59. So, on the basis of the Wald test, we would once again reject the hypothesis that the same coefficient vector applies in the two subperiods 1953 to 1973 and 1974 to 2004. We should note that the Wald statistic is valid only in large samples, and our samples of 21 and 31

**TABLE 6.7** Gasoline Consumption Functions

| Coefficients | 1953–2004 | Pooled | Preshock | Postshock |
|---|---|---|---|---|
| Constant | −26.6787 | −24.9009 | −22.1647 | |
| Constant | | −24.8167 | | −15.3283 |
| ln *Income/Pop* | 1.6250 | 1.4562 | 9.8482 | 0.3739 |
| ln *PG* | −0.05392 | −0.1132 | −0.03227 | −0.1240 |
| ln *PNC* | −0.08343 | −0.1044 | 0.6988 | −0.001146 |
| ln *PUC* | −0.08467 | −0.08646 | −0.2905 | −0.02167 |
| Year | −0.01393 | −0.009232 | 0.01006 | 0.004492 |
| $R^2$ | 0.9649 | 0.9683 | 0.9975 | 0.9529 |
| Standard error | 0.04709 | 0.04524 | 0.01161 | 0.01689 |
| Sum of squares | 0.101997 | 0.092082 | 0.00202244 | 0.007127899 |

observations hardly meet that standard. We have tested the hypothesis that the regression model for the gasoline market changed in 1973, and on the basis of the $F$ test (Chow test) we strongly rejected the hypothesis of model stability.

## 6.4.5   PREDICTIVE TEST

The hypothesis test defined in (6-15) in Section 6.4.2 is equivalent to $H_0 : \boldsymbol{\beta}_2 = \boldsymbol{\beta}_1$ in the "model"

$$y_t = \mathbf{x}_t' \boldsymbol{\beta}_1 + \varepsilon_t, \quad t = 1, \dots, T_1$$
$$y_t = \mathbf{x}_t' \boldsymbol{\beta}_2 + \varepsilon_t, \quad t = T_1 + 1, \dots, T_1 + T_2.$$

(Note that the disturbance variance is assumed to be the same in both subperiods.) An alternative formulation of the model (the one used in the example) is

$$\begin{bmatrix} \mathbf{y}_1 \\ \mathbf{y}_2 \end{bmatrix} = \begin{bmatrix} \mathbf{X}_1 & \mathbf{0} \\ \mathbf{X}_2 & \mathbf{I} \end{bmatrix} \begin{pmatrix} \boldsymbol{\beta} \\ \boldsymbol{\gamma} \end{pmatrix} + \begin{bmatrix} \boldsymbol{\varepsilon}_1 \\ \boldsymbol{\varepsilon}_2 \end{bmatrix}.$$

This formulation states that

$$y_t = \mathbf{x}_t' \boldsymbol{\beta}_1 + \varepsilon_t, \quad t = 1, \dots, T_1$$
$$y_t = \mathbf{x}_t' \boldsymbol{\beta}_2 + \gamma_t + \varepsilon_t, \quad t = T_1 + 1, \dots, T_1 + T_2.$$

Because each $\gamma_t$ is unrestricted, this alternative formulation states that the regression model of the first $T_1$ periods ceases to operate in the second subperiod (and, in fact, no systematic model operates in the second subperiod). A test of the hypothesis $\boldsymbol{\gamma} = \mathbf{0}$ in this framework would thus be a test of model stability. The least squares coefficients for this regression can be found by using the formula for the partitioned inverse matrix

$$\begin{pmatrix} \mathbf{b} \\ \mathbf{c} \end{pmatrix} = \begin{bmatrix} \mathbf{X}_1'\mathbf{X}_1 + \mathbf{X}_2'\mathbf{X}_2 & \mathbf{X}_2' \\ \mathbf{X}_2 & \mathbf{I} \end{bmatrix}^{-1} \begin{bmatrix} \mathbf{X}_1'\mathbf{y}_1 + \mathbf{X}_2'\mathbf{y}_2 \\ \mathbf{y}_2 \end{bmatrix}$$

$$= \begin{bmatrix} (\mathbf{X}_1'\mathbf{X}_1)^{-1} & -(\mathbf{X}_1'\mathbf{X}_1)^{-1}\mathbf{X}_2' \\ -\mathbf{X}_2(\mathbf{X}_1'\mathbf{X}_1)^{-1} & \mathbf{I} + \mathbf{X}_2(\mathbf{X}_1'\mathbf{X}_1)^{-1}\mathbf{X}_2' \end{bmatrix} \begin{bmatrix} \mathbf{X}_1'\mathbf{y}_1 + \mathbf{X}_2'\mathbf{y}_2 \\ \mathbf{y}_2 \end{bmatrix}$$

$$= \begin{pmatrix} \mathbf{b}_1 \\ \mathbf{c}_2 \end{pmatrix}$$

where $\mathbf{b}_1$ is the least squares slopes based on the first $T_1$ observations and $\mathbf{c}_2$ is $\mathbf{y}_2 - \mathbf{X}_2\mathbf{b}_1$. The covariance matrix for the full set of estimates is $s^2$ times the bracketed matrix. The two subvectors of residuals in this regression are $\mathbf{e}_1 = \mathbf{y}_1 - \mathbf{X}_1\mathbf{b}_1$ and $\mathbf{e}_2 = \mathbf{y}_2 - (\mathbf{X}_2\mathbf{b}_1 + \mathbf{I}\mathbf{c}_2) = \mathbf{0}$, so the sum of squared residuals in this least squares regression is just $\mathbf{e}_1'\mathbf{e}_1$. This is the same sum of squares as appears in (6-15). The degrees of freedom for the denominator is $[T_1 + T_2 - (K + T_2)] = T_1 - K$ as well, and the degrees of freedom for the numerator is the number of elements in $\boldsymbol{\gamma}$ which is $T_2$. The restricted regression with $\boldsymbol{\gamma} = \mathbf{0}$ is the pooled model, which is likewise the same as appears in (6-15). This implies that the $F$ statistic for testing the null hypothesis in this model is precisely that which appeared earlier in (6-15), which suggests why the test is labeled the "predictive test."

## 6.5 SUMMARY AND CONCLUSIONS

This chapter has discussed the functional form of the regression model. We examined the use of dummy variables and other transformations to build nonlinearity into the model. We then considered other nonlinear models in which the parameters of the nonlinear model could be recovered from estimates obtained for a linear regression. The final sections of the chapter described hypothesis tests designed to reveal whether the assumed model had changed during the sample period, or was different for different groups of observations.

### Key Terms and Concepts

- Binary variable
- Chow test
- Dummy variable
- Dummy variable trap
- Exactly identified
- Identification condition
- Interaction term
- Intrinsically linear

- Knots
- Loglinear model
- Marginal effect
- Nonlinear restriction
- Overidentified
- Piecewise continuous
- Predictive test
- Qualification indices

- Response
- Semilog model
- Spline
- Structural change
- Threshold effect
- Time profile
- Treatment
- Wald test

### Exercises

1. A regression model with $K = 16$ independent variables is fit using a panel of seven years of data. The sums of squares for the seven separate regressions and the pooled regression are shown below. The model with the pooled data allows a separate constant for each year. Test the hypothesis that the same coefficients apply in every year.

|  | *1954* | *1955* | *1956* | *1957* | *1958* | *1959* | *1960* | *All* |
|---|---|---|---|---|---|---|---|---|
| Observations | 65 | 55 | 87 | 95 | 103 | 87 | 78 | 570 |
| $e'e$ | 104 | 88 | 206 | 144 | 199 | 308 | 211 | 1425 |

2. *Reverse regression.* A common method of analyzing statistical data to detect discrimination in the workplace is to fit the regression

$$y = \alpha + \mathbf{x}'\boldsymbol{\beta} + \gamma d + \varepsilon, \tag{1}$$

where $y$ is the wage rate and $d$ is a dummy variable indicating either membership ($d = 1$) or nonmembership ($d = 0$) in the class toward which it is suggested the discrimination is directed. The regressors $\mathbf{x}$ include factors specific to the particular type of job as well as indicators of the qualifications of the individual. The hypothesis of interest is $H_0 : \gamma \geq 0$ versus $H_1 : \gamma < 0$. The regression seeks to answer the question, "In a given job, are individuals in the class ($d = 1$) paid less than equally qualified individuals not in the class ($d = 0$)?" Consider an alternative approach. Do individuals in the class in the same job as others, and receiving the same wage, uniformly have higher qualifications? If so, this might also be viewed as a form of discrimination. To analyze this question, Conway and Roberts (1983) suggested the following procedure:

1. Fit (1) by ordinary least squares. Denote the estimates $a$, $\mathbf{b}$, and $c$.
2. Compute the set of **qualification indices,**

$$\mathbf{q} = a\mathbf{i} + \mathbf{Xb}. \tag{2}$$

Note the omission of $c\mathbf{d}$ from the fitted value.

3. Regress $\mathbf{q}$ on a constant, $\mathbf{y}$ and $\mathbf{d}$. The equation is

$$\mathbf{q} = \alpha_* + \beta_*\mathbf{y} + \gamma_*\mathbf{d} + \varepsilon_*. \tag{3}$$

The analysis suggests that if $\gamma < 0$, $\gamma_* > 0$.

a. Prove that the theory notwithstanding, the least squares estimates $c$ and $c_*$ are related by

$$c_* = \frac{(\bar{y}_1 - \bar{y})(1 - R^2)}{(1 - P)(1 - r_{yd}^2)} - c, \tag{4}$$

where

$\bar{y}_1$ = mean of $y$ for observations with $d = 1$,
$\bar{y}$ = mean of $y$ for all observations,
$P$ = mean of $d$,
$R^2$ = coefficient of determination for (1),
$r_{yd}^2$ = squared correlation between $y$ and $d$.

[Hint: The model contains a constant term. Thus, to simplify the algebra, assume that all variables are measured as deviations from the overall sample means and use a partitioned regression to compute the coefficients in (3). Second, in (2), use the result that based on the least squares results $\mathbf{y} = a\mathbf{i} + \mathbf{Xb} + c\mathbf{d} + \mathbf{e}$, so $\mathbf{q} = \mathbf{y} - c\mathbf{d} - \mathbf{e}$. From here on, we drop the constant term. Thus, in the regression in (3) you are regressing $[\mathbf{y} - c\mathbf{d} - \mathbf{e}]$ on $\mathbf{y}$ and $\mathbf{d}$.

b. Will the sample evidence necessarily be consistent with the theory? [Hint: Suppose that $c = 0$.]

A symposium on the Conway and Roberts paper appeared in the *Journal of Business and Economic Statistics* in April, 1983.

3. *Reverse regression continued.* This and the next exercise continue the analysis of Exercise 2. In Exercise 2, interest centered on a particular dummy variable in which the regressors were accurately measured. Here we consider the case in which the crucial regressor in the model is measured with error. The paper by Kamlich and Polachek (1982) is directed toward this issue.

Consider the simple errors in the variables model,

$$y = \alpha + \beta x^* + \varepsilon, \quad x = x^* + u,$$

where $u$ and $\varepsilon$ are uncorrelated and $x$ is the erroneously measured, observed counterpart to $x^*$.

a. Assume that $x^*$, $u$, and $\varepsilon$ are all normally distributed with means $\mu^*$, 0, and 0, variances $\sigma_*^2$, $\sigma_u^2$, and $\sigma_\varepsilon^2$, and zero covariances. Obtain the probability limits of the least squares estimators of $\alpha$ and $\beta$.

b. As an alternative, consider regressing $x$ on a constant and $y$, and then computing the reciprocal of the estimate. Obtain the probability limit of this estimator.

c. Do the "direct" and "reverse" estimators bound the true coefficient?

4. *Reverse regression continued.* Suppose that the model in Exercise 3 is extended to $y = \beta x^* + \gamma d + \varepsilon, x = x^* + u$. For convenience, we drop the constant term. Assume that $x^*, \varepsilon$, and $u$ are independent normally distributed with zero means. Suppose that $d$ is a random variable that takes the values one and zero with probabilities $\pi$ and $1 - \pi$ in the population and is independent of all other variables in the model. To put this formulation in context, the preceding model (and variants of it) have appeared in the literature on discrimination. We view $y$ as a "wage" variable, $x^*$ as "qualifications," and $x$ as some imperfect measure such as education. The dummy variable $d$ is membership ($d = 1$) or nonmembership ($d = 0$) in some protected class. The hypothesis of discrimination turns on $\gamma < 0$ versus $\gamma \geq 0$.

a. What is the probability limit of $c$, the least squares estimator of $\gamma$, in the least squares regression of $y$ on $x$ and $d$? [Hints: The independence of $x^*$ and $d$ is important. Also, plim $\mathbf{d}'\mathbf{d}/n = \text{Var}[d] + E^2[d] = \pi(1 - \pi) + \pi^2 = \pi$. This minor modification does not affect the model substantively, but it greatly simplifies the algebra.] Now suppose that $x^*$ and $d$ are not independent. In particular, suppose that $E[x^* \mid d = 1] = \mu^1$ and $E[x^* \mid d = 0] = \mu^0$. Repeat the derivation with this assumption.

b. Consider, instead, a regression of $x$ on $y$ and $d$. What is the probability limit of the coefficient on $d$ in this regression? Assume that $x^*$ and $d$ are independent.

c. Suppose that $x^*$ and $d$ are not independent, but $\gamma$ is, in fact, less than zero. Assuming that both preceding equations still hold, what is estimated by $(\bar{y} \mid d = 1) - (\bar{y} \mid d = 0)$? What does this quantity estimate if $\gamma$ does equal zero?

## Applications

1. In Application 1 in Chapter 3 and Application 1 in Chapter 5, we examined Koop and Tobias's data on wages, education, ability, and so on. We continue the analysis here. (The source, location and configuration of the data are given in the earlier application.) We consider the model

$$\ln Wage = \beta_1 + \beta_2 \ Educ + \beta_3 \ Ability + \beta_4 \ Experience$$
$$+ \beta_5 \ Mother's \ education + \beta_6 \ Father's \ education + \beta_7 \ Broken \ home$$
$$+ \beta_8 \ Siblings + \varepsilon.$$

a. Compute the full regression by least squares and report your results. Based on your results, what is the estimate of the marginal value, in \$/hour, of an additional year of education, for someone who has 12 years of education when all other variables are at their means and *Broken home* = 0?

b. We are interested in possible nonlinearities in the effect of education on ln *Wage*. (Koop and Tobias focused on experience. As before, we are not attempting to replicate their results.) A histogram of the education variable shows values from 9 to 20, a huge spike at 12 years (high school graduation) and, perhaps surprisingly, a second at 15—intuition would have anticipated it at 16. Consider aggregating the education variable into a set of dummy variables:

$$HS = 1 \text{ if } Educ \leq 12, 0 \text{ otherwise}$$

$$Col = 1 \text{ if } Educ > 12 \text{ and } Educ \leq 16, 0 \text{ otherwise}$$

$$Grad = 1 \text{ if } Educ > 16, 0 \text{ otherwise.}$$

Replace *Educ* in the model with (*Col, Grad*), making high school (*HS*) the base category, and recompute the model. Report all results. How do the results change? Based on your results, what is the marginal value of a college degree? (This is actually the marginal value of having 16 years of education—in recent years, college graduation has tended to require somewhat more than four years on average.) What is the marginal impact on ln *Wage* of a graduate degree?

c. The aggregation in part b actually loses quite a bit of information. Another way to introduce nonlinearity in education is through the function itself. Add $Educ^2$ to the equation in part a and recompute the model. Again, report all results. What changes are suggested? Test the hypothesis that the quadratic term in the equation is not needed—i.e., that its coefficient is zero. Based on your results, sketch a profile of log wages as a function of education.

d. One might suspect that the value of education is enhanced by greater ability. We could examine this effect by introducing an interaction of the two variables in the equation. Add the variable

$$Educ\_Ability = Educ \times Ability$$

to the base model in part a. Now, what is the marginal value of an additional year of education? The sample mean value of ability is 0.052374. Compute a confidence interval for the marginal impact on ln *Wage* of an additional year of education for a person of average ability.

e. Combine the models in c and d. Add both $Educ^2$ and *Educ_Ability* to the base model in part a and reestimate. As before, report all results and describe your findings. If we define "low ability" as less than the mean and "high ability" as greater than the mean, the sample averages are $-0.798563$ for the 7,864 low-ability individuals in the sample and $+0.717891$ for the 10,055 high-ability individuals in the sample. Using the formulation in part c, with this new functional form, sketch, describe, and compare the log wage profiles for low- and high-ability individuals.

2. (An extension of Application 1.) Here we consider whether different models as specified in Application 1 would apply for individuals who reside in "Broken homes." Using the results in Sections 6.4.1 and 6.4.4, test the hypothesis that the same model (not including the *Broken home* dummy variable) applies to both groups of individuals, those with *Broken home* $= 0$ and with *Broken home* $= 1$.

3. In Solow's classic (1957) study of technical change in the U.S. economy, he suggests the following aggregate production function: $q(t) = A(t) f[k(t)]$, where $q(t)$ is aggregate output per work hour, $k(t)$ is the aggregate capital labor ratio, and $A(t)$ is the technology index. Solow considered four static models, $q/A = \alpha + \beta \ln k$, $q/A = \alpha - \beta/k$, $\ln(q/A) = \alpha + \beta \ln k$, and $\ln(q/A) = \alpha + \beta/k$. Solow's data for the years 1909 to 1949 are listed in Appendix Table F6.3.

a. Use these data to estimate the $\alpha$ and $\beta$ of the four functions listed above. (Note: Your results will not quite match Solow's. See the next exercise for resolution of the discrepancy.)

b. In the aforementioned study, Solow states:

> A scatter of $q/A$ against $k$ is shown in Chart 4. Considering the amount of a priori doctoring which the raw figures have undergone, the fit is remarkably tight. Except, that is, for the layer of points which are obviously too high. These maverick observations relate to the seven last years of the period, 1943–1949. From the way they lie almost exactly parallel to the main scatter, one is tempted to conclude that in 1943 the aggregate production function simply shifted.

Compute a scatter diagram of $q/A$ against $k$ and verify the result he notes above.

c. Estimate the four models you estimated in the previous problem including a dummy variable for the years 1943 to 1949. How do your results change? (Note: These results match those reported by Solow, although he did not report the coefficient on the dummy variable.)

d. Solow went on to surmise that, in fact, the data were fundamentally different in the years before 1943 than during and after. Use a Chow test to examine the difference in the two subperiods using your four functional forms. Note that with the dummy variable, you can do the test by introducing an interaction term between the dummy and whichever function of $k$ appears in the regression. Use an $F$ test to test the hypothesis.

4. Data on the number of incidents of wave damage to a sample of ships, with the type of ship and the period when it was constructed, are given in Table 6.8. There are five types of ships and four different periods of construction. Use $F$ tests and dummy variable regressions to test the hypothesis that there is no significant "ship type effect" in the expected number of incidents. Now, use the same procedure to test whether there is a significant "period effect."

**TABLE 6.8**  Ship Damage Incidents

| Ship Type | Period Constructed | | | |
|---|---|---|---|---|
| | *1960–1964* | *1965–1969* | *1970–1974* | *1975–1979* |
| A | 0 | 4 | 18 | 11 |
| B | 29 | 53 | 44 | 18 |
| C | 1 | 1 | 2 | 1 |
| D | 0 | 0 | 11 | 4 |
| E | 0 | 7 | 12 | 1 |

*Source:* Data from McCullagh and Nelder (1983, p. 137).

# 7

# SPECIFICATION ANALYSIS
# AND MODEL SELECTION

## 7.1 INTRODUCTION

Chapter 6 presented results that were primarily focused on sharpening the functional form of the model. Functional form and hypothesis testing are directed toward improving the specification of the model or using that model to draw generally narrow inferences about the population. In this chapter we turn to some broader techniques that relate to choosing a specific model when there is more than one competing candidate. Section 7.2 describes some larger issues related to the use of the multiple regression model—specifically the impacts of an incomplete or excessive specification on estimation and inference. Sections 7.3 and 7.4 turn to the broad question of statistical methods for choosing among alternative models. Some larger methodological issues are examined in Section 7.5.

## 7.2 SPECIFICATION ANALYSIS AND MODEL BUILDING

Our analysis has been based on the assumption that the correct specification of the regression model is known to be

$$\mathbf{y} = \mathbf{X}\boldsymbol{\beta} + \boldsymbol{\varepsilon}. \tag{7-1}$$

There are numerous types of errors that one might make in the specification of the estimated equation. Perhaps the most common ones are the **omission of relevant variables** and the **inclusion of superfluous variables.**

### 7.2.1 BIAS CAUSED BY OMISSION OF RELEVANT VARIABLES

Suppose that a correctly specified regression model would be

$$\mathbf{y} = \mathbf{X}_1\boldsymbol{\beta}_1 + \mathbf{X}_2\boldsymbol{\beta}_2 + \boldsymbol{\varepsilon}, \tag{7-2}$$

where the two parts of $\mathbf{X}$ have $K_1$ and $K_2$ columns, respectively. If we regress $\mathbf{y}$ on $\mathbf{X}_1$ without including $\mathbf{X}_2$, then the estimator is

$$\mathbf{b}_1 = (\mathbf{X}_1'\mathbf{X}_1)^{-1}\mathbf{X}_1'\mathbf{y} = \boldsymbol{\beta}_1 + (\mathbf{X}_1'\mathbf{X}_1)^{-1}\mathbf{X}_1'\mathbf{X}_2\boldsymbol{\beta}_2 + (\mathbf{X}_1'\mathbf{X}_1)^{-1}\mathbf{X}_1'\boldsymbol{\varepsilon}. \tag{7-3}$$

Taking the expectation, we see that unless $\mathbf{X}_1'\mathbf{X}_2 = \mathbf{0}$ or $\boldsymbol{\beta}_2 = \mathbf{0}$, $\mathbf{b}_1$ is biased. The well-known result is the **omitted variable formula:**

$$E[\mathbf{b}_1 \mid \mathbf{X}] = \boldsymbol{\beta}_1 + \mathbf{P}_{1.2}\boldsymbol{\beta}_2, \tag{7-4}$$

where

$$\mathbf{P}_{1.2} = (\mathbf{X}_1'\mathbf{X}_1)^{-1}\mathbf{X}_1'\mathbf{X}_2. \tag{7-5}$$

Each column of the $K_1 \times K_2$ matrix $\mathbf{P}_{1.2}$ is the column of slopes in the least squares regression of the corresponding column of $\mathbf{X}_2$ on the columns of $\mathbf{X}_1$.

### Example 7.1  Omitted Variables

If a demand equation is estimated without the relevant income variable, then (7-4) shows how the estimated price elasticity will be biased. Letting $b$ be the estimator, we obtain

$$E[b \mid price, income] = \beta + \frac{\text{Cov}[price, income]}{\text{Var}[price]}\gamma,$$

where $\gamma$ is the income coefficient. In aggregate data, it is unclear whether the missing co-variance would be positive or negative. The sign of the bias in $b$ would be the same as this covariance, however, because Var[$price$] and $\gamma$ would be positive for a normal good such as gasoline. (See Example 2.3.)

The gasoline market data we have examined in Examples 2.3 and 6.7 provide a striking example. Figure 6.5 showed a simple plot of per capita gasoline consumption, $G/Pop$ against the price index $P_G$. The plot is considerably at odds with what one might expect. But a look at the data in Appendix Table F2.2 shows clearly what is at work. Holding per capita income, $Income/Pop$, and other prices constant, these data might well conform to expectations. In these data, however, income is persistently growing, and the simple correlations between $G/Pop$ and $Income/Pop$ and between $P_G$ and $Income/Pop$ are 0.938 and 0.934, respectively, which are quite large. To see if the expected relationship between price and consumption shows up, we will have to purge our data of the intervening effect of $Income/Pop$. To do so, we rely on the Frisch–Waugh result in Theorem 3.3. The regression results appear in Table 6.7. The first column shows the full regression model, with ln $P_G$, ln $Income$, and several other variables. The estimated demand elasticity is $-0.0539$, which conforms with expectations. If income is omitted from this equation, the estimated price elasticity is $+0.06788$ which has the wrong sign, but is what we would expect given the theoretical results above.

In this development, it is straightforward to deduce the directions of bias when there is a single included variable and one omitted variable. It is important to note, however, that if more than one variable is included, then the terms in the omitted variable formula involve multiple regression coefficients, which themselves have the signs of partial, not simple, correlations. For example, in the demand equation of the previous example, if the price of a closely related product had been included as well, then the simple correlation between price and income would be insufficient to determine the direction of the bias in the price elasticity. What would be required is the sign of the correlation between price and income net of the effect of the other price. This requirement might not be obvious, and it would become even less so as more regressors were added to the equation.

### 7.2.2  PRETEST ESTIMATION

The variance of $\mathbf{b}_1$ is that of the third term in (7-3), which is

$$\text{Var}[\mathbf{b}_1 \mid \mathbf{X}] = \sigma^2(\mathbf{X}_1'\mathbf{X}_1)^{-1}. \tag{7-6}$$

If we had computed the correct regression, including $\mathbf{X}_2$, then the slopes on $\mathbf{X}_1$ would have been unbiased and would have had a covariance matrix equal to the upper left block of $\sigma^2(\mathbf{X}'\mathbf{X})^{-1}$. This matrix is

$$\text{Var}[\mathbf{b}_{1.2} \mid \mathbf{X}] = \sigma^2(\mathbf{X}_1'\mathbf{M}_2\mathbf{X}_1)^{-1}, \tag{7-7}$$

where

$$\mathbf{M}_2 = \mathbf{I} - \mathbf{X}_2(\mathbf{X}_2'\mathbf{X}_2)^{-1}\mathbf{X}_2',$$

or

$$\text{Var}[\mathbf{b}_{1.2} \mid \mathbf{X}] = \sigma^2[\mathbf{X}_1'\mathbf{X}_1 - \mathbf{X}_1'\mathbf{X}_2(\mathbf{X}_2'\mathbf{X}_2)^{-1}\mathbf{X}_2'\mathbf{X}_1]^{-1}.$$

We can compare the covariance matrices of $\mathbf{b}_1$ and $\mathbf{b}_{1.2}$ more easily by comparing their inverses [see result (A-120)];

$$\text{Var}[\mathbf{b}_1 \mid \mathbf{X}]^{-1} - \text{Var}[\mathbf{b}_{1.2} \mid \mathbf{X}]^{-1} = (1/\sigma^2)\mathbf{X}_1'\mathbf{X}_2(\mathbf{X}_2'\mathbf{X}_2)^{-1}\mathbf{X}_2'\mathbf{X}_1,$$

which is nonnegative definite. We conclude that although $\mathbf{b}_1$ is **biased,** its variance is never larger than that of $\mathbf{b}_{1.2}$ (because the inverse of its variance is at least as large).

Suppose, for instance, that $\mathbf{X}_1$ and $\mathbf{X}_2$ are each a single column and that the variables are measured as deviations from their respective means. Then

$$\text{Var}[b_1 \mid \mathbf{X}] = \frac{\sigma^2}{s_{11}}, \quad \text{where } s_{11} = \sum_{i=1}^{n} (x_{i1} - \bar{x}_1)^2,$$

whereas

$$\text{Var}[b_{1.2} \mid \mathbf{X}] = \sigma^2[\mathbf{x}_1'\mathbf{x}_1 - \mathbf{x}_1'\mathbf{x}_2(\mathbf{x}_2'\mathbf{x}_2)^{-1}\mathbf{x}_2'\mathbf{x}_1]^{-1} = \frac{\sigma^2}{s_{11}(1 - r_{12}^2)}, \tag{7-8}$$

where

$$r_{12}^2 = \frac{(\mathbf{x}_1'\mathbf{x}_2)^2}{\mathbf{x}_1'\mathbf{x}_1\mathbf{x}_2'\mathbf{x}_2}$$

is the squared sample correlation between $\mathbf{x}_1$ and $\mathbf{x}_2$. The more highly correlated $\mathbf{x}_1$ and $\mathbf{x}_2$ are, the larger is the variance of $b_{1.2}$ compared with that of $b_1$. Therefore, it is possible that $b_1$ is a more precise estimator based on the **mean-squared error** criterion.

The result in the preceding paragraph poses a bit of a dilemma for applied researchers. The situation arises frequently in the search for a model specification. Faced with a variable that a researcher suspects should be in their model, but that is causing a problem of collinearity, the analyst faces a choice of omitting the relevant variable or including it and estimating its (and all the other variables') coefficient imprecisely. This presents a choice between two estimators, $b_1$ and $b_{1.2}$. In fact, what researchers usually do actually creates a third estimator. It is common to include the problem variable provisionally. If its $t$ ratio is sufficiently large, it is retained; otherwise it is discarded. This third estimator is called a **pretest estimator.** What is known about pretest estimators is not encouraging. Certainly they are biased. How badly depends on the unknown parameters. Analytical results suggest that the pretest estimator is the least precise of the three when the researcher is most likely to use it. [See Judge et al. (1985).]

### 7.2.3 INCLUSION OF IRRELEVANT VARIABLES

If the regression model is correctly given by

$$\mathbf{y} = \mathbf{X}_1\boldsymbol{\beta}_1 + \boldsymbol{\varepsilon} \tag{7-9}$$

and we estimate it as if (7-2) were correct (i.e., we include some extra variables), then it might seem that the same sorts of problems considered earlier would arise. In fact, this case is not true. We can view the omission of a set of relevant variables as equivalent to imposing an incorrect restriction on (7-2). In particular, omitting $\mathbf{X}_2$ is equivalent to *incorrectly* estimating (7-2) subject to the restriction $\boldsymbol{\beta}_2 = \mathbf{0}$. As we discovered, incorrectly imposing a restriction produces a biased estimator. Another way to view this error is to note that it amounts to incorporating incorrect information in our estimation. Suppose, however, that our error is simply a failure to use some information that is *correct*.

The inclusion of the irrelevant variables $\mathbf{X}_2$ in the regression is equivalent to failing to impose $\boldsymbol{\beta}_2 = \mathbf{0}$ on (7-2) in estimation. But (7-2) is not incorrect; it simply fails to incorporate $\boldsymbol{\beta}_2 = \mathbf{0}$. Therefore, we do not need to prove formally that the least squares estimator of $\boldsymbol{\beta}$ in (7-2) is unbiased *even given* the restriction; we have already proved it. We can assert on the basis of all our earlier results that

$$E[\mathbf{b} \mid \mathbf{X}] = \begin{bmatrix} \boldsymbol{\beta}_1 \\ \boldsymbol{\beta}_2 \end{bmatrix} = \begin{bmatrix} \boldsymbol{\beta}_1 \\ \mathbf{0} \end{bmatrix}. \tag{7-10}$$

By the same reasoning, $s^2$ is also unbiased:

$$E\left[\frac{\mathbf{e'e}}{n - K_1 - K_2} \,\middle|\, \mathbf{X}\right] = \sigma^2. \tag{7-11}$$

Then where is the problem? It would seem that one would generally want to "overfit" the model. From a theoretical standpoint, the difficulty with this view is that the failure to use correct information is always costly. In this instance, the cost is the reduced precision of the estimates. As we have shown, the covariance matrix in the short regression (omitting $\mathbf{X}_2$) is never larger than the covariance matrix for the estimator obtained in the presence of the superfluous variables.[1] Consider again the single-variable comparison given earlier. If $\mathbf{x}_2$ is highly correlated with $\mathbf{x}_1$, then incorrectly including it in the regression will greatly inflate the variance of the estimator.

### 7.2.4 MODEL BUILDING—A GENERAL TO SIMPLE STRATEGY

There has been a shift in the general approach to model building in the past 20 years or so, partly based on the results in the previous two sections. With an eye toward maintaining simplicity, model builders would generally begin with a small specification and gradually build up the model ultimately of interest by adding variables. But, based on the preceding results, we can surmise that just about any criterion that would be used to decide whether to add a variable to a current specification would be tainted by the biases caused by the incomplete specification at the early steps. Omitting variables from the equation seems generally to be the worse of the two errors. Thus, the **simple-to-general** approach to model building has little to recommend it. Building on the work

---

[1]There is no loss if $\mathbf{X}_1'\mathbf{X}_2 = \mathbf{0}$, which makes sense in terms of the information about $\mathbf{X}_1$ contained in $\mathbf{X}_2$ (here, none). This situation is not likely to occur in practice, however.

of Hendry [e.g., (1995)] and aided by advances in estimation hardware and software, researchers are now more comfortable beginning their specification searches with large elaborate models involving many variables and perhaps long and complex lag structures. The attractive strategy is then to adopt a **general-to-simple,** downward reduction of the model to the preferred specification. (This approach has been completely automated in Hendry's PCGets computer program. [See, e.g., Hendry and Kotzis (2001).].). Of course, this must be tempered by two related considerations. In the "kitchen sink" regression, which contains every variable that might conceivably be relevant, the adoption of a fixed probability for the type I error, say, 5 percent, ensures that in a big enough model, some variables will appear to be significant, even if "by accident." Second, the problems of pretest estimation and **stepwise model building** also pose some risk of ultimately misspecifying the model. To cite one unfortunately common example, the statistics involved often produce unexplainable lag structures in dynamic models with many lags of the dependent or independent variables.

## 7.3 CHOOSING BETWEEN NONNESTED MODELS

The classical testing procedures that we have been using have been shown to be most powerful for the types of hypotheses we have considered.[2] Although use of these procedures is clearly desirable, the requirement that we express the hypotheses in the form of restrictions on the model $\mathbf{y} = \mathbf{X}\boldsymbol{\beta} + \boldsymbol{\varepsilon}$,

$$H_0 : \mathbf{R}\boldsymbol{\beta} = \mathbf{q}$$

versus

$$H_1 : \mathbf{R}\boldsymbol{\beta} \neq \mathbf{q},$$

can be limiting. Two common exceptions are the general problem of determining which of two possible sets of regressors is more appropriate and whether a linear or loglinear model is more appropriate for a given analysis. For the present, we are interested in comparing two competing linear models:

$$H_0 : \mathbf{y} = \mathbf{X}\boldsymbol{\beta} + \boldsymbol{\varepsilon}_0 \tag{7-12a}$$

and

$$H_1 : \mathbf{y} = \mathbf{Z}\boldsymbol{\gamma} + \boldsymbol{\varepsilon}_1. \tag{7-12b}$$

The classical procedures we have considered thus far provide no means of forming a preference for one model or the other. The general problem of testing nonnested hypotheses such as these has attracted an impressive amount of attention in the theoretical literature and has appeared in a wide variety of empirical applications.[3]

---

[2]See, for example, Stuart and Ord (1989, Chap. 27).

[3]Recent surveys on this subject are White (1982a, 1983), Gourieroux and Monfort (1994), McAleer (1995), and Pesaran and Weeks (2001). McAleer's survey tabulates an array of applications, while Gourieroux and Monfort focus on the underlying theory.

### 7.3.1 TESTING NONNESTED HYPOTHESES

A useful distinction between hypothesis testing as discussed in the preceding chapters and model selection as considered here will turn on the asymmetry between the null and alternative hypotheses that is a part of the classical testing procedure.[4] Because, by construction, the classical procedures seek evidence in the sample to refute the "null" hypothesis, how one frames the null can be crucial to the outcome. Fortunately, the Neyman–Pearson methodology provides a prescription; the null is usually cast as the narrowest model in the set under consideration. On the other hand, the classical procedures never reach a sharp conclusion. Unless the significance level of the testing procedure is made so high as to exclude all alternatives, there will always remain the possibility of a Type 1 error. As such, the null hypothesis is never rejected with certainty, but only with a prespecified degree of confidence. Model selection tests, in contrast, give the competing hypotheses equal standing. There is no natural null hypothesis. However, the end of the process is a firm decision—in testing (7-12a, b), one of the models will be rejected and the other will be retained; the analysis will then proceed in the framework of that one model and not the other. Indeed, it cannot proceed until one of the models is discarded. It is common, for example, in this new setting for the analyst first to test with one model cast as the null, then with the other. Unfortunately, given the way the tests are constructed, it can happen that both or neither model is rejected; in either case, further analysis is clearly warranted. As we shall see, the science is a bit inexact.

The earliest work on nonnested hypothesis testing, notably Cox (1961, 1962), was done in the framework of sample likelihoods and maximum likelihood procedures. Recent developments have been structured around a common pillar labeled the **encompassing principle** [Mizon and Richard (1986)]. In the large, the principle directs attention to the question of whether a maintained model can explain the features of its competitors, that is, whether the maintained model encompasses the alternative. Yet a third approach is based on forming a **comprehensive model** that contains both competitors as special cases. When possible, the test between models can be based, essentially, on classical (-like) testing procedures. We will examine tests that exemplify all three approaches.

### 7.3.2 AN ENCOMPASSING MODEL

The encompassing approach is one in which the ability of one model to explain features of another is tested. Model 0 "encompasses" Model 1 if the features of Model 1 can be explained by Model 0 but the reverse is not true.[5] Because $H_0$ cannot be written as a restriction on $H_1$, none of the procedures we have considered thus far is appropriate. One possibility is an artificial nesting of the two models. Let $\overline{\mathbf{X}}$ be the set of variables in $\mathbf{X}$ that are not in $\mathbf{Z}$, define $\overline{\mathbf{Z}}$ likewise with respect to $\mathbf{X}$, and let $\mathbf{W}$ be the variables that the models have in common. Then $H_0$ and $H_1$ could be combined in a "supermodel":

$$\mathbf{y} = \overline{\mathbf{X}}\,\overline{\beta} + \overline{\mathbf{Z}}\,\overline{\gamma} + \mathbf{W}\delta + \varepsilon.$$

---

[4]See Granger and Pesaran (2000) for discussion.

[5]See Deaton (1982), Dastoor (1983), Gourieroux, et al. (1983, 1995) and, especially, Mizon and Richard (1986).

In principle, $H_1$ is rejected if it is found that $\overline{\gamma} = \mathbf{0}$ by a conventional $F$ test, whereas $H_0$ is rejected if it is found that $\overline{\beta} = \mathbf{0}$. There are two problems with this approach. First, $\delta$ remains a mixture of parts of $\beta$ and $\gamma$, and it is not established by the $F$ test that either of these parts is zero. Hence, this test does not really distinguish between $H_0$ and $H_1$; it distinguishes between $H_1$ and a hybrid model. Second, this compound model may have an extremely large number of regressors. In a time-series setting, the problem of collinearity may be severe.

Consider an alternative approach. If $H_0$ is correct, then $\mathbf{y}$ will, apart from the random disturbance $\boldsymbol{\varepsilon}$, be fully explained by $\mathbf{X}$. Suppose we then attempt to estimate $\gamma$ by regression of $\mathbf{y}$ on $\mathbf{Z}$. Whatever set of parameters is estimated by this regression, say, $\mathbf{c}$, if $H_0$ is correct, then we should estimate exactly the same coefficient vector if we were to regress $\mathbf{X}\beta$ on $\mathbf{Z}$, since $\boldsymbol{\varepsilon}_0$ is random noise under $H_0$. Because $\beta$ must be estimated, suppose that we use $\mathbf{Xb}$ instead and compute $\mathbf{c}_0$. A test of the proposition that Model 0 "encompasses" Model 1 would be a test of the hypothesis that $E[\mathbf{c} - \mathbf{c}_0] = \mathbf{0}$. It is straightforward to show [see Davidson and MacKinnon (2004, pp. 671–672)] that the test can be carried out by using a standard $F$ test to test the hypothesis that $\gamma_1 = \mathbf{0}$ in the augmented regression,

$$\mathbf{y} = \mathbf{X}\beta + \mathbf{Z}_1\gamma_1 + \boldsymbol{\varepsilon}_1,$$

where $\mathbf{Z}_1$ is the variables in $\mathbf{Z}$ that are not in $\mathbf{X}$. (Of course, a line of manipulation reveals that $\overline{\mathbf{Z}}$ and $\mathbf{Z}_1$ are the same, so the tests are also.)

### 7.3.3 COMPREHENSIVE APPROACH—THE $J$ TEST

The underpinnings of the comprehensive approach are tied to the density function as the characterization of the data generating process. Let $f_0(y_i \mid data, \beta_0)$ be the assumed density under Model 0 and define the alternative likewise as $f_1(y_i \mid data, \beta_1)$. Then, a comprehensive model which subsumes both of these is

$$f_c(y_i \mid data, \beta_0, \beta_1) = \frac{[f_0(y_i \mid data, \beta_0)]^{1-\lambda}[f_1(y_i \mid data, \beta_1)]^{\lambda}}{\int_{\text{range of } y_i} [f_0(y_i \mid data, \beta_0)]^{1-\lambda}[f_1(y_i \mid data, \beta_1)]^{\lambda} \, dy_i}.$$

Estimation of the comprehensive model followed by a test of $\lambda = 0$ or 1 is used to assess the validity of Model 0 or 1, respectively.[6]

The $J$ **test** proposed by Davidson and MacKinnon (1981) can be shown [see Pesaran and Weeks (2001)] to be an application of this principle to the linear regression model. Their suggested alternative to the preceding compound model is

$$\mathbf{y} = (1 - \lambda)\mathbf{X}\beta + \lambda(\mathbf{Z}\gamma) + \boldsymbol{\varepsilon}.$$

In this model, a test of $\lambda = 0$ would be a test against $H_1$. The problem is that $\lambda$ cannot be separately estimated in this model; it would amount to a redundant scaling of the regression coefficients. Davidson and MacKinnon's $J$ test consists of estimating $\gamma$ by a least squares regression of $\mathbf{y}$ on $\mathbf{Z}$ followed by a least squares regression of $\mathbf{y}$ on $\mathbf{X}$ and $\mathbf{Z}\hat{\gamma}$, the fitted values in the first regression. A valid test, at least asymptotically, of $H_1$ is to test $H_0 : \lambda = 0$. If $H_0$ is true, then plim $\hat{\lambda} = 0$. Asymptotically, the ratio $\hat{\lambda}/se(\hat{\lambda})$ (i.e., the usual $t$ ratio) is distributed as standard normal and may be referred to

---

[6]Silva (2001) presents an application to the choice of probit or logit model for binary choice.

the standard table to carry out the test. Unfortunately, in testing $H_0$ versus $H_1$ and vice versa, all four possibilities (reject both, neither, or either one of the two hypotheses) could occur. This issue, however, is a finite sample problem. Davidson and MacKinnon show that as $n \to \infty$, if $H_1$ is true, then the probability that $\hat{\lambda}$ will differ significantly from 0 approaches 1.

**Example 7.2** **J Test for a Consumption Function**
Gaver and Geisel (1974) propose two forms of a consumption function:

$$H_0 : C_t = \beta_1 + \beta_2 Y_t + \beta_3 Y_{t-1} + \varepsilon_{0t}$$

and

$$H_1 : C_t = \gamma_1 + \gamma_2 Y_t + \gamma_3 C_{t-1} + \varepsilon_{1t}.$$

The first model states that consumption responds to changes in income over two periods, whereas the second states that the effects of changes in income on consumption persist for many periods. Quarterly data on aggregate U.S. real consumption and real disposable income are given in Appendix Table F5.1. Here we apply the *J* test to these data and the two proposed specifications. First, the two models are estimated separately (using observations 1950.2 through 2000.4). The least squares regression of *C* on a constant, *Y*, lagged *Y*, and the fitted values from the second model produces an estimate of $\lambda$ of 1.0145 with a *t* ratio of 62.861. Thus, $H_0$ should be rejected in favor of $H_1$. But reversing the roles of $H_0$ and $H_1$, we obtain an estimate of $\lambda$ of $-10.677$ with a *t* ratio of $-7.188$. Thus, $H_1$ is rejected as well.[7]

### 7.3.4 VUONG'S TEST AND THE KULLBACK–LEIBLER INFORMATION CRITERION

Vuong's (1989) approach to testing **nonnested models** is also based on the likelihood ratio statistic.[8] The logic of the test is similar to that which motivates the likelihood ratio test in general. Suppose that $f(y_i \mid \mathbf{Z}_i, \boldsymbol{\theta})$ and $g(y_i \mid \mathbf{Z}_i, \boldsymbol{\gamma})$ are two competing models for the density of the random variable $y_i$, with $f$ being the null model, $H_0$, and $g$ being the alternative, $H_1$. For instance, in Example 7.2, both densities are (by assumption now) normal, $y_i$ is consumption, $C_t$, $\mathbf{Z}_i$ is $[1, Y_t, Y_{t-1}, C_{t-1}]$, $\boldsymbol{\theta}$ is $(\beta_1, \beta_2, \beta_3, 0, \sigma^2)$, $\boldsymbol{\gamma}$ is $(\gamma_1, \gamma_2, 0, \gamma_3, \omega^2)$, and $\sigma^2$ and $\omega^2$ are the respective conditional variances of the disturbances, $\varepsilon_{0t}$ and $\varepsilon_{1t}$. The crucial element of Vuong's analysis is that it need not be the case that either competing model is "true"; they may both be incorrect. What we want to do is attempt to use the data to determine which competitor is closer to the truth, that is, closer to the correct (unknown) model.

We assume that observations in the sample (disturbances) are conditionally independent. Let $L_{i,0}$ denote the $i$th contribution to the likelihood function under the null hypothesis. Thus, the log likelihood function under the null hypothesis is $\Sigma_i \ln L_{i,0}$. Define $L_{i,1}$ likewise for the alternative model. Now, let $m_i$ equal $\ln L_{i,1} - \ln L_{i,0}$. If we were using the familiar likelihood ratio test, then, the likelihood ratio statistic would be simply $LR = 2\Sigma_i m_i = 2n\overline{m}$ when $L_{i,0}$ and $L_{i,1}$ are computed at the respective maximum likelihood estimators. When the competing models are nested—$H_0$ is a restriction on $H_1$—we know that $\Sigma_i m_i \geq 0$. The restrictions of the null hypothesis will never increase

---

[7]For related discussion of this possibility, see McAleer, Fisher, and Volker (1982).

[8]Once again, it is necessary to rely on results that we will develop more fully in Chapter 16. But, this discussion of nonnested models is a convenient point at which to introduce Vuong's useful statistic, and we will not be returning to the topic of nonnested models save for a short application in Chapter 24.

the likelihood function. (In the linear regression model with normally distributed disturbances that we have examined so far, the log likelihood and these results are all based on the sum of squared residuals, and as we have seen, imposing restrictions never reduces the sum of squares.) The limiting distribution of the $LR$ statistic under the assumption of the null hypothesis is chi squared with degrees of freedom equal to the reduction in the number of dimensions of the parameter space of the alternative hypothesis that results from imposing the restrictions.

Vuong's analysis is concerned with nonnested models for which $\Sigma_i\, m_i$ need not be positive. Formalizing the test requires us to look more closely at what is meant by the "right" model (and provides a convenient departure point for the discussion in the next two sections). In the context of nonnested models, Vuong allows for the possibility that neither model is "true" in the absolute sense. We maintain the classical assumption that there does exist a "true" model, $h(y_i \mid \mathbf{Z}_i, \boldsymbol{\alpha})$ where $\boldsymbol{\alpha}$ is the "true" parameter vector, but possibly neither hypothesized model is that true model. The **Kullback–Leibler Information Criterion** (KLIC) measures the distance between the true model (distribution) and a hypothesized model in terms of the likelihood function. Loosely, the KLIC is the log likelihood function under the hypothesis of the true model minus the log likelihood function for the (misspecified) hypothesized model under the assumption of the true model. Formally, for the model of the null hypothesis,

$$\text{KLIC} = E[\ln h(y_i \mid \mathbf{Z}_i, \boldsymbol{\alpha}) \mid h \text{ is true}] - E[\ln f(y_i \mid \mathbf{Z}_i, \boldsymbol{\theta}) \mid h \text{ is true}]. \qquad \textbf{(7-13)}$$

The first term on the right hand side is what we would estimate with $(1/n)\ln L$ if we maximized the log likelihood for the true model, $h(y_i \mid \mathbf{Z}_i, \boldsymbol{\alpha})$. The second term is what is estimated by $(1/n) \ln L$ assuming (incorrectly) that $f(y_i \mid \mathbf{Z}_i, \boldsymbol{\theta})$ is the correct model.[9] In the context of the model in the previous example, suppose the "true" model is $\mathbf{y} = \mathbf{X}\boldsymbol{\beta} + \boldsymbol{\varepsilon}$, with normally distributed disturbances and $\mathbf{y} = \mathbf{Z}\boldsymbol{\delta} + \mathbf{w}$ is the proposed competing model. The KLIC would be the expected log likelihood function for the true model minus the expected log likelihood function for the second model, still assuming that the first one is the truth. By construction, the KLIC is positive. We will now say that one model is "better" than another if it is closer to the "truth" based on the KLIC. If we take the difference of the two KLICs for two models, the true log likelihood function falls out, and we are left with

$$\text{KLIC}_1 - \text{KLIC}_0 = E[\ln f(y_i \mid \mathbf{Z}_i, \boldsymbol{\theta}) \mid h \text{ is true}] - E[\ln g(y_i \mid \mathbf{Z}_i, \boldsymbol{\gamma}) \mid h \text{ is true}].$$

To compute this using a sample, we would simply compute the likelihood ratio statistic, $n\overline{m}$ (without multiplying by 2) again. Thus, this provides an interpretation of the LR statistic. But, in this context, the statistic can be negative—we don't know which competing model is closer to the truth.

---

[9]Notice that $f(y_i \mid \mathbf{Z}_i, \boldsymbol{\theta})$ is written in terms of a parameter vector, $\boldsymbol{\theta}$. Because $\boldsymbol{\alpha}$ is the "true" parameter vector, it is perhaps ambiguous what is meant by the parameterization, $\boldsymbol{\theta}$. Vuong (p. 310) calls this the "pseudotrue" parameter vector. It is the vector of constants that the estimator converges to when one uses the estimator implied by $f(y_i \mid \mathbf{Z}_i, \boldsymbol{\theta})$. In Example 7.2, if $H_0$ gives the correct model, this formulation assumes that the least squares estimator in $H_1$ would converge to some vector of pseudo-true parameters. But, these are not the parameters of the correct model—they would be the slopes in the population linear projection of $C_t$ on $[1, Y_t, C_{t-1}]$. (See Section 4.2.2.)

Vuong's general result for nonnested models (his Theorem 5.1) describes the behavior of the statistic

$$V = \frac{\sqrt{n}\left(\frac{1}{n}\sum_{i=1}^{n} m_i\right)}{\sqrt{\frac{1}{n}\sum_{i=1}^{n}(m_i - \bar{m})^2}} = \sqrt{n}(\bar{m}/s_m), \quad m_i = \ln L_{i,0} - \ln L_{i,1}. \tag{7-14}$$

He finds:

(1) Under the hypothesis that the models are "equivalent", $V \xrightarrow{D} N[0, 1]$

(2) Under the hypothesis that $f(y_i \mid \mathbf{Z}_i, \boldsymbol{\theta})$ is "better", $V \xrightarrow{A.S.} +\infty$

(3) Under the hypothesis that $g(y_i \mid \mathbf{Z}_i, \boldsymbol{\gamma})$ is "better", $V \xrightarrow{A.S.} -\infty$.

This test is directional. Large positive values favor the null model while large negative values favor the alternative. The intermediate values (e.g., between $-1.96$ and $+1.96$ for 95 percent significance) are an inconclusive region.

### Example 7.3 Vuong Test for a Consumption Function
We conclude Example 7.2 by applying the **Vuong test** to the consumption data. For the linear model, $\mathbf{y} = \mathbf{X}\beta + \varepsilon$ with normally distributed disturbances,

$$\ln L_i = -1/2\left[\ln \sigma^2 + \ln 2\pi + (y_i - \mathbf{x}_i'\beta)^2/\sigma^2\right] \tag{7-15}$$

and the maximum likelihood estimators of $\beta$ and $\sigma^2$ are $\mathbf{b}$ and $\mathbf{e}'\mathbf{e}/n$. For the time-series data in Example 7.2, define for $H_0$, $e_{t0} = C_t - b_1 - b_2 Y_t - b_3 Y_{t-1}$ and $\mathbf{e}_0'\mathbf{e}_0 = \Sigma_t e_{t0}^2$. Define $e_{t1}$ and $\mathbf{e}_0'\mathbf{e}_1$ likewise for $H_1$. Then, based on (7-14), we will have

$$\hat{m}_t = -1/2[\ln(\mathbf{e}_0'\mathbf{e}_0/\mathbf{e}_1'\mathbf{e}_1) + (e_{t0}^2/(\mathbf{e}_0'\mathbf{e}_0/T) - e_{t1}^2/(\mathbf{e}_0'\mathbf{e}_1/T))], \quad t = 1950.2, \ldots, 2000.4$$

(where $T = 203$). The Vuong statistic is $-13.604$, which once again strongly favors the alternative, $H_1$.

## 7.4 MODEL SELECTION CRITERIA

The preceding discussion suggested some approaches to model selection based on nonnested hypothesis tests. Fit measures and testing procedures based on the sum of squared residuals, such as $R^2$ and the Cox test, are useful when interest centers on the within-sample fit or within-sample prediction of the dependent variable. When the model building is directed toward forecasting, within-sample measures are not necessarily optimal. As we have seen, $R^2$ cannot fall when variables are added to a model, so there is a built-in tendency to overfit the model. This criterion may point us away from the best forecasting model, because adding variables to a model may increase the variance of the forecast error (see Section 5.6) despite the improved fit to the data. With this thought in mind, the **adjusted** $R^2$,

$$\bar{R}^2 = 1 - \frac{n-1}{n-K}(1 - R^2) = 1 - \frac{n-1}{n-K}\left(\frac{\mathbf{e}'\mathbf{e}}{\sum_{i=1}^{n}(y_i - \bar{y})^2}\right), \tag{7-16}$$

has been suggested as a fit measure that appropriately penalizes the loss of degrees of freedom that result from adding variables to the model. Note that $\bar{R}^2$ may fall when a variable is added to a model if the sum of squares does not fall fast enough. (The applicable result appears in Theorem 3.7; $\bar{R}^2$ does not rise when a variable is added to a model unless the $t$ ratio associated with that variable exceeds one in absolute value.)

The adjusted $R^2$ has been found to be a preferable fit measure for assessing the fit of forecasting models. [See Diebold (2003), who argues that the simple $R^2$ has a downward bias as a measure of the out-of-sample, one-step-ahead prediction error variance.]

The adjusted $R^2$ penalizes the loss of degrees of freedom that occurs when a model is expanded. There is, however, some question about whether the penalty is sufficiently large to ensure that the criterion will necessarily lead the analyst to the correct model (assuming that it is among the ones considered) as the sample size increases. Two alternative fit measures that have seen suggested are the **Akaike Information Criterion,**

$$\text{AIC}(K) = s_y^2(1 - R^2)e^{2K/n} \tag{7-17}$$

and the Schwarz or **Bayesian Information Criterion,**

$$\text{BIC}(K) = s_y^2(1 - R^2)n^{K/n}. \tag{7-18}$$

(There is no degrees of freedom correction in $s_y^2$.) Both measures improve (decline) as $R^2$ increases (decreases), but, everything else constant, degrade as the model size increases. Like $\bar{R}^2$, these measures place a premium on achieving a given fit with a smaller number of parameters per observation, $K/n$. Logs are usually more convenient; the measures reported by most software are

$$\text{AIC}(K) = \ln\left(\frac{\mathbf{e}'\mathbf{e}}{n}\right) + \frac{2K}{n} \tag{7-19}$$

$$\text{BIC}(K) = \ln\left(\frac{\mathbf{e}'\mathbf{e}}{n}\right) + \frac{K\ln n}{n}. \tag{7-20}$$

Both **prediction criteria** have their virtues, and neither has an obvious advantage over the other. [See Diebold (2003).] The **Schwarz criterion,** with its heavier penalty for degrees of freedom lost, will lean toward a simpler model. All else given, simplicity does have some appeal.

## 7.5  MODEL SELECTION

The preceding has laid out a number of choices for **model selection,** but, at the same time, has posed some uncomfortable propositions. The pretest estimation aspects of specification search are based on the model builder's knowledge of "the truth" and the consequences of failing to use that knowledge. While the cautions about blind search for statistical significance are well taken, it does seem optimistic to assume that the correct model is likely to be known with hard certainty at the outset of the analysis. The bias documented in (7-4) is well worth the modeler's attention. But, in practical terms, knowing anything about the magnitude presumes that we know what variables are in $\mathbf{X}_2$, which need not be the case. While we can agree that the model builder will omit income from a demand equation at their peril, we could also have some sympathy for the analyst faced with finding the right specification for their forecasting model among dozens of choices. The tests for nonnested models would seem to free the modeler from having to claim that the specified set of models contain "the truth." But, a moment's thought should suggest that the cost of this is the possibly deflated power of these procedures to point toward that truth, The *J* test may provide a sharp choice between two alternatives, but it neglects the third possibility, that both models are wrong. Vuong's test does but, of course, it suffers from the fairly large inconclusive region, which is a symptom of its relatively low power against many alternatives. The upshot of all of this is that there remains much to be accomplished in the area of model selection. Recent commentary has provided suggestions from two perspective, classical and Bayesian.

### 7.5.1 CLASSICAL MODEL SELECTION

Hansen (2005) lists four shortcomings of the methodology we have considered here:

**(1)** parametric vision
**(2)** assuming a true data generating process
**(3)** evaluation based on fit
**(4)** ignoring model uncertainty

All four of these aspects have framed the analysis of the preceding sections. Hansen's view is that the analysis considered here is too narrow, and stands in the way of progress in model discovery.

All of the model selection procedures considered here are based on the likelihood function, which requires a specific distributional assumption. Hansen argues for a focus, instead, on semiparametric structures. For regression analysis, this points toward generalized method of moments estimators. Casualties of this reorientation will be distributionally based test statistics such as the Cox and Vuong statistics, and even the AIC and BIC measures, which are transformations of the likelihood function. However, alternatives have been proposed [e.g, by Hong, Preston, and Shum (2000)]. The second criticism is one we have addressed. The assumed "true" model can be a straight-jacket. Rather (he argues), we should view our specifications as approximations to the underlying true data generating process—this greatly widens the specification search, to one for a model which provides the best approximation. Of course, that now forces the question of what is "best." So far, we have focused on the likelihood function, which in the classical regression can be viewed as an increasing function of $R^2$. The author argues for a more "focused" information criterion (FIC) that examines directly the parameters of interest, rather than the fit of the model to the data. Each of these suggestions seeks to improve the process of model selection based on familiar criteria, such as test statistics based on fit measures and on characteristics of the model.

A (perhaps *the*) crucial issue remaining is uncertainty about the model itself. The search for the correct model is likely to have the same kinds of impacts on statistical inference as the search for a specification given the form of the model (see Section 7.2). Unfortunately, incorporation of this kind of uncertainty in statistical inference procedures remains an unsolved problem. Hansen suggests one potential route would be the Bayesian model averaging methods discussed next although he does express some skepticism about Bayesian methods in general.

### 7.5.2 BAYESIAN MODEL AVERAGING

If we have doubts as to which of two models is appropriate, then we might well be convinced to concede that possibly neither one is really "the truth." We have painted ourselves into a corner with our "left or right" approach to testing. The Bayesian approach to this question would treat it as a problem of comparing the two hypotheses rather than testing for the validity of one over the other. We enter our sampling experiment with a set of prior probabilities about the relative merits of the two hypotheses, which is summarized in a "prior odds ratio," $P_{01} = \text{Prob}[H_0]/\text{Prob}[H_1]$. After gathering our data, we construct the Bayes factor, which summarizes the weight of the sample evidence in favor of one model or the other. After the data have been analyzed, we have our "posterior odds ratio," $P_{01}\,|\,\text{data} = \text{Bayes factor} \times P_{01}$. The upshot is that ex post, neither model is discarded; we have merely revised our assessment of the comparative likelihood of the two in the face of the sample data. Of course, this still leaves the specification question open. Faced with a choice among models, how can we best use the information we have? Recent work on **Bayesian model averaging** [Hoeting et al. (1999)] has suggested an answer.

An application by Wright (2003) provides an interesting illustration. Recent advances such as Bayesian VARs have improved the forecasting performance of econometric models. Stock and Watson (2001, 2004) report that striking improvements in predictive performance of international inflation can be obtained by averaging a large number of forecasts from different models and sources. The result is remarkably consistent across subperiods and countries. Two ideas are suggested by this outcome. First, the idea of blending different models is very much in the spirit of Hansen's fourth point. Second, note that the focus of the improvement is not on the fit of the model (point 3), but its predictive ability. Stock and Watson suggested that simple equal-weighted averaging, while one could not readily explain why, seems to bring large improvements. Wright proposed Bayesian model averaging as a means of making the choice of the weights for the average more systematic and of gaining even greater predictive performance.

Leamer (1978) appears to be the first to propose Bayesian model averaging as a means of combining models. The idea has been studied more recently by Min and Zellner (1993) for output growth forecasting, Doppelhofer et al. (2000) for cross-country growth regressions, Koop and Potter (2004) for macroeconomic forecasts, and others. Assume that there are $M$ models to be considered, indexed by $m = 1, \dots, M$. For simplicity, we will write the $m$th model in a simple form, $f_m(\mathbf{y}\,|\,\mathbf{Z}, \boldsymbol{\theta}_m)$ where $f(.)$ is the density, $\mathbf{y}$ and $\mathbf{Z}$ are the data, and $\boldsymbol{\theta}_m$ is the parameter vector for model $m$. Assume, as well, that model $m^*$, is the true model, unknown to the analyst. The analyst has priors $\pi_m$ over the probabilities that model $m$ is the correct model, so $\pi_m$ is the prior probability that $m = m^*$. The posterior probabilities for the models are

$$\Pi_m = \text{Prob}(m = m^* \,|\, \mathbf{y}, \mathbf{Z}) = \frac{P(\mathbf{y}, \mathbf{Z}\,|\,m)\pi_m}{\sum_{r=1}^{M} P(\mathbf{y}, \mathbf{Z}\,|\,r)\pi_r}, \tag{7-21}$$

where $P(\mathbf{y}, \mathbf{Z}\,|\,m)$ is the marginal likelihood for the $m$th model,

$$P(\mathbf{y}, \mathbf{Z}\,|\,m) = \int_{\theta_m} P(\mathbf{y}, \mathbf{Z}\,|\,\theta_m, m)\,P(\theta_m)d\theta_m, \tag{7-22}$$

while $P(\mathbf{y}, \mathbf{Z}\,|\,\theta_m, m)$ is the conditional (on $\theta_m$) likelihood for the $m$th model and $P(\theta_m)$ is the analyst's prior over the parameters of the $m$th model. This provides an alternative set of weights to the $\Pi_m = 1/M$ suggested by Stock and Watson. Let $\hat{\theta}_m$ denote the

Bayesian estimate (posterior mean) of the parameters of model $m$. (See Chapter 18.) Each model provides an appropriate posterior forecast density, $f^*(\mathbf{y} \mid \mathbf{Z}, \hat{\theta}_m, m)$. The Bayesian model averaged forecast density would then be

$$\bar{f}^* = \sum_{m=1}^{M} f^*(\mathbf{y} \mid \mathbf{Z}, \hat{\theta}, m) \Pi_m. \tag{7-23}$$

A point forecast would be a similarly weighted average of the forecasts from the individual models.

### Example 7.4  Bayesian Averaging of Classical Estimates

Many researchers have expressed skepticism of Bayesian methods because of the apparent arbitrariness of the specifications of prior densities over unknown parameters. In the Bayesian model averaging setting, the analyst requires prior densities over not only the model probabilities, $\pi_m$, but also the model specific parameters, $\theta_m$. In their application, Doppelhofer, Miller, and Sala-i-Martin (2000) were interested in the appropriate set of regressors to include in a long-term macroeconomic (income) growth equation. With 32 candidates, $M$ for their application was $2^{32}$ (minus one if the zero regressors model is ignored), or roughly four billion. Forming this many priors would be optimistic in the extreme. The authors proposed a novel method of weighting a large subset (roughly 21 million) of the $2^M$ possible (classical) least squares regressions. The weights are formed using a Bayesian procedure, however, the estimates that are weighted are the classical least squares estimates. While this saves considerable computational effort, it still requires the computation of millions of least squares coefficient vectors. [See Sala-i-Martin (1997).] The end result is a model with 12 independent variables.

## 7.6  SUMMARY AND CONCLUSIONS

This is the last of six chapters that we have devoted specifically to the most heavily used tool in econometrics, the classical linear regression model. We began in Chapter 2 with a statement of the regression model. Chapter 3 then described computation of the parameters by least squares—a purely algebraic exercise. Chapter 4 reinterpreted least squares as an estimator of an unknown parameter vector, and described the finite sample and large sample characteristics of the sampling distribution of the estimator. Chapters 5 and 6 were devoted to building and sharpening the regression model, with tools for developing the functional form and statistical results for testing hypotheses about the underlying population. In this chapter, we have examined some broad issues related to model specification and selection of a model among a set of competing alternatives. The concepts considered here are tied very closely to one of the pillars of the paradigm of econometrics, that underlying the model is a theoretical construction, a set of true behavioral relationships that constitute *the model*. It is only on this notion that the concepts of bias and biased estimation and model selection make any sense—"bias" as a concept can only be described with respect to some underlying "model" against which an estimator can be said to be biased. That is, there must be a yardstick. This concept is a central result in the analysis of specification, where we considered the implications of underfitting (omitting variables) and overfitting (including superfluous variables) the model. We concluded this chapter (and our discussion of the classical linear regression model) with an examination of procedures that are used to choose among competing model specifications.

## Key Terms and Concepts

- Adjusted R-squared
- Akaike Information Criterion
- Bayesian model averaging
- Bayesian Information Criterion
- Biased estimator
- Comprehensive model
- Encompassing principle
- General-to-simple strategy

- Inclusion of superfluous variables
- $J$ test
- Kullback–Leibler Information Criterion
- Mean-squared error
- Model selection
- Nonnested models
- Omission of relevant variables

- Omitted variable formula
- Prediction criterion
- Pretest estimator
- Schwarz criterion
- Simple-to-general
- Specification analysis
- Stepwise model building
- Vuong's test

## Exercises

1. Suppose the true regression model is given by (7-2). The result in (7-4) shows that if either $\mathbf{P}_{1.2}$ is nonzero or $\boldsymbol{\beta}_2$ is nonzero, then regression of $\mathbf{y}$ on $\mathbf{X}_1$ alone produces a biased and inconsistent estimator of $\boldsymbol{\beta}_1$. Suppose the objective is to forecast $\mathbf{y}$, not to estimate the parameters. Consider regression of $\mathbf{y}$ on $\mathbf{X}_1$ alone to estimate $\boldsymbol{\beta}_1$ with $\mathbf{b}_1$ (which is biased). Is the forecast of $\mathbf{y}$ computed using $\mathbf{X}_1\mathbf{b}_1$ also biased? Assume that $E[\mathbf{X}_2 \mid \mathbf{X}_1]$ is a linear function of $\mathbf{X}_1$. Discuss your findings generally. What are the implications for prediction when variables are omitted from a regression?

2. Compare the mean squared errors of $b_1$ and $b_{1.2}$ in Section 7.2.2. (Hint: the comparison depends on the data and the model parameters, but you can devise a compact expression for the two quantities.)

3. An individual term in the log likelihood function for the linear regression model with normally distributed disturbances is shown in (7-15). Show that at the maximum likelihood estimators of $\mathbf{b}$ for $\boldsymbol{\beta}$ and $\mathbf{e}'\mathbf{e}/n$ for $\sigma^2$, the log likelihood is an increasing function of $R^2$ for the model.

4. Show that the model of the alternative hypothesis in Example 7.2 can be written

$$H_1: \; C_t = \theta_1 + \theta_2 Y_t + \theta_3 Y_{t-1} + \sum_{s=2}^{\infty} \theta_{s+2} Y_{t-s} + \varepsilon_{it} + \sum_{s=1}^{\infty} \lambda_s \varepsilon_{t-s}.$$

As such, it does appear that $H_0$ is a restriction on $H_1$. However, because there are an infinite number of constraints, this does not reduce the test to a standard test of restrictions. It does suggest the connections between the two formulations. (We will revisit models of this sort in Chapter 20.)

## Applications

1. The $J$ test in Example 7.2 is carried out using more than 50 years of data. It is optimistic to hope that the underlying structure of the economy did not change in 50 years. Does the result of the test carried out in Example 7.2 persist if it is based on data only from 1980 to 2000? Repeat the computation with this subset of the data.

# 8

# THE GENERALIZED
# REGRESSION MODEL AND
# HETEROSCEDASTICITY

―――=☙☙☙=―――

## 8.1 INTRODUCTION

In this and the next several chapters, we will extend the multiple regression model to disturbances that violate assumption A4 of the classical regression model. The **generalized linear regression model** is

$$\mathbf{y} = \mathbf{X}\boldsymbol{\beta} + \boldsymbol{\varepsilon},$$

$$E[\boldsymbol{\varepsilon} \mid \mathbf{X}] = \mathbf{0},$$

$$E[\boldsymbol{\varepsilon}\boldsymbol{\varepsilon}' \mid \mathbf{X}] = \sigma^2 \boldsymbol{\Omega} = \boldsymbol{\Sigma},$$

(8-1)

where $\boldsymbol{\Omega}$ is a positive definite matrix. (The covariance matrix is written in the form $\sigma^2\boldsymbol{\Omega}$ at several points so that we can obtain the classical model, $\sigma^2\mathbf{I}$, as a convenient special case.)

The two leading cases we will consider in detail are **heteroscedasticity** and **autocorrelation.** Disturbances are heteroscedastic when they have different variances. Heteroscedasticity arises in volatile high-frequency time-series data such as daily observations in financial markets and in cross-section data where the scale of the dependent variable and the explanatory power of the model tend to vary across observations. Microeconomic data such as expenditure surveys are typical. The disturbances are still assumed to be uncorrelated across observations, so $\sigma^2\boldsymbol{\Omega}$ would be

$$\sigma^2 \boldsymbol{\Omega} = \sigma^2 \begin{bmatrix} \omega_1 & 0 & \cdots & 0 \\ 0 & \omega_2 & \cdots & 0 \\ & & \vdots & \\ 0 & 0 & \cdots & \omega_n \end{bmatrix} = \begin{bmatrix} \sigma_1^2 & 0 & \cdots & 0 \\ 0 & \sigma_2^2 & \cdots & 0 \\ & & \vdots & \\ 0 & 0 & \cdots & \sigma_n^2 \end{bmatrix}.$$

(The first mentioned situation involving financial data is more complex than this, and is examined in detail in Chapter 19.)

Autocorrelation is usually found in time-series data. Economic time series often display a "memory" in that variation around the regression function is not independent from one period to the next. The seasonally adjusted price and quantity series published by government agencies are examples. Time-series data are usually homoscedastic, so $\sigma^2\boldsymbol{\Omega}$ might be

$$\sigma^2\boldsymbol{\Omega} = \sigma^2 \begin{bmatrix} 1 & \rho_1 & \cdots & \rho_{n-1} \\ \rho_1 & 1 & \cdots & \rho_{n-2} \\ & & \vdots & \\ \rho_{n-1} & \rho_{n-2} & \cdots & 1 \end{bmatrix}.$$

The values that appear off the diagonal depend on the model used for the disturbance. In most cases, consistent with the notion of a fading memory, the values decline as we move away from the diagonal.

    **Panel data** sets, consisting of cross sections observed at several points in time, may exhibit both characteristics. We shall consider them in Chapter 9. This chapter presents some general results for this extended model. We will examine the model of heteroscedasticity in this chapter and in Chapter 16. A general model of autocorrelation appears in Chapter 19. Chapters 9 and 10 examine in detail specific types of generalized regression models.

    Our earlier results for the classical model will have to be modified. We will take the following approach on general results and in the specific cases of heteroscedasticity and serial correlation:

1. We first consider the consequences for the least squares estimator of the more general form of the regression model. This will include assessing the effect of ignoring the complication of the generalized model and of devising an appropriate estimation strategy, still based on least squares.
2. We will examine alternative estimation approaches that can make better use of the characteristics of the model. Minimal assumptions about $\boldsymbol{\Omega}$ are made at this point.
3. We then narrow the assumptions and begin to look for methods of detecting the failure of the classical model—that is, we formulate procedures for testing the specification of the classical model against the generalized regression.
4. The final step in the analysis is to formulate **parametric models** that make specific assumptions about $\boldsymbol{\Omega}$. Estimators in this setting are some form of generalized least squares or maximum likelihood which is developed in Chapter 16.

The model is examined in general terms in this chapter. Major applications to panel data and multiple equation systems are considered in Chapters 9 and 10.

## 8.2   LEAST SQUARES ESTIMATION

The essential results for the classical model with **spherical disturbances**

$$E[\boldsymbol{\varepsilon} \mid \mathbf{X}] = \mathbf{0}$$

and

$$E[\boldsymbol{\varepsilon}\boldsymbol{\varepsilon}' \mid \mathbf{X}] = \sigma^2 \mathbf{I} \tag{8-2}$$

are presented in Chapters 2 through 7. To reiterate, we found that the **ordinary least squares (OLS) estimator**

$$\mathbf{b} = (\mathbf{X'X})^{-1}\mathbf{X'y} = \boldsymbol{\beta} + (\mathbf{X'X})^{-1}\mathbf{X'\varepsilon} \tag{8-3}$$

is best linear unbiased (BLU), consistent and asymptotically normally distributed (CAN), and if the disturbances are normally distributed, like other maximum likelihood estimators considered in Chapter 16, asymptotically efficient among all CAN estimators. We now consider which of these properties continue to hold in the model of (8-1).

To summarize, the least squares estimators retain only some of their desirable properties in this model. Least squares remains unbiased, consistent, and asymptotically normally distributed. It will, however, no longer be efficient—this claim remains to be verified—and the usual inference procedures are no longer appropriate.

### 8.2.1 FINITE-SAMPLE PROPERTIES OF ORDINARY LEAST SQUARES

By taking expectations on both sides of (8-3), we find that if $E[\varepsilon \mid \mathbf{X}] = \mathbf{0}$, then

$$E[\mathbf{b}] = E_{\mathbf{X}}[E[\mathbf{b} \mid \mathbf{X}]] = \boldsymbol{\beta}. \tag{8-4}$$

Therefore, we have the following theorem.

---

**THEOREM 8.1** **Finite-Sample Properties of b in the Generalized Regression Model**

*If the regressors and disturbances are uncorrelated, then the unbiasedness of least squares is unaffected by violations of assumption (8-2). The least squares estimator is unbiased in the generalized regression model. With nonstochastic regressors, or conditional on* $\mathbf{X}$, *the sampling variance of the least squares estimator is*

$$
\begin{aligned}
\text{Var}[\mathbf{b} \mid \mathbf{X}] &= E[(\mathbf{b} - \boldsymbol{\beta})(\mathbf{b} - \boldsymbol{\beta})' \mid \mathbf{X}] \\
&= E[(\mathbf{X'X})^{-1}\mathbf{X'\varepsilon\varepsilon'X}(\mathbf{X'X})^{-1} \mid \mathbf{X}] \\
&= (\mathbf{X'X})^{-1}\mathbf{X'}(\sigma^2\boldsymbol{\Omega})\mathbf{X}(\mathbf{X'X})^{-1} \\
&= \frac{\sigma^2}{n}\left(\frac{1}{n}\mathbf{X'X}\right)^{-1}\left(\frac{1}{n}\mathbf{X'\Omega X}\right)\left(\frac{1}{n}\mathbf{X'X}\right)^{-1}.
\end{aligned} \tag{8-5}
$$

*If the regressors are stochastic, then the unconditional variance is* $E_{\mathbf{X}}[\text{Var}[\mathbf{b} \mid \mathbf{X}]]$. *In (8-3),* $\mathbf{b}$ *is a linear function of* $\varepsilon$. *Therefore, if* $\varepsilon$ *is normally distributed, then*

$$\mathbf{b} \mid \mathbf{X} \sim N[\boldsymbol{\beta}, \sigma^2(\mathbf{X'X})^{-1}(\mathbf{X'\Omega X})(\mathbf{X'X})^{-1}].$$

---

The end result is that **b** has properties that are similar to those in the classical regression case. Because the variance of the least squares estimator is not $\sigma^2(\mathbf{X'X})^{-1}$, however, statistical inference based on $s^2(\mathbf{X'X})^{-1}$ may be misleading. Not only is this the wrong matrix to be used, but $s^2$ may be a biased estimator of $\sigma^2$. There is usually no way to know whether $\sigma^2(\mathbf{X'X})^{-1}$ is larger or smaller than the true variance of **b**, so even with a good estimator of $\sigma^2$, the conventional estimator of $\text{Var}[\mathbf{b} \mid \mathbf{X}]$ may not be particularly useful. Finally, because we have dispensed with the fundamental underlying assumption, the familiar inference procedures based on the $F$ and $t$ distributions will no longer be appropriate. One issue we will explore at several points following is how badly one is likely to go awry if the result in (8-5) is ignored and if the use of the familiar procedures based on $s^2(\mathbf{X'X})^{-1}$ is continued.

### 8.2.2 ASYMPTOTIC PROPERTIES OF LEAST SQUARES

If $\text{Var}[\mathbf{b} \mid \mathbf{X}]$ converges to zero, then $\mathbf{b}$ is mean square consistent. With well-behaved regressors, $(\mathbf{X'X}/n)^{-1}$ will converge to a constant matrix. But $(\sigma^2/n)(\mathbf{X'\Omega X}/n)$ need not converge at all. By writing this product as

$$\frac{\sigma^2}{n}\left(\frac{\mathbf{X'\Omega X}}{n}\right) = \left(\frac{\sigma^2}{n}\right)\left(\frac{\sum_{i=1}^{n}\sum_{j=1}^{n}\omega_{ij}\mathbf{x}_i\mathbf{x}_j'}{n}\right) \tag{8-6}$$

we see that though the leading constant will, by itself, converge to zero, the matrix is a sum of $n^2$ terms, divided by $n$. Thus, the product is a scalar that is $O(1/n)$ times a matrix that is, at least at this juncture, $O(n)$, which is $O(1)$. So, it does appear at first blush that if the product in (8-6) does converge, it might converge to a matrix of nonzero constants. In this case, the covariance matrix of the least squares estimator would not converge to zero, and consistency would be difficult to establish. We will examine in some detail, the conditions under which the matrix in (8-6) converges to a constant matrix.[1] If it does, then because $\sigma^2/n$ does vanish, ordinary least squares is consistent as well as unbiased.

---

**THEOREM 8.2** **Consistency of OLS in the Generalized Regression Model**

*If $\mathbf{Q} = \text{plim}(\mathbf{X'X}/n)$ and $\text{plim}(\mathbf{X'\Omega X}/n)$ are both finite positive definite matrices, then $\mathbf{b}$ is consistent for $\beta$. Under the assumed conditions,*

$$\text{plim}\,\mathbf{b} = \beta. \tag{8-7}$$

---

The conditions in Theorem 8.2 depend on both $\mathbf{X}$ and $\mathbf{\Omega}$. An alternative formula[2] that separates the two components is as follows. Ordinary least squares is consistent in the generalized regression model if:

1. The smallest characteristic root of $\mathbf{X'X}$ increases without bound as $n \to \infty$, which implies that $\text{plim}(\mathbf{X'X})^{-1} = \mathbf{0}$. If the regressors satisfy the Grenander conditions **G1** through **G3** of Section 4.9.1, then they will meet this requirement.
2. The largest characteristic root of $\mathbf{\Omega}$ is finite for all $n$. For the heteroscedastic model, the variances are the characteristic roots, which requires them to be finite. For models with autocorrelation, the requirements are that the elements of $\mathbf{\Omega}$ be finite and that the off-diagonal elements not be too large relative to the diagonal elements. We will examine this condition at several points below.

---
[1] In order for the product in (8-6) to vanish, it would be sufficient for $(\mathbf{X'\Omega X}/n)$ to be $O(n^\delta)$ where $\delta < 1$.

[2] Amemiya (1985, p. 184).

The least squares estimator is asymptotically normally distributed if the limiting distribution of

$$\sqrt{n}(\mathbf{b} - \boldsymbol{\beta}) = \left(\frac{\mathbf{X}'\mathbf{X}}{n}\right)^{-1} \frac{1}{\sqrt{n}}\mathbf{X}'\boldsymbol{\varepsilon} \tag{8-8}$$

is normal. If $\text{plim}(\mathbf{X}'\mathbf{X}/n) = \mathbf{Q}$, then the limiting distribution of the right-hand side is the same as that of

$$\mathbf{v}_{n,LS} = \mathbf{Q}^{-1}\frac{1}{\sqrt{n}}\mathbf{X}'\boldsymbol{\varepsilon} = \mathbf{Q}^{-1}\frac{1}{\sqrt{n}}\sum_{i=1}^{n}\mathbf{x}_i\varepsilon_i, \tag{8-9}$$

where $\mathbf{x}_i'$ is a row of $\mathbf{X}$ (assuming, of course, that the limiting distribution exists at all). The question now is whether a central limit theorem can be applied directly to $\mathbf{v}$. If the disturbances are merely heteroscedastic and still uncorrelated, then the answer is generally yes. In fact, we already showed this result in Section 4.9.2 when we invoked the Lindeberg–Feller central limit theorem (D.19) or the Lyapounov theorem (D.20). The theorems allow unequal variances in the sum. The exact variance of the sum is

$$E_{\mathbf{x}}\left[\text{Var}\left[\frac{1}{\sqrt{n}}\sum_{i=1}^{n}\mathbf{x}_i\varepsilon_i\right]\bigg|\mathbf{x}_i\right] = \frac{\sigma^2}{n}\sum_{i=1}^{n}\omega_i\mathbf{Q}_i,$$

which, for our purposes, we would require to converge to a positive definite matrix. In our analysis of the classical model, the heterogeneity of the variances arose because of the regressors, but we still achieved the limiting normal distribution in (4-27) through (4-33). All that has changed here is that the variance of $\varepsilon$ varies across observations *as well*. Therefore, *the proof of asymptotic normality in Section 4.9.2 is general enough to include this model without modification.* As long as $\mathbf{X}$ is well behaved and the diagonal elements of $\boldsymbol{\Omega}$ are finite and well behaved, the least squares estimator is asymptotically normally distributed, with the covariance matrix given in (8-5). That is:

> *In the heteroscedastic case, if the variances of $\varepsilon_i$ are finite and are not dominated by any single term, so that the conditions of the Lindeberg–Feller central limit theorem apply to $\mathbf{v}_{n,LS}$ in (8-9), then the least squares estimator is asymptotically normally distributed with covariance matrix*

$$\text{Asy. Var}[\mathbf{b}] = \frac{\sigma^2}{n}\mathbf{Q}^{-1}\text{plim}\left(\frac{1}{n}\mathbf{X}'\boldsymbol{\Omega}\mathbf{X}\right)\mathbf{Q}^{-1}. \tag{8-10}$$

For the most general case, asymptotic normality is much more difficult to establish because the sums in (8-9) are not necessarily sums of independent or even uncorrelated random variables. Nonetheless, Amemiya (1985, p. 187) and Anderson (1971) have established the asymptotic normality of $\mathbf{b}$ in a model of autocorrelated disturbances general enough to include most of the settings we are likely to meet in practice. We will revisit this issue in Chapters 19 and 20 when we examine time-series modeling. We can conclude that, except in particularly unfavorable cases, we have the following theorem.

> **THEOREM 8.3**  **Asymptotic Distribution of b in the GR Model**
> *If the regressors are sufficiently well behaved and the off-diagonal terms in $\boldsymbol{\Omega}$ diminish sufficiently rapidly, then the least squares estimator is asymptotically normally distributed with mean $\boldsymbol{\beta}$ and covariance matrix given in (8-10).*

### 8.2.3  ROBUST ESTIMATION OF ASYMPTOTIC COVARIANCE MATRICES

There is a remaining question regarding all the preceding results. In view of (8-5), is it necessary to discard ordinary least squares as an estimator? Certainly if $\boldsymbol{\Omega}$ is known, then, as shown in Section 8.6, there is a simple and efficient estimator available based on it, and the answer is yes. If $\boldsymbol{\Omega}$ is unknown but its structure is known and we can estimate $\boldsymbol{\Omega}$ using sample information, then the answer is less clear-cut. In many cases, basing estimation of $\boldsymbol{\beta}$ on some alternative procedure that uses an $\hat{\boldsymbol{\Omega}}$ will be preferable to ordinary least squares. This subject is covered in Chapters 9 and 10. The third possibility is that $\boldsymbol{\Omega}$ is completely unknown, both as to its structure and the specific values of its elements. In this situation, least squares or instrumental variables may be the only estimator available, and as such, the only available strategy is to try to devise an estimator for the appropriate asymptotic covariance matrix of **b**.

If $\sigma^2\boldsymbol{\Omega}$ were known, then the *estimator* of the asymptotic covariance matrix of **b** in (8-10) would be

$$\mathbf{V}_{\mathrm{OLS}} = \frac{1}{n}\left(\frac{1}{n}\mathbf{X}'\mathbf{X}\right)^{-1}\left(\frac{1}{n}\mathbf{X}'[\sigma^2\boldsymbol{\Omega}]\mathbf{X}\right)\left(\frac{1}{n}\mathbf{X}'\mathbf{X}\right)^{-1}.$$

The matrix of sums of squares and cross products in the left and right matrices are sample data that are readily estimable. The problem is the center matrix that involves the unknown $\sigma^2\boldsymbol{\Omega}$. For estimation purposes, note that $\sigma^2$ is not a separate unknown parameter. Because $\boldsymbol{\Omega}$ is an unknown matrix, it can be scaled arbitrarily, say, by $\kappa$, and with $\sigma^2$ scaled by $1/\kappa$, the same product remains. In our applications, we will remove the indeterminacy by assuming that $\mathrm{tr}(\boldsymbol{\Omega}) = n$, as it is when $\sigma^2\boldsymbol{\Omega} = \sigma^2\mathbf{I}$ in the classical model. For now, just let $\boldsymbol{\Sigma} = \sigma^2\boldsymbol{\Omega}$. It might seem that to estimate $(1/n)\mathbf{X}'\boldsymbol{\Sigma}\mathbf{X}$, an estimator of $\boldsymbol{\Sigma}$, which contains $n(n+1)/2$ unknown parameters, is required. But fortunately (because with $n$ observations, this method is going to be hopeless), this observation is not quite right. What is required is an estimator of the $K(K+1)/2$ unknown elements in the matrix

$$\mathrm{plim}\,\mathbf{Q}_* = \mathrm{plim}\frac{1}{n}\sum_{i=1}^{n}\sum_{j=1}^{n}\sigma_{ij}\mathbf{x}_i\mathbf{x}_j'.$$

The point is that $\mathbf{Q}_*$ is a matrix of sums of squares and cross products that involves $\sigma_{ij}$ *and* the rows of **X**. The least squares estimator **b** is a consistent estimator of $\boldsymbol{\beta}$, which implies that the least squares residuals $e_i$ are "pointwise" consistent estimators of their population counterparts $\varepsilon_i$. The general approach, then, will be to use **X** and **e** to devise an estimator of $\mathbf{Q}_*$.

This (perhaps somewhat counterintuitive) principle is exceedingly useful in modern research. Most important applications, including general models of heteroscedasticity, autocorrelation, and a variety of panel data models, can be estimated in this fashion. The payoff is that the estimator frees the analyst from the necessity to assume a particular structure for $\boldsymbol{\Omega}$. With tools such as the robust covariance estimator in hand, one of the distinct trends in current research is away from narrow assumptions and toward broad, robust models such as these. The heteroscedasticity and autocorrelation cases are considered in Section 8.4.4 and Chapter 19, respectively, while several models for panel data are detailed in Chapter 9.

## 8.3 EFFICIENT ESTIMATION BY GENERALIZED LEAST SQUARES

Efficient estimation of $\boldsymbol{\beta}$ in the generalized regression model requires knowledge of $\boldsymbol{\Omega}$. To begin, it is useful to consider cases in which $\boldsymbol{\Omega}$ is a known, symmetric, positive definite matrix. This assumption will occasionally be true, though in most models, $\boldsymbol{\Omega}$ will contain unknown parameters that must also be estimated. We shall examine this case in Section 8.7.

### 8.3.1 GENERALIZED LEAST SQUARES (GLS)

Because $\boldsymbol{\Omega}$ is a positive definite symmetric matrix, it can be factored into

$$\boldsymbol{\Omega} = \mathbf{C}\boldsymbol{\Lambda}\mathbf{C}',$$

where the columns of $\mathbf{C}$ are the characteristic vectors of $\boldsymbol{\Omega}$ and the characteristic roots of $\boldsymbol{\Omega}$ are arrayed in the diagonal matrix $\boldsymbol{\Lambda}$. Let $\boldsymbol{\Lambda}^{1/2}$ be the diagonal matrix with $i$th diagonal element $\sqrt{\lambda_i}$, and let $\mathbf{T} = \mathbf{C}\boldsymbol{\Lambda}^{1/2}$. Then $\boldsymbol{\Omega} = \mathbf{T}\mathbf{T}'$. Also, let $\mathbf{P}' = \mathbf{C}\boldsymbol{\Lambda}^{-1/2}$, so $\boldsymbol{\Omega}^{-1} = \mathbf{P}'\mathbf{P}$. Premultiply the model in (8-1) by $\mathbf{P}$ to obtain

$$\mathbf{P}\mathbf{y} = \mathbf{P}\mathbf{X}\boldsymbol{\beta} + \mathbf{P}\boldsymbol{\varepsilon}$$

or

$$\mathbf{y}_* = \mathbf{X}_*\boldsymbol{\beta} + \boldsymbol{\varepsilon}_*. \tag{8-11}$$

The conditional variance of $\boldsymbol{\varepsilon}_*$ is

$$E[\boldsymbol{\varepsilon}_*\boldsymbol{\varepsilon}_*' \mid \mathbf{X}_*] = \mathbf{P}\sigma^2\boldsymbol{\Omega}\mathbf{P}' = \sigma^2\mathbf{I},$$

so the classical regression model applies to this transformed model. Because $\boldsymbol{\Omega}$ is assumed to be known, $\mathbf{y}_*$ and $\mathbf{X}_*$ are observed data. In the classical model, ordinary least squares is efficient; hence,

$$\hat{\boldsymbol{\beta}} = (\mathbf{X}_*'\mathbf{X}_*)^{-1}\mathbf{X}_*'\mathbf{y}_*$$
$$= (\mathbf{X}'\mathbf{P}'\mathbf{P}\mathbf{X})^{-1}\mathbf{X}'\mathbf{P}'\mathbf{P}\mathbf{y}$$
$$= (\mathbf{X}'\boldsymbol{\Omega}^{-1}\mathbf{X})^{-1}\mathbf{X}'\boldsymbol{\Omega}^{-1}\mathbf{y}$$

is the **efficient estimator** of $\boldsymbol{\beta}$. This estimator is the **generalized least squares (GLS)** or Aitken (1935) estimator of $\boldsymbol{\beta}$. This estimator is in contrast to the ordinary least squares (OLS) estimator, which uses a "weighting matrix," $\mathbf{I}$, instead of $\boldsymbol{\Omega}^{-1}$. By appealing to the classical regression model in (8-11), we have the following theorem, which includes the generalized regression model analogs to our results of Chapter 4:

---

**THEOREM 8.4**   **Properties of the Generalized Least Squares Estimator**

*If $E[\boldsymbol{\varepsilon}_* \mid \mathbf{X}_*] = \mathbf{0}$, then*

$$E[\hat{\boldsymbol{\beta}} \mid \mathbf{X}_*] = E[(\mathbf{X}'_*\mathbf{X}_*)^{-1}\mathbf{X}'_*\mathbf{y}_* \mid \mathbf{X}_*] = \boldsymbol{\beta} + E[(\mathbf{X}'_*\mathbf{X}_*)^{-1}\mathbf{X}'_*\boldsymbol{\varepsilon}_* \mid \mathbf{X}_*] = \boldsymbol{\beta}.$$

*The GLS estimator $\hat{\boldsymbol{\beta}}$ is unbiased. This result is equivalent to $E[\mathbf{P}\boldsymbol{\varepsilon} \mid \mathbf{P}\mathbf{X}] = \mathbf{0}$, but because $\mathbf{P}$ is a matrix of known constants, we return to the familiar requirement $E[\boldsymbol{\varepsilon} \mid \mathbf{X}] = \mathbf{0}$. The requirement that the regressors and disturbances be uncorrelated is unchanged.*

*The GLS estimator is consistent if $\operatorname{plim}(1/n)\mathbf{X}'_*\mathbf{X}_* = \mathbf{Q}_*$, where $\mathbf{Q}_*$ is a finite positive definite matrix. Making the substitution, we see that this implies*

$$\operatorname{plim}[(1/n)\mathbf{X}'\boldsymbol{\Omega}^{-1}\mathbf{X}]^{-1} = \mathbf{Q}_*^{-1}. \tag{8-12}$$

*We require the transformed data $\mathbf{X}_* = \mathbf{P}\mathbf{X}$, not the original data $\mathbf{X}$, to be well behaved.[3] Under the assumption in (8-1), the following hold:*

*The GLS estimator is asymptotically normally distributed, with mean $\boldsymbol{\beta}$ and sampling variance*

$$\operatorname{Var}[\hat{\boldsymbol{\beta}} \mid \mathbf{X}_*] = \sigma^2(\mathbf{X}'_*\mathbf{X}_*)^{-1} = \sigma^2(\mathbf{X}'\boldsymbol{\Omega}^{-1}\mathbf{X})^{-1}. \tag{8-13}$$

*The GLS estimator $\hat{\boldsymbol{\beta}}$ is the minimum variance linear unbiased estimator in the generalized regression model. This statement follows by applying the Gauss–Markov theorem to the model in (8-11). The result in Theorem 8.4 is **Aitken's** (1935) **theorem**, and $\hat{\boldsymbol{\beta}}$ is sometimes called the Aitken estimator. This broad result includes the Gauss–Markov theorem as a special case when $\boldsymbol{\Omega} = \mathbf{I}$.*

---

For testing hypotheses, we can apply the full set of results in Chapter 5 to the transformed model in (8-11). For testing the $J$ linear restrictions, $\mathbf{R}\boldsymbol{\beta} = \mathbf{q}$, the appropriate statistic is

$$F[J, n-K] = \frac{(\mathbf{R}\hat{\boldsymbol{\beta}} - \mathbf{q})'[\mathbf{R}\hat{\sigma}^2(\mathbf{X}'_*\mathbf{X}_*)^{-1}\mathbf{R}']^{-1}(\mathbf{R}\hat{\boldsymbol{\beta}} - \mathbf{q})}{J} = \frac{(\hat{\boldsymbol{\varepsilon}}'_c\hat{\boldsymbol{\varepsilon}}_c - \hat{\boldsymbol{\varepsilon}}'\hat{\boldsymbol{\varepsilon}})/J}{\hat{\sigma}^2},$$

where the residual vector is

$$\hat{\boldsymbol{\varepsilon}} = \mathbf{y}_* - \mathbf{X}_*\hat{\boldsymbol{\beta}}$$

and

$$\hat{\sigma}^2 = \frac{\hat{\boldsymbol{\varepsilon}}'\hat{\boldsymbol{\varepsilon}}}{n-K} = \frac{(\mathbf{y} - \mathbf{X}\hat{\boldsymbol{\beta}})'\boldsymbol{\Omega}^{-1}(\mathbf{y} - \mathbf{X}\hat{\boldsymbol{\beta}})}{n-K}. \tag{8-14}$$

---

[3] Once again, to allow a time trend, we could weaken this assumption a bit.

The constrained GLS residuals, $\hat{\boldsymbol{\varepsilon}}_c = \mathbf{y}_* - \mathbf{X}_* \hat{\boldsymbol{\beta}}_c$, are based on

$$\hat{\boldsymbol{\beta}}_c = \hat{\boldsymbol{\beta}} - [\mathbf{X}'\boldsymbol{\Omega}^{-1}\mathbf{X}]^{-1}\mathbf{R}'[\mathbf{R}(\mathbf{X}'\boldsymbol{\Omega}^{-1}\mathbf{X})^{-1}\mathbf{R}']^{-1}(\mathbf{R}\hat{\boldsymbol{\beta}} - \mathbf{q}).[4]$$

To summarize, all the results for the classical model, including the usual inference procedures, apply to the transformed model in (8-11).

There is no precise counterpart to $R^2$ in the generalized regression model. Alternatives have been proposed, but care must be taken when using them. For example, one choice is the $R^2$ in the transformed regression, (8-11). But this regression need not have a constant term, so the $R^2$ is not bounded by zero and one. Even if there is a constant term, the transformed regression is a computational device, not the model of interest. That a good (or bad) fit is obtained in the "model" in (8-11) may be of no interest; the dependent variable in that model, $y_*$, is different from the one in the model as originally specified. The usual $R^2$ often suggests that the fit of the model is improved by a correction for heteroscedasticity and degraded by a correction for autocorrelation, but both changes can often be attributed to the computation of $y_*$. A more appealing fit measure might be based on the residuals from the original model once the GLS estimator is in hand, such as

$$R_G^2 = 1 - \frac{(\mathbf{y} - \mathbf{X}\hat{\boldsymbol{\beta}})'(\mathbf{y} - \mathbf{X}\hat{\boldsymbol{\beta}})}{\sum_{i=1}^{n}(y_i - \bar{y})^2}.$$

Like the earlier contender, however, this measure is not bounded in the unit interval. In addition, this measure cannot be reliably used to compare models. The generalized least squares estimator minimizes the **generalized sum of squares**

$$\boldsymbol{\varepsilon}_*'\boldsymbol{\varepsilon}_* = (\mathbf{y} - \mathbf{X}\boldsymbol{\beta})'\boldsymbol{\Omega}^{-1}(\mathbf{y} - \mathbf{X}\boldsymbol{\beta}),$$

not $\boldsymbol{\varepsilon}'\boldsymbol{\varepsilon}$. As such, there is no assurance, for example, that dropping a variable from the model will result in a decrease in $R_G^2$, as it will in $R^2$. Other goodness-of-fit measures, designed primarily to be a function of the sum of squared residuals (raw or weighted by $\boldsymbol{\Omega}^{-1}$) and to be bounded by zero and one, have been proposed.[5] Unfortunately, they all suffer from at least one of the previously noted shortcomings. The $R^2$-like measures in this setting are purely descriptive. That being the case, the squared sample correlation between the actual and predicted values, $r_{y,\hat{y}}^2 = corr^2(y, \hat{y}) = corr^2(y, \mathbf{x}'\hat{\boldsymbol{\beta}})$, would likely be a useful descriptor. Note, though, that this is not a proportion of variation explained, as is $R^2$; it is a measure of the agreement of the model predictions with the actual data.

### 8.3.2 FEASIBLE GENERALIZED LEAST SQUARES (FGLS)

To use the results of Section 8.3.1, $\boldsymbol{\Omega}$ must be known. If $\boldsymbol{\Omega}$ contains unknown parameters that must be estimated, then generalized least squares is not feasible. But with an unrestricted $\boldsymbol{\Omega}$, there are $n(n + 1)/2$ additional parameters in $\sigma^2\boldsymbol{\Omega}$. This number is far too many to estimate with $n$ observations. Obviously, some structure must be imposed on the model if we are to proceed.

---

[4]Note that this estimator is the constrained OLS estimator using the transformed data. [See (5-14).]

[5]See, example, Judge et al. (1985, p. 32) and Buse (1973).

The typical problem involves a small set of parameters $\theta$ such that $\boldsymbol{\Omega} = \boldsymbol{\Omega}(\theta)$. For example, a commonly used formula in time-series settings is

$$\boldsymbol{\Omega}(\rho) = \begin{bmatrix} 1 & \rho & \rho^2 & \rho^3 & \cdots & \rho^{n-1} \\ \rho & 1 & \rho & \rho^2 & \cdots & \rho^{n-2} \\ & & & & \vdots & \\ \rho^{n-1} & \rho^{n-2} & & \cdots & & 1 \end{bmatrix},$$

which involves only one additional unknown parameter. A model of heteroscedasticity that also has only one new parameter is

$$\sigma_i^2 = \sigma^2 z_i^\theta. \tag{8-15}$$

Suppose, then, that $\hat{\theta}$ is a consistent estimator of $\theta$. (We consider later how such an estimator might be obtained.) To make GLS estimation feasible, we shall use $\hat{\boldsymbol{\Omega}} = \boldsymbol{\Omega}(\hat{\theta})$ instead of the true $\boldsymbol{\Omega}$. The issue we consider here is whether using $\boldsymbol{\Omega}(\hat{\theta})$ requires us to change any of the results of Section 8.3.1.

It would seem that if plim $\hat{\theta} = \theta$, then using $\hat{\boldsymbol{\Omega}}$ is asymptotically equivalent to using the true $\boldsymbol{\Omega}$.[6] Let the **feasible generalized least squares (FGLS)** estimator be denoted

$$\hat{\hat{\boldsymbol{\beta}}} = (\mathbf{X}'\hat{\boldsymbol{\Omega}}^{-1}\mathbf{X})^{-1}\mathbf{X}'\hat{\boldsymbol{\Omega}}^{-1}\mathbf{y}.$$

Conditions that imply that $\hat{\hat{\boldsymbol{\beta}}}$ is asymptotically equivalent to $\hat{\boldsymbol{\beta}}$ are

$$\text{plim}\left[\left(\frac{1}{n}\mathbf{X}'\hat{\boldsymbol{\Omega}}^{-1}\mathbf{X}\right) - \left(\frac{1}{n}\mathbf{X}'\boldsymbol{\Omega}^{-1}\mathbf{X}\right)\right] = \mathbf{0} \tag{8-16}$$

and

$$\text{plim}\left[\left(\frac{1}{\sqrt{n}}\mathbf{X}'\hat{\boldsymbol{\Omega}}^{-1}\boldsymbol{\varepsilon}\right) - \left(\frac{1}{\sqrt{n}}\mathbf{X}'\boldsymbol{\Omega}^{-1}\boldsymbol{\varepsilon}\right)\right] = \mathbf{0}. \tag{8-17}$$

The first of these equations states that if the weighted sum of squares matrix based on the true $\boldsymbol{\Omega}$ converges to a positive definite matrix, then the one based on $\hat{\boldsymbol{\Omega}}$ converges to the same matrix. We are assuming that this is true. In the second condition, if the *transformed* regressors are well behaved, then the right-hand-side sum will have a limiting normal distribution. This condition is exactly the one we used in Chapter 4 to obtain the asymptotic distribution of the least squares estimator; here we are using the same results for $\mathbf{X}_*$ and $\boldsymbol{\varepsilon}_*$. Therefore, (8-17) requires the same condition to hold when $\boldsymbol{\Omega}$ is replaced with $\hat{\boldsymbol{\Omega}}$.[7]

These conditions, in principle, must be verified on a case-by-case basis. Fortunately, in most familiar settings, they are met. If we assume that they are, then the FGLS estimator based on $\hat{\theta}$ has the same asymptotic properties as the GLS estimator. This result is extremely useful. Note, especially, the following theorem.

---

[6]This equation is sometimes denoted plim $\hat{\boldsymbol{\Omega}} = \boldsymbol{\Omega}$. Because $\boldsymbol{\Omega}$ is $n \times n$, it cannot have a probability limit. We use this term to indicate convergence element by element.

[7]The condition actually requires only that if the right-hand sum has *any* limiting distribution, then the left-hand one has the same one. Conceivably, this distribution might not be the normal distribution, but that seems unlikely except in a specially constructed, theoretical case.

---

**THEOREM 8.5** Efficiency of the FGLS Estimator

*An asymptotically efficient FGLS estimator does not require that we have an efficient estimator of $\boldsymbol{\theta}$; only a consistent one is required to achieve full efficiency for the FGLS estimator.*

---

Except for the simplest cases, the finite-sample properties and exact distributions of FGLS estimators are unknown. The asymptotic efficiency of FGLS estimators may not carry over to small samples because of the variability introduced by the estimated $\boldsymbol{\Omega}$. Some analyses for the case of heteroscedasticity are given by Taylor (1977). A model of autocorrelation is analyzed by Griliches and Rao (1969). In both studies, the authors find that, over a broad range of parameters, FGLS is more efficient than least squares. But if the departure from the classical assumptions is not too severe, then least squares may be more efficient than FGLS in a small sample.

## 8.4 HETEROSCEDASTICITY

Regression disturbances whose variances are not constant across observations are **heteroscedastic.** Heteroscedasticity arises in numerous applications, in both cross-section and time-series data. For example, even after accounting for firm sizes, we expect to observe greater variation in the profits of large firms than in those of small ones. The variance of profits might also depend on product diversification, research and development expenditure, and industry characteristics and therefore might also vary across firms of similar sizes. When analyzing family spending patterns, we find that there is greater variation in expenditure on certain commodity groups among high-income families than low ones due to the greater discretion allowed by higher incomes.[8]

In the heteroscedastic regression model,

$$\text{Var}[\varepsilon_i \mid \mathbf{X}] = \sigma_i^2, \quad i = 1, \ldots, n.$$

We continue to assume that the disturbances are pairwise uncorrelated. Thus,

$$E[\boldsymbol{\varepsilon}\boldsymbol{\varepsilon}' \mid \mathbf{X}] = \sigma^2 \boldsymbol{\Omega} = \sigma^2 \begin{bmatrix} \omega_1 & 0 & 0 & \cdots & 0 \\ 0 & \omega_2 & 0 & \cdots & \\ & & & \vdots & \\ 0 & 0 & 0 & \cdots & \omega_n \end{bmatrix} = \begin{bmatrix} \sigma_1^2 & 0 & 0 & \cdots & 0 \\ 0 & \sigma_2^2 & 0 & \cdots & \\ & & & \vdots & \\ 0 & 0 & 0 & \cdots & \sigma_n^2 \end{bmatrix}.$$

It will sometimes prove useful to write $\sigma_i^2 = \sigma^2 \omega_i$. This form is an arbitrary scaling which allows us to use a normalization,

$$\text{tr}(\boldsymbol{\Omega}) = \sum_{i=1}^{n} \omega_i = n.$$

This makes the classical regression with homoscedastic disturbances a simple special case with $\omega_i = 1, i = 1, \ldots, n$. Intuitively, one might then think of the $\omega$'s as weights that are scaled in such a way as to reflect only the variety in the disturbance variances. The scale factor $\sigma^2$ then provides the overall scaling of the disturbance process.

---

[8]Prais and Houthakker (1955).

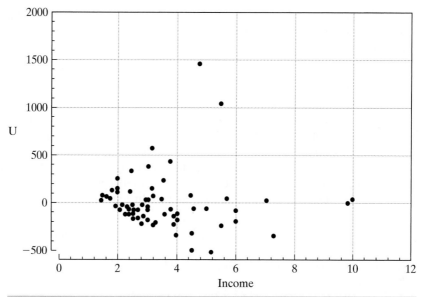

**FIGURE 8.1** Plot of Residuals Against Income.

**Example 8.1 Heteroscedastic Regression**
The data in Appendix Table F8.1 give monthly credit card expenditure for 100 individuals, sampled from a larger sample of 13,444 people. Linear regression of monthly expenditure on a constant, age, income and its square, and a dummy variable for home ownership using the 72 observations for which expenditure was nonzero produces the residuals plotted in Figure 8.1. The pattern of the residuals is characteristic of a regression with heteroscedasticity.

We will examine the heteroscedastic regression model, first in general terms, then with some specific forms of the disturbance covariance matrix. We begin by examining the consequences of heteroscedasticity for least squares estimation. We then consider **robust estimation.** Section 8.4.4 presents appropriate estimators of the asymptotic covariance matrix of the least squares estimator. Specification tests for heteroscedasticity are considered in Section 8.5. Sections 8.6 and 8.7 consider generalized (weighted) least squares, which requires knowledge at least of the form of $\mathbf{\Omega}$. Finally, two common applications are examined in Section 8.8.

## 8.4.1 ORDINARY LEAST SQUARES ESTIMATION

We showed in Section 8.2 that in the presence of heteroscedasticity, the least squares estimator $\mathbf{b}$ is still unbiased, consistent, and asymptotically normally distributed. The asymptotic covariance matrix is

$$\text{Asy. Var}[\mathbf{b}] = \frac{\sigma^2}{n}\left(\text{plim}\,\frac{1}{n}\,\mathbf{X}'\mathbf{X}\right)^{-1}\left(\text{plim}\,\frac{1}{n}\mathbf{X}'\mathbf{\Omega}\mathbf{X}\right)\left(\text{plim}\,\frac{1}{n}\mathbf{X}'\mathbf{X}\right)^{-1}.$$

Estimation of the asymptotic covariance matrix would be based on

$$\text{Var}[\mathbf{b}\mid\mathbf{X}] = (\mathbf{X}'\mathbf{X})^{-1}\left(\sigma^2\sum_{i=1}^{n}\omega_i\mathbf{x}_i\mathbf{x}_i'\right)(\mathbf{X}'\mathbf{X})^{-1}. \qquad \textbf{(8-18)}$$

[See (8-5).] Assuming, as usual, that the regressors are well behaved, so that $(\mathbf{X'X}/n)^{-1}$ converges to a positive definite matrix, we find that the mean square consistency of $\mathbf{b}$ depends on the limiting behavior of the matrix:

$$\mathbf{Q}_n^* = \frac{\mathbf{X'\Omega X}}{n} = \frac{1}{n} \sum_{i=1}^{n} \omega_i \mathbf{x}_i \mathbf{x}_i'.$$

If $\mathbf{Q}_n^*$ converges to a positive definite matrix $\mathbf{Q}^*$, then as $n \to \infty$, $\mathbf{b}$ will converge to $\boldsymbol{\beta}$ in mean square. Under most circumstances, if $\omega_i$ is finite for all $i$, then we would expect this result to be true. Note that $\mathbf{Q}_n^*$ is a weighted sum of the squares and cross products of $\mathbf{x}$ with weights $\omega_i/n$, which sum to 1. We have already assumed that another weighted sum, $\mathbf{X'X}/n$, in which the weights are $1/n$, converges to a positive definite matrix $\mathbf{Q}$, so it would be surprising if $\mathbf{Q}_n^*$ did not converge as well. In general, then, we would expect that

$$\mathbf{b} \stackrel{a}{\sim} N\left[\boldsymbol{\beta}, \frac{\sigma^2}{n}\mathbf{Q}^{-1}\mathbf{Q}^*\mathbf{Q}^{-1}\right], \quad \text{with } \mathbf{Q}^* = \text{plim } \mathbf{Q}_n^*.$$

A formal proof is based on Section 4.9 with $\mathbf{Q}_i = \omega_i \mathbf{x}_i \mathbf{x}_i'$.

### 8.4.2 INEFFICIENCY OF LEAST SQUARES

It follows from our earlier results that $\mathbf{b}$ is inefficient relative to the GLS estimator. By how much will depend on the setting, but there is some generality to the pattern. As might be expected, the greater is the dispersion in $\omega_i$ across observations, the greater the efficiency of GLS over OLS. The impact of this on the efficiency of estimation will depend crucially on the nature of the disturbance variances. In the usual cases, in which $\omega_i$ depends on variables that appear elsewhere in the model, the greater is the dispersion in these variables, the greater will be the gain to using GLS. It is important to note, however, that both these comparisons are based on knowledge of $\boldsymbol{\Omega}$. In practice, one of two cases is likely to be true. If we do have detailed knowledge of $\boldsymbol{\Omega}$, the performance of the inefficient estimator is a moot point. We will use GLS or feasible GLS anyway. In the more common case, we will not have detailed knowledge of $\boldsymbol{\Omega}$, so the comparison is not possible.

### 8.4.3 THE ESTIMATED COVARIANCE MATRIX OF b

If the type of heteroscedasticity is known with certainty, then the ordinary least squares estimator is undesirable; we should use generalized least squares instead. The precise form of the heteroscedasticity is usually unknown, however. In that case, generalized least squares is not usable, and we may need to salvage what we can from the results of ordinary least squares.

The conventionally estimated covariance matrix for the least squares estimator $\sigma^2(\mathbf{X'X})^{-1}$ is inappropriate; the appropriate matrix is $\sigma^2(\mathbf{X'X})^{-1}(\mathbf{X'\Omega X})(\mathbf{X'X})^{-1}$. It is unlikely that these two would coincide, so the usual estimators of the standard errors are likely to be erroneous. In this section, we consider how erroneous the conventional estimator is likely to be.

As usual,

$$s^2 = \frac{\mathbf{e'e}}{n-K} = \frac{\boldsymbol{\varepsilon'M\varepsilon}}{n-K}, \tag{8-19}$$

where $\mathbf{M} = \mathbf{I} - \mathbf{X}(\mathbf{X}'\mathbf{X})^{-1}\mathbf{X}'$. Expanding this equation, we obtain

$$s^2 = \frac{\boldsymbol{\varepsilon}'\boldsymbol{\varepsilon}}{n - K} - \frac{\boldsymbol{\varepsilon}'\mathbf{X}(\mathbf{X}'\mathbf{X})^{-1}\mathbf{X}'\boldsymbol{\varepsilon}}{n - K}. \tag{8-20}$$

Taking the two parts separately yields

$$E\left[\frac{\boldsymbol{\varepsilon}'\boldsymbol{\varepsilon}}{n - K} \,\middle|\, \mathbf{X}\right] = \frac{\operatorname{tr} E[\boldsymbol{\varepsilon}\boldsymbol{\varepsilon}' \mid \mathbf{X}]}{n - K} = \frac{n\sigma^2}{n - K}. \tag{8-21}$$

[We have used the scaling $\operatorname{tr}(\boldsymbol{\Omega}) = n$.] In addition,

$$E\left[\frac{\boldsymbol{\varepsilon}'\mathbf{X}(\mathbf{X}'\mathbf{X})^{-1}\mathbf{X}'\boldsymbol{\varepsilon}}{n - K} \,\middle|\, \mathbf{X}\right] = \frac{\operatorname{tr}\{E[(\mathbf{X}'\mathbf{X})^{-1}\mathbf{X}'\boldsymbol{\varepsilon}\boldsymbol{\varepsilon}'\mathbf{X} \mid \mathbf{X}]\}}{n - K}$$

$$= \frac{\operatorname{tr}\left[\sigma^2 \left(\dfrac{\mathbf{X}'\mathbf{X}}{n}\right)^{-1} \left(\dfrac{\mathbf{X}'\boldsymbol{\Omega}\mathbf{X}}{n}\right)\right]}{n - K} = \frac{\sigma^2}{n - K} \operatorname{tr}\left[\left(\frac{\mathbf{X}'\mathbf{X}}{n}\right)^{-1} \mathbf{Q}_n^*\right], \tag{8-22}$$

where $\mathbf{Q}_n^*$ is defined after (8-18). As $n \to \infty$, the term in (8-21) will converge to $\sigma^2$. The term in (8-22) will converge to zero if $\mathbf{b}$ is consistent because both matrices in the product are finite. Therefore:

If $\mathbf{b}$ is consistent, then $\lim\limits_{n \to \infty} E[s^2] = \sigma^2$.

It can also be shown—we leave it as an exercise—that if the fourth moment of every disturbance is finite and all our other assumptions are met, then

$$\lim_{n \to \infty} \operatorname{Var}\left[\frac{\mathbf{e}'\mathbf{e}}{n - K}\right] = \lim_{n \to \infty} \operatorname{Var}\left[\frac{\boldsymbol{\varepsilon}'\boldsymbol{\varepsilon}}{n - K}\right] = 0.$$

This result implies, therefore, that:

If $\operatorname{plim} \mathbf{b} = \boldsymbol{\beta}$, then $\operatorname{plim} s^2 = \sigma^2$.

Before proceeding, it is useful to pursue this result. The normalization $\operatorname{tr}(\boldsymbol{\Omega}) = n$ implies that

$$\sigma^2 = \overline{\sigma}^2 = \frac{1}{n}\sum_i \sigma_i^2 \quad \text{and} \quad \omega_i = \frac{\sigma_i^2}{\overline{\sigma}^2}.$$

Therefore, our previous convergence result implies that the least squares estimator $s^2$ converges to $\operatorname{plim} \overline{\sigma}^2$, that is, the probability limit of the average variance of the disturbances, *assuming that this probability limit exists*. Thus, some further assumption about these variances is necessary to obtain the result.

The difference between the conventional estimator and the appropriate (true) covariance matrix for $\mathbf{b}$ is

$$\text{Est. Var}[\mathbf{b} \mid \mathbf{X}] - \operatorname{Var}[\mathbf{b} \mid \mathbf{X}] = s^2(\mathbf{X}'\mathbf{X})^{-1} - \sigma^2(\mathbf{X}'\mathbf{X})^{-1}(\mathbf{X}'\boldsymbol{\Omega}\mathbf{X})(\mathbf{X}'\mathbf{X})^{-1}. \tag{8-23}$$

In a large sample (so that $s^2 \approx \sigma^2$), this difference is approximately equal to

$$\mathbf{D} = \frac{\sigma^2}{n}\left(\frac{\mathbf{X}'\mathbf{X}}{n}\right)^{-1}\left[\frac{\mathbf{X}'\mathbf{X}}{n} - \frac{\mathbf{X}'\boldsymbol{\Omega}\mathbf{X}}{n}\right]\left(\frac{\mathbf{X}'\mathbf{X}}{n}\right)^{-1}. \tag{8-24}$$

The difference between the two matrices hinges on

$$\Delta = \frac{\mathbf{X'X}}{n} - \frac{\mathbf{X'\Omega X}}{n} = \sum_{i=1}^{n} \left(\frac{1}{n}\right)\mathbf{x}_i\mathbf{x}_i' - \sum_{i=1}^{n} \left(\frac{\omega_i}{n}\right)\mathbf{x}_i\mathbf{x}_i' = \frac{1}{n}\sum_{i=1}^{n}(1-\omega_i)\mathbf{x}_i\mathbf{x}_i', \quad \textbf{(8-25)}$$

where $\mathbf{x}_i'$ is the $i$th row of $\mathbf{X}$. These are two weighted averages of the matrices $\mathbf{Q}_i = \mathbf{x}_i\mathbf{x}_i'$, using weights 1 for the first term and $\omega_i$ for the second. The scaling $\text{tr}(\mathbf{\Omega}) = n$ implies that $\sum_i(\omega_i/n) = 1$. Whether the weighted average based on $\omega_i/n$ differs much from the one using $1/n$ depends on the weights. If the weights are related to the values in $\mathbf{x}_i$, then the difference can be considerable. If the weights are uncorrelated with $\mathbf{x}_i\mathbf{x}_i'$, however, then the weighted average will tend to equal the unweighted average.[9]

Therefore, the comparison rests on whether the heteroscedasticity is related to any of $x_k$ or $x_j \times x_k$. The conclusion is that, in general: *If the heteroscedasticity is not correlated with the variables in the model, then at least in large samples, the ordinary least squares computations, although not the optimal way to use the data, will not be misleading.* For example, in the groupwise heteroscedasticity model of Section 8.8.1, if the observations are grouped in the subsamples in a way that is unrelated to the variables in $\mathbf{X}$, then the usual OLS estimator of $\text{Var}[\mathbf{b}]$ will, at least in large samples, provide a reliable estimate of the appropriate covariance matrix. It is worth remembering, however, that the least squares estimator will be inefficient, the more so the larger are the differences among the variances of the groups.[10]

The preceding is a useful result, but one should not be overly optimistic. First, it remains true that ordinary least squares is demonstrably inefficient. Second, if the primary assumption of the analysis—that the heteroscedasticity is unrelated to the variables in the model—is incorrect, then the conventional standard errors may be quite far from the appropriate values.

### 8.4.4 ESTIMATING THE APPROPRIATE COVARIANCE MATRIX FOR ORDINARY LEAST SQUARES

It is clear from the preceding that heteroscedasticity has some potentially serious implications for inferences based on the results of least squares. The application of more appropriate estimation techniques requires a detailed formulation of $\mathbf{\Omega}$, however. It may well be that the form of the heteroscedasticity is unknown. White (1980a) has shown that it is still possible to obtain an appropriate estimator for the variance of the least squares estimator, even if the heteroscedasticity is related to the variables in $\mathbf{X}$. Referring to (8-18), we seek an estimator of

$$\mathbf{Q}_* = \frac{1}{n}\sum_{i=1}^{n}\sigma_i^2\mathbf{x}_i\mathbf{x}_i'.$$

---

[9]Suppose, for example, that $\mathbf{X}$ contains a single column and that both $\mathbf{x}_i$ and $\omega_i$ are independent and identically distributed random variables. Then $\mathbf{x'x}/n$ converges to $E[x_i^2]$, whereas $\mathbf{x'\Omega x}/n$ converges to $\text{Cov}[\omega_i, x_i^2] + E[\omega_i]E[x_i^2]$. $E[\omega_i] = 1$, so if $\omega$ and $x^2$ are uncorrelated, then the sums have the same probability limit.

[10]Some general results, including analysis of the properties of the estimator based on estimated variances, are given in Taylor (1977).

White (1980a) shows that under very general conditions, the estimator

$$\mathbf{S}_0 = \frac{1}{n} \sum_{i=1}^{n} e_i^2 \mathbf{x}_i \mathbf{x}_i' \tag{8-26}$$

has

$$\text{plim } \mathbf{S}_0 = \text{plim } \mathbf{Q}_*.^{[11]}$$

We can sketch a proof of this result using the results we obtained in Section 4.9.[12] Note first that $\mathbf{Q}_*$ is not a parameter matrix in itself. It is a weighted sum of the outer products of the rows of $\mathbf{X}$ (or $\mathbf{Z}$ for the instrumental variables case). Thus, we seek not to "estimate" $\mathbf{Q}_*$, but to find a function of the sample data that will be arbitrarily close to this function of the population parameters as the sample size grows large. The distinction is important. We are not estimating the middle matrix in (8-10) or (8-18); we are attempting to construct a matrix from the sample data that will behave the same way that this matrix behaves. In essence, if $\mathbf{Q}_*$ converges to a finite positive matrix, then we would be looking for a function of the sample data that converges to the same matrix. Suppose that the true disturbances $\varepsilon_i$ could be observed. Then each term in $\mathbf{Q}_*$ would equal $E[\varepsilon_i^2 \mathbf{x}_i \mathbf{x}_i' \mid \mathbf{x}_i]$. With some fairly mild assumptions about $\mathbf{x}_i$, then, we could invoke a law of large numbers (see Theorems D.4 through D.9) to state that if $\mathbf{Q}_*$ has a probability limit, then

$$\text{plim} \frac{1}{n} \sum_{i=1}^{n} \sigma_i^2 \mathbf{x}_i \mathbf{x}_i' = \text{plim} \frac{1}{n} \sum_{i=1}^{n} \varepsilon_i^2 \mathbf{x}_i \mathbf{x}_i'.$$

The final detail is to justify the replacement of $\varepsilon_i$ with $e_i$ in $\mathbf{S}_0$. The consistency of $\mathbf{b}$ for $\boldsymbol{\beta}$ is sufficient for the argument. (Actually, residuals based on *any* consistent estimator of $\boldsymbol{\beta}$ would suffice for this estimator, but as of now, $\mathbf{b}$ or $\mathbf{b}_{IV}$ is the only one in hand.) The end result is that the **White heteroscedasticity consistent estimator**

$$\text{Est. Asy. Var}[\mathbf{b}] = \frac{1}{n} \left( \frac{1}{n} \mathbf{X}'\mathbf{X} \right)^{-1} \left( \frac{1}{n} \sum_{i=1}^{n} e_i^2 \mathbf{x}_i \mathbf{x}_i' \right) \left( \frac{1}{n} \mathbf{X}'\mathbf{X} \right)^{-1}$$

$$= n(\mathbf{X}'\mathbf{X})^{-1} \mathbf{S}_0 (\mathbf{X}'\mathbf{X})^{-1} \tag{8-27}$$

can be used to estimate the asymptotic covariance matrix of $\mathbf{b}$.

This result is extremely important and useful.[13] It implies that without actually specifying the type of heteroscedasticity, we can still make appropriate inferences based on the results of least squares. This implication is especially useful if we are unsure of the precise nature of the heteroscedasticity (which is probably most of the time). We will pursue some examples in Section 8.8.

A number of studies have sought to improve on the White estimator for OLS.[14] The asymptotic properties of the estimator are unambiguous, but its usefulness in small samples is open to question. The possible problems stem from the general result that

---

[11] See also Eicker (1967), Horn, Horn, and Duncan (1975), and MacKinnon and White (1985).

[12] We will give only a broad sketch of the proof. Formal results appear in White (1980) and (2001).

[13] Further discussion and some refinements may be found in Cragg (1982). Cragg shows how White's observation can be extended to devise an estimator that improves on the efficiency of ordinary least squares.

[14] See, e.g., MacKinnon and White (1985) and Messer and White (1984).

**TABLE 8.1** Least Squares Regression Results

|  | *Constant* | *Age* | *OwnRent* | *Income* | *Income*$^2$ |
|---|---|---|---|---|---|
| Sample mean |  | 32.08 | 0.36 | 3.369 |  |
| Coefficient | −237.15 | −3.0818 | 27.941 | 234.35 | −14.997 |
| Standard error | 199.35 | 5.5147 | 82.922 | 80.366 | 7.4693 |
| *t* ratio | −1.10 | −0.5590 | 0.337 | 2.916 | −2.008 |
| White S.E. | 212.99 | 3.3017 | 92.188 | 88.866 | 6.9446 |
| D. and M. (1) | 220.79 | 3.4227 | 95.566 | 92.122 | 7.1991 |
| D. and M. (2) | 221.09 | 3.4477 | 95.632 | 92.083 | 7.1995 |

$$R^2 = 0.243578, \quad s = 284.75080$$

Mean expenditure = $262.53. Income is ×$10,000
Tests for heteroscedasticity: White = 14.329,
Breusch–Pagan = 41.920, Koenker–Bassett = 6.187.
(Two degrees of freedom. $\chi^2_* = 5.99$.)

the squared OLS residuals tend to underestimate the squares of the true disturbances. [That is why we use $1/(n - K)$ rather than $1/n$ in computing $s^2$.] The end result is that in small samples, at least as suggested by some Monte Carlo studies [e.g., MacKinnon and White (1985)], the White estimator is a bit too optimistic; the matrix is a bit too small, so asymptotic $t$ ratios are a little too large. Davidson and MacKinnon (1993, p. 554) suggest a number of fixes, which include (1) scaling up the end result by a factor $n/(n - K)$ and (2) using the squared residual scaled by its true variance, $e_i^2/m_{ii}$, instead of $e_i^2$, where $m_{ii} = 1 - \mathbf{x}_i'(\mathbf{X}'\mathbf{X})^{-1}\mathbf{x}_i$.[15] [See Exercise 8.6.b.] On the basis of their study, Davidson and MacKinnon strongly advocate one or the other correction. Their admonition "One should *never* use [the White estimator] because [(2)] *always* performs better" seems a bit strong, but the point is well taken. The use of sharp asymptotic results in small samples can be problematic. The last two rows of Table 8.1 show the recomputed standard errors with these two modifications.

### Example 8.2 The White Estimator

Using White's estimator for the regression in Example 8.1 produces the results in the row labeled "White S. E." in Table 8.1. The two income coefficients are individually and jointly statistically significant based on the individual $t$ ratios and $F(2, 67) = [(0.244 - 0.064)/2]/[0.776/(72 - 5)] = 7.771$. The 1 percent critical value is 4.94.

The differences in the estimated standard errors seem fairly minor given the extreme heteroscedasticity. One surprise is the decline in the standard error of the age coefficient. The $F$ test is no longer available for testing the joint significance of the two income coefficients because it relies on homoscedasticity. A **Wald test**, however, may be used in any event. The chi-squared test is based on

$$W = (\mathbf{Rb})'\left[\mathbf{R}\left(\text{Est. Asy. Var}[\mathbf{b}]\right)\mathbf{R}'\right]^{-1}(\mathbf{Rb}) \quad \text{where } \mathbf{R} = \begin{bmatrix} 0 & 0 & 0 & 1 & 0 \\ 0 & 0 & 0 & 0 & 1 \end{bmatrix},$$

and the estimated asymptotic covariance matrix is the White estimator. The $F$ statistic based on least squares is 7.771. The Wald statistic based on the White estimator is 20.604; the 95 percent critical value for the chi-squared distribution with two degrees of freedom is 5.99, so the conclusion is unchanged.

---

[15]They also suggest a third correction, $e_i^2/m_{ii}^2$, as an approximation to an estimator based on the "jackknife" technique, but their advocacy of this estimator is much weaker than that of the other two.

## 8.5   TESTING FOR HETEROSCEDASTICITY

Heteroscedasticity poses potentially severe problems for inferences based on least squares. One can rarely be certain that the disturbances are heteroscedastic however, and unfortunately, what form the heteroscedasticity takes if they are. As such, it is useful to be able to test for homoscedasticity and, if necessary, modify our estimation procedures accordingly.[16] Several types of tests have been suggested. They can be roughly grouped in descending order in terms of their generality and, as might be expected, in ascending order in terms of their power.[17] We will examine the two most commonly used tests.

Tests for heteroscedasticity are based on the following strategy. Ordinary least squares is a consistent estimator of $\beta$ even in the presence of heteroscedasticity. As such, the ordinary least squares residuals will mimic, albeit imperfectly because of sampling variability, the heteroscedasticity of the true disturbances. Therefore, tests designed to detect heteroscedasticity will, in general, be applied to the ordinary least squares residuals.

### 8.5.1   WHITE'S GENERAL TEST

To formulate most of the available tests, it is necessary to specify, at least in rough terms, the nature of the heteroscedasticity. It would be desirable to be able to test a general hypothesis of the form

$$H_0 : \sigma_i^2 = \sigma^2 \quad \text{for all } i,$$

$$H_1 : \text{Not } H_0.$$

In view of our earlier findings on the difficulty of estimation in a model with $n$ unknown parameters, this is rather ambitious. Nonetheless, such a test has been devised by White (1980b). The correct covariance matrix for the least squares estimator is

$$\text{Var}[\mathbf{b} \mid \mathbf{X}] = \sigma^2 [\mathbf{X}'\mathbf{X}]^{-1} [\mathbf{X}'\mathbf{\Omega}\mathbf{X}][\mathbf{X}'\mathbf{X}]^{-1},$$

which, as we have seen, can be estimated using (8-27). The conventional estimator is $\mathbf{V} = s^2 [\mathbf{X}'\mathbf{X}]^{-1}$. If there is no heteroscedasticity, then $\mathbf{V}$ will give a consistent estimator of $\text{Var}[\mathbf{b} \mid \mathbf{X}]$, whereas if there is, then it will not. White has devised a statistical test based on this observation. A simple operational version of his test is carried out by obtaining $nR^2$ in the regression of $e_i^2$ on a constant and all unique variables contained in $\mathbf{x}$ and all the squares and cross products of the variables in $\mathbf{x}$. The statistic is asymptotically distributed as chi-squared with $P - 1$ degrees of freedom, where $P$ is the number of regressors in the equation, including the constant.

The **White test** is extremely general. To carry it out, we need not make any specific assumptions about the nature of the heteroscedasticity. Although this characteristic is

---

[16]There is the possibility that a preliminary test for heteroscedasticity will incorrectly lead us to use weighted least squares or fail to alert us to heteroscedasticity and lead us improperly to use ordinary least squares. Some limited results on the properties of the resulting estimator are given by Ohtani and Toyoda (1980). Their results suggest that it is best to test first for heteroscedasticity rather than merely to assume that it is present.

[17]A study that examines the power of several tests for heteroscedasticity is Ali and Giaccotto (1984).

a virtue, it is, at the same time, a potentially serious shortcoming. The test may reveal heteroscedasticity, but it may instead simply identify some other specification error (such as the omission of $x^2$ from a simple regression).[18] Except in the context of a specific problem, little can be said about the power of White's test; it may be very low against some alternatives. In addition, unlike some of the other tests we shall discuss, the White test is **nonconstructive.** If we reject the null hypothesis, then the result of the test gives no indication of what to do next.

### 8.5.2 THE BREUSCH–PAGAN/GODFREY LM TEST

Breusch and Pagan[19] have devised a **Lagrange multiplier test** of the hypothesis that $\sigma_i^2 = \sigma^2 f(\alpha_0 + \boldsymbol{\alpha'z}_i)$, where $\mathbf{z}_i$ is a vector of independent variables.[20] The model is homoscedastic if $\boldsymbol{\alpha} = \mathbf{0}$. The test can be carried out with a simple regression:

$$LM = \frac{1}{2} \text{ explained sum of squares in the regression of } e_i^2/(\mathbf{e'e}/n) \text{ on } \mathbf{z}_i.$$

For computational purposes, let $\mathbf{Z}$ be the $n \times P$ matrix of observations on $(1, \mathbf{z}_i)$, and let $\mathbf{g}$ be the vector of observations of $g_i = e_i^2/(\mathbf{e'e}/n) - 1$. Then

$$LM = \frac{1}{2}[\mathbf{g'Z(Z'Z)}^{-1}\mathbf{Z'g}]. \tag{8-28}$$

Under the null hypothesis of homoscedasticity, LM has a limiting chi-squared distribution with degrees of freedom equal to the number of variables in $\mathbf{z}_i$. This test can be applied to a variety of models, including, for example, those examined in Example 8.3 (2) and in Sections 8.8.1 and 8.8.2.[21]

It has been argued that the **Breusch–Pagan Lagrange multiplier test** is sensitive to the assumption of normality. Koenker (1981) and Koenker and Bassett (1982) suggest that the computation of LM be based on a more **robust estimator** of the variance of $\varepsilon_i^2$,

$$V = \frac{1}{n} \sum_{i=1}^{n} \left[ e_i^2 - \frac{\mathbf{e'e}}{n} \right]^2.$$

The variance of $\varepsilon_i^2$ is not necessarily equal to $2\sigma^4$ if $\varepsilon_i$ is not normally distributed. Let $\mathbf{u}$ equal $(e_1^2, e_2^2, \ldots, e_n^2)$ and $\mathbf{i}$ be an $n \times 1$ column of 1s. Then $\bar{u} = \mathbf{e'e}/n$. With this change, the computation becomes

$$LM = \left[\frac{1}{V}\right](\mathbf{u} - \bar{u}\,\mathbf{i})'\mathbf{Z(Z'Z)}^{-1}\mathbf{Z'}(\mathbf{u} - \bar{u}\,\mathbf{i}).$$

Under normality, this modified statistic will have the same asymptotic distribution as the Breusch–Pagan statistic, but absent normality, there is some evidence that it provides a more powerful test. Waldman (1983) has shown that if the variables in $\mathbf{z}_i$ are the same as those used for the White test described earlier, then the two tests are algebraically the same.

---

[18]Thursby (1982) considers this issue in detail.

[19]Breusch and Pagan (1979).

[20]Lagrange multiplier tests are discussed in Section 16.6.3.

[21]The model $\sigma_i^2 = \sigma^2 \exp(\boldsymbol{\alpha'z}_i)$ is one of these cases. In analyzing this model specifically, Harvey (1976) derived the same test statistic.

***Example 8.3    Testing for Heteroscedasticity***
**1. White's Test:** For the data used in Example 8.1, there are 15 variables in $\mathbf{x} \otimes \mathbf{x}$ including the constant term. But since Ownrent$^2$ = OwnRent and Income × Income = Income$^2$, only 13 are unique. Regression of the squared least squares residuals on these 13 variables produces $R^2 = 0.199013$. The chi-squared statistic is therefore $72(0.199013) = 14.329$. The 95 percent critical value of chi-squared with 12 degrees of freedom is 21.03, so despite what might seem to be obvious in Figure 8.1, the hypothesis of homoscedasticity is not rejected by this test.
**2. Breusch–Pagan Test:** This test requires a specific alternative hypothesis. For this purpose, we specify the test based on $\mathbf{z} = [1, \text{Income}, \text{Income}^2]$. Using the least squares residuals, we compute $g_i = e_i^2 / (\mathbf{e}'\mathbf{e}/72) - 1$; then LM $= \frac{1}{2}\mathbf{g}'\mathbf{Z}(\mathbf{Z}'\mathbf{Z})^{-1}\mathbf{Z}'\mathbf{g}$. The sum of squares is 5,432,562.033. The computation produces LM = 41.920. The critical value for the chi-squared distribution with two degrees of freedom is 5.99, so the hypothesis of homoscedasticity is rejected. The Koenker and Bassett variant of this statistic is only 6.187, which is still significant but much smaller than the LM statistic. The wide difference between these two statistics suggests that the assumption of normality is erroneous. Absent any knowledge of the heteroscedasticity, we might use the Bera and Jarque (1981, 1982) and Kiefer and Salmon (1983) test for normality,

$$\chi^2[2] = n[(m_3/s^3)^2 + ((m_4 - 3)/s^4)^2]$$

where $m_j = (1/n)\sum_i e_i^j$. Under the null hypothesis of *homoscedastic* and normally distributed disturbances, this statistic has a limiting chi-squared distribution with two degrees of freedom. Based on the least squares residuals, the value is 482.12, which certainly does lead to rejection of the hypothesis. Some caution is warranted here, however. It is unclear what part of the hypothesis should be rejected. We have convincing evidence in Figure 8.1 that the disturbances are heteroscedastic, so the assumption of homoscedasticity underlying this test is questionable. This does suggest the need to examine the data before applying a **specification test** such as this one.

## 8.6   WEIGHTED LEAST SQUARES WHEN $\Omega$ IS KNOWN

Having tested for and found evidence of heteroscedasticity, the logical next step is to revise the estimation technique to account for it. The GLS estimator is

$$\hat{\beta} = (\mathbf{X}'\Omega^{-1}\mathbf{X})^{-1}\mathbf{X}'\Omega^{-1}\mathbf{y}. \tag{8-29}$$

Consider the most general case, $\text{Var}[\varepsilon_i \mid \mathbf{X}] = \sigma_i^2 = \sigma^2\omega_i$. Then $\Omega^{-1}$ is a diagonal matrix whose $i$th diagonal element is $1/\omega_i$. The GLS estimator is obtained by regressing

$$\mathbf{Py} = \begin{bmatrix} y_1/\sqrt{\omega_1} \\ y_2/\sqrt{\omega_2} \\ \vdots \\ y_n/\sqrt{\omega_n} \end{bmatrix} \quad \text{on} \quad \mathbf{PX} = \begin{bmatrix} \mathbf{x}_1'/\sqrt{\omega_1} \\ \mathbf{x}_2'/\sqrt{\omega_2} \\ \vdots \\ \mathbf{x}_n'/\sqrt{\omega_n} \end{bmatrix}.$$

Applying ordinary least squares to the transformed model, we obtain the **weighted least squares (WLS)** estimator.

$$\hat{\beta} = \left[\sum_{i=1}^{n} w_i \mathbf{x}_i \mathbf{x}_i'\right]^{-1} \left[\sum_{i=1}^{n} w_i \mathbf{x}_i y_i\right],$$

where $w_i = 1/\omega_i$.[22] The logic of the computation is that observations with smaller variances receive a larger weight in the computations of the sums and therefore have greater influence in the estimates obtained.

A common specification is that the variance is proportional to one of the regressors or its square. Our earlier example of family expenditures is one in which the relevant variable is usually income. Similarly, in studies of firm profits, the dominant variable is typically assumed to be firm size. If

$$\sigma_i^2 = \sigma^2 x_{ik}^2,$$

then the transformed regression model for GLS is

$$\frac{y}{x_k} = \beta_k + \beta_1 \left( \frac{x_1}{x_k} \right) + \beta_2 \left( \frac{x_2}{x_k} \right) + \cdots + \frac{\varepsilon}{x_k}. \tag{8-30}$$

If the variance is proportional to $x_k$ instead of $x_k^2$, then the weight applied to each observation is $1/\sqrt{x_k}$ instead of $1/x_k$.

In (8-30), the coefficient on $x_k$ becomes the constant term. But if the variance is proportional to any power of $x_k$ other than two, then the transformed model will no longer contain a constant, and we encounter the problem of interpreting $R^2$ mentioned earlier. For example, no conclusion should be drawn if the $R^2$ in the regression of $y/z$ on $1/z$ and $x/z$ is higher than in the regression of $y$ on a constant and $x$ for any $z$, including $x$. The good fit of the weighted regression might be due to the presence of $1/z$ on both sides of the equality.

It is rarely possible to be certain about the nature of the heteroscedasticity in a regression model. In one respect, this problem is only minor. The weighted least squares estimator

$$\hat{\beta} = \left[ \sum_{i=1}^{n} w_i \mathbf{x}_i \mathbf{x}_i' \right]^{-1} \left[ \sum_{i=1}^{n} w_i \mathbf{x}_i y_i \right]$$

is consistent regardless of the weights used, as long as the weights are uncorrelated with the disturbances.

But using the wrong set of weights has two other consequences that may be less benign. First, the improperly weighted least squares estimator is inefficient. This point might be moot if the correct weights are unknown, but the GLS standard errors will also be incorrect. The asymptotic covariance matrix of the estimator

$$\hat{\beta} = [\mathbf{X}'\mathbf{V}^{-1}\mathbf{X}]^{-1}\mathbf{X}'\mathbf{V}^{-1}\mathbf{y} \tag{8-31}$$

is

$$\text{Asy. Var}[\hat{\beta}] = \sigma^2 [\mathbf{X}'\mathbf{V}^{-1}\mathbf{X}]^{-1}\mathbf{X}'\mathbf{V}^{-1}\mathbf{\Omega}\mathbf{V}^{-1}\mathbf{X}[\mathbf{X}'\mathbf{V}^{-1}\mathbf{X}]^{-1}. \tag{8-32}$$

This result may or may not resemble the usual estimator, which would be the matrix in brackets, and underscores the usefulness of the White estimator in (8-27).

The standard approach in the literature is to use OLS with the White estimator or some variant for the asymptotic covariance matrix. One could argue both flaws and

---

[22]The weights are often denoted $w_i = 1/\sigma_i^2$. This expression is consistent with the equivalent $\hat{\beta} = [\mathbf{X}'(\sigma^2\mathbf{\Omega})^{-1}\mathbf{X}]^{-1}\mathbf{X}'(\sigma^2\mathbf{\Omega})^{-1}\mathbf{y}$. The $\sigma^2$'s cancel, leaving the expression given previously.

virtues in this approach. In its favor, **robustness to unknown heteroscedasticity** is a compelling virtue. In the clear presence of heteroscedasticity, however, least squares can be extremely inefficient. The question becomes whether using the wrong weights is better than using no weights at all. There are several layers to the question. If we use one of the models mentioned earlier—Harvey's, for example, is a versatile and flexible candidate—then we may use the wrong set of weights and, in addition, estimation of the variance parameters introduces a new source of variation into the slope estimators for the model. A heteroscedasticity robust estimator for weighted least squares can be formed by combining (8-32) with the White estimator. The weighted least squares estimator in (8-31) is consistent with any set of weights $\mathbf{V} = \text{diag}[v_1, v_2, \ldots, v_n]$. Its asymptotic covariance matrix can be estimated with

$$\text{Est. Asy. Var}[\hat{\beta}] = (\mathbf{X}'\mathbf{V}^{-1}\mathbf{X})^{-1} \left[ \sum_{i=1}^{n} \left( \frac{e_i^2}{v_i^2} \right) \mathbf{x}_i \mathbf{x}_i' \right] (\mathbf{X}'\mathbf{V}^{-1}\mathbf{X})^{-1}. \qquad \textbf{(8-33)}$$

Any consistent estimator can be used to form the residuals. The weighted least squares estimator is a natural candidate.

## 8.7 ESTIMATION WHEN $\mathbf{\Omega}$ CONTAINS UNKNOWN PARAMETERS

The general form of the heteroscedastic regression model has too many parameters to estimate by ordinary methods. Typically, the model is restricted by formulating $\sigma^2 \mathbf{\Omega}$ as a function of a few parameters, as in $\sigma_i^2 = \sigma^2 x_i^\alpha$ or $\sigma_i^2 = \sigma^2 [\mathbf{x}_i'\alpha]^2$. Write this as $\mathbf{\Omega}(\alpha)$. FGLS based on a consistent estimator of $\mathbf{\Omega}(\alpha)$ (meaning a consistent estimator of $\alpha$) is asymptotically equivalent to full GLS. The new problem is that we must first find consistent estimators of the unknown parameters in $\mathbf{\Omega}(\alpha)$. Two methods are typically used, two-step GLS and maximum likelihood. We consider the two-step estimator here and the maximum likelihood estimator in Chapter 16.

For the heteroscedastic model, the GLS estimator is

$$\hat{\beta} = \left[ \sum_{i=1}^{n} \left( \frac{1}{\sigma_i^2} \right) \mathbf{x}_i \mathbf{x}_i' \right]^{-1} \left[ \sum_{i=1}^{n} \left( \frac{1}{\sigma_i^2} \right) \mathbf{x}_i y_i \right]. \qquad \textbf{(8-34)}$$

The **two-step estimators** are computed by first obtaining estimates $\hat{\sigma}_i^2$, usually using some function of the ordinary least squares residuals. Then, $\hat{\hat{\beta}}$ uses (8-34) and $\hat{\sigma}_i^2$. The ordinary least squares estimator of $\beta$, although inefficient, is still consistent. As such, statistics computed using the ordinary least squares residuals, $e_i = (y_i - \mathbf{x}_i'\mathbf{b})$, will have the same asymptotic properties as those computed using the true disturbances, $\varepsilon_i = (y_i - \mathbf{x}_i'\beta)$. This result suggests a regression approach for the true disturbances and variables $\mathbf{z}_i$ that may or may not coincide with $\mathbf{x}_i$. Now $E[\varepsilon_i^2 \mid \mathbf{z}_i] = \sigma_i^2$, so

$$\varepsilon_i^2 = \sigma_i^2 + v_i,$$

where $v_i$ is just the difference between $\varepsilon_i^2$ and its conditional expectation. Because $\varepsilon_i$ is unobservable, we would use the least squares residual, for which $e_i = \varepsilon_i - \mathbf{x}_i'(\mathbf{b} - \beta) = \varepsilon_i + u_i$. Then, $e_i^2 = \varepsilon_i^2 + u_i^2 + 2\varepsilon_i u_i$. But, in large samples, as $\mathbf{b} \xrightarrow{p} \beta$, terms in $u_i$ will become negligible, so that at least approximately,[23]

$$e_i^2 = \sigma_i^2 + v_i^*.$$

The procedure suggested is to treat the variance function as a regression and use the squares or some other functions of the least squares residuals as the dependent variable.[24] For example, if $\sigma_i^2 = \mathbf{z}_i'\alpha$, then a consistent estimator of $\alpha$ will be the least squares slopes, $\mathbf{a}$, in the "model,"

$$e_i^2 = \mathbf{z}_i'\alpha + v_i^*.$$

In this model, $v_i^*$ is both heteroscedastic and autocorrelated, so $\mathbf{a}$ is consistent but inefficient. But, consistency is all that is required for asymptotically efficient estimation of $\beta$ using $\Omega(\hat{\alpha})$. It remains to be settled whether improving the estimator of $\alpha$ in this and the other models we will consider would improve the small sample properties of the two-step estimator of $\beta$.[25]

The two-step estimator may be iterated by recomputing the residuals after computing the FGLS estimates and then reentering the computation. The asymptotic properties of the iterated estimator are the same as those of the two-step estimator, however. In some cases, this sort of iteration will produce the maximum likelihood estimator at convergence. Yet none of the estimators based on regression of squared residuals on other variables satisfy the requirement. Thus, iteration in this context provides little additional benefit, if any.

## 8.8 APPLICATIONS

This section will present two common applications of the heteroscedastic regression model, Harvey's model of **multiplicative heteroscedasticity** and a model of **groupwise heteroscedasticity** that extends to the disturbance variance some concepts that are usually associated with variation in the regression function.

### 8.8.1 MULTIPLICATIVE HETEROSCEDASTICITY

Harvey's (1976) model of multiplicative heteroscedasticity is a very flexible, general model that includes most of the useful formulations as special cases. The general formulation is

$$\sigma_i^2 = \sigma^2 \exp(\mathbf{z}_i'\alpha).$$

A model with heteroscedasticity of the form

$$\sigma_i^2 = \sigma^2 \prod_{m=1}^{M} z_{im}^{\alpha_m}$$

---

[23] See Amemiya (1985) and Harvey (1976) for formal analyses.

[24] See, for example, Jobson and Fuller (1980).

[25] Fomby, Hill, and Johnson (1984, pp. 177–186) and Amemiya (1985, pp. 203–207; 1977a) examine this model.

results if the logs of the variables are placed in $\mathbf{z}_i$. The groupwise heteroscedasticity model described in Example 8.4 is produced by making $\mathbf{z}_i$ a set of group dummy variables (one must be omitted). In this case, $\sigma^2$ is the disturbance variance for the base group whereas for the other groups, $\sigma_g^2 = \sigma^2 \exp(\alpha_g)$.

### Example 8.4   Multiplicative Heteroscedasticity.

In Example 6.2, we fit a cost function for the U.S. airline industry of the form

$$\ln C_{it} = \beta_1 + \beta_2 \ln Q_{it} + \beta_3 [\ln Q_{it}]^2 + \beta_4 \ln P_{fuel,i,t} + \beta_5 \, Loadfactor_{i,t} + \varepsilon_{i,t}$$

where $C_{i,t}$ is total cost, $Q_{i,t}$ is output, and $P_{fuel,i,t}$ is the price of fuel and the 90 observations in the data set are for six firms observed for 15 years. (The model also included dummy variables for firm and year, which we will omit for simplicity.) We now consider a revised model in which the load factor appears in the variance of $\varepsilon_{i,t}$ rather than in the regression function. The model is

$$\sigma_{i,t}^2 = \sigma^2 \exp(\gamma \, Loadfactor_{i,t})$$
$$= \exp(\gamma_1 + \gamma_2 \, Loadfactor_{i,t}).$$

The constant in the implied regression is $\gamma_1 = \ln \sigma^2$. Figure 8.2 shows a plot of the least squares residuals against *Load factor* for the 90 observations. The figure does suggest the presence of heteroscedasticity. (The dashed lines are placed to highlight the effect.) We computed the LM statistic using (8-28). The chi-squared statistic is 2.946. This is smaller than the critical value of 3.84 for one degree of freedom, so on this basis, the null hypothesis of homoscedasticity with respect to the load factor is not rejected.

To begin, we use OLS to estimate the parameters of the cost function and the set of residuals, $e_{i,t}$. Regression of $\log(e_{it}^2)$ on a constant and the load factor provides estimates of $\gamma_1$ and $\gamma_2$, denoted $c_1$ and $c_2$. The results are shown in Table 8.2. As Harvey notes, $\exp(c_1)$ does not necessarily estimate $\sigma^2$ consistently—for normally distributed disturbances, it is low by a factor of 1.2704. However, as seen in (8-29), the estimate of $\sigma^2$ (biased or otherwise) is not needed to compute the FGLS estimator. Weights $w_{i,t} = \exp(-c_1 - c_2 Loadfactor_{i,t})$ are

**FIGURE 8.2**    Plot of Residuals Against Load Factor

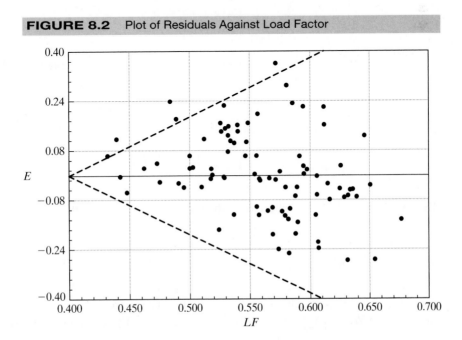

**TABLE 8.2** Multiplicative Heteroscedasticity Model

| | Constant | Ln Q | Ln² Q | Ln Pf | R² | Sum of Squares |
|---|---|---|---|---|---|---|
| OLS | 9.1382 | 0.92615 | 0.029145 | 0.41006 | | |
| | 0.24507[a] | 0.032306 | 0.012304 | 0.018807 | 0.9861674[c] | 1.577479[d] |
| | 0.22595[b] | 0.030128 | 0.011346 | 0.017524 | | |
| Two step | 9.2463 | 0.92136 | 0.024450 | 0.40352 | 0.986119 | 1.612938 |
| | 0.21896 | 0.033028 | 0.011412 | 0.016974 | | |
| Iterated[e] | 9.2774 | 0.91609 | 0.021643 | 0.40174 | 0.986071 | 1.645693 |
| | 0.20977 | 0.032993 | 0.011017 | 0.016332 | | |

[a]Conventional OLS standard errors
[b]White robust standard errors
[c]Squared correlation between actual and fitted values
[d]Sum of squared residuals
[e]Values of $c_2$ by iteration: 8.254344, 11.622473, 11.705029, 11.710618, 11.711012, 11.711040, 11.711042

computed using these estimates, then weighted least squares using (8-30) is used to obtain the FGLS estimates of $\beta$. The results of the computations are shown in Table 8.2.

We might consider iterating the procedure. Using the results of FGLS at step 2, we can recompute the residuals, then recompute $c_1$ and $c_2$ and the weights, and then reenter the iteration. The process converges when the estimate of $c_2$ stabilizes. This requires seven iterations. The results are shown in Table 8.2. As noted earlier, iteration does not produce any gains here. The second step estimator is already fully efficient. Moreover, this does not produce the MLE, either. That would be obtained by regressing $[e_{i,t}^2 / \exp(c_1 + c_2 Loadfactor_{i,t}) - 1]$ on the constant and load factor at each iteration to obtain the new estimates. We will revisit this in Chapter 16.

### 8.8.2 GROUPWISE HETEROSCEDASTICITY

A groupwise heteroscedastic regression has the structural equations

$$y_i = \mathbf{x}_i'\boldsymbol{\beta} + \varepsilon_i, \quad i = 1, \ldots, n,$$

$$E[\varepsilon_i \mid \mathbf{x}_i] = 0, \quad i = 1, \ldots, n.$$

The $n$ observations are grouped into $G$ groups, each with $n_g$ observations. The slope vector is the same in all groups, but within group $g$:

$$\text{Var}[\varepsilon_{ig} \mid \mathbf{x}_{ig}] = \sigma_g^2, \quad i = 1, \ldots, n_g.$$

If the variances are known, then the GLS estimator is

$$\hat{\boldsymbol{\beta}} = \left[\sum_{g=1}^{G} \left(\frac{1}{\sigma_g^2}\right) \mathbf{X}_g'\mathbf{X}_g\right]^{-1} \left[\sum_{g=1}^{G} \left(\frac{1}{\sigma_g^2}\right) \mathbf{X}_g'\mathbf{y}_g\right]. \tag{8-35}$$

Because $\mathbf{X}_g'\mathbf{y}_g = \mathbf{X}_g'\mathbf{X}_g\mathbf{b}_g$, where $\mathbf{b}_g$ is the OLS estimator in the $g$th subset of observations,

$$\hat{\boldsymbol{\beta}} = \left[\sum_{g=1}^{G} \left(\frac{1}{\sigma_g^2}\right) \mathbf{X}_g'\mathbf{X}_g\right]^{-1} \left[\sum_{g=1}^{G} \left(\frac{1}{\sigma_g^2}\right) \mathbf{X}_g'\mathbf{X}_g\mathbf{b}_g\right] = \left[\sum_{g=1}^{G} \mathbf{V}_g\right]^{-1} \left[\sum_{g=1}^{G} \mathbf{V}_g\mathbf{b}_g\right] = \sum_{g=1}^{G} \mathbf{W}_g\mathbf{b}_g.$$

This result is a matrix weighted average of the $G$ least squares estimators. The weighting matrices are $\mathbf{W}_g = \left[\sum_{g=1}^{G} (\text{Var}[\mathbf{b}_g])^{-1}\right]^{-1} (\text{Var}[\mathbf{b}_g])^{-1}$. The estimator with the smaller covariance matrix therefore receives the larger weight. (If $\mathbf{X}_g$ is the same in every group, then the matrix $\mathbf{W}_g$ reduces to the simple, $w_g\mathbf{I} = (h_g/\sum_g h_g)\mathbf{I}$ where $h_g = 1/\sigma_g^2$.)

The preceding is a useful construction of the estimator, but it relies on an algebraic result that might be unusable. If the number of observations in any group is smaller than the number of regressors, then the group specific OLS estimator cannot be computed. But, as can be seen in (8-35), that is not what is needed to proceed; what is needed are the weights. As always, pooled least squares is a consistent estimator, which means that using the group specific subvectors of the OLS residuals,

$$\hat{\sigma}_g^2 = \frac{\mathbf{e}_g'\mathbf{e}_g}{n_g} \tag{8-36}$$

provides the needed estimator for the group specific disturbance variance. Thereafter, (8-35) is the estimator and the inverse matrix in that expression gives the estimator of the asymptotic covariance matrix.

Continuing this line of reasoning, one might consider iterating the estimator by returning to (8-36) with the two-step FGLS estimator, recomputing the weights, then returning to (8-35) to recompute the slope vector. This can be continued until convergence. It can be shown [see Oberhofer and Kmenta (1974)] that so long as (8-36) is used without a degrees of freedom correction, then if this does converge, it will do so at the maximum likelihood estimator (with normally distributed disturbances).

For testing the homoscedasticity assumption, both White's test and the LM test are straightforward. The variables thought to enter the conditional variance are simply a set of group dummy variables, not including one of them (to avoid the dummy variable trap), which we'll denote $\mathbf{Z}$. Because the columns of $\mathbf{Z}$ are binary and orthogonal, to carry out White's test, we need only regress the squared least squares residuals on a constant and $\mathbf{Z}$, and compute $NR^2$ where $N = \sum_g n_g$. The LM test is also straightforward. In (8-28), the vector $\mathbf{g}$ is $G$-1 subvectors where each subvector is the $n_g$ elements of $(e_{ig}^2/\hat{\sigma}^2 - 1)$ and $\hat{\sigma}^2 = \mathbf{e}'\mathbf{e}/N$. By multiplying it out, we find that $\mathbf{g}'\mathbf{Z}$ is the $G - 1$ vector with elements $n_g(\hat{\sigma}_g^2/\hat{\sigma}^2 - 1)$ while $(\mathbf{Z}'\mathbf{Z})^{-1}$ is the $(G-1) \times (G-1)$ matrix with diagonal elements $1/n_g$. It follows that

$$LM = \frac{1}{2}\mathbf{g}'\mathbf{Z}(\mathbf{Z}'\mathbf{Z})^{-1}\mathbf{Z}'\mathbf{g} = \frac{1}{2}\sum_{g=2}^{G} n_g \left(\frac{\hat{\sigma}_g^2}{\hat{\sigma}^2} - 1\right)^2. \tag{8-37}$$

Both statistics have limiting chi squared distributions with $G$-1 degrees of freedom under the null hypothesis of homoscedasticity.

### Example 8.5  Groupwise Heteroscedasticity

Baltagi and Griffin (1983) is a study of gasoline usage in 18 of the 30 OECD countries. The model analyzed in the paper is

$$\ln\,(Gasoline\ usage/car)_{i,t} = \beta_1 + \beta_2 \ln\,(Per\ capita\ income)_{i,t} + \beta_3 \ln Price_{i,t} + \varepsilon_{i,t}$$

where $i$ = country and $t$ = 1960, ..., 1978. This is a balanced panel (see Section 9.2) with 19(18) = 342 observations in total. The data are given in Table F8.2.

Figure 8.3 displays the OLS residuals from least squares estimates of the model above with the addition of 17 country dummy variables (2–18). (The country dummy variables are used so that the country-specific residuals will have mean zero. The $F$ statistic for testing the null hypothesis that all the constants are equal is 232.736. The critical value from the $F$ table with 17 and 322 degrees of freedom is 1.645.) The regression results are given in Table 8.3.

**TABLE 8.3**   Estimated Gasoline Consumption Equations

|  | OLS | | | FGLS | |
| --- | --- | --- | --- | --- | --- |
|  | *Coefficient* | *Std. Error* | *White Std. Err.* | *Coefficient* | *Std. Error* |
| Income | −0.82771 | 0.038879 | 0.062742 | −0.70312 | 0.027898 |
| Price | −0.25725 | 0.068772 | 0.067946 | −0.24180 | 0.043580 |
| Constant | −1.13378 | 0.25695 | 0.40047 | −0.36379 | 0.18247 |
| Country 2 | 0.12823 | 0.050251 | 0.050434 | 0.092447 | 0.045811 |
| Country 3 | 1.11015 | 0.058294 | 0.065694 | 1.05124 | 0.056393 |
| Country 4 | 0.46674 | 0.050812 | 0.048357 | 0.41954 | 0.041046 |
| Country 5 | 0.028432 | 0.051859 | 0.061009 | −0.0067462 | 0.057571 |
| Country 6 | 0.055864 | 0.047854 | 0.051152 | 0.022173 | 0.048597 |
| Country 7 | 0.53554 | 0.054621 | 0.055420 | 0.58920 | 0.047796 |
| Country 8 | −0.061854 | 0.048287 | 0.047687 | −0.023875 | 0.044996 |
| Country 9 | −0.43201 | 0.051115 | 0.045110 | −0.40842 | 0.041434 |
| Country 10 | 0.58760 | 0.048404 | 0.084495 | 0.60060 | 0.086526 |
| Country 11 | 0.21880 | 0.048706 | 0.053574 | 0.19216 | 0.051130 |
| Country 12 | 0.41001 | 0.052771 | 0.051592 | 0.36116 | 0.043067 |
| Country 13 | 0.721119 | 0.105434 | 0.10535 | 0.64091 | 0.076633 |
| Country 14 | −2.02670 | 0.19764 | 0.21721 | −1.78096 | 0.12723 |
| Country 15 | 0.23328 | 0.053597 | 0.046908 | 0.21574 | 0.043099 |
| Country 16 | 0.71876 | 0.065289 | 0.089370 | 0.86945 | 0.059205 |
| Country 17 | 0.021290 | 0.047105 | 0.040347 | 0.0078929 | 0.039544 |
| Country 18 | 1.13233 | 0.064527 | 0.069356 | 1.05989 | 0.055362 |

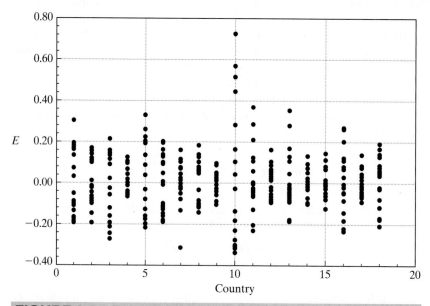

**FIGURE 8.3**   Plot of OLS Residuals by Country.

(The OLS results seem odd enough to suggest that gasoline is a strongly inferior good. We have no explanation for this result, and we leave it for other researchers to resolve.) The figure does convincingly suggest the presence of groupwise heteroscedasticity. The White and LM statistics are 120.179 and 160.576, respectively. The critical value from the chi-squared distribution with 17 degrees of freedom is 27.587. So, we reject the hypothesis of homoscedasticity and proceed to fit the model by feasible GLS. The two-step estimators are shown in Table 8.3. Comparing the White standard errors to the two step estimators, we see that in this instance, there is a substantial gain to using feasible generalized least squares.

## 8.9   SUMMARY AND CONCLUSIONS

This chapter has introduced a major extension of the classical linear model. By allowing for heteroscedasticity and autocorrelation in the disturbances, we expand the range of models to a large array of frameworks. We will explore these in the next several chapters. The formal concepts introduced in this chapter include how this extension affects the properties of the least squares estimator, how an appropriate estimator of the asymptotic covariance matrix of the least squares estimator can be computed in this extended modeling framework and, finally, how to use the information about the variances and covariances of the disturbances to obtain an estimator that is more efficient than ordinary least squares.

We have analyzed in detail one form of the generalized regression model, the model of heteroscedasticity. We first considered least squares estimation. The primary result for least squares estimation is that it retains its consistency and asymptotic normality, but some correction to the estimated asymptotic covariance matrix may be needed for appropriate inference. The White estimator is the standard approach for this computation. After examining two general tests for heteroscedasticity, we then narrowed the model to some specific parametric forms, and considered weighted (generalized) least squares for efficient estimation and maximum likelihood estimation. If the form of the heteroscedasticity is known but involves unknown parameters, then it remains uncertain whether FGLS corrections are better than OLS. Asymptotically, the comparison is clear, but in small or moderately sized samples, the additional variation incorporated by the estimated variance parameters may offset the gains to GLS.

## Key Terms and Concepts

- Aitken's theorem
- Asymptotic properties
- Autocorrelation
- Breusch–Pagan Lagrange multiplier test
- Efficient estimator
- Feasible generalized least squares (FGLS)
- Finite-sample properties
- Generalized least squares (GLS)
- Generalized linear regression model
- Generalized sum of squares
- Groupwise heteroscedasticity
- Heteroscedasticity
- Kruskal's theorem
- Lagrange multiplier test
- Multiplicative heteroscedasticity
- Nonconstructive test
- Ordinary least squares (OLS)
- Panel data
- Parametric model
- Robust estimation
- Robust estimator
- Robustness to unknown heteroscedasticity
- Semiparametric model
- Specification test
- Spherical disturbances
- Two-step estimator
- Wald test
- Weighted least squares (WLS)
- White heteroscedasticity consistent estimator
- White test

## Exercises

1. What is the covariance matrix, $\text{Cov}[\hat{\beta}, \hat{\beta} - \mathbf{b}]$, of the GLS estimator $\hat{\beta} = (\mathbf{X}'\boldsymbol{\Omega}^{-1}\mathbf{X})^{-1}\mathbf{X}'\boldsymbol{\Omega}^{-1}\mathbf{y}$ and the difference between it and the OLS estimator, $\mathbf{b} = (\mathbf{X}'\mathbf{X})^{-1}\mathbf{X}'\mathbf{y}$? The result plays a pivotal role in the development of specification tests in Hausman (1978).

2. This and the next two exercises are based on the test statistic usually used to test a set of $J$ linear restrictions in the generalized regression model

$$F[J, n - K] = \frac{(\mathbf{R}\hat{\beta} - \mathbf{q})'[\mathbf{R}(\mathbf{X}'\boldsymbol{\Omega}^{-1}\mathbf{X})^{-1}\mathbf{R}']^{-1}(\mathbf{R}\hat{\beta} - \mathbf{q})/J}{(\mathbf{y} - \mathbf{X}\hat{\beta})'\boldsymbol{\Omega}^{-1}(\mathbf{y} - \mathbf{X}\hat{\beta})/(n - K)},$$

where $\hat{\beta}$ is the GLS estimator. Show that if $\boldsymbol{\Omega}$ is known, if the disturbances are normally distributed and if the null hypothesis, $\mathbf{R}\beta = \mathbf{q}$, is true, then this statistic is exactly distributed as $F$ with $J$ and $n - K$ degrees of freedom. What assumptions about the regressors are needed to reach this conclusion? Need they be non-stochastic?

3. Now suppose that the disturbances are not normally distributed, although $\boldsymbol{\Omega}$ is still known. Show that the limiting distribution of previous statistic is $(1/J)$ times a chi-squared variable with $J$ degrees of freedom. (Hint: The denominator converges to $\sigma^2$.) Conclude that in the generalized regression model, the limiting distribution of the Wald statistic

$$W = (\mathbf{R}\hat{\beta} - \mathbf{q})'\{\mathbf{R}(\text{Est. Var}[\hat{\beta}])\mathbf{R}'\}^{-1}(\mathbf{R}\hat{\beta} - \mathbf{q})$$

is chi-squared with $J$ degrees of freedom, regardless of the distribution of the disturbances, as long as the data are otherwise well behaved. Note that in a finite sample, the true distribution may be approximated with an $F[J, n - K]$ distribution. It is a bit ambiguous, however, to interpret this fact as implying that the statistic is asymptotically distributed as $F$ with $J$ and $n - K$ degrees of freedom, because the limiting distribution used to obtain our result is the chi-squared, not the $F$. In this instance, the $F[J, n - K]$ is a random variable that tends asymptotically to the chi-squared variate.

4. Finally, suppose that $\boldsymbol{\Omega}$ must be estimated, but that assumptions (8-16) and (8-17) are met by the estimator. What changes are required in the development of the previous problem?

5. In the generalized regression model, if the $K$ columns of $\mathbf{X}$ are characteristic vectors of $\boldsymbol{\Omega}$, then ordinary least squares and generalized least squares are identical. (The result is actually a bit broader; $\mathbf{X}$ may be any linear combination of exactly $K$ characteristic vectors. This result is **Kruskal's theorem.**)
   a. Prove the result directly using matrix algebra.
   b. Prove that if $\mathbf{X}$ contains a constant term and if the remaining columns are in deviation form (so that the column sum is zero), then the model of Exercise 8 below is one of these cases. (The seemingly unrelated regressions model with identical regressor matrices, discussed in Chapter 10, is another.)

6. In the generalized regression model, suppose that $\boldsymbol{\Omega}$ is known.
   a. What is the covariance matrix of the OLS and GLS estimators of $\beta$?
   b. What is the covariance matrix of the OLS residual vector $\mathbf{e} = \mathbf{y} - \mathbf{X}\mathbf{b}$?

c. What is the covariance matrix of the GLS residual vector $\hat{\boldsymbol{\varepsilon}} = \mathbf{y} - \mathbf{X}\hat{\boldsymbol{\beta}}$?

d. What is the covariance matrix of the OLS and GLS residual vectors?

7. Suppose that $y$ has the pdf $f(y \mid \mathbf{x}) = (1/\mathbf{x}'\boldsymbol{\beta})e^{-y/(\boldsymbol{\beta}'\mathbf{x})}$, $y > 0$.

   Then $E[y \mid \mathbf{x}] = \boldsymbol{\beta}'\mathbf{x}$ and $\mathrm{Var}[y \mid \mathbf{x}] = (\boldsymbol{\beta}'\mathbf{x})^2$. For this model, prove that GLS and MLE are the same, even though this distribution involves the same parameters in the conditional mean function and the disturbance variance.

8. Suppose that the regression model is $y = \mu + \varepsilon$, where $\varepsilon$ has a zero mean, constant variance, and equal correlation $\rho$ across observations. Then $\mathrm{Cov}[\varepsilon_i, \varepsilon_j] = \sigma^2\rho$ if $i \neq j$. Prove that the least squares estimator of $\mu$ is inconsistent. Find the characteristic roots of $\boldsymbol{\Omega}$ and show that Condition 2 after Theorem 8.2 is violated.

9. Suppose that the regression model is $y_i = \mu + \varepsilon_i$, where

$$E[\varepsilon_i \mid x_i] = 0, \ \mathrm{Cov}[\varepsilon_i, \varepsilon_j \mid x_i, x_j] = 0 \quad \text{for } i = j, \text{ but } \mathrm{Var}[\varepsilon_i \mid x_i] = \sigma^2 x_i^2, x_i > 0.$$

   a. Given a sample of observations on $y_i$ and $x_i$, what is the most efficient estimator of $\mu$? What is its variance?

   b. What is the OLS estimator of $\mu$, and what is the variance of the ordinary least squares estimator?

   c. Prove that the estimator in part a is at least as efficient as the estimator in part b.

10. For the model in Exercise 9, what is the probability limit of $s^2 = \frac{1}{n}\sum_{i=1}^{n}(y_i - \bar{y})^2$? Note that $s^2$ is the least squares estimator of the residual variance. It is also $n$ times the conventional estimator of the variance of the OLS estimator,

$$\text{Est. Var}\,[\bar{y}] = s^2(\mathbf{X}'\mathbf{X})^{-1} = \frac{s^2}{n}.$$

   How does this equation compare with the true value you found in part b of Exercise 9? Does the conventional estimator produce the correct estimator of the true asymptotic variance of the least squares estimator?

11. For the model in Exercise 9, suppose that $\varepsilon$ is normally distributed, with mean zero and variance $\sigma^2[1 + (\gamma x)^2]$. Show that $\sigma^2$ and $\gamma^2$ can be consistently estimated by a regression of the least squares residuals on a constant and $x^2$. Is this estimator efficient?

12. Two samples of 50 observations each produce the following moment matrices. (In each case, $\mathbf{X}$ is a constant and one variable.)

|  | Sample 1 | Sample 2 |
|---|---|---|
| $\mathbf{X}'\mathbf{X}$ | $\begin{bmatrix} 50 & 300 \\ 300 & 2100 \end{bmatrix}$ | $\begin{bmatrix} 50 & 300 \\ 300 & 2100 \end{bmatrix}$ |
| $\mathbf{y}'\mathbf{X}$ | $[300 \quad 2000]$ | $[300 \quad 2200]$ |
| $\mathbf{y}'\mathbf{y}$ | $[2100]$ | $[2800]$ |

   a. Compute the least squares regression coefficients and the residual variances $s^2$ for each data set. Compute the $R^2$ for each regression.

   b. Compute the OLS estimate of the coefficient vector assuming that the coefficients and disturbance variance are the same in the two regressions. Also compute the estimate of the asymptotic covariance matrix of the estimate.

   c. Test the hypothesis that the variances in the two regressions are the same without assuming that the coefficients are the same in the two regressions.

   d. Compute the two-step FGLS estimator of the coefficients in the regressions, assuming that the constant and slope are the same in both regressions. Compute the estimate of the covariance matrix and compare it with the result of part b.

## Applications

1. This application is based on the following data set.

| | | | 50 Observations on y: | | | | | |
|---|---|---|---|---|---|---|---|---|
| −1.42 | 2.75 | 2.10 | −5.08 | 1.49 | 1.00 | 0.16 | −1.11 | 1.66 |
| −0.26 | −4.87 | 5.94 | 2.21 | −6.87 | 0.90 | 1.61 | 2.11 | −3.82 |
| −0.62 | 7.01 | 26.14 | 7.39 | 0.79 | 1.93 | 1.97 | −23.17, | −2.52 |
| −1.26 | −0.15 | 3.41 | −5.45 | 1.31 | 1.52 | 2.04 | 3.00 | 6.31 |
| 5.51 | −15.22 | −1.47 | −1.48 | 6.66 | 1.78 | 2.62 | −5.16 | −4.71 |
| −0.35 | −0.48 | 1.24 | 0.69 | 1.91 | | | | |

| | | | 50 Observations on $x_1$: | | | | | |
|---|---|---|---|---|---|---|---|---|
| −1.65 | 1.48 | 0.77 | 0.67 | 0.68 | 0.23 | −0.40 | −1.13 | 0.15 |
| −0.63 | 0.34 | 0.35 | 0.79 | 0.77 | −1.04 | 0.28 | 0.58 | −0.41 |
| −1.78 | 1.25 | 0.22 | 1.25 | −0.12 | 0.66 | 1.06 | −0.66 | −1.18 |
| −0.80 | −1.32 | 0.16 | 1.06 | −0.60 | 0.79 | 0.86 | 2.04 | −0.51 |
| 0.02 | 0.33 | −1.99 | 0.70 | −0.17 | 0.33 | 0.48 | 1.90 | −0.18 |
| −0.18 | −1.62 | 0.39 | 0.17 | 1.02 | | | | |

| | | | 50 Observations on $x_2$: | | | | | |
|---|---|---|---|---|---|---|---|---|
| −0.67 | 0.70 | 0.32 | 2.88 | −0.19 | −1.28 | −2.72 | −0.70 | −1.55 |
| −0.74 | −1.87 | 1.56 | 0.37 | −2.07 | 1.20 | 0.26 | −1.34 | −2.10 |
| 0.61 | 2.32 | 4.38 | 2.16 | 1.51 | 0.30 | −0.17 | 7.82 | −1.15 |
| 1.77 | 2.92 | −1.94 | 2.09 | 1.50 | −0.46 | 0.19 | −0.39 | 1.54 |
| 1.87 | −3.45 | −0.88 | −1.53 | 1.42 | −2.70 | 1.77 | −1.89 | −1.85 |
| 2.01 | 1.26 | −2.02 | 1.91 | −2.23 | | | | |

   a. Compute the ordinary least squares regression of $y$ on a constant, $x_1$, and $x_2$. Be sure to compute the conventional estimator of the asymptotic covariance matrix of the OLS estimator as well.
   b. Compute the White estimator of the appropriate asymptotic covariance matrix for the OLS estimates.
   c. Test for the presence of heteroscedasticity using White's general test. Do your results suggest the nature of the heteroscedasticity?
   d. Use the Breusch–Pagan/Godfrey Lagrange multiplier test to test for heteroscedasticity.
   e. Reestimate the parameters using a two-step FGLS estimator. Use Harvey's formulation, $\text{Var}[\varepsilon_i \mid x_{i1}, x_{i2}] = \sigma^2 \exp(\gamma_1 x_{i1} + \gamma_2 x_{i2})$.

2. In the study of gasoline consumption in Example 8.6 using Baltagi and Griffin's data, we did not use another variable in the data set, LCARPCAP, which is the log of the number of cars per capita in the country. Repeat the analysis after adding this variable to the model. First determine whether this variable "belongs" in the model—that is, using an appropriate standard error, test the significance of the coefficient on this variable in the model.

3.  (We look ahead to our use of maximum likelihood to estimate the models discussed in this chapter in Chapter 16.) In Example 8.5, we computed an iterated FGLS estimator using the airline data and the model $\mathrm{Var}[\varepsilon_{it} \,|\, \textit{Loadfactor}] = \exp(\gamma_1 + \gamma_2$ Loadfactor). The weights computed at each iteration were computed by estimating $(\gamma_1, \gamma_2)$ by least squares regression of $\ln \hat{\varepsilon}^2_{i,t}$ on a constant and Loadfactor. The maximum likelihood estimator would proceed along similar lines, however the weights would be computed by regression of $[\hat{\varepsilon}^2_{i,t} / \hat{\sigma}^2_{i,t} - 1]$ on a constant and Loadfactor instead. Use this alternative procedure to estimate the model. Do you get different results?

# 9

# MODELS FOR PANEL DATA

## 9.1 INTRODUCTION

Data sets that combine time series and cross sections are common in economics. For example, the published statistics of the OECD contain numerous series of economic aggregates observed yearly for many countries. Recently constructed **longitudinal data sets** contain observations on thousands of individuals or families, each observed at several points in time. Other empirical studies have analyzed time-series data on sets of firms, states, countries, or industries simultaneously. These data sets provide rich sources of information about the economy. Modeling in this setting, however, calls for some complex stochastic specifications. In this chapter, we will survey the most commonly used techniques for time-series cross-section data analyses in single equation models.

## 9.2 PANEL DATA MODELS

Many recent studies have analyzed **panel,** or longitudinal, data sets. Two very famous ones are the National Longitudinal Survey of Labor Market Experience (NLS, http://www.bls.gov/nls/nlsdoc.htm) and the Michigan Panel Study of Income Dynamics (PSID, http://psidonline.isr.umich.edu/). In these data sets, very large cross sections, consisting of thousands of microunits, are followed through time, but the number of periods is often quite small. The PSID, for example, is a study of roughly 6,000 families and 15,000 individuals who have been interviewed periodically from 1968 to the present. An ongoing study in the United Kingdom is the British Household Panel Survey (BHPS, http://www.iser.essex.ac.uk/ulsc/bhps/) which was begun in 1991 and is now in its 15th wave. The survey follows several thousand households (currently over 5,000) for several years. Many very rich data sets have recently been developed in the area of health care and health economics, including the German Socioeconomic Panel (GSOEP, http://dpls.dacc.wisc.edu/apdu/GSOEP/gsoep_cd_data.html) and the Medical Expenditure Panel Survey (MEPS, http://www.meps.ahrq.gov/). Constructing long, evenly spaced time series in contexts such as these would be prohibitively expensive, but for the purposes for which these data are typically used, it is unnecessary. Time effects are often viewed as "transitions" or discrete changes of state. The Current Population Survey (CPS, http://www.census.gov/cps/), for example, is a monthly survey of about 50,000 households that interviews households monthly for four months, waits for eight months, then reinterviews. This two-wave, **rotating panel** format allows analysis of short-term changes as well as a more general analysis of the U.S. national labor market. They are typically modeled as specific to the period in which they occur and are not carried across periods within a cross-sectional unit.[1] Panel data sets are more oriented toward cross-section analyses; they are wide but typically short. Heterogeneity across units is an integral part—indeed, often the central focus—of the analysis.

The analysis of panel or longitudinal data is the subject of one of the most active and innovative bodies of literature in econometrics,[2] partly because panel data provide such a rich environment for the development of estimation techniques and theoretical results. In more practical terms, however, researchers have been able to use time-series cross-sectional data to examine issues that could not be studied in either cross-sectional or time-series settings alone. Two examples are as follows.

**1.** In a widely cited study of labor supply, Ben-Porath (1973) observes that at a certain point in time, in a cohort of women, 50 percent may appear to be working. It is ambiguous whether this finding implies that, in this cohort, one-half of the women on average will be working or that the same one-half will be working in every period. These have very different implications for policy and for the interpretation of any statistical results. Cross-sectional data alone will not shed any light on the question.

**2.** A long-standing problem in the analysis of production functions has been the inability to separate economies of scale and technological change.[3] Cross-sectional data provide information only about the former, whereas time-series data muddle the two effects, with no prospect of separation. It is common, for example, to assume constant returns to scale so as to reveal the technical change.[4] Of course, this practice assumes away the problem. A panel of data on costs or output for a number of firms each observed over several years can provide estimates of both the rate of technological change (as time progresses) and economies of scale (for the sample of different sized firms at each point in time).

Recent applications have allowed researchers to study the impact of health policy changes [e.g., Riphahn, et al's. (2003) analysis of reforms in German public health insurance regulations] and more generally the dynamics of labor market behavior. In principle, the methods of Chapters 6 and 20 can be applied to longitudinal data sets. In the typical panel, however, there are a large number of cross-sectional units and

---

[1]Formal time-series modeling for panel data is briefly examined in Section 22.5.

[2]The panel data literature rivals the received research on unit roots and cointegration in econometrics in its rate of growth. A compendium of the earliest literature is Maddala (1993). Book-length surveys on the econometrics of panel data include Hsiao (2003), Dielman (1989), Matyas and Sevestre (1996), Raj and Baltagi (1992), Nerlove (2002), Arellano (2003), and Baltagi (2001, 2005). There are also lengthy surveys devoted to specific topics, such as limited dependent variable models [Hsiao, Lahiri, Lee, and Pesaran (1999)] and semiparametric methods [Lee (1998)]. An extensive bibliography is given in Baltagi (2005).

[3]The distinction between these two effects figured prominently in the policy question of whether it was appropriate to break up the AT&T Corporation in the 1980s and, ultimately, to allow competition in the provision of long-distance telephone service.

[4]In a classic study of this issue, Solow (1957) states: "From time series of $\Delta Q/Q$, $w_K$, $\Delta K/K$, $w_L$ and $\Delta L/L$ or their discrete year-to-year analogues, we could estimate $\Delta A/A$ and thence $A(t)$ itself. Actually an amusing thing happens here. Nothing has been said so far about returns to scale. But if all factor inputs are classified either as $K$ or $L$, then the available figures always show $w_K$ and $w_L$ adding up to one. Since we have assumed that factors are paid their marginal products, this amounts to assuming the hypothesis of Euler's theorem. The calculus being what it is, we might just as well assume the conclusion, namely, the $F$ is homogeneous of degree one."

only a few periods. Thus, the time-series methods discussed there may be somewhat problematic. Recent work has generally concentrated on models better suited to these short and wide data sets. The techniques are focused on cross-sectional variation, or heterogeneity. In this chapter, we shall examine in detail the most widely used models and look briefly at some extensions.

### 9.2.1 GENERAL MODELING FRAMEWORK FOR ANALYZING PANEL DATA

The fundamental advantage of a panel data set over a cross section is that it will allow the researcher great flexibility in modeling differences in behavior across individuals. The basic framework for this discussion is a regression model of the form

$$y_{it} = \mathbf{x}'_{it}\boldsymbol{\beta} + \mathbf{z}'_i\boldsymbol{\alpha} + \varepsilon_{it}$$
$$= \mathbf{x}'_{it}\boldsymbol{\beta} + c_i + \varepsilon_{it}.$$

**(9-1)**

There are $K$ regressors in $\mathbf{x}_{it}$, *not including a constant term*. The **heterogeneity**, or **individual effect** is $\mathbf{z}'_i\boldsymbol{\alpha}$ where $\mathbf{z}_i$ contains a constant term and a set of individual or group specific variables, which may be observed, such as race, sex, location, etc, or unobserved, such as family specific characteristics, individual heterogeneity in skill or preferences, and so on, all of which are taken to be constant over time $t$. As it stands, this model is a classical regression model. If $\mathbf{z}_i$ is observed for all individuals, then the entire model can be treated as an ordinary linear model and fit by least squares. The complications arise when $c_i$ is unobserved, which will be the case in most applications. Consider, for example, analyses of the effect of education and experience on earnings from which "ability" will always be a missing and unobservable variable. In health care studies, for example of usage of the health care system, "health" and "health care" will be unobservable factors in the analysis.

The main objective of the analysis will be consistent and efficient estimation of the **partial effects,**

$$\boldsymbol{\beta} = \partial E[y_{it} \mid \mathbf{x}_{it}]/\partial \mathbf{x}_{it}.$$

Whether this is possible depends on the assumptions about the unobserved effects. We begin with a **strict exogeneity** assumption for the independent variables,

$$E[\varepsilon_{it} \mid \mathbf{x}_{i1}, \mathbf{x}_{i2}, \dots, ] = 0.$$

That is, the current disturbance is uncorrelated with the independent variables in every period, past, present and future. The crucial aspect of the model concerns the heterogeneity. A particularly convenient assumption would be **mean independence,**

$$E[c_i \mid \mathbf{x}_{i1}, \mathbf{x}_{i2}, \dots] = \alpha.$$

If the missing variable(s) are uncorrelated with the included variables, then, as we shall see, they may be included in the disturbance of the model. This is the assumption that underlies the random effects model, as we will explore below. It is, however, a particularly strong assumption—it would be unlikely in the labor market and health care examples mentioned above. The alternative would be

$$E[c_i \mid \mathbf{x}_{i1}, \mathbf{x}_{i2}, \ldots,] = h(\mathbf{x}_{i1}, \mathbf{x}_{i2}, \ldots)$$
$$= h(\mathbf{X}_i).$$

This formulation is more general, but at the same time, considerably more complicated, the more so since it may require yet further assumptions about the nature of the function.

### 9.2.2  MODEL STRUCTURES

We will examine a variety of different models for panel data. Broadly, they can be arranged as follows:

1.  **Pooled Regression:** If $\mathbf{z}_i$ contains only a constant term, then ordinary least squares provides consistent and efficient estimates of the common $\alpha$ and the slope vector $\boldsymbol{\beta}$.

2.  **Fixed Effects:** If $\mathbf{z}_i$ is unobserved, but correlated with $\mathbf{x}_{it}$, then the least squares estimator of $\boldsymbol{\beta}$ is biased and inconsistent as a consequence of an omitted variable. However, in this instance, the model

$$y_{it} = \mathbf{x}'_{it}\boldsymbol{\beta} + \alpha_i + \varepsilon_{it},$$

where $\alpha_i = \mathbf{z}'_i\boldsymbol{\alpha}$, embodies all the observable effects and specifies an estimable conditional mean. This **fixed effects** approach takes $\alpha_i$ to be a group-specific constant term in the regression model. It should be noted that the term "fixed" as used here signifies the correlation of $c_i$ and $\mathbf{x}_{it}$, not that $c_i$ is nonstochastic.

3.  **Random Effects:** If the unobserved individual heterogeneity, however formulated, can be assumed to be uncorrelated with the included variables, then the model may be formulated as

$$y_{it} = \mathbf{x}'_{it}\boldsymbol{\beta} + E[\mathbf{z}'_i\boldsymbol{\alpha}] + \{\mathbf{z}'_i\boldsymbol{\alpha} - E[\mathbf{z}'_i\boldsymbol{\alpha}]\} + \varepsilon_{it}$$
$$= \mathbf{x}'_{it}\boldsymbol{\beta} + \alpha + u_i + \varepsilon_{it},$$

that is, as a linear regression model with a compound disturbance that may be consistently, albeit inefficiently, estimated by least squares. This **random effects** approach specifies that $u_i$ is a group-specific random element, similar to $\varepsilon_{it}$ except that for each group, there is but a single draw that enters the regression identically in each period. Again, the crucial distinction between fixed and random effects is whether the unobserved individual effect embodies elements that are correlated with the regressors in the model, not whether these effects are stochastic or not. We will examine this basic formulation, then consider an extension to a dynamic model.

4.  **Random Parameters:** The random effects model can be viewed as a regression model with a random constant term. With a sufficiently rich data set, we may extend this idea to a model in which the other coefficients vary randomly across individuals as well. The extension of the model might appear as

$$y_{it} = \mathbf{x}'_{it}(\boldsymbol{\beta} + \mathbf{h}_i) + (\alpha + u_i) + \varepsilon_{it},$$

where $\mathbf{h}_i$ is a random vector that induces the variation of the parameters across individuals. This random parameters model was proposed quite early in this literature, but has only fairly recently enjoyed widespread attention in several fields. It represents a natural extension in which researchers broaden the amount of heterogeneity across individuals while retaining some commonalities—the parameter vectors still share a common mean. Some recent applications have extended this yet another step by allowing the mean value of the parameter distribution to be person-specific, as in

$$y_{it} = \mathbf{x}'_{it}(\boldsymbol{\beta} + \boldsymbol{\Delta}\mathbf{z}_i + \boldsymbol{h}_i) + (\alpha + u_i) + \varepsilon_{it},$$

where $\mathbf{z}_i$ is a set of observable, person specific variables, and $\boldsymbol{\Delta}$ is a matrix of parameters to be estimated. As we will examine later, this **hierarchical model** is extremely versatile.

### 9.2.3 EXTENSIONS

The short list of model types provided earlier only begins to suggest the variety of applications of panel data methods in econometrics. We will begin in this chapter to study some of the formulations and uses of linear models. The random and fixed effects models and random parameters models have also been widely used in models of censoring, binary, and other discrete choices, and models for event counts. We will examine all of these in the chapters to follow. In some cases, such as the models for count data in Chapter 25 the extension of random and fixed effects models is straightforward, if somewhat more complicated computationally. In others, such as in binary choice models in Chapter 23 and censoring models in Chapter 24, these panel data models have been used, but not before overcoming some significant methodological and computational obstacles.

### 9.2.4 BALANCED AND UNBALANCED PANELS

By way of preface to the analysis to follow, we note an important aspect of panel data analysis. As suggested by the preceding, a "panel" data set will consist of $n$ sets of observations on individuals to be denoted $i = 1, \ldots, n$. If each individual in the data set is observed the same number of times, usually denoted $T$, the data set is a **balanced panel.** An **unbalanced panel** data set is one in which individuals may be observed different numbers of times. We will denote this $T_i$. A **fixed panel** is one in which the same set of individuals is observed for the duration of the study. The data sets we will examine in this chapter, while not all balanced, are fixed. A rotating panel is one in which the cast of individuals changes from one period to the next. For example, Gonzalez and Maloney (1999) examined self-employment decisions in Mexico using the National Urban Employment Survey. This is a quarterly data set drawn from 1987 to 1993 in which individuals are interviewed five times. Each quarter, one-fifth of the individuals is rotated out of the data set. We will not treat rotating panels in this text. Some discussion and numerous references may be found in Baltagi (2005).

 The development to follow is structured so that the distinction between balanced and unbalanced panels will entail nothing more than a trivial change in notation—where for convenience we write $T$ suggesting a balanced panel, merely changing $T$ to $T_i$ generalizes the results. We will note specifically when this is not the case, such as in Breusch and Pagan's (1980) LM statistic.

## 9.3 THE POOLED REGRESSION MODEL

We begin the analysis by assuming the simplest version of the model, the **pooled model,**

$$y_{it} = \alpha + \mathbf{x}'_{it}\boldsymbol{\beta} + \varepsilon_{it}, i = 1, \ldots, n, t = 1, \ldots, T_i,$$

$$E[\varepsilon_{it} \mid \mathbf{x}_{i1}, \mathbf{x}_{i2}, \ldots, \mathbf{x}_{iT_i}] = 0,$$

$$Var[\varepsilon_{it} \mid \mathbf{x}_{i1}, \mathbf{x}_{i2}, \ldots, \mathbf{x}_{iT_i}] = \sigma_\varepsilon^2,$$

$$Cov[\varepsilon_{it}, \varepsilon_{js} \mid \mathbf{x}_{i1}, \mathbf{x}_{i2}, \ldots, \mathbf{x}_{iT_i}] = 0 \text{ if } i \neq j \text{ or } t \neq s.$$

**(9-2)**

(In the panel data context, this is also called the **population averaged model** under the assumption that any latent heterogeneity has been averaged out.) In this form, if the remaining assumptions of the classical model are met (zero conditional mean of $\varepsilon_{it}$, homoscedasticity, independence across observations, $i$, and strict exogeneity of $\mathbf{x}_{it}$), then no further analysis beyond the results of Chapter 4 is needed. Ordinary least squares is the efficient estimator and inference can reliably proceed along the lines developed in Chapter 5.

### 9.3.1 LEAST SQUARES ESTIMATION OF THE POOLED MODEL

The crux of the panel data analysis in this chapter is that the assumptions underlying ordinary least squares estimation of the pooled model are unlikely to be met. The question, then, is what can be expected of the estimator when the heterogeneity does differ across individuals? The fixed effects case is obvious. As we will examine later, omitting (or ignoring) the heterogeneity when the fixed effects model is appropriate renders the least squares estimator inconsistent—sometimes wildly so. In the random effects case, in which the true model is

$$y_{it} = c_i + \mathbf{x}'_{it}\boldsymbol{\beta} + \varepsilon_{it},$$

where $E[c_i \mid \mathbf{X}_i] = \alpha$, we can write the model

$$y_{it} = \alpha + \mathbf{x}'_{it}\boldsymbol{\beta} + \varepsilon_{it} + (c_i - E[c_i \mid \mathbf{X}_i])$$

$$= \alpha + \mathbf{x}'_{it}\boldsymbol{\beta} + \varepsilon_{it} + u_i$$

$$= \alpha + \mathbf{x}'_{it}\boldsymbol{\beta} + w_{it}.$$

In this form, we can see that the unobserved heterogeneity induces **autocorrelation;** $E[w_{it}w_{is}] = \sigma_u^2$ when $t \neq s$. As we explored in Chapter 8—we will revisit it in Chapter 19—the ordinary least squares estimator in the generalized regression model may be consistent, but the conventional estimator of its asymptotic variance is likely to underestimate the true variance of the estimator.

### 9.3.2 ROBUST COVARIANCE MATRIX ESTIMATION

Suppose we consider the model more generally than this. Stack the $T_i$ observations for individual $i$ in a single equation,

$$\mathbf{y}_i = \mathbf{X}_i\boldsymbol{\beta} + \mathbf{w}_i,$$

where $\boldsymbol{\beta}$ now includes the constant term. In this setting, there may be heteroscedasticity across individuals. However, in a panel data set, the more substantive problem is cross-observation correlation, or autocorrelation. In a longitudinal data set, the group of observations may all pertain to the same individual, so any latent effects left out of the model will carry across all periods. Suppose, then, we assume that the disturbance vector consists of $\varepsilon_{it}$ plus these omitted components. Then,

$$\text{Var}[\mathbf{w}_i \mid \mathbf{X}_i] = \sigma_\varepsilon^2 \mathbf{I}_{Ti} + \Sigma_i$$

$$= \Omega_i.$$

The ordinary least squares estimator of $\beta$ is

$$\mathbf{b} = (\mathbf{X}'\mathbf{X})^{-1}\mathbf{X}'\mathbf{y}$$

$$= \left[\sum_{i=1}^{n} \mathbf{X}_i'\mathbf{X}_i\right]^{-1} \sum_{i=1}^{n} \mathbf{X}_i'\mathbf{y}_i$$

$$= \left[\sum_{i=1}^{n} \mathbf{X}_i'\mathbf{X}_i\right]^{-1} \sum_{i=1}^{n} \mathbf{X}_i'(\mathbf{X}_i\beta + \mathbf{w}_i)$$

$$= \beta + \left[\sum_{i=1}^{n} \mathbf{X}_i'\mathbf{X}_i\right]^{-1} \sum_{i=1}^{n} \mathbf{X}_i'\mathbf{w}_i.$$

Consistency can be established along the lines developed in Chapter 4. The true asymptotic covariance matrix would take the form we saw for the generalized regression model in (8-10),

$$\text{Asy. Var}[\mathbf{b}] = \frac{1}{n}\text{plim}\left[\frac{1}{n}\sum_{i=1}^{n}\mathbf{X}_i'\mathbf{X}_i\right]^{-1}\text{plim}\left[\frac{1}{n}\sum_{i=1}^{n}\mathbf{X}_i'\mathbf{w}_i\mathbf{w}_i'\mathbf{X}_i\right]\text{plim}\left[\frac{1}{n}\sum_{i=1}^{n}\mathbf{X}_i'\mathbf{X}_i\right]^{-1}$$

$$= \frac{1}{n}\text{plim}\left[\frac{1}{n}\sum_{i=1}^{n}\mathbf{X}_i'\mathbf{X}_i\right]^{-1}\text{plim}\left[\frac{1}{n}\sum_{i=1}^{n}\mathbf{X}_i'\Omega_i\mathbf{X}_i\right]\text{plim}\left[\frac{1}{n}\sum_{i=1}^{n}\mathbf{X}_i'\mathbf{X}_i\right]^{-1}.$$

This result provides the counterpart to (8-28). As before, the center matrix must be estimated. In the same spirit as the White estimator, we can estimate this matrix with

$$\text{Est. Asy. Var}[\mathbf{b}] = \frac{1}{n}\left[\frac{1}{n}\sum_{i=1}^{n}\mathbf{X}_i'\mathbf{X}_i\right]^{-1}\left[\frac{1}{n}\sum_{i=1}^{n}\mathbf{X}_i'\hat{\mathbf{w}}_i\hat{\mathbf{w}}_i'\mathbf{X}_i\right]\left[\frac{1}{n}\sum_{i=1}^{n}\mathbf{X}_i'\mathbf{X}_i\right]^{-1}, \qquad \text{(9-3)}$$

where $\hat{\mathbf{w}}'$ is the vector of $T_i$ residuals for individual $i$. In fact, the logic of the White estimator *does* carry over to this estimator. Note, however, this is not quite the same as (8-27). It is quite likely that the more important issue for appropriate estimation of the asymptotic covariance matrix is the correlation across observations, not heteroscedasticity. As such, it is quite likely that the White estimator in (8-27) is not the solution to the inference problem here. Example 9.1 shows this effect at work.

### Example 9.1  Wage Equation
Cornwell and Rupert (1988) analyzed the returns to schooling in a (balanced) panel of 595 observations on heads of households. The sample data are drawn from years 1976–1982 from the "Non-Survey of Economic Opportunity" from the Panel Study of Income Dynamics.

The estimating equation is

$$\ln Wage_{it} = \beta_1 + \beta_2 Exp_{it} + \beta_3 Exp_{it}^2 + \beta_4 Wks_{it} + \beta_5 Occ_{it}$$
$$+ \beta_6 Ind_{it} + \beta_7 South_{it} + \beta_8 SMSA_{it} + \beta_9 MS_{it}$$
$$+ \beta_{10} Union_{it} + \beta_{11} Ed_i + \beta_{12} Fem_i + \beta_{13} Blk_i + \varepsilon_{it}$$

where the variables are

| | |
|---|---|
| *Exp* | = years of full time work experience, 0 if not, |
| *Wks* | = weeks worked, 0 if not, |
| *Occ* | = 1 if blue collar occupation, 0 if not, |
| *Ind* | = 1 if the individual works in a manufacturing industry, 0 if not, |
| *South* | = 1 if the individual resides in the south, 0 if not, |
| *SMSA* | = 1 if the individual resides in an SMSA, 0 if not, |
| *MS* | = 1 if the individual is married, 0 if not, |
| *Union* | = 1 if the individual wage is set by a union contract, 0 if not, |
| *Ed* | = years of education, |
| *Fem* | = 1 if the individual is female, 0 if not, |
| *Blk* | = 1 if the individual is black, 0 if not. |

Note that *Ed*, *Fem*, and *Blk* are **time-invariant**. See Appendix Table F9.1 for the data source. The main interest of the study, beyond comparing various estimation methods, is $\beta_{11}$, the return to education. Table 9.1 reports the least squares estimates based on the full sample of 4,165 observations. [The authors do not report OLS estimates. However, they do report linear least squares estimates of the fixed effects model, which are simple least squares using deviations from individual means. (See Section 9.4.) It was not possible to match their reported results for these or any of their other reported results. Because our purpose is to compare the various estimators to each other, we have not attempted to resolve the discrepancy.] The conventional OLS standard errors are given in the second column of results. The third column gives the robust standard errors computed using (9-3). For these data, the computation is

$$\text{Est. Asy. Var}[\mathbf{b}] = \left[\sum_{i=1}^{595} \mathbf{X}_i'\mathbf{X}_i\right]^{-1} \left[\sum_{i=1}^{595}\left(\sum_{t=1}^{7}\mathbf{x}_{it}e_{it}\right)\left(\sum_{t=1}^{7}\mathbf{x}_{it}e_{it}\right)'\right]\left[\sum_{i=1}^{595}\mathbf{X}_i'\mathbf{X}_i\right]^{-1}.$$

**TABLE 9.1** Wage Equation Estimated by OLS

| Coefficient | Estimated Coefficient | OLS Standard Error | Panel Robust Standard Error | White Hetero. Consistent Std. Error |
|---|---|---|---|---|
| $\beta_1$: Constant | 5.2511 | 0.07129 | 0.1233 | 0.07435 |
| $\beta_2$: Exp | 0.04010 | 0.002159 | 0.004067 | 0.002158 |
| $\beta_3$: Exp$^2$ | −0.0006734 | 0.00004744 | 0.00009111 | 0.00004789 |
| $\beta_4$: Wks | 0.004216 | 0.001081 | 0.001538 | 0.001143 |
| $\beta_5$: Occ | −0.1400 | 0.01466 | 0.02718 | 0.01494 |
| $\beta_6$: Ind | 0.04679 | 0.01179 | 0.02361 | 0.01199 |
| $\beta_7$: South | −0.05564 | 0.01253 | 0.02610 | 0.01274 |
| $\beta_8$: SMSA | 0.1517 | 0.01207 | 0.02405 | 0.01208 |
| $\beta_9$: MS | 0.04845 | 0.02057 | 0.04085 | 0.02049 |
| $\beta_{10}$: Union | 0.09263 | 0.01280 | 0.02362 | 0.01233 |
| $\beta_{11}$: Ed | 0.05670 | 0.002613 | 0.005552 | 0.002726 |
| $\beta_{12}$: Fem | −0.3678 | 0.02510 | 0.04547 | 0.02310 |
| $\beta_{13}$: Blk | −0.1669 | 0.02204 | 0.04423 | 0.02075 |

The robust standard errors are generally about twice the uncorrected ones. In contrast, the White robust standard errors are almost the same as the uncorrected ones. This suggests that for this model, ignoring the within group correlations does, indeed, substantially affect the inferences one would draw.

### 9.3.3  CLUSTERING AND STRATIFICATION

Many recent studies have analyzed survey data sets, such as the Current Population Survey (CPS). Survey data are often drawn in "clusters," partly to reduce costs. For example, interviewers might visit all the families in a particular block. In other cases, effects that resemble the common random effects in panel data treatments might arise naturally in the sampling setting. Consider, for example, a study of student test scores across several states. Common effects could arise at many levels in such a data set. Education curriculum or funding policies in a state could cause a "state effect;" there could be school district effects, school effects within districts, and even teacher effects within a particular school. Each of these is likely to induce correlation across observations that resembles the random (or fixed) effects we have identified above. One might be reluctant to assume that a tightly structured model such as the simple random effects specification is at work. But, as we saw in Example 9.1, ignoring common effects can lead to serious inference errors. The robust estimator suggested in Section 9.3.2 provides a useful approach.

For a two-level model, such as might arise in a sample of firms that are grouped by industry, or students who share teachers in particular schools, a natural approach to this "clustering" would be the robust common effects approach shown earlier. The resemblance of the now standard **cluster estimator** for a one level model to the common effects panel model considered above is more than coincidental. A refinement to (9-1) is often employed to account for small sample effects when the number of clusters is likely to be a significant proportion of a finite total, such as the number of school districts in a state. A degrees of freedom correction as shown in (9-4) is often employed for this purpose. The robust covariance matrix estimator would be

$$
\textit{Est. Asy. Var}[\mathbf{b}] = \left[\sum_{g=1}^{G}\mathbf{X}_g'\mathbf{X}_g\right]^{-1}\left[\frac{G}{G-1}\sum_{g=1}^{G}\mathbf{X}_g'\hat{\mathbf{w}}_g\hat{\mathbf{w}}_g'\mathbf{X}_g\right]\left[\sum_{g=1}^{G}\mathbf{X}_g'\mathbf{X}_g\right]^{-1}, \quad \textbf{(9-4)}
$$

where $G$ is the number of clusters in the sample and each cluster consists of $n_g, g = 1, \ldots, G$ observations. [Note that this matrix is simply $G/(G-1)$ times the matrix in (9-3).] Many further refinements for more complex samples—consider the test scores example—have been suggested. For a detailed analysis, see Cameron and Trivedi (2005, Chapter 24).

### 9.3.4  ROBUST ESTIMATION USING GROUP MEANS

The pooled regression model can be estimated using the sample means of the data. The implied regression model is obtained by premultiplying each group by $(1/T)\mathbf{i}'$ where $\mathbf{i}'$ is a row vector of ones;

$$
(1/T)\mathbf{i}'\mathbf{y}_i = (1/T)\mathbf{i}'\mathbf{X}_i\boldsymbol{\beta} + (1/T)\mathbf{i}'\mathbf{w}_i
$$

or

$$\bar{y}_{i.} = \bar{\mathbf{x}}'_{i.}\boldsymbol{\beta} + \bar{w}_i.$$

In the transformed linear regression, the disturbances continue to have zero conditional means but heteroscedastic variances $\sigma_i^2 = (1/T^2)\mathbf{i}'\boldsymbol{\Omega}_i\mathbf{i}$. With $\boldsymbol{\Omega}_i$ unspecified, this is a heteroscedastic regression for which we would use the White estimator for appropriate inference. Why might one want to use this estimator when the full data set is available? If the classical assumptions are met, then it is straightforward to show that the asymptotic covariance matrix for the group means estimator is unambiguously larger, and the answer would be that there is no benefit. But, failure of the classical assumptions is what brought us to this point, and then the issue is less clear-cut. In the presence of unstructured cluster effects the efficiency of least squares can be considerably diminished, as we saw in the preceding example. The loss of information that occurs through the averaging might be relatively small, though in principle, the disaggregated data should still be better.

We emphasize, using **group means** does not solve the problem that is addressed by the fixed effects estimator. Consider the general model,

$$\mathbf{y}_i = \mathbf{X}_i\boldsymbol{\beta} + c_i\mathbf{i} + \mathbf{w}_i,$$

where as before, $c_i$ is the latent effect. If the mean independence assumption, $E[c_i \mid \mathbf{X}_i] = \alpha$, is not met, then, the effect will be transmitted to the group means as well. In this case, $E[c_i \mid \mathbf{X}_i] = h(\mathbf{X}_i)$. A common specification is Mundlak's (1978),

$$E[c_i \mid \mathbf{X}_i] = \bar{\mathbf{x}}'_{i.}\boldsymbol{\gamma}.$$

(We will revisit this specification in Section 9.5.5.) Then,

$$
\begin{aligned}
y_{it} &= \mathbf{x}'_{it}\boldsymbol{\beta} + c_i + \varepsilon_{it} \\
&= \mathbf{x}'_{it}\boldsymbol{\beta} + \bar{\mathbf{x}}'_{i.}\boldsymbol{\gamma} + [\varepsilon_{it} + c_i - E[c_i \mid \mathbf{X}_i]] \\
&= \mathbf{x}'_{it}\boldsymbol{\beta} + \bar{\mathbf{x}}'_{i.}\boldsymbol{\gamma} + u_{it}
\end{aligned}
$$

where by construction, $E[u_{it} \mid \mathbf{X}_i] = 0$. Taking means as before,

$$
\begin{aligned}
\bar{y}_{i.} &= \bar{\mathbf{x}}'_{i.}\boldsymbol{\beta} + \bar{\mathbf{x}}'_{i.}\boldsymbol{\gamma} + \bar{u}_{i.} \\
&= \bar{\mathbf{x}}'_{i.}(\boldsymbol{\beta} + \boldsymbol{\gamma}) + \bar{u}_{i.}.
\end{aligned}
$$

The implication is that the group means estimator estimates not $\boldsymbol{\beta}$, but $\boldsymbol{\beta} + \boldsymbol{\gamma}$. Averaging the observations in the group collects the entire set of effects, observed and latent, in the group means.

One consideration that remains, which, unfortunately, we cannot resolve analytically, is the possibility of **measurement error.** If the regressors are measured with error, then, as we will explore in Section 12.5, the least squares estimator is inconsistent and, as a consequence, efficiency is a moot point. In the panel data setting, if the measurement error is random, then using group means would work in the direction of averaging it out—indeed, in this instance, assuming the benchmark case $x_{itk} = x^*_{itk} + u_{itk}$, one could show that the group means estimator would be consistent as $T \to \infty$ while the OLS estimator would not.

**TABLE 9.2** Wage Equation Estimated by OLS

| Coefficient | OLS Estimated Coefficient | Panel Robust Standard Error | Group Means Estimates | White Robust Standard Error |
|---|---|---|---|---|
| $\beta_1$: Constant | 5.2511 | 0.1233 | 5.1214 | 0.2078 |
| $\beta_2$: Exp | 0.04010 | 0.004067 | 0.03190 | 0.004597 |
| $\beta_3$: Exp$^2$ | −0.0006734 | 0.00009111 | −0.0005656 | 0.0001020 |
| $\beta_4$: Wks | 0.004216 | 0.001538 | 0.009189 | 0.003578 |
| $\beta_5$: Occ | −0.1400 | 0.02718 | −0.1676 | 0.03338 |
| $\beta_6$: Ind | 0.04679 | 0.02361 | 0.05792 | 0.02636 |
| $\beta_7$: South | −0.05564 | 0.02610 | −0.05705 | 0.02660 |
| $\beta_8$: SMSA | 0.1517 | 0.02405 | 0.1758 | 0.02541 |
| $\beta_9$: MS | 0.04845 | 0.04085 | 0.1148 | 0.04989 |
| $\beta_{10}$: Union | 0.09263 | 0.02362 | 0.1091 | 0.02830 |
| $\beta_{11}$: Ed | 0.05670 | 0.005552 | 0.05144 | 0.005862 |
| $\beta_{12}$: Fem | −0.3678 | 0.04547 | −0.3171 | 0.05105 |
| $\beta_{13}$: Blk | −0.1669 | 0.04423 | −0.1578 | 0.04352 |

**Example 9.2   Robust Estimators of the Wage Equation**
Table 9.2 shows the group means estimator of the wage equation shown in Example 9.1 with the original least squares estimates. In both cases, a robust estimator is used for the covariance matrix of the estimator. It appears that similar results are obtained with the means.

### 9.3.5 ESTIMATION WITH FIRST DIFFERENCES

First differencing is another approach to estimation. Here, the intent would explicitly be to transform latent heterogeneity out of the model. The base case would be

$$y_{it} = c_i + \mathbf{x}_{it}'\boldsymbol{\beta} + \varepsilon_{it},$$

which implies the first differences equation

$$\Delta y_{it} = \Delta c_i + (\Delta \mathbf{x}_{it})'\boldsymbol{\beta} + \Delta \varepsilon_{it},$$

or

$$\Delta y_{it} = (\Delta \mathbf{x}_{it})'\boldsymbol{\beta} + \varepsilon_{it} - \varepsilon_{i,t-1}$$

$$= (\Delta \mathbf{x}_{it})'\boldsymbol{\beta} + u_{it}.$$

The advantage of the **first difference** approach is that it removes the latent heterogeneity from the model whether the fixed or random effects model is appropriate. The disadvantage is that the differencing also removes any time-invariant variables from the model. In our example, we had three, *Ed*, *Fem*, and *Blk*. If the time-invariant variables in the model are of no interest, then this is a robust approach that can estimate the parameters of the time-varying variables consistently. Of course, this is not helpful for the application in the example, because the impact of *Ed* on ln *Wage* was the primary object of the analysis. Note, as well, that the differencing procedure trades the cross-observation correlation in $c_i$ for a moving average (MA) disturbance, $u_{i,t} = \varepsilon_{i,t} - \varepsilon_{i,t-1}$. The new disturbance, $u_{i,t}$ is autocorrelated, though across only one period. Procedures are available for using two-step feasible GLS for an MA disturbance (see Chapter 19). Alternatively, this model is a natural candidate for OLS with the Newey–West robust covariance estimator, since the right number of lags (one) is known. (See Section 19.5.2.)

As a general observation, with a variety of approaches available, the first difference estimator does not have much to recommend it, save for one very important application. Many studies involve two period "panels," a before and after treatment. In these cases, as often as not, the phenomenon of interest may well specifically be the change in the outcome variable—the "treatment effect." Consider the model

$$y_{it} = c_i + \mathbf{x}'_{it}\boldsymbol{\beta} + \theta S_{it} + \varepsilon_{it},$$

where $t = 1, 2$ and $S_{it} = 0$ in period 1 and 1 in period 2; $S_{it}$ indicates a "treatment" that takes place between the two observations. The "treatment effect" would be

$$E[\Delta y_i \mid (\Delta \mathbf{x}_i = 0)] = \theta,$$

which is precisely the constant term in the first difference regression,

$$\Delta y_i = \theta + (\Delta \mathbf{x}_i)'\boldsymbol{\beta} + u_i.$$

We will examine cases like these in detail in Section 24.5.

### 9.3.6 THE WITHIN- AND BETWEEN-GROUPS ESTIMATORS

We can formulate the pooled regression model in three ways. First, the original formulation is

$$y_{it} = \alpha + \mathbf{x}'_{it}\boldsymbol{\beta} + \varepsilon_{it}. \tag{9-4a}$$

In terms of the group means,

$$\overline{y}_{i.} = \alpha + \overline{\mathbf{x}}'_{i.}\boldsymbol{\beta} + \overline{\varepsilon}_{i.}, \tag{9-4b}$$

while in terms of deviations from the group means,

$$y_{it} - \overline{y}_{i.} = (\mathbf{x}_{it} - \overline{\mathbf{x}}_{i.})'\boldsymbol{\beta} + \varepsilon_{it} - \overline{\varepsilon}_{i.}. \tag{9-4c}$$

[We are assuming there are no time-invariant variables, such as $Ed$ in Example 9.1, in $\mathbf{x}_{it}$. These would become all zeros in (9-4c).] All three are classical regression models, and in principle, all three could be estimated, at least consistently if not efficiently, by ordinary least squares. [Note that (9-4b) defines only $n$ observations, the group means.] Consider then the matrices of sums of squares and cross products that would be used in each case, where we focus only on estimation of $\boldsymbol{\beta}$. In (9-4a), the moments would accumulate variation about the overall means, $\overline{\overline{y}}$ and $\overline{\overline{\mathbf{x}}}$, and we would use the total sums of squares and cross products,

$$\mathbf{S}^{total}_{xx} = \sum_{i=1}^{n}\sum_{t=1}^{T}(\mathbf{x}_{it} - \overline{\overline{\mathbf{x}}})(\mathbf{x}_{it} - \overline{\overline{\mathbf{x}}})' \quad \text{and} \quad \mathbf{S}^{total}_{xy} = \sum_{i=1}^{n}\sum_{t=1}^{T}(\mathbf{x}_{it} - \overline{\overline{\mathbf{x}}})(y_{it} - \overline{\overline{y}}). \tag{9-5}$$

For (9-4c), because the data are in deviations already, the means of $(y_{it} - \overline{y}_{i.})$ and $(\mathbf{x}_{it} - \overline{\mathbf{x}}_{i.})$ are zero. The moment matrices are **within-groups** (i.e., variation around group means) sums of squares and cross products,

$$\mathbf{S}^{within}_{xx} = \sum_{i=1}^{n}\sum_{t=1}^{T}(\mathbf{x}_{it} - \overline{\mathbf{x}}_{i.})(\mathbf{x}_{it} - \overline{\mathbf{x}}_{i.})' \quad \text{and} \quad \mathbf{S}^{within}_{xy} = \sum_{i=1}^{n}\sum_{t=1}^{T}(\mathbf{x}_{it} - \overline{\mathbf{x}}_{i.})(y_{it} - \overline{y}_{i.}).$$

Finally, for (9-4b), the mean of group means is the overall mean. The moment matrices are the **between-groups** sums of squares and cross products—that is, the variation of the group means around the overall means;

$$\mathbf{S}_{xx}^{between} = \sum_{i=1}^{n} T(\overline{\mathbf{x}}_{i.} - \overline{\overline{\mathbf{x}}})(\overline{\mathbf{x}}_{i.} - \overline{\overline{\mathbf{x}}})' \quad \text{and} \quad \mathbf{S}_{xy}^{between} = \sum_{i=1}^{n} T(\overline{\mathbf{x}}_{i.} - \overline{\overline{\mathbf{x}}})(\overline{y}_{i.} - \overline{\overline{y}}).$$

It is easy to verify that

$$\mathbf{S}_{xx}^{total} = \mathbf{S}_{xx}^{within} + \mathbf{S}_{xx}^{between} \quad \text{and} \quad \mathbf{S}_{xy}^{total} = \mathbf{S}_{xy}^{within} + \mathbf{S}_{xy}^{between}.$$

Therefore, there are three possible least squares estimators of $\beta$ corresponding to the decomposition. The least squares estimator is

$$\mathbf{b}^{total} = \left[\mathbf{S}_{xx}^{total}\right]^{-1} \mathbf{S}_{xy}^{total} = \left[\mathbf{S}_{xx}^{within} + \mathbf{S}_{xx}^{between}\right]^{-1} \left[\mathbf{S}_{xy}^{within} + \mathbf{S}_{xy}^{between}\right]. \tag{9-6}$$

The **within-groups estimator** is

$$\mathbf{b}^{within} = \left[\mathbf{S}_{xx}^{within}\right]^{-1} \mathbf{S}_{xy}^{within}. \tag{9-7}$$

This is the dummy variable estimator developed in Section 9.4. An alternative estimator would be the **between-groups estimator,**

$$\mathbf{b}^{between} = \left[\mathbf{S}_{xx}^{between}\right]^{-1} \mathbf{S}_{xy}^{between}. \tag{9-8}$$

This is the **group means estimator.** This least squares estimator of (9-4b) is based on the $n$ sets of groups means. (Note that we are assuming that $n$ is at least as large as $K$.) From the preceding expressions (and familiar previous results),

$$\mathbf{S}_{xy}^{within} = \mathbf{S}_{xx}^{within} \mathbf{b}^{within} \quad \text{and} \quad \mathbf{S}_{xy}^{between} = \mathbf{S}_{xx}^{between} \mathbf{b}^{between}.$$

Inserting these in (9-6), we see that the least squares estimator is a **matrix weighted average** of the within- and between-groups estimators:

$$\mathbf{b}^{total} = \mathbf{F}^{within} \mathbf{b}^{within} + \mathbf{F}^{between} \mathbf{b}^{between}, \tag{9-9}$$

where

$$\mathbf{F}^{within} = \left[\mathbf{S}_{xx}^{within} + \mathbf{S}_{xx}^{between}\right]^{-1} \mathbf{S}_{xx}^{within} = \mathbf{I} - \mathbf{F}^{between}.$$

The form of this result resembles the Bayesian estimator in the classical model discussed in Chapter 18. The resemblance is more than passing; it can be shown [see, e.g., Judge et al. (1985)] that

$$\mathbf{F}^{within} = \left\{\left[\text{Asy. Var}(\mathbf{b}^{within})\right]^{-1} + \left[\text{Asy. Var}(\mathbf{b}^{between})\right]^{-1}\right\}^{-1} \left[\text{Asy. Var}(\mathbf{b}^{within})\right]^{-1},$$

which is essentially the same mixing result we have for the Bayesian estimator. In the weighted average, the estimator with the smaller variance receives the greater weight.

### Example 9.3 Analysis of Covariance and the World Health Organization Data

The decomposition of the total variation in Section 9.3.6 extends to the linear regression model the familiar "analysis of variance," or ANOVA, that is often used to decompose the variation in a variable in a clustered or stratified sample, or in a panel data set. One of the useful features of panel data analysis as we are doing here is the ability to analyze the

**TABLE 9.3** Analysis of Variance for WHO Data on Health Care Attainment

| Variable | Within-Groups Variation | Between-Groups Variation |
|---|---|---|
| *DALE* | 5.645% | 94.355% |
| *COMP* | 0.150% | 99.850% |
| *Expenditure* | 0.635% | 99.365% |
| *Education* | 0.178% | 99.822% |

between-groups variation (heterogeneity) to learn about the main regression relationships and the within-groups variation to learn about dynamic effects.

The World Health Organization data used in Example 6.6 is an unbalanced panel data set—we used only one year of the data in Example 6.6. Of the 191 countries in the sample, 140 are observed in the full five years, one is observed four times, and 50 are observed only once. The original WHO studies (2000a, 2000b) analyzed these data using the fixed effects model developed in the next section. The estimator is that in (9-4c). It is easy to see that groups with one observation will fall out of the computation, because if $T_i = 1$, then the observation equals the group mean. These data have been used by many researchers in similar panel data analyses. [See, e.g., Greene (2004c) and several references.] Gravelle et al. (2002a) have strongly criticized these analyses, arguing that the WHO data are much more like a cross section than a panel data set.

From Example 6.6, the model used by the researchers at WHO was

$$\ln DALE_{it} = \alpha_i + \beta_1 \ln Health\ Expenditure_{it} + \beta_2 \ln Education_{it} + \beta_3 \ln^2 Education_{it} + \varepsilon_{it}.$$

Additional models were estimated using WHO's composite measure of health care attainment, *COMP*. The analysis of variance for a variable $x_{it}$ is based on the decomposition

$$\sum_{i=1}^{n}\sum_{t=1}^{T_i}(x_{it} - \overline{\overline{x}})^2 = \sum_{i=1}^{n}\sum_{t=1}^{T_i}(x_{it} - \overline{x}_{i.})^2 + \sum_{t=1}^{n}T_i(\overline{x}_{i.} - \overline{\overline{x}})^2.$$

Dividing both sides of the equation by the left hand side produces the decomposition:

$$1 = \textit{Within-groups proportion} + \textit{Between-groups proportion}.$$

The first term on the right-hand side is the within-group variation that differentiates a panel data set from a cross section (or simply multiple observations on the same variable). Table 9.3 lists the decomposition of the variation in the variables used in the WHO studies.

The results suggest the reasons for the authors' concern about the data. For all but DALE, virtually all the variation in the data is between groups—that is cross-sectional variation. As the authors argue, these data are only slightly different from a cross section.

## 9.4 THE FIXED EFFECTS MODEL

The fixed effects model arises from the assumption that the omitted effects, $c_i$, in the general model,

$$y_{it} = \mathbf{x}'_{it}\boldsymbol{\beta} + c_i + \varepsilon_{it},$$

are correlated with the included variables. In a general form,

$$E[c_i \mid \mathbf{X}_i] = h(\mathbf{X}_i). \tag{9-10}$$

Because the conditional mean is the same in every period, we can write the model as

$$y_{it} = \mathbf{x}'_{it}\boldsymbol{\beta} + h(\mathbf{X}_i) + \varepsilon_{it} + [c_i - h(\mathbf{X}_i)]$$
$$= \mathbf{x}'_{it}\boldsymbol{\beta} + \alpha_i \quad + \varepsilon_{it} + [c_i - h(\mathbf{X}_i)].$$

By construction, the bracketed term is uncorrelated with $\mathbf{X}_i$, so we may absorb it in the disturbance, and write the model as

$$y_{it} = \mathbf{x}'_{it}\boldsymbol{\beta} + \alpha_i + \varepsilon_{it}. \tag{9-11}$$

A further assumption (usually unstated) is that $\text{Var}[c_i \mid \mathbf{X}_i]$ is constant. With this assumption, (9-11) becomes a classical linear regression model. (We will reconsider the homoscedasticity assumption shortly.) We emphasize, it is (9-10) that signifies the "fixed effects" model, not that any variable is "fixed" in this context and random elsewhere. The fixed effects formulation implies that differences across groups can be captured in differences in the constant term.[5] Each $\alpha_i$ is treated as an unknown parameter to be estimated.

Before proceeding, we note once again a major shortcoming of the fixed effects approach. Any **time invariant** variables in $\mathbf{x}_{it}$ will mimic the individual specific constant term. Consider the application of Examples 9.1 and 9.2. We could write the fixed effects formulation as

$$\ln Wage_{it} = \mathbf{x}'_{it}\boldsymbol{\beta} + [\beta_{10} Ed_i + \beta_{11} Fem_i + \beta_{12} Blk_i + c_i] + \varepsilon_{it}.$$

The fixed effects formulation of the model will absorb the last four terms in the regression in $\alpha_i$. The coefficients on the time-invariant variables cannot be estimated. This lack of identification is the price of the robustness of the specification to unmeasured correlation between the common effect and the exogenous variables.

### 9.4.1 LEAST SQUARES ESTIMATION

Let $\mathbf{y}_i$ and $\mathbf{X}_i$ be the $T$ observations for the $i$th unit, $\mathbf{i}$ be a $T \times 1$ column of ones, and let $\boldsymbol{\varepsilon}_i$ be the associated $T \times 1$ vector of disturbances.[6] Then,

$$\mathbf{y}_i = \mathbf{X}_i \boldsymbol{\beta} + \mathbf{i}\alpha_i + \boldsymbol{\varepsilon}_i.$$

Collecting these terms gives

$$\begin{bmatrix} \mathbf{y}_1 \\ \mathbf{y}_2 \\ \vdots \\ \mathbf{y}_n \end{bmatrix} = \begin{bmatrix} \mathbf{X}_1 \\ \mathbf{X}_2 \\ \vdots \\ \mathbf{X}_n \end{bmatrix} \boldsymbol{\beta} + \begin{bmatrix} \mathbf{i} & \mathbf{0} & \cdots & \mathbf{0} \\ \mathbf{0} & \mathbf{i} & \cdots & \mathbf{0} \\ & & \vdots & \\ \mathbf{0} & \mathbf{0} & \cdots & \mathbf{i} \end{bmatrix} \begin{bmatrix} \alpha_1 \\ \alpha_2 \\ \vdots \\ \alpha_n \end{bmatrix} + \begin{bmatrix} \boldsymbol{\varepsilon}_1 \\ \boldsymbol{\varepsilon}_2 \\ \vdots \\ \boldsymbol{\varepsilon}_n \end{bmatrix}$$

or

$$\mathbf{y} = [\mathbf{X} \quad \mathbf{d}_1 \quad \mathbf{d}_2 \ldots \mathbf{d}_n] \begin{bmatrix} \boldsymbol{\beta} \\ \boldsymbol{\alpha} \end{bmatrix} + \boldsymbol{\varepsilon}, \tag{9-12}$$

---

[5]It is also possible to allow the slopes to vary across $i$, but this method introduces some new methodological issues, as well as considerable complexity in the calculations. A study on the topic is Cornwell and Schmidt (1984).

[6]The assumption of a fixed group size, $T$, at this point is purely for convenience. As noted in Section 9.2.4, the unbalanced case is a minor variation.

where $\mathbf{d}_i$ is a dummy variable indicating the $i$th unit. Let the $nT \times n$ matrix $\mathbf{D} = [\mathbf{d}_1, \mathbf{d}_2, \dots, \mathbf{d}_n]$. Then, assembling all $nT$ rows gives

$$\mathbf{y} = \mathbf{X}\boldsymbol{\beta} + \mathbf{D}\boldsymbol{\alpha} + \boldsymbol{\varepsilon}.$$

This model is usually referred to as the **least squares dummy variable (LSDV) model** (although the "least squares" part of the name refers to the technique usually used to estimate it, not to the model itself).

This model is a classical regression model, so no new results are needed to analyze it. If $n$ is small enough, then the model can be estimated by ordinary least squares with $K$ regressors in $\mathbf{X}$ and $n$ columns in $\mathbf{D}$, as a multiple regression with $K + n$ parameters. Of course, if $n$ is thousands, as is typical, then this model is likely to exceed the storage capacity of any computer. But, by using familiar results for a partitioned regression, we can reduce the size of the computation.[7] We write the least squares estimator of $\boldsymbol{\beta}$ as

$$\mathbf{b} = [\mathbf{X}'\mathbf{M_D}\mathbf{X}]^{-1}[\mathbf{X}'\mathbf{M_D}\mathbf{y}] = \mathbf{b}^{within}, \tag{9-13}$$

where

$$\mathbf{M_D} = \mathbf{I} - \mathbf{D}(\mathbf{D}'\mathbf{D})^{-1}\mathbf{D}'.$$

This amounts to a least squares regression using the transformed data $\mathbf{X}_* = \mathbf{M_D}\mathbf{X}$ and $\mathbf{y}_* = \mathbf{M_D}\mathbf{y}$. The structure of $\mathbf{D}$ is particularly convenient; its columns are orthogonal, so

$$\mathbf{M_D} = \begin{bmatrix} \mathbf{M}^0 & \mathbf{0} & \mathbf{0} & \cdots & \mathbf{0} \\ \mathbf{0} & \mathbf{M}^0 & \mathbf{0} & \cdots & \mathbf{0} \\ & & \cdots & & \\ \mathbf{0} & \mathbf{0} & \mathbf{0} & \cdots & \mathbf{M}^0 \end{bmatrix}.$$

Each matrix on the diagonal is

$$\mathbf{M}^0 = \mathbf{I}_T - \frac{1}{T}\mathbf{i}\mathbf{i}'. \tag{9-14}$$

Premultiplying any $T \times 1$ *vector* $\mathbf{z}_i$ by $\mathbf{M}^0$ creates $\mathbf{M}^0\mathbf{z}_i = \mathbf{z}_i - \bar{z}\mathbf{i}$. (Note that the mean is taken over only the $T$ observations for unit $i$.) Therefore, the least squares regression of $\mathbf{M_D}\mathbf{y}$ on $\mathbf{M_D}\mathbf{X}$ is equivalent to a regression of $[y_{it} - \bar{y}_{i.}]$ on $[\mathbf{x}_{it} - \bar{\mathbf{x}}_{i.}]$, where $\bar{y}_{i.}$ and $\bar{\mathbf{x}}_{i.}$ are the scalar and $K \times 1$ vector of means of $y_{it}$ and $\mathbf{x}_{it}$ over the $T$ observations for group $i$.[8] The dummy variable coefficients can be recovered from the other normal equation in the partitioned regression:

$$\mathbf{D}'\mathbf{D}\mathbf{a} + \mathbf{D}'\mathbf{X}\mathbf{b} = \mathbf{D}'\mathbf{y}$$

or

$$\mathbf{a} = [\mathbf{D}'\mathbf{D}]^{-1}\mathbf{D}'(\mathbf{y} - \mathbf{X}\mathbf{b}).$$

This implies that for each $i$,

$$a_i = \bar{y}_{i.} - \bar{\mathbf{x}}_{i.}'\mathbf{b}. \tag{9-15}$$

---

[7]See Theorem 3.3.

[8]An interesting special case arises if $T = 2$. In the two-period case, you can show—we leave it as an exercise—that this least squares regression is done with $nT/2$ first difference observations, by regressing observation $(y_{i2} - y_{i1})$ (and its negative) on $(\mathbf{x}_{i2} - \mathbf{x}_{i1})$ (and its negative).

The appropriate estimator of the asymptotic covariance matrix for **b** is

$$\text{Est. Asy. Var}[\mathbf{b}] = s^2[\mathbf{X}'\mathbf{M_D}\mathbf{X}]^{-1} = s^2[\mathbf{S}_{xx}^{within}]^{-1}, \tag{9-16}$$

which uses the second moment matrix with **x**'s now expressed as deviations from their respective group means. The disturbance variance estimator is

$$s^2 = \frac{\sum_{i=1}^{n}\sum_{t=1}^{T}(y_{it} - \mathbf{x}_{it}'\mathbf{b} - a_i)^2}{nT - n - K} = \frac{(\mathbf{M_D}\mathbf{y} - \mathbf{M_D}\mathbf{X}\mathbf{b})'(\mathbf{M_D}\mathbf{y} - \mathbf{M_D}\mathbf{X}\mathbf{b})}{nT - n - K}. \tag{9-17}$$

The $it$th residual used in this computation is

$$e_{it} = y_{it} - \mathbf{x}_{it}'\mathbf{b} - a_i = y_{it} - \mathbf{x}_{it}'\mathbf{b} - (\bar{y}_{i.} - \bar{\mathbf{x}}_{i.}'\mathbf{b}) = (y_{it} - \bar{y}_{i.}) - (\mathbf{x}_{it} - \bar{\mathbf{x}}_{i.})'\mathbf{b}.$$

Thus, the numerator in $s^2$ is exactly the sum of squared residuals using the least squares slopes and the data in group mean deviation form. But, done in this fashion, one might then use $nT - K$ instead of $nT - n - K$ for the denominator in computing $s^2$, so a correction would be necessary. For the individual effects,

$$\text{Asy. Var}[a_i] = \frac{\sigma_\varepsilon^2}{T} + \bar{\mathbf{x}}_{i.}'\{\text{Asy. Var}[\mathbf{b}]\}\bar{\mathbf{x}}_{i.}, \tag{9-18}$$

so a simple estimator based on $s^2$ can be computed.

### 9.4.2 SMALL $T$ ASYMPTOTICS

From (9-16), we find

$$\text{Asy. Var}[\mathbf{b}] = \sigma_\varepsilon^2[\mathbf{X}'\mathbf{M_D}\mathbf{X}]^{-1}$$

$$= \frac{\sigma_\varepsilon^2}{n}\left[\frac{1}{n}\sum_{i=1}^{n}\mathbf{X}_i'\mathbf{M}^0\mathbf{X}_i\right]^{-1}$$

$$= \frac{\sigma_\varepsilon^2}{n}\left[\frac{1}{n}\sum_{i=1}^{n}\sum_{t=1}^{T}(\mathbf{x}_{it} - \bar{\mathbf{x}}_{i.})(\mathbf{x}_{it} - \bar{\mathbf{x}}_{i.})'\right]^{-1} \tag{9-19}$$

$$= \frac{\sigma_\varepsilon^2}{n}\left[T\frac{1}{n}\sum_{i=1}^{n}\frac{1}{T}\sum_{t=1}^{T}(\mathbf{x}_{it} - \bar{\mathbf{x}}_{i.})(\mathbf{x}_{it} - \bar{\mathbf{x}}_{i.})'\right]^{-1}$$

$$= \frac{\sigma_\varepsilon^2}{n}\left[T\bar{S}_{xx,i}\right]^{-1}.$$

Since least squares is unbiased in this model, the question of (mean square) consistency turns on the covariance matrix. Does the matrix above converge to zero? It is necessary to be specific about what is meant by convergence. In this setting, increasing sample size refers to increasing $n$, that is, increasing the number of groups. The group size, $T$, is assumed fixed. The leading scalar clearly vanishes with increasing $n$. The matrix in the square brackets is $T$ times the average over the $n$ groups of the within groups covariance matrices of the variables in $\mathbf{X}_i$. So long as the data are well behaved, we can assume that the bracketed matrix does not converge to a zero matrix (or a matrix with zeros on the diagonal). On this basis, we can expect consistency of the least squares estimator. In practical terms, this requires within-groups variation of the data. Notice that the result falls apart if there are time invariant variables in $\mathbf{X}_i$, because then there are zeros on the diagonals of the bracketed matrix. This result also suggests the nature of the problem of the WHO data in Example 9.3 as analyzed by Gravelle et al. (2002).

Now, consider the result in (9-18) for the asymptotic variance of $a_i$. Assume that **b** is consistent, as shown above. Then, with increasing $n$, the asymptotic variance of $a_i$ declines to a lower bound of $\sigma_\varepsilon^2/T$ *which does not converge to zero*. The constant term estimators in the fixed effects model are not consistent estimators of $\alpha_i$. They are not inconsistent because they gravitate toward the wrong parameter. They are so because their asymptotic variances do not converge to zero, even as the sample size grows. It is easy to see why this is the case. From (9-15), we see that each $a_i$ is estimated using only $T$ observations—assume $n$ were infinite, so that $\boldsymbol{\beta}$ were known. Because $T$ is not assumed to be increasing, we have the surprising result. The constant terms are inconsistent unless $T \to \infty$, which is not part of the model.

### 9.4.3 TESTING THE SIGNIFICANCE OF THE GROUP EFFECTS

The $t$ ratio for $a_i$ can be used for a test of the hypothesis that $\alpha_i$ equals zero. This hypothesis about one specific group, however, is typically not useful for testing in this regression context. If we are interested in differences across groups, then we can test the hypothesis that the constant terms are all equal with an $F$ test. Under the null hypothesis of equality, the efficient estimator is pooled least squares. The $F$ ratio used for this test is

$$F(n-1, nT-n-K) = \frac{\left(R_{LSDV}^2 - R_{Pooled}^2\right)/(n-1)}{\left(1 - R_{LSDV}^2\right)/(nT-n-K)}, \tag{9-20}$$

where $LSDV$ indicates the dummy variable model and $Pooled$ indicates the pooled or restricted model with only a single overall constant term. Alternatively, the model may have been estimated with an overall constant and $n-1$ dummy variables instead. All other results (i.e., the least squares slopes, $s^2$, $R^2$) will be unchanged, but rather than estimate $\alpha_i$, each dummy variable coefficient will now be an estimate of $\alpha_i - \alpha_1$ where group "1" is the omitted group. The $F$ test that the coefficients on these $n-1$ dummy variables are zero is identical to the one above. It is important to keep in mind, however, that although the statistical results are the same, the interpretation of the dummy variable coefficients in the two formulations is different.[9]

### 9.4.4 FIXED TIME AND GROUP EFFECTS

The least squares dummy variable approach can be extended to include a time-specific effect as well. One way to formulate the extended model is simply to add the time effect, as in

$$y_{it} = \mathbf{x}_{it}'\boldsymbol{\beta} + \alpha_i + \delta_t + \varepsilon_{it}. \tag{9-21}$$

This model is obtained from the preceding one by the inclusion of an additional $T-1$ dummy variables. (One of the time effects must be dropped to avoid perfect collinearity—the group effects and time effects both sum to one.) If the number of variables is too large to handle by ordinary regression, then this model can also be

---

[9]For a discussion of the differences, see Suits (1984).

estimated by using the partitioned regression.[10] There is an asymmetry in this formulation, however, since each of the group effects is a group-specific intercept, whereas the time effects are **contrasts**—that is, comparisons to a base period (the one that is excluded). A symmetric form of the model is

$$y_{it} = \mathbf{x}'_{it}\boldsymbol{\beta} + \mu + \alpha_i + \delta_t + \varepsilon_{it}, \tag{9-21'}$$

where a full $n$ and $T$ effects are included, but the restrictions

$$\sum_i \alpha_i = \sum_t \delta_t = 0$$

are imposed. Least squares estimates of the slopes in this model are obtained by regression of

$$y_{*it} = y_{it} - \bar{y}_{i.} - \bar{y}_{.t} + \bar{\bar{y}} \tag{9-22}$$

on

$$\mathbf{x}_{*it} = \mathbf{x}_{it} - \bar{\mathbf{x}}_{i.} - \bar{\mathbf{x}}_{.t} + \bar{\bar{\mathbf{x}}},$$

where the period-specific and overall means are

$$\bar{y}_{.t} = \frac{1}{n}\sum_{i=1}^{n} y_{it} \quad \text{and} \quad \bar{\bar{y}} = \frac{1}{nT}\sum_{i=1}^{n}\sum_{t=1}^{T} y_{it},$$

and likewise for $\bar{\mathbf{x}}_{.t}$ and $\bar{\bar{\mathbf{x}}}$. The overall constant and the dummy variable coefficients can then be recovered from the normal equations as

$$\hat{\mu} = m = \bar{\bar{y}} - \bar{\bar{\mathbf{x}}}'\mathbf{b},$$

$$\hat{\alpha}_i = a_i = (\bar{y}_{i.} - \bar{\bar{y}}) - (\bar{\mathbf{x}}_{i.} - \bar{\bar{\mathbf{x}}})'\mathbf{b}, \tag{9-23}$$

$$\hat{\delta}_t = d_t = (\bar{y}_{.t} - \bar{\bar{y}}) - (\bar{\mathbf{x}}_{.t} - \bar{\bar{\mathbf{x}}})'\mathbf{b}.$$

The estimated asymptotic covariance matrix for $\mathbf{b}$ is computed using the sums of squares and cross products of $\mathbf{x}_{*it}$ computed in (9-22) and

$$s^2 = \frac{\sum_{i=1}^{n}\sum_{t=1}^{T}(y_{it} - \mathbf{x}'_{it}\mathbf{b} - m - a_i - d_t)^2}{nT - (n-1) - (T-1) - K - 1} \tag{9-24}$$

If one of $n$ or $T$ is small and the other is large, then it may be simpler just to treat the smaller set as an ordinary set of variables and apply the previous results to the one-way fixed effects model defined by the larger set. Although more general, this model is infrequently used in practice. There are two reasons. First, the cost in terms of degrees of freedom is often not justified. Second, in those instances in which a model of the timewise evolution of the disturbance is desired, a more general model than this simple dummy variable formulation is usually used.

---

[10] The matrix algebra and the theoretical development of two-way effects in panel data models are complex. See, for example, Baltagi (2005). Fortunately, the practical application is much simpler. The number of periods analyzed in most panel data sets is rarely more than a handful. Because modern computer programs uniformly allow dozens (or even hundreds) of regressors, almost any application involving a second fixed effect can be handled just by literally including the second effect as a set of actual dummy variables.

**TABLE 9.4**    Fixed Effects Estimates of the Wage Equation

| Variable | Pooled Estimate | Pooled Std.Err.[a] | Time Effects Estimate | Time Effects Std.Err.[a] | Individual Effects Estimate | Individual Effects Std. Err. (Robust) | Time and Individual Effects Estimate | Time and Individual Effects Std.Err. |
|---|---|---|---|---|---|---|---|---|
| Constant | 5.8802 | 0.09654 | 5.6963 | 0.09425 | | | | |
| Exp | 0.03611 | 0.0045241 | 0.02738 | 0.004556 | 0.1132 | 0.002471 (0.00404) | 0.1114 | 0.002618 |
| Exp² | −0.00066 | 0.0001013 | −0.00053 | 0.000101 | −0.00042 | 0.55e−4 (0.82e−4) | −0.00004 | 0.54e−04 |
| Wks | 0.00446 | 0.001725 | 0.00409 | 0.001694 | 0.00084 | 0.000600 (0.00086) | 0.00068 | 0.0005991 |
| Occ | −0.3176 | 0.02721 | −0.3045 | 0.02684 | −0.02148 | 0.01378 (0.01896) | −0.01916 | 0.01375 |
| Ind | 0.03213 | 0.02521 | 0.04010 | 0.02489 | 0.01921 | 0.01545 (0.02264) | 0.02076 | 0.1540 |
| South | −0.1137 | 0.028626 | −0.1157 | 0.02834 | −0.00186 | 0.03430 (0.08913) | 0.00309 | 0.03419 |
| SMSA | 0.1586 | 0.025967 | 0.1722 | 0.02566 | −0.04247 | 0.01942 (0.02682) | −0.04188 | 0.01937 |
| MS | 0.3203 | 0.03487 | 0.3425 | 0.03459 | −0.02973 | 0.01898 (0.02943) | −0.02856 | 0.018918 |
| Union | 0.06975 | 0.026618 | 0.06272 | 0.02578 | 0.03278 | 0.01492 (0.02502) | 0.02952 | 0.01488 |
| Year2 | | | 0.07812 | 0.006860 | | | −0.00775 | 0.008167 |
| Year3 | | | 0.2050 | 0.01072 | | | 0.02557 | 0.007769 |
| Year4 | | | 0.2926 | 0.01125 | | | 0.02845 | 0.007639 |
| Year5 | | | 0.3724 | 0.01095 | | | 0.02418 | 0.007772 |
| Year6 | | | 0.4498 | 0.01245 | | | 0.00737 | 0.008161 |
| Year7 | | | 0.5422 | 0.013015 | | | | |
| e′e | 607.1265 | | 475.6659 | | 82.26732 | | 81.52012 | |
| s | 0.3822558 | | 0.3385940 | | 0.1519944 | | 0.1514089 | |
| R² | 0.3154548 | | 0.4636788 | | 0.9072422 | | 0.9080847 | |

[a] Robust standard errors computed using (9-3)

### Example 9.4    Fixed Effects Wage Equation

Table 9.4 presents the estimated wage equation with individual effects for the Cornwell and Rupert data used in Examples 9.1 and 9.2. The model includes three time-invariant variables, *Ed*, *Fem*, *Blk*, that must be dropped from the equation. As a consequence, the fixed effects estimates computed here are not comparable to the results for the pooled model already examined. For comparison, the least squares estimates with panel robust standard errors are also presented. We have also added a set of time dummy variables to the model. The *F* statistic for testing the significance of the individual effects based on the $R^2$s for the equations is

$$F[594,3561] = \frac{(0.9072422 - 0.3154548) / 594}{(1 - 0.9072422) / (4165 - 9 - 595)} = 38.247.$$

The critical value for the *F* table with 594 and 3561 degrees of freedom is 1.106, so the evidence is strongly in favor of an individual-specific effect. As often happens, the fit of the model increases greatly when the individual effects are added. We have also added time effects to the model. The model with time effects without the individual effects are in the second column results. The $F$ statistic for testing the significance of the time effects (in the absence of the individual effects) is

$$F[6,4149] = \frac{(0.4636788 - 0.3154548)/6}{(1 - 0.4636788)/(4165 - 10 - 6)} = 191.11.$$

The critical value from the $F$ table is 2.101, so the hypothesis that the time effects are zero is also rejected. The last column of results shows the model with both time and individual effects. For this model it is necessary to drop a second time effect because the experience variable, *Exp*, is an individual specific time trend. The *Exp* variable can be expressed as

$$Exp_{i,t} = E_{i,0} + (t - 1), t = 1, \ldots, 7.$$

which can be expressed as a linear combination of the individual dummy variable and the six time variables. For the last model, we have dropped the first and last of the time effects. In this model, the $F$ statistic for testing the significance of the time effects is

$$F[5,3556] = \frac{(0.9080847 - 0.9072422)/5}{(1 - 0.9080847)/(4165 - 9 - 5 - 595)} = 6.519.$$

The time effects remain significant—the critical value is 2.217—, but the test statistic is considerably reduced. The time effects reveal a striking pattern. In the equation without the individual effects, we find a steady increase in wages of 7–9 percent per year. But, when the individual effects are added to the model, this progression disappears.

It might seem appropriate to compute the robust standard errors for the fixed effects estimator as well as for the pooled estimator. However, in principle, that should be unnecessary. If the model is correct and completely specified, then the individual effects should be capturing the omitted heterogeneity, and what remains is a classical, homoscedastic, nonautocorrelated disturbance. This does suggest a rough indicator of the appropriateness of the model specification. If the conventional asymptotic covariance matrix in (9-16) and the robust estimator in (9-3), with $X_i$ replaced with the data in group mean deviations form, give very different estimates, one might question the model specification. [This is the logic that underlies White's (1982a) information matrix test (and the extensions by Newey (1985a) and Tauchen (1985).] The robust standard errors are shown in parentheses under those for the fixed effects estimates in the sixth column of Table 9.4. They are considerably higher than the uncorrected standard errors—50 percent to 100 percent—which might suggest that the fixed effects specification should be reconsidered.

## 9.5 RANDOM EFFECTS

The fixed effects model allows the unobserved individual effects to be correlated with the included variables. We then modeled the differences between units strictly as parametric shifts of the regression function. This model might be viewed as applying only to the cross-sectional units in the study, not to additional ones outside the sample. For example, an intercountry comparison may well include the full set of countries for which it is reasonable to assume that the model is constant. If the individual effects are strictly uncorrelated with the regressors, then it might be appropriate to model the individual specific constant terms as randomly distributed across cross-sectional units. This view would be appropriate if we believed that sampled cross-sectional units were drawn from a large population. It would certainly be the case for the longitudinal data sets listed in the introduction to this chapter.[11] The payoff to this form is that it greatly reduces

---

[11]This distinction is not hard and fast; it is purely heuristic. We shall return to this issue later. See Mundlak (1978) for methodological discussion of the distinction between fixed and random effects.

the number of parameters to be estimated. The cost is the possibility of inconsistent estimates, should the assumption turn out to be inappropriate.

Consider, then, a reformulation of the model

$$y_{it} = \mathbf{x}'_{it}\boldsymbol{\beta} + (\alpha + u_i) + \varepsilon_{it}, \tag{9-25}$$

where there are $K$ regressors including a constant and now the single constant term is the mean of the unobserved heterogeneity, $E[\mathbf{z}'_i\boldsymbol{\alpha}]$. The component $u_i$ is the random heterogeneity specific to the $i$th observation and is constant through time; recall from Section 9.2.1, $u_i = \{\mathbf{z}'_i\boldsymbol{\alpha} - E[\mathbf{z}'_i\boldsymbol{\alpha}]\}$. For example, in an analysis of families, we can view $u_i$ as the collection of factors, $\mathbf{z}'_i\boldsymbol{\alpha}$, not in the regression that are specific to that family. We continue to assume strict exogeneity:

$$E[\varepsilon_{it} \mid \mathbf{X}] = E[u_i \mid \mathbf{X}] = 0,$$
$$E\left[\varepsilon_{it}^2 \mid \mathbf{X}\right] = \sigma_\varepsilon^2,$$
$$E\left[u_i^2 \mid \mathbf{X}\right] = \sigma_u^2,$$
$$E[\varepsilon_{it}u_j \mid \mathbf{X}] = 0 \quad \text{for all } i, t, \text{ and } j, \tag{9-26}$$
$$E[\varepsilon_{it}\varepsilon_{js} \mid \mathbf{X}] = 0 \quad \text{if } t \neq s \text{ or } i \neq j,$$
$$E[u_iu_j \mid \mathbf{X}] = 0 \quad \text{if } i \neq j.$$

As before, it is useful to view the formulation of the model in blocks of $T$ observations for group $i$, $\mathbf{y}_i$, $\mathbf{X}_i$, $u_i\mathbf{i}$, and $\boldsymbol{\varepsilon}_i$. For these $T$ observations, let

$$\eta_{it} = \varepsilon_{it} + u_i$$

and

$$\boldsymbol{\eta}_i = [\eta_{i1}, \eta_{i2}, \ldots, \eta_{iT}]'.$$

In view of this form of $\eta_{it}$, we have what is often called an **error components model.** For this model,

$$E\left[\eta_{it}^2 \mid \mathbf{X}\right] = \sigma_\varepsilon^2 + \sigma_u^2,$$
$$E[\eta_{it}\eta_{is} \mid \mathbf{X}] = \sigma_u^2, \quad t \neq s \tag{9-27}$$
$$E[\eta_{it}\eta_{js} \mid \mathbf{X}] = 0 \quad \text{for all } t \text{ and } s \text{ if } i \neq j.$$

For the $T$ observations for unit $i$, let $\boldsymbol{\Sigma} = E[\boldsymbol{\eta}_i\boldsymbol{\eta}'_i \mid \mathbf{X}]$. Then

$$\boldsymbol{\Sigma} = \begin{bmatrix} \sigma_\varepsilon^2 + \sigma_u^2 & \sigma_u^2 & \sigma_u^2 & \cdots & \sigma_u^2 \\ \sigma_u^2 & \sigma_\varepsilon^2 + \sigma_u^2 & \sigma_u^2 & \cdots & \sigma_u^2 \\ & & \cdots & & \\ \sigma_u^2 & \sigma_u^2 & \sigma_u^2 & \cdots & \sigma_\varepsilon^2 + \sigma_u^2 \end{bmatrix} = \sigma_\varepsilon^2\mathbf{I}_T + \sigma_u^2\mathbf{i}_T\mathbf{i}'_T, \tag{9-28}$$

where $\mathbf{i}_T$ is a $T \times 1$ column vector of 1s. Because observations $i$ and $j$ are independent, the disturbance covariance matrix for the full $nT$ observations is

$$\mathbf{\Omega} = \begin{bmatrix} \mathbf{\Sigma} & \mathbf{0} & \mathbf{0} & \cdots & \mathbf{0} \\ \mathbf{0} & \mathbf{\Sigma} & \mathbf{0} & \cdots & \mathbf{0} \\ & & & \vdots & \\ \mathbf{0} & \mathbf{0} & \mathbf{0} & \cdots & \mathbf{\Sigma} \end{bmatrix} = \mathbf{I}_n \otimes \mathbf{\Sigma}. \tag{9-29}$$

### 9.5.1 GENERALIZED LEAST SQUARES

The generalized least squares estimator of the slope parameters is

$$\hat{\boldsymbol{\beta}} = (\mathbf{X}'\mathbf{\Omega}^{-1}\mathbf{X})^{-1}\mathbf{X}'\mathbf{\Omega}^{-1}\mathbf{y} = \left( \sum_{i=1}^{n} \mathbf{X}_i'\mathbf{\Sigma}^{-1}\mathbf{X}_i \right)^{-1} \left( \sum_{i=1}^{n} \mathbf{X}_i'\mathbf{\Sigma}^{-1}\mathbf{y}_i \right).$$

To compute this estimator as we did in Chapter 8 by transforming the data and using ordinary least squares with the transformed data, we will require $\mathbf{\Omega}^{-1/2} = [\mathbf{I}_n \otimes \mathbf{\Sigma}]^{-1/2}$. We need only find $\mathbf{\Sigma}^{-1/2}$, which is

$$\mathbf{\Sigma}^{-1/2} = \frac{1}{\sigma_\varepsilon} \left[ \mathbf{I} - \frac{\theta}{T}\mathbf{i}_T\mathbf{i}_T' \right],$$

where

$$\theta = 1 - \frac{\sigma_\varepsilon}{\sqrt{\sigma_\varepsilon^2 + T\sigma_u^2}}.$$

The transformation of $\mathbf{y}_i$ and $\mathbf{X}_i$ for GLS is therefore

$$\mathbf{\Sigma}^{-1/2}\mathbf{y}_i = \frac{1}{\sigma_\varepsilon} \begin{bmatrix} y_{i1} - \theta\bar{y}_{i.} \\ y_{i2} - \theta\bar{y}_{i.} \\ \vdots \\ y_{iT} - \theta\bar{y}_{i.} \end{bmatrix}, \tag{9-30}$$

and likewise for the rows of $\mathbf{X}_i$.[12] For the data set as a whole, then, generalized least squares is computed by the regression of these partial deviations of $y_{it}$ on the same transformations of $x_{it}$. Note the similarity of this procedure to the computation in the LSDV model, which uses $\theta = 1$ in (9-14). (One could interpret $\theta$ as the effect that would remain if $\sigma_\varepsilon$ were zero, because the only effect would then be $u_i$. In this case, the fixed and random effects models would be indistinguishable, so this result makes sense.)

It can be shown that the GLS estimator is, like the pooled OLS estimator, a matrix weighted average of the within- and between-units estimators:

$$\hat{\boldsymbol{\beta}} = \hat{\mathbf{F}}^{within}\mathbf{b}^{within} + (\mathbf{I} - \hat{\mathbf{F}}^{within})\mathbf{b}^{between},^{13} \tag{9-31}$$

---

[12]This transformation is a special case of the more general treatment in Nerlove (1971b).

[13]An alternative form of this expression, in which the weighing matrices are proportional to the covariance matrices of the two estimators, is given by Judge et al. (1985).

where now,

$$\hat{\mathbf{F}}^{within} = \left[\mathbf{S}_{xx}^{within} + \lambda\mathbf{S}_{xx}^{between}\right]^{-1}\mathbf{S}_{xx}^{within},$$

$$\lambda = \frac{\sigma_\varepsilon^2}{\sigma_\varepsilon^2 + T\sigma_u^2} = (1 - \theta)^2.$$

To the extent that $\lambda$ differs from one, we see that the inefficiency of ordinary least squares will follow from an inefficient weighting of the two estimators. Compared with generalized least squares, ordinary least squares places too much weight on the between-units variation. It includes it all in the variation in $\mathbf{X}$, rather than apportioning some of it to random variation across groups attributable to the variation in $u_i$ across units.

Unbalanced panels add a layer of difficulty in the random effects model. The first problem can be seen in (9-29). The matrix $\mathbf{\Omega}$ is no longer $\mathbf{I}_n \otimes \mathbf{\Sigma}$ because the diagonal blocks in $\mathbf{\Omega}$ are of different sizes. There is also groupwise heteroscedasticity in (9-30), because the $i$th diagonal block in $\mathbf{\Omega}^{-1/2}$ is

$$\mathbf{\Sigma}_i^{-1/2} = \mathbf{I}_{T_i} - \frac{\theta_i}{T_i}\mathbf{i}_{T_i}\mathbf{i}'_{T_i}, \qquad \theta_i = 1 - \frac{\sigma_\varepsilon}{\sqrt{\sigma_\varepsilon^2 + T_i\sigma_u^2}}.$$

In principle, estimation is still straightforward, because the source of the groupwise heteroscedasticity is only the unequal group sizes. Thus, for GLS, or FGLS with estimated variance components, it is necessary only to use the group specific $\theta_i$ in the transformation in (9-30).

### 9.5.2 FEASIBLE GENERALIZED LEAST SQUARES WHEN Σ IS UNKNOWN

If the variance components are known, generalized least squares can be computed as shown earlier. Of course, this is unlikely, so as usual, we must first estimate the disturbance variances and then use an FGLS procedure. A heuristic approach to estimation of the variance components is as follows:

$$y_{it} = \mathbf{x}'_{it}\boldsymbol{\beta} + \alpha + \varepsilon_{it} + u_i \tag{9-32}$$

and

$$\bar{y}_{i.} = \bar{\mathbf{x}}'_{i.}\boldsymbol{\beta} + \alpha + \bar{\varepsilon}_{i.} + u_i.$$

Therefore, taking deviations from the group means removes the heterogeneity:

$$y_{it} - \bar{y}_{i.} = [\mathbf{x}_{it} - \bar{\mathbf{x}}_{i.}]'\boldsymbol{\beta} + [\varepsilon_{it} - \bar{\varepsilon}_{i.}]. \tag{9-33}$$

Because

$$E\left[\sum_{t=1}^{T}(\varepsilon_{it} - \bar{\varepsilon}_{i.})^2\right] = (T-1)\sigma_\varepsilon^2,$$

if $\boldsymbol{\beta}$ were observed, then an unbiased estimator of $\sigma_\varepsilon^2$ based on $T$ observations in group $i$ would be

$$\hat{\sigma}_\varepsilon^2(i) = \frac{\sum_{t=1}^{T}(\varepsilon_{it} - \bar{\varepsilon}_{i.})^2}{T-1}. \tag{9-34}$$

Because $\beta$ must be estimated—(9-33) implies that the LSDV estimator is consistent, indeed, unbiased in general—we make the degrees of freedom correction and use the LSDV residuals in

$$s_e^2(i) = \frac{\sum_{t=1}^T (e_{it} - \bar{e}_{i.})^2}{T - K - 1}. \tag{9-35}$$

(Note that based on the LSDV estimates, $\bar{e}_{i.}$ is actually zero. We will carry it through nonetheless to maintain the analogy to (9-34) where $\bar{\varepsilon}_{i.}$ is not zero but is an estimator of $E[\varepsilon_{it}] = 0$.) We have $n$ such estimators, so we average them to obtain

$$\bar{s}_e^2 = \frac{1}{n} \sum_{i=1}^n s_e^2(i) = \frac{1}{n} \sum_{i=1}^n \left[ \frac{\sum_{t=1}^T (e_{it} - \bar{e}_{i.})^2}{T - K - 1} \right] = \frac{\sum_{i=1}^n \sum_{t=1}^T (e_{it} - \bar{e}_{i.})^2}{nT - nK - n}. \tag{9-36}$$

The degrees of freedom correction in $\bar{s}_e^2$ is excessive because it assumes that $\alpha$ and $\beta$ are reestimated for each $i$. The estimated parameters are the $n$ means $\bar{y}_{i.}$ and the $K$ slopes. Therefore, we propose the unbiased estimator[14]

$$\hat{\sigma}_\varepsilon^2 = s_{LSDV}^2 = \frac{\sum_{i=1}^n \sum_{t=1}^T (e_{it} - \bar{e}_{i.})^2}{nT - n - K}. \tag{9-37}$$

This is the variance estimator in the fixed effects model in (9-17), appropriately corrected for degrees of freedom. It remains to estimate $\sigma_u^2$. Return to the original model specification in (9-32). In spite of the correlation across observations, this is a classical regression model in which the ordinary least squares slopes and variance estimators are both consistent and, in most cases, unbiased. Therefore, using the ordinary least squares residuals from the model with only a single overall constant, we have

$$\text{plim } s_{Pooled}^2 = \text{plim } \frac{e'e}{nT - K - 1} = \sigma_\varepsilon^2 + \sigma_u^2. \tag{9-38}$$

This provides the two estimators needed for the variance components; the second would be $\hat{\sigma}_u^2 = s_{Pooled}^2 - s_{LSDV}^2$. A possible complication is that this second estimator could be negative. But, recall that for feasible generalized least squares, we do not need an unbiased estimator of the variance, only a consistent one. As such, we may drop the degrees of freedom corrections in (9-37) and (9-38). If so, then the two variance estimators must be nonnegative, since the sum of squares in the LSDV model cannot be larger than that in the simple regression with only one constant term. Alternative estimators have been proposed, all based on this principle of using two different sums of squared residuals.[15] This is a point on which modern software varies greatly. Generally, programs begin with (9-37) and (9-38) to estimate the variance components. What they do next when the estimate of $\sigma_u^2$ is nonpositive is far from uniform. Dropping the degrees of freedom correction is a frequently used strategy, but at least one widely used program simply sets $\sigma_u^2$ to zero, and others resort to different strategies based on, for example, the group means estimator. The unfortunate implication for the unwary is that different programs can systematically produce different results using the same model and the

---

[14] A formal proof of this proposition may be found in Maddala (1971) or in Judge et al. (1985, p. 551).

[15] See, for example, Wallace and Hussain (1969), Maddala (1971), Fuller and Battese (1974), and Amemiya (1971).

same data. The practitioner is strongly advised to consult the program documentation for resolution.

There is a remaining complication. If there are any regressors that do not vary within the groups, the LSDV estimator cannot be computed. For example, in a model of family income or labor supply, one of the regressors might be a dummy variable for location, family structure, or living arrangement. Any of these could be perfectly collinear with the fixed effect for that family, which would prevent computation of the LSDV estimator. In this case, it is still possible to estimate the random effects variance components. Let $[\mathbf{b}, a]$ be any consistent estimator of $[\boldsymbol{\beta}, \alpha]$ in (9-32), such as the ordinary least squares estimator. Then, (9-38) provides a consistent estimator of $m_{ee} = \sigma_\varepsilon^2 + \sigma_u^2$. The mean squared residuals using a regression based only on the $n$ group means in (9-32) provides a consistent estimator of $m_{**} = \sigma_u^2 + (\sigma_\varepsilon^2 / T)$, so we can use

$$\hat{\sigma}_\varepsilon^2 = \frac{T}{T-1}(m_{ee} - m_{**})$$

$$\hat{\sigma}_u^2 = \frac{T}{T-1}m_{**} - \frac{1}{T-1}m_{ee} = \omega m_{**} + (1-\omega)m_{ee},$$

where $\omega > 1$. As before, this estimator can produce a negative estimate of $\sigma_u^2$ that, once again, calls the specification of the model into question. [Note, finally, that the residuals in (9-37) and (9-38) could be based on the same coefficient vector.]

There is, perhaps surprisingly, a simpler way out of the dilemma posed by time-invariant regressors. In (9-33), we find that the group mean deviations estimator still provides a consistent estimator of $\sigma_\varepsilon^2$. The time-invariant variables fall out of the model so it is not possible to estimate the full coefficient vector $\boldsymbol{\beta}$. But, recall, estimation of $\boldsymbol{\beta}$ is not the objective at this step, estimation of $\sigma_\varepsilon^2$ is. Therefore, it follows that the residuals from the group mean deviations (LSDV) estimator can still be used to estimate $\sigma_\varepsilon^2$. By the same logic, the first differences could also be used. (See Section 9.3.5.) The residual variance in the first difference regression would estimate $2\sigma_\varepsilon^2$. These outcomes are irrespective of whether there are time-invariant regressors in the model.

### 9.5.3   TESTING FOR RANDOM EFFECTS

Breusch and Pagan (1980) have devised a **Lagrange multiplier test** for the random effects model based on the OLS residuals.[16] For

$$H_0: \sigma_u^2 = 0 \quad (\text{or } \text{Corr}[\eta_{it}, \eta_{is}] = 0),$$

$$H_1: \sigma_u^2 \neq 0,$$

the test statistic is

$$\text{LM} = \frac{nT}{2(T-1)}\left[\frac{\sum_{i=1}^{n}\left[\sum_{t=1}^{T}e_{it}\right]^2}{\sum_{i=1}^{n}\sum_{t=1}^{T}e_{it}^2} - 1\right]^2 = \frac{nT}{2(T-1)}\left[\frac{\sum_{i=1}^{n}(T\bar{e}_{i.})^2}{\sum_{i=1}^{n}\sum_{t=1}^{T}e_{it}^2} - 1\right]^2. \quad \textbf{(9-39)}$$

---

[16]We have focused thus far strictly on generalized least squares and moments based consistent estimation of the variance components. The LM test is based on maximum likelihood estimation, instead. See Maddala (1971) and Balestra and Nerlove (1966, 2003) for this approach to estimation.

Under the null hypothesis, the limiting distribution of LM is chi-squared with one degree of freedom.

### Example 9.5  Testing for Random Effects

We are interested in comparing the random and fixed effects estimators in the Cornwell and Rupert wage equation. As we saw earlier, there are three time-invariant variables in the equation: *Ed*, *Fem*, and *Blk*. As such, we cannot directly compare the two estimators. The **random effects model** can provide separate estimates of the parameters on the time-invariant variables while the fixed effects estimator cannot. For purposes of the illustration, then, we will for the present time confine attention to the restricted common effects model,

$$\ln Wage_{it} = \beta_1 Exp_{it} + \beta_2 Exp_{it}^2 + \beta_3 Wks_{it} + \beta_4 Occ_{it} + \beta_5 Ind_{it} + \beta_6 South_{it}$$
$$+ \beta_7 SMSA_{it} + \beta_8 MS_{it} + \beta_9 Union_{it} + c_i + \varepsilon_{it}.$$

The fixed and random effects models differ in the treatment of $c_i$.

Least squares estimates of the parameters including a constant term appear in Table 9.5. We then computed the group mean residuals for the seven observations for each individual. The sum of squares of the means is 53.824384. The total sum of squared residuals for the regression is 607.1265. With $T$ and $n$ equal to 7 and 595, respectively, (9-39) produces a chi-squared statistic of 3881.34. This far exceeds the 95 percent critical value for the chi-squared distribution with one degree of freedom, 3.84. At this point, we conclude that the classical regression model with a single constant term is inappropriate for these data. The result of the test is to reject the null hypothesis in favor of the random effects model. But, it is best to reserve judgment on that, because there is another competing specification that might induce these same results, the fixed effects model. We will examine this possibility in the subsequent examples.

### TABLE 9.5  Estimates of the Wage Equation

| Variable | Pooled Least Squares Estimate | Std. Error[a] | Fixed Effects LSDV Estimate | Std. Error | Random Effects FGLS Estimate | Std. Error |
|---|---|---|---|---|---|---|
| *Exp* | 0.0361 | 0.004533 | 0.1132 | 0.002471 | 0.08906 | 0.002280 |
| *Exp²* | −0.0006550 | 0.0001016 | −0.0004184 | 0.0000546 | −0.0007577 | 0.00005036 |
| *Wks* | 0.004461 | 0.001728 | 0.0008359 | 0.0005997 | 0.001066 | 0.0005939 |
| *Occ* | −0.3176 | 0.02726 | −0.02148 | 0.01378 | −0.1067 | 0.01269 |
| *Ind* | 0.03213 | 0.02526 | 0.01921 | 0.01545 | −0.01637 | 0.01391 |
| *South* | −0.1137 | 0.02868 | −0.001861 | 0.03430 | −0.06899 | 0.02354 |
| *SMSA* | 0.1586 | 0.02602 | −0.04247 | 0.01943 | −0.01530 | 0.01649 |
| *MS* | 0.3203 | 0.03494 | −0.02973 | 0.01898 | −0.02398 | 0.01711 |
| *Union* | 0.06975 | 0.02667 | 0.03278 | 0.01492 | 0.03597 | 0.01367 |
| *Constant* | 5.8802 | 0.09673 | | | 5.3455 | 0.04361 |
| | | | **Mundlak: Group Means** | | **Mundlak: Time Varying** | |
| *Exp* | | | −0.08574 | 0.005821 | 0.1132 | 0.002474 |
| *Exp²* | | | −0.0001168 | 0.0001281 | −0.0004184 | 0.00005467 |
| *Wks* | | | 0.008020 | 0.004006 | 0.0008359 | 0.0006004 |
| *Occ* | | | −0.3321 | 0.03363 | −0.02148 | 0.01380 |
| *Ind* | | | 0.02677 | 0.03203 | 0.01921 | 0.01547 |
| *South* | | | −0.1064 | 0.04444 | −0.001861 | 0.03434 |
| *SMSA* | | | 0.2239 | 0.03421 | 0.04247 | 0.01945 |
| *MS* | | | 0.4134 | 0.03984 | −0.02972 | 0.01901 |
| *Union* | | | 0.05637 | 0.03549 | 0.03278 | 0.01494 |
| *Constant* | | | | | 5.7222 | 0.1906 |

[a] Robust standard errors

With the variance estimators in hand, FGLS can be used to estimate the parameters of the model. All of our earlier results for FGLS estimators apply here. In particular, all that is needed for efficient estimation of the model parameters are consistent estimators of the variance components, and there are several. [See Hsiao (2003), Baltagi (2005), Nerlove (2002), Berzeg (1979), and Maddala and Mount (1973).]

### Example 9.6   Estimates of the Random Effects Model

In the previous example, we found the total sum of squares for the least squares estimator was 607.1265. The fixed effects (LSDV) estimates for this model appear in Table 9.4 (and 9.5), where the sum of squares given is 82.26732. Therefore, the moment estimators of the parameters are

$$\hat{\sigma}_\varepsilon^2 + \hat{\sigma}_u^2 = \frac{607.1265}{4165 - 10} = 0.1461195.$$

and

$$\hat{\sigma}_\varepsilon^2 = \frac{82.26732}{4165 - 595 - 9} = 0.0231023.$$

The implied estimator of $\sigma_u^2$ is 0.12301719. (No problem of negative variance components has emerged.) The estimate of $\theta$ for FGLS is

$$\hat{\theta} = 1 - \sqrt{\frac{0.0231023}{0.0231023 + 7(0.12301719)}} = 0.8383608.$$

FGLS estimates are computed by regressing the partial differences of In $Wage_{it}$ on the partial differences of the constant and the 9 regressors, using this estimate of $\theta$ in (9-30). Estimates of the parameters using the OLS, fixed effects and random effects estimators appear in Table 9.5.

None of the desirable properties of the estimators in the random effects model rely on $T$ going to infinity.[17] Indeed, $T$ is likely to be quite small. The estimator of $\sigma_\varepsilon^2$ is equal to an average of $n$ estimators, each based on the $T$ observations for unit $i$. [See (9-36).] Each component in this average is, in principle, consistent. That is, its variance is of order $1/T$ or smaller. Because $T$ is small, this variance may be relatively large. But, each term provides some information about the parameter. The average over the $n$ cross-sectional units has a variance of order $1/(nT)$, which will go to zero if $n$ increases, even if we regard $T$ as fixed. The conclusion to draw is that nothing in this treatment relies on $T$ growing large. Although it can be shown that some consistency results will follow for $T$ increasing, the typical panel data set is based on data sets for which it does not make sense to assume that $T$ increases without bound or, in some cases, at all.[18] As a general proposition, it is necessary to take some care in devising estimators whose properties hinge on whether $T$ is large or not. The widely used conventional ones we have discussed here do not, but we have not exhausted the possibilities.

The random effects model was developed by Balestra and Nerlove (1966). Their formulation included a time-specific component, $\kappa_t$, as well as the individual effect:

$$y_{it} = \alpha + \boldsymbol{\beta}' \mathbf{x}_{it} + \varepsilon_{it} + u_i + \kappa_t.$$

---

[17]See Nickell (1981).

[18]In this connection, Chamberlain (1984) provided some innovative treatments of panel data that, in fact, take $T$ as given in the model and that base consistency results solely on $n$ increasing. Some additional results for dynamic models are given by Bhargava and Sargan (1983).

The extended formulation is rather complicated analytically. In Balestra and Nerlove's study, it was made even more so by the presence of a lagged dependent variable. A full set of results for this extended model, including a method for handling the lagged dependent variable, has been developed.[19] We will turn to this in Section 9.8.

### 9.5.4 HAUSMAN'S SPECIFICATION TEST FOR THE RANDOM EFFECTS MODEL

At various points, we have made the distinction between fixed and random effects models. An inevitable question is, Which should be used? From a purely practical standpoint, the dummy variable approach is costly in terms of degrees of freedom lost. On the other hand, the fixed effects approach has one considerable virtue. There is little justification for treating the individual effects as uncorrelated with the other regressors, as is assumed in the random effects model. The random effects treatment, therefore, may suffer from the inconsistency due to this correlation between the included variables and the random effect.[20]

The **specification test** devised by Hausman (1978)[21] is used to test for orthogonality of the common effects and the regressors. The test is based on the idea that under the hypothesis of no correlation, both OLS in the LSDV model and GLS are consistent, but OLS is inefficient,[22] whereas under the alternative, OLS is consistent, but GLS is not. Therefore, under the null hypothesis, the two estimates should not differ systematically, and a test can be based on the difference. The other essential ingredient for the test is the covariance matrix of the difference vector, $[\mathbf{b} - \hat{\boldsymbol{\beta}}]$:

$$\text{Var}[\mathbf{b} - \hat{\boldsymbol{\beta}}] = \text{Var}[\mathbf{b}] + \text{Var}[\hat{\boldsymbol{\beta}}] - \text{Cov}[\mathbf{b}, \hat{\boldsymbol{\beta}}] - \text{Cov}[\hat{\boldsymbol{\beta}}, \mathbf{b}]. \tag{9-40}$$

Hausman's essential result is that *the covariance of an efficient estimator with its difference from an inefficient estimator is zero,* which implies that

$$\text{Cov}[(\mathbf{b} - \hat{\boldsymbol{\beta}}), \hat{\boldsymbol{\beta}}] = \text{Cov}[\mathbf{b}, \hat{\boldsymbol{\beta}}] - \text{Var}[\hat{\boldsymbol{\beta}}] = \mathbf{0}$$

or that

$$\text{Cov}[\mathbf{b}, \hat{\boldsymbol{\beta}}] = \text{Var}[\hat{\boldsymbol{\beta}}].$$

Inserting this result in (9-40) produces the required covariance matrix for the test,

$$\text{Var}[\mathbf{b} - \hat{\boldsymbol{\beta}}] = \text{Var}[\mathbf{b}] - \text{Var}[\hat{\boldsymbol{\beta}}] = \boldsymbol{\Psi}.$$

The chi-squared test is based on the Wald criterion:

$$W = \chi^2[K - 1] = [\mathbf{b} - \hat{\boldsymbol{\beta}}]'\hat{\boldsymbol{\Psi}}^{-1}[\mathbf{b} - \hat{\boldsymbol{\beta}}]. \tag{9-41}$$

For $\hat{\boldsymbol{\Psi}}$, we use the estimated covariance matrices of the slope estimator in the LSDV model and the estimated covariance matrix in the random effects model, excluding the

---

[19]See Balestra and Nerlove (1966), Fomby, Hill, and Johnson (1984), Judge et al. (1985), Hsiao (1986), Anderson and Hsiao (1982), Nerlove (1971a, 2002), and Baltagi (2005).

[20]See Hausman and Taylor (1981) and Chamberlain (1978).

[21]Related results are given by Baltagi (1986).

[22]Referring to the GLS matrix weighted average given earlier, we see that the efficient weight uses $\theta$, whereas OLS sets $\theta = 1$.

constant term. Under the null hypothesis, $W$ has a limiting chi-squared distribution with $K - 1$ degrees of freedom.

The **Hausman test** is a useful device for determining the preferred specification of the common effects model. As developed here, it has one practical shortcoming. The construction in (9-40) conforms to the theory of the test. However, it does not guarantee that the difference of the two covariance matrices will be positive definite in a finite sample. The implication is that nothing prevents the statistic from being negative when it is computed according to (9-41). One can, in that event, conclude that the random effects model is not rejected, since the similarity of the covariance matrices is what is causing the problem, and under the alternative (fixed effects) hypothesis, they would be significantly different. There are, however, several alternative methods of computing the statistic for the Hausman test, some asymptotically equivalent and others actually numerically identical. Baltagi (2005, pp. 65–73) provides an extensive analysis. One particularly convenient form of the test finesses the practical problem noted here. An asymptotically equivalent test statistic is given by

$$H' = (\hat{\beta}_{LSDV} - \hat{\beta}_{MEANS})' \left[ Asy.Var[\hat{\beta}_{LSDV}] + Asy.Var[\hat{\beta}_{MEANS}] \right]^{-1} (\hat{\beta}_{LSDV} - \hat{\beta}_{MEANS})$$

$$\textbf{(9-42)}$$

where $\hat{\beta}_{MEANS}$ is the group means estimator discussed in Section 9.3.4. As noted, this is one of several equivalent forms of the test. The advantage of this form is that the covariance matrix will always be nonnegative definite.

### Example 9.7 Hausman Test for Fixed versus Random Effects

Using the results of the preceding example, we retrieved the coefficient vector and estimated asymptotic covariance matrix, $\mathbf{b}_{FE}$ and $\mathbf{V}_{FE}$ from the fixed effects results and the first nine elements of $\hat{\beta}_{RE}$ and $\mathbf{V}_{RE}$ (excluding the constant term). The test statistic is

$$H = (\mathbf{b}_{FE} - \hat{\beta}_{RE})'[\mathbf{V}_{FE} - \mathbf{V}_{RE}]^{-1}(\mathbf{b}_{FE} - \hat{\beta}_{RE})$$

The value of the test statistic is 2,636.08. The critical value from the chi-squared table is 14.07, so the null hypothesis of the random effects model is rejected. We conclude that the fixed effects model is the preferred specification for these data. This is an unfortunate turn of events, as the main object of the study is the impact of education, which is a time-invariant variable in this sample. Using (9-42) instead, we obtain a test statistic of 3,177.58. Of course, this does not change the conclusion.

### 9.5.5 EXTENDING THE UNOBSERVED EFFECTS MODEL: MUNDLAK'S APPROACH

Even with the Hausman test available, choosing between the fixed and random effects specifications presents a bit of a dilemma. Both specifications have unattractive short-comings. The fixed effects approach is robust to correlation between the omitted heterogeneity and the regressors, but it proliferates parameters and cannot accommodate time-invariant regressors. The random effects model hinges on an unlikely assumption, that the omitted heterogeneity is uncorrelated with the regressors.

Several authors have suggested modifications of the random effects model that would at least partly overcome its deficit. The failure of the random effects approach is that the mean independence assumption, $E[c_i \mid \mathbf{X}_i] = 0$, is untenable. **Mundlak's** (1978)

**approach** would suggest the specification

$$E[c_i \mid \mathbf{X}_i] = \bar{\mathbf{x}}'_{i.}\boldsymbol{\gamma}.^{23}$$

Substituting this in the random effects model, we obtain

$$
\begin{aligned}
y_{it} &= \mathbf{x}'_{it}\boldsymbol{\beta} + c_i + \varepsilon_{it} \\
&= \mathbf{x}'_{it}\boldsymbol{\beta} + \bar{\mathbf{x}}'_{i.}\boldsymbol{\gamma} + \varepsilon_{it} + (c_i - E[c_i \mid \mathbf{X}_i]) \\
&= \mathbf{x}'_{it}\boldsymbol{\beta} + \bar{\mathbf{x}}'_{i.}\boldsymbol{\gamma} + \varepsilon_{it} + u_i.
\end{aligned}
\tag{9-43}
$$

This preserves the specification of the random effects model, but (one hopes) deals directly with the problem of correlation of the effects and the regressors. Note that the additional terms in $\bar{\mathbf{x}}'_{i.}\boldsymbol{\gamma}$ will only include the time-varying variables—the time invariant variables are already group means. This additional set of estimates is shown in the lower panel of Table 9.5 in Example 9.6.

Mundlak's approach is frequently used as a compromise between the fixed and random effects models. One side benefit of the specification is that it provides another convenient approach to the Hausman test. As the model is formulated above, the difference between the "fixed effects" model and the "random effects" model is the nonzero $\boldsymbol{\gamma}$. As such, a statistical test of the null hypothesis that $\boldsymbol{\gamma}$ equals zero should provide an alternative approach to the two methods suggested earlier.

**Example 9.8  Variable Addition Test for Fixed versus Random Effects**
Using the results in Example 9.6, we recovered the subvector of the estimates in the lower half of Table 9.5 corresponding to $\boldsymbol{\gamma}$, and the corresponding submatrix of the full covariance matrix. The test statistic is

$$H' = \hat{\boldsymbol{\gamma}}'[\text{Est. Asy. Var}(\hat{\boldsymbol{\gamma}})]^{-1}\hat{\boldsymbol{\gamma}}$$

The value of the test statistic is 297.17. The critical value from the chi-squared table for nine degrees of freedom is 14.07, so the null hypothesis of the random effects model is rejected. We conclude as before that the fixed effects estimator is the preferred specification for this model.

## 9.6  NONSPHERICAL DISTURBANCES AND ROBUST COVARIANCE ESTIMATION

Because the models considered here are extensions of the classical regression model, we can treat heteroscedasticity in the same way that we did in Chapter 8. That is, we can compute the ordinary or feasible generalized least squares estimators and obtain an appropriate robust covariance matrix estimator, or we can impose some structure on the disturbance variances and use generalized least squares. In the panel data settings,

---

[23] Other analyses, e.g., Chamberlain (1982) and Wooldridge (2002a), interpret the linear function as the *projection* of $c_i$ on the group means, rather than the conditional mean. The difference is that we need not make any particular assumptions about the conditional mean function while there always exists a linear projection. The conditional mean interpretation does impose an additional assumption on the model, but brings considerable simplification. Several authors have analyzed the extension of the model to projection on the full set of individual observations rather than the means. The additional generality provides the bases of several other estimators including minimum distance [Chamberlain (1982)], GMM [Arellano and Bover (1995)], and constrained seemingly unrelated regressions and three-stage least squares [Wooldridge (2002a)].

there is greater flexibility for the second of these without making strong assumptions about the nature of the heteroscedasticity.

### 9.6.1 ROBUST ESTIMATION OF THE FIXED EFFECTS MODEL

As noted in Section 9.3.2, in a panel data set, the correlation across observations within a group is likely to be a more substantial influence on the estimated covariance matrix of the least squares estimator than is heteroscedasticity. This is evident in the estimates in Table 9.1. In the fixed (or random) effects model, the intent of explicitly including the common effect in the model is to account for the source of this correlation. However, accounting for the common effect in the model does not remove heteroscedasticity—it centers the conditional mean properly. Here, we consider the straightforward extension of White's estimator to the fixed and random effects models.

In the fixed effects model, the full regressor matrix is $\mathbf{Z} = [\mathbf{X}, \mathbf{D}]$. The White heteroscedasticity consistent covariance matrix for OLS—that is, for the fixed effects estimator—is the lower right block of the partitioned matrix

$$\text{Est. Asy. Var}[\mathbf{b}, \mathbf{a}] = (\mathbf{Z}'\mathbf{Z})^{-1}\mathbf{Z}'\mathbf{E}^2\mathbf{Z}(\mathbf{Z}'\mathbf{Z})^{-1},$$

where $\mathbf{E}$ is a diagonal matrix of least squares (fixed effects estimator) residuals. This computation promises to be formidable, but fortunately, it works out very simply. The White estimator for the slopes is obtained just by using the data in group mean deviation form [see (9-14) and (9-17)] in the familiar computation of $\mathbf{S}_0$ [see (8-26) and (8-27)]. Also, the disturbance variance estimator in (9-17) is the counterpart to the one in (8-20), which we showed that after the appropriate scaling of $\boldsymbol{\Omega}$ was a consistent estimator of $\sigma^2 = \text{plim}[1/(nT)]\sum_{i=1}^{n}\sum_{t=1}^{T}\sigma_{it}^2$. The implication is that we may still use (9-17) to estimate the variances of the fixed effects.

A somewhat less general but useful simplification of this result can be obtained if we assume that the disturbance variance is constant within the $i$th group. If $E[\varepsilon_{it}^2 | \mathbf{Z}_i] = \sigma_i^2$, then, with a panel of data, $\sigma_i^2$ is estimable by $\mathbf{e}_i'\mathbf{e}_i / T$ using the least squares residuals. The center matrix in Est. Asy. Var$[\mathbf{b}, \mathbf{a}]$ may be replaced with $\sum_i (\mathbf{e}_i'\mathbf{e}_i / T)\mathbf{Z}_i'\mathbf{Z}_i$. Whether this estimator is preferable is unclear. If the groupwise model is correct, then it and the White estimator will estimate the same matrix. On the other hand, if the disturbance variances do vary within the groups, then this revised computation may be inappropriate.

Arellano (1987) and Arellano and Bover (1995) have taken this analysis a step further. If one takes the $i$th group as a whole, then we can treat the observations in

$$\mathbf{y}_i = \mathbf{X}_i\boldsymbol{\beta} + \alpha_i\mathbf{i}_T + \boldsymbol{\varepsilon}_i$$

as a generalized regression model with disturbance covariance matrix $\boldsymbol{\Omega}_i$. We saw in Section 8.3.2 that a model this general, with no structure on $\boldsymbol{\Omega}$, offered little hope for estimation, robust or otherwise. But the problem is more manageable with a panel data set where correlation across units can be assumed to be zero. As before, let $\mathbf{X}_{i*}$ denote the data in group mean deviation form. The counterpart to $\mathbf{X}'\boldsymbol{\Omega}\mathbf{X}$ here is

$$\mathbf{X}_*'\boldsymbol{\Omega}\mathbf{X}_* = \sum_{i=1}^{n}(\mathbf{X}_{i*}'\boldsymbol{\Omega}_i\mathbf{X}_{i*}).$$

By the same reasoning that we used to construct the White estimator in Chapter 8, we can consider estimating $\boldsymbol{\Omega}_i$ with the sample of one, $\mathbf{e}_i\mathbf{e}_i'$. As before, it is not consistent estimation of the individual $\boldsymbol{\Omega}_i$s that is at issue, but estimation of the sum. If $n$ is large enough, then we could argue that

$$\text{plim} \frac{1}{nT}\mathbf{X}'_*\boldsymbol{\Omega}\mathbf{X}_* = \text{plim} \frac{1}{nT}\sum_{i=1}^{n}\mathbf{X}'_{i*}\boldsymbol{\Omega}_i\mathbf{X}_{*i}$$

$$= \text{plim} \frac{1}{n}\sum_{i=1}^{n}\frac{1}{T}\mathbf{X}'_{*i}\mathbf{e}_i\mathbf{e}'_i\mathbf{X}_{*i} \qquad \textbf{(9-44)}$$

$$= \text{plim} \frac{1}{n}\sum_{i=1}^{n}\left(\frac{1}{T}\sum_{t=1}^{T}\sum_{s=1}^{T} e_{it}e_{is}\mathbf{x}_{*it}\mathbf{x}'_{*is}\right).$$

This is the extension of (9-3) to the fixed effects case.

### 9.6.2 HETEROSCEDASTICITY IN THE RANDOM EFFECTS MODEL

Because the random effects model is a generalized regression model with a known structure, OLS with a robust estimator of the asymptotic covariance matrix is not the best use of the data. The GLS estimator is efficient whereas the OLS estimator is not. If a perfectly general covariance structure is assumed, then one might simply use Arellano's estimator described in the preceding section with a single overall constant term rather than a set of fixed effects. But, within the setting of the random effects model, $\eta_{it} = \varepsilon_{it} + u_i$, allowing the disturbance variance to vary across groups would seem to be a useful extension.

A series of papers, notably Mazodier and Trognon (1978), Baltagi and Griffin (1988), and the recent monograph by Baltagi (2005, pp. 77–79) suggest how one might allow the group-specific component $u_i$ to be heteroscedastic. But, empirically, there is an insurmountable problem with this approach. In the final analysis, all estimators of the variance components must be based on sums of squared residuals, and, in particular, an estimator of $\sigma_{ui}^2$ would be estimated using a set of residuals from the distribution of $u_i$. However, the data contain only a single observation on $u_i$ repeated in each observation in group $i$. So, the estimators presented, for example, in Baltagi (2001), use, in effect, one residual in each case to estimate $\sigma_{ui}^2$. What appears to be a mean squared residual is only $(1/T)\sum_{t=1}^{T}\hat{u}_i^2 = \hat{u}_i^2$. The properties of this estimator are ambiguous, but efficiency seems unlikely. The estimators do not converge to any population figure as the sample size, even $T$, increases. [The counterpoint is made in Hsiao (2003, p. 56).] Heteroscedasticity in the unique component, $\varepsilon_{it}$ represents a more tractable modeling possibility.

In Section 9.5.1, we introduced heteroscedasticity into estimation of the random effects model by allowing the group sizes to vary. But the estimator there (and its feasible counterpart in the next section) would be the same if, instead of $\theta_i = 1 - \sigma_\varepsilon/(T_i\sigma_u^2+\sigma_\varepsilon^2)^{1/2}$, we were faced with

$$\theta_i = 1 - \frac{\sigma_{\varepsilon i}}{\sqrt{\sigma_{\varepsilon i}^2 + T_i\sigma_u^2}}.$$

Therefore, for computing the appropriate feasible generalized least squares estimator, once again we need only devise consistent estimators for the variance components and then apply the GLS transformation shown earlier. One possible way to proceed is as follows: Because pooled OLS is still consistent, OLS provides a usable set of residuals. Using the OLS residuals for the specific groups, we would have, for each group,

$$\widehat{\sigma_{\varepsilon i}^2 + u_i^2} = \frac{\mathbf{e}_i'\mathbf{e}_i}{T}.$$

The residuals from the dummy variable model are purged of the individual specific effect, $u_i$, so $\sigma_{\varepsilon i}^2$ may be consistently (in $T$) estimated with

$$\widehat{\sigma_{\varepsilon i}^2} = \frac{\mathbf{e}_i^{lsdv\prime}\mathbf{e}_i^{lsdv}}{T}$$

where $e_{it}^{lsdv} = y_{it} - \mathbf{x}_{it}'\mathbf{b}^{lsdv} - a_i$. Combining terms, then,

$$\hat{\sigma}_u^2 = \frac{1}{n}\sum_{i=1}^{n}\left[\left(\frac{\mathbf{e}_i^{ols\prime}\mathbf{e}_i^{ols}}{T}\right) - \left(\frac{\mathbf{e}_i^{lsdv\prime}\mathbf{e}_i^{lsdv}}{T}\right)\right] = \frac{1}{n}\sum_{i=1}^{n}\widehat{(u_i^2)}.$$

We can now compute the FGLS estimator as before.

### 9.6.3   AUTOCORRELATION IN PANEL DATA MODELS

Serial correlation of regression disturbances will be considered in detail in Chapter 19. Rather than defer the topic in connection to panel data to Chapter 19, we will briefly note it here. As we saw in Section 9.3.2 and Example 9.1, "autocorrelation"—that is, correlation across the observations in the groups in a panel—is likely to be a substantive feature of the model. Our treatment of the effect there, however, was meant to accommodate autocorrelation in its broadest sense, that is, nonzero covariances across observations in a group. The results there would apply equally to clustered observations, as observed in Section 9.3.3. An important element of that specification was that with clustered data, there might be no obvious structure to the autocorrelation. When the panel data set consists explicitly of groups of time series, and especially if the time series are relatively long as in Example 9.9, one might want to begin to invoke the more detailed, structured time series models which are discussed in Chapter 19.

## 9.7   EXTENSIONS OF THE RANDOM EFFECTS MODEL

In spite of its strong assumption of mean independence of the individual effects and the regressors, the random effects model, perhaps augmented with Mundlak's extension (Section 9.5.5), provides the preferred framework for much of the empirical literature. (As we will explore in several applications later in the book, the fixed effects model has a significant shortcoming of its own.) This section will describe a few common extensions of the model. The nested random effects model was suggested earlier as an approach for analyzing hierarchical data sets. We will describe some of the received estimation techniques and applications for nested effects. Spatial autocorrelation is a natural application of panel models in which the correlation across observations relates to their distance from each other in space rather than time. Finally, we will take a brief look at dynamic panel data models and nonstationary panels.

### 9.7.1 NESTED RANDOM EFFECTS[24]

Consider, once again, a data set on test scores for multiple school districts in a state. To establish a notation for this complex model, we define a four-level unbalanced structure,

$$z_{ijkt} = \text{test score for student } t, \text{ teacher } k, \text{ school } j, \text{ district } i,$$

$$L = \text{school districts}, i = 1, \ldots, L,$$

$$M_i = \text{schools in each district}, j = 1, \ldots, M_i,$$

$$N_{ij} = \text{teachers in each school}, k = 1, \ldots, N_{ij}$$

$$T_{ijk} = \text{students in each class}, t = 1, \ldots, T_{ijk}.$$

Thus, from the outset, we allow the model to be unbalanced at all levels. In general terms, then, the random effects regression model would be

$$y_{ijkt} = \mathbf{x}'_{ijkt}\boldsymbol{\beta} + u_{ijk} + v_{ij} + w_i + \varepsilon_{ijkt}.$$

Strict exogeneity of the regressors is assumed at all levels. All parts of the disturbance are also assumed to be uncorrelated. (A normality assumption will be added later as well.) From the structure of the disturbances, we can see that the overall covariance matrix, $\boldsymbol{\Omega}$, is block-diagonal over $i$, with each diagonal block itself block-diagonal in turn over $j$, each of these is block-diagonal over $k$, and, at the lowest level, the blocks, e.g., for the class in our example, have the form for the random effects model that we saw earlier.

Generalized least squares has been well worked out for the balanced case. [See, e.g., Baltagi, Song, and Jung (2001), who also provide results for the three-level unbalanced case.] Define the following to be constructed from the variance components, $\sigma_\varepsilon^2, \sigma_u^2, \sigma_v^2$, and $\sigma_w^2$:

$$\sigma_1^2 = T\sigma_u^2 + \sigma_\varepsilon^2,$$

$$\sigma_2^2 = NT\sigma_v^2 + T\sigma_u^2 + \sigma_\varepsilon^2 = \sigma_1^2 + NT\sigma_v^2,$$

$$\sigma_3^2 = MNT\sigma_w^2 + NT\sigma_v^2 + T\sigma_u^2 + \sigma_\varepsilon^2 = \sigma_2^2 + MNT\sigma_w^2.$$

Then, full generalized least squares is equivalent to OLS regression of

$$\tilde{y}_{ijkt} = y_{ijkt} - \left(1 - \frac{\sigma_\varepsilon}{\sigma_1}\right)\bar{y}_{ijk\cdot} - \left(\frac{\sigma_\varepsilon}{\sigma_1} - \frac{\sigma_\varepsilon}{\sigma_2}\right)\bar{y}_{ij\cdot\cdot} - \left(\frac{\sigma_\varepsilon}{\sigma_2} - \frac{\sigma_\varepsilon}{\sigma_3}\right)\bar{y}_{i\cdots} \qquad \textbf{(9-45)}$$

on the same transformation of $\mathbf{x}_{ijkt}$. FGLS estimates are obtained by three groupwise between estimators and the within estimator for the innermost grouping.

The counterparts for the unbalanced case can be derived [see Baltagi et al. (2001)], but the degree of complexity rises dramatically. As Antwiler (2001) shows, however, if one is willing to assume normality of the distributions, then the log likelihood is very tractable. (We note an intersection of practicality with nonrobustness.) Define the variance ratios

$$\rho_u = \frac{\sigma_u^2}{\sigma_\varepsilon^2}, \rho_v = \frac{\sigma_v^2}{\sigma_\varepsilon^2}, \rho_w = \frac{\sigma_w^2}{\sigma_\varepsilon^2}.$$

---

[24]This development is based on maximum likelihood estimation, which is presented in Chapter 16.

Construct the following intermediate results:

$$\theta_{ijk} = 1 + T_{ijk}\rho_u, \; \phi_{ij} = \sum_{k=1}^{N_{ij}} \frac{T_{ijk}}{\theta_{ijk}}, \; \theta_{ij} = 1 + \phi_{ij}\rho_v, \; \phi_i = \sum_{j=1}^{M_i} \frac{\phi_{ij}}{\theta_{ij}}, \; \theta_i = 1 + \rho_w\phi_i$$

and sums of squares of the disturbances $e_{ijkt} = y_{ijkt} - \mathbf{x}'_{ijkt}\boldsymbol{\beta}$,

$$A_{ijk} = \sum_{t=1}^{T_{ijk}} e_{ijkt}^2,$$

$$B_{ijk} = \sum_{t=1}^{T_{ijk}} e_{ijkt}, \; B_{ij} = \sum_{k=1}^{N_{ij}} \frac{B_{ijk}}{\theta_{ijk}}, \; B_i = \sum_{j=1}^{M_i} \frac{B_{ij}}{\theta_{ij}}.$$

The log likelihood is

$$\ln L = -\frac{1}{2} H \ln (2\pi\sigma_\varepsilon^2) - \frac{1}{2} \left[ \sum_{i=1}^{L} \left\{ \ln \theta_i + \sum_{j=1}^{M_i} \left\{ \ln \theta_{ij} + \sum_{k=1}^{N_{ij}} \right. \right. \right.$$

$$\left. \left. \left\{ \ln \theta_{ijk} + \frac{A_{ijk}}{\sigma_\varepsilon^2} - \frac{\rho_u}{\theta_{ijk}} \frac{B_{ijk}^2}{\sigma_\varepsilon^2} \right\} - \frac{\rho_v}{\theta_{ij}} \frac{B_{ij}^2}{\sigma_\varepsilon^2} \right\} - \frac{\rho_w}{\theta_i} \frac{B_i^2}{\sigma_\varepsilon^2} \right\} \right],$$

where $H$ is the total number of observations. (For three levels, $L = 1$ and $\rho_w = 0$.) Antwiler (2001) provides the first derivatives of the log likelihood function needed to maximize $\ln L$. However, he does suggest that the complexity of the results might make numerical differentiation attractive. On the other hand, he finds the second derivatives of the function intractable and resorts to numerical second derivatives in his application. The complex part of the Hessian is the cross derivatives between $\boldsymbol{\beta}$ and the variance parameters, and the lower right part for the variance parameters themselves. However, these are not needed. As in any generalized regression model, the variance estimators and the slope estimators are asymptotically uncorrelated. As such, one need only invert the part of the matrix with respect to $\boldsymbol{\beta}$ to get the appropriate asymptotic covariance matrix. The relevant block is

$$-\frac{\partial^2 \ln L}{\partial\boldsymbol{\beta}\partial\boldsymbol{\beta}'} = \frac{1}{\sigma_\varepsilon^2} \sum_{i=1}^{L}\sum_{j=1}^{M_i}\sum_{k=1}^{N_{ij}}\sum_{t=1}^{T_{ijk}} \mathbf{x}_{ijkt}\mathbf{x}'_{ijkt} - \frac{\rho_w}{\sigma_\varepsilon^2} \sum_{i=1}^{L}\sum_{j=1}^{M_i}\sum_{k=1}^{N_{ij}} \frac{1}{\theta_{ijk}} \left(\sum_{t=1}^{T_{ijk}} \mathbf{x}_{ijkt}\right) \left(\sum_{t=1}^{T_{ijk}} \mathbf{x}'_{ijkt}\right)$$

$$-\frac{\rho_v}{\sigma_\varepsilon^2} \sum_{i=1}^{L}\sum_{j=1}^{M_i} \frac{1}{\theta_{ij}} \left(\sum_{k=1}^{N_{ij}} \frac{1}{\theta_{ijk}} \left(\sum_{t=1}^{T_{ijk}} \mathbf{x}_{ijkt}\right)\right) \left(\sum_{k=1}^{N_{ij}} \frac{1}{\theta_{ijk}} \left(\sum_{t=1}^{T_{ijk}} \mathbf{x}'_{ijkt}\right)\right) \qquad \textbf{(9-46)}$$

$$-\frac{\rho_u}{\sigma_\varepsilon^2} \sum_{i=1}^{L} \left(\sum_{j=1}^{M_i} \frac{1}{\theta_{ij}} \left(\sum_{k=1}^{N_{ij}} \frac{1}{\theta_{ijk}} \left(\sum_{t=1}^{T_{ijk}} \mathbf{x}_{ijkt}\right)\right)\right) \left(\sum_{j=1}^{M_i} \frac{1}{\theta_{ij}} \left(\sum_{k=1}^{N_{ij}} \frac{1}{\theta_{ijk}} \left(\sum_{t=1}^{T_{ijk}} \mathbf{x}'_{ijkt}\right)\right)\right).$$

The maximum likelihood estimator of $\boldsymbol{\beta}$ is FGLS based on the maximum likelihood estimators of the variance parameters. Thus, expression (9-46) provides the appropriate covariance matrix for the GLS or maximum likelihood estimator. The difference will be in how the variance components are computed. Baltagi et al. (2001) suggest a variety of methods for the three-level model. For more than three levels, the MLE becomes more attractive.

Given the complexity of the results, one might prefer simply to use OLS in spite of its inefficiency. As might be expected, the standard errors will be biased owing to the correlation across observations; there is evidence that the bias is downward. [See Moulton (1986).] In that event, the robust estimator in (9-3) would be the natural alternative. In the example given earlier, the nesting structure was obvious. In other cases, such as our application in Example 9.10, that might not be true. In Example 9.9 [and in the application in Baltagi (2005)], statewide observations are grouped into regions based on intuition. The impact of an incorrect grouping is unclear. Both OLS and FGLS would remain consistent—both are equivalent to GLS with the wrong weights, which we considered earlier. However, the impact on the asymptotic covariance matrix for the estimator remains to be analyzed.

### Example 9.9   Statewide Productivity

Munell (1990) analyzed the productivity of public capital at the state level using a Cobb–Douglas production function. We will use the data from that study to estimate a three-level log linear regression model,

$$\ln gsp_{jkt} = \alpha + \beta_1 \ln p\_cap_{jkt} + \beta_2 \ln hwy_{jkt} + \beta_3 \ln water_{jkt}$$
$$+ \beta_4 \ln util_{jkt} + \beta_5 \ln emp_{jkt} + \beta_6 unemp_{jkt} + \varepsilon_{jkt} + u_{jk} + v_j,$$
$$j = 1, \ldots, 9; t = 1, \ldots, 17, k = 1, \ldots, N_j,$$

where the variables in the model are

| | | |
|---|---|---|
| $gsp$ | = | gross state product, |
| $p\_cap$ | = | public capital, |
| $hwy$ | = | highway capital, |
| $water$ | = | water utility capital, |
| $util$ | = | utility capital, |
| $pc$ | = | private capital, |
| $emp$ | = | employment (labor), |
| $unemp$ | = | unemployment rate, |

and there are M = 9 regions each consisting of a group of the 48 continental states:

| | |
|---|---|
| *Gulf* | = AL, FL, LA, MS, |
| *Midwest* | = IL, IN, KY, MI, MN, OH, WI, |
| *Mid Atlantic* | = DE, MD, NJ, NY, PA, VA, |
| *Mountain* | = CO, ID, MT, ND, SD, WY, |
| *New England* | = CD, ME, MA, NH, RI, VT, |
| *South* | = GA, NC, SC, TN, WV, |
| *Southwest* | = AZ, NV, NM, TX, UT, |
| *Tornado Alley* | = AK, IA, KS, MS, NE, OK, |
| *West Coast* | = CA, OR, WA. |

For each state, we have 17 years of data, from 1970 to 1986.[25] The two- and three-level random effects models were estimated by maximum likelihood. The two-level model was also fit by FGLS using the methods developed in Section 9.5.2.

---

[25]The data were downloaded from the website for Baltagi (2005) at http://www.wiley.com/legacy/wileychi/baltagi3e/. See Appendix Table F9.2.

**TABLE 9.6**   Estimated Statewide Production Function

| | OLS Estimate | OLS Std. Err.[a] | Fixed Effects Estimate (Std. Err.) | Random Effects FGLS Estimate (Std. Err.) | Random Effects ML Estimate (Std. Err.) | Nested Random Effects Estimate (Std. Err.) |
|---|---|---|---|---|---|---|
| $\alpha$ | 1.9260 | 0.05250 (0.2143) | | 2.1608 (0.1380) | 2.1759 (0.1477) | 2.1348 (0.1514) |
| $\beta_1$ | 0.3120 | 0.01109 (0.04678) | 0.2350 (0.02621) | 0.2755 (0.01972) | 0.2703 (0.02110) | 0.2724 (0.02141) |
| $\beta_2$ | 0.05888 | 0.01541 (0.05078) | 0.07675 (0.03124) | 0.06167 (0.02168) | 0.06268 (0.02269) | 0.06645 (0.02287) |
| $\beta_3$ | 0.1186 | 0.01236 (0.03450) | 0.0786 (0.0150) | 0.07572 (0.01381) | 0.07545 (0.01397) | 0.07392 (0.01399) |
| $\beta_4$ | 0.00856 | 0.01235 (0.04062) | −0.11478 (0.01814) | −0.09672 (0.01683) | −0.1004 (0.01730) | −0.1004 (0.01698) |
| $\beta_5$ | 0.5497 | 0.01554 (0.06770) | 0.8011 (0.02976) | 0.7450 (0.02482) | 0.7542 (0.02664) | 0.7539 (0.02613) |
| $\beta_6$ | −0.00727 | 0.001384 (0.002946) | −0.005179 (0.000980) | −0.005963 (0.0008814) | −0.005809 (0.0009014) | −0.005878 (0.0009002) |
| $\sigma_\varepsilon$ | 0.985422 | | 0.03676493 | 0.0367649 | 0.0366974 | 0.0366964 |
| $\sigma_u$ | | | | 0.0771064 | 0.0875682 | 0.0791243 |
| $\sigma_v$ | | | | | | 0.0386299 |
| ln $L$ | 853.1372 | | 1565.501 | | 1429.075 | 1430.30576 |

[a]Robust (cluster) standard errors in parentheses

Table 9.6 presents the estimates of the production function using pooled OLS, OLS for the fixed effects model and both FGLS and maximum likelihood for the random effects models. Overall, the estimates are similar, though the OLS estimates do stand somewhat apart. This suggests, as one might suspect, that there are omitted effects in the pooled model. The $F$ statistic for testing the significance of the fixed effects is 76.712 with 47 and 762 degrees of freedom. The critical value from the table is 1.379, so on this basis, one would reject the hypothesis of no common effects. Note, as well, the extremely large differences between the conventional OLS standard errors and the robust (cluster) corrected values. The three or four fold differences strongly suggest that there are latent effects at least at the state level. It remains to consider which approach, fixed or random effects is preferred. The Hausman test for fixed vs. random effects produces a chi-squared value of 18.987. The critical value is 12.592. This would imply that the fixed effects model would be the preferred specification. When we repeat the calculation of the Hausman statistic using the three-level estimates in the last column of Table 9.6, the statistic falls slightly to 15.327. Finally, note the similarity of all three sets of random effects estimates. In fact, under the hypothesis of mean independence, all three are consistent estimators. It is tempting at this point to carry out a likelihood ratio test of the hypothesis of the two-level model against the broader alternative three-level model. The test statistic would be twice the difference of the log likelihoods, which is 2.46. For one degree of freedom, the critical chi-squared with one degree of freedom is 3.84, so on this basis, we would not reject the hypothesis of the two-level model. We note, however, that there is a problem with this testing procedure. The hypothesis that a variance is zero is not well defined for the likelihood ratio test—the parameter under the null hypothesis is on the boundary of the parameter space ($\sigma_v^2 \geq 0$). In this instance, the familiar distribution theory does not apply. We will revisit this issue in Chapter 16 in our study of the method of maximum likelihood.

### 9.7.2 SPATIAL AUTOCORRELATION

The nested random effects structure in Example 9.9 was motivated by an expectation that effects of neighboring states would spill over into each other, creating a sort of correlation across space, rather than across time as we have focused on thus far. The effect should be common in cross-region studies, such as in agriculture, urban economics, and regional science. Recent studies of the phenomenon include Case's (1991) study of expenditure patterns, Bell and Bockstael's (2000) study of real estate prices, and Baltagi and Li's (2001) analysis of R&D spillovers. Models of **spatial autocorrelation** [see Anselin (1988, 2001) for the canonical reference], are constructed to formalize this notion.

A model with spatial autocorrelation can be formulated as follows: The regression model takes the familiar panel structure,

$$y_{it} = \mathbf{x}'_{it}\boldsymbol{\beta} + \varepsilon_{it} + u_i, i = 1, \ldots, n; t = 1, \ldots, T.$$

The common $u_i$ is the usual unit (e.g., country) effect. The correlation across space is implied by the spatial autocorrelation structure

$$\varepsilon_{it} = \lambda \sum_{j=1}^{n} W_{ij}\varepsilon_{jt} + v_t.$$

The scalar $\lambda$ is the **spatial autoregression coefficient.** The elements $W_{ij}$ are spatial (or **contiguity**) weights that are assumed known. The elements that appear in the sum above are a row of the spatial weight or **contiguity matrix**, $\mathbf{W}$, so that for the $n$ units, we have

$$\boldsymbol{\varepsilon}_t = \lambda \mathbf{W}\boldsymbol{\varepsilon}_t + \mathbf{v}_t, \mathbf{v}_t = v_t\mathbf{i}.$$

The structure of the model is embodied in the symmetric weight matrix, $\mathbf{W}$. Consider for an example counties or states arranged geographically on a grid or some linear scale such as a line from one coast of the country to another. Typically $W_{ij}$ will equal one for $i, j$ pairs that are neighbors and zero otherwise. Alternatively, $W_{ij}$ may reflect distances across space, so that $W_{ij}$ decreases with increases in $|i - j|$. This would be similar to a temporal autocorrelation matrix. Assuming that $|\lambda|$ is less than one, and that the elements of $\mathbf{W}$ are such that $(\mathbf{I} - \lambda\mathbf{W})$ is nonsingular, we may write

$$\boldsymbol{\varepsilon}_t = (\mathbf{I}_n - \lambda\mathbf{W})^{-1}\mathbf{v}_t,$$

so for the $n$ observations at time $t$,

$$\mathbf{y}_t = \mathbf{X}_t\boldsymbol{\beta} + (\mathbf{I}_n - \lambda\mathbf{W})^{-1}\mathbf{v}_t + \mathbf{u}.$$

We further assume that $u_i$ and $v_i$ have zero means, variances $\sigma_u^2$ and $\sigma_v^2$ and are independent across countries and of each other. It follows that a generalized regression model applies to the $n$ observations at time $t$;

$$E[\mathbf{y}_t \mid \mathbf{X}_t] = \mathbf{X}_t\boldsymbol{\beta},$$

$$\text{Var}[\mathbf{y}_t \mid \mathbf{X}_t] = (\mathbf{I}_n - \lambda\mathbf{W})^{-1}[\sigma_v^2\mathbf{i}\mathbf{i}'](\mathbf{I}_n - \lambda\mathbf{W})^{-1} + \sigma_u^2\mathbf{I}_n.$$

At this point, estimation could proceed along the lines of Chapter 8, save for the need to estimate $\lambda$. There is no natural residual based estimator of $\lambda$. Recent treatments of this model have added a normality assumption and employed maximum likelihood methods. [The log likelihood function for this model and numerous references appear in Baltagi (2005, p. 196). Extensive analysis of the estimation problem is given in Bell and Bockstael (2000).]

A natural first step in the analysis is a test for spatial effects. The standard procedure for a cross section is Moran's (1950) $I$ statistic, which would be computed for each set of residuals, $\mathbf{e}_t$, using

$$I_t = \frac{n \sum_{i=1}^{n} \sum_{j=1}^{n} W_{ij}(e_{it} - \bar{e}_t)(e_{jt} - \bar{e}_t)}{\left( \sum_{i=1}^{n} \sum_{j=1}^{n} W_{i,j} \right) \sum_{i=1}^{n} (e_{it} - \bar{e}_t)^2}.$$

For a panel of $T$ independent sets of observations, $\bar{I} = \frac{1}{T} \sum_{t=1}^{T} I_t$ would use the full set of information. A large sample approximation to the variance of the statistic under the null hypothesis of no spatial autocorrelation is

$$V^2 = \frac{1}{T} \frac{n^2 \sum_{i=1}^{n} \sum_{j=1}^{n} W_{ij}^2 + 3 \left( \sum_{i=1}^{n} \sum_{j=1}^{n} W_{ij} \right)^2 - n \sum_{i=1}^{n} \left( \sum_{j=1}^{n} W_{ij} \right)^2}{(n^2 - 1) \left( \sum_{i=1}^{n} \sum_{j=1}^{n} W_{ij} \right)^2}.$$

The statistic $\bar{I}/V$ will converge to standard normality under the null hypothesis and can form the basis of the test. (The assumption of independence across time is likely to be dubious at best, however.) Baltagi, Song, and Koh (2003) identify a variety of LM tests based on the assumption of normality. Two that apply to cross section analysis [See Bell and Bockstael (2000, p. 78)] are

$$LM(1) = \frac{(\mathbf{e}'\mathbf{W}\mathbf{e}/s^2)^2}{tr(\mathbf{W}'\mathbf{W} + \mathbf{W}^2)}$$

for spatial autocorrelation and

$$LM(2) = \frac{(\mathbf{e}'\mathbf{W}\mathbf{y}/s^2)^2}{\mathbf{b}'\mathbf{X}'\mathbf{W}\mathbf{M}\mathbf{W}\mathbf{X}\mathbf{b}/s^2 + tr(\mathbf{W}'\mathbf{W} + \mathbf{W}^2)}$$

for spatially lagged dependent variables, where $\mathbf{e}$ is the vector of OLS residuals, $s^2 = \mathbf{e}'\mathbf{e}/n$ and $\mathbf{M} = \mathbf{I} - \mathbf{X}(\mathbf{X}'\mathbf{X})^{-1}\mathbf{X}'$. [See Anselin and Hudak (1992).]

Anselin (1988) identifies several possible extensions of the spatial model to dynamic regressions. A "pure space-recursive model" specifies that the autocorrelation pertains to neighbors in the previous period:

$$y_{it} = \gamma [\mathbf{W}\mathbf{y}_{t-1}]_i + \mathbf{x}_{it}'\boldsymbol{\beta} + \varepsilon_{it}.$$

A "time-space recursive model" specifies dependence that is purely autoregressive with respect to neighbors in the previous period:

$$y_{it} = \rho y_{i,t-1} + \gamma [\mathbf{W}\mathbf{y}_{t-1}]_i + \mathbf{x}_{it}'\boldsymbol{\beta} + \varepsilon_{it}.$$

A "time-space simultaneous" model specifies that the spatial dependence is with respect to neighbors in the current period:

$$y_{it} = \rho y_{i,t-1} + [\lambda \mathbf{W}\mathbf{y}_t]_i + \mathbf{x}_{it}'\boldsymbol{\beta} + \varepsilon_{it}.$$

Finally, a "time-space dynamic model" specifies that autoregression depends on neighbors in both the current and last period:

$$y_{it} = \rho y_{i,t-1} + [\lambda \mathbf{W} \mathbf{y}_t]_i + \gamma [\mathbf{W} \mathbf{y}_{t-1}]_i + \mathbf{x}_{it}' \boldsymbol{\beta} + \varepsilon_{it}.$$

### Example 9.10    Spatial Autocorrelation in Real Estate Sales

Bell and Bockstael analyzed the problem of modeling spatial autocorrelation in large samples. This is likely to become an increasingly common problem with GIS (geographic information system) data sets. The central problem is maximization of a likelihood function that involves a sparse matrix, $(\mathbf{I} - \lambda \mathbf{W})$. Direct approaches to the problem can encounter severe inaccuracies in evaluation of the inverse and determinant. Kelejian and Prucha (1999) have developed a moment-based estimator for $\lambda$ that helps to alleviate the problem. Once the estimate of $\lambda$ is in hand, estimation of the spatial autocorrelation model is done by FGLS. The authors applied the method to analysis of a cross section of 1,000 residential sales in Anne Arundel County, Maryland, from 1993 to 1996. The parcels sold all involved houses built within one year prior to the sale. GIS software was used to measure attributes of interest.

The model is

$\ln Price = \alpha + \beta_1 \ln Assessed\ value\ (LIV)$

$\qquad + \beta_2 \ln Lot\ size\ (LLT)$

$\qquad + \beta_3 \ln Distance\ in\ km\ to\ Washington,\ DC\ (LDC)$

$\qquad + \beta_4 \ln Distance\ in\ km\ to\ Baltimore\ (LBA)$

$\qquad + \beta_5 \%\ land\ surrounding\ parcel\ in\ publicly\ owned\ space\ (POPN)$

$\qquad + \beta_6 \%\ land\ surrounding\ parcel\ in\ natural\ privately\ owned\ space\ (PNAT)$

$\qquad + \beta_7 \%\ land\ surrounding\ parcel\ in\ intensively\ developed\ use\ (PDEV)$

$\qquad + \beta_8 \%\ land\ surrounding\ parcel\ in\ low\ density\ residential\ use\ (PLOW)$

$\qquad + \beta_9 Public\ sewer\ service\ (1\ if\ existing\ or\ planned,\ 0\ if\ not)\ (PSEW)$

$\qquad + \varepsilon.$

(Land surrounding the parcel is all parcels in the GIS data whose centroids are within 500 meters of the transacted parcel.) For the full model, the specification is

$$\mathbf{y} = \mathbf{X}\boldsymbol{\beta} + \boldsymbol{\varepsilon},$$

$$\boldsymbol{\varepsilon} = \lambda \mathbf{W} \boldsymbol{\varepsilon} + \mathbf{v}.$$

The authors defined four contiguity matrices:

W1: $W_{ij}$ = 1/distance between i and j if distance < 600 meters, 0 otherwise,

W2: $W_{ij}$ = 1 if distance between i and j < 200 meters, 0 otherwise,

W3: $W_{ij}$ = 1 if distance between i and j < 400 meters, 0 otherwise,

W4: $W_{ij}$ = 1 if distance between i and j < 600 meters, 0 othewise.

All contiguity matrices were row-standardized. That is, elements in each row are scaled so that the row sums to one. One of the objectives of the study was to examine the impact of row standardization on the estimation. It is done to improve the numerical stability of the optimization process. Because the estimates depend numerically on the normalization, it is not completely innocent.

Test statistics for spatial autocorrelation based on the OLS residuals are shown in Table 9.7. (These are taken from the authors' Table 3.) The Moran statistics are distributed as standard normal while the LM statistics are distributed as chi-squared with one degree of freedom. All but the LM(2) statistic for W3 are larger than the 99% critical value from the respective table, so we would conclude that there is evidence of spatial autocorrelation. Estimates from some of the regressions are shown in Table 9.8. In the remaining results in the study, the

**TABLE 9.7**   Test Statistics for Spatial Autocorrelation

|            | *W1*  | *W2*  | *W3*   | *W4*  |
|------------|-------|-------|--------|-------|
| Moran's $I$ | 7.89  | 9.67  | 13.66  | 6.88  |
| LM(1)      | 49.95 | 84.93 | 156.48 | 36.46 |
| LM(2)      | 7.40  | 17.22 | 2.33   | 7.42  |

**TABLE 9.8**   Estimated Spatial Regression Models

|           | OLS | | FGLS[a] | | Spatial based on W1 ML | | Spatial based on W1 Gen. Moments | |
|-----------|----------|----------|----------|----------|----------|----------|----------|----------|
| *Parameter* | *Estimate* | *Std. Err.* | *Estimate* | *Std. Err.* | *Estimate* | *Std. Err.* | *Estimate* | *Std. Err.* |
| $\alpha$   | 4.7332  | 0.2047 | 4.7380  | 0.2048 | 5.1277  | 0.2204 | 5.0648  | 0.2169 |
| $\beta_1$  | 0.6926  | 0.0124 | 0.6924  | 0.0214 | 0.6537  | 0.0135 | 0.6638  | 0.0132 |
| $\beta_2$  | 0.0079  | 0.0052 | 0.0078  | 0.0052 | 0.0002  | 0.0052 | 0.0020  | 0.0053 |
| $\beta_3$  | −0.1494 | 0.0195 | −0.1501 | 0.0195 | −0.1774 | 0.0245 | −0.1691 | 0.0230 |
| $\beta_4$  | −0.0453 | 0.0114 | −0.0455 | 0.0114 | −0.0169 | 0.0156 | −0.0278 | 0.0143 |
| $\beta_5$  | −0.0493 | 0.0408 | −0.0484 | 0.0408 | −0.0149 | 0.0414 | −0.0269 | 0.0413 |
| $\beta_6$  | 0.0799  | 0.0177 | 0.0800  | 0.0177 | 0.0586  | 0.0213 | 0.0644  | 0.0204 |
| $\beta_7$  | 0.0677  | 0.0180 | 0.0680  | 0.0180 | 0.0253  | 0.0221 | 0.0394  | 0.0211 |
| $\beta_8$  | −0.0166 | 0.0194 | −0.0168 | 0.0194 | −0.0374 | 0.0224 | −0.0313 | 0.0215 |
| $\beta_9$  | −0.1187 | 0.0173 | −0.1192 | 0.0174 | −0.0828 | 0.0180 | −0.0939 | 0.0179 |
| $\lambda$  | —       | —      | —       | —      | 0.4582  | 0.0454 | 0.3517  | —      |

[a]The author reports using a heteroscedasticity model $\sigma_i^2 \times f(LIV_i, LIV_i^2)$. The function $f(.)$ is not identified.

authors find that the outcomes are somewhat sensitive to the specification of the spatial weight matrix, but not particularly so to the method of estimating $\lambda$.

### Example 9.11   Spatial Lags in Health Expenditures

Moscone, Knapp, and Tosetti (2007) investigated the determinants of mental health expenditure over six years in 148 British local authorities using two forms of the spatial correlation model to incorporate possible interaction among authorities as well as unobserved spatial heterogeneity. The models estimated, in addition to pooled regression and a random effects model, were as follows. The first is a model with **spatial lags:**

$$\mathbf{y}_t = \gamma_t \mathbf{i} + \rho \mathbf{W} \mathbf{y}_t + \mathbf{X}_t \boldsymbol{\beta} + \mathbf{u} + \boldsymbol{\varepsilon}_t,$$

where **u** is a 148 × 1 vector of random effects and **i** is a 148 × 1 column of ones. For each local authority,

$$y_{it} = \gamma_t + \rho(\mathbf{w}_i' \mathbf{y}_t) + \mathbf{x}_{it}' \boldsymbol{\beta} + u_i + \varepsilon_{it},$$

where $\mathbf{w}_i'$ is the $i$th row of the contiguity matrix, **W**. Contiguities were defined in **W** as one if the locality shared a border or vertex and zero otherwise. (The authors also experimented with other contiguity matrices based on "sociodemographic" differences.) The second model estimated is of **spatial error correlation**

$$\mathbf{y}_t = \gamma_t \mathbf{i} + \mathbf{X}_t \boldsymbol{\beta} + \mathbf{u} + \boldsymbol{\varepsilon}_t,$$

$$\boldsymbol{\varepsilon}_t = \lambda \mathbf{W} \boldsymbol{\varepsilon}_t + \mathbf{v}_t.$$

For each local authority, this model implies

$$y_{it} = \gamma_t + \mathbf{x}'_{it}\boldsymbol{\beta} + u_i + \lambda \Sigma_j w_{ij}\varepsilon_{jt} + v_{it}.$$

The authors use maximum likelihood to estimate the parameters of the model. To simplify the computations, they note that the maximization can be done using a two-step procedure. As we have seen in other applications, when $\boldsymbol{\Omega}$ in a generalized regression model is known, the appropriate estimator is GLS. For both of these models, with known spatial autocorrelation parameter, a GLS transformation of the data produces a classical regression model. [See (8-11).] The method used is to iterate back and forth between simple OLS estimation of $\gamma_t$, $\boldsymbol{\beta}$ and $\sigma^2_\varepsilon$ and maximization of the "concentrated log likelihood" function which, given the other estimates, is a function of the spatial autocorrelation parameter, $\rho$ or $\lambda$, and the variance of the heterogeneity, $\sigma^2_u$.

The dependent variable in the models is the log of per capita mental health expenditures. The covariates are the percentage of males and of people under 20 in the area, average mortgage rates, numbers of unemployment claims, employment, average house price, median weekly wage, percent of single parent households, dummy variables for Labour party or Liberal Democrat party authorities, and the density of population ("to control for supply-side factors"). The estimated spatial autocorrelation coefficients for the two models are 0.1579 and 0.1220, both more than twice as large as the estimated standard error. Based on the simple Wald tests, the hypothesis of no spatial correlation would be rejected. The log likelihood values for the two spatial models were +206.3 and +202.8, compared to −211.1 for the model with no spatial effects or region effects, so the results seem to favor the spatial models based on a chi-squared test statistic (with one degree of freedom) of twice the difference. However, there is an ambiguity in this result as the improved "fit" could be due to the region effects rather than the spatial effects. A simple random effects model shows a log likelihood value of +202.3, which bears this out. Measured against this value, the spatial lag model seems the preferred specification, whereas the spatial autocorrelation model does not add significantly to the log likelihood function compared to the basic random effects model.

## 9.8 PARAMETER HETEROGENEITY

The treatment so far has essentially treated the slope parameters of the model as fixed constants, and the intercept as varying randomly from group to group. An equivalent formulation of the pooled, fixed, and random effects model is

$$y_{it} = (\alpha + u_i) + \mathbf{x}'_{it}\boldsymbol{\beta} + \varepsilon_{it},$$

where $u_i$ is a person-specific random variable with conditional variance zero in the pooled model, positive in the others, and conditional mean dependent on $\mathbf{X}_i$ in the fixed effects model and constant in the random effects model. By any of these, the heterogeneity in the model shows up as variation in the constant terms in the regression model. There is ample evidence in many studies—we will examine two later—that suggests that the other parameters in the model also vary across individuals. In the dynamic model we consider in Section 9.8.5, cross-country variation in the slope parameter in a production function is the central focus of the analysis. This section will consider several approaches to analyzing parameter heterogeneity in panel data models. The model will be extended to multiple equations in Section 10.3.

## 9.8.1 THE RANDOM COEFFICIENTS MODEL

Parameter heterogeneity across individuals or groups can me modeled as stochastic variation.[26] Suppose that we write

$$y_i = X_i\beta_i + \varepsilon_i, \tag{9-47}$$

$$E[\varepsilon_i \mid X_i] = 0,$$

$$E[\varepsilon_i\varepsilon_i' \mid X_i] = \sigma_\varepsilon^2 I_T,$$

where

$$\beta_i = \beta + u_i \tag{9-48}$$

and

$$E[u_i \mid X_i] = 0,$$
$$E[u_i u_i' \mid X_i] = \Gamma. \tag{9-49}$$

(Note that if only the constant term in $\beta$ is random in this fashion and the other parameters are fixed as before, then this reproduces the random effects model we studied in Section 9.5.) Assume for now that there is no autocorrelation or cross-section correlation in $\varepsilon_i$. We also assume for now that $T > K$, so that when desired, it is possible to compute the linear regression of $y_i$ on $X_i$ for each group. Thus, the $\beta_i$ that applies to a particular cross-sectional unit is the outcome of a random process with mean vector $\beta$ and covariance matrix $\Gamma$.[27] By inserting (9-48) into (9-47) and expanding the result, we obtain a generalized regression model for each block of observations:

$$y_i = X_i\beta + (\varepsilon_i + X_i u_i),$$

so

$$\Omega_{ii} = E[(y_i - X_i\beta)(y_i - X_i\beta)' \mid X_i] = \sigma_\varepsilon^2 I_T + X_i\Gamma X_i'.$$

For the system as a whole, the disturbance covariance matrix is block diagonal, with $T \times T$ diagonal block $\Omega_{ii}$. We can write the GLS estimator as a matrix weighted average of the group specific OLS estimators:

$$\hat{\beta} = (X'\Omega^{-1}X)^{-1}X'\Omega^{-1}y = \sum_{i=1}^n W_i b_i, \tag{9-50}$$

where

$$W_i = \left[\sum_{i=1}^n \left(\Gamma + \sigma_\varepsilon^2(X_i'X_i)^{-1}\right)^{-1}\right]^{-1} \left(\Gamma + \sigma_\varepsilon^2(X_i'X_i)^{-1}\right)^{-1}.$$

[26]The most widely cited studies are Hildreth and Houck (1968), Swamy (1970, 1971, 1974), Hsiao (1975), and Chow (1984). See also Breusch and Pagan (1979). Some recent discussions are Swamy and Tavlas (1995, 2001) and Hsiao (2003). The model bears some resemblance to the Bayesian approach of Chapter 18. But, the similarity is only superficial. We are maintaining the classical approach to estimation throughout.

[27]Swamy and Tavlas (2001) label this the "first-generation random coefficients model" (RCM). We will examine the "second generation" (the current generation) of random coefficients models in the next section.

Empirical implementation of this model requires an estimator of $\mathbf{\Gamma}$. One approach [see, e.g., Swamy (1971)] is to use the empirical variance of the set of $n$ least squares estimates, $\mathbf{b}_i$ minus the average value of $s_i^2(\mathbf{X}_i'\mathbf{X}_i)^{-1}$:

$$\mathbf{G} = [1/(n-1)]\left[\Sigma_i \mathbf{b}_i \mathbf{b}_i' - n\bar{\mathbf{b}}\,\bar{\mathbf{b}}'\right] - (1/N)\Sigma_i \mathbf{V}_i, \tag{9-51}$$

where

$$\bar{\mathbf{b}} = (1/n)\Sigma_i \mathbf{b}_i$$

and

$$\mathbf{V}_i = s_i^2(\mathbf{X}_i'\mathbf{X}_i)^{-1}.$$

This matrix may not be positive definite, however, in which case [as Baltagi (2005) suggests], one might drop the second term.

A chi-squared test of the random coefficients model against the alternative of the classical regression (no randomness of the coefficients) can be based on

$$C = \Sigma_i (\mathbf{b}_i - \mathbf{b}_*)' \mathbf{V}_i^{-1} (\mathbf{b}_i - \mathbf{b}_*),$$

where

$$\mathbf{b}_* = \left[\Sigma_i \mathbf{V}_i^{-1}\right]^{-1} \Sigma_i \mathbf{V}_i^{-1} \mathbf{b}_i.$$

Under the null hypothesis of homogeneity, $C$ has a limiting chi-squared distribution with $(n-1)K$ degrees of freedom. The best linear unbiased individual predictors of the group-specific coefficient vectors are matrix weighted averages of the GLS estimator, $\hat{\boldsymbol{\beta}}$, and the group specific OLS estimates, $\mathbf{b}_i$,[28]

$$\hat{\boldsymbol{\beta}}_i = \mathbf{Q}_i \hat{\boldsymbol{\beta}} + [\mathbf{I} - \mathbf{Q}_i]\mathbf{b}_i,$$

where $\qquad\qquad\qquad\qquad\qquad\qquad\qquad\qquad\qquad\qquad\qquad\qquad$ (9-52)

$$\mathbf{Q}_i = \left[(1/s_i^2)\mathbf{X}_i'\mathbf{X}_i + \mathbf{G}^{-1}\right]^{-1}\mathbf{G}^{-1}.$$

### Example 9.12   Random Coefficients Model
In Example 9.9, we examined Munell's production model for gross state product,

$$\ln gsp_{it} = \beta_1 + \beta_2 \ln p\_cap_{it} + \beta_3 \ln hwy_{it} + \beta_4 \ln water_{it}$$
$$+ \beta_5 \ln util_{it} + \beta_6 \ln emp_{it} + \beta_7 unemp_{it} + \varepsilon_{it}, \quad i = 1,\dots,48; t = 1,\dots,17.$$

The panel consists of state level data for 17 years. The model in Example 9.9 (and Munnell's) provide no means for parameter heterogeneity save for the constant term. We have reestimated the model using the Hildreth and Houck approach. The OLS, Feasible GLS and maximum likelihood estimates are given in Table 9.9. The chi-squared statistic for testing the null hypothesis of parameter homogeneity is 25,556.26, with 7(47) = 329 degrees of freedom. The critical value from the table is 372.299, so the hypothesis would be rejected.

Unlike the other cases we have examined in this chapter, the FGLS estimates are very different from OLS in these estimates, in spite of the fact that both estimators are consistent and the sample is fairly large. The underlying standard deviations are computed using **G** as the covariance matrix. [For these data, subtracting the second matrix rendered **G** not positive

---

[28]See Hsiao (2003, pp. 144–149).

**TABLE 9.9**    Estimated Random Coefficients Models

| Variable | Least Squares | | Feasible GLS | | | Maximum Simulated Likelihood | |
| | Estimate | Standard Error | Estimate | Standard Error | Popn. Std. Deviation | Estimate | Std. Error |
|---|---|---|---|---|---|---|---|
| Constant | 1.9260 | 0.05250 | 1.6533 | 1.08331 | 7.0782 | 1.9463 (0.0411) | 0.03569 |
| ln p_cap | 0.3120 | 0.01109 | 0.09409 | 0.05152 | 0.3036 | 0.2962 (0.0730) | 0.00882 |
| ln hwy | 0.05888 | 0.01541 | 0.1050 | 0.1736 | 1.1112 | 0.09515 (0.146) | 0.01157 |
| ln water | 0.1186 | 0.01236 | 0.07672 | 0.06743 | 0.4340 | 0.2434 (0.343) | 0.01929 |
| ln util | 0.00856 | 0.01235 | −0.01489 | 0.09886 | 0.6322 | −0.1855 (0.281) | 0.02713 |
| ln emp | 0.5497 | 0.01554 | 0.9190 | 0.1044 | 0.6595 | 0.6795 (0.121) | 0.02274 |
| unemp | −0.00727 | 0.001384 | −0.004706 | 0.002067 | 0.01266 | −0.02318 (0.0308) | 0.002712 |
| $\sigma_\varepsilon$ | 0.08542 | | 0.2129 | | | 0.02748 | |
| ln L | 853.1372 | | | | | 1567.233 | |

definite, so in the table, the standard deviations are based on the estimates using only the first term in (9-51).] The increase in the standard errors is striking. This suggests that there is considerable variation in the parameters across states. We have used (9-52) to compute the estimates of the state specific coefficients. Figure 9.1 shows a histogram for the coefficient on private capital. As suggested, there is a wide variation in the estimates.

**FIGURE 9.1**    Estimates of Coefficients on Private Capital.

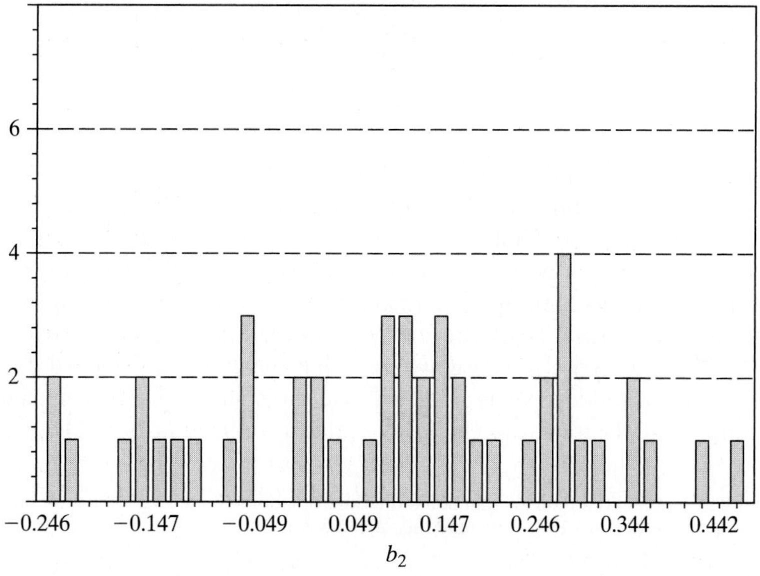

### 9.8.2 RANDOM PARAMETERS AND SIMULATION-BASED ESTIMATION[29]

The random parameters model accommodates an important shortcoming of the basic regression model: individual heterogeneity not only in the constant term, but also in the remaining coefficients. It does have two shortcomings of its own. It is rather inflexible in terms of the model specification compared to the hierarchical models described in the next section. In more practical terms, panels are often short and there may be too few observations to compute $\mathbf{b}_i$. More recent applications of random parameter variation have taken a completely different approach based on simulation estimation. [McFadden and Train (2000), Train (2003) and Greene (2001).] We will develop this technique in detail in Section 17.5. However, this is a useful point to introduce the topic in a familiar setting.

We begin with assumptions (9-47)–(9-49) and in addition, $\mathbf{u}_i \sim N[\mathbf{0}, \mathbf{\Gamma}]$ and $\varepsilon_{it} \sim N[0, \sigma_\varepsilon^2]$. Conditioned on $\mathbf{X}_i$ and on the specific $\boldsymbol{\beta}_i$,

$$y_{it} = \mathbf{x}'_{it}\boldsymbol{\beta}_i + \varepsilon_{it}.$$

For the given $\boldsymbol{\beta}_i$ and with conditional normality, it follows that $y_{it}, t = 1, \ldots, T$ are mutually independent as well as uncorrelated. Thus, the density for $y_{it} \mid \mathbf{x}_{it}, \boldsymbol{\beta}_i$ is $N[\mathbf{x}'_{it}\boldsymbol{\beta}_i, \sigma_\varepsilon^2]$. With independence and joint normality, the log likelihood function for the $T$ observations in group $i$ is the sum of the logs of the densities,

$$\ln f(y_{i1}, y_{i2}, \ldots, y_{iT} \mid \mathbf{X}_i, \boldsymbol{\beta}_i) = \ln L_i \mid \mathbf{X}_i, \boldsymbol{\beta}_i$$
$$= -T/2 \ln 2\pi - T/2 \ln \sigma_\varepsilon^2 - 1/2 \Sigma_t (y_{it} - \mathbf{x}'_{it}\boldsymbol{\beta}_i)^2/\sigma_\varepsilon^2. \quad \textbf{(9-53)}$$

The log likelihood for the full sample is

$$\ln L = \sum_i \ln L_i \mid \mathbf{X}_i, \boldsymbol{\beta}_i.$$

Inserting the expression for $\boldsymbol{\beta}_i = \boldsymbol{\beta} + \mathbf{u}_i$, we obtain

$$\ln L \mid (\mathbf{X}_i, \mathbf{u}_i, i = 1, \ldots, n) = \sum_i \left\{ -T/2 \ln 2\pi - T/2 \ln \sigma_\varepsilon^2 - \frac{1}{2}\Sigma_t[y_{it} - \mathbf{x}'_{it}(\boldsymbol{\beta} + \mathbf{u}_i)^2]/\sigma_\varepsilon^2 \right\}.$$
$$\textbf{(9-54)}$$

In principle, we would estimate the unknown parameters of the model by maximizing this log likelihood function with respect to $\boldsymbol{\beta}$ and $\sigma_\varepsilon^2$. However, there are two problems with that prescription. First, $\ln L$ contains the unobserved $\mathbf{u}_i$, so it cannot be computed. Second, the covariance matrix of $\mathbf{u}_i$, which is $\mathbf{\Gamma}$ in (9-49) does not appear in the log likelihood to be maximized. The second of these problems is straightforward to solve. In the univariate case, if $u_i$ is a normally distributed variable with zero mean and variance $\gamma^2$, then we can write $u_i = \gamma v_i$ where $v_i$ has mean 0 and standard deviation 1. To do likewise for a random vector, we will use the square root of $\mathbf{\Gamma}$ in the same fashion. Because in application, the Cholesky matrix (see Section A.6.11) is more convenient,

---

[29]This development relies on maximum likelihood estimation. The reader who is not familiar with the MLE should examine Chapter 16 as they read this section.

we will use it instead, and write $\mathbf{u}_i = \boldsymbol{\Lambda}\mathbf{v}_i$ where $\boldsymbol{\Lambda}\boldsymbol{\Lambda}' = \boldsymbol{\Gamma}$ and $\mathbf{v}_i$ is a normally distributed vector with mean vector $\mathbf{0}$ and covariance matrix $\mathbf{I}$. Insert this result in (9-54) to obtain the full (still conditional) log likelihood,

$$\ln L \,|\, (\mathbf{X}_i, \mathbf{v}_i, i = 1, \ldots, n) = \sum_i -T/2 \ln 2\pi - T/2 \ln \sigma_\varepsilon^2$$
$$- 1/2\, \Sigma_t \left[ y_{it} - \mathbf{x}'_{it}(\boldsymbol{\beta} + \boldsymbol{\Lambda}\mathbf{v}_i) \right]^2 / \sigma_\varepsilon^2. \qquad \textbf{(9-55)}$$

This solves the second problem, but the first remains. The conditional log likelihood function now involves the unobserved $\mathbf{v}_i$. In order to estimate the parameters by maximizing the log likelihood, we require the unconditional log likelihood, which is obtained by integrating $\mathbf{v}_i$ out of the conditional function. Thus,

$$\ln L \,|\, (\mathbf{X}_i, i = 1, \ldots, n) = \sum_i \int_{\mathbf{v}_i} \left\{ -T/2 \ln 2\pi - T/2 \ln \sigma_\varepsilon^2 \right.$$
$$\left. - 1/2\Sigma_t \left[ y_{it} - \mathbf{x}'_{it}(\boldsymbol{\beta} + \boldsymbol{\Lambda}\mathbf{v}_i) \right]^2 / \sigma_\varepsilon^2 \right\} f(\mathbf{v}_i)\, d\mathbf{v}_i, \qquad \textbf{(9-56)}$$

where $f(\mathbf{v}_i)$ is the joint density of the elements of $\mathbf{v}_i$ — the standard normal. The parameters of the model are estimated by maximizing the function in (9-56) with respect to $\boldsymbol{\beta}, \boldsymbol{\Lambda}$ and $\sigma_\varepsilon^2$.

Integrals of the form in (9-56) typically do not exist in closed form. (In fact, this one does, but we will not need the analytic solution. The closed form does not exist for the other models we will examine in Chapter 17.) Researchers have found that integrals of this form can be satisfactorily evaluated by simulation methods. We will pursue simulation based estimation methods in detail in Chapter 17, so we will only sketch the result here. For this particular problem, we would evaluate the integral for each $i$ by drawing a random sample of vectors $\mathbf{v}_i$ from the standard normal population and averaging the function values computed using these draws. More formally, the **simulated log likelihood** that corresponds to (9-56) is

$$\ln L_S \,|\, (\mathbf{X}_i, i = 1, \ldots, n) = \sum_{i=1}^{n} \frac{1}{R} \sum_{r=1}^{R} \left\{ -T/2 \ln 2\pi - T/2 \ln \sigma_\varepsilon^2 \right.$$
$$\left. - 1/2 \sum_t \left[ y_{it} - \mathbf{x}'_{it}(\boldsymbol{\beta} + \boldsymbol{\Lambda}\mathbf{v}_{ir}) \right]^2 / \sigma_\varepsilon^2 \right\}. \qquad \textbf{(9-57)}$$

Notice how the integration (which is the expectation of the function in curled brackets in (9-56)) is replaced with summation, and $\mathbf{v}_{ir}$ are $R$ multivariate standard normal draws obtained using a random number generator. The function in (9-57) is now maximized with respect to $\boldsymbol{\beta}, \boldsymbol{\Lambda}$ and $\sigma_\varepsilon^2$. This is called the **maximum simulated likelihood estimator.** (The mechanical aspects and a fuller development of the theory appear in Chapter 17.)

The solutions to the maximization problem are found by equating the derivatives to zero. For the least squares problem in (9-57), these are found as follows. Let $\boldsymbol{\lambda}'_k$ denote the $k$th row of $\mathbf{\Lambda}$. Then

$$\frac{\partial \ln L_S(\mathbf{X}_i, i = 1, \ldots, n)}{\partial \boldsymbol{\beta}} = \sum_{i=1}^{n} \frac{1}{R} \sum_{r=1}^{R} \frac{-1}{\sigma_{\varepsilon}^2} (y_{it} - \mathbf{x}'_{it}(\boldsymbol{\beta} + \mathbf{\Lambda}\mathbf{v}_{ir}))(-\mathbf{x}_{it}) = \mathbf{0},$$

$$\frac{\partial \ln L_S(\mathbf{X}_i, i = 1, \ldots, n)}{\partial \lambda_k} = \sum_{i=1}^{n} \frac{1}{R} \sum_{r=1}^{R} \frac{-1}{\sigma_{\varepsilon}^2} (y_{it} - \mathbf{x}'_{it}(\boldsymbol{\beta} + \mathbf{\Lambda}\mathbf{v}_{ir}))(-x_{itk}\mathbf{v}_{ir}) = 0.$$

(9-58)

[The derivatives with respect to all the rows of $\mathbf{\Lambda}$ can be collected in one expression by replacing $(-x_{itk}\mathbf{v}_{ir})$ with $(\mathbf{x}_{it} \otimes \mathbf{v}_{ir})$.] Note that $\sigma_{\varepsilon}^2$ does not affect the solutions to the likelihood equations in (9-58). To see this, multiply both equations by $-\sigma_{\varepsilon}^2$ and the same solution emerges independently of $\sigma_{\varepsilon}^2$. Thus, we can view the solution as the counterpart to least squares, which we might call minimum simulated sum of squares. Once the simulated sum of squares is minimized with respect to $\boldsymbol{\beta}$ and $\mathbf{\Lambda}$, then the solution for $\sigma_{\varepsilon}^2$ can be obtained via the likelihood equation

$$\frac{\partial \ln L_S(\mathbf{X}_i, i = 1, \ldots, n)}{\partial \sigma_{\varepsilon}^2} = \sum_{i=1}^{n} \frac{1}{R} \sum_{r=1}^{R} \frac{-T}{2\sigma_{\varepsilon}^2} + \frac{\sum_{t=1}^{T} (y_{it} - \mathbf{x}'_{it}(\boldsymbol{\beta} + \mathbf{\Lambda}\mathbf{v}_{ir}))^2}{2\sigma_{\varepsilon}^4} = 0.$$

Multiply both sides of this equation by $-2\sigma_{\varepsilon}^4 / T$ to obtain the equivalent condition,

$$\sum_{i=1}^{n} \frac{1}{R} \sum_{r=1}^{R} \left[ \sigma_{\varepsilon}^2 - \frac{\sum_{t=1}^{T} (y_{it} - \mathbf{x}'_{it}(\boldsymbol{\beta} + \mathbf{\Lambda}\mathbf{v}_{ir}))^2}{T} \right] = 0.$$

This implies that the solution for $\sigma_{\varepsilon}^2$ is obtained by

$$\hat{\sigma}_{\varepsilon}^2 = \frac{1}{n} \sum_{i=1}^{n} \frac{1}{R} \sum_{r=1}^{R} \frac{\sum_{t=1}^{T} (y_{it} - \mathbf{x}'_{it}(\boldsymbol{\beta} + \mathbf{\Lambda}\mathbf{v}_{ir}))^2}{T}$$

$$= \frac{1}{n} \sum_{i=1}^{n} \frac{1}{R} \sum_{r=1}^{R} \hat{\sigma}_{\varepsilon,ir}^2.$$

Minimization of the sum of squares is a nonlinear optimization problem. The solution for $\sigma_{\varepsilon}^2$ is then obtained as a function of the estimates of $\boldsymbol{\beta}$ and $\mathbf{\Lambda}$.

### Example 9.13  Minimum Simulated Sum of Squares Estimates of the Production Function

The rightmost columns of Table 9.9 present the maximum simulated likelihood estimates of the random parameters production function model. They somewhat resemble the OLS estimates, more so than the FGLS estimates, which are computed by an entirely different method. The values in parentheses under the parameter estimates are the estimates of the standard deviations of the distribution of $u_i$, the square roots of the diagonal elements of $\mathbf{\Gamma}$. These are obtained by computing the square roots of the diagonal elements of $\mathbf{\Lambda}\mathbf{\Lambda}'$. The estimate of $\mathbf{\Lambda}$ is shown here.

$$\hat{\mathbf{\Lambda}} = \begin{bmatrix} 0.04114 & 0 & 0 & 0 & 0 & 0 & 0 \\ 0.00715 & 0.07266 & 0 & 0 & 0 & 0 & 0 \\ -0.02446 & 0.12392 & 0.07247 & 0 & 0 & 0 & 0 \\ 0.09972 & -0.00644 & 0.31916 & 0.07614 & 0 & 0 & 0 \\ -0.08928 & 0.02143 & -0.25105 & 0.07583 & 0.04053 & 0 & 0 \\ 0.03842 & -0.06321 & -0.03992 & -0.06693 & -0.05490 & 0.00857 & 0 \\ -0.00833 & -0.00257 & -0.02478 & 0.01594 & 0.00102 & -0.00185 & 0.0018. \end{bmatrix}$$

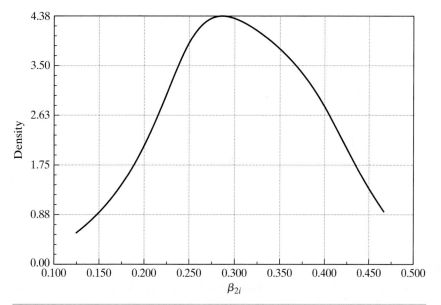

**FIGURE 9.2**   Kernel Density Estimate for the Distribution of Means of $\beta_{2i}$.

An estimate of the correlation matrix for the parameters is likely to be more informative. This is also derived from $\hat{\Lambda}$ by computing $\hat{\Gamma}$ then transforming the covariances to correlations by dividing by the products of the respective standard deviations (the values in parentheses in Table 9.9). The result is

$$
\mathbf{R} = \begin{array}{llllllll}
1 & & & & & & \\
0.0979 & 1 & & & & & \\
-0.1680 & 0.83040 & 1 & & & & \\
0.2907 & 0.00980 & 0.3983 & 1 & & & \\
-0.3180 & 0.04481 & -0.3266 & -0.8659 & 1 & & \\
0.3176 & -0.48890 & -0.6622 & -0.3277 & -0.06073 & 1 & \\
-0.2700 & -0.10940 & -0.4253 & -0.7097 & 0.94190 & -0.08228 & 1.
\end{array}
$$

Section 17.5 presents a method of computing an estimator of $E[\beta_i \mid \mathbf{y}_i, \mathbf{X}_i]$. This would be the counterpart to the best linear predictor in (9-52), though this computation uses more information—it uses the information on $\mathbf{y}_i$ as well as $\mathbf{X}_i$. We have computed the estimates of $E[\beta_{2i} \mid \mathbf{y}_i, \mathbf{X}_i]$ for the 48 states in the sample. Figure 9.2 shows a kernel density estimate based on these estimates. The figure is not directly comparable to 9.1 because 9.2 shows the distribution of conditional means while 9.1 shows the distribution of predictions of the coefficients themselves. By construction, the variation in the means will be much less than the variation in the estimated parameters. Nonetheless, Figure 9.2 does confirm the suggestion of the statistical results, that there is a very large amount of variation in the coefficients across states. Finally, a likelihood ratio test of the null hypothesis of the pooled model would be based on chi squared = $2(\ln L_{MSL} - \ln_{OLS}) = 1428.192$, with 7(8)/2 = 28 degrees of freedom. The critical value is 41.337, so the hypothesis is once again rejected.

### 9.8.3   TWO-STEP ESTIMATION OF PANEL DATA MODELS

The preceding sections have suggested an extension of the common effects model to variation across individuals of the slope parameters as well as the constant terms. At various points, we have suggested other similar possibilities. Our initial definition of the common effects model in (9-1) was

$$y_{it} = \mathbf{x}'_{it}\boldsymbol{\beta} + \mathbf{z}'_i\boldsymbol{\alpha} + \varepsilon_{it}, \tag{9-59}$$

where $\mathbf{z}_i$ could contain both observed and unobserved time invariant variables. It is the treatment of the *unobservables* in $\mathbf{z}_i$ that lies behind the fixed and random effects formulations considered above. To this point, observables in $\mathbf{z}_i$ have simply been included in the model as time-invariant variables. We then considered the practical implications of time-invariant variables for fixed and random effects estimation. The Mundlak and Chamberlain approaches, for example, treated $c_i = \mathbf{z}'_i\boldsymbol{\alpha}$ as a single unknown random variable, and formulated the model around the projection of $c_i$ on either the group means of $\mathbf{x}_{it}$ (Mundlak's approach) or all observations on $\mathbf{x}_{it}$ (Chamberlain's model). In this section, we consider more structured arrangements in which the "time-invariant" effects are also part of the model structure.

Consider, first, the basic common effects model,

$$y_{it} = \mathbf{x}'_{it}\boldsymbol{\beta} + c_i + \varepsilon_{it}, \tag{9-60}$$

which we extend to a simple **hierarchical linear model** in which all variables in $\mathbf{z}_i$ are observed and

$$c_i = \mathbf{z}'_i\boldsymbol{\alpha} + u_i,$$
$$E[u_i \mid \mathbf{z}_i] = 0, \tag{9-61}$$
$$E[u_i^2 \mid \mathbf{z}_i] = \sigma_u^2.$$

The problem accommodated by the fixed effects approach is the possibility that $E[u_i \mid \mathbf{X}_i]$ is a function of $\mathbf{X}_i$. As such, merely inserting (9-61) in (9-60) and estimating the parameters as a random effects model with time invariant effects does not solve the problem of estimating $\boldsymbol{\beta}$ because we have not assumed that $E[u_i \mid \mathbf{X}_i] = 0$; the unobservables may still be correlated with the regressors. Consider an alternative, fixed effects approach,

$$y_{it} = \mathbf{x}'_{it}\boldsymbol{\beta} + \alpha_i + \varepsilon_{it},$$

where, as before, $\alpha_i = \mathbf{z}'_i\boldsymbol{\alpha} + u_i$. The fixed effects (LSDV) estimator is a consistent estimator of $\boldsymbol{\beta}$ regardless of whether $E[u_i \mid \mathbf{X}_i] = 0$ or not. For the LSDV estimator of $\alpha_i$, [see (9-15)], we have

$$\begin{aligned} a_i &= \alpha_i + w_i \\ &= \mathbf{z}'_i\boldsymbol{\alpha} + u_i + w_i, \end{aligned} \tag{9-62}$$

where $w_i$ is the sampling variation, i.e., estimation error in $\alpha_i$. From (9-15), the fixed effects estimator of $\alpha_i$ is

$$a_i = \bar{y}_i - \bar{\mathbf{x}}'_i\mathbf{b},$$

where $\mathbf{b}$ is the (consistent and unbiased) LSDV estimator of $\boldsymbol{\beta}$. It follows that

$$\begin{aligned} a_i &= \bar{\mathbf{x}}'_i\boldsymbol{\beta} + \alpha_i. + \bar{\varepsilon}_i. - \bar{\mathbf{x}}'_i\mathbf{b} \\ &= \mathbf{z}'_i\boldsymbol{\alpha} + u_i + \bar{\varepsilon}_i. + \bar{\mathbf{x}}'_i(\boldsymbol{\beta} - \mathbf{b}). \end{aligned}$$

**TABLE 9.10**   Random Effects and Two-Step Estimates of a Wage Equation

| | Random Effects | | Hierarchical | |
|---|---|---|---|---|
| | *Estimate* | *Standard Error* | *Estimate* | *Standard Error* |
| *Exp* | 008748 | 0.002246 | 0.1132 | 0.002471 |
| *Exp²* | −0.0007644 | 0.00004957 | −0.0004183 | 0.00005459 |
| *Wks* | 0.0009572 | 0.0005930 | 0.0008359 | 0.0005997 |
| *Occ* | −0.04322 | 0.01299 | −0.02145 | 0.01378 |
| *Ind* | 0.003776 | 0.01373 | 0.01921 | 0.01545 |
| *South* | −0.008250 | 0.02246 | −0.001861 | 0.03430 |
| *SMSA* | −0.02840 | 0.01616 | −0.04247 | 0.01943 |
| *MS* | −0.07090 | 0.01793 | −0.02973 | 0.01898 |
| *Union* | 0.05835 | 0.01350 | 0.03278 | 0.01492 |
| *Constant* | 4.0414 | 0.08330 | 2.8286* | 0.1860 |
| *Ed* | 0.1071 | 0.005112 | 0.1444* | 0.01403 |
| *Fem* | −0.3094 | 0.04554 | −0.1300* | 0.1256 |
| *Blk* | −0.2195 | 0.05252 | −0.2751* | 0.1544 |

*Second step estimates.

For large $n$, the sampling variation in **b** diminishes as it is a consistent estimator. Therefore, for estimation of $\alpha$, linear regression of $a_i$ on $z_i$ will be consistent in $n$.[30] We emphasize, this is not a general remedy for fixed effects with time invariant variables. The presence of unobserved heterogeneity in (9-61) has the same impact that it had before. What has changed here is our additional assumption that the linear regression model in (9-61) applies to the relationship between the common effect and all of the time-invariant variables in the model.

### Example 9.14   Two-Step Estimation of Cornwell and Rupert's Wage Equation

Fixed and random effects estimates of the wage equation using only the time-varying variables in the Cornwell and Rupert data appear in Table 9.5 in Example 9.6. Here, we will estimate a hierarchical model using the two-step procedure suggested preceding. The estimates appear in Table 9.10. They are rather different, as might be expected. The hierarchical model estimator is consistent in all cases. The random effects estimator is only consistent if the unobservables are not correlated with the regressors. But, on the basis of the Hausman test in Example 9.7, we convincingly rejected that hypothesis.

Many researchers have employed this sort of two-step approach to estimate two-level models. In a common form of the application, a panel data set is employed to estimate the two level model,

$$y_{it} = \mathbf{x}'_{it}\boldsymbol{\beta}_i + \varepsilon_{it}, i = 1, \ldots, n, \ t = 1, \ldots, T,$$

$$\beta_{i,k} = \mathbf{z}'_i\boldsymbol{\alpha}_k + u_i, \ i = 1, \ldots, n.$$

---

[30]Early references on two-step estimation are Hanuschek (1999) and Saxonhouse (1976). The latter explores the case in which heteroscedasticity in the counterpart to (9-61) is passed on to the second step model in (9-62). A recent exploration of two step estimators is Achen (2005). Borjas and Sueyoshi (1994) and Jusko (2005) considered two step procedures in which the effects are associated with a binary choice model rather than a linear regression.

Assuming the panel is long enough, the first equation is estimated $n$ times, once for each individual $i$, then the estimated coefficient on $x_{itk}$ in each regression forms an observation for the second step regression.[31]

### Example 9.15  Fannie Mae's Pass Through

Fannie Mae is the popular name for the Federal National Mortgage Corporation. Fannie Mae is the secondary provider for mortgage money for nearly all of the small and moderate-sized home mortgages in the United States. Loans in the study described here are termed "small" if they are for less than $100,000. A loan is termed a "conforming" in the language of the literature on this market if (as of 2004), it was for no more than $333,700. A larger than conforming loan is called a "jumbo" mortgage. Fannie Mae provides the capital for nearly all conforming loans and no nonconforming loans. The question pursued in the study described here was whether the clearly observable spread between the rates on jumbo loans and conforming loans reflects the cost of raising the capital in the market.

Fannie Mae is a "Government Sponsored Enterprice" (GSE). It was created by the U.S. Congress, but it is not an arm of the government; it is a private corporation. In spite of, or perhaps because of this ambiguous relationship to the government, apparently, capital markets believe that there is some benefit to Fannie Mae in raising capital. Purchasers of the GSE's debt securities seem to believe that the debt is implicitly backed by the government—this in spite of the fact that Fannie Mae explicitly states otherwise in its publications. This emerges as a "funding advantage" (GFA) estimated by the authors of the study of about 17 basis points (hundredths of one percent). In a study of the residential mortgage market, Passmore (2005) and Passmore, Sherlund, and Burgess (2005) sought to determine whether this implicit subsity to the GSE was passed on to the mortgagees or was, instead, passed on to the stockholders. Their approach utilitized a very large data set and a two-level, two-step estimation procedure.

The first step equation estimated was a mortgage rate equation using a sample of roughly 1 million closed mortgages. All were conventional 30-year fixed-rate loans closed between April 1997 and May 2003. The dependent variable of interest is the rate on the mortgage, $RM_{it}$. The first level equation is

$$RM_{it} = \beta_{1i} + \beta_{2,i} J_{it} + \text{terms for "loan to value ratio,"}$$
$$\text{"new home dummy variable,"}$$
$$\text{"small mortgage"}$$
$$+ \text{ terms for "fees charged" and}$$
$$\text{whether the mortgage was originated}$$
$$\text{by a mortgage company}$$
$$+ \varepsilon_{it}.$$

The main variable of interest in this model is $J_{it}$, which is a dummy variable for whether the loan is a jumbo mortgage. The "$i$" in this setting is a (state, time) pair for California, New Jersey, Maryland, Virginia, and all other states, and months from April 1997 to May 2003. There were 370 groups in total. The regression model was estimated for each group. At the second step, the coefficient of interest is $\beta_{2,i}$. On overall average, the spread between jumbo and conforming loans at the time was roughly 16 basis points. The second level equation is

$$\beta_{2,i} = \alpha_1 + \alpha_2 \text{GFA}_i + \alpha_3 \text{ one-year treasury rate}$$
$$+ \alpha_4 \text{ ten-year treasure rate}$$
$$+ \alpha_5 \text{ credit risk}$$
$$+ \alpha_6 \text{ prepayment risk}$$
$$+ \text{ measures of maturity mismatch risk}$$
$$+ \text{ quarter and state fixed effects}$$
$$+ \text{ mortgage market capacity}$$
$$+ \text{ mortgage market development}$$
$$+ u_i$$

---

[31] An extension of the model in which $u_i$ is heteroscedastic is developed at length in Saxonhouse (1976) and revisited by Achen (2005).

The result ultimately of interest is the coefficient on GFA, $\alpha_2$, which is interpreted as the fraction of the GSE funding advantage that is passed through to the mortgage holders.

Four different estimates of $\alpha_2$ were obtained, based on four different measures of corporate debt liquidity; the estimated values were $(\hat{\alpha}_2^1, \hat{\alpha}_2^2, \hat{\alpha}_2^3, \hat{\alpha}_2^4) = (0.07, 0.31, 0.17, 0.10)$. The four estimates were averaged using a **minimum distance estimator.** Let $\hat{\Omega}$ denote the estimated $4 \times 4$ asymptotic covariance matrix for the estimators. Denote the distance vector

$$\mathbf{d} = (\hat{\alpha}_2^1 - \alpha_2, \hat{\alpha}_2^2 - \alpha_2, \hat{\alpha}_2^3 - \alpha_2, \hat{\alpha}_2^4 - \alpha_2)'.$$

The minimum distance estimator is the value for $\alpha_2$ that minimizes $\mathbf{d}'\hat{\Omega}^{-1}\mathbf{d}$. For this study, $\hat{\Omega}$ is a diagonal matrix. It is straighforward to show that in this case, the MDE is

$$\hat{\alpha}_2 = \sum_{j=1}^{4} \hat{\alpha}_2^j \left( \frac{1/\hat{\omega}_j}{\sum_{m=1}^{4} 1/\hat{\omega}_m} \right).$$

The final answer is roughly 16%. By implication, then, the authors estimated that 84% of the GSE funding advantage was kept within the company or passed through to stockholders.

### 9.8.4  HIERARCHICAL LINEAR MODELS

Recent research in many fields has extended the idea of hierarchical modeling to the full set of parameters in the model. (Depending on the field studied, the reader may find these labeled "hierarchical models," **mixed models,** "random parameters models," or "random effects models." The last of these generalizes our notion of random effects.) A two level formulation of the model in (9-47) might appear as

$$\mathbf{y}_i = \mathbf{X}_i \boldsymbol{\beta}_i + \boldsymbol{\varepsilon}_i,$$

$$\boldsymbol{\beta}_i = \boldsymbol{\beta} + \boldsymbol{\Delta}\mathbf{z}_i + \mathbf{u}_i.$$

This model retains the earlier stochastic specification but adds the measurement equation to the generation of the random parameters. In principle, this is actually only a minor extension of the model used thus far. The model of the previous section now becomes

$$y_{it} = \mathbf{x}_{it}'(\boldsymbol{\beta} + \boldsymbol{\Delta}\mathbf{z}_i + \mathbf{u}_i) + \varepsilon_{it}$$

$$= \mathbf{x}_{it}'\boldsymbol{\beta} + \mathbf{x}_{it}'\boldsymbol{\Delta}\mathbf{z}_i + \mathbf{x}_{it}'\mathbf{u}_i + \varepsilon_{it},$$

which is essentially the same as our earlier model in (9-47)–(9-49) with the addition of product terms of the form $\delta_{kl}x_{itk}z_{il}$. The heteroscedasticity induced by the latter random terms remains. What differs in the contemporary treatment is the method of estimation. The need to be able to fit the model with each unit and then average the results is a significant shortcoming of that treatment. More recent analyses have overcome this limitation by using simulation based methods, as in Section 9.8.2.

The hierarchical model can be extended in several useful directions. Recent analyses, for example, have expanded the model to accommodate multilevel stratification in data sets such as those we considered in the treatment of nested random effects in Section 9.7.1.

***Example 9.16  Hierarchical Linear Model of Home Prices***
Beron, Murdoch, and Thayer (1999) used a hedonic pricing model to analyze the sale prices of 76,343 homes in four California counties: Los Angeles, San Bernardino, Riverside, and Orange. The data set is stratified into 2,185 census tracts and 131 school districts. Home

prices are modeled using a three-level random parameters pricing model. (We will change their notation somewhat to make roles of the components of the model more obvious.) Let *site* denote the specific location (sale), *nei* denote the neighborhood, and *com* denote the community, the highest level of aggregation. The pricing equation is

$$\ln Price_{site,nei,com} = \pi_{nei,com}^0 + \sum_{k=1}^{K} \pi_{nei,com}^k x_{k,site,nei,com} + \varepsilon_{site,nei,com},$$

$$\pi_{nei,com}^k = \beta_{com}^{0,k} + \sum_{l=1}^{L} \beta_{com}^{l,k} z_{k,nei,com} + r_{nei,com}^k, k = 0, \ldots, K,$$

$$\beta_{com}^{l,k} = \gamma^{0,l,k} + \sum_{m=1}^{M} \gamma^{m,l,k} e_{m,com} + u_{com}^{l,k}, l = 1, \ldots, L.$$

There are $K$ level one variables, $x_k$, and a constant in the main equation, $L$ level two variables, $z_l$, and a constant in the second-level equations, and $M$ level three variables, $e_m$, and a constant in the third-level equations. The variables in the model are as follows. The level one variables define the hedonic pricing model,

**x** = house size, number of bathrooms, lot size, presence of central heating, presence of air conditioning, presence of a pool, quality of the view, age of the house, distance to the nearest beach.

Levels two and three are measured at the neighborhood and community levels

**z** = percentage of the neighborhood below the poverty line, racial makeup of the neighborhood, percentage of residents over 65, average time to travel to work

and

**e** = FBI crime index, average achievement test score in school district, air quality measure, visibility index.

The model is estimated by maximum simulated likelihood.

The **hierarchical linear model** analyzed in this section is also called a "mixed model" and "random parameters" model. Although the three terms are usually used interchangeably, each highlights a different aspect of the structural model in (9-63). The "hierarchical" aspect of the model refers to the layering of coefficients that is built into stratified and panel data structures, such as in Example 9.16. The random parameters feature is a signature feature of the model that relates to the modeling of heterogeneity across units in the sample. Note that the model in (9-63) or Beron et al.'s application could be formulated without the random terms in the lower level equations. This would then provide a convenient way to introduce interactions of variables in the linear regression model. The addition of the random component is motivated on precisely the same basis that $u_i$ appears in the familiar random effects model in Section 9.5. (The random effects model is the special case of (9-63) when only the constant term is random.) It is important to bear in mind, in all these structures, strict mean independence is maintained between $u_i$, and all other variables in the model. In most treatments, we go yet a step further and assume a particular distribution for $u_i$, typically joint normal. Finally, the "mixed" model aspect of the specification relates to (9-56). The unconditional estimated model is a mixture of the underlying models, where the weights in the mixture are provided by the underlying density of the random component.

Hierarchical, or random parameter models have been applied in many frameworks beyond the linear regression. (We will explore several of these later in the text.) The linear model with normally distributed effects can be fit by generalized least squares. Nonlinear models (and, often, linear ones) are fit by the simulation technique used in Section 9.8.2. Example 9.17 illustrates.

### Example 9.17   Mixed Linear Model for Wages

Koop and Tobias (2004) analyzed a panel of 17,919 observations in their study of the relationship between wages and education, ability and family characteristics. (See the end of chapter applications in Chapters 3 and 5 and Appendix Table F3.2 for details on the location of the data.) The variables used in the analysis are

> *Person id,*
> *Education,*                (time varying)
> *Log of hourly wage,*       (time varying)
> *Potential experience,*     (time varying)
> *Time trend,*               (time varying)
> *Ability,*                  (time invariant)
> *Mother's education,*       (time invariant)
> *Father's education,*       (time invariant)
> *Dummy variable for residence in a broken home,* (time invariant)
> *Number of siblings.*       (time invariant)

This is an unbalanced panel of 2,178 individuals; Figure 9.3 shows a frequency count of the numbers of observations in the sample.

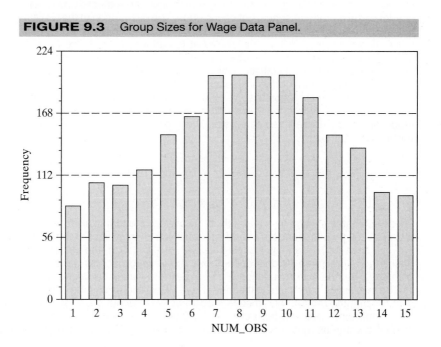

**FIGURE 9.3**   Group Sizes for Wage Data Panel.

We will estimate the following hierarchical wage model

$$\ln Wage_{it} = \beta_{1,i} + \beta_{2,i} \, Education_{it} + \beta_3 \, Experience_{it} + \beta_4 \, Experience_{it}^2$$
$$+ \beta_5 \, Broken \, Home_i + \beta_6 \, Siblings_i + \varepsilon_{it},$$

$$\beta_{1,i} = \alpha_{1,1} + \alpha_{1,2} \, Ability_i + \alpha_{1,3} \, Mother's \, education_i + \alpha_{1,4} \, Father's \, education_i + u_{1,i},$$

$$\beta_{2,i} = \alpha_{2,1} + \alpha_{2,2} \, Ability_i + \alpha_{2,3} \, Mother's \, education_i + \alpha_{2,4} \, Father's \, education_i + u_{2,i}.$$

Estimates are computed using the maximum simulated likelihood method described in Section 9.8.2. Estimates of the model parameters appear in Table 9.11.

The four models in Table 9.11 are the pooled OLS estimates, the random effects model, and the random parameters models first assuming that the random parameters are uncorrelated ($\Gamma_{21} = 0$), then allowing free correlation ($\Gamma_{21} = $ nonzero). The differences between the conventional and the robust standard errors in the pooled model are fairly large, which suggests the presence of latent common effects. The formal estimates of the random effects model confirm this. There are only minor differences between the FGLS and the ML estimates of the random effects model. But, the hypothesis of the pooled model is soundly rejected by the likelihood ratio test. The LM statistic [Section 9.5.3 and (9-39)] is 11,709.7, which is far larger than the critical value of 3.84. So, the hypothesis of the pooled model is firmly rejected. The likelihood ratio statistic based on the MLEs is $2(10,840.18-(-885.674)) = 23,451.71$, which produces the same conclusion. An alternative approach would be to test the hypothesis that $\sigma_u^2 = 0$ using a Wald statistic—the standard $t$ test. The software used for this exercise reparameterizes the log likelihood in terms of $\theta_1 = \sigma_u^2/\sigma_\varepsilon^2$ and $\theta_2 = 1/\sigma_\varepsilon^2$. One approach, based on the delta method (see Section 4.9.4) would be to estimate $\sigma_u^2$ with the MLE of $\theta_1/\theta_2$. The asymptotic variance of this estimator would be estimated using Theorem 4.6. Alternatively, we might note that $\sigma_\varepsilon^2$ must be positive in this model, so it is sufficient simply to test the hypothesis that $\theta_1 = 0$. Our MLE of $\theta_1$ is 0.999206 and the estimated asymptotic standard error is 0.03934. Following this logic, then, the test statistic is $0.999206/0.03934 = 25.397$. This is far larger than the critical value of 1.96, so, once again, the hypothesis is rejected. We do note a problem with the LR and Wald tests. The hypothesis that $\sigma_u^2 = 0$ produces a nonstandard test under the null hypothesis, because $\sigma_u^2 = 0$ is on the boundary of the parameter space. Our standard theory for likelihood ratio testing (see Chapter 16) requires the restricted parameters to be in the interior of the parameter space, not on the edge. The distribution of the test statistic under the null hypothesis is not the familiar chi squared. This issue is confronted in Breusch and Pagan (1980) and Godfrey (1988) and analyzed at (great) length by Andrews (1998, 1999, 2000, 2001, 2002) and Andrews and Ploberger (1994, 1995). The simple expedient in this complex situation is to use the LM statistic, which remains consistent with the earlier conclusion.

The third and fourth models in Table 9.11 present the mixed model estimates. The first of them imposes the restriction that $\Lambda_{21} = 0$ [see the text above (9-55)], which is equivalent to $\Gamma_{21} = 0$ in (9-49), or that the two random parameters are uncorrelated. The second mixed model allows $\Lambda_{21}$ to be a free parameter. The implied estimators for $\sigma_{u1}$, $\sigma_{u2}$ and $\sigma_{u,21}$ are the elements of $\Lambda\Lambda'$, or

$$\sigma_{u1}^2 = \Lambda_{11}^2,$$
$$\sigma_{u,21} = \Lambda_{11}\Lambda_{21},$$
$$\sigma_{u2}^2 = \Lambda_{21}^2 + \Lambda_{22}^2.$$

These estimates are shown separately in the table. Note that in all three random parameters models (including the random effects model which is equivalent to the mixed model with all $\alpha_{lm} = 0$ save for $\alpha_{1,1}$ and $\alpha_{2,1}$ as well as $\Lambda_{21} = \Lambda_{22} = 0.0$), the estimate of $\sigma_\varepsilon$ is relatively unchanged. The three models decompose the variation across groups in the parameters differently, but the overall variation of the dependent variable is largely the same.

The interesting coefficient in the model is $\beta_{2,i}$. Reading across the row for *Educ*, one might suspect that the random parameters model has washed out the impact of education, since the "coefficient" declines from 0.04072 to 0.007607. However, in the mixed models, the "mean" parameter, $\alpha_{2,1}$, is not the coefficient of interest. The coefficient on education in the

**TABLE 9.11**  Estimated Random Parameter Models

| Variable | Pooled OLS Estimate | Std.Err. (Robust) | Random Effects FGLS [Random Effects MLE] Estimate [MLE] | Std.Err. [MLE] | Random Parameters Estimate (Std.Err.) | Random Parameters Estimate (Std.Err.) |
|---|---|---|---|---|---|---|
| Exp | 0.04157 | 0.001819 (0.002242) | 0.04698 [0.04715] | 0.001468 [0.001481] | 0.04758 (0.001108) | 0.04802 (0.001118) |
| $Exp^2$ | −0.00144 | 0.0001002 (0.000126) | −0.00172 [−0.00172] | 0.0000805 [0.000081] | −0.001750 (0.000063) | −0.001761 (0.0000631) |
| Broken | −0.02781 | 0.005296 (0.01074) | −0.03185 [−0.03224] | 0.01089 [0.01172] | −0.01236 (0.003669) | −0.01980 (0.003534) |
| Sibs | −0.00120 | 0.0009143 (0.001975) | −0.002999 [−0.00310] | 0.001925 [0.002071] | 0.0000496 (0.000662) | −0.001953 (0.0006599) |
| Constant | 0.09728 | 0.01589 (0.02783) | 0.03281 [0.03306] | 0.02438 [0.02566] | 0.3277 (0.03803) | 0.3935 (0.03778) |
| Ability |  |  |  |  | 0.04232 (0.01064) | 0.1107 (0.01077) |
| MEd |  |  |  |  | −0.01393 (0.0040) | −0.02887 (0.003990) |
| FEd |  |  |  |  | −0.007548 (0.003252) | 0.002657 (0.003299) |
| $\sigma_{u1}$ |  |  | 0.172278 [0.18767] |  | 0.004187 (0.001320) | 0.5026 |
| Educ | 0.03854 | 0.001040 (0.002013) | 0.04072 [0.04061] | 0.001758 [0.001853] | 0.01253 (0.003015) | 0.007607 (0.002973) |
| Ability |  |  |  |  | −0.0002560 (0.000869) | −0.005316 (0.0008751) |
| MEd |  |  |  |  | 0.001054 (0.000321) | 0.002142 (0.0003165) |
| Fed |  |  |  |  | 0.0007754 (0.000255) | 0.00006752 (0.00001354) |
| $\sigma_{u2}$ |  |  |  |  | 0.01622 (0.000114) | 0.03365 |
| $\sigma_{u,12}$ |  |  |  |  | 0.0000 | −0.01560 |
|  |  |  |  |  | 0.0000 | −0.92259 |
| $\sigma_\varepsilon$ | 0.2542736 |  | 0.187017 [0.187742] |  | 0.192741 | 0.1919182 |
| $\Lambda_{11}$ |  |  |  |  | 0.004187 (0.001320) 0.0000 (0) | 0.5026 (0.008775) −0.03104 (0.0001114) |
| $\Lambda_{21}$ |  |  |  |  |  |  |
| $\Lambda_{22}$ |  |  |  |  | 0.01622 (0.000113) | 0.01298 (0.0006841) |
| ln $L$ | −885.6740 |  | [10480.18] |  | 3550.594 | 3587.611 |

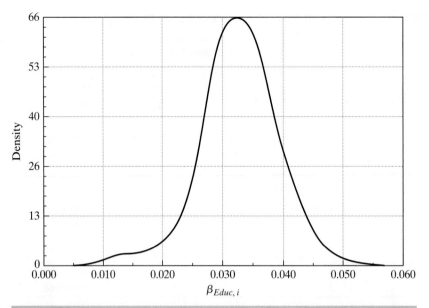

**FIGURE 9.4**   Kernel Density Estimate for Education Coefficient.

model is $\beta_{2,i} = \alpha_{2,1} + \alpha_{2,2}$ *Ability* $+ \beta_{2,3}$ *Mother's education* $+ \beta_{2,4}$ *Father's education* $+ u_{2,i}$. A rough indication of the magnitude of this result can be seen by inserting the sample means for these variables, 0.052374, 11.4719, and 11.7092, respectively. With these values, the mean value for the education coefficient is approximately 0.0327. This is comparable, though somewhat smaller, than the estimates for the pooled and random effects model. Of course, variation in this parameter across the sample individuals was the objective of this specification. Figure 9.4 plots a kernel density estimate for the 2,178 sample individuals. The figure shows the very wide range of variation in the sample estimates.

### 9.8.5   PARAMETER HETEROGENEITY AND DYNAMIC PANEL DATA MODELS

The analysis so far has involved static models and relatively straightforward estimation problems. We have seen as this section has progressed that parameter heterogeneity introduces a fair degree of complexity to the treatment. Dynamic effects in the model, with or without heterogeneity, also raise complex new issues in estimation and inference. There are numerous cases in which dynamic effects and parameter heterogeneity coincide in panel data models. This section will explore a few of the specifications and some applications. The familiar estimation techniques (OLS, FGLS, etc.) are not effective in these cases. The proposed solutions are developed in Chapter 12 where we present the technique of instrumental variables and in Chapter 15 where we present the GMM estimator and its application to **dynamic panel data models.**

*Example 9.18   Dynamic Panel Data Models*
The antecedent of much of the current research on panel data is Balestra and Nerlove's (1966) study of the natural gas market. [See, also, Nerlove (2002, Chapter 2).] The model is a stock-flow description of the derived demand for fuel for gas using appliances. The central equation is a model for total demand,

$$G_{it} = G_{it}^* + (1-r)G_{i,t-1},$$

where $G_{it}$ is current total demand. Current demand consists of new demand, $G_{it}^*$, that is created by additions to the stock of appliances plus old demand which is a proportion of the previous period's demand, $r$ being the depreciation rate for gas using appliances. New demand is due to net increases in the stock of gas using appliances, which is modeled as

$$G_{it}^* = \beta_0 + \beta_1 Price_{it} + \beta_2 \Delta Pop_{it} + \beta_3 Pop_{it} + \beta_4 \Delta Income_{it} + \beta_5 Income_{it} + \varepsilon_{it},$$

where $\Delta$ is the first difference (change) operator, $\Delta X_t = X_t - X_{t-1}$. The reduced form of the model is a dynamic equation,

$$G_{it} = \beta_0 + \beta_1 Price_{it} + \beta_2 \Delta Pop_{it} + \beta_3 Pop_{it} + \beta_4 \Delta Income_{it} + \beta_5 Income_{it} + \gamma G_{i,t-1} + \varepsilon_{it}.$$

The authors analyzed a panel of 36 states over a six-year period (1957–1962). Both fixed effects and random effects approaches were considered.

An equilibrium model for steady state growth has been used by numerous authors [e.g., Robertson and Symons (1992), Pesaran and Smith (1995), Lee, Pesaran, and Smith (1997), Pesaran, Shin, and Smith (1999), Nerlove (2002) and Hsiao, Pesaran, and Tahmiscioglu (2002)] for cross industry or country comparisons. Robertson and Symons modeled real wages in 13 OECD countries over the period 1958 to 1986 with a wage equation

$$W_{it} = \alpha_i + \beta_{1i} k_{it} + \beta_{2i} \Delta wedge_{it} + \gamma_i W_{i,t-1} + \varepsilon_{it},$$

where $W_{it}$ is the real product wage for country $i$ in year $t$, $k_{it}$ is the capital-labor ratio, and *wedge* is the "tax and import price wedge."

Lee, Pesaran, and Smith (1997) compared income growth across countries with a steady-state income growth model of the form

$$\ln y_{it} = \alpha_i + \theta_i t + \lambda_i \ln y_{i,t-1} + \varepsilon_{it},$$

where $\theta_i = (1 - \lambda_i)\delta_i$, $\delta_i$ is the technological growth rate for country $i$ and $\lambda_i$ is the convergence parameter. The rate of convergence to a steady state is $1 - \lambda_i$.

Pesaran and Smith (1995) analyzed employment in a panel of 38 UK industries observed over 29 years, 1956–1984. The main estimating equation was

$$\ln e_{it} = \alpha_i + \beta_{1i} t + \beta_{2i} \ln y_{it} + \beta_{3i} \ln y_{i,t-1} + \beta_{4i} \ln \bar{y}_t + \beta_{5i} \ln \bar{y}_{t-1}$$

$$+ \beta_{6i} \ln w_{it} + \beta_{7i} \ln w_{i,t-1} + \gamma_{1i} \ln e_{i,t-1} + \gamma_{2i} \ln e_{i,t-2} + \varepsilon_{it},$$

where $y_{it}$ is industry output, $\bar{y}_t$ is total (not average) output, and $w_{it}$ is real wages.

In the growth models, a quantity of interest is the **long run multiplier** or **long-run elasticity.** Long-run effects are derived through the following conceptual experiment. The essential feature of the models above is a dynamic equation of the form

$$y_t = \alpha + \beta x_t + \gamma y_{t-1}.$$

Suppose at time $t$, $x_t$ is fixed from that point forward at $\bar{x}$. The value of $y_t$ at that time will then be $\alpha + \beta \bar{x} + \gamma y_{t-1}$, given the previous value. If this process continues, and if $|\gamma| < 1$, then eventually $y_s$ will reach an equilibrium at a value such that $y_s = y_{s-1} = \bar{y}$. If so, then $\bar{y} = \alpha + \beta \bar{x} + \gamma \bar{y}$, from which we can deduce that $\bar{y} = (\alpha + \bar{x})/(1 - \gamma)$. (We will analyze this computation at length in Chapter 13.) The path to this equilibrium from time $t$ into the future is governed by the **adjustment equation**

$$y_s - \bar{y} = (y_t - \bar{y})\gamma^{s-t}, s \geq t.$$

The experiment, then, is to ask: What is the impact on the equilibrium of a change in the input, $\bar{x}$? The result is $\partial \bar{y}/\partial \bar{x} = \beta/(1 - \gamma)$. This is the long-run multiplier, or **equilibrium multiplier** in the model. In the Pesaran and Smith model preceding, the inputs are in logarithms, so the multipliers are long-run elasticities. For example, with two lags of ln $e_{it}$ in Pesaran and Smith's model, the long-run effects for wages are

$$\phi_i = (\beta_{6i} + \beta_{7i})/(1 - \gamma_{1i} - \gamma_{2i}).$$

In this setting, in contrast to the preceding treatments, the number of units, $n$, is generally taken to be fixed, though often it will be fairly large. The Penn World Tables (http://pwt.econ.upenn.edu/php_site/pwt_index.php) that provide the database for many of these analyses now contain information on almost 200 countries for well over 50 years. Asymptotic results for the estimators are with respect to increasing $T$, though we will consider in general, cases in which $T$ is small. Surprisingly, increasing $T$ and $n$ at the same time need not simplify the derivations. We will revisit this issue in the next section.

The parameter of interest in many studies is the average long-run effect, say $\bar{\phi} = (1/n)\Sigma_i\phi_i$, in the Pesaran and Smith example. Because $n$ is taken to be fixed, the "parameter" $\bar{\phi}$ is a definable object of estimation—that is, with $n$ fixed, we can speak of $\bar{\phi}$ as a parameter rather than as an estimator of a parameter. There are numerous approaches one might take. For estimation purposes, pooling, fixed effects, random effects, group means, or separate regressions are all possibilities. (Unfortunately, nearly all are inconsistent.) In addition, there is a choice to be made whether to compute the average of long-run effects or compute the long-run effect from averages of the parameters. The choice of the average of functions, $\bar{\phi}$ versus the function of averages,

$$\bar{\phi}* = \frac{\frac{1}{n}\sum_{i=1}^{n}(\hat{\beta}_{6i} + \hat{\beta}_{7i})}{1 - \frac{1}{n}\sum_{i=1}^{n}(\hat{\gamma}_{1i} + \hat{\gamma}_{2i})}$$

turns out to be of substance. For their UK industry study, Pesaran and Smith report estimates of $-0.33$ for $\bar{\phi}$ and $-0.45$ for $\bar{\phi}*$. (The authors do not express a preference for one over the other.)

The development to this point is implicitly based on estimation of separate models for each unit (country, industry, etc.). There are also a variety of other estimation strategies one might consider. We will assume for the moment that the data series are stationary in the dimension of $T$. (See Chapter 22.) This is a transparently false assumption, as revealed by a simple look at the trends in macroeconomic data, but maintaining it for the moment allows us to proceed. We will reconsider it later.

We consider the generic, dynamic panel data model,

$$y_{it} = \alpha_i + \beta_i x_{it} + \gamma_i y_{i,t-1} + \varepsilon_{it}. \tag{9-63}$$

Assume that $T$ is large enough that the individual regressions can be computed. In the absence of autocorrelation in $\varepsilon_{it}$, it has been shown [e.g., Griliches (1961), Maddala and Rao (1973)] that the OLS estimator of $\gamma_i$ is biased downward, but consistent in $T$. Thus, $E[\hat{\gamma}_i - \gamma_i] = \theta_i/T$ for some $\theta_i$. The implication for the individual estimator of the long-run multiplier, $\phi_i = \beta_i/(1 - \gamma_i)$, is unclear in this case, however. The denominator is overestimated. But it is not clear whether the estimator of $\beta_i$ is overestimated or underestimated. It is true that whatever bias there is O(1/$T$). For this application, $T$ is fixed and possibly quite small. The end result is that it is unlikely that the individual estimator of $\phi_i$ is unbiased, and by construction, it is inconsistent, because $T$ cannot be assumed to be increasing. If that is the case, then $\hat{\bar{\phi}}$ is likewise inconsistent for $\bar{\phi}$. We are averaging $n$ estimators, each of which has bias and variance that are O(1/$T$). The variance of the mean is, therefore, O(1/$nT$) which goes to zero, but the bias remains O(1/$T$). It follows that the average of the $n$ means is not converging to $\bar{\phi}$; it is converging to the average of whatever these biased estimators are estimating. The problem vanishes with large $T$, but that is not relevant to the current context. However, in the Pesaran and Smith study, $T$ was 29, which is large enough that these effects are probably moderate. For macroeconomic cross-country studies such as those based on the Penn World Tables, the data series might be yet longer than this.

One might consider aggregating the data to improve the results. Smith and Pesaran (1995) suggest an average based on country means. Averaging the observations over $T$ in (9-63) produces

$$\bar{y}_{i.} = \alpha_i + \beta_i \bar{x}_{i.} + \gamma_i \bar{y}_{-1,i} + \bar{\varepsilon}_{i.}. \tag{9-64}$$

A linear regression using the $n$ observations would be inconsistent for two reasons: First, $\bar{\varepsilon}_{i.}$ and $\bar{y}_{-1,i}$ must be correlated. Second, because of the parameter heterogeneity, it is not clear without further assumptions what the OLS slopes estimate under the false assumption that all coefficients are equal. But $\bar{y}_{i.}$ and $\bar{y}_{-1,i}$ differ by only the first and last observations; $\bar{y}_{-1,i} = \bar{y}_{i.} - (y_{iT} - y_{i0})/T = \bar{y}_{i.} - [\Delta_T(y)/T]$. Inserting this in (9-64) produces

$$\bar{y}_{i.} = \alpha_i + \beta_i \bar{x}_{i.} + \gamma_i \bar{y}_{i.} - \gamma_i [\Delta_T(y)/T] + \bar{\varepsilon}_{i.}$$

$$= \frac{\alpha_i}{1-\gamma_i} + \frac{\beta_i}{1-\gamma_i}\bar{x}_{i.} - \frac{\gamma_i}{1-\gamma_i}[\Delta_T(y)/T] + \bar{\varepsilon}_{i.} \tag{9-65}$$

$$= \delta_i + \phi_i \bar{x}_{i.} + \tau_i [\Delta_T(y)/T] + \bar{\varepsilon}_{i.}.$$

We still seek to estimate $\bar{\phi}$. The form in (9-65) does not solve the estimation problem, since the regression suggested using the group means is still heterogeneous. If it could be assumed that the individual long run coefficients differ randomly from the averages in the fashion of the random parameters model of the previous section, so $\delta_i = \bar{\delta} + u_{\delta,i}$ and likewise for the other parameters, then the model could be written

$$\bar{y}_{i.} = \bar{\delta} + \bar{\phi}\bar{x}_{i.} + \bar{\tau}[\Delta_T(y)/T]_i + \bar{\varepsilon}_{i.} + \{u_{\delta,i} + u_{\phi,i}\bar{x}_i + u_{\tau,i}[\Delta_T(y)/T]_i\}$$

$$= \bar{\delta} + \bar{\phi}\bar{x}_{i.} + \bar{\tau}[\Delta_T(y)/T]_i + \bar{\varepsilon}_i + w_i.$$

At this point, the equation appears to be a heteroscedastic regression amenable to least squares estimation, but for one loose end. Consistency follows if the terms $[\Delta_T(y)/T]_i$ and $\bar{\varepsilon}_i$ are uncorrelated. Because the first is a rate of change and the second is in levels, this should generally be the case. Another interpretation that serves the same purpose is that the rates of change in $[\Delta_T(y)/T]_i$ should be uncorrelated with the levels in $\bar{x}_{i.}$, in which case, the regression can be partitioned, and simple linear regression of the country means of $y_{it}$ on the country means of $x_{it}$ and a constant produces consistent estimates of $\bar{\phi}$ and $\bar{\delta}$.

Alternatively, consider a time-series approach. We average the observation in (9-63) across countries at each time period rather than across time within countries. In this case, we have

$$\bar{y}_{.t} = \bar{\alpha} + \frac{1}{n}\sum_{i=1}^{n}\beta_i x_{it} + \frac{1}{n}\sum_{i=1}^{n}\gamma_i y_{i,t-1} + \frac{1}{n}\sum_{i=1}^{n}\varepsilon_{it}.$$

Let $\bar{\gamma} = \frac{1}{n}\sum_{i=1}^{n}\gamma_i$ so that $\gamma_i = \bar{\gamma} + (\gamma_i - \bar{\gamma})$ and $\beta_i = \bar{\beta} + (\beta_i - \bar{\beta})$. Then,

$$\bar{y}_{.t} = \bar{\alpha} + \bar{\beta}\bar{x}_{.t} + \bar{\gamma}\,\bar{y}_{-1,t} + [\bar{\varepsilon}_{.t} + (\beta_i - \bar{\beta})\bar{x}_{.t} + (\gamma_i - \bar{\gamma})\bar{y}_{-1,t}]$$

$$= \bar{\alpha} + \bar{\beta}\bar{x}_{.t} + \bar{\gamma}\,\bar{y}_{-1,t} + \bar{\varepsilon}_{.t} + w_{.t}.$$

Unfortunately, the regressor, $\overline{\gamma}\,\overline{y}_{-1,t}$ is surely correlated with $w_{,t}$, so neither OLS or GLS will provide a consistent estimator for this model. (One might consider an instrumental variable estimator, however, there is no natural instrument available in the model as constructed.) Another possibility is to pool the entire data set, possibly with random or fixed effects for the constant terms. Because pooling, even with country-specific constant terms, imposes homogeneity on the other parameters, the same problems we have just observed persist.

Finally, returning to (9-63), one might treat it as a formal random parameters model,

$$
\begin{aligned}
y_{it} &= \alpha_i + \beta_i x_{it} + \gamma_i y_{i,t-1} + \varepsilon_{it}, \\
\alpha_i &= \alpha + u_{\alpha,i}, \\
\beta_i &= \beta + u_{\beta,i}, \\
\gamma_i &= \gamma + u_{\gamma,i}.
\end{aligned}
\tag{9-63$'$}
$$

The assumptions needed to formulate the model in this fashion are those of the previous section. As Pesaran and Smith (1995) observe, this model can be estimated using the "Swamy (1971)" estimator, which is the matrix weighted average of the least squares estimators discussed in Section 9.8.1. The estimator requires that $T$ be large enough to fit each country regression by least squares. That has been the case for the received applications. Indeed, for the applications we have examined, both $n$ and $T$ are relatively large. If not, then one could still use the mixed models approach developed in Section 9.8.2. A compromise that appears to work well for panels with moderate sized $n$ and $T$ is the "mixed-fixed" model suggested in Hsiao (1986, 2003) and Weinhold (1999). The dynamic model in (9-63) is formulated as a partial fixed effects model,

$$
\begin{aligned}
y_{it} &= \alpha_i d_{it} + \beta_i x_{it} + \gamma_i d_{it} y_{i,t-1} + \varepsilon_{it}, \\
\beta_i &= \beta + u_{\beta,i},
\end{aligned}
$$

where $d_{it}$ is a dummy variable that equals one for country $i$ in every period and zero otherwise (i.e., the usual fixed effects approach). Note that $d_{it}$ also appears with $y_{i,t-1}$. As stated, the model has "fixed effects," one random coefficient, and a total of $2n+1$ coefficients to estimate, in addition to the two variance components, $\sigma_\varepsilon^2$ and $\sigma_u^2$. The model could be estimated inefficiently by using ordinary least squares—the random coefficient induces heteroscedasticity (see Section 9.8.1)—by using the Hildreth–Houck–Swamy approach, or with the mixed linear model approach developed in Section 9.8.2.

### Example 9.19  A Mixed Fixed Growth Model for Developing Countries

Weinhold (1996) and Nair–Reichert and Weinhold (2001) analyzed growth and development in a panel of 24 developing countries observed for 25 years, 1971–1995. The model they employed was a variant of the mixed-fixed model proposed by Hsiao (1986, 2003). In their specification,

$$
\begin{aligned}
GGDP_{i,t} = {}& \alpha_i d_{it} + \gamma_i d_{it} GGDP_{i,t-1} \\
& + \beta_{1i} GGDI_{i,t-1} + \beta_{2i} GFDI_{i,t-1} + \beta_{3i} GEXP_{i,t-1} + \beta_4 INFL_{i,t-1} + \varepsilon_{it},
\end{aligned}
$$

where

$$
\begin{aligned}
GGDP &= \text{Growth rate of gross domestic product,} \\
GGDI &= \text{Growth rate of gross domestic investment,} \\
GFDI &= \text{Growth rate of foreign direct investment (inflows),} \\
GEXP &= \text{Growth rate of exports of goods and services,} \\
INFL &= \text{Inflation rate.}
\end{aligned}
$$

The constant terms and coefficients on the lagged dependent variable are country specific. The remaining coefficients are treated as random, normally distributed, with means $\beta_k$ and unrestricted variances. They are modeled as uncorrelated, so in (9-49), $\Gamma$ is diagonal. [In the form of the model in Section 9.8.2, the diagonal matrix would be $\Lambda$ in (9-55).] The model was estimated using a modification of the Hildreth–Houck–Swamy method described in Section 9.8.1.

### 9.8.6   NONSTATIONARY DATA AND PANEL DATA MODELS

Some of the discussion thus far (and to follow) focuses on "small $T$" statistical results. Panels are taken to contain a fixed and small $T$ observations on a large $n$ individual units. Recent research using cross-country data sets such as the Penn World Tables (http://pwt.econ.upenn.edu/php_site/pwt_index.php), which now include data on nearly 200 countries for well over 50 years, have begun to analyze panels with $T$ sufficiently large that the time-series properties of the data become an important consideration. In particular, the recognition and accommodation of nonstationarity that is now a standard part of single time-series analyses (as in Chapter 22) are now seen to be appropriate for large scale cross-country studies, such as income growth studies based on the Penn World Tables, cross-country studies of health care expenditure and analyses of purchasing power parity.

The analysis of long panels, such as in the growth and convergence literature, typically involves dynamic models, such as

$$y_{it} = \alpha_i + \gamma_i y_{i,t-1} + \mathbf{x}'_{it}\boldsymbol{\beta}_i + \varepsilon_{it}. \tag{9-66}$$

In single time-series analysis involving low-frequency macroeconomic flow data such as income, consumption, investment, the current account deficit, etc., it has long been recognized that estimated regression relations can be distorted by nonstationarity in the data. What appear to be persistent and strong regression relationships can be entirely spurious and due to underlying characteristics of the time-series processes rather than actual connections among the variables. Hypothesis tests about long-run effects will be considerably distorted by unit roots in the data. It has become evident that the same influences, with the same deleterious effects, will be found in long panel data sets. The panel data application is further complicated by the possible heterogeneity of the parameters. The coefficients of interest in many cross-country studies are the lagged effects, such as $\gamma_i$ in (9-66), and it is precisely here that the received results on nonstationary data have revealed the problems of estimation and inference. Valid tests for unit roots in panel data have been proposed in many studies. Three that are frequently cited are Levin and Lin (1992), Im, Pesaran, and Shin (2003) and Maddala and Wu (1999).

There have been numerous empirical applications of time series methods for nonstationary data in panel data settings, including Frankel and Rose's (1996) and Pedroni's (2001) studies of purchasing power parity, Fleissig and Strauss (1997) on real wage stationarity, Culver and Papell (1997) on inflation, Wu (2000) on the current account balance, McCoskey and Selden (1998) on health care expenditure, Sala-i-Martin (1996) on growth and convergence, McCoskey and Kao (1999) on urbanization and production, and Coakely et al. (1996) on savings and investment.[32]

---

[32] A more complete enumeration appears in Baltagi (2005, Chapter 12).

A subtle problem arises in obtaining results useful for characterizing the properties of estimators of the model in (9-66). The asymptotic results based on large $n$ and large $T$ are not necessarily obtainable simultaneously, and great care is needed in deriving the asymptotic behavior of useful statistics. Phillips and Moon (1999, 2000) are standard references on the subject.

We will return to the topic of nonstationary data in Chapter 22. This is an emerging literature, most of which is well beyond the level of this text. We will rely on the several detailed received surveys, such as Bannerjee (1999), Smith (2000), and Baltagi and Kao (2000) to fill in the details.

## 9.9 CONSISTENT ESTIMATION OF DYNAMIC PANEL DATA MODELS

As prelude to the further developments of Chapters 12 and 13, we return to a homogeneous dynamic panel data model,

$$y_{it} = \gamma y_{i,t-1} + \mathbf{x}'_{it}\boldsymbol{\beta} + c_i + \varepsilon_{it}, \tag{9-67}$$

where $c_i$ is, as in the preceding sections of this chapter, individual unmeasured heterogeneity, that may or may not be correlated with $\mathbf{x}_{it}$. We consider methods of estimation for this model when $T$ is fixed and relatively small, and $n$ may be large and increasing.

Pooled OLS is obviously inconsistent. Rewrite (9-67) as

$$y_{it} = \gamma y_{i,t-1} + \mathbf{x}'_{it}\boldsymbol{\beta} + w_{it}. \tag{9-68}$$

The disturbance in this pooled regression may be correlated with $\mathbf{x}_{it}$, but either way, it is surely correlated with $y_{i,t-1}$. By substitution,

$$\text{Cov}[y_{i,t-1}, (c_i + \varepsilon_{it})] = \sigma_c^2 + \gamma \text{Cov}[y_{i,t-2}, (c_i + \varepsilon_{it})],$$

and so on. By repeated substitution, it can be seen that for $|\gamma| < 1$ and moderately large $T$,

$$\text{Cov}[y_{i,t-1}, (c_i + \varepsilon_{it})] \approx \sigma_c^2/(1 - \gamma). \tag{9-69}$$

[It is useful to obtain this result from a different direction. If the stochastic process that is generating $(y_{it}, c_i)$ is *stationary*, then $\text{Cov}[y_{i,t-1}, c_i] = \text{Cov}[y_{i,t-2}, c_i]$, from which we would obtain (9-69) directly. The assumption $|\gamma| < 1$ would be required for stationarity. We will return to this subject in Chapters 20 and 21.] Consequently, OLS and GLS are inconsistent. The fixed effects approach does not solve the problem either. Taking deviations from individual means, we have

$$y_{it} - \overline{y}_{i.} = (\mathbf{x}_{it} - \overline{\mathbf{x}}_{i.})'\boldsymbol{\beta} + \gamma(y_{i,t-1} - \overline{y}_{i.}) + (\varepsilon_{it} - \overline{\varepsilon}_{i.}).$$

Anderson and Hsiao (1981, 1982) show that

$$\text{Cov}[(y_{it} - \overline{y}_{i.}), (\varepsilon_{it} - \overline{\varepsilon}_{i.})] \approx \frac{-\sigma_\varepsilon^2}{T(1-\gamma)^2}\left[\frac{(T-1) - T\gamma + \gamma^T}{T}\right]$$

$$= \frac{-\sigma_\varepsilon^2}{T(1-\gamma)^2}\left[(1-\gamma) - \frac{1-\gamma^T}{T}\right]. \tag{9-70}$$

This does converge to zero as $T$ increases, but, again, we are considering cases in which $T$ is small or moderate, say 5 to 15, in which case, the bias in the OLS estimator could be 15 percent to 60 percent. The implication is that the "within" transformation does not produce a consistent estimator.

It is easy to see that taking first differences is likewise ineffective. The first differences of the observations are

$$y_{it} - y_{i,t-1} = (\mathbf{x}_{it} - \mathbf{x}_{i,t-1})'\boldsymbol{\beta} + \gamma(y_{i,t-1} - y_{i,t-2}) + (\varepsilon_{it} - \varepsilon_{i,t-1}). \qquad \textbf{(9-71)}$$

As before, the correlation between the last regressor and the disturbance persists, so OLS or GLS based on first differences would also be inconsistent. There is another approach. Write the regression in differenced form as

$$\Delta y_{it} = \Delta \mathbf{x}'_{it}\boldsymbol{\beta} + \gamma \Delta y_{i,t-1} + \Delta \varepsilon_{it}$$

or, defining $\mathbf{x}^*_{it} = [\Delta \mathbf{x}_{it}, \Delta y_{i,t-1}]$, $\varepsilon^*_{it} = \Delta \varepsilon_{it}$ and $\theta = [\boldsymbol{\beta}', \gamma]'$

$$y^*_{it} = \mathbf{x}^{*\prime}_{it}\theta + \varepsilon^*_{it}.$$

For the pooled sample, beginning with $t = 3$, write this as

$$\mathbf{y}^* = \mathbf{X}^*\theta + \boldsymbol{\varepsilon}^*.$$

The least squares estimator based on the first differenced data is

$$\hat{\theta} = \left[\frac{1}{n(T-3)}\mathbf{X}^{*\prime}\mathbf{X}^*\right]^{-1}\left(\frac{1}{n(T-3)}\mathbf{X}^{*\prime}\mathbf{y}^*\right)$$

$$= \theta + \left[\frac{1}{n(T-3)}\mathbf{X}^{*\prime}\mathbf{X}^*\right]^{-1}\left(\frac{1}{n(T-3)}\mathbf{X}^{*\prime}\boldsymbol{\varepsilon}^*\right).$$

Assuming that the inverse matrix in brackets converges to a positive definite matrix— that remains to be shown—the inconsistency in this estimator arises because the vector in parentheses does not converge to zero. The last element is $\text{plim}_{n \to \infty}[1/(n(T-3))]$ $\sum_{i=1}^{n}\sum_{t=3}^{T}(y_{i,t-1} - y_{i,t-2})(\varepsilon_{it} - \varepsilon_{i,t-1})$ which is not zero.

Suppose there were a variable $z^*$ such that $\text{plim}[1/(n(T-3))]\mathbf{z}^{*\prime}\boldsymbol{\varepsilon}^* = 0$ and $\text{plim}[1/(n(T-3))]\mathbf{z}^{*\prime}\mathbf{X}^* \neq \mathbf{0}$. Let $\mathbf{Z} = [\Delta \mathbf{X}, \mathbf{z}^*]$; $z^*_{it}$ replaces $\Delta y_{i,t-1}$ in $\mathbf{x}^*_{it}$. By this construction, it appears we have a consistent estimator. Consider

$$\hat{\theta}_{\text{IV}} = (\mathbf{Z}'\mathbf{X}^*)^{-1}\mathbf{Z}'\mathbf{y}^*.$$

$$= (\mathbf{Z}'\mathbf{X}^*)^{-1}\mathbf{Z}'(\mathbf{X}^*\theta + \boldsymbol{\varepsilon}^*)$$

$$= \theta + (\mathbf{Z}'\mathbf{X}^*)^{-1}\mathbf{Z}'\boldsymbol{\varepsilon}^*.$$

Then, after multiplying throughout by $1/(n(T-3))$ as before, we find

$$\text{Plim } \hat{\theta}_{\text{IV}} = \theta + \text{plim}\{[1/(n(T-3))](\mathbf{Z}'\mathbf{X}^*)\}^{-1} \times \mathbf{0},$$

which seems to solve the problem of consistent estimation.

The variable $z^*$ is an **instrumental variable,** and the estimator is an **instrumental variable estimator** (hence the subscript on the preceding estimator). Finding suitable, valid instruments, that is, variables that satisfy the necessary assumptions, for models in which the right-hand variables are correlated with omitted factors is often challenging. In this setting, there is a natural candidate—in fact, there are several. From (9-71), we have at period $t = 3$

$$y_{i3} - y_{i2} = (\mathbf{x}_{i3} - \mathbf{x}_{i2})'\boldsymbol{\beta} + \gamma(y_{i2} - y_{i1}) + (\varepsilon_{i3} - \varepsilon_{i2}). \tag{9-72}$$

We could use $y_{i1}$ as the needed variable, because it is not correlated $\varepsilon_{i3} - \varepsilon_{i2}$. Continuing in this fashion, we see that for $t = 3, 4, \ldots, T$, $y_{i,t-2}$ appears to satisfy our requirements. Alternatively, beginning from period $t = 4$, we can see that $z_{it} = (y_{i,t-2} - y_{i,t-3})$ once again satisfies our requirements. This is Anderson and Hsiao's (1981) result for instrumental variable estimation of the dynamic panel data model. It now becomes a question of which approach, levels ($y_{i,t-2}, t = 3, \ldots, T$), or differences ($y_{i,t-2} - y_{i,t-3}, t = 4, \ldots, T$) is a preferable approach. Kiviet (1995) obtains results that suggest that the estimator based on levels is more efficient.

This application has sketched the method of instrumental variables. There are numerous aspects yet to be considered, including a fuller development of the assumptions, the asymptotic distribution of the estimator, and what to use for an asymptotic covariance matrix to allow inference. We will return to the development of the method of instrumental variables in Chapter 12.

## 9.10 SUMMARY AND CONCLUSIONS

The preceding has shown a few of the extensions of the classical model that can be obtained when panel data are available. In principle, any of the models we have examined before this chapter and all those we will consider later, including the multiple equation models, can be extended in the same way. The main advantage, as we noted at the outset, is that with panel data, one can formally model the heterogeneity across groups that is typical in microeconomic data.

We will find in Chapter 10 that to some extent this model of heterogeneity can be misleading. What might have appeared at one level to be differences in the variances of the disturbances across groups may well be due to heterogeneity of a different sort, associated with the coefficient vectors. We will consider this possibility in the next chapter. We will also examine some additional models for disturbance processes that arise naturally in a multiple equations context but are actually more general cases of some of the models we looked at earlier, such as the model of groupwise heteroscedasticity.

### Key Terms and Concepts

- Adjustment equation
- Autocorrelation
- Balanced panel
- Between groups
- Cluster estimator
- Contiguity
- Contiguity matrix
- Contrasts
- Dynamic panel data model
- Equilibrium multiplier
- Error components model
- First difference
- Fixed effects
- Fixed panel
- Group means
- Group means estimator
- Hausman specification test
- Heterogeneity
- Hierarchical linear model
- Hierarchical model
- Individual effect
- Instrumental variable
- Instrumental variable estimator
- Lagrange multiplier test
- Least squares dummy variable estimator
- Long run elasticity
- Long run multiplier
- Longitudinal data sets
- Matrix weighted average
- Maximum simulated likelihood estimator
- Mean independence
- Measurement error
- Minimum distance estimator
- Mixed model
- Mundlak's approach

| • Nested random effects | • Random parameters | • Spatial lags |
| • Panel data | • Robust covariance matrix | • Specification test |
| • Parameter heterogeneity | • Rotating panel | • Strict exogeneity |
| • Partial effects | • Simulated log-likelihood | • Time invariant |
| • Pooled model | • Simulation based estimation | • Two-step estimation |
| • Pooled regression | • Small $T$ asymptotics | • Unbalanced panel |
| • Population averaged model | • Spatial autocorrelation | • Variable addition test |
| • Random coefficients model | • Spatial autoregression | • Within groups |
| • Random effects | coefficient | |

## Exercises

1. The following is a panel of data on investment ($y$) and profit ($x$) for $n = 3$ firms over $T = 10$ periods.

| | $i = 1$ | | $i = 2$ | | $i = 3$ | |
|---|---|---|---|---|---|---|
| t | y | x | y | x | y | x |
| 1 | 13.32 | 12.85 | 20.30 | 22.93 | 8.85 | 8.65 |
| 2 | 26.30 | 25.69 | 17.47 | 17.96 | 19.60 | 16.55 |
| 3 | 2.62 | 5.48 | 9.31 | 9.16 | 3.87 | 1.47 |
| 4 | 14.94 | 13.79 | 18.01 | 18.73 | 24.19 | 24.91 |
| 5 | 15.80 | 15.41 | 7.63 | 11.31 | 3.99 | 5.01 |
| 6 | 12.20 | 12.59 | 19.84 | 21.15 | 5.73 | 8.34 |
| 7 | 14.93 | 16.64 | 13.76 | 16.13 | 26.68 | 22.70 |
| 8 | 29.82 | 26.45 | 10.00 | 11.61 | 11.49 | 8.36 |
| 9 | 20.32 | 19.64 | 19.51 | 19.55 | 18.49 | 15.44 |
| 10 | 4.77 | 5.43 | 18.32 | 17.06 | 20.84 | 17.87 |

   a. Pool the data and compute the least squares regression coefficients of the model $y_{it} = \alpha + \beta x_{it} + \varepsilon_{it}$.
   b. Estimate the fixed effects model of (9-12), and then test the hypothesis that the constant term is the same for all three firms.
   c. Estimate the random effects model of (9-26), and then carry out the Lagrange multiplier test of the hypothesis that the classical model without the common effect applies.
   d. Carry out Hausman's specification test for the random versus the fixed effect model.

2. Suppose that the fixed effects model is formulated with an overall constant term and $n - 1$ dummy variables (dropping, say, the last one). Investigate the effect that this supposition has on the set of dummy variable coefficients and on the least squares estimates of the slopes.

3. *Unbalanced design for random effects.* Suppose that the random effects model of Section 9.5 is to be estimated with a panel in which the groups have different numbers of observations. Let $T_i$ be the number of observations in group $i$.
   a. Show that the pooled least squares estimator is unbiased and consistent despite this complication.
   b. Show that the estimator in (9-37) based on the pooled least squares estimator of $\beta$ (or, for that matter, *any* consistent estimator of $\beta$) is a consistent estimator of $\sigma_\varepsilon^2$.

4. What are the probability limits of $(1/n)$LM, where LM is defined in (9-39) under the null hypothesis that $\sigma_u^2 = 0$ and under the alternative that $\sigma_u^2 \neq 0$?

5. *A two-way fixed effects model.* Suppose that the fixed effects model is modified to include a time-specific dummy variable as well as an individual-specific variable. Then $y_{it} = \alpha_i + \gamma_t + \mathbf{x}'_{it}\boldsymbol{\beta} + \varepsilon_{it}$. At every observation, the individual- and time-specific dummy variables sum to 1, so there are some redundant coefficients. The discussion in Section 9.4.4 shows that one way to remove the redundancy is to include an overall constant and drop one of the time specific *and* one of the time-dummy variables. The model is, thus,

$$y_{it} = \mu + (\alpha_i - \alpha_1) + (\gamma_t - \gamma_1) + \mathbf{x}'_{it}\boldsymbol{\beta} + \varepsilon_{it}.$$

(Note that the respective time- or individual-specific variable is zero when $t$ or $i$ equals one.) Ordinary least squares estimates of $\boldsymbol{\beta}$ are then obtained by regression of $y_{it} - \bar{y}_{i.} - \bar{y}_{.t} + \bar{\bar{y}}$ on $\mathbf{x}_{it} - \bar{\mathbf{x}}_{i.} - \bar{\mathbf{x}}_{.t} + \bar{\bar{\mathbf{x}}}$. Then $(\alpha_i - \alpha_1)$ and $(\gamma_t - \gamma_1)$ are estimated using the expressions in (9-23) while $m = \bar{\bar{y}} - \bar{\bar{\mathbf{x}}}'\mathbf{b}$. Using the following data, estimate the full set of coefficients for the least squares dummy variable model:

| | $t = 1$ | $t = 2$ | $t = 3$ | $t = 4$ | $t = 5$ | $t = 6$ | $t = 7$ | $t = 8$ | $t = 9$ | $t = 10$ |
|---|---|---|---|---|---|---|---|---|---|---|
| | | | | | $i = 1$ | | | | | |
| $y$ | 21.7 | 10.9 | 33.5 | 22.0 | 17.6 | 16.1 | 19.0 | 18.1 | 14.9 | 23.2 |
| $x_1$ | 26.4 | 17.3 | 23.8 | 17.6 | 26.2 | 21.1 | 17.5 | 22.9 | 22.9 | 14.9 |
| $x_2$ | 5.79 | 2.60 | 8.36 | 5.50 | 5.26 | 1.03 | 3.11 | 4.87 | 3.79 | 7.24 |
| | | | | | $i = 2$ | | | | | |
| $y$ | 21.8 | 21.0 | 33.8 | 18.0 | 12.2 | 30.0 | 21.7 | 24.9 | 21.9 | 23.6 |
| $x_1$ | 19.6 | 22.8 | 27.8 | 14.0 | 11.4 | 16.0 | 28.8 | 16.8 | 11.8 | 18.6 |
| $x_2$ | 3.36 | 1.59 | 6.19 | 3.75 | 1.59 | 9.87 | 1.31 | 5.42 | 6.32 | 5.35 |
| | | | | | $i = 3$ | | | | | |
| $y$ | 25.2 | 41.9 | 31.3 | 27.8 | 13.2 | 27.9 | 33.3 | 20.5 | 16.7 | 20.7 |
| $x_1$ | 13.4 | 29.7 | 21.6 | 25.1 | 14.1 | 24.1 | 10.5 | 22.1 | 17.0 | 20.5 |
| $x_2$ | 9.57 | 9.62 | 6.61 | 7.24 | 1.64 | 5.99 | 9.00 | 1.75 | 1.74 | 1.82 |
| | | | | | $i = 4$ | | | | | |
| $y$ | 15.3 | 25.9 | 21.9 | 15.5 | 16.7 | 26.1 | 34.8 | 22.6 | 29.0 | 37.1 |
| $x_1$ | 14.2 | 18.0 | 29.9 | 14.1 | 18.4 | 20.1 | 27.6 | 27.4 | 28.5 | 28.6 |
| $x_2$ | 4.09 | 9.56 | 2.18 | 5.43 | 6.33 | 8.27 | 9.16 | 5.24 | 7.92 | 9.63 |

Test the hypotheses that (1) the "period" effects are all zero, (2) the "group" effects are all zero, and (3) both period and group effects are zero. Use an $F$ test in each case.

6. *Two-way random effects model.* We modify the random effects model by the addition of a time-specific disturbance. Thus,

$$y_{it} = \alpha + \mathbf{x}'_{it}\boldsymbol{\beta} + \varepsilon_{it} + u_i + v_t,$$

where

$$E[\varepsilon_{it} \mid \mathbf{X}] = E[u_i \mid \mathbf{X}] = E[v_t \mid \mathbf{X}] = 0,$$

$$E[\varepsilon_{it}u_j \mid \mathbf{X}] = E[\varepsilon_{it}v_s \mid \mathbf{X}] = E[u_i v_t \mid \mathbf{X}] = 0 \quad \text{for all } i, j, t, s$$

$$\text{Var}[\varepsilon_{it} \mid \mathbf{X}] = \sigma_\varepsilon^2, \quad \text{Cov}[\varepsilon_{it}, \varepsilon_{js} \mid \mathbf{X}] = 0 \quad \text{for all } i, j, t, s$$

$$\text{Var}[u_i \mid \mathbf{X}] = \sigma_u^2, \quad \text{Cov}[u_i, u_j \mid \mathbf{X}] = 0 \quad \text{for all } i, j$$

$$\text{Var}[v_t \mid \mathbf{X}] = \sigma_v^2, \quad \text{Cov}[v_t, v_s \mid \mathbf{X}] = 0 \quad \text{for all } t, s.$$

Write out the full disturbance covariance matrix for a data set with $n = 2$ and $T = 2$.

7. The model

$$
\begin{bmatrix} \mathbf{y}_1 \\ \mathbf{y}_2 \end{bmatrix} = \begin{bmatrix} \mathbf{x}_1 \\ \mathbf{x}_2 \end{bmatrix} \beta + \begin{bmatrix} \boldsymbol{\varepsilon}_1 \\ \boldsymbol{\varepsilon}_2 \end{bmatrix}
$$

satisfies the groupwise heteroscedastic regression model of Section 8.8.2. All variables have zero means. The following sample second-moment matrix is obtained from a sample of 20 observations:

|       | $y_1$ | $y_2$ | $x_1$ | $x_2$ |
|-------|----|----|----|----|
| $y_1$ | 20 | 6  | 4  | 3  |
| $y_2$ | 6  | 10 | 3  | 6  |
| $x_1$ | 4  | 3  | 5  | 2  |
| $x_2$ | 3  | 6  | 2  | 10 |

a. Compute the two separate OLS estimates of $\beta$, their sampling variances, the estimates of $\sigma_1^2$ and $\sigma_2^2$, and the $R^2$'s in the two regressions.
b. Carry out the Lagrange multiplier test of the hypothesis that $\sigma_1^2 = \sigma_2^2$.
c. Compute the two-step FGLS estimate of $\beta$ and an estimate of its sampling variance. Test the hypothesis that $\beta$ equals 1.
d. Carry out the Wald test of equal disturbance variances.
e. Compute the maximum likelihood estimates of $\beta$, $\sigma_1^2$, and $\sigma_2^2$ by iterating the FGLS estimates to convergence.
f. Carry out a likelihood ratio test of equal disturbance variances.

8. Suppose that in the groupwise heteroscedasticity model of Section 8.8.2, $\mathbf{X}_i$ is the same for all $i$. What is the generalized least squares estimator of $\boldsymbol{\beta}$? How would you compute the estimator if it were necessary to estimate $\sigma_i^2$?

9. The following table presents a hypothetical panel of data:

|    | $i=1$ |       | $i=2$ |       | $i=3$ |       |
|----|-------|-------|-------|-------|-------|-------|
| t  | y     | x     | y     | x     | y     | x     |
| 1  | 30.27 | 24.31 | 38.71 | 28.35 | 37.03 | 21.16 |
| 2  | 35.59 | 28.47 | 29.74 | 27.38 | 43.82 | 26.76 |
| 3  | 17.90 | 23.74 | 11.29 | 12.74 | 37.12 | 22.21 |
| 4  | 44.90 | 25.44 | 26.17 | 21.08 | 24.34 | 19.02 |
| 5  | 37.58 | 20.80 | 5.85  | 14.02 | 26.15 | 18.64 |
| 6  | 23.15 | 10.55 | 29.01 | 20.43 | 26.01 | 18.97 |
| 7  | 30.53 | 18.40 | 30.38 | 28.13 | 29.64 | 21.35 |
| 8  | 39.90 | 25.40 | 36.03 | 21.78 | 30.25 | 21.34 |
| 9  | 20.44 | 13.57 | 37.90 | 25.65 | 25.41 | 15.86 |
| 10 | 36.85 | 25.60 | 33.90 | 11.66 | 26.04 | 13.28 |

a. Estimate the groupwise heteroscedastic model of Section 8.8.2. Include an estimate of the asymptotic variance of the slope estimator. Use a two-step procedure, basing the FGLS estimator at the second step on residuals from the pooled least squares regression.
b. Carry out the Wald and Lagrange multiplier tests of the hypothesis that the variances are all equal.

## Applications

As usual, the applications below require econometric software. The computations can be done with any modern software package, so no specific program is recommended.

1. The data in Appendix Table F9.3 were used by Grunfeld (1958) and dozens of researchers since, including Zellner (1962, 1963) and Zellner and Huang (1962), to study different estimators for panel data and linear regression systems. The model is an investment equation

$$I_{it} = \beta_1 + \beta_2 F_{it} + \beta_3 C_{it} + \varepsilon_{it}, t = 1, \ldots, 20, i = 1, \ldots, 10,$$

where

$$I_{it} = \text{real gross investment for firm } i \text{ in year } t,$$

$$F_{it} = \text{real value of the firm—shares outstanding,}$$

$$C_{it} = \text{real value of the capital stock.}$$

For present purposes, this is a balanced panel data set.
   a. Fit the pooled regression model.
   b. Referring to the results in part a, is there evidence of within groups correlation? Compute the robust standard errors for your pooled OLS estimator and compare them to the conventional ones.
   c. Compute the fixed effects estimator for these data, then, using an $F$ test, test the hypothesis that the constants for the 10 firms are all the same.
   d. Use a Lagrange multiplier statistic to test for the presence of common effects in the data.
   e. Compute the one-way random effects estimator and report all estimation results. Explain the difference between this specification and the one in part c.
   f. Use a Hausman test to determine whether a fixed or random effects specification is preferred for these data.

2. The data in Appendix Table F6.1 are an unbalanced panel on 25 U.S. airlines in the pre-deregulation days of the 1970s and 1980s. The group sizes range from 2 to 15. Data in the file are the following variables. (Variable names contained in the data file are constructed to indicate the variable contents.)

   Total cost,
   Expenditures on Capital, Labor, Fuel, Materials, Property, and Equipment,
   Price measures for the six inputs,
   Quantity measures for the six inputs,
   Output measured in revenue passenger miles, converted to an index number for the airline,
   Load factor = the average percentage capacity utilization of the airline's fleet,
   Stage      = the average flight (stage) length in miles,
   Points     = the number of points served by the airline,
   Year       = the calendar year,
   T          = Year—1969,
   TI         = the number of observations for the airline, repeated for each year.

Use these data to build a cost model for airline service. Allow for cross-airline heterogeneity in the constants in the model. Use both random and fixed effects specifications, and use available statistical tests to determine which is the preferred model. An appropriate cost model to begin the analysis with would be

$$\ln cost_{it} = \alpha_i + \sum_{k=1}^{6} \beta_k \ln Price_{k,it} + \gamma \ln Output_{it} + \varepsilon_{it}.$$

It is necessary to impose linear homogeneity in the input prices on the cost function, which you would do by dividing five of the six prices and the total cost by the sixth price (choose any one), then using $\ln(cost/P_6)$ and $\ln(P_k/P_6)$ in the regression. You might also generalize the cost function by including a quadratic term in the log of output in the function. A translog model would include the unique squares and cross products of the input prices and products of log output with the logs of the prices. The data include three additional factors that may influence costs, stage length, load factor and number of points served. Include them in your model, and use the appropriate test statistic to test whether they are, indeed, relevant to the determination of (log) total cost.

# 10
# SYSTEMS OF REGRESSION EQUATIONS

—◦◦◦—

## 10.1 INTRODUCTION

There are many settings in which the single equation models of the previous chapters apply to a group of related variables. In these contexts, it makes sense to consider the several models jointly. Some examples follow.

1.  In a classic application that lays the foundation for the literature discussed in this chapter, Grunfeld (1958), Boot and de Witt (1960), and Zellner (1962, 1963) examined investment by a set of firms, each of which makes decisions based on variables that reflect anticipated profit and replacement of the capital stock;

    $$I_{it} = \beta_{1i} + \beta_{2i} F_{it} + \beta_{3i} C_{it} + \varepsilon_{it}.$$

    Whether the parameter vector should be the same for all firms is a question that we shall study in this chapter. But the disturbances in the investment equations certainly include factors that are common to all of the firms, such as the perceived general health of the economy, as well as factors that are specific to the particular firm or industry.

2.  The capital asset pricing model of finance specifies that for a given security,

    $$r_{it} - r_{ft} = \alpha_i + \beta_i(r_{mt} - r_{ft}) + \varepsilon_{it},$$

    where $r_{it}$ is the return over period $t$ on security $i$, $r_{ft}$ is the return on a risk-free security, $r_{mt}$ is the market return, and $\beta_i$ is the security's beta coefficient. The disturbances are obviously correlated across securities. The knowledge that the return on security $i$ exceeds the risk-free rate by a given amount gives some information about the excess return of security $j$, at least for some $j$'s. It will be useful to estimate the equations jointly rather than ignore this connection.

3.  In Example 9.12 (the data are described in Example 9.9), we examined Munnell's (1990) model for output by the 48 continental U.S. states,

    $$\ln GSP_{it} = \beta_{1i} + \beta_{2i} \ln p\_cap_{it} + \beta_{3i} \ln hwy_{it} + \beta_{4i} \ln water_{it} + \beta_{5i} \ln util_{it}$$
    $$+ \beta_{6i} \ln emp_{it} + \beta_{7i}\, unemp_{it} + \varepsilon_{it}.$$

    Taken one state at a time, this provides a set of 48 linear regression models. The application develops a model in which the observations are correlated across time within a state. An important question pursued here and in the applications in the next example is whether it is valid to assume that the coefficient vector is the same for all states (individuals) in the sample.

4. In Example 9.18, we examined Pesaran and Smith's (1995) dynamic model for wage determination in 38 UK industries. The central equation is of the form

$$y_{it} = \alpha_i + \mathbf{x}'_{it}\boldsymbol{\beta}_i + \gamma_i y_{i,t-1} + \varepsilon_{it}.$$

Nair-Reichert and Weinhold's (2001) cross-country analysis of growth of developing countries takes the same form. In both cases, each group (industry, country) could be analyzed separately. However, the connections across groups and the interesting question of "poolability"—that is, whether it is valid to assume identical coefficients—is a central part of the analysis. The lagged dependent variable in the model produces a substantial complication.

5. In a model of production, the optimization conditions of economic theory imply that if a firm faces a set of factor prices $\mathbf{p}$, then its set of cost-minimizing factor demands for producing output $Q$ will be a set of equations of the form $x_m = f_m(Q, \mathbf{p})$. The empirical model is

$$x_1 = f_1(Q, \mathbf{p} \,|\, \boldsymbol{\theta}) + \varepsilon_1,$$
$$x_2 = f_2(Q, \mathbf{p} \,|\, \boldsymbol{\theta}) + \varepsilon_2,$$
$$\cdots$$
$$x_M = f_M(Q, \mathbf{p} \,|\, \boldsymbol{\theta}) + \varepsilon_M,$$

where $\boldsymbol{\theta}$ is a vector of parameters that are part of the technology and $\varepsilon_m$ represents errors in optimization. Once again, the disturbances should be correlated. In addition, the same parameters of the production technology will enter all the demand equations, so the set of equations have cross-equation restrictions. Estimating the equations separately will waste the information that the same set of parameters appears in all the equations.

All these examples have a common multiple equation structure, which we may write as

$$\begin{aligned}
\mathbf{y}_1 &= \mathbf{X}_1\boldsymbol{\beta}_1 + \boldsymbol{\varepsilon}_1, \\
\mathbf{y}_2 &= \mathbf{X}_2\boldsymbol{\beta}_2 + \boldsymbol{\varepsilon}_2, \\
&\cdots \\
\mathbf{y}_M &= \mathbf{X}_M\boldsymbol{\beta}_M + \boldsymbol{\varepsilon}_M.
\end{aligned} \tag{10-1}$$

There are $M$ equations and $T$ observations in the sample of data used to estimate them.[1] The second and third examples embody different types of constraints across equations and different structures of the disturbances. A basic set of principles will apply to them all, however.[2]

Section 10.2 examines the general model in which each equation has its own fixed set of parameters, and it examines efficient estimation techniques. Section 10.2.8 examines the special case of the model suggested in illustrations 3 and 4 preceding, the "pooled" model with identical coefficients in all equations. Production and consumer demand models are a special case of the general model in which the equations of the model obey an adding up constraint that has important implications for specification and estimation.

---

[1] The use of $T$ is not necessarily meant to imply any connection to time series. For instance, in the fifth example above, the data might be cross-sectional.

[2] See the surveys by Srivastava and Dwivedi (1979), Srivastava and Giles (1987), and Fiebig (2001).

Some general results for demand systems are considered in Section 10.3. In Section 10.4, we examine a classic application of the model in Section 10.3 that illustrates a number of the interesting features of the current genre of demand studies in the applied literature.

### Example 10.1  Munnell's Statewide Production Data

In Examples 9.9 and 9.12, we examined Munnell's (1990) study of productivity of public capital at the state level. The central equation of the analysis that we will extend here is a Cobb–Douglas production function,

$$\ln gsp_{it} = \alpha_i + \beta_{1i} \ln p\_cap_{it} + \beta_{2i} \ln hwy_{it} + \beta_{3i} \ln water_{it}$$
$$+ \beta_{4i} \ln util_{it} + \beta_{5i} \ln emp_{it} + \beta_{6i} unemp_{it} + \varepsilon_{it},$$

where the variables in the model, measured for the lower 48 U.S. states and years 1970–1986, are

$$
\begin{aligned}
gsp &= \text{gross state product,} \\
p\_cap &= \text{public capital,} \\
hwy &= \text{highway capital,} \\
water &= \text{water utility capital,} \\
util &= \text{utility capital,} \\
pc &= \text{private capital,} \\
emp &= \text{employment (labor),} \\
unemp &= \text{unemployment rate.}
\end{aligned}
$$

In Example 9.9, we defined nine regions consisting of groups of the 48 states:

1. GF  = *Gulf*         = AL, FL, LA, MS,
2. MW = *Midwest*       = IL, IN, KY, MI, MN, OH, WI,
3. MA  = *Mid Atlantic* = DE, MD, NJ, NY, PA, VA,
4. MT  = *Mountain*     = CO, ID, MT, ND, SD, WY,
5. NE  = *New England*  = CT, ME, MA, NH, RI, VT,
6. SO  = *South*        = GA, NC, SC, TN, WV,
7. SW  = *Southwest*    = AZ, NV, NM, TX, UT,
8. CN  = *Central*      = AK, IA, KS, MS, NE, OK,
9. WC = *West Coast*    = CA, OR, WA.

For our application in this chapter, we will use the aggregated data to analyze a nine-region (equation) model. Data on output, the capital stocks, and employment are aggregated simply by summing the values for the individual states (before taking logarithms). The unemployment rate for each region, $m$, at time $t$ is determined by a weighted average of the unemployment rates for the states in the region, where the weights are

$$w_{it} = emp_{it} / \Sigma_j emp_{jt}.$$

Then, the unemployment rate for region $m$ at time $t$ is the following average of the unemployment rates of the states ($j$) in region ($m$) at time $t$:

$$unemp_{mt} = \Sigma_j w_{jt}(m) \, unemp_{jt}(m).$$

## 10.2  THE SEEMINGLY UNRELATED REGRESSIONS MODEL

The **seemingly unrelated regressions** (SUR) model in (10-1) is

$$\mathbf{y}_i = \mathbf{X}_i \boldsymbol{\beta}_i + \boldsymbol{\varepsilon}_i, \quad i = 1, \dots, M, \tag{10-2}$$

where

$$\boldsymbol{\varepsilon} = [\boldsymbol{\varepsilon}_1', \boldsymbol{\varepsilon}_2', \ldots, \boldsymbol{\varepsilon}_M']'.$$

We assume strict exogeneity of $\mathbf{X}_i$,

$$E[\boldsymbol{\varepsilon} \mid \mathbf{X}_1, \mathbf{X}_2, \ldots, \mathbf{X}_M] = \mathbf{0},$$

and homoscedasticity

$$E[\boldsymbol{\varepsilon}_m \boldsymbol{\varepsilon}_m' \mid \mathbf{X}_1, \mathbf{X}_2, \ldots, \mathbf{X}_M] = \sigma_{mm}\mathbf{I}_T.$$

We assume that a total of $T$ observations are used in estimating the parameters of the $M$ equations.[3] Each equation involves $K_i$ regressors, for a total of $K = \sum_{i=1}^{M} K_i$. We will require $T > K_i$. The data are assumed to be well behaved, as described in Section 4.9.1, and we shall not treat the issue separately here. For the present, we also assume that disturbances are uncorrelated across observations but correlated across equations. Therefore,

$$E[\varepsilon_{it}\varepsilon_{js} \mid \mathbf{X}_1, \mathbf{X}_2, \ldots, \mathbf{X}_M] = \sigma_{ij}, \quad \text{if } t = s \text{ and 0 otherwise.}$$

The disturbance formulation is, therefore,

$$E[\boldsymbol{\varepsilon}_i \boldsymbol{\varepsilon}_j' \mid \mathbf{X}_1, \mathbf{X}_2, \ldots, \mathbf{X}_M] = \sigma_{ij}\mathbf{I}_T,$$

or

$$E[\boldsymbol{\varepsilon}\boldsymbol{\varepsilon}' \mid \mathbf{X}_1, \mathbf{X}_2, \ldots, \mathbf{X}_M] = \boldsymbol{\Omega} = \begin{bmatrix} \sigma_{11}\mathbf{I} & \sigma_{12}\mathbf{I} & \cdots & \sigma_{1M}\mathbf{I} \\ \sigma_{21}\mathbf{I} & \sigma_{22}\mathbf{I} & \cdots & \sigma_{2M}\mathbf{I} \\ & & \vdots & \\ \sigma_{M1}\mathbf{I} & \sigma_{M2}\mathbf{I} & \cdots & \sigma_{MM}\mathbf{I} \end{bmatrix}. \tag{10-3}$$

Note that when the data matrices are group-specific observations on the same variables, as in Example 10.1, the specification of this model is precisely that of the covariance structures model of Section 10.2.8 save for the extension here that allows the parameter vector to vary across groups. The covariance structures model is, therefore, a testable special case.[4]

It will be convenient in the discussion below to have a term for the particular kind of model in which the data matrices are group specific data sets on the same set of variables. The Grunfeld model noted in the introduction is such a case. This special case of the seemingly unrelated regressions model is a **multivariate regression model.** In contrast, the cost function model examined in Section 10.4.1 is not of this type—it consists of a cost function that involves output and prices and a set of cost share equations that have only a set of constant terms. We emphasize, this is merely a convenient term for a specific form of the SUR model, not a modification of the model itself.

---

[3]There are a few results for unequal numbers of observations, such as Schmidt (1977), Baltagi, Garvin, and Kerman (1989), Conniffe (1985), Hwang (1990), and Im (1994). But, the case of fixed $T$ is the norm in practice.

[4]This is the test of "Aggregation Bias" that is the subject of Zellner (1962, 1963). (The bias results if parameter equality is incorrectly assumed.) We will examine this issue in detail in Section 10.2.4.

### 10.2.1 GENERALIZED LEAST SQUARES

Each equation is, by itself, a classical regression. Therefore, the parameters could be estimated consistently, if not efficiently, one equation at a time by ordinary least squares. The **generalized regression model** applies to the stacked model,

$$
\begin{bmatrix} \mathbf{y}_1 \\ \mathbf{y}_2 \\ \vdots \\ \mathbf{y}_M \end{bmatrix} = \begin{bmatrix} \mathbf{X}_1 & \mathbf{0} & \cdots & \mathbf{0} \\ \mathbf{0} & \mathbf{X}_2 & \cdots & \mathbf{0} \\ & & \vdots & \\ \mathbf{0} & \mathbf{0} & \cdots & \mathbf{X}_M \end{bmatrix} \begin{bmatrix} \boldsymbol{\beta}_1 \\ \boldsymbol{\beta}_2 \\ \vdots \\ \boldsymbol{\beta}_M \end{bmatrix} + \begin{bmatrix} \boldsymbol{\varepsilon}_1 \\ \boldsymbol{\varepsilon}_2 \\ \vdots \\ \boldsymbol{\varepsilon}_M \end{bmatrix} = \mathbf{X}\boldsymbol{\beta} + \boldsymbol{\varepsilon}. \qquad \textbf{(10-4)}
$$

Therefore, the efficient estimator is generalized least squares.[5] The model has a particularly convenient form. For the $t$th observation, the $M \times M$ covariance matrix of the disturbances is

$$
\boldsymbol{\Sigma} = \begin{bmatrix} \sigma_{11} & \sigma_{12} & \cdots & \sigma_{1M} \\ \sigma_{21} & \sigma_{22} & \cdots & \sigma_{2M} \\ & & \vdots & \\ \sigma_{M1} & \sigma_{M2} & \cdots & \sigma_{MM} \end{bmatrix}, \qquad \textbf{(10-5)}
$$

so, in (10-3),

$$
\boldsymbol{\Omega} = \boldsymbol{\Sigma} \otimes \mathbf{I} \qquad \textbf{(10-6)}
$$

and

$$
\boldsymbol{\Omega}^{-1} = \boldsymbol{\Sigma}^{-1} \otimes \mathbf{I}.
$$

Denoting the $ij$th element of $\boldsymbol{\Sigma}^{-1}$ by $\sigma^{ij}$, we find that the GLS estimator is

$$
\hat{\boldsymbol{\beta}} = [\mathbf{X}'\boldsymbol{\Omega}^{-1}\mathbf{X}]^{-1}\mathbf{X}'\boldsymbol{\Omega}^{-1}\mathbf{y} = [\mathbf{X}'(\boldsymbol{\Sigma}^{-1} \otimes \mathbf{I})\mathbf{X}]^{-1}\mathbf{X}'(\boldsymbol{\Sigma}^{-1} \otimes \mathbf{I})\mathbf{y}. \qquad \textbf{(10-7)}
$$

Expanding the **Kronecker products** produces

$$
\hat{\boldsymbol{\beta}} = \begin{bmatrix} \sigma^{11}\mathbf{X}_1'\mathbf{X}_1 & \sigma^{12}\mathbf{X}_1'\mathbf{X}_2 & \cdots & \sigma^{1M}\mathbf{X}_1'\mathbf{X}_M \\ \sigma^{21}\mathbf{X}_2'\mathbf{X}_1 & \sigma^{22}\mathbf{X}_2'\mathbf{X}_2 & \cdots & \sigma^{2M}\mathbf{X}_2'\mathbf{X}_M \\ & & \vdots & \\ \sigma^{M1}\mathbf{X}_M'\mathbf{X}_1 & \sigma^{M2}\mathbf{X}_M'\mathbf{X}_2 & \cdots & \sigma^{MM}\mathbf{X}_M'\mathbf{X}_M \end{bmatrix}^{-1} \begin{bmatrix} \sum_{j=1}^{M} \sigma^{1j}\mathbf{X}_1'\mathbf{y}_j \\ \sum_{j=1}^{M} \sigma^{2j}\mathbf{X}_2'\mathbf{y}_j \\ \vdots \\ \sum_{j=1}^{M} \sigma^{Mj}\mathbf{X}_M'\mathbf{y}_j \end{bmatrix}.
$$

The asymptotic covariance matrix for the GLS estimator is the bracketed inverse matrix in (10-7). All the results of Chapter 8 for the generalized regression model extend to this model (which has both **heteroscedasticity** and **autocorrelation**).

This estimator is obviously different from ordinary least squares. At this point, however, the equations are linked only by their disturbances—hence the name *seemingly unrelated* regressions model—so it is interesting to ask just how much efficiency is gained by using generalized least squares instead of ordinary least squares. Zellner (1962) and Dwivedi and Srivastava (1978) have analyzed some special cases in detail.

---

[5]See Zellner (1962) and Telser (1964).

1. If the equations are *actually* unrelated—that is, if $\sigma_{ij} = 0$ for $i \neq j$—then there is obviously no payoff to GLS estimation of the full set of equations. Indeed, full GLS is equation by equation OLS.[6]
2. If the equations have **identical explanatory variables**—that is, if $\mathbf{X}_i = \mathbf{X}_j$—then OLS and GLS are identical. We will turn to this case in Section 10.2.2.[7]
3. If the regressors in one block of equations are a subset of those in another, then GLS brings no efficiency gain over OLS in estimation of the smaller set of equations; thus, GLS and OLS are once again identical. We will look at an application of this result in Section 20.6.5.[8]

In the more general case, with unrestricted correlation of the disturbances and different regressors in the equations, the results are complicated and dependent on the data. Two propositions that apply generally are as follows:

1. The greater is the correlation of the disturbances, the greater is the efficiency gain accruing to GLS.
2. The less correlation there is between the $\mathbf{X}$ matrices, the greater is the gain in efficiency in using GLS.[9]

## 10.2.2    SEEMINGLY UNRELATED REGRESSIONS WITH IDENTICAL REGRESSORS

The case of **identical regressors** is quite common, notably in the capital asset pricing model in empirical finance—see the Introduction and Chapter 20. In this special case, generalized least squares is equivalent to equation by equation ordinary least squares. Impose the assumption that $\mathbf{X}_i = \mathbf{X}_j = \mathbf{X}$, so that $\mathbf{X}_i'\mathbf{X}_j = \mathbf{X}'\mathbf{X}$ for all $i$ and $j$ in (10-7). The inverse matrix on the right-hand side now becomes $[\mathbf{\Sigma}^{-1} \otimes \mathbf{X}'\mathbf{X}]^{-1}$, which, using (A-76), equals $[\mathbf{\Sigma} \otimes (\mathbf{X}'\mathbf{X})^{-1}]$. Also on the right-hand side, each term $\mathbf{X}_i'\mathbf{y}_j$ equals $\mathbf{X}'\mathbf{y}_j$, which, in turn equals $\mathbf{X}'\mathbf{X}\mathbf{b}_j$. With these results, after moving the common $\mathbf{X}'\mathbf{X}$ out of the summations on the right-hand side, we obtain

$$
\hat{\beta} = \begin{bmatrix} \sigma_{11}(\mathbf{X}'\mathbf{X})^{-1} & \sigma_{12}(\mathbf{X}'\mathbf{X})^{-1} & \cdots & \sigma_{1M}(\mathbf{X}'\mathbf{X})^{-1} \\ \sigma_{21}(\mathbf{X}'\mathbf{X})^{-1} & \sigma_{22}(\mathbf{X}'\mathbf{X})^{-1} & \cdots & \sigma_{2M}(\mathbf{X}'\mathbf{X})^{-1} \\ & & \vdots & \\ \sigma_{M1}(\mathbf{X}'\mathbf{X})^{-1} & \sigma_{M2}(\mathbf{X}'\mathbf{X})^{-1} & \cdots & \sigma_{MM}(\mathbf{X}'\mathbf{X})^{-1} \end{bmatrix} \begin{bmatrix} (\mathbf{X}'\mathbf{X})\sum_{l=1}^{M} \sigma^{1l}\mathbf{b}_l \\ (\mathbf{X}'\mathbf{X})\sum_{l=1}^{M} \sigma^{2l}\mathbf{b}_l \\ \vdots \\ (\mathbf{X}'\mathbf{X})\sum_{l=1}^{M} \sigma^{Ml}\mathbf{b}_l \end{bmatrix}. \quad \textbf{(10-8)}
$$

---

[6] See also Baltagi (1989) and Bartels and Fiebig (1992) for other cases in which OLS = GLS.

[7] An intriguing result, albeit probably of negligible practical significance, is that the result also applies if the $\mathbf{X}$'s are all nonsingular, and not necessarily identical, linear combinations of the same set of variables. The formal result which is a corollary of Kruskal's theorem [see Davidson and MacKinnon (1993, p. 294)] is that OLS and GLS will be the same if the $K$ columns of $\mathbf{X}$ are a linear combination of exactly $K$ characteristic vectors of $\mathbf{\Omega}$. By showing the equality of OLS and GLS here, we have verified the conditions of the corollary. The general result is pursued in the exercises. The intriguing result cited is now an obvious case.

[8] The result was analyzed by Goldberger (1970) and later by Revankar (1974) and Conniffe (1982a, b).

[9] See also Binkley (1982) and Binkley and Nelson (1988).

Now, we isolate one of the subvectors, say the first, from $\hat{\boldsymbol{\beta}}$. After multiplication, the moment matrices cancel, and we are left with

$$\hat{\boldsymbol{\beta}}_1 = \sum_{j=1}^{M} \sigma_{1j} \sum_{l=1}^{M} \sigma^{jl} \mathbf{b}_l = \mathbf{b}_1 \left( \sum_{j=1}^{M} \sigma_{1j} \sigma^{j1} \right) + \mathbf{b}_2 \left( \sum_{j=1}^{M} \sigma_{1j} \sigma^{j2} \right) + \cdots + \mathbf{b}_M \left( \sum_{j=1}^{M} \sigma_{1j} \sigma^{jM} \right).$$

The terms in parentheses are the elements of the first row of $\boldsymbol{\Sigma}\boldsymbol{\Sigma}^{-1} = \mathbf{I}$, so the end result is $\hat{\boldsymbol{\beta}}_1 = \mathbf{b}_1$. For the remaining subvectors, which are obtained the same way, $\hat{\boldsymbol{\beta}}_i = \mathbf{b}_i$, which is the result we sought.[10]

To reiterate, the important result we have here is that in the SUR model, when all equations have the same regressors, the efficient estimator is single-equation ordinary least squares; OLS is the same as GLS. Also, the asymptotic covariance matrix of $\hat{\boldsymbol{\beta}}$ for this case is given by the large inverse matrix in brackets in (10-8), which would be estimated by

$$\text{Est. Asy. Cov}[\hat{\boldsymbol{\beta}}_i, \hat{\boldsymbol{\beta}}_j] = \hat{\sigma}_{ij}(\mathbf{X}'\mathbf{X})^{-1}, \quad i, j = 1, \ldots, M, \quad \text{where } \hat{\boldsymbol{\Sigma}}_{ij} = \hat{\sigma}_{ij} = \frac{1}{T}\mathbf{e}_i'\mathbf{e}_j.$$

Except in some special cases, this general result is lost if there are any restrictions on $\boldsymbol{\beta}$, either within or across equations. We will examine one of those cases, the block of zeros restriction, in Section 20.6.5.

### 10.2.3 FEASIBLE GENERALIZED LEAST SQUARES

The preceding discussion assumes that $\boldsymbol{\Sigma}$ is known, which, as usual, is unlikely to be the case. FGLS estimators have been devised, however.[11] The least squares residuals may be used (of course) to estimate consistently the elements of $\boldsymbol{\Sigma}$ with

$$\hat{\sigma}_{ij} = s_{ij} = \frac{\mathbf{e}_i'\mathbf{e}_j}{T}. \tag{10-9}$$

The consistency of $s_{ij}$ follows from that of $\mathbf{b}_i$ and $\mathbf{b}_j$.[12] A degrees of freedom correction in the divisor is occasionally suggested. Two possibilities that are unbiased when $i = j$ are

$$s_{ij}^* = \frac{\mathbf{e}_i'\mathbf{e}_j}{[(T - K_i)(T - K_j)]^{1/2}} \quad \text{and} \quad s_{ij}^{**} = \frac{\mathbf{e}_i'\mathbf{e}_j}{T - \max(K_i, K_j)}.^{[13]} \tag{10-10}$$

Whether unbiasedness of the estimator of $\boldsymbol{\Sigma}$ used for FGLS is a virtue here is uncertain. The asymptotic properties of the **feasible GLS** estimator, $\hat{\hat{\boldsymbol{\beta}}}$ do not rely on an unbiased estimator of $\boldsymbol{\Sigma}$; only consistency is required. All our results from Chapters 8 and 9 for FGLS estimators extend to this model, with no modification. We shall use (10-9)

---

[10]See Hashimoto and Ohtani (1990) for discussion of hypothesis testing in this case.

[11]See Zellner (1962) and Zellner and Huang (1962). The FGLS estimator for this model is also labeled **Zellner's efficient estimator,** or ZEF, in reference to Zellner (1962) where it was introduced.

[12]Perhaps surprisingly, if it is assumed that the density of $\boldsymbol{\varepsilon}$ is symmetric, as it would be with normality, then $\mathbf{b}_i$ is also unbiased. See Kakwani (1967).

[13]See, as well, Judge et al. (1985), Theil (1971), and Srivastava and Giles (1987).

in what follows. With

$$S = \begin{bmatrix} s_{11} & s_{12} & \cdots & s_{1M} \\ s_{21} & s_{22} & \cdots & s_{2M} \\ & & \vdots & \\ s_{M1} & s_{M2} & \cdots & s_{MM} \end{bmatrix} \tag{10-11}$$

in hand, FGLS can proceed as usual.

### Example 10.2  Estimated SUR Model for Regional Output

We initially estimated the nine equations of the regional productivity model separately by OLS. The OLS estimates are shown in Table 10.1. The correlation matrix for the OLS residuals is as follows:

|       |    | GF      | MW      | MA      | MT      | NE      | SO     | SW     | CN     | WC     |
|-------|----|---------|---------|---------|---------|---------|--------|--------|--------|--------|
|       | GF | 1.0000  |         |         |         |         |        |        |        |        |
|       | MW | −0.1782 | 1.0000  |         |         |         |        |        |        |        |
|       | MA | 0.0816  | 0.8362  | 1.0000  |         |         |        |        |        |        |
| R =   | MT | 0.6418  | 0.4746  | 0.6837  | 1.0000  |         |        |        |        |        |
|       | NE | −0.0250 | 0.0797  | −0.1736 | −0.1873 | 1.0000  |        |        |        |        |
|       | SO | 0.0654  | −0.4630 | −0.0436 | −0.1190 | −0.5338 | 1.0000 |        |        |        |
|       | SW | −0.1032 | −0.4845 | −0.1709 | −0.3502 | −0.3041 | 0.9339 | 1.0000 |        |        |
|       | CN | 0.6194  | −0.8034 | −0.4376 | 0.1160  | −0.1924 | 0.4745 | 0.3507 | 1.0000 |        |
|       | WC | 0.6759  | −0.1774 | 0.2312  | 0.6723  | −0.1261 | 0.3124 | 0.1525 | 0.6845 | 1.0000 |

The values in **R** are large enough to suggest that there is substantial correlation of the disturbances across regions. As noted in Section 10.2.7, we do not have a standard test of the specification of the SUR model against the alternative hypothesis of uncorrelated disturbances for the general SUR model without an assumption of normality. The Breusch and Pagan (1980) Lagrange multiplier test based on the correlation matrix does have some intuitive appeal. For the correlation matrix shown earlier, the chi-squared statistic equals 215.88 with $8(9)/2 = 36$ degrees of freedom. The critical value from the chi-squared table is 50.998, so the null hypothesis that the seemingly unrelated regressions are actually unrelated is rejected.

Table 10.1 presents estimates of the parameters of the SUR model for regional output. The table lists the OLS as well as the FGLS parameter estimates. (The pooled results that are also presented are discussed in Section 10.2.8.) The correlations listed earlier suggest that there is likely to be considerable benefit to using FGLS in terms of efficiency of the estimator. The individual equation OLS estimators are consistent, but they neglect the cross equation correlation. The substantially lower estimated standard errors for the FGLS results with each equation appear to confirm that expectation.

### 10.2.4   TESTING HYPOTHESES

For testing a hypothesis about $\beta$, a statistic analogous to the $F$ ratio in multiple regression analysis is

$$F[J, MT - K] = \frac{(\mathbf{R}\hat{\beta} - \mathbf{q})'[\mathbf{R}(\mathbf{X}'\hat{\mathbf{\Omega}}^{-1}\mathbf{X})^{-1}\mathbf{R}']^{-1}(\mathbf{R}\hat{\beta} - \mathbf{q})/J}{\hat{\varepsilon}'\hat{\mathbf{\Omega}}^{-1}\hat{\varepsilon}/(MT - K)}. \tag{10-12}$$

The computation requires the unknown $\mathbf{\Omega}$. If we insert the FGLS estimate $\hat{\mathbf{\Omega}}$ based on (10-9) and use the result that the denominator converges to one, then, in large samples,

**TABLE 10.1** Estimated SUR Model for Regional Output. (standard errors in parentheses)

| Region | Estimator | $\alpha$ | $\beta_1$ | $\beta_2$ | $\beta_3$ | $\beta_4$ | $\beta_5$ | $\beta_6$ | $\sigma_m$ | $R^2$ |
|---|---|---|---|---|---|---|---|---|---|---|
| GF | OLS | 12.1458 (3.3154) | −0.007117 (0.01114) | −2.1352 (0.8677) | 0.1161 (0.06278) | 1.4247 (0.5944) | 0.7851 (0.1493) | −0.00742 (0.00316) | 0.01075 | 0.9971 |
| | FGLS | 10.4792 (1.5912) | −0.003160 (0.005391) | −1.5448 (0.3888) | 0.1139 (0.03651) | 0.8987 (0.2516) | 0.8886 (0.07715) | −0.005299 (0.00182) | 0.008745 | 0.9967 |
| MW | OLS | 3.0282 (1.7834) | 0.1635 (0.1660) | −0.07471 (0.2205) | −0.1689 (0.09896) | 0.6372 (0.2078) | 0.3622 (0.1650) | −0.01736 (0.004741) | 0.009942 | 0.9984 |
| | FGLS | 4.1206 (1.0091) | 0.06370 (0.08739) | −0.1275 (0.1284) | −0.1292 (0.06152) | 0.5144 (0.1118) | 0.5497 (0.08597) | −0.01545 (0.00252) | 0.008608 | 0.9980 |
| MA | OLS | −11.2110 (3.5867) | 0.4120 (0.2281) | 2.1355 (0.5571) | 0.5122 (0.1192) | −0.4740 (0.2519) | −0.4620 (0.3529) | −0.03022 (0.00853) | 0.01040 | 0.9950 |
| | FGLS | −9.1438 (2.2025) | 0.3511 (0.1077) | 1.7972 (0.3410) | 0.5168 (0.06405) | −0.3616 (0.1294) | −0.3391 (0.1997) | −0.02954 (0.00474) | 0.008625 | 0.9946 |
| MT | OLS | 3.5902 (6.9490) | 0.2948 (0.2054) | 0.1740 (0.2082) | −0.2257 (0.3840) | −0.2144 (0.9712) | 0.9166 (0.3772) | −0.008143 (0.00839) | 0.01688 | 0.9940 |
| | FGLS | 2.8150 (3.4428) | 0.1843 (0.09220) | 0.1164 (0.1165) | −0.3811 (0.1774) | 0.01648 (0.4654) | 1.1032 (0.1718) | −0.005507 (0.00422) | 0.01321 | 0.9938 |
| NE | OLS | 6.3783 (2.3823) | −0.1526 (0.08403) | −0.1233 (0.2850) | 0.3065 (0.08917) | −0.5326 (0.2375) | 1.3437 (0.1876) | 0.005098 (0.00517) | 0.008601 | 0.9986 |
| | FGLS | 3.5331 (1.3388) | −0.1097 (0.04570) | 0.1637 (0.1676) | 0.2459 (0.04974) | −0.3155 (0.1194) | 1.0828 (0.09248) | −0.000664 (0.00263) | 0.007249 | 0.9983 |
| SO | OLS | −13.7297 (18.0199) | −0.02040 (0.2856) | 0.6621 (1.8111) | −0.9693 (0.2843) | −0.1074 (0.5634) | 3.3803 (1.1643) | 0.03378 (0.02150) | 0.02241 | 0.9851 |
| | FGLS | −13.1186 (7.6009) | 0.1007 (0.1280) | 0.9923 (0.7827) | −0.5851 (0.1373) | −0.3029 (0.2412) | 2.5897 (0.4665) | 0.02143 (0.00809) | 0.01908 | 0.9817 |

| Region | Estimator | $\alpha$ | $\beta_1$ | $\beta_2$ | $\beta_3$ | $\beta_4$ | $\beta_5$ | $\beta_6$ | $\sigma_m$ | $R^2$ |
|---|---|---|---|---|---|---|---|---|---|---|
| SW | OLS | −22.8553 (4.8739) | −0.3776 (0.1673) | 3.3478 (1.8584) | −0.2637 (0.4317) | −1.7783 (1.1757) | 2.6732 (1.0325) | 0.02592 (0.01727) | 0.01293 | 0.9864 |
| | FGLS | −19.9917 (2.8649) | −0.3386 (0.08943) | 3.2821 (0.8894) | −0.1105 (0.1993) | −1.7812 (0.5609) | 2.2510 (0.4802) | 0.01846 (0.00793) | 0.01055 | 0.9846 |
| CN | OLS | 3.4425 (1.2571) | 0.05040 (0.2662) | −0.5938 (0.3219) | 0.06351 (0.3333) | −0.01294 (0.3787) | 1.5731 (0.4125) | 0.006125 (0.00892) | 0.01753 | 0.9936 |
| | FGLS | 2.8172 (0.8434) | 0.01412 (0.08833) | −0.5086 (0.1869) | −0.02685 (0.1405) | 0.1165 (0.1774) | 1.5339 (0.1762) | 0.006499 (0.00421) | 0.01416 | 0.9930 |
| WC | OLS | 9.1108 (3.9704) | 0.2334 (0.2062) | 1.6043 (0.7449) | 0.7174 (0.1613) | −0.3563 (0.3153) | −0.2592 (0.3029) | −0.03416 (0.00629) | 0.01085 | 0.9895 |
| | FGLS | −10.2989 (2.4189) | 0.03734 (0.1107) | 1.8176 (0.4503) | 0.6572 (0.1011) | −0.4358 (0.1912) | 0.02904 (0.1828) | −0.02867 (0.00373) | 0.008837 | 0.9881 |
| Pooled | OLS | 3.1567 (0.1377) | 0.08692 (0.01058) | −0.02956 (0.03405) | 0.4922 (0.04167) | 0.06092 (0.03833) | 0.3676 (0.04018) | −0.01746 (0.00304) | 0.05558 | 0.9926 |
| | FGLS | 3.1089 (0.0208) | 0.08076 (0.005148) | −0.01797 (0.006186) | 0.3728 (0.01311) | 0.1221 (0.00557) | 0.4206 (0.01442) | −0.01506 (0.00101) | NA | 0.9882[a] |
| | FGLS Het. | 3.0977 (0.1233) | 0.08646 (0.01144) | −0.02141 (0.02830) | 0.03874 (0.03529) | 0.1215 (0.02805) | 0.4032 (0.03410) | −0.01529 (0.00256) | NA | 0.9875[a] |

[a] $R^2$ for models fit by FGLS is computed using $1 - 9/\mathrm{tr}(\mathbf{S}^{-1}\mathbf{S}_{yy})$

the statistic will behave the same as

$$\hat{F} = \frac{1}{J}(\mathbf{R}\hat{\hat{\beta}} - \mathbf{q})'[\mathbf{R}\,\widehat{\text{Var}}[\hat{\hat{\beta}}]\mathbf{R}']^{-1}(\mathbf{R}\hat{\hat{\beta}} - \mathbf{q}). \qquad \textbf{(10-13)}$$

This can be referred to the standard $F$ table. Because it uses the estimated $\Sigma$, even with normally distributed disturbances, the $F$ distribution is only valid approximately. In general, the statistic $F[J, n]$ converges to $1/J$ times a chi-squared $[J]$ as $n \to \infty$. Therefore, an alternative test statistic that has a limiting chi-squared distribution with $J$ degrees of freedom when the null hypothesis is true is

$$J\hat{F} = (\mathbf{R}\,\hat{\hat{\beta}} - \mathbf{q})'[\mathbf{R}\widehat{\text{Var}}[\hat{\hat{\beta}}]\mathbf{R}']^{-1}(\mathbf{R}\hat{\hat{\beta}} - \mathbf{q}). \qquad \textbf{(10-14)}$$

This can be recognized as a **Wald statistic** that measures the distance between $\mathbf{R}\hat{\hat{\beta}}$ and $\mathbf{q}$. Both statistics are valid asymptotically, but (10-13) may perform better in a small or moderately sized sample.[14] Once again, the divisor used in computing $\hat{\sigma}_{ij}$ may make a difference, but there is no general rule.

A hypothesis of particular interest is the **homogeneity restriction** of equal coefficient vectors in the multivariate regression model. That case is fairly common in this setting. The homogeneity restriction is that $\beta_i = \beta_M, i = 1, \ldots, M-1$. Consistent with (10-13)–(10-14), we would form the hypothesis as

$$\mathbf{R}\beta = \begin{bmatrix} \mathbf{I} & \mathbf{0} & \cdots & \mathbf{0} & -\mathbf{I} \\ \mathbf{0} & \mathbf{I} & \cdots & \mathbf{0} & -\mathbf{I} \\ & & \cdots & & \\ \mathbf{0} & \mathbf{0} & \cdots & \mathbf{I} & -\mathbf{I} \end{bmatrix} \begin{pmatrix} \beta_1 \\ \beta_2 \\ \cdots \\ \beta_M \end{pmatrix} = \begin{pmatrix} \beta_1 - \beta_M \\ \beta_2 - \beta_M \\ \cdots \\ \beta_{M-1} - \beta_M \end{pmatrix} = \mathbf{0}. \qquad \textbf{(10-15)}$$

This specifies a total of $(M-1)K$ restrictions on the $KM \times 1$ parameter vector. Denote the estimated asymptotic covariance for $(\hat{\beta}_i, \hat{\beta}_j)$ as $\hat{\mathbf{V}}_{ij}$. The bracketed matrix in (10-13) would have typical block

$$[\mathbf{R}\,\widehat{\text{Var}}[\hat{\hat{\beta}}]\mathbf{R}']_{ij} = \hat{\mathbf{V}}_{ij} - \hat{\mathbf{V}}_{iM} - \hat{\mathbf{V}}_{Mj} + \hat{\mathbf{V}}_{MM}$$

This may be a considerable amount of computation. The test will be simpler if the model has been fit by maximum likelihood, as we examine in Section 16.9.3.

### Example 10.3   Hypothesis Tests in the SUR Model
We used (10-14) to construct test statistics for two hypotheses. The "pooling" restriction for the multivariate regression (same variables—not necessarily the same data, as in our example) is formulated as

$$H_0: \quad \beta_1 = \beta_2 = \cdots = \beta_M,$$

$$H_1: \quad \text{Not } H_0.$$

For this hypothesis, the **R** matrix is shown in (10-15). The test statistic is in (10-14). For our model with nine equations and seven parameters in each, the null hypothesis imposes $8(7) = 56$ restrictions. The computed test statistic is 10,554.77, which is far larger than the critical value from the table, 74.468. So, the hypothesis of homogeneity is rejected.

---

[14]See Judge et al. (1985, p. 476). The Wald statistic often performs poorly in the small sample sizes typical in this area. Fiebig (2001, pp. 108–110) surveys a recent literature on methods of improving the power of testing procedures in SUR models.

We also tested the hypothesis of constant returns to scale throughout the system. Constant returns to scale would require that the coefficients on the inputs, $\beta_2$ through $\beta_6$ (four capital variables and the labor variable) sum to 1.0. The $9 \times 9(7)$ matrix, **R**, for (10-14) would have rows equal to

$$R_1 = (0,1,1,1,1,0) \quad \mathbf{0}' \quad \mathbf{0}' \quad \mathbf{0}' \quad \mathbf{0}' \quad \mathbf{0}' \quad \mathbf{0}' \quad \mathbf{0}' \quad \mathbf{0}'$$

$$R_2 = \mathbf{0}' \quad (0,1,1,1,1,0) \quad \mathbf{0}' \quad \mathbf{0}' \quad \mathbf{0}' \quad \mathbf{0}' \quad \mathbf{0}' \quad \mathbf{0}' \quad \mathbf{0}'$$

and so on. In (10-14), we would have $\mathbf{q}' = (1,1,1,1,1,1,1,1,1)$. This hypothesis imposes nine restrictions. The computed chi-squared is 148.418. The critical value is 16.919, so this hypothesis is rejected as well. The discrepancy vector for these results is

$$(\mathbf{R}\hat{\beta} - \mathbf{q})' = (-0.64674, -0.12883, 0.96435, 0.03930, 0.06710, 1.79472, 2.30283, .12907, 1.10534).$$

The distance is quite large for some regions, so the hypothesis of constant returns to scale (to the extent it is meaningful at this level of aggregation) does appear to be inconsistent with the data (results).

### 10.2.5  HETEROSCEDASTICITY

In principle, the SUR model can accommodate heteroscedasticity as well as autocorrelation. Bartels and Fiebig (1992) suggested the generalized SUR model, $\mathbf{\Omega} = \mathbf{A}[\mathbf{\Sigma} \otimes \mathbf{I}]\mathbf{A}'$ where **A** is a block diagonal matrix. Ideally, **A** is made a function of measured characteristics of the individual and a separate parameter vector, $\boldsymbol{\theta}$, so that the model can be estimated in stages. In a first step, OLS residuals could be used to form a preliminary estimator of $\boldsymbol{\theta}$, then the data are transformed to homoscedasticity, leaving $\mathbf{\Sigma}$ and $\boldsymbol{\beta}$ to be estimated at subsequent steps using transformed data. One application along these lines is the random parameters model of Fiebig, Bartels, and Aigner (1991); (9-50) shows how the random parameters model induces heteroscedasticity. Another application is Mandy and Martins-Filho (1993), who specified $\sigma_{ij}(t) = \mathbf{z}_{ij}(t)'\boldsymbol{\alpha}_{ij}$. (The linear specification of a variance does present some problems, as a negative value is not precluded.) Kumbhakar and Heshmati (1996) proposed a cost and demand system that combined the translog model of Section 10.4.2 with the complete equation system in 10.4.1. In their application, only the cost equation was specified to include a heteroscedastic disturbance.

### 10.2.6  AUTOCORRELATION

Autocorrelation in the disturbances of regression models usually arises as a particular feature of the time-series model. It is among the properties of the time series. (We will explore this aspect of the model specification in detail in Chapter 19.) In the multiple equation models examined in this chapter, the time-series properties of the data are usually not the main focus of the investigation. The main advantage of the SUR specification is its treatment of the correlation *across* observations at a particular point in time. Frequently, panel data specifications, such as those in examples 3 and 4 in the Introduction, can also be analyzed in the framework of the SUR model of this chapter. In these cases, there may be persistent effects in the disturbances, but here, again, those effects are often viewed as a consequence of the presence of latent, time invariant heterogeneity. Nonetheless, because the multiple equations models examined in this chapter often do involve moderately long time series, it is appropriate to deal at least somewhat more formally with autocorrelation. Opinions differ on the appropriateness of "corrections" for autocorrelation. At one extreme is Mizon (1995) who argues forcefully that autocorrelation arises as a consequence of a remediable failure to include dynamic effects in the model. However, in a system of equations, the analysis that leads to this conclusion is going to be far more complex than in a single equation model.[15] Suffice to say, the issue remains to be settled conclusively.

### 10.2.7 A SPECIFICATION TEST FOR THE SUR MODEL

It is of interest to assess statistically whether the off diagonal elements of $\Sigma$ are zero. If so, then the efficient estimator for the full parameter vector, absent heteroscedasticity or autocorrelation, is equation by equation ordinary least squares. There is no standard test for the general case of the SUR model unless the additional assumption of normality of the disturbances is imposed in (10-2) and (10-3). With normally distributed disturbances, the standard trio of tests, Wald, **likelihood ratio,** and **Lagrange multiplier,** can be used. For reasons we will turn to shortly, the Wald test is likely to be too cumbersome to apply. With normally distributed disturbances, the likelihood ratio statistic for testing the null hypothesis that the matrix $\Sigma$ in (10-5) is a diagonal matrix against the alternative that $\Sigma$ is simply an unrestricted positive definite matrix would be

$$\lambda_{LR} = T[\ln |\mathbf{S}_0| - \ln |\mathbf{S}_1|], \qquad (10\text{-}16)$$

where $\mathbf{S}_h$ is the residual covariance matrix defined in (10-9) (without a degrees of freedom correction). The residuals are computed using maximum likelihood estimates of the parameters, not FGLS.[16] Under the null hypothesis, the model would be efficiently estimated by individual equation OLS, so

$$\ln |\mathbf{S}_0| = \sum_{i=1}^{M} \ln (\mathbf{e}_i' \mathbf{e}_i / T),$$

where $\mathbf{e}_i = \mathbf{y}_i - \mathbf{X}_i \mathbf{b}_i$. The limiting distribution of the likelihood ratio statistic under the null hypothesis would be chi-squared with $M(M-1)/2$ degrees of freedom.

The likelihood ratio statistic requires the unrestricted MLE to compute the residual covariance matrix under the alternative, so it is can be cumbersome to compute. A simpler alternative is the Lagrange multiplier statistic developed by Breusch and

---

[15] Dynamic SUR models in the spirit of Mizon's admonition were proposed by Anderson and Blundell (1982). A few recent applications are Kiviet, Phillips, and Schipp (1995) and DesChamps (1998). However, relatively little work has been done with dynamic SUR models. The VAR models in Section 20.6 are an important group of applications, but they come from a different analytical framework. Likewise, the panel data applications noted in the Introduction and in Section 9.8.5 would fit into the modeling framework we are developing here. However, in these applications, the regressions are "actually" unrelated—the authors did not model the cross-unit correlation that is the central focus of this chapter. Related results may be found in Guilkey and Schmidt (1973), Guilkey (1974), Berndt and Savin (1977), Moschino and Moro (1994), McLaren (1996), and Holt (1998).

[16] In the SUR model of this chapter, the MLE for normally distributed disturbances can be computed by iterating the FGLS procedure, back and forth between (10-7) and (10-9) until the estimates are no longer changing. We note, this procedure produces the MLE when it converges, but it is not guaranteed to converge, nor is it assured that there is a unique MLE. For our regional data set, the iterated FGLS procedure does not converge after 1,000 iterations. The Oberhofer–Kmenta (1974) result implies that if the iteration converges, it reaches the MLE. It does not guarantee that the iteration will converge, however. The problem with this application may be the very small sample size, 17 observations. One would not normally use the technique of maximum likelihood with a sample this small.

Pagan (1980) which is

$$\lambda_{LM} = T\sum_{i=2}^{M}\sum_{j=1}^{i-1} r_{ij}^2$$

$$= (T/2)[trace(\mathbf{R}'\mathbf{R}) - M],$$

(10-17)

where $\mathbf{R}$ is the sample correlation matrix of the $M$ sets of $T$ OLS residuals. This has the same large sample distribution under the null hypothesis as the likelihood ratio statistic, but is obviously easier to compute, as it only requires the OLS residuals.

### Example 10.4   Testing for Cross-Equation Correlation

We used (10-17) to compute the LM statistic for the 9 equation model reported in Table 10.1. The chi-squared statistic is 215.879 with $9(8)/2 = 36$ degrees of freedom. The critical value is 50.998, so we conclude that the disturbances in the regional model are not actually unrelated. The null hypothesis that $\sigma_{ij} = 0$ for all $i \neq j$ is rejected. To investigate a bit further, we repeated the test with the completely disaggregated (statewide) data. The corresponding chi-squared statistic is 2455.71 with $48(47)/2 = 1,128$ degrees of freedom. The critical value is 1,207.25, so the null hypothesis is rejected at the state level as well.

The third test statistic in the trio is the Wald statistic. In principle, the Wald statistic for the SUR model would be computed using

$$W = \hat{\sigma}'[Asy.\ Var(\hat{\sigma})]^{-1}\hat{\sigma},$$

where $\hat{\sigma}$ is the $M(M-1)/2$ length vector containing the estimates of the off-diagonal (lower triangle) elements of $\Sigma$, and the asymptotic covariance matrix of the estimator appears in the brackets. Under normality, the asymptotic covariance matrix contains the corresponding elements of $2\Sigma \otimes \Sigma/T$. It would be possible to estimate the covariance term more generally using a moment-based estimator. Because

$$\hat{\sigma}_{ij} = \frac{1}{T}\sum_{t=1}^{T} e_{it}e_{jt}$$

is a mean of $T$ observations, one might use the conventional estimator of its variance and its covariance with $\hat{\sigma}_{lm}$, which would be

$$f_{ij,lm} = \frac{1}{T}\frac{1}{T-1}\sum_{t=1}^{T}(e_{it}e_{jt} - \hat{\sigma}_{ij})(e_{lt}e_{mt} - \hat{\sigma}_{lm}).$$

(10-18)

The modified Wald statistic would then be

$$W' = \hat{\sigma}'[\mathbf{F}]^{-1}\hat{\sigma}$$

where the elements of $\mathbf{F}$ are the corresponding values in (10-18). This computation is obviously more complicated than the other two. However, it does have the virtue that it does not require an assumption of normality of the disturbances in the model. What would be required is (a) consistency of the estimators of $\boldsymbol{\beta}_i$ so that the we can assert (b) consistency of the estimators of $\sigma_{ij}$ and, finally, (c) asymptotic normality of the estimators in (b) so that we can apply Theorem 4.5. All three requirements should be met in the SUR model with well behaved regressors.

Alternative approaches that have been suggested [see, e.g., Johnson and Wichern (2005, p. 424)] are based on the following general strategy: Under the alternative hypothesis of an unrestricted $\Sigma$, the sample estimate of $\Sigma$ will be $\hat{\Sigma} = [\hat{\sigma}_{ij}]$ as defined in (10-9). Under any restrictive null hypothesis, the estimator of $\Sigma$ will be $\hat{\Sigma}_0$, a matrix that by construction will be larger than $\hat{\Sigma}_1$ in the matrix sense defined in Appendix A. Statistics based on the "excess variation," such as $T(\hat{\Sigma}_0 - \hat{\Sigma}_1)$ are suggested for the testing procedure. One of these is the likelihood ratio test in (10-16).

### 10.2.8 THE POOLED MODEL

If the variables in $\mathbf{X}_i$ are all the same and the coefficient vectors in (10-2) are assumed all to be equal, the **pooled model**,

$$y_{it} = \mathbf{x}'_{it}\boldsymbol{\beta} + \varepsilon_{it}$$

results. This differs from the panel data treatment in Chapter 9, however, in that the correlation across observations is assumed to occur at time $t$, not within group $i$. (Of course, by a minor rearrangement of the data, the same model results. However, the interpretation differs, so we will maintain the distinction.) Collecting the $T$ observations for group $i$, we obtain

$$\mathbf{y}_i = \mathbf{X}_i\boldsymbol{\beta} + \boldsymbol{\varepsilon}_i$$

or, for all $n$ groups,

$$\begin{bmatrix} \mathbf{y}_1 \\ \mathbf{y}_2 \\ \vdots \\ \mathbf{y}_n \end{bmatrix} = \begin{bmatrix} \mathbf{X}_1 \\ \mathbf{X}_2 \\ \vdots \\ \mathbf{X}_n \end{bmatrix}\boldsymbol{\beta} + \begin{bmatrix} \boldsymbol{\varepsilon}_1 \\ \boldsymbol{\varepsilon}_2 \\ \vdots \\ \boldsymbol{\varepsilon}_n \end{bmatrix} = \mathbf{X}\boldsymbol{\beta} + \boldsymbol{\varepsilon}, \tag{10-19}$$

where

$$E[\boldsymbol{\varepsilon}_i \mid \mathbf{X}] = \mathbf{0},$$
$$E[\boldsymbol{\varepsilon}_i\boldsymbol{\varepsilon}'_j \mid \mathbf{X}] = \sigma_{ij}\boldsymbol{\Omega}_{ij}. \tag{10-20}$$

If $\boldsymbol{\Omega}_{ij} = \mathbf{I}$, then this is equivalent to the SUR model of (10-2) with identical coefficient vectors. The generalized least squares estimator under this **covariance structures model** assumption is

$$\hat{\boldsymbol{\beta}} = [\mathbf{X}'(\boldsymbol{\Sigma} \otimes \mathbf{I})^{-1}\mathbf{X}]^{-1}[\mathbf{X}'(\boldsymbol{\Sigma} \otimes \mathbf{I})^{-1}\mathbf{y}]$$

$$= \left[\sum_{i=1}^{n}\sum_{j=1}^{n}\sigma^{ij}\mathbf{X}'_i\mathbf{X}_j\right]^{-1}\left[\sum_{i=1}^{n}\sum_{j=1}^{n}\sigma^{ij}\mathbf{X}'_i\mathbf{y}_j\right]. \tag{10-21}$$

where $\sigma^{ij}$ denotes the $ij$th element of $\boldsymbol{\Sigma}^{-1}$. The FGLS estimator can be computed using (10-9), where $\mathbf{e}_i$ can either be computed using group-specific OLS residuals or it can be a subvector of the pooled OLS residual vector using all $nT$ observations.

There is an important consideration to note in feasible GLS estimation of this model. The computation requires inversion of the matrix $\hat{\boldsymbol{\Sigma}}$ where the $ij$th element is given by (10-9). This matrix is $n \times n$. It is computed from the least squares residuals using

$$\hat{\boldsymbol{\Sigma}} = \frac{1}{T}\sum_{t=1}^{T}\mathbf{e}_t\mathbf{e}'_t = \frac{1}{T}\mathbf{E}'\mathbf{E},$$

where $\mathbf{e}'_t$ is a $1 \times n$ vector containing all $n$ residuals for the $n$ groups at time $t$, placed as the $t$th row of the $T \times n$ matrix of residuals, $\mathbf{E}$. The rank of this matrix cannot be larger than $T$. Note what happens if $n > T$. In this case, the $n \times n$ matrix has rank $T$, which is less than $n$, so it must be singular, and the FGLS estimator cannot be computed. Consider Example 10.2. We aggregated the 48 states into $n = 9$ regions. It would not be possible to fit a full model for the $n = 48$ states with only $T = 17$ observations. This result is a deficiency of the data set, not the model. The population matrix, $\Sigma$ is positive definite. But, if there are not enough observations, then the data set is too short to obtain a positive definite estimate of the matrix.

## 10.3 PANEL DATA APPLICATIONS

Extensions of the SUR model to panel data applications have been made in two directions. Several studies have layered the familiar random effects treatment of Section 9.5 on top of the generalized regression. An alternative treatment of the fixed and random effects models as a form of seemingly unrelated regressions model suggested by Chamberlain (1982, 1984) has provided some of the foundation of recent treatments of dynamic panel data models.

### 10.3.1 RANDOM EFFECTS SUR MODELS

Avery (1977) suggested a natural extension of the random effects model to multiple equations,

$$y_{it,j} = \mathbf{x}'_{it,j}\boldsymbol{\beta}_j + \varepsilon_{it,j} + u_{i,j}$$

where $j$ indexes the equation, $i$ indexes individuals, and $t$ is the time index as before. Each equation can be treated as a random effects model. In this instance, however, the efficient estimator when the equations are *actually* unrelated (that is, $\text{Cov}[\varepsilon_{it,m}, \varepsilon_{it,l} \mid \mathbf{X}] = 0$ and $\text{Cov}[u_{i,m}, u_{i,l} \mid \mathbf{X}] = 0$) is equation by equation GLS as developed in Section 9.5, not OLS. That is, without the cross-equation correlation, each equation constitutes a random effects model. The cross-equation correlation takes the form

$$E[\varepsilon_{it,j}\varepsilon_{it,l} \mid \mathbf{X}] = \sigma_{jl}$$

and

$$E[u_{i,j}u_{i,l} \mid \mathbf{X}] = \theta_{jl}.$$

Observations remain uncorrelated across individuals, $(\varepsilon_{it,j}, \varepsilon_{rs,l})$ and $(u_{ij}, u_{r,l})$ when $i \neq r$. The "noise" terms, $\varepsilon_{it,j}$ are also uncorrelated across time for all individuals and across individuals. Correlation over time arises through the influence of the common effect, which produces persistent random effects for the given individual, both within the equation and across equations through $\theta_{jl}$. Avery developed a two-step estimator for the model. At the first step, as usual, estimates of the variance components are based on OLS residuals. The second step is FGLS. Subsequent studies have added features to the model. Magnus (1982) derived the log likelihood function for normally distributed disturbances, the likelihood equations for the MLE, and a method of estimation. Verbon (1980) added heteroscedasticity to the model.

There have also been a handful of applications, including Howrey and Varian's (1984) analysis of electricity pricing and the impact of time of day rates, Brown et al.'s

(1983) treatment of a form of the capital asset pricing model (CAPM), Sickles's (1985) analysis of airline costs, and Wan et al.'s (1992) development of a nonlinear panel data SUR model for agricultural output.

### Example 10.5  Demand for Electricity and Gas

Beierlein, Dunn, and McConnon (1981) proposed a dynamic panel data SUR model for demand for electricity and natural gas in the northeastern U.S. The central equation of the model is

$$\ln Q_{it,j} = \beta_0 + \beta_1 \ln P\_natural\ gas_{it,j} + \beta_2 \ln P\_electricity_{it,j} + \beta_3 \ln P\_fuel\ oil_{it,j}$$
$$ + \beta_4 \ln per\ capita\ income_{it,j} + \beta_5 \ln Q_{i,t-1,j} + w_{it,j}$$
$$w_{it,j} = \varepsilon_{it,j} + u_{i,j} + v_{t,j}$$

where

$j$ = consuming sectors (natural gas, electricity) × (residential, comercial, industrial)

$i$ = state (New England plus New York, New Jersey, Pennsylvania)

$t$ = year, 1957,...,1977.

Note that this model has both time and state random effects and a lagged dependent variable in each equation.

### 10.3.2  THE RANDOM AND FIXED EFFECTS MODELS

The linear unobserved effects model is

$$y_{it} = c_i + \mathbf{x}'_{it}\boldsymbol{\beta} + \varepsilon_{it}. \tag{10-22}$$

The **random effects** model assumes that $E[c_i \mid \mathbf{X}_i] = \alpha$, where the $T$ rows of $\mathbf{X}_i$ are $\mathbf{x}'_{it}$. As we saw in Section 9.5, this model can be estimated consistently by ordinary least squares. Regardless of how $\varepsilon_{it}$ is modeled, there is autocorrelation induced by the common, unobserved $c_i$, so the generalized regression model applies. The random effects formulation is based on the assumption $E[\mathbf{w}_i\mathbf{w}'_i \mid \mathbf{X}_i] = \sigma_\varepsilon^2\mathbf{I}_T + \sigma_u^2\mathbf{ii}'$, where $w_{it} = (\varepsilon_{it} + u_i)$. We developed the GLS and FGLS estimators for this formulation as well as a strategy for robust estimation of the OLS covariance matrix. Among the implications of the development of Section 10.2.8 is that this formulation of the disturbance covariance matrix is more restrictive than necessary, given the information contained in the data. The assumption that $E[\boldsymbol{\varepsilon}_i\boldsymbol{\varepsilon}'_i \mid \mathbf{X}_i] = \sigma_\varepsilon^2\mathbf{I}_T$ assumes that the correlation across periods is equal for all pairs of observations, and arises solely through the persistent $c_i$. In Section 10.2.8, we estimated the equivalent model with an unrestricted covariance matrix, $E[\boldsymbol{\varepsilon}_i\boldsymbol{\varepsilon}'_i \mid \mathbf{X}_i] = \boldsymbol{\Sigma}$. The implication is that the random effects treatment includes two restrictive assumptions, mean independence, $E[c_i \mid \mathbf{X}_i] = \alpha$, and homoscedasticity, $E[\boldsymbol{\varepsilon}_i\boldsymbol{\varepsilon}'_i \mid \mathbf{X}_i] = \sigma_\varepsilon^2\mathbf{I}_T$. [We do note, dropping the second assumption will cost us the identification of $\sigma_u^2$ as an estimable parameter. This makes sense—if the correlation across periods $t$ and $s$ can arise from either their common $u_i$ or from correlation of $(\varepsilon_{it}, \varepsilon_{is})$ then there is no way for us separately to estimate a variance for $u_i$ apart from the covariances of $\varepsilon_{it}$ and $\varepsilon_{is}$.] It is useful to note, however, that the panel data model can be viewed and formulated as a seemingly unrelated regressions model with common coefficients in which each period constitutes an equation, Indeed, it is possible, aibeit unnecessary, to impose the restriction $E[\mathbf{w}_i\mathbf{w}'_i \mid \mathbf{X}_i] = \sigma_\varepsilon^2\mathbf{I}_T + \sigma_u^2\mathbf{ii}'$.

The mean independence assumption is the major shortcoming of the **random effects model.** The central feature of the fixed effects model in Section 9.4 is the possibility that $E[c_i \mid \mathbf{X}_i]$ is a nonconstant $g(\mathbf{X}_i)$. As such, least squares regression of $y_{it}$ on $\mathbf{x}_{it}$ produces an inconsistent estimator of $\boldsymbol{\beta}$. The dummy variable model considered in Section 9.4 is the natural alternative. The **fixed effects** approach has the advantage of dispensing with the unlikely assumption that $c_i$ and $\mathbf{x}_{it}$ are uncorrelated. However, it has the shortcoming of requiring estimation of the $n$ "parameters," $\alpha_i$.

Chamberlain (1982, 1984) and Mundlak (1978) suggested alternative approaches that lie between these two. Their modifications of the fixed effects model augment it with the **projections** of $c_i$ on all the rows of $\mathbf{X}_i$ (Chamberlain) or the group means (Mundlak). (See Sections 4.2.2 and 9.5.5.) Consider the first of these, and assume (as it requires) a **balanced panel** of $T$ observations per group. For purposes of this development, we will assume $T = 3$. The generalization will be obvious at the conclusion. Then, the projection suggested by Chamberlain is

$$c_i = \alpha + \mathbf{x}'_{i1}\boldsymbol{\gamma}_1 + \mathbf{x}'_{i2}\boldsymbol{\gamma}_2 + \mathbf{x}'_{i3}\boldsymbol{\gamma}_3 + r_i \tag{10-23}$$

where now, by construction, $r_i$ is orthogonal to $\mathbf{x}_{it}$.[17] Insert (10-23) into (10-22) to obtain

$$y_{it} = \alpha + \mathbf{x}'_{i1}\boldsymbol{\gamma}_1 + \mathbf{x}'_{i2}\boldsymbol{\gamma}_2 + \mathbf{x}'_{i3}\boldsymbol{\gamma}_3 + \mathbf{x}'_{it}\boldsymbol{\beta} + \varepsilon_{it} + r_i.$$

Estimation of the $1 + 3K + K$ parameters of this model presents a number of complications. [We do note, this approach has the potential to (wildly) proliferate parameters. For our quite small regional productivity model in Example 10.2, the original model with six main coefficients plus the treatment of the constants becomes a model with $1 + 6 + 17(6) = 109$ parameters to be estimated.]

If only the $n$ observations for period 1 are used, then the parameter vector,

$$\boldsymbol{\theta}_1 = \alpha, (\boldsymbol{\beta} + \boldsymbol{\gamma}_1), \boldsymbol{\gamma}_2, \boldsymbol{\gamma}_3 = \alpha, \boldsymbol{\pi}_1, \boldsymbol{\gamma}_2, \boldsymbol{\gamma}_3, \tag{10-24}$$

can be estimated consistently, albeit inefficiently, by ordinary least squares. The "model" is

$$y_{i1} = \mathbf{z}'_{i1}\boldsymbol{\theta}_1 + w_{i1}, \ i = 1, \dots, n.$$

Collecting the $n$ observations, we have

$$\mathbf{y}_1 = \mathbf{Z}_1\boldsymbol{\theta}_1 + \mathbf{w}_1.$$

If, instead, only the $n$ observations from period 2 or period 3 are used, then OLS estimates, in turn,

$$\boldsymbol{\theta}_2 = \alpha, \boldsymbol{\gamma}_1, (\boldsymbol{\beta} + \boldsymbol{\gamma}_2), \boldsymbol{\gamma}_3 = \alpha, \boldsymbol{\gamma}_1, \boldsymbol{\pi}_2, \boldsymbol{\gamma}_3,$$

or

$$\boldsymbol{\theta}_3 = \alpha, \boldsymbol{\gamma}_1, \boldsymbol{\gamma}_2, (\boldsymbol{\beta} + \boldsymbol{\gamma}_3) = \alpha, \boldsymbol{\gamma}_1, \boldsymbol{\gamma}_2, \boldsymbol{\pi}_3.$$

---

[17]There are some fine points here that can only be resolved theoretically. If the projection in (10-23) is not the conditional mean, then we have $E[r_i \times \mathbf{x}_{it}] = 0, t = 1, \dots, T$ but not $E[r_i \mid \mathbf{X}_i] = 0$. This does not affect the asymptotic properties of the FGLS estimator to be developed here, although it does have implications, e.g., for unbiasedness. Consistency will hold regardless. The assumptions behind (10-23) do not include that $\text{Var}[r_i \mid \mathbf{X}_i]$ is homoscedastic. It might not be. This *could* be investigated empirically. The implication here concerns efficiency, not consistency. The FGLS estimator to be developed here would remain consistent, but a GMM estimator would be more efficient—see Chapter 15. Moreover, without homoscedasticity, it is not certain that the FGLS estimator suggested here is more efficient than OLS (with a robust covariance matrix estimator). Our intent is to begin the investigation here. Further details can be found in Chamberlain (1984) and, e.g., Im, Ahn, Schmidt, and Wooldridge (1999).

It remains to reconcile the multiple estimates of the same parameter vectors. In terms of the preceding layouts above, we have the following:

OLS Estimates: $\quad a_1, \mathbf{p}_1, \mathbf{c}_{2,1}, \mathbf{c}_{3,1}, \qquad a_2\, \mathbf{c}_{1,2}, \mathbf{p}_2, \mathbf{c}_{3,2}, \qquad a_3, \mathbf{c}_{1,3}, \mathbf{c}_{2,3}, \mathbf{p}_3;$
Estimated Parameters: $\alpha, (\beta + \gamma_1), \gamma_2, \gamma_3, \quad \alpha, \gamma_1, (\beta + \gamma_2), \gamma_3, \quad \alpha, \gamma_1, \gamma_2, (\beta + \gamma_3);$
Structural Parameters: $\alpha, \beta, \gamma_1, \gamma_2, \gamma_3.$

$$(10\text{-}25)$$

Chamberlain suggested a minimum distance estimator (MDE). For this problem, the MDE is essentially a weighted average of the several estimators of each part of the parameter vector. We will examine the MDE for this application in more detail in Chapter 15. (For another simpler application of minimum distance estimation that shows the "weighting" procedure at work, see the reconciliation of four competing estimators of a single parameter at the end of Example 9.15.) There is an alternative way to formulate the estimator that is a bit more transparent. For the first period,

$$\mathbf{y}_1 = \begin{pmatrix} y_{1,1} \\ y_{2,1} \\ \vdots \\ y_{n,1} \end{pmatrix} = \begin{bmatrix} 1 & \mathbf{x}_{1,1} & \mathbf{x}_{1,1} & \mathbf{x}_{1,2} & \mathbf{x}_{1,3} \\ 1 & \mathbf{x}_{2,2} & \mathbf{x}_{2,1} & \mathbf{x}_{2,2} & \mathbf{x}_{2,3} \\ \vdots & \vdots & \vdots & \vdots & \vdots \\ 1 & \mathbf{x}_{n,1} & \mathbf{x}_{n,1} & \mathbf{x}_{n,1} & \mathbf{x}_{n,1} \end{bmatrix} \begin{pmatrix} \alpha \\ \beta \\ \gamma_1 \\ \gamma_2 \\ \gamma_3 \end{pmatrix} + \begin{pmatrix} r_{1,1} \\ r_{2,1} \\ \vdots \\ r_{n,1} \end{pmatrix} = \tilde{\mathbf{X}}_1\theta + \mathbf{r}_1. \qquad (10\text{-}26)$$

We treat this as the first equation in a $T$ equation seemingly unrelated regressions model. The second equation, for period 2, is the same (same coefficients), with the data from the second period appearing in the blocks, then likewise for period 3 (and periods $4, \ldots, T$ in the general case). Stacking the data for the $T$ equations (periods), we have

$$\begin{pmatrix} \mathbf{y}_1 \\ \mathbf{y}_2 \\ \vdots \\ \mathbf{y}_T \end{pmatrix} = \begin{pmatrix} \tilde{\mathbf{X}}_1 \\ \tilde{\mathbf{X}}_2 \\ \vdots \\ \tilde{\mathbf{X}}_T \end{pmatrix} \begin{pmatrix} \alpha \\ \beta \\ \gamma_1 \\ \vdots \\ \gamma_T \end{pmatrix} + \begin{pmatrix} \mathbf{r}_1 \\ \mathbf{r}_2 \\ \vdots \\ \mathbf{r}_T \end{pmatrix} = \tilde{\mathbf{X}}\theta + \mathbf{r}, \qquad (10\text{-}27)$$

where $E[\tilde{\mathbf{X}}'\mathbf{r}] = \mathbf{0}$ and (by assumption), $E[\mathbf{rr}' \mid \tilde{\mathbf{X}}] = \Sigma \otimes \mathbf{I}_n$. With the homoscedasticity assumption for $r_{i,t}$, this is precisely the application in Section 10.2.8. The parameters can be estimated by FGLS as shown in Section 10.2.8.

### Example 10.6 Hospital Costs
Carey (1997) examined hospital costs for a sample of 1,733 hospitals observed in five years, 1987–1991. The model estimated is

$$\begin{aligned}
\ln(TC/P)_{it} = {}& \alpha_i + \beta_D\, DIS_{it} + \beta_O\, OPV_{it} + \beta_3\, ALS_{it} + \beta_4\, CM_{it} \\
& + \beta_5\, DIS_{it}^2 + \beta_6\, DIS_{it}^3 + \beta_7\, OPV_{it}^2 + \beta_8\, OPV_{it}^3 \\
& + \beta_9\, ALS_{it}^2 + \beta_{10}\, ALS_{it}^3 + \beta_{11}\, DIS_{it} \times OPV_{it} \\
& + \beta_{12}\, FA_{it} + \beta_{13}\, HI_{it} + \beta_{14}\, HT_i + \beta_{15}\, LT_i + \beta_{16}\, Large_i \\
& + \beta_{17}\, Small_i + \beta_{18}\, NonProfit_i + \beta_{19}\, Profit_i \\
& + \varepsilon_{it},
\end{aligned}$$

where

|         |                                                           |
|---------|-----------------------------------------------------------|
| TC      | = total cost,                                             |
| P       | = input price index,                                     |
| DIS     | = discharges,                                            |
| OPV     | = outpatient visits,                                     |
| ALS     | = average length of stay,                                |
| CM      | = case mix index,                                        |
| FA      | = fixed assets,                                          |
| HI      | = Hirfindahl index of market concentration at county level, |
| HT      | = dummy for high teaching load hospital,                 |
| LT      | = dummy variable for low teaching load hospital,         |
| Large   | = dummy variable for large urban area,                   |
| Small   | = dummy variable for small urban area,                   |
| Nonprofit | = dummy variable for nonprofit hospital,               |
| Profit  | = dummy variable for for profit hospital.                |

We have used subscripts "D" and "O" for the coefficients on DIS and OPV as these will be isolated in the following discussion. The model employed in the study is that in (10-22) and (10-23). Initial OLS estimates are obtained for the full cost function in each year. SUR estimates are then obtained using a restricted version of the Chamberlain system. This second step involved a hybrid model that modified (10-24) so that in each period the coefficient vector was

$$\boldsymbol{\theta}_t = [\alpha_t, \beta_{Dt}(\boldsymbol{\gamma}), \beta_{Ot}(\boldsymbol{\gamma}), \beta_{3t}(\boldsymbol{\gamma}), \beta_{4t}(\boldsymbol{\gamma}), \beta_{5t}, \ldots, \beta_{19t}]$$

where $\beta_{Dt}(\boldsymbol{\gamma})$ indicates that all five years of the variable $(DIS_{it})$ are included in the equation and, likewise for $\beta_{Ot}(\boldsymbol{\gamma})(OPV)$, $\beta_{3t}(\boldsymbol{\gamma})(ALS)$ and $\beta_{4t}(\boldsymbol{\gamma})(CM)$. This is equivalent to using

$$c_i = \alpha + \Sigma_{t=1987}^{1991}(DIS, OPV, ALS, CM)'_{it}\boldsymbol{\gamma}_t + r_i$$

in (10-23).

The unrestricted SUR system estimated at the second step provides multiple estimates of the various model parameters. For example, each of the five equations provides an estimate of $(\beta_5, \ldots, \beta_{19})$. The author added one more layer to the model in allowing the coefficients on $DIS_{it}$ and $OPV_{it}$ to vary over time. Therefore, the structural parameters of interest are $(\beta_{D1}, \ldots, \beta_{D5}), (\gamma_{D1} \ldots, \gamma_{D5})$ (the coefficients on DIS) and $(\beta_{O1}, \ldots, \beta_{O5}), (\gamma_{O1} \ldots, \gamma_{O5})$ (the coefficients on OPV). There are, altogether, 20 parameters of interest. The SUR estimates produce, in each year (equation), parameters on DIS for the five years and on OPV for the five years, so there are a total of 50 estimates. Reconciling all of them means imposing a total of 30 restrictions. Table 10.2 shows the relationships for the time varying parameter on $DIS_{it}$ in the five-equation model. The numerical values reported by the author are shown following the theoretical results. A similar table would apply for the coefficients on OPV, ALS, and CM. (In the latter two, the $\beta$ coefficient was not assumed to be time varying.) It can be seen in the table, for example, that there are directly four different estimates of $\gamma_{D,87}$ in the second to fifth equations, and likewise for each of the other parameters. Combining the entries in Table 10.2 with the counterpart for the coefficients on OPV, we see 50 SUR/FGLS estimates to be used to estimate 20 underlying parameters. The author used a minimum distance approach to reconcile the different estimates. We will return to this example in Chapter 15, where we will develop the MDE in more detail.

**TABLE 10.2**   Coefficient Estimates in SUR Model for Hospital Costs

| Equation | Coefficient on Variable in the Equation | | | | |
|---|---|---|---|---|---|
| | DIS87 | DIS88 | DIS89 | DIS90 | DIS91 |
| SUR87 | $\beta_{D,87} + \gamma_{D,87}$ <br> 1.76 | $\gamma_{D,88}$ <br> 0.116 | $\gamma_{D,89}$ <br> $-0.0881$ | $\gamma_{D,90}$ <br> 0.0570 | $\gamma_{D,91}$ <br> $-0.0617$ |
| SUR88 | $\gamma_{D,87}$ <br> 0.254 | $\beta_{D,88} + \gamma_{D,88}$ <br> 1.61 | $\gamma_{D,89}$ <br> $-0.0934$ | $\gamma_{D,90}$ <br> 0.0610 | $\gamma_{D,91}$ <br> $-0.0514$ |
| SUR89 | $\gamma_{D,87}$ <br> 0.217 | $\gamma_{D,88}$ <br> 0.0846 | $\beta_{D,89} + \gamma_{D,89}$ <br> 1.51 | $\gamma_{D,90}$ <br> 0.0454 | $\gamma_{D,91}$ <br> $-0.0253$ |
| SUR90 | $\gamma_{D,87}$ <br> 0.179 | $\gamma_{D,88}$ <br> 0.0822[a] | $\gamma_{D,89}$ <br> 0.0295 | $\beta_{D,90} + \gamma_{D,90}$ <br> 1.57 | $\gamma_{D,91}$ <br> 0.0244 |
| SUR91 | $\gamma_{D,87}$ <br> 0.153 | $\gamma_{D,88}$ <br> 0.0363 | $\gamma_{D,89}$ <br> $-0.0422$ | $\gamma_{D,90}$ <br> 0.0813 | $\beta_{D,91} + \gamma_{D,91}$ <br> 1.70 |

[a]The value reported in the published paper is 8.22. The correct value is 0.0822. (Personal communication from the author.)

## 10.4 SYSTEMS OF DEMAND EQUATIONS: SINGULAR SYSTEMS

Most of the recent applications of the multivariate regression model[18] have been in the context of **systems of demand equations,** either commodity demands or factor demands in studies of production.

### Example 10.7   Stone's Expenditure System
Stone's expenditure system[19] based on a set of logarithmic commodity demand equations, income $Y$, and commodity prices $p_n$ is

$$\log q_i = \alpha_i + \eta_i \log \left( \frac{Y}{P} \right) + \sum_{j=1}^{M} \eta_{ij}^* \log \left( \frac{p_j}{P} \right),$$

where $P$ is a generalized (share-weighted) price index, $\eta_i$ is an income elasticity, and $\eta_{ij}^*$ is a compensated price elasticity. We can interpret this system as the demand equation in real expenditure and real prices. The resulting set of equations constitutes an econometric model in the form of a set of seemingly unrelated regressions. In estimation, we must account for a number of restrictions including homogeneity of degree one in income, $\Sigma_i S_i \eta_i = 1$, and symmetry of the matrix of compensated price elasticities, $\eta_{ij}^* = \eta_{ji}^*$, where $S_i$ is the budget share for good $i$.

Other examples include the system of factor demands and factor cost shares from production, which we shall consider again later. In principle, each is merely a particular application of the model of the Section 10.2. But some special problems arise in these settings. First, the parameters of the systems are generally constrained across equations. That is, the unconstrained model is inconsistent with the underlying

---

[18]Note the distinction between the multi*variate* or multiple-equation model discussed here and the *multiple* regression model.

[19]A very readable survey of the estimation of systems of commodity demands is Deaton and Muellbauer (1980). The example discussed here is taken from their Chapter 3 and the references to Stone's (1954a,b) work cited therein. Deaton (1986) is another useful survey. A counterpart for production function modeling is Chambers (1988). More recent developments in the specification of systems of demand equations include Chavez and Segerson (1987), Brown and Walker (1995), and Fry, Fry, and McLaren (1996).

theory.[20] The numerous constraints in the system of demand equations presented earlier give an example. A second intrinsic feature of many of these models is that the disturbance covariance matrix $\mathbf{\Sigma}$ is singular.[21]

### 10.4.1 COBB–DOUGLAS COST FUNCTION (EXAMPLE 6.3 CONTINUED)

Consider a **Cobb–Douglas** production function,

$$Q = \alpha_0 \prod_{i=1}^{M} x_i^{\alpha_i}.$$

Profit maximization with an exogenously determined output price calls for the firm to maximize output for a given cost level $C$ (or minimize costs for a given output $Q$). The Lagrangean for the maximization problem is

$$\Lambda = \alpha_0 \prod_{i=1}^{M} x_i^{\alpha_i} + \lambda(C - \mathbf{p}'\mathbf{x}),$$

where $\mathbf{p}$ is the vector of $M$ factor prices. The necessary conditions for maximizing this function are

$$\frac{\partial \Lambda}{\partial x_i} = \frac{\alpha_i Q}{x_i} - \lambda p_i = 0 \quad \text{and} \quad \frac{\partial \Lambda}{\partial \lambda} = C - \mathbf{p}'\mathbf{x} = 0.$$

The joint solution provides $x_i(Q, \mathbf{p})$ and $\lambda(Q, \mathbf{p})$. The total cost of production is

$$\sum_{i=1}^{M} p_i x_i = \sum_{i=1}^{M} \frac{\alpha_i Q}{\lambda}.$$

The cost share allocated to the $i$th factor is

$$\frac{p_i x_i}{\sum_{i=1}^{M} p_i x_i} = \frac{\alpha_i}{\sum_{i=1}^{M} \alpha_i} = \beta_i. \tag{10-28}$$

The full model is[22]

$$\ln C = \beta_0 + \beta_q \ln Q + \sum_{i=1}^{M} \beta_i \ln p_i + \varepsilon_c, \tag{10-29}$$

$$s_i = \beta_i + \varepsilon_i, \quad i = 1, \ldots, M.$$

---

[20]This inconsistency does not imply that the theoretical restrictions are not testable or that the unrestricted model cannot be estimated. Sometimes, the meaning of the model is ambiguous without the restrictions, however. Statistically rejecting the restrictions implied by the theory, which were used to derive the econometric model in the first place, can put us in a rather uncomfortable position. For example, in a study of utility functions, Christensen, Jorgenson, and Lau (1975), after rejecting the cross-equation symmetry of a set of commodity demands, stated, "With this conclusion we can terminate the test sequence, since these results invalidate the theory of demand" (p. 380). See Silver and Ali (1989) for discussion of testing symmetry restrictions. The theory and the model may also conflict in other ways. For example, Stone's loglinear expenditure system in Example 10.7 does not conform to any theoretically valid utility function. See Goldberger (1987).

[21]Denton (1978) examines several of these cases.

[22]We leave as an exercise the derivation of $\beta_0$, which is a mixture of all the parameters, and $\beta_q$, which equals $1/\Sigma_m \alpha_m$.

By construction, $\sum_{i=1}^{M} \beta_i = 1$ and $\sum_{i=1}^{M} s_i = 1$. (This is the cost function analysis begun in Example 6.3. We will return to that application below.) The cost shares will also sum identically to one in the data. It therefore follows that $\sum_{i=1}^{M} \varepsilon_i = 0$ at every data point, so the system is singular. For the moment, ignore the cost function. Let the $M \times 1$ disturbance vector from the shares be $\boldsymbol{\varepsilon} = [\varepsilon_1, \varepsilon_2, \ldots, \varepsilon_M]'$. Because $\boldsymbol{\varepsilon}'\mathbf{i} = 0$, where $\mathbf{i}$ is a column of 1s, it follows that $E[\boldsymbol{\varepsilon}\boldsymbol{\varepsilon}'\mathbf{i}] = \boldsymbol{\Sigma}\mathbf{i} = \mathbf{0}$, which implies that $\boldsymbol{\Sigma}$ is singular. Therefore, the methods of the previous sections cannot be used here. (You should verify that the *sample* covariance matrix of the OLS residuals will also be singular.)

The solution to the singularity problem appears to be to drop one of the equations, estimate the remainder, and solve for the last parameter from the other $M - 1$. The constraint $\sum_{i=1}^{M} \beta_i = 1$ states that the cost function must be homogeneous of degree one in the prices, a theoretical necessity. If we impose the constraint

$$\beta_M = 1 - \beta_1 - \beta_2 - \cdots - \beta_{M-1}, \tag{10-30}$$

then the system is reduced to a nonsingular one:

$$\ln\left(\frac{C}{p_M}\right) = \beta_0 + \beta_q \ln Q + \sum_{i=1}^{M-1} \beta_i \ln\left(\frac{p_i}{p_M}\right) + \varepsilon_c,$$

$$s_i = \beta_i + \varepsilon_i, \quad i = 1, \ldots, M - 1.$$

This system provides estimates of $\beta_0$, $\beta_q$, and $\beta_1, \ldots, \beta_{M-1}$. The last parameter is estimated using (10-30). It is immaterial which factor is chosen as the numeraire. Both FGLS and **maximum likelihood,** which can be obtained by iterating FGLS or by direct maximum likelihood estimation, are **invariant** to which factor is chosen as the numeraire.[23]

Nerlove's (1963) study of the electric power industry that we examined in Example 6.3 provides an application of the Cobb–Douglas cost function model. His ordinary least squares estimates of the parameters were listed in Example 6.3. Among the results are (unfortunately) a negative capital coefficient in three of the six regressions. Nerlove also found that the simple Cobb–Douglas model did not adequately account for the relationship between output and average cost. Christensen and Greene (1976) further analyzed the Nerlove data and augmented the data set with cost share data to estimate the complete **demand system.** Appendix Table F10.1 lists Nerlove's 145 observations with Christensen and Greene's cost share data. Cost is the total cost of generation in millions of dollars, output is in millions of kilowatt-hours, the capital price is an index of construction costs, the wage rate is in dollars per hour for production and maintenance, the fuel price is an index of the cost per Btu of fuel purchased by the firms, and the data reflect the 1955 costs of production. The regression estimates are given in Table 10.3.

Least squares estimates of the Cobb–Douglas cost function are given in the first column.[24] The coefficient on capital is negative. Because $\beta_i = \beta_q \partial \ln Q / \partial \ln x_i$—that is, a positive multiple of the output elasticity of the $i$th factor—this finding is troubling.

---

[23]The invariance result is proved in Barten (1969). Some additional results on the method are given by Revankar (1976), Deaton (1986), Powell (1969), and McGuire et al. (1968).

[24]Results based on Nerlove's full data set are given in Example 6.3. We have recomputed the values given in Table 10.5. Note that Nerlove used base 10 logs while we have used natural logs in our computations.

**TABLE 10.3**   Regression Estimates (standard errors in parentheses)

| | *Ordinary Least Squares* | | | | *Multivariate Regression* | | | |
|---|---|---|---|---|---|---|---|---|
| $\beta_0$ | −4.686 | (0.885) | −3.764 | (0.702) | −7.069 | (0.107) | −5.707 | (0.165) |
| $\beta_q$ | 0.721 | (0.0174) | 0.153 | (0.0618) | 0.766 | (0.0154) | 0.238 | (0.0587) |
| $\beta_{qq}$ | — | | 0.0505 | (0.00536) | — | | 0.0451 | (0.00508) |
| $\beta_k$ | −0.00847 | (0.191) | 0.0739 | (0.150) | 0.424 | (0.00946) | 0.424 | (0.00944) |
| $\beta_l$ | 0.594 | (0.205) | 0.481 | (0.161) | 0.106 | (0.00386) | 0.106 | (0.00382) |
| $\beta_f$ | 0.414 | (0.0989) | 0.445 | (0.0777) | 0.470 | (0.0101) | 0.470 | (0.0100) |
| $R^2$ | 0.9316 | | 0.9581 | | — | | — | |
| | — | | — | | | | | |

The third column presents the constrained FGLS estimates. To obtain the constrained estimator, we set up the model in the form of the pooled SUR estimator in (10-19);

$$
\mathbf{y} = \begin{bmatrix} \ln(C/P_f) \\ s_k \\ s_l \end{bmatrix} = \begin{bmatrix} \mathbf{i} & \ln\mathbf{Q} & \ln(\mathbf{P}_k/\mathbf{P}_f) & \ln(\mathbf{P}_l/\mathbf{P}_f) \\ \mathbf{0} & \mathbf{0} & \mathbf{i} & \mathbf{0} \\ \mathbf{0} & \mathbf{0} & \mathbf{0} & \mathbf{i} \end{bmatrix} \begin{pmatrix} \beta_0 \\ \beta_q \\ \beta_k \\ \beta_l \end{pmatrix} + \begin{bmatrix} \boldsymbol{\varepsilon}_c \\ \boldsymbol{\varepsilon}_k \\ \boldsymbol{\varepsilon}_l \end{bmatrix}
$$

[There are 3(145) = 435 observations in the data matrices.] The estimator is then FGLS as shown in (10-21). An additional column is added for the log quadratic model. Two things to note are the dramatically smaller standard errors and the now positive (and reasonable) estimate of the capital coefficient. The estimates of economies of scale in the basic Cobb–Douglas model are $1/\beta_q = 1.39$ (column 1) and 1.31 (column 3), which suggest some increasing returns to scale. Nerlove, however, had found evidence that at extremely large firm sizes, economies of scale diminished and eventually disappeared. To account for this (essentially a classical U-shaped average cost curve), he appended a quadratic term in log output in the cost function. The single equation and multivariate regression estimates are given in the second and fourth sets of results.

The quadratic output term gives the cost function the expected U-shape. We can determine the point where average cost reaches its minimum by equating $\partial \ln C / \partial \ln Q$ to 1. This is $Q^* = \exp[(1 - \beta_q)/(2\beta_{qq})]$. For the multivariate regression, this value is $Q^* = 4665$. About 85 percent of the firms in the sample had output less than this, so by these estimates, most firms in the sample had not yet exhausted the available economies of scale. Figure 10.1 shows predicted and actual average costs for the sample. (To obtain a reasonable scale, the smallest one third of the firms are omitted from the figure.) Predicted average costs are computed at the sample averages of the input prices. The figure does reveal that that beyond a quite small scale, the economies of scale, while perhaps statistically significant, are economically quite small.

### 10.4.2   FLEXIBLE FUNCTIONAL FORMS: THE TRANSLOG COST FUNCTION

The literatures on production and cost and on utility and demand have evolved in several directions. In the area of models of producer behavior, the classic paper by Arrow et al. (1961) called into question the inherent restriction of the Cobb–Douglas model that all elasticities of factor substitution are equal to 1. Researchers have since developed

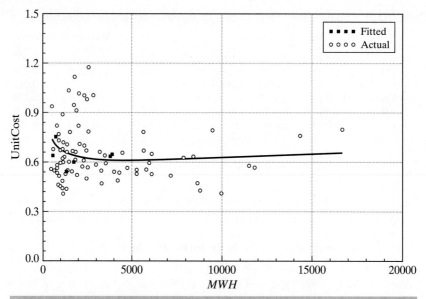

**FIGURE 10.1** Predicted and Actual Average Costs.

numerous **flexible functions** that allow substitution to be unrestricted (i.e., not even constant).[25] Similar strands of literature have appeared in the analysis of commodity demands.[26] In this section, we examine in detail a model of production.

Suppose that production is characterized by a production function, $Q = f(\mathbf{x})$. The solution to the problem of minimizing the cost of producing a specified output rate given a set of factor prices produces the cost-minimizing set of factor demands $x_i = x_i(Q, \mathbf{p})$. The total cost of production is given by the cost function,

$$C = \sum_{i=1}^{M} p_i x_i(Q, \mathbf{p}) = C(Q, \mathbf{p}). \qquad \textbf{(10-31)}$$

If there are **constant returns to scale,** then it can be shown that $C = Qc(\mathbf{p})$ or

$$C/Q = c(\mathbf{p}),$$

where $c(\mathbf{p})$ is the unit or average cost function.[27] The cost-minimizing factor demands are obtained by applying **Shephard's** (1970) **lemma,** which states that if $C(Q, \mathbf{p})$ gives the minimum total cost of production, then the cost-minimizing set of factor demands

---

[25]See, in particular, Berndt and Christensen (1973). Two useful surveys of the topic are Jorgenson (1983) and Diewert (1974).

[26]See, for example, Christensen, Jorgenson, and Lau (1975) and two surveys, Deaton and Muellbauer (1980) and Deaton (1983). Berndt (1990) contains many useful results.

[27]The Cobb–Douglas function of the previous section gives an illustration. The restriction of constant returns to scale is $\beta_q = 1$, which is equivalent to $C = Qc(\mathbf{p})$. Nerlove's more general version of the cost function allows nonconstant returns to scale. See Christensen and Greene (1976) and Diewert (1974) for some of the formalities of the cost function and its relationship to the structure of production.

is given by

$$x_i^* = \frac{\partial C(Q, \mathbf{p})}{\partial p_i} = \frac{Q \partial c(\mathbf{p})}{\partial p_i}. \tag{10-32}$$

Alternatively, by differentiating logarithmically, we obtain the cost-minimizing factor cost shares:

$$s_i = \frac{\partial \ln C(Q, \mathbf{p})}{\partial \ln p_i} = \frac{p_i x_i}{C}. \tag{10-33}$$

With constant returns to scale, $\ln C(Q, \mathbf{p}) = \ln Q + \ln c(\mathbf{p})$, so

$$s_i = \frac{\partial \ln c(\mathbf{p})}{\partial \ln p_i}. \tag{10-34}$$

In many empirical studies, the objects of estimation are the elasticities of factor substitution and the own price elasticities of demand, which are given by

$$\theta_{ij} = \frac{c(\partial^2 c / \partial p_i \partial p_j)}{(\partial c / \partial p_i)(\partial c / \partial p_j)}$$

and

$$\eta_{ii} = s_i \theta_{ii}.$$

By suitably parameterizing the cost function (10-31) and the cost shares (10-34), we obtain an $M$ or $M+1$ equation econometric model that can be used to estimate these quantities.[28]

The transcendental logarithmic, or **translog function** is the most frequently used flexible function in empirical work.[29] By expanding $\ln c(\mathbf{p})$ in a second-order **Taylor series** about the point $\ln \mathbf{p} = \mathbf{0}$, we obtain

$$\ln c \approx \beta_0 + \sum_{i=1}^{M} \left( \frac{\partial \ln c}{\partial \ln p_i} \right) \log p_i + \frac{1}{2} \sum_{i=1}^{M} \sum_{j=1}^{M} \left( \frac{\partial^2 \ln c}{\partial \ln p_i \, \partial \ln p_j} \right) \ln p_i \ln p_j, \tag{10-35}$$

where all derivatives are evaluated at the expansion point. If we treat these derivatives as the coefficients, then the cost function becomes

$$\ln c = \beta_0 + \beta_1 \ln p_1 + \cdots + \beta_M \ln p_M + \delta_{11} \left( \tfrac{1}{2} \ln^2 p_1 \right) + \delta_{12} \ln p_1 \ln p_2$$
$$+ \delta_{22} \left( \tfrac{1}{2} \ln^2 p_2 \right) + \cdots + \delta_{MM} \left( \tfrac{1}{2} \ln^2 p_M \right). \tag{10-36}$$

---

[28]The cost function is only one of several approaches to this study. See Jorgenson (1983) for a discussion.

[29]See Example 2.4. The function was developed by Kmenta (1967) as a means of approximating the CES production function and was introduced formally in a series of papers by Berndt, Christensen, Jorgenson, and Lau, including Berndt and Christensen (1973) and Christensen et al. (1975). The literature has produced something of a competition in the development of exotic functional forms. The translog function has remained the most popular, however, and by one account, Guilkey, Lovell, and Sickles (1983) is the most reliable of several available alternatives. See also Example 5.2.

This is the translog cost function. If $\delta_{ij}$ equals zero, then it reduces to the Cobb–Douglas function we looked at earlier. The cost shares are given by

$$
s_1 = \frac{\partial \ln c}{\partial \ln p_1} = \beta_1 + \delta_{11} \ln p_1 + \delta_{12} \ln p_2 + \cdots + \delta_{1M} \ln p_M,
$$

$$
s_2 = \frac{\partial \ln c}{\partial \ln p_2} = \beta_2 + \delta_{21} \ln p_1 + \delta_{22} \ln p_2 + \cdots + \delta_{2M} \ln p_M, \qquad \textbf{(10-37)}
$$

$$
\vdots
$$

$$
s_M = \frac{\partial \ln c}{\partial \ln p_M} = \beta_M + \delta_{M1} \ln p_1 + \delta_{M2} \ln p_2 + \cdots + \delta_{MM} \ln p_M.
$$

The cost shares must sum to 1, which requires,

$$
\beta_1 + \beta_2 + \cdots + \beta_M = 1,
$$

$$
\sum_{i=1}^{M} \delta_{ij} = 0 \quad \text{(column sums equal zero)}, \qquad \textbf{(10-38)}
$$

$$
\sum_{j=1}^{M} \delta_{ij} = 0 \quad \text{(row sums equal zero)}.
$$

We will also impose the (theoretical) symmetry restriction, $\delta_{ij} = \delta_{ji}$.

The system of **share equations** provides a seemingly unrelated regressions model that can be used to estimate the parameters of the model.[30] To make the model operational, we must impose the restrictions in (10-38) and solve the problem of **singularity of the disturbance covariance matrix** of the share equations. The first is accomplished by dividing the first $M-1$ prices by the $M$th, thus eliminating the last term in each row and column of the parameter matrix. As in the Cobb–Douglas model, we obtain a nonsingular system by dropping the $M$th share equation. We compute maximum likelihood estimates of the parameters to ensure **invariance** with respect to the choice of which share equation we drop. For the translog cost function, the elasticities of substitution are particularly simple to compute once the parameters have been estimated:

$$
\theta_{ij} = \frac{\delta_{ij} + s_i s_j}{s_i s_j}, \quad \theta_{ii} = \frac{\delta_{ii} + s_i (s_i - 1)}{s_i^2}. \qquad \textbf{(10-39)}
$$

These elasticities will differ at every data point. It is common to compute them at some central point such as the means of the data.[31]

### Example 10.8 A Cost Function for U.S. Manufacturing

A number of recent studies using the translog methodology have used a four-factor model, with capital $K$, labor $L$, energy $E$, and materials $M$, the factors of production. Among the first studies to employ this methodology was Berndt and Wood's (1975) estimation of a translog

---

[30] The cost function may be included, if desired, which will provide an estimate of $\beta_0$ but is otherwise inessential. Absent the assumption of constant returns to scale, however, the cost function will contain parameters of interest that do not appear in the share equations. As such, one would want to include it in the model. See Christensen and Greene (1976) for an application.

[31] They will also be highly nonlinear functions of the parameters and the data. A method of computing asymptotic standard errors for the estimated elasticities is presented in Anderson and Thursby (1986). Krinsky and Robb (1986, 1990) (see Example 4.8) proposed their method as an alternative approach to this computation.

**TABLE 10.4** Parameter Estimates (standard errors in parentheses)

| | | | | | |
|---|---|---|---|---|---|
| $\beta_K$ | 0.05682 | (0.00131) | $\delta_{KM}$ | -0.02169* | (0.00963) |
| $\beta_L$ | 0.25355 | (0.001987) | $\delta_{LL}$ | 0.07488 | (0.00639) |
| $\beta_E$ | 0.04383 | (0.00105) | $\delta_{LE}$ | -0.00321 | (0.00275) |
| $\beta_M$ | 0.64580* | (0.00299) | $\delta_{LM}$ | -0.07169* | (0.00941) |
| $\delta_{KK}$ | 0.02987 | (0.00575) | $\delta_{EE}$ | 0.02938 | (0.00741) |
| $\delta_{KL}$ | 0.0000221 | (0.00367) | $\delta_{EM}$ | -0.01797* | (0.01075) |
| $\delta_{KE}$ | -0.00820 | (0.00406) | $\delta_{MM}$ | 0.11134* | (0.02239) |

*Estimated indirectly using (10-38).

cost function for the U.S. manufacturing sector. The three factor shares used to estimate the model are

$$s_K = \beta_K + \delta_{KK} \ln\left(\frac{p_K}{p_M}\right) + \delta_{KL} \ln\left(\frac{p_L}{p_M}\right) + \delta_{KE} \ln\left(\frac{p_E}{p_M}\right),$$

$$s_L = \beta_L + \delta_{KL} \ln\left(\frac{p_K}{p_M}\right) + \delta_{LL} \ln\left(\frac{p_L}{p_M}\right) + \delta_{LE} \ln\left(\frac{p_E}{p_M}\right),$$

$$s_E = \beta_E + \delta_{KE} \ln\left(\frac{p_K}{p_M}\right) + \delta_{LE} \ln\left(\frac{p_L}{p_M}\right) + \delta_{EE} \ln\left(\frac{p_E}{p_M}\right).$$

Berndt and Wood's data are reproduced in Appendix Table F10.2. Constrained FGLS estimates of the parameters presented in Table 10.4 were obtained by constructing the "pooled regression" in (10-19) with data matrices

$$\mathbf{y} = \begin{bmatrix} s_K \\ s_L \\ s_E \end{bmatrix},$$

$$\mathbf{X} = \begin{bmatrix} \mathbf{i} & 0 & 0 & \ln P_K/P_M & \ln P_L/P_M & \ln P_E/P_M & 0 & 0 & 0 \\ 0 & \mathbf{i} & 0 & 0 & \ln P_K/P_M & 0 & \ln P_L/P_M & \ln P_E/P_M & 0 \\ 0 & 0 & \mathbf{i} & 0 & 0 & \ln P_K/P_M & 0 & \ln P_L/P_M & \ln P_E/P_M \end{bmatrix},$$

$$\boldsymbol{\beta}' = (\beta_K, \beta_L, \beta_E, \delta_{KK}, \delta_{KL}, \delta_{KE}, \delta_{LL}, \delta_{LE}, \delta_{EE}).$$

(10-40)

Estimates are then obtained using the two-step procedure in (10-7) and (10-9).[32] The full set of estimates are given in Table 10.5. The parameters not estimated directly in (10-36) are computed using (10-38).

The implied estimates of the elasticities of substitution and demand for 1959 (the central year in the data) are derived in Table 10.5 using the fitted cost shares and the estimated parameters in (10-39). The departure from the Cobb–Douglas model with unit elasticities is substantial. For example, the results suggest almost no substitutability between energy and labor and some complementarity between capital and energy.[33]

---

[32] These estimates do not match those reported by Berndt and Wood. They used an iterative estimator whereas ours is two steps FGLS. To purge their data of possible correlation with the disturbances, they first regressed the prices on 10 exogenous macroeconomic variables, such as U.S. population, government purchases of labor services, real exports of durable goods and U.S. tangible capital stock, and then based their analysis on the fitted values. The estimates given here are, in general quite close to those given by Berndt and Wood. For example, their estimates of the first five parameters are 0.0564, 0.2539, 0.0442, 0.6455, and 0.0254.

[33] Berndt and Wood's estimate of $\theta_{EL}$ for 1959 is 0.64.

**TABLE 10.5**   Estimated Elasticities

|  | Capital | Labor | Energy | Materials |
|---|---|---|---|---|
| **Cost Shares for 1959** | | | | |
| Fitted shares | 0.05646 | 0.27454 | 0.04424 | 0.62476 |
| Actual shares | 0.06185 | 0.27303 | 0.04563 | 0.61948 |
| **Implied Elasticities of Substitution, 1959** | | | | |
| Capital | −7.34124 | | | |
| Labor | 1.0014 | −1.64902 | | |
| Energy | −2.28422 | 0.73556 | −6.59124 | |
| Materials | 0.34994 | 0.58205 | 0.38512 | −0.19702 |
| **Implied Own Price Elasticities** | | | | |
|  | −0.41448 | −0.45274 | −0.29161 | −0.19702 |

## 10.5   SUMMARY AND CONCLUSIONS

This chapter has surveyed use of the seemingly unrelated regressions model. The SUR model is an application of the generalized regression model introduced in Chapter 8. The advantage of the SUR formulation is the rich variety of behavioral models that fit into this framework. We began with estimation and inference with the SUR model, treating it essentially as a generalized regression. The major difference between this set of results and the single equation model in Chapter 8 is practical. While the SUR model is, in principle a single equation GR model with an elaborate covariance structure, special problems arise when we explicitly recognize its intrinsic nature as a set of equations linked by their disturbances. The major result for estimation at this step is the feasible GLS estimator. In spite of its apparent complexity, we can estimate the SUR model by a straightforward two-step GLS approach that is similar to the one we used for models with heteroscedasticity in Chapter 8. We also extended the SUR model to autocorrelation and heteroscedasticity. Once again, the multiple equation nature of the model complicates these applications. Maximum likelihood is an alternative method that is useful for systems of demand equations. This chapter examined a number of applications of the SUR model. Some panel data applications were presented in Section 10.3. Section 10.4 presented one of the most common recent applications of the seemingly unrelated regressions model, the estimation of demand systems. One of the signature features of this literature is the seamless transition from the theoretical models of optimization of consumers and producers to the sets of empirical demand equations derived from Roy's identity for consumers and Shephard's lemma for producers.

### Key Terms and Concepts

- Autocorrelation
- Balanced panel
- Cobb-Douglas model
- Constant returns to scale
- Covariance structures model
- Demand system
- Feasible GLS
- Fixed effects
- Flexible functional form
- Generalized regression model
- Heteroscedasticity
- Homogeneity restriction
- Identical explanatory variables
- Identical regressors
- Invariance
- Kronecker product

- Lagrange multiplier test
- Likelihood ratio test
- Maximum likelihood
- Multivariate regression model
- Pooled model
- Projection

- Random effects model
- Seemingly unrelated regressions
- Share equations
- Shephard's lemma
- Singular disturbance covariance matrix

- System of demand equations
- Taylor series
- Translog function
- Wald statistic
- Zellner's efficient estimator

## Exercises

1.  A sample of 100 observations produces the following sample data:

$$\bar{y}_1 = 1, \quad \bar{y}_2 = 2,$$
$$\mathbf{y}_1'\mathbf{y}_1 = 150,$$
$$\mathbf{y}_2'\mathbf{y}_2 = 550,$$
$$\mathbf{y}_1'\mathbf{y}_2 = 260.$$

The underlying bivariate regression model is

$$y_1 = \mu + \varepsilon_1,$$
$$y_2 = \mu + \varepsilon_2.$$

a. Compute the OLS estimate of $\mu$, and estimate the sampling variance of this estimator.

b. Compute the FGLS estimate of $\mu$ and the sampling variance of the estimator.

2.  Consider estimation of the following two-equation model:

$$y_1 = \beta_1 + \varepsilon_1,$$
$$y_2 = \beta_2 x + \varepsilon_2.$$

A sample of 50 observations produces the following moment matrix:

|       | 1   | $y_1$ | $y_2$ | $x$ |
|-------|-----|-----|-----|-----|
| 1     | 50  |     |     |     |
| $y_1$ | 150 | 500 |     |     |
| $y_2$ | 50  | 40  | 90  |     |
| $x$   | 100 | 60  | 50  | 100 |

a. Write the explicit formula for the GLS estimator of $[\beta_1, \beta_2]$. What is the asymptotic covariance matrix of the estimator?

b. Derive the OLS estimator and its sampling variance in this model.

c. Obtain the OLS estimates of $\beta_1$ and $\beta_2$, and estimate the sampling covariance matrix of the two estimates. Use $n$ instead of $(n-1)$ as the divisor to compute the estimates of the disturbance variances.

d. Compute the FGLS estimates of $\beta_1$ and $\beta_2$ and the estimated sampling covariance matrix.

e. Test the hypothesis that $\beta_2 = 1$.

3. The model

$$y_1 = \beta_1 x_1 + \varepsilon_1,$$
$$y_2 = \beta_2 x_2 + \varepsilon_2$$

satisfies all the assumptions of the classical multivariate regression model. All variables have zero means. The following sample second-moment matrix is obtained from a sample of 20 observations:

$$
\begin{array}{c c}
 & \begin{array}{c c c c} y_1 & y_2 & x_1 & x_2 \end{array} \\
\begin{array}{c} y_1 \\ y_2 \\ x_1 \\ x_2 \end{array} &
\begin{bmatrix}
20 & 6 & 4 & 3 \\
6 & 10 & 3 & 6 \\
4 & 3 & 5 & 2 \\
3 & 6 & 2 & 10
\end{bmatrix}.
\end{array}
$$

a. Compute the FGLS estimates of $\beta_1$ and $\beta_2$.
b. Test the hypothesis that $\beta_1 = \beta_2$.
c. Compute the maximum likelihood estimates of the model parameters.
d. Use the likelihood ratio test to test the hypothesis in part b.

4. Prove that in the model

$$\mathbf{y}_1 = \mathbf{X}_1 \boldsymbol{\beta}_1 + \boldsymbol{\varepsilon}_1,$$
$$\mathbf{y}_2 = \mathbf{X}_2 \boldsymbol{\beta}_2 + \boldsymbol{\varepsilon}_2,$$

generalized least squares is equivalent to equation-by-equation ordinary least squares if $\mathbf{X}_1 = \mathbf{X}_2$. Does your result hold if it is also known that $\boldsymbol{\beta}_1 = \boldsymbol{\beta}_2$?

5. Consider the two-equation system

$$y_1 = \beta_1 x_1 \qquad\quad + \varepsilon_1,$$
$$y_2 = \qquad \beta_2 x_2 + \beta_3 x_3 + \varepsilon_2.$$

Assume that the disturbance variances and covariance are known. Now suppose that the analyst of this model applies GLS but erroneously omits $x_3$ from the second equation. What effect does this specification error have on the consistency of the estimator of $\beta_1$?

6. Consider the system

$$y_1 = \alpha_1 + \beta x + \varepsilon_1,$$
$$y_2 = \alpha_2 \qquad\quad + \varepsilon_2.$$

The disturbances are freely correlated. Prove that GLS applied to the system leads to the OLS estimates of $\alpha_1$ and $\alpha_2$ but to a mixture of the least squares slopes in the regressions of $y_1$ and $y_2$ on $x$ as the estimator of $\beta$. What is the mixture? To simplify the algebra, assume (with no loss of generality) that $\bar{x} = 0$.

7. For the model

$$y_1 = \alpha_1 + \beta x + \varepsilon_1,$$
$$y_2 = \alpha_2 \qquad\quad + \varepsilon_2,$$
$$y_3 = \alpha_3 \qquad\quad + \varepsilon_3,$$

assume that $y_{i2} + y_{i3} = 1$ at every observation. Prove that the sample covariance matrix of the least squares residuals from the three equations will be singular, thereby precluding computation of the FGLS estimator. How could you proceed in this case?

## Applications

1.  Continuing the analysis of Section 10.4.2, we find that a translog cost function for one output and three factor inputs that does not impose constant returns to scale is

$$\ln C = \alpha + \beta_1 \ln p_1 + \beta_2 \ln p_2 + \beta_3 \ln p_3 + \delta_{11}\tfrac{1}{2}\ln^2 p_1 + \delta_{12}\ln p_1 \ln p_2$$

$$+ \delta_{13}\ln p_1 \ln p_3 + \delta_{22}\tfrac{1}{2}\ln^2 p_2 + \delta_{23}\ln p_2 \ln p_3 + \delta_{33}\tfrac{1}{2}\ln^2 p_3$$

$$+ \gamma_{q1}\ln Q \ln p_1 + \gamma_{q2}\ln Q \ln p_2 + \gamma_{q3}\ln Q \ln p_3$$

$$+ \beta_q \ln Q + \beta_{qq}\tfrac{1}{2}\ln^2 Q + \varepsilon_c.$$

    The factor share equations are

$$S_1 = \beta_1 + \delta_{11}\ln p_1 + \delta_{12}\ln p_2 + \delta_{13}\ln p_3 + \gamma_{q1}\ln Q + \varepsilon_1,$$

$$S_2 = \beta_2 + \delta_{12}\ln p_1 + \delta_{22}\ln p_2 + \delta_{23}\ln p_3 + \gamma_{q2}\ln Q + \varepsilon_2,$$

$$S_3 = \beta_3 + \delta_{13}\ln p_1 + \delta_{23}\ln p_2 + \delta_{33}\ln p_3 + \gamma_{q3}\ln Q + \varepsilon_3.$$

    [See Christensen and Greene (1976) for analysis of this model.]
    a.  The three factor shares must add identically to 1. What restrictions does this requirement place on the model parameters?
    b.  Show that the adding-up condition in (10-38) can be imposed directly on the model by specifying the translog model in $(C/p_3)$, $(p_1/p_3)$, and $(p_2/p_3)$ and dropping the third share equation. (See Example 10.8.) Notice that this reduces the number of free parameters in the model to 10.
    c.  Continuing part b, the model as specified with the symmetry and equality restrictions has 15 parameters. By imposing the constraints, you reduce this number to 10 in the estimating equations. How would you obtain estimates of the parameters not estimated directly?
    The remaining parts of this exercise will require specialized software. The **E-Views, TSP, Stata** or **LIMDEP,** programs noted in the preface are four that could be used. All estimation is to be done using the data used in Section 10.4.1
    d.  Estimate each of the three equations you obtained in part b by ordinary least squares. Do the estimates appear to satisfy the cross-equation equality and symmetry restrictions implied by the theory?
    e.  Using the data in Section 10.4.1, estimate the full system of three equations (cost and the two independent shares), imposing the symmetry and cross-equation equality constraints.
    f.  Using your parameter estimates, compute the estimates of the elasticities in (10-39) at the means of the variables.
    g.  Use a likelihood ratio statistic to test the joint hypothesis that $\gamma_{qi} = 0$, $i = 1, 2, 3$. [Hint: Just drop the relevant variables from the model.]
2.  The Grunfeld investment data in Appendix Table F9.3 are a classic data set that have been used for decades to develop and demonstrate estimators for seemingly unrelated regressions.[34] Although somewhat dated at this juncture, they remain an ideal application of the techniques presented in this chapter.[35] The data consist of

---

[34] See Grunfeld (1958), Grunfeld and Griliches (1960), and Boot and de Witt (1960).

[35] See, in particular, Zellner (1962, 1963) and Zellner and Huang (1962).

time series of 20 yearly observations on ten firms. The three variables are

$I_{it}$ = gross investment,

$F_{it}$ = market value of the firm at the end of the previous year,

$C_{it}$ = value of the stock of plant and equipment at the end of the previous year.

The main equation in the studies noted is

$$I_{it} = \beta_1 + \beta_2 F_{it} + \beta_3 C_{it} + \varepsilon_{it}.[36]$$

a. Fit the ten equations separately by ordinary least squares and report your results.
b. Use a Wald (Chow) test to test the "aggregation" restriction that the ten coefficient vectors are the same.
c. Use the seemingly unrelated regressions (FGLS) estimator to reestimate the parameters of the model, once again, allowing the coefficients to differ across the ten equations. Now, use the pooled model and, again, FGLS to estimate the constrained equation with equal parameter vectors, and test the aggregation hypothesis.
d. Using the OLS residuals from the separate regression, use the LM statistic in (10-17) to test for the presence of cross equation correlation.
e. An alternative specification to the model in part c. that focuses on the variances rather than the means is the groupwise heteroscedasticity model of Section 8.8.2. For the current application, you can fit this model using (10-19), (10-20), and (10-21) while imposing the much simpler model with $\sigma_{ij} = 0$ when $i \neq j$. Do the results of the pooled model differ in the three cases considered, simple OLS, groupwise heteroscedasticity and full unrestricted covariances [which would be (10-20)] with $\Omega_{ij} = I$?

---

[36]Note that the model specifies investment, a flow, as a function of two stocks. This could be a theoretical misspecification. It might be preferable to specify the model in terms of planned investment. But, 50 years after the fact, we'll take the specified model as it is.

# 11

# NONLINEAR REGRESSIONS AND NONLINEAR LEAST SQUARES

———⚬⚬⚬———

## 11.1 INTRODUCTION

Although the linear model is flexible enough to allow great variety in the shape of the regression, it still rules out many useful functional forms. In this chapter, we examine regression models that are intrinsically nonlinear in their parameters. This allows a much wider range of functional forms than the linear model can accommodate.[1]

## 11.2 NONLINEAR REGRESSION MODELS

The general form of the nonlinear regression model is

$$y_i = h(\mathbf{x}_i, \boldsymbol{\beta}) + \varepsilon_i. \tag{11-1}$$

The linear model is obviously a special case. Moreover, some models which appear to be nonlinear, such as

$$y = e^{\beta_0} x_1^{\beta_1} x_2^{\beta_2} e^{\varepsilon},$$

become linear after a transformation, in this case after taking logarithms. In this chapter, we are interested in models for which there is no such transformation, such as the ones in the following examples.

### Example 11.1  CES Production Function
In Example 6.5, we examined a constant elasticity of substitution production function model:

$$\ln y = \ln \gamma - \frac{v}{\rho} \ln[\delta K^{-\rho} + (1 - \delta) L^{-\rho}] + \varepsilon.$$

No transformation renders this equation linear in the parameters. We did find, however, that a linear Taylor series approximation to this function around the point $\rho = 0$ produced an intrinsically linear equation that could be fit by least squares. Nonetheless, the true model is nonlinear in the sense that interests us in this chapter.

---

[1] A complete discussion of this subject can be found in Amemiya (1985). Other important references are Jennrich (1969), Malinvaud (1970), and especially Goldfeld and Quandt (1971, 1972). A very lengthy authoritative treatment is the text by Davidson and MacKinnon (1993).

*Example 11.2*  *Translog Demand System*

Christensen, Jorgenson, and Lau (1975), proposed the translog **indirect utility function** for a consumer allocating a budget among $K$ commodities:

$$-\ln V = \beta_0 + \sum_{k=1}^{K} \beta_k \ln(p_k/M) + \sum_{k=1}^{K} \sum_{l=1}^{K} \gamma_{kl} \ln(p_k/M) \ln(p_l/M),$$

where $V$ is indirect utility, $p_k$ is the price for the $k$th commodity, and $M$ is income. **Roy's identity** applied to this logarithmic function produces a budget share equation for the $k$th commodity that is of the form

$$S_k = -\frac{\partial \ln V/\partial \ln p_k}{\partial \ln V/\partial \ln M} = \frac{\beta_k + \sum_{j=1}^{K} \gamma_{kj} \ln(p_j/M)}{\beta_M + \sum_{j=1}^{K} \gamma_{Mj} \ln(p_j/M)} + \varepsilon, \quad k = 1, \ldots, K,$$

where $\beta_M = \sum_k \beta_k$ and $\gamma_{Mj} = \sum_k \gamma_{kj}$. No transformation of the budget share equation produces a linear model. This is an intrinsically nonlinear regression model. (It is also one among a system of equations, an aspect we will ignore for the present.)

## 11.2.1 ASSUMPTIONS OF THE NONLINEAR REGRESSION MODEL

We shall require a somewhat more formal definition of a nonlinear regression model. Sufficient for our purposes will be the following, which include the linear model as the special case noted earlier. We assume that there is an underlying probability distribution, or data generating process (DGP) for the observable $y_i$ and a true parameter vector, $\boldsymbol{\beta}$, which is a characteristic of that DGP. The following are the assumptions of the nonlinear regression model:

1. **Functional form:** The conditional mean function for $y_i$ given $\mathbf{x}_i$ is

$$E[y_i \mid \mathbf{x}_i] = h(\mathbf{x}_i, \boldsymbol{\beta}), \quad i = 1, \ldots, n,$$

   where $h(\mathbf{x}_i, \boldsymbol{\beta})$ is a continuously differentiable function of $\boldsymbol{\beta}$.
2. **Identifiability of the model parameters:** The parameter vector in the model is identified (estimable) if there is no nonzero parameter $\boldsymbol{\beta}^0 \neq \boldsymbol{\beta}$ such that $h(\mathbf{x}_i, \boldsymbol{\beta}^0) = h(\mathbf{x}_i, \boldsymbol{\beta})$ for all $\mathbf{x}_i$. In the linear model, this was the full rank assumption, but the simple absence of "multicollinearity" among the variables in $\mathbf{x}$ is not sufficient to produce this condition in the nonlinear regression model. Note that the model given in Example 11.2 is not identified. If the parameters in the model are all multiplied by the same nonzero constant, the same conditional mean function results. This condition persists even if all the variables in the model are linearly independent. The indeterminacy was removed in the study cited by imposing the **normalization** $\beta_M = 1$.
3. **Zero mean of the disturbance:** It follows from Assumption 1 that we may write

$$y_i = h(\mathbf{x}_i, \boldsymbol{\beta}) + \varepsilon_i.$$

   where $E[\varepsilon_i \mid h(\mathbf{x}_i, \boldsymbol{\beta})] = 0$. This states that the disturbance at observation $i$ is uncorrelated with the conditional mean function for all observations in the sample. This is not quite the same as assuming that the disturbances and the exogenous variables are uncorrelated, which is the familiar assumption, however.
4. **Homoscedasticity and nonautocorrelation:** As in the linear model, we assume conditional homoscedasticity,

$$E\left[\varepsilon_i^2 \mid h(\mathbf{x}_j, \boldsymbol{\beta}), \; j = 1, \ldots, n\right] = \sigma^2, \quad \text{a finite constant,} \tag{11-2}$$

and nonautocorrelation

$$E[\varepsilon_i \varepsilon_j \mid h(\mathbf{x}_i, \boldsymbol{\beta}), h(\mathbf{x}_j, \boldsymbol{\beta}), \ j = 1, \ldots, n] = 0 \quad \text{for all } j \neq i.$$

5. **Data-generating process:** The data-generating process for $\mathbf{x}_i$ is assumed to be a well-behaved population such that first and second moments of the data can be assumed to converge to fixed, finite population counterparts. The crucial assumption is that the process generating $\mathbf{x}_i$ is strictly exogenous to that generating $\varepsilon_i$. The data on $\mathbf{x}_i$ are assumed to be "well behaved."

6. **Underlying probability model:** There is a well-defined probability distribution generating $\varepsilon_i$. At this point, we assume only that this process produces a sample of uncorrelated, identically (marginally) distributed random variables $\varepsilon_i$ with mean 0 and variance $\sigma^2$ conditioned on $h(\mathbf{x}_i, \boldsymbol{\beta})$. Thus, at this point, our statement of the model is **semiparametric.** (See Section 14.3.) We will not be assuming any particular distribution for $\varepsilon_i$. The conditional moment assumptions in 3 and 4 will be sufficient for the results in this chapter. In Chapter 16, we will fully parameterize the model by assuming that the disturbances are normally distributed. This will allow us to be more specific about certain test statistics and, in addition, allow some generalizations of the regression model. The assumption is not necessary here.

### 11.2.2 THE ORTHOGONALITY CONDITION AND THE SUM OF SQUARES

Assumptions 1 and 3 imply that $E[\varepsilon_i \mid h(\mathbf{x}_i, \boldsymbol{\beta})] = 0$. In the linear model, it follows, *because of the linearity of the conditional mean,* that $\varepsilon_i$ and $\mathbf{x}_i$, itself, are uncorrelated. However, *uncorrelatedness* of $\varepsilon_i$ with a particular *nonlinear* function of $\mathbf{x}_i$ (the regression function) does not necessarily imply uncorrelatedness with $\mathbf{x}_i$, itself, nor, for that matter, with other nonlinear functions of $\mathbf{x}_i$. On the other hand, the results we will obtain for the behavior of the estimator in this model are couched not in terms of $\mathbf{x}_i$ but in terms of certain functions of $\mathbf{x}_i$ (the derivatives of the regression function), so, in point of fact, $E[\boldsymbol{\varepsilon} \mid \mathbf{X}] = \mathbf{0}$ is not even the assumption we need.

The foregoing is not a theoretical fine point. Dynamic models, which are very common in the contemporary literature, would greatly complicate this analysis. If it can be assumed that $\varepsilon_i$ is strictly uncorrelated with any *prior information* in the model, including previous disturbances, then perhaps a treatment analogous to that for the linear model would apply. But the convergence results needed to obtain the asymptotic properties of the estimator still have to be strengthened. The dynamic nonlinear regression model is beyond the reach of our treatment here. Strict independence of $\varepsilon_i$ and $\mathbf{x}_i$ would be sufficient for uncorrelatedness of $\varepsilon_i$ and every function of $\mathbf{x}_i$, but, again, in a dynamic model, this assumption might be questionable. Some commentary on this aspect of the nonlinear regression model may be found in Davidson and MacKinnon (1993, 2004).

If the disturbances in the nonlinear model are normally distributed, then the log of the normal density for the $i$th observation will be

$$\ln f(y_i \mid \mathbf{x}_i, \boldsymbol{\beta}, \sigma^2) = -(1/2)\big[\ln 2\pi + \ln \sigma^2 + \varepsilon_i^2 / \sigma^2\big]. \tag{11-3}$$

For this special case, we have from item D.2 in Theorem 16.2 (on maximum likelihood estimation), that the derivatives of the log density with respect to the parameters have mean zero. That is,

$$E\left[\frac{\partial \ln f(y_i \mid \mathbf{x}_i, \boldsymbol{\beta}, \sigma^2)}{\partial \boldsymbol{\beta}}\right] = E\left[\frac{1}{\sigma^2}\left(\frac{\partial h(\mathbf{x}_i, \boldsymbol{\beta})}{\partial \boldsymbol{\beta}}\right)\varepsilon_i\right] = \mathbf{0}, \tag{11-4}$$

so, in the normal case, the derivatives and the disturbances are uncorrelated. Whether this can be assumed to hold in other cases is going to be model specific, but under reasonable conditions, we would assume so. [See Ruud (2000, p. 540).]

In the context of the linear model, the **orthogonality condition** $E[\mathbf{x}_i \varepsilon_i] = 0$ produces least squares as a **GMM estimator** for the model. (See Chapter 15.) The orthogonality condition is that the regressors and the disturbance in the model are uncorrelated. In this setting, the same condition applies to the first derivatives of the conditional mean function. The result in (11-4) produces a moment condition which will define the nonlinear least squares estimator as a GMM estimator.

### Example 11.3   First-Order Conditions for a Nonlinear Model
The first-order conditions for estimating the parameters of the nonlinear model,

$$y_i = \beta_1 + \beta_2 e^{\beta_3 x_i} + \varepsilon_i,$$

by nonlinear least squares [see (11-10)] are

$$\frac{\partial S(\mathbf{b})}{\partial b_1} = -\sum_{i=1}^{n}\left[y_i - b_1 - b_2 e^{b_3 x_i}\right] = 0,$$

$$\frac{\partial S(\mathbf{b})}{\partial b_2} = -\sum_{i=1}^{n}\left[y_i - b_1 - b_2 e^{b_3 x_i}\right]e^{b_3 x_i} = 0,$$

$$\frac{\partial S(\mathbf{b})}{\partial b_3} = -\sum_{i=1}^{n}\left[y_i - b_1 - b_2 e^{b_3 x_i}\right]b_2 x_i e^{b_3 x_i} = 0.$$

These equations do not have an explicit solution.

Conceding the potential for ambiguity, we define a nonlinear regression model at this point as follows.

> **DEFINITION 11.1**   Nonlinear Regression Model
> *A **nonlinear regression model** is one for which the first-order conditions for least squares estimation of the parameters are nonlinear functions of the parameters.*

Thus, nonlinearity is defined in terms of the techniques needed to estimate the parameters, not the shape of the regression function. Later we shall broaden our definition to include other techniques besides least squares.

### 11.2.3   THE LINEARIZED REGRESSION

The nonlinear regression model is $y = h(\mathbf{x}, \boldsymbol{\beta}) + \varepsilon$. (To save some notation, we have dropped the observation subscript.) The sampling theory results that have been obtained for nonlinear regression models are based on a linear Taylor series approximation to

$h(\mathbf{x}, \boldsymbol{\beta})$ at a particular value for the parameter vector, $\boldsymbol{\beta}^0$:

$$h(\mathbf{x}, \boldsymbol{\beta}) \approx h(\mathbf{x}, \boldsymbol{\beta}^0) + \sum_{k=1}^{K} \frac{\partial h(\mathbf{x}, \boldsymbol{\beta}^0)}{\partial \beta_k^0}(\beta_k - \beta_k^0). \qquad \textbf{(11-5)}$$

This form of the equation is called the **linearized regression model.** By collecting terms, we obtain

$$h(\mathbf{x}, \boldsymbol{\beta}) \approx \left[h(\mathbf{x}, \boldsymbol{\beta}^0) - \sum_{k=1}^{K} \beta_k^0\left(\frac{\partial h(\mathbf{x}, \boldsymbol{\beta}^0)}{\partial \beta_k^0}\right)\right] + \sum_{k=1}^{K} \beta_k\left(\frac{\partial h(\mathbf{x}, \boldsymbol{\beta}^0)}{\partial \beta_k^0}\right). \qquad \textbf{(11-6)}$$

Let $x_k^0$ equal the $k$th partial derivative,[2] $\partial h(\mathbf{x}, \boldsymbol{\beta}^0)/\partial \beta_k^0$. For a given value of $\boldsymbol{\beta}^0$, $x_k^0$ is a function only of the data, not of the unknown parameters. We now have

$$h(\mathbf{x}, \boldsymbol{\beta}) \approx \left[h^0 - \sum_{k=1}^{K} x_k^0 \beta_k^0\right] + \sum_{k=1}^{K} x_k^0 \beta_k,$$

which may be written

$$h(\mathbf{x}, \boldsymbol{\beta}) \approx h^0 - \mathbf{x}^{0\prime}\boldsymbol{\beta}^0 + \mathbf{x}^{0\prime}\boldsymbol{\beta},$$

which implies that

$$y \approx h^0 - \mathbf{x}^{0\prime}\boldsymbol{\beta}^0 + \mathbf{x}^{0\prime}\boldsymbol{\beta} + \varepsilon.$$

By placing the known terms on the left-hand side of the equation, we obtain a linear equation:

$$y^0 = y - h^0 + \mathbf{x}^{0\prime}\boldsymbol{\beta}^0 = \mathbf{x}^{0\prime}\boldsymbol{\beta} + \varepsilon^0. \qquad \textbf{(11-7)}$$

Note that $\varepsilon^0$ contains both the true disturbance, $\varepsilon$, and the error in the first order Taylor series approximation to the true regression, shown in (11-6). That is,

$$\varepsilon^0 = \varepsilon + \left[h(\mathbf{x}, \boldsymbol{\beta}) - \left\{h^0 - \sum_{k=1}^{K} x_k^0 \beta_k^0 + \sum_{k=1}^{K} x_k^0 \beta_k\right\}\right]. \qquad \textbf{(11-8)}$$

Because all the errors are accounted for, (11-7) is an equality, not an approximation. With a value of $\boldsymbol{\beta}^0$ in hand, we could compute $y^0$ and $\mathbf{x}^0$ and then estimate the parameters of (11-7) by linear least squares. (Whether this estimator is consistent or not remains to be seen.)

### Example 11.4   Linearized Regression
For the model in Example 11.3, the regressors in the linearized equation would be

$$x_1^0 = \frac{\partial h(.)}{\partial \beta_1^0} = 1,$$

$$x_2^0 = \frac{\partial h(.)}{\partial \beta_2^0} = e^{\beta_3^0 x},$$

$$x_3^0 = \frac{\partial h(.)}{\partial \beta_3^0} = \beta_2^0 x e^{\beta_3^0 x}.$$

---

[2] You should verify that for the linear regression model, these derivatives are the independent variables.

With a set of values of the parameters $\beta^0$,

$$y^0 = y - h\left(x, \beta_1^0, \beta_2^0, \beta_3^0\right) + \beta_1^0 x_1^0 + \beta_2^0 x_2^0 + \beta_3^0 x_3^0$$

could be linearly regressed on the three variables previously defined to estimate $\beta_1$, $\beta_2$, and $\beta_3$.

### 11.2.4  LARGE SAMPLE PROPERTIES OF THE NONLINEAR LEAST SQUARES ESTIMATOR

Numerous analytical results have been obtained for the nonlinear least squares estimator, such as consistency and asymptotic normality. We cannot be sure that nonlinear least squares is the most efficient estimator, except in the case of normally distributed disturbances. (This conclusion is the same one we drew for the linear model.) But, in the semiparametric setting of this chapter, we can ask whether this estimator is optimal in some sense given the information that we do have; the answer turns out to be yes. Some examples that follow will illustrate the points.

It is necessary to make some assumptions about the regressors. The precise requirements are discussed in some detail in Judge et al. (1985), Amemiya (1985), and Davidson and MacKinnon (2004). In the linear regression model, to obtain our asymptotic results, we assume that the sample moment matrix $(1/n)\mathbf{X}'\mathbf{X}$ converges to a positive definite matrix $\mathbf{Q}$. By analogy, we impose the same condition on the derivatives of the regression function, which are called the **pseudoregressors** in the linearized model *when they are computed at the true parameter values*. Therefore, for the nonlinear regression model, the analog to (4-21) is

$$\operatorname{plim} \frac{1}{n}\mathbf{X}^{0\prime}\mathbf{X}^0 = \operatorname{plim} \frac{1}{n}\sum_{i=1}^{n}\left(\frac{\partial h(\mathbf{x}_i, \boldsymbol{\beta}_0)}{\partial \boldsymbol{\beta}_0}\right)\left(\frac{\partial h(\mathbf{x}_i, \boldsymbol{\beta}_0)}{\partial \boldsymbol{\beta}_0'}\right) = \mathbf{Q}^0, \qquad \textbf{(11-9)}$$

where $\mathbf{Q}^0$ is a positive definite matrix. To establish consistency of $\mathbf{b}$ in the linear model, we required $\operatorname{plim}(1/n)\mathbf{X}'\boldsymbol{\varepsilon} = \mathbf{0}$. We will use the counterpart to this for the pseudoregressors:

$$\operatorname{plim} \frac{1}{n}\sum_{i=1}^{n}\mathbf{x}_i^0 \varepsilon_i = \mathbf{0}.$$

This is the orthogonality condition noted earlier in (4-24). In particular, note that orthogonality of the disturbances and the data is not the same condition. Finally, asymptotic normality can be established under general conditions if

$$\frac{1}{\sqrt{n}}\sum_{i=1}^{n}\mathbf{x}_i^0 \varepsilon_i \xrightarrow{d} N[\mathbf{0}, \sigma^2 \mathbf{Q}^0].$$

With these in hand, the asymptotic properties of the nonlinear least squares estimator have been derived. They are, in fact, essentially those we have already seen for the linear model, except that in this case we place the derivatives of the linearized function evaluated at $\beta$, $\mathbf{X}^0$ in the role of the regressors. [See Amemiya (1985).]

The nonlinear least squares criterion function is

$$S(\mathbf{b}) = \frac{1}{2}\sum_{i=1}^{n}[y_i - h(\mathbf{x}_i, \mathbf{b})]^2 = \frac{1}{2}\sum_{i=1}^{n}e_i^2, \qquad \textbf{(11-10)}$$

where we have inserted what will be the solution value, **b**. The values of the parameters that minimize (one half of) the sum of squared deviations are the **nonlinear least squares** estimators. The first-order conditions for a minimum are

$$\mathbf{g}(\mathbf{b}) = -\sum_{i=1}^{n}[y_i - h(\mathbf{x}_i, \mathbf{b})]\frac{\partial h(\mathbf{x}_i, \mathbf{b})}{\partial \mathbf{b}} = \mathbf{0}. \qquad \textbf{(11-11)}$$

In the linear model of Chapter 3, this produces a set of linear equations, the normal equations (3-4). But in this more general case, (11-11) is a set of nonlinear equations that do not have an explicit solution. Note that $\sigma^2$ is not relevant to the solution [nor was it in (3-4)]. At the solution,

$$\mathbf{g}(\mathbf{b}) = -\mathbf{X}^{0\prime}\mathbf{e} = \mathbf{0},$$

which is the same as (3-12) for the linear model.

Given our assumptions, we have the following general results:

---

**THEOREM 11.1** **Consistency of the Nonlinear Least Squares Estimator**

*If the following assumptions hold:*

**a.** *The parameter space containing $\boldsymbol{\beta}$ is compact (has no gaps or nonconcave regions),*

**b.** *For any vector $\boldsymbol{\beta}^0$ in that parameter space, plim $(1/n)S(\boldsymbol{\beta}^0) = q(\boldsymbol{\beta}^0)$, a continuous and differentiable function,*

**c.** *$q(\boldsymbol{\beta}^0)$ has a unique minimum at the true parameter vector, $\boldsymbol{\beta}$,*

*then, the nonlinear least squares estimator defined by (11-10) and (11-11) is consistent. We will sketch the proof, then consider why the theorem and the proof differ as they do from the apparently simpler counterpart for the linear model. The proof, notwithstanding the underlying subtleties of the assumptions, is straightforward. The estimator, say, $\mathbf{b}^0$, minimizes $(1/n)S(\boldsymbol{\beta}^0)$. If $(1/n)S(\boldsymbol{\beta}^0)$ is minimized for every n, then it is minimized by $\mathbf{b}^0$ as n increases without bound. We also assumed that the minimizer of $q(\boldsymbol{\beta}^0)$ is uniquely $\boldsymbol{\beta}$. If the minimum value of plim $(1/n)S(\boldsymbol{\beta}^0)$ equals the probability limit of the minimized value of the sum of squares, the theorem is proved. This equality is produced by the continuity in assumption b.*

---

In the linear model, consistency of the least squares estimator could be established based on plim$(1/n)\mathbf{X}'\mathbf{X} = \mathbf{Q}$ and plim$(1/n)\mathbf{X}'\boldsymbol{\varepsilon} = \mathbf{0}$. To follow that approach here, we would use the linearized model, and take essentially the same result. The loose end in that argument would be that the linearized model is not the true model, and there remains an approximation. For this line of reasoning to be valid, it must also be either assumed or shown that plim$(1/n)\mathbf{X}^{0\prime}\boldsymbol{\delta} = \mathbf{0}$ where $\delta_i = h(\mathbf{x}_i, \boldsymbol{\beta})$ minus the Taylor series approximation. An argument to this effect appears in Mittelhammer et al. (2000, p. 190–191).

> **THEOREM 11.2** **Asymptotic Normality of the Nonlinear Least Squares Estimator**
>
> *If the pseudoregressors defined in (11-9) are "well behaved," then*
>
> $$\mathbf{b} \overset{a}{\sim} N\left[\boldsymbol{\beta}, \frac{\sigma^2}{n}(\mathbf{Q}^0)^{-1}\right],$$
>
> *where*
>
> $$\mathbf{Q}^0 = \text{plim}\frac{1}{n}\mathbf{X}^{0\prime}\mathbf{X}^0.$$
>
> *The sample estimator of the asymptotic covariance matrix is*
>
> $$\text{Est. Asy. Var}[\mathbf{b}] = \hat{\sigma}^2(\mathbf{X}^{0\prime}\mathbf{X}^0)^{-1}. \tag{11-12}$$

Asymptotic efficiency of the nonlinear least squares estimator is difficult to establish without a distributional assumption. There is an indirect approach that is one possibility. The assumption of the orthogonality of the pseudoregressors and the true disturbances implies that the nonlinear least squares estimator is a GMM estimator in this context. With the assumptions of homoscedasticity and nonautocorrelation, the optimal weighting matrix is the one that we used, which is to say that in the class of GMM estimators for this model, nonlinear least squares uses the optimal weighting matrix. As such, it is asymptotically efficient in the class of GMM estimators.

The requirement that the matrix in (11-9) converges to a positive definite matrix implies that the columns of the regressor matrix $\mathbf{X}^0$ must be linearly independent. This **identification condition** is analogous to the requirement that the independent variables in the linear model be linearly independent. Nonlinear regression models usually involve several independent variables, and at first blush, it might seem sufficient to examine the data directly if one is concerned with multicollinearity. However, this situation is not the case. Example 11.5 gives an application.

### 11.2.5 COMPUTING THE NONLINEAR LEAST SQUARES ESTIMATOR

Minimizing the sum of squares is a standard problem in nonlinear optimization that can be solved by a number of methods. (See Section E.3.) The method of Gauss–Newton is often used. In the linearized regression model, if a value of $\boldsymbol{\beta}^0$ is available, then the linearized regression model shown in (11-7) can be estimated by linear least squares. Once a parameter vector is obtained, it can play the role of a new $\boldsymbol{\beta}^0$, and the computation can be done again. The **iteration** can continue until the difference between successive parameter vectors is small enough to assume convergence. One of the main virtues of this method is that at the last iteration the estimate of $(\mathbf{Q}^0)^{-1}$ will, apart from the scale factor $\hat{\sigma}^2/n$, provide the correct estimate of the asymptotic covariance matrix for the parameter estimator.

This iterative solution to the minimization problem is

$$
\mathbf{b}_{t+1} = \left[ \sum_{i=1}^{n} \mathbf{x}_i^0 \mathbf{x}_i^{0\prime} \right]^{-1} \left[ \sum_{i=1}^{n} \mathbf{x}_i^0 \left( y_i - h_i^0 + \mathbf{x}_i^{0\prime} \mathbf{b}_t \right) \right]
$$

$$
= \mathbf{b}_t + \left[ \sum_{i=1}^{n} \mathbf{x}_i^0 \mathbf{x}_i^{0\prime} \right]^{-1} \left[ \sum_{i=1}^{n} \mathbf{x}_i^0 \left( y_i - h_i^0 \right) \right]
$$

$$
= \mathbf{b}_t + (\mathbf{X}^{0\prime} \mathbf{X}^0)^{-1} \mathbf{X}^{0\prime} \mathbf{e}^0
$$

$$
= \mathbf{b}_t + \boldsymbol{\Delta}_t,
$$

where all terms on the right-hand side are evaluated at $\mathbf{b}_t$ and $\mathbf{e}^0$ is the vector of non-linear least squares residuals. This algorithm has some intuitive appeal as well. For each iteration, we update the previous parameter estimates by regressing the nonlinear least squares residuals on the derivatives of the regression functions. The process will have converged (i.e., the update will be $\mathbf{0}$) when $\mathbf{X}^{0\prime} \mathbf{e}^0$ is close enough to $\mathbf{0}$. This derivative has a direct counterpart in the normal equations for the linear model, $\mathbf{X}' \mathbf{e} = \mathbf{0}$.

As usual, when using a digital computer, we will not achieve exact convergence with $\mathbf{X}^{0\prime} \mathbf{e}^0$ exactly equal to zero. A useful, scale-free counterpart to the convergence criterion discussed in Section E.3.6 is $\delta = \mathbf{e}^{0\prime} \mathbf{X}^0 (\mathbf{X}^{0\prime} \mathbf{X}^0)^{-1} \mathbf{X}^{0\prime} \mathbf{e}^0$. [See (11-22).] We note, finally, that iteration of the linearized regression, although a very effective algorithm for many problems, does not always work. As does Newton's method, this algorithm sometimes "jumps off" to a wildly errant second iterate, after which it may be impossible to compute the residuals for the next iteration. The choice of starting values for the iterations can be crucial. There is art as well as science in the computation of nonlinear least squares estimates. [See McCullough and Vinod (1999).] In the absence of information about starting values, a workable strategy is to try the Gauss–Newton iteration first. If it fails, go back to the initial starting values and try one of the more general algorithms, such as BFGS, treating minimization of the sum of squares as an otherwise ordinary optimization problem.

A consistent estimator of $\sigma^2$ is based on the residuals:

$$
\hat{\sigma}^2 = \frac{1}{n} \sum_{i=1}^{n} [y_i - h(\mathbf{x}_i, \mathbf{b})]^2. \tag{11-13}
$$

A degrees of freedom correction, $1/(n - K)$, where $K$ is the number of elements in $\boldsymbol{\beta}$, is not strictly necessary here, because all results are asymptotic in any event. Davidson and MacKinnon (2004) argue that on average, (11-13) will underestimate $\sigma^2$, and one should use the degrees of freedom correction. Most software in current use for this model does, but analysts will want to verify which is the case for the program they are using. With this in hand, the estimator of the asymptotic covariance matrix for the nonlinear least squares estimator is given in (11-12).

Once the nonlinear least squares estimates are in hand, inference and hypothesis tests can proceed in the same fashion as prescribed in Chapter 5. A minor problem can arise in evaluating the fit of the regression in that the familiar measure,

$$
R^2 = 1 - \frac{\sum_{i=1}^{n} e_i^2}{\sum_{i=1}^{n} (y_i - \bar{y})^2}, \tag{11-14}
$$

is no longer guaranteed to be in the range of 0 to 1. It does, however, provide a useful descriptive measure.

## 11.3 APPLICATIONS

We will examine two applications. The first is a nonlinear extension of the consumption function examined in Examples 2.1, 3.2 and 7.2–7.4. The Box–Cox transformation presented in Section 11.3.2 is a device used to search for functional form in regression.

### 11.3.1 A NONLINEAR CONSUMPTION FUNCTION

The linear consumption function analyzed at the beginning of Chapter 2 is a restricted version of the more general consumption function

$$C = \alpha + \beta Y^\gamma + \varepsilon,$$

in which $\gamma$ equals 1. With this restriction, the model is linear. If $\gamma$ is free to vary, however, then this version becomes a nonlinear regression. The next example considers nonlinear least squares estimation of this nonlinear regression model.

#### Example 11.5  Analysis of a Nonlinear Consumption Function
The linearized model is

$$C - \left(\alpha^0 + \beta^0 Y^{\gamma^0}\right) + \left(\alpha^0 1 + \beta^0 Y^{\gamma^0} + \gamma^0 \beta^0 Y^{\gamma^0} \ln Y\right) = \alpha + \beta\left(Y^{\gamma^0}\right) + \gamma\left(\beta^0 Y^{\gamma^0} \ln Y\right) + \varepsilon.$$

The nonlinear least squares procedure reduces to iterated regression of

$$C^0 = C + \gamma^0 \beta^0 Y^{\gamma^0} \ln Y \text{ on } \mathbf{x}^0 = \left[\frac{\partial h(.)}{\partial \alpha} \quad \frac{\partial h(.)}{\partial \beta} \quad \frac{\partial h(.)}{\partial \gamma}\right]' = \left[\begin{array}{c} 1 \\ Y^{\gamma^0} \\ \beta^0 Y^{\gamma^0} \ln Y \end{array}\right].$$

Quarterly data on consumption, real disposable income, and several other variables for 1950 to 2000 are listed in Appendix Table F5.1. We will use these to fit the nonlinear consumption function. This turns out to be a particularly straightforward estimation problem. The **iterations** are begun at the least squares estimates for $\alpha$ and $\beta$ and 1 for $\gamma$. As shown here, the solution is reached in eight iterations, after which any further iteration is merely "fine tuning" the hidden digits (i.e., those that the analyst would not be reporting to their reader). ("Gradient" is the scale-free convergence measure noted earlier.)

   Begin NLSQ iterations. Linearized regression.

Iteration = 1;  Sum of squares = 1536321.88;        Gradient = 996103.930
Iteration = 2;  Sum of squares = 0.184780956E+12;  Gradient = 0.184780452E+12 ( × $10^{12}$)
Iteration = 3;  Sum of squares = 20406917.6;        Gradient = 19902415.7
Iteration = 4;  Sum of squares = 581703.598;        Gradient = 77299.6342
Iteration = 5;  Sum of squares = 504403.969;        Gradient = 0.752189847
Iteration = 6;  Sum of squares = 504403.216;        Gradient = 0.526642396E-04
Iteration = 7;  Sum of squares = 504403.216;        Gradient = 0.511324981E-07
Iteration = 8;  Sum of squares = 504403.216;        Gradient = 0.606793426E-10

The linear and nonlinear least squares regression results are shown in Table 11.1.
   Finding the **starting values** for a nonlinear procedure can be difficult. Simply trying a convenient set of values can be unproductive. Unfortunately, there are no good rules for starting values, except that they should be as close to the final values as possible (not particularly helpful). When it is possible, an initial consistent estimator of $\beta$ will be a good starting value. In many cases, however, the only consistent estimator available is the one we are trying to compute by least squares. For better or worse, trial and error is the most frequently used procedure. For the present model, a natural set of values can be obtained because a simple linear model is a special case. Thus, we can start $\alpha$ and $\beta$ at the linear least squares values that would result in the special case of $\gamma = 1$ and use 1 for the starting value for $\gamma$.

**TABLE 11.1**    Estimated Consumption Functions

| Parameter | Linear Model | | Nonlinear Model | |
|---|---|---|---|---|
| | Estimate | Standard Error | Estimate | Standard Error |
| $\alpha$ | −80.3547 | 14.3059 | 458.7990 | 22.5014 |
| $\beta$ | 0.9217 | 0.003872 | 0.10085 | 0.01091 |
| $\gamma$ | 1.0000 | — | 1.24483 | 0.01205 |
| e′e | 1,536,321.881 | | 504,403.1725 | |
| $\sigma$ | 87.20983 | | 50.0946 | |
| $R^2$ | 0.996448 | | 0.998834 | |
| Var[b] | — | | 0.000119037 | |
| Var[c] | — | | 0.00014532 | |
| Cov[b, c] | — | | −0.000131491 | |

The procedures outlined earlier are used at the last iteration to obtain the asymptotic standard errors and an estimate of $\sigma^2$. (To make this comparable to $s^2$ in the linear model, the value includes the degrees of freedom correction.) The estimates for the linear model are shown in Table 11.1 as well. Eight iterations are required for convergence. The value of $\delta$ is shown at the right. Note that the coefficient vector takes a very errant step after the first iteration—the sum of squares becomes huge—but the iterations settle down after that and converge routinely.

For hypothesis testing and confidence intervals, the familiar procedures can be used, with the proviso that all results are only asymptotic. As such, for testing a restriction, the chi-squared statistic rather than the $F$ ratio is likely to be more appropriate. For example, for testing the hypothesis that $\gamma$ is different from 1, an asymptotic $t$ test, based on the standard normal distribution, is carried out, using

$$z = \frac{1.24483 - 1}{0.01205} = 20.3178.$$

This result is larger than the critical values of 1.96 for the 5 percent significance level, and we thus reject the linear model in favor of the nonlinear regression. We are also interested in the marginal propensity to consume. In this expanded model, $H_0 : \gamma = 1$ is a test that the marginal propensity to consume is constant, not that it is 1. (That would be a joint test of both $\gamma = 1$ and $\beta = 1$.) In this model, the marginal propensity to consume is

$$\text{MPC} = \frac{dC}{dY} = \beta \gamma Y^{\gamma-1},$$

which varies with $Y$. To test the hypothesis that this value is 1, we require a particular value of $Y$. Because it is the most recent value, we choose $DPI_{2000.4} = 6634.9$. At this value, the MPC is estimated as 0.86971. We estimate its standard error using the delta method, with the square root of

$$[\partial\text{MPC}/\partial b \quad \partial\text{MPC}/\partial c] \begin{bmatrix} \text{Var}[b] & \text{Cov}[b, c] \\ \text{Cov}[b, c] & \text{Var}[c] \end{bmatrix} \begin{bmatrix} \partial\text{MPC}/\partial b \\ \partial\text{MPC}/\partial c \end{bmatrix}$$

$$= [cY^{c-1} \quad bY^{c-1}(1 + c \ln Y)] \begin{bmatrix} 0.000119037 & -0.000131491 \\ -0.000131491 & 0.00014532 \end{bmatrix} \begin{bmatrix} cY^{c-1} \\ bY^{c-1}(1 + c \ln Y) \end{bmatrix}$$

$$= 0.00007469,$$

which gives a standard error of 0.0086423. For testing the hypothesis that the MPC is equal to 1.0 in 2000.4 we would refer

$$z = \frac{0.86971 - 1}{0.0086423} = -15.076$$

to a standard normal table. This difference is certainly statistically significant, so we would reject the hypothesis.

### Example 11.6  Multicollinearity in Nonlinear Regression

In the preceding example, there is no question of collinearity in the data matrix $\mathbf{X} = [\mathbf{i}, \mathbf{y}]$; the variation in $Y$ is obvious on inspection. But, at the final parameter estimates, the $R^2$ in the regression is 0.998834 and the correlation between the two pseudoregressors $x_2^0 = Y^\gamma$ and $x_3^0 = \beta Y^\gamma \ln Y$ is 0.999752. The condition number for the normalized matrix of sums of squares and cross products is 208.306. (The condition number is computed by computing the square root of the ratio of the largest to smallest characteristic root of $\mathbf{D}^{-1}\mathbf{X}^{0\prime}\mathbf{X}^0\mathbf{D}^{-1}$ where $x_1^0 = 1$ and $\mathbf{D}$ is the diagonal matrix containing the square roots of $\mathbf{x}_k^{0\prime}\mathbf{x}_k^0$ on the diagonal.) Recall that 20 was the benchmark for a problematic data set. By the standards discussed in Section 4.8.1, the collinearity problem in this "data set" is severe.

### 11.3.2  THE BOX–COX TRANSFORMATION

The **Box–Cox transformation** is a device for generalizing the linear model. The transformation is[3]

$$x^{(\lambda)} = \frac{x^\lambda - 1}{\lambda}.$$

In a regression model, the analysis can be done *conditionally*. For a given value of $\lambda$, the model,

$$y = \alpha + \sum_{k=1}^{K} \beta_k x_k^{(\lambda)} + \varepsilon, \tag{11-15}$$

is a linear regression that can be estimated by least squares.[4] In principle, each regressor could be transformed by a different value of $\lambda$, but, in most applications, this level of generality becomes excessively cumbersome, and $\lambda$ is assumed to be the same for all the variables in the model.[5] At the same time, it is also possible to transform $y$, say, by $y^{(\theta)}$. Transformation of the dependent variable, however, amounts to a specification of the whole model, not just the functional form.

### Example 11.7  Flexible Cost Function

Caves, Christensen, and Trethaway (1980) analyzed the costs of production for railroads providing freight and passenger service. Continuing a long line of literature on the costs of production in regulated industries, a translog cost function (see Section 10.4.2) would be a natural choice for modeling this multiple-output technology. Several of the firms in the study, however, produced no passenger service, which would preclude the use of the translog model. (This model would require the log of zero.) An alternative is the Box–Cox transformation, which is computable for zero output levels. A constraint must still be placed on $\lambda$ in their model, as $0^{(\lambda)}$ is defined only if $\lambda$ is strictly positive. A positive value of $\lambda$ is not assured. A question does arise in this context (and other similar ones) as to whether zero outputs should be treated the same as nonzero outputs or whether an output of zero represents a discrete corporate decision distinct from other variations in the output levels.

---

[3]Box and Cox (1964). To be defined for all values of $\lambda$, $x$ must be strictly positive. See also Zarembka (1974).

[4]In most applications, some of the regressors—for example, a dummy variable—will not be transformed. For such a variable, say $v_k$, $v_k^{(\lambda)} = v_k$, and the relevant derivatives in (11-16) will be zero.

[5]See, for example, Seaks and Layson (1983).

In addition, as can be seen in (11-16), this solution is only partial. The zero values of the regressors preclude computation of appropriate standard errors.

If $\lambda$ in (11-15) is taken to be an unknown parameter, then the regression becomes nonlinear in the parameters. Although no transformation will reduce it to linearity, nonlinear least squares is straightforward. In most instances, we can expect to find the least squares value of $\lambda$ between $-2$ and $2$. Typically, then, $\lambda$ is estimated by scanning this range for the value that minimizes the sum of squares. When $\lambda$ equals zero, the transformation is, by L'Hôpital's rule,

$$\lim_{\lambda \to 0} \frac{x^\lambda - 1}{\lambda} = \lim_{\lambda \to 0} \frac{d(x^\lambda - 1)/d\lambda}{1} = \lim_{\lambda \to 0} x^\lambda \times \ln x = \ln x.$$

Once the optimal value of $\lambda$ is located, the least squares estimates, the mean squared residual, and this value of $\lambda$ constitute the nonlinear least squares estimates of the parameters.

After determining the optimal value of $\lambda$, it is sometimes treated as if it were a *known* value in the least squares results. But $\hat{\lambda}$ is an estimate of an unknown parameter. It is not hard to show that the least squares standard errors will always underestimate the correct asymptotic standard errors.[6] To get the appropriate values, we need the derivatives of the right-hand side of (11-15) with respect to $\alpha$, $\boldsymbol{\beta}$, and $\lambda$. In the notation of Section 11.2.3, these are

$$\frac{\partial h(.)}{\partial \alpha} = 1,$$

$$\frac{\partial h(.)}{\partial \beta_k} = x_k^{(\lambda)}, \qquad\qquad\qquad \textbf{(11-16)}$$

$$\frac{\partial h(.)}{\partial \lambda} = \sum_{k=1}^{K} \beta_k \frac{\partial x_k^{(\lambda)}}{\partial \lambda} = \sum_{k=1}^{K} \beta_k \left[ \frac{1}{\lambda} \left( x_k^\lambda \ln x_k - x_k^{(\lambda)} \right) \right].$$

We can now use (11-12) and (11-13) to estimate the asymptotic covariance matrix of the parameter estimates. Note that $\ln x_k$ appears in $\partial h(.)/\partial \lambda$. If $x_k = 0$, then this matrix cannot be computed. This was the point noted at the end of Example 11.7.

It is important to remember that the coefficients in a nonlinear model are not equal to the slopes (i.e., here the demand elasticities) with respect to the variables. For the particular Box–Cox model,[7]

$$\ln Y = \alpha + \beta \left[ \frac{X^\lambda - 1}{\lambda} \right] + \varepsilon,$$

$$\frac{dE[\ln Y \mid X]}{d \ln X} = \beta X^\lambda = \eta. \qquad\qquad \textbf{(11-17)}$$

Standard errors for these estimates can be obtained using the **delta method.** The derivatives are $\partial \eta / \partial \beta = \eta / \beta$ and $\partial \eta / \partial \lambda = \eta \ln X$. Collecting terms, we obtain

$$\text{Asy. Var}[\hat{\eta}] = (\eta/\beta)^2 \left\{ \text{Asy. Var}[\hat{\beta}] + (\beta \ln X)^2 \text{Asy. Var}[\hat{\lambda}] + (2\beta \ln X)\text{Asy. Cov}[\hat{\beta}, \hat{\lambda}] \right\}.$$

---

[6]See Fomby, Hill, and Johnson (1984, pp. 426–431).

[7]We have used the result $d \ln Y / d \ln X = X d \ln Y / dX$.

## 11.4 HYPOTHESIS TESTING AND PARAMETRIC RESTRICTIONS

In most cases, the sorts of hypotheses one would test in this context will involve fairly simple linear restrictions. The tests can be carried out using the usual formulas discussed in Chapter 5 and the asymptotic covariance matrix presented earlier. For more involved hypotheses and for nonlinear restrictions, the procedures are a bit less clear-cut. Two principal testing procedures were discussed in Section 5.4: the Wald and Lagrange multiplier tests. For the linear model, these statistics are transformations of the standard $F$ statistic (see Section 16.9.1), so the tests are essentially identical. In the nonlinear case, they are equivalent only asymptotically. We will work through the Wald and Lagrange multiplier tests for the general case and then apply them to the example of the previous section. Since we have not assumed normality of the disturbances (yet), we will postpone treatment of the likelihood ratio statistic until we revisit this model in Section 16.9.5.

### 11.4.1 SIGNIFICANCE TESTS FOR RESTRICTIONS: F AND WALD STATISTICS

The hypothesis to be tested is

$$H_0 : \mathbf{r}(\boldsymbol{\beta}) = \mathbf{q}, \tag{11-18}$$

where $\mathbf{r}(\boldsymbol{\beta})$ is a column vector of $J$ continuous functions of the elements of $\boldsymbol{\beta}$. These restrictions may be linear or nonlinear. It is necessary, however, that they be **overidentifying restrictions.** Thus, in formal terms, if the original parameter vector has $K$ free elements, then the hypothesis $\mathbf{r}(\boldsymbol{\beta}) - \mathbf{q}$ must impose at least one functional relationship on the parameters. If there is more than one restriction, then they must be functionally independent. These two conditions imply that the $J \times K$ **Jacobian,**

$$\mathbf{R}(\boldsymbol{\beta}) = \frac{\partial \mathbf{r}(\boldsymbol{\beta})}{\partial \boldsymbol{\beta}'}, \tag{11-19}$$

must have full row rank and that $J$, the number of restrictions, must be strictly less than $K$. This situation is analogous to the linear model, in which $\mathbf{R}(\boldsymbol{\beta})$ would be the matrix of coefficients in the restrictions. (See, as well, Section 5.5, where the methods examined here are applied to the linear model.)

Let $\mathbf{b}$ be the unrestricted, nonlinear least squares estimator, and let $\mathbf{b}_*$ be the estimator obtained when the constraints of the hypothesis are imposed.[8] Which test statistic one uses depends on how difficult the computations are. Unlike the linear model, the various testing procedures vary in complexity. For instance, in our example, the Lagrange multiplier is by far the simplest to compute. Of the four methods we will consider, only this test does not require us to compute a nonlinear regression.

The nonlinear analog to the familiar $F$ statistic based on the fit of the regression (i.e., the sum of squared residuals) would be

$$F[J, n - K] = \frac{[S(\mathbf{b}_*) - S(\mathbf{b})]/J}{S(\mathbf{b})/(n - K)}. \tag{11-20}$$

---

[8] This computational problem may be extremely difficult in its own right, especially if the constraints are nonlinear. We assume that the estimator has been obtained by whatever means are necessary.

This equation has the appearance of our earlier $F$ ratio. In the nonlinear setting, however, neither the numerator nor the denominator has exactly the necessary chi-squared distribution, so the $F$ distribution is only approximate. Note that this $F$ statistic requires that both the restricted and unrestricted models be estimated.

The Wald test is based on the distance between $\mathbf{r}(\mathbf{b})$ and $\mathbf{q}$. If the unrestricted estimates fail to satisfy the restrictions, then doubt is cast on the validity of the restrictions. The statistic is

$$
\begin{aligned}
W &= [\mathbf{r}(\mathbf{b}) - \mathbf{q}]'\{\text{Est. Asy. Var}[\mathbf{r}(\mathbf{b}) - \mathbf{q}]\}^{-1}[\mathbf{r}(\mathbf{b}) - \mathbf{q}] \\
&= [\mathbf{r}(\mathbf{b}) - \mathbf{q}]'\{\mathbf{R}(\mathbf{b})\hat{\mathbf{V}}\mathbf{R}'(\mathbf{b})\}^{-1}[\mathbf{r}(\mathbf{b}) - \mathbf{q}],
\end{aligned}
\tag{11-21}
$$

where

$$
\hat{\mathbf{V}} = \text{Est. Asy. Var}[\mathbf{b}],
$$

and $\mathbf{R}(\mathbf{b})$ is evaluated at $\mathbf{b}$, the estimate of $\boldsymbol{\beta}$.

Under the null hypothesis, this statistic has a limiting chi-squared distribution with $J$ degrees of freedom. If the restrictions are correct, the Wald statistic and $J$ times the $F$ statistic are asymptotically equivalent. The Wald statistic can be based on the estimated covariance matrix obtained earlier using the unrestricted estimates, which may provide a large savings in computing effort if the restrictions are nonlinear. It should be noted that the small-sample behavior of $W$ can be erratic, and the more conservative $F$ statistic may be preferable if the sample is not large.

The caveat about Wald statistics that applied in the linear case applies here as well. Because it is a pure significance test that does not involve the alternative hypothesis, the Wald statistic is not invariant to how the hypothesis is framed. In cases in which there are more than one equivalent ways to specify $\mathbf{r}(\boldsymbol{\beta}) = \mathbf{q}$, $W$ can give different answers depending on which is chosen.

### 11.4.2 TESTS BASED ON THE LM STATISTIC

The **Lagrange multiplier test** is based on the decrease in the sum of squared residuals that would result if the restrictions in the restricted model were released. The formalities of the test are given in Section 16.6.3. For the nonlinear regression model, the test has a particularly appealing form.[9] Let $\mathbf{e}_*$ be the vector of residuals $y_i - h(\mathbf{x}_i, \mathbf{b}_*)$ computed using the restricted estimates. Recall that we defined $\mathbf{X}^0$ as an $n \times K$ matrix of derivatives computed at a particular parameter vector in (11-6). Let $\mathbf{X}_*^0$ be this matrix *computed at the restricted estimates*. Then the Lagrange multiplier statistic for the nonlinear regression model is

$$
\text{LM} = \frac{\mathbf{e}_*'\mathbf{X}_*^0[\mathbf{X}_*^{0\prime}\mathbf{X}_*^0]^{-1}\mathbf{X}_*^{0\prime}\mathbf{e}_*}{\mathbf{e}_*'\mathbf{e}_*/n}.
\tag{11-22}
$$

Under $H_0$, this statistic has a limiting chi-squared distribution with $J$ degrees of freedom. What is especially appealing about this approach is that it requires only the restricted estimates. This method may provide some savings in computing effort if, as in our example, the restrictions result in a linear model. Note, also, that the Lagrange multiplier

---

[9]This test is derived in Judge et al. (1985). A lengthy discussion appears in Mittelhammer et al. (2000).

statistic is $n$ times the uncentered $R^2$ in the regression of $\mathbf{e}_*$ on $\mathbf{X}_*^0$. Many Lagrange multiplier statistics are computed in this fashion.

### Example 11.8 Hypothesis Tests in a Nonlinear Regression Model
We test the hypothesis $H_0 : \gamma = 1$ in the consumption function of Section 11.3.1.

- **F statistic.** The $F$ statistic is

$$F[1, 204 - 3] = \frac{(1{,}536{,}321.881 - 504{,}403.17) / 1}{504{,}403.17 / (204 - 3)} = 411.29.$$

The critical value from the tables is 3.84, so the hypothesis is rejected.
- **Wald statistic.** For our example, the Wald statistic is based on the distance of $\hat{\gamma}$ from 1 and is simply the square of the asymptotic $t$ ratio we computed in the example:

$$W = \frac{(1.244827 - 1)^2}{0.01205^2} = 412.805.$$

The critical value from the chi-squared table is 3.84.
- **Lagrange multiplier.** For our example, the elements in $\mathbf{x}_i^*$ are

$$\mathbf{x}_i^* = [1, Y^\gamma, \beta\gamma Y^\gamma \ln Y].$$

To compute this at the restricted estimates, we use the ordinary least squares estimates for $\alpha$ and $\beta$ and 1 for $\gamma$ so that

$$\mathbf{x}_i^* = [1, Y, \beta Y \ln Y].$$

The residuals are the least squares residuals computed from the linear regression. Inserting the values given earlier, we have

$$\text{LM} = \frac{996{,}103.9}{(1{,}536{,}321.881 / 204)} = 132.267.$$

As expected, this statistic is also larger than the critical value from the chi-squared table.

## 11.5 NONLINEAR SYSTEMS OF EQUATIONS

We now consider estimation of nonlinear systems of equations. The underlying theory is essentially the same as that for linear systems. As such, most of the following will describe practical aspects of estimation. Consider estimation of the parameters of the equation system

$$\begin{aligned}
\mathbf{y}_1 &= \mathbf{h}_1(\boldsymbol{\beta}, \mathbf{X}) + \boldsymbol{\varepsilon}_1, \\
\mathbf{y}_2 &= \mathbf{h}_2(\boldsymbol{\beta}, \mathbf{X}) + \boldsymbol{\varepsilon}_2, \\
&\vdots \\
\mathbf{y}_M &= \mathbf{h}_M(\boldsymbol{\beta}, \mathbf{X}) + \boldsymbol{\varepsilon}_M.
\end{aligned} \tag{11-23}$$

[Note the analogy to (10-19).]

There are $M$ equations in total, to be estimated with $t = 1, \ldots, T$ observations. There are $K$ parameters in the model. No assumption is made that each equation has "its own" parameter vector; we simply use some of or all the $K$ elements in $\boldsymbol{\beta}$ in each equation. Likewise, there is a set of $T$ observations on each of $P$ independent variables $\mathbf{x}_p, p = 1, \ldots, P$, some of or all that appear in each equation. For convenience, the equations are written generically in terms of the full $\boldsymbol{\beta}$ and $\mathbf{X}$. The disturbances are assumed to have zero means and contemporaneous covariance matrix $\boldsymbol{\Sigma}$. We will leave the extension to autocorrelation for more advanced treatments.

In the multivariate regression model, if $\boldsymbol{\Sigma}$ is known, then the generalized least squares estimator of $\boldsymbol{\beta}$ is the vector that minimizes the generalized sum of squares

$$\boldsymbol{\varepsilon}(\boldsymbol{\beta})'\boldsymbol{\Omega}^{-1}\boldsymbol{\varepsilon}(\boldsymbol{\beta}) = \sum_{i=1}^{M}\sum_{j=1}^{M}\sigma^{ij}[\mathbf{y}_i - \mathbf{h}_i(\boldsymbol{\beta}, \mathbf{X})]'[\mathbf{y}_j - \mathbf{h}_j(\boldsymbol{\beta}, \mathbf{X})], \qquad \textbf{(11-24)}$$

where $\boldsymbol{\varepsilon}(\boldsymbol{\beta})$ is an $MT \times 1$ vector of disturbances obtained by stacking the equations, $\boldsymbol{\Omega} = \boldsymbol{\Sigma} \otimes \mathbf{I}$, and $\sigma^{ij}$ is the $ij$th element of $\boldsymbol{\Sigma}^{-1}$. [See (10-7).] As we did in Section 11.2, define the pseudoregressors as the derivatives of the $\mathbf{h}(\boldsymbol{\beta}, \mathbf{X})$ functions with respect to $\boldsymbol{\beta}$. That is, linearize each of the equations. Then the first-order condition for minimizing this sum of squares is

$$\frac{\partial\boldsymbol{\varepsilon}(\boldsymbol{\beta})'\boldsymbol{\Omega}^{-1}\boldsymbol{\varepsilon}(\boldsymbol{\beta})}{\partial\boldsymbol{\beta}} = \sum_{i=1}^{M}\sum_{j=1}^{M}\sigma^{ij}\left[2\mathbf{X}_i^{0\prime}(\boldsymbol{\beta})\boldsymbol{\varepsilon}_j(\boldsymbol{\beta})\right] = \mathbf{0}, \qquad \textbf{(11-25)}$$

where $\mathbf{X}_i^0(\boldsymbol{\beta})$ is the $T \times K$ matrix of pseudoregressors from the linearization of the $i$th equation. (See Section 11.2.3.) If any of the parameters in $\boldsymbol{\beta}$ do not appear in the $i$th equation, then the corresponding column of $\mathbf{X}_i^0(\boldsymbol{\beta})$ will be a column of zeros.

This problem of estimation is doubly complex. In almost any circumstance, solution will require an iteration using one of the methods discussed in Appendix E. Second, of course, is that $\boldsymbol{\Sigma}$ is not known and must be estimated. Remember that efficient estimation in the multivariate regression model does not require an efficient estimator of $\boldsymbol{\Sigma}$, only a consistent one. Therefore, one approach would be to estimate the parameters of each equation separately using nonlinear least squares. This method will be inefficient if any of the equations share parameters, since that information will be ignored. But at this step, consistency is the objective, not efficiency. The resulting residuals can then be used to compute

$$\mathbf{S} = \frac{1}{T}\mathbf{E}'\mathbf{E}. \qquad \textbf{(11-26)}$$

The second step of FGLS is the solution of (11-25), which will require an iterative procedure once again and can be based on $\mathbf{S}$ instead of $\boldsymbol{\Sigma}$. With well-behaved pseudore-gressors, this second-step estimator is fully efficient. Once again, the same theory used for FGLS in the linear, single-equation case applies here.[10] Once the FGLS estimator is obtained, the appropriate asymptotic covariance matrix is estimated with

$$\text{Est. Asy. Var}[\hat{\boldsymbol{\beta}}] = \left[\sum_{i=1}^{M}\sum_{j=1}^{M}s^{ij}\mathbf{X}_i^0(\boldsymbol{\beta})'\mathbf{X}_j^0(\boldsymbol{\beta})\right]^{-1}. \qquad \textbf{(11-27)}$$

---

[10]Neither the nonlinearity nor the multiple equation aspect of this model brings any new statistical issues to the fore. By stacking the equations, we see that this model is simply a variant of the nonlinear regression model with the added complication of a nonscalar disturbance covariance matrix, which we analyzed in Chapter 8. The new complications are primarily practical.

There is a possible flaw in the strategy just outlined. It may not be possible to fit all the equations individually by nonlinear least squares. It is conceivable that identification of some of the parameters requires joint estimation of more than one equation. But as long as the full system identifies all parameters, there is a simple way out of this problem. Recall that all we need for our first step is a consistent set of estimators of the elements of $\boldsymbol{\beta}$. It is easy to show that the preceding defines a GMM estimator (see Chapter 15.) We can use this result to devise an alternative, simple strategy. The weighting of the sums of squares and cross products in (11-24) by $\sigma^{ij}$ produces an efficient estimator of $\boldsymbol{\beta}$. Any other weighting based on some positive definite $\mathbf{A}$ would produce consistent, although inefficient, estimates. At this step, though, efficiency is secondary, so the choice of $\mathbf{A} = \mathbf{I}$ is a convenient candidate. Thus, for our first step, we can find $\boldsymbol{\beta}$ to minimize

$$\boldsymbol{\varepsilon}(\boldsymbol{\beta})'\boldsymbol{\varepsilon}(\boldsymbol{\beta}) = \sum_{i=1}^{M}[\mathbf{y}_i - \mathbf{h}_i(\boldsymbol{\beta}, \mathbf{X})]'[\mathbf{y}_i - \mathbf{h}_i(\boldsymbol{\beta}, \mathbf{X})] = \sum_{i=1}^{M}\sum_{t=1}^{T}[y_{it} - h_i(\boldsymbol{\beta}, \mathbf{x}_{it})]^2.$$

(This estimator is just pooled nonlinear least squares, where the regression function varies across the sets of observations.) This step will produce the $\hat{\boldsymbol{\beta}}$ we need to compute $\mathbf{S}$.

## 11.6 TWO-STEP NONLINEAR LEAST SQUARES ESTIMATION

In this section, we consider the case in which the nonlinear regression model depends on a second set of parameters that is estimated separately.

The model is

$$y = h(\mathbf{x}, \boldsymbol{\beta}, \mathbf{w}, \boldsymbol{\gamma}) + \varepsilon.$$

We consider cases in which the auxiliary parameter $\boldsymbol{\gamma}$ is estimated separately in a model that depends on an additional set of variables $\mathbf{w}$. This first step might be a least squares regression, a nonlinear regression, or a maximum likelihood estimation. The parameters $\boldsymbol{\gamma}$ will usually enter $h(.)$ through some function of $\boldsymbol{\gamma}$ and $\mathbf{w}$, such as an expectation. The second step then consists of a nonlinear regression of $y$ on $h(\mathbf{x}, \boldsymbol{\beta}, \mathbf{w}, \mathbf{c})$ in which $\mathbf{c}$ is the first-round estimate of $\boldsymbol{\gamma}$. To put this in context, we will develop an example.

The estimation procedure is as follows.

1. Estimate $\boldsymbol{\gamma}$ by least squares, nonlinear least squares, or maximum likelihood. We assume that this estimator, however obtained, denoted $\mathbf{c}$, is consistent and asymptotically normally distributed with asymptotic covariance matrix $\frac{1}{n}\mathbf{V}_c$. Let $\hat{\mathbf{V}}_c$ be any appropriate estimator of $\mathbf{V}_c$.

2. Estimate $\boldsymbol{\beta}$ by nonlinear least squares regression of $y$ on $h(\mathbf{x}, \boldsymbol{\beta}, \mathbf{w}, \mathbf{c})$. Let $\frac{\sigma^2}{n}\mathbf{V}_b$ be the asymptotic covariance matrix of this estimator of $\boldsymbol{\beta}$, assuming $\boldsymbol{\gamma}$ is known and let $\frac{s^2}{n}\hat{\mathbf{V}}_b$ be any appropriate estimator of $\frac{\sigma^2}{n}\mathbf{V}_b = \frac{\sigma^2}{n}\left(\frac{\mathbf{X}^{0\prime}\mathbf{X}^0}{n}\right)^{-1}$, where $\mathbf{X}^0$ is the matrix of pseudoregressors evaluated at the true parameter values $\mathbf{x}_i^0 = \partial h(\mathbf{x}_i, \boldsymbol{\beta}, \mathbf{w}_i, \boldsymbol{\gamma})/\partial\boldsymbol{\beta}$.

The argument for consistency of **b** is based on the Slutsky theorem, theorem D.12, as we treat **b** as a function of **c** and the data. We require, as usual, well-behaved pseudo-regressors. As long as **c** is consistent for $\gamma$, the large-sample behavior of the estimator of $\beta$ conditioned on **c** is the same as that conditioned on $\gamma$, that is, as if $\gamma$ were known. Asymptotic normality is obtained along similar lines (albeit with greater difficulty). The asymptotic covariance matrix for the two-step estimator is provided by the following theorem.

---

**THEOREM 11.3** **Asymptotic Distribution of the Two-Step Nonlinear[11] Least Squares Estimator [Murphy and Topel (2002)]**

*Under the standard conditions assumed for the nonlinear least squares estimator, the second-step estimator of $\beta$ is consistent and asymptotically normally distributed with asymptotic covariance matrix*

$$\mathbf{V}_b^* = \frac{1}{n} \left[ \sigma^2 \mathbf{V}_b + \mathbf{V}_b \left( \mathbf{C}\mathbf{V}_c\mathbf{C}' - \mathbf{C}\mathbf{V}_c\mathbf{R}' - \mathbf{R}\mathbf{V}_c\mathbf{C}' \right) \mathbf{V}_b \right],$$

*where*

$$\mathbf{C} = \text{plim} \frac{1}{n} \sum_{i=1}^{n} \mathbf{x}_i^0 \hat{\varepsilon}_i^2 \left( \frac{\partial h(\mathbf{x}_i, \beta, \mathbf{w}_i, \gamma)}{\partial \gamma'} \right)$$

*and*

$$\mathbf{R} = \text{plim} \frac{1}{n} \sum_{i=1}^{n} \mathbf{x}_i^0 \hat{\varepsilon}_i \left( \frac{\partial g(\mathbf{w}_i, \gamma)}{\partial \gamma'} \right).$$

*The function $\partial g(.)/\partial \gamma$ in the definition of $\mathbf{R}$ is the gradient of the ith term in the log-likelihood function if $\gamma$ is estimated by maximum likelihood. (The precise form is shown here.) If $\gamma$ appears as the parameter vector in a regression model,*

$$z_i = f(\mathbf{w}_i, \gamma) + u_i, \tag{11-28}$$

*then $\partial g(.)/\partial \gamma$ will be a derivative of the sum of squared deviations function,*

$$\frac{\partial g(.)}{\partial \gamma} = u_i \frac{\partial f(\mathbf{w}_i, \gamma)}{\partial \gamma}.$$

*If this is a linear regression, then the derivative vector is just $u_i \mathbf{w}_i$.*

---

Implementation of the theorem requires that the asymptotic covariance matrix computed as usual for the second-step estimator based on **c** instead of the true $\gamma$ must be corrected for the presence of the estimator **c** in **b**.

---

[11] Murphy and Topel (2002) was originally published in 1985 in *The Journal of Business and Economic Statistics* and republished in 2002.

Before developing the application, we note how some important special cases are handled. If $\gamma$ enters $h(.)$ as the coefficient vector in a prediction of another variable in a regression model, then we have the following useful results.

**Case 1 Linear regression models.** If $h(.) = \mathbf{x}_i'\boldsymbol{\beta} + \delta E[z_i \mid \mathbf{w}_i] + \varepsilon_i$, where $E[z_i \mid \mathbf{w}_i] = \mathbf{w}_i'\gamma$, then the two models are just fit by linear least squares as usual. The regression for $y$ includes an additional variable, $\mathbf{w}_i'\mathbf{c}$. Let $d$ be the coefficient on this new variable. Then

$$\hat{\mathbf{C}} = \frac{d}{n} \sum_{i=1}^{n} e_i^2 \mathbf{x}_i \mathbf{w}_i' \tag{11-29}$$

and

$$\hat{\mathbf{R}} = \frac{1}{n} \sum_{i=1}^{n} (e_i u_i) \mathbf{x}_i \mathbf{w}_i'. \tag{11-30}$$

**Case 2 Uncorrelated linear regression models.** In Case 1, if the two regression disturbances are uncorrelated, then $\mathbf{R} = \mathbf{0}$.

Case 2 is general. The terms in $\mathbf{R}$ vanish asymptotically if the regressions have uncorrelated disturbances, whether either or both of them are linear. This situation will be quite common.

**Case 3 Prediction from a nonlinear model.** In Cases 1 and 2, if $E[z_i \mid \mathbf{w}_i]$ is a nonlinear function rather than a linear function, then it is only necessary to change $\mathbf{w}_i$ to $\mathbf{w}_i^0 = \partial E[z_i \mid \mathbf{w}_i]/\partial\gamma$—a vector of pseudoregressors—in the definitions of $\mathbf{C}$ and $\mathbf{R}$.

**Case 4 Subset of regressors.** In case 2 (but not in case 1), if $\mathbf{w}$ contains all the variables that are in $\mathbf{x}$, then the appropriate estimator is simply

$$\mathbf{V}_b^* = \frac{s_e^2}{n} \left(1 + \frac{c^2 s_u^2}{s_e^2}\right) \left(\frac{\mathbf{X}^{*'}\mathbf{X}^*}{n}\right)^{-1}, \tag{11-31}$$

where $\mathbf{X}^*$ includes all the variables in $\mathbf{x}$ as well as the prediction for $z$.

All these cases carry over to the case of a nonlinear regression function for $y$. It is only necessary to replace $\mathbf{x}_i$, the actual regressors in the linear model, with $\mathbf{x}_i^0$, the pseudoregressors.

### Example 11.9 Two-Step Estimation of a Credit Scoring Model

Greene (1994) estimates a model of consumer behavior in which the dependent variable of interest is the number of major derogatory reports recorded in the credit history of a sample of applicants for a type of credit card. In fact, this particular variable is one of the most significant determinants of whether an application for a loan or a credit card will be accepted. This dependent variable $y$ is a discrete variable that at any time, for most consumers, will equal zero, but for a significant fraction who have missed several revolving credit payments, it will take a positive value. The typical values are 0, 1, or 2, but values up to, say, 10 are not unusual. This count variable is modeled using a Poisson regression model. This model appears in Sections 25.2–25.5. The probability density function for this discrete random variable is

$$\text{Prob}[y_i = j] = \frac{e^{-\lambda_i} \lambda_i^j}{j!}.$$

The expected value of $y_i$ is $\lambda_i$, so depending on how $\lambda_i$ is specified and despite the unusual nature of the dependent variable, this model is a linear or nonlinear regression model. We will consider both cases, the linear model $E[y_i \mid \mathbf{x}_i] = \mathbf{x}_i' \beta$ and the more common **loglinear model** $E[y_i \mid \mathbf{x}_i] = e^{\mathbf{x}_i' \beta}$, where $\mathbf{x}_i$ might include such covariates as age, income, and typical monthly credit account expenditure. This model is usually estimated by maximum likelihood. But because it is a bona fide regression model, least squares, either linear or nonlinear, is a consistent, if inefficient, estimator.

In Greene's study, a secondary model is fit for the outcome of the credit card application. Let $z_i$ denote this outcome, coded 1 if the application is accepted, 0 if not. For purposes of this example, we will model this outcome using a **logit model** (see the extensive development in Chapter 23). Thus

$$\text{Prob}[z_i = 1] = P(\mathbf{w}_i, \gamma) = \frac{e^{\mathbf{w}_i' \gamma}}{1 + e^{\mathbf{w}_i' \gamma}},$$

where $\mathbf{W}_i$ might include age, income, whether the applicant owns their own home, and whether they are self-employed; these are the sorts of variables that "credit scoring" agencies examine.

Finally, we suppose that the probability of acceptance enters the regression model as an additional explanatory variable. (We concede that the power of the underlying theory wanes a bit here.) Thus, our nonlinear regression model is

$$E[y_i \mid \mathbf{x}_i] = \mathbf{x}_i' \beta + \delta P(\mathbf{w}_i, \gamma) \quad \text{(linear)},$$

or

$$E[y_i \mid \mathbf{x}_i] = e^{\mathbf{x}_i' \beta + \delta P(\mathbf{w}_i, \gamma)} \quad \text{(loglinear, nonlinear)}.$$

The two-step estimation procedure consists of estimation of $\gamma$ by maximum likelihood, then computing $\hat{P}_i = P(\mathbf{w}_i, \mathbf{c})$ where $\mathbf{c}$ is the estimate of $\gamma$, and finally estimating by either linear or nonlinear least squares $[\beta, \delta]$ using $\hat{P}_i$ as a constructed regressor. We will develop the theoretical background for the estimator and then continue with implementation of the estimator.

For the Poisson regression model, when the conditional mean function is linear, $\mathbf{x}_i^0 = \mathbf{x}_i$. If it is loglinear, then

$$\mathbf{x}_i^0 = \partial \lambda_i / \partial \beta = \partial \exp(\mathbf{x}_i' \beta) / \partial \beta = \lambda_i \mathbf{x}_i,$$

which is simple to compute. When $P(\mathbf{w}_i, \gamma)$ is included in the model, the pseudoregressor vector $\mathbf{x}_i^0$ includes this variable and the coefficient vector is $[\beta, \delta]$. Then

$$\hat{V}_b = \frac{1}{n} \sum_{i=1}^{n} [y_i - h(\mathbf{x}_i, \mathbf{b}, \mathbf{w}_i, \mathbf{c})]^2 \times \left( \frac{\hat{\mathbf{X}}^{0'} \hat{\mathbf{X}}^0}{n} \right)^{-1},$$

where $\hat{\mathbf{X}}^0$ is computed at $[\mathbf{b}, d, \mathbf{c}]$, the final estimates.

For the logit model, the gradient of the log-likelihood and the estimator of $\mathbf{V}_c$ are given in Section 23.4. They are

$$\partial \ln f(z_i \mid \mathbf{w}_i, \gamma) / \partial \gamma = [z_i - P(\mathbf{w}_i, \gamma)] \mathbf{w}_i,$$

and

$$\hat{V}_c = \left[ \frac{1}{n} \sum_{i=1}^{n} [z_i - P(\mathbf{w}_i, \hat{\gamma})]^2 \mathbf{w}_i \mathbf{w}_i' \right]^{-1}.$$

Note that for this model, we are actually inserting a prediction from a regression model of sorts, since $E[z_i \mid \mathbf{w}_i] = P(\mathbf{w}_i, \gamma)$. To compute $\mathbf{C}$, we will require

$$\partial h(\cdot) / \partial \gamma = \lambda_i \delta \partial P_i / \partial \gamma = \lambda_i \delta P_i (1 - P_i) \mathbf{w}_i.$$

The remaining parts of the corrected covariance matrix are computed using

$$\hat{\mathbf{C}} = \frac{1}{n}\sum_{i=1}^{n}(\hat{\lambda}_i\hat{\mathbf{x}}_i^0\hat{\varepsilon}_i^2)[\hat{\lambda}_i\hat{\delta}\hat{P}_i(1-\hat{P}_i)]\mathbf{w}_i'$$

and

$$\mathbf{R} = \frac{1}{n}\sum_{i=1}^{n}(\hat{\lambda}_i\mathbf{x}_i^0\varepsilon_i)(z_i - P_i)\mathbf{w}_i'.$$

(If the regression model is linear, then the three occurrences of $\hat{\lambda}_i$ are omitted.)

Data used in the application are listed in Appendix Table F8.1. We use the following model:

$$\text{Prob}[z_i = 1] = P(\text{age, income, own home, self-employed}),$$

$$E[y_i] = h(\text{age, income, expend}).$$

We have used 100 of the 1,319 observations used in the original study. Table 11.2 reports the results of the various regressions and computations. The column denoted St.Er.* contains the corrected standard error. The column marked St.Er. contains the standard errors that would be computed ignoring the two-step nature of the computations. For the linear model, we used $\mathbf{e}'\mathbf{e}/n$ to estimate $\sigma^2$. As expected, accounting for the variability in $\hat{\mathbf{y}}$ increases the standard errors of the second-step estimator.

The linear model appears to give quite different results from the nonlinear model. But this can be deceiving. In the linear model, $\partial E[y_i \mid \mathbf{x}_i, P_i]/\partial\mathbf{x}_i = \boldsymbol{\beta}$ whereas in the nonlinear model, the counterpart is not $\boldsymbol{\beta}$ but $\lambda_i\boldsymbol{\beta}$. The value of $\lambda_i$ at the mean values of all the variables in the second-step model is roughly 0.36 (the mean of the dependent variable), so the marginal effects in the nonlinear model are [0.02876, −0.04774, −0.1061, 2.5145], respectively, including $P_i$, but not the constant, which are reasonably similar to those for the linear model. To compute an asymptotic covariance matrix for the estimated marginal effects, we would use the delta method from Sections D.2.7 and D.3.1. For convenience, let $\mathbf{b}_p = [\mathbf{b}', d]'$, and let $\mathbf{v}_i = [\mathbf{x}_i', \hat{P}_i]'$, which just adds $\hat{P}_i$ to the regressor vector so we need not treat it separately. Then the vector of marginal effects is

$$\mathbf{m} = \exp(\mathbf{v}_i'\mathbf{b}_p) \times \mathbf{b}_p = \lambda_i\mathbf{b}_p.$$

The matrix of derivatives is

$$\mathbf{G} = \partial\mathbf{m}/\partial\mathbf{b}_p' = \lambda_i(\mathbf{I} + \mathbf{b}_p\mathbf{v}_i'),$$

**TABLE 11.2** Two-Step Estimates of a Credit Scoring Model

| Variable | Step 1. $P(\mathbf{w}_i, \gamma)$ Est. | St.Er. | Step 2. $E[y_i \mid x_i] = x_i'\beta + \delta P_i$ Est. | St.Er. | St.Er.* | Step 2. $E[y_i \mid x_i] = e^{x_i'\beta + \delta P_i}$ Est. | St.Er. | St.Er.* |
|---|---|---|---|---|---|---|---|---|
| Constant | 2.7236 | 1.0970 | −1.0628 | 1.1907 | 1.2084 | −7.1896 | 6.2687 | 7.95116 |
| Age | −0.07328 | 0.02962 | 0.021661 | 0.018756 | 0.019144 | 0.079885 | 0.08132 | 0.10139 |
| Income | 0.21920 | 0.14296 | 0.03473 | 0.07266 | 0.078240 | −0.132609 | 0.21374 | 0.282928 |
| Self-empl | −1.9439 | 1.01270 | | | | | | |
| Own Rent | 0.18937 | 0.49817 | | | | | | |
| Expend | | | −0.000787 | 0.000368 | 0.000393 | −0.294712 | 1.12573 | 1.12577 |
| $P(\mathbf{W}_i, \gamma)$ | | | 1.0408 | 1.0653 | 1.122120 | 6.98463 | 5.79595 | 7.58521 |
| ln $L$ | | −53.924 | | | | | | |
| $\mathbf{e}'\mathbf{e}$ | | | 95.5506 | | | 80.31053 | | |
| $s$ | | | 0.977496 | | | 0.89616 | | |
| $R^2$ | | | 0.05433 | | | 0.20516 | | |
| Mean | | 0.73 | 0.36 | | | 0.36 | | |

so the estimator of the asymptotic covariance matrix for **m** is

$$\text{Est. Asy. Var}[\mathbf{m}] = \mathbf{G}\mathbf{V}_b^*\mathbf{G}'.$$

One might be tempted to treat $\lambda_i$ as a constant, in which case only the first term in the quadratic form would appear and the computation would amount simply to multiplying the asymptotic standard errors for $\mathbf{b}_p$ by $\lambda_i$. This approximation would leave the asymptotic $t$ ratios unchanged, whereas making the full correction will change the entire covariance matrix. The approximation will generally lead to an understatement of the correct standard errors.

## 11.7   PANEL DATA APPLICATIONS

The extension of the panel data models of Chapter 9 to the nonlinear regression case is, perhaps surprisingly, not at all straightforward. Thus far, to accommodate the non-linear model, we have generally applied familiar results to the linearized regression. This approach will carry forward to the case of clustered data. (See Section 9.3.3) Un-fortunately, this will not work with the standard panel data methods. The nonlinear regression will be the first of numerous panel data applications that we will consider in which the widsom of the linear regression model cannot be extended to the more general framework.

### 11.7.1   A ROBUST COVARIANCE MATRIX FOR NONLINEAR LEAST SQUARES

The counterpart to (9-3) or (9-4) would simply replace $\mathbf{X}_i$ with $\hat{\mathbf{X}}_i^0$ where the rows are the pseudoregressors for cluster $i$ as defined in (11-9) and "^" indicates that it is computed using the nonlinear least squares estimates of the parameters.

#### Example 11.10   Health Care Utilization
The recent literature in health economics includes many studies of health care utilization. A common measure of the dependent variable of interest is a count of the number of encounters with the health care system, either through visits to a physician or to a hospital. These counts of occurrences are usually studied with the Poisson regression model described in Example 11.9. The nonlinear regression model is

$$E[y_i \mid \mathbf{x}_i] = \exp(\mathbf{x}_i'\boldsymbol{\beta}).$$

A recent study in this genre is "Incentive Effects in the Demand for Health Care: A Bivariate Panel Count Data Estimation" by Riphahn, Wambach, and Million (2003). The authors were interested in counts of physician visits and hospital visits. In this application, they were par-ticularly interested in the impact that the presence of private insurance had on the utilization counts of interest, i.e., whether the data contain evidence of moral hazard.

The raw data are published on the *Journal of Applied Econometrics* data archive website, The URL for the data file is http://qed.econ.queensu.ca/jae/2003-v18.4/riphahn-wambach-million/. The variables in the data file are listed in Appendix Table F11.1. The sample is an unbalanced panel of 7,293 households, the German Socioeconomic Panel data set. The number of observations varies from one to seven (1,525; 1,079; 825; 926; 1,311; 1,000; 887) with a total number of observations of 27,326. We will use these data in several examples here and later in the book.

The following model uses a simple specification for the count of number of visits to the physican in the observation year,

$$\mathbf{x}_{it} = (1, age_{it}, educ_{it}, income_{it}, kids_{it})$$

| TABLE 11.3 | Nonlinear Least Squares Estimates of a Utilization Equation |
|---|---|

Begin NLSQ iterations. Linearized regression.
Iteration = 1;  Sum of squares = 1014865.00; Gradient = 156281.794
Iteration = 2;  Sum of squares = 8995221.17; Gradient = 8131951.67
Iteration = 3;  Sum of squares = 1757006.18; Gradient = 897066.012
Iteration = 4;  Sum of squares = 930876.806; Gradient = 73036.2457
Iteration = 5;  Sum of squares = 860068.332; Gradient = 2430.80472
Iteration = 6;  Sum of squares = 857614.333; Gradient = 12.8270683
Iteration = 7;  Sum of squares = 857600.927; Gradient = 0.411851239E-01
Iteration = 8;  Sum of squares = 857600.883; Gradient = 0.190628165E-03
Iteration = 9;  Sum of squares = 857600.883; Gradient = 0.904650588E-06
Iteration = 10; Sum of squares = 857600.883; Gradient = 0.430441193E-08
Iteration = 11; Sum of squares = 857600.883; Gradient = 0.204875467E-10

Convergence achieved

| Variable | Estimate | Standard Error | Robust Standard Error |
|---|---|---|---|
| Constant | 0.9801 | 0.08927 | 1.01613 |
| Age | 0.01873 | 0.001053 | 0.01107 |
| Education | −0.03613 | 0.005732 | 0.06881 |
| Income | −0.5911 | 0.07173 | 0.7182 |
| Kids | −0.1692 | 0.02642 | 0.2735 |

Table 11.3 details the nonlinear least squares iterations and the results. The convergence criterion for the iterations is $\mathbf{e}^{0\prime}\mathbf{X}^0(\mathbf{X}^{0\prime}\mathbf{X}^0)\mathbf{X}^{0\prime}\mathbf{e}^0 < 10^{-10}$. Although this requires 11 iterations, the function actually reaches the minimum in seven. The estimates of the asymptotic standard errors are computed using the conventional method, $s^2(\hat{\mathbf{X}}^{0\prime}\hat{\mathbf{X}}^0)^{-1}$ and then by the cluster correction in (9-4). The corrected standard errors are considerably larger, as might be expected given that these are panel data set.

### 11.7.2 FIXED EFFECTS

The nonlinear panel data regression model would appear

$$y_{it} = h(\mathbf{x}_{it}, \boldsymbol{\beta}) + \varepsilon_{it}, t = 1, \ldots, T_i, i = 1, \ldots, n.$$

Consider a model with latent heterogeneity, $c_i$. An ambiguity immediately emerges; how should heterogeneity enter the model. Building on the linear model, an additive term might seem natural, as in

$$y_{it} = h(\mathbf{x}_{it}, \boldsymbol{\beta}) + c_i + \varepsilon_{it}, t = 1, \ldots, T_i, i = 1, \ldots, n. \tag{11-32}$$

But we can see in the previous application that this is likely to be inappropriate. The loglinear model of the previous section is constrained to ensure that $E[y_{it} \mid \mathbf{x}_{it}]$ is positive. But an additive random term $c_i$ as in (11-32) could subvert this; unless the range of $c_i$ is restricted, the conditional mean could be negative. The most common application of nonlinear models is the **index function model,**

$$y_{it} = h(\mathbf{x}_{it}'\boldsymbol{\beta} + c_i) + \varepsilon_{it}.$$

This is the natural extension of the linear model, but only in the appearance of the conditional mean. Neither the fixed effects nor the random effects model can be estimated as they were in the linear case in Chapter 9.

Consider the fixed effects model first. We would write this as

$$y_{it} = h(\mathbf{x}'_{it}\boldsymbol{\beta} + \alpha_i) + \varepsilon_{it},$$

where the parameters to be estimated are $\boldsymbol{\beta}$ and $\alpha_i, i = 1, \ldots, n$. Transforming the data to deviations from group means does not remove the fixed effects from the model. For example,

$$y_{it} - \bar{y}_{i.} = h(\mathbf{x}'_{it}\boldsymbol{\beta} + \alpha_i) - \frac{1}{T_i} \sum_{s=1}^{T_i} h(\mathbf{x}'_{is}\boldsymbol{\beta} + \alpha_i), \tag{11-33}$$

which does not simplify things at all. Transforming the regressors to deviations is likewise pointless. To estimate the parameters, it is necessary to minimize the sum of squares with respect to all $n + K$ parameters simultaneously. Because the number of dummy variable coefficients can be huge—the preceding example is based on a data set with 7,293 groups—this can be a difficult or impractical computation. A method of maximizing a function (such as the negative of the sum of squares) that contains an unlimited number of dummy variable coefficients is shown in Chapter 23. As we will examine later in the book, the difficulty with nonlinear models that contain large numbers of dummy variable coefficients is not necessarily the practical one of computing the estimates. That is generally a solvable problem. The difficulty with such models is an intriguing phenomenon known as the **incidental parameters problem.** In most (not all, as we shall find) nonlinear panel data models that contain $n$ dummy variable coefficients, such as the one in (11-33), as a consequence of the fact that the number of parameters increases with the number of individuals in the sample, the estimator of $\boldsymbol{\beta}$ is biased and inconsistent, to a degree that is $O(1/T)$. Because $T$ is only 7 or less in our application, this would seem to be a case in point.

### Example 11.11    Exponential Model with Fixed Effects

The exponential model of the preceding example is actually one of a small handful of known special cases in which it is possible to "condition" out the dummy variables. Consider the sum of squared residuals,

$$S_n = \frac{1}{2} \sum_{i=1}^{n} \sum_{t=1}^{T_i} [y_{it} - \exp(\mathbf{x}'_{it}\boldsymbol{\beta} + \alpha_i)]^2.$$

The first order condition for minimizing $S_n$ with respect to $\alpha_i$ is

$$\frac{\partial S_n}{\partial \alpha_i} = \sum_{t=1}^{T_i} -[y_{it} - \exp(\mathbf{x}'_{it}\boldsymbol{\beta} + \alpha_i)]\exp(\mathbf{x}'_{it}\boldsymbol{\beta} + \alpha_i) = 0. \tag{11-34}$$

Let $\gamma_i = \exp(\alpha_i)$. Then, an equivalent necessary condition would be

$$\frac{\partial S_n}{\partial \gamma_i} = \sum_{t=1}^{T_i} -[y_{it} - \gamma_i \exp(\mathbf{x}'_{it}\boldsymbol{\beta})][\gamma_i \exp(\mathbf{x}'_{it}\boldsymbol{\beta})] = 0,$$

or

$$\gamma_i \sum_{t=1}^{T_i} [y_{it} \exp(\mathbf{x}'_{it}\boldsymbol{\beta})] = \gamma_i^2 \sum_{t=1}^{T_i} [\exp(\mathbf{x}'_{it}\boldsymbol{\beta})]^2.$$

Obviously, if we can solve the equation for $\gamma_i$, we can obtain $\alpha_i = \ln\gamma_i$. The preceding equation can, indeed, be solved for $\gamma_i$, at least conditionally. At the minimum of the sum of squares, it will be true that

$$\hat{\gamma}_i = \frac{\sum_{t=1}^{T_i} y_{it} \exp(\mathbf{x}'_{it}\hat{\boldsymbol{\beta}})}{\sum_{t=1}^{T_i} [\exp(\mathbf{x}'_{it}\hat{\boldsymbol{\beta}})]^2}. \tag{11-35}$$

We can now insert (11-35) into (11-34) to eliminate $\alpha_i$. (This is a counterpart to taking deviations from means in the linear case. As noted, this is possible only for a very few special models—this happens to be one of them. The process is also known as "concentrating out" the parameters $\gamma_i$. Note that at the solution, $\hat{\gamma}_i$, is obtained as the slope in a regression without a constant term of $y_{it}$ on $\hat{z}_{it} = \exp(\mathbf{x}'_{it}\hat{\boldsymbol{\beta}})$ using $T_i$ observations.) The result in (11-35) must hold at the solution. Thus, (11-35) inserted in (11-34) restricts the search for $\boldsymbol{\beta}$ to those values that satisfy the restrictions in (11-35). The resulting sum of squares function is now a function only of the data and $\boldsymbol{\beta}$, and can be minimized with respect to this vector of $K$ parameters. With the estimate of $\boldsymbol{\beta}$ in hand, $\alpha_i$ can be estimated using the log of the result in (11-35) (which is positive by construction).

The preceding presents a mixed picture for the fixed effects model. In nonlinear cases, two problems emerge that were not present earlier, the practical one of actually computing the dummy variable parameters and the theoretical incidental parameters problem that we have yet to investigate, but which promises to be a significant shortcoming of the fixed effects model. We also note, we have focused on a particular form of the model, the "single index" function, in which the conditional mean is a nonlinear function of a linear function. In more general cases, it may be unclear how the unobserved heterogeneity should enter the regression function.

### 11.7.3 RANDOM EFFECTS

The random effects nonlinear model also presents complications both for specification and for estimation. We might begin with a general model

$$y_{it} = h(\mathbf{x}_{it}, \boldsymbol{\beta}, u_i) + \varepsilon_{it}. \tag{11-36}$$

The "random effects" assumption would be, as usual, mean independence,

$$E[u_i \mid \mathbf{X}_i] = 0.$$

Unlike the linear model, the nonlinear regression cannot be consistently estimated by (nonlinear) least squares. In practical terms, we can see why in (11-5)–(11-7). In the linearized regression, the conditional mean at the expansion point $\boldsymbol{\beta}^0$ [see (11-5)] as well as the pseudoregressors are both functions of the unobserved $u_i$. This is true in the general case (11-36) as well as the simpler case of a single index model,

$$y_{it} = h(\mathbf{x}'_{it}\boldsymbol{\beta} + u_i) + \varepsilon_{it}.$$

Thus, it is not possible to compute the iterations for nonlinear least squares. As in the fixed effects case, neither deviations from group means nor first differences solves the problem. Ignoring the problem—that is, simply computing the nonlinear least squares estimator without accounting for heterogeneity—does not produce a consistent estimator, for the same reasons. In general, the benign effect of latent heterogeneity (random effects) that we observe in the linear model only carries over to a very few nonlinear models and, unfortunately, this is not one of them.

An approach that can be used, albeit at the cost of an additional assumption, is the simulation based estimator in Section 9.8.2. If we assume that $u_i$ is normally distributed with mean zero and variance $\sigma_u^2$, then an analog to (9-57) for least squares would be

$$S_n^S = \frac{1}{2} \sum_{i=1}^{n} \frac{1}{R} \sum_{r=1}^{R} \sum_{t=1}^{T_i} [y_{it} - h(\mathbf{x}_{it}, \boldsymbol{\beta}, \sigma_u v_{ir})]^2 \qquad \textbf{(11-37)}$$

The approach from this point would be the same as in Section 9.8.2. [If it is further assumed that $\varepsilon_{it}$ is normally distributed, then after incorporating $\sigma_\varepsilon^2$ in the criterion function, (11-37) would actually be the extension of (9-57) to a nonlinear regression function. The random parameter vector there is specialized here to a nonrandom constant term.]

## 11.8 SUMMARY AND CONCLUSIONS

In this chapter, we extended the regression model to a form that allows nonlinearity in the parameters in the regression function. The results for interpretation, estimation, and hypothesis testing are quite similar to those for the linear model. The two crucial differences between the two models are, first, the more involved estimation procedures needed for the nonlinear model and, second, the ambiguity of the interpretation of the coefficients in the nonlinear model (because the derivatives of the regression are often nonconstant, in contrast to those in the linear model). Finally, we added an additional level of generality to the model. Two-step nonlinear least squares is suggested as a method of allowing a model to be fit while including functions of previously estimated parameters.

### Key Terms and Concepts

- Box–Cox transformation
- Delta method
- GMM estimator
- Identification condition
- Incidental parameters problem
- Index function model
- Indirect utility function
- Iteration
- Jacobian
- Linearized regression model
- Lagrange multiplier test
- Logit model
- Loglinear model
- Nonlinear regression model
- Normalization
- Nonlinear least squares
- Orthogonality condition
- Overidentifying restrictions
- Pseudoregressors
- Roy's identity
- Semiparametric
- Starting values
- Two-step estimation
- Wald test

### Exercises

1. Describe how to obtain nonlinear least squares estimates of the parameters of the model $y = \alpha x^\beta + \varepsilon$.

2. Verify the following differential equation, which applies to the Box–Cox transformation:

$$\frac{d^i x^{(\lambda)}}{d\lambda^i} = \left(\frac{1}{\lambda}\right) \left[x^\lambda (\ln x)^i - \frac{i d^{i-1} x^{(\lambda)}}{d\lambda^{i-1}}\right]. \qquad \textbf{(11-38)}$$

Show that the limiting sequence for $\lambda = 0$ is

$$\lim_{\lambda \to 0} \frac{d^i x^{(\lambda)}}{d\lambda^i} = \frac{(\ln x)^{i+1}}{i+1}.$$ **(11-39)**

These results can be used to great advantage in deriving the actual second derivatives of the log-likelihood function for the Box–Cox model.

## Applications

1. The data in Appendix table F5.2 present 27 statewide observations on value added (output), labor input (labor), and capital stock (capital) for SIC 33 (primary metals). We are interested in determining whether a linear or loglinear production model is more appropriate for these data. Use MacKinnon, White, and Davidson's (1983) $P_E$ test to determine whether a linear or log-linear production model is preferred.

2. Using the Box–Cox transformation, we may specify an alternative to the Cobb–Douglas model as

$$\ln Y = \alpha + \beta_k \frac{(K^\lambda - 1)}{\lambda} + \beta_l \frac{(L^\lambda - 1)}{\lambda} + \varepsilon.$$

Using Zellner and Revankar's data in Appendix Table F14.1, estimate $\alpha$, $\beta_k$, $\beta_l$, and $\lambda$ by using the scanning method suggested in Section 11.3.2. (Do not forget to scale $Y$, $K$, and $L$ by the number of establishments.) Use (11-16), (11-12), and (11-13) to compute the appropriate asymptotic standard errors for your estimates. Compute the two output elasticities, $\partial \ln Y / \partial \ln K$ and $\partial \ln Y / \partial \ln L$, at the sample means of $K$ and $L$. (Hint: $\partial \ln Y / \partial \ln K = K \partial \ln Y / \partial K$.)

3. For the model in Application 2, test the hypothesis that $\lambda = 0$ using a Wald test and a Lagrange multiplier test. Note that the restricted model is the Cobb–Douglas log-linear model. The LM test statistic is shown in (11-22). To carry out the test, you will need to compute the elements of the fourth column of $\mathbf{X}^0$, the pseudoregressor corresponding to $\lambda$ is $\partial E[y \mid x] / \partial \lambda \mid \lambda = 0$. Result (11-39) will be useful.

4. The National Institute of Standards and Technology (NIST) has created a Web site that contains a variety of estimation problems, with data sets, designed to test the accuracy of computer programs. (The URL is http://www.itl.nist.gov/div898/strd/.) One of the five suites of test problems is a set of 27 nonlinear least squares problems, divided into three groups: easy, moderate, and difficult. We have chosen one of them for this application. You might wish to try the others (perhaps to see if the software you are using can solve the problems). This is the Misralc problem (http://www.itl.nist.gov/div898/strd/nls/data/misralc.shtml). The nonlinear regression model is

$$y_i = h(x, \beta) + \varepsilon$$

$$= \beta_1 \left( 1 - \frac{1}{\sqrt{1 + 2\beta_2 x_i}} \right) + \varepsilon_i$$

The data are as follows:

| Y | X |
|-------|-------|
| 10.07 | 77.6 |
| 14.73 | 114.9 |
| 17.94 | 141.1 |
| 23.93 | 190.8 |
| 29.61 | 239.9 |
| 35.18 | 289.0 |
| 40.02 | 332.8 |
| 44.82 | 378.4 |
| 50.76 | 434.8 |
| 55.05 | 477.3 |
| 61.01 | 536.8 |
| 66.40 | 593.1 |
| 75.47 | 689.1 |
| 81.78 | 760.0 |

For each problem posed, NIST also provides the "certified solution," (i.e., the right answer). For the Misralc problem, the solutions are as follows:

| | *Estimate* | *Estimated Standard Error* |
|---|---|---|
| $\beta_1$ | 6.3642725809E + 02 | 4.6638326572E + 00 |
| $\beta_2$ | 2.0813627256E − 04 | 1.7728423155E − 06 |
| **e′e** | | 4.0966836971E − 02 |
| $s^2 = $ **e′e**$/(n - K)$ | | 5.8428615257E − 02 |

Finally, NIST provides two sets of starting values for the iterations, generally one set that is "far" from the solution and a second that is "close" from the solution. For this problem, the starting values provided are $\boldsymbol{\beta}^1 = (500, 0.0001)$ and $\boldsymbol{\beta}^2 = (600, 0.0002)$. The exercise here is to reproduce the NIST results with your software. [For a detailed analysis of the NIST nonlinear least squares benchmarks with several well-known computer programs, see McCullough (1999).]

# 12

# INSTRUMENTAL VARIABLES
# ESTIMATION

=⟨⟨⟨⟩⟩⟩=

## 12.1 INTRODUCTION

The assumption that $\mathbf{x}_i$ and $\varepsilon_i$ are uncorrelated in the linear regression model,

$$y_i = \mathbf{x}_i'\boldsymbol{\beta} + \varepsilon_i, \tag{12-1}$$

has been crucial in the development thus far. But, there are many applications in economics in which this assumption is untenable. Examples include models that contain variables that are measured with error and most dynamic models involving expectations. Without this assumption, none of the proofs of consistency or unbiasedness of the least squares estimator (ordinary or generalized) that were obtained will remain valid, so least squares loses its attractiveness as an estimator.

### Example 12.1    Models in Which Least Squares Is Inconsistent
The following models will appear at various points in this book. In general, least squares will not be a suitable estimator.

**Dynamic Panel Data Models:** In Example 9.18, we examined a random effects dynamic model of the form $y_{it} = x_{it}\beta + \gamma y_{i,t-1} + \varepsilon_{it} + u_i$. Clearly in this case, the regressor $y_{i,t-1}$ is correlated with the disturbance, $(\varepsilon_{it} + u_i)$. In Chapter 15, we will examine a model for municipal expenditure of the form $S_{it} = f(S_{it-1}, \ldots) + \varepsilon_{it}$. The disturbances are assumed to be freely correlated across periods, so both $S_{i,t-1}$ and $\varepsilon_{i,t}$ are correlated with $\varepsilon_{i,t-1}$. It follows that they are correlated with each other, which means that this model, even with a linear specification, does not satisfy the assumptions of the classical model. The regressors and disturbances are correlated.

**Dynamic Regression:** In Chapters 19–21, we will examine a variety of time-series models which are of the form $y_t = f(y_{t-1}, \ldots) + \varepsilon_t$ in which $\varepsilon_t$ is correlated with its past values. This case is essentially the same as the one we just considered. Because the disturbances are autocorrelated, it follows that the dynamic regression implies correlation between the disturbance and a right hand side variable. Once again, least squares will be inconsistent.

**Consumption Function:** We (and many another authors) have used a macroeconomic version of the consumption function at various points to illustrate least squares estimation of the classical regression model. But, by construction, the model violates the assumptions of the classical regression model. The national income data are assembled around some basic accounting identities, including "$Y = C + investment + government\ spending + net\ exports$." Therefore, although the precise relationship between consumption $C$, and income $Y$, $C = f(Y, \varepsilon)$, is ambiguous and is a suitable candidate for modeling, it is clear that consumption (and therefore $\varepsilon$) is one of the main determinants of $Y$. The model $C_t = \alpha + \beta Y_t + \varepsilon_t$ does not fit our assumptions for the classical model if $\text{Cov}[Y_t, \varepsilon_t] \neq 0$. But it is reasonable to assume (at least for now) that $\varepsilon_t$ is uncorrelated with past values of $C$ and $Y$. Therefore, in this model, we might consider $Y_{t-1}$ and $C_{t-1}$ as suitable instrumental variables.

**Measurement Error:** In Section 12.5, we will examine an application in which an earnings equation $y_{i,t} = f(Education_{i,t}, \ldots) + \varepsilon_{i,t}$ is specified for sibling pairs (twins) $t = 1, 2$ for $n$ individuals. Because education is a variable that is measured with error, it will emerge (in a way that will be established following) that this is, once again, a case in which the disturbance and an independent variable are correlated.

None of these models can be consistently estimated by least squares—the method of instrumental variables is the standard approach.

There is an alternative method of estimation called the method of **instrumental variables** (IV). The least squares estimator is a special case, but the IV method is far more general. The method of instrumental variables is developed around the following general extension of the estimation strategy in the classical regression model: Suppose that in the classical model of (12-1), the $K$ variables $\mathbf{x}_i$ may be correlated with $\varepsilon_i$. Suppose as well that there exists a set of $L$ variables $\mathbf{z}_i$, where $L$ is at least as large as $K$, such that $\mathbf{z}_i$ is correlated with $\mathbf{x}_i$ but not with $\varepsilon_i$. We cannot estimate $\boldsymbol{\beta}$ consistently by using the familiar least squares estimator. But we can construct a consistent estimator of $\boldsymbol{\beta}$ by using the assumed relationships among $\mathbf{z}_i$, $\mathbf{x}_i$, and $\varepsilon_i$.

## 12.2  ASSUMPTIONS OF THE MODEL

The assumptions of the classical regression model, laid out in Chapters 2 and 4 are

**A1.  Linearity:** $y_i = x_{i1}\beta_1 + x_{i2}\beta_2 + \cdots + x_{iK}\beta_K + \varepsilon_i$.
**A2.  Full rank:** The $n \times K$ sample data matrix, $\mathbf{X}$ has full column rank
**A3.  Exogeneity of the independent variables:** $E[\varepsilon_i | x_{j1}, x_{j2}, \ldots, x_{jk}] = 0, i,$
  $j = 1, \ldots, n$. There is no correlation between the disturbances and the independent variables.
**A4.  Homoscedasticity and nonautocorrelation:** Each disturbance, $\varepsilon_i$, has the same finite variance, $\sigma^2$ and is uncorrelated with every other disturbance, $\varepsilon_j$, conditioned on $\mathbf{X}$.
**A5.  Stochastic or nonstochastic data:** $(x_{i1}, x_{i2}, \ldots, x_{iK})\, i = 1, \ldots, n$.
**A6.  Normal distribution:** The disturbances are normally distributed.

We will maintain the important result that plim $(\mathbf{X}'\mathbf{X}/n) = \mathbf{Q}_{xx}$. The basic assumptions of the regression model have changed, however. First, A3 (no correlation between $\mathbf{x}$ and $\varepsilon$) is, under our new assumptions,

$$\text{\textbf{AI3.}} \quad E[\varepsilon_i \mid \mathbf{x}_i] = \eta_i.$$

We interpret Assumption AI3 to mean that the regressors now provide information about the expectations of the disturbances. The important implication of AI3 is that the disturbances and the regressors are now correlated. Assumption AI3 implies that

$$E[\mathbf{x}_i \varepsilon_i] = \boldsymbol{\gamma} \tag{12-2}$$

for some nonzero $\boldsymbol{\gamma}$. If the data are "well behaved," then we can apply Theorem D.5 (Khinchine's theorem) to assert that

$$\text{plim } (1/n)\mathbf{X}'\boldsymbol{\varepsilon} = \boldsymbol{\gamma}. \tag{12-3}$$

Notice that the original model results if $\eta_i = 0$. The implication of (12-3) is that the regressors, $\mathbf{X}$, are no longer exogenous.

We now assume that there is an additional set of variables, $\mathbf{Z}$, that have two properties:

1. **Exogeneity:** They are uncorrelated with the disturbance.
2. **Relevance:** They are correlated with the independent variables, $\mathbf{X}$.

We will formalize these notions as we proceed. In the context of our model, variables that have these two properties are instrumental variables. We assume the following:

**AI7.** $[\mathbf{x}_i, \mathbf{z}_i, \varepsilon_i], i = 1, \ldots, n$, are an i.i.d. sequence of random variables.
**AI8a.** $E[x_{ik}^2] = \mathbf{Q}_{xx,kk} < \infty$, a finite constant, $k = 1, \ldots, K$.
**AI8b.** $E[z_{il}^2] = \mathbf{Q}_{zz,ll} < \infty$, a finite constant, $l = 1, \ldots, L$.
**AI8c.** $E[z_{il}x_{ik}] = \mathbf{Q}_{zx,lk} < \infty$, a finite constant, $l = 1, \ldots, L, k = 1, \ldots, K$.
**AI9.** $E[\varepsilon_i \mid \mathbf{z}_i] = 0$.

In later work in time series models, it will be important to relax assumption AI7. Finite means of $\mathbf{z}_l$ follows from AI8b. Using the same analysis as in Section 4.9, we have

$$\text{plim} \, (1/n)\mathbf{Z}'\mathbf{Z} = \mathbf{Q}_{zz}, \text{ a finite, positive definite matrix } (\textit{well behaved data}),$$

$$\text{plim} \, (1/n)\mathbf{Z}'\mathbf{X} = \mathbf{Q}_{zx}, \text{ a finite, } L \times K \text{ matrix with rank } K(\textit{relevance}),$$

$$\text{plim} \, (1/n)\mathbf{Z}'\boldsymbol{\varepsilon} = \mathbf{0} \, (\textit{exogeneity}).$$

In our statement of the classical regression model, we have assumed thus far the special case of $\eta_i = 0; \boldsymbol{\gamma} = \mathbf{0}$ follows. There is no need to dispense with Assumption AI7—it may well continue to be true—but in this special case, it becomes irrelevant.

## 12.3 ESTIMATION

For this more general model of (12-3), we lose most of the useful results we had for least squares. We will consider the implications for least squares, then construct an alternative estimator for $\boldsymbol{\beta}$ in this extended model.

### 12.3.1 ORDINARY LEAST SQUARES

The estimator $\mathbf{b}$ is no longer unbiased;

$$E[\mathbf{b} \mid \mathbf{X}] = \boldsymbol{\beta} + (\mathbf{X}'\mathbf{X})^{-1}\mathbf{X}'\boldsymbol{\eta} \neq \boldsymbol{\beta},$$

so the Gauss–Markov theorem no longer holds. It is also inconsistent;

$$\text{plim} \, \mathbf{b} = \boldsymbol{\beta} + \text{plim} \left(\frac{\mathbf{X}'\mathbf{X}}{n}\right)^{-1} \text{plim} \left(\frac{\mathbf{X}'\boldsymbol{\varepsilon}}{n}\right) = \boldsymbol{\beta} + \mathbf{Q}_{xx}^{-1}\boldsymbol{\gamma} \neq \boldsymbol{\beta}. \tag{12-4}$$

(The asymptotic distribution is considered in the exercises.)

### 12.3.2 THE INSTRUMENTAL VARIABLES ESTIMATOR

Because $E[\mathbf{z}_i\varepsilon_i] = \mathbf{0}$ and all terms have finite variances, it follows that

$$\text{plim} \left(\frac{\mathbf{Z}'\boldsymbol{\varepsilon}}{n}\right) = \text{plim} \left(\frac{\mathbf{Z}'\mathbf{y}}{n}\right) - \text{plim} \left(\frac{\mathbf{Z}'\mathbf{X}\boldsymbol{\beta}}{n}\right) = \mathbf{0}.$$

Therefore,

$$\text{plim}\left(\frac{\mathbf{Z}'\mathbf{y}}{n}\right) = \left[\text{plim}\left(\frac{\mathbf{Z}'\mathbf{X}}{n}\right)\right]\boldsymbol{\beta} + \text{plim}\left(\frac{\mathbf{Z}'\boldsymbol{\varepsilon}}{n}\right) = \left[\text{plim}\left(\frac{\mathbf{Z}'\mathbf{X}}{n}\right)\right]\boldsymbol{\beta}. \qquad \text{(12-5)}$$

Suppose that $\mathbf{Z}$ has the same number of variables as $\mathbf{X}$. For example, suppose in our consumption function that $\mathbf{x}_t = [1, Y_t]$ when $\mathbf{z}_t = [1, Y_{t-1}]$. We have assumed that the rank of $\mathbf{Z}'\mathbf{X}$ is $K$, so now $\mathbf{Z}'\mathbf{X}$ is a square matrix. It follows that

$$\left[\text{plim}\left(\frac{\mathbf{Z}'\mathbf{X}}{n}\right)\right]^{-1}\text{plim}\left(\frac{\mathbf{Z}'\mathbf{y}}{n}\right) = \boldsymbol{\beta},$$

which leads us to the **instrumental variable estimator,**

$$\mathbf{b}_{\text{IV}} = (\mathbf{Z}'\mathbf{X})^{-1}\mathbf{Z}'\mathbf{y}.$$

We have already proved that $\mathbf{b}_{\text{IV}}$ is consistent. We now turn to the **asymptotic distribution.** We will use the same method as in Section 4.9.2. First,

$$\sqrt{n}(\mathbf{b}_{\text{IV}} - \boldsymbol{\beta}) = \left(\frac{\mathbf{Z}'\mathbf{X}}{n}\right)^{-1}\frac{1}{\sqrt{n}}\mathbf{Z}'\boldsymbol{\varepsilon},$$

which has the same **limiting distribution** as $\mathbf{Q}_{zx}^{-1}[(1/\sqrt{n})\mathbf{Z}'\boldsymbol{\varepsilon}]$. Our analysis of $(1/\sqrt{n})\mathbf{Z}'\boldsymbol{\varepsilon}$ can be the same as that of $(1/\sqrt{n})\mathbf{X}'\boldsymbol{\varepsilon}$ in Section 4.9.2, so it follows that

$$\left(\frac{1}{\sqrt{n}}\mathbf{Z}'\boldsymbol{\varepsilon}\right) \xrightarrow{d} N[\mathbf{0}, \sigma^2\mathbf{Q}_{zz}],$$

and

$$\left(\frac{\mathbf{Z}'\mathbf{X}}{n}\right)^{-1}\left(\frac{1}{\sqrt{n}}\mathbf{Z}'\boldsymbol{\varepsilon}\right) \xrightarrow{d} N[\mathbf{0}, \sigma^2\mathbf{Q}_{zx}^{-1}\mathbf{Q}_{zz}\mathbf{Q}_{xz}^{-1}].$$

This step completes the derivation for the next theorem.

---

**THEOREM 12.1** **Asymptotic Distribution of the Instrumental Variables Estimator**

*If Assumptions A1, A2, AI3, A4, A5, AI7, AI8a–c, and AI9 all hold for $[y_i, \mathbf{x}_i, \mathbf{z}_i, \varepsilon_i]$, where $\mathbf{z}$ is a valid set of $L = K$ instrumental variables, then the asymptotic distribution of the instrumental variables estimator $\mathbf{b}_{\text{IV}} = (\mathbf{Z}'\mathbf{X})^{-1}\mathbf{Z}'\mathbf{y}$ is*

$$\mathbf{b}_{\text{IV}} \stackrel{a}{\sim} N\left[\boldsymbol{\beta}, \frac{\sigma^2}{n}\mathbf{Q}_{zx}^{-1}\mathbf{Q}_{zz}\mathbf{Q}_{xz}^{-1}\right]. \qquad \text{(12-6)}$$

*where $\mathbf{Q}_{zx} = \text{plim}(\mathbf{Z}'\mathbf{X}/n)$ and $\mathbf{Q}_{zz} = \text{plim}(\mathbf{Z}'\mathbf{Z}/n)$.*

---

To estimate the **asymptotic covariance matrix,** we will require an estimator of $\sigma^2$. The natural estimator is

$$\hat{\sigma}^2 = \frac{1}{n}\sum_{i=1}^{n}(y_i - \mathbf{x}_i'\mathbf{b}_{\text{IV}})^2.$$

A correction for degrees of freedom is superfluous, as all results here are asymptotic, and $\hat{\sigma}^2$ would not be unbiased in any event. (Nonetheless, it is standard practice in most software to make the degrees of freedom correction.) Write the vector of residuals as

$$\mathbf{y} - \mathbf{X}\mathbf{b}_{\text{IV}} = \mathbf{y} - \mathbf{X}(\mathbf{Z}'\mathbf{X})^{-1}\mathbf{Z}'\mathbf{y}.$$

Substitute $\mathbf{y} = \mathbf{X}\boldsymbol{\beta} + \boldsymbol{\varepsilon}$ and collect terms to obtain $\hat{\boldsymbol{\varepsilon}} = [\mathbf{I} - \mathbf{X}(\mathbf{Z}'\mathbf{X})^{-1}\mathbf{Z}']\boldsymbol{\varepsilon}$. Now,

$$\hat{\sigma}^2 = \frac{\hat{\boldsymbol{\varepsilon}}'\hat{\boldsymbol{\varepsilon}}}{n}$$

$$= \frac{\boldsymbol{\varepsilon}'\boldsymbol{\varepsilon}}{n} + \left(\frac{\boldsymbol{\varepsilon}'\mathbf{Z}}{n}\right)\left(\frac{\mathbf{X}'\mathbf{Z}}{n}\right)^{-1}\left(\frac{\mathbf{X}'\mathbf{X}}{n}\right)\left(\frac{\mathbf{Z}'\mathbf{X}}{n}\right)^{-1}\left(\frac{\mathbf{Z}'\boldsymbol{\varepsilon}}{n}\right) - 2\left(\frac{\boldsymbol{\varepsilon}'\mathbf{X}}{n}\right)\left(\frac{\mathbf{Z}'\mathbf{X}}{n}\right)^{-1}\left(\frac{\mathbf{Z}'\boldsymbol{\varepsilon}}{n}\right).$$

We found earlier that we could (after a bit of manipulation) apply the product result for probability limits to obtain the probability limit of an expression such as this. Without repeating the derivation, we find that $\hat{\sigma}^2$ is a **consistent estimator** of $\sigma^2$, by virtue of the first term. The second and third product terms converge to zero. To complete the derivation, then, we will estimate Asy. Var$[\mathbf{b}_{\text{IV}}]$ with

$$\text{Est. Asy. Var}[\mathbf{b}_{\text{IV}}] = \frac{1}{n}\left\{\left(\frac{\hat{\boldsymbol{\varepsilon}}'\hat{\boldsymbol{\varepsilon}}}{n}\right)\left(\frac{\mathbf{Z}'\mathbf{X}}{n}\right)^{-1}\left(\frac{\mathbf{Z}'\mathbf{Z}}{n}\right)\left(\frac{\mathbf{X}'\mathbf{Z}}{n}\right)^{-1}\right\} \qquad \textbf{(12-7)}$$

$$= \hat{\sigma}^2(\mathbf{Z}'\mathbf{X})^{-1}(\mathbf{Z}'\mathbf{Z})(\mathbf{X}'\mathbf{Z})^{-1}.$$

### 12.3.3 TWO-STAGE LEAST SQUARES

There is a remaining detail. If $\mathbf{Z}$ contains more variables than $\mathbf{X}$, then much of the preceding is unusable, because $\mathbf{Z}'\mathbf{X}$ will be $L \times K$ with rank $K < L$ and will thus not have an inverse. The crucial result in all the preceding is $\text{plim}(\mathbf{Z}'\boldsymbol{\varepsilon}/n) = \mathbf{0}$. That is, every column of $\mathbf{Z}$ is asymptotically uncorrelated with $\boldsymbol{\varepsilon}$. That also means that every linear combination of the columns of $\mathbf{Z}$ is also uncorrelated with $\boldsymbol{\varepsilon}$, which suggests that one approach would be to choose $K$ linear combinations of the columns of $\mathbf{Z}$. Which to choose? One obvious possibility is simply to choose $K$ variables among the $L$ in $\mathbf{Z}$. But intuition correctly suggests that throwing away the information contained in the remaining $L - K$ columns is inefficient. A better choice is the projection of the columns of $\mathbf{X}$ in the column space of $\mathbf{Z}$:

$$\hat{\mathbf{X}} = \mathbf{Z}(\mathbf{Z}'\mathbf{Z})^{-1}\mathbf{Z}'\mathbf{X}.$$

We will return shortly to the virtues of this choice. With this choice of instrumental variables, $\hat{\mathbf{X}}$ for $\mathbf{Z}$, we have

$$\mathbf{b}_{\text{IV}} = (\hat{\mathbf{X}}'\mathbf{X})^{-1}\hat{\mathbf{X}}'\mathbf{y}$$

$$= [\mathbf{X}'\mathbf{Z}(\mathbf{Z}'\mathbf{Z})^{-1}\mathbf{Z}'\mathbf{X}]^{-1}\mathbf{X}'\mathbf{Z}(\mathbf{Z}'\mathbf{Z})^{-1}\mathbf{Z}'\mathbf{y}. \qquad \textbf{(12-8)}$$

The estimator of the asymptotic covariance matrix will be $\hat{\sigma}^2$ times the bracketed matrix in (12-8). The proofs of consistency and asymptotic normality for this estimator are exactly the same as before, because our proof was generic for any valid set of instruments, and $\hat{\mathbf{X}}$ qualifies.

There are two reasons for using this estimator—one practical, one theoretical. If any column of $\mathbf{X}$ also appears in $\mathbf{Z}$, then that column of $\mathbf{X}$ is reproduced exactly in

$\hat{\mathbf{X}}$. This is easy to show. In the expression for $\hat{\mathbf{X}}$, if the $k$th column in $\mathbf{X}$ is one of the columns in $\mathbf{Z}$, say the $l$th, then the $k$th column in $(\mathbf{Z}'\mathbf{Z})^{-1}\mathbf{Z}'\mathbf{X}$ will be the $l$th column of an $L \times L$ identity matrix. This result means that the $k$th column in $\hat{\mathbf{X}} = \mathbf{Z}(\mathbf{Z}'\mathbf{Z})^{-1}\mathbf{Z}'\mathbf{X}$ will be the $l$th column in $\mathbf{Z}$, which is the $k$th column in $\mathbf{X}$. This result is important and useful. Consider what is probably the typical application. Suppose that the regression contains $K$ variables, only one of which, say, the $k$th, is correlated with the disturbances. We have one or more instrumental variables in hand, as well as the other $K-1$ variables that certainly qualify as instrumental variables in their own right. Then what we would use is $\mathbf{Z} = [\mathbf{X}_{(k)}, \mathbf{z}_1, \mathbf{z}_2, \ldots]$, where we indicate omission of the $k$th variable by $(k)$ in the subscript. Another useful interpretation of $\hat{\mathbf{X}}$ is that each column is the set of fitted values when the corresponding column of $\mathbf{X}$ is regressed on all the columns of $\mathbf{Z}$, which is obvious from the definition. It also makes clear why each $\mathbf{x}_k$ that appears in $\mathbf{Z}$ is perfectly replicated. Every $\mathbf{x}_k$ provides a perfect predictor for itself, without any help from the remaining variables in $\mathbf{Z}$. In the example, then, every column of $\mathbf{X}$ except the one that is omitted from $\mathbf{X}_{(k)}$ is replicated exactly, whereas the one that *is* omitted is replaced in $\hat{\mathbf{X}}$ by the predicted values in the regression of this variable on all the $\mathbf{z}$'s.

Of all the different linear combinations of $\mathbf{Z}$ that we might choose, $\hat{\mathbf{X}}$ is the most efficient in the sense that the asymptotic covariance matrix of an IV estimator based on a linear combination $\mathbf{ZF}$ is smaller when $\mathbf{F} = (\mathbf{Z}'\mathbf{Z})^{-1}\mathbf{Z}'\mathbf{X}$ than with any other $\mathbf{F}$ that uses all $L$ columns of $\mathbf{Z}$; a fortiori, this result eliminates linear combinations obtained by dropping any columns of $\mathbf{Z}$. This important result was proved in a seminal paper by Brundy and Jorgenson (1971). [See, also, Wooldridge (2002a, pp. 96–97).]

We close this section with some practical considerations in the use of the instrumental variables estimator. By just multiplying out the matrices in the expression, you can show that

$$\begin{aligned}
\mathbf{b}_{\text{IV}} &= (\hat{\mathbf{X}}'\mathbf{X})^{-1}\hat{\mathbf{X}}'\mathbf{y} \\
&= (\mathbf{X}'(\mathbf{I} - \mathbf{M}_Z)\mathbf{X})^{-1}\mathbf{X}'(\mathbf{I} - \mathbf{M}_Z)\mathbf{y} \\
&= (\hat{\mathbf{X}}'\hat{\mathbf{X}})^{-1}\hat{\mathbf{X}}'\mathbf{y}
\end{aligned} \tag{12-9}$$

because $\mathbf{I} - \mathbf{M}_Z$ is idempotent. Thus, when (*and only when*) $\hat{\mathbf{X}}$ is the set of instruments, the IV estimator is computed by least squares regression of $\mathbf{y}$ on $\hat{\mathbf{X}}$. This conclusion suggests (only logically; one need not actually do this in two steps), that $\mathbf{b}_{\text{IV}}$ can be computed in two steps, first by computing $\hat{\mathbf{X}}$, then by the least squares regression. For this reason, this is called the **two-stage least squares** (2SLS) estimator. We will revisit this form of estimator at great length at several points later, particularly in our discussion of simultaneous equations models. One should be careful of this approach, however, in the computation of the asymptotic covariance matrix; $\hat{\sigma}^2$ should not be based on $\hat{\mathbf{X}}$. The estimator

$$s_{\text{IV}}^2 = \frac{(\mathbf{y} - \hat{\mathbf{X}}\mathbf{b}_{\text{IV}})'(\mathbf{y} - \hat{\mathbf{X}}\mathbf{b}_{\text{IV}})}{n}$$

is inconsistent for $\sigma^2$, with or without a correction for degrees of freedom.

An obvious question is where one is likely to find a suitable set of instrumental variables. In many time-series settings, lagged values of the variables in the model provide natural candidates. In other cases, the answer is less than obvious. The asymptotic covariance matrix of the IV estimator can be rather large if $\mathbf{Z}$ is not highly correlated with $\mathbf{X}$; the elements of $(\mathbf{Z}'\mathbf{X})^{-1}$ grow large. (See Section 12.9 on "weak" instruments.) Unfortunately, there usually is not much choice in the selection of instrumental variables. The choice of $\mathbf{Z}$ is often ad hoc.[1] There is a bit of a dilemma in this result. It would seem to suggest that the best choices of instruments are variables that are highly correlated with $\mathbf{X}$. But the more highly correlated a variable is with the problematic columns of $\mathbf{X}$, the less defensible the claim that these same variables are *uncorrelated* with the disturbances.

### Example 12.2  Streams as Instruments

In Hoxby (2000), the author was interested in the effect of the amount of school "choice" in a school "market" on educational achievement in the market. The equations of interest were of the form

$$\frac{A_{ikm}}{\ln E_{km}} = \beta_1 C_m + \mathbf{x}'_{ikm}\boldsymbol{\beta}_2 + \bar{\mathbf{x}}'_{\cdot km}\boldsymbol{\beta}_3 + \bar{\mathbf{x}}'_{\cdot\cdot m}\boldsymbol{\beta}_4 + \cdots + \varepsilon_{ikm} + \varepsilon_{km} + \varepsilon_m$$

where "$ikm$" denotes household $i$ in district $k$ in market $m$, $A_{ikm}$ is a measure of achievement and $E_{ikm}$ is per capita expenditures. The equation contains individual level data, district means, and market means. Note as well that the model specifies the nested random effects model of Section 9.7.1 as well as the Mundlak treatment discussed in Section 9.5.5. The exogenous variables are intended to capture the different sources of heterogeneity at all three levels of aggregation. Reasoning that the amount of choice available to students, $C_m$, would be endogenous in this equation, the author sought a valid instrumental variable that would "explain" (be correlated with) $C_m$ but uncorrelated with the disturbances in the equation. In the U.S. market, to a large degree, school district boundaries were set in the late 18th and through the 19th centuries, and handed down to present-day administrators by historical precedent. In the formative years, the author noted, district boundaries were set in response to natural travel barriers, such as rivers and streams. It follows, as she notes, that "the number of districts in a given land area is an increasing function of the number of natural barriers"; hence, the number of streams in the physical market area provides the needed instrumental variable. [The controversial topic of the study and the unconventional choice of instruments caught the attention of the popular press, for example, http://www.economicprincipals.com/issues/05.10.30.html, and academic observers, see, e.g., Rothstein (2004).]

### Example 12.3  Labor Supply Model

A leading example of a model in which correlation between regressor and disturbance is likely to arise is in market equilibrium models. In Example 9.1, we built a "reduced form" wage equation,

$$\ln Wage_{it} = \beta_1 + \beta_2 Exp_{it} + \beta_3 Exp_{it}^2 + \beta_4 Wks_{it} + \beta_5 Occ_{it} + \beta_6 Ind_{it} + \beta_7 South_{it}$$

$$+ \beta_8 SMSA_{it} + \beta_9 MS_{it} + \beta_{10} Union_{it} + \beta_{11} Ed_i + \beta_{12} Fem_i + \beta_{13} Blk_i + \varepsilon_{it}.$$

We will return to the idea of reduced forms in the setting of simultaneous equations models in Chapter 13. For the present, the implication for our estimated model is that this market equilibrium equation represents the outcome of the interplay of supply and demand in a labor market. Arguably, the supply side of this market might consist of a household labor supply equation such as

$$Wks_{it} = \gamma_1 + \gamma_2 \ln Wage_{it} + \gamma_3 Ed_i + \gamma_4 Union_{it} + \gamma_5 Fem_i + u_{it}$$

(One might prefer a different set of right-hand-side variables in this structural equation. Structural equations are more difficult to specify than reduced forms, which simply contain all the

---

[1]Results on "optimal instruments" appear in White (2001) and Hansen (1982). In the other direction, there is a contemporary literature on "weak" instruments, such as Staiger and Stock (1997), which we will explore in Section 12.9.

**TABLE 12.1**    Estimated Labor Supply Equation

| | OLS | | IV with $Z_1$ | | IV with $Z_2$ | |
|---|---|---|---|---|---|---|
| *Variable* | *Estimate* | *Std. Error* | *Estimate* | *Std. Error* | *Estimate* | *Std. Error* |
| Constant | 44.7665 | 1.2153 | 18.8987 | 13.0590 | 30.7044 | 4.9997 |
| ln Wage | 0.7326 | 0.1972 | 5.1828 | 2.2454 | 3.1518 | 0.8572 |
| Education | −0.1532 | 0.03206 | −0.4600 | 0.1578 | −0.3200 | 0.06607 |
| Union | −1.9960 | 0.1701 | −2.3602 | 0.2567 | −2.1940 | 0.1860 |
| Female | −1.3498 | 0.2642 | 0.6957 | 1.0650 | −0.2378 | 0.4679 |

variables in the model.) If the number of weeks worked and the accepted wage offer are determined jointly, then ln *Wage* and $u_{it}$ in this equation are correlated. We consider two instrumental variable estimators based on

$$\mathbf{Z}_1 = [1, Ind_{it}, Ed_i, Union_{it}, Fem_i]$$

and

$$\mathbf{Z}_2 = [1, Ind_{it}, Ed_i, Union_{it}, Fem_i, SMSA_{it}]$$

Table 12.1 presents the three sets of estimates. The OLS results are computed using the standard results in Chapters 3 and 4. One noteworthy result is the very small coefficient on the log wage variable. The second set of results is the instrumental variable estimate developed in Section 12.3.2. As might be expected, the log wage coefficient becomes considerably larger. The other coefficients are, perhaps, contradictory. One have might different expectations about all three coefficients. The third set of coefficients are the two-stage least squares estimates based on the larger set of instrumental variables.

## 12.4 THE HAUSMAN AND WU SPECIFICATION TESTS AND AN APPLICATION TO INSTRUMENTAL VARIABLE ESTIMATION

It might not be obvious that the regressors in the model are correlated with the disturbances or that the regressors are measured with error. If not, there would be some benefit to using the least squares estimator rather than the IV estimator. Consider a comparison of the two covariance matrices *under the hypothesis that both are consistent, that is, assuming* plim $(1/n)\mathbf{X}'\boldsymbol{\varepsilon} = \mathbf{0}$. The difference between the asymptotic covariance matrices of the two estimators is

$$\text{Asy. Var}[\mathbf{b}_{IV}] - \text{Asy. Var}[\mathbf{b}_{LS}] = \frac{\sigma^2}{n}\text{plim}\left(\frac{\mathbf{X}'\mathbf{Z}(\mathbf{Z}'\mathbf{Z})^{-1}\mathbf{Z}'\mathbf{X}}{n}\right)^{-1} - \frac{\sigma^2}{n}\text{plim}\left(\frac{\mathbf{X}'\mathbf{X}}{n}\right)^{-1}$$

$$= \frac{\sigma^2}{n}\text{ plim } n\left[(\mathbf{X}'\mathbf{Z}(\mathbf{Z}'\mathbf{Z})^{-1}\mathbf{Z}'\mathbf{X})^{-1} - (\mathbf{X}'\mathbf{X})^{-1}\right].$$

To compare the two matrices in the brackets, we can compare their inverses. The inverse of the first is $\mathbf{X}'\mathbf{Z}(\mathbf{Z}'\mathbf{Z})^{-1}\mathbf{Z}'\mathbf{X} = \mathbf{X}'(\mathbf{I} - \mathbf{M_Z})\mathbf{X} = \mathbf{X}'\mathbf{X} - \mathbf{X}'\mathbf{M_Z}\mathbf{X}$. Because $\mathbf{M_Z}$ is a nonnegative definite matrix, it follows that $\mathbf{X}'\mathbf{M_Z}\mathbf{X}$ is also. So, $\mathbf{X}'\mathbf{Z}(\mathbf{Z}'\mathbf{Z})^{-1}\mathbf{Z}'\mathbf{X}$ equals $\mathbf{X}'\mathbf{X}$ minus a nonnegative definite matrix. Because $\mathbf{X}'\mathbf{Z}(\mathbf{Z}'\mathbf{Z})^{-1}\mathbf{Z}'\mathbf{X}$ is smaller, in the matrix sense, than $\mathbf{X}'\mathbf{X}$, its inverse is larger. Under the hypothesis, the asymptotic covariance matrix of the LS estimator is never larger than that of the IV estimator, and it will actually be smaller unless all the columns of $\mathbf{X}$ are perfectly predicted by regressions on $\mathbf{Z}$. Thus, we have established that if $\text{plim}(1/n)\mathbf{X}'\boldsymbol{\varepsilon} = \mathbf{0}$—that is, if LS is consistent—then it is a preferred estimator. (Of course, we knew that from all our earlier results on the virtues of least squares.)

Our interest in the difference between these two estimators goes beyond the question of efficiency. The null hypothesis of interest will usually be specifically whether $\text{plim}(1/n)\mathbf{X}'\boldsymbol{\varepsilon} = \mathbf{0}$. Seeking the covariance between $\mathbf{X}$ and $\boldsymbol{\varepsilon}$ through $(1/n)\mathbf{X}'\mathbf{e}$ is fruitless, of course, because the normal equations produce $(1/n)\mathbf{X}'\mathbf{e} = \mathbf{0}$. In a seminal paper, Hausman (1978) suggested an alternative testing strategy. [Earlier work by Wu (1973) and Durbin (1954) produced what turns out to be the same test.] The logic of Hausman's approach is as follows. Under the null hypothesis, we have two consistent estimators of $\boldsymbol{\beta}$, $\mathbf{b}_{\text{LS}}$ and $\mathbf{b}_{\text{IV}}$. Under the alternative hypothesis, only one of these, $\mathbf{b}_{\text{IV}}$, is consistent. The suggestion, then, is to examine $\mathbf{d} = \mathbf{b}_{\text{IV}} - \mathbf{b}_{\text{LS}}$. Under the null hypothesis, $\text{plim } \mathbf{d} = \mathbf{0}$, whereas under the alternative, $\text{plim } \mathbf{d} \neq \mathbf{0}$. Using a strategy we have used at various points before, we might test this hypothesis with a Wald statistic,

$$H = \mathbf{d}'\big\{\text{Est. Asy. Var}[\mathbf{d}]\big\}^{-1}\mathbf{d}.$$

The asymptotic covariance matrix we need for the test is

$$\text{Asy. Var}[\mathbf{b}_{\text{IV}} - \mathbf{b}_{\text{LS}}] = \text{Asy. Var}[\mathbf{b}_{\text{IV}}] + \text{Asy. Var}[\mathbf{b}_{\text{LS}}]$$
$$- \text{Asy. Cov}[\mathbf{b}_{\text{IV}}, \mathbf{b}_{\text{LS}}] - \text{Asy. Cov}[\mathbf{b}_{\text{LS}}, \mathbf{b}_{\text{IV}}].$$

At this point, the test is straightforward, save for the considerable complication that we do not have an expression for the covariance term. Hausman gives a fundamental result that allows us to proceed. Paraphrased slightly,

*the covariance between an efficient estimator, $\mathbf{b}_E$, of a parameter vector, $\boldsymbol{\beta}$, and its difference from an inefficient estimator, $\mathbf{b}_I$, of the same parameter vector, $\mathbf{b}_E - \mathbf{b}_I$, is zero.*

For our case, $\mathbf{b}_E$ is $\mathbf{b}_{\text{LS}}$ and $\mathbf{b}_I$ is $\mathbf{b}_{\text{IV}}$. By Hausman's result we have

$$\text{Cov}[\mathbf{b}_E, \mathbf{b}_E - \mathbf{b}_I] = \text{Var}[\mathbf{b}_E] - \text{Cov}[\mathbf{b}_E, \mathbf{b}_I] = \mathbf{0}$$

or

$$\text{Cov}[\mathbf{b}_E, \mathbf{b}_I] = \text{Var}[\mathbf{b}_E],$$

so,

$$\text{Asy. Var}[\mathbf{b}_{\text{IV}} - \mathbf{b}_{\text{LS}}] = \text{Asy. Var}[\mathbf{b}_{\text{IV}}] - \text{Asy. Var}[\mathbf{b}_{\text{LS}}].$$

Inserting this useful result into our Wald statistic and reverting to our empirical estimates of these quantities, we have

$$H = (\mathbf{b}_{\text{IV}} - \mathbf{b}_{\text{LS}})'\big\{\text{Est. Asy. Var}[\mathbf{b}_{\text{IV}}] - \text{Est. Asy. Var}[\mathbf{b}_{\text{LS}}]\big\}^{-1}(\mathbf{b}_{\text{IV}} - \mathbf{b}_{\text{LS}}).$$

Under the null hypothesis, we are using two different, but consistent, estimators of $\sigma^2$. If we use $s^2$ as the common estimator, then the statistic will be

$$H = \frac{\mathbf{d}'[(\hat{\mathbf{X}}'\hat{\mathbf{X}})^{-1} - (\mathbf{X}'\mathbf{X})^{-1}]^{-1}\mathbf{d}}{s^2}.$$

It is tempting to invoke our results for the full rank quadratic form in a normal vector and conclude the degrees of freedom for this chi-squared statistic is $K$. But that method will usually be incorrect, and worse yet, *unless* **X** *and* **Z** *have no variables in common, the rank of the matrix in this statistic is less than K, and the ordinary inverse will not even exist.* In most cases, at least some of the variables in **X** will also appear in **Z**. (In almost any application, **X** and **Z** will both contain the constant term.) That is, some of the variables in **X** are known to be uncorrelated with the disturbances. For example, the usual case will involve a single variable that is thought to be problematic or that is measured with error. In this case, our hypothesis, $\text{plim}(1/n)\mathbf{X}'\boldsymbol{\varepsilon} = \mathbf{0}$, does not really involve all $K$ variables, because a subset of the elements in this vector, say, $K_0$, are known to be zero. As such, the quadratic form in the Wald test is being used to test only $K^* = K - K_0$ hypotheses. It is easy (and useful) to show that, in fact, $H$ is a rank $K^*$ quadratic form. Since $\mathbf{Z}(\mathbf{Z}'\mathbf{Z})^{-1}\mathbf{Z}'$ is an idempotent matrix, $(\hat{\mathbf{X}}'\hat{\mathbf{X}}) = \hat{\mathbf{X}}'\mathbf{X}$. Using this result and expanding **d**, we find

$$\mathbf{d} = (\hat{\mathbf{X}}'\hat{\mathbf{X}})^{-1}\hat{\mathbf{X}}'\mathbf{y} - (\mathbf{X}'\mathbf{X})^{-1}\mathbf{X}'\mathbf{y}$$
$$= (\hat{\mathbf{X}}'\hat{\mathbf{X}})^{-1}[\hat{\mathbf{X}}'\mathbf{y} - (\hat{\mathbf{X}}'\hat{\mathbf{X}})(\mathbf{X}'\mathbf{X})^{-1}\mathbf{X}'\mathbf{y}]$$
$$= (\hat{\mathbf{X}}'\hat{\mathbf{X}})^{-1}\hat{\mathbf{X}}'(\mathbf{y} - \mathbf{X}(\mathbf{X}'\mathbf{X})^{-1}\mathbf{X}'\mathbf{y})$$
$$= (\hat{\mathbf{X}}'\hat{\mathbf{X}})^{-1}\hat{\mathbf{X}}'\mathbf{e},$$

where **e** is the vector of least squares residuals. Recall that $K_0$ of the columns in $\hat{\mathbf{X}}$ are the original variables in **X**. Suppose that these variables are the first $K_0$. Thus, the first $K_0$ rows of $\hat{\mathbf{X}}'\mathbf{e}$ are the same as the first $K_0$ rows of $\mathbf{X}'\mathbf{e}$, which are, of course **0**. (This statement does not mean that the first $K_0$ elements of **d** are zero.) So, we can write **d** as

$$\mathbf{d} = (\hat{\mathbf{X}}'\hat{\mathbf{X}})^{-1}\begin{bmatrix}\mathbf{0}\\\hat{\mathbf{X}}^{*'}\mathbf{e}\end{bmatrix} = (\hat{\mathbf{X}}'\hat{\mathbf{X}})^{-1}\begin{bmatrix}\mathbf{0}\\\mathbf{q}^*\end{bmatrix}$$

where $\mathbf{X}^*$ is the $K^*$ variables in **x** that are not in **z**.

Finally, denote the entire matrix in $H$ by **W**. (Because that ordinary inverse may not exist, this matrix will have to be a generalized inverse; see Section A.6.12.) Then, denoting the whole matrix product by **P**, we obtain

$$H = [\mathbf{0}' \ \mathbf{q}^{*'}](\hat{\mathbf{X}}'\hat{\mathbf{X}})^{-1}\mathbf{W}(\hat{\mathbf{X}}'\hat{\mathbf{X}})^{-1}\begin{bmatrix}\mathbf{0}\\\mathbf{q}^*\end{bmatrix} = [\mathbf{0}' \ \mathbf{q}^{*'}]\mathbf{P}\begin{bmatrix}\mathbf{0}\\\mathbf{q}^*\end{bmatrix} = \mathbf{q}^{*'}\mathbf{P}_{**}\mathbf{q}^*,$$

where $\mathbf{P}_{**}$ is the lower right $K^* \times K^*$ submatrix of **P**. We now have the end result. Algebraically, $H$ is actually a quadratic form in a $K^*$ vector, so $K^*$ is the degrees of freedom for the test.

The preceding Wald test requires a generalized inverse [see Hausman and Taylor (1981)], so it is going to be a bit cumbersome. In fact, one need not actually approach the test in this form, and it can be carried out with any regression program. The alternative **variable addition test** approach devised by Wu (1973) is simpler. An $F$ statistic with $K^*$ and $n - K - K^*$ degrees of freedom can be used to test the joint significance of the elements of $\boldsymbol{\gamma}$ in the augmented regression

$$\mathbf{y} = \mathbf{X}\boldsymbol{\beta} + \hat{\mathbf{X}}^*\boldsymbol{\gamma} + \boldsymbol{\varepsilon}^*, \tag{12-10}$$

where $\hat{\mathbf{X}}^*$ are the fitted values in regressions of the variables in $\mathbf{X}^*$ on $\mathbf{Z}$. This result is equivalent to the Hausman test for this model. [Algebraic derivations of this result can be found in the articles and in Davidson and MacKinnon (2004, Section 8.7).]

### Example 12.3    (Continued) Labor Supply Model

For the labor supply equation estimated in Example 12.3, we used the Wu (variable addition) test to examine the endogeneity of the ln *Wage* variable. For the first step, ln $Wage_{it}$ is regressed on $\mathbf{z}_{1,it}$. The predicted value from this equation is then added to the least squares regression of $Wks_{it}$ on $\mathbf{x}_{it}$. The results of this regression are

$$\widehat{Wks}_{it} = 18.8987 + 0.6938 \ln Wage_{it} - 0.4600 \, Ed_i - 2.3602 \, Union_{it}$$

$$(12.3284) \quad (0.1980) \qquad\quad (0.1490) \qquad\quad (0.2423)$$

$$+ \; 0.6958 \, Fem_i + 4.4891 \ln \widehat{Wage}_{it} + u_{it},$$

$$(1.0054) \qquad\quad (2.1290)$$

where the estimated standard errors are in parentheses. The *t* ratio on the fitted log wage coefficient is 2.108, which is larger than the critical value from the standard normal table of 1.96. Therefore, the hypothesis of exogeneity of the log *Wage* variable is rejected.

Although most of the preceding results are specific to this test of correlation between some of the columns of $\mathbf{X}$ and the disturbances, $\boldsymbol{\varepsilon}$, the Hausman test is general. To reiterate, when we have a situation in which we have a pair of estimators, $\hat{\boldsymbol{\theta}}_E$ and $\hat{\boldsymbol{\theta}}_I$, such that under $H_0\!: \hat{\boldsymbol{\theta}}_E$ and $\hat{\boldsymbol{\theta}}_I$ are both consistent and $\hat{\boldsymbol{\theta}}_E$ is efficient relative to $\hat{\boldsymbol{\theta}}_I$, while under $H_1\!: \hat{\boldsymbol{\theta}}_I$ remains consistent while $\hat{\boldsymbol{\theta}}_E$ is inconsistent, then we can form a test of the hypothesis by referring the **Hausman statistic,**

$$H = (\hat{\boldsymbol{\theta}}_I - \hat{\boldsymbol{\theta}}_E)' \big\{ \text{Est. Asy. Var}[\hat{\boldsymbol{\theta}}_I] - \text{Est. Asy. Var}[\hat{\boldsymbol{\theta}}_E] \big\}^{-1} (\hat{\boldsymbol{\theta}}_I - \hat{\boldsymbol{\theta}}_E) \xrightarrow{d} \chi^2[J],$$

to the appropriate critical value for the chi-squared distribution. The appropriate degrees of freedom for the test, $J$, will depend on the context. Moreover, some sort of generalized inverse matrix may be needed for the matrix, although in at least one common case, the random effects regression model (see Chapter 9), the appropriate approach is to extract some rows and columns from the matrix instead. The short rank issue is not general. Many applications can be handled directly in this form with a full rank quadratic form. Moreover, the Wu approach *is* specific to this application. Another applications that we will consider, the independence from irrelevant alternatives test for the multinomial logit model, does not lend itself to the regression approach and is typically handled using the Wald statistic and the full rank quadratic form. As a final note, observe that the short rank of the matrix in the Wald statistic is an algebraic result. The failure of the matrix in the Wald statistic to be positive definite, however, is sometimes a finite sample problem that is not part of the model structure. In such a case, forcing a solution by using a generalized inverse may be misleading. Hausman suggests that in this instance, the appropriate conclusion might be simply to take the result as zero and, by implication, not reject the null hypothesis.

### Example 12.4    Hausman Test for a Consumption Function

Quarterly data for 1950.1 to 2000.4 on a number of macroeconomic variables appear in Appendix Table F5.1. A consumption function of the form $C_t = \alpha + \beta Y_t + \varepsilon_t$ is estimated using the 203 observations on aggregate U.S. real consumption and real disposable personal income, omitting the first. In Example 12.1, this model is suggested as a candidate for the possibility of bias due to correlation between $Y_t$ and $\varepsilon_t$. Consider instrumental variables estimation using $Y_{t-1}$ and $C_{t-1}$ as the instruments for $Y_t$, and, of course, the constant term is its own instrument. One observation is lost because of the lagged values, so the results are based on 203 quarterly observations. The Hausman statistic can be computed in two ways:

1. Use the Wald statistic for $H$ with the Moore–Penrose generalized inverse. The common $s^2$ is the one computed by least squares under the null hypothesis of no correlation. With this computation, $H = 8.481$. There is $K^* = 1$ degree of freedom. The 95 percent critical value from the chi-squared table is 3.84. Therefore, we reject the null hypothesis of no correlation between $Y_t$ and $\varepsilon_t$.
2. Using the Wu statistic based on (12-10), we regress $C_t$ on a constant, $Y_t$, and the predicted value in a regression of $Y_t$ on a constant, $Y_{t-1}$ and $C_{t-1}$. The $t$ ratio on the prediction is 2.968, so the $F$ statistic with 1 and 201 degrees of freedom is 8.809. The critical value for this $F$ distribution is 4.15, so, again, the null hypothesis is rejected.

## 12.5  MEASUREMENT ERROR

Thus far, it has been assumed (at least implicitly) that the data used to estimate the parameters of our models are true measurements on their theoretical counterparts. In practice, this situation happens only in the best of circumstances. All sorts of measurement problems creep into the data that must be used in our analyses. Even carefully constructed survey data do not always conform exactly to the variables the analysts have in mind for their regressions. Aggregate statistics such as GDP are only estimates of their theoretical counterparts, and some variables, such as depreciation, the services of capital, and "the interest rate," do not even exist in an agreed-upon theory. At worst, there may be no physical measure corresponding to the variable in our model; intelligence, education, and permanent income are but a few examples. Nonetheless, they all have appeared in very precisely defined regression models.

### 12.5.1  LEAST SQUARES ATTENUATION

In this section, we examine some of the received results on regression analysis with badly measured data. The general assessment of the problem is not particularly optimistic. The biases introduced by measurement error can be rather severe. There are almost no known finite-sample results for the models of measurement error; nearly all the results that have been developed are asymptotic.[2] The following presentation will use a few simple asymptotic results for the classical regression model.

The simplest case to analyze is that of a regression model with a single regressor and no constant term. Although this case is admittedly unrealistic, it illustrates the essential concepts, and we shall generalize it presently. Assume that the model,

$$y^* = \beta x^* + \varepsilon, \tag{12-11}$$

conforms to all the assumptions of the classical normal regression model. If data on $y^*$ and $x^*$ were available, then $\beta$ would be estimable by least squares. Suppose, however, that the observed data are only imperfectly measured versions of $y^*$ and $x^*$. In the context of an example, suppose that $y^*$ is ln(output/labor) and $x^*$ is ln(capital/labor). Neither factor input can be measured with precision, so the observed $y$ and $x$ contain

---

[2]See, for example, Imbens and Hyslop (2001).

errors of measurement. We assume that

$$y = y^* + v \quad \text{with } v \sim N[0, \sigma_v^2], \tag{12-12a}$$

$$x = x^* + u \quad \text{with } u \sim N[0, \sigma_u^2]. \tag{12-12b}$$

Assume, as well, that $u$ and $v$ are independent of each other and of $y^*$ and $x^*$. (As we shall see, adding these restrictions is not sufficient to rescue a bad situation.)

As a first step, insert (12-12a) into (12-11), assuming for the moment that only $y^*$ is measured with error:

$$y = \beta x^* + \varepsilon + v = \beta x^* + \varepsilon'.$$

This result conforms to the assumptions of the classical regression model. As long as the regressor is measured properly, measurement error on the dependent variable can be absorbed in the disturbance of the regression and ignored. To save some cumbersome notation, therefore, we shall henceforth assume that the measurement error problems concern only the independent variables in the model.

Consider, then, the regression of $y$ on the observed $x$. By substituting (12-12b) into (12-11), we obtain

$$y = \beta x + [\varepsilon - \beta u] = \beta x + w. \tag{12-13}$$

Because $x$ equals $x^* + u$, the regressor in (12-13) is correlated with the disturbance:

$$\text{Cov}[x, w] = \text{Cov}[x^* + u, \varepsilon - \beta u] = -\beta \sigma_u^2. \tag{12-14}$$

This result violates one of the central assumptions of the classical model, so we can expect the least squares estimator,

$$b = \frac{(1/n) \sum_{i=1}^{n} x_i y_i}{(1/n) \sum_{i=1}^{n} x_i^2},$$

to be inconsistent. To find the probability limits, insert (12-11) and (12-12b) and use the Slutsky theorem:

$$\text{plim } b = \frac{\text{plim}(1/n) \sum_{i=1}^{n} (x_i^* + u_i)(\beta x_i^* + \varepsilon_i)}{\text{plim}(1/n) \sum_{i=1}^{n} (x_i^* + u_i)^2}.$$

Because $x^*$, $\varepsilon$, and $u$ are mutually independent, this equation reduces to

$$\text{plim } b = \frac{\beta Q^*}{Q^* + \sigma_u^2} = \frac{\beta}{1 + \sigma_u^2/Q^*}, \tag{12-15}$$

where $Q^* = \text{plim}(1/n) \sum_i x_i^{*2}$. As long as $\sigma_u^2$ is positive, $b$ is inconsistent, with a persistent bias toward zero. Clearly, the greater the variability in the measurement error, the worse the bias. The effect of biasing the coefficient toward zero is called **attenuation.**

In a multiple regression model, matters only get worse. Suppose, to begin, we assume that $\mathbf{y} = \mathbf{X}^* \boldsymbol{\beta} + \boldsymbol{\varepsilon}$ and $\mathbf{X} = \mathbf{X}^* + \mathbf{U}$, allowing every observation on every variable to be measured with error. The extension of the earlier result is

$$\text{plim}\left(\frac{\mathbf{X'X}}{n}\right) = \mathbf{Q}^* + \boldsymbol{\Sigma}_{uu}, \quad \text{and} \quad \text{plim}\left(\frac{\mathbf{X'y}}{n}\right) = \mathbf{Q}^* \boldsymbol{\beta}.$$

Hence,

$$\text{plim } \mathbf{b} = [\mathbf{Q}^* + \boldsymbol{\Sigma}_{uu}]^{-1}\mathbf{Q}^*\boldsymbol{\beta} = \boldsymbol{\beta} - [\mathbf{Q}^* + \boldsymbol{\Sigma}_{uu}]^{-1}\boldsymbol{\Sigma}_{uu}\boldsymbol{\beta}. \tag{12-16}$$

This probability limit is a mixture of all the parameters in the model. In the same fashion as before, bringing in outside information could lead to **identification.** The amount of information necessary is extremely large, however, and this approach is not particularly promising.

It is common for only a single variable to be measured with error. One might speculate that the problems would be isolated to the single coefficient. Unfortunately, this situation is not the case. For a single bad variable—assume that it is the first—the matrix $\boldsymbol{\Sigma}_{uu}$ is of the form

$$\boldsymbol{\Sigma}_{uu} = \begin{bmatrix} \sigma_u^2 & 0 & \cdots & 0 \\ 0 & 0 & \cdots & 0 \\ & & \vdots & \\ 0 & 0 & \cdots & 0 \end{bmatrix}.$$

It can be shown that for this special case,

$$\text{plim } b_1 = \frac{\beta_1}{1 + \sigma_u^2 q^{*11}} \tag{12-17a}$$

[note the similarity of this result to (12-15)], and, for $k \neq 1$,

$$\text{plim } b_k = \beta_k - \beta_1 \left[ \frac{\sigma_u^2 q^{*k1}}{1 + \sigma_u^2 q^{*11}} \right], \tag{12-17b}$$

where $q^{*k1}$ is the $(k, 1)$th element in $(\mathbf{Q}^*)^{-1}$.[3] This result depends on several unknowns and cannot be estimated. The coefficient on the badly measured variable is still biased toward zero. The other coefficients are all biased as well, although in unknown directions. A badly measured variable contaminates all least squares estimates.[4] If more than one variable is measured with error, there is very little that can be said.[5] Although expressions can be derived for the biases in a few of these cases, they generally depend on numerous parameters whose signs and magnitudes are unknown and, presumably, unknowable.

## 12.5.2   INSTRUMENTAL VARIABLES ESTIMATION

An alternative set of results for estimation in this model (and numerous others) is built around the method of instrumental variables. Consider once again the errors in variables model in (12-11) and (12-12a,b). The parameters, $\beta, \sigma_\varepsilon^2, q^*$, and $\sigma_u^2$ are not identified in terms of the moments of $x$ and $y$. Suppose, however, that there exists a variable $z$ such that $z$ is correlated with $x^*$ but not with $u$. For example, in surveys of families, income is notoriously badly reported, partly deliberately and partly because respondents often

---

[3]Use (A-66) to invert $[\mathbf{Q}^* + \boldsymbol{\Sigma}_{uu}] = [\mathbf{Q}^* + (\sigma_u\mathbf{e}_1)(\sigma_u\mathbf{e}_1)']$, where $\mathbf{e}_1$ is the first column of a $K \times K$ identity matrix. The remaining results are then straightforward.

[4]This point is important to remember when the presence of measurement error is suspected.

[5]Some firm analytic results have been obtained by Levi (1973), Theil (1961), Klepper and Leamer (1983), Garber and Klepper (1980), Griliches (1986), and Cragg (1997).

neglect some minor sources. Suppose, however, that one could determine the total amount of checks written by the head(s) of the household. It is quite likely that this $z$ would be highly correlated with income, but perhaps not significantly correlated with the errors of measurement. If $\text{Cov}[x^*, z]$ is not zero, then the parameters of the model become estimable, as

$$\text{plim} \frac{(1/n) \sum_i y_i z_i}{(1/n) \sum_i x_i z_i} = \frac{\beta \, \text{Cov}[x^*, z]}{\text{Cov}[x^*, z]} = \beta. \tag{12-18}$$

For the general case, $\mathbf{y} = \mathbf{X}^* \boldsymbol{\beta} + \boldsymbol{\varepsilon}$, $\mathbf{X} = \mathbf{X}^* + \mathbf{U}$, suppose that there exists a matrix of variables $\mathbf{Z}$ that is not correlated with the disturbances or the measurement error but is correlated with regressors, $\mathbf{X}$. Then the instrumental variables estimator based on $\mathbf{Z}$, $\mathbf{b}_{IV} = (\mathbf{Z}'\mathbf{X})^{-1}\mathbf{Z}'\mathbf{y}$, is consistent and asymptotically normally distributed with asymptotic covariance matrix that is estimated with

$$\text{Est. Asy. Var}[\mathbf{b}_{IV}] = \hat{\sigma}^2 [\mathbf{Z}'\mathbf{X}]^{-1} [\mathbf{Z}'\mathbf{Z}][\mathbf{X}'\mathbf{Z}]^{-1}. \tag{12-19}$$

For more general cases, Theorem 12.1 and the results in Section 12.3 apply.

### 12.5.3 PROXY VARIABLES

In some situations, a variable in a model simply has no observable counterpart. Education, intelligence, ability, and like factors are perhaps the most common examples. In this instance, unless there is some observable indicator for the variable, the model will have to be treated in the framework of missing variables. Usually, however, such an indicator can be obtained; for the factors just given, years of schooling and test scores of various sorts are familiar examples. The usual treatment of such variables is in the measurement error framework. If, for example,

$$\text{income} = \beta_1 + \beta_2 \, \text{education} + \varepsilon$$

and

$$\text{years of schooling} = \text{education} + u,$$

then the model of Section 12.5.1 applies. The only difference here is that the true variable in the model is "latent." No amount of improvement in reporting or measurement would bring the proxy closer to the variable for which it is proxying.

The preceding is a pessimistic assessment, perhaps more so than necessary. Consider a **structural model,**

$$\text{Earnings} = \beta_1 + \beta_2 \, \text{Experience} + \beta_3 \, \text{Industry} + \beta_4 \, \text{Ability} + \varepsilon.$$

*Ability* is unobserved, but suppose that an indicator, say, $IQ$, is. If we suppose that $IQ$ is related to *Ability* through a relationship such as

$$IQ = \alpha_1 + \alpha_2 \, \text{Ability} + v,$$

then we may solve the second equation for *Ability* and insert it in the first to obtain the
**reduced form equation**

$$Earnings = (\beta_1 - \beta_4\alpha_1/\alpha_2) + \beta_2 \; Experience + \beta_3 \; Industry + (\beta_4/\alpha_2)IQ + (\varepsilon - v\beta_4/\alpha_2).$$

This equation is intrinsically linear and can be estimated by least squares. We do not have
consistent estimators of $\beta_1$ and $\beta_4$, but we do have them for the coefficients of interest,
$\beta_2$ and $\beta_3$. This would appear to "solve" the problem. We should note the essential
ingredients; we require that the **indicator,** *IQ*, not be related to the other variables in
the model, and we also require that $v$ not be correlated with any of the variables. In
this instance, some of the parameters of the structural model are identified in terms of
observable data. Note, though, that *IQ* is not a proxy variable, it is an indicator of the
latent variable, *Ability*. This form of modeling has figured prominently in the education
and educational psychology literature. Consider, in the preceding small model how one
might proceed with not just a single indicator, but say with a battery of test scores, all
of which are indicators of the same latent ability variable.

It is to be emphasized that a proxy variable is not an instrument (or the reverse).
Thus, in the instrumental variables framework, it is implied that we do not regress **y** on
**Z** to obtain the estimates. To take an extreme example, suppose that the full model was

$$\mathbf{y} = \mathbf{X}^*\boldsymbol{\beta} + \boldsymbol{\varepsilon},$$

$$\mathbf{X} = \mathbf{X}^* + \mathbf{U},$$

$$\mathbf{Z} = \mathbf{X}^* + \mathbf{W}.$$

That is, we happen to have two badly measured estimates of $\mathbf{X}^*$. The parameters of this
model can be estimated without difficulty if **W** is uncorrelated with **U** and $\mathbf{X}^*$, *but not
by regressing* **y** *on* **Z**. The instrumental variables technique is called for.

When the model contains a variable such as education or ability, the question that
naturally arises is: If interest centers on the other coefficients in the model, why not
just discard the problem variable?[6] This method produces the familiar problem of an
omitted variable, compounded by the least squares estimator in the full model being
inconsistent anyway. Which estimator is worse? McCallum (1972) and Wickens (1972)
show that the asymptotic bias (actually, degree of inconsistency) is worse if the proxy
is omitted, even if it is a bad one (has a high proportion of measurement error). This
proposition neglects, however, the precision of the estimates. Aigner (1974) analyzed
this aspect of the problem and found, as might be expected, that it could go either way.
He concluded, however, that "there is evidence to broadly support use of the proxy."

### Example 12.5   Income and Education in a Study of Twins

The traditional model used in labor economics to study the effect of education on income is
an equation of the form

$$y_i = \beta_1 + \beta_2 \; age_i + \beta_3 \; age_i^2 + \beta_4 \; education_i + \mathbf{x}_i'\boldsymbol{\beta}_5 + \varepsilon_i,$$

where $y_i$ is typically a wage or yearly income (perhaps in log form) and $\mathbf{x}_i$ contains other
variables, such as an indicator for sex, region of the country, and industry. The literature

---

[6]This discussion applies to the measurement error and latent variable problems equally.

contains discussion of many possible problems in estimation of such an equation by least squares using measured data. Two of them are of interest here:

1. Although "education" is the variable that appears in the equation, the data available to researchers usually include only "years of schooling." This variable is a proxy for education, so an equation fit in this form will be tainted by this problem of measurement error. Perhaps surprisingly so, researchers also find that reported data on years of schooling are themselves subject to error, so there is a second source of measurement error. For the present, we will not consider the first (much more difficult) problem.
2. Other variables, such as "ability"—we denote these $\mu_i$—will also affect income and are surely correlated with education. If the earnings equation is estimated in the form shown above, then the estimates will be further biased by the absence of this "omitted variable." For reasons we will explore in Chapter 24, this bias has been called the **selectivity effect** in recent studies.

Simple cross-section studies will be considerably hampered by these problems. But, in a recent study, Ashenfelter and Kreuger (1994) analyzed a data set that allowed them, with a few simple assumptions, to ameliorate these problems.

Annual "twins festivals" are held at many places in the United States. The largest is held in Twinsburg, Ohio. The authors interviewed about 500 individuals over the age of 18 at the August 1991 festival. Using pairs of twins as their observations enabled them to modify their model as follows: Let $(y_{ij}, A_{ij})$ denote the earnings and age for twin $j$, $j = 1, 2$, for pair $i$. For the education variable, only self-reported "schooling" data, $S_{ij}$, are available. The authors approached the measurement problem in the schooling variable, $S_{ij}$, by asking each twin how much schooling they had and how much schooling their sibling had. Denote reported schooling *by* sibling $m$ of sibling $j$ by $S_{ij}(m)$. So, the self-reported years of schooling of twin 1 is $S_{i1}(1)$. When asked how much schooling twin 1 has, twin 2 reports $S_{i1}(2)$. The measurement error model for the schooling variable is

$$S_{ij}(m) = S_{ij} + u_{ij}(m), \quad j, m = 1, 2, \text{ where } S_{ij} = \text{"true" schooling for twin } j \text{ of pair } i.$$

We assume that the two sources of measurement error, $u_{ij}(m)$, are uncorrelated and they and $S_{ij}$ have zero means. Now, consider a simple bivariate model such as the one in (12-11):

$$y_{ij} = \beta S_{ij} + \varepsilon_{ij}.$$

As we saw earlier, a least squares estimate of $\beta$ using the reported data will be attenuated:

$$\text{plim } b = \frac{\beta \times \text{Var}[S_{ij}]}{\text{Var}[S_{ij}] + \text{Var}[u_{ij}(j)]} = \beta q.$$

(Because there is no natural distinction between twin 1 and twin 2, the assumption that the variances of the two measurement errors are equal is innocuous.) The factor $q$ is sometimes called the reliability ratio. In this simple model, if the reliability ratio were known, then $\beta$ could be consistently estimated. In fact, the construction of this model allows just that. Since the two measurement errors are uncorrelated,

$$\text{Corr}[S_{i1}(1), S_{i1}(2)] = \text{Corr}[S_{i2}(1), S_{i2}(2)]$$

$$= \frac{\text{Var}[S_{i1}]}{\{\{\text{Var}[S_{i1}] + \text{Var}[u_{i1}(1)]\} \times \{\text{Var}[S_{i1}] + \text{Var}[u_{i1}(2)]\}\}^{1/2}} = q.$$

In words, the correlation between the two reported education attainments measures the reliability ratio. The authors obtained values of 0.920 and 0.877 for 298 pairs of identical twins and 0.869 and 0.951 for 92 pairs of fraternal twins, thus providing a quick assessment of the extent of measurement error in their schooling data.

The earnings equation is a multiple regression, so this result is useful for an overall assessment of the problem, but the numerical values are not sufficient to undo the overall biases in the least squares regression coefficients. An instrumental variables estimator was used for that purpose. The estimating equation for $y_{ij} = \ln Wage_{ij}$ with the least squares (LS) and instrumental variable (IV) estimates is as follows:

$$y_{ij} = \beta_1 + \beta_2 \, age_i + \beta_3 \, age_i^2 + \beta_4 \, S_{ij}(j) + \beta_5 \, S_{im}(m) + \beta_6 \, sex_i + \beta_7 \, race_i + \varepsilon_{ij}$$

| | | | | | | |
|---|---|---|---|---|---|---|
| LS | (0.088) | (−0.087) | (0.084) | | (0.204) | (−0.410) |
| IV | (0.088) | (−0.087) | (0.116) | (−0.037) | (0.206) | (−0.428). |

In the equation, $S_{ij}(j)$ is the person's report of his or her own years of schooling and $S_{im}(m)$ is the sibling's report of the sibling's own years of schooling. The problem variable is schooling. To obtain a consistent estimator, the method of instrumental variables was used, using each sibling's report of the other sibling's years of schooling as a pair of instrumental variables. The estimates reported by the authors are shown below the equation. (The constant term was not reported, and for reasons not given, the second schooling variable was not included in the equation when estimated by LS.) This preliminary set of results is presented to give a comparison to other results in the literature. The age, schooling, and gender effects are comparable with other received results, whereas the effect of race is vastly different, −40 percent here compared with a typical value of +9 percent in other studies. The effect of using the instrumental variable estimator on the estimates of $\beta_4$ is of particular interest. Recall that the reliability ratio was estimated at about 0.9, which suggests that the IV estimate would be roughly 11 percent higher (1/0.9). Because this result is a multiple regression, that estimate is only a crude guide. The estimated effect shown above is closer to 38 percent.

The authors also used a different estimation approach. Recall the issue of selection bias caused by unmeasured effects. The authors reformulated their model as

$$y_{ij} = \beta_1 + \beta_2 \, age_i + \beta_3 \, age_i^2 + \beta_4 \, S_{ij}(j) + \beta_6 \, sex_i + \beta_7 \, race_i + \mu_i + \varepsilon_{ij}.$$

Unmeasured latent effects, such as "ability," are contained in $\mu_i$. Because $\mu_i$ is not observable but is, it is assumed, correlated with other variables in the equation, the least squares regression of $y_{ij}$ on the other variables produces a biased set of coefficient estimates. [This is a "fixed effects model—See Section 9.4. The assumption that the latent effect, "ability" is common between the twins and fully accounted for is a controversial assumption that ability is accounted for by "nature" rather than "nurture." See, e.g., Behrman and Taubman (1989). A search of the internet on the subject of the "nature versus nurture debate" will turn up millions of citations. We will not visit the subject here.] The difference between the two earnings equations is

$$y_{i1} - y_{i2} = \beta_4[S_{i1}(1) - S_{i2}(2)] + \varepsilon_{i1} - \varepsilon_{i2}.$$

This equation removes the latent effect but, it turns out, worsens the measurement error problem. As before, $\beta_4$ can be estimated by instrumental variables. There are two instrumental variables available, $S_{i2}(1)$ and $S_{i1}(2)$. (It is not clear in the paper whether the authors used the two separately or the difference of the two.) The least squares estimate is 0.092, which is comparable to the earlier estimate. The instrumental variable estimate is 0.167, which is nearly 82 percent higher. The two reported standard errors are 0.024 and 0.043, respectively. With these figures, it is possible to carry out Hausman's test;

$$H = \frac{(0.167 - 0.092)^2}{0.043^2 - 0.024^2} = 4.418.$$

The 95 percent critical value from the chi-squared distribution with one degree of freedom is 3.84, so the hypothesis that the LS estimator is consistent would be rejected. (The square root of $H$, 2.102, would be treated as a value from the standard normal distribution, from which the critical value would be 1.96. The authors reported a $t$ statistic for this regression of 1.97. The source of the difference is unclear.)

## 12.6 ESTIMATION OF THE GENERALIZED REGRESSION MODEL

We have considered cases in which the regressors, $\mathbf{X}$, are correlated with the disturbances, $\boldsymbol{\varepsilon}$. In this case, $\mathbf{b}$ is neither unbiased nor consistent.[7] In the classical model considered so far, we have constructed an estimator around a set of variables $\mathbf{Z}$ that were uncorrelated with $\boldsymbol{\varepsilon}$,

$$\mathbf{b}_{IV} = [\mathbf{X}'\mathbf{Z}(\mathbf{Z}'\mathbf{Z})^{-1}\mathbf{Z}'\mathbf{X}]^{-1}\mathbf{X}'\mathbf{Z}(\mathbf{Z}'\mathbf{Z})^{-1}\mathbf{Z}'\mathbf{y} \tag{12-20}$$

$$= \boldsymbol{\beta} + [\mathbf{X}'\mathbf{Z}(\mathbf{Z}'\mathbf{Z})^{-1}\mathbf{Z}'\mathbf{X}]^{-1}\mathbf{X}'\mathbf{Z}(\mathbf{Z}'\mathbf{Z})^{-1}\mathbf{Z}'\boldsymbol{\varepsilon}.$$

We now consider the extension to the generalized regression model, $E[\boldsymbol{\varepsilon}\boldsymbol{\varepsilon}' \mid \mathbf{X}] = \sigma^2 \boldsymbol{\Omega}$. Suppose that $\mathbf{X}$ and $\mathbf{Z}$ are well behaved as assumed in Section 12.2. That is,

$$\text{plim}(1/n)\mathbf{Z}'\mathbf{Z} = \mathbf{Q}_{ZZ}, \text{ a positive definite matrix,}$$

$$\text{plim}(1/n)\mathbf{Z}'\mathbf{X} = \mathbf{Q}_{ZX} = \mathbf{Q}'_{XZ}, \text{ a nonzero matrix,}$$

$$\text{plim}(1/n)\mathbf{X}'\mathbf{X} = \mathbf{Q}_{XX}, \text{ a positive definite matrix.}$$

To avoid a string of matrix computations that may not fit on a single line, for convenience let

$$\mathbf{Q}_{XX.Z} = \left[\mathbf{Q}_{XZ}\mathbf{Q}_{ZZ}^{-1}\mathbf{Q}_{ZX}\right]^{-1}\mathbf{Q}_{XZ}\mathbf{Q}_{ZZ}^{-1}$$

$$= \text{plim}\left[\left(\frac{1}{n}\mathbf{X}'\mathbf{Z}\right)\left(\frac{1}{n}\mathbf{Z}'\mathbf{Z}\right)^{-1}\left(\frac{1}{n}\mathbf{Z}'\mathbf{X}\right)\right]^{-1}\left(\frac{1}{n}\mathbf{X}'\mathbf{Z}\right)\left(\frac{1}{n}\mathbf{Z}'\mathbf{Z}\right)^{-1}.$$

If $\mathbf{Z}$ is a valid set of instrumental variables, that is, if the second term in (12-20) vanishes asymptotically, then

$$\text{plim}\,\mathbf{b}_{IV} = \boldsymbol{\beta} + \mathbf{Q}_{XX.Z}\,\text{plim}\left(\frac{1}{n}\mathbf{Z}'\boldsymbol{\varepsilon}\right) = \boldsymbol{\beta}.$$

This result is exactly the same one we had before. We might note that at the several points where we have established unbiasedness or consistency of the least squares or instrumental variables estimator, the covariance matrix of the disturbance vector has played no role; unbiasedness is a property of the means. As such, this result should come as no surprise. The large sample behavior of $\mathbf{b}_{IV}$ depends on the behavior of

$$\mathbf{v}_{n,IV} = \frac{1}{\sqrt{n}}\sum_{i=1}^{n}\mathbf{z}_i\varepsilon_i.$$

This result is exactly the one we analyzed in Section 4.9.2. If the sampling distribution of $\mathbf{v}_n$ converges to a normal distribution, then we will be able to construct the asymptotic distribution for $\mathbf{b}_{IV}$. This set of conditions is the same that was necessary for $\mathbf{X}$ when we just considered $\mathbf{b}$, with $\mathbf{Z}$ in place of $\mathbf{X}$. We will once again rely on the results of

---

[7]It may be asymptotically normally distributed, but around a mean that differs from $\boldsymbol{\beta}$.

Anderson (1971) or Amemiya (1985) that under very general conditions,

$$\frac{1}{\sqrt{n}} \sum_{i=1}^{n} \mathbf{z}_i \varepsilon_i \xrightarrow{d} \mathbf{N} \left[ \mathbf{0}, \sigma^2 \text{plim} \left( \frac{1}{n} \mathbf{Z}' \mathbf{\Omega} \mathbf{Z} \right) \right].$$

With the other results already in hand, we now have the following.

---

**THEOREM 12.2  Asymptotic Distribution of the IV Estimator in the Generalized Regression Model**

*If the regressors and the instrumental variables are well behaved in the fashions just discussed, then*

$$\mathbf{b}_{\text{IV}} \overset{a}{\sim} N[\boldsymbol{\beta}, \mathbf{V}_{\text{IV}}],$$

*where* $\qquad\qquad\qquad\qquad\qquad\qquad\qquad\qquad\qquad\qquad$ **(12-21)**

$$\mathbf{V}_{\text{IV}} = \frac{\sigma^2}{n} (\mathbf{Q}_{\mathbf{XX.Z}}) \, \text{plim} \left( \frac{1}{n} \mathbf{Z}' \mathbf{\Omega} \mathbf{Z} \right) (\mathbf{Q}'_{\mathbf{XX.Z}}).$$

---

## 12.7 NONLINEAR INSTRUMENTAL VARIABLES ESTIMATION

In Section 12.2, we extended the linear regression model to allow for the possibility that the regressors might be correlated with the disturbances. The same problem can arise in nonlinear models. The consumption function estimated in Section 11.3.1 is almost surely a case in point, and we reestimated it using the instrumental variables technique for linear models in Example 12.4. In this section, we will extend the method of instrumental variables to nonlinear regression models.

In the nonlinear model,

$$y_i = h(\mathbf{x}_i, \boldsymbol{\beta}) + \varepsilon_i,$$

the covariates $\mathbf{x}_i$ may be correlated with the disturbances. We would expect this effect to be transmitted to the pseudoregressors, $\mathbf{x}_i^0 = \partial h(\mathbf{x}_i, \boldsymbol{\beta}) / \partial \boldsymbol{\beta}$. If so, then the results that we derived for the linearized regression would no longer hold. Suppose that there is a set of variables $[\mathbf{z}_1, \ldots, \mathbf{z}_L]$ such that

$$\text{plim}(1/n)\mathbf{Z}'\boldsymbol{\varepsilon} = \mathbf{0} \qquad\qquad\qquad \text{(12-22)}$$

and

$$\text{plim}(1/n)\mathbf{Z}'\mathbf{X}^0 = \mathbf{Q}_{\mathbf{zx}}^0 \neq \mathbf{0},$$

where $\mathbf{X}^0$ is the matrix of pseudoregressors in the linearized regression, evaluated at the true parameter values. If the analysis that we used for the linear model in Section 12.3 can be applied to this set of variables, then we will be able to construct a consistent estimator for $\boldsymbol{\beta}$ using the instrumental variables. As a first step, we will attempt to replicate the approach that we used for the linear model. The linearized regression model is given in (11-7),

$$\mathbf{y} = \mathbf{h}(\mathbf{X}, \boldsymbol{\beta}) + \boldsymbol{\varepsilon} \approx \mathbf{h}^0 + \mathbf{X}^0(\boldsymbol{\beta} - \boldsymbol{\beta}^0) + \boldsymbol{\varepsilon}$$

or

$$\mathbf{y}^0 \approx \mathbf{X}^0\boldsymbol{\beta} + \boldsymbol{\varepsilon},$$

where

$$\mathbf{y}^0 = \mathbf{y} - \mathbf{h}^0 + \mathbf{X}^0\boldsymbol{\beta}^0.$$

For the moment, we neglect the approximation error in linearizing the model. In (12-22), we have assumed that

$$\text{plim}(1/n)\mathbf{Z}'\mathbf{y}^0 = \text{plim }(1/n)\mathbf{Z}'\mathbf{X}^0\boldsymbol{\beta}. \tag{12-23}$$

Suppose, as we assumed before, that there are the same number of instrumental variables as there are parameters, that is, columns in $\mathbf{X}^0$. (Note: This number need not be the number of variables.) Then the "estimator" used before is suggested:

$$\mathbf{b}_{\text{IV}} = (\mathbf{Z}'\mathbf{X}^0)^{-1}\mathbf{Z}'\mathbf{y}^0. \tag{12-24}$$

The logic is sound, but there is a problem with this estimator. The unknown parameter vector $\boldsymbol{\beta}$ appears on both sides of (12-23). We might consider the approach we used for our first solution to the nonlinear regression model. That is, with some initial estimator in hand, iterate back and forth between the instrumental variables regression and recomputing the pseudoregressors until the process converges to the fixed point that we seek. Once again, the logic is sound, and in principle, this method does produce the estimator we seek.

If we add to our preceding assumptions

$$\frac{1}{\sqrt{n}}\mathbf{Z}'\boldsymbol{\varepsilon} \xrightarrow{d} N[\mathbf{0}, \sigma^2\mathbf{Q}_{zz}],$$

then we will be able to use the same form of the asymptotic distribution for this estimator that we did for the linear case. Before doing so, we must fill in some gaps in the preceding. First, despite its intuitive appeal, the suggested procedure for finding the estimator is very unlikely to be a good algorithm for locating the estimates. Second, we do not wish to limit ourselves to the case in which we have the same number of instrumental variables as parameters. So, we will consider the problem in general terms. The estimation criterion for nonlinear instrumental variables is a quadratic form,

$$\text{Min}_{\boldsymbol{\beta}} \; S(\boldsymbol{\beta}) = \tfrac{1}{2}\{[\mathbf{y} - \mathbf{h}(\mathbf{X}, \boldsymbol{\beta})]'\mathbf{Z}\}(\mathbf{Z}'\mathbf{Z})^{-1}\{\mathbf{Z}'[\mathbf{y} - \mathbf{h}(\mathbf{X}, \boldsymbol{\beta})]\}$$

$$= \tfrac{1}{2}\boldsymbol{\varepsilon}(\boldsymbol{\beta})'\mathbf{Z}(\mathbf{Z}'\mathbf{Z})^{-1}\mathbf{Z}'\boldsymbol{\varepsilon}(\boldsymbol{\beta}).^{8} \tag{12-25}$$

---

[8]Perhaps the more natural point to begin the minimization would be $S^0(\boldsymbol{\beta}) = [\boldsymbol{\varepsilon}(\boldsymbol{\beta})'\mathbf{Z}][\mathbf{Z}'\boldsymbol{\varepsilon}(\boldsymbol{\beta})]$. We have bypassed this step because the criterion in (12-25) and the estimator in (12-26) will turn out (following and in Chapter 15) to be a simple yet more efficient GMM estimator.

The first-order conditions for minimization of this weighted sum of squares are

$$\frac{\partial S(\boldsymbol{\beta})}{\partial \boldsymbol{\beta}} = -\mathbf{X}^{0\prime}\mathbf{Z}(\mathbf{Z}'\mathbf{Z})^{-1}\mathbf{Z}'\boldsymbol{\varepsilon}(\boldsymbol{\beta}) = \mathbf{0}. \tag{12-26}$$

This result is the same one we had for the linear model with $\mathbf{X}^0$ in the role of $\mathbf{X}$. This problem, however, is highly nonlinear in most cases, and the repeated least squares approach is unlikely to be effective. But it is a straightforward minimization problem in the frameworks of Appendix E, and instead, we can just treat estimation here as a problem in nonlinear optimization.

We have approached the formulation of this instrumental variables estimator more or less strategically. However, there is a more structured approach. The **orthogonality condition**

$$\text{plim}(1/n)\mathbf{Z}'\boldsymbol{\varepsilon} = \mathbf{0}$$

defines a GMM estimator. With the homoscedasticity and nonautocorrelation assumption, the resultant **minimum distance estimator** produces precisely the criterion function suggested above. We will revisit this estimator in this context, in Chapter 15.

With well-behaved *pseudoregressors* and instrumental variables, we have the general result for the nonlinear instrumental variables estimator; this result is discussed at length in Davidson and MacKinnon (2004).

---

**THEOREM 12.3**    **Asymptotic Distribution of the Nonlinear Instrumental Variables Estimator**

*With well-behaved instrumental variables and pseudoregressors,*

$$\mathbf{b}_{\text{IV}} \overset{a}{\sim} N\big[\boldsymbol{\beta}, (\sigma^2/n)\big(\mathbf{Q}^0_{\mathbf{xz}}(\mathbf{Q}_{\mathbf{zz}})^{-1}\mathbf{Q}^0_{\mathbf{zx}}\big)^{-1}\big].$$

*We estimate the asymptotic covariance matrix with*

$$\text{Est. Asy. Var}[\mathbf{b}_{\text{IV}}] = \hat{\sigma}^2[\hat{\mathbf{X}}^{0\prime}\mathbf{Z}(\mathbf{Z}'\mathbf{Z})^{-1}\mathbf{Z}'\hat{\mathbf{X}}^0]^{-1},$$

*where $\hat{\mathbf{X}}^0$ is $\mathbf{X}^0$ computed using $\mathbf{b}_{\text{IV}}$.*

---

As a final observation, note that the "two-stage least squares" interpretation of the instrumental variables estimator for the linear model still applies here, with respect to the IV estimator. That is, at the final estimates, the first-order conditions (normal equations) imply that

$$\mathbf{X}^{0\prime}\mathbf{Z}(\mathbf{Z}'\mathbf{Z})^{-1}\mathbf{Z}'\mathbf{y} = \mathbf{X}^{0\prime}\mathbf{Z}(\mathbf{Z}'\mathbf{Z})^{-1}\mathbf{Z}'\mathbf{X}^0\boldsymbol{\beta},$$

which says that the estimates satisfy the normal equations for a linear regression of $\mathbf{y}$ (not $\mathbf{y}^0$) on the predictions obtained by regressing the columns of $\mathbf{X}^0$ on $\mathbf{Z}$. The interpretation is not quite the same here, because to compute the predictions of $\mathbf{X}^0$, we must have the estimate of $\boldsymbol{\beta}$ in hand. Thus, this two-stage least squares approach does not show *how to compute* $\mathbf{b}_{\text{IV}}$; it shows a characteristic of $\mathbf{b}_{\text{IV}}$.

**TABLE 12.2** Nonlinear Least Squares and Instrumental Variable Estimates

| Parameter | Instrumental Variables | | Least Squares | |
|---|---|---|---|---|
| | Estimate | Standard Error | Estimate | Standard Error |
| $\alpha$ | 627.031 | 26.6063 | 468.215 | 22.788 |
| $\beta$ | 0.040291 | 0.006050 | 0.0971598 | 0.01064 |
| $\gamma$ | 1.34738 | 0.016816 | 1.24892 | 0.1220 |
| $\sigma$ | 57.1681 | — | 49.87998 | — |
| $\mathbf{e'e}$ | 650,369.805 | — | 495,114.490 | — |

***Example 12.6  Instrumental Variables Estimates of the
Consumption Function***
The consumption function in Section 11.3.1 was estimated by nonlinear least squares without accounting for the nature of the data that would certainly induce correlation between $\mathbf{X}^0$ and $\varepsilon$. As we did earlier, we will reestimate this model using the technique of instrumental variables. For this application, we will use the one-period lagged value of consumption and one- and two-period lagged values of income as instrumental variables estimates. Table 12.2 reports the nonlinear least squares and instrumental variables estimates. Because we are using two periods of lagged values, two observations are lost. Thus, the least squares estimates are not the same as those reported earlier.

The instrumental variable estimates differ considerably from the least squares estimates. The differences can be deceiving, however. Recall that the MPC in the model is $\beta\gamma Y^{\gamma-1}$. The 2000.4 value for *DPI* that we examined earlier was 6634.9. At this value, the instrumental variables and least squares estimates of the MPC are 1.1543 with an estimated standard error of 0.01234 and 1.08406 with an estimated standard error of 0.008694, respectively. These values do differ a bit but less than the quite large differences in the parameters might have led one to expect. We do note that the IV estimate is considerably greater than the estimate in the linear model, 0.9217 (and greater than one, which seems a bit implausible).

## 12.8  PANEL DATA APPLICATIONS

Recent **panel data** applications have relied heavily on the methods of instrumental variables that we are developing here. We will develop this methodology in detail in Chapter 15 where we consider generalized method of moments (GMM) estimation. At this point, we can examine two major building blocks in this set of methods, Hausman and Taylor's (1981) estimator for the random effects model and Bhargava and Sargan's (1983) proposals for estimating a dynamic panel data model. These two tools play a significant role in the GMM estimators of dynamic panel models in Chapter 15.

### 12.8.1  INSTRUMENTAL VARIABLES ESTIMATION OF THE RANDOM EFFECTS MODEL—THE HAUSMAN AND TAYLOR ESTIMATOR

Recall the original specification of the linear model for panel data in (9-1):

$$y_{it} = \mathbf{x}'_{it}\boldsymbol{\beta} + \mathbf{z}'_i\boldsymbol{\alpha} + \varepsilon_{it}. \tag{12-27}$$

The random effects model is based on the assumption that the unobserved person-specific effects, $\mathbf{z}_i$, are uncorrelated with the included variables, $\mathbf{x}_{it}$. This assumption is a major shortcoming of the model. However, the random effects treatment does allow the model to contain observed time invariant characteristics, such as demographic characteristics, while the fixed effects model does not—if present, they are simply absorbed into the fixed effects. **Hausman and Taylor's** (1981) **estimator** for the random effects model suggests a way to overcome the first of these while accommodating the second.

Their model is of the form:

$$y_{it} = \mathbf{x}'_{1it}\boldsymbol{\beta}_1 + \mathbf{x}'_{2it}\boldsymbol{\beta}_2 + \mathbf{z}'_{1i}\boldsymbol{\alpha}_1 + \mathbf{z}'_{2i}\boldsymbol{\alpha}_2 + \varepsilon_{it} + u_i$$

where $\boldsymbol{\beta} = (\boldsymbol{\beta}'_1, \boldsymbol{\beta}'_2)'$ and $\boldsymbol{\alpha} = (\boldsymbol{\alpha}'_1, \boldsymbol{\alpha}'_2)'$. In this formulation, all individual effects denoted $\mathbf{z}_i$ are observed. As before, unobserved individual effects that are contained in $\mathbf{z}'_i\boldsymbol{\alpha}$ in (12-27) are contained in the person specific random term, $u_i$. Hausman and Taylor define four sets of *observed* variables in the model:

$\mathbf{x}_{1it}$ is $K_1$ variables that are time varying and uncorrelated with $u_i$,
$\mathbf{z}_{1i}$ is $L_1$ variables that are time invariant and uncorrelated with $u_i$,
$\mathbf{x}_{2it}$ is $K_2$ variables that are time varying and are correlated with $u_i$,
$\mathbf{z}_{2i}$ is $L_2$ variables that are time invariant and are correlated with $u_i$.

The assumptions about the random terms in the model are

$$E[u_i \mid \mathbf{x}_{1it}, \mathbf{z}_{1i}] = 0 \text{ though } E[u_i \mid \mathbf{x}_{2it}, \mathbf{z}_{2i}] \neq 0,$$

$$\mathrm{Var}[u_i \mid \mathbf{x}_{1it}, \mathbf{z}_{1i}, \mathbf{x}_{2it}, \mathbf{z}_{2i}] = \sigma_u^2,$$

$$\mathrm{Cov}[\varepsilon_{it}, u_i \mid \mathbf{x}_{1it}, \mathbf{z}_{1i}, \mathbf{x}_{2it}, \mathbf{z}_{2i}] = 0,$$

$$\mathrm{Var}[\varepsilon_{it} + u_i \mid \mathbf{x}_{1it}, \mathbf{z}_{1i}, \mathbf{x}_{2it}, \mathbf{z}_{2i}] = \sigma^2 = \sigma_\varepsilon^2 + \sigma_u^2,$$

$$\mathrm{Corr}[\varepsilon_{it} + u_i, \varepsilon_{is} + u_i \mid \mathbf{x}_{1it}, \mathbf{z}_{1i}, \mathbf{x}_{2it}, \mathbf{z}_{2i}] = \rho = \sigma_u^2/\sigma^2.$$

Note the crucial assumption that one can distinguish sets of variables $\mathbf{x}_1$ and $\mathbf{z}_1$ that are uncorrelated with $u_i$ from $\mathbf{x}_2$ and $\mathbf{z}_2$ which are not. The likely presence of $\mathbf{x}_2$ and $\mathbf{z}_2$ is what complicates specification and estimation of the random effects model in the first place.

By construction, any OLS or GLS estimators of this model are inconsistent when the model contains variables that are correlated with the random effects. Hausman and Taylor have proposed an instrumental variables estimator that uses only the information within the model (i.e., as already stated). The strategy for estimation is based on the following logic: First, by taking deviations from group means, we find that

$$y_{it} - \bar{y}_{i.} = (\mathbf{x}_{1it} - \bar{\mathbf{x}}_{1i.})'\boldsymbol{\beta}_1 + (\mathbf{x}_{2it} - \bar{\mathbf{x}}_{2i.})'\boldsymbol{\beta}_2 + \varepsilon_{it} - \bar{\varepsilon}_{i.}, \qquad \textbf{(12-28)}$$

which implies that $\boldsymbol{\beta}$ can be consistently estimated by least squares, *in spite of the correlation between* $\mathbf{x}_2$ *and u*. This is the familiar, fixed effects, least squares dummy variable estimator—the transformation to deviations from group means removes from the model the part of the disturbance that is correlated with $\mathbf{x}_{2it}$. Now, in the original model, Hausman and Taylor show that the group mean deviations can be used as $(K_1 + K_2)$ instrumental variables for estimation of $(\boldsymbol{\beta}, \boldsymbol{\alpha})$. That is the implication of (12-28). Because $\mathbf{z}_1$ is uncorrelated with the disturbances, it can likewise serve as a set of $L_1$ instrumental variables. That leaves a necessity for $L_2$ instrumental variables. The authors show that the group means for $\mathbf{x}_1$ can serve as these remaining instruments, and the model will be identified so long as $K_1$ is greater than or equal to $L_2$. *For identification purposes, then,* $K_1$ *must be at least as large as* $L_2$. As usual, **feasible GLS** is better than OLS, and available. Likewise, FGLS is an improvement over simple instrumental variable estimation of the model, which is consistent but inefficient.

The authors propose the following set of steps for consistent and efficient estimation:

**Step 1.** Obtain the LSDV (fixed effects) estimator of $\beta = (\beta_1', \beta_2')'$ based on $\mathbf{x}_1$ and $\mathbf{x}_2$. The residual variance estimator from this step is a consistent estimator of $\sigma_\varepsilon^2$.

**Step 2.** Form the within-groups residuals, $e_{it}$, from the LSDV regression at step 1. Stack the group means of these residuals in a full sample length data vector. Thus,

$$e_{it}^* = \bar{e}_{i.} = \frac{1}{T}\sum_{t=1}^{T}(y_{it} - \mathbf{x}_{it}'\mathbf{b}_w), \ t = 1, \ldots, T, i = 1, \ldots, n.$$ (The individual constant term, $a_i$, is not included in $e_{it}^*$.) These group means are used as the dependent variable in an instrumental variable regression on $\mathbf{z}_1$ and $\mathbf{z}_2$ with instrumental variables $\mathbf{z}_1$ and $\mathbf{x}_1$. (Note the identification requirement that $K_1$, the number of variables in $\mathbf{x}_1$ be at least as large as $L_2$, the number of variables in $\mathbf{z}_2$.) The time invariant variables are each repeated $T$ times in the data matrices in this regression. This provides a consistent estimator of $\alpha$.

**Step 3.** The residual variance in the regression in step 2 is a consistent estimator of $\sigma^{*2} = \sigma_u^2 + \sigma_\varepsilon^2/T$. From this estimator and the estimator of $\sigma_\varepsilon^2$ in step 1, we deduce an estimator of $\sigma_u^2 = \sigma^{*2} - \sigma_\varepsilon^2/T$. We then form the weight for feasible GLS in this model by forming the estimate of

$$\theta = 1 - \sqrt{\frac{\sigma_\varepsilon^2}{\sigma_\varepsilon^2 + T\sigma_u^2}}.$$

**Step 4.** The final step is a weighted instrumental variable estimator. Let the full set of variables in the model be

$$\mathbf{w}_{it}' = (\mathbf{x}_{1it}', \mathbf{x}_{2it}', \mathbf{z}_{1i}', \mathbf{z}_{2i}').$$

Collect these $nT$ observations in the rows of data matrix $\mathbf{W}$. The transformed variables for GLS are, as before when we first fit the random effects model,

$$\mathbf{w}_{it}^{*'} = \mathbf{w}_{it}' - \hat{\theta}\bar{\mathbf{w}}_{i.}' \quad \text{and} \quad y_{it}^* = y_{it} - \hat{\theta}\bar{y}_{i.}$$

where $\hat{\theta}$ denotes the sample estimate of $\theta$. The transformed data are collected in the rows data matrix $\mathbf{W}^*$ and in column vector $\mathbf{y}^*$. Note in the case of the time invariant variables in $\mathbf{w}_{it}$, the group mean is the original variable, and the transformation just multiplies the variable by $1 - \hat{\theta}$. The instrumental variables are

$$\mathbf{v}_{it}' = [(\mathbf{x}_{1it} - \bar{\mathbf{x}}_{1i.})', (\mathbf{x}_{2it} - \bar{\mathbf{x}}_{2i.})', \mathbf{z}_{1i}' \ \bar{\mathbf{x}}_{1i.}'].$$

These are stacked in the rows of the $nT \times (K_1 + K_2 + L_1 + K_1)$ matrix $\mathbf{V}$. Note for the third and fourth sets of instruments, the time invariant variables and group means are repeated for each member of the group. The instrumental variable estimator would be

$$(\hat{\beta}', \hat{\alpha}')_{\text{IV}}' = [(\mathbf{W}^{*'}\mathbf{V})(\mathbf{V}'\mathbf{V})^{-1}(\mathbf{V}'\mathbf{W}^*)]^{-1}[(\mathbf{W}^{*'}\mathbf{V})(\mathbf{V}'\mathbf{V})^{-1}(\mathbf{V}'\mathbf{y}^*)].^{[9]} \qquad \textbf{(12-29)}$$

---

[9]Note that the FGLS random effects estimator would be $(\hat{\beta}', \hat{\alpha}')_{RE}' = [\mathbf{W}^{*'}\mathbf{W}^*]^{-1}\mathbf{W}^{*'}\mathbf{y}^*$.

The instrumental variable estimator is consistent if the data are not weighted, that is, if $\mathbf{W}$ rather than $\mathbf{W}^*$ is used in the computation. But, this is inefficient, in the same way that OLS is consistent but inefficient in estimation of the simpler random effects model.

### Example 12.7 The Returns to Schooling

The economic returns to schooling have been a frequent topic of study by econometricians. The PSID and NLS data sets have provided a rich source of panel data for this effort. In wage (or log wage) equations, it is clear that the economic benefits of schooling are correlated with latent, unmeasured characteristics of the individual such as innate ability, intelligence, drive, or perseverance. As such, there is little question that simple random effects models based on panel data will suffer from the effects noted earlier. The fixed effects model is the obvious alternative, but these rich data sets contain many useful variables, such as race, union membership, and marital status, which are generally time invariant. Worse yet, the variable most of interest, years of schooling, is also time invariant. Hausman and Taylor (1981) proposed the estimator described here as a solution to these problems. The authors studied the effect of schooling on (the log of) wages using a random sample from the PSID of 750 men aged 25–55, observed in two years, 1968 and 1972. The two years were chosen so as to minimize the effect of serial correlation apart from the persistent unmeasured individual effects. The variables used in their model were as follows:

Experience = age − years of schooling − 5,
Years of schooling,
Bad Health = a dummy variable indicating general health,
Race = a dummy variable indicating nonwhite (70 of 750 observations),
Union = a dummy variable indicating union membership,
Unemployed = a dummy variable indicating previous year's unemployment.

The model also included a constant term and a period indicator. [The coding of the latter is not given, but any two distinct values, including 0 for 1968 and 1 for 1972, would produce identical results. (Why?)]

The primary focus of the study is the coefficient on schooling in the log wage equation. Because schooling and, probably, Experience and Unemployed are correlated with the latent effect, there is likely to be serious bias in conventional estimates of this equation. Table 12.3 reports some of their reported results. The OLS and random effects GLS results in the first two columns provide the benchmark for the rest of the study. The schooling coefficient is estimated at 0.0669, a value which the authors suspected was far too small. As we saw earlier, even in the presence of correlation between measured and latent effects, in this model, the LSDV estimator provides a consistent estimator of the coefficients on the time varying variables. Therefore, we can use it in the **Hausman specification test** for correlation between the included variables and the latent heterogeneity. The calculations are shown in Section 9.5.4, result (9-42). Because there are three variables remaining in the LSDV equation, the chi-squared statistic has three degrees of freedom. The reported value of 20.2 is far larger than the 95 percent critical value of 7.81, so the results suggest that the random effects model is misspecified.

Hausman and Taylor proceeded to reestimate the log wage equation using their proposed estimator. The fourth and fifth sets of results in Table 12.3 present the instrumental variable estimates. The specification test given with the fourth set of results suggests that the procedure has produced the desired result. The hypothesis of the modified random effects model is now not rejected; the chi-squared value of 2.24 is much smaller than the critical value. The schooling variable is treated as endogenous (correlated with $u_i$) in both cases. The difference between the two is the treatment of Unemployed and Experience. In the preferred equation, they are included in $\mathbf{x}_2$ rather than $\mathbf{x}_1$. The end result of the exercise is, again, the coefficient on schooling, which has risen from 0.0669 in the worst specification (OLS) to 0.2169 in the last one, a difference of over 200 percent. As the authors note, at the same time, the measured effect of race nearly vanishes.

**TABLE 12.3** Estimated Log Wage Equations

| | Variables | OLS | GLS/RE | LSDV | HT/IV-GLS | HT/IV-GLS |
|---|---|---|---|---|---|---|
| $x_1$ | Experience | 0.0132 | 0.0133 | 0.0241 | 0.0217 | |
| | | (0.0011)[a] | (0.0017) | (0.0042) | (0.0031) | |
| | Bad health | −0.0843 | −0.0300 | −0.0388 | −0.0278 | −0.0388 |
| | | (0.0412) | (0.0363) | (0.0460) | (0.0307) | (0.0348) |
| | Unemployed | −0.0015 | −0.0402 | −0.0560 | −0.0559 | |
| | Last Year | (0.0267) | (0.0207) | (0.0295) | (0.0246) | |
| | Time | NR[b] | NR | NR | NR | NR |
| $x_2$ | Experience | | | | | 0.0241 |
| | | | | | | (0.0045) |
| | Unemployed | | | | | −0.0560 |
| | | | | | | (0.0279) |
| $z_1$ | Race | −0.0853 | −0.0878 | | −0.0278 | −0.0175 |
| | | (0.0328) | (0.0518) | | (0.0752) | (0.0764) |
| | Union | 0.0450 | 0.0374 | | 0.1227 | 0.2240 |
| | | (0.0191) | (0.0296) | | (0.0473) | (0.2863) |
| | Schooling | 0.0669 | 0.0676 | | | |
| | | (0.0033) | (0.0052) | | | |
| | Constant | NR | NR | NR | NR | NR |
| $z_2$ | Schooling | | | | 0.1246 | 0.2169 |
| | | | | | (0.0434) | (0.0979) |
| | $\sigma_\varepsilon$ | 0.321 | 0.192 | 0.160 | 0.190 | 0.629 |
| | $\rho = \sqrt{\sigma_u^2/(\sigma_u^2 + \sigma_\varepsilon^2)}$ | | 0.632 | | 0.661 | 0.817 |
| | Spec. Test [3] | | 20.2 | | 2.24 | 0.00 |

[a]Estimated asymptotic standard errors are given in parentheses.
[b]NR indicates that the coefficient estimate was not reported in the study.

### 12.8.2 DYNAMIC PANEL DATA MODELS—THE ANDERSON/HSIAO AND ARELLANO/BOND ESTIMATORS

A leading contemporary application of the methods of this chapter and Chapter 9 is the **dynamic panel data model,** which we now write

$$y_{it} = \mathbf{x}'_{it}\boldsymbol{\beta} + \delta y_{i,t-1} + c_i + \varepsilon_{it}.$$

Several applications are described in Example 9.18. The basic assumptions of the model are

1. Strict exogeneity: $E[\varepsilon_{it} \mid \mathbf{X}_i, c_i] = 0,$
2. Homoscedasticity: $E[\varepsilon_{it}^2 \mid \mathbf{X}_i, c_i] = \sigma_\varepsilon^2,$
3. Nonautocorrelation: $E[\varepsilon_{it}\varepsilon_{is} \mid \mathbf{X}_i, c_i] = 0$ if $t \neq s,$
4. Uncorrelated observations: $E[\varepsilon_{it}\varepsilon_{js} \mid \mathbf{X}_i, c_i, \mathbf{X}_j, c_j] = 0$ for $i \neq j$ and for all $t$ and $s,$

where the rows of the $T \times K$ data matrix $\mathbf{X}_i$ are $\mathbf{x}'_{it}$. We will not assume mean independence. The "effects" may be fixed or random, so we allow

$$E[c_i \mid \mathbf{X}_i] = g(\mathbf{X}_i).$$

(See Section 9.2.1.) We will also assume a fixed number of periods, $T$, for convenience. The treatment here (and in the literature) can be modified to accommodate unbalanced panels, but it is a bit inconvenient. (It involves the placement of zeros at various places in the data matrices defined below and, of course, changing the terminal indexes in summations from 1 to $T$.)

The presence of the lagged dependent variable in this model presents a considerable obstacle to estimation. Consider, first, the straightforward application of assumption AI3 in Section 12.2. The compound disturbance in the model is $(c_i + \varepsilon_{it})$. The correlation between $y_{i,t-1}$ and $(c_i + \varepsilon_{i,t})$ is obviously nonzero because $y_{i,t-1} = \mathbf{x}'_{i,t-1}\boldsymbol{\beta} + \delta y_{i,t-2} + c_i + \varepsilon_{i,t-1}$:

$$\text{Cov}[y_{i,t-1}, (c_i + \varepsilon_{it})] = \sigma_c^2 + \delta \, \text{Cov}[y_{i,t-2}, (c_i + \varepsilon_{it})].$$

If $T$ is large and $-1 < \delta < 1$, then this covariance will be approximately $\sigma_c^2/(1-\delta)$. The large $T$ assumption is not going to be met in most cases. But, because $\delta$ will generally be positive, we can expect that this covariance will be at least larger than $\sigma_c^2$. The implication is that both (pooled) OLS and GLS in this model will be inconsistent. Unlike the case for the static model ($\delta = 0$), the fixed effects treatment does not solve the problem. Taking group mean differences, we obtain

$$y_{i,t} - \bar{y}_{i.} = (\mathbf{x}_{i,t} - \bar{\mathbf{x}}_{i.})'\boldsymbol{\beta} + \delta(y_{i,t-1} - \bar{y}_{i.}) + (\varepsilon_{i,t} - \bar{\varepsilon}_{i.}). \tag{12-30}$$

As shown in Anderson and Hsiao (1981, 1982),

$$\text{Cov}[(y_{i,t-1} - \bar{y}_{i.}), (\varepsilon_{i,t} - \bar{\varepsilon}_{i.})] \approx \frac{-\sigma_\varepsilon^2}{T^2} \frac{(T-1) - T\delta + \delta^T}{(1-\delta)^2}. \tag{12-31}$$

This result is $O(1/T)$, which would generally be no problem if the asymptotics in our model were with respect to increasing $T$. But, in this panel data model, $T$ is assumed to be fixed and relatively small. For conventional values of $T$, say 5 to 15, the proportional bias in estimation of $\delta$ could be on the order of, say, 15 to 60 percent.

Neither OLS nor GLS are useful as estimators. There are, however, instrumental variables available within the structure of the model. Anderson and Hsiao (1981, 1982) proposed an approach based on first differences rather than differences from group means,

$$y_{it} - y_{i,t-1} = (\mathbf{x}_{it} - \mathbf{x}_{i,t-1})'\boldsymbol{\beta} + \delta(y_{i,t-1} - y_{i,t-2}) + \varepsilon_{it} - \varepsilon_{i,t-1}.$$

For the first full observation,

$$y_{i3} - y_{i2} = (\mathbf{x}_{i3} - \mathbf{x}_{i2})'\boldsymbol{\beta} + \delta(y_{i2} - y_{i1}) + \varepsilon_{i3} - \varepsilon_{i2}, \tag{12-32}$$

the variable $y_{i1}$ (assuming initial point $t = 0$ is where our data generating process begins) satisfies the requirements, because $\varepsilon_{i1}$ is predetermined with respect to $(\varepsilon_{i3} - \varepsilon_{i2})$. [That is, if we used only the data from periods 1 to 3 constructed as in (12-32), then the instrumental variables for $(y_{i2} - y_{i1})$ would be $\mathbf{z}_{i(3)}$ where $\mathbf{z}_{i(3)} = (y_{1,1}, y_{2,1}, \ldots, y_{n,1})$ for the $n$ observations.] For the next observation,

$$y_{i4} - y_{i3} = (\mathbf{x}_{i4} - \mathbf{x}_{i3})'\boldsymbol{\beta} + \delta(y_{i3} - y_{i2}) + \varepsilon_{i4} - \varepsilon_{i3}, \tag{12-33}$$

variables $y_{i2}$ and $(y_{i2} - y_{i1})$ are both available. It then becomes a question whether the twice lagged levels or the twice lagged first differences will be preferable. Arellano (1989) and Kiviet (1995) find evidence that suggests that the asymptotic variance of the estimator is smaller with the levels as instruments than with the differences.

Based on the preceding paragraph, one might begin to suspect that there is, in fact, rather than a paucity of instruments, a large surplus. In this limited development, we have a choice between differences and levels. Indeed, we could use both and, moreover, in any period after the fourth, not only is $y_{i2}$ available as an instrument, but so also is $y_{i1}$, and so on. This is the essential observation behind the Arellano, Bover, and Bond (1991, 1995) estimators, which are based on the very large number of candidates for instrumental variables in this panel data model. To begin, with the model in first differences form, for $y_{i3} - y_{i2}$, variable $y_{i1}$ is available. For $y_{i4} - y_{i3}$, $y_{i1}$ and $y_{i2}$ are both available; for $y_{i5} - y_{i4}$, we have $y_{i1}$, $y_{i2}$, and $y_{i3}$, etc. Consider, as well, that we have not used the exogenous variables. With strictly exogenous regressors, not only are all lagged values of $y_{is}$ for $s$ previous to $t - 1$, but all values of $\mathbf{x}_{it}$ are also available as instruments. For example, for $y_{i4} - y_{i3}$, the candidates are $y_{i1}$, $y_{i2}$ and $(\mathbf{x}'_{i1}, \mathbf{x}'_{i2}, \ldots, \mathbf{x}'_{iT})$ for all $T$ periods. The number of candidates for instruments is, in fact, potentially huge. [See Ahn and Schmidt (1995) for a very detailed analysis.] If the exogenous variables are only predetermined, rather than strictly exogenous, then only $E[\varepsilon_{it} \mid \mathbf{x}_{i,t}, \mathbf{x}_{i,t-1}, \ldots, \mathbf{x}_{i1}] = 0$, and only vectors $\mathbf{x}_{is}$ from 1 to $t - 1$ will be valid instruments in the differenced equation that contains $\varepsilon_{it} - \varepsilon_{i,t-1}$. [See Baltagi and Levin (1986) for an application.] This is hardly a limitation, given that in the end, for a moderate sized model, we may be considering potentially hundreds or thousands of instrumental variables for estimation of what is usually a small handful of parameters.

We now formulate the model in a more familiar form, so we can apply the instrumental variable estimator. In terms of the differenced data, the basic equation is

$$y_{it} - y_{i,t-1} = (\mathbf{x}_{it} - \mathbf{x}_{i,t-1})'\boldsymbol{\beta} + \delta(y_{i,t-1} - y_{i,t-2}) + \varepsilon_{it} - \varepsilon_{i,t-1},$$

or

$$\Delta y_{it} = (\Delta \mathbf{x}_{it})'\boldsymbol{\beta} + \delta(\Delta y_{i,t-1}) + \Delta \varepsilon_{it}, \tag{12-34}$$

where $\Delta$ is the first difference operator, $\Delta a_t = a_t - a_{t-1}$ for any time-series variable (or vector) $a_t$. (It should be noted that a constant term and any time-invariant variables in $\mathbf{x}_{it}$ will fall out of the first differences. We will recover these below after we develop the estimator for $\boldsymbol{\beta}$.) The parameters of the model to be estimated are $\boldsymbol{\theta} = (\boldsymbol{\beta}', \delta)'$ and $\sigma_\varepsilon^2$. For convenience, write the model as

$$\tilde{y}_{it} = \tilde{\mathbf{x}}'_{it}\boldsymbol{\theta} + \tilde{\varepsilon}_{it}$$

We are going to define an instrumental variable estimator along the lines of (12-8) and (12-9). Because our data set is a panel, the counterpart to

$$\mathbf{Z}'\tilde{\mathbf{X}} = \sum_{i=1}^{n} \mathbf{z}_i \tilde{\mathbf{x}}'_i \tag{12-35}$$

in the cross-section case would seem to be

$$\mathbf{Z}'\tilde{\mathbf{X}} = \sum_{i=1}^{n} \sum_{t=3}^{T} \mathbf{z}_{it} \tilde{\mathbf{x}}'_{it} = \sum_{i=1}^{n} \mathbf{Z}'_i \tilde{\mathbf{X}}_i \tag{12-36}$$

$$\tilde{\mathbf{y}}_i = \begin{bmatrix} \Delta y_{i3} \\ \Delta y_{i4} \\ \vdots \\ \Delta y_{iT_i} \end{bmatrix}, \quad \tilde{\mathbf{X}}_i = \begin{bmatrix} \Delta \mathbf{x}'_{i3} & \Delta y_{i2} \\ \Delta \mathbf{x}'_{i4} & \Delta y_{i3} \\ \cdots \\ \Delta \mathbf{x}'_{iT} & \Delta y_{i,T-1} \end{bmatrix},$$

where there are $(T - 2)$ observations (rows) and $K + 1$ columns in $\tilde{\mathbf{X}}_i$. There is a complication, however, in that the number of instruments we have defined may vary by period, so the matrix computation in (12-36) appears to sum matrices of different sizes.

Consider an alternative approach. If we used only the first full observations defined in (12-34), then the cross-section version would apply, and the set of instruments $\mathbf{Z}$ in (12-35) with strictly exogenous variables would be the $n \times (1 + KT)$ matrix

$$
\mathbf{Z}_{(3)} = \begin{bmatrix} y_{1,1}, \mathbf{x}'_{1,1}, \mathbf{x}'_{1,2}, \dots \mathbf{x}'_{1,T} \\ y_{2,1}, \mathbf{x}'_{2,1}, \mathbf{x}'_{2,2}, \dots \mathbf{x}'_{2,T} \\ \vdots \\ y_{n,1}, \mathbf{x}'_{n,1}, \mathbf{x}'_{n,2}, \dots \mathbf{x}'_{n,T} \end{bmatrix},
$$

and the instrumental variable estimator of (12-8) would be based on

$$
\tilde{\mathbf{X}}_{(3)} = \begin{bmatrix} \mathbf{x}'_{1,3} - \mathbf{x}'_{1,2} & y_{1,4} - y_{1,3} \\ \mathbf{x}'_{2,3} - \mathbf{x}'_{2,2} & y_{2,4} - y_{2,3} \\ \vdots & \vdots \\ \mathbf{x}'_{n,3} - \mathbf{x}'_{n,2} & y_{n,4} - y_{n,3} \end{bmatrix} \text{ and } \tilde{\mathbf{y}}_{(3)} = \begin{bmatrix} y_{1,3} - y_{1,2} \\ y_{2,3} - y_{2,2} \\ \vdots \\ y_{n,3} - y_{n,2} \end{bmatrix}.
$$

The subscript "(3)" indicates the first observation used for the left-hand side of the equation. Neglecting the other observations, then, we could use these data to form the IV estimator in (12-8), which we label for the moment $\hat{\boldsymbol{\theta}}_{\text{IV}(3)}$. Now, repeat the construction using the next (fourth) observation as the first, and, again, using only a single year of the panel. The data matrices are now

$$
\tilde{\mathbf{X}}_{(4)} = \begin{bmatrix} \mathbf{x}'_{1,4} - \mathbf{x}'_{1,3} & y_{1,3} - y_{1,2} \\ \mathbf{x}'_{2,4} - \mathbf{x}'_{2,3} & y_{2,3} - y_{2,2} \\ \vdots & \vdots \\ \mathbf{x}'_{n,4} - \mathbf{x}'_{n,3} & y_{n,3} - y_{n,2} \end{bmatrix}, \tilde{\mathbf{y}}_{(4)} = \begin{bmatrix} y_{1,4} - y_{1,3} \\ y_{2,4} - y_{2,3} \\ \vdots \\ y_{n,4} - y_{n,3} \end{bmatrix}, \text{ and}
$$

$$
\mathbf{Z}_{(4)} = \begin{bmatrix} y_{1,1}, y_{1,2}, \mathbf{x}'_{1,1}, \mathbf{x}'_{1,2}, \dots \mathbf{x}'_{1,T} \\ y_{2,1}, y_{2,2}, \mathbf{x}'_{2,1}, \mathbf{x}'_{2,2}, \dots \mathbf{x}'_{2,T} \\ \vdots \\ y_{n,1}, y_{n,2}, \mathbf{x}'_{n,1}, \mathbf{x}'_{n,2}, \dots \mathbf{x}'_{n,T} \end{bmatrix}
$$

$$\tag{12-37}$$

and we have a second IV estimator, $\hat{\boldsymbol{\theta}}_{\text{IV}(4)}$, also based on $n$ observations, but, now, $2 + KT$ instruments. And so on.

We now need to reconcile the $T - 2$ estimators of $\boldsymbol{\theta}$ that we have constructed, $\hat{\boldsymbol{\theta}}_{\text{IV}(3)}$, $\hat{\boldsymbol{\theta}}_{\text{IV}(4)}, \dots, \hat{\boldsymbol{\theta}}_{\text{IV}(T)}$. We faced this problem in Section 10.3.2 where we examined Chamberlain's formulation of the fixed effects model. The minimum distance estimator suggested there and used in Carey's (1997) study of hospital costs in Example 10.6 provides a means of efficiently "averaging" the multiple estimators of the parameter vector. We will (as promised) return to the MDE in Chapter 15. For the present, we consider, instead, **Arellano and Bond's** (1991) [and Arellano and Bover's (1995)] **approach** to this problem. We will collect the full set of estimators in a counterpart to (10-26) and (10-27). First, combine the sets of instruments in a single matrix, $\mathbf{Z}$, where for each individual, we obtain the $(T - 2) \times L$ matrix $\mathbf{Z}_i$. The definition of the rows of $\mathbf{Z}_i$ depend on whether the regressors are assumed to be strictly exogenous or predetermined. For strictly exogenous variables,

$$\mathbf{Z}_i = \begin{bmatrix} y_{i,1}, \mathbf{x}'_{i,1}, \mathbf{x}'_{i,2}, \dots \mathbf{x}'_{i,T} & 0 & \dots & 0 \\ 0 & y_{i,1}, y_{i,2}, \mathbf{x}'_{i,1}, \mathbf{x}'_{i,2}, \dots \mathbf{x}'_{i,T} & \dots & 0 \\ \dots & \dots & \dots & \dots \\ 0 & 0 & \dots & y_{i,1}, y_{i,2}, \dots, y_{i,T-2}, \mathbf{x}'_{i,1}, \mathbf{x}'_{i,2}, \dots \mathbf{x}'_{i,T} \end{bmatrix},$$

(12-38a)

and $L = \sum_{i=1}^{T-2}(i + TK) = (T-2)(T-1)/2 + (T-2)TK$. For only predetermined variables, the matrix of instrumental variables is

$$\mathbf{Z}_i = \begin{bmatrix} y_{i,1}, \mathbf{x}'_{i,1}, \mathbf{x}'_{i,2} & 0 & \dots & 0 \\ 0 & y_{i,1}, y_{i,2}, \mathbf{x}'_{i,1}, \mathbf{x}'_{i,2}, \mathbf{x}'_{i,3} & \dots & 0 \\ \dots & \dots & \dots & \dots \\ 0 & 0 & \dots & y_{i,1}, y_{i,2}, \dots, y_{i,T-2}, \mathbf{x}'_{i,1}, \mathbf{x}'_{i,2}, \dots \mathbf{x}'_{i,T-1} \end{bmatrix},$$

(12-38b)

and $L = \sum_{i=1}^{T-2}(i(K+1)+K) = [(T-2)(T-1)/2](1+K)+(T-2)K$. This construction does proliferate instruments (moment conditions, as we will see in Chapter 15). In the application in Example 12.8, we have a small panel with only $T = 7$ periods, and we fit a model with only $K = 4$ regressors in $\mathbf{x}_{it}$, plus the lagged dependent variable. The strict exogeneity assumption produces a $\mathbf{Z}_i$ matrix that is $(5 \times 135)$ for this case. With only the assumption of predetermined $\mathbf{x}_{it}$, $\mathbf{Z}_i$ collapses slightly to $(5 \times 95)$. For purposes of the illustration, we have used only the two previous observations on $\mathbf{x}_{it}$. This further reduces the matrix to

$$\mathbf{Z}_i = \begin{bmatrix} y_{i,1}, \mathbf{x}'_{i,1}, \mathbf{x}'_{i,2} & 0 & \dots & 0 \\ 0 & y_{i,1}, y_{i,2}, \mathbf{x}_{i,2}, \mathbf{x}'_{i,3} & \dots & 0 \\ \dots & \dots & \dots & \dots \\ 0 & 0 & \dots & y_{i,1}, y_{i,2}, \dots, y_{i,T-2}, \mathbf{x}'_{i,T-2}, \mathbf{x}'_{i,T-1} \end{bmatrix},$$

(12-38c)

which, with $T = 7$ and $K = 4$, will be $(5 \times 55)$. [Baltagi (2005, Chapter 8) presents some alternative configurations of $\mathbf{Z}_i$ that allow for mixtures of strictly exogenous and predetermined variables.]

Now, we can compute the two-stage least squares estimator in (12-8) using our definitions of the data matrices $\mathbf{Z}_i$, $\tilde{\mathbf{X}}_i$, and $\tilde{\mathbf{y}}_i$ and (12-36). This will be

$$\hat{\boldsymbol{\theta}}_{IV} = \left[ \left( \sum_{i=1}^{n} \tilde{\mathbf{X}}'_i \mathbf{Z}_i \right) \left( \sum_{i=1}^{n} \mathbf{Z}'_i \mathbf{Z}_i \right)^{-1} \left( \sum_{i=1}^{n} \mathbf{Z}'_i \tilde{\mathbf{X}}_i \right) \right]^{-1}$$

$$\times \left[ \left( \sum_{i=1}^{n} \tilde{\mathbf{X}}'_i \mathbf{Z}_i \right) \left( \sum_{i=1}^{n} \mathbf{Z}'_i \mathbf{Z}_i \right)^{-1} \left( \sum_{i=1}^{n} \mathbf{Z}'_i \tilde{\mathbf{y}}_i \right) \right]. \quad (12\text{-}39)$$

The natural estimator of the asymptotic covariance matrix for the estimator would be

$$\text{Est. Asy. Var}\left[\hat{\boldsymbol{\theta}}_{IV}\right] = \hat{\sigma}^2_{\Delta\varepsilon} \left[ \left( \sum_{i=1}^{n} \tilde{\mathbf{X}}'_i \mathbf{Z}_i \right) \left( \sum_{i=1}^{n} \mathbf{Z}'_i \mathbf{Z}_i \right)^{-1} \left( \sum_{i=1}^{n} \mathbf{Z}'_i \mathbf{X}_i \right) \right]^{-1}, \quad (12\text{-}40)$$

where

$$\hat{\sigma}_{\Delta\varepsilon}^2 = \frac{\sum_{i=1}^n \sum_{t=3}^T [(y_{it} - y_{i,t-1}) - (\mathbf{x}_{it} - \mathbf{x}_{i,t-1})'\hat{\boldsymbol{\beta}} - \hat{\delta}(y_{i,t-1} - y_{i,t-2})]^2}{n(T-2)}. \qquad \textbf{(12-41)}$$

However, this variance estimator is likely to understate the true asymptotic variance because the observations are autocorrelated for one period. Because $(y_{it} - y_{i,t-1}) = \tilde{\mathbf{x}}_{it}'\boldsymbol{\theta} + (\varepsilon_{it} - \varepsilon_{i,t-1}) = \tilde{\mathbf{x}}_{it}'\boldsymbol{\theta} + v_{it}$,

$$\text{Cov}[v_{it}, v_{i,t-1}] = \text{Cov}[v_{it}, v_{i,t+1}] = -\sigma_\varepsilon^2.$$

Covariances at longer lags or leads are zero. In the differenced model, though the disturbance covariance matrix is not $\sigma_v^2\mathbf{I}$, it does take a particularly simple form.

$$\text{Cov}\begin{pmatrix} \varepsilon_{i,3} - \varepsilon_{i,2} \\ \varepsilon_{i,4} - \varepsilon_{i,3} \\ \varepsilon_{i,5} - \varepsilon_{i,4} \\ \cdots \\ \varepsilon_{i,T} - \varepsilon_{i,T-1} \end{pmatrix} = \sigma_\varepsilon^2 \begin{bmatrix} 2 & -1 & 0 & \cdots & 0 \\ -1 & 2 & -1 & \cdots & 0 \\ 0 & -1 & 2 & \cdots & 0 \\ \cdots & \cdots & -1 & \cdots & -1 \\ 0 & 0 & \cdots & -1 & 2 \end{bmatrix} = \sigma_\varepsilon^2 \boldsymbol{\Omega}_i. \qquad \textbf{(12-42)}$$

The implication is that the estimator in (12-41) estimates not $\sigma_\varepsilon^2$ but $2\sigma_\varepsilon^2$. However, simply dividing the estimator by two does not produce the correct asymptotic covariance matrix because the observations themselves are autocorrelated. As such, the matrix in (12-40) is inappropriate. (We encountered this issue in Theorem 8.1 and in Sections 8.2.3, 8.4.3, and 9.3.2.) An appropriate correction can be based on the counterpart to the White estimator that we developed in Chapter 9, in (9-3). For simplicity, let

$$\hat{\mathbf{A}} = \left[ \left( \sum_{i=1}^n \tilde{\mathbf{X}}_i'\mathbf{Z}_i \right) \left( \sum_{i=1}^n \mathbf{Z}_i'\mathbf{Z}_i \right)^{-1} \left( \sum_{i=1}^n \mathbf{Z}_i'\tilde{\mathbf{X}}_i \right) \right]^{-1}.$$

Then, a robust covariance matrix that accounts for the autocorrelation would be

$$\hat{\mathbf{A}} \left[ \left( \sum_{i=1}^n \tilde{\mathbf{X}}_i'\mathbf{Z}_i \right) \left( \sum_{i=1}^n \mathbf{Z}_i'\mathbf{Z}_i \right)^{-1} \left( \sum_{i=1}^n \mathbf{Z}_i'\hat{\mathbf{v}}_i\hat{\mathbf{v}}_i'\mathbf{Z}_i \right) \left( \sum_{i=1}^n \mathbf{Z}_i'\mathbf{Z}_i \right)^{-1} \left( \sum_{i=1}^n \mathbf{Z}_i'\tilde{\mathbf{X}}_i \right) \right] \hat{\mathbf{A}}. \qquad \textbf{(12-43)}$$

[One could also replace the $\hat{\mathbf{v}}_i\hat{\mathbf{v}}_i'$ in (12-43) with $\hat{\sigma}_\varepsilon^2\boldsymbol{\Omega}_i$ in (12-42) because this is the known expectation.]

It will be useful to digress briefly and examine the estimator in (12-39). The computations are less formidable than it might appear. Note that the rows of $\mathbf{Z}_i$ in (12-38a,b,c) are orthogonal. It follows that the matrix

$$\mathbf{F} = \sum_{i=1}^n \mathbf{Z}_i'\mathbf{Z}_i$$

in (12-39) is block-diagonal with $T-2$ blocks. The specific blocks in $\mathbf{F}$ are

$$\mathbf{F}_t = \sum_{i=1}^n \mathbf{z}_{it}\mathbf{z}_{it}'$$

$$= \mathbf{Z}_{(t)}'\mathbf{Z}_{(t)},$$

for $t = 3, \ldots, T$. Because the number of instruments is different in each period—see (12-38)—these blocks are of different sizes, say, $(L_t \times L_t)$. The same construction shows that the matrix $\sum_{i=1}^{n} \tilde{\mathbf{X}}_i' \mathbf{Z}_i$ is actually a partitioned matrix of the form

$$\sum_{i=1}^{n} \tilde{\mathbf{X}}_i' \mathbf{Z}_i = \left[ \tilde{\mathbf{X}}_{(3)}' \mathbf{Z}_{(3)} \quad \tilde{\mathbf{X}}_{(4)}' \mathbf{Z}_{(4)} \quad \cdots \quad \tilde{\mathbf{X}}_{(T)}' \mathbf{Z}_{(T)} \right],$$

where, again, the matrices are of different sizes; there are $T - 2$ rows in each but the number of columns differs. It follows that the inverse matrix, $(\sum_{i=1}^{n} \mathbf{Z}_i' \mathbf{Z}_i)^{-1}$, is also block-diagonal, and that the matrix quadratic form in (12-39) can be written

$$\left( \sum_{i=1}^{n} \tilde{\mathbf{X}}_i' \mathbf{Z}_i \right) \left( \sum_{i=1}^{n} \tilde{\mathbf{Z}}_i' \mathbf{Z}_i \right)^{-1} \left( \sum_{i=1}^{n} \mathbf{Z}_i' \tilde{\mathbf{X}}_i \right) = \sum_{t=3}^{T} \left( \tilde{\mathbf{X}}_{(t)}' \mathbf{Z}_{(t)} \right) \left( \mathbf{Z}_{(t)}' \mathbf{Z}_{(t)} \right)^{-1} \left( \mathbf{Z}_{(t)}' \tilde{\mathbf{X}}_{(t)} \right)$$

$$= \sum_{t=3}^{T} \left( \hat{\tilde{\mathbf{X}}}_{(t)}' \hat{\tilde{\mathbf{X}}}_{(t)} \right)$$

$$= \sum_{t=3}^{T} \mathbf{W}_{(t)},$$

[see (12-8) and the preceding result]. Continuing in this fashion, we find

$$\left( \sum_{i=1}^{n} \tilde{\mathbf{X}}_i' \mathbf{Z}_i \right) \left( \sum_{i=1}^{n} \tilde{\mathbf{Z}}_i' \mathbf{Z}_i \right)^{-1} \left( \sum_{i=1}^{n} \mathbf{Z}_i' \tilde{\mathbf{y}}_i \right) = \sum_{t=3}^{T} \hat{\tilde{\mathbf{X}}}_{(t)}' \mathbf{y}_{(t)}.$$

From (12-9), we can see that

$$\hat{\tilde{\mathbf{X}}}_{(t)}' \mathbf{y}_{(t)} = \left( \hat{\tilde{\mathbf{X}}}_{(t)}' \hat{\tilde{\mathbf{X}}}_{(t)} \right) \hat{\boldsymbol{\theta}}_{\text{IV}(t)}$$

$$= \mathbf{W}_{(t)} \hat{\boldsymbol{\theta}}_{\text{IV}(t)}.$$

Combining the terms constructed thus far, we find that the estimator in (12-39) can be written in the form

$$\hat{\boldsymbol{\theta}}_{\text{IV}} = \left( \sum_{t=3}^{T} \mathbf{W}_{(t)} \right)^{-1} \left( \sum_{t=3}^{T} \mathbf{W}_{(t)} \hat{\boldsymbol{\theta}}_{\text{IV}(t)} \right)$$

$$= \sum_{t=3}^{T} \mathbf{R}_{(t)} \hat{\boldsymbol{\theta}}_{\text{IV}(t)},$$

where

$$\mathbf{R}_{(t)} = \left( \sum_{t=3}^{T} \mathbf{W}_{(t)} \right)^{-1} \mathbf{W}_{(t)} \quad \text{and} \quad \sum_{i=3}^{T} \mathbf{R}_{(t)} = \mathbf{I}.$$

In words, we find that, as might be expected, the Arellano and Bond estimator of the parameter vector is a matrix weighted average of the $T - 2$ period specific two-stage least squares estimators, where the instruments used in each period may differ. Because the estimator is an average of estimators, a question arises, is it an efficient average—are the weights chosen to produce an efficient estimator? This is precisely the question that arose, with a similar estimation problem, in Section 10.3.2, and Example 10.6 where we considered pooling a set of estimators for a generalized regression model. Perhaps not surprisingly, the answer for this $\hat{\theta}$ is no; there is a more efficient set of weights that can be constructed for this model. We will assemble them when we examine the generalized method of moments estimator in Chapter 15.

There remains a loose end in the preceding. After (12-34), it was noted that this treatment discards a constant term and any time invariant variables that appear in the model. The Hausman and Taylor (1981) approach developed in the preceding section suggests a means by which the model could be completed to accommodate this possibility. Expand the basic formulation to include the time-invariant effects, as

$$y_{it} = \mathbf{x}'_{it}\boldsymbol{\beta} + \delta y_{i,t-1} + \alpha + \mathbf{f}'_i\boldsymbol{\gamma} + c_i + \varepsilon_{it}, \qquad \textbf{(12-44)}$$

where $\mathbf{f}_i$ is the set of time-invariant variables and $\boldsymbol{\gamma}$ is the parameter vector yet to be estimated. This model is consistent with the entire preceding development, as the component $\alpha + \mathbf{f}'_i\boldsymbol{\gamma}$ would have fallen out of the differenced equation along with $c_i$ at the first step at (12-30). Having developed a consistent estimator for $\boldsymbol{\theta} = (\boldsymbol{\beta}', \delta)'$, we now turn to estimation of $(\alpha, \boldsymbol{\gamma}')'$. The residuals from the IV regression (12-39),

$$w_{it} = \mathbf{x}'_{it}\hat{\boldsymbol{\beta}}_{IV} - \hat{\delta}_{IV} y_{i,t-1}$$

are pointwise consistent estimators of

$$\omega_{it} = \alpha + \mathbf{f}'_i\boldsymbol{\gamma} + c_i + \varepsilon_{it}.$$

Thus, the group means of the residuals can form the basis of a second-step regression;

$$\overline{w}_i = \alpha + \mathbf{f}'_i\boldsymbol{\gamma} + c_i + \overline{\varepsilon}_i + \eta_i \qquad \textbf{(12-45)}$$

where $\eta_i = (\overline{w}_i. - \overline{\omega}_i.)$ is the estimation error that converges to zero as $\hat{\boldsymbol{\theta}}$ converges to $\boldsymbol{\theta}$. The implication would seem to be that we can now linearly regress these group mean residuals on a constant and the time invariant variables $\mathbf{f}_i$ to estimate $\alpha$ and $\boldsymbol{\gamma}$. The flaw in the strategy, however, is that the initial assumptions of the model do not state that $c_i$ is uncorrelated with the other variables in the model, including the implicit time invariant terms, $\mathbf{f}_i$. Therefore, least squares is not a usable estimator here unless the random effects model is assumed, which we specifically sought to avoid at the outset. As in Hausman and Taylor's treatment, there is a workable strategy if it can be assumed that there are some variables in the model, including possibly some among the $\mathbf{f}_i$ as well as others among $\mathbf{x}_{it}$ that are uncorrelated with $c_i$ and $\varepsilon_{it}$. These are the $\mathbf{z}_1$ and $\mathbf{x}_1$ in the Hausman and Taylor estimator (see Step 2 in the development of the preceding section). Assuming that these variables are available—this is an identification assumption that must be added to the model—then we do have a usable instrumental variable estimator, using as instruments the constant term (1), any variables in $\mathbf{f}_i$ that are uncorrelated with the latent effects or the disturbances (call this $\mathbf{f}_{i1}$), and the group means of any variables in $\mathbf{x}_{it}$ that are also exogenous. There must be enough of these to provide a sufficiently large set of instruments to fit all the parameters in (12-45). This is, once again, the same identification we saw in step 2 of the Hausman and Taylor estimator, $K_1$, the number of exogenous variables in $\mathbf{x}_{it}$ must be at least as large as $L_2$, which is the number of endogenous variables in $\mathbf{f}_i$. With all this in place, we then have the instrumental variable estimator in which the dependent variable is $\overline{w}_i.$, the right-hand-side variables are $(1, \mathbf{f}_i)$, and the instrumental variables are $(1, \mathbf{f}_{i1}, \overline{\mathbf{x}}_{i1}.)$.

There is yet another direction that we might extend this estimation method. In (12-43), we have implicitly allowed a more general covariance matrix to govern the generation of the disturbances $\varepsilon_{it}$ and computed a robust covariance matrix for the simple IV estimator. We could take this a step further and look for a more efficient estimator. As a library of recent studies have shown, panel data sets are rich in information that allows the analyst to specify highly general models and to exploit the implied relationships among the variables to construct much more efficient generalized method of moments (GMM) estimators. [See, in particular, Arellano and Bover (1995) and Blundell and Bond (1998).] We will return to this development in Chapter 15.

### Example 12.8    Dynamic Labor Supply Equation

In Example 12.3, we used instrumental variables fit a labor supply equation,

$$Wks_{it} = \gamma_1 + \gamma_2 \ln Wage_{it} + \gamma_3 Ed_i + \gamma_4 Union_{it} + \gamma_5 Fem_i + u_{it}.$$

To illustrate the computations of this section, we will extend this model as follows:

$$Wks_{it} = \beta_1 \ln Wage_{it} + \beta_2 Union_{it} + \beta_3 Occ_{it} + \beta_4 Exp_{it} + \delta Wks_{i,t-1}$$
$$+ \alpha + \gamma_1 Ed_i + \gamma_2 Fem_i + c_i + \varepsilon_{it}.$$

(We have rearranged the variables and parameter names to conform to the notation in this section.) We note, in theoretical terms, as suggested in the earlier example, it may not be appropriate to treat $\ln Wage_{it}$ as uncorrelated with $\varepsilon_{it}$ or $c_i$. However, we will be analyzing the model in first differences. It may well be appropriate to treat changes in wages as exogenous. That will depend on the theoretical underpinnings of the model. We will treat the variable as predetermined here, and proceed. There are two time-invariant variables in the model, $Fem_i$, which is clearly exogenous, and $Ed_i$, which might be endogenous. The identification requirement for estimation of $(\alpha, \gamma_1, \gamma_2)$ is met by the presence of three exogenous variables, $Union_{it}$, $Occ_{it}$, and $Exp_{it}$ ($K_1 = 3$ and $L_2 = 1$).

The differenced equation analyzed at the first step is

$$\Delta Wks_{it} = \beta_1 \Delta \ln Wage_{it} + \beta_2 \Delta Union_{it} + \beta_3 \Delta Occ_{it} + \beta_4 \Delta Exp_{it} + \delta \Delta Wks_{i,t-1} + \varepsilon_{it}.$$

We estimated the parameters and the asymptotic covariance matrix according to (12-39) and (12-43). For specification of the instrumental variables, we used the two previous observations on $\mathbf{x}_{it}$, as shown in the text.[10] Table 12.4 presents the computations with several other inconsistent estimators.

The various estimates are quite far apart. In the absence of the common effects (and autocorrelation of the disturbances), all five estimators shown would be consistent. Given the very wide disparities, one might suspect that common effects are an important feature of the data. The second standard errors given with the IV estimates are based on the uncorrected matrix in (12-40) with $\hat{\sigma}_{\Delta\varepsilon}^2$ in (12-41) divided by two. We found the estimator to be quite volatile, as can be seen in the table. The estimator is also very sensitive to the choice of instruments that comprise $\mathbf{Z}_i$. Using (12-38a) instead of (12-38b) produces wild swings in the estimates and, in fact, produces implausible results. One possible explanation in this particular example is that the instrumental variables we are using are dummy variables that have relatively little variation over time.

---

[10]This estimator and the GMM estimators in Chapter 15 are built into some contemporary computer programs, including *NLOGIT* and *Stata*. Many researchers use Gauss programs that are distributed by M. Arellano, http://www.cemfi.es/%7Earellano/#dpd, or program the calculations themselves using *MatLab* or *R*. We have programmed the matrix computations directly for this application using the matrix package in *NLOGIT*.

**TABLE 12.4** Estimated Dynamic Panel Data Model Using Arellano and Bond's Estimator

| Variable | OLS, Full Eqn. | | OLS, Differenced | | IV, Differenced | | Random Effects | | Fixed Effects | |
|---|---|---|---|---|---|---|---|---|---|---|
| | Estimate | Std. Err. | Estimate | Std. Err. | Estimate | Std. Err. | Estimate | Std. Err. | Estimate | Std. Err. |
| ln Wage | 0.2966 | 0.2052 | −0.1100 | 0.4565 | −1.1402 | 0.2639 / 0.8768 | 0.2281 | 0.2405 | 0.5886 | 0.4790 |
| Union | −1.2945 | 0.1713 | 1.1640 | 0.4222 | 2.7089 | 0.3684 / 0.8676 | −1.4104 | 0.2199 | 0.1444 | 0.4369 |
| Occ | 0.4163 | 0.2005 | 0.8142 | 0.3924 | 2.2808 | 1.3105 / 0.7220 | 0.5191 | 0.2484 | 1.0064 | 0.4030 |
| Exp | −0.0295 | 0.00728 | −0.0742 | 0.0975 | −0.0208 | 0.1126 / 0.1104 | −0.0353 | 0.01021 | −0.1683 | 0.05954 |
| $Wks_{t-1}$ | 0.3804 | 0.01477 | −0.3527 | 0.01609 | 0.1304 | 0.04760 / 0.02131 | 0.2100 | 0.01511 | 0.0148 | 0.01705 |
| Constant | 28.918 | 1.4490 | | | −0.4110 | 0.3364 | 37.461 | 1.6778 | | |
| Ed | −0.0690 | 0.03703 | | | 0.0321 | 0.02587 | −0.0657 | 0.04988 | | |
| Fem | −0.8607 | 0.2544 | | | −0.0122 | 0.1554 | −1.1463 | 0.3513 | | |
| Sample | $t = 2 - 7$ $n = 595$ | | $t = 3 - 7$ $n = 595$ | | $t = 3 - 7; n = 595$ Means used $t = 7$ | | $t = 2 - 7$ $n = 595$ | | $t = 2 - 7$ $n = 595$ | |

## 12.9 WEAK INSTRUMENTS

Our analysis thus far has focused on the "identification" condition for IV estimation, that is, the "exogeneity assumption," AI9, which produces

$$\text{plim } (1/n)\mathbf{Z}'\boldsymbol{\varepsilon} = \mathbf{0}. \tag{12-46}$$

Taking the "relevance" assumption,

$$\text{plim } (1/n)\mathbf{Z}'\mathbf{X} = \mathbf{Q}_{\mathbf{ZX}}, \text{ a finite, nonzero, } L \times K \text{ matrix with rank } K, \tag{12-47}$$

as given produces a consistent IV estimator. In absolute terms, with (12-46) in place, (12-47) is sufficient to assert consistency. As such, researchers have focused on *exogeneity* as the defining problem to be solved in constructing the IV estimator. A growing literature has argued that greater attention needs to be given to the relevance condition. While strictly speaking, (12-47) is indeed sufficient for the asymptotic results we have claimed, the common case of "weak instruments," in which (12-47) is only barely true has attracted considerable scrutiny. In practical terms, instruments are "weak" when they are only slightly correlated with the right-hand-side variables, $\mathbf{X}$; that is, $(1/n)\mathbf{Z}'\mathbf{X}$ is *close* to zero. (We will quantify this theoretically when we revisit the issue in Chapter 13.) Researchers have begun to examine these cases, finding in some an explanation for perverse and contradictory empirical results.[11]

Superficially, the problem of weak instruments shows up in the asymptotic covariance matrix of the IV estimator,

$$\text{Asy. Var}[\mathbf{b}_{\text{IV}}] = \frac{\sigma_\varepsilon^2}{n} \left[ \left( \frac{\mathbf{X}'\mathbf{Z}}{n} \right) \left( \frac{\mathbf{Z}'\mathbf{Z}}{n} \right)^{-1} \left( \frac{\mathbf{Z}'\mathbf{X}}{n} \right) \right]^{-1},$$

which will be "large" when the instruments are weak, and, other things equal, larger the weaker they are. However, the problems run deeper than that. Hahn and Hausman (2003) list two implications: (i) the two stage least squares estimator is badly biased toward the ordinary least squares estimator, which is known to be inconsistent, and (ii) the standard first order asymptotics (such as those we have used in the preceding) will not give an accurate framework for statistical inference. Thus, the problem is worse than simply lack of precision. There is also at least some evidence that the issue goes well beyond "small sample problems." [See Bound, Jaeger, and Baker (1995).]

Current research offers several prescriptions for detecting weakness in instrumental variables. For a single endogenous variable ($\mathbf{x}$ that is correlated with $\boldsymbol{\varepsilon}$), the standard approach is based on the first step least squares regression of two-stage least squares. The conventional $F$ statistic for testing the hypothesis that all the coefficients in the regression

$$x_i = \mathbf{z}_i'\boldsymbol{\pi} + v_i$$

are zero is used to test the "hypothesis" that the instruments are weak. An $F$ statistic less than 10 signals the problem. [See Staiger and Stock (1997) and Stock and Watson (2007, Chapter 12) for motivation of this specific test.] When there are more than one

---

[11]Important references are Staiger and Stock (1997), Stock, Wright, and Yogo (2002), Hahn and Hausman (2002, 2003), Kleibergen (2002), Stock and Yogo (2005), and Hausman, Stock, and Yogo (2005).

endogenous variable in the model, testing each one separately using this test is not sufficient, since collinearity among the variables could impact the result, but would not show up in either test. Shea (1997) proposes a four step multivariate procedure that can be used. Godfrey (1999) derived a surprisingly simple alternative method of doing the computation. For endogenous variable $k$, the Godfrey statistic is the ratio of the estimated variances of the two estimators, OLS and 2SLS,

$$R_k^2 = \frac{v_k(OLS)/\mathbf{e}'\mathbf{e}(OLS)}{v_k(2SLS)/\mathbf{e}'\mathbf{e}(2SLS)}$$

where $v_k(OLS)$ is the $k$th diagonal element of $[\mathbf{e}'\mathbf{e}(OLS)/(n-K)](\mathbf{X}'\mathbf{X})^{-1}$ and $v_k(2SLS)$ is defined likewise. With the scalings, the statistic reduces to

$$R_k^2 = \frac{(\mathbf{X}'\mathbf{X})^{kk}}{(\hat{\mathbf{X}}'\hat{\mathbf{X}})^{kk}}$$

where the superscript indicates the element of the inverse matrix. The $F$ statistic can then be based on this measure; $F = [R_k^2/(L-1)]/[(1-R_k^2)/(n-L)]$ assuming that $\mathbf{Z}$ contains a constant term.

It is worth noting that the test for weak instruments is not a specification test, nor is it a constructive test for building the model. Rather, it is a strategy for helping the researcher avoid basing inference on unreliable statistics whose properties are not well represented by the familiar asymptotic results, e.g., distributions under assumed null model specifications. Several extensions are of interest. Other statistical procedures are proposed in Hahn and Hausman (2002) and Kleibergen (2002). We are also interested in cases of more than a single endogenous variable. We will take another look at this issue in Chapter 13, where we can cast the modeling framework as a simultaneous equations model.

The stark results of this section call the IV estimator into question. In a fairly narrow circumstance, an alternative estimator is the "moment"-free LIML estimator discussed in the next chapter. Another, perhaps somewhat unappealing, approach is to revert to least squares. The OLS estimator is not without virtue. The asymptotic variance of the OLS estimator

$$\text{Asy. Var}[\mathbf{b}_{LS}] = (\sigma^2/n)\mathbf{Q}_{\mathbf{XX}}^{-1}$$

is unambiguously smaller than the asymptotic variance of the IV estimator

$$\text{Asy. Var}[\mathbf{b}_{IV}] = (\sigma^2/n)(\mathbf{Q}_{\mathbf{XZ}}\mathbf{Q}_{\mathbf{ZZ}}^{-1}\mathbf{Q}_{\mathbf{ZX}})^{-1}.$$

(The proof is considered in the exercises.) Given the preceding results, it could be far smaller. The OLS estimator is inconsistent, however,

$$\text{plim } \mathbf{b}_{LS} - \boldsymbol{\beta} = \mathbf{Q}_{\mathbf{XX}}^{-1}\boldsymbol{\gamma}$$

[see (12-4)]. By a mean squared error comparison, it is unclear whether the OLS estimator with

$$M(\mathbf{b}_{LS} \mid \boldsymbol{\beta}) = (\sigma^2/n)\mathbf{Q}_{\mathbf{XX}}^{-1} + \mathbf{Q}_{\mathbf{XX}}^{-1}\boldsymbol{\gamma}\boldsymbol{\gamma}'\mathbf{Q}_{\mathbf{XX}}^{-1},$$

or the IV estimator, with

$$M(\mathbf{b}_{IV} \mid \boldsymbol{\beta}) = (\sigma^2/n)(\mathbf{Q}_{\mathbf{XZ}}\mathbf{Q}_{\mathbf{ZZ}}^{-1}\mathbf{Q}_{\mathbf{ZX}})^{-1},$$

is more precise. The natural recourse in the face of weak instruments is to drop the endogenous variable from the model or improve the instrument set. Each of these is a specification issue. Strictly in terms of estimation strategy within the framework of the data and specification in hand, there is scope for OLS to be the preferred strategy.

## 12.10 SUMMARY AND CONCLUSIONS

The instrumental variable (IV) estimator, in various forms, is among the most fundamental tools in econometrics. Broadly interpreted, it encompasses most of the estimation methods that we will examine in this book. This chapter has developed the basic results for IV estimation of linear models. The essential departure point is the exogeneity and relevance assumptions that define an instrumental variable. We then analyzed linear IV estimation in the form of the two-stage least squares estimator. With only a few special exceptions related to simultaneous equations models with two variables, almost no finite sample properties have been established for the IV estimator. (We temper that, however, with the results in Section 12.9 on weak instruments, where we saw evidence that whatever the finite sample properties of the IV estimator might be, under some well-discernible circumstances, these properties are not attractive.) We then examined the asymptotic properties of the IV estimator for linear and nonlinear regression models. Two important applications of the IV estimator are Hausman and Taylor's (1981) method of fitting the random effects model with endogenous regressors and Anderson and Hsiao's (1981) and Arellano and Bond's (1991) strategies for fitting dynamic panel data models. Finally, some cautionary notes about using IV estimators when the instruments are only weakly relevant in the model are examined in Section 12.9.

### Key Terms and Concepts

- Anderson and Hsiao estimator
- Arellano and Bond estimator
- Asymptotic distribution
- Asymptotic covariance matrix
- Attenuation
- Consistent estimator
- Dynamic panel data model
- Exogeneity
- Feasible GLS
- Generalized regression model
- Hausman and Taylor's estimator
- Hausman's specification test
- Identification
- Indicator
- Instrumental variables
- Instrumental variable estimator
- Limiting distribution
- Minimum distance estimator
- Orthogonality condition
- Panel data
- Proxy variable
- Relevance
- Reliability ratio
- Reduced form equation
- Selectivity effect
- Specification test
- Structural model
- Two-stage least squares
- Variable addition test
- Weak instruments
- Wu test

### Exercises

1. In the discussion of the instrumental variable estimator, we showed that the least squares estimator, $\mathbf{b}_{LS}$, is biased and inconsistent. Nonetheless, $\mathbf{b}_{LS}$ does estimate something—see (12-4). Derive the asymptotic covariance matrix of $\mathbf{b}_{LS}$ and show that $\mathbf{b}_{LS}$ is asymptotically normally distributed.

2.  For the measurement error model in (12-11) and (12-12), prove that when only $x$ is measured with error, the squared correlation between $y$ and $x$ is less than that between $y^*$ and $x^*$. (Note the assumption that $y^* = y$.) Does the same hold true if $y^*$ is also measured with error?

3.  Derive the results in (12-17a) and (12-17b) for the measurement error model. Note the hint in footnote 3 in Section 12.5.1 that suggests you use result (A-66) when you need to invert

$$[\mathbf{Q}^* + \mathbf{\Sigma}_{uu}] = [\mathbf{Q}^* + (\sigma_u \mathbf{e}_1)(\sigma_u \mathbf{e}_1)'].$$

4.  At the end of Section 12.9, it is suggested that the OLS estimator could have a smaller mean squared error than the 2SLS estimator. Using (12-4), the results of Exercise 1, and Theorem 12.1, show that the result will be true if

$$\mathbf{Q}_{XX} - \mathbf{Q}_{XZ}\mathbf{Q}_{ZZ}^{-1}\mathbf{Q}_{ZX} \gg \frac{1}{(\sigma^2/n) + \gamma'\mathbf{Q}_{XX}^{-1}\gamma}\gamma\gamma'.$$

How can you verify that this is at least possible? The right-hand-side is a rank one, nonnegative definite matrix. What can be said about the left-hand-side?

5.  Consider the linear model $y_i = \alpha + \beta x_i + \varepsilon_i$ in which $\text{Cov}[x_i, \varepsilon_i] = \gamma \neq 0$. Let $z$ be an exogenous, relevant instrumental variable for this model. Assume, as well, that $z$ is binary—it takes only values 1 and 0. Show the algebraic forms of the LS estimator and the IV estimator for both $\alpha$ and $\beta$.

## Application

1.  In Example 12.3, we have suggested a model of a labor market. From the "reduced form" equation given first, you can see the full set of variables that appears in the model—that is the "endogenous variables," ln $Wage_{it}$ and $Wks_{it}$ and all other exogenous variables. The labor supply equation suggested next contains these two variables and three of the exogenous variables. From these facts, you can deduce what variables would appear in a labor "demand" equation for ln $Wage_{it}$. Assume (for purpose of our example) that ln $Wage_{it}$ is determined by $Wks_{it}$ and the remaining appropriate exogenous variables. (We should emphasize that this exercise is purely to illustrate the computations—the structure here would not provide a theoretically sound model for labor market equilibrium.)
    a.  What is the labor demand equation implied by the preceding?
    b.  Estimate the parameters of this equation by OLS and by 2SLS and compare the results. (Ignore the panel nature of the data set. Just pool the data.)
    c.  Are the instruments used in this equation relevant? How do you know?

# 13
# SIMULTANEOUS EQUATIONS MODELS

$\overbrace{\phantom{xxxxx}}$

## 13.1 INTRODUCTION

Although most of our work thus far has been in the context of single-equation models, even a cursory look through almost any economics textbook shows that much of the theory is built on sets, or *systems*, of relationships. Familiar examples include market equilibrium, models of the macroeconomy, and sets of factor or commodity demand equations. Whether one's interest is only in a particular part of the system or in the system as a whole, the interaction of the variables in the model will have important implications for both interpretation and estimation of the model's parameters. The implications of simultaneity for econometric estimation were recognized long before the apparatus discussed in this chapter was developed.[1] The subsequent research in the subject, continuing to the present, is among the most extensive in econometrics.

This chapter considers the issues that arise in interpreting and estimating multiple-equations models. Section 13.2 describes the general framework used for analyzing systems of simultaneous equations. Most of the discussion of these models centers on problems of estimation. But before estimation can even be considered, the fundamental question of whether the parameters of interest in the model are even estimable must be resolved. This **problem of identification** is discussed in Section 13.3. Sections 13.4 to 13.7 then discuss methods of estimation. Section 13.8 is concerned with specification tests. In Section 13.9, the special characteristics of dynamic models are examined.

## 13.2 FUNDAMENTAL ISSUES IN SIMULTANEOUS EQUATIONS MODELS

In this section, we describe the basic terminology and statistical issues in the analysis of simultaneous equations models. We begin with some simple examples and then present a general framework.

### 13.2.1 ILLUSTRATIVE SYSTEMS OF EQUATIONS

A familiar example of a system of simultaneous equations is a model of market equilibrium, consisting of the following:

$$\text{demand equation:} \quad q_{d,t} = \alpha_1 p_t + \alpha_2 x_t + \varepsilon_{d,t},$$
$$\text{supply equation:} \quad q_{s,t} = \beta_1 p_t \qquad\quad + \varepsilon_{s,t},$$
$$\text{equilibrium condition:} \quad q_{d,t} = q_{s,t} = q_t.$$

---

[1]See, for example, Working (1926) and Haavelmo (1943).

These equations are **structural equations** in that they are derived from theory and each purports to describe a particular aspect of the economy.[2] Because the model is one of the joint determination of price and quantity, they are labeled **jointly dependent** or **endogenous** variables. Income, $x$, is assumed to be determined outside of the model, which makes it **exogenous.** The disturbances are added to the usual textbook description to obtain an **econometric model.** All three equations are needed to determine the equilibrium price and quantity, so the system is **interdependent.** Finally, because an equilibrium solution for price and quantity in terms of income and the disturbances is, indeed, implied (unless $\alpha_1$ equals $\beta_1$), the system is said to be a **complete system of equations.** *The completeness of the system requires that the number of equations equal the number of endogenous variables.* As a general rule, it is not possible to estimate all the parameters of incomplete systems (although it may be possible to estimate some of them).

Suppose that interest centers on estimating the demand elasticity $\alpha_1$. For simplicity, assume that $\varepsilon_d$ and $\varepsilon_s$ are well behaved, classical disturbances with

$$E[\varepsilon_{d,t} \mid x_t] = E[\varepsilon_{s,t} \mid x_t] = 0,$$
$$E[\varepsilon_{d,t}^2 \mid x_t] = \sigma_d^2,$$
$$E[\varepsilon_{s,t}^2 \mid x_t] = \sigma_s^2,$$
$$E[\varepsilon_{d,t}\varepsilon_{s,t} \mid x_t] = 0.$$

All variables are mutually uncorrelated with observations at different time periods. Price, quantity, and income are measured in logarithms in deviations from their sample means. Solving the equations for $p$ and $q$ in terms of $x$, $\varepsilon_d$, and $\varepsilon_s$ produces the **reduced form** of the model

$$p = \frac{\alpha_2 x}{\beta_1 - \alpha_1} + \frac{\varepsilon_d - \varepsilon_s}{\beta_1 - \alpha_1} = \pi_1 x + v_1,$$

$$q = \frac{\beta_1 \alpha_2 x}{\beta_1 - \alpha_1} + \frac{\beta_1 \varepsilon_d - \alpha_1 \varepsilon_s}{\beta_1 - \alpha_1} = \pi_2 x + v_2.$$

**(13-1)**

(Note the role of the "completeness" requirement that $\alpha_1$ not equal $\beta_1$.)

It follows that $\text{Cov}[p, \varepsilon_d] = \sigma_d^2 / (\beta_1 - \alpha_1)$ and $\text{Cov}[p, \varepsilon_s] = -\sigma_s^2 / (\beta_1 - \alpha_1)$ so neither the demand nor the supply equation satisfies the assumptions of the classical regression model. The price elasticity of demand cannot be consistently estimated by least squares regression of $q$ on $x$ and $p$. This result is characteristic of simultaneous-equations models. Because the endogenous variables are all correlated with the disturbances, the least squares estimators of the parameters of equations with endogenous variables on the right-hand side are inconsistent.[3]

Suppose that we have a sample of $T$ observations on $p$, $q$, and $x$ such that

$$\text{plim}(1 / T)\mathbf{x}'\mathbf{x} = \sigma_x^2.$$

---

[2]The distinction between **structural** and **nonstructural** models is sometimes drawn on this basis. See, for example, Cooley and LeRoy (1985).

[3]This failure of least squares is sometimes labeled **simultaneous equations bias.**

Since least squares is inconsistent, we might instead use an **instrumental variable estimator.**[4] The only variable in the system that is not correlated with the disturbances is $x$. Consider, then, the IV estimator, $\hat{\beta}_1 = \mathbf{q'x}/\mathbf{p'x}$. This estimator has

$$\text{plim } \hat{\beta}_1 = \text{plim } \frac{\mathbf{q'x}/T}{\mathbf{p'x}/T} = \frac{\sigma_x^2 \beta_1 \alpha_2 / (\beta_1 - \alpha_1)}{\sigma_x^2 \alpha_2 / (\beta_1 - \alpha_1)} = \beta_1.$$

Evidently, the parameter of the supply curve can be estimated by using an instrumental variable estimator. In the least squares regression of $\mathbf{p}$ on $\mathbf{x}$, the predicted values are $\hat{\mathbf{p}} = (\mathbf{p'x}/\mathbf{x'x})\mathbf{x}$. It follows that in the instrumental variable regression the instrument is $\hat{\mathbf{p}}$. That is,

$$\hat{\beta}_1 = \frac{\hat{\mathbf{p}}'\mathbf{q}}{\hat{\mathbf{p}}'\mathbf{p}}.$$

Because $\hat{\mathbf{p}}'\mathbf{p} = \hat{\mathbf{p}}'\hat{\mathbf{p}}$, $\hat{\beta}_1$ is also the slope in a regression of $q$ on these predicted values. This interpretation defines the **two-stage least squares estimator.**

It would be desirable to use a similar device to estimate the parameters of the demand equation, but unfortunately, we have exhausted the information in the sample. Not only does least squares fail to estimate the demand equation, but without some further assumptions, the sample contains no other information that can be used. This example illustrates the **problem of identification** alluded to in the introduction to this chapter.

A second example is the following simple model of income determination.

### Example 13.1   A Small Macroeconomic Model
Consider the model

consumption:   $c_t = \alpha_0 + \alpha_1 y_t + \alpha_2 c_{t-1} + \varepsilon_{t1},$

investment:   $i_t = \beta_0 + \beta_1 r_t + \beta_2 (y_t - y_{t-1}) + \varepsilon_{t2},$

demand:   $y_t = c_t + i_t + g_t.$

The model contains an autoregressive consumption function, an investment equation based on interest and the growth in output, and an equilibrium condition. The model determines the values of the three endogenous variables $c_t$, $i_t$, and $y_t$. This model is a **dynamic model.** In addition to the exogenous variables $r_t$ and $g_t$, it contains two **predetermined variables,** $c_{t-1}$ and $y_{t-1}$. These are obviously not exogenous, but with regard to the current values of the endogenous variables, they may be regarded as having already been determined. The deciding factor is whether or not they are uncorrelated with the current disturbances, which we might assume. The reduced form of this model is

$Ac_t = \alpha_0(1 - \beta_2) + \beta_0\alpha_1 + \alpha_1\beta_1 r_t + \alpha_1 g_t + \alpha_2(1 - \beta_2)c_{t-1} - \alpha_1\beta_2 y_{t-1} + (1 - \beta_2)\varepsilon_{t1} + \alpha_1\varepsilon_{t2},$

$Ai_t = \alpha_0\beta_2 + \beta_0(1 - \alpha_1) + \beta_1(1 - \alpha_1)r_t + \beta_2 g_t + \alpha_2\beta_2 c_{t-1} - \beta_2(1 - \alpha_1)y_{t-1} + \beta_2\varepsilon_{t1} + (1 - \alpha_1)\varepsilon_{t2},$

$Ay_t = \alpha_0 + \beta_0 + \beta_1 r_t + g_t + \alpha_2 c_{t-1} - \beta_2 y_{t-1} + \varepsilon_{t1} + \varepsilon_{t2},$

where $A = 1 - \alpha_1 - \beta_2$. Note that the reduced form preserves the equilibrium condition.

The preceding two examples illustrate systems in which there are **behavioral equations** and **equilibrium conditions.** The latter are distinct in that even in an econometric model, they have no disturbances. Another model, which illustrates nearly all the concepts to be discussed in this chapter, is shown in the next example.

---

[4]See Section 12.1.

*Example 13.2   Klein's Model I*
A widely used example of a simultaneous equations model of the economy is Klein's (1950) *Model I*. The model may be written

$$C_t = \alpha_0 + \alpha_1 P_t + \alpha_2 P_{t-1} + \alpha_3 \left(W_t^p + W_t^g\right) + \varepsilon_{1t} \quad \text{(consumption)},$$

$$I_t = \beta_0 + \beta_1 P_t + \beta_2 P_{t-1} + \beta_3 K_{t-1} \qquad\qquad + \varepsilon_{2t} \quad \text{(investment)},$$

$$W_t^p = \gamma_0 + \gamma_1 X_t + \gamma_2 X_{t-1} + \gamma_3 A_t \qquad\qquad + \varepsilon_{3t} \quad \text{(private wages)},$$

$$X_t = C_t + I_t + G_t \qquad\qquad\qquad\qquad\qquad\quad \text{(equilibrium demand)},$$

$$P_t = X_t - T_t - W_t^p \qquad\qquad\qquad\qquad\qquad \text{(private profits)},$$

$$K_t = K_{t-1} + I_t \qquad\qquad\qquad\qquad\qquad\qquad \text{(capital stock)}.$$

The endogenous variables are each on the left-hand side of an equation and are labeled on the right. The exogenous variables are $G_t$ = government nonwage spending, $T_t$ = indirect business taxes plus net exports, $W_t^g$ = government wage bill, $A_t$ = time trend measured as years from 1931, and the constant term. There are also three predetermined variables: the lagged values of the capital stock, private profits, and total demand. The model contains three behavioral equations, an equilibrium condition and two accounting identities. This model provides an excellent example of a small, dynamic model of the economy. It has also been widely used as a test ground for simultaneous equations estimators. Klein estimated the parameters using yearly data for 1921 to 1941. The data are listed in Appendix Table F13.1.

### 13.2.2   ENDOGENEITY AND CAUSALITY

The distinction between "exogenous" and "endogenous" variables in a model is a subtle and sometimes controversial complication. It is the subject of a long literature.[5] We have drawn the distinction in a useful economic fashion at a few points in terms of whether a variable in the model could reasonably be expected to vary "autonomously," independently of the other variables in the model. Thus, in a model of supply and demand, the weather variable in a supply equation seems obviously to be exogenous in a pure sense to the determination of price and quantity, whereas the current price clearly is "endogenous" by any reasonable construction. Unfortunately, this neat classification is of fairly limited use in macroeconomics, where almost no variable can be said to be truly exogenous in the fashion that most observers would understand the term. To take a common example, the estimation of consumption functions by ordinary least squares, as we did in some earlier examples, is usually treated as a respectable enterprise, even though most macroeconomic models (including the examples given here) depart from a consumption function in which income is exogenous. This departure has led analysts, for better or worse, to draw the distinction largely on statistical grounds.

The methodological development in the literature has produced some consensus on this subject. As we shall see, the definitions formalize the economic characterization we drew earlier. We will loosely sketch a few results here for purposes of our derivations to follow. The interested reader is referred to the literature (and forewarned of some challenging reading).

---

[5]See, for example, Zellner (1979), Sims (1977), Granger (1969), and especially Engle, Hendry, and Richard (1983).

Engle, Hendry, and Richard (1983) define a set of variables $\mathbf{x}_t$ in a parameterized model to be **weakly exogenous** if the full model can be written in terms of a marginal probability distribution for $\mathbf{x}_t$ and a conditional distribution for $\mathbf{y}_t \mid \mathbf{x}_t$ such that estimation of the parameters of the conditional distribution is no less efficient than estimation of the full set of parameters of the joint distribution. This case will be true if none of the parameters in the conditional distribution appears in the marginal distribution for $\mathbf{x}_t$. In the present context, we will need this sort of construction to derive reduced forms the way we did previously.

With reference to time-series applications (although the notion extends to cross sections as well), variables $\mathbf{x}_t$ are said to be **predetermined** in the model if $\mathbf{x}_t$ is independent of all *subsequent* structural disturbances $\varepsilon_{t+s}$ for $s \geq 0$. Variables that are predetermined in a model can be treated, at least asymptotically, as if they were exogenous in the sense that consistent estimators can be derived when they appear as regressors. We used this result in Section 12.8.2 as well, when we derived the properties of regressions containing lagged values of the dependent variable.

A related concept is **Granger causality.** Granger causality (a kind of statistical feedback) is absent when $f(\mathbf{x}_t \mid \mathbf{x}_{t-1}, \mathbf{y}_{t-1})$ equals $f(\mathbf{x}_t \mid \mathbf{x}_{t-1})$. The definition states that in the conditional distribution, lagged values of $\mathbf{y}_t$ add no information to explanation of movements of $\mathbf{x}_t$ beyond that provided by lagged values of $\mathbf{x}_t$ itself. This concept is useful in the construction of forecasting models. Finally, if $\mathbf{x}_t$ is weakly exogenous and if $\mathbf{y}_{t-1}$ does not Granger cause $\mathbf{x}_t$, then $\mathbf{x}_t$ is **strongly exogenous.**

### 13.2.3  A GENERAL NOTATION FOR LINEAR SIMULTANEOUS EQUATIONS MODELS[6]

The **structural form** of the model is[7]

$$\gamma_{11} y_{t1} + \gamma_{21} y_{t2} + \cdots + \gamma_{M1} y_{tM} + \beta_{11} x_{t1} + \cdots + \beta_{K1} x_{tK} = \varepsilon_{t1},$$

$$\gamma_{12} y_{t1} + \gamma_{22} y_{t2} + \cdots + \gamma_{M2} y_{tM} + \beta_{12} x_{t1} + \cdots + \beta_{K2} x_{tK} = \varepsilon_{t2},$$

$$\vdots$$

$$\gamma_{1M} y_{t1} + \gamma_{2M} y_{t2} + \cdots + \gamma_{MM} y_{tM} + \beta_{1M} x_{t1} + \cdots + \beta_{KM} x_{tK} = \varepsilon_{tM}.$$

**(13-2)**

There are $M$ equations and $M$ endogenous variables, denoted $y_1, \ldots, y_M$. There are $K$ exogenous variables, $x_1, \ldots, x_K$, that may include predetermined values of $y_1, \ldots, y_M$ as well. The first element of $\mathbf{x}_t$ will usually be the constant, 1. Finally, $\varepsilon_{t1}, \ldots, \varepsilon_{tM}$ are the **structural disturbances.** The subscript $t$ will be used to index observations, $t = 1, \ldots, T$.

---

[6]We will be restricting our attention to linear models in this chapter. **Nonlinear systems** occupy another strand of literature in this area. Nonlinear systems bring forth numerous complications beyond those discussed here and are beyond the scope of this text. Gallant (1987), Gallant and Holly (1980), Gallant and White (1988), Davidson and MacKinnon (2004), and Wooldridge (2002a) provide further discussion.

[7]For the present, it is convenient to ignore the special nature of lagged endogenous variables and treat them the same as the strictly exogenous variables.

In matrix terms, the system may be written

$$[y_1 \quad y_2 \quad \cdots \quad y_M]_t \begin{bmatrix} \gamma_{11} & \gamma_{12} & \cdots & \gamma_{1M} \\ \gamma_{21} & \gamma_{22} & \cdots & \gamma_{2M} \\ & & \vdots & \\ \gamma_{M1} & \gamma_{M2} & \cdots & \gamma_{MM} \end{bmatrix}$$

$$+ [x_1 \quad x_2 \quad \cdots \quad x_K]_t \begin{bmatrix} \beta_{11} & \beta_{12} & \cdots & \beta_{1M} \\ \beta_{21} & \beta_{22} & \cdots & \beta_{2M} \\ & & \vdots & \\ \beta_{K1} & \beta_{K2} & \cdots & \beta_{KM} \end{bmatrix} = [\varepsilon_1 \quad \varepsilon_2 \quad \cdots \quad \varepsilon_M]_t,$$

or

$$\mathbf{y}_t'\mathbf{\Gamma} + \mathbf{x}_t'\mathbf{B} = \boldsymbol{\varepsilon}_t'.$$

Each column of the parameter matrices is the vector of coefficients in a particular equation, whereas each row applies to a specific endogenous variable.

The underlying theory will imply a number of restrictions on $\mathbf{\Gamma}$ and $\mathbf{B}$. One of the variables in each equation is labeled the *dependent* variable so that its coefficient in the model will be 1. Thus, there will be at least one "1" in each column of $\mathbf{\Gamma}$. This **normalization** is not a substantive restriction. The relationship defined for a given equation will be unchanged if every coefficient in the equation is multiplied by the same constant. Choosing a "dependent variable" simply removes this indeterminacy. If there are any identities, then the corresponding columns of $\mathbf{\Gamma}$ and $\mathbf{B}$ will be completely known, and there will be no disturbance for that equation. Because not all variables appear in all equations, some of the parameters will be zero. The theory may also impose other types of restrictions on the parameter matrices.

If $\mathbf{\Gamma}$ is an upper triangular matrix, then the system is said to be **triangular.** In this case, the model is of the form

$$y_{t1} = f_1(\mathbf{x}_t) + \varepsilon_{t1},$$

$$y_{t2} = f_2(y_{t1}, \mathbf{x}_t) + \varepsilon_{t2},$$

$$\vdots$$

$$y_{tM} = f_M(y_{t1}, y_{t2}, \ldots, y_{t,M-1}, \mathbf{x}_t) + \varepsilon_{tM}.$$

The joint determination of the variables in this model is **recursive.** The first is completely determined by the exogenous factors. Then, given the first, the second is likewise determined, and so on.

The solution of the system of equations determining $\mathbf{y}_t$ in terms of $\mathbf{x}_t$ and $\boldsymbol{\varepsilon}_t$ is the **reduced form** of the model,

$$\mathbf{y}'_t = [x_1 \quad x_2 \quad \cdots \quad x_K]_t \begin{bmatrix} \pi_{11} & \pi_{12} & \cdots & \pi_{1M} \\ \pi_{21} & \pi_{22} & \cdots & \pi_{2M} \\ & & \vdots & \\ \pi_{K1} & \pi_{K2} & \cdots & \pi_{KM} \end{bmatrix} + [v_1 \quad \cdots \quad v_M]_t$$

$$= -\mathbf{x}'_t \mathbf{B}\boldsymbol{\Gamma}^{-1} + \boldsymbol{\varepsilon}'_t \boldsymbol{\Gamma}^{-1}$$

$$= \mathbf{x}'_t \boldsymbol{\Pi} + \mathbf{v}'_t.$$

For this solution to exist, the model must satisfy the **completeness condition** for simultaneous equations systems: $\boldsymbol{\Gamma}$ must be nonsingular.

### Example 13.3  Structure and Reduced Form

For the small model in Example 15.1, $\mathbf{y}' = [c, i, y]$, $\mathbf{x}' = [1, r, g, c_{-1}, y_{-1}]$, and

$$\boldsymbol{\Gamma} = \begin{bmatrix} 1 & 0 & -1 \\ 0 & 1 & -1 \\ -\alpha_1 & -\beta_2 & 1 \end{bmatrix}, \quad \mathbf{B} = \begin{bmatrix} -\alpha_0 & -\beta_0 & 0 \\ 0 & -\beta_1 & 0 \\ 0 & 0 & -1 \\ -\alpha_2 & 0 & 0 \\ 0 & \beta_2 & 0 \end{bmatrix}, \quad \boldsymbol{\Gamma}^{-1} = \frac{1}{\Delta} \begin{bmatrix} 1-\beta_2 & \beta_2 & 1 \\ \alpha_1 & 1-\alpha_1 & 1 \\ \alpha_1 & \beta_2 & 1 \end{bmatrix},$$

$$\boldsymbol{\Pi}' = \frac{1}{\Delta} \begin{bmatrix} \alpha_0(1-\beta_2+\beta_0\alpha_1) & \alpha_1\beta_1 & \alpha_1 & \alpha_2(1-\beta_2) & -\beta_2\alpha_1 \\ \alpha_0\beta_2+\beta_0(1-\alpha_1) & \beta_1(1-\alpha_1) & \beta_2 & \alpha_2\beta_2 & -\beta_2(1-\alpha_1) \\ \alpha_0+\beta_0 & \beta_1 & 1 & \alpha_2 & -\beta_2 \end{bmatrix},$$

where $\Delta = 1 - \alpha_1 - \beta_2$. The completeness condition is that $\alpha_1$ and $\beta_2$ do not sum to one.

The structural disturbances are assumed to be randomly drawn from an $M$-variate distribution with

$$E[\boldsymbol{\varepsilon}_t \mid \mathbf{x}_t] = \mathbf{0} \quad \text{and} \quad E[\boldsymbol{\varepsilon}_t \boldsymbol{\varepsilon}'_t \mid \mathbf{x}_t] = \boldsymbol{\Sigma}.$$

For the present, we assume that

$$E[\boldsymbol{\varepsilon}_t \boldsymbol{\varepsilon}'_s \mid \mathbf{x}_t, \mathbf{x}_s] = \mathbf{0}, \quad \forall t, s.$$

Later, we will drop this assumption to allow for heteroscedasticity and autocorrelation. It will occasionally be useful to assume that $\boldsymbol{\varepsilon}_t$ has a multivariate normal distribution, but we shall postpone this assumption until it becomes necessary. It may be convenient to retain the identities without disturbances as separate equations. If so, then one way to proceed with the stochastic specification is to place rows and columns of zeros in the appropriate places in $\boldsymbol{\Sigma}$. It follows that the **reduced-form disturbances, $\mathbf{v}'_t = \boldsymbol{\varepsilon}'_t \boldsymbol{\Gamma}^{-1}$** have

$$E[\mathbf{v}_t \mid \mathbf{x}_t] = (\boldsymbol{\Gamma}^{-1})'\mathbf{0} = \mathbf{0},$$

$$E[\mathbf{v}_t \mathbf{v}'_t \mid \mathbf{x}_t] = (\boldsymbol{\Gamma}^{-1})'\boldsymbol{\Sigma}\boldsymbol{\Gamma}^{-1} = \boldsymbol{\Omega}.$$

This implies that

$$\boldsymbol{\Sigma} = \boldsymbol{\Gamma}'\boldsymbol{\Omega}\boldsymbol{\Gamma}.$$

The preceding formulation describes the model as it applies to an observation $[\mathbf{y}', \mathbf{x}', \boldsymbol{\varepsilon}']_t$ at a particular point in time or in a cross section. In a sample of data, each joint observation will be one row in a data matrix,

$$[\mathbf{Y} \quad \mathbf{X} \quad \mathbf{E}] = \begin{bmatrix} \mathbf{y}'_1 & \mathbf{x}'_1 & \boldsymbol{\varepsilon}'_1 \\ \mathbf{y}'_2 & \mathbf{x}'_2 & \boldsymbol{\varepsilon}'_2 \\ & \vdots & \\ \mathbf{y}'_T & \mathbf{x}'_T & \boldsymbol{\varepsilon}'_T \end{bmatrix}.$$

In terms of the full set of $T$ observations, the structure is

$$\mathbf{Y}\boldsymbol{\Gamma} + \mathbf{X}\mathbf{B} = \mathbf{E},$$

with

$$E[\mathbf{E} \mid \mathbf{X}] = \mathbf{0} \quad \text{and} \quad E[(1/T)\mathbf{E}'\mathbf{E} \mid \mathbf{X}] = \boldsymbol{\Sigma}.$$

Under general conditions, we can strengthen this structure to

$$\text{plim}[(1/T)\mathbf{E}'\mathbf{E}] = \boldsymbol{\Sigma}.$$

An important assumption, comparable with the one made in Chapter 4 for the classical regression model, is

$$\text{plim}(1/T)\mathbf{X}'\mathbf{X} = \mathbf{Q}, \quad \text{a finite positive definite matrix.} \tag{13-3}$$

We also assume that

$$\text{plim}(1/T)\mathbf{X}'\mathbf{E} = \mathbf{0}. \tag{13-4}$$

This assumption is what distinguishes the predetermined variables from the endogenous variables. The reduced form is

$$\mathbf{Y} = \mathbf{X}\boldsymbol{\Pi} + \mathbf{V}, \quad \text{where } \mathbf{V} = \mathbf{E}\boldsymbol{\Gamma}^{-1}.$$

Combining the earlier results, we have

$$\text{plim} \frac{1}{T} \begin{bmatrix} \mathbf{Y}' \\ \mathbf{X}' \\ \mathbf{V}' \end{bmatrix} [\mathbf{Y} \quad \mathbf{X} \quad \mathbf{V}] = \begin{bmatrix} \boldsymbol{\Pi}'\mathbf{Q}\boldsymbol{\Pi} + \boldsymbol{\Omega} & \boldsymbol{\Pi}'\mathbf{Q} & \boldsymbol{\Omega} \\ \mathbf{Q}\boldsymbol{\Pi} & \mathbf{Q} & \mathbf{0}' \\ \boldsymbol{\Omega} & \mathbf{0} & \boldsymbol{\Omega} \end{bmatrix}. \tag{13-5}$$

## 13.3   THE PROBLEM OF IDENTIFICATION

Solving the problem to be considered here, the identification problem, logically precedes estimation. We ask at this point whether there is *any* way to obtain estimates of the parameters of the model. We have in hand a certain amount of information upon which to base any inference about its underlying structure. If more than one theory is consistent with the same "data," then the theories are said to be **observationally equivalent** and there is no way of distinguishing them. The structure is said to be *unidentified*.[8]

---

[8] A useful survey of this issue is Hsiao (1983).

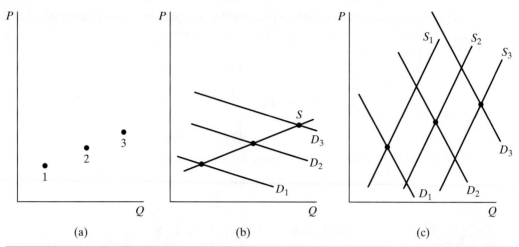

**FIGURE 13.1** Market Equilibria.

### Example 13.4  Observational Equivalence[9]

The *observed* data consist of the market outcomes shown in Figure 13.1a. We have no knowledge of the conditions of supply and demand beyond our belief that the data represent *equilibria*. Unfortunately, parts (b) and (c) of Figure 13.1 both show *structures*—that is, true underlying supply and demand curves—which are consistent with the data in Figure 13.1a. With only the data in Figure 13.1a, we have no way of determining which of theories 13.1b or c is the right one. Thus, the structure underlying the data in Figure 13.1a is unidentified. To suggest where our discussion is headed, suppose that we add to the preceding the known fact that the conditions of supply were unchanged during the period over which the data were drawn. This rules out 13.1c and identifies 13.1b as the correct structure. Note how this scenario relates to Example 13.1 and to the discussion following that example.

The identification problem is not one of sampling properties or the size of the sample. To focus ideas, it is even useful to suppose that we have at hand an infinite-sized sample of observations on the variables in the model. Now, with this sample and our prior theory, what information do we have? In the reduced form,

$$\mathbf{y}_t' = \mathbf{x}_t'\mathbf{\Pi} + \mathbf{v}_t', \qquad E[\mathbf{v}_t\mathbf{v}_t' \mid \mathbf{x}_t] = \mathbf{\Omega},$$

the predetermined variables are uncorrelated with the disturbances. Thus, we can "observe"

$$\text{plim}(1/T)\mathbf{X}'\mathbf{X} = \mathbf{Q} \text{ [assumed; see (13-3)]},$$

$$\text{plim}(1/T)\mathbf{X}'\mathbf{Y} = \text{plim}(1/T)\mathbf{X}'(\mathbf{X}\mathbf{\Pi} + \mathbf{V}) = \mathbf{Q}\mathbf{\Pi},$$

$$\text{plim}(1/T)\mathbf{Y}'\mathbf{Y} = \text{plim}(1/T)(\mathbf{\Pi}'\mathbf{X}' + \mathbf{V}')(\mathbf{X}\mathbf{\Pi} + \mathbf{V}) = \mathbf{\Pi}'\mathbf{Q}\mathbf{\Pi} + \mathbf{\Omega}.$$

Therefore, $\mathbf{\Pi}$, the matrix of reduced-form coefficients, is observable:

$$\mathbf{\Pi} = \left[\text{plim}\left(\frac{\mathbf{X}'\mathbf{X}}{T}\right)\right]^{-1} \left[\text{plim}\left(\frac{\mathbf{X}'\mathbf{Y}}{T}\right)\right].$$

---

[9]This example paraphrases the classic argument of Working (1926).

This estimator is simply the equation-by-equation least squares regression of **Y** on **X**. Because **Π** is observable, **Ω** is also:

$$\mathbf{\Omega} = \text{plim}\,\frac{\mathbf{Y}'\mathbf{Y}}{T} - \text{plim}\left[\frac{\mathbf{Y}'\mathbf{X}}{T}\right]\left[\frac{\mathbf{X}'\mathbf{X}}{T}\right]^{-1}\left[\frac{\mathbf{X}'\mathbf{Y}}{T}\right].$$

This result should be recognized as the matrix of least squares residual variances and covariances. Therefore,

**Π** *and* **Ω** *can be estimated consistently by least squares regression of* **Y** *on* **X**.

The information in hand, therefore, consists of **Π**, **Ω**, and whatever other nonsample information we have about the structure.[10] Now, can we deduce the structural parameters from the reduced form?

The correspondence between the structural and reduced-form parameters is the relationships

$$\mathbf{\Pi} = -\mathbf{B}\mathbf{\Gamma}^{-1} \quad \text{and} \quad \mathbf{\Omega} = E[\mathbf{v}\mathbf{v}'] = (\mathbf{\Gamma}^{-1})'\mathbf{\Sigma}\mathbf{\Gamma}^{-1}.$$

If **Γ** were known, then we could deduce **B** as $-\mathbf{\Pi}\mathbf{\Gamma}$ and **Σ** as $\mathbf{\Gamma}'\mathbf{\Omega}\mathbf{\Gamma}$. It would appear, therefore, that our problem boils down to obtaining **Γ**, which makes sense. If **Γ** were known, then we could rewrite (13-2), collecting the endogenous variables times their respective coefficients on the left-hand side of a regression, and estimate the remaining unknown coefficients on the predetermined variables by ordinary least squares.[11]

The identification question we will pursue can be posed as follows: We can "observe" the reduced form. We must deduce the structure from what we know about the reduced form. If there is more than one structure that can lead to the same reduced form, then we cannot say that we can "estimate the structure." Which structure would that be? Suppose that the "true" structure is [**Γ**, **B**, **Σ**]. Now consider a different structure, $\mathbf{y}'\tilde{\mathbf{\Gamma}}+\mathbf{x}'\tilde{\mathbf{B}} = \tilde{\boldsymbol{\varepsilon}}'$, that is obtained by postmultiplying the first structure by some nonsingular matrix **F**. Thus, $\tilde{\mathbf{\Gamma}} = \mathbf{\Gamma}\mathbf{F}$, $\tilde{\mathbf{B}} = \mathbf{B}\mathbf{F}$, $\tilde{\boldsymbol{\varepsilon}}' = \boldsymbol{\varepsilon}'\mathbf{F}$. The reduced form that corresponds to this new structure is, unfortunately, the same as the one that corresponds to the old one;

$$\tilde{\mathbf{\Pi}} = -\tilde{\mathbf{B}}\tilde{\mathbf{\Gamma}}^{-1} = -\mathbf{B}\mathbf{F}\mathbf{F}^{-1}\mathbf{\Gamma}^{-1} = \mathbf{\Pi},$$

and, in the same fashion, $\tilde{\mathbf{\Omega}} = \mathbf{\Omega}$. The false structure looks just like the true one, at least in terms of the information we have. Statistically, there is no way we can tell them apart. The structures are observationally equivalent.

Because **F** was chosen arbitrarily, we conclude that *any* nonsingular transformation of the original structure has the same reduced form. Any reason for optimism that we might have had should be abandoned. As the model stands, there is no means by which the structural parameters can be deduced from the reduced form. The practical implication is that if the only information that we have is the reduced-form parameters, then the structural model is not estimable. So how were we able to identify the models

---

[10]We have not necessarily shown that this is *all* the information in the sample. In general, we observe the conditional distribution $f(\mathbf{y}_t \,|\, \mathbf{x}_t)$, which constitutes the likelihood for the reduced form. With normally distributed disturbances, this distribution is a function of **Π**, **Ω**. (See Section 13.6.2.) With other distributions, other or higher moments of the variables might provide additional information. See, for example, Goldberger (1964, p. 311), Hausman (1983, pp. 402–403), and especially Reirsøl (1950).

[11]This method is precisely the approach of the LIML estimator. See Section 13.5.4.

in the earlier examples? The answer is by bringing to bear our **nonsample information,** namely our theoretical restrictions. Consider the following examples:

### Example 13.5 Identification

Consider a market in which $q$ is quantity of $Q$, $p$ is price, and $z$ is the price of $Z$, a related good. We assume that $z$ enters both the supply and demand equations. For example, $Z$ might be a crop that is purchased by consumers and that will be grown by farmers instead of $Q$ if its price rises enough relative to $p$. Thus, we would expect $\alpha_2 > 0$ and $\beta_2 < 0$. So,

$$q_d = \alpha_0 + \alpha_1 p + \alpha_2 z + \varepsilon_d \quad (demand),$$

$$q_s = \beta_0 + \beta_1 p + \beta_2 z + \varepsilon_s \quad (supply),$$

$$q_d = q_s = q \quad (equilibrium).$$

The reduced form is

$$q = \frac{\alpha_1 \beta_0 - \alpha_0 \beta_1}{\alpha_1 - \beta_1} + \frac{\alpha_1 \beta_2 - \alpha_2 \beta_1}{\alpha_1 - \beta_1} z + \frac{\alpha_1 \varepsilon_s - \alpha_2 \varepsilon_d}{\alpha_1 - \beta_1} = \pi_{11} + \pi_{21} z + v_q,$$

$$p = \frac{\beta_0 - \alpha_0}{\alpha_1 - \beta_1} + \frac{\beta_2 - \alpha_2}{\alpha_1 - \beta_1} z + \frac{\varepsilon_s - \varepsilon_d}{\alpha_1 - \beta_1} = \pi_{12} + \pi_{22} z + v_p.$$

With only four reduced-form coefficients and six structural parameters, it is obvious that there will not be a complete solution for all six structural parameters in terms of the four reduced parameters. Suppose, though, that it is known that $\beta_2 = 0$ (farmers do not substitute the alternative crop for this one). Then the solution for $\beta_1$ is $\pi_{21} / \pi_{22}$. After a bit of manipulation, we also obtain $\beta_0 = \pi_{11} - \pi_{12}\pi_{21} / \pi_{22}$. The restriction identifies the supply parameters. But this step is as far as we can go.

Now, suppose that income $x$, rather than $z$, appears in the demand equation. The revised model is

$$q = \alpha_0 + \alpha_1 p + \alpha_2 x + \varepsilon_1,$$

$$q = \beta_0 + \beta_1 p + \beta_2 z + \varepsilon_2.$$

The structure is now

$$[q \quad p] \begin{bmatrix} 1 & 1 \\ -\alpha_1 & -\beta_1 \end{bmatrix} + [1 \quad x \quad z] \begin{bmatrix} -\alpha_0 & -\beta_0 \\ -\alpha_2 & 0 \\ 0 & -\beta_2 \end{bmatrix} = [\varepsilon_1 \quad \varepsilon_2].$$

The reduced form is

$$[q \quad p] = [1 \quad x \quad z] \begin{bmatrix} (\alpha_1 \beta_0 - \alpha_0 \beta_1) / \Delta & (\beta_0 - \alpha_0) / \Delta \\ -\alpha_2 \beta_1 / \Delta & -\alpha_2 / \Delta \\ \alpha_1 \beta_2 / \Delta & \beta_2 / \Delta \end{bmatrix} + [v_1 \quad v_2],$$

where $\Delta = (\alpha_1 - \beta_1)$. Every false structure has the same reduced form. But in the coefficient matrix,

$$\tilde{\mathbf{B}} = \mathbf{BF} = \begin{bmatrix} \alpha_0 f_{11} + \beta_0 f_{21} & \alpha_0 f_{12} + \beta_0 f_{22} \\ \alpha_2 f_{11} & \alpha_2 f_{12} \\ \beta_2 f_{21} & \beta_2 f_{22} \end{bmatrix},$$

if $f_{12}$ is not zero, then the imposter will have income appearing in the supply equation, which our theory has ruled out. Likewise, if $f_{21}$ is not zero, then $z$ will appear in the demand equation, which is also ruled out by our theory. Thus, although all false structures have the same reduced form as the true one, the only one that is consistent with our theory (i.e., is **admissible**) and has coefficients of 1 on $q$ in both equations (examine $\mathbf{\Gamma F}$) is $\mathbf{F} = \mathbf{I}$. This transformation just produces the original structure.

The unique solutions for the structural parameters in terms of the reduced-form parameters are now

$$\alpha_0 = \pi_{11} - \pi_{12}\left(\frac{\pi_{31}}{\pi_{32}}\right), \quad \beta_0 = \pi_{11} - \pi_{12}\left(\frac{\pi_{21}}{\pi_{22}}\right),$$

$$\alpha_1 = \frac{\pi_{31}}{\pi_{32}}, \qquad\qquad \beta_1 = \frac{\pi_{21}}{\pi_{22}},$$

$$\alpha_2 = \pi_{22}\left(\frac{\pi_{21}}{\pi_{22}} - \frac{\pi_{31}}{\pi_{32}}\right), \quad \beta_2 = \pi_{32}\left(\frac{\pi_{31}}{\pi_{32}} - \frac{\pi_{21}}{\pi_{22}}\right).$$

The preceding discussion has considered two equivalent methods of establishing identifiability. If it is possible to deduce the structural parameters from the known reduced form parameters, then the model is identified. Alternatively, if it can be shown that no false structure is admissible—that is, satisfies the theoretical restrictions—then the model is identified.[12]

### 13.3.1    THE RANK AND ORDER CONDITIONS FOR IDENTIFICATION

It is useful to summarize what we have determined thus far. The unknown structural parameters consist of

$\mathbf{\Gamma}$ = an $M \times M$ nonsingular matrix,

$\mathbf{B}$ = a $K \times M$ parameter matrix,

$\mathbf{\Sigma}$ = an $M \times M$ symmetric positive definite matrix.

The known, reduced-form parameters are

$\mathbf{\Pi}$ = a $K \times M$ reduced-form coefficients matrix,

$\mathbf{\Omega}$ = an $M \times M$ reduced-form covariance matrix.

Simply counting parameters in the structure and reduced forms yields an excess of

$$l = M^2 + KM + \tfrac{1}{2}M(M+1) - KM - \tfrac{1}{2}M(M+1) = M^2,$$

which is, as might be expected from the earlier results, the number of unknown elements in $\mathbf{\Gamma}$. Without further information, identification is clearly impossible. The additional information comes in several forms.

**1.** *Normalizations.* In each equation, one variable has a coefficient of 1. This normalization is a necessary scaling of the equation that is logically equivalent to putting one variable on the left-hand side of a regression. For purposes of identification (and some estimation methods), the choice among the endogenous variables is arbitrary. But at the time the model is formulated, each equation will usually have some natural dependent variable. The normalization does not identify the dependent variable in any formal

[12]For other interpretations, see Amemiya (1985, p. 230) and Gabrielsen (1978). Some deeper theoretical results on identification of parameters in econometric models are given by Bekker and Wansbeek (2001).

or causal sense. For example, in a model of supply and demand, both the "demand" equation, $Q = f(P, \mathbf{x})$, and the "inverse demand" equation, $P = g(Q, \mathbf{x})$, are appropriate specifications of the relationship between price and quantity. We note, though, the following:

> With the normalizations, there are $M(M-1)$, not $M^2$, undetermined values in $\boldsymbol{\Gamma}$ and this many indeterminacies in the model to be resolved through nonsample information.

**2.** *Identities.* In some models, variable definitions or equilibrium conditions imply that all the coefficients in a particular equation are known. In the preceding market example, there are three equations, but the third is the equilibrium condition $q_d = q_s$. Klein's Model I (Example 13.3) contains six equations, including two accounting identities and the equilibrium condition. There is no question of identification with respect to identities. They may be carried as additional equations in the model, as we do with Klein's Model I in several later examples, or built into the model a priori, as is typical in models of supply and demand.

The substantive nonsample information that will be used in identifying the model will consist of the following:

**3.** *Exclusions.* The omission of variables from an equation places zeros in $\mathbf{B}$ and $\boldsymbol{\Gamma}$. In Example 13.5, the exclusion of income from the supply equation served to identify its parameters.

**4.** *Linear restrictions.* **Restrictions** on the structural parameters may also serve to rule out false structures. For example, a long-standing problem in the estimation of production models using time-series data is the inability to disentangle the effects of economies of scale from those of technological change. In some treatments, the solution is to assume that there are constant returns to scale, thereby identifying the effects due to technological change.

**5.** *Restrictions on the disturbance covariance matrix.* In the identification of a model, these are similar to restrictions on the slope parameters. For example, if the previous market model were to apply to a microeconomic setting, then it would probably be reasonable to assume that the structural disturbances in these supply and demand equations are uncorrelated. Section 13.5.1 shows a case in which a covariance restriction identifies an otherwise unidentified model.

To formalize the identification criteria, we require a notation for a single equation. The coefficients of the $j$th equation are contained in the $j$th columns of $\boldsymbol{\Gamma}$ and $\mathbf{B}$. The $j$th equation is

$$\mathbf{y}'\boldsymbol{\Gamma}_j + \mathbf{x}'\mathbf{B}_j = \varepsilon_j. \tag{13-6}$$

(For convenience, we have dropped the observation subscript.) In this equation, we know that (1) one of the elements in $\boldsymbol{\Gamma}_j$ is one and (2) some variables that appear elsewhere in the model are excluded from this equation. Table 13.1 defines the notation used to incorporate these restrictions in (13-6).

Equation $j$ may be written

$$y_j = \mathbf{Y}'_j\boldsymbol{\gamma}_j + \mathbf{Y}^{*'}_j\boldsymbol{\gamma}^*_j + \mathbf{x}'_j\boldsymbol{\beta}_j + \mathbf{x}^{*'}_j\boldsymbol{\beta}^*_j + \varepsilon_j.$$

**TABLE 13.1**    Components of Equation $j$ (Dependent Variable $= y_j$)

|  | *Endogenous Variables* | *Exogenous Variables* |
|---|---|---|
| Included | $\mathbf{Y}_j = M_j$ variables | $\mathbf{x}_j = K_j$ variables |
| Excluded | $\mathbf{Y}_j^* = M_j^*$ variables | $\mathbf{x}_j^* = K_j^*$ variables |

The number of equations is $M_j + M_j^* + 1 = M$.
The number of exogenous variables is $K_j + K_j^* = K$.
The coefficient on $y_j$ in equation $j$ is 1.
*$s$ will always be associated with excluded variables.

The exclusions imply that $\boldsymbol{\gamma}_j^* = \mathbf{0}$ and $\boldsymbol{\beta}_j^* = \mathbf{0}$. Thus,

$$\boldsymbol{\Gamma}_j' = [1 \ -\boldsymbol{\gamma}_j' \ \ \mathbf{0}'] \quad \text{and} \quad \mathbf{B}_j' = [-\boldsymbol{\beta}_j' \ \ \mathbf{0}'].$$

(Note the sign convention.) For this equation, we partition the reduced-form coefficient matrix in the same fashion:

$$(1) \ (M_j) \ (M_j^*)$$

$$[\mathbf{y}_j \ \ \mathbf{Y}_j' \ \ \mathbf{Y}_j^{*\prime}] = [\mathbf{x}_j' \ \ \mathbf{x}_j^{*\prime}] \begin{bmatrix} \pi_j & \boldsymbol{\Pi}_j & \overline{\boldsymbol{\Pi}}_j \\ \pi_j^* & \boldsymbol{\Pi}_j^* & \overline{\boldsymbol{\Pi}}_j^* \end{bmatrix} + [\mathbf{v}_j \ \ \mathbf{V}_j \ \ \mathbf{V}_j^*] \begin{matrix} [K_j \text{ rows}] \\ [K_j^* \text{ rows}]. \end{matrix} \quad \textbf{(13-7)}$$

The reduced-form coefficient matrix is

$$\boldsymbol{\Pi} = -\mathbf{B}\boldsymbol{\Gamma}^{-1},$$

which implies that

$$\boldsymbol{\Pi}\boldsymbol{\Gamma} = -\mathbf{B}.$$

The $j$th column of this matrix equation applies to the $j$th equation,

$$\boldsymbol{\Pi}\boldsymbol{\Gamma}_j = -\mathbf{B}_j.$$

Inserting the parts from Table 13.1 yields

$$\begin{bmatrix} \pi_j & \boldsymbol{\Pi}_j & \overline{\boldsymbol{\Pi}}_j \\ \pi_j^* & \boldsymbol{\Pi}_j^* & \overline{\boldsymbol{\Pi}}_j^* \end{bmatrix} \begin{bmatrix} 1 \\ -\boldsymbol{\gamma}_j \\ \mathbf{0} \end{bmatrix} = \begin{bmatrix} \boldsymbol{\beta}_j \\ \mathbf{0} \end{bmatrix}.$$

Now extract the two subequations,

$$\pi_j - \boldsymbol{\Pi}_j\boldsymbol{\gamma}_j = \boldsymbol{\beta}_j \quad (K_j \text{ equations}), \quad \textbf{(13-8)}$$

$$\pi_j^* - \boldsymbol{\Pi}_j^*\boldsymbol{\gamma}_j = \mathbf{0} \quad (K_j^* \text{ equations}), \quad \textbf{(13-9)}$$

$$(1) \quad (M_j).$$

The solution for $\mathbf{B}$ in terms of $\boldsymbol{\Gamma}$ that we observed at the beginning of this discussion is in (13-8). Equation (13-9) may be written

$$\boldsymbol{\Pi}_j^*\boldsymbol{\gamma}_j = \pi_j^*. \quad \textbf{(13-10)}$$

This system is $K_j^*$ equations in $M_j$ unknowns. If they can be solved for $\boldsymbol{\gamma}_j$, then (13-8) gives the solution for $\boldsymbol{\beta}_j$ and the equation is identified. For there to be a solution, there must be at least as many equations as unknowns, which leads to the following condition.

---

**DEFINITION 13.1** Order Condition for Identification of Equation $j$

$$K_j^* \geq M_j. \tag{13-11}$$

*The number of exogenous variables excluded from equation $j$ must be at least as large as the number of endogenous variables included in equation $j$.*

---

The order condition is only a counting rule. It is a necessary but not sufficient condition for identification. It ensures that (13-10) has at least one solution, but it does not ensure that it has only one solution. The sufficient condition for uniqueness follows.

---

**DEFINITION 13.2** Rank Condition for Identification

$$\text{rank}[\boldsymbol{\pi}_j^*, \boldsymbol{\Pi}_j^*] = \text{rank}[\boldsymbol{\Pi}_j^*] = M_j.$$

*This condition imposes a restriction on a submatrix of the reduced-form coefficient matrix.*

---

The rank condition ensures that there is exactly one solution for the structural parameters given the reduced-form parameters. Our alternative approach to the identification problem was to use the prior restrictions on $[\boldsymbol{\Gamma}, \mathbf{B}]$ to eliminate all false structures. An equivalent condition based on this approach is simpler to apply and has more intuitive appeal. We first rearrange the structural coefficients in the matrix

$$\mathbf{A} = \begin{bmatrix} \boldsymbol{\Gamma} \\ \mathbf{B} \end{bmatrix} = \begin{bmatrix} 1 & \mathbf{A}_1 \\ -\boldsymbol{\gamma}_j & \mathbf{A}_2 \\ \mathbf{0} & \mathbf{A}_3 \\ -\boldsymbol{\beta}_j & \mathbf{A}_4 \\ \mathbf{0} & \mathbf{A}_5 \end{bmatrix} = [\mathbf{a}_j \quad \mathbf{A}_j]. \tag{13-12}$$

The $j$th column in a false structure $[\boldsymbol{\Gamma}\mathbf{F}, \mathbf{B}\mathbf{F}]$ (i.e., the imposter for our equation $j$) would be $[\boldsymbol{\Gamma}\mathbf{f}_j, \mathbf{B}\mathbf{f}_j]$, where $\mathbf{f}_j$ is the $j$th column of $\mathbf{F}$. This new $j$th equation is to be built up as a linear combination of the old one and the other equations in the model. Thus, partitioning as previously,

$$\tilde{\mathbf{a}}_j = \begin{bmatrix} 1 & \mathbf{A}_1 \\ -\boldsymbol{\gamma}_j & \mathbf{A}_2 \\ \mathbf{0} & \mathbf{A}_3 \\ -\boldsymbol{\beta}_j & \mathbf{A}_4 \\ \mathbf{0} & \mathbf{A}_5 \end{bmatrix} \begin{bmatrix} f^0 \\ \mathbf{f}^1 \end{bmatrix} = \begin{bmatrix} 1 \\ \tilde{\boldsymbol{\gamma}}_j \\ \mathbf{0} \\ \tilde{\boldsymbol{\beta}}_j \\ \mathbf{0} \end{bmatrix}.$$

If this hybrid is to have the same variables as the original, then it must have nonzero elements in the same places, which can be ensured by taking $f^0 = 1$, and zeros in the same positions as the original $\mathbf{a}_j$. Extracting the third and fifth blocks of rows, if $\tilde{\mathbf{a}}_j$ is to be **admissible,** then it must meet the requirement

$$\begin{bmatrix} \mathbf{A}_3 \\ \mathbf{A}_5 \end{bmatrix} \mathbf{f}^1 = \mathbf{0}.$$

This equality is not possible if the $(M_j^* + K_j^*) \times (M - 1)$ matrix in brackets has full column rank, so we have the equivalent rank condition,

$$\operatorname{rank} \begin{bmatrix} \mathbf{A}_3 \\ \mathbf{A}_5 \end{bmatrix} = M - 1.$$

The corresponding order condition is that the matrix in brackets must have at least as many rows as columns. Thus, $M_j^* + K_j^* \geq M - 1$. But because $M = M_j + M_j^* + 1$, this condition is the same as the order condition in (13-11). The equivalence of the two rank conditions is pursued in the exercises.

The preceding provides a simple method for checking the rank and order conditions. We need only arrange the structural parameters in a tableau and examine the relevant submatrices one at a time; $\mathbf{A}_3$ and $\mathbf{A}_5$ are the structural coefficients in the other equations on the variables that are excluded from equation $j$.

One rule of thumb is sometimes useful in checking the rank and order conditions of a model: *If every equation has its own predetermined variable, the entire model is identified.* The proof is simple and is left as an exercise. For a final example, we consider a somewhat larger model.

### Example 13.6  Identification of Klein's Model I

The structural coefficients in the six equations of Klein's Model I, transposed and multiplied by −1 for convenience, are listed in Table 13.2. Identification of the consumption function requires that the matrix $[\mathbf{A}_3', \mathbf{A}_5']$ have rank 5. The columns of this matrix are contained in boxes in the table. None of the columns indicated by arrows can be formed as linear combinations of the other columns, so the rank condition is satisfied. Verification of the rank and order conditions for the other two equations is left as an exercise.

It is unusual for a model to pass the order but not the rank condition. Generally, either the conditions are obvious or the model is so large and has so many predetermined

---

**TABLE 13.2**  Klein's Model I, Structural Coefficients

| | $\mathbf{\Gamma}'$ | | | | | | $\mathbf{B}'$ | | | | | | | |
| | $C$ | $I$ | $W^p$ | $X$ | $P$ | $K$ | $1$ | $W^g$ | $G$ | $T$ | $A$ | $P_{-1}$ | $K_{-1}$ | $X_{-1}$ |
|---|---|---|---|---|---|---|---|---|---|---|---|---|---|---|
| $C$ | $-1$ | $0$ | $\alpha_3$ | $0$ | $\alpha_1$ | $0$ | $\alpha_0$ | $\alpha_3$ | $0$ | $0$ | $0$ | $\alpha_2$ | $0$ | $0$ |
| $I$ | $0$ | $-1$ | $0$ | $0$ | $\beta_1$ | $0$ | $\beta_0$ | $0$ | $0$ | $0$ | $0$ | $\beta_2$ | $\beta_3$ | $0$ |
| $W^p$ | $0$ | $0$ | $-1$ | $\gamma_1$ | $0$ | $0$ | $\gamma_0$ | $0$ | $0$ | $0$ | $\gamma_3$ | $0$ | $0$ | $\gamma_2$ |
| $X$ | $1$ | $1$ | $0$ | $-1$ | $0$ | $0$ | $0$ | $0$ | $1$ | $0$ | $0$ | $0$ | $0$ | $0$ |
| $P$ | $0$ | $0$ | $-1$ | $1$ | $-1$ | $0$ | $0$ | $0$ | $0$ | $-1$ | $0$ | $0$ | $0$ | $0$ |
| $K$ | $0$ | $1$ | $0$ | $0$ | $0$ | $-1$ | $0$ | $0$ | $0$ | $0$ | $0$ | $0$ | $1$ | $0$ |
| | | | $\mathbf{A}_3'$ | ↑ | ↑ | | | | $\mathbf{A}_5'$ | ↑ | ↑ | ↑ | | |

variables that the conditions are met trivially. In practice, it is simple to check both conditions for a small model. For a large model, frequently only the order condition is verified. We distinguish three cases:

1. **Underidentified.** $K_j^* < M_j$ or rank condition fails.
2. **Exactly identified.** $K_j^* = M_j$ and rank condition is met.
3. **Overidentified.** $K_j^* > M_j$ and rank condition is met.

### 13.3.2 IDENTIFICATION THROUGH OTHER NONSAMPLE INFORMATION

The rank and order conditions given in the preceding section apply to identification of an equation through **exclusion restrictions.** Intuition might suggest that other types of nonsample information should be equally useful in securing identification. To take a specific example, suppose that in Example 13.5, it is known that $\beta_2$ equals 2, not 0. The second equation could then be written as

$$\mathbf{q}_s - 2\mathbf{z} = \mathbf{q}_s^* = \beta_0 + \beta_1 \mathbf{p} + \beta_j^* \mathbf{z} + \varepsilon_2.$$

But we know that $\beta_j^* = 0$, so the supply equation is identified by this restriction. As this example suggests, a linear restriction on the parameters *within* an equation is, for identification purposes, essentially the same as an exclusion.[13] By an appropriate manipulation—that is, by "solving out" the restriction—we can turn the restriction into one more exclusion. The order condition that emerges is

$$n_j \geq M - 1,$$

where $n_j$ is the total number of restrictions. Because $M - 1 = M_j + M_j^*$ and $n_j$ is the number of exclusions plus $r_j$, the number of additional restrictions, this condition is equivalent to

$$r_j + K_j^* + M_j^* \geq M_j + M_j^*,$$

or

$$r_j + K_j^* \geq M_j.$$

This result is the same as (13-11) save for the addition of the number of restrictions, which is the result suggested previously.

## 13.4 METHODS OF ESTIMATION

It is possible to estimate the reduced-form parameters, $\mathbf{\Pi}$ and $\mathbf{\Omega}$, consistently by ordinary least squares. But except for forecasting $\mathbf{y}$ given $\mathbf{x}$, these are generally not the parameters of interest; $\mathbf{\Gamma}, \mathbf{B}$, and $\mathbf{\Sigma}$ are. The ordinary least squares (OLS) estimators of the structural parameters are inconsistent, ostensibly because the included endogenous variables in each equation are correlated with the disturbances. Still, it is at

---

[13] The analysis is more complicated if the restrictions are *across* equations, that is, involve the parameters in more than one equation. Kelly (1975) contains a number of results and examples.

least of passing interest to examine what is estimated by ordinary least squares, particularly in view of its widespread use (despite its inconsistency). The proof of identification was based on solving for $\mathbf{\Gamma}$, $\mathbf{B}$, and $\mathbf{\Sigma}$ from $\mathbf{\Pi}$ and $\mathbf{\Omega}$, so one way to proceed is to apply our finding to the sample estimates, $\mathbf{P}$ and $\mathbf{W}$. This **indirect least squares** approach is feasible but inefficient. Worse, there will usually be more than one possible estimator and no obvious means of choosing among them. There are two approaches for direct estimation, both based on the principle of instrumental variables. It is possible to estimate each equation separately using a **limited information** estimator. But the same principle that suggests that joint estimation brings efficiency gains in the seemingly unrelated regressions setting of Chapter 10 is at work here, so we shall also consider **full information** or system methods of estimation.

## 13.5   SINGLE EQUATION: LIMITED INFORMATION ESTIMATION METHODS

Estimation of the system one equation at a time has the benefit of computational simplicity. But because these methods neglect information contained in the other equations, they are labeled limited information methods.

### 13.5.1   ORDINARY LEAST SQUARES

For all $T$ observations, the nonzero terms in the $j$th equation are

$$\mathbf{y}_j = \mathbf{Y}_j \boldsymbol{\gamma}_j + \mathbf{X}_j \boldsymbol{\beta}_j + \boldsymbol{\varepsilon}_j$$
$$= \mathbf{Z}_j \boldsymbol{\delta}_j + \boldsymbol{\varepsilon}_j.$$

The $M$ reduced-form equations are $\mathbf{Y} = \mathbf{X}\mathbf{\Pi} + \mathbf{V}$. For the included endogenous variables $\mathbf{Y}_j$, the reduced forms are the $M_j$ appropriate columns of $\mathbf{\Pi}$ and $\mathbf{V}$, written

$$\mathbf{Y}_j = \mathbf{X}\mathbf{\Pi}_j + \mathbf{V}_j. \tag{13-13}$$

[Note that $\mathbf{\Pi}_j$ is the middle part of $\mathbf{\Pi}$ shown in (13-7).] Likewise, $\mathbf{V}_j$ is $M_j$ columns of $\mathbf{V} = \mathbf{E}\mathbf{\Gamma}^{-1}$. This least squares estimator is

$$\mathbf{d}_j = [\mathbf{Z}_j'\mathbf{Z}_j]^{-1}\mathbf{Z}_j'\mathbf{y}_j = \boldsymbol{\delta}_j + \begin{bmatrix} \mathbf{Y}_j'\mathbf{Y}_j & \mathbf{Y}_j'\mathbf{X}_j \\ \mathbf{X}_j'\mathbf{Y}_j & \mathbf{X}_j'\mathbf{X}_j \end{bmatrix}^{-1} \begin{bmatrix} \mathbf{Y}_j'\boldsymbol{\varepsilon}_j \\ \mathbf{X}_j'\boldsymbol{\varepsilon}_j \end{bmatrix}.$$

None of the terms in the inverse matrix converge to $\mathbf{0}$. Although $\text{plim}(1/T)\mathbf{X}_j'\boldsymbol{\varepsilon}_j = \mathbf{0}$, $\text{plim}(1/T)\mathbf{Y}_j'\boldsymbol{\varepsilon}_j$ is nonzero, which means that both parts of $\mathbf{d}_j$ are inconsistent. (This is the "simultaneous equations bias" of least squares.) Although we can say with certainty that $\mathbf{d}_j$ is inconsistent, we cannot state how serious this problem is. OLS does have the virtue of computational simplicity, although with modern software, this virtue is extremely modest. For better or worse, OLS is a very commonly used estimator in this context. We will return to this issue later in a comparison of several estimators.

An intuitively appealing form of simultaneous equations model is the triangular system that we examined in Section 13.2.3,

$$
\begin{aligned}
(1) \ y_1 &= \mathbf{x}'\boldsymbol{\beta}_1 && + \varepsilon_1, \\
(2) \ y_2 &= \mathbf{x}'\boldsymbol{\beta}_2 + \gamma_{12}y_1 && + \varepsilon_2, \\
(3) \ y_3 &= \mathbf{x}'\boldsymbol{\beta}_3 + \gamma_{13}y_1 + \gamma_{23}y_2 + \varepsilon_3,
\end{aligned}
$$

and so on. If $\boldsymbol{\Gamma}$ is triangular and $\boldsymbol{\Sigma}$ is diagonal, so that the disturbances are uncorrelated, then the system is a **fully recursive model.** (No restrictions are placed on **B**.) It is easy to see that in this case, the entire system may be estimated consistently (and, as we shall show later, efficiently) by ordinary least squares. The first equation is a classical regression model. In the second equation, $\text{Cov}(y_1, \varepsilon_2) = \text{Cov}(\mathbf{x}'\boldsymbol{\beta}_1 + \varepsilon_1, \varepsilon_2) = 0$, so it too may be estimated by ordinary least squares. Proceeding in the same fashion to (3), it is clear that $y_1$ and $\varepsilon_3$ are uncorrelated. Likewise, if we substitute (1) in (2) and then the result for $y_2$ in (3), then we find that $y_2$ is also uncorrelated with $\varepsilon_3$. Continuing in this way, we find that in every equation the full set of right-hand variables is uncorrelated with the respective disturbance. The result is that *the fully recursive model may be consistently estimated using equation-by-equation ordinary least squares.* (In the more general case, in which $\boldsymbol{\Sigma}$ is not diagonal, the preceding argument does not apply.)

### 13.5.2 ESTIMATION BY INSTRUMENTAL VARIABLES

In the next several sections, we will discuss various methods of consistent and efficient estimation. As will be evident quite soon, there is a surprisingly long menu of choices. It is a useful result that all of the methods in general use can be placed under the umbrella of instrumental variable (IV) estimators.

Returning to the structural form, we first consider direct estimation of the $j$th equation,

$$
\begin{aligned}
\mathbf{y}_j &= \mathbf{Y}_j \boldsymbol{\gamma}_j + \mathbf{X}_j \boldsymbol{\beta}_j + \boldsymbol{\varepsilon}_j \\
&= \mathbf{Z}_j \boldsymbol{\delta}_j + \boldsymbol{\varepsilon}_j.
\end{aligned} \tag{13-14}
$$

As we saw previously, the OLS estimator of $\boldsymbol{\delta}_j$ is inconsistent because of the correlation of $\mathbf{Z}_j$ and $\boldsymbol{\varepsilon}_j$. A general method of obtaining **consistent estimators** is the method of instrumental variables. (See Chapter 12.) Let $\mathbf{W}_j$ be a $T \times (M_j + K_j)$ matrix that satisfies the requirements for an IV estimator,

$$
\text{plim}(1 / T)\mathbf{W}_j'\mathbf{Z}_j = \boldsymbol{\Sigma}_{wz} = \text{a finite nonsingular matrix}, \tag{13-15a}
$$

$$
\text{plim}(1 / T)\mathbf{W}_j'\boldsymbol{\varepsilon}_j = \mathbf{0}, \tag{13-15b}
$$

$$
\text{plim}(1 / T)\mathbf{W}_j'\mathbf{W}_j = \boldsymbol{\Sigma}_{ww} = \text{a positive definite matrix}. \tag{13-15c}
$$

Then the IV estimator,

$$
\hat{\boldsymbol{\delta}}_{j,\text{IV}} = [\mathbf{W}_j'\mathbf{Z}_j]^{-1}\mathbf{W}_j'\mathbf{y}_j,
$$

will be consistent and have asymptotic covariance matrix

$$\text{Asy. Var}[\hat{\boldsymbol{\delta}}_{j,\text{IV}}] = \frac{\sigma_{jj}}{T}\text{plim}\left[\frac{1}{T}\mathbf{W}_j'\mathbf{Z}_j\right]^{-1}\left[\frac{1}{T}\mathbf{W}_j'\mathbf{W}_j\right]\left[\frac{1}{T}\mathbf{Z}_j'\mathbf{W}_j\right]^{-1}$$

$$= \frac{\sigma_{jj}}{T}\left[\boldsymbol{\Sigma}_{wz}^{-1}\boldsymbol{\Sigma}_{ww}\boldsymbol{\Sigma}_{zw}^{-1}\right]. \tag{13-16}$$

A consistent estimator of $\sigma_{jj}$ is

$$\hat{\sigma}_{jj} = \frac{(\mathbf{y}_j - \mathbf{Z}_j\hat{\boldsymbol{\delta}}_{j,\text{IV}})'(\mathbf{y}_j - \mathbf{Z}_j\hat{\boldsymbol{\delta}}_{j,\text{IV}})}{T}, \tag{13-17}$$

which is the familiar sum of squares of the estimated disturbances. A degrees of freedom correction for the denominator, $T - M_j - K_j$, is sometimes suggested. Asymptotically, the correction is immaterial. Whether it is beneficial in a small sample remains to be settled. The resulting estimator is not unbiased in any event, as it would be in the classical regression model. In the interest of simplicity (only), we shall omit the degrees of freedom correction in what follows. Current practice in most applications is to make the correction.

The various estimators that have been developed for simultaneous equations models are all IV estimators. They differ in the choice of instruments and in whether the equations are estimated one at a time or jointly. We divide them into two classes, limited information or full information, on this basis.

### 13.5.3 TWO-STAGE LEAST SQUARES

The method of two-stage least squares is the most common method used for estimating simultaneous equations models. We developed the full set of results for this estimator in Section 12.3.3. By merely changing notation slightly, the results of Section 12.3.3 are exactly the derivation of the estimator we will describe here. Thus, you might want to review this section before continuing.

The two-stage least squares (2SLS) method consists of using as the instruments for $\mathbf{Y}_j$ the predicted values in a regression of $\mathbf{Y}_j$ on *all* the $x$'s in the system:

$$\hat{\mathbf{Y}}_j = \mathbf{X}[(\mathbf{X}'\mathbf{X})^{-1}\mathbf{X}'\mathbf{Y}_j] = \mathbf{X}\mathbf{P}_j. \tag{13-18}$$

It can be shown that absent heteroscedasticity or autocorrelation, this produces the most efficient IV estimator that can be formed using only the columns of $\mathbf{X}$. Note the emulation of $E[\mathbf{Y}_j \mid \mathbf{X}] = \mathbf{X}\boldsymbol{\Pi}_j$ in the result. The 2SLS estimator is, thus,

$$\hat{\boldsymbol{\delta}}_{j,\text{2SLS}} = \begin{bmatrix} \hat{\mathbf{Y}}_j'\mathbf{Y}_j & \hat{\mathbf{Y}}_j'\mathbf{X}_j \\ \mathbf{X}_j'\mathbf{Y}_j & \mathbf{X}_j'\mathbf{X}_j \end{bmatrix}^{-1} \begin{bmatrix} \hat{\mathbf{Y}}_j'\mathbf{y}_j \\ \mathbf{X}_j'\mathbf{y}_j \end{bmatrix}. \tag{13-19}$$

Before proceeding, it is important to emphasize the role of the identification condition in this result. In the matrix $[\hat{\mathbf{Y}}_j, \mathbf{X}_j]$, which has $M_j + K_j$ columns, all columns are linear functions of the $K$ columns of $\mathbf{X}$. There exist, at most, $K$ linearly independent combinations of the columns of $\mathbf{X}$. If the equation is not identified, then $M_j + K_j$ is greater than $K$, and $[\hat{\mathbf{Y}}_j, \mathbf{X}_j]$ will not have full column rank. In this case, the 2SLS estimator cannot be computed. If, however, the order condition but not the rank condition is met, then although the 2SLS estimator can be computed, it is not a consistent estimator. There are a few useful simplifications. First, because $\mathbf{X}(\mathbf{X}'\mathbf{X})^{-1}\mathbf{X}' = (\mathbf{I} - \mathbf{M})$ is idempotent, $\hat{\mathbf{Y}}_j'\mathbf{Y}_j = \hat{\mathbf{Y}}_j'\hat{\mathbf{Y}}_j$. Second, $\mathbf{X}_j'\mathbf{X}(\mathbf{X}'\mathbf{X})^{-1}\mathbf{X}' = \mathbf{X}_j'$ implies that $\mathbf{X}_j'\mathbf{Y}_j = \mathbf{X}_j'\hat{\mathbf{Y}}_j$. Thus, (13-19) can also be written

$$\hat{\boldsymbol{\delta}}_{j,2SLS} = \begin{bmatrix} \hat{\mathbf{Y}}_j'\hat{\mathbf{Y}}_j & \hat{\mathbf{Y}}_j'\mathbf{X}_j \\ \mathbf{X}_j'\hat{\mathbf{Y}}_j & \mathbf{X}_j'\mathbf{X}_j \end{bmatrix}^{-1} \begin{bmatrix} \hat{\mathbf{Y}}_j'\mathbf{y}_j \\ \mathbf{X}_j'\mathbf{y}_j \end{bmatrix}. \tag{13-20}$$

The 2SLS estimator is obtained by ordinary least squares regression of $\mathbf{y}_j$ on $\hat{\mathbf{Y}}_j$ and $\mathbf{X}_j$. Thus, the name stems from the two regressions in the procedure:

1. *Stage 1.* Obtain the least squares predictions from regression of $\mathbf{Y}_j$ on $\mathbf{X}$.
2. *Stage 2.* Estimate $\boldsymbol{\delta}_j$ by least squares regression of $\mathbf{y}_j$ on $\hat{\mathbf{Y}}_j$ and $\mathbf{X}_j$.

A direct proof of the consistency of the 2SLS estimator requires only that we establish that it is a valid IV estimator. For (13-15a), we require

$$\text{plim} \begin{bmatrix} \hat{\mathbf{Y}}_j'\mathbf{Y}_j / T & \hat{\mathbf{Y}}_j'\mathbf{X}_j / T \\ \mathbf{X}_j'\mathbf{Y}_j / T & \mathbf{X}_j'\mathbf{X}_j / T \end{bmatrix} = \text{plim} \begin{bmatrix} \mathbf{P}_j'\mathbf{X}'(\mathbf{X}\mathbf{\Pi}_j + \mathbf{V}_j) / T & \mathbf{P}_j'\mathbf{X}'\mathbf{X}_j / T \\ \mathbf{X}_j'(\mathbf{X}\mathbf{\Pi}_j + \mathbf{V}_j) / T & \mathbf{X}_j'\mathbf{X}_j / T \end{bmatrix}$$

to be a finite nonsingular matrix. We have used (13-13) for $\mathbf{Y}_j$, which is a continuous function of $\mathbf{P}_j$, which has plim $\mathbf{P}_j = \mathbf{\Pi}_j$. The Slutsky theorem thus allows us to substitute $\mathbf{\Pi}_j$ for $\mathbf{P}_j$ in the probability limit. That the parts converge to a finite matrix follows from (13-3) and (13-5). It will be nonsingular if $\mathbf{\Pi}_j$ has full column rank, which, in turn, will be true if the equation is identified.[14] For (13-15b), we require that

$$\text{plim} \frac{1}{T} \begin{bmatrix} \hat{\mathbf{Y}}_j'\boldsymbol{\varepsilon}_j \\ \mathbf{X}_j'\boldsymbol{\varepsilon}_j \end{bmatrix} = \begin{bmatrix} \mathbf{0} \\ \mathbf{0} \end{bmatrix}.$$

The second part is assumed in (13-4). For the first, by direct substitution,

$$\text{plim} \frac{1}{T}\mathbf{Y}_j'\mathbf{X}(\mathbf{X}'\mathbf{X})^{-1}\mathbf{X}'\boldsymbol{\varepsilon}_j = \text{plim} \left( \frac{\mathbf{Y}_j'\mathbf{X}}{T} \right) \left( \frac{\mathbf{X}'\mathbf{X}}{T} \right)^{-1} \left( \frac{\mathbf{X}'\boldsymbol{\varepsilon}_j}{T} \right).$$

The third part on the right converges to zero, whereas the other two converge to finite matrices, which confirms the result. Because $\hat{\boldsymbol{\delta}}_{j,2SLS}$ is an IV estimator, we can just invoke Theorem 12.1 for the asymptotic distribution. A proof of asymptotic efficiency requires the establishment of the benchmark, which we shall do in the discussion of the MLE.

As a final shortcut that is useful for programming purposes, we note that if $\mathbf{X}_j$ is regressed on $\mathbf{X}$, then a perfect fit is obtained, so $\hat{\mathbf{X}}_j = \mathbf{X}_j$. Using the idempotent matrix $(\mathbf{I} - \mathbf{M})$, (13-20) becomes

$$\hat{\boldsymbol{\delta}}_{j,2SLS} = \begin{bmatrix} \mathbf{Y}_j'(\mathbf{I} - \mathbf{M})\mathbf{Y}_j & \mathbf{Y}_j'(\mathbf{I} - \mathbf{M})\mathbf{X}_j \\ \mathbf{X}_j'(\mathbf{I} - \mathbf{M})\mathbf{Y}_j & \mathbf{X}_j'(\mathbf{I} - \mathbf{M})\mathbf{X}_j \end{bmatrix}^{-1} \begin{bmatrix} \mathbf{Y}_j'(\mathbf{I} - \mathbf{M})\mathbf{y}_j \\ \mathbf{X}_j'(\mathbf{I} - \mathbf{M})\mathbf{y}_j \end{bmatrix}.$$

---

[14]Schmidt (1976, pp. 150–151) provides a proof of this result.

Thus,

$$
\begin{aligned}
\hat{\boldsymbol{\delta}}_{j,2\text{SLS}} &= [\hat{\mathbf{Z}}'_j\hat{\mathbf{Z}}_j]^{-1}\hat{\mathbf{Z}}'_j\mathbf{y}_j \\
&= [(\mathbf{Z}'_j\mathbf{X})(\mathbf{X}'\mathbf{X})^{-1}(\mathbf{X}'\mathbf{Z}_j)]^{-1}(\mathbf{Z}'_j\mathbf{X})(\mathbf{X}'\mathbf{X})^{-1}\mathbf{X}'\mathbf{y}_j,
\end{aligned}
\tag{13-21}
$$

where all columns of $\hat{\mathbf{Z}}'_j$ are obtained as predictions in a regression of the corresponding column of $\mathbf{Z}_j$ on $\mathbf{X}$. This equation also results in a useful simplification of the estimated asymptotic covariance matrix,

$$
\text{Est. Asy. Var}[\hat{\boldsymbol{\delta}}_{j,2\text{SLS}}] = \hat{\sigma}_{jj}[\hat{\mathbf{Z}}'_j\hat{\mathbf{Z}}_j]^{-1}.
$$

It is important to note that $\sigma_{jj}$ is estimated by

$$
\hat{\sigma}_{jj} = \frac{(\mathbf{y}_j - \mathbf{Z}_j\hat{\boldsymbol{\delta}}_j)'(\mathbf{y}_j - \mathbf{Z}_j\hat{\boldsymbol{\delta}}_j)}{T},
$$

using the original data, not $\hat{\mathbf{Z}}_j$.

### 13.5.4 LIMITED INFORMATION MAXIMUM LIKELIHOOD AND THE $K$ CLASS OF ESTIMATORS

The **limited information maximum likelihood (LIML) estimator** is based on a single equation under the assumption of normally distributed disturbances; LIML is efficient among single-equation estimators. (We treat the LIML estimator here and the FIML estimator in Section 13.6.2 rather than in Chapter 16 because in both cases, the estimators provide more than just an alternative estimation strategy. As will emerge shortly, the maximum likelihood estimators for linear simultaneous equations models provide a useful theoretical benchmark for analyzing the other estimators we are analyzing here. In the LIML case, the technique has, as well, found recent use in a new setting, the analysis of weak instruments. We will return to this application in the next section.) A full (lengthy) derivation of the log-likelihood is provided in Theil (1971) and Davidson and MacKinnon (2004). We will proceed to the practical aspects of this estimator and refer the reader to these sources for the background formalities. A result that emerges from the derivation is that the LIML estimator has the same asymptotic distribution as the 2SLS estimator, and the latter does not rely on an assumption of normality. This raises the question why one would use the LIML technique given the availability of the more robust (and computationally simpler) alternative. Small sample results are sparse, but they would favor 2SLS as well. [See Phillips (1983).] The one significant virtue of LIML is its invariance to the normalization of the equation. Consider an example in a system of equations,

$$
y_1 = y_2\gamma_2 + y_3\gamma_3 + x_1\beta_1 + x_2\beta_2 + \varepsilon_1.
$$

An equivalent equation would be

$$
\begin{aligned}
y_2 &= y_1(1/\gamma_2) + y_3(-\gamma_3/\gamma_2) + x_1(-\beta_1/\gamma_2) + x_2(-\beta_2/\gamma_2) + \varepsilon_1(-1/\gamma_2) \\
&= y_1\tilde{\gamma}_1 + y_3\tilde{\gamma}_3 + x_1\tilde{\beta}_1 + x_2\tilde{\beta}_2 + \tilde{\varepsilon}_1.
\end{aligned}
$$

The parameters of the second equation can be manipulated to produce those of the first. But, as you can easily verify, the 2SLS estimator is not invariant to the normalization of the equation—2SLS would produce numerically different answers. LIML would give the same numerical solutions to both estimation problems suggested earlier.

The LIML, or **least variance ratio** estimator, can be computed as follows.[15] Let

$$\mathbf{W}_j^0 = \mathbf{E}_j^{0\prime}\mathbf{E}_j^0, \tag{13-22}$$

where

$$\mathbf{Y}_j^0 = [\mathbf{y}_j, \mathbf{Y}_j],$$

and

$$\mathbf{E}_j^0 = \mathbf{M}_j\mathbf{Y}_j^0 = [\mathbf{I} - \mathbf{X}_j(\mathbf{X}_j'\mathbf{X}_j)^{-1}\mathbf{X}_j']\mathbf{Y}_j^0. \tag{13-23}$$

Each column of $\mathbf{E}_j^0$ is a set of least squares residuals in the regression of the corresponding column of $\mathbf{Y}_j^0$ on $\mathbf{X}_j$, that is, the exogenous variables that appear in the $j$th equation. Thus, $\mathbf{W}_j^0$ is the matrix of sums of squares and cross products of these residuals. Define

$$\mathbf{W}_j^1 = \mathbf{E}_j^{1\prime}\mathbf{E}_j^1 = \mathbf{Y}_j^{0\prime}[\mathbf{I} - \mathbf{X}(\mathbf{X}'\mathbf{X})^{-1}\mathbf{X}']\mathbf{Y}_j^0. \tag{13-24}$$

That is, $\mathbf{W}_j^1$ is defined like $\mathbf{W}_j^0$ except that the regressions are on all the $x$'s in the model, not just the ones in the $j$th equation. Let

$$\lambda_1 = \text{smallest characteristic root of } \left(\mathbf{W}_j^1\right)^{-1}\mathbf{W}_j^0. \tag{13-25}$$

This matrix is asymmetric, but all its roots are real and greater than or equal to 1. Depending on the available software, it may be more convenient to obtain the identical smallest root of the symmetric matrix $\mathbf{D} = (\mathbf{W}_j^1)^{-1/2}\mathbf{W}_j^0(\mathbf{W}_j^1)^{-1/2}$. Now partition $\mathbf{W}_j^0$ into $\mathbf{W}_j^0 = \begin{bmatrix} w_{jj}^0 & \mathbf{w}_j^{0\prime} \\ \underline{\mathbf{w}}_j^0 & \mathbf{W}_{jj}^0 \end{bmatrix}$ corresponding to $[\mathbf{y}_j, \mathbf{Y}_j]$, and partition $\mathbf{W}_j^1$ likewise. Then, with these parts in hand,

$$\hat{\boldsymbol{\gamma}}_{j,\text{LIML}} = \left[\mathbf{W}_{jj}^0 - \lambda_1\mathbf{W}_{jj}^1\right]^{-1}\left(\mathbf{w}_j^0 - \lambda_1\mathbf{w}_j^1\right) \tag{13-26}$$

and

$$\hat{\boldsymbol{\beta}}_{j,\text{LIML}} = [\mathbf{X}_j'\mathbf{X}_j]^{-1}\mathbf{X}_j'(\mathbf{y}_j - \mathbf{Y}_j\hat{\boldsymbol{\gamma}}_{j,\text{LIML}}).$$

Note that $\boldsymbol{\beta}_j$ is estimated by a simple least squares regression. [See (3-18).] The asymptotic covariance matrix for the LIML estimator is identical to that for the 2SLS

---

[15]The least variance ratio estimator is derived in Johnston (1984). The LIML estimator was derived by Anderson and Rubin (1949, 1950). The LIML estimator has, since its derivation by Anderson and Rubin in 1949 and 1950, been of largely theoretical interest only. The much simpler and equally efficient two-stage least squares estimator has stood as the estimator of choice. But LIML and the A-R specification test have been rediscovered and reinvigorated with their use in the analysis of weak instruments. See Hahn and Hausman (2002, 2003) and Sections 12.9 and 13.5.5.

estimator.[16] The implication is that with normally distributed disturbances, 2SLS is fully efficient.

The **k class** of estimators is defined by the following form

$$\hat{\delta}_{j,k} = \begin{bmatrix} \mathbf{Y}'_j\mathbf{Y}_j - k\mathbf{V}'_j\mathbf{V}_j & \mathbf{Y}'_j\mathbf{X}_j \\ \mathbf{X}'_j\mathbf{Y}_j & \mathbf{X}'_j\mathbf{X}_j \end{bmatrix}^{-1} \begin{bmatrix} \mathbf{Y}'_j\mathbf{y}_j - k\mathbf{V}'_j\mathbf{v}_j \\ \mathbf{X}'_j\mathbf{y}_j \end{bmatrix}.$$

We have already considered three members of the class, OLS with $k = 0$, 2SLS with $k = 1$, and, it can be shown, LIML with $k = \lambda_1$. [This last result follows from (13-26).] There have been many other $k$-class estimators derived; Davidson and MacKinnon (2004, pp. 537–538 and 548–549) and Mariano (2001) give discussion. It has been shown that all members of the $k$ class for which $k$ converges to 1 at a rate faster than $1/\sqrt{n}$ have the same asymptotic distribution as that of the 2SLS estimator that we examined earlier. These are largely of theoretical interest, given the pervasive use of 2SLS or OLS, save for an important consideration. The large sample properties of all $k$-class estimators are the same, but the finite-sample properties are possibly very different. Davidson and MacKinnon (2004, pp. 537–538 and 548–549) and Mariano (1982, 2001) suggest that some evidence favors LIML when the sample size is small or moderate and the number of overidentifying restrictions is relatively large.

### 13.5.5   TESTING IN THE PRESENCE OF WEAK INSTRUMENTS

In Section 12.9, we introduced the problems of estimation and inference with instrumental variables in the presence of weak instruments. The first-stage regression method of Staiger and Stock (1997) is often used to detect the condition. Other tests have also been proposed, notably that of Hahn and Hausman (2002, 2003). Consider an equation with a single endogenous variable on the right-hand side,

$$y_1 = \gamma y_2 + \mathbf{x}'_1\boldsymbol{\beta}_1 + \varepsilon_1.$$

Given the way the model has been developed, the placement of $y_1$ on the left-hand side of this equation and $y_2$ on the right represents nothing more than a normalization of the coefficient matrix $\boldsymbol{\Gamma}$ in (13-2). (Note point 1 in Section 13.3.1.) For the moment, label this the "forward" equation. If we renormalize the model in terms of $y_2$, we obtain the completely equivalent equation

$$y_2 = (1/\gamma)y_1 + \mathbf{x}'_1(\boldsymbol{\beta}_1/\gamma) + \varepsilon_1/\gamma$$
$$= \theta y_1 + \mathbf{x}'_1\lambda_1 + v_1,$$

which we [i.e., Hahn and Hausman (2002)] label the "reverse equation," In principle, for estimation of $\gamma$, it should make no difference which form we estimate; we can estimate $\gamma$ directly in the first equation or indirectly through $1/\theta$ in the second. However, in practice, of all the $k$-class estimators listed in Section 13.5.4, which includes all the estimators we have examined, only the LIML estimator is invariant to this renormalization; certainly the 2SLS estimator is not. If we consider the forward 2SLS estimator, $\hat{\gamma}$, and the reverse estimator, $1/\hat{\theta}$, we should in principle obtain similar estimates. But there

---

[16]This is proved by showing that both estimators are members of the "$k$ class" of estimators, all of which have the same asymptotic covariance matrix. Details are given in Theil (1971) and Schmidt (1976).

is a bias in the 2SLS estimator that becomes more pronounced as the instruments become weaker. The Hahn and Hausman test statistic is based on the difference between these two estimators (corrected for the known bias of the 2SLS estimator in this case). [Research on this and other tests is ongoing. Hausman, Stock, and Yogo (2005) do report rather disappointing results for the power of this test in the presence of irrelevant instruments.]

The problem of inference remains. The upshot of the development so far is that the usual test statistics are likely to be unreliable. Some useful results have been obtained for devising inference procedures that are more robust than the standard first order asymptotics that we have employed (for example, in Theorem 12.1 and Section 13.5.3). Kleibergen (2002) has constructed a class of test statistics based on Anderson and Rubin's (1949, 1950) results that appears to offer some progress. An intriguing aspect of this strand of research is that the Anderson and Rubin test was developed in their 1949 and 1950 studies and predates by several years the development of two-stage least squares by Theil (1953) and Basmann (1957). [See Stock and Trebbi (2003) for discussion of the early development of the method of instrumental variables.] A lengthy description of Kleibergen's method and several extensions appears in the survey by Dufour (2003), which we draw on here for a cursory look at the Anderson and Rubin statistic.

The simultaneous equations model in terms of equation 1 is written

$$\mathbf{y}_1 = \mathbf{X}_1\boldsymbol{\beta}_1 + \mathbf{Y}_1\boldsymbol{\gamma}_1 + \boldsymbol{\varepsilon}_1,$$
$$\mathbf{Y}_1 = \mathbf{X}_1\boldsymbol{\Pi}_1 + \mathbf{X}_1^*\boldsymbol{\Pi}_1^* + \mathbf{V}_1, \tag{13-27}$$

where $\mathbf{y}_1$ is the $n$ observations on the left-hand variable in the equation of interest, $\mathbf{Y}_1$ is the $n$ observations on $M_1$ endogenous variables in this equation, $\boldsymbol{\gamma}_1$ is the structural parameter vector in this equation, and $\mathbf{X}_1$ is the $K_1$ included exogenous variables in equation 1. (See Table 13.1.) The second equation is the set of $M_1$ reduced form equations for the included endogenous variables that appear in equation 1. (Note that $M_1^*$ endogenous variables, $\mathbf{Y}_1^*$, are excluded from equation 1.) The full set of exogenous variables in the model is

$$\mathbf{X} = [\mathbf{X}_1, \mathbf{X}_1^*],$$

where $X_1^*$ is the $K_1^*$ exogenous variables that are excluded from equation 1. (We are changing Dufour's notation slightly to conform to the conventions used in our development of the model.) Note that the second equation represents the first stage of the two-stage least squares procedure.

We are interested in inference about $\boldsymbol{\gamma}_1$. We must first assume that the model is identified. We will invoke the rank and order conditions as usual. The order condition is that there must be at least as many excluded exogenous variables as there are included endogenous variables, which is that $K_1^* \geq M_1$. (With the model in the preceding form, it is easy to see the logic of this condition. If we are going to apply 2SLS by regressing $\mathbf{y}_1$ on a prediction for $\mathbf{Y}_1$ that is a linear combination of the variables in $\mathbf{X}$, then in order for the resulting regressor matrix to have full column rank, the predicted $\mathbf{Y}_1$ in equation 1 above must involve at least enough variables that it is linearly independent of $\mathbf{X}_1$.) For the rank condition to be met, we must have

$$\boldsymbol{\pi}_1^* - \boldsymbol{\Pi}_1^*\boldsymbol{\gamma}_1 = \mathbf{0},$$

where $\pi_1^*$ is the second part of the coefficient vector in the reduced form equation for $\mathbf{y}_1$, that is,

$$\mathbf{y}_1 = \mathbf{X}_1\boldsymbol{\pi}_1 + \mathbf{X}_1^*\boldsymbol{\pi}_1^* + \mathbf{v}_1.$$

This is equation (13-10). For this result to hold, $\boldsymbol{\Pi}_1$ must have full column rank, $K_1^*$. The weak instruments problem is embodied in $\boldsymbol{\Pi}_1^*$. If this matrix has short rank, the parameter vector $\boldsymbol{\gamma}_1$ is not identified. The weak instruments problem arises when $\boldsymbol{\Pi}_1^*$ is nearly short ranked. The important aspect of that observation is that the weak instruments can be characterized as an identification problem.

Anderson and Rubin (1949, 1950) (AR) proposed a method of testing $H_0: \boldsymbol{\gamma}_1 = \boldsymbol{\gamma}_1^0$. The AR statistic is constructed as follows: Combining the two equations in (13-27), we have

$$\mathbf{y}_1 = \mathbf{X}_1\boldsymbol{\beta}_1 + \mathbf{X}_1\boldsymbol{\Pi}_1\boldsymbol{\gamma}_1 + \mathbf{X}_1^*\boldsymbol{\Pi}_1^*\boldsymbol{\gamma}_1 + \boldsymbol{\varepsilon}_1 + \mathbf{V}_1\boldsymbol{\gamma}_1.$$

Using (13-27) again, subtract $\mathbf{Y}_1\boldsymbol{\gamma}_1^0$ from both sides of this equation to obtain

$$
\begin{aligned}
\mathbf{y}_1 - \mathbf{Y}_1\boldsymbol{\gamma}_1^0 &= \mathbf{X}_1\boldsymbol{\beta}_1 + \mathbf{X}_1\boldsymbol{\Pi}_1\boldsymbol{\gamma}_1 + \mathbf{X}_1^*\boldsymbol{\Pi}_1^*\boldsymbol{\gamma}_1 + \boldsymbol{\varepsilon}_1 + \mathbf{V}_1\boldsymbol{\gamma}_1 \\
&\quad - \mathbf{X}_1\boldsymbol{\Pi}_1\boldsymbol{\gamma}_1^0 - \mathbf{X}_1^*\boldsymbol{\Pi}_1^*\boldsymbol{\gamma}_1^0 - \mathbf{V}_1\boldsymbol{\gamma}_1^0 \\
&= \mathbf{X}_1[\boldsymbol{\beta}_1 + \boldsymbol{\Pi}_1(\boldsymbol{\gamma}_1 - \boldsymbol{\gamma}_1^0)] + \mathbf{X}_1^*[\boldsymbol{\Pi}_1^*(\boldsymbol{\gamma}_1 - \boldsymbol{\gamma}_1^0)] + \boldsymbol{\varepsilon}_1 + \mathbf{V}_1(\boldsymbol{\gamma}_1 - \boldsymbol{\gamma}_1^0) \\
&= \mathbf{X}_1\boldsymbol{\theta}_1 + \mathbf{X}_1^*\boldsymbol{\theta}_1^* + \mathbf{w}_1.
\end{aligned}
$$

Under the null hypothesis, this equation reduces to

$$\mathbf{y}_1 - \mathbf{Y}_1\boldsymbol{\gamma}_1^0 = \mathbf{X}_1\boldsymbol{\theta}_1 + \mathbf{w}_1,$$

so a test of the null hypothesis can be carried out by testing the hypothesis that $\boldsymbol{\theta}_1^*$ equals zero in the preceding partial reduced-form equation. Anderson and Rubin proposed a simple $F$ test,

$$
\begin{aligned}
\mathrm{AR}(\boldsymbol{\gamma}_1^0) &= \frac{[(\mathbf{y}_1 - \mathbf{Y}_1\boldsymbol{\gamma}_1^0)'\mathbf{M}_1(\mathbf{y}_1 - \mathbf{Y}_1\boldsymbol{\gamma}_1^0) - (\mathbf{y}_1 - \mathbf{Y}_1\boldsymbol{\gamma}_1^0)'\mathbf{M}(\mathbf{y}_1 - \mathbf{Y}_1\boldsymbol{\gamma}_1^0)]/K_1^*}{(\mathbf{y}_1 - \mathbf{Y}_1\boldsymbol{\gamma}_1^0)'\mathbf{M}(\mathbf{y}_1 - \mathbf{Y}_1\boldsymbol{\gamma}_1^0)/(n-K)} \\
&\sim F[K_1^*, n - K],
\end{aligned}
$$

where $\mathbf{M}_1 = [\mathbf{I} - \mathbf{X}_1(\mathbf{X}_1'\mathbf{X}_1)^{-1}\mathbf{X}_1']$ and $\mathbf{M} = [\mathbf{I} - \mathbf{X}(\mathbf{X}'\mathbf{X})^{-1}\mathbf{X}']$. This is the standard $F$ statistic for testing the hypothesis that the set of coefficients is zero in the classical linear regression. [See (5-20).] [Dufour (2003) shows how the statistic can be extended to allow more general restrictions that also include $\boldsymbol{\beta}_1$.]

There are several striking features of this approach, beyond the fact that it has been available since 1949: (1) its distribution is free of the model parameters in finite samples (assuming normality of the disturbances); (2) *it is robust to the weak instruments problem;* (3) it is robust to the exclusion of other instruments; and (4) it is robust to specification errors in the structural equations for $\mathbf{Y}_1$, the other variables in the equation. There are some shortcomings as well, namely: (1) the tests developed by this method are only applied to the full parameter vector; (2) the power of the test may diminish as more (and too many more) instrumental variables are added; (3) it relies on a normality assumption for the disturbances; and (4) there does not appear to be a counterpart for nonlinear systems of equations.

As noted earlier, analysis of problems of estimation and inference in structural equation models is one of the bedrock platforms of research in econometrics. The analysis sketched here continues that line of inquiry.

### 13.5.6 TWO-STAGE LEAST SQUARES IN MODELS THAT ARE NONLINEAR IN VARIABLES

The analysis of simultaneous equations becomes considerably more complicated when the equations are nonlinear. Amemiya presents a general treatment of nonlinear models.[17] A case that is broad enough to include many practical applications is the one analyzed by Kelejian (1971),

$$\mathbf{y}_j = \gamma_{1j}\mathbf{f}_{1j}(\mathbf{y}, \mathbf{x}) + \gamma_{2j}\mathbf{f}_{2j}(\mathbf{y}, \mathbf{x}) + \cdots + \mathbf{X}_j\boldsymbol{\beta}_j + \boldsymbol{\varepsilon}_j,$$[18]

which is an extension of (6-4). Ordinary least squares will be inconsistent for the same reasons as before, but an IV estimator, if one can be devised, should have the familiar properties. Because of the nonlinearity, it may not be possible to solve for the reduced-form equations (assuming that they exist), $h_{ij}(\mathbf{x}) = E[f_{ij} \mid \mathbf{x}]$. Kelejian shows that 2SLS based on a Taylor series approximation to $h_{ij}$, using the linear terms, higher powers, and cross-products of the variables in $\mathbf{x}$, will be consistent. The analysis of 2SLS presented earlier then applies to the $\mathbf{Z}_j$ consisting of $[\hat{\mathbf{f}}_{1j}, \hat{\mathbf{f}}_{2j}, \ldots, \mathbf{X}_j]$. [The alternative approach of using fitted values for $\mathbf{y}$ appears to be inconsistent. See Kelejian (1971) and Goldfeld and Quandt (1968).]

In a linear model, if an equation fails the order condition, then it cannot be estimated by 2SLS. This statement is not true of Kelejian's approach, however, because taking higher powers of the regressors creates many more linearly independent instrumental variables. If an equation in a linear model fails the rank condition but not the order condition, then the 2SLS estimates can be computed in a finite sample but will fail to exist asymptotically because $\mathbf{X}\boldsymbol{\Pi}_j$ will have short rank. Unfortunately, to the extent that Kelejian's approximation never exactly equals the true reduced form unless it happens to be the polynomial in $\mathbf{x}$ (unlikely), this built-in control need not be present, even asymptotically.

## 13.6 SYSTEM METHODS OF ESTIMATION

We may formulate the full system of equations as

$$\begin{bmatrix} \mathbf{y}_1 \\ \mathbf{y}_2 \\ \vdots \\ \mathbf{y}_M \end{bmatrix} = \begin{bmatrix} \mathbf{Z}_1 & \mathbf{0} & \cdots & \mathbf{0} \\ \mathbf{0} & \mathbf{Z}_2 & \cdots & \mathbf{0} \\ \vdots & \vdots & \vdots & \vdots \\ \mathbf{0} & \mathbf{0} & \cdots & \mathbf{Z}_M \end{bmatrix} \begin{bmatrix} \boldsymbol{\delta}_1 \\ \boldsymbol{\delta}_2 \\ \vdots \\ \boldsymbol{\delta}_M \end{bmatrix} + \begin{bmatrix} \boldsymbol{\varepsilon}_1 \\ \boldsymbol{\varepsilon}_2 \\ \vdots \\ \boldsymbol{\varepsilon}_M \end{bmatrix}$$

or

$$\mathbf{y} = \mathbf{Z}\boldsymbol{\delta} + \boldsymbol{\varepsilon},$$

---

[17]Amemiya (1985, pp. 245–265). See, as well, Wooldridge (2002a, ch. 9).

[18]2SLS for models that are nonlinear in the parameters is discussed in Chapter 15 in connection with GMM estimators.

where

$$E[\boldsymbol{\varepsilon} \mid \mathbf{X}] = \mathbf{0}, \quad \text{and} \quad E[\boldsymbol{\varepsilon}\boldsymbol{\varepsilon}' \mid \mathbf{X}] = \overline{\boldsymbol{\Sigma}} = \boldsymbol{\Sigma} \otimes \mathbf{I}. \tag{13-28}$$

[See (10-3).] The least squares estimator,

$$\mathbf{d} = [\mathbf{Z}'\mathbf{Z}]^{-1}\mathbf{Z}'\mathbf{y},$$

is equation-by-equation ordinary least squares and is inconsistent. But even if ordinary least squares were consistent, we know from our results for the seemingly unrelated regressions model in Chapter 10 that it would be inefficient compared with an estimator that makes use of the cross-equation correlations of the disturbances. For the first issue, we turn once again to an IV estimator. For the second, as we did in Chapter 10, we use a generalized least squares approach. Thus, assuming that the matrix of instrumental variables, $\overline{\mathbf{W}}$ satisfies the requirements for an IV estimator, a consistent though inefficient estimator would be

$$\hat{\boldsymbol{\delta}}_{\text{IV}} = [\overline{\mathbf{W}}'\mathbf{Z}]^{-1}\overline{\mathbf{W}}'\mathbf{y}. \tag{13-29}$$

Analogous to the seemingly unrelated regressions model, a more efficient estimator would be based on the generalized least squares principle,

$$\hat{\boldsymbol{\delta}}_{\text{IV,GLS}} = [\overline{\mathbf{W}}'(\boldsymbol{\Sigma}^{-1} \otimes \mathbf{I})\mathbf{Z}]^{-1}\overline{\mathbf{W}}'(\boldsymbol{\Sigma}^{-1} \otimes \mathbf{I})\mathbf{y}, \tag{13-30}$$

or, where $\mathbf{W}_j$ is the set of instrumental variables for the $j$th equation,

$$\hat{\boldsymbol{\delta}}_{\text{IV,GLS}} = \begin{bmatrix} \sigma^{11}\mathbf{W}_1'\mathbf{Z}_1 & \sigma^{12}\mathbf{W}_1'\mathbf{Z}_2 & \cdots & \sigma^{1M}\mathbf{W}_1'\mathbf{Z}_M \\ \sigma^{21}\mathbf{W}_2'\mathbf{Z}_1 & \sigma^{22}\mathbf{W}_2'\mathbf{Z}_2 & \cdots & \sigma^{2M}\mathbf{W}_2'\mathbf{Z}_M \\ & & \vdots & \\ \sigma^{M1}\mathbf{W}_M'\mathbf{Z}_1 & \sigma^{M2}\mathbf{W}_M'\mathbf{Z}_2 & \cdots & \sigma^{MM}\mathbf{W}_M'\mathbf{Z}_M \end{bmatrix}^{-1} \begin{bmatrix} \sum_{j=1}^{M}\sigma^{1j}\mathbf{W}_1'\mathbf{y}_j \\ \sum_{j=1}^{M}\sigma^{2j}\mathbf{W}_2'\mathbf{y}_j \\ \vdots \\ \sum_{j=1}^{M}\sigma^{Mj}\mathbf{W}_M'\mathbf{y}_j \end{bmatrix}.$$

Three techniques are generally used for joint estimation of the entire system of equations: three-stage least squares, GMM, and full information maximum likelihood.

### 13.6.1    THREE-STAGE LEAST SQUARES

Consider the IV estimator formed from

$$\overline{\mathbf{W}} = \hat{\mathbf{Z}} = \text{diag}[\mathbf{X}(\mathbf{X}'\mathbf{X})^{-1}\mathbf{X}'\mathbf{Z}_1, \ldots, \mathbf{X}(\mathbf{X}'\mathbf{X})^{-1}\mathbf{X}'\mathbf{Z}_M] = \begin{bmatrix} \hat{\mathbf{Z}}_1 & \mathbf{0} & \cdots & \mathbf{0} \\ \mathbf{0} & \hat{\mathbf{Z}}_2 & \cdots & \mathbf{0} \\ \vdots & \vdots & \vdots & \vdots \\ \mathbf{0} & \mathbf{0} & \cdots & \hat{\mathbf{Z}}_M \end{bmatrix}.$$

The IV estimator,

$$\hat{\boldsymbol{\delta}}_{\text{IV}} = [\hat{\mathbf{Z}}'\mathbf{Z}]^{-1}\hat{\mathbf{Z}}'\mathbf{y},$$

is simply equation-by-equation 2SLS. We have already established the consistency of 2SLS. By analogy to the seemingly unrelated regressions model of Chapter 10, however, we would expect this estimator to be less efficient than a GLS estimator. A natural candidate would be

$$\hat{\boldsymbol{\delta}}_{\text{3SLS}} = [\hat{\mathbf{Z}}'(\boldsymbol{\Sigma}^{-1} \otimes \mathbf{I})\mathbf{Z}]^{-1}\hat{\mathbf{Z}}'(\boldsymbol{\Sigma}^{-1} \otimes \mathbf{I})\mathbf{y}.$$

For this estimator to be a valid IV estimator, we must establish that

$$\text{plim} \, \frac{1}{T} \hat{\mathbf{Z}}' (\mathbf{\Sigma}^{-1} \otimes \mathbf{I}) \boldsymbol{\varepsilon} = \mathbf{0},$$

which is $M$ sets of equations, each one of the form

$$\text{plim} \, \frac{1}{T} \sum_{j=1}^{M} \sigma^{ij} \hat{\mathbf{Z}}_i' \boldsymbol{\varepsilon}_j = \mathbf{0}.$$

Each is the sum of vectors all of which converge to zero, as we saw in the development of the 2SLS estimator. The second requirement, that

$$\text{plim} \, \frac{1}{T} \hat{\mathbf{Z}}' (\mathbf{\Sigma}^{-1} \otimes \mathbf{I}) \mathbf{Z} \neq \mathbf{0},$$

and that the matrix be nonsingular, can be established along the lines of its counterpart for 2SLS. Identification of every equation by the rank condition is sufficient. [But, see Mariano (2001) on the subject of "weak instruments."]

Once again using the idempotency of $\mathbf{I} - \mathbf{M}$, we may also interpret this estimator as a GLS estimator of the form

$$\hat{\boldsymbol{\delta}}_{3SLS} = [\hat{\mathbf{Z}}' (\mathbf{\Sigma}^{-1} \otimes \mathbf{I}) \hat{\mathbf{Z}}]^{-1} \hat{\mathbf{Z}}' (\mathbf{\Sigma}^{-1} \otimes \mathbf{I}) \mathbf{y}. \tag{13-31}$$

The appropriate asymptotic covariance matrix for the estimator is

$$\text{Asy. Var}[\hat{\boldsymbol{\delta}}_{3SLS}] = [\overline{\mathbf{Z}}' (\mathbf{\Sigma}^{-1} \otimes \mathbf{I}) \overline{\mathbf{Z}}]^{-1}, \tag{13-32}$$

where $\overline{\mathbf{Z}} = \text{diag}[\mathbf{X}\mathbf{\Pi}_j, \mathbf{X}_j]$. This matrix would be estimated with the bracketed inverse matrix in (13-31).

Using sample data, we find that $\overline{\mathbf{Z}}$ may be estimated with $\hat{\mathbf{Z}}$. The remaining difficulty is to obtain an estimate of $\mathbf{\Sigma}$. In estimation of the multivariate regression model, for efficient estimation (that remains to be shown), any consistent estimator of $\mathbf{\Sigma}$ will do. The designers of the 3SLS method, Zellner and Theil (1962), suggest the natural choice arising out of the two-stage least estimates. The **three-stage least squares (3SLS) estimator** is thus defined as follows:

1. Estimate $\mathbf{\Pi}$ by ordinary least squares and compute $\hat{\mathbf{Y}}_j$ for each equation.
2. Compute $\hat{\boldsymbol{\delta}}_{j,2SLS}$ for each equation; then

$$\hat{\sigma}_{ij} = \frac{(\mathbf{y}_i - \mathbf{Z}_i \hat{\boldsymbol{\delta}}_i)'(\mathbf{y}_j - \mathbf{Z}_j \hat{\boldsymbol{\delta}}_j)}{T}. \tag{13-33}$$

3. Compute the GLS estimator according to (13-31) and an estimate of the asymptotic covariance matrix according to (13-32) using $\hat{\mathbf{Z}}$ and $\hat{\mathbf{\Sigma}}$.

It is also possible to iterate the 3SLS computation. Unlike the seemingly unrelated regressions estimator, however, this method does not provide the maximum likelihood estimator, nor does it improve the asymptotic efficiency.[19]

By showing that the 3SLS estimator satisfies the requirements for an IV estimator, we have established its consistency. The question of asymptotic efficiency remains. It can

---

[19] A Jacobian term needed to maximize the log-likelihood is not treated by the 3SLS estimator. See Dhrymes (1973).

be shown that among all IV estimators that use only the sample information embodied in the system, 3SLS is asymptotically efficient.[20] For normally distributed disturbances, it can also be shown that 3SLS has the same asymptotic distribution as the full information maximum likelihood estimator, which is asymptotically efficient among all estimators. A direct proof based on the information matrix is possible, but we shall take a much simpler route by simply exploiting a handy result due to Hausman in the next section.

### 13.6.2  FULL INFORMATION MAXIMUM LIKELIHOOD

Because of their simplicity and asymptotic efficiency, 2SLS and 3SLS are used almost exclusively (when ordinary least squares is not used) for the estimation of simultaneous equations models. Nonetheless, it is occasionally useful to obtain maximum likelihood estimates directly. The **full information maximum likelihood (FIML) estimator** is based on the entire system of equations. With normally distributed disturbances, FIML is efficient among all estimators. (Like the LIML estimator in Section 13.5.4, the FIML estimator for linear simultaneous equations models stands somewhat apart from the other maximum likelihood applications developed in Chapter 16. The practical interest in the estimator is rather limited because the 3SLS estimator is equally efficient, much easier to compute, and does not impose a normality assumption. On the other hand, like the LIML estimator, the FIML estimator presents a useful theoretical benchmark. As such, it is more useful to present it here, while the background theory for the ML methodology can be found in Chapter 16.)

The FIML estimator treats all equations and all parameters jointly. To formulate the appropriate log-likelihood function, we begin with the reduced form,

$$\mathbf{Y} = \mathbf{X}\mathbf{\Pi} + \mathbf{V},$$

where each row of $\mathbf{V}$ is assumed to be multivariate normally distributed, with $E[\mathbf{v}_t \mid \mathbf{X}] = \mathbf{0}$ and covariance matrix, $E[\mathbf{v}_t \mathbf{v}_t' \mid \mathbf{X}] = \mathbf{\Omega}$. The log-likelihood for this model is precisely that of the seemingly unrelated regressions model of Chapter 10. (See Section 16.9.3.b.) For the moment, we can ignore the relationship between the structural and reduced-form parameters. The log-likelihood function is

$$\ln L = -\frac{T}{2}[M \ln(2\pi) + \ln|\mathbf{\Omega}| + \mathrm{tr}(\mathbf{\Omega}^{-1}\mathbf{W})],$$

where

$$\mathbf{W}_{ij} = \frac{1}{T}\left(\mathbf{y} - \mathbf{X}\boldsymbol{\pi}_i^0\right)'\left(\mathbf{y} - \mathbf{X}\boldsymbol{\pi}_j^0\right),$$

and

$$\boldsymbol{\pi}_j^0 = j\text{th column of } \mathbf{\Pi}.$$

This function is to be maximized subject to all the restrictions imposed by the structure. Make the substitutions $\mathbf{\Pi} = -\mathbf{B}\mathbf{\Gamma}^{-1}$ and $\mathbf{\Omega} = (\mathbf{\Gamma}^{-1})'\mathbf{\Sigma}\mathbf{\Gamma}^{-1}$ so that $\mathbf{\Omega}^{-1} = \mathbf{\Gamma}\mathbf{\Sigma}^{-1}\mathbf{\Gamma}'$. Thus,

$$\ln L = -\frac{T}{2}\left[M\ln(2\pi) + \ln|(\mathbf{\Gamma}^{-1})'\mathbf{\Sigma}\mathbf{\Gamma}^{-1}| + \mathrm{tr}\left\{\frac{1}{T}[\mathbf{\Gamma}\mathbf{\Sigma}^{-1}\mathbf{\Gamma}'(\mathbf{Y} + \mathbf{X}\mathbf{B}\mathbf{\Gamma}^{-1})'(\mathbf{Y} + \mathbf{X}\mathbf{B}\mathbf{\Gamma}^{-1})]\right\}\right],$$

---

[20]See Schmidt (1976) for a proof of its efficiency relative to 2SLS.

which can be simplified. First,

$$-\frac{T}{2}\ln|(\mathbf{\Gamma}^{-1})'\mathbf{\Sigma}\mathbf{\Gamma}^{-1}| = -\frac{T}{2}\ln|\mathbf{\Sigma}| + T\ln|\mathbf{\Gamma}|.$$

(The term $\mathbf{T}\ln|\mathbf{\Gamma}|$ is the Jacobian term noted in footnote 19.) Second, $\mathbf{\Gamma}'(\mathbf{Y}+\mathbf{XB}\,\mathbf{\Gamma}^{-1})' = \mathbf{\Gamma}'\mathbf{Y}' + \mathbf{B}'\mathbf{X}'$. By permuting $\mathbf{\Gamma}$ from the beginning to the end of the trace and collecting terms,

$$\text{tr}(\mathbf{\Omega}^{-1}\mathbf{W}) = \text{tr}\left[\frac{\mathbf{\Sigma}^{-1}(\mathbf{Y\Gamma} + \mathbf{XB})'(\mathbf{Y\Gamma} + \mathbf{XB})}{T}\right].$$

Therefore, the log-likelihood is

$$\ln L = -\frac{T}{2}[M\ln(2\pi) - 2\ln|\mathbf{\Gamma}| + \text{tr}(\mathbf{\Sigma}^{-1}\mathbf{S}) + \ln|\mathbf{\Sigma}|],$$

where

$$s_{ij} = \frac{1}{T}(\mathbf{Y\Gamma}_i + \mathbf{XB}_i)'(\mathbf{Y\Gamma}_j + \mathbf{XB}_j).$$

[In terms of nonzero parameters, $s_{ij}$ is $\hat{\sigma}_{ij}$ of (13-33).]

In maximizing $\ln L$, it is necessary to impose all the additional restrictions on the structure. The trace may be written in the form

$$\text{tr}(\mathbf{\Sigma}^{-1}\mathbf{S}) = \sum_{i=1}^{M}\sum_{j=1}^{M}\sigma^{ij}\frac{(\mathbf{y}_i - \mathbf{Y}_i\boldsymbol{\gamma}_i - \mathbf{X}_i\boldsymbol{\beta}_i)'(\mathbf{y}_j - \mathbf{Y}_j\boldsymbol{\gamma}_j - \mathbf{X}_j\boldsymbol{\beta}_j)}{T}. \tag{13-34}$$

Maximizing $\ln L$ subject to the exclusions in (13-34) and any other restrictions, if necessary, produces the FIML estimator. This has all the desirable asymptotic properties of maximum likelihood estimators and, therefore, is asymptotically efficient among estimators of the simultaneous equations model. The asymptotic covariance matrix for the FIML estimator is the same as that for the 3SLS estimator.

A useful interpretation of the FIML estimator is provided by Dhrymes (1973, p. 360) and Hausman (1975, 1983). They show that the FIML estimator of $\boldsymbol{\delta}$ is also an IV estimator. The asymptotic covariance matrix for the FIML estimator follows directly from its form as an IV estimator. Because this matrix is the same as that of the 3SLS estimator, we conclude that with normally distributed disturbances, 3SLS has the same asymptotic distribution as maximum likelihood. The practical usefulness of this important result has not gone unnoticed by practitioners. The 3SLS estimator is far easier to compute than the FIML estimator. The benefit in computational cost comes at no cost in asymptotic efficiency. As always, the small-sample properties remain ambiguous, but by and large, where a systems estimator is used, 3SLS dominates FIML nonetheless.[21] (One reservation arises from the fact that the 3SLS estimator is robust to nonnormality whereas, because of the term $\ln|\mathbf{\Gamma}|$ in the log-likelihood, the FIML estimator is not. In fact, the 3SLS and FIML estimators are usually quite different numerically.)

---

[21]PC-GIVE, SAS, and TSP are three computer programs that are widely used. A survey is given in Silk (1996).

## 13.7 COMPARISON OF METHODS—KLEIN'S MODEL I

The preceding has described a large number of estimators for simultaneous equations models. As an example, Table 13.3 presents limited and full information estimates for Klein's Model I based on the original data for 1920–1941. (The data are given in Appendix Table F13.1) The H3SLS estimates for the system were computed in two pairs, $(C, I)$ and $(C, W^p)$, because there were insufficient observations to fit the system as a whole. The first of these are reported for the $C$ equation.[22]

**TABLE 13.3** Estimates of Klein's Model I (Estimated Asymptotic Standard Errors in Parentheses)

| | *Limited Information Estimates* | | | | *Full Information Estimates* | | | |
|---|---|---|---|---|---|---|---|---|
| | **2SLS** | | | | **3SLS** | | | |
| $C$ | 16.6 | 0.017 | 0.216 | 0.810 | 16.4 | 0.125 | 0.163 | 0.790 |
| | (1.32) | (0.118) | (0.107) | (0.040) | (1.30) | (0.108) | (0.100) | (0.038) |
| $I$ | 20.3 | 0.150 | 0.616 | −0.158 | 28.2 | −0.013 | 0.756 | −0.195 |
| | (7.54) | (0.173) | (0.162) | (0.036) | (6.79) | (0.162) | (0.153) | (0.033) |
| $W^p$ | 1.50 | 0.439 | 0.147 | 0.130 | 1.80 | 0.400 | 0.181 | 0.150 |
| | (1.15) | (0.036) | (0.039) | (0.029) | (1.12) | (0.032) | (0.034) | (0.028) |
| | **LIML** | | | | **FIML** | | | |
| $C$ | 17.1 | −0.222 | 0.396 | 0.823 | 18.3 | −0.232 | 0.388 | 0.802 |
| | (1.84) | (0.202) | (0.174) | (0.055) | (2.49) | (0.312) | (0.217) | (0.036) |
| $I$ | 22.6 | 0.075 | 0.680 | −0.168 | 27.3 | −0.801 | 1.052 | −0.146 |
| | (9.24) | (0.219) | (0.203) | (0.044) | (7.94) | (0.491) | (0.353) | (0.30) |
| $W^p$ | 1.53 | 0.434 | 0.151 | 0.132 | 5.79 | 0.234 | 0.285 | 0.235 |
| | (2.40) | (0.137) | (0.135) | (0.065) | (1.80) | (0.049) | (0.045) | (0.035) |
| | **GMM (H2SLS)** | | | | **GMM (H3SLS)** | | | |
| $C$ | 14.3 | 0.090 | 0.143 | 0.864 | 15.7 | 0.068 | 0.167 | 0.829 |
| | (0.897) | (0.062) | (0.065) | (0.029) | (0.951) | (0.091) | (0.080) | (0.033) |
| $I$ | 23.5 | 0.146 | 0.591 | −0.171 | 20.6 | 0.213 | −0.520 | −0.157 |
| | (6.40) | (0.120) | (0.129) | (0.031) | (4.89) | (0.087) | (0.099) | (0.025) |
| $W^p$ | 3.06 | 0.455 | 0.106 | 0.130 | 2.09 | 0.446 | 0.131 | 0.112 |
| | (0.64) | (0.028) | (0.030) | (0.022) | (0.510) | (0.019) | (0.021) | (0.021) |
| | **OLS** | | | | **I3SLS** | | | |
| $C$ | 16.2 | 0.193 | 0.090 | 0.796 | 16.6 | 0.165 | 0.177 | 0.766 |
| | (1.30) | (0.091) | (0.091) | (0.040) | (1.22) | (0.096) | (0.090) | (0.035) |
| $I$ | 10.1 | 0.480 | 0.333 | −0.112 | 42.9 | −0.356 | 1.01 | −0.260 |
| | (5.47) | (0.097) | (0.101) | (0.027) | (10.6) | (0.260) | (0.249) | (0.051) |
| $W^p$ | 1.50 | 0.439 | 0.146 | 0.130 | 2.62 | 0.375 | 0.194 | 0.168 |
| | (1.27) | (0.032) | (0.037) | (0.032) | (1.20) | (0.031) | (0.032) | (0.029) |

---

[22]The asymptotic covariance matrix for the LIML estimator will differ from that for the 2SLS estimator in a finite sample because the estimator of $\sigma_{jj}$ that multiplies the inverse matrix will differ and because in computing the matrix to be inverted, the value of "$k$" (see the equation after (13-26)) is one for 2SLS and the smallest root in (13-25) for LIML. Asymptotically, $k$ equals one and the estimators of $\sigma_{jj}$ are equivalent. The H2SLS and H3SLS estimators are generalized method of moments (GMM) estimators. Because these will be developed in Section 15.6.4, we will postpone discussion of the estimates until then. They are listed in Table 13.3 purely for convenience in comparing them to the results from the other estimators.

It might seem, in light of the entire discussion, that one of the structural estimators described previously should always be preferred to ordinary least squares, which, alone among the estimators considered here, is inconsistent. Unfortunately, the issue is not so clear. First, it is often found that the OLS estimator is surprisingly close to the structural estimator. It can be shown that at least in some cases, OLS has a smaller variance about its mean than does 2SLS about its mean, leading to the possibility that OLS might be more precise in a mean-squared-error sense.[23] But this result must be tempered by the finding that the OLS standard errors are, in all likelihood, not useful for inference purposes.[24] Nonetheless, OLS is a frequently used estimator. Obviously, this discussion is relevant only to finite samples. Asymptotically, 2SLS must dominate OLS, and in a correctly specified model, any full information estimator must dominate any limited information one. The finite sample properties are of crucial importance. Most of what we know is asymptotic properties, but most applications are based on rather small or moderately sized samples.

The large difference between the inconsistent OLS and the other estimates suggests the bias discussed earlier. On the other hand, the incorrect sign on the LIML and FIML estimate of the coefficient on $P$ and the even larger difference of the coefficient on $P_{-1}$ in the $C$ equation are striking. Assuming that the equation is properly specified, these anomalies would likewise be attributed to finite sample variation, because LIML and 2SLS are asymptotically equivalent. The GMM estimator is also striking. The estimated standard errors are noticeably smaller for all the coefficients. It should be noted, however, that this estimator is based on a presumption of heteroscedasticity when in this time series, there is little evidence of its presence. The results are broadly suggestive, but the appearance of having achieved something for nothing is deceiving. Our earlier results on the efficiency of 2SLS are intact. If there is heteroscedasticity, then 2SLS is no longer fully efficient, but, then again, neither is H2SLS. The latter is more efficient than the former in the presence of heteroscedasticity, but it is equivalent to 2SLS in its absence. (See Section 15.6.4.)

Intuition would suggest that systems methods, 3SLS, GMM, and FIML, are to be preferred to single-equation methods, 2SLS and LIML. Indeed, if the advantage is so transparent, why would one ever choose a single-equation estimator? The proper analogy is to the use of single-equation OLS versus GLS in the SURE model of Chapter 10. An obvious practical consideration is the computational simplicity of the single-equation methods. But the current state of available software has all but eliminated this advantage.

Although the systems methods are asymptotically better, they have two problems. First, any specification error in the structure of the model will be propagated throughout the system by 3SLS or FIML. The limited information estimators will, by and large, confine a problem to the particular equation in which it appears. Second, in the same fashion as the SURE model, the finite-sample variation of the estimated covariance matrix is transmitted throughout the system. Thus, the finite-sample variance of 3SLS may well be as large as or larger than that of 2SLS. Although they are only single estimates, the results for Klein's Model I give a striking example. The upshot would

---

[23] See Goldberger (1964, pp. 359–360).

[24] Cragg (1967).

appear to be that the advantage of the systems estimators in finite samples may be more modest than the asymptotic results would suggest. Monte Carlo studies of the issue have tended to reach the same conclusion.[25]

## 13.8 SPECIFICATION TESTS

In a strident criticism of structural estimation, Liu (1960) argued that all simultaneous equations models of the economy were truly unidentified and that only reduced forms could be estimated. Although his criticisms may have been exaggerated (and never gained wide acceptance), modelers have been interested in testing the restrictions that overidentify an econometric model.

The first procedure for testing the overidentifying restrictions in a model was developed by Anderson and Rubin (1950). Their likelihood ratio test statistic is a by-product of LIML estimation:

$$\text{LR} = \chi^2[K_j^* - M_j] = T(\lambda_j - 1),$$

where $\lambda_j$ is the root used to find the LIML estimator. [See (13-25).] The statistic has a limiting chi-squared distribution with degrees of freedom equal to the number of overidentifying restrictions. A large value is taken as evidence that there are exogenous variables in the model that have been inappropriately omitted from the equation being examined. If the equation is exactly identified, then $K_j^* - M_j = 0$, but at the same time, the root will be 1. An alternative based on the Lagrange multiplier principle was proposed by Hausman (1983, p. 433). Operationally, the test requires only the calculation of $TR^2$, where the $R^2$ is the uncentered $R^2$ in the regression of $\hat{\boldsymbol{\varepsilon}}_j = \mathbf{y}_j - \mathbf{Z}_j \hat{\boldsymbol{\delta}}_j$ on all the predetermined variables in the model. The estimated parameters may be computed using 2SLS, LIML, or any other *efficient* limited information estimator. The statistic has a limiting chi-squared distribution with $K_j^* - M_j$ degrees of freedom under the assumed specification of the model.

Another specification error occurs if the variables assumed to be exogenous in the system are, in fact, correlated with the structural disturbances. Since all the asymptotic properties claimed earlier rest on this assumption, this specification error would be quite serious. Several authors have studied this issue.[26] The **specification test** devised by Hausman that we used in Section 12.4 in the errors in variables model provides a method of testing for exogeneity in a simultaneous equations model. Suppose that the variable $x^e$ is in question. The test is based on the existence of two estimators, say, $\hat{\boldsymbol{\delta}}$ and $\hat{\boldsymbol{\delta}}^*$, such that

under $H_0$: ($x^e$ is exogenous), both $\hat{\boldsymbol{\delta}}$ and $\hat{\boldsymbol{\delta}}^*$ are consistent and $\hat{\boldsymbol{\delta}}^*$ is asymptotically efficient,

under $H_1$: ($x^e$ is endogenous), $\hat{\boldsymbol{\delta}}$ is consistent, but $\hat{\boldsymbol{\delta}}^*$ is inconsistent.

Hausman bases his version of the test on $\hat{\boldsymbol{\delta}}$ being the 2SLS estimator and $\hat{\boldsymbol{\delta}}^*$ being the 3SLS estimator. A shortcoming of the procedure is that it requires an arbitrary choice of

---

[25]See Cragg (1967) and the many related studies listed by Judge et al. (1985, pp. 646–653).

[26]Wu (1973), Durbin (1954), Hausman (1978), Nakamura and Nakamura (1981), and Dhrymes (1994).

some equation that does not contain $x^e$ for the test. For instance, consider the exogeneity of $X_{-1}$ in the third equation of Klein's Model I. To apply this test, we must use one of the other two equations.

A single-equation version of the test has been devised by Spencer and Berk (1981). We suppose that $x^e$ appears in equation $j$, so that for the $n$ observations,

$$\mathbf{y}_j = \mathbf{Y}_j\boldsymbol{\gamma}_j + \mathbf{X}_j\boldsymbol{\beta}_j + \mathbf{x}^e\theta + \boldsymbol{\varepsilon}_j$$
$$= [\mathbf{Y}_j, \mathbf{X}_j, \mathbf{x}^e]\boldsymbol{\delta}_j + \boldsymbol{\varepsilon}_j.$$

Then $\hat{\boldsymbol{\delta}}^*$ is the 2SLS estimator, treating $x^e$ as an exogenous variable in the system, whereas $\hat{\boldsymbol{\delta}}$ is the IV estimator based on regressing $\mathbf{y}_j$ on $\hat{\mathbf{Y}}_j, \mathbf{X}_j, \hat{\mathbf{x}}^e$, where the least squares fitted values are based on all the remaining exogenous variables, excluding $\mathbf{x}^e$. The test statistic is then

$$w = (\hat{\boldsymbol{\delta}}^* - \hat{\boldsymbol{\delta}})'\left\{\text{Est. Var}[\hat{\boldsymbol{\delta}}^*] - \text{Est. Var}[\hat{\boldsymbol{\delta}}]\right\}^{-1}(\hat{\boldsymbol{\delta}}^* - \hat{\boldsymbol{\delta}}), \qquad \textbf{(13-35)}$$

which is the Wald statistic based on the difference of the two estimators. The statistic has one degree of freedom. (The extension to a set of variables is direct.)

### Example 13.7  Testing Overidentifying Restrictions

For Klein's Model I, the test statistics and critical values for the chi-squared distribution for the overidentifying restrictions for the three equations are given in Table 13.4. There are 21 observations used to estimate the model and eight predetermined variables. The overidentifying restrictions for the wage equation are rejected by both single-equation tests. There are two possibilities. The equation may well be misspecified. Or, as Liu suggests, in a dynamic model, if there is autocorrelation of the disturbances, then the treatment of lagged endogenous variables as if they were exogenous is a specification error.

The preceding results suggest a specification problem in the third equation of Klein's Model I. To pursue that finding, we now apply the Spencer and Berk procedure to test the exogeneity of $X_{-1}$. The two estimated parameter vectors are

$$\hat{\boldsymbol{\delta}}^* = [1.5003, 0.43886, 0.14667, 0.13040] \text{ (i.e., 2SLS)}$$

and

$$\hat{\boldsymbol{\delta}} = [1.2524, 0.42277, 0.167614, 0.13062].$$

Using the Wald criterion, the chi-squared statistic is 1.3977. Thus, the hypothesis (such as it is) is not rejected.

**TABLE 13.4**  Test Statistics and Critical Values

|  | $\lambda$ | **LR** | $TR^2$ | $K_j^* - M_j$ | Chi-Squared Critical Values | $\chi^2[4]$ |
|---|---|---|---|---|---|---|
| Consumption | 1.499 | 10.48 | 9.21 | 4 | | |
| Investment | 1.086 | 1.81 | 1.90 | 4 | 5% | 9.49 |
| Wages | 2.466 | 30.77 | 13.11 | 4 | 1% | 13.28 |

## 13.9 PROPERTIES OF DYNAMIC MODELS

In models with lagged endogenous variables, the entire previous time path of the exogenous variables and disturbances, not just their current values, determines the current value of the endogenous variables. The intrinsic dynamic properties of the autoregressive model, such as **stability** and the existence of an equilibrium value, are embodied in their autoregressive parameters. In this section, we are interested in long- and short-run multipliers, stability properties, and simulated time paths of the dependent variables.

### 13.9.1 DYNAMIC MODELS AND THEIR MULTIPLIERS

The structural form of a dynamic model is

$$\mathbf{y}_t'\boldsymbol{\Gamma} + \mathbf{x}_t'\mathbf{B} + \mathbf{y}_{t-1}'\boldsymbol{\Phi} = \boldsymbol{\varepsilon}_t'. \tag{13-36}$$

If the model contains additional lags, then we can add additional equations to the system of the form $\mathbf{y}_{t-1}' = \mathbf{y}_{t-1}'$. For example, a model with two periods of lags would be written

$$[\mathbf{y}_t \quad \mathbf{y}_{t-1}]'\begin{bmatrix} \boldsymbol{\Gamma} & \mathbf{0} \\ \mathbf{0} & \mathbf{I} \end{bmatrix} + \mathbf{x}_t'[\mathbf{B} \quad \mathbf{0}] + [\mathbf{y}_{t-1} \quad \mathbf{y}_{t-2}]'\begin{bmatrix} \boldsymbol{\Phi}_1 & \mathbf{I} \\ \boldsymbol{\Phi}_2 & \mathbf{0} \end{bmatrix} = [\boldsymbol{\varepsilon}_t' \quad \mathbf{0}'],$$

which can be treated as a model with only a single lag—this is in the form of (13-36). The reduced form is

$$\mathbf{y}_t' = \mathbf{x}_t'\boldsymbol{\Pi} + \mathbf{y}_{t-1}'\boldsymbol{\Delta} + \mathbf{v}_t',$$

where

$$\boldsymbol{\Pi} = -\mathbf{B}\boldsymbol{\Gamma}^{-1},$$

and

$$\boldsymbol{\Delta} = -\boldsymbol{\Phi}\boldsymbol{\Gamma}^{-1}.$$

From the reduced form,

$$\frac{\partial y_{t,m}}{\partial x_{t,k}} = \Pi_{km}.$$

The short-run effects are the coefficients on the current $x$'s, so $\boldsymbol{\Pi}$ is the matrix of **impact multipliers.** By substituting for $\mathbf{y}_{t-1}$ in (13-36), we obtain

$$\mathbf{y}_t' = \mathbf{x}_t'\boldsymbol{\Pi} + \mathbf{x}_{t-1}'\boldsymbol{\Pi}\boldsymbol{\Delta} + \mathbf{y}_{t-2}'\boldsymbol{\Delta}^2 + (\mathbf{v}_t' + \mathbf{v}_{t-1}'\boldsymbol{\Delta}).$$

(This manipulation can easily be done with the lag operator—see Section 20.2.2—but it is just as convenient to proceed in this fashion for the present.) Continuing this method for the full $t$ periods, we obtain

$$\mathbf{y}_t' = \sum_{s=0}^{t-1}[\mathbf{x}_{t-s}'\boldsymbol{\Pi}\boldsymbol{\Delta}^s] + \mathbf{y}_0'\boldsymbol{\Delta}^t + \sum_{s=0}^{t-1}\mathbf{v}_{t-s}'\boldsymbol{\Delta}^s. \tag{13-37}$$

This shows how the **initial conditions, $\mathbf{y}_0$,** and the subsequent time path of the exogenous variables and disturbances completely determine the current values of the endogenous variables. The coefficient matrices in the bracketed sum are the **dynamic multipliers,**

$$\frac{\partial y_{t,m}}{\partial x_{t-s,k}} = (\mathbf{\Pi}\mathbf{\Delta}^s)_{km}.$$

The **cumulative multipliers** are obtained by adding the matrices of dynamic multipliers. If we let $s$ go to infinity in (13-37), then we obtain the **final form** of the model,[27]

$$\mathbf{y}_t' = \sum_{s=0}^{\infty} [\mathbf{x}_{t-s}' \mathbf{\Pi}\mathbf{\Delta}^s] + \sum_{s=0}^{\infty} [\mathbf{v}_{t-s}' \mathbf{\Delta}^s].$$

Assume for the present that $\lim_{t\to\infty} \mathbf{\Delta}^t = \mathbf{0}$. (This says that $\mathbf{\Delta}$ is nilpotent.) Then the matrix of cumulated multipliers in the final form is

$$\mathbf{\Pi}[\mathbf{I} + \mathbf{\Delta} + \mathbf{\Delta}^2 + \cdots] = \mathbf{\Pi}[\mathbf{I} - \mathbf{\Delta}]^{-1}.$$

These coefficient matrices are the long-run or **equilibrium multipliers.** We can also obtain the cumulated multipliers for $s$ periods as

$$\text{cumulative multipliers} = \mathbf{\Pi}[\mathbf{I} - \mathbf{\Delta}]^{-1}[\mathbf{I} - \mathbf{\Delta}^s].$$

Suppose that the values of $\mathbf{x}$ were permanently fixed at $\bar{\mathbf{x}}$. Then the final form shows that if there are no disturbances, the equilibrium value of $\mathbf{y}_t$ would be

$$\bar{\mathbf{y}}' = \sum_{s=0}^{\infty} [\bar{\mathbf{x}}' \mathbf{\Pi}\mathbf{\Delta}^s] = \bar{\mathbf{x}}' \sum_{s=0}^{\infty} \mathbf{\Pi}\mathbf{\Delta}^s = \bar{\mathbf{x}}' \mathbf{\Pi}[\mathbf{I} - \mathbf{\Delta}]^{-1}. \tag{13-38}$$

Therefore, the equilibrium multipliers are

$$\frac{\partial \bar{y}_m}{\partial \bar{x}_k} = [\mathbf{\Pi}(\mathbf{I} - \mathbf{\Delta})^{-1}]_{km}.$$

Some examples are shown later for Klein's Model I.

### 13.9.2 STABILITY

It remains to be shown that the matrix of multipliers in the final form converges. For the analysis to proceed, it is necessary for the matrix $\mathbf{\Delta}^t$ to converge to a zero matrix. Although $\mathbf{\Delta}$ is not a symmetric positive definite matrix, it will still have a spectral decomposition of the form

$$\mathbf{\Delta} = \mathbf{C}\mathbf{\Lambda}\mathbf{C}^{-1}, \tag{13-39}$$

where $\mathbf{\Lambda}$ is a diagonal matrix containing the characteristic roots of $\mathbf{\Delta}$ and each column of $\mathbf{C}$ is a right characteristic vector,

$$\mathbf{\Delta}\mathbf{c}_m = \lambda_m \mathbf{c}_m. \tag{13-40}$$

Because $\mathbf{\Delta}$ is not symmetric, the elements of $\mathbf{\Lambda}$ (and $\mathbf{C}$) may be complex. Nonetheless, (A-105) continues to hold:

$$\mathbf{\Delta}^2 = \mathbf{C}\mathbf{\Lambda}\mathbf{C}^{-1}\mathbf{C}\mathbf{\Lambda}\mathbf{C}^{-1} = \mathbf{C}\mathbf{\Lambda}^2\mathbf{C}^{-1}, \tag{13-41}$$

---

[27] In some treatments, (13-38) is labeled the final form instead. Both forms eliminate the lagged values of the dependent variables from the current value. The dependence of the first form on the initial values may make it simpler to interpret than the second form.

and

$$\boldsymbol{\Delta}^t = \mathbf{C}\boldsymbol{\Lambda}^t\mathbf{C}^{-1}.$$

It is apparent that whether or not $\boldsymbol{\Delta}^t$ vanishes as $t \to \infty$ depends on its characteristic roots. The condition is $|\lambda_m| < 1$. For the case of a complex root, $|\lambda_m| = |a + bi| = \sqrt{a^2 + b^2}$. For a given model, the stability may be established by examining the largest or **dominant root.**

With many endogenous variables in the model but only a few lagged variables, $\boldsymbol{\Delta}$ is a large but sparse matrix. Finding the characteristic roots of large, asymmetric matrices is a rather complex computation problem (although there exists specialized software for doing so). There is a way to make the problem a bit more compact. In the context of an example, in Klein's Model I, $\boldsymbol{\Delta}$ is $6 \times 6$, but with three rows of zeros, it has only rank three and three nonzero roots. (See Table 13.5 in Example 13.8 following.) The following partitioning is useful. Let $\mathbf{y}_{t1}$ be the set of endogenous variables that appear in both current and lagged form, and let $\mathbf{y}_{t2}$ be those that appear only in current form. Then the model may be written

$$[\mathbf{y}'_{t1} \quad \mathbf{y}'_{t2}] = \mathbf{x}'_t[\boldsymbol{\Pi}_1 \quad \boldsymbol{\Pi}_2] + [\mathbf{y}'_{t-1,1} \quad \mathbf{y}'_{t-1,2}]\begin{bmatrix} \boldsymbol{\Delta}_1 & \boldsymbol{\Delta}_2 \\ \mathbf{0} & \mathbf{0} \end{bmatrix} + [\mathbf{v}'_{t1} \quad \mathbf{v}'_{t2}]. \qquad \textbf{(13-42)}$$

The characteristic roots of $\boldsymbol{\Delta}$ are defined by the characteristic polynomial, $|\boldsymbol{\Delta} - \lambda\mathbf{I}| = 0$. For the partitioned model, this result is

$$\begin{vmatrix} \boldsymbol{\Delta}_1 - \lambda\mathbf{I} & \boldsymbol{\Delta}_2 \\ 0 & -\lambda\mathbf{I} \end{vmatrix} = 0.$$

We may use (A-72) to obtain

$$|\boldsymbol{\Delta} - \lambda\mathbf{I}| = (-\lambda)^{M_2}|\boldsymbol{\Delta}_1 - \lambda\mathbf{I}| = 0,$$

where $M_2$ is the number of variables in $\mathbf{y}_2$. Consequently, we need only concern ourselves with the submatrix of $\boldsymbol{\Delta}$ that defines explicit autoregressions. The part of the reduced form defined by $\mathbf{y}'_{t2} = \mathbf{x}'_t\boldsymbol{\Pi}_2 + \mathbf{y}'_{t-1,1}\boldsymbol{\Delta}_2$ is not directly relevant.

### 13.9.3    ADJUSTMENT TO EQUILIBRIUM

The adjustment of a dynamic model to an equilibrium involves the following conceptual experiment. We assume that the exogenous variables $\mathbf{x}_t$ have been fixed at a level $\bar{\mathbf{x}}$ for a long enough time that the endogenous variables have fully adjusted to their equilibrium $\bar{\mathbf{y}}$ [defined in (13-38)]. In some arbitrarily chosen period, labeled period 0, an exogenous one-time shock hits the system, so that in period $t = 0$, $\mathbf{x}_t = \mathbf{x}_0 \neq \bar{\mathbf{x}}$. Thereafter, $\mathbf{x}_t$ returns to its former value $\bar{\mathbf{x}}$, and $\mathbf{x}_t = \bar{\mathbf{x}}$ for all $t > 0$. We know from the expression for the final form that, if disturbed, $\mathbf{y}_t$ will ultimately return to the equilibrium. That situation is ensured by the stability condition. Here we consider the time path of the adjustment. Because our only concern at this point is with the exogenous shock, we will ignore the disturbances in the analysis.

At time 0, $\mathbf{y}'_0 = \mathbf{x}'_0\boldsymbol{\Pi} + \mathbf{y}'_{-1}\boldsymbol{\Delta}$. But prior to time 0, the system was in equilibrium, so $\mathbf{y}'_0 = \mathbf{x}'_0\boldsymbol{\Pi} + \bar{\mathbf{y}}'\boldsymbol{\Delta}$. The initial displacement due to the shock to $\bar{\mathbf{x}}$ is

$$\mathbf{y}'_0 - \bar{\mathbf{y}}' = \mathbf{x}'_0\boldsymbol{\Pi} - \bar{\mathbf{y}}'(\mathbf{I} - \boldsymbol{\Delta}).$$

Substituting $\bar{\mathbf{x}}'\boldsymbol{\Pi} = \bar{\mathbf{y}}'(\mathbf{I} - \boldsymbol{\Delta})$ produces

$$\mathbf{y}_0' - \bar{\mathbf{y}}' = (\mathbf{x}_0' - \bar{\mathbf{x}}')\boldsymbol{\Pi}. \tag{13-43}$$

As might be expected, the initial displacement is determined entirely by the exogenous shock occurring in that period. Because $\mathbf{x}_t = \bar{\mathbf{x}}$ after period 0, (13-37) implies that

$$
\begin{aligned}
\mathbf{y}_t' &= \sum_{s=0}^{t-1} \bar{\mathbf{x}}'\boldsymbol{\Pi}\boldsymbol{\Delta}^s + \mathbf{y}_0'\boldsymbol{\Delta}^t \\
&= \bar{\mathbf{x}}'\boldsymbol{\Pi}(\mathbf{I} - \boldsymbol{\Delta})^{-1}(\mathbf{I} - \boldsymbol{\Delta}^t) + \mathbf{y}_0'\boldsymbol{\Delta}^t \\
&= \bar{\mathbf{y}}' - \bar{\mathbf{y}}'\boldsymbol{\Delta}^t + \mathbf{y}_0'\boldsymbol{\Delta}^t \\
&= \bar{\mathbf{y}}' + (\mathbf{y}_0' - \bar{\mathbf{y}}')\boldsymbol{\Delta}^t.
\end{aligned}
$$

Thus, the entire time path is a function of the initial displacement. By inserting (13-43), we see that

$$\mathbf{y}_t' = \bar{\mathbf{y}}' + (\mathbf{x}_0' - \bar{\mathbf{x}}')\boldsymbol{\Pi}\boldsymbol{\Delta}^t. \tag{13-44}$$

Because $\lim_{t\to\infty}\boldsymbol{\Delta}^t = \mathbf{0}$, the path back to the equilibrium subsequent to the exogenous shock $(\mathbf{x}_0 - \bar{\mathbf{x}})$ is defined. The stability condition imposed on $\boldsymbol{\Delta}$ ensures that if the system is disturbed at some point by a one-time shock, then barring further shocks or disturbances, it will return to its equilibrium. Because $\mathbf{y}_0$, $\bar{\mathbf{x}}$, $\mathbf{x}_0$, and $\boldsymbol{\Pi}$ are fixed for all time, the shape of the path is completely determined by the behavior of $\boldsymbol{\Delta}^t$, which we now examine.

In the preceding section, in (13-39) to (13-42), we used the characteristic roots of $\boldsymbol{\Delta}$ to infer the (lack of) stability of the model. The spectral decomposition of $\boldsymbol{\Delta}^t$ given in (13-41) may be written

$$\boldsymbol{\Delta}^t = \sum_{m=1}^{M} \lambda_m^t \mathbf{c}_m \mathbf{d}_m',$$

where $\mathbf{c}_m$ is the $m$th column of $\mathbf{C}$ and $\mathbf{d}_m'$ is the $m$th row of $\mathbf{C}^{-1}$.[28] Inserting this result in (13-44), gives

$$
\begin{aligned}
(\mathbf{y}_t - \bar{\mathbf{y}})' &= [(\mathbf{x}_0 - \bar{\mathbf{x}})'\boldsymbol{\Pi}] \sum_{m=1}^{M} \lambda_m^t \mathbf{c}_m \mathbf{d}_m' \\
&= \sum_{m=1}^{M} \lambda_m^t [(\mathbf{x}_0 - \bar{\mathbf{x}})'\boldsymbol{\Pi}\mathbf{c}_m \mathbf{d}_m'] = \sum_{m=1}^{M} \lambda_m^t \mathbf{g}_m'.
\end{aligned}
$$

(Note that this equation may involve fewer than $M$ terms, because some of the roots may be zero. For Klein's Model I, $M = 6$, but there are only three nonzero roots.) Because $\mathbf{g}_m$ depends only on the initial conditions and the parameters of the model, the behavior of the time path of $(\mathbf{y}_t - \bar{\mathbf{y}})$ is completely determined by $\lambda_m^t$. In each period, the deviation from the equilibrium is a sum of $M$ terms of powers of $\lambda_m$ times a constant.

---

[28] See Section A.6.9.

(Each variable has its own set of constants.) The terms in the sum behave as follows:

$$\lambda_m \text{ real} > 0, \quad \lambda_m^t \text{ adds a damped exponential term,}$$
$$\lambda_m \text{ real} < 0, \quad \lambda_m^t \text{ adds a damped sawtooth term,}$$
$$\lambda_m \text{ complex,} \quad \lambda_m^t \text{ adds a damped sinusoidal term.}$$

If we write the complex root $\lambda_m = a + bi$ in polar form, then $\lambda = A[\cos B + i \sin B]$, where $A = [a^2 + b^2]^{1/2}$ and $B = \arccos(a / A)$ (in radians), the sinusoidal components each have amplitude $A^t$ and period $2\pi / B$.[29]

***Example 13.8 Dynamic Model***

The 2SLS estimates of the structure and reduced form of Klein's Model I are given in Table 13.5. (Only the nonzero rows of $\hat{\mathbf{\Phi}}$ and $\hat{\mathbf{\Delta}}$ are shown.) For the 2SLS estimates of Klein's Model I, the relevant submatrix of $\hat{\mathbf{\Delta}}$ is

$$\hat{\mathbf{\Delta}}_1 = \begin{array}{c} \begin{matrix} X & P & K \end{matrix} \\ \begin{bmatrix} 0.172 & -0.051 & -0.008 \\ 1.511 & 0.848 & 0.743 \\ -0.287 & -0.161 & 0.818 \end{bmatrix} \end{array} \begin{matrix} X_{-1} \\ P_{-1} \\ K_{-1} \end{matrix}.$$

**TABLE 13.5 2SLS Estimates of Coefficient Matrices in Klein's Model I**

| | | *Equation* | | | | | |
|---|---|---|---|---|---|---|---|
| ***Variable*** | | **C** | **I** | **W^p** | **X** | **P** | **K** |
| $\hat{\mathbf{\Gamma}} =$ | $C$ | 1 | 0 | 0 | −1 | 0 | 0 |
| | $I$ | 0 | 1 | 0 | −1 | 0 | −1 |
| | $W^p$ | −0.810 | 0 | 1 | 0 | 1 | 0 |
| | $X$ | 0 | 0 | −0.439 | 1 | −1 | 0 |
| | $P$ | −0.017 | −0.15 | 0 | 0 | 1 | 0 |
| | $K$ | 0 | 0 | 0 | 0 | 0 | 1 |
| $\hat{\mathbf{B}} =$ | 1 | −16.555 | −20.278 | −1.5 | 0 | 0 | 0 |
| | $W^g$ | −0.810 | 0 | 0 | 0 | 0 | 0 |
| | $T$ | 0 | 0 | 0 | 0 | 1 | 0 |
| | $G$ | 0 | 0 | 0 | −1 | 0 | 0 |
| | $A$ | 0 | 0 | −0.13 | 0 | 0 | 0 |
| $\hat{\mathbf{\Phi}} =$ | $X_{-1}$ | 0 | 0 | −0.147 | 0 | 0 | 0 |
| | $P_{-1}$ | −0.216 | −0.6160 | 0 | 0 | 0 | 0 |
| | $K_{-1}$ | 0 | 0.158 | 0 | 0 | 0 | −1 |
| $\hat{\mathbf{\Pi}} =$ | 1 | 42.80 | 25.83 | 31.63 | 68.63 | 37.00 | 25.83 |
| | $W^g$ | 1.35 | 0.124 | 0.646 | 1.47 | 0.825 | 0.125 |
| | $T$ | −0.128 | −0.176 | −0.133 | −0.303 | −1.17 | −0.176 |
| | $G$ | 0.663 | 0.153 | 0.797 | 1.82 | 1.02 | 0.153 |
| | $A$ | 0.159 | −0.007 | 0.197 | 0.152 | −0.045 | −0.007 |
| $\hat{\mathbf{\Delta}} =$ | $X_{-1}$ | 0.179 | −0.008 | 0.222 | 0.172 | −0.051 | −0.008 |
| | $P_{-1}$ | 0.767 | 0.743 | 0.663 | 1.511 | 0.848 | 0.743 |
| | $K_{-1}$ | −0.105 | −0.182 | −0.125 | −0.287 | −0.161 | 0.818 |

[29] Goldberger (1964, p. 378).

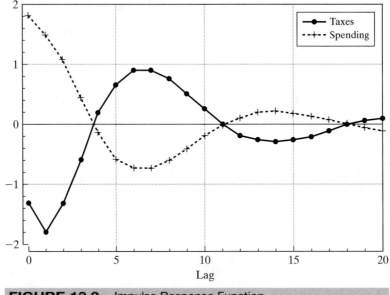

**FIGURE 13.2**   Impulse Response Function.

The characteristic roots of this matrix are 0.2995 and the complex pair $0.7692 \pm 0.3494i = 0.8448$ [cos 0.4263 $\pm i$ sin 0.4263]. The moduli of the complex roots are 0.8448, so we conclude that the model is stable. The period for the oscillations is $2\pi / 0.4263 = 14.73$ periods (years). (See Figure 13.2.)

For a particular variable or group of variables, the various multipliers are submatrices of the multiplier matrices. The dynamic multipliers based on the estimates in Table 13.5 for the effects of the policy variables $T$ and $G$ on output, $X$, are plotted in Figure 13.2 for current and 20 lagged values. A plot of the period multipliers against the lag length is called the **impulse response function.** The policy effects on output are shown in Figure 13.2. The damped sine wave pattern is characteristic of a dynamic system with imaginary roots. When the roots are real, the impulse response function is a monotonically declining function, instead.

This model has the interesting feature that the long-run multipliers of both policy variables for investment are zero. This is intrinsic to the model. The estimated long-run *balanced-budget multiplier* for equal increases in spending and taxes is $2.10 + (-1.48) = 0.62$.

## 13.10   SUMMARY AND CONCLUSIONS

The models surveyed in this chapter involve most of the issues that arise in analysis of linear equations in econometrics. Before one embarks on the process of estimation, it is necessary to establish that the sample data actually contain sufficient information to provide estimates of the parameters in question. This is the question of identification. Identification involves both the statistical properties of estimators and the role of theory in the specification of the model. Once identification is established, there are numerous methods of estimation. We considered a number of single-equation techniques, including least squares, instrumental variables, and maximum likelihood. Fully efficient use of the sample data will require joint estimation of all the equations in the system. Once again, there are several techniques—these are extensions of the single-equation methods including three stage least squares, and full information maximum likelihood. In both frameworks, this is one of those benign situations in which the computationally simplest estimator is generally the most efficient one. In the final section of this chapter, we examined the special properties of dynamic models. An important consideration in this analysis was the stability of the equations. Modern macroeconometrics involves many models in which one or more roots of the dynamic system equal one, so that these models, in the simple autoregressive form are unstable. In terms of the analysis in Section 13.9.3, in such a model, a shock to the system is permanent—the effects do not die out. We will examine a model of monetary policy with these characteristics in Section 20.6.8.

## Key Terms and Concepts

- Admissible
- Behavioral equation
- Causality
- Complete system
- Completeness condition
- Consistent estimators
- Cumulative multiplier
- Dominant root
- Dynamic model
- Dynamic multiplier
- Econometric model
- Endogenous
- Equilibrium condition
- Equilibrium multipliers
- Exactly identified model
- Exclusion restrictions
- Exogenous
- FIML
- Final form
- Full information
- Full information maximum likelihood

- Fully recursive model
- Granger causality
- Identification
- Impact multiplier
- Impulse response function
- Indirect least squares
- Initial conditions
- Instrumental variable estimator
- Interdependent
- Jointly dependent
- $k$ class
- Least variance ratio
- Limited information
- LIML
- Nonlinear systems
- Nonsample information
- Nonstructural
- Normalization
- Observationally equivalent
- Order condition
- Overidentification

- Predetermined variable
- Problem of identification
- Rank condition
- Recursive model
- Reduced form
- Reduced form disturbance
- Restrictions
- Simultaneous equations bias
- Specification test
- Stability
- Strongly exogenous
- Structural disturbance
- Structural equation
- Structural form
- System methods of estimation
- Three-stage least squares
- Triangular system
- Two-stage least squares
- Underidentified
- Weak instruments
- Weakly exogenous

## Exercises

1. Consider the following two-equation model:

$$y_1 = \gamma_1 y_2 + \beta_{11} x_1 + \beta_{21} x_2 + \beta_{31} x_3 + \varepsilon_1,$$
$$y_2 = \gamma_2 y_1 + \beta_{12} x_1 + \beta_{22} x_2 + \beta_{32} x_3 + \varepsilon_2.$$

a. Verify that, as stated, neither equation is identified.

b. Establish whether or not the following restrictions are sufficient to identify (or partially identify) the model:

(1) $\beta_{21} = \beta_{32} = 0$,

(2) $\beta_{12} = \beta_{22} = 0$,

(3) $\gamma_1 = 0$,

(4) $\gamma_1 = \gamma_2$ and $\beta_{32} = 0$,

(5) $\sigma_{12} = 0$ and $\beta_{31} = 0$,

(6) $\gamma_1 = 0$ and $\sigma_{12} = 0$,

(7) $\beta_{21} + \beta_{22} = 1$,

(8) $\sigma_{12} = 0$, $\beta_{21} = \beta_{22} = \beta_{31} = \beta_{32} = 0$,

(9) $\sigma_{12} = 0$, $\beta_{11} = \beta_{21} = \beta_{22} = \beta_{31} = \beta_{32} = 0$.

2. Verify the rank and order conditions for identification of the second and third behavioral equations in Klein's Model I.

3. Check the identifiability of the parameters of the following model:

$$
[y_1 \quad y_2 \quad y_3 \quad y_4]
\begin{bmatrix}
1 & \gamma_{12} & 0 & 0 \\
\gamma_{21} & 1 & \gamma_{23} & \gamma_{24} \\
0 & \gamma_{32} & 1 & \gamma_{34} \\
\gamma_{41} & \gamma_{42} & 0 & 1
\end{bmatrix}
$$

$$
+ [x_1 \quad x_2 \quad x_3 \quad x_4 \quad x_5]
\begin{bmatrix}
0 & \beta_{12} & \beta_{13} & \beta_{14} \\
\beta_{21} & 1 & 0 & \beta_{24} \\
\beta_{31} & \beta_{32} & \beta_{33} & 0 \\
0 & 0 & \beta_{43} & \beta_{44} \\
0 & \beta_{52} & 0 & 0
\end{bmatrix}
= [\varepsilon_1 \quad \varepsilon_2 \quad \varepsilon_3 \quad \varepsilon_4].
$$

4. Obtain the reduced form for the model in Exercise 1 under each of the assumptions made in parts a and in parts b1 and b9.

5. The following model is specified:

$$y_1 = \gamma_1 y_2 + \beta_{11} x_1 + \varepsilon_1,$$

$$y_2 = \gamma_2 y_1 + \beta_{22} x_2 + \beta_{32} x_3 + \varepsilon_2.$$

All variables are measured as deviations from their means. The sample of 25 observations produces the following matrix of sums of squares and cross products:

|       | $y_1$ | $y_2$ | $x_1$ | $x_2$ | $x_3$ |
|-------|-------|-------|-------|-------|-------|
| $y_1$ | 20    | 6     | 4     | 3     | 5     |
| $y_2$ | 6     | 10    | 3     | 6     | 7     |
| $x_1$ | 4     | 3     | 5     | 2     | 3     |
| $x_2$ | 3     | 6     | 2     | 10    | 8     |
| $x_3$ | 5     | 7     | 3     | 8     | 15    |

a. Estimate the two equations by OLS.
b. Estimate the parameters of the two equations by 2SLS. Also estimate the asymptotic covariance matrix of the 2SLS estimates.
c. Obtain the LIML estimates of the parameters of the first equation.
d. Estimate the two equations by 3SLS.
e. Estimate the reduced form coefficient matrix by OLS and indirectly by using your structural estimates from part b.

6. For the model

$$y_1 = \gamma_1 y_2 + \beta_{11} x_1 + \beta_{21} x_2 + \varepsilon_1,$$

$$y_2 = \gamma_2 y_1 + \beta_{32} x_3 + \beta_{42} x_4 + \varepsilon_2,$$

show that there are two restrictions on the reduced form coefficients. Describe a procedure for estimating the model while incorporating the restrictions.

7. An updated version of Klein's Model I was estimated. The relevant submatrix of $\Delta$ is

$$\Delta_1 = \begin{bmatrix} -0.1899 & -0.9471 & -0.8991 \\ 0 & 0.9287 & 0 \\ -0.0656 & -0.0791 & 0.0952 \end{bmatrix}.$$

Is the model stable?

8. Prove that

$$\text{plim} \frac{\mathbf{Y}'_j \boldsymbol{\varepsilon}_j}{T} = \boldsymbol{\omega}_j - \boldsymbol{\Omega}_{jj} \boldsymbol{\gamma}_j.$$

9. Prove that an underidentified equation cannot be estimated by 2SLS.

## Application

The data in Appendix Table F5.1 may be used to estimate a small macroeconomic model. Use these data to estimate the model in Example 13.1. Estimate the parameters of the two equations by two-stage and three-stage least squares. Then, using the two-stage least squares results, examine the dynamic properties of the model. Using the results in Section 13.9, determine if the dominant root of the system is less than one.

# 14

# ESTIMATION FRAMEWORKS IN ECONOMETRICS

## 14.1 INTRODUCTION

This chapter begins our treatment of methods of estimation. Contemporary econometrics offers the practitioner a remarkable variety of estimation methods, ranging from tightly parameterized likelihood-based techniques at one end to thinly stated nonparametric methods that assume little more than mere association between variables at the other, and a rich variety in between. Even the experienced researcher could be forgiven for wondering how they should choose from this long menu. It is certainly beyond our scope to answer this question here, but a few principles can be suggested. Recent research has leaned when possible toward methods that require few (or fewer) possibly unwarranted or improper assumptions. This explains the ascendance of the GMM estimator in situations where strong likelihood-based parameterizations can be avoided and robust estimation can be done in the presence of heteroscedasticity and serial correlation. (It is intriguing to observe that this is occurring at a time when advances in computation have helped bring about *increased* acceptance of very heavily parameterized Bayesian methods.)

As a general proposition, the progression from full to semi- to non-**parametric estimation** relaxes strong assumptions, but at the cost of weakening the conclusions that can be drawn from the data. As much as anywhere else, this is clear in the analysis of discrete choice models, which provide one of the most active literatures in the field. (A sampler appears in Chapter 23.) A formal probit or logit model allows estimation of probabilities, marginal effects, and a host of ancillary results, but at the cost of imposing the normal or logistic distribution on the data. **Semiparametric** and **nonparametric estimators** allow one to relax the restriction, but often provide, in return, only ranges of probabilities, if that, and in many cases, preclude estimation of probabilities or useful marginal effects. One does have the virtue of robustness in the conclusions, however. [See, e.g., the symposium in Angrist (2001) for a spirited discussion on these points.]

Estimation properties is another arena in which the different approaches can be compared. Within a class of estimators, one can define "the best" (most efficient) means of using the data. (See Example 14.2 for an application.) Sometimes comparisons can be made across classes as well. For example, when they are estimating the same parameters—this remains to be established—the best parametric estimator will generally outperform the best semiparametric estimator. That is the value of the information, of course. The other side of the comparison, however, is that the semiparametric estimator will carry the day if the parametric model is misspecified in a fashion to which the semiparametric estimator is robust (and the parametric model is not).

Schools of thought have entered this conversation for a long time. Proponents of **Bayesian estimation** often took an almost theological viewpoint in their criticism of their classical colleagues. [See, for example, Poirier (1995).] Contemporary practitioners are usually more pragmatic than this. Bayesian estimation has gained currency as a set of techniques that can, in very many cases, provide both elegant and tractable solutions to problems that have heretofore been out of reach. Thus, for example, the **simulation-based estimation** advocated in the many papers of Chib and Greenberg (e.g., 1996) have provided solutions to a variety of computationally challenging problems.[1] Arguments as to the methodological virtue of one approach or the other have received much less attention than before.

Chapters 2 through 7 and 11 of this book have focused on the classical regression model and a particular estimator, least squares (linear and nonlinear). In this and the next four chapters, we will examine several general estimation strategies that are used in a wide variety of situations. This chapter will survey a few methods in the three broad areas we have listed. Chapter 15 discusses the **generalized method of moments,** which has emerged as the centerpiece of semiparametric estimation. Chapter 16 presents the method of **maximum likelihood,** the broad platform for parametric, classical estimation in econometrics. Chapter 17 discusses simulation-based estimation and bootstrapping. This is a recently developed body of techniques that have been made feasible by advances in estimation technology and which has made quite straightforward many estimators which were previously only scarcely used because of the sheer difficulty of the computations. Finally, Chapter 18 introduces the methods of Bayesian econometrics.

The list of techniques presented here is far from complete. We have chosen a set that constitute the mainstream of econometrics. Certainly there are others that might be considered. [See, for example, Mittelhammer, Judge, and Miller (2000) for a lengthy catalog.] Virtually all of them are the subject of excellent monographs on the subject. In this chapter we will present several applications, some from the literature, some home grown, to demonstrate the range of techniques that are current in econometric practice. We begin in Section 14.2 with parametric approaches, primarily maximum likelihood. Because this is the subject of much of the remainder of this book, this section is brief. Section 14.2 also introduces Bayesian estimation, which in its traditional form, is as heavily parameterized as maximum likelihood estimation. Section 14.3 is on semiparametric estimation. GMM estimation is the subject of all of Chapter 15, so it is only introduced here. The technique of least absolute deviations is presented here as well. A range of applications from the recent literature is also surveyed. Section 14.4 describes nonparametric estimation. The fundamental tool, the kernel density estimator is developed, then applied to a problem in regression analysis. Two applications are presented here as well. Being focused on application, this chapter will say very little about the

---

[1]The penetration of Bayesian econometrics could be overstated. It is fairly well represented in current journals such as the *Journal of Econometrics, Journal of Applied Econometrics, Journal of Business and Economic Statistics,* and so on. On the other hand, in the six major general treatments of econometrics published in 2000, four (Hayashi, Ruud, Patterson, Davidson) do not mention Bayesian methods at all, a buffet of 32 essays (Baltagi) devotes only one to the subject, and the one that displays any preference (Mittelhammer et al.) devotes nearly 10 percent (70) of its pages to Bayesian estimation, but all to the broad metatheory or the linear regression model and none to the more elaborate applications that form the received applications in the many journals in the field.

statistical theory for of these techniques—such as their asymptotic properties. (The results are developed at length in the literature, of course.) We will turn to the subject of the properties of estimators briefly at the end of the chapter, in Section 14.5, then in greater detail in Chapters 15 through 18.

## 14.2 PARAMETRIC ESTIMATION AND INFERENCE

Parametric estimation departs from a full statement of the **density** or probability model that provides the **data-generating mechanism** for a random variable of interest. For the sorts of applications we have considered thus far, we might say that the joint density of a scalar random variable, "$y$" and a random vector, "$\mathbf{x}$" of interest can be specified by

$$f(y, \mathbf{x}) = g(y \mid \mathbf{x}, \boldsymbol{\beta}) \times h(\mathbf{x} \mid \boldsymbol{\theta}), \tag{14-1}$$

with unknown parameters $\boldsymbol{\beta}$ and $\boldsymbol{\theta}$. To continue the application that has occupied us since Chapter 2, consider the linear regression model with normally distributed disturbances. The assumption produces a full statement of the **conditional density** that is the population from which an observation is drawn;

$$y_i \mid \mathbf{x}_i \sim N[\mathbf{x}_i' \boldsymbol{\beta}, \sigma^2].$$

All that remains for a full definition of the population is knowledge of the specific values taken by the *unknown* but *fixed* parameters. With those in hand, the conditional probability distribution for $y_i$ is completely defined—mean, variance, probabilities of certain events, and so on. (The marginal density for the conditioning variables is usually not of particular interest.) Thus, the signature features of this modeling platform are specifications of both the density and the features (parameters) of that density.

The **parameter space** for the parametric model is the set of allowable values of the parameters that satisfy some prior specification of the model. For example, in the regression model specified previously, the $K$ regression slopes may take any real value, but the variance must be a positive number. Therefore, the parameter space for that model is $[\boldsymbol{\beta}, \sigma^2] \in \mathbb{R}^K \times \mathbb{R}_+$. "Estimation" in this context consists of specifying a criterion for ranking the points in the parameter space, then choosing that point (a point estimate) or a set of points (an interval estimate) that optimizes that criterion, that is, has the best ranking. Thus, for example, we chose linear least squares as one **estimation criterion** for the linear model. "Inference" in this setting is a process by which some regions of the (already specified) parameter space are deemed not to contain the unknown parameters, though, in more practical terms, we typically define a criterion and then, state that, by that criterion, certain regions are *unlikely* to contain the true parameters.

### 14.2.1 CLASSICAL LIKELIHOOD-BASED ESTIMATION

The most common (by far) class of parametric estimators used in econometrics is the maximum likelihood estimators. The underlying philosophy of this class of estimators is the idea of "sample information." When the density of a sample of observations is completely specified, apart from the unknown parameters, then the joint density of those observations (assuming they are independent), is the **likelihood function**

$$f(y_1, y_2, \ldots, \mathbf{x}_1, \mathbf{x}_2, \ldots) = \prod_{i=1}^{n} f(y_i, \mathbf{x}_i \mid \boldsymbol{\beta}, \boldsymbol{\theta}). \qquad \textbf{(14-2)}$$

This function contains all the information available in the sample about the population from which those observations were drawn. The strategy by which that information is used in estimation constitutes the estimator.

The **maximum likelihood estimator** [Fisher (1925)] is the function of the data that (as its name implies) maximizes the likelihood function (or, because it is usually more convenient, the log of the likelihood function). The motivation for this approach is most easily visualized in the setting of a discrete random variable. In this case, the likelihood function gives the joint probability for the observed sample observations, and the maximum likelihood estimator is the function of the sample information that makes the observed data most probable (at least by that criterion). Though the analogy is most intuitively appealing for a discrete variable, it carries over to continuous variables as well. Since this estimator is the subject of Chapter 16, which is quite lengthy, we will defer any formal discussion until then, and consider instead two applications to illustrate the techniques and underpinnings.

### Example 14.1   The Linear Regression Model
Least squares weighs negative and positive deviations equally and gives disproportionate weight to large deviations in the calculation. This property can be an advantage or a disadvantage, depending on the data-generating process. For normally distributed disturbances, this method is precisely the one needed to use the data most efficiently. If the data are generated by a normal distribution, then the log of the likelihood function is

$$\ln L = -\frac{n}{2}\ln 2\pi - \frac{n}{2}\ln \sigma^2 - \frac{1}{2\sigma^2}(\mathbf{y} - \mathbf{X}\boldsymbol{\beta})'(\mathbf{y} - \mathbf{X}\boldsymbol{\beta}).$$

You can easily show that least squares is the estimator of choice for this model. Maximizing the function means minimizing the exponent, which is done by least squares for $\beta$, then $\mathbf{e}'\mathbf{e}/n$ follows as the estimator for $\sigma^2$.

If the appropriate distribution is deemed to be something other than normal—perhaps on the basis of an observation that the tails of the disturbance distribution are too thick—see Example 4.9 and Section 16.9.5.a—then there are three ways one might proceed. First, as we have observed, the consistency of least squares is robust to this failure of the specification, so long as the conditional mean of the disturbances is still zero. Some correction to the standard errors is necessary for proper inferences. Second, one might want to proceed to an estimator with better finite sample properties. The least absolute deviations estimator discussed in Section 14.3.2 is a candidate. Finally, one might consider some other distribution which accommodates the observed discrepancy. For example, Ruud (2000) examines in some detail a linear regression model with disturbances distributed according to the $t$ distribution with $v$ degrees of freedom. As long as $v$ is finite, this random variable will have a larger variance than the normal. Which way should one proceed? The third approach is the least appealing. Surely if the normal distribution is inappropriate, then it would be difficult to come up with a plausible mechanism whereby the $t$ distribution would not be. The LAD estimator might well be preferable if the sample were small. If not, then least squares would probably remain the estimator of choice, with some allowance for the fact that standard inference tools would probably be misleading. Current practice is generally to adopt the first strategy.

### Example 14.2   The Stochastic Frontier Model

The **stochastic frontier** model, discussed in detail in Section 16.9.5.a, is a regression-like model with a disturbance distribution that is asymmetric and distinctly nonnormal. (See Figure 16.4.) The conditional density for the dependent variable in this model is

$$f(y \mid \mathbf{x}, \beta, \sigma, \lambda) = \frac{\sqrt{2}}{\sigma\sqrt{\pi}} \exp\left[\frac{-(y - \alpha - \mathbf{x}'\beta)^2}{2\sigma^2}\right] \Phi\left(\frac{-\lambda(y - \alpha - \mathbf{x}'\beta)}{\sigma}\right).$$

This produces a log-likelihood function for the model,

$$\ln L = -n \ln \sigma - \frac{n}{2}\ln\frac{2}{\pi} - \frac{1}{2}\sum_{i=1}^{n}\left(\frac{\varepsilon_i}{\sigma}\right)^2 + \sum_{i=1}^{n}\ln\Phi\left(\frac{-\lambda\varepsilon_i}{\sigma}\right).$$

There are at least two fully parametric estimators for this model. The maximum likelihood estimator is discussed in Section 16.9.5.a. Greene (2007) presents the following **method of moments** estimator: For the regression slopes, excluding the constant term, use least squares. For the parameters $\alpha, \sigma$, and $\lambda$, based on the second and third moments of the least squares residuals and least squares constant, solve

$$m_2 = \sigma_v^2 + [1 - 2/\pi]\sigma_u^2,$$

$$m_3 = (2/\pi)^{1/2}[1 - 4/\pi]\sigma_u^3,$$

$$a = \alpha + (2/\pi)^2\sigma_u,$$

where $\lambda = \sigma_u/\sigma_v$ and $\sigma^2 = \sigma_u^2 + \sigma_v^2$.

Both estimators are fully parametric. The maximum likelihood estimator is for the reasons discussed earlier. The method of moments estimators (see Section 15.2) are appropriate only for this distribution. Which is preferable? As we will see in Chapter 16, both estimators are consistent and asymptotically normally distributed. By virtue of the Cramér–Rao theorem, the maximum likelihood estimator has a smaller asymptotic variance. Neither has any small sample optimality properties. Thus, the only virtue of the method of moments estimator is that one can compute it with any standard regression/statistics computer package and a hand calculator whereas the maximum likelihood estimator requires specialized software (only somewhat—it is reasonably common).

### 14.2.2   MODELING JOINT DISTRIBUTIONS WITH COPULA FUNCTIONS

Specifying the likelihood function commits the analyst to a possibly strong assumption about the distribution of the random variable of interest. The payoff, of course, is the stronger inferences that this permits. However, when there are more than one random variable of interest, such as in a joint household decision on health care usage in the example to follow, formulating the full likelihood involves specifying the marginal distributions, which might be comfortable, and a full specification of the joint distribution, which is likely to be less so. In the typical situation, the model might involve two similar random variables and an ill-formed specification of correlation between them. Implicitly, this case involves specification of the marginal distributions. The joint distribution is an empirical necessity to allow the correlation to be nonzero. The **copula function** approach provides a mechanism that the researcher can use to steer around this situation.

Trivedi and Zimmer (2007) suggest a variety of applications that fit this description:

• Financial institutions are often concerned with the prices of different, related (dependent) assets. The typical multivariate normality assumption is problematic because of GARCH effects (see Section 19.13) and thick tails in the distributions. While specifying appropriate marginal distributions may be reasonably straightforward, specifying the joint distribution is anything but that. Klugman and Parsa (2000) is an application.

- There are many microeconometric applications in which straightforward marginal distributions cannot be readily combined into a natural joint distribution. The bivariate event count model analyzed in Munkin and Trivedi (1999) and in the next example is an application.

- In the linear self-selection model of Chapter 24, the necessary joint distribution is part of a larger model. The likelihood function for the observed outcome involves the joint distribution of a variable of interest, hours, wages, income, etc., and the probability of observation. The typical application is based on a joint normal distribution. Smith (2003, 2005) suggests some applications in which a flexible copula representation is more appropriate. [In an intriguing early application of copula modeling that was not labeled as such, since it greatly predates the econometric literature, Lee (1983) modeled the outcome variable in a selectivity model as normal, the observation probability as logistic, and the connection between them using what amounted to the "Gaussian" copula function shown next.]

Although the antecedents in the statistics literature date to Sklar's (1973) derivations, the applications in econometrics and finance are quite recent, with most applications appearing since 2000. [See the excellent survey by Trivedi and Zimmer (2007) for an extensive description.]

Consider a modeling problem in which the marginal cdfs of two random variables can be fully specified as $F_1(y_1 \mid \bullet)$ and $F_2(y_2 \mid \bullet)$, where we condition on sample information (data) and parameters denoted "$\bullet$." For the moment, assume these are continuous random variables that obey all the axioms of probability. The bivariate cdf is $F_{12}(y_1, y_2 \mid \bullet)$. A (bivariate) copula function (the results also extend to multivariate functions) is a function $C(u_1, u_2)$ defined over the unit square $[(0 \leq u_1 \leq 1) \times (0 \leq u_2 \leq 1)]$ that satisfies

(1)  $C(1, u_2) = u_2$ and $C(u_1, 1) = u_1$,

(2)  $C(0, u_2) = C(u_1, 0) = 0$,

(3)  $\partial C(u_1, u_2)/\partial u_1 \geq 0$ and $\partial C(u_1, u_2)/\partial u_2 \geq 0$.

These are properties of bivariate cdfs for random variables $u_1$ and $u_2$ that are bounded in the unit square. It follows that the copula function is a two-dimensional cdf defined over the unit square that has one-dimensional marginal distributions that are standard uniform in the unit interval [that is, property (1)]. To make profitable use of this relationship, we note that the cdf of a random variable, $F_1(y_1 \mid \bullet)$, is, itself, a uniformly distributed random variable. This is the **fundamental probability transform** that we use for generating random numbers. (See Section 17.2.) In **Sklar's** (1973) **theorem,** the marginal cdfs play the roles of $u_1$ and $u_2$. The theorem states that there exists a copula function, $C(.,.)$ such that

$$F_{12}(y_1, y_2 \mid \bullet) = C[F_1(y_1 \mid \bullet), F_2(y_2 \mid \bullet)].$$

If $F_{12}(y_1, y_2 \mid \bullet) = C[F_1(y_1 \mid \bullet), F_2(y_2 \mid \bullet)]$ is continuous and if the marginal cdfs have quantile (inverse) functions $F_j^{-1}(u_j)$ where $0 \leq u_j \leq 1$, then the copula function can be expressed as

$$F_{12}(y_1, y_2 \mid \bullet) = F_{12}[F_1^{-1}(u_1 \mid \bullet), F_2^{-1}(u_2 \mid \bullet)]$$
$$= \text{Prob}[U_1 \leq u_1, U_2 \leq u_2]$$
$$= C(u_1, u_2).$$

In words, the theorem implies that the joint density can be written as the copula function evaluated at the two cumulative probability functions.

Copula functions allow the analyst to assemble joint distributions when only the marginal distributions can be specified. To fill in the desired element of correlation between the random variables, the copula function is written

$$F_{12}(y_1, y_2 \mid \bullet) = C[F_1(y_1 \mid \bullet), F_2(y_2 \mid \bullet), \theta],$$

where $\theta$ is a "dependence parameter." For continuous random variables, the joint pdf is then the mixed partial derivative,

$$f_{12}(y_1, y_2 \mid \bullet) = c_{12}[F_1(y_1 \mid \bullet), F_2(y_2 \mid \bullet), \theta]$$
$$= \partial^2 C[F_1(y_1 \mid \bullet), F_2(y_2 \mid \bullet), \theta]/\partial y_1 \partial y_2 \qquad \textbf{(14-3)}$$
$$= [\partial^2 C(., ., \theta)/\partial F_1 \partial F_2] f_1(y_1 \mid \bullet) f_2(y_2 \mid \bullet).$$

A log-likelihood function can now be constructed using the logs of the right-hand sides of (14-3). Taking logs of (14-3) reveals the utility of the copula approach. The contribution of the joint observation to the log likelihood is

$$\ln f_{12}(y_1, y_2 \mid \bullet) = \ln[\partial^2 C(., ., \theta)/\partial F_1 \partial F_2] + \ln f_1(y_1 \mid \bullet) + \ln f_2(y_2 \mid \bullet).$$

Some of the common copula functions that have been used in applications are as follows:

Product: $\quad C[u_1, u_2, \theta] = u_1 \times u_2,$

FGM: $\quad C[u_1, u_2, \theta] = u_1 u_2[1 + \theta(1 - u_1)(1 - u_2)],$

Gaussian: $\quad C[u_1, u_2, \theta] = \Phi_2[\Phi^{-1}(u_1), \Phi^{-1}(u_2), \theta],$

Clayton: $\quad C[u_1, u_2, \theta] = [u_1^{-\theta} + u_2^{-\theta} - 1]^{-1/\theta},$

Frank: $\quad C[u_1, u_2, \theta] = \dfrac{1}{\theta} \ln\left[1 + \dfrac{\exp(\theta u_1 - 1)\exp(\theta u_2 - 1)}{\exp(\theta) - 1}\right].$

The product copula implies that the random variables are independent, because it implies that the joint cdf is the product of the marginals. In the FGM (Fairlie, Gumbel, Morgenstern) copula, it can be seen that $\theta = 0$ implies the product copula, or independence. The same result can be shown for the Clayton copula. In the Gaussian function, the copula is the bivariate normal cdf if the marginals happen to be normal to begin with. The essential point is that the marginals need not be normal to construct the copula function, so long as the marginal cdfs can be specified. (The dependence parameter is not the correlation between the variables. Trivedi and Zimmer provide transformations of $\theta$ that are closely related to correlations for each copula function listed.)

The essence of the copula technique is that the researcher can specify and analyze the marginals and the copula functions separately. The likelihood function is obtained by formulating the cdfs [or the densities, because the differentiation in (14-3) will reduce the joint density to a convenient function of the marginal densities] and the copula.

**Example 14.3  Joint Modeling of a Pair of Event Counts**

The standard regression modeling approach for a random variable, $y$, that is a count of events is the Poisson regression model,

$$\text{Prob}[Y = y \mid \mathbf{x}] = \exp(-\lambda)\lambda^y / y!, \text{ where } \lambda = \exp(\mathbf{x}'\beta), y = 0, 1, \dots.$$

More intricate specifications use the negative binomial model (version 2, NB2),

$$\text{Prob}[Y = y \mid \mathbf{x}] = \frac{\Gamma(y+\alpha)}{\Gamma(\alpha)\Gamma(y+1)} \left( \frac{\alpha}{\lambda+\alpha} \right)^{\alpha} \left( \frac{\lambda}{\lambda+\alpha} \right)^{y}, y = 0, 1, \dots,$$

where $\alpha$ is an overdispersion parameter. (See Chapter 25.) A satisfactory, appropriate specification for bivariate outcomes has been an ongoing topic of research. Early suggestions were based on a latent mixture model,

$$y_1 = z + w_1,$$

$$y_2 = z + w_2,$$

where $w_1$ and $w_2$ have the Poisson or NB2 distributions specified earlier with conditional means $\lambda_1$ and $\lambda_2$ and $z$ is taken to be an unobserved Poisson or NB variable. This formulation induces correlation between the variables, but is unsatisfactory because that correlation must be positive. In a natural application, $y_1$ is doctor visits and $y_2$ is hospital visits. These could be negatively correlated. Munkin and Trivedi (1999) specified the jointness in the conditional mean functions, in the form of latent, common heterogeneity;

$$\lambda_j = \exp(\mathbf{x}_j'\beta_j + \varepsilon)$$

where $\varepsilon$ is common to the two functions. Cameron et al. (2004) used a bivariate copula approach to analyze Australian data on self reported and actual physician visits (the latter maintained by the Health Insurance Commission). They made two adjustments to the model we developed above. First, they adapted the basic copula formulation to these discrete random variables. Second, the variable of interest to them was not the actual or self-reported count, but the difference. Both of these are straightforward modifications of the basic copula model.

## 14.3  SEMIPARAMETRIC ESTIMATION

Semiparametric estimation is based on fewer assumptions than parametric estimation. In general, the distributional assumption is removed, and an estimator is devised from certain more general characteristics of the population. Intuition suggests two (correct) conclusions. First, the semiparametric estimator will be more robust than the parametric estimator—it will retain its properties, notably consistency across a greater range of specifications. Consider our most familiar example. The least squares slope estimator is consistent whenever the data are well behaved and the disturbances and the regressors are uncorrelated. This is even true for the frontier function in Example 14.2, which has an asymmetric, nonnormal disturbance. But, second, this robustness comes at a cost. The distributional assumption usually makes the preferred estimator more efficient than a robust one. The best robust estimator in its class will usually be inferior to the parametric estimator when the assumption of the distribution is correct. Once again, in the frontier function setting, least squares may be robust for the slopes, and it is the most efficient estimator that uses only the orthogonality of the disturbances and the regressors, but it will be inferior to the maximum likelihood estimator when the two-part normal distribution is the correct assumption.

### 14.3.1 GMM ESTIMATION IN ECONOMETRICS

Recent applications in economics include many that base estimation on the **method of moments.** The generalized method of moments departs from a set of model based moment equations, $E[\mathbf{m}(y_i, \mathbf{x}_i, \boldsymbol{\beta})] = \mathbf{0}$, where the set of equations specifies a relationship known to hold in the population. We used one of these in the preceding paragraph. The least squares estimator can be motivated by noting that the essential assumption is that $E[\mathbf{x}_i(y_i - \mathbf{x}_i'\boldsymbol{\beta})] = \mathbf{0}$. The estimator is obtained by seeking a parameter estimator, $\mathbf{b}$, which mimics the population result; $(1/n)\Sigma_i[\mathbf{x}_i(y_i - \mathbf{x}_i'\mathbf{b})] = \mathbf{0}$. These are, of course, the normal equations for least squares. Note that the estimator is specified without benefit of any distributional assumption. Method of moments estimation is the subject of Chapter 15, so we will defer further analysis until then.

### 14.3.2 LEAST ABSOLUTE DEVIATIONS ESTIMATION

Least squares can be severely distorted by outlying observations. Recent applications in microeconomics and financial economics involving thick-tailed disturbance distributions, for example, are particularly likely to be affected by precisely these sorts of observations. (Of course, in those applications in finance involving hundreds of thousands of observations, which are becoming commonplace, this discussion is moot.) These applications have led to the proposal of "robust" estimators that are unaffected by outlying observations.[2] In this section, we will examine one of these, the least absolute deviations, or LAD estimator.

That least squares gives such large weight to large deviations from the regression causes the results to be particularly sensitive to small numbers of atypical data points when the sample size is small or moderate. The **least absolute deviations** (LAD) estimator has been suggested as an alternative that remedies (at least to some degree) the problem. The LAD estimator is the solution to the optimization problem,

$$\text{Min}_{\mathbf{b}_0} \sum_{i=1}^{n} |y_i - \mathbf{x}_i'\mathbf{b}_0|.$$

The LAD estimator's history predates least squares (which itself was proposed over 200 years ago). It has seen little use in econometrics, primarily for the same reason that Gauss's method (LS) supplanted LAD at its origination; LS is vastly easier to compute. Moreover, in a more modern vein, its statistical properties are more firmly established than LAD's and samples are usually large enough that the small sample advantage of LAD is not needed.

---

[2]For some applications, see Taylor (1974), Amemiya (1985, pp. 70–80), Andrews (1974), Koenker and Bassett (1978), and a survey written at a very accessible level by Birkes and Dodge (1993). A somewhat more rigorous treatment is given by Hardle (1990).

The LAD estimator is a special case of the quantile regression:

$$\text{Prob}[y_i \leq \mathbf{x}_i'\boldsymbol{\beta}] = q.$$

The LAD estimator estimates the *median regression*. That is, it is the solution to the quantile regression when $q = 0.5$. Koenker and Bassett (1978, 1982), Huber (1967), and Rogers (1993) have analyzed this regression.[3] Their results suggest an estimator for the asymptotic covariance matrix of the **quantile regression** estimator,

$$\text{Est. Asy. Var}[\mathbf{b}_q] = (\mathbf{X}'\mathbf{X})^{-1}\mathbf{X}'\mathbf{D}\mathbf{X}(\mathbf{X}'\mathbf{X})^{-1},$$

where $\mathbf{D}$ is a diagonal matrix containing weights

$$d_i = \left[\frac{q}{f(0)}\right]^2 \text{ if } y_i - \mathbf{x}_i'\boldsymbol{\beta} \text{ is positive and } \left[\frac{1-q}{f(0)}\right]^2 \text{ otherwise,}$$

and $f(0)$ is the true density of the disturbances evaluated at $0$.[4] [It remains to obtain an estimate of $f(0)$.] There is a useful symmetry in this result. Suppose that the true density were normal with variance $\sigma^2$. Then the preceding would reduce to $\sigma^2(\pi/2)(\mathbf{X}'\mathbf{X})^{-1}$, which is the result we used in Example 17.4 to compare estimates of the median and the mean in a simple situation of random sampling. For more general cases, some other empirical estimate of $f(0)$ is going to be required. Nonparametric methods of density estimation are available [see Section 14.4 and, e.g., Johnston and DiNardo (1997, pp. 370–375)]. But for the small sample situations in which techniques such as this are most desirable (our application below involves 25 observations), nonparametric kernel density estimation of a single ordinate is optimistic; these are, after all, asymptotic results. But asymptotically, as suggested by Example 17.4, the results begin overwhelmingly to favor least squares. For better or worse, a convenient estimator would be a **kernel density estimator** as described in Section 14.4.1. Looking ahead, the computation would be

$$\hat{f}(0) = \frac{1}{n}\sum_{i=1}^{n}\frac{1}{h}K\left[\frac{e_i}{h}\right]$$

where $h$ is the **bandwidth** (to be discussed shortly), K[.] is a weighting, or kernel function and $e_i, i = 1, \ldots, n$ is the set of residuals. There are no hard and fast rules for choosing $h$; one popular choice is that used by Stata (2006), $h = .9s/n^{1/5}$. The kernel function is likewise discretionary, though it rarely matters much which one chooses; the logit kernel (see Table 14.2) is a common choice.

The **bootstrap** method of inferring statistical properties is well suited for this application. Since the efficacy of the bootstrap has been established for this purpose, the search for a formula for standard errors of the LAD estimator is not really

---

[3]Powell (1984) has extended the LAD estimator to produce a robust estimator for the case in which data on the dependent variable are censored, that is, when negative values of $y_i$ are recorded as zero. See Example 14.7 for discussion and Melenberg and van Soest (1996) for an application. For some related results on other semiparametric approaches to regression, see Butler et al. (1990) and McDonald and White (1993).

[4]Koenker suggests that for independent and identically distributed observations, one should replace $d_i$ with the constant $a = q(1 - q)/[f(F^{-1}(q))]^2 = [.50/f(0)]^2$ for the median (LAD) estimator. This reduces the expression to the true asymptotic covariance matrix, $a(\mathbf{X}'\mathbf{X})^{-1}$. The one given is a sample estimator which will behave the same in large samples. (Personal communication to the author.)

necessary. The bootstrap estimator for the asymptotic covariance matrix can be computed as follows:

$$\text{Est. Var}[\mathbf{b}_{LAD}] = \frac{1}{R}\sum_{r=1}^{R}(\mathbf{b}_{LAD}(r) - \mathbf{b}_{LAD})(\mathbf{b}_{LAD}(r) - \mathbf{b}_{LAD})',$$

where $\mathbf{b}_{LAD}$ is the LAD estimator and $\mathbf{b}_{LAD}(r)$ is the $r$th LAD estimate of $\boldsymbol{\beta}$ based on a sample of $n$ observations, drawn with replacement, from the original data set.

### Example 14.4  LAD Estimation of a Cobb–Douglas Production Function

Zellner and Revankar (1970) proposed a generalization of the Cobb–Douglas production function that allows economies of scale to vary with output. Their statewide data on $Y =$ value added (output), $K =$ capital, $L =$ labor, and $N =$ the number of establishments in the transportation industry are given in Appendix Table F14.1. For this application, estimates of the Cobb–Douglas production function,

$$\ln(Y_i/N_i) = \beta_1 + \beta_2 \ln(K_i/N_i) + \beta_3 \ln(L_i/N_i) + \varepsilon_i,$$

are obtained by least squares and LAD. The standardized least squares residuals shown in Figure 14.1 suggest that two observations (Florida and Kentucky) are outliers by the usual construction. The least squares coefficient vectors with and without these two observations are (2.293, 0.279, 0.927) and (2.205, 0.261, 0.879), respectively, which bears out the suggestion that these two points do exert considerable influence. Table 14.1 presents the LAD estimates of the same parameters, with standard errors based on 500 bootstrap replications. The LAD estimates with and without these two observations are identical, so only the former are presented. Using the simple approximation of multiplying the corresponding OLS standard error by $(\pi/2)^{1/2} = 1.2533$ produces a surprisingly close estimate of the bootstrap estimated standard errors for the two slope parameters (0.102, 0.123) compared with the bootstrap estimates of (0.124, 0.121). The second set of estimated standard errors are based on Koenker's suggested estimator, $.25/f^2(0) = 0.25/1.5467^2 = 0.104502$. The bandwidth and kernel function are those suggested earlier. The results are surprisingly consistent given the small sample size.

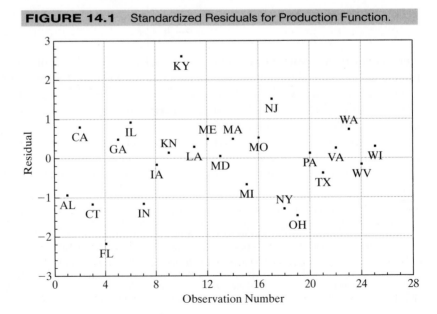

**FIGURE 14.1**  Standardized Residuals for Production Function.

**TABLE 14.1**   LS and LAD Estimates of a Production Function

| | Least Squares | | | LAD | | | | |
| | | | | | Bootstrap | | Kernel Density | |
| Coefficient | Estimate | Standard Error | t Ratio | Estimate | Std. Error | t Ratio | Std. Error | t Ratio |
|---|---|---|---|---|---|---|---|---|
| Constant | 2.293 | 0.107 | 21.396 | 2.275 | 0.202 | 11.246 | 0.183 | 12.374 |
| $\beta_k$ | 0.279 | 0.081 | 3.458 | 0.261 | 0.124 | 2.099 | 0.138 | 1.881 |
| $\beta_l$ | 0.927 | 0.098 | 9.431 | 0.927 | 0.121 | 7.637 | 0.169 | 5.498 |
| $\Sigma e^2$ | 0.7814 | | | 0.7984 | | | | |
| $\Sigma|e|$ | 3.3652 | | | 3.2541 | | | | |

### 14.3.3  PARTIALLY LINEAR REGRESSION

The proper functional form in the linear regression is an important specification issue. We examined this in detail in Chapter 6. Some approaches, including the use of dummy variables, logs, quadratics, and so on, were considered as means of capturing nonlinearity. The translog model in particular (Example 2.4) is a well-known approach to approximating an unknown nonlinear function. Even with these approaches, the researcher might still be interested in relaxing the assumption of functional form in the model. The **partially linear model** [analyzed in detail by Yatchew (1998, 2000)] is another approach. Consider a regression model in which one variable, $x$, is of particular interest, and the functional form with respect to $x$ is problematic. Write the model as

$$y_i = f(x_i) + \mathbf{z}_i'\boldsymbol{\beta} + \varepsilon_i,$$

where the data are assumed to be well behaved and, save for the functional form, the assumptions of the classical model are met. The function $f(x_i)$ remains unspecified. As stated, estimation by least squares is not feasible until $f(x_i)$ is specified. Suppose the data were such that they consisted of pairs of observations $(y_{j1}, y_{j2})$, $j = 1, \ldots, n/2$, in which $x_{j1} = x_{j2}$ within every pair. If so, then estimation of $\boldsymbol{\beta}$ could be based on the simple transformed model

$$y_{j2} - y_{j1} = (\mathbf{z}_{j2} - \mathbf{z}_{j1})'\boldsymbol{\beta} + (\varepsilon_{j2} - \varepsilon_{j1}), \quad j = 1, \ldots, n/2.$$

As long as observations are independent, the constructed disturbances, $v_i$ still have zero mean, variance now $2\sigma^2$, and remain uncorrelated across pairs, so a classical model applies and least squares is actually optimal. Indeed, with the estimate of $\boldsymbol{\beta}$, say, $\hat{\boldsymbol{\beta}}_d$ in hand, a noisy estimate of $f(x_i)$ could be estimated with $y_i - \mathbf{z}_i'\hat{\boldsymbol{\beta}}_d$ (the estimate contains the estimation error as well as $\varepsilon_i$).[5]

The problem, of course, is that the enabling assumption is heroic. Data would not behave in that fashion unless they were generated experimentally. The logic of the partially linear regression estimator is based on this observation nonetheless. Suppose that the observations are sorted so that $x_1 < x_2 < \cdots < x_n$. Suppose, as well, that this variable is well behaved in the sense that as the sample size increases, this sorted data vector more tightly and uniformly fills the space within which $x_i$ is assumed to vary. Then, intuitively, the difference is "almost" right, and becomes better as the sample size

---

[5]See Estes and Honoré (1995) who suggest this approach (with simple differencing of the data).

grows. [Yatchew (1997, 1998) goes more deeply into the underlying theory.] A theory is also developed for a better differencing of groups of two or more observations. The transformed observation is $y_{d,i} = \sum_{m=0}^{M} d_m y_{i-m}$ where $\sum_{m=0}^{M} d_m = 0$ and $\sum_{m=0}^{M} d_m^2 = 1$. (The data are not separated into nonoverlapping groups for this transformation—we merely used that device to motivate the technique.) The pair of weights for $M = 1$ is obviously $\pm\sqrt{0.5}$—this is just a scaling of the simple difference, 1, −1. Yatchew [1998, p. 697)] tabulates "optimal" differencing weights for $M = 1, \ldots, 10$. The values for $M = 2$ are $(0.8090, -0.500, -0.3090)$ and for $M = 3$ are $(0.8582, -0.3832, -0.2809, -0.1942)$. This estimator is shown to be consistent, asymptotically normally distributed, and have asymptotic covariance matrix[6]

$$\text{Asy. Var}[\hat{\boldsymbol{\beta}}_d] = \left(1 + \frac{1}{2M}\right) \frac{\sigma_v^2}{n} E_x[\text{Var}[\mathbf{z} \mid x]].$$

The matrix can be estimated using the sums of squares and cross products of the differenced data. The residual variance is likewise computed with

$$\hat{\sigma}_v^2 = \frac{\sum_{i=M+1}^{n} (y_{d,i} - \mathbf{z}_{d,i}' \hat{\boldsymbol{\beta}}_d)^2}{n - M}.$$

Yatchew suggests that the partial residuals, $y_{d,i} - \mathbf{z}_{d,i}' \hat{\boldsymbol{\beta}}_d$ be smoothed with a kernel density estimator to provide an improved estimator of $f(x_i)$.

### Example 14.5  Partially Linear Translog Cost Function

Yatchew (1998, 2000) applied this technique to an analysis of scale effects in the costs of electricity supply. The cost function, following Nerlove (1963) and Christensen and Greene (1976) was specified to be a translog model (see Example 2.4 and Section 10.4.2) involving labor and capital input prices, other characteristics of the utility and the variable of interest, the number of customers in the system, $C$. We will carry out a similar analysis using Christensen and Greene's 1970 electricity supply data. The data are given in Appendix Table F4.3. (See Section 10.4.1 for description of the data.) There are 158 observations in the data set, but the last 35 are holding companies which are comprised of combinations of the others. In addition, there are several extremely small New England utilities whose costs are clearly unrepresentative of the best practice in the industry. We have done the analysis using firms 6–123 in the data set. Variables in the data set include $Q =$ output, $C =$ total cost, and $PK, PL,$ and $PF =$ unit cost measures for capital, labor, and fuel, respectively. The parametric model specified is a restricted version of the Christensen and Greene model,

$$\ln c = \beta_1 k + \beta_2 l + \beta_3 q + \beta_4(q^2/2) + \beta_5 + \varepsilon.$$

where $c = \ln[C/(Q \times PF)], k = \ln(PK/PF), l = \ln(PL/PF),$ and $q = \ln Q$. The partially linear model substitutes $f(Q)$ for the last three terms. The division by $PF$ ensures that average cost is homogeneous of degree one in the prices, a theoretical necessity. The estimated equations, with estimated standard errors, are shown here.

(parametric)　　$c = -6.83 + 0.168k + 0.146l - 0.590q + 0.061q^2/2 + \varepsilon,$
　　　　　　　　　(0.353)　(0.042)　(0.048)　(0.075)　(0.010) $s = 0.13383$

(partially linear) $c_d =$ 　　　　$0.170k_d + 0.127l_d + f(q) + v$
　　　　　　　　　　　　　　　(0.049)　(0.057)　　　　　　　$s = 0.14044$

---

[6]Yatchew (2000, p. 191) denotes this covariance matrix $E[\text{Cov}[\mathbf{z} \mid x]]$.

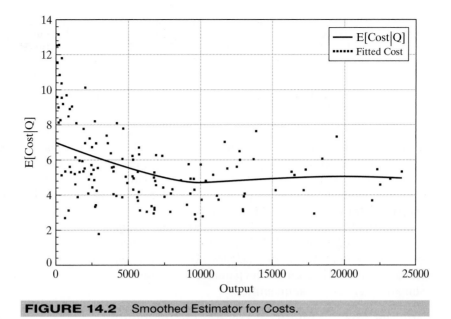

**FIGURE 14.2**   Smoothed Estimator for Costs.

Yatchew's suggested smoothed kernel density estimator for the relationship between average cost and output is shown in Figure 14.2 with the unsmoothed partial residuals. We find (as did Christensen and Greene in the earlier study) that in the relatively low ranges of output, there is a fairly strong relationship between scale and average cost.

### 14.3.4   KERNEL DENSITY METHODS

The kernel density estimator is an inherently nonparametric tool, so it fits more appropriately into the next section. But some models that use kernel methods are not completely nonparametric. The partially linear model in the preceding example is a case in point. Many models retain an index function formulation, that is, build the specification around a linear function, $\mathbf{x}'\boldsymbol{\beta}$, which makes them at least semiparametric, but nonetheless still avoid distributional assumptions by using kernel methods. Lewbel's (2000) estimator for the binary choice model is another example.

*Example 14.6   Semiparametric Estimator for Binary Choice Models*
The core binary choice model analyzed in Section 23.4, the probit model, is a fully parametric specification. Under the assumptions of the model, maximum likelihood is the efficient (and appropriate) estimator. However, as documented in a voluminous literature, the estimator of $\beta$ is fragile with respect to failures of the distributional assumption. We will examine a few semiparametric and nonparametric estimators in Section 23.6. To illustrate the nature of the modeling process, we consider an estimator recently suggested by Lewbel (2000). The probit model is based on the normal distribution, with $\text{Prob}[y_i = 1 \mid \mathbf{x}_i] = \text{Prob}[\mathbf{x}_i'\boldsymbol{\beta} + \varepsilon_i > 0]$ where $\varepsilon_i \sim N[0, 1]$. The estimator of $\beta$ under this specification will be inconsistent if the distribution is not normal or if $\varepsilon_i$ is heteroscedastic. Lewbel suggests the following: If (a) it can be assumed that $\mathbf{x}_i$ contains a "special" variable, $v_i$, whose coefficient has a known sign—a method is developed for determining the sign and (b) the density of $\varepsilon_i$ is independent of this variable, then a consistent estimator of $\beta$ can be obtained by *linear regression* of $[y_i - s(v_i)] / f(v_i \mid \mathbf{x}_i)$ on $\mathbf{x}_i$ where $s(v_i) = 1$ if $v_i > 0$ and $0$ otherwise and $f(v_i \mid \mathbf{x}_i)$ is a kernel density estimator

of the density of $v_i \mid \mathbf{x}_i$. Lewbel's estimator is robust to heteroscedasticity and distribution. A method is also suggested for estimating the distribution of $\varepsilon_i$. Note that Lewbel's estimator is semiparametric. His underlying model is a function of the parameters $\beta$, but the distribution is unspecified.

### 14.3.5 COMPARING PARAMETRIC AND SEMIPARAMETRIC ANALYSES

It is often of interest to compare the outcomes of parametric and semiparametric models. As we have noted earlier, the strong assumptions of the fully parametric model come at a cost; the inferences from the model are only as robust as the underlying assumptions. Of course, the other side of that equation is that when the assumptions are met, parametric models represent efficient strategies for analyzing the data. The alternative, semiparametric approaches relax assumptions such as normality and homoscedasticity. It is important to note that the model extensions to which semiparametric estimators are typically robust render the more heavily parameterized estimators inconsistent. The comparison is not just one of efficiency. As a consequence, comparison of parameter estimates can be misleading—the parametric and semiparametric estimators are often estimating very different quantities.

#### Example 14.7  A Model of Vacation Expenditures

Melenberg and van Soest (1996) analyzed the 1981 vacation expenditures of a sample of 1,143 Dutch families. The important feature of the data that complicated the analysis was that 37 percent (423) of the families reported zero expenditures. A linear regression that ignores this feature of the data would be heavily skewed toward underestimating the response of expenditures to the covariates such as total family expenditures (budget), family size, age, or education. (See Section 24.3.) The standard parametric approach to analyzing data of this sort is the "Tobit," or censored, regression model:

$$y_i^* = \mathbf{x}_i'\beta + \varepsilon_i, \ \varepsilon_i \sim N[0, \sigma^2],$$

$$y_i = \max(0, y_i^*).$$

(Maximum likelihood estimation of this model is examined in detail in Section 24.3.) The model rests on two strong assumptions, normality and homoscedasticity. Both assumptions can be relaxed in a more elaborate parametric framework, but the authors found that test statistics persistently rejected one or both of the assumptions even with the extended specifications. An alternative approach that is robust to both is Powell's (1984, 1986a, b) censored least absolute deviations estimator, which is a more technically demanding computation based on the LAD estimator in Section 14.3.2. Not surprisingly, the parameter estimates produced by the two approaches vary widely. The authors computed a variety of estimators of $\beta$. A useful exercise that they did not undertake would be to compare the partial effects from the different models. This is a benchmark on which the differences between the different estimators can sometimes be reconciled. In the Tobit model, $\partial E[y_i \mid \mathbf{x}_i] / \partial \mathbf{x}_i = \Phi(\mathbf{x}_i'\beta / \sigma)\beta$ (see Section 24.3). It is unclear how to compute the counterpart in the semiparametric model, since the underlying specification holds only that $\text{Med}[\varepsilon_i \mid \mathbf{x}_i] = 0$. (The authors report on the *Journal of Applied Econometrics* data archive site that these data are proprietary. As such, we were unable to extend the analysis to obtain estimates of partial effects.) This highlights a significant difficulty with the semiparametric approach to estimation. In a nonlinear model such as this one, it is often the partial effects that are of interest, not the coefficients. But, one of the byproducts of the more "robust" specification is that the partial effects are undefined.

In a second stage of the analysis, the authors decomposed their expenditure equation into a "participation" equation that modeled probabilities for the binary outcome "expenditure = 0 or > 0" and a conditional expenditure equation for those with positive expenditure. [In Chapter 25, we will label this a "hurdle" model. See Mullahy (1986).] For this step, the authors

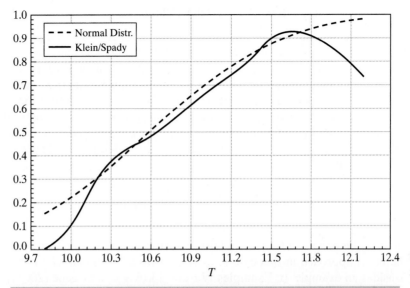

**FIGURE 14.3** Predicted Probabilities of Positive Expenditure.

once again used a parametric model based on the normal distribution (the probit model—see Section 23.3) and a semiparametric model that is robust to distribution and heteroscedasticity developed by Klein and Spady (1993). As before, the coefficient estimates differ substantially. However, in this instance, the specification tests are considerably more sympathetic to the parametric model. Figure 14.3, which reproduces their Figure 2, compares the predicted probabilities from the two models. The dashed curve is the probit model. Within the range of most of the data, the models give quite similar predictions. Once again, however, it is not possible to compare partial effects. The interesting outcome from this part of the analysis seems to be that the failure of the parametric specification resides more in the modeling of the continuous expenditure variable than with the model that separates the two subsamples based on zero or positive expenditures.

## 14.4 NONPARAMETRIC ESTIMATION

Researchers have long held reservations about the strong assumptions made in parametric models fit by maximum likelihood. The linear regression model with normal disturbances is a leading example. Splines, translog models, and polynomials all represent attempts to generalize the functional form. Nonetheless, questions remain about how much generality can be obtained with such approximations. The techniques of nonparametric estimation discard essentially all fixed assumptions about functional form and distribution. Given their very limited structure, it follows that nonparametric specifications rarely provide very precise inferences. The benefit is that what information is provided is extremely robust. The centerpiece of this set of techniques is the kernel density estimator that we have used in the preceding examples. We will examine some examples, then examine an application to a bivariate regression.[7]

---

[7]The set of literature in this area of econometrics is large and rapidly growing. Major references which provide an applied and theoretical foundation are Härdle (1990), Pagan and Ullah (1999), and Li and Racine (2007).

### 14.4.1 KERNEL DENSITY ESTIMATION

Sample statistics such as a mean, variance, and range give summary information about the values that a random variable may take. But, they do not suffice to show the distribution of values that the random variable takes, and these may be of interest as well. The density of the variable is used for this purpose. A fully parametric approach to density estimation begins with an assumption about the form of a distribution. Estimation of the density is accomplished by estimation of the parameters of the distribution. To take the canonical example, if we decide that a variable is generated by a normal distribution with mean $\mu$ and variance $\sigma^2$, then the density is fully characterized by these parameters. It follows that

$$\hat{f}(x) = f(x \mid \hat{\mu}, \hat{\sigma}^2) = \frac{1}{\hat{\sigma}} \frac{1}{\sqrt{2\pi}} \exp\left[-\frac{1}{2}\left(\frac{x - \hat{\mu}}{\hat{\sigma}}\right)^2\right].$$

One may be unwilling to make a narrow distributional assumption about the density. The usual approach in this case is to begin with a **histogram** as a descriptive device. Consider an example. In Examples 17.6 and 23.16 and in Greene (2004a), we estimate a model that produces a conditional estimator of a slope vector for each of the 1,270 firms in our sample. We might be interested in the distribution of these estimators across firms. In particular, the conditional estimates of the estimated slope on ln *sales* for the 1,270 firms have a sample mean of 0.3428, a standard deviation of 0.08919, a minimum of 0.2361 and a maximum of 0.5664. This tells us little about the distribution of values, though the fact that the mean is well below the midrange of .4013 might suggest some skewness. The histogram in Figure 14.4 is much more revealing. Based

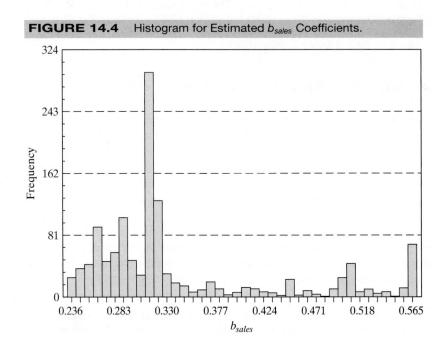

**FIGURE 14.4** Histogram for Estimated $b_{sales}$ Coefficients.

on what we see thus far, an assumption of normality might not be appropriate. The distribution seems to be bimodal, but certainly no particular functional form seems natural.

The histogram is a crude density estimator. The rectangles in the figure are called bins. By construction, they are of equal width. (The parameters of the histogram are the number of bins, the bin width, and the leftmost starting point. Each is important in the shape of the end result.) Because the frequency count in the bins sums to the sample size, by dividing each by $n$, we have a density estimator that satisfies an obvious requirement for a density; it sums (integrates) to one. We can formalize this by laying out the method by which the frequencies are obtained. Let $x_k$ be the midpoint of the $k$th bin and let $h$ be the width of the bin—we will shortly rename $h$ to be the bandwidth for the density estimator. The distance to the left and right boundaries of the bins are $h/2$. The frequency count in each bin is the number of observations in the sample which fall in the range $x_k \pm h/2$. Collecting terms, we have our "estimator"

$$\hat{f}(x) = \frac{1}{n} \frac{\text{frequency in bin}_x}{\text{width of bin}_x} = \frac{1}{n} \sum_{i=1}^{n} \frac{1}{h} \mathbf{1}\left(x - \frac{h}{2} < x_i < x + \frac{h}{2}\right),$$

where $\mathbf{1}(statement)$ denotes an indicator function which equals 1 if the statement is true and 0 if it is false and $\text{bin}_x$ denotes the bin which has $x$ as its midpoint. We see, then, that the histogram is an estimator, at least in some respects, like other estimators we have encountered. The event in the indicator can be rearranged to produce an equivalent form

$$\hat{f}(x) = \frac{1}{n} \sum_{i=1}^{n} \frac{1}{h} \mathbf{1}\left(-\frac{1}{2} < \frac{x_i - x}{h} < \frac{1}{2}\right).$$

This form of the estimator simply counts the number of points that are within one half bin width of $x_k$.

Albeit rather crude, this "naive" (its formal name in the literature) estimator is in the form of **kernel density estimators** that we have met at various points;

$$\hat{f}(x) = \frac{1}{n} \sum_{i=1}^{n} \frac{1}{h} K\left[\frac{x_i - x}{h}\right], \quad \text{where } K[z] = \mathbf{1}[-1/2 < z < 1/2].$$

The naive estimator has several shortcomings. It is neither smooth nor continuous. Its shape is partly determined by where the leftmost and rightmost terminals of the histogram are set. (In constructing a histogram, one often chooses the bin width to be a specified fraction of the sample range. If so, then the terminals of the lowest and highest bins will equal the minimum and maximum values in the sample, and this will partly determine the shape of the histogram. If, instead, the bin width is set irrespective of the sample values, then this problem is resolved.) More importantly, the shape of the histogram will be crucially dependent on the bandwidth itself. (Unfortunately, this problem remains even with more sophisticated specifications.)

The crudeness of the weighting function in the estimator is easy to remedy. Rosenblatt's (1956) suggestion was to substitute for the naive estimator some other weighting function which is continuous and which also integrates to one. A number of

**TABLE 14.2**  Kernels for Density Estimation

| Kernel | Formula K[z] |
|---|---|
| Epanechnikov | $0.75(1 - 0.2z^2)/2.236$ if $|z| \leq 5$, 0 else |
| Normal | $\phi(z)$ (normal density), |
| Logit | $\Lambda(z)[1 - \Lambda(z)]$ (logistic density) |
| Uniform | $0.5$ if $|z| \leq 1$, 0 else |
| Beta | $0.75(1 - z)(1 + z)$ if $|z| \leq 1$, 0 else |
| Cosine | $1 + \cos(2\pi z)$ if $|z| \leq 0.5$, 0 else |
| Triangle | $1 - |z|$, if $|z| \leq 1$, 0 else |
| Parzen | $4/3 - 8z^2 + 8|z|^3$ if $|z| \leq 0.5$, $8(1 - |z|)^3/3$ if $0.5 < |z| \leq 1$, 0 else. |

candidates have been suggested, including the (long) list in Table 14.2. Each of these is smooth, continuous, symmetric, and equally attractive. The logit and normal kernels are defined so that the weight only asymptotically falls to zero whereas the others fall to zero at specific points. It has been observed that in constructing a density estimator, the choice of kernel function is rarely crucial, and is usually minor in importance compared to the more difficult problem of choosing the bandwidth. (The logit and normal kernels appear to be the default choice in many applications.)

The kernel density function is an estimator. For any specific $x$, $\hat{f}(x)$ is a sample statistic,

$$\hat{f}(z) = \frac{1}{n}\sum_{i=1}^{n} g(x_i \mid z, h).$$

Because $g(x_i \mid z, h)$ is nonlinear, we should expect a bias in a finite sample. It is tempting to apply our usual results for sample moments, but the analysis is more complicated because the bandwidth is a function of $n$. Pagan and Ullah (1999) have examined the properties of kernel estimators in detail and found that under certain assumptions, the estimator is consistent and asymptotically normally distributed but biased in finite samples. The bias is a function of the bandwidth but for an appropriate choice of $h$, the bias does vanish asymptotically. As intuition might suggest, the larger is the bandwidth, the greater is the bias, but at the same time, the smaller is the variance. This might suggest a search for an optimal bandwidth. After a lengthy analysis of the subject, however, the authors' conclusion provides little guidance for finding one. One consideration does seem useful. For the proportion of observations captured in the bin to converge to the corresponding area under the density, the width itself must shrink more slowly than $1/n$. Common applications typically use a **bandwidth** equal to some multiple of $n^{-1/5}$ for this reason. Thus, the one we used earlier is $h = 0.9 \times s/n^{1/5}$. To conclude the illustration begun earlier, Figure 14.5 is a logit-based kernel density estimator for the distribution of slope estimates for the model estimated earlier. The resemblance to the histogram in Figure 14.4 is to be expected.

### 14.4.2  NONPARAMETRIC REGRESSION

The regression function of a variable $y$ on a single variable $x$ is specified as

$$y = \mu(x) + \varepsilon.$$

No assumptions about distribution, homoscedasticity, serial correlation or, most importantly, functional form are made at the outset; $\mu(x)$ may be quite nonlinear. Because this is the conditional mean, the only substantive restriction would be that deviations

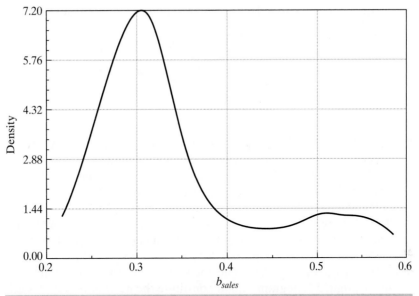

**FIGURE 14.5** Kernel Density for $b_{sales}$ Coefficients.

from the conditional mean function are not a function of (correlated with) $x$. We have already considered several possible strategies for allowing the conditional mean to be nonlinear, including spline functions, polynomials, logs, dummy variables, and so on. But, each of these is a "global" specification. The functional form is still the same for all values of $x$. Here, we are interested in methods that do not assume any particular functional form.

The simplest case to analyze would be one in which several (different) observations on $y_i$ were made with each specific value of $x_i$. Then, the conditional mean function could be estimated naturally using the simple group means. The approach has two shortcomings, however. Simply connecting the points of means, $(x_i, \bar{y} \mid x_i)$ does not produce a smooth function. The method would still be assuming something specific about the function between the points, which we seek to avoid. Second, this sort of data arrangement is unlikely to arise except in an experimental situation. Given that data are not likely to be grouped, another possibility is a piecewise regression in which we define "neighborhoods" of points around each $x$ of interest and fit a separate linear or quadratic regression in each neighborhood. This returns us to the problem of continuity that we noted earlier, but the method of splines is actually designed specifically for this purpose. Still, unless the number of neighborhoods is quite large, such a function is still likely to be crude.

Smoothing techniques are designed to allow construction of an estimator of the conditional mean function without making strong assumptions about the behavior of the function between the points. They retain the usefulness of the **nearest neighbor** concept, but use more elaborate schemes to produce smooth, well behaved functions. The general class may be defined by a conditional mean estimating function

$$\hat{\mu}(x^*) = \sum_{i=1}^{n} w_i(x^* \mid x_1, x_2, \ldots, x_n)y_i = \sum_{i=1}^{n} w_i(x^* \mid \mathbf{x})y_i,$$

where the weights sum to 1. The linear least squares regression line is such an estimator. The predictor is

$$\hat{\mu}(x^*) = a + bx^*,$$

where $a$ and $b$ are the least squares constant and slope. For this function, you can show that

$$w_i(x^* \mid \mathbf{x}) = \frac{1}{n} + \frac{x^*(x_i - \bar{x})}{\sum_{i=1}^{n}(x_i - \bar{x})^2}.$$

The problem with this particular weighting function, which we seek to avoid here, is that it allows every $x_i$ to be in the neighborhood of $x^*$, but it does not reduce the weight of any $x_i$ when it is far from $x^*$. A number of **smoothing functions** have been suggested that are designed to produce a better behaved regression function. [See Cleveland (1979) and Schimek (2000).] We will consider two.

The locally weighted smoothed regression estimator ("loess" or "lowess" depending on your source) is based on explicitly defining a neighborhood of points that is close to $x^*$. This requires the choice of a bandwidth, $h$. The neighborhood is the set of points for which $|x^* - x_i|$ is small. For example, the set of points that are within the range $x^* \pm h/2$ (as in our original histogram) might constitute the neighborhood. A suitable weight is then required. Cleveland (1979) recommends the tricube weight,

$$T_i(x^* \mid \mathbf{x}, h) = \left[ 1 - \left( \frac{|x_i - x^*|}{h} \right)^3 \right]^3.$$

Combining terms, then the weight for the loess smoother is

$$w_i(x^* \mid \mathbf{x}, h) = \mathbf{1}(x_i \text{ in the neighborhood}) \times T_i(x^* \mid \mathbf{x}).$$

As always, the bandwidth is crucial. A wider neighborhood will produce a smoother function. But the wider neighborhood will track the data less closely than a narrower one. A second possibility, similar to the first, is to allow the neighborhood to be all points, but make the weighting function decline smoothly with the distance between $x^*$ and any $x_i$. Any of the kernel functions suggested earlier will serve this purpose. This produces the kernel weighted regression estimator,

$$\hat{\mu}(x^* \mid \mathbf{x}, h) = \frac{\sum_{i=1}^{n} \frac{1}{h} K\left[ \frac{x_i - x^*}{h} \right] y_i}{\sum_{i=1}^{n} \frac{1}{h} K\left[ \frac{x_i - x^*}{h} \right]},$$

which has become a standard tool in nonparametric analysis.

### Example 14.8   A Nonparametric Average Cost Function
In Example 14.5, we fit a partially linear regression for the relationship between average cost and output for electricity supply. Figures 14.6 and Figure 14.7 show the less ambitious nonparametric regressions of average cost on output. The overall picture is the same as in the earlier example. The kernel function is the logit density in both cases. The function in Figure 14.6 uses a bandwidth of 2,000. Because this is a fairly large proportion of the range of variation of output, the function is quite smooth. The regression in Figure 14.7 uses a bandwidth of only 200. The function tracks the data better, but at an obvious cost. The example demonstrates what we and others have noted often; the choice of bandwidth in this exercise is crucial.

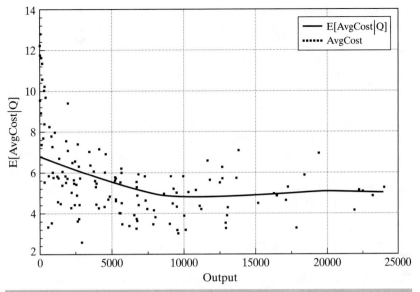

**FIGURE 14.6**　Nonparametric Cost Function.

**FIGURE 14.7**　Nonparametric Cost Function.

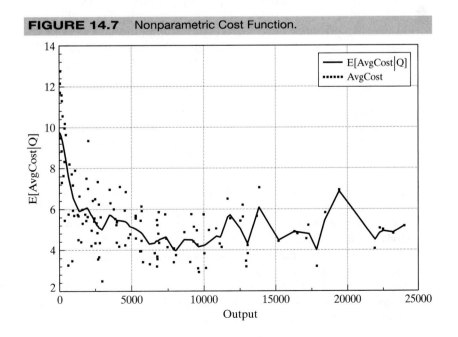

Data smoothing is essentially data driven. As with most nonparametric techniques, inference is not part of the analysis—this body of results is largely descriptive. As can be seen in the example, nonparametric regression can reveal interesting characteristics of the data set. For the econometrician, however, there are a few drawbacks. There is no danger of misspecifying the conditional mean function, for example. But, the great generality of the approach limits the ability to test one's specification or the underlying theory. [See, for example, Blundell, Browning, and Crawford's (2003) extensive study of British expenditure patterns.] Most relationships are more complicated than a simple conditional mean of one variable. In the example just given, some of the variation in average cost relates to differences in factor prices (particularly fuel) and in load factors. Extensions of the fully nonparametric regression to more than one variable is feasible, but very cumbersome. [See Härdle (1990) and Li and Racine (2007).] A promising approach is the partially linear model considered earlier.

## 14.5 PROPERTIES OF ESTIMATORS

The preceding has been concerned with methods of estimation. We have surveyed a variety of techniques that have appeared in the applied literature. We have not yet examined the statistical properties of these estimators. Although, as noted earlier, we will leave extensive analysis of the asymptotic theory for more advanced treatments, it is appropriate to spend at least some time on the fundamental theoretical platform which underlies these techniques.

### 14.5.1 STATISTICAL PROPERTIES OF ESTIMATORS

Properties that we have considered are as follows:

- **Unbiasedness:** This is a finite sample property that can be established in only a very small number of cases. Strict unbiasedness is rarely of central importance outside the linear regression model. However, "asymptotic unbiasedness" (whereby the expectation of an estimator converges to the true parameter as the sample size grows), might be of interest. [See, e.g., Pagan and Ullah (1999, Section 2.5.1 on the subject of the kernel density estimator).] In most cases, however, discussions of asymptotic unbiasedness are actually directed toward consistency, which is a more desirable property.
- **Consistency:** This is a much more important property. Econometricians are rarely willing to place much credence in an estimator for which consistency cannot be established.
- **Asymptotic normality:** This property forms the platform for most of the statistical inference that is done with common estimators. When asymptotic normality cannot be established, it sometimes becomes difficult to find a method of progressing beyond simple presentation of the numerical values of estimates (with caveats). However, most of the contemporary literature in macroeconomics and time-series analysis is strongly focused on estimators that are decidedly not asymptotically normally distributed. The implication is that this property takes its importance only in context, not as an absolute virtue.
- **Asymptotic efficiency:** Efficiency can rarely be established in absolute terms. Efficiency within a class often can, however. Thus, for example, a great deal can

be said about the relative efficiency of maximum likelihood and GMM estimators in the class of consistent and asymptotically normally distributed (CAN) estimators. There are two important practical considerations in this setting. First, the researcher will want to know that he or she has not made demonstrably suboptimal use of the data. (The literature contains discussions of GMM estimation of fully specified parametric probit models—GMM estimation in this context is unambiguously inferior to maximum likelihood.) Thus, when possible, one would want to avoid obviously inefficient estimators. On the other hand, it will usually be the case that the researcher is not choosing from a list of available estimators; he or she has one at hand, and questions of relative efficiency are moot.

### 14.5.2    EXTREMUM ESTIMATORS

An **extremum estimator** is one that is obtained as the optimizer of a **criterion function** $q(\theta \mid \text{data})$. Three that have occupied much of our effort thus far are

- Least squares: $\hat{\theta}_{LS} = \text{Argmax}\left[-(1/n)\sum_{i=1}^{n}(y_i - h(\mathbf{x}_i, \theta_{LS}))^2\right]$,
- Maximum likelihood: $\hat{\theta}_{ML} = \text{Argmax}\left[(1/n)\sum_{i=1}^{n} \ln f(y_i \mid \mathbf{x}_i, \theta_{ML})\right]$, and
- GMM: $\hat{\theta}_{GMM} = \text{Argmax}[-\bar{\mathbf{m}}(\text{data}, \theta_{GMM})'\mathbf{W}\bar{\mathbf{m}}(\text{data}, \theta_{GMM})]$.

(We have changed the signs of the first and third only for convenience so that all three may be cast as the same type of optimization problem.) The least squares and maximum likelihood estimators are examples of **M estimators,** which are defined by optimizing over a sum of terms. Most of the familiar theoretical results developed here and in other treatises concern the behavior of extremum estimators. Several of the estimators considered in this chapter are extremum estimators, but a few—including the Bayesian estimators, some of the semiparametric estimators and all of the nonparametric estimators—are not. Nonetheless. we are interested in establishing the properties of estimators in all these cases, whenever possible. The end result for the practitioner will be the set of statistical properties that will allow him or her to draw with confidence conclusions about the data-generating process(es) that have motivated the analysis in the first place.

Derivations of the behavior of extremum estimators are pursued at various levels in the literature. (See, for example, any of the sources mentioned in Footnote 1 of this chapter.) Amemiya (1985) and Davidson and MacKinnon (2004) are very accessible treatments. Newey and McFadden (1994) is a rigorous analysis that provides a current, standard source. Our discussion at this point will only suggest the elements of the analysis. The reader is referred to one of these sources for detailed proofs and derivations.

### 14.5.3    ASSUMPTIONS FOR ASYMPTOTIC PROPERTIES OF EXTREMUM ESTIMATORS

Some broad results are needed in order to establish the asymptotic properties of the classical (not Bayesian) conventional extremum estimators noted above.

1. **The parameter space** (see Section 14.2) must be convex and the parameter vector that is the object of estimation must be a point in its interior. The first requirement rules out ill-defined estimation problems such as estimating a parameter which can only take one of a finite discrete set of values. Thus, searching for the date of

a structural break in a time-series model as if it were a conventional parameter leads to a nonconvexity. Some proofs in this context are simplified by assuming that the parameter space is compact. (A compact set is closed and bounded.) However, assuming compactness is usually restrictive, so we will opt for the weaker requirement.

2. **The criterion function** must be concave in the parameters. (See Section A.8.2.) This assumption implies that with a given data set, the objective function has an interior optimum and that we can locate it. Criterion functions need not be "globally concave"; they may have multiple optima. But, if they are not at least "locally concave," then we cannot speak meaningfully about optimization. One would normally only encounter this problem in a badly structured model, but it is possible to formulate a model in which the estimation criterion is monotonically increasing or decreasing in a parameter. Such a model would produce a nonconcave criterion function.[8] The distinction between compactness and concavity in the preceding condition is relevant at this point. If the criterion function is strictly continuous in a compact parameter space, then it has a maximum in that set and assuming concavity is not necessary. The problem for estimation, however, is that this does not rule out having that maximum occur on the (assumed) boundary of the parameter space. This case interferes with proofs of consistency and asymptotic normality. The overall problem is solved by assuming that the criterion function is concave in the neighborhood of the true parameter vector.

3. **Identifiability of the parameters.** Any statement that begins with "the true parameters of the model, $\boldsymbol{\theta}_0$ are identified if . . ." is problematic because if the parameters are "not identified" then arguably, they are not *the* parameters of the (any) model. (For example, there is no "true" parameter vector in the unidentified model of Example 2.5.) A useful way to approach this question that avoids the ambiguity of trying to define *the* true parameter vector first and then asking if it is identified (estimable) is as follows, where we borrow from Davidson and MacKinnon (1993, p. 591): Consider the parameterized model, $\boldsymbol{M}$, and the set of allowable data-generating processes for the model, $\mu$. Under a particular parameterization $\mu$, let there be an assumed "true" parameter vector, $\boldsymbol{\theta}(\mu)$. Consider any parameter vector $\boldsymbol{\theta}$ in the parameter space, $\boldsymbol{\Theta}$. Define

$$q_\mu(\mu, \boldsymbol{\theta}) = \text{plim}_\mu q_n(\boldsymbol{\theta} \mid \textbf{data}).$$

This function is the probability limit of the objective function under the assumed parameterization $\mu$. If this probability limit exists (is a finite constant) and moreover, if

$$q_\mu[\mu, \boldsymbol{\theta}(\mu)] > q_\mu(\mu, \boldsymbol{\theta}) \quad \text{if } \boldsymbol{\theta} \neq \boldsymbol{\theta}(\mu),$$

then, if the parameter space is compact, the parameter vector is identified by the criterion function. We have not assumed compactness. For a convex parameter

---

[8]In their Exercise 23.6, Griffiths, Hill, and Judge (1993), based (alas) on the first edition of this text, suggest a probit model for statewide voting outcomes that includes dummy variables for region: Northeast, Southeast, West, and Mountain. One would normally include three of the four dummy variables in the model, but Griffiths et al. carefully dropped two of them because in addition to the dummy variable trap, the Southeast variable is always zero when the dependent variable is zero. Inclusion of this variable produces a nonconcave likelihood function—the parameter on this variable diverges. Analysis of a closely related case appears as a caveat on page 272 of Amemiya (1985).

space, we would require the additional condition that there exist no sequences without limit points $\boldsymbol{\theta}^m$ such that $q(\mu, \boldsymbol{\theta}^m)$ converges to $q[\mu, \boldsymbol{\theta}(\mu)]$.

The approach taken here is to assume first that the model has *some* set of parameters. The identifiability criterion states that assuming this is the case, the probability limit of the criterion is maximized at these parameters. This result rests on convergence of the criterion function to a finite value at any point in the interior of the parameter space. Because the criterion function is a function of the data, this convergence requires a statement of the properties of the data—for example, well behaved in some sense. Leaving that aside for the moment, interestingly, the results to this point already establish the consistency of the M estimator. In what might seem to be an extremely terse fashion, Amemiya (1985) defined identifiability simply as "existence of a consistent estimator." We see that identification and the conditions for consistency of the M estimator are substantively the same.

This form of identification is necessary, in theory, to establish the consistency arguments. In any but the simplest cases, however, it will be extremely difficult to verify in practice. Fortunately, there are simpler ways to secure identification that will appeal more to the intuition:

- For the least squares estimator, a sufficient condition for identification is that any two different parameter vectors, $\boldsymbol{\theta}$ and $\boldsymbol{\theta}_0$, must be able to produce different values of the conditional mean function. This means that for any two different parameter vectors, there must be an $\mathbf{x}_i$ that produces different values of the conditional mean function. You should verify that for the linear model, this is the full rank assumption A.2. For the model in Example 2.5, we have a regression in which $x_2 = x_3 + x_4$. In this case, any parameter vector of the form $(\beta_1, \beta_2 - a, \beta_3 + a, \beta_4 + a)$ produces the same conditional mean as $(\beta_1, \beta_2, \beta_3, \beta_4)$ regardless of $\mathbf{x}_i$, so this model is not identified. The full rank assumption is needed to preclude this problem. For nonlinear regressions, the problem is much more complicated, and there is no simple generality. Example 11.2 shows a nonlinear regression model that is not identified and how the lack of identification is remedied.

- For the maximum likelihood estimator, a condition similar to that for the regression model is needed. For any two parameter vectors, $\boldsymbol{\theta} \neq \boldsymbol{\theta}_0$, it must be possible to produce different values of the density $f(y_i \mid \mathbf{x}_i, \boldsymbol{\theta})$ for some data vector $(y_i, \mathbf{x}_i)$. Many econometric models that are fit by maximum likelihood are "index function" models that involve densities of the form $f(y_i \mid \mathbf{x}_i, \boldsymbol{\theta}) = f(y_i \mid \mathbf{x}_i'\boldsymbol{\theta})$. When this is the case, the same full rank assumption that applies to the regression model may be sufficient. (If there are no other parameters in the model, then it will be sufficient.)

- For the GMM estimator, not much simplicity can be gained. A sufficient condition for identification is that $E[\bar{\mathbf{m}}(\mathbf{data}, \boldsymbol{\theta})] \neq \mathbf{0}$ if $\boldsymbol{\theta} \neq \boldsymbol{\theta}_0$.

4.  **Behavior of the data** has been discussed at various points in the preceding text. The estimators are based on means of functions of observations. (You can see this in all three of the preceding definitions. Derivatives of these criterion functions will likewise be means of functions of observations.) Analysis of their large sample behaviors will turn on determining conditions under which certain sample means of functions of observations will be subject to laws of large numbers such as the Khinchine (D.5) or Chebychev (D.6) theorems, and what must be assumed in order

to assert that "root-$n$" times sample means of functions will obey central limit theorems such as the Lindeberg–Feller (D.19) or Lyapounov (D.20) theorems for cross sections or the Martingale Difference Central Limit theorem for dependent observations (Theorem 19.3). Ultimately, this is the issue in establishing the statistical properties. The convergence property claimed above must occur in the context of the data. These conditions have been discussed in Sections 4.9.1 and 4.9.2 under the heading of "well-behaved data." At this point, we will assume that the data are well behaved.

### 14.5.4 ASYMPTOTIC PROPERTIES OF ESTIMATORS

With all this apparatus in place, the following are the standard results on asymptotic properties of M estimators:

---

**THEOREM 14.1** **Consistency of M Estimators**

*If (a) the parameter space is convex and the true parameter vector is a point in its interior, (b) the criterion function is concave, (c) the parameters are identified by the criterion function, and (d) the data are well behaved, then the M estimator converges in probability to the true parameter vector.*

---

Proofs of consistency of M estimators rely on a fundamental convergence result that, itself, rests on assumptions (a) through (d) in Theorem 14.1. We have assumed identification. The fundamental device is the following: Because of its dependence on the data, $q(\boldsymbol{\theta} \mid \mathbf{data})$ is a random variable. We assumed in (c) that plim $q(\boldsymbol{\theta} \mid \mathbf{data}) = q_0(\boldsymbol{\theta})$ for any point in the parameter space. Assumption (c) states that the maximum of $q_0(\boldsymbol{\theta})$ occurs at $q_0(\boldsymbol{\theta}_0)$, so $\boldsymbol{\theta}_0$ is the maximizer of the probability limit. By its definition, the estimator $\hat{\boldsymbol{\theta}}$, is the maximizer of $q(\boldsymbol{\theta} \mid \mathbf{data})$. Therefore, consistency requires the limit of the maximizer, $\hat{\boldsymbol{\theta}}$ be equal to the maximizer of the limit, $\boldsymbol{\theta}_0$. Our identification condition establishes this. We will use this approach in somewhat greater detail in Section 16.4.5.a where we establish consistency of the maximum likelihood estimator.

---

**THEOREM 14.2** **Asymptotic Normality of M Estimators**

*If*

*(i)* $\hat{\boldsymbol{\theta}}$ *is a consistent estimator of $\boldsymbol{\theta}_0$ where $\boldsymbol{\theta}_0$ is a point in the interior of the parameter space;*

*(ii)* $q(\boldsymbol{\theta} \mid \mathbf{data})$ *is concave and twice continuously differentiable in $\boldsymbol{\theta}$ in a neighborhood of $\boldsymbol{\theta}_0$;*

*(iii)* $\sqrt{n}[\partial q(\boldsymbol{\theta}_0 \mid \mathbf{data})/\partial \boldsymbol{\theta}_0] \xrightarrow{d} N[\mathbf{0},\, \boldsymbol{\Phi}]$;

*(iv)* *for any $\boldsymbol{\theta}$ in $\boldsymbol{\Theta}$,* $\lim_{n\to\infty} \Pr[|(\partial^2 q(\boldsymbol{\theta} \mid \mathbf{data})/\partial\theta_k\partial\theta_m) - h_{km}(\boldsymbol{\theta})| > \varepsilon] = 0\ \forall\ \varepsilon > 0$
*where $h_{km}(\boldsymbol{\theta})$ is a continuous finite valued function of $\boldsymbol{\theta}$;*

*(v)* *the matrix of elements $\mathbf{H}(\boldsymbol{\theta})$ is nonsingular at $\boldsymbol{\theta}_0$, then*
$$\sqrt{n}(\hat{\boldsymbol{\theta}} - \boldsymbol{\theta}_0) \xrightarrow{d} N\{\mathbf{0},\, [\mathbf{H}^{-1}(\boldsymbol{\theta}_0)\boldsymbol{\Phi}\mathbf{H}^{-1}(\boldsymbol{\theta}_0)]\}.$$

---

The proof of asymptotic normality is based on the mean value theorem from calculus and a Taylor series expansion of the derivatives of the maximized criterion function around the true parameter vector;

$$\sqrt{n}\frac{\partial q(\hat{\theta}\mid \mathbf{data})}{\partial \hat{\theta}} = \mathbf{0} = \sqrt{n}\frac{\partial q(\theta_0\mid \mathbf{data})}{\partial \theta_0} + \frac{\partial^2 q(\bar{\theta}\mid \mathbf{data})}{\partial \bar{\theta}\partial \bar{\theta}'}\sqrt{n}(\hat{\theta}-\theta_0).$$

The second derivative is evaluated at a point $\bar{\theta}$ that is between $\hat{\theta}$ and $\theta_0$, that is, $\bar{\theta} = w\hat{\theta} + (1-w)\theta_0$ for some $0 < w < 1$. Because we have assumed plim $\hat{\theta} = \theta_0$, we see that the matrix in the second term on the right must be converging to $\mathbf{H}(\theta_0)$. The assumptions in the theorem can be combined to produce the claimed normal distribution. Formal proof of this set of results appears in Newey and McFadden (1994). A somewhat more detailed analysis based on this theorem appears in Section 16.4.5.b, where we establish the asymptotic normality of the maximum likelihood estimator.

The preceding was restricted to M estimators, so it remains to establish counterparts for the important GMM estimator. Consistency follows along the same lines used earlier, but asymptotic normality is a bit more difficult to establish. We will return to this issue in Chapter 15, where, once again, we will sketch the formal results and refer the reader to a source such as Newey and McFadden (1994) for rigorous derivation.

The preceding results are not straightforward in all estimation problems. For example, the least absolute deviations (LAD) is not among the estimators noted earlier, but it is an M estimator and it shares the results given here. The analysis is complicated because the criterion function is not continuously differentiable. Nonetheless, consistency and asymptotic normality have been established. [See Koenker and Bassett (1982) and Amemiya (1985, pp. 152–154).] Some of the semiparametric and all of the nonparametric estimators noted require somewhat more intricate treatments. For example, Pagan and Ullah (Section 2.5 and 2.6) are able to establish the familiar desirable properties for the kernel density estimator $\hat{f}(x^*)$, but it requires a somewhat more involved analysis of the function and the data than is necessary, say, for the linear regression or binomial logit model. The interested reader can find many lengthy and detailed analyses of asymptotic properties of estimators in, for example, Amemiya (1985), Newey and McFadden (1994), Davidson and MacKinnon (2004) and Hayashi (2000). In practical terms, it is rarely possible to verify the conditions for an estimation problem at hand, and they are usually simply assumed. However, finding violations of the conditions is sometimes more straightforward, and this is worth pursuing. For example, lack of parametric identification can often be detected by analyzing the model itself.

### 14.5.5 TESTING HYPOTHESES

The preceding describes a set of results that (more or less) unifies the theoretical underpinnings of three of the major classes of estimators in econometrics, least squares, maximum likelihood, and GMM. A similar body of theory has been produced for the familiar test statistics, Wald, likelihood ratio (LR), and Lagrange multiplier (LM). [See Newey and McFadden (1994).] All of these have been laid out in practical terms elsewhere in this text, so in the interest of brevity, we will refer the interested reader to the background sources listed for the technical details.

## 14.6 SUMMARY AND CONCLUSIONS

This chapter has presented a short overview of estimation in econometrics. There are various ways to approach such a survey. The current literature can be broadly grouped by three major types of estimators—parametric, semiparametric, and nonparametric. It has been suggested that the overall drift in the literature is from the first toward the third of these, but on a closer look, we see that this is probably not the case. Maximum likelihood is still the estimator of choice in many settings. New applications have been found for the GMM estimator, but at the same time, new Bayesian and simulation estimators, all fully parametric, are emerging at a rapid pace. Certainly, the range of tools that can be applied in any setting is growing steadily.

### Key Terms and Concepts

- Bandwidth
- Bayesian estimation
- Bootstrap
- Conditional density
- Copula function
- Criterion function
- Data generating mechanism
- Density
- Estimation criterion
- Extremum estimator
- Fundamental probability transform
- Generalized method of moments
- Histogram
- Identifiability
- Kernel density estimator
- Least absolute deviations (LAD)
- Likelihood function
- M estimator
- Maximum likelihood estimator
- Method of moments
- Nearest neighbor
- Nonparametric estimators
- Parameter space
- Parametric estimation
- Partially linear model
- Quantile regression
- Semiparametric estimation
- Simulation-based estimation
- Sklar's theorem
- Smoothing function
- Stochastic frontier model

### Exercise and Question

1.  Compare the fully parametric and semiparametric approaches to estimation of a discrete choice model such as the multinomial logit model discussed in Chapter 23. What are the benefits and costs of the semiparametric approach?

### Applications

The following exercises require specific software. The relevant techniques are available in several packages that might be in use, such as SAS, Stata, or LIMDEP. The exercises are suggested as departure points for explorations using a few of the many estimation techniques listed in this chapter.

1.  Using the gasoline market data in Appendix Table F2.2, use the partially linear regression method in Section 14.3.3 to fit an equation of the form

$$\ln(G/Pop) = \beta_1 \ln(Income) + \beta_2 \ln P_{new\ cars} + \beta_3 \ln P_{used\ cars} + g(\ln P_{gasoline}) + \varepsilon$$

2.  To continue the analysis in Question 1, consider a nonparametric regression of $G/Pop$ on the price. Using the nonparametric estimation method in Section 14.4.2, fit the nonparametric estimator using a range of bandwidth values to explore the effect of bandwidth.

3. (You might find it useful to read the early sections of Chapter 24 for this exercise.) The extramarital affairs data analyzed in Section 25.5.2 can be reinterpreted in the context of a binary choice model. The dependent variable in the analysis is a count of events. Using these data, first recode the dependent variable 0 for none and 1 for more than zero. Now, first using the binary probit estimator, fit a binary choice model using the same independent variables as in the example discussed in Section 25.5.2. Then using a semiparametric or nonparametric estimator, estimate the same binary choice model. A model for binary choice can be fit for at least two purposes, for estimation of interesting coefficients or for prediction of the dependent variable. Use your estimated models for these two purposes and compare the two models.

# 15

# MINIMUM DISTANCE ESTIMATION AND THE GENERALIZED METHOD OF MOMENTS

## 15.1 INTRODUCTION

The **maximum likelihood estimator** presented in Chapter 16 is fully efficient among consistent and asymptotically normally distributed estimators, *in the context of the specified parametric model*. The possible shortcoming in this result is that to attain that efficiency, it is necessary to make possibly strong, restrictive assumptions about the distribution, or data-generating process. The generalized method of moments (GMM) estimators discussed in this chapter move away from parametric assumptions, toward estimators that are robust to some variations in the underlying data-generating process.

This chapter will present a number of fairly general results on parameter estimation. We begin with perhaps the oldest formalized theory of estimation, the classical theory of the method of moments. This body of results dates to the pioneering work of Fisher (1925). The use of sample moments as the building blocks of estimating equations is fundamental in econometrics. GMM is an extension of this technique that, as will be clear shortly, encompasses nearly all the familiar estimators discussed in this book. Section 15.2 will introduce the estimation framework with the method of moments. The technique of minimum distance estimation is developed in Section 15.3. Formalities of the GMM estimator are presented in Section 15.4. Section 15.5 discusses hypothesis testing based on moment equations. Major applications, including dynamic panel data models, are described in Section 15.6.

### Example 15.1  Euler Equations and Life Cycle Consumption

One of the most often-cited applications of the GMM principle for estimating econometric models is Hall's (1978) permanent income model of consumption. The original form of the model (with some small changes in notation) posits a hypothesis about the optimizing behavior of a consumer over the life cycle. Consumers are hypothesized to act according to the model:

$$\text{Maximize } E_t \left[ \sum_{\tau=0}^{T-t} \left( \frac{1}{1+\delta} \right)^{\tau} U(c_{t+\tau}) \,|\, \Omega_t \right] \text{ subject to } \sum_{\tau=0}^{T-t} \left( \frac{1}{1+r} \right)^{\tau} (c_{t+\tau} - w_{t+\tau}) = A_t.$$

The information available at time $t$ is denoted $\Omega_t$ so that $E_t$ denotes the expectation formed at time $t$ based on the information set $\Omega_t$. The maximand is the expected discounted stream of future utility from consumption from time $t$ until the end of life at time $T$. The individual's subjective rate of time preference is $\beta = 1/(1+\delta)$. The real rate of interest, $r \geq \delta$ is assumed to be constant. The utility function $U(c_t)$ is assumed to be strictly concave and time separable (as shown in the model). One period's consumption is $c_t$. The intertemporal budget constraint states that the present discounted excess of $c_t$ over earnings, $w_t$, over the lifetime equals total assets $A_t$ not including human capital. In this model, it is claimed that the only source of uncertainty is $w_t$. No assumption is made about the stochastic properties of $w_t$ except that there exists an expected future earnings, $E_t[w_{t+\tau} \mid \Omega_t]$. Successive values are not assumed to be independent and $w_t$ is not assumed to be stationary.

Hall's major "theorem" in the paper is the solution to the optimization problem, which states

$$E_t[U'(c_{t+1}) \mid \Omega_t] = \frac{1+\delta}{1+r} U'(c_t).$$

For our purposes, the major conclusion of the paper is "Corollary 1" which states "No information available in time $t$ apart from the level of consumption, $c_t$, helps predict future consumption, $c_{t+1}$, in the sense of affecting the expected value of marginal utility. In particular, income or wealth in periods $t$ or earlier are irrelevant once $c_t$ is known." We can use this as the basis of a model that can be placed in the GMM framework. To proceed, it is necessary to assume a form of the utility function. A common (convenient) form of the utility function is $U(c_t) = c_t^{1-\alpha}/(1-\alpha)$, which is monotonic, $U' = c_t^{-\alpha} > 0$ and concave, $U''/U' = -\alpha/c_t < 0$. Inserting this form into the solution, rearranging the terms, and reparameterizing it for convenience, we have

$$E_t\left[(1+r)\left(\frac{1}{1+\delta}\right)\left(\frac{c_{t+1}}{c_t}\right)^{-\alpha} - 1 \mid \Omega_t\right] = E_t\left[\beta(1+r)R_{t+1}^\lambda - 1 \mid \Omega_t\right] = 0,$$

where $R_{t+1} = c_{t+1}/c_t$ and $\lambda = -\alpha$.

Hall assumed that $r$ was constant over time. Other applications of this modeling framework [for example, Hansen and Singleton (1982)] have modified the framework so as to involve a forecasted interest rate, $r_{t+1}$. How one proceeds from here depends on what is in the information set. The unconditional mean does not identify the two parameters. The corollary states that the only relevant information in the information set is $c_t$. Given the form of the model, the more natural instrument might be $R_t$. This assumption exactly identifies the two parameters in the model:

$$E_t\left[\left(\beta(1+r_{t+1})R_{t+1}^\lambda - 1\right)\begin{pmatrix}1 \\ R_t\end{pmatrix}\right] = \begin{bmatrix}0 \\ 0\end{bmatrix}.$$

As stated, the model has no testable implications. These two moment equations would exactly identify the two unknown parameters. Hall hypothesized several models involving income and consumption which would overidentify and thus place restrictions on the model.

## 15.2 CONSISTENT ESTIMATION: THE METHOD OF MOMENTS

Sample statistics such as the mean and variance can be treated as simple descriptive measures. In our discussion of estimation in Appendix C, however, we argue that, in general, sample statistics each have a counterpart in the population, for example, the correspondence between the sample mean and the population expected value. The natural (perhaps obvious) next step in the analysis is to use this analogy to justify using the sample "moments" as estimators of these population parameters. What remains to establish is whether this approach is the best, or even a good way to use the sample data to infer the characteristics of the population.

The basis of the **method of moments** is as follows: In random sampling, under generally benign assumptions, a sample statistic will converge in probability to some constant. For example, with i.i.d. random sampling, $\overline{m}_2' = (1/n)\sum_{i=1}^n y_i^2$ will converge in mean square to the variance plus the square of the mean of the random variable, $y_i$. This constant will, in turn, be a function of the unknown parameters of the distribution. To estimate $K$ parameters, $\theta_1, \ldots, \theta_K$, we can compute $K$ such statistics, $\overline{m}_1, \ldots, \overline{m}_K$, whose **probability limits** are known functions of the parameters. These $K$ moments are equated to the $K$ functions, and the functions are inverted to express the parameters as functions of the moments. The moments will be consistent by virtue of a law of large numbers (Theorems D.4–D.9). They will be asymptotically normally distributed by virtue of the Lindeberg–Levy **Central Limit theorem** (D.18). The derived parameter estimators will inherit consistency by virtue of the Slutsky theorem (D.12) and asymptotic normality by virtue of the delta method (Theorem D.21).

This section will develop this technique in some detail, partly to present it in its own right and partly as a prelude to the discussion of the generalized method of moments, or GMM, estimation technique, which is treated in Section 15.4.

### 15.2.1 RANDOM SAMPLING AND ESTIMATING THE PARAMETERS OF DISTRIBUTIONS

Consider independent, identically distributed random sampling from a distribution $f(y \mid \theta_1, \ldots, \theta_K)$ with finite moments up to $E[y^{2K}]$. The **random sample** consists of $n$ observations, $y_1, \ldots, y_n$. The $k$th "raw" or **uncentered moment** is

$$\overline{m}'_k = \frac{1}{n} \sum_{i=1}^{n} y_i^k.$$

By Theorem D.4,

$$E[\overline{m}'_k] = \mu'_k = E\left[y_i^k\right],$$

and

$$\text{Var}[\overline{m}'_k] = \frac{1}{n} \text{Var}\left[y_i^k\right] = \frac{1}{n}\left(\mu'_{2k} - \mu'^2_k\right).$$

By convention, $\mu'_1 = E[y_i] = \mu$. By the Khinchine theorem, D.5,

$$\text{plim } \overline{m}'_k = \mu'_k = E\left[y_i^k\right].$$

Finally, by the Lindeberg–Levy Central Limit theorem,

$$\sqrt{n}(\overline{m}'_k - \mu'_k) \xrightarrow{d} N\left[0, \ \mu'_{2k} - \mu'^2_k\right].$$

In general, $\mu'_k$ will be a function of the underlying parameters. By computing $K$ raw moments and equating them to these functions, we obtain $K$ equations that can (in principle) be solved to provide estimates of the $K$ unknown parameters.

***Example 15.2  Method of Moments Estimator for N[μ, σ²]***
In random sampling from $N[\mu, \sigma^2]$,

$$\text{plim } \frac{1}{n} \sum_{i=1}^{n} y_i = \text{plim } \overline{m}'_1 = E[y_i] = \mu,$$

and

$$\text{plim} \frac{1}{n} \sum_{i=1}^{n} y_i^2 = \text{plim} \, \overline{m}_2' = \text{Var}[y_i] + \mu^2 = \sigma^2 + \mu^2.$$

Equating the right- and left-hand sides of the probability limits gives moment estimators

$$\hat{\mu} = \overline{m}_1' = \overline{y},$$

and

$$\hat{\sigma}^2 = \overline{m}_2' - \overline{m}_1'^2 = \left( \frac{1}{n} \sum_{i=1}^{n} y_i^2 \right) - \left( \frac{1}{n} \sum_{i=1}^{n} y_i \right)^2 = \frac{1}{n} \sum_{i=1}^{n} (y_i - \overline{y})^2.$$

Note that $\hat{\sigma}^2$ is biased, although both estimators are consistent.

Although the moments based on powers of $y$ provide a natural source of information about the parameters, other functions of the data may also be useful. Let $m_k(\cdot)$ be a continuous and differentiable function not involving the sample size $n$, and let

$$\overline{m}_k = \frac{1}{n} \sum_{i=1}^{n} m_k(y_i), \quad k = 1, 2, \ldots, K.$$

These are also "moments" of the data. It follows from Theorem D.4 and the corollary, (D-5), that

$$\text{plim} \, \overline{m}_k = E[m_k(y_i)] = \mu_k(\theta_1, \ldots, \theta_K).$$

We assume that $\mu_k(\cdot)$ involves some of or all the parameters of the distribution. With $K$ parameters to be estimated, the $K$ **moment equations,**

$$\overline{m}_1 - \mu_1(\theta_1, \ldots, \theta_K) = 0,$$

$$\overline{m}_2 - \mu_2(\theta_1, \ldots, \theta_K) = 0,$$

$$\ldots$$

$$\overline{m}_K - \mu_K(\theta_1, \ldots, \theta_K) = 0,$$

provide $K$ equations in $K$ unknowns, $\theta_1, \ldots, \theta_K$. If the equations are continuous and functionally independent, then **method of moments estimators** can be obtained by solving the system of equations for

$$\hat{\theta}_k = \hat{\theta}_k[\overline{m}_1, \ldots, \overline{m}_K].$$

As suggested, there may be more than one set of moments that one can use for estimating the parameters, or there may be more moment equations available than are necessary.

### Example 15.3 *Inverse Gaussian (Wald) Distribution*

The inverse Gaussian distribution is used to model survival times, or elapsed times from some beginning time until some kind of transition takes place. The standard form of the density for this random variable is

$$f(y) = \sqrt{\frac{\lambda}{2\pi y^3}} \exp\left[-\frac{\lambda(y - \mu)^2}{2\mu^2 y}\right], \quad y > 0, \lambda > 0, \mu > 0.$$

The mean is $\mu$ while the variance is $\mu^3/\lambda$. The efficient maximum likelihood estimators of the two parameters are based on $(1/n)\sum_{i=1}^{n} y_i$ and $(1/n)\sum_{i=1}^{n}(1/y_i)$. Because the mean and variance are simple functions of the underlying parameters, we can also use the sample mean and sample variance as moment estimators of these functions. Thus, an alternative pair of method of moments estimators for the parameters of the Wald distribution can be based on $(1/n) \sum_{i=1}^{n} y_i$ and $(1/n) \sum_{i=1}^{n} y_i^2$. The precise formulas for these two pairs of estimators is left as an exercise.

### Example 15.4  Mixtures of Normal Distributions

Quandt and Ramsey (1978) analyzed the problem of estimating the parameters of a mixture of normal distributions. Suppose that each observation in a random sample is drawn from one of two different normal distributions. The probability that the observation is drawn from the first distribution, $N[\mu_1, \sigma_1^2]$, is $\lambda$, and the probability that it is drawn from the second is $(1 - \lambda)$. The density for the observed $y$ is

$$f(y) = \lambda N\left[\mu_1, \sigma_1^2\right] + (1 - \lambda) N\left[\mu_2, \sigma_2^2\right], \quad 0 \le \lambda \le 1$$

$$= \frac{\lambda}{\left(2\pi\sigma_1^2\right)^{1/2}} e^{-1/2[(y-\mu_1)/\sigma_1]^2} + \frac{1 - \lambda}{\left(2\pi\sigma_2^2\right)^{1/2}} e^{-1/2[(y-\mu_2)/\sigma_2]^2}.$$

The sample mean and second through fifth **central moments,**

$$\overline{m}_k = \frac{1}{n} \sum_{i=1}^{n} (y_i - \overline{y})^k, \quad k = 2, 3, 4, 5,$$

provide five equations in five unknowns that can be solved (via a ninth-order polynomial) for consistent estimators of the five parameters. Because $\overline{y}$ converges in probability to $E[y_i] = \mu$, the theorems given earlier for $\overline{m}_k'$ as an estimator of $\mu_k'$ apply as well to $\overline{m}_k$ as an estimator of

$$\mu_k = E[(y_i - \mu)^k].$$

For the mixed normal distribution, the mean and variance are

$$\mu = E[y_i] = \lambda\mu_1 + (1 - \lambda)\mu_2,$$

and

$$\sigma^2 = \text{Var}[y_i] = \lambda\sigma_1^2 + (1 - \lambda)\sigma_2^2 + 2\lambda(1 - \lambda)(\mu_1 - \mu_2)^2,$$

which suggests how complicated the familiar method of moments is likely to become. An alternative method of estimation proposed by the authors is based on

$$E[e^{ty_i}] = \lambda e^{t\mu_1 + t^2\sigma_1^2/2} + (1 - \lambda)e^{t\mu_2 + t^2\sigma_2^2/2} = \Lambda_t,$$

where $t$ is any value not necessarily an integer. Quandt and Ramsey (1978) suggest choosing five values of $t$ that are not too close together and using the statistics

$$\overline{M}_t = \frac{1}{n} \sum_{i=1}^{n} e^{ty_i}$$

to estimate the parameters. The moment equations are $\overline{M}_t - \Lambda_t(\mu_1, \mu_2, \sigma_1^2, \sigma_2^2, \lambda) = 0$. They label this procedure the **method of moment generating functions.** (See Section B.6 for definition of the moment generating function.)

In most cases, method of moments estimators are not efficient. The exception is in random sampling from **exponential families** of distributions.

---

**DEFINITION 15.1**  **Exponential Family**

*An exponential (parametric) family of distributions is one whose log-likelihood is of the form*

$$\ln L(\boldsymbol{\theta} \mid \mathbf{data}) = a(\mathbf{data}) + b(\boldsymbol{\theta}) + \sum_{k=1}^{K} c_k(\mathbf{data})s_k(\boldsymbol{\theta}),$$

*where $a(\cdot)$, $b(\cdot)$, $c_k(\cdot)$, and $s_k(\cdot)$ are functions. The members of the "family" are distinguished by the different parameter values.*

---

If the log-likelihood function is of this form, then the functions $c_k(\cdot)$ are called **sufficient statistics.**[1] When sufficient statistics exist, method of moments estimator(s) can be functions of them. In this case, the method of moments estimators will also be the maximum likelihood estimators, so, of course, they will be efficient, at least asymptotically. We emphasize, in this case, the probability distribution is fully specified. Because the normal distribution is an exponential family with sufficient statistics $\overline{m}'_1$ and $\overline{m}'_2$, the estimators described in Example 15.2 are fully efficient. (They are the maximum likelihood estimators.) The mixed normal distribution is not an exponential family. We leave it as an exercise to show that the Wald distribution in Example 15.3 is an exponential family. You should be able to show that the sufficient statistics are the ones that are suggested in Example 15.3 as the bases for the MLEs of $\mu$ and $\lambda$.

*Example 15.5  Gamma Distribution*

The gamma distribution (see Section B.4.5) is

$$f(y) = \frac{\lambda^P}{\Gamma(P)} e^{-\lambda y} y^{P-1}, \quad y \geq 0, P > 0, \lambda > 0.$$

The log-likelihood function for this distribution is

$$\frac{1}{n} \ln L = [P \ln \lambda - \ln \Gamma(P)] - \lambda \frac{1}{n} \sum_{i=1}^{n} y_i + (P-1) \frac{1}{n} \sum_{i=1}^{n} \ln y_i.$$

This function is an exponential family with $a(\mathbf{data}) = 0$, $b(\boldsymbol{\theta}) = n[P \ln \lambda - \ln \Gamma(P)]$ and two sufficient statistics, $\frac{1}{n} \sum_{i=1}^{n} y_i$ and $\frac{1}{n} \sum_{i=1}^{n} \ln y_i$. The method of moments estimators based on $\frac{1}{n} \sum_{i=1}^{n} y_i$ and $\frac{1}{n} \sum_{i=1}^{n} \ln y_i$ would be the maximum likelihood estimators. But, we also have

$$\text{plim} \frac{1}{n} \sum_{i=1}^{n} \begin{bmatrix} y_i \\ y_i^2 \\ \ln y_i \\ 1/y_i \end{bmatrix} = \begin{bmatrix} P/\lambda \\ P(P+1)/\lambda^2 \\ \Psi(P) - \ln \lambda \\ \lambda/(P-1) \end{bmatrix}.$$

(The functions $\Gamma(P)$ and $\Psi(P) = d \ln \Gamma(P)/dP$ are discussed in Section E.2.3.) Any two of these can be used to estimate $\lambda$ and $P$.

---

[1] Stuart and Ord (1989, pp. 1–29) give a discussion of sufficient statistics and exponential families of distributions. A result that we will use in Chapter 23 is that if the statistics, $c_k(\mathbf{data})$ are sufficient statistics, then the conditional density $f[y_1, \ldots, y_n \mid c_k(\mathbf{data}), k = 1, \ldots, K]$ is not a function of the parameters.

For the income data in Example C.1, the four moments listed earlier are

$$(\overline{m}_1', \overline{m}_2', \overline{m}_*', \overline{m}_{-1}') = \frac{1}{n} \sum_{i=1}^{n} \left[ y_i, y_i^2, \ln y_i, \frac{1}{y_i} \right] = [31.278, 1453.96, 3.22139, 0.050014].$$

The method of moments estimators of $\theta = (P, \lambda)$ based on the six possible pairs of these moments are as follows:

$$(\hat{P}, \hat{\lambda}) = \begin{bmatrix} & \overline{m}_1' & \overline{m}_2' & \overline{m}_{-1}' \\ \overline{m}_2' & 2.05682, 0.065759 & & \\ \overline{m}_{-1}' & 2.77198, 0.0886239 & 2.60905, 0.080475 & \\ \overline{m}_*' & 2.4106, 0.0770702 & 2.26450, 0.071304 & 3.03580, 0.1018202 \end{bmatrix}.$$

The maximum likelihood estimates are $\hat{\theta}(\overline{m}_1', \overline{m}_*') = (2.4106, 0.0770702)$.

## 15.2.2 ASYMPTOTIC PROPERTIES OF THE METHOD OF MOMENTS ESTIMATOR

In a few cases, we can obtain the exact distribution of the method of moments estimator. For example, in sampling from the normal distribution, $\hat{\mu}$ has mean $\mu$ and variance $\sigma^2/n$ and is normally distributed, while $\hat{\sigma}^2$ has mean $[(n-1)/n]\sigma^2$ and variance $[(n-1)/n]^2 2\sigma^4/(n-1)$ and is exactly distributed as a multiple of a chi-squared variate with $(n-1)$ degrees of freedom. If sampling is not from the normal distribution, the exact variance of the sample mean will still be $\text{Var}[y]/n$, whereas an asymptotic variance for the moment estimator of the population variance could be based on the leading term in (D-27), in Example D.10, but the precise distribution may be intractable.

There are cases in which no explicit expression is available for the variance of the underlying sample moment. For instance, in Example 15.4, the underlying sample statistic is

$$\overline{M}_t = \frac{1}{n} \sum_{i=1}^{n} e^{t y_i} = \frac{1}{n} \sum_{i=1}^{n} M_{it}.$$

The exact variance of $\overline{M}_t$ is known only if $t$ is an integer. But if sampling is random, and if $\overline{M}_t$ is a sample mean: we can estimate its variance with $1/n$ times the sample variance of the observations on $M_{it}$. We can also construct an estimator of the covariance of $\overline{M}_t$ and $\overline{M}_s$:

$$\text{Est. Asy. Cov}[\overline{M}_t, \overline{M}_s] = \frac{1}{n} \left\{ \frac{1}{n} \sum_{i=1}^{n} [(e^{t y_i} - \overline{M}_t)(e^{s y_i} - \overline{M}_s)] \right\}.$$

In general, when the moments are computed as

$$\overline{m}_{n,k} = \frac{1}{n} \sum_{i=1}^{n} m_k(\mathbf{y}_i), \quad k = 1, \dots, K,$$

where $\mathbf{y}_i$ is an observation on a vector of variables, an appropriate estimator of the asymptotic covariance matrix of $\overline{\mathbf{m}}_n = [\overline{m}_{n,1}, \dots, \overline{m}_{n,k}]$ can be computed using

$$\frac{1}{n} \mathbf{F}_{jk} = \frac{1}{n} \left\{ \frac{1}{n} \sum_{i=1}^{n} [(m_j(\mathbf{y}_i) - \overline{m}_j)(m_k(\mathbf{y}_i) - \overline{m}_k)] \right\}, \quad j, k = 1, \dots, K.$$

(One might divide the inner sum by $n - 1$ rather than $n$. Asymptotically it is the same.) This estimator provides the asymptotic covariance matrix for the moments used in computing the estimated parameters. Under the assumption of i.i.d. random sampling from a distribution with finite moments, $n\mathbf{F}$ will converge in probability to the appropriate covariance matrix of the normalized vector of moments, $\mathbf{\Phi} = \text{Asy.Var}[\sqrt{n}\,\overline{\mathbf{m}}_n(\boldsymbol{\theta})]$. Finally, under our assumptions of random sampling, although the precise distribution is likely to be unknown, we can appeal to the Lindeberg–Levy Central Limit theorem (D.18) to obtain an asymptotic approximation.

To formalize the remainder of this derivation, refer back to the moment equations, which we will now write

$$\overline{m}_{n,k}(\theta_1, \theta_2, \ldots, \theta_K) = 0, \quad k = 1, \ldots, K.$$

The subscript $n$ indicates the dependence on a data set of $n$ observations. We have also combined the sample statistic (sum) and function of parameters, $\mu(\theta_1, \ldots, \theta_K)$ in this general form of the moment equation. Let $\overline{\mathbf{G}}_n(\boldsymbol{\theta})$ be the $K \times K$ matrix whose $k$th row is the vector of partial derivatives

$$\overline{\mathbf{G}}'_{n,k} = \frac{\partial \overline{m}_{n,k}}{\partial \boldsymbol{\theta}'}.$$

Now, expand the set of solved moment equations around the true values of the parameters $\boldsymbol{\theta}_0$ in a linear **Taylor series.** The linear approximation is

$$\mathbf{0} \approx [\overline{\mathbf{m}}_n(\boldsymbol{\theta}_0)] + \overline{\mathbf{G}}'_n(\boldsymbol{\theta}_0)(\hat{\boldsymbol{\theta}} - \boldsymbol{\theta}_0).$$

Therefore,

$$\sqrt{n}(\hat{\boldsymbol{\theta}} - \boldsymbol{\theta}_0) \approx -[\overline{\mathbf{G}}_n(\boldsymbol{\theta}_0)]^{-1}\sqrt{n}[\overline{\mathbf{m}}_n(\boldsymbol{\theta}_0)]. \tag{15-1}$$

(We have treated this as an approximation because we are not dealing formally with the higher order term in the Taylor series. We will make this explicit in the treatment of the GMM estimator in Section 15.4.) The argument needed to characterize the large sample behavior of the estimator, $\hat{\boldsymbol{\theta}}$, is discussed in Appendix D. We have from Theorem D.18 (the Central Limit theorem) that $\sqrt{n}\,\overline{\mathbf{m}}_n(\boldsymbol{\theta}_0)$ has a limiting normal distribution with mean vector $\mathbf{0}$ and covariance matrix equal to $\mathbf{\Phi}$. Assuming that the functions in the moment equation are continuous and functionally independent, we can expect $\overline{\mathbf{G}}_n(\boldsymbol{\theta}_0)$ to converge to a nonsingular matrix of constants, $\mathbf{\Gamma}(\boldsymbol{\theta}_0)$. Under general conditions, the limiting distribution of the right-hand side of (15-1) will be that of a linear function of a normally distributed vector. Jumping to the conclusion, we expect the asymptotic distribution of $\hat{\boldsymbol{\theta}}$ to be normal with mean vector $\boldsymbol{\theta}_0$ and covariance matrix $(1/n) \times \{-[\mathbf{\Gamma}(\boldsymbol{\theta}_0)]^{-1}\}\mathbf{\Phi}\{-[\mathbf{\Gamma}'(\boldsymbol{\theta}_0)]^{-1}\}$. Thus, the asymptotic covariance matrix for the method of moments estimator may be estimated with

$$\text{Est. Asy. Var}[\hat{\boldsymbol{\theta}}] = \frac{1}{n}[\overline{\mathbf{G}}'_n(\hat{\boldsymbol{\theta}})\mathbf{F}^{-1}\overline{\mathbf{G}}_n(\hat{\boldsymbol{\theta}})]^{-1}.$$

***Example 15.5   (Continued)***
Using the estimates $\hat{\boldsymbol{\theta}}(m'_1, m'_*) = (2.4106, \; 0.0770702)$,

$$\hat{\overline{\mathbf{G}}} = \begin{bmatrix} -1/\hat{\lambda} & \hat{P}/\hat{\lambda}^2 \\ -\hat{\Psi}' & 1/\hat{\lambda} \end{bmatrix} = \begin{bmatrix} -12.97515 & 405.8353 \\ -0.51241 & 12.97515 \end{bmatrix}.$$

[The function $\Psi'$ is $d^2 \ln \Gamma(P)/dP^2 = (\Gamma\Gamma'' - \Gamma'^2)/\Gamma^2$. With $\hat{P} = 2.4106$, $\hat{\Gamma} = 1.250832$, $\hat{\Psi} = 0.658347$, and $\hat{\Psi}' = 0.512408$].[2] The matrix **F** is the sample covariance matrix of $y$ and $\ln y$ (using 19 as the divisor),

$$\mathbf{F} = \begin{bmatrix} 25.034 & 0.7155 \\ 0.7155 & 0.023873 \end{bmatrix}.$$

The product is

$$\frac{1}{n} \left[ \hat{\mathbf{G}}' \mathbf{F}^{-1} \hat{\mathbf{G}} \right]^{-1} = \begin{bmatrix} 0.38978 & 0.014605 \\ 0.014605 & 0.00068747 \end{bmatrix}.$$

For the maximum likelihood estimator, the estimate of the asymptotic covariance matrix based on the expected (and actual) Hessian is

$$\frac{1}{n}[-\mathbf{H}]^{-1} = \frac{1}{n} \begin{bmatrix} \Psi' & -1/\lambda \\ -1/\lambda & P/\lambda^2 \end{bmatrix}^{-1} = \begin{bmatrix} 0.51203 & 0.01637 \\ 0.01637 & 0.00064654 \end{bmatrix}.$$

The Hessian has the same elements as **G** because we chose to use the sufficient statistics for the moment estimators, so the moment equations that we differentiated are, apart from a sign change, also the derivatives of the log-likelihood. The estimates of the two variances are 0.51203 and 0.00064654, respectively, which agrees reasonably well with the method of moments estimates. The difference would be due to sampling variability in a finite sample and the presence of **F** in the first variance estimator.

### 15.2.3 SUMMARY—THE METHOD OF MOMENTS

In the simplest cases, the method of moments is robust to differences in the specification of the data generating process (DGP). A sample mean or variance estimates its population counterpart (assuming it exists), regardless of the underlying process. It is this freedom from unnecessary distributional assumptions that has made this method so popular in recent years. However, this comes at a cost. If more is known about the DGP, its specific distribution for example, then the method of moments may not make use of all of the available information. Thus, in Example 15.3, the natural estimators of the parameters of the distribution based on the sample mean and variance turn out to be inefficient. The method of maximum likelihood, which remains the foundation of much work in econometrics, is an alternative approach which utilizes this out of sample information and is, therefore, more efficient.

## 15.3 MINIMUM DISTANCE ESTIMATION

The preceding analysis has considered **exactly identified cases.** In each example, there were $K$ parameters to estimate and we used $K$ moments to estimate them. In Example 15.5, we examined the gamma distribution, a two-parameter family, and considered different pairs of moments that could be used to estimate the two parameters. (The most efficient estimator for the parameters of this distribution will be based on $(1/n)\Sigma_i y_i$ and $(1/n)\Sigma_i \ln y_i$. This does raise a general question: How should we proceed if we have more moments than we need? It would seem counterproductive to simply discard the

---

[2]$\Psi'$ is the trigamma function. Values for $\Gamma(P)$, $\Psi(P)$, and $\Psi'(P)$ are tabulated in Abramovitz and Stegun (1971). The values given were obtained using the IMSL computer program library.

additional information. In this case, logically, the sample information provides more than one estimate of the model parameters, and it is now necessary to reconcile those competing estimators.

We have encountered this situation in several earlier examples: In Example 9.15, in Passmore's (2005) study of Fannie Mae, we have four independent estimators of a single parameter, $\hat{\alpha}_j$, with estimated asymptotic variance $\hat{V}_j$, $j = 1, \ldots, 4$. The estimators were combined using a **criterion function:**

$$\text{minimize with respect to } \alpha : q = \sum_{j=i}^{4} \frac{(\hat{\alpha}_j - \alpha)^2}{\hat{V}_j}.$$

The solution to this minimization problem is

$$\hat{\alpha}_{\text{MDE}} = \sum_{j=1}^{4} w_j \hat{\alpha}_j, w_j = \frac{1/\hat{V}_j}{\sum_{s=1}^{4}(1/\hat{V}_s)}, j = 1, \ldots, 4 \text{ and } \sum_{j=1}^{4} w_j = 1.$$

In forming the two-stage least squares estimator of the parameters in a dynamic panel data model in Section 12.8.2, we obtained $T - 2$ instrumental variable estimators of the parameter vector $\theta$ by forming different instruments for each period for which we had sufficient data. The $T - 2$ estimators of the same parameter vector are $\hat{\theta}_{\text{IV}(t)}$. The Arellano–Bond estimator of the single parameter vector in this setting is

$$\hat{\theta}_{\text{IV}} = \left( \sum_{t=3}^{T} \mathbf{W}_{(t)} \right)^{-1} \left( \sum_{t=3}^{T} \mathbf{W}_{(t)} \hat{\theta}_{\text{IV}(t)} \right)$$

$$= \sum_{t=3}^{T} \mathbf{R}_{(t)} \hat{\theta}_{\text{IV}(t)},$$

where

$$\mathbf{W}_{(t)} = \left( \hat{\mathbf{X}}'_{(t)} \hat{\mathbf{X}}_{(t)} \right)$$

and

$$\mathbf{R}_{(t)} = \left( \sum_{t=3}^{T} \mathbf{W}_{(t)} \right)^{-1} \mathbf{W}_{(t)} \text{ and } \sum_{t=3}^{T} \mathbf{R}_{(t)} = \mathbf{I}.$$

Finally, Carey's (1997) analysis of hospital costs that we examined in Example 10.6 involved a seemingly unrelated regressions model that produced multiple estimates of several of the model parameters. We will revisit this application in Example 15.6.

A **minimum distance estimator** (MDE) is defined as follows: Let $\overline{m}_{n,l}$ denote a sample statistic based on $n$ observations such that

$$\text{plim } \overline{m}_{n,l} = g_l(\theta_0), l = 1, \ldots, L,$$

where $\theta_0$ is a vector of $K \leq L$ parameters to be estimated. Arrange these moments and functions in $L \times 1$ vectors $\overline{\mathbf{m}}_n$ and $\mathbf{g}(\theta_0)$ and further assume that the statistics are jointly asymptotically normally distributed with plim $\overline{\mathbf{m}}_n = \mathbf{g}(\theta)$ and Asy. $\text{Var}[\overline{\mathbf{m}}_n] = (1/n)\mathbf{\Phi}$.

Define the criterion function

$$q = [\overline{\mathbf{m}}_n - \mathbf{g}(\boldsymbol{\theta})]'\mathbf{W}[\overline{\mathbf{m}}_n - \mathbf{g}(\boldsymbol{\theta})]$$

for a positive definite **weighting matrix, W**. The minimum distance estimator is the $\hat{\boldsymbol{\theta}}_{\text{MDE}}$ that minimizes $q$. Different choices of **W** will produce different estimators, but the estimator has the following properties for any **W**:

---

**THEOREM 15.1** **Asymptotic Distribution of the Minimum Distance Estimator**

*Under the assumption that $\sqrt{n}[\overline{\mathbf{m}}_n - \mathbf{g}(\boldsymbol{\theta}_0)] \xrightarrow{d} N[\mathbf{0}, \boldsymbol{\Phi}]$, the asymptotic properties of the minimum distance estimator are as follows:*

$$\text{plim}\ \hat{\boldsymbol{\theta}}_{\text{MDE}} = \boldsymbol{\theta}_0,$$

$$\text{Asy. Var}\left[\hat{\boldsymbol{\theta}}_{\text{MDE}}\right] = \frac{1}{n}[\boldsymbol{\Gamma}(\boldsymbol{\theta}_0)'\mathbf{W}(\boldsymbol{\Gamma}\boldsymbol{\theta}_0)]^{-1}[\boldsymbol{\Gamma}(\boldsymbol{\theta}_0)'\mathbf{W}\boldsymbol{\Phi}\mathbf{W}\boldsymbol{\Gamma}(\boldsymbol{\theta}_0)][\boldsymbol{\Gamma}(\boldsymbol{\theta}_0)'\mathbf{W}\boldsymbol{\Gamma}(\boldsymbol{\theta}_0)]^{-1}$$

$$= \frac{1}{n}\mathbf{V},$$

*where*

$$\boldsymbol{\Gamma}(\boldsymbol{\theta}_0) = \text{plim}\ \mathbf{G}(\hat{\boldsymbol{\theta}}_{\text{MDE}}) = \text{plim}\frac{\partial \mathbf{g}(\hat{\boldsymbol{\theta}}_{\text{MDE}})}{\partial \hat{\boldsymbol{\theta}}'_{\text{MDE}}},$$

*and*

$$\hat{\boldsymbol{\theta}}_{\text{MDE}} \xrightarrow{a} N\left[\boldsymbol{\theta}_0, \frac{1}{n}\mathbf{V}\right].$$

---

Proofs may be found in Malinvaud (1970) and Amemiya (1985). For our purposes, we can note that the MDE is an extension of the method of moments presented in the preceding section. One implication is that the estimator is consistent for any **W**, but the asymptotic covariance matrix is a function of **W**. This suggests that the choice of **W** might be made with an eye toward the size of the covariance matrix and that there might be an optimal choice. That does indeed turn out to be the case. For minimum distance estimation, the weighting matrix that produces the smallest variance is

$$\text{optimal weighting matrix: } \mathbf{W}^* = \left[Asy.\ Var.\sqrt{n}\{\overline{\mathbf{m}}_n - \mathbf{g}(\boldsymbol{\theta})\}\right]^{-1}$$

$$= \boldsymbol{\Phi}^{-1}.$$

[See Hansen (1982) for discussion.] With this choice of **W**,

$$\text{Asy. Var}\left[\hat{\boldsymbol{\theta}}_{\text{MDE}}\right] = \frac{1}{n}\left[\boldsymbol{\Gamma}(\boldsymbol{\theta}_0)'\boldsymbol{\Phi}^{-1}\boldsymbol{\Gamma}(\boldsymbol{\theta}_0)\right]^{-1},$$

which is the result we had earlier for the method of moments estimator.

The solution to the MDE estimation problem is found by locating the $\hat{\theta}_{\text{MDE}}$ such that

$$\frac{\partial q}{\partial \hat{\theta}_{\text{MDE}}} = -\mathbf{G}(\hat{\theta}_{\text{MDE}})'\mathbf{W}\left[\overline{\mathbf{m}}_n - \mathbf{g}(\hat{\theta}_{\text{MDE}})\right] = \mathbf{0}.$$

An important aspect of the MDE arises in the exactly identified case. If $K$ equals $L$, and if the functions $g_l(\theta)$ are functionally independent, that is, $\mathbf{G}(\theta)$ has full row rank, $K$, then it is possible to solve the moment equations exactly. That is, the minimization problem becomes one of simply solving the $K$ moment equations, $\overline{m}_{n,l} = g_l(\theta_0)$ in the $K$ unknowns, $\hat{\theta}_{\text{MDE}}$. This is the method of moments estimator examined in the preceding section. In this instance, the weighting matrix, $\mathbf{W}$, is irrelevant to the solution, because the MDE will now satisfy the moment equations

$$\left[\overline{\mathbf{m}}_n - \mathbf{g}(\hat{\theta}_{\text{MDE}})\right] = \mathbf{0}.$$

For the examples listed earlier, which are all for **overidentified cases,** the minimum distance estimators are defined by

$$q = \left((\hat{\alpha}_1 - \alpha)\ (\hat{\alpha}_2 - \alpha)\ (\hat{\alpha}_3 - \alpha)\ (\hat{\alpha}_4 - \alpha)\right) \begin{bmatrix} \hat{V}_1 & 0 & 0 & 0 \\ 0 & \hat{V}_2 & 0 & 0 \\ 0 & 0 & \hat{V}_3 & 0 \\ 0 & 0 & 0 & \hat{V}_4 \end{bmatrix}^{-1} \begin{pmatrix} (\hat{\alpha}_1 - \alpha) \\ (\hat{\alpha}_2 - \alpha) \\ (\hat{\alpha}_3 - \alpha) \\ (\hat{\alpha}_4 - \alpha) \end{pmatrix}$$

for Passmore's analysis of Fannie Mae, and

$$q = \left((\mathbf{b}_{\text{IV}(3)} - \theta)\ \cdots\ (\mathbf{b}_{\text{IV}(T)} - \theta)\right)' \begin{bmatrix} \left(\hat{\tilde{\mathbf{X}}}'_{(3)}\hat{\tilde{\mathbf{X}}}_{(3)}\right) & \cdots & \mathbf{0} \\ \vdots & \ddots & \vdots \\ \mathbf{0} & \cdots & \left(\hat{\tilde{\mathbf{X}}}'_{(T)}\hat{\tilde{\mathbf{X}}}_{(T)}\right) \end{bmatrix}^{-1} \begin{pmatrix} (\mathbf{b}_{\text{IV}(3)} - \theta) \\ \vdots \\ (\mathbf{b}_{\text{IV}(T)} - \theta) \end{pmatrix}$$

for the Arellano–Bond estimator of the dynamic panel data model.

### Example 15.6   Minimum Distance Estimation of a Hospital Cost Function

In Carey's (1997) study of hospital costs in Example 10.8, Chamberlain's (1984) seemingly un-related regressions approach to a panel data model produces five period-specific estimates of a parameter vector, $\theta_t$. Some of the parameters are specific to the year while others (it is hypothesized) are common to all five years. There are two specific parameters of interest, $\beta_D$ and $\beta_O$, that are allowed to vary by year, but are each estimated multiple times by the SUR model. We focus on just these parameters. The model states

$$y_{it} = \alpha_i + A_{it} + \beta_{D,t}\,DIS_{it} + \beta_{O,t}\,OUT_{it} + \varepsilon_{it},$$

where

$$\alpha_i = B_i + \Sigma_t \gamma_{D,t}\,DIS_{it} + \Sigma_t \gamma_{O,t}\,OUT_{it} + u_i, t = 1987, \ldots, 1991,$$

$DIS_{it}$ is patient discharges, and $OUT_{it}$ is outpatient visits. (We are changing Carey's notation slightly and suppressing parts of the model that are extraneous to the development here. The terms $A_{it}$ and $B_i$ contain those additional components.) The preceding model is estimated by inserting the expression for $\alpha_i$ in the main equation, then fitting an unrestricted seemingly un-related regressions model by FGLS. There are five years of data, hence five sets of estimates. Note, however, with respect to the discharge variable, $DIS$, although each equation provides separate estimates of $(\gamma_{D,1}, \ldots, (\beta_{D,t} + \gamma_{D,t}), \ldots, \gamma_{D,5})$, a total of five parameter estimates in each each equation (year), there are only 10, not 25 parameters to be estimated in total.

**TABLE 15.1a** Coefficient Estimates for DIS in SUR Model for Hospital Costs

*Coefficient on Variable in the Equation*

| Equation | DIS87 | DIS88 | DIS89 | DIS90 | DIS91 |
|---|---|---|---|---|---|
| SUR87 | $\beta_{D,87} + \gamma_{D,87}$<br>1.76 | $\gamma_{D,88}$<br>0.116 | $\gamma_{D,89}$<br>−0.0881 | $\gamma_{D,90}$<br>0.0570 | $\gamma_{D,91}$<br>−0.0617 |
| SUR88 | $\gamma_{D,87}$<br>0.254 | $\beta_{D,88} + \gamma_{D,88}$<br>1.61 | $\gamma_{D,89}$<br>−0.0934 | $\gamma_{D,90}$<br>0.0610 | $\gamma_{D,91}$<br>−0.0514 |
| SUR89 | $\gamma_{D,87}$<br>0.217 | $\gamma_{D,88}$<br>0.0846 | $\beta_{D,89} + \gamma_{D,89}$<br>1.51 | $\gamma_{D,90}$<br>0.0454 | $\gamma_{D,91}$<br>−0.0253 |
| SUR90 | $\gamma_{D,87}$<br>0.179 | $\gamma_{D,88}$<br>0.0822 | $\gamma_{D,89}$<br>0.0295 | $\beta_{D,90} + \gamma_{D,90}$<br>1.57 | $\gamma_{D,91}$<br>0.0244 |
| SUR91 | $\gamma_{D,87}$<br>0.153 | $\gamma_{D,88}$<br>0.0363 | $\gamma_{D,89}$<br>−0.0422 | $\gamma_{D,90}$<br>0.0813 | $\beta_{D,91} + \gamma_{D,91}$<br>1.70 |
| MDE | $\beta = 1.50$<br>$\gamma = 0.219$ | $\beta = 1.58$<br>$\gamma = 0.0666$ | $\beta = 1.54$<br>$\gamma = -0.0539$ | $\beta = 1.57$<br>$\gamma = 0.0690$ | $\beta = 1.63$<br>$\gamma = -0.0213$ |

**TABLE 15.1b** Coefficient Estimates for OUT in SUR Model for Hospital Costs

*Coefficient on Variable in the Equation*

| Equation | OUT87 | OUT88 | OUT89 | OUT90 | OUT91 |
|---|---|---|---|---|---|
| SUR87 | $\beta_{O,87} + \gamma_{D,87}$<br>0.0139 | $\gamma_{O,88}$<br>0.00292 | $\gamma_{O,89}$<br>0.00157 | $\gamma_{O,90}$<br>0.000951 | $\gamma_{O,91}$<br>0.000678 |
| SUR88 | $\gamma_{O,87}$<br>0.00347 | $\beta_{O,88} + \gamma_{O,88}$<br>0.0125 | $\gamma_{O,89}$<br>0.00501 | $\gamma_{O,90}$<br>0.00550 | $\gamma_{O,91}$<br>0.00503 |
| SUR89 | $\gamma_{O,87}$<br>0.00118 | $\gamma_{O,88}$<br>0.00159 | $\beta_{O,89} + \gamma_{O,89}$<br>0.00832 | $\gamma_{O,90}$<br>−0.00220 | $\gamma_{O,91}$<br>−0.00156 |
| SUR90 | $\gamma_{O,87}$<br>−0.00226 | $\gamma_{O,88}$<br>−0.00155 | $\gamma_{O,89}$<br>0.000401 | $\beta_{O,90} + \gamma_{O,90}$<br>0.00897 | $\gamma_{O,91}$<br>0.000450 |
| SUR91 | $\gamma_{O,87}$<br>0.00278 | $\gamma_{O,88}$<br>0.00255 | $\gamma_{O,89}$<br>0.00233 | $\gamma_{O,90}$<br>0.00305 | $\beta_{O,91} + \gamma_{O,91}$<br>0.0105 |
| MDE | $\beta = 0.0112$<br>$\gamma = 0.00177$ | $\beta = 0.00999$<br>$\gamma = 0.00408$ | $\beta = 0.0100$<br>$\gamma = -0.00011$ | $\beta = 0.00915$<br>$\gamma = -0.00073$ | $\beta = 0.00793$<br>$\gamma = 0.00267$ |

The parameters on $OUT_{it}$ are likewise overidentified. Table 15.1 reproduces the estimates in Table 10.2 for the discharge coefficients and adds the estimates for the outpatient variable.

Looking at the tables we see that the SUR model provides four direct estimates of $\gamma_{D,87}$, based on the 1988–1991 equations. It also implicitly provides four estimates of $\beta_{D,87}$ since any of the four estimates of $\gamma_{D,87}$ from the last four equations can be subtracted from the coefficient on DIS in the 1987 equation to estimate $\beta_{D,87}$. There are 50 parameter estimates of different functions of the 20 underlying parameters

$$\theta = (\beta_{D,87}, \ldots, \beta_{D,91}), (\gamma_{D,87}, \ldots, \gamma_{D,91}), (\beta_{O,87}, \ldots, \beta_{O,91}), (\gamma_{O,87}, \ldots, \gamma_{O,91}),$$

and, therefore, 30 constraints to impose in finding a common, restricted estimator. An MDE was used to reconcile the competing estimators.

Let $\hat{\beta}_t$ denote the $10 \times 1$ period-specific estimator of the model parameters. Unlike the other cases we have examined, the individual estimates here are not uncorrelated. In the SUR model, the estimated asymptotic covariance matrix is the partitioned matrix given in

(10-7). For the estimators of two equations,

$$
\text{Est. Asy. Cov}\left[\hat{\beta}_t, \hat{\beta}_s\right] = \text{the } t, s \text{ block of } \begin{bmatrix} \hat{\sigma}^{11}\mathbf{X}_1'\mathbf{X}_1 & \hat{\sigma}^{12}\mathbf{X}_1'\mathbf{X}_2 & \cdots & \hat{\sigma}^{15}\mathbf{X}_1'\mathbf{X}_5 \\ \hat{\sigma}^{21}\mathbf{X}_2'\mathbf{X}_1 & \hat{\sigma}^{22}\mathbf{X}_2'\mathbf{X}_2 & \cdots & \hat{\sigma}^{25}\mathbf{X}_2'\mathbf{X}_5 \\ \vdots & \vdots & \ddots & \vdots \\ \hat{\sigma}^{51}\mathbf{X}_5'\mathbf{X}_1 & \hat{\sigma}^{52}\mathbf{X}_5'\mathbf{X}_2 & \cdots & \hat{\sigma}^{55}\mathbf{X}_5'\mathbf{X}_5 \end{bmatrix}^{-1} = \hat{\mathbf{V}}_{ts}
$$

where $\hat{\sigma}^{ts}$ is the t,s element of $\hat{\boldsymbol{\Sigma}}^{-1}$. (We are extracting a submatrix of the relevant matrices here since Carey's SUR model contained 26 other variables in each equation in addition to the five periods of DIS and OUT). The $50 \times 50$ weighting matrix for the MDE is

$$
\mathbf{W} = \begin{bmatrix} \hat{\mathbf{V}}_{87,87} & \hat{\mathbf{V}}_{87,88} & \hat{\mathbf{V}}_{87,89} & \hat{\mathbf{V}}_{87,90} & \hat{\mathbf{V}}_{87,91} \\ \hat{\mathbf{V}}_{88,87} & \hat{\mathbf{V}}_{88,88} & \hat{\mathbf{V}}_{88,89} & \hat{\mathbf{V}}_{88,90} & \hat{\mathbf{V}}_{88,91} \\ \hat{\mathbf{V}}_{89,87} & \hat{\mathbf{V}}_{89,88} & \hat{\mathbf{V}}_{89,89} & \hat{\mathbf{V}}_{89,90} & \hat{\mathbf{V}}_{89,91} \\ \hat{\mathbf{V}}_{90,87} & \hat{\mathbf{V}}_{90,88} & \hat{\mathbf{V}}_{90,89} & \hat{\mathbf{V}}_{90,90} & \hat{\mathbf{V}}_{90,91} \\ \hat{\mathbf{V}}_{91,87} & \hat{\mathbf{V}}_{91,88} & \hat{\mathbf{V}}_{91,89} & \hat{\mathbf{V}}_{91,90} & \hat{\mathbf{V}}_{91,91} \end{bmatrix}^{-1} = \left[\hat{\mathbf{V}}^{ts}\right].
$$

The vector of the quadratic form is a stack of five $10 \times 1$ vectors; the first is

$$
\overline{\mathbf{m}}_{n,87} - \mathbf{g}_{87}(\boldsymbol{\theta})
$$

$$
= \begin{bmatrix} \left\{\hat{\beta}_{D,87}^{87} - (\beta_{D,87} + \gamma_{D,87})\right\}, \left\{\hat{\beta}_{D,88}^{87} - \gamma_{D,88}\right\}, \left\{\hat{\beta}_{D,89}^{87} - \gamma_{D,89}\right\}, \left\{\hat{\beta}_{D,90}^{87} - \gamma_{D,90}\right\}, \left\{\hat{\beta}_{D,91}^{87} - \gamma_{D,90}\right\}, \\ \left\{\hat{\beta}_{O,87}^{87} - (\beta_{O,87} + \gamma_{O,87})\right\}, \left\{\hat{\beta}_{O,88}^{87} - \gamma_{O,88}\right\}, \left\{\hat{\beta}_{O,89}^{87} - \gamma_{D,89}\right\}, \left\{\hat{\beta}_{O,90}^{87} - \gamma_{O,90}\right\}, \left\{\hat{\beta}_{O,91}^{87} - \gamma_{O,90}\right\} \end{bmatrix}
$$

for the 1987 equation and likewise for the other four equations. The MDE criterion function for this model is

$$
q = \sum_{t=1987}^{1991} \sum_{s=1997}^{1981} [\overline{\mathbf{m}}_t - \mathbf{g}_t(\boldsymbol{\theta})]' \hat{\mathbf{V}}^{ts} [\overline{\mathbf{m}}_s - \mathbf{g}_s(\boldsymbol{\theta})].
$$

Note, there are 50 estimated parameters from the SUR equations (those are listed in Table 15.1) and 20 unknown parameters to be calibrated in the criterion function. The reported minimum distance estimates are shown in the last row of each table.

## 15.4 THE GENERALIZED METHOD OF MOMENTS (GMM) ESTIMATOR

A large proportion of the recent empirical work in econometrics, particularly in macro-economics and finance, has employed GMM estimators. As we shall see, this broad class of estimators, in fact, includes most of the estimators discussed elsewhere in this book.

The GMM estimation technique is an extension of the minimum distance technique described in Section 15.3.[3] In the following, we will extend the generalized method of moments to other models beyond the generalized linear regression, and we will fill in some gaps in the derivation in Section 15.2.

---

[3]Formal presentation of the results required for this analysis are given by Hansen (1982); Hansen and Singleton (1988); Chamberlain (1987); Cumby, Huizinga, and Obstfeld (1983); Newey (1984, 1985a, 1985b); Davidson and MacKinnon (1993); and Newey and McFadden (1994). Useful summaries of GMM estimation and other developments in econometrics are provided by Pagan and Wickens (1989) and Matyas (1999). An application of some of these techniques that contains useful summaries is Pagan and Vella (1989). Some further discussion can be found in Davidson and MacKinnon (2004). Ruud (2000) provides many of the theoretical details. Hayashi (2000) is another extensive treatment of estimation centered on GMM estimators.

### 15.4.1 ESTIMATION BASED ON ORTHOGONALITY CONDITIONS

Consider the least squares estimator of the parameters in the classical linear regression model. An important assumption of the model is

$$E[\mathbf{x}_i \varepsilon_i] = E[\mathbf{x}_i(y_i - \mathbf{x}_i'\boldsymbol{\beta})] = \mathbf{0}.$$

The sample analog is

$$\frac{1}{n}\sum_{i=1}^{n}\mathbf{x}_i\hat{\varepsilon}_i = \frac{1}{n}\sum_{i=1}^{n}\mathbf{x}_i(y_i - \mathbf{x}_i'\hat{\boldsymbol{\beta}}) = \mathbf{0}.$$

The estimator of $\boldsymbol{\beta}$ is the one that satisfies these moment equations, which are just the normal equations for the least squares estimator. So, we see that the OLS estimator is a method of moments estimator.

For the instrumental variables estimator of Chapter 12, we relied on a large sample analog to the moment condition,

$$\text{plim}\left(\frac{1}{n}\sum_{i=1}^{n}\mathbf{z}_i\varepsilon_i\right) = \text{plim}\left(\frac{1}{n}\sum_{i=1}^{n}\mathbf{z}_i(y_i - \mathbf{x}_i'\boldsymbol{\beta})\right) = \mathbf{0}.$$

We resolved the problem of having more instruments than parameters by solving the equations

$$\left(\frac{1}{n}\mathbf{X}'\mathbf{Z}\right)\left(\frac{1}{n}\mathbf{Z}'\mathbf{Z}\right)^{-1}\left(\frac{1}{n}\mathbf{Z}'\hat{\boldsymbol{\varepsilon}}\right) = \frac{1}{n}\hat{\mathbf{X}}'\hat{\boldsymbol{\varepsilon}} = \frac{1}{n}\sum_{i=1}^{n}\hat{\mathbf{x}}_i\hat{\varepsilon}_i = \mathbf{0},$$

where the columns of $\hat{\mathbf{X}}$ are the fitted values in regressions on all the columns of $\mathbf{Z}$ (that is, the projections of these columns of $\mathbf{X}$ into the column space of $\mathbf{Z}$). (See Section 12.3.3 for further details.)

The nonlinear least squares estimator was defined similarly, although in this case, the normal equations are more complicated because the estimator is only implicit. The population **orthogonality condition** for the nonlinear regression model is $E[\mathbf{x}_i^0 \varepsilon_i] = \mathbf{0}$. The **empirical moment equation** is

$$\frac{1}{n}\sum_{i=1}^{n}\left(\frac{\partial E[y_i \mid \mathbf{x}_i, \boldsymbol{\beta}]}{\partial \boldsymbol{\beta}}\right)(y_i - E[y_i \mid \mathbf{x}_i, \boldsymbol{\beta}]) = \mathbf{0}.$$

Maximum likelihood estimators are obtained by equating the derivatives of a log-likelihood to zero. The scaled log-likelihood function is

$$\frac{1}{n}\ln L = \frac{1}{n}\sum_{i=1}^{n}\ln f(y_i \mid \mathbf{x}_i, \boldsymbol{\theta}),$$

where $f(\cdot)$ is the density function and $\boldsymbol{\theta}$ is the parameter vector. For densities that satisfy the regularity conditions [see Chapter 16],

$$E\left[\frac{\partial \ln f(y_i \mid \mathbf{x}_i, \boldsymbol{\theta})}{\partial \boldsymbol{\theta}}\right] = \mathbf{0}.$$

The maximum likelihood estimator is obtained by equating the sample analog to zero:

$$\frac{1}{n}\frac{\partial \ln L}{\partial \hat{\boldsymbol{\theta}}} = \frac{1}{n}\sum_{i=1}^{n}\frac{\partial \ln f(y_i \mid \mathbf{x}_i, \hat{\boldsymbol{\theta}})}{\partial \hat{\boldsymbol{\theta}}} = \mathbf{0}.$$

(Dividing by $n$ to make this result comparable to our earlier ones does not change the solution.) The upshot is that nearly all the estimators we have discussed and will encounter later can be construed as method of moments estimators. [Manski's (1992) treatment of **analog estimation** provides some interesting extensions and methodological discourse.]

As we extend this line of reasoning, it will emerge that most of the estimators defined in this book can be viewed as generalized method of moments estimators.

### 15.4.2  GENERALIZING THE METHOD OF MOMENTS

The preceding examples all have a common aspect. In each case listed, save for the general case of the instrumental variable estimator, there are exactly as many moment equations as there are parameters to be estimated. Thus, each of these are **exactly identified** cases. There will be a single solution to the moment equations, and at that solution, the equations will be exactly satisfied.[4] But there are cases in which there are more moment equations than parameters, so the system is overdetermined. In Example 15.5, we defined four sample moments,

$$\bar{\mathbf{g}} = \frac{1}{n}\sum_{i=1}^{n}\left[y_i,\, y_i^2,\, \frac{1}{y_i},\, \ln y_i\right]$$

with probability limits $P/\lambda$, $P(P+1)/\lambda^2$, $\lambda/(P-1)$, and $\psi(P) - \ln \lambda$, respectively. Any pair could be used to estimate the two parameters, but as shown in the earlier example, the six pairs produce six somewhat different estimates of $\boldsymbol{\theta} = (P, \lambda)$.

In such a case, to use all the information in the sample it is necessary to devise a way to reconcile the conflicting estimates that may emerge from the overdetermined system. More generally, suppose that the model involves $K$ parameters, $\boldsymbol{\theta} = (\theta_1, \theta_2, \ldots, \theta_K)'$, and that the theory provides a set of $L > K$ moment conditions,

$$E[m_l(y_i, \mathbf{x}_i, \mathbf{z}_i, \boldsymbol{\theta})] = E[m_{il}(\boldsymbol{\theta})] = 0,$$

where $y_i$, $\mathbf{x}_i$, and $\mathbf{z}_i$ are variables that appear in the model and the subscript $i$ on $m_{il}(\boldsymbol{\theta})$ indicates the dependence on $(y_i, \mathbf{x}_i, \mathbf{z}_i)$. Denote the corresponding sample means as

$$\bar{m}_l(\mathbf{y}, \mathbf{X}, \mathbf{Z}, \boldsymbol{\theta}) = \frac{1}{n}\sum_{i=1}^{n} m_l(y_i, \mathbf{x}_i, \mathbf{z}_i, \boldsymbol{\theta}) = \frac{1}{n}\sum_{i=1}^{n} m_{il}(\boldsymbol{\theta}).$$

Unless the equations are functionally dependent, the system of $L$ equations in $K$ unknown parameters,

$$\bar{m}_l(\boldsymbol{\theta}) = \frac{1}{n}\sum_{i=1}^{n} m_l(y_i, \mathbf{x}_i, \mathbf{z}_i, \boldsymbol{\theta}) = 0, \quad l = 1, \ldots, L,$$

---

[4]That is, of course if there is *any* solution. In the regression model with multicollinearity, there are $K$ parameters but fewer than $K$ independent moment equations.

will not have a unique solution.[5] For convenience, the moment equations are defined implicitly here as opposed to equalities of moments to functions as in Section 15.3. It will be necessary to reconcile the $\binom{L}{K}$ different sets of estimates that can be produced. One possibility is to minimize a criterion function, such as the sum of squares,[6]

$$q = \sum_{l=1}^{L} \overline{m}_l^2 = \overline{\mathbf{m}}(\boldsymbol{\theta})' \overline{\mathbf{m}}(\boldsymbol{\theta}). \tag{15-2}$$

It can be shown [see, e.g., Hansen (1982)] that under the assumptions we have made so far, specifically that plim $\overline{\mathbf{m}}(\boldsymbol{\theta}) = E[\overline{\mathbf{m}}(\boldsymbol{\theta})] = \mathbf{0}$, the minimizer of $q$ in (15-2) produces a consistent (albeit, as we shall see, possibly inefficient) estimator of $\boldsymbol{\theta}$. We can, in fact, use as the criterion a weighted sum of squares,

$$q = \overline{\mathbf{m}}(\boldsymbol{\theta})' \mathbf{W}_n \overline{\mathbf{m}}(\boldsymbol{\theta}),$$

where $\mathbf{W}_n$ is *any* positive definite matrix that may depend on the data but is not a function of $\boldsymbol{\theta}$, such as $\mathbf{I}$ in (15-2), to produce a consistent estimator of $\boldsymbol{\theta}$.[7] For example, we might use a diagonal matrix of weights if some information were available about the importance (by some measure) of the different moments. We do make the additional assumption that plim $\mathbf{W}_n = $ a positive definite matrix, $\mathbf{W}$.

By the same logic that makes generalized least squares preferable to ordinary least squares, it should be beneficial to use a weighted criterion in which the weights are inversely proportional to the variances of the moments. Let $\mathbf{W}$ be a diagonal matrix whose diagonal elements are the reciprocals of the variances of the individual moments,

$$w_{ll} = \frac{1}{\text{Asy. Var}[\sqrt{n}\,\overline{m}_l]} = \frac{1}{\phi_{ll}}.$$

(We have written it in this form to emphasize that the right-hand side involves the variance of a sample mean which is of order $(1/n)$.) Then, a **weighted least squares** estimator would minimize

$$q = \overline{\mathbf{m}}(\boldsymbol{\theta})' \boldsymbol{\Phi}^{-1} \overline{\mathbf{m}}(\boldsymbol{\theta}). \tag{15-3}$$

In general, the $L$ elements of $\overline{\mathbf{m}}$ are freely correlated. In (15-3), we have used a diagonal $\mathbf{W}$ that ignores this correlation. To use generalized least squares, we would define the full matrix,

$$\mathbf{W} = \left\{ \text{Asy. Var}[\sqrt{n}\,\overline{\mathbf{m}}] \right\}^{-1} = \boldsymbol{\Phi}^{-1}. \tag{15-4}$$

The estimators defined by choosing $\boldsymbol{\theta}$ to minimize

$$q = \overline{\mathbf{m}}(\boldsymbol{\theta})' \mathbf{W}_n \overline{\mathbf{m}}(\boldsymbol{\theta})$$

---

[5]It may if $L$ is greater than the sample size, $n$. We assume that $L$ is strictly less than $n$.

[6]This approach is one that Quandt and Ramsey (1978) suggested for the problem in Example 15.4.

[7]In principle, the weighting matrix can be a function of the parameters as well. See Hansen, Heaton, and Yaron (1996) for discussion. Whether this provides any benefit in terms of the asymptotic properties of the estimator seems unlikely. The one payoff the authors do note is that certain estimators become invariant to the sort of normalization that is discussed in Example 16.1. In practical terms, this is likely to be a consideration only in a fairly small class of cases.

are minimum distance estimators as defined in Section 15.3. The general result is that if $\mathbf{W}_n$ is a positive definite matrix and if

$$\text{plim } \overline{\mathbf{m}}(\boldsymbol{\theta}) = \mathbf{0},$$

then the minimum distance (generalized method of moments, or GMM) estimator of $\boldsymbol{\theta}$ is consistent.[8] Because the OLS criterion in (15-2) uses $\mathbf{I}$, this method produces a consistent estimator, as does the weighted least squares estimator and the full GLS estimator. What remains to be decided is the best $\mathbf{W}$ to use. Intuition might suggest (correctly) that the one defined in (15-4) would be optimal, once again based on the logic that motivates generalized least squares. This result is the now-celebrated one of Hansen (1982).

The asymptotic covariance matrix of this **generalized method of moments estimator** is

$$\mathbf{V}_{GMM} = \frac{1}{n}[\mathbf{\Gamma}'\mathbf{W}\mathbf{\Gamma}]^{-1} = \frac{1}{n}[\mathbf{\Gamma}'\mathbf{\Phi}^{-1}\mathbf{\Gamma}]^{-1}, \tag{15-5}$$

where $\mathbf{\Gamma}$ is the matrix of derivatives with $j$th row equal to

$$\mathbf{\Gamma}^j = \text{plim } \frac{\partial \overline{m}_j(\boldsymbol{\theta})}{\partial \boldsymbol{\theta}'},$$

and $\mathbf{\Phi} = \text{Asy. Var}[\sqrt{n}\,\overline{\mathbf{m}}]$. Finally, by virtue of the central limit theorem applied to the sample moments and the **Slutsky theorem** applied to this manipulation, we can expect the estimator to be asymptotically normally distributed. We will revisit the asymptotic properties of the estimator in Section 15.4.3.

### Example 15.7   GMM Estimation of the Parameters of a Gamma Distribution

Referring once again to our earlier results in Example 15.5, we consider how to use all four of our sample moments to estimate the parameters of the gamma distribution.[9] The four moment equations are

$$E\begin{bmatrix} y_i - P/\lambda \\ y_i^2 - P(P+1)/\lambda^2 \\ \ln y_i - \Psi(P) + \ln\lambda \\ 1/y_i - \lambda/(P-1) \end{bmatrix} = \begin{bmatrix} 0 \\ 0 \\ 0 \\ 0 \end{bmatrix}.$$

The sample means of these will provide the moment equations for estimation. Let $y_1 = y$, $y_2 = y^2$, $y_3 = \ln y$, and $y_4 = 1/y$. Then

$$\overline{m}_1(P, \lambda) = \frac{1}{n}\sum_{i=l}^{n}(y_{i1} - P/\lambda) = \frac{1}{n}\sum_{i=1}^{n}[y_{i1} - \mu_1(P, \lambda)] = \overline{y}_1 - \mu_1(P, \lambda),$$

and likewise for $\overline{m}_2(P, \lambda)$, $\overline{m}_3(P, \lambda)$, and $\overline{m}_4(P, \lambda)$.

---

[8]In the most general cases, a number of other subtle conditions must be met so as to assert consistency and the other properties we discuss. For our purposes, the conditions given will suffice. Minimum distance estimators are discussed in Malinvaud (1970), Hansen (1982), and Amemiya (1985).

[9]We emphasize that this example is constructed only to illustrate the computation of a GMM estimator. The gamma model is fully specified by the likelihood function, and the MLE is fully efficient. We will examine other cases that involve less detailed specifications later in this chapter.

For our initial set of estimates, we will use ordinary least squares. The optimization problem is

$$\text{Minimize}_{P,\lambda} \sum_{l=1}^{4} \overline{m}_l(P,\lambda)^2 = \sum_{l=1}^{4} [\overline{y}_l - \mu_l(P,\lambda)]^2 = \overline{\mathbf{m}}(P,\lambda)'\overline{\mathbf{m}}(P,\lambda).$$

This estimator will be the minimum distance estimator with $\mathbf{W} = \mathbf{I}$. This nonlinear optimization problem must be solved iteratively. As starting values for the iterations, we used the maximum likelihood estimates from Example 15.5, $\hat{P}_{ML} = 2.4106$ and $\hat{\lambda}_{ML} = 0.0770702$. The least squares values that result from this procedure are $\hat{P} = 2.0582996$ and $\hat{\lambda} = 0.06579888$. We can now use these to form our estimate of $\mathbf{W}$. GMM estimation usually requires a first-step estimation such as this one to obtain the weighting matrix $\mathbf{W}$. With these new estimates in hand, we obtained

$$\hat{\mathbf{\Phi}} = \left\{ \frac{1}{20} \sum_{i=1}^{20} \begin{bmatrix} y_{i1} - \hat{P}/\hat{\lambda} \\ y_{i2} - \hat{P}(\hat{P}+1)/\hat{\lambda}^2 \\ y_{i3} - \Psi(\hat{P}) + \ln\hat{\lambda} \\ y_{i4} - \hat{\lambda}/(\hat{P}-1) \end{bmatrix} \begin{bmatrix} y_{i1} - \hat{P}/\hat{\lambda} \\ y_{i2} - \hat{P}(\hat{P}+1)/\hat{\lambda}^2 \\ y_{i3} - \Psi(\hat{P}) + \ln\hat{\lambda} \\ y_{i4} - \hat{\lambda}/(\hat{P}-1) \end{bmatrix}' \right\}.$$

(Note, we could have computed $\hat{\mathbf{\Phi}}$ using the maximum likelihood estimates.) The GMM estimator is now obtained by minimizing

$$q = \overline{\mathbf{m}}(P,\lambda)'\hat{\mathbf{\Phi}}^{-1}\overline{\mathbf{m}}(P,\lambda).$$

The two estimates are $\hat{P}_{GMM} = 3.35894$ and $\hat{\lambda}_{GMM} = 0.124489$. At these two values, the value of the function is $q = 1.97522$. To obtain an asymptotic covariance matrix for the two estimates, we first recompute $\hat{\mathbf{\Phi}}$ as shown in the preceding matrix.

$$\frac{1}{20}\hat{\mathbf{\Phi}} = \begin{bmatrix} 24.7051 & & & \\ 2307.126 & 229{,}609.5 & & \\ 0.6974 & 58.8148 & 0.2302 & \\ -0.02881 & -2.14227 & -0.0011 & 0.000065414 \end{bmatrix}.$$

To complete the computation, we will require the derivatives matrix,

$$\mathbf{\Gamma}'(\boldsymbol{\theta}) = \begin{bmatrix} \partial\overline{m}_1/\partial P & \partial\overline{m}_2/\partial P & \partial\overline{m}_3/\partial P & \partial\overline{m}_4/\partial P \\ \partial\overline{m}_1/\partial\lambda & \partial\overline{m}_2/\partial\lambda & \partial\overline{m}_3/\partial\lambda & \partial\overline{m}_4/\partial\lambda \end{bmatrix}$$

$$= \begin{bmatrix} -1/\lambda & -(2P+1)/\lambda^2 & -\Psi'(P) & \lambda/(P-1)^2 \\ P/\lambda^2 & 2P(P+1)/\lambda^3 & 1/\lambda & -1/(P-1) \end{bmatrix}.$$

The estimate is

$$\overline{\mathbf{G}}'(\hat{\boldsymbol{\theta}}) = \begin{bmatrix} -8.0328 & -498.01 & -0.34635 & 0.022372 \\ 216.74 & 15178.2 & 8.0328 & -0.42392 \end{bmatrix} = \hat{\mathbf{G}}.$$

Finally,

$$\frac{1}{20}[\hat{\mathbf{G}}'\hat{\mathbf{\Phi}}^{-1}\hat{\mathbf{G}}]^{-1} = \begin{bmatrix} 0.202084 & 0.0117284 \\ 0.0117284 & 0.000846541 \end{bmatrix}$$

gives the estimated asymptotic covariance matrix for the estimators. Recall that in Example 15.5, we obtained maximum likelihood estimates of the same parameters. Table 15.2 summarizes.

| TABLE 15.2 | Estimates of the Parameters of a Gamma Distribution | |
|---|---|---|
| *Parameter* | *Maximum Likelihood* | *Generalized Method of Moments* |
| P | 2.4106 | 3.35894 |
| Standard Error | (0.87682) | (0.449538) |
| λ | 0.0770702 | 0.124489 |
| Standard Error | (0.02707) | (0.029095) |

### 15.4.3   PROPERTIES OF THE GMM ESTIMATOR

We will now examine the properties of the GMM estimator in some detail. Because the GMM estimator includes other familiar estimators that we have already encountered, including least squares (linear and nonlinear), and instrumental variables, these results will extend to those cases. The discussion given here will only sketch the elements of the formal proofs. The assumptions we make here are somewhat narrower than a fully general treatment might allow; but they are broad enough to include the situations likely to arise in practice. More detailed and rigorous treatments may be found in, for example, Newey and McFadden (1994), White (2001), Hayashi (2000), Mittelhammer et al. (2000), or Davidson (2000).

The GMM estimator is based on the set of population orthogonality conditions,

$$E[\mathbf{m}_i(\boldsymbol{\theta}_0)] = \mathbf{0},$$

where we denote the true parameter vector by $\boldsymbol{\theta}_0$. The subscript $i$ on the term on the left-hand side indicates dependence on the observed data, $(y_i, \mathbf{x}_i, \mathbf{z}_i)$. Averaging this over the sample observations produces the sample moment equation

$$E[\overline{\mathbf{m}}_n(\boldsymbol{\theta}_0)] = \mathbf{0},$$

where

$$\overline{\mathbf{m}}_n(\boldsymbol{\theta}_0) = \frac{1}{n}\sum_{i=1}^{n} \mathbf{m}_i(\boldsymbol{\theta}_0).$$

This moment is a set of $L$ equations involving the $K$ parameters. We will assume that this expectation exists and that the sample counterpart converges to it. The definitions are cast in terms of the population parameters and are indexed by the sample size. To fix the ideas, consider, once again, the empirical moment equations that define the instrumental variable estimator for a linear or nonlinear regression model.

*Example 15.8   Empirical Moment Equation for Instrumental Variables*
For the IV estimator in the linear or nonlinear regression model, we assume

$$E[\overline{\mathbf{m}}_n(\boldsymbol{\beta})] = E\left[\frac{1}{n}\sum_{i=1}^{n} \mathbf{z}_i[y_i - h(\mathbf{x}_i, \boldsymbol{\beta})]\right] = \mathbf{0}.$$

There are $L$ instrumental variables in $\mathbf{z}_i$ and $K$ parameters in $\boldsymbol{\beta}$. This statement defines $L$ moment equations, one for each instrumental variable.

We make the following assumptions about the model and these empirical moments:

---

ASSUMPTION 15.1. **Convergence of the Empirical Moments:** *The data generating process is assumed to meet the conditions for a law of large numbers to apply, so that we may assume that the empirical moments converge in probability to their expectation. Appendix D lists several different laws of large numbers that increase in generality. What is required for this assumption is that*

$$\overline{\mathbf{m}}_n(\boldsymbol{\theta}_0) = \frac{1}{n} \sum_{i=1}^{n} \mathbf{m}_i(\boldsymbol{\theta}_0) \xrightarrow{p} \mathbf{0}.$$

---

The laws of large numbers that we examined in Appendix D accommodate cases of independent observations. Cases of dependent or correlated observations can be gathered under the **Ergodic theorem** (19.1). For this more general case, then, we would assume that the sequence of observations $\mathbf{m}(\boldsymbol{\theta})$ constitutes a jointly $(L \times 1)$ stationary and ergodic process.

The empirical moments are assumed to be continuous and continuously differentiable functions of the parameters. For our earlier example, this would mean that the conditional mean function, $h(\mathbf{x}_i, \boldsymbol{\beta})$ is a continuous function of $\boldsymbol{\beta}$ (although not necessarily of $\mathbf{x}_i$). With continuity and differentiability, we will also be able to assume that the derivatives of the moments,

$$\overline{\mathbf{G}}_n(\boldsymbol{\theta}_0) = \frac{\partial \overline{\mathbf{m}}_n(\boldsymbol{\theta}_0)}{\partial \boldsymbol{\theta}_0'} = \frac{1}{n} \sum_{i=1}^{n} \frac{\partial \mathbf{m}_{i,n}(\boldsymbol{\theta}_0)}{\partial \boldsymbol{\theta}_0'},$$

converge to a probability limit, say, plim $\overline{\mathbf{G}}_n(\boldsymbol{\theta}_0) = \overline{\mathbf{G}}(\boldsymbol{\theta}_0)$. [See (15-1), (15-5), and Theorem 15.1.] For sets of *independent* observations, the continuity of the functions and the derivatives will allow us to invoke the Slutsky theorem to obtain this result. For the more general case of sequences of *dependent* observations, Theorem 19.2, Ergodicity of Functions, will provide a counterpart to the Slutsky theorem for time series data. In sum, if the moments themselves obey a law of large numbers, then it is reasonable to assume that the derivatives do as well.

---

ASSUMPTION 15.2. **Identification:** *For any $n \geq K$, if $\boldsymbol{\theta}_1$ and $\boldsymbol{\theta}_2$ are two different parameter vectors, then there exist data sets such that $\overline{\mathbf{m}}_n(\boldsymbol{\theta}_1) \neq \overline{\mathbf{m}}_n(\boldsymbol{\theta}_2)$. Formally, in Section 14.5.3, identification is defined to imply that the probability limit of the GMM criterion function is uniquely minimized at the true parameters, $\boldsymbol{\theta}_0$.*

---

Assumption 15.2 is a practical prescription for identification. More formal conditions are discussed in Section 14.5.3. We have examined two violations of this crucial assumption. In the linear regression model, one of the assumptions is full rank of the matrix of exogenous variables—the absence of multicollinearity in $\mathbf{X}$. In our discussion of the maximum likelihood estimator, we will encounter a case (Example 16.1) in which a normalization is needed to identify the vector of parameters. [See Hansen et al.

(1996) for discussion of this case.] Both of these cases are included in this assumption. The identification condition has three important implications:

1. **Order condition.** The number of moment conditions is at least as large as the number of parameters; $L \geq K$. This is necessary but not sufficient for identification.
2. **Rank condition.** The $L \times K$ matrix of derivatives, $\overline{\mathbf{G}}_n(\boldsymbol{\theta}_0)$ will have row rank equal to $K$. (Again, note that the number of rows must equal or exceed the number of columns.)
3. **Uniqueness.** With the continuity assumption, the identification assumption implies that the parameter vector that satisfies the population moment condition is unique. We know that at the true parameter vector, $\text{plim}\, \overline{\mathbf{m}}_n(\boldsymbol{\theta}_0) = \mathbf{0}$. If $\boldsymbol{\theta}_1$ is any parameter vector that satisfies this condition, then $\boldsymbol{\theta}_1$ must equal $\boldsymbol{\theta}_0$.

Assumptions 15.1 and 15.2 characterize the parameterization of the model. Together they establish that the parameter vector will be estimable. We now make the statistical assumption that will allow us to establish the properties of the GMM estimator.

---

ASSUMPTION 15.3. **Asymptotic Distribution of Empirical Moments:** *We assume that the empirical moments obey a central limit theorem. This assumes that the moments have a finite asymptotic covariance matrix,* $(1/n)\boldsymbol{\Phi}$, *so that*

$$\sqrt{n}\,\overline{\mathbf{m}}_n(\boldsymbol{\theta}_0) \xrightarrow{d} N[\mathbf{0}, \boldsymbol{\Phi}].$$

---

The underlying requirements on the data for this assumption to hold will vary and will be complicated if the observations comprising the empirical moment are not independent. For samples of independent observations, we assume the conditions underlying the Lindeberg–Feller (D.19) or Liapounov Central Limit theorem (D.20) will suffice. For the more general case, it is once again necessary to make some assumptions about the data. We have assumed that

$$E[\mathbf{m}_i(\boldsymbol{\theta}_0)] = \mathbf{0}.$$

If we can go a step further and assume that the functions $\mathbf{m}_i(\boldsymbol{\theta}_0)$ are an ergodic, stationary **martingale difference series,**

$$E[\mathbf{m}_i(\boldsymbol{\theta}_0) \mid \mathbf{m}_{i-1}(\boldsymbol{\theta}_0), \mathbf{m}_{i-2}(\boldsymbol{\theta}_0) \ldots] = \mathbf{0},$$

then we can invoke Theorem 19.3, the Central Limit Theorem for Martingale Difference Series. It will generally be fairly complicated to verify this assumption for nonlinear models, so it will usually be assumed outright. On the other hand, the assumptions are likely to be fairly benign in a typical application. For regression models, the assumption takes the form

$$E[\mathbf{z}_i \varepsilon_i \mid \mathbf{z}_{i-1}\varepsilon_{i-1}, \ldots] = \mathbf{0}$$

which will often be part of the central structure of the model.

With the assumptions in place, we have

---

**THEOREM 15.2**   **Asymptotic Distribution of the GMM Estimator**
*Under the preceding assumptions,*

$$\hat{\boldsymbol{\theta}}_{GMM} \xrightarrow{p} \boldsymbol{\theta}_0,$$

$$\hat{\boldsymbol{\theta}}_{GMM} \stackrel{a}{\sim} N[\boldsymbol{\theta}_0, \mathbf{V}_{GMM}], \tag{15-6}$$

*where $\mathbf{V}_{GMM}$ is defined in (15-5).*

---

We will now sketch a proof of Theorem 15.2. The GMM estimator is obtained by minimizing the criterion function

$$q_n(\boldsymbol{\theta}) = \overline{\mathbf{m}}_n(\boldsymbol{\theta})' \mathbf{W}_n \overline{\mathbf{m}}_n(\boldsymbol{\theta}),$$

where $\mathbf{W}_n$ is the weighting matrix used. Consistency of the estimator that minimizes this criterion can be established by the same logic that will be used for the maximum likelihood estimator. It must first be established that $q_n(\boldsymbol{\theta})$ converges to a value $q_0(\boldsymbol{\theta})$. By our assumptions of strict continuity and Assumption 15.1, $q_n(\boldsymbol{\theta}_0)$ converges to 0. (We could apply the Slutsky theorem to obtain this result.) We will assume that $q_n(\boldsymbol{\theta})$ converges to $q_0(\boldsymbol{\theta})$ for other points in the parameter space as well. Because $\mathbf{W}_n$ is positive definite, for any finite $n$, we know that

$$0 \leq q_n(\hat{\boldsymbol{\theta}}_{GMM}) \leq q_n(\boldsymbol{\theta}_0). \tag{15-7}$$

That is, in the finite sample, $\hat{\boldsymbol{\theta}}_{GMM}$ actually minimizes the function, so the sample value of the criterion is not larger at $\hat{\boldsymbol{\theta}}_{GMM}$ than at any other value, including the true parameters. But, at the true parameter values, $q_n(\boldsymbol{\theta}_0) \xrightarrow{p} 0$. So, if (15-7) is true, then it must follow that $q_n(\hat{\boldsymbol{\theta}}_{GMM}) \xrightarrow{p} 0$ as well because of the identification assumption, 15.2. As $n \rightarrow \infty$, $q_n(\hat{\boldsymbol{\theta}}_{GMM})$ and $q_n(\boldsymbol{\theta})$ converge to the same limit. It must be the case, then, that as $n \rightarrow \infty$, $\overline{\mathbf{m}}_n(\hat{\boldsymbol{\theta}}_{GMM}) \rightarrow \overline{\mathbf{m}}_n(\boldsymbol{\theta}_0)$, because the function is quadratic and $\mathbf{W}$ is positive definite. The identification condition that we assumed earlier now assures that as $n \rightarrow \infty$, $\hat{\boldsymbol{\theta}}_{GMM}$ must equal $\boldsymbol{\theta}_0$. This establishes consistency of the estimator.

We will now sketch a proof of the asymptotic normality of the estimator: The first-order conditions for the GMM estimator are

$$\frac{\partial q_n(\hat{\boldsymbol{\theta}}_{GMM})}{\partial \hat{\boldsymbol{\theta}}_{GMM}} = 2\overline{\mathbf{G}}_n(\hat{\boldsymbol{\theta}}_{GMM})' \mathbf{W}_n \overline{\mathbf{m}}_n(\hat{\boldsymbol{\theta}}_{GMM}) = \mathbf{0}. \tag{15-8}$$

(The leading 2 is irrelevant to the solution, so it will be dropped at this point.) The orthogonality equations are assumed to be continuous and continuously differentiable. This allows us to employ the **mean value theorem** as we expand the empirical moments in a linear Taylor series around the true value, $\boldsymbol{\theta}_0$

$$\overline{\mathbf{m}}_n(\hat{\boldsymbol{\theta}}_{GMM}) = \overline{\mathbf{m}}_n(\boldsymbol{\theta}_0) + \overline{\mathbf{G}}_n(\overline{\boldsymbol{\theta}})(\hat{\boldsymbol{\theta}}_{GMM} - \boldsymbol{\theta}_0), \tag{15-9}$$

where $\overline{\boldsymbol{\theta}}$ is a point between $\hat{\boldsymbol{\theta}}_{GMM}$ and the true parameters, $\boldsymbol{\theta}_0$. Thus, for each element $\overline{\theta}_k = w_k \hat{\theta}_{k,GMM} + (1 - w_k)\theta_{0,k}$ for some $w_k$ such that $0 < w_k < 1$. Insert (15-9) in (15-8) to obtain

$$\overline{\mathbf{G}}_n(\hat{\boldsymbol{\theta}}_{GMM})'\mathbf{W}_n\overline{\mathbf{m}}_n(\boldsymbol{\theta}_0) + \overline{\mathbf{G}}_n(\hat{\boldsymbol{\theta}}_{GMM})'\mathbf{W}_n\overline{\mathbf{G}}_n(\overline{\boldsymbol{\theta}})(\hat{\boldsymbol{\theta}}_{GMM} - \boldsymbol{\theta}_0) = \mathbf{0}.$$

Solve this equation for the estimation error and multiply by $\sqrt{n}$. This produces

$$\sqrt{n}(\hat{\boldsymbol{\theta}}_{GMM} - \boldsymbol{\theta}_0) = -[\overline{\mathbf{G}}_n(\hat{\boldsymbol{\theta}}_{GMM})'\mathbf{W}_n\overline{\mathbf{G}}_n(\overline{\boldsymbol{\theta}})]^{-1}\overline{\mathbf{G}}_n(\hat{\boldsymbol{\theta}}_{GMM})'\mathbf{W}_n\sqrt{n}\,\overline{\mathbf{m}}_n(\boldsymbol{\theta}_0).$$

Assuming that they have them, the quantities on the left- and right-hand sides have the same limiting distributions. By the consistency of $\hat{\boldsymbol{\theta}}_{GMM}$, we know that $\hat{\boldsymbol{\theta}}_{GMM}$ and $\overline{\boldsymbol{\theta}}$ both converge to $\boldsymbol{\theta}_0$. By the strict continuity assumed, it must also be the case that

$$\overline{\mathbf{G}}_n(\overline{\boldsymbol{\theta}}) \xrightarrow{p} \overline{\mathbf{G}}(\boldsymbol{\theta}_0) \text{ and } \overline{\mathbf{G}}_n(\hat{\boldsymbol{\theta}}_{GMM}) \xrightarrow{p} \overline{\mathbf{G}}(\boldsymbol{\theta}_0).$$

We have also assumed that the weighting matrix, $\mathbf{W}_n$, converges to a matrix of constants, $\mathbf{W}$. Collecting terms, we find that the limiting distribution of the vector on the left-hand side must be the same as that on the right-hand side in (15-10),

$$\sqrt{n}(\hat{\boldsymbol{\theta}}_{GMM} - \boldsymbol{\theta}_0) \xrightarrow{p} \{[\overline{\mathbf{G}}(\boldsymbol{\theta}_0)'\mathbf{W}\overline{\mathbf{G}}(\boldsymbol{\theta}_0)]^{-1}\overline{\mathbf{G}}(\boldsymbol{\theta}_0)'\mathbf{W}\}\sqrt{n}\,\overline{\mathbf{m}}_n(\boldsymbol{\theta}_0). \qquad \textbf{(15-10)}$$

We now invoke Assumption 15.3. The matrix in curled brackets is a set of constants. The last term has the normal limiting distribution given in Assumption 15.3. The mean and variance of this limiting distribution are zero and $\boldsymbol{\Phi}$, respectively. Collecting terms, we have the result in Theorem 15.2, where

$$\mathbf{V}_{GMM} = \frac{1}{n}[\overline{\mathbf{G}}(\boldsymbol{\theta}_0)'\mathbf{W}\overline{\mathbf{G}}(\boldsymbol{\theta}_0)]^{-1}\overline{\mathbf{G}}(\boldsymbol{\theta}_0)'\mathbf{W}\boldsymbol{\Phi}\mathbf{W}\overline{\mathbf{G}}(\boldsymbol{\theta}_0)[\overline{\mathbf{G}}(\boldsymbol{\theta}_0)'\mathbf{W}\overline{\mathbf{G}}(\boldsymbol{\theta}_0)]^{-1}. \qquad \textbf{(15-11)}$$

The final result is a function of the choice of weighting matrix, $\mathbf{W}$. If the optimal weighting matrix, $\mathbf{W} = \boldsymbol{\Phi}^{-1}$, is used, then the expression collapses to

$$\mathbf{V}_{GMM,optimal} = \frac{1}{n}[\overline{\mathbf{G}}(\boldsymbol{\theta}_0)'\boldsymbol{\Phi}^{-1}\overline{\mathbf{G}}(\boldsymbol{\theta}_0)]^{-1}. \qquad \textbf{(15-12)}$$

Returning to (15-11), there is a special case of interest. If we use least squares or instrumental variables with $\mathbf{W} = \mathbf{I}$, then

$$\mathbf{V}_{GMM} = \frac{1}{n}(\overline{\mathbf{G}}'\overline{\mathbf{G}})^{-1}\overline{\mathbf{G}}'\boldsymbol{\Phi}\overline{\mathbf{G}}(\overline{\mathbf{G}}'\overline{\mathbf{G}})^{-1}.$$

This equation prescibes essentially the White or **Newey-West estimator,** which returns us to our departure point and provides a neat symmetry to the GMM principle. We will formalize this in Section 15.6.1.

## 15.5 TESTING HYPOTHESES IN THE GMM FRAMEWORK

The estimation framework developed in the previous section provides the basis for a convenient set of statistics for testing hypotheses. We will consider three groups of tests. The first is a pair of statistics that is used for testing the validity of the restrictions that produce the moment equations. The second is a trio of tests that correspond to the familiar Wald, LM, and LR tests. The third is a class of tests based on the theoretical underpinnings of the conditional moments that we used earlier to devise the GMM estimator.

### 15.5.1 TESTING THE VALIDITY OF THE MOMENT RESTRICTIONS

In the exactly identified cases we examined earlier (least squares, instrumental variables, maximum likelihood), the criterion for GMM estimation

$$q = \overline{\mathbf{m}}(\boldsymbol{\theta})' \mathbf{W} \overline{\mathbf{m}}(\boldsymbol{\theta})$$

would be exactly zero because we can find a set of estimates for which $\overline{\mathbf{m}}(\boldsymbol{\theta})$ is exactly zero. Thus in the exactly identified case when there are the same number of moment equations as there are parameters to estimate, the weighting matrix $\mathbf{W}$ is irrelevant to the solution. But if the parameters are overidentified by the moment equations, then these equations imply substantive restrictions. As such, if the hypothesis of the model that led to the moment equations in the first place is incorrect, at least some of the sample moment restrictions will be systematically violated. This conclusion provides the basis for a test of the **overidentifying restrictions.** By construction, when the optimal weighting matrix is used,

$$nq = \left[ \sqrt{n}\, \overline{\mathbf{m}}(\hat{\boldsymbol{\theta}})' \right] \left\{ \text{Est. Asy. Var}[\sqrt{n}\, \overline{\mathbf{m}}(\hat{\boldsymbol{\theta}})] \right\}^{-1} \left[ \sqrt{n}\, \overline{\mathbf{m}}(\hat{\boldsymbol{\theta}}) \right],$$

so $nq$ is a Wald statistic. Therefore, under the hypothesis of the model,

$$nq \xrightarrow{d} \chi^2[L - K].$$

(For the exactly identified case, there are zero degrees of freedom and $q = 0$.)

#### Example 15.9  Overidentifying Restrictions
In Hall's consumption model, two orthogonality conditions noted in Example 15.1 exactly identify the two parameters. But his analysis of the model suggests a way to test the specification. The conclusion, "No information available in time $t$ apart from the level of consumption, $c_t$, helps predict future consumption, $c_{t+1}$, in the sense of affecting the expected value of marginal utility. In particular, income or wealth in periods $t$ or earlier are irrelevant once $c_t$ is known" suggests how one might test the model. If lagged values of income ($Y_t$ might equal the ratio of current income to the previous period's income) are added to the set of instruments, then the model is now overidentified by the orthogonality conditions;

$$E_t \left[ \left( \beta(1 + r_{t+1}) R_{t+1}^{\lambda} - 1 \right) \times \begin{pmatrix} 1 \\ R_t \\ Y_{t-1} \\ Y_{t-2} \end{pmatrix} \right] = \begin{bmatrix} 0 \\ 0 \end{bmatrix}.$$

A simple test of the overidentifying restrictions would be suggestive of the validity of the corollary. Rejecting the restrictions casts doubt on the original model. Hall's proposed tests to distinguish the life cycle–permanent income model from other theories of consumption involved adding two lags of income to the information set. Hansen and Singleton (1982) operated directly on this form of the model. Other studies, for example, Campbell and Mankiw's (1989) as well as Hall's, used the model's implications to formulate more conventional instrumental variable regression models.

The preceding is a **specification test,** not a test of parametric restrictions. However, there is a symmetry between the moment restrictions and restrictions on the parameter vector. Suppose $\boldsymbol{\theta}$ is subjected to $J$ restrictions (linear or nonlinear) which restrict the number of free parameters from $K$ to $K - J$. (That is, reduce the dimensionality of the parameter space from $K$ to $K - J$.) The nature of the GMM estimation problem we have posed is not changed at all by the restrictions. The constrained problem may be stated in terms of

$$q_R = \overline{\mathbf{m}}(\boldsymbol{\theta}_R)'\mathbf{W}\overline{\mathbf{m}}(\boldsymbol{\theta}_R).$$

Note that the weighting matrix, $\mathbf{W}$, is unchanged. The precise nature of the solution method may be changed—the restrictions mandate a constrained optimization. However, the criterion is essentially unchanged. It follows then that

$$nq_R \xrightarrow{d} \chi^2[L - (K - J)].$$

This result suggests a method of testing the restrictions, although the distribution theory is not obvious. The weighted sum of squares with the restrictions imposed, $nq_R$, must be larger than the weighted sum of squares obtained without the restrictions, $nq$. The difference is

$$(nq_R - nq) \xrightarrow{d} \chi^2[J]. \tag{15-13}$$

The test is attributed to Newey and West (1987b). This provides one method of testing a set of restrictions. (The small-sample properties of this test will be the central focus of the application discussed in Section 15.6.5.) We now consider several alternatives.

### 15.5.2   GMM COUNTERPARTS TO THE WALD, LM, AND LR TESTS

Section 16.6 describes a trio of testing procedures that can be applied to a hypothesis in the context of maximum likelihood estimation. To reiterate, let the hypothesis to be tested be a set of $J$ possibly nonlinear restrictions on $K$ parameters $\boldsymbol{\theta}$ in the form $H_0: \mathbf{r}(\boldsymbol{\theta}) = \mathbf{0}$. Let $\mathbf{c}_1$ be the maximum likelihood estimates of $\boldsymbol{\theta}$ estimated without the restrictions, and let $\mathbf{c}_0$ denote the restricted maximum likelihood estimates, that is, the estimates obtained while imposing the null hypothesis. The three statistics, which are asymptotically equivalent, are obtained as follows:

$$\text{LR} = \text{likelihood ratio} = -2(\ln L_0 - \ln L_1),$$

where

$$\ln L_j = \log \text{ likelihood function evaluated at } \mathbf{c}_j, \quad j = 0, 1.$$

The **likelihood ratio statistic** requires that both estimates be computed. The Wald statistic is

$$W = \text{Wald} = [\mathbf{r}(\mathbf{c}_1)]' \{\text{Est. Asy. Var}[\mathbf{r}(\mathbf{c}_1)]\}^{-1} [\mathbf{r}(\mathbf{c}_1)]. \tag{15-14}$$

The **Wald statistic** is the distance measure for the degree to which the unrestricted estimator fails to satisfy the restrictions. The usual estimator for the asymptotic covariance matrix would be

$$\text{Est. Asy. Var}[\mathbf{r}(\mathbf{c}_1)] = \mathbf{R}_1 \{\text{Est. Asy. Var}[\mathbf{c}_1]\} \mathbf{R}_1', \tag{15-15}$$

where

$$\mathbf{R}_1 = \partial \mathbf{r}(\mathbf{c}_1)/\partial \mathbf{c}_1' \quad (\mathbf{R}_1 \text{ is a } J \times K \text{ matrix}).$$

The Wald statistic can be computed using only the unrestricted estimate. The LM statistic is

$$\text{LM} = \text{Lagrange multiplier} = \mathbf{g}_1'(\mathbf{c}_0)\big\{\text{Est. Asy. Var}[\mathbf{g}_1(\mathbf{c}_0)]\big\}^{-1}\mathbf{g}_1(\mathbf{c}_0), \qquad \textbf{(15-16)}$$

where

$$\mathbf{g}_1(\mathbf{c}_0) = \partial \ln L_1(\mathbf{c}_0)/\partial \mathbf{c}_0,$$

that is, the first derivatives of the *unconstrained* log-likelihood computed at the *restricted* estimates. The term Est. Asy. Var$[\mathbf{g}_1(\mathbf{c}_0)]$ is the inverse of any of the usual estimators of the asymptotic covariance matrix of the maximum likelihood estimators of the parameters, computed using the restricted estimates. The most convenient choice is usually the BHHH estimator. The LM statistic is based on the restricted estimates.

Newey and West (1987b) have devised counterparts to these test statistics for the GMM estimator. The Wald statistic is computed identically, using the results of GMM estimation rather than maximum likelihood.[10] That is, in (15-14), we would use the unrestricted GMM estimator of $\boldsymbol{\theta}$. The appropriate asymptotic covariance matrix is (15-12). The computation is exactly the same. The counterpart to the LR statistic is the difference in the values of $nq$ in (15-13). It is necessary to use the same weighting matrix, $\mathbf{W}$, in both restricted and unrestricted estimators. Because the unrestricted estimator is consistent under both $H_0$ and $H_1$, a consistent, unrestricted estimator of $\boldsymbol{\theta}$ is used to compute $\mathbf{W}$. Label this $\boldsymbol{\Phi}_1^{-1} = \big\{\text{Asy. Var}[\sqrt{n}\,\overline{\mathbf{m}}_1(\mathbf{c}_1)]\big\}^{-1}$. In each occurrence, the subscript 1 indicates reference to the unrestricted estimator. Then $q$ is minimized without restrictions to obtain $q_1$ and then subject to the restrictions to obtain $q_0$. The statistic is then $(nq_0 - nq_1)$.[11] Because we are using the same $\mathbf{W}$ in both cases, this statistic is necessarily nonnegative. (This is the statistic discussed in Section 15.5.1.)

Finally, the counterpart to the LM statistic would be

$$\text{LM}_{GMM} = n\big[\overline{\mathbf{m}}_1(\mathbf{c}_0)'\hat{\boldsymbol{\Phi}}_1^{-1}\overline{\mathbf{G}}_1(\mathbf{c}_0)\big]\big[\overline{\mathbf{G}}_1(\mathbf{c}_0)'\hat{\boldsymbol{\Phi}}_1^{-1}\overline{\mathbf{G}}_1(\mathbf{c}_0)\big]^{-1}\big[\overline{\mathbf{G}}_1(\mathbf{c}_0)'\hat{\boldsymbol{\Phi}}_1^{-1}\overline{\mathbf{m}}_1(\mathbf{c}_0)\big].$$

The logic for this LM statistic is the same as that for the MLE. The derivatives of the minimized criterion $q$ in (15-3) evaluated at the restricted estimator are

$$\mathbf{g}_1(\mathbf{c}_0) = \frac{\partial q}{\partial \mathbf{c}_0} = 2\overline{\mathbf{G}}_1(\mathbf{c}_0)'\hat{\boldsymbol{\Phi}}_1^{-1}\overline{\mathbf{m}}(\mathbf{c}_0).$$

The **LM statistic,** $\text{LM}_{GMM}$, is a Wald statistic for testing the hypothesis that this vector equals zero under the restrictions of the null hypothesis. From our earlier results, we would have

$$\text{Est. Asy. Var}[\mathbf{g}_1(\mathbf{c}_0)] = \frac{4}{n}\overline{\mathbf{G}}_1(\mathbf{c}_0)'\hat{\boldsymbol{\Phi}}_1^{-1}\big\{\text{Est. Asy. Var}[\sqrt{n}\,\overline{\mathbf{m}}(\mathbf{c}_0)]\big\}\hat{\boldsymbol{\Phi}}_1^{-1}\overline{\mathbf{G}}_1(\mathbf{c}_0).$$

The estimated asymptotic variance of $\sqrt{n}\,\overline{\mathbf{m}}(\mathbf{c}_0)$ is $\hat{\boldsymbol{\Phi}}_1$, so

$$\text{Est. Asy. Var}[\mathbf{g}_1(\mathbf{c}_0)] = \frac{4}{n}\overline{\mathbf{G}}_1(\mathbf{c}_0)'\hat{\boldsymbol{\Phi}}_1^{-1}\overline{\mathbf{G}}_1(\mathbf{c}_0).$$

---

[10]See Burnside and Eichenbaum (1996) for some small-sample results on this procedure. Newey and McFadden (1994) have shown the asymptotic equivalence of the three procedures.

[11]Newey and West label this test the *D* test.

The Wald statistic would be

$$
\begin{aligned}
\text{Wald} &= \mathbf{g}_1(\mathbf{c}_0)'\big\{\text{Est. Asy. Var}[\mathbf{g}_1(\mathbf{c}_0)]\big\}^{-1}\mathbf{g}_1(\mathbf{c}_0) \\
&= n\,\overline{\mathbf{m}}_1'(\mathbf{c}_0)\hat{\boldsymbol{\Phi}}_1^{-1}\overline{\mathbf{G}}_1(\mathbf{c}_0)\big\{\overline{\mathbf{G}}_1(\mathbf{c}_0)'\hat{\boldsymbol{\Phi}}_1^{-1}\overline{\mathbf{G}}_1(\mathbf{c}_0)\big\}^{-1}\overline{\mathbf{G}}_1(\mathbf{c}_0)'\hat{\boldsymbol{\Phi}}_1^{-1}\overline{\mathbf{m}}_1(\mathbf{c}_0).
\end{aligned} \tag{15-17}
$$

## 15.6  GMM ESTIMATION OF ECONOMETRIC MODELS

The preceding has suggested that the GMM approach to estimation broadly encompasses most of the estimators we will encounter in this book. We have implicitly examined least squares and the general method of instrumental variables in the process. In this section, we will formalize more specifically the GMM estimators for several of the estimators that appear in the earlier chapters. Section 15.6.1 examines the generalized regression model of Chapter 8. Section 15.6.2 describes a relatively minor extension of the GMM/IV estimator to nonlinear regressions. Sections 15.6.3 and 15.6.4 describe the GMM estimators for our models of systems of equations, the seemingly unrelated regressions (SUR) model and models of simultaneous equations. In the latter, as we did in Chapter 13, we consider both limited (single-equation) and full information (multiple-equation) estimators. Finally, in Section 15.6.5, we develop one of the major applications of GMM estimation, the Arellano–Bond–Bover estimator for dynamic panel data models.

### 15.6.1  SINGLE-EQUATION LINEAR MODELS

It is useful to confine attention to the instrumental variables case, as it is fairly general and we can easily specialize it to the simpler regression models if that is appropriate. Thus, we depart from the usual linear model (12-1), but we no longer require that $E[\varepsilon_i \mid \mathbf{x}_i] = 0$. Instead, we adopt the instrumental variables formulation in Section 12.6. That is, our model is

$$
y_i = \mathbf{x}_i'\boldsymbol{\beta} + \varepsilon_i
$$

$$
E[\mathbf{z}_i\varepsilon_i] = \mathbf{0}
$$

for $K$ variables in $\mathbf{x}_i$ and for some set of $L$ instrumental variables, $\mathbf{z}_i$, where $L \geq K$. The earlier case of the generalized regression model arises if $\mathbf{z}_i = \mathbf{x}_i$, and the classical regression form results if we add $\boldsymbol{\Omega} = \mathbf{I}$ as well, so this is a convenient encompassing model framework.

In Chapter 8 on generalized least squares estimation, we considered two cases, first one with a known $\boldsymbol{\Omega}$, then one with an unknown $\boldsymbol{\Omega}$ that must be estimated. In estimation by the generalized method of moments, neither of these approaches is relevant because we begin with much less (assumed) knowledge about the data generating process. We will consider three cases:

- Classical regression: $\text{Var}[\varepsilon_i \mid \mathbf{X}, \mathbf{Z}] = \sigma^2$,
- Heteroscedasticity: $\text{Var}[\varepsilon_i \mid \mathbf{X}, \mathbf{Z}] = \sigma_i^2$,
- Generalized model: $\text{Cov}[\varepsilon_t, \varepsilon_s \mid \mathbf{X}, \mathbf{Z}] = \sigma^2\omega_{ts}$,

where $\mathbf{Z}$ and $\mathbf{X}$ are the $n \times L$ and $n \times K$ observed data matrices. (We assume, as will often be true, that the fully general case will apply in a time-series setting. Hence the change in the subscripts.) *No specific distribution is assumed for the disturbances, conditional or unconditional.*

The assumption $E[\mathbf{z}_i \varepsilon_i] = \mathbf{0}$ implies the following **orthogonality condition:**

$$\text{Cov}[\mathbf{z}_i, \varepsilon_i] = \mathbf{0}, \quad \text{or} \quad E[\mathbf{z}_i(y_i - \mathbf{x}_i'\boldsymbol{\beta})] = \mathbf{0}.$$

By summing the terms, we find that this further implies the **population moment equation,**

$$E\left[\frac{1}{n}\sum_{i=1}^{n}\mathbf{z}_i(y_i - \mathbf{x}_i'\boldsymbol{\beta})\right] = E[\overline{\mathbf{m}}(\boldsymbol{\beta})] = \mathbf{0}. \tag{15-18}$$

This relationship suggests how we might now proceed to estimate $\boldsymbol{\beta}$. Note, in fact, that if $\mathbf{z}_i = \mathbf{x}_i$, then this is just the population counterpart to the least squares normal equations. So, as a guide to estimation, this would return us to least squares. Suppose, we now translate this population expectation into a sample analog and use that as our guide for estimation. That is, if the population relationship holds for the true parameter vector, $\boldsymbol{\beta}$, suppose we attempt to mimic this result with a sample counterpart, or empirical moment equation,

$$\left[\frac{1}{n}\sum_{i=1}^{n}\mathbf{z}_i(y_i - \mathbf{x}_i'\hat{\boldsymbol{\beta}})\right] = \left[\frac{1}{n}\sum_{i=1}^{n}\mathbf{m}_i(\hat{\boldsymbol{\beta}})\right] = \overline{\mathbf{m}}(\hat{\boldsymbol{\beta}}) = \mathbf{0}. \tag{15-19}$$

In the absence of other information about the data generating process, we can use the empirical moment equation as the basis of our estimation strategy.

The empirical moment condition is $L$ equations (the number of variables in $\mathbf{Z}$) in $K$ unknowns (the number of parameters we seek to estimate). There are three possibilities to consider:

1.   **Underidentified:** $L < K$. If there are fewer moment equations than there are parameters, then it will not be possible to find a solution to the equation system in (15-19). With no other information, such as restrictions that would reduce the number of free parameters, there is no need to proceed any further with this case.

For the identified cases, it is convenient to write (15-19) as

$$\overline{\mathbf{m}}(\hat{\boldsymbol{\beta}}) = \left(\frac{1}{n}\mathbf{Z}'\mathbf{y}\right) - \left(\frac{1}{n}\mathbf{Z}'\mathbf{X}\right)\hat{\boldsymbol{\beta}}. \tag{15-20}$$

2.   **Exactly identified.** If $L = K$, then you can easily show (we leave it as an exercise) that the single solution to our equation system is the familiar instrumental variables estimator from Section 12.3.2,

$$\hat{\boldsymbol{\beta}} = (\mathbf{Z}'\mathbf{X})^{-1}\mathbf{Z}'\mathbf{y}. \tag{15-21}$$

3.   **Overidentified.** If $L > K$, then there is no unique solution to the equation system $\overline{\mathbf{m}}(\hat{\boldsymbol{\beta}}) = \mathbf{0}$. In this instance, we need to formulate some strategy to choose an estimator. One intuitively appealing possibility which has served well thus far is "least squares." In this instance, that would mean choosing the estimator based on the criterion function

$$\text{Min}_{\boldsymbol{\beta}} \; q = \overline{\mathbf{m}}(\hat{\boldsymbol{\beta}})'\overline{\mathbf{m}}(\hat{\boldsymbol{\beta}}).$$

We do keep in mind that we will only be able to minimize this at some positive value; there is no exact solution to (15-19) in the overidentified case. Also, you can verify that if we treat the exactly identified case as if it were overidentified, that is, use least squares anyway, we will still obtain the IV estimator shown in (15-21) for the solution to case (2). For the overidentified case, the first-order conditions are

$$\frac{\partial q}{\partial \boldsymbol{\beta}} = 2 \left( \frac{\partial \overline{\mathbf{m}}'(\hat{\boldsymbol{\beta}})}{\partial \boldsymbol{\beta}} \right) \overline{\mathbf{m}}(\hat{\boldsymbol{\beta}}) = 2\overline{\mathbf{G}}(\hat{\boldsymbol{\beta}})' \overline{\mathbf{m}}(\hat{\boldsymbol{\beta}})$$

$$= 2 \left( \frac{1}{n} \mathbf{X}'\mathbf{Z} \right) \left( \frac{1}{n} \mathbf{Z}'\mathbf{y} - \frac{1}{n} \mathbf{Z}'\mathbf{X}\hat{\boldsymbol{\beta}} \right) = \mathbf{0}.$$

(15-22)

We leave as exercise to show that the solution in both cases (2) and (3) is now

$$\hat{\boldsymbol{\beta}} = [(\mathbf{X}'\mathbf{Z})(\mathbf{Z}'\mathbf{X})]^{-1}(\mathbf{X}'\mathbf{Z})(\mathbf{Z}'\mathbf{y}).$$

(15-23)

The estimator in (15-23) is a hybrid that we have not encountered before, though if $L = K$, then it does reduce to the earlier one in (15-21). (In the overidentified case, (15-21) is not an IV estimator, it is, as we have sought, a **method of moments estimator.**)

It remains to establish consistency and to obtain the asymptotic distribution and an asymptotic covariance matrix for the estimator. The intermediate results we need are Assumptions 15.1, 15.2 and 15.3 in Section 15.4.3:

- **Convergence of the moments.** The sample moment converges in probability to its population counterpart. That is, $\overline{\mathbf{m}}(\boldsymbol{\beta}) \rightarrow \mathbf{0}$. Different circumstances will produce different kinds of convergence, but we will require it in some form. For the simplest cases, such as a model of heteroscedasticity, this will be convergence in mean square. Certain time-series models that involve correlated observations will necessitate some other form of convergence. But, in any of the cases we consider, we will require the general result: plim $\overline{\mathbf{m}}(\boldsymbol{\beta}) = \mathbf{0}$.
- **Identification.** The parameters are identified in terms of the moment equations. Identification means, essentially, that a large enough sample will contain sufficient information for us actually to estimate $\boldsymbol{\beta}$ consistently using the sample moments. There are two conditions which must be met—an **order condition,** which we have already assumed ($L \geq K$), and a **rank condition,** which states that the moment equations are not redundant. The rank condition implies the order condition, so we need only formalize it:
- **Identification condition for GMM estimation:** The $L \times K$ matrix

$$\boldsymbol{\Gamma}(\boldsymbol{\beta}) = E[\overline{\mathbf{G}}(\boldsymbol{\beta})] = \text{plim }\overline{\mathbf{G}}(\boldsymbol{\beta}) = \text{plim} \frac{\partial \overline{\mathbf{m}}}{\partial \boldsymbol{\beta}'} = \text{plim} \frac{1}{n} \sum_{i=1}^{n} \frac{\partial \mathbf{m}_i}{\partial \boldsymbol{\beta}'}$$

must have row rank equal to $K$.[12] Because this requires $L \geq K$, this implies the order condition. This assumption means that this derivative matrix converges in probability to its expectation. Note that we have assumed, in addition, that the

---

[12]We require that the row rank be at least as large as $K$. There could be redundant, that is, functionally dependent, moments, so long as there are at least $K$ that are functionally independent.

derivatives, like the moments themselves, obey a law of large numbers—they converge in probability to their expectations.

• **Limiting Normal Distribution for the Sample Moments.** The population moment obeys a central limit theorem or some similar variant. Since we are studying a generalized regression model, Lindeberg–Levy (D.18.) will be too narrow—the observations will have different variances. Lindeberg–Feller (D.19.A) suffices in the heteroscedasticity case, but in the general case, we will ultimately require something more general. See Section 15.4.3.

It will follow from Assumptions 15.1–15.3 (again, at this point we do this without proof) that the GMM estimators that we obtain are, in fact, consistent. By virtue of the Slutsky theorem, we can transfer our limiting results to the empirical moment equations.

To obtain the asymptotic covariance matrix we will simply invoke the general result for GMM estimators in Section 15.4.3. That is,

$$\text{Asy. Var}[\hat{\beta}] = \frac{1}{n}[\boldsymbol{\Gamma}'\boldsymbol{\Gamma}]^{-1}\boldsymbol{\Gamma}'\left\{\text{Asy. Var}[\sqrt{n}\,\overline{\mathbf{m}}(\beta)]\right\}\boldsymbol{\Gamma}[\boldsymbol{\Gamma}'\boldsymbol{\Gamma}]^{-1}.$$

For the particular model we are studying here,

$$\overline{\mathbf{m}}(\beta) = (1/n)(\mathbf{Z}'\mathbf{y} - \mathbf{Z}'\mathbf{X}\beta),$$

$$\overline{\mathbf{G}}(\beta) = (1/n)\mathbf{Z}'\mathbf{X},$$

$$\boldsymbol{\Gamma}(\beta) = \mathbf{Q_{ZX}} \text{ (see Section 12.3.2)}.$$

(You should check in the preceding expression that the dimensions of the particular matrices and the dimensions of the various products produce the correctly configured matrix that we seek.) The remaining detail, which is the crucial one for the model we are examining, is for us to determine

$$\mathbf{V} = \text{Asy. Var}[\sqrt{n}\,\overline{\mathbf{m}}(\beta)].$$

Given the form of $\overline{\mathbf{m}}(\beta)$,

$$\mathbf{V} = \frac{1}{n}\text{Var}\left[\sum_{i=1}^{n}\mathbf{z}_i\varepsilon_i\right] = \frac{1}{n}\sum_{i=1}^{n}\sum_{j=1}^{n}\sigma^2\omega_{ij}\mathbf{z}_i\mathbf{z}_j' = \sigma^2\frac{\mathbf{Z}'\boldsymbol{\Omega}\mathbf{Z}}{n}$$

for the most general case. Note that this is precisely the expression that appears in (8-6), so the question that arose there arises here once again. That is, under what conditions will this converge to a constant matrix? We take the discussion there as given. The only remaining detail is how to estimate this matrix. The answer appears in Section 8.2.3, where we pursued this same question in connection with robust estimation of the asymptotic covariance matrix of the least squares estimator. To review then, what we have achieved to this point is to provide a theoretical foundation for the instrumental variables estimator. As noted earlier, this specializes to the least squares estimator. The estimators of **V** for our three cases will be

• Classical regression:

$$\hat{\mathbf{V}} = \frac{(\mathbf{e}'\mathbf{e}/n)}{n}\sum_{i=1}^{n}\mathbf{z}_i\mathbf{z}_i' = \frac{(\mathbf{e}'\mathbf{e}/n)}{n}\mathbf{Z}'\mathbf{Z}.$$

- Heteroscedastic regression:

$$\hat{\mathbf{V}} = \frac{1}{n} \sum_{i=1}^{n} e_i^2 \mathbf{z}_i \mathbf{z}_i'. \tag{15-24}$$

- Generalized regression:

$$\hat{\mathbf{V}} = \frac{1}{n} \left[ \sum_{t=1}^{n} e_t^2 \mathbf{z}_t \mathbf{z}_t' + \sum_{\ell=1}^{p} \left( 1 - \frac{\ell}{(p+1)} \right) \sum_{t=\ell+1}^{n} e_t e_{t-\ell} (\mathbf{z}_t \mathbf{z}_{t-\ell}' + \mathbf{z}_{t-\ell} \mathbf{z}_t') \right].$$

We should observe that in each of these cases, we have actually used some information about the structure of $\mathbf{\Omega}$. If it is known only that the terms in $\overline{\mathbf{m}}(\boldsymbol{\beta})$ are uncorrelated, then there is a convenient estimator available,

$$\hat{\mathbf{V}} = \frac{1}{n} \sum_{i=1}^{n} \mathbf{m}_i(\hat{\boldsymbol{\beta}}) \mathbf{m}_i(\hat{\boldsymbol{\beta}})',$$

that is, the natural, empirical variance estimator. Note that this is what is being used in the heteroscedasticity case directly preceding.

Collecting all the terms so far, then, we have

$$\text{Est. Asy. Var}[\hat{\boldsymbol{\beta}}] = \frac{1}{n} [\overline{\mathbf{G}}(\hat{\boldsymbol{\beta}})' \overline{\mathbf{G}}(\hat{\boldsymbol{\beta}})]^{-1} \overline{\mathbf{G}}(\hat{\boldsymbol{\beta}})' \hat{\mathbf{V}} \overline{\mathbf{G}}(\hat{\boldsymbol{\beta}}) [\overline{\mathbf{G}}(\hat{\boldsymbol{\beta}})' \overline{\mathbf{G}}(\hat{\boldsymbol{\beta}})]^{-1}$$

$$= n[(\mathbf{X}'\mathbf{Z})(\mathbf{Z}'\mathbf{X})]^{-1}(\mathbf{X}'\mathbf{Z})\hat{\mathbf{V}}(\mathbf{Z}'\mathbf{X})[(\mathbf{X}'\mathbf{Z})(\mathbf{Z}'\mathbf{X})]^{-1}. \tag{15-25}$$

The preceding might seem to endow the least squares or method of moments estimators with some degree of optimality, but that is not the case. We have only provided them with a different statistical motivation (and established consistency). We now consider the question of whether, because this is the generalized regression model, there is some better (more efficient) means of using the data.

The class of minimum distance estimators for this model is defined by the solutions to the criterion function

$$\text{Min}_{\boldsymbol{\beta}} \; q = \overline{\mathbf{m}}(\boldsymbol{\beta})' \mathbf{W} \overline{\mathbf{m}}(\boldsymbol{\beta}),$$

where $\mathbf{W}$ is *any* positive definite **weighting matrix.** Based on the assumptions just made, we can invoke Theorem 15.1 to obtain

$$\text{Asy. Var} \left[ \hat{\boldsymbol{\beta}}_{MD} \right] = \frac{1}{n} \left[ \overline{\mathbf{G}}' \mathbf{W} \overline{\mathbf{G}} \right]^{-1} \overline{\mathbf{G}}' \mathbf{W} \mathbf{V} \mathbf{W} \overline{\mathbf{G}} \left[ \overline{\mathbf{G}}' \mathbf{W} \overline{\mathbf{G}} \right]^{-1}.$$

Note that our entire preceding analysis was of the simplest minimum distance estimator, which has $\mathbf{W} = \mathbf{I}$. The obvious question now arises, if any $\mathbf{W}$ produces a consistent estimator, is any $\mathbf{W}$ better than any other one, or is it simply arbitrary? There is a firm answer, for which we have to consider two cases separately:

- **Exactly identified case.** If $L = K$; that is, if the number of moment conditions is the same as the number of parameters being estimated, then $\mathbf{W}$ is irrelevant to the solution, so on the basis of simplicity alone, the optimal $\mathbf{W}$ is $\mathbf{I}$.
- **Overidentified case.** In this case, the "optimal" weighting matrix, that is, the $\mathbf{W}$ that produces the most efficient estimator, is $\mathbf{W} = \mathbf{V}^{-1}$. The best weighting matrix is the inverse of the asymptotic covariance of the moment vector. In this case,

the MDE will be the GMM estimator with

$$\hat{\boldsymbol{\beta}}_{GMM} = [(\mathbf{X}'\mathbf{Z})\hat{\mathbf{V}}^{-1}(\mathbf{Z}'\mathbf{X})]^{-1}(\mathbf{X}'\mathbf{Z})\hat{\mathbf{V}}^{-1}(\mathbf{Z}'\mathbf{y}),$$

and

$$\text{Asy. Var}\big[\hat{\boldsymbol{\beta}}_{GMM}\big] = \frac{1}{n}[\overline{\mathbf{G}}'\mathbf{V}^{-1}\overline{\mathbf{G}}]^{-1}$$
$$= [(\mathbf{X}'\mathbf{Z})\mathbf{V}^{-1}(\mathbf{Z}'\mathbf{X})]^{-1}.$$

We conclude this discussion by tying together what should seem to be a loose end. The GMM estimator is computed as the solution to

$$\text{Min}_{\beta} \; q = \overline{\mathbf{m}}(\boldsymbol{\beta})' \left\{ \text{Asy. Var}[\sqrt{n}\,\overline{\mathbf{m}}(\boldsymbol{\beta})] \right\}^{-1} \overline{\mathbf{m}}(\boldsymbol{\beta}),$$

which might suggest that the weighting matrix is a function of the thing we are trying to estimate. The process of GMM estimation will have to proceed in two steps: Step 1 is to obtain an estimate of $\mathbf{V}$; Step 2 will consist of using the inverse of this $\mathbf{V}$ as the weighting matrix in computing the GMM estimator. The following is a common strategy:

**Step 1.** Use $\mathbf{W} = \mathbf{I}$ to obtain a consistent estimator of $\boldsymbol{\beta}$. Then, estimate $\mathbf{V}$ with

$$\hat{\mathbf{V}} = \frac{1}{n} \sum_{i=1}^{n} e_i^2 \mathbf{z}_i \mathbf{z}_i'$$

in the heteroscedasticity case (i.e., the White estimator) or, for the more general case, the Newey-West estimator.

**Step 2.** Use $\mathbf{W} = \hat{\mathbf{V}}^{-1}$ to compute the GMM estimator.

By this point, the observant reader should have noticed that in all of the preceding, we have never actually encountered the two-stage least squares estimator that we introduced in Section 12.3.3. To obtain this estimator, we must revert back to the classical, that is, homoscedastic, and nonautocorrelated disturbances case. In that instance, the weighting matrix in Theorem 15.2 will be $\mathbf{W} = (\mathbf{Z}'\mathbf{Z})^{-1}$ and we will obtain the apparently missing result.

The **GMM estimator** in the heteroscedastic regression model is produced by the empirical moment equations

$$\frac{1}{n} \sum_{i=1}^{n} \mathbf{x}_i \big( y_i - \mathbf{x}_i'\hat{\boldsymbol{\beta}}_{GMM} \big) = \frac{1}{n}\mathbf{X}'\hat{\boldsymbol{\varepsilon}}\big(\hat{\boldsymbol{\beta}}_{GMM}\big) = \overline{\mathbf{m}}\big(\hat{\boldsymbol{\beta}}_{GMM}\big) = \mathbf{0}. \tag{15-26}$$

The estimator is obtained by minimizing

$$q = \overline{\mathbf{m}}'\big(\hat{\boldsymbol{\beta}}_{GMM}\big)\mathbf{W}\overline{\mathbf{m}}\big(\hat{\boldsymbol{\beta}}_{GMM}\big),$$

where $\mathbf{W}$ is a positive definite weighting matrix. The optimal weighting matrix would be

$$\mathbf{W} = \left\{ \text{Asy. Var}[\sqrt{n}\,\overline{\mathbf{m}}(\boldsymbol{\beta})] \right\}^{-1},$$

which is the inverse of

$$\text{Asy. Var}[\sqrt{n}\overline{\mathbf{m}}(\boldsymbol{\beta})] = \text{Asy. Var}\left[ \frac{1}{\sqrt{n}} \sum_{i=1}^{n} \mathbf{x}_i \varepsilon_i \right] = \plim_{n \to \infty} \frac{1}{n} \sum_{i=1}^{n} \sigma^2 \omega_i \mathbf{x}_i \mathbf{x}_i' = \sigma^2 \mathbf{Q}^*.$$

[See Section 8.4.1.] The optimal weighting matrix would be $[\sigma^2 \mathbf{Q}^*]^{-1}$. But recall that this minimization problem is an exactly identified case, so the weighting matrix is irrelevant to the solution. You can see the result in the moment equation—that equation is simply the normal equations for ordinary least squares. We can solve the moment equations exactly, so there is no need for the weighting matrix. *Regardless of the covariance matrix of the moments, the GMM estimator for the heteroscedastic regression model is ordinary least squares.* We can use the results we have already obtained to find its asymptotic covariance matrix. The implied estimator is the White estimator in (8-27). [Once again, see Theorem 15.2.] The conclusion to be drawn at this point is that until we make some specific assumptions about the variances, we do not have a more efficient estimator than least squares, but we do have to modify the estimated asymptotic covariance matrix.

### 15.6.2  SINGLE-EQUATION NONLINEAR MODELS

Suppose that the theory specifies a relationship

$$y_i = h(\mathbf{x}_i, \boldsymbol{\beta}) + \varepsilon_i,$$

where $\boldsymbol{\beta}$ is a $K \times 1$ parameter vector that we wish to estimate. This may not be a regression relationship, because it is possible that

$$\text{Cov}[\varepsilon_i, h(\mathbf{x}_i, \boldsymbol{\beta})] \neq 0,$$

or even

$$\text{Cov}[\varepsilon_i, \mathbf{x}_j] \neq 0 \text{ for all } i \text{ and } j.$$

Consider, for example, a model that contains lagged dependent variables and autocorrelated disturbances. (See Section 19.9.3.) For the present, we assume that

$$E[\boldsymbol{\varepsilon} \mid \mathbf{X}] \neq \mathbf{0},$$

and

$$E[\boldsymbol{\varepsilon}\boldsymbol{\varepsilon}' \mid \mathbf{X}] = \sigma^2 \boldsymbol{\Omega} = \boldsymbol{\Sigma},$$

where $\boldsymbol{\Sigma}$ is symmetric and positive definite but otherwise unrestricted. The disturbances may be heteroscedastic and/or autocorrelated. But for the possibility of correlation between regressors and disturbances, this model would be a generalized, possibly nonlinear, regression model. Suppose that at each observation $i$ we observe a vector of $L$ variables, $\mathbf{z}_i$, such that $\mathbf{z}_i$ is uncorrelated with $\varepsilon_i$. You will recognize $\mathbf{z}_i$ as a set of **instrumental variables.** The assumptions thus far have implied a set of orthogonality conditions,

$$E[\mathbf{z}_i \varepsilon_i] = \mathbf{0},$$

which may be sufficient to identify (if $L = K$) or even overidentify (if $L > K$) the parameters of the model.

For convenience, define

$$\mathbf{e}(\mathbf{X}, \hat{\boldsymbol{\beta}}) = y_i - h(\mathbf{x}_i, \hat{\boldsymbol{\beta}}), \quad i = 1, \ldots, n,$$

and

$$\mathbf{Z} = n \times L \text{ matrix whose ith row is } \mathbf{z}_i'.$$

By a straightforward extension of our earlier results, we can produce a GMM estimator of $\boldsymbol{\beta}$. The sample moments will be

$$\bar{\mathbf{m}}_n(\boldsymbol{\beta}) = \frac{1}{n} \sum_{i=1}^{n} \mathbf{z}_i e(\mathbf{x}_i, \boldsymbol{\beta}) = \frac{1}{n} \mathbf{Z}' \mathbf{e}(\mathbf{X}, \boldsymbol{\beta}).$$

The minimum distance estimator will be the $\hat{\boldsymbol{\beta}}$ that minimizes

$$q = \bar{\mathbf{m}}_n(\hat{\boldsymbol{\beta}})' \mathbf{W} \bar{\mathbf{m}}_n(\hat{\boldsymbol{\beta}}) = \left( \frac{1}{n} [\mathbf{e}(\mathbf{X}, \hat{\boldsymbol{\beta}})' \mathbf{Z}] \right) \mathbf{W} \left( \frac{1}{n} [\mathbf{Z}' \mathbf{e}(\mathbf{X}, \hat{\boldsymbol{\beta}})] \right) \tag{15-27}$$

for some choice of $\mathbf{W}$ that we have yet to determine. The criterion given earlier produces the **nonlinear instrumental variable estimator.** If we use $\mathbf{W} = (\mathbf{Z}'\mathbf{Z})^{-1}$, then we have exactly the estimation criterion we used in Section 12.7, where we defined the nonlinear instrumental variables estimator. Apparently (15-27) is more general, because we are not limited to this choice of $\mathbf{W}$. For any given choice of $\mathbf{W}$, as long as there are enough orthogonality conditions to identify the parameters, estimation by minimizing $q$ is, at least in principle, a straightforward problem in nonlinear optimization. The optimal choice of $\mathbf{W}$ for this estimator is

$$\begin{aligned} \mathbf{W}_{\text{GMM}} &= \left\{ \text{Asy. Var}[\sqrt{n}\, \bar{\mathbf{m}}_n(\boldsymbol{\beta})] \right\}^{-1} \\ &= \left\{ \text{Asy. Var}\left[ \frac{1}{\sqrt{n}} \sum_{i=1}^{n} \mathbf{z}_i \varepsilon_i \right] \right\}^{-1} = \left\{ \text{Asy. Var}\left[ \frac{1}{\sqrt{n}} \mathbf{Z}' \mathbf{e}(\mathbf{X}, \boldsymbol{\beta}) \right] \right\}^{-1}. \end{aligned} \tag{15-28}$$

For our model, this is

$$\mathbf{W} = \left[ \frac{1}{n} \sum_{i=1}^{n} \sum_{j=1}^{n} \text{Cov}[\mathbf{z}_i \varepsilon_i, \mathbf{z}_j \varepsilon_j] \right]^{-1} = \left[ \frac{1}{n} \sum_{i=1}^{n} \sum_{j=1}^{n} \sigma_{ij} \mathbf{z}_i \mathbf{z}_j' \right]^{-1} = \left[ \frac{\mathbf{Z}' \boldsymbol{\Sigma} \mathbf{Z}}{n} \right]^{-1}.$$

If we insert this result in (15-27), we obtain the criterion for the GMM estimator:

$$q = \left[ \left( \frac{1}{n} \right) \mathbf{e}(\mathbf{X}, \hat{\boldsymbol{\beta}})' \mathbf{Z} \right] \left( \frac{\mathbf{Z}' \boldsymbol{\Sigma} \mathbf{Z}}{n} \right)^{-1} \left[ \left( \frac{1}{n} \right) \mathbf{Z}' \mathbf{e}(\mathbf{X}, \hat{\boldsymbol{\beta}}) \right].$$

There is a possibly difficult detail to be considered. The GMM estimator involves

$$\frac{1}{n} \mathbf{Z}' \boldsymbol{\Sigma} \mathbf{Z} = \frac{1}{n} \sum_{i=1}^{n} \sum_{j=1}^{n} \mathbf{z}_i \mathbf{z}_j' \text{Cov}[\varepsilon_i, \varepsilon_j] = \frac{1}{n} \sum_{i=1}^{n} \sum_{j=1}^{n} \mathbf{z}_i \mathbf{z}_j' \text{Cov}[(y_i - h(\mathbf{x}_i, \boldsymbol{\beta})), (y_j - h(\mathbf{x}_j, \boldsymbol{\beta}))].$$

The conditions under which such a double sum might converge to a positive definite matrix are sketched in Section 8.2.2. Assuming that they do hold, estimation appears to require that an estimate of $\boldsymbol{\beta}$ be in hand already, even though it is the object of estimation.

It may be that a consistent but inefficient estimator of $\beta$ is available. Suppose for the present that one is. If observations are uncorrelated, then the cross-observation terms may be omitted, and what is required is

$$\frac{1}{n}\mathbf{Z}'\mathbf{\Sigma}\mathbf{Z} = \frac{1}{n}\sum_{i=1}^{n}\mathbf{z}_i\mathbf{z}_i'\mathrm{Var}[(y_i - h(\mathbf{x}_i, \boldsymbol{\beta}))].$$

We can use a counterpart to the White (1980) estimator discussed in Section 8.4.4 for this case:

$$\mathbf{S}_0 = \frac{1}{n}\sum_{i=1}^{n}\mathbf{z}_i\mathbf{z}_i'(y_i - h(\mathbf{x}_i, \hat{\boldsymbol{\beta}}))^2. \tag{15-29}$$

If the disturbances are autocorrelated but the process is stationary, then Newey and West's (1987a) estimator is available (assuming that the autocorrelations are sufficiently small at a reasonable lag, $p$):

$$\mathbf{S} = \left[\mathbf{S}_0 + \frac{1}{n}\sum_{\ell=1}^{p}w(\ell)\sum_{i=\ell+1}^{n}e_ie_{i-\ell}(\mathbf{z}_i\mathbf{z}_{i-\ell}' + \mathbf{z}_{i-\ell}\mathbf{z}_i')\right] = \sum_{\ell=0}^{p}w(\ell)\mathbf{S}_\ell, \tag{15-30}$$

where

$$w(\ell) = 1 - \frac{\ell}{p+1}.$$

The maximum lag length $p$ must be determined in advance. We will require that observations that are far apart in time—that is, for which $|i - \ell|$ is large—must have increasingly smaller covariances for us to establish the convergence results that justify OLS, GLS, and now GMM estimation. The choice of $p$ is a reflection of how far back in time one must go to consider the autocorrelation negligible for purposes of estimating $(1/n)\mathbf{Z}'\mathbf{\Sigma}\mathbf{Z}$. Current practice suggests using the smallest integer greater than or equal to $n^{1/4}$.

Still left open is the question of where the initial consistent estimator should be obtained. One possibility is to obtain an inefficient but consistent GMM estimator by using $\mathbf{W} = \mathbf{I}$ in (15-27). That is, use a nonlinear (or linear, if the equation is linear) instrumental variables estimator. This first-step estimator can then be used to construct $\mathbf{W}$, which, in turn, can then be used in the GMM estimator. Another possibility is that $\beta$ may be consistently estimable by some straightforward procedure other than GMM.

Once the GMM estimator has been computed, its asymptotic covariance matrix and asymptotic distribution can be estimated based on Theorem 15.2. Recall that

$$\overline{\mathbf{m}}_n(\boldsymbol{\beta}) = \frac{1}{n}\sum_{i=1}^{n}\mathbf{z}_i\varepsilon_i,$$

which is a sum of $L \times 1$ vectors. The derivative, $\partial\overline{\mathbf{m}}_n(\boldsymbol{\beta})/\partial\boldsymbol{\beta}'$, is a sum of $L \times K$ matrices, so

$$\overline{\mathbf{G}}(\boldsymbol{\beta}) = \partial\overline{\mathbf{m}}(\boldsymbol{\beta})/\partial\boldsymbol{\beta}' = \frac{1}{n}\sum_{i=1}^{n}\mathbf{G}_i(\boldsymbol{\beta}) = \frac{1}{n}\sum_{i=1}^{n}\mathbf{z}_i\left[\frac{\partial\varepsilon_i}{\partial\boldsymbol{\beta}'}\right]. \tag{15-31}$$

In the model we are considering here,

$$\frac{\partial \varepsilon_i}{\partial \boldsymbol{\beta}'} = \frac{-\partial h(\mathbf{x}_i, \boldsymbol{\beta})}{\partial \boldsymbol{\beta}'}.$$

The derivatives are the pseudoregressors in the linearized regression model that we examined in Section 11.2.3. Using the notation defined there,

$$\frac{\partial \varepsilon_i}{\partial \boldsymbol{\beta}} = -\mathbf{x}_i^0,$$

so

$$\overline{\mathbf{G}}(\boldsymbol{\beta}) = \frac{1}{n} \sum_{i=1}^n \mathbf{G}_i(\boldsymbol{\beta}) = \frac{1}{n} \sum_{i=1}^n -\mathbf{z}_i \mathbf{x}_i^{0\prime} = -\frac{1}{n} \mathbf{Z}' \mathbf{X}^0. \qquad \textbf{(15-32)}$$

With this matrix in hand, the estimated asymptotic covariance matrix for the GMM estimator is

$$\text{Est. Asy. Var}[\hat{\boldsymbol{\beta}}] = \left[ \overline{\mathbf{G}}(\hat{\boldsymbol{\beta}})' \left( \frac{1}{n} \mathbf{Z}' \hat{\boldsymbol{\Sigma}} \mathbf{Z} \right)^{-1} \overline{\mathbf{G}}(\hat{\boldsymbol{\beta}}) \right]^{-1} = [(\mathbf{X}^{0\prime} \mathbf{Z})(\mathbf{Z}' \hat{\boldsymbol{\Sigma}} \mathbf{Z})^{-1}(\mathbf{Z}' \mathbf{X}^0)]^{-1}.$$

$$\textbf{(15-33)}$$

(The two minus signs, a $1/n^2$, and an $n^2$, all fall out of the result.)

If the $\boldsymbol{\Sigma}$ that appears in (15-33) were $\sigma^2 \mathbf{I}$, then (15-33) would be precisely the asymptotic covariance matrix that appears in Theorem 12.2 for linear models and Theorem 12.3 for nonlinear models. But there is an interesting distinction between this estimator and the IV estimators discussed earlier. In the earlier cases, when there were more instrumental variables than parameters, we resolved the overidentification by specifically choosing a set of $K$ instruments, the $K$ projections of the columns of $\mathbf{X}$ or $\mathbf{X}^0$ into the column space of $\mathbf{Z}$. Here, in contrast, we do not attempt to resolve the overidentification; we simply use all the instruments and minimize the GMM criterion. Now, you should be able to show that when $\boldsymbol{\Sigma} = \sigma^2 \mathbf{I}$ *and we use this information*, when all is said and done, the same parameter estimates will be obtained. But, if we use a weighting matrix that differs from $\mathbf{W} = (\mathbf{Z}' \mathbf{Z}/n)^{-1}$, then they are not.

### 15.6.3 SEEMINGLY UNRELATED REGRESSION MODELS

In Section 11.5, we considered FGLS estimation of the equation system

$$\mathbf{y}_1 = \mathbf{h}_1(\mathbf{X}, \boldsymbol{\beta}) + \boldsymbol{\varepsilon}_1,$$

$$\mathbf{y}_2 = \mathbf{h}_2(\mathbf{X}, \boldsymbol{\beta}) + \boldsymbol{\varepsilon}_2,$$

$$\vdots$$

$$\mathbf{y}_M = \mathbf{h}_M(\mathbf{X}, \boldsymbol{\beta}) + \boldsymbol{\varepsilon}_M.$$

The development there extends backwards to the linear system as well. However, none of the estimators considered are consistent if the pseudoregressors, $\mathbf{x}_{tm}^0$, or the actual regressors, $\mathbf{x}_{tm}$ for the linear model, are correlated with the disturbances, $\varepsilon_{tm}$. Suppose we allow for this correlation both within and across equations. (If it is, in fact, absent, then the GMM estimator developed here will remain consistent.) For simplicity in this section, we will denote observations with subscript $t$ and equations with subscripts $i$ and $j$. Suppose, as well, that there are a set of instrumental variables, $\mathbf{z}_t$, such that

$$E[\mathbf{z}_t \varepsilon_{tm}] = \mathbf{0}, t = 1, \ldots, T \text{ and } m = 1, \ldots, M. \tag{15-34}$$

(We could allow a separate set of instrumental variables for each equation, but it would needlessly complicate the presentation.)

Under these assumptions, the nonlinear FGLS and ML estimators given earlier will be inconsistent. But a relatively minor extension of the instrumental variables technique developed for the single-equation case in Section 12.4 can be used instead. The sample analog to (15-34) is

$$\frac{1}{T} \sum_{t=1}^{T} \mathbf{z}_t [y_{ti} - h_i(\mathbf{x}_t, \boldsymbol{\beta})] = \mathbf{0}, \quad i = 1, \ldots, M.$$

If we use this result for each equation in the system, one at a time, then we obtain exactly the GMM estimator discussed in Section 15.6.2. But, in addition to the efficiency loss that results from not imposing the cross-equation constraints in $\boldsymbol{\beta}$, we would also neglect the correlation between the disturbances. Let

$$\frac{1}{T} \mathbf{Z}' \boldsymbol{\Omega}_{ij} \mathbf{Z} = E\left[\frac{\mathbf{Z}' \boldsymbol{\varepsilon}_i \boldsymbol{\varepsilon}'_j \mathbf{Z}}{T}\right]. \tag{15-35}$$

The GMM criterion for estimation in this setting is

$$q = \sum_{i=1}^{M} \sum_{j=1}^{M} [(\mathbf{y}_i - \mathbf{h}_i(\mathbf{X}, \boldsymbol{\beta}))' \mathbf{Z}/T][\mathbf{Z}' \boldsymbol{\Omega}_{ij} \mathbf{Z}/T]^{ij} [\mathbf{Z}'(\mathbf{y}_j - \mathbf{h}_j(\mathbf{X}, \boldsymbol{\beta}))/T]$$

$$= \sum_{i=1}^{M} \sum_{j=1}^{M} [\boldsymbol{\varepsilon}_i(\boldsymbol{\beta})' \mathbf{Z}/T][\mathbf{Z}' \boldsymbol{\Omega}_{ij} \mathbf{Z}/T]^{ij} [\mathbf{Z}' \boldsymbol{\varepsilon}_j(\boldsymbol{\beta})/T], \tag{15-36}$$

where $[\mathbf{Z}' \boldsymbol{\Omega}_{ij} \mathbf{Z}/T]^{ij}$ denotes the $ij$th block of the inverse of the matrix with the $ij$th block equal to $\mathbf{Z}' \boldsymbol{\Omega}_{ij} \mathbf{Z}/T$. (This matrix is laid out in full in Section 15.6.4.)

GMM estimation would proceed in several passes. To compute any of the variance parameters, we will require an initial consistent estimator of $\boldsymbol{\beta}$. This step can be done with equation-by-equation nonlinear instrumental variables—see Section 12.7—although if equations have parameters in common, then a choice must be made as to which to use. At the next step, the familiar White or Newey-West technique is used to compute, block by block, the matrix in (15-35). Because it is based on a consistent estimator of $\boldsymbol{\beta}$ (we assume), this matrix need not be recomputed. Now, with this result in hand, an iterative solution to the maximization problem in (15-36) can be sought, for example, using the methods of Appendix E. The first-order conditions are

$$\frac{\partial q}{\partial \boldsymbol{\beta}} = -2 \sum_{i=1}^{M} \sum_{j=1}^{M} [\mathbf{X}_i^0(\boldsymbol{\beta})' \mathbf{Z}/T][\mathbf{Z}' \mathbf{W}_{ij} \mathbf{Z}/T]^{ij} [\mathbf{Z}' \boldsymbol{\varepsilon}_j(\boldsymbol{\beta})/T] = \mathbf{0}. \tag{15-37}$$

Note again that the blocks of the inverse matrix in the center are extracted from the larger constructed matrix *after inversion*. [This brief discussion might understate the complexity of the optimization problem in (15-36), but that is inherent in the procedure.] At completion, the asymptotic covariance matrix for the GMM estimator is estimated with

$$
\mathbf{V}_{\text{GMM}} = \frac{1}{T} \left[ \sum_{i=1}^{M} \sum_{j=1}^{M} \left[ \mathbf{X}_i^0(\boldsymbol{\beta})' \mathbf{Z}/T \right] \left[ \mathbf{Z}' \mathbf{W}_{ij} \mathbf{Z}/T \right]^{ij} \left[ \mathbf{Z}' \mathbf{X}_j^0(\boldsymbol{\beta})/T \right] \right]^{-1}.
$$

### 15.6.4 SIMULTANEOUS EQUATIONS MODELS WITH HETEROSCEDASTICITY

The GMM estimator in Section 15.6.1 is, with a minor change of notation, precisely the set of procedures we used in Section 13.5 to estimate the equations in a simultaneous equations model. Using a GMM estimator, however, will allow us to generalize the covariance structure for the disturbances. We assume that

$$
y_{tj} = \mathbf{z}_{tj}' \boldsymbol{\delta}_j + \varepsilon_{tj}, \quad t = 1, \ldots, T,
$$

where $\mathbf{z}_{tj} = [\mathbf{Y}_{tj}, \mathbf{x}_{tj}]$. (We use the capital $\mathbf{Y}_{tj}$ to denote the $L_j$ included endogenous variables. Note, as well, that to maintain consistency with Chapter 13, the roles of the symbols $\mathbf{x}$ and $\mathbf{z}$ are reversed here; $\mathbf{x}$ is now the vector of exogenous variables.) We have assumed that $\varepsilon_{tj}$ in the $j$th equation is neither heteroscedastic nor autocorrelated. There is no need to impose those assumptions at this point. Autocorrelation in the context of a simultaneous equations model is a substantial complication, however. For the present, we will consider the heteroscedastic case only.

The assumptions of the model provide the orthogonality conditions,

$$
E[\mathbf{x}_t \varepsilon_{tj}] = E[\mathbf{x}_t(y_{tj} - \mathbf{z}_{tj}' \boldsymbol{\delta}_j)] = \mathbf{0}.
$$

If $\mathbf{x}_t$ is taken to be the full set of exogenous variables in the model, then we obtain the criterion for the GMM estimator for the $j$th equation,

$$
q = \left[ \frac{\mathbf{e}(\mathbf{z}_t, \boldsymbol{\delta}_j)' \mathbf{X}}{T} \right] \mathbf{W}_{jj}^{-1} \left[ \frac{\mathbf{X}' \mathbf{e}(\mathbf{z}_t, \boldsymbol{\delta}_j)}{T} \right]
$$

$$
= \overline{\mathbf{m}}(\boldsymbol{\delta}_j)' \mathbf{W}_{jj}^{-1} \overline{\mathbf{m}}(\boldsymbol{\delta}_j),
$$

where

$$
\overline{\mathbf{m}}(\boldsymbol{\delta}_j) = \frac{1}{T} \sum_{t=1}^{T} \mathbf{x}_t(y_{tj} - \mathbf{z}_{tj}' \boldsymbol{\delta}_j) \quad \text{and} \quad \mathbf{W}_{jj}^{-1} = \text{the GMM weighting matrix.}
$$

Once again, this is precisely the estimator defined in Section 15.6.1. If the disturbances are assumed to be homoscedastic and nonautocorrelated, then the optimal weighting matrix will be an estimator of the inverse of

$$
\mathbf{W}_{jj} = \text{Asy. Var}[\sqrt{T} \, \overline{\mathbf{m}}(\boldsymbol{\delta}_j)]
$$

$$
= \text{plim} \left[ \frac{1}{T} \sum_{t=1}^{T} \mathbf{x}_t \mathbf{x}_t' (y_{tj} - \mathbf{z}_{tj}' \boldsymbol{\delta}_j)^2 \right]
$$

$$
= \text{plim} \frac{1}{T} \sum_{t=1}^{T} \sigma_{jj} \mathbf{x}_t \mathbf{x}_t'
$$

$$
= \text{plim} \, \sigma_{jj} \left( \frac{\mathbf{X}' \mathbf{X}}{T} \right).
$$

The constant $\sigma_{jj}$ is irrelevant to the solution. If we use $(\mathbf{X}'\mathbf{X})^{-1}$ as the weighting matrix, then the GMM estimator that minimizes $q$ is the 2SLS estimator.

The extension that we can obtain here is to allow for heteroscedasticity of unknown form. There is no need to rederive the earlier result. If the disturbances are heteroscedastic, then

$$\mathbf{W}_{jj} = \text{plim} \frac{1}{T} \sum_{t=1}^{T} \omega_{jj,t} \mathbf{x}_t \mathbf{x}_t' = \text{plim} \frac{\mathbf{X}' \boldsymbol{\Omega}_{jj} \mathbf{X}}{T}.$$

The weighting matrix can be estimated with White's heteroscedasticity consistent estimator—see (15-24)—if a consistent estimator of $\boldsymbol{\delta}_j$ is in hand with which to compute the residuals. One is, because 2SLS ignoring the heteroscedasticity is consistent, albeit inefficient. The conclusion then is that under these assumptions, there is a way to improve on 2SLS by adding another step. The name 3SLS is reserved for the systems estimator of this sort. When choosing between 2.5-stage least squares and Davidson and MacKinnon's suggested "heteroscedastic 2SLS," or **H2SLS**, we chose to opt for the latter. The estimator is based on the initial two-stage least squares procedure. Thus,

$$\hat{\boldsymbol{\delta}}_{j,\text{H2SLS}} = [\mathbf{Z}_j' \mathbf{X}(\mathbf{S}_{0,jj})^{-1} \mathbf{X}' \mathbf{Z}_j]^{-1} [\mathbf{Z}_j' \mathbf{X}(\mathbf{S}_{0,jj})^{-1} \mathbf{X}' \mathbf{y}_j],$$

where

$$\mathbf{S}_{0,jj} = \sum_{t=1}^{T} \mathbf{x}_t \mathbf{x}_t' (y_{tj} - \mathbf{z}_{tj}' \hat{\boldsymbol{\delta}}_{j,\text{2SLS}})^2.$$

The asymptotic covariance matrix is estimated with

$$\text{Est. Asy. Var}[\hat{\boldsymbol{\delta}}_{j,\text{H2SLS}}] = [\mathbf{Z}_j' \mathbf{X}(\mathbf{S}_{0,jj})^{-1} \mathbf{X}' \mathbf{Z}_j]^{-1}.$$

Extensions of this estimator were suggested by Cragg (1983) and Cumby, Huizinga, and Obstfeld (1983). The H2SLS estimates for Klein's Model I appear in the third panel of results in Table 13.3. Note that the estimated standard errors for these estimates are considerably smaller than those for 2SLS or LIML.

The GMM estimator for a system of equations is described in Section 15.6.3. As in the single-equation case, a minor change in notation produces the estimators for a simultaneous equations model. As before, we will consider the case of unknown heteroscedasticity only. The extension to autocorrelation is quite complicated. [See Cumby, Huizinga, and Obstfeld (1983).] The orthogonality conditions defined in (15-34) are

$$E[\mathbf{x}_t \varepsilon_{tj}] = E[\mathbf{x}_t (y_{tj} - \mathbf{z}_{tj}' \boldsymbol{\delta}_j)] = \mathbf{0}.$$

If we consider all the equations jointly, then we obtain the criterion for estimation of all the model's parameters,

$$q = \sum_{j=1}^{M} \sum_{l=1}^{M} \left[ \frac{\mathbf{e}(\mathbf{z}_t, \boldsymbol{\delta}_j)' \mathbf{X}}{T} \right] [\mathbf{W}]^{jl} \left[ \frac{\mathbf{X}' \mathbf{e}(\mathbf{z}_t, \boldsymbol{\delta}_l)}{T} \right]$$

$$= \sum_{j=1}^{M} \sum_{l=1}^{M} \overline{\mathbf{m}}(\boldsymbol{\delta}_j)' [\mathbf{W}]^{jl} \overline{\mathbf{m}}(\boldsymbol{\delta}_l),$$

where

$$\overline{\mathbf{m}}(\boldsymbol{\delta}_j) = \frac{1}{T} \sum_{t=1}^{T} \mathbf{x}_t (y_{tj} - \mathbf{z}_{tj}' \boldsymbol{\delta}_j),$$

and

$$[\mathbf{W}]^{jl} = \text{block } jl \text{ of the weighting matrix, } \mathbf{W}^{-1}.$$

As before, we consider the optimal weighting matrix obtained as the asymptotic covariance matrix of the empirical moments, $\overline{\mathbf{m}}(\boldsymbol{\delta}_j)$. These moments are stacked in a single vector $\overline{\mathbf{m}}(\boldsymbol{\delta})$. Then, the $jl$th block of Asy. Var$[\sqrt{T}\,\overline{\mathbf{m}}(\boldsymbol{\delta})]$ is

$$\boldsymbol{\Phi}_{jl} = \text{plim}\left\{\frac{1}{T}\sum_{t=1}^{T}[\mathbf{x}_t\mathbf{x}_t'(y_{tj} - \mathbf{z}_{tj}'\boldsymbol{\delta}_j)(y_{tl} - \mathbf{z}_{tl}'\boldsymbol{\delta}_l)]\right\} = \text{plim}\left(\frac{1}{T}\sum_{t=1}^{T}\omega_{jl,t}\mathbf{x}_t\mathbf{x}_t'\right).$$

If the disturbances are homoscedastic, then $\boldsymbol{\Phi}_{jl} = \sigma_{jl}[\text{plim}(\mathbf{X}'\mathbf{X}/T)]$ is produced. Otherwise, we obtain a matrix of the form $\boldsymbol{\Phi}_{jl} = \text{plim}[\mathbf{X}'\boldsymbol{\Omega}_{jl}\mathbf{X}/T]$. Collecting terms, then, the criterion function for GMM estimation is

$$q = \begin{bmatrix} [\mathbf{X}'(\mathbf{y}_1 - \mathbf{Z}_1\boldsymbol{\delta}_1)]/T \\ [\mathbf{X}'(\mathbf{y}_2 - \mathbf{Z}_2\boldsymbol{\delta}_2)]/T \\ \vdots \\ [\mathbf{X}'(\mathbf{y}_M - \mathbf{Z}_M\boldsymbol{\delta}_M)]/T \end{bmatrix}' \begin{bmatrix} \boldsymbol{\Phi}_{11} & \boldsymbol{\Phi}_{12} & \cdots & \boldsymbol{\Phi}_{1M} \\ \boldsymbol{\Phi}_{21} & \boldsymbol{\Phi}_{22} & \cdots & \boldsymbol{\Phi}_{2M} \\ \vdots & \vdots & \cdots & \vdots \\ \boldsymbol{\Phi}_{M1} & \boldsymbol{\Phi}_{M2} & \cdots & \boldsymbol{\Phi}_{MM} \end{bmatrix}^{-1} \begin{bmatrix} [\mathbf{X}'(\mathbf{y}_1 - \mathbf{Z}_1\boldsymbol{\delta}_1)]/T \\ [\mathbf{X}'(\mathbf{y}_2 - \mathbf{Z}_2\boldsymbol{\delta}_2)]/T \\ \vdots \\ [\mathbf{X}'(\mathbf{y}_M - \mathbf{Z}_M\boldsymbol{\delta}_M)]/T \end{bmatrix}.$$

For implementation, $\boldsymbol{\Phi}_{jl}$ can be estimated with

$$\hat{\boldsymbol{\Phi}}_{jl} = \frac{1}{T}\sum_{t=1}^{T}\mathbf{x}_t\mathbf{x}_t'(y_{tj} - \mathbf{z}_{tj}'\mathbf{d}_j)(y_{tl} - \mathbf{z}_{tl}'\mathbf{d}_l),$$

where $\mathbf{d}_j$ is a consistent estimator of $\boldsymbol{\delta}_j$. The two-stage least squares estimator is a natural choice. For the diagonal blocks, this choice is the White estimator as usual. For the off-diagonal blocks, it is a simple extension. With this result in hand, the first-order conditions for GMM estimation are

$$\frac{\partial\hat{q}}{\partial\boldsymbol{\delta}_j} = -2\sum_{l=1}^{M}\left(\frac{\mathbf{Z}_j'\mathbf{X}}{T}\right)\hat{\boldsymbol{\Phi}}^{jl}\left[\frac{\mathbf{X}'(\mathbf{y}_l - \mathbf{Z}_l\boldsymbol{\delta}_l)}{T}\right],$$

where $\hat{\boldsymbol{\Phi}}^{jl}$ is the $jl$th block in the inverse of the estimate of the center matrix in $q$.

The solution is

$$\begin{bmatrix} \hat{\boldsymbol{\delta}}_{1,\text{GMM}} \\ \hat{\boldsymbol{\delta}}_{2,\text{GMM}} \\ \vdots \\ \hat{\boldsymbol{\delta}}_{M,\text{GMM}} \end{bmatrix} = \begin{bmatrix} \mathbf{Z}_1'\mathbf{X}\hat{\boldsymbol{\Phi}}^{11}\mathbf{X}'\mathbf{Z}_1 & \mathbf{Z}_1'\mathbf{X}\hat{\boldsymbol{\Phi}}^{12}\mathbf{X}'\mathbf{Z}_2 & \cdots & \mathbf{Z}_1'\mathbf{X}\hat{\boldsymbol{\Phi}}^{1M}\mathbf{X}'\mathbf{Z}_M \\ \mathbf{Z}_2'\mathbf{X}\hat{\boldsymbol{\Phi}}^{21}\mathbf{X}'\mathbf{Z}_1 & \mathbf{Z}_2'\mathbf{X}\hat{\boldsymbol{\Phi}}^{22}\mathbf{X}'\mathbf{Z}_2 & \cdots & \mathbf{Z}_2'\mathbf{X}\hat{\boldsymbol{\Phi}}^{2M}\mathbf{X}'\mathbf{Z}_M \\ \vdots & \vdots & \cdots & \vdots \\ \mathbf{Z}_M'\mathbf{X}\hat{\boldsymbol{\Phi}}^{M1}\mathbf{X}'\mathbf{Z}_1 & \mathbf{Z}_M'\mathbf{X}\hat{\boldsymbol{\Phi}}^{M2}\mathbf{X}'\mathbf{Z}_2 & \cdots & \mathbf{Z}_M'\mathbf{X}\hat{\boldsymbol{\Phi}}^{MM}\mathbf{X}'\mathbf{Z}_M \end{bmatrix}^{-1} \begin{bmatrix} \sum_{j=1}^{M}\mathbf{Z}_1'\mathbf{X}\hat{\boldsymbol{\Phi}}^{1j}\mathbf{y}_j \\ \sum_{j=1}^{M}\mathbf{Z}_2'\mathbf{X}\hat{\boldsymbol{\Phi}}^{2j}\mathbf{y}_j \\ \vdots \\ \sum_{j=1}^{M}\mathbf{Z}_M'\mathbf{X}\hat{\boldsymbol{\Phi}}^{Mj}\mathbf{y}_j \end{bmatrix}.$$

The asymptotic covariance matrix for the estimator would be estimated with $T$ times the large inverse matrix in brackets.

Several of the estimators we have already considered are special cases:

- If $\hat{\boldsymbol{\Phi}}_{jj} = \hat{\sigma}_{jj}(\mathbf{X}'\mathbf{X}/T)$ and $\hat{\boldsymbol{\Phi}}_{jl} = \mathbf{0}$ for $j \neq l$, then $\hat{\boldsymbol{\delta}}_j$ is 2SLS.
- If $\hat{\boldsymbol{\Phi}}_{jl} = \mathbf{0}$ for $j \neq l$, then $\hat{\boldsymbol{\delta}}_j$ is H2SLS, the single-equation GMM estimator.
- If $\hat{\boldsymbol{\Phi}}_{jl} = \hat{\sigma}_{jl}(\mathbf{X}'\mathbf{X}/T)$, then $\hat{\boldsymbol{\delta}}_j$ is 3SLS.

As before, the GMM estimator brings efficiency gains in the presence of heteroscedasticity. If the disturbances are homoscedastic, then it is asymptotically the same as 3SLS, [although in a finite sample, it will differ numerically because $\mathbf{S}_{jl}$ will not be identical to $\hat{\sigma}_{jl}(\mathbf{X}'\mathbf{X})$]. These H3SLS estimates for Klein's Model I appear in Table 13.3 with the other full information estimates. As noted there, the sample is too small to fit all three equations jointly, so they are analyzed in pairs.

### 15.6.5    GMM ESTIMATION OF DYNAMIC PANEL DATA MODELS

Panel data are well suited for examining dynamic effects, as in the first-order model,

$$y_{it} = \mathbf{x}_{it}'\boldsymbol{\beta} + \delta y_{i,t-1} + c_i + \varepsilon_{it}$$
$$= \mathbf{w}_{it}'\boldsymbol{\theta} + \alpha_i + \varepsilon_{it},$$

where the set of right-hand-side variables, $\mathbf{w}_{it}$, now includes the lagged dependent variable, $y_{i,t-1}$. Adding dynamics to a model in this fashion creates a major change in the interpretation of the equation. Without the lagged variable, the "independent variables" represent the full set of information that produce observed outcome $y_{it}$. With the lagged variable, we now have in the equation the entire history of the right-hand-side variables, so that any measured influence is conditioned on this history; in this case, any impact of $\mathbf{x}_{it}$ represents the effect of *new* information. Substantial complications arise in estimation of such a model. In both the fixed and random effects settings, the difficulty is that the lagged dependent variable is correlated with the disturbance, even if it is assumed that $\varepsilon_{it}$ is not itself autocorrelated. For the moment, consider the fixed effects model as an ordinary regression with a lagged dependent variable. We considered this case in Section 4.9.6 as a regression with a stochastic regressor that is dependent across observations. In that dynamic regression model, the estimator based on $T$ observations is biased in finite samples, but it is consistent in $T$. That conclusion was the main result of Section 4.9.6. The finite sample bias is of order $1/T$. The same result applies here, but the difference is that whereas before we obtained our large sample results by allowing $T$ to grow large, in this setting, $T$ is assumed to be small and fixed, and large-sample results are obtained with respect to $n$ growing large, not $T$. The fixed effects estimator of $\boldsymbol{\theta} = [\boldsymbol{\beta}, \delta]$ can be viewed as an average of $n$ such estimators. Assume for now that $T \geq K + 1$ where $K$ is the number of variables in $\mathbf{x}_{it}$. Then, from (9-13),

$$\hat{\boldsymbol{\theta}} = \left[\sum_{i=1}^{n} \mathbf{W}_i'\mathbf{M}^0\mathbf{W}_i\right]^{-1}\left[\sum_{i=1}^{n} \mathbf{W}_i'\mathbf{M}^0\mathbf{y}_i\right]$$

$$= \left[\sum_{i=1}^{n} \mathbf{W}_i'\mathbf{M}^0\mathbf{W}_i\right]^{-1}\left[\sum_{i=1}^{n} \mathbf{W}_i'\mathbf{M}^0\mathbf{W}_i\mathbf{d}_i\right]$$

$$= \sum_{i=1}^{n} \mathbf{F}_i\mathbf{d}_i,$$

where the rows of the $T \times (K+1)$ matrix $\mathbf{W}_i$ are $\mathbf{w}'_{it}$ and $\mathbf{M}^0$ is the $T \times T$ matrix that creates deviations from group means [see (9-14)]. Each group-specific estimator, $\mathbf{d}_i$, is inconsistent, as it is biased in finite samples and its variance does not go to zero as $n$ increases. This matrix weighted average of $n$ inconsistent estimators will also be inconsistent. (This analysis is only heuristic. If $T < K+1$, then the individual coefficient vectors cannot be computed.[13])

The problem is more transparent in the random effects model. In the model

$$y_{it} = \mathbf{x}'_{it}\boldsymbol{\beta} + \delta y_{i,t-1} + u_i + \varepsilon_{it},$$

the lagged dependent variable is correlated with the compound disturbance in the model, since the same $u_i$ enters the equation for every observation in group $i$.

Neither of these results renders the model inestimable, but they do make necessary some technique other than our familiar LSDV or FGLS estimators. The general approach, which has been developed in several stages in the literature,[14] relies on instrumental variables estimators and, most recently [by **Arellano and Bond** (1991) and **Arellano and Bover** (1995)] on a **GMM estimator.** For example, in either the fixed or random effects cases, the heterogeneity can be swept from the model by taking first differences, which produces

$$y_{it} - y_{i,t-1} = (\mathbf{x}_{it} - \mathbf{x}_{i,t-1})'\boldsymbol{\beta} + \delta(y_{i,t-1} - y_{i,t-2}) + (\varepsilon_{it} - \varepsilon_{i,t-1}).$$

This model is still complicated by correlation between the lagged dependent variable and the disturbance (and by its first-order moving average disturbance). But without the group effects, there is a simple instrumental variables estimator available. Assuming that the time series is long enough, one could use the lagged differences, $(y_{i,t-2} - y_{i,t-3})$, or the lagged levels, $y_{i,t-2}$ and $y_{i,t-3}$, as one or two instrumental variables for $(y_{i,t-1} - y_{i,t-2})$. (The other variables can serve as their own instruments.) This is the Anderson and Hsiao estimator developed for this model in Section 12.8.2. By this construction, then, the treatment of this model is a standard application of the instrumental variables technique that we developed in Section 12.8.2.[15] This illustrates the flavor of an instrumental variable approach to estimation. But, as Arellano et al. and Ahn and Schmidt (1995) have shown, there is still more information in the sample that can be brought to bear on estimation, in the context of a GMM estimator, which we now consider.

We can extend the Hausman and Taylor (HT) formulation of the random effects model in Section 12.8.1 to include the lagged dependent variable;

$$\begin{aligned} y_{it} &= \delta y_{i,t-1} + \mathbf{x}'_{1it}\boldsymbol{\beta}_1 + \mathbf{x}'_{2it}\boldsymbol{\beta}_2 + \mathbf{z}'_{1i}\boldsymbol{\alpha}_1 + \mathbf{z}'_{2i}\boldsymbol{\alpha}_2 + \varepsilon_{it} + u_i \\ &= \boldsymbol{\theta}'\mathbf{w}_{it} + \varepsilon_{it} + u_i \\ &= \boldsymbol{\theta}'\mathbf{w}_{it} + \eta_{it}, \end{aligned}$$

---

[13]Further discussion is given by Nickell (1981), Ridder and Wansbeek (1990), and Kiviet (1995).

[14]The model was first proposed in this form by Balestra and Nerlove (1966). See, for example, Anderson and Hsiao (1981, 1982), Bhargava and Sargan (1983), Arellano (1989), Arellano and Bond (1991), Arellano and Bover (1995), Ahn and Schmidt (1995), and Nerlove (2003).

[15]There is a question as to whether one should use differences or levels as instruments. Arellano (1989) and Kiviet (1995) give evidence that the latter is preferable.

where

$$\mathbf{w}_{it} = [y_{i,t-1}, \mathbf{x}'_{1it}, \mathbf{x}'_{2it}, \mathbf{z}'_{1i}, \mathbf{z}'_{2i}]'$$

is now a $(1+K_1+K_2+L_1+L_2) \times 1$ vector. The terms in the equation are the same as in the Hausman and Taylor model. Instrumental variables estimation of the model without the lagged dependent variable is discussed in Section 12.8.1 on the HT estimator. Moreover, by just including $y_{i,t-1}$ in $\mathbf{x}_{2it}$, we see that the HT approach extends to this setting as well, essentially without modification. Arellano et al. suggest a GMM estimator and show that efficiency gains are available by using a larger set of moment conditions. In the previous treatment, we used a GMM estimator constructed as follows: The set of moment conditions we used to formulate the instrumental variables were

$$E\left[\begin{pmatrix}\mathbf{x}_{1it}\\\mathbf{x}_{2it}\\\mathbf{z}_{1i}\\\overline{\mathbf{x}}_{1i.}\end{pmatrix}(\eta_{it}-\overline{\eta}_i)\right] = E\left[\begin{pmatrix}\mathbf{x}_{1it}\\\mathbf{x}_{2it}\\\mathbf{z}_{1i}\\\overline{\mathbf{x}}_{1i.}\end{pmatrix}(\varepsilon_{it}-\overline{\varepsilon}_i)\right] = \mathbf{0}.$$

This moment condition is used to produce the instrumental variable estimator. We could ignore the nonscalar variance of $\eta_{it}$ and use simple instrumental variables at this point. However, by accounting for the random effects formulation and using the counterpart to feasible GLS, we obtain the more efficient estimator in (12-29). As usual, this can be done in two steps. The inefficient estimator is computed to obtain the residuals needed to estimate the variance components. This is Hausman and Taylor's steps 1 and 2. Steps 3 and 4 are the GMM estimator based on these estimated variance components.

Arellano et al. suggest that the preceding does not exploit all the information in the sample. In simple terms, within the $T$ observations in group $i$, we have not used the fact that

$$E\left[\begin{pmatrix}\mathbf{x}_{1it}\\\mathbf{x}_{2it}\\\mathbf{z}_{1i}\\\overline{\mathbf{x}}_{1i.}\end{pmatrix}(\eta_{is}-\overline{\eta}_i)\right] = \mathbf{0} \text{ for some } s \neq t.$$

Thus, for example, not only are disturbances at time $t$ uncorrelated with these variables at time $t$, arguably, they are uncorrelated with the same variables at time $t-1, t-2$, possibly $t+1$, and so on. In principle, the number of valid instruments is potentially enormous. Suppose, for example, that the set of instruments listed above is strictly exogenous with respect to $\eta_{it}$ in every period including current, lagged, and future. Then, there are a total of $[T(K_1+K_2)+L_1+K_1)]$ moment conditions for every observation. On this basis alone. Consider, for example, a panel with two periods. We would have for the two periods,

$$E\left[\begin{pmatrix}\mathbf{x}_{1i1}\\\mathbf{x}_{2i1}\\\mathbf{x}_{1i2}\\\mathbf{x}_{2i2}\\\mathbf{z}_{1i}\\\overline{\mathbf{x}}_{1i.}\end{pmatrix}(\eta_{i1}-\overline{\eta}_i)\right] = \mathbf{0} \quad \text{and} \quad E\left[\begin{pmatrix}\mathbf{x}_{1i1}\\\mathbf{x}_{2i1}\\\mathbf{x}_{1i2}\\\mathbf{x}_{2i2}\\\mathbf{z}_{1i}\\\overline{\mathbf{x}}_{1i.}\end{pmatrix}(\eta_{i2}-\overline{\eta}_i)\right] = \mathbf{0}. \qquad \textbf{(15-38)}$$

How much useful information is brought to bear on estimation of the parameters is uncertain, as it depends on the correlation of the instruments with the included exogenous variables in the equation. The farther apart in time these sets of variables become the less information is likely to be present. (The literature on this subject contains reference to "strong" versus "weak" instrumental variables.[16]) To proceed, as noted, we can include the lagged dependent variable in $\mathbf{x}_{2i}$. This set of instrumental variables can be used to construct the estimator, actually whether the lagged variable is present or not. We note, at this point, that on this basis, Hausman and Taylor's estimator did not actually use all the information available in the sample. We now have the elements of the Arellano et al. estimator in hand; what remains is essentially the (unfortunately, fairly involved) algebra, which we now develop.

Let

$$\mathbf{W}_i = \begin{bmatrix} \mathbf{w}'_{i1} \\ \mathbf{w}'_{i2} \\ \vdots \\ \mathbf{w}'_{iT} \end{bmatrix} = \text{the full set of rhs data for group } i, \quad \text{and} \quad \mathbf{y}_i = \begin{bmatrix} y_{i1} \\ y_{i2} \\ \vdots \\ y_{iT} \end{bmatrix}.$$

Note that $\mathbf{W}_i$ is assumed to be, a $T \times (1 + K_1 + K_2 + L_1 + L_2)$ matrix. Because there is a lagged dependent variable in the model, it must be assumed that there are actually $T + 1$ observations available on $y_{it}$. To avoid a cumbersome, cluttered notation, we will leave this distinction embedded in the notation for the moment. Later, when necessary, we will make it explicit. It will reappear in the formulation of the instrumental variables. A total of $T$ observations will be available for constructing the IV estimators. We now form a matrix of instrumental variables. [Different approaches to this have been considered by Hausman and Taylor (1981), Arellano et al. (1991, 1995, 1999), Ahn and Schmidt (1995) and Amemiya and MaCurdy (1986), among others.] We will form a matrix $\mathbf{V}_i$ consisting of $T_i - 1$ rows constructed the same way for $T_i - 1$ observations and a final row that will be different, as discussed later. [This is to exploit a useful algebraic result discussed by Arellano and Bover (1995).] The matrix will be of the form

$$\mathbf{V}_i = \begin{bmatrix} \mathbf{v}'_{i1} & \mathbf{0}' & \cdots & \mathbf{0}' \\ \mathbf{0}' & \mathbf{v}'_{i2} & \cdots & \mathbf{0}' \\ \vdots & \vdots & \ddots & \vdots \\ \mathbf{0}' & \mathbf{0}' & \cdots & \mathbf{a}'_i \end{bmatrix}. \tag{15-39}$$

The instrumental variable sets contained in $\mathbf{v}'_{it}$ which have been suggested might include the following from within the model:

$\mathbf{x}_{it}$ and $\mathbf{x}_{i,t-1}$ (i.e., current and one lag of all the time varying variables),

$\mathbf{x}_{i1}, \ldots, \mathbf{x}_{iT}$ (i.e., all current, past and future values of all the time varying variables),

$\mathbf{x}_{i1}, \ldots, \mathbf{x}_{it}$ (i.e., all current and past values of all the time varying variables).

The time-invariant variables that are uncorrelated with $u_i$, that is $\mathbf{z}_{1i}$, are appended at the end of the nonzero part of each of the first $T - 1$ rows. It may seem that including $\mathbf{x}_2$ in the instruments would be invalid. However, we will be converting the disturbances to deviations from group means which are free of the latent effects—that is, this set of moment conditions will ultimately be converted to what appears in (15-38). While the variables are correlated with $u_i$ by construction, they are not correlated with

---

[16]See West (2001).

$\varepsilon_{it} - \bar{\varepsilon}_i$. The final row of $\mathbf{V}_i$ is important to the construction. Two possibilities have been suggested:

$\mathbf{a}'_i = [\mathbf{z}'_{1i} \quad \bar{\mathbf{x}}_{i1}]$ (produces the Hausman and Taylor estimator),

$\mathbf{a}'_i = [\mathbf{z}'_{1i} \quad \mathbf{x}'_{1i1}, \mathbf{x}'_{1i2}, \ldots, \mathbf{x}_{1iT}]$ (produces Amemiya and MaCurdy's estimator).

Note that the $\mathbf{a}$ variables are exogenous time-invariant variables, $\mathbf{z}_{1i}$ and the exogenous time-varying variables, either condensed into the single group mean or in the raw form, with the full set of $T$ observations.

To construct the estimator, we will require a transformation matrix, $\mathbf{H}$, constructed as follows. Let $\mathbf{M}^{01}$ denote the first $T - 1$ rows of $\mathbf{M}^0$, the matrix that creates deviations from group means. Then,

$$\mathbf{H} = \begin{bmatrix} \mathbf{M}^{01} \\ \dfrac{1}{T}\mathbf{i}'_T \end{bmatrix}.$$

Thus, $\mathbf{H}$ replaces the last row of $\mathbf{M}^0$ with a row of $1/T$. The effect is as follows: if $\mathbf{q}$ is $T$ observations on a variable, then $\mathbf{Hq}$ produces $\mathbf{q}^*$ in which the first $T - 1$ observations are converted to deviations from group means and the last observation is the group mean. In particular, let the $T \times 1$ column vector of disturbances

$$\boldsymbol{\eta}_i = [\eta_{i1}, \eta_{i2}, \ldots, \eta_{iT}] = [(\varepsilon_{i1} + u_i), (\varepsilon_{i2} + u_i), \ldots, (\varepsilon_{iT} + u_i)]',$$

then

$$\mathbf{H}\boldsymbol{\eta} = \begin{bmatrix} \eta_{i1} - \bar{\eta}_i \\ \vdots \\ \eta_{i,T-1} - \bar{\eta}_i \\ \bar{\eta}_i \end{bmatrix}.$$

We can now construct the moment conditions. With all this machinery in place, we have the result that appears in (15-40), that is

$$E[\mathbf{V}'_i \mathbf{H}\boldsymbol{\eta}_i] = E[\mathbf{g}_i] = \mathbf{0}.$$

It is useful to expand this for a particular case. Suppose $T = 3$ and we use as instruments the current values in period 1, and the current and previous values in period 2 and the Hausman and Taylor form for the invariant variables. Then the preceding is

$$E\left[\begin{pmatrix} \mathbf{x}_{1i1} & \mathbf{0} & \mathbf{0} \\ \mathbf{x}_{2i1} & \mathbf{0} & \mathbf{0} \\ \mathbf{z}_{1i} & \mathbf{0} & \mathbf{0} \\ \mathbf{0} & \mathbf{x}_{1i1} & \mathbf{0} \\ \mathbf{0} & \mathbf{x}_{2i1} & \mathbf{0} \\ \mathbf{0} & \mathbf{x}_{1i2} & \mathbf{0} \\ \mathbf{0} & \mathbf{x}_{2i2} & \mathbf{0} \\ \mathbf{0} & \mathbf{z}_{1i} & \mathbf{0} \\ \mathbf{0} & \mathbf{0} & \mathbf{z}_{1i} \\ \mathbf{0} & \mathbf{0} & \bar{\mathbf{x}}_{1i} \end{pmatrix} \begin{pmatrix} \eta_{i1} - \bar{\eta}_i \\ \eta_{i2} - \bar{\eta}_i \\ \bar{\eta}_i \end{pmatrix}\right] = \mathbf{0}. \qquad \textbf{(15-40)}$$

This is the same as (15-38).[17] The empirical moment condition that follows from this is

$$\text{plim}\frac{1}{n}\sum_{i=1}^{n}\mathbf{V}_i'\mathbf{H}\boldsymbol{\eta}_i$$

$$= \text{plim}\frac{1}{n}\sum_{i=1}^{n}\mathbf{V}_i'\mathbf{H}\begin{pmatrix} y_{i1} - \delta y_{i0} - \mathbf{x}_{1i1}'\boldsymbol{\beta}_1 - \mathbf{x}_{2i1}'\boldsymbol{\beta}_2 - \mathbf{z}_{1i}'\boldsymbol{\alpha}_1 - \mathbf{z}_{2i}'\boldsymbol{\alpha}_2 \\ y_{i2} - \delta y_{i1} - \mathbf{x}_{1i2}'\boldsymbol{\beta}_1 - \mathbf{x}_{2i2}'\boldsymbol{\beta}_2 - \mathbf{z}_{1i}'\boldsymbol{\alpha}_1 - \mathbf{z}_{2i}'\boldsymbol{\alpha}_2 \\ \vdots \\ y_{iT} - \delta y_{i,T-1} - \mathbf{x}_{1iT}'\boldsymbol{\beta}_1 - \mathbf{x}_{2iT}'\boldsymbol{\beta}_2 - \mathbf{z}_{1i}'\boldsymbol{\alpha}_1 - \mathbf{z}_{2i}'\boldsymbol{\alpha}_2 \end{pmatrix} = \mathbf{0}.$$

Write this as

$$\text{plim}\frac{1}{n}\sum_{i=1}^{n}\mathbf{m}_i = \text{plim}\,\overline{\mathbf{m}} = \mathbf{0}.$$

The GMM estimator $\hat{\boldsymbol{\theta}}$ is then obtained by minimizing

$$q = \overline{\mathbf{m}}'\mathbf{A}\overline{\mathbf{m}}$$

with an appropriate choice of the weighting matrix, $\mathbf{A}$. The optimal weighting matrix will be the inverse of the asymptotic covariance matrix of $\sqrt{n}\,\overline{\mathbf{m}}$. With a consistent estimator of $\boldsymbol{\theta}$ in hand, this can be estimated empirically using

$$\text{Est. Asy. Var}[\sqrt{n}\,\overline{\mathbf{m}}] = \frac{1}{n}\sum_{i=1}^{n}\hat{\mathbf{m}}_i\hat{\mathbf{m}}_i' = \frac{1}{n}\sum_{i=1}^{n}\mathbf{V}_i'\mathbf{H}\hat{\boldsymbol{\eta}}_i\hat{\boldsymbol{\eta}}_i'\mathbf{H}'\mathbf{V}_i.$$

This is a robust estimator that allows an unrestricted $T \times T$ covariance matrix for the $T$ disturbances, $\varepsilon_{it} + u_i$. But, we have assumed that this covariance matrix is the $\boldsymbol{\Sigma}$ defined in (9-28) for the random effects model. To use this information we would, instead, use the residuals in

$$\hat{\boldsymbol{\eta}}_i = \mathbf{y}_i - \mathbf{W}_i\hat{\boldsymbol{\theta}}$$

to estimate $\sigma_u^2$ and $\sigma_\varepsilon^2$ and then $\boldsymbol{\Sigma}$, which produces

$$\text{Est. Asy. Var}[\sqrt{n}\,\overline{\mathbf{m}}] = \frac{1}{n}\sum_{i=1}^{n}\mathbf{V}_i'\mathbf{H}\hat{\boldsymbol{\Sigma}}\mathbf{H}'\mathbf{V}_i.$$

We now have the full set of results needed to compute the GMM estimator. The solution to the optimization problem of minimizing $q$ with respect to the parameter vector $\boldsymbol{\theta}$ is

$$\hat{\boldsymbol{\theta}}_{GMM} = \left[\left(\sum_{i=1}^{n}\mathbf{W}_i'\mathbf{H}\mathbf{V}_i\right)\left(\sum_{i=1}^{n}\mathbf{V}_i'\mathbf{H}'\hat{\boldsymbol{\Sigma}}\mathbf{H}\mathbf{V}_i\right)^{-1}\left(\sum_{i=1}^{n}\mathbf{V}_i'\mathbf{H}'\mathbf{W}_i\right)\right]^{-1}$$

$$\times \left(\sum_{i=1}^{n}\mathbf{W}_i'\mathbf{H}\mathbf{V}_i\right)\left(\sum_{i=1}^{n}\mathbf{V}_i'\mathbf{H}'\hat{\boldsymbol{\Sigma}}\mathbf{H}\mathbf{V}_i\right)^{-1}\left(\sum_{i=1}^{n}\mathbf{V}_i'\mathbf{H}'\mathbf{y}_i\right). \qquad \textbf{(15-41)}$$

The estimator of the asymptotic covariance matrix for $\hat{\boldsymbol{\theta}}_{GMM}$ is the inverse matrix in brackets.

---

[17]In some treatments [e.g., Blundell and Bond (1998)], an additional condition is assumed for the initial value, $y_{i0}$, namely $E[y_{i0} \mid \text{exogenous data}] = \mu_0$. This would add a row at the top of the matrix in (15-40) containing $[(y_{i0} - \mu_0), 0, 0]$.

The remaining loose end is how to obtain the consistent estimator of $\hat{\theta}$ to compute $\Sigma$. Recall that the GMM estimator is consistent with any positive definite weighting matrix, $\mathbf{A}$, in our preceding expression. Therefore, for an initial estimator, we could set $\mathbf{A} = \mathbf{I}$ and use the simple instrumental variables estimator,

$$\hat{\theta}_{IV} = \left[ \left( \sum_{i=1}^{n} \mathbf{W}'_i \mathbf{H} \mathbf{V}_i \right) \left( \sum_{i=1}^{n} \mathbf{V}'_i \mathbf{H} \mathbf{W}_i \right) \right]^{-1} \left( \sum_{i=1}^{n} \mathbf{W}'_i \mathbf{H} \mathbf{V}_i \right) \left( \sum_{i=1}^{n} \mathbf{V}'_i \mathbf{H} \mathbf{y}_i \right).$$

It is more common to proceed directly to the "two-stage least squares" estimator (see Sections 12.3.3 and 12.8.2), which uses

$$\mathbf{A} = \left( \frac{1}{n} \sum_{i=1}^{n} \mathbf{V}'_i \mathbf{H}' \mathbf{H} \mathbf{V}_i \right)^{-1}.$$

The estimator is, then, the one given earlier in (15-41) with $\hat{\Sigma}$ replaced by $\mathbf{I}_T$. Either estimator is a function of the sample data only and provides the initial estimator we need.

Ahn and Schmidt (among others) observed that the IV estimator proposed here, as extensive as it is, still neglects quite a lot of information and is therefore (relatively) inefficient. For example, in the first differenced model,

$$E[y_{is}(\varepsilon_{it} - \varepsilon_{i,t-1})] = 0, \quad s = 0, \ldots, t - 2, \quad t = 2, \ldots, T.$$

That is, the *level* of $y_{is}$ is uncorrelated with the differences of disturbances that are at least two periods subsequent.[18] (The differencing transformation, as the transformation to deviations from group means, removes the individual effect.) The corresponding moment equations that can enter the construction of a GMM estimator are

$$\frac{1}{n} \sum_{i=1}^{n} y_{is}[(y_{it} - y_{i,t-1}) - \delta(y_{i,t-1} - y_{i,t-2}) - (\mathbf{x}_{it} - \mathbf{x}_{i,t-1})'\boldsymbol{\beta}] = 0$$

$$s = 0, \ldots, t - 2, \quad t = 2, \ldots, T.$$

Altogether, Ahn and Schmidt identify $T(T-1)/2 + T - 2$ such equations that involve mixtures of the levels and differences of the variables. The main conclusion that they demonstrate is that in the dynamic model, there is a large amount of information to be gleaned not only from the familiar relationships among the levels of the variables but also from the implied relationships between the levels and the first differences. The issue of correlation between the transformed $y_{it}$ and the deviations of $\varepsilon_{it}$ is discussed in the papers cited. [As Ahn and Schmidt show, there are potentially huge numbers of additional orthogonality conditions in this model owing to the relationship between first differences and second moments. We do not consider those. The matrix $\mathbf{V}_i$ could be huge. Consider a model with 10 time-varying right-hand-side variables and suppose $T_i$ is 15. Then, there are 15 rows and roughly $15 \times (10 \times 15)$ or 2,250 columns. The Ahn and Schmidt estimator, which involves potentially thousands of instruments in a model containing only a handful of parameters, may become a bit impractical at this point. The

---

[18]This is the approach suggested by Holtz-Eakin (1988) and Holtz-Eakin, Newey, and Rosen (1988).

common approach is to use only a small subset of the available instrumental variables. The order of the computation grows as the number of parameters times the square of $T$.]

The number of orthogonality conditions (instrumental variables) used to estimate the parameters of the model is determined by the number of variables in $\mathbf{v}_{it}$ and $\mathbf{a}_i$ in (15-39). In most cases, the model is vastly overidentified—there are far more orthogonality conditions than parameters. As usual in GMM estimation, a test of the overidentifying restrictions can be based on $q$, the estimation criterion. At its minimum, the limiting distribution of $nq$ is chi-squared with degrees of freedom equal to the number of instrumental variables in total minus $(1 + K_1 + K_2 + L_1 + L_2)$.[19]

### Example 15.10  GMM Estimation of a Dynamic Panel Data Model of Local Government Expenditures

Dahlberg and Johansson (2000) estimated a model for the local government expenditure of several hundred municipalities in Sweden observed over the nine-year period $t = 1979$ to 1987. The equation of interest is

$$S_{i,t} = \alpha_t + \sum_{j=1}^{m} \beta_j S_{i,t-j} + \sum_{j=1}^{m} \gamma_j R_{i,t-j} + \sum_{j=1}^{m} \delta_j G_{i,t-j} + f_i + \varepsilon_{it},$$

for $i = 1, \ldots, n = 265$, and $t = m+1, \ldots, 9$. (We have changed their notation slightly to make it more convenient.) $S_{i,t}$, $R_{i,t}$, and $G_{i,t}$ are municipal spending, receipts (taxes and fees), and central government grants, respectively. Analogous equations are specified for the current values of $R_{i,t}$ and $G_{i,t}$. The appropriate lag length, $m$, is one of the features of interest to be determined by the empirical study. The model contains a municipality specific effect, $f_i$, which is not specified as being either "fixed" or "random." To eliminate the individual effect, the model is converted to first differences. The resulting equation is

$$\Delta S_{i,t} = \lambda_t + \sum_{j=1}^{m} \beta_j \Delta S_{i,t-j} + \sum_{j=1}^{m} \gamma_j \Delta R_{i,t-j} + \sum_{j=1}^{m} \delta_j \Delta G_{i,t-j} + u_{it},$$

or

$$y_{i,t} = \mathbf{x}'_{i,t} \boldsymbol{\theta} + u_{i,t},$$

where $\Delta S_{i,t} = S_{i,t} - S_{i,t-1}$ and so on and $u_{i,t} = \varepsilon_{i,t} - \varepsilon_{i,t-1}$. This removes the group effect and leaves the time effect. Because the time effect was unrestricted to begin with, $\Delta \alpha_t = \lambda_t$ remains an unrestricted time effect, which is treated as "fixed" and modeled with a time-specific dummy variable. The maximum lag length is set at $m = 3$. With nine years of data, this leaves usable observations from 1983 to 1987 for estimation, that is, $t = m+2, \ldots, 9$. Similar equations were fit for $R_{i,t}$ and $G_{i,t}$.

The orthogonality conditions claimed by the authors are

$$E[S_{i,s}u_{i,t}] = E[R_{i,s}u_{i,t}] = E[G_{i,s}u_{i,t}] = 0, \quad s = 1, \ldots, t - 2.$$

The orthogonality conditions are stated in terms of the levels of the financial variables and the differences of the disturbances. The issue of this formulation as opposed to, for example, $E[\Delta S_{i,s}\Delta \varepsilon_{i,t}] = 0$ (which is implied) is discussed by Ahn and Schmidt (1995). As we shall see, this set of orthogonality conditions implies a total of 80 instrumental variables. The authors use only the first of the three sets listed, which produces a total of 30. For the five observations, using the formulation developed in Section 15.6.5, we have the following matrix

---

[19]This is true generally in GMM estimation. It was proposed for the dynamic panel data model by Bhargava and Sargan (1983).

of instrumental variables for the orthogonality conditions

$$
\mathbf{Z}_i = \begin{bmatrix}
S_{81-79} & d_{83} & \mathbf{0}' & 0 & \mathbf{0}' & 0 & \mathbf{0}' & 0 & \mathbf{0}' & 0 \\
\mathbf{0}' & 0 & S_{82-79} & d_{84} & \mathbf{0}' & 0 & \mathbf{0}' & 0 & \mathbf{0}' & 0 \\
\mathbf{0}' & 0 & \mathbf{0}' & 0 & S_{83-79} & d_{85} & \mathbf{0}' & 0 & \mathbf{0}' & 0 \\
\mathbf{0}' & 0 & \mathbf{0}' & 0 & \mathbf{0}' & 0 & S_{84-79} & d_{86} & \mathbf{0}' & 0 \\
\mathbf{0}' & 0 & \mathbf{0}' & 0 & \mathbf{0}' & 0 & \mathbf{0}' & 0 & S_{85-79} & d_{87}
\end{bmatrix}
\begin{matrix}
1983 \\ 1984 \\ 1985 \\ 1986 \\ 1987
\end{matrix}
$$

where the notation $S_{t1-t0}$ indicates the range of years for that variable. For example, $S_{83-79}$ denotes $[S_{i,1983}, S_{i,1982}, S_{i,1981}, S_{i,1980}, S_{i,1979}]$ and $d_{\text{year}}$ denotes the year-specific dummy variable. Counting columns in $\mathbf{Z}_i$ we see that using only the lagged values of the dependent variable and the time dummy variables, we have $(3+1)+(4+1)+(5+1)+(6+1)+(7+1)=30$ instrumental variables. Using the lagged values of the other two variables in each equation would add 50 more, for a total of 80 if all the orthogonality conditions suggested earlier were employed. Given the preceding construction, the orthogonality conditions are now

$$
E[\mathbf{Z}_i'\mathbf{u}_i] = \mathbf{0},
$$

where $\mathbf{u}_i = [u_{i,1987}, u_{i,1986}, u_{i,1985}, u_{i,1984}, u_{i,1983}]'$. The empirical moment equation is

$$
\text{plim}\left[\frac{1}{n}\sum_{i=1}^{n}\mathbf{Z}_i'\mathbf{u}_i\right] = \text{plim}\,\overline{\mathbf{m}}(\boldsymbol{\theta}) = \mathbf{0}.
$$

The parameters are vastly overidentified. Using only the lagged values of the dependent variable in each of the three equations estimated, there are 30 moment conditions and 14 parameters being estimated when $m = 3$, 11 when $m = 2$, 8 when $m = 1$, and 5 when $m = 0$. (As we do our estimation of each of these, we will retain the same matrix of instrumental variables in each case.) GMM estimation proceeds in two steps. In the first step, basic, unweighted instrumental variables is computed using

$$
\hat{\boldsymbol{\theta}}_{IV}' = \left[\left(\sum_{i=1}^{n}\mathbf{X}_i'\mathbf{Z}_i\right)\left(\sum_{i=1}^{n}\mathbf{Z}_i'\mathbf{Z}_i\right)^{-1}\left(\sum_{i=1}^{n}\mathbf{Z}_i'\mathbf{X}_i\right)\right]^{-1}\left(\sum_{i=1}^{n}\mathbf{X}_i'\mathbf{Z}_i\right)\left(\sum_{i=1}^{n}\mathbf{Z}_i'\mathbf{Z}_i\right)^{-1}\left(\sum_{i=1}^{n}\mathbf{Z}_i'\mathbf{y}_i\right),
$$

where

$$
\mathbf{y}_i' = (\Delta S_{83} \quad \Delta S_{84} \quad \Delta S_{85} \quad \Delta S_{86} \quad \Delta S_{87}),
$$

and

$$
\mathbf{X}_i = \begin{bmatrix}
\Delta S_{82} & \Delta S_{81} & \Delta S_{80} & \Delta R_{82} & \Delta R_{81} & \Delta R_{80} & \Delta G_{82} & \Delta G_{81} & \Delta G_{80} & 1 & 0 & 0 & 0 & 0 \\
\Delta S_{83} & \Delta S_{82} & \Delta S_{81} & \Delta R_{83} & \Delta R_{82} & \Delta R_{81} & \Delta G_{83} & \Delta G_{82} & \Delta G_{81} & 0 & 1 & 0 & 0 & 0 \\
\Delta S_{84} & \Delta S_{83} & \Delta S_{82} & \Delta R_{84} & \Delta R_{83} & \Delta R_{82} & \Delta G_{84} & \Delta G_{83} & \Delta G_{82} & 0 & 0 & 1 & 0 & 0 \\
\Delta S_{85} & \Delta S_{84} & \Delta S_{83} & \Delta R_{85} & \Delta R_{84} & \Delta R_{83} & \Delta G_{85} & \Delta G_{84} & \Delta G_{83} & 0 & 0 & 0 & 1 & 0 \\
\Delta S_{86} & \Delta S_{85} & \Delta S_{84} & \Delta R_{86} & \Delta R_{85} & \Delta R_{84} & \Delta G_{86} & \Delta G_{85} & \Delta G_{84} & 0 & 0 & 0 & 0 & 1
\end{bmatrix}.
$$

The second step begins with the computation of the new weighting matrix,

$$
\hat{\boldsymbol{\Phi}} = \text{Est. Asy. Var}[\sqrt{n}\,\overline{\mathbf{m}}] = \frac{1}{N}\sum_{i=1}^{n}\mathbf{Z}_i'\hat{\mathbf{u}}_i\hat{\mathbf{u}}_i'\mathbf{Z}_i.
$$

After multiplying and dividing by the implicit $(1/n)$ in the outside matrices, we obtain the estimator,

$$\theta'_{GMM} = \left[ \left( \sum_{i=1}^{n} \mathbf{X}'_i \mathbf{Z}_i \right) \left( \sum_{i=1}^{n} \mathbf{Z}'_i \hat{\mathbf{u}}_i \hat{\mathbf{u}}'_i \mathbf{Z}_i \right)^{-1} \left( \sum_{i=1}^{n} \mathbf{Z}'_i \mathbf{X}_i \right) \right]^{-1}$$
$$\times \left( \sum_{i=1}^{n} \mathbf{X}'_i \mathbf{Z}_i \right) \left( \sum_{i=1}^{n} \mathbf{Z}'_i \hat{\mathbf{u}}_i \hat{\mathbf{u}}'_i \mathbf{Z}_i \right)^{-1} \left( \sum_{i=1}^{n} \mathbf{Z}'_i \mathbf{y}_i \right)$$
$$= \left[ \left( \sum_{i=1}^{n} \mathbf{X}'_i \mathbf{Z}_i \right) \mathbf{W} \left( \sum_{i=1}^{n} \mathbf{Z}'_i \mathbf{X}_i \right) \right]^{-1} \left( \sum_{i=1}^{n} \mathbf{X}'_i \mathbf{Z}_i \right) \mathbf{W} \left( \sum_{i=1}^{n} \mathbf{Z}'_i \mathbf{y}_i \right).$$

The estimator of the asymptotic covariance matrix for the estimator is the inverse matrix in square brackets in the first line of the result.

The primary focus of interest in the study was not the estimator itself, but the lag length and whether certain lagged values of the independent variables appeared in each equation. These restrictions would be tested by using the GMM criterion function, which in this formulation would be (based on recomputing the residuals after GMM estimation)

$$q = \left( \sum_{i=1}^{n} \hat{\mathbf{u}}'_i \mathbf{Z}_i \right) \mathbf{W} \left( \sum_{i=1}^{n} \mathbf{Z}'_i \hat{\mathbf{u}}_i \right).$$

Note that the weighting matrix is not (necessarily) recomputed. For purposes of testing hypotheses, the same weighting matrix should be used.

At this point, we will consider the appropriate lag length, $m$. The specification can be reduced simply by redefining $\mathbf{X}$ to change the lag length. To test the specification, the weighting matrix must be kept constant for all restricted versions ($m = 2$ and $m = 1$) of the model.

The Dahlberg and Johansson data may be downloaded from the *Journal of Applied Econometrics* Web site—see Appendix Table F15.1. The authors provide the summary statistics for the raw data that are given in Table 15.3. The data used in the study and provided in the internet source are nominal values in Swedish Kroner, deflated by a municipality-specific price index then converted to per capita values. Descriptive statistics for the raw data appear in Table 15.3.[20] Equations were estimated for all three variables, with maximum lag lengths of $m = 1$, 2, and 3. (The authors did not provide the actual estimates.) Estimation is done using the methods developed by Ahn and Schmidt (1995), Arellano and Bover (1995), and Holtz-Eakin, Newey, and Rosen (1988), as described. The estimates of the first specification provided are given in Table 15.4.

Table 15.5 contains estimates of the model parameters for each of the three equations, and for the three lag lengths, as well as the value of the GMM criterion function for each model estimated. The base case for each model has $m = 3$. There are three restrictions implied by

**TABLE 15.3** Descriptive Statistics for Local Expenditure Data

| Variable | Mean | Std. Deviation | Minimum | Maximum |
|----------|------|----------------|---------|---------|
| Spending | 18478.51 | 3174.36 | 12225.68 | 33883.25 |
| Revenues | 13422.56 | 3004.16 | 6228.54 | 29141.62 |
| Grants | 5236.03 | 1260.97 | 1570.64 | 12589.14 |

---

[20]The data provided on the Web site and used in our computations were further transformed by dividing by 100,000.

**TABLE 15.4**    Estimated Spending Equation

| Variable | Estimate | Standard Error | t Ratio |
|---|---|---|---|
| Year 1983 | −0.0036578 | 0.0002969 | −12.32 |
| Year 1984 | −0.00049670 | 0.0004128 | −1.20 |
| Year 1985 | 0.00038085 | 0.0003094 | 1.23 |
| Year 1986 | 0.00031469 | 0.0003282 | 0.96 |
| Year 1987 | 0.00086878 | 0.0001480 | 5.87 |
| Spending $(t-1)$ | 1.15493 | 0.34409 | 3.36 |
| Revenues $(t-1)$ | −1.23801 | 0.36171 | −3.42 |
| Grants $(t-1)$ | 0.016310 | 0.82419 | 0.02 |
| Spending $(t-2)$ | −0.0376625 | 0.22676 | −0.17 |
| Revenues $(t-2)$ | 0.0770075 | 0.27179 | 0.28 |
| Grants $(t-2)$ | 1.55379 | 0.75841 | 2.05 |
| Spending $(t-3)$ | −0.56441 | 0.21796 | −2.59 |
| Revenues $(t-3)$ | 0.64978 | 0.26930 | 2.41 |
| Grants $(t-3)$ | 1.78918 | 0.69297 | 2.58 |

each reduction in the lag length. The critical chi-squared value for three degrees of freedom is 7.81 for 95 percent significance, so at this level, we find that the two-level model is just barely accepted for the spending equation, but clearly appropriate for the other two—the difference between the two criteria is 7.62. Conditioned on $m = 2$, only the revenue model rejects the restriction of $m = 1$. As a final test, we might ask whether the data suggest that perhaps no lag structure at all is necessary. The GMM criterion value for the three equations with only the time dummy variables are 45.840, 57.908, and 62.042, respectively. Therefore, all three zero lag models are rejected.

   Among the interests in this study were the appropriate critical values to use for the specification test of the moment restriction. With 16 degrees of freedom, the critical chi-squared value for 95 percent significance is 26.3, which would suggest that the revenues equation is misspecified. Using a bootstrap technique, the authors find that a more appropriate critical value leaves the specification intact. Finally, note that the three-equation model in the $m = 3$ columns of Table 15.5 imply a **vector autoregression** of the form

$$\mathbf{y}_t = \mathbf{\Gamma}_1\mathbf{y}_{t-1} + \mathbf{\Gamma}_2\mathbf{y}_{t-2} + \mathbf{\Gamma}_3\mathbf{y}_{t-3} + \mathbf{v}_t,$$

where $\mathbf{y}_t = (\Delta S_t, \Delta R_t, \Delta G_t)'$. We will explore the properties and characteristics of equation systems such as this in our discussion of time-series models in Chapter 21.

**TABLE 15.5**    Estimated Lag Equations for Spending, Revenue, and Grants

| | Expenditure Model | | | Revenue Model | | | Grant Model | | |
|---|---|---|---|---|---|---|---|---|---|
| | m = 3 | m = 2 | m = 1 | m = 3 | m = 2 | m = 1 | m = 3 | m = 2 | m = 1 |
| $S_{t-1}$ | 1.155 | 0.8742 | 0.5562 | −0.1715 | −0.3117 | −0.1242 | −0.1675 | −0.1461 | −0.1958 |
| $S_{t-2}$ | −0.0377 | 0.2493 | — | 0.1621 | −0.0773 | — | −0.0303 | −0.0304 | — |
| $S_{t-3}$ | −0.5644 | — | — | −0.1772 | — | — | −0.0955 | — | — |
| $R_{t-1}$ | −1.2380 | −0.8745 | −0.5328 | −0.0176 | 0.1863 | −0.0245 | 0.1578 | 0.1453 | 0.2343 |
| $R_{t-2}$ | 0.0770 | −0.2776 | — | −0.0309 | 0.1368 | — | 0.0485 | 0.0175 | — |
| $R_{t-3}$ | 0.6497 | — | — | 0.0034 | — | — | 0.0319 | — | — |
| $G_{t-1}$ | 0.0163 | −0.4203 | 0.1275 | −0.3683 | 0.5425 | −0.0808 | −0.2381 | −0.2066 | −0.0559 |
| $G_{t-2}$ | 1.5538 | 0.1866 | — | −2.7152 | 2.4621 | — | −0.0492 | −0.0804 | — |
| $G_{t-3}$ | 1.7892 | — | — | 0.0948 | — | — | 0.0598 | — | — |
| $q$ | 22.8287 | 30.4526 | 34.4986 | 30.5398 | 34.2590 | 53.2506 | 17.5810 | 20.5416 | 27.5927 |

## 15.7 SUMMARY AND CONCLUSIONS

The generalized method of moments provides an estimation framework that includes least squares, nonlinear least squares, instrumental variables, and maximum likelihood, and a general class of estimators that extends beyond these. But it is more than just a theoretical umbrella. The GMM provides a method of formulating models and implied estimators without making strong distributional assumptions. Hall's model of household consumption is a useful example that shows how the optimization conditions of an underlying economic theory produce a set of distribution-free estimating equations. In this chapter, we first examined the classical method of moments. GMM as an estimator is an extension of this strategy that allows the analyst to use additional information beyond that necessary to identify the model, in an optimal fashion. After defining and establishing the properties of the estimator, we then turned to inference procedures. It is convenient that the GMM procedure provides counterparts to the familiar trio of test statistics: Wald, LM, and LR. In the final section, we specialized the GMM estimator for linear and nonlinear equations and multiple-equation models. We then developed an example that appears at many points in the recent applied literature, the dynamic panel data model with individual specific effects, and lagged values of the dependent variable.

### Key Terms and Concepts

- Analog estimation
- Arellano and Bover estimator
- Central limit theorem
- Central moments
- Criterion function
- Dynamic panel data model
- Empirical moment equation
- Ergodic theorem
- Euler equation
- Exactly identified
- Exactly defined cases
- Exponential family
- Generalized method of moments
- GMM estimator
- Identification
- Instrumental variables
- Likelihood ratio statistic
- LM statistic
- Martingale difference series
- Maximum likelihood estimator
- Mean value theorem
- Method of moment generating functions
- Method of moments
- Method of moments estimators
- Minimum distance estimator (MDE)
- Moment equation
- Newey-West estimator
- Nonlinear instrumental variable estimator
- Optimal weighting matrix
- Order condition
- Orthogonality conditions
- Overidentifying restrictions
- Overidentified cases
- Population moment equation
- Probability limit
- Random sample
- Rank condition
- Slutsky theorem
- Specification test
- Sufficient statistic
- Taylor series
- Uncentered moment
- Vector autoregression
- Wald statistic
- Weighted least squares
- Weighting matrix

### Exercises

1. For the normal distribution $\mu_{2k} = \sigma^{2k}(2k)!/(k!2^k)$ and $\mu_{2k+1} = 0$, $k = 0, 1, \ldots$. Use this result to analyze the two estimators

$$\sqrt{b_1} = \frac{m_3}{m_2^{3/2}} \quad \text{and} \quad b_2 = \frac{m_4}{m_2^2},$$

where $m_k = \frac{1}{n}\sum_{i=1}^{n}(x_i - \bar{x})^k$. The following result will be useful:

$$\text{Asy. Cov}[\sqrt{n}m_j, \sqrt{n}m_k] = \mu_{j+k} - \mu_j\mu_k + jk\mu_2\mu_{j-1}\mu_{k-1} - j\mu_{j-1}\mu_{k+1} - k\mu_{k-1}\mu_{j+1}.$$

Use the delta method to obtain the asymptotic variances and covariance of these two functions, assuming the data are drawn from a normal distribution with mean $\mu$ and variance $\sigma^2$. (Hint: Under the assumptions, the sample mean is a consistent estimator of $\mu$, so for purposes of deriving asymptotic results, the difference between $\bar{x}$ and $\mu$ may be ignored. As such, no generality is lost by assuming the mean is zero, and proceeding from there.) Obtain **V**, the $3 \times 3$ covariance matrix for the three moments, then use the delta method to show that the covariance matrix for the two estimators is

$$\mathbf{JVJ'} = \begin{bmatrix} 6/n & 0 \\ 0 & 24/n \end{bmatrix},$$

where **J** is the $2 \times 3$ matrix of derivatives.

2. Using the results in Example 15.7, estimate the asymptotic covariance matrix of the method of moments estimators of $P$ and $\lambda$ based on $m_1'$ and $m_2'$. [Note: You will need to use the data in Example C.1 to estimate **V**.]

3. **Exponential Families of Distributions.** For each of the following distributions, determine whether it is an exponential family by examining the log-likelihood function. Then, identify the sufficient statistics.
   a. Normal distribution with mean $\mu$ and variance $\sigma^2$.
   b. The Weibull distribution in Exercise 4 in Chapter 16.
   c. The mixture distribution in Exercise 3 in Chapter 16.

4. In the classical regression model with heteroscedasticity, which is more efficient, ordinary least squares or GMM? Obtain the two estimators and their respective asymptotic covariance matrices, then prove your assertion.

5. Consider the probit model analyzed in Chapter 23. The model states that for given vector of independent variables,

$$\text{Prob}[y_i = 1 \,|\, \mathbf{x}_i] = \Phi[\mathbf{x}_i'\boldsymbol{\beta}], \quad \text{Prob}[y_i = 0 \,|\, \mathbf{x}_i] = 1 - \text{Prob}[y_i = 1 \,|\, \mathbf{x}_i].$$

Consider a GMM estimator based on the result that

$$E[y_i \,|\, \mathbf{x}_i] = \Phi(\mathbf{x}_i'\boldsymbol{\beta}).$$

This suggests that we might base estimation on the orthogonality conditions

$$E[(y_i - \Phi(\mathbf{x}_i'\boldsymbol{\beta}))\mathbf{x}_i] = \mathbf{0}.$$

Construct a GMM estimator based on these results. Note that this is not the non-linear least squares estimator. Explain—what would the orthogonality conditions be for nonlinear least squares estimation of this model?

6. Consider GMM estimation of a regression model as shown at the beginning of Example 15.8. Let $\mathbf{W}_1$ be the optimal weighting matrix based on the moment equations. Let $\mathbf{W}_2$ be some other positive definite matrix. Compare the asymptotic covariance matrices of the two proposed estimators. Show conclusively that the asymptotic covariance matrix of the estimator based on $\mathbf{W}_1$ is not larger than that based on $\mathbf{W}_2$.

# 16

# MAXIMUM LIKELIHOOD
# ESTIMATION

## 16.1  INTRODUCTION

The generalized method of moments discussed in Chapter 15 and the semiparametric, nonparametric, and Bayesian estimators discussed in Chapters 14 and 18 are becoming widely used by model builders. Nonetheless, the maximum likelihood estimator discussed in this chapter remains the preferred estimator in many more settings than the others listed. As such, we focus our discussion of generally applied estimation methods on this technique. Sections 16.2 through 16.6 present basic statistical results for estimation and hypothesis testing based on the maximum likelihood principle. Sections 16.7 and 16.8 present two extensions of the method, two-step estimation and pseudo maximum likelihood estimation. After establishing the general results for this method of estimation, we will then apply them to the more familiar setting of econometric models. The applications presented in Section 16.9 apply the maximum likelihood method to most of the models in the preceding chapters and several others that illustrate different uses of the technique.

## 16.2  THE LIKELIHOOD FUNCTION AND IDENTIFICATION OF THE PARAMETERS

The probability density function, or pdf, for a random variable, $y$, conditioned on a set of parameters, $\boldsymbol{\theta}$, is denoted $f(y \mid \boldsymbol{\theta})$.[1] This function identifies the data-generating process that underlies an observed sample of data and, at the same time, provides a mathematical description of the data that the process will produce. The joint density of $n$ *independent* and *identically distributed* (i.i.d.) observations from this process is the product of the individual densities;

$$f(y_1, \ldots, y_n \mid \boldsymbol{\theta}) = \prod_{i=1}^{n} f(y_i \mid \boldsymbol{\theta}) = L(\boldsymbol{\theta} \mid \mathbf{y}). \qquad \textbf{(16-1)}$$

This joint density is the **likelihood function,** defined as a function of the unknown parameter vector, $\boldsymbol{\theta}$, where $\mathbf{y}$ is used to indicate the collection of sample data. Note that we write the joint density as a function of the data conditioned on the parameters whereas when we form the likelihood function, we will write this function in reverse,

---

[1] Later we will extend this to the case of a random vector, $\mathbf{y}$, with a multivariate density, but at this point, that would complicate the notation without adding anything of substance to the discussion.

as a function of the parameters, conditioned on the data. Though the two functions are the same, it is to be emphasized that the likelihood function is written in this fashion to highlight our interest in the parameters and the information about them that is contained in the observed data. However, it is understood that the likelihood function is not meant to represent a probability density for the parameters as it is in Chapter 18. In this classical estimation framework, the parameters are assumed to be fixed constants that we hope to learn about from the data.

It is usually simpler to work with the log of the likelihood function:

$$\ln L(\boldsymbol{\theta} \mid \mathbf{y}) = \sum_{i=1}^{n} \ln f(y_i \mid \boldsymbol{\theta}). \tag{16-2}$$

Again, to emphasize our interest in the parameters, given the observed data, we denote this function $L(\boldsymbol{\theta} \mid \mathbf{data}) = L(\boldsymbol{\theta} \mid \mathbf{y})$. The likelihood function and its logarithm, evaluated at $\boldsymbol{\theta}$, are sometimes denoted simply $L(\boldsymbol{\theta})$ and $\ln L(\boldsymbol{\theta})$, respectively, or, where no ambiguity can arise, just $L$ or $\ln L$.

It will usually be necessary to generalize the concept of the likelihood function to allow the density to depend on other conditioning variables. To jump immediately to one of our central applications, suppose the disturbance in the classical linear regression model is normally distributed. Then, conditioned on its specific $\mathbf{x}_i$, $y_i$ is normally distributed with mean $\mu_i = \mathbf{x}_i'\boldsymbol{\beta}$ and variance $\sigma^2$. That means that the observed random variables are not i.i.d.; they have different means. Nonetheless, the observations are independent, and as we will examine in closer detail,

$$\ln L(\boldsymbol{\theta} \mid \mathbf{y}, \mathbf{X}) = \sum_{i=1}^{n} \ln f(y_i \mid \mathbf{x}_i, \boldsymbol{\theta}) = -\frac{1}{2} \sum_{i=1}^{n} [\ln \sigma^2 + \ln(2\pi) + (y_i - \mathbf{x}_i'\boldsymbol{\beta})^2/\sigma^2], \tag{16-3}$$

where $\mathbf{X}$ is the $n \times K$ matrix of data with $i$th row equal to $\mathbf{x}_i'$.

The rest of this chapter will be concerned with obtaining estimates of the parameters, $\boldsymbol{\theta}$, and in testing hypotheses about them and about the data-generating process. Before we begin that study, we consider the question of whether estimation of the parameters is possible at all—the question of **identification.** Identification is an issue related to the formulation of the model. The issue of identification must be resolved before estimation can even be considered. The question posed is essentially this: Suppose we had an infinitely large sample—that is, for current purposes, all the information there is to be had about the parameters. Could we uniquely determine the values of $\boldsymbol{\theta}$ from such a sample? As will be clear shortly, the answer is sometimes no.

---

**DEFINITION 16.1**  **Identification**

*The parameter vector $\boldsymbol{\theta}$ is identified (**estimable**) if for any other parameter vector, $\boldsymbol{\theta}^* \neq \boldsymbol{\theta}$, for some data $\mathbf{y}$, $L(\boldsymbol{\theta}^* \mid \mathbf{y}) \neq L(\boldsymbol{\theta} \mid \mathbf{y})$.*

---

This result will be crucial at several points in what follows. We consider two examples, the first of which will be very familiar to you by now.

### Example 16.1    Identification of Parameters

For the regression model specified in (16-3), suppose that there is a nonzero vector **a** such that $\mathbf{x}_i'\mathbf{a} = 0$ for every $\mathbf{x}_i$. Then there is another "parameter" vector, $\boldsymbol{\gamma} = \boldsymbol{\beta} + \mathbf{a} \neq \boldsymbol{\beta}$ such that $\mathbf{x}_i'\boldsymbol{\beta} = \mathbf{x}_i'\boldsymbol{\gamma}$ for every $\mathbf{x}_i$. You can see in (16-3) that if this is the case, then the log-likelihood is the same whether it is evaluated at $\boldsymbol{\beta}$ or at $\boldsymbol{\gamma}$. As such, it is not possible to consider estimation of $\boldsymbol{\beta}$ in this model because $\boldsymbol{\beta}$ cannot be distinguished from $\boldsymbol{\gamma}$. This is the case of perfect collinearity in the regression model, which we ruled out when we first proposed the linear regression model with "Assumption 2. Identifiability of the Model Parameters."

The preceding dealt with a necessary characteristic of the sample data. We now consider a model in which identification is secured by the specification of the parameters in the model. (We will study this model in detail in Chapter 23.) Consider a simple form of the regression model considered earlier, $y_i = \beta_1 + \beta_2 x_i + \varepsilon_i$, where $\varepsilon_i \,|\, x_i$ has a normal distribution with zero mean and variance $\sigma^2$. To put the model in a context, consider a consumer's purchases of a large commodity such as a car where $x_i$ is the consumer's income and $y_i$ is the difference between what the consumer is willing to pay for the car, $p_i^*$, and the price tag on the car, $p_i$. Suppose rather than observing $p_i^*$ or $p_i$, we observe only whether the consumer actually purchases the car, which, we assume, occurs when $y_i = p_i^* - p_i$ is positive. Collecting this information, our model states that they will purchase the car if $y_i > 0$ and not purchase it if $y_i \leq 0$. Let us form the likelihood function for the observed data, which are purchase (or not) and income. The random variable in this model is "purchase" or "not purchase"—there are only two outcomes. The probability of a purchase is

$$
\begin{aligned}
\text{Prob}(\text{purchase} \,|\, \beta_1, \beta_2, \sigma, x_i) &= \text{Prob}(y_i > 0 \,|\, \beta_1, \beta_2, \sigma, x_i) \\
&= \text{Prob}(\beta_1 + \beta_2 x_i + \varepsilon_i > 0 \,|\, \beta_1, \beta_2, \sigma, x_i) \\
&= \text{Prob}[\varepsilon_i > -(\beta_1 + \beta_2 x_i) \,|\, \beta_1, \beta_2, \sigma, x_i] \\
&= \text{Prob}[\varepsilon_i/\sigma > -(\beta_1 + \beta_2 x_i)/\sigma \,|\, \beta_1, \beta_2, \sigma, x_i] \\
&= \text{Prob}[z_i > -(\beta_1 + \beta_2 x_i)/\sigma \,|\, \beta_1, \beta_2, \sigma, x_i]
\end{aligned}
$$

where $z_i$ has a standard normal distribution. The probability of not purchase is just one minus this probability. The likelihood function is

$$
\prod_{i=purchased} [\text{Prob}(\text{purchase} \,|\, \beta_1, \beta_2, \sigma, x_i)] \prod_{i=not\ purchased} [1 - \text{Prob}(\text{purchase} \,|\, \beta_1, \beta_2, \sigma, x_i)].
$$

We need go no further to see that the parameters of this model are not identified. If $\beta_1$, $\beta_2$, and $\sigma$ are all multiplied by the same nonzero constant, regardless of what it is, then Prob(purchase) is unchanged, $1 - \text{Prob}(\text{purchase})$ is also, and the likelihood function does not change. This model requires a **normalization**. The one usually used is $\sigma = 1$, but some authors [e.g., Horowitz (1993)] have used $\beta_1 = 1$ instead.

## 16.3    EFFICIENT ESTIMATION: THE PRINCIPLE OF MAXIMUM LIKELIHOOD

The principle of **maximum likelihood** provides a means of choosing an asymptotically efficient estimator for a parameter or a set of parameters. The logic of the technique is easily illustrated in the setting of a discrete distribution. Consider a random sample of the following 10 observations from a Poisson distribution: 5, 0, 1, 1, 0, 3, 2, 3, 4, and 1. The density for each observation is

$$
f(y_i \,|\, \theta) = \frac{e^{-\theta}\theta^{y_i}}{y_i!}.
$$

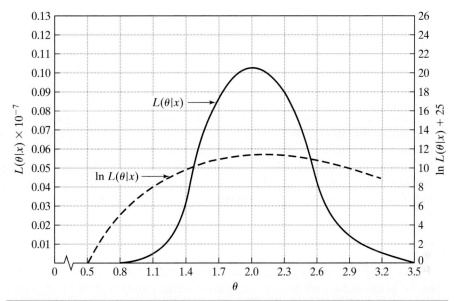

**FIGURE 16.1**   Likelihood and Log-Likelihood Functions for a Poisson Distribution.

Because the observations are independent, their joint density, which is the likelihood for this sample, is

$$f(y_1, y_2, \ldots, y_{10} \mid \theta) = \prod_{i=1}^{10} f(y_i \mid \theta) = \frac{e^{-10\theta}\theta^{\sum_{i=1}^{10} y_i}}{\prod_{i=1}^{10} y_i!} = \frac{e^{-10\theta}\theta^{20}}{207,360}.$$

The last result gives the probability of observing *this particular sample*, assuming that a Poisson distribution with as yet unknown parameter $\theta$ generated the data. What value of $\theta$ would make this sample most probable? Figure 16.1 plots this function for various values of $\theta$. It has a single mode at $\theta = 2$, which would be the **maximum likelihood estimate,** or MLE, of $\theta$.

Consider maximizing $L(\theta \mid \mathbf{y})$ with respect to $\theta$. Because the log function is monotonically increasing and easier to work with, we usually maximize $\ln L(\theta \mid \mathbf{y})$ instead; in sampling from a Poisson population,

$$\ln L(\theta \mid \mathbf{y}) = -n\theta + \ln\theta \sum_{i=1}^{n} y_i - \sum_{i=1}^{n} \ln(y_i!),$$

$$\frac{\partial \ln L(\theta \mid \mathbf{y})}{\partial \theta} = -n + \frac{1}{\theta}\sum_{i=1}^{n} y_i = 0 \Rightarrow \hat{\theta}_{\mathrm{ML}} = \bar{y}_n.$$

For the assumed sample of observations,

$$\ln L(\theta \mid \mathbf{y}) = -10\theta + 20\ln\theta - 12.242,$$

$$\frac{d \ln L(\theta \mid \mathbf{y})}{d\theta} = -10 + \frac{20}{\theta} = 0 \Rightarrow \hat{\theta} = 2,$$

and

$$\frac{d^2 \ln L(\theta \mid \mathbf{y})}{d\theta^2} = \frac{-20}{\theta^2} < 0 \Rightarrow \text{this is a maximum.}$$

The solution is the same as before. Figure 16.1 also plots the log of $L(\theta \mid \mathbf{y})$ to illustrate the result.

The reference to the probability of observing the given sample is not exact in a continuous distribution, because a particular sample has probability zero. Nonetheless, the principle is the same. The values of the parameters that maximize $L(\theta \mid \mathbf{data})$ or its log are the maximum likelihood estimates, denoted $\hat{\theta}$. The logarithm is a monotonic function, so the values that maximize $L(\theta \mid \mathbf{data})$ are the same as those that maximize $\ln L(\theta \mid \mathbf{data})$. The necessary condition for maximizing $\ln L(\theta \mid \mathbf{data})$ is

$$\frac{\partial \ln L(\theta \mid \mathbf{data})}{\partial \theta} = 0. \tag{16-4}$$

This is called the **likelihood equation.** The general result then is that the MLE is a root of the likelihood equation. The application to the parameters of the dgp for a discrete random variable are suggestive that maximum likelihood is a "good" use of the data. It remains to establish this as a general principle. We turn to that issue in the next section.

**Example 16.2   Log-Likelihood Function and Likelihood Equations
for the Normal Distribution**
In sampling from a normal distribution with mean $\mu$ and variance $\sigma^2$, the log-likelihood function and the likelihood equations for $\mu$ and $\sigma^2$ are

$$\ln L(\mu, \sigma^2) = -\frac{n}{2} \ln(2\pi) - \frac{n}{2} \ln \sigma^2 - \frac{1}{2} \sum_{i=1}^{n} \left[ \frac{(y_i - \mu)^2}{\sigma^2} \right], \tag{16-5}$$

$$\frac{\partial \ln L}{\partial \mu} = \frac{1}{\sigma^2} \sum_{i=1}^{n} (y_i - \mu) = 0, \tag{16-6}$$

$$\frac{\partial \ln L}{\partial \sigma^2} = -\frac{n}{2\sigma^2} + \frac{1}{2\sigma^4} \sum_{i=1}^{n} (y_i - \mu)^2 = 0. \tag{16-7}$$

To solve the likelihood equations, multiply (16-6) by $\sigma^2$ and solve for $\hat{\mu}$, then insert this solution in (16-7) and solve for $\sigma^2$. The solutions are

$$\hat{\mu}_{ML} = \frac{1}{n} \sum_{i=1}^{n} y_i = \bar{y}_n \quad \text{and} \quad \hat{\sigma}^2_{ML} = \frac{1}{n} \sum_{i=1}^{n} (y_i - \bar{y}_n)^2. \tag{16-8}$$

## 16.4   PROPERTIES OF MAXIMUM LIKELIHOOD ESTIMATORS

Maximum likelihood estimators (MLEs) are most attractive because of their large-sample or asymptotic properties.

---

**DEFINITION 16.2** **Asymptotic Efficiency**
*An estimator is asymptotically efficient if it is consistent, asymptotically normally distributed (CAN), and has an asymptotic covariance matrix that is not larger than the asymptotic covariance matrix of any other consistent, asymptotically normally distributed estimator.*[2]

---

If certain regularity conditions are met, the MLE will have these properties. The finite sample properties are sometimes less than optimal. For example, the MLE may be biased; the MLE of $\sigma^2$ in Example 16.2 is biased downward. The occasional statement that the properties of the MLE are *only* optimal in large samples is not true, however. It can be shown that when sampling is from an exponential family of distributions (see Definition 15.1), there will exist sufficient statistics. If so, MLEs will be functions of them, which means that when minimum variance unbiased estimators exist, they will be MLEs. [See Stuart and Ord (1989).] Most applications in econometrics do not involve exponential families, so the appeal of the MLE remains primarily its asymptotic properties.

We use the following notation: $\hat{\theta}$ is the maximum likelihood estimator; $\theta_0$ denotes the true value of the parameter vector; $\theta$ denotes another possible value of the parameter vector, not the MLE and not necessarily the true values. Expectation based on the true values of the parameters is denoted $E_0[.]$. If we assume that the regularity conditions discussed momentarily are met by $f(\mathbf{x}, \theta_0)$, then we have the following theorem.

---

**THEOREM 16.1** **Properties of an MLE**
*Under regularity, the maximum likelihood estimator (MLE) has the following asymptotic properties:*

**M1.** **Consistency:** $\text{plim} \, \hat{\theta} = \theta_0$.

**M2.** **Asymptotic normality:** $\hat{\theta} \stackrel{a}{\sim} N[\theta_0, \{\mathbf{I}(\theta_0)\}^{-1}]$, *where*

$$\mathbf{I}(\theta_0) = -E_0[\partial^2 \ln L / \partial \theta_0 \partial \theta_0'].$$

**M3.** **Asymptotic efficiency:** $\hat{\theta}$ *is asymptotically efficient and achieves the* **Cramér–Rao lower bound** *for consistent estimators, given in M2 and Theorem C.2.*

**M4.** **Invariance:** *The maximum likelihood estimator of* $\gamma_0 = \mathbf{c}(\theta_0)$ *is* $\mathbf{c}(\hat{\theta})$ *if* $\mathbf{c}(\theta_0)$ *is a continuous and continuously differentiable function.*

---

### 16.4.1 REGULARITY CONDITIONS

To sketch proofs of these results, we first obtain some useful properties of probability density functions. We assume that $(y_1, \ldots, y_n)$ is a random sample from the population

---

[2]*Not larger* is defined in the sense of (A-118): The covariance matrix of the less efficient estimator equals that of the efficient estimator plus a nonnegative definite matrix.

with density function $f(y_i \mid \boldsymbol{\theta}_0)$ and that the following **regularity conditions** hold. [Our statement of these is informal. A more rigorous treatment may be found in Stuart and Ord (1989) or Davidson and MacKinnon (2004).]

---

**DEFINITION 16.3** Regularity Conditions

**R1.** *The first three derivatives of $\ln f(y_i \mid \boldsymbol{\theta})$ with respect to $\boldsymbol{\theta}$ are continuous and finite for almost all $y_i$ and for all $\boldsymbol{\theta}$. This condition ensures the existence of a certain Taylor series approximation and the finite variance of the derivatives of $\ln L$.*

**R2.** *The conditions necessary to obtain the expectations of the first and second derivatives of $\ln f(y_i \mid \boldsymbol{\theta})$ are met.*

**R3.** *For all values of $\boldsymbol{\theta}$, $|\partial^3 \ln f(y_i \mid \boldsymbol{\theta})/\partial\theta_j \partial\theta_k \partial\theta_l|$ is less than a function that has a finite expectation. This condition will allow us to truncate the Taylor series.*

---

With these regularity conditions, we will obtain the following fundamental characteristics of $f(y_i \mid \boldsymbol{\theta})$: D1 is simply a consequence of the definition of the likelihood function. D2 leads to the moment condition which defines the maximum likelihood estimator. On the one hand, the MLE is found as the maximizer of a function, which mandates finding the vector that equates the gradient to zero. On the other, D2 is a more fundamental relationship that places the MLE in the class of generalized method of moments estimators. D3 produces what is known as the **information matrix equality.** This relationship shows how to obtain the asymptotic covariance matrix of the MLE.

### 16.4.2 PROPERTIES OF REGULAR DENSITIES

Densities that are "regular" by Definition 16.3 have three properties that are used in establishing the properties of maximum likelihood estimators:

---

**THEOREM 16.2** Moments of the Derivatives of the Log-Likelihood

**D1.** $\ln f(y_i \mid \boldsymbol{\theta})$, $\mathbf{g}_i = \partial \ln f(y_i \mid \boldsymbol{\theta})/\partial\boldsymbol{\theta}$, *and* $\mathbf{H}_i = \partial^2 \ln f(y_i \mid \boldsymbol{\theta})/\partial\boldsymbol{\theta}\partial\boldsymbol{\theta}'$, $i = 1, \ldots, n$, *are all random samples of random variables. This statement follows from our assumption of random sampling. The notation $\mathbf{g}_i(\boldsymbol{\theta}_0)$ and $\mathbf{H}_i(\boldsymbol{\theta}_0)$ indicates the derivative evaluated at $\boldsymbol{\theta}_0$.*

**D2.** $E_0[\mathbf{g}_i(\boldsymbol{\theta}_0)] = \mathbf{0}$.

**D3.** $\text{Var}[\mathbf{g}_i(\boldsymbol{\theta}_0)] = -E[\mathbf{H}_i(\boldsymbol{\theta}_0)]$.

*Condition D1 is simply a consequence of the definition of the density.*

---

For the moment, we allow the range of $y_i$ to depend on the parameters; $A(\boldsymbol{\theta}_0) \leq y_i \leq B(\boldsymbol{\theta}_0)$. (Consider, for example, finding the maximum likelihood estimator of $\theta_0$

for a continuous uniform distribution with range $[0, \theta_0]$.) (In the following, the single integral $\int \ldots dy_i$, would be used to indicate the multiple integration over all the elements of a multivariate of $y_i$ if that were necessary.) By definition,

$$\int_{A(\theta_0)}^{B(\theta_0)} f(y_i \mid \theta_0) \, dy_i = 1.$$

Now, differentiate this expression with respect to $\theta_0$. Leibnitz's theorem gives

$$\frac{\partial \int_{A(\theta_0)}^{B(\theta_0)} f(y_i \mid \theta_0) \, dy_i}{\partial \theta_0} = \int_{A(\theta_0)}^{B(\theta_0)} \frac{\partial f(y_i \mid \theta_0)}{\partial \theta_0} \, dy_i + f(B(\theta_0) \mid \theta_0) \frac{\partial B(\theta_0)}{\partial \theta_0}$$

$$- f(A(\theta_0) \mid \theta_0) \frac{\partial A(\theta_0)}{\partial \theta_0}$$

$$= \mathbf{0}.$$

If the second and third terms go to zero, then we may interchange the operations of differentiation and integration. The necessary condition is that $\lim_{y_i \to A(\theta_0)} f(y_i \mid \theta_0) = \lim_{y_i \to B(\theta_0)} f(y_i \mid \theta_0) = 0$. (Note that the uniform distribution suggested earlier violates this condition.) Sufficient conditions are that the range of the observed random variable, $y_i$, does not depend on the parameters, which means that $\partial A(\theta_0)/\partial \theta_0 = \partial B(\theta_0)/\partial \theta_0 = \mathbf{0}$ or that the density is zero at the terminal points. This condition, then, is regularity condition R2. The latter is usually assumed, and we will assume it in what follows. So,

$$\frac{\partial \int f(y_i \mid \theta_0) \, dy_i}{\partial \theta_0} = \int \frac{\partial f(y_i \mid \theta_0)}{\partial \theta_0} \, dy_i = \int \frac{\partial \ln f(y_i \mid \theta_0)}{\partial \theta_0} f(y_i \mid \theta_0) \, dy_i$$

$$= E_0 \left[ \frac{\partial \ln f(y_i \mid \theta_0)}{\partial \theta_0} \right] = \mathbf{0}.$$

This proves D2.

Because we may interchange the operations of integration and differentiation, we differentiate under the integral once again to obtain

$$\int \left[ \frac{\partial^2 \ln f(y_i \mid \theta_0)}{\partial \theta_0 \partial \theta_0'} f(y_i \mid \theta_0) + \frac{\partial \ln f(y_i \mid \theta_0)}{\partial \theta_0} \frac{\partial f(y_i \mid \theta_0)}{\partial \theta_0'} \right] dy_i = \mathbf{0}.$$

But

$$\frac{\partial f(y_i \mid \theta_0)}{\partial \theta_0'} = f(y_i \mid \theta_0) \frac{\partial \ln f(y_i \mid \theta_0)}{\partial \theta_0'},$$

and the integral of a sum is the sum of integrals. Therefore,

$$-\int \left[ \frac{\partial^2 \ln f(y_i \mid \theta_0)}{\partial \theta_0 \partial \theta_0'} \right] f(y_i \mid \theta_0) \, dy_i = \int \left[ \frac{\partial \ln f(y_i \mid \theta_0)}{\partial \theta_0} \frac{\partial \ln f(y_i \mid \theta_0)}{\partial \theta_0'} \right] f(y_i \mid \theta_0) \, dy_i.$$

The left-hand side of the equation is the negative of the expected second derivatives matrix. The right-hand side is the expected square (outer product) of the first derivative vector. But, because this vector has expected value $\mathbf{0}$ (we just showed this), the right-hand side is the variance of the first derivative vector, which proves D3:

$$\text{Var}_0 \left[ \frac{\partial \ln f(y_i \mid \theta_0)}{\partial \theta_0} \right] = E_0 \left[ \left( \frac{\partial \ln f(y_i \mid \theta_0)}{\partial \theta_0} \right) \left( \frac{\partial \ln f(y_i \mid \theta_0)}{\partial \theta_0'} \right) \right] = -E \left[ \frac{\partial^2 \ln f(y_i \mid \theta_0)}{\partial \theta_0 \partial \theta_0'} \right].$$

### 16.4.3   THE LIKELIHOOD EQUATION

The log-likelihood function is

$$\ln L(\boldsymbol{\theta} \mid \mathbf{y}) = \sum_{i=1}^{n} \ln f(y_i \mid \boldsymbol{\theta}).$$

The first derivative vector, or **score vector,** is

$$\mathbf{g} = \frac{\partial \ln L(\boldsymbol{\theta} \mid \mathbf{y})}{\partial \boldsymbol{\theta}} = \sum_{i=1}^{n} \frac{\partial \ln f(y_i \mid \boldsymbol{\theta})}{\partial \boldsymbol{\theta}} = \sum_{i=1}^{n} \mathbf{g}_i. \tag{16-9}$$

Because we are just adding terms, it follows from D1 and D2 that at $\boldsymbol{\theta}_0$,

$$E_0 \left[ \frac{\partial \ln L(\boldsymbol{\theta}_0 \mid \mathbf{y})}{\partial \boldsymbol{\theta}_0} \right] = E_0[\mathbf{g}_0] = \mathbf{0}. \tag{16-10}$$

which is the **likelihood equation** mentioned earlier.

### 16.4.4   THE INFORMATION MATRIX EQUALITY

The Hessian of the log-likelihood is

$$\mathbf{H} = \frac{\partial^2 \ln L(\boldsymbol{\theta} \mid \mathbf{y})}{\partial \boldsymbol{\theta} \partial \boldsymbol{\theta}'} = \sum_{i=1}^{n} \frac{\partial^2 \ln f(y_i \mid \boldsymbol{\theta})}{\partial \boldsymbol{\theta} \partial \boldsymbol{\theta}'} = \sum_{i=1}^{n} \mathbf{H}_i.$$

Evaluating once again at $\boldsymbol{\theta}_0$, by taking

$$E_0[\mathbf{g}_0 \mathbf{g}_0'] = E_0 \left[ \sum_{i=1}^{n} \sum_{j=1}^{n} \mathbf{g}_{0i} \mathbf{g}_{0j}' \right],$$

and, because of D1, dropping terms with unequal subscripts we obtain

$$E_0[\mathbf{g}_0 \mathbf{g}_0'] = E_0 \left[ \sum_{i=1}^{n} \mathbf{g}_{0i} \mathbf{g}_{0i}' \right] = E_0 \left[ \sum_{i=1}^{n} (-\mathbf{H}_{0i}) \right] = -E_0[\mathbf{H}_0],$$

so that

$$\text{Var}_0 \left[ \frac{\partial \ln L(\boldsymbol{\theta}_0 \mid \mathbf{y})}{\partial \boldsymbol{\theta}_0} \right] = E_0 \left[ \left( \frac{\partial \ln L(\boldsymbol{\theta}_0 \mid \mathbf{y})}{\partial \boldsymbol{\theta}_0} \right) \left( \frac{\partial \ln L(\boldsymbol{\theta}_0 \mid \mathbf{y})}{\partial \boldsymbol{\theta}_0'} \right) \right]$$

$$= -E_0 \left[ \frac{\partial^2 \ln L(\boldsymbol{\theta}_0 \mid \mathbf{y})}{\partial \boldsymbol{\theta}_0 \partial \boldsymbol{\theta}_0'} \right]. \tag{16-11}$$

This very useful result is known as the **information matrix equality.**

### 16.4.5   ASYMPTOTIC PROPERTIES OF THE MAXIMUM LIKELIHOOD ESTIMATOR

We can now sketch a derivation of the asymptotic properties of the MLE. Formal proofs of these results require some fairly intricate mathematics. Two widely cited derivations are those of Cramér (1948) and Amemiya (1985). To suggest the flavor of the exercise, we will sketch an analysis provided by Stuart and Ord (1989) for a simple case, and indicate where it will be necessary to extend the derivation if it were to be fully general.

### 16.4.5.a  Consistency

We assume that $f(\mathbf{y}_i \mid \boldsymbol{\theta}_0)$ is a possibly multivariate density that at this point does not depend on covariates, $\mathbf{x}_i$. Thus, this is the i.i.d., random sampling case. Because $\hat{\boldsymbol{\theta}}$ is the MLE, in any finite sample, for any $\boldsymbol{\theta} \neq \hat{\boldsymbol{\theta}}$ (including the true $\boldsymbol{\theta}_0$) it must be true that

$$\ln L(\hat{\boldsymbol{\theta}}) \geq \ln L(\boldsymbol{\theta}). \tag{16-12}$$

Consider, then, the random variable $L(\boldsymbol{\theta})/L(\boldsymbol{\theta}_0)$. Because the log function is strictly concave, from Jensen's Inequality (Theorem D.13.), we have

$$E_0\left[\ln \frac{L(\boldsymbol{\theta})}{L(\boldsymbol{\theta}_0)}\right] < \ln E_0\left[\frac{L(\boldsymbol{\theta})}{L(\boldsymbol{\theta}_0)}\right]. \tag{16-13}$$

The expectation on the right-hand side is exactly equal to one, as

$$E_0\left[\frac{L(\boldsymbol{\theta})}{L(\boldsymbol{\theta}_0)}\right] = \int \left(\frac{L(\boldsymbol{\theta})}{L(\boldsymbol{\theta}_0)}\right) L(\boldsymbol{\theta}_0)\, d\mathbf{y} = 1 \tag{16-14}$$

is simply the integral of a joint density. Now, take logs on both sides of (16-13), insert the result of (16-14), then divide by $n$ to produce

$$E_0[1/n \ln L(\boldsymbol{\theta})] - E_0[1/n \ln L(\boldsymbol{\theta}_0)] < 0. \tag{16-15}$$

This produces a central result:

---

**THEOREM 16.3**   **Likelihood Inequality**

$E_0[(1/n) \ln L(\theta_0)] > E_0[(1/n) \ln L(\theta)]$   for any $\boldsymbol{\theta} \neq \boldsymbol{\theta}_0$ (including $\hat{\boldsymbol{\theta}}$).

*This result is (16-15).*

---

In words, *the expected value of the log-likelihood is maximized at the true value of the parameters.*

For any $\boldsymbol{\theta}$, including $\hat{\boldsymbol{\theta}}$,

$$[(1/n) \ln L(\boldsymbol{\theta})] = (1/n) \sum_{i=1}^{n} \ln f(y_i \mid \boldsymbol{\theta})$$

is the sample mean of $n$ i.i.d. random variables, with expectation $E_0[(1/n) \ln L(\boldsymbol{\theta})]$. Because the sampling is i.i.d. by the regularity conditions, we can invoke the Khinchine theorem, D.5; the sample mean converges in probability to the population mean. Using $\boldsymbol{\theta} = \hat{\boldsymbol{\theta}}$, it follows from Theorem 16.3 that as $n \to \infty$, $\lim \text{Prob}\{[(1/n) \ln L(\hat{\boldsymbol{\theta}})] < [(1/n) \ln L(\boldsymbol{\theta}_0)]\} = 1$ if $\hat{\boldsymbol{\theta}} \neq \boldsymbol{\theta}_0$. But, $\hat{\boldsymbol{\theta}}$ is the MLE, so for every $n$, $(1/n) \ln L(\hat{\boldsymbol{\theta}}) \geq (1/n) \ln L(\boldsymbol{\theta}_0)$. The only way these can both be true is if $(1/n)$ times the sample log-likelihood evaluated at the MLE converges to the population expectation of $(1/n)$ times the log-likelihood evaluated at the true parameters. There remains one final step. Does $(1/n) \ln L(\hat{\boldsymbol{\theta}}) \to (1/n) \ln L(\boldsymbol{\theta}_0)$ imply that $\hat{\boldsymbol{\theta}} \to \boldsymbol{\theta}_0$? If there is a single parameter and the likelihood function is one to one, then clearly so. For more general cases, this requires a further characterization of the likelihood function. If the likelihood is strictly continuous and twice differentiable, which we assumed in the regularity conditions, and if the parameters of the model are identified which we assumed at the beginning of this discussion, then yes, it does, so we have the result.

This is a heuristic proof. As noted, formal presentations appear in more advanced treatises than this one. We should also note, we have assumed at several points that sample means converged to the population expectations. This is likely to be true for the sorts of applications usually encountered in econometrics, but a fully general set of results would look more closely at this condition. Second, we have assumed i.i.d. sampling in the preceding—that is, the density for $\mathbf{y}_i$ does not depend on any other variables, $\mathbf{x}_i$. This will almost never be true in practice. Assumptions about the behavior of these variables will enter the proofs as well. For example, in assessing the large sample behavior of the least squares estimator, we have invoked an assumption that the data are "well behaved." The same sort of consideration will apply here as well. We will return to this issue shortly. With all this in place, we have property M1, plim $\hat{\boldsymbol{\theta}} = \boldsymbol{\theta}_0$.

### 16.4.5.b Asymptotic Normality

At the maximum likelihood estimator, the gradient of the log-likelihood equals zero (by definition), so

$$\mathbf{g}(\hat{\boldsymbol{\theta}}) = \mathbf{0}.$$

(This is the sample statistic, not the expectation.) Expand this set of equations in a Taylor series around the true parameters $\boldsymbol{\theta}_0$. We will use the mean value theorem to truncate the Taylor series at the second term,

$$\mathbf{g}(\hat{\boldsymbol{\theta}}) = \mathbf{g}(\boldsymbol{\theta}_0) + \mathbf{H}(\bar{\boldsymbol{\theta}})(\hat{\boldsymbol{\theta}} - \boldsymbol{\theta}_0) = \mathbf{0}.$$

The Hessian is evaluated at a point $\bar{\boldsymbol{\theta}}$ that is between $\hat{\boldsymbol{\theta}}$ and $\boldsymbol{\theta}_0$ [$\bar{\boldsymbol{\theta}} = w\hat{\boldsymbol{\theta}} + (1 - w)\boldsymbol{\theta}_0$ for some $0 < w < 1$]. We then rearrange this function and multiply the result by $\sqrt{n}$ to obtain

$$\sqrt{n}(\hat{\boldsymbol{\theta}} - \boldsymbol{\theta}_0) = [-\mathbf{H}(\bar{\boldsymbol{\theta}})]^{-1}[\sqrt{n}\mathbf{g}(\boldsymbol{\theta}_0)].$$

Because plim$(\hat{\boldsymbol{\theta}} - \boldsymbol{\theta}_0) = \mathbf{0}$, plim$(\hat{\boldsymbol{\theta}} - \bar{\boldsymbol{\theta}}) = \mathbf{0}$ as well. The second derivatives are continuous functions. Therefore, if the limiting distribution exists, then

$$\sqrt{n}(\hat{\boldsymbol{\theta}} - \boldsymbol{\theta}_0) \xrightarrow{d} [-\mathbf{H}(\boldsymbol{\theta}_0)]^{-1}[\sqrt{n}\mathbf{g}(\boldsymbol{\theta}_0)].$$

By dividing $\mathbf{H}(\boldsymbol{\theta}_0)$ and $\mathbf{g}(\boldsymbol{\theta}_0)$ by $n$, we obtain

$$\sqrt{n}(\hat{\boldsymbol{\theta}} - \boldsymbol{\theta}_0) \xrightarrow{d} \left[-\tfrac{1}{n}\mathbf{H}(\boldsymbol{\theta}_0)\right]^{-1}[\sqrt{n}\,\bar{\mathbf{g}}(\boldsymbol{\theta}_0)].$$

We may apply the Lindeberg–Levy central limit theorem (D.18) to $[\sqrt{n}\,\bar{\mathbf{g}}(\boldsymbol{\theta}_0)]$, because it is $\sqrt{n}$ times the mean of a random sample; we have invoked D1 again. The limiting variance of $[\sqrt{n}\,\bar{\mathbf{g}}(\boldsymbol{\theta}_0)]$ is $-E_0[(1/n)\mathbf{H}(\boldsymbol{\theta}_0)]$, so

$$\sqrt{n}\,\bar{\mathbf{g}}(\boldsymbol{\theta}_0) \xrightarrow{d} N\left\{\mathbf{0}, -E_0\left[\tfrac{1}{n}\mathbf{H}(\boldsymbol{\theta}_0)\right]\right\}.$$

By virtue of Theorem D.2, plim$[-(1/n)\mathbf{H}(\boldsymbol{\theta}_0)] = -E_0[(1/n)\mathbf{H}(\boldsymbol{\theta}_0)]$. This result is a constant matrix, so we can combine results to obtain

$$\left[-\tfrac{1}{n}\mathbf{H}(\boldsymbol{\theta}_0)\right]^{-1}\sqrt{n}\,\bar{\mathbf{g}}(\boldsymbol{\theta}_0) \xrightarrow{d} N\left[\mathbf{0}, \left\{-E_0\left[\tfrac{1}{n}\mathbf{H}(\boldsymbol{\theta}_0)\right]\right\}^{-1}\left\{-E_0\left[\tfrac{1}{n}\mathbf{H}(\boldsymbol{\theta}_0)\right]\right\}\left\{-E_0\left[\tfrac{1}{n}\mathbf{H}(\boldsymbol{\theta}_0)\right]\right\}^{-1}\right],$$

or

$$\sqrt{n}(\hat{\boldsymbol{\theta}} - \boldsymbol{\theta}_0) \xrightarrow{d} N\big[\mathbf{0}, \big\{-E_0\big[\tfrac{1}{n}\mathbf{H}(\boldsymbol{\theta}_0)\big]\big\}^{-1}\big],$$

which gives the asymptotic distribution of the MLE:

$$\hat{\boldsymbol{\theta}} \overset{a}{\sim} N[\boldsymbol{\theta}_0, \{\mathbf{I}(\boldsymbol{\theta}_0)\}^{-1}].$$

This last step completes M2.

### Example 16.3   Information Matrix for the Normal Distribution
For the likelihood function in Example 16.2, the second derivatives are

$$\frac{\partial^2 \ln L}{\partial \mu^2} = \frac{-n}{\sigma^2},$$

$$\frac{\partial^2 \ln L}{\partial (\sigma^2)^2} = \frac{n}{2\sigma^4} - \frac{1}{\sigma^6}\sum_{i=1}^{n}(y_i - \mu)^2,$$

$$\frac{\partial^2 \ln L}{\partial \mu \partial \sigma^2} = \frac{-1}{\sigma^4}\sum_{i=1}^{n}(y_i - \mu).$$

For the **asymptotic variance** of the maximum likelihood estimator, we need the expectations of these derivatives. The first is nonstochastic, and the third has expectation 0, as $E[y_i] = \mu$. That leaves the second, which you can verify has expectation $-n/(2\sigma^4)$ because each of the $n$ terms $(y_i - \mu)^2$ has expected value $\sigma^2$. Collecting these in the information matrix, reversing the sign, and inverting the matrix gives the asymptotic covariance matrix for the maximum likelihood estimators:

$$\left\{-E_0\left[\frac{\partial^2 \ln L}{\partial \boldsymbol{\theta}_0 \, \partial \boldsymbol{\theta}_0'}\right]\right\}^{-1} = \begin{bmatrix} \sigma^2/n & 0 \\ 0 & 2\sigma^4/n \end{bmatrix}.$$

### 16.4.5.c   Asymptotic Efficiency
Theorem C.2 provides the lower bound for the variance of an unbiased estimator. Because the asymptotic variance of the MLE achieves this bound, it seems natural to extend the result directly. There is, however, a loose end in that the MLE is almost never unbiased. As such, we need an asymptotic version of the bound, which was provided by Cramér (1948) and Rao (1945) (hence the name):

---

**THEOREM 16.4   Cramér–Rao Lower Bound**
*Assuming that the density of $y_i$ satisfies the regularity conditions R1–R3, the asymptotic variance of a consistent and asymptotically normally distributed estimator of the parameter vector $\boldsymbol{\theta}_0$ will always be at least as large as*

$$[\mathbf{I}(\boldsymbol{\theta}_0)]^{-1} = \left(-E_0\left[\frac{\partial^2 \ln L(\boldsymbol{\theta}_0)}{\partial \boldsymbol{\theta}_0 \, \partial \boldsymbol{\theta}_0'}\right]\right)^{-1} = \left(E_0\left[\left(\frac{\partial \ln L(\boldsymbol{\theta}_0)}{\partial \boldsymbol{\theta}_0}\right)\left(\frac{\partial \ln L(\boldsymbol{\theta}_0)}{\partial \boldsymbol{\theta}_0}\right)'\right]\right)^{-1}.$$

---

The asymptotic variance of the MLE is, in fact, equal to the Cramér–Rao Lower Bound for the variance of a consistent, asymptotically normally distributed estimator, so this completes the argument.[3]

### 16.4.5.d Invariance

Last, the invariance property, M4, is a mathematical result of the method of computing MLEs; it is not a statistical result as such. More formally, the MLE is invariant to *one-to-one* transformations of $\theta$. Any transformation that is not one to one either renders the model inestimable if it is one to many or imposes restrictions if it is many to one. Some theoretical aspects of this feature are discussed in Davidson and MacKinnon (2004, pp. 446, 539–540). For the practitioner, the result can be extremely useful. For example, when a parameter appears in a likelihood function in the form $1/\theta_j$, it is usually worthwhile to reparameterize the model in terms of $\gamma_j = 1/\theta_j$. In an important application, Olsen (1978) used this result to great advantage. (See Section 24.3.3.) Suppose that the normal log-likelihood in Example 16.2 is parameterized in terms of the **precision parameter,** $\theta^2 = 1/\sigma^2$. The log-likelihood becomes

$$\ln L(\mu, \theta^2) = -(n/2)\ln(2\pi) + (n/2)\ln\theta^2 - \frac{\theta^2}{2}\sum_{i=1}^{n}(y_i - \mu)^2.$$

The MLE for $\mu$ is clearly still $\bar{x}$. But the likelihood equation for $\theta^2$ is now

$$\partial \ln L(\mu, \theta^2)/\partial\theta^2 = \frac{1}{2}\left[n/\theta^2 - \sum_{i=1}^{n}(y_i - \mu)^2\right] = 0,$$

which has solution $\hat{\theta}^2 = n/\sum_{i=1}^{n}(y_i - \hat{\mu})^2 = 1/\hat{\sigma}^2$, as expected. There is a second implication. If it is desired to analyze a function of an MLE, then the function of $\hat{\theta}$ will, itself, be the MLE.

### 16.4.5.e Conclusion

These four properties explain the prevalence of the maximum likelihood technique in econometrics. The second greatly facilitates hypothesis testing and the construction of interval estimates. The third is a particularly powerful result. The MLE has the minimum variance achievable by a consistent and asymptotically normally distributed estimator.

### 16.4.6 ESTIMATING THE ASYMPTOTIC VARIANCE OF THE MAXIMUM LIKELIHOOD ESTIMATOR

The asymptotic covariance matrix of the maximum likelihood estimator is a matrix of parameters that must be estimated (i.e., it is a function of the $\theta_0$ that is being estimated). If the form of the expected values of the second derivatives of the

---

[3]A result reported by LeCam (1953) and recounted in Amemiya (1985, p. 124) suggests that, in principle, there do exist CAN functions of the data with smaller variances than the MLE. But, the finding is a narrow result with no practical implications. For practical purposes, the statement may be taken as given.

log-likelihood is known, then

$$[\mathbf{I}(\boldsymbol{\theta}_0)]^{-1} = \left\{ -E_0 \left[ \frac{\partial^2 \ln L(\boldsymbol{\theta}_0)}{\partial \boldsymbol{\theta}_0 \, \partial \boldsymbol{\theta}_0'} \right] \right\}^{-1} \tag{16-16}$$

can be evaluated at $\hat{\boldsymbol{\theta}}$ to estimate the covariance matrix for the MLE. This estimator will rarely be available. The second derivatives of the log-likelihood will almost always be complicated nonlinear functions of the data whose exact expected values will be unknown. There are, however, two alternatives. A second estimator is

$$[\hat{\mathbf{I}}(\hat{\boldsymbol{\theta}})]^{-1} = \left( -\frac{\partial^2 \ln L(\hat{\boldsymbol{\theta}})}{\partial \hat{\boldsymbol{\theta}} \, \partial \hat{\boldsymbol{\theta}}'} \right)^{-1}. \tag{16-17}$$

This estimator is computed simply by evaluating the actual (not expected) second derivatives matrix of the log-likelihood function at the maximum likelihood estimates. It is straightforward to show that this amounts to estimating the expected second derivatives of the density with the sample mean of this quantity. Theorem D.4 and Result (D-5) can be used to justify the computation. The only shortcoming of this estimator is that the second derivatives can be complicated to derive and program for a computer. A third estimator based on result D3 in Theorem 16.2, that the expected second derivatives matrix is the covariance matrix of the first derivatives vector, is

$$[\hat{\mathbf{I}}(\hat{\boldsymbol{\theta}})]^{-1} = \left[ \sum_{i=1}^{n} \hat{\mathbf{g}}_i \hat{\mathbf{g}}_i' \right]^{-1} = [\hat{\mathbf{G}}' \hat{\mathbf{G}}]^{-1}, \tag{16-18}$$

where

$$\hat{\mathbf{g}}_i = \frac{\partial \ln f(\mathbf{x}_i, \hat{\boldsymbol{\theta}})}{\partial \hat{\boldsymbol{\theta}}},$$

and

$$\hat{\mathbf{G}} = [\hat{\mathbf{g}}_1, \hat{\mathbf{g}}_2, \dots, \hat{\mathbf{g}}_n]'.$$

$\hat{\mathbf{G}}$ is an $n \times K$ matrix with $i$th row equal to the transpose of the $i$th vector of derivatives in the terms of the log-likelihood function. For a single parameter, this estimator is just the reciprocal of the sum of squares of the first derivatives. This estimator is extremely convenient, in most cases, because it does not require any computations beyond those required to solve the likelihood equation. It has the added virtue that it is always non-negative definite. For some extremely complicated log-likelihood functions, sometimes because of rounding error, the *observed* Hessian can be indefinite, even at the maximum of the function. The estimator in (16-18) is known as the **BHHH** estimator[4] and the **outer product of gradients,** or **OPG,** estimator.

　　None of the three estimators given here is preferable to the others on statistical grounds; all are asymptotically equivalent. In most cases, the BHHH estimator will be the easiest to compute. One caution is in order. As the following example illustrates, these estimators can give different results in a finite sample. This is an unavoidable finite sample problem that can, in some cases, lead to different statistical conclusions. The example is a case in point. Using the usual procedures, we would reject the hypothesis that $\beta = 0$ if either of the first two variance estimators were used, but not if the third were used. The estimator in (16-16) is usually unavailable, as the exact expectation of

---

[4]It appears to have been advocated first in the econometrics literature in Berndt et al. (1974).

the Hessian is rarely known. Available evidence suggests that in small or moderate-sized samples, (16-17) (the Hessian) is preferable.

### Example 16.4   Variance Estimators for an MLE

The sample data in Example C.1 are generated by a model of the form

$$f(y_i, x_i, \beta) = \frac{1}{\beta + x_i} e^{-y_i/(\beta + x_i)},$$

where $y = $ income and $x = $ education. To find the maximum likelihood estimate of $\beta$, we maximize

$$\ln L(\beta) = -\sum_{i=1}^{n} \ln(\beta + x_i) - \sum_{i=1}^{n} \frac{y_i}{\beta + x_i}.$$

The likelihood equation is

$$\frac{\partial \ln L(\beta)}{\partial \beta} = -\sum_{i=1}^{n} \frac{1}{\beta + x_i} + \sum_{i=1}^{n} \frac{y_i}{(\beta + x_i)^2} = 0, \tag{16-19}$$

which has the solution $\hat{\beta} = 15.602727$. To compute the asymptotic variance of the MLE, we require

$$\frac{\partial^2 \ln L(\beta)}{\partial \beta^2} = \sum_{i=1}^{n} \frac{1}{(\beta + x_i)^2} - 2 \sum_{i=1}^{n} \frac{y_i}{(\beta + x_i)^3}. \tag{16-20}$$

Because the function $E(y_i) = \beta + x_i$ is known, the exact form of the expected value in (16-20) is known. Inserting $\hat{\beta} + x_i$ for $y_i$ in (16-20) and taking the negative of the reciprocal yields the first variance estimate, 44.2546. Simply inserting $\hat{\beta} = 15.602727$ in (16-20) and taking the negative of the reciprocal gives the second estimate, 46.16337. Finally, by computing the reciprocal of the sum of squares of first derivatives of the densities evaluated at $\hat{\beta}$,

$$[\hat{\mathbf{I}}(\hat{\beta})]^{-1} = \frac{1}{\sum_{i=1}^{n} [-1/(\hat{\beta} + x_i) + y_i/(\hat{\beta} + x_i)^2]^2},$$

we obtain the BHHH estimate, 100.5116.

## 16.5   CONDITIONAL LIKELIHOODS, ECONOMETRIC MODELS, AND THE GMM ESTIMATOR

All of the preceding results form the statistical underpinnings of the technique of maximum likelihood estimation. But, for our purposes, a crucial element is missing. We have done the analysis in terms of the density of an observed random variable and a vector of parameters, $f(y_i \mid \boldsymbol{\alpha})$. But econometric models will involve exogenous or predetermined variables, $\mathbf{x}_i$, so the results must be extended. A workable approach is to treat this modeling framework the same as the one in Chapter 4, where we considered the large sample properties of the linear regression model. Thus, we will allow $\mathbf{x}_i$ to denote a mix of random variables and constants that enter the conditional density of $y_i$. By partitioning the joint density of $y_i$ and $\mathbf{x}_i$ into the product of the conditional and the marginal, the log-likelihood function may be written

$$\ln L(\boldsymbol{\alpha} \mid \mathbf{data}) = \sum_{i=1}^{n} \ln f(y_i, \mathbf{x}_i \mid \boldsymbol{\alpha}) = \sum_{i=1}^{n} \ln f(y_i \mid \mathbf{x}_i, \boldsymbol{\alpha}) + \sum_{i=1}^{n} \ln g(\mathbf{x}_i \mid \boldsymbol{\alpha}),$$

where any nonstochastic elements in $\mathbf{x}_i$ such as a time trend or dummy variable are being carried as constants. To proceed, we will assume as we did before that the process generating $\mathbf{x}_i$ takes place outside the model of interest. For present purposes, that means that the parameters that appear in $g(\mathbf{x}_i \mid \boldsymbol{\alpha})$ do not overlap with those that appear in $f(y_i \mid \mathbf{x}_i, \boldsymbol{\alpha})$. Thus, we partition $\boldsymbol{\alpha}$ into $[\boldsymbol{\theta}, \boldsymbol{\delta}]$ so that the log-likelihood function may be written

$$\ln L(\boldsymbol{\theta}, \boldsymbol{\delta} \mid \mathbf{data}) = \sum_{i=1}^{n} \ln f(y_i, \mathbf{x}_i \mid \boldsymbol{\alpha}) = \sum_{i=1}^{n} \ln f(y_i \mid \mathbf{x}_i, \boldsymbol{\theta}) + \sum_{i=1}^{n} \ln g(\mathbf{x}_i \mid \boldsymbol{\delta}).$$

As long as $\boldsymbol{\theta}$ and $\boldsymbol{\delta}$ have no elements in common and no restrictions connect them (such as $\theta + \delta = 1$), then the two parts of the log likelihood may be analyzed separately. In most cases, the marginal distribution of $\mathbf{x}_i$ will be of secondary (or no) interest.

Asymptotic results for the maximum conditional likelihood estimator must now account for the presence of $\mathbf{x}_i$ in the functions and derivatives of $\ln f(y_i \mid \mathbf{x}_i, \boldsymbol{\theta})$. We will proceed under the assumption of well-behaved data so that sample averages such as

$$(1/n) \ln L(\boldsymbol{\theta} \mid \mathbf{y}, \mathbf{X}) = \frac{1}{n} \sum_{i=1}^{n} \ln f(y_i \mid \mathbf{x}_i, \boldsymbol{\theta})$$

and its gradient with respect to $\boldsymbol{\theta}$ will converge in probability to their population expectations. We will also need to invoke central limit theorems to establish the asymptotic normality of the gradient of the log likelihood, so as to be able to characterize the MLE itself. We will leave it to more advance treatises such as Amemiya (1985) and Newey and McFadden (1994) to establish specific conditions and fine points that must be assumed to claim the "usual" properties for maximum likelihood estimators. For present purposes (and the vast bulk of empirical applications), the following minimal assumptions should suffice:

- **Parameter space.** Parameter spaces that have gaps and nonconvexities in them will generally disable these procedures. An estimation problem that produces this failure is that of "estimating" a parameter that can take only one among a discrete set of values. For example, this set of procedures does not include "estimating" the timing of a structural change in a model. The likelihood function must be a continuous function of a convex parameter space. We allow unbounded parameter spaces, such as $\sigma > 0$ in the regression model, for example.
- **Identifiability.** Estimation must be feasible. This is the subject of Definition 16.1 concerning identification and the surrounding discussion.
- **Well-behaved data.** Laws of large numbers apply to sample means involving the data and some form of central limit theorem (generally Lyapounov) can be applied to the gradient. Ergodic stationarity is broad enough to encompass any situation that is likely to arise in practice, though it is probably more general than we need for most applications, because we will not encounter dependent observations specifically until later in the book. The definitions in Chapter 4 are assumed to hold generally.

With these in place, analysis is essentially the same in character as that we used in the linear regression model in Chapter 4 and follows precisely along the lines of Section 14.5.

## 16.6 HYPOTHESIS AND SPECIFICATION TESTS AND FIT MEASURES

The next several sections will discuss the most commonly used test procedures: the likelihood ratio, Wald, and Lagrange multiplier tests. [Extensive discussion of these procedures is given in Godfrey (1988).] We consider maximum likelihood estimation of a parameter $\theta$ and a test of the hypothesis $H_0: c(\theta) = 0$. The logic of the tests can be seen in Figure 16.2.[5] The figure plots the log-likelihood function $\ln L(\theta)$, its derivative with respect to $\theta$, $d \ln L(\theta)/d\theta$, and the constraint $c(\theta)$. There are three approaches to testing the hypothesis suggested in the figure:

- **Likelihood ratio test.** If the restriction $c(\theta) = 0$ is valid, then imposing it should not lead to a large reduction in the log-likelihood function. Therefore, we base the test on the difference, $\ln L_U - \ln L_R$, where $L_U$ is the value of the likelihood function at the unconstrained value of $\theta$ and $L_R$ is the value of the likelihood function at the restricted estimate.
- **Wald test.** If the restriction is valid, then $c(\hat{\theta}_{MLE})$ should be close to zero because the MLE is consistent. Therefore, the test is based on $c(\hat{\theta}_{MLE})$. We reject the hypothesis if this value is significantly different from zero.
- **Lagrange multiplier test.** If the restriction is valid, then the restricted estimator should be near the point that maximizes the log-likelihood. Therefore, the slope of the log-likelihood function should be near zero at the restricted estimator. The test is based on the slope of the log-likelihood at the point where the function is maximized subject to the restriction.

These three tests are asymptotically equivalent under the null hypothesis, but they can behave rather differently in a small sample. Unfortunately, their small-sample properties are unknown, except in a few special cases. As a consequence, the choice among them is typically made on the basis of ease of computation. The likelihood ratio test requires calculation of both restricted and unrestricted estimators. If both are simple to compute, then this way to proceed is convenient. The Wald test requires only the unrestricted estimator, and the Lagrange multiplier test requires only the restricted estimator. In some problems, one of these estimators may be much easier to compute than the other. For example, a linear model is simple to estimate but becomes nonlinear and cumbersome if a nonlinear constraint is imposed. In this case, the Wald statistic might be preferable. Alternatively, restrictions sometimes amount to the removal of nonlinearities, which would make the Lagrange multiplier test the simpler procedure.

### 16.6.1 THE LIKELIHOOD RATIO TEST

Let $\boldsymbol{\theta}$ be a vector of parameters to be estimated, and let $H_0$ specify some sort of restriction on these parameters. Let $\hat{\boldsymbol{\theta}}_U$ be the maximum likelihood estimator of $\boldsymbol{\theta}$ obtained without regard to the constraints, and let $\hat{\boldsymbol{\theta}}_R$ be the constrained maximum likelihood estimator. If $\hat{L}_U$ and $\hat{L}_R$ are the likelihood functions evaluated at these two estimates, then the

---

[5]See Buse (1982). Note that the scale of the vertical axis would be different for each curve. As such, the points of intersection have no significance.

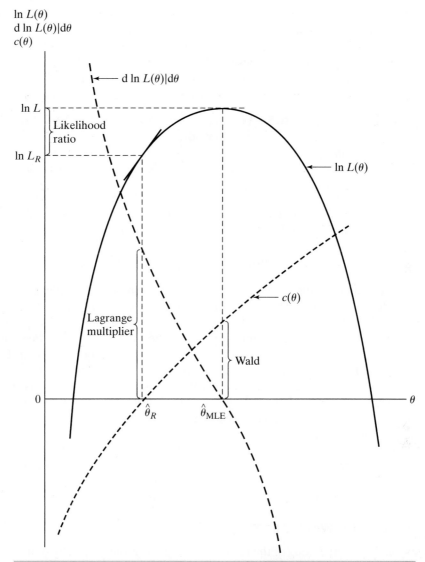

**FIGURE 16.2**    Three Bases for Hypothesis Tests.

**likelihood ratio** is

$$\lambda = \frac{\hat{L}_R}{\hat{L}_U}. \tag{16-21}$$

This function must be between zero and one. Both likelihoods are positive, and $\hat{L}_R$ cannot be larger than $\hat{L}_U$. (A restricted optimum is never superior to an unrestricted one.) If $\lambda$ is too small, then doubt is cast on the restrictions.

An example from a discrete distribution helps to fix these ideas. In estimating from a sample of 10 from a Poisson distribution at the beginning of Section 16.3, we found the

MLE of the parameter $\theta$ to be 2. At this value, the likelihood, which is the probability of observing the sample we did, is $0.104 \times 10^{-7}$. Are these data consistent with $H_0: \theta = 1.8$? $L_R = 0.936 \times 10^{-8}$, which is, as expected, smaller. This particular sample is somewhat less probable under the hypothesis.

The formal test procedure is based on the following result.

---

**THEOREM 16.5** **Limiting Distribution of the Likelihood Ratio Test Statistic**

*Under regularity and under $H_0$, the large sample distribution of $-2 \ln \lambda$ is chi-squared, with degrees of freedom equal to the number of restrictions imposed.*

---

The null hypothesis is rejected if this value exceeds the appropriate critical value from the chi-squared tables. Thus, for the Poisson example,

$$-2 \ln \lambda = -2 \ln \left( \frac{0.0936}{0.104} \right) = 0.21072.$$

This chi-squared statistic with one degree of freedom is not significant at any conventional level, so we would not reject the hypothesis that $\theta = 1.8$ on the basis of this test.[6]

It is tempting to use the likelihood ratio test to test a simple null hypothesis against a simple alternative. For example, we might be interested in the Poisson setting in testing $H_0: \theta = 1.8$ against $H_1: \theta = 2.2$. But the test cannot be used in this fashion. The degrees of freedom of the chi-squared statistic for the likelihood ratio test equals the reduction in the number of dimensions in the parameter space that results from imposing the restrictions. In testing a simple null hypothesis against a simple alternative, this value is zero.[7] Second, one sometimes encounters an attempt to test one distributional assumption against another with a likelihood ratio test; for example, a certain model will be estimated assuming a normal distribution and then assuming a $t$ distribution. The ratio of the two likelihoods is then compared to determine which distribution is preferred. This comparison is also inappropriate. The parameter spaces, and hence the likelihood functions of the two cases, are unrelated.

### 16.6.2 THE WALD TEST

A practical shortcoming of the likelihood ratio test is that it usually requires estimation of both the restricted and unrestricted parameter vectors. In complex models, one or the other of these estimates may be very difficult to compute. Fortunately, there are two alternative testing procedures, the Wald test and the Lagrange multiplier test, that circumvent this problem. Both tests are based on an estimator that is asymptotically normally distributed.

These two tests are based on the distribution of the full rank quadratic form considered in Section B.11.6. Specifically,

$$\text{If } \mathbf{x} \sim N_J[\boldsymbol{\mu}, \boldsymbol{\Sigma}], \text{ then } (\mathbf{x} - \boldsymbol{\mu})'\boldsymbol{\Sigma}^{-1}(\mathbf{x} - \boldsymbol{\mu}) \sim \text{chi-squared}[J]. \qquad \textbf{(16-22)}$$

---

[6] Of course, our use of the large-sample result in a sample of 10 might be questionable.

[7] Note that because both likelihoods are restricted in this instance, there is nothing to prevent $-2 \ln \lambda$ from being negative.

In the setting of a hypothesis test, under the hypothesis that $E(\mathbf{x}) = \boldsymbol{\mu}$, the quadratic form has the chi-squared distribution. If the hypothesis that $E(\mathbf{x}) = \boldsymbol{\mu}$ is false, however, then the quadratic form just given will, on average, be larger than it would be if the hypothesis were true.[8] This condition forms the basis for the test statistics discussed in this and the next section.

Let $\hat{\boldsymbol{\theta}}$ be the vector of parameter estimates obtained without restrictions. We hypothesize a set of restrictions

$$H_0\colon \mathbf{c}(\boldsymbol{\theta}) = \mathbf{q}.$$

If the restrictions are valid, then at least approximately $\hat{\boldsymbol{\theta}}$ should satisfy them. If the hypothesis is erroneous, however, then $\mathbf{c}(\hat{\boldsymbol{\theta}}) - \mathbf{q}$ should be farther from $\mathbf{0}$ than would be explained by sampling variability alone. The device we use to formalize this idea is the Wald test.

---

**THEOREM 16.6**  **Limiting Distribution of the Wald Test Statistic**
*The Wald statistic is*

$$W = [\mathbf{c}(\hat{\boldsymbol{\theta}}) - \mathbf{q}]' \left(\text{Asy.Var}[\mathbf{c}(\hat{\boldsymbol{\theta}}) - \mathbf{q}]\right)^{-1} [\mathbf{c}(\hat{\boldsymbol{\theta}}) - \mathbf{q}].$$

*Under $H_0$, in large samples, $W$ has a chi-squared distribution with degrees of freedom equal to the number of restrictions [i.e., the number of equations in $\mathbf{c}(\hat{\boldsymbol{\theta}}) - \mathbf{q} = \mathbf{0}$]. A derivation of the limiting distribution of the Wald statistic appears in Theorem 5.1.*

---

This test is analogous to the chi-squared statistic in (16-22) if $\mathbf{c}(\hat{\boldsymbol{\theta}}) - \mathbf{q}$ is normally distributed with the hypothesized mean of $\mathbf{0}$. A large value of $W$ leads to rejection of the hypothesis. Note, finally, that $W$ only requires computation of the unrestricted model. One must still compute the covariance matrix appearing in the preceding quadratic form. This result is the variance of a possibly nonlinear function, which we treated earlier.

$$\text{Est. Asy. Var}[\mathbf{c}(\hat{\boldsymbol{\theta}}) - \mathbf{q}] = \hat{\mathbf{C}} \text{ Est. Asy. Var}[\hat{\boldsymbol{\theta}}]\hat{\mathbf{C}}',$$

$$\hat{\mathbf{C}} = \left[\frac{\partial \mathbf{c}(\hat{\boldsymbol{\theta}})}{\partial \hat{\boldsymbol{\theta}}'}\right]. \tag{16-23}$$

That is, $\mathbf{C}$ is the $J \times K$ matrix whose $j$th row is the derivatives of the $j$th constraint with respect to the $K$ elements of $\boldsymbol{\theta}$. A common application occurs in testing a set of linear restrictions.

For testing a set of linear restrictions $\mathbf{R}\boldsymbol{\theta} = \mathbf{q}$, the Wald test would be based on

$$H_0\colon \mathbf{c}(\boldsymbol{\theta}) - \mathbf{q} = \mathbf{R}\boldsymbol{\theta} - \mathbf{q} = \mathbf{0},$$

$$\hat{\mathbf{C}} = \left[\frac{\partial \mathbf{c}(\hat{\boldsymbol{\theta}})}{\partial \hat{\boldsymbol{\theta}}'}\right] = \mathbf{R}', \tag{16-24}$$

$$\text{Est. Asy. Var}[\mathbf{c}(\hat{\boldsymbol{\theta}}) - \mathbf{q}] = \mathbf{R} \text{ Est. Asy. Var}[\hat{\boldsymbol{\theta}}]\mathbf{R}',$$

---

[8]If the mean is not $\boldsymbol{\mu}$, then the statistic in (16-22) will have a **noncentral chi-squared distribution**. This distribution has the same basic shape as the central chi-squared distribution, with the same degrees of freedom, but lies to the right of it. Thus, a random draw from the noncentral distribution will tend, on average, to be larger than a random observation from the central distribution.

and

$$W = [\mathbf{R}\hat{\boldsymbol{\theta}} - \mathbf{q}]'[\mathbf{R} \text{ Est. Asy. Var}(\hat{\boldsymbol{\theta}})\mathbf{R}']^{-1}[\mathbf{R}\hat{\boldsymbol{\theta}} - \mathbf{q}].$$

The degrees of freedom is the number of rows in $\mathbf{R}$.

If $\mathbf{c}(\boldsymbol{\theta}) = \mathbf{q}$ is a single restriction, then the Wald test will be the same as the test based on the confidence interval developed previously. If the test is

$$H_0{:}\,\theta = \theta_0 \quad \text{versus} \quad H_1{:}\,\theta \neq \theta_0,$$

then the earlier test is based on

$$z = \frac{|\hat{\theta} - \theta_0|}{s(\hat{\theta})}, \tag{16-25}$$

where $s(\hat{\theta})$ is the estimated asymptotic standard error. The test statistic is compared to the appropriate value from the standard normal table. The Wald test will be based on

$$W = [(\hat{\theta} - \theta_0) - 0](\text{Asy. Var}[(\hat{\theta} - \theta_0) - 0])^{-1}[(\hat{\theta} - \theta_0) - 0] = \frac{(\hat{\theta} - \theta_0)^2}{\text{Asy. Var}[\hat{\theta}]} = z^2. \tag{16-26}$$

Here $W$ has a chi-squared distribution with one degree of freedom, which is the distribution of the square of the standard normal test statistic in (16-25).

To summarize, the Wald test is based on measuring the extent to which the unrestricted estimates fail to satisfy the hypothesized restrictions. There are two shortcomings of the Wald test. First, it is a pure significance test against the null hypothesis, not necessarily for a specific alternative hypothesis. As such, its power may be limited in some settings. In fact, the test statistic tends to be rather large in applications. The second shortcoming is not shared by either of the other test statistics discussed here. The Wald statistic is not invariant to the formulation of the restrictions. For example, for a test of the hypothesis that a function $\theta = \beta/(1 - \gamma)$ equals a specific value $q$ there are two approaches one might choose. A Wald test based directly on $\theta - q = 0$ would use a statistic based on the variance of this nonlinear function. An alternative approach would be to analyze the linear restriction $\beta - q(1 - \gamma) = 0$, which is an equivalent, but linear, restriction. The Wald statistics for these two tests could be different and might lead to different inferences. These two shortcomings have been widely viewed as compelling arguments against use of the Wald test. But, in its favor, the Wald test does not rely on a strong distributional assumption, as do the likelihood ratio and Lagrange multiplier tests. The recent econometrics literature is replete with applications that are based on distribution free estimation procedures, such as the GMM method. As such, in recent years, the Wald test has enjoyed a redemption of sorts.

### 16.6.3 THE LAGRANGE MULTIPLIER TEST

The third test procedure is the **Lagrange multiplier (LM)** or **efficient score** (or just **score**) test. It is based on the restricted model instead of the unrestricted model. Suppose that we maximize the log-likelihood subject to the set of constraints $\mathbf{c}(\boldsymbol{\theta}) - \mathbf{q} = \mathbf{0}$. Let $\boldsymbol{\lambda}$ be a vector of Lagrange multipliers and define the Lagrangean function

$$\ln L^*(\boldsymbol{\theta}) = \ln L(\boldsymbol{\theta}) + \boldsymbol{\lambda}'(\mathbf{c}(\boldsymbol{\theta}) - \mathbf{q}).$$

The solution to the constrained maximization problem is the root of

$$\frac{\partial \ln L^*}{\partial \boldsymbol{\theta}} = \frac{\partial \ln L(\boldsymbol{\theta})}{\partial \boldsymbol{\theta}} + \mathbf{C}'\boldsymbol{\lambda} = \mathbf{0},$$

$$\frac{\partial \ln L^*}{\partial \boldsymbol{\lambda}} = \mathbf{c}(\boldsymbol{\theta}) - \mathbf{q} = \mathbf{0},$$

(16-27)

where $\mathbf{C}'$ is the transpose of the derivatives matrix in the second line of (16-23). If the restrictions are valid, then imposing them will not lead to a significant difference in the maximized value of the likelihood function. In the first-order conditions, the meaning is that the second term in the derivative vector will be small. In particular, $\boldsymbol{\lambda}$ will be small. We could test this directly, that is, test $H_0: \boldsymbol{\lambda} = \mathbf{0}$, which leads to the Lagrange multiplier test. There is an equivalent simpler formulation, however. At the restricted maximum, the derivatives of the log-likelihood function are

$$\frac{\partial \ln L(\hat{\boldsymbol{\theta}}_R)}{\partial \hat{\boldsymbol{\theta}}_R} = -\hat{\mathbf{C}}'\hat{\boldsymbol{\lambda}} = \hat{\mathbf{g}}_R.$$

(16-28)

If the restrictions are valid, at least within the range of sampling variability, then $\hat{\mathbf{g}}_R = \mathbf{0}$. That is, the derivatives of the log-likelihood evaluated at the restricted parameter vector will be approximately zero. The vector of first derivatives of the log-likelihood is the vector of **efficient scores.** Because the test is based on this vector, it is called the **score test** as well as the Lagrange multiplier test. The variance of the first derivative vector is the information matrix, which we have used to compute the asymptotic covariance matrix of the MLE. The test statistic is based on reasoning analogous to that underlying the Wald test statistic.

---

**THEOREM 16.7   Limiting Distribution of the Lagrange Multiplier Statistic**

*The Lagrange multiplier test statistic is*

$$\text{LM} = \left(\frac{\partial \ln L(\hat{\boldsymbol{\theta}}_R)}{\partial \hat{\boldsymbol{\theta}}_R}\right)' [\mathbf{I}(\hat{\boldsymbol{\theta}}_R)]^{-1} \left(\frac{\partial \ln L(\hat{\boldsymbol{\theta}}_R)}{\partial \hat{\boldsymbol{\theta}}_R}\right).$$

*Under the null hypothesis, LM has a limiting chi-squared distribution with degrees of freedom equal to the number of restrictions. All terms are computed at the restricted estimator.*

---

The LM statistic has a useful form. Let $\hat{\mathbf{g}}_{iR}$ denote the $i$th term in the gradient of the log-likelihood function. Then,

$$\hat{\mathbf{g}}_R = \sum_{i=1}^{n} \hat{\mathbf{g}}_{iR} = \hat{\mathbf{G}}_R'\mathbf{i},$$

where $\hat{\mathbf{G}}_R$ is the $n \times K$ matrix with $i$th row equal to $\hat{\mathbf{g}}_{iR}'$ and $\mathbf{i}$ is a column of 1s. If we use the BHHH (outer product of gradients) estimator in (16-18) to estimate the Hessian, then

$$[\hat{\mathbf{I}}(\hat{\boldsymbol{\theta}})]^{-1} = [\hat{\mathbf{G}}'_R\hat{\mathbf{G}}_R]^{-1},$$

and

$$\text{LM} = \mathbf{i}'\hat{\mathbf{G}}_R[\hat{\mathbf{G}}'_R\hat{\mathbf{G}}_R]^{-1}\hat{\mathbf{G}}'_R\mathbf{i}.$$

Now, because $\mathbf{i}'\mathbf{i}$ equals $n$, $\text{LM} = n(\mathbf{i}'\hat{\mathbf{G}}_R[\hat{\mathbf{G}}'_R\hat{\mathbf{G}}_R]^{-1}\hat{\mathbf{G}}'_R\mathbf{i}/n) = nR_\mathbf{i}^2$, which is $n$ times the uncentered squared multiple correlation coefficient in a linear regression of a column of 1s on the derivatives of the log-likelihood function computed at the restricted estimator. We will encounter this result in various forms at several points in the book.

### 16.6.4 AN APPLICATION OF THE LIKELIHOOD-BASED TEST PROCEDURES

Consider, again, the data in Example C.1. In Example 16.4, the parameter $\beta$ in the model

$$f(y_i \mid x_i, \beta) = \frac{1}{\beta + x_i}e^{-y_i/(\beta+x_i)} \tag{16-29}$$

was estimated by maximum likelihood. For convenience, let $\beta_i = 1/(\beta + x_i)$. This exponential density is a restricted form of a more general gamma distribution,

$$f(y_i \mid x_i, \beta, \rho) = \frac{\beta_i^\rho}{\Gamma(\rho)}y_i^{\rho-1}e^{-y_i\beta_i}. \tag{16-30}$$

The restriction is $\rho = 1$.[9] We consider testing the hypothesis

$$H_0: \rho = 1 \quad \text{versus} \quad H_1: \rho \neq 1$$

using the various procedures described previously. The log-likelihood and its derivatives are

$$\ln L(\beta, \rho) = \rho\sum_{i=1}^{n}\ln \beta_i - n\ln\Gamma(\rho) + (\rho - 1)\sum_{i=1}^{n}\ln y_i - \sum_{i=1}^{n}y_i\beta_i,$$

$$\frac{\partial \ln L}{\partial \beta} = -\rho\sum_{i=1}^{n}\beta_i + \sum_{i=1}^{n}y_i\beta_i^2, \qquad \frac{\partial \ln L}{\partial \rho} = \sum_{i=1}^{n}\ln\beta_i - n\Psi(\rho) + \sum_{i=1}^{n}\ln y_i, \quad \textbf{(16-31)}$$

$$\frac{\partial^2\ln L}{\partial\beta^2} = \rho\sum_{i=1}^{n}\beta_i^2 - 2\sum_{i=1}^{n}y_i\beta_i^3, \qquad \frac{\partial^2 \ln L}{\partial\rho^2} = -n\Psi'(\rho), \qquad \frac{\partial^2 \ln L}{\partial\beta\partial\rho} = -\sum_{i=1}^{n}\beta_i.$$

[Recall that $\Psi(\rho) = d\ln\Gamma(\rho)/d\rho$ and $\Psi'(\rho) = d^2\ln\Gamma(\rho)/d\rho^2$.] Unrestricted maximum likelihood estimates of $\beta$ and $\rho$ are obtained by equating the two first derivatives to zero. The restricted maximum likelihood estimate of $\beta$ is obtained by equating $\partial\ln L/\partial\beta$ to zero while fixing $\rho$ at one. The results are shown in Table 16.1. Three estimators are available for the asymptotic covariance matrix of the estimators of $\boldsymbol{\theta} = (\beta, \rho)'$. Using the actual Hessian as in (16-17), we compute $\mathbf{V} = [-\Sigma_i\partial^2\ln f(y_i \mid x_i, \beta, \rho)/\partial\boldsymbol{\theta}\partial\boldsymbol{\theta}']^{-1}$ at the maximum likelihood estimates. For this model, it is easy to show that

---

[9]The gamma function $\Gamma(\rho)$ and the gamma distribution are described in Sections B.4.5 and E2.3.

| TABLE 16.1 | Maximum Likelihood Estimates | |
|---|---|---|
| **Quantity** | **Unrestricted Estimate[a]** | **Restricted Estimate** |
| $\beta$ | −4.7198 (2.344) | 15.6052 (6.794) |
| $\rho$ | 3.1517 (0.7943) | 1.0000 (0.000) |
| $\ln L$ | −82.91444 | −88.43771 |
| $\partial \ln L/\partial\beta$ | 0.0000 | 0.0000 |
| $\partial \ln L/\partial\rho$ | 0.0000 | 7.9162 |
| $\partial^2 \ln L/\partial\beta^2$ | −0.85628 | −0.021659 |
| $\partial^2 \ln L/\partial\rho^2$ | −7.4569 | −32.8987 |
| $\partial^2 \ln L/\partial\beta\partial\rho$ | −2.2423 | −0.66885 |

[a]Estimated asymptotic standard errors based on **V** are given in parentheses.

$E[y_i \mid x_i] = \rho(\beta + x_i)$ (either by direct integration or, more simply, by using the result that $E[\partial \ln L/\partial\beta] = 0$ to deduce it). Therefore, we can also use the expected Hessian as in (16-16) to compute $\mathbf{V}_E = \{-\Sigma_i E[\partial^2 \ln f(y_i \mid x_i, \beta, \rho)/\partial\boldsymbol{\theta}\partial\boldsymbol{\theta}']\}^{-1}$. Finally, by using the sums of squares and cross products of the first derivatives, we obtain the BHHH estimator in (16-18), $\mathbf{V}_B = [\Sigma_i(\partial \ln f(y_i \mid x_i, \beta, \rho)/\partial\boldsymbol{\theta})(\partial \ln f(y_i \mid x_i, \beta, \rho)/\partial\boldsymbol{\theta}')]^{-1}$. Results in Table 16.1 are based on **V**.

The three estimators of the asymptotic covariance matrix produce notably different results:

$$\mathbf{V} = \begin{bmatrix} 5.495 & -1.652 \\ -1.652 & 0.6309 \end{bmatrix}, \quad \mathbf{V}_E = \begin{bmatrix} 4.897 & -1.473 \\ -1.473 & 0.5770 \end{bmatrix}, \quad \mathbf{V}_B = \begin{bmatrix} 13.35 & -4.314 \\ -4.314 & 1.535 \end{bmatrix}.$$

Given the small sample size, the differences are to be expected. Nonetheless, the striking difference of the BHHH estimator is typical of its erratic performance in small samples.

- **Confidence interval test:** A 95 percent confidence interval for $\rho$ based on the unrestricted estimates is $3.1517 \pm 1.96\sqrt{0.6309} = [1.5942, 4.7085]$. This interval does not contain $\rho = 1$, so the hypothesis is rejected.
- **Likelihood ratio test:** The LR statistic is $\lambda = -2[-88.43771 - (-82.91444)] = 11.0465$. The table value for the test, with one degree of freedom, is 3.842. The computed value is larger than this critical value, so the hypothesis is again rejected.
- **Wald test:** The Wald test is based on the unrestricted estimates. For this restriction, $c(\boldsymbol{\theta}) - q = \rho - 1$, $dc(\hat{\rho})/d\hat{\rho} = 1$, Est. Asy. Var$[c(\hat{\rho}) - q] =$ Est. Asy. Var$[\hat{\rho}] = 0.6309$, so $W = (3.1517 - 1)^2/[0.6309] = 7.3384$. The critical value is the same as the previous one. Hence, $H_0$ is once again rejected. Note that the Wald statistic is the square of the corresponding test statistic that would be used in the confidence interval test, $|3.1517 - 1|/\sqrt{0.6309} = 2.70895$.
- **Lagrange multiplier test:** The Lagrange multiplier test is based on the restricted estimators. The estimated asymptotic covariance matrix of the derivatives used to compute the statistic can be any of the three estimators discussed earlier. The BHHH estimator, $\mathbf{V}_B$, is the empirical estimator of the variance of the gradient and is the one usually used in practice. This computation produces

$$LM = \begin{bmatrix} 0.0000 & 7.9162 \end{bmatrix} \begin{bmatrix} 0.0099438 & 0.26762 \\ 0.26762 & 11.197 \end{bmatrix}^{-1} \begin{bmatrix} 0.0000 \\ 7.9162 \end{bmatrix} = 15.687.$$

The conclusion is the same as before. Note that the same computation done using $\mathbf{V}$ rather than $\mathbf{V}_B$ produces a value of 5.1182. As before, we observe substantial small sample variation produced by the different estimators.

The latter three test statistics have substantially different values. It is possible to reach different conclusions, depending on which one is used. For example, if the test had been carried out at the 1 percent level of significance instead of 5 percent and LM had been computed using $\mathbf{V}$, then the critical value from the chi-squared statistic would have been 6.635 and the hypothesis would not have been rejected by the LM test. Asymptotically, all three tests are equivalent. But, in a finite sample such as this one, differences are to be expected.[10] Unfortunately, there is no clear rule for how to proceed in such a case, which highlights the problem of relying on a particular significance level and drawing a firm reject or accept conclusion based on sample evidence.

### 16.6.5 COMPARING MODELS AND COMPUTING MODEL FIT

The test statistics described in Sections 16.6.1–16.6.3 are available for assessing the validity of restrictions on the parameters in a model. When the models are nested, any of the three mentioned testing procedures can be used. For nonnested models, the computation is a comparison of one model to another based on an estimation criterion to discern which is to be preferred. Two common measures that are based on the same logic as the adjusted $R$-squared for the linear model are

$$\textbf{Akaike information criterion (AIC)} \qquad = -2\ln L + 2K,$$

$$\textbf{Bayes (Schwarz) information criterion (BIC)} = -2\ln L + K\ln n,$$

where $K$ is the number of parameters in the model. Choosing a model based on the lowest AIC is logically the same as using $\bar{R}^2$ in the linear model; nonstatistical, albeit widely accepted. Another means of comparing nonnested models that is valid in some circumstances is the **Vuong statistic** (see Section 7.3.4).

$$V = \frac{\sqrt{n}\,\bar{m}}{s_m}, \text{ where } m_i = \ln L_i(1) - \ln L_i(2),$$

and $L_i(j)$ is the contribution of individual $i$ to the log-likelihood under the assumption that model $j$ is correct. We use this test in Example 16.10 to choose between a geometric and a Poisson regression model for a count dependent variable.

The AIC and BIC are information criteria, not fit measures as such. This does leave open the question of how to assess the "fit" of the model. Only the case of a linear least squares regression in a model with a constant term produces an $R^2$, which measures the proportion of variation explained by the regression. The ambiguity in $R^2$ as a fit measure arose immediately when we moved from the linear regression model to the generalized regression model in Chapter 8. The problem is yet more acute in the context of the models we consider in this chapter. For example, the estimators of the models for count data in Example 16.10 make no use of the "variation" in the dependent variable and there is no obvious measure of "explained variation."

A measure of "fit" that was originally proposed for discrete choice models in McFadden (1974), but surprisingly has gained wide currency throughout the empirical

---

[10]For further discussion of this problem, see Berndt and Savin (1977).

literature is the **likelihood ratio index,** which has come to be known as the **Pseudo** $R^2$. It is computed as

$$\text{Pseudo } R^2 = 1 - (\ln L)/(\ln L_0)$$

where $\ln L$ is the log-likelihood for the model estimated and $\ln L_0$ is the log-likelihood for the same model with only a constant term. The statistic does resemble the $R^2$ in a linear regression. The choice of name is for this statistic is unfortunate, however, because even in the discrete choice context for which it was proposed, it has no connection to the fit of the model to the data. In discrete choice settings in which log-likelihoods must be negative, the pseudo $R^2$ must be between zero and one and rises as variables are added to the model. It can obviously be zero, but is usually bounded below one. In the linear model with normally distributed disturbances, the maximized log-likelihood is

$$\ln L = (-n/2)[1 + \ln 2\pi + \ln(\mathbf{e}'\mathbf{e}/n)].$$

With a small amount of manipulation, we find that the pseudo $R^2$ for the linear regression model is

$$\text{Pseudo } R^2 = \frac{-\ln(1 - R^2)}{1 + \ln 2\pi + \ln s_y^2},$$

while the "true" $R^2$ is $1 - \mathbf{e}'\mathbf{e}/\mathbf{e}_0'\mathbf{e}_0$. Because $s_y^2$ can vary independently of $R^2$—multiplying $\mathbf{y}$ by any scalar, $A$, leaves $R^2$ unchanged but multiplies $s_y^2$ by $A^2$—although the upper limit is one, there is no lower limit on this measure. This same problem arises in any model that uses information on the scale of a dependent variable, such as the tobit model (Chapter 24). The computation makes even less sense as a fit measure in multinomial models such as the ordered probit model (Chapter 23) or the multinomial logit model. For discrete choice models, there are a variety of such measures discussed in Chapter 23. For limited dependent variable and many loglinear models, some other measure that is related to a correlation between a prediction and the actual value would be more useable. Nonetheless, the measure seems to have gained currency in the contemporary literature. [The popular software package, *Stata*, reports the pseudo $R^2$ with every model fit by MLE, but at the same time, admonishes its users not to interpret it as anything meaningful. See, e.g., http://www.stata.com/support/faqs/stat/pseudor2.html. Cameron and Trivedi (2005) document the pseudo $R^2$ at length, then give similar cautions about it and urge their readers to seek a more meaningful measure of the correlation between model predictions and the outcome variable of interest. Wooldridge (2002a) dismisses it summarily, and argues that coefficients are more interesting.]

## 16.7  TWO-STEP MAXIMUM LIKELIHOOD ESTIMATION

The applied literature contains a large and increasing number of models in which one model is embedded in another, which produces what are broadly known as "two-step" estimation problems. Consider an (admittedly contrived) example in which we have the following.

    **Model 1.** Expected number of children $= E[y_1 \mid \mathbf{x}_1, \boldsymbol{\theta}_1]$.
    **Model 2.** Decision to enroll in job training $= y_2$, a function of $(\mathbf{x}_2, \boldsymbol{\theta}_2, E[y_1 \mid \mathbf{x}_1, \boldsymbol{\theta}_1])$.

There are two parameter vectors, $\boldsymbol{\theta}_1$ and $\boldsymbol{\theta}_2$. The first appears in the second model, although not the reverse. In such a situation, there are two ways to proceed. **Full information maximum likelihood (FIML)** estimation would involve forming the joint distribution $f(y_1, y_2 \mid \mathbf{x}_1, \mathbf{x}_2, \boldsymbol{\theta}_1, \boldsymbol{\theta}_2)$ of the two random variables and then maximizing the full log-likelihood function,

$$\ln L = \sum_{i=1}^{n} f(y_{i1}, y_{i2} \mid \mathbf{x}_{i1}, \mathbf{x}_{i2}, \boldsymbol{\theta}_1, \boldsymbol{\theta}_2).$$

A second, or two-step, **limited information maximum likelihood (LIML)** procedure for this kind of model could be done by estimating the parameters of model 1, because it does not involve $\boldsymbol{\theta}_2$, and then maximizing a conditional log-likelihood function using the estimates from step 1:

$$\ln \hat{L} = \sum_{i=1}^{n} f[y_{i2} \mid \mathbf{x}_{i2}, \boldsymbol{\theta}_2, (\mathbf{x}_{i1}, \hat{\boldsymbol{\theta}}_1)].$$

There are at least two reasons one might proceed in this fashion. First, it may be straightforward to formulate the two separate log-likelihoods, but very complicated to derive the joint distribution. This situation frequently arises when the two variables being modeled are from different kinds of populations, such as one discrete and one continuous (which is a very common case in this framework). The second reason is that maximizing the separate log-likelihoods may be fairly straightforward, but maximizing the joint log-likelihood may be numerically complicated or difficult.[11] We will consider a few examples. Although we will encounter FIML problems at various points later in the book, for now we will present some basic results for two-step estimation. Proofs of the results given here can be found in an important reference on the subject, Murphy and Topel (2002).

Suppose, then, that our model consists of the two marginal distributions, $f_1(y_1 \mid \mathbf{x}_1, \boldsymbol{\theta}_1)$ and $f_2(y_2 \mid \mathbf{x}_1, \mathbf{x}_2, \boldsymbol{\theta}_1, \boldsymbol{\theta}_2)$. Estimation proceeds in two steps.

1. Estimate $\boldsymbol{\theta}_1$ by maximum likelihood in model 1. Let $\hat{\mathbf{V}}_1$ be $n$ times any of the estimators of the asymptotic covariance matrix of this estimator that were discussed in Section 16.4.6.
2. Estimate $\boldsymbol{\theta}_2$ by maximum likelihood in model 2, with $\hat{\boldsymbol{\theta}}_1$ inserted in place of $\boldsymbol{\theta}_1$ as if it were known. Let $\hat{\mathbf{V}}_2$ be $n$ times any appropriate estimator of the asymptotic covariance matrix of $\hat{\boldsymbol{\theta}}_2$.

The argument for consistency of $\hat{\boldsymbol{\theta}}_2$ is essentially that if $\boldsymbol{\theta}_1$ *were* known, then all our results for MLEs would apply for estimation of $\boldsymbol{\theta}_2$, and because plim $\hat{\boldsymbol{\theta}}_1 = \boldsymbol{\theta}_1$, asymptotically, this line of reasoning is correct. But the same line of reasoning is not sufficient to justify using $(1/n)\hat{\mathbf{V}}_2$ as the estimator of the asymptotic covariance matrix of $\hat{\boldsymbol{\theta}}_2$. Some correction is necessary to account for an estimate of $\boldsymbol{\theta}_1$ being used in estimation of $\boldsymbol{\theta}_2$. The essential result is the following.

---

[11] There is a third possible motivation. If either model is misspecified, then the FIML estimates of both models will be inconsistent. But if only the second is misspecified, at least the first will be estimated consistently. Of course, this result is only "half a loaf," but it may be better than none.

**THEOREM 16.8   Asymptotic Distribution of the Two-Step MLE
[Murphy and Topel (2002)]**

*If the standard regularity conditions are met for both log-likelihood functions, then
the second-step maximum likelihood estimator of $\theta_2$ is consistent and asymptotically normally distributed with asymptotic covariance matrix*

$$\mathbf{V}_2^* = \frac{1}{n}\big[\mathbf{V}_2 + \mathbf{V}_2[\mathbf{CV}_1\mathbf{C}' - \mathbf{RV}_1\mathbf{C}' - \mathbf{CV}_1\mathbf{R}']\mathbf{V}_2\big],$$

*where*

$$\mathbf{V}_1 = \text{Asy. Var}[\sqrt{n}(\hat{\boldsymbol{\theta}}_1 - \boldsymbol{\theta}_1)] \text{ based on } \ln L_1,$$

$$\mathbf{V}_2 = \text{Asy. Var}[\sqrt{n}(\hat{\boldsymbol{\theta}}_2 - \boldsymbol{\theta}_2)] \text{ based on } \ln L_2 \mid \boldsymbol{\theta}_1,$$

$$\mathbf{C} = E\left[\frac{1}{n}\left(\frac{\partial \ln L_2}{\partial \boldsymbol{\theta}_2}\right)\left(\frac{\partial \ln L_2}{\partial \boldsymbol{\theta}_1'}\right)\right], \quad \mathbf{R} = E\left[\frac{1}{n}\left(\frac{\partial \ln L_2}{\partial \boldsymbol{\theta}_2}\right)\left(\frac{\partial \ln L_1}{\partial \boldsymbol{\theta}_1'}\right)\right].$$

*The correction of the asymptotic covariance matrix at the second step requires
some additional computation. Matrices $\mathbf{V}_1$ and $\mathbf{V}_2$ are estimated by the respective
uncorrected covariance matrices. Typically, the BHHH estimators,*

$$\hat{\mathbf{V}}_1 = \left[\frac{1}{n}\sum_{i=1}^{n}\left(\frac{\partial \ln f_{i1}}{\partial \hat{\boldsymbol{\theta}}_1}\right)\left(\frac{\partial \ln f_{i1}}{\partial \hat{\boldsymbol{\theta}}_1'}\right)\right]^{-1}$$

*and*

$$\hat{\mathbf{V}}_2 = \left[\frac{1}{n}\sum_{i=1}^{n}\left(\frac{\partial \ln f_{i2}}{\partial \hat{\boldsymbol{\theta}}_2}\right)\left(\frac{\partial \ln f_{i2}}{\partial \hat{\boldsymbol{\theta}}_2'}\right)\right]^{-1}$$

*are used. The matrices $\mathbf{R}$ and $\mathbf{C}$ are obtained by summing the individual obser-
vations on the cross products of the derivatives. These are estimated with*

$$\hat{\mathbf{C}} = \frac{1}{n}\sum_{i=1}^{n}\left(\frac{\partial \ln f_{i2}}{\partial \hat{\boldsymbol{\theta}}_2}\right)\left(\frac{\partial \ln f_{i2}}{\partial \hat{\boldsymbol{\theta}}_1'}\right)$$

*and*

$$\hat{\mathbf{R}} = \frac{1}{n}\sum_{i=1}^{n}\left(\frac{\partial \ln f_{i2}}{\partial \hat{\boldsymbol{\theta}}_2}\right)\left(\frac{\partial \ln f_{i1}}{\partial \hat{\boldsymbol{\theta}}_1'}\right).$$

### Example 16.5   Two-Step ML Estimation

Continuing the example discussed at the beginning of this section, we suppose that $y_{i2}$ is a
binary indicator of the choice whether to enroll in the program ($y_{i2} = 1$) or not ($y_{i2} = 0$) and
that the probabilities of the two outcomes are

$$\text{Prob}[y_{i2} = 1 \mid \mathbf{x}_{i1}, \mathbf{x}_{i2}] = \frac{e^{\mathbf{x}_{i2}'\beta + \gamma E[y_{i1} \mid \mathbf{x}_{i1}']}}{1 + e^{\mathbf{x}_{i2}'\beta + \gamma E[y_{i1} \mid \mathbf{x}_{i1}']}}$$

and $\text{Prob}[y_{i2} = 0 | \mathbf{x}_{i1}, \mathbf{x}_{i2}] = 1 - \text{Prob}[y_{i2} = 1 | \mathbf{x}_{i1}, \mathbf{x}_{i2}]$, where $\mathbf{x}_{i2}$ is some covariates that might influence the decision, such as marital status or age and $\mathbf{x}_{i1}$ are determinants of family size. This setup is a **logit model.** We will develop this model more fully in Chapter 23. The *expected value* of $y_{i1}$ appears in the probability. (Remark: The expected, rather than the actual, value was chosen deliberately. Otherwise, the models would differ substantially. In our case, we might view the difference as that between an ex ante decision and an ex post one.) Suppose that the number of children can be described by a Poisson distribution (see Section B.4.8) dependent on some variables $\mathbf{x}_{i1}$ such as education, age, and so on. Then

$$\text{Prob}[y_{i1} = j | \mathbf{x}_{i1}] = \frac{e^{-\lambda_i} \lambda_i^j}{j!}, \quad j = 0, 1, \ldots,$$

and suppose, as is customary, that

$$E[y_{i1}] = \lambda_i = \exp(\mathbf{x}_{i1}' \delta).$$

The models involve $\theta = [\delta, \beta, \gamma]$, where $\theta_1 = \delta$. In fact, it is unclear what the joint distribution of $y_1$ and $y_2$ might be, but two-step estimation is straightforward. For model 1, the log-likelihood and its first derivatives are

$$\ln L_1 = \sum_{i=1}^{n} \ln f_1(y_{i1} | \mathbf{x}_{i1}, \delta)$$

$$= \sum_{i=1}^{n} [-\lambda_i + y_{i1} \ln \lambda_i - \ln y_{i1}!] = \sum_{i=1}^{n} [-\exp(\mathbf{x}_{i1}' \delta) + y_{i1}(\mathbf{x}_{i1}' \delta) - \ln y_{i1}!],$$

$$\frac{\partial \ln L_1}{\partial \delta} = \sum_{i=1}^{n} (y_{i1} - \lambda_i) \mathbf{x}_{i1} = \sum_{i=1}^{n} u_i \mathbf{x}_{i1}.$$

Computation of the estimates is developed in Chapter 25. Any of the three estimators of $\mathbf{V}_1$ is also easy to compute, but the BHHH estimator is most convenient, so we use

$$\hat{\mathbf{V}}_1 = \left[ \frac{1}{n} \sum_{i=1}^{n} \hat{u}_i^2 \mathbf{x}_{i1} \mathbf{x}_{i1}' \right]^{-1}.$$

[In this and the succeeding summations, we are actually estimating expectations of the various matrices.]

We can write the density function for the second model as

$$f_2(y_{i2} | \mathbf{x}_{i1}, \mathbf{x}_{i2}, \beta, \gamma, \delta) = P_i^{y_{i2}} \times (1 - P_i)^{1 - y_{i2}},$$

where $P_i = \text{Prob}[y_{i2} = 1 | \mathbf{x}_{i1}, \mathbf{x}_{i2}]$ as given earlier. Then

$$\ln L_2 = \sum_{i=1}^{n} y_{i2} \ln P_i + (1 - y_{i2}) \ln(1 - P_i).$$

For convenience, let $\hat{\mathbf{x}}_{i2}^* = [\mathbf{x}_{i2}', \exp(\mathbf{x}_{i1}' \hat{\delta})]'$, and recall that $\theta_2 = [\beta, \gamma]'$. Then

$$\ln \hat{L}_2 = \sum_{i=1}^{n} y_{i2} [\hat{\mathbf{x}}_{i2}^{*'} \theta_2 - \ln(1 + \exp(\hat{\mathbf{x}}_{i2}^{*'} \theta_2))] + (1 - y_{i2})[-\ln(1 + \exp(\hat{\mathbf{x}}_{i2}^{*'} \theta_2))].$$

So, at the second step, we create the additional variable, append it to $\mathbf{x}_{i2}$, and estimate the logit model as if $\delta$ (and this additional variable) were actually observed instead of estimated. The maximum likelihood estimates of $[\beta, \gamma]$ are obtained by maximizing this function. (See

Chapter 23.) After a bit of manipulation, we find the convenient result that

$$\frac{\partial \ln \hat{L}_2}{\partial \theta_2} = \sum_{i=1}^{n} (y_{i2} - P_i)\hat{\mathbf{x}}_{i2}^* = \sum_{i=1}^{n} v_i \hat{\mathbf{x}}_{i2}^*.$$

Once again, any of the three estimators could be used for estimating the asymptotic covariance matrix, but the BHHH estimator is convenient, so we use

$$\hat{\mathbf{V}}_2 = \left[\frac{1}{n}\sum_{i=1}^{n} \hat{v}_i^2 \hat{\mathbf{x}}_{i2}^* \hat{\mathbf{x}}_{i2}^{*\prime}\right]^{-1}.$$

For the final step, we must correct the asymptotic covariance matrix using $\hat{\mathbf{C}}$ and $\hat{\mathbf{R}}$. What remains to derive—the few lines are left for the reader—is

$$\frac{\partial \ln L_2}{\partial \delta} = \sum_{i=1}^{n} v_i [\gamma \exp(\mathbf{x}_{i1}'\delta)]\mathbf{x}_{i1}.$$

So, using our estimates,

$$\hat{\mathbf{C}} = \frac{1}{n}\sum_{i=1}^{n} \hat{v}_i^2 [\gamma \exp(\mathbf{x}_{i1}'\hat{\delta})]\hat{\mathbf{x}}_{i2}^* \mathbf{x}_{i1}', \quad \text{and} \quad \hat{\mathbf{R}} = \frac{1}{n}\sum_{i=1}^{n} \hat{u}_i \hat{v}_i \hat{\mathbf{x}}_{i2}^* \mathbf{x}_{i1}'.$$

We can now compute the correction.

In many applications, the covariance of the two gradients, $\mathbf{R}$, converges to zero. When the first and second step estimates are based on different samples, $\mathbf{R}$ is exactly zero. For example, in our earlier application, $\mathbf{R} = \sum_{i=1}^{n} u_i v_i \mathbf{x}_{i2}^* \mathbf{x}_{i1}'$. The two "residuals," $u$ and $v$, may well be uncorrelated. This assumption must be checked on a model-by-model basis, but in such an instance, the third and fourth terms in $\mathbf{V}_2^*$ vanish asymptotically and what remains is the simpler alternative,

$$\mathbf{V}_2^{**} = (1/n)[\mathbf{V}_2 + \mathbf{V}_2\mathbf{C}\mathbf{V}_1\mathbf{C}'\mathbf{V}_2].$$

We will examine some additional applications of this technique (including an empirical implementation of the preceding example) later in the book. Perhaps the most common application of two-step maximum likelihood estimation in the current literature, especially in regression analysis, involves inserting a prediction of one variable into a function that describes the behavior of another.

## 16.8 PSEUDO-MAXIMUM LIKELIHOOD ESTIMATION AND ROBUST ASYMPTOTIC COVARIANCE MATRICES

Maximum likelihood estimation requires complete specification of the distribution of the observed random variable. If the correct distribution is something other than what we assume, then the likelihood function is misspecified and the desirable properties of the MLE might not hold. This section considers a set of results on an estimation approach that is robust to some kinds of model misspecification. For example, we have found that in a model, if the conditional mean function is $E[y \mid \mathbf{x}] = \mathbf{x}'\boldsymbol{\beta}$, then certain estimators, such as least squares, are "robust" to specifying the wrong distribution of the disturbances. That is, LS is MLE if the disturbances are normally distributed, but we can still claim some desirable properties for LS, including consistency, even if the disturbances are not normally distributed. This section will discuss some results that relate to what happens if we maximize the "wrong" log-likelihood function, and for those cases in which the estimator is consistent despite this, how to compute an appropriate asymptotic covariance matrix for it.[12]

### 16.8.1    MAXIMUM LIKELIHOOD AND GMM ESTIMATION

Let $f(y_i \mid \mathbf{x}_i, \boldsymbol{\beta})$ be the true probability density for a random variable $y_i$ given a set of covariates $\mathbf{x}_i$ and parameter vector $\boldsymbol{\beta}$. The log-likelihood function is $(1/n) \ln L(\boldsymbol{\beta} \mid \mathbf{y}, \mathbf{X}) = (1/n) \sum_{i=1}^{n} \ln f(y_i \mid \mathbf{x}_i, \boldsymbol{\beta})$. The MLE, $\hat{\boldsymbol{\beta}}_{\text{ML}}$, is the sample statistic that maximizes this function. (The division of $\ln L$ by $n$ does not affect the solution.) We maximize the log-likelihood function by equating its derivatives to zero, so the MLE is obtained by solving the set of empirical moment equations

$$\frac{1}{n} \sum_{i=1}^{n} \frac{\partial \ln f(y_i \mid \mathbf{x}_i, \hat{\boldsymbol{\beta}}_{\text{ML}})}{\partial \hat{\boldsymbol{\beta}}_{\text{ML}}} = \frac{1}{n} \sum_{i=1}^{n} \mathbf{d}_i(\hat{\boldsymbol{\beta}}_{\text{ML}}) = \bar{\mathbf{d}}(\hat{\boldsymbol{\beta}}_{\text{ML}}) = \mathbf{0}.$$

The population counterpart to the sample moment equation is

$$E\left[\frac{1}{n} \frac{\partial \ln L}{\partial \boldsymbol{\beta}}\right] = E\left[\frac{1}{n} \sum_{i=1}^{n} \mathbf{d}_i(\boldsymbol{\beta})\right] = E[\bar{\mathbf{d}}(\boldsymbol{\beta})] = \mathbf{0}.$$

Using what we know about GMM estimators, if $E[\bar{\mathbf{d}}(\boldsymbol{\beta})] = \mathbf{0}$, then $\hat{\boldsymbol{\beta}}_{\text{ML}}$ is consistent and asymptotically normally distributed, with asymptotic covariance matrix equal to

$$\mathbf{V}_{\text{ML}} = [\mathbf{G}(\boldsymbol{\beta})'\mathbf{G}(\boldsymbol{\beta})]^{-1} \mathbf{G}(\boldsymbol{\beta})' \{\text{Var}[\bar{\mathbf{d}}(\boldsymbol{\beta})]\} \mathbf{G}(\boldsymbol{\beta})[\mathbf{G}(\boldsymbol{\beta})'\mathbf{G}(\boldsymbol{\beta})]^{-1},$$

where $\mathbf{G}(\boldsymbol{\beta}) = \text{plim} \, \partial \bar{\mathbf{d}}(\boldsymbol{\beta})/\partial \boldsymbol{\beta}'$. Because $\bar{\mathbf{d}}(\boldsymbol{\beta})$ is the derivative vector, $\mathbf{G}(\boldsymbol{\beta})$ is $1/n$ times the expected Hessian of $\ln L$; that is, $(1/n)E[\mathbf{H}(\boldsymbol{\beta})] = \bar{\mathbf{H}}(\boldsymbol{\beta})$. As we saw earlier, $\text{Var}[\partial \ln L/\partial \boldsymbol{\beta}] = -E[\mathbf{H}(\boldsymbol{\beta})]$. Collecting all seven appearances of $(1/n)E[\mathbf{H}(\boldsymbol{\beta})]$, we obtain the familiar result $\mathbf{V}_{\text{ML}} = \{-E[\mathbf{H}(\boldsymbol{\beta})]\}^{-1}$. [All the $n$s cancel and $\text{Var}[\bar{\mathbf{d}}] = (1/n)\bar{\mathbf{H}}(\boldsymbol{\beta})$.] Note that this result depends crucially on the result $\text{Var}[\partial \ln L/\partial \boldsymbol{\beta}] = -E[\mathbf{H}(\boldsymbol{\beta})]$.

### 16.8.2    MAXIMUM LIKELIHOOD AND *M* ESTIMATION

The maximum likelihood estimator is obtained by maximizing the function $\bar{h}_n(\mathbf{y}, \mathbf{X}, \boldsymbol{\beta}) = (1/n) \sum_{i=1}^{n} \ln f(y_i, \mathbf{x}_i, \boldsymbol{\beta})$. This function converges to its expectation as $n \to \infty$. Because this function is the log-likelihood for the sample, it is also the case (not proven here) that as $n \to \infty$, it attains its unique maximum at the true parameter vector, $\boldsymbol{\beta}$. (We used this result in proving the consistency of the maximum likelihood estimator.) Since $\text{plim} \, \bar{h}_n(\mathbf{y}, \mathbf{X}, \boldsymbol{\beta}) = E[\bar{h}_n(\mathbf{y}, \mathbf{X}, \boldsymbol{\beta})]$, it follows (by interchanging differentiation and the expectation operation) that $\text{plim} \, \partial \bar{h}_n(\mathbf{y}, \mathbf{X}, \boldsymbol{\beta})/\partial \boldsymbol{\beta} = E[\partial \bar{h}_n(\mathbf{y}, \mathbf{X}, \boldsymbol{\beta})/\partial \boldsymbol{\beta}]$. But, if this

---

[12]The following will sketch a set of results related to this estimation problem. The important references on this subject are White (1982a); Gourieroux, Monfort, and Trognon (1984); Huber (1967); and Amemiya (1985). A recent work with a large amount of discussion on the subject is Mittelhammer et al. (2000). The derivations in these works are complex, and we will only attempt to provide an intuitive introduction to the topic.

function achieves its *maximum* at $\boldsymbol{\beta}$, then it must be the case that plim $\partial \overline{h}_n(\mathbf{y}, \mathbf{X}, \boldsymbol{\beta})/\partial \boldsymbol{\beta} = \mathbf{0}$.

An estimator that is obtained by maximizing a criterion function is called an **M estimator** [Huber (1967)] or an extremum estimator [Amemiya (1985)]. Suppose that we obtain an estimator by maximizing some other function, $M_n(\mathbf{y}, \mathbf{X}, \boldsymbol{\beta})$ that, although not the log-likelihood function, also attains its unique maximum at the true $\boldsymbol{\beta}$ as $n \to \infty$. Then the preceding argument might produce a consistent estimator with a known asymptotic distribution. For example, the log-likelihood for a linear regression model with normally distributed disturbances with *different* variances, $\sigma^2 \omega_i$, is

$$\overline{h}_n(\mathbf{y}, \mathbf{X}, \boldsymbol{\beta}) = \frac{1}{n} \sum_{i=1}^{n} \left\{ \frac{-1}{2} \left[ \ln(2\pi\sigma^2\omega_i) + \frac{(y_i - \mathbf{x}_i'\boldsymbol{\beta})^2}{\sigma^2\omega_i} \right] \right\}.$$

By maximizing this function, we obtain the maximum likelihood estimator. But we also examined another estimator, simple least squares, which maximizes $M_n(\mathbf{y}, \mathbf{X}, \boldsymbol{\beta}) = -(1/n) \sum_{i=1}^{n}(y_i - \mathbf{x}_i'\boldsymbol{\beta})^2$. As we showed earlier, least squares is consistent and asymptotically normally distributed even with this extension, so it qualifies as an $M$ estimator of the sort we are considering here.

Now consider the general case. Suppose that we estimate $\boldsymbol{\beta}$ by maximizing a criterion function

$$M_n(\mathbf{y} \mid \mathbf{X}, \boldsymbol{\beta}) = \frac{1}{n} \sum_{i=1}^{n} \ln g(y_i \mid \mathbf{x}_i, \boldsymbol{\beta}).$$

Suppose as well that plim $M_n(\mathbf{y}, \mathbf{X}, \boldsymbol{\beta}) = E[M_n(\mathbf{y} \mid \mathbf{X}, \boldsymbol{\beta})]$ and that as $n \to \infty$, $E[M_n(\mathbf{y} \mid \mathbf{X}, \boldsymbol{\beta})]$ attains its unique maximum at $\boldsymbol{\beta}$. Then, by the argument we used earlier for the MLE, plim $\partial M_n(\mathbf{y} \mid \mathbf{X}, \boldsymbol{\beta})/\partial \boldsymbol{\beta} = E[\partial M_n(\mathbf{y} \mid \mathbf{X}, \boldsymbol{\beta})/\partial \boldsymbol{\beta}] = \mathbf{0}$. Once again, we have a set of moment equations for estimation. Let $\hat{\boldsymbol{\beta}}_E$ be the estimator that maximizes $M_n(\mathbf{y} \mid \mathbf{X}, \boldsymbol{\beta})$. Then the estimator is defined by

$$\frac{\partial M_n(\mathbf{y} \mid \mathbf{X}, \hat{\boldsymbol{\beta}}_E)}{\partial \hat{\boldsymbol{\beta}}_E} = \frac{1}{n} \sum_{i=1}^{n} \frac{\partial \ln g(y_i \mid \mathbf{x}_i, \hat{\boldsymbol{\beta}}_E)}{\partial \hat{\boldsymbol{\beta}}_E} = \overline{\mathbf{m}}(\hat{\boldsymbol{\beta}}_E) = \mathbf{0}.$$

Thus, $\hat{\boldsymbol{\beta}}_E$ is a GMM estimator. Using the notation of our earlier discussion, $\mathbf{G}(\hat{\boldsymbol{\beta}}_E)$ is the symmetric Hessian of $E[M_n(\mathbf{y}, \mathbf{X}, \boldsymbol{\beta})]$, which we will denote $(1/n)E[\mathbf{H}_M(\hat{\boldsymbol{\beta}}_E)] = \overline{\mathbf{H}}_M(\hat{\boldsymbol{\beta}}_E)$. Proceeding as we did above to obtain $\mathbf{V}_{\mathrm{ML}}$, we find that the appropriate asymptotic covariance matrix for the extremum estimator would be

$$\mathbf{V}_E = [\overline{\mathbf{H}}_M(\boldsymbol{\beta})]^{-1} \left( \frac{1}{n} \boldsymbol{\Phi} \right) [\overline{\mathbf{H}}_M(\boldsymbol{\beta})]^{-1},$$

where $\boldsymbol{\Phi} = \mathrm{Var}[\partial \log g(y_i \mid \mathbf{x}_i, \boldsymbol{\beta})/\partial \boldsymbol{\beta}]$, and, as before, the asymptotic distribution is normal.

The Hessian in $\mathbf{V}_E$ can easily be estimated by using its empirical counterpart,

$$\mathrm{Est.}[\overline{\mathbf{H}}_M(\hat{\boldsymbol{\beta}}_E)] = \frac{1}{n} \sum_{i=1}^{n} \frac{\partial^2 \ln g(y_i \mid \mathbf{x}_i, \hat{\boldsymbol{\beta}}_E)}{\partial \hat{\boldsymbol{\beta}}_E \partial \hat{\boldsymbol{\beta}}_E'}.$$

But, $\boldsymbol{\Phi}$ remains to be specified, and it is unlikely that we would know what function to use. The important difference is that in this case, the variance of the first derivatives vector need not equal the Hessian, so $\mathbf{V}_E$ does not simplify. We can, however, consistently estimate $\boldsymbol{\Phi}$ by using the sample variance of the first derivatives,

$$\hat{\boldsymbol{\Phi}} = \frac{1}{n} \sum_{i=1}^{n} \left[ \frac{\partial \ln g(y_i \mid \mathbf{x}_i, \hat{\boldsymbol{\beta}})}{\partial \hat{\boldsymbol{\beta}}} \right] \left[ \frac{\partial \ln g(y_i \mid \mathbf{x}_i, \hat{\boldsymbol{\beta}})}{\partial \hat{\boldsymbol{\beta}}'} \right].$$

If this were the maximum likelihood estimator, then $\hat{\boldsymbol{\Phi}}$ would be the OPG estimator that we have used at several points. For example, for the least squares estimator in the heteroscedastic linear regression model, the criterion is $M_n(\mathbf{y}, \mathbf{X}, \boldsymbol{\beta}) = -(1/n) \sum_{i=1}^{n} (y_i - \mathbf{x}_i'\boldsymbol{\beta})^2$, the solution is $\mathbf{b}$, $\mathbf{G}(\mathbf{b}) = (-2/n)\mathbf{X}'\mathbf{X}$, and

$$\hat{\boldsymbol{\Phi}} = \frac{1}{n} \sum_{i=1}^{n} [2\mathbf{x}_i(y_i - \mathbf{x}_i'\boldsymbol{\beta})][2\mathbf{x}_i(y_i - \mathbf{x}_i'\boldsymbol{\beta})]' = \frac{4}{n} \sum_{i=1}^{n} e_i^2 \mathbf{x}_i \mathbf{x}_i'.$$

Collecting terms, the 4s cancel and we are left precisely with the White estimator of (8-27)!

### 16.8.3 SANDWICH ESTIMATORS

At this point, we consider the motivation for all this weighty theory. One disadvantage of maximum likelihood estimation is its requirement that the density of the observed random variable(s) be fully specified. The preceding discussion suggests that in some situations, we can make somewhat fewer assumptions about the distribution than a full specification would require. The extremum estimator is robust to some kinds of specification errors. One useful result to emerge from this derivation is an estimator for the asymptotic covariance matrix of the extremum estimator that is robust at least to some misspecification. In particular, if we obtain $\hat{\boldsymbol{\beta}}_E$ by maximizing a criterion function that satisfies the other assumptions, then the appropriate estimator of the asymptotic covariance matrix is

$$\text{Est. } \mathbf{V}_E = \frac{1}{n} [\overline{\mathbf{H}}(\hat{\boldsymbol{\beta}}_E)]^{-1} \hat{\boldsymbol{\Phi}}(\hat{\boldsymbol{\beta}}_E) [\overline{\mathbf{H}}(\hat{\boldsymbol{\beta}}_E)]^{-1}.$$

If $\hat{\boldsymbol{\beta}}_E$ is the true MLE, then $\mathbf{V}_E$ simplifies to $\{-[\mathbf{H}(\hat{\boldsymbol{\beta}}_E)]\}^{-1}$. In the current literature, this estimator has been called the **sandwich estimator.** There is a trend in the current literature to compute this estimator routinely, regardless of the likelihood function. It is worth noting that if the log-likelihood is not specified correctly, then the parameter estimators are likely to be inconsistent, save for the cases such as those noted below, so robust estimation of the asymptotic covariance matrix may be misdirected effort. But if the likelihood function is correct, then the sandwich estimator is unnecessary. This method is not a general patch for misspecified models. Not every likelihood function qualifies as a consistent extremum estimator *for the parameters of interest in the model.*

One might wonder at this point how likely it is that the conditions needed for all this to work will be met. There are applications in the literature in which this machinery has been used that probably do not meet these conditions, such as the tobit model of Chapter 24. We have seen one important case. Least squares in the generalized regression model passes the test. Another important application is models of "individual heterogeneity" in cross-section data. Evidence suggests that simple models often overlook unobserved sources of variation across individuals in cross sections, such as unmeasurable "family effects" in studies of earnings or employment. Suppose that the correct model for a variable is $h(y_i \mid \mathbf{x}_i, \mathbf{v}_i, \boldsymbol{\beta}, \theta)$, where $\mathbf{v}_i$ is a random term that is not observed and $\theta$ is a parameter of the distribution of $\mathbf{v}$. The correct log-likelihood function is $\Sigma_i \ln f(y_i \mid \mathbf{x}_i, \boldsymbol{\beta}, \theta) = \Sigma_i \ln \int_v h(y_i \mid \mathbf{x}_i, \mathbf{v}_i, \boldsymbol{\beta}, \theta) f(\mathbf{v}_i) \, dv_i$. Suppose that we maximize some other **pseudo-log-likelihood function**, $\Sigma_i \ln g(y_i \mid \mathbf{x}_i, \boldsymbol{\beta})$ and then use the sandwich estimator to estimate the asymptotic covariance matrix of $\hat{\boldsymbol{\beta}}$. Does this produce a consistent estimator of the true parameter vector? Surprisingly, sometimes it does, even though it has ignored the nuisance parameter, $\theta$. We saw one case, using OLS in the GR model with heteroscedastic disturbances. Inappropriately fitting a Poisson model when the negative binomial model is correct—see Chapter 26—is another case. For some specifications, using the wrong likelihood function in the probit model with proportions data is a third. [These examples are suggested, with several others, by Gourieroux, Monfort, and Trognon (1984).] We do emphasize once again that the sandwich estimator, in and of itself, is not necessarily of any virtue if the likelihood function is misspecified and the other conditions for the $M$ estimator are not met.

### 16.8.4    CLUSTER ESTIMATORS

Micro-level, or individual, data are often grouped or "clustered." A model of production or economic success at the firm level might be based on a group of industries, with multiple firms in each industry. Analyses of student educational attainment might be based on samples of entire classes, or schools, or statewide averages of schools within school districts. And, of course, such "clustering" is the defining feature of a panel data set. We considered several of these types of applications in our analysis of panel data in Chapter 9. The recent literature contains many studies of clustered data in which the analyst has estimated a pooled model but sought to accommodate the expected correlation across observations with a correction to the asymptotic covariance matrix. We used this approach in computing a robust covariance matrix for the pooled least squares estimator in a panel data model [see (9-3) and Example 9.1 in Section 9.3.2].

For the normal linear regression model, the log-likelihood that we maximize with the pooled least squares estimator is

$$\ln L = \sum_{i=1}^{n} \sum_{t=1}^{T_i} \left[ -\frac{1}{2} \ln 2\pi - \frac{1}{2} \ln \sigma^2 - \frac{1}{2} \frac{(y_{it} - \mathbf{x}_{it}'\boldsymbol{\beta})^2}{\sigma^2} \right].$$

[See (16-34).] The "cluster-robust" estimator in (9-3) can be written

$$\mathbf{W} = \left( \sum_{i=1}^{n} \mathbf{X}_i'\mathbf{X}_i \right)^{-1} \left[ \sum_{i=1}^{n} (\mathbf{X}_i'\mathbf{e}_i)(\mathbf{e}_i'\mathbf{X}_i) \right] \left( \sum_{i=1}^{n} \mathbf{X}_i'\mathbf{X}_i \right)^{-1}$$

$$= \left( -\frac{1}{\hat{\sigma}^2} \sum_{i=1}^{n} \sum_{t=1}^{T_i} \mathbf{x}_{it}\mathbf{x}_{it}' \right)^{-1} \left[ \sum_{i=1}^{n} \left( \sum_{t=1}^{T_i} \frac{1}{\hat{\sigma}^2} \mathbf{x}_{it} e_{it} \right) \left( \sum_{t=1}^{T_i} \frac{1}{\hat{\sigma}^2} e_{it} \mathbf{x}_{it}' \right) \right] \left( -\frac{1}{\hat{\sigma}^2} \sum_{i=1}^{n} \sum_{t=1}^{T_i} \mathbf{x}_{it}\mathbf{x}_{it}' \right)^{-1}$$

$$= \left( \sum_{i=1}^{n} \sum_{t=1}^{T_i} \frac{\partial^2 \ln f_{it}}{\partial \hat{\boldsymbol{\beta}} \partial \hat{\boldsymbol{\beta}}'} \right)^{-1} \left[ \sum_{i=1}^{n} \left( \sum_{t=1}^{T_i} \frac{\partial \ln f_{it}}{\partial \hat{\boldsymbol{\beta}}} \right) \left( \sum_{t=1}^{T_i} \frac{\partial \ln f_{it}}{\partial \hat{\boldsymbol{\beta}}'} \right) \right] \left( \sum_{i=1}^{n} \sum_{t=1}^{T_i} \frac{\partial^2 \ln f_{it}}{\partial \hat{\boldsymbol{\beta}} \partial \hat{\boldsymbol{\beta}}'} \right)^{-1},$$

where $f_{it}$ is the normal density with mean $\mathbf{x}'_{it}\boldsymbol{\beta}$ and variance $\sigma^2$. This is precisely the "cluster-corrected" robust covariance matrix that appears elsewhere in the literature [minus an ad hoc "finite population correction" as in (9-4)].

In the generalized linear regression model (as in others), the OLS estimator is consistent, and will have asymptotic covariance matrix equal to

$$\text{Asy. Var}[\mathbf{b}] = (\mathbf{X}'\mathbf{X})^{-1}[\mathbf{X}'(\sigma^2\boldsymbol{\Omega})\mathbf{X}](\mathbf{X}'\mathbf{X})^{-1}.$$

(See Theorem 8.1.) The center matrix in the sandwich for the panel data case can be written

$$\mathbf{X}'(\sigma^2\boldsymbol{\Omega})\,\mathbf{X} = \sum_{i=1}^{n} \mathbf{X}'_i \boldsymbol{\Sigma} \mathbf{X}_i,$$

which motivates the preceding robust estimator. Whereas when we first encountered it, we motivated the cluster estimator with an appeal to the same logic that leads to the White estimator for heteroscedasticity, we now have an additional result that appears to justify the estimator in terms of the likelihood function.

Consider the specification error that the estimator is intended to accommodate. Suppose that the observations in group $i$ were multivariate normally distributed with disturbance mean vector $\mathbf{0}$ and unrestricted $T_i \times T_i$ covariance matrix, $\boldsymbol{\Sigma}_i$. Then, the appropriate log-likelihood function would be

$$\ln L = \sum_{i=1}^{n} \left( -T_i/2 \ln 2\pi - \tfrac{1}{2} \ln |\boldsymbol{\Sigma}_i| - \tfrac{1}{2} \boldsymbol{\varepsilon}'_i \boldsymbol{\Sigma}_i^{-1} \boldsymbol{\varepsilon}_i \right),$$

where $\boldsymbol{\varepsilon}_i$ is the $T_i \times 1$ vector of disturbances for individual $i$. Therefore, we have maximized the wrong likelihood function. Indeed, the $\boldsymbol{\beta}$ that maximizes this log likelihood function is the GLS estimator, not the OLS estimator. OLS, and the cluster corrected estimator given earlier, "work" in the sense that (1) the least squares estimator is consistent in spite of the misspecification and (2) the robust estimator does, indeed, estimate the appropriate asymptotic covariance matrix.

Now, consider the more general case. Suppose the data set consists of $n$ multivariate observations, $[y_{i,1}, \ldots, y_{i,T_i}], i = 1, \ldots, n$. Each cluster is a draw from joint density $f_i(\mathbf{y}_i \mid \mathbf{X}_i, \boldsymbol{\theta})$. Once again, to preserve the generality of the result, we will allow the cluster sizes to differ. The appropriate log likelihood for the sample is

$$\ln L = \sum_{i=1}^{n} \ln f_i(\mathbf{y}_i \mid \mathbf{X}_i, \boldsymbol{\theta}).$$

Instead of maximizing $\ln L$, we maximize a pseudo-log-likelihood

$$\ln L_P = \sum_{i=1}^{n} \sum_{t=1}^{T_i} \ln g\left( y_{it} \mid \mathbf{x}_{it}, \boldsymbol{\theta} \right),$$

where we make the possibly unreasonable assumption that the same parameter vector, $\boldsymbol{\theta}$ enters the pseudo-log-likelihood as enters the correct one. Assume that it does. Using our familiar first-order asymptotics, the **pseudo-maximum likelihood estimator** will satisfy

$$\left(\hat{\boldsymbol{\theta}}_{P,ML} - \boldsymbol{\theta}\right) \approx \left(\frac{1}{\sum_{i=1}^{n} T_i} \sum_{i=1}^{n} \sum_{t=1}^{T_i} \frac{\partial^2 \ln f_{it}}{\partial \boldsymbol{\theta} \partial \boldsymbol{\theta}'}\right)^{-1} \left(\frac{1}{\sum_{i=1}^{n} T_i} \sum_{i=1}^{n} \sum_{t=1}^{T_i} \frac{\partial \ln f_{it}}{\partial \boldsymbol{\theta}}\right) + (\boldsymbol{\theta} - \boldsymbol{\beta})$$

$$= \left(\frac{1}{\sum_{i=1}^{n} T_i} \sum_{i=1}^{n} \sum_{t=1}^{T_i} H_{it}\right)^{-1} \left(\sum_{i=1}^{n} w_i \bar{\mathbf{g}}_i\right) + (\boldsymbol{\theta} - \boldsymbol{\beta}),$$

where $w_i = T_i / \sum_{i=1}^{n} T_i$ and $\bar{\mathbf{g}}_i = (1/T_i) \sum_{t=1}^{T_i} \partial \ln f_{it}/\partial \boldsymbol{\theta}$. The trailing term in the expression is included to allow for the possibility that plim $\hat{\boldsymbol{\theta}}_{P,ML} = \boldsymbol{\beta}$, which may not equal $\boldsymbol{\theta}$. [Note, for example, Cameron and Trivedi (2005, p. 842) specifically assume consistency in the generic model they describe.] Taking the expected outer product of this expression to estimate the asymptotic mean squared deviation will produce two terms—the cross term vanishes. The first will be the cluster-corrected matrix that is ubiquitous in the current literature. The second will be the squared error that may persist as $n$ increases because the pseudo-MLE need not estimate the parameters of the model of interest.

We draw two conclusions. We can justify the cluster estimator based on this approximation. In general, it will estimate the expected squared variation of the pseudo-MLE around its probability limit. Whether it measures the variation around the appropriate parameters of the model hangs on whether the second term equals zero. In words, perhaps not surprisingly, this apparatus only works if the estimator is consistent. Is that likely? Certainly not if the pooled model is ignoring unobservable fixed effects. Moreover, it will be inconsistent in most cases in which the misspecification is to ignore latent random effects as well. The pseudo-MLE is only consistent for random effects in a few special cases, such as the linear model and Poisson and negative binomial models discussed in Chapter 25. It is not consistent in the probit and logit models in which this approach often used. In the end, the cases in which the estimator are consistent are rarely, if ever, enumerated. The upshot is stated succinctly by Freedman (2006, p. 302): "The sandwich algorithm, under stringent regularity conditions, yields variances for the MLE that are asymptotically correct even when the specification—and hence the likelihood function—are incorrect. However, it is quite another thing to ignore bias. It remains unclear why applied workers should care about the variance of an estimator for the wrong parameter."

## 16.9 APPLICATIONS OF MAXIMUM LIKELIHOOD ESTIMATION

We will now examine several applications of the maximum likelihood estimator (MLE). We begin by developing the ML counterparts to most of the estimators for the classical and generalized regression models in Chapters 4 through 12. (Generally, the development for dynamic models becomes more involved than we are able to pursue here. The one exception we will consider is the standard model of autocorrelation.) We emphasize, in each of these cases, that we have already developed an efficient, generalized method of moments estimator that has the same asymptotic properties as the MLE under the assumption of normality. In more general cases, we will sometimes find that the GMM estimator is actually preferred to the MLE because of its robustness to failures of the distributional assumptions or its freedom from the necessity to make those assumptions in the first place. However, for the extensions of the classical model based on generalized least sqaures that are treated here, that is not the case. It might be argued that in these cases, the MLE is superfluous. There are occasions when the MLE will be preferred for other reasons, such as its invariance to transformation in nonlinear models and, possibly, its small sample behavior (although that is usually not the case). And, we will examine some nonlinear models in which there is no linear, method of moments counterpart, so the MLE is the natural estimator. Finally, in each case, we will find some useful aspect of the estimator, itself, including the development of algorithms such as Newton's method and the EM method for latent class models.

### 16.9.1  THE NORMAL LINEAR REGRESSION MODEL

The linear regression model is

$$y_i = \mathbf{x}_i'\boldsymbol{\beta} + \varepsilon_i.$$

The likelihood function for a sample of $n$ independent, identically and normally distributed disturbances is

$$L = (2\pi\sigma^2)^{-n/2}e^{-\boldsymbol{\varepsilon}'\boldsymbol{\varepsilon}/(2\sigma^2)}. \tag{16-32}$$

The transformation from $\varepsilon_i$ to $y_i$ is $\varepsilon_i = y_i - \mathbf{x}_i'\boldsymbol{\beta}$, so the **Jacobian** for each observation, $|\partial\varepsilon_i/\partial y_i|$, is one.[13] Making the transformation, we find that the likelihood function for the $n$ observations on the observed random variables is

$$L = (2\pi\sigma^2)^{-n/2}e^{(-1/(2\sigma^2))(\mathbf{y}-\mathbf{X}\boldsymbol{\beta})'(\mathbf{y}-\mathbf{X}\boldsymbol{\beta})}. \tag{16-33}$$

To maximize this function with respect to $\boldsymbol{\beta}$, it will be necessary to maximize the exponent or minimize the familiar sum of squares. Taking logs, we obtain the log-likelihood function for the classical regression model:

$$\ln L = -\frac{n}{2}\ln 2\pi - \frac{n}{2}\ln\sigma^2 - \frac{(\mathbf{y}-\mathbf{X}\boldsymbol{\beta})'(\mathbf{y}-\mathbf{X}\boldsymbol{\beta})}{2\sigma^2}. \tag{16-34}$$

The necessary conditions for maximizing this log-likelihood are

$$\begin{bmatrix} \dfrac{\partial\ln L}{\partial\boldsymbol{\beta}} \\[2mm] \dfrac{\partial\ln L}{\partial\sigma^2} \end{bmatrix} = \begin{bmatrix} \dfrac{\mathbf{X}'(\mathbf{y}-\mathbf{X}\boldsymbol{\beta})}{\sigma^2} \\[2mm] \dfrac{-n}{2\sigma^2} + \dfrac{(\mathbf{y}-\mathbf{X}\boldsymbol{\beta})'(\mathbf{y}-\mathbf{X}\boldsymbol{\beta})}{2\sigma^4} \end{bmatrix} = \begin{bmatrix} \mathbf{0} \\ 0 \end{bmatrix}. \tag{16-35}$$

The values that satisfy these equations are

$$\hat{\boldsymbol{\beta}}_{\mathrm{ML}} = (\mathbf{X}'\mathbf{X})^{-1}\mathbf{X}'\mathbf{y} = \mathbf{b} \quad\text{and}\quad \hat{\sigma}^2_{\mathrm{ML}} = \frac{\mathbf{e}'\mathbf{e}}{n}. \tag{16-36}$$

---

[13]See (B-41) in Section B.5. The analysis to follow is conditioned on $\mathbf{X}$. To avoid cluttering the notation, we will leave this aspect of the model implicit in the results. As noted earlier, we assume that the data generating process for $\mathbf{X}$ does not involve $\boldsymbol{\beta}$ or $\sigma^2$ and that the data are well behaved as discussed in Chapter 4.

The slope estimator is the familiar one, whereas the variance estimator differs from the least squares value by the divisor of $n$ instead of $n - K$.[14]

The Cramér–Rao bound for the variance of an unbiased estimator is the negative inverse of the expectation of

$$
\begin{bmatrix}
\dfrac{\partial^2 \ln L}{\partial \boldsymbol{\beta} \partial \boldsymbol{\beta}'} & \dfrac{\partial^2 \ln L}{\partial \boldsymbol{\beta} \partial \sigma^2} \\[2mm]
\dfrac{\partial^2 \ln L}{\partial \sigma^2 \partial \boldsymbol{\beta}'} & \dfrac{\partial^2 \ln L}{\partial (\sigma^2)^2}
\end{bmatrix}
=
\begin{bmatrix}
-\dfrac{\mathbf{X}'\mathbf{X}}{\sigma^2} & -\dfrac{\mathbf{X}'\boldsymbol{\varepsilon}}{\sigma^4} \\[2mm]
-\dfrac{\boldsymbol{\varepsilon}'\mathbf{X}}{\sigma^4} & \dfrac{n}{2\sigma^4} - \dfrac{\boldsymbol{\varepsilon}'\boldsymbol{\varepsilon}}{\sigma^6}
\end{bmatrix} .
\tag{16-37}
$$

In taking expected values, the off-diagonal term vanishes, leaving

$$
[\mathbf{I}(\boldsymbol{\beta}, \sigma^2)]^{-1} =
\begin{bmatrix}
\sigma^2 (\mathbf{X}'\mathbf{X})^{-1} & \mathbf{0} \\
\mathbf{0}' & 2\sigma^4/n
\end{bmatrix} .
\tag{16-38}
$$

The least squares slope estimator is the maximum likelihood estimator for this model. Therefore, it inherits all the desirable *asymptotic* properties of maximum likelihood estimators.

We showed earlier that $s^2 = \mathbf{e}'\mathbf{e}/(n - K)$ is an unbiased estimator of $\sigma^2$. Therefore, the maximum likelihood estimator is biased toward zero:

$$
E[\hat{\sigma}^2_{\text{ML}}] = \frac{n - K}{n}\sigma^2 = \left(1 - \frac{K}{n}\right)\sigma^2 < \sigma^2.
\tag{16-39}
$$

Despite its small-sample bias, the maximum likelihood estimator of $\sigma^2$ has the same desirable asymptotic properties. We see in (16-39) that $s^2$ and $\hat{\sigma}^2$ differ only by a factor $-K/n$, which vanishes in large samples. It is instructive to formalize the asymptotic equivalence of the two. From (16-38), we know that

$$
\sqrt{n}\big(\hat{\sigma}^2_{\text{ML}} - \sigma^2\big) \xrightarrow{d} N[0, 2\sigma^4].
$$

It follows that

$$
z_n = \left(1 - \frac{K}{n}\right)\sqrt{n}\big(\hat{\sigma}^2_{\text{ML}} - \sigma^2\big) + \frac{K}{\sqrt{n}}\sigma^2 \xrightarrow{d} \left(1 - \frac{K}{n}\right)N[0, 2\sigma^4] + \frac{K}{\sqrt{n}}\sigma^2.
$$

But $K/\sqrt{n}$ and $K/n$ vanish as $n \to \infty$, so the limiting distribution of $z_n$ is also $N[0, 2\sigma^4]$. Because $z_n = \sqrt{n}(s^2 - \sigma^2)$, we have shown that the asymptotic distribution of $s^2$ is the same as that of the maximum likelihood estimator.

The standard test statistic for assessing the validity of a set of linear restrictions in the linear model, $\mathbf{R}\boldsymbol{\beta} - \mathbf{q} = \mathbf{0}$, is the $F$ ratio,

$$
F[J, n - K] = \frac{(\mathbf{e}'_*\mathbf{e}_* - \mathbf{e}'\mathbf{e})/J}{\mathbf{e}'\mathbf{e}/(n - K)} = \frac{(\mathbf{R}\mathbf{b} - \mathbf{q})'[\mathbf{R}s^2(\mathbf{X}'\mathbf{X})^{-1}\mathbf{R}']^{-1}(\mathbf{R}\mathbf{b} - \mathbf{q})}{J}.
$$

With normally distributed disturbances, the $F$ test is valid in any sample size. There remains a problem with nonlinear restrictions of the form $\mathbf{c}(\boldsymbol{\beta}) = \mathbf{0}$, since the counterpart to $F$, which we will examine here, has validity only asymptotically even with normally distributed disturbances. In this section, we will reconsider the Wald statistic and examine two related statistics, the likelihood ratio statistic and the Lagrange multiplier

---

[14] As a general rule, maximum likelihood estimators do not make corrections for degrees of freedom.

statistic. These statistics are both based on the likelihood function and, like the Wald statistic, are generally valid only asymptotically.

No simplicity is gained by restricting ourselves to linear restrictions at this point, so we will consider general hypotheses of the form

$$H_0: \mathbf{c}(\boldsymbol{\beta}) = \mathbf{0},$$

$$H_1: \mathbf{c}(\boldsymbol{\beta}) \neq \mathbf{0}.$$

The **Wald statistic** for testing this hypothesis and its limiting distribution under $H_0$ would be

$$W = \mathbf{c}(\mathbf{b})'\{\mathbf{C}(\mathbf{b})[\hat{\sigma}^2(\mathbf{X}'\mathbf{X})^{-1}]\mathbf{C}(\mathbf{b})'\}^{-1}\mathbf{c}(\mathbf{b}) \xrightarrow{d} \chi^2[J], \qquad \textbf{(16-40)}$$

where

$$\mathbf{C}(\mathbf{b}) = [\partial \mathbf{c}(\mathbf{b})/\partial \mathbf{b}']. \qquad \textbf{(16-41)}$$

The **likelihood ratio (LR) test** is carried out by comparing the values of the log-likelihood function with and without the restrictions imposed. We leave aside for the present how the restricted estimator $\mathbf{b}_*$ is computed (except for the linear model, which we saw earlier). The test statistic and it's limiting distribution under $H_0$ are

$$\text{LR} = -2[\ln L_* - \ln L] \xrightarrow{d} \chi^2[J]. \qquad \textbf{(16-42)}$$

The log-likelihood for the regression model is given in (16-34). The first-order conditions imply that regardless of how the slopes are computed, the estimator of $\sigma^2$ without restrictions on $\boldsymbol{\beta}$ will be $\hat{\sigma}^2 = (\mathbf{y} - \mathbf{Xb})'(\mathbf{y} - \mathbf{Xb})/n$ and likewise for a restricted estimator $\hat{\sigma}_*^2 = (\mathbf{y} - \mathbf{Xb}_*)'(\mathbf{y} - \mathbf{Xb}_*)/n = \mathbf{e}_*'\mathbf{e}_*/n$. The **concentrated log-likelihood**[15] will be

$$\ln L_c = -\frac{n}{2}[1 + \ln 2\pi + \ln(\mathbf{e}'\mathbf{e}/n)]$$

and likewise for the restricted case. If we insert these in the definition of LR, then we obtain

$$\text{LR} = n\ln[\mathbf{e}_*'\mathbf{e}_*/\mathbf{e}'\mathbf{e}] = n(\ln \hat{\sigma}_*^2 - \ln \hat{\sigma}^2) = n\ln(\hat{\sigma}_*^2/\hat{\sigma}^2). \qquad \textbf{(16-43)}$$

The **Lagrange multiplier (LM) test** is based on the gradient of the log-likelihood function. The principle of the test is that if the hypothesis is valid, then at the restricted estimator, the derivatives of the log-likelihood function should be close to zero. There are two ways to carry out the LM test. The log-likelihood function can be maximized subject to a set of restrictions by using

$$\ln L_{\text{LM}} = -\frac{n}{2}\left[\ln 2\pi + \ln \sigma^2 + \frac{[(\mathbf{y} - \mathbf{X}\boldsymbol{\beta})'(\mathbf{y} - \mathbf{X}\boldsymbol{\beta})]/n}{\sigma^2}\right] + \boldsymbol{\lambda}'\mathbf{c}(\boldsymbol{\beta}).$$

---

[15] See Section E4.3.

The first-order conditions for a solution are

$$\begin{bmatrix} \dfrac{\partial \ln L_{\text{LM}}}{\partial \boldsymbol{\beta}} \\[2ex] \dfrac{\partial \ln L_{\text{LM}}}{\partial \sigma^2} \\[2ex] \dfrac{\partial \ln L_{\text{LM}}}{\partial \boldsymbol{\lambda}} \end{bmatrix} = \begin{bmatrix} \dfrac{\mathbf{X}'(\mathbf{y} - \mathbf{X}\boldsymbol{\beta})}{\sigma^2} + \mathbf{C}(\boldsymbol{\beta})'\boldsymbol{\lambda} \\[2ex] \dfrac{-n}{2\sigma^2} + \dfrac{(\mathbf{y} - \mathbf{X}\boldsymbol{\beta})'(\mathbf{y} - \mathbf{X}\boldsymbol{\beta})}{2\sigma^4} \\[2ex] \mathbf{c}(\boldsymbol{\beta}) \end{bmatrix} = \begin{bmatrix} \mathbf{0} \\[1ex] 0 \\[1ex] \mathbf{0} \end{bmatrix}. \tag{16-44}$$

The solutions to these equations give the restricted least squares estimator, $\mathbf{b}_*$; the usual variance estimator, now $\mathbf{e}'_*\mathbf{e}_*/n$; and the Lagrange multipliers. There are now two ways to compute the test statistic. In the setting of the classical linear regression model, when we actually compute the Lagrange multipliers, a convenient way to proceed is to test the hypothesis that the multipliers equal zero. For this model, the solution for $\boldsymbol{\lambda}_*$ is $\boldsymbol{\lambda}_* = [\mathbf{R}(\mathbf{X}'\mathbf{X})^{-1}\mathbf{R}']^{-1}(\mathbf{R}\mathbf{b}-\mathbf{q})$. This equation is a linear function of the least squares estimator. If we carry out a *Wald* test of the hypothesis that $\boldsymbol{\lambda}_*$ equals $\mathbf{0}$, then the statistic will be

$$\text{LM} = \boldsymbol{\lambda}'_*\{\text{Est. Var}[\boldsymbol{\lambda}_*]\}^{-1}\boldsymbol{\lambda}_* = (\mathbf{R}\mathbf{b} - \mathbf{q})'[\mathbf{R}\,s_*^2(\mathbf{X}'\mathbf{X})^{-1}\mathbf{R}']^{-1}(\mathbf{R}\mathbf{b} - \mathbf{q}). \tag{16-45}$$

The disturbance variance estimator, $s_*^2$, based on the restricted slopes is $\mathbf{e}'_*\mathbf{e}_*/n$.

An alternative way to compute the LM statistic often produces interesting results. In most situations, we maximize the log-likelihood function without actually computing the vector of Lagrange multipliers. (The restrictions are usually imposed some other way.) An alternative way to compute the statistic is based on the (general) result that under the hypothesis being tested,

$$E[\partial \ln L/\partial \boldsymbol{\beta}] = E[(1/\sigma^2)\mathbf{X}'\boldsymbol{\varepsilon}] = \mathbf{0}$$

and[16]

$$\text{Asy. Var}[\partial \ln L/\partial \boldsymbol{\beta}] = -E[\partial^2 \ln L/\partial \boldsymbol{\beta}\partial \boldsymbol{\beta}']^{-1} = \sigma^2(\mathbf{X}'\mathbf{X})^{-1}. \tag{16-46}$$

We can test the hypothesis that at the restricted estimator, the derivatives are equal to zero. The statistic would be

$$\text{LM} = \dfrac{\mathbf{e}'_*\mathbf{X}(\mathbf{X}'\mathbf{X})^{-1}\mathbf{X}'\mathbf{e}_*}{\mathbf{e}'_*\mathbf{e}_*/n} = nR_*^2. \tag{16-47}$$

In this form, the LM statistic is $n$ times the coefficient of determination in a regression of the residuals $e_{i*} = (y_i - \mathbf{x}'_i\mathbf{b}_*)$ on the full set of regressors.

With some manipulation we can show that $W = [n/(n - K)]JF$ and LR and LM are approximately equal to this function of $F$.[17] All three statistics converge to $JF$ as $n$ increases. The linear model is a special case in that the LR statistic is based only on the unrestricted estimator and does not actually require computation of the restricted least squares estimator, although computation of $F$ does involve most of the computation of $\mathbf{b}_*$. Because the log function is concave, and $W/n \geq \ln(1 + W/n)$, Godfrey (1988) also shows that $W \geq \text{LR} \geq \text{LM}$, so for the linear model, we have a firm ranking of the three statistics.

---

[16]This makes use of the fact that the Hessian is block diagonal.

[17]See Godfrey (1988, pp. 49–51).

There is ample evidence that the asymptotic results for these statistics are problematic in small or moderately sized samples. [See, e.g., Davidson and MacKinnon (2004, pp. 424–428).] The true distributions of all three statistics involve the data and the unknown parameters and, as suggested by the algebra, converge to the $F$ distribution *from above.* The implication is that critical values from the chi-squared distribution are likely to be too small; that is, using the limiting chi-squared distribution in small or moderately sized samples is likely to exaggerate the significance of empirical results. Thus, in applications, the more conservative $F$ statistic (or $t$ for one restriction) is likely to be preferable unless one's data are plentiful.

### 16.9.2 THE GENERALIZED REGRESSION MODEL

For the generalized regression model of Section 8.1,

$$y_i = \mathbf{x}_i'\boldsymbol{\beta} + \varepsilon_i, i = 1, \ldots, n,$$
$$E[\boldsymbol{\varepsilon} \mid \mathbf{X}] = \mathbf{0},$$
$$E[\boldsymbol{\varepsilon}\boldsymbol{\varepsilon}' \mid \mathbf{X}] = \sigma^2\boldsymbol{\Omega},$$

as before, we first assume that $\boldsymbol{\Omega}$ is a matrix of known constants. If the disturbances are multivariate normally distributed, then the log-likelihood function for the sample is

$$\ln L = -\frac{n}{2}\ln(2\pi) - \frac{n}{2}\ln\sigma^2 - \frac{1}{2\sigma^2}(\mathbf{y} - \mathbf{X}\boldsymbol{\beta})'\boldsymbol{\Omega}^{-1}(\mathbf{y} - \mathbf{X}\boldsymbol{\beta}) - \frac{1}{2}\ln|\boldsymbol{\Omega}|. \qquad \textbf{(16-48)}$$

Because $\boldsymbol{\Omega}$ is a matrix of known constants, the maximum likelihood estimator of $\boldsymbol{\beta}$ is the vector that minimizes the **generalized sum of squares,**

$$S_*(\boldsymbol{\beta}) = (\mathbf{y} - \mathbf{X}\boldsymbol{\beta})'\boldsymbol{\Omega}^{-1}(\mathbf{y} - \mathbf{X}\boldsymbol{\beta})$$

(hence the name *generalized least squares*). The necessary conditions for maximizing $L$ are

$$\frac{\partial \ln L}{\partial \boldsymbol{\beta}} = \frac{1}{\sigma^2}\mathbf{X}'\boldsymbol{\Omega}^{-1}(\mathbf{y} - \mathbf{X}\boldsymbol{\beta}) = \frac{1}{\sigma^2}\mathbf{X}_*'(\mathbf{y}_* - \mathbf{X}_*\boldsymbol{\beta}) = \mathbf{0},$$

$$\frac{\partial \ln L}{\partial \sigma^2} = -\frac{n}{2\sigma^2} + \frac{1}{2\sigma^4}(\mathbf{y} - \mathbf{X}\boldsymbol{\beta})'\boldsymbol{\Omega}^{-1}(\mathbf{y} - \mathbf{X}\boldsymbol{\beta}) \qquad \textbf{(16-49)}$$

$$= -\frac{n}{2\sigma^2} + \frac{1}{2\sigma^4}(\mathbf{y}_* - \mathbf{X}_*\boldsymbol{\beta})'(\mathbf{y}_* - \mathbf{X}_*\boldsymbol{\beta}) = 0.$$

The solutions are the OLS estimators using the transformed data:

$$\hat{\boldsymbol{\beta}}_{\text{ML}} = (\mathbf{X}_*'\mathbf{X}_*)^{-1}\mathbf{X}_*'\mathbf{y}_* = (\mathbf{X}'\boldsymbol{\Omega}^{-1}\mathbf{X})^{-1}\mathbf{X}'\boldsymbol{\Omega}^{-1}\mathbf{y}, \qquad \textbf{(16-50)}$$

$$\hat{\sigma}_{\text{ML}}^2 = \frac{1}{n}(\mathbf{y}_* - \mathbf{X}_*\hat{\boldsymbol{\beta}})'(\mathbf{y}_* - \mathbf{X}_*\hat{\boldsymbol{\beta}})$$

$$\qquad\qquad\qquad\qquad\qquad \textbf{(16-51)}$$

$$= \frac{1}{n}(\mathbf{y} - \mathbf{X}\hat{\boldsymbol{\beta}})'\boldsymbol{\Omega}^{-1}(\mathbf{y} - \mathbf{X}\hat{\boldsymbol{\beta}}),$$

which implies that with normally distributed disturbances, generalized least squares is also maximum likelihood. As in the classical regression model, the maximum likelihood estimator of $\sigma^2$ is biased. An unbiased estimator is the one in (8-14). The conclusion, which would be expected, is that when $\mathbf{\Omega}$ is known, the maximum likelihood estimator is generalized least squares.

When $\mathbf{\Omega}$ is unknown and must be estimated, then it is necessary to maximize the log-likelihood in (16-48) with respect to the full set of parameters $[\boldsymbol{\beta}, \sigma^2, \mathbf{\Omega}]$ simultaneously. Because an unrestricted $\mathbf{\Omega}$ alone contains $n(n+1)/2 - 1$ parameters, it is clear that some restriction will have to be placed on the structure of $\mathbf{\Omega}$ for estimation to proceed. We will examine several applications in which $\mathbf{\Omega} = \mathbf{\Omega}(\boldsymbol{\theta})$ for some smaller vector of parameters in the next several sections. We note only a few general results at this point.

1. For a given value of $\boldsymbol{\theta}$ the estimator of $\boldsymbol{\beta}$ would be feasible GLS and the estimator of $\sigma^2$ would be the estimator in (16-51).
2. The likelihood equations for $\boldsymbol{\theta}$ will generally be complicated functions of $\boldsymbol{\beta}$ and $\sigma^2$, so joint estimation will be necessary. However, in many cases, for given values of $\boldsymbol{\beta}$ and $\sigma^2$, the estimator of $\boldsymbol{\theta}$ is straightforward. For example, in the model of (8-15), the iterated estimator of $\theta$ when $\boldsymbol{\beta}$ and $\sigma^2$ and a prior value of $\theta$ are given is the prior value plus the slope in the regression of $(e_i^2/\hat{\sigma}_i^2 - 1)$ on $z_i$.

The second step suggests a sort of back and forth iteration for this model that will work in many situations—starting with, say, OLS, iterating back and forth between 1 and 2 until convergence will produce the joint maximum likelihood estimator. This situation was examined by Oberhofer and Kmenta (1974), who showed that under some fairly weak requirements, most importantly that $\theta$ not involve $\sigma^2$ or any of the parameters in $\boldsymbol{\beta}$, this procedure would produce the maximum likelihood estimator. Another implication of this formulation which is simple to show (we leave it as an exercise) is that under the Oberhofer and Kmenta assumption, the asymptotic covariance matrix of the estimator is the same as the GLS estimator. This is the same whether $\mathbf{\Omega}$ is known or estimated, which means that if $\theta$ and $\boldsymbol{\beta}$ have no parameters in common, then *exact knowledge of $\mathbf{\Omega}$ brings no gain in asymptotic efficiency in the estimation of $\boldsymbol{\beta}$ over estimation of $\boldsymbol{\beta}$ with a consistent estimator of $\mathbf{\Omega}$.*

We will now examine the two primary, single-equation applications: heteroscedasticity and autocorrelation.

### 16.9.2.a  Multiplicative Heteroscedasticity

Harvey's (1976) model of multiplicative heteroscedasticity is a very flexible, general model that includes most of the useful formulations as special cases. The general formulation is

$$\sigma_i^2 = \sigma^2 \exp(\mathbf{z}_i'\boldsymbol{\alpha}). \tag{16-52}$$

A model with heteroscedasticity of the form

$$\sigma_i^2 = \sigma^2 \prod_{m=1}^{M} z_{im}^{\alpha_m} \tag{16-53}$$

results if the logs of the variables are placed in $z_i$. The groupwise heteroscedasticity model described in Section 8.8.2 is produced by making $\mathbf{z}_i$ a set of group dummy variables (one must be omitted). In this case, $\sigma^2$ is the disturbance variance for the base group whereas for the other groups, $\sigma_g^2 = \sigma^2 \exp(\alpha_g)$.

We begin with a useful simplification. Let $\mathbf{z}_i$ include a constant term so that $\mathbf{z}_i' = [1, \mathbf{q}_i']$, where $\mathbf{q}_i$ is the original set of variables, and let $\boldsymbol{\gamma}' = [\ln \sigma^2, \boldsymbol{\alpha}']$. Then, the model is simply $\sigma_i^2 = \exp(\mathbf{z}_i' \boldsymbol{\gamma})$. Once the full parameter vector is estimated, $\exp(\gamma_1)$ provides the estimator of $\sigma^2$. (This estimator uses the invariance result for maximum likelihood estimation. See Section 16.4.5.d.)

The log-likelihood is

$$
\begin{aligned}
\ln L &= -\frac{n}{2} \ln(2\pi) - \frac{1}{2} \sum_{i=1}^{n} \ln \sigma_i^2 - \frac{1}{2} \sum_{i=1}^{n} \frac{\varepsilon_i^2}{\sigma_i^2} \\
&= -\frac{n}{2} \ln(2\pi) - \frac{1}{2} \sum_{i=1}^{n} \mathbf{z}_i' \boldsymbol{\gamma} - \frac{1}{2} \sum_{i=1}^{n} \frac{\varepsilon_i^2}{\exp(\mathbf{z}_i' \boldsymbol{\gamma})}.
\end{aligned}
\tag{16-54}
$$

The likelihood equations are

$$
\frac{\partial \ln L}{\partial \boldsymbol{\beta}} = \sum_{i=1}^{n} \mathbf{x}_i \frac{\varepsilon_i}{\exp(\mathbf{z}_i' \boldsymbol{\gamma})} = \mathbf{X}' \boldsymbol{\Omega}^{-1} \boldsymbol{\varepsilon} = \mathbf{0},
$$

$$
\frac{\partial \ln L}{\partial \boldsymbol{\gamma}} = \frac{1}{2} \sum_{i=1}^{n} \mathbf{z}_i \left( \frac{\varepsilon_i^2}{\exp(\mathbf{z}_i' \boldsymbol{\gamma})} - 1 \right) = \mathbf{0}.
\tag{16-55}
$$

For this model, the method of scoring turns out to be a particularly convenient way to maximize the log-likelihood function. The terms in the Hessian are

$$
\frac{\partial^2 \ln L}{\partial \boldsymbol{\beta} \, \partial \boldsymbol{\beta}'} = -\sum_{i=1}^{n} \frac{1}{\exp(\mathbf{z}_i' \boldsymbol{\gamma})} \mathbf{x}_i \mathbf{x}_i' = -\mathbf{X}' \boldsymbol{\Omega}^{-1} \mathbf{X},
\tag{16-56}
$$

$$
\frac{\partial^2 \ln L}{\partial \boldsymbol{\beta} \, \partial \boldsymbol{\gamma}'} = -\sum_{i=1}^{n} \frac{\varepsilon_i}{\exp(\mathbf{z}_i' \boldsymbol{\gamma})} \mathbf{x}_i \mathbf{z}_i',
\tag{16-57}
$$

$$
\frac{\partial^2 \ln L}{\partial \boldsymbol{\gamma} \, \partial \boldsymbol{\gamma}'} = -\frac{1}{2} \sum_{i=1}^{n} \frac{\varepsilon_i^2}{\exp(\mathbf{z}_i' \boldsymbol{\gamma})} \mathbf{z}_i \mathbf{z}_i'.
\tag{16-58}
$$

The expected value of $\partial^2 \ln L / \partial \boldsymbol{\beta} \partial \boldsymbol{\gamma}'$ is $\mathbf{0}$ because $E[\varepsilon_i | \mathbf{x}_i, \mathbf{z}_i] = 0$. The expected value of the fraction in $\partial^2 \ln L / \partial \boldsymbol{\gamma} \partial \boldsymbol{\gamma}'$ is $E[\varepsilon_i^2 / \sigma_i^2 | \mathbf{x}_i, \mathbf{z}_i] = 1$. Let $\boldsymbol{\delta} = [\boldsymbol{\beta}, \boldsymbol{\gamma}]$. Then

$$
-E\left( \frac{\partial^2 \ln L}{\partial \boldsymbol{\delta} \, \partial \boldsymbol{\delta}'} \right) = \begin{bmatrix} \mathbf{X}' \boldsymbol{\Omega}^{-1} \mathbf{X} & \mathbf{0} \\ \mathbf{0}' & \frac{1}{2} \mathbf{Z}' \mathbf{Z} \end{bmatrix} = -\overline{\mathbf{H}}.
\tag{16-59}
$$

The **method of scoring** is an algorithm for finding an iterative solution to the likelihood equations. The iteration is

$$
\boldsymbol{\delta}_{t+1} = \boldsymbol{\delta}_t - \overline{\mathbf{H}}^{-1} \mathbf{g}_t,
$$

where $\boldsymbol{\delta}_t$ (i.e., $\boldsymbol{\beta}_t$, $\boldsymbol{\gamma}_t$, and $\boldsymbol{\Omega}_t$) is the estimate at iteration $t$, $\mathbf{g}_t$ is the two-part vector of first derivatives $[\partial \ln L / \partial \boldsymbol{\beta}_t', \partial \ln L / \partial \boldsymbol{\gamma}_t']'$, and $\overline{\mathbf{H}}$ is partitioned likewise. [**Newton's method** uses the actual second derivatives in (16-56)–(16-58) rather than their expectations in (16-59). The scoring method exploits the convenience of the zero expectation of the off-diagonal block (cross derivative) in (16-57).] Because $\overline{\mathbf{H}}$ is block diagonal, the iteration can be written as separate equations:

$$
\begin{aligned}
\boldsymbol{\beta}_{t+1} &= \boldsymbol{\beta}_t + (\mathbf{X}'\boldsymbol{\Omega}_t^{-1}\mathbf{X})^{-1}(\mathbf{X}'\boldsymbol{\Omega}_t^{-1}\boldsymbol{\varepsilon}_t) \\
&= \boldsymbol{\beta}_t + (\mathbf{X}'\boldsymbol{\Omega}_t^{-1}\mathbf{X})^{-1}\mathbf{X}'\boldsymbol{\Omega}_t^{-1}(\mathbf{y} - \mathbf{X}\boldsymbol{\beta}_t) \quad\quad \textbf{(16-60)} \\
&= (\mathbf{X}'\boldsymbol{\Omega}_t^{-1}\mathbf{X})^{-1}\mathbf{X}'\boldsymbol{\Omega}_t^{-1}\mathbf{y} \text{ (of course).}
\end{aligned}
$$

Therefore, the updated coefficient vector $\boldsymbol{\beta}_{t+1}$ is computed by FGLS using the previously computed estimate of $\boldsymbol{\gamma}$ to compute $\boldsymbol{\Omega}$. We use the same approach for $\boldsymbol{\gamma}$:

$$
\boldsymbol{\gamma}_{t+1} = \boldsymbol{\gamma}_t + [2(\mathbf{Z}'\mathbf{Z})^{-1}]\left[\frac{1}{2}\sum_{i=1}^{n}\mathbf{z}_i\left(\frac{\varepsilon_i^2}{\exp(\mathbf{z}_i'\boldsymbol{\gamma})} - 1\right)\right]. \quad\quad \textbf{(16-61)}
$$

The 2 and $\frac{1}{2}$ cancel. The updated value of $\boldsymbol{\gamma}$ is computed by adding the vector of coefficients in the least squares regression of $[\varepsilon_i^2/\exp(\mathbf{z}_i'\boldsymbol{\gamma}) - 1]$ on $\mathbf{z}_i$ to the old one. Note that the correction is $2(\mathbf{Z}'\mathbf{Z})^{-1}\mathbf{Z}'(\partial \ln L/\partial\boldsymbol{\gamma})$, so convergence occurs when the derivative is zero.

The remaining detail is to determine the starting value for the iteration. Because any consistent estimator will do, the simplest procedure is to use OLS for $\boldsymbol{\beta}$ and the slopes in a regression of the logs of the squares of the least squares residuals on $\mathbf{z}_i$ for $\boldsymbol{\gamma}$. Harvey (1976) shows that this method will produce an inconsistent estimator of $\gamma_1 = \ln\sigma^2$, but the inconsistency can be corrected just by adding 1.2704 to the value obtained.[18] Thereafter, the iteration is simply:

1. Estimate the disturbance variance $\sigma_i^2$ with $\exp(\mathbf{z}_i'\boldsymbol{\gamma})$.
2. Compute $\boldsymbol{\beta}_{t+1}$ by FGLS.[19]
3. Update $\boldsymbol{\gamma}_t$ using the regression described in the preceding paragraph.
4. Compute $\mathbf{d}_{t+1} = [\boldsymbol{\beta}_{t+1}, \boldsymbol{\gamma}_{t+1}] - [\boldsymbol{\beta}_t, \boldsymbol{\gamma}_t]$. If $\mathbf{d}_{t+1}$ is large, then return to step 1.

If $\mathbf{d}_{t+1}$ at step 4 is sufficiently small, then exit the iteration. The asymptotic covariance matrix is simply $-\mathbf{H}^{-1}$, which is block diagonal with blocks

$$
\text{Asy. Var}[\hat{\boldsymbol{\beta}}_{ML}] = (\mathbf{X}'\boldsymbol{\Omega}^{-1}\mathbf{X})^{-1},
$$
$$
\text{Asy. Var}[\hat{\boldsymbol{\gamma}}_{ML}] = 2(\mathbf{Z}'\mathbf{Z})^{-1}.
$$

If desired, then $\hat{\sigma}^2 = \exp(\hat{\gamma}_1)$ can be computed. The asymptotic variance would be $[\exp(\gamma_1)]^2(\text{Asy. Var}[\hat{\gamma}_{1,ML}])$.

Testing the null hypothesis of homoscedasticity in this model,

$$
\text{H}_0: \boldsymbol{\alpha} = \mathbf{0}
$$

in (16-52), is particularly simple. The Wald test will be carried out by testing the hypothesis that the last M elements of $\boldsymbol{\gamma}$ are zero. Thus, the statistic will be

$$
\lambda_{WALD} = (0 \quad \hat{\boldsymbol{\alpha}}')\left[\frac{1}{2}(\mathbf{Z}'\mathbf{Z})\right]^{-1}\begin{pmatrix}0\\\hat{\boldsymbol{\alpha}}\end{pmatrix}.
$$

---

[18]He also presents a correction for the asymptotic covariance matrix for this first step estimator of $\boldsymbol{\gamma}$.

[19]The two-step estimator obtained by stopping here would be fully efficient if the starting value for $\boldsymbol{\gamma}$ were consistent, but it would not be the maximum likelihood estimator.

Because the first column in $\mathbf{Z}$ is a constant term, this reduces to

$$\lambda_{WALD} = 2\hat{\boldsymbol{\alpha}}'(\mathbf{Z}_1'\mathbf{M}^0\mathbf{Z}_1)^{-1}\hat{\boldsymbol{\alpha}}$$

where $\mathbf{Z}_1$ is the last $M$ columns of $\mathbf{Z}$, not including the column of ones, and $\mathbf{M}^0$ creates deviations from means. The likelihood ratio statistic is computed based on (16-54). Under both the null hypothesis (homoscedastic—using OLS) and the alternative (heteroscedastic—using MLE), the third term in $\ln L$ reduces to $-n/2$. Therefore, the statistic is simply

$$\lambda_{LR} = 2(\ln L_1 - \ln L_0) = n \ln s^2 - \sum_{i=1}^{n} \ln \hat{\sigma}_i^2,$$

where $s^2 = \mathbf{e}'\mathbf{e}/n$ using the OLS residuals. To compute the LM statistic, we will use the expected Hessian in (16-59). Under the null hypothesis, the part of the derivative vector in (16-55) that corresponds to $\boldsymbol{\beta}$ is $(1/s^2)\mathbf{X}'\mathbf{e} = \mathbf{0}$. Therefore, using (16-55), the LM statistic is

$$\lambda_{LM} = \left[ \frac{1}{2} \sum_{i=1}^{n} \left( \frac{e_i^2}{s^2} - 1 \right) \binom{1}{\mathbf{z}_{i1}} \right]' \left[ \frac{1}{2}(\mathbf{Z}'\mathbf{Z}) \right]^{-1} \left[ \frac{1}{2} \sum_{i=1}^{n} \left( \frac{e_i^2}{s^2} - 1 \right) \binom{1}{\mathbf{z}_{i1}} \right].$$

The first element in the derivative vector is zero, because $\sum_i e_i^2 = ns^2$. Therefore, the expression reduces to

$$\lambda_{LM} = \frac{1}{2} \left[ \sum_{i=1}^{n} \left( \frac{e_i^2}{s^2} - 1 \right) \mathbf{z}_{i1} \right]' (\mathbf{Z}_1'\mathbf{M}^0\mathbf{Z}_1)^{-1} \left[ \sum_{i=1}^{n} \left( \frac{e_i^2}{s^2} - 1 \right) \mathbf{z}_{i1} \right].$$

This is one-half times the explained sum of squares in the linear regression of the variable $h_i = (e_i^2/s^2 - 1)$ on $\mathbf{Z}$, which is the Breusch–Pagan/Godfrey LM statistic from Section 8.5.2.

### Example 16.6    Multiplicative Heteroscedasticity
In Example 6.2, we fit a cost function for the U.S. airline industry of the form

$$\ln C_{it} = \beta_1 + \beta_2 \ln Q_{it} + \beta_3 [\ln Q_{it}]^2 + \beta_4 \ln P_{fuel,i,t} + \beta_5 \, Loadfactor_{i,t} + \varepsilon_{i,t},$$

where $C_{i,t}$ is total cost, $Q_{i,t}$ is output, and $P_{fuel,i,t}$ is the price of fuel and the 90 observations in the data set are for six firms observed for 15 years. (The model also included dummy variables for firm and year, which we will omit for simplicity.) In Example 8.4, we fit a revised model in which the load factor appears in the variance of $\varepsilon_{i,t}$ rather than in the regression function. The model is

$$\sigma_{i,t}^2 = \sigma^2 \exp(\alpha \, Loadfactor_{i,t})$$

$$= \exp(\gamma_1 + \gamma_2 \, Loadfactor_{i,t}).$$

Estimates were obtained by iterating the weighted least squares procedure using weights $W_{i,t} = \exp(-c_1 - c_2 \, Loadfactor_{i,t})$. The estimates of $\gamma_1$ and $\gamma_2$ were obtained at each iteration by regressing the logs of the squared residuals on a constant and $Loadfactor_{it}$. It was noted at the end of the example [and is evident in (16-61)] that these would be the wrong weights to use for the iterated weighted least if we wish to compute the MLE. Table 16.2 reproduces the results from Example 8.4 and adds the MLEs produced using Harvey's method. The MLE of $\gamma_2$ is substantially different from the earlier result. The Wald statistic for testing the

**TABLE 16.2** Multiplicative Heteroscedasticity Model

| | Constant | Ln Q | Ln² Q | Ln P_f | R² | Sum of Squares |
|---|---|---|---|---|---|---|
| OLS | 9.1382 | 0.92615 | 0.029145 | 0.41006 | | |
| ln L = 54.2747 | 0.24507[a] | 0.032306 | 0.012304 | 0.018807 | 0.9861674[c] | 1.577479[d] |
| | 0.22595[b] | 0.030128 | 0.011346 | 0.017524 | | |
| Two-step | 9.2463 | 0.92136 | 0.024450 | 0.40352 | | |
| | 0.21896 | 0.033028 | 0.011412 | 0.016974 | 0.986119 | 1.612938 |
| Iterated[e] | 9.2774 | 0.91609 | 0.021643 | 0.40174 | | |
| | 0.20977 | 0.032993 | 0.011017 | 0.016332 | 0.986071 | 1.645693 |
| MLE[f] | 9.2611 | 0.91931 | 0.023281 | 0.40266 | | |
| ln L = 57.3122 | 0.2099 | 0.032295 | 0.010987 | 0.016304 | 0.986100 | 1.626301 |

[a] Conventional OLS standard errors
[b] White robust standard errors
[c] Squared correlation between actual and fitted values
[d] Sum of squared residuals
[e] Values of $c_2$ by iteration: 8.254344, 11.622473, 11.705029, 11.710618, 11.711012, 11.711040, 11.711042
[f] Estimate of $\gamma_2$ is 9.78076 (2.839).

homoscedasticity restriction ($\alpha = 0$) is $(9.78076/2.839)^2 = 11.869$, which is greater than 3.84, so the null hypothesis would be rejected. The likelihood ratio statistic is $-2(54.2747 - 57.3122) = 6.075$, which produces the same conclusion. However, the LM statistic is 2.96, which conflicts. This is a finite sample result that is not uncommon.

### 16.9.2.b   Autocorrelation

At various points in the preceding sections, we have considered models in which there is correlation across observations, including the spatial autocorrelation case in Section 9.7.2, autocorrelated disturbances in panel data models [Section 9.6.3 and in (9-28)], and in the seemingly unrelated regressions model in Section 10.2.6. The first order autoregression model examined there will be formalized in detail in Chapter 19. We will briefly examine it here to highlight some useful results about the maximum likelihood estimator.

The linear regression model with first order autoregressive [AR(1)] disturbances is

$$y_t = \mathbf{x}_t'\boldsymbol{\beta} + \varepsilon_t, t = 1, \ldots, T,$$

$$\varepsilon_t = \rho\varepsilon_t + u_t, |\rho| < 1,$$

$$E[u_t \mid \mathbf{X}] = 0$$

$$E[u_t u_s \mid \mathbf{X}] = \sigma_u^2 \quad \text{if } t = s \quad \text{and 0 otherwise.}$$

Feasible GLS estimation of the parameters of this model is examined in detail in Chapter 19. We now add the assumption of normality; $u_t \sim N[0, \sigma_u^2]$, and construct the maximum likelihood estimator.

Because every observation on $y_t$ is correlated with every other observation, in principle, to form the likelihood function, we have the joint density of one $T$-variate observation. The Prais and Winsten (1954) transformation in (19-28) suggests a useful way to reformulate this density. We can write

$$f(y_1, y_2, \ldots, y_T) = f(y_1) f(y_2 \mid y_1), \; f(y_3 \mid y_2) \ldots, f(y_T \mid y_{T-1}).$$

Because

$$\sqrt{1 - \rho^2}\, y_1 = \sqrt{1 - \rho^2}\, \mathbf{x}_1' \boldsymbol{\beta} + u_1$$

$$y_t \mid y_{t-1} = \rho y_{t-1} + (\mathbf{x}_t - \rho \mathbf{x}_{t-1})' \boldsymbol{\beta} + u_t, \tag{16-62}$$

and the observations on $u_t$ are independently normally distributed, we can use these results to form the log-likelihood function,

$$\ln L = \left[ -\frac{1}{2} \ln 2\pi - \frac{1}{2} \ln \sigma_u^2 - \frac{1}{2} \ln(1 - \rho^2) - \frac{(1 - \rho^2)(y_1 - \mathbf{x}_1' \boldsymbol{\beta})^2}{2\sigma_u^2} \right]$$

$$+ \sum_{t=2}^{T} \left[ -\frac{1}{2} \ln 2\pi - \frac{1}{2} \ln \sigma_u^2 - \frac{[(y_t - \rho y_{t-1}) - (\mathbf{x}_t - \rho \mathbf{x}_{t-1})' \boldsymbol{\beta}]^2}{2\sigma_v^2} \right]. \tag{16-63}$$

As usual, the MLE of $\boldsymbol{\beta}$ is GLS based on the MLEs of $\sigma_u^2$ and $\rho$, and the MLE for $\sigma_u^2$ will be $\mathbf{u}'\mathbf{u}/T$ given $\boldsymbol{\beta}$ and $\rho$. The complication is how to compute $\rho$. As we will note in Chapter 19, there is a strikingly large number of choices for consistently estimating $\rho$ in the AR(1) model. It is tempting to choose the most convenient, then begin the back and forth iterations between $\boldsymbol{\beta}$ and $(\sigma_u^2, \rho)$ to obtain the MLE. However, this strategy will not (in general) locate the MLE unless the intermediate estimates of the variance parameters also satisfy the likelihood equation, which for $\rho$ is

$$\frac{\partial \ln L}{\partial \rho} = \frac{\rho \varepsilon_1}{\sigma_u^2} - \frac{\rho}{1 - \rho^2} + \sum_{t=2}^{T} \frac{u_t \varepsilon_{t-1}}{\sigma_u^2}.$$

One could sidestep the problem simply by scanning the range of $\rho$ of $(-1, +1)$ and computing the other estimators at every point, to locate the maximum of the likelihood function by brute force. With modern computers, even with long time series, the amount of computation involved would be minor (if a bit inelegant and inefficient). Beach and MacKinnon (1978a) developed a more systematic algorithm for searching for $\rho$ in this model. The iteration is then defined between $\rho$ and $(\boldsymbol{\beta}, \sigma_u^2)$ as usual.

The information matrix for this log-likelihood is

$$-E \left[ \frac{\partial^2 \ln L}{\partial \begin{pmatrix} \boldsymbol{\beta} \\ \sigma_u^2 \\ \rho \end{pmatrix} \partial (\boldsymbol{\beta}' \sigma_u^2 \, \rho)} \right] = \begin{bmatrix} \dfrac{1}{\sigma_u^2} \mathbf{X}' \boldsymbol{\Omega}^{-1} \mathbf{X} & \mathbf{0} & \mathbf{0} \\[2mm] \mathbf{0}' & \dfrac{T}{2\sigma_u^4} & \dfrac{\rho}{\sigma_u^2(1 - \rho^2)} \\[2mm] \mathbf{0}' & \dfrac{\rho}{\sigma_u^2(1 - \rho^2)} & \dfrac{T - 2}{1 - \rho^2} + \dfrac{1 + \rho^2}{(1 - \rho^2)^2} \end{bmatrix}. \tag{16-64}$$

Note that the diagonal elements in the matrix are $O(T)$. But the $(2, 3)$ and $(3, 2)$ elements are constants of $O(1)$ that will, like the second part of the $(3, 3)$ element, become minimal as $T$ increases. Dropping these "end effects" (and treating $T - 2$ as the same as $T$ when $T$ increases) produces a diagonal matrix from which we extract the

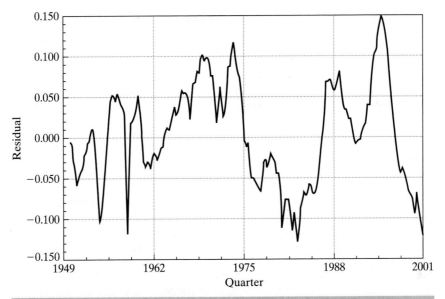

**FIGURE 16.3** Residuals from Estimated Money Demand Equation.

standard approximations for the MLEs in this model:

$$\text{Asy. Var}[\hat{\boldsymbol{\beta}}] = \sigma_u^2 (\mathbf{X}'\boldsymbol{\Omega}^{-1}\mathbf{X})^{-1},$$

$$\text{Asy. Var}[\hat{\sigma}_u^2] = \frac{2\sigma_u^4}{T}, \qquad (16\text{-}65)$$

$$\text{Asy. Var}[\hat{\rho}] = \frac{1 - \rho^2}{T}.$$

***Example 16.7  Autocorrelation in a Money Demand Equation***
Using the macroeconomic data in Table F5.1, we fit a money demand equation,

$$\ln(M1/CPI\_u)_t = \beta_1 + \beta_2 \ln Real\ GDP_t + \beta_3 \ln T\text{-}bill\ rate_t + \varepsilon_t.$$

The least squares residuals shown in Figure 16.3 display the typical pattern for a highly autocorrelated series.

The simple first-order autocorrelation of the ordinary least squares residuals is $r = 0.9557002$. We then refit the model using the Prais and Winsten FGLS estimator and the maximum likelihood estimator using the Beach and MacKinnon algorithm. The results are shown in Table 16.3. Although the OLS estimator is consistent in this model, nonetheless, the FGLS and ML estimates are quite different.

### 16.9.3  SEEMINGLY UNRELATED REGRESSION MODELS

The general form of the seemingly unrelated regression (SUR) model is given in (10-1)–(10-3);

$$\mathbf{y}_i = \mathbf{X}_i \boldsymbol{\beta}_i + \boldsymbol{\varepsilon}_i, i = 1, \ldots, M,$$

$$E[\boldsymbol{\varepsilon}_i \mid \mathbf{X}_1, \ldots, \mathbf{X}_M] = 0, \qquad (16\text{-}66)$$

$$E[\boldsymbol{\varepsilon}_i \boldsymbol{\varepsilon}_j' \mid \mathbf{X}_1, \ldots, \mathbf{X}_M] = \sigma_{ij}\mathbf{I}$$

**TABLE 16.3** Estimates of Money Demand Equation: $T = 204$

| Variable | OLS | | Prais and Winsten | | Maximum Likelihood | |
|---|---|---|---|---|---|---|
| | Estimate | Std. Error | Estimate | Std. Error | Estimate | Std. Error |
| Constant | −2.1316 | 0.09100 | −1.4755 | 0.2550 | −1.6319 | 0.4296 |
| Ln real GDP | 0.3519 | 0.01205 | 0.2549 | 0.03097 | 0.2731 | 0.0518 |
| Ln T-bill rate | −0.1249 | 0.009841 | −0.02666 | 0.007007 | −0.02522 | 0.006941 |
| $\sigma_\varepsilon$ | | 0.06185 | | 0.07767 | | 0.07571 |
| $\sigma_u$ | | 0.06185 | | 0.01298 | | 0.01273 |
| $\rho$ | 0. | 0. | 0.9557 | 0.02061 | 0.9858 | 0.01180 |

FGLS estimation of this model is examined in detail in Section 10.2.3. We will now add the assumption of normally distributed disturbances to the model and develop the maximum likelihood estimators. Given the covariance structure defined in (16-66), the joint normality assumption applies to the vector of $M$ disturbances observed at time $t$, which we write as

$$\boldsymbol{\varepsilon}_t \mid \mathbf{X}_1, \ldots, \mathbf{X}_M \sim N[\mathbf{0}, \boldsymbol{\Sigma}], t = 1, \ldots, T. \tag{16-67}$$

### 16.9.3.a The Pooled Model

The pooled model, in which all coefficient vectors are equal, provides a convenient starting point. With the assumption of equal coefficient vectors, the regression model becomes

$$y_{it} = \mathbf{x}_{it}\boldsymbol{\beta} + \varepsilon_{it},$$

$$E[\varepsilon_{it} \mid \mathbf{X}_1, \ldots, \mathbf{X}_M] = 0, \tag{16-68}$$

$$E[\varepsilon_{it}\varepsilon_{js} \mid \mathbf{X}_1, \ldots, \mathbf{X}_M] = \sigma_{ij} \quad \text{if} \quad t = s, \quad \text{and} \quad 0 \quad \text{if} \quad t \neq s.$$

This is a model of heteroscedasticity and cross-sectional correlation. With multivariate normality, the log likelihood is

$$\ln L = \sum_{t=1}^{T} \left[ -\frac{M}{2} \ln 2\pi - \frac{1}{2} \ln |\boldsymbol{\Sigma}| - \frac{1}{2} \boldsymbol{\varepsilon}_t' \boldsymbol{\Sigma}^{-1} \boldsymbol{\varepsilon}_t \right]. \tag{16-69}$$

As we saw earlier, the efficient estimator for this model is GLS as shown in (10-21). Because the elements of $\boldsymbol{\Sigma}$ must be estimated, the FGLS estimator based on (10-9) is used.

As we have seen in several applications now, the maximum likelihood estimator of $\boldsymbol{\beta}$, given $\boldsymbol{\Sigma}$, is GLS, based on (10-21). The maximum likelihood estimator of $\boldsymbol{\Sigma}$ is

$$\hat{\sigma}_{ij} = \frac{\left(\mathbf{y}_i' - \mathbf{X}_i \hat{\boldsymbol{\beta}}_{ML}\right)'\left(\mathbf{y}_j - \mathbf{X}_j \hat{\boldsymbol{\beta}}_{ML}\right)}{T} = \frac{\hat{\boldsymbol{\varepsilon}}_i' \hat{\boldsymbol{\varepsilon}}_j}{T} \tag{16-70}$$

based on the MLE of $\boldsymbol{\beta}$. If each MLE requires the other, how can we proceed to obtain both? The answer is provided by **Oberhofer and Kmenta** (1974), who show that for certain models, including this one, one can iterate back and forth between the two estimators. Thus, the MLEs are obtained by iterating to convergence between

(16-70) and

$$\hat{\hat{\beta}} = [\mathbf{X}'\hat{\Omega}^{-1}\mathbf{X}]^{-1}[\mathbf{X}'\hat{\Omega}^{-1}\mathbf{y}]. \tag{16-71}$$

The process may begin with the (consistent) ordinary least squares estimator, then (16-70), and so on. The computations are simple, using basic matrix algebra. Hypothesis tests about $\beta$ may be done using the familiar Wald statistic. The appropriate estimator of the asymptotic covariance matrix is the inverse matrix in brackets in (10-21).

For testing the hypothesis that the off-diagonal elements of $\Sigma$ are zero—that is, that there is no correlation across firms—there are three approaches. The likelihood ratio test is based on the statistic

$$\lambda_{LR} = T(\ln|\hat{\Sigma}_{heteroscedastic}| - \ln|\hat{\Sigma}_{general}|) = T\left(\sum_{i=1}^{M}\ln\hat{\sigma}_i^2 - \ln|\hat{\Sigma}|\right), \tag{16-72}$$

where $\hat{\sigma}_i^2$ are the estimates of $\sigma_i^2$ obtained from the maximum likelihood estimates of the groupwise heteroscedastic model and $\hat{\Sigma}$ is the maximum likelihood estimator in the unrestricted model. (Note how the excess variation produced by the restrictive model is used to construct the test.) The large-sample distribution of the statistic is chi-squared with $M(M-1)/2$ degrees of freedom. The Lagrange multiplier test developed by Breusch and Pagan (1980) provides an alternative. The general form of the statistic is

$$\lambda_{LM} = T\sum_{i=2}^{n}\sum_{j=1}^{i-1}r_{ij}^2, \tag{16-73}$$

where $r_{ij}^2$ is the $ij$th residual correlation coefficient. If every equation had a different parameter vector, then equation specific ordinary least squares would be efficient (and ML) and we would compute $r_{ij}$ from the OLS residuals (assuming that there are sufficient observations for the computation). Here, however, we are assuming only a single-parameter vector. Therefore, the appropriate basis for computing the correlations is the residuals from the iterated estimator in the groupwise heteroscedastic model, that is, the same residuals used to compute $\hat{\sigma}_i^2$. (An asymptotically valid approximation to the test can be based on the FGLS residuals instead.) Note that this is not a procedure for testing all the way down to the classical, homoscedastic regression model. That case involves different LM and LR statistics based on the groupwise heteroscedasticity model. If either the LR statistic in (16-72) or the LM statistic in (16-73) are smaller than the critical value from the table, the conclusion, based on this test, is that the appropriate model is the groupwise heteroscedastic model.

### 16.9.3.b    The SUR Model

The Oberhofer–Kmenta (1974) conditions are met for the seemingly unrelated regressions model, so maximum likelihood estimates can be obtained by iterating the FGLS procedure. We note, once again, that this procedure presumes the use of (10-9) for estimation of $\sigma_{ij}$ at each iteration. Maximum likelihood enjoys no advantages over FGLS in its asymptotic properties.[20] Whether it would be preferable in a small sample is an open question whose answer will depend on the particular data set.

---

[20]Jensen (1995) considers some variation on the computation of the asymptotic covariance matrix for the estimator that allows for the possibility that the normality assumption might be violated.

### 16.9.3.c    Exclusion Restrictions

By simply inserting the special form of $\boldsymbol{\Omega}$ in the log-likelihood function for the generalized regression model in (16-48), we can consider direct maximization instead of iterated FGLS. It is useful, however, to reexamine the model in a somewhat different formulation. This alternative construction of the likelihood function appears in many other related models in a number of literatures.

Consider one observation on each of the $M$ dependent variables and their associated regressors. We wish to arrange this observation horizontally instead of vertically. The model for this observation can be written

$$[y_1 \quad y_2 \quad \cdots \quad y_M]_t = [\mathbf{x}_t^*]'[\boldsymbol{\pi}_1 \quad \boldsymbol{\pi}_2 \quad \cdots \quad \boldsymbol{\pi}_M] + [\varepsilon_1 \quad \varepsilon_2 \quad \cdots \quad \varepsilon_M]_t$$

$$= [\mathbf{x}_t^*]'\boldsymbol{\Pi} + \mathbf{E}, \tag{16-74}$$

where $\mathbf{x}_t^*$ is the full set of all $K^*$ *different* independent variables that appear in the model. The parameter matrix then has one column for each equation, but the columns are not the same as $\boldsymbol{\beta}_i$ in (16-66) unless every variable happens to appear in every equation. Otherwise, in the $i$th equation, $\boldsymbol{\pi}_i$ will have a number of zeros in it, each one imposing an **exclusion restriction.** For example, consider a two-equation model for production costs for two airlines,

$$C_{1t} = \alpha_1 + \beta_{1P} P_{1t} + \beta_{1L} LF_{1t} + \varepsilon_{1t},$$

$$C_{2t} = \alpha_2 + \beta_{2P} P_{2t} + \beta_{2L} LF_{2t} + \varepsilon_{2t},$$

where $C$ is cost, $P$ is fuel price, and $LF$ is load factor. The $t$th observation would be

$$[C_1 \quad C_2]_t = [1 \quad P_1 \quad LF_1 \quad P_2 \quad LF_2]_t \begin{bmatrix} \alpha_1 & \alpha_2 \\ \beta_{1P} & 0 \\ \beta_{1L} & 0 \\ 0 & \beta_{2P} \\ 0 & \beta_{2L} \end{bmatrix} + [\varepsilon_1 \quad \varepsilon_2]_t.$$

This vector is one observation. Let $\boldsymbol{\varepsilon}_t$ be the vector of $M$ disturbances for this observation arranged, for now, in a column. Then $E[\boldsymbol{\varepsilon}_t \boldsymbol{\varepsilon}_t'] = \boldsymbol{\Sigma}$. The log of the joint normal density of these $M$ disturbances is

$$\ln L_t = -\frac{M}{2} \ln(2\pi) - \frac{1}{2} \ln|\boldsymbol{\Sigma}| - \frac{1}{2} \boldsymbol{\varepsilon}_t' \boldsymbol{\Sigma}^{-1} \boldsymbol{\varepsilon}_t. \tag{16-75}$$

The log-likelihood for a sample of $T$ joint observations is the sum of these over $t$:

$$\ln L = \sum_{t=1}^{T} \ln L_t = -\frac{MT}{2} \ln(2\pi) - \frac{T}{2} \ln|\boldsymbol{\Sigma}| - \frac{1}{2} \sum_{t=1}^{T} \boldsymbol{\varepsilon}_t' \boldsymbol{\Sigma}^{-1} \boldsymbol{\varepsilon}_t. \tag{16-76}$$

The term in the summation in (16-76) is a scalar that equals its trace. We can always permute the matrices in a trace, so

$$\sum_{t=1}^{T} \boldsymbol{\varepsilon}_t' \boldsymbol{\Sigma}^{-1} \boldsymbol{\varepsilon}_t = \sum_{t=1}^{T} \text{tr}(\boldsymbol{\varepsilon}_t' \boldsymbol{\Sigma}^{-1} \boldsymbol{\varepsilon}_t) = \sum_{t=1}^{T} \text{tr}(\boldsymbol{\Sigma}^{-1} \boldsymbol{\varepsilon}_t \boldsymbol{\varepsilon}_t'). \tag{16-77}$$

This can be further simplified. The sum of the traces of $T$ matrices equals the trace of the sum of the matrices [see (A-91)]. We will now also be able to move the constant matrix, $\Sigma^{-1}$, outside the summation. Finally, it will prove useful to multiply and divide by $T$. Combining all three steps, we obtain

$$\sum_{t=1}^{T} \text{tr}(\Sigma^{-1}\varepsilon_t \varepsilon_t') = T \, \text{tr}\left[\Sigma^{-1}\left(\frac{1}{T}\right)\sum_{t=1}^{T}\varepsilon_t \varepsilon_t'\right] = T \, \text{tr}(\Sigma^{-1}\mathbf{W}), \qquad \textbf{(16-78)}$$

where

$$\mathbf{W}_{ij} = \frac{1}{T}\sum_{t=1}^{T}\varepsilon_{ti}\varepsilon_{tj}.$$

Because this step uses actual disturbances, $E[\mathbf{W}_{ij}] = \sigma_{ij}$; $\mathbf{W}$ is the $M \times M$ matrix we would use to estimate $\Sigma$ if the $\varepsilon$'s were actually observed. Inserting this result in the log-likelihood, we have

$$\ln L = -\frac{T}{2}[M\ln(2\pi) + \ln|\Sigma| + \text{tr}(\Sigma^{-1}\mathbf{W})]. \qquad \textbf{(16-79)}$$

We now consider maximizing this function.

It has been shown[21] that

$$\frac{\partial \ln L}{\partial \mathbf{\Pi}'} = \frac{T}{2}\mathbf{X}^{*\prime}\mathbf{E}\Sigma^{-1},$$

$$\frac{\partial \ln L}{\partial \Sigma} = -\frac{T}{2}\Sigma^{-1}(\Sigma - \mathbf{W})\Sigma^{-1}. \qquad \textbf{(16-80)}$$

where the $\mathbf{x}_t^{*\prime}$ in (16-74) is row $t$ of $\mathbf{X}^*$. Equating the second of these derivatives to a zero matrix, we see that given the maximum likelihood estimates of the slope parameters, the maximum likelihood estimator of $\Sigma$ is $\mathbf{W}$, the matrix of mean residual sums of squares and cross products—that is, the matrix we have used for FGLS. [Notice that there is no correction for degrees of freedom; $\partial \ln L/\partial \Sigma = \mathbf{0}$ implies (10-9).]

We also know that because this model is a generalized regression model, the maximum likelihood estimator of the parameter matrix $[\boldsymbol{\beta}]$ must be equivalent to the FGLS estimator we discussed earlier.[22] It is useful to go a step further. If we insert our solution for $\Sigma$ in the likelihood function, then we obtain the **concentrated log-likelihood,**

$$\ln L_c = -\frac{T}{2}[M(1 + \ln(2\pi)) + \ln|\mathbf{W}|]. \qquad \textbf{(16-81)}$$

We have shown, therefore, that the criterion for choosing the maximum likelihood estimator of $\boldsymbol{\beta}$ is

$$\hat{\boldsymbol{\beta}}_{\text{ML}} = \text{Min}_{\boldsymbol{\beta}} \tfrac{1}{2} \ln|\mathbf{W}|, \qquad \textbf{(16-82)}$$

*subject to the exclusion restrictions.* This important result reappears in many other models and settings. This minimization must be done subject to the constraints in the parameter matrix. In our two-equation example, there are two blocks of zeros in the

---

[21] See, for example, Joreskog (1973).

[22] This equivalence establishes the Oberhofer–Kmenta conditions.

parameter matrix, which must be present in the MLE as well. The estimator of $\beta$ is the set of nonzero elements in the parameter matrix in (16-74).

The **likelihood ratio statistic** is an alternative to the $F$ statistic discussed earlier for testing hypotheses about $\beta$. The likelihood ratio statistic is[23]

$$\lambda = -2(\log L_r - \log L_u) = T(\log|\hat{\mathbf{W}}_r| - \log|\hat{\mathbf{W}}_u|), \tag{16-83}$$

where $\hat{\mathbf{W}}_r$ and $\hat{\mathbf{W}}_u$ are the residual sums of squares and cross-product matrices using the constrained and unconstrained estimators, respectively. Under the null hypothesis of the restrictions, the limiting distribution of the likelihood ratio statistic is chi-squared with degrees of freedom equal to the number of restrictions. This procedure can also be used to test the homogeneity restriction in the multivariate regression model. The restricted model is the pooled model discussed in the preceding section.

It may also be of interest to test whether $\Sigma$ is a diagonal matrix. Two possible approaches were suggested in Section 16.9.3a [see (16-72) and (16-73)]. The unrestricted model is the one we are using here, whereas the restricted model is the groupwise heteroscedastic model of Section 8.8.2 (Example 8.5), without the restriction of equal-parameter vectors. As such, the restricted model reduces to separate regression models, estimable by ordinary least squares. The likelihood ratio statistic would be

$$\lambda_{\mathrm{LR}} = T\left[\sum_{i=1}^{M} \log \hat{\sigma}_i^2 - \log|\hat{\Sigma}|\right], \tag{16-84}$$

where $\hat{\sigma}_i^2$ is $\mathbf{e}_i'\mathbf{e}_i/T$ from the individual least squares regressions and $\hat{\Sigma}$ is the maximum likelihood estimate of $\Sigma$. This statistic has a limiting chi-squared distribution with $M(M-1)/2$ degrees of freedom under the hypothesis. The alternative suggested by Breusch and Pagan (1980) is the **Lagrange multiplier statistic,**

$$\lambda_{\mathrm{LM}} = T\sum_{i=2}^{M}\sum_{j=1}^{i-1} r_{ij}^2, \tag{16-85}$$

where $r_{ij}$ is the estimated correlation $\hat{\sigma}_{ij}/[\hat{\sigma}_{ii}\hat{\sigma}_{jj}]^{1/2}$. This statistic also has a limiting chi-squared distribution with $M(M-1)/2$ degrees of freedom. This test has the advantage that it does not require computation of the maximum likelihood estimator of $\Sigma$, because it is based on the OLS residuals.

### Example 16.8  ML Estimates of a Seemingly Unrelated Regressions Model

Although a bit dated, the Grunfeld data used in Application 9.1 have withstood the test of time and are still the standard data set used to demonstrate the SUR model. The data in Appendix Table F9.3 are for 10 firms and 20 years (1935–1954). For the purpose of this illustration, we will use the first four firms. [The data are downloaded from the website for Baltagi (2005), at http://www.wiley.com/legacy/wileychi/baltagi/supp/Grunfeld.fil.]

The model is an investment equation:

$$I_{it} = \beta_{1i} + \beta_{2i} F_{it} + \beta_{3i} C_{it} + \varepsilon_{it}, t = 1, \dots, 20, i = 1, \dots, 10,$$

---

[23] See Attfield (1998) for refinements of this calculation to improve the small sample performance.

where

$$I_{it} = \text{real gross investment for firm } i \text{ in year } t,$$
$$F_{it} = \text{real value of the firm-shares outstanding,}$$
$$C_{it} = \text{real value of the capital stock.}$$

The OLS estimates for the four equations are shown in the left panel of Table 16.4. The correlation matrix for the four OLS residual vectors is

$$\mathbf{R_e} = \begin{bmatrix} 1 & -0.261 & 0.279 & -0.273 \\ -0.261 & 1 & 0.428 & 0.338 \\ 0.279 & 0.428 & 1 & -0.0679 \\ -0.273 & 0.338 & -0.0679 & 1 \end{bmatrix}.$$

Before turning to the FGLS and MLE estimates, we carry out the LM test against the null hypothesis that the regressions are actually unrelated. We leave as an exercise to show that the LM statistic in (16-85) can be computed as

$$\lambda_{LM} = (T/2)[\text{trace}(\mathbf{R'_e R_e}) - M] = 10.451.$$

The 95 percent critical value from the chi squared distribution with 6 degrees of freedom is 12.59, so at this point, it appears that the null hypothesis is not rejected. We will proceed in spite of this finding.

The next step is to compute the covariance matrix for the OLS residuals using

$$\mathbf{W} = (1/T)\mathbf{E'E} = \begin{bmatrix} \mathbf{7160.29} & -1967.05 & 607.533 & -282.756 \\ -1967.05 & \mathbf{7904.66} & 978.45 & 367.84 \\ 607.533 & 978.45 & \mathbf{660.829} & -21.3757 \\ -282.756 & 367.84 & -21.3757 & \mathbf{149.872} \end{bmatrix},$$

where $\mathbf{E}$ is the $20 \times 4$ matrix of OLS residuals. Stacking the data in the partitioned matrices

$$\mathbf{X} = \begin{bmatrix} \mathbf{X_1} & \mathbf{0} & \mathbf{0} & \mathbf{0} \\ \mathbf{0} & \mathbf{X_2} & \mathbf{0} & \mathbf{0} \\ \mathbf{0} & \mathbf{0} & \mathbf{X_3} & \mathbf{0} \\ \mathbf{0} & \mathbf{0} & \mathbf{0} & \mathbf{X_4} \end{bmatrix} \quad \text{and} \quad \mathbf{y} = \begin{bmatrix} \mathbf{y_1} \\ \mathbf{y_2} \\ \mathbf{y_3} \\ \mathbf{y_4} \end{bmatrix},$$

we now compute $\hat{\mathbf{\Omega}} = \mathbf{W} \otimes \mathbf{I}_{20}$ and the FGLS estimates,

$$\hat{\beta} = [\mathbf{X'}\hat{\mathbf{\Omega}}^{-1}\mathbf{X}]^{-1}\mathbf{X'}\hat{\mathbf{\Omega}}^{-1}\mathbf{y}.$$

The estimated asymptotic covariance matrix for the FGLS estimates is the bracketed inverse matrix. These results are shown in the center panel in Table 16.4.

To compute the MLE, we will take advantage of the Oberhofer and Kmenta (1974) result and iterate the FGLS estimator. Using the FGLS coefficient vector, we recompute the residuals, then recompute $\mathbf{W}$, then reestimate $\beta$. The iteration is repeated until the estimated parameter vector converges. We use as our convergence measure the following criterion based on the change in the estimated parameter from iteration $(s-1)$ to iteration $(s)$:

$$\delta = [\hat{\beta}(s) - \hat{\beta}(s-1)][\mathbf{X'}[\hat{\mathbf{\Omega}}(s)]^{-1}\mathbf{X}][\hat{\beta}(s) - \hat{\beta}(s-1)].$$

The sequence of values of this criterion function are: 0.21922, 0.16318, 0.00662, 0.00037, 0.00002367825, 0.000001563348, 0.1041980 × 10⁻⁶. We exit the iterations after iteration 7. The ML estimates are shown in the right panel of Table 16.4.

We then carry out the likelihood ratio test of the null hypothesis of a diagonal covariance matrix. The maximum likelihood estimate of $\Sigma$ is

$$\hat{\Sigma} = \begin{bmatrix} \mathbf{7235.46} & -2455.13 & 615.167 & -325.413 \\ -2455.13 & \mathbf{8146.41} & 1288.66 & 427.011 \\ 615.167 & 1288.66 & \mathbf{702.268} & 2.51786 \\ -325.413 & 427.011 & 2.51786 & \mathbf{153.889} \end{bmatrix}$$

**TABLE 16.4** Estimated Investment Equations

| Firm | Variable | OLS Estimate | OLS St. Er. | FGLS Estimate | FGLS St. Er. | MLE Estimate | MLE St. Er. |
|------|----------|----------|----------|----------|----------|----------|----------|
| 1 | Constant | −149.78 | 97.58 | −160.68 | 90.41 | −179.41 | 86.66 |
| | F | 0.1192 | 0.02382 | 0.1205 | 0.02187 | 0.1248 | 0.02086 |
| | C | 0.3714 | 0.03418 | 0.3800 | 0.03311 | 0.3802 | 0.03266 |
| 2 | Constant | −49.19 | 136.52 | 21.16 | 116.18 | 36.46 | 106.18 |
| | F | 0.1749 | 0.06841 | 0.1304 | 0.05737 | 0.1244 | 0.05191 |
| | C | 0.3896 | 0.1312 | 0.4485 | 0.1225 | 0.4367 | 0.1171 |
| 3 | Constant | −9.956 | 28.92 | −19.72 | 26.58 | −24.10 | 25.80 |
| | F | 0.02655 | 0.01435 | 0.03464 | 0.01279 | 0.03808 | 0.01217 |
| | C | 0.1517 | 0.02370 | 0.1368 | 0.02249 | 0.1311 | 0.02223 |
| 4 | Constant | −6.190 | 12.45 | 0.9366 | 11.59 | 2.581 | 11.54 |
| | F | 0.07795 | 0.01841 | 0.06785 | 0.01705 | 0.06564 | 0.01698 |
| | C | 0.3157 | 0.02656 | 0.3146 | 0.02606 | 0.3137 | 0.02617 |

The estimate for the constrained model is the diagonal matrix formed from the diagonals of $\mathbf{W}$ shown earlier for the OLS results. (The estimates are shown in boldface in the preceding matrix.) The test statistic is then

$$\text{LR} = T(\ln|\text{diag}(\mathbf{W})| - \ln|\hat{\boldsymbol{\Sigma}}|) = 18.55.$$

Recall that the critical value is 12.59. The results contradict the LM statistic. The hypothesis of diagonal covariance matrix is now rejected.

Note that aside from the constants, the four sets of coefficient estimates are fairly similar. Because of the constants, there seems little doubt that the pooling restriction will be rejected. To find out, we compute the Wald statistic based on the MLE results. For testing

$$H_0: \boldsymbol{\beta}_1 = \boldsymbol{\beta}_2 = \boldsymbol{\beta}_3 = \boldsymbol{\beta}_4,$$

we can formulate the hypothesis as

$$H_0: \boldsymbol{\beta}_1 - \boldsymbol{\beta}_4 = \mathbf{0}, \boldsymbol{\beta}_2 - \boldsymbol{\beta}_4 = \mathbf{0}, \boldsymbol{\beta}_3 - \boldsymbol{\beta}_4 = \mathbf{0}.$$

The Wald statistic is

$$\lambda_W = (\mathbf{R}\hat{\boldsymbol{\beta}} - \mathbf{q})'[\mathbf{R}\mathbf{V}\mathbf{R}']^{-1}(\mathbf{R}\hat{\boldsymbol{\beta}} - \mathbf{q}) = 2190.96$$

where $\mathbf{R} = \begin{bmatrix} \mathbf{I}_3 & \mathbf{0} & \mathbf{0} & -\mathbf{I}_3 \\ \mathbf{0} & \mathbf{I}_3 & \mathbf{0} & -\mathbf{I}_3 \\ \mathbf{0} & \mathbf{0} & \mathbf{I}_3 & -\mathbf{I}_3 \end{bmatrix}$, $\mathbf{q} = \begin{bmatrix} \mathbf{0} \\ \mathbf{0} \\ \mathbf{0} \end{bmatrix}$, and $\mathbf{V} = [\mathbf{X}'\hat{\boldsymbol{\Omega}}^{-1}\mathbf{X}]^{-1}$. Under the null hypothesis, the Wald statistic has a limiting chi-squared distribution with 9 degrees of freedom. The critical value is 16.92, so, as expected, the hypothesis is rejected. It may be that the difference is due to the different constant terms. To test the hypothesis that the four pairs of slope coefficients are equal, we replaced the $\mathbf{I}_3$ in $\mathbf{R}$ with $[\mathbf{0}, \mathbf{I}_2]$, the $\mathbf{0}$s with $2 \times 3$ zero matrices and $\mathbf{q}$ with a $6 \times 1$ zero vector, The resulting chi-squared statistic equals 229.005. The critical value is 12.59, so this hypothesis is rejected also.

### 16.9.4 SIMULTANEOUS EQUATIONS MODELS

In Chapter 13, we noted two approaches to maximum likelihood estimation in the equation system

$$\mathbf{y}_t'\boldsymbol{\Gamma} + \mathbf{x}_t'\mathbf{B} = \boldsymbol{\varepsilon}_t',$$

$$\boldsymbol{\varepsilon}_t \mid \mathbf{X} \sim N[\mathbf{0}, \boldsymbol{\Sigma}].$$

**(16-86)**

The limited information maximum likelihood (LIML) estimator is a single-equation approach that estimates the parameters one equation at a time. The full information maximum likelihood (FIML) estimator analyzes the full set of equations at one step.

Derivation of the LIML estimator is quite complicated. Lengthy treatments appear in Anderson and Rubin (1948), Theil (1971), and Davidson and MacKinnon (1993, Chapter 18). The mechanics of the computation are surprisingly simple, as shown earlier (Section 13.5.4). The LIML estimates for Klein's Model I appear in Table 13.3 (Section 13.7) with the other single-equation and system estimators. For the practitioner, a useful result is that the asymptotic variance of the two-stage least squares (2SLS) estimator, which is yet simpler to compute, is the same as that of the LIML estimator. For practical purposes, this would generally render the LIML estimator, with its additional normality assumption, moot. The virtue of the LIML is largely theoretical—it provides a useful benchmark for the analysis of the properties of single-equation estimators. The single exception would be the invariance of the estimator to normalization of the equation (i.e., which variable appears on the left of the equals sign). This turns out to be useful in the context of analysis in the presence of weak instruments. (See Sections 12.9 and 13.5.5.)

The FIML estimator is much simpler to derive than the LIML and considerably more difficult to implement. The log-likelihood is derived and analyzed in Section 13.6.2. To obtain the needed results, we first operated on the reduced form

$$\mathbf{y}'_t = \mathbf{x}'_t \Pi + \mathbf{v}'_t,$$

$$\mathbf{v}_t \mid \mathbf{X} \sim N[\mathbf{0}, \mathbf{\Omega}], \tag{16-87}$$

which is the seemingly unrelated regressions model analyzed at length in Chapter 12 and in Section 16.9.3. The complication is the restrictions imposed on the parameters,

$$\Pi = -\mathbf{B}\Gamma^{-1} \quad \text{and} \quad \mathbf{\Omega} = (\Gamma^{-1})'\mathbf{\Sigma}(\Gamma^{-1}). \tag{16-88}$$

As is now familiar from several applications, given estimates of $\Gamma$ and $\mathbf{B}$ in (16-86), the estimator of $\mathbf{\Sigma}$ is $(1/T)\mathbf{E}'\mathbf{E}$ based on the residuals. We can even show fairly easily that given $\Gamma$ and $\mathbf{\Sigma}$, the estimator of $(-\mathbf{B})$ in (16-86) would be provided by the results for the SUR model in Section 16.9.3.c (where we estimate the model subject to the zero restrictions in the coefficient matrix). The complication in estimation is brought by $\Gamma$; this is a Jacobian. The term $\ln |\Gamma|$ appears in the log-likelihood function in Section 13.6.2. Nonlinear optimization over the nonzero elements in a function that includes this term is exceedingly complicated. However, three-stage least squares (3SLS) has the same asymptotic efficiency as the FIML estimator, again without the normality assumption and without the practical complications.

The end result is that for the practitioner, the LIML and FIML estimators have been supplanted in the literature by much simpler GMM estimators, 2SLS, H2SLS, 3SLS, and H3SLS. Interest remains in these estimators, but largely as a component of the ongoing theoretical development.

### 16.9.5 MAXIMUM LIKELIHOOD ESTIMATION OF NONLINEAR REGRESSION MODELS

In Chapter 11, we considered nonlinear regression models in which the nonlinearity in the parameters appeared entirely on the right-hand side of the equation. Maximum likelihood is used when the disturbances in a regression, or the dependent variable, more generally, is not normally distributed. We now consider two applications.

### 16.9.5.a    Nonnormal Disturbances—The Stochastic Frontier Model

This application will examine a regressionlike model in which the disturbances do not have a normal distribution. The model developed here also presents a convenient platform on which to illustrate the use of the invariance property of maximum likelihood estimators to simplify the estimation of the model.

A lengthy literature commencing with theoretical work by Knight (1933), Debreu (1951), and Farrell (1957) and the pioneering empirical study by Aigner, Lovell, and Schmidt (1977) has been directed at models of production that specifically account for the textbook proposition that a production function is a theoretical ideal.[24] If $y = f(\mathbf{x})$ defines a production relationship between inputs, $\mathbf{x}$, and an output, $y$, then for any given $\mathbf{x}$, the observed value of $y$ must be less than or equal to $f(\mathbf{x})$. The implication for an empirical regression model is that in a formulation such as $y = h(\mathbf{x}, \boldsymbol{\beta}) + u, u$ must be negative. Because the theoretical production function is an ideal—the frontier of efficient production—any nonzero disturbance must be interpreted as the result of inefficiency. A strictly orthodox interpretation embedded in a Cobb–Douglas production model might produce an empirical frontier production model such as

$$\ln y = \beta_1 + \Sigma_k \beta_k \ln x_k - u, \quad u \geq 0.$$

The gamma model described in Example 4.9 was an application. One-sided disturbances such as this one present a particularly difficult estimation problem. The primary theoretical problem is that any measurement error in $\ln y$ must be embedded in the disturbance. The practical problem is that the entire estimated function becomes a slave to any single errantly measured data point.

Aigner, Lovell, and Schmidt proposed instead a formulation within which observed deviations from the production function could arise from two sources: (1) productive inefficiency, as we have defined it earlier and that would necessarily be negative, and (2) idiosyncratic effects that are specific to the firm and that could enter the model with either sign. The end result was what they labeled the **stochastic frontier**:

$$\ln y = \beta_1 + \Sigma_k \beta_k \ln x_k - u + v, \quad u \geq 0, \quad v \sim N[0, \sigma_v^2].$$
$$= \beta_1 + \Sigma_k \beta_k \ln x_k + \varepsilon.$$

The frontier for any particular firm is $h(\mathbf{x}, \boldsymbol{\beta}) + v$, hence the name *stochastic frontier*. The inefficiency term is $u$, a random variable of particular interest in this setting. Because the data are in log terms, $u$ is a measure of the percentage by which the particular observation fails to achieve the frontier, ideal production rate.

To complete the specification, they suggested two possible distributions for the inefficiency term: the absolute value of a normally distributed variable and an exponentially distributed variable. The density functions for these two compound variables are given by Aigner, Lovell, and Schmidt; let $\varepsilon = v - u, \lambda = \sigma_u/\sigma_v, \sigma = (\sigma_u^2 + \sigma_v^2)^{1/2}$,

---

[24]A survey by Greene (2007a) appears in Fried, Lovell, and Schmidt (2007). Kumbhakar and Lovell (2000) is a comprehensive reference on the subject.

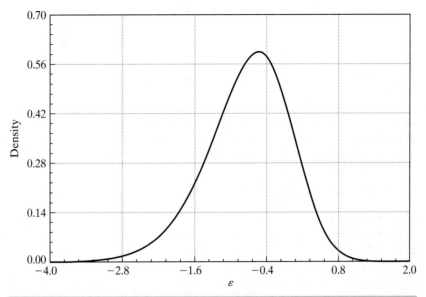

**FIGURE 16.4**    Density for the Disturbance in the Stochastic Frontier Model.

and $\Phi(z)$ = the probability to the left of $z$ in the standard normal distribution (see Section B.4.1). For the "half-normal" model,

$$\ln h(\varepsilon_i \mid \boldsymbol{\beta}, \lambda, \sigma) = \left[ -\ln \sigma + \left( \frac{1}{2} \right) \ln \frac{2}{\pi} - \frac{1}{2} \left( \frac{\varepsilon_i}{\sigma} \right)^2 + \ln \Phi \left( \frac{-\varepsilon_i \lambda}{\sigma} \right) \right],$$

whereas for the exponential model

$$\ln h(\varepsilon_i \mid \boldsymbol{\beta}, \theta, \sigma_v) = \left[ \ln \theta + \frac{1}{2} \theta^2 \sigma_v^2 + \theta \varepsilon_i + \ln \Phi \left( -\frac{\varepsilon_i}{\sigma_v} - \theta \sigma_v \right) \right].$$

Both these distributions are asymmetric. We thus have a regression model with a nonnormal distribution specified for the disturbance. The disturbance, $\varepsilon$, has a nonzero mean as well; $E[\varepsilon] = -\sigma_u (2/\pi)^{1/2}$ for the half-normal model and $-1/\theta$ for the exponential model. Figure 16.4 illustrates the density for the half-normal model with $\sigma = 1$ and $\lambda = 2$. By writing $\beta_0 = \beta_1 + E[\varepsilon]$ and $\varepsilon^* = \varepsilon - E[\varepsilon]$, we obtain a more conventional formulation

$$\ln y = \beta_0 + \Sigma_k \beta_k \ln x_k + \varepsilon^*,$$

which does have a disturbance with a zero mean but an asymmetric, nonnormal distribution. The asymmetry of the distribution of $\varepsilon^*$ does not negate our basic results for least squares in this classical regression model. This model satisfies the assumptions of the Gauss–Markov theorem, so least squares is unbiased and consistent (save for the constant term) and efficient among linear unbiased estimators. In this model, however, the maximum likelihood estimator is not linear, and it is more efficient than least squares.

We will work through maximum likelihood estimation of the half-normal model in detail to illustrate the technique. The log-likelihood is

$$\ln L = -n\ln\sigma + \frac{n}{2}\ln\frac{2}{\pi} - \frac{1}{2}\sum_{i=1}^{n}\left(\frac{\varepsilon_i}{\sigma}\right)^2 + \sum_{i=1}^{n}\ln\Phi\left(\frac{-\varepsilon_i\lambda}{\sigma}\right).$$

This is not a particularly difficult log-likelihood to maximize numerically. Nonetheless, it is instructive to make use of a convenience that we noted earlier. Recall that maximum likelihood estimators are invariant to one-to-one transformation. If we let $\theta = 1/\sigma$ and $\gamma = (1/\sigma)\beta$, the log-likelihood function becomes

$$\ln L = n\ln\theta + \frac{n}{2}\ln\frac{2}{\pi} - \frac{1}{2}\sum_{i=1}^{n}(\theta y_i - \mathbf{x}_i'\gamma)^2 + \sum_{i=1}^{n}\ln\Phi[-\lambda(\theta y_i - \mathbf{x}_i'\gamma)].$$

As you could verify by trying the derivations, this transformation brings a dramatic simplification in the manipulation of the log-likelihood and its derivatives. We will make repeated use of the functions

$$\alpha_i = \varepsilon_i/\sigma = \theta y_i - \mathbf{x}_i'\gamma,$$

$$\delta(y_i, \mathbf{x}_i, \lambda, \theta, \gamma) = \frac{\phi[-\lambda\alpha_i]}{\Phi[-\lambda\alpha_i]} = \delta_i.$$

$$\Delta_i = -\delta_i(-\lambda\alpha_i + \delta_i)$$

(The second of these is the derivative of the function in the final term in $\ln L$. The third is the derivative of $\delta_i$ with respect to its argument; $\Delta_i < 0$ for all values of $\lambda\alpha_i$.) It will also be convenient to define the $(K+1)\times 1$ columns vectors $\mathbf{z}_i = (\mathbf{x}_i', -y_i)'$ and $\mathbf{t}_i = (\mathbf{0}', 1/\theta)'$. The likelihood equations are

$$\frac{\partial\ln L}{\partial(\gamma', \theta)'} = \sum_{i=1}^{n}\mathbf{t}_i + \sum_{i=1}^{n}\alpha_i\mathbf{z}_i + \lambda\sum_{i=1}^{n}\delta_i\mathbf{z}_i = \mathbf{0},$$

$$\frac{\partial\ln L}{\partial\lambda} = -\sum_{i=1}^{n}\delta_i\alpha_i = 0,$$

and the second derivatives are

$$\mathbf{H}(\gamma, \theta, \lambda) = \sum_{i=1}^{n}\left\{\begin{bmatrix} (\lambda^2\Delta_i - 1)\mathbf{z}_i\mathbf{z}_i' & (\delta_i - \lambda\alpha_i\Delta_i)\mathbf{z}_i \\ (\delta_i - \lambda\alpha_i\Delta_i)\mathbf{z}_i' & \alpha_i^2\Delta_i \end{bmatrix} - \begin{bmatrix} \mathbf{t}_i\mathbf{t}_i' & \mathbf{0} \\ \mathbf{0}' & 0 \end{bmatrix}\right\}.$$

The estimator of the asymptotic covariance matrix for the directly estimated parameters is

$$\text{Est. Asy. Var}[\hat{\gamma}', \hat{\theta}, \hat{\lambda}]' = \{-\mathbf{H}[\hat{\gamma}', \hat{\theta}, \hat{\lambda}]\}^{-1}.$$

There are two sets of transformations of the parameters in our formulation. To recover estimates of the original structural parameters $\sigma = 1/\theta$ and $\beta = \gamma/\theta$ we need only transform the MLEs. Because these transformations are one to one, the MLEs of $\sigma$ and $\beta$ are $1/\hat{\theta}$ and $\hat{\gamma}/\hat{\theta}$. To compute an asymptotic covariance matrix for these estimators we will use the delta method, which will use the derivative matrix

$$\mathbf{G} = \begin{bmatrix} \partial\hat{\boldsymbol{\beta}}/\partial\hat{\boldsymbol{\gamma}}' & \partial\hat{\boldsymbol{\beta}}/\partial\hat{\theta} & \partial\hat{\boldsymbol{\beta}}/\partial\hat{\lambda} \\ \partial\hat{\sigma}/\partial\hat{\boldsymbol{\gamma}}' & \partial\hat{\sigma}/\partial\hat{\theta} & \partial\hat{\sigma}/\partial\hat{\lambda} \\ \partial\hat{\lambda}/\partial\hat{\boldsymbol{\gamma}}' & \partial\hat{\lambda}/\partial\hat{\theta} & \partial\hat{\lambda}/\partial\hat{\lambda} \end{bmatrix} = \begin{bmatrix} (1/\hat{\theta})\mathbf{I} & -(1/\hat{\theta}^2)\hat{\boldsymbol{\gamma}} & \mathbf{0} \\ \mathbf{0}' & -(1/\hat{\theta}^2) & 0 \\ \mathbf{0}' & 0 & 1 \end{bmatrix}.$$

Then, for the recovered parameters, we use

$$\text{Est. Asy. Var}[\hat{\boldsymbol{\beta}}', \hat{\sigma}, \hat{\lambda}]' = \mathbf{G} \times \left\{ -\mathbf{H}[\hat{\boldsymbol{\gamma}}', \hat{\theta}, \hat{\lambda}] \right\}^{-1} \times \mathbf{G}'.$$

For the half-normal model, we would also rely on the invariance of maximum likelihood estimators to recover estimates of the deeper variance parameters, $\sigma_v^2 = \sigma^2/(1+\lambda^2)$ and $\sigma_u^2 = \sigma^2\lambda^2/(1+\lambda^2)$.

The stochastic frontier model is a bit different from those we have analyzed previously in that the disturbance is the central focus of the analysis rather than the catchall for the unknown and unknowable factors omitted from the equation. Ideally, we would like to estimate $u_i$ for each firm in the sample to compare them on the basis of their productive efficiency. (The parameters of the production function are usually of secondary interest in these studies.) Unfortunately, the data do not permit a direct estimate, because with estimates of $\boldsymbol{\beta}$ in hand, we are only able to compute a direct estimate of $\varepsilon = y - \mathbf{x}'\boldsymbol{\beta}$. Jondrow et al. (1982), however, have derived a useful approximation that is now the standard measure in these settings,

$$E[u \mid \varepsilon] = \frac{\sigma\lambda}{1+\lambda^2}\left[\frac{\phi(z)}{1-\Phi(z)} - z\right], \quad z = \frac{\varepsilon\lambda}{\sigma},$$

for the half-normal model, and

$$E[u \mid \varepsilon] = z + \sigma_v\frac{\phi(z/\sigma_v)}{\Phi(z/\sigma_v)}, \quad z = -\varepsilon - \theta\sigma_v^2,$$

for the exponential model. These values can be computed using the maximum likelihood estimates of the structural parameters in the model. In addition, a structural parameter of interest is the proportion of the total variance of $\varepsilon$ that is due to the inefficiency term. For the half-normal model, $\text{Var}[\varepsilon] = \text{Var}[u] + \text{Var}[v] = (1 - 2/\pi)\sigma_u^2 + \sigma_v^2$, whereas for the exponential model, the counterpart is $1/\theta^2 + \sigma_v^2$.

### Example 16.9  Stochastic Frontier Model

Appendix Table F14.1 lists 25 statewide observations used by Zellner and Revankar (1970) to study production in the transportation equipment manufacturing industry. We have used these data to estimate the stochastic frontier models. Results are shown in Table 16.5.[25] The Jondrow et al. (1982) estimates of the inefficiency terms are listed in Table 16.6. The estimates of the parameters of the production function, $\beta_1$, $\beta_2$, and $\beta_3$ are fairly similar, but the variance parameters, $\sigma_u$ and $\sigma_v$, appear to be quite different. Some of the parameter difference is illusory, however. The variance components for the half-normal model are $(1 - 2/\pi)\sigma_u^2 = 0.0179$ and $\sigma_v^2 = 0.0361$, whereas those for the exponential model are $1/\theta^2 = 0.0183$ and $\sigma_v^2 = 0.0293$. In each case, about one-third of the total variance of $\varepsilon$ is accounted for by the variance of $u$.

---

[25]$N$ is the number of establishments in the state Zellner and Revankar used per establishment data in their study. The stochastic frontier model has the intriguing property that if the least squares residuals are skewed in the positive direction, then least squares with $\lambda = 0$ maximizes the log-likelihood. This property, in fact, characterizes the preceding data when scaled by $N$. Because that leaves a not particularly interesting example and it does not occur when the data are not normalized, for the purposes of this illustration we have used the unscaled data to produce Table 16.5. We do note that this result is a common, vexing occurrence in practice.

**TABLE 16.5** Estimated Stochastic Frontier Functions

| Coefficient | Least Squares | | | Half-Normal Model | | | Exponential Model | | |
|---|---|---|---|---|---|---|---|---|---|
| | Estimate | Standard Error | t Ratio | Estimate | Standard Error[a] | t Ratio | Estimate | Standard Error[a] | t Ratio |
| Constant | 1.844 | 0.234 | 7.896 | 2.081 | 0.422 | 4.933 | 2.069 | 0.290 | 7.135 |
| $\beta_k$ | 0.245 | 0.107 | 2.297 | 0.259 | 0.144 | 1.800 | 0.262 | 0.120 | 2.184 |
| $\beta_l$ | 0.805 | 0.126 | 6.373 | 0.780 | 0.170 | 4.595 | 0.770 | 0.138 | 5.581 |
| $\sigma$ | 0.236 | | | 0.282 | 0.087 | 3.237 | | | |
| $\sigma_u$ | — | | | 0.222 | | | 0.136 | | |
| $\sigma_v$ | — | | | 0.175 | | | 0.171 | 0.054 | 3.170 |
| $\lambda$ | — | | | 1.265 | 1.620 | 0.781 | | | |
| $\theta$ | — | | | | | | 7.398 | 3.931 | 1.882 |
| $\log L$ | 2.2537 | | | 2.4695 | | | 2.8605 | | |

[a] Based on BHHH estimator. Using second derivatives, standard errors would be (0.232, 0.098, 0.116, 0.0082, 0.557) for the half-normal and (0.236, 0.092, 0.111, 0.038, 3.431) for the exponential. The t ratios would be adjusted accordingly.

**TABLE 16.6** Estimated Inefficiencies

| State | Half-Normal | Exponential | State | Half-Normal | Exponential |
|---|---|---|---|---|---|
| Alabama | 0.2011 | 0.1459 | Maryland | 0.1353 | 0.0925 |
| California | 0.1448 | 0.0972 | Massachusetts | 0.1564 | 0.1093 |
| Connecticut | 0.1903 | 0.1348 | Michigan | 0.1581 | 0.1076 |
| Florida | 0.5175 | 0.5903 | Missouri | 0.1029 | 0.0704 |
| Georgia | 0.1040 | 0.0714 | New Jersey | 0.0958 | 0.0659 |
| Illinois | 0.1213 | 0.0830 | New York | 0.2779 | 0.2225 |
| Indiana | 0.2113 | 0.1545 | Ohio | 0.2291 | 0.1698 |
| Iowa | 0.2493 | 0.2007 | Pennsylvania | 0.1501 | 0.1030 |
| Kansas | 0.1010 | 0.0686 | Texas | 0.2030 | 0.1455 |
| Kentucky | 0.0563 | 0.0415 | Virginia | 0.1400 | 0.0968 |
| Louisiana | 0.2033 | 0.1507 | Washington | 0.1105 | 0.0753 |
| Maine | 0.2226 | 0.1725 | West Virginia | 0.1556 | 0.1124 |
| Wisconsin | 0.1407 | 0.0971 | | | |

### 16.9.5.b ML Estimation of a Geometric Regression Model for Count Data

The standard approach to modeling counts of events begins with the Poisson regression model,

$$\text{Prob}[Y = y_i \mid \mathbf{x}_i] = \frac{\exp(-\lambda_i)\lambda_i^{y_i}}{y_i!}, \; \lambda_i = \exp(\mathbf{x}_i'\boldsymbol{\beta}), \; y_i = 0, 1, \dots$$

which has **loglinear conditional mean** function $E[y_i \mid \mathbf{x}_i] = \lambda_i$. (The Poisson regression model and other specifications for data on counts are discussed at length in Chapter 25. We introduce the topic here to begin development of the MLE in a fairly straightforward, typical nonlinear setting.) Appendix Table F11.1 presents the Riphahn et al. (2003) data, which we will use to analyze a count variable, *DocVis*, the number of visits to physicians in the survey year. The histogram in Figure 16.5 shows a distinct spike at zero followed by rapidly declining frequencies. While the Poisson distribution, which

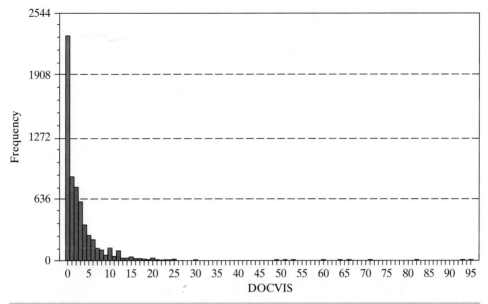

**FIGURE 16.5**   Histogram for Doctor Visits.

is typically hump-shaped, can accommodate this configuration if $\lambda_i$ is less than one, the shape is nonetheless somewhat "non-Poisson." [So-called Zero Inflation models (discussed in Chapter 25) are often used for this situation.]

The geometric distribution,

$$f(y_i \mid \mathbf{x}_i) = \theta_i(1 - \theta_i)^{y_i}, \theta_i = 1/(1 + \lambda_i), \lambda_i = \exp(\mathbf{x}_i'\boldsymbol{\beta}), y_i = 0, 1, \ldots,$$

is a convenient specification that produces the effect shown in Figure 16.5. (Note that, formally, the specification is used to model the number of failures before the first success in successive independent trials each with success probability $\theta_i$, so in fact, it is misspecified as a model for counts. The model does provide a convenient and useful illustration, however.) The conditional mean function is also $E[y_i \mid \mathbf{x}_i] = \lambda_i$. The partial effects in the model are

$$\frac{\partial E[y_i \mid \mathbf{x}_i]}{\partial \mathbf{x}_i} = \lambda_i \boldsymbol{\beta},$$

so this is a distinctly nonlinear regression model. We will construct a maximum likelihood estimator, then compare the MLE to the **nonlinear least squares** and (misspecified) linear least squares estimates.

The log-likelihood function is

$$\ln L = \sum_{i=1}^{n} \ln f(y_i \mid \mathbf{x}_i, \boldsymbol{\beta}) = \sum_{i=1}^{n} \ln \theta_i + y_i \ln(1 - \theta_i).$$

The likelihood equations are

$$\frac{\partial \ln L}{\partial \boldsymbol{\beta}} = \sum_{i=1}^{n} \left( \frac{1}{\theta_i} - \frac{y_i}{1-\theta_i} \right) \frac{d\theta_i}{d\lambda_i} \frac{\partial \lambda_i}{\partial \boldsymbol{\beta}}.$$

Because

$$\frac{d\theta_i}{d\lambda_i} \frac{\partial \lambda_i}{\partial \boldsymbol{\beta}} = \left( \frac{-1}{(1+\lambda_i)^2} \right) \lambda_i \mathbf{x}_i = -\theta_i(1-\theta_i)\mathbf{x}_i,$$

the likelihood equations simplify to

$$\frac{\partial \ln L}{\partial \boldsymbol{\beta}} = \sum_{i=1}^{n} (\theta_i y_i - (1-\theta_i))\mathbf{x}_i$$

$$= \sum_{i=1}^{n} (\theta_i(1+y_i) - 1)\mathbf{x}_i.$$

To estimate the asymptotic covariance matrix, we can use any of the three estimators of Asy. Var $[\hat{\boldsymbol{\beta}}_{\mathrm{MLE}}]$. The BHHH estimator would be

$$\text{Est. Asy. Var}_{\mathrm{BHHH}}[\hat{\boldsymbol{\beta}}_{\mathrm{MLE}}] = \left[ \sum_{i=1}^{n} \left( \frac{\partial \ln f(y_i \mid \mathbf{x}_i, \hat{\boldsymbol{\beta}})}{\partial \hat{\boldsymbol{\beta}}} \right) \left( \frac{\partial \ln f(y_i \mid \mathbf{x}_i, \hat{\boldsymbol{\beta}})}{\partial \hat{\boldsymbol{\beta}}} \right)' \right]^{-1}$$

$$= \left[ \sum_{i=1}^{n} (\hat{\theta}_i(1+y_i) - 1)^2 \mathbf{x}_i \mathbf{x}_i' \right].$$

The negative inverse of the second derivatives matrix evaluated at the MLE is

$$\left[ -\frac{\partial^2 \ln L}{\partial \hat{\boldsymbol{\beta}} \partial \hat{\boldsymbol{\beta}}'} \right]^{-1} = \left[ \sum_{i=1}^{n} (1+y_i)\hat{\theta}_i(1-\hat{\theta}_i)\mathbf{x}_i \mathbf{x}_i' \right]^{-1}.$$

Finally, as noted earlier, $E[y_i \mid \mathbf{x}_i] = \lambda_i = (1-\theta_i)/\theta_i$, is known, so we can also use the negative inverse of the expected second derivatives matrix,

$$\left[ -E\left( \frac{\partial^2 \ln L}{\partial \hat{\boldsymbol{\beta}} \partial \hat{\boldsymbol{\beta}}'} \right) \right]^{-1} = \left[ \sum_{i=1}^{n} (1-\hat{\theta}_i)\mathbf{x}_i \mathbf{x}_i' \right]^{-1}.$$

To compute the estimates of the parameters, either **Newton's method**,

$$\hat{\boldsymbol{\beta}}^{t+1} = \hat{\boldsymbol{\beta}}^t - \left[ \hat{\mathbf{H}}^t \right]^{-1} \hat{\mathbf{g}}^t,$$

or the method of scoring,

$$\hat{\boldsymbol{\beta}}^{t+1} = \hat{\boldsymbol{\beta}}^t - \left\{ E[\hat{\mathbf{H}}^t] \right\}^{-1} \hat{\mathbf{g}}^t,$$

can be used, where $\mathbf{H}$ and $\mathbf{g}$ are the second and first derivatives that will be evaluated at the current estimates of the parameters. Like many models of this sort, there is a convenient set of starting values, assuming the model contains a constant term. Because $E[y_i \mid x_i] = \lambda_i$, if we start the slope parameters at zero, then a natural starting value for the constant term is the log of $\bar{y}$.

### Example 16.10 Geometric Model for Doctor Visits

In Example 11.10, we considered nonlinear least squares estimation of a loglinear model for the number of doctor visits variable shown in Figure 16.5. The data are drawn from the Riphahn et al. (2003) data set in Appendix Table F11.1. We will continue that analysis here by fitting a more detailed model for the count variable *DocVis*. The conditional mean analyzed here is

$$\ln E[DocVis_{it} \mid \mathbf{x}_{it}] = \beta_1 + \beta_2\, Age_{it} + \beta_3\, Educ_{it} + \beta_4\, Income_{it} + \beta_5\, Kids_{it}$$

(This differs slightly from the model in Example 11.10. For this exercise, with an eye toward the fixed effects model in Example 16.13, we have specified a model that does not contain any time invariant variables, such as $Female_i$.) Sample means for the variables in the model are given in Table 16.7. Note, these data are a panel. In this exercise, we are ignoring that fact, and fitting a pooled model. We will turn to panel data treatments in the next section, and revisit this application.

We used Newton's method for the optimization, with starting values as suggested earlier. The five iterations are as follows:

| Variable | Constant | Age | Educ | Income | Kids |
|---|---|---|---|---|---|
| Start values: | .11580e+01 | .00000e+00 | .00000e+00 | .00000e+00 | .00000e+00 |
| 1st derivs. | −.25191e−08 | −.61777e+05 | .73202e+04 | .42575e+04 | .16464e+04 |
| Parameters: | .11580e+01 | .00000e+00 | .00000e+00 | .00000e+00 | .00000e+00 |
| Iteration 1 F = | .6287e+05 | g′inv(H)g = | .4367e+02 | | |
| 1st derivs. | .48616e+03 | −.22449e+05 | −.57162e+04 | −.17112e+04 | −.16521e+03 |
| Parameters: | .11186e+01 | .17563e−01 | −.50263e−01 | −.46274e−01 | −.15609e+00 |
| Iteration 2 F = | .6192e+05 | g′inv(H)g = | .3547e+01 | | |
| 1st derivs. | −.31284e+01 | −.15595e+03 | −.37197e+02 | −.10630e+02 | −.77186e+00 |
| Parameters: | .10922e+01 | .17981e−01 | −.47303e−01 | −.46739e−01 | −.15683e+00 |
| Iteration 3 F= | .6192e+05 | g′inv(H)g = | .2598e−01 | | |
| 1st derivs. | −.18417e−03 | −.99368e−02 | −.21992e−02 | −.59354e−03 | −.25994e−04 |
| Parameters: | .10918e+01 | .17988e−01 | −.47274e−01 | −.46751e−01 | −.15686e+00 |
| Iteration 4 F= | .6192e+05 | g′inv(H)g = | .1831e−05 | | |
| 1st derivs. | −.35727e−11 | .86745e−10 | −.26302e−10 | −.61006e−11 | −.15620e−11 |
| Parameters: | .10918e+01 | .17988e−01 | −.47274e−01 | −.46751e−01 | −.15686e+00 |
| Iteration 5 F= | .6192e+05 | g′inv(H)g = | .1772e−12 | | |

Convergence based on the LM criterion, $\mathbf{g'H}^{-1}\mathbf{g}$ is achieved after the fourth iteration. Note that the derivatives at this point are extremely small, albeit not absolutely zero. Table 16.7 presents the maximum likelihood estimates of the parameters. Several sets of standard errors are presented. The three sets based on different estimators of the information matrix are presented first. The fourth set are based on the cluster corrected covariance matrix discussed in Section 16.8.4. Because this is actually an (unbalanced) panel data set, we anticipate correlation across observations. Not surprisingly, the standard errors rise substantially. The

**TABLE 16.7** Estimated Geometric Regression Model Dependent Variable: DocVis: Mean = 3.18352, Standard Deviation = 5.68969

| Variable | Estimate | St. Er. H | St. Er. E[H] | St. Er. BHHH | St. Er. Cluster | APE | PE Mean | OLS | Mean |
|---|---|---|---|---|---|---|---|---|---|
| Constant | 1.0918 | 0.0524 | 0.0524 | 0.0354 | 0.1112 | — | — | 2.656 | |
| Age | 0.0180 | 0.0007 | 0.0007 | 0.0005 | 0.0013 | 0.0572 | 0.0547 | 0.061 | 43.52 |
| Education | −0.0473 | 0.0033 | 0.0033 | 0.0023 | 0.0069 | −0.150 | −0.144 | −0.121 | 11.32 |
| Income | −0.0468 | 0.0041 | 0.0042 | 0.0023 | 0.0075 | −0.149 | −0.142 | −0.162 | 3.52 |
| Kids | −0.1569 | 0.0156 | 0.0155 | 0.0103 | 0.0319 | −0.499 | −0.477 | −0.517 | 0.40 |

partial effects listed next are computed in two ways. The "Average Partial Effect" is computed by averaging $\lambda_i \boldsymbol{\beta}$ across the individuals in the sample. The "Partial Effect" is computed for the average individual by computing $\lambda$ at the means of the data. The next-to-last column contains the ordinary least squares coefficients. In this model, there is no reason to expect ordinary least squares to provide a consistent estimator of $\boldsymbol{\beta}$. The question might arise, What does ordinary least squares estimate? The answer is the slopes of the linear projection of DocVis on $\boldsymbol{x}_{it}$. The resemblance of the OLS coefficients to the estimated partial effects is more than coincidental, and suggests an answer to the question.

The analysis in the table suggests three competing approaches to modeling DocVis. The results for the geometric regression model are given in Table 16.7. At the beginning of this section, we noted that the more conventional approach to modeling a count variable such as DocVis is with the Poisson regression model. The log-likelihood function and its derivatives are even simpler than the geometric model,

$$\ln L = \sum_{i=1}^{n} y_i \ln \lambda_i - \lambda_i - \ln y_i!,$$

$$\partial \ln L / \partial \boldsymbol{\beta} = \sum_{i=1}^{n} (y_i - \lambda_i) \boldsymbol{x}_i,$$

$$\partial^2 \ln L / \partial \boldsymbol{\beta} \partial \boldsymbol{\beta}' = \sum_{i=1}^{n} -\lambda_i \boldsymbol{x}_i \boldsymbol{x}_i'.$$

A third approach might be a semiparametric, nonlinear regression model,

$$y_{it} = \exp(\boldsymbol{x}_{it}' \boldsymbol{\beta}) + \varepsilon_{it}.$$

This is, in fact, the model that applies to both the geometric and Poisson cases. Under either distributional assumption, nonlinear least squares is inefficient compared to MLE. But, the distributional assumption can be dropped altogether, and the model fit as a simple exponential regression. Table 16.8 presents the three sets of estimates.

It is not obvious how to choose among the alternatives. Of the three, the Poisson model is used most often by far. The Poisson and geometric models are not nested, so we cannot use a simple parametric test to choose between them. However, these two models will surely fit the conditions for the Vuong test described in Section 7.3.4. To implement the test, we first computed

$$V_{it} = \ln f_{it} \mid \text{geometric} - \ln f_{it} \mid \text{Poisson}$$

using the respective MLEs of the parameters. The test statistic given in (7-14) is then

$$V = \frac{\left( \sqrt{\sum_{i=1}^{n} T_i} \right) \overline{V}}{s_V}.$$

**TABLE 16.8** Estimates of Three Models for DOCVIS

| Variable | *Geometric Model* | | *Poisson Model* | | *Nonlinear Reg.* | |
|---|---|---|---|---|---|---|
| | *Estimate* | *St. Er* | *Estimate* | *St. Er.* | *Estimate* | *St. Er.* |
| Constant | 1.0918 | 0.0524 | 1.0480 | 0.0272 | 0.9801 | 0.0893 |
| Age | 0.0180 | 0.0007 | 0.0184 | 0.0003 | 0.0187 | 0.0011 |
| Education | −0.0473 | 0.0033 | −0.0433 | 0.0017 | −0.0361 | 0.0057 |
| Income | −0.0468 | 0.0041 | −0.0520 | 0.0022 | −0.0591 | 0.0072 |
| Kids | −0.1569 | 0.0156 | −0.1609 | 0.0080 | −0.1692 | 0.0264 |

This statistic converges to standard normal under the underlying assumptions. A large positive value favors the geometric model. The computed sample value is 37.885, which strongly favors the geometric model over the Poisson.

### 16.9.6 PANEL DATA APPLICATIONS

Application of panel data methods to the linear panel data models we have considered so far is a fairly marginal extension. For the random effects linear model, considered in the following Section 16.9.6.a, the MLE of $\beta$ is, as always, FGLS given the MLEs of the variance parameters. The latter produce a fairly substantial complication, as we shall see. This extension does provide a convenient, interesting application to see the payoff to the invariance property of the MLE—we will reparameterize a fairly complicated log-likelihood function to turn it into a simple one. Where the method of maximum likelihood becomes essential is in analysis of fixed and random effects in nonlinear models. We will develop two general methods for handling these situations in generic terms in Sections 16.9.6.b and 16.9.6.c, then apply them in several models later in the book.

#### 16.9.6.a ML Estimation of the Linear Random Effects Model

The contribution of the $i$th individual to the log-likelihood for the random effects model [(9-26) to (9-29)] with normally distributed disturbances is

$$
\ln L_i\left(\beta, \sigma_\varepsilon^2, \sigma_u^2\right) = \frac{-1}{2}\left[T_i \ln 2\pi + \ln |\Omega_i| + (y_i - X_i\beta)'\Omega_i^{-1}(y_i - X_i\beta)\right]
$$
$$
= \frac{-1}{2}\left[T_i \ln 2\pi + \ln |\Omega_i| + \varepsilon_i'\Omega_i^{-1}\varepsilon_i\right],
$$
(16-89)

where

$$
\Omega_i = \sigma_\varepsilon^2 I_{Ti} + \sigma_u^2 ii',
$$

and $i$ denotes a $T_i \times 1$ column of ones. Note that the $\Omega_i$ varies over $i$ because it is $T_i \times T_i$. Baltagi (2005, pp. 19–20) presents a convenient and compact estimator for this model that involves iteration between an estimator of $\phi^2 = \left[\sigma_\varepsilon^2/(\sigma_\varepsilon^2 + T\sigma_u^2)\right]$, based on sums of squared residuals, and $(\alpha, \beta, \sigma_\varepsilon^2)$ ($\alpha$ is the constant term) using FGLS. Unfortunately, the convenience and compactness come unraveled in the unbalanced case. We consider, instead, what Baltagi labels a "brute force" approach, that is, direct maximization of the log-likelihood function in (16-89). (See, op. cit, pp. 169–170.)

Using (A-66), we find (in (9-28) that

$$
\Omega_i^{-1} = \frac{1}{\sigma_\varepsilon^2}\left[I_{T_i} - \frac{\sigma_u^2}{\sigma_\varepsilon^2 + T_i\sigma_u^2}ii'\right].
$$

We will also need the determinant of $\Omega_i$. To obtain this, we will use the product of its characteristic roots. First, write

$$
|\Omega_i| = \left(\sigma_\varepsilon^2\right)^{T_i}|I + \gamma ii'|,
$$

where $\gamma = \sigma_u^2/\sigma_\varepsilon^2$. To find the characteristic roots of the matrix, use the definition

$$
[I + \gamma ii']c = \lambda c,
$$

where $\mathbf{c}$ is a characteristic vector and $\lambda$ is the associated characteristic root. The equation implies that $\gamma \mathbf{i} \mathbf{i}' \mathbf{c} = (\lambda - 1)\mathbf{c}$. Premultiply by $\mathbf{i}'$ to obtain $\gamma (\mathbf{i}' \mathbf{i})(\mathbf{i}' \mathbf{c}) = (\lambda - 1)(\mathbf{i}' \mathbf{c})$. Any vector $\mathbf{c}$ with elements that sum to zero will satisfy this equality. There will be $T_i - 1$ such vectors and the associated characteristic roots will be $(\lambda - 1) = 0$ or $\lambda = 1$. For the remaining root, divide by the nonzero $(\mathbf{i}' \mathbf{c})$ and note that $\mathbf{i}' \mathbf{i} = T_i$, so the last root is $T_i \gamma = \lambda - 1$ or $\lambda = (1 + T_i \gamma)$. [26] It follows that the determinant is

$$\ln |\mathbf{\Omega}_i| = T_i \ln \sigma_\varepsilon^2 + \ln(1 + T_i \gamma).$$

Expanding the parts and multiplying out the third term gives the log-likelihood function

$$\ln L = \sum_{i=1}^n \ln L_i$$

$$= -\frac{1}{2} \left[ (\ln 2\pi + \ln \sigma_\varepsilon^2) \sum_{i=1}^n T_i + \sum_{i=1}^n \ln(1 + T_i \gamma) \right] - \frac{1}{2\sigma_\varepsilon^2} \sum_{i=1}^n \left[ \boldsymbol{\varepsilon}_i' \boldsymbol{\varepsilon}_i - \frac{\sigma_u^2 (T_i \bar{\varepsilon}_i)^2}{\sigma_\varepsilon^2 + T_i \sigma_u^2} \right].$$

Note that in the third term, we can write $\sigma_\varepsilon^2 + T_i \sigma_u^2 = \sigma_\varepsilon^2 (1 + T_i \gamma)$ and $\sigma_u^2 = \sigma_\varepsilon^2 \gamma$. After inserting these, two appearances of $\sigma_\varepsilon^2$ in the square brackets will cancel, leaving

$$\ln L = -\frac{1}{2} \sum_{i=1}^n \left( T_i (\ln 2\pi + \ln \sigma_\varepsilon^2) + \ln(1 + T_i \gamma) + \frac{1}{\sigma_\varepsilon^2} \left[ \boldsymbol{\varepsilon}_i' \boldsymbol{\varepsilon}_i - \frac{\gamma (T_i \bar{\varepsilon}_i)^2}{1 + T_i \gamma} \right] \right).$$

Now, let $\theta = 1/\sigma_\varepsilon^2$, $R_i = 1 + T_i \gamma$, and $Q_i = \gamma / R_i$. The individual contribution to the log likelihood becomes

$$\ln L_i = -\frac{1}{2} [\theta (\boldsymbol{\varepsilon}_i' \boldsymbol{\varepsilon}_i - Q_i (T_i \bar{\varepsilon}_i)^2) + \ln R_i + T_i \ln \theta + T_i \ln 2\pi].$$

The likelihood equations are

$$\frac{\partial \ln L_i}{\partial \boldsymbol{\beta}} = \theta \left[ \sum_{t=1}^{T_i} \mathbf{x}_{it} \varepsilon_{it} \right] - \theta \left[ Q_i \left( \sum_{t=1}^{T_i} \mathbf{x}_{it} \right) \left( \sum_{t=1}^{T_i} \varepsilon_{it} \right) \right],$$

$$\frac{\partial \ln L_i}{\partial \theta} = -\frac{1}{2} \left[ \left( \sum_{t=1}^{T_i} \varepsilon_{it}^2 \right) - Q_i \left( \sum_{t=1}^{T_i} \varepsilon_{it} \right)^2 - \frac{T_i}{\theta} \right],$$

$$\frac{\partial \ln L_i}{\partial \gamma} = \frac{1}{2} \left[ \theta \left( \frac{1}{R_i^2} \left( \sum_{t=1}^{T_i} \varepsilon_{it} \right)^2 \right) - \frac{T_i}{R_i} \right].$$

These will be sufficient for programming an optimization algorithm such as DFP or BFGS. (See Section E3.3.) We could continue to derive the second derivatives for computing the asymptotic covariance matrix, but this is unnecessary. For $\hat{\boldsymbol{\beta}}_{\text{MLE}}$, we know that because this is a generalized regression model, the appropriate asymptotic

---

[26] By this derivation, we have established a useful general result. The characteristic roots of a $T \times T$ matrix of the form $\mathbf{A} = (\mathbf{I} + a \mathbf{b} \mathbf{b}')$ are 1 with multiplicity $(T - 1)$ and $a \mathbf{b}' \mathbf{b}$ with multiplicity 1. The proof follows precisely along the lines of our earlier derivation.

covariance matrix is

$$\text{Asy. Var}[\hat{\boldsymbol{\beta}}_{\text{MLE}}] = \left[\sum_{i=1}^{n} \mathbf{X}_i' \hat{\boldsymbol{\Omega}}_i^{-1} \mathbf{X}_i\right]^{-1}.$$

(See Section 9.5.1.) We also know that the MLEs of the variance components estimators will be asymptotically uncorrelated with that of $\boldsymbol{\beta}$. In principle, we could continue to estimate the asymptotic variances of the MLEs of $\sigma_\varepsilon^2$ and $\sigma_u^2$. It would be necessary to derive these from the estimators of $\theta$ and $\gamma$, which one would typically do in any event. However, statistical inference about the disturbance variance, $\sigma_\varepsilon^2$ in a regression model, is typically of no interest. On the other hand, one might want to test the hypothesis that $\sigma_u^2$ equals zero, or $\gamma = 0$. Breusch and Pagan's (1979) LM statistic in (9-39) extended to the unbalanced panel case considered here would be

$$LM = \frac{\left(\sum_{i=1}^{N} T_i\right)^2}{\left[2\sum_{i=1}^{N} T_i(T_i - 1)\right]} \left[\frac{\sum_{i=1}^{N}(T_i\bar{e}_i)^2}{\sum_{i=1}^{N}\sum_{t=1}^{T_i} e_{it}^2} - 1\right]^2$$

$$= \frac{\left(\sum_{i=1}^{N} T_i\right)^2}{\left[2\sum_{i=1}^{N} T_i(T_i - 1)\right]} \left[\frac{\sum_{i=1}^{N}[(T_i\bar{e}_i)^2 - \mathbf{e}_i'\mathbf{e}_i]}{\sum_{i=1}^{N} \mathbf{e}_i'\mathbf{e}_i}\right]^2.$$

### Example 16.11  Maximum Likelihood and FGLS Estimates of a Wage Equation

Example 9.6 presented FGLS estimates of a wage equation using Cornwell and Rupert's panel data. We have reestimated the wage equation using maximum likelihood instead of FGLS. The parameter estimates appear in Table 16.9, with the FGLS and pooled OLS estimates. The estimates of the variance components are shown in the table as well. The similarity of the MLEs and FGLS estimates is to be expected given the large sample size. The LM statistic for testing for the presence of the common effects is 3,881.34, which is far larger than the critical value of 3.84. With the MLE, we can also use an LR test to test for

**TABLE 16.9**  Estimates of the Wage Equation

| Variable | Pooled Least Squares | | Random Effects MLE | | Random Effects FGLS | |
|---|---|---|---|---|---|---|
| | Estimate | Std. Error[a] | Estimate | Std. Error | Estimate | Std. Error |
| Exp | 0.0361 | 0.004533 | 0.1078 | 0.002480 | 0.08906 | 0.002280 |
| Exp$^2$ | −0.0006550 | 0.0001016 | −0.0005054 | 0.00005452 | −0.0007577 | 0.00005036 |
| Wks | 0.004461 | 0.001728 | 0.0008663 | 0.0006031 | 0.001066 | 0.0005939 |
| Occ | −0.3176 | 0.02726 | −0.03954 | 0.01374 | −0.1067 | 0.01269 |
| Ind | 0.03213 | 0.02526 | 0.008807 | 0.01531 | −0.01637 | 0.01391 |
| South | −0.1137 | 0.02868 | −0.01615 | 0.03201 | −0.06899 | 0.02354 |
| SMSA | 0.1586 | 0.02602 | −0.04019 | 0.01901 | −0.01530 | 0.01649 |
| MS | 0.3203 | 0.03494 | −0.03540 | 0.01880 | −0.02398 | 0.01711 |
| Union | 0.06975 | 0.02667 | 0.03306 | 0.01482 | 0.03597 | 0.01367 |
| Constant | 5.8802 | 0.09673 | 4.8197 | 0.06035 | 5.3455 | 0.04361 |
| $\sigma_\varepsilon^2$ | 0.146119 | | 0.023436 ($\theta = 42.66926$) | | 0.023102 | |
| $\sigma_u^2$ | 0 | | 0.876517 ($\gamma = 37.40035$) | | 0.838361 | |
| ln $L$ | −1899.537 | | 2162.938 | | — | |

[a] Robust standard errors

random effects against the null hypothesis of no effects. The chi-squared statistic based on the two log-likelihoods is 8,124.949, which leads to the same conclusion.

### 16.9.6.b   Random Effects in Nonlinear Models: MLE using Quadrature

Section 16.9.5.b describes a nonlinear model for panel data, the geometric regression model,

$$\text{Prob}[Y_{it} = y_{it} \mid \mathbf{x}_{it}] = \theta_{it}(1 - \theta_{it})^{y_{it}}, \; y_{it} = 0, 1, \ldots; i = 1, \ldots, n, t = 1, \ldots, T_i,$$

$$\theta_{it} = 1/(1 + \lambda_{it}), \lambda_{it} = \exp(\mathbf{x}_{it}'\boldsymbol{\beta}).$$

As noted, this is a panel data model, although as stated, it has none of the features we have used for the panel data in the linear case. It is a regression model,

$$E[y_{it} \mid \mathbf{x}_{it}] = \lambda_{it},$$

which implies that

$$y_{it} = \lambda_{it} + \varepsilon_{it}.$$

This is simply a tautology that defines the deviation of $y_{it}$ from its conditional mean. It might seem natural at this point to introduce a common fixed or random effect, as we did earlier in the linear case, as in

$$y_{it} = \lambda_{it} + \varepsilon_{it} + c_i.$$

However, the difficulty in this specification is that whereas $\varepsilon_{it}$ is defined residually just as the difference between $y_{it}$ and its mean, $c_i$ is a freely varying random variable. Without extremely complex constraints on how $c_i$ varies, the model as stated cannot prevent $y_{it}$ from being negative. When building the specification for a nonlinear model, greater care must be taken to preserve the internal consistency of the specification. A frequent approach in **index function models** such as this one is to introduce the common effect in the conditional mean function. The random effects geometric regression model, for example, might appear

$$\text{Prob}[Y_{it} = y_{it} \mid \mathbf{x}_{it}] = \theta_{it}(1 - \theta_{it})^{y_{it}}, \; y_{it} = 0, 1, \ldots; i = 1, \ldots, n, t = 1, \ldots, T_i,$$

$$\theta_{it} = 1/(1 + \lambda_{it}), \lambda_{it} = \exp(\mathbf{x}_{it}'\boldsymbol{\beta} + u_i),$$

$f(u_i) = $ the specification of the distribution of random effects    **(16-90)**
over individuals.

By this specification, it is now appropriate to state the model specification as

$$\text{Prob}[Y_{it} = y_{it} \mid \mathbf{x}_{it}, u_i] = \theta_{it}(1 - \theta_{it})^{y_{it}}.$$

That is, our statement of the probability is now conditioned on both the observed data and the unobserved random effect. The random common effect can then vary freely and the inherent characteristics of the model are preserved.

Two questions now arise:

- How does one obtain maximum likelihood estimates of the parameters of the model? We will pursue that question now.

● If we ignore the individual heterogeneity and simply estimate the pooled model, will we obtain consistent estimators of the model parameters? The answer is sometimes, but usually not. The favorable cases are the simple loglinear models such as the geometric and Poisson models that we consider in this chapter. The unfavorable cases are most of the other common applications in the literature, including, notably, models for binary choice, censored regressions, sample selection, and, generally, nonlinear models that do not have simple exponential means. [Note that this is the crucial issue in the consideration of robust covariance matrix estimation in Sections 16.8.3 and 16.8.4. See, as well, Freedman (2006).]

We will now develop a maximum likelihood estimator for a nonlinear random effects model. To set up the methodology for applications later in the book, we will do this in a generic specification, then return to the specific application of the geometric regression model in Example 16.12. Assume, then, that the panel data model defines the probability distribution of a random variable, $y_{it}$, conditioned on a data vector, $\mathbf{x}_{it}$, and an unobserved common random effect, $u_i$. As always, there are $T_i$ observations in the group, and the data on $\mathbf{x}_{it}$ and now $u_i$ are assumed to be strictly exogenously determined. Our model for one individual is, then,

$$p(y_{it} \mid \mathbf{x}_{it}, u_i) = f(y_{it} \mid \mathbf{x}_{it}, u_i, \boldsymbol{\theta}),$$

where $p(y_{it} \mid \mathbf{x}_{it}, u_i)$ indicates that we are defining a conditional density while $f(y_{it} \mid \mathbf{x}_{it}, u_i, \theta)$ defines the functional form and emphasizes the vector of parameters to be estimated. We are also going to assume that, but for the common $u_i$, observations within a group would be independent—the dependence of observations in the group arises through the presence of the common $u_i$. The joint density of the $T_i$ observations on $y_{it}$ given $u_i$ under these assumptions would be

$$p(y_{i1}, y_{i2}, \ldots, y_{i,T_i} \mid \mathbf{X}_i, u_i) = \prod_{t=1}^{T_i} f(y_{it} \mid \mathbf{x}_{it}, u_i, \boldsymbol{\theta}),$$

because conditioned on $u_i$, the observations are independent. But because $u_i$ is part of the observation on the group, to construct the log-likelihood, we will require

$$p(y_{i1}, y_{i2}, \ldots, y_{i,T_i}, u_i \mid \mathbf{X}_i) = \left[ \prod_{t=1}^{T_i} f(y_{it} \mid \mathbf{x}_{it}, u_i, \boldsymbol{\theta}) \right] f(u_i).$$

The likelihood function is the joint density for the observed random variables. Because $u_i$ is an unobserved random effect, to construct the likelihood function, we will then have to integrate it out of the joint density. Thus,

$$p(y_{i1}, y_{i2}, \ldots, y_{i,T_i} \mid \mathbf{X}_i) = \int_{u_i} \left[ \prod_{t=1}^{T_i} f(y_{it} \mid \mathbf{x}_{it}, u_i, \boldsymbol{\theta}) \right] f(u_i) du_i.$$

The contribution to the log-likelihood function of group $i$ is, then,

$$\ln L_i = \ln \int_{u_i} \left[ \prod_{t=1}^{T_i} f(y_{it} \mid \mathbf{x}_{it}, u_i, \boldsymbol{\theta}) \right] f(u_i) du_i.$$

There are two practical problems to be solved to implement this estimator. First, it will be rare that the integral will exist in closed form. (It does when the density of $y_{it}$ is normal with linear conditional mean and the random effect is normal, because, as we have seen, this is the random effects linear model.) As such, the practical complication that arises is how the integrals are to be computed. Second, it remains to specify the distribution of $u_i$ over which the integration is taken. The distribution of the common effect is part of the model specification. Several approaches for this model have now appeared in the literature. The one we will develop here extends the random effects model with normally distributed effects that we have analyzed in the previous section. The technique is **Butler and Moffitt's** (1982) **method.** It was originally proposed for extending the random effects model to a binary choice setting (see Chapter 23), but, as we shall see presently, it is straightforward to extend it to a wide range of other models. The computations center on a technique for approximating integrals known as **Gauss–Hermite quadrature.**

We assume that $u_i$ is normally distributed with mean zero and variance $\sigma_u^2$. Thus,

$$f(u_i) = \frac{1}{\sqrt{2\pi\sigma_u^2}} \exp\left(-\frac{u_i^2}{2\sigma_u^2}\right).$$

With this assumption, the $i$th term in the log-likelihood is

$$\ln L_i = \ln \int_{-\infty}^{\infty} \left[\prod_{t=1}^{T_i} f(y_{it} \mid \mathbf{x}_{it}, u_i, \boldsymbol{\theta})\right] \frac{1}{\sqrt{2\pi\sigma_u^2}} \exp\left(-\frac{u_i^2}{2\sigma_i^2}\right) du_i.$$

To put this function in a form that will be convenient for us later, we now let $w_i = u_i/(\sigma_u\sqrt{2})$ so that $u_i = \sigma_u\sqrt{2}w_i = \phi w_i$ and the Jacobian of the transformation from $u_i$ to $w_i$ is $du_i = \phi dw_i$. Now, we make the change of variable in the integral, to produce the function

$$\ln L_i = \ln \frac{1}{\sqrt{\pi}} \int_{-\infty}^{\infty} \left[\prod_{t=1}^{T_i} f(y_{it} \mid \mathbf{x}_{it}, \phi w_i, \boldsymbol{\theta})\right] \exp\left(-w_i^2\right) dw_i.$$

For the moment, let

$$g(w_i) = \prod_{t=1}^{T_i} f(y_{it} \mid \mathbf{x}_{it}, \phi w_i, \boldsymbol{\theta}).$$

Then, the function we are manipulating is

$$\ln L_i = \ln \frac{1}{\sqrt{\pi}} \int_{-\infty}^{\infty} g(w_i) \exp\left(-w_i^2\right) dw_i.$$

The payoff to all this manipulation is that integrals of this form can be computed very accurately by Gauss–Hermite quadrature. Gauss–Hermite quadrature replaces the integration with a weighted sum of the functions evaluated at a specific set of points. For the general case, this is

$$\int_{-\infty}^{\infty} g(w_i) \exp\left(-w_i^2\right) dw_i \approx \sum_{h=1}^{H} z_h g(v_h)$$

where $z_h$ is the weight and $v_h$ is the node. Tables of the weights and nodes are found in popular sources such as Abramovitz and Stegun (1971). For example, the nodes and weights for a four-point quadrature are

$$v_h = \pm 0.52464762327529002 \text{ and } \pm 1.6506801238857849,$$

$$z_h = \quad 0.80491409000549996 \quad \text{and} \quad 0.081312835447250001.$$

In practice, it is common to use eight or more points, up to a practical limit of about 96. Assembling all of the parts, we obtain the approximation to the contribution to the log-likelihood,

$$\ln L_i = \ln \frac{1}{\sqrt{\pi}} \sum_{h=1}^{H} z_h \left[ \prod_{t=1}^{T_i} f(y_{it} \mid \mathbf{x}_{it}, \phi v_h, \boldsymbol{\theta}) \right].$$

The Hermite approximation to the log-likelihood function is

$$\ln L = \frac{1}{\sqrt{\pi}} \sum_{i=1}^{n} \ln \sum_{h=1}^{H} z_h \left[ \prod_{t=1}^{T_i} f(y_{it} \mid \mathbf{x}_{it}, \phi v_h, \boldsymbol{\theta}) \right].$$

This function is now to be maximized with respect to $\boldsymbol{\theta}$ and $\phi$. Maximization is a complex problem. However, it has been automated in contemporary software for some models, notably the binary choice models mentioned earlier, and is in fact quite straightforward to implement in many other models as well. The first and second derivatives of the log-likelihood function are correspondingly complex but still computable using quadrature. The estimate of $\sigma_u$ and an appropriate standard error are obtained from $\hat{\phi}$ using the result $\phi = \sigma_u \sqrt{2}$. The hypothesis of no cross-period correlation can be tested, in principle, using any of the three standard testing procedures.

### Example 16.12   Random Effects Geometric Regression Model

We will use the preceding to construct a random effects model for the *DocVis* count variable analyzed in Example 16.10. Using (16-90), the approximate log-likelihood function will be

$$\ln L_H = \frac{1}{\sqrt{\pi}} \sum_{i=1}^{n} \ln \sum_{h=1}^{H} z_h \left[ \prod_{t=1}^{T_i} \theta_{it} (1 - \theta_{it})^{y_{it}} \right],$$

$$\theta_{it} = 1/(1 + \lambda_{it}), \lambda_{it} = \exp(\mathbf{x}'_{it} \boldsymbol{\beta} + \phi v_h).$$

The derivatives of the log-likelihood are approximated as well. The following is the general result—development is left as an exercise:

$$\frac{\partial \log L}{\partial \binom{\boldsymbol{\beta}}{\phi}} = \sum_{i=1}^{n} \frac{1}{L_i} \frac{\partial L_i}{\partial \binom{\boldsymbol{\beta}}{\phi}}$$

$$\approx \sum_{i=1}^{n} \frac{\left\{ \dfrac{1}{\sqrt{\pi}} \displaystyle\sum_{h=1}^{H} z_h \left[ \displaystyle\prod_{t=1}^{T_i} f(y_{it} \mid \mathbf{x}_{it}, \phi v_h, \boldsymbol{\beta}) \right] \left[ \displaystyle\sum_{t=1}^{T_i} \dfrac{\partial \log f(y_{it} \mid \mathbf{x}_{it}, \phi v_h, \boldsymbol{\beta})}{\partial \binom{\boldsymbol{\beta}}{\phi}} \right] \right\}}{\left\{ \dfrac{1}{\sqrt{\pi}} \displaystyle\sum_{h=1}^{H} z_h \left[ \displaystyle\prod_{t=1}^{T_i} f(y_{it} \mid \mathbf{x}_{it}, \phi v_h, \boldsymbol{\beta}) \right] \right\}}.$$

It remains only to specialize this to our geometric regression model. For this case, the density is given earlier. The missing components of the preceding derivatives are the partial derivatives with respect to $\beta$ and $\phi$ that were obtained in Section 16.9.5.b. The necessary result is

$$\frac{\partial \ln f(y_{it} \mid \mathbf{x}_{it}, \phi v_h, \beta)}{\partial \begin{pmatrix} \beta \\ \phi \end{pmatrix}} = [\theta_{it}(1 + y_{it}) - 1]\begin{pmatrix} \mathbf{x}_{it} \\ v_h \end{pmatrix}.$$

Maximum likelihood estimates of the parameters of the random effects geometric regression model are given in Example 16.13 with the fixed effects estimates for this model.

### 16.9.6.c  Fixed Effects in Nonlinear Models: Full MLE

Using the same modeling framework that we used in the previous section, we now define a fixed effects model as an index function model with a group-specific constant term. As before, the "model" is the assumed density for a random variable,

$$p(y_{it} \mid d_{it}, \mathbf{x}_{it}) = f(y_{it} \mid \alpha_i d_{it} + \mathbf{x}'_{it}\beta),$$

where $d_{it}$ is a dummy variable that takes the value one in every period for individual $i$ and zero otherwise. (In more involved models, such as the censored regression model we examine in Chapter 24, there might be other parameters, such as a variance. For now, it is convenient to omit them—the development can be extended to add them later.) For convenience, we have redefined $\mathbf{x}_{it}$ to be the nonconstant variables in the model.[27] The parameters to be estimated are the $K$ elements of $\beta$ and the $n$ individual constant terms. The log-likelihood function for the fixed effects model is

$$\ln L = \sum_{i=1}^{n} \sum_{t=1}^{T_i} \ln f(y_{it} \mid \alpha_i + \mathbf{x}'_{it}\beta),$$

where $f(.)$ is the probability density function of the observed outcome, for example, the geometric regression model that we used in our previous example. It will be convenient to let $z_{it} = \alpha_i + \mathbf{x}'_{it}\beta$ so that $p(y_{it} \mid d_{it}, \mathbf{x}_{it}) = f(y_{it} \mid z_{it})$.

In the fixed effects linear regression case, we found that estimation of the parameters was made possible by a transformation of the data to deviations from group means that eliminated the person-specific constants from the equation. (See Section 9.4.1.) In a few cases of nonlinear models, it is also possible to eliminate the fixed effects from the likelihood function, although in general not by taking deviations from means. One example is the **exponential regression model** that is used for lifetimes of electronic components and electrical equipment such as light bulbs:

$$f(y_{it} \mid \alpha_i + \mathbf{x}'_{it}\beta) = \theta_{it} \exp(-\theta_{it} y_{it}), \theta_{it} = \exp(\alpha_i + \mathbf{x}'_{it}\beta), y_{it} \geq 0.$$

It will be convenient to write $\theta_{it} = \gamma_i \exp(\mathbf{x}'_{it}\beta) = \gamma_i \Delta_{it}$. We are exploiting the invariance property of the MLE—estimating $\gamma_i = \exp(\alpha_i)$ is the same as estimating $\alpha_i$. The

---

[27] In estimating a fixed effects linear regression model in Section 9.4, we found that it was not possible to analyze models with time-invariant variables. The same limitation applies in the nonlinear case, for essentially the same reasons. The time-invariant effects are absorbed in the constant term. In estimation, the columns of the data matrix with time-invariant variables will be transformed to columns of zeros when we compute derivatives of the log-likelihood function.

log-likelihood is

$$\ln L = \sum_{i=1}^{n} \sum_{t=1}^{T_i} \ln \theta_{it} - \theta_{it} y_{it}$$

$$= \sum_{i=1}^{n} \sum_{t=1}^{T_i} \ln(\gamma_i \mathbf{\Delta}_{it}) - (\gamma_i \mathbf{\Delta}_{it}) y_{it}.$$

(16-91)

The MLE will be found by equating the $n + K$ partial derivatives with respect to $\gamma_i$ and $\boldsymbol{\beta}$ to zero. For each constant term,

$$\frac{\partial \ln L}{\partial \gamma_i} = \sum_{t=1}^{T_i} \left( \frac{1}{\gamma_i} - \mathbf{\Delta}_{it} y_{it} \right).$$

Equating this to zero provides a solution for $\gamma_i$ in terms of the data and $\boldsymbol{\beta}$,

$$\gamma_i = \frac{T_i}{\sum_{t=1}^{T_i} \mathbf{\Delta}_{it} y_{it}}.$$

(16-92)

[Note the analogous result for the linear model in (9-15).] Inserting this solution back in the log-likelihood function in (16-91), we obtain the concentrated log-likelihood,

$$\ln L_C = \sum_{i=1}^{n} \sum_{t=1}^{T_i} \ln \left( \frac{T_i \mathbf{\Delta}_{it}}{\sum_{s=1}^{T_i} \mathbf{\Delta}_{is} y_{is}} \right) - \left( \frac{T_i \mathbf{\Delta}_{it}}{\sum_{s=1}^{T_i} \mathbf{\Delta}_{is} y_{is}} \right) y_{it},$$

which is now only a function of $\boldsymbol{\beta}$. This function can now be maximized with respect to $\boldsymbol{\beta}$ alone. The MLEs for $\alpha_i$ are then found as the logs of the results of (16-91). Note, once again, we have eliminated the constants from the estimation problem, but not by computing deviations from group means. That is specific to the linear model.

The concentrated log-likelihood is only obtainable in only a small handful of cases, including the linear model, the exponential model (as just shown), the Poisson regression model, and a few others. Lancaster (2000) lists some of these and discusses the underlying methodological issues. In most cases, if one desires to estimate the parameters of a fixed effects model, it will be necessary to actually compute the possibly huge number of constant terms, $\alpha_i$, at the same time as the main parameters, $\boldsymbol{\beta}$. This has widely been viewed as a practical obstacle to estimation of this model because of the need to invert a potentially large second derivatives matrix, but this is a misconception. [See, e.g., Maddala (1987), p. 317.] The likelihood equations for the fixed effects model are

$$\frac{\partial \ln L}{\partial \alpha_i} = \sum_{t=1}^{T_i} \frac{\partial \ln f(y_{it} \mid z_{it})}{\partial z_{it}} \frac{\partial z_{it}}{\partial \alpha_i} = \sum_{t=1}^{T_i} g_{it} = g_{ii} = 0,$$

and

$$\frac{\partial \ln L}{\partial \boldsymbol{\beta}} = \sum_{i=1}^{n} \sum_{t=1}^{T_i} \frac{\partial \ln f(y_{it} \mid z_{it})}{\partial z_{it}} \frac{\partial z_{it}}{\partial \boldsymbol{\beta}} = \sum_{i=1}^{n} \sum_{t=1}^{T_i} g_{it} \mathbf{x}_{it} = \mathbf{0}.$$

The second derivatives matrix is

$$
\frac{\partial^2 \ln L}{\partial \alpha_i^2} = \sum_{t=1}^{T_i} \frac{\partial^2 \ln f(y_{it} \mid z_{it})}{\partial z_{it}^2} = \sum_{t=1}^{T_i} h_{it} = h_{i.} < 0,
$$

$$
\frac{\partial^2 \ln L}{\partial \boldsymbol{\beta} \partial \alpha_i} = \sum_{t=1}^{T_i} h_{it} \mathbf{x}_{it},
$$

$$
\frac{\partial^2 \ln L}{\partial \boldsymbol{\beta} \partial \boldsymbol{\beta}'} = \sum_{i=1}^{n} \sum_{t=1}^{T_i} h_{it} \mathbf{x}_{it} \mathbf{x}_{it}' = \mathbf{H}_{\boldsymbol{\beta}\boldsymbol{\beta}'},
$$

where $\mathbf{H}_{\boldsymbol{\beta}\boldsymbol{\beta}'}$ is a negative definite matrix. The likelihood equations are a large system, but the solution turns out to be surprisingly straightforward. [See Greene (2001).]

By using the formula for the partitioned inverse, we find that the $K \times K$ submatrix of the inverse of the Hessian that corresponds to $\boldsymbol{\beta}$, which would provide the asymptotic covariance matrix for the MLE, is

$$
\mathbf{H}^{\boldsymbol{\beta}\boldsymbol{\beta}'} = \left\{ \sum_{i=1}^{n} \left[ \sum_{t=1}^{T_i} h_{it} \mathbf{x}_{it} \mathbf{x}_{it}' - \frac{1}{h_{i.}} \left( \sum_{t=1}^{T_i} h_{it} \mathbf{x}_{it} \right) \left( \sum_{t=1}^{T_i} h_{it} \mathbf{x}_{it}' \right) \right] \right\}^{-1},
$$

$$
= \left\{ \sum_{i=1}^{n} \left[ \sum_{t=1}^{T_i} h_{it} (\mathbf{x}_{it} - \bar{\mathbf{x}}_i)(\mathbf{x}_{it} - \bar{\mathbf{x}}_i)' \right] \right\}^{-1}, \quad \text{where} \quad \bar{\mathbf{x}}_i = \frac{\sum_{t=1}^{T_i} h_{it} \mathbf{x}_{it}}{h_{i.}}.
$$

Note the striking similarity to the result we had in (9-18) for the fixed effects model in the linear case. [A similar result is noted briefly in Chamberlain (1984).] By assembling the Hessian as a partitioned matrix for $\boldsymbol{\beta}$ and the full vector of constant terms, then using (A-66b) and the preceding definitions to isolate one diagonal element, we find

$$
\mathbf{H}^{\alpha_i \alpha_i} = \frac{1}{h_{i.}} + \bar{\mathbf{x}}_i' \mathbf{H}^{\boldsymbol{\beta}\boldsymbol{\beta}'} \bar{\mathbf{x}}_i.
$$

Once again, the result has the same format as its counterpart in the linear model. [See (9-18).] In principle, the negatives of these would be the estimators of the asymptotic variances of the maximum likelihood estimators. (Asymptotic properties in this model are problematic, as we consider shortly.)

All of these can be computed quite easily once the parameter estimates are in hand, so that in fact, practical estimation of the model is not really the obstacle. [This must be qualified, however. Consider the likelihood equation for one of the constants in the geometric regression model. This would be

$$
\sum_{t=1}^{T_i} [\theta_{it}(1 + y_{it}) - 1] = 0.
$$

Suppose $y_{it}$ equals zero in every period for individual $i$. Then, the solution occurs where $\Sigma_i(\theta_{it} - 1) = 0$. But $\theta_{it}$ is between zero and one, so the sum must be negative and cannot equal zero. The likelihood equation has no solution with finite coefficients. Such groups would have to be removed from the sample to fit this model.]

It is shown in Greene (2001) in spite of the potentially large number of parameters in the model, Newton's method can be used with the following iteration, which uses only the $K \times K$ matrix computed earlier and a few $K \times 1$ vectors:

$$\hat{\boldsymbol{\beta}}^{(s+1)} = \hat{\boldsymbol{\beta}}^{(s)} - \left\{ \sum_{i=1}^{n} \left[ \sum_{t=1}^{T_i} h_{it}(\mathbf{x}_{it} - \bar{\mathbf{x}}_i)(\mathbf{x}_{it} - \bar{\mathbf{x}}_i)' \right] \right\}^{-1} \left\{ \sum_{i=1}^{n} \left[ \sum_{t=1}^{T_i} g_{it}(\mathbf{x}_{it} - \bar{\mathbf{x}}_i) \right] \right\}$$

$$= \hat{\boldsymbol{\beta}}^{(s)} + \boldsymbol{\Delta}_{\boldsymbol{\beta}}^{(s)},$$

and

$$\hat{\alpha}_i^{(s+1)} = \hat{\alpha}_i^{(s)} - \left[ (g_{ii}/h_{ii}) + \bar{\mathbf{x}}_i' \boldsymbol{\Delta}_{\boldsymbol{\beta}}^{(s)} \right].^{[28]}$$

This is a large amount of computation involving many summations, but it is linear in the number of parameters and does not involve any $n \times n$ matrices.

In addition to the theoretical virtues and shortcomings of this model, we note the practical aspect of estimation of what are possibly a huge number of parameters, $n + K$. In the fixed effects case, $n$ is not limited, and could be in the thousands in a typical application. [In Example 16.13, $n$ is 7,293. As of this writing, the largest application of the method described here that we are aware of is Kingdon and Cassen's (2007) study in which they fit a fixed effects probit model with well over 140,000 dummy variable coefficients.] The problems with the fixed effects estimator are statistical, not practical.[29] The estimator relies on $T_i$ increasing for the constant terms to be consistent—in essence, each $\alpha_i$ is estimated with $T_i$ observations. In this setting, not only is $T_i$ fixed, it is likely to be quite small. As such, the estimators of the constant terms are not consistent (not because they converge to something other than what they are trying to estimate, but because they do not converge at all). There is, as well, a small sample (small $T_i$) bias in the slope estimators. This is the **incidental parameters problem.** [See Neyman and Scott (1948) and Lancaster (2000).] We will examine the incidental parameters problem in a bit more detail with a Monte Carlo study in Section 17.4.

### Example 16.13   *Fixed and Random Effects Geometric Regression*
Example 16.10 presents pooled estimates for the geometric regression model

$$f(y_{it} \mid \mathbf{x}_{it}) = \theta_{it}(1 - \theta_{it})^{y_{it}}, \theta_{it} = 1/(1 + \lambda_{it}), \lambda_{it} = \exp(c_i + \mathbf{x}_{it}'\beta), y_{it} = 0, 1, \ldots$$

We will now reestimate the model under the assumptions of the random and fixed effects specifications. The methods of the preceding two sections are applied directly—no modification of the procedures was required. Table 16.10 presents the three sets of maximum likelihood estimates. The estimates vary considerably. The average group size is about five. This implies that the fixed effects estimator may well be subject to a small sample bias. Save for the coefficient on *Kids*, the fixed effects and random effects estimates are quite similar. On the other hand, the two panel models give similar results to the pooled model except for the *Income* coefficient. On this basis, it is difficult to see, based solely on the results, which should be the preferred model. The model is nonlinear to begin with, so the pooled model, which might otherwise be preferred on the basis of computational ease, now has no

---

[28]Similar results appear in Prentice and Gloeckler (1978) who attribute it to Rao (1973) and Chamberlain (1980, 1984).

[29]See Vytlacil, Aakvik, and Heckman (2005), Chamberlain (1980, 1984), Newey (1994), Bover and Arellano (1997), and Chen (1998) for some extensions of parametric and semiparametric forms of the binary choice models with fixed effects.

**TABLE 16.10**  Panel Data Estimates of a Geometric Regression for DOCVIS

| | Pooled | | Random Effects[a] | | Fixed Effects | |
|---|---|---|---|---|---|---|
| *Variable* | *Estimate* | *St. Er.* | *Estimate* | *St. Er.* | *Estimate* | *St. Er.* |
| Constant | 1.0918 | 0.1112 | 0.3998 | 0.09531 | | |
| Age | 0.0180 | 0.0013 | 0.02208 | 0.001220 | 0.04845 | 0.003511 |
| Education | −0.0473 | 0.0069 | −0.04507 | 0.006262 | −0.05437 | 0.03721 |
| Income | −0.0468 | 0.0075 | −0.1959 | 0.06103 | −0.1892 | 0.09127 |
| Kids | −0.1569 | 0.0319 | −0.1242 | 0.02336 | −0.002543 | 0.03687 |

[a]Estimated $\sigma_u = 0.9542921$.

redeeming virtues. None of the three models is robust to misspecification. Unlike the linear model, in this and other nonlinear models, the fixed effects estimator is inconsistent when $T$ is small in both random and fixed effects models. The random effects estimator is consistent in the random effects model, but, as usual, not in the fixed effects model. The pooled estimator is inconsistent in both random and fixed effects cases (which calls into question the virtue of the robust covariance matrix). It might be tempting to use a Hausman specification test (see Section 9.5.4); however, the conditions that underlie the test are not met—unlike the linear model where the fixed effects is consistent in both cases, here it is inconsistent in both cases. For better or worse, that leaves the analyst with the need to choose the model based on the underlying theory.

### 16.9.7  LATENT CLASS AND FINITE MIXTURE MODELS

The latent class model specifies that the distribution of the observed data is a mixture of a finite number of underlying distributions. The model can be motivated in several ways:

- In the classic application of the technique, the observed data are drawn from a mix of distinct underlying populations. Consider, for example, a historical or fossilized record of the intersection (or collision) of two populations. The anthropological record consists of measurements on some variable that would differ distinctly between the populations. However, the analyst has no definitive marker for which subpopulation an observation is drawn from. Given a sample of observations, they are interested in two statistical problems: (1) estimate the parameters of the underlying populations and (2) classify observations in hand as having originated in which population. In another contemporary application, Lambert (1992) studied the number of defective outcomes in a production process. When a "zero defectives" condition is observed, it could indicate either regime 1, "the process is under control," or regime 2, "the process is not under control but just happens to produce a zero observation."

- In a narrower sense, one might view parameter heterogeneity in a population as a form of discrete mixing. We have modeled parameter heterogeneity using continuous distributions in Chapter 9. The "finite mixture" approach takes the distribution of parameters across individuals to be discrete. (Of course, this is another way to interpret the first point.)

- The finite mixing approach is a means by which a distribution (model) can be constructed from a mixture of underlying distributions. Goldfeld and Quandt's mixture of normals model in Example 15.4 is a case in which a nonnormal distribution is created by mixing two normal distributions with different parameters.

### 16.9.7.a A Finite Mixture Model

To lay the foundation for the more fully developed model that follows, we revisit the mixture of normals model from Example 15.4. Consider a population that consists of a latent mixture of two underlying normal distributions. Neglecting for the moment that it is unknown which applies to a given individual, we have, for individual $i$,

$$f(y_i \mid class_i = 1) = N[\mu_1, \sigma_1^2] = \frac{\exp\left[-\frac{1}{2}(y_i - \mu_1)^2/\sigma_1^2\right]}{\sigma_1\sqrt{2\pi}},$$

and

$$f(y_i \mid class_i = 2) = N[\mu_2, \sigma_2^2] = \frac{\exp\left[-\frac{1}{2}(y_i - \mu_2)^2/\sigma_2^2\right]}{\sigma_2\sqrt{2\pi}}.$$

**(16-93)**

The contribution to the likelihood function is $f(y_i \mid class_i = 1)$ for an individual in class 1 and $f(y_i \mid class = 2)$ for an individual in class 2. Assume that there is a true proportion $\lambda = \text{Prob}(class_i = 1)$ of individuals in the population that are in class 1, and $(1 - \lambda)$ in class 2. Then the unconditional (marginal) density for individual $i$ is

$$f(y_i) = \lambda f(y_i \mid class_i = 1) + (1 - \lambda) f(y_i \mid class_i = 2)$$

**(16-94)**

$$= E_{classes} f(y_i \mid class_i).$$

The parameters to be estimated are $\lambda$, $\mu_1$, $\mu_2$, $\sigma_1$, and $\sigma_2$. Combining terms, the log-likelihood for a sample of $n$ individual observations would be

$$\ln L = \sum_{i=1}^{n} \ln \left( \frac{\lambda \exp\left[-\frac{1}{2}(y_i - \mu_1)^2/\sigma_1^2\right]}{\sigma_1\sqrt{2\pi}} + \frac{(1 - \lambda) \exp\left[-\frac{1}{2}(y_i - \mu_2)^2/\sigma_2^2\right]}{\sigma_2\sqrt{2\pi}} \right).$$

**(16-95)**

This is the mixture density that we saw in Example 15.4. We suggested the method of moments as an estimator of the five parameters in that example. However, this appears to be a straightforward problem in maximum likelihood estimation.

#### Example 16.14 Latent Class Model for Grade Point Averages

Appendix Table F16.1 contains a data set of 32 observations used by Spector and Mazzeo (1980) to study whether a new method of teaching economics, the Personalized System of Instruction (PSI), significantly influenced performance in later economics courses. Variables in the data set include

| | |
|---|---|
| *GPA_i* | = the student's grade point average, |
| *GRADE_i* | = dummy variable for whether the student's grade in intermediate macroeconomics was higher than in the principles course, |
| *PSI_i* | = dummy variable for whether the individual participated in the PSI, |
| *TUCE_i* | = the student's score on a pretest in economics. |

We will use these data to develop a finite mixture normal model for the distribution of grade point averages.

We begin by computing maximum likelihood estimates of the parameters in (16-95). To estimate the parameters using an iterative method, it is necessary to devise a set of starting values. It is might seem natural to use the simple values from a one-class model, $\bar{y}$ and $s_y$, and a value such as 1/2 for $\lambda$. However, the optimizer will immediately stop on these values, as the derivatives will be zero at this point. Rather, it is common to use some value near these—perturbing them slightly (a few percent), just to get the iterations started. Table 16.11 contains the estimates for this two-class finite mixture model. The estimates for the one-class model are the sample mean and standard deviations of *GPA*. [Because these are the MLEs,

**TABLE 16.11**   Estimated Normal Mixture Model

| Parameter | One Class | | Latent Class 1 | | Latent Class 2 | |
|---|---|---|---|---|---|---|
| | *Estimate* | *Std. Err.* | *Estimate* | *Std. Err.* | *Estimate* | *Std. Err.* |
| $\mu$ | 3.1172 | 0.08251 | 3.64187 | 0.3452 | 2.8894 | 0.2514 |
| $\sigma$ | 0.4594 | 0.04070 | 0.2524 | 0.2625 | 0.3218 | 0.1095 |
| *Probability* | 1.0000 | 0.0000 | 0.3028 | 0.3497 | 0.6972 | 0.3497 |
| *ln L* | −20.51274 | | | −19.63654 | | |

$\hat{\sigma}^2 = \frac{1}{n}\sum_{i=1}^{n}(GPA_i - \overline{GPA})^2$.] The means and standard deviations of the two classes are noticeably different—the model appears to be revealing a distinct splitting of the data into two classes. (Whether two is the appropriate number of classes is considered in Section 16.9.7.e). It is tempting at this point to identify the two classes with some other covariate, either in the data set or not, such as *PSI*. However, at this point, there is no basis for doing so—the classes are "latent." As the analysis continues, however, we will want to investigate whether any observed data help to predict the class membership.

### 16.9.7.b   Measured and Unmeasured Heterogeneity

The development thus far has assumed that the analyst has no information about class membership. Estimation of the "prior" probabilities ($\lambda$ in the preceding example) is part of the estimation problem. There may be some, albeit imperfect, information about class membership in the sample as well. For our earlier example of grade point averages, we also know the individual's score on a test of economic literacy *(TUCE)*. Use of this information might sharpen the estimates of the class probabilities. The mixture of normals problem, for example, might be formulated

$$f(y_i \mid \mathbf{z}_i) = \left( \frac{\text{Prob}(class = 1 \mid \mathbf{z}_i)\exp\left[-\frac{1}{2}(y_i - \mu_1)^2/\sigma_1^2\right]}{\sigma_1\sqrt{2\pi}} + \frac{[1 - \text{Prob}(class = 1 \mid \mathbf{z}_i)]\exp\left[-\frac{1}{2}(y_i - \mu_2)^2/\sigma_2^2\right]}{\sigma_2\sqrt{2\pi}} \right),$$

where $\mathbf{z}_i$ is the vector of variables that help to explain the class probabilities. To make the mixture model amenable to estimation, it is necessary to parameterize the probabilities. The logit probability model is a common device. (See Section 23.4. For applications, see Greene (2007d, Section 2.3.3) and references cited.) For the two-class case, this might appear as follows:

$$\text{Prob}(class = 1 \mid \mathbf{z}_i) = \frac{\exp(\mathbf{z}_i'\boldsymbol{\theta})}{1 + \exp(\mathbf{z}_i'\boldsymbol{\theta})}, \quad \text{Prob}(class = 2 \mid \mathbf{z}_i) = 1 - \text{Prob}(class = 1 \mid \mathbf{z}_i).$$

**(16-96)**

(The more general *J* class case is shown in Section 16.9.7f.) The log-likelihood for our mixture of two normals example becomes

$$\ln L = \sum_{i=1}^{n} \ln L_i$$

$$= \sum_{i=1}^{n} \ln \left( \left(\frac{\exp(\mathbf{z}_i'\boldsymbol{\theta})}{1 + \exp(\mathbf{z}_i'\boldsymbol{\theta})}\right) \frac{\exp\left[-\frac{1}{2}(y_i - \mu_1)^2/\sigma_1^2\right]}{\sigma_1\sqrt{2\pi}} + \left(\frac{1}{1 + \exp(\mathbf{z}_i'\boldsymbol{\theta})}\right) \frac{\exp\left[-\frac{1}{2}(y_i - \mu_2)^2/\sigma_2^2\right]}{\sigma_2\sqrt{2\pi}} \right).$$

**(16-97)**

The log-likelihood is now maximized with respect to $\mu_1, \sigma_1, \mu_2, \sigma_2$, and $\theta$. If $\mathbf{z}_i$ contains a constant term and some other observed variables, then the earlier model returns if the coefficients on those other variables all equal zero. In this case, it follows that $\lambda = \ln[\theta/(1-\theta)]$. (This device is usually used to ensure that $0 < \lambda < 1$ in the earlier model.)

### 16.9.7.c  Predicting Class Membership

The model in (16-97) now characterizes two random variables, $y_i$, the outcome variable of interest, and $class_i$, the indicator of which class the individual resides in. We have a joint distribution, $f(y_i, class_i)$, which we are modeling in terms of the conditional density, $f(y_i \mid class_i)$ in (16-93), and the marginal density of $class_i$ in (16-96). We have initially assumed the latter to be a simple Bernoulli distribution with $\text{Prob}(class_i = 1) = \lambda$, but then modified in the previous section to equal $\text{Prob}(class_i = 1 \mid \mathbf{z}_i) = \Lambda(\mathbf{z}_i'\boldsymbol{\theta})$. These can be viewed as the "prior" probabilities in a Bayesian sense. If we wish to make a prediction as to which class the individual came from, using all the information that we have on that individual, then the prior probability is going to waste some information. The "posterior," or conditional (on the remaining data) probability,

$$\text{Prob}(class_i = 1 \mid \mathbf{z}_i \, y_i) = \frac{f(y_i, class = 1 \mid \mathbf{z}_i)}{f(y_i)}, \tag{16-98}$$

will be based on more information than the marginal probabilities. We have the elements that we need to compute this conditional probability. Use **Bayes theorem** to write this as

$$\text{Prob}(class_i = 1 \mid \mathbf{z}_i, \, y_i)$$
$$= \frac{f(y_i \mid class_i = 1, \mathbf{z}_i)\text{Prob}(class_i = 1 \mid \mathbf{z}_i)}{f(y_i \mid class_i = 1, \mathbf{z}_i)\text{Prob}(class_i = 1 \mid \mathbf{z}_i) + f(y_i \mid class_i = 2, \mathbf{z}_i)\text{Prob}(class_i = 2 \mid \mathbf{z}_i)}. \tag{16-99}$$

The denominator is $L_i$ (not $\ln L_i$) from (16-97). The numerator is the first term in $L_i$. To continue our mixture of two normals example, the conditional (posterior) probability is

$$\text{Prob}(class_i = 1 \mid \mathbf{z}_i, \, y_i) = \frac{\left(\dfrac{\exp(\mathbf{z}_i'\boldsymbol{\theta})}{1 + \exp(\mathbf{z}_i'\boldsymbol{\theta})}\right)\dfrac{\exp\left[-\frac{1}{2}(y_i - \mu_1)^2/\sigma_1^2\right]}{\sigma_1\sqrt{2\pi}}}{L_i}, \tag{16-100}$$

while the unconditional probability is in (16-96). The conditional probability for the second class is computed using the other two marginal densities in the numerator (or by subtraction from one). Note that the conditional probabilities are functions of the data even if the unconditional ones are not. To come to the problem suggested at the outset, then, the natural predictor of $class_i$ is the class associated with the largest estimated posterior probability.

### 16.9.7.d  A Conditional Latent Class Model

To complete the construction of the latent class model, we note that the means (and, in principle, the variances) in the original model could be conditioned on observed data as well. For our normal mixture models, we might make the marginal mean, $\mu_j$, a conditional mean:

$$\mu_{ij} = \mathbf{x}_i' \boldsymbol{\beta}_j.$$

In the data of Example 16.14, we also observe an indicator of whether the individual has participated in a special program designed to enhance the economics program (PSI). We might modify the model,

$$f(y_i \mid class_i = 1, PSI_i) = N\left[\mu_{i1}, \sigma_1^2\right] = \frac{\exp\left[-\frac{1}{2}(y_i - \beta_{1,1} - \beta_{2,1}PSI_i)^2/\sigma_1^2\right]}{\sigma_1\sqrt{2\pi}},$$

and similarly for $f(y_i \mid class_i = 2, PSI_i)$. The model is now a **latent class linear regression** model.

More generally, as we will see shortly, the latent class, or **finite mixture model** for a variable $y_i$ can be formulated as

$$f(y_i \mid class_i = j, \mathbf{x}_i) = h_j(y_i, \mathbf{x}_i, \boldsymbol{\gamma}_j),$$

where $h_j$ denotes the density conditioned on class $j$—indexed by $j$ to indicate, for example, the $j$th parameter vector $\boldsymbol{\gamma}_j = (\boldsymbol{\beta}_j, \sigma_j)$ and so on. The marginal class probabilities are

$$\text{Prob}(class_i = j \mid \mathbf{z}_i) = p_j(j, \mathbf{z}_i, \boldsymbol{\theta}).$$

The methodology can be applied to any model for $y_i$. In the example in Section 16.9.7.f, we will model a binary dependent variable with a probit model. The methodology has been applied in many other settings, such as stochastic frontier models [Orea and Kumbhakar (2004), Greene (2004)], Poisson regression models [Wedel et al. (1993)], and a wide variety of count, discrete choice, and limited dependent variable models [McLachlan and Peel (2000), Greene (2007b)].

### Example 16.15  Latent Class Regression Model for Grade Point Averages

Combining 16.9.7.b and 16.9.7.d, we have a latent class model for grade point averages,

$$f(GPA_i \mid class_i = j, PSI_i) = \frac{\exp\left[-\frac{1}{2}(y_i - \beta_{1j} - \beta_{2j}PSI_i)^2/\sigma_j^2\right]}{\sigma_j\sqrt{2\pi}}, j = 1, 2,$$

$$\text{Prob}(class_i = 1 \mid TUCE_i) = \frac{\exp(\theta_1 + \theta_2 TUCE_i)}{1 + \exp(\theta_1 + \theta_2 TUCE_i)},$$

$$\text{Prob}(class_i = 2 \mid TUCE_i) = 1 - \text{Prob}(class = 1 \mid TUCE_i).$$

The log-likelihood is now

$$\ln L = \sum_{i=1}^{n} \ln \left( \left( \frac{\exp(\theta_1 + \theta_2 TUCE_i)}{1 + \exp(\theta_1 + \theta_2 TUCE_i)} \right) \frac{\exp\left[-\frac{1}{2}(y_i - \beta_{1,1} - \beta_{2,1}PSI_i)^2/\sigma_1^2\right]}{\sigma_1\sqrt{2\pi}} + \left( \frac{1}{1 + \exp(\theta_1 + \theta_2 TUCE_i)} \right) \frac{\exp\left[-\frac{1}{2}(y_i - \beta_{1,2} - \beta_{2,2}PSI_i)^2/\sigma_2^2\right]}{\sigma_2\sqrt{2\pi}} \right).$$

Maximum likelihood estimates of the parameters are given in Table 16.12.

Table 16.13 lists the observations sorted by GPA. The predictions of class membership reflect what one might guess from the coefficients in the table of coefficients. Class 2 members on average have lower GPAs than in class 1. The listing in Table 16.13 shows this clustering. It also suggests how the latent class model is using the sample information. If the results in

**TABLE 16.12** Estimated Latent Class Linear Regression Model for GPA

| Parameter | One Class | | Latent Class 1 | | Latent Class 2 | |
|---|---|---|---|---|---|---|
| | *Estimate* | *Std. Err.* | *Estimate* | *Std. Err.* | *Estimate* | *Std. Err.* |
| $\beta_1$ | 3.1011 | 0.1117 | 3.3928 | 0.1733 | 2.7926 | 0.04988 |
| $\beta_2$ | 0.03675 | 0.1689 | −0.1074 | 0.2006 | −0.5703 | 0.07553 |
| $\sigma = \mathbf{e}'\mathbf{e}/n$ | 0.4443 | 0.0003086 | 0.3812 | 0.09337 | 0.1119 | 0.04487 |
| $\theta_1$ | 0.0000 | 0.0000 | −6.8392 | 3.07867 | 0.0000 | 0.0000 |
| $\theta_2$ | 0.0000 | 0.0000 | 0.3518 | 0.1601 | 0.0000 | 0.0000 |
| $Prob\,|\,\overline{TUCE}$ | 1.0000 | | 0.7063 | | 0.2937 | |
| $\ln L$ | −20.48752 | | −13.39966 | | | |

**TABLE 16.13** Estimated Latent Class Probabilities

| GPA | TUCE | PSI | CLASS | P1 | P1* | P2 | P2* |
|---|---|---|---|---|---|---|---|
| 2.06 | 22 | 1 | 2 | 0.7109 | 0.0116 | 0.2891 | 0.9884 |
| 2.39 | 19 | 1 | 2 | 0.4612 | 0.0467 | 0.5388 | 0.9533 |
| 2.63 | 20 | 0 | 2 | 0.5489 | 0.1217 | 0.4511 | 0.8783 |
| 2.66 | 20 | 0 | 2 | 0.5489 | 0.1020 | 0.4511 | 0.8980 |
| 2.67 | 24 | 1 | 1 | 0.8325 | 0.9992 | 0.1675 | 0.0008 |
| 2.74 | 19 | 0 | 2 | 0.4612 | 0.0608 | 0.5388 | 0.9392 |
| 2.75 | 25 | 0 | 2 | 0.8760 | 0.3499 | 0.1240 | 0.6501 |
| 2.76 | 17 | 0 | 2 | 0.2975 | 0.0317 | 0.7025 | 0.9683 |
| 2.83 | 19 | 0 | 2 | 0.4612 | 0.0821 | 0.5388 | 0.9179 |
| 2.83 | 27 | 1 | 1 | 0.9345 | 1.0000 | 0.0655 | 0.0000 |
| 2.86 | 17 | 0 | 2 | 0.2975 | 0.0532 | 0.7025 | 0.9468 |
| 2.87 | 21 | 0 | 2 | 0.6336 | 0.2013 | 0.3664 | 0.7987 |
| 2.89 | 14 | 1 | 1 | 0.1285 | 1.0000 | 0.8715 | 0.0000 |
| 2.89 | 22 | 0 | 2 | 0.7109 | 0.3065 | 0.2891 | 0.6935 |
| 2.92 | 12 | 0 | 2 | 0.0680 | 0.0186 | 0.9320 | 0.9814 |
| 3.03 | 25 | 0 | 1 | 0.8760 | 0.9260 | 0.1240 | 0.0740 |
| 3.10 | 21 | 1 | 1 | 0.6336 | 1.0000 | 0.3664 | 0.0000 |
| 3.12 | 23 | 1 | 1 | 0.7775 | 1.0000 | 0.2225 | 0.0000 |
| 3.16 | 25 | 1 | 1 | 0.8760 | 1.0000 | 0.1240 | 0.0000 |
| 3.26 | 25 | 0 | 1 | 0.8760 | 0.9999 | 0.1240 | 0.0001 |
| 3.28 | 24 | 0 | 1 | 0.8325 | 0.9999 | 0.1675 | 0.0001 |
| 3.32 | 23 | 0 | 1 | 0.7775 | 1.0000 | 0.2225 | 0.0000 |
| 3.39 | 17 | 1 | 1 | 0.2975 | 1.0000 | 0.7025 | 0.0000 |
| 3.51 | 26 | 1 | 1 | 0.9094 | 1.0000 | 0.0906 | 0.0000 |
| 3.53 | 26 | 0 | 1 | 0.9094 | 1.0000 | 0.0906 | 0.0000 |
| 3.54 | 24 | 1 | 1 | 0.8325 | 1.0000 | 0.1675 | 0.0000 |
| 3.57 | 23 | 0 | 1 | 0.7775 | 1.0000 | 0.2225 | 0.0000 |
| 3.62 | 28 | 1 | 1 | 0.9530 | 1.0000 | 0.0470 | 0.0000 |
| 3.65 | 21 | 1 | 1 | 0.6336 | 1.0000 | 0.3664 | 0.0000 |
| 3.92 | 29 | 0 | 1 | 0.9665 | 1.0000 | 0.0335 | 0.0000 |
| 4.00 | 21 | 0 | 1 | 0.6336 | 1.0000 | 0.3664 | 0.0000 |
| 4.00 | 23 | 1 | 1 | 0.7775 | 1.0000 | 0.2225 | 0.0000 |

Table 16.11—just estimating the means, constant class probabilities—are used to produce the same table, when sorted, the highest 10 GPAs are in class 1 and the remainder are in class 2. The more elaborate model is adding information on *TUCE* to the computation. A low *TUCE* score can push a high GPA individual into class 2. (Of course, this is largely what multiple linear regression does as well).

### 16.9.7.e    Determining the Number of Classes

There is an unsolved inference issue remaining in the specification of the model. The number of classes has been taken as a known parameter—two in our main example thus far, three in the following application. Ideally, one would like to determine the appropriate number of classes statistically. However, $J$ is not a parameter in the model. A likelihood ratio test, for example, will not provide a valid result. Consider the original model in Example 16.14. The model has two classes and five parameters in total. It would seem natural to test down to a one-class model that contains only the mean and variance using the LR test. However, the number of restrictions here is actually ambiguous. If $\mu_1 = \mu_2$ and $\sigma_1 = \sigma_2$, then the mixing probability is irrelevant—the two class densities are the same, and it is a one-class model. Thus, the number of restrictions needed to get from the two-class model to the one-class model is ambiguous. It is neither two nor three. One strategy that has been suggested is to test upward, adding classes until the marginal class insignificantly changes the log-likelihood or one of the information criteria such as the AIC or BIC (see Section 16.6.5). Unfortunately, this approach is likewise problematic because the estimates from any specification that is too short are inconsistent. The alternative would be to test down from a specification known to be too large. Heckman and Singer (1984b) discuss this possibility and note that when the number of classes becomes larger than appropriate, the estimator should break down. In our Example 16.14, if we expand to four classes, the optimizer breaks down, and it is no longer possible to compute the estimates. A five-class model does produce estimates, but some are nonsensical. This does provide at least the directions to seek a viable strategy. The authoritative treatise on finite mixture models by McLachlan and Peel (2000, Chapter 6) contains extensive discussion of this issue.

### 16.9.7.f    A Panel Data Application

The latent class model is a useful framework for applications in panel data. The class probabilities partly play the role of common random effects, as we will now explore. The latent class model can be interpreted as a random parameters model, as suggested in Section 9.8.2, with a discrete distribution of the parameters.

Suppose that $\boldsymbol{\beta}_j$ is generated from a discrete distribution with $J$ outcomes, or classes, so that the distribution of $\boldsymbol{\beta}_j$ is over these classes. Thus, the model states that an individual belongs to one of the $J$ latent classes, indexed by the parameter vector, but it is unknown from the sample data exactly which one. We will use the sample data to estimate the parameter vectors, the parameters of the underlying probability distribution and the probabilities of class membership. The corresponding model formulation is now

$$f(y_{it} \mid \mathbf{x}_{it}, \mathbf{z}_i, \boldsymbol{\Delta}, \boldsymbol{\beta}_1, \boldsymbol{\beta}_2, \ldots, \boldsymbol{\beta}_J) = \sum_{j=1}^{J} p_{ij}(\mathbf{z}_i, \boldsymbol{\Delta}) f(y_{it} \mid class = j, \mathbf{x}_{it}, \boldsymbol{\beta}_j),$$

where it remains to parameterize the class probabilities, $p_{ij}$, and the structural model, $f(y_{it} \mid class = j, \mathbf{x}_{it}, \boldsymbol{\beta}_j)$. The parameter matrix, $\boldsymbol{\Delta}$, contains the parameters of the discrete probability distribution. It has $J$ rows, one for each class, and $M$ columns, for the $M$ variables in $\mathbf{z}_i$. At a minimum, $M = 1$ and $\mathbf{z}_i$ contains a constant term if the class probabilities are fixed parameters as in Example 16.14. Finally, to accommodate the panel data nature of the sampling situation, we suppose that conditioned on $\boldsymbol{\beta}_j$, that is, on membership in class $j$, which is fixed over time, the observations on $y_{it}$ are independent. Therefore, for a group of $T_i$ observations, the joint density is

$$f(y_{i1}, y_{i2}, \ldots, y_{t,T_i} \mid class = j, \mathbf{x}_{i1}, \mathbf{x}_{i2}, \ldots, \mathbf{x}_{i,T_i}, \boldsymbol{\beta}_j) = \prod_{t=1}^{T_i} f(y_{it} \mid class = j, \mathbf{x}_{it}, \boldsymbol{\beta}_j).$$

The log-likelihood function for a panel of data is

$$\ln L = \sum_{i=1}^{n} \ln \left[ \sum_{j=1}^{J} p_{ij}(\boldsymbol{\Delta}, \mathbf{z}_i) \prod_{t=1}^{T_i} f(y_{it} \mid class = j, \mathbf{x}_{it}, \boldsymbol{\beta}_j) \right].$$

The class probabilities must be constrained to sum to 1. The approach that is usually used is to reparameterize them as a set of logit probabilities, as we did in the preceding examples. Then,

$$p_{ij}(\mathbf{z}_i, \boldsymbol{\Delta}) = \frac{\exp(\theta_{ij})}{\sum_{j=1}^{J} \exp(\theta_{ij})}, J = 1, \ldots, J, \theta_{ij} = \mathbf{z}_i' \boldsymbol{\delta}_j, \theta_{iJ} = 0\,(\boldsymbol{\delta}_J = \mathbf{0}). \quad \textbf{(16-101)}$$

(See Section 23.11 for development of this model for the set of probabilities.) Note the restriction on $\theta_{ij}$. This is an identification restriction. Without it, the same set of probabilities will arise if an arbitrary vector is added to every $\boldsymbol{\delta}_j$. The resulting log likelihood is a continuous function of the parameters $\boldsymbol{\beta}_1, \ldots, \boldsymbol{\beta}_J$ and $\boldsymbol{\delta}_1, \ldots, \boldsymbol{\delta}_J$. For all its apparent complexity, estimation of this model by direct maximization of the log-likelihood is not especially difficult. [See Section E.3 and Greene (2001, 2007b). The EM algorithm discussed in Section E.3.7 is especially well suited for estimating the parameters of latent class models. See McLachlan and Peel (2000).] The number of classes that can be identified is likely to be relatively small (on the order of 5 or 10 at most), however, which has been viewed as a drawback of the approach. In general, the more complex the model for $y_{it}$, the more difficult it becomes to expand the number of classes. Also, as might be expected, the less rich the data set in terms of cross-group variation, the more difficult it is to estimate latent class models.

Estimation produces values for the structural parameters, $(\boldsymbol{\beta}_j, \boldsymbol{\delta}_j), j = 1, \ldots, J$. With these in hand, we can compute the prior class probabilities, $p_{ij}$ using (16-101). For prediction purposes, we are also interested in the posterior (on the data) class probabilities, which we can compute using Bayes theorem [see (16-99)]. The conditional probability is

$$
\begin{aligned}
&\text{Prob}(class = j \mid \text{observation } i) \\
&= \frac{f(\text{observation } i \mid \text{class} = j)\text{Prob}(\text{class } j)}{\sum_{j=1}^{J} f(\text{observation } i \mid \text{class} = j)\text{Prob}(\text{class } j)} \\
&= \frac{f(y_{i1}, y_{i2}, \ldots, y_{i,T_i} \mid \mathbf{x}_{i1}, \mathbf{x}_{i2}, \ldots, \mathbf{x}_{i,T_i}, \boldsymbol{\beta}_j)p_{ij}(\mathbf{z}_j, \boldsymbol{\Delta})}{\sum_{j=1}^{J} f(y_{i1}, y_{i2}, \ldots, y_{i,T_i} \mid \mathbf{x}_{i1}, \mathbf{x}_{i2}, \ldots, \mathbf{x}_{i,T_i}, \boldsymbol{\beta}_j)p_{ij}(\mathbf{z}_j, \boldsymbol{\Delta})} \\
&= w_{ij}.
\end{aligned}
\quad \textbf{(16-102)}
$$

The set of probabilities, $\mathbf{w}_i = (w_{i1}, w_{i2}, \ldots, w_{iJ})$ gives the posterior density over the distribution of values of $\boldsymbol{\beta}$, that is, $[\boldsymbol{\beta}_1, \boldsymbol{\beta}_2, \ldots, \boldsymbol{\beta}_J]$.

**TABLE 16.14**  Panel Data Estimates of a Geometric Regression for DocVis

| | Pooled MLE (Nonlinear Least Squares) | | Random Effects[a] | | Fixed Effects | |
|---|---|---|---|---|---|---|
| Variable | Estimate | St. Er | Estimate | St. Er. | Estimate | St. Er. |
| Constant | 1.0918 (0.9801) | 0.1082 (0.1813) | 0.3998 | 0.09531 | | |
| Age | 0.0180 (0.01873) | 0.0013 (0.00198) | 0.02208 | 0.001220 | 0.04845 | 0.003511 |
| Education | −0.0473 (−0.03613) | 0.0067 (0.01228) | −0.04507 | 0.006262 | −0.05437 | 0.03721 |
| Income | −0.4687 (−0.5911) | 0.0726 (0.1282) | −0.1959 | 0.06103 | −0.1982 | 0.09127 |
| Kids | −0.1569 (−0.1692) | 0.0306 (0.04882) | −0.1242 | 0.02336 | −0.002543 | 0.03687 |

[a]Estimated $\sigma_u = 0.9542921$.

### Example 16.16  Latent Class Model for Health Care Utilization

In Example 11.10, we proposed an exponential regression model,

$$y_{it} = DocVis_{it} = \exp(\mathbf{x}_{it}'\beta) + \varepsilon_{it},$$

for the variable DocVis, the number of visits to the doctor, in the German health care data. (See Example 11.10 for details.) The regression results for the specification,

$$\mathbf{x}_{it} = (1, Age_{it}, Education_{it}, Income_{it}, Kids_{it})$$

are repeated (in parentheses) in Table 16.14 for convenience. The nonlinear least squares estimator is only semiparametric; it makes no assumption about the distribution of $DocVis_{it}$ or about $\varepsilon_{it}$. We do see striking increases in the standard errors when the "cluster robust" asymptotic covariance matrix is used. (The estimates are given in Example 11.10.) The analysis at this point assumes that the nonlinear least squares estimator remains consistent in the presence of the cross-observation correlation. Given the way the model is specified, that is, only in terms of the conditional mean function, this is probably reasonable. The extension would imply a nonlinear generalized regression as opposed to a nonlinear ordinary regression. In Example 16.10, we narrowed this model by assuming that the observations on doctor visits were generated by a geometric distribution,

$$f(y_i \mid \mathbf{x}_i) = \theta_i(1 - \theta_i)^{y_i}, \theta_i = 1/(1 + \lambda_i), \lambda_i = \exp(\mathbf{x}_i'\beta), y_i = 0, 1, \dots.$$

The conditional mean is still $\exp(\mathbf{x}_{it}'\beta)$, but this specification adds the structure of a particular distribution for outcomes. The pooled model was estimated in Example 16.10. Example 16.13 added the panel data assumptions of random then fixed effects to the model. The model is now

$$f(y_{it} \mid \mathbf{x}_{it}) = \theta_{it}(1 - \theta_{it})^{y_{it}}, \theta_{it} = 1/(1 + \lambda_{it}), \lambda_{it} = \exp(c_i + \mathbf{x}_{it}'\beta), y_{it} = 0, 1, \dots.$$

The pooled, random effects and fixed effects estimates appear in Table 16.14. The pooled estimates, where the standard errors are corrected for the panel data grouping, are comparable to the nonlinear least squares estimates with the robust standard errors. The parameter estimates are similar—both are consistent and this is a very large sample. The smaller standard errors seen for the MLE are the product of the more detailed specification.

We will now relax the specification by assuming a two-class finite mixture model. We also specify that the class probabilities are functions of gender and marital status. For the latent

**TABLE 16.15** Estimated Latent Class Linear Regression Model for GPA

| Parameter | One Class | | Latent Class 1 | | Latent Class 2 | |
|---|---|---|---|---|---|---|
| | *Estimate* | *Std. Err.* | *Estimate* | *Std. Err.* | *Estimate* | *Std. Err.* |
| $\beta_1$ | 1.0918 | 0.1082 | 1.6423 | 0.05351 | −0.3344 | 0.09288 |
| $\beta_2$ | 0.0180 | 0.0013 | 0.01691 | 0.0007324 | 0.02649 | 0.001248 |
| $\beta_3$ | −0.0473 | 0.0067 | −0.04473 | 0.003451 | −0.06502 | 0.005739 |
| $\beta_4$ | −0.4687 | 0.0726 | −0.4567 | 0.04688 | 0.01395 | 0.06964 |
| $\beta_5$ | −0.1569 | 0.0306 | −0.1177 | 0.01611 | −0.1388 | 0.02738 |
| $\theta_1$ | 0.0000 | 0.0000 | −0.4280 | 0.06938 | 0.0000 | 0.0000 |
| $\theta_2$ | 0.0000 | 0.0000 | 0.8255 | 0.06322 | 0.0000 | 0.0000 |
| $\theta_3$ | 0.0000 | 0.0000 | −0.07829 | 0.07143 | 0.0000 | 0.0000 |
| $Prob \mid \bar{z}$ | 1.0000 | | 0.47697 | | 0.52303 | |
| ln $L$ | −61917.97 | | | −58708.63 | | |

**TABLE 16.16** Descriptive Statistics for Doctor Visits

| Class | Mean | Standard Deviation |
|---|---|---|
| *All*, $n = 27{,}326$ | 3.18352 | 7.47579 |
| *Class 1*, $n = 12{,}349$ | 5.80347 | 1.63076 |
| *Class 2*, $n = 14{,}977$ | 1.02330 | 3.18352 |

class specification,

$$\text{Prob}(class_i = 1 \mid \mathbf{z}_i) = \Lambda(\theta_1 + \theta_2\,Female_i + \theta_3\,Married_i).$$

The model structure is the geometric regression as before. Estimates of the parameters of the latent class model are shown in Table 16.15.

Deb and Trivedi (2002) suggested that a meaningful distinction between groups of health care system users would be between "infrequent" and "frequent" users. To investigate whether our latent class model is picking up this distinction in the data, we used (16-102) to predict the class memberships (class 1 or 2). We then linearly regressed $DocVis_{it}$ on a constant and a dummy variable for class 2. The results are

$$DocVis_{it} = 5.8034\,(0.0465) - 4.7801\,(0.06282)\,Class2_i + e_{it},$$

where estimated standard errors are in parentheses. The linear regression suggests that the class membership dummy variable is strongly segregating the observations into frequent and infrequent users. The information in the regression is summarized in the descriptive statistics in Table 16.16.

## 16.10 SUMMARY AND CONCLUSIONS

This chapter has presented the theory and several applications of maximum likelihood estimation, which is the most frequently used estimation technique in econometrics after least squares. The maximum likelihood estimators are consistent, asymptotically normally distributed, and efficient among estimators that have these properties. The drawback to the technique is that it requires a fully parametric, detailed specification of the data generating process. As such, it is vulnerable to misspecification problems. The previous chapter considered GMM estimation techniques which are less parametric, but more robust to variation in the underlying data generating process. Together, ML and GMM estimation account for the large majority of empirical estimation in econometrics.

## Key Terms and Concepts

- AIC
- Asymptotic efficiency
- Asymptotic normality
- Asymptotic variance
- Autocorrelation
- Bayes theorem
- BHHH estimator
- BIC
- Butler and Moffitt's model
- Cluster estimator
- Concentrated log-likelihood
- Conditional likelihood
- Consistency
- Cramér–Rao lower bound
- Efficient score
- Estimable parameters
- Exclusion restriction
- Exponential regression model
- Finite mixture
- Fixed effects
- Full information maximum likelihood
- Gauss–Hermite quadrature
- Generalized sum of squares
- Geometric regression
- GMM estimator
- Identification
- Incidental parameters problem
- Index function model
- Information matrix
- Information matrix equality
- Invariance
- Jacobian
- Lagrange multiplier statistic
- Lagrange multiplier test
- Latent class model
- Latent class regression model
- Likelihood equation
- Likelihood function
- Likelihood inequality
- Likelihood ratio index
- Likelihood ratio statistic
- Likelihood ratio test
- Limited information maximum likelihood
- Logit model
- Loglinear conditional mean
- Maximum likelihood
- Maximum likelihood estimator
- $M$ estimator
- Method of scoring
- Murphy and Topel estimator
- Newton's method
- Nonlinear least squares
- Noncentral chi-squared distribution
- Normalization
- Oberhofer–Kmenta estimator
- Outer product of gradients estimator (OPG)
- Parameter space
- Pseudo-log likelihood function
- Pseudo MLE
- Pseudo R squared
- Quadrature
- Random effects
- Regularity conditions
- Sandwich estimator
- Score test
- Score vector
- Stochastic frontier
- Two-step maximum likelihood
- Wald statistic
- Wald test
- Vuong test

## Exercises

1. Assume that the distribution of $x$ is $f(x) = 1/\theta, 0 \le x \le \theta$. In random sampling from this distribution, prove that the sample maximum is a consistent estimator of $\theta$. Note: You can prove that the maximum is the maximum likelihood estimator of $\theta$. But the usual properties do not apply here. Why not? (Hint: Attempt to verify that the expected first derivative of the log-likelihood with respect to $\theta$ is zero.)

2. In random sampling from the exponential distribution $f(x) = (1/\theta)e^{-x/\theta}, x \ge 0$, $\theta > 0$, find the maximum likelihood estimator of $\theta$ and obtain the asymptotic distribution of this estimator.

3. *Mixture distribution.* Suppose that the joint distribution of the two random variables $x$ and $y$ is

$$f(x, y) = \frac{\theta e^{-(\beta+\theta)y}(\beta y)^x}{x!}, \quad \beta, \theta > 0, y \ge 0, x = 0, 1, 2, \ldots.$$

a. Find the maximum likelihood estimators of $\beta$ and $\theta$ and their asymptotic joint distribution.
b. Find the maximum likelihood estimator of $\theta/(\beta + \theta)$ and its asymptotic distribution.
c. Prove that $f(x)$ is of the form

$$f(x) = \gamma(1 - \gamma)^x, \quad x = 0, 1, 2, \ldots,$$

and find the maximum likelihood estimator of $\gamma$ and its asymptotic distribution.
d. Prove that $f(y \mid x)$ is of the form

$$f(y \mid x) = \frac{\lambda e^{-\lambda y}(\lambda y)^x}{x!}, \quad y \geq 0, \lambda > 0.$$

Prove that $f(y \mid x)$ integrates to 1. Find the maximum likelihood estimator of $\lambda$ and its asymptotic distribution. (Hint: In the conditional distribution, just carry the $x$'s along as constants.)
e. Prove that

$$f(y) = \theta e^{-\theta y}, \quad y \geq 0, \quad \theta > 0.$$

Find the maximum likelihood estimator of $\theta$ and its asymptotic variance.
f. Prove that

$$f(x \mid y) = \frac{e^{-\beta y}(\beta y)^x}{x!}, \quad x = 0, 1, 2, \ldots, \beta > 0.$$

Based on this distribution, what is the maximum likelihood estimator of $\beta$?

4. Suppose that $x$ has the Weibull distribution

$$f(x) = \alpha \beta x^{\beta-1} e^{-\alpha x^\beta}, \quad x \geq 0, \alpha, \beta > 0.$$

a. Obtain the log-likelihood function for a random sample of $n$ observations.
b. Obtain the likelihood equations for maximum likelihood estimation of $\alpha$ and $\beta$. Note that the first provides an explicit solution for $\alpha$ in terms of the data and $\beta$. But, after inserting this in the second, we obtain only an implicit solution for $\beta$. How would you obtain the maximum likelihood estimators?
c. Obtain the second derivatives matrix of the log-likelihood with respect to $\alpha$ and $\beta$. The exact expectations of the elements involving $\beta$ involve the derivatives of the gamma function and are quite messy analytically. Of course, your exact result provides an empirical estimator. How would you estimate the asymptotic covariance matrix for your estimators in part b?
d. Prove that $\alpha\beta\text{Cov}[\ln x, x^\beta] = 1$. (Hint: The expected first derivatives of the log-likelihood function are zero.)

5. The following data were generated by the Weibull distribution of Exercise 4:

| | | | | | | |
|---|---|---|---|---|---|---|
| 1.3043 | 0.49254 | 1.2742 | 1.4019 | 0.32556 | 0.29965 | 0.26423 |
| 1.0878 | 1.9461 | 0.47615 | 3.6454 | 0.15344 | 1.2357 | 0.96381 |
| 0.33453 | 1.1227 | 2.0296 | 1.2797 | 0.96080 | 2.0070 | |

a. Obtain the maximum likelihood estimates of $\alpha$ and $\beta$, and estimate the asymptotic covariance matrix for the estimates.
b. Carry out a Wald test of the hypothesis that $\beta = 1$.
c. Obtain the maximum likelihood estimate of $\alpha$ under the hypothesis that $\beta = 1$.

   d. Using the results of Parts a and c, carry out a likelihood ratio test of the hypothesis that $\beta = 1$.

   e. Carry out a Lagrange multiplier test of the hypothesis that $\beta = 1$.

6. **Limited Information Maximum Likelihood Estimation.** Consider a bivariate distribution for $x$ and $y$ that is a function of two parameters, $\alpha$ and $\beta$. The joint density is $f(x, y \mid \alpha, \beta)$. We consider maximum likelihood estimation of the two parameters. The full information maximum likelihood estimator is the now familiar maximum likelihood estimator of the two parameters. Now, suppose that we can factor the joint distribution as done in Exercise 3, but in this case, we have $f(x, y \mid \alpha, \beta) = f(y \mid x, \alpha, \beta) f(x \mid \alpha)$. That is, the conditional density for $y$ is a function of both parameters, but the marginal distribution for $x$ involves only $\alpha$.

   a. Write down the general form for the log-likelihood function using the joint density.

   b. Because the joint density equals the product of the conditional times the marginal, the log-likelihood function can be written equivalently in terms of the factored density. Write this down, in general terms.

   c. The parameter $\alpha$ can be estimated by itself using only the data on $x$ and the log likelihood formed using the marginal density for $x$. It can also be estimated with $\beta$ by using the full log-likelihood function and data on both $y$ and $x$. Show this.

   d. Show that the first estimator in part c has a larger asymptotic variance than the second one. This is the difference between a limited information maximum likelihood estimator and a full information maximum likelihood estimator.

   e. Show that if $\partial^2 \ln f(y \mid x, \alpha, \beta)/\partial\alpha\partial\beta = 0$, then the result in part d is no longer true.

7. Show that the likelihood inequality in Theorem 16.3 holds for the Poisson distribution used in Section 16.3 by showing that $E[(1/n) \ln L(\theta \mid y)]$ is uniquely maximized at $\theta = \theta_0$. (Hint: First show that the expectation is $-\theta + \theta_0 \ln \theta - E_0[\ln y_i!]$.)

8. Show that the likelihood inequality in Theorem 16.3 holds for the normal distribution.

9. For random sampling from the classical regression model in (16-3), reparameterize the likelihood function in terms of $\eta = 1/\sigma$ and $\delta = (1/\sigma)\beta$. Find the maximum likelihood estimators of $\eta$ and $\delta$ and obtain the asymptotic covariance matrix of the estimators of these parameters.

10. Consider sampling from a multivariate normal distribution with mean vector $\mu = (\mu_1, \mu_2, \ldots, \mu_M)$ and covariance matrix $\sigma^2 \mathbf{I}$. The log-likelihood function is

$$\ln L = \frac{-nM}{2} \ln(2\pi) - \frac{nM}{2} \ln \sigma^2 - \frac{1}{2\sigma^2} \sum_{i=1}^{n} (\mathbf{y}_i - \mu)'(\mathbf{y}_i - \mu).$$

Show that the maximum likelihood estimates of the parameters are $\hat{\mu} = \bar{y}_m$, and

$$\hat{\sigma}_{ML}^2 = \frac{\sum_{i=1}^{n} \sum_{m=1}^{M} (y_{im} - \bar{y}_m)^2}{nM} = \frac{1}{M} \sum_{m=1}^{M} \frac{1}{n} \sum_{i=1}^{n} (y_{im} - \bar{y}_m)^2 = \frac{1}{M} \sum_{m=1}^{M} \hat{\sigma}_m^2.$$

Derive the second derivatives matrix and show that the asymptotic covariance matrix for the maximum likelihood estimators is

$$\left\{ -E\left[ \frac{\partial^2 \ln L}{\partial\boldsymbol{\theta}\partial\boldsymbol{\theta}'} \right] \right\}^{-1} = \begin{bmatrix} \sigma^2 \mathbf{I}/n & \mathbf{0} \\ \mathbf{0} & 2\sigma^4/(nM) \end{bmatrix}.$$

Suppose that we wished to test the hypothesis that the means of the $M$ distributions were all equal to a particular value $\mu^0$. Show that the Wald statistic would be

$$\mathbf{W} = (\bar{\mathbf{y}} - \mu^0 \mathbf{i})' \left( \frac{\hat{\sigma}^2}{n} \mathbf{I} \right)^{-1} (\bar{\mathbf{y}} - \mu^0 \mathbf{i}) = \left( \frac{n}{s^2} \right) (\bar{\mathbf{y}} - \mu^0 \mathbf{i})'(\bar{\mathbf{y}} - \mu^0 \mathbf{i}),$$

where $\bar{\mathbf{y}}$ is the vector of sample means.
11. Prove the result claimed in Example 4.9.

## Applications

1. **Binary Choice.** This application will be based on the health care data analyzed in Example 16.15 and several others. Details on obtaining the data are given in Example 11.10. We consider analysis of a dependent variable, $y_{it}$, that takes values and 1 and 0 with probabilities $F(\mathbf{x}_i'\boldsymbol{\beta})$ and $1 - F(\mathbf{x}_i'\boldsymbol{\beta})$, where $F$ is a function that defines a probability. The dependent variable, $y_{it}$, is constructed from the count variable *DocVis*, which is the number of visits to the doctor in the given year. Construct the binary variable

$$y_{it} = 1 \text{ if } DocVis_{it} > 0, 0 \text{ otherwise.}$$

We will build a model for the probability that $y_{it}$ equals one. The independent variables of interest will be,

$$\mathbf{x}_{it} = (1, age_{it}, educ_{it}, female_{it}, married_{it}, hsat_{it}).$$

a. According to the model, the theoretical density for $y_{it}$ is

$$f(y_{it} \mid \mathbf{x}_{it}) = F(\mathbf{x}_{it}'\boldsymbol{\beta}) \text{ for } y_{it} = 1 \text{ and } 1 - F(\mathbf{x}_{it}'\boldsymbol{\beta}) \text{ for } y_{it} = 0.$$

We will assume that a "logit model" (see Section 23.4) is appropriate, so that

$$F(\mathbf{x}_{it}'\boldsymbol{\beta}) = \Lambda(\mathbf{x}_{it}'\boldsymbol{\beta}) = \frac{\exp(\mathbf{x}_{it}'\boldsymbol{\beta})}{1 - \exp(\mathbf{x}_{it}'\boldsymbol{\beta})}.$$

Show that for the two outcomes, the probabilities may be may be combined into the density function

$$f(y_{it} \mid \mathbf{x}_{it}) = g(y_{it}, \mathbf{x}_{it}, \boldsymbol{\beta}) = \Lambda[(2y_{it} - 1)\mathbf{x}_{it}'\boldsymbol{\beta}].$$

Now, use this result to construct the log-likelihood function for a sample of data on $(y_{it}, \mathbf{x}_{it})$. (Note that we will be ignoring the panel aspect of the data set. Build the model as if this were a cross section.)
b. Derive the likelihood equations for estimation of $\boldsymbol{\beta}$.
c. Derive the second derivatives matrix of the log likelihood function. (Hint: The following will prove useful in the derivation: $d\Lambda(t)/dt = \Lambda(t)[1 - \Lambda(t)]$.)
d. Show how to use Newton's method to estimate the parameters of the model.
e. Does the method of scoring differ from Newton's method? Derive the negative of the expectation of the second derivatives matrix.
f. Obtain maximum likelihood estimates of the parameters for the data and variables noted. Report your results: estimates, standard errors, etc., as well as the value of the log-likelihood.

    g. Test the hypothesis that the coefficients on female and marital status are zero. Show how to do the test using Wald, LM, and LR tests, then carry out the tests.

    h. Test the hypothesis that all the coefficients in the model save for the constant term are equal to zero.

2. **Stochastic Frontier Model.** Section 10.4.1 presents estimates of a Cobb-Douglas cost function using Nerlove's 1955 data on the U.S. electric power industry. Christensen and Greene's 1976 update of this study used 1970 data for this industry. The Christensen and Greene data are given in Appendix Table F4.3. These data have provided a standard test data set for estimating different forms of production and cost functions, including the stochastic frontier model examined in Example 16.9. It has been suggested that one explanation for the apparent finding of economies of scale in these data is that the smaller firms were inefficient for other reasons. The stochastic frontier might allow one to disentangle these effects. Use these data to fit a frontier cost function which includes a quadratic term in log output in addition to the linear term and the factor prices. Then examine the estimated Jondrow et al. residuals to see if they do indeed vary negatively with output, as suggested. (This will require either some programming on your part or specialized software. The stochastic frontier model is provided as an option in Stata, TSP and LIMDEP. Or, the likelihood function can be programmed fairly easily for RATS, MatLab or GAUSS. Note, for a cost frontier as opposed to a production frontier, it is necessary to reverse the sign on the argument in the $\Phi$ function that appears in the log-likelihood.)

# 17

# SIMULATION-BASED
# ESTIMATION AND
# INFERENCE

## 17.1 INTRODUCTION

Familiar estimation and inference methods, such as least squares and maximum likelihood, rely on "closed form" expressions that can be evaluated exactly [at least in principle—likelihood equations such as (16-4) may require an iterative solution]. Model building and analysis often require evaluation of expressions that cannot be computed directly. Familiar examples include expectations that involve integrals with no closed form such as the random effects probit model presented in Section 23.5.1. To an increasing degree, analysts frequently rely on random sampling methods to obtain these results. In Section 9.8.2, for example, we relied on simulation to estimate a model with random parameters. Section 16.9.6.b discussed estimation of a random effects model in which it is necessary to approximate an integral, in that case using Hermite quadrature. The computation could also have been done using simulation, as we consider here.

This chapter will survey some of the (increasingly) more common applications of simulation methods in econometrics. Sections 17.2 and 17.3 begin with the essential tools of this area, random number generation and simulation-based evaluation of integrals. Sections 17.4 to 17.6 then examine three leading applications. Monte Carlo studies of the properties of estimators and test statistics are described in Section 17.4. Maximum simulated likelihood and the method of simulated moments are discussed in Section 17.5. The technique is applied to estimation of random parameters (mixed) models. Section 17.6 then considers the method of bootstrapping to infer the properties of estimators. A fourth major (perhaps *the* major) application of simulation-based estimation in the current literature is Bayesian analysis using Markov Chain Monte Carlo (MCMC or MC$^2$) methods. Bayesian methods are discussed separately in Chapter 18.

## 17.2 RANDOM NUMBER GENERATION

The data used in an econometric study can be broadly characterized as either real or simulated. "Real" data consist of actual measurements on some physical phenomenon such as the level of activity of an economy or the behavior of real consumers. For present purposes, the defining characteristic of such data is that they are generated outside the context of the empirical study and are gathered for the purpose of measuring some aspect of their real-world counterpart, such as an elasticity of some aspect of consumer behavior. The alternative is simulated data, produced by the analyst with a random number generator, usually for the purpose of studying the behavior of econometric estimators for which the statistical properties are unknown or impossible to derive. This section will consider a few aspects of the manipulation of data with a computer.

### 17.2.1 GENERATING PSEUDO-RANDOM NUMBERS

Monte Carlo methods and Monte Carlo studies of estimators are enjoying a flowering in the econometrics literature. In these studies, data are generated internally in the computer using **pseudo–random number generators.** These computer programs generate sequences of values that appear to be strings of draws from a specified probability distribution. There are many types of random number generators, but most take advantage of the inherent inaccuracy of the digital representation of real numbers. The method of generation is usually by the following steps:

1. Set a **seed.**
2. Update the seed by $\text{seed}_j = \text{seed}_{j-1} \times s$ value.
3. $x_j = \text{seed}_j \times x$ value.
4. Transform $x_j$ if necessary, then move $x_j$ to desired place in memory.
5. Return to step 2, or exit if no additional values are needed.

Random number generators produce sequences of values that resemble strings of random draws from the specified distribution. In fact, the sequence of values produced by the preceding method is not truly random at all; it is a deterministic **Markov chain** of values. The set of 32 bits in the random value only appear random when subjected to certain tests. [See Press et al. (1986).] Because the series is, in fact, deterministic, at any point that a generator produces a value it has produced before, it must thereafter replicate the entire sequence. Because modern digital computers typically use 32-bit double precision variables to represent numbers, it follows that the longest string of values that this kind of generator can produce is $2^{32} - 1$ (about 4.3 billion). This length is the **period** of a random number generator. (A generator with a shorter period than this would be inefficient, because it is possible to achieve this period with some fairly simple algorithms.) Some improvements in the periodicity of a generator can be achieved by the method of *shuffling*. By this method, a set of, say, 128 values is maintained in an array. The random draw is used to select one of these 128 positions from which the draw is taken and then the value in the array is replaced with a draw from the generator. The period of the generator can also be increased by combining several generators. [See L'Ecuyer (1998), Gentle (2002, 2003), and Greene (2001).]

The deterministic nature of pseudo–random number generators is both a flaw and a virtue. Many Monte Carlo studies require billions of draws, so the finite period of any generator represents a nontrivial consideration. On the other hand, being able to reproduce a sequence of values just by resetting the seed to its initial value allows the researcher to replicate a study.[1] The seed itself can be a problem. It is known that certain seeds in particular generators will produce shorter series or series that do not pass randomness tests. For example, *congruential* generators of the sort just discussed should be started from odd seeds.

---

[1] Current trends in the econometrics literature dictate that readers of empirical studies be able to replicate applied work. In Monte Carlo studies, at least in principle, data can be replicated efficiently merely by providing the random number generator and the seed.

### 17.2.2 SAMPLING FROM A STANDARD UNIFORM POPULATION

When sampling from a standard uniform, $U[0, 1]$ population, the sequence is a kind of difference equation, because given the initial seed, $x_j$ is ultimately a function of $x_{j-1}$. In most cases, the result at step 3 is a pseudo-draw from the continuous uniform distribution in the range zero to one, which can then be transformed to a draw from another distribution by using the fundamental probability transformation.

### 17.2.3 SAMPLING FROM CONTINUOUS DISTRIBUTIONS

As soon as the sequence of $U[0, 1]$ values is obtained, there are several ways to transform them to a sample from the desired distribution. A common approach is to use the **fundamental probability transform.** For continuous distributions, this is done by treating the draw, $F$, as if $F$ were $F(x)$, where $F$ is the cdf of $x$. For example, if we desire draws from the exponential distribution with known $\theta$, then $F(x) = 1 - \exp(-\theta x)$. The inverse transform is $x = (-1/\theta) \ln(1 - F)$. For example, for a draw of 0.4 with $\theta = 5$, the associated $x$ would be 0.1022. One of the most common applications is the draws from the standard normal distribution, which is complicated because there is no closed form for $\Phi^{-1}(F)$. There are several ways to proceed. One is to approximate the inverse function. A well-known approximation is given in Abramovitz and Stegun (1971):

$$\Phi^{-1}(F) = x \approx T - \frac{c_0 + c_1 T + c_2 T^2}{1 + d_1 T + d_2 T^2 + d_3 T^3},$$

where $T = [\ln(1/H^2)]^{1/2}$ and $H = F$ if $F > 0.5$ and $1 - F$ otherwise. The sign is then reversed if $F < 0.5$. A second method is to transform the $U[0, 1]$ values directly to a standard normal value. The Box–Muller (1958) method is $z = (-2 \ln x_1)^{1/2} \cos(2\pi x_2)$, where $x_1$ and $x_2$ are two independent $U[0, 1]$ draws. A second $N[0, 1]$ draw can be obtained from the same two values by replacing cos with sin in the transformation. The Marsagila–Bray (1964) generator, $z_i = x_i (-(2/v) \ln v)^{1/2}$, where $x_i = 2w_i - 1$, $w_i$ is a random draw from $U[0, 1]$ and $v = x_1^2 + x_2^2, i = 1, 2$, is often used as well. (The pair of draws must be rejected and redrawn if $v \geq 1$.) Sequences of draws from the standard normal distribution can be transformed easily into draws from other distributions by making use of the results in Section B.4. The square of a standard normal has chi-squared [1], and the sum of $K$ chi-squareds is chi-squared [K]. From this relationship, it is possible to produce samples from the chi-squared, $t$, $F$, and beta distributions. A related problem is obtaining draws from the truncated normal distribution. An obviously inefficient (albeit effective) method of drawing values from the truncated normal $[\mu, \sigma^2]$ distribution in the range $[L, U]$ is simply to draw $F$ from the $U[0, 1]$ distribution and transform it first to a standard normal variate as discussed previously and then to the $N[\mu, \sigma^2]$ variate by using $x = \mu + \sigma \Phi^{-1}(F)$. Finally, the value $x$ is retained if it falls in the range $[L, U]$ and discarded otherwise. This rejection method will require, on average, $1/[\Phi(U) - \Phi(L)]$ draws per observation, which could be substantial. A direct transformation that requires only one draw is as follows. Let $P_j = \Phi[(j - \mu)/\sigma], j = L, U$. Then

$$x = \mu + \sigma \Phi^{-1}[P_L + F \times (P_U - P_L)]. \tag{17-1}$$

### 17.2.4 SAMPLING FROM A MULTIVARIATE NORMAL POPULATION

A common application involves draws from a multivariate normal distribution with specified mean $\mu$ and covariance matrix $\Sigma$. To sample from this $K$-variate distribution, we begin with a draw, $\mathbf{z}$, from the $K$-variate standard normal distribution just by stacking $K$ independent draws from the univariate standard normal distribution. Let $\mathbf{T}$ be the square root of $\Sigma$ such that $\mathbf{TT'} = \Sigma$.[2] The desired draw is then just $\mathbf{x} = \mu + \mathbf{Tz}$. A draw from a Wishart distribution of order $K$ (which is a multivariate generalization of the chi-squared distribution, see Section B.4.8) can be produced by computing $\mathbf{X'M^0X}$, where each row of $\mathbf{X}$ is a draw from the multivariate normal distribution. Note that the Wishart "variable" is a matrix-variate random variable and that a sample of $M$ draws from the Wishart distribution ultimately requires $M \times N \times K$ draws from the standard normal distribution, however generated.

### 17.2.5 SAMPLING FROM A DISCRETE POPULATION

Discrete distributions, such as the Poisson, present a different problem. There is no obvious inverse transformation for most of these. One inefficient, albeit unfortunately, unavoidable method for some distributions is to draw the $F$ and then search sequentially for the discrete value that has cdf equal to or greater than $F$. This procedure makes intuitive sense, but it can involve a lot of computation. The **rejection method** described by Press et al. (1986, pp. 203–209) will be more efficient (although not more accurate) for some distributions.

## 17.3 MONTE CARLO INTEGRATION

The quadrature methods presented in Sections E2.4, 16.9.6.b, and 23.5.1 have proved very useful in empirical research and are surprisingly accurate even for a small number of points. There are integrals that defy treatment in this form, however. Recent work has brought many advances in techniques for evaluating complex integrals by using Monte Carlo methods rather than direct numerical approximations.

#### Example 17.1  Fractional Moments of the Truncated Normal Distribution

The following function appeared in Greene's (1990) study of the stochastic frontier model:

$$h(r, \varepsilon) = \frac{\int_0^\infty z^r \frac{1}{\sigma} \phi \left[ \frac{z - (-\varepsilon - \theta\sigma^2)}{\sigma} \right] dz}{\int_0^\infty \frac{1}{\sigma} \phi \left[ \frac{z - (-\varepsilon - \theta\sigma^2)}{\sigma} \right] dz}.$$

(See Section 24.2.1.) If we let $\mu = -(\varepsilon + \theta\sigma^2)$, we can show that the denominator is just $1 - \Phi(-\mu/\sigma)$, which is a value from the standard normal cdf. But the numerator is complex. It does not fit into a form that lends itself to Gauss–Laguerre integration (see Section E.2.4) because the exponential function involves both $z$ and $z^2$. An alternative form that has potential is obtained by making the change of variable to $w = (z - \mu)/\sigma$, which produces the right

---

[2]In practice, this is usually done with a Cholesky decomposition in which $\mathbf{T}$ is a lower triangular matrix. See Section A.6.11.

weighting function. But now the range of integration is not $-\infty$ to $+\infty$; it is $-\mu/\sigma$ to $+\infty$. There is another approach. Suppose that $z$ is a random variable with $N[\mu, \sigma^2]$ distribution. Then the density of the truncated normal (at zero) distribution for $z$ is

$$f(z \mid z > 0) = \frac{f(z)}{\text{Prob}[z > 0]} = \frac{\frac{1}{\sigma} \phi \left[ \frac{z - \mu}{\sigma} \right]}{\int_0^\infty \frac{1}{\sigma} \phi \left[ \frac{z - \mu}{\sigma} \right] dz}.$$

This result is exactly the weighting function that appears in $h(r, \varepsilon)$, and the function being weighted is $z^r$. Therefore, $h(r, \varepsilon)$ is the expected value of $z^r$ given that $z$ is greater than zero. That is, $h(r, \varepsilon)$ is a possibly fractional moment—we do not restrict $r$ to integer values—from the truncated (at zero) normal distribution when the untruncated variable has mean $-(\varepsilon + \theta\sigma^2)$ and variance $\sigma^2$.

Now that we have identified the function, how do we compute it? We have already concluded that the familiar quadrature methods will not suffice. (And, no one has previously derived closed forms for the fractional moments of the normal distribution, truncated or not.) But, if we can draw a random sample of observations from this truncated normal distribution $\{z_i\}$, then the sample mean of $w_i = z_i^r$ will converge in probability (mean square) to its population counterpart. [The remaining detail is to establish that this expectation is finite, which it is for the truncated normal distribution; see Amemiya (1973).] Because we showed earlier how to draw observations from a truncated normal distribution, this remaining step is simple.

The preceding is a fairly straightforward application of **Monte Carlo integration.** In certain cases, an integral can be approximated by computing the sample average of a set of function values. The approach taken here was to interpret the integral as an expected value. We then had to establish that the mean we were computing was finite. Our basic statistical result for the behavior of sample means implies that with a large enough sample, we can approximate the integral as closely as we like. The general approach is widely applicable in Bayesian econometrics and has begun to appear in classical statistics and econometrics as well.[3]

### 17.3.1 HALTON SEQUENCES AND RANDOM DRAWS FOR SIMULATION-BASED INTEGRATION

Monte Carlo integration is used to evaluate the expectation

$$E[g(x)] = \int_x g(x) f(x) \, dx$$

where $f(x)$ is the density of the random variable $x$ and $g(x)$ is a smooth function. The Monte Carlo approximation is

$$\widehat{E[g(x)]} = \frac{1}{R} \sum_{r=1}^R g(x_r).$$

Convergence of the approximation to the expectation is based on the law of large numbers—a random sample of draws on $g(x)$ will converge in probability to its expectation. The standard approach to simulation-based integration is to use random draws from the specified distribution. Conventional simulation-based estimation uses

---

[3]See Geweke (1986, 1988, 1989) for discussion and applications. A number of other references are given in Poirier (1995, p. 654).

a random number generator to produce the draws from a specified distribution. The central component of this approach is draws from the standard continuous uniform distribution, $U[0, 1]$. Draws from other distributions are obtained from these draws by using transformations. In particular, for a draw from the normal distribution, where $u_i$ is one draw from $U[0, 1]$, $v_i = \Phi^{-1}(u_i)$. Given that the initial draws satisfy the necessary assumptions, the central issue for purposes of specifying the simulation is the number of draws. Good performance in this connection requires very large numbers of draws. Results differ on the number needed in a given application, but the general finding is that when simulation is done in this fashion, the number is large (hundreds or thousands). A consequence of this is that for large-scale problems, the amount of computation time in simulation-based estimation can be extremely long.

Procedures have recently been devised in the numerical analysis literature for taking "intelligent" draws from the uniform distribution, rather than random ones. [See Train (1999, 2003) and Bhat (1999) for extensive discussion and further references.] An emerging literature has documented dramatic speed gains with no degradation in simulation performance through the use of a small number of **Halton draws** or other constructed, nonrandom sequences instead of a large number of random draws. These procedures appear vastly to reduce the number of draws needed for estimation (sometimes by a factor of 90% or more) and reduce the simulation error associated with a given number of draws. In one application of the method to be discussed here, Bhat (1999) found that 100 Halton draws (discussed later) produced lower simulation error than 1,000 random numbers.

A sequence of Halton draws is generated as follows: Let $r$ be a prime number larger than two. Expand the sequence of integers $g = 1, 2, \ldots$ in terms of the base $r$ as

$$g = \sum_{i=0}^{I} b_i r^i \text{ where, by construction, } 0 \le b_i \le r - 1 \text{ and } r^I \le g < r^{I+1}.$$

The Halton sequence of values that corresponds to this series is

$$H(g) = \sum_{i=0}^{I} b_i r^{-i-1}.$$

For example, using base 5, the integer 37 has $b_0 = 2$, $b_1 = 2$, and $b_3 = 1$. Then

$$H_5(37) = 2 \times 5^{-1} + 2 \times 5^{-2} + 1 \times 5^{-3} = 0.448.$$

The sequence of Halton values is efficiently spread over the unit interval. The sequence is not random as the sequence of pseudo-random numbers is; it is a well-defined deterministic sequence. But, randomness is not the key to obtaining accurate approximations to integrals. Uniform coverage of the support of the random variable is the central requirement. The large numbers of random draws are required to obtain smooth and dense coverage of the unit interval. Figures 17.1 and 17.2 show two sequences of 1,000 Halton draws and two sequences of 1,000 pseudo-random draws. The Halton draws are based on $r = 7$ and $r = 9$. The clumping evident in the first figure is the feature (among others) that mandates large samples for simulations.

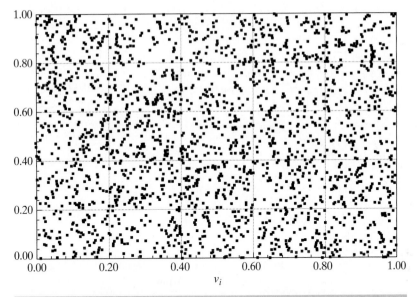

**FIGURE 17.1**    Bivariate Distribution of Random Uniform Draws.

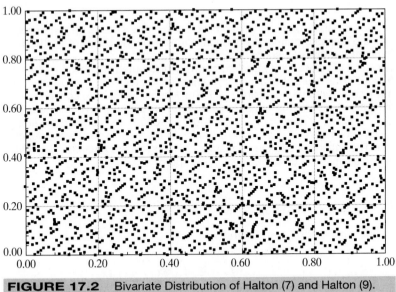

**FIGURE 17.2**    Bivariate Distribution of Halton (7) and Halton (9).

***Example 17.2    Estimating the Lognormal Mean***
We are interested in estimating the mean of a standard lognormally distributed variable. Formally, this is

$$E[y] = \int_{-\infty}^{\infty} \exp(x) \frac{1}{\sqrt{2\pi}} \exp\left[-\frac{1}{2}x^2\right] dx = 1.649.$$

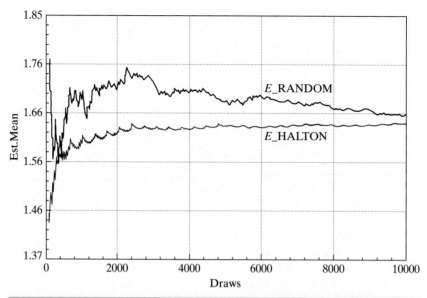

**FIGURE 17.3**   Estimates of $E[\exp(x)]$ Based on Random Draws and Halton Sequences, by Sample Size.

To use simulation for the estimation, we will average $n$ draws on $y = \exp(x)$ where $x$ is drawn from the standard normal distribution. To examine the behavior of the Halton sequence as compared to that of a set of random draws, we did the following experiment. Let $x_{i,t}$ = the sequence of values for a standard normally distributed variable. We draw $t = 1, \ldots, 10{,}000$ draws. For $i = 1$, we used a random number generator. For $i = 2$, we used the sequence of the first 10,000 Halton draws using $r = 7$. The Halton draws were converted to standard normal using the inverse normal transformation. To finish preparation of the data, we transformed $x_{i,t}$ to $y_{i,t} = \exp(x_{i,t})$ Then, for $n = 100, 110, \ldots, 10000$, we averaged the first $n$ observations in the sample. Figure 17.3 plots the evolution of the sample means as a function of the sample size. The ligher trace is the sequence of Halton-based means. The greater stability of the Halton estimator is clearly evident in the figure.

### 17.3.2   IMPORTANCE SAMPLING

Consider the general computation

$$F(x) = \int_{L}^{U} f(x)\, g(x)\, dx,$$

where $g(x)$ is a continuous function in the range $[L, U]$. (We could achieve greater generality by allowing more complicated functions, but for current purposes, we limit ourselves to straightforward cases.) Now, suppose that $g(x)$ is nonnegative in the entire range $[L, U]$. To normalize the weighting function, we suppose, as well, that

$$K = \int_{L}^{U} g(x)\, dx$$

is a known constant. Then $h(x) = g(x)/K$ is a probability density function in the range because it satisfies the axioms of probability.[4] Let

$$H(x) = \int_L^x h(t)\, dt.$$

Then $H(L) = 0$, $H(U) = 1$, $H'(x) = h(x) > 0$, and so on. Then

$$\int_L^U f(x)g(x)\, dx = K \int_L^U f(x)\frac{g(x)}{K}\, dx = K E_{h(x)}[f(x)],$$

where we use the notation $E_{h(x)}[f(x)]$ to denote the expected value of the function $f(x)$ when $x$ is drawn from the population with probability density function $h(x)$. We assume that this expected value is a finite constant. This set of results defines the computation. We now assume that we are able to draw (pseudo)random samples from the population $h(x)$. Because $K$ is a known constant and the means of random samples are unbiased and consistent estimators of their population counterparts, the sample mean of the functions,

$$\hat{F}(x) = K \times \frac{1}{n}\sum_{i=1}^n f(x_i^h),$$

where $x_i^h$ is a random draw from $h(.)$, is a consistent estimator of the integral. [The claim is based on the Corollary to Theorem D.4, as the integral is equal to the expected value of the function $f(x)$.]

Suppose that the problem is well defined as stated earlier, but that it is not possible to draw random samples from the population $h(.)$. If there is another probability density function that resembles $h(\cdot)$, say, $I(x)$, then there may be an alternative strategy. We can rewrite our computation in the form

$$F(x) = K \int_L^U f(x)\, h(x)\, dx = K \int_L^U \left[\frac{f(x)\, h(x)}{I(x)}\right] I(x)\, dx.$$

Then we can interpret our integral as the expected value of $[f(x)h(x)]/I(x)$ when the population has density $I(x)$. The new density $I(x)$ is called an **importance function.** The same strategy works if certain fairly benign conditions are imposed on the importance function. [See Geweke (1989).] The range of variation is an important consideration, for example. If the range of $x$ is, say, $(-\infty, +\infty)$, and we choose an importance function that is nonzero only in the range $(0, +\infty)$, then our strategy is likely to come to some difficulties.

### Example 17.3 *Mean of a Lognormal Distribution (Continued)*
Consider computing the mean of a lognormal distribution. If $x \sim N[0, 1]$, then $e^x$ is distributed as lognormal and has density

$$g(x) = \frac{1}{x\sqrt{2\pi}}e^{-1/2(\ln x)^2}, \quad x > 0$$

(see Section B.4.4). The expected value is $\int xg(x)\, dx$, so $f(x) = x$. Suppose that we did not know how to draw a random sample from this lognormal distribution (by just exponentiating our draws from the standard normal distribution) [or that the true mean is $\exp(0.5) = 1.649$]. Consider using a $\chi^2[1]$ as an importance function, instead. This chi-squared distribution is a

---

[4]In many applications, $K$ will already be part of the desired integral.

gamma distribution with parameters $P = \lambda = \frac{1}{2}$ [see (B-39)], so

$$l(x) = \frac{\frac{1}{2}^{1/2}}{\Gamma\left(\frac{1}{2}\right)}x^{-1/2}e^{-(1/2)x}.$$

After a bit of manipulation, we find that

$$\frac{f(x)g(x)}{l(x)} = q(x) = e^{(1/2)[x-(\ln x)^2]}x^{1/2}.$$

Therefore, to estimate the mean of this lognormal distribution, we can draw a random sample of values $x_i$ from the $\chi^2[1]$ distribution, which we can do by squaring the draws in a sample from the standard normal distribution, then computing the average of the sample of values, $q(x_i)$.

We carried out this experiment with 1,000 draws from a standard normal distribution. The mean of our sample was 1.6974, compared with a true mean of 1.649, so the error was less than 3 percent.

### 17.3.3 COMPUTING MULTIVARIATE NORMAL PROBABILITIES USING THE GHK SIMULATOR

The computation of bivariate normal probabilities requires a large amount of computing effort. Quadrature methods have been developed for trivariate probabilities as well, but the amount of computing effort needed at this level is enormous. For integrals of level greater than three, satisfactory (in terms of speed and accuracy) direct approximations remain to be developed. Our work thus far does suggest an alternative approach. Suppose that $\mathbf{x}$ has a $K$-variate normal distribution with mean vector $\mathbf{0}$ and covariance matrix $\boldsymbol{\Sigma}$. (No generality is sacrificed by the assumption of a zero mean, because we could just subtract a nonzero mean from the random vector wherever it appears in any result.) We wish to compute the $K$-variate probability, $\text{Prob}[a_1 < x_1 < b_1, a_2 < x_2 < b_2, \ldots, a_K < x_K < b_K]$. Our Monte Carlo integration technique is well suited for this well-defined problem. As a first approach, consider sampling $R$ observations, $\mathbf{x}_r, r = 1, \ldots, R$, from this multivariate normal distribution, using the method described in Section 17.2.4. Now, define

$$d_r = \mathbf{1}[a_1 < x_{r1} < b_1, a_2 < x_{r2} < b_2, \ldots, a_K < x_{rK} < b_K].$$

(That is, $d_r = 1$ if the condition is true and 0 otherwise.) Based on our earlier results, it follows that

$$\text{plim}\,\bar{d} = \text{plim}\frac{1}{R}\sum_{r=1}^{R} d_r = \text{Prob}[a_1 < x_1 < b_1, a_2 < x_2 < b_2, \ldots, a_K < x_K < b_K].^5$$

This method is valid in principle, but in practice it has proved to be unsatisfactory for several reasons. For large-order problems, it requires an enormous number of draws from the distribution to give reasonable accuracy. Also, even with large numbers of draws, it appears to be problematic when the desired tail area is very small. Nonetheless, the idea is sound, and recent research has built on this idea to produce some quite

---

[5]This method was suggested by Lerman and Manski (1981).

accurate and efficient simulation methods for this computation. A survey of the methods is given in McFadden and Ruud (1994).[6]

Among the simulation methods examined in the survey, the **GHK smooth recursive simulator** appears to be the most accurate.[7] The method is surprisingly simple. The general approach uses

$$\text{Prob}[a_1 < x_1 < b_1, a_2 < x_2 < b_2, \ldots, a_K < x_K < b_K] \approx \frac{1}{R} \sum_{r=1}^{R} \prod_{k=1}^{K} Q_{rk},$$

where $Q_{rk}$ are easily computed univariate probabilities. The probabilities $Q_{rk}$ are computed according to the following recursion: We first factor $\Sigma$ using the **Cholesky factorization** $\Sigma = \mathbf{LL}'$, where $\mathbf{L}$ is a lower triangular matrix (see Section A.6.11). The elements of $\mathbf{L}$ are $l_{km}$, where $l_{km} = 0$ if $m > k$. Then we begin the recursion with

$$Q_{r1} = \Phi(b_1/l_{11}) - \Phi(a_1/l_{11}).$$

Note that $l_{11} = \sigma_{11}$, so this is just the marginal probability, $\text{Prob}[a_1 < x_1 < b_1]$. Now, we generate a random observation $\varepsilon_{r1}$ from the truncated standard normal distribution in the range

$$A_{r1} \text{ to } B_{r1} = a_1/l_{11} \text{ to } b_1/l_{11}.$$

(Note, again, that the range is standardized since $l_{11} = \sigma_{11}$.) The draw can be obtained from a $U[0, 1]$ observation using (17-1). For steps $k = 2, \ldots, K$, compute

$$A_{rk} = \left[ a_k - \sum_{m=1}^{k-1} l_{km}\varepsilon_{rm} \right] \Big/ l_{kk},$$

$$B_{rk} = \left[ b_k - \sum_{m=1}^{k-1} l_{km}\varepsilon_{rm} \right] \Big/ l_{kk}.$$

Then

$$Q_{rk} = \Phi(B_{rk}) - \Phi(A_{rk}).$$

Finally, in preparation for the next step in the recursion, we generate a random draw from the truncated standard normal distribution in the range $A_{rk}$ to $B_{rk}$. This process is replicated $R$ times, and the estimated probability is the sample average of the simulated probabilities.

The GHK simulator has been found to be impressively fast and accurate for fairly moderate numbers of replications. Its main usage has been in computing functions and derivatives for maximum likelihood estimation of models that involve multivariate normal integrals. We will revisit this in the context of the method of simulated moments when we examine the probit model in Chapter 23. (See Example 23.16 and Section 23.11.5.)

---

[6]A symposium on the topic of simulation methods appears in *Review of Economic Statistics*, Vol. 76, November 1994. See, especially, McFadden and Ruud (1994), Stern (1994), Geweke, Keane, and Runkle (1994), and Breslaw (1994). See, as well, Gourieroux and Monfort (1996).

[7]See Geweke (1989), Hajivassiliou (1990), and Keane (1994). Details on the properties of the simulator are given in Börsch-Supan and Hajivassiliou (1990).

## 17.4 MONTE CARLO STUDIES

Simulated data generated by the methods of the preceding sections have various uses in econometrics. One of the more common applications is the derivation of the properties of estimators or in obtaining comparisons of the properties of estimators. For example, in time-series settings, most of the known results for characterizing the sampling distributions of estimators are asymptotic, large-sample results. But the typical time series is not very long, and descriptions that rely on $T$, the number of observations, going to infinity may not be very accurate. Exact, finite sample properties are usually intractable, however, which leaves the analyst with only the choice of learning about the behavior of the estimators experimentally.

In the typical application, one would either compare the properties of two or more estimators while holding the sampling conditions fixed or study how the properties of an estimator are affected by changing conditions such as the sample size or the value of an underlying parameter.

### Example 17.4   Monte Carlo Study of the Mean Versus the Median
In Example D.8, we compared the asymptotic distributions of the sample mean and the sample median in random sampling from the normal distribution. The basic result is that both estimators are consistent, but the mean is asymptotically more efficient by a factor of

$$\frac{\text{Asy. Var[Median]}}{\text{Asy. Var[Mean]}} = \frac{\pi}{2} = 1.5708.$$

This result is useful, but it does not tell which is the better estimator in small samples, nor does it suggest how the estimators would behave in some other distribution. It is known that the mean is affected by outlying observations whereas the median is not. The effect is averaged out in large samples, but the small sample behavior might be very different. To investigate the issue, we constructed the following experiment: We sampled 500 observations from the $t$ distribution with $d$ degrees of freedom by sampling $d + 1$ values from the standard normal distribution and then computing

$$t_{ir} = \frac{z_{ir,d+1}}{\sqrt{\frac{1}{d} \sum_{l=1}^{d} z_{ir,l}^2}}, \quad i = 1, \ldots, 500, \quad r = 1, \ldots, 100.$$

The $t$ distribution with a low value of $d$ was chosen because it has very thick tails and because large, outlying values have high probability. For each value of $d$, we generated $R = 100$ replications. For each of the 100 replications, we obtained the mean and median. Because both are unbiased, we compared the mean squared errors around the true expectations using

$$M_d = \frac{(1/R) \sum_{r=1}^{R} (\text{median}_r - 0)^2}{(1/R) \sum_{r=1}^{R} (\bar{x}_r - 0)^2}.$$

We obtained ratios of 0.6761, 1.2779, and 1.3765 for $d = 3, 6$, and 10, respectively. (You might want to repeat this experiment with different degrees of freedom.) These results agree with what intuition would suggest. As the degrees of freedom parameter increases, which brings the distribution closer to the normal distribution, the sample mean becomes more efficient—the ratio should approach its limiting value of 1.5708 as $d$ increases. What might be surprising is the apparent overwhelming advantage of the median when the distribution is very nonnormal even in a sample as large as 500.

The preceding is a very small, straightforward application of the technique. In a typical study, there are many more parameters to be varied and more dimensions upon which the results are to be studied. One of the practical problems in this setting is how to organize the results. There is a tendency in Monte Carlo work to proliferate tables indiscriminately. It is incumbent on the analyst to collect the results in a fashion that is useful to the reader. For example, this requires some judgment on how finely one should vary the parameters of interest. One useful possibility that will often mimic the thought process of the reader is to collect the results of bivariate tables in carefully designed contour plots.

There are any number of situations in which Monte Carlo simulation offers the only method of learning about finite sample properties of estimators. Still, there are a number of problems with Monte Carlo studies. To achieve any level of generality, the number of parameters that must be varied and hence the amount of information that must be distilled can become enormous. Second, they are limited by the design of the experiments, so the results they produce are rarely generalizable. For our example, we may have learned something about the $t$ distribution. But the results that would apply in other distributions remain to be described. And, unfortunately, real data will rarely conform to any specific distribution, so no matter how many other distributions we analyze, our results would still only be suggestive. In more general terms, this problem of **specificity** [Hendry (1984)] limits most Monte Carlo studies to quite narrow ranges of applicability. There are very few that have proved general enough to have provided a widely cited result.[8]

### 17.4.1   A MONTE CARLO STUDY: BEHAVIOR OF A TEST STATISTIC

Monte Carlo methods are often used to study the behavior of test statistics when their true properties are uncertain. This is often the case with Lagrange Multiplier statistics. For example, Baltagi (2005) reports on the development of several new test statistics for panel data models such as a test for serial correlation. Examining the behavior of a test statistic is fairly straightforward. We are interested in two characeristics: the **true size of the test**—that is, the probability that it rejects the null hypothesis when that hypothesis is actually true (the probability of a type 1 error) and the **power of the test**—that is the probability that it will correctly reject a false null hypothesis (one minus the probability of a type 2 error). As we will see, the power of a test is a function of the alternative against which the null is tested.

To illustrate a Monte Carlo study of a test statistic, we consider how a familiar procedure behaves when the model assumptions are incorrect. Consider the linear regression model

$$y_i = \alpha + \beta x_i + \gamma z_i + \varepsilon_i, \quad \varepsilon_i \mid (x_i, z_i) \sim N[0, \sigma^2].$$

The Lagrange multiplier statistic for testing the null hypothesis that $\gamma$ equals zero for this model is

$$LM = \mathbf{e}_0' \mathbf{X} (\mathbf{X}'\mathbf{X})^{-1} \mathbf{X}' \mathbf{e}_0 / (\mathbf{e}_0' \mathbf{e}_0 / n)$$

where $\mathbf{X} = (\mathbf{1}, \mathbf{x}, \mathbf{z})$ and $\mathbf{e}_0$ is the vector of least squares residuals obtained from the regression of $\mathbf{y}$ on the constant and $\mathbf{x}$ (and not $\mathbf{z}$). (See Section 16.6.3.) Under the assumptions of the model above, the large sample distribution of the LM statistic is chi squared with one degree of freedom. Thus, our testing procedure is to compute LM, then reject the null hypothesis $\gamma = 0$ if LM is greater than the critical value. We

---

[8]Two that have withstood the test of time are Griliches and Rao (1969) and Kmenta and Gilbert (1968).

**TABLE 17.1** Size and Power Functions for LM Test

| Model | 0.0 | 0.1 −0.1 | 0.2 −0.2 | 0.3 −0.3 | 0.4 −0.4 | 0.5 −0.5 | 0.6 −0.6 | 0.7 −0.7 | 0.8 −0.8 | 0.9 −0.9 | 1.0 −1.0 |
|---|---|---|---|---|---|---|---|---|---|---|---|
| Normal | 0.059 | 0.090 | 0.235 | 0.464 | 0.691 | 0.859 | 0.957 | 0.989 | 0.998 | 1.000 | 1.000 |
|  |  | 0.103 | 0.236 | 0.451 | 0.686 | 0.863 | 0.961 | 0.989 | 0.999 | 1.000 | 1.000 |
| $t(5)$ | 0.052 | 0.083 | 0.169 | 0.320 | 0.508 | 0.680 | 0.816 | 0.911 | 0.956 | 0.976 | 0.994 |
|  |  | 0.080 | 0.177 | 0.312 | 0.500 | 0.677 | 0.822 | 0.921 | 0.953 | 0.984 | 0.993 |
| Het. | 0.071 | 0.098 | 0.249 | 0.457 | 0.666 | 0.835 | 0.944 | 0.984 | 0.995 | 0.998 | 1.000 |
|  |  | 0.107 | 0.239 | 0.442 | 0.651 | 0.832 | 0.940 | 0.985 | 0.996 | 1.000 | 1.000 |

*(Column header group: **Gamma**)*

will use a nominal size of 0.05, so the critical value is 3.84. The theory for the statistic is well developed when the specification of the model is correct. [See, for example, Godfrey (1988).] We are interested in two specification errors. First, how does the statistic behave if the normality assumption is not met? Because the LM statistic is based on the likelihood function, if some distribution other than the normal governs $\varepsilon_i$, then the LM statistic would not be based on the OLS estimator. We will examine the behavior of the statistic under the true specification that $\varepsilon_i$ comes from a $t$ distribution with 5 degrees of freedom. Second, how does the statistic behave if the homoscedasticity assumption is not met? The statistic is entirely wrong if the disturbances are heteroscedastic. We will examine the case in which the conditional variance is $\mathrm{Var}[\varepsilon_i \mid (x_i, z_i)] = \sigma^2 [\exp(0.2x_i)]^2$.

The design of the experiment is as follows: We will base the analysis on a sample of 50 observations. We draw 50 observations on $x_i$ and $z_i$ from independent N[0, 1] populations at the outset of each cycle. For each of 1,000 replications, we draw a sample of 50 $\varepsilon_i$s according to the assumed specification. The LM statistic is computed and the proportion of the computed statistics that exceed 3.84 is recorded. The experiment is repeated for $\gamma = 0$ to ascertain the true size of the test and for values of $\gamma$ including $-1, \ldots, -0.2, -0.1, 0, 0.1, 0.2, \ldots, 1.0$ to assess the power of the test. The cycle of tests is repeated for the two scenarios, the $t(5)$ distribution and the model with heteroscedasticity.

Table 17.1 lists the results of the experiment. The first row shows the expected results for the LM statistic under the model assumptions for which is is appropriate. The size of the test appears to be in line with the theoretical results. Comparing the first and third rows, it appears that the presence of heteroscedasticity seems not to degrade the power of the statistic. But the different distributional assumption does. Figure 17.4 plots the values in the table, and displays the characteristic form of the power function for a test statistic.

### 17.4.2 A MONTE CARLO STUDY: THE INCIDENTAL PARAMETERS PROBLEM

Section 16.9.6.c examines the maximum likelihood estimator of a panel data model with fixed effects,

$$f(y_{it} \mid \mathbf{x}_{it}) = g(y_{it}, \mathbf{x}'_{it}\boldsymbol{\beta} + \alpha_i, \boldsymbol{\theta})$$

where the individual effects may be correlated with $x_{it}$. The extra parameter vector $\boldsymbol{\theta}$ represents $M$ other parameters that might appear in the model, such as the disturbance

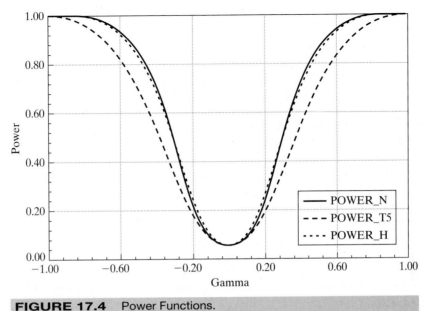

**FIGURE 17.4**    Power Functions.

variance, $\sigma_\varepsilon^2$, in a linear regression model with normally distributed disturbance. The development there considers the mechanical problem of maximizing the log-likelihood

$$\ln L = \sum_{i=1}^{n} \sum_{t=1}^{T_i} \ln g(y_{it}, \mathbf{x}_{it}'\boldsymbol{\beta} + \alpha_i, \boldsymbol{\theta})$$

with respect to the $n + K + M$ parameters $(\alpha_1, \ldots, \alpha_n, \boldsymbol{\beta}, \boldsymbol{\theta})$. A statistical problem with this estimator that was suggested there is a phenomenon labeled the **incidental parameters problem** [see Neyman and Scott (1948), Lancaster (2000)]. With the exception of a very small number of specific models (such as the Poisson regression model in Section 25.3.2), the "brute force," unconditional maximum likelihood estimator of the parameters in this model is inconsistent. The result is strightforward to visualize with respect to the individual effects. Suppose that $\boldsymbol{\beta}$ and $\boldsymbol{\theta}$ were actually known. Then, each $\alpha_i$ would be estimated with $T_i$ observations. Because $T_i$ is assumed to be fixed (and small), there is no asymptotic result to provide consistency for the MLE of $\alpha_i$. But, $\boldsymbol{\beta}$ and $\boldsymbol{\theta}$ are estimated with $\Sigma_i T_i = N$ observations, so their large sample behavior is less transparent. One known result concerns the logit model for binary choice (see Section 23.2–23.5). Kalbfleisch and Sprott (1970), Andersen (1973), Hsiao (1996), and Abrevaya (1997) have established that in the binary logit model, if $T_i = 2$, then plim $\hat{\boldsymbol{\beta}}_{\text{MLE}} = 2\boldsymbol{\beta}$. Two other cases are known with certainty. In the linear regression model with fixed effects and normally distributed disturbances, the slope estimator, $\mathbf{b}_{\text{LSDV}}$ is unbiased and consistent, however, the MLE of the variance, $\sigma^2$ converges to $(T - 1)\sigma^2/T$. (The degrees of freedom correction will adjust for this, but the MLE does not correct for degrees of freedom.) Finally, in the Poisson regression model (Section 25.3.2), the unconditional MLE is consistent [see Cameron and Trivedi (1988)]. Almost nothing else is known with certainty—that is, as a firm theoretical result—about the behavior of the maximum likelihood estimator in the presence of fixed effects. The literature appears to take as given the qualitative wisdom of Hsiao and Abrevaya, that the FE/MLE is inconsistent with $T$ is small and fixed. (The implication that the severity of the inconsistency declines as $T$ increases makes sense, but, again, remains to be shown analytically.)

The result for the two-period binary logit model is a standard result for discrete choice estimation. Several authors, all using Monte Carlo methods have pursued the result for the logit model for larger values of $T$. [See, for example, Katz (2001).] Greene (2004) analyzed the incidental parameters problem for other discrete choice models using Monte Carlo methods. We will examine part of that study.

The current studies are preceded by a small study in Heckman (1981) which examined the behavior of the fixed effects MLE in the following experiment:

$$z_{it} = 0.1t + 0.5z_{i,t-1} + u_{it}, z_{i0} = 5 + 10.0U_{i0},$$

$$U_{it} \sim U[-0.5, 0.5], i = 1, \ldots, 100, t = 0, \ldots, 8,$$

$$Y_{it} = \sigma_\tau \tau_i + \beta z_{it} + \varepsilon_{it}, \tau_i \sim N[0, 1], \varepsilon_{it} \sim N[0, 1],$$

$$y_{it} = 1 \text{ if } Y_{it} > 0, 0 \text{ otherwise.}$$

Heckman attempted to learn something about the behavior of the MLE for the probit model with $T = 8$. He used values of $\beta = -1.0, -0.1,$ and $1.0$ and $\sigma_\tau = 0.5, 1.0,$ and $3.0$. The mean values of the maximum likelihood estimates of $\beta$ for the 9 cases are as follows:

|                    | $\beta = -1.0$ | $\beta = -0.1$ | $\beta = 1.0$ |
|--------------------|----------------|----------------|---------------|
| $\sigma_\tau = 0.5$ | $-0.96$        | $-0.10$        | $0.93$        |
| $\sigma_\tau = 1.0$ | $-0.95$        | $-0.09$        | $0.91$        |
| $\sigma_\tau = 3.0$ | $-0.96$        | $-0.10$        | $0.90.$       |

The findings here disagree with the received wisdom. Where there appears to be a bias (that is, excluding the center column), it seems to be quite small, and toward, not away from zero.

The Heckman study used a very small sample and, moreover, analyzed the fixed effects estimator in a random effects model (note that $\tau_i$ is independent of $z_{it}$). Greene (2004a), using the same parameter values, number of replications, and sample design found persistent biases away from zero on the order of 15–20 percent. Numerous authors have extended the logit result for $T = 2$ with larger values of $T$, and likewise persistently found biases, away from zero, that diminish with increases in $T$. Greene (2004a) redid the experiment for the logit model, then replicated it for the probit and ordered probit models. The experiment is designed as follows: All models are based on the same index function

$$w_{it} = \alpha_i + \beta x_{it} + \delta d_{it}, \quad \text{where } \beta = \delta = 1,$$

$$x_{it} \sim N[0, 1], d_{it} = \mathbf{1}[x_{it} + h_{it} > 0], \quad \text{where } h_{it} \sim N[0, 1],$$

$$\alpha_i = \sqrt{T}\bar{x}_i + a_i, a_i \sim N[0, 1].$$

The regressors $d_{it}$ and $x_{it}$ are constructed to be correlated. The random term $h_{it}$ is used to produce independent variation in $d_{it}$. There is, however, no within group correlation in $x_{it}$ or $d_{it}$ built into the data generator. (Other experiments suggested that the marginal distribution of $x_{it}$ mattered little to the outcome of the experiment.) The correlations between the variables are approximately 0.7 between $x_{it}$ and $d_{it}$, 0.4 between $\alpha_i$ and $x_{it}$, and 0.2 between $\alpha_i$ and $d_{it}$. The individual effect is produced from independent

**TABLE 17.2** Means of Empirical Sampling Distributions, $N = 1,000$ Individuals Based on 200 Replications

| | T = 2 | | T = 3 | | T = 5 | | T = 8 | | T = 10 | | T = 20 | |
|---|---|---|---|---|---|---|---|---|---|---|---|---|
| | $\beta$ | $\delta$ | $\beta$ | $\delta$ | $\beta$ | $\delta$ | $\beta$ | $\delta$ | $\beta$ | $\delta$ | $\beta$ | $\delta$ |
| Logit Coeff | 2.020 | 2.027 | 1.698 | 1.668 | 1.379 | 1.323 | 1.217 | 1.156 | 1.161 | 1.135 | 1.069 | 1.062 |
| Logit M.E.[a] | 1.676 | 1.660 | 1.523 | 1.477 | 1.319 | 1.254 | 1.191 | 1.128 | 1.140 | 1.111 | 1.034 | 1.052 |
| Probit Coeff | 2.083 | 1.938 | 1.821 | 1.777 | 1.589 | 1.407 | 1.328 | 1.243 | 1.247 | 1.169 | 1.108 | 1.068 |
| Probit M.E.[a] | 1.474 | 1.388 | 1.392 | 1.354 | 1.406 | 1.231 | 1.241 | 1.152 | 1.190 | 1.110 | 1.088 | 1.047 |
| Ord. Probit | 2.328 | 2.605 | 1.592 | 1.806 | 1.305 | 1.415 | 1.166 | 1.220 | 1.131 | 1.158 | 1.058 | 1.068 |

[a] Average ratio of estimated marginal effect to true marginal effect.

variation, $\alpha_i$ as well as the group mean of $x_{it}$. The latter is scaled by $\sqrt{T}$ to maintain the unit variances of the two parts—without the scaling, the covariance between $\alpha_i$ and $x_{it}$ falls to zero as $T$ increases and $\bar{x}_i$ converges to its mean of zero). Thus, the data generator for the index function satisfies the assumptions of the fixed effects model. The sample used for the results below contains $n = 1,000$ individuals. The data-generating processes for the discrete dependent variables are as follows:

$$\text{probit:} \qquad y_{it} = \mathbf{1}[w_{it} + \varepsilon_{it} > 0], \varepsilon_{it} \sim N[0, 1],$$

$$\text{ordered probit:} \quad y_{it} = \mathbf{1}[w_{it} + \varepsilon_{it} > 0] + \mathbf{1}[w_{it} + \varepsilon_{it} > 3], \varepsilon_{it} \sim N[0, 1],$$

$$\text{logit:} \qquad y_{it} = \mathbf{1}[w_{it} + v_{it} > 0], v_{it} = \log[u_{it}/(1 - u_{it})], u_{it} \sim U[0, 1].$$

(The three discrete dependent variables are described in Chapter 23.)

Table 17.2 reports the results of computing the MLE with 200 replications. Models were fit with $T = 2, 3, 5, 8, 10$, and 20. (Note that this includes Heckman's experiment.) Each model specification and group size ($T$) is fit 200 times with random draws for $\varepsilon_{it}$ or $u_{it}$. The data on the regressors were drawn at the beginning of each experiment (that is, for each $T$) and held constant for the replications. The table contains the average estimate of the coefficient and, for the binary choice models, the partial effects. The value at the extreme left corresponds to the received result, the 100 percent bias in the $T = 2$ case. The remaining values show, as intuition would suggest, that the bias decreases with increasing $T$. The benchmark case of $T = 8$, appears to be less benign than Heckman's results suggested. One encouraging finding for the model builder is that the biases in the estimated marginal effects appears to be somewhat less than for the coefficients. [Greene (2004b) extends this analysis to some other models, including the tobit and truncated regression models discussed in Chapter 24. The results there suggest that the conventional wisdom for the tobit model may not be correct—the incidental parameters problem seems to appear in the estimator of $\sigma^2$ in the tobit model, not in the estimators of the slopes. This is consistent with the linear regression model, but not with the binary choice models.]

## 17.5 SIMULATION-BASED ESTIMATION

The technique of maximum simulated likelihood (MSL) is essentially a classical sampling theory counterpart to the hierarchical Bayesian estimator considered in Chapter 18. Since the celebrated paper of Berry, Levinsohn, and Pakes (1995), and a related literature advocated by McFadden and Train (2000), maximum simulated likelihood estimation has been used in a large and growing number of studies based on log-likelihoods that involve integrals that are expectations.[9] In this section, we will lay out some general results for MSL estimation by developing a particular application, the random parameters model. This general modeling framework has been used in the majority of the received applications. We will then continue the application to the discrete choice model for panel data that we began in Section 16.9.6. A related technique, the **method of simulated moments** is described at the end of this section.

### 17.5.1 MAXIMUM SIMULATED LIKELIHOOD ESTIMATION OF RANDOM PARAMETERS MODELS

One of the most common applications of simulation-based estimation is the computation of random parameters models. The randomness to be integrated out of the log-likelihood function is produced by the heterogeneity of parameters among individuals, usually in a panel data set. The latent class model uses a discrete distribution to model this heterogeneity. We now consider an approach that assumes that parameters are randomly distributed with a continuous distribution.

The density of $y_{it}$ when the parameter vector is $\boldsymbol{\beta}_i$ is $f(y_{it} \mid \mathbf{x}_{it}, \boldsymbol{\beta}_i)$. The parameter vector $\boldsymbol{\beta}_i$ is randomly distributed over individuals according to

$$\boldsymbol{\beta}_i = \boldsymbol{\beta} + \boldsymbol{\Delta}\mathbf{z}_i + \mathbf{v}_i,$$

where $\boldsymbol{\beta} + \boldsymbol{\Delta}\mathbf{z}_i$ is the mean of the distribution, which depends on time-invariant individual characteristics as well as parameters yet to be estimated, and the random variation comes from the individual heterogeneity, $\mathbf{v}_i$. This random vector is assumed to have mean zero and covariance matrix, $\boldsymbol{\Sigma}$. The conditional density of the parameters is denoted

$$g(\boldsymbol{\beta}_i \mid \mathbf{z}_i, \boldsymbol{\beta}, \boldsymbol{\Delta}, \boldsymbol{\Sigma}) = g(\mathbf{v}_i + \boldsymbol{\beta} + \boldsymbol{\Delta}\mathbf{z}_i, \boldsymbol{\Sigma}),$$

where $g(.)$ is the underlying marginal density of the heterogeneity. For the $T_i \geq 1$ observations in group $i$, the joint conditional density is

$$f(\mathbf{y}_i \mid \mathbf{X}_i, \boldsymbol{\beta}_i) = \prod_{t=1}^{T_i} f(y_{it} \mid \mathbf{x}_{it}, \boldsymbol{\beta}_i). \tag{17-2}$$

The unconditional density for $\mathbf{y}_i$ is obtained by integrating over $\boldsymbol{\beta}_i$,

$$f(\mathbf{y}_i \mid \mathbf{X}_i, \mathbf{z}_i, \boldsymbol{\beta}, \boldsymbol{\Delta}, \boldsymbol{\Sigma}) = E_{\boldsymbol{\beta}_i}[f(\mathbf{y}_i \mid \mathbf{X}_i, \boldsymbol{\beta}_i)] = \int_{\boldsymbol{\beta}_i} f(\mathbf{y}_i \mid \mathbf{X}_i, \boldsymbol{\beta}_i)g(\boldsymbol{\beta}_i \mid \mathbf{z}_i, \boldsymbol{\beta}, \boldsymbol{\Delta}, \boldsymbol{\Sigma})d\boldsymbol{\beta}_i.$$

---

[9]Two major references for this set of techniques are Gourieroux and Monfort (1996) and Train (2003). A survey that is oriented toward applications is given in Cameron and Trivedi (2005, Chapter 12).

Collecting terms, and making the transformation from $\boldsymbol{\beta}_i$ to $\mathbf{v}_i$, the true log-likelihood would be

$$
\ln L = \sum_{i=1}^{n} \ln \left\{ \int_{\mathbf{v}_i} \left[ \prod_{t=1}^{T_i} f(y_{it} \mid \mathbf{x}_{it}, \boldsymbol{\beta} + \boldsymbol{\Delta}\mathbf{z}_i + \mathbf{v}_i) \right] g(\mathbf{v}_i \mid \boldsymbol{\Sigma}) d\mathbf{v}_i \right\}
$$

$$
= \sum_{i=1}^{n} \ln \left\{ \int_{\mathbf{v}_i} f(\mathbf{y}_i \mid \mathbf{X}_i, \boldsymbol{\beta} + \boldsymbol{\Delta}\mathbf{z}_i + \mathbf{v}_i) g(\mathbf{v}_i \mid \boldsymbol{\Sigma}) d\mathbf{v}_i \right\}. \tag{17-3}
$$

Each of the $n$ terms involves an expectation over $\mathbf{v}_i$. The end result of the integration is a function of $(\boldsymbol{\beta}, \boldsymbol{\Delta}, \boldsymbol{\Sigma})$, which is then maximized.

It will not be possible to maximize the log-likelihood in this form because there is no closed form for the integral. There are several approaches to maximizing such a log-likelihood. In the latent class formulation, it is assumed that the parameter vector takes one of a discrete set of values, and the log-likelihood is maximized over this discrete distribution as well as the structural parameters. (See Section 16.9.7.) The hierarchical Bayes procedure uses Markov Chain–Monte Carlo methods to sample from the joint posterior distribution of the underlying parameters and uses the empirical mean of the sample of draws as the estimator. (See Chapter 18.) We now consider a third approach to estimating the parameters of a model of this form, maximum simulated likelihood estimation.

The terms in the log-likelihood are each of the form

$$
\ln L_i = E_{\mathbf{v}_i}[f(\mathbf{y}_i \mid \mathbf{X}_i, \boldsymbol{\beta} + \boldsymbol{\Delta}\mathbf{z}_i + \mathbf{v}_i)].
$$

As noted, we do not have a closed form for this function, so we cannot compute it directly. Suppose we could sample randomly from the distribution of $\mathbf{v}_i$. If an appropriate law of large numbers can be applied, then

$$
\lim_{R \to \infty} \frac{1}{R} \sum_{r=1}^{R} f(\mathbf{y}_i \mid \mathbf{X}_i, \boldsymbol{\beta} + \boldsymbol{\Delta}\mathbf{z}_i + \mathbf{v}_{ir}) = E_{\mathbf{v}_i}[f(\mathbf{y}_i \mid \mathbf{X}_i, \boldsymbol{\beta} + \boldsymbol{\Delta}\mathbf{z}_i + \mathbf{v}_i)],
$$

where $\mathbf{v}_{ir}$ is the $r$th random draw from the distribution. This suggests a strategy for computing the log-likelihood. We can substitute this approximation to the expectation into the log-likelihood function. With sufficient random draws, the approximation can be made as close to the true function as desired. [The theory for this approach is discussed in Gourieroux and Monfort (1996), Bhat (1999), and Train (1999, 2002, 2003). Practical details on applications of the method are given in Greene (2001).] A detail to add concerns how to sample from the distribution of $\mathbf{v}_i$. [See Hensher and Greene (2003).] There are many possibilities, but for now, we consider the simplest case, the multivariate normal distribution. Write $\boldsymbol{\Sigma}$ in the Cholesky form $\boldsymbol{\Sigma} = \mathbf{L}\mathbf{L}'$ where $\mathbf{L}$ is a lower triangular matrix. Now, let $\mathbf{u}_{ir}$ be a vector of $K$ independent draws from the standard normal distribution. Then a draw from the multivariate distribution with covariance matrix $\boldsymbol{\Sigma}$ is simply $\mathbf{v}_{ir} = \mathbf{L}\mathbf{u}_{ir}$. The simulated log-likelihood is

$$
\ln L_S = \sum_{i=1}^{n} \ln \left\{ \frac{1}{R} \sum_{r=1}^{R} \left[ \prod_{t=1}^{T} f(y_{it} \mid \mathbf{x}_{it}, \boldsymbol{\beta} + \boldsymbol{\Delta}\mathbf{z}_i + \mathbf{L}\mathbf{u}_{ir}) \right] \right\}. \tag{17-4}
$$

The resulting function is maximized with respect to $\beta$, $\Delta$, and $\mathbf{L}$. This is obviously not a simple calculation, but it is feasible, and much easier than trying to manipulate the integrals directly. In fact, for most problems to which this method has been applied, the computations are surprisingly simple. The intricate part is obtaining the function and its derivatives. But, the functions are usually index function models that involve $\mathbf{x}'_{it}\beta_i$ which greatly simplifies the derivations.

Inference in this setting does not involve any new results. The estimated asymptotic covariance matrix for the estimated parameters is computed by manipulating the derivatives of the simulated log-likelihood. The Wald and likelihood ratio statistics are also computed the way they would usually be. As before, we are interested in estimating person-specific parameters. A prior estimate might simply use $\beta + \Delta\mathbf{z}_i$, but this would not use all the information in the sample. A posterior estimate would compute

$$\hat{E}_{\mathbf{v}_i}[\beta_i \mid \beta, \Delta, \mathbf{y}_i, \mathbf{X}_i, \mathbf{z}_i, \Sigma] = \frac{\sum_{r=1}^{R} \hat{\beta}_{ir} f(\mathbf{y}_i \mid \mathbf{X}_i, \hat{\beta}_{ir})}{\sum_{r=1}^{R} f(\mathbf{y}_i \mid \mathbf{X}_i, \hat{\beta}_{ir})}, \qquad \hat{\beta}_{ir} = \hat{\beta} + \hat{\Delta}\mathbf{z}_i + \hat{\mathbf{L}}\mathbf{u}_{ir}. \quad \textbf{(17-5)}$$

Mechanical details on computing the MSLE are omitted. The interested reader is referred to Gourieroux and Monfort (1996), Train (2001, 2002, 2003), and Greene (2001, 2002) for details.

A question remains about the number of draws, $R$, required for the maximum simulated likelihood estimator to be consistent. In (17-3), the approximated function,

$$\hat{E}_{u_i}[f(\mathbf{y}_i \mid \mathbf{X}_i, \beta + \Delta\mathbf{z}_i + \Gamma\mathbf{u}_i)] = \frac{1}{R}\sum_{r=1}^{R} f(\mathbf{y}_i \mid \mathbf{X}_i, \beta + \Delta\mathbf{z}_i + \Gamma\mathbf{u}_{i,r}),$$

is an unbiased estimator of $E_{u_i}[f(\mathbf{y}_i \mid \mathbf{X}_i, \beta + \Delta\mathbf{z}_i + \Gamma\mathbf{u}_i)]$. However, what appears in the simulated log-likelihood is $\ln E_{u_i}[f(\mathbf{y}_i \mid \mathbf{X}_i, \beta + \Delta\mathbf{z}_i + \Gamma\mathbf{u}_i)]$, and the log of the estimator is a biased estimator of the log of its expectation. To maintain the asymptotic equivalence of the MSL estimator of $(\beta, \Delta, \Gamma)$ and the true MLE (if $u_i$ were observed), it is necessary for the estimators of these terms in the log-likelihood to converge to their expectations faster than the expectation of $\ln L$ converges to its expectation. The requirement [see Gourieroux and Monfort (1996)] is that $\sqrt{n}/R \to 0$. The estimator remains consistent if $\sqrt{n}$ and $R$ increase at the same rate; however, the asymptotic covariance matrix of the MSL estimator is larger than that of the MLE if so. In practical terms, this suggests that the number of draws be on the order of $n^{.5+\delta}$ for some positive $\delta$. [This does not state, however, what $R$ should be for a given $n$; it only establishes the properties of the MSL estimator as $n$ increases. For better or worse, researchers who have one sample of $n$ observations often rely on the numerical stability of the estimator with respect to changes in $R$ as their guide. Hajivassiliou (2000) gives some suggestions.] Note, as well, that the use of Halton sequences or any other autocorrelated sequences for the simulation, which is itself becoming more prevalent, interrupts this result. The appropriate counterpart to the Gourieroux and Monfort result for random sampling remains to be derived. One might suspect that the convergence result would persist, however.

### Example 17.5   Random Effects Geometric Regression

A random effects model is equivalent to a random parameters model in which the one random parameter is the constant term. We will use that result to fit a random effects model using simulation as an alternative to the Butler and Moffitt (1982) quadrature method.

**TABLE 17.3** Panel Data Estimates of a Geometric Regression for DOCVIS

| Variable | Pooled Estimate | St. Err. | Random Effects[a] Butler and Moffitt Estimate | St. Err. | Random Effects[b] Maximum Sim. Like. Estimate | St. Err. |
|---|---|---|---|---|---|---|
| Constant | 1.0918 | 0.1112 | 0.3998 | 0.09531 | 0.3999 | 0.05642 |
| Age | 0.0180 | 0.0013 | 0.02208 | 0.001220 | 0.02209 | 0.00072 |
| Education | −0.0473 | 0.0069 | −0.04507 | 0.006262 | −0.04528 | 0.003532 |
| Income | −0.0468 | 0.0075 | −0.1959 | 0.06103 | −0.1903 | 0.04407 |
| Kids | −0.1569 | 0.0319 | −0.1242 | 0.02336 | −0.1236 | 0.01635 |

[a] Estimated $\sigma_u = 0.9542921$.
[b] Estimated $\sigma_u = 0.9552153$.

Example 16.12 presents random effects estimates for the geometric regression model,

$$f(y_{it} \mid \mathbf{x}_{it}) = \theta_{it}(1 - \theta_{it})^{y_{it}}, \theta_{it} = 1/(1 + \lambda_{it}), \lambda_{it} = \exp(c_i + \mathbf{x}'_{it}\boldsymbol{\beta}), y_{it} = 0, 1, \ldots,$$

computed using the Hermite quadrature method. The simulation based estimator uses the simulated log-likelihood

$$\ln L_s = \sum_{i=1}^{n} \ln \frac{1}{R} \sum_{r=1}^{R} \left[ \prod_{t=1}^{T_i} \theta_{it,r}(1 - \theta_{it,r})^{y_{it}} \right],$$

$$\theta_{it,r} = 1/(1 + \lambda_{it,r}), \lambda_{it,r} = \exp(\mathbf{x}'_{it}\boldsymbol{\beta} + \sigma_u u_{ir}).$$

We recomputed the random effects estimates in Example 16.18 using maximum simulated likelihood. We used a Halton sequence with 100 points. The results appear in Table 17.3. As expected, the estimates are essentially the same as the ones computed using Hermite quadrature. The different methods of computing the standard errors does appear to produce a noticeable difference.

One of the most common applications of simulation-based estimation is for random parameters ("mixed") models. Model builders have been able to extend the methodology to many formulations. We have examined a few cases for linear models in Chapter 9. The application to nonlinear models is straightforward, as the next example suggests.

### Example 17.6  Maximum Simulated Likelihood Estimation of a Binary Choice Model

Bertschek and Lechner (1998) analyzed the product innovations of a sample of German manufacturing firms. They used a probit model (Sections 23.2–23.4) to study firm innovations. The model is for $\text{Prob}[y_{it} = 1 \mid \mathbf{x}_{it}, \boldsymbol{\beta}_i]$ where

$y_{it} = 1$ if firm $i$ realized a product innovation in year $t$ and 0 if not.

The independent variables in the model are

$X_{it1}$ = constant,

$X_{it2}$ = log of sales,

$X_{it3}$ = relative size = ratio of employment in business unit to employment in the industry,

$X_{it4}$ = ratio of industry imports to (industry sales + imports),

$X_{it5}$ = ratio of industry foreign direct investment to (industry sales + imports),

$X_{it6}$ = productivity = ratio of industry value added to industry employment,

$X_{it7}$ = dummy variable indicating firm is in the raw materials sector,

$X_{it8}$ = dummy variable indicating firm is in the investment goods sector.

| TABLE 17.4 | Estimated Random Parameters Model | | | |
|---|---|---|---|---|
| | *Probit* | *RP Mean* | *RP Std. Dev.* | *Empirical Distn.* |
| Constant | −1.96 | −3.91 | 2.70 | −3.27 |
| | (0.23) | (0.20) | | (0.57) |
| In Sales | 0.18 | 0.36 | 0.28 | 0.32 |
| | (0.022) | (0.019) | | (0.15) |
| Relative Size | 1.07 | 6.01 | 5.99 | 3.33 |
| | (0.14) | (0.22) | | (2.25) |
| Import | 1.13 | 1.51 | 0.84 | 2.01 |
| | (0.15) | (0.13) | | (0.58) |
| FDI | 2.85 | 3.81 | 6.51 | 3.76 |
| | (0.40) | (0.33) | | (1.69) |
| Productivity | −2.34 | −5.10 | 13.03 | −8.15 |
| | (0.72) | (0.73) | | (8.29) |
| Raw Materials | −0.28 | −0.31 | 1.65 | −0.18 |
| | (0.081) | (0.075) | | (0.57) |
| Investment | 0.19 | 0.27 | 1.42 | 0.27 |
| | (0.039) | (0.032) | | (0.38) |
| ln $L$ | −4114.05 | | −3498.654 | |

The sample consists of 1,270 German firms observed for five years, 1984–1988. (See Appendix Table F17.1.) The density that enters the log-likelihood is

$$f(y_{it} \mid \mathbf{x}_{it}, \boldsymbol{\beta}_i) = \text{Prob}[y_{it} \mid \mathbf{x}'_{it}\boldsymbol{\beta}_i] = \Phi[(2y_{it} - 1)\mathbf{x}'_{it}\boldsymbol{\beta}_i], \quad y_{it} = 0, 1.$$

where

$$\boldsymbol{\beta}_i = \boldsymbol{\beta} + \mathbf{v}_i, \quad \mathbf{v}_i \sim N[\mathbf{0}, \Sigma].$$

To be consistent with Bertschek and Lechner (1998) we did not fit any firm specific, time invariant components in the main equation for $\beta_i$.[10] (See Example 23.15 for further details about the model and the data set.)

Table 17.4 presents the estimated coefficients for the basic probit model in the first column. These are the values reported in the 1998 study. The estimates of the means, $\boldsymbol{\beta}$, are shown in the second column. There appear to be large differences in the parameter estimates, although this can be misleading as there is large variation across the firms in the posterior estimates. The third column presents the square roots of the implied diagonal elements of $\Sigma$ computed as the diagonal elements of $\mathbf{LL'}$. These estimated standard deviations are for the underlying distribution of the parameter in the model—they are not estimates of the standard deviation of the sampling distribution of the estimator. For the mean parameter, that is shown in the second column. The fourth column presents the sample means and standard deviations of the 1,270 estimated conditional estimates of the coefficients.

The latent class formulation developed in Section 16.9.7 provides an alternative approach for modeling latent parameter heterogeneity.[11] To illustrate the specification, we will reestimate the random parameters innovation model using a three-class latent class model. Estimates of the model parameters are presented in Table 17.5. The estimated conditional mean shown, which is comparable to the empirical means in the rightmost column in Table 17.4 for the random parameters model, are the sample average and standard deviation of the 1,270

---

[10]Apparently they did not use the second derivatives to compute the standard errors—we could not replicate these. Those show in the Table 17.4 are our results.

[11][See Greene (2001) for a survey.] For two examples, Nagin and Land (1993) employed the model to study age transitions through stages of criminal careers and Wang et al. (1998) and Wedel et al. (1993) and used the Poisson regression model to study counts of patents.

**TABLE 17.5** Estimated Latent Class Model

|  | Class 1 | Class 2 | Class 3 | Posterior |
|---|---|---|---|---|
| Constant | −2.32 | −2.71 | −8.97 | −3.38 |
|  | (0.59) | (0.69) | (2.20) | (2.14) |
| ln Sales | 0.32 | 0.23 | 0.57 | 0.34 |
|  | (0.061) | (0.072) | (0.18) | (0.09) |
| Relative Size | 4.38 | 0.72 | 1.42 | 2.58 |
|  | (0.89) | (0.37) | (0.76) | (1.30) |
| Import | 0.94 | 2.26 | 3.12 | 1.81 |
|  | (0.37) | (0.53) | (1.38) | (0.74) |
| FDI | 2.20 | 2.81 | 8.37 | 3.63 |
|  | (1.16) | (1.11) | (1.93) | (1.98) |
| Productivity | −5.86 | −7.70 | −0.91 | −5.48 |
|  | (2.70) | (4.69) | (6.76) | (1.78) |
| Raw Materials | −0.11 | −0.60 | 0.86 | −0.08 |
|  | (0.24) | (0.42) | (0.70) | (0.37) |
| Investment | 0.13 | 0.41 | 0.47 | 0.29 |
|  | (0.11) | (0.12) | (0.26) | (0.13) |
| ln L |  | −3503.55 |  |  |
| Class Prob (Prior) | 0.469 | 0.331 | 0.200 |  |
|  | (0.0352) | (0.0333) | (0.0246) |  |
| Class Prob (Posterior) | 0.469 | 0.331 | 0.200 |  |
|  | (0.394) | (0.289) | (0.325) |  |
| Pred. Count | 649 | 366 | 255 |  |

firm-specific posterior mean parameter vectors. They are computed using $\hat{\boldsymbol{\beta}}_i = \sum_{j=1}^{3} \hat{\pi}_{ij}\hat{\boldsymbol{\beta}}_j$ where $\hat{\pi}_{ij}$ is the conditional estimator of the class probabilities in (16-102). These estimates differ considerably from the probit model, but they are quite similar to the empirical means in Table 17.4. In each case, a confidence interval around the posterior mean contains the one-class, pooled probit estimator. Finally, the (identical) prior and average of the sample posterior class probabilities are shown at the bottom of the table. The much larger empirical standard deviations reflect that the posterior estimates are based on aggregating the sample data and involve, as well, complicated functions of all the model parameters. The estimated numbers of class members are computed by assigning to each firm the predicted class associated with the highest posterior class probability.

## 17.5.2 THE METHOD OF SIMULATED MOMENTS

As we saw in the development of the GMM estimator, one can view the likelihood equations as a set of $K$ moment equations. In the same fashion, the simulated likelihood equations can be viewed as a set of simulated moments, and the maximum simulated likelihood (MSL) estimator can be viewed as a generalized method of simulated moments estimator. Consider a (perhaps somewhat simpler) counterpart for a nonlinear regression model with latent heterogeneity, perhaps in the form of a random constant term in the model, to be estimated using instrumental variables. Suppose the model is

$$y_i = f(\mathbf{x}_i, \boldsymbol{\beta} \mid u_i) + \varepsilon_i,$$

such that

$$E[(y_i - E_u f(\mathbf{x}_i, \boldsymbol{\beta} \mid u_i))\mathbf{z}_i] = \mathbf{0}.$$

The empirical counterpart would be

$$(1/n)\Sigma_i[(y_i - E_u f(\mathbf{x}_i, \boldsymbol{\beta} \mid u_i))\mathbf{z}_i] = \mathbf{0}.$$

We could use the methods developed in Chapter 15 for GMM estimation, but for the presence of the unobserved $u_i$ in the moment equation. The **method of simulated moments** proposed by Pakes and Pollard (1989) and McFadden (1989) replaces the unobserved expectation in the moment equation, $E_u f(\mathbf{x}_i, \boldsymbol{\beta} \mid u_i)$, with a simulation estimator

$$\hat{E}[f(\mathbf{x}_i, \boldsymbol{\beta} \mid u_i)] = \frac{1}{R} \sum_{r=1}^{R} f(\mathbf{x}_i, \boldsymbol{\beta} \mid u_{i,r}).$$

The method of simulated moments estimator is then the minimizer of

$$q = \left[ (1/n) \sum_{i=1}^{n} \left( y_i - \frac{1}{R} \sum_{r=1}^{R} f(\mathbf{x}_i, \boldsymbol{\beta} \mid u_{i,r}) \right) \mathbf{z}_i \right]' \left[ (1/n) \sum_{i=1}^{n} \left( y_i - \frac{1}{R} \sum_{r=1}^{R} f(\mathbf{x}_i, \boldsymbol{\beta} \mid u_{i,r}) \right) \mathbf{z}_i \right].$$

If the number of instruments is equal to the number of parameters, then the moment equations can be satisfied exactly, and $q$ equals zero. Otherwise, $q$ is minimized with respect to $\boldsymbol{\beta}$. As in the MSL case, it is crucial to use the same set of random draws for every function evaluation. The practical solution is to create and associate with observation $i$ a vector of simulated draws, $\mathbf{u}_{S,i} = (u_{iS,1}, \ldots, u_{iS,R})$ at the beginning of the optimization and reuse it for every function evaluation. The amount of computation is comparable to the MSL estimator. The use of Halton sequences or other intelligent methods of simulating the integration would have the same payoff here that it did with the MSL estimator.

The preceding defines a GMM estimator with weighting matrix $\mathbf{I}$. In the same fashion as before, an efficient estimator can be produced by taking a second pass, re-computing the estimator using a weighting that estimates the inverse of the asymptotic covariance matrix of the vector of empirical moments. The estimator of the weighting matrix would be

$$\mathbf{W} = \left[ (1/n) \sum_{i=1}^{n} \left( y_i - \frac{1}{R} \sum_{r=1}^{R} f(\mathbf{x}_i, \hat{\boldsymbol{\beta}} \mid u_{i,r}) \right)^2 \mathbf{z}_i \mathbf{z}_i' \right]^{-1},$$

where $\hat{\boldsymbol{\beta}}$ is the estimated parameter vector computed at the first step.

## 17.6 BOOTSTRAPPING

The technique of **bootstrapping** is used to obtain a description of the sampling properties of empirical estimators using the sample data themselves, rather than broad theoretical results.[12] Suppose that $\hat{\theta}_n$ is an estimator of a parameter vector $\theta$ based on a sample $\mathbf{X} = (\mathbf{x}_1, \ldots, \mathbf{x}_n)$. An approximation to the statistical properties of $\hat{\theta}_n$ can be obtained by studying a sample of bootstrap estimators $\hat{\theta}(b)_m$, $b = 1, \ldots, B$, obtained by sampling $m$ observations, *with replacement,* from $\mathbf{X}$ and recomputing $\hat{\theta}$ with each sample. After

---

[12]See Efron (1979), Efron and Tibshirani (1994), and Davidson and Hinkley (1997).

a total of $B$ times, the desired sampling characteristic is computed from

$$\hat{\Theta} = [\hat{\theta}(1)_m, \ldots, \hat{\theta}(B)_m].$$

For example, if it were known that the estimator were consistent and if $n$ were reasonably large, then one might approximate the asymptotic covariance matrix of the estimator $\hat{\theta}$ by using

$$\text{Est. Asy. Var}[\hat{\theta}] = \frac{1}{B} \sum_{b=1}^{B} [\hat{\theta}(b)_m - \hat{\theta}_n][\hat{\theta}(b)_m - \hat{\theta}_n]'.$$

This technique was developed by Efron (1979) and has been appearing with increasing frequency in the applied econometrics literature. [See, for example, Veall (1987, 1992), Vinod (1993), and Vinod and Raj (1994). Extensive surveys of uses and methods in econometrics appear in Cameron and Trivedi (2005), Horowitz (2001), and Davidson and MacKinnon (2006).] An application of this technique to the least absolute deviations in the linear model is shown in the following example and in Chapter 4, and to a model of binary choice in Section 23.6.1.

### Example 17.7   Bootstrapping the Variance of the Median

As discussed earlier, there are few cases in which an exact expression for the sampling variance of the median are known. In Example 17.4, we examined the case of the median of a sample of 500 observations from the $t$ distribution with 10 degrees of freedom. This is one of those cases in which there is no exact formula for the asymptotic variance of the median. However, we can use the bootstrap technique to estimate one empirically. (You might want to replicate this experiment.) To demonstrate, consider the same data as used in the preceding example. We have a sample of 500 observations, for which we have computed the median, $-0.00786$. We drew 100 samples of 500 with replacement from this sample and recomputed the median with each of these samples. The empirical square root of the mean squared deviation around this estimate of $-0.00786$ was 0.056. In contrast, consider the same calculation for the mean. The sample mean is $-0.07247$. The sample standard deviation is 1.08469, so the standard error of the mean is 0.04657. (The bootstrap estimate of the standard error of the mean was 0.052.) This agrees with our expectation in that the sample mean should generally be a more efficient estimator of the mean of the distribution in a large sample.

There is another approach we might take in this situation. Consider the regression model

$$y_i = \alpha + \varepsilon_i$$

where $\varepsilon_i$ has a symmetric distribution with finite variance. As discussed in Section 14.3.2, the least absolute deviations estimator of the coefficient in this model is an estimator of the median (which equals the mean) of the distribution. So, this presents another estimator. Once again, the bootstrap estimator must be used to estimate the asymptotic variance of the estimator. Using the same data, we fit this regression model using the LAD estimator. The coefficient estimate is $-.05397$ with a bootstrap estimated standard error of 0.05872. The estimated standard error agrees with the earlier one. The difference in the estimated coefficient stems from the different computations—the regression estimate is the solution to a linear programming problem while the earlier estimate is the actual sample median.

The bootstrap estimation procedure has also been suggested as a method of reducing bias. The revised estimator would be

$$\hat{\theta}_B = \hat{\theta} + \left[ \hat{\theta} - \frac{1}{B} \sum_{b=1}^{B} \hat{\theta}(b)_m \right].$$

Davidson and MacKinnon (2006) argue that the smaller bias of the corrected estimator is offset by an increased variance compared to the uncorrected estimator. [See, as well, Cameron and Trivedi (2005).] The authors offer some other cautions for practitioners contemplating use of this technique. First, perhaps obviously, the extension of the method to samples with dependent observations presents some obstacles. For time-series data, the technique makes little sense—none of the bootstrapped samples will be a time series, so the properties of the resulting estimators will not satisfy the underlying the assumptions needed to make the technique appropriate. Second, there are many additional considerations involved in using the bootstrapped estimates for construction of test statistics and confidence intervals. Davidson and MacKinnon (2006) and Cameron and Trivedi (2005) present the analysis in great detail.

## 17.7 SUMMARY AND CONCLUSIONS

This chapter has outlined several applications in which analytic solutions to a necessary expectation cannot be derived, but simulations based on random samples can be used to obtain the result. The essential ingredient in any of these applications is a random number generator. We examined the most common method of generating what appear to be samples of random draws from a population—in fact, they are deterministic Markov chains that only appear to be random. Random number generators are used directly to obtain draws from the standard uniform distribution. The inverse probability transformation is then used to transform these to draws from other distributions. We examined several major applications involving random sampling:

- Many integrals that do not have closed forms can be transformed into expectations of random variables that can be sampled with a random number generator. This produces the technique of Monte Carlo integration.
- Monte Carlo studies are used to examine the behavior of statistics when the precise sampling distribution of the statistic cannot be derived. We examined the behavior of a certain test statistic and of the maximum likelihood estimator in a fixed effects model.
- The technique of maximum simulated likelihood estimation allows the researcher to formulate likelihood functions (and other criteria such as moment equations) that involve expectations that can be integrated out of the function using Monte Carlo techniques. We used the method to fit a random parameters model.
- Random sampling, in the form of bootstrapping, allows us to infer the characteristics of the sampling distribution of an estimator, in particular its asymptotic variance. We used this result to examine the sampling variance of the median in random sampling from a nonnormal population.

The techniques suggested here open up a vast range of applications of Bayesian statistics and econometrics in which the characteristics of a posterior distribution are deduced from random samples from the distribution, rather than brute force derivation of the analytic form. Bayesian methods based on this principle are discussed in the next chapter.

## Key Terms and Concepts

- Bootstrapping
- Cholesky factorization
- Fundamental probability transformation
- GHK simulator
- Halton sequence
- Importance function
- Importance sampling
- Incidental parameters problem

- Markov chain
- Maximum simulated likelihood
- Method of simulated moments
- Monte Carlo integration
- Monte Carlo study
- Period
- Power of a test

- Pseudo–random number generator
- Random parameters
- Rejection method
- Seed
- Simulation
- Size of a test
- Specificity

## Exercises

1. The exponential distribution has density $\theta \exp(-\theta x)$. How would you obtain a random sample of observations from an exponential population? The Weibull population has survival function $S(x) = \lambda p \exp(-(\lambda x)^p)$. How would you obtain a random sample of observations from a Weibull population?

2. Suppose $x$ and $y$ are bivariate normally distributed with zero means, variances equal to one and correlation equal to $\rho$. Show how to use a Gibbs sampler to extimate $E[x^2 \exp(y) + y^2 \exp(x)]$.

## Application

1. Does the Wald statistic reject the null too often? Construct a Monte Carlo study of the behavior of the Wald statistic for testing the hypothesis that $\gamma$ equals zero in the model of Section 17.4.1. Recall, the Wald statistic is the square of the $t$ ratio on the parameter in question. The procedure of the test is to reject the null hypothesis if the Wald statistic is greater than 3.84, the critical value from the chi squared distribution with one degree of freedom. Replicate the study in Section 17.4.1, that is for all three assumptions about the underlying data.

# 18

# BAYESIAN ESTIMATION
# AND INFERENCE

## 18.1 INTRODUCTION

The preceding chapters (and those that follow this one) are focused primarily on parametric specifications and classical estimation methods. These elements of the econometric method present a bit of a methodological dilemma for the researcher. They appear to straightjacket the analyst into a fixed and immutable specification of the model. But in any analysis, there is uncertainty as to the magnitudes, sometimes the signs and, at the extreme, even the meaning of parameters. It is rare that the presentation of a set of empirical results has not been preceded by at least some exploratory analysis. Proponents of the Bayesian methodology argue that the process of "estimation" is not one of deducing the values of fixed parameters, but rather, in accordance with the scientific method, one of continually updating and sharpening our subjective beliefs about the state of the world. Of course, this adherence to a subjective approach to model building is not necessarily a virtue. If one holds that "models" and "parameters" represent objective truths that the analyst seeks to discover, then the subjectivity of Bayesian methods may be less than perfectly comfortable.

Contemporary applications of Bayesian methods typically advance little of this theological debate. The modern practice of Bayesian econometrics is much more pragmatic. As we will see below in several examples, Bayesian methods have produced some remarkably efficient solutions to difficult estimation problems. Researchers often choose the techniques on practical grounds, rather than in adherence to their philosophical basis; indeed, for some, the Bayesian estimator is merely an algorithm.[1]

Bayesian methods have have been employed by econometricians since well before Zellner's classic (1971) presentation of the methodology to economists, but until fairly recently, were more or less at the margin of the field. With recent advances in technique (notably the Gibbs sampler) and the advance of computer software and hardware that has made simulation-based estimation routine, Bayesian methods that rely heavily on both have become widespread throughout the social sciences. There are libraries of work on Bayesian econometrics and a rapidly expanding applied

---

[1]For example, from the home website of MLWin, a widely used program for multilevel (random parameters) modeling, http://www.cmm.bris.ac.uk/MLwiN/features/mcmc.shtml, we find "Markov Chain Monte Carlo (MCMC) methods allow Bayesian models to be fitted, where prior distributions for the model parameters are specified. By default *MLwiN* sets diffuse priors which can be used to approximate maximum likelihood estimation." Train (2001) is an interesting application that compares Bayesian and classical estimators of a random parameters model.

literature.[2] This chapter will introduce the vocabulary and techniques of Bayesian econometrics. Section 18.2 lays out the essential foundation for the method. The canonical application, the linear regression model, is developed in Section 18.3. Section 18.4 continues the methodological development. The fundamental tool of contemporary Bayesian econometrics, the Gibbs sampler, is presented in Section 18.5. Three applications and several more limited examples are presented in Sections 18.6, 18.7, and 18.8. Section 18.6 shows how to use the Gibbs sampler to estimate the parameters of a probit model without maximizing the likelihood function. This application also introduces the technique of data augmentation. Bayesian counterparts to the panel data random and fixed effects models are presented in Section 18.7. A hierarchical Bayesian treatment of the random parameters model is presented in Section 18.8 with a comparison to the classical treatment of the same model. Some conclusions are drawn in Section 18.9. The presentation here is nontechnical. A much more extensive entry level presentation is given by Lancaster (2004). Intermediate-level presentations appear in Cameron and Trivedi (2005, Chapter 13), and Koop (2003). A more challenging treatment is offered in Geweke (2005). The other sources listed in footnote 2 are oriented to applications.

## 18.2 BAYES THEOREM AND THE POSTERIOR DENSITY

The centerpiece of the Bayesian methodology is the **Bayes theorem:** for events $A$ and $B$, the conditional probability of event $A$ given that $B$ has occurred is

$$P(A \mid B) = \frac{P(B \mid A) P(A)}{P(B)}. \tag{18-1}$$

Paraphrased for our applications here, we would write

$$P(\text{parameters} \mid \text{data}) = \frac{P(\text{data} \mid \text{parameters}) P(\text{parameters})}{P(\text{data})}.$$

In this setting, the data are viewed as constants whose distributions do not involve the parameters of interest. For the purpose of the study, we treat the data as only a fixed set of additional information to be used in updating our beliefs about the parameters. Note the similarity to (14-1). Thus, we write

$$P(\text{parameters} \mid \text{data}) \propto P(\text{data} \mid \text{parameters}) P(\text{parameters})$$
$$= \textbf{Likelihood function} \times \textbf{Prior density}. \tag{18-2}$$

The symbol $\propto$ means "is proportional to." In the preceding equation, we have dropped the marginal density of the data, so what remains is not a proper density until it is scaled by what will be an inessential proportionality constant. The first term on the right is the joint distribution of the observed random variables $\mathbf{y}$, given the parameters. As we

---

[2]Recent additions to the dozens of books on the subject include Gelman et al. (2004), Geweke (2005), Gill (2002), Koop (2003), Lancaster (2004), Congdon (2005), and Rossi et al. (2005). Readers with an historical bent will find Zellner (1971) and Leamer (1978) worthwhile reading. There are also many methodological surveys. Poirier and Tobias (2006) as well as Poirier (1988, 1995) sharply focus the nature of the methodological distinctions between the classical (frequentist) and Bayesian approaches.

shall analyze it here, this distribution is the normal distribution we have used in our previous analysis—see (14-1). The second term is the **prior beliefs** of the analyst. The left-hand side is the **posterior density** of the parameters, given the current body of data, or our *revised* beliefs about the distribution of the parameters after "seeing" the data. The posterior is a mixture of the prior information and the "current information," that is, the data. Once obtained, this posterior density is available to be the prior density function when the next body of data or other usable information becomes available. The principle involved, which appears nowhere in the classical analysis, is one of continual accretion of knowledge about the parameters.

Traditional Bayesian estimation is heavily parameterized. The prior density and the likelihood function are crucial elements of the analysis, and both must be fully specified for estimation to proceed. The Bayesian "estimator" is the mean of the posterior density of the parameters, a quantity that is usually obtained either by integration (when closed forms exist), approximation of integrals by numerical techniques, or by Monte Carlo methods, which are discussed in Section 17.3.

### Example 18.1 Bayesian Estimation of a Probability

Consider estimation of the probability that a production process will produce a defective product. In case 1, suppose the sampling design is to choose $N = 25$ items from the production line and count the number of defectives. If the probability that any item is defective is a constant $\theta$ between zero and one, then the likelihood for the sample of data is

$$L(\theta \mid \textbf{data}) = \theta^D (1 - \theta)^{25-D},$$

where $D$ is the number of defectives, say, 8. The maximum likelihood estimator of $\theta$ will be $p = D/25 = 0.32$, and the asymptotic variance of the maximum likelihood estimator is estimated by $p(1 - p)/25 = 0.008704$.

Now, consider a Bayesian approach to the same analysis. The posterior density is obtained by the following reasoning:

$$p(\theta \mid \textbf{data}) = \frac{p(\theta, \textbf{data})}{p(\textbf{data})} = \frac{p(\theta, \textbf{data})}{\int_\theta p(\theta, \textbf{data})d\theta} = \frac{p(\textbf{data} \mid \theta)p(\theta)}{p(\textbf{data})}$$

$$= \frac{Likelihood(\textbf{data} \mid \theta) \times p(\theta)}{p(\textbf{data})}$$

where $p(\theta)$ is the prior density assumed for $\theta$. [We have taken some license with the terminology, since the likelihood function is conventionally defined as $L(\theta \mid \textbf{data})$.] Inserting the results of the sample first drawn, we have the posterior density:

$$p(\theta \mid \textbf{data}) = \frac{\theta^D(1 - \theta)^{N-D}p(\theta)}{\int_\theta \theta^D(1 - \theta)^{N-D}p(\theta)d\theta}.$$

What follows depends on the assumed prior for $\theta$. Suppose we begin with a "noninformative" prior that treats all *allowable* values of $\theta$ as equally likely. This would imply a uniform distribution over (0,1). Thus, $p(\theta) = 1, 0 \le \theta \le 1$. The denominator with this assumption is a beta integral (see Section E2.3) with parameters $a = D + 1$ and $b = N - D + 1$, so the posterior density is

$$p(\theta \mid \textbf{data}) = \frac{\theta^D(1 - \theta)^{N-D}}{\left(\dfrac{\Gamma(D + 1)\Gamma(N - D + 1)}{\Gamma(D + 1 + N - D + 1)}\right)} = \frac{\Gamma(N + 2)\theta^D(1 - \theta)^{N-D}}{\Gamma(D + 1)\Gamma(N - D + 1)}.$$

This is the density of a random variable with a beta distribution with parameters $(\alpha, \beta) = (D+1, N-D+1)$. (See Section B.4.6.) The mean of this random variable is $(D+1)/(N+2) = 9/27 = 0.3333$ (as opposed to 0.32, the MLE). The posterior variance is $[(D+1)/(N-D+1)]/[(N+3)(N+2)^2] = 0.007936$.

There is a loose end in this example. If the uniform prior were noninformative, that would mean that the only information we had was in the likelihood function. Why didn't the Bayesian estimator and the MLE coincide? The reason is that the uniform prior over [0,1] is not really noninformative. It did introduce the information that $\theta$ must fall in the unit interval. The prior mean is 0.5 and the prior variance is 1/12. The posterior mean is an average of the MLE and the prior mean. Another less than obvious aspect of this result is the smaller variance of the Bayesian estimator. The principle that lies behind this (aside from the fact that the prior did in fact introduce some certainty in the estimator) is that the Bayesian estimator is conditioned on the specific sample data. The theory behind the classical MLE implies that it averages over the entire population that generates the data. This will always introduce a greater degree of "uncertainty" in the classical estimator compared to its Bayesian counterpart.

## 18.3 BAYESIAN ANALYSIS OF THE CLASSICAL REGRESSION MODEL

The complexity of the algebra involved in Bayesian analysis is often extremely burdensome. For the linear regression model, however, many fairly straightforward results have been obtained. To provide some of the flavor of the techniques, we present the full derivation only for some simple cases. In the interest of brevity, and to avoid the burden of excessive algebra, we refer the reader to one of the several sources that present the full derivation of the more complex cases.[3]

The classical normal regression model we have analyzed thus far is constructed around the conditional multivariate normal distribution $N[\mathbf{X}\boldsymbol{\beta}, \sigma^2\mathbf{I}]$. The interpretation is different here. In the sampling theory setting, this distribution embodies the information about the observed sample data *given* the assumed distribution and the fixed, albeit unknown, parameters of the model. In the Bayesian setting, this function summarizes the information that a particular realization of the data provides about the assumed distribution of the model parameters. To underscore that idea, we rename this joint density the *likelihood for $\boldsymbol{\beta}$ and $\sigma^2$ given the data,* so

$$L(\boldsymbol{\beta}, \sigma^2 \mid \mathbf{y}, \mathbf{X}) = [2\pi\sigma^2]^{-n/2}e^{-[(1/(2\sigma^2))(\mathbf{y}-\mathbf{X}\boldsymbol{\beta})'(\mathbf{y}-\mathbf{X}\boldsymbol{\beta})]}. \tag{18-3}$$

For purposes of the results below, some reformulation is useful. Let $d = n - K$ (the degrees of freedom parameter), and substitute

$$\mathbf{y} - \mathbf{X}\boldsymbol{\beta} = \mathbf{y} - \mathbf{Xb} - \mathbf{X}(\boldsymbol{\beta} - \mathbf{b}) = \mathbf{e} - \mathbf{X}(\boldsymbol{\beta} - \mathbf{b})$$

in the exponent. Expanding this produces

$$\left(-\frac{1}{2\sigma^2}\right)(\mathbf{y} - \mathbf{X}\boldsymbol{\beta})'(\mathbf{y} - \mathbf{X}\boldsymbol{\beta}) = \left(-\frac{1}{2}ds^2\right)\left(\frac{1}{\sigma^2}\right) - \frac{1}{2}(\boldsymbol{\beta} - \mathbf{b})'\left(\frac{1}{\sigma^2}\mathbf{X}'\mathbf{X}\right)(\boldsymbol{\beta} - \mathbf{b}).$$

After a bit of manipulation (note that $n/2 = d/2 + K/2$), the likelihood may be written

$$L(\boldsymbol{\beta}, \sigma^2 \mid \mathbf{y}, \mathbf{X})$$
$$= [2\pi]^{-d/2}[\sigma^2]^{-d/2}e^{-(d/2)(s^2/\sigma^2)}[2\pi]^{-K/2}[\sigma^2]^{-K/2}e^{-(1/2)(\boldsymbol{\beta}-\mathbf{b})'[\sigma^2(\mathbf{X}'\mathbf{X})^{-1}]^{-1}(\boldsymbol{\beta}-\mathbf{b})}.$$

---

[3]These sources include Judge et al. (1982, 1985), Maddala (1977a), Mittelhammer et al. (2000), and the canonical reference for econometricians, Zellner (1971). A remarkable feature of the current literature is the degree to which the analytical components have become ever simpler while the applications have become progressively more complex. This will become evident in Sections 18.5–18.7.

This density embodies all that we have to learn about the parameters from the observed data. Because the data are taken to be constants in the joint density, we may multiply this joint density by the (very carefully chosen), inessential (because it does not involve $\beta$ or $\sigma^2$) constant function of the observations,

$$A = \frac{\left(\frac{d}{2}s^2\right)^{(d/2)+1}}{\Gamma\left(\frac{d}{2}+1\right)}[2\pi]^{(d/2)}|\mathbf{X'X}|^{-1/2}.$$

For convenience, let $v = d/2$. Then, multiplying $L(\beta, \sigma^2 | \mathbf{y}, \mathbf{X})$ by $A$ gives

$$L(\beta, \sigma^2 | \mathbf{y}, \mathbf{X}) \propto \frac{[vs^2]^{v+1}}{\Gamma(v+1)}\left(\frac{1}{\sigma^2}\right)^v e^{-vs^2(1/\sigma^2)}[2\pi]^{-K/2}|\sigma^2(\mathbf{X'X})^{-1}|^{-1/2}$$

$$\times e^{-(1/2)(\beta-\mathbf{b})'[\sigma^2(\mathbf{X'X})^{-1}]^{-1}(\beta-\mathbf{b})}. \tag{18-4}$$

The likelihood function is proportional to the product of a gamma density for $z = 1/\sigma^2$ with parameters $\lambda = vs^2$ and $P = v + 1$ [see (B-39); this is an **inverted gamma distribution**] and a $K$-variate normal density for $\beta | \sigma^2$ with mean vector $\mathbf{b}$ and covariance matrix $\sigma^2(\mathbf{X'X})^{-1}$. The reason will be clear shortly.

### 18.3.1 ANALYSIS WITH A NONINFORMATIVE PRIOR

The departure point for the Bayesian analysis of the model is the specification of a **prior distribution.** This distribution gives the analyst's prior beliefs about the parameters of the model. One of two approaches is generally taken. If no prior information is known about the parameters, then we can specify a **noninformative prior** that reflects that. We do this by specifying a "flat" prior for the parameter in question:[4]

$$g(\text{parameter}) \propto \text{constant}.$$

There are different ways that one might characterize the lack of prior information. The implication of a flat prior is that within the range of valid values for the parameter, all intervals of equal length—hence, in principle, all values—are equally likely. The second possibility, an **informative prior,** is treated in the next section. The posterior density is the result of combining the likelihood function with the prior density. Because it pools the full set of information available to the analyst, *once the data have been drawn,* the posterior density would be interpreted the same way the prior density was before the data were obtained.

To begin, we analyze the case in which $\sigma^2$ is assumed to be known. This assumption is obviously unrealistic, and we do so only to establish a point of departure. Using Bayes Theorem, we construct the posterior density,

$$f(\beta | \mathbf{y}, \mathbf{X}, \sigma^2) = \frac{L(\beta | \sigma^2, \mathbf{y}, \mathbf{X})g(\beta | \sigma^2)}{f(\mathbf{y})} \propto L(\beta | \sigma^2, \mathbf{y}, \mathbf{X})g(\beta | \sigma^2),$$

---

[4]That this "improper" density might not integrate to one is only a minor difficulty. Any constant of integration would ultimately drop out of the final result. See Zellner (1971, pp. 41–53) for a discussion of noninformative priors.

assuming that the distribution of $\mathbf{X}$ does not depend on $\boldsymbol{\beta}$ or $\sigma^2$. Because $g(\boldsymbol{\beta} \mid \sigma^2) \propto$ a constant, this density is the one in (18-4). For now, write

$$f(\boldsymbol{\beta} \mid \sigma^2, \mathbf{y}, \mathbf{X}) \propto h(\sigma^2)[2\pi]^{-K/2} |\sigma^2(\mathbf{X}'\mathbf{X})^{-1}|^{-1/2} e^{-(1/2)(\boldsymbol{\beta}-\mathbf{b})'[\sigma^2(\mathbf{X}'\mathbf{X})^{-1}]^{-1}(\boldsymbol{\beta}-\mathbf{b})}, \quad \textbf{(18-5)}$$

where

$$h(\sigma^2) = \frac{[vs^2]^{v+1}}{\Gamma(v+1)} \left[\frac{1}{\sigma^2}\right]^v e^{-vs^2(1/\sigma^2)}. \quad \textbf{(18-6)}$$

For the present, we treat $h(\sigma^2)$ simply as a constant that involves $\sigma^2$, not as a probability density; (18-5) is *conditional* on $\sigma^2$. Thus, the posterior density $f(\boldsymbol{\beta} \mid \sigma^2, \mathbf{y}, \mathbf{X})$ is proportional to a multivariate normal distribution with mean $\mathbf{b}$ and covariance matrix $\sigma^2(\mathbf{X}'\mathbf{X})^{-1}$.

This result is familiar, but it is interpreted differently in this setting. First, we have combined our prior information about $\boldsymbol{\beta}$ (in this case, no information) and the sample information to obtain a *posterior distribution*. Thus, on the basis of the sample data in hand, we obtain a distribution for $\boldsymbol{\beta}$ with mean $\mathbf{b}$ and covariance matrix $\sigma^2(\mathbf{X}'\mathbf{X})^{-1}$. The result is dominated by the sample information, as it should be if there is no prior information. In the absence of any prior information, the mean of the posterior distribution, which is a type of Bayesian point estimate, is the sampling theory estimator.

To generalize the preceding to an unknown $\sigma^2$, we specify a noninformative prior distribution for $\ln \sigma$ over the entire real line.[5] By the change of variable formula, if $g(\ln \sigma)$ is constant, then $g(\sigma^2)$ is proportional to $1/\sigma^2$.[6] Assuming that $\boldsymbol{\beta}$ and $\sigma^2$ are independent, we now have the noninformative joint prior distribution:

$$g(\boldsymbol{\beta}, \sigma^2) = g_{\boldsymbol{\beta}}(\boldsymbol{\beta})g_{\sigma^2}(\sigma^2) \propto \frac{1}{\sigma^2}.$$

We can obtain the **joint posterior distribution** for $\boldsymbol{\beta}$ and $\sigma^2$ by using

$$f(\boldsymbol{\beta}, \sigma^2 \mid \mathbf{y}, \mathbf{X}) = L(\boldsymbol{\beta} \mid \sigma^2, \mathbf{y}, \mathbf{X})g_{\sigma^2}(\sigma^2) \propto L(\boldsymbol{\beta} \mid \sigma^2, \mathbf{y}, \mathbf{X}) \times \frac{1}{\sigma^2}. \quad \textbf{(18-7)}$$

For the same reason as before, we multiply $g_{\sigma^2}(\sigma^2)$ by a well-chosen constant, this time $vs^2\Gamma(v+1)/\Gamma(v+2) = vs^2/(v+1)$. Multiplying (18-5) by this constant times $g_{\sigma^2}(\sigma^2)$ and inserting $h(\sigma^2)$ gives the joint posterior for $\boldsymbol{\beta}$ and $\sigma^2$, given $\mathbf{y}$ and $\mathbf{X}$:

$$f(\boldsymbol{\beta}, \sigma^2 \mid \mathbf{y}, \mathbf{X}) \propto \frac{[vs^2]^{v+2}}{\Gamma(v+2)} \left[\frac{1}{\sigma^2}\right]^{v+1} e^{-vs^2(1/\sigma^2)}[2\pi]^{-K/2} |\sigma^2(\mathbf{X}'\mathbf{X})^{-1}|^{-1/2}$$

$$\times e^{-(1/2)(\boldsymbol{\beta}-\mathbf{b})'[\sigma^2(\mathbf{X}'\mathbf{X})^{-1}]^{-1}(\boldsymbol{\beta}-\mathbf{b})}.$$

To obtain the marginal posterior distribution for $\boldsymbol{\beta}$, it is now necessary to integrate $\sigma^2$ out of the joint distribution (and vice versa to obtain the marginal distribution for $\sigma^2$). By collecting the terms, $f(\boldsymbol{\beta}, \sigma^2 \mid \mathbf{y}, \mathbf{X})$ can be written as

$$f(\boldsymbol{\beta}, \sigma^2 \mid \mathbf{y}, \mathbf{X}) \propto A \times \left(\frac{1}{\sigma^2}\right)^{P-1} e^{-\lambda(1/\sigma^2)},$$

---

[5]See Zellner (1971) for justification of this prior distribution.

[6]Many treatments of this model use $\sigma$ rather than $\sigma^2$ as the parameter of interest. The end results are identical. We have chosen this parameterization because it makes manipulation of the likelihood function with a gamma prior distribution especially convenient. See Zellner (1971, pp. 44–45) for discussion.

where

$$A = \frac{[vs^2]^{v+2}}{\Gamma(v+2)}[2\pi]^{-K/2}|(\mathbf{X'X})^{-1}|^{-1/2},$$

$$P = v + 2 + K/2 = (n-K)/2 + 2 + K/2 = (n+4)/2,$$

and

$$\lambda = vs^2 + \tfrac{1}{2}(\boldsymbol{\beta} - \mathbf{b})'\mathbf{X'X}(\boldsymbol{\beta} - \mathbf{b}),$$

so the marginal posterior distribution for $\boldsymbol{\beta}$ is

$$\int_0^\infty f(\boldsymbol{\beta}, \sigma^2 \mid \mathbf{y}, \mathbf{X})d\sigma^2 \propto A \int_0^\infty \left(\frac{1}{\sigma^2}\right)^{P-1} e^{-\lambda(1/\sigma^2)}d\sigma^2.$$

To do the integration, we have to make a change of variable; $d(1/\sigma^2) = -(1/\sigma^2)^2 d\sigma^2$, so $d\sigma^2 = -(1/\sigma^2)^{-2} d(1/\sigma^2)$. Making the substitution—the sign of the integral changes twice, once for the Jacobian and back again because the integral from $\sigma^2 = 0$ to $\infty$ is the negative of the integral from $(1/\sigma^2) = 0$ to $\infty$—we obtain

$$\int_0^\infty f(\boldsymbol{\beta}, \sigma^2 \mid \mathbf{y}, \mathbf{X})d\sigma^2 \propto A \int_0^\infty \left(\frac{1}{\sigma^2}\right)^{P-3} e^{-\lambda(1/\sigma^2)}d\left(\frac{1}{\sigma^2}\right)$$

$$= A \times \frac{\Gamma(P-2)}{\lambda^{P-2}}.$$

Reinserting the expressions for $A$, $P$, and $\lambda$ produces

$$f(\boldsymbol{\beta} \mid \mathbf{y}, \mathbf{X}) \propto \frac{\frac{[vs^2]^{v+2}\Gamma(v+K/2)}{\Gamma(v+2)}[2\pi]^{-K/2}|\mathbf{X'X}|^{-1/2}}{\left[vs^2 + \frac{1}{2}(\boldsymbol{\beta} - \mathbf{b})'\mathbf{X'X}(\boldsymbol{\beta} - \mathbf{b})\right]^{v+K/2}}. \tag{18-8}$$

This density is proportional to a **multivariate $t$ distribution**[7] and is a generalization of the familiar univariate distribution we have used at various points. This distribution has a degrees of freedom parameter, $d = n - K$, mean $\mathbf{b}$, and covariance matrix $(d/(d-2))\times [s^2(\mathbf{X'X})^{-1}]$. Each element of the $K$-element vector $\boldsymbol{\beta}$ has a marginal distribution that is the univariate $t$ distribution with degrees of freedom $n - K$, mean $b_k$, and variance equal to the $k$th diagonal element of the covariance matrix given earlier. Once again, this is the same as our sampling theory result. The difference is a matter of interpretation. In the current context, the estimated distribution is for $\boldsymbol{\beta}$ and is centered at $\mathbf{b}$.

## 18.3.2 ESTIMATION WITH AN INFORMATIVE PRIOR DENSITY

Once we leave the simple case of noninformative priors, matters become quite complicated, both at a practical level and, methodologically, in terms of just where the prior comes from. The integration of $\sigma^2$ out of the posterior in (18-7) is complicated by itself. It is made much more so if the prior distributions of $\boldsymbol{\beta}$ and $\sigma^2$ are at all involved. Partly to offset these difficulties, researchers usually use what is called a **conjugate prior**, which

---

[7]See, for example, Judge et al. (1985) for details. The expression appears in Zellner (1971, p. 67). Note that the exponent in the denominator is $v + K/2 = n/2$.

is one that has the same form as the conditional density and is therefore amenable to the integration needed to obtain the marginal distributions.[8]

### Example 18.2 Estimation with a Conjugate Prior

We continue Example 18.1, but we now assume a conjugate prior. For likelihood functions involving proportions, the beta prior is a common device, for reasons that will emerge shortly. The beta prior is

$$p(\theta) = \frac{\Gamma(\alpha + \beta)\theta^{\alpha-1}(1 - \theta)^{\beta-1}}{\Gamma(\alpha)\Gamma(\beta)}.$$

Then, the posterior density becomes

$$\frac{\theta^D(1 - \theta)^{N-D}\dfrac{\Gamma(\alpha + \beta)\theta^{\alpha-1}(1 - \theta)^{\beta-1}}{\Gamma(\alpha)\Gamma(\beta)}}{\displaystyle\int_0^1 \theta^D(1 - \theta)^{N-D}\dfrac{\Gamma(\alpha + \beta)\theta^{\alpha-1}(1 - \theta)^{\beta-1}}{\Gamma(\alpha)\Gamma(\beta)}d\theta} = \frac{\theta^{D+\alpha-1}(1 - \theta)^{N-D+\beta-1}}{\displaystyle\int_0^1 \theta^{D+\alpha-1}(1 - \theta)^{N-D+\beta-1}d\theta}.$$

The posterior density is, once again, a beta distribution, with parameters $(D + \alpha, N - D + \beta)$. The posterior mean is

$$E[\theta \mid \mathbf{data}] = \frac{D + \alpha}{N + \alpha + \beta}.$$

(Our previous choice of the uniform density was equivalent to $\alpha = \beta = 1$.) Suppose we choose a prior that conforms to a prior mean of 0.5, but with less mass near zero and one than in the center, such as $\alpha = \beta = 2$. Then, the posterior mean would be $(8 + 2)/(25 + 3) = 0.33571$. (This is yet larger than the previous estimator. The reason is that the prior variance is now smaller than 1/12, so the prior mean, still 0.5, receives yet greater weight than it did in the previous example.)

Suppose that we assume that the prior beliefs about $\boldsymbol{\beta}$ may be summarized in a $K$-variate normal distribution with mean $\boldsymbol{\beta}_0$ and variance matrix $\boldsymbol{\Sigma}_0$. Once again, it is illuminating to begin with the case in which $\sigma^2$ is assumed to be known. Proceeding in exactly the same fashion as before, we would obtain the following result: The posterior density of $\boldsymbol{\beta}$ conditioned on $\sigma^2$ and the data will be normal with

$$E[\boldsymbol{\beta} \mid \sigma^2, \mathbf{y}, \mathbf{X}] = \left\{\boldsymbol{\Sigma}_0^{-1} + [\sigma^2(\mathbf{X}'\mathbf{X})^{-1}]^{-1}\right\}^{-1}\left\{\boldsymbol{\Sigma}_0^{-1}\boldsymbol{\beta}_0 + [\sigma^2(\mathbf{X}'\mathbf{X})^{-1}]^{-1}\mathbf{b}\right\} \tag{18-9}$$

$$= \mathbf{F}\boldsymbol{\beta}_0 + (\mathbf{I} - \mathbf{F})\mathbf{b},$$

where

$$\mathbf{F} = \left\{\boldsymbol{\Sigma}_0^{-1} + [\sigma^2(\mathbf{X}'\mathbf{X})^{-1}]^{-1}\right\}^{-1}\boldsymbol{\Sigma}_0^{-1}$$

$$= \left\{[\text{prior variance}]^{-1} + [\text{conditional variance}]^{-1}\right\}^{-1}[\text{prior variance}]^{-1}. \tag{18-10}$$

This vector is a matrix weighted average of the prior and the least squares (sample) coefficient estimates, where the weights are the inverses of the prior and the conditional

---

[8]Our choice of noninformative prior for $\ln \sigma$ led to a convenient prior for $\sigma^2$ in our derivation of the posterior for $\boldsymbol{\beta}$. The idea that the prior can be specified arbitrarily in whatever form is mathematically convenient is very troubling; it is supposed to represent the accumulated prior belief about the parameter. On the other hand, it could be argued that the conjugate prior is the posterior of a previous analysis, which could justify its form. The issue of how priors should be specified is one of the focal points of the methodological debate. "Non-Bayesians" argue that it is disingenuous to claim the methodological high ground and then base the crucial prior density in a model purely on the basis of mathematical convenience. In a small sample, this assumed prior is going to dominate the results, whereas in a large one, the sampling theory estimates will dominate anyway.

covariance matrices.[9] The smaller the variance of the estimator, the larger its weight, which makes sense. Also, still taking $\sigma^2$ as known, we can write the variance of the posterior normal distribution as

$$\text{Var}[\boldsymbol{\beta} \mid \mathbf{y}, \mathbf{X}, \sigma^2] = \left\{ \boldsymbol{\Sigma}_0^{-1} + [\sigma^2(\mathbf{X}'\mathbf{X})^{-1}]^{-1} \right\}^{-1}. \tag{18-11}$$

Notice that the posterior variance combines the prior and conditional variances on the basis of their inverses.[10] We may interpret the noninformative prior as having infinite elements in $\boldsymbol{\Sigma}_0$. This assumption would reduce this case to the earlier one.

Once again, it is necessary to account for the unknown $\sigma^2$. If our prior over $\sigma^2$ is to be informative as well, then the resulting distribution can be extremely cumbersome. A conjugate prior for $\boldsymbol{\beta}$ and $\sigma^2$ that can be used is

$$g(\boldsymbol{\beta}, \sigma^2) = g_{\boldsymbol{\beta} \mid \sigma^2}(\boldsymbol{\beta} \mid \sigma^2) g_{\sigma^2}(\sigma^2), \tag{18-12}$$

where $g_{\boldsymbol{\beta} \mid \sigma^2}(\boldsymbol{\beta} \mid \sigma^2)$ is normal, with mean $\boldsymbol{\beta}^0$ and variance $\sigma^2 \mathbf{A}$ and

$$g_{\sigma^2}(\sigma^2) = \frac{[m\sigma_0^2]^{m+1}}{\Gamma(m+1)} \left( \frac{1}{\sigma^2} \right)^m e^{-m\sigma_0^2(1/\sigma^2)}. \tag{18-13}$$

This distribution is an inverted gamma distribution. It implies that $1/\sigma^2$ has a gamma distribution. The prior mean for $\sigma^2$ is $\sigma_0^2$ and the prior variance is $\sigma_0^4/(m-1)$.[11] The product in (18-12) produces what is called a **normal-gamma prior,** which is the natural conjugate prior for this form of the model. By integrating out $\sigma^2$, we would obtain the prior marginal for $\boldsymbol{\beta}$ alone, which would be a multivariate $t$ distribution.[12] Combining (18-12) with (18-13) produces the joint posterior distribution for $\boldsymbol{\beta}$ and $\sigma^2$. Finally, the marginal posterior distribution for $\boldsymbol{\beta}$ is obtained by integrating out $\sigma^2$. It has been shown that this posterior distribution is multivariate $t$ with

$$E[\boldsymbol{\beta} \mid \mathbf{y}, \mathbf{X}] = \left\{ [\overline{\sigma}^2 \mathbf{A}]^{-1} + [\overline{\sigma}^2(\mathbf{X}'\mathbf{X})^{-1}]^{-1} \right\}^{-1} \left\{ [\overline{\sigma}^2 \mathbf{A}]^{-1} \boldsymbol{\beta}_0 + [\overline{\sigma}^2(\mathbf{X}'\mathbf{X})^{-1}]^{-1} \mathbf{b} \right\} \tag{18-14}$$

and

$$\text{Var}[\boldsymbol{\beta} \mid \mathbf{y}, \mathbf{X}] = \left( \frac{j}{j-2} \right) \left\{ [\overline{\sigma}^2 \mathbf{A}]^{-1} + [\overline{\sigma}^2(\mathbf{X}'\mathbf{X})^{-1}]^{-1} \right\}^{-1}, \tag{18-15}$$

where $j$ is a degrees of freedom parameter and $\overline{\sigma}^2$ is the Bayesian estimate of $\sigma^2$. The prior degrees of freedom $m$ is a parameter of the prior distribution for $\sigma^2$ that would have been determined at the outset. (See the following example.) Once again, it is clear that as the amount of data increases, the posterior density, and the estimates thereof, converge to the sampling theory results.

---

[9]Note that it will not follow that individual elements of the posterior mean vector lie between those of $\boldsymbol{\beta}_0$ and $\mathbf{b}$. See Judge et al. (1985, pp. 109–110) and Chamberlain and Leamer (1976).

[10]Precisely this estimator was proposed by Theil and Goldberger (1961) as a way of combining a previously obtained estimate of a parameter and a current body of new data. They called their result a "mixed estimator." The term "mixed estimation" takes an entirely different meaning in the current literature, as we saw in Chapter 17.

[11]You can show this result by using gamma integrals. Note that the density is a function of $1/\sigma^2 = 1/x$ in the formula of (B-39), so to obtain $E[\sigma^2]$, we use the analog of $E[1/x] = \lambda/(P-1)$ and $E[(1/x)^2] = \lambda^2/[(P-1)(P-2)]$. In the density for $(1/\sigma^2)$, the counterparts to $\lambda$ and $P$ are $m\sigma_0^2$ and $m+1$.

[12]Full details of this (lengthy) derivation appear in Judge et al. (1985, pp. 106–110) and Zellner (1971).

| TABLE 18.1 | Estimates of the MPC | | | |
|---|---|---|---|---|
| *Years* | *Estimated MPC* | *Variance of* b | *Degrees of Freedom* | *Estimated* $\sigma$ |
| 1940–1950 | 0.6848014 | 0.061878 | 9 | 24.954 |
| 1950–2000 | 0.92481 | 0.000065865 | 49 | 92.244 |

### Example 18.3 Bayesian Estimate of the Marginal Propensity to Consume

In Example 3.2, an estimate of the marginal propensity to consume is obtained using 11 observations from 1940 to 1950, with the results shown in the top row of Table 18.1. A classical 95 percent confidence interval for $\beta$ based on these estimates is (0.1221, 1.2475). (The very wide interval probably results from the obviously poor specification of the model.) Based on noninformative priors for $\beta$ and $\sigma^2$, we would estimate the posterior density for $\beta$ to be univariate $t$ with 9 degrees of freedom, with mean 0.6848014 and variance (11/9)0.061878 = 0.075628. An HPD interval for $\beta$ would coincide with the confidence interval. Using the fourth quarter (yearly) values of the 1950–2000 data used in Example 5.3, we obtain the new estimates that appear in the second row of the table.

We take the first estimate and its estimated distribution as our prior for $\beta$ and obtain a posterior density for $\beta$ based on an informative prior instead. We assume for this exercise that $\sigma^2$ may be taken as known at the sample value of 24.954. Then,

$$\bar{b} = \left[ \frac{1}{0.000065865} + \frac{1}{0.061878} \right]^{-1} \left[ \frac{0.92481}{0.000065865} + \frac{0.6848014}{0.061878} \right] = 0.92455$$

The weighted average is overwhelmingly dominated by the far more precise sample estimate from the larger sample. The posterior variance is the inverse in brackets, which is 0.000065795. This is close to the variance of the latter estimate. An HPD interval can be formed in the familiar fashion. It will be slightly narrower than the confidence interval, because the variance of the posterior distribution is slightly smaller than the variance of the sampling estimator. This reduction is the value of the prior information. (As we see here, the prior is not particularly informative.)

## 18.4 BAYESIAN INFERENCE

The posterior density is the Bayesian counterpart to the likelihood function. It embodies the information that is available to make inference about the econometric model. As we have seen, the mean and variance of the posterior distribution correspond to the classical (sampling theory) point estimator and asymptotic variance, although they are interpreted differently. Before we examine more intricate applications of Bayesian inference, it is useful to formalize some other components of the method, point and interval estimation and the Bayesian equivalent of testing a hypothesis.[13]

### 18.4.1 POINT ESTIMATION

The posterior density function embodies the prior and the likelihood and therefore contains all the researcher's information about the parameters. But for purposes of presenting results, the density is somewhat imprecise, and one normally prefers a point

---

[13]We do not include prediction in this list. The Bayesian approach would treat the prediction problem as one of estimation in the same fashion as "parameter" estimation. The value to be forecasted is among the unknown elements of the model that would be characterized by a prior and would enter the posterior density in a symmetric fashion along with the other parameters.

or interval estimate. The natural approach would be to use the mean of the posterior distribution as the estimator. For the noninformative prior, we use **b**, the **sampling theory** estimator.

One might ask at this point, why bother? These Bayesian point estimates are identical to the sampling theory estimates. All that has changed is our interpretation of the results. This situation is, however, exactly the way it should be. Remember that we entered the analysis with noninformative priors for $\beta$ and $\sigma^2$. Therefore, the only information brought to bear on estimation is the sample data, and it would be peculiar if anything other than the sampling theory estimates emerged at the end. The results do change when our prior brings out of sample information into the estimates, as we shall see below.

The results will also change if we change our motivation for estimating $\beta$. The parameter estimates have been treated thus far as if they were an end in themselves. But in some settings, parameter estimates are obtained so as to enable the analyst to make a decision. Consider then, a **loss function,** $H(\hat{\beta}, \beta)$, which quantifies the cost of basing a decision on an estimate $\hat{\beta}$ when the parameter is $\beta$. The expected, or average loss is

$$E_\beta[H(\hat{\beta}, \beta)] = \int_\beta H(\hat{\beta}, \beta) f(\beta \mid \mathbf{y}, \mathbf{X}) d\beta, \qquad \textbf{(18-16)}$$

where the weighting function is the marginal posterior density. (The joint density for $\beta$ and $\sigma^2$ would be used if the loss were defined over both.) The Bayesian point estimate is the parameter vector that minimizes the expected loss. If the loss function is a quadratic form in $(\hat{\beta} - \beta)$, then the mean of the posterior distribution is the "minimum expected loss" (MELO) estimator. The proof is simple. For this case,

$$E[H(\hat{\beta}, \beta) \mid \mathbf{y}, \mathbf{X}] = E\left[\tfrac{1}{2}(\hat{\beta} - \beta)'\mathbf{W}(\hat{\beta} - \beta) \mid \mathbf{y}, \mathbf{X}\right].$$

To minimize this, we can use the result that

$$\partial E[H(\hat{\beta}, \beta) \mid \mathbf{y}, \mathbf{X}]/\partial \hat{\beta} = E[\partial H(\hat{\beta}, \beta)/\partial \hat{\beta} \mid \mathbf{y}, \mathbf{X}]$$
$$= E[-\mathbf{W}(\hat{\beta} - \beta) \mid \mathbf{y}, \mathbf{X}].$$

The minimum is found by equating this derivative to **0**, whence, because $-\mathbf{W}$ is irrelevant, $\hat{\beta} = E[\beta \mid \mathbf{y}, \mathbf{X}]$. This kind of loss function would state that errors in the positive and negative direction are equally bad, and large errors are much worse than small errors. If the loss function were a linear function instead, then the MELO estimator would be the median of the posterior distribution. These results are the same in the case of the noninformative prior that we have just examined.

## 18.4.2 INTERVAL ESTIMATION

The counterpart to a confidence interval in this setting is an interval of the posterior distribution that contains a specified probability. Clearly, it is desirable to have this interval be as narrow as possible. For a unimodal density, this corresponds to an interval within which the density function is higher than any points outside it, which justifies the term **highest posterior density (HPD) interval.** For the case we have analyzed, which involves a symmetric distribution, we would form the HPD interval for $\beta$ around the least squares estimate **b**, with terminal values taken from the standard $t$ tables.

### 18.4.3    HYPOTHESIS TESTING

The Bayesian methodology treats the classical approach to hypothesis testing with a large amount of skepticism. Two issues are especially problematic. First, a close examination of only the work we have done in Chapter 5 will show that because we are using consistent estimators, with a large enough sample, we will ultimately reject any (nested) hypothesis unless we adjust the significance level of the test downward as the sample size increases. Second, the all-or-nothing approach of either rejecting or not rejecting a hypothesis provides no method of simply sharpening our beliefs. Even the most committed of analysts might be reluctant to discard a strongly held prior based on a single sample of data, yet this is what the sampling methodology mandates. (Note, for example, the uncomfortable dilemma this creates in footnote 20 in Chapter 10.) The Bayesian approach to hypothesis testing is much more appealing in this regard. Indeed, the approach might be more appropriately called "comparing hypotheses," because it essentially involves only making an assessment of which of two hypotheses has a higher probability of being correct.

The Bayesian approach to hypothesis testing bears large similarity to Bayesian estimation.[14] We have formulated two hypotheses, a "null," denoted $H_0$, and an alternative, denoted $H_1$. These need not be complementary, as in $H_0$: "statement $A$ is true" versus $H_1$: "statement $A$ is not true," since the intent of the procedure is not to reject one hypothesis in favor of the other. For simplicity, however, we will confine our attention to hypotheses about the parameters in the regression model, which often are complementary. Assume that before we begin our experimentation (data gathering, statistical analysis) we are able to assign **prior probabilities** $P(H_0)$ and $P(H_1)$ to the two hypotheses. The **prior odds ratio** is simply the ratio

$$\text{Odds}_{prior} = \frac{P(H_0)}{P(H_1)}. \tag{18-17}$$

For example, one's uncertainty about the sign of a parameter might be summarized in a prior odds over $H_0$: $\beta \geq 0$ versus $H_1$: $\beta < 0$ of $0.5/0.5 = 1$. After the sample evidence is gathered, the prior will be modified, so the posterior is, in general,

$$\text{Odds}_{posterior} = B_{01} \times \text{Odds}_{prior}.$$

The value $B_{01}$ is called the **Bayes factor** for comparing the two hypotheses. It summarizes the effect of the sample data on the prior odds. The end result, $\text{Odds}_{posterior}$, is a new odds ratio that can be carried forward as the prior in a subsequent analysis.

The Bayes factor is computed by assessing the likelihoods of the data observed under the two hypotheses. We return to our first departure point, the likelihood of the data, given the parameters:

$$f(\mathbf{y} \mid \boldsymbol{\beta}, \sigma^2, \mathbf{X}) = [2\pi\sigma^2]^{-n/2} e^{(-1/(2\sigma^2))(\mathbf{y}-\mathbf{X}\boldsymbol{\beta})'(\mathbf{y}-\mathbf{X}\boldsymbol{\beta})}. \tag{18-18}$$

Based on our priors for the parameters, the expected, or average likelihood, assuming that hypothesis $j$ is true ($j = 0, 1$), is

$$f(\mathbf{y} \mid \mathbf{X}, H_j) = E_{\boldsymbol{\beta},\sigma^2}[f(\mathbf{y} \mid \boldsymbol{\beta}, \sigma^2, \mathbf{X}, H_j)] = \int_{\sigma^2} \int_{\boldsymbol{\beta}} f(\mathbf{y} \mid \boldsymbol{\beta}, \sigma^2, \mathbf{X}, H_j) g(\boldsymbol{\beta}, \sigma^2) \, d\boldsymbol{\beta} \, d\sigma^2.$$

---

[14]For extensive discussion, see Zellner and Siow (1980) and Zellner (1985, pp. 275–305).

(This conditional density is also the **predictive density** for **y**.) Therefore, based on the observed data, we use Bayes theorem to reassess the probability of $H_j$; the posterior probability is

$$P(H_j \mid \mathbf{y}, \mathbf{X}) = \frac{f(\mathbf{y} \mid \mathbf{X}, H_j) P(H_j)}{f(\mathbf{y})}.$$

The posterior odds ratio is $P(H_0 \mid \mathbf{y}, \mathbf{X})/P(H_1 \mid \mathbf{y}, \mathbf{X})$, so the Bayes factor is

$$B_{01} = \frac{f(\mathbf{y} \mid \mathbf{X}, H_0)}{f(\mathbf{y} \mid \mathbf{X}, H_1)}.$$

### Example 18.4  Posterior Odds for the Classical Regression Model

Zellner (1971) analyzes the setting in which there are two possible explanations for the variation in a dependent variable $y$:

$$\text{Model 0: } y = \mathbf{x}_0' \boldsymbol{\beta}_0 + \varepsilon_0$$

and

$$\text{Model 1: } y = \mathbf{x}_1' \boldsymbol{\beta}_1 + \varepsilon_1.$$

We will briefly sketch his results. We form *informative priors* for $[\boldsymbol{\beta}, \sigma^2]_j$, $j = 0, 1$, as specified in (18-12) and (18-13), that is, multivariate normal and inverted gamma, respectively. Zellner then derives the Bayes factor for the posterior odds ratio. The derivation is lengthy and complicated, but for large $n$, with some simplifying assumptions, a useful formulation emerges. First, assume that the priors for $\sigma_0^2$ and $\sigma_1^2$ are the same. Second, assume that $[|\mathbf{A}_0^{-1}|/|\mathbf{A}_0^{-1} + \mathbf{X}_0'\mathbf{X}_0|]/[|\mathbf{A}_1^{-1}|/|\mathbf{A}_1^{-1} + \mathbf{X}_1'\mathbf{X}_1|] \to 1$. The first of these would be the usual situation, in which the uncertainty concerns the covariation between $y_i$ and $\mathbf{x}_i$, not the amount of residual variation (lack of fit). The second concerns the relative amounts of information in the prior (**A**) versus the likelihood (**X'X**). These matrices are the inverses of the covariance matrices, or the **precision matrices.** [Note how these two matrices form the matrix weights in the computation of the posterior mean in (18-9).] Zellner (p. 310) discusses this assumption at some length. With these two assumptions, he shows that as $n$ grows large,[15]

$$B_{01} \approx \left(\frac{s_0^2}{s_1^2}\right)^{-(n+m)/2} = \left(\frac{1 - R_0^2}{1 - R_1^2}\right)^{-(n+m)/2}.$$

Therefore, the result favors the model that provides the better fit using $R^2$ as the fit measure. If we stretch Zellner's analysis a bit by interpreting model 1 as "the model" and model 0 as "no model" (that is, the relevant part of $\boldsymbol{\beta}_0 = \mathbf{0}$, so $R_0^2 = 0$), then the ratio simplifies to

$$B_{01} = \left(1 - R_1^2\right)^{(n+m)/2}.$$

Thus, the better the fit of the regression, the lower the Bayes factor in favor of model 0 (no model), which makes intuitive sense.

Zellner and Siow (1980) have continued this analysis with noninformative priors for $\boldsymbol{\beta}$ and $\sigma_j^2$. Specifically, they use the flat prior for $\ln \sigma$ [see (18-7)] and a multivariate Cauchy prior (which has infinite variances) for $\boldsymbol{\beta}$. Their main result (3.10) is

$$B_{01} = \frac{\frac{1}{2}\sqrt{\pi}}{\Gamma[(k+1)/2]} \left(\frac{n - K}{2}\right)^{k/2} (1 - R^2)^{(n-K-1)/2}.$$

This result is very much like the previous one, with some slight differences due to degrees of freedom corrections and the several approximations used to reach the first one.

---

[15]A ratio of exponentials that appears in Zellner's result (his equation 10.50) is omitted. To the order of approximation in the result, this ratio vanishes from the final result. (Personal correspondence from A. Zellner to the author.)

### 18.4.4  LARGE SAMPLE RESULTS

Although all statistical results for Bayesian estimators are necessarily "finite sample" (they are conditioned on the sample data), it remains of interest to consider how the estimators behave in large samples.[16] Do Bayesian estimators "converge" to something? To do this exercise, it is useful to envision having a sample that is the entire population. Then, the posterior distribution would characterize this entire population, not a sample from it. It stands to reason in this case, at least intuitively, that the posterior distribution should coincide with the likelihood function. It will (as usual), save for the influence of the prior. But as the sample size grows, one should expect the likelihood function to overwhelm the prior. It will, unless the strength of the prior grows with the sample size (that is, for example, if the prior variance is of order $1/n$). An informative prior will still fade in its influence on the posterior unless it becomes *more* informative as the sample size grows.

The preceding suggests that the posterior mean will converge to the maximum likelihood estimator. The MLE is the parameter vector that is at the mode of the likelihood function. The Bayesian estimator is the **posterior mean,** not the mode, so a remaining question concerns the relationship between these two features. The **Bernstein–von Mises "theorem"** [See Cameron and Trivedi (2005, p. 433) and Train (2003, Chapter 12)] states that the posterior mean and the maximum likelihood estimator will coverge to the same probability limit and have the same limiting normal distribution. A form of **central limit theorem** is at work.

But for remaining philosophical questions, the results suggest that for large samples, the choice between Bayesian and frequentist methods can be one of computational efficiency. (This is the thrust of the application in Section 18.8. Note, as well, footnote 1 at the beginning of this chapter. In an infinite sample, the maintained "uncertainty" of the Bayesian estimation framework would have to arise from deeper questions about the model. For example, the mean of the entire population is its mean; there is no uncertainty about the "parameter.")

## 18.5  POSTERIOR DISTRIBUTIONS AND THE GIBBS SAMPLER

The preceding analysis has proceeded along a set of steps that includes formulating the likelihood function (the model), the prior density over the objects of estimation, and the posterior density. To complete the inference step, we then analytically derived the characteristics of the posterior density of interest, such as the mean or mode, and the variance. The complicated element of any of this analysis is determining the moments of the posterior density, for example, the mean:

$$\hat{\theta} = E[\theta \mid \textbf{data}] = \int_{\theta} \theta \, p(\theta \mid \textbf{data}) d\theta. \tag{18-19}$$

---

[16]The standard preamble in econometric studies, that the analysis to follow is "exact" as opposed to approximate or "large sample," refers to this aspect—the analysis is conditioned on and, by implication, applies only to the sample data in hand. Any inference outside the sample, for example, to hypothesized random samples is, like the sampling theory counterpart, approximate.

There are relatively few applications for which integrals such as this can be derived in closed form. (This is one motivation for conjugate priors.) The modern approach to Bayesian inference takes a different strategy. The result in (18-19) is an expectation. Suppose it were possible to obtain a random sample, as large as desired, from the population defined by $p(\boldsymbol{\theta} \,|\, \textbf{data})$. Then, using the same strategy we used throughout Chapter 17 for simulation-based estimation, we could use that sample's characteristics, such as mean, variance, quantiles, and so on, to infer the characteristics of the posterior distribution. Indeed, with an (essentially) infinite sample, we would be freed from having to limit our attention to a few simple features such as the mean and variance, we could view any features of the posterior distribution that we like. The (much less) complicated part of the analysis is the formulation of the posterior density.

It remains to determine how the sample is to be drawn from the posterior density. This element of the strategy is provided by a remarkable (and remarkably useful) result known as the **Gibbs sampler.** [See Casella and George (1992).] The central result of the Gibbs sampler is as follows: We wish to draw a random sample from the joint population $(x, y)$. The joint distribution of $x$ and $y$ is either unknown or intractable and it is not possible to sample from the joint distribution. However, assume that the conditional distributions $f(x \,|\, y)$ and $f(y \,|\, x)$ are known and simple enough that it is possible to draw univariate random samples from both of them. The following iteration will produce a bivariate random sample from the joint distribution:

Gibbs sampler:
1. Begin the cycle with a value of $x_0$ that is in the right range of $x \,|\, y$,
2. Draw an observation $y_0 \,|\, x_0$,
3. Draw an observation $x_t \,|\, y_{t-1}$,
4. Draw an observation $y_t \,|\, x_t$.

Iteration of steps 3 and 4 for several thousand cycles will eventually produce a random sample from the joint distribution. (The first several thousand draws are discarded to avoid the influence of the initial conditions—this is called the **burn in.**) [Some technical details on the procedure appear in Cameron and Trivedi (Chapter Section 13.5).]

***Example 18.5   Gibbs Sampling from the Normal Distribution***
To illustrate the mechanical aspects of the Gibbs sampler, consider random sampling from the joint normal distribution. We consider the bivariate normal distribution first. Suppose we wished to draw a random sample from the population

$$\begin{pmatrix} x_1 \\ x_2 \end{pmatrix} \sim N\left[ \begin{pmatrix} 0 \\ 0 \end{pmatrix}, \begin{pmatrix} 1 & \rho \\ \rho & 1 \end{pmatrix} \right].$$

As we have seen in Chapter 17, a direct approach is to use the fact that linear functions of normally distributed variables are normally distributed. [See (B-80).] Thus, we might transform a series of independent normal draws $(u_1, u_2)'$ by the Cholesky decomposition of the covariance matrix

$$\begin{pmatrix} x_1 \\ x_2 \end{pmatrix}_i = \begin{bmatrix} 1 & 0 \\ \theta_1 & \theta_2 \end{bmatrix} \begin{pmatrix} u_1 \\ u_2 \end{pmatrix}_i = \textbf{L}\textbf{u}_i,$$

where $\theta_1 = \rho$ and $\theta_2 = \sqrt{1 - \rho^2}$. The Gibbs sampler would take advantage of the result

$$x_1 \,|\, x_2 \sim N[\rho x_2, (1 - \rho^2)],$$

and

$$x_2 \,|\, x_1 \sim N[\rho x_1, (1 - \rho^2)].$$

To sample from a trivariate, or multivariate population, we can expand the Gibbs sequence in the natural fashion. For example, to sample from a trivariate population, we would use the Gibbs sequence

$$x_1 \,|\, x_2, x_3 \sim N[\beta_{1,2}x_2 + \beta_{1,3}x_3, \Sigma_{1|2,3}],$$

$$x_2 \,|\, x_1, x_3 \sim N[\beta_{2,1}x_1 + \beta_{2,3}x_3, \Sigma_{2|1,3}],$$

$$x_3 \,|\, x_1, x_2 \sim N[\beta_{3,1}x_1 + \beta_{3,2}x_2, \Sigma_{3|1,2}],$$

where the conditional means and variances are given in Theorem B.7. This defines a three-step cycle.

The availability of the Gibbs sampler frees the researcher from the necessity of deriving the analytical properties of the full, joint posterior distribution. Because the formulation of conditional priors is straightforward, and the derivation of the *conditional* posteriors is only slightly less so, this tool has facilitated a vast range of applications that previously were intractable. For an example, consider, once again, the classical normal regression model. From (18-7), the joint posterior for $(\beta, \sigma^2)$ is

$$p(\beta, \sigma^2 \,|\, \mathbf{y}, \mathbf{X}) \propto \frac{[vs^2]^{v+2}}{\Gamma(v + 2)} \left[\frac{1}{\sigma^2}\right]^{v+1} \exp(-vs^2/\sigma^2)[2\pi]^{-K/2} |\sigma^2(\mathbf{X}'\mathbf{X})^{-1}|^{-1/2}$$

$$\times \exp(-(1/2)(\beta - \mathbf{b})'[\sigma^2(\mathbf{X}'\mathbf{X})^{-1}]^{-1}(\beta - \mathbf{b}).$$

If we wished to use a simulation approach to characterizing the posterior distribution, we would need to draw a $K + 1$ variate sample of observations from this intractable distribution. However, with the assumed priors, we found the conditional posterior for $\beta$ in (18-5):

$$p(\beta \,|\, \sigma^2, \mathbf{y}, \mathbf{X}) = N[\mathbf{b}, \sigma^2(\mathbf{X}'\mathbf{X})^{-1}].$$

From (18-6), we can deduce that the conditional posterior for $\sigma^2 \,|\, \beta, \mathbf{y}, \mathbf{X}$ is an inverted gamma distribution with parameters $m\sigma_0^2 = v\hat{\sigma}^2$ and $m = v$ in (18-13):

$$p(\sigma^2 \,|\, \beta, \mathbf{y}, \mathbf{X}) = \frac{[v\hat{\sigma}^2]^{v+1}}{\Gamma(v + 1)} \left[\frac{1}{\sigma^2}\right]^v \exp(-v\hat{\sigma}^2/\sigma^2), \quad \hat{\sigma}^2 = \frac{\Sigma_{i=1}(y_i - \mathbf{x}_i'\beta)^2}{n - K}.$$

This sets up a Gibbs sampler for sampling from the joint posterior of $\beta$ and $\sigma^2$. We would cycle between random draws from the multivariate normal for $\beta$ and the inverted gamma distribution for $\sigma^2$ to obtain a $K + 1$ variate sample on $(\beta, \sigma^2)$. [Of course, for this application, we do know the marginal posterior distribution for $\beta$—see (18-8).]

The Gibbs sampler is not truly a random sampler; it is a Markov chain—each "draw" from the distribution is a function of the draw that precedes it. The random input at each cycle provides the randomness, which leads to the popular name for this strategy, **Markov–Chain Monte Carlo** or **MCMC** or **MC²** (pick one) estimation. In its simplest form, it provides a remarkably efficient tool for studying the posterior distributions in very complicated models. The example in the next section shows a striking example of how to locate the MLE for a probit model without computing the likelihood function or its derivatives. In Section 18.8, we will examine an extension and refinement of the strategy, the Metropolis–Hasting algorithm.

In the next several sections, we will present some applications of Bayesian inference. In Section 18.9, we will return to some general issues in classical and Bayesian estimation and inference.

## 18.6 APPLICATION: BINOMIAL PROBIT MODEL

Consider inference about the binomial probit model for a dependent variable that is generated as follows (see Sections 23.2–23.4):

$$y_i^* = \mathbf{x}_i'\boldsymbol{\beta} + \varepsilon_i, \ \varepsilon_i \sim N[0, 1], \tag{18-20}$$

$$y_i = 1 \text{ if } y_i^* > 0, \text{ otherwise } y_i = 0. \tag{18-21}$$

(Theoretical moivation for the model appears in Section 23.3.) The data consist of $(\mathbf{y}, \mathbf{X}) = (y_i, \mathbf{x}_i), i = 1, \dots, n$. The random variable $y_i$ has a Bernoulli distribution with probabilities

$$\text{Prob}[y_i = 1 \mid \mathbf{x}_i] = \Phi(\mathbf{x}_i'\boldsymbol{\beta}),$$

$$\text{Prob}[y_i = 0 \mid \mathbf{x}_i] = 1 - \Phi(\mathbf{x}_i'\boldsymbol{\beta}).$$

The likelihood function for the observed data is

$$L(\mathbf{y} \mid \mathbf{X}, \boldsymbol{\beta}) = \prod_{i=1}^{n} [\Phi(\mathbf{x}_i'\boldsymbol{\beta})]^{y_i} [1 - \Phi(\mathbf{x}_i'\boldsymbol{\beta})]^{1-y_i}.$$

(Once again, we cheat a bit on the notation—the likelihood function is actually the joint density for the data, given $\mathbf{X}$ and $\boldsymbol{\beta}$.) Classical maximum likelihood estimation of $\boldsymbol{\beta}$ is developed in Section 23.4. To obtain the posterior mean (Bayesian estimator), we assume a noninformative, flat (improper) prior for $\boldsymbol{\beta}$,

$$p(\boldsymbol{\beta}) \propto 1.$$

The posterior density would be

$$p(\boldsymbol{\beta} \mid \mathbf{y}, \mathbf{X}) = \frac{\prod_{i=1}^{n} [\Phi(\mathbf{x}_i'\boldsymbol{\beta})]^{y_i} [1 - \Phi(\mathbf{x}_i'\boldsymbol{\beta})]^{1-y_i} (1)}{\int_{\boldsymbol{\beta}} \prod_{i=1}^{n} [\Phi(\mathbf{x}_i'\boldsymbol{\beta})]^{y_i} [1 - \Phi(\mathbf{x}_i'\boldsymbol{\beta})]^{1-y_i} (1) d\boldsymbol{\beta}},$$

and the estimator would be the posterior mean,

$$\hat{\boldsymbol{\beta}} = E[\boldsymbol{\beta} \mid \mathbf{y}, \mathbf{X}] = \frac{\int_{\boldsymbol{\beta}} \boldsymbol{\beta} \prod_{i=1}^{n} [\Phi(\mathbf{x}_i'\boldsymbol{\beta})]^{y_i} [1 - \Phi(\mathbf{x}_i'\boldsymbol{\beta})]^{1-y_i} d\boldsymbol{\beta}}{\int_{\boldsymbol{\beta}} \prod_{i=1}^{n} [\Phi(\mathbf{x}_i'\boldsymbol{\beta})]^{y_i} [1 - \Phi(\mathbf{x}_i'\boldsymbol{\beta})]^{1-y_i} d\boldsymbol{\beta}}. \tag{18-22}$$

Evaluation of the integrals in (18-22) is hopelessly complicated, but a solution using the Gibbs sampler and a technique known as **data augmentation,** pioneered by Albert and Chib (1993a) is surprisingly simple. We begin by treating the unobserved $y_i^*$s as unknowns to be estimated, along with $\boldsymbol{\beta}$. Thus, the $(K + n) \times 1$ parameter vector is $\boldsymbol{\theta} = (\boldsymbol{\beta}, \mathbf{y}^*)$. We now construct a Gibbs sampler. Consider, first, $p(\boldsymbol{\beta} \mid \mathbf{y}^*, \mathbf{y}, \mathbf{X})$. If $y_i^*$ is known, then $y_i$ is known [see (18-21)]. It follows that

$$p(\boldsymbol{\beta} \mid \mathbf{y}^*, \mathbf{y}, \mathbf{X}) = p(\boldsymbol{\beta} \mid \mathbf{y}^*, \mathbf{X}).$$

This posterior defines a linear regression model with normally distributed disturbances and known $\sigma^2 = 1$. It is precisely the model we saw in Section 18.3.1, and the posterior we need is in (18-5), with $\sigma^2 = 1$. So, based on our earlier results, it follows that

$$p(\boldsymbol{\beta} \mid \mathbf{y}^*, \mathbf{y}, \mathbf{X}) = N[\mathbf{b}^*, (\mathbf{X}'\mathbf{X})^{-1}], \tag{18-23}$$

where

$$\mathbf{b}^* = (\mathbf{X}'\mathbf{X})^{-1}\mathbf{X}'\mathbf{y}^*.$$

For $y_i^*$, ignoring $y_i$ for the moment, it would follow immediately from (18-20) that

$$p(y_i^* \mid \boldsymbol{\beta}, \mathbf{X}) = N[\mathbf{x}_i'\boldsymbol{\beta}, 1].$$

However, $y_i$ is informative about $y_i^*$. If $y_i$ equals one, we know that $y_i^* > 0$ and if $y_i$ equals zero, then $y_i^* \le 0$. The implication is that conditioned on $\boldsymbol{\beta}$, $\mathbf{X}$, and $\mathbf{y}$, $y_i^*$ has the truncated (above or below zero) normal distribution that is developed in Sections 24.2.1 and 24.2.2. The standard notation for this is

$$p(y_i^* \mid y_i = 1, \boldsymbol{\beta}, \mathbf{x}_i) = N^+[\mathbf{x}_i'\boldsymbol{\beta}, 1],$$

$$p(y_i^* \mid y_i = 0, \boldsymbol{\beta}, \mathbf{x}_i) = N^-[\mathbf{x}_i'\boldsymbol{\beta}, 1]. \tag{18-24}$$

Results (18-23) and (18-24) set up the components for a Gibbs sampler that we can use to estimate the posterior means $E[\boldsymbol{\beta} \mid \mathbf{y}, \mathbf{X}]$ and $E[\mathbf{y}^* \mid \mathbf{y}, \mathbf{X}]$. The following is our algorithm:

*Gibbs Sampler for the Binomial Probit Model*
1. Compute $\mathbf{X}'\mathbf{X}$ once at the outset and obtain $\mathbf{L}$ such that $\mathbf{LL}' = (\mathbf{X}'\mathbf{X})^{-1}$.
2. Start $\boldsymbol{\beta}$ at any value such as $\mathbf{0}$.
3. Result (17-1) shows how to transform a draw from $U[0, 1]$ to a draw from the truncated normal with underlying mean $\mu$ and standard deviation $\sigma$. For this application, the draw is

$$y_{i,r}^*(r) = \mathbf{x}_i'\boldsymbol{\beta}_{r-1} + \Phi^{-1}[1 - (1 - U)\Phi(\mathbf{x}_i'\boldsymbol{\beta}_{r-1})] \text{ if } y_i = 1,$$

$$y_{i,r}^*(r) = \mathbf{x}_i'\boldsymbol{\beta}_{r-1} + \Phi^{-1}[U\Phi(-\mathbf{x}_i'\boldsymbol{\beta}_{r-1})] \text{ if } y_i = 0.$$

This step is used to draw the $n$ observations on $y_{i,r}^*(r)$.
4. Section 17.2.4 shows how to draw an observation from the multivariate normal population. For this application, we use the results at step 3 to compute $\mathbf{b}^* = (\mathbf{X}'\mathbf{X})^{-1}\mathbf{X}'\mathbf{y}^*(r)$. We obtain a vector, $\mathbf{v}$, of $K$ draws from the $N[0, 1]$ population, then $\boldsymbol{\beta}(r) = \mathbf{b}^* + \mathbf{Lv}$.

The iteration cycles between steps 3 and 4. This should be repeated several thousand times, discarding the burn-in draws, then the estimator of $\boldsymbol{\beta}$ is the sample mean of the retained draws. The posterior variance is computed with the variance of the retained draws. Posterior estimates of $y_i^*$ would typically not be useful.

| TABLE 18.2 | Probit Estimates for Grade Equation | | | |
|---|---|---|---|---|
| | **Maximum Likelihood** | | **Posterior Means and Std. Devs** | |
| *Variable* | *Estimate* | *Standard Error* | *Posterior Mean* | *Posterior S.D.* |
| Constant | −7.4523 | 2.5425 | −8.6286 | 2.7995 |
| GPA | 1.6258 | 0.6939 | 1.8754 | 0.7668 |
| TUCE | 0.05173 | 0.08389 | 0.06277 | 0.08695 |
| PSI | 1.4263 | 0.5950 | 1.6072 | 0.6257 |

### Example 18.6 Gibbs Sampler for a Probit Model

In Examples 16.14 and 16.15, we examined Spector and Mazzeo's (1980) widely traveled data on a binary choice outcome. (The example used the data for a different model.) The binary probit model studied in the paper was

$$\text{Prob}(GRADE_i = 1 \mid \boldsymbol{\beta}, \mathbf{x}_i) = \Phi(\beta_1 + \beta_2 GPA_i + \beta_3 TUCE_i + \beta_4 PSI_i).$$

The variables are defined in Example 16.14. Their probit model is studied in Example 23.3. The sample contains 32 observations. Table 18.2 presents the maximum likelihood estimates and the posterior means and standard deviations for the probit model. For the Gibbs sampler, we used 5,000 draws, and discarded the first 1,000.

The results in Table 18.2 suggest the similarity of the posterior mean estimated with the Gibbs sampler to the maximum likelihood estimate. However, the sample is quite small, and the differences between the coefficients are still fairly substantial. For a striking example of the behavior of this procedure, we now revisit the German health care data examined in Examples 11.10, 11.11 and 16.16, and several other examples throughout the book. The probit model to be estimated is

$$\text{Prob}(Doctor\ visits_{it} > 0) = \Phi(\beta_1 + \beta_2\ Age_{it} + \beta_3\ Education_{it} + \beta_4\ Income_{it}$$

$$+ \beta_5\ Kids_{it} + \beta_6\ Married_{it} + \beta_7\ Female_{it}).$$

The sample contains data on 7,293 families and a total of 27,326 observations. We are pooling the data for this application. Table 18.3 presents the probit results for this model using the same procedure as before. (We used only 500 draws, and discarded the first 100.)

The similarity is what one would expect given the large sample size. We note before proceeding to other applications, notwithstanding the striking similarity of the Gibbs sampler to the MLE, that this is not an efficient method of estimating the parameters of a probit model. The estimator requires generation of thousands of samples of potentially thousands of observations. We used only 500 replications to produce Table 18.3. The computations took about five minutes. Using Newton's method to maximize the log-likelihood directly took less than five seconds. Unless one is wedded to the Bayesian paradigm, on strictly practical grounds, the MLE would be the preferred estimator.

| TABLE 18.3 | Probit Estimates for Doctor Visits Equation | | | |
|---|---|---|---|---|
| | **Maximum Likelihood** | | **Posterior Means and Std. Devs** | |
| *Variable* | *Estimate* | *Standard Error* | *Posterior Mean* | *Posterior S.D.* |
| Constant | −0.12433 | 0.058146 | −0.12628 | 0.054759 |
| Age | 0.011892 | 0.00079568 | 0.011979 | 0.00080073 |
| Education | −0.014966 | 0.0035747 | −0.015142 | 0.0036246 |
| Income | −0.13242 | 0.046552 | −0.12669 | 0.047979 |
| Kids | −0.15212 | 0.018327 | −0.15149 | 0.018400 |
| Married | 0.073522 | 0.020644 | 0.071977 | 0.020852 |
| Female | 0.35591 | 0.016017 | 0.35582 | 0.015913 |

This application of the Gibbs sampler demonstrates in an uncomplicated case how the algorithm can provide an alternative to actually maximizing the log-likelihood. We do note that the similarity of the method to the EM algorithm in Section E.3.7 is not coincidental. Both procedures use an estimate of the unobserved, censored data, and both estimate $\beta$ by using OLS using the predicted data.

## 18.7  PANEL DATA APPLICATION: INDIVIDUAL EFFECTS MODELS

We consider a panel data model with common individual effects,

$$y_{it} = \alpha_i + \mathbf{x}'_{it}\boldsymbol{\beta} + \varepsilon_{it}, \quad \varepsilon_{it} \sim N[0, \sigma_\varepsilon^2].$$

In the Bayesian framework, there is no need to distinguish between fixed and random effects. The classical distinction results from an asymmetric treatment of the data and the parameters. So, we will leave that unspecified for the moment. The implications will emerge later when we specify the prior densities over the model parameters.

The likelihood function for the sample under normality of $\varepsilon_{it}$ is

$$p(\mathbf{y} \mid \alpha_1, \ldots, \alpha_n, \boldsymbol{\beta}, \sigma_\varepsilon^2, \mathbf{X}) = \prod_{i=1}^{n} \prod_{t=1}^{T_i} \frac{1}{\sigma_\varepsilon \sqrt{2\pi}} \exp\left(-\frac{(y_{it} - \alpha_i - \mathbf{x}'_{it}\boldsymbol{\beta})^2}{2\sigma_\varepsilon^2}\right).$$

The remaining analysis hinges on the specification of the prior distributions. We will consider three cases. Each illustrates an aspect of the methodology.

First, group the full set of location (regression) parameters in one $(n + K) \times 1$ slope vector, $\boldsymbol{\gamma}$. Then, with the disturbance variance, $\boldsymbol{\theta} = (\boldsymbol{\alpha}, \boldsymbol{\beta}, \sigma_\varepsilon^2) = (\boldsymbol{\gamma}, \sigma_\varepsilon^2)$. Define a conformable data matrix, $\mathbf{Z} = (\mathbf{D}, \mathbf{X})$, where $\mathbf{D}$ contains the $n$ dummy variables so that we may write the model,

$$\mathbf{y} = \mathbf{Z}\boldsymbol{\gamma} + \boldsymbol{\varepsilon}$$

in the familiar fashion for our common effects linear regression. (See Chapter 9.) We now assume the **uniform–inverse gamma prior** that we used in our earlier treatment of the linear model,

$$p(\boldsymbol{\gamma}, \sigma_\varepsilon^2) \propto 1/\sigma_\varepsilon^2.$$

The resulting (marginal) posterior density for $\boldsymbol{\gamma}$ is precisely that in (18-8) (where now the slope vector includes the elements of $\boldsymbol{\alpha}$). The density is an $(n + K)$ variate $t$ with mean equal to the OLS estimator and covariance matrix $[(\Sigma_i T_i - n - K)/(\Sigma_i T_i - n - K - 2)]s^2(\mathbf{Z}'\mathbf{Z})^{-1}$. Because OLS in this model as stated means the within estimator, the implication is that with this noninformative prior over $(\boldsymbol{\alpha}, \boldsymbol{\beta})$, the model is equivalent to the fixed effects model. Note, again, this is not a consequence of any assumption about correlation between effects and included variables. That has remained unstated; though, by implication, we would allow correlation between $\mathbf{D}$ and $\mathbf{X}$.

Some observers are uncomfortable with the idea of a **uniform prior** over the entire real line. [See, e.g., Koop (2003, pp. 22–23).] Others, e.g., Zellner (1971, p. 20), are less concerned. Cameron and Trivedi (2005, pp. 425–427) suggest a middle ground.] Formally, our assumption of a uniform prior over the entire real line is an **improper**

**prior,** because it cannot have a positive density and integrate to one over the entire real line. As such, the posterior appears to be ill defined. However, note that the "improper" uniform prior will, in fact, fall out of the posterior, because it appears in both numerator and denominator. [Zellner (1971, p. 20) offers some more methodological commentary.] The practical solution for location parameters, such as a vector of regression slopes, is to assume a nearly flat, "almost uninformative" prior. The usual choice is a conjugate normal prior with an arbitrarily large variance. (It should be noted, of course, that as long as that variance is finite, even if it is large, the prior is informative. We return to this point in Section 18.9.)

Consider, then, the conventional **normal-gamma prior** over $(\gamma, \sigma_\varepsilon^2)$ where the conditional (on $\sigma_\varepsilon^2$) prior normal density for the slope parameters has mean $\gamma_0$ and covariance matrix $\sigma_\varepsilon^2 \mathbf{A}$, where the $(n + K) \times (n + K)$ matrix, $\mathbf{A}$, is yet to be specified. [See the discussion after (18-13).] The marginal posterior mean and variance for $\gamma$ for this set of assumptions are given in (18-14) and (18-15). We reach a point that presents two rather serious dilemmas for the researcher. The posterior was simple with our uniform, noninformative prior. Now, it is necessary actually to specify $\mathbf{A}$, which is potentially large. (In one of our main applications in this text, we are analyzing models with $n = 7,293$ constant terms and about $K = 7$ regressors.) It is hopelessly optimistic to expect to be able to specify all the variances and covariances in a matrix this large, unless we actually have the results of an earlier study (in which case we would also have a prior estimate of $\gamma$). A practical solution that is frequently chosen is to specify $\mathbf{A}$ to be a diagonal matrix with extremely large diagonal elements, thus emulating a uniform prior without having to commit to one. The second practical issue then becomes dealing with the actual computation of the order $(n + K)$ inverse matrix in (18-14) and (18-15). Under the strategy chosen, to make $\mathbf{A}$ a multiple of the identity matrix, however, there are forms of partitioned inverse matrices that will allow solution to the actual computation.

Thus far, we have assumed that each $\alpha_i$ is generated by a different normal distribution, $-\gamma_0$ and $\mathbf{A}$, however specified, have (potentially) different means and variances for the elements of $\alpha$. The third specification we consider is one in which all $\alpha_i$s in the model are assumed to be draws from the same population. To produce this specification, we use a **hierarchical prior** for the individual effects. The full model will be

$$y_{it} = \alpha_i + \mathbf{x}'_{it}\boldsymbol{\beta} + \varepsilon_{it}, \varepsilon_{it} \sim \mathrm{N}[0, \sigma_\varepsilon^2],$$
$$p(\boldsymbol{\beta} \mid \sigma_\varepsilon^2) = \mathrm{N}[\boldsymbol{\beta}_0, \sigma_\varepsilon^2 \mathbf{A}],$$
$$p(\sigma_\varepsilon^2) = \mathrm{Gamma}(\sigma_0^2, \mathrm{m}),$$
$$p(\alpha_i) = \mathrm{N}[\mu_\alpha, \tau_\alpha^2],$$
$$p(\mu_\alpha) = \mathrm{N}[a, Q],$$
$$p(\tau_\alpha^2) = \mathrm{Gamma}(\tau_0^2, v).$$

We will not be able to derive the posterior density (joint or marginal) for the parameters of this model. However, it is possible to set up a Gibbs sampler that can be used to infer the characteristics of the posterior densities statistically. The sampler will be driven by conditional normal posteriors for the location parameters, $[\boldsymbol{\beta} \mid \boldsymbol{\alpha}, \sigma_\varepsilon^2, \mu_\alpha, \tau_\alpha^2]$, $[\alpha_i \mid \boldsymbol{\beta}, \sigma_\varepsilon^2, \mu_\alpha, \tau_\alpha^2]$, and $[\mu_\alpha \mid \boldsymbol{\beta}, \boldsymbol{\alpha}, \sigma_\varepsilon^2, \tau_\alpha^2]$ and conditional gamma densities for the scale (variance) parameters, $[\sigma_\varepsilon^2 \mid \boldsymbol{\alpha}, \boldsymbol{\beta}, \mu_\alpha, \tau_\alpha^2]$ and $[\tau_\alpha^2 \mid \boldsymbol{\alpha}, \boldsymbol{\beta}, \sigma_\varepsilon^2, \mu_\alpha]$. [The procedure is developed at length by Koop (2003, pp. 152–153).] The assumption of a common distribution for the individual effects and an independent prior for $\boldsymbol{\beta}$ produces a Bayesian counterpart to the random effects model.

## 18.8 HIERARCHICAL BAYES ESTIMATION OF A RANDOM PARAMETERS MODEL

We now consider a Bayesian approach to estimation of the random parameters model.[17] For an individual $i$, the conditional density for the dependent variable in period $t$ is $f(y_{it} \mid \mathbf{x}_{it}, \boldsymbol{\beta}_i)$ where $\boldsymbol{\beta}_i$ is the individual specific $K \times 1$ parameter vector and $\mathbf{x}_{it}$ is individual specific data that enter the probability density.[18] For the sequence of $T$ observations, assuming conditional (on $\boldsymbol{\beta}_i$) independence, person $i$'s contribution to the likelihood for the sample is

$$f(\mathbf{y}_i \mid \mathbf{X}_i, \boldsymbol{\beta}_i) = \prod_{t=1}^{T} f(y_{it} \mid \mathbf{x}_{it}, \boldsymbol{\beta}_i). \tag{18-25}$$

where $\mathbf{y}_i = (y_{i1}, \ldots, y_{iT})$ and $\mathbf{X}_i = [\mathbf{x}_{i1}, \ldots, \mathbf{x}_{iT}]$. We will suppose that $\boldsymbol{\beta}_i$ is distributed normally with mean $\boldsymbol{\beta}$ and covariance matrix $\boldsymbol{\Sigma}$. (This is the "hierarchical" aspect of the model.) The unconditional density would be the expected value over the possible values of $\boldsymbol{\beta}_i$;

$$f(\mathbf{y}_i \mid \mathbf{X}_i, \boldsymbol{\beta}, \boldsymbol{\Sigma}) = \int_{\boldsymbol{\beta}_i} \prod_{t=1}^{T} f(y_{it} \mid \mathbf{x}_{it}, \boldsymbol{\beta}_i) \phi_K[\boldsymbol{\beta}_i \mid \boldsymbol{\beta}, \boldsymbol{\Sigma}] \, d\boldsymbol{\beta}_i, \tag{18-26}$$

where $\phi_K[\boldsymbol{\beta}_i \mid \boldsymbol{\beta}, \boldsymbol{\Sigma}]$ denotes the $K$ variate normal prior density for $\boldsymbol{\beta}_i$ given $\boldsymbol{\beta}$ and $\boldsymbol{\Sigma}$. Maximum likelihood estimation of this model, which entails estimation of the "deep" parameters, $\boldsymbol{\beta}, \boldsymbol{\Sigma}$, then estimation of the individual specific parameters, $\boldsymbol{\beta}_i$ is considered in Section 17.5. We now consider the Bayesian approach to estimation of the parameters of this model.

To approach this from a Bayesian viewpoint, we will assign noninformative prior densities to $\boldsymbol{\beta}$ and $\boldsymbol{\Sigma}$. As is conventional, we assign a flat (noninformative) prior to $\boldsymbol{\beta}$. The variance parameters are more involved. If it is assumed that the elements of $\boldsymbol{\beta}_i$ are conditionally independent, then each element of the (now) diagonal matrix $\boldsymbol{\Sigma}$ may be assigned the inverted gamma prior that we used in (18-13). A full matrix $\boldsymbol{\Sigma}$ is handled by assigning to $\boldsymbol{\Sigma}$ an **inverted Wishart** prior density with parameters scalar $K$ and matrix $K \times \mathbf{I}$. [The Wishart density is a multivariate counterpart to the chi-squared

---

[17]Note that, there is occasional confusion as to what is meant by "random parameters" in a random parameters (RP) model. In the Bayesian framework we discuss in this chapter, the "randomness" of the random parameters in the model arises from the "uncertainty" of the analyst. As developed at several points in this book (and in the literature), the randomness of the parameters in the RP model is a characterization of the heterogeneity of parameters across individuals. Consider, for example, in the Bayesian framework of this section, in the RP model, each vector $\boldsymbol{\beta}_i$ is a random vector with a distribution (defined hierarchically). In the classical framework, each $\boldsymbol{\beta}_i$ represents a single draw from a parent population.

[18]To avoid a layer of complication, we will embed the time-invariant effect $\Delta \mathbf{z}_i$ in $\mathbf{x}'_{it} \boldsymbol{\beta}$. A full treatment in the same fashion as the latent class model would be substantially more complicated in this setting (although it is quite straightforward in the maximum simulated likelihood approach discussed in Section 17.5.1).

distribution. Discussion may be found in Zellner (1971, pp. 389–394).] This produces the joint posterior density,

$$\Lambda(\boldsymbol{\beta}_1, \ldots, \boldsymbol{\beta}_n, \boldsymbol{\beta}, \boldsymbol{\Sigma} \mid \text{all data}) = \left\{ \prod_{i=1}^{n} \prod_{t=1}^{T} f(y_{it} \mid \mathbf{x}_{it}, \boldsymbol{\beta}_i) \phi_K[\boldsymbol{\beta}_i \mid \boldsymbol{\beta}, \boldsymbol{\Sigma}] \right\} \times p(\boldsymbol{\beta}, \boldsymbol{\Sigma}).$$

**(18-27)**

This gives the joint density of all the unknown parameters conditioned on the observed data. Our Bayesian estimators of the parameters will be the posterior means for these $(n + 1)K + K(K + 1)/2$ parameters. In principle, this requires integration of (18-27) with respect to the components. As one might guess at this point, that integration is hopelessly complex and not remotely feasible.

However, the techniques of Markov Chain Monte Carlo (MCMC) simulation estimation (the Gibbs sampler) and the **Metropolis–Hastings algorithm** enable us to sample from the (hopelessly complex) joint density $\Lambda(\boldsymbol{\beta}_1, \ldots, \boldsymbol{\beta}_n, \boldsymbol{\beta}, \boldsymbol{\Sigma} \mid \textbf{all data})$ in a remarkably simple fashion. Train (2001 and 2002, Chapter 12) describe how to use these results for this random parameters model.[19] The usefulness of this result for our current problem is that it is, indeed, possible to partition the joint distribution, and we can easily sample from the conditional distributions. We begin by partitioning the parameters into $\boldsymbol{\gamma} = (\boldsymbol{\beta}, \boldsymbol{\Sigma})$ and $\boldsymbol{\delta} = (\boldsymbol{\beta}_1, \ldots, \boldsymbol{\beta}_n)$. Train proposes the following strategy: To obtain a draw from $\boldsymbol{\gamma} \mid \boldsymbol{\delta}$, we will use the Gibbs sampler to obtain a draw from the distribution of $(\boldsymbol{\beta} \mid \boldsymbol{\Sigma}, \boldsymbol{\delta})$ then one from the distribution of $(\boldsymbol{\Sigma} \mid \boldsymbol{\beta}, \boldsymbol{\delta})$. We will lay out this first, then turn to sampling from $\boldsymbol{\delta} \mid \boldsymbol{\beta}, \boldsymbol{\Sigma}$.

Conditioned on $\boldsymbol{\delta}$ and $\boldsymbol{\Sigma}$, $\boldsymbol{\beta}$ has a $K$-variate normal distribution with mean $\bar{\boldsymbol{\beta}} = (1/n)|\Sigma_{i=1}^{n}\boldsymbol{\beta}_i$ and covariance matrix $(1/n)\boldsymbol{\Sigma}$. To sample from this distribution we will first obtain the Cholesky factorization of $\boldsymbol{\Sigma} = \mathbf{LL}'$ where $\mathbf{L}$ is a lower triangular matrix. [See Section A.6.11.] Let $\mathbf{v}$ be a vector of $K$ draws from the standard normal distribution. Then, $\bar{\boldsymbol{\beta}} + \mathbf{Lv}$ has mean vector $\bar{\boldsymbol{\beta}} + \mathbf{L} \times \mathbf{0} = \bar{\boldsymbol{\beta}}$ and covariance matrix $\mathbf{LIL}' = \boldsymbol{\Sigma}$, which is exactly what we need. So, this shows how to sample a draw from the conditional distribution $\boldsymbol{\beta}$.

To obtain a random draw from the distribution of $\boldsymbol{\Sigma} \mid \boldsymbol{\beta}, \boldsymbol{\delta}$, we will require a random draw from the inverted Wishart distribution. The marginal posterior distribution of $\boldsymbol{\Sigma} \mid \boldsymbol{\beta}, \boldsymbol{\delta}$ is inverted Wishart with parameters scalar $K + n$ and matrix $\mathbf{W} = (K\mathbf{I} + n\mathbf{V})$, where $\mathbf{V} = (1/n)\sum_{i=1}^{n}(\boldsymbol{\beta}_i - \bar{\boldsymbol{\beta}})(\boldsymbol{\beta}_i - \bar{\boldsymbol{\beta}})'$. Train (2001) suggests the following strategy for sampling a matrix from this distribution: Let $\mathbf{M}$ be the lower triangular Cholesky factor of $\mathbf{W}^{-1}$, so $\mathbf{MM}' = \mathbf{W}^{-1}$. Obtain $K + n$ draws of $\mathbf{v}_k = K$ standard normal variates. Then, obtain $\mathbf{S} = \mathbf{M}\left(\sum_{k=1}^{K+n} \mathbf{v}_k\mathbf{v}'_k\right)\mathbf{M}'$. Then, $\boldsymbol{\Sigma}^j = \mathbf{S}^{-1}$ is a draw from the inverted Wishart distribution. [This is fairly straightforward, as it involves only random sampling from the standard normal distribution. For a diagonal $\boldsymbol{\Sigma}$ matrix, that is, uncorrelated parameters in $\boldsymbol{\beta}_i$, it simplifies a bit further. A draw for the nonzero $k$th diagonal element can be obtained using $(1 + n\mathbf{V}_{kk})/\sum_{r=1}^{K+n} v_{rk}^2$.]

---

[19] Train describes use of this method for "mixed (random parameters) multinomial logit" models. By writing the densities in generic form, we have extended his result to any general setting that involves a parameter vector in the fashion described above. The classical version of this appears in Section 17.5.1 for the binomial probit model and in Section 23.11.6 for the mixed logit model.

The difficult step is sampling $\boldsymbol{\beta}_i$. For this step, we use the Metropolis–Hastings (M-H) algorithm suggested by Chib and Greenberg (1995, 1996) and Gelman et al. (2004). The procedure involves the following steps:

1. Given $\boldsymbol{\beta}$ and $\boldsymbol{\Sigma}$ and "tuning constant" $\tau$ (to be described below), compute $\mathbf{d} = \tau \mathbf{L} \mathbf{v}$ where $\mathbf{L}$ is the Cholesky factorization of $\boldsymbol{\Sigma}$ and $\mathbf{v}$ is a vector of $K$ independent standard normal draws.
2. Create a trial value $\boldsymbol{\beta}_{i1} = \boldsymbol{\beta}_{i0} + \mathbf{d}$ where $\boldsymbol{\beta}_{i0}$ is the previous value.
3. The posterior distribution for $\boldsymbol{\beta}_i$ is the likelihood that appears in (18-26) times the joint normal prior density, $\phi_K[\boldsymbol{\beta}_i \mid \boldsymbol{\beta}, \boldsymbol{\Sigma}]$. Evaluate this posterior density at the trial value $\boldsymbol{\beta}_{i1}$ and the previous value $\boldsymbol{\beta}_{i0}$. Let

$$R_{10} = \frac{f(\mathbf{y}_i \mid \mathbf{X}_i, \boldsymbol{\beta}_{i1}) \phi_K(\boldsymbol{\beta}_{i1} \mid \boldsymbol{\beta}, \boldsymbol{\Sigma})}{f(\mathbf{y}_i \mid \mathbf{X}_i, \boldsymbol{\beta}_{i0}) \phi_K(\boldsymbol{\beta}_{i0} \mid \boldsymbol{\beta}, \boldsymbol{\Sigma})}.$$

4. Draw one observation, $u$, from the standard uniform distribution, $U[0, 1]$.
5. If $u < R_{10}$, then accept the trial (new) draw. Otherwise, reuse the old one.

This M-H iteration converges to a sequence of draws from the desired density. Overall, then, the algorithm uses the Gibbs sampler and the Metropolis–Hastings algorithm to produce the sequence of draws for all the parameters in the model. The sequence is repeated a large number of times to produce each draw from the joint posterior distribution. The entire sequence must then be repeated $N$ times to produce the sample of $N$ draws, which can then be analyzed, for example, by computing the posterior mean.

Some practical details remain. The tuning constant, $\tau$ is used to control the iteration. A smaller $\tau$ increases the acceptance rate. But at the same time, a smaller $\tau$ makes new draws look more like old draws so this slows down the process. Gelman et al. (2004) suggest $\tau = 0.4$ for $K = 1$ and smaller values down to about 0.23 for higher dimensions, as will be typical. Each multivariate draw takes many runs of the MCMC sampler. The process must be started somewhere, though it does not matter much where. Nonetheless, a "burn-in" period is required to eliminate the influence of the starting value. Typical applications use several draws for this burn in period for each run of the sampler. How many sample observations are needed for accurate estimation is not certain, though several hundred would be a minimum. This means that there is a huge amount of computation done by this estimator. However, the computations are fairly simple. The only complicated step is computation of the acceptance criterion at step 3 of the M-H iteration. Depending on the model, this may, like the rest of the calculations, be quite simple.

## 18.9 SUMMARY AND CONCLUSIONS

This chapter has introduced the major elements of the Bayesian approach to estimation and inference. The contrast between Bayesian and classical, or frequentist, approaches to the analysis has been the subject of a decades-long dialogue among practitioners and philosophers. As the frequency of applications of Bayesian methods have grown dramatically in the modern literature, however, the approach to the body of techniques has typically become more pragmatic. The Gibbs sampler and related techniques including the Metropolis–Hastings algorithm have enabled some remarkable simplifications of heretofore intractable problems. For example, recent developments in commercial software have produced a wide choice of "mixed" estimators which are various implementations of the maximum likelihood procedures and hierarchical Bayes procedures (such as the Sawtooth and MLWin programs). Unless one is dealing with a small sample, the choice between these can be based on convenience. There is little methodological difference. This returns us to the practical point noted earlier. The choice between the Bayesian approach and the sampling theory method in this application would not be based on a fundamental methodological criterion, but on purely practical considerations—the end result is the same.

This chapter concludes our survey of estimation and inference methods in econometrics. We will now turn to two major areas of applications, time series and (broadly) macroeconometrics, and microeconometrics which is primarily oriented to cross section and panel data applications.

## Key Terms and Concepts

- Bayes factor
- Bayes theorem
- Bernstein–von Mises theorem
- Burn in
- Central limit theorem
- Conjugate prior
- Data augmentation
- Gibbs sampler
- Hierarchical Bayes
- Hierarchical prior
- Highest posterior density (HPD)
- Improper prior
- Informative prior
- Inverted gamma distribution
- Inverted Wishart
- Joint posterior
- Likelihood
- Loss function
- Markov–Chain Monte Carlo (MCMC)
- Metropolis–Hastings algorithm
- Multivariate $t$ distribution
- Noninformative prior
- Normal-gamma prior
- Posterior density
- Posterior mean
- Posterior odds
- Precision matrix
- Predictive density
- Prior beliefs
- Prior density
- Prior distribution
- Prior odds ratio
- Prior probabilities
- Sampling theory
- Uniform prior
- Uniform-inverse gamma prior

## Exercise

1. Suppose the distribution of $y_i \mid \lambda$ is Poisson,

$$f(y_i \mid \lambda) = \frac{\exp(-\lambda)\lambda^{y_i}}{y_i!} = \frac{\exp(-\lambda)\lambda^{y_i}}{\Gamma(y_i + 1)}, \quad y_i = 0, 1, \ldots, \lambda > 0.$$

We will obtain a sample of observations, $y_i, \ldots, y_n$. Suppose our prior for $\lambda$ is the inverted gamma, which will imply

$$p(\lambda) \propto \frac{1}{\lambda}.$$

a. Construct the likelihood function, $p(y_1, \ldots, y_n \mid \lambda)$.
b. Construct the posterior density

$$p(\lambda \mid y_1, \ldots, y_n) = \frac{p(y_1, \ldots, y_n \mid \lambda)p(\lambda)}{\displaystyle\int_0^\infty p(y_1, \ldots, y_n \mid \lambda)p(\lambda)d\lambda}.$$

c. Prove that the Bayesian estimator of $\lambda$ is the posterior mean, $E[\lambda \mid y_1, \ldots, y_n] = \overline{y}$.
d. Prove that the posterior variance is $\mathrm{Var}[\lambda \mid y_l, \ldots, y_n] = \overline{y}/n$.

(Hint: You will make heavy use of gamma integrals in solving this problem. Also, you will find it convenient to use $\Sigma_i y_i = n\bar{y}$.)

## Application

1. Consider a model for the mix of male and female children in families. Let $K_i$ denote the family size (number of children), $K_i = 1, \ldots$. Let $F_i$ denote the number of female children, $F_i = 0, \ldots, K_i$. Suppose the density for the number of female children in a family with $K_i$ children is binomial with constant success probability $\theta$:

$$p(F_i|K_i, \theta) = \binom{K_i}{F_i} \theta^{F_i}(1 - \theta)^{K_i - F_i}.$$

We are interested in analyzing the "probability," $\theta$. Suppose the (conjugate) prior over $\theta$ is a beta distribution with parameters $a$ and $b$:

$$p(\theta) = \frac{\Gamma(a + b)}{\Gamma(a)\Gamma(b)} \theta^{a-1}(1 - \theta)^{b-1}.$$

Your sample of 25 observations is given here:

| $K_i$ | 2 | 1 | 1 | 5 | 5 | 4 | 4 | 5 | 1 | 2 | 4 | 4 | 2 | 4 | 3 | 2 | 3 | 2 | 3 | 5 | 3 | 2 | 5 | 4 | 1 |
|---|---|---|---|---|---|---|---|---|---|---|---|---|---|---|---|---|---|---|---|---|---|---|---|---|---|
| $F_i$ | 1 | 1 | 1 | 3 | 2 | 3 | 2 | 4 | 0 | 2 | 3 | 1 | 1 | 3 | 2 | 1 | 3 | 1 | 2 | 4 | 2 | 1 | 1 | 4 | 1 |

a. Compute the classical maximum likelihood estimate of $\theta$.
b. Form the posterior density for $\theta$ given $(K_i, F_i), i = 1, \ldots, 25$ conditioned on $a$ and $b$.
c. Using your sample of data, compute the posterior mean assuming $a = b = 1$.
d. Using your sample of data, compute the posterior mean assuming $a = b = 2$.
e. Using your sample of data, compute the posterior mean assuming $a = 1$ and $b = 2$.

# 19

# SERIAL CORRELATION

## 19.1 INTRODUCTION

Time-series data often display **autocorrelation,** or serial correlation of the disturbances across periods. Consider, for example, the plot of the least squares residuals in the following example.

### Example 19.1  Money Demand Equation

Appendix Table F5.1 contains quarterly data from 1950.1 to 2000.4 on the U.S. money stock (M1) and output (real GDP) and the price level (CPI_U). Consider a simple (extremely) model of money demand,[1]

$$\ln M1_t = \beta_1 + \beta_2 \ln GDP_t + \beta_3 \ln CPI_t + \varepsilon_t.$$

A plot of the least squares residuals is shown in Figure 19.1. The pattern in the residuals suggests that knowledge of the sign of a residual in one period is a good indicator of the sign of the residual in the next period. This knowledge suggests that the effect of a given disturbance is carried, at least in part, across periods. This sort of "memory" in the disturbances creates the long, slow swings from positive values to negative ones that is evident in Figure 19.1. One might argue that this pattern is the result of an obviously naive model, but that is one of the important points in this discussion. Patterns such as this usually do not arise spontaneously; to a large extent, they are, indeed, a result of an incomplete or flawed model specification.

One explanation for autocorrelation is that relevant factors omitted from the time-series regression, like those included, are correlated across periods. This fact may be due to serial correlation in factors that should be in the regression model. It is easy to see why this situation would arise. Example 19.2 shows an obvious case.

### Example 19.2  Autocorrelation Induced by Misspecification of the Model

In Examples 2.3 and 6.7, we examined yearly time-series data on the U.S. gasoline market from 1953 to 2004. The evidence in the examples was convincing that a regression model of variation in $\ln G/Pop$ should include, at a minimum, a constant, $\ln P_G$ and ln income/Pop. Other price variables and a time trend also provide significant explanatory power, but these two are a bare minimum. Moreover, we also found on the basis of a Chow test of structural change that apparently this market changed structurally after 1974. Figure 19.2 displays plots of four sets of least squares residuals. Parts (a) through (c) show clearly that as the specification of the regression is expanded, the autocorrelation in the "residuals" diminishes. Part (c) shows the effect of forcing the coefficients in the equation to be the same both before and after the structural shift. In part (d), the residuals in the two subperiods 1953 to 1974 and 1975 to 2004 are produced by separate unrestricted regressions. This latter set of residuals is almost nonautocorrelated. (Note also that the range of variation of the residuals falls as

---

[1]Because this chapter deals exclusively with time-series data, we shall use the index $t$ for observations and $T$ for the sample size throughout.

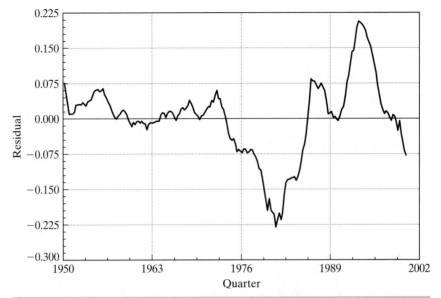

**FIGURE 19.1** Autocorrelated Least Squares Residuals.

the model is improved, i.e., as its fit improves.) The full equation is

$$\ln \frac{G_t}{Pop_t} = \beta_1 + \beta_2 \ln P_{Gt} + \beta_3 \ln \frac{I_t}{Pop_t} + \beta_4 \ln P_{NCt} + \beta_5 \ln P_{UCt}$$
$$+ \beta_6 \ln P_{PTt} + \beta_7 \ln P_{Nt} + \beta_8 \ln P_{Dt} + \beta_9 \ln P_{St} + \beta_{10}t + \varepsilon_t.$$

Finally, we consider an example in which serial correlation is an anticipated part of the model.

### Example 19.3 Negative Autocorrelation in the Phillips Curve

The Phillips curve [Phillips (1957)] has been one of the most intensively studied relationships in the macroeconomics literature. As originally proposed, the model specifies a negative relationship between wage inflation and unemployment in the United Kingdom over a period of 100 years. Recent research has documented a similar relationship between unemployment and price inflation. It is difficult to justify the model when cast in simple levels; labor market theories of the relationship rely on an uncomfortable proposition that markets persistently fall victim to money illusion, even when the inflation can be anticipated. Current research [e.g., Staiger et al. (1996)] has reformulated a short run (disequilibrium) "expectations augmented Phillips curve" in terms of unexpected inflation and unemployment that deviates from a long run equilibrium or "natural rate." The **expectations-augmented Phillips curve** can be written as

$$\Delta p_t - E[\Delta p_t \mid \Psi_{t-1}] = \beta[u_t - u^*] + \varepsilon_t$$

where $\Delta p_t$ is the rate of inflation in year $t$, $E[\Delta p_t \mid \Psi_{t-1}]$ is the forecast of $\Delta p_t$ made in period $t-1$ based on information available at time $t-1$, $\Psi_{t-1}$, $u_t$ is the unemployment rate and $u^*$ is the natural, or equilibrium rate. (Whether $u^*$ can be treated as an unchanging parameter, as we are about to do, is controversial.) By construction, $[u_t - u^*]$ is disequilibrium, or cyclical unemployment. In this formulation, $\varepsilon_t$ would be the supply shock (i.e., the stimulus that produces the disequilibrium situation). To complete the model, we require a model for the expected inflation. We will revisit this in some detail in Example 20.2. For the present, we'll

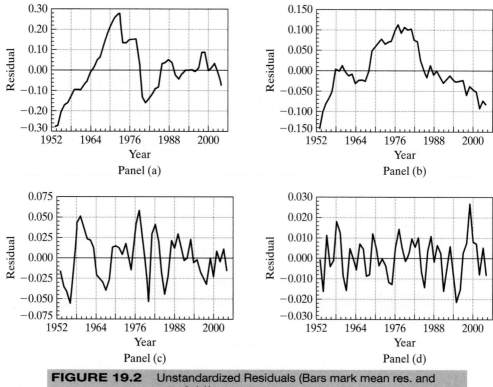

**FIGURE 19.2** Unstandardized Residuals (Bars mark mean res. and +/− 2s(e)).

assume that economic agents are rank empiricists. The forecast of next year's inflation is simply this year's value. This produces the estimating equation

$$\Delta p_t - \Delta p_{t-1} = \beta_1 + \beta_2 u_t + \varepsilon_t$$

where $\beta_2 = \beta$ and $\beta_1 = -\beta u^*$. Note that there is an implied estimate of the natural rate of unemployment embedded in the equation. After estimation, $u^*$ can be estimated by $-b_1/b_2$. The equation was estimated with the 1950.1–2000.4 data in Appendix Table F5.1 that were used in Example 19.1 (minus two quarters for the change in the rate of inflation). Least squares estimates (with standard errors in parentheses) are as follows:

$$\Delta p_t - \Delta p_{t-1} = 0.49189 - 0.090136\, u_t + e_t$$

$$(0.7405) \quad (0.1257) \quad R^2 = 0.002561, \ T = 201.$$

The implied estimate of the natural rate of unemployment is 5.46 percent, which is in line with other recent estimates. The estimated asymptotic covariance of $b_1$ and $b_2$ is −0.08973. Using the delta method, we obtain a standard error of 2.2062 for this estimate, so a confidence interval for the natural rate is 5.46 percent ±1.96 (2.21 percent) = (1.13 percent, 9.79 percent) (which seems fairly wide, but, again, whether it is reasonable to treat this as a parameter is at least questionable). The regression of the least squares residuals on their past values gives a slope of −0.4263 with a highly significant $t$ ratio of −6.725. We thus conclude that the residuals (and, apparently, the disturbances) in this model are highly negatively autocorrelated. This is consistent with the striking pattern in Figure 19.3.

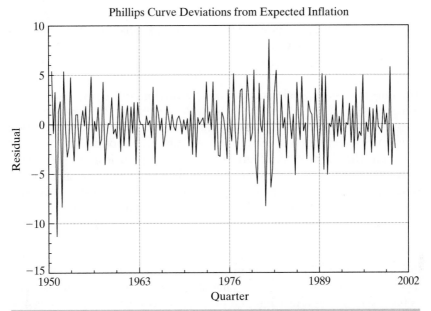

**FIGURE 19.3**  Negatively Autocorrelated Residuals.

The problems for estimation and inference caused by autocorrelation are similar to (although, unfortunately, more involved than) those caused by heteroscedasticity. As before, least squares is inefficient, and inference based on the least squares estimates is adversely affected. Depending on the underlying process, however, GLS and FGLS estimators can be devised that circumvent these problems. There is one qualitative difference to be noted. In Chapter 8, we examined models in which the generalized regression model can be viewed as an extension of the regression model to the conditional second moment of the dependent variable. In the case of autocorrelation, the phenomenon arises in almost all cases from a misspecification of the model. Views differ on how one should react to this failure of the classical assumptions, from a pragmatic one that treats it as another "problem" in the data to an orthodox methodological view that it represents a major specification issue—see, for example, "A Simple Message to Autocorrelation Correctors: Don't" [Mizon (1995).]

We should emphasize that the models we shall examine here are quite far removed from the classical regression. The exact or small-sample properties of the estimators are rarely known, and only their asymptotic properties have been derived.

## 19.2  THE ANALYSIS OF TIME-SERIES DATA

The treatment in this chapter will be the first structured analysis of time-series data in the text. (We had a brief encounter in Section 4.9.6 where we established some conditions under which moments of time-series data would converge.) Time-series analysis requires some revision of the interpretation of both data generation and sampling that we have maintained thus far.

A time-series model will typically describe the path of a variable $y_t$ in terms of contemporaneous (and perhaps lagged) factors $\mathbf{x}_t$, disturbances (**innovations**), $\varepsilon_t$, and its own past, $y_{t-1}, \ldots$ . For example,

$$y_t = \beta_1 + \beta_2 x_t + \beta_3 y_{t-1} + \varepsilon_t.$$

The time series is a single occurrence of a random event. For example, the quarterly series on real output in the United States from 1950 to 2000 that we examined in Example 19.1 is a single realization of a process, $\text{GDP}_t$. The entire history over this period constitutes a realization of the process. At least in economics, the process could not be repeated. There is no counterpart to repeated sampling in a cross section or replication of an experiment involving a time-series process in physics or engineering. Nonetheless, were circumstances different at the end of World War II, the observed history *could* have been different. In principle, a completely different realization of the entire series might have occurred. The sequence of observations, $\{y_t\}_{t=-\infty}^{t=\infty}$ is a **time-series process,** which is characterized by its time ordering and its systematic correlation between observations in the sequence. The signature characteristic of a time-series process is that empirically, the data generating mechanism produces exactly one realization of the sequence. Statistical results based on sampling characteristics concern not random sampling from a population, but from distributions of statistics constructed from sets of observations taken from this realization in a **time window,** $t = 1, \ldots, T$. Asymptotic distribution theory in this context concerns behavior of statistics constructed from an increasingly long window in this sequence.

The properties of $y_t$ as a random variable in a cross section are straightforward and are conveniently summarized in a statement about its mean and variance or the probability distribution generating $y_t$. The statement is less obvious here. It is common to assume that innovations are generated independently from one period to the next, with the familiar assumptions

$$E[\varepsilon_t] = 0,$$

$$\text{Var}[\varepsilon_t] = \sigma_\varepsilon^2,$$

and

$$\text{Cov}[\varepsilon_t, \varepsilon_s] = 0 \quad \text{for } t \neq s.$$

In the current context, this distribution of $\varepsilon_t$ is said to be **covariance stationary** or **weakly stationary.** Thus, although the substantive notion of "random sampling" must be extended for the time series $\varepsilon_t$, the mathematical results based on that notion apply here. It can be said, for example, that $\varepsilon_t$ is generated by a time-series process whose mean and variance are not changing over time. As such, by the method we will discuss in this chapter, we could, at least in principle, obtain sample information and use it to characterize the distribution of $\varepsilon_t$. Could the same be said of $y_t$? There is an obvious difference between the series $\varepsilon_t$ and $y_t$; observations on $y_t$ at different points in time are necessarily correlated. Suppose that the $y_t$ series *is* weakly stationary and that, for the moment, $\beta_2 = 0$. Then we could say that

$$E[y_t] = \beta_1 + \beta_3 E[y_{t-1}] + E[\varepsilon_t] = \beta_1/(1 - \beta_3)$$

and

$$\text{Var}[y_t] = \beta_3^2 \, \text{Var}[y_{t-1}] + \text{Var}[\varepsilon_t],$$

or

$$\gamma_0 = \beta_3^2 \gamma_0 + \sigma_\varepsilon^2,$$

so that

$$\gamma_0 = \frac{\sigma_\varepsilon^2}{1 - \beta_3^2}.$$

Thus, $\gamma_0$, the variance of $y_t$, is a fixed characteristic of the process generating $y_t$. Note how the stationarity assumption, which apparently includes $|\beta_3| < 1$, has been used. The assumption that $|\beta_3| < 1$ is needed to ensure a finite and positive variance.[2] Finally, the same results can be obtained for nonzero $\beta_2$ if it is further assumed that $x_t$ is a weakly stationary series.[3]

Alternatively, consider simply repeated substitution of lagged values into the expression for $y_t$:

$$y_t = \beta_1 + \beta_3(\beta_1 + \beta_3 y_{t-2} + \varepsilon_{t-1}) + \varepsilon_t \tag{19-1}$$

and so on. We see that, in fact, the current $y_t$ is an accumulation of the entire history of the innovations, $\varepsilon_t$. So if we wish to characterize the distribution of $y_t$, then we might do so in terms of sums of random variables. By continuing to substitute for $y_{t-2}$, then $y_{t-3}, \ldots$ in (19-1), we obtain an explicit representation of this idea,

$$y_t = \sum_{i=0}^{\infty} \beta_3^i (\beta_1 + \varepsilon_{t-i}).$$

Do sums that reach back into infinite past make any sense? We might view the process as having begun generating data at some remote, effectively "infinite" past. As long as distant observations become progressively less important, the extension to an infinite past is merely a mathematical convenience. The diminishing importance of past observations is implied by $|\beta_3| < 1$. Notice that, not coincidentally, this requirement is the same as that needed to solve for $\gamma_0$ in the preceding paragraphs. A second possibility is to assume that the *observation* of *this* time series begins at some time 0 [with $(x_0, \varepsilon_0)$ called the **initial conditions**], by which time the underlying process has reached a state such that the mean and variance of $y_t$ are not (or are no longer) changing over time. The mathematics are slightly different, but we are led to the same characterization of the random process generating $y_t$. In fact, the same weak stationarity assumption ensures both of them.

Except in very special cases, we would expect all the elements in the $T$ component random vector $(y_1, \ldots, y_T)$ to be correlated. In this instance, said correlation is called "autocorrelation." As such, the results pertaining to estimation with independent or uncorrelated observations that we used in the previous chapters are no longer usable. In point of fact, we have a sample of but one observation on the multivariate random variable $[y_t, t = 1, \ldots, T]$. There is a counterpart to the cross-sectional notion of parameter estimation, but only under assumptions (e.g., weak stationarity) that establish that parameters in the familiar sense even exist. Even with stationarity, it will emerge that for estimation and inference, none of our earlier finite sample results are usable. Consistency and asymptotic normality of estimators are somewhat more difficult to

---

[2]The current literature in macroeconometrics and time series analysis is dominated by analysis of cases in which $\beta_3 = 1$ (or counterparts in different models). We will return to this subject in Chapter 22.

[3]See Section 19.4.1 on the stationarity assumption.

establish in time-series settings because results that require independent observations, such as the central limit theorems, are no longer usable. Nonetheless, counterparts to our earlier results have been established for most of the estimation problems we consider here and in Chapters 20 and 21.

## 19.3 DISTURBANCE PROCESSES

The preceding section has introduced a bit of the vocabulary and aspects of time-series specification. To obtain the theoretical results, we need to draw some conclusions about autocorrelation and add some details to that discussion.

### 19.3.1 CHARACTERISTICS OF DISTURBANCE PROCESSES

In the usual time-series setting, the disturbances are assumed to be homoscedastic but correlated across observations, so that

$$E[\boldsymbol{\varepsilon}\boldsymbol{\varepsilon}' \mid \mathbf{X}] = \sigma^2 \boldsymbol{\Omega},$$

where $\sigma^2 \boldsymbol{\Omega}$ is a full, positive definite matrix with a constant $\sigma^2 = \text{Var}[\varepsilon_t \mid \mathbf{X}]$ on the diagonal. As will be clear in the following discussion, we shall also assume that $\boldsymbol{\Omega}_{ts}$ is a function of $|t - s|$, but not of $t$ or $s$ alone, which is a **stationarity** assumption. (See the preceding section.) It implies that the covariance between observations $t$ and $s$ is a function only of $|t - s|$, the distance apart in time of the observations. Because $\sigma^2$ is not restricted, we normalize $\boldsymbol{\Omega}_{tt} = 1$. We define the **autocovariances:**

$$\text{Cov}[\varepsilon_t, \varepsilon_{t-s} \mid \mathbf{X}] = \text{Cov}[\varepsilon_{t+s}, \varepsilon_t \mid \mathbf{X}] = \sigma^2 \boldsymbol{\Omega}_{t,t-s} = \gamma_s = \gamma_{-s}.$$

Note that $\sigma^2 \boldsymbol{\Omega}_{tt} = \gamma_0$. The correlation between $\varepsilon_t$ and $\varepsilon_{t-s}$ is their autocorrelation,

$$\text{Corr}[\varepsilon_t, \varepsilon_{t-s} \mid \mathbf{X}] = \frac{\text{Cov}[\varepsilon_t, \varepsilon_{t-s} \mid \mathbf{X}]}{\sqrt{\text{Var}[\varepsilon_t \mid \mathbf{X}]\text{Var}[\varepsilon_{t-s} \mid \mathbf{X}]}} = \frac{\gamma_s}{\gamma_0} = \rho_s = \rho_{-s}.$$

We can then write

$$E[\boldsymbol{\varepsilon}\boldsymbol{\varepsilon}' \mid \mathbf{X}] = \boldsymbol{\Gamma} = \gamma_0 \mathbf{R},$$

where $\boldsymbol{\Gamma}$ is an **autocovariance matrix** and $\mathbf{R}$ is an **autocorrelation matrix**—the $ts$ element is an **autocorrelation coefficient**

$$\rho_{ts} = \frac{\gamma_{|t-s|}}{\gamma_0}.$$

(Note that the matrix $\boldsymbol{\Gamma} = \gamma_0 \mathbf{R}$ is the same as $\sigma^2 \boldsymbol{\Omega}$. The name change conforms to standard usage in the literature.) We will usually use the abbreviation $\rho_s$ to denote the autocorrelation between observations $s$ periods apart.

Different types of processes imply different patterns in $\mathbf{R}$. For example, the most frequently analyzed process is a **first-order autoregression** or **AR(1)** process,

$$\varepsilon_t = \rho \varepsilon_{t-1} + u_t,$$

where $u_t$ is a stationary, nonautocorrelated (**white noise**) process and $\rho$ is a parameter. We will verify later that for this process, $\rho_s = \rho^s$. Higher-order **autoregressive processes** of the form

$$\varepsilon_t = \theta_1 \varepsilon_{t-1} + \theta_2 \varepsilon_{t-2} + \cdots + \theta_p \varepsilon_{t-p} + u_t$$

imply more involved patterns, including, for some values of the parameters, cyclical behavior of the autocorrelations.[4] Stationary autoregressions are structured so that the influence of a given disturbance fades as it recedes into the more distant past but vanishes only asymptotically. For example, for the AR(1), $\text{Cov}[\varepsilon_t, \varepsilon_{t-s}]$ is never zero, but it does become negligible if $|\rho|$ is less than 1. **Moving-average processes,** conversely, have a short memory. For the MA(1) process,

$$\varepsilon_t = u_t - \lambda u_{t-1},$$

the memory in the process is only one period: $\gamma_0 = \sigma_u^2(1 + \lambda^2)$, $\gamma_1 = -\lambda \sigma_u^2$, but $\gamma_s = 0$ if $s > 1$.

### 19.3.2 AR(1) DISTURBANCES

Time-series processes such as the ones listed here can be characterized by their order, the values of their parameters, and the behavior of their autocorrelations.[5] We shall consider various forms at different points. The received empirical literature is overwhelmingly dominated by the AR(1) model, which is partly a matter of convenience. Processes more involved than this model are usually extremely difficult to analyze. There is, however, a more practical reason. It is very optimistic to expect to know precisely the correct form of the appropriate model for the disturbance in any given situation. The first-order autoregression has withstood the test of time and experimentation as a reasonable *model* for underlying processes that probably, in truth, are impenetrably complex. AR(1) works as a first pass—higher order models are often constructed as a refinement—as in the following example.

The first-order autoregressive disturbance, or AR(1) process, is represented in the **autoregressive form** as

$$\varepsilon_t = \rho \varepsilon_{t-1} + u_t, \tag{19-2}$$

where

$$E[u_t \mid \mathbf{X}] = 0,$$

$$E[u_t^2 \mid \mathbf{X}] = \sigma_u^2,$$

and

$$\text{Cov}[u_t, u_s \mid \mathbf{X}] = 0 \quad \text{if } t \neq s.$$

Because $u_t$ is white noise, the conditional moments equal the unconditional moments. Thus $E[\varepsilon_t \mid \mathbf{X}] = E[\varepsilon_t]$ and so on.

By repeated substitution, we have

$$\varepsilon_t = u_t + \rho u_{t-1} + \rho^2 u_{t-2} + \cdots. \tag{19-3}$$

From the preceding **moving-average form,** it is evident that each disturbance $\varepsilon_t$ embodies the entire past history of the $u$'s, with the most recent observations receiving greater weight than those in the distant past. Depending on the sign of $\rho$, the series will exhibit

---

[4]This model is considered in more detail in Chapter 21.
[5]See Box and Jenkins (1984) for an authoritative study.

clusters of positive and then negative observations or, if $\rho$ is negative, regular oscillations of sign (as in Example 19.3).

Because the successive values of $u_t$ are uncorrelated, the variance of $\varepsilon_t$ is the variance of the right-hand side of (19-3):

$$\text{Var}[\varepsilon_t] = \sigma_u^2 + \rho^2 \sigma_u^2 + \rho^4 \sigma_u^2 + \cdots. \tag{19-4}$$

To proceed, a restriction must be placed on $\rho$,

$$|\rho| < 1, \tag{19-5}$$

because otherwise, the right-hand side of (19-4) will become infinite. This result is the stationarity assumption discussed earlier. With (19-5), which implies that $\lim_{s \to \infty} \rho^s = 0$, $E[\varepsilon_t] = 0$ and

$$\text{Var}[\varepsilon_t] = \frac{\sigma_u^2}{1 - \rho^2} = \sigma_\varepsilon^2. \tag{19-6}$$

With the stationarity assumption, there is an easier way to obtain the variance

$$\text{Var}[\varepsilon_t] = \rho^2 \, \text{Var}[\varepsilon_{t-1}] + \sigma_u^2$$

because $\text{Cov}[u_t, \varepsilon_s] = 0$ if $t > s$. With stationarity, $\text{Var}[\varepsilon_{t-1}] = \text{Var}[\varepsilon_t]$, which implies (19-6). Proceeding in the same fashion,

$$\text{Cov}[\varepsilon_t, \varepsilon_{t-1}] = E[\varepsilon_t \varepsilon_{t-1}] = E[\varepsilon_{t-1}(\rho \varepsilon_{t-1} + u_t)] = \rho \, \text{Var}[\varepsilon_{t-1}] = \frac{\rho \sigma_u^2}{1 - \rho^2}. \tag{19-7}$$

By repeated substitution in (19-2), we see that for any $s$,

$$\varepsilon_t = \rho^s \varepsilon_{t-s} + \sum_{i=0}^{s-1} \rho^i u_{t-i}$$

(e.g., $\varepsilon_t = \rho^3 \varepsilon_{t-3} + \rho^2 u_{t-2} + \rho u_{t-1} + u_t$). Therefore, because $\varepsilon_s$ is not correlated with any $u_t$ for which $t > s$ (i.e., any subsequent $u_t$), it follows that

$$\text{Cov}[\varepsilon_t, \varepsilon_{t-s}] = E[\varepsilon_t \varepsilon_{t-s}] = \frac{\rho^s \sigma_u^2}{1 - \rho^2}. \tag{19-8}$$

Dividing by $\gamma_0 = \sigma_u^2/(1 - \rho^2)$ provides the autocorrelations:

$$\text{Corr}[\varepsilon_t, \varepsilon_{t-s}] = \rho_s = \rho^s. \tag{19-9}$$

With the stationarity assumption, the autocorrelations fade over time. Depending on the sign of $\rho$, they will either be declining in geometric progression or alternating in sign if $\rho$ is negative. Collecting terms, we have

$$\sigma^2 \Omega = \frac{\sigma_u^2}{1 - \rho^2} \begin{bmatrix} 1 & \rho & \rho^2 & \rho^3 & \cdots & \rho^{T-1} \\ \rho & 1 & \rho & \rho^2 & \cdots & \rho^{T-2} \\ \rho^2 & \rho & 1 & \rho & \cdots & \rho^{T-3} \\ \vdots & \vdots & \vdots & \vdots & \cdots & \rho \\ \rho^{T-1} & \rho^{T-2} & \rho^{T-3} & \cdots & \rho & 1 \end{bmatrix}. \tag{19-10}$$

## 19.4 SOME ASYMPTOTIC RESULTS FOR ANALYZING TIME-SERIES DATA

Because $\Omega$ is not equal to $\mathbf{I}$, the now-familiar complications will arise in establishing the properties of estimators of $\beta$, in particular of the least squares estimator. The finite sample properties of the OLS and GLS estimators remain intact. Least squares will continue to be unbiased; the earlier general proof allows for autocorrelated disturbances. The Aitken theorem (Theorem 8.4) and the distributional results for normally distributed disturbances can still be established conditionally on $\mathbf{X}$. (However, even these will be complicated when $\mathbf{X}$ contains lagged values of the dependent variable.) But, finite sample properties are of very limited usefulness in time-series contexts. Nearly all that can be said about estimators involving time-series data is based on their asymptotic properties.

As we saw in our analysis of heteroscedasticity, whether least squares is consistent or not, depends on the matrices

$$\mathbf{Q}_T = (1/T)\mathbf{X}'\mathbf{X},$$

and

$$\mathbf{Q}_T^* = (1/T)\mathbf{X}'\Omega\mathbf{X}.$$

In our earlier analyses, we were able to argue for convergence of $\mathbf{Q}_T$ to a positive definite matrix of constants, $\mathbf{Q}$, by invoking laws of large numbers. But, these theorems assume that the observations in the sums are independent, which as suggested in Section 19.2, is surely not the case here. Thus, we require a different tool for this result. We can expand the matrix $\mathbf{Q}_T^*$ as

$$\mathbf{Q}_T^* = \frac{1}{T}\sum_{t=1}^{T}\sum_{s=1}^{T}\rho_{ts}\mathbf{x}_t\mathbf{x}_s', \tag{19-11}$$

where $\mathbf{x}_t'$ and $\mathbf{x}_s'$ are rows of $\mathbf{X}$ and $\rho_{ts}$ is the autocorrelation between $\varepsilon_t$ and $\varepsilon_s$. Sufficient conditions for this matrix to converge are that $\mathbf{Q}_T$ converge and that the correlations between disturbances die off reasonably rapidly as the observations become further apart in time. For example, if the disturbances follow the AR(1) process described earlier, then $\rho_{ts} = \rho^{|t-s|}$ and if $\mathbf{x}_t$ is sufficiently well behaved, $\mathbf{Q}_T^*$ will converge to a positive definite matrix $\mathbf{Q}^*$ as $T \to \infty$.

**Asymptotic normality** of the least squares and GLS estimators will depend on the behavior of sums such as

$$\sqrt{T}\,\overline{\mathbf{w}}_T = \sqrt{T}\left(\frac{1}{T}\sum_{t=1}^{T}\mathbf{x}_t\varepsilon_t\right) = \sqrt{T}\left(\frac{1}{T}\mathbf{X}'\boldsymbol{\varepsilon}\right).$$

Asymptotic normality of least squares is difficult to establish for this general model. The central limit theorems we have relied on thus far do not extend to sums of *dependent* observations. The results of Amemiya (1985), Mann and Wald (1943), and Anderson (1971) do carry over to most of the familiar types of autocorrelated disturbances, including those that interest us here, so we shall ultimately conclude that ordinary least squares, GLS, and instrumental variables continue to be consistent and asymptotically normally distributed, and, in the case of OLS, inefficient. This section will provide a brief introduction to some of the underlying principles that are used to reach these conclusions.

### 19.4.1 CONVERGENCE OF MOMENTS—THE ERGODIC THEOREM

The discussion thus far has suggested (appropriately) that stationarity (or its absence) is an important characteristic of a process. The points at which we have encountered this notion concerned requirements that certain sums converge to finite values. In particular, for the AR(1) model, $\varepsilon_t = \rho \varepsilon_{t-1} + u_t$, for the variance of the process to be finite, we require $|\rho| < 1$, which is a sufficient condition. However, this result is only a byproduct. Stationarity (at least, the weak stationarity we have examined) is only a characteristic of the sequence of moments of a distribution.

---

**DEFINITION 19.1** Strong Stationarity
*A time-series process, $\{z_t\}_{t=-\infty}^{t=\infty}$ is strongly stationary, or "stationary," if the joint probability distribution of any set of k observations in the sequence $[z_t, z_{t+1}, \ldots, z_{t+k}]$ is the same regardless of the origin, t, in the time scale.*

---

For example, in (19-2), if we add $u_t \sim N[0, \sigma_u^2]$, then the resulting process $\{\varepsilon_t\}_{t=-\infty}^{t=\infty}$ can easily be shown to be strongly stationary.

---

**DEFINITION 19.2** Weak Stationarity
*A time-series process, $\{z_t\}_{t=-\infty}^{t=\infty}$ is weakly stationary (or covariance stationary) if $E[z_t]$ is finite and is the same for all t and if the covariances between any two observations (labeled their autocovariance), $\text{Cov}[z_t, z_{t-k}]$, is a finite function only of model parameters and their distance apart in time, k, but not of the absolute location of either observation on the time scale.*

---

Weak stationary is obviously implied by strong stationary, although it requires less because the distribution can, at least in principle, be changing on the time axis. The distinction is rarely necessary in applied work. In general, save for narrow theoretical examples, it will be difficult to come up with a process that is weakly but not strongly stationary. The reason for the distinction is that in much of our work, only weak stationary is required, and, as always, when possible, econometricians will dispense with unnecessary assumptions.

As we will discover shortly, stationarity is a crucial characteristic at this point in the analysis. If we are going to proceed to parameter estimation in this context, we will also require another characteristic of a time series, **ergodicity.** There are various ways to delineate this characteristic, none of them particularly intuitive. We borrow one definition from Davidson and MacKinnon (1993, p. 132) which comes close:

---

**DEFINITION 19.3** Ergodicity
*A strongly stationary time-series process, $\{z_t\}_{t=-\infty}^{t=\infty}$, is ergodic if for any two bounded functions that map vectors in the a and b dimensional real vector spaces to real scalars, $f: \mathbf{R}^a \to \mathbf{R}^1$ and $g: \mathbf{R}^b \to \mathbf{R}^1$,*

$$\lim_{k \to \infty} |E[f(z_t, z_{t+1}, \ldots, z_{t+a})g(z_{t+k}, z_{t+k+1}, \ldots, z_{t+k+b})]|$$
$$= |E[f(z_t, z_{t+1}, \ldots, z_{t+a})]| \, |E[g(z_{t+k}, z_{t+k+1}, \ldots, z_{t+k+b})]|.$$

---

The definition states essentially that if events are separated far enough in time, then they are "asymptotically independent." An implication is that in a time series, every observation will contain at least some unique information. Ergodicity is a crucial element of our theory of estimation. When a time series has this property (with stationarity), then we can consider estimation of parameters in a meaningful sense.[6] The analysis relies heavily on the following theorem:

---

**THEOREM 19.1   The Ergodic Theorem**

*If $\{z_t\}_{t=-\infty}^{t=\infty}$ is a time-series process that is strongly stationary and ergodic and $E[|z_t|]$ is a finite constant, and if $\bar{z}_T = (1/T)\sum_{t=1}^{T} z_t$, then $\bar{z}_T \xrightarrow{a.s.} \mu$, where $\mu = E[z_t]$. Note that the convergence is almost surely not in probability (which is implied) or in mean square (which is also implied). [See White (2001, p. 44) and Davidson and MacKinnon (1993, p. 133).]*

---

What we have in the Ergodic theorem is, for sums of dependent observations, a counterpart to the laws of large numbers that we have used at many points in the preceding chapters. Note, once again, the need for this extension is that to this point, our laws of large numbers have required sums of independent observations. But, in this context, by design, observations are distinctly not independent.

For this result to be useful, we will require an extension.

---

**THEOREM 19.2   Ergodicity of Functions**

*If $\{z_t\}_{t=-\infty}^{t=\infty}$ is a time-series process that is strongly stationary and ergodic and if $y_t = f\{z_t\}$ is a measurable function in the probability space that defines $z_t$, then $y_t$ is also stationary and ergodic. Let $\{\mathbf{z}_t\}_{t=-\infty}^{t=\infty}$ define a $K \times 1$ vector valued stochastic process—each element of the vector is an ergodic and stationary series, and the characteristics of ergodicity and stationarity apply to the joint distribution of the elements of $\{\mathbf{z}_t\}_{t=-\infty}^{t=\infty}$. Then, the Ergodic theorem applies to functions of $\{\mathbf{z}_t\}_{t=-\infty}^{t=\infty}$. [See White (2001, pp. 44–45) for discussion.]*

---

Theorem 19.2 produces the results we need to characterize the least squares (and other) estimators. In particular, our minimal assumptions about the data are

---

ASSUMPTION 19.1   **Ergodic Data Series:** In the regression model, $y_t = \mathbf{x}_t'\boldsymbol{\beta} + \varepsilon_t$, $[\mathbf{x}_t, \varepsilon_t]_{t=-\infty}^{t=\infty}$ is a jointly stationary and ergodic process.

---

[6]Much of the analysis in later chapters will encounter nonstationary series, which are the focus of most of the current literature—tests for nonstationarity largely dominate the recent study in time-series analysis. Ergodicity is a much more subtle and difficult concept. For any process that we will consider, ergodicity will have to be a given, at least at this level. A classic reference on the subject is Doob (1953). Another authoritative treatise is Billingsley (1995). White (2001) provides a concise analysis of many of these concepts as used in econometrics, and some useful commentary.

By analyzing terms element by element we can use these results directly to assert that averages of $\mathbf{w}_t = \mathbf{x}_t \varepsilon_t$, $\mathbf{Q}_{tt} = \mathbf{x}_t \mathbf{x}_t'$, and $\mathbf{Q}_{tt}^* = \varepsilon_t^2 \mathbf{x}_t \mathbf{x}_t'$ will converge to their population counterparts, $\mathbf{0}$, $\mathbf{Q}$ and $\mathbf{Q}^*$.

### 19.4.2 CONVERGENCE TO NORMALITY—A CENTRAL LIMIT THEOREM

To form a distribution theory for least squares, GLS, ML, and GMM, we will need a counterpart to the central limit theorem. In particular, we need to establish a large sample distribution theory for quantities of the form

$$\sqrt{T} \left( \frac{1}{T} \sum_{t=1}^{T} \mathbf{x}_t \varepsilon_t \right) = \sqrt{T} \, \overline{\mathbf{w}}.$$

As noted earlier, we cannot invoke the familiar central limit theorems (Lindeberg–Levy, Lindeberg–Feller, Liapounov) because the observations in the sum are not independent. But, with the assumptions already made, we do have an alternative result. Some needed preliminaries are as follows:

---

**DEFINITION 19.4**  Martingale Sequence
*A vector sequence $\mathbf{z}_t$ is a martingale sequence if $E[\mathbf{z}_t \mid \mathbf{z}_{t-1}, \mathbf{z}_{t-2}, \ldots] = \mathbf{z}_{t-1}$.*

---

An important example of a martingale sequence is the **random walk,**

$$z_t = z_{t-1} + u_t,$$

where $\text{Cov}[u_t, u_s] = 0$ for all $t \neq s$. Then

$$E[z_t \mid z_{t-1}, z_{t-2}, \ldots] = E[z_{t-1} \mid z_{t-1}, z_{t-2}, \ldots] + E[u_t \mid z_{t-1}, z_{t-2}, \ldots] = z_{t-1} + 0 = z_{t-1}.$$

---

**DEFINITION 19.5**  Martingale Difference Sequence
*A vector sequence $\mathbf{z}_t$ is a martingale difference sequence if $E[\mathbf{z}_t \mid \mathbf{z}_{t-1}, \mathbf{z}_{t-2}, \ldots]$ $= \mathbf{0}$.*

---

With Definition 19.5, we have the following broadly encompassing result:

---

**THEOREM 19.3**  Martingale Difference Central Limit Theorem
*If $\mathbf{z}_t$ is a vector valued stationary and ergodic martingale difference sequence, with $E[\mathbf{z}_t \mathbf{z}_t'] = \Sigma$, where $\Sigma$ is a finite positive definite matrix, and if $\overline{\mathbf{z}}_T = (1/T) \sum_{t=1}^{T} \mathbf{z}_t$, then $\sqrt{T} \, \overline{\mathbf{z}}_T \xrightarrow{d} N[\mathbf{0}, \Sigma]$. [For discussion, see Davidson and MacKinnon (1993, Sections. 4.7 and 4.8).][7]*

---

[7] For convenience, we are bypassing a step in this discussion—establishing multivariate normality requires that the result first be established for the marginal normal distribution of each component, then that every linear combination of the variables also be normally distributed (See Theorems D.17 and D.18A.). Our interest at this point is merely to collect the useful end results. Interested users may find the detailed discussions of the many subtleties and narrower points in White (2001) and Davidson and MacKinnon (1993, Chapter 4).

Theorem 19.3 is a generalization of the Lindeberg–Levy central limit theorem. It is not yet broad enough to cover cases of autocorrelation, but it does go beyond Lindeberg–Levy, for example, in extending to the GARCH model of Section 19.13.3. [Forms of the theorem that surpass Lindeberg–Feller (D.19) and Liapounov (Theorem D.20) by allowing for different variances at each time, $t$, appear in Ruud (2000, p. 479) and White (2001, p. 133). These variants extend beyond our requirements in this treatment.] But, looking ahead, this result encompasses what will be a very important application. Suppose in the classical linear regression model, $\{\mathbf{x}_t\}_{t=-\infty}^{t=\infty}$ is a stationary and ergodic multivariate stochastic process and $\{\varepsilon_t\}_{t=-\infty}^{t=\infty}$ is an i.i.d. process—that is, not autocorrelated and not heteroscedastic. Then, this is the most general case of the classical model that still maintains the assumptions about $\varepsilon_t$ that we made in Chapter 2. In this case, the process $\{\mathbf{w}_t\}_{t=-\infty}^{t=\infty} = \{\mathbf{x}_t \varepsilon_t\}_{t=-\infty}^{t=\infty}$ is a martingale difference sequence, so that with sufficient assumptions on the moments of $\mathbf{x}_t$ we could use this result to establish consistency and asymptotic normality of the least squares estimator. [See, e.g., Hamilton (1994, pp. 208–212).]

We now consider a central limit theorem that is broad enough to include the case that interested us at the outset, stochastically dependent observations on $\mathbf{x}_t$ and autocorrelation in $\varepsilon_t$.[8] Suppose as before that $\{\mathbf{z}_t\}_{t=-\infty}^{t=\infty}$ is a stationary and ergodic stochastic process. We consider $\sqrt{T}\,\bar{\mathbf{z}}_T$. The following conditions are assumed:[9]

1.  **Asymptotic uncorrelatedness:** $E[\mathbf{z}_t \mid \mathbf{z}_{t-k}, \mathbf{z}_{t-k-1}, \ldots]$ converges in mean square to zero as $k \to \infty$. Note that is similar to the condition for ergodicity. White (2001) demonstrates that a (nonobvious) implication of this assumption is $E[\mathbf{z}_t] = \mathbf{0}$.

2.  **Summability of autocovariances:** With dependent observations,

$$\lim_{T \to \infty} \text{Var}[\sqrt{T}\,\bar{\mathbf{z}}_T] = \sum_{t=0}^{\infty} \sum_{s=0}^{\infty} \text{Cov}[\mathbf{z}_t, \mathbf{z}_s'] = \sum_{k=-\infty}^{\infty} \mathbf{\Gamma}_k = \mathbf{\Gamma}^*.$$

To begin, we will need to assume that this matrix is finite, a condition called **summability.** Note this is the condition needed for convergence of $\mathbf{Q}_T^*$ in (19-11). If the sum is to be finite, then the $k = 0$ term must be finite, which gives us a necessary condition

$$E[\mathbf{z}_t \mathbf{z}_t'] = \mathbf{\Gamma}_0, \text{ a finite matrix.}$$

3.  **Asymptotic negligibility of innovations:** Let

$$\mathbf{r}_{tk} = E[\mathbf{z}_t \mid \mathbf{z}_{t-k}, \mathbf{z}_{t-k-1}, \ldots] - E[\mathbf{z}_t \mid \mathbf{z}_{t-k-1}, \mathbf{z}_{t-k-2}, \ldots].$$

An observation $\mathbf{z}_t$ may be viewed as the accumulated information that has entered the process since it began up to time $t$. Thus, it can be shown that

$$\mathbf{z}_t = \sum_{s=0}^{\infty} \mathbf{r}_{ts}.$$

The vector $\mathbf{r}_{tk}$ can be viewed as the information in this accumulated sum that entered the process at time $t - k$. The condition imposed on the process is that $\sum_{s=0}^{\infty} \sqrt{E[\mathbf{r}_{ts}' \mathbf{r}_{ts}]}$ be finite. In words, condition (3) states that information eventually becomes negligible as it fades far back in time from the current observation. The AR(1) model (as usual)

---

[8]Detailed analysis of this case is quite intricate and well beyond the scope of this book. Some fairly terse analysis may be found in White (2001, pp. 122–133) and Hayashi (2000).

[9]See Hayashi (2000, p. 405) who attributes the results to Gordin (1969).

helps to illustrate this point. If $z_t = \rho z_{t-1} + u_t$, then

$$r_{t0} = E[z_t \mid z_t, z_{t-1}, \ldots] - E[z_t \mid z_{t-1}, z_{t-2}, \ldots] = z_t - \rho z_{t-1} = u_t$$

$$r_{t1} = E[z_t \mid z_{t-1}, z_{t-2} \ldots] - E[z_t \mid z_{t-2}, z_{t-3} \ldots]$$

$$= E[\rho z_{t-1} + u_t \mid z_{t-1}, z_{t-2} \ldots] - E[\rho(\rho z_{t-2} + u_{t-1}) + u_t \mid z_{t-2}, z_{t-3}, \ldots]$$

$$= \rho(z_{t-1} - \rho z_{t-2})$$

$$= \rho u_{t-1}.$$

By a similar construction, $r_{tk} = \rho^k u_{t-k}$ from which it follows that $z_t = \sum_{s=0}^{\infty} \rho^s u_{t-s}$, which we saw earlier in (19-3). You can verify that if $|\rho| < 1$, the negligibility condition will be met.

With all this machinery in place, we now have the theorem we will need:

---

**THEOREM 19.4**   **Gordin's Central Limit Theorem**
*If $\mathbf{z}_t$ is strongly stationary and ergodic and if conditions (1)–(3) are met, then*
$$\sqrt{T}\,\bar{\mathbf{z}}_T \xrightarrow{d} N[\mathbf{0}, \mathbf{\Gamma}^*].$$

---

We will be able to employ these tools when we consider the least squares, IV, and GLS estimators in the discussion to follow.

## 19.5   LEAST SQUARES ESTIMATION

The least squares estimator is

$$\mathbf{b} = (\mathbf{X}'\mathbf{X})^{-1}\mathbf{X}'\mathbf{y} = \boldsymbol{\beta} + \left(\frac{\mathbf{X}'\mathbf{X}}{T}\right)^{-1} \left(\frac{\mathbf{X}'\boldsymbol{\varepsilon}}{T}\right).$$

Unbiasedness follows from the results in Chapter 4—no modification is needed. We know from Chapter 8 that the Gauss–Markov theorem has been lost—assuming it exists (that remains to be established), the GLS estimator is efficient and OLS is not. How much information is lost by using least squares instead of GLS depends on the data. Broadly, least squares fares better in data that have long periods and little cyclical variation, such as aggregate output series. As might be expected, the greater is the autocorrelation in $\varepsilon$, the greater will be the benefit to using generalized least squares (when this is possible). Even if the disturbances are normally distributed, the usual $F$ and $t$ statistics do not have those distributions. So, not much remains of the finite sample properties we obtained in Chapter 4. The asymptotic properties remain to be established.

### 19.5.1   ASYMPTOTIC PROPERTIES OF LEAST SQUARES

The asymptotic properties of $\mathbf{b}$ are straightforward to establish given our earlier results. If we assume that the process generating $\mathbf{x}_t$ is stationary and ergodic, then by Theorems 19.1 and 19.2, $(1/T)(\mathbf{X}'\mathbf{X})$ converges to $\mathbf{Q}$ and we can apply the Slutsky theorem to the inverse. If $\varepsilon_t$ is not serially correlated, then $\mathbf{w}_t = \mathbf{x}_t \varepsilon_t$ is a martingale difference sequence, so $(1/T)(\mathbf{X}'\boldsymbol{\varepsilon})$ converges to zero. This establishes consistency for the simple case. On the other hand, if $[\mathbf{x}_t, \varepsilon_t]$ are jointly stationary and ergodic, then we can invoke the Ergodic theorems 19.1 and 19.2 for both moment matrices and establish consistency. Asymptotic normality is a bit more subtle. For the case without serial correlation in $\varepsilon_t$, we can employ Theorem 19.3 for $\sqrt{T}\,\bar{\mathbf{w}}$. The involved case is the one that interested us at the outset of this discussion, that is, where there is autocorrelation in $\varepsilon_t$ and dependence in $\mathbf{x}_t$. Theorem 19.4 is in place for this case. Once again, the conditions described in the preceding section must apply and, moreover, the assumptions needed will have to be established both for $\mathbf{x}_t$ and $\varepsilon_t$. Commentary on these cases may be found in Davidson and MacKinnon (1993), Hamilton (1994), White (2001), and Hayashi (2000). Formal presentation extends beyond the scope of this text, so at this point, we will proceed, and assume that the conditions underlying Theorem 19.4 are met. The results suggested here are quite general, albeit only sketched for the general case. For the remainder of our examination, at least in this chapter, we will confine attention to fairly simple processes in which the necessary conditions for the asymptotic distribution theory will be fairly evident.

There is an important exception to the results in the preceding paragraph. If the regression contains any lagged values of the dependent variable, then least squares will no longer be unbiased or consistent. To take the simplest case, suppose that

$$y_t = \beta y_{t-1} + \varepsilon_t,$$
$$\varepsilon_t = \rho\varepsilon_{t-1} + u_t, \tag{19-12}$$

and assume $|\beta| < 1$, $|\rho| < 1$. In this model, the regressor and the disturbance are correlated. There are various ways to approach the analysis. One useful way is to rearrange (19-12) by subtracting $\rho y_{t-1}$ from $y_t$. Then,

$$y_t = (\beta + \rho)y_{t-1} - \beta\rho y_{t-2} + u_t, \tag{19-13}$$

which is a classical regression with stochastic regressors. Because $u_t$ is an innovation in period $t$, it is uncorrelated with both regressors, and least squares regression of $y_t$ on $(y_{t-1}, y_{t-2})$ estimates $\rho_1 = (\beta + \rho)$ and $\rho_2 = -\beta\rho$. What is estimated by regression of $y_t$ on $y_{t-1}$ alone? Let $\gamma_k = \text{Cov}[y_t, y_{t-k}] = \text{Cov}[y_t, y_{t+k}]$. By stationarity, $\text{Var}[y_t] = \text{Var}[y_{t-1}]$, and $\text{Cov}[y_t, y_{t-1}] = \text{Cov}[y_{t-1}, y_{t-2}]$, and so on. These and (19-13) imply the following relationships:

$$\gamma_0 = \rho_1\gamma_1 + \rho_2\gamma_2 + \sigma_u^2,$$
$$\gamma_1 = \rho_1\gamma_0 + \rho_2\gamma_1, \tag{19-14}$$
$$\gamma_2 = \rho_1\gamma_1 + \rho_2\gamma_0.$$

(These are the **Yule–Walker equations** for this model. See Section 21.2.3.) The slope in the simple regression estimates $\gamma_1/\gamma_0$, which can be found in the solutions to these three equations. (An alternative approach is to use the left-out variable formula, which is a useful way to interpret this estimator.) In this case, we see that the slope in the short regression is an estimator of $(\beta + \rho) - \beta\rho(\gamma_1/\gamma_0)$. In either case, solving the three equations in (19-14) for $\gamma_0$, $\gamma_1$, and $\gamma_2$ in terms of $\rho_1$, $\rho_2$, and $\sigma_u^2$ produces

$$\text{plim } b = \frac{\beta + \rho}{1 + \beta\rho}. \tag{19-15}$$

This result is between $\beta$ (when $\rho = 0$) and 1 (when both $\beta$ and $\rho = 1$). Therefore, least squares is inconsistent unless $\rho$ equals zero. The more general case that includes regressors, $\mathbf{x}_t$, involves more complicated algebra, but gives essentially the same result. This is a general result; when the equation contains a lagged dependent variable in the presence of autocorrelation, OLS and GLS are inconsistent. The problem can be viewed as one of an omitted variable.

### 19.5.2 ESTIMATING THE VARIANCE OF THE LEAST SQUARES ESTIMATOR

As usual, $s^2(\mathbf{X}'\mathbf{X})^{-1}$ is an inappropriate estimator of $\sigma^2(\mathbf{X}'\mathbf{X})^{-1}(\mathbf{X}'\mathbf{\Omega}\mathbf{X})(\mathbf{X}'\mathbf{X})^{-1}$, both because $s^2$ is a biased estimator of $\sigma^2$ and because the matrix is incorrect. Generalities are scarce, but in general, for economic time series that are positively related to their past values, the standard errors conventionally *estimated* by least squares are likely to be too small. For slowly changing, trending aggregates such as output and consumption, this is probably the norm. For highly variable data such as inflation, exchange rates, and market returns, the situation is less clear. Nonetheless, as a general proposition, one would normally not want to rely on $s^2(\mathbf{X}'\mathbf{X})^{-1}$ as an estimator of the asymptotic covariance matrix of the least squares estimator.

In view of this situation, if one is going to use least squares, then it is desirable to have an appropriate estimator of the covariance matrix of the least squares estimator. There are two approaches. If the form of the autocorrelation is known, then one can estimate the parameters of $\mathbf{\Omega}$ directly and compute a consistent estimator. Of course, if so, then it would be more sensible to use feasible generalized least squares instead and not waste the sample information on an inefficient estimator. The second approach parallels the use of the White estimator for heteroscedasticity.

The extension of White's result to the more general case of autocorrelation is much more difficult than in the heteroscedasticity case. The natural counterpart for estimating

$$\mathbf{Q}_* = \frac{1}{n} \sum_{i=1}^{n} \sum_{j=1}^{n} \sigma_{ij} \mathbf{x}_i \mathbf{x}'_j$$

(19-16)

in Section 8.2.3 would be

$$\hat{\mathbf{Q}}_* = \frac{1}{T} \sum_{t=1}^{T} \sum_{s=1}^{T} e_t e_s \mathbf{x}_t \mathbf{x}'_s.$$

But there are two problems with this estimator, one theoretical, which applies to $\mathbf{Q}_*$ as well, and one practical, which is specific to the latter.

Unlike the heteroscedasticity case, the matrix in (19-16) is $1/T$ times a sum of $T^2$ terms, so it is difficult to conclude yet that it will converge to anything at all. This application is most likely to arise in a time-series setting. To obtain convergence, it is necessary to assume that the terms involving unequal subscripts in (19-16) diminish in importance as $T$ grows. A sufficient condition is that terms with subscript pairs $|t - s|$ grow smaller as the distance between them grows larger. In practical terms, observation pairs are progressively less correlated as their separation in time grows. Intuitively, if one can think of weights with the diagonal elements getting a weight of 1.0, then in the sum, the weights in the sum grow smaller as we move away from the diagonal. If we think of the sum of the weights rather than just the number of terms, then this sum falls off sufficiently rapidly that as $n$ grows large, the sum is of order $T$ rather than $T^2$. Thus,

**TABLE 19.1** Robust Covariance Estimation

| Variable | OLS Estimate | OLS SE | Corrected SE |
|----------|-------------|--------|--------------|
| Constant | −1.6331 | 0.2286 | 0.3335 |
| ln Output | 0.2871 | 0.04738 | 0.07806 |
| ln CPI | 0.9718 | 0.03377 | 0.06585 |

$R^2 = 0.98952$, $d = 0.02477$, $r = 0.98762$.

we achieve convergence of $\mathbf{Q}_*$ by assuming that the rows of $\mathbf{X}$ are well behaved and that the correlations diminish with increasing separation in time. (See Sections 4.9.6 and 21.2.5 for a more formal statement of this condition.)

The practical problem is that $\hat{\mathbf{Q}}_*$ need not be positive definite. Newey and West (1987a) have devised an estimator that overcomes this difficulty:

$$\hat{\mathbf{Q}}_* = \mathbf{S}_0 + \frac{1}{T} \sum_{l=1}^{L} \sum_{t=l+1}^{T} w_l e_t e_{t-l} (\mathbf{x}_t \mathbf{x}'_{t-l} + \mathbf{x}_{t-l} \mathbf{x}'_t),$$

$$w_l = 1 - \frac{l}{(L+1)}.$$

(19-17)

[See (8-26).] The **Newey–West autocorrelation consistent covariance estimator** is surprisingly simple and relatively easy to implement.[10] There is a final problem to be solved. It must be determined in advance how large $L$ is to be. In general, there is little theoretical guidance. Current practice specifies $L \approx T^{1/4}$. Unfortunately, the result is not quite as crisp as that for the heteroscedasticity consistent estimator.

We have the result that $\mathbf{b}$ and $\mathbf{b}_{IV}$ are asymptotically normally distributed, and we have an appropriate estimator for the asymptotic covariance matrix. We have not specified the distribution of the disturbances, however. Thus, for inference purposes, the $F$ statistic is approximate at best. Moreover, for more involved hypotheses, the likelihood ratio and Lagrange multiplier tests are unavailable. That leaves the Wald statistic, including asymptotic "$t$ ratios," as the main tool for statistical inference. We will examine a number of applications in the chapters to follow.

The White and Newey–West estimators are standard in the econometrics literature. We will encounter them at many points in the discussion to follow.

---

**Example 19.4** *Autocorrelation Consistent Covariance Estimation*
For the model shown in Example 19.1, the regression results with the uncorrected standard errors and the Newey–West autocorrelation robust covariance matrix for lags of five quarters are shown in Table 19.1. The effect of the very high degree of autocorrelation is evident.

## 19.6 GMM ESTIMATION

The **GMM estimator** in the regression model with autocorrelated disturbances is produced by the empirical moment equations

$$\frac{1}{T} \sum_{t=1}^{T} \mathbf{x}_t \left( y_t - \mathbf{x}'_t \hat{\boldsymbol{\beta}}_{GMM} \right) = \frac{1}{T} \mathbf{X}' \hat{\boldsymbol{\varepsilon}} \left( \hat{\boldsymbol{\beta}}_{GMM} \right) = \overline{\mathbf{m}} \left( \hat{\boldsymbol{\beta}}_{GMM} \right) = \mathbf{0}.$$

(19-18)

---

[10]Both estimators are now standard features in modern econometrics computer programs. Further results on different weighting schemes may be found in Hayashi (2000, pp. 406–410).

The estimator is obtained by minimizing

$$q = \overline{\mathbf{m}}'(\hat{\boldsymbol{\beta}}_{GMM})\mathbf{W}\,\overline{\mathbf{m}}(\hat{\boldsymbol{\beta}}_{GMM})$$

where $\mathbf{W}$ is a positive definite weighting matrix. The optimal weighting matrix would be

$$\mathbf{W} = \left\{\text{Asy. Var}[\sqrt{T}\,\overline{\mathbf{m}}(\boldsymbol{\beta})]\right\}^{-1},$$

which is the inverse of

$$\text{Asy. Var}[\sqrt{T}\,\overline{\mathbf{m}}(\boldsymbol{\beta})] = \text{Asy. Var}\left[\frac{1}{\sqrt{T}}\sum_{i=1}^{n}\mathbf{x}_i\varepsilon_i\right] = \underset{n\to\infty}{\text{plim}}\,\frac{1}{T}\sum_{t=1}^{T}\sum_{s=1}^{T}\sigma^2\rho_{ts}\mathbf{x}_t\mathbf{x}_s' = \sigma^2\mathbf{Q}^*.$$

The optimal weighting matrix would be $[\sigma^2\mathbf{Q}^*]^{-1}$. As in the heteroscedasticity case, this minimization problem is an exactly identified case, so, the weighting matrix is actually irrelevant to the solution. *The GMM estimator for the regression model with autocorrelated disturbances is ordinary least squares.* We can use the results in Section 19.5.2 to construct the asymptotic covariance matrix. We will require the assumptions in Section 19.4 to obtain convergence of the moments and asymptotic normality. We will wish to extend this simple result in one instance. In the common case in which $\mathbf{x}_t$ contains lagged values of $y_t$, we will want to use an instrumental variable estimator. We will return to that estimation problem in Section 19.9.3.

## 19.7   TESTING FOR AUTOCORRELATION

The available tests for autocorrelation are based on the principle that if the true disturbances are autocorrelated, then this fact can be detected through the autocorrelations of the least squares residuals. The simplest indicator is the slope in the artificial regression

$$e_t = re_{t-1} + v_t,$$
$$e_t = y_t - \mathbf{x}_t'\mathbf{b},$$

$$r = \left(\sum_{t=2}^{T}e_te_{t-1}\right)\bigg/\left(\sum_{t=1}^{T-1}e_t^2\right). \tag{19-19}$$

If there is autocorrelation, then the slope in this regression will be an estimator of $\rho = \text{Corr}[\varepsilon_t, \varepsilon_{t-1}]$. The complication in the analysis lies in determining a formal means of evaluating when the estimator is "large," that is, on what statistical basis to reject the null hypothesis that $\rho$ equals zero. As a first approximation, treating (19-19) as a classical linear model and using a $t$ or $F$ (squared $t$) test to test the hypothesis is a valid way to proceed based on the Lagrange multiplier principle. We used this device in Example 19.3. The tests we consider here are refinements of this approach.

### 19.7.1   LAGRANGE MULTIPLIER TEST

The Breusch (1978)–Godfrey (1978) test is a Lagrange multiplier test of $H_0$: no autocorrelation versus $H_1\!:\varepsilon_t = \text{AR}(P)$ or $\varepsilon_t = \text{MA}(P)$. The same test is used for either structure. The test statistic is

$$\text{LM} = T\left(\frac{\mathbf{e}'\mathbf{X}_0(\mathbf{X}_0'\mathbf{X}_0)^{-1}\mathbf{X}_0'\mathbf{e}}{\mathbf{e}'\mathbf{e}}\right) = TR_0^2, \tag{19-20}$$

where $\mathbf{X}_0$ is the original $\mathbf{X}$ matrix augmented by $P$ additional columns containing the lagged OLS residuals, $e_{t-1}, \ldots, e_{t-P}$. The test can be carried out simply by regressing the ordinary least squares residuals $e_t$ on $\mathbf{x}_{t0}$ (filling in missing values for lagged residuals with zeros) and referring $TR_0^2$ to the tabled critical value for the chi-squared distribution with $P$ degrees of freedom.[11] Because $\mathbf{X}'\mathbf{e} = \mathbf{0}$, the test is equivalent to regressing $e_t$ on the part of the lagged residuals that is unexplained by $\mathbf{X}$. There is therefore a compelling logic to it; if any fit is found, then it is due to correlation between the current and lagged residuals. The test is a joint test of the first $P$ autocorrelations of $\varepsilon_t$, not just the first.

### 19.7.2 BOX AND PIERCE'S TEST AND LJUNG'S REFINEMENT

An alternative test that is asymptotically equivalent to the LM test when the null hypothesis, $\rho = 0$, is true and when $\mathbf{X}$ does not contain lagged values of $y$ is due to Box and Pierce (1970). The **Q test** is carried out by referring

$$Q = T\sum_{j=1}^{P} r_j^2, \tag{19-21}$$

where $r_j = (\sum_{t=j+1}^{T} e_t e_{t-j})/(\sum_{t=1}^{T} e_t^2)$, to the critical values of the chi-squared table with $P$ degrees of freedom. A refinement suggested by Ljung and Box (1979) is

$$Q' = T(T+2)\sum_{j=1}^{P} \frac{r_j^2}{T-j}. \tag{19-22}$$

The essential difference between the Godfrey–Breusch and the Box–Pierce tests is the use of partial correlations (controlling for $\mathbf{X}$ and the other variables) in the former and simple correlations in the latter. Under the null hypothesis, there is no autocorrelation in $\varepsilon_t$, and no correlation between $\mathbf{x}_t$ and $\varepsilon_s$ in any event, so the two tests are asymptotically equivalent. On the other hand, because it does not condition on $\mathbf{x}_t$, the Box–Pierce test is less powerful than the LM test when the null hypothesis is false, as intuition might suggest.

### 19.7.3 THE DURBIN–WATSON TEST

The Durbin–Watson statistic[12] was the first formal procedure developed for testing for autocorrelation using the least squares residuals. The test statistic is

$$d = \frac{\sum_{t=2}^{T}(e_t - e_{t-1})^2}{\sum_{t=1}^{T} e_t^2} = 2(1-r) - \frac{e_1^2 + e_T^2}{\sum_{t=1}^{T} e_t^2}, \tag{19-23}$$

where $r$ is the same first-order autocorrelation that underlies the preceding two statistics. If the sample is reasonably large, then the last term will be negligible, leaving

---

[11] A warning to practitioners: Current software varies on whether the lagged residuals are filled with zeros or the first $P$ observations are simply dropped when computing this statistic. In the interest of replicability, users should determine which is the case before reporting results.

[12] Durbin and Watson (1950, 1951, 1971).

$d \approx 2(1 - r)$. The statistic takes this form because the authors were able to determine the exact distribution of this transformation of the autocorrelation and could provide tables of critical values. Usable critical values that depend only on $T$ and $K$ are presented in tables such as those at the end of this book. The one-sided test for $H_0$: $\rho = 0$ against $H_1$: $\rho > 0$ is carried out by comparing $d$ to values $d_L(T, K)$ and $d_U(T, K)$. If $d < d_L$, the null hypothesis is rejected; if $d > d_U$, the hypothesis is not rejected. If $d$ lies between $d_L$ and $d_U$, then no conclusion is drawn.

### 19.7.4 TESTING IN THE PRESENCE OF A LAGGED DEPENDENT VARIABLE

The Durbin–Watson test is not likely to be valid when there is a lagged dependent variable in the equation.[13] The statistic will usually be biased toward a finding of no autocorrelation. Three alternatives have been devised. The LM and Q tests can be used whether or not the regression contains a lagged dependent variable. (In the absence of a lagged dependent variable, they are asymptotically equivalent.) As an alternative to the standard test, Durbin (1970) derived a Lagrange multiplier test that is appropriate in the presence of a lagged dependent variable. The test may be carried out by referring

$$h = r\sqrt{T/(1 - Ts_c^2)}, \tag{19-24}$$

where $s_c^2$ is the estimated variance of the least squares regression coefficient on $y_{t-1}$, to the standard normal tables. Large values of $h$ lead to rejection of $H_0$. The test has the virtues that it can be used even if the regression contains additional lags of $y_t$, and it can be computed using the standard results from the initial regression without any further regressions. If $s_c^2 > 1/T$, however, then it cannot be computed. An alternative is to regress $e_t$ on $\mathbf{x}_t$, $y_{t-1}, \ldots, e_{t-1}$, and any additional lags that are appropriate for $e_t$ and then to test the joint significance of the coefficient(s) on the lagged residual(s) with the standard $F$ test. This method is a minor modification of the Breusch–Godfrey test. Under $H_0$, the coefficients on the remaining variables will be zero, so the tests are the same asymptotically.

### 19.7.5 SUMMARY OF TESTING PROCEDURES

The preceding has examined several testing procedures for locating autocorrelation in the disturbances. In all cases, the procedure examines the least squares residuals. We can summarize the procedures as follows:

**LM test.** $LM = TR^2$ in a regression of the least squares residuals on $[\mathbf{x}_t, e_{t-1}, \ldots$ $e_{t-P}]$. Reject $H_0$ if $LM > \chi_*^2[P]$. This test examines the covariance of the residuals with lagged values, controlling for the intervening effect of the independent variables.

**Q test.** $Q = T(T - 2)\sum_{j=1}^{P} r_j^2/(T - j)$. Reject $H_0$ if $Q > \chi_*^2[P]$. This test examines the raw correlations between the residuals and $P$ lagged values of the residuals.

**Durbin–Watson test.** $d = 2(1 - r)$. Reject $H_0$: $\rho = 0$ if $d < d_L^*$. This test looks directly at the first-order autocorrelation of the residuals.

---

[13]This issue has been studied by Nerlove and Wallis (1966), Durbin (1970), and Dezhbaksh (1990).

**Durbin's test.** $F_D =$ the $F$ statistic for the joint significance of $P$ lags of the residuals in the regression of the least squares residuals on $[\mathbf{x}_t, y_{t-1}, \ldots y_{t-R}, e_{t-1}, \ldots e_{t-P}]$. Reject $H_0$ if $F_D > F_*[P, T - K - P]$. This test examines the partial correlations between the residuals and the lagged residuals, controlling for the intervening effect of the independent variables and the lagged dependent variable.

The Durbin–Watson test has some major shortcomings. The inconclusive region is large if $T$ is small or moderate. The bounding distributions, while free of the parameters $\beta$ and $\sigma$, do depend on the data (and assume that $\mathbf{X}$ is nonstochastic). An exact version based on an algorithm developed by Imhof (1980) avoids the inconclusive region, but is rarely used. The LM and Box–Pierce statistics do not share these shortcomings—their limiting distributions are chi-squared independently of the data and the parameters. For this reason, the LM test has become the standard method in applied research.

## 19.8 EFFICIENT ESTIMATION WHEN Ω IS KNOWN

As a prelude to deriving feasible estimators for $\beta$ in this model, we consider full generalized least squares estimation assuming that $\mathbf{\Omega}$ is known. In the next section, we will turn to the more realistic case in which $\mathbf{\Omega}$ must be estimated as well.

If the parameters of $\mathbf{\Omega}$ are known, then the GLS estimator,

$$\hat{\beta} = (\mathbf{X}'\mathbf{\Omega}^{-1}\mathbf{X})^{-1}(\mathbf{X}'\mathbf{\Omega}^{-1}\mathbf{y}), \tag{19-25}$$

and the estimate of its sampling variance,

$$\text{Est. Var}[\hat{\beta}] = \hat{\sigma}_\varepsilon^2[\mathbf{X}'\mathbf{\Omega}^{-1}\mathbf{X}]^{-1}, \tag{19-26}$$

where

$$\hat{\sigma}_\varepsilon^2 = \frac{(\mathbf{y} - \mathbf{X}\hat{\beta})'\mathbf{\Omega}^{-1}(\mathbf{y} - \mathbf{X}\hat{\beta})}{T} \tag{19-27}$$

can be computed in one step. For the AR(1) case, data for the transformed model are

$$\mathbf{y}_* = \begin{bmatrix} \sqrt{1-\rho^2}\,y_1 \\ y_2 - \rho y_1 \\ y_3 - \rho y_2 \\ \vdots \\ y_T - \rho y_{T-1} \end{bmatrix}, \quad \mathbf{X}_* = \begin{bmatrix} \sqrt{1-\rho^2}\,\mathbf{x}_1 \\ \mathbf{x}_2 - \rho\mathbf{x}_1 \\ \mathbf{x}_3 - \rho\mathbf{x}_2 \\ \vdots \\ \mathbf{x}_T - \rho\mathbf{x}_{T-1} \end{bmatrix}. \tag{19-28}$$

These transformations are variously labeled **partial differences, quasi differences,** or **pseudo-differences.** Note that in the transformed model, every observation except the first contains a constant term. What was the column of 1s in $\mathbf{X}$ is transformed to $[(1 - \rho^2)^{1/2}, (1 - \rho), (1 - \rho), \ldots]$. Therefore, if the sample is relatively small, then the problems with measures of fit noted in Section 3.5 will reappear.

The variance of the transformed disturbance is

$$\text{Var}[\varepsilon_t - \rho\varepsilon_{t-1}] = \text{Var}[u_t] = \sigma_u^2.$$

The variance of the first disturbance is also $\sigma_u^2$; [see (19-6)]. This can be estimated using $(1 - \rho^2)\hat{\sigma}_\varepsilon^2$.

Corresponding results have been derived for higher-order autoregressive processes. For the AR(2) model,

$$\varepsilon_t = \theta_1 \varepsilon_{t-1} + \theta_2 \varepsilon_{t-2} + u_t, \qquad \text{(19-29)}$$

the transformed data for generalized least squares are obtained by

$$\mathbf{z}_{*1} = \left[ \frac{(1 + \theta_2)\left[(1 - \theta_2)^2 - \theta_1^2\right]}{1 - \theta_2} \right]^{1/2} \mathbf{z}_1,$$

$$\mathbf{z}_{*2} = \left(1 - \theta_2^2\right)^{1/2} \mathbf{z}_2 - \frac{\theta_1\left(1 - \theta_1^2\right)^{1/2}}{1 - \theta_2} \mathbf{z}_1, \qquad \text{(19-30)}$$

$$\mathbf{z}_{*t} = \mathbf{z}_t - \theta_1 \mathbf{z}_{t-1} - \theta_2 \mathbf{z}_{t-2}, \quad t > 2,$$

where $\mathbf{z}_t$ is used for $y_t$ or $\mathbf{x}_t$. The transformation becomes progressively more complex for higher-order processes.[14]

Note that in both the AR(1) and AR(2) models, the transformation to $y_*$ and $\mathbf{X}_*$ involves "starting values" for the processes that depend only on the first one or two observations. We can view the process as having begun in the infinite past. Because the sample contains only $T$ observations, however, it is convenient to treat the first one or two (or $P$) observations as shown and consider them as "initial values." Whether we view the process as having begun at time $t = 1$ or in the infinite past is ultimately immaterial in regard to the asymptotic properties of the estimators.

The asymptotic properties for the GLS estimator are quite straightforward given the apparatus we assembled in Section 19.4. We begin by assuming that $\{\mathbf{x}_t, \varepsilon_t\}$ are jointly an ergodic, stationary process. Then, after the GLS transformation, $\{\mathbf{x}_{*t}, \varepsilon_{*t}\}$ is also stationary and ergodic. Moreover, $\varepsilon_{*t}$ is nonautocorrelated by construction. In the transformed model, then, $\{\mathbf{w}_{*t}\} = \{\mathbf{x}_{*t} \varepsilon_{*t}\}$ is a stationary and ergodic martingale difference series. We can use the ergodic theorem to establish consistency and the central limit theorem for martingale difference sequences to establish asymptotic normality for GLS in this model. Formal arrangement of the relevant results is left as an exercise.

## 19.9  ESTIMATION WHEN Ω IS UNKNOWN

For an unknown $\boldsymbol{\Omega}$, there are a variety of approaches. Any consistent estimator of $\boldsymbol{\Omega}(\rho)$ will suffice—recall from Theorem (8.5) in Section 8.3.2, all that is needed for efficient estimation of $\boldsymbol{\beta}$ is a consistent estimator of $\boldsymbol{\Omega}(\rho)$. The complication arises, as might be expected, in estimating the autocorrelation parameter(s).

### 19.9.1  AR(1) DISTURBANCES

The AR(1) model is the one most widely used and studied. The most common procedure is to begin FGLS with a natural estimator of $\rho$, the autocorrelation of the residuals. Because **b** is consistent, we can use $r$. Others that have been suggested include Theil's (1971) estimator, $r[(T-K)/(T-1)]$ and Durbin's (1970), the slope on $y_{t-1}$ in a regression

---

[14] See Box and Jenkins (1984) and Fuller (1976).

of $y_t$ on $y_{t-1}$, $\mathbf{x}_t$ and $\mathbf{x}_{t-1}$. The second step is FGLS based on (19-25)–(19-28). This is the **Prais and Winsten** (1954) **estimator.** The **Cochrane and Orcutt** (1949) **estimator** (based on computational ease) omits the first observation.

It is possible to iterate any of these estimators to convergence. Because the estimator is asymptotically efficient at every iteration, nothing is gained by doing so. Unlike the heteroscedastic model, iterating when there is autocorrelation does not produce the maximum likelihood estimator. The iterated FGLS estimator, regardless of the estimator of $\rho$, does not account for the term $(1/2)\ln(1 - \rho^2)$ in the log-likelihood function [see the following (19-31)].

Maximum likelihood estimators can be obtained by maximizing the log-likelihood with respect to $\boldsymbol{\beta}$, $\sigma_u^2$, and $\rho$. The log-likelihood function may be written

$$\ln L = -\frac{\sum_{t=1}^{T} u_t^2}{2\sigma_u^2} + \frac{1}{2}\ln(1 - \rho^2) - \frac{T}{2}(\ln 2\pi + \ln \sigma_u^2), \qquad \textbf{(19-31)}$$

where, as before, the first observation is computed differently from the others using (19-28). The MLE for this model is developed in Section 16.9.2.d. Based on the MLE, the standard approximations to the asymptotic variances of the estimators are:

$$\text{Est. Asy. Var}[\hat{\boldsymbol{\beta}}_{ML}] = \hat{\sigma}_{\varepsilon,ML}^2[\mathbf{X}'\hat{\boldsymbol{\Omega}}_{ML}^{-1}\mathbf{X}]^{-1},$$

$$\text{Est. Asy. Var}[\hat{\sigma}_{u,ML}^2] = 2\hat{\sigma}_{u,ML}^4/T, \qquad \textbf{(19-32)}$$

$$\text{Est. Asy. Var}[\hat{\rho}_{ML}] = (1 - \hat{\rho}_{ML}^2)/T.$$

All the foregoing estimators have the same asymptotic properties. The available evidence on their small-sample properties comes from Monte Carlo studies and is, unfortunately, only suggestive. Griliches and Rao (1969) find evidence that if the sample is relatively small and $\rho$ is not particularly large, say, less than 0.3, then least squares is as good as or better than FGLS. The problem is the additional variation introduced into the sampling variance by the variance of $r$. Beyond these, the results are rather mixed. Maximum likelihood seems to perform well in general, but the Prais–Winsten estimator is evidently nearly as efficient. Both estimators have been incorporated in all contemporary software. In practice, the Prais and Winsten (1954) and Beach and MacKinnon (1978a) maximum likelihood estimators are probably the most common choices.

### 19.9.2 APPLICATION: ESTIMATION OF A MODEL WITH AUTOCORRELATION

The model of the U.S. gasoline market that appears in Example 6.7 is

$$\ln \frac{G_t}{pop_t} = \beta_1 + \beta_2 \ln \frac{I_t}{pop_t} + \beta_3 \ln P_{G,t} + \beta_4 \ln P_{NC,t} + \beta_5 \ln P_{UC,t} + \beta_6 t + \varepsilon_t.$$

The results in Figure 19.2 suggest that the specification may be incomplete, and, if so, there may be autocorrelation in the disturbances in this specification. Least squares estimates of the parameters using the data in Appendix Table F2.2 appear in the first row of Table 19.2. [The dependent variable is $\ln(Gas\ expenditure / (price \times population))$. These are the OLS results reported in Example 6.7.] The first five autocorrelations of the least squares residuals are 0.667, 0.438, 0.142, −0.018, and −0.198. This produces Box–Pierce

**TABLE 19.2** Parameter Estimates (standard errors in parentheses)

| | $\beta_1$ | $\beta_2$ | $\beta_3$ | $\beta_4$ | $\beta_5$ | $\beta_6$ | $\rho$ |
|---|---|---|---|---|---|---|---|
| OLS | −26.43 | 1.6017 | −0.06166 | −0.1408 | −0.001293 | −0.01518 | 0.0000 |
| $R^2 = 0.96780$ | (1.835) | (0.1790) | (0.03872) | (0.1628) | (0.09664) | (0.004393) | (0.0000) |
| Prais– | −18.58 | 0.7447 | −0.1138 | −0.1364 | −0.008956 | 0.006689 | 0.9567 |
| Winsten | (1.768) | (0.1761) | (0.03689) | (0.1528) | (0.07213) | (0.004974) | (0.04078) |
| Cochrane– | −18.76 | 0.7300 | −0.1080 | −0.06675 | 0.04190 | −0.0001653 | 0.9695 |
| Orcutt | (1.382) | (0.1377) | (0.02885) | (0.1201) | (0.05713) | (0.004082) | (0.03434) |
| Maximum | −16.25 | 0.4690 | −0.1387 | −0.09682 | −0.001485 | 0.01280 | 0.9792 |
| Likelihood | (1.391) | (0.1350) | (0.02794) | (0.1270) | (0.05198) | (0.004427) | (0.02844) |
| AR(2) | −19.45 | 0.8116 | −0.09538 | −0.09099 | 0.04091 | −0.001374 | 0.8610 |
| | (1.495) | (0.1502) | (0.03117) | (0.1297) | (0.06558) | (0.004227) | (0.07053) |

and Box–Ljung statistics of 36.217 and 38.789, respectively, both of which are larger than the critical value from the chi-squared table of 11.01. We regressed the least squares residuals on the independent variables and five lags of the residuals. (The missing values in the first five years were filled with zeros.) The coefficients on the lagged residuals and the associated $t$ statistics are 0.741 (4.635), 0.153 (0.789), −0.246 (−1.262), 0.0942 (0.472), and −0.125 (−0.658). The $R^2$ in this regression is 0.549086, which produces a chi-squared value of 28.55. This is larger than the critical value of 11.01, so once again, the null hypothesis of zero autocorrelation is rejected. Finally, the Durbin–Watson statistic is 0.425007. For 5 regressors and 52 observations, the critical value of $d_L$ is 1.36, so on this basis as well, the null hypothesis $\rho = 0$ would pe rejected. The plot of the residuals shown in Figure 19.4 seems consistent with this conclusion.

**FIGURE 19.4** Least Squares Residuals.

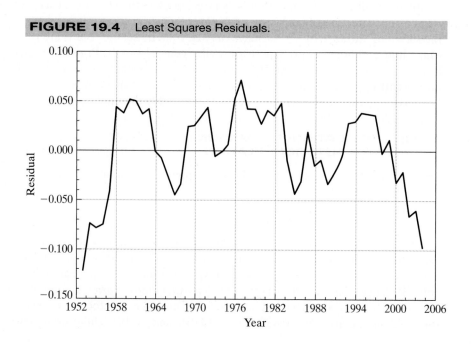

The Prais and Winsten FGLS estimates appear in the second row of Table 19.2 followed by the Cochrane and Orcutt results then the maximum likelihood estimates. [The autocorrelation coefficient computed using (19-19) is 0.78750. The MLE is computed using the Beach and MacKinnon algorithm. See Section 16.9.2.b.] Finally, we fit the AR(2) model by first regressing the least squares residuals, $e_t$, on $e_{t-1}$ and $e_{t-2}$ (without a constant term and filling the first two observations with zeros). The two estimates are 0.751941 and $-0.022464$, respectively. With the estimates of $\theta_1$ and $\theta_2$, we transformed the data using $y_t^* = y_t - \theta_1 y_{t-1} - \theta_2 y_{t-2}$ and likewise for each regressor. Two observations are then discarded, so the AR(2) regression uses 50 observations while the Prais–Winsten estimator uses 52 and the Cochrane–Orcutt regression uses 51. In each case, the autocorrelation of the FGLS residuals is computed and reported in the last column of the table.

One might want to examine the residuals after estimation to ascertain whether the AR(1) model is appropriate. In the results just presented, there are two large autocorrelation coefficients listed with the residual based tests, and in computing the LM statistic, we found that the first two coefficients were statistically significant. If the AR(1) model is appropriate, then one should find that only the coefficient on the first lagged residual is statistically significant in this auxiliary, second-step regression. Another indicator is provided by the FGLS residuals, themselves. After computing the FGLS regression, the estimated residuals,

$$\hat{\varepsilon} = y_t - \mathbf{x}_t'\hat{\boldsymbol{\beta}}$$

will still be autocorrelated. In our results using the Prais–Winsten estimates, the autocorrelation of the FGLS residuals is 0.957. The associated Durbin–Watson statistic is 0.0867. This is to be expected. However, if the model is correct, then the transformed residuals

$$\hat{u}_t = \hat{\varepsilon}_t - \hat{\rho}\hat{\varepsilon}_{t-1}$$

should be at least close to nonautocorrelated. But, for our data, the autocorrelation of these adjusted residuals is only 0.292 with a Durbin–Watson statistic of 1.416. The value of $d_L$ for one regressor ($u_{t-1}$) and 50 observations is 1.50. It appears on this basis that, in fact, the AR(1) model has largely completed the specification.

### 19.9.3 ESTIMATION WITH A LAGGED DEPENDENT VARIABLE

In Section 19.5.1, we considered the problem of estimation by least squares when the model contains both autocorrelation and lagged dependent variable(s). Because the OLS estimator is inconsistent, the residuals on which an estimator of $\rho$ would be based are likewise inconsistent. Therefore, $\hat{\rho}$ will be inconsistent as well. The consequence is that the FGLS estimators described earlier are not usable in this case. There is, however, an alternative way to proceed, based on the method of instrumental variables. The method of instrumental variables was introduced in Section 12.3. To review, the general problem is that in the regression model, if

$$\text{plim}(1/T)\mathbf{X}'\boldsymbol{\varepsilon} \neq \mathbf{0},$$

then the least squares estimator is not consistent. A consistent estimator is

$$\mathbf{b}_{\text{IV}} = (\mathbf{Z}'\mathbf{X})^{-1}(\mathbf{Z}'\mathbf{y}),$$

where $\mathbf{Z}$ is a set of $K$ variables chosen such that $\text{plim}(1/T)\mathbf{Z}'\boldsymbol{\varepsilon} = \mathbf{0}$ but $\text{plim}(1/T)\mathbf{Z}'\mathbf{X} \neq \mathbf{0}$. For the purpose of consistency only, any such set of instrumental variables will suffice. The relevance of that here is that the obstacle to consistent FGLS is, at least for the present, is the lack of a consistent estimator of $\rho$. By using the technique of instrumental variables, we may estimate $\boldsymbol{\beta}$ consistently, then estimate $\rho$ and proceed.

Hatanaka (1974, 1976) has devised an efficient two-step estimator based on this principle. To put the estimator in the current context, we consider estimation of the model

$$y_t = \mathbf{x}'_t \boldsymbol{\beta} + \gamma y_{t-1} + \varepsilon_t,$$
$$\varepsilon_t = \rho \varepsilon_{t-1} + u_t.$$

To get to the second step of FGLS, we require a consistent estimator of the slope parameters. These estimates can be obtained using an IV estimator, where the column of $\mathbf{Z}$ corresponding to $y_{t-1}$ is the only one that need be different from that of $\mathbf{X}$. An appropriate instrument can be obtained by using the fitted values in the regression of $y_t$ on $\mathbf{x}_t$ and $\mathbf{x}_{t-1}$. The residuals from the IV regression are then used to construct

$$\hat{\rho} = \frac{\sum_{t=3}^{T} \hat{\varepsilon}_t \hat{\varepsilon}_{t-1}}{\sum_{t=3}^{T} \hat{\varepsilon}_t^2}, \tag{19-33}$$

where

$$\hat{\varepsilon}_t = y_t - \mathbf{b}'_{IV}\mathbf{x}_t - c_{IV}y_{t-1}.$$

FGLS estimates may now be computed by regressing $y_{*_t} = y_t - \hat{\rho} y_{t-1}$ on

$$\mathbf{x}_{*_t} = \mathbf{x}_t - \hat{\rho}\mathbf{x}_{t-1},$$
$$y_{*_{t-1}} = y_{t-1} - \hat{\rho} y_{t-2},$$
$$\hat{\varepsilon}_{t-1} = y_{t-1} - \mathbf{b}'_{IV}\mathbf{x}_{t-1} - c_{IV}y_{t-2}.$$

Let $d$ be the coefficient on $\hat{\varepsilon}_{t-1}$ in this regression. The efficient estimator of $\rho$ is

$$\hat{\hat{\rho}} = \hat{\rho} + d.$$

Appropriate asymptotic standard errors for the estimators, including $\hat{\hat{\rho}}$, are obtained from the $s^2[\mathbf{X}'_*\mathbf{X}_*]^{-1}$ computed at the second step. Hatanaka shows that these estimators are asymptotically equivalent to maximum likelihood estimators.

## 19.10 AUTOCORRELATION IN PANEL DATA

The extension of the AR(1) model to stationary panel data would mirror the procedures for a single time series. The standard model is

$$y_{it} = \mathbf{x}'_{it}\boldsymbol{\beta} + c_i + \varepsilon_{it}, \varepsilon_{it} = \rho\varepsilon_{i,t-1} + v_{it}, i = 1, \ldots, n, t = 1, \ldots, T_i.$$

[See, e.g., Baltagi (2005, Section 5.2).] The same considerations would apply to the fixed and random effects cases, so we have left the model in generic form. The practical issues are how to obtain an estimate of $\rho$ and how to carry out an FGLS procedure.

Assuming for the moment that $\rho$ is known, the Prais and Winsten transformation,

$$y_{i1}^* = (1 - \rho^2)^{1/2} y_{i1}, \qquad \mathbf{x}_{i1}^* = (1 - \rho^2)^{1/2} \mathbf{x}_{i1},$$
$$y_{it}^* = y_{it} - \rho y_{i,t-1}, \qquad \mathbf{x}_{it}^* = \mathbf{x}_{it} - \rho \mathbf{x}_{i,t-1}, \tag{19-34}$$

produces the transformed model

$$y_{it}^* = (\mathbf{x}_{it}^*)' \boldsymbol{\beta} + c_{it}^* + v_{it}, \, v_{it} \mid \mathbf{X}_i \sim 0, \sigma_v^2. \tag{19-35}$$

[See (19-28).] This would seem to restore the original panel data model, save for a potentially complicated loose end. The common effect in the transformed model, $c_{it}^*$, is treated differently for the first observation from the remaining $T_i - 1$, hence the necessity for the double subscript in (19-35). The resulting model is no longer a "common effect" model. Baltagi and Li (1991) have devised a full FGLS treatment for the balanced panel random effects case, including the asymmetric treatment of $c_i$. The method is shown in detail in Baltagi (2005, pp. 84–85). The procedure as documented can be generalized to the unbalanced case fairly easily, but overall is quite complicated, again owing to the special treatment of the first observation. FGLS estimation of the fixed effects model is more complicated yet, because there is no simple transformation comparable to differences from group means that will remove the common effect in (19-35). For least squares estimation of $\boldsymbol{\beta}$ in (19-35), we would have to use brute force, with $c_{it}^* = \alpha_i d_{it}$ where $d_{it} = (1 - \rho^2)^{1/2}$ for individual $i$ and $t = 1$ and $d_{it} = 1 - \rho$ for individual $i$ and $t > 1$. (In principle, the Frisch–Waugh result could be applied group by group to transform the observations for estimation of $\boldsymbol{\beta}$. However, the application would involve a different tranformation for the first observation and the mean of observations $2 - T_i$ rather than the full group mean.)

For better or worse, dropping the first observation is a practical compromise that produces a large payoff. The different approaches based on $T_i - 1$ observations remain consistent in $n$, just as in the single time-series case. The question of efficiency might be raised here as it was in an earlier literature in the time-series case [see, e.g., Maeshiro (1979)]. In a given panel, $T_i$ may well be fairly small. However, with the assumption of common $\rho$, this case is likely to be much more favorable than the single time-series case, because the way the model is structured, estimation of $\boldsymbol{\beta}$ based on the Cochrane–Orcutt transformation becomes analogous to the random effects case with $\sum_{i=1}^n (T_i - 1)$ observations. If $n$ is even moderately sized, the efficiency question is likely to be a moot point.

There remains the problem of estimation of $\rho$. For either fixed or random effects case, the within (dummy variables) estimator produces a consistent estimator of $\boldsymbol{\beta}$ and a usable set of residuals, $e_{it}$ that can be used to estimate $\rho$ with $\left[ \sum_{i=1}^n \sum_{t=2}^{T_i} e_{it} e_{i,t-1} \right] / \left[ \sum_{i=1}^n \sum_{t=2}^{T_i} e_{i,t}^2 \right]$. [Baltagi and Li (1991a) suggest some alternative estimators that may have better small sample properties.]

### Example 19.5  Panel Data Models with Autocorrelation

Munnell (1990) analyzed the productivity of public capital at the state level using a Cobb–Douglas production function. We will use the data from that study to estimate a log-linear regression model

$$\ln gsp_{it} = \alpha + \beta_1 \ln p\_cap_{it} + \beta_2 \ln hwy_{it} + \beta_3 \ln water_{it}$$
$$+ \beta_4 \ln util_{it} + \beta_5 \ln emp_{it} + \beta_6 unemp_{it} + \varepsilon_{it} + u_i,$$

**TABLE 19.3** Estimated Statewide Production Function.

| | OLS | | Fixed Effects | | Random Effects FGLS | |
|---|---|---|---|---|---|---|
| | $\rho = 0$ | AR(1) | $\rho = 0$ | AR(1) | $\rho = 0$ | AR(1) |
| | Estimate (Std. Err.[a]) | Estimate (Std. Err.) | Estimate (Std. Err.) | Estimate (Std. Err.) | Estimate (Std. Err.) | Estimate (Std. Err.) |
| $\alpha$ | 1.9260 (0.2143) | 2.1463 (0.01806) | | | 2.1608 (0.1380) | 2.8226 (0.1537) |
| $\beta_1$ | 0.3120 (0.04678) | 0.2615 (0.01338) | 0.2350 (0.02621) | 0.04041 (0.02383) | 0.2755 (0.01972) | 0.1342 (0.01943) |
| $\beta_2$ | 0.05888 (0.05078) | 0.06788 (0.01802) | 0.07675 (0.03124) | −0.05831 (0.06101) | 0.06167 (0.02168) | 0.04585 (0.03044) |
| $\beta_3$ | 0.1186 (0.0345) | 0.09225 (0.01464) | 0.0786 (0.0150) | 0.04934 (0.02098) | 0.07572 (0.01381) | 0.04879 (0.01911) |
| $\beta_4$ | 0.00856 (0.0406) | −0.006299 (0.01432) | −0.11478 (0.01814) | −0.07459 (0.02759) | −0.09672 (0.01683) | −0.07977 (0.02273) |
| $\beta_5$ | 0.5497 (0.0677) | 0.6337 (0.01916) | 0.8011 (0.02976) | 1.0534 (0.03677) | 0.7450 (0.02482) | 0.08931 (0.03011) |
| $\beta_6$ | −0.00727 (0.002946) | −0.009327 (0.00083) | −0.005179 (0.000980) | −0.002924 (0.000817) | −0.005963 (0.0008814) | −0.005374 (0.0007513) |
| $\sigma_\varepsilon$ | 0.0854228 | 0.105407 | 0.0367649 | 0.074687 | .0366974[b] | 0.074687[c] |
| $\sigma_u$ | | | | | .0875682[b] | 0.074380[c] |

[a] Robust (cluster) standard errors in parentheses
[b] Based on OLS and LSDV residuals
[c] Based on OLS/AR(1) and LSDV/AR(1) residuals

where the variables in the model are

$$
\begin{aligned}
gsp &= \text{gross state product,}\\
p\_cap &= \text{public capital,}\\
hwy &= \text{highway capital,}\\
water &= \text{water utility capital,}\\
util &= \text{utility capital,}\\
pc &= \text{private capital,}\\
emp &= \text{employment (labor),}\\
unemp &= \text{unemployment rate.}
\end{aligned}
$$

In Example 9.9, we estimated the parameters of the model under the fixed and random effects assumptions. The results are repeated in Table 19.3. Using the fixed effects residuals, the estimate of $\rho$ is 0.717897, which is quite large. We reestimated the two models using the Cochrane–Orcutt transformation. The results are shown at the right in Table 19.3. The estimates of $\sigma_\varepsilon$ and $\sigma_u$ in each case are obtained as $1/(1-r)^2$ times the estimated variances in the transformed model.

There are several strategies available for testing for serial correlation in a panel data set. [See Baltagi (2005, pp. 93–103).] In general, an obstacle to a simple test against the null hypothesis of no autocorrelation is the possible presence of a time-invariant common effect in the model,

$$y_{it} = c_i + \mathbf{x}'_{it}\boldsymbol{\beta} + \varepsilon_{it}.$$

Under the alternative hypothesis, $\text{Corr}(\varepsilon_{it}, \varepsilon_{i,t-1}) = \rho$. Many variants of the model, based on $AR(1)$, $MA(1)$, and other specifications have been analyzed. We consider the first, as it is the standard framework in the absence of a specific model that suggests another process. The LM statistic is based on the within-groups (LSDV) residuals from the fixed effects specification,

$$\text{LM} = \left( \frac{NT^2}{T-1} \right) \left( \frac{\sum_{i=1}^{n} \sum_{t=2}^{T} e_{it} e_{i,t-1}}{\sum_{i=1}^{n} \sum_{t=1}^{T} e_{it}^2} \right)^2.$$

Under the null hypothesis that $\rho = 0$, the limiting distribution of LM is chi-squared with one degree of freedom. The Durbin–Watson statistic is obtained by omitting $[NT^2/(T-1)]$ and replacing $e_{it} e_{i,t-1}$ with $(e_{it} - e_{i,t-1})^2$. Bhargava et al. (1982) showed that the Durbin–Watson version of the test is locally most powerful in the neighborhood of $\rho = 0$. In the typical panel, the data set is large enough that the advantage over the simpler LM statistic is unlikely to be substantial. Both tests will suffer from a loss of power if the model is a random effects model. Baltagi and Li (1991a,b) have devised several test statistics that are appropriate for the random effects specification. Wooldridge (2002a) proposes an alternative approach based on first differences that will be invariant to the presence of fixed or random effects.

## 19.11 COMMON FACTORS

We saw in Example 19.2 that misspecification of an equation could create the appearance of serially correlated disturbances when, in fact, there are none. An orthodox (perhaps somewhat optimistic) purist might argue that autocorrelation is *always* an artifact of misspecification. Although this view might be extreme [see, e.g., Hendry (1980) for a more moderate, but still strident statement], it does suggest a useful point. It might be useful if we could examine the specification of a model statistically with this consideration in mind. The test for **common factors** is such a test. [See, as well, the aforementioned paper by Mizon (1995).]

The assumption that the correctly specified model is

$$y_t = \mathbf{x}_t'\boldsymbol{\beta} + \varepsilon_t, \quad \varepsilon_t = \rho \varepsilon_{t-1} + u_t, \quad t = 1, \ldots, T$$

implies the "reduced form,"

$$M_0: y_t = \rho y_{t-1} + (\mathbf{x}_t - \rho \mathbf{x}_{t-1})'\boldsymbol{\beta} + u_t, \quad t = 2, \ldots, T,$$

where $u_t$ is free from serial correlation. The second of these is actually a restriction on the model

$$M_1: y_t = \rho y_{t-1} + \mathbf{x}_t'\boldsymbol{\beta} + \mathbf{x}_{t-1}'\boldsymbol{\alpha} + u_t, \quad t = 2, \ldots, T,$$

in which, once again, $u_t$ is a classical disturbance. The second model contains $2K+1$ parameters, but if the model is correct, then $\boldsymbol{\alpha} = -\rho\boldsymbol{\beta}$ and there are only $K+1$ parameters and $K$ restrictions. Both $M_0$ and $M_1$ can be estimated by least squares, although $M_0$ is a nonlinear model. One might then test the restrictions of $M_0$ using an $F$ test. This test will be valid asymptotically, although its exact distribution in finite samples will not be precisely $F$. In large samples, $KF$ will converge to a chi-squared statistic, so we use the $F$ distribution as usual to be conservative. There is a minor practical complication in implementing this test. Some elements of $\alpha$ may not be estimable. For example, if $\mathbf{x}_t$ contains a constant term, then the one in $\alpha$ is unidentified. If $\mathbf{x}_t$ contains both current and lagged values of a variable, then the one period lagged value will appear twice in $M_1$, once in $\mathbf{x}_t$ as the lagged value and once in $\mathbf{x}_{t-1}$ as the current value. There are other combinations that will be problematic, so the actual number of restrictions that appear in the test is reduced to the number of identified parameters in $\alpha$.

### Example 19.6   Test for Common Factors

We will reexamine the model estimated in Section 19.9.2. The base model is

$$\ln \frac{G_t}{Pop_t} = \beta_1 + \beta_2 \ln \frac{I_t}{Pop_t} + \beta_3 \ln P_{G,t} + \beta_4 \ln P_{NC,t} + \beta_5 \ln P_{UC,t} + \beta_6 t + \varepsilon_t.$$

If the AR(1) model is appropriate for $\varepsilon_t$, that is, $\varepsilon_t = \rho \varepsilon_{t-1} + u_t$, then the restricted model,

$$\ln \frac{G_t}{Pop_t} = \rho \left( \ln \frac{G_{t-1}}{Pop_{t-1}} \right) + \beta_1 + \beta_2 \left( \ln \frac{I_t}{Pop_t} - \rho \ln \frac{I_{t-1}}{Pop_{t-1}} \right) + \beta_3 \left( \ln P_{G,t} - \rho \ln P_{G,t-1} \right)$$

$$+ \beta_4 \left( \ln P_{NC,t} - \rho \ln P_{NC,t-1} \right) + \beta_5 \left( \ln P_{UC,t} - \rho \ln P_{UC,t-1} \right) + \beta_6 \left[ t - \rho(t-1) \right] + u_t,$$

with 7 free coefficients will not significantly degrate the fit of the unrestricted model,

$$\ln \frac{G_t}{Pop_t} = \rho \left( \ln \frac{G_{t-1}}{Pop_{t-1}} \right) + \beta_1 + \alpha_1 + \beta_2 \ln \frac{I_t}{Pop_t} + \alpha_2 \ln \frac{I_{t-1}}{Pop_{t-1}} + \beta_3 \ln P_{G,t} + \alpha_3 \ln P_{G,t-1}$$

$$+ \beta_4 \ln P_{NC,t} + \alpha_4 \ln P_{NC,t-1} + \beta_5 \ln P_{UC,t} + \alpha_5 \ln P_{UC,t-1} + \beta_6 t + \alpha_6(t-1) + u_t,$$

which has 13 coefficients. Note, however, that $\alpha_1$ and $\alpha_6$ are not identified [because $t = (t-1) + 1$]. Thus, the common factor restriction imposes four restrictions on the model. We fit the unrestricted model [minus one constant and $(t-1)$] by ordinary least squares and obtained a sum of squared residuals of 0.00737717. We fit the restricted model by nonlinear least squares, using the OLS coefficients from the base model as starting values for $\beta$ and zero for $\rho$. (See Section 11.2.5.) The sum of squared residuals is 0.01084939. This produces an $F$ statistic of

$$\frac{(0.10184939 - 0.00737717)/4}{0.00737717/(51 - 11)} = 4.707,$$

which is larger than the critical value with 4 and 40 degrees of freedom of 2.606. Thus, we would conclude that the AR(1) model would not be appropriate for this specification and these data.

## 19.12   FORECASTING IN THE PRESENCE OF AUTOCORRELATION

For purposes of forecasting, we refer first to the transformed model,

$$y_{*_t} = \mathbf{x}'_{*_t} \beta + \varepsilon_{*_t}.$$

Suppose that the process generating $\varepsilon_t$ is an AR(1) and that $\rho$ is known. This model is a classical regression model, so the results of Section 5.6 may be used. The optimal forecast of $y^0_{*_{T+1}}$, given $\mathbf{x}^0_{T+1}$ and $\mathbf{x}_T$ (i.e., $\mathbf{x}^0_{*_{T+1}} = \mathbf{x}^0_{T+1} - \rho \mathbf{x}_T$), is

$$\hat{y}^0_{*_{T+1}} = \mathbf{x}^{0\prime}_{*_{T+1}} \hat{\beta}.$$

Disassembling $\hat{y}^0_{*T+1}$, we find that

$$\hat{y}^0_{T+1} - \rho y_T = \mathbf{x}^{0\prime}_{T+1}\hat{\boldsymbol{\beta}} - \rho \mathbf{x}'_T \hat{\boldsymbol{\beta}},$$

or

$$\hat{y}^0_{T+1} = \mathbf{x}^{0\prime}_{T+1}\hat{\boldsymbol{\beta}} + \rho(y_T - \mathbf{x}'_T \hat{\boldsymbol{\beta}})$$
$$= \mathbf{x}^{0\prime}_{T+1}\hat{\boldsymbol{\beta}} + \rho e_T. \qquad \textbf{(19-36)}$$

Thus, we carry forward a proportion $\rho$ of the estimated disturbance in the preceding period. This step can be justified by reference to

$$E[\varepsilon_{T+1} \mid \varepsilon_T] = \rho \varepsilon_T.$$

It can also be shown that to forecast $n$ periods ahead, we would use

$$\hat{y}^0_{T+n} = \mathbf{x}^{0\prime}_{T+n}\hat{\boldsymbol{\beta}} + \rho^n e_T.$$

The extension to higher-order autoregressions is direct. For a second-order model, for example,

$$\hat{y}^0_{T+n} = \hat{\boldsymbol{\beta}}'\mathbf{x}^0_{T+n} + \theta_1 e_{T+n-1} + \theta_2 e_{T+n-2}. \qquad \textbf{(19-37)}$$

For residuals that are outside the sample period, we use the recursion

$$e_s = \theta_1 e_{s-1} + \theta_2 e_{s-2}, \qquad \textbf{(19-38)}$$

beginning with the last two residuals within the sample.

Moving average models are somewhat simpler, as the autocorrelation lasts for only $Q$ periods. For an MA(1) model, for the first postsample period,

$$\hat{y}^0_{T+1} = \mathbf{x}^0_{T+1}{}'\hat{\boldsymbol{\beta}} + \hat{\varepsilon}_{T+1},$$

where

$$\hat{\varepsilon}_{T+1} = \hat{u}_{T+1} - \lambda \hat{u}_T.$$

Therefore, a forecast of $\varepsilon_{T+1}$ will use all previous residuals. One way to proceed is to accumulate $\hat{\varepsilon}_{T+1}$ from the recursion

$$\hat{u}_t = \hat{\varepsilon}_t + \lambda \hat{u}_{t-1},$$

with $\hat{u}_{T+1} = \hat{u}_0 = 0$ and $\hat{\varepsilon}_t = (y_t - \mathbf{x}'_t \hat{\boldsymbol{\beta}})$. After the first postsample period,

$$\hat{\varepsilon}_{T+n} = \hat{u}_{T+n} - \lambda \hat{u}_{T+n-1} = 0.$$

If the parameters of the disturbance process are known, then the variances for the forecast errors can be computed using the results of Section 5.6. For an AR(1) disturbance, the estimated variance would be

$$s^2_f = \hat{\sigma}^2_\varepsilon + (\mathbf{x}_t - \rho \mathbf{x}_{t-1})'\{\text{Est. Var}[\hat{\boldsymbol{\beta}}]\}(\mathbf{x}_t - \rho \mathbf{x}_{t-1}). \qquad \textbf{(19-39)}$$

For a higher-order process, it is only necessary to modify the calculation of $\mathbf{x}_{*_t}$ accordingly. The forecast variances for an MA(1) process are somewhat more involved. Details may be found in Judge et al. (1985) and Hamilton (1994). If the parameters of the disturbance process, $\rho, \lambda, \theta_j$, and so on, are estimated as well, then the forecast variance will be greater. For an AR(1) model, the necessary correction to the forecast variance of the $n$-period-ahead forecast error is $\hat{\sigma}_\varepsilon^2 n^2 \rho^{2(n-1)}/T$. [For a one-period-ahead forecast, this merely adds a term, $\hat{\sigma}_\varepsilon^2 / T$ in (19-39)]. Higher-order AR and MA processes are analyzed in Baillie (1979). Finally, if the regressors are stochastic, the expressions become more complex by another order of magnitude.

If $\rho$ is known, then (19-36) provides the best linear unbiased forecast of $y_{t+1}$.[15] If, however, $\rho$ must be estimated, then this assessment must be modified. There is information about $\varepsilon_{t+1}$ embodied in $e_t$. Having to estimate $\rho$, however, implies that some or all the value of this information is offset by the variation introduced into the forecast by including the stochastic component $\hat{\rho} e_t$.[16] Whether (19-36) is preferable to the obvious expedient $\hat{y}^0_{T+n} = \hat{\boldsymbol{\beta}}' \mathbf{x}^0_{T+n}$ in a small sample when $\rho$ is estimated remains to be settled.

## 19.13 AUTOREGRESSIVE CONDITIONAL HETEROSCEDASTICITY

Heteroscedasticity is often associated with cross-sectional data, whereas time series are usually studied in the context of homoscedastic processes. In analyses of macroeconomic data, Engle (1982, 1983) and Cragg (1982) found evidence that for some kinds of data, the disturbance variances in time-series models were less stable than usually assumed. Engle's results suggested that in models of inflation, large and small forecast errors appeared to occur in clusters, suggesting a form of heteroscedasticity in which the variance of the forecast error depends on the size of the previous disturbance. He suggested the autoregressive, conditionally heteroscedastic, or ARCH, model as an alternative to the usual time-series process. More recent studies of financial markets suggest that the phenomenon is quite common. The ARCH model has proven to be useful in studying the volatility of inflation [Coulson and Robins (1985)], the term structure of interest rates [Engle, Hendry, and Trumble (1985)], the volatility of stock market returns [Engle, Lilien, and Robins (1987)], and the behavior of foreign exchange markets [Domowitz and Hakkio (1985) and Bollerslev and Ghysels (1996)], to name but a few. This section will describe specification, estimation, and testing, in the basic formulations of the ARCH model and some extensions.[17]

### Example 19.7 Stochastic Volatility
Figure 19.5 shows Bollerslev and Ghysel's 1974 data on the daily percentage nominal return for the Deutschmark/Pound exchange rate. (These data are given in Appendix Table F19.1.) The variation in the series appears to be fluctuating, with several clusters of large and small movements.

---

[15]See Goldberger (1962).

[16]See Baillie (1979).

[17]Engle and Rothschild (1992) give a survey of this literature which describes many extensions. Mills (1993) also presents several applications. See, as well, Bollerslev (1986) and Li, Ling, and McAleer (2001). See McCullough and Renfro (1999) for discussion of estimation of this model.

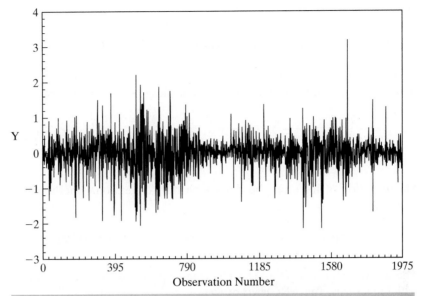

**FIGURE 19.5**   Nominal Exchange Rate Returns.

### 19.13.1   THE ARCH(1) MODEL

The simplest form of this model is the ARCH(1) model,

$$y_t = \mathbf{x}_t'\boldsymbol{\beta} + \varepsilon_t,$$

$$\varepsilon_t = u_t\sqrt{\alpha_0 + \alpha_1\varepsilon_{t-1}^2},$$

$$(19\text{-}40)$$

where $u_t$ is distributed as standard normal.[18] It follows that $E[\varepsilon_t \mid \mathbf{x}_t, \varepsilon_{t-1}] = 0$, so that $E[\varepsilon_t \mid \mathbf{x}_t] = 0$ and $E[y_t \mid \mathbf{x}_t] = \mathbf{x}_t'\boldsymbol{\beta}$. Therefore, this model is a classical regression model. But

$$\text{Var}[\varepsilon_t \mid \varepsilon_{t-1}] = E[\varepsilon_t^2 \mid \varepsilon_{t-1}] = E[u_t^2][\alpha_0 + \alpha_1\varepsilon_{t-1}^2] = \alpha_0 + \alpha_1\varepsilon_{t-1}^2,$$

so $\varepsilon_t$ is *conditionally heteroscedastic*, not with respect to $\mathbf{x}_t$ as we considered in Chapter 8, but with respect to $\varepsilon_{t-1}$. The unconditional variance of $\varepsilon_t$ is

$$\text{Var}[\varepsilon_t] = \text{Var}\{E[\varepsilon_t \mid \varepsilon_{t-1}]\} + E\{\text{Var}[\varepsilon_t \mid \varepsilon_{t-1}]\} = \alpha_0 + \alpha_1 E[\varepsilon_{t-1}^2] = \alpha_0 + \alpha_1\text{Var}[\varepsilon_{t-1}].$$

If the process generating the disturbances is weakly (covariance) stationary (see Definition 19.2),[19] then the unconditional variance is not changing over time so

$$\text{Var}[\varepsilon_t] = \text{Var}[\varepsilon_{t-1}] = \alpha_0 + \alpha_1\text{Var}[\varepsilon_{t-1}] = \frac{\alpha_0}{1-\alpha_1}.$$

For this ratio to be finite and positive, $|\alpha_1|$ must be less than 1. Then, unconditionally, $\varepsilon_t$ is distributed with mean zero and variance $\sigma^2 = \alpha_0/(1-\alpha_1)$. Therefore, the model

---

[18]The assumption that $u_t$ has unit variance is not a restriction. The scaling implied by any other variance would be absorbed by the other parameters.

[19]This discussion will draw on the results and terminology of time-series analysis in Section 19.3 and Chapter 21. The reader may wish to peruse this material at this point.

obeys the classical assumptions, and ordinary least squares is the most efficient *linear* unbiased estimator of $\beta$.

But there is a more efficient *nonlinear* estimator. The log-likelihood function for this model is given by Engle (1982). Conditioned on starting values $y_0$ and $\mathbf{x}_0$ (and $\varepsilon_0$), the conditional log-likelihood for observations $t = 1, \ldots, T$ is the one we examined in Section 16.9.2.a for the general heteroscedastic regression model [see (16-52)],

$$
\ln L = -\frac{T}{2}\ln(2\pi) - \frac{1}{2}\sum_{t=1}^{T}\ln\left(\alpha_0 + \alpha_1\varepsilon_{t-1}^2\right) - \frac{1}{2}\sum_{t=1}^{T}\frac{\varepsilon_t^2}{\alpha_0 + \alpha_1\varepsilon_{t-1}^2}, \quad \varepsilon_t = y_t - \beta'\mathbf{x}_t.
$$

$$(19\text{-}41)$$

Maximization of $\log L$ can be done with the conventional methods, as discussed in Appendix E.[20]

### 19.13.2 ARCH($q$), ARCH-IN-MEAN, AND GENERALIZED ARCH MODELS

The natural extension of the ARCH(1) model presented before is a more general model with longer lags. The ARCH($q$) process,

$$
\sigma_t^2 = \alpha_0 + \alpha_1\varepsilon_{t-1}^2 + \alpha_2\varepsilon_{t-2}^2 + \cdots + \alpha_q\varepsilon_{t-q}^2,
$$

is a $q$th order moving average [MA($q$)] process. (Much of the analysis of the model parallels the results in Chapter 21 for more general time-series models.) [Once again, see Engle (1982).] This section will generalize the ARCH($q$) model, as suggested by Bollerslev (1986), in the direction of the autoregressive-moving average (ARMA) models of Section 21.2.1. The discussion will parallel his development, although many details are omitted for brevity. The reader is referred to that paper for background and for some of the less critical details.

Among the many variants of the capital asset pricing model (CAPM) is an intertemporal formulation by Merton (1980) that suggests an approximate linear relationship between the return and variance of the market portfolio. One of the possible flaws in this model is its assumption of a constant variance of the market portfolio. In this connection, then, the **ARCH-in-Mean,** or ARCH-M, model suggested by Engle, Lilien, and Robins (1987) is a natural extension. The model states that

$$
y_t = \beta'\mathbf{x}_t + \delta\sigma_t^2 + \varepsilon_t,
$$

$$
\text{Var}[\varepsilon_t \mid \Psi_t] = \text{ARCH}(q).
$$

Among the interesting implications of this modification of the standard model is that under certain assumptions, $\delta$ is the coefficient of relative risk aversion. The ARCH-M model has been applied in a wide variety of studies of volatility in asset returns, including the daily Standard and Poor's Index [French, Schwert, and Stambaugh (1987)] and

---

[20]Engle (1982) and Judge et al. (1985, pp. 441–444) suggest a four-step procedure based on the method of scoring that resembles the two-step method we used for the multiplicative heteroscedasticity model in Section 8.8.1. However, the full MLE is now incorporated in most modern software, so the simple regression based methods, which are difficult to generalize, are less attractive in the current literature. But, see McCullough and Renfro (1999) and Fiorentini, Calzolari, and Panattoni (1996) for commentary and some cautions related to maximum likelihood estimation.

weekly New York Stock Exchange returns [Chou (1988)]. A lengthy list of applications is given in Bollerslev, Chou, and Kroner (1992).

The ARCH-M model has several noteworthy statistical characteristics. Unlike the standard regression model, misspecification of the variance function does affect the consistency of estimators of the parameters of the mean. [See Pagan and Ullah (1988) for formal analysis of this point.] Recall that in the classical regression setting, weighted least squares is consistent even if the weights are misspecified as long as the weights are uncorrelated with the disturbances. That is not true here. If the ARCH part of the model is misspecified, then conventional estimators of $\beta$ and $\delta$ will not be consistent. Bollerslev, Chou, and Kroner (1992) list a large number of studies that called into question the specification of the ARCH-M model, and they subsequently obtained quite different results after respecifying the model. A closely related practical problem is that the mean and variance parameters in this model are no longer uncorrelated. In analysis up to this point, we made quite profitable use of the block diagonality of the Hessian of the log-likelihood function for the model of heteroscedasticity. But the Hessian for the ARCH-M model is not block diagonal. In practical terms, the estimation problem cannot be segmented as we have done previously with the heteroscedastic regression model. All the parameters must be estimated simultaneously.

The model of generalized autoregressive conditional heteroscedasticity (GARCH) is defined as follows.[21] The underlying regression is the usual one in (19-40). *Conditioned on an information set at time t*, denoted $\Psi_t$, the distribution of the disturbance is assumed to be

$$\varepsilon_t \mid \Psi_t \sim N[0, \sigma_t^2],$$

where the conditional variance is

$$\sigma_t^2 = \alpha_0 + \delta_1 \sigma_{t-1}^2 + \delta_2 \sigma_{t-2}^2 + \cdots + \delta_p \sigma_{t-p}^2 + \alpha_1 \varepsilon_{t-1}^2 + \alpha_2 \varepsilon_{t-2}^2 + \cdots + \alpha_q \varepsilon_{t-q}^2. \quad \textbf{(19-42)}$$

Define

$$\mathbf{z}_t = \left[1, \sigma_{t-1}^2, \sigma_{t-2}^2, \ldots, \sigma_{t-p}^2, \varepsilon_{t-1}^2, \varepsilon_{t-2}^2, \ldots, \varepsilon_{t-q}^2\right]'$$

and

$$\boldsymbol{\gamma} = [\alpha_0, \delta_1, \delta_2, \ldots, \delta_p, \alpha_1, \ldots, \alpha_q]' = [\alpha_0, \boldsymbol{\delta}', \boldsymbol{\alpha}']'.$$

Then

$$\sigma_t^2 = \boldsymbol{\gamma}' \mathbf{z}_t.$$

Notice that the conditional variance is defined by an autoregressive-moving average [ARMA $(p, q)$] process in the innovations $\varepsilon_t^2$, exactly as in Section 21.2.1. The difference here is that the *mean* of the random variable of interest $y_t$ is described completely by a heteroscedastic, but otherwise ordinary, regression model. The *conditional variance,* however, evolves over time in what might be a very complicated manner, depending on the parameter values and on $p$ and $q$. The model in (19-42) is a GARCH($p, q$) model,

---

[21] As have most areas in time-series econometrics, the line of literature on GARCH models has progressed rapidly in recent years and will surely continue to do so. We have presented Bollerslev's model in some detail, despite many recent extensions, not only to introduce the topic as a bridge to the literature, but also because it provides a convenient and interesting setting in which to discuss several related topics such as double-length regression and pseudo–maximum likelihood estimation.

where $p$ refers, as before, to the order of the autoregressive part.[22] As Bollerslev (1986) demonstrates with an example, the virtue of this approach is that a GARCH model with a small number of terms appears to perform as well as or better than an ARCH model with many.

The **stationarity conditions** discussed in Section 21.2.2 are important in this context to ensure that the moments of the normal distribution are finite. The reason is that higher moments of the normal distribution are finite powers of the variance. A normal distribution with variance $\sigma_t^2$ has fourth moment $3\sigma_t^4$, sixth moment $15\sigma_t^6$, and so on. [The precise relationship of the even moments of the normal distribution to the variance is $\mu_{2k} = (\sigma^2)^k (2k)!/(k!2^k)$.] Simply ensuring that $\sigma_t^2$ is stable does not ensure that higher powers are as well.[23] Bollerslev presents a useful figure that shows the conditions needed to ensure stability for moments up to order 12 for a GARCH(1, 1) model and gives some additional discussion. For example, for a GARCH(1, 1) process, for the fourth moment to exist, $3\alpha_1^2 + 2\alpha_1\delta_1 + \delta_1^2$ must be less than 1.

It is convenient to write (19-42) in terms of polynomials in the lag operator (see Section 20.2.2):

$$\sigma_t^2 = \alpha_0 + D(L)\sigma_t^2 + A(L)\varepsilon_t^2.$$

As discussed in Section 20.2.2, the stationarity condition for such an equation is that the roots of the characteristic equation, $1 - D(z) = 0$, must lie outside the unit circle. For the present, we will assume that this case is true for the model we are considering and that $A(1) + D(1) < 1$. [This assumption is stronger than that needed to ensure stationarity in a higher-order autoregressive model, which would depend only on $D(L)$.] The implication is that the GARCH process is covariance stationary with $E[\varepsilon_t] = 0$ (unconditionally), $\text{Var}[\varepsilon_t] = \alpha_0/[1 - A(1) - D(1)]$, and $\text{Cov}[\varepsilon_t, \varepsilon_s] = 0$ for all $t \neq s$. Thus, unconditionally the model is the classical regression model that we examined in Chapters 2–7.

The usefulness of the GARCH specification is that it allows the variance to evolve over time in a way that is much more general than the simple specification of the ARCH model. The comparison between simple finite-distributed lag models and the dynamic regression model discussed in Chapter 20 is analogous. For the example discussed in his paper, Bollerslev reports that although Engle and Kraft's (1983) ARCH(8) model for the rate of inflation in the GNP deflator appears to remove all ARCH effects, a closer look reveals GARCH effects at several lags. By fitting a GARCH(1, 1) model to the same data, Bollerslev finds that the ARCH effects out to the same eight-period lag as fit by Engle and Kraft and his observed GARCH effects are all satisfactorily accounted for.

### 19.13.3 MAXIMUM LIKELIHOOD ESTIMATION OF THE GARCH MODEL

Bollerslev describes a method of estimation based on the BHHH algorithm. As he shows, the method is relatively simple, although with the line search and first derivative method that he suggests, it probably involves more computation and more iterations

---

[22]We have changed Bollerslev's notation slightly so as not to conflict with our previous presentation. He used $\beta$ instead of our $\delta$ in (19-42) and **b** instead of our $\beta$ in (19-40).

[23]The conditions cannot be imposed a priori. In fact, there is no nonzero set of parameters that guarantees stability of *all* moments, even though the normal distribution has finite moments of all orders. As such, the normality assumption must be viewed as an approximation.

than necessary. Following the suggestions of Harvey (1976), it turns out that there is a simpler way to estimate the GARCH model that is also very illuminating. This model is actually very similar to the more conventional model of multiplicative heteroscedasticity that we examined in Section 16.9.2.b.

For normally distributed disturbances, the log-likelihood for a sample of $T$ observations is[24]

$$\ln L = \sum_{t=1}^{T} -\frac{1}{2}\left[\ln(2\pi) + \ln \sigma_t^2 + \frac{\varepsilon_t^2}{\sigma_t^2}\right] = \sum_{t=1}^{T} \ln f_t(\boldsymbol{\theta}) = \sum_{t=1}^{T} l_t(\boldsymbol{\theta}),$$

where $\varepsilon_t = y_t - \mathbf{x}_t'\boldsymbol{\beta}$ and $\boldsymbol{\theta} = (\boldsymbol{\beta}', \alpha_0, \boldsymbol{\alpha}', \boldsymbol{\delta}')' = (\boldsymbol{\beta}', \boldsymbol{\gamma}')'$. Derivatives of $\ln L$ are obtained by summation. Let $l_t$ denote $\ln f_t(\boldsymbol{\theta})$. The first derivatives with respect to the variance parameters are

$$\frac{\partial l_t}{\partial \boldsymbol{\gamma}} = -\frac{1}{2}\left[\frac{1}{\sigma_t^2} - \frac{\varepsilon_t^2}{(\sigma_t^2)^2}\right]\frac{\partial \sigma_t^2}{\partial \boldsymbol{\gamma}} = \frac{1}{2}\left(\frac{1}{\sigma_t^2}\right)\frac{\partial \sigma_t^2}{\partial \boldsymbol{\gamma}}\left(\frac{\varepsilon_t^2}{\sigma_t^2} - 1\right) = \frac{1}{2}\left(\frac{1}{\sigma_t^2}\right)\mathbf{g}_t v_t = \mathbf{b}_t v_t.$$
$$(19\text{-}43)$$

Note that $E[v_t] = 0$. Suppose, for now, that there are no regression parameters. Newton's method for estimating the variance parameters would be

$$\hat{\boldsymbol{\gamma}}^{i+1} = \hat{\boldsymbol{\gamma}}^i - \mathbf{H}^{-1}\mathbf{g}, \qquad (19\text{-}44)$$

where $\mathbf{H}$ indicates the Hessian and $\mathbf{g}$ is the first derivatives vector. Following Harvey's suggestion (see Section 16.9.2.a), we will use the method of scoring instead. To do this, we make use of $E[v_t] = 0$ and $E[\varepsilon_t^2/\sigma_t^2] = 1$. After taking expectations in (19-43), the iteration reduces to a linear regression of $v_{*_t} = (1/\sqrt{2})v_t$ on regressors $\mathbf{w}_{*_t} = (1/\sqrt{2})\mathbf{g}_t/\sigma_t^2$. That is,

$$\hat{\boldsymbol{\gamma}}^{i+1} = \hat{\boldsymbol{\gamma}}^i + [\mathbf{W}_*'\mathbf{W}_*]^{-1}\mathbf{W}_*'\mathbf{v}_* = \hat{\boldsymbol{\gamma}}^i + [\mathbf{W}_*'\mathbf{W}_*]^{-1}\left(\frac{\partial \ln L}{\partial \boldsymbol{\gamma}}\right), \qquad (19\text{-}45)$$

where row $t$ of $\mathbf{W}_*$ is $\mathbf{w}_{*_t}'$. The iteration has converged when the slope vector is zero, which happens when the first derivative vector is zero. When the iterations are complete, the estimated asymptotic covariance matrix is simply

$$\text{Est. Asy. Var}[\hat{\boldsymbol{\gamma}}] = [\hat{\mathbf{W}}_*'\mathbf{W}_*]^{-1}$$

based on the estimated parameters.

The usefulness of the result just given is that $E[\partial^2 \ln L/\partial\boldsymbol{\gamma}\,\partial\boldsymbol{\beta}']$ is, in fact, zero. Because the expected Hessian is block diagonal, applying the method of scoring to the full parameter vector can proceed in two parts, exactly as it did in Section 16.9.2.a for the multiplicative heteroscedasticity model. That is, the updates for the mean and variance parameter vectors can be computed separately. Consider then the slope parameters, $\boldsymbol{\beta}$.

---

[24]There are three minor errors in Bollerslev's derivation that we note here to avoid the apparent inconsistencies. In his (22), $\frac{1}{2}h_t$ should be $\frac{1}{2}h_t^{-1}$. In (23), $-2h_t^{-2}$ should be $-h_t^{-2}$. In (28), $h\,\partial h/\partial \omega$ should, in each case, be $(1/h)\,\partial h/\partial \omega$. [In his (8), $\alpha_0\alpha_1$ should be $\alpha_0 + \alpha_1$, but this has no implications for our derivation.]

The same type of modified scoring method as used earlier produces the iteration

$$\hat{\beta}^{i+1} = \hat{\beta}^i + \left[\sum_{t=1}^{T} \frac{\mathbf{x}_t \mathbf{x}_t'}{\sigma_t^2} + \frac{1}{2}\left(\frac{\mathbf{d}_t}{\sigma_t^2}\right)\left(\frac{\mathbf{d}_t}{\sigma_t^2}\right)'\right]^{-1} \left[\sum_{t=1}^{T} \frac{\mathbf{x}_t \varepsilon_t}{\sigma_t^2} + \frac{1}{2}\left(\frac{\mathbf{d}_t}{\sigma_t^2}\right)v_t\right]$$

$$= \hat{\beta}^i + \left[\sum_{t=1}^{T} \frac{\mathbf{x}_t \mathbf{x}_t'}{\sigma_t^2} + \frac{1}{2}\left(\frac{\mathbf{d}_t}{\sigma_t^2}\right)\left(\frac{\mathbf{d}_t}{\sigma_t^2}\right)'\right]^{-1} \left(\frac{\partial \ln L}{\partial \beta}\right) \qquad \textbf{(19-46)}$$

$$= \hat{\beta}^i + \mathbf{h}^i,$$

which has been referred to as a **double-length regression.** [See Orme (1990) and Davidson and MacKinnon (1993, Chapter 14).] The update vector $\mathbf{h}^i$ is the vector of slopes in an augmented or double-length generalized regression,

$$\mathbf{h}^i = [\mathbf{C}'\mathbf{\Omega}^{-1}\mathbf{C}]^{-1}[\mathbf{C}'\mathbf{\Omega}^{-1}\mathbf{a}], \qquad \textbf{(19-47)}$$

where $\mathbf{C}$ is a $2T \times K$ matrix whose first $T$ rows are the $\mathbf{X}$ from the original regression model and whose next $T$ rows are $(1/\sqrt{2})\mathbf{d}_t'/\sigma_t^2, t = 1, \ldots, T$; $\mathbf{a}$ is a $2T \times 1$ vector whose first $T$ elements are $\varepsilon_t$ and whose next $T$ elements are $(1/\sqrt{2})v_t/\sigma_t^2, t = 1, \ldots, T$; and $\mathbf{\Omega}$ is a diagonal matrix with $1/\sigma_t^2$ in positions $1, \ldots, T$ and ones below observation $T$. At convergence, $[\mathbf{C}'\mathbf{\Omega}^{-1}\mathbf{C}]^{-1}$ provides the asymptotic covariance matrix for the MLE. The resemblance to the familiar result for the generalized regression model is striking, but note that this result is based on the double-length regression.

The iteration is done simply by computing the update vectors to the current parameters as defined earlier.[25] An important consideration is that to apply the scoring method, the estimates of $\beta$ and $\gamma$ are updated simultaneously. That is, one does not use the updated estimate of $\gamma$ in (19-45) to update the weights for the GLS regression to compute the new $\beta$ in (19-46). The same estimates (the results of the prior iteration) are used on the right-hand sides of both (19-45) and (19-46). The remaining problem is to obtain starting values for the iterations. One obvious choice is $\mathbf{b}$, the OLS estimator, for $\beta$, $\mathbf{e}'\mathbf{e}/T = s^2$ for $\alpha_0$, and zero for all the remaining parameters. The OLS slope vector will be consistent under all specifications. A useful alternative in this context would be to start $\alpha$ at the vector of slopes in the least squares regression of $e_t^2$, the squared OLS residual, on a constant and $q$ lagged values.[26] As discussed later, an LM test for the presence of GARCH effects is then a by-product of the first iteration. In principle, the updated result of the first iteration is an **efficient two-step estimator** of all the parameters. But having gone to the full effort to set up the iterations, nothing is gained by not iterating to convergence. One virtue of allowing the procedure to iterate to convergence is that the resulting log-likelihood function can be used in likelihood ratio tests.

### 19.13.4 TESTING FOR GARCH EFFECTS

The preceding development appears fairly complicated. In fact, it is not, because at each step, nothing more than a linear least squares regression is required. The intricate part

---

[25] See Fiorentini et al. (1996) on computation of derivatives in GARCH models.

[26] A test for the presence of $q$ ARCH effects against none can be carried out by carrying $TR^2$ from this regression into a table of critical values for the chi-squared distribution. But in the presence of GARCH effects, this procedure loses its validity.

of the computation is setting up the derivatives. On the other hand, it does take a fair amount of programming to get this far.[27] As Bollerslev suggests, it might be useful to test for GARCH effects first.

The simplest approach is to examine the squares of the least squares residuals. The autocorrelations (correlations with lagged values) of the squares of the residuals provide evidence about ARCH effects. An LM test of ARCH($q$) against the hypothesis of no ARCH effects [ARCH(0), the classical model] can be carried out by computing $\chi^2 = TR^2$ in the regression of $e_t^2$ on a constant and $q$ lagged values. Under the null hypothesis of no ARCH effects, the statistic has a limiting chi-squared distribution with $q$ degrees of freedom. Values larger than the critical table value give evidence of the presence of ARCH (or GARCH) effects.

Bollerslev suggests a Lagrange multiplier statistic that is, in fact, surprisingly simple to compute. The LM test for GARCH($p, 0$) against GARCH($p, q$) can be carried out by referring $T$ times the $R^2$ in the linear regression defined in (19-45) to the chi-squared critical value with $q$ degrees of freedom. There is, unfortunately, an indeterminacy in this test procedure. The test for ARCH($q$) against GARCH($p, q$) is exactly the same as that for ARCH($p$) against ARCH($p + q$). For carrying out the test, one can use as starting values a set of estimates that includes $\delta = 0$ and any consistent estimators for $\beta$ and $\alpha$. Then $TR^2$ for the regression at the initial iteration provides the test statistic.[28]

A number of recent papers have questioned the use of test statistics based solely on normality. Wooldridge (1991) is a useful summary with several examples.

### Example 19.8   GARCH Model for Exchange Rate Volatility

Bollerslev and Ghysels analyzed the exchange rate data in Example 19.7 using a GARCH(1, 1) model,

$$y_t = \mu + \varepsilon_t,$$

$$E[\varepsilon_t \mid \varepsilon_{t-1}] = 0,$$

$$\text{Var}[\varepsilon_t \mid \varepsilon_{t-1}] = \sigma_t^2 = \alpha_0 + \alpha_1 \varepsilon_{t-1}^2 + \delta \sigma_{t-1}^2.$$

The least squares residuals for this model are simply $e_t = y_t - \bar{y}$. Regression of the squares of these residuals on a constant and 10 lagged squared values using observations 11–1974 produces an $R^2 = 0.09795$. With $T = 1964$, the chi-squared statistic is 192.37, which is larger than the critical value from the table of 18.31. We conclude that there is evidence of GARCH effects in these residuals. The maximum likelihood estimates of the GARCH model are given in Table 19.4. Note the resemblance between the OLS unconditional variance (0.221128) and the estimated equilibrium variance from the GARCH model, 0.2631.

---

[27]Because this procedure is available as a preprogrammed procedure in many computer programs, including TSP, E-Views, Stata, RATS, LIMDEP, and Shazam, this warning might itself be overstated.

[28]Bollerslev argues that in view of the complexity of the computations involved in estimating the GARCH model, it is useful to have a test for GARCH effects. This case is one (as are many other maximum likelihood problems) in which the apparatus for carrying out the test is the same as that for estimating the model. Having computed the LM statistic for GARCH effects, one can proceed to estimate the model just by allowing the program to iterate to convergence. There is no additional cost beyond waiting for the answer.

**TABLE 19.4** Maximum Likelihood Estimates of a GARCH(1, 1) Model[29]

| | $\mu$ | $\alpha_0$ | $\alpha_1$ | $\delta$ | $\alpha_0/(1 - \alpha_1 - \delta)$ |
|---|---|---|---|---|---|
| Estimate | −0.006190 | 0.01076 | 0.1531 | 0.8060 | 0.2631 |
| Std. Error | 0.00873 | 0.00312 | 0.0273 | 0.0302 | 0.594 |
| $t$ ratio | −0.709 | 3.445 | 5.605 | 26.731 | 0.443 |

$\ln L = -1106.61$, $\ln L_{OLS} = -1311.09$, $\bar{y} = -0.01642$, $s^2 = 0.221128$

### 19.13.5 PSEUDO–MAXIMUM LIKELIHOOD ESTIMATION

We now consider an implication of nonnormality of the disturbances. Suppose that the assumption of normality is weakened to only

$$E[\varepsilon_t \mid \Psi_t] = 0, \quad E\left[\frac{\varepsilon_t^2}{\sigma_t^2} \,\middle|\, \Psi_t\right] = 1, \quad E\left[\frac{\varepsilon_t^4}{\sigma_t^4} \,\middle|\, \Psi_t\right] = \kappa < \infty,$$

where $\sigma_t^2$ is as defined earlier. Now the normal log-likelihood function is inappropriate. In this case, the nonlinear (ordinary or weighted) least squares estimator would have the properties discussed in Chapter 11. It would be more difficult to compute than the MLE discussed earlier, however. It has been shown [see White (1982a) and Weiss (1982)] that the **pseudo-MLE** obtained by maximizing the same log-likelihood as if it were correct produces a consistent estimator despite the misspecification.[30] The asymptotic covariance matrices for the parameter estimators must be adjusted, however.

The general result for cases such as this one [see Gourieroux, Monfort, and Trognon (1984)] is that the appropriate asymptotic covariance matrix for the pseudo-MLE of a parameter vector $\boldsymbol{\theta}$ would be

$$\text{Asy. Var}[\hat{\boldsymbol{\theta}}] = \mathbf{H}^{-1}\mathbf{F}\mathbf{H}^{-1}, \tag{19-48}$$

where

$$\mathbf{H} = -E\left[\frac{\partial^2 \ln L}{\partial \boldsymbol{\theta} \, \partial \boldsymbol{\theta}'}\right],$$

and

$$\mathbf{F} = E\left[\left(\frac{\partial \ln L}{\partial \boldsymbol{\theta}}\right)\left(\frac{\partial \ln L}{\partial \boldsymbol{\theta}'}\right)\right]$$

(i.e., the BHHH estimator), and $\ln L$ is the used but inappropriate log-likelihood function. For current purposes, $\mathbf{H}$ and $\mathbf{F}$ are still block diagonal, so we can treat the mean and variance parameters separately. In addition, $E[v_t]$ is still zero, so the second derivative terms in both blocks are quite simple. (The parts involving $\partial^2 \sigma_t^2/\partial \boldsymbol{\gamma} \, \partial \boldsymbol{\gamma}'$ and $\partial^2 \sigma_t^2/\partial \boldsymbol{\beta} \, \partial \boldsymbol{\beta}'$ fall out of the expectation.) Taking expectations and inserting the parts produces the

---

[29]These data have become a standard data set for the evaluation of software for estimating GARCH models. The values given are the benchmark estimates. Standard errors differ substantially from one method to the next. Those given are the Bollerslev and Wooldridge (1992) results. See McCullough and Renfro (1999).

[30]White (1982a) gives some additional requirements for the true underlying density of $\varepsilon_t$. Gourieroux, Monfort, and Trognon (1984) also consider the issue. Under the assumptions given, the expectations of the matrices in (19-42) and (19-47) remain the same as under normality. The consistency and asymptotic normality of the pseudo-MLE can be argued under the logic of GMM estimators.

corrected asymptotic covariance matrix for the variance parameters:

$$\text{Asy. Var}[\hat{\boldsymbol{\gamma}}_{\text{PMLE}}] = [\mathbf{W}_*'\mathbf{W}_*]^{-1}\mathbf{B}'\mathbf{B}[\mathbf{W}_*'\mathbf{W}_*]^{-1},$$

where the rows of $\mathbf{W}^*$ are defined in (19-45) and those of $\mathbf{B}$ are in (19-43). For the slope parameters, the adjusted asymptotic covariance matrix would be

$$\text{Asy. Var}[\hat{\boldsymbol{\beta}}_{\text{PMLE}}'] = [\mathbf{C}'\boldsymbol{\Omega}^{-1}\mathbf{C}]^{-1}\left[\sum_{t=1}^{T}\mathbf{b}_t\mathbf{b}_t'\right][\mathbf{C}'\boldsymbol{\Omega}^{-1}\mathbf{C}]^{-1},$$

where the outer matrix is defined in (19-47) and, from the first derivatives given in (19-43) and (19-46),[31]

$$\mathbf{b}_t = \frac{\mathbf{x}_t\varepsilon_t}{\sigma_t^2} + \frac{1}{2}\left(\frac{v_t}{\sigma_t^2}\right)\mathbf{d}_t.$$

## 19.14 SUMMARY AND CONCLUSIONS

This chapter has examined the generalized regression model with serial correlation in the disturbances. We began with some general results on analysis of time-series data. When we consider dependent observations and serial correlation, the laws of large numbers and central limit theorems used to analyze independent observations no longer suffice. We presented some useful tools that extend these results to time-series settings. We then considered estimation and testing in the presence of autocorrelation. As usual, OLS is consistent but inefficient. The Newey–West estimator is a robust estimator for the asymptotic covariance matrix of the OLS estimator. This pair of estimators also constitute the GMM estimator for the regression model with autocorrelation. We then considered two-step feasible generalized least squares and maximum likelihood estimation for the special case usually analyzed by practitioners, the AR(1) model. The model with a correction for autocorrelation is a restriction on a more general model with lagged values of both dependent and independent variables. We considered a means of testing this specification as an alternative to "fixing" the problem of autocorrelation. The final section, on ARCH and GARCH effects, describes an extension of the models of autoregression to the conditional variance of $\varepsilon$ as opposed to the conditional mean. This model embodies elements of both autocorrelation and heteroscedasticity. The set of methods plays a fundamental role in the modern analysis of volatility in financial data.

## Key Terms and Concepts

- AR(1)
- ARCH
- ARCH-in-mean
- Asymptotic negligibility
- Asymptotic normality
- Autocorrelation
- Autocorrelation matrix
- Autocovariance
- Autocovariance matrix
- Autoregressive form
- Autoregressive processes
- Cochrane–Orcutt estimator
- Common factor model
- Covariance stationarity
- Double-length regression

---

[31]McCullough and Renfro (1999) examined several approaches to computing an appropriate asymptotic covariance matrix for the GARCH model, including the conventional Hessian and BHHH estimators and three sandwich style estimators, including the one suggested earlier and two based on the method of scoring suggested by Bollerslev and Wooldridge (1992). None stand out as obviously better, but the Bollerslev and QMLE estimator based on an actual Hessian appears to perform well in Monte Carlo studies.

- Durbin–Watson test
- Efficient two-step estimator
- Ergodicity
- Ergodic theorem
- Expectations-augmented Phillips curve
- First-order autoregression
- GARCH
- GMM estimator
- Initial conditions
- Innovation
- Lagrange multiplier test

- Martingale sequence
- Martingale difference sequence
- Moving average form
- Moving-average process
- Newey–West robust covariance matrix estimator
- Partial difference
- Prais–Winsten estimator
- Pseudo-differences
- Pseudo-MLE
- $Q$ test

- Quasi differences
- Random walk
- Stationarity
- Stationarity conditions
- Summability
- Time-series process
- Time window
- Weakly stationary
- White noise
- Yule–Walker equations

## Exercises

1. Does first differencing reduce autocorrelation? Consider the models $y_t = \boldsymbol{\beta}'\mathbf{x}_t + \varepsilon_t$, where $\varepsilon_t = \rho\varepsilon_{t-1} + u_t$ and $\varepsilon_t = u_t - \lambda u_{t-1}$. Compare the autocorrelation of $\varepsilon_t$ in the original model with that of $v_t$ in $y_t - y_{t-1} = \boldsymbol{\beta}'(\mathbf{x}_t - \mathbf{x}_{t-1}) + v_t$, where $v_t = \varepsilon_t - \varepsilon_{t-1}$.

2. Derive the disturbance covariance matrix for the model

$$y_t = \boldsymbol{\beta}'\mathbf{x}_t + \varepsilon_t,$$

$$\varepsilon_t = \rho\varepsilon_{t-1} + u_t - \lambda u_{t-1}.$$

What parameter is estimated by the regression of the OLS residuals on their lagged values?

3. The following regression is obtained by ordinary least squares, using 21 observations. (Estimated asymptotic standard errors are shown in parentheses.)

$$y_t = 1.3 + 0.97y_{t-1} + 2.31x_t, \quad D - W = 1.21.$$
$$\quad\ \ (0.3)\ \ (0.18) \qquad (1.04)$$

Test for the presence of autocorrelation in the disturbances.

4. It is commonly asserted that the Durbin–Watson statistic is only appropriate for testing for first-order autoregressive disturbances. What combination of the coefficients of the model is estimated by the Durbin–Watson statistic in each of the following cases: AR(1), AR(2), MA(1)? In each case, assume that the regression model does not contain a lagged dependent variable. Comment on the impact on your results of relaxing this assumption.

## Applications

1. The data used to fit the expectations augmented Phillips curve in Example 19.3 are given in Appendix Table F5.1. Using these data, reestimate the model given in the example. Carry out a formal test for first-order autocorrelation using the LM statistic. Then, reestimate the model using an AR(1) model for the disturbance process. Because the sample is large, the Prais–Winsten and Cochrane–Orcutt estimators should give essentially the same answer. Do they? After fitting the model, obtain the transformed residuals and examine them for first-order autocorrelation. Does the AR(1) model appear to have adequately "fixed" the problem?

2. Data for fitting an improved Phillips curve model can be obtained from many sources, including the Bureau of Economic Analysis's (BEA) own Web site, www.economagic.com, and so on. Obtain the necessary data and expand the model of Example 19.3. Does adding additional explanatory variables to the model reduce the extreme pattern of the OLS residuals that appears in Figure 19.3?

3. (This exercise requires appropriate computer software. The computations required can be done with RATS, EViews, Stata, TSP, LIMDEP, and a variety of other software using only preprogrammed procedures.) Quarterly data on the consumer price index for 1950.1 to 2000.4 are given in Appendix Table F5.1. Use these data to fit the model proposed by Engle and Kraft (1983). The model is

$$\pi_t = \beta_0 + \beta_1 \pi_{t-1} + \beta_2 \pi_{t-2} + \beta_3 \pi_{t-3} + \beta_4 \pi_{t-4} + \varepsilon_t,$$

where $\pi_t = 100 \ln[p_t / p_{t-1}]$ and $p_t$ is the price index.

a. Fit the model by ordinary least squares, then use the tests suggested in the text to see if ARCH effects appear to be present.

b. The authors fit an ARCH(8) model with declining weights,

$$\sigma_t^2 = \alpha_0 + \sum_{i=1}^{8} \left( \frac{9-i}{36} \right) \varepsilon_{t-i}^2.$$

Fit this model. If the software does not allow constraints on the coefficients, you can still do this with a two-step least squares procedure, using the least squares residuals from the first step. What do you find?

c. Bollerslev (1986) recomputed this model as a GARCH(1,1). Use the GARCH(1,1) form and refit your model.

# 20

# MODELS WITH LAGGED
# VARIABLES

〜〜〜

## 20.1 INTRODUCTION

This chapter begins our introduction to the analysis of economic time series. By most views, this field has become synonymous with empirical macroeconomics and the analysis of financial markets.[1] In this and the next chapter, we will consider a number of models and topics in which time and relationships through time play an explicit part in the formulation. Consider the **dynamic regression model**

$$y_t = \beta_1 + \beta_2 x_t + \beta_3 x_{t-1} + \gamma y_{t-1} + \varepsilon_t. \tag{20-1}$$

Models of this form specifically include as right-hand-side variables previous as well as contemporaneous values of the regressors. It is also in this context that lagged values of the dependent variable appear as a consequence of the theoretical basis of the model rather than as a computational means of removing autocorrelation. There are several reasons lagged effects might appear in an empirical model:

- In modeling the response of economic variables to policy stimuli, it is expected that there will be possibly long lags between policy changes and their impacts. The length of lag between changes in monetary policy and its impact on important economic variables such as output and investment has been a subject of analysis for several decades.
- Either the dependent variable or one of the independent variables is based on expectations. **Expectations** about economic events are usually formed by aggregating new information and past experience. Thus, we might write the expectation of a future value of variable $x$, formed this period, as

$$x_t = E_t[x_{t+1}^* \mid z_t, x_{t-1}, x_{t-2}, \ldots] = g(z_t, x_{t-1}, x_{t-2}, \ldots).$$

---

[1] The literature in this area has grown at an impressive rate, and, more so than in any other area, it has become impossible to provide comprehensive surveys in general textbooks such as this one. Fortunately, specialized volumes have been produced that can fill this need at any level. Harvey (1990) has been in wide use for some time. Among the many other books, three very useful works are Enders (2003), which presents the basics of time-series analysis at an introductory level with several very detailed applications; Hamilton (1994), which gives a relatively technical but quite comprehensive survey of the field; and Lutkepohl (2005), which provides an extremely detailed treatment of the topics presented at the end of this chapter. Hamilton also surveys a number of the applications in the contemporary literature. Two references that are focused on financial econometrics are Mills (1993) and Tsay (2005). There are also a number of important references that are primarily limited to forecasting, including Diebold (1998a, 2003) and Granger and Newbold (1996). A survey of research in many areas of time-series analysis is Engle and McFadden (1994). An extensive, fairly advanced treatise that analyzes in great depth all the issues we touch on in this chapter is Hendry (1995). Finally, Patterson (2000) surveys most of the practical issues in time series and presents a large variety of useful and very detailed applications.

For example, forecasts of prices and income enter demand equations and consumption equations. (See Example 15.1 for an influential application.)

- Certain economic decisions are explicitly driven by a history of related activities. For example, energy demand by individuals is clearly a function not only of current prices and income, but also the accumulated stocks of energy using capital. Even energy demand in the macroeconomy behaves in this fashion—the stock of automobiles and its attendant demand for gasoline is clearly driven by past prices of gasoline and automobiles. Other classic examples are the dynamic relationship between investment decisions and past appropriation decisions and the consumption of addictive goods such as cigarettes and theater performances.

We begin with a general discussion of models containing **lagged variables.** In Section 20.2, we consider some methodological issues in the specification of dynamic regressions. In Sections 20.3 and 20.4, we describe a general dynamic model that encompasses some of the extensions and more formal models for time-series data that are presented in Chapter 21. Section 20.5 takes a closer look at some of issues in model specification. Finally, Section 20.6 considers systems of dynamic equations. These are largely extensions of the models that we examined at the end of Chapter 13. But the interpretation is rather different here. This chapter is generally not about methods of estimation. OLS and GMM estimation are usually routine in this context. Because we are examining time-series data, conventional assumptions including ergodicity and stationarity will be made at the outset. In particular, in the general framework, we will assume that the multivariate stochastic process $(y_t, \mathbf{x}_t, \varepsilon_t)$ are a **stationary** and ergodic process. As such, without further analysis, we will invoke the theorems discussed in Chapters 4, 15, 16, and 19 that support least squares and GMM as appropriate estimate techniques in this context. In most of what follows, in fact, in practical terms, the dynamic regression model can be treated as a linear regression model and estimated by conventional methods (e.g., ordinary least squares or instrumental variables if $\varepsilon_t$ is autocorrelated). As noted, we will generally not return to the issue of estimation and inference theory except where new results are needed, such as in the discussion of nonstationary processes.

## 20.2 DYNAMIC REGRESSION MODELS

In some settings, economic agents respond not only to current values of independent variables but to past values as well. When effects persist over time, an appropriate model will include lagged variables. Example 20.1 illustrates a familiar case.

### Example 20.1 A Structural Model of the Demand for Gasoline
Drivers demand gasoline not for direct consumption but as fuel for cars to provide a source of energy for transportation. Per capita demand for gasoline in any period, $G/Pop$, is determined partly by the current price, $P_g$, and per capita income, $Y/Pop$, which influence how intensively the existing stock of gasoline using "capital," $K$, is used and partly by the size and composition of the stock of cars and other vehicles. The capital stock is determined, in turn, by income, $Y/Pop$; prices of the equipment such as new and used cars, $Pnc$ and $Puc$; the price of alternative modes of transportation such as public transportation, $Ppt$; and past prices of gasoline as they influence forecasts of future gasoline prices. A structural model of

these effects might appear as follows:

per capita demand: $\quad\quad\quad\quad\quad G_t/Pop_t = \alpha + \beta Pg_t + \delta Y_t/Pop_t + \gamma K_t + u_t,$

stock of vehicles: $\quad\quad\quad\quad\quad K_t = (1 - \Delta)K_{t-1} + I_t, \Delta = $ depreciation rate,

investment in new vehicles: $\quad I_t = \theta Y_t/Pop_t + \phi E_t[Pg_{t+1}] + \lambda_1 Pnc_t + \lambda_2 Puc_t + \lambda_3 Ppt_t$

expected price of gasoline: $\quad E_t[Pg_{t+1}] = w_0 Pg_t + w_1 Pg_{t-1} + w_2 Pg_{t-2}.$

The capital stock is the sum of all past investments, so it is evident that not only current income and prices, but all past values, play a role in determining $K$. When income or the price of gasoline changes, the immediate effect will be to cause drivers to use their vehicles more or less intensively. But, over time, vehicles are added to the capital stock, and some cars are replaced with more or less efficient ones. These changes take some time, so the full impact of income and price changes will not be felt for several periods. Two episodes in the recent history have shown this effect clearly. For well over a decade following the 1973 oil shock, drivers gradually replaced their large, fuel-inefficient cars with smaller, less-fuel-intensive models. In the late 1990s in the United States, this process has visibly worked in reverse. As American drivers have become accustomed to steadily rising incomes and steadily falling real gasoline prices, the downsized, efficient coupes and sedans of the 1980s have yielded the highways to a tide of ever-larger, six- and eight-cylinder sport utility vehicles, whose size and power can reasonably be characterized as astonishing.

### 20.2.1 LAGGED EFFECTS IN A DYNAMIC MODEL

The general form of a dynamic regression model is

$$y_t = \alpha + \sum_{i=0}^{\infty} \beta_i x_{t-i} + \varepsilon_t. \quad\quad\quad\quad \textbf{(20-2)}$$

In this model, a one-time change in $x$ at any point in time will affect $E[y_s \mid x_t, x_{t-1}, \ldots]$ in every period thereafter. When it is believed that the duration of the lagged effects is extremely long—for example, in the analysis of monetary policy—**infinite lag** models that have effects that gradually fade over time are quite common. But models are often constructed in which changes in $x$ cease to have any influence after a fairly small number of periods. We shall consider these **finite lag** models first.

Marginal effects in the static classical regression model are one-time events. The response of $y$ to a change in $x$ is assumed to be immediate and to be complete at the end of the period of measurement. In a dynamic model, the counterpart to a marginal effect is the effect of a one-time change in $x_t$ on the **equilibrium** of $y_t$. If the level of $x_t$ has been unchanged from, say, $\bar{x}$ for many periods prior to time $t$, then the equilibrium value of $E[y_t \mid x_t, x_{t-1}, \ldots]$ (assuming that it exists) will be

$$\bar{y} = \alpha + \sum_{i=0}^{\infty} \beta_i \bar{x} = \alpha + \bar{x} \sum_{i=0}^{\infty} \beta_i, \quad\quad\quad\quad \textbf{(20-3)}$$

where $\bar{x}$ is the permanent value of $x_t$. For this value to be finite, we require that

$$\left| \sum_{i=0}^{\infty} \beta_i \right| < \infty. \quad\quad\quad\quad \textbf{(20-4)}$$

Consider the effect of a unit change in $\bar{x}$ occurring in period $s$. To focus ideas, consider the earlier example of demand for gasoline and suppose that $x_t$ is the unit price. Prior to the oil shock, demand had reached an equilibrium consistent with accumulated habits,

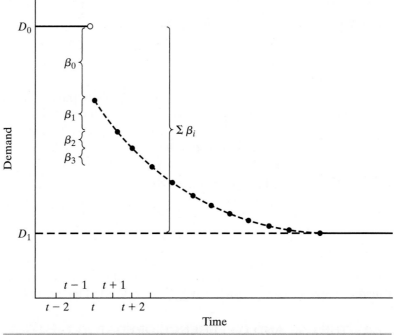

**FIGURE 20.1**  Lagged Adjustment.

experience with stable real prices, and the accumulated stocks of vehicles. Now suppose that the price of gasoline, $Pg$, rises permanently from $\overline{Pg}$ to $\overline{Pg} + 1$ in period $s$. The path to the new equilibrium might appear as shown in Figure 20.1. The short-run effect is the one that occurs in the same period as the change in $x$. This effect is $\beta_0$ in the figure.

---

**DEFINITION 20.1  Impact Multiplier**
$\beta_0 = $ *impact multiplier* $=$ *short-run multiplier.*

---

**DEFINITION 20.2  Cumulated Effect**
*The accumulated effect $\tau$ periods later of an impulse at time t is $\boldsymbol{\beta}_\tau = \sum_{i=0}^{\tau} \beta_i$.*

---

In Figure 20.1, we see that the total effect of a price change in period $t$ after three periods have elapsed will be $\beta_0 + \beta_1 + \beta_2 + \beta_3$.

The difference between the old equilibrium $D_0$ and the new one $D_1$ is the sum of the individual period effects. The **long-run multiplier** is this total effect.

---

> **DEFINITION 20.3** Equilibrium Multiplier
> $\beta = \sum_{i=0}^{\infty} \beta_i = equilibrium\ multiplier = long\text{-}run\ multiplier.$

---

Because the lag coefficients are regression coefficients, their scale is determined by the scales of the variables in the model. As such, it is often useful to define the

$$\text{lag weights: } w_i = \frac{\beta_i}{\sum_{j=0}^{\infty} \beta_j}, \tag{20-5}$$

so that $\sum_{i=0}^{\infty} w_i = 1$, and to rewrite the model as

$$y_t = \alpha + \beta \sum_{i=0}^{\infty} w_i x_{t-i} + \varepsilon_t. \tag{20-6}$$

(Note the equation for the expected price in Example 20.1.) Two useful statistics, based on the lag weights, that characterize the period of adjustment to a new equilibrium are the **median lag** = smallest $q^*$ such that $\sum_{i=0}^{q^*} w_i \geq 0.5$ and the **mean lag** = $\sum_{i=0}^{\infty} i w_i.$[2]

### 20.2.2 THE LAG AND DIFFERENCE OPERATORS

A convenient device for manipulating lagged variables is the **lag operator,**

$$L x_t = x_{t-1}.$$

Some basic results are $La = a$ if $a$ is a constant and $L(L x_t) = L^2 x_t = x_{t-2}$. Thus, $L^p x_t = x_{t-p}$, $L^q(L^p x_t) = L^{p+q} x_t = x_{t-p-q}$, and $(L^p + L^q) x_t = x_{t-p} + x_{t-q}$. By convention, $L^0 x_t = 1 x_t = x_t$. A related operation is the first difference,

$$\Delta x_t = x_t - x_{t-1}.$$

Obviously, $\Delta x_t = (1 - L) x_t$ and $x_t = x_{t-1} + \Delta x_t$. These two operations can be usefully combined, for example, as in

$$\Delta^2 x_t = (1 - L)^2 x_t = (1 - 2L + L^2) x_t = x_t - 2 x_{t-1} + x_{t-2}.$$

Note that

$$(1 - L)^2 x_t = (1 - L)(1 - L) x_t = (1 - L)(x_t - x_{t-1}) = (x_t - x_{t-1}) - (x_{t-1} - x_{t-2}).$$

The dynamic regression model can be written

$$y_t = \alpha + \sum_{i=0}^{\infty} \beta_i L^i x_t + \varepsilon_t = \alpha + B(L) x_t + \varepsilon_t,$$

---

[2] If the lag coefficients do not all have the same sign, then these results may not be meaningful. In some contexts, lag coefficients with different signs may be taken as an indication that there is a flaw in the specification of the model.

where $B(L)$ is a polynomial in $L$, $B(L) = \beta_0 + \beta_1 L + \beta_2 L^2 + \cdots$. A **polynomial in the lag operator** that reappears in many contexts is

$$A(L) = 1 + aL + (aL)^2 + (aL)^3 + \cdots = \sum_{i=0}^{\infty} (aL)^i.$$

If $|a| < 1$, then

$$A(L) = \frac{1}{1 - aL}.$$

A **distributed lag** model in the form

$$y_t = \alpha + \beta \sum_{i=0}^{\infty} \gamma^i L^i x_t + \varepsilon_t$$

can be written

$$y_t = \alpha + \beta(1 - \gamma L)^{-1} x_t + \varepsilon_t,$$

if $|\gamma| < 1$. This form is called the **moving-average form** or **distributed lag form.** If we multiply through by $(1 - \gamma L)$ and collect terms, then we obtain the **autoregressive form,**

$$y_t = \alpha(1 - \gamma) + \beta x_t + \gamma y_{t-1} + (1 - \gamma L)\varepsilon_t.$$

In more general terms, consider the $p$th order **autoregressive model,**

$$y_t = \alpha + \beta x_t + \gamma_1 y_{t-1} + \gamma_2 y_{t-2} + \cdots + \gamma_p y_{t-p} + \varepsilon_t,$$

which may be written

$$C(L)y_t = \alpha + \beta x_t + \varepsilon_t,$$

where

$$C(L) = (1 - \gamma_1 L - \gamma_2 L^2 - \cdots - \gamma_p L^p).$$

Can this equation be "inverted" so that $y_t$ is written as a function only of current and past values of $x_t$ and $\varepsilon_t$? By successively substituting the corresponding autoregressive equation for $y_{t-1}$ in that for $y_t$, then likewise for $y_{t-2}$ and so on, it would appear so. However, it is also clear that the resulting distributed lag form will have an infinite number of coefficients. Formally, the operation just described amounts to writing

$$y_t = [C(L)]^{-1}(\alpha + \beta x_t + \varepsilon_t) = A(L)(\alpha + \beta x_t + \varepsilon_t).$$

It will be of interest to be able to solve for the elements of $A(L)$ (see, for example, Section 20.6.6). By this arrangement, it follows that $C(L)A(L) = 1$ where

$$A(L) = (\alpha_0 L^0 - \alpha_1 L - \alpha_2 L^2 - \cdots).$$

By collecting like powers of $L$ in

$$(1 - \gamma_1 L - \gamma_2 L^2 - \cdots - \gamma_p L^p)(\alpha_0 L^0 + \alpha_1 L + \alpha_2 L^2 - \cdots) = 1,$$

we find that a recursive solution for the $\alpha$ coefficients is

$$
\begin{aligned}
L^0: &\ \alpha_0 & = 1 \\
L^1: &\ \alpha_1 - \gamma_1\alpha_0 & = 0 \\
L^2: &\ \alpha_2 - \gamma_1\alpha_1 - \gamma_2\alpha_0 & = 0 \\
L^3: &\ \alpha_3 - \gamma_1\alpha_2 - \gamma_2\alpha_1 - \gamma_3\alpha_0 & = 0 \\
L^4: &\ \alpha_4 - \gamma_1\alpha_3 - \gamma_2\alpha_2 - \gamma_3\alpha_1 - \gamma_4\alpha_0 & = 0 \\
&\ \cdots \\
L^p: &\ \alpha_p - \gamma_1\alpha_{p-1} - \gamma_2\alpha_{p-2} - \cdots - \gamma_p\alpha_0 & = 0
\end{aligned}
\tag{20-7}
$$

and, thereafter,

$$
L^q: \ \alpha_q - \gamma_1\alpha_{q-1} - \gamma_2\alpha_{q-2} - \cdots - \gamma_p\alpha_{q-p} = 0.
$$

After a set of $p-1$ starting values, the $\alpha$ coefficients obey the same difference equation as $y_t$ does in the dynamic equation. One problem remains. For the given set of values, the preceding gives no assurance that the solution for $\alpha_q$ does not ultimately explode. The preceding equation system is not necessarily stable for all values of $\gamma_j$ (although it certainly is for some). If the system is stable in this sense, then the polynomial $C(L)$ is said to be **invertible.** The necessary conditions are precisely those discussed in Section 20.4.3, so we will defer completion of this discussion until then.

Finally, two useful results are

$$
B(1) = \beta_0 1^0 + \beta_1 1^1 + \beta_2 1^2 + \cdots = \beta = \text{long-run multiplier},
$$

and

$$
B'(1) = [dB(L)/dL]_{|L=1} = \sum_{i=0}^{\infty} i\beta_i.
$$

It follows that $B'(1)/B(1) = \text{mean lag}$.

### 20.2.3 SPECIFICATION SEARCH FOR THE LAG LENGTH

Various procedures have been suggested for determining the appropriate lag length in a dynamic model such as

$$
y_t = \alpha + \sum_{i=0}^{p} \beta_i x_{t-i} + \varepsilon_t.
\tag{20-8}
$$

One must be careful about a purely significance based specification search. Let us suppose that there is an appropriate, "true" value of $p > 0$ that we seek. A **simple-to-general approach** to finding the right lag length would depart from a model with only the current value of the independent variable in the regression and add deeper lags until a simple $t$ test suggested that the last one added is statistically insignificant. The problem with such an approach is that at any level at which the number of included lagged variables is less than $p$, the estimator of the coefficient vector is biased and inconsistent. [See the omitted variable formula (7-4).] The asymptotic covariance matrix is biased as well, so statistical inference on this basis is unlikely to be successful. A **general-to-simple approach** would begin from a model that contains more than $p$ lagged values—it is assumed that although the precise value of $p$ is unknown, the analyst can posit a maintained value that should be larger than $p$. Least squares or instrumental variables regression of $y$ on a constant and $(p + d)$ lagged values of $x$ consistently estimates $\theta = [\alpha, \beta_0, \beta_1, \ldots, \beta_p, 0, 0, \ldots]$.

Because models with lagged values are often used for forecasting, researchers have tended to look for measures that have produced better results for assessing "out of sample" prediction properties. The adjusted $R^2$ [see Section 3.5.1] is one possibility. Others include the Akaike (1973) information criterion, AIC($p$),

$$\text{AIC}(p) = \ln\frac{\mathbf{e'e}}{T} + \frac{2p}{T}, \tag{20-9}$$

and Schwarz's criterion, SC($p$):

$$\text{SC}(p) = \text{AIC}(p) + \left(\frac{p}{T}\right)(\ln T - 2). \tag{20-10}$$

(See Section 7.4.) If some maximum $P$ is known, then $p < P$ can be chosen to minimize AIC($p$) or SC($p$).[3] An alternative approach, also based on a known $P$, is to do sequential $F$ tests on the last $P > p$ coefficients, stopping when the test rejects the hypothesis that the coefficients are jointly zero. Each of these approaches has its flaws and virtues. The Akaike information criterion retains a positive probability of leading to overfitting even as $T \to \infty$. In contrast, SC($p$) has been seen to lead to underfitting in some finite sample cases. They do avoid, however, the inference problems of sequential estimators. The sequential $F$ tests require successive revision of the significance level to be appropriate, but they do have a statistical underpinning.[4]

## 20.3  SIMPLE DISTRIBUTED LAG MODELS

Before examining some very general specifications of the dynamic regression, we briefly consider an **infinite lag model,** which emerges from a simple model of expectations.

There are cases in which the distributed lag models the accumulation of information. The formation of expectations is an example. In these instances, intuition suggests that the most recent past will receive the greatest weight and that the influence of past observations will fade uniformly with the passage of time. The geometric lag model is often used for these settings. The general form of the model is

$$y_t = \alpha + \beta \sum_{i=0}^{\infty} (1 - \lambda)\lambda^i x_{t-i} + \varepsilon_t, \quad 0 < \lambda < 1,$$

$$= \alpha + \beta B(L)x_t + \varepsilon_t, \tag{20-11}$$

where

$$B(L) = (1 - \lambda)(1 + \lambda L + \lambda^2 L^2 + \lambda^3 L^3 + \cdots) = \frac{1 - \lambda}{1 - \lambda L}.$$

[3]For further discussion and some alternative measures, see Geweke and Meese (1981), Amemiya (1985, pp. 146–147), Diebold (1998, pp. 85–91), and Judge et al. (1985, pp. 353–355).

[4]See Pagano and Hartley (1981) and Trivedi and Pagan (1979).

The lag coefficients are $\beta_i = \beta(1 - \lambda)\lambda^i$. The model incorporates **infinite lags,** but it assigns arbitrarily small weights to the distant past. The lag weights decline geometrically;

$$w_i = (1 - \lambda)\lambda^i, \quad 0 \le w_i < 1.$$

The **mean lag** is

$$\overline{w} = \frac{B'(1)}{B(1)} = \frac{\lambda}{1 - \lambda}.$$

The **median lag** is $p^*$ such that $\sum_{i=0}^{p^*-1} w_i = 0.5$. We can solve for $p^*$ by using the result

$$\sum_{i=0}^{p} \lambda^i = \frac{1 - \lambda^{p+1}}{1 - \lambda}.$$

Thus,

$$p^* = \frac{\ln 0.5}{\ln \lambda} - 1.$$

The impact multiplier is $\beta(1 - \lambda)$. The long-run multiplier is $\beta \sum_{i=0}^{\infty} (1 - \lambda)\lambda^i = \beta$. The equilibrium value of $y_t$ would be found by fixing $x_t$ at $\overline{x}$ and $\varepsilon_t$ at zero in (20-11), which produces $\overline{y} = \alpha + \beta\overline{x}$.

The geometric lag model can be motivated with an economic model of expectations. We begin with a regression in an expectations variable such as an expected future price based on information available at time $t$, $x_{t+1|t}^*$, and perhaps a second regressor, $w_t$,

$$y_t = \alpha + \beta x_{t+1|t}^* + \delta w_t + \varepsilon_t,$$

and a mechanism for the formation of the expectation,

$$x_{t+1|t}^* = \lambda x_{t|t-1}^* + (1 - \lambda)x_t = \lambda L x_{t+1|t}^* + (1 - \lambda)x_t. \tag{20-12}$$

The currently formed expectation is a weighted average of the expectation in the previous period and the most recent observation. The parameter $\lambda$ is the adjustment coefficient. If $\lambda$ equals 1, then the current datum is ignored and expectations are never revised. A value of zero characterizes a strict pragmatist who forgets the past immediately. The expectation variable can be written as

$$x_{t+1|t}^* = \frac{1 - \lambda}{1 - \lambda L}x_t = (1 - \lambda)[x_t + \lambda x_{t-1} + \lambda^2 x_{t-2} + \cdots]. \tag{20-13}$$

Inserting (20-13) into (20-12) produces the geometric distributed lag model,

$$y_t = \alpha + \beta(1 - \lambda)[x_t + \lambda x_{t-1} + \lambda^2 x_{t-2} + \cdots] + \delta w_t + \varepsilon_t.$$

The geometric lag model can be estimated by nonlinear least squares. Rewrite it as

$$y_t = \alpha + \gamma z_t(\lambda) + \delta w_t + \varepsilon_t, \quad \gamma = \beta(1 - \lambda). \tag{20-14}$$

The constructed variable $z_t(\lambda)$ obeys the recursion $z_t(\lambda) = x_t + \lambda z_{t-1}(\lambda)$. For the first observation, we use $z_1(\lambda) = x_{1|0}^* = x_1/(1 - \lambda)$. If the sample is moderately long, then assuming that $x_t$ was in long-run equilibrium, although it is an approximation, will not unduly affect the results. One can then scan over the range of $\lambda$ from zero to one to locate the value that minimizes the sum of squares. Once the minimum is located, an estimate of the asymptotic covariance matrix of the estimators of $(\alpha, \gamma, \delta, \lambda)$ can be found using (11-12) and Theorem 11.2. For the regression function $h_t(\text{data} \mid \alpha, \gamma, \delta, \lambda)$, $x_{t1}^0 = 1$, $x_{t2}^0 = z_t(\lambda)$, and $x_{t3}^0 = w_t$. The derivative with respect to $\lambda$ can be computed by using the recursion $d_t(\lambda) = \partial z_t(\lambda)/\partial \lambda = z_{t-1}(\lambda) + \lambda \partial z_{t-1}(\lambda)/\partial \lambda$. If $z_1 = x_1/(1 - \lambda)$, then $d_1(\lambda) = z_1/(1 - \lambda)$. Then, $x_{t4}^0 = d_t(\lambda)$. Finally, we estimate $\beta$ from the relationship $\beta = \gamma/(1 - \lambda)$ and use the delta method to estimate the asymptotic standard error.

For purposes of estimating long- and short-run elasticities, researchers often use a different form of the geometric lag model. The **partial adjustment** model describes the *desired* level of $y_t$,

$$y_t^* = \alpha + \beta x_t + \delta w_t + \varepsilon_t,$$

and an *adjustment equation*,

$$y_t - y_{t-1} = (1 - \lambda)(y_t^* - y_{t-1}).$$

If we solve the second equation for $y_t$ and insert the first expression for $y_t^*$, then we obtain

$$y_t = \alpha(1 - \lambda) + \beta(1 - \lambda)x_t + \delta(1 - \lambda)w_t + \lambda y_{t-1} + (1 - \lambda)\varepsilon_t$$
$$= \alpha' + \beta' x_t + \delta' w_t + \lambda y_{t-1} + \varepsilon_t'.$$

This formulation offers a number of significant practical advantages. It is intrinsically linear in the parameters (unrestricted), and its disturbance is nonautocorrelated if $\varepsilon_t$ was to begin with. As such, the parameters of this model can be estimated consistently and efficiently by ordinary least squares. In this revised formulation, the short-run multipliers for $x_t$ and $w_t$ are $\beta'$ and $\delta'$. The long-run effects are $\beta = \beta'/(1 - \lambda)$ and $\delta = \delta'/(1 - \lambda)$. With the variables in logs, these effects are the short- and long-run elasticities.

### Example 20.2 Expectations-Augmented Phillips Curve

In Example 19.3, we estimated an expectations-augmented Phillips curve of the form

$$\Delta p_t - E[\Delta p_t \mid \Psi_{t-1}] = \beta[u_t - u^*] + \varepsilon_t.$$

Our model assumed a particularly simple model of expectations, $E[\Delta p_t \mid \Psi_{t-1}] = \Delta p_{t-1}$. The least squares results for this equation were

$$\Delta p_t - \Delta p_{t-1} = 0.49189 - 0.090136 u_t + e_t$$

$$(0.7405) \quad (0.1257) \quad R^2 = 0.002561, T = 201.$$

The implied estimate of the natural rate of unemployment is $-(0.49189/-0.090136)$ or about 5.46 percent. Suppose we allow expectations to be formulated less pragmatically with the expectations model in (20-12). For this setting, this would be

$$E[\Delta p_t \mid \Psi_{t-1}] = \lambda E[\Delta p_{t-1} \mid \Psi_{t-2}] + (1 - \lambda)\Delta p_{t-1}.$$

The strict pragmatist has $\lambda = 0.0$. Using the method set out earlier, we would compute this for different values of $\lambda$, recompute the dependent variable in the regression, and locate the value of $\lambda$ which produces the lowest sum of squares. Figure 20.2 shows the sum of squares for the values of $\lambda$ ranging from 0.0 to 1.0.

The minimum value of the sum of squares occurs at $\lambda = 0.66$. The least squares regression results are

$$\Delta p_t - \widehat{\Delta p_{t-1}} = 1.69453 - 0.30427 u_t + e_t$$

$$(0.6617) \quad (0.11125) \quad T = 201.$$

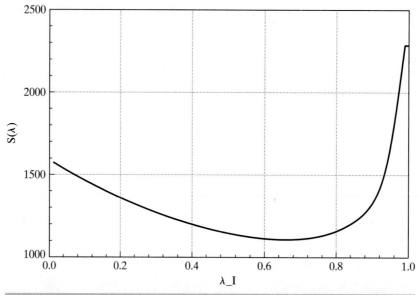

**FIGURE 20.2**  Residuals Sums of Squares for Phillips Curve Estimates.

The estimated standard errors are computed using the method described earlier for the nonlinear regression. The extra variable described in the paragraph after (20-14) accounts for the estimated $\lambda$. The estimated asymptotic covariance matrix is then computed using $(\mathbf{e}'\mathbf{e}/201)[\mathbf{W}'\mathbf{W}]^{-1}$ where $w_1 = 1, w_2 = u_t$ and $w_3 = \partial\widehat{\Delta p_{t-1}}/\partial\lambda$. The estimated standard error for $\lambda$ is 0.04610. Because this is highly statistically significantly different from zero ($t = 14.315$), we would reject the simple model. Finally, the implied estimate of the natural rate of unemployment is $-(-1.69453/0.30427)$ or about 5.57 percent. The estimated asymptotic covariance of the slope and constant term is $-0.0720293$, so, using this value and the estimated standard errors given earlier and the delta method, we obtain an estimated standard error for this estimate of 0.5467. Thus, a confidence interval for the natural rate of unemployment based on these results would be (4.49 percent, 6.64 percent), which is in line with our prior expectations. There are two things to note about these results. First, because the dependent variables are different, we cannot compare the $R^2$s of the models with $\lambda = 0.00$ and $\lambda = 0.66$. But, the sum of squares for the two models can be compared (they are 1592.32 and 1112.89), so the second model fits far better. One of the payoffs is the much narrower confidence interval for the natural rate. The counterpart to the one given earlier when $\lambda = 0.00$ is (1.13%, 9.79%). No doubt the model could be improved still further by expanding the equation. (This is considered in the exercises.)

### Example 20.3  Price and Income Elasticities of Demand for Gasoline

We have extended the gasoline demand equation estimated in Examples 19.2 and 19.6 to allow for dynamic effects. Table 20.1 presents estimates of three distributed lag models for gasoline consumption. The unrestricted model allows five years of adjustment in the price and income effects. The expectations model includes the same distributed lag ($\lambda$) on price and income but different long-run multipliers ($\beta_{Pg}$ and $\beta_I$). [Note, for this formulation, that the extra regressor used in computing the asymptotic covariance matrix is $d_t(\lambda) = \beta_{Pg}d_{price}(\lambda) + \beta_I d_{income}(\lambda)$.] Finally, the partial adjustment model implies lagged effects for all the variables in the model. To facilitate comparison, the constant and the first four slope coefficients in the partial adjustment model have been divided by the estimate of $(1-\lambda)$. The implied long- and short-run price and income **elasticities** are shown in Table 20.2.

**TABLE 20.1** Estimated Distributed Lag Models

| Coefficient | Unrestricted | Expectations | | Partial Adjustment | |
|---|---|---|---|---|---|
| | | *Estimated* | *Derived* | *Estimated* | *Derived* |
| Constant | −28.5512 | −16.1867 | | −4.9489 | |
| ln Pnc | 0.01738 | −0.1050 | | −0.1429 | |
| ln Puc | 0.07602 | 0.02815 | | 0.09435 | |
| ln Ppt | 0.04770 | 0.2550 | | 0.03243 | |
| Trend | −0.02297 | 0.02064 | | −0.004029 | |
| ln Pg | −0.08282 | −0.06702* | −0.06702* | −0.07627 | −0.07627 |
| ln Pg[−1] | −0.07152 | | −0.06233 | | −0.06116 |
| ln Pg[−2] | 0.03669 | | −0.05797 | | −0.04904 |
| ln Pg[−3] | −0.04814 | | −0.05391 | | −0.03933 |
| ln Pg[−4] | 0.02958 | | −0.05013 | | −0.03153 |
| ln Pg[−5] | −0.1481 | | −0.04663 | | −0.02529 |
| ln Income | 1.1074 | 0.04372* | 0.04372* | 0.3135 | 0.3135 |
| ln Income[−1] | 0.3776 | | 0.04066 | | 0.2514 |
| ln Income[−2] | −0.01255 | | 0.03781 | | 0.2016 |
| ln Income[−3] | −0.03919 | | 0.03517 | | 0.1616 |
| ln Income[−4] | 0.2737 | | 0.03270 | | 0.1296 |
| ln Income[−5] | 0.09350 | | 0.03042 | | 0.1039 |
| $Z_t$(Price) | — | −0.06702 | | | |
| $Z_t$(Income) | — | 0.04372 | | | |
| ln (G/Pop)[−1] | — | | | 0.80188 | |
| β | — | −0.9574 | | | |
| γ | — | 0.6245 | | | |
| λ | — | 0.9300 | | 0.80188 | |
| **e′e** | 0.01565356 | 0.03911383 | | .01151860 | |
| T | 47 | 52 | | 51 | |

*Estimated directly

**TABLE 20.2** Estimated Elasticities

| | Short-Run | | Long-Run | |
|---|---|---|---|---|
| | *Price* | *Income* | *Price* | *Income* |
| Unrestricted model | −0.08282 | 1.1074 | −0.2843 | 1.8004 |
| Expectations model | −0.06702 | 0.04372 | −0.9574 | 0.6246 |
| Partial adjustment model | −0.07628 | 0.3135 | −0.3850 | 1.5823 |

## 20.4 AUTOREGRESSIVE DISTRIBUTED LAG MODELS

Both the finite lag models and the geometric lag model impose strong, possibly incorrect restrictions on the lagged response of the dependent variable to changes in an independent variable. A very general compromise that also provides a useful platform for studying a number of interesting methodological issues is the **autoregressive distributed lag (ARDL)** model,

$$y_t = \mu + \sum_{i=1}^{p} \gamma_i y_{t-i} + \sum_{j=0}^{r} \beta_j x_{t-j} + \delta w_t + \varepsilon_t, \tag{20-15}$$

in which $\varepsilon_t$ is assumed to be serially uncorrelated and homoscedastic (we will relax both these assumptions in Chapter 21). We can write this more compactly as

$$C(L)y_t = \mu + B(L)x_t + \delta w_t + \varepsilon_t$$

by defining polynomials in the lag operator,

$$C(L) = 1 - \gamma_1 L - \gamma_2 L^2 - \cdots - \gamma_p L^p,$$

and

$$B(L) = \beta_0 + \beta_1 L + \beta_2 L^2 + \cdots + \beta_r L^r.$$

The model in this form is denoted ARDL$(p, r)$ to indicate the orders of the two polynomials in $L$. The partial adjustment model estimated in the previous section is the special case in which $p$ equals 1 and $r$ equals 0. A number of other special cases are also interesting, including the familiar model of **autocorrelation** $(p = 1, r = 1, \beta_1 = -\gamma_1\beta_0)$, the classical regression model $(p = 0, r = 0)$, and so on.

### 20.4.1 ESTIMATION OF THE ARDL MODEL

Save for the presence of the stochastic right-hand-side variables, the ARDL is a linear model with a classical disturbance. As such, ordinary least squares is the efficient estimator. The lagged dependent variable does present a complication, but we considered this in Chapter 19. Absent any obvious violations of the assumptions there, least squares continues to be the estimator of choice. Conventional testing procedures are, as before, asymptotically valid as well. Thus, for testing linear restrictions, the Wald statistic can be used, although the $F$ statistic is generally preferable in finite samples because of its more conservative critical values.

One subtle complication in the model has attracted a large amount of attention in the recent literature. If $C(1) = 0$, then the model is actually inestimable. This fact is evident in the distributed lag form, which includes a term $\mu/C(1)$. If the equivalent condition $\Sigma_i \gamma_i = 1$ holds, then the stochastic difference equation is unstable and a host of other problems arise as well. This implication suggests that one might be interested in testing this specification as a hypothesis in the context of the model. This restriction might seem to be a simple linear constraint on the alternative (unrestricted) model in (20-15). Under the null hypothesis, however, the conventional test statistics do not have the familiar distributions. The formal derivation is complicated [in the extreme, see Dickey and Fuller (1979) for an example], but intuition should suggest the reason. Under the null hypothesis, the difference equation is explosive, so our assumptions about well behaved data cannot be met. Consider a simple ARDL$(1, 0)$ example and simplify it even further with $B(L) = 0$. Then,

$$y_t = \mu + \gamma y_{t-1} + \varepsilon_t.$$

If $\gamma$ equals 1, then

$$y_t = \mu + y_{t-1} + \varepsilon_t.$$

Assuming we start the time series at time $t = 1$,

$$y_t = t\mu + \Sigma_s \varepsilon_s = t\mu + v_t.$$

to be a simple hypothesis to test in the framework of the ARDL model. Instead, we find the explosive case that we examined in Section 20.4.1, so the hypothesis is more complicated than it first appears. To reiterate, under the null hypothesis that $C(1) = 0$, it is not possible for the standard $F$ statistic to have a central $F$ distribution because of the behavior of the variables in the model. We will return to this case shortly.

The **univariate autoregression,**

$$y_t = \mu + \gamma_1 y_{t-1} + \gamma_2 y_{t-2} + \cdots + \gamma_p y_{t-p} + \varepsilon_t,$$

can be augmented with the $p - 1$ equations

$$y_{t-1} = y_{t-1},$$

$$y_{t-2} = y_{t-2},$$

and so on to give a **vector autoregression, VAR** (to be considered in the next section):

$$\mathbf{y}_t = \boldsymbol{\mu} + \mathbf{C}\mathbf{y}_{t-1} + \boldsymbol{\varepsilon}_t,$$

where $\mathbf{y}_t$ has $p$ elements, $\boldsymbol{\varepsilon}_t = (\varepsilon_t, 0, \ldots)'$, and $\boldsymbol{\mu} = (\mu, 0, 0, \ldots)'$. It will ultimately not be relevant to the solution, so we will let $\varepsilon_t$ equal its expected value of zero. Now, by successive substitution, we obtain

$$\mathbf{y}_t = \boldsymbol{\mu} + \mathbf{C}\boldsymbol{\mu} + \mathbf{C}^2\boldsymbol{\mu} + \cdots,$$

which may or may not converge. Write $\mathbf{C}$ in the spectral form $\mathbf{C} = \mathbf{P}\boldsymbol{\Lambda}\mathbf{Q}$, where $\mathbf{QP} = \mathbf{I}$ and $\boldsymbol{\Lambda}$ is a diagonal matrix of the characteristic roots. (Note that the characteristic roots in $\boldsymbol{\Lambda}$ and vectors in $\mathbf{P}$ and $\mathbf{Q}$ may be complex.) We then obtain

$$\mathbf{y}_t = \left[\sum_{i=0}^{\infty} \mathbf{P}\boldsymbol{\Lambda}^i \mathbf{Q}\right]\boldsymbol{\mu}. \tag{20-19}$$

If all the roots of $\mathbf{C}$ are less than one in absolute value, then this vector will converge to the equilibrium

$$\mathbf{y}_\infty = (\mathbf{I} - \mathbf{C})^{-1}\boldsymbol{\mu}.$$

Nonexplosion of the powers of the roots of $\mathbf{C}$ is equivalent to $|\lambda_p| < 1$, or $|1/\lambda_p| > 1$, which was our original requirement. Note finally that because $\boldsymbol{\mu}$ is a multiple of the first column of $\mathbf{I}_p$, it must be the case that each element in the first column of $(\mathbf{I} - \mathbf{C})^{-1}$ is the same. At equilibrium, therefore, we must have $y_t = y_{t-1} = \cdots = y_\infty$.

### Example 20.4   A Rational Lag Model

Appendix Table F5.1 lists quarterly data on a number of macroeconomic variables including consumption and real GDP for the U.S. economy for the years 1950 to 2000, a total of 204 quarters. The model

$$c_t = \delta + \beta_0 y_t + \beta_1 y_{t-1} + \beta_2 y_{t-2} + \beta_3 y_{t-3} + \gamma_1 c_{t-1} + \gamma_2 c_{t-2} + \gamma_3 c_{t-3} + \varepsilon_t$$

is estimated using the logarithms of real consumption and real GDP, denoted $c_t$ and $y_t$. Ordinary least squares estimates of the parameters of the ARDL(3,3) model are

$$c_t = 0.7233 c_{t-1} + 0.3914 c_{t-2} - 0.2337 c_{t-3}$$

$$+ 0.5651 y_t - 0.3909 y_{t-1} - 0.2379 y_{t-2} + 0.1902 y_{t-3} + e_t.$$

| TABLE 20.3 | Lag Coefficients in a Rational Lag Model | | | | | | |
|---|---|---|---|---|---|---|---|
| Lag | 0 | 1 | 2 | 3 | 4 | 5 | 6 | 7 |
| ARDL | 0.565 | 0.018 | −0.004 | 0.062 | 0.039 | 0.054 | 0.039 | 0.041 |
| Unrestricted | 0.954 | −0.090 | −0.063 | 0.100 | −0.024 | 0.057 | −0.112 | 0.236 |

(A full set of quarterly dummy variables is omitted.) The Durbin–Watson statistic is 1.78597, so remaining autocorrelation seems unlikely to be a consideration. The lag coefficients are given by the equality

$$(\alpha_0 + \alpha_1 L + \alpha_2 L^2 + \cdots)(1 - \gamma_1 L - \gamma_2 L^2 - \gamma_3 L^3) = (\beta_0 + \beta_1 L + \beta_2 L^2 + \beta_3 L^3).$$

Note that $A(L)$ is an infinite polynomial. The lag coefficients are

$$1: \quad \alpha_0 \qquad\qquad\qquad\qquad = \beta_0 \text{ (which will always be the case)},$$

$$L^1: -\alpha_0\gamma_1 + \alpha_1 \qquad\qquad = \beta_1 \text{ or } \alpha_1 = \beta_1 + \alpha_0\gamma_1,$$

$$L^2: -\alpha_0\gamma_2 - \alpha_1\gamma_1 + \alpha_2 \qquad = \beta_2 \text{ or } \alpha_2 = \beta_2 + \alpha_0\gamma_2 + \alpha_1\gamma_1,$$

$$L^3: -\alpha_0\gamma_3 - \alpha_1\gamma_2 - \alpha_2\gamma_1 + \alpha_3 = \beta_3 \text{ or } \alpha_3 = \beta_3 + \alpha_0\gamma_3 + \alpha_1\gamma_2 + \alpha_2\gamma_1,$$

$$L^4: -\alpha_1\gamma_3 - \alpha_2\gamma_2 - \alpha_3\gamma_1 + \alpha_4 = 0 \text{ or } \alpha_4 = \gamma_1\alpha_3 + \gamma_2\alpha_2 + \gamma_3\alpha_1,$$

$$L^j: -\alpha_{j-3}\gamma_3 - \alpha_{j-2}\gamma_2 - \alpha_{j-1}\gamma_1 + \alpha_j = 0 \text{ or } \alpha_j = \gamma_1\alpha_{j-1} + \gamma_2\alpha_{j-2} + \gamma_3\alpha_{j-3}, \quad j = 5, 6, \ldots,$$

and so on. From the fourth term onward, the series of lag coefficients follows the recursion $\alpha_j = \gamma_1\alpha_{j-1} + \gamma_2\alpha_{j-2} + \gamma_3\alpha_{j-3}$, which is the same as the autoregressive part of the ARDL model. The series of lag weights follows the same difference equation as the current and lagged values of $y_t$ after $r$ initial values, where $r$ is the order of the DL part of the ARDL model. The three characteristic roots of the **C** matrix are 0.8631, −0.5949, and 0.4551. Because all are less than one, we conclude that the stochastic difference equation is stable.

The first seven lag coefficients of the estimated ARDL model are listed in Table 20.3 with the first seven coefficients in an unrestricted lag model. The coefficients from the ARDL model only vaguely resemble those from the unrestricted model, but the erratic swings of the latter are prevented by the smooth equation from the distributed lag model. The estimated long-term effects (with standard errors in parentheses) from the two models are 1.0634 (0.00791) from the ARDL model and 1.0570 (0.002135) from the unrestricted model. Surprisingly, in view of the large and highly significant estimated coefficients, the lagged effects fall off essentially to zero after the initial impact.

### 20.4.4 FORECASTING

Consider, first, a **one-period-ahead forecast** of $y_t$ in the ARDL($p, r$) model. It will be convenient to collect the terms in $\mu$, $x_t$, $w_t$, and so on in a single term,

$$\mu_t = \mu + \sum_{j=0}^{r} \beta_j x_{t-j} + \delta w_t.$$

Now, the ARDL model is just

$$y_t = \mu_t + \gamma_1 y_{t-1} + \cdots + \gamma_p y_{t-p} + \varepsilon_t.$$

Conditioned on the full set of information available up to time $T$ and on forecasts of the exogenous variables, the one-period-ahead forecast of $y_t$ would be

$$\hat{y}_{T+1|T} = \hat{\mu}_{T+1|T} + \gamma_1 y_T + \cdots + \gamma_p y_{T-p+1} + \hat{\varepsilon}_{T+1|T}.$$

To form a prediction interval, we will be interested in the variance of the forecast error,

$$e_{T+1|T} = \hat{y}_{T+1|T} - y_{T+1}.$$

This error will arise from three sources. First, in forecasting $\mu_t$, there will be two sources of error. The parameters, $\mu$, $\delta$, and $\beta_0, \ldots, \beta_r$ will have been estimated, so $\hat{\mu}_{T+1|T}$ will differ from $\mu_{T+1}$ because of the sampling variation in these estimators. Second, if the exogenous variables, $x_{T+1}$ and $w_{T+1}$ have been forecasted, then to the extent that these forecasts are themselves imperfect, yet another source of error to the forecast will result. Finally, although we will forecast $\varepsilon_{T+1}$ with its expectation of zero, we would not assume that the actual realization will be zero, so this step will be a third source of error. In principle, an estimate of the forecast variance, $\text{Var}[e_{T+1|T}]$, would account for all three sources of error. In practice, handling the second of these errors is largely intractable, while the first is merely extremely difficult. [See Harvey (1990) and Hamilton (1994, especially Section 11.7) for useful discussion. McCullough (1996) presents results that suggest that "intractable" may be too pessimistic.] For the moment, we will concentrate on the third source and return to the other issues briefly at the end of the section.

Ignoring for the moment the variation in $\hat{\mu}_{T+1|T}$—that is, assuming that the parameters are known and the exogenous variables are forecasted perfectly—the variance of the forecast error will be simply

$$\text{Var}[e_{T+1|T} \mid x_{T+1}, w_{T+1}, \mu, \boldsymbol{\beta}, \delta, y_T, \ldots] = \text{Var}[\varepsilon_{T+1}] = \sigma^2,$$

so at least within these assumptions, forming the forecast and computing the forecast variance are straightforward. Also, at this first step, given the data used for the forecast, the first part of the variance is also tractable. Let $\mathbf{z}_{T+1} = [1, x_{T+1}, x_T, \ldots, x_{T-r+1}, w_T, y_T, y_{T-1}, \ldots, y_{T-p+1}]$, and let $\hat{\boldsymbol{\theta}}$ denote the full estimated parameter vector. Then we would use

$$\text{Est. Var}[e_{T+1|T} \mid z_{T+1}] = s^2 + \mathbf{z}'_{T+1}\{\text{Est. Asy. Var}[\hat{\boldsymbol{\theta}}]\}\mathbf{z}_{T+1}.$$

Now, consider forecasting further out beyond the sample period:

$$\hat{y}_{T+2|T} = \hat{\mu}_{T+2|T} + \gamma_1 \hat{y}_{T+1|T} + \cdots + \gamma_p y_{T-p+2} + \hat{\varepsilon}_{T+2|T}.$$

Note that for period $T + 1$, the forecasted $y_{T+1}$ is used. Making the substitution for $\hat{y}_{T+1|T}$, we have

$$\hat{y}_{T+2|T} = \hat{\mu}_{T+2|T} + \gamma_1(\hat{\mu}_{T+1|T} + \gamma_1 y_T + \cdots + \gamma_p y_{T-p+1} + \hat{\varepsilon}_{T+1|T}) + \cdots + \gamma_p y_{T-p+2} + \hat{\varepsilon}_{T+2|T},$$

and, likewise, for subsequent periods. Our method will be simplified considerably if we use the device we constructed in the previous section. For the first forecast period, write the forecast with the previous $p$ lagged values as

$$
\begin{bmatrix} \hat{y}_{T+1|T} \\ y_T \\ y_{T-1} \\ \vdots \end{bmatrix} = \begin{bmatrix} \hat{\mu}_{T+1|T} \\ 0 \\ 0 \\ \vdots \end{bmatrix} + \begin{bmatrix} \gamma_1 & \gamma_2 & \cdots & \gamma_p \\ 1 & 0 & \cdots & 0 \\ 0 & 1 & \cdots & 0 \\ 0 & \cdots & 1 & 0 \end{bmatrix} \begin{bmatrix} y_T \\ y_{T-1} \\ y_{T-2} \\ \vdots \end{bmatrix} + \begin{bmatrix} \hat{\varepsilon}_{T+1|T} \\ 0 \\ 0 \\ \vdots \end{bmatrix}.
$$

The coefficient matrix on the right-hand side is $\mathbf{C}$, which we defined in (20-18). To maintain the thread of the discussion, we will continue to use the notation $\hat{\mu}_{T+1|T}$ for the forecast of the deterministic part of the model, although for the present, we are assuming that this value, as well as $\mathbf{C}$, is known with certainty. With this modification, then, our forecast is the top element of the vector of forecasts,

$$\hat{\mathbf{y}}_{T+1|T} = \hat{\boldsymbol{\mu}}_{T+1|T} + \mathbf{C}\mathbf{y}_T + \hat{\boldsymbol{\varepsilon}}_{T+1|T}.$$

We are assuming that everything on the right-hand side is known except the period $T + 1$ disturbance, so the covariance matrix for this $p + 1$ vector is

$$E\left[(\hat{\mathbf{y}}_{T+1|T} - \mathbf{y}_{T+1})(\hat{\mathbf{y}}_{T+1|T} - \mathbf{y}_{T+1})'\right] = \begin{bmatrix} \sigma^2 & 0 & \cdots \\ 0 & 0 & \vdots \\ \vdots & \cdots & \ddots \end{bmatrix},$$

and the forecast variance for $\hat{y}_{T+1|T}$ is just the upper left element, $\sigma^2$.

Now, extend this notation to forecasting out to periods $T + 2$, $T + 3$, and so on:

$$\hat{\mathbf{y}}_{T+2|T} = \hat{\boldsymbol{\mu}}_{T+2|T} + \mathbf{C}\hat{\mathbf{y}}_{T+1|T} + \hat{\boldsymbol{\varepsilon}}_{T+2|T}$$

$$= \hat{\boldsymbol{\mu}}_{T+2|T} + \mathbf{C}\hat{\boldsymbol{\mu}}_{T+1|T} + \mathbf{C}^2\mathbf{y}_T + \hat{\boldsymbol{\varepsilon}}_{T+2|T} + \mathbf{C}\hat{\boldsymbol{\varepsilon}}_{T+1|T}.$$

Once again, the only unknowns are the disturbances, so the forecast variance for this two-period-ahead forecasted vector is

$$\text{Var}[\hat{\boldsymbol{\varepsilon}}_{T+2|T} + \mathbf{C}\hat{\boldsymbol{\varepsilon}}_{T+1|T}] = \begin{bmatrix} \sigma^2 & 0 & \cdots \\ 0 & 0 & \vdots \\ \vdots & \cdots & \ddots \end{bmatrix} + \mathbf{C}\begin{bmatrix} \sigma^2 & 0 & \cdots \\ 0 & 0 & \vdots \\ \vdots & \cdots & \ddots \end{bmatrix}\mathbf{C}'.$$

Thus, the forecast variance for the two-step-ahead forecast is $\sigma^2[1 + \boldsymbol{\Psi}(1)_{11}]$, where $\boldsymbol{\Psi}(1)_{11}$ is the $(1, 1)$ element of $\boldsymbol{\Psi}(1) = \mathbf{C}\mathbf{j}\mathbf{j}'\mathbf{C}'$, where $\mathbf{j}' = [\sigma, 0, \ldots, 0]$. By extending this device to a forecast $F$ periods beyond the sample period, we obtain

$$\hat{\mathbf{y}}_{T+F|T} = \sum_{f=1}^{F} \mathbf{C}^{f-1}\hat{\boldsymbol{\mu}}_{T+F-(f-1)|T} + \mathbf{C}^F\mathbf{y}_T + \sum_{f=1}^{F} \mathbf{C}^{f-1}\hat{\boldsymbol{\varepsilon}}_{T+F-(f-1)|T}. \tag{20-20}$$

This equation shows how to compute the forecasts, which is reasonably simple. We also obtain our expression for the conditional forecast variance,

$$\text{Conditional Var}[\hat{y}_{T+F|T}] = \sigma^2[1 + \boldsymbol{\Psi}(1)_{11} + \boldsymbol{\Psi}(2)_{11} + \cdots + \boldsymbol{\Psi}(F-1)_{11}], \tag{20-21}$$

where $\boldsymbol{\Psi}(i) = \mathbf{C}^i\mathbf{j}\mathbf{j}'\mathbf{C}^{i'}$.

The general form of the $F$-period-ahead forecast shows how the forecasts will behave as the forecast period extends further out beyond the sample period. If the equation is stable—that is, if all roots of the matrix $\mathbf{C}$ are less than one in absolute value—then $\mathbf{C}^F$ will converge to zero, and because the forecasted disturbances are zero, the forecast will be dominated by the sum in the first term. If we suppose, in addition, that the forecasts of the exogenous variables are just the period $T + 1$ forecasted values and not revised, then, as we found at the end of the previous section, the forecast will ultimately converge to

$$\lim_{F \to \infty} \hat{\mathbf{y}}_{T+F|T} \mid \hat{\boldsymbol{\mu}}_{T+1|T} = [\mathbf{I} - \mathbf{C}]^{-1}\hat{\boldsymbol{\mu}}_{T+1|T}.$$

To account fully for all sources of variation in the forecasts, we would have to revise the forecast variance to include the variation in the forecasts of the exogenous variables and the variation in the parameter estimates. As noted, the first of these is likely to be intractable. For the second, this revision will be extremely difficult, the more so when we also account for the matrix $\mathbf{C}$, as well as the vector $\boldsymbol{\mu}$, being built up from the estimated parameters. The level of difficulty in this case falls from impossible to merely extremely difficult. In principle, what is required is

$$\text{Est. Conditional Var}[\hat{y}_{T+F|T}] = \sigma^2[1 + \boldsymbol{\Psi}(1)_{11} + \boldsymbol{\Psi}(2)_{11} + \cdots + \boldsymbol{\Psi}(F-1)_{11}]$$
$$+ \mathbf{g}'\text{Est. Asy. Var}[\hat{\boldsymbol{\mu}}, \hat{\boldsymbol{\beta}}, \hat{\boldsymbol{\gamma}}]\mathbf{g},$$

where

$$\mathbf{g} = \frac{\partial \hat{y}_{T+F}}{\partial[\hat{\boldsymbol{\mu}}, \hat{\boldsymbol{\beta}}, \hat{\boldsymbol{\gamma}}]}.$$

[See Hamilton (1994, Appendix to Chapter 11) for formal derivation.]

One possibility is to use the bootstrap method. For this application, bootstrapping would involve sampling new sets of disturbances from the estimated distribution of $\varepsilon_t$, and then repeatedly rebuilding the within-sample time series of observations on $y_t$ by using

$$\hat{y}_t = \hat{\mu}_t + \gamma_1 y_{t-1} + \cdots + \gamma_p y_{t-p} + e_{bt}(m),$$

where $e_{bt}(m)$ is the estimated "bootstrapped" disturbance in period $t$ during replication $m$. The process is repeated $M$ times, with new parameter estimates and a new forecast generated in each replication. The variance of these forecasts produces the estimated forecast variance.[6]

## 20.5 METHODOLOGICAL ISSUES IN THE ANALYSIS OF DYNAMIC MODELS

### 20.5.1 AN ERROR CORRECTION MODEL

Consider the ARDL(1, 1) model, which has become a workhorse of the modern literature on time-series analysis. By defining the first differences $\Delta y_t = y_t - y_{t-1}$ and $\Delta x_t = x_t - x_{t-1}$ we can rearrange

$$y_t = \mu + \gamma_1 y_{t-1} + \beta_0 x_t + \beta_1 x_{t-1} + \varepsilon_t$$

to obtain

$$\Delta y_t = \mu + \beta_0 \Delta x_t + (\gamma_1 - 1)(y_{t-1} - \theta x_{t-1}) + \varepsilon_t, \tag{20-22}$$

where $\theta = -(\beta_0 + \beta_1)/(\gamma_1 - 1)$. This form of the model is in the **error correction** form. In this form, we have an **equilibrium relationship,** $\Delta y_t = \mu + \beta_0 \Delta x_t + \varepsilon_t$, and the **equilibrium error,** $(\gamma_1 - 1)(y_{t-1} - \theta x_{t-1})$, which account for the deviation of the pair of variables from that equilibrium. The model states that the change in $y_t$ from the previous period consists of the change associated with movement with $x_t$ along the

---

[6]Bernard and Veall (1987) give an application of this technique. See, also, McCullough (1996).

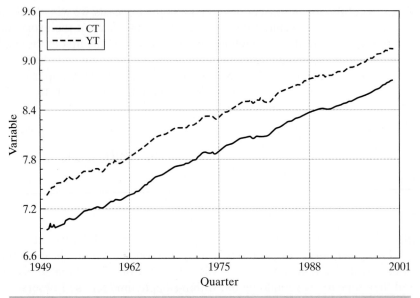

**FIGURE 20.3** Consumption and Income Data.

long-run equilibrium path plus a part $(\gamma_1 - 1)$ of the deviation $(y_{t-1} - \theta x_{t-1})$ from the equilibrium. With a model in logs, this relationship would be in proportional terms.

It is useful at this juncture to jump ahead a bit—we will return to this topic in some detail in Chapter 21—and explore why the error correction form might be such a useful formulation of this simple model. Consider the logged consumption and income data plotted in Figure 20.3. It is obvious on inspection of the figure that a simple regression of the log of consumption on the log of income would suggest a highly significant relationship; in fact, the simple linear regression produces a slope of 1.0567 with a $t$ ratio of 440.5 (!) and an $R^2$ of 0.99896. The disturbing result of a line of literature in econometrics that begins with Granger and Newbold (1974) and continues to the present is that this seemingly obvious and powerful relationship might be entirely spurious. Equally obvious from the figure is that both $c_t$ and $y_t$ are trending variables. If, in fact, both variables unconditionally were random walks with drift of the sort that we met at the end of Section 20.4.1—that is, $c_t = t\mu_c + v_t$ and likewise for $y_t$—then we would almost certainly observe a figure such as 20.3 and compelling regression results such as those, *even if there were no relationship at all*. In addition, there is ample evidence in the recent literature that low-frequency (infrequently observed, aggregated over long periods) flow variables such as consumption and output are, indeed, often well described as random walks. In such data, the ARDL(1, 1) model might appear to be entirely appropriate even if it is not. So, how is one to distinguish between the spurious regression and a genuine relationship as shown in the ARDL(1, 1)? The first difference of consumption produces $\Delta c_t = \mu_c + v_t - v_{t-1}$. If the random walk proposition is indeed correct, then the spurious appearance of regression will not survive the first differencing, whereas if there is a relationship between $c_t$ and $y_t$, then it will be preserved in the error correction model. We will return to this issue in Chapter 21, when we examine the issue of integration and cointegration of economic variables.

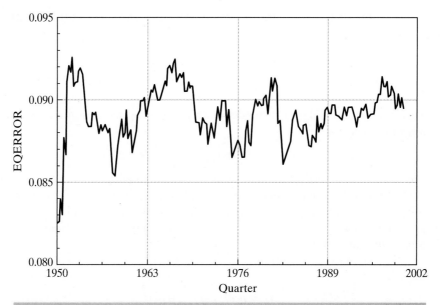

**FIGURE 20.4** Consumption–Income Equilibrium Errors.

### Example 20.5   An Error Correction Model for Consumption

The error correction model is a nonlinear regression model, although in fact it is intrinsically linear and can be deduced simply from the unrestricted form directly above it. Because the parameter $\theta$ is actually of some interest, it might be more convenient to use nonlinear least squares and fit the second form directly. (The model is intrinsically linear, so the nonlinear least squares estimates will be identical to the derived linear least squares estimates.) The logs of consumption and income data in Appendix Table F5.1 are plotted in Figure 20.3. Not surprisingly, the two variables are drifting upward together.

The estimated error correction model, with estimated standard errors in parentheses, is

$$c_t - c_{t-1} = -0.08533 + (0.90458 - 1)[c_{t-1} - 1.06034 y_{t-1}] + 0.58421(y_t - y_{t-1}).$$
$$\quad\;\;(0.02899) \qquad (0.03029) \qquad\qquad (0.01052) \qquad (0.05090)$$

The estimated equilibrium errors are shown in Figure 20.4. Note that they are all positive, but that in each period, the adjustment is in the opposite direction. Thus (according to this model), when consumption is below its equilibrium value, the adjustment is upward, as might be expected.

### 20.5.2   AUTOCORRELATION

The disturbance in the error correction model is assumed to be nonautocorrelated. As we saw in Chapter 19, autocorrelation in a model can be induced by misspecification. An orthodox view of the modeling process might state, in fact, that this misspecification is the *only* source of autocorrelation. Although admittedly a bit optimistic in its implication, this misspecification does raise an interesting methodological question. Consider once again the simplest model of autocorrelation from Chapter 19 (with a small change in notation to make it consistent with the present discussion),

$$y_t = \beta x_t + v_t, \qquad v_t = \rho v_{t-1} + \varepsilon_t, \tag{20-23}$$

where $\varepsilon_t$ is nonautocorrelated. As we found earlier, this model can be written as

$$y_t - \rho y_{t-1} = \beta(x_t - \rho x_{t-1}) + \varepsilon_t, \qquad (20\text{-}24)$$

or

$$y_t = \rho y_{t-1} + \beta x_t - \beta \rho x_{t-1} + \varepsilon_t. \qquad (20\text{-}25)$$

This model is an ARDL(1, 1) model in which $\beta_1 = -\gamma_1 \beta_0$. Thus, we can view (20-25) as a restricted version of

$$y_t = \gamma_1 y_{t-1} + \beta_0 x_t + \beta_1 x_{t-1} + \varepsilon_t. \qquad (20\text{-}26)$$

The crucial point here is that the (nonlinear) restriction on (20-26) is testable, so there is no compelling reason to proceed to (20-23) first without establishing that the restriction is in fact consistent with the data. The upshot is that the AR(1) disturbance model, as a general proposition, is a testable restriction on a simpler, linear model, not necessarily a structure unto itself.

Now, let us take this argument to its logical conclusion. The AR($p$) disturbance model,

$$v_t = \rho_1 v_{t-1} + \cdots + \rho_p v_{t-p} + \varepsilon_t,$$

or $R(L)v_t = \varepsilon_t$, can be written in its moving average form as

$$v_t = \frac{\varepsilon_t}{R(L)}.$$

[Recall, in the AR(1) model, that $\varepsilon_t = u_t + \rho u_{t-1} + \rho^2 u_{t-2} + \cdots.$] The regression model with this AR($p$) disturbance is, therefore,

$$y_t = \beta x_t + \frac{\varepsilon_t}{R(L)}.$$

But consider instead the ARDL($p, p$) model

$$C(L)y_t = \beta B(L)x_t + \varepsilon_t.$$

These coefficients are the same model if $B(L) = C(L)$. The implication is that *any model with an AR($p$) disturbance can be interpreted as a nonlinearly restricted version of an ARDL($p, p$) model.*

The preceding discussion is a rather orthodox view of autocorrelation. It is predicated on the AR($p$) model. Researchers have found that a more involved model for the process generating $\varepsilon_t$ is sometimes called for. If the time-series structure of $\varepsilon_t$ is not autoregressive, much of the preceding analysis will become intractable. As such, there remains room for disagreement with the strong conclusions. We will turn to models whose disturbances are mixtures of autoregressive and moving-average terms, which would be beyond the reach of this apparatus, in Chapter 21.

### 20.5.3 SPECIFICATION ANALYSIS

The usual explanation of autocorrelation is serial correlation in omitted variables. The preceding discussion and our results in Chapter 19 suggest another candidate: misspecification of what would otherwise be an unrestricted ARDL model. Thus, upon finding evidence of autocorrelation on the basis of a Durbin–Watson statistic or an LM statistic, we might find that relaxing the nonlinear restrictions on the ARDL model is a preferable next step to "correcting" for the autocorrelation by imposing the restrictions and refitting the model by FGLS. Because an ARDL$(p, r)$ model with AR disturbances, even with $p = 0$, is implicitly an ARDL$(p + d, r + d)$ model, where $d$ is usually one, the approach suggested is just to add additional lags of the dependent variable to the model. Thus, one might even ask why we would ever use the familiar FGLS procedures. [See, e.g., Mizon (1995).] The payoff is that the restrictions imposed by the FGLS procedure produce a more efficient estimator than other methods. If the restrictions are in fact appropriate, then not imposing them amounts to not using information.

A related question now arises, apart from the issue of autocorrelation. In the context of the ARDL model, how should one do the specification search? (This question is not specific to the ARDL or even to the time-series setting.) Is it better to start with a small model and expand it until conventional fit measures indicate that additional variables are no longer improving the model, or is it better to start with a large model and pare away variables that conventional statistics suggest are superfluous? The first strategy, going from a *simple model to a general model,* is likely to be problematic, because the statistics computed for the narrower model are biased and inconsistent if the hypothesis is incorrect. Consider, for example, an LM test for autocorrelation in a model from which important variables have been omitted. The results are biased in favor of a finding of autocorrelation. The alternative approach is to proceed from a *general model to a simple one.* Thus, one might overfit the model and then subject it to whatever battery of tests are appropriate to produce the correct specification at the end of the procedure. In this instance, the estimates and test statistics computed from the overfit model, although inefficient, are not generally systematically biased. (We have encountered this issue at several points.)

The latter approach is common in modern analysis, but some words of caution are needed. The procedure routinely leads to overfitting the model. A typical time-series analysis might involve specifying a model with deep lags on all the variables and then paring away the model as conventional statistics indicate. The danger is that the resulting model might have an autoregressive structure with peculiar holes in it that would be hard to justify with any theory. Thus, a model for quarterly data that includes lags of 2, 3, 6, and 9 on the dependent variable would look suspiciously like the end result of a computer-driven fishing trip and, moreover, might not survive even moderate changes in the estimation sample. [As Hendry (1995) notes, a model in which the largest and most significant lag coefficient occurs at the last lag is surely misspecified.]

## 20.6   VECTOR AUTOREGRESSIONS

The preceding discussions can be extended to sets of variables. The resulting autoregressive model is

$$\mathbf{y}_t = \boldsymbol{\mu} + \boldsymbol{\Gamma}_1 \mathbf{y}_{t-1} + \cdots + \boldsymbol{\Gamma}_p \mathbf{y}_{t-p} + \boldsymbol{\varepsilon}_t, \tag{20-27}$$

where $\boldsymbol{\varepsilon}_t$ is a vector of nonautocorrelated disturbances (innovations) with zero means and contemporaneous covariance matrix $E[\boldsymbol{\varepsilon}_t \boldsymbol{\varepsilon}_t'] = \boldsymbol{\Omega}$. This equation system is a vector

**autoregression,** or VAR. Equation (20-27) may also be written as

$$\mathbf{\Gamma}(L)\mathbf{y}_t = \boldsymbol{\mu} + \boldsymbol{\varepsilon}_t$$

where $\mathbf{\Gamma}(L)$ is a matrix of polynomials in the lag operator. The individual equations are

$$y_{mt} = \mu_m + \sum_{j=1}^{p}(\mathbf{\Gamma}_j)_{m1}y_{1,t-j} + \sum_{j=1}^{p}(\mathbf{\Gamma}_j)_{m2}y_{2,t-j} + \cdots + \sum_{j=1}^{p}(\mathbf{\Gamma}_j)_{mM}y_{M,t-j} + \varepsilon_{mt},$$

where $(\mathbf{\Gamma}_j)_{ml}$ indicates the $(m, l)$ element of $\mathbf{\Gamma}_j$.

VARs have been used primarily in macroeconomics. Early in their development, it was argued by some authors [e.g., Sims (1980), Litterman (1979, 1986)] that VARs would forecast better than the sort of structural equation models discussed in Chapter 13. One could argue that as long as $\boldsymbol{\mu}$ includes the current observations on the (truly) relevant exogenous variables, the VAR is simply an overfit reduced form of some simultaneous equations model. [See Hamilton (1994, pp. 326–327).] The overfitting results from the possible inclusion of more lags than would be appropriate in the original model. (See Example 20.7 for a detailed discussion of one such model.) On the other hand, one of the virtues of the VAR is that it obviates a decision as to what contemporaneous variables are exogenous; it has only lagged (predetermined) variables on the right-hand side, and all variables are endogenous.

The motivation behind VARs in macroeconomics runs deeper than the statistical issues.[7] The large structural equations models of the 1950s and 1960s were built on a theoretical foundation that has not proved satisfactory. That the forecasting performance of VARs surpassed that of large structural models—some of the later counterparts to Klein's Model I ran to hundreds of equations—signaled to researchers a more fundamental problem with the underlying methodology. The Keynesian style systems of equations describe a structural model of decisions (consumption, investment) that seem loosely to mimic individual behavior; see Keynes's formulation of the consumption function in Example 1.1 that is, perhaps, the canonical example. In the end, however, these decision rules are fundamentally ad hoc, and there is little basis on which to assume that they would aggregate to the macroeconomic level anyway. On a more practical level, the high inflation and high unemployment experienced in the 1970s were very badly predicted by the Keynesian paradigm. From the point of view of the underlying paradigm, the most troubling criticism of the structural modeling approach comes in the form of "the Lucas critique" (1976), in which the author argued that the *parameters* of the "decision rules" embodied in the systems of structural equations would not remain stable when economic policies changed, even if the rules themselves were appropriate. Thus, the paradigm underlying the systems of equations approach to macroeconomic modeling is arguably fundamentally flawed. More recent research has reformulated the basic equations of macroeconomic models in terms of a microeconomic optimization foundation and has, at the same time, been much less ambitious in specifying the interrelationships among economic variables.

The preceding arguments have drawn researchers to less structured equation systems for forecasting. Thus, it is not just the form of the equations that has changed. The

---

[7]An extremely readable, nontechnical discussion of the paradigm shift in macroeconomic forecasting is given in Diebold (2003). See also Stock and Watson (2001).

variables in the equations have changed as well; the VAR is not just the reduced form of some structural model. For purposes of analyzing and forecasting macroeconomic activity and tracing the effects of policy changes and external stimuli on the economy, researchers have found that simple, small-scale VARs without a possibly flawed theoretical foundation have proved as good as or better than large-scale structural equation systems. In addition to forecasting, VARs have been used for two primary functions: testing Granger causality and studying the effects of policy through impulse response characteristics.

### 20.6.1   MODEL FORMS

To simplify things for the present, we note that the $p$th order VAR can be written as a first-order VAR as follows:

$$
\begin{pmatrix} \mathbf{y}_t \\ \mathbf{y}_{t-1} \\ \cdots \\ \mathbf{y}_{t-p+1} \end{pmatrix} = \begin{pmatrix} \boldsymbol{\mu} \\ \mathbf{0} \\ \cdots \\ \mathbf{0} \end{pmatrix} + \begin{bmatrix} \boldsymbol{\Gamma}_1 & \boldsymbol{\Gamma}_2 & \cdots & \boldsymbol{\Gamma}_p \\ \mathbf{I} & \mathbf{0} & \cdots & \mathbf{0} \\ \cdots & \cdots & \cdots & \mathbf{0} \\ \mathbf{0} & \cdots & \mathbf{I} & \mathbf{0} \end{bmatrix} \begin{pmatrix} \mathbf{y}_{t-1} \\ \mathbf{y}_{t-2} \\ \cdots \\ \mathbf{y}_{t-p} \end{pmatrix} + \begin{pmatrix} \boldsymbol{\varepsilon}_t \\ \mathbf{0} \\ \cdots \\ \mathbf{0} \end{pmatrix}.
$$

[See, e.g., (20-18).] This means that we do not lose any generality in casting the treatment in terms of a first-order model

$$ \mathbf{y}_t = \boldsymbol{\mu} + \boldsymbol{\Gamma}\mathbf{y}_{t-1} + \boldsymbol{\varepsilon}_t. $$

In Example 15.10, we examined Dahlberg and Johansson's model for municipal finances in Sweden, in which $\mathbf{y}_t = [\Delta S_t, \Delta R_t, \Delta G_t]'$, where $S_t$ is spending, $R_t$ is receipts, $G_t$ is grants from the central government, and $p = 3$. We will continue that application in Example 20.7.

In principle, the VAR model is a seemingly unrelated regressions model—indeed, a particularly simple one because each equation has the same set of regressors. This is the traditional form of the model as originally proposed, for example, by Sims (1980). The VAR may also be viewed as the reduced form of a simultaneous equations model; the corresponding structure would then be

$$ \boldsymbol{\Theta}\mathbf{y}_t = \boldsymbol{\alpha} + \boldsymbol{\Psi}\mathbf{y}_{t-1} + \boldsymbol{\omega}_t, $$

where $\boldsymbol{\Theta}$ is a nonsingular matrix and $\mathrm{Var}[\boldsymbol{\omega}_t] = \boldsymbol{\Sigma}$. In one of Cecchetti and Rich's (2001) formulations, for example, $\mathbf{y}_t = [\Delta y_t, \Delta \pi_t]'$ where $y_t$ is the log of aggregate real output, $\pi_t$ is the inflation rate from time $t-1$ to time $t$, $\boldsymbol{\Theta} = \begin{bmatrix} 1 & -\theta_{12} \\ -\theta_{21} & 1 \end{bmatrix}$, and $p = 8$. (We will examine their model in Section 20.6.8.) In this form, we have a conventional simultaneous equations model, which we analyzed in detail in Chapter 13. As we saw, for such a model to be identified—that is, estimable—certain restrictions must be placed on the structural coefficients. The reason for this is that ultimately, only the original VAR form, now the reduced form, is estimated from the data; the structural parameters must be deduced from these coefficients. In this model, to deduce these structural parameters, they must be extracted from the reduced form parameters, $\boldsymbol{\Gamma} = \boldsymbol{\Theta}^{-1}\boldsymbol{\Psi}$, $\boldsymbol{\mu} = \boldsymbol{\Theta}^{-1}\boldsymbol{\alpha}$, and $\boldsymbol{\Omega} = \boldsymbol{\Theta}^{-1}\boldsymbol{\Sigma}\boldsymbol{\Theta}^{-1\prime}$. We analyzed this issue in detail in Section 13.3. The results would be the same here. In Cecchetti and Rich's application, certain restrictions were placed on the lag coefficients in order to secure identification.

### 20.6.2 ESTIMATION

In the form of (20-27)—that is, without autocorrelation of the disturbances—VARs are particularly simple to estimate. Although the equation system can be exceedingly large, it is, in fact, a seemingly unrelated regressions model with identical regressors. As such, the equations should be estimated separately by ordinary least squares. (See Section 10.2.2 for discussion of SUR systems with identical regressors.) The disturbance covariance matrix can then be estimated with average sums of squares or cross-products of the least squares residuals. If the disturbances are normally distributed, then these least squares estimators are also maximum likelihood. If not, then OLS remains an efficient GMM estimator. The extension to instrumental variables and GMM is a bit more complicated, as the model now contains multiple equations (see Section 15.6.3), but since the equations are all linear, the necessary extensions are at least relatively straightforward. GMM estimation of the VAR system is a special case of the model discussed in Section 15.6.3. (We will examine an application in Example 20.7.)

The proliferation of parameters in VARs has been cited as a major disadvantage of their use. Consider, for example, a VAR involving five variables and three lags. Each $\mathbf{\Gamma}$ has 25 unconstrained elements, and there are three of them, for a total of 75 free parameters, plus any others in $\boldsymbol{\mu}$, plus $5(6)/2 = 15$ free parameters in $\mathbf{\Omega}$. On the other hand, each single equation has only 25 parameters, and at least given sufficient degrees of freedom—there's the rub—a linear regression with 25 parameters is simple work. Moreover, applications rarely involve even as many as four variables, so the model-size issue may well be exaggerated.

### 20.6.3 TESTING PROCEDURES

Formal testing in the VAR setting usually centers either on determining the appropriate lag length (a specification search) or on whether certain blocks of zeros in the coefficient matrices are zero (a simple linear restriction on the collection of slope parameters). Both types of hypotheses may be treated as sets of linear restrictions on the elements in $\boldsymbol{\gamma} = \text{vec}[\boldsymbol{\mu}, \mathbf{\Gamma}_1, \mathbf{\Gamma}_2, \ldots, \mathbf{\Gamma}_p]$.

We begin by assuming that the disturbances have a joint normal distribution. Let $\mathbf{W}$ be the $M \times M$ residual covariance matrix based on a restricted model, and let $\mathbf{W}^*$ be its counterpart when the model is unrestricted. Then the likelihood ratio statistic,

$$\lambda = T(\ln|\mathbf{W}| - \ln|\mathbf{W}^*|),$$

can be used to test the hypothesis. The statistic would have a limiting chi-squared distribution with degrees of freedom equal to the number of restrictions. In principle, one might base a specification search for the right lag length on this calculation. The procedure would be to test down from, say, lag $q$ to lag $p$. The *general-to-simple* principle discussed in Section 20.5.3 would be to set the maximum lag length and test down from it until deletion of the last set of lags leads to a significant loss of fit. At each step at which the alternative lag model has excess terms, the estimators of the superfluous coefficient matrices would have probability limits of zero and the likelihood function would (again, asymptotically) resemble that of the model with the correct number of lags. Formally, suppose the appropriate lag length is $p$ but the model is fit with $q \geq p+1$ lagged terms.

Then, under the null hypothesis,

$$\lambda_q = T[\ln|\mathbf{W}(\boldsymbol{\mu}, \boldsymbol{\Gamma}_1, \ldots, \boldsymbol{\Gamma}_{q-1})| - \ln|\mathbf{W}^*(\boldsymbol{\mu}, \boldsymbol{\Gamma}_1, \ldots, \boldsymbol{\Gamma}_q)|] \xrightarrow{d} \chi^2[M^2].$$

The same approach would be used to test other restrictions. Thus, the Granger causality test noted in Section 20.6.5 would fit the model with and without certain blocks of zeros in the coefficient matrices, then refer the value of $\lambda$ once again to the chi-squared distribution.

For specification searches for the right lag, the suggested procedure may be less effective than one based on the information criteria suggested for other linear models (see Section 7.4). Lutkepohl (2005, pp. 128–135) suggests an alternative approach based on the minimizing functions of the information criteria we have considered earlier;

$$\lambda^* = \ln(|\mathbf{W}|) + (pM^2 + M)\mathrm{IC}(T)/T,$$

where $T$ is the sample size, $p$ is the number of lags, $M$ is the number of equations, and $\mathrm{IC}(T) = 2$ for the Akaike information criterion and $\ln T$ for the Schwarz (Bayesian) information criterion. We should note that this is not a test statistic; it is a diagnostic tool that we are using to conduct a specification search. Also, as in all such cases, the testing procedure should be from a larger model to a smaller one to avoid the misspecification problems induced by a lag length that is smaller than the appropriate one.

The preceding has relied heavily on the normality assumption. Because most recent applications of these techniques have either treated the least squares estimators as robust (distribution-free) estimators, or used GMM (as we did in Chapter 15), it is necessary to consider a different approach that does not depend on normality. An alternative approach that should be robust to variations in the underlying distributions is the Wald statistic. [See Lutkepohl (2005, pp. 93–95).] The full set of coefficients in the model may be arrayed in a single coefficient vector, $\boldsymbol{\gamma}$. Let $\mathbf{c}$ be the sample estimator of $\boldsymbol{\gamma}$ and let $\mathbf{V}$ denote the estimated asymptotic covariance matrix. Then, the hypothesis in question (lag length, or other linear restriction) can be cast in the form $\mathbf{R}\boldsymbol{\gamma} - \mathbf{q} = \mathbf{0}$. The Wald statistic for testing the null hypothesis is

$$W = (\mathbf{Rc} - \mathbf{q})'[\mathbf{RVR}']^{-1}(\mathbf{Rc} - \mathbf{q}).$$

Under the null hypothesis, this statistic has a limiting chi-squared distribution with degrees of freedom equal to $J$, the number of restrictions (rows in $\mathbf{R}$). For the specification search for the appropriate lag length (or the Granger causality test discussed in the next section), the null hypothesis will be that a certain subvector of $\boldsymbol{\gamma}$, say $\boldsymbol{\gamma}_0$, equals zero. In this case, the statistic will be

$$W_0 = \mathbf{c}_0' \mathbf{V}_{00}^{-1} \mathbf{c}_0,$$

where $\mathbf{V}_{00}$ denotes the corresponding submatrix of $\mathbf{V}$.

Because time-series data sets are often only moderately long, use of the limiting distribution for the test statistic may be a bit optimistic. Also, the Wald statistic does not account for the fact that the asymptotic covariance matrix is estimated using a finite sample. In our analysis of the classical linear regression model, we accommodated these considerations by using the $F$ distribution instead of the limiting chi-squared. (See Section 5.4.) The adjustment made was to refer $W/J$ to the $F[J, T - K]$ distribution. This produces a more conservative test—the corresponding critical values of $JF$ converge of to those of the chi-squared *from above*. A remaining complication is to decide what degrees of freedom to use for the denominator. It might seem natural to use $MT$ minus the number of parameters, which would be correct if the restrictions are imposed on all equations simultaneously, because there are that many "observations." In testing for causality, as in Section 20.6.5 below, Lutkepohl (2005, p. 95) argues that $MT$ is excessive, because the restrictions are not imposed on all equations. When the causality test involves testing for zero restrictions within a single equation, the appropriate degrees of freedom would be $T - Mp - 1$ for that one equation.

### 20.6.4 EXOGENEITY

In the classical regression model with nonstochastic regressors, there is no ambiguity about which is the independent or conditioning or "exogenous" variable in the model

$$y_t = \beta_1 + \beta_2 x_t + \varepsilon_t. \tag{20-28}$$

This is the kind of characterization that might apply in an experimental situation in which the analyst is choosing the values of $x_t$. But, the case of nonstochastic regressors has little to do with the sort of modeling that will be of interest in this and the next chapter. There is no basis for the narrow assumption of nonstochastic regressors, and, in fact, in most of the analysis that we have done to this point, we have left this assumption far behind. With stochastic regressor(s), the regression relationship such as the preceding one becomes a conditional mean in a bivariate distribution. In this more realistic setting, what constitutes an "exogenous" variable becomes ambiguous. Assuming that the regression relationship is linear, (20-28) can be written (trivially) as

$$y_t = E[y_t \mid x_t] + (y_t - E[y_t \mid x_t]),$$

where the familiar moment condition $E[x_t \varepsilon_t] = 0$ follows by construction. But, this form of the model is no more the "correct" equation than would be

$$x_t = \delta_1 + \delta_2 y_t + \omega_t,$$

which is (we assume)

$$x_t = E[x_t \mid y_t] + (x_t - E[x_t \mid y_t]),$$

and now, $E[y_t \omega_t] = 0$. Both equations are correctly specified in the context of the bivariate distribution, so there is nothing to define one variable or the other as "exogenous." This might seem puzzling, but it is, in fact, at the heart of the matter when one considers modeling in a world in which variables are jointly determined. The definition of exogeneity depends on the analyst's understanding of the world they are modeling, and, in the final analysis, on the purpose to which the model is to be put.

The methodological platform on which this discussion rests is the classic paper by Engle, Hendry, and Richard (1983), where they point out that exogeneity is not an absolute concept at all; it is defined in the context of the model. The central idea, which will be very useful to us here, is that we define a variable (set of variables) as exogenous *in the context of our model* if the joint density may be written

$$f(y_t, x_t) = f(y_t \mid \boldsymbol{\beta}, x_t) \times f(x_t \mid \boldsymbol{\theta})$$

where the parameters in the conditional distribution do not appear in and are functionally unrelated to those in the marginal distribution of $x_t$. By this arrangement, we can think of "autonomous variation" of the parameters of interest, $\boldsymbol{\beta}$. The parameters in the conditional model for $y_t \mid x_t$ can be analyzed as if they could vary independently of those in the marginal distribution of $x_t$. If this condition does not hold, then we cannot think of variation of those parameters without linking that variation to some effect in the marginal distribution of $x_t$. In this case, it makes little sense to think of $x_t$ as somehow being determined "outside" the (conditional) model. (We considered this issue in Section 13.8 in the context of a simultaneous equations model.)

A second form of exogeneity we will consider is **strong exogeneity,** which is sometimes called **Granger noncausality.** Granger noncausality can be superficially defined by the assumption

$$E[y_t \mid y_{t-1}, x_{t-1}, x_{t-2}, \ldots] = E[y_t \mid y_{t-1}].$$

That is, lagged values of $x_t$ do not provide information about the conditional mean of $y_t$ once lagged values of $y_t$, itself, are accounted for. We will consider this issue at the end of this chapter. For the present, we note that most of the models we will examine will explicitly fail this assumption.

To put this back in the context of our model, we will be assuming that in the model

$$y_t = \beta_1 + \beta_2 x_t + \beta_3 x_{t-1} + \gamma y_{t-1} + \varepsilon_t,$$

and the extensions that we will consider, $x_t$ is weakly exogenous—we can meaningfully estimate the parameters of the regression equation independently of the marginal distribution of $x_t$, but we will allow for Granger causality between $x_t$ and $y_t$, thus generally not assuming strong exogeneity.

### 20.6.5 TESTING FOR GRANGER CAUSALITY

Causality in the sense defined by Granger (1969) and Sims (1972) is inferred when lagged values of a variable, say, $x_t$, have explanatory power in a regression of a variable $y_t$ on lagged values of $y_t$ and $x_t$. (See Section 13.2.2.) The VAR can be used to test the hypothesis.[8] Tests of the restrictions can be based on simple $F$ tests in the single equations of the VAR model. That the unrestricted equations have identical regressors means that these tests can be based on the results of simple OLS estimates. The notion can be extended in a system of equations to attempt to ascertain if a given variable is weakly exogenous to the system. If lagged values of a variable $x_t$ have no explanatory power for *any* of the variables in a system, then we would view $x_t$ as weakly exogenous to the system. Once again, this specification can be tested with a likelihood ratio test as described later—the restriction will be to put "holes" in one or more $\boldsymbol{\Gamma}$ matrices—or with a form of $F$ test constructed by stacking the equations.

### Example 20.6 Granger Causality[9]
All but one of the major recessions in the U.S. economy since World War II have been preceded by large increases in the price of crude oil. Does movement of the price of oil *cause* movements in U.S. GDP in the Granger sense? Let $\mathbf{y}_t = $ [GDP, crude oil price]$'_t$. Then,

---

[8]See Geweke, Meese, and Dent (1983), Sims (1980), and Stock and Watson (2001).

[9]This example is adapted from Hamilton (1994, pp. 307–308).

a simple VAR would be

$$\mathbf{y}_t = \begin{bmatrix} \mu_1 \\ \mu_2 \end{bmatrix} + \begin{bmatrix} \alpha_1 & \alpha_2 \\ \beta_1 & \beta_2 \end{bmatrix} \mathbf{y}_{t-1} + \begin{bmatrix} \varepsilon_{1t} \\ \varepsilon_{2t} \end{bmatrix}.$$

To assert a causal relationship between oil prices and GDP, we must find that $\alpha_2$ is not zero; previous movements in oil prices do help explain movements in GDP even in the presence of the lagged value of GDP. Consistent with our earlier discussion, this fact, in itself, is not sufficient to assert a causal relationship. We would also have to demonstrate that there were no other intervening explanations that would explain movements in oil prices *and* GDP. (We will examine a more extensive application in Example 20.7.)

To establish the general result, it will prove useful to write the VAR in the multivariate regression format we used in Section 16.9.3.b. Partition the two data vectors $\mathbf{y}_t$ and $\mathbf{x}_t$ into $[\mathbf{y}_{1t}, \mathbf{y}_{2t}]$ and $[\mathbf{x}_{1t}, \mathbf{x}_{2t}]$. Consistent with our earlier discussion, $\mathbf{x}_1$ is lagged values of $\mathbf{y}_1$ and $\mathbf{x}_2$ is lagged values of $\mathbf{y}_2$. The VAR with this partitioning would be

$$\begin{bmatrix} \mathbf{y}_1 \\ \mathbf{y}_2 \end{bmatrix} = \begin{bmatrix} \mathbf{\Gamma}_{11} & \mathbf{\Gamma}_{12} \\ \mathbf{\Gamma}_{21} & \mathbf{\Gamma}_{22} \end{bmatrix} \begin{bmatrix} \mathbf{x}_1 \\ \mathbf{x}_2 \end{bmatrix} + \begin{bmatrix} \boldsymbol{\varepsilon}_1 \\ \boldsymbol{\varepsilon}_2 \end{bmatrix}, \quad \text{Var} \begin{bmatrix} \boldsymbol{\varepsilon}_{1t} \\ \boldsymbol{\varepsilon}_{2t} \end{bmatrix} = \begin{bmatrix} \mathbf{\Sigma}_{11} & \mathbf{\Sigma}_{12} \\ \mathbf{\Sigma}_{21} & \mathbf{\Sigma}_{22} \end{bmatrix}.$$

We would still obtain the unrestricted maximum likelihood estimates by least squares regressions. For testing Granger causality, the hypothesis $\mathbf{\Gamma}_{12} = \mathbf{0}$ is of interest. (See Example 20.6.) For testing the hypothesis of interest, $\mathbf{\Gamma}_{12} = \mathbf{0}$, the second set of equations is irrelevant. For testing for Granger causality in the VAR model, only the restricted equations are relevant. The hypothesis can be tested using the likelihood ratio statistic. For the present application, testing means computing

$\mathbf{S}_{11} =$ residual covariance matrix when current values of $\mathbf{y}_1$ are regressed on values of both $\mathbf{x}_1$ and $\mathbf{x}_2$,

$\mathbf{S}_{11}(0) =$ residual covariance matrix when current values of $\mathbf{y}_1$ are regressed only on values of $\mathbf{x}_1$.

The likelihood ratio statistic is then

$$\lambda = T(\ln|\mathbf{S}_{11}(0)| - \ln|\mathbf{S}_{11}|).$$

The number of degrees of freedom is the number of zero restrictions.

The fact that this test is wedded to the normal distribution limits its generality. The Wald test or its transformation to an approximate $F$ statistic as described in Section 20.6.3 is an alternative that should be more generally applicable. When the equation system is fit by GMM, as in Example 20.7, the simplicity of the likelihood ratio test is lost. The Wald statistic remains usable, however. Another possibility is to use the GMM counterpart to the likelihood ratio statistic (see Section 15.5.2) based on the GMM criterion functions. This is just the difference in the GMM criteria. Fitting both restricted and unrestricted models in this framework may be burdensome, but having set up the GMM estimator for the (larger) unrestricted model, imposing the zero restrictions of the smaller model should require only a minor modification.

There is a complication in these causality tests. The VAR can be motivated by the Wold representation theorem (see Section 21.2.5, Theorem 21.1), although with assumed nonautocorrelated disturbances, the motivation is incomplete. On the other hand, there is no formal theory behind the formulation. As such, the causality tests are predicated on a model that may, in fact, be missing either intervening variables or additional lagged effects that should be present but are not. For the first of these, the problem is that a finding of causal effects might equally well result from the omission of a variable that is correlated with both (or all) of the left-hand-side variables.

### 20.6.6   IMPULSE RESPONSE FUNCTIONS

Any VAR can be written as a first-order model by augmenting it, if necessary, with additional identity equations. For example, the model

$$\mathbf{y}_t = \boldsymbol{\mu} + \boldsymbol{\Gamma}_1 \mathbf{y}_{t-1} + \boldsymbol{\Gamma}_2 \mathbf{y}_{t-2} + \mathbf{v}_t$$

can be written

$$\begin{bmatrix} \mathbf{y}_t \\ \mathbf{y}_{t-1} \end{bmatrix} = \begin{bmatrix} \boldsymbol{\mu} \\ \mathbf{0} \end{bmatrix} + \begin{bmatrix} \boldsymbol{\Gamma}_1 & \boldsymbol{\Gamma}_2 \\ \mathbf{I} & \mathbf{0} \end{bmatrix} \begin{bmatrix} \mathbf{y}_{t-1} \\ \mathbf{y}_{t-2} \end{bmatrix} + \begin{bmatrix} \mathbf{v}_t \\ \mathbf{0} \end{bmatrix},$$

which is a first-order model. We can study the dynamic characteristics of the model in either form, but the second is more convenient, as will soon be apparent.

As we analyzed earlier, in the model

$$\mathbf{y}_t = \boldsymbol{\mu} + \boldsymbol{\Gamma} \mathbf{y}_{t-1} + \mathbf{v}_t,$$

dynamic stability is achieved if the characteristic roots of $\boldsymbol{\Gamma}$ have modulus less than one. (The roots may be complex, because $\boldsymbol{\Gamma}$ need not be symmetric. See Section 20.4.3 for the case of a single equation and Section 13.9 for analysis of essentially this model in a simultaneous equations context.)

Assuming that the equation system is stable, the equilibrium is found by obtaining the final form of the system. We can do this step by repeated substitution, or more simply by using the lag operator to write

$$\mathbf{y}_t = \boldsymbol{\mu} + \boldsymbol{\Gamma}(L)\mathbf{y}_t + \mathbf{v}_t,$$

or

$$[\mathbf{I} - \boldsymbol{\Gamma}(L)]\mathbf{y}_t = \boldsymbol{\mu} + \mathbf{v}_t.$$

With the stability condition, we have

$$\begin{aligned} \mathbf{y}_t &= [\mathbf{I} - \boldsymbol{\Gamma}(L)]^{-1}(\boldsymbol{\mu} + \mathbf{v}_t) \\ &= (\mathbf{I} - \boldsymbol{\Gamma})^{-1}\boldsymbol{\mu} + \sum_{i=0}^{\infty} \boldsymbol{\Gamma}^i \mathbf{v}_{t-i} \\ &= \bar{\mathbf{y}} + \sum_{i=0}^{\infty} \boldsymbol{\Gamma}^i \mathbf{v}_{t-i} \\ &= \bar{\mathbf{y}} + \mathbf{v}_t + \boldsymbol{\Gamma} \mathbf{v}_{t-1} + \boldsymbol{\Gamma}^2 \mathbf{v}_{t-2} + \cdots. \end{aligned} \tag{20-29}$$

The coefficients in the powers of $\boldsymbol{\Gamma}$ are the multipliers in the system. In fact, by renaming things slightly, this set of results is precisely the one we examined in Section 13.9 in our discussion of dynamic simultaneous equations models. We will change the interpretation slightly here, however. As we did in Section 13.9, we consider the conceptual experiment of disturbing a system in equilibrium. Suppose that $\mathbf{v}$ has equaled $\mathbf{0}$ for long enough that $\mathbf{y}$ has reached equilibrium, $\bar{\mathbf{y}}$. Now we consider injecting a shock to the system by changing one of the $v$'s, for one period, and then returning it to zero thereafter.

As we saw earlier, $y_{mt}$ will move away from, then return to, its equilibrium. The path whereby the variables return to the equilibrium is called the **impulse response** of the VAR.[10]

In the autoregressive form of the model, we can identify each **innovation,** $v_{mt}$, with a particular variable in $\mathbf{y}_t$, say, $y_{mt}$. Consider then the effect of a one-time shock to the system, $dv_{mt}$. As compared with the equilibrium, we will have, in the current period,

$$y_{mt} - \bar{y}_m = dv_{mt} = \phi_{mm}(0)dv_t.$$

One period later, we will have

$$y_{m,t+1} - \bar{y}_m = (\mathbf{\Gamma})_{mm}dv_{mt} = \phi_{mm}(1)dv_t.$$

Two periods later,

$$y_{m,t+2} - \bar{y}_m = (\mathbf{\Gamma}^2)_{mm}dv_{mt} = \phi_{mm}(2)dv_t,$$

and so on. The function, $\phi_{mm}(i)$ gives the impulse response characteristics of variable $y_m$ to innovations in $v_m$. A useful way to characterize the system is to plot the impulse response functions. The preceding traces through the effect on variable $m$ of a one-time innovation in $v_m$. We could also examine the effect of a one-time innovation of $v_l$ on variable $m$. The impulse response function would be

$$\phi_{ml}(i) = \text{element } (m, l) \text{ in } \mathbf{\Gamma}^i.$$

Point estimation of $\phi_{ml}(i)$ using the estimated model parameters is straightforward. Confidence intervals present a more difficult problem because the estimated functions $\hat{\phi}_{ml}(i, \hat{\beta})$ are so highly nonlinear in the original parameter estimates. The delta method has thus proved unsatisfactory. Killian (1998) presents results that suggest that bootstrapping may be the more productive approach to statistical inference regarding impulse response functions.

### 20.6.7   STRUCTURAL VARs

The VAR approach to modeling dynamic behavior of economic variables has provided some interesting insights and appears [see Litterman (1986)] to bring some real benefits for forecasting. The method has received some strident criticism for its atheoretical approach, however. The "unrestricted" nature of the lag structure in (20-27) could be synonymous with "unstructured." With no theoretical input to the model, it is difficult to claim that its output provides much of a theoretically justified result. For example, how are we to interpret the impulse response functions derived in the previous section? What lies behind much of this discussion is the idea that there is, in fact, a structure underlying the model, and the VAR that we have specified is a mere hodgepodge of all its components. Of course, that is exactly what reduced forms are. As such, to respond to this sort of criticism, analysts have begun to cast VARs formally as reduced forms and thereby attempt to deduce the structure that they had in mind all along.

A VAR model $\mathbf{y}_t = \mu + \mathbf{\Gamma}\mathbf{y}_{t-1} + \mathbf{v}_t$ could, in principle, be viewed as the reduced form of the dynamic **structural model**

$$\mathbf{\Theta}\mathbf{y}_t = \alpha + \mathbf{\Phi}\mathbf{y}_{t-1} + \varepsilon_t,$$

---

[10]See Hamilton (1994, pp. 318–323 and 336–350) for discussion and a number of related results.

where we have embedded any exogenous variables $x_t$ in the vector of constants $\boldsymbol{\alpha}$. Thus, $\boldsymbol{\Gamma} = \boldsymbol{\Theta}^{-1}\boldsymbol{\Phi}, \boldsymbol{\mu} = \boldsymbol{\Theta}^{-1}\boldsymbol{\alpha}, \mathbf{v} = \boldsymbol{\Theta}^{-1}\boldsymbol{\varepsilon}$, and $\boldsymbol{\Omega} = \boldsymbol{\Theta}^{-1}\boldsymbol{\Sigma}(\boldsymbol{\Theta}^{-1})'$. Perhaps it is the structure, specified by an underlying theory, that is of interest. For example, we can discuss the impulse response characteristics of this system. For particular configurations of $\boldsymbol{\Theta}$, such as a triangular matrix, we can meaningfully interpret innovations, $\boldsymbol{\varepsilon}$. As we explored at great length in the previous chapter, however, as this model stands, there is not sufficient information contained in the reduced form as just stated to deduce the structural parameters. A possibly large number of restrictions must be imposed on $\boldsymbol{\Theta}, \boldsymbol{\Phi}$, and $\boldsymbol{\Sigma}$ to enable us to deduce structural forms from reduced-form estimates, which are always obtainable. The recent work on **structural VARs** centers on the types of restrictions and forms of the theory that can be brought to bear to allow this analysis to proceed. See, for example, the survey in Hamilton (1994, Chapter 11). At this point, the literature on this subject has come full circle because the contemporary development of "unstructured VARs" becomes very much the analysis of quite conventional dynamic structural simultaneous equations models. Indeed, current research [e.g., Diebold (1998)] brings the literature back into line with the structural modeling tradition by demonstrating how VARs can be derived formally as the reduced forms of dynamic structural models. That is, the most recent applications have begun with structures and derived the reduced forms as VARs, rather than departing from the VAR as a reduced form and attempting to deduce a structure from it by layering on restrictions.

### 20.6.8  APPLICATION: POLICY ANALYSIS WITH A VAR

Cecchetti and Rich (2001) used a structural VAR to analyze the effect of recent disinflationary policies of the Fed on aggregate output in the U.S. economy. The Fed's policy of the last two decades has leaned more toward controlling inflation and less toward stimulation of the economy. The authors argue that the long-run benefits of this policy include economic stability and increased long-term trend output growth. But, there is a short-term cost in lost output. Their study seeks to estimate the "sacrifice ratio," which is a measure of the cumulative cost of this policy. The specific indicator they study measures the cumulative output loss after $\tau$ periods of a policy shock at time $t$, where the (persistent) shock is measured as the change in the level of inflation.

#### 20.6.8.a  A VAR Model for the Macroeconomic Variables
The model proposed for estimating the ratio is a structural VAR,

$$\Delta y_t = \sum_{i=1}^{p} b_{11}^i \Delta y_{t-i} + b_{12}^0 \Delta \pi_t + \sum_{i=1}^{p} b_{12}^i \Delta \pi_{t-i} + \varepsilon_t^y,$$

$$\Delta \pi_t = b_{21}^0 \Delta y_t + \sum_{i=1}^{p} b_{21}^i \Delta y_{t-i} + \sum_{i=1}^{p} b_{22}^i \Delta \pi_{t-i} + \varepsilon_t^\pi,$$

where $y_t$ is aggregate real output in period $t$ and $\pi_t$ is the rate of inflation from period $t-1$ to $t$ and the model is cast in terms of rates of changes of these two variables. (Note, therefore, that sums of $\Delta \pi_t$ measure accumulated changes in the rate of inflation, not changes in the CPI.) The vector of innovations, $\boldsymbol{\varepsilon}_t = (\varepsilon_t^y, \varepsilon_t^\pi)'$ is assumed to have mean $\mathbf{0}$, contemporaneous covariance matrix $E[\boldsymbol{\varepsilon}_t\boldsymbol{\varepsilon}_t'] = \boldsymbol{\Omega}$ and to be strictly nonautocorrelated. (We have retained Cecchetti and Rich's notation for most of this discussion, save for the number of lags, which is denoted $n$ in their paper and $p$ here, and some other minor changes which will be noted in passing where necessary.)[11] The equation system may also be written

$$\mathbf{B}(L)\begin{bmatrix} \Delta y_t \\ \Delta \pi_t \end{bmatrix} = \begin{bmatrix} \varepsilon_t^y \\ \varepsilon_t^\pi \end{bmatrix},$$

where $\mathbf{B}(L)$ is a $2 \times 2$ matrix of polynomials in the lag operator. The components of the disturbance (innovation) vector $\boldsymbol{\varepsilon}_t$ are identified as shocks to aggregate supply and aggregate demand, respectively.

### 20.6.8.b  The Sacrifice Ratio

Interest in the study centers on the impact over time of structural shocks to output and the rate of inflation. To calculate these, the authors use the **vector moving average** (VMA) form of the model, which would be

$$\begin{bmatrix} \Delta y_t \\ \Delta \pi_t \end{bmatrix} = [\mathbf{B}(L)]^{-1} \begin{bmatrix} \varepsilon_t^y \\ \varepsilon_t^\pi \end{bmatrix} = \mathbf{A}(L) \begin{bmatrix} \varepsilon_t^y \\ \varepsilon_t^\pi \end{bmatrix} = \begin{bmatrix} A_{11}(L) & A_{12}(L) \\ A_{21}(L) & A_{22}(L) \end{bmatrix} \begin{bmatrix} \varepsilon_t^y \\ \varepsilon_t^\pi \end{bmatrix}$$

$$= \begin{bmatrix} \sum_{i=0}^{\infty} a_{11}^i \varepsilon_{t-i}^y & \sum_{i=0}^{\infty} a_{12}^i \varepsilon_{t-i}^\pi \\ \sum_{i=0}^{\infty} a_{21}^i \varepsilon_{t-i}^y & \sum_{i=0}^{\infty} a_{22}^i \varepsilon_{t-i}^\pi \end{bmatrix}.$$

(Note that the superscript "$i$" in the last form of the preceding model is not an exponent; it is the index of the sequence of coefficients.) The impulse response functions for the model corresponding to (20-27) are precisely the coefficients in $\mathbf{A}(L)$. In particular, the effect on the change in inflation $\tau$ periods later of a change in $\varepsilon_t^\pi$ in period $t$ is $a_{22}^\tau$. The total effect from time $t+0$ to time $t+\tau$ would be the sum of these, $\sum_{i=0}^{\tau} a_{22}^i$. The counterparts for the rate of output would be $\sum_{i=0}^{\tau} a_{12}^i$. However, what is needed is not the effect only on period $\tau$'s output, but the cumulative effect on output from the time of the shock up to period $\tau$. That would be obtained by summing these period-specific effects, to obtain $\sum_{i=0}^{\tau} \sum_{j=0}^{i} a_{12}^j$. Combining terms, the sacrifice ratio is

$$S_{\varepsilon^\pi}(\tau) = \frac{\sum_{j=0}^{\tau} \dfrac{\partial y_{t+j}}{\partial \varepsilon_t^\pi}}{\dfrac{\partial \pi_{t+\tau}}{\partial \varepsilon_t^\pi}} = \frac{\sum_{i=0}^{0} a_{12}^j + \sum_{i=0}^{1} a_{12}^j + \cdots + \sum_{i=0}^{\tau} a_{12}^j}{\sum_{i=0}^{\tau} a_{22}^i} = \frac{\sum_{i=0}^{\tau} \sum_{j=0}^{i} a_{12}^j}{\sum_{i=0}^{\tau} a_{22}^i}.$$

The function $S(\tau)$ is then examined over long periods to study the long-term effects of monetary policy.

### 20.6.8.c  Identification and Estimation of a Structural VAR Model

Estimation of this model requires some manipulation. The **structural model** is a conventional linear simultaneous equations model of the form,

$$\mathbf{B}_0 \mathbf{y}_t = \mathbf{B} \mathbf{x}_t + \boldsymbol{\varepsilon}_t,$$

---

[11] The authors examine two other VAR models, a three-equation model of Shapiro and Watson (1988), which adds an equation in real interest rates ($i_t - \pi_t$) and a four-equation model by Gali (1992), which models $\Delta y_t$, $\Delta i_t$, $(i_t - \pi_t)$, and the real money stock, $(\Delta m_t - \pi_t)$. Among the foci of Cecchetti and Rich's paper was the surprisingly large variation in estimates of the sacrifice ratio produced by the three models. In the interest of brevity, we will restrict our analysis to Cecchetti's (1994) two-equation model.

where $\mathbf{y}_t$ is $(\Delta y_t, \Delta \pi_t)'$ and $\mathbf{x}_t$ is the lagged values on the right-hand side. As we saw in Section 13.3, without further restrictions, a model such as this is not identified (estimable). A total of $M^2$ restrictions—$M$ is the number of equations, here two—are needed to identify the model. In the familiar cases of simultaneous equations models that we examined in Chapter 13, identification is usually secured through exclusion restrictions (i.e., zero restrictions), either in $\mathbf{B}_0$ or $\mathbf{B}$. This type of exclusion restriction would be unnatural in a model such as this one—there would be no basis for poking specific holes in the coefficient matrices. The authors take a different approach, which requires us to look more closely at the different forms the time-series model can take.

Write the structural form as

$$\mathbf{B}_0\mathbf{y}_t = \mathbf{B}_1\mathbf{y}_{t-1} + \mathbf{B}_2\mathbf{y}_{t-2} + \cdots + \mathbf{B}_p\mathbf{y}_{t-p} + \boldsymbol{\varepsilon}_t,$$

where

$$\mathbf{B}_0 = \begin{bmatrix} 1 & -b_{12}^0 \\ -b_{21}^0 & 1 \end{bmatrix}.$$

As noted, this is in the form of a conventional simultaneous equations model. Assuming that $\mathbf{B}_0$ is nonsingular, which for this two-equation system requires only that $1 - b_{12}^0 b_{21}^0$ not equal zero, we can obtain the reduced form of the model as

$$
\begin{aligned}
\mathbf{y}_t &= \mathbf{B}_0^{-1}\mathbf{B}_1\mathbf{y}_{t-1} + \mathbf{B}_0^{-1}\mathbf{B}_2\mathbf{y}_{t-2} + \cdots + \mathbf{B}_0^{-1}\mathbf{B}_p\mathbf{y}_{t-p} + \mathbf{B}_0^{-1}\boldsymbol{\varepsilon}_t \\
&= \mathbf{D}_1\mathbf{y}_{t-1} + \mathbf{D}_2\mathbf{y}_{t-2} + \cdots + \mathbf{D}_p\mathbf{y}_{t-p} + \boldsymbol{\mu}_t,
\end{aligned}
\tag{20-30}
$$

where $\boldsymbol{\mu}_t$ is the vector of reduced form innovations. Now, collect the terms in the equivalent form

$$[\mathbf{I} - \mathbf{D}_1 L - \mathbf{D}_2 L^2 - \cdots]\mathbf{y}_t = \boldsymbol{\mu}_t.$$

The moving-average form that we obtained earlier is

$$\mathbf{y}_t = [\mathbf{I} - \mathbf{D}_1 L - \mathbf{D}_2 L^2 - \cdots]^{-1}\boldsymbol{\mu}_t.$$

Assuming stability of the system, we can also write this as

$$
\begin{aligned}
\mathbf{y}_t &= [\mathbf{I} - \mathbf{D}_1 L - \mathbf{D}_2 L^2 - \cdots]^{-1}\boldsymbol{\mu}_t \\
&= [\mathbf{I} - \mathbf{D}_1 L - \mathbf{D}_2 L^2 - \cdots]^{-1}\mathbf{B}_0^{-1}\boldsymbol{\varepsilon}_t \\
&= [\mathbf{I} + \mathbf{C}_1 L + \mathbf{C}_2 L^2 + \cdots]\boldsymbol{\mu}_t \\
&= \boldsymbol{\mu}_t + \mathbf{C}_1\boldsymbol{\mu}_{t-1} + \mathbf{C}_2\boldsymbol{\mu}_{t-2}\cdots \\
&= \mathbf{B}_0^{-1}\boldsymbol{\varepsilon}_t + \mathbf{C}_1\boldsymbol{\mu}_{t-1} + \mathbf{C}_2\boldsymbol{\mu}_{t-2}\cdots.
\end{aligned}
$$

So, the $\mathbf{C}_j$ matrices correspond to our $\mathbf{A}_j$ matrices in the original formulation. But this manipulation has added something. We can see that $\mathbf{A}_0 = \mathbf{B}_0^{-1}$. Looking ahead, the reduced form equations can be estimated by least squares. Whether the structural parameters, and thereafter, the VMA parameters can as well depends entirely on whether $\mathbf{B}_0$ can be estimated. From (20-30) we can see that if $\mathbf{B}_0$ can be estimated, then $\mathbf{B}_1 \ldots \mathbf{B}_p$ can also just by premultiplying the reduced form coefficient matrices by this estimated

$\mathbf{B}_0$. So, we must now consider this issue. (This is precisely the conclusion we drew at the beginning of Section 13.3.)

Recall the initial assumption that $E[\boldsymbol{\varepsilon}_t \boldsymbol{\varepsilon}_t'] = \boldsymbol{\Omega}$. In the reduced form, we assume $E[\boldsymbol{\mu}_t \boldsymbol{\mu}_t'] = \boldsymbol{\Sigma}$. As we know, reduced forms are always estimable (indeed, by least squares if the assumptions of the model are correct). That means that $\boldsymbol{\Sigma}$ is estimable by the least squares residual variances and covariance. From the earlier derivation, we have that $\boldsymbol{\Sigma} = \mathbf{B}_0^{-1} \boldsymbol{\Omega} (\mathbf{B}_0^{-1})' = \mathbf{A}_0 \boldsymbol{\Omega} \mathbf{A}_0'$. (Again, see the beginning of Section 13.3.) The authors have secured identification of the model through this relationship. In particular, they assume first that $\boldsymbol{\Omega} = \mathbf{I}$. Assuming that $\boldsymbol{\Omega} = \mathbf{I}$, we now have that $\mathbf{A}_0 \mathbf{A}_0' = \boldsymbol{\Sigma}$, where $\boldsymbol{\Sigma}$ is an estimable matrix with three free parameters. Because $\mathbf{A}_0$ is $2 \times 2$, one more restriction is needed to secure identification. At this point, the authors, invoking Blanchard and Quah (1989), assume that "demand shocks have no permanent effect on the level of output. This is equivalent to $A_{12}(1) = \sum_{i=0}^{\infty} a_{12}^i = 0$." This might seem like a cumbersome restriction to impose. But, the matrix $\mathbf{A}(1)$ is $[\mathbf{I} - \mathbf{D}_1 - \mathbf{D}_2 - \cdots - \mathbf{D}_p]^{-1} \mathbf{A}_0 = \mathbf{F} \mathbf{A}_0$ and the components, $\mathbf{D}_j$, have been estimated as the reduced form coefficient matrices, so $A_{12}(1) = 0$ assumes only that the upper right element of this matrix is zero. We now obtain the equations needed to solve for $\mathbf{A}_0$. First,

$$\mathbf{A}_0 \mathbf{A}_0' = \boldsymbol{\Sigma} \Rightarrow \begin{bmatrix} \left(a_{11}^0\right)^2 + \left(a_{12}^0\right)^2 & a_{11}^0 a_{21}^0 + a_{12}^0 a_{22}^0 \\ a_{11}^0 a_{21}^0 + a_{12}^0 a_{22}^0 & \left(a_{21}^0\right)^2 + \left(a_{22}^0\right)^2 \end{bmatrix} = \begin{bmatrix} \sigma_{11} & \sigma_{12} \\ \sigma_{12} & \sigma_{11} \end{bmatrix}, \quad \text{(20-31)}$$

which provides three equations. Second, the theoretical restriction is

$$\mathbf{F} \mathbf{A}_0 = \begin{bmatrix} * & f_{11} a_{12}^0 + f_{12} a_{22}^0 \\ * & * \end{bmatrix} = \begin{bmatrix} * & 0 \\ * & * \end{bmatrix}.$$

This provides the four equations needed to identify the four elements in $\mathbf{A}_0$.[12]

Collecting results, the estimation strategy is first to estimate $\mathbf{D}_1, \ldots, \mathbf{D}_p$ and $\boldsymbol{\Sigma}$ in the reduced form, by least squares. (They set $p = 8$.) Then use the restrictions and (20-31) to obtain the elements of $\mathbf{A}_0 = \mathbf{B}_0^{-1}$ and, finally, $\mathbf{B}_j = \mathbf{A}_0^{-1} \mathbf{D}_j$.

The last step is estimation of the matrices of impulse responses, which can be done as follows: We return to the reduced form which, using our augmentation trick, we

---

[12] At this point, an intriguing loose end arises. We have carried this discussion in the form of the original papers by Blanchard and Quah (1989) and Cecchetti and Rich (2001). Returning to the original structure, we see that because $\mathbf{A}_0 = \mathbf{B}_0^{-1}$, if $\mathbf{B}_0$ has ones on the diagonal, then $\mathbf{A}_0$ actually does not have four unrestricted and unknown elements, it has two. The model is thus overidentified. We could have predicted this at the outset. In our conventional simultaneous equations model, the normalizations in $\mathbf{B}_0$ (ones on the diagonal) provide two restrictions of the $M^2 = 4$ required for identification. Assuming that $\boldsymbol{\Omega} = \mathbf{I}$ provides three more, and the theoretical restriction provides a sixth. Therefore, the four unknown elements in an unrestricted $\mathbf{B}_0$ are overidentified. It might seem convenient at this point to forego the theoretical restriction on long-term impacts, but it seems more natural to omit the restrictions on the scaling of $\boldsymbol{\Omega}$. With the two normalizations already in place, assuming that the innovations are uncorrelated ($\boldsymbol{\Omega}$ is diagonal) and "demand shocks have no permanent effect on the level of output" together suffice to identify the model. Blanchard and Quah appear to reach the same conclusion (page 656), but then they also assume the unit variances [page 657, equation (1)]. They argue that the assumption of unit variances is just a convenient normalization, which for their model is actually the case, because they do not assume that $\mathbf{B}_0$ is diagonal. Cecchetti and Rich, however, *do* appear to normalize $\mathbf{B}_0$ in their equation (1). They then (evidently) drop the assumption after (10), however, "[B]ecause $\mathbf{A}_0$ has $(n \times n)$ unique elements . . . ." This would imply that the normalization they impose on their (1) has not, in fact, been carried through the later manipulations, so, once again, the model is exactly identified.

write as

$$\begin{bmatrix} \mathbf{y}_t \\ \mathbf{y}_{t-1} \\ \cdots \\ \mathbf{y}_{t-p+1} \end{bmatrix} = \begin{bmatrix} \mathbf{D}_1 & \mathbf{D}_2 & \cdots & \mathbf{D}_p \\ \mathbf{I} & \mathbf{0} & \cdots & \mathbf{0} \\ \cdots & \cdots & \cdots & \mathbf{0} \\ \mathbf{0} & \cdots & \mathbf{I} & \mathbf{0} \end{bmatrix} \begin{bmatrix} \mathbf{y}_{t-1} \\ \mathbf{y}_{t-2} \\ \cdots \\ \mathbf{y}_{t-p} \end{bmatrix} + \begin{bmatrix} \mathbf{A}_0\boldsymbol{\varepsilon}_t \\ \mathbf{0} \\ \cdots \\ \mathbf{0} \end{bmatrix}. \qquad \textbf{(20-32)}$$

For convenience, arrange this result as

$$\mathbf{Y}_t = (\mathbf{D}L)\mathbf{Y}_t + \mathbf{w}_t.$$

Now, solve this for $\mathbf{Y}_t$ to obtain the final form

$$\mathbf{Y}_t = [\mathbf{I} - \mathbf{D}L]^{-1}\mathbf{w}_t.$$

Write this in the spectral form and expand as we did earlier, to obtain

$$\mathbf{Y}_t = \sum_{i=0}^{\infty} \mathbf{P}\boldsymbol{\Lambda}^i\mathbf{Q}\mathbf{w}_{t-i}. \qquad \textbf{(20-33)}$$

We will be interested in the uppermost subvector of $\mathbf{Y}_t$, so we expand (20-33) to yield

$$\begin{bmatrix} \mathbf{y}_t \\ \mathbf{y}_{t-1} \\ \cdots \\ \mathbf{y}_{t-p+1} \end{bmatrix} = \begin{bmatrix} \sum_{i=0}^{\infty} \mathbf{P}\boldsymbol{\Lambda}^i\mathbf{Q} \begin{bmatrix} \mathbf{A}_0\boldsymbol{\varepsilon}_{t-i} \\ \mathbf{0} \\ \cdots \\ \mathbf{0} \end{bmatrix} \end{bmatrix}.$$

The matrix in the summation is $Mp \times Mp$. The impact matrices we seek are the $M \times M$ matrices in the upper left corner of the spectral form, multiplied by $\mathbf{A}_0$.

### 20.6.8.d  Inference

As noted at the end of Section 20.6.6, obtaining usable standard errors for estimates of impulse responses is a difficult (as yet unresolved) problem. Killian (1998) has suggested that bootstrapping is a preferable approach to using the delta method. Cecchetti and Rich reach the same conclusion and likewise resort to a bootstrapping procedure. Their bootstrap procedure is carried out as follows: Let $\hat{\boldsymbol{\delta}}$ and $\hat{\boldsymbol{\Sigma}}$ denote the full set of estimated coefficients and estimated reduced form covariance matrix based on direct estimation. As suggested by Doan (2007), they construct a sequence of $N$ draws for the reduced form parameters, then recompute the entire set of impulse responses. The narrowest interval, which contains 90 percent of these draws, is taken to be a confidence interval for an estimated impulse function.

### 20.6.8.e  Empirical Results

Cecchetti and Rich used quarterly observations on real aggregate output and the consumer price index. Their data set spanned 1959.1 to 1997.4. This is a subset of the data described in the Appendix Table F5.1. Before beginning their analysis, they subjected the data to the standard tests for stationarity. Figures 20.5–20.7 show the log of real output, the rate of inflation, and the changes in these two variables. The

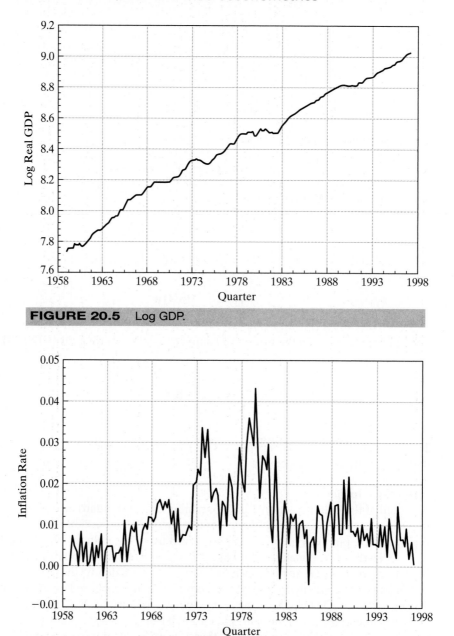

**FIGURE 20.5** Log GDP.

**FIGURE 20.6** The Quarterly Rate of Inflation.

first two figures do suggest that neither variable is stationary. On the basis of the Dickey–Fuller (1981) test (see Section 22.2.4), they found (as might be expected) that the $y_t$ and $\pi_t$ series both contain unit roots. They conclude that because output has a unit root, the identification restriction that the long-run effect of aggregate demand shocks on output is well defined and meaningful. The unit root in inflation allows for

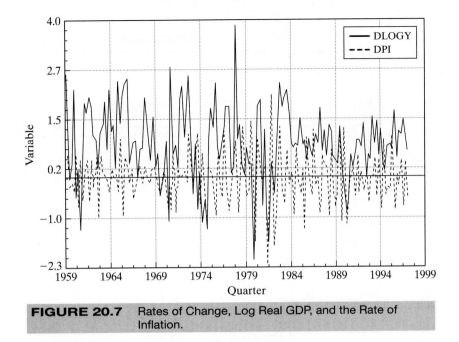

**FIGURE 20.7**    Rates of Change, Log Real GDP, and the Rate of Inflation.

permanent shifts in its level. The lag length for the model is set at $p = 8$. Long-run impulse response function are truncated at 20 years (80 quarters). Analysis is based on the rate of change data shown in Figure 20.7.

As a final check on the model, the authors examined the data for the possibility of a structural shift using the tests described in Andrews (1993) and Andrews and Ploberger (1994). None of the Andrews/Quandt supremum LM test, Andrews/Ploberger exponential LM test, or the Andrews/Ploberger average LM test suggested that the underlying structure had changed (in spite of what seems likely to have been a major shift in Fed policy in the 1970s). On this basis, they concluded that the VAR is stable over the sample period.

Figure 20.8 (Figures 3A and 3B taken from the article) shows their two separate estimated impulse response functions. The dotted lines in the figures show the bootstrap-generated confidence bounds. Estimates of the sacrifice ratio for Cecchetti's model are 1.3219 for $\tau = 4$, 1.3204 for $\tau = 8$, 1.5700 for $\tau = 12$, 1.5219 for $\tau = 16$, and 1.3763 for $\tau = 20$.

The authors also examined the forecasting performance of their model compared to Shapiro and Watson's and Gali's. The device used was to produce one step ahead, period $T + 1 \mid T$ forecasts for the model estimated using periods $1 \ldots, T$. The first reduced form of the model is fit using 1959.1 to 1975.1 and used to forecast 1975.2. Then, it is reestimated using 1959.1 to 1975.2 and used to forecast 1975.3, and so on. Finally, the root mean squared error of these out of sample forecasts is compared for three models. In each case, the level, rather than the rate of change of the inflation rate is forecasted. Overall, the results suggest that the smaller model does a better job of estimating the impulse responses (has smaller confidence bounds and conforms more

A: Dynamic Response to a Monetary Policy Shock

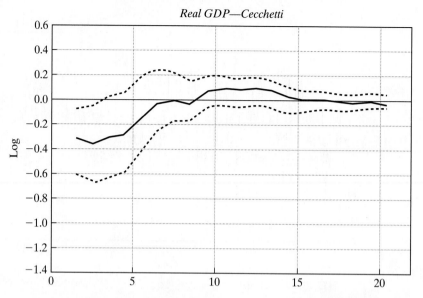

*Real GDP—Cecchetti*

B: Dynamic Response to a Monetary Policy Shock

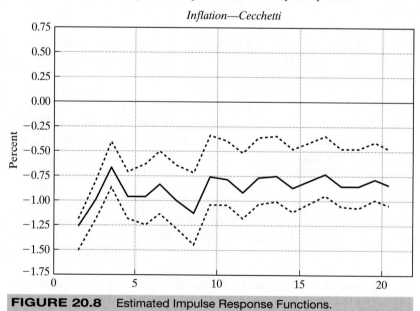

*Inflation—Cecchetti*

**FIGURE 20.8**   Estimated Impulse Response Functions.

nearly with theoretical predictions) but performs worst of the three (slightly) in terms of the mean squared error of the out-of-sample forecasts. Because the unrestricted reduced form model is being used for the latter, this comes as no surprise. The end result follows essentially from the result that adding variables to a regression model improves its fit.

### 20.6.9  VARs IN MICROECONOMICS

VARs have appeared in the microeconometrics literature as well. Chamberlain (1980) suggested that a useful approach to the analysis of panel data would be to treat each period's observation as a separate equation. For the case of $T = 2$, we would have

$$y_{i1} = \alpha_i + \mathbf{x}_{i1}'\boldsymbol{\beta} + \varepsilon_{i1},$$

$$y_{i2} = \alpha_i + \mathbf{x}_{i2}'\boldsymbol{\beta} + \varepsilon_{i2},$$

where $i$ indexes individuals and $\alpha_i$ are unobserved individual effects. This specification produces a multivariate regression, to which Chamberlain added restrictions related to the individual effects. Holtz-Eakin, Newey, and Rosen's (1988) approach is to specify the equation as

$$y_{it} = \alpha_{0t} + \sum_{l=1}^{m} \alpha_{lt} y_{i,t-l} + \sum_{l=1}^{m} \delta_{lt} x_{i,t-l} + \Psi_t f_i + \mu_{it}.$$

In their study, $y_{it}$ is hours worked by individual $i$ in period $t$ and $x_{it}$ is the individual's wage in that period. A second equation for earnings is specified with lagged values of hours and earnings on the right-hand side. The individual, unobserved effects are $f_i$. This model is similar to the VAR in (20-27), but it differs in several ways as well. The number of periods is quite small (14 yearly observations for each individual), but there are nearly 1,000 individuals. The dynamic equation is specified for a specific period, however, so the relevant sample size in each case is $n$, not $T$. Also, the number of lags in the model used is relatively small; the authors fixed it at three. They thus have a two-equation VAR containing 12 unknown parameters, six in each equation. The authors used the model to analyze causality, measurement error, and parameter stability—that is, constancy of $\alpha_{lt}$ and $\delta_{lt}$ across time.

### Example 20.7  VAR for Municipal Expenditures
In Example 15.10, we examined a model of municipal expenditures proposed by Dahlberg and Johansson (2000): Their equation of interest is

$$\Delta S_{i,t} = \mu_t + \sum_{j=1}^{m} \beta_j \Delta S_{i,t-j} + \sum_{j=1}^{m} \gamma_j \Delta R_{i,t-j} + \sum_{j=1}^{m} \delta_j \Delta G_{i,t-j} + u_{i,t}^S$$

for $i = 1, \ldots, N = 265$ and $t = m + 1, \ldots, 9$. $S_{i,t}$, $R_{i,t}$, and $G_{i,t}$ are municipal spending, receipts (taxes and fees), and central government grants, respectively. Analogous equations are specified for the current values of $R_{i,t}$ and $G_{i,t}$. This produces a vector autoregression for each municipality,

$$
\begin{bmatrix} \Delta S_{i,t} \\ \Delta R_{i,t} \\ \Delta G_{i,t} \end{bmatrix} = \begin{pmatrix} \mu_{S,t} \\ \mu_{R,t} \\ \mu_{G,t} \end{pmatrix} + \begin{pmatrix} \beta_{S,1} & \gamma_{S,1} & \delta_{S,1} \\ \beta_{R,1} & \gamma_{R,1} & \delta_{R,1} \\ \beta_{G,1} & \gamma_{G,1} & \delta_{G,1} \end{pmatrix} \begin{bmatrix} \Delta S_{i,t-1} \\ \Delta R_{i,t-1} \\ \Delta G_{i,t-1} \end{bmatrix} + \cdots
$$

$$
+ \begin{pmatrix} \beta_{S,m} & \gamma_{S,m} & \delta_{S,m} \\ \beta_{R,m} & \gamma_{R,m} & \delta_{R,m} \\ \beta_{G,m} & \gamma_{G,m} & \delta_{G,m} \end{pmatrix} \begin{bmatrix} \Delta S_{i,t-m} \\ \Delta R_{i,t-m} \\ \Delta G_{i,t-m} \end{bmatrix} + \begin{bmatrix} u_{i,t}^S \\ u_{i,t}^R \\ u_{i,t}^G \end{bmatrix}.
$$

The model was estimated by GMM, so the discussion at the end of the preceding section applies here. We will be interested in testing whether changes in municipal spending, $\Delta S_{i,t}$, are Granger-caused by changes in revenues, $\Delta R_{i,t}$, and grants, $\Delta G_{i,t}$. The hypothesis to be tested is $\gamma_{S,j} = \delta_{S,j} = 0$ for all $j$. This hypothesis can be tested in the context of only the first equation. Parameter estimates and diagnostic statistics are given in Example 15.10. We can carry out the test in two ways. In the unrestricted equation with all three lagged values of all three variables, the minimized GMM criterion is $q = 22.8287$. If the lagged values of $\Delta R$ and $\Delta G$ are omitted from the $\Delta S$ equation, the criterion rises to 42.9182.[13] There are six restrictions. The difference is 20.090 so the $F$ statistic is $20.09/6 = 3.348$. We have more than 1,000 degrees of freedom for the denominator, with 265 municipalities and 5 years, so we can use the limiting value for the critical value. This is 2.10, so we may reject the hypothesis of noncausality and conclude that changes in revenues and grants do Granger cause changes in spending. (This hardly seems surprising.) The alternative approach is to use a Wald statistic to test the six restrictions. Using the full GMM results for the $\Delta S$ equation with 14 coefficients we obtain a Wald statistic of 15.3030. The critical chi-squared would be $6 \times 2.1 = 12.6$, so once again, the hypothesis is rejected.

Dahlberg and Johansson approach the causality test somewhat differently by using a sequential testing procedure. (See their page 413 for discussion.) They suggest that the intervening variables be dropped in turn. By dropping first $G$, then $R$ and $G$, and then first $R$ then $G$ and $R$, they conclude that grants do not Granger-cause changes in spending ($\Delta q =$ only 0.07) but in the absence of grants, revenues do ($\Delta q |$grants excluded) $= 24.6$. The reverse order produces test statistics of 12.2 and 12.4, respectively. Our own calculations of the four values of $q$ yields 22.829 for the full model, 23.1302 with only grants excluded, 23.0894 with only $R$ excluded, and 42.9182 with both excluded, which disagrees with their results but is consistent with our earlier ones.

### Instability of a VAR Model

The coefficients for the three-variable VAR model in Example 20.7 appear in Table 15.5. The characteristic roots of the $9 \times 9$ coefficient matrix are $-0.6025$, $0.2529$, $0.0840$, $(1.4586 \pm 0.6584i)$, $(-0.6992 \pm 0.2019i)$, and $(0.0611 \pm 0.6291i)$. The first pair of complex roots has modulus greater than one, so the estimated VAR is unstable. The data do not appear to be consistent with this result, though with only five usable years of data, that conclusion is a bit fragile. One might suspect that the model is overfit. Because the disturbances are assumed to be uncorrelated across equations, the three equations have been estimated separately. The GMM criterion for the system is then the sum of those for the three equations. For $p = 3, 2$, and 1, respectively, these are $(22.8287 + 30.5398 + 17.5810) = 70.9495$, $(30.4526 + 34.2590 + 20.5416) = 85.2532$, and $(34.4986 + 53.2506 + 27.5927) = 115.6119$. The difference statistic for testing down from three lags to two is 14.3037. The critical chi-squared for nine degrees of freedom is 19.62, so it would appear that $m = 3$ may be too large. The results clearly reject the hypothesis that $m = 1$, however. The coefficients for a model with two lags instead of one appear in Table 15.5. If we construct $\Gamma$ from these results instead, we obtain a $6 \times 6$ matrix whose characteristic roots are $1.5817$, $-0.2196$, $-0.3509 \pm 0.4362i$, and $0.0968 \pm 0.2791i$. The system remains unstable.

## 20.7   SUMMARY AND CONCLUSIONS

This chapter has surveyed a particular type of regression model, the dynamic regression. The signature feature of the dynamic model is effects that are delayed or that persist through time. In a static regression setting, effects embodied in coefficients are assumed to take place all at once. In the dynamic model, the response to an innovation is distributed through several periods. The first three sections of this chapter examined several different forms of single-equation models that contained lagged effects. The

---

[13]Once again, these results differ from those given by Dahlberg and Johansson. As before, the difference results from our use of the same weighting matrix for all GMM computations in contrast to their recomputation of the matrix for each new coefficient vector estimated.

progression, which mirrors the current literature, is from tightly structured lag "models" (which were sometimes formulated to respond to a shortage of data rather than to correspond to an underlying theory) to unrestricted models with multiple period lag structures. We also examined several hybrids of these two forms, models that allow long lags but build some regular structure into the lag weights. Thus, our model of the formation of expectations of inflation is reasonably flexible, but does assume a specific behavioral mechanism. We then examined several methodological issues. In this context as elsewhere, there is a preference in the methods toward forming broad unrestricted models and using familiar inference tools to reduce them to the final appropriate specification. The second half of the chapter was devoted to a type of seemingly unrelated regressions model. The vector autoregression, or VAR, has been a major tool in recent research. After developing the econometric framework, we examined two applications, one in macroeconomics centered on monetary policy and one from microeconomics.

## Key Terms and Concepts

- Autocorrelation
- Autoregression
- Autoregressive distributed lag
- Autoregressive form
- Autoregressive model
- Characteristic equation
- Distributed lag
- Dynamic regression model
- Elasticity
- Equilibrium
- Equilibrium error
- Equilibrium multiplier
- Equilibrium relationship
- Error correction
- Exogeneity
- Expectation
- Finite lags

- General-to-simple method
- Granger causality
- Impact multiplier
- Impulse response
- Infinite lag model
- Infinite lags
- Innovation
- Invertible
- Lagged variables
- Lag operator
- Lag weight
- Long-run multiplier
- Mean lag
- Median lag
- Moving-average form
- One-period-ahead forecast
- Partial adjustment
- Phillips curve

- Polynomial in lag operator
- Random walk with drift
- Rational lag
- Simple-to-general approach
- Specification
- Stability
- Stationary
- Strong exogeneity
- Structural model
- Structural VAR
- Superconsistent
- Univariate autoregression
- Vector autoregression (VAR)
- Vector moving average (VMA)

## Exercises

1. Obtain the mean lag and the long- and short-run multipliers for the following distributed lag models:

   a. $y_t = 0.55(0.02x_t + 0.15x_{t-1} + 0.43x_{t-2} + 0.23x_{t-3} + 0.17x_{t-4}) + e_t$.

   b. The model in Exercise 3.

   c. The model in Exercise 4. (Do for either $x$ or $z$.)

2. Expand the rational lag model $y_t = [(0.6 + 2L)/(1 - 0.6L + 0.5L^2)]x_t + e_t$. What are the coefficients on $x_t$, $x_{t-1}$, $x_{t-2}$, $x_{t-3}$, and $x_{t-4}$?

3. Suppose that the model of Exercise 2 were specified as

$$y_t = \alpha + \frac{\beta + \gamma L}{1 - \delta_1 L - \delta_2 L^2} x_t + e_t.$$

Describe a method of estimating the parameters. Is ordinary least squares consistent?

4. Describe how to estimate the parameters of the model

$$y_t = \alpha + \beta \frac{x_t}{1 - \gamma L} + \delta \frac{z_t}{1 - \phi L} + \varepsilon_t,$$

where $\varepsilon_t$ is a serially uncorrelated, homoscedastic, classical disturbance.

## Applications

1. We are interested in the long-run multiplier in the model

$$y_t = \beta_0 + \sum_{j=0}^{6} \beta_j x_{t-j} + \varepsilon_t.$$

Assume that $x_t$ is an autoregressive series, $x_t = r x_{t-1} + v_t$ where $|r| < 1$.

a. What is the long run multiplier in this model?

b. How would you estimate the long-run multiplier in this model?

c. Suppose you knew that the preceding is the true model but you linearly regress $y_t$ only on a constant and the first five lags of $x_t$. How does this affect your estimate of the long run multiplier?

d. Same as c. for four lags instead of five.

e. Using the macroeconomic data in Appendix Table F5.1, let $y_t$ be the log of real investment and $x_t$ be the log of real output. Carry out the computations suggested and report your findings. Specifically, how does the omission of a lagged value affect estimates of the short-run and long-run multipliers in the unrestricted lag model?

2. Explain how to estimate the parameters of the following model:

$$y_t = \alpha + \beta x_t + \gamma y_{t-1} + \delta y_{t-2} + e_t,$$

$$e_t = \rho e_{t-1} + u_t.$$

Is there any problem with ordinary least squares? Let $y_t$ be consumption and let $x_t$ be disposable income. Using the method you have described, fit the previous model to the data in Appendix Table F5.1. Report your results.

21

# TIME-SERIES MODELS

## 21.1 INTRODUCTION

For forecasting purposes, a simple model that *describes* the behavior of a variable (or a set of variables) in terms of past values, without the benefit of a well-developed theory, may well prove quite satisfactory. Researchers have observed that the large simultaneous equations macroeconomic models constructed in the 1960s frequently have poorer forecasting performance than fairly simple, univariate time-series models based on just a few parameters and compact specifications. It is just this observation that has raised to prominence the univariate time-series forecasting models pioneered by Box and Jenkins (1984).

In this chapter, we introduce some of the tools employed in the analysis of time-series data.[1] Section 21.2 describes stationary stochastic processes. We encountered this body of theory in Chapters 19 and 20, where we discovered that certain assumptions were required to ascribe familiar properties to a time series of data. We continue that discussion by defining several characteristics of a stationary time series. The recent literature in macroeconometrics has seen an explosion of studies of nonstationary time series. Nonstationarity mandates a revision of the standard inference tools we have used thus far. Chapter 22 introduces some extensions of the results of this chapter to nonstationary time series.

Some of the concepts to be discussed here were introduced in Section 19.2. Section 19.2 also contains a cursory introduction to the nature of time-series processes. It will be useful to review that material before proceeding with the rest of this chapter. Finally, Sections 13.6 on estimation and 13.9.2 and 20.4.3 on stability of dynamic models will be especially useful for the latter sections of this chapter.

---

[1]Each topic discussed here is the subject of a vast literature with articles and book-length treatments at all levels. For example, two survey papers on the subject of unit roots in economic time-series data, Diebold and Nerlove (1990) and Campbell and Perron (1991), cite between them more than 200 basic sources on the subject. The literature on unit roots and cointegration is almost surely the most rapidly moving target in econometrics. Stock's (1994) survey adds hundreds of references to those in the aforementioned surveys and brings the literature up to date as of then. Useful basic references on the subjects of this chapter are Box and Jenkins (1984); Judge et al. (1985); Mills (1990); Granger and Newbold (1996); Granger and Watson (1984); Hendry, Pagan, and Sargan (1984); Geweke (1984); and especially Harvey (1989, 1990); Enders (2004); Tsay (2005); Hamilton (1994); and Patterson (2000). There are also many survey style and pedagogical articles on these subjects. The aforementioned paper by Diebold and Nerlove is a useful tour guide through some of the literature. We recommend Dickey, Bell, and Miller (1986) and Dickey, Jansen, and Thorton (1991) as well. The latter is an especially clear introduction at a very basic level of the fundamental tools for empirical researchers.

## 21.2 STATIONARY STOCHASTIC PROCESSES

The essential building block for the models to be discussed in this chapter is the **white noise** time-series process,

$$\{\varepsilon_t\}, t = -\infty, +\infty,$$

where each element in the sequence has $E[\varepsilon_t] = 0$, $E[\varepsilon_t^2] = \sigma_\varepsilon^2$, and $\text{Cov}[\varepsilon_t, \varepsilon_s] = 0$ for all $s \neq t$. Each element in the series is a random draw from a population with zero mean and constant variance. It is occasionally assumed that the draws are independent or normally distributed, although for most of our analysis, neither assumption will be essential.

A **univariate time-series model** describes the behavior of a variable in terms of its own past values. Consider, for example, the autoregressive disturbance models introduced in Chapter 19,

$$u_t = \rho u_{t-1} + \varepsilon_t. \tag{21-1}$$

Autoregressive disturbances are generally the residual variation in a regression model built up from what may be an elaborate underlying theory, $y_t = \mathbf{x}_t' \boldsymbol{\beta} + u_t$. The theory usually stops short of stating what enters the disturbance. But the presumption that some time-series process generates $\mathbf{x}_t$ should extend equally to $u_t$. There are two ways to interpret this simple series. As stated, $u_t$ equals the previous value of $u_t$ plus an "innovation," $\varepsilon_t$. Alternatively, by manipulating the series, we showed that $u_t$ could be interpreted as an aggregation of the entire history of the $\varepsilon_t$'s.

Occasionally, statistical evidence is convincing that a more intricate process is at work in the disturbance. Perhaps a second-order **autoregression,**

$$u_t = \rho_1 u_{t-1} + \rho_2 u_{t-2} + \varepsilon_t, \tag{21-2}$$

better explains the movement of the disturbances in the regression. The model may not arise naturally from an underlying behavioral theory. But in the face of certain kinds of statistical evidence, one might conclude that the more elaborate model would be preferable.[2] This section will describe several alternatives to the AR(1) model that we have relied on in most of the preceding applications.

### 21.2.1 AUTOREGRESSIVE MOVING-AVERAGE PROCESSES

The variable $y_t$ in the model

$$y_t = \mu + \gamma y_{t-1} + \varepsilon_t \tag{21-3}$$

is said to be **autoregressive** (or **self-regressive**) because under certain assumptions,

$$E[y_t \mid y_{t-1}] = \mu + \gamma y_{t-1}.$$

A more general $p$th-order autoregression or AR($p$) process would be written

$$y_t = \mu + \gamma_1 y_{t-1} + \gamma_2 y_{t-2} + \cdots + \gamma_p y_{t-p} + \varepsilon_t. \tag{21-4}$$

---

[2]For example, the estimates of $\varepsilon_t$ computed after a correction for first-order autocorrelation may fail tests of randomness such as the LM (Section 19.7.1) test.

The analogy to the classical regression is clear. Now consider the first-order moving average, or MA(1) specification[3]

$$y_t = \mu + \varepsilon_t - \theta \varepsilon_{t-1}. \tag{21-5}$$

By writing

$$y_t = \mu + (1 - \theta L)\varepsilon_t,$$

or

$$\frac{y_t}{1 - \theta L} = \frac{\mu}{1 - \theta} + \varepsilon_t,$$

we find that

$$y_t = \frac{\mu}{1 - \theta} - \theta y_{t-1} - \theta^2 y_{t-2} - \cdots + \varepsilon_t.$$

Once again, the effect is to represent $y_t$ as a function of its own past values.

An extremely general model that encompasses (21-4) and (21-5) is the **autoregressive moving average,** or ARMA($p, q$), model:

$$y_t = \mu + \gamma_1 y_{t-1} + \gamma_2 y_{t-2} + \cdots + \gamma_p y_{t-p} + \varepsilon_t - \theta_1 \varepsilon_{t-1} - \cdots - \theta_q \varepsilon_{t-q}. \tag{21-6}$$

Note the convention that the ARMA($p, q$) process has $p$ autoregressive (lagged dependent-variable) terms and $q$ lagged **moving average** terms. Researchers have found that models of this sort with relatively small values of $p$ and $q$ have proved quite effective as forecasting models.

The disturbances $\varepsilon_t$ are labeled the **innovations** in the model. The term is fitting because the only new information that enters the processes in period $t$ is this innovation. Consider, then, the AR(1) process

$$y_t = \mu + \gamma y_{t-1} + \varepsilon_t. \tag{21-7}$$

Either by successive substitution or by using the lag operator, we obtain

$$(1 - \gamma L)y_t = \mu + \varepsilon_t,$$

or

$$y_t = \frac{\mu}{1 - \gamma} + \sum_{i=0}^{\infty} \gamma^i \varepsilon_{t-i}.^{[4]} \tag{21-8}$$

The observed series is a particular type of aggregation of the history of the innovations. The moving average, MA($q$) model,

$$y_t = \mu + \varepsilon_t - \theta_1 \varepsilon_{t-1} - \cdots - \theta_q \varepsilon_{t-q} = \mu + D(L)\varepsilon_t, \tag{21-9}$$

is yet another, particularly simple form of aggregation in that only information from the $q$ most recent periods is retained. The general result is that many time-series processes can be viewed either as regressions on lagged values with additive disturbances or as aggregations of a history of innovations. They differ from one to the next in the form of that aggregation.

---

[3]The lag operator is discussed in Section 20.2.2. Because $\mu$ is a constant, $(1 - \theta L)^{-1}\mu = \mu + \theta\mu + \theta^2\mu + \cdots = \mu/(1 - \theta)$. The lag operator may be set equal to one when it operates on a constant.

[4]See Section 20.3 for discussion of models with infinite lag structures.

More involved processes can be similarly represented in either an autoregressive or moving-average form. (We will turn to the mathematical requirements later.) Consider, for example, the ARMA(2, 1) process,

$$y_t = \mu + \gamma_1 y_{t-1} + \gamma_2 y_{t-2} + \varepsilon_t - \theta \varepsilon_{t-1},$$

which we can write as

$$(1 - \theta L)\varepsilon_t = y_t - \mu - \gamma_1 y_{t-1} - \gamma_2 y_{t-2}.$$

If $|\theta| < 1$, then we can divide both sides of the equation by $(1 - \theta L)$ and obtain

$$\varepsilon_t = \sum_{i=0}^{\infty} \theta^i (y_{t-i} - \mu - \gamma_1 y_{t-i-1} - \gamma_2 y_{t-i-2}).$$

After some tedious manipulation, this equation produces the autoregressive form,

$$y_t = \frac{\mu}{1-\theta} + \sum_{i=1}^{\infty} \pi_i y_{t-i} + \varepsilon_t,$$

where

$$\pi_1 = \gamma_1 - \theta \quad \text{and} \quad \pi_j = -(\theta^j - \gamma_1 \theta^{j-1} - \gamma_2 \theta^{j-2}), \quad j = 2, 3, \ldots. \quad \textbf{(21-10)}$$

Alternatively, by similar (yet more tedious) manipulation, we can write

$$y_t = \frac{\mu}{1 - \gamma_1 - \gamma_2} + \left[ \frac{1 - \theta L}{1 - \gamma_1 L - \gamma_2 L^2} \right] \varepsilon_t = \frac{\mu}{1 - \gamma_1 - \gamma_2} + \sum_{i=0}^{\infty} \delta_i \varepsilon_{t-i}. \quad \textbf{(21-11)}$$

In each case, the weights, $\pi_i$ in the **autoregressive form** and $\delta_i$ in the **moving-average form,** are complicated functions of the original parameters. But nonetheless, each is just an alternative representation of the same time-series process that produces the current value of $y_t$. This result is a fundamental property of certain time series. We will return to the issue after we formally define the assumption that we have used at the preceding several steps that allows these transformations.

### 21.2.2 STATIONARITY AND INVERTIBILITY

At several points in the preceding, we have alluded to the notion of **stationarity,** either directly or indirectly by making certain assumptions about the parameters in the model. In Section 19.3.2, we characterized an AR(1) disturbance process

$$u_t = \rho u_{t-1} + \varepsilon_t,$$

as stationary if $|\rho| < 1$ and $\varepsilon_t$ is **white noise.** Then

$$E[u_t] = 0 \quad \text{for all } t,$$

$$\text{Var}[u_t] = \frac{\sigma_\varepsilon^2}{1 - \rho^2},$$

$$\text{Cov}[u_t, u_s] = \frac{\rho^{|t-s|} \sigma_\varepsilon^2}{1 - \rho^2}. \quad \textbf{(21-12)}$$

If $|\rho| \geq 1$, then the variance and covariances are undefined.

In the following, we use $\varepsilon_t$ to denote the white noise innovations in the process. The ARMA($p, q$) process will be denoted as in (21-6).

> **DEFINITION 21.1**  Covariance Stationarity
>
> *A stochastic process $y_t$ is **weakly stationary** or **covariance stationary** if it satisfies the following requirements:*[5]
>
> **1.** $E[y_t]$ *is independent of $t$.*
> **2.** $\text{Var}[y_t]$ *is a finite, positive constant, independent of $t$.*
> **3.** $\text{Cov}[y_t, y_s]$ *is a finite function of $|t - s|$, but not of $t$ or $s$.*

The third requirement is that the covariance between observations in the series is a function only of how far apart they are in time, not the time at which they occur. These properties clearly hold for the AR(1) process shown earlier. Whether they apply for the other models we have examined remains to be seen.

We define the **autocovariance** at lag $k$ as

$$\lambda_k = \text{Cov}[y_t, y_{t-k}].$$

Note that

$$\lambda_{-k} = \text{Cov}[y_t, y_{t+k}] = \lambda_k.$$

Stationarity implies that autocovariances are a function of $k$, but not of $t$. For example, in (21-12), we see that the autocovariances of the AR(1) process $y_t = \mu + \gamma y_{t-1} + \varepsilon_t$ are

$$\text{Cov}[y_t, y_{t-k}] = \frac{\gamma^k \sigma_\varepsilon^2}{1 - \gamma^2}, \quad k = 0, 1 \dots . \tag{21-13}$$

If $|\gamma| < 1$, then this process is stationary. For any MA($q$) series,

$$y_t = \mu + \varepsilon_t - \theta_1 \varepsilon_{t-1} - \cdots - \theta_q \varepsilon_{t-q},$$

$$E[y_t] = \mu + E[\varepsilon_t] - \theta_1 E[\varepsilon_{t-1}] - \cdots - \theta_q E[\varepsilon_{t-q}] = \mu,$$

$$\text{Var}[y_t] = \left(1 + \theta_1^2 + \cdots + \theta_q^2\right) \sigma_\varepsilon^2, \tag{21-14}$$

$$\text{Cov}[y_t, y_{t-1}] = (-\theta_1 + \theta_1 \theta_2 + \theta_2 \theta_3 + \cdots + \theta_{q-1} \theta_q) \sigma_\varepsilon^2,$$

and so on until

$$\text{Cov}[y_t, y_{t-(q-1)}] = [-\theta_{q-1} + \theta_1 \theta_q] \sigma_\varepsilon^2,$$

$$\text{Cov}[y_t, y_{t-q}] = -\theta_q \sigma_\varepsilon^2,$$

and, for lags greater than $q$, the autocovariances are zero. It follows, therefore, that finite moving-average processes are stationary regardless of the values of the parameters. The MA(1) process $y_t = \varepsilon_t - \theta \varepsilon_{t-1}$ is an important special case that has $\text{Var}[y_t] = (1 + \theta^2)\sigma_\varepsilon^2$, $\lambda_1 = -\theta \sigma_\varepsilon^2$, and $\lambda_k = 0$ for $|k| > 1$.

For the AR(1) process, the stationarity requirement is that $|\gamma| < 1$, which in turn, implies that the variance of the moving average representation in (21-8) is finite.

---

[5] *Strong* stationarity requires that the joint distribution of all sets of observations $(y_t, y_{t-1}, \dots)$ be invariant to when the observations are made. For practical purposes in econometrics, this statement is a theoretical fine point. Although weak stationary suffices for our applications, we would not normally analyze weakly stationary time series that were not **strongly stationary** as well. Indeed, we often go even beyond this step and assume joint normality.

Consider the AR(2) process

$$y_t = \mu + \gamma_1 y_{t-1} + \gamma_2 y_{t-2} + \varepsilon_t.$$

Write this equation as

$$C(L)y_t = \mu + \varepsilon_t,$$

where

$$C(L) = 1 - \gamma_1 L - \gamma_2 L^2.$$

Then, if it is possible, we invert this result to produce

$$y_t = [C(L)]^{-1}(\mu + \varepsilon_t).$$

Whether the inversion of the polynomial in the lag operator leads to a convergent series depends on the values of $\gamma_1$ and $\gamma_2$. If so, then the moving-average representation will be

$$y_t = \sum_{i=0}^{\infty} \delta_i (\mu + \varepsilon_{t-i}),$$

so that

$$\text{Var}[y_t] = \sum_{i=0}^{\infty} \delta_i^2 \sigma_\varepsilon^2.$$

Whether this result is finite or not depends on whether the series of $\delta_i s$ is exploding or converging. For the AR(2) case, the series converges if $|\gamma_2| < 1$, $\gamma_1 + \gamma_2 < 1$, and $\gamma_2 - \gamma_1 < 1$.[6]

For the more general case, the autoregressive process is stationary if the roots of the **characteristic equation,**

$$C(z) = 1 - \gamma_1 z - \gamma_2 z^2 - \cdots - \gamma_p z^p = 0,$$

have modulus greater than one, or "lie outside the **unit circle.**"[7] It follows that if a stochastic process is stationary, it has an infinite moving-average representation (and, if not, it does not). The AR(1) process is the simplest case. The characteristic equation is

$$C(z) = 1 - \gamma z = 0,$$

and its single root is $1/\gamma$. This root lies outside the unit circle if $|\gamma| < 1$, which we saw earlier.

Finally, consider the inversion of the moving-average process in (21-9). Whether this inversion is possible depends on the coefficients in $D(L)$ in the same fashion that stationarity hinges on the coefficients in $C(L)$. This counterpart to stationarity of an autoregressive process is called **invertibility.** For it to be possible to invert a moving-average process to produce an autoregressive representation, the roots of $D(L) = 0$ must be outside the unit circle. Notice, for example, that in (21-5), the inversion of the

---

[6]This requirement restricts $(\gamma_1, \gamma_2)$ to within a triangle with points at $(2, -1)$, $(-2, -1)$, and $(0, 1)$.

[7]The roots may be complex. (See Sections 13.9.2 and 20.4.3.) They are of the form $a \pm bi$, where $i = \sqrt{-1}$. The unit circle refers to the two-dimensional set of values of $a$ and $b$ defined by $a^2 + b^2 = 1$, which defines a circle centered at the origin with radius 1.

moving-average process is possible only if $|\theta| < 1$. Because the characteristic equation for the MA(1) process is $1 - \theta L = 0$, the root is $1/\theta$, which must be larger than one.

If the roots of the characteristic equation of a moving-average process all lie outside the unit circle, then the series is said to be invertible. Note that invertibility has no bearing on the stationarity of a process. All moving-average processes with finite coefficients are stationary. Whether an ARMA process is stationary or not depends only on the AR part of the model.

### 21.2.3   AUTOCORRELATIONS OF A STATIONARY STOCHASTIC PROCESS

The function

$$\lambda_k = \text{Cov}[y_t, y_{t-k}]$$

is called the **autocovariance function** of the process $y_t$. The **autocorrelation function,** or **ACF,** is obtained by dividing by the variance, $\lambda_0$, to obtain

$$\rho_k = \frac{\lambda_k}{\lambda_0}, \quad -1 \leq \rho_k \leq 1.$$

For a stationary process, the ACF will be a function of $k$ and the parameters of the process. The ACF is a useful device for describing a time-series process in much the same way that the moments are used to describe the distribution of a random variable. One of the characteristics of a stationary stochastic process is an autocorrelation function that either abruptly drops to zero at some finite lag or eventually tapers off to zero. The AR(1) process provides the simplest example, because

$$\rho_k = \gamma^k,$$

which is a geometric series that either declines monotonically from $\rho_0 = 1$ if $\gamma$ is positive or with a damped sawtooth pattern if $\gamma$ is negative. Note as well that for the process $y_t = \gamma y_{t-1} + \varepsilon_t$,

$$\rho_k = \gamma \rho_{k-1}, \quad k \geq 1,$$

which bears a noteworthy resemblance to the process itself.

For higher-order autoregressive series, the autocorrelations may decline monotonically or may progress in the fashion of a damped sine wave.[8] Consider, for example, the second-order autoregression, where we assume without loss of generality that $\mu = 0$ (because we are examining second moments in deviations from the mean):

$$y_t = \gamma_1 y_{t-1} + \gamma_2 y_{t-2} + \varepsilon_t.$$

If the process is stationary, then $\text{Var}[y_t] = \text{Var}[y_{t-s}]$ for all $s$. Also, $\text{Var}[y_t] = \text{Cov}[y_t, y_t]$, and $\text{Cov}[\varepsilon_t, y_{t-s}] = 0$ if $s > 0$. These relationships imply that

$$\lambda_0 = \gamma_1 \lambda_1 + \gamma_2 \lambda_2 + \sigma_\varepsilon^2.$$

---

[8]The behavior is a function of the roots of the characteristic equation. This aspect is discussed in Section 13.9 and especially 13.9.3.

Now, using additional lags, we find that

$$\lambda_1 = \gamma_1\lambda_0 + \gamma_2\lambda_1,$$

and

$$\lambda_2 = \gamma_1\lambda_1 + \gamma_2\lambda_0.$$

(21-15)

These three equations provide the solution:

$$\lambda_0 = \sigma_\varepsilon^2 \frac{[(1-\gamma_2)/(1+\gamma_2)]}{(1-\gamma_2)^2 - \gamma_1^2}.$$

The variance is unchanging, so we can divide throughout by $\lambda_0$ to obtain the relationships for the autocorrelations,

$$\rho_1 = \gamma_1\rho_0 + \gamma_2\rho_1.$$

Because $\rho_0 = 1$, $\rho_1 = \gamma_1/(1-\gamma_2)$. Using the same procedure for additional lags, we find that

$$\rho_2 = \gamma_1\rho_1 + \gamma_2,$$

so $\rho_2 = \gamma_1^2/(1-\gamma_2) + \gamma_2$. Generally, then, for lags of two or more,

$$\rho_k = \gamma_1\rho_{k-1} + \gamma_2\rho_{k-2}.$$

Once again, the autocorrelations follow the same difference equation as the series itself. The behavior of this function depends on $\gamma_1$, $\gamma_2$, and $k$, although not in an obvious way. The inherent behavior of the autocorrelation function can be deduced from the characteristic equation.[9] For the second-order process we are examining, the autocorrelations are of the form

$$\rho_k = \phi_1(1/z_1)^k + \phi_2(1/z_2)^k,$$

where the two roots are[10]

$$1/z = \tfrac{1}{2}\left[\gamma_1 \pm \sqrt{\gamma_1^2 + 4\gamma_2}\right].$$

If the two roots are real, then we know that their reciprocals will be less than one in absolute value, so that $\rho_k$ will be the sum of two terms that are decaying to zero. If the two roots are complex, then $\rho_k$ will be the sum of two terms that are oscillating in the form of a damped sine wave.

Applications that involve autoregressions of order greater than two are relatively unusual. Nonetheless, higher-order models can be handled in the same fashion. For the AR($p$) process

$$y_t = \gamma_1 y_{t-1} + \gamma_2 y_{t-2} + \cdots + \gamma_p y_{t-p} + \varepsilon_t,$$

the autocovariances will obey the **Yule–Walker equations**

$$\lambda_0 = \gamma_1\lambda_1 + \gamma_2\lambda_2 + \cdots + \gamma_p\lambda_p + \sigma_\varepsilon^2,$$
$$\lambda_1 = \gamma_1\lambda_0 + \gamma_2\lambda_1 + \cdots + \gamma_p\lambda_{p-1},$$

---

[9]The set of results that we would use to derive this result are exactly those we used in Section 20.4.3 to analyze the stability of a dynamic equation, which makes sense, of course, because the equation linking the autocorrelations is a simple difference equation.

[10]We used the device in Section 20.4.3 to find the characteristic roots. For a second-order equation, the quadratic is easy to manipulate.

and so on. The autocorrelations will once again follow the same difference equation as the original series,

$$\rho_k = \gamma_1\rho_{k-1} + \gamma_2\rho_{k-2} + \cdots + \gamma_p\rho_{k-p}.$$

The ACF for a moving-average process is very simple to obtain. For the first-order process,

$$y_t = \varepsilon_t - \theta\varepsilon_{t-1},$$
$$\lambda_0 = (1 + \theta^2)\sigma_\varepsilon^2,$$
$$\lambda_1 = -\theta\sigma_\varepsilon^2,$$

then $\lambda_k = 0$ for $k > 1$. Higher-order processes appear similarly. For the MA(2) process, by multiplying out the terms and taking expectations, we find that

$$\lambda_0 = \left(1 + \theta_1^2 + \theta_2^2\right)\sigma_\varepsilon^2,$$
$$\lambda_1 = (-\theta_1 + \theta_1\theta_2)\sigma_\varepsilon^2,$$
$$\lambda_2 = -\theta_2\sigma_\varepsilon^2,$$
$$\lambda_k = 0, \quad k > 2.$$

The pattern for the general MA($q$) process $y_t = \varepsilon_t - \theta_1\varepsilon_{t-1} - \theta_2\varepsilon_{t-2} - \cdots - \theta_q\varepsilon_{t-q}$ is analogous. The signature of a moving-average process is an autocorrelation function that abruptly drops to zero at one lag past the order of the process. As we will explore later, this sharp distinction provides a statistical tool that will help us distinguish between these two types of processes empirically.

The mixed process, ARMA($p, q$), is more complicated because it is a mixture of the two forms. For the ARMA(1, 1) process

$$y_t = \gamma y_{t-1} + \varepsilon_t - \theta\varepsilon_{t-1},$$

the Yule–Walker equations are

$$\lambda_0 = E\left[y_t(\gamma y_{t-1} + \varepsilon_t - \theta\varepsilon_{t-1})\right] = \gamma\lambda_1 + \sigma_\varepsilon^2 - \sigma_\varepsilon^2(\theta\gamma - \theta^2),$$
$$\lambda_1 = \gamma\lambda_0 - \theta\sigma_\varepsilon^2,$$

and

$$\lambda_k = \gamma\lambda_{k-1}, \quad k > 1.$$

The general characteristic of ARMA processes is that when the moving-average component is of order $q$, then in the series of autocorrelations there will be an initial $q$ terms that are complicated functions of both the AR and MA parameters, but after $q$ periods,

$$\rho_k = \gamma_1\rho_{k-1} + \gamma_2\rho_{k-2} + \cdots + \gamma_p\rho_{k-p}, \quad k > q.$$

### 21.2.4 PARTIAL AUTOCORRELATIONS OF A STATIONARY STOCHASTIC PROCESS

The autocorrelation function ACF($k$) gives the gross correlation between $y_t$ and $y_{t-k}$. But as we saw in our analysis of the classical regression model in Section 3.4, a gross correlation such as this one can mask a completely different underlying relationship. In this setting, we observe, for example, that a correlation between $y_t$ and $y_{t-2}$ could arise primarily because both variables are correlated with $y_{t-1}$. Consider the AR(1) process $y_t = \gamma y_{t-1} + \varepsilon_t$, where $E[\varepsilon_t] = 0$ so $E[y_t] = E[y_t]/(1 - \gamma) = 0$. The second gross autocorrelation is $\rho_2 = \gamma^2$. But in the same spirit, we might ask what is the correlation between $y_t$ and $y_{t-2}$ *net of the intervening effect of* $y_{t-1}$? In this model, if we remove the effect of $y_{t-1}$ from $y_t$, then only $\varepsilon_t$ remains, and this disturbance is uncorrelated with $y_{t-2}$. We would conclude that the **partial autocorrelation** between $y_t$ and $y_{t-2}$ in this model is zero.

---

**DEFINITION 21.2** Partial Autocorrelation Coefficient

*The partial correlation between $y_t$ and $y_{t-k}$ is the simple correlation between $y_{t-k}$ and $y_t$ minus that part explained linearly by the intervening lags. That is,*

$$\rho_k^* = \text{Corr}[y_t - E^*(y_t \mid y_{t-1}, \ldots, y_{t-k+1}), y_{t-k}],$$

*where $E^*(y_t \mid y_{t-1}, \ldots, y_{t-k+1})$ is the minimum mean-squared error predictor of $y_t$ by $y_{t-1}, \ldots, y_{t-k+1}$.*

---

The function $E^*(.)$ might be the linear regression if the conditional mean happened to be linear, but it might not. The optimal *linear* predictor *is* the linear regression, however, so what we have is

$$\rho_k^* = \text{Corr}[y_t - \beta_1 y_{t-1} - \beta_2 y_{t-2} - \cdots - \beta_{k-1} y_{t-k+1}, y_{t-k}],$$

where $\boldsymbol{\beta} = [\beta_1, \beta_2, \ldots, \beta_{k-1}] = \{\text{Var}[y_{t-1}, y_{t-2}, \ldots, y_{t-k+1}]\}^{-1} \times \text{Cov}[y_t, (y_{t-1}, y_{t-2}, \ldots, y_{t-k+1})]'$. This equation will be recognized as a vector of regression coefficients. As such, what we are computing here (of course) is the correlation between a vector of residuals and $y_{t-k}$. There are various ways to formalize this computation [see, e.g., Enders (2004)]. One intuitively appealing approach is suggested by the equivalent definition (which is also a prescription for computing it), as follows.

---

**DEFINITION 21.3** Partial Autocorrelation Coefficient

*The partial correlation between $y_t$ and $y_{t-k}$ is the last coefficient in the linear projection of $y_t$ on $[y_{t-1}, y_{t-2}, \ldots, y_{t-k}]$,*

$$\begin{bmatrix} \beta_1 \\ \beta_2 \\ \vdots \\ \beta_{k-1} \\ \rho_k^* \end{bmatrix} = \begin{bmatrix} \lambda_0 & \lambda_1 & \cdots & \lambda_{k-2} & \lambda_{k-1} \\ \lambda_1 & \lambda_0 & \cdots & \lambda_{k-3} & \lambda_{k-2} \\ & & \cdots & \vdots & \cdots \\ \lambda_{k-1} & \lambda_{k-2} & \cdots & \lambda_1 & \lambda_0 \end{bmatrix}^{-1} \begin{bmatrix} \lambda_1 \\ \lambda_2 \\ \vdots \\ \lambda_k \end{bmatrix}.$$

---

As before, there are some distinctive patterns for particular time-series processes. Consider first the autoregressive processes,

$$y_t = \gamma_1 y_{t-1} + \gamma_2 y_{t-2} + \cdots + \gamma_p y_{t-p} + \varepsilon_t.$$

We are interested in the last coefficient in the projection of $y_t$ on $y_{t-1}$, then on $[y_{t-1}, y_{t-2}]$, and so on. The first of these is the simple regression coefficient of $y_t$ on $y_{t-1}$, so

$$\rho_1^* = \frac{\text{Cov}[y_t, y_{t-1}]}{\text{Var}[y_{t-1}]} = \frac{\lambda_1}{\lambda_0} = \rho_1.$$

The first partial autocorrelation coefficient for any process equals the first autocorrelation coefficient.

Without doing the messy algebra, we also observe that for the $\text{AR}(p)$ process, $\rho_1^*$ is a mixture of all the $\gamma$ coefficients. Of course, if $p$ equals 1, then $\rho_1^* = \rho_1 = \gamma$. For the higher-order processes, the autocorrelations are likewise mixtures of the autoregressive coefficients until we reach $\rho_p^*$. In view of the form of the $\text{AR}(p)$ model, the last coefficient in the linear projection on $p$ lagged values is $\gamma_p$. Also, we can see the signature pattern of the $\text{AR}(p)$ process, any additional partial autocorrelations must be zero, because they will be simply $\rho_k^* = \text{Corr}[\varepsilon_t, y_{t-k}] = 0$ if $k > p$.

Combining results thus far, we have the characteristic pattern for an autoregressive process. The ACF, $\rho_k$, will gradually decay to zero, either monotonically if the characteristic roots are real or in a sinusoidal pattern if they are complex. The PACF, $\rho_k^*$, will be irregular out to lag $p$, when they abruptly drop to zero and remain there.

The moving-average process has the mirror image of this pattern. We have already examined the ACF for the $\text{MA}(q)$ process; it has $q$ irregular spikes, then it falls to zero and stays there. For the PACF, write the model as

$$y_t = (1 - \theta_1 L - \theta_2 L^2 - \cdots - \theta_q L^q)\varepsilon_t.$$

If the series is invertible, which we will assume throughout, then we have

$$\frac{y_t}{1 - \theta_1 L - \cdots - \theta_q L^q} = \varepsilon_t,$$

or

$$y_t = \pi_1 y_{t-1} + \pi_2 y_{t-2} + \cdots + \varepsilon_t$$

$$= \sum_{i=1}^{\infty} \pi_i y_{t-i} + \varepsilon_t.$$

The autoregressive form of the $\text{MA}(q)$ process has an infinite number of terms, which means that the PACF will not fall off to zero the way that the PACF of the AR process does. Rather, the PACF of an MA process will resemble the ACF of an AR process. For example, for the $\text{MA}(1)$ process $y_t = \varepsilon_t - \theta \varepsilon_{t-1}$, the AR representation is

$$y_t = \theta y_{t-1} + \theta^2 y_{t-2} + \cdots + \varepsilon_t,$$

which is the familiar form of an $\text{AR}(1)$ process. Thus, the PACF of an $\text{MA}(1)$ process is identical to the ACF of an $\text{AR}(1)$ process, $\rho_k^* = \theta^k$.

The $\text{ARMA}(p, q)$ is a mixture of the two types of processes, so its ACF and PACF are likewise mixtures of the two forms discussed above. Generalities are difficult to draw, but normally, the ACF of an ARMA process will have a few distinctive spikes in the early lags corresponding to the number of MA terms, followed by the characteristic smooth pattern of the AR part of the model. High-order MA processes are relatively uncommon in general, and high-order AR processes (greater than two) seem primarily to arise in the form of the nonstationary processes described in the next section. For a stationary process, the workhorses of the applied literature are the (2, 0) and (1, 1) processes. For the ARMA(1, 1) process, both the ACF and the PACF will display a distinctive spike at lag 1 followed by an exponentially decaying pattern thereafter.

### 21.2.5  MODELING UNIVARIATE TIME SERIES

The preceding discussion is largely descriptive. There is no underlying economic theory that states *why* a compact ARMA$(p, q)$ representation should adequately describe the movement of a given economic time series. Nonetheless, as a methodology for building forecasting models, this set of tools and its empirical counterpart have proved as good as and even superior to much more elaborate specifications (perhaps to the consternation of the builders of large macroeconomic models).[11] Box and Jenkins (1984) pioneered a forecasting framework based on the preceding that has been used in a great many fields and that has, certainly in terms of numbers of applications, largely supplanted the use of large integrated econometric models.

Box and Jenkins's approach to modeling a stochastic process can be motivated by the following.

---

**THEOREM 21.1**  Wold's Decomposition Theorem

*Every zero-mean covariance stationary stochastic process can be represented in the form*

$$y_t = E^*[y_t \mid y_{t-1}, y_{t-2}, \dots, y_{t-p}] + \sum_{i=0}^{\infty} \pi_i \varepsilon_{t-i},$$

*where $\varepsilon_t$ is white noise, $\pi_0 = 1$, and the weights are **square summable**—that is,*

$$\sum_{i=1}^{\infty} \pi_i^2 < \infty$$

*$-E^*[y_t \mid y_{t-1}, y_{t-2}, \dots, y_{t-p}]$ is the optimal linear predictor of $y_t$ based on its lagged values, and the predictor $E_t^*$ is uncorrelated with $\varepsilon_{t-i}$.*

---

Thus, the theorem decomposes the process generating $y_t$ into

$$E_t^* = E^*[y_t \mid y_{t-1}, y_{t-2}, \dots, y_{t-p}] = \text{the \textbf{linearly deterministic component}}$$

and

$$\sum_{i=0}^{\infty} \pi_i \varepsilon_{t-i} = \text{the \textbf{linearly indeterministic component.}}$$

---

[11] This observation can be overstated. Even the most committed advocate of the Box–Jenkins methods would concede that an ARMA model of, for example, housing starts will do little to reveal the link between the interest rate policies of the Federal Reserve and their variable of interest. That is, the *covariation* of economic variables remains as interesting as ever.

The theorem states that for any stationary stochastic process, for a given choice of $p$, there is a Wold representation of the stationary series

$$y_t = \sum_{i=1}^{p} \gamma_i y_{t-i} + \sum_{i=0}^{\infty} \pi_i \varepsilon_{t-i}.$$

Note that for a specific ARMA$(P, Q)$ process, if $p \geq P$, then $\pi_i = 0$ for $i > Q$. For practical purposes, the problem with the Wold representation is that we cannot estimate the infinite number of parameters needed to produce the full right-hand side, and, of course, $P$ and $Q$ are unknown. The compromise, then, is to base an estimate of the representation on a model with a finite number of moving-average terms. We can seek the one that best fits the data in hand.

It is important to note that neither the ARMA representation of a process nor the Wold representation is unique. In general terms, suppose that the process generating $y_t$ is

$$\Gamma(L)y_t = \Theta(L)\varepsilon_t.$$

We assume that $\Gamma(L)$ is finite but $\Theta(L)$ need not be. Let $\Phi(L)$ be some other polynomial in the lag operator with roots that are outside the unit circle. Then

$$\left[\frac{\Phi(L)}{\Gamma(L)}\right]\Gamma(L)y_t = \left[\frac{\Phi(L)}{\Gamma(L)}\right]\Theta(L)\varepsilon_t,$$

or

$$\Phi(L)y_t = \Pi(L)\varepsilon_t.$$

The new representation is fully equivalent to the old one, but it might have a different number of autoregressive parameters, which is exactly the point of the Wold decomposition. The implication is that part of the model-building process will be to determine the lag structures. Further discussion on the methodology is given by Box and Jenkins (1984).

The Box–Jenkins approach to modeling stochastic processes consists of the following steps:

1.  Satisfactorily transform the data so as to obtain a stationary series. This step will usually mean taking first differences, logs, or both to obtain a series whose autocorrelation function eventually displays the characteristic exponential decay of a stationary series.
2.  Estimate the parameters of the resulting ARMA model, generally by nonlinear least squares.
3.  Generate the set of residuals from the estimated model and verify that they satisfactorily resemble a white noise series. If not, respecify the model and return to step 2.
4.  The model can now be used for forecasting purposes.

Space limitations prevent us from giving a full presentation of the set of techniques. Because this methodology has spawned a mini-industry of its own, however, there is no shortage of book length analyses and prescriptions to which the reader may refer. Five to consider are the canonical source, Box and Jenkins (1984), Granger and Newbold

(1996), Mills (1993), Enders (2004), and Patterson (2000). Some of the aspects of the estimation and analysis steps do have broader relevance for our work here, so we will continue to examine them in some detail.

### 21.2.6 ESTIMATION OF THE PARAMETERS OF A UNIVARIATE TIME SERIES

The broad problem of regression estimation with time-series data, which carries through to all the discussions of this chapter, is that the consistency and asymptotic normality results that we derived based on random sampling will no longer apply. For example, for a stationary series, we have assumed that $\text{Var}[y_t] = \lambda_0$ regardless of $t$. But we have yet to establish that an estimated variance,

$$c_0 = \frac{1}{T-1} \sum_{t=1}^{T} (y_t - \overline{y})^2,$$

will converge to $\lambda_0$, or anything else for that matter. It is necessary to assume that the process is **ergodic.** (We first encountered this assumption in Section 19.4.1—see Definition 19.3.) Ergodicity is a crucial element of our theory of estimation. When a time series has this property (with stationarity), then we can consider estimation of parameters in a meaningful sense. If the process is stationary and ergodic, then, by the Ergodic theorem (Theorems 19.1 and 19.2), moments such as $\overline{y}$ and $c_0$ converge to their population counterparts $\mu$ and $\lambda_0$.[12] The essential component of the condition is one that we have met at many points in this discussion, that autocovariances must decline sufficiently rapidly as the separation in time increases. It is possible to construct theoretical examples of processes that are stationary but not ergodic, but for practical purposes, a stationarity assumption will be sufficient for us to proceed with estimation. For example, in our models of stationary processes, if we assume that $\varepsilon_t \sim N[0, \sigma^2]$, which is common, then the stationary processes are ergodic as well.

Estimation of the parameters of a time-series process must begin with a determination of the type of process that we have in hand. (Box and Jenkins label this the **identification** step. But identification is a term of art in econometrics, so we will steer around that admittedly standard name.) For this purpose, the empirical estimates of the autocorrelation and partial autocorrelation functions are useful tools.

The sample counterpart to the ACF is the **correlogram,**

$$r_k = \frac{\sum_{t=k+1}^{T} (y_t - \overline{y})(y_{t-k} - \overline{y})}{\sum_{t=1}^{T} (y_t - \overline{y})^2}.$$

A plot of $r_k$ against $k$ provides a description of a process and can be used to help discern what type of process is generating the data. The sample PACF is the counterpart to the ACF, but net of the intervening lags; that is,

$$r_k^* = \frac{\sum_{t=k+1}^{T} y_t^* y_{t-k}^*}{\sum_{t=k+1}^{T} (y_{t-k}^*)^2},$$

---

[12]The formal conditions for ergodicity are quite involved; see Davidson and MacKinnon (1993) or Hamilton (1994, Chapter 7).

where $y_t^*$ and $y_{t-k}^*$ are residuals from the regressions of $y_t$ and $y_{t-k}$ on $[1, y_{t-1}, y_{t-2}, \ldots,$ $y_{t-k+1}]$. We have seen this at many points before; $r_k^*$ is simply the last linear least squares regression coefficient in the regression of $y_t$ on $[1, y_{t-1}, y_{t-2}, \ldots, y_{t-k+1}, y_{t-k}]$. Plots of the ACF and PACF of a series are usually presented together. Because the sample estimates of the autocorrelations and partial autocorrelations are not likely to be identically zero even when the population values are, we use diagnostic tests to discern whether a time series appears to be nonautocorrelated.[13] Individual sample autocorrelations will be approximately distributed with mean zero and variance $1/T$ under the hypothesis that the series is white noise. The Box–Pierce (1970) statistic

$$Q = T \sum_{k=1}^{p} r_k^2$$

is commonly used to test whether a series is white noise. Under the null hypothesis that the series is white noise, $Q$ has a limiting chi-squared distribution with $p$ degrees of freedom. A refinement that appears to have better finite-sample properties is the Ljung–Box (1979) statistic,

$$Q' = T(T+2) \sum_{k=1}^{p} \frac{r_k^2}{T-k}.$$

The limiting distribution of $Q'$ is the same as that of $Q$.

The process of finding the appropriate specification is essentially trial and error. An initial specification based on the sample ACF and PACF can be found. The parameters of the model can then be estimated by least squares. For pure $AR(p)$ processes, the estimation step is simple. The parameters can be estimated by linear least squares. If there are moving-average terms, then linear least squares is inconsistent, but the parameters of the model can be fit by nonlinear least squares. Once the model has been estimated, a set of residuals is computed to assess the adequacy of the specification. In an AR model, the residuals are just the deviations from the regression line.

The adequacy of the specification can be examined by applying the foregoing techniques to the estimated residuals. If they appear satisfactorily to mimic a white noise process, then analysis can proceed to the forecasting step. If not, a new specification should be considered.

### Example 21.1   ACF and PACF for a Series of Bond Yields
Appendix Table F21.1 lists five years of monthly averages of the yield on a Moody's Aaa-rated corporate bond. (Note: In previous editions of this text, the second observation in the data file was incorrectly recorded as 9.72. The correct value is 9.22. Computations to follow are based on the corrected value.) The series is plotted in Figure 21.1. From the figure, it would appear that stationarity may not be a reasonable assumption. We will return to this question below. The ACF and PACF for the original series are shown in Table 21.1, with the diagnostic statistics discussed earlier.

Based on the two spikes in the PACF, the results appear to be consistent with an AR(2) process, although the ACF at longer lags seems a bit more persistent than might have been expected. Once again, this condition may indicate that the series is not stationary. Maintaining that assumption for the present, we computed the residuals from an AR(2) model and

---

[13]The LM test discussed in Section 19.7.1 is one of these.

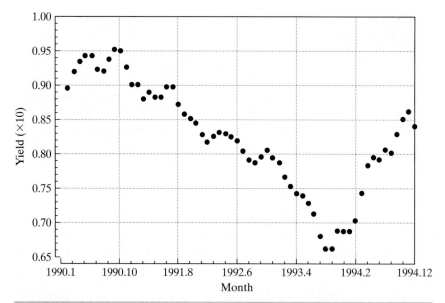

**FIGURE 21.1**  Monthly Data on Bond Yields.

subjected them to the same test as the original series. To compute the regression, we first subtracted the overall mean from all 60 obserations. We then fit the AR(2) without the first two observations. The coefficients of the AR(2) process are 1.4970 and −0.4986, which also satisfy the restrictions for stationarity given in Section 21.2.2. Despite the earlier suggestions, the residuals do appear to resemble a stationary process. (See Table 21.2.)

---

**TABLE 21.1**  ACF and PACF for Bond Yields

Time-series identification for YIELD
Box–Pierce statistic = 326.0507          Box–Ljung statistic = 364.6475
Degrees of freedom = 14                   Degrees of freedom = 14
Significance level = 0.0000               Significance level = 0.0000
∗ ⇒ |coefficient| > 2/sqrt($N$) or > 95% significant.
PACF is computed using Yule–Walker equations.

| Lag | Autocorrelation Function | | Box/Prc | Partial Autocorrelations X | | |
|-----|------------|-------------|---------|---------|--------|-------------|
| 1 | 0.973* | ********** | 56.81* | 0.973* | | ********** |
| 2 | 0.922* | ********** | 107.76* | −0.477* | ****** | |
| 3 | 0.863* | ********* | 152.47* | 0.057 | | * |
| 4 | 0.806* | ********* | 191.43* | 0.021 | | * |
| 5 | 0.745* | ******** | 224.71* | −0.186 | *** | |
| 6 | 0.679* | ******* | 252.39* | −0.046 | * | |
| 7 | 0.606* | ******* | 274.44* | −0.174 | *** | |
| 8 | 0.529* | ****** | 291.22* | −0.039 | * | |
| 9 | 0.450* | ***** | 303.37* | −0.049 | * | |
| 10 | 0.379* | **** | 311.98* | 0.146 | | ** |
| 11 | 0.316* | *** | 317.95* | −0.023 | * | |
| 12 | 0.259* | *** | 321.97* | −0.001 | * | |
| 13 | 0.205 | ** | 324.49* | −0.018 | * | |
| 14 | 0.161 | ** | 326.05* | 0.185 | | *** |

Note, *s in first column and bars in the right-hand panel have changed from earlier edition.

**TABLE 21.2**   ACF and PACF for Residuals

Time series identification for U

| | |
|---|---|
| Box–Pierce statistic = 10.7650 | Box–Ljung statistic = 12.4641 |
| Degrees of freedom = 14 | Degrees of freedom = 14 |
| Significance level = 0.7044 | Significance level = 0.5691 |

$* \Rightarrow |\text{coefficient}| > 2/\text{sqrt}(N)$ or $> 95\%$ significant.
PACF is computed using Yule–Walker equations.

| Lag | Autocorrelation Function | | | Box/Prc | Partial Autocorrelations X | | |
|-----|--------|------|------|---------|--------|------|------|
| 1 | 0.084 | | ** | 0.41 | 0.084 | | * |
| 2 | −0.120 | ** | | 1.25 | −0.138 | ** | |
| 3 | −0.241 | *** | | 4.61 | −0.242 | *** | |
| 4 | 0.095 | | * | 5.12 | 0.137 | | ** |
| 5 | 0.137 | | ** | 6.22 | 0.104 | | * |
| 6 | 0.121 | | * | 7.06 | 0.102 | | * |
| 7 | −0.084 | * | | 7.46 | −0.048 | * | |
| 8 | 0.049 | | * | 7.60 | 0.184 | | *** |
| 9 | −0.169 | ** | | 9.26 | −0.327* | **** | |
| 10 | 0.025 | | * | 9.30 | 0.025 | | * |
| 11 | −0.005 | * | | 9.30 | 0.037 | | * |
| 12 | 0.003 | | * | 9.30 | −0.100 | ** | |
| 13 | −0.137 | ** | | 10.39 | −0.203 | *** | |
| 14 | −0.081 | * | | 10.77 | −0.167 | *** | |

Note, * in third column and bars in both panels have changed from earlier edition.

## 21.3   THE FREQUENCY DOMAIN

For the analysis of macroeconomic flow data such as output and consumption, and aggregate economic index series such as the price level and the rate of unemployment, the tools described in the previous sections have proved quite satisfactory. The low frequency of observation (yearly, quarterly, or, occasionally, monthly) and very significant aggregation (both across time and of individuals) make these data relatively smooth and straightforward to analyze. Much contemporary economic analysis, especially financial econometrics, has dealt with more disaggregated, microlevel data, observed at far greater frequency. Some important examples are stock market data for which daily returns data are routinely available, and exchange rate movements, which have been tabulated on an almost continuous basis. In these settings, analysts have found that the tools of spectral analysis, and the frequency domain, have provided many useful results and have been applied to great advantage. This section introduces a small amount of the terminology of spectral analysis to acquaint the reader with a few basic features of the technique. For those who desire further detail, Fuller (1976), Granger and Newbold (1996), Hamilton (1994), Chatfield (1996), Shumway (1988), and Hatanaka (1996) (among many others with direct application in economics) are excellent introductions. Most of the following is based on Chapter 6 of Hamilton (1994).

In this framework, we view an observed time series as a weighted sum of underlying series that have different cyclical patterns. For example, aggregate retail sales and construction data display several different kinds of cyclical variation, including a regular seasonal pattern and longer frequency variation associated with variation in the economy as a whole over the business cycle. The total variance of an observed time series may thus be viewed as a sum of the contributions of these underlying series, which vary at different frequencies. The standard application we consider is how spectral analysis is used to decompose the variance of a time series.

### 21.3.1 Theoretical Results

Let $\{y_t\}_{t=-\infty,\infty}$ define a zero-mean, stationary time-series process. The autocovariance at lag $k$ was defined in Section 21.2.2 as

$$\lambda_k = \lambda_{-k} = \text{Cov}[y_t, y_{t-k}].$$

We assume that the series $\lambda_k$ is *absolutely summable*; $\sum_{i=0}^{\infty} |\lambda_k|$ is finite. The **autocovariance generating function** for this time-series process is

$$g_Y(z) = \sum_{k=-\infty}^{\infty} \lambda_k z^k.$$

We evaluate this function at the complex value $z = \exp(i\omega)$, where $i = \sqrt{-1}$ and $\omega$ is a real number, and divide by $2\pi$ to obtain the **spectrum,** or **spectral density function,** of the time-series process,

$$h_Y(\omega) = \frac{1}{2\pi} \left( \sum_{k=-\infty}^{\infty} \lambda_k e^{-i\omega k} \right). \tag{21-16}$$

The spectral density function is a characteristic of the time-series process very much like the sequence of autocovariances (or the sequence of moments for a probability distribution). For a time-series process that has the set of autocovariances $\lambda_k$, the spectral density can be computed at any particular value of $\omega$. Several results can be combined to simplify $h_Y(\omega)$:

1. Symmetry of the autocovariances, $\lambda_k = \lambda_{-k}$;
2. DeMoivre's theorem, $\exp(\pm i\omega k) = \cos(\omega k) \pm i \sin(\omega k)$;
3. Polar values, $\cos(0) = 1$, $\cos(\pi) = -1$, $\sin(0) = 0$, $\sin(\pi) = 0$;
4. Symmetries of sin and cos functions, $\sin(-\omega) = -\sin(\omega)$ and $\cos(-\omega) = \cos(\omega)$.

One of the convenient consequences of result 2 is $\exp(i\omega k) + \exp(-i\omega k) = 2\cos(\omega k)$, which is always real. These equations can be combined to simplify the spectrum,

$$h_Y(\omega) = \frac{1}{2\pi} \left[ \lambda_0 + 2 \sum_{k=1}^{\infty} \lambda_k \cos(\omega k) \right], \quad \omega \in [0, \pi]. \tag{21-17}$$

This is a strictly real-valued, continuous function of $\omega$. Because the cosine function is cyclic with period $2\pi$, $h_Y(\omega) = h_Y(\omega + M2\pi)$ for any integer $M$, which implies that the entire spectrum is known if its values for $\omega$ from 0 to $\pi$ are known. [Because $\cos(-\omega) = \cos(\omega)$, $h_Y(\omega) = h_Y(-\omega)$, so the values of the spectrum for $\omega$ from 0 to $-\pi$ are the same as those from 0 to $+\pi$.] There is also a correspondence between the spectrum and the autocovariances,

$$\lambda_k = \int_{-\pi}^{\pi} h_Y(\omega) \cos(k\omega) \, d\omega,$$

which we can interpret as indicating that the sequence of autocovariances and the spectral density function just produce two different ways of looking at the same time-series process (in the first case, in the "time domain," and in the second case, in the "frequency domain," hence the name for this analysis).

The spectral density function is a function of the infinite sequence of autocovariances. For ARMA processes, however, the autocovariances are functions of the usually small numbers of parameters, so $h_Y(\omega)$ will generally simplify considerably. For the ARMA$(p, q)$ process defined in (21-6),

$$(y_t - \mu) = \gamma_1(y_{t-1} - \mu) + \cdots + \gamma_p(y_{t-p} - \mu) + \varepsilon_t - \theta_1\varepsilon_{t-1} - \cdots - \theta_q\varepsilon_{t-q},$$

or

$$\Gamma(L)(y_t - \mu) = \Theta(L)\varepsilon_t,$$

the autocovariance generating function is

$$g_Y(z) = \frac{\sigma^2\Theta(z)\Theta(1/z)}{\Gamma(z)\Gamma(1/z)} = \sigma^2\Pi(z)\Pi(1/z),$$

where $\Pi(z)$ gives the sequence of coefficients in the infinite moving-average representation of the series, $\Theta(z)/\Gamma(z)$. In some cases, this result can be used explicitly to derive the spectral density function. The spectral density function can be obtained from this relationship through

$$h_Y(\omega) = \frac{\sigma^2}{2\pi}\Pi(e^{-i\omega})\Pi(e^{i\omega}).$$

### Example 21.2  Spectral Density Function for an AR(1) Process

For an AR(1) process with autoregressive parameter $\rho$, $y_t = \rho y_{t-1} + \varepsilon_t$, $\varepsilon_t \sim N[0, 1]$, the lag polynomials are $\Theta(z) = 1$ and $\Gamma(z) = 1 - \rho z$. The autocovariance generating function is

$$g_Y(z) = \frac{\sigma^2}{(1 - \rho z)(1 - \rho/z)}$$

$$= \frac{\sigma^2}{1 + \rho^2 - \rho(z + 1/z)}$$

$$= \frac{\sigma^2}{1 + \rho^2}\sum_{i=0}^{\infty}\left(\frac{\rho}{1 + \rho^2}\right)^i\left(\frac{1 + z^2}{z}\right)^i.$$

The spectral density function is

$$h_Y(\omega) = \frac{\sigma^2}{2\pi}\frac{1}{[1 - \rho\exp(-i\omega)][1 - \rho\exp(i\omega)]} = \frac{\sigma^2}{2\pi}\frac{1}{[1 + \rho^2 - 2\rho\cos(\omega)]}.$$

For the general case suggested at the outset, $\Gamma(L)(y_t - \mu) = \Theta(L)\varepsilon_t$, there is a template we can use, which, if not simple, is at least transparent. Let $\alpha_i$ be the reciprocal of a root of the characteristic polynomial for the autoregressive part of the model, $\Gamma(\alpha_i) = 0, i = 1, \ldots, p$, and let $\delta_j, j = 1, \ldots, q$, be the same for the moving-average part of the model. Then

$$h_Y(\omega) = \frac{\sigma^2}{2\pi}\frac{\prod_{j=1}^{q}\left[1 + \delta_j^2 - 2\delta_j\cos(\omega)\right]}{\prod_{i=1}^{p}\left[1 + \alpha_i^2 - 2\alpha_i\cos(\omega)\right]}.$$

Some of the roots of either polynomial may be complex pairs, but in this case, the product for adjacent pairs $(a \pm bi)$ is real, so the function is always real valued. [Note also that $(a \pm bi)^{-1} = (a \mp bi)/(a^2 + b^2).$]

For purposes of our initial objective, decomposing the variance of the time series, our final useful theoretical result is

$$\int_{-\pi}^{\pi} h_Y(\omega) \, d\omega = \lambda_0.$$

Thus, the total variance can be viewed as the sum of the spectral densities over all possible frequencies. (More precisely, it is the area under the spectral density.) Once again exploiting the symmetry of the cosine function, we can rewrite this equation in the form

$$2 \int_0^{\pi} h_Y(\omega) \, d\omega = \lambda_0.$$

Consider, then, integration over only some of the frequencies;

$$\frac{2}{\lambda_0} \int_0^{\omega_j} h_Y(\omega) \, d\omega = \tau(\omega_j), \quad 0 < \omega_j \leq \pi, 0 < \tau(\omega_j) \leq 1.$$

Thus, $\tau(\omega_j)$ can be interpreted as the proportion of the total variance of the time series that is associated with frequencies less than or equal to $\omega_j$.

### 21.3.2 Empirical Counterparts

We have in hand a sample of observations, $y_t, t = 1, \ldots, T$. The first task is to establish a correspondence between the frequencies $0 < \omega \leq \pi$ and something of interest in the sample. The lowest frequency we could observe would be once in the entire sample period, so we map $\omega_1$ to $2\pi/T$. The highest would then be $\omega_T = 2\pi$, and the intervening values will be $2\pi j/T, j = 2, \ldots, T - 1$. It may be more convenient to think in terms of period rather than frequency. The number of periods per cycle will correspond to $T/j = 2\pi/\omega_j$. Thus, the lowest frequency, $\omega_1$, corresponds to the highest period, $T$ "dates" (months, quarters, years, etc.).

There are a number of ways to estimate the population spectral density function. The obvious way is the sample counterpart to the population spectrum. The sample of $T$ observations provides the variance and $T - 1$ distinct sample autocovariances

$$c_k = c_{-k} = \frac{1}{T} \sum_{t=k+1}^{T} (y_t - \bar{y})(y_{t-k} - \bar{y}), \qquad \bar{y} = \frac{1}{T} \sum_{t=1}^{T} y_t, \quad k = 0, 1, \ldots, T - 1,$$

so we can compute the **sample periodogram,** which is

$$\hat{h}_Y(\omega) = \frac{1}{2\pi} \left[ c_0 + 2 \sum_{k=1}^{T-1} c_k \cos(\omega k) \right].$$

The sample periodogram is a natural estimator of the spectrum, but it has a statistical flaw. With the sample variance and the $T - 1$ autocovariances, we are estimating $T$ parameters with $T$ observations. The periodogram is, in the end, $T$ transformations of these $T$ estimates. As such, there are no "degrees of freedom"; the estimator does not improve as the sample size increases. A number of methods have been suggested for improving the behavior of the estimator. Two common ways are truncation and windowing [see Chatfield (1996, pp. 139–143)]. The truncated estimator of the peri-odogram is based on a subset of the first $L < T$ autocovariances. The choice of $L$ is a problem because there is no theoretical guidance. Chatfield (1996) suggests $L$ approxi-mately equal to $2\sqrt{T}$ is large enough to provide resolution while removing some of the sampling variation induced by the long lags in the untruncated estimator. The second mechanism for improving the properties of the estimator is a set of weights called a **lag window.** The revised estimator is

$$\hat{h}_Y(\omega) = \frac{1}{2\pi}\left[w_0 c_0 + 2\sum_{k=1}^{L} w_k c_k \cos(\omega k)\right],$$

where the set of weights, $\{w_k, k = 0, \ldots, L\}$, is the lag window. One choice for the weights is the Bartlett window, which produces

$$\hat{h}_{Y,\text{Bartlett}}(\omega) = \frac{1}{2\pi}\left[c_0 + 2\sum_{k=1}^{L} w(k, L)c_k \cos(\omega k)\right], \qquad w(k, L) = 1 - \frac{k}{L+1}.$$

Note that this result is the same set of weights used in the Newey–West robust covariance matrix estimator in Chapter 19, with essentially the same motivation. Two others that are commonly used are the Tukey window, which has $w_k = \frac{1}{2}[1 + \cos(\pi k/L)]$, and the Parzen window, $w_k = 1 - 6[(k/L)^2 - (k/L)^3]$, if $k \le L/2$, and $w_k = 2(1-k/L)^3$ otherwise.

If the series has been modeled as an ARMA process, we can instead compute the fully parametric estimator based on our sample estimates of the roots of the autore-gressive and moving-average polynomials. This second estimator would be

$$\hat{h}_{Y,\text{ARMA}}(\omega) = \frac{\hat{\sigma}^2}{2\pi}\frac{\prod_{j=1}^{q}\left[1 + d_j^2 - 2d_j \cos(\omega k)\right]}{\prod_{i=1}^{p}\left[1 + a_i^2 - 2a_i \cos(\omega k)\right]}.$$

Others have been suggested. [See Chatfield (1996, Chapter 7).]

Finally, with the empirical estimate of the spectrum, the variance decomposition can be approximated by summing the values around the frequencies of interest.

### Example 21.3  *Spectral Analysis of the Growth Rate of Real GNP*
Appendix Table F21.2 lists quarterly observations on U.S. GNP and the implicit price defla-tor for GNP for 1950 through 1983. The GNP series, with its upward trend, is obviously nonstationary. We will analyze instead the quarterly growth rate, $100[\log(GNP_t/price_t) - \log(GNP_{t-1}/price_{t-1})]$. Figure 21.2 shows the resulting data. The differenced series has 135 observations.

Figure 21.3 plots the sample periodogram, with frequencies scaled so that $\omega_j = (j/T)2\pi$. The figure shows the sample periodogram for $j = 1, \ldots, 67$ (because values of the spectrum for $j = 68, \ldots, 134$) are a mirror image of the first half, we have omitted them). Figure 21.3 shows peaks at several frequencies. The effect is more easily visualized in terms of the periods of these cyclical components. The second row of labels shows the periods, computed as quarters $= T/(2j)$, where $T = 67$ quarters. There are distinct masses around 2 to 3 years that correspond roughly to the "business cycle" of this era. One might also expect seasonal effects in these quarterly data, and there are discernible spikes in the periodogram at about 0.3 year (one quarter). These spikes, however, are minor compared with the other effects in the figure. This is to be expected, because the data are seasonally adjusted already. Finally, there is a pronounced spike at about 6 years in the periodogram. The original data in Figure 21.2 do seem consistent with this result, with substantial recessions coming at intervals of 5 to 7 years from 1953 to 1980.

To underscore these results, consider what we would obtain if we analyzed the original (log) real GNP series instead of the growth rates. Figure 21.4 shows the raw data. Although there does appear to be some short-run (high-frequency) variation (around a long-run trend, for example), the cyclical variation of this series is obviously dominated by the upward trend. If this series were viewed as a single periodic series, then we would surmise that the period of this cycle would be the entire sample interval. The frequency of the dominant part of this time series seems to be quite close to zero. The periodogram for this series, shown in Figure 21.5, is consistent with that suspicion. By far, the largest component of the spectrum is provided by frequencies close to zero.

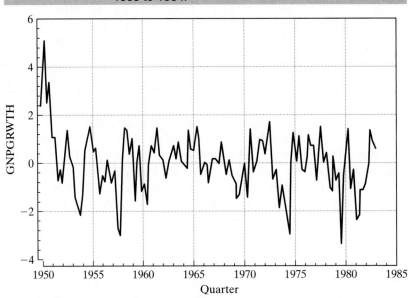

**FIGURE 21.2**    Growth Rate of U.S. Real GNP, Quarterly, 1953 to 1984.

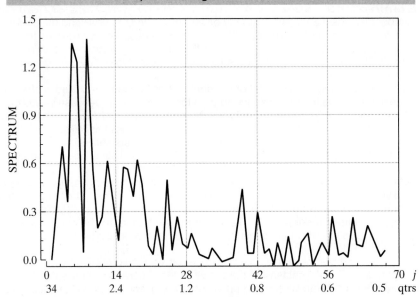

**FIGURE 21.3**    Sample Periodogram.

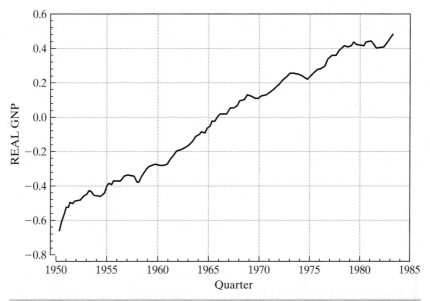

**FIGURE 21.4**    Quarterly Data on Real GNP.

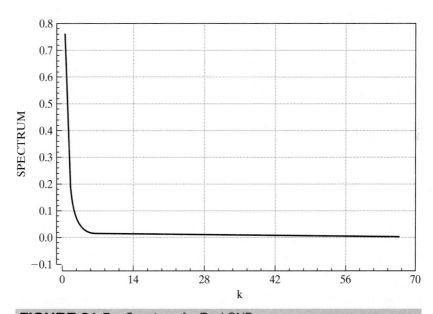

**FIGURE 21.5**    Spectrum for Real GNP.

**A Computational Note**    The computation in (21-16) or (21-17) is the **discrete Fourier transform** of the series of autocovariances. In principle, it involves an enormous amount of computation, on the order of $T^2$ *sets* of computations. For ordinary time series involving up to a few hundred observations, this work is not particularly onerous. (The preceding computations involving 135 observations took a total of perhaps 20 seconds of computing time.) For series involving multiple thousands of observations, such as daily market returns, or far more, such as in recorded exchange rates and forward premiums, the amount of computation could become prohibitive. However, the computation can be done using an important tool, the fast Fourier transform (FFT), that reduces the computational level to $O(T \log_2 T)$, which is many orders of magnitude less than $T^2$. The FFT is programmed in some econometric software packages, such as RATS and Matlab. [See Press et al. (1986) for further discussion.]

## 21.4 SUMMARY AND CONCLUSIONS

This chapter has developed the standard tools for analyzing a stationary time series. The analysis takes place in one of two frameworks, the time domain or the frequency domain. The analysis in the time domain focuses on the different representations of the series in terms of autoregressive and moving-average components. This interpretation of the time series is closely related to the concept of regression—though in this case it is "auto" or self-regression, that is, on past values of the random variable itself. The autocorrelations and partial autocorrelations are the central tools for characterizing a time series in this framework. Constructing a time series in this fashion allows the analyst to construct forecasting equations that exploit the internal structure of the time series. (We have left for additional courses and the many references on the subject the embellishments of these models in terms of seasonal patterns, differences, and so on, that are the staples of Box–Jenkins model building.) The other approach to time-series analysis is in the frequency domain. In this representation, the time series is decomposed into a sum of components that vary cyclically with different periods (and frequencies). The different components that vary at different frequencies provide a view of how the different components contribute to the overall variation of the series.

The analysis in this chapter, of modern economic time-series analysis, is a prelude to the analysis of nonstationary series in the next chapter. Nonstationarity is, in large measure, the norm in recent time-series modeling.

### Key Terms and Concepts

- Autocorrelation function
- Autocovariance
- Autocovariance function
- Autocovariance generating function
- Autoregression
- Autoregressive
- Autoregressive form
- Autoregressive moving average
- Characteristic equation
- Correlogram
- Covariance stationarity
- Discrete Fourier transform
- Ergodic
- Frequency domain
- Identification
- Innovations
- Invertibility
- Lag window
- Linearly deterministic component
- Linearly indeterministic component
- Moving average
- Moving-average form
- Nonstationarity
- Partial autocorrelation
- Periodogram
- Sample periodogram
- Self-regressive
- Spectral density function
- Square summable
- Stationarity
- Strong stationarity
- Unit circle
- Univariate time-series model
- Weak stationarity
- White noise
- Wold's decomposition theorem
- Yule–Walker equations

# 22
# NONSTATIONARY DATA
## ⟨≈≈⟩

## 22.1 INTRODUCTION

Most economic variables that exhibit strong trends, such as GDP, consumption, or the price level, are not stationary and are thus not amenable to the analysis of the previous three chapters. In many cases, stationarity can be achieved by simple differencing or some other simple transformation. But, new statistical issues arise in analyzing nonstationary series that are understated by this superficial observation. This chapter will survey a few of the major issues in the analysis of nonstationary data.[1] We begin in Section 22.2 with results on analysis of a single nonstationary time series. Section 22.3 examines the implications of nonstationarity for analyzing regression relationship. Finally, Section 22.4 turns to the extension of the time-series results to panel data.

## 22.2 NONSTATIONARY PROCESSES AND UNIT ROOTS

This section will begin the analysis of nonstationary time series with some basic results for univariate time series. The fundamental results concern the characteristics of nonstationary series and statistical tests for identification of nonstationarity in observed data.

### 22.2.1 INTEGRATED PROCESSES AND DIFFERENCING

A process that figures prominently in recent work is the **random walk with drift,**

$$y_t = \mu + y_{t-1} + \varepsilon_t.$$

By direct substitution,

$$y_t = \sum_{i=0}^{\infty} (\mu + \varepsilon_{t-i}).$$

That is, $y_t$ is the simple sum of what will eventually be an infinite number of random variables, possibly with nonzero mean. If the innovations are being generated by the same zero-mean, constant-variance distribution, then the variance of $y_t$ would obviously

---

[1] With panel data, this is one of the rapidly growing areas in econometrics, and the literature advances rapidly. We can only scratch the surface. Several recent surveys and books provide useful extensions. Two that will be very helpful are Enders (2004) and Tsay (2005).

be infinite. As such, the random walk is clearly a **nonstationary process,** even if $\mu$ equals zero. On the other hand, the first difference of $y_t$,

$$z_t = y_t - y_{t-1} = \mu + \varepsilon_t,$$

is simply the innovation plus the mean of $z_t$, which we have already assumed is stationary.

The series $y_t$ is said to be **integrated of order one,** denoted $I(1)$, because taking a first difference produces a stationary process. A nonstationary series is integrated of order $d$, denoted $I(d)$, if it becomes stationary after being first differenced $d$ times. A further generalization of the ARMA model discussed in Section 21.2.1 would be the series

$$z_t = (1 - L)^d y_t = \Delta^d y_t.$$

The resulting model is denoted an **autoregressive integrated moving-average** model, or **ARIMA** $(p, d, q)$.[2] In full, the model would be

$$\Delta^d y_t = \mu + \gamma_1 \Delta^d y_{t-1} + \gamma_2 \Delta^d y_{t-2} + \cdots + \gamma_p \Delta^d y_{t-p} + \varepsilon_t - \theta_1 \varepsilon_{t-1} - \cdots - \theta_q \varepsilon_{t-q},$$

where

$$\Delta y_t = y_t - y_{t-1} = (1 - L) y_t.$$

This result may be written compactly as

$$C(L)[(1 - L)^d y_t] = \mu + D(L)\varepsilon_t,$$

where $C(L)$ and $D(L)$ are the polynomials in the lag operator and $(1 - L)^d y_t = \Delta^d y_t$ is the $d$th difference of $y_t$.

An $I(1)$ series in its raw (undifferenced) form will typically be constantly growing, or wandering about with no tendency to revert to a fixed mean. Most macroeconomic flows and stocks that relate to population size, such as output or employment, are $I(1)$. An $I(2)$ series is growing at an ever-increasing rate. The price-level data in Appendix Table F21.2 and shown later appear to be $I(2)$. Series that are $I(3)$ or greater are extremely unusual, but they do exist. Among the few manifestly $I(3)$ series that could be listed, one would find, for example, the money stocks or price levels in hyperinflationary economies such as interwar Germany or Hungary after World War II.

### Example 22.1   A Nonstationary Series

The nominal GNP and price deflator variables in Appendix Table F21.2 are strongly trended, so the mean is changing over time. Figures 22.1 through 22.3 plot the log of the GNP deflator series in Table F21.2 and its first and second differences. The original series and first differences are obviously nonstationary, but the second differencing appears to have rendered the series stationary.

The first 10 autocorrelations of the log of the GNP deflator series are shown in Table 22.1. The autocorrelations of the original series show the signature of a strongly trended, nonstationary series. The first difference also exhibits nonstationarity, because the autocorrelations are still very large after a lag of 10 periods. The second difference appears to be stationary, with mild negative autocorrelation at the first lag, but essentially none after that. Intuition might suggest that further differencing would reduce the autocorrelation further, but that would be incorrect. We leave as an exercise to show that, in fact, for values of $\gamma$ less than about 0.5, first differencing of an AR(1) process actually increases autocorrelation.

---

[2]There are yet further refinements one might consider, such as removing seasonal effects from $z_t$ by differencing by quarter or month. See Harvey (1990) and Davidson and MacKinnon (1993). Some recent work has relaxed the assumption that $d$ is an integer. The **fractionally integrated** series, or ARFIMA has been used to model series in which the very long-run multipliers decay more slowly than would be predicted otherwise.

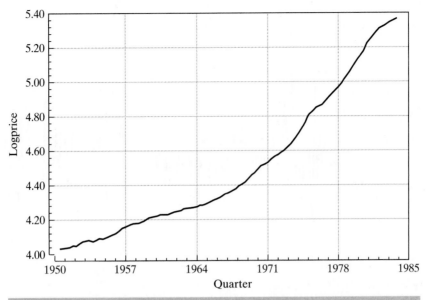

**FIGURE 22.1**  Quarterly Data on log GNP Deflator.

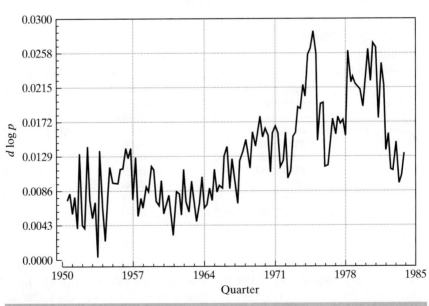

**FIGURE 22.2**  First Difference of log GNP Deflator.

## 22.2.2  RANDOM WALKS, TRENDS, AND SPURIOUS REGRESSIONS

In a seminal paper, Granger and Newbold (1974) argued that researchers had not paid sufficient attention to the warning of very high autocorrelation in the residuals from conventional regression models. Among their conclusions were that macroeconomic data, as a rule, were integrated and that in regressions involving the levels of such

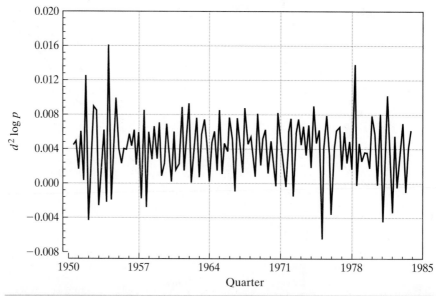

**FIGURE 22.3** Second Difference of log GNP Deflator.

**TABLE 22.1** Autocorrelations for ln GNP Deflator

| Lag | Autocorrelation Function Original Series, log Price | | Autocorrelation Function First Difference of log Price | | Autocorrelation Function Second Difference of log Price | |
|---|---|---|---|---|---|---|
| 1 | 1.000 | ▬▬ | 0.812 | ▬▬ | −0.395 | ▬ |
| 2 | 1.000 | ▬▬ | 0.765 | ▬▬ | −0.112 | ▪ |
| 3 | 0.999 | ▬▬ | 0.776 | ▬▬ | 0.258 | ▬ |
| 4 | 0.999 | ▬▬ | 0.682 | ▬▬ | −0.101 | ▪ |
| 5 | 0.999 | ▬▬ | 0.631 | ▬▬ | −0.022 | ▪ |
| 6 | 0.998 | ▬▬ | 0.592 | ▬▬ | 0.076 | ▪ |
| 7 | 0.998 | ▬▬ | 0.523 | ▬▬ | −0.163 | ▪ |
| 8 | 0.997 | ▬▬ | 0.513 | ▬▬ | 0.052 | ▪ |
| 9 | 0.997 | ▬▬ | 0.488 | ▬▬ | −0.054 | ▪ |
| 10 | 0.997 | ▬▬ | 0.491 | ▬▬ | 0.062 | ▪ |

data, the standard significance tests were usually misleading. The conventional $t$ and $F$ tests would tend to reject the hypothesis of no relationship when, in fact, there might be none. The general result at the center of these findings is that conventional linear regression, ignoring serial correlation, of one random walk on another is virtually certain to suggest a significant relationship, even if the two are, in fact, independent. Among their extreme conclusions, Granger and Newbold suggested that researchers use a critical $t$ value of 11.2 rather than the standard normal value of 1.96 to assess the significance of a coefficient estimate. Phillips (1986) took strong issue with this conclusion. Based on a more general model and on an analytical rather than a Monte Carlo approach, he suggested that the normalized statistic $t_\beta/\sqrt{T}$ be used for testing purposes rather than $t_\beta$ itself. For the 50 observations used by Granger and Newbold, the appropriate critical value would be close to 15! If anything, Granger and Newbold were too optimistic.

The random walk with drift,

$$z_t = \mu + z_{t-1} + \varepsilon_t, \tag{22-1}$$

and the **trend stationary process,**

$$z_t = \mu + \beta t + \varepsilon_t, \tag{22-2}$$

where, in both cases, $\varepsilon_t$ is a white noise process, appear to be reasonable characterizations of many macroeconomic time series.[3] Clearly both of these will produce strongly trended, nonstationary series,[4] so it is not surprising that regressions involving such variables almost always produce significant relationships. The strong correlation would seem to be a consequence of the underlying trend, whether or not there really is any regression at work. But Granger and Newbold went a step further. The intuition is less clear if there is a pure **random walk** at work,

$$z_t = z_{t-1} + \varepsilon_t, \tag{22-3}$$

but even here, they found that regression "relationships" appear to persist even in unrelated series.

Each of these three series is characterized by a **unit root.** In each case, the **data-generating process (DGP)** can be written

$$(1 - L)z_t = \alpha + v_t, \tag{22-4}$$

where $\alpha = \mu, \beta$, and 0, respectively, and $v_t$ is a stationary process. Thus, the characteristic equation has a single root equal to one, hence the name. The upshot of Granger and Newbold's and Phillips's findings is that the use of data characterized by unit roots has the potential to lead to serious errors in inferences.

In all three settings, differencing or detrending would seem to be a natural first step. On the other hand, it is not going to be immediately obvious which is the correct way to proceed—the data are strongly trended in all three cases—and taking the incorrect approach will not necessarily improve matters. For example, first differencing in (22-1) or (22-3) produces a white noise series, but first differencing in (22-2) trades the trend for autocorrelation in the form of an MA(1) process. On the other hand, detrending—that is, computing the residuals from a regression on time—is obviously counterproductive in (22-1) and (22-3), even though the regression of $z_t$ on a trend will appear to be significant for the reasons we have been discussing, whereas detrending in (22-2) appears to be the right approach.[5] Because none of these approaches is likely to

---

[3]The analysis to follow has been extended to more general disturbance processes, but that complicates matters substantially. In this case, in fact, our assumption does cost considerable generality, but the extension is beyond the scope of our work. Some references on the subject are Phillips and Perron (1988) and Davidson and MacKinnon (1993).

[4]The constant term $\mu$ produces the deterministic trend in the random walk with drift. For convenience, suppose that the process starts at time zero. Then $z_t = \sum_{s=0}^{t}(\mu + \varepsilon_s) = \mu t + \sum_{s=0}^{t}\varepsilon_s$. Thus, $z_t$ consists of a deterministic trend plus a stochastic trend consisting of the sum of the innovations. The result is a variable with increasing variance around a linear trend.

[5]See Nelson and Kang (1984).

be obviously preferable at the outset, some means of choosing is necessary. Consider nesting all three models in a single equation,

$$z_t = \mu + \beta t + z_{t-1} + \varepsilon_t.$$

Now subtract $z_{t-1}$ from both sides of the equation and introduce the artificial parameter $\gamma$.

$$
\begin{aligned}
z_t - z_{t-1} &= \mu\gamma + \beta\gamma t + (\gamma - 1)z_{t-1} + \varepsilon_t \\
&= \alpha_0 + \alpha_1 t + (\gamma - 1)z_{t-1} + \varepsilon_t,
\end{aligned}
\tag{22-5}
$$

where, by hypothesis, $\gamma = 1$. Equation (22-5) provides the basis for a variety of tests for unit roots in economic data. In principle, a test of the hypothesis that $\gamma - 1$ equals zero gives confirmation of the random walk with drift, because if $\gamma$ equals 1 (and $\alpha_1$ equals zero), then (22-1) results. If $\gamma - 1$ is less than zero, then the evidence favors the trend stationary (or some other) model, and detrending (or some alternative) is the preferable approach. The practical difficulty is that standard inference procedures based on least squares and the familiar test statistics are not valid in this setting. The issue is discussed in the next section.

### 22.2.3  TESTS FOR UNIT ROOTS IN ECONOMIC DATA

The implications of unit roots in macroeconomic data are, at least potentially, profound. If a structural variable, such as real output, is truly $I(1)$, then shocks to it will have permanent effects. If confirmed, then this observation would mandate some rather serious reconsideration of the analysis of macroeconomic policy. For example, the argument that a change in monetary policy could have a transitory effect on real output would vanish.[6] The literature is not without its skeptics, however. This result rests on a razor's edge. Although the literature is thick with tests that have failed to reject the hypothesis that $\gamma = 1$, many have also not rejected the hypothesis that $\gamma \geq 0.95$, and at 0.95 (or even at 0.99), the entire issue becomes moot.[7]

Consider the simple AR(1) model with zero-mean, white noise innovations,

$$y_t = \gamma y_{t-1} + \varepsilon_t.$$

The downward bias of the least squares estimator when $\gamma$ approaches one has been widely documented.[8] For $|\gamma| < 1$, however, the least squares estimator

$$c = \frac{\sum_{t=2}^{T} y_t y_{t-1}}{\sum_{t=2}^{T} y_{t-1}^2}$$

does have

$$\text{plim } c = \gamma$$

---

[6]The 1980s saw the appearance of literally hundreds of studies, both theoretical and applied, of unit roots in economic data. An important example is the seminal paper by Nelson and Plosser (1982). There is little question but that this observation is an early part of the radical paradigm shift that has occurred in empirical macroeconomics.

[7]A large number of issues are raised in Maddala (1992, pp. 582–588).

[8]See, for example, Evans and Savin (1981, 1984).

and

$$\sqrt{T}(c - \gamma) \xrightarrow{d} N[0, 1 - \gamma^2].$$

Does the result hold up if $\gamma = 1$? The case is called the unit root case, because in the ARMA representation $C(L)y_t = \varepsilon_t$, the characteristic equation $1 - \gamma z = 0$ has one root equal to one. That the limiting variance appears to go to zero should raise suspicions. The literature on the questions dates back to Mann and Wald (1943) and Rubin (1950). But for econometric purposes, the literature has a focal point at the celebrated papers of Dickey and Fuller (1979, 1981). They showed that if $\gamma$ equals one, then

$$T(c - \gamma) \xrightarrow{d} v,$$

where $v$ is a random variable with finite, positive variance, and in finite samples, $E[c] < 1$.[9]

There are two important implications in the Dickey–Fuller results. First, the estimator of $\gamma$ is biased downward if $\gamma$ equals one. Second, the OLS estimator of $\gamma$ converges to its probability limit more rapidly than the estimators to which we are accustomed. That is, the variance of $c$ under the null hypothesis is $O(1/T^2)$, not $O(1/T)$. (In a mean squared error sense, the OLS estimator is superconsistent.) It turns out that the implications of this finding for the regressions with trended data are considerable.

We have already observed that in some cases, differencing or detrending is required to achieve stationarity of a series. Suppose, though, that the preceding AR(1) model is fit to an $I(1)$ series, despite that fact. The upshot of the preceding discussion is that the conventional measures will tend to hide the true value of $\gamma$; the sample estimate is biased downward, and by dint of the very small *true* sampling variance, the conventional $t$ test will tend, incorrectly, to reject the hypothesis that $\gamma = 1$. The practical solution to this problem devised by Dickey and Fuller was to derive, through Monte Carlo methods, an appropriate set of critical values for testing the hypothesis that $\gamma$ equals one in an AR(1) regression when there truly is a unit root. One of their general results is that the test may be carried out using a conventional $t$ statistic, but the critical values for the test must be revised; the standard $t$ table is inappropriate. A number of variants of this form of testing procedure have been developed. We will consider several of them.

### 22.2.4   THE DICKEY–FULLER TESTS

The simplest version of the of the model to be analyzed is the random walk,

$$y_t = \gamma y_{t-1} + \varepsilon_t, \quad \varepsilon_t \sim N[0, \sigma^2], \quad \text{and} \quad \text{Cov}[\varepsilon_t, \varepsilon_s] = 0 \,\forall\, t \neq s.$$

Under the null hypothesis that $\gamma = 1$, there are two approaches to carrying out the test. The conventional $t$ ratio

$$\text{DF}_t = \frac{\hat{\gamma} - 1}{\text{Est. Std. Error}(\hat{\gamma})}$$

---

[9]A full derivation of this result is beyond the scope of this book. For the interested reader, a fairly comprehensive treatment at an accessible level is given in Chapter 17 of Hamilton (1994, pp. 475–542).

**TABLE 22.2** Critical Values for the Dickey–Fuller DF$_\tau$ Test

| | Sample Size | | | |
|---|---|---|---|---|
| | *25* | *50* | *100* | *∞* |
| *F* ratio (D–F)[a] | 7.24 | 6.73 | 6.49 | 6.25 |
| *F* ratio (standard) | 3.42 | 3.20 | 3.10 | 3.00 |
| AR model[b] (random walk) | | | | |
| 0.01 | −2.66 | −2.62 | −2.60 | −2.58 |
| 0.025 | −2.26 | −2.25 | −2.24 | −2.23 |
| 0.05 | −1.95 | −1.95 | −1.95 | −1.95 |
| 0.10 | −1.60 | −1.61 | −1.61 | −1.62 |
| 0.975 | 1.70 | 1.66 | 1.64 | 1.62 |
| AR model with constant (random walk with drift) | | | | |
| 0.01 | −3.75 | −3.59 | −3.50 | −3.42 |
| 0.025 | −3.33 | −3.23 | −3.17 | −3.12 |
| 0.05 | −2.99 | −2.93 | −2.90 | −2.86 |
| 0.10 | −2.64 | −2.60 | −2.58 | −2.57 |
| 0.975 | 0.34 | 0.29 | 0.26 | 0.23 |
| AR model with constant and time trend (trend stationary) | | | | |
| 0.01 | −4.38 | −4.15 | −4.04 | −3.96 |
| 0.025 | −3.95 | −3.80 | −3.69 | −3.66 |
| 0.05 | −3.60 | −3.50 | −3.45 | −3.41 |
| 0.10 | −3.24 | −3.18 | −3.15 | −3.13 |
| 0.975 | −0.50 | −0.58 | −0.62 | −0.66 |

[a] From Dickey and Fuller (1981, p. 1063). Degrees of freedom are 2 and $T - p - 3$.
[b] From Fuller (1976, p. 373 and 1996, Table 10.A.2).

with the revised set of critical values may be used for a one-sided test. Critical values for this test are shown in the top panel of Table 22.2. Note that in general, the critical value is considerably larger in absolute value than its counterpart from the $t$ distribution. The second approach is based on the statistic

$$\text{DF}_\gamma = T(\hat{\gamma} - 1).$$

Critical values for this test are shown in the top panel of Table 22.2.

The simple random walk model is inadequate for many series. Consider the rate of inflation from 1950.2 to 2000.4 (plotted in Figure 22.4) and the log of GDP over the same period (plotted in Figure 22.5). The first of these may be a random walk, but it is clearly drifting. The log GDP series, in contrast, has a strong trend. For the first of these, a random walk with drift may be specified,

$$y_t = \mu + z_t,$$
$$z_t = \gamma z_{t-1} + \varepsilon_t,$$

or

$$y_t = \mu(1 - \gamma) + \gamma y_{t-1} + \varepsilon_t.$$

For the second type of series, we may specify the trend stationary form,

$$y_t = \mu + \beta t + z_t,$$
$$z_t = \gamma z_{t-1} + \varepsilon_t$$

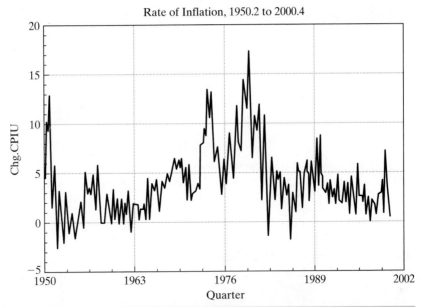

**FIGURE 22.4**    Rate of Inflation in the Consumer Price Index.

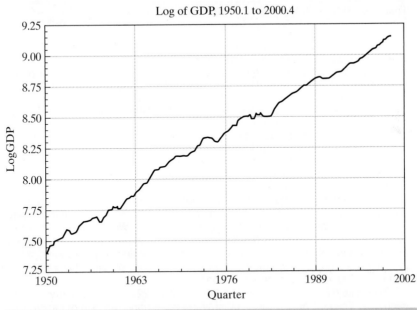

**FIGURE 22.5**    Log of Gross Domestic Product.

or

$$y_t = [\mu(1 - \gamma) + \gamma\beta] + \beta(1 - \gamma) + \gamma y_{t-1} + \varepsilon_t.$$

The tests for these forms may be carried out in the same fashion. For the model with drift only, the center panels of Tables 22.2 and 22.3 are used. When the trend is included, the lower panel of each table is used.

**TABLE 22.3** Critical Values for the Dickey–Fuller $DF_y$ Test

| | | Sample Size | | |
|---|---|---|---|---|
| | *25* | *50* | *100* | *∞* |
| **AR model[a] (random walk)** | | | | |
| 0.01 | −11.8 | −12.8 | −13.3 | −13.8 |
| 0.025 | −9.3 | −9.9 | −10.2 | −10.5 |
| 0.05 | −7.3 | −7.7 | −7.9 | −8.1 |
| 0.10 | −5.3 | −5.5 | −5.6 | −5.7 |
| 0.975 | 1.78 | 1.69 | 1.65 | 1.60 |
| **AR model with constant (random walk with drift)** | | | | |
| 0.01 | −17.2 | −18.9 | −19.8 | −20.7 |
| 0.025 | −14.6 | −15.7 | −16.3 | −16.9 |
| 0.05 | −12.5 | −13.3 | −13.7 | −14.1 |
| 0.10 | −10.2 | −10.7 | −11.0 | −11.3 |
| 0.975 | 0.65 | 0.53 | 0.47 | 0.41 |
| **AR model with constant and time trend (trend stationary)** | | | | |
| 0.01 | −22.5 | −25.8 | −27.4 | −29.4 |
| 0.025 | −20.0 | −22.4 | −23.7 | −24.4 |
| 0.05 | −17.9 | −19.7 | −20.6 | −21.7 |
| 0.10 | −15.6 | −16.8 | −17.5 | −18.3 |
| 0.975 | −1.53 | −1.667 | −1.74 | −1.81 |

[a]From Fuller (1976, p. 373 and 1996, Table 10.A.1).

### Example 22.2    Tests for Unit Roots

In Section 20.6.8, we examined Cecchetti and Rich's study of the effect of recent monetary policy on the U.S. economy. The data used in their study were the following variables:

$$\pi = \text{one period rate of inflation} = \text{the rate of change in the CPI,}$$
$$y = \text{log of real GDP,}$$
$$i = \text{nominal interest rate} = \text{the quarterly average yield on a 90-day T-bill,}$$
$$\Delta m = \text{change in the log of the money stock, M1,}$$
$$i - \pi = \text{ex post real interest rate,}$$
$$\Delta m - \pi = \text{real growth in the money stock.}$$

Data used in their analysis were from the period 1959.1 to 1997.4. As part of their analysis, they checked each of these series for a unit root and suggested that the hypothesis of a unit root could only be rejected for the last two variables. We will reexamine these data for the longer interval, 1950.2 to 2000.4. The data are in Appendix Table F5.1. Figures 22.6 through 22.9 show the behavior of the last four variables. The first two are shown in Figures 22.4 and 22.5. Only the real output figure shows a strong trend, so we will use the random walk with drift for all the variables except this one.

The Dickey–Fuller tests are carried out in Table 22.3. There are 202 observations used in each one. The first observation is lost when computing the rate of inflation and the change in the money stock, and one more is lost for the difference term in the regression. The critical values from interpolating to the second row, last column in each panel for 95 percent significance and a one-tailed test are −3.68 and −24.2, respectively, for $DF_\tau$ and $DF_y$ for the output equation, which contains the time trend, and −3.14 and −16.8 for the other equations, which contain a constant but no trend. For the output equation ($y$), the test statistics are

$$DF_\tau = \frac{0.9584940384 - 1}{.017880922} = -2.32 > -3.44,$$

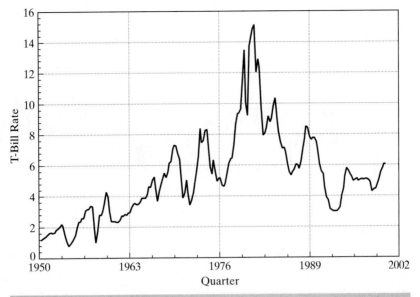

**FIGURE 22.6** T-Bill Rate.

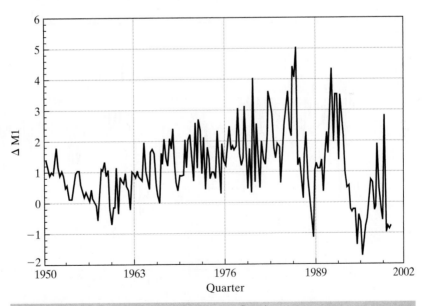

**FIGURE 22.7** Change in the Money Stock.

and

$$DF_y = 202(0.9584940384 - 1) = -8.38 > -21.2.$$

Neither is less than the critical value, so we conclude (as have others) that there is a unit root in the log GDP process. The results of the other tests are shown in Table 22.4. Surprisingly,

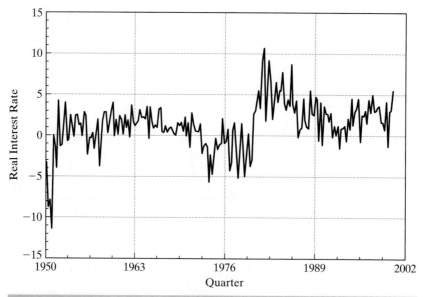

**FIGURE 22.8**   Ex Post Real T-Bill Rate.

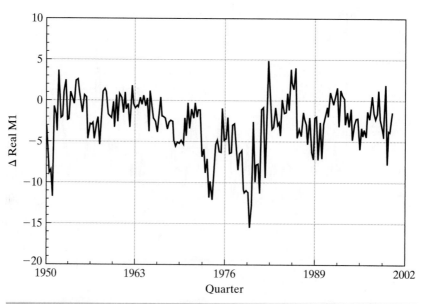

**FIGURE 22.9**   Change in the Real Money Stock.

these results do differ sharply from those obtained by Cecchetti and Rich (2001) for $\pi$ and $\Delta m$. The sample period appears to matter; if we repeat the computation using Cecchetti and Rich's interval, 1959.4 to 1997.4, then $DF_\tau$ equals $-3.51$. This is borderline, but less contradictory. For $\Delta m$ we obtain a value of $-4.204$ for $DF_\tau$ when the sample is restricted to the shorter interval.

**TABLE 22.4** Unit Root Tests (Standard errors of estimates in parentheses)

|  | $\mu$ | $\beta$ | $\gamma$ | $DF_\tau$ | $DF_\gamma$ | *Conclusion* |
|---|---|---|---|---|---|---|
| $\pi$ | 0.332 (0.0696) | | 0.659 (0.0532) | −6.40 $R^2 = 0.432, s = 0.643$ | −68.88 | Reject $H_0$ |
| $y$ | 0.320 (0.134) | 0.00033 (0.00015) | 0.958 (0.0179) | −2.35 $R^2 = 0.999, s = 0.001$ | −8.48 | Do not reject $H_0$ |
| $i$ | 0.228 (0.109) | | 0.961 (0.0182) | −2.14 $R^2 = 0.933, s = 0.743$ | −7.88 | Do not reject $H_0$ |
| $\Delta m$ | 0.448 (0.0923) | | 0.596 (0.0573) | −7.05 $R^2 = 0.351, s = 0.929$ | −81.61 | Reject $H_0$ |
| $i - \pi$ | 0.615 (0.185) | | 0.557 (0.0585) | −7.57 $R^2 = 0.311, s = 2.395$ | −89.49 | Reject $H_0$ |
| $\Delta m - \pi$ | 0.0700 (0.0833) | | 0.490 (0.0618) | −8.25 $R^2 = 0.239, s = 1.176$ | −103.02 | Reject $H_0$ |

The Dickey–Fuller tests described in this section assume that the disturbances in the model as stated are white noise. An extension which will accommodate some forms of serial correlation is the **augmented Dickey–Fuller test.** The augmented Dickey–Fuller test is the same one as described earlier, carried out in the context of the model

$$y_t = \mu + \beta t + \gamma y_{t-1} + \gamma_1 \Delta y_{t-1} + \cdots + \gamma_p \Delta y_{t-p} + \varepsilon_t.$$

The random walk form is obtained by imposing $\mu = 0$ and $\beta = 0$; the random walk with drift has $\beta = 0$; and the trend stationary model leaves both parameters free. The two test statistics are

$$DF_\tau = \frac{\hat{\gamma} - 1}{\text{Est. Std. Error}(\hat{\gamma})},$$

exactly as constructed before, and

$$DF_\gamma = \frac{T(\hat{\gamma} - 1)}{1 - \hat{\gamma}_1 - \cdots - \hat{\gamma}_p}.$$

The advantage of this formulation is that it can accommodate higher-order autoregressive processes in $\varepsilon_t$.

An alternative formulation may prove convenient. By subtracting $y_{t-1}$ from both sides of the equation, we obtain

$$\Delta y_t = \mu + \gamma^* y_{t-1} + \sum_{j=1}^{p-1} \phi_j \Delta y_{t-j} + \varepsilon_t,$$

where

$$\phi_j = -\sum_{k=j+1}^{p} \gamma_k \quad \text{and} \quad \gamma^* = \left( \sum_{i=1}^{p} \gamma_i \right) - 1.$$

The unit root test is carried out as before by testing the null hypothesis $\gamma^* = 0$ against $\gamma^* < 0$.[10] The $t$ test, $DF_\tau$, may be used. If the failure to reject the unit root is taken as evidence that a unit root is present, that is, $\gamma^* = 0$, then the model specializes to the AR$(p-1)$ model in the first differences which is an ARIMA$(p-1,1,0)$ model for $y_t$. For a model with a time trend,

$$\Delta y_t = \mu + \beta t + \gamma^* y_{t-1} + \sum_{j=1}^{p-1} \phi_j \Delta y_{t-j} + \varepsilon_t,$$

the test is carried out by testing the joint hypothesis that $\beta = \gamma^* = 0$. Dickey and Fuller (1981) present counterparts to the critical $F$ statistics for testing the hypothesis. Some of their values are reproduced in the first row of Table 22.2. (Authors frequently focus on $\gamma^*$ and ignore the time trend, maintaining it only as part of the appropriate formulation. In this case, one may use the simple test of $\gamma^* = 0$ as before, with the $DF_\tau$ critical values.)

The lag length, $p$, remains to be determined. As usual, we are well advised to test down to the right value instead of up. One can take the familiar approach and sequentially examine the $t$ statistic on the last coefficient—the usual $t$ test is appropriate. An alternative is to combine a measure of model fit, such as the regression $s^2$ with one of the information criteria. The Akaike and Schwarz (Bayesian) information criteria would produce the two information measures

$$IC(p) = \ln\left(\frac{\mathbf{e}'\mathbf{e}}{T - p_{\max} - K^*}\right) + (p + K^*)\left(\frac{A^*}{T - p_{\max} - K^*}\right),$$

$K^* = 1$ for random walk, 2 for random walk with drift, 3 for trend stationary,

$A^* = 2$ for Akaike criterion, $\ln(T - p_{\max} - K^*)$ for Bayesian criterion,

$p_{\max} =$ the largest lag length being considered.

The remaining detail is to decide upon $p_{\max}$. The theory provides little guidance here. On the basis of a large number of simulations, Schwert (1989) found that

$$p_{\max} = \text{integer part of } [12 \times (T/100)^{.25}]$$

gave good results.

Many alternatives to the Dickey–Fuller tests have been suggested, in some cases to improve on the finite sample properties and in others to accommodate more general modeling frameworks. The Phillips (1987) and Phillips and Perron (1988) statistic may be computed for the same three functional forms,

$$y_t = \delta_t + \gamma y_{t-1} + \gamma_1 \Delta y_{t-1} + \cdots + \gamma_p \Delta y_{t-p} + \varepsilon_t, \tag{22-6}$$

where $\delta_t$ may be 0, $\mu$, or $\mu + \beta t$. The procedure modifies the two Dickey–Fuller statistics we previously examined:

$$Z_\tau = \sqrt{\frac{c_0}{a}}\left(\frac{\hat{\gamma} - 1}{v}\right) - \frac{1}{2}(a - c_0)\frac{Tv}{\sqrt{as^2}},$$

$$Z_\gamma = \frac{T(\hat{\gamma} - 1)}{1 - \hat{\gamma}_1 - \cdots - \hat{\gamma}_p} - \frac{1}{2}\left(\frac{T^2 v^2}{s^2}\right)(a - c_0),$$

---

[10]It is easily verified that one of the roots of the characteristic polynomial is $1/(\gamma_1 + \gamma_2 + \cdots + \gamma_p)$.

where

$$s^2 = \frac{\sum_{t=1}^{T} e_t^2}{T - K},$$

$v^2 =$ estimated asymptotic variance of $\hat{\gamma}$,

$$c_j = \frac{1}{T} \sum_{s=j+1}^{T} e_t e_{t-s}, \quad j = 0, \ldots, p = j\text{th autocovariance of residuals},$$

$$c_0 = [(T - K)/T]s^2,$$

$$a = c_0 + 2 \sum_{j=1}^{L} \left(1 - \frac{j}{L+1}\right) c_j.$$

[Note the Newey–West (Bartlett) weights in the computation of $a$. As before, the analyst must choose $L$.] The test statistics are referred to the same Dickey–Fuller tables we have used before.

Elliot, Rothenberg, and Stock (1996) have proposed a method they denote the ADF-GLS procedure, which is designed to accommodate more general formulations of $\varepsilon$; the process generating $\varepsilon_t$ is assumed to be an $I(0)$ stationary process, possibly an ARMA$(r, s)$. The null hypothesis, as before, is $\gamma = 1$ in (22-6) where $\delta_t = \mu$ or $\mu + \beta t$. The method proceeds as follows:

**Step 1.** Linearly regress

$$\mathbf{y}^* = \begin{bmatrix} y_1 \\ y_2 - \bar{r} y_1 \\ \cdots \\ y_T - \bar{r} y_{T-1} \end{bmatrix} \quad \text{on} \quad \mathbf{X}^* = \begin{bmatrix} 1 \\ 1 - \bar{r} \\ \cdots \\ 1 - \bar{r} \end{bmatrix} \quad \text{or} \quad \mathbf{X}^* = \begin{bmatrix} 1 & 1 \\ 1 - \bar{r} & 2 - \bar{r} \\ \cdots & \\ 1 - \bar{r} & T - \bar{r}(T-1) \end{bmatrix}$$

for the random walk with drift and trend stationary cases, respectively. (Note that the second column of the matrix is simply $\bar{r} + (1 - \bar{r})t$.) Compute the residuals from this regression, $\tilde{y}_t = y_t - \hat{\delta}_t$. $\bar{r} = 1 - 7/T$ for the random walk model and $1 - 13.5/T$ for the model with a trend.

**Step 2.** The Dickey–Fuller DF$_\tau$ test can now be carried out using the model

$$\tilde{y}_t = \gamma \tilde{y}_{t-1} + \gamma_1 \Delta \tilde{y}_{t-1} + \cdots + \gamma_p \Delta \tilde{y}_{t-p} + \eta_t.$$

If the model does not contain the time trend, then the $t$ statistic for $(\gamma - 1)$ may be referred to the critical values in the center panel of Table 22.2. For the trend stationary model, the critical values are given in a table presented in Elliot et al. The 97.5 percent critical values for a one-tailed test from their table is $-3.15$.

As in many such cases of a new technique, as researchers develop large and small modifications of these tests, the practitioner is likely to have some difficulty deciding how to proceed. The Dickey–Fuller procedures have stood the test of time as robust tools that appear to give good results over a wide range of applications. The **Phillips–Perron tests** are very general, but appear to have less than optimal small sample properties. Researchers continue to examine it and the others such as Elliot et al. method. Other tests are catalogued in Maddala and Kim (1998).

### Example 22.3   Augmented Dickey–Fuller Test for a Unit Root in GDP

The Dickey–Fuller 1981 JASA paper is a classic in the econometrics literature—it is probably the single most frequently cited paper in the field. It seems appropriate, therefore, to revisit at least some of their work. Dickey and Fuller apply their methodology to a model for the log of a quarterly series on output, the Federal Reserve Board Production Index. The model used is

$$y_t = \mu + \beta t + \gamma y_{t-1} + \phi(y_{t-1} - y_{t-2}) + \varepsilon_t. \tag{22-7}$$

The test is carried out by testing the joint hypothesis that both $\beta$ and $\gamma^*$ are zero in the model

$$y_t - y_{t-1} = \mu^* + \beta t + \gamma^* y_{t-1} + \phi(y_{t-1} - y_{t-2}) + \varepsilon_t.$$

(If $\gamma = 0$, then $\mu^*$ will also by construction.) We will repeat the study with our data on real GDP from Appendix Table F5.1 using observations 1950.1 to 2000.4.

We will use the augmented Dickey–Fuller test first. Thus, the first step is to determine the appropriate lag length for the augmented regression. Using Schwert's suggestion, we find that the maximum lag length should be allowed to reach $p_{max} = \{$the integer part of $12[204/100]^{.25}\} = 14$. The specification search uses observations 18 to 204, because as many as 17 coefficients will be estimated in the equation

$$y_t = \mu + \beta t + \gamma y_{t-1} + \sum_{j=1}^{p} \gamma_j \Delta y_{t-j} + \varepsilon_t.$$

In the sequence of 14 regressions with $j = 14, 13, \ldots$, the only statistically significant lagged difference is the first one, in the last regression, so it would appear that the model used by Dickey and Fuller would be chosen on this basis. The two information criteria produce a similar conclusion. Both of them decline monotonically from $j = 14$ all the way down to $j = 1$, so on this basis, we end the search with $j = 1$, and proceed to analyze Dickey and Fuller's model.

The linear regression results for the equation in (22-7) are

$$y_t = 0.368 + 0.000391t + 0.952y_{t-1} + 0.36025\Delta y_{t-1} + e_t, \quad s = 0.00912$$
$$\quad\ (0.125)\ \ (0.000138)\ \ (0.0167)\quad\ \ (0.0647) \qquad\qquad R^2 = 0.999647.$$

The two test statistics are

$$DF_\tau = \frac{0.95166 - 1}{0.016716} = -2.892$$

and

$$DF_\gamma = \frac{201(0.95166 - 1)}{1 - 0.36025} = -15.263.$$

Neither statistic is less than the respective critical values, which are $-3.70$ and $-24.5$. On this basis, we conclude, as have many others, that there is a unit root in log GDP.

For the Phillips and Perron statistic, we need several additional intermediate statistics. Following Hamilton (1994, p. 512), we choose $L = 4$ for the long-run variance calculation. Other values we need are $T = 201$, $\hat{\gamma} = 0.9516613$, $s^2 = 0.00008311488$, $v^2 = 0.00027942647$, and the first five autocovariances, $c_0 = 0.000081469$, $c_1 = -0.00000351162$, $c_2 = 0.00000688053$, $c_3 = 0.000000597305$, and $c_4 = -0.00000128163$. Applying these to the weighted sum produces $a = 0.0000840722$, which is only a minor correction to $c_0$. Collecting the results, we obtain the Phillips–Perron statistics, $Z_\tau = -2.89921$ and $Z_\gamma = -15.44133$. Because these are applied to the same critical values in the Dickey–Fuller tables, we reach the same conclusion as before—we do not reject the hypothesis of a unit root in log GDP.

## 22.2.5 THE KPSS TEST OF STATIONARITY

Kwitkowski et al. (1992) (KPSS) have devised an alternative to the Dickey–Fuller test for stationarity of a time series. The procedure is a test of nonstationarity against the null hypothesis of stationarity in the model

$$y_t = \alpha + \beta t + \gamma \sum_{i=1}^{t} z_i + \varepsilon_t, \quad t = 1, \ldots, T$$

$$= \alpha + \beta t + \gamma Z_t + \varepsilon_t,$$

where $\varepsilon_t$ is a stationary series and $z_t$ is an i.i.d. stationary series with mean zero and variance one. (These are merely convenient normalizations because a nonzero mean would move to $\alpha$ and a nonunit variance is absorbed in $\gamma$.) If $\gamma$ equals zero, then the process is stationary if $\beta = 0$ and trend stationary if $\beta \neq 0$. Because $Z_t$, is $I(1)$, $y_t$ is nonstationary if $\gamma$ is nonzero.

The KPSS test of the null hypothesis, $H_0$: $\gamma = 0$, against the alternative that $\gamma$ is nonzero reverses the strategy of the Dickey–Fuller statistic (which tests the null hypothesis $\gamma < 1$ against the alternative $\gamma = 1$). Under the null hypothesis, $\alpha$ and $\beta$ can be estimated by OLS. Let $e_t$ denote the $t$th OLS residual,

$$e_t = y_t - a - bt,$$

and let the sequence of partial sums be

$$E_t = \sum_{i=1}^{t} e_i, \quad t = 1, \ldots, T.$$

(Note $E_T = 0$.) The KPSS statistic is

$$\text{KPSS} = \frac{\sum_{t=1}^{T} E_t^2}{T^2 \hat{\sigma}^2},$$

where

$$\hat{\sigma}^2 = \frac{\sum_{t=1}^{T} e_t^2}{T} + 2 \sum_{j=1}^{L} \left(1 - \frac{j}{L+1}\right) r_j \quad \text{and} \quad r_j = \frac{\sum_{s=j+1}^{T} e_s e_{s-j}}{T},$$

and $L$ is chosen by the analyst. [See (19-17).] Under normality of the disturbances, $\varepsilon_t$, the KPSS statistic is an LM statistic. The authors derive the statistic under more general conditions. Critical values for the test statistic are estimated by simulation. Table 22.5 gives the values reported by the authors (in their Table 1, p. 166).

### Example 22.4 Is There a Unit Root in GDP?
Using the data used for the Dickey–Fuller tests in Example 21.6, we repeated the procedure using the KPSS test with $L = 10$. The two statistics are 1.953 without the trend and 0.312

**TABLE 22.5** Critical Values for the KPSS Test

| Critical Value | Upper Tail Percentiles | | | |
|---|---|---|---|---|
| | *0.100* | *0.050* | *0.025* | *0.010* |
| $\beta = 0$ | 0.347 | 0.463 | 0.573 | 0.739 |
| $\beta \neq 0$ | 0.119 | 0.146 | 0.176 | 0.216 |

with it. Comparing these results to the values in Table 22.4 we conclude (again) that there is, indeed, a unit root in ln GDP. Or, more precisely, we conclude that ln GDP is not a stationary series, nor even a trend stationary series.

## 22.3 COINTEGRATION

Studies in empirical macroeconomics almost always involve nonstationary and trending variables, such as income, consumption, money demand, the price level, trade flows, and exchange rates. Accumulated wisdom and the results of the previous sections suggest that the appropriate way to manipulate such series is to use differencing and other transformations (such as seasonal adjustment) to reduce them to stationarity and then to analyze the resulting series as VARs or with the methods of Box and Jenkins. But recent research and a growing literature has shown that there are more interesting, appropriate ways to analyze trending variables.

In the *fully specified* regression model

$$y_t = \beta x_t + \varepsilon_t,$$

there is a presumption that the disturbances $\varepsilon_t$ are a stationary, white noise series.[11] But this presumption is unlikely to be true if $y_t$ and $x_t$ are integrated series. Generally, if two series are integrated to different orders, then linear combinations of them will be integrated to the higher of the two orders. Thus, if $y_t$ and $x_t$ are $I(1)$—that is, if both are trending variables—then we would normally expect $y_t - \beta x_t$ to be $I(1)$ regardless of the value of $\beta$, not $I(0)$ (i.e., not stationary). If $y_t$ and $x_t$ are each drifting upward with their own trend, then unless there is some relationship between those trends, the difference between them should also be growing, with yet another trend. There must be some kind of inconsistency in the model. On the other hand, if the two series are both $I(1)$, then there *may* be a $\beta$ such that

$$\varepsilon_t = y_t - \beta x_t$$

is $I(0)$. Intuitively, if the two series are both $I(1)$, then this partial difference between them might be stable around a fixed mean. The implication would be that the series are drifting together at roughly the same rate. Two series that satisfy this requirement are said to be **cointegrated,** and the vector $[1, -\beta]$ (or any multiple of it) is a **cointegrating vector.** In such a case, we can distinguish between a long-run relationship between $y_t$ and $x_t$, that is, the manner in which the two variables drift upward together, and the short-run dynamics, that is, the relationship between deviations of $y_t$ from its long-run trend and deviations of $x_t$ from its long-run trend. If this is the case, then differencing of the data would be counterproductive, since it would obscure the long-run relationship between $y_t$ and $x_t$. Studies of cointegration and a related technique, **error correction,** are concerned with methods of estimation that preserve the information about both forms of covariation.[12]

---

[11] If there is autocorrelation in the model, then it has been removed through an appropriate transformation.

[12] See, for example, Engle and Granger (1987) and the lengthy literature cited in Hamilton (1994). A survey paper on VARs and cointegration is Watson (1994).

### Example 22.5    Cointegration in Consumption and Output

Consumption and income provide one of the more familiar examples of the phenomenon described above. The logs of GDP and consumption for 1950.1 to 2000.4 are plotted in Figure 22.10. Both variables are obviously nonstationary. We have already verified that there is a unit root in the income data. We leave as an exercise for the reader to verify that the consumption variable is likewise $I(1)$. Nonetheless, there is a clear relationship between consumption and output. To see where this discussion of relationships among variables is going, consider a simple regression of the log of consumption on the log of income, where both variables are manipulated in mean deviation form (so, the regression includes a constant). The slope in that regression is 1.056765. The residuals from the regression, $u_t = [\text{lnCons}^*, \text{lnGDP}^*][1, -1.056765]'$ (where the "*" indicates mean deviations) are plotted in Figure 22.11. The trend is clearly absent from the residuals. But, it remains to verify whether the series of residuals is stationary. In the ADF regression of the least squares residuals on a constant (random walk with drift), the lagged value and the lagged first difference, the coefficient on $u_{t-1}$ is 0.838488 (0.0370205) and that on $u_{t-1} - u_{t-2}$ is $-0.098522$. (The constant differs trivially from zero because two observations are lost in computing the ADF regression.) With 202 observations, we find $DF_\tau = -4.63$ and $DF_\gamma = -29.55$. Both are well below the critical values, which suggests that the residual series does not contain a unit root. We conclude (at least it appears so) that even after accounting for the trend, although neither of the original variables is stationary, there is a linear combination of them that is. If this conclusion holds up after a more formal treatment of the testing procedure, we will state that logGDP and log consumption are cointegrated.

### Example 22.6    Several Cointegrated Series

The theory of purchasing power parity specifies that in long-run equilibrium, exchange rates will adjust to erase differences in purchasing power across different economies. Thus, if $p_1$ and $p_0$ are the price levels in two countries and $E$ is the exchange rate between the two currencies, then in equilibrium,

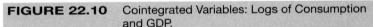

$$v_t = E_t \frac{p_{1t}}{p_{0t}} = \mu, \quad \text{a constant.}$$

**FIGURE 22.10**    Cointegrated Variables: Logs of Consumption and GDP.

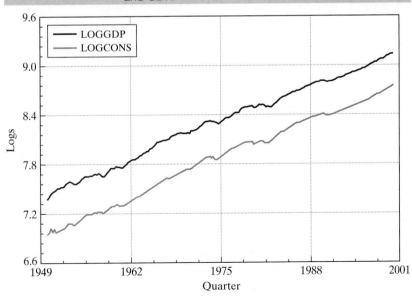

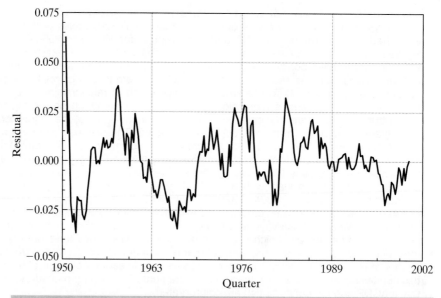

**FIGURE 22.11** Residuals from Consumption—Income Regression.

The price levels in any two countries are likely to be strongly trended. But allowing for short-term deviations from equilibrium, the theory suggests that for a particular $\boldsymbol{\beta} = (\ln \mu, -1, 1)$, in the model

$$\ln E_t = \beta_1 + \beta_2 \ln p_{1t} + \beta_3 \ln p_{0t} + \varepsilon_t,$$

$\varepsilon_t = \ln v_t$ would be a stationary series, which would imply that the logs of the three variables in the model are cointegrated.

We suppose that the model involves $M$ variables, $\mathbf{y}_t = [y_{1t}, \ldots, y_{Mt}]'$, which individually may be $I(0)$ or $I(1)$, and a long-run equilibrium relationship,

$$\mathbf{y}_t'\boldsymbol{\gamma} - \mathbf{x}_t'\boldsymbol{\beta} = 0.$$

The "regressors" may include a constant, exogenous variables assumed to be $I(0)$, and/or a time trend. The vector of parameters $\boldsymbol{\gamma}$ is the cointegrating vector. In the short run, the system may deviate from its equilibrium, so the relationship is rewritten as

$$\mathbf{y}_t'\boldsymbol{\gamma} - \mathbf{x}_t'\boldsymbol{\beta} = \varepsilon_t,$$

where the **equilibrium error** $\varepsilon_t$ must be a stationary series. In fact, because there are $M$ variables in the system, at least in principle, there could be more than one cointegrating vector. In a system of $M$ variables, there can only be up to $M - 1$ linearly independent cointegrating vectors. A proof of this proposition is very simple, but useful at this point.

**Proof:** Suppose that $\boldsymbol{\gamma}_i$ is a cointegrating vector and that there are $M$ linearly independent cointegrating vectors. Then, neglecting $\mathbf{x}_t'\boldsymbol{\beta}$ for the moment, for every $\boldsymbol{\gamma}_i$, $\mathbf{y}_t'\boldsymbol{\gamma}_i$ is a stationary series $v_{ti}$. Any linear combination of a set of stationary series is stationary, so it follows that every linear combination of the cointegrating vectors is also a cointegrating vector. If there are $M$ such $M \times 1$ linearly independent vectors, then they form a basis for the $M$-dimensional space, so any $M \times 1$ vector can be formed from these cointegrating vectors, including the columns of an $M \times M$ identity matrix. Thus, the first column of an identity matrix would be a cointegrating vector, or $y_{t1}$ is $I(0)$. This result is a contradiction, because we are allowing $y_{t1}$ to be $I(1)$. It follows that there can be at most $M - 1$ cointegrating vectors.

The number of linearly independent cointegrating vectors that exist in the equilibrium system is called its **cointegrating rank.** The cointegrating rank may range from 1 to $M - 1$. If it exceeds one, then we will encounter an interesting identification problem. As a consequence of the observation in the preceding proof, we have the unfortunate result that, in general, *if the cointegrating rank of a system exceeds one,* then without out-of-sample, *exact* information, it is not possible to estimate behavioral relationships as cointegrating vectors. Enders (1995) provides a useful example.

### Example 22.7   Multiple Cointegrating Vectors

We consider the logs of four variables, money demand $m$, the price level $p$, real income $y$, and an interest rate $r$. The basic relationship is

$$m = \gamma_0 + \gamma_1 p + \gamma_2 y + \gamma_3 r + \varepsilon.$$

The price level and real income are assumed to be $I(1)$. The existence of long-run equilibrium in the money market implies a cointegrating vector $\alpha_1$. If the Fed follows a certain feedback rule, increasing the money stock when *nominal* income $(y + p)$ is low and decreasing it when nominal income is high—which might make more sense in terms of rates of growth—then there is a second cointegrating vector in which $\gamma_1 = \gamma_2$ and $\gamma_3 = 0$. Suppose that we label this vector $\alpha_2$. The parameters in the money demand equation, notably the interest elasticity, are interesting quantities, and we might seek to estimate $\alpha_1$ to learn the value of this quantity. But since every linear combination of $\alpha_1$ and $\alpha_2$ is a cointegrating vector, to this point we are only able to estimate a hash of the two cointegrating vectors.

In fact, the parameters of this model *are* identifiable from sample information (in principle). We have specified two cointegrating vectors,

$$\alpha_1 = [1, -\gamma_{10}, -\gamma_{11}, -\gamma_{12}, -\gamma_{13}]$$

and

$$\alpha_2 = [1, -\gamma_{20}, \gamma_{21}, \gamma_{21}, 0]'.$$

Although it is true that every linear combination of $\alpha_1$ and $\alpha_2$ is a cointegrating vector, only the original two vectors, as they are, have a 1 in the first position of both and a 0 in the last position of the second. (The equality restriction actually overidentifies the parameter matrix.) This result is, of course, exactly the sort of analysis that we used in establishing the identifiability of a simultaneous equations system.

### 22.3.1   COMMON TRENDS

If two $I(1)$ variables are cointegrated, then some linear combination of them is $I(0)$. Intuition should suggest that the linear combination does not mysteriously create a well-behaved new variable; rather, something present in the original variables must be missing from the aggregated one. Consider an example. Suppose that two $I(1)$ variables have a linear trend,

$$y_{1t} = \alpha + \beta t + u_t,$$

$$y_{2t} = \gamma + \delta t + v_t,$$

where $u_t$ and $v_t$ are white noise. A linear combination of $y_{1t}$ and $y_{2t}$ with vector $(1, \theta)$ produces the new variable,

$$z_t = (\alpha + \theta \gamma) + (\beta + \theta \delta)t + u_t + \theta v_t,$$

which, in general, is still $I(1)$. In fact, the only way the $z_t$ series can be made stationary is if $\theta = -\beta/\delta$. If so, then the effect of combining the two variables linearly is *to remove the common linear trend,* which is the basis of Stock and Watson's (1988) analysis of the problem. But their observation goes an important step beyond this one. *The only way that $y_{1t}$ and $y_{2t}$ can be cointegrated to begin with is if they have a common trend of some sort.* To continue, suppose that instead of the linear trend $t$, the terms on the right-hand side, $y_1$ and $y_2$, are functions of a random walk, $w_t = w_{t-1} + \eta_t$, where $\eta_t$ is white noise. The analysis is identical. But now suppose that each variable $y_{it}$ has its own random walk component $w_{it}, i = 1, 2$. Any linear combination of $y_{1t}$ and $y_{2t}$ must involve *both* random walks. It is clear that they cannot be cointegrated unless, in fact, $w_{1t} = w_{2t}$. That is, once again, they must have a **common trend.** Finally, suppose that $y_{1t}$ and $y_{2t}$ share two common trends,

$$y_{1t} = \alpha + \beta t + \lambda w_t + u_t,$$

$$y_{2t} = \gamma + \delta t + \pi w_t + v_t.$$

We place no restriction on $\lambda$ and $\pi$. Then, a bit of manipulation will show that it is not possible to find a linear combination of $y_{1t}$ and $y_{2t}$ that is cointegrated, even though they share common trends. The end result for this example is that if $y_{1t}$ and $y_{2t}$ are cointegrated, then they must share exactly one common trend.

As Stock and Watson determined, the preceding is the crux of the cointegration of economic variables. A set of $M$ variables that are cointegrated can be written as a stationary component plus linear combinations of a smaller set of common trends. If the cointegrating rank of the system is $r$, then there can be up to $M - r$ linear trends and $M - r$ common random walks. [See Hamilton (1994, p. 578).] (The two-variable case is special. In a two-variable system, there can be only one common trend in total.) The effect of the cointegration is to purge these common trends from the resultant variables.

### 22.3.2 ERROR CORRECTION AND VAR REPRESENTATIONS

Suppose that the two $I(1)$ variables $y_t$ and $z_t$ are cointegrated and that the cointegrating vector is $[1, -\theta]$. Then all three variables, $\Delta y_t = y_t - y_{t-1}$, $\Delta z_t$, and $(y_t - \theta z_t)$ are $I(0)$. The **error correction model**

$$\Delta y_t = \mathbf{x}_t' \boldsymbol{\beta} + \gamma(\Delta z_t) + \lambda(y_{t-1} - \theta z_{t-1}) + \varepsilon_t$$

describes the variation in $y_t$ around its long-run trend in terms of a set of $I(0)$ exogenous factors $\mathbf{x}_t$, the variation of $z_t$ around its long-run trend, and the error correction $(y_t - \theta z_t)$, which is the equilibrium error in the model of cointegration. There is a tight connection between models of cointegration and models of error correction. The model in this form is reasonable as it stands, but in fact, it is only internally consistent if the two variables are cointegrated. If not, then the third term, and hence the right-hand side, cannot be $I(0)$, even though the left-hand side must be. The upshot is that the same assumption that we make to produce the cointegration implies (and is implied by) the existence of an error correction model.[13] As we will examine in the next section, the utility of this representation is that it suggests a way to build an elaborate model of the long-run variation in $y_t$ as well as a test for cointegration. Looking ahead, the preceding suggests that residuals from an estimated cointegration model—that is, estimated equilibrium errors—can be included in an elaborate model of the long-run covariation of $y_t$ and $z_t$. Once again, we have the foundation of Engel and Granger's approach to analyzing cointegration.

Consider the VAR representation of the model

$$\mathbf{y}_t = \mathbf{\Gamma}\mathbf{y}_{t-1} + \varepsilon_t,$$

where the vector $\mathbf{y}_t$ is $[y_t, z_t]'$. Now take first differences to obtain

$$\mathbf{y}_t - \mathbf{y}_{t-1} = (\mathbf{\Gamma} - \mathbf{I})\mathbf{y}_{t-1} + \varepsilon_t,$$

or

$$\Delta\mathbf{y}_t = \mathbf{\Pi}\mathbf{y}_{t-1} + \varepsilon_t.$$

If all variables are $I(1)$, then all $M$ variables on the left-hand side are $I(0)$. Whether those on the right-hand side are $I(0)$ remains to be seen. The matrix $\mathbf{\Pi}$ produces linear combinations of the variables in $\mathbf{y}_t$. But as we have seen, not all linear combinations can be cointegrated. The number of such independent linear combinations is $r < M$. Therefore, although there must be a VAR representation of the model, cointegration implies a restriction on the rank of $\mathbf{\Pi}$. It cannot have full rank; its rank is $r$. From another viewpoint, a different approach to discerning cointegration is suggested. Suppose that we estimate this model as an unrestricted VAR. The resultant coefficient matrix should be short-ranked. The implication is that if we fit the VAR model and impose short rank on the coefficient matrix as a restriction—how we could do that remains to be seen— then if the variables really are cointegrated, this restriction should not lead to a loss of fit. This implication is the basis of Johansen's (1988) and Stock and Watson's (1988) analysis of cointegration.

### 22.3.3   TESTING FOR COINTEGRATION

A natural first step in the analysis of cointegration is to establish that it is indeed a characteristic of the data. Two broad approaches for testing for cointegration have been developed. The Engle and Granger (1987) method is based on assessing whether single-equation estimates of the equilibrium errors appear to be stationary. The second approach, due to Johansen (1988, 1991) and Stock and Watson (1988), is based on the VAR approach. As noted earlier, if a set of variables is truly cointegrated, then we should be able to detect the implied restrictions in an otherwise unrestricted VAR. We will examine these two methods in turn.

Let $\mathbf{y}_t$ denote the set of $M$ variables that are believed to be cointegrated. Step one of either analysis is to establish that the variables are indeed integrated to the same order. The Dickey–Fuller tests discussed in Section 22.2.4 can be used for this purpose. If the evidence suggests that the variables are integrated to different orders or not at all, then the specification of the model should be reconsidered.

---

[13]The result in its general form is known as the Granger representation theorem. See Hamilton (1994, p. 582).

If the cointegration rank of the system is $r$, then there are $r$ independent vectors, $\boldsymbol{\gamma}_i = [1, -\boldsymbol{\theta}_i]$, where each vector is distinguished by being normalized on a different variable. If we suppose that there are also a set of $I(0)$ exogenous variables, including a constant, in the model, then each cointegrating vector produces the equilibrium relationship

$$\mathbf{y}_t' \boldsymbol{\gamma}_i = \mathbf{x}_t' \boldsymbol{\beta} + \varepsilon_{it},$$

which we may rewrite as

$$y_{it} = \mathbf{Y}_{it}' \boldsymbol{\theta}_i + \mathbf{x}_t' \boldsymbol{\beta} + \varepsilon_{it}.$$

We can obtain estimates of $\boldsymbol{\theta}_i$ by least squares regression. If the theory is correct *and* if this OLS estimator is consistent, then residuals from this regression should estimate the equilibrium errors. There are two obstacles to consistency. First, because both sides of the equation contain $I(1)$ variables, the problem of spurious regressions appears. Second, a moment's thought should suggest that what we have done is extract an equation from an otherwise ordinary simultaneous equations model and propose to estimate its parameters by ordinary least squares. As we examined in Chapter 13, consistency is unlikely in that case. It is one of the extraordinary results of this body of theory that in this setting, neither of these considerations is a problem. In fact, as shown by a number of authors [see, e.g., Davidson and MacKinnon (1993)], not only is $\mathbf{c}_i$, the OLS estimator of $\boldsymbol{\theta}_i$, consistent, it is **superconsistent** in that its asymptotic variance is $O(1/T^2)$ rather than $O(1/T)$ as in the usual case. Consequently, the problem of spurious regressions disappears as well. Therefore, the next step is to estimate the cointegrating vector(s), by OLS. Under all the assumptions thus far, the residuals from these regressions, $e_{it}$, are estimates of the equilibrium errors, $\varepsilon_{it}$. As such, they should be $I(0)$. The natural approach would be to apply the familiar Dickey–Fuller tests to these residuals. The logic is sound, but the Dickey–Fuller tables are inappropriate for these estimated errors. Estimates of the appropriate critical values for the tests are given by Engle and Granger (1987), Engle and Yoo (1987), Phillips and Ouliaris (1990), and Davidson and MacKinnon (1993). If autocorrelation in the equilibrium errors is suspected, then an augmented Engle and Granger test can be based on the template

$$\Delta e_{it} = \delta e_{i,t-1} + \phi_1(\Delta e_{i,t-1}) + \cdots + u_t.$$

If the null hypothesis that $\delta = 0$ cannot be rejected (against the alternative $\delta < 0$), then we conclude that the variables are not cointegrated. (Cointegration can be rejected by this method. Failing to reject does not confirm it, of course. But having failed to reject the presence of cointegration, we will proceed as if our finding had been affirmative.)

### Example 22.8 *(Continued) Cointegration in Consumption and Output*

In the example presented at the beginning of this discussion, we proposed precisely the sort of test suggested by Phillips and Ouliaris (1990) to determine if (log) consumption and (log) GDP are cointegrated. As noted, the logic of our approach is sound, but a few considerations remain. The Dickey–Fuller critical values suggested for the test are appropriate only in a few cases, and not when several trending variables appear in the equation. For the case of only a pair of trended variables, as we have here, one may use infinite sample values in the Dickey–Fuller tables for the trend stationary form of the equation. (The drift and trend would have been removed from the residuals by the original regression, which would have these terms either embedded in the variables or explicitly in the equation.) Finally, there remains an issue of how many lagged differences to include in the ADF regression. We have specified one, although further analysis might be called for. [A lengthy discussion of this set of issues appears in Hayashi (2000, pp. 645–648).] Thus, but for the possibility of this specification issue, the ADF approach suggested in the introduction does pass muster. The sample value found earlier was −4.63. The critical values from the table are −3.45 for 5 percent and −3.67 for 2.5 percent. Thus, we conclude (as have many other analysts) that log consumption and log GDP are cointegrated.

The Johansen (1988, 1992) and Stock and Watson (1988) methods are similar, so we will describe only the first one. The theory is beyond the scope of this text, although the operational details are suggestive. To carry out the Johansen test, we first formulate the VAR:

$$\mathbf{y}_t = \boldsymbol{\Gamma}_1 \mathbf{y}_{t-1} + \boldsymbol{\Gamma}_2 \mathbf{y}_{t-2} + \cdots + \boldsymbol{\Gamma}_p \mathbf{y}_{t-p} + \boldsymbol{\varepsilon}_t.$$

The order of the model, $p$, must be determined in advance. Now, let $\mathbf{z}_t$ denote the vector of $M(p-1)$ variables,

$$\mathbf{z}_t = [\Delta \mathbf{y}_{t-1}, \Delta \mathbf{y}_{t-2}, \ldots, \Delta \mathbf{y}_{t-p+1}].$$

That is, $\mathbf{z}_t$ contains the lags 1 to $p-1$ of the first differences of all $M$ variables. Now, using the $T$ available observations, we obtain two $T \times M$ matrices of least squares residuals:

$$\mathbf{D} = \text{the residuals in the regressions of } \Delta \mathbf{y}_t \text{ on } \mathbf{z}_t,$$

$$\mathbf{E} = \text{the residuals in the regressions of } \mathbf{y}_{t-p} \text{ on } \mathbf{z}_t.$$

We now require the $M^2$ **canonical correlations** between the columns in $\mathbf{D}$ and those in $\mathbf{E}$. To continue, we will digress briefly to define the canonical correlations. Let $\mathbf{d}_1^*$ denote a linear combination of the columns of $\mathbf{D}$, and let $\mathbf{e}_1^*$ denote the same from $\mathbf{E}$. We wish to choose these two linear combinations so as to maximize the correlation between them. This pair of variables are the first canonical variates, and their correlation $r_1^*$ is the first canonical correlation. In the setting of cointegration, this computation has some intuitive appeal. Now, with $\mathbf{d}_1^*$ and $\mathbf{e}_1^*$ in hand, we seek a second pair of variables $\mathbf{d}_2^*$ and $\mathbf{e}_2^*$ to maximize *their* correlation, subject to the constraint that this second variable in each pair be orthogonal to the first. This procedure continues for all $M$ pairs of variables. It turns out that the computation of all these is quite simple. We will not need to compute the coefficient vectors for the linear combinations. The squared canonical correlations are simply the ordered characteristic roots of the matrix

$$\mathbf{R}^* = \mathbf{R}_{DD}^{-1/2} \mathbf{R}_{DE} \mathbf{R}_{EE}^{-1} \mathbf{R}_{ED} \mathbf{R}_{DD}^{-1/2},$$

where $\mathbf{R}_{ij}$ is the (cross-) correlation matrix between variables in set $i$ and set $j$, for $i, j = D, E$.

Finally, the null hypothesis that there are $r$ or fewer cointegrating vectors is tested using the test statistic

$$\text{TRACE TEST} = -T \sum_{i=r+1}^{M} \ln[1 - (r_i^*)^2].$$

If the correlations based on actual disturbances had been observed instead of estimated, then we would refer this statistic to the chi-squared distribution with $M - r$ degrees of freedom. Alternative sets of appropriate tables are given by Johansen and Juselius (1990) and Osterwald-Lenum (1992). Large values give evidence against the hypothesis of $r$ or fewer cointegrating vectors.

### 22.3.4 ESTIMATING COINTEGRATION RELATIONSHIPS

Both of the testing procedures discussed earlier involve actually estimating the cointegrating vectors, so this additional section is actually superfluous. In the Engle and Granger framework, at a second step after the cointegration test, we can use the residuals from the static regression as an error correction term in a dynamic, first-difference regression, as shown in Section 22.4.2. One can then "test down" to find a satisfactory structure. In the Johansen test shown earlier, the characteristic vectors corresponding to the canonical correlations are the sample estimates of the cointegrating vectors. Once again, computation of an error correction model based on these first step results is a natural next step. We will explore these in an application.

### 22.3.5 APPLICATION: GERMAN MONEY DEMAND

The demand for money has provided a convenient and well targeted illustration of methods of cointegration analysis. The central equation of the model is

$$m_t - p_t = \mu + \beta y_t + \gamma i_t + \varepsilon_t, \tag{22-8}$$

where $m_t$, $p_t$, and $y_t$ are the logs of nominal money demand, the price level, and output, and $i$ is the nominal interest rate (not the log of). The equation involves trending variables ($m_t$, $p_t$, $y_t$), and one that we found earlier appears to be a random walk with drift ($i_t$). As such, the usual form of statistical inference for estimation of the income elasticity and interest semielasticity based on stationary data is likely to be misleading.

Beyer (1998) analyzed the demand for money in Germany over the period 1975 to 1994. A central focus of the study was whether the 1990 reunification produced a structural break in the long-run demand function. (The analysis extended an earlier study by the same author that was based on data that predated the reunification.) One of the interesting questions pursued in this literature concerns the stability of the long-term demand equation,

$$(m - p)_t - y_t = \mu + \gamma i_t + \varepsilon_t. \tag{22-9}$$

The left-hand side is the log of the inverse of the velocity of money, as suggested by Lucas (1988). An issue to be confronted in this specification is the exogeneity of the interest variable—exogeneity [in the Engle, Hendry, and Richard (1993) sense] of income is moot in the long-run equation as its coefficient is assumed (per Lucas) to equal one. Beyer explored this latter issue in the framework developed by Engle et al. (see Section 22.3.5) and through the Granger causality testing methods discussed in Section 20.6.5.

The analytical platform of Beyer's study is a long-run function for the real money stock M3 (we adopt the author's notation)

$$(m - p)^* = \delta_0 + \delta_1 y + \delta_2 RS + \delta_3 RL + \delta_4 \Delta_4 p, \tag{22-10}$$

where $RS$ is a short-term interest rate, $RL$ is a long-term interest rate, and $\Delta_4 p$ is the annual inflation rate—the data are quarterly. The first step is an examination of the data. Augmented Dickey–Fuller tests suggest that for these German data in this period, $m_t$ and $p_t$ are $I(2)$, while $(m_t - p_t)$, $y_t$, $\Delta_4 p_t$, $RS_t$, and $RL_t$ are all $I(1)$. Some of Beyer's results which produced these conclusions are shown in Table 22.6. Note that although both $m_t$ and $p_t$ appear to be $I(2)$, their simple difference (linear combination) is $I(1)$,

**TABLE 22.6**  Augmented Dickey–Fuller Tests for Variables in the Beyer Model

| *Variable* | **m** | **Δm** | **Δ²m** | **p** | **Δp** | **Δ²p** | **Δ₄p** | **ΔΔ₄p** |
|---|---|---|---|---|---|---|---|---|
| Spec. | TS | RW | RW | TS | RW/D | RW | RW/D | RW |
| lag | 0 | 4 | 3 | 4 | 3 | 2 | 2 | 2 |
| DF$_\tau$ | −1.82 | −1.61 | −6.87 | −2.09 | −2.14 | −10.6 | −2.66 | −5.48 |
| Crit. Value | −3.47 | −1.95 | −1.95 | −3.47 | −2.90 | −1.95 | −2.90 | −1.95 |

| *Variable* | **y** | **Δy** | **RS** | **ΔRS** | **RL** | **ΔRL** | **(m − p)** | **Δ(m − p)** |
|---|---|---|---|---|---|---|---|---|
| Spec. | TS | RW/D | TS | RW | TS | RW | RW/D | RW/D |
| lag | 4 | 3 | 1 | 0 | 1 | 0 | 0 | 0 |
| DF$_\tau$ | −1.83 | −2.91 | −2.33 | −5.26 | −2.40 | −6.01 | −1.65 | −8.50 |
| Crit. Value | −3.47 | −2.90 | −2.90 | −1.95 | −2.90 | −1.95 | −3.47 | −2.90 |

that is, integrated to a lower order. That produces the long-run specification given by (22-10). The Lucas specification is layered onto this to produce the model for the long-run velocity

$$(m - p - y)^* = \delta_0^* + \delta_2^* RS + \delta_3^* RL + \delta_4^* \Delta_4 p. \qquad \textbf{(22-11)}$$

### 22.3.5.a  Cointegration Analysis and a Long-Run Theoretical Model

For (22-10) to be a valid model, there must be at least one cointegrating vector that transforms $\mathbf{z}_t = [(m_t - p_t), y_t, RS_t, RL_t, \Delta_4 p_t]$ to stationarity. The Johansen trace test described in Section 22.3.3 was applied to the VAR consisting of these five $I(1)$ variables. A lag length of two was chosen for the analysis. The results of the trace test are a bit ambiguous; the hypothesis that $r = 0$ is rejected, albeit not strongly (sample value = 90.17 against a 95 percent critical value = 87.31) while the hypothesis that $r \le 1$ is not rejected (sample value = 60.15 against a 95 percent critical value of 62.99). (These borderline results follow from the result that Beyer's first three eigenvalues—canonical correlations in the trace test statistic—are nearly equal. Variation in the test statistic results from variation in the correlations.) On this basis, it is concluded that the cointegrating rank equals one. The unrestricted cointegrating vector for the equation, with a time trend added is found to be

$$(m - p) = 0.936y - 1.780\Delta_4 p + 1.601 RS - 3.279 RL + 0.002t. \qquad \textbf{(22-12)}$$

(These are the coefficients from the first characteristic vector of the canonical correlation analysis in the Johansen computations detailed in Section 22.3.3.) An exogeneity test— we have not developed this in detail; see Beyer (1998, p. 59), Hendry and Ericsson (1991), and Engle and Hendry (1993)—confirms weak exogeneity of all four right-hand-side variables in this specification. The final specification test is for the Lucas formulation and elimination of the time trend, both of which are found to pass, producing the cointegration vector

$$(m - p - y) = -1.832\Delta_4 p + 4.352 RS - 10.89 RL.$$

The conclusion drawn from the cointegration analysis is that a single-equation model for the long-run money demand is appropriate and a valid way to proceed. A last step before this analysis is a series of Granger causality tests for feedback between changes in the money stock and the four right-hand-side variables in (22-12) (not including the trend). (See Section 20.6.5.) The test results are generally favorable, with some mixed results for exogeneity of GDP.

### 22.3.5.b Testing for Model Instability

Let $\mathbf{z}_t = [(m_t - p_t), y_t, \Delta_4 p_t, RS_t, RL_t]$ and let $\mathbf{z}_{t-1}^0$ denote the entire history of $\mathbf{z}_t$ up to the previous period. The joint distribution for $\mathbf{z}_t$, conditioned on $\mathbf{z}_{t-1}^0$ and a set of parameters $\Psi$ factors one level further into

$$f\left(\mathbf{z}_t \mid \mathbf{z}_{t-1}^0, \Psi\right) = f\left[(m - p)_t \mid y_t, \Delta_4 p_t, RS_t, RL_t, \mathbf{z}_{t-1}^0, \Psi_1\right]$$
$$\times g\left(y_t, \Delta_4 p_t, RS_t, RL_t \mid \mathbf{z}_{t-1}^0, \Psi_2\right).$$

The result of the exogeneity tests carried out earlier implies that the conditional distribution may be analyzed apart from the marginal distribution—that is, the implication of the Engle, Hendry, and Richard results noted earlier. Note the partitioning of the parameter vector. Thus, the conditional model is represented by an error correction form that explains $\Delta(m - p)_t$ in terms of its own lags, the error correction term and contemporaneous and lagged changes in the (now established) weakly exogenous variables as well as other terms such as a constant term, trend, and certain dummy variables which pick up particular events. The error correction model specified is

$$\Delta(m - p)_t = \sum_{i=1}^{4} c_i \Delta(m - p)_{t-i} + \sum_{i=0}^{4} d_{1,i} \Delta\left(\Delta_4 p_{t-i}\right) + \sum_{i=0}^{4} d_{2,i} \Delta y_{t-i}$$

$$+ \sum_{i=0}^{4} d_{3,i} \Delta RS_{t-i} + \sum_{i=0}^{4} d_{4,i} \Delta RL_{t-i} + \lambda(m - p - y)_{t-1} \quad \textbf{(22-13)}$$

$$+ \gamma_1 RS_{t-1} + \gamma_2 RL_{t-1} + \mathbf{d}_t' \boldsymbol{\phi} + \omega_t,$$

where $\mathbf{d}_t$ is the set of additional variables, including the constant and five one-period dummy variables that single out specific events such as a currency crisis in September, 1992 [Beyer (1998, p. 62, fn. 4)]. The model is estimated by least squares, "stepwise simplified and reparameterized." (The number of parameters in the equation is reduced from 32 to 15.[14])

The estimated form of (22-13) is an autoregressive distributed lag model. We proceed to use the model to solve for the long-run, steady-state growth path of the real money stock, (22-10). The annual growth rates $\Delta_4 m = g_m, \Delta_4 p = g_p, \Delta_4 y = g_y$ and (assumed) $\Delta_4 RS = g_{RS} = \Delta_4 RL = g_{RL} = 0$ are used for the solution[15]

$$\frac{1}{4}(g_m - g_p) = \frac{c_4}{4}(g_m - g_p) - d_{1,1} g_p + \frac{d_{2,2}}{2} g_y + \gamma_1 RS + \gamma_2 RL + \lambda(m - p - y).$$

This equation is solved for $(m - p)^*$ under the assumption that $g_m = (g_y + g_p)$,

$$(m - p)^* = \hat{\delta}_0 + \hat{\delta}_1 g_y + y + \hat{\delta}_2 \Delta_4 p + \hat{\delta}_3 RS + \hat{\delta}_4 RL.$$

Analysis then proceeds based on this estimated long-run relationship.

---

[14]The equation ultimately used is $\Delta(m_t - p_t) = h[\Delta(m - p)_{t-4}, \Delta\Delta_4 p_t, \Delta^2 y_{t-2}, \Delta RS_{t-1} + \Delta RS_{t-3}, \Delta^2 RL_t,$ $RS_{t-1}, RL_{t-1}, \Delta_4 p_{t-1}, (m - p - y)_{t-1}, \mathbf{d}_t]$.

[15]The division of the coefficients is done because the intervening lags do not appear in the estimated equation.

The primary interest of the study is the stability of the demand equation pre- and postunification. A comparison of the parameter estimates from the same set of procedures using the period 1976–1989 shows them to be surprisingly similar, $[(1.22 - 3.67g_y), 1, -3.67, 3.67, -6.44]$ for the earlier period and $[(1.25 - 2.09g_y), 1, -3.625, 3.5, -7.25]$ for the later one. This suggests, albeit informally, that the function has not changed (at least by much). A variety of testing procedures for structural break led to the conclusion that in spite of the dramatic changes of 1990, the long-run money demand function had not materially changed in the sample period.

## 22.4 NONSTATIONARY PANEL DATA

In Section 9.8.5, we began to examine panel data settings in which $T$, the number of observations in each group (e.g., country), became large as well as $n$. Applications include cross-country studies of growth using the Penn World Tables [Im, Pesaran, and Shin (2003) and Sala-i-Martin (1996)], studies of purchasing power parity [Pedroni (2001)], and analyses of health care expenditures [McCoskey and Selden (1998)]. In the small $T$ cases of longitudinal, microeconomic data sets, the time-series properties of the data are a side issue that is usually of little interest. But when $T$ is growing at essentially the same rate as $n$, for example, in the cross-country studies, these properties become a central focus of the analysis.

The large $T$, large $n$ case presents several complications for the analyst. In the longitudinal analysis, pooling of the data is usually a given, although we developed several extensions of the models to accommodate parameter heterogeneity (see Section 9.8.5). In a long-term cross-country model, any type of pooling would be especially suspect. The time series are long, so this would seem to suggest that the appropriate modeling strategy would be simply to analyze each country separately. But this would neglect the hypothsized commonalities across countries such as a (proposed) common growth rate. Thus, the recent "time-series panel data" literature seeks to reconcile these opposing features of the data.

As in the single time-series cases examined earlier in this chapter, long-term aggregate series are usually nonstationary, which calls conventional methods (such as those in Section 9.8.5) into question. A focus of the recent literature, for example, is on testing for unit roots in an analog to the platform for the augmented Dickey–Fuller tests (Section 22.2),

$$\Delta y_{it} = \rho_i y_{i,t-1} + \sum_{m=1}^{L_i} \gamma_{im} \Delta y_{i,t-m} + \alpha_i + \beta_i t + \varepsilon_{it}.$$

Different formulations of this model have been analyzed, for example, by Levin, Lin, and Chu (2002), who assume $\rho_i = \rho$; Im, Pesaran, and Shin (2003), who relax that restriction; and Breitung (2000), who considers various mixtures of the cases. An extension of the KPSS test in Section 22.2.5 that is particularly simple to compute is Hadri's (2000) LM statistic,

$$\text{LM} = \frac{1}{n} \sum_{i=1}^{n} \left( \frac{\sum_{t=1}^{T} E_{it}^2}{T^2 \hat{\sigma}_\varepsilon^2} \right) = \frac{\sum_{i=1}^{n} KPSS_i}{n}.$$

This is the sample average of the KPSS statistics for the $n$ countries. Note that it includes two assumptions: that the countries are independent and that there is a common $\sigma_\varepsilon^2$ for all countries. An alternative is suggested that allows $\sigma_\varepsilon^2$ to vary across countries.

As it stands, the preceding model would suggest that separate analyses for each country would be appropriate. An issue to consider, then, would be how to combine, if possible, the separate results in some optimal fashion. Maddala and Wu (1999), for example, suggested a "Fisher-type" chi-squared test based on $P = -2\Sigma_i \ln p_i$, where $p_i$ is the $p$-value from the individual tests. Under the null hypothesis that $\rho_i$ equals zero, the limiting distribution is chi-squared with $2n$ degrees of freedom.

Analysis of cointegration, and models of cointegrated series in the panel data setting, parallel the single time-series case, but also differ in a crucial respect. [See, e.g., Kao (1999), McCoskey and Kao (1999), and Pedroni (2000, 2004)]. Whereas in the single time-series case, the analysis of cointegration focuses on the long-run relationships between, say, $x_t$ and $z_t$ for two variables for the same country, in the panel data setting, say, in the analysis of exchange rates, inflation, purchasing power parity or international R & D spillovers, interest may focus on a long-run relationship between $x_{it}$ and $x_{mt}$ for two different countries (or $n$ countries). This substantially complicates the analyses. It is also well beyond the scope of this text. Extensive surveys of these issues may be found in Baltagi (2005, Chapter 12) and Smith (2000).

## 22.5 SUMMARY AND CONCLUSIONS

This chapter has completed our survey of techniques for the analysis of time-series data. While Chapters 20 and 21 were about extensions of regression modeling to time-series setting, most of the results in this chapter focus on the internal structure of the individual time series, themselves. Chapter 21 presented the standard models for time-series processes. While the empirical distinction between, say, $AR(p)$ and $MA(q)$ series may seem ad hoc, the Wold decomposition assures that with enough care, a variety of models can be used to analyze a time series. This chapter described what is arguably the fundamental tool of modern macroeconometrics: the tests for nonstationarity. Contemporary econometric analysis of macroeconomic data has added considerable structure and formality to trending variables, which are more common than not in that setting. The variants of the Dickey–Fuller and KPSS tests for unit roots are an indispensable tool for the analyst of time-series data. Section 22.4 then considered the subject of cointegration. This modeling framework is a distinct extension of the regression modeling where this discussion began. Cointegrated relationships and equilibrium relationships form the basis of the time-series counterpart to regression relationships. But, in this case, it is not the conditional mean as such that is of interest. Here, both the long-run equilibrium and short-run relationships around trends are of interest and are studied in the data.

### Key Terms and Concepts

- Autoregressive integrated moving-average (ARIMA) process
- Augmented Dickey-Fuller test
- Canonical correlation
- Cointegration
- Cointegration rank
- Cointegration relationship
- Cointegrating vector
- Common trend
- Data generating process (DGP)
- Dickey-Fuller test
- Equilibrium error

- Error correction model
- Fractional integration
- Integrated of order one
- KPSS test
- Phillips-Perron test
- Random walk
- Random walk with drift
- Spurious regression
- Superconsistent
- Trend stationary process
- Unit root

## Exercise

1. Find the autocorrelations and partial autocorrelations for the MA(2) process

$$\varepsilon_t = v_t - \theta_1 v_{t-1} - \theta_2 v_{t-2}.$$

## Applications

1. Carry out the ADF test for a unit root in the bond yield data of Example 21.1.
2. Using the macroeconomic data in Appendix Table F5.1, estimate by least squares the parameters of the model

$$c_t = \beta_0 + \beta_1 y_t + \beta_2 c_{t-1} + \beta_3 c_{t-2} + \varepsilon_t,$$

   where $c_t$ is the log of real consumption and $y_t$ is the log of real disposable income.
   a. Use the Breusch and Pagan test to examine the residuals for autocorrelation.
   b. Is the estimated equation stable? What is the characteristic equation for the autoregressive part of this model? What are the roots of the characteristic equation, using your estimated parameters?
   c. What is your implied estimate of the short-run (impact) multiplier for change in $y_t$ on $c_t$? Compute the estimated long-run multiplier.
3. Carry out an ADF test for a unit root in the rate of inflation using the subset of the data in Appendix Table F5.1 since 1974.1. (This is the first quarter after the oil shock of 1973.)
4. Estimate the parameters of the model in Example 13.1 using two-stage least squares. Obtain the residuals from the two equations. Do these residuals appear to be white noise series? Based on your findings, what do you conclude about the specification of the model?

# 23

# MODELS FOR DISCRETE CHOICE

---∾∾∾---

## 23.1 INTRODUCTION

There are many settings in which the economic outcome we seek to model is a discrete choice among a set of alternatives, rather than a continuous measure of some activity. Consider, for example, modeling labor force participation, the decision of whether or not to make a major purchase, or the decision of which candidate to vote for in an election. For the first of these examples, intuition would suggest that factors such as age, education, marital status, number of children, and some economic data would be relevant in explaining whether an individual chooses to seek work or not in a given period. But something is obviously lacking if this example is treated as the same sort of regression model we used to analyze consumption or the costs of production or the movements of exchange rates. In this chapter, we shall examine a variety of what have come to be known as **qualitative response (QR)** models. There are numerous different types that apply in different situations. What they have in common is that they are models in which the dependent variable is an indicator of a discrete choice, such as a "yes or no" decision. In general, conventional regression methods are inappropriate in these cases.

This chapter is a lengthy but far from complete survey of topics in estimating QR models. Almost none of these models can be consistently estimated with linear regression methods. Therefore, readers interested in the mechanics of estimation may want to review the material in Appendices D and E before continuing. In most cases, the method of estimation is **maximum likelihood.** The various properties of maximum likelihood estimators are discussed in Chapter 16. We shall assume throughout this chapter that the necessary conditions behind the optimality properties of maximum likelihood estimators are met and, therefore, we will not derive or establish these properties specifically for the QR models. Detailed proofs for most of these models can be found in surveys by Amemiya (1981), McFadden (1984), Maddala (1983), and Dhrymes (1984). Additional commentary on some of the issues of interest in the contemporary literature is given by Maddala and Flores-Lagunes (2001). Cameron and Trivedi (2005) contains numerous applications. Greene (2008) provides a general survey.

## 23.2 DISCRETE CHOICE MODELS

The general class of models we shall consider are those for which the dependent variable takes values $0, 1, 2, \ldots$. In a few cases, the values will themselves be meaningful, as in the following:

**1.** Number of patents: $y = 0, 1, 2, \ldots$. These are count data.

In most of the cases we shall study, the values taken by the dependent variables are merely a coding for some qualitative outcome. Some examples are as follows:

2.  Labor force participation: We equate "no" with 0 and "yes" with 1. These decisions are **qualitative choices.** The 0/1 coding is a mere convenience.
3.  Opinions of a certain type of legislation: Let 0 represent "strongly opposed," 1 "opposed," 2 "neutral," 3 "support," and 4 "strongly support." These numbers are **rankings,** and the values chosen are not quantitative but merely an ordering. The difference between the outcomes represented by 1 and 0 is not necessarily the same as that between 2 and 1.
4.  The occupational field chosen by an individual: Let 0 be clerk, 1 engineer, 2 lawyer, 3 politician, and so on. These data are merely categories, giving neither a ranking nor a count.
5.  Consumer choice among alternative shopping areas: This case has the same characteristics as number 4, but the appropriate model is a bit different. These two examples will differ in the extent to which the choice is based on characteristics of the individual, which are probably dominant in the occupational choice, as opposed to attributes of the choices, which is likely the more important consideration in the choice of shopping venue.

None of these situations lends itself readily to our familiar type of regression analysis. Nonetheless, in each case, we can construct models that link the decision or outcome to a set of factors, at least in the spirit of regression. Our approach will be to analyze each of them in the general framework of probability models:

$$\text{Prob(event } j \text{ occurs)} = \text{Prob}(Y = j) = F[\text{relevant effects, parameters}]. \quad \textbf{(23-1)}$$

The study of qualitative choice focuses on appropriate specification, estimation, and use of models for the probabilities of events, where in most cases, the "event" is an individual's choice among a set of alternatives.

### Example 23.1  Labor Force Participation Model

In Example 4.3 we estimated an earnings equation for the subsample of 428 married women who participated in the formal labor market taken from a full sample of 753 observations. The semilog earnings equation is of the form

$$\ln earnings = \beta_1 + \beta_2\, age + \beta_3\, age^2 + \beta_4\, education + \beta_5\, kids + \varepsilon$$

where *earnings* is *hourly wage* times *hours worked*, *education* is measured in years of schooling, and *kids* is a binary variable which equals one if there are children under 18 in the household. What of the other 325 individuals? The underlying labor supply model described a market in which labor force participation was the outcome of a market process whereby the demanders of labor services were willing to offer a wage based on expected marginal product and individuals themselves made a decision whether or not to accept the offer depending on whether it exceeded their own reservation wage. The first of these depends on, among other things, education, while the second (we assume) depends on such variables as age, the presence of children in the household, other sources of income (husband's), and marginal tax rates on labor income. The sample we used to fit the earnings equation contains data on all these other variables. The models considered in this chapter would be appropriate for modeling the outcome $y_i = 1$ if in the labor force, and 0 if not.

## 23.3 MODELS FOR BINARY CHOICE

Models for explaining a binary (0/1) dependent variable typically arise in two contexts. In many cases, the analyst is essentially interested in a regressionlike model of the sort considered in Chapters 2 through 7. With data on the variable of interest and a set of covariates, the analyst is interested in specifying a relationship between the former and the latter, more or less along the lines of the models we have already studied. The relationship between voting behavior and income is typical. In other cases, the **binary choice model** arises in the context of a model in which the nature of the observed data dictate the special treatment of a binary choice model. For example, in a model of the demand for tickets for sporting events, in which the variable of interest is number of tickets, it could happen that the observation consists only of whether the sports facility was filled to capacity (demand greater than or equal to capacity so $Y=1$) or not ($Y=0$). It will generally turn out that the models and techniques used in both cases are the same. Nonetheless, it is useful to examine both of them.

### 23.3.1 THE REGRESSION APPROACH

To focus ideas, consider the model of labor force participation suggested in Example 23.1.[1] The respondent either works or seeks work ($Y=1$) or does not ($Y=0$) in the period in which our survey is taken. We believe that a set of factors, such as age, marital status, education, and work history, gathered in a vector $\mathbf{x}$ explain the decision, so that

$$\text{Prob}(Y = 1 \mid \mathbf{x}) = F(\mathbf{x}, \boldsymbol{\beta})$$
$$\text{Prob}(Y = 0 \mid \mathbf{x}) = 1 - F(\mathbf{x}, \boldsymbol{\beta}). \tag{23-2}$$

The set of parameters $\boldsymbol{\beta}$ reflects the impact of changes in $\mathbf{x}$ on the probability. For example, among the factors that might interest us is the marginal effect of marital status on the probability of labor force participation. The problem at this point is to devise a suitable model for the right-hand side of the equation.

One possibility is to retain the familiar linear regression,

$$F(\mathbf{x}, \boldsymbol{\beta}) = \mathbf{x}'\boldsymbol{\beta}.$$

Because $E[y \mid \mathbf{x}] = F(\mathbf{x}, \boldsymbol{\beta})$, we can construct the regression model,

$$y = E[y \mid \mathbf{x}] + (y - E[y \mid \mathbf{x}]) = \mathbf{x}'\boldsymbol{\beta} + \varepsilon. \tag{23-3}$$

The **linear probability model** has a number of shortcomings. A minor complication arises because $\varepsilon$ is heteroscedastic in a way that depends on $\boldsymbol{\beta}$. Because $\mathbf{x}'\boldsymbol{\beta} + \varepsilon$ must equal 0 or 1, $\varepsilon$ equals either $-\mathbf{x}'\boldsymbol{\beta}$ or $1 - \mathbf{x}'\boldsymbol{\beta}$, with probabilities $1 - F$ and $F$, respectively. Thus, you can easily show that

$$\text{Var}[\varepsilon \mid \mathbf{x}] = \mathbf{x}'\boldsymbol{\beta}(1 - \mathbf{x}'\boldsymbol{\beta}). \tag{23-4}$$

We could manage this complication with an FGLS estimator in the fashion of Chapter 8. A more serious flaw is that without some ad hoc tinkering with the disturbances, we cannot be assured that the predictions from this model will truly look like probabilities.

---

[1]Models for qualitative dependent variables can now be found in most disciplines in economics. A frequent use is in labor economics in the analysis of microlevel data sets.

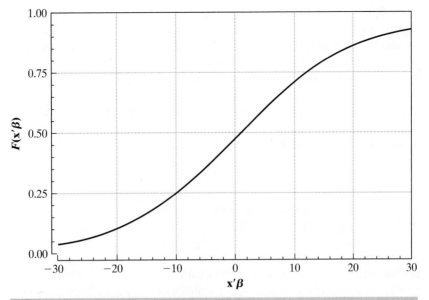

**FIGURE 23.1**    Model for a Probability.

We cannot constrain $\mathbf{x}'\boldsymbol{\beta}$ to the 0–1 interval. Such a model produces both nonsense probabilities and negative variances. For these reasons, the linear model is becoming less frequently used except as a basis for comparison to some other more appropriate models.[2]

Our requirement, then, is a model that will produce predictions consistent with the underlying theory in (23-1). For a given regressor vector, we would expect

$$\lim_{\mathbf{x}'\boldsymbol{\beta}\to+\infty} \text{Prob}(Y=1\,|\,\mathbf{x}) = 1$$

$$\lim_{\mathbf{x}'\boldsymbol{\beta}\to-\infty} \text{Prob}(Y=1\,|\,\mathbf{x}) = 0.$$

(23-5)

See Figure 23.1. In principle, any proper, continuous probability distribution defined over the real line will suffice. The normal distribution has been used in many analyses, giving rise to the **probit** model,

$$\text{Prob}(Y=1\,|\,\mathbf{x}) = \int_{-\infty}^{\mathbf{x}'\boldsymbol{\beta}} \phi(t)\,dt = \Phi(\mathbf{x}'\boldsymbol{\beta}).$$

(23-6)

The function $\Phi(.)$ is a commonly used notation for the standard normal distribution function. Partly because of its mathematical convenience, the logistic distribution,

$$\text{Prob}(Y=1\,|\,\mathbf{x}) = \frac{e^{\mathbf{x}'\boldsymbol{\beta}}}{1+e^{\mathbf{x}'\boldsymbol{\beta}}} = \Lambda(\mathbf{x}'\boldsymbol{\beta}),$$

(23-7)

---

[2]The linear model is not beyond redemption. Aldrich and Nelson (1984) analyze the properties of the model at length. Judge et al. (1985) and Fomby, Hill, and Johnson (1984) give interesting discussions of the ways we may modify the model to force internal consistency. But the fixes are sample dependent, and the resulting estimator, such as it is, may have no known sampling properties. Additional discussion of weighted least squares appears in Amemiya (1977) and Mullahy (1990). Finally, its shortcomings notwithstanding, the linear probability model is applied by Caudill (1988), Heckman and MaCurdy (1985), and Heckman and Snyder (1997). An exchange on the usefulness of the approach is Angrist (2001) and Moffitt (2001).

has also been used in many applications. We shall use the notation $\Lambda(.)$ to indicate the logistic cumulative distribution function. This model is called the **logit** model for reasons we shall discuss in the next section. Both of these distributions have the familiar bell shape of symmetric distributions. Other models which do not assume symmetry, such as the **Gumbel model,**

$$\text{Prob}(Y = 1 \mid \mathbf{x}) = \exp[-\exp(-\mathbf{x}'\boldsymbol{\beta})],$$

and complementary log log model,

$$\text{Prob}(Y = 1 \mid \mathbf{x}) = 1 - \exp[\exp(\mathbf{x}'\boldsymbol{\beta})],$$

have also been employed. Still other distributions have been suggested,[3] but the probit and logit models are still the most common frameworks used in econometric applications.

The question of which distribution to use is a natural one. The logistic distribution is similar to the normal except in the tails, which are considerably heavier. (It more closely resembles a $t$ distribution with seven degrees of freedom.) Therefore, for intermediate values of $\mathbf{x}'\boldsymbol{\beta}$ (say, between $-1.2$ and $+1.2$), the two distributions tend to give similar probabilities. The logistic distribution tends to give larger probabilities to $Y = 1$ when $\mathbf{x}'\boldsymbol{\beta}$ is extremely small (and smaller probabilities to $Y = 1$ when $\mathbf{x}'\boldsymbol{\beta}$ is very large) than the normal distribution. It is difficult to provide practical generalities on this basis, however, as they would require knowledge of $\boldsymbol{\beta}$. We should expect different predictions from the two models, however, if the sample contains (1) very few responses ($Y$'s equal to 1) or very few nonresponses ($Y$'s equal to 0) and (2) very wide variation in an important independent variable, particularly if (1) is also true. There are practical reasons for favoring one or the other in some cases for mathematical convenience, but it is difficult to justify the choice of one distribution or another on theoretical grounds. Amemiya (1981) discusses a number of related issues, but as a general proposition, the question is unresolved. In most applications, the choice between these two seems not to make much difference. However, as seen in the example below, the symmetric and asymmetric distributions can give substantively different results, and here, the guidance on how to choose is unfortunately sparse.

The probability model is a regression:

$$E[y \mid \mathbf{x}] = 0[1 - F(\mathbf{x}'\boldsymbol{\beta})] + 1[F(\mathbf{x}'\boldsymbol{\beta})] = F(\mathbf{x}'\boldsymbol{\beta}). \tag{23-8}$$

Whatever distribution is used, it is important to note that the parameters of the model, like those of any nonlinear regression model, are not necessarily the marginal effects we are accustomed to analyzing. In general,

$$\frac{\partial E[y \mid \mathbf{x}]}{\partial \mathbf{x}} = \left\{ \frac{dF(\mathbf{x}'\boldsymbol{\beta})}{d(\mathbf{x}'\boldsymbol{\beta})} \right\} \boldsymbol{\beta} = f(\mathbf{x}'\boldsymbol{\beta})\boldsymbol{\beta}, \tag{23-9}$$

---

[3]See, for example, Maddala (1983, pp. 27–32), Aldrich and Nelson (1984), and Greene (2001).

where $f(.)$ is the density function that corresponds to the cumulative distribution, $F(.)$. For the normal distribution, this result is

$$\frac{\partial E[y \mid \mathbf{x}]}{\partial \mathbf{x}} = \phi(\mathbf{x}'\boldsymbol{\beta})\boldsymbol{\beta}, \qquad (23\text{-}10)$$

where $\phi(t)$ is the standard normal density. For the logistic distribution,

$$\frac{d\Lambda(\mathbf{x}'\boldsymbol{\beta})}{d(\mathbf{x}'\boldsymbol{\beta})} = \frac{e^{\mathbf{x}'\boldsymbol{\beta}}}{(1 + e^{\mathbf{x}'\boldsymbol{\beta}})^2} = \Lambda(\mathbf{x}'\boldsymbol{\beta})[1 - \Lambda(\mathbf{x}'\boldsymbol{\beta})]. \qquad (23\text{-}11)$$

Thus, in the logit model,

$$\frac{\partial E[y \mid \mathbf{x}]}{\partial \mathbf{x}} = \Lambda(\mathbf{x}'\boldsymbol{\beta})[1 - \Lambda(\mathbf{x}'\boldsymbol{\beta})]\boldsymbol{\beta}. \qquad (23\text{-}12)$$

It is obvious that these values will vary with the values of $\mathbf{x}$. In interpreting the estimated model, it will be useful to calculate this value at, say, the means of the regressors and, where necessary, other pertinent values. For convenience, it is worth noting that the same scale factor applies to all the slopes in the model.

For computing **marginal effects,** one can evaluate the expressions at the sample means of the data or evaluate the marginal effects at every observation and use the sample average of the individual marginal effects. The functions are continuous with continuous first derivatives, so Theorem D.12 (the Slutsky theorem) and assuming that the data are "well behaved" a law of large numbers (Theorems D.4 and D.5) apply; in large samples these will give the same answer. But that is not so in small or moderate-sized samples. Current practice favors averaging the individual marginal effects when it is possible to do so.

Another complication for computing marginal effects in a binary choice model arises because $\mathbf{x}$ will often include dummy variables—for example, a labor force participation equation will often contain a dummy variable for marital status. Because the derivative is with respect to a small change, it is not appropriate to apply (23-10) for the effect of a change in a dummy variable, or change of state. The appropriate marginal effect for a binary independent variable, say, $d$, would be

$$\text{Marginal effect} = \text{Prob}\big[Y = 1 \mid \overline{\mathbf{x}}_{(d)}, \, d = 1\big] - \text{Prob}\big[Y = 1 \mid \overline{\mathbf{x}}_{(d)}, \, d = 0\big],$$

where $\overline{\mathbf{x}}_{(d)}$, denotes the means of all the other variables in the model. Simply taking the derivative with respect to the binary variable as if it were continuous provides an approximation that is often surprisingly accurate. In Example 23.3, for the binary variable *PSI*, the difference in the two probabilities for the probit model is $(0.5702 - 0.1057) = 0.4645$, whereas the derivative approximation reported in Table 23.1 is 0.468. Nonetheless, it might be optimistic to rely on this outcome. We will revisit this computation in the examples and discussion to follow.

### 23.3.2   LATENT REGRESSION—INDEX FUNCTION MODELS

Discrete dependent-variable models are often cast in the form of **index function models.** We view the outcome of a discrete choice as a reflection of an underlying regression. As an often-cited example, consider the decision to make a large purchase. The theory states that the consumer makes a marginal benefit/marginal cost calculation based on the utilities achieved by making the purchase and by not making the purchase and by using the money for something else. We model the difference between benefit and cost as an unobserved variable $y^*$ such that

$$y^* = \mathbf{x}'\boldsymbol{\beta} + \varepsilon.$$

We assume that $\varepsilon$ has mean zero and has either a standardized logistic with (known) variance $\pi^2/3$ [see (23-7)] or a standard normal distribution with variance one [see (23-6)]. We do not observe the net benefit of the purchase, only whether it is made or not. Therefore, our observation is

$$
\begin{aligned}
y &= 1 \quad \text{if } y^* > 0, \\
y &= 0 \quad \text{if } y^* \le 0.
\end{aligned}
$$

In this formulation, $\mathbf{x}'\boldsymbol{\beta}$ is called the index function.

Two aspects of this construction merit our attention. First, the assumption of known variance of $\varepsilon$ is an innocent normalization. Suppose the variance of $\varepsilon$ is scaled by an unrestricted parameter $\sigma^2$. The **latent regression** will be $y^* = \mathbf{x}'\boldsymbol{\beta} + \sigma\varepsilon$. But, $(y^*/\sigma) = \mathbf{x}'(\boldsymbol{\beta}/\sigma) + \varepsilon$ is the same model with the same data. The observed data will be unchanged; $y$ is still 0 or 1, depending only on the sign of $y^*$ not on its scale. This means that there is no information about $\sigma$ in the data so it cannot be estimated. Second, the assumption of zero for the threshold is likewise innocent if the model contains a constant term (and not if it does not).[4] Let $a$ be the supposed nonzero threshold and $\alpha$ be an unknown constant term and, for the present, $\mathbf{x}$ and $\boldsymbol{\beta}$ contain the rest of the index not including the constant term. Then, the probability that $y$ equals one is

$$\text{Prob}(y^* > a \mid \mathbf{x}) = \text{Prob}(\alpha + \mathbf{x}'\boldsymbol{\beta} + \varepsilon > a \mid \mathbf{x}) = \text{Prob}[(\alpha - a) + \mathbf{x}'\boldsymbol{\beta} + \varepsilon > 0 \mid \mathbf{x}].$$

Because $\alpha$ is unknown, the difference $(\alpha - a)$ remains an unknown parameter. With the two normalizations,

$$\text{Prob}(y^* > 0 \mid \mathbf{x}) = \text{Prob}(\varepsilon > -\mathbf{x}'\boldsymbol{\beta} \mid \mathbf{x}).$$

If the distribution is symmetric, as are the normal and logistic, then

$$\text{Prob}(y^* > 0 \mid \mathbf{x}) = \text{Prob}(\varepsilon < \mathbf{x}'\boldsymbol{\beta} \mid \mathbf{x}) = F(\mathbf{x}'\boldsymbol{\beta}),$$

which provides an underlying structural model for the probability.

### Example 23.2  Structural Equations for a Probit Model

Nakosteen and Zimmer (1980) analyze a model of migration based on the following structure:[5] For individual $i$, the market wage that can be earned at the present location is

$$y_p^* = \mathbf{x}_p'\boldsymbol{\beta} + \varepsilon_p.$$

Variables in the equation include age, sex, race, growth in employment, and growth in per capita income. If the individual migrates to a new location, then his or her market wage would be

$$y_m^* = \mathbf{x}_m'\boldsymbol{\gamma} + \varepsilon_m.$$

---

[4] Unless there is some compelling reason, binomial probability models should not be estimated without constant terms.

[5] A number of other studies have also used variants of this basic formulation. Some important examples are Willis and Rosen (1979) and Robinson and Tomes (1982). The study by Tunali (1986) examined in Example 23.6 is another example. The now standard approach, in which "participation" equals one if wage offer $(\mathbf{x}_w'\boldsymbol{\beta}_w + \varepsilon_w)$ minus reservation wage $(\mathbf{x}_r'\boldsymbol{\beta}_r + \varepsilon_r)$ is positive, is also used in Fernandez and Rodriguez-Poo (1997). Brock and Durlauf (2000) describe a number of models and situations involving individual behavior that give rise to binary choice models.

Migration, however, entails costs that are related both to the individual and to the labor market:

$$C^* = \mathbf{z}'\boldsymbol{\alpha} + u.$$

Costs of moving are related to whether the individual is self-employed and whether that person recently changed his or her industry of employment. They migrate if the benefit $y_m^* - y_p^*$ is greater than the cost $C^*$. The net benefit of moving is

$$
\begin{aligned}
M^* &= y_m^* - y_p^* - C^* \\
&= \mathbf{x}_m'\boldsymbol{\gamma} - \mathbf{x}_p'\boldsymbol{\beta} - \mathbf{z}'\boldsymbol{\alpha} + (\varepsilon_m - \varepsilon_p - u) \\
&= \mathbf{w}'\boldsymbol{\delta} + \varepsilon.
\end{aligned}
$$

Because $M^*$ is unobservable, we cannot treat this equation as an ordinary regression. The individual either moves or does not. After the fact, we observe only $y_m^*$ if the individual has moved or $y_p^*$ if he or she has not. But we do observe that $M = 1$ for a move and $M = 0$ for no move. If the disturbances are normally distributed, then the probit model we analyzed earlier is produced. Logistic disturbances produce the logit model instead.

### 23.3.3  RANDOM UTILITY MODELS

An alternative interpretation of data on individual choices is provided by the **random utility model.** Suppose that in the Nakosteen–Zimmer framework, $y_m$ and $y_p$ represent the individual's utility of two choices, which we might denote $U^a$ and $U^b$. For another example, $U^a$ might be the utility of rental housing and $U^b$ that of home ownership. The observed choice between the two reveals which one provides the greater utility, but not the unobservable utilities. Hence, the observed indicator equals 1 if $U^a > U^b$ and 0 if $U^a \leq U^b$. A common formulation is the linear random utility model,

$$U^a = \mathbf{x}'\boldsymbol{\beta}_a + \varepsilon_a \quad \text{and} \quad U^b = \mathbf{x}'\boldsymbol{\beta}_b + \varepsilon_b. \tag{23-13}$$

Then, if we denote by $Y = 1$ the consumer's choice of alternative $a$, we have

$$
\begin{aligned}
\text{Prob}[Y = 1 \mid \mathbf{x}] &= \text{Prob}[U^a > U^b] \\
&= \text{Prob}[\mathbf{x}'\boldsymbol{\beta}_a + \varepsilon_a - \mathbf{x}'\boldsymbol{\beta}_b - \varepsilon_b > 0 \mid \mathbf{x}] \\
&= \text{Prob}[\mathbf{x}'(\boldsymbol{\beta}_a - \boldsymbol{\beta}_b) + \varepsilon_a - \varepsilon_b > 0 \mid \mathbf{x}] \\
&= \text{Prob}[\mathbf{x}'\boldsymbol{\beta} + \varepsilon > 0 \mid \mathbf{x}],
\end{aligned}
\tag{23-14}
$$

once again.

## 23.4  ESTIMATION AND INFERENCE IN BINARY CHOICE MODELS

With the exception of the linear probability model, estimation of binary choice models is usually based on the method of maximum likelihood. Each observation is treated as a single draw from a Bernoulli distribution (binomial with one draw). The model with success probability $F(\mathbf{x}'\boldsymbol{\beta})$ and independent observations leads to the joint probability, or likelihood function,

$$\text{Prob}(Y_1 = y_1, Y_2 = y_2, \ldots, Y_n = y_n \mid \mathbf{X}) = \prod_{y_i=0}[1 - F(\mathbf{x}_i'\boldsymbol{\beta})] \prod_{y_i=1} F(\mathbf{x}_i'\boldsymbol{\beta}), \tag{23-15}$$

where $\mathbf{X}$ denotes $[\mathbf{x}_i]_{i=1,\ldots,n}$. The likelihood function for a sample of $n$ observations can be conveniently written as

$$L(\boldsymbol{\beta} \mid \text{data}) = \prod_{i=1}^{n}[F(\mathbf{x}_i'\boldsymbol{\beta})]^{y_i}[1 - F(\mathbf{x}_i'\boldsymbol{\beta})]^{1-y_i}. \tag{23-16}$$

Taking logs, we obtain

$$\ln L = \sum_{i=1}^{n}\left\{y_i \ln F(\mathbf{x}_i'\boldsymbol{\beta}) + (1 - y_i)\ln[1 - F(\mathbf{x}_i'\boldsymbol{\beta})]\right\}.^6 \tag{23-17}$$

The **likelihood equations** are

$$\frac{\partial \ln L}{\partial \boldsymbol{\beta}} = \sum_{i=1}^{n}\left[\frac{y_i f_i}{F_i} + (1 - y_i)\frac{-f_i}{(1 - F_i)}\right]\mathbf{x}_i = \mathbf{0}, \tag{23-18}$$

where $f_i$ is the density, $dF_i/d(\mathbf{x}_i'\boldsymbol{\beta})$. [In (23-18) and later, we will use the subscript $i$ to indicate that the function has an argument $\mathbf{x}_i'\boldsymbol{\beta}$.] The choice of a particular form for $F_i$ leads to the empirical model.

Unless we are using the linear probability model, the likelihood equations in (23-18) will be nonlinear and require an iterative solution. All of the models we have seen thus far are relatively straightforward to analyze. For the logit model, by inserting (23-7) and (23-11) in (23-18), we get, after a bit of manipulation, the likelihood equations

$$\frac{\partial \ln L}{\partial \boldsymbol{\beta}} = \sum_{i=1}^{n}(y_i - \Lambda_i)\mathbf{x}_i = \mathbf{0}. \tag{23-19}$$

Note that if $\mathbf{x}_i$ contains a constant term, the first-order conditions imply that the average of the predicted probabilities must equal the proportion of ones in the sample.[7] This implication also bears some similarity to the least squares normal equations if we view the term $y_i - \Lambda_i$ as a residual.[8] For the normal distribution, the log-likelihood is

$$\ln L = \sum_{y_i=0}\ln[1 - \Phi(\mathbf{x}_i'\boldsymbol{\beta})] + \sum_{y_i=1}\ln \Phi(\mathbf{x}_i'\boldsymbol{\beta}). \tag{23-20}$$

The first-order conditions for maximizing $\ln L$ are

$$\frac{\partial \ln L}{\partial \boldsymbol{\beta}} = \sum_{y_i=0}\frac{-\phi_i}{1 - \Phi_i}\mathbf{x}_i + \sum_{y_i=1}\frac{\phi_i}{\Phi_i}\mathbf{x}_i = \sum_{y_i=0}\lambda_{0i}\mathbf{x}_i + \sum_{y_i=1}\lambda_{1i}\mathbf{x}_i.$$

Using the device suggested in footnote 6, we can reduce this to

$$\frac{\partial \log L}{\partial \boldsymbol{\beta}} = \sum_{i=1}^{n}\left[\frac{q_i\phi(q_i\mathbf{x}_i'\boldsymbol{\beta})}{\Phi(q_i\mathbf{x}_i'\boldsymbol{\beta})}\right]\mathbf{x}_i = \sum_{i=1}^{n}\lambda_i\mathbf{x}_i = \mathbf{0}, \tag{23-21}$$

where $q_i = 2y_i - 1$.

---

[6] If the distribution is symmetric, as the normal and logistic are, then $1 - F(\mathbf{x}'\boldsymbol{\beta}) = F(-\mathbf{x}'\boldsymbol{\beta})$. There is a further simplification. Let $q = 2y - 1$. Then $\ln L = \Sigma_i \ln F(q_i\mathbf{x}_i'\boldsymbol{\beta})$. See (23-21).

[7] The same result holds for the linear probability model. Although regularly observed in practice, the result has not been verified for the probit model.

[8] This sort of construction arises in many models. The first derivative of the log-likelihood with respect to the constant term produces the **generalized residual** in many settings. See, for example, Chesher, Lancaster, and Irish (1985) and the equivalent result for the tobit model in Section 24.3.4.d.

The actual second derivatives for the logit model are quite simple:

$$\mathbf{H} = \frac{\partial^2 \ln L}{\partial \boldsymbol{\beta} \partial \boldsymbol{\beta}'} = -\sum_i \Lambda_i (1 - \Lambda_i) \mathbf{x}_i \mathbf{x}_i'. \tag{23-22}$$

The second derivatives do not involve the random variable $y_i$, so Newton's method is also the **method of scoring** for the logit model. Note that the Hessian is always negative definite, so the log-likelihood is globally concave. Newton's method will usually converge to the maximum of the log-likelihood in just a few iterations unless the data are especially badly conditioned. The computation is slightly more involved for the probit model. A useful simplification is obtained by using the variable $\lambda(y_i, \boldsymbol{\beta}' \mathbf{x}_i) = \lambda_i$ that is defined in (23-21). The second derivatives can be obtained using the result that for any $z$, $d\phi(z)/dz = -z\phi(z)$. Then, for the probit model,

$$\mathbf{H} = \frac{\partial^2 \ln L}{\partial \boldsymbol{\beta} \partial \boldsymbol{\beta}'} = \sum_{i=1}^{n} -\lambda_i (\lambda_i + \mathbf{x}_i'\boldsymbol{\beta}) \mathbf{x}_i \mathbf{x}_i'. \tag{23-23}$$

This matrix is also negative definite for all values of $\boldsymbol{\beta}$. The proof is less obvious than for the logit model.[9] It suffices to note that the scalar part in the summation is $\mathrm{Var}[\varepsilon \mid \varepsilon \leq \boldsymbol{\beta}'\mathbf{x}]$ $-1$ when $y = 1$ and $\mathrm{Var}[\varepsilon \mid \varepsilon \geq -\boldsymbol{\beta}'\mathbf{x}] - 1$ when $y = 0$. The unconditional variance is one. Because truncation always reduces variance—see Theorem 24.2—in both cases, the variance is between zero and one, so the value is negative.[10]

The asymptotic covariance matrix for the maximum likelihood estimator can be estimated by using the inverse of the Hessian evaluated at the maximum likelihood estimates. There are also two other estimators available. The Berndt, Hall, Hall, and Hausman estimator [see (16-18) and Example 16.4] would be

$$\mathbf{B} = \sum_{i=1}^{n} g_i^2 \mathbf{x}_i \mathbf{x}_i',$$

where $g_i = (y_i - \Lambda_i)$ for the logit model [see (23-19)] and $g_i = \lambda_i$ for the probit model [see (23-21)]. The third estimator would be based on the expected value of the Hessian. As we saw earlier, the Hessian for the logit model does not involve $y_i$, so $\mathbf{H} = E[\mathbf{H}]$. But because $\lambda_i$ is a function of $y_i$ [see (23-21)], this result is not true for the probit model. Amemiya (1981) showed that for the probit model,

$$E\left[\frac{\partial^2 \ln L}{\partial \boldsymbol{\beta} \, \partial \boldsymbol{\beta}'}\right]_{\text{probit}} = \sum_{i=1}^{n} \lambda_{0i} \lambda_{1i} \mathbf{x}_i \mathbf{x}_i'. \tag{23-24}$$

Once again, the scalar part of the expression is always negative [see (23-21) and note that $\lambda_{0i}$ is always negative and $\lambda_{i1}$ is always positive]. The estimator of the asymptotic covariance matrix for the maximum likelihood estimator is then the negative inverse of whatever matrix is used to estimate the expected Hessian. Since the actual Hessian is generally used for the iterations, this option is the usual choice. As we shall see later, though, for certain hypothesis tests, the BHHH estimator is a more convenient choice.

---

[9]See, for example, Amemiya (1985, pp. 273–274) and Maddala (1983, p. 63).

[10]See Johnson and Kotz (1993) and Heckman (1979). We will make repeated use of this result in Chapter 24.

### 23.4.1  ROBUST COVARIANCE MATRIX ESTIMATION

The probit maximum likelihood estimator is often labeled a **quasi-maximum likelihood estimator** (QMLE) in view of the possibility that the normal probability model might be misspecified. White's (1982a) robust "sandwich" estimator for the asymptotic covariance matrix of the QMLE (see Section 16.8 for discussion),

$$\text{Est. Asy. Var}[\hat{\boldsymbol{\beta}}] = [\hat{\mathbf{H}}]^{-1}\hat{\mathbf{B}}[\hat{\mathbf{H}}]^{-1},$$

has been used in a number of recent studies based on the probit model [e.g., Fernandez and Rodriguez-Poo (1997), Horowitz (1993), and Blundell, Laisney, and Lechner (1993)]. If the probit model is correctly specified, then $\text{plim}(1/n)\hat{\mathbf{B}} = \text{plim}(1/n)(-\hat{\mathbf{H}})$ and either single matrix will suffice, so the robustness issue is moot (of course). On the other hand, the probit ($Q$-) maximum likelihood estimator is *not* consistent in the presence of any form of heteroscedasticity, unmeasured heterogeneity, omitted variables (even if they are orthogonal to the included ones), nonlinearity of the functional form of the index, or an error in the distributional assumption [with some narrow exceptions as described by Ruud (1986)]. Thus, in almost any case, the sandwich estimator provides an appropriate asymptotic covariance matrix for an estimator that is biased in an unknown direction. [See Section 16.8 and Freedman (2006).] White raises this issue explicitly, although it seems to receive little attention in the literature: "It is the consistency of the QMLE for the parameters of interest in a wide range of situations which insures its usefulness as the basis for robust estimation techniques" (1982a, p. 4). His very useful result is that if the quasi-maximum likelihood estimator converges to a probability limit, then the sandwich estimator can, under certain circumstances, be used to estimate the asymptotic covariance matrix of that estimator. But there is no guarantee that the QMLE *will* converge to anything interesting or useful. Simply computing a robust covariance matrix for an otherwise inconsistent estimator does not give it redemption. Consequently, the virtue of a robust covariance matrix in this setting is unclear.

### 23.4.2  MARGINAL EFFECTS AND AVERAGE PARTIAL EFFECTS

The predicted probabilities, $F(\mathbf{x}'\hat{\boldsymbol{\beta}}) = \hat{F}$ and the estimated marginal effects $f(\mathbf{x}'\hat{\boldsymbol{\beta}}) \times \hat{\boldsymbol{\beta}} = \hat{f}\hat{\boldsymbol{\beta}}$ are nonlinear functions of the parameter estimates. To compute standard errors, we can use the linear approximation approach (delta method) discussed in Section 4.9.4. For the predicted probabilities,

$$\text{Asy. Var}[\hat{F}] = [\partial\hat{F}/\partial\hat{\boldsymbol{\beta}}]'\mathbf{V}[\partial\hat{F}/\partial\hat{\boldsymbol{\beta}}],$$

where

$$\mathbf{V} = \text{Asy. Var}[\hat{\boldsymbol{\beta}}].$$

The estimated asymptotic covariance matrix of $\hat{\boldsymbol{\beta}}$ can be any of the three described earlier. Let $z = \mathbf{x}'\hat{\boldsymbol{\beta}}$. Then the derivative vector is

$$[\partial\hat{F}/\partial\hat{\boldsymbol{\beta}}] = [d\hat{F}/dz][\partial z/\partial\hat{\boldsymbol{\beta}}] = \hat{f}\mathbf{x}.$$

Combining terms gives

$$\text{Asy. Var}[\hat{F}] = \hat{f}^2\mathbf{x}'\,\mathbf{V}\mathbf{x},$$

which depends, of course, on the particular $\mathbf{x}$ vector used. This result is useful when a marginal effect is computed for a dummy variable. In that case, the estimated effect is

$$\Delta \hat{F} = \hat{F} \mid (d=1) - \hat{F} \mid (d=0). \tag{23-25}$$

The asymptotic variance would be

$$\text{Asy. Var}[\Delta \hat{F}] = [\partial \Delta \hat{F} / \partial \hat{\boldsymbol{\beta}}]' \mathbf{V}[\partial \Delta \hat{F} / \partial \hat{\boldsymbol{\beta}}],$$

where $\hspace{11cm}$ **(23-26)**

$$[\partial \Delta \hat{F} / \partial \hat{\boldsymbol{\beta}}] = \hat{f}_1 \begin{pmatrix} \overline{\mathbf{x}}_{(d)} \\ 1 \end{pmatrix} - \hat{f}_0 \begin{pmatrix} \overline{\mathbf{x}}_{(d)} \\ 0 \end{pmatrix}.$$

For the other marginal effects, let $\hat{\boldsymbol{\gamma}} = \hat{f} \hat{\boldsymbol{\beta}}$. Then

$$\text{Asy. Var}[\hat{\boldsymbol{\gamma}}] = \left[ \frac{\partial \hat{\boldsymbol{\gamma}}}{\partial \hat{\boldsymbol{\beta}}'} \right] \mathbf{V} \left[ \frac{\partial \hat{\boldsymbol{\gamma}}}{\partial \hat{\boldsymbol{\beta}}'} \right]'.$$

The matrix of derivatives is

$$\hat{f} \left( \frac{\partial \hat{\boldsymbol{\beta}}}{\partial \hat{\boldsymbol{\beta}}'} \right) + \hat{\boldsymbol{\beta}} \left( \frac{d\hat{f}}{dz} \right) \left( \frac{\partial z}{\partial \hat{\boldsymbol{\beta}}'} \right) = \hat{f} \mathbf{I} + \left( \frac{d\hat{f}}{dz} \right) \hat{\boldsymbol{\beta}} \mathbf{x}'.$$

For the probit model, $df/dz = -z\phi$, so

$$\text{Asy. Var}[\hat{\boldsymbol{\gamma}}] = \phi^2 [\mathbf{I} - (\mathbf{x}'\boldsymbol{\beta})\boldsymbol{\beta}\mathbf{x}'] \mathbf{V}[\mathbf{I} - (\mathbf{x}'\boldsymbol{\beta})\boldsymbol{\beta}\mathbf{x}']'.$$

For the logit model, $\hat{f} = \hat{\Lambda}(1 - \hat{\Lambda})$, so

$$\frac{d\hat{f}}{dz} = (1 - 2\hat{\Lambda}) \left( \frac{d\hat{\Lambda}}{dz} \right) = (1 - 2\hat{\Lambda})\hat{\Lambda}(1 - \hat{\Lambda}).$$

Collecting terms, we obtain

$$\text{Asy. Var}[\hat{\boldsymbol{\gamma}}] = [\Lambda(1 - \Lambda)]^2 [\mathbf{I} + (1 - 2\Lambda)\boldsymbol{\beta}\mathbf{x}'] \mathbf{V}[\mathbf{I} + (1 - 2\Lambda)\mathbf{x}\boldsymbol{\beta}'].$$

As before, the value obtained will depend on the $\mathbf{x}$ vector used.

### Example 23.3  Probability Models

The data listed in Appendix Table F16.1 were taken from a study by Spector and Mazzeo (1980), which examined whether a new method of teaching economics, the Personalized System of Instruction (*PSI*), significantly influenced performance in later economics courses. The "dependent variable" used in our application is *GRADE*, which indicates the whether a student's grade in an intermediate macroeconomics course was higher than that in the principles course. The other variables are *GPA*, their grade point average; *TUCE*, the score on a pretest that indicates entering knowledge of the material; and *PSI*, the binary variable indicator of whether the student was exposed to the new teaching method. (Spector and Mazzeo's specific equation was somewhat different from the one estimated here.)

Table 23.1 presents four sets of parameter estimates. The slope parameters and derivatives were computed for four probability models: linear, probit, logit, and Gumbel. The last three sets of estimates are computed by maximizing the appropriate log-likelihood function. Estimation is discussed in the next section, so standard errors are not presented here. The scale factor given in the last row is the density function evaluated at the means of the variables. Also, note that the slope given for *PSI* is the derivative, not the change in the function with *PSI* changed from zero to one with other variables held constant.

**TABLE 23.1** Estimated Probability Models

| | Linear | | Logistic | | Probit | | Gumbel | |
|---|---|---|---|---|---|---|---|---|
| Variable | Coefficient | Slope | Coefficient | Slope | Coefficient | Slope | Coefficient | Slope |
| Constant | −1.498 | — | −13.021 | — | −7.452 | — | −10.631 | — |
| GPA | 0.464 | 0.464 | 2.826 | 0.534 | 1.626 | 0.533 | 2.293 | 0.477 |
| TUCE | 0.010 | 0.010 | 0.095 | 0.018 | 0.052 | 0.017 | 0.041 | 0.009 |
| PSI | 0.379 | 0.379 | 2.379 | 0.450 | 1.426 | 0.468 | 1.562 | 0.325 |
| $f(\overline{\mathbf{x}}'\hat{\beta})$ | 1.000 | | 0.189 | | 0.328 | | 0.208 | |

If one looked only at the coefficient estimates, then it would be natural to conclude that the four models had produced radically different estimates. But a comparison of the columns of slopes shows that this conclusion is clearly wrong. The models are very similar; in fact, the logit and probit models results are nearly identical.

The data used in this example are only moderately unbalanced between 0s and 1s for the dependent variable (21 and 11). As such, we might expect similar results for the probit and logit models.[11] One indicator is a comparison of the coefficients. In view of the different variances of the distributions, one for the normal and $\pi^2/3$ for the logistic, we might expect to obtain comparable estimates by multiplying the probit coefficients by $\pi/\sqrt{3} \approx 1.8$. Amemiya (1981) found, through trial and error, that scaling by 1.6 instead produced better results. This proportionality result is frequently cited. The result in (23-9) may help to explain the finding. The index $\mathbf{x}'\beta$ is not the random variable. (See Section 23.3.2.) The marginal effect in the probit model for, say, $x_k$ is $\phi(\mathbf{x}'\beta_p)\beta_{pk}$, whereas that for the logit is $\Lambda(1-\Lambda)\beta_{lk}$. (The subscripts $p$ and $l$ are for probit and logit.) Amemiya suggests that his approximation works best at the center of the distribution, where $F = 0.5$, or $\mathbf{x}'\beta = 0$ for either distribution. Suppose it is. Then $\phi(0) = 0.3989$ and $\Lambda(0)[1 - \Lambda(0)] = 0.25$. If the marginal effects are to be the same, then $0.3989\,\beta_{pk} = 0.25\beta_{lk}$, or $\beta_{lk} = 1.6\beta_{pk}$, which is the regularity observed by Amemiya. Note, though, that as we depart from the center of the distribution, the relationship will move away from 1.6. Because the logistic density descends more slowly than the normal, for unbalanced samples such as ours, the ratio of the logit coefficients to the probit coefficients will tend to be larger than 1.6. The ratios for the ones in Table 23.1 are closer to 1.7 than 1.6.

The computation of the derivatives of the conditional mean function is useful when the variable in question is continuous and often produces a reasonable approximation for a dummy variable. Another way to analyze the effect of a dummy variable on the whole distribution is to compute Prob($Y = 1$) over the range of $\mathbf{x}'\beta$ (using the sample estimates) and with the two values of the binary variable. Using the coefficients from the probit model in Table 23.1, we have the following probabilities as a function of *GPA*, at the mean of TUCE:

$$PSI = 0: \text{Prob}(GRADE = 1) = \Phi[-7.452 + 1.626GPA + 0.052(21.938)],$$

$$PSI = 1: \text{Prob}(GRADE = 1) = \Phi[-7.452 + 1.626GPA + 0.052(21.938) + 1.426].$$

Figure 23.2 shows these two functions plotted over the range of *GRADE* observed in the sample, 2.0 to 4.0. The marginal effect of *PSI* is the difference between the two functions, which ranges from only about 0.06 at *GPA* = 2 to about 0.50 at *GPA* of 3.5. This effect shows that the probability that a student's grade will increase after exposure to *PSI* is far greater for students with high *GPAs* than for those with low *GPAs*. At the sample mean of *GPA* of 3.117, the effect of *PSI* on the probability is 0.465. The simple derivative calculation of (23-9) is given in Table 23.1; the estimate is 0.468. But, of course, this calculation does not show the wide range of differences displayed in Figure 23.2.

---

[11] One might be tempted in this case to suggest an asymmetric distribution for the model, such as the Gumbel distribution. However, the asymmetry in the model, to the extent that it is present at all, refers to the values of $\varepsilon$, not to the observed sample of values of the dependent variable.

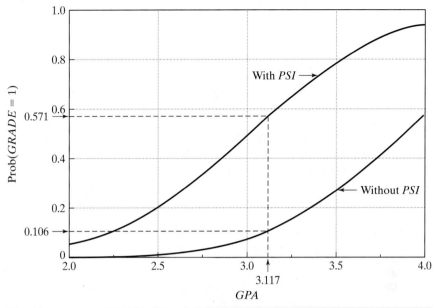

**FIGURE 23.2**    Effect of *PSI* on Predicted Probabilities.

Table 23.2 presents the estimated coefficients and marginal effects for the probit and logit models in Table 23.2. In both cases, the asymptotic covariance matrix is computed from the negative inverse of the actual Hessian of the log-likelihood. The standard errors for the estimated marginal effect of *PSI* are computed using (23-25) and (23-26) since *PSI* is a binary variable. In comparison, the simple derivatives produce estimates and standard errors of (0.449, 0.181) for the logit model and (0.464, 0.188) for the probit model. These differ only slightly from the results given in the table.

The preceding has emphasized computing the partial effects for the average individual in the sample. Current practice has many applications based, instead, on "average partial effects." [See, e.g., Wooldridge (2002a).] The underlying logic is that the quantity

**TABLE 23.2**    Estimated Coefficients and Standard Errors (standard errors in parentheses)

| Variable | Logistic | | | | Probit | | | |
|---|---|---|---|---|---|---|---|---|
| | *Coefficient* | *t Ratio* | *Slope* | *t Ratio* | *Coefficient* | *t Ratio* | *Slope* | *t Ratio* |
| Constant | −13.021 | −2.641 | — | — | −7.452 | −2.931 | — | — |
| | (4.931) | | | | (2.542) | | | |
| GPA | 2.826 | 2.238 | 0.534 | 2.252 | 1.626 | 2.343 | 0.533 | 2.294 |
| | (1.263) | | (0.237) | | (0.694) | | (0.232) | |
| TUCE | 0.095 | 0.672 | 0.018 | 0.685 | 0.052 | 0.617 | 0.017 | 0.626 |
| | (0.142) | | (0.026) | | (0.084) | | (0.027) | |
| PSI | 2.379 | 2.234 | 0.456 | 2.521 | 1.426 | 2.397 | 0.464 | 2.727 |
| | (1.065) | | (0.181) | | (0.595) | | (0.170) | |
| log-likelihood | | | −12.890 | | | | −12.819 | |

of interest is

$$APE = E_x \left[ \frac{\partial E[y \mid \mathbf{x}]}{\partial \mathbf{x}} \right].$$

In practical terms, this suggests the computation

$$\widehat{APE} = \bar{\hat{\gamma}} = \frac{1}{n} \sum_{i=1}^{n} f(\mathbf{x}_i' \hat{\boldsymbol{\beta}}) \hat{\boldsymbol{\beta}}.$$

This does raise two questions. Because the computation is (marginally) more burdensome than the simple marginal effects at the means, one might wonder whether this produces a noticeably different answer. That will depend on the data. Save for small sample variation, the difference in these two results is likely to be small. Let

$$\bar{\gamma}_k = APE_k = \frac{1}{n} \sum_{i=1}^{n} \frac{\partial \Pr(y_i = 1 \mid \mathbf{x}_i)}{\partial x_{ik}} = \frac{1}{n} \sum_{i=1}^{n} F'(\mathbf{x}_i' \boldsymbol{\beta}) \beta_k = \frac{1}{n} \sum_{i=1}^{N} \gamma_k(\mathbf{x}_i)$$

denote the computation of the average partial effect. We compute this at the MLE, $\hat{\boldsymbol{\beta}}$. Now, expand this function in a second-order Taylor series around the point of sample means, $\bar{\mathbf{x}}$, to obtain

$$\begin{aligned}
\bar{\gamma}_k = \frac{1}{n} \sum_{i=1}^{n} \Bigg[ & \gamma_k(\bar{\mathbf{x}}) + \sum_{m=1}^{k} \frac{\partial \gamma_k(\bar{\mathbf{x}})}{\partial \bar{x}_m} (x_{im} - \bar{x}_m) \\
& + \frac{1}{2} \sum_{l=1}^{K} \sum_{m=1}^{K} \frac{\partial^2 \gamma_k(\bar{\mathbf{x}})}{\partial \bar{x}_l \partial \bar{x}_m} (x_{il} - \bar{x}_l)(x_{im} - \bar{x}_m) \Bigg] + \Delta,
\end{aligned}$$

where $\Delta$ is the remaining higher-order terms. The first of the three terms is the marginal effect computed at the sample means. The second term is zero by construction. That leaves the remainder plus an average of a term that is a function of the variances and covariances of the data and the curvature of the probability function at the means. Little can be said to characterize these two terms in any particular sample, but one might guess they are likely to be small. We will examine an application in Example 23.4.

Computing the individual effects, then using the natural estimator to estimate the variance of the mean,

$$\text{Est. Var}[\bar{\hat{\gamma}}_k] = \frac{1}{n} \left[ \frac{1}{n-1} \sum_{i=1}^{N} \left( \hat{\gamma}_k(\mathbf{x}_i) - \bar{\hat{\gamma}}_k \right)^2 \right],$$

may badly estimate the asymptotic variance of the average partial effect. [See, e.g. Contoyannis et al. (2004, p. 498).] The reason is that the observations in the $APE$ are highly correlated—they all use the same estimate of $\boldsymbol{\beta}$—but this variance computation treats them as a random sample. The following example shows the difference, which is substantial. To use the delta method to estimate asymptotic standard errors for the average partial effects, we would use

$$\begin{aligned}
\text{Est. Asy. Var}[\bar{\hat{\gamma}}] &= \frac{1}{n^2} \text{Est. Asy. Var} \left[ \sum_{i=1}^{n} \hat{\gamma}_i \right] \\
&= \frac{1}{n^2} \sum_{i=1}^{n} \sum_{j=1}^{n} \text{Est. Asy. Cov}[\hat{\gamma}_i, \hat{\gamma}_j] \\
&= \frac{1}{n^2} \sum_{i=1}^{n} \sum_{j=1}^{n} \mathbf{G}_i(\hat{\boldsymbol{\beta}}) \hat{\mathbf{V}} \mathbf{G}_j'(\hat{\boldsymbol{\beta}}),
\end{aligned}$$

where $\mathbf{G}_i(\hat{\boldsymbol{\beta}}) = \partial F(\mathbf{x}_i'\hat{\boldsymbol{\beta}})$ and $\hat{\mathbf{V}}$ is the estimated asymptotic covariance matrix for $\hat{\boldsymbol{\beta}}$. (The terms with equal subscripts are the same computation we did earlier with the sample means.) This looks like a formidable amount of computation—Example 23.4 uses a sample of 27,326 observations, so at first blush, it appears we need a double sum of roughly 750 million terms. The computation is actually linear in $n$, not quadratic, however, because the same matrix is used in the center of each product. Moving the first derivative matrix outside the inner summation and using the $1/n$ twice, we find that the estimator of the asymptotic covariance matrix for the $APE$ is simply

$$\text{Est. Asy. Var}[\bar{\boldsymbol{\gamma}}] = \bar{\mathbf{G}}(\hat{\boldsymbol{\beta}})\hat{\mathbf{V}}\bar{\mathbf{G}}'(\hat{\boldsymbol{\beta}}).$$

The appropriate covariance matrix is computed by making the same adjustment as in the partial effects—the derivatives are averaged over the observations rather than being computed at the means of the data.

**Example 23.4   Average Partial Effects**
We estimated a binary logit model for $y = 1(DocVis > 0)$ using the German health care utilization data examined in Example 11.10 (and in Examples 11.11, 16.10, 16.12, 16.13, 16.16, and 18.6). The model is

$$\text{Prob}(DocVis_{it} > 0) = \Lambda(\beta_1 + \beta_2 Age_{it} + \beta_3 Income_{it} + \beta_4 Kids_{it}$$
$$+ \beta_5 Education_{it} + \beta_6 Married_{it})$$

No account of the panel nature of the data set was taken for this exercise. The sample contains 27,326 observations, which should be large enough to reveal the large sample behavior of the computations. Table 23.3 presents the parameter estimates for the logit probability model and both the marginal effects and the average partial effects, each with standard errors computed using the results given earlier. The results do suggest the similarity of the computations. The values in parentheses are based on the naive estimator that ignores the covariances.

### 23.4.3   HYPOTHESIS TESTS

For testing hypotheses about the coefficients, the full menu of procedures is available. The simplest method for a single restriction would be based on the usual $t$ tests, using the standard errors from the information matrix. Using the normal distribution of the estimator, we would use the standard normal table rather than the $t$ table for critical points. For more involved restrictions, it is possible to use the Wald test. For a set of

**TABLE 23.3**    Estimated Parameters and Partial Effects

| Variable | Parameter Estimates | | Marginal Effects | | Average Partial Effects | |
|---|---|---|---|---|---|---|
| | Estimate | Std. Error | Estimate | Std. Error | Estimate | Std. Error |
| Constant | 0.25111 | 0.091135 | | | | |
| Age | 0.020709 | 0.0012852 | 0.0048133 | 0.00029819 | 0.0047109 | 0.00028727 (0.00042971) |
| Income | −0.18592 | 0.075064 | −0.043213 | 0.017446 | −0.042294 | 0.017069 (0.0038579) |
| Kids | −0.22947 | 0.029537 | −0.053335 | 0.0068626 | −0.052201 | 0.0066921 (0.0047615) |
| Education | −0.045588 | 0.0056465 | −0.010596 | 0.0013122 | −0.010370 | 0.0012787 (0.00094595) |
| Married | 0.085293 | 0.033286 | 0.019824 | 0.0077362 | 0.019403 | 0.0075686 (0.0017698) |

restrictions $\mathbf{R}\boldsymbol{\beta} = \mathbf{q}$, the statistic is

$$W = (\mathbf{R}\hat{\boldsymbol{\beta}} - \mathbf{q})'\{\mathbf{R}(\text{Est. Asy. Var}[\hat{\boldsymbol{\beta}}])\mathbf{R}'\}^{-1}(\mathbf{R}\hat{\boldsymbol{\beta}} - \mathbf{q}).$$

For example, for testing the hypothesis that a subset of the coefficients, say, the last $M$, are zero, the Wald statistic uses $\mathbf{R} = [\mathbf{0} \,|\, \mathbf{I}_M]$ and $\mathbf{q} = \mathbf{0}$. Collecting terms, we find that the test statistic for this hypothesis is

$$W = \hat{\boldsymbol{\beta}}'_M \mathbf{V}_M^{-1} \hat{\boldsymbol{\beta}}_M, \tag{23-27}$$

where the subscript $M$ indicates the subvector or submatrix corresponding to the $M$ variables and $\mathbf{V}$ is the estimated asymptotic covariance matrix of $\hat{\boldsymbol{\beta}}$.

Likelihood ratio and Lagrange multiplier statistics can also be computed. The likelihood ratio statistic is

$$\text{LR} = -2[\ln \hat{L}_R - \ln \hat{L}_U],$$

where $\hat{L}_R$ and $\hat{L}_U$ are the log-likelihood functions evaluated at the restricted and unrestricted estimates, respectively. A common test, which is similar to the $F$ test that all the slopes in a regression are zero, is the **likelihood ratio test** that all the slope coefficients in the probit or logit model are zero. For this test, the constant term remains unrestricted. In this case, the restricted log-likelihood is the same for both probit and logit models,

$$\ln L_0 = n[P \ln P + (1 - P) \ln(1 - P)], \tag{23-28}$$

where $P$ is the proportion of the observations that have dependent variable equal to 1.

It might be tempting to use the likelihood ratio test to choose between the probit and logit models. But there is no restriction involved, and the test is not valid for this purpose. To underscore the point, there is nothing in its construction to prevent the chi-squared statistic for this "test" from being negative.

The **Lagrange multiplier test** statistic is $\text{LM} = \mathbf{g}'\mathbf{Vg}$, where $\mathbf{g}$ is the first derivatives of the *unrestricted* model evaluated at the *restricted* parameter vector and $\mathbf{V}$ is any of the three estimators of the asymptotic covariance matrix of the maximum likelihood estimator, once again computed using the restricted estimates. Davidson and MacKinnon (1984) find evidence that $E[\mathbf{H}]$ is the best of the three estimators to use, which gives

$$\text{LM} = \left(\sum_{i=1}^{n} g_i \mathbf{x}_i\right)' \left[\sum_{i=1}^{n} E[-h_i]\mathbf{x}_i\mathbf{x}_i'\right]^{-1} \left(\sum_{i=1}^{n} g_i \mathbf{x}_i\right), \tag{23-29}$$

where $E[-h_i]$ is defined in (23-22) for the logit model and in (23-24) for the probit model.

For the logit model, when the hypothesis is that all the slopes are zero,

$$\text{LM} = nR^2,$$

where $R^2$ is the uncentered coefficient of determination in the regression of $(y_i - \bar{y})$ on $\mathbf{x}_i$ and $\bar{y}$ is the proportion of 1s in the sample. An alternative formulation based on the BHHH estimator, which we developed in Section 16.6.3 is also convenient. For any of the models (probit, logit, Gumbel, etc.), the first derivative vector can be written as

$$\frac{\partial \ln L}{\partial \boldsymbol{\beta}} = \sum_{i=1}^{n} g_i \mathbf{x}_i = \mathbf{X}'\mathbf{Gi},$$

where $\mathbf{G}(n \times n) = \text{diag}[g_1, g_2, \ldots, g_n]$ and $\mathbf{i}$ is an $n \times 1$ column of 1s. The BHHH estimator of the Hessian is $(\mathbf{X}'\mathbf{G}'\mathbf{G}\mathbf{X})$, so the LM statistic based on this estimator is

$$\text{LM} = n \left[ \frac{1}{n} \mathbf{i}'(\mathbf{G}\mathbf{X})(\mathbf{X}'\mathbf{G}'\mathbf{G}\mathbf{X})^{-1}(\mathbf{X}'\mathbf{G}')\mathbf{i} \right] = n R_\mathbf{i}^2, \qquad \textbf{(23-30)}$$

where $R_\mathbf{i}^2$ is the uncentered coefficient of determination in a regression of a column of ones on the first derivatives of the logs of the individual probabilities.

All the statistics listed here are asymptotically equivalent and under the null hypothesis of the restricted model have limiting chi-squared distributions with degrees of freedom equal to the number of restrictions being tested. We consider some examples in the next section.

### 23.4.4 SPECIFICATION TESTS FOR BINARY CHOICE MODELS

In the linear regression model, we considered two important specification problems: the effect of omitted variables and the effect of heteroscedasticity. In the classical model, $\mathbf{y} = \mathbf{X}_1\boldsymbol{\beta}_1 + \mathbf{X}_2\boldsymbol{\beta}_2 + \boldsymbol{\varepsilon}$, when least squares estimates $\mathbf{b}_1$ are computed omitting $\mathbf{X}_2$,

$$E[\mathbf{b}_1] = \boldsymbol{\beta}_1 + [\mathbf{X}_1'\mathbf{X}_1]^{-1}\mathbf{X}_1'\mathbf{X}_2\boldsymbol{\beta}_2.$$

Unless $\mathbf{X}_1$ and $\mathbf{X}_2$ are orthogonal or $\boldsymbol{\beta}_2 = \mathbf{0}$, $\mathbf{b}_1$ is biased. If we ignore heteroscedasticity, then although the least squares estimator is still unbiased and consistent, it is inefficient and the usual estimate of its sampling covariance matrix is inappropriate. Yatchew and Griliches (1984) have examined these same issues in the setting of the probit and logit models. Their general results are far more pessimistic. In the context of a binary choice model, they find the following:

1. If $x_2$ is omitted from a model containing $x_1$ and $x_2$, (i.e. $\boldsymbol{\beta}_2 \neq 0$) then

$$\text{plim } \hat{\boldsymbol{\beta}}_1 = c_1\boldsymbol{\beta}_1 + c_2\boldsymbol{\beta}_2,$$

   where $c_1$ and $c_2$ are complicated functions of the unknown parameters. The implication is that even if the omitted variable is uncorrelated with the included one, the coefficient on the included variable will be inconsistent.
2. If the disturbances in the underlying regression are heteroscedastic, then the maximum likelihood estimators are inconsistent and the covariance matrix is inappropriate.

The second result is particularly troubling because the probit model is most often used with microeconomic data, which are frequently heteroscedastic.

Any of the three methods of hypothesis testing discussed here can be used to analyze these specification problems. The Lagrange multiplier test has the advantage that it can be carried out using the estimates from the restricted model, which sometimes brings a large saving in computational effort. This situation is especially true for the test for **heteroscedasticity.**[12]

To reiterate, the Lagrange multiplier statistic is computed as follows. Let the null hypothesis, $H_0$, be a specification of the model, and let $H_1$ be the alternative. For example,

---

[12]The results in this section are based on Davidson and MacKinnon (1984) and Engle (1984). A symposium on the subject of specification tests in discrete choice models is Blundell (1987).

$H_0$ might specify that only variables $\mathbf{x}_1$ appear in the model, whereas $H_1$ might specify that $\mathbf{x}_2$ appears in the model as well. The statistic is

$$\mathrm{LM} = \mathbf{g}_0' \mathbf{V}_0^{-1} \mathbf{g}_0,$$

where $\mathbf{g}_0$ is the vector of derivatives of the log-likelihood as specified by $H_1$ but evaluated at the maximum likelihood estimator of the parameters assuming that $H_0$ is true, and $\mathbf{V}_0^{-1}$ is any of the three consistent estimators of the asymptotic variance matrix of the maximum likelihood estimator under $H_1$, also computed using the maximum likelihood estimators based on $H_0$. The statistic is asymptotically distributed as chi-squared with degrees of freedom equal to the number of restrictions.

### 23.4.4.a Omitted Variables

The hypothesis to be tested is

$$\begin{aligned} H_0: y^* &= \mathbf{x}_1' \boldsymbol{\beta}_1 && +\varepsilon, \\ H_1: y^* &= \mathbf{x}_1' \boldsymbol{\beta}_1 + \mathbf{x}_2' \boldsymbol{\beta}_2 &&+\varepsilon, \end{aligned} \tag{23-31}$$

so the test is of the null hypothesis that $\boldsymbol{\beta}_2 = \mathbf{0}$. The Lagrange multiplier test would be carried out as follows:

1. Estimate the model in $H_0$ by maximum likelihood. The restricted coefficient vector is $[\hat{\boldsymbol{\beta}}_1, \mathbf{0}]$.
2. Let $\mathbf{x}$ be the compound vector, $[\mathbf{x}_1, \mathbf{x}_2]$.

The statistic is then computed according to (23-29) or (23-30). It is noteworthy that in this case as in many others, the Lagrange multiplier is the coefficient of determination in a regression. The likelihood ratio test is equally straightforward. Using the estimates of the two models, the statistic is simply $2(\ln L_1 - \ln L_0)$.

### 23.4.4.b Heteroscedasticity

We use the general formulation analyzed by Harvey (1976) (see Section 16.9.2.a),[13]

$$\mathrm{Var}[\varepsilon] = [\exp(\mathbf{z}'\boldsymbol{\gamma})]^2.$$

This model can be applied equally to the probit and logit models. We will derive the results specifically for the probit model; the logit model is essentially the same. Thus,

$$\begin{aligned} y^* &= \mathbf{x}'\boldsymbol{\beta} + \varepsilon, \\ \mathrm{Var}[\varepsilon \mid \mathbf{x}, \mathbf{z}] &= [\exp(\mathbf{z}'\boldsymbol{\gamma})]^2. \end{aligned} \tag{23-32}$$

The presence of heteroscedasticity makes some care necessary in interpreting the coefficients for a variable $w_k$ that could be in $\mathbf{x}$ or $\mathbf{z}$ or both,

$$\frac{\partial\, \mathrm{Prob}(Y=1 \mid \mathbf{x}, \mathbf{z})}{\partial w_k} = \phi\left[\frac{\mathbf{x}'\boldsymbol{\beta}}{\exp(\mathbf{z}'\boldsymbol{\gamma})}\right] \frac{\beta_k - (\mathbf{x}'\boldsymbol{\beta})\gamma_k}{\exp(\mathbf{z}'\boldsymbol{\gamma})}.$$

Only the first (second) term applies if $w_k$ appears only in $\mathbf{x}$ ($\mathbf{z}$). This implies that the simple coefficient may differ radically from the effect that is of interest in the estimated model. This effect is clearly visible in the next example.

---

[13] See Knapp and Seaks (1992) for an application. Other formulations are suggested by Fisher and Nagin (1981), Hausman and Wise (1978), and Horowitz (1993).

The log-likelihood is

$$
\ln L = \sum_{i=1}^{n} \left\{ y_i \ln F\left( \frac{\mathbf{x}_i'\boldsymbol{\beta}}{\exp(\mathbf{z}_i'\boldsymbol{\gamma})} \right) + (1 - y_i) \ln \left[ 1 - F\left( \frac{\mathbf{x}_i'\boldsymbol{\beta}}{\exp(\mathbf{z}_i'\boldsymbol{\gamma})} \right) \right] \right\}. \qquad \textbf{(23-33)}
$$

To be able to estimate all the parameters, $\mathbf{z}$ cannot have a constant term. The derivatives are

$$
\frac{\partial \ln L}{\partial \boldsymbol{\beta}} = \sum_{i=1}^{n} \left[ \frac{f_i(y_i - F_i)}{F_i(1 - F_i)} \right] \exp(-\mathbf{z}_i'\boldsymbol{\gamma})\mathbf{x}_i,
$$

$$
\frac{\partial \ln L}{\partial \boldsymbol{\gamma}} = \sum_{i=1}^{n} \left[ \frac{f_i(y_i - F_i)}{F_i(1 - F_i)} \right] \exp(-\mathbf{z}_i'\boldsymbol{\gamma})\mathbf{z}_i(-\mathbf{x}_i'\boldsymbol{\beta}),
\qquad \textbf{(23-34)}
$$

which implies a difficult log-likelihood to maximize. But if the model is estimated assuming that $\boldsymbol{\gamma} = \mathbf{0}$, then we can easily test for homoscedasticity. Let

$$
\mathbf{w}_i = \begin{bmatrix} \mathbf{x}_i \\ (-\mathbf{x}_i'\hat{\boldsymbol{\beta}})\mathbf{z}_i \end{bmatrix}, \qquad \textbf{(23-35)}
$$

computed at the maximum likelihood estimator, assuming that $\boldsymbol{\gamma} = \mathbf{0}$. Then (23-29) or (23-30) can be used as usual for the Lagrange multiplier statistic.

Davidson and MacKinnon carried out a Monte Carlo study to examine the true sizes and power functions of these tests. As might be expected, the test for omitted variables is relatively powerful. The test for heteroscedasticity may well pick up some other form of misspecification, however, including perhaps the simple omission of $\mathbf{z}$ from the index function, so its power may be problematic. It is perhaps not surprising that the same problem arose earlier in our test for heteroscedasticity in the linear regression model.

### Example 23.5 Specification Tests in a Labor Force Participation Model

Using the data described in Example 23.1, we fit a probit model for labor force participation based on the specification

$$
\text{Prob}[LFP = 1] = F(constant, age, age^2, family\ income, education, kids).
$$

For these data, $P = 428/753 = 0.568393$. The restricted (all slopes equal zero, free constant term) log-likelihood is $325 \times \ln(325/753) + 428 \times \ln(428/753) = -514.8732$. The unrestricted log-likelihood for the probit model is $-490.8478$. The chi-squared statistic is, therefore, 48.05072. The critical value from the chi-squared distribution with 5 degrees of freedom is 11.07, so the joint hypothesis that the coefficients on $age$, $age^2$, $family\ income$, and $kids$ are all zero is rejected.

Consider the alternative hypothesis, that the constant term and the coefficients on $age$, $age^2$, $family\ income$, and $education$ are the same whether $kids$ equals one or zero, against the alternative that an altogether different equation applies for the two groups of women, those with $kids = 1$ and those with $kids = 0$. To test this hypothesis, we would use a counterpart to the **Chow test** of Section 6.4 and Example 6.7. The restricted model in this instance would be based on the pooled data set of all 753 observations. The log-likelihood for the pooled model—which has a constant term, $age$, $age^2$, $family\ income$, and $education$ is $-496.8663$. The log-likelihoods for this model based on the 524 observations with $kids = 1$ and the 229 observations with $kids = 0$ are $-347.87441$ and $-141.60501$, respectively. The log-likelihood for the unrestricted model with separate coefficient vectors is thus the sum, $-489.47942$. The chi-squared statistic for testing the five restrictions of the pooled model is twice the difference, $LR = 2[-489.47942 - (-496.8663)] = 14.7738$. The 95 percent critical value from the chi-squared distribution with 5 degrees of freedom is 11.07, so at this significance level, the hypothesis that the constant terms and the coefficients on $age$, $age^2$, $family\ income$, and $education$ are the same is rejected. (The 99 percent critical value is 15.09.)

**TABLE 23.4** Estimated Coefficients

| | | Estimate (Std. Er) | Marg. Effect* | Estimate (St. Er.) | Marg. Effect* |
|---|---|---|---|---|---|
| Constant | $\beta_1$ | −4.157(1.402) | — | −6.030(2.498) | — |
| Age | $\beta_2$ | 0.185(0.0660) | −0.0079(0.0027) | 0.264(0.118) | −0.0088(0.00251) |
| Age$^2$ | $\beta_3$ | −0.0024(0.00077) | — | −0.0036(0.0014) | — |
| Income | $\beta_4$ | 0.0458(0.0421) | 0.0180(0.0165) | 0.424(0.222) | 0.0552(0.0240) |
| Education | $\beta_5$ | 0.0982(0.0230) | 0.0385(0.0090) | 0.140(0.0519) | 0.0289(0.00869) |
| Kids | $\beta_6$ | −0.449(0.131) | −0.171(0.0480) | −0.879(0.303) | −0.167(0.0779) |
| Kids | $\gamma_1$ | 0.000 | — | −0.141(0.324) | — |
| Income | $\gamma_2$ | 0.000 | — | 0.313(0.123) | — |
| ln $L$ | | −490.8478 | | −487.6356 | |
| Correct Preds. | | 0s: 106, 1s: 357 | | 0s: 115, 1s: 358 | |

*Marginal effect and estimated standard error include both mean ($\beta$) and variance ($\gamma$) effects.

Table 23.4 presents estimates of the probit model with a correction for heteroscedasticity of the form

$$\text{Var}[\varepsilon_i] = \exp(\gamma_1 kids + \gamma_2 family\ income).$$

The three tests for homoscedasticity give

$$LR = 2[-487.6356 - (-490.8478)] = 6.424,$$

$$LM = 2.236 \text{ based on the BHHH estimator},$$

$$Wald = 6.533\,(2\text{ restrictions}).$$

The 99 percent critical value for two restrictions is 5.99, so the LM statistic conflicts with the other two.

### 23.4.5 MEASURING GOODNESS OF FIT

There have been many fit measures suggested for QR models.[14] At a minimum, one should report the maximized value of the log-likelihood function, ln $L$. Because the hypothesis that all the slopes in the model are zero is often interesting, the log-likelihood computed with only a constant term, ln $L_0$ [see (23-28)], should also be reported. An analog to the $R^2$ in a conventional regression is McFadden's (1974) likelihood ratio index,

$$\text{LRI} = 1 - \frac{\ln L}{\ln L_0}.$$

This measure has an intuitive appeal in that it is bounded by zero and one. (See Section 16.6.5.) If all the slope coefficients are zero, then it equals zero. There is no way to make LRI equal 1, although one can come close. If $F_i$ is always one when $y$ equals one and zero when $y$ equals zero, then ln $L$ equals zero (the log of one) and LRI equals one. It has been suggested that this finding is indicative of a "perfect fit" and that LRI increases as the fit of the model improves. To a degree, this point is true (see the analysis in Section 23.8.4). Unfortunately, the values between zero and one have no natural interpretation. If $F(\mathbf{x}_i'\boldsymbol{\beta})$ is a proper pdf, then even with many regressors the model cannot fit perfectly unless $\mathbf{x}_i'\boldsymbol{\beta}$ goes to $+\infty$ or $-\infty$. As a practical matter, it does happen. But when it does, it

---

[14]See, for example, Cragg and Uhler (1970), Amemiya (1981), Maddala (1983), McFadden (1974), Ben-Akiva and Lerman (1985), Kay and Little (1986), Veall and Zimmermann (1992), Zavoina and McKelvey (1975), Efron (1978), and Cramer (1999). A survey of techniques appears in Windmeijer (1995).

indicates a flaw in the model, not a good fit. If the range of one of the independent variables contains a value, say, $x^*$, such that the sign of $(x - x^*)$ predicts $y$ perfectly and vice versa, then the model will become a perfect predictor. This result also holds in general if the sign of $\mathbf{x}'\boldsymbol{\beta}$ gives a perfect predictor for some vector $\boldsymbol{\beta}$.[15] For example, one might mistakenly include as a regressor a dummy variables that is identical, or nearly so, to the dependent variable. In this case, the maximization procedure will break down precisely because $\mathbf{x}'\boldsymbol{\beta}$ is diverging during the iterations. [See McKenzie (1998) for an application and discussion.] Of course, this situation is not at all what we had in mind for a good fit.

Other fit measures have been suggested. Ben-Akiva and Lerman (1985) and Kay and Little (1986) suggested a fit measure that is keyed to the prediction rule,

$$R^2_{\mathrm{BL}} = \frac{1}{n} \sum_{i=1}^{n} \left[ y_i \hat{F}_i + (1 - y_i)(1 - \hat{F}_i) \right],$$

which is the average probability of correct prediction by the prediction rule. The difficulty in this computation is that in unbalanced samples, the less frequent outcome will usually be predicted very badly by the standard procedure, and this measure does not pick up that point. Cramer (1999) has suggested an alternative measure that directly measures this failure,

$$\lambda = (\text{average}\,\hat{F} \mid y_i = 1) - (\text{average}\,\hat{F} \mid y_i = 0)$$

$$= (\text{average}(1 - \hat{F}) \mid y_i = 0) - (\text{average}(1 - \hat{F}) \mid y_i = 1).$$

Cramer's measure heavily penalizes the incorrect predictions, and because each proportion is taken within the subsample, it is not unduly influenced by the large proportionate size of the group of more frequent outcomes. Some of the other proposed fit measures are Efron's (1978)

$$R^2_{\mathrm{Ef}} = 1 - \frac{\sum_{i=1}^{n} (y_i - \hat{p}_i)^2}{\sum_{i=1}^{n} (y_i - \overline{y})^2},$$

Veall and Zimmermann's (1992)

$$R^2_{\mathrm{VZ}} = \left( \frac{\delta - 1}{\delta - \mathrm{LRI}} \right) \mathrm{LRI}, \quad \delta = \frac{n}{2 \log L_0},$$

and Zavoina and McKelvey's (1975)

$$R^2_{\mathrm{MZ}} = \frac{\sum_{i=1}^{n} \left( \mathbf{x}'_i \hat{\boldsymbol{\beta}} - \overline{\mathbf{x}}' \hat{\boldsymbol{\beta}} \right)^2}{n + \sum_{i=1}^{n} \left( \mathbf{x}'_i \hat{\boldsymbol{\beta}} - \overline{\mathbf{x}}' \hat{\boldsymbol{\beta}} \right)^2}.$$

The last of these measures corresponds to the regression variation divided by the total variation in the latent index function model, where the disturbance variance is $\sigma^2 = 1$. The values of several of these statistics are given with the model results in Table 23.15 with the application in Section 23.8.4 for illustration.

A useful summary of the predictive ability of the model is a $2 \times 2$ table of the hits and misses of a prediction rule such as

$$\hat{y} = 1 \quad \text{if } \hat{F} > F^* \text{ and 0 otherwise.} \tag{23-36}$$

---

[15] See McFadden (1984) and Amemiya (1985). If this condition holds, then gradient methods *will* find that $\boldsymbol{\beta}$.

The usual threshold value is 0.5, on the basis that we should predict a one if the model says a one is more likely than a zero. It is important not to place too much emphasis on this measure of goodness of fit, however. Consider, for example, the naive predictor

$$\hat{y} = 1 \quad \text{if } P > 0.5 \text{ and } 0 \text{ otherwise,} \tag{23-37}$$

where $P$ is the simple proportion of ones in the sample. This rule will always predict correctly $100P$ percent of the observations, which means that the naive model does not have zero fit. In fact, if the proportion of ones in the sample is very high, it is possible to construct examples in which the second model will generate more correct predictions than the first! Once again, this flaw is not in the model; it is a flaw in the fit measure.[16] The important element to bear in mind is that the coefficients of the estimated model are not chosen so as to maximize this (or any other) fit measure, as they are in the linear regression model where **b** maximizes $R^2$. (The **maximum score estimator** discussed in Example 23.12 addresses this issue directly.)

Another consideration is that 0.5, although the usual choice, may not be a very good value to use for the threshold. If the sample is **unbalanced**—that is, has many more ones than zeros, or vice versa—then by this prediction rule it might never predict a one (or zero). To consider an example, suppose that in a sample of 10,000 observations, only 1,000 have $Y = 1$. We know that the average predicted probability in the sample will be 0.10. As such, it may require an extreme configuration of regressors even to produce an $F$ of 0.2, to say nothing of 0.5. In such a setting, the prediction rule may fail every time to predict when $Y = 1$. The obvious adjustment is to reduce $F^*$. Of course, this adjustment comes at a cost. If we reduce the threshold $F^*$ so as to predict $y = 1$ more often, then we will increase the number of correct classifications of observations that do have $y = 1$, but we will also increase the number of times that we *incorrectly* classify as ones observations that have $y = 0$.[17] In general, any prediction rule of the form in (23-36) will make two types of errors: It will incorrectly classify zeros as ones and ones as zeros. In practice, these errors need not be symmetric in the costs that result. For example, in a credit scoring model [see Boyes, Hoffman, and Low (1989)], incorrectly classifying an applicant as a bad risk is not the same as incorrectly classifying a bad risk as a good one. Changing $F^*$ will always reduce the probability of one type of error while increasing the probability of the other. There is no correct answer as to the best value to choose. It depends on the setting and on the criterion function upon which the prediction rule depends.

The likelihood ratio index and Veall and Zimmermann's modification of it are obviously related to the likelihood ratio statistic for testing the hypothesis that the coefficient vector is zero. Efron's and Cramer's measures listed previously are oriented more toward the relationship between the fitted probabilities and the actual values. Efron's and Cramer's statistics are usefully tied to the standard prediction rule $\hat{y} = \mathbf{1}[\hat{F} > 0.5]$. The McKelvey and Zavoina measure is an analog to the regression coefficient of determination, based on the underlying regression $y^* = \mathbf{x}'\boldsymbol{\beta} + \varepsilon$. Whether these have a close relationship to any type of fit in the familiar sense is a question that needs to be

---

[16]See Amemiya (1981).

[17]The technique of **discriminant analysis** is used to build a procedure around this consideration. In this setting, we consider not only the number of correct and incorrect classifications, but the cost of each type of misclassification.

studied. In some cases, it appears so. But the maximum likelihood estimator, on which all the fit measures are based, is not chosen so as to maximize a fitting criterion based on prediction of $y$ as it is in the classical regression (which maximizes $R^2$). It is chosen to maximize the joint density of the observed dependent variables. It remains an interesting question for research whether fitting $y$ well or obtaining good parameter estimates is a preferable estimation criterion. Evidently, they need not be the same thing.

### Example 23.6 Prediction with a Probit Model

Tunali (1986) estimated a probit model in a study of migration, subsequent remigration, and earnings for a large sample of observations of male members of households in Turkey. Among his results, he reports the summary shown here for a probit model: The estimated model is highly significant, with a likelihood ratio test of the hypothesis that the coefficients (16 of them) are zero based on a chi-squared value of 69 with 16 degrees of freedom.[18] The model predicts 491 of 690, or 71.2 percent, of the observations correctly, although the likelihood ratio index is only 0.083. A naive model, which always predicts that $y = 0$ because $P < 0.5$, predicts 487 of 690, or 70.6 percent, of the observations correctly. This result is hardly suggestive of no fit. The maximum likelihood estimator produces several significant influences on the probability but makes only four more correct predictions than the naive predictor.[19]

|        |         | Predicted | | |
|--------|---------|-----------|-------|-------|
|        |         | **D = 0** | **D = 1** | **Total** |
| *Actual* | $D = 0$ | 471 | 16 | 487 |
|        | $D = 1$ | 183 | 20 | 203 |
|        | Total | 654 | 36 | 690 |

### 23.4.6 CHOICE-BASED SAMPLING

In some studies [e.g., Boyes, Hoffman, and Low (1989), Greene (1992)], the mix of ones and zeros in the observed sample of the dependent variable is deliberately skewed in favor of one outcome or the other to achieve a more balanced sample than random sampling would produce. The sampling is said to be **choice based.** In the studies noted, the dependent variable measured the occurrence of loan default, which is a relatively uncommon occurrence. To enrich the sample, observations with $y = 1$ (default) were oversampled. Intuition should suggest (correctly) that the bias in the sample should be transmitted to the parameter estimates, which will be estimated so as to mimic the sample, not the population, which is known to be different. Manski and Lerman (1977) derived the weighted endogenous sampling maximum likelihood (WESML) estimator for this situation. The estimator requires that the true population proportions, $\omega_1$ and $\omega_0$, be known. Let $p_1$ and $p_0$ be the sample proportions of ones and zeros. Then the estimator is obtained by maximizing a weighted log-likelihood,

$$\ln L = \sum_{i=1}^{n} w_i \ln F(q_i \mathbf{x}_i' \boldsymbol{\beta}),$$

---

[18]This view actually understates slightly the significance of his model, because the preceding predictions are based on a bivariate model. The likelihood ratio test fails to reject the hypothesis that a univariate model applies, however.

[19]It is also noteworthy that nearly all the correct predictions of the maximum likelihood estimator are the zeros. It hits only 10 percent of the ones in the sample.

where $w_i = y_i(\omega_1/p_1) + (1 - y_i)(\omega_0/p_0)$. Note that $w_i$ takes only two different values. The derivatives and the Hessian are likewise weighted. A final correction is needed after estimation; the appropriate estimator of the asymptotic covariance matrix is the sandwich estimator discussed in Section 23.4.1, $\mathbf{H}^{-1}\mathbf{B}\mathbf{H}^{-1}$ (with weighted $\mathbf{B}$ and $\mathbf{H}$), instead of $\mathbf{B}$ or $\mathbf{H}$ alone. (The weights are not squared in computing $\mathbf{B}$.)[20]

### 23.4.7 DYNAMIC BINARY CHOICE MODELS

A random or fixed effects model that explicitly allows for lagged effects would be

$$y_{it} = \mathbf{1}(\mathbf{x}_{it}'\boldsymbol{\beta} + \alpha_i + \gamma y_{i,t-1} + \varepsilon_{it} > 0).$$

Lagged effects, or **persistence,** in a binary choice setting can arise from three sources, serial correlation in $\varepsilon_{it}$, the **heterogeneity,** $\alpha_i$, or true **state dependence** through the term $\gamma y_{i,t-1}$. Chiappori (1998) [and see Arellano (2001)] suggests an application to the French automobile insurance market in which the incentives built into the pricing system are such that having an accident in one period should lower the probability of having one in the next (state dependence), but, some drivers remain more likely to have accidents than others in every period, which would reflect the heterogeneity instead. State dependence is likely to be particularly important in the typical panel which has only a few observations for each individual. Heckman (1981a) examined this issue at length. Among his findings were that the somewhat muted small sample bias in fixed effects models with $T = 8$ was made much worse when there was state dependence. A related problem is that with a relatively short panel, the **initial conditions,** $y_{i0}$, have a crucial impact on the entire path of outcomes. Modeling dynamic effects and initial conditions in binary choice models is more complex than in the linear model, and by comparison there are relatively fewer firm results in the applied literature.[21]

Much of the contemporary literature has focused on methods of avoiding the strong parametric assumptions of the probit and logit models. Manski (1987) and Honore and Kyriazidou (2000) show that Manski's (1986) maximum score estimator can be applied to the differences of unequal pairs of observations in a two period panel with fixed effects. However, the limitations of the maximum score estimator have motivated research on other approaches. An extension of lagged effects to a parametric model is Chamberlain (1985), Jones and Landwehr (1988), and Magnac (1997), who added state dependence to Chamberlain's fixed effects logit estimator. Unfortunately, once the identification issues are settled, the model is only operational if there are no other exogenous variables in it, which limits is usefulness for practical application. Lewbel (2000) has extended his fixed effects estimator to dynamic models as well. In this framework, the narrow assumptions about the independent variables somewhat

---

[20]WESML and the choice-based sampling estimator are not the free lunch they may appear to be. That which the biased sampling does, the weighting undoes. It is common for the end result to be very large standard errors, which might be viewed as unfortunate, insofar as the purpose of the biased sampling was to balance the data precisely to avoid this problem.

[21]A survey of some of these results is given by Hsiao (2003). Most of Hsiao (2003) is devoted to the linear regression model. A number of studies specifically focused on discrete choice models and panel data have appeared recently, including Beck, Epstein, Jackman and O'Halloran (2001), Arellano (2001) and Greene (2001). Vella and Verbeek (1998) provide an application to the joint determination of wages and union membership.

limit its practical applicability. Honore and Kyriazidou (2000) have combined the logic of the **conditional logit model** and Manski's maximum score estimator. They specify

$$\text{Prob}(y_{i0} = 1 \mid \mathbf{x}_i, \alpha_i) = p_0(\mathbf{x}_i, \alpha_i) \quad \text{where } \mathbf{x}_i = (\mathbf{x}_{i1}, \mathbf{x}_{i2}, \dots, \mathbf{x}_{iT}),$$

$$\text{Prob}(y_{it} = 1 \mid \mathbf{x}_i, \alpha_i, y_{i0}, y_{i1}, \dots, y_{i,t-1}) = F(\mathbf{x}'_{it}\boldsymbol{\beta} + \alpha_i + \gamma y_{i,t-1}) \quad t = 1, \dots, T.$$

The analysis assumes a single regressor and focuses on the case of $T = 3$. The resulting estimator resembles Chamberlain's but relies on observations for which $\mathbf{x}_{it} = \mathbf{x}_{i,t-1}$, which rules out direct time effects as well as, for practical purposes, any continuous variable. The restriction to a single regressor limits the generality of the technique as well. The need for observations with equal values of $\mathbf{x}_{it}$ is a considerable restriction, and the authors propose a kernel density estimator for the difference, $\mathbf{x}_{it} - \mathbf{x}_{i,t-1}$, instead which does relax that restriction a bit. The end result is an estimator that converges (they conjecture) but to a nonnormal distribution and at a rate slower than $n^{-1/3}$.

Semiparametric estimators for dynamic models at this point in the development are still primarily of theoretical interest. Models that extend the parametric formulations to include state dependence have a much longer history, including Heckman (1978, 1981a, 1981b), Heckman and MaCurdy (1980), Jakubson (1988), Keane (1993), and Beck et al. (2001) to name a few.[22] In general, even without heterogeneity, dynamic models ultimately involve modeling the joint outcome $(y_{i0}, \dots, y_{iT})$, which necessitates some treatment involving multivariate integration. Example 23.7 describes a recent application. Stewart (2006) provides another.

### Example 23.7  An Intertemporal Labor Force Participation Equation

Hyslop (1999) presents a model of the labor force participation of married women. The focus of the study is the high degree of persistence in the participation decision. Data used in the study were the years 1979–1985 of the Panel Study of Income Dynamics. A sample of 1,812 continuously married couples were studied. Exogenous variables that appeared in the model were measures of permanent and transitory income and fertility captured in yearly counts of the number of children from 0–2, 3–5, and 6–17 years old. Hyslop's formulation, in general terms, is

(initial condition) $y_{i0} = 1(\mathbf{x}'_{i0}\boldsymbol{\beta}_0 + v_{i0} > 0),$

(dynamic model) $y_{it} = 1(\mathbf{x}'_{it}\boldsymbol{\beta} + \gamma y_{i,t-1} + \alpha_i + v_{it} > 0)$

(heterogeneity correlated with participation) $\alpha_i = \mathbf{z}'_i\boldsymbol{\delta} + \eta_i,$

(stochastic specification)

$$\eta_i \mid \mathbf{X}_i \sim N[0, \sigma_\eta^2],$$

$$v_{i0} \mid \mathbf{X}_i \sim N[0, \sigma_0^2],$$

$$w_{it} \mid \mathbf{X}_i \sim N[0, \sigma_w^2],$$

$$v_{it} = \rho v_{i,t-1} + w_{it}, \sigma_\eta^2 + \sigma_w^2 = 1.$$

$$\text{Corr}[v_{i0}, v_{it}] = \rho^t, \quad t = 1, \dots, T - 1.$$

---

[22] Beck et al. (2001) is a bit different from the others mentioned in that in their study of "state failure," they observe a large sample of countries (147) observed over a fairly large number of years, 40. As such, they are able to formulate their models in a way that makes the asymptotics with respect to $T$ appropriate. They can analyze the data essentially in a time-series framework. Sepanski (2000) is another application that combines state dependence and the random coefficient specification of Akin, Guilkey, and Sickles (1979).

The presence of the autocorrelation and state dependence in the model invalidate the simple maximum likelihood procedures we examined earlier. The appropriate likelihood function is constructed by formulating the probabilities as

$$\text{Prob}(y_{i0}, y_{i1}, \ldots) = \text{Prob}(y_{i0}) \times \text{Prob}(y_{i1} \mid y_{i0}) \times \cdots \times \text{Prob}(y_{iT} \mid y_{i,T-1}).$$

This still involves a $T = 7$ order normal integration, which is approximated in the study using a simulator similar to the GHK simulator discussed in 17.3.3. Among Hyslop's results are a comparison of the model fit by the simulator for the multivariate normal probabilities with the same model fit using the maximum simulated likelihood technique described in Section 17.5.1.

## 23.5 BINARY CHOICE MODELS FOR PANEL DATA

Qualitative response models have been a growth industry in econometrics. The recent literature, particularly in the area of panel data analysis, has produced a number of new techniques. The availability of high-quality panel data sets on microeconomic behavior has maintained an interest in extending the models of Chapter 9 to binary (and other discrete choice) models. In this section, we will survey a few results from this rapidly growing literature.

The structural model for a possibly unbalanced panel of data would be written

$$y_{it}^* = \mathbf{x}_{it}'\boldsymbol{\beta} + \varepsilon_{it}, \quad i = 1, \ldots, n, t = 1, \ldots, T_i,$$

$$y_{it} = 1 \quad \text{if } y_{it}^* > 0, \text{and 0 otherwise,}$$

The second line of this definition is often written

$$y_{it} = \mathbf{1}(\mathbf{x}_{it}'\boldsymbol{\beta} + \varepsilon_{it} > 0)$$

to indicate a variable that equals one when the condition in parentheses is true and zero when it is not. Ideally, we would like to specify that $\varepsilon_{it}$ and $\varepsilon_{is}$ are freely correlated within a group, but uncorrelated across groups. But doing so will involve computing joint probabilities from a $T_i$ variate distribution, which is generally problematic.[23] (We will return to this issue later.) A more promising approach is an effects model,

$$y_{it}^* = \mathbf{x}_{it}'\boldsymbol{\beta} + v_{it} + u_i, \quad i = 1, \ldots, n, t = 1, \ldots, T_i,$$

$$y_{it} = 1 \quad \text{if } y_{it}^* > 0, \text{and 0 otherwise,}$$

where, as before (see Section 9.5), $u_i$ is the unobserved, individual specific heterogeneity. Once again, we distinguish between "random" and "fixed" effects models by the relationship between $u_i$ and $\mathbf{x}_{it}$. The assumption that $u_i$ is unrelated to $\mathbf{x}_{it}$, so that the conditional distribution $f(u_i \mid \mathbf{x}_{it})$ is not dependent on $\mathbf{x}_{it}$, produces the **random effects model.** Note that this places a restriction on the distribution of the heterogeneity.

---

[23] A "limited information" approach based on the GMM estimation method has been suggested by Avery, Hansen, and Hotz (1983). With recent advances in simulation-based computation of multinormal integrals (see Section 17.5.1), some work on such a panel data estimator has appeared in the literature. See, for example, Geweke, Keane, and Runkle (1994, 1997). The GEE estimator of Diggle, Liang, and Zeger (1994) [see also, Liang and Zeger (1986) and Stata (2006)] seems to be another possibility. However, in all these cases, it must be remembered that the procedure specifies estimation of a correlation matrix for a $T_i$ vector of unobserved variables based on a dependent variable that takes only two values. We should not be too optimistic about this if $T_i$ is even moderately large.

If that distribution is unrestricted, so that $u_i$ and $\mathbf{x}_{it}$ may be correlated, then we have what is called the **fixed effects model.** The distinction does not relate to any intrinsic characteristic of the effect, itself.

As we shall see shortly, this is a modeling framework that is fraught with difficulties and unconventional estimation problems. Among them are the following: estimation of the random effects model requires very strong assumptions about the heterogeneity; the fixed effects model encounters an **incidental parameters problem** that renders the maximum likelihood estimator inconsistent.

### 23.5.1 Random Effects Models

A specification that has the same structure as the random effects model of Section 9.5 has been implemented by Butler and Moffitt (1982). We will sketch the derivation to suggest how random effects can be handled in discrete and limited dependent variable models such as this one. Full details on estimation and inference may be found in Butler and Moffitt (1982) and Greene (1995a). We will then examine some extensions of the Butler and Moffitt model.

The random effects model specifies

$$\varepsilon_{it} = v_{it} + u_i,$$

where $v_{it}$ and $u_i$ are independent random variables with

$$E[v_{it} \mid \mathbf{X}] = 0; \; \mathrm{Cov}[v_{it}, v_{js} \mid \mathbf{X}] = \mathrm{Var}[v_{it} \mid \mathbf{X}] = 1, \quad \text{if } i = j \text{ and } t = s; 0 \text{ otherwise,}$$

$$E[u_i \mid \mathbf{X}] = 0; \; \mathrm{Cov}[u_i, u_j \mid \mathbf{X}] = \mathrm{Var}[u_i \mid \mathbf{X}] = \sigma_u^2, \quad \text{if } i = j; 0 \text{ otherwise,}$$

$$\mathrm{Cov}[v_{it}, u_j \mid \mathbf{X}] = 0 \text{ for all } i, t, j,$$

and $\mathbf{X}$ indicates all the exogenous data in the sample, $\mathbf{x}_{it}$ for all $i$ and $t$.[24] Then,

$$E[\varepsilon_{it} \mid \mathbf{X}] = 0,$$

$$\mathrm{Var}[\varepsilon_{it} \mid \mathbf{X}] = \sigma_v^2 + \sigma_u^2 = 1 + \sigma_u^2,$$

and

$$\mathrm{Corr}[\varepsilon_{it}, \varepsilon_{is} \mid \mathbf{X}] = \rho = \frac{\sigma_u^2}{1 + \sigma_u^2}.$$

The new free parameter is $\sigma_u^2 = \rho/(1 - \rho)$.

Recall that in the cross-section case, the probability associated with an observation is

$$P(y_i \mid \mathbf{x}_i) = \int_{L_i}^{U_i} f(\varepsilon_i) d\varepsilon_i, \; (L_i, U_i) = (-\infty, -\mathbf{x}_i'\boldsymbol{\beta}) \quad \text{if } y_i = 0 \text{ and } (-\mathbf{x}_i'\boldsymbol{\beta}, +\infty) \quad \text{if } y_i = 1.$$

This simplifies to $\Phi[(2y_i - 1)\mathbf{x}_i'\boldsymbol{\beta}]$ for the normal distribution and $\Lambda[(2y_i - 1)\mathbf{x}_i'\boldsymbol{\beta}]$ for the logit model. In the fully general case with an unrestricted covariance matrix, the contribution of group $i$ to the likelihood would be the joint probability for all $T_i$ observations;

$$L_i = P(y_{i1}, \ldots, y_{iT_i} \mid \mathbf{X}) = \int_{L_{iT_i}}^{U_{iT_i}} \cdots \int_{L_{i1}}^{U_{i1}} f(\varepsilon_{i1}, \varepsilon_{i2}, \ldots, \varepsilon_{iT_i}) d\varepsilon_{i1} d\varepsilon_{i2} \ldots d\varepsilon_{iT_i}. \quad \textbf{(23-38)}$$

---

[24]See Wooldridge (1999) for discussion of this assumption.

The integration of the joint density, as it stands, is impractical in most cases. The special nature of the random effects model allows a simplification, however. We can obtain the joint density of the $v_{it}$'s by integrating $u_i$ out of the joint density of $(\varepsilon_{i1}, \ldots, \varepsilon_{iT_i}, u_i)$ which is

$$f(\varepsilon_{i1}, \ldots, \varepsilon_{iT_i}, u_i) = f(\varepsilon_{i1}, \ldots, \varepsilon_{iT_i} \mid u_i) f(u_i).$$

So,

$$f(\varepsilon_{i1}, \varepsilon_{i2}, \ldots, \varepsilon_{iT_i}) = \int_{-\infty}^{+\infty} f(\varepsilon_{i1}, \varepsilon_{i2}, \ldots, \varepsilon_{iT_i} \mid u_i) f(u_i) \, du_i.$$

The advantage of this form is that conditioned on $u_i$, the $\varepsilon_{it}$'s are independent, so

$$f(\varepsilon_{i1}, \varepsilon_{i2}, \ldots, \varepsilon_{iT_i}) = \int_{-\infty}^{+\infty} \prod_{t=1}^{T_i} f(\varepsilon_{it} \mid u_i) f(u_i) \, du_i.$$

Inserting this result in (23-38) produces

$$L_i = P[y_{i1}, \ldots, y_{iT_i} \mid \mathbf{X}] = \int_{L_{iT_i}}^{U_{iT_i}} \cdots \int_{L_{i1}}^{U_{i1}} \int_{-\infty}^{+\infty} \prod_{t=1}^{T_i} f(\varepsilon_{it} \mid u_i) f(u_i) \, du_i \, d\varepsilon_{i1} \, d\varepsilon_{i2} \ldots d\varepsilon_{iT_i}.$$

This may not look like much simplification, but in fact, it is. Because the ranges of integration are independent, we may change the order of integration;

$$L_i = P[y_{i1}, \ldots, y_{iT_i} \mid \mathbf{X}] = \int_{-\infty}^{+\infty} \left[ \int_{L_{iT_i}}^{U_{iT_i}} \cdots \int_{L_{i1}}^{U_{i1}} \prod_{t=1}^{T_i} f(\varepsilon_{it} \mid u_i) \, d\varepsilon_{i1} \, d\varepsilon_{i2} \ldots d\varepsilon_{iT_i} \right] f(u_i) \, du_i.$$

Conditioned on the common $u_i$, the $\varepsilon$'s are independent, so the term in square brackets is just the product of the individual probabilities. We can write this as

$$L_i = P[y_{i1}, \ldots, y_{iT_i} \mid \mathbf{X}] = \int_{-\infty}^{+\infty} \left[ \prod_{t=1}^{T_i} \left( \int_{L_{it}}^{U_{it}} f(\varepsilon_{it} \mid u_i) \, d\varepsilon_{it} \right) \right] f(u_i) \, du_i. \qquad \textbf{(23-39)}$$

Now, consider the individual densities in the product. Conditioned on $u_i$, these are the now-familiar probabilities for the individual observations, computed now at $\mathbf{x}_{it}'\boldsymbol{\beta} + u_i$. This produces a general model for random effects for the binary choice model. Collecting all the terms, we have reduced it to

$$L_i = P[y_{i1}, \ldots, y_{iT_i} \mid \mathbf{X}] = \int_{-\infty}^{+\infty} \left[ \prod_{t=1}^{T_i} \text{Prob}(Y_{it} = y_{it} \mid \mathbf{x}_{it}'\boldsymbol{\beta} + u_i) \right] f(u_i) \, du_i. \qquad \textbf{(23-40)}$$

It remains to specify the distributions, but the important result thus far is that the entire computation requires only one-dimensional integration. The inner probabilities may be any of the models we have considered so far, such as probit, logit, Gumbel, and so on. The intricate part that remains is to determine how to do the outer integration. **Butler and Moffitt's method** assuming that $u_i$ is normally distributed is detailed in Section 16.9.6.b.

A number of authors have found the Butler and Moffitt formulation to be a satisfactory compromise between a fully unrestricted model and the cross-sectional variant that ignores the correlation altogether. An application that includes both group and time effects is Tauchen, Witte, and Griesinger's (1994) study of arrests and criminal behavior. The Butler and Moffitt approach has been criticized for the restriction of equal correlation across periods. But it does have a compelling virtue that the model can be efficiently estimated even with fairly large $T_i$ using conventional computational methods. [See Greene (2007b).]

A remaining problem with the Butler and Moffitt specification is its assumption of normality. In general, other distributions are problematic because of the difficulty of finding either a closed form for the integral or a satisfactory method of approximating the integral. An alternative approach that allows some flexibility is the method of **maximum simulated likelihood** (MSL), which was discussed in Section 9.8.2 and Chapter 17. The transformed likelihood we derived in (23-40) is an expectation;

$$
L_i = \int_{-\infty}^{+\infty} \left[ \prod_{t=1}^{T_i} \text{Prob}(Y_{it} = y_{it} \mid \mathbf{x}'_{it}\boldsymbol{\beta} + u_i) \right] f(u_i)\, du_i
$$

$$
= E_{u_i} \left[ \prod_{t=1}^{T_i} \text{Prob}(Y_{it} = y_{it} \mid \mathbf{x}'_{it}\boldsymbol{\beta} + u_i) \right].
$$

This expectation can be approximated by simulation rather than **quadrature.** First, let $\theta$ now denote the scale parameter in the distribution of $u_i$. This would be $\sigma_u$ for a normal distribution, for example, or some other scaling for the logistic or uniform distribution. Then, write the term in the likelihood function as

$$
L_i = E_{u_i} \left[ \prod_{t=1}^{T_i} F(y_{it}, \mathbf{x}'_{it}\boldsymbol{\beta} + \theta u_i) \right] = E_{u_i}[h(u_i)].
$$

The function is smooth, continuous, and continuously differentiable. If this expectation is finite, then the conditions of the law of large numbers should apply, which would mean that for a sample of observations $u_{i1}, \ldots, u_{iR}$,

$$
\text{plim}\, \frac{1}{R} \sum_{r=1}^{R} h(u_{ir}) = E_u[h(u_i)].
$$

This suggests, based on the results in Chapter 17, an alternative method of maximizing the log-likelihood for the random effects model. A sample of person-specific draws from the population $u_i$ can be generated with a random number generator. For the Butler and Moffitt model with normally distributed $u_i$, the simulated log-likelihood function is

$$
\ln L_{Simulated} = \sum_{i=1}^{n} \ln \left\{ \frac{1}{R} \sum_{r=1}^{R} \left[ \prod_{t=1}^{T_i} F\left[ q_{it}(\mathbf{x}'_{it}\boldsymbol{\beta} + \sigma_u u_{ir}) \right] \right] \right\}. \tag{23-41}
$$

This function is maximized with respect $\boldsymbol{\beta}$ and $\sigma_u$. Note that in the preceding, as in the quadrature approximated log-likelihood, the model can be based on a probit, logit, or any other functional form desired. There is an additional degree of flexibility in this approach. The Hermite quadrature approach is essentially limited by its functional form to the normal distribution. But, in the simulation approach, $u_{ir}$ can come from some other distribution. For example, it might be believed that the dispersion of the heterogeneity is greater than implied by a normal distribution. The logistic distribution might be preferable. A random sample from the logistic distribution can be created by sampling $(w_{i1}, \ldots, w_{iR})$ from the standard uniform $[0, 1]$ distribution; then $u_{ir} = \ln[w_{ir}/(1 - w_{ir})]$. Other distributions, such as the uniform itself, are also possible.

We have examined two approaches to estimation of a probit model with random effects. GMM estimation is another possibility. Avery, Hansen, and Hotz (1983), Bertschek and Lechner (1998), and Inkmann (2000) examine this approach; the latter two offer some comparison with the quadrature and simulation-based estimators considered here. (Our application in Example 23.16 will use the Bertschek and Lechner data.)

The preceding opens another possibility. The random effects model can be cast as a model with a random constant term;

$$y_{it}^* = \alpha_i + \mathbf{x}_{it}'\boldsymbol{\beta} + \varepsilon_{it}, \quad i = 1, \ldots, n, \ t = 1, \ldots, T_i,$$

$$y_{it} = 1 \ \text{ if } y_{it}^* > 0, \text{ and } 0 \text{ otherwise},$$

where $\alpha_i = \alpha + \sigma_u u_i$. This is simply a reinterpretation of the model we just analyzed. We might, however, now extend this formulation to the full parameter vector. The resulting structure is

$$y_{it}^* = \mathbf{x}_{it}'\boldsymbol{\beta}_i + \varepsilon_{it}, \quad i = 1, \ldots, n, \ t = 1, \ldots, T_i,$$

$$y_{it} = 1 \ \text{ if } y_{it}^* > 0, \text{ and } 0 \text{ otherwise},$$

where $\boldsymbol{\beta}_i = \boldsymbol{\beta} + \boldsymbol{\Gamma}\mathbf{u}_i$ where $\boldsymbol{\Gamma}$ is a nonnegative definite diagonal matrix—some of its diagonal elements could be zero for nonrandom parameters. The method of estimation is essentially the same as before. The simulated log-likelihood is now

$$\ln L_{Simulated} = \sum_{i=1}^{n} \ln \left\{ \frac{1}{R} \sum_{r=1}^{R} \left[ \prod_{t=1}^{T_i} F[q_{it}(\mathbf{x}_{it}'(\boldsymbol{\beta} + \boldsymbol{\Gamma}\mathbf{u}_{ir}))] \right] \right\}.$$

The simulation now involves $R$ draws from the multivariate distribution of $\mathbf{u}$. Because the draws are uncorrelated—$\boldsymbol{\Gamma}$ is diagonal—this is essentially the same estimation problem as the random effects model considered previously. This model is estimated in Example 23.11. Example 23.11 also presents a similar model that assumes that the distribution of $\boldsymbol{\beta}_i$ is discrete rather than continuous.

### 23.5.2 Fixed Effects Models

The fixed effects model is

$$y_{it}^* = \alpha_i d_{it} + \mathbf{x}_{it}'\boldsymbol{\beta} + \varepsilon_{it}, \quad i = 1, \ldots, n, \ t = 1, \ldots, T_i,$$

$$y_{it} = 1 \ \text{ if } y_{it}^* > 0, \text{ and } 0 \text{ otherwise},$$

where $d_{it}$ is a dummy variable that takes the value one for individual $i$ and zero otherwise. For convenience, we have redefined $\mathbf{x}_{it}$ to be the nonconstant variables in the model. The parameters to be estimated are the $K$ elements of $\boldsymbol{\beta}$ and the $n$ individual constant terms. Before we consider the several virtues and shortcomings of this model, we consider the practical aspects of estimation of what are possibly a huge number of parameters, $(n + K) - n$ is not limited here, and could be in the thousands in a typical application. The log-likelihood function for the fixed effects model is

$$\ln L = \sum_{i=1}^{n} \sum_{t=1}^{T_i} \ln P(y_{it} \mid \alpha_i + \mathbf{x}_{it}'\boldsymbol{\beta}),$$

where $P(.)$ is the probability of the observed outcome, for example, $\Phi[q_{it}(\alpha_i + \mathbf{x}_{it}'\boldsymbol{\beta})]$ for the probit model or $\Lambda[q_{it}(\alpha_i + \mathbf{x}_{it}'\boldsymbol{\beta})]$ for the logit model. What follows can be extended to any index function model, but for the present, we'll confine our attention to symmetric distributions such as the normal and logistic, so that the probability can be conveniently written as $\text{Prob}(Y_{it} = y_{it} \mid \mathbf{x}_{it}) = P[q_{it}(\alpha_i + \mathbf{x}'_{it}\boldsymbol{\beta})]$. It will be convenient to let $z_{it} = \alpha_i + \mathbf{x}'_{it}\boldsymbol{\beta}$ so $\text{Prob}(Y_{it} = y_{it} \mid \mathbf{x}_{it}) = P(q_{it}z_{it})$.

In our previous application of this model, in the linear regression case, we found that estimation of the parameters was made possible by a transformation of the data to deviations from group means which eliminated the person specific constants from the estimator. (See Section 9.4.1.) Save for the special case discussed later, that will not be possible here, so that if one desires to estimate the parameters of this model, it will be necessary actually to compute the possibly huge number of constant terms at the same time. This has been widely viewed as a practical obstacle to estimation of this model because of the need to invert a potentially large second derivatives matrix, but this is a misconception. [See, e.g., Maddala (1987), p. 317.] The method for estimation of nonlinear fixed effects models such as the probit and logit models is detailed in Section 16.9.6.c.

The problems with the fixed effects estimator are statistical, not practical. The estimator relies on $T_i$ increasing for the constant terms to be consistent—in essence, each $\alpha_i$ is estimated with $T_i$ observations. But, in this setting, not only is $T_i$ fixed, it is likely to be quite small. As such, the estimators of the constant terms are not consistent (not because they converge to something other than what they are trying to estimate, but because they do not converge at all). The estimator of $\boldsymbol{\beta}$ is a function of the estimators of $\alpha$, which means that the MLE of $\boldsymbol{\beta}$ is not consistent either. This is the incidental parameters problem. [See Neyman and Scott (1948) and Lancaster (2000).] There is, as well, a small sample (small $T_i$) bias in the estimators. How serious this bias is remains a question in the literature. Two pieces of received wisdom are Hsiao's (1986) results for a binary logit model [with additional results in Abrevaya (1997)] and Heckman and MaCurdy's (1980) results for the probit model. Hsiao found that for $T_i = 2$, the bias in the MLE of $\boldsymbol{\beta}$ is 100 percent, which is extremely pessimistic. Heckman and MaCurdy found in a Monte Carlo study that in samples of $n = 100$ and $T = 8$, the bias appeared to be on the order of 10 percent, which is substantive, but certainly less severe than Hsiao's results suggest. No other theoretical results have been shown for other models, although in *very* few cases, it can be shown that there is no incidental parameters problem. (The Poisson model mentioned in Chapter 16 is one of these special cases.) The fixed effects approach does have some appeal in that it does not require an assumption of orthogonality of the independent variables and the heterogeneity. An ongoing pursuit in the literature is concerned with the severity of the tradeoff of this virtue against the incidental parameters problem. Some commentary on this issue appears in Arellano (2001). Results of our own investigation appear in Chapter 17 and Greene (2004).

### Example 23.8  Binary Choice Models for Panel Data

In Example 23.4, we fit a pooled binary logit model $y = 1(DocVis > 0)$ using the German health care utilization data examined in Example 11.11. The model is

$$\text{Prob}(DocVis_{it} > 0) = \Lambda(\beta_1 + \beta_2\,Age_{it} + \beta_3\,Income_{it} + \beta_4\,Kids_{it}$$
$$+ \beta_5\,Education_{it} + \beta_6\,Married_{it}).$$

No account of the panel nature of the data set was taken in that exercise. The sample contains a total of 27,326 observations on 7,293 families with $T_i$ dispersed from one to seven. (See Example 11.11 for details.) Table 23.5 lists estimates of parameter estimates and estimated standard errors for probit and logit random and fixed effects models. There is a surprising amount of variation across the estimators. The coefficients are in bold to facilitate reading the table. It is generally difficult to compare across the estimators. The three estimators would

**TABLE 23.5** Estimated Parameters for Panel Data Binary Choice Models

| Model | Estimate | ln L | Variable | | | | | |
|---|---|---|---|---|---|---|---|---|
| | | | Constant | Age | Income | Kids | Education | Married |
| Logit Pooled | β | −17673.10 | 0.25112 | 0.020709 | −0.18592 | −0.22947 | −0.045587 | 0.085293 |
| | St.Err. | | 0.091135 | 0.0012852 | 0.075064 | 0.029537 | 0.005646 | 0.033286 |
| | Rob.SE[e] | | 0.12827 | 0.0017429 | 0.091546 | 0.038313 | 0.008075 | 0.045314 |
| Logit R.E. ρ = 0.41607 | β | −15261.90 | −0.13460 | 0.039267 | 0.021914 | −0.21598 | −0.063578 | 0.025071 |
| | St.Err. | | 0.17764 | 0.0024659 | 0.11866 | 0.047738 | 0.011322 | 0.056282 |
| Logit F.E.(U)[a] | β | −9458.64 | | 0.10475 | −0.060973 | −0.088407 | −0.11671 | −0.057318 |
| | St.Err. | | | 0.0072548 | 0.17829 | 0.074399 | 0.066749 | 0.10609 |
| Logit F.E.(C)[b] | β | −6299.02 | | 0.084760 | −0.050383 | −0.077764 | −0.090816 | −0.052072 |
| | St.Err. | | | 0.0065022 | 0.15888 | 0.066282 | 0.056673 | 0.093044 |
| Probit Pooled | β | −17670.94 | 0.15500 | 0.012835 | −0.11643 | −0.14118 | −0.028115 | 0.052260 |
| | St.Err. | | 0.056516 | 0.0007903 | 0.046329 | 0.018218 | 0.003503 | 0.020462 |
| | Rob.SE[e] | | 0.079591 | 0.0010739 | 0.056543 | 0.023614 | 0.005014 | 0.027904 |
| Probit:RE[c] ρ = 0.44789 | β | −16273.96 | 0.034113 | 0.020143 | −0.003176 | −0.15379 | −0.033694 | 0.016325 |
| | St.Err. | | 0.096354 | 0.0013189 | 0.066672 | 0.027043 | 0.006289 | 0.031347 |
| Probit:RE[d] ρ = 0.44799 | β | −16279.97 | 0.033290 | 0.020078 | −0.002973 | −0.153579 | −0.033489 | 0.016826 |
| | St.Err. | | 0.063229 | 0.0009013 | 0.052012 | 0.020286 | 0.003931 | 0.022771 |
| Probit F.E.(U) | β | −9453.71 | | 0.062528 | −0.034328 | −0.048270 | −0.072189 | −0.032774 |
| | St.Err. | | | 0.0043219 | 0.10745 | 0.044559 | 0.040731 | 0.063627 |

[a] Unconditional fixed effects estimator
[b] Conditional fixed effects estimator
[c] Butler and Moffitt estimator
[d] Maximum simulated likelihood estimator
[e] Robust, "cluster" corrected standard error

**TABLE 23.6**    Estimated Partial Effects for Panel Data Binary Choice Models

| Model | Age | Income | Kids | Education | Married |
|---|---|---|---|---|---|
| Logit, P[a] | 0.0048133 | −0.043213 | −0.053598 | −0.010596 | 0.019936 |
| Logit: RE,Q[b] | 0.0064213 | 0.0035835 | −0.035448 | −0.010397 | 0.0041049 |
| Logit: F,U[c] | 0.024871 | −0.014477 | −0.020991 | −0.027711 | −0.013609 |
| Logit: F,C[d] | 0.0072991 | −0.0043387 | −0.0066967 | −0.0078206 | −0.0044842 |
| Probit, P[a] | 0.0048374 | −0.043883 | −0.053414 | −0.010597 | 0.019783 |
| Probit RE.Q[b] | 0.0056049 | −0.0008836 | −0.042792 | −0.0093756 | 0.0045426 |
| Probit:RE,S[e] | 0.0071455 | −0.0010582 | −0.054655 | −0.011917 | 0.0059878 |
| Probit: F,U[c] | 0.023958 | −0.013152 | −0.018495 | −0.027659 | −0.012557 |

[a]Pooled estimator
[b]Butler and Moffitt estimator
[c]Unconditional fixed effects estimator
[d]Conditional fixed effects estimator
[e]Maximum simulated likelihood estimator

be expected to produce very different estimates in any of the three specifications—recall, for example, the pooled estimator is inconsistent in either the fixed or random effects cases. The logit results include two fixed effects estimators. The line market "U" is the unconditional (inconsistent) estimator. The one marked "C" is Chamberlain's consistent estimator. Note for all three fixed effects estimators, it is necessary to drop from the sample any groups that have $DocVis_{it}$ equal to zero or one for every period. There were 3,046 such groups, which is about 42 percent of the sample. We also computed the probit random effects model in two ways, first by using the Butler and Moffitt method, then by using maximum simulated likelihood estimation. In this case, the estimators are very similar, as might be expected. The estimated correlation coefficient, $\rho$, is computed as $\sigma_u^2/(\sigma_\varepsilon^2+\sigma_u^2)$. For the probit model, $\sigma_\varepsilon^2 = 1$. The MSL estimator computes $s_u = 0.9088376$, from which we obtained $\rho$. The estimated partial effects for the models are shown in Table 23.6. The average of the fixed effects constant terms is used to obtain a constant term for the fixed effects case. Once again there is a considerable amount of variation across the different estimators. On average, the fixed effects models tend to produce much larger values than the pooled or random effects models.

Why did the incidental parameters problem arise here and not in the linear regression model? Recall that estimation in the regression model was based on the deviations from group means, not the original data as it is here. The result we exploited there was that although $f(y_{it} \mid \mathbf{X}_i)$ is a function of $\alpha_i$, $f(y_{it} \mid \mathbf{X}_i, \bar{y}_i)$ is not a function of $\alpha_i$, and we used the latter in estimation of $\boldsymbol{\beta}$. In that setting, $\bar{y}_i$ is a **minimal sufficient statistic** for $\alpha_i$. Sufficient statistics are available for a few distributions that we will examine, but not for the probit model. They are available for the logit model, as we now examine.

A fixed effects binary logit model is

$$\text{Prob}(y_{it} = 1 \mid \mathbf{x}_{it}) = \frac{e^{\alpha_i + \mathbf{x}'_{it}\boldsymbol{\beta}}}{1 + e^{\alpha_i + \mathbf{x}'_{it}\boldsymbol{\beta}}}.$$

The unconditional likelihood for the $nT$ independent observations is

$$L = \prod_i \prod_t (F_{it})^{y_{it}} (1 - F_{it})^{1-y_{it}}.$$

Chamberlain (1980) [following Rasch (1960) and Andersen (1970)] observed that the **conditional likelihood function,**

$$L^c = \prod_{i=1}^{n} \text{Prob}\left( Y_{i1} = y_{i1}, Y_{i2} = y_{i2}, \ldots, Y_{iT_i} = y_{iT_i} \,\middle|\, \sum_{t=1}^{T_i} y_{it} \right),$$

is free of the incidental parameters, $\alpha_i$. The joint likelihood for each set of $T_i$ observations conditioned on the number of ones in the set is

$$\text{Prob}\left(Y_{i1} = y_{i1}, Y_{i2} = y_{i2}, \ldots, Y_{iT_i} = y_{iT_i} \,\Bigg|\, \sum_{t=1}^{T_i} y_{it}, \text{data}\right)$$

$$= \frac{\exp\left(\sum_{t=1}^{T_i} y_{it}\mathbf{x}'_{it}\boldsymbol{\beta}\right)}{\sum_{\Sigma_t d_{it}=S_i} \exp\left(\sum_{t=1}^{T_i} d_{it}\mathbf{x}'_{it}\boldsymbol{\beta}\right)}.$$

The function in the denominator is summed over the set of all $\binom{T_i}{S_i}$ different sequences of $T_i$ zeros and ones that have the same sum as $S_i = \sum_{t=1}^{T_i} y_{it}$.[25]

Consider the example of $T_i = 2$. The unconditional likelihood is

$$L = \prod_i \text{Prob}(Y_{i1} = y_{i1})\text{Prob}(Y_{i2} = y_{i2}).$$

For each pair of observations, we have these possibilities:

1.  $y_{i1} = 0$ and $y_{i2} = 0$. Prob$(0, 0 \,|\, \text{sum} = 0) = 1$.
2.  $y_{i1} = 1$ and $y_{i2} = 1$. Prob$(1, 1 \,|\, \text{sum} = 2) = 1$.

The $i$th term in $L^c$ for either of these is just one, so they contribute nothing to the conditional likelihood function.[26] When we take logs, these terms (and these observations) will drop out. But suppose that $y_{i1} = 0$ and $y_{i2} = 1$. Then

3.  $\text{Prob}(0, 1 \,|\, \text{sum} = 1) = \dfrac{\text{Prob}(0, 1 \text{ and } \text{sum} = 1)}{\text{Prob}(\text{sum} = 1)} = \dfrac{\text{Prob}(0, 1)}{\text{Prob}(0, 1) + \text{Prob}(1, 0)}.$

Therefore, for this pair of observations, the conditional probability is

$$\frac{\dfrac{1}{1 + e^{\alpha_i + \mathbf{x}'_{i1}\boldsymbol{\beta}}} \dfrac{e^{\alpha_i + \mathbf{x}'_{i2}\boldsymbol{\beta}}}{1 + e^{\alpha_i + \mathbf{x}'_{i2}\boldsymbol{\beta}}}}{\dfrac{1}{1 + e^{\alpha_i + \mathbf{x}'_{i1}\boldsymbol{\beta}}} \dfrac{e^{\alpha_i + \mathbf{x}'_{i2}\boldsymbol{\beta}}}{1 + e^{\alpha_i + \mathbf{x}'_{i2}\boldsymbol{\beta}}} + \dfrac{e^{\alpha_i + \mathbf{x}'_{i1}\boldsymbol{\beta}}}{1 + e^{\alpha_i + \mathbf{x}'_{i1}\boldsymbol{\beta}}} \dfrac{1}{1 + e^{\alpha_i + \mathbf{x}'_{i2}\boldsymbol{\beta}}}} = \frac{e^{\mathbf{x}'_{i2}\boldsymbol{\beta}}}{e^{\mathbf{x}'_{i1}\boldsymbol{\beta}} + e^{\mathbf{x}'_{i2}\boldsymbol{\beta}}}.$$

By conditioning on the sum of the two observations, we have removed the heterogeneity. Therefore, we can construct the conditional likelihood function as the product of these terms for the pairs of observations for which the two observations are $(0, 1)$. Pairs of observations with one and zero are included analogously. The product of the terms such as the preceding, for those observation sets for which the sum is not zero or $T_i$, constitutes the conditional likelihood. Maximization of the resulting function is straightforward and may be done by conventional methods.

As in the linear regression model, it is of some interest to test whether there is indeed heterogeneity. With homogeneity ($\alpha_i = \alpha$), there is no unusual problem, and the

---

[25]The enumeration of all these computations stands to be quite a burden—see Arellano (2000, p. 47) or Baltagi (2005, p. 235). In fact, using a recursion suggested by Krailo and Pike (1984), the computation even with $T_i$ up to 100 is routine.

[26]Recall that in the probit model when we encountered this situation, the individual constant term could not be estimated and the group was removed from the sample. The same effect is at work here.

model can be estimated, as usual, as a logit model. It is not possible to test the hypothesis using the likelihood ratio test, however, because the two likelihoods are not comparable. (The conditional likelihood is based on a restricted data set.) None of the usual tests of restrictions can be used because the individual effects are never actually estimated.[27] Hausman's (1978) specification test is a natural one to use here, however. Under the null hypothesis of homogeneity, both Chamberlain's conditional maximum likelihood estimator (CMLE) and the usual maximum likelihood estimator are consistent, but Chamberlain's is inefficient. (It fails to use the information that $\alpha_i = \alpha$, and it may not use all the data.) Under the alternative hypothesis, the unconditional maximum likelihood estimator is inconsistent,[28] whereas Chamberlain's estimator is consistent and efficient. The Hausman test can be based on the chi-squared statistic

$$\chi^2 = (\hat{\boldsymbol{\beta}}_{\text{CML}} - \hat{\boldsymbol{\beta}}_{\text{ML}})'(\text{Var}[\text{CML}] - \text{Var}[\text{ML}])^{-1}(\hat{\boldsymbol{\beta}}_{\text{CML}} - \hat{\boldsymbol{\beta}}_{\text{ML}}). \qquad \textbf{(23-42)}$$

The estimated covariance matrices are those computed for the two maximum likelihood estimators. For the unconditional maximum likelihood estimator, the row and column corresponding to the constant term are dropped. A large value will cast doubt on the hypothesis of homogeneity. (There are $K$ degrees of freedom for the test.) It is possible that the covariance matrix for the maximum likelihood estimator will be larger than that for the conditional maximum likelihood estimator. If so, then the difference matrix in brackets is assumed to be a zero matrix, and the chi-squared statistic is therefore zero.

### Example 23.9   Fixed Effects Logit Models: Magazine Prices Revisited
The fixed effects model does have some appeal, but the incidental parameters problem is a significant shortcoming of the unconditional probit and logit estimators. The conditional MLE for the fixed effects logit model is a fairly common approach. A widely cited application of the model is Cecchetti's (1986) analysis of changes in newsstand prices of magazines. Cecchetti's model was

$$\text{Prob}(\textit{Price change in year i of magazine t}) = \Lambda(\alpha_j + \mathbf{x}'_{it}\boldsymbol{\beta}),$$

where the variables in $\mathbf{x}_{it}$ are (1) time since last price change, (2) inflation since last change, (3) previous fixed price change, (4) current inflation, (5) industry sales growth, and (6) sales volatility. The fixed effect in the model is indexed "$j$" rather than "$i$" as it is defined as a three-year interval for magazine $i$. Thus, a magazine that had been on the newsstands for nine years would have three constants, not just one. In addition to estimating several specifications of the price change model, Cecchetti used the Hausman test in (23-42) to test for the existence of the common effects. Some of Cecchetti's results appear in Table 23.7.

Willis (2006) argued that Cecchetti's estimates were inconsistent and the Hausman test is invalid because right-hand-side variables (1), (2), and (6) are all functions of lagged dependent variables. This state dependence invalidates the use of the sum of the observations for the group as a sufficient statistic in the Chamberlain estimator and the Hausman tests. He proposes, instead, a method suggested by Heckman and Singer (1984b) to incorporate the unobserved heterogeneity in the *unconditional* likelihood function. The Heckman and Singer model can be formulated as a latent class model (see Sections 16.9.7 and 23.5.3) in which the classes are defined by different constant terms—the remaining parameters in the model are constrained to be equal across classes. Willis fit the Heckman and Singer model with

---

[27]This produces a difficulty for this estimator that is shared by the semiparametric estimators discussed in the next section. Because the fixed effects are not estimated, it is not possible to compute probabilities or marginal effects with these estimated coefficients, and it is a bit ambiguous what one can do with the results of the computations. The brute force estimator that actually computes the individual effects might be preferable.

[28]Hsiao (2003) derives the result explicitly for some particular cases.

**TABLE 23.7** Models for Magazine Price Changes (standard errors in parentheses)

|  | Pooled | Unconditional FE | Conditional FE Cecchetti | Conditional FE Willis | Heckman and Singer |
|---|---|---|---|---|---|
| $\beta_1$ | −1.10 (0.03) | −0.07 (0.03) | 1.12 (3.66) | 1.02 (0.28) | −0.09 (0.04) |
| $\beta_2$ | 6.93 (1.12) | 8.83 (1.25) | 11.57 (1.68) | 19.20 (7.51) | 8.23 (1.53) |
| $\beta_5$ | −0.36 (0.98) | −1.14 (1.06) | 5.85 (1.76) | 7.60 (3.46) | −0.13 (1.14) |
| Constant 1 | −1.90 (0.14) |  |  |  | −1.94 (0.20) |
| Constant 2 |  |  |  |  | −29.15 (1.1e11) |
| ln $L$ | −500.45 | −473.18 | −82.91 | −83.72 | −499.65 |
| Sample size | 1026 | 1026 |  | 543 | 1026 |

two classes to a restricted version of Cecchetti's model using variables (1), (2), and (5). The results in Table 23.7 show some of the results from Willis's Table I. (Willis reports that he could not reproduce Cecchetti's results—the ones in Cecchetti's second column would be the counterparts—because of some missing values. In fact, Willis's estimates are quite far from Cecchetti's results, so it will be difficult to compare them. Both are reported here.)

The two "mass points" reported by Willis are shown in Table 23.7. He reports that these two values (−1.94 and −29.15) correspond to class probabilities of 0.88 and 0.12, though it is difficult to make the translation based on the reported values. He does note that the change in the log-likelihood in going from one mass point (pooled logit model) to two is marginal, only from −500.45 to −499.65. There is another anomaly in the results that is consistent with this finding. The reported standard error for the second "mass point" is $1.1 \times 10^{11}$, or essentially $+\infty$. The finding is consistent with overfitting the latent class model. The results suggest that the better model is a one-class (pooled) model.

### 23.5.3 MODELING HETEROGENEITY

The panel data analysis considered thus far has focused on modeling heterogeneity with the fixed and random effects specifications. Both assume that the heterogeneity is continuously distributed among individuals. The random effects model is fully parametric, requiring a full specification of the likelihood for estimation. The fixed effects model is essentially semiparametric. It requires no specific distributional assumption, however, it does require that the realizations of the latent heterogeneity be treated as parameters, either estimated in the unconditional fixed effects estimator or conditioned out of the likelihood function when possible. As noted in the preceding example, Heckman and Singer's (1984b) model provides a less stringent model specification based on a discrete distribution of the latent heterogeneity. A straightforward method of implementing their model is to cast it as a latent class model in which the classes are distinguished by different constant terms and the associated probabilities. The class probabilities are treated as parameters to be estimated with the model parameters.

*Example 23.10  Semiparametric Models of Heterogeneity*
We have extended the random effects and fixed effects logit models in Example 23.8 by fitting the Heckman and Singer (1984b) model. Table 23.8 shows the specification search and the results under different specifications. The first column of results shows the estimated fixed effects model from Example 23.8. The conditional estimates are shown in parentheses. Of the 7,293 groups in the sample, 3,056 are not used in estimation of the fixed effects models because the sum of $Doctor_{it}$ is either 0 or $T_i$ for the group. The mean and standard deviation of the estimated underlying heterogeneity distribution are computed using the estimates of

**TABLE 23.8** Estimated Heterogeneity Models

| | Fixed Effect | Number of Classes | | | | |
| | | 1 | 2 | 3 | 4 | 5 |
|---|---|---|---|---|---|---|
| $\beta_1$ | 0.10475 | 0.020708 | 0.030325 | 0.033684 | 0.034083 | 0.034159 |
| | (0.084760) | | | | | |
| $\beta_2$ | −0.060973 | −0.18592 | 0.025550 | −0.0058013 | −0.0063516 | −0.013627 |
| | (−0.050383) | | | | | |
| $\beta_3$ | −0.088407 | −0.22947 | −0.24708 | −0.26388 | −0.26590 | −0.26626 |
| | (−0.077764) | | | | | |
| $\beta_4$ | −0.11671 | −0.045588 | −0.050924 | −0.058022 | −0.059751 | −0.059176 |
| | (−0.090816) | | | | | |
| $\beta_5$ | −0.057318 | 0.085293 | 0.042974 | 0.037944 | 0.029227 | 0.030699 |
| | (−0.52072) | | | | | |
| $\alpha_1$ | −2.62334 | 0.25111 | 0.91764 | 1.71669 | 1.94536 | 2.76670 |
| | | (1.00000) | (0.62681) | (0.34838) | (0.29309) | (0.11633) |
| $\alpha_2$ | | | −1.47800 | −2.23491 | −1.76371 | 1.18323 |
| | | | (0.37319) | (0.18412) | (0.21714) | (0.26468) |
| $\alpha_3$ | | | | −0.28133 | −0.036739 | −1.96750 |
| | | | | (0.46749) | (0.46341) | (0.19573) |
| $\alpha_4$ | | | | | −4.03970 | −0.25588 |
| | | | | | (0.026360) | (0.40930) |
| $\alpha_5$ | | | | | | −6.48191 |
| | | | | | | (0.013960) |
| Mean | −2.62334 | 0.00000 | 0.023613 | 0.055059 | 0.063685 | 0.054705 |
| Std. Dev. | 3.13415 | 0.00000 | 1.158655 | 1.40723 | 1.48707 | 1.62143 |
| ln L | −9458.638 | −17673.10 | −16353.14 | −16278.56 | −16276.07 | −16275.85 |
| | (−6299.02) | | | | | |
| AIC | 1.00349 | 1.29394 | 1.19748 | 1.19217 | 1.19213 | 1.19226 |

$\alpha_i$ for the remaining 4,237 groups. The remaining five columns in the table show the results for different numbers of latent classes in the Heckman and Singer model. The listed constant terms are the "mass points" of the underlying distributions. The associated class probabilities are shown in parentheses under them. The mean and standard deviation are derived from the 2- to 5-point discrete distributions shown. It is noteworthy that the mean of the distribution is relatively stable, but the standard deviation rises monotonically. The search for the best model would be based on the AIC. As noted in Section 16.9.6, using a likelihood ratio test in this context is dubious, as the number of degrees of freedom is ambiguous. Based on the AIC, the four-class model is the preferred specification.

### 23.5.4 PARAMETER HETEROGENEITY

In Chapter 9, we examined specifications that extend the underlying heterogeneity to all the parameters of the model. We have considered two approaches. The random parameters, or mixed models discussed in Chapter 17 allow parameters to be distributed continuously across individuals. The latent class model in Section 16.9.6 specifies a discrete distribution instead. (The Heckman and Singer model in the previous section applies this method to the constant term.) Most of the focus to this point, save for Example 16.16, has been on linear models. However, as the next example demonstrates, the same methods can be applied to nonlinear models, such as the discrete choice models.

**TABLE 23.9** Estimated Heterogeneous Parameter Models

| Variable | Pooled Estimate: $\beta$ | Random Parameters Estimate: $\beta$ | Random Parameters Estimate: $\sigma$ | Latent Class Estimate: $\beta$ | Latent Class Estimate: $\beta$ | Latent Class Estimate: $\beta$ |
|---|---|---|---|---|---|---|
| Constant | 0.25111 | −0.034964 | 0.81651 | 0.96605 | −0.18579 | −1.52595 |
| | (0.091135) | (0.075533) | (0.016542) | (0.43757) | (0.23907) | (0.43498) |
| Age | 0.020709 | 0.026306 | 0.025330 | 0.049058 | 0.032248 | 0.019981 |
| | (0.0012852) | (0.0011038) | (0.0004226) | (0.0069455) | (0.0031462) | (0.0062550) |
| Income | −0.18592 | −0.0043649 | 0.10737 | −0.27917 | −0.068633 | 0.45487 |
| | (0.075064) | (0.062445) | (0.038276) | (0.37149) | (0.16748) | (0.31153) |
| Kids | −0.22947 | −0.17461 | 0.55520 | −0.28385 | −0.28336 | −0.11708 |
| | (0.029537) | (0.024522) | (0.023866) | (0.14279) | (0.066404) | (0.12363) |
| Education | −0.045588 | −0.040510 | 0.037915 | −0.025301 | −0.057335 | −0.09385 |
| | (0.0056465) | (0.0047520) | (0.0013416) | (0.027768) | (0.012465) | (0.027965) |
| Married | 0.085293 | 0.014618 | 0.070696 | −0.10875 | 0.025331 | 0.23571 |
| | (0.033286) | (0.027417) | (0.017362) | (0.17228) | (0.075929) | (0.14369) |
| Class Prob. | 1.00000 | 1.00000 | | 0.34833 | 0.46181 | 0.18986 |
| | (0.00000) | (0.00000) | | (0.038495) | (0.028062) | (0.022335) |
| ln $L$ | −17673.10 | −16271.72 | | −16265.59 | | |

### Example 23.11 Parameter Heterogeneity in a Binary Choice Model

We have extended the logit model for doctor visits from Example 23.10 to allow the parameters to vary randomly across individuals. The random parameters logit model is

$$\text{Prob}(Doctor_{it} = 1) = \Lambda(\beta_{1i} + \beta_{2i}\, Age_{it} + \beta_{3i}\, Income_{it} + \beta_{4i}\, Kids_{it} + \beta_{5i}\, Educ_{it} + \beta_{6i}\, Married_{it}),$$

where the two models for the parameter variation we have employed are:

Continuous: $\beta_{ki} = \beta_k + \sigma_k u_{ki}, u_{ki} \sim N[0, 1], k = 1, \ldots, 6, \text{Cov}[u_{ki}, u_{mi}] = 0,$

Discrete: $\beta_{ki} = \beta_k^1$ with probability $\pi_1$

$\beta_k^2$ with probability $\pi_2$

$\beta_k^3$ with probability $\pi_3$.

We have chosen a three-class latent class model for the illustration. In an application, one might undertake a systematic search, such as in Example 23.10, to find a preferred specification. Table 23.9 presents the fixed parameter (pooled) logit model and the two random parameters versions. (There are infinite variations on these specifications that one might explore—See Chapter 17 for discussion—we have shown only the simplest to illustrate the models.[29] A more elaborate specification appears in Section 23.11.7.)

Figure 23.3 shows the implied distribution for the coefficient on age. For the continuous distribution, we have simply plotted the normal density. For the discrete distribution, we first obtained the mean (0.0358) and standard deviation (0.0107). Notice that the distribution is tighter than the estimated continuous normal (mean, 0.026, standard deviation, 0.0253). To suggest the variation of the parameter (purely for purpose of the display, because the distribution is discrete), we placed the mass of the center interval, 0.462, between the midpoints of the intervals between the center mass point and the two extremes. With a width of 0.0145 the density is 0.461 / 0.0145 = 31.8. We used the same interval widths for the outer segments. This range of variation covers about five standard deviations of the distribution.

---

[29]We have arrived (once again) at a point where the question of replicability arises. Nonreplicability is an ongoing challenge in empirical work in economics. (See, e.g., Example 23.9.) The problem is particularly acute in analyses that involve simulation such as Monte Carlo studies and random parameter models. In the interest of replicability, we note that the random parameter estimates in Table 23.9 were computed with NLOGIT [Econometric Software (2007)] and are based on 50 Halton draws. We used the first six sequences (prime numbers 2, 3, 5, 7, 11, 13) and discarded the first 10 draws in each sequence.

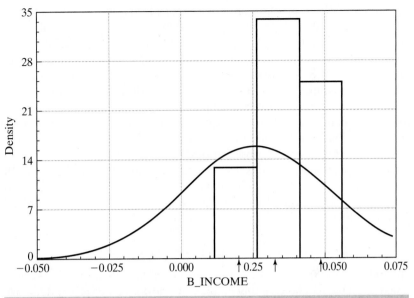

**FIGURE 23.3** Distributions of Income Coefficient.

## 23.6 SEMIPARAMETRIC ANALYSIS

In his survey of qualitative response models, Amemiya (1981) reports the following widely cited approximations for the linear probability (LP) model: Over the range of probabilities of 30 to 70 percent,

$$\hat{\beta}_{\text{LP}} \approx 0.4\beta_{\text{probit}} \text{ for the slopes,}$$

$$\hat{\beta}_{\text{LP}} \approx 0.25\beta_{\text{logit}} \text{ for the slopes.}$$

Aside from confirming our intuition that least squares approximates the nonlinear model and providing a quick comparison for the three models involved, the practical usefulness of the formula is somewhat limited. Still, it is a striking result.[30] A series of studies has focused on reasons why the least squares estimates should be proportional to the probit and logit estimates. A related question concerns the problems associated with assuming that a probit model applies when, in fact, a logit model is appropriate or vice versa.[31] The approximation would seem to suggest that with this type of misspecification, we would once again obtain a scaled version of the correct coefficient vector. (Amemiya also reports the widely observed relationship $\hat{\beta}_{\text{logit}} = 1.6\hat{\beta}_{\text{probit}}$, which follows from the results for the linear probability model.)

---

[30]This result does not imply that it is useful to report 2.5 times the linear probability estimates with the probit estimates for comparability. The linear probability estimates are already in the form of marginal effects, whereas the probit coefficients must be scaled *downward*. If the sample proportion happens to be close to 0.5, then the right scale factor will be roughly $\phi[\Phi^{-1}(0.5)] = 0.3989$. But the density falls rapidly as $P$ moves away from 0.5.

[31]See Ruud (1986) and Gourieroux et al. (1987).

Greene (1983), building on Goldberger (1981), finds that if the probit model is correctly specified and if the regressors are themselves joint normally distributed, then the probability limit of the least squares estimator is a multiple of the true coefficient vector.[32] Greene's result is useful only for the same purpose as Amemiya's quick correction of OLS. Multivariate normality is obviously inconsistent with most applications. For example, nearly all applications include at least one dummy variable. Ruud (1982) and Chung and Goldberger (1984), however, have shown that much weaker conditions than joint normality will produce the same proportionality result. For a probit model, Chung and Goldberger require only that $E[\mathbf{x} \mid y^*]$ be linear in $y^*$. Several authors have built on these observations to pursue the issue of what circumstances will lead to proportionality results such as these. Ruud (1986) and Stoker (1986) have extended them to a very wide class of models that goes well beyond those of Chung and Goldberger. Curiously enough, Stoker's results rule out dummy variables, but it is those for which the proportionality result seems to be most robust.[33]

### 23.6.1 SEMIPARAMETRIC ESTIMATION

The fully parametric probit and logit models remain by far the mainstays of empirical research on binary choice. Fully nonparametric discrete choice models are fairly exotic and have made only limited inroads in the literature, and much of that literature is theoretical [e.g., Matzkin (1993)]. The primary obstacle to application is their paucity of interpretable results. (See Example 23.12.) Of course, one could argue on this basis that the firm results produced by the fully parametric models are merely fragile artifacts of the detailed specification, not genuine reflections of some underlying truth. [In this connection, see Manski (1995).] But that orthodox view raises the question of what motivates the study to begin with and what one hopes to learn by embarking upon it. The intent of model building to approximate reality so as to draw useful conclusions is hardly limited to the analysis of binary choices. Semiparametric estimators represent a middle ground between these extreme views.[34] The single index model of Klein and Spady (1993) has been used in several applications, including Gerfin (1996), Horowitz (1993), and Fernandez and Rodriguez-Poo (1997).[35]

The single index formulation departs from a linear "regression" formulation,

$$E[y_i \mid \mathbf{x}_i] = E[y_i \mid \mathbf{x}_i' \boldsymbol{\beta}].$$

Then

$$\text{Prob}(y_i = 1 \mid \mathbf{x}_i) = F(\mathbf{x}_i' \boldsymbol{\beta} \mid \mathbf{x}_i) = G(\mathbf{x}_i' \boldsymbol{\beta}),$$

where $G$ is an unknown continuous distribution function whose range is $[0, 1]$. The function $G$ is not specified a priori; it is estimated along with the parameters. (Since $G$ as well as $\boldsymbol{\beta}$ is to be estimated, a constant term is not identified; essentially, $G$ provides

---

[32]The scale factor is estimable with the sample data, so under these assumptions, a method of moments estimator is available.

[33]See Greene (1983).

[34]Recent proposals for semiparametric estimators in addition to the one developed here include Lewbel (1997, 2000), Lewbel and Honorè (2001), and Altonji and Matzkin (2001). In spite of nearly 10 years of development, this is a nascent literature. The theoretical development tends to focus on root-n consistent coefficient estimation in models which provide no means of computation of probabilities or marginal effects.

[35]A symposium on the subject is Hardle and Manski (1993).

the location for the index that would otherwise be provided by a constant.) The criterion function for estimation, in which subscripts $n$ denote estimators of their unsubscripted counterparts, is

$$\ln L_n = \frac{1}{n} \sum_{i=1}^{n} \left\{ y_i \ln G_n(\mathbf{x}_i'\boldsymbol{\beta}_n) + (1 - y_i) \ln[1 - G_n(\mathbf{x}_i'\boldsymbol{\beta}_n)] \right\}.$$

The estimator of the probability function, $G_n$, is computed at each iteration using a nonparametric kernel estimator of the density of $\mathbf{x}'\boldsymbol{\beta}_n$; we did this calculation in Section 14.4. For the Klein and Spady estimator, the nonparametric regression estimator is

$$G_n(z_i) = \frac{\overline{y} g_n(z_i \mid y_i = 1)}{\overline{y} g_n(z_i \mid y_i = 1) + (1 - \overline{y}) g_n(z_i \mid y_i = 0)},$$

where $g_n(z_i \mid y_i)$ is the **kernel density estimator** of the density of $z_i = \mathbf{x}_i'\boldsymbol{\beta}_n$. This result is

$$g_n(z_i \mid y_i = 1) = \frac{1}{n \overline{y} h_n} \sum_{j=1}^{n} y_j K\left( \frac{z_i - \mathbf{x}_j'\boldsymbol{\beta}_n}{h_n} \right);$$

$g_n(z_i \mid y_i = 0)$ is obtained by replacing $\overline{y}$ with $1 - \overline{y}$ in the leading scalar and $y_j$ with $1 - y_j$ in the summation. As before, $h_n$ is the bandwidth. There is no firm theory for choosing the kernel function or the bandwidth. Both Horowitz and Gerfin used the standard normal density. Two different methods for choosing the bandwidth are suggested by them.[36] Klein and Spady provide theoretical background for computing asymptotic standard errors.

### Example 23.12   A Comparison of Binary Choice Estimators

Gerfin (1996) did an extensive analysis of several binary choice estimators, the probit model, Klein and Spady's single index model, and Horowitz's smoothed maximum score (MSCORE) estimator. [The MSCORE estimator is the (nonunique) vector $\mathbf{b}_M$ computed such that the sign of $\mathbf{x}_i'\mathbf{b}_M$ is the same as that of $(2y_i - 1)$ the maximum number of times. See Manski and Thompson (1986).] (A fourth "seminonparametric" estimator was also examined, but in the interest of brevity, we confine our attention to the three more widely used procedures.) The several models were all fit to two data sets on labor force participation of married women, one from Switzerland and one from Germany. Variables included in the equation were (our notation), $x_1 =$ a constant, $x_2 =$ age, $x_3 =$ age$^2$, $x_4 =$ education, $x_5 =$ number of young children, $x_6 =$ number of older children, $x_7 =$ log of yearly nonlabor income, and $x_8 =$ a dummy variable for permanent foreign resident (Swiss data only). Coefficient estimates for the models are not directly comparable. We suggested in Example 23.3 that they could be made comparable by transforming them to marginal effects. Neither MSCORE nor the single index model, however, produces a marginal effect (which does suggest a question of interpretation). The author obtained comparability by dividing all coefficients by the absolute value of the coefficient on $x_7$. The set of normalized coefficients estimated for the Swiss data appears in Table 23.10, with estimated standard errors (from Gerfin's Table III) shown in parentheses.

Given the very large differences in the models, the agreement of the estimates is impressive. [A similar comparison of the same estimators with comparable concordance may be found in Horowitz (1993, p. 56).] In every case, the standard error of the probit estimator is smaller than that of the others. It is tempting to conclude that it is a more efficient estimator, but that is true only if the normal distribution assumed for the model is correct. In any event,

---

[36] The function $G_n(z)$ involves an enormous amount of computation, on the order of $n^2$, in principle. As Gerfin (1996) observes, however, computation of the kernel estimator can be cast as a Fourier transform, for which the fast Fourier transform reduces the amount of computation to the order of $n \log_2 n$. This value is only slightly larger than linear in $n$. See Press et al. (1986) and Gerfin (1996).

**TABLE 23.10**  Estimated Parameters for Semiparametric Models

|  | $x_1$ | $x_2$ | $x_3$ | $x_4$ | $x_5$ | $x_6$ | $x_7$ | $x_8$ | $h$ |
|---|---|---|---|---|---|---|---|---|---|
| Probit | 5.62 | 3.11 | −0.44 | 0.03 | −1.07 | −0.22 | −1.00 | 1.07 | — |
|  | (1.35) | (0.77) | (0.10) | (0.03) | (0.26) | (0.09) | — | (0.29) |  |
| Single | — | 2.98 | −0.44 | 0.02 | −1.32 | −0.25 | −1.00 | 1.06 | 0.40 |
| index | — | (0.90) | (0.12) | (0.03) | (0.33) | (0.11) | — | (0.32) |  |
| MSCORE | 5.83 | 2.84 | −0.40 | 0.03 | −0.80 | −0.16 | −1.00 | 0.91 | 0.70 |
|  | (1.78) | (0.98) | (0.13) | (0.05) | (0.43) | (0.20) | — | (0.57) |  |

the smaller standard error is the payoff to the sharper specification of the distribution. This payoff could be viewed in much the same way that parametric restrictions in the classical regression make the asymptotic covariance matrix of the restricted least squares estimator smaller than its unrestricted counterpart, even if the restrictions are incorrect.

Gerfin then produced plots of $F(z)$ for $z$ in the range of the sample values of $\mathbf{x'b}$. Once again, the functions are surprisingly close. In the German data, however, the Klein–Spady estimator is nonmonotonic over a sizable range, which would cause some difficult problems of interpretation. The maximum score estimator does not produce an estimate of the probability, so it is excluded from this comparison. Another comparison is based on the predictions of the observed response. Two approaches are tried, first counting the number of cases in which the predicted probability exceeds 0.5. ($\mathbf{x'b} > 0$ for MSCORE) and second by summing the sample values of $F(\mathbf{x'b})$. (Once again, MSCORE is excluded.) By the second approach, the estimators are almost indistinguishable, but the results for the first differ widely. Of 401 ones (out of 873 observations), the counts of predicted ones are 389 for probit, 382 for Klein/Spady, and 355 for MSCORE. (The results do not indicate how many of these counts are correct predictions.)

### 23.6.2  A KERNEL ESTIMATOR FOR A NONPARAMETRIC REGRESSION FUNCTION

As noted, one unsatisfactory aspect of semiparametric formulations such as MSCORE is that the amount of information that the procedure provides about the population is limited; this aspect is, after all, the purpose of dispensing with the firm (parametric) assumptions of the probit and logit models. Thus, in the preceding example, there is little that one can say about the population that generated the data based on the MSCORE "estimates" in the table. The estimates do allow predictions of the response variable. But there is little information about any relationship between the response and the independent variables based on the "estimation" results. Even the **mean-squared deviation** matrix is suspect as an estimator of the asymptotic covariance matrix of the MSCORE coefficients.

The authors of the technique have proposed a secondary analysis of the results. Let

$$F_\beta(z_i) = E[y_i \mid \mathbf{x}_i'\boldsymbol{\beta} = z_i]$$

denote a smooth regression function for the response variable. Based on a parameter vector $\boldsymbol{\beta}$, the authors propose to estimate the regression by the **method of kernels** as follows. For the $n$ observations in the sample and for the given $\boldsymbol{\beta}$ (e.g., $\mathbf{b}_n$ from MSCORE), let

$$z_i = \mathbf{x}_i'\boldsymbol{\beta},$$

$$s = \left[ \frac{1}{n} \sum_{i=1}^{n} (z_i - \bar{z})^2 \right]^{1/2}.$$

For a particular value $z^*$, we compute a set of $n$ weights using the **kernel function,**

$$w_i(z^*) = K[(z^* - z_i)/(\lambda s)],$$

where

$$K(r_i) = P(r_i)[1 - P(r_i)],$$

and

$$P(r_i) = [1 + \exp(-cr_i)]^{-1}.$$

The constant $c = (\pi/\sqrt{3})^{-1} \approx 0.55133$ is used to standardize the logistic distribution that is used for the kernel function. (See Section 14.4.1.) The parameter $\lambda$ is the smoothing (bandwidth) parameter. Large values will flatten the estimated function through $\bar{y}$, whereas values close to zero will allow greater variation in the function but might cause it to be unstable. There is no good theory for the choice, but some suggestions have been made based on descriptive statistics. [See Wong (1983) and Manski (1986).] Finally, the function value is estimated with

$$F(z^*) \approx \frac{\sum_{i=1}^n w_i(z^*) y_i}{\sum_{i=1}^n w_i(z^*)}.$$

The nonparametric estimator displays a relationship between $\mathbf{x}'\boldsymbol{\beta}$ and $E[y_i]$. At first blush, this relationship might suggest that we could deduce the marginal effects, but unfortunately, that is not the case. The coefficients in this setting are not meaningful, so all we can deduce is an estimate of the density, $f(z)$, by using first differences of the estimated regression function. It might seem, therefore, that the analysis has produced relatively little payoff for the effort. But that should come as no surprise if we reconsider the assumptions we have made to reach this point. The only assumptions made thus far are that for a given vector of covariates $\mathbf{x}_i$ and coefficient vector $\boldsymbol{\beta}$ (i.e., *any* $\boldsymbol{\beta}$), there exists a smooth function $F(\mathbf{x}'\boldsymbol{\beta}) = E[y_i \mid z_i]$. We have also assumed, at least implicitly, that the coefficients carry some information about the covariation of $\mathbf{x}'\boldsymbol{\beta}$ and the response variable. The technique will approximate any such function [see Manski (1986)].

There is a large and burgeoning literature on kernel estimation and nonparametric estimation in econometrics. [A recent application is Melenberg and van Soest (1996).] As this simple example suggests, with the radically different forms of the specified model, the information that is culled from the data changes radically as well. The general principle now made evident is that the fewer assumptions one makes about the population, the less precise the information that can be deduced by statistical techniques. That tradeoff is inherent in the methodology.

## 23.7 ENDOGENOUS RIGHT-HAND-SIDE VARIABLES IN BINARY CHOICE MODELS

The analysis in Example 23.10 (Magazine Prices Revisited) suggests that the presence of endogenous right-hand-side variables in a binary choice model presents familiar problems for estimation. The problem is made worse in nonlinear models because even if one has an instrumental variable readily at hand, it may not be immediately clear what is to be done with it. The instrumental variable estimator described in Chapter 12 is based on moments of the data, variances, and covariances. In this binary choice setting, we are not using any form of least squares to estimate the parameters, so the IV method would appear not to apply. Generalized method of moments is a possibility. (This will figure prominently in the analysis in Section 23.9.) Consider the model

$$y_i^* = \mathbf{x}_i'\boldsymbol{\beta} + \gamma w_i + \varepsilon_i,$$
$$y_i = 1(y_i^* > 0),$$
$$E[\varepsilon_i \mid w_i] = g(w_i) \neq 0.$$

Thus, $w_i$ is endogenous in this model. The maximum likelihood estimators considered earlier will not consistently estimate $(\boldsymbol{\beta}, \gamma)$. [Without an additional specification that allows us to formalize $\text{Prob}(y_i = 1 \mid \mathbf{x}_i, w_i)$, we cannot state what the MLE will, in fact, estimate.] Suppose that we have a "relevant" (see Section 12.2) instrumental variable, $z_i$ such that

$$E[\varepsilon_i \mid z_i, \mathbf{x}_i] = 0,$$
$$E[w_i z_i] \neq 0.$$

A natural instrumental variable estimator would be based on the "moment" condition

$$E\left[(y_i^* - \mathbf{x}_i'\boldsymbol{\beta} - \gamma w_i)\begin{pmatrix}\mathbf{x}_i \\ z_i\end{pmatrix}\right] = \mathbf{0}.$$

However, $y_i^*$ is not observed, $y_i$ is. But the "residual," $y_i - \mathbf{x}_i'\boldsymbol{\beta} - \gamma w_i$, would have no meaning even if the true parameters were known.[37] One approach that was used in Avery et al. (1983), Butler and Chatterjee (1997), and Bertschek and Lechner (1998) is to assume that the instrumental variable is orthogonal to the residual $[y - \Phi(\mathbf{x}_i'\boldsymbol{\beta} + \gamma w_i)]$; that is,

$$E\left[[y_i - \Phi(\mathbf{x}_i'\boldsymbol{\beta} + \gamma w_i)]\begin{pmatrix}\mathbf{x}_i \\ z_i\end{pmatrix}\right] = \mathbf{0}.$$

This form of the moment equation, based on observables, can form the basis of a straight-forward two-step GMM estimator. (See Chapter 15 for details.)

The GMM estimator is not less parametric than the full information maximum likelihood estimator described following because the probit model based on the normal distribution is still invoked to specify the moment equation.[38] Nothing is gained in simplicity or robustness of this approach to full information maximum likelihood estimation, which we now consider. (As Bertschek and Lechner argue, however, the gains might come in terms of practical implementation and computation time. The same considerations motivated Avery et al.)

This maximum likelihood estimator requires a full specification of the model, including the assumption that underlies the endogeneity of $w_i$. This becomes essentially

---

[37] One would proceed in precisely this fashion if the central specification were a linear probability model (LPM) to begin with. See, for example, Eisenberg and Rowe (2006) or Angrist (2001) for an application and some analysis of this case.

[38] This is precisely the platform that underlies the GLIM/GEE treatment of binary choice models in, for example, the widely used programs *SAS* and *Stata*.

a simultaneous equations model. The model equations are

$$y_i^* = \mathbf{x}_i'\boldsymbol{\beta} + \gamma w_i + \varepsilon_i, y_i = 1[y_i^* > 0],$$
$$w_i = \mathbf{z}_i'\boldsymbol{\alpha} + u_i,$$
$$(\varepsilon_i, u_i) \sim N\left[\begin{pmatrix} 0 \\ 0 \end{pmatrix}, \begin{pmatrix} 1 & \rho\sigma_u \\ \rho\sigma_u & \sigma_u^2 \end{pmatrix}\right].$$

(We are assuming that there is a vector of instrumental variables, $\mathbf{z}_i$.) Probit estimation based on $y_i$ and $(\mathbf{x}_i, w_i)$ will not consistently estimate $(\boldsymbol{\beta}, \gamma)$ because of the correlation between $w_i$ and $\varepsilon_i$ induced by the correlation between $u_i$ and $\varepsilon_i$. Several methods have been proposed for estimation of this model. One possibility is to use the partial reduced form obtained by inserting the second equation in the first. This becomes a probit model with probability $\text{Prob}(y_i = 1 | \mathbf{x}_i, \mathbf{z}_i) = \Phi(\mathbf{x}_i'\boldsymbol{\beta}^* + \mathbf{z}_i'\boldsymbol{\alpha}^*)$. This will produce consistent estimates of $\boldsymbol{\beta}^* = \boldsymbol{\beta}/(1 + \gamma^2\sigma_u^2 + 2\gamma\sigma_u\rho)^{1/2}$ and $\boldsymbol{\alpha}^* = \gamma\boldsymbol{\alpha}/(1 + \gamma^2\sigma_u^2 + 2\gamma\sigma_u\rho)^{1/2}$ as the coefficients on $\mathbf{x}_i$ and $\mathbf{z}_i$, respectively. (The procedure will estimate a mixture of $\boldsymbol{\beta}^*$ and $\boldsymbol{\alpha}^*$ for any variable that appears in both $\mathbf{x}_i$ and $\mathbf{z}_i$.) In addition, linear regression of $w_i$ on $\mathbf{z}_i$ produces estimates of $\boldsymbol{\alpha}$ and $\sigma_u^2$, but there is no method of moments estimator of $\rho$ or $\gamma$ produced by this procedure, so this estimator is incomplete. Newey (1987) suggested a "minimum chi-squared" estimator that does estimate all parameters. A more direct, and actually simpler approach is full information maximum likelihood.

The log-likelihood is built up from the joint density of $y_i$ and $w_i$, which we write as the product of the conditional and the marginal densities,

$$f(y_i, w_i) = f(y_i | w_i) f(w_i).$$

To derive the conditional distribution, we use results for the bivariate normal, and write

$$\varepsilon_i | u_i = \left[(\rho\sigma_u)/\sigma_u^2\right] u_i + v_i,$$

where $v_i$ is normally distributed with $\text{Var}[v_i] = (1 - \rho^2)$. Inserting this in the first equation, we have

$$y_i^* | w_i = \mathbf{x}_i'\boldsymbol{\beta} + \gamma w_i + (\rho/\sigma_u)u_i + v_i.$$

Therefore,

$$\text{Prob}[y_i = 1 | \mathbf{x}_i, w_i] = \Phi\left[\frac{\mathbf{x}_i'\boldsymbol{\beta} + \gamma w_i + (\rho/\sigma_u)u_i}{\sqrt{1 - \rho^2}}\right]. \tag{23-43}$$

Inserting the expression for $u_i = (w_i - \mathbf{z}_i'\boldsymbol{\alpha})$, and using the normal density for the marginal distribution of $w_i$ in the second equation, we obtain the log-likelihood function for the sample,

$$\ln L = \sum_{i=1}^{n} \ln \Phi\left[(2y_i - 1)\left(\frac{\mathbf{x}_i'\boldsymbol{\beta} + \gamma w_i + (\rho/\sigma_u)(w_i - \mathbf{z}_i'\boldsymbol{\alpha})}{\sqrt{1 - \rho^2}}\right)\right] + \ln\left[\frac{1}{\sigma_u}\phi\left(\frac{w_i - \mathbf{z}_i'\boldsymbol{\alpha}}{\sigma_u}\right)\right].$$

### Example 23.13   Labor Supply Model
In Examples 4.3 and 23.1, we examined a labor suppy model for married women using Mroz's (1987) data on labor supply. The wife's labor force participation equation suggested in Example 23.1 is

$$\text{Prob}(LFP_i = 1) = \Phi(\beta_1 + \beta_2 Age_i + \beta_3 Age_i^2 + \beta_4 Education_i + \beta_5 Kids_i).$$

**TABLE 23.11** Estimated Labor Supply Model

| | *Probit* | | *Regression* | | *Maximum Likelihood* | |
|---|---|---|---|---|---|---|
| Constant | −3.86704 | (1.41153) | | | −5.08405 | (1.43134) |
| Age | 0.18681 | (0.065901) | | | 0.17108 | (0.063321) |
| Age$^2$ | −0.00243 | (0.000774) | | | −0.00219 | (0.0007629) |
| Education | 0.11098 | (0.021663) | | | 0.09037 | (0.029041) |
| Kids | −0.42652 | (0.13074) | | | −0.40202 | (0.12967) |
| Husband hours | −0.000173 | (0.0000797) | | | 0.00055 | (0.000482) |
| Constant | | | 2325.38 | (167.515) | 2424.90 | (158.152) |
| Husband age | | | −6.71056 | (2.73573) | −7.3343 | (2.57979) |
| Husband education | | | 9.29051 | (7.87278) | 2.1465 | (7.28048) |
| Family income | | | 55.72534 | (19.14917) | 63.4669 | (18.61712) |
| $\sigma_u$ | | | 588.2355 | | 586.994 | |
| $\rho$ | | | 0.0000 | | −0.4221 | (0.26931) |
| ln $L$ | | −489.0766 | −5868.432 | | −6357.093 | |

A natural extension of this model would be to include the husband's hours in the equation,

$$\text{Prob}(LFP_i = 1) = \Phi(\beta_1 + \beta_2 Age_i + \beta_3 Age_i^2 + \beta_4 Education_i + \beta_5 Kids_i + \gamma HHrs_i).$$

It would also be natural to assume that the husband's hours would be correlated with the determinants (observed and unobserved) of the wife's labor force participation. The auxiliary equation might be

$$HHrs_i = \alpha_1 + \alpha_2 HAge_i + \alpha_3 HEducation_i + \alpha_4 Family\ Income_i + u_i.$$

As before, we use the Mroz (1987) labor supply data described in Example 4.3. Table 23.11 reports the single-equation and maximum likelihood estimates of the parameters of the two equations. Comparing the two sets of probit estimates, it appears that the (assumed) endogeneity of the husband's hours is not substantially affecting the estimates. There are two simple ways to test the hypothesis that $\rho$ equals zero. The FIML estimator produces an estimated asymptotic standard error with the estimate of $\rho$, so a Wald test can be carried out. For the preceding results, the Wald statistic would be $(−0.4221/0.26921)^2 = 2.458$. The critical value from the chi-squared table for one degree of freedom would be 3.84, so we would not reject the hypothesis. The second approach would use the likelihood ratio test. Under the null hypothesis of exogeneity, the probit model and the regression equation can be estimated independently. The log-likelihood for the full model would be the sum of the two log-likelihoods, which would be −6357.508 based on the following results. Without the restriction $\rho = 0$, the combined log likelihood is −6357.093. Twice the difference is 0.831, which is also well under the 3.84 critical value, so on this basis as well, we would not reject the null hypothesis that $\rho = 0$.

Blundell and Powell (2004) label the foregoing the **control function** approach to accommodating the endogeneity. As noted, the estimator is fully parametric. They propose an alternative semiparametric approach that retains much of the functional form specification, but works around the specific distributional assumptions. Adapting their model to our earlier notation, their departure point is a general specification that produces, once again, a control function,

$$E[y_i \mid \mathbf{x}_i, w_i, u_i] = F(\mathbf{x}_i'\boldsymbol{\beta} + \gamma w_i, u_i).$$

Note that (23-43) satisfies the assumption; however, they reach this point without assuming either joint or marginal normality. The authors propose a three-step, semiparametric approach to estimating the structural parameters. In an application somewhat similar to Example 23.13, they apply the technique to a labor force participation model for British men in which a variable of interest is a dummy variable for education greater than 16 years, the endogenous variable in the participation equation, also of interest, is earned income of the spouse, and an instrumental variable is a welfare benefit entitlement. Their findings are rather more substantial than ours; they find that when the endogeneity of other family income is accommodated in the equation, the education coefficient increases by 40 percent and remains significant, but the coefficient on other income increases by more than tenfold.

The case in which the endogenous variable in the main equation is, itself, a binary variable occupies a large segment of the recent literature. Consider the model

$$y_i^* = \mathbf{x}_i'\boldsymbol{\beta} + \gamma T_i + \varepsilon_i,$$
$$y_i = 1(y_i^* > 0),$$
$$E[\varepsilon_i \mid T_i] \neq 0,$$

where $T_i$ is a binary variable indicating some kind of program participation (e.g., graduating from high school or college, receiving some kind of job training, etc.). The model in this form (and several similar ones) is a "treatment effects" model. The main object of estimation is $\gamma$ (at least superficially). In these settings, the observed outcome may be $y_i^*$ (e.g., income or hours) or $y_i$ (e.g., labor force participation). The preceding analysis has suggested that problems of endogeneity will intervene in either case. The subject of treatment effects models is surveyed in many studies, including Angrist (2001). We will examine this model in some detail in Chapter 24.

## 23.8 BIVARIATE PROBIT MODELS

In Chapter 10, we analyzed a number of different multiple-equation extensions of the classical and generalized regression model. A natural extension of the probit model would be to allow more than one equation, with correlated disturbances, in the same spirit as the seemingly unrelated regressions model. The general specification for a two-equation model would be

$$
\begin{aligned}
&y_1^* = \mathbf{x}_1'\boldsymbol{\beta}_1 + \varepsilon_1, \quad y_1 = 1 \quad \text{if } y_1^* > 0, 0 \text{ otherwise,} \\
&y_2^* = \mathbf{x}_2'\boldsymbol{\beta}_2 + \varepsilon_2, \quad y_2 = 1 \quad \text{if } y_2^* > 0, 0 \text{ otherwise,} \\
&E[\varepsilon_1 \mid \mathbf{x}_1, \mathbf{x}_2] = E[\varepsilon_2 \mid \mathbf{x}_1, \mathbf{x}_2] = 0, \\
&\text{Var}[\varepsilon_1 \mid \mathbf{x}_1, \mathbf{x}_2] = \text{Var}[\varepsilon_2 \mid \mathbf{x}_1, \mathbf{x}_2] = 1, \\
&\text{Cov}[\varepsilon_1, \varepsilon_2 \mid \mathbf{x}_1, \mathbf{x}_2] = \rho.
\end{aligned}
\tag{23-44}
$$

### 23.8.1 MAXIMUM LIKELIHOOD ESTIMATION

The bivariate normal cdf is

$$\text{Prob}(X_1 < x_1, X_2 < x_2) = \int_{-\infty}^{x_2} \int_{-\infty}^{x_1} \phi_2(z_1, z_2, \rho) \, dz_1 dz_2,$$

which we denote $\Phi_2(x_1, x_2, \rho)$. The density is[39]

$$\phi_2(x_1, x_2, \rho) = \frac{e^{-(1/2)(x_1^2+x_2^2-2\rho x_1 x_2)/(1-\rho^2)}}{2\pi(1-\rho^2)^{1/2}}.$$

To construct the log-likelihood, let $q_{i1} = 2y_{i1} - 1$ and $q_{i2} = 2y_{i2} - 1$. Thus, $q_{ij} = 1$ if $y_{ij} = 1$ and $-1$ if $y_{ij} = 0$ for $j = 1$ and 2. Now let

$$z_{ij} = \mathbf{x}'_{ij}\boldsymbol{\beta}_j \quad \text{and} \quad w_{ij} = q_{ij}z_{ij}, \quad j = 1, 2,$$

and

$$\rho_{i*} = q_{i1}q_{i2}\rho.$$

Note the notational convention. The subscript 2 is used to indicate the bivariate normal distribution in the density $\phi_2$ and cdf $\Phi_2$. In all other cases, the subscript 2 indicates the variables in the second equation. As before, $\phi(.)$ and $\Phi(.)$ without subscripts denote the univariate standard normal density and cdf.

The probabilities that enter the likelihood function are

$$\text{Prob}(Y_1 = y_{i1}, Y_2 = y_{i2} \mid \mathbf{x}_1, \mathbf{x}_2) = \Phi_2(w_{i1}, w_{i2}, \rho_{i*}),$$

which accounts for all the necessary sign changes needed to compute probabilities for $y$'s equal to zero and one. Thus,[40]

$$\ln L = \sum_{i=1}^{n} \ln \Phi_2(w_{i1}, w_{i2}, \rho_{i*}).$$

The derivatives of the log-likelihood then reduce to

$$\frac{\partial \ln L}{\partial \boldsymbol{\beta}_j} = \sum_{i=1}^{n} \left(\frac{q_{ij}g_{ij}}{\Phi_2}\right)\mathbf{x}_{ij}, \quad j = 1, 2,$$

(23-45)

$$\frac{\partial \ln L}{\partial \rho} = \sum_{i=1}^{n} \frac{q_{i1}q_{i2}\phi_2}{\Phi_2},$$

where

$$g_{i1} = \phi(w_{i1})\Phi\left[\frac{w_{i2} - \rho_{i*}w_{i1}}{\sqrt{1-\rho_{i*}^2}}\right]$$

(23-46)

and the subscripts 1 and 2 in $g_{i1}$ are reversed to obtain $g_{i2}$. Before considering the Hessian, it is useful to note what becomes of the preceding if $\rho = 0$. For $\partial \ln L/\partial \boldsymbol{\beta}_1$, if $\rho = \rho_{i*} = 0$, then $g_{i1}$ reduces to $\phi(w_{i1})\Phi(w_{i2})$, $\phi_2$ is $\phi(w_{i1})\phi(w_{i2})$, and $\Phi_2$ is $\Phi(w_{i1})\Phi(w_{i2})$. Inserting these results in (23-45) with $q_{i1}$ and $q_{i2}$ produces (23-21). Because both functions in $\partial \ln L/\partial \rho$ factor into the product of the univariate functions, $\partial \ln L/\partial \rho$ reduces to $\sum_{i=1}^{n} \lambda_{i1}\lambda_{i2}$, where $\lambda_{ij}$, $j = 1, 2$, is defined in (23-21). (This result will reappear in the LM statistic shown later.)

The maximum likelihood estimates are obtained by simultaneously setting the three derivatives to zero. The second derivatives are relatively straightforward but tedious.

---

[39]See Section B.9.

[40]To avoid further ambiguity, and for convenience, the observation subscript will be omitted from $\Phi_2 = \Phi_2(w_{i1}, w_{i2}, \rho_{i*})$ and from $\phi_2 = \phi_2(w_{i1}, w_{i2}, \rho_{i*})$.

Some simplifications are useful. Let

$$\delta_i = \frac{1}{\sqrt{1-\rho_{i*}^2}},$$

$$v_{i1} = \delta_i(w_{i2} - \rho_{i*}w_{i1}), \quad \text{so } g_{i1} = \phi(w_{i1})\Phi(v_{i1}),$$

$$v_{i2} = \delta_i(w_{i1} - \rho_{i*}w_{i2}), \quad \text{so } g_{i2} = \phi(w_{i2})\Phi(v_{i2}).$$

By multiplying it out, you can show that

$$\delta_i\phi(w_{i1})\phi(v_{i1}) = \delta_i\phi(w_{i2})\phi(v_{i2}) = \phi_2.$$

Then

$$\frac{\partial^2 \log L}{\partial\boldsymbol{\beta}_1\partial\boldsymbol{\beta}_1'} = \sum_{i=1}^{n} \mathbf{x}_{i1}\mathbf{x}_{i1}' \left[\frac{-w_{i1}g_{i1}}{\Phi_2} - \frac{\rho_{i*}\phi_2}{\Phi_2} - \frac{g_{i1}^2}{\Phi_2^2}\right],$$

$$\frac{\partial^2 \log L}{\partial\boldsymbol{\beta}_1\partial\boldsymbol{\beta}_2'} = \sum_{i=1}^{n} q_{i1}q_{i2}\mathbf{x}_{i1}\mathbf{x}_{i2}' \left[\frac{\phi_2}{\Phi_2} - \frac{g_{i1}g_{i2}}{\Phi_2^2}\right],$$

$$\frac{\partial^2 \log L}{\partial\boldsymbol{\beta}_1\partial\rho} = \sum_{i=1}^{n} q_{i2}\mathbf{x}_{i1}\frac{\phi_2}{\Phi_2} \left[\rho_{i*}\delta_i v_{i1} - w_{i1} - \frac{g_{i1}}{\Phi_2}\right], \quad \text{(23-47)}$$

$$\frac{\partial^2 \log L}{\partial\rho^2} = \sum_{i=1}^{n} \frac{\phi_2}{\Phi_2} \left[\delta_i^2\rho_{i*}(1 - \mathbf{w}_i'\mathbf{R}_i^{-1}\mathbf{w}_i) + \delta_i^2 w_{i1}w_{i2} - \frac{\phi_2}{\Phi_2}\right],$$

where $\mathbf{w}_i'\mathbf{R}_i^{-1}\mathbf{w}_i = \delta_i^2(w_{i1}^2 + w_{i2}^2 - 2\rho_{i*}w_{i1}w_{i2})$. (For $\boldsymbol{\beta}_2$, change the subscripts in $\partial^2 \ln L/\partial\boldsymbol{\beta}_1\partial\boldsymbol{\beta}_1'$ and $\partial^2 \ln L/\partial\boldsymbol{\beta}_1\partial\rho$ accordingly.) The complexity of the second derivatives for this model makes it an excellent candidate for the Berndt et al. estimator of the variance matrix of the maximum likelihood estimator.

### Example 23.14  Tetrachoric Correlation
Returning once again to the health care application of Examples 11.11, 16.16, 23.4, and 23.8, we now consider a second binary variable,

$$Hospital_{it} = 1 \text{ if } HospVis_{it} > 0 \text{ and } 0 \text{ otherwise.}$$

Our previous analyses have focused on

$$Doctor_{it} = 1 \text{ if } DocVis_{it} > 0 \text{ and } 0 \text{ otherwise.}$$

A simple bivariate frequency count for these two variables is

|  | **Hospital** | | |
| --- | --- | --- | --- |
| **Doctor** | **0** | **1** | **Total** |
| 0 | 9,715 | 420 | 10,135 |
| 1 | 15,216 | 1,975 | 17,191 |
| Total | 24,931 | 2,395 | 27,326 |

Looking at the very large value in the lower-left cell, one might surmise that these two binary variables (and the underlying phenomena that they represent) are negatively correlated. The usual Pearson, product moment correlation would be inappropriate as a measure of this correlation since it is used for continuous variables. Consider, instead, a bivariate probit "model,"

$$H_{it}^* = \mu_1 + \varepsilon_{1,it}, \quad Hospital_{it} = 1(H_{it}^* > 0),$$

$$D_{it}^* = \mu_2 + \varepsilon_{2,it}, \quad Doctor_{it} = 1(D_{it}^* > 0),$$

where $(\varepsilon_1, \varepsilon_2)$ have a bivariate normal distribution with means (0, 0), variances (1, 1) and correlation $\rho$. This is the model in (23-44) without independent variables. In this representation, the **tetrachoric correlation,** which is a correlation measure for a pair of binary variables, is precisely the $\rho$ in this model—it is the correlation that would be measured between the underlying continuous variables if they could be observed. This suggests an interpretation of the correlation coefficient in a bivariate probit model—as the conditional tetrachoric correlation. It also suggests a method of easily estimating the tetrachoric correlation coefficient using a program that is built into nearly all commercial software packages.

Applied to the hospital/doctor data defined earlier, we obtained an estimate of $\rho$ of 0.31106, with an estimated asymptotic standard error of 0.01357. Apparently, our earlier intuition was incorrect.

### 23.8.2 TESTING FOR ZERO CORRELATION

The Lagrange multiplier statistic is a convenient device for testing for the absence of correlation in this model. Under the null hypothesis that $\rho$ equals zero, the model consists of independent probit equations, which can be estimated separately. Moreover, in the multivariate model, all the bivariate (or multivariate) densities and probabilities factor into the products of the marginals if the correlations are zero, which makes construction of the test statistic a simple matter of manipulating the results of the independent probits. The Lagrange multiplier statistic for testing $H_0$: $\rho = 0$ in a bivariate probit model is[41]

$$\text{LM} = \frac{\left[ \sum_{i=1}^{n} q_{i1} q_{i2} \dfrac{\phi(w_{i1})\phi(w_{i2})}{\Phi(w_{i1})\Phi(w_{i2})} \right]^2}{\sum_{i=1}^{n} \dfrac{[\phi(w_{i1})\phi(w_{i2})]^2}{\Phi(w_{i1})\Phi(-w_{i1})\Phi(w_{i2})\Phi(-w_{i2})}}.$$

As usual, the advantage of the LM statistic is that it obviates computing the bivariate probit model. But the full unrestricted model is now fairly common in commercial software, so that advantage is minor. The likelihood ratio or Wald test can often be used with equal ease. To carry out the likelihood ratio test, we note first that if $\rho$ equals zero, then the bivariate probit model becomes two independent univariate probits models. The log-likelihood in that case would simply be the sum of the two separate log-likelihoods. The test statistic would be

$$\lambda_{\text{LR}} = 2[\ln L_{\text{BIVARIATE}} - (\ln L_1 + \ln L_2)].$$

This would converge to a chi-squared variable with one degree of freedom. The Wald test is carried out by referring

$$\lambda_{\text{WALD}} = \left[ \hat{\rho}_{MLE} / \sqrt{\text{Est. Asy. Var}[\hat{\rho}_{MLE}]} \right]^2$$

to the chi-squared distribution with one degree of freedom. For 95 percent significance, the critical value is 3.84 (or one can refer the positive square root to the standard normal critical value of 1.96). Example 23.14 demonstrates.

---

[41] This is derived in Kiefer (1982).

### 23.8.3  MARGINAL EFFECTS

There are several "marginal effects" one might want to evaluate in a bivariate probit model.[42] A natural first step would be the derivatives of $\text{Prob}[y_1 = 1, y_2 = 1 \mid \mathbf{x}_1, \mathbf{x}_2]$. These can be deduced from (23-45) by multiplying by $\Phi_2$, removing the sign carrier, $q_{ij}$ and differentiating with respect to $\mathbf{x}_j$ rather than $\boldsymbol{\beta}_j$. The result is

$$\frac{\partial \Phi_2(\mathbf{x}_1'\boldsymbol{\beta}_1, \mathbf{x}_2'\boldsymbol{\beta}_2, \rho)}{\partial \mathbf{x}_1} = \phi(\mathbf{x}_1'\boldsymbol{\beta}_1) \Phi\left(\frac{\mathbf{x}_2'\boldsymbol{\beta}_2 - \rho \mathbf{x}_1'\boldsymbol{\beta}_1}{\sqrt{1-\rho^2}}\right) \boldsymbol{\beta}_1.$$

Note, however, the bivariate probability, albeit possibly of interest in its own right, is not a conditional mean function. As such, the preceding does not correspond to a regression coefficient or a slope of a conditional expectation.

For convenience in evaluating the conditional mean and its partial effects, we will define a vector $\mathbf{x} = \mathbf{x}_1 \cup \mathbf{x}_2$ and let $\mathbf{x}_1'\boldsymbol{\beta}_1 = \mathbf{x}'\boldsymbol{\gamma}_1$. Thus, $\boldsymbol{\gamma}_1$ contains all the nonzero elements of $\boldsymbol{\beta}_1$ and possibly some zeros in the positions of variables in $\mathbf{x}$ that appear only in the other equation; $\boldsymbol{\gamma}_2$ is defined likewise. The bivariate probability is

$$\text{Prob}[y_1 = 1, y_2 = 1 \mid \mathbf{x}] = \Phi_2[\mathbf{x}'\boldsymbol{\gamma}_1, \mathbf{x}'\boldsymbol{\gamma}_2, \rho].$$

Signs are changed appropriately if the probability of the zero outcome is desired in either case. (See 23-44.) The marginal effects of changes in $\mathbf{x}$ on this probability are given by

$$\frac{\partial \Phi_2}{\partial \mathbf{x}} = g_1 \boldsymbol{\gamma}_1 + g_2 \boldsymbol{\gamma}_2,$$

where $g_1$ and $g_2$ are defined in (23-46). The familiar univariate cases will arise if $\rho = 0$, and effects specific to one equation or the other will be produced by zeros in the corresponding position in one or the other parameter vector. There are also some conditional mean functions to consider. The unconditional mean functions are given by the univariate probabilities:

$$E[y_j \mid \mathbf{x}] = \Phi(\mathbf{x}'\boldsymbol{\gamma}_j), \quad j = 1, 2,$$

so the analysis of (23-9) and (23-10) applies. One pair of conditional mean functions that might be of interest are

$$E[y_1 \mid y_2 = 1, \mathbf{x}] = \text{Prob}[y_1 = 1 \mid y_2 = 1, \mathbf{x}] = \frac{\text{Prob}[y_1 = 1, y_2 = 1 \mid \mathbf{x}]}{\text{Prob}[y_2 = 1 \mid \mathbf{x}]}$$

$$= \frac{\Phi_2(\mathbf{x}'\boldsymbol{\gamma}_1, \mathbf{x}'\boldsymbol{\gamma}_2, \rho)}{\Phi(\mathbf{x}'\boldsymbol{\gamma}_2)}$$

and similarly for $E[y_2 \mid y_1 = 1, \mathbf{x}]$. The marginal effects for this function are given by

$$\frac{\partial E[y_1 \mid y_2 = 1, \mathbf{x}]}{\partial \mathbf{x}} = \left(\frac{1}{\Phi(\mathbf{x}'\boldsymbol{\gamma}_2)}\right)\left[g_1 \boldsymbol{\gamma}_1 + \left(g_2 - \Phi_2 \frac{\phi(\mathbf{x}'\boldsymbol{\gamma}_2)}{\Phi(\mathbf{x}'\boldsymbol{\gamma}_2)}\right) \boldsymbol{\gamma}_2\right].$$

Finally, one might construct the nonlinear conditional mean function

$$E[y_1 \mid y_2, \mathbf{x}] = \frac{\Phi_2[\mathbf{x}'\boldsymbol{\gamma}_1, (2y_2 - 1)\mathbf{x}'\boldsymbol{\gamma}_2, (2y_2 - 1)\rho]}{\Phi[(2y_2 - 1)\mathbf{x}'\boldsymbol{\gamma}_2]}.$$

---

[42]See Greene (1996b) and Christofides et al. (1997, 2000).

The derivatives of this function are the same as those presented earlier, with sign changes in several places if $y_2 = 0$ is the argument.

### Example 23.15    Bivariate Probit Model for Health Care Utilization

We have extended the bivariate probit model of the previous example by specifying a set of independent variables,

$$\mathbf{x}_i = Constant, Female_i, Age_{it}, Income_{it}, Kids_{it}, Education_{it}, Married_{it}.$$

We have specified that the same exogenous variables appear in both equations. (There is no requirement that different variables appear in the equations, nor that a variable be excluded from each equation.) The correct analogy here is to the seemingly unrelated regressions model, not to the linear simultaneous equations model. Unlike the SUR model of Chapter 10, it is not the case here that having the same variables in the two equations implies that the model can be fit equation by equation, one equation at a time. That result only applies to the estimation of sets of linear regression equations.

Table 23.12 contains the estimates of the parameters of the univariate and bivariate probit models. The tests of the null hypothesis of zero correlation strongly reject the hypothesis that $\rho$ equals zero. The t statistic for $\rho$ based on the full model is $0.2981 / 0.0139 = 21.446$, which is much larger than the critical value of 1.96. For the likelihood ratio test, we compute

$$\lambda_{LR} = 2\{-25285.07 - [-17422.72 - (-8073.604)]\} = 422.508.$$

Once again, the hypothesis is rejected. (The Wald statistic is $21.446^2 = 459.957$.) The LM statistic is 383.953. The coefficient estimates agree with expectations. The income coefficient is statistically significant in the doctor equation but not in the hospital equation, suggesting, perhaps, that physican visits are at least to some extent discretionary while hospital visits occur on an emergency basis that would be much less tied to income. The table also contains the decomposition of the partial effects for $E[y_1 \mid y_2 = 1]$. The direct effect is $[g_1/\Phi(\mathbf{x}'\gamma_2)]\gamma_1$ in the definition given earlier. The mean estimate of $E[y_1 \mid y_2 = 1]$ is 0.821285. In the table in Example 23.13, this would correspond to the raw proportion $P(D = 1, H = 1) / P(H = 1) = (1975 / 27326) / 2395 / 27326) = 0.8246$.

**TABLE 23.12**    Estimated Bivariate Probit Model

| | Doctor | | | | | Hospital | |
| | Model Estimates | | Partial Effects | | | Model Estimates | |
| Variable | Univariate | Bivariate | Direct | Indirect | Total | Univariate | Bivariate |
|---|---|---|---|---|---|---|---|
| Constant | −0.1243 | −0.1243 | | | | −1.3328 | −1.3385 |
| | (0.05815) | (0.05814) | | | | (0.08320) | (0.07957) |
| Female | 0.3559 | 0.3551 | 0.09650 | −0.00724 | 0.08926 | 0.1023 | 0.1050 |
| | (0.01602) | (0.01604) | (0.004957) | (0.001515) | (0.005127) | (0.02195) | (0.02174) |
| Age | 0.01189 | 0.01188 | 0.003227 | −0.00032 | 0.002909 | 0.004605 | 0.00461 |
| | (0.0007957) | (0.000802) | (0.000231) | (0.000073) | (0.000238) | (0.001082) | (0.001058) |
| Income | −0.1324 | −0.1337 | −0.03632 | −0.003064 | −0.03939 | 0.03739 | 0.04441 |
| | (0.04655) | (0.04628) | (0.01260) | (0.004105) | (0.01254) | (0.06329) | (0.05946) |
| Kids | −0.1521 | −0.1523 | −0.04140 | 0.001047 | −0.04036 | −0.01714 | −0.01517 |
| | (0.01833) | (0.01825) | (0.005053) | (0.001773) | (0.005168) | (0.02562) | (0.02570) |
| Education | −0.01497 | −0.01484 | −0.004033 | 0.001512 | −0.002521 | −0.02196 | −0.02191 |
| | (0.003575) | (0.003575) | (0.000977) | (0.00035) | (0.0010) | (0.005215) | (0.005110) |
| Married | 0.07352 | 0.07351 | 0.01998 | 0.003303 | 0.02328 | −0.04824 | −0.04789 |
| | (0.02064) | (0.02063) | (0.005626) | (0.001917) | (0.005735) | (0.02788) | (0.02777) |

### 23.8.4  RECURSIVE BIVARIATE PROBIT MODELS

Burnett (1997) proposed the following bivariate probit model for the presence of a gender economics course in the curriculum of a liberal arts college:

$$\text{Prob}[y_1 = 1, y_2 = 1 \mid \mathbf{x}_1, \mathbf{x}_2] = \Phi_2(\mathbf{x}_1'\boldsymbol{\beta}_1 + \gamma y_2, \mathbf{x}_2'\boldsymbol{\beta}_2, \rho).$$

The dependent variables in the model are

$y_1$ = presence of a gender economics course,

$y_2$ = presence of a women's studies program on the campus.

The independent variables in the model are

$z_1$ = constant term;

$z_2$ = academic reputation of the college, coded 1 (best), 2, ... to 141;

$z_3$ = size of the full-time economics faculty, a count;

$z_4$ = percentage of the economics faculty that are women, proportion (0 to 1);

$z_5$ = religious affiliation of the college, 0 = no, 1 = yes;

$z_6$ = percentage of the college faculty that are women, proportion (0 to 1);

$z_7$–$z_{10}$ = regional dummy variables, South, Midwest, Northeast, West.

The regressor vectors are

$$\mathbf{x}_1 = z_1, z_2, z_3, z_4, z_5, \quad \mathbf{x}_2 = z_2, z_6, z_5, z_7\text{–}z_{10}.$$

Burnett's model illustrates a number of interesting aspects of the bivariate probit model. Note that this model is qualitatively different from the bivariate probit model in (23-44); the second dependent variable, $y_2$, appears on the right-hand side of the first equation.[43] This model is a **recursive,** simultaneous-equations model. Surprisingly, the endogenous nature of one of the variables on the right-hand side of the first equation can be ignored in formulating the log-likelihood. [The model appears in Maddala (1983, p. 123).] We can establish this fact with the following (admittedly trivial) argument: The term that enters the log-likelihood is $P(y_1 = 1, y_2 = 1) = P(y_1 = 1 \mid y_2 = 1)P(y_2 = 1)$. Given the model as stated, the marginal probability for $y_2$ is just $\Phi(\mathbf{x}_2'\boldsymbol{\beta}_2)$, whereas the conditional probability is $\Phi_2(\ldots)/\Phi(\mathbf{x}_2'\boldsymbol{\beta}_2)$. The product returns the probability we had earlier. The other three terms in the log-likelihood are derived similarly, which produces (Maddala's results with some sign changes):

$$P_{11} = \Phi_2(\mathbf{x}_1'\boldsymbol{\beta}_1 + \gamma y_2, \mathbf{x}_2'\boldsymbol{\beta}_2, \rho), \qquad P_{10} = \Phi_2(\mathbf{x}_1'\boldsymbol{\beta}_1, -\mathbf{x}_2'\boldsymbol{\beta}_2, -\rho)$$

$$P_{01} = \Phi_2[-(\mathbf{x}_1'\boldsymbol{\beta}_1 + \gamma y_2), \boldsymbol{\beta}_2'\mathbf{x}_2, -\rho], \quad P_{00} = \Phi_2(-\mathbf{x}_1'\boldsymbol{\beta}_1, -\mathbf{x}_2'\boldsymbol{\beta}_2, \rho).$$

These terms are exactly those of (23-44) that we obtain just by carrying $y_2$ in the first equation with no special attention to its endogenous nature. We can ignore the simultaneity in this model and we cannot in the linear regression model because, in this instance, we are maximizing the log-likelihood, whereas in the linear regression case, we are manipulating certain sample moments that do not converge to the necessary population parameters in the presence of simultaneity.

---

[43]Eisenberg and Rowe (2006) is another application of this model. In their study, they analyzed the joint (recursive) effect of $y_2$ = veteran status on $y_1$, smoking behavior. The estimator they used was two-stage least squares and GMM. (The GMM estimator is the H2SLS estimator described in Section 15.6.4.)

The marginal effects in this model are fairly involved, and as before, we can consider several different types. Consider, for example, $z_2$, academic reputation. There is a direct effect produced by its presence in the first equation, but there is also an indirect effect. Academic reputation enters the women's studies equation and, therefore, influences the probability that $y_2$ equals one. Because $y_2$ appears in the first equation, this effect is transmitted back to $y_1$. The total effect of academic reputation and, likewise, religious affiliation is the sum of these two parts. Consider first the gender economics variable, $y_1$. The conditional mean is

$$E[y_1 \mid \mathbf{x}_1, \mathbf{x}_2] = \text{Prob}[y_2 = 1]E[y_1 \mid y_2 = 1, \mathbf{x}_1, \mathbf{x}_2] + \text{Prob}[y_2 = 0]E[y_1 \mid y_2 = 0, \mathbf{x}_1, \mathbf{x}_2]$$
$$= \Phi_2(\mathbf{x}_1'\boldsymbol{\beta}_1 + \gamma y_2, \mathbf{x}_2'\boldsymbol{\beta}_2, \rho) + \Phi_2(\mathbf{x}_1'\boldsymbol{\beta}_1, -\mathbf{x}_2'\boldsymbol{\beta}_2, -\rho).$$

Derivatives can be computed using our earlier results. We are also interested in the effect of religious affiliation. Because this variable is binary, simply differentiating the conditional mean function may not produce an accurate result. Instead, we would compute the conditional mean function with this variable set to one and then zero, and take the difference. Finally, what is the effect of the presence of a women's studies program on the probability that the college will offer a gender economics course? To compute this effect, we would compute $\text{Prob}[y_1 = 1 \mid y_2 = 1, \mathbf{x}_1, \mathbf{x}_2] - \text{Prob}[y_1 = 1 \mid y_2 = 0, \mathbf{x}_1, \mathbf{x}_2]$. In all cases, standard errors for the estimated marginal effects can be computed using the delta method.

Maximum likelihood estimates of the parameters of Burnett's model were computed by Greene (1998) using her sample of 132 liberal arts colleges; 31 of the schools offer gender economics, 58 have women's studies, and 29 have both. (See Appendix Table F23.1.) The estimated parameters are given in Table 23.13. Both bivariate probit

**TABLE 23.13** Estimates of a Recursive Simultaneous Bivariate Probit Model (estimated standard errors in parentheses)

| Variable | Single Equation | | Bivariate Probit | |
|---|---|---|---|---|
| | Coefficient | Standard Error | Coefficient | Standard Error |
| **Gender Economics Equation** | | | | |
| Constant | −1.4176 | (0.8768) | −1.1911 | (2.2155) |
| AcRep | −0.01143 | (0.003610) | −0.01233 | (0.007937) |
| WomStud | 1.1095 | (0.4699) | 0.8835 | (2.2603) |
| EconFac | 0.06730 | (0.05687) | 0.06769 | (0.06952) |
| PctWecon | 2.5391 | (0.8997) | 2.5636 | (1.0144) |
| Relig | −0.3482 | (0.4212) | −0.3741 | (0.5264) |
| **Women's Studies Equation** | | | | |
| AcRep | −0.01957 | (0.004117) | −0.01939 | (0.005704) |
| PctWfac | 1.9429 | (0.9001) | 1.8914 | (0.8714) |
| Relig | −0.4494 | (0.3072) | −0.4584 | (0.3403) |
| South | 1.3597 | (0.5948) | 1.3471 | (0.6897) |
| West | 2.3386 | (0.6449) | 2.3376 | (0.8611) |
| North | 1.8867 | (0.5927) | 1.9009 | (0.8495) |
| Midwest | 1.8248 | (0.6595) | 1.8070 | (0.8952) |
| $\rho$ | 0.0000 | (0.0000) | 0.1359 | (1.2539) |
| $\ln L$ | −85.6458 | | −85.6317 | |

and the single-equation estimates are given. The estimate of $\rho$ is only 0.1359, with a standard error of 1.2359. The Wald statistic for the test of the hypothesis that $\rho$ equals zero is $(0.1359 / 1.2539)^2 = 0.011753$. For a single restriction, the critical value from the chi-squared table is 3.84, so the hypothesis cannot be rejected. The likelihood ratio statistic for the same hypothesis is $2[-85.6317 - (-85.6458)] = 0.0282$, which leads to the same conclusion. The Lagrange multiplier statistic is 0.003807, which is consistent. This result might seem counterintuitive, given the setting. Surely "gender economics" and "women's studies" are highly correlated, but this finding does not contradict that proposition. The correlation coefficient measures the correlation between the disturbances in the equations, the omitted factors. That is, $\rho$ measures (roughly) the correlation between the outcomes after the influence of the included factors is accounted for. Thus, the value 0.1359 measures the effect after the influence of women's studies is already accounted for. As discussed in the next paragraph, the proposition turns out to be right. The single most important determinant (at least within this model) of whether a gender economics course will be offered is indeed whether the college offers a women's studies program.

Table 23.14 presents the estimates of the marginal effects and some descriptive statistics for the data. The calculations were simplified slightly by using the restricted model with $\rho = 0$. Computations of the marginal effects still require the preceding decomposition, but they are simplified by the result that if $\rho$ equals zero, then the bivariate probabilities factor into the products of the marginals. Numerically, the strongest effect appears to be exerted by the representation of women on the faculty; its coefficient of $+0.4491$ is by far the largest. This variable, however, cannot change by a full unit because it is a proportion. An increase of 1 percent in the presence of women on the faculty raises the probability by only $+0.004$, which is comparable in scale to the effect of academic reputation. The effect of women on the faculty is likewise fairly small, only 0.0013 per 1 percent change. As might have been expected, the single most important influence is the presence of a women's studies program, which increases the likelihood of a gender economics course by a full 0.1863. Of course, the raw data would have anticipated this result; of the 31 schools that offer a gender economics course, 29 also have a women's studies program and only two do not. Note finally that the effect of religious affiliation (whatever it is) is mostly direct.

**TABLE 23.14**    Marginal Effects in Gender Economics Model

| | Direct | Indirect | Total | (Std. Error) | (Type of Variable, Mean) | |
|---|---|---|---|---|---|---|
| **Gender Economics Equation** | | | | | | |
| AcRep | −0.002022 | −0.001453 | −0.003476 | (0.001126) | (Continuous, | 119.242) |
| PctWecon | +0.4491 | | +0.4491 | (0.1568) | (Continuous, | 0.24787) |
| EconFac | +0.01190 | | +0.1190 | (0.01292) | (Continuous, | 6.74242) |
| Relig | −0.06327 | −0.02306 | −0.08632 | (0.08220) | (Binary, | 0.57576) |
| WomStud | +0.1863 | | +0.1863 | (0.0868) | (Endogenous, | 0.43939) |
| PctWfac | | +0.14434 | +0.14434 | (0.09051) | (Continuous, | 0.35772) |
| **Women's Studies Equation** | | | | | | |
| AcRep | −0.00780 | | −0.00780 | (0.001654) | (Continuous, | 119.242) |
| PctWfac | +0.77489 | | +0.77489 | (0.3591) | (Continuous, | 0.35772) |
| Relig | −0.17777 | | −0.17777 | (0.11946) | (Binary, | 0.57576) |

**TABLE 23.15**   Binary Choice Fit Measures

| Measure | (1) | (2) | (3) | (4) | (5) | (6) | (7) |
|---|---|---|---|---|---|---|---|
| LRI | 0.573 | 0.535 | 0.495 | 0.407 | 0.279 | 0.206 | 0.000 |
| $R^2_{BL}$ | 0.844 | 0.844 | 0.823 | 0.797 | 0.754 | 0.718 | 0.641 |
| $\lambda$ | 0.565 | 0.560 | 0.526 | 0.444 | 0.319 | 0.216 | 0.000 |
| $R^2_{EF}$ | 0.561 | 0.558 | 0.530 | 0.475 | 0.343 | 0.216 | 0.000 |
| $R^2_{VZ}$ | 0.708 | 0.707 | 0.672 | 0.589 | 0.447 | 0.352 | 0.000 |
| $R^2_{MZ}$ | 0.687 | 0.679 | 0.628 | 0.567 | 0.545 | 0.329 | 0.000 |
| Predictions | $\begin{bmatrix} 92 & 9 \\ 5 & 26 \end{bmatrix}$ | $\begin{bmatrix} 93 & 8 \\ 5 & 26 \end{bmatrix}$ | $\begin{bmatrix} 92 & 9 \\ 8 & 23 \end{bmatrix}$ | $\begin{bmatrix} 94 & 7 \\ 8 & 23 \end{bmatrix}$ | $\begin{bmatrix} 98 & 3 \\ 16 & 15 \end{bmatrix}$ | $\begin{bmatrix} 101 & 0 \\ 31 & 0 \end{bmatrix}$ | $\begin{bmatrix} 101 & 0 \\ 31 & 0 \end{bmatrix}$ |

Before closing this application, we can use this opportunity to examine the fit measures listed in Section 23.4.5. We computed the various fit measures using seven different specifications of the gender economics equation:

1. Single-equation probit estimates, $z_1, z_2, z_3, z_4, z_5, y_2$
2. Bivariate probit model estimates, $z_1, z_2, z_3, z_4, z_5, y_2$
3. Single-equation probit estimates, $z_1, z_2, z_3, z_4, z_5$
4. Single-equation probit estimates, $z_1, \quad z_3, \quad z_5, y_2$
5. Single-equation probit estimates, $z_1, \quad z_3, \quad z_5$
6. Single-equation probit estimates, $z_1, \quad\quad z_5$
7. Single-equation probit estimates $z_1$ (constant only).

The specifications are in descending "quality" because we removed the most statistically significant variables from the model at each step. The values are listed in Table 23.15. The matrix below each column is the table of "hits" and "misses" of the prediction rule $\hat{y} = 1$ if $\hat{P} > 0.5$, 0 otherwise. [Note that by construction, model (7) must predict all ones or all zeros.] The column is the actual count and the row is the prediction. Thus, for model (1), 92 of 101 zeros were predicted correctly, whereas 5 of 31 ones were predicted incorrectly. As one would hope, the fit measures decline as the more significant variables are removed from the model. The Ben-Akiva measure has an obvious flaw in that with only a constant term, the model still obtains a "fit" of 0.641. From the prediction matrices, it is clear that the explanatory power of the model, such as it is, comes from its ability to predict the ones correctly. The poorer the model, the greater the number of correct predictions of $y = 0$. But as this number rises, the number of incorrect predictions rises and the number of correct predictions of $y = 1$ declines. All the fit measures appear to react to this feature to some degree. The Efron and Cramer measures, which are nearly identical, and McFadden's LRI appear to be most sensitive to this, with the remaining two only slightly less consistent.

## 23.9   A MULTIVARIATE PROBIT MODEL

In principle, a multivariate probit model would simply extend (23-44) to more than two outcome variables just by adding equations. The resulting equation system, again analogous to the seemingly unrelated regressions model, would be

$$y_m^* = \mathbf{x}_m' \boldsymbol{\beta}_m + \varepsilon_m, \ y_m = 1 \text{ if } y_m^* > 0, 0 \text{ otherwise}, m = 1, \ldots, M,$$
$$E[\varepsilon_m \mid \mathbf{x}_1, \ldots, \mathbf{x}_M] = 0,$$
$$\text{Var}[\varepsilon_m \mid \mathbf{x}_1, \ldots, \mathbf{x}_M] = 1,$$
$$\text{Cov}[\varepsilon_j, \varepsilon_m \mid \mathbf{x}_1, \ldots, \mathbf{x}_M] = \rho_{jm},$$
$$(\varepsilon_1, \ldots, \varepsilon_M) \sim N_M[\mathbf{0}, \mathbf{R}].$$

The joint probabilities of the observed events, $[y_{i1}, y_{i2} \ldots, y_{iM} \mid \mathbf{x}_{i1}, \mathbf{x}_{i2}, \ldots, \mathbf{x}_{iM}], i = 1, \ldots, n$ that from the basis for the log-likelihood function are the $M$-variate normal probabilities,

$$L_i = \Phi_M(q_{i1}\mathbf{x}_{i1}'\beta_1, \ldots, q_{iM}\mathbf{x}_{iM}'\beta_M, \mathbf{R}^*),$$

where

$$q_{im} = 2y_{im} - 1,$$
$$\mathbf{R}_{jm}^* = q_{ij}q_{im}\rho_{jm}.$$

The practical obstacle to this extension is the evaluation of the $M$-variate normal integrals and their derivatives. Some progress has been made on using quadrature for trivariate integration (see Section 16.9.6.b), but existing results are not sufficient to allow accurate and efficient evaluation for more than two variables in a sample of even moderate size. However, given the speed of modern computers, simulation-based integration using the GHK simulator or simulated likelihood methods (see Chapter 17) do allow for estimation of relatively large models. We consider an application in Example 23.16.[44]

The multivariate probit model in another form presents a useful extension of the random effects probit model for panel data (Section 23.5.1). If the parameter vectors in all equations are constrained to be equal, we obtain what Bertschek and Lechner (1998) call the "panel probit model,"

$$y_{it}^* = \mathbf{x}_{it}'\boldsymbol{\beta} + \varepsilon_{it}, \ y_{it} = 1 \text{ if } y_{it}^* > 0, 0 \text{ otherwise}, i = 1, \ldots, n, t = 1, \ldots, T,$$
$$(\varepsilon_{i1}, \ldots, \varepsilon_{iT}) \sim N[\mathbf{0}, \mathbf{R}].$$

The Butler and Moffitt (1982) approach for this model (see Section 23.5.1) has proved useful in many applications. But, their underlying assumption that $\text{Cov}[\varepsilon_{it}, \varepsilon_{is}] = \rho$ is a substantive restriction. By treating this structure as a multivariate probit model with the restriction that the coefficient vector be the same in every period, one can obtain a model with free correlations across periods.[45] Hyslop (1999), Bertschek and Lechner (1998), Greene (2004 and Example 23.16), and Cappellari and Jenkins (2006) are applications.

---

[44] Studies that propose improved methods of simulating probabilities include Pakes and Pollard (1989) and especially Börsch-Supan and Hajivassiliou (1990), Geweke (1989), and Keane (1994). A symposium in the November 1994 issue of *Review of Economics and Statistics* presents discussion of numerous issues in specification and estimation of models based on simulation of probabilities. Applications that employ simulation techniques for evaluation of multivariate normal integrals are now fairly numerous. See, for example, Hyslop (1999) (Example 23.7) which applies the technique to a panel data application with $T = 7$. Example 23.16 develops a five-variate application.

[45] By assuming the coefficient vectors are the same in all periods, we actually obviate the normalization that the diagonal elements of $\mathbf{R}$ are all equal to one as well. The restriction identifies $T - 1$ relative variances $\rho_{tt} = \sigma_T^2/\sigma_T^2$. This aspect is examined in Greene (2004).

### Example 23.16 A Multivariate Probit Model for Product Innovations

Bertschek and Lechner applied the panel probit model to an analysis of the product innovation activity of 1,270 German firms observed in five years, 1984–1988, in response to imports and foreign direct investment. [See Bertschek (1995).] The probit model to be estimated is based on the latent regression

$$y_{it}^* = \beta_1 + \sum_{k=2}^{8} x_{k,it}\beta_k + \varepsilon_{it}, \ y_{it} = 1(y_{it}^* > 0), i = 1, \ldots, 1,270, t = 1984, \ldots, 1988,$$

where

$y_{it}$ = 1 if a product innovation was realized by firm $i$ in year $t$, 0 otherwise,

$x_{2,it}$ = Log of industry sales in DM,

$x_{3,it}$ = Import share = ratio of industry imports to (industry sales plus imports),

$x_{4,it}$ = Relative firm size = ratio of employment in business unit to employment in the industry (times 30),

$x_{5,it}$ = FDI share = Ratio of industry foreign direct investment to (industry sales plus imports),

$x_{6,it}$ = Productivity = Ratio of industry value added to industry employment,

$x_{7,it}$ = Raw materials sector = 1 if the firm is in this sector,

$x_{8,it}$ = Investment goods sector = 1 if the firm is in this sector.

The coefficients on import share ($\beta_3$) and FDI share ($\beta_5$) were of particular interest. The objectives of the study were the empirical investigation of innovation and the methodological development of an estimator that could obviate computing the five-variate normal probabilities necessary for a full maximum likelihood estimation of the model.

Table 23.16 presents the single-equation, pooled probit model estimates.[46] Given the structure of the model, the parameter vector could be estimated consistently with any single

**TABLE 23.16**   Estimated Pooled Probit Model

| Variable | Estimate[a] | Estimated Standard Errors | | | | Marginal Effects | | |
|---|---|---|---|---|---|---|---|---|
| | | SE(1)[b] | SE(2)[c] | SE(3)[d] | SE(4)[e] | Partial | Std. Err. | t ratio |
| Constant | −1.960 | 0.239 | 0.377 | 0.230 | 0.373 | — | — | — |
| log Sales | 0.177 | 0.0250 | 0.0375 | 0.0222 | 0.0358 | 0.0683[f] | 0.0138 | 4.96 |
| Rel Size | 1.072 | 0.206 | 0.306 | 0.142 | 0.269 | 0.413[f] | 0.103 | 4.01 |
| Imports | 1.134 | 0.153 | 0.246 | 0.151 | 0.243 | 0.437[f] | 0.0938 | 4.66 |
| FDI | 2.853 | 0.467 | 0.679 | 0.402 | 0.642 | 1.099[f] | 0.247 | 4.44 |
| Prod. | −2.341 | 1.114 | 1.300 | 0.715 | 1.115 | −0.902[f] | 0.429 | −2.10 |
| Raw Mtl | −0.279 | 0.0966 | 0.133 | 0.0807 | 0.126 | −0.110[g] | 0.0503 | −2.18 |
| Inv Good | 0.188 | 0.0404 | 0.0630 | 0.0392 | 0.0628 | 0.0723[g] | 0.0241 | 3.00 |

[a]Recomputed. Only two digits were reported in the earlier paper.
[b]Obtained from results in Bertschek and Lechner, Table 9.
[c]Based on the Avery et al. (1983) GMM estimator.
[d]Square roots of the diagonals of the negative inverse of the Hessian
[e]Based on the cluster estimator.
[f]Coefficient scaled by the density evaluated at the sample means
[g]Computed as the difference in the fitted probability with the dummy variable equal to one, then zero.

---

[46]We are grateful to the authors of this study who have generously loaned us their data for our continued analysis. The data are proprietary and cannot be made publicly available, unlike the other data sets used in our examples.

period's data, Hence, pooling the observations, which produces a mixture of the estimators, will also be consistent. Given the panel data nature of the data set, however, the conventional standard errors from the pooled estimator are dubious. Because the marginal distribution will produce a consistent estimator of the parameter vector, this is a case in which the cluster estimator (see Section 16.8.4) provides an appropriate asymptotic covariance matrix. Note that the standard errors in column SE(4) of the table are considerably higher than the uncorrected ones in columns 1–3.

The pooled estimator is consistent, so the further development of the estimator is a matter of (1) obtaining a more efficient estimator of $\beta$ and (2) computing estimates of the cross-period correlation coefficients. The authors proposed a set of GMM estimators based on the orthogonality conditions implied by the single-equation conditional mean functions:

$$E\{[y_{it} - \Phi(\mathbf{x}'_{it}\beta)] \mid \mathbf{X}_i\} = 0.$$

The orthogonality conditions are

$$E\left[ \mathbf{A}(\mathbf{X}_i) \begin{pmatrix} [y_{i1} - \Phi(\mathbf{x}'_{i1}\beta)] \\ [y_{i2} - \Phi(\mathbf{x}'_{i2}\beta)] \\ \vdots \\ [y_{iT} - \Phi(\mathbf{x}'_{iT}\beta)] \end{pmatrix} \right] = \mathbf{0},$$

where $\mathbf{A}(\mathbf{X}_1)$ is a $P \times T$ matrix of instrumental variables constructed from the exogenous data for individual $i$.

Using only the raw data as $\mathbf{A}(\mathbf{X}_i)$, strong exogeneity of the regressors in every period would provide $TK$ moment equations of the form $E[\mathbf{x}_{it}(y_{is} - \Phi(\mathbf{x}'_{is}\beta))] = \mathbf{0}$ for each pair of periods, or a total of $T^2K$ moment equations altogether for estimation of $K$ parameters in $\beta$. [See Wooldridge (1995).] The full set of such orthogonality conditions would be $E[(\mathbf{I}_T \otimes \mathbf{x}_i)\mathbf{u}_i] = \mathbf{0}$, where $\mathbf{x}_i = [\mathbf{x}'_{i1}, \ldots, \mathbf{x}'_{iT}]'$, $\mathbf{u}_i = (u_{i1}, \ldots, u_{iT})'$ and $u_{it} = y_{it} - \Phi(\mathbf{x}'_{it}\beta)$. This produces 200 orthogonality conditions for the estimation of the 8 parameters. The empirical counterpart to the left-hand side of (6) is

$$\mathbf{g}_N(\beta) = \frac{1}{N} \sum_{i=1}^{N} \left[ \mathbf{A}(\mathbf{X}_i) \begin{pmatrix} [y_{i1} - \Phi(\mathbf{x}'_{i1}\beta)] \\ [y_{i2} - \Phi(\mathbf{x}'_{i2}\beta)] \\ \vdots \\ [y_{iT} - \Phi(\mathbf{x}'_{iT}\beta)] \end{pmatrix} \right].$$

The various GMM estimators are the solutions to

$$\beta_{GMM,A,W} = \arg \min_{\beta}[\mathbf{g}_N(\beta)]'\mathbf{W}[\mathbf{g}_N(\beta)].$$

The specific estimator is defined by the choice of instrument matrix $\mathbf{A}(\mathbf{X}_i)$ and weighting matrix, $\mathbf{W}$; the authors suggest several. In their application (see p. 337), only data from period $t$ are used in the $t$th moment condition. This reduces the number of moment conditions from 200 to 40.

As noted, the FIML estimates of the model can be computed using the GHK simulator.[47] The FIML estimates, Bertschek and Lechner's GMM estimates, and the random effects model using the Butler and Moffit (1982) quadrature method are reported in Table 23.17: The FIML and GMM estimates are strikingly similar. This would be expected because both are consistent estimators and the sample is fairly large. The correlations reported are based on the FIML estimates. [They are not estimated with the GMM estimator. As the authors note, an inefficient estimator of the correlation matrix is available by fitting pairs of equations (years)

---

[47]The full computation required about one hour of computing time. Computation of the single-equation (pooled) estimators required only about 1/100 of the time reported by the authors for the same models, which suggests that the evolution of computing technology may play a significant role in advancing the FIML estimators.

**TABLE 23.17** Estimated Constrained Multivariate Probit Model (estimated standard errors in parentheses)

| Coefficients | Full Maximum Likelihood Using GHK Simulator | | BL GMM[a] | | Random Effects $\rho = 0.578$ (0.0189) | |
|---|---|---|---|---|---|---|
| Constant | −1.797** | (0.341) | −1.74** | (0.37) | −2.839 | (0.533) |
| log Sales | 0.154** | (0.0334) | 0.15** | (0.034) | 0.244 | (0.0522) |
| Relative size | 0.953** | (0.160) | 0.95** | (0.20) | 1.522 | (0.257) |
| Imports | 1.155** | (0.228) | 1.14** | (0.24) | 1.779 | (0.360) |
| FDI | 2.426** | (0.573) | 2.59** | (0.59) | 3.652 | (0.870) |
| Productivity | −1.578 | (1.216) | −1.91* | (0.82) | −2.307 | (1.911) |
| Raw material | −0.292** | (0.130) | −0.28* | (0.12) | −0.477 | (0.202) |
| Investment goods | 0.224** | (0.0605) | 0.21** | (0.063) | 0.578 | (0.0189) |
| log-likelihood | −3522.85 | | | | −3535.55 | |

**Estimated Correlations**

| | | |
|---|---|---|
| 1984, 1985 | 0.460** | (0.0301) |
| 1984, 1986 | 0.599** | (0.0323) |
| 1985, 1986 | 0.643** | (0.0308) |
| 1984, 1987 | 0.540** | (0.0308) |
| 1985, 1987 | 0.546** | (0.0348) |
| 1986, 1987 | 0.610** | (0.0322) |
| 1984, 1988 | 0.483** | (0.0364) |
| 1985, 1988 | 0.446** | (0.0380) |
| 1986, 1988 | 0.524** | (0.0355) |
| 1987, 1988 | 0.605** | (0.0325) |

**Estimated Correlation Matrix**

| | 1984 | 1985 | 1986 | 1987 | 1988 |
|---|---|---|---|---|---|
| **1984** | 1.000 | (0.658) | (0.599) | (0.540) | (0.483) |
| **1985** | 0.460 | 1.000 | (0.644) | (0.558) | (0.441) |
| **1986** | 0.599 | 0.643 | 1.000 | (0.602) | (0.537) |
| **1987** | 0.540 | 0.546 | 0.610 | 1.000 | (0.621) |
| **1988** | 0.483 | 0.446 | 0.524 | 0.605 | 1.000 |

[a]Estimates are BL's WNP-joint uniform estimates with $k = 880$. Estimates are from their Table 9, standard errors from their Table 10.
*Indicates significant at 95 percent level, ** indicates significant at 99 percent level based on a two-tailed test.

**TABLE 23.18** Unrestricted Five-Period Multivariate Probit Model (estimated standard errors in parentheses)

| Coefficients | 1984 | 1985 | 1986 | 1987 | 1988 | Constrained |
|---|---|---|---|---|---|---|
| Constant | −1.802** | −2.080** | −2.630** | −1.721** | −1.729** | −1.797** |
| | (0.532) | (0.519) | (0.542) | (0.534) | (0.523) | (0.341) |
| log Sales | 0.167** | 0.178** | 0.274** | 0.163** | 0.130** | 0.154** |
| | (0.0538) | (0.0565) | (0.0584) | (0.0560) | (0.0519) | (0.0334) |
| Relative size | 0.658** | 1.280** | 1.739** | 1.085** | 0.826** | 0.953** |
| | (0.323) | (0.330) | (0.431) | (0.351) | (0.263) | (0.160) |
| Imports | 1.118** | 0.923** | 0.936** | 1.091** | 1.301** | 1.155** |
| | (0.377) | (0.361) | (0.370) | (0.338) | (0.342) | (0.228) |
| FDI | 2.070** | 1.509* | 3.759** | 3.718** | 3.834** | 2.426** |
| | (0.835) | (0.769) | (0.990) | (1.214) | (1.106) | (0.573) |
| Productivity | −2.615 | −0.252 | −5.565 | −3.905 | −0.981 | −1.578 |
| | (4.110) | (3.802) | (3.537) | (3.188) | (2.057) | (1.216) |
| Raw material | −0.346 | −0.357 | −0.260 | 0.0261 | −0.294 | −0.292 |
| | (0.283) | (0.247) | (0.299) | (0.288) | (0.218) | (0.130) |
| Investment goods | 0.239** | 0.177* | 0.0467 | 0.218* | 0.280** | 0.224** |
| | (0.0864) | (0.0875) | (0.0891) | (0.0955) | (0.0923) | (0.0605) |

as bivariate probit models.] Also noteworthy in Table 23.17 is the divergence of the random effects estimates from the other two sets. The log-likelihood function is −3535.55 for the random effects model and −3522.85 for the unrestricted model. The chi-squared statistic for the 9 restrictions of the equicorrelation model is 25.4. The critical value from the chi-squared table for 9 degrees of freedom is 16.9 for 95 percent and 21.7 for 99 percent significance, so the hypothesis of the random effects model would be rejected.

Table 23.18 reports the coefficients of a fully unrestricted model that allows the coefficients to vary across the periods. (The correlations in parentheses in Table 23.17 are computed using this model.) There is a surprising amount of variation in the parameter vector. The log-likelihood for the full unrestricted model is −3494.57. The chi-squared statistic for testing the 32 restrictions of the homogeneity hypothesis is twice the difference, or 56.56. The critical value from the chi-squared table with 32 degrees of freedom is 46.19, so the hypothesis of homogeneity would be rejected statistically. It does seem questionable whether, in theoretical terms, the relationship estimated in this application should be this volatile, however.

# 23.10 ANALYSIS OF ORDERED CHOICES

Some multinomial-choice variables are inherently ordered. Examples that have appeared in the literature include the following:

1. Bond ratings
2. Results of taste tests
3. Opinion surveys
4. The assignment of military personnel to job classifications by skill level
5. Voting outcomes on certain programs
6. The level of insurance coverage taken by a consumer: none, part, or full
7. Employment: unemployed, part time, or full time

In each of these cases, although the outcome is discrete, the multinomial logit or probit model would fail to account for the ordinal nature of the dependent variable.[48] Ordinary regression analysis would err in the opposite direction, however. Take the outcome of an opinion survey. If the responses are coded 0, 1, 2, 3, or 4, then linear regression would treat the difference between a 4 and a 3 the same as that between a 3 and a 2, whereas in fact they are only a ranking.

### 23.10.1 THE ORDERED PROBIT MODEL

The ordered probit and logit models have come into fairly wide use as a framework for analyzing such responses [Zavoina and McElvey (1975)]. The model is built around a latent regression in the same manner as the binomial probit model. We begin with

$$y^* = \mathbf{x}'\boldsymbol{\beta} + \varepsilon.$$

---

[48] In two papers, Beggs, Cardell, and Hausman (1981) and Hausman and Ruud (1986), the authors analyze a richer specification of the logit model when respondents provide their rankings of the full set of alternatives in addition to the identity of the most preferred choice. This application falls somewhere between the conditional logit model and the ones we shall discuss here in that, rather than provide a single choice among $J$ either unordered or ordered alternatives, the consumer chooses one of the $J!$ possible orderings of the set of unordered alternatives.

As usual, $y^*$ is unobserved. What we do observe is

$$
\begin{aligned}
y &= 0 && \text{if } y^* \leq 0 \\
&= 1 && \text{if } 0 < y^* \leq \mu_1 \\
&= 2 && \text{if } \mu_1 < y^* \leq \mu_2 \\
&\;\;\vdots \\
&= J && \text{if } \mu_{J-1} \leq y^*,
\end{aligned}
$$

which is a form of censoring. The $\mu$'s are unknown parameters to be estimated with $\boldsymbol{\beta}$. Consider, for example, an opinion survey. The respondents have their own intensity of feelings, which depends on certain measurable factors $\mathbf{x}$ and certain unobservable factors $\varepsilon$. In principle, they could respond to the questionnaire with their own $y^*$ if asked to do so. Given only, say, five possible answers, they choose the cell that most closely represents their own feelings on the question.

As before, we assume that $\varepsilon$ is normally distributed across observations.[49] For the same reasons as in the binomial probit model (which is the special case of $J = 1$), we normalize the mean and variance of $\varepsilon$ to zero and one. We then have the following probabilities:

$$
\text{Prob}(y = 0 \,|\, \mathbf{x}) = \Phi(-\mathbf{x}'\boldsymbol{\beta}),
$$
$$
\text{Prob}(y = 1 \,|\, \mathbf{x}) = \Phi(\mu_1 - \mathbf{x}'\boldsymbol{\beta}) - \Phi(-\mathbf{x}'\boldsymbol{\beta}),
$$
$$
\text{Prob}(y = 2 \,|\, \mathbf{x}) = \Phi(\mu_2 - \mathbf{x}'\boldsymbol{\beta}) - \Phi(\mu_1 - \mathbf{x}'\boldsymbol{\beta}),
$$
$$
\vdots
$$
$$
\text{Prob}(y = J \,|\, \mathbf{x}) = 1 - \Phi(\mu_{J-1} - \mathbf{x}'\boldsymbol{\beta}).
$$

For all the probabilities to be positive, we must have

$$
0 < \mu_1 < \mu_2 < \cdots < \mu_{J-1}.
$$

Figure 23.4 shows the implications of the structure. This is an extension of the univariate probit model we examined earlier. The log-likelihood function and its derivatives can be obtained readily, and optimization can be done by the usual means.

As usual, the marginal effects of the regressors $\mathbf{x}$ on the probabilities are not equal to the coefficients. It is helpful to consider a simple example. Suppose there are three categories. The model thus has only one unknown threshold parameter. The three probabilities are

$$
\text{Prob}(y = 0 \,|\, \mathbf{x}) = 1 - \Phi(\mathbf{x}'\boldsymbol{\beta}),
$$
$$
\text{Prob}(y = 1 \,|\, \mathbf{x}) = \Phi(\mu - \mathbf{x}'\boldsymbol{\beta}) - \Phi(-\mathbf{x}'\boldsymbol{\beta}),
$$
$$
\text{Prob}(y = 2 \,|\, \mathbf{x}) = 1 - \Phi(\mu - \mathbf{x}'\boldsymbol{\beta}).
$$

---

[49] Other distributions, particularly the logistic, could be used just as easily. We assume the normal purely for convenience. The logistic and normal distributions generally give similar results in practice.

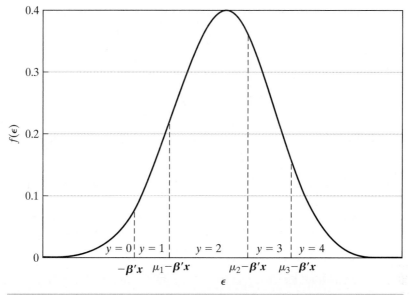

**FIGURE 23.4** Probabilities in the Ordered Probit Model.

For the three probabilities, the marginal effects of changes in the regressors are

$$\frac{\partial \text{Prob}(y = 0 \mid \mathbf{x})}{\partial \mathbf{x}} = -\phi(\mathbf{x}'\boldsymbol{\beta})\boldsymbol{\beta},$$

$$\frac{\partial \text{Prob}(y = 1 \mid \mathbf{x})}{\partial \mathbf{x}} = [\phi(-\mathbf{x}'\boldsymbol{\beta}) - \phi(\mu - \mathbf{x}'\boldsymbol{\beta})]\boldsymbol{\beta},$$

$$\frac{\partial \text{Prob}(y = 2 \mid \mathbf{x})}{\partial \mathbf{x}} = \phi(\mu - \mathbf{x}'\boldsymbol{\beta})\boldsymbol{\beta}.$$

Figure 23.5 illustrates the effect. The probability distributions of $y$ and $y^*$ are shown in the solid curve. Increasing one of the $x$'s while holding $\boldsymbol{\beta}$ and $\mu$ constant is equivalent to shifting the distribution slightly to the right, which is shown as the dashed curve. The effect of the shift is unambiguously to shift some mass out of the leftmost cell. Assuming that $\boldsymbol{\beta}$ is positive (for this $x$), $\text{Prob}(y = 0 \mid \mathbf{x})$ must decline. Alternatively, from the previous expression, it is obvious that the derivative of $\text{Prob}(y = 0 \mid \mathbf{x})$ has the opposite sign from $\boldsymbol{\beta}$. By a similar logic, the change in $\text{Prob}(y = 2 \mid \mathbf{x})$ [or $\text{Prob}(y = J \mid \mathbf{x})$ in the general case] must have the same sign as $\boldsymbol{\beta}$. Assuming that the particular $\boldsymbol{\beta}$ is positive, we are shifting some probability into the rightmost cell. But what happens to the middle cell is ambiguous. It depends on the two densities. In the general case, relative to the signs of the coefficients, only the signs of the changes in $\text{Prob}(y = 0 \mid \mathbf{x})$ and $\text{Prob}(y = J \mid \mathbf{x})$ are unambiguous! The upshot is that we must be very careful in interpreting the coefficients in this model. Indeed, without a fair amount of extra calculation, it is quite unclear how the coefficients in the ordered probit model should be interpreted.[50]

---

[50]This point seems uniformly to be overlooked in the received literature. Authors often report coefficients and $t$ ratios, occasionally with some commentary about significant effects, but rarely suggest upon what or in what direction those effects are exerted.

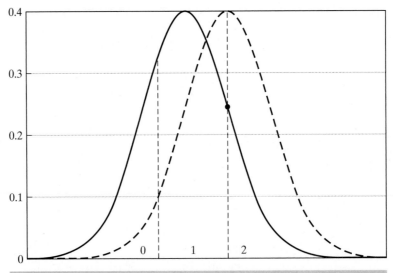

**FIGURE 23.5**  Effects of Change in *x* on Predicted Probabilities.

### Example 23.17  Rating Assignments

Marcus and Greene (1985) estimated an ordered probit model for the job assignments of new Navy recruits. The Navy attempts to direct recruits into job classifications in which they will be most productive. The broad classifications the authors analyzed were technical jobs with three clearly ranked skill ratings: "medium skilled," "highly skilled," and "nuclear qualified/highly skilled." Because the assignment is partly based on the Navy's own assessment and needs and partly on factors specific to the individual, an ordered probit model was used with the following determinants: (1) ENSPE = a dummy variable indicating that the individual entered the Navy with an "A school" (technical training) guarantee, (2) EDMA = educational level of the entrant's mother, (3) AFQT = score on the Armed Forces Qualifying Test, (4) EDYRS = years of education completed by the trainee, (5) MARR = a dummy variable indicating that the individual was married at the time of enlistment, and (6) AGEAT = trainee's age at the time of enlistment. (The data used in this study are not available for distribution.) The sample size was 5,641. The results are reported in Table 23.19. The extremely large *t* ratio on the AFQT score is to be expected, as it is a primary sorting device used to assign job classifications.

**TABLE 23.19**  Estimated Rating Assignment Equation

| Variable | Estimate | t Ratio | Mean of Variable |
|----------|----------|---------|------------------|
| Constant | −4.34 | — | — |
| ENSPA | 0.057 | 1.7 | 0.66 |
| EDMA | 0.007 | 0.8 | 12.1 |
| AFQT | 0.039 | 39.9 | 71.2 |
| EDYRS | 0.190 | 8.7 | 12.1 |
| MARR | −0.48 | −9.0 | 0.08 |
| AGEAT | 0.0015 | 0.1 | 18.8 |
| $\mu$ | 1.79 | 80.8 | — |

**TABLE 23.20**   Marginal Effect of a Binary Variable

|  | $-\hat{\beta}'\mathbf{x}$ | $\hat{\mu} - \hat{\beta}'\mathbf{x}$ | *Prob*[y = 0] | *Prob*[y = 1] | *Prob*[y = 2] |
|---|---|---|---|---|---|
| MARR = 0 | −0.8863 | 0.9037 | 0.187 | 0.629 | 0.184 |
| MARR = 1 | −0.4063 | 1.3837 | 0.342 | 0.574 | 0.084 |
| Change |  |  | 0.155 | −0.055 | −0.100 |

To obtain the marginal effects of the continuous variables, we require the standard normal density evaluated at $-\bar{\mathbf{x}}'\hat{\beta} = -0.8479$ and $\hat{\mu} - \bar{\mathbf{x}}'\hat{\beta} = 0.9421$. The predicted probabilities are $\Phi(-0.8479) = 0.198$, $\Phi(0.9421) - \Phi(-0.8479) = 0.628$, and $1 - \Phi(0.9421) = 0.174$. (The actual frequencies were 0.25, 0.52, and 0.23.) The two densities are $\phi(-0.8479) = 0.278$ and $\phi(0.9421) = 0.255$. Therefore, the derivatives of the three probabilities with respect to AFQT, for example, are

$$\frac{\partial P_0}{\partial \text{AFQT}} = (-0.278)0.039 = -0.01084,$$

$$\frac{\partial P_1}{\partial \text{AFQT}} = (0.278 - 0.255)0.039 = 0.0009,$$

$$\frac{\partial P_2}{\partial \text{AFQT}} = 0.255(0.039) = 0.00995.$$

Note that the marginal effects sum to zero, which follows from the requirement that the probabilities add to one. This approach is not appropriate for evaluating the effect of a dummy variable. We can analyze a dummy variable by comparing the probabilities that result when the variable takes its two different values with those that occur with the other variables held at their sample means. For example, for the MARR variable, we have the results given in Table 23.20.

## 23.10.2   BIVARIATE ORDERED PROBIT MODELS

There are several extensions of the ordered probit model that follow the logic of the bivariate probit model we examined in Section 23.8. A direct analog to the base case two-equation model is used in the study in Example 23.18.

### Example 23.18   Calculus and Intermediate Economics Courses
Butler et al. (1994) analyzed the relationship between the level of calculus attained and grades in intermediate economics courses for a sample of Vanderbilt students. The two-step estimation approach involved the following strategy. (We are stylizing the precise formulation a bit to compress the description.) Step 1 involved a direct application of the ordered probit model of Section 23.10.1 to the level of calculus achievement, which is coded 0, 1, . . . , 6:

$$m_i^* = \mathbf{x}_i'\beta + \varepsilon_i, \; \varepsilon_i \mid \mathbf{x}_i \sim N[0, 1],$$
$$m_i = 0 \text{ if } -\infty < m_i^* \leq 0$$
$$= 1 \text{ if } 0 < m_i^* \leq \mu_1$$
$$\cdots$$
$$= 6 \text{ if } \mu_5 < m_i^* < +\infty.$$

The authors argued that although the various calculus courses can be ordered discretely by the material covered, the differences between the levels cannot be measured directly. Thus, this is an application of the ordered probit model. The independent variables in this first step model included SAT scores, foreign language proficiency, indicators of intended major, and several other variables related to areas of study.

The second step of the estimator involves regression analysis of the grade in the intermediate microeconomics or macroeconomics course. Grades in these courses were translated to a granular continuous scale (A = 4.0, A- = 3.7, etc.). A linear regression is specified,

$$Grade_i = \mathbf{z}_i'\delta + u_i, \quad \text{where} \quad u_i \mid \mathbf{z}_i \sim N\left[0, \sigma_u^2\right].$$

Independent variables in this regression include, among others, (1) dummy variables for which outcome in the ordered probit model applies to the student (with the zero reference case omitted), (2) grade in the last calculus course, (3) several other variables related to prior courses, (4) class size, (5) freshman GPA, etc. The unobservables in the *Grade* equation and the math attainment are clearly correlated, a feature captured by the additional assumption that $(\varepsilon_i, u_i \mid \mathbf{x}_i, \mathbf{z}_i) \sim N_2[(0, 0), (1, \sigma_u^2), \rho\sigma_u]$. A nonzero $\rho$ captures this "selection" effect. With this in place, the dummy variables in (1) have now become endogenous. The solution is a "selection" correction that we will examine in detail in Chapter 24. The modified equation becomes

$$Grade_i \mid m_i = \mathbf{z}_i'\delta + E[u_i \mid m_i] + v_i$$
$$= \mathbf{z}_i'\delta + (\rho\sigma_u)[\lambda(\mathbf{x}_i'\boldsymbol{\beta}, \mu_1, \ldots, \mu_5)] + v_i.$$

They thus adopt a "control function" approach to accommodate the endogeneity of the math attainment dummy variables. [See Section 23.7 and (23-43) for another application of this method.] The term $\lambda(\mathbf{x}_i'\boldsymbol{\beta}, \mu_1, \ldots, \mu_5)$ is a generalized residual that is constructed using the estimates from the first-stage ordered probit model. [A precise statement of the form of this variable is given in Li and Tobias (2006).] Linear regression of the course grade on $\mathbf{z}_i$ and this constructed regressor is computed at the second step. The standard errors at the second step must be corrected for the use of the estimated regressor using what amounts to a Murphy and Topel (2002) correction. (See Section 16.7.)

Li and Tobias (2006) in a replication of and comment on Butler et al. (1994), after roughly replicating the classical estimation results with a Bayesian estimator, observe that the *Grade* equation above could also be treated as an ordered probit model. The resulting **bivariate ordered probit** model would be

$$m_i^* = \mathbf{x}_i'\boldsymbol{\beta} + \varepsilon_i, \qquad \text{and} \qquad g_i^* = \mathbf{z}_i'\delta + u_i,$$
$$m_i = 0 \text{ if } -\infty < m_i^* \leq 0 \qquad\qquad g_i = 0 \text{ if } -\infty < g_i^* \leq 0$$
$$= 1 \text{ if } 0 < m_i^* \leq \mu_1 \qquad\qquad = 1 \text{ if } 0 < g_i^* \leq \alpha_1$$
$$\cdots \qquad\qquad\qquad\qquad \cdots$$
$$= 6 \text{ if } \mu_5 < m_i^* < +\infty. \qquad\qquad = 11 \text{ if } \mu_9 < g_i^* < +\infty$$

where

$$(\varepsilon_i, u_i \mid \mathbf{x}_i, \mathbf{z}_i) \sim N_2\left[(0, 0), \left(1, \sigma_u^2\right), \rho\sigma_u\right].$$

Li and Tobias extended their analysis to this case simply by "transforming" the dependent variable in Butler et al.'s second equation. Computing the log-likelihood using sets of bivariate normal probabilities is fairly straightforward for the bivariate ordered probit model. [See Greene (2007).] However, the classical study of these data using the bivariate ordered approach remains to be done, so a side-by-side comparison to Li and Tobias's Bayesian alternative estimator is not possible. The endogeneity of the calculus dummy variables in (1) remains a feature of the model, so both the MLE and the Bayesian posterior are less straightforward than they might appears. Whether the results in Section 23.8.4 on the recursive bivariate probit model extend to this case also remains to be determined.

The bivariate ordered probit model has been applied in a number of settings in the recent empirical literature, including husband and wife's education levels [Magee et al. (2000)], family size [(Calhoun (1991)], and many others. In two early contributions to the field of pet econometrics, Butler and Chatterjee analyze ownership of cats and dogs (1995) and dogs and televisions (1997).

### 23.10.3 PANEL DATA APPLICATIONS

The ordered probit model is used to model discrete scales that represent indicators of a continuous underlying variable such as strength of preference, performance, or level of attainment. Many of the recently assembled national panel data sets contain survey questions that ask about subjective assessments of health, satisfaction, or well-being, all of which are applications of this interpretation. Examples include:

- The European Community Household Panel (ECHP) includes questions about job satisfaction [see D'Addio (2004)].
- The British Household Panel Survey (BHPS) includes questions about health status [see Contoyannis et al. (2004)].
- The German Socioeconomic Household Panel (GSOEP) includes questions about subjective well being [see Winkelmann (2004)] and subjective assessment of health satisfaction [see Riphahn et al. (2003) and Example 23.19.]

Ostensibly, the applications would fit well into the ordered probit frameworks already described. However, given the panel nature of the data, it will be desirable to augment the model with some accommodation of the individual heterogeneity that is likely to be present. The two standard models, fixed and random effects, have both been applied to the analyses of these survey data.

### 23.10.3.a Ordered Probit Models with Fixed Effects

D'Addio et al. (2003), using methodology developed by Frijters et al. (2004) and Ferrer-i-Carbonel et al. (2004), analyzed survey data on job satisfaction using the Danish component of the European Community Household Panel. Their estimator for an ordered logit model is built around the logic of Chamberlain's estimator for the binary logit model. [See Section 23.5.2.] Because the approach is robust to individual specific threshold parameters and allows time-invariant variables, it differs sharply from the fixed effects models we have considered thus far as well as from the ordered probit model of Section 23.10.1.[51] Unlike Chamberlain's estimator for the binary logit model, however, their conditional estimator is not a function of minimal sufficient statistics. As such, the incidental parameters problem remains an issue.

Das and van Soest (2000) proposed a somewhat simpler approach. [See, as well, Long's (1997) discussion of the "parallel regressions assumption," which employs this device in a cross-section framework]. Consider the base case ordered logit model with fixed effects,

$$y_{it}^* = \alpha_i + \mathbf{x}_{it}'\boldsymbol{\beta} + \varepsilon_{it}, \, \varepsilon_{it} \mid \mathbf{X}_i \sim N[0, 1],$$

$$y_{it} = j \quad \text{if} \quad \mu_{j-1} < y_{it}^* < \mu_j, \, j = 0, 1, \ldots, J \quad \text{and} \quad \mu_{-1} = -\infty, \mu_0 = 0, \mu_J = +\infty.$$

The model assumptions imply that

$$\text{Prob}(y_{it} = j \mid \mathbf{X}_i) = \Lambda(\mu_j - \alpha_i - \mathbf{x}_{it}'\boldsymbol{\beta}) - \Lambda(\mu_{j-1} - \alpha_i - \mathbf{x}_{it}'\boldsymbol{\beta}),$$

where $\Lambda(t)$ is the cdf of the logistic distribution. Now, define a binary variable

$$w_{it,j} = 1 \text{ if } y_{it} > j, \quad j = 0, \ldots, J - 1.$$

---

[51] Cross-section versions of the ordered probit model with individual specific thresholds appear in Terza (1985a), Pudney and Shields (2000), and Greene (2007).

It follows that

$$\text{Prob}[w_{it,j} = 1 \mid \mathbf{X}_i] = \Lambda(\alpha_i - \mu_j + \mathbf{x}'_{it}\boldsymbol{\beta})$$
$$= \Lambda(\theta_i + x'_{it}\boldsymbol{\beta}).$$

The "$j$" specific constant, which is the same for all individuals, is absorbed in $\theta_i$. Thus, a fixed effects binary logit model applies to each of the $J - 1$ binary random variables, $w_{it,j}$. The method in Section 23.5.2 can now be applied to each of the $J - 1$ random samples. This provides $J - 1$ estimators of the parameter vector $\boldsymbol{\beta}$ (but no estimator of the threshold parameters). The authors propose to reconcile these different estimators by using a minimum distance estimator of the common true $\boldsymbol{\beta}$. (See Section 15.3.) The minimum distance estimator at the second step is chosen to minimize

$$q = \sum_{j=0}^{J-1} \sum_{m=0}^{J-1} (\hat{\boldsymbol{\beta}}_j - \boldsymbol{\beta})' [\mathbf{V}_{jm}^{-1}] (\hat{\boldsymbol{\beta}}_m - \boldsymbol{\beta}),$$

where $[\mathbf{V}_{jm}^{-1}]$ is the $j, m$ block of the inverse of the $(J - 1)K \times (J - 1)K$ partitioned matrix $\mathbf{V}$ that contains Asy. Cov$[\hat{\boldsymbol{\beta}}_j, \hat{\boldsymbol{\beta}}_m]$. The appropriate form of this matrix for a set of cross-section estimators is given in Brant (1990). Das and van Soest (2000) used the counterpart for Chamberlain's fixed effects estimator but do not provide the specifics for computing the off-diagonal blocks in $\mathbf{V}$.

The full ordered probit model with fixed effects, including the individual specific constants, can be estimated by unconditional maximum likelihood using the results in Section 16.9.6.c. The likelihood function is concave [see Pratt (1981)], so despite its superficial complexity, the estimation is straightforward. (In the following application, with more than 27,000 observations and 7,293 individual effects, estimation of the full model required roughly five seconds of computation.) No theoretical counterpart to the Hsiao (1986, 2003) and Abrevaya (1997) results on the small $T$ bias (incidental parameters problem) of the MLE in the presence of fixed effects has been derived for the ordered probit model. The Monte Carlo results in Greene (2004) (see, as well, Chapter 17), suggest that biases comparable to those in the binary choice models persist in the ordered probit model as well. As in the binary choice case, the complication of the fixed effects model is the small sample bias, not the computation. The Das and van Soest approach finesses this problem—their estimator is consistent—but at the cost of losing the information needed to compute partial effects or predicted probabilities.

### 23.10.3.b Ordered Probit Models with Random Effects

The random effects ordered probit model model has been much more widely used than the fixed effects model. Applications include Groot and van den Brink (2003), who studied training levels of employees, with firm effects; Winkelmann (2003b), who examined subjective measures of well being with individual and family effects; Contoyannis et al. (2004), who analyzed self-reported measures of health status; and numerous others. In the simplest case, the method of the Butler and Moffitt (1982) quadrature method (Section 16.9.6.b) can be extended to this model.

### Example 23.19   Health Satisfaction

The GSOEP German Health Care data that we have used in Examples 11.11, 16.16, and others includes a self-reported measure of health satisfaction, *HSAT*, that takes values

0, 1, ..., 10.[52] This is a typical application of a scale variable that reflects an underlying continuous variable, "health." The frequencies and sample proportions for the reported values are as follows:

| HSAT | Frequency | Proportion |
|---|---|---|
| 0 | 447 | 1.6% |
| 1 | 255 | 0.9% |
| 2 | 642 | 2.3% |
| 3 | 1173 | 4.2% |
| 4 | 1390 | 5.0% |
| 5 | 4233 | 15.4% |
| 6 | 2530 | 9.2% |
| 7 | 4231 | 15.4% |
| 8 | 6172 | 22.5% |
| 9 | 3061 | 11.2% |
| 10 | 3192 | 11.6% |

We have fit pooled and panel data versions of the ordered probit model to these data. The model used is

$$y_{it}^* = \beta_1 + \beta_2\, Age_{it} + \beta_3\, Income_{it} + \beta_4\, Education_{it} + \beta_5\, Married_{it} + \beta_6\, Working_{it} + \varepsilon_{it} + c_i,$$

where $c_i$ will be the common fixed or random effect. (We are interested in comparing the fixed and random effects estimators, so we have not included any time-invariant variables such as gender in the equation.) Table 23.21 lists five estimated models. (Standard errors for the estimated threshold parameters are omitted.) The first is the pooled ordered probit model. The second and third are fixed effects. Column 2 shows the unconditional fixed effects estimates using the results of Section 16.9.6.c. Column 3 shows the Das and van Soest estimator. For the minimum distance estimator, we used an inefficient weighting matrix, the block-diagonal matrix in which the $j$th block is the inverse of the $j$th asymptotic covariance matrix for the individual logit estimators. With this weighting matrix, the estimator is

$$\hat{\boldsymbol{\beta}}_{MDE} = \left[\sum_{j=0}^{9} \mathbf{V}_j^{-1}\right]^{-1} \sum_{j=0}^{9} \mathbf{V}_j^{-1}\hat{\boldsymbol{\beta}}_j,$$

and the estimator of the asymptotic covariance matrix is approximately equal to the bracketed inverse matrix. The fourth set of results is the random effects estimator computed using the maximum simulated likelihood method. This model can be estimated using Butler and Moffitt's quadrature method; however, we found that even with a large number of nodes, the quadrature estimator converged to a point where the log-likelihood was far lower than the MSL estimator, and at parameter values that were implausibly different from the other estimates. Using different starting values and different numbers of quadrature points did not change this outcome. The MSL estimator for a random constant term (see Section 17.5) is considerably slower, but produces more reasonable results. The fifth set of results is the Mundlak form of the random effects model, which includes the group means in the models as controls to accommodate possible correlation between the latent heterogeneity and the included variables. As noted in Example 23.17, the components of the ordered choice model must be interpreted with some care. By construction, the partial effects of the variables on the probabilities of the outcomes must change sign, so the simple coefficients do not show the complete picture implied by the estimated model. Table 23.22 shows the partial effects for the pooled model to illustrate the computations.

---

[52] In the original data set, 40 (of 27,326) observations on this variable were coded with noninteger values between 6 and 7. For purposes of our example, we have recoded all 40 observations to 7.

**TABLE 23.21** Estimated Ordered Probit Models for Health Satisfaction

| Variable | (1) Pooled | (2) Fixed Effects Unconditional | (3) Fixed Effects Conditional | (4) Random Effects | (5) Random Effects Mundlak Controls Variables | Means |
|---|---|---|---|---|---|---|
| Constant | 2.4739 (0.04669) | | | 3.8577 (0.05072) | 3.2603 (0.05323) | |
| Age | −0.01913 (0.00064) | −0.07162 (0.002743) | −0.1011 (0.002878) | −0.03319 (0.00065) | −0.06282 (0.00234) | 0.03940 (0.002442) |
| Income | 0.1811 (0.03774) | 0.2992 (0.07058) | 0.4353 (0.07462) | 0.09436 (0.03632) | 0.2618 (0.06156) | 0.1461 (0.07695) |
| Kids | 0.06081 (0.01459) | −0.06385 (0.02837) | −0.1170 (0.03041) | 0.01410 (0.01421) | −0.05458 (0.02566) | 0.1854 (0.03129) |
| Education | 0.03421 (0.002828) | 0.02590 (0.02677) | 0.06013 (0.02819) | 0.04728 (0.002863) | 0.02296 (0.02793) | 0.02257 (0.02807) |
| Married | 0.02574 (0.01623) | 0.05157 (0.04030) | 0.08505 (0.04181) | 0.07327 (0.01575) | 0.04605 (0.03506) | −0.04829 (0.03963) |
| Working | 0.1292 (0.01403) | −0.02659 (0.02758) | −0.007969 (0.02830) | 0.07108 (0.01338) | −0.02383 (0.02311) | 0.2702 (0.02856) |
| $\mu_1$ | 0.1949 | 0.3249 | | 0.2726 | 0.2752 | |
| $\mu_2$ | 0.5029 | 0.8449 | | 0.7060 | 0.7119 | |
| $\mu_3$ | 0.8411 | 1.3940 | | 1.1778 | 1.1867 | |
| $\mu_4$ | 1.111 | 1.8230 | | 1.5512 | 1.5623 | |
| $\mu_5$ | 1.6700 | 2.6992 | | 2.3244 | 2.3379 | |
| $\mu_6$ | 1.9350 | 3.1272 | | 2.6957 | 2.7097 | |
| $\mu_7$ | 2.3468 | 3.7923 | | 3.2757 | 3.2911 | |
| $\mu_8$ | 3.0023 | 4.8436 | | 4.1967 | 4.2168 | |
| $\mu_9$ | 3.4615 | 5.5727 | | 4.8308 | 4.8569 | |
| $\sigma_u$ | 0.0000 | 0.0000 | | 1.0078 | 0.9936 | |
| ln $L$ | −56813.52 | −41875.63 | | −53215.54 | −53070.43 | |

Winkelmann (2003b) used the random effects approach to analyze the subjective well being (SWB) question (also coded 0 to 10) in the German Socioeconomic Panel (GSOEP) data set. The ordered probit model in this study is based on the latent regression

$$y_{imt}^* = \mathbf{x}_{imt}'\boldsymbol{\beta} + \varepsilon_{imt} + u_{im} + v_i.$$

**TABLE 23.22** Estimated Marginal Effects: Pooled Model

| HSAT | Age | Income | Kids | Education | Married | Working |
|---|---|---|---|---|---|---|
| 0 | 0.0006 | −0.0061 | −0.0020 | −0.0012 | −0.0009 | −0.0046 |
| 1 | 0.0003 | −0.0031 | −0.0010 | −0.0006 | −0.0004 | −0.0023 |
| 2 | 0.0008 | −0.0072 | −0.0024 | −0.0014 | −0.0010 | −0.0053 |
| 3 | 0.0012 | −0.0113 | −0.0038 | −0.0021 | −0.0016 | −0.0083 |
| 4 | 0.0012 | −0.0111 | −0.0037 | −0.0021 | −0.0016 | −0.0080 |
| 5 | 0.0024 | −0.0231 | −0.0078 | −0.0044 | −0.0033 | −0.0163 |
| 6 | 0.0008 | −0.0073 | −0.0025 | −0.0014 | −0.0010 | −0.0050 |
| 7 | 0.0003 | −0.0024 | −0.0009 | −0.0005 | −0.0003 | −0.0012 |
| 8 | −0.0019 | 0.0184 | 0.0061 | 0.0035 | 0.0026 | 0.0136 |
| 9 | −0.0021 | 0.0198 | 0.0066 | 0.0037 | 0.0028 | 0.0141 |
| 10 | −0.0035 | 0.0336 | 0.0114 | 0.0063 | 0.0047 | 0.0233 |

The independent variables include age, gender, employment status, income, family size, and an indicator for good health. An unusual feature of the model is the nested random effects (see Section 9.7.1), which include a family effect, $v_i$, as well as the individual family member ($i$ in family $m$) effect, $u_{im}$. The GLS/MLE approach we applied to the linear regression model in Section 9.7.1 is unavailable in this nonlinear setting. Winkelmann instead employed a Hermite quadrature procedure to maximize the log-likelihood function.

Contoyannis, Jones, and Rice (2004) analyzed a self-assessed health scale that ranged from 1 (very poor) to 5 (excellent) in the British Household Panel Survey. Their model accommodated a variety of complications in survey data. The latent regression underlying their ordered probit model is

$$h_{it}^* = \mathbf{x}_{it}'\boldsymbol{\beta} + \mathbf{H}_{i,t-1}'\boldsymbol{\gamma} + \alpha_i + \varepsilon_{it},$$

where $\mathbf{x}_{it}$ includes marital status, race, education, household size, age, income, and number of children in the household. The lagged value, $\mathbf{H}_{i,t-1}$, is a set of binary variables for the observed health status in the previous period. (This is the same device that was used by Butler et al. in Example 23.18.) In this case, the lagged values capture state dependence—the assumption that the health outcome is redrawn randomly in each period is inconsistent with evident runs in the data. The initial formulation of the regression is a fixed effects model. To control for the possible correlation between the effects, $\alpha_i$, and the regressors, and the initial conditions problem that helps to explain the state dependence, they use a hybrid of Mundlak's (1978) correction and a suggestion by Wooldridge (2002a) for modeling the initial conditions,

$$\alpha_i = \alpha_0 + \bar{\mathbf{x}}'\boldsymbol{\alpha}_1 + \mathbf{H}_{i,1}'\boldsymbol{\delta} + u_i,$$

where $u_i$ is exogenous. Inserting the second equation into the first produces a random effects model that can be fit using the quadrature method we considered earlier.

## 23.11  MODELS FOR UNORDERED MULTIPLE CHOICES

Some studies of multiple-choice settings include the following:

1. Hensher (1986, 1991), McFadden (1974), and many others have analyzed the travel mode of urban commuters.
2. Schmidt and Strauss (1975a,b) and Boskin (1974) have analyzed occupational choice among multiple alternatives.
3. Terza (1985a) has studied the assignment of bond ratings to corporate bonds as a choice among multiple alternatives.
4. Rossi and Allenby (1999, 2003) studied consumer brand choices in a repeated choice (panel data) model.
5. Train (2003) studied the choice of electricity supplier by a sample of California electricity customers.
6. Hensher, Rose, and Greene (2006) analyzed choices of automobile models by a sample of consumers offered a hypothetical menu of features.

These are all distinct from the multivariate probit model we examined earlier. In that setting, there were several decisions, each between two alternatives. Here there is a single decision among two or more alternatives. We will encounter two broad types of choice sets, **ordered choice models** and **unordered choice models.** The choice among means of getting to work—by car, bus, train, or bicycle—is clearly unordered. A bond rating is, by design, a ranking; that is its purpose. Quite different techniques are used for the two types of models. We examined models for ordered choices in Section 23.10. This section will examine models for unordered choice sets.[53] General references on the topics discussed here include Hensher, Louviere, and Swait (2000); Train (2003); and Hensher, Rose, and Greene (2006).

Unordered choice models can be motivated by a random utility model. For the $i$th consumer faced with $J$ choices, suppose that the utility of choice $j$ is

$$U_{ij} = \mathbf{z}'_{ij}\boldsymbol{\theta} + \varepsilon_{ij}.$$

If the consumer makes choice $j$ in particular, then we assume that $U_{ij}$ is the maximum among the $J$ utilities. Hence, the statistical model is driven by the probability that choice $j$ is made, which is

$$\text{Prob}(U_{ij} > U_{ik}) \quad \text{for all other } k \neq j.$$

The model is made operational by a particular choice of distribution for the disturbances. As in the binary choice case, two models are usually considered, logit and probit. Because of the need to evaluate multiple integrals of the normal distribution, the probit model has found rather limited use in this setting. The logit model, in contrast, has been widely used in many fields, including economics, market research, politics, finance, and transportation engineering. Let $Y_i$ be a random variable that indicates the choice made. McFadden (1974a) has shown that if (and only if) the $J$ disturbances are independent and identically distributed with Gumbel (type 1 extreme value) distribution,

$$F(\varepsilon_{ij}) = \exp(-\exp(-\varepsilon_{ij})), \tag{23-48}$$

then

$$\text{Prob}(Y_i = j) = \frac{\exp(\mathbf{z}'_{ij}\boldsymbol{\theta})}{\sum_{j=1}^{J} \exp(\mathbf{z}'_{ij}\boldsymbol{\theta})}, \tag{23-49}$$

which leads to what is called the **conditional logit model.** (It is often labeled the **multinomial logit model,** but this wording conflicts with the usual name for the model discussed in the next section, which differs slightly. Although the distinction turns out to be purely artificial, we will maintain it for the present.)

Utility depends on $\mathbf{z}_{ij}$, which includes aspects specific to the individual as well as to the choices. It is useful to distinguish them. Let $\mathbf{z}_{ij} = [\mathbf{x}_{ij}, \mathbf{w}_i]$ and partition $\boldsymbol{\theta}$ conformably into $[\boldsymbol{\beta}', \boldsymbol{\alpha}']'$. Then $\mathbf{x}_{ij}$ varies across the choices and possibly across the individuals as well. The components of $\mathbf{x}_{ij}$ are typically called the **attributes** of the choices. But $\mathbf{w}_i$ contains the **characteristics** of the individual and is, therefore, the same

---

[53] A hybrid case occurs in which consumers reveal their own specific ordering for the choices in an unordered choice set. Beggs, Cardell, and Hausman (1981) studied consumers' rankings of different automobile types, for example.

for all choices. If we incorporate this fact in the model, then (23-49) becomes

$$\text{Prob}(Y_i = j) = \frac{\exp(\mathbf{x}'_{ij}\boldsymbol{\beta} + \mathbf{w}'_i\boldsymbol{\alpha})}{\sum_{j=1}^{J} \exp(\mathbf{x}'_{ij}\boldsymbol{\beta} + \mathbf{w}'_i\boldsymbol{\alpha})} = \frac{[\exp(\mathbf{x}'_{ij}\boldsymbol{\beta})]\exp(\mathbf{w}'_i\boldsymbol{\alpha})}{\left[\sum_{j=1}^{J} \exp(\mathbf{x}'_{ij}\boldsymbol{\beta})\right]\exp(\mathbf{w}'_i\boldsymbol{\alpha})}. \tag{23-50}$$

Terms that do not vary across alternatives—that is, those specific to the individual—fall out of the probability. Evidently, if the model is to allow individual specific effects, then it must be modified. One method is to create a set of dummy variables, $A_j$, for the choices and multiply each of them by the common $\mathbf{w}$. We then allow the coefficient to vary across the choices instead of the characteristics. Analogously to the linear model, a complete set of interaction terms creates a singularity, so one of them must be dropped. For example, a model of a shopping center choice by individuals in various cities might specify that the choice depends on attributes of the shopping centers such as number of stores, $S_{ij}$, and distance from the central business district, $D_{ij}$, and income, which varies across individuals but not across the choices. Suppose that there were three choices in each city. The three attribute/characteristic vectors would be as follows:

| | | | | |
|---|---|---|---|---|
| Choice 1: | Stores | Distance | Income | 0 |
| Choice 2: | Stores | Distance | 0 | Income |
| Choice 3: | Stores | Distance | 0 | 0 |

The probabilities for this model would be

$$\text{Prob}(Y_i = j)$$
$$= \frac{\exp(\beta_1 S_{ij} + \beta_2 D_{ij} + \alpha_1 A_1\,Income_i + \alpha_2 A_2\,Income_i + \alpha_3 A_3\,Income_i)}{\sum_{j=1}^{3} \exp(\beta_1 S_{ij} + \beta_2 D_{ij} + \alpha_1 A_1\,Income_i + \alpha_2 A_2\,Income_i + \alpha_3 A_3\,Income_i)}, \quad \alpha_3 = 0.$$

The nonexperimental data sets typically analyzed by economists do not contain mixtures of individual- and choice-specific attributes. Such data would be far too costly to gather for most purposes. When they do, the preceding framework can be used. For the present, it is useful to examine the two types of data separately and consider aspects of the model that are specific to the two types of applications.

### 23.11.1 THE MULTINOMIAL LOGIT MODEL

To set up the model that applies when data are individual specific, it will help to consider an example. Schmidt and Strauss (1975a, b) estimated a model of occupational choice based on a sample of 1,000 observations drawn from the Public Use Sample for three years: 1960, 1967, and 1970. For each sample, the data for each individual in the sample consist of the following:

1. *Occupation:* $0 =$ menial, $1 =$ blue collar, $2 =$ craft, $3 =$ white collar, $4 =$ professional. (Note the slightly different numbering convention, starting at zero, which is standard.)
2. *Characteristics:* constant, education, experience, race, sex.

The model for occupational choice is

$$\text{Prob}(Y_i = j \mid \mathbf{w}_i) = \frac{\exp(\mathbf{w}'_i\boldsymbol{\alpha}_j)}{\sum_{j=0}^{4} \exp(\mathbf{w}'_i\boldsymbol{\alpha}_j)}, \quad j = 0, 1, \ldots, 4. \tag{23-51}$$

(The binomial logit model in Sections 23.3 and 23.4 is conveniently produced as the special case of $J = 1$.)

The model in (23-51) is a **multinomial logit model**.[54] The estimated equations provide a set of probabilities for the $J + 1$ choices for a decision maker with characteristics $\mathbf{w}_i$. Before proceeding, we must remove an indeterminacy in the model. If we define $\boldsymbol{\alpha}_j^* = \boldsymbol{\alpha}_j + \mathbf{q}$ for any vector $\mathbf{q}$, then recomputing the probabilities defined later using $\boldsymbol{\alpha}_j^*$ instead of $\boldsymbol{\alpha}_j$ produces the identical set of probabilities because all the terms involving $\mathbf{q}$ drop out. A convenient normalization that solves the problem is $\boldsymbol{\alpha}_0 = \mathbf{0}$. (This arises because the probabilities sum to one, so only $J$ parameter vectors are needed to determine the $J + 1$ probabilities.) Therefore, the probabilities are

$$\text{Prob}(Y_i = j \mid \mathbf{w}_i) = P_{ij} = \frac{\exp(\mathbf{w}_i'\boldsymbol{\alpha}_j)}{1 + \sum_{k=1}^{J} \exp(\mathbf{w}_i'\boldsymbol{\alpha}_k)}, \quad j = 0, 1, \ldots, J, \quad \boldsymbol{\alpha}_0 = \mathbf{0}. \quad \textbf{(23-52)}$$

The form of the binomial model examined in Section 23.4 results if $J = 1$. The model implies that we can compute $J$ **log-odds ratios**

$$\ln\left[\frac{P_{ij}}{P_{ik}}\right] = \mathbf{w}_i'(\boldsymbol{\alpha}_j - \boldsymbol{\alpha}_k) = \mathbf{w}_i'\boldsymbol{\alpha}_j \quad \text{if } k = 0.$$

From the point of view of estimation, it is useful that the odds ratio, $P_{ij}/P_{ik}$, does not depend on the other choices, which follows from the independence of the disturbances in the original model. From a behavioral viewpoint, this fact is not very attractive. We shall return to this problem in Section 23.11.3.

The log-likelihood can be derived by defining, for each individual, $d_{ij} = 1$ if alternative $j$ is chosen by individual $i$, and 0 if not, for the $J + 1$ possible outcomes. Then, for each $i$, one and only one of the $d_{ij}$'s is 1. The log-likelihood is a generalization of that for the binomial probit or logit model:

$$\ln L = \sum_{i=1}^{n} \sum_{j=0}^{J} d_{ij} \ln \text{Prob}(Y_i = j \mid \mathbf{w}_i).$$

The derivatives have the characteristically simple form

$$\frac{\partial \ln L}{\partial \boldsymbol{\alpha}_j} = \sum_{i=1}^{n} (d_{ij} - P_{ij})\mathbf{w}_i \quad \text{for } j = 1, \ldots, J.$$

The exact second derivatives matrix has $J^2 K \times K$ blocks,[55]

$$\frac{\partial^2 \ln L}{\partial \boldsymbol{\alpha}_j \partial \boldsymbol{\alpha}_l'} = -\sum_{i=1}^{n} P_{ij}[\mathbf{1}(j = l) - P_{il}]\mathbf{w}_i\mathbf{w}_i',$$

where $\mathbf{1}(j = l)$ equals 1 if $j$ equals $l$ and 0 if not. Because the Hessian does not involve $d_{ij}$, these are the expected values, and Newton's method is equivalent to the method of scoring. It is worth noting that the number of parameters in this model proliferates

---

[54] Nerlove and Press (1973).

[55] If the data were in the form of proportions, such as market shares, then the appropriate log-likelihood and derivatives are $\Sigma_i \Sigma_j n_i p_{ij}$ and $\Sigma_i \Sigma_j n_i (p_{ij} - P_{ij})\mathbf{w}_i$, respectively. The terms in the Hessian are multiplied by $n_i$.

with the number of choices, which is inconvenient because the typical cross section sometimes involves a fairly large number of regressors.

The coefficients in this model are difficult to interpret. It is tempting to associate $\alpha_j$ with the $j$th outcome, but that would be misleading. By differentiating (23-52), we find that the marginal effects of the characteristics on the probabilities are

$$\delta_{ij} = \frac{\partial P_{ij}}{\partial \mathbf{w}_i} = P_{ij} \left[ \alpha_j - \sum_{k=0}^{J} P_{ik} \alpha_k \right] = P_{ij}[\alpha_j - \bar{\alpha}]. \tag{23-53}$$

Therefore, every subvector of $\alpha$ enters every marginal effect, both through the probabilities and through the weighted average that appears in $\delta_{ij}$. These values can be computed from the parameter estimates. Although the usual focus is on the coefficient estimates, equation (23-53) suggests that there is at least some potential for confusion. Note, for example, that for any particular $w_{ik}$, $\partial P_{ij}/\partial w_{ik}$ need not have the same sign as $\alpha_{jk}$. Standard errors can be estimated using the delta method. (See Section 4.9.4.) For purposes of the computation, let $\alpha = [\mathbf{0}, \alpha_1', \alpha_2', \ldots, \alpha_J']'$. We include the fixed $\mathbf{0}$ vector for outcome 0 because although $\alpha_0 = \mathbf{0}$, $\delta_{i0} = -P_{i0}\bar{\alpha}$, which is not $\mathbf{0}$. Note as well that Asy. $\text{Cov}[\hat{\alpha}_0, \hat{\alpha}_j] = \mathbf{0}$ for $j = 0, \ldots, J$. Then

$$\text{Asy. Var}[\hat{\delta}_{ij}] = \sum_{l=0}^{J} \sum_{m=0}^{J} \left( \frac{\partial \delta_{ij}}{\partial \alpha_l'} \right) \text{Asy. Cov}[\hat{\alpha}_l', \hat{\alpha}_m'] \left( \frac{\partial \delta_{ij}'}{\partial \alpha_m} \right),$$

$$\frac{\partial \delta_{ij}}{\partial \alpha_l} = [\mathbf{1}(j = l) - P_{il}][P_{ij}\mathbf{I} + \delta_{ij}\mathbf{w}_i'] + P_{ij}[\delta_{il}\mathbf{w}_i'].$$

Finding adequate fit measures in this setting presents the same difficulties as in the binomial models. As before, it is useful to report the log-likelihood. If the model contains no covariates and no constant term, then the log-likelihood will be

$$\ln L_c = \sum_{j=0}^{J} n_j \ln \left( \frac{1}{J+1} \right)$$

where $n_j$ is the number of individuals who choose outcome $j$. If the characteristic vector includes only a constant term, then the restricted log-likelihood is

$$\ln L_0 = \sum_{j=0}^{J} n_j \ln \left( \frac{n_j}{n} \right) = \sum_{j=0}^{J} n_j \ln p_j,$$

where $p_j$ is the sample proportion of observations that make choice $j$. A useful table will give a listing of hits and misses of the prediction rule "predict $Y_i = j$ if $\hat{P}_{ij}$ is the maximum of the predicted probabilities."[56]

---

[56] It is common for this rule to predict all observation with the same value in an unbalanced sample or a model with little explanatory power. This is not a contradiction of an estimated model with many "significant" coefficients, because the coefficients are not estimated so as to maximize the number of correct predictions.

### 23.11.2 THE CONDITIONAL LOGIT MODEL

When the data consist of choice-specific attributes instead of individual-specific characteristics, the appropriate model is

$$\text{Prob}(Y_i = j \mid \mathbf{x}_{i1}, \mathbf{x}_{i2}, \ldots, \mathbf{x}_{iJ}) = \text{Prob}(Y_i = j \mid \mathbf{X}_i) = P_{ij} = \frac{\exp(\mathbf{x}'_{ij}\boldsymbol{\beta})}{\sum_{j=1}^{J} \exp(\mathbf{x}'_{ij}\boldsymbol{\beta})}. \quad \textbf{(23-54)}$$

Here, in accordance with the convention in the literature, we let $j = 1, 2, \ldots, J$ for a total of $J$ alternatives. The model is otherwise essentially the same as the multinomial logit. Even more care will be required in interpreting the parameters, however. Once again, an example will help to focus ideas.

In this model, the coefficients are not directly tied to the marginal effects. The marginal effects for continuous variables can be obtained by differentiating (23-54) with respect to a particular $\mathbf{x}_m$ to obtain

$$\frac{\partial P_{ij}}{\partial \mathbf{x}_{im}} = [P_{ij}(\mathbf{1}(j = m) - P_{im})]\boldsymbol{\beta}, \quad m = 1, \ldots, J.$$

It is clear that through its presence in $P_{ij}$ and $P_{im}$, every attribute set $\mathbf{x}_m$ affects all the probabilities. Hensher (1991) suggests that one might prefer to report elasticities of the probabilities. The effect of attribute $k$ of choice $m$ on $P_{ij}$ would be

$$\frac{\partial \ln P_j}{\partial \ln x_{mk}} = x_{mk}[\mathbf{1}(j = m) - P_{im}]\beta_k.$$

Because there is no ambiguity about the scale of the probability itself, whether one should report the derivatives or the elasticities is largely a matter of taste. Some of Hensher's elasticity estimates are given in Table 23.29 later on in this chapter.

Estimation of the conditional logit model is simplest by Newton's method or the method of scoring. The log-likelihood is the same as for the multinomial logit model. Once again, we define $d_{ij} = 1$ if $Y_i = j$ and 0 otherwise. Then

$$\ln L = \sum_{i=1}^{n} \sum_{j=1}^{J} d_{ij} \ln \text{Prob}(Y_i = j).$$

Market share and frequency data are common in this setting. If the data are in this form, then the only change needed is, once again, to define $d_{ij}$ as the proportion or frequency.

Because of the simple form of $L$, the gradient and Hessian have particularly convenient forms: Let $\bar{\mathbf{x}}_i = \sum_{j=1}^{J} P_{ij}\mathbf{x}_{ij}$. Then,

$$\frac{\partial \log L}{\partial \boldsymbol{\beta}} = \sum_{i=1}^{n} \sum_{j=1}^{J} d_{ij}(\mathbf{x}_{ij} - \bar{\mathbf{x}}_i),$$

$$\frac{\partial^2 \log L}{\partial \boldsymbol{\beta} \partial \boldsymbol{\beta}'} = -\sum_{i=1}^{n} \sum_{j=1}^{J} P_{ij}(\mathbf{x}_{ij} - \bar{\mathbf{x}}_i)(\mathbf{x}_{ij} - \bar{\mathbf{x}}_i)', \quad \textbf{(23-55)}$$

The usual problems of fit measures appear here. The log-likelihood ratio and tabulation of actual versus predicted choices will be useful. There are two possible constrained log-likelihoods. The model cannot contain a constant term, so the constraint $\boldsymbol{\beta} = \mathbf{0}$ renders all probabilities equal to $1/J$. The constrained log-likelihood for this constraint is then $L_c = -n \ln J$. Of course, it is unlikely that this hypothesis would fail to be rejected. Alternatively, we could fit the model with only the $J - 1$ choice-specific constants, which makes the constrained log-likelihood the same as in the multinomial logit model, $\ln L_0^* = \sum_j n_j \ln p_j$ where, as before, $n_j$ is the number of individuals who choose alternative $j$.

### 23.11.3   THE INDEPENDENCE FROM IRRELEVANT ALTERNATIVES ASSUMPTION

We noted earlier that the odds ratios in the multinomial logit or conditional logit models are independent of the other alternatives. This property is convenient as regards estimation, but it is not a particularly appealing restriction to place on consumer behavior. The property of the logit model whereby $P_{ij}/P_{im}$ is independent of the remaining probabilities is called the **independence from irrelevant alternatives (IIA).**

The independence assumption follows from the initial assumption that the disturbances are independent and homoscedastic. Later we will discuss several models that have been developed to relax this assumption. Before doing so, we consider a test that has been developed for testing the validity of the assumption. Hausman and McFadden (1984) suggest that if a subset of the choice set truly is irrelevant, omitting it from the model altogether will not change parameter estimates systematically. Exclusion of these choices will be inefficient but will not lead to inconsistency. But if the remaining odds ratios are not truly independent from these alternatives, then the parameter estimates obtained when these choices are excluded will be inconsistent. This observation is the usual basis for Hausman's specification test. The statistic is

$$\chi^2 = (\hat{\boldsymbol{\beta}}_s - \hat{\boldsymbol{\beta}}_f)'[\hat{\mathbf{V}}_s - \hat{\mathbf{V}}_f]^{-1}(\hat{\boldsymbol{\beta}}_s - \hat{\boldsymbol{\beta}}_f),$$

where $s$ indicates the estimators based on the restricted subset, $f$ indicates the estimator based on the full set of choices, and $\hat{\mathbf{V}}_s$ and $\hat{\mathbf{V}}_f$ are the respective estimates of the asymptotic covariance matrices. The statistic has a limiting chi-squared distribution with $K$ degrees of freedom.[57]

### 23.11.4   NESTED LOGIT MODELS

If the independence from irrelevant alternatives test fails, then an alternative to the multinomial logit model will be needed. A natural alternative is a multivariate probit model:

$$U_{ij} = \mathbf{x}_{ij}'\boldsymbol{\beta} + \varepsilon_{ij}, \quad j = 1, \ldots, J, [\varepsilon_{i1}, \varepsilon_{i2}, \ldots, \varepsilon_{iJ}] \sim N[\mathbf{0}, \boldsymbol{\Sigma}].$$

We had considered this model earlier but found that as a general model of consumer choice, its failings were the practical difficulty of computing the multinormal integral and estimation of an unrestricted correlation matrix. Hausman and Wise (1978) point out that for a model of consumer choice, the probit model may not be as impractical as it might seem. First, for $J$ choices, the comparisons implicit in $U_{ij} > U_{im}$ for $m \neq j$ involve the $J - 1$ differences, $\varepsilon_j - \varepsilon_m$. Thus, starting with a $J$-dimensional problem, we need only consider derivatives of $(J - 1)$-order probabilities. Therefore, to come to a concrete example, a model with four choices requires only the evaluation of bivariate

---

[57]McFadden (1987) shows how this hypothesis can also be tested using a Lagrange multiplier test.

normal integrals, which, albeit still complicated to estimate, is well within the received technology. (We will examine the multivariate probit model in Section 23.11.5.) For larger models, however, other specifications have proved more useful.

One way to relax the homoscedasticity assumption in the conditional logit model that also provides an intuitively appealing structure is to group the alternatives into subgroups that allow the variance to differ across the groups while maintaining the IIA assumption within the groups. This specification defines a **nested logit model.** To fix ideas, it is useful to think of this specification as a two- (or more) level choice problem (although, once again, the model arises as a modification of the stochastic specification in the original conditional logit model, not necessarily as a model of behavior). Suppose, then, that the $J$ alternatives can be divided into $B$ subgroups (branches) such that the choice set can be written

$$[c_1, \ldots, c_J] = [(c_{1|1}, \ldots, c_{J_1|1}), (c_{1|2}, \ldots, c_{J_2|2}) \ldots, (c_{1|B}, \ldots, c_{J_B|B})].$$

Logically, we may think of the choice process as that of choosing among the $B$ choice sets and then making the specific choice within the chosen set. This method produces a tree structure, which for two branches and, say, five choices (twigs) might look as follows:

Suppose as well that the data consist of observations on the attributes of the choices $\mathbf{x}_{ij|b}$ and attributes of the choice sets $\mathbf{z}_{ib}$.

To derive the mathematical form of the model, we begin with the unconditional probability

$$\text{Prob}[twig_j, branch_b] = P_{ijb} = \frac{\exp(\mathbf{x}'_{ij|b}\boldsymbol{\beta} + \mathbf{z}'_{ib}\boldsymbol{\gamma})}{\sum_{b=1}^{B} \sum_{j=1}^{J_b} \exp(\mathbf{x}'_{ij|b}\boldsymbol{\beta} + \mathbf{z}'_{ib}\boldsymbol{\gamma})}.$$

Now write this probability as

$$P_{ijb} = P_{ij|b} P_b$$

$$= \left(\frac{\exp(\mathbf{x}'_{ij|b}\boldsymbol{\beta})}{\sum_{j=1}^{J_b} \exp(\mathbf{x}'_{ij|b}\boldsymbol{\beta})}\right) \left(\frac{\exp(\mathbf{z}'_{ib}\boldsymbol{\gamma})}{\sum_{l=1}^{L} \exp(\mathbf{z}'_{ib}\boldsymbol{\gamma})}\right) \frac{\left(\sum_{j=1}^{J_b} \exp(\mathbf{x}'_{ij|b}\boldsymbol{\beta})\right) \left(\sum_{l=1}^{L} \exp(\mathbf{z}'_{ib}\boldsymbol{\gamma})\right)}{\left(\sum_{l=1}^{L} \sum_{j=1}^{J_l} \exp(\mathbf{x}'_{ij|b}\boldsymbol{\beta} + \mathbf{z}'_{ib}\boldsymbol{\gamma})\right)}.$$

Define the **inclusive value** for the $l$th branch as

$$IV_{ib} = \ln \left(\sum_{j=1}^{J_b} \exp(\mathbf{x}'_{ij|b}\boldsymbol{\beta})\right).$$

Then, after canceling terms and using this result, we find

$$P_{ij|b} = \frac{\exp(\mathbf{x}'_{ij|b}\boldsymbol{\beta})}{\sum_{j=1}^{J_b} \exp(\mathbf{x}'_{ij|b}\boldsymbol{\beta})} \quad \text{and} \quad P_b = \frac{\exp[\tau_b(\mathbf{z}'_{ib}\boldsymbol{\gamma} + IV_{ib})]}{\sum_{b=1}^{B} \exp[\tau_b(\mathbf{z}'_{ib}\boldsymbol{\gamma} + IV_{ib})]},$$

where the new parameters $\tau_l$ must equal 1 to produce the original model. Therefore, we use the restriction $\tau_l = 1$ to recover the conditional logit model, and the preceding equation just writes this model in another form. The nested logit model arises if this restriction is relaxed. The inclusive value coefficients, unrestricted in this fashion, allow the model to incorporate some degree of heteroscedasticity. Within each branch, the IIA restriction continues to hold. The equal variance of the disturbances within the $j$th branch are now[58]

$$\sigma_b^2 = \frac{\pi^2}{6\tau_b}.$$

With $\tau_j = 1$, this reverts to the basic result for the multinomial logit model.

As usual, the coefficients in the model are not directly interpretable. The derivatives that describe covariation of the attributes and probabilities are

$$\frac{\partial \ln \text{Prob}[choice = m, branch = b]}{\partial x(k) \text{ in } choice \text{ } M \text{ and } branch \text{ } B}$$

$$= \{\mathbf{1}(b = B)[\mathbf{1}(m = M) - P_{M|B}] + \tau_B[\mathbf{1}(b = B) - P_B]P_{M|B}\}\boldsymbol{\beta}_k.$$

The nested logit model has been extended to three and higher levels. The complexity of the model increases rapidly with the number of levels. But the model has been found to be extremely flexible and is widely used for modeling consumer choice in the marketing and transportation literatures, to name a few.

There are two ways to estimate the parameters of the nested logit model. A **limited information,** two-step maximum likelihood approach can be done as follows:

1.  Estimate $\boldsymbol{\beta}$ by treating the choice within branches as a simple conditional logit model.
2.  Compute the inclusive values for all the branches in the model. Estimate $\boldsymbol{\gamma}$ and the $\tau$ parameters by treating the choice among branches as a conditional logit model with attributes $\mathbf{z}_{ib}$ and $I_{ib}$.

Because this approach is a two-step estimator, the estimate of the asymptotic covariance matrix of the estimates at the second step must be corrected. [See Section 16.7 and McFadden (1984).] For **full information maximum likelihood** (FIML) estimation of the model, the log-likelihood is

$$\ln L = \sum_{i=1}^{n} \ln[\text{Prob}(twig \mid branch)_i \times \text{Prob}(branch)_i].$$

[See Hensher (1986, 1991) and Greene (2007a).] The information matrix is not block diagonal in $\boldsymbol{\beta}$ and $(\boldsymbol{\gamma}, \tau)$, so FIML estimation will be more efficient than two-step estimation. The FIML estimator is now available in several commercial computer packages. The two-step estimator is rarely used in current research.

To specify the nested logit model, it is necessary to partition the choice set into branches. Sometimes there will be a natural partition, such as in the example given by Maddala (1983) when the choice of residence is made first by community, then by

---

[58]See Hensher, Louviere, and Swaite (2000). See Greene and Hensher (2002) for alternative formulations of the nested logit model.

dwelling type within the community. In other instances, however, the partitioning of the choice set is ad hoc and leads to the troubling possibility that the results might be dependent on the branches so defined. (Many studies in this literature present several sets of results based on different specifications of the tree structure.) There is no well-defined testing procedure for discriminating among tree structures, which is a problematic aspect of the model.

### 23.11.5 THE MULTINOMIAL PROBIT MODEL

A natural alternative model that relaxes the independence restrictions built into the multinomial logit (MNL) model is the **multinomial probit model** (MNP). The structural equations of the MNP model are

$$U_{ij} = \mathbf{x}'_{ij}\boldsymbol{\beta} + \varepsilon_{ij}, \quad j = 1, \ldots, J, \ [\varepsilon_{i1}, \varepsilon_{i2}, \ldots, \varepsilon_{iJ}] \sim N[\mathbf{0}, \boldsymbol{\Sigma}].$$

The term in the log-likelihood that corresponds to the choice of alternative $q$ is

$$\text{Prob}[\text{choice}_{iq}] = \text{Prob}[U_{iq} > U_{ij}, \ j = 1, \ldots, J, j \neq q].$$

The probability for this occurrence is

$$\text{Prob}[\text{choice}_i q] = \text{Prob}[\varepsilon_{i1} - \varepsilon_{iq} < (\mathbf{x}_{iq} - \mathbf{x}_{i1})'\boldsymbol{\beta}, \ldots, \varepsilon_{iJ} - \varepsilon_{iq} < (\mathbf{x}_{iq} - \mathbf{x}_{iJ})'\boldsymbol{\beta}]$$

for the $J - 1$ other choices, which is a cumulative probability from a $(J - 1)$-variate normal distribution. Because we are only making comparisons, one of the variances in this $J - 1$ variate structure—that is, one of the diagonal elements in the reduced $\boldsymbol{\Sigma}$—must be normalized to 1.0. Because only comparisons are ever observable in this model, for identification, $J - 1$ of the covariances must also be normalized, to zero. The MNP model allows an unrestricted $(J - 1) \times (J - 1)$ correlation structure and $J - 2$ free standard deviations for the disturbances in the model. (Thus, a two-choice model returns to the univariate probit model of Section 23.2.) For more than two choices, this specification is far more general than the MNL model, which assumes that $\boldsymbol{\Sigma} = \mathbf{I}$. (The scaling is absorbed in the coefficient vector in the MNL model.) It adds the unrestricted correlations to the heteroscedastic model of the previous section.

The main obstacle to implementation of the MNP model has been the difficulty in computing the multivariate normal probabilities for any dimensionality higher than 2. Recent results on accurate simulation of multinormal integrals, however, have made estimation of the MNP model feasible. (See Section 17.3.3 and a symposium in the November 1994 issue of the *Review of Economics and Statistics*.) Yet some practical problems remain. Computation is exceedingly time consuming. It is also necessary to ensure that $\boldsymbol{\Sigma}$ remain a positive definite matrix. One way often suggested is to construct the Cholesky decomposition of $\boldsymbol{\Sigma}, \mathbf{LL}'$, where $\mathbf{L}$ is a lower triangular matrix, and estimate the elements of $\mathbf{L}$. The normalizations and zero restrictions can be imposed by making the last row of the $J \times J$ matrix $\boldsymbol{\Sigma}$ equal $(0, 0, \ldots, 1)$ and using $\mathbf{LL}'$ to create the upper $(J - 1) \times (J - 1)$ matrix. The additional normalization restriction is obtained by imposing $\mathbf{L}_{11} = 1$. This is straightforward to implement for an otherwise unrestricted $\boldsymbol{\Sigma}$. A remaining problem, however, is that it is now difficult by this method to impose any other restrictions, such as a zero in a specific location in $\boldsymbol{\Sigma}$, which is common. An alternative approach is estimate the correlations, $\mathbf{R}$, and a diagonal matrix of standard deviations, $\mathbf{S} = \text{diag}(\sigma_1, \ldots, \sigma_{J-2}, 1, 1)$, separately. The normalizations, $\mathbf{R}_{jj} = 1$, and exclusions, $\mathbf{R}_{Jl} = 0$, are then simple to impose, and $\boldsymbol{\Sigma}$ is just **SRS**. The resulting matrix must still be symmetric and positive definite. The restriction $-1 < \mathbf{R}_{jl} < +1$ is necessary but still not sufficient to ensure definiteness. The full set of restrictions is difficult to enumerate explicitly and involves sets of inequalities that would be difficult to impose in estimation. (Typically when this method is employed, the matrix is estimated without the explicit restrictions.) Identification appears to be a serious problem with the MNP model. Although the unrestricted MNP model is fully identified in principle, convergence to satisfactory results in applications with more than three choices appears to require many additional restrictions on the standard deviations and correlations, such as zero restrictions or equality restrictions in the case of the standard deviations.

### 23.11.6 THE MIXED LOGIT MODEL

Another variant of the multinomial logit model is the **random parameters logit model** (RPL) (also called the **mixed logit model**). [See Revelt and Train (1996); Bhat (1996); Berry, Levinsohn, and Pakes (1995); Jain, Vilcassim, and Chintagunta (1994); and Hensher and Greene (2004).] Train's (2003) formulation of the RPL model (which encompasses the others) is a modification of the MNL model. The model is a **random coefficients** formulation. The change to the basic MNL model is the parameter specification in the distribution of the parameters across individuals, $i$;

$$\beta_{ik} = \beta_k + \mathbf{z}_i' \boldsymbol{\theta}_k + \sigma_k u_{ik}, \tag{23-56}$$

where $u_{ik}, k = 1, \ldots, K$, is multivariate normally distributed with correlation matrix $\mathbf{R}$, $\sigma_k$ is the standard deviation of the $k$th distribution, $\beta_k + \mathbf{z}_i' \boldsymbol{\theta}_k$ is the mean of the distribution, and $\mathbf{z}_i$ is a vector of person specific characteristics (such as age and income) that do not vary across choices. This formulation contains all the earlier models. For example, if $\boldsymbol{\theta}_k = \mathbf{0}$ for all the coefficients and $\sigma_k = 0$ for all the coefficients except for choice-specific constants, then the original MNL model with a normal-logistic mixture for the random part of the MNL model arises (hence the name).

The model is estimated by simulating the log-likelihood function rather than direct integration to compute the probabilities, which would be infeasible because the mixture distribution composed of the original $\varepsilon_{ij}$ and the random part of the coefficient is unknown. For any individual,

$$\text{Prob[choice } q \mid \mathbf{u}_i] = \text{MNL probability} \mid \beta_i(\mathbf{u}_i),$$

with all restrictions imposed on the coefficients. The appropriate probability is

$$E_u[\text{Prob(choice } q \mid \mathbf{u})] = \int_{u_1, \ldots, u_k} \text{Prob[choice } q \mid \mathbf{u}] f(\mathbf{u}) d\mathbf{u},$$

which can be estimated by simulation, using

$$\text{Est. } E_u[\text{Prob(choice } q \mid \mathbf{u})] = \frac{1}{R} \sum_{r=1}^{R} \text{Prob[choice } q \mid \beta_i(\mathbf{u}_{ir})],$$

where $\mathbf{u}_{ir}$ is the $r$th of $R$ draws for observation $i$. (There are $nkR$ draws in total. The draws for observation $i$ must be the same from one computation to the next, which can be accomplished by assigning to each individual their own seed for the random number generator and restarting it each time the probability is to be computed.) By this method, the log-likelihood and its derivatives with respect to $(\beta_k, \theta_k, \sigma_k), k = 1, \ldots, K$ and $\mathbf{R}$ are simulated to find the values that maximize the simulated log-likelihood. (See Section 17.5 and Example 23.8.)

The mixed model enjoys two considerable advantages not available in any of the other forms suggested. In a panel data or repeated-choices setting (see Section 23.11.8), one can formulate a random effects model simply by making the variation in the coefficients time invariant. Thus, the model is changed to

$$U_{ijt} = \mathbf{x}'_{ijt}\boldsymbol{\beta}_{it} + \varepsilon_{ijt}, \quad i = 1, \ldots, n, \quad j = 1, \ldots, J, \quad t = 1, \ldots, T,$$

$$\boldsymbol{\beta}_{it,k} = \beta_k + \mathbf{z}'_{it}\boldsymbol{\theta}_k + \sigma_k u_{ik}.$$

The time variation in the coefficients is provided by the choice-invariant variables, which may change through time. Habit persistence is carried by the time-invariant random effect, $u_{ik}$. If only the constant terms vary and they are assumed to be uncorrelated, then this is logically equivalent to the familiar random effects model. But, much greater generality can be achieved by allowing the other coefficients to vary randomly across individuals and by allowing correlation of these effects.[59] A second degree of flexibility is in (23-56). The random components, $u_i$ are not restricted to normality. Other distributions that can be simulated will be appropriate when the range of parameter variation consistent with consumer behavior must be restricted, for example to narrow ranges or to positive values.

### 23.11.7 APPLICATION: CONDITIONAL LOGIT MODEL FOR TRAVEL MODE CHOICE

Hensher and Greene [Greene (2007a)] report estimates of a model of travel mode choice for travel between Sydney and Melbourne, Australia. The data set contains 210 observations on choice among four travel modes, *air*, *train*, *bus*, and *car*. (See Appendix Table F23.2.) The attributes used for their example were: choice-specific constants; two choice-specific continuous measures; *GC*, a measure of the generalized cost of the travel that is equal to the sum of in-vehicle cost, *INVC*, and a wagelike measure times *INVT*, the amount of time spent traveling; and *TTME*, the terminal time (zero for car); and for the choice between air and the other modes, *HINC*, the household income. A summary of the sample data is given in Table 23.23. The sample is **choice based** so as to balance it among the four choices—the true population allocation, as shown in the last column of Table 23.23, is dominated by drivers.

The model specified is

$$U_{ij} = \alpha_{air}d_{i,air} + \alpha_{train}d_{i,train} + \alpha_{bus}d_{i,bus} + \beta_G GC_{ij} + \beta_T TTME_{ij} + \gamma_H d_{i,air}HINC_i + \varepsilon_{ij},$$

where for each $j$, $\varepsilon_{ij}$ has the same independent, type 1 extreme value distribution,

$$F_\varepsilon(\varepsilon_{ij}) = \exp(-\exp(-\varepsilon_{ij})),$$

which has standard deviation $\pi^2/6$. The mean is absorbed in the constants. Estimates of the conditional logit model are shown in Table 23.24. The model was fit with and

---

[59]See Hensher (2001) for an application to transportation mode choice in which each individual is observed in several choice situations. A stated choice experiment in which consumers make several choices in sequence about automobile features appears in Hensher, Rost, and Greene (2006).

**TABLE 23.23**    Summary Statistics for Travel Mode Choice Data

|  | GC | TTME | INVC | INVT | HINC | *Number Choosing* | p | *True Prop.* |
|---|---|---|---|---|---|---|---|---|
| Air | 102.648 | 61.010 | 85.522 | 133.710 | 34.548 | 58 | 0.28 | 0.14 |
|  | 113.522 | 46.534 | 97.569 | 124.828 | 41.274 |  |  |  |
| Train | 130.200 | 35.690 | 51.338 | 608.286 | 34.548 | 63 | 0.30 | 0.13 |
|  | 106.619 | 28.524 | 37.460 | 532.667 | 23.063 |  |  |  |
| Bus | 115.257 | 41.650 | 33.457 | 629.462 | 34.548 | 30 | 0.14 | 0.09 |
|  | 108.133 | 25.200 | 33.733 | 618.833 | 29.700 |  |  |  |
| Car | 94.414 | 0 | 20.995 | 573.205 | 34.548 | 59 | 0.28 | 0.64 |
|  | 89.095 | 0 | 15.694 | 527.373 | 42.220 |  |  |  |

*Note:* The upper figure is the average for all 210 observations. The lower figure is the mean for the observations that made that choice.

**TABLE 23.24**    Parameter Estimates

|  | *Unweighted Sample* | | *Choice-Based Weighting* | |
|---|---|---|---|---|
|  | *Estimate* | *t Ratio* | *Estimate* | *t Ratio* |
| $\beta_G$ | −0.15501 | −3.517 | −0.01333 | −2.724 |
| $\beta_T$ | −0.09612 | −9.207 | −0.13405 | −7.164 |
| $\gamma_H$ | 0.01329 | 1.295 | −0.00108 | −0.087 |
| $\alpha_{air}$ | 5.2074 | 6.684 | 6.5940 | 5.906 |
| $\alpha_{train}$ | 3.8690 | 8.731 | 3.6190 | 7.447 |
| $\alpha_{bus}$ | 3.1632 | 7.025 | 3.3218 | 5.698 |
| Log-likelihood at $\beta = 0$ |  | −291.1218 |  | −291.1218 |
| Log-likelihood (sample shares) |  | −283.7588 |  | −223.0578 |
| Log-likelihood at convergence |  | −199.1284 |  | −147.5896 |

without the corrections for choice-based sampling. Because the sample shares do not differ radically from the population proportions, the effect on the estimated parameters is fairly modest. Nonetheless, it is apparent that the choice-based sampling is not completely innocent. A cross tabulation of the predicted versus actual outcomes is given in Table 23.25. The predictions are generated by tabulating the integer parts of $m_{jk} = \sum_{i=1}^{210} \hat{p}_{ij} d_{ik}$, $j, k =$ *air, train, bus, car*, where $\hat{p}_{ij}$ is the predicted probability of outcome $j$ for observation $i$ and $d_{ik}$ is the binary variable which indicates if individual $i$ made choice $k$.

Are the odds ratios *train/bus* and *car/bus* really independent from the presence of the *air* alternative? To use the Hausman test, we would eliminate choice *air,* from the

**TABLE 23.25**    Predicted Choices Based on Model Probabilities (predictions based on choice-based sampling in parentheses)

|  | *Air* | *Train* | *Bus* | *Car* | *Total (Actual)* |
|---|---|---|---|---|---|
| Air | 32 (30) | 8 (3) | 5 (3) | 13 (23) | 58 |
| Train | 7 (3) | 37 (30) | 5 (3) | 14 (27) | 63 |
| Bus | 3 (1) | 5 (2) | 15 (4) | 6 (12) | 30 |
| Car | 16 (5) | 13 (5) | 6 (3) | 25 (45) | 59 |
| Total (Predicted) | 58 (39) | 63 (40) | 30 (23) | 59 (108) | 210 |

**TABLE 23.26** Results for IIA Test

| | Full-Choice Set | | | | Restricted-Choice Set | | | |
|---|---|---|---|---|---|---|---|---|
| | $\beta_G$ | $\beta_T$ | $\alpha_{train}$ | $\alpha_{bus}$ | $\beta_G$ | $\beta_T$ | $\alpha_{train}$ | $\alpha_{bus}$ |
| Estimate | −0.0155 | −0.0961 | 3.869 | 3.163 | −0.0639 | −0.0699 | 4.464 | 3.105 |
| | Estimated Asymptotic Covariance Matrix | | | | Estimated Asymptotic Covariance Matrix | | | |
| $\beta_G$ | 0.194e-5 | | | | 0.000101 | | | |
| $\beta_T$ | −0.46e-7 | 0.000110 | | | −0.0000013 | 0.000221 | | |
| $\alpha_{train}$ | −0.00060 | −0.0038 | 0.196 | | −0.000244 | −0.00759 | 0.410 | |
| $\alpha_{bus}$ | −0.00026 | −0.0037 | 0.161 | 0.203 | −0.000113 | −0.00753 | 0.336 | 0.371 |

*Note:* 0.nnne-$p$ indicates times 10 to the negative $p$ power.
$H = 33.3363$. Critical chi-squared[4] = 9.488.

choice set and estimate a three-choice model. Because 58 respondents chose this mode, we would lose 58 observations. In addition, for every data vector left in the sample, the air-specific constant and the interaction, $d_{i,air} \times HINC_i$ would be zero for every remaining individual. Thus, these parameters could not be estimated in the restricted model. We would drop these variables. The test would be based on the two estimators of the remaining four coefficients in the model, $[\beta_G, \beta_T, \alpha_{train}, \alpha_{bus}]$. The results for the test are as shown in Table 23.26.

The hypothesis that the odds ratios for the other three choices are independent from *air* would be rejected based on these results, as the chi-squared statistic exceeds the critical value.

Because IIA was rejected, they estimated a nested logit model of the following type:

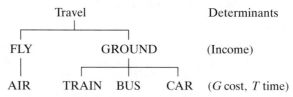

Note that one of the branches has only a single choice, so the conditional probability, $P_{j|fly} = P_{air|fly} = 1$. The estimates marked "unconditional" in Table 23.27 are the simple conditional (multinomial) logit (MNL) model for choice among the four alternatives that was reported earlier. Both inclusive value parameters are constrained (by construction) to equal 1.0000. The FIML estimates are obtained by maximizing the full log-likelihood for the nested logit model. In this model,

$$\text{Prob}(choice\,|\,branch) = P(\alpha_{air}d_{air} + \alpha_{train}d_{train} + \alpha_{bus}d_{bus} + \beta_G GC + \beta_T TTME),$$
$$\text{Prob}(branch) = P(\gamma d_{air}HINC + \tau_{fly}IV_{fly} + \tau_{ground}IV_{ground}),$$
$$\text{Prob}(choice, branch) = \text{Prob}(choice\,|\,branch) \times \text{Prob}(branch).$$

The likelihood ratio statistic for the nesting (heteroscedasticity) against the null hypothesis of homoscedasticity is $-2[-199.1284 - (-193.6561)] = 10.945$. The 95 percent critical value from the chi-squared distribution with two degrees of freedom is 5.99, so the hypothesis is rejected. We can also carry out a Wald test. The asymptotic covariance matrix for the two inclusive value parameters is $[0.01977 / 0.009621, 0.01529]$. The Wald

**TABLE 23.27**    Estimates of a Mode Choice Model (standard errors in parentheses)

| Parameter | FIML Estimate | | Unconditional | |
|---|---|---|---|---|
| $\alpha_{air}$ | 6.042 | (1.199) | 5.207 | (0.779) |
| $\alpha_{bus}$ | 4.096 | (0.615) | 3.163 | (0.450) |
| $\alpha_{train}$ | 5.065 | (0.662) | 3.869 | (0.443) |
| $\beta_{GC}$ | −0.03159 | (0.00816) | −0.1550 | (0.00441) |
| $\beta_{TTME}$ | −0.1126 | (0.0141) | −0.09612 | (0.0104) |
| $\gamma_H$ | 0.01533 | (0.00938) | 0.01329 | (0.0103) |
| $\tau_{fly}$ | 0.5860 | (0.141) | 1.0000 | (0.000) |
| $\tau_{ground}$ | 0.3890 | (0.124) | 1.0000 | (0.000) |
| $\sigma_{fly}$ | 2.1886 | (0.525) | 1.2825 | (0.000) |
| $\sigma_{ground}$ | 3.2974 | (1.048) | 1.2825 | (0.000) |
| $\ln L$ | −193.6561 | | −199.1284 | |

statistic for the joint test of the hypothesis that $\tau_{fly} = \tau_{ground} = 1$, is

$$W = \begin{pmatrix} 0.586 - 1.0 & 0.389 - 1.0 \end{pmatrix} \begin{bmatrix} 0.1977 & 0.009621 \\ 0.009621 & 0.01529 \end{bmatrix}^{-1} \begin{pmatrix} 0.586 - 1.0 \\ 0.389 - 1.0 \end{pmatrix} = 24.475.$$

The hypothesis is rejected, once again.

The choice model was reestimated under the assumptions of the heteroscedastic extreme value (HEV) model. [See Greene (2007b).] This model allows a separate variance, $\sigma_j^2 = \pi^2/(6\theta_j^2)$ for each $\varepsilon_{ij}$ in (23-48). The results are shown in Table 23.28. This model is

**TABLE 23.28**    Estimates of a Heteroscedastic Extreme Value Model (standard errors in parentheses)

| Parameter | HEV Model | | Heteroscedastic HEV Model | | Restricted HEV Model | | Nested Logit Model | |
|---|---|---|---|---|---|---|---|---|
| $\alpha_{air}$ | 7.8326 | (10.951) | 5.1815 | (6.042) | 2.973 | (0.995) | 6.062 | (1.199) |
| $\alpha_{bus}$ | 7.1718 | (9.135) | 5.1302 | (5.132) | 4.050 | (0.494) | 4.096 | (0.615) |
| $\alpha_{train}$ | 6.8655 | (8.829) | 4.8654 | (5.071) | 3.042 | (0.429) | 5.065 | (0.662) |
| $\beta_{GC}$ | −0.05156 | (0.0694) | −0.03326 | (0.0378) | −0.0289 | (0.00580) | −0.03159 | (0.00816) |
| $\beta_{TTME}$ | −0.1968 | (0.288) | −0.1372 | (0.164) | −0.0828 | (0.00576) | −0.1126 | (0.0141) |
| $\gamma$ | 0.04024 | (0.0607) | 0.03557 | (0.0451) | 0.0238 | (0.0186) | 0.01533 | (0.00938) |
| $\tau_{fly}$ | | | | | | | 0.5860 | (0.141) |
| $\tau_{ground}$ | | | | | | | 0.3890 | (0.124) |
| $\theta_{air}$ | 0.2485 | (0.369) | 0.2890 | (0.321) | 0.4959 | (0.124) | | |
| $\theta_{train}$ | 0.2595 | (0.418) | 0.3629 | (0.482) | 1.0000 | (0.000) | | |
| $\theta_{bus}$ | 0.6065 | (1.040) | 0.6895 | (0.945) | 1.0000 | (0.000) | | |
| $\theta_{car}$ | 1.0000 | (0.000) | 1.0000 | (0.000) | 1.0000 | (0.000) | | |
| $\phi$ | 0.0000 | (0.000) | 0.00552 | (0.00573) | 0.0000 | (0.000) | | |
| *Implied Standard Deviations* | | | | | | | | |
| $\sigma_{air}$ | 5.161 | (7.667) | | | | | | |
| $\sigma_{train}$ | 4.942 | (7.978) | | | | | | |
| $\sigma_{bus}$ | 2.115 | (3.623) | | | | | | |
| $\sigma_{car}$ | 1.283 | (0.000) | | | | | | |
| $\ln L$ | −195.6605 | | −194.5107 | | −200.3791 | | −193.6561 | |

less restrictive than the nested logit model. To make them comparable, we note that we found that $\sigma_{air} = \pi/(\tau_{fly}\sqrt{6}) = 2.1886$ and $\sigma_{train} = \sigma_{bus} = \sigma_{car} = \pi/(\tau_{ground}\sqrt{6}) = 3.2974$. The heteroscedastic extreme value (HEV) model thus relaxes one variance restriction, because it has three free variance parameters instead of two. On the other hand, the important degree of freedom here is that the HEV model does not impose the IIA assumption anywhere in the choice set, whereas the nested logit does, within each branch.

A primary virtue of the HEV model, the nested logit model, and other alternative models is that they relax the IIA assumption. This assumption has implications for the cross elasticities between attributes in the different probabilities. Table 23.29 lists the estimated elasticities of the estimated probabilities with respect to changes in the generalized cost variable. Elasticities are computed by averaging the individual sample values rather than computing them once at the sample means. The implication of the IIA assumption can be seen in the table entries. Thus, in the estimates for the multinomial logit (MNL) model, the cross elasticities for each attribute are all equal. In the nested logit model, the IIA property only holds within the branch. Thus, in the first column, the effect of GC of air affects all ground modes equally, whereas the effect of GC for train is the same for bus and car but different from these two for air. All these elasticities vary freely in the HEV model.

Table 23.29 lists the estimates of the parameters of the multinomial probit and random parameters logit models. For the multinomial probit model, we fit three specifications: (1) free correlations among the choices, which implies an unrestricted $3 \times 3$ correlation matrix and two free standard deviations; (2) uncorrelated disturbances, but free standard deviations, a model that parallels the heteroscedastic extreme value model; and (3) uncorrelated disturbances and equal standard deviations, a model that is the same as the original conditional logit model save for the normal distribution of the disturbances instead of the extreme value assumed in the logit model. In this case,

**TABLE 23.29** Estimated Elasticities with Respect to Generalized Cost

| | Cost Is That of Alternative | | | |
| --- | --- | --- | --- | --- |
| *Effect on* | *Air* | *Train* | *Bus* | *Car* |
| *Multinomial Logit* | | | | |
| Air | −1.136 | 0.498 | 0.238 | 0.418 |
| Train | 0.456 | −1.520 | 0.238 | 0.418 |
| Bus | 0.456 | 0.498 | −1.549 | 0.418 |
| Car | 0.456 | 0.498 | 0.238 | −1.061 |
| *Nested Logit* | | | | |
| Air | −0.858 | 0.332 | 0.179 | 0.308 |
| Train | 0.314 | −4.075 | 0.887 | 1.657 |
| Bus | 0.314 | 1.595 | −4.132 | 1.657 |
| Car | 0.314 | 1.595 | 0.887 | −2.498 |
| *Heteroscedastic Extreme Value* | | | | |
| Air | −1.040 | 0.367 | 0.221 | 0.441 |
| Train | 0.272 | −1.495 | 0.250 | 0.553 |
| Bus | 0.688 | 0.858 | −6.562 | 3.384 |
| Car | 0.690 | 0.930 | 1.254 | −2.717 |

the scaling of the utility functions is different by a factor of $(\pi^2/6)^{1/2} = 1.283$, as the probit model assumes $\varepsilon_j$ has a standard deviation of 1.0.

We also fit three variants of the random parameters logit. In these cases, the choice-specific variance for each utility function is $\sigma_j^2 + \theta_j^2$ where $\sigma_j^2$ is the contribution of the logit model, which is $\pi^2/6 = 1.645$, and $\theta_j^2$ is the estimated constant specific variance estimated in the random parameters model. The combined estimated standard deviations are given in the table. The estimates of the specific parameters, $\theta_j$, are given in the footnotes. The estimated models are (1) unrestricted variation and correlation among the three intercept parameters—this parallels the general specification of the multinomial probit model; (2) only the constant terms randomly distributed but uncorrelated, a model that is parallel to the multinomial probit model with no cross-equation correlation and to the heteroscedastic extreme value model shown in Table 23.28; and (3) random but uncorrelated parameters. This model is more general than the others, but is somewhat restricted as the parameters are assumed to be uncorrelated. Identification of the correlation matrix is weak in this model—after all, we are attempting to estimate a $6 \times 6$ correlation matrix for all unobserved variables. Only the estimated parameters are shown in Table 23.30. Estimated standard errors are similar to (although generally somewhat larger than) those for the basic multinomial logit model.

The standard deviations and correlations shown for the multinomial probit model are parameters of the distribution of $\varepsilon_{ij}$, the overall randomness in the model. The counterparts in the random parameters model apply to the distributions of the parameters. Thus, the full disturbance in the model in which only the constants are random is $\varepsilon_{iair} + u_{air}$ for air, and likewise for train and bus. Likewise, the correlations shown

**TABLE 23.30**  Parameter Estimates for Normal-Based Multinomial Choice Models

| Parameter | Multinomial Probit | | | Random Parameters Logit | | |
|---|---|---|---|---|---|---|
| | *Unrestricted* | *Homoscedastic* | *Uncorrelated* | *Unrestricted* | *Constants* | *Uncorrelated* |
| $\alpha_{air}$ | 1.358 | 3.005 | 3.171 | 5.519 | 4.807 | 12.603 |
| $\sigma_{air}$ | 4.940 | 1.000[a] | 3.629 | 4.009[d] | 3.225[b] | 2.803[c] |
| $\alpha_{train}$ | 4.298 | 2.409 | 4.277 | 5.776 | 5.035 | 13.504 |
| $\sigma_{train}$ | 1.899 | 1.000[a] | 1.581 | 1.904 | 1.290[b] | 1.373 |
| $\alpha_{bus}$ | 3.609 | 1.834 | 3.533 | 4.813 | 4.062 | 11.962 |
| $\sigma_{bus}$ | 1.000[a] | 1.000[a] | 1.000[a] | 1.424 | 3.147[b] | 1.287 |
| $\alpha_{car}$ | 0.000[a] | 0.000[a] | 0.000[a] | 0.000[a] | 0.000[a] | 0.000 |
| $\sigma_{car}$ | 1.000[a] | 1.000 | 1.000[a] | 1.283[a] | 1.283[a] | 1.283[a] |
| $\beta_G$ | −0.0351 | −0.0113 | −0.0325 | −0.0326 | −0.0317 | −0.0544 |
| $\sigma_{\beta G}$ | — | — | — | 0.000[a] | 0.000[a] | 0.00561 |
| $\beta_T$ | −0.0769 | −0.0563 | −0.0918 | −0.126 | −0.112 | −0.2822 |
| $\sigma_{\beta T}$ | — | — | — | 0.000[a] | 0.000[a] | 0.182 |
| $\gamma_H$ | 0.0593 | 0.0126 | 0.0370 | 0.0334 | 0.0319 | 0.0846 |
| $\sigma_{\gamma}$ | — | — | — | 0.000[a] | 0.000[a] | 0.0768 |
| $\rho_{AT}$ | 0.581 | 0.000[a] | 0.000[a] | 0.543 | 0.000[a] | 0.000[a] |
| $\rho_{AB}$ | 0.576 | 0.000[a] | 0.000[a] | 0.532 | 0.000[a] | 0.000[a] |
| $\rho_{BT}$ | 0.718 | 0.000[a] | 0.000[a] | 0.993 | 0.000[a] | 0.000[a] |
| log $L$ | −196.9244 | −208.9181 | −199.7623 | −193.7160 | −199.0073 | −175.5333 |

[a]Restricted to this fixed value.
[b]Computed as the square root of $(\pi^2/6 + \theta_j^2)$, $\theta_{air} = 2.959$, $\theta_{train} = 0.136$, $\theta_{bus} = 0.183$, $\theta_{car} = 0.000$.
[c]$\theta_{air} = 2.492$, $\theta_{train} = 0.489$, $\theta_{bus} = 0.108$, $\theta_{car} = 0.000$.
[d]Derived standard deviations for the random constants are $\theta_{air} = 3.798$, $\theta_{train} = 1.182$, $\theta_{bus} = 0.0712$, $\theta_{car} = 0.000$.

for the first two models are directly comparable, although it should be noted that in the random parameters model, the disturbances have a distribution that is that of a sum of an extreme value and a normal variable, while in the probit model, the disturbances are normally distributed. With these considerations, the "unrestricted" models in each case are comparable and are, in fact, fairly similar.

None of this discussion suggests a preference for one model or the other. The likelihood values are not comparable, so a direct test is precluded. Both relax the IIA assumption, which is a crucial consideration. The random parameters model enjoys a significant practical advantage, as discussed earlier, and also allows a much richer specification of the utility function itself. But, the question still warrants additional study. Both models are making their way into the applied literature.

### 23.11.8 PANEL DATA AND STATED CHOICE EXPERIMENTS

Panel data in the unordered discrete choice setting typically come in the form of sequential choices. Train (2003, Chapter 6) reports an analysis of the site choices of 258 anglers who chose among 59 possible fishing sites for total of 962 visits. Allenby and Rossi (1999) modeled brand choice for a sample of shoppers who made multiple store trips. The mixed logit model is a framework that allows the counterpart to a random effects model. The random utility model would appear

$$U_{ij,t} = \mathbf{x}'_{ij,t}\boldsymbol{\beta}_i + \varepsilon_{ij,t},$$

where conditioned on $\boldsymbol{\beta}_i$, a multinomial logit model applies. The random coefficients carry the common effects across choice situations. For example, if the random co-efficients include choice-specific constant terms, then the random utility model becomes essentially a random effects model. A modification of the model that resembles Mundlak's correction for the random effects model is

$$\boldsymbol{\beta}_i = \boldsymbol{\beta}^0 + \boldsymbol{\Delta}\mathbf{z}_i + \boldsymbol{\Gamma}\mathbf{u}_i,$$

where, typically, $\mathbf{z}_i$ would contain demographic and socioeconomic information.

The **stated choice experiment** is similar to the repeated choice situation, with a crucial difference. In a stated choice survey, the respondent is asked about his or her preferences over a series of hypothetical choices, often including one or more that are actually available and others that might not be available (yet). Hensher, Rose, and Greene (2006) describe a survey of Australian commuters who were asked about hypothetical commutation modes in a choice set that included the one they currently took and a variety of alternatives. Revelt and Train (2000) analyzed a stated choice experiment in which California electricity consumers were asked to choose among alternative hypothetical energy suppliers. The advantage of the stated choice experiment is that it allows the analyst to study choice situations over a range of variation of the attributes or a range of choices that might not exist within the observed, actual outcomes. Thus, the original work on the MNL by McFadden et al. concerned survey data on whether commuters would ride a (then-hypothetical) underground train system to work in the San Francisco Bay area. The disadvantage of **stated choice data** is that they are hypothetical. Particularly when they are mixed with **revealed preference data,** the researcher must assume that the same preference patterns govern both types of outcomes. This is likely to be a dubious assumption. One method of accommodating the mixture of underlying preferences is to build different scaling parameters into the model for the stated and revealed preference components of the model. Greene and Hensher (2007) suggest a nested logit model that groups the hypothetical choices in one branch of a tree and the observed choices in another.

## 23.12  SUMMARY AND CONCLUSIONS

This chapter has surveyed techniques for modeling discrete choice. We examined three classes of models: binary choice, ordered choice, and multinomial choice. These are quite far removed from the regression models (linear and nonlinear) that have been the focus of the preceding 22 chapters. The most important difference concerns the modeling approach. Up to this point, we have been primarily interested in modeling the conditional mean function for outcomes that vary continuously. In this chapter, we have shifted our approach to one of modeling the conditional probabilities of events.

Modeling binary choice—the decision between two alternatives—is a growth area in the applied econometrics literature. Maximum likelihood estimation of fully parameterized models remains the mainstay of the literature. But, we also considered semiparametric and nonparametric forms of the model and examined models for time series and panel data. The ordered choice model is a natural extension of the binary choice setting and also a convenient bridge between models of choice between two alternatives and more complex models of choice among multiple alternatives. Multinomial choice modeling is likewise a large field, both within economics and, especially, in many other fields, such as marketing, transportation, political science, and so on. The multinomial logit model and many variations of it provide an especially rich framework within which modelers have carefully matched behavioral modeling to empirical specification and estimation.

### Key Terms and Concepts

- Attributes
- Binary choice model
- Bivariate ordered probit
- Bivariate probit
- Bootstrapping
- Butler and Moffitt method
- Characteristics
- Choice-based sampling
- Chow test
- Conditional likelihood function
- Conditional logit model
- Control function
- Discriminant analysis
- Fixed effects model
- Full information maximum likelihood (FIML)
- Generalized residual

- Goodness of fit measure
- Gumbel model
- Heterogeneity
- Heteroscedasticity
- Incidental parameters problem
- Inclusive value
- Independence from irrelevant alternatives
- Index function model
- Initial conditions
- Kernel density estimator
- Kernel function
- Lagrange multiplier test
- Latent regression
- Likelihood equations
- Likelihood ratio test
- Limited information ML

- Linear probability model
- Logit
- Log-odds ratios
- Marginal effects
- Maximum likelihood
- Maximum score estimator
- Maximum simulated likelihood
- Mean-squared deviation
- Method of kernels
- Method of scoring
- Minimal sufficient statistic
- Mixed logit model
- Multinomial logit model
- Multinomial probit model
- Multivariate probit
- Negative binomial model

- Nested logit model
- Nonnested models
- Normit
- Ordered choice model
- Persistence
- Probit
- Quadrature
- Qualitative choice
- Qualitative response

- Quasi-MLE
- Random coefficients
- Random effects model
- Random parameters logit model
- Random utility model
- Ranking
- Recursive model
- Revealed preference data

- Robust covariance estimation
- Semiparametric estimation
- State dependence
- Stated choice data
- Stated choice experiment
- Tetrachoric correlation
- Unbalanced sample
- Unordered choice

## Exercises

1. A binomial probability model is to be based on the following index function model:

$$y^* = \alpha + \beta d + \varepsilon,$$
$$y = 1, \quad \text{if } y^* > 0,$$
$$y = 0 \quad \text{otherwise.}$$

   The only regressor, $d$, is a dummy variable. The data consist of 100 observations that have the following:

   |       | $y$ |    |
   |-------|-----|----|
   |       | 0   | 1  |
   | $d$  0 | 24  | 28 |
   |       1 | 32  | 16 |

   Obtain the maximum likelihood estimators of $\alpha$ and $\beta$, and estimate the asymptotic standard errors of your estimates. Test the hypothesis that $\beta$ equals zero by using a Wald test (asymptotic $t$ test) and a likelihood ratio test. Use the probit model and then repeat, using the logit model. Do your results change? (Hint: Formulate the log-likelihood in terms of $\alpha$ and $\delta = \alpha + \beta$.)

2. Suppose that a linear probability model is to be fit to a set of observations on a dependent variable $y$ that takes values zero and one, and a single regressor $x$ that varies continuously across observations. Obtain the exact expressions for the least squares slope in the regression in terms of the mean(s) and variance of $x$, and interpret the result.

3. Given the data set

   | $y$ | 1 | 0 | 0 | 1 | 1 | 0 | 0 | 1 | 1 | 1 |
   |-----|---|---|---|---|---|---|---|---|---|---|
   | $x$ | 9 | 2 | 5 | 4 | 6 | 7 | 3 | 5 | 2 | 6' |

   estimate a probit model and test the hypothesis that $x$ is not influential in determining the probability that $y$ equals one.

4. Construct the Lagrange multiplier statistic for testing the hypothesis that all the slopes (but not the constant term) equal zero in the binomial logit model. Prove that the Lagrange multiplier statistic is $nR^2$ in the regression of $(y_i = p)$ on the $x$'s, where $p$ is the sample proportion of 1's.

5. We are interested in the ordered probit model. Our data consist of 250 observations, of which the response are

| y | 0 | 1 | 2 | 3 | 4 |
|---|---|---|---|---|---|
| n | 50 | 40 | 45 | 80 | 35 |

Using the preceding data, obtain maximum likelihood estimates of the unknown parameters of the model. (Hint: Consider the probabilities as the unknown parameters.)

6. The following hypothetical data give the participation rates in a particular type of recycling program and the number of trucks purchased for collection by 10 towns in a small mid-Atlantic state:

| Town | 1 | 2 | 3 | 4 | 5 | 6 | 7 | 8 | 9 | 10 |
|---|---|---|---|---|---|---|---|---|---|---|
| Trucks | 160 | 250 | 170 | 365 | 210 | 206 | 203 | 305 | 270 | 340 |
| Participation% | 11 | 74 | 8 | 87 | 62 | 83 | 48 | 84 | 71 | 79 |

The town of Eleven is contemplating initiating a recycling program but wishes to achieve a 95 percent rate of participation. Using a probit model for your analysis,

a. How many trucks would the town expect to have to purchase to achieve its goal? (Hint: You can form the log likelihood by replacing $y_i$ with the participation rate (e.g., 0.11 for observation 1) and $(1 - y_i)$ with 1—the rate in (23-33).

b. If trucks cost $20,000 each, then is a goal of 90 percent reachable within a budget of $6.5 million? (That is, should they *expect* to reach the goal?)

c. According to your model, what is the marginal value of the 301st truck in terms of the increase in the percentage participation?

7. A data set consists of $n = n_1 + n_2 + n_3$ observations on y and x. For the first $n_1$ observations, $y = 1$ and $x = 1$. For the next $n_2$ observations, $y = 0$ and $x = 1$. For the last $n_3$ observations, $y = 0$ and $x = 0$. Prove that neither (23-19) nor (23-21) has a solution.

8. Prove (23-28).

9. In the panel data models estimated in Section 23.5, neither the logit nor the probit model provides a framework for applying a Hausman test to determine whether fixed or random effects is preferred. Explain. (Hint: Unlike our application in the linear model, the incidental parameters problem persists here.)

## Applications

1. Appendix Table F24.1 provides Fair's (1978) *Redbook* survey on extramarital affairs. The data are described in Application 1 at the end of Chapter 24 and in Appendix F. The variables in the data set are as follows:

   $id$ = an identification number,
   $C$ = constant, value = 1,
   $yrb$ = a constructed measure of time spent in extramarital affairs,

$v1$ = a rating of the marriage, coded 1 to 4,
$v2$ = age, in years, aggregated,
$v3$ = number of years married,
$v4$ = number of children, top coded at 5,
$v5$ = religiosity, 1 to 4, 1 = not, 4 = very,
$v6$ = education, coded 9, 12, 14, 16, 17, 20,
$v7$ = occupation,
$v8$ = husband's occupation,

and three other variables that are not used. The sample contains a survey of 6,366 married women, conducted by *Redbook* magazine. For this exercise, we will analyze, first, the binary variable

$$A = 1 \text{ if } yrb > 0, 0 \text{ otherwise.}$$

The regressors of interest are $v1$ to $v8$; however, not necessarily all of them belong in your model. Use these data to build a binary choice model for $A$. Report all computed results for the model. Compute the marginal effects for the variables you choose. Compare the results you obtain for a probit model to those for a logit model. Are there any substantial differences in the results for the two models?

2. Continuing the analysis of the first application, we now consider the self-reported rating, $v1$. This is a natural candidate for an ordered choice model, because the simple four-item coding is a censored version of what would be a continuous scale on some subjective satisfaction variable. Analyze this variable using an ordered probit model. What variables appear to explain the response to this survey question? (Note, the variable is coded 1, 2, 3, 4. Some programs accept data for ordered choice modeling in this form, e.g., *Stata*, while others require the variable to be coded 0, 1, 2, 3, e.g., *LIMDEP*. Be sure to determine which is appropriate for the program you are using and transform the data if necessary.) Can you obtain the partial effects for your model? Report them as well. What do they suggest about the impact of the different independent variables on the reported ratings?

# 24

# TRUNCATION, CENSORING, AND SAMPLE SELECTION

## 24.1 INTRODUCTION

This chapter is concerned with truncation and censoring.[1] The effect of truncation occurs when sample data are drawn from a subset of a larger population of interest. For example, studies of income based on incomes above or below some poverty line may be of limited usefulness for inference about the whole population. Truncation is essentially a characteristic of the distribution from which the sample data are drawn. Censoring is a more common feature of recent studies. To continue the example, suppose that instead of being unobserved, all incomes below the poverty line are reported as if they were *at* the poverty line. The censoring of a range of values of the variable of interest introduces a distortion into conventional statistical results that is similar to that of truncation. Unlike truncation, however, censoring is essentially a defect in the sample data. Presumably, if they were not censored, the data would be a representative sample from the population of interest.

This chapter will discuss three broad topics: truncation, censoring, and a form of truncation called the **sample selection** problem. Although most empirical work in this area involves censoring rather than truncation, we will study the simpler model of truncation first. It provides most of the theoretical tools we need to analyze models of censoring and sample selection.[2]

## 24.2 TRUNCATION

In this section, we are concerned with inferring the characteristics of a full population from a sample drawn from a restricted part of that population.

### 24.2.1 TRUNCATED DISTRIBUTIONS

A **truncated distribution** is the part of an untruncated distribution that is above or below some specified value. For instance, in Example 24.2, we are given a characteristic of the distribution of incomes above $100,000. This subset is a part of the full distribution of incomes which range from zero to (essentially) infinity.

---

[1]Five of the many surveys of these topics are Dhrymes (1984), Maddala (1977b, 1983, 1984), and Amemiya (1984). The last is part of a symposium on censored and truncated regression models. Surveys that are oriented toward applications and techniques are Long (1997), deMaris (2004), and Greene (2006). Some recent results on non- and semiparametric estimation appear in Lee (1996).

[2]Although sample selection can be viewed formally as merely a type of truncation, it is useful to treat the methodological aspects separately.

> **THEOREM 24.1  Density of a Truncated Random Variable**
> *If a continuous random variable $x$ has pdf $f(x)$ and $a$ is a constant, then*[3]
> $$f(x \mid x > a) = \frac{f(x)}{\text{Prob}(x > a)}.$$
> *The proof follows from the definition of conditional probability and amounts merely to scaling the density so that it integrates to one over the range above $a$. Note that the truncated distribution is a conditional distribution.*

Most recent applications based on continuous random variables use the **truncated normal distribution.** If $x$ has a normal distribution with mean $\mu$ and standard deviation $\sigma$, then

$$\text{Prob}(x > a) = 1 - \Phi\left(\frac{a - \mu}{\sigma}\right) = 1 - \Phi(\alpha),$$

where $\alpha = (a - \mu)/\sigma$ and $\Phi(.)$ is the standard normal cdf. The density of the truncated normal distribution is then

$$f(x \mid x > a) = \frac{f(x)}{1 - \Phi(\alpha)} = \frac{(2\pi\sigma^2)^{-1/2}e^{-(x-\mu)^2/(2\sigma^2)}}{1 - \Phi(\alpha)} = \frac{\frac{1}{\sigma}\phi\left(\frac{x - \mu}{\sigma}\right)}{1 - \Phi(\alpha)},$$

where $\phi(.)$ is the standard normal pdf. The **truncated standard normal distribution,** with $\mu = 0$ and $\sigma = 1$, is illustrated for $a = -0.5, 0,$ and $0.5$ in Figure 24.1. Another truncated distribution that has appeared in the recent literature, this one for a discrete random variable, is the truncated at zero Poisson distribution,

$$\text{Prob}[Y = y \mid y > 0] = \frac{(e^{-\lambda}\lambda^y)/y!}{\text{Prob}[Y > 0]} = \frac{(e^{-\lambda}\lambda^y)/y!}{1 - \text{Prob}[Y = 0]}$$

$$= \frac{(e^{-\lambda}\lambda^y)/y!}{1 - e^{-\lambda}}, \quad \lambda > 0, y = 1, \ldots$$

This distribution is used in models of uses of recreation and other kinds of facilities where observations of zero uses are discarded.[4]

For convenience in what follows, we shall call a random variable whose distribution is truncated a **truncated random variable.**

## 24.2.2  MOMENTS OF TRUNCATED DISTRIBUTIONS

We are usually interested in the mean and variance of the truncated random variable. They would be obtained by the general formula:

$$E[x \mid x > a] = \int_a^\infty x f(x \mid x > a)\, dx$$

for the mean and likewise for the variance.

---

[3]The case of truncation from above instead of below is handled in an analogous fashion and does not require any new results.

[4]See Shaw (1988).

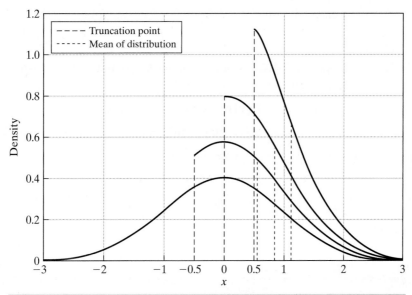

**FIGURE 24.1**   Truncated Normal Distributions.

### Example 24.1   Truncated Uniform Distribution

If $x$ has a *standard* uniform distribution, denoted $U(0, 1)$, then

$$f(x) = 1, \quad 0 \le x \le 1.$$

The truncated at $x = \frac{1}{3}$ distribution is also uniform;

$$f\left(x \mid x > \frac{1}{3}\right) = \frac{f(x)}{\mathrm{Prob}\left(x > \frac{1}{3}\right)} = \frac{1}{\left(\frac{2}{3}\right)} = \frac{3}{2}, \quad \frac{1}{3} \le x \le 1.$$

The expected value is

$$E\left[x \mid x > \frac{1}{3}\right] = \int_{1/3}^{1} x\left(\frac{3}{2}\right) dx = \frac{2}{3}.$$

For a variable distributed uniformly between $L$ and $U$, the variance is $(U - L)^2/12$. Thus,

$$\mathrm{Var}\left[x \mid x > \tfrac{1}{3}\right] = \tfrac{1}{27}.$$

The mean and variance of the untruncated distribution are $\frac{1}{2}$ and $\frac{1}{12}$, respectively.

Example 24.1 illustrates two results.

1. If the truncation is from below, then the mean of the truncated variable is greater than the mean of the original one. If the truncation is from above, then the mean of the truncated variable is smaller than the mean of the original one. This is clearly visible in Figure 24.1.
2. Truncation reduces the variance compared with the variance in the untruncated distribution.

Henceforth, we shall use the terms **truncated mean** and **truncated variance** to refer to the mean and variance of the random variable with a truncated distribution.

For the truncated normal distribution, we have the following theorem:[5]

---

**THEOREM 24.2**   **Moments of the Truncated Normal Distribution**
*If $x \sim N[\mu, \sigma^2]$ and a is a constant, then*

$$E[x \mid \text{truncation}] = \mu + \sigma\lambda(\alpha), \qquad \textbf{(24-1)}$$

$$\text{Var}[x \mid \text{truncation}] = \sigma^2[1 - \delta(\alpha)], \qquad \textbf{(24-2)}$$

*where $\alpha = (a - \mu)/\sigma$, $\phi(\alpha)$ is the standard normal density and*

$$\lambda(\alpha) = \phi(\alpha)/[1 - \Phi(\alpha)] \quad \text{if truncation is } x > a, \qquad \textbf{(24-3a)}$$

$$\lambda(\alpha) = -\phi(\alpha)/\Phi(\alpha) \qquad \text{if truncation is } x < a, \qquad \textbf{(24-3b)}$$

*and*

$$\delta(\alpha) = \lambda(\alpha)[\lambda(\alpha) - \alpha]. \qquad \textbf{(24-4)}$$

---

An important result is

$$0 < \delta(\alpha) < 1 \quad \text{for all values of } \alpha,$$

which implies point 2 after Example 24.1. A result that we will use at several points below is $d\phi(\alpha)/d\alpha = -\alpha\phi(\alpha)$. The function $\lambda(\alpha)$ is called the **inverse Mills ratio.** The function in (24-3a) is also called the **hazard function** for the standard normal distribution.

### Example 24.2   A Truncated Lognormal Income Distribution

"The typical 'upper affluent American' . . . makes $142,000 per year. . . . The people surveyed had household income of at least $100,000."[6] Would this statistic tell us anything about the "typical American"? As it stands, it probably does not (popular impressions notwithstanding). The 1987 article where this appeared went on to state, "If you're in that category, pat yourself on the back—only 2 percent of American households make the grade, according to the survey." Because the **degree of truncation** in the sample is 98 percent, the $142,000 was probably quite far from the mean in the full population.

Suppose that incomes, $x$, in the population were lognormally distributed—see Section B.4.4. Then, the log of income, $y$, had a normal distribution with, say, mean $\mu$ and standard deviation, $\sigma$. Suppose that the survey was large enough for us to treat the sample average as the true mean. Assuming so, we'll deduce $\mu$ and $\sigma$ then determine the population mean income.

Two useful numbers for this example are ln 100 = 4.605 and ln 142 = 4.956. The article states that

$$\text{Prob}[x \geq 100] = \text{Prob}[\exp(y) \geq 100] = 0.02,$$

or

$$\text{Prob}(y < 4.605) = 0.98.$$

---

[5]Details may be found in Johnson, Kotz, and Balakrishnan (1994, pp. 156–158).
[6]See *New York Post* (1987).

This implies that

$$\text{Prob}[(y - \mu)/\sigma < (4.605 - \mu)/\sigma] = 0.98.$$

Because $\Phi[(4.605 - \mu)/\sigma] = 0.98$, we know that

$$\Phi^{-1}(0.98) = 2.054 = (4.605 - \mu)/\sigma,$$

or

$$4.605 = \mu + 2.054\sigma.$$

The article also states that

$$E[x \mid x > 100] = E[\exp(y) \mid \exp(y) > 100] = 142,$$

or

$$E[\exp(y) \mid y > 4.645] = 142.$$

To proceed, we need another result for the lognormal distribution:

> If $y \sim N[\mu, \sigma^2]$, then $E[\exp(y) \mid y > a] = \exp(\mu + \sigma^2/2) \times \dfrac{\Phi(\sigma - (a - \mu)/\sigma)}{1 - \Phi((a - \mu)/\sigma)}.$

[See Johnson, Kotz and Balakrishnan (1995, p. 241).] For our application, we would equate this expression to 142, and a to ln 100 = 4.605. This provides a second equation. To estimate the two parameters, we used the method of moments. We solved the minimization problem

$$\text{Minimize}_{\mu,\sigma} \, [4.605 - (\mu + 2.054\sigma)]^2 + [142\Phi((\mu - 4.605)/\sigma) - \exp(\mu + \sigma^2/2)\,\Phi(\sigma - (4.605 - \mu)/\sigma)]^2.$$

The two solutions are 2.89372 and 0.83314 for $\mu$ and $\sigma$, respectively. To obtain the mean income, we now use the result that if $y \sim N[\mu, \sigma^2]$ and $x = \exp(y)$, then $E[x] = \exp(\mu + \sigma^2/2)$. Inserting our values for $\mu$ and $\sigma$ gives $E[x] = \$25,554$. The 1987 Statistical Abstract of the United States gives the mean of household incomes across all groups for the United States as about \$25,000. So, the estimate based on surprisingly little information would have been relatively good. These meager data did, indeed, tell us something about the average American.

### 24.2.3 THE TRUNCATED REGRESSION MODEL

In the model of the earlier examples, we now assume that

$$\mu_i = \mathbf{x}_i'\boldsymbol{\beta}$$

is the deterministic part of the classical regression model. Then

$$y_i = \mathbf{x}_i'\boldsymbol{\beta} + \varepsilon_i,$$

where

$$\varepsilon_i \mid \mathbf{x}_i \sim N[0, \sigma^2],$$

so that

$$y_i \mid \mathbf{x}_i \sim N[\mathbf{x}_i'\boldsymbol{\beta}, \sigma^2]. \tag{24-5}$$

We are interested in the distribution of $y_i$ given that $y_i$ is greater than the truncation point $a$. This is the result described in Theorem 24.2. It follows that

$$E[y_i \mid y_i > a] = \mathbf{x}_i'\boldsymbol{\beta} + \sigma \frac{\phi[(a - \mathbf{x}_i'\boldsymbol{\beta})/\sigma]}{1 - \Phi[(a - \mathbf{x}_i'\boldsymbol{\beta})/\sigma]}. \tag{24-6}$$

The conditional mean is therefore a nonlinear function of $a, \sigma, \mathbf{x}$, and $\boldsymbol{\beta}$.

The marginal effects in this model *in the subpopulation* can be obtained by writing

$$E[y_i \mid y_i > a] = \mathbf{x}_i'\boldsymbol{\beta} + \sigma\lambda(\alpha_i), \tag{24-7}$$

where now $\alpha_i = (a - \mathbf{x}_i'\boldsymbol{\beta})/\sigma$. For convenience, let $\lambda_i = \lambda(\alpha_i)$ and $\delta_i = \delta(\alpha_i)$. Then

$$\begin{aligned}
\frac{\partial E[y_i \mid y_i > a]}{\partial \mathbf{x}_i} &= \boldsymbol{\beta} + \sigma(d\lambda_i/d\alpha_i)\frac{\partial \alpha_i}{\partial \mathbf{x}_i} \\
&= \boldsymbol{\beta} + \sigma(\lambda_i^2 - \alpha_i\lambda_i)(-\boldsymbol{\beta}/\sigma) \\
&= \boldsymbol{\beta}(1 - \lambda_i^2 + \alpha_i\lambda_i) \\
&= \boldsymbol{\beta}(1 - \delta_i).
\end{aligned} \tag{24-8}$$

Note the appearance of the scale factor $1 - \delta_i$ from the truncated variance. Because $(1 - \delta_i)$ is between zero and one, we conclude that for every element of $\mathbf{x}_i$, the marginal effect is less than the corresponding coefficient. There is a similar **attenuation** of the variance. In the subpopulation $y_i > a$, the regression variance is not $\sigma^2$ but

$$\mathrm{Var}[y_i \mid y_i > a] = \sigma^2(1 - \delta_i). \tag{24-9}$$

Whether the marginal effect in (24-7) or the coefficient $\boldsymbol{\beta}$ itself is of interest depends on the intended inferences of the study. If the analysis is to be confined to the subpopulation, then (24-7) is of interest. If the study is intended to extend to the entire population, however, then it is the coefficients $\boldsymbol{\beta}$ that are actually of interest.

One's first inclination might be to use ordinary least squares to estimate the parameters of this regression model. For the subpopulation from which the data are drawn, we could write (24-6) in the form

$$y_i \mid y_i > a = E[y_i \mid y_i > a] + u_i = \mathbf{x}_i'\boldsymbol{\beta} + \sigma\lambda_i + u_i, \tag{24-10}$$

where $u_i$ is $y_i$ minus its conditional expectation. By construction, $u_i$ has a zero mean, but it is heteroscedastic:

$$\mathrm{Var}[u_i] = \sigma^2(1 - \lambda_i^2 + \lambda_i\alpha_i) = \sigma^2(1 - \delta_i),$$

which is a function of $\mathbf{x}_i$. If we estimate (24-10) by ordinary least squares regression of $\mathbf{y}$ on $\mathbf{X}$, then we have omitted a variable, the nonlinear term $\lambda_i$. All the biases that arise because of an omitted variable can be expected.[7]

Without some knowledge of the distribution of $\mathbf{x}$, it is not possible to determine how serious the bias is likely to be. A result obtained by Chung and Goldberger (1984) is broadly suggestive. If $E[\mathbf{x} \mid y]$ in the full population is a linear function of $y$, then plim $\mathbf{b} = \boldsymbol{\beta}\tau$ for some proportionality constant $\tau$. This result is consistent with the widely observed (albeit rather rough) proportionality relationship between least squares estimates

---

[7] See Heckman (1979) who formulates this as a "specification error."

of this model and maximum likelihood estimates.[8] The proportionality result appears to be quite general. In applications, it is usually found that, compared with consistent maximum likelihood estimates, the OLS estimates are biased toward zero. (See Example 24.4.)

## 24.3 CENSORED DATA

A very common problem in microeconomic data is **censoring** of the dependent variable. When the dependent variable is censored, values in a certain range are all transformed to (or reported as) a single value. Some examples that have appeared in the empirical literature are as follows:[9]

1. Household purchases of durable goods [Tobin (1958)],
2. The number of extramarital affairs [Fair (1977, 1978)],
3. The number of hours worked by a woman in the labor force [Quester and Greene (1982)],
4. The number of arrests after release from prison [Witte (1980)],
5. Household expenditure on various commodity groups [Jarque (1987)],
6. Vacation expenditures [Melenberg and van Soest (1996)].

Each of these studies analyzes a dependent variable that is zero for a significant fraction of the observations. Conventional regression methods fail to account for the qualitative difference between *limit* (zero) observations and *nonlimit* (continuous) observations.

### 24.3.1 THE CENSORED NORMAL DISTRIBUTION

The relevant distribution theory for a **censored variable** is similar to that for a truncated one. Once again, we begin with the normal distribution, as much of the received work has been based on an assumption of normality. We also assume that the censoring point is zero, although this is only a convenient normalization. In a truncated distribution, only the part of distribution above $y = 0$ is relevant to our computations. To make the distribution integrate to one, we scale it up by the probability that an observation in the untruncated population falls in the range that interests us. When data are censored, the distribution *that applies to the sample data* is a mixture of discrete and continuous distributions. Figure 24.2 illustrates the effects.

To analyze this distribution, we define a new random variable $y$ transformed from the original one, $y^*$, by

$$y = 0 \quad \text{if } y^* \leq 0,$$
$$y = y^* \quad \text{if } y^* > 0.$$

The distribution that applies if $y^* \sim N[\mu, \sigma^2]$ is $\text{Prob}(y=0) = \text{Prob}(y^* \leq 0) = \Phi(-\mu/\sigma) = 1 - \Phi(\mu/\sigma)$, and if $y^* > 0$, then $y$ has the density of $y^*$.

This distribution is a mixture of discrete and continuous parts. The total probability is one, as required, but instead of scaling the second part, we simply assign the full probability in the censored region to the censoring point, in this case, zero.

---

[8]See the appendix in Hausman and Wise (1977) and Greene (1983) as well.

[9]More extensive listings may be found in Amemiya (1984) and Maddala (1983).

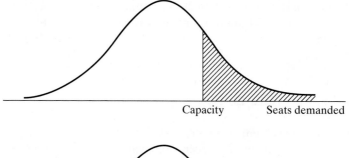

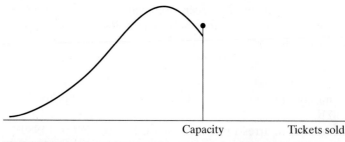

**FIGURE 24.2** Partially Censored Distribution.

**THEOREM 24.3** **Moments of the Censored Normal Variable**
*If* $y^* \sim N[\mu, \sigma^2]$ *and* $y = a$ *if* $y^* \le a$ *or else* $y = y^*$, *then*

$$E[y] = \Phi a + (1 - \Phi)(\mu + \sigma\lambda),$$

*and*

$$\mathrm{Var}[y] = \sigma^2(1 - \Phi)[(1 - \delta) + (\alpha - \lambda)^2\Phi],$$

*where*

$$\Phi[(a - \mu)/\sigma] = \Phi(\alpha) = \mathrm{Prob}(y^* \le a) = \Phi, \quad \lambda = \phi/(1 - \Phi),$$

*and*

$$\delta = \lambda^2 - \lambda\alpha.$$

**Proof:** *For the mean,*

$$\begin{aligned} E[y] &= \mathrm{Prob}(y = a) \times E[y \mid y = a] + \mathrm{Prob}(y > a) \times E[y \mid y > a] \\ &= \mathrm{Prob}(y^* \le a) \times a + \mathrm{Prob}(y^* > a) \times E[y^* \mid y^* > a] \\ &= \Phi a + (1 - \Phi)(\mu + \sigma\lambda) \end{aligned}$$

*using Theorem 24.2. For the variance, we use a counterpart to the decomposition in (B-69), that is,* $\mathrm{Var}[y] = E[\text{conditional variance}] + \mathrm{Var}[\text{conditional mean}]$, *and Theorem 24.2.*

For the special case of $a = 0$, the mean simplifies to

$$E[y \mid a = 0] = \Phi(\mu/\sigma)(\mu + \sigma\lambda), \quad \text{where } \lambda = \frac{\phi(\mu/\sigma)}{\Phi(\mu/\sigma)}.$$

For censoring of the upper part of the distribution instead of the lower, it is only necessary to reverse the role of $\Phi$ and $1 - \Phi$ and redefine $\lambda$ as in Theorem 24.2.

### Example 24.3   Censored Random Variable

We are interested in the number of tickets *demanded* for events at a certain arena. Our only measure is the number actually *sold*. Whenever an event sells out, however, we know that the actual number demanded is larger than the number sold. The number of tickets demanded is censored when it is transformed to obtain the number sold. Suppose that the arena in question has 20,000 seats and, in a recent season, sold out 25 percent of the time. If the average attendance, including sellouts, was 18,000, then what are the mean and standard deviation of the demand for seats? According to Theorem 24.3, the 18,000 is an estimate of

$$E[\text{sales}] = 20{,}000(1 - \Phi) + [\mu + \sigma\lambda]\Phi.$$

Because this is censoring from above, rather than below, $\lambda = -\phi(\alpha)/\Phi(\alpha)$. The argument of $\Phi$, $\phi$, and $\lambda$ is $\alpha = (20{,}000 - \mu)/\sigma$. If 25 percent of the events are sellouts, then $\Phi = 0.75$. Inverting the standard normal at 0.75 gives $\alpha = 0.675$. In addition, if $\alpha = 0.675$, then $-\phi(0.675)/0.75 = \lambda = -0.424$. This result provides two equations in $\mu$ and $\sigma$, (a) $18{,}000 = 0.25(20{,}000) + 0.75(\mu - 0.424\sigma)$ and (b) $0.675\sigma = 20{,}000 - \mu$. The solutions are $\sigma = 2426$ and $\mu = 18{,}362$.

For comparison, suppose that we were told that the mean of 18,000 applies only to the events that were *not* sold out and that, on average, the arena sells out 25 percent of the time. Now our estimates would be obtained from the equations (a) $18{,}000 = \mu - 0.424\sigma$ and (b) $0.675\sigma = 20{,}000 - \mu$. The solutions are $\sigma = 1820$ and $\mu = 18{,}772$.

### 24.3.2   THE CENSORED REGRESSION (TOBIT) MODEL

The regression model based on the preceding discussion is referred to as the **censored regression model** or the **tobit model.** [In reference to Tobin (1958), where the model was first proposed.] The regression is obtained by making the mean in the preceding correspond to a classical regression model. The general formulation is usually given in terms of an index function,

$$
\begin{aligned}
y_i^* &= \mathbf{x}_i'\boldsymbol{\beta} + \varepsilon_i, \\
y_i &= 0 \quad \text{if } y_i^* \leq 0, \\
y_i &= y_i^* \quad \text{if } y_i^* > 0.
\end{aligned}
\tag{24-11}
$$

There are potentially three conditional mean functions to consider, depending on the purpose of the study. For the index variable, sometimes called the *latent variable,* $E[y_i^* \mid \mathbf{x}_i]$ is $\mathbf{x}_i'\boldsymbol{\beta}$. If the data are always censored, however, then this result will usually not be useful. Consistent with Theorem 24.3, for an observation randomly drawn from the population, which may or may not be censored,

$$E[y_i \mid \mathbf{x}_i] = \Phi\left(\frac{\mathbf{x}_i'\boldsymbol{\beta}}{\sigma}\right)(\mathbf{x}_i'\boldsymbol{\beta} + \sigma\lambda_i),$$

where

$$\lambda_i = \frac{\phi[(0 - \mathbf{x}_i'\boldsymbol{\beta})/\sigma]}{1 - \Phi[(0 - \mathbf{x}_i'\boldsymbol{\beta})/\sigma]} = \frac{\phi(\mathbf{x}_i'\boldsymbol{\beta}/\sigma)}{\Phi(\mathbf{x}_i'\boldsymbol{\beta}/\sigma)}.\tag{24-12}$$

Finally, if we intend to confine our attention to uncensored observations, then the results for the truncated regression model apply. The limit observations should not be discarded, however, because the truncated regression model is no more amenable to least squares than the censored data model. It is an unresolved question which of these functions should be used for computing predicted values from this model. Intuition suggests that $E[y_i \mid \mathbf{x}_i]$ is correct, but authors differ on this point. For the setting in Example 24.3, for predicting the number of tickets sold, say, to plan for an upcoming event, the censored mean is obviously the relevant quantity. On the other hand, if the objective is to study the need for a new facility, then the mean of the latent variable $y_i^*$ would be more interesting.

There are differences in the marginal effects as well. For the index variable,

$$\frac{\partial E[y_i^* \mid \mathbf{x}_i]}{\partial \mathbf{x}_i} = \boldsymbol{\beta}.$$

But this result is not what will usually be of interest, because $y_i^*$ is unobserved. For the observed data, $y_i$, the following general result will be useful:[10]

---

**THEOREM 24.4** **Marginal Effects in the Censored Regression Model**

*In the censored regression model with latent regression $y^* = \mathbf{x}'\boldsymbol{\beta} + \varepsilon$ and observed dependent variable, $y = a$ if $y^* \leq a$, $y = b$ if $y^* \geq b$, and $y = y^*$ otherwise, where $a$ and $b$ are constants, let $f(\varepsilon)$ and $F(\varepsilon)$ denote the density and cdf of $\varepsilon$. Assume that $\varepsilon$ is a continuous random variable with mean 0 and variance $\sigma^2$, and $f(\varepsilon \mid \mathbf{x}) = f(\varepsilon)$. Then*

$$\frac{\partial E[y \mid \mathbf{x}]}{\partial \mathbf{x}} = \boldsymbol{\beta} \times \mathrm{Prob}[a < y^* < b].$$

*Proof: By definition,*

$$E[y \mid \mathbf{x}] = a \, \mathrm{Prob}[y^* \leq a \mid \mathbf{x}] + b \, \mathrm{Prob}[y^* \geq b \mid \mathbf{x}]$$
$$+ \mathrm{Prob}[a < y^* < b \mid \mathbf{x}] E[y^* \mid a < y^* < b \mid \mathbf{x}].$$

*Let $\alpha_j = (j - \mathbf{x}'\boldsymbol{\beta})/\sigma$, $F_j = F(\alpha_j)$, $f_j = f(\alpha_j)$, and $j = a, b$. Then*

$$E[y \mid \mathbf{x}] = a F_a + b(1 - F_b) + (F_b - F_a) E[y^* \mid a < y^* < b, \mathbf{x}].$$

*Because $y^* = \mathbf{x}'\boldsymbol{\beta} + \sigma[(y^* - \boldsymbol{\beta}'\mathbf{x})/\sigma]$, the conditional mean may be written*

$$E[y^* \mid a < y^* < b, \mathbf{x}] = \mathbf{x}'\boldsymbol{\beta} + \sigma E\left[\frac{y^* - \mathbf{x}'\boldsymbol{\beta}}{\sigma} \,\middle|\, \frac{a - \mathbf{x}'\boldsymbol{\beta}}{\sigma} < \frac{y^* - \mathbf{x}'\boldsymbol{\beta}}{\sigma} < \frac{b - \mathbf{x}'\boldsymbol{\beta}}{\sigma}\right]$$

$$= \mathbf{x}'\boldsymbol{\beta} + \sigma \int_{\alpha_a}^{\alpha_b} \frac{(\varepsilon/\sigma) f(\varepsilon/\sigma)}{F_b - F_a} d\left(\frac{\varepsilon}{\sigma}\right).$$

---

[10]See Greene (1999) for the general result and Rosett and Nelson (1975) and Nakamura and Nakamura (1983) for applications based on the normal distribution.

> **THEOREM 24.4** (Continued)
>
> *Collecting terms, we have*
>
> $$E[y \mid \mathbf{x}] = a F_a + b(1 - F_b) + (F_b - F_a)\boldsymbol{\beta}'\mathbf{x} + \sigma \int_{\alpha_a}^{\alpha_b} \left(\frac{\varepsilon}{\sigma}\right) f\left(\frac{\varepsilon}{\sigma}\right) d\left(\frac{\varepsilon}{\sigma}\right).$$
>
> *Now, differentiate with respect to* **x**. *The only complication is the last term, for which the differentiation is with respect to the limits of integration. We use Leibnitz's theorem and use the assumption that* $f(\varepsilon)$ *does not involve* **x**. *Thus,*
>
> $$\frac{\partial E[y \mid \mathbf{x}]}{\partial \mathbf{x}} = \left(\frac{-\boldsymbol{\beta}}{\sigma}\right) a f_a - \left(\frac{-\boldsymbol{\beta}}{\sigma}\right) b f_b + (F_b - F_a)\boldsymbol{\beta} + (\mathbf{x}'\boldsymbol{\beta})(f_b - f_a)\left(\frac{-\boldsymbol{\beta}}{\sigma}\right)$$
>
> $$+ \sigma[\alpha_b f_b - \alpha_a f_a]\left(\frac{-\boldsymbol{\beta}}{\sigma}\right).$$
>
> *After inserting the definitions of* $\alpha_a$ *and* $\alpha_b$, *and collecting terms, we find all terms sum to zero save for the desired result,*
>
> $$\frac{\partial E[y \mid \mathbf{x}]}{\partial \mathbf{x}} = (F_b - F_a)\boldsymbol{\beta} = \boldsymbol{\beta} \times \text{Prob}[a < y_i^* < b].$$

Note that this general result includes censoring in either or both tails of the distribution, and it does not assume that $\varepsilon$ is normally distributed. For the standard case with censoring at zero and normally distributed disturbances, the result specializes to

$$\frac{\partial E[y_i \mid \mathbf{x}_i]}{\partial \mathbf{x}_i} = \boldsymbol{\beta} \Phi\left(\frac{\mathbf{x}_i'\boldsymbol{\beta}}{\sigma}\right).$$

Although not a formal result, this does suggest a reason why, in general, least squares estimates of the coefficients in a tobit model usually resemble the MLEs times the proportion of nonlimit observations in the sample.

McDonald and Moffitt (1980) suggested a useful decomposition of $\partial E[y_i \mid \mathbf{x}_i]/\partial \mathbf{x}_i$,

$$\frac{\partial E[y_i \mid \mathbf{x}_i]}{\partial \mathbf{x}_i} = \boldsymbol{\beta} \times \left\{ \Phi_i[1 - \lambda_i(\alpha_i + \lambda_i)] + \phi_i(\alpha_i + \lambda_i) \right\},$$

where $\alpha_i = \mathbf{x}_i'\boldsymbol{\beta}/\sigma$, $\Phi_i = \Phi(\alpha_i)$ and $\lambda_i = \phi_i/\Phi_i$. Taking the two parts separately, this result decomposes the slope vector into

$$\frac{\partial E[y_i \mid \mathbf{x}_i]}{\partial \mathbf{x}_i} = \text{Prob}[y_i > 0] \frac{\partial E[y_i \mid \mathbf{x}_i, y_i > 0]}{\partial \mathbf{x}_i} + E[y_i \mid \mathbf{x}_i, y_i > 0] \frac{\partial \text{Prob}[y_i > 0]}{\partial \mathbf{x}_i}.$$

Thus, a change in $\mathbf{x}_i$ has two effects: It affects the conditional mean of $y_i^*$ in the positive part of the distribution, and it affects the probability that the observation will fall in that part of the distribution.

### Example 24.4  Estimated Tobit Equations for Hours Worked
In their study of the number of hours worked in a survey year by a large sample of wives, Quester and Greene (1982) were interested in whether wives whose marriages were statistically more likely to dissolve hedged against that possibility by spending, on average, more time working. They reported the tobit estimates given in Table 24.1. The last figure in the

**TABLE 24.1**  Tobit Estimates of an Hours Worked Equation

| | White Wives | | Black Wives | | Least | Scaled |
|---|---|---|---|---|---|---|
| | *Coefficient* | *Slope* | *Coefficient* | *Slope* | *Squares* | *OLS* |
| Constant | −1803.13 | | −2753.87 | | | |
| | (−8.64) | | (−9.68) | | | |
| Small kids | −1324.84 | −385.89 | −824.19 | −376.53 | −352.63 | −766.56 |
| | (−19.78) | | (−10.14) | | | |
| Education | −48.08 | −14.00 | 22.59 | 10.32 | 11.47 | 24.93 |
| difference | (−4.77) | | (1.96) | | | |
| Relative wage | 312.07 | 90.90 | 286.39 | 130.93 | 123.95 | 269.46 |
| | (5.71) | | (3.32) | | | |
| Second marriage | 175.85 | 51.51 | 25.33 | 11.57 | 13.14 | 28.57 |
| | (3.47) | | (0.41) | | | |
| Mean divorce | 417.39 | 121.58 | 481.02 | 219.75 | 219.22 | 476.57 |
| probability | (6.52) | | (5.28) | | | |
| High divorce | 670.22 | 195.22 | 578.66 | 264.36 | 244.17 | 530.80 |
| probability | (8.40) | | (5.33) | | | |
| $\sigma$ | 1559 | 618 | 1511 | 826 | | |
| Sample size | 7459 | | 2798 | | | |
| Proportion working | 0.29 | | 0.46 | | | |

table implies that a very large proportion of the women reported zero hours, so least squares regression would be inappropriate.

The figures in parentheses are the ratio of the coefficient estimate to the estimated asymptotic standard error. The dependent variable is hours worked in the survey year. "Small kids" is a dummy variable indicating whether there were children in the household. The "education difference" and "relative wage" variables compare husband and wife on these two dimensions. The wage rate used for wives was predicted using a previously estimated regression model and is thus available for all individuals, whether working or not. "Second marriage" is a dummy variable. Divorce probabilities were produced by a large microsimulation model presented in another study [Orcutt, Caldwell, and Wertheimer (1976)]. The variables used here were dummy variables indicating "mean" if the predicted probability was between 0.01 and 0.03 and "high" if it was greater than 0.03. The "slopes" are the marginal effects described earlier.

Note the marginal effects compared with the tobit coefficients. Likewise, the estimate of $\sigma$ is quite misleading as an estimate of the standard deviation of hours worked.

The effects of the divorce probability variables were as expected and were quite large. One of the questions raised in connection with this study was whether the divorce probabilities could reasonably be treated as independent variables. It might be that for these individuals, the number of hours worked was a significant determinant of the probability.

## 24.3.3 ESTIMATION

Estimation of this model is very similar to that of truncated regression. The tobit model has become so routine and been incorporated in so many computer packages that despite formidable obstacles in years past, estimation is now essentially on the level of ordinary linear regression.[11] The log-likelihood for the censored regression model is

$$\ln L = \sum_{y_i > 0} -\frac{1}{2}\left[\log(2\pi) + \ln \sigma^2 + \frac{(y_i - \mathbf{x}_i'\boldsymbol{\beta})^2}{\sigma^2}\right] + \sum_{y_i = 0} \ln\left[1 - \Phi\left(\frac{\mathbf{x}_i'\boldsymbol{\beta}}{\sigma}\right)\right]. \quad \text{(24-13)}$$

---

[11] See Hall (1984).

The two parts correspond to the classical regression for the nonlimit observations and the relevant probabilities for the limit observations, respectively. This likelihood is a nonstandard type, because it is a mixture of discrete and continuous distributions. In a seminal paper, Amemiya (1973) showed that despite the complications, proceeding in the usual fashion to maximize ln $L$ would produce an estimator with all the familiar desirable properties attained by MLEs.

The log-likelihood function is fairly involved, but **Olsen's** (1978) **reparameterization** simplifies things considerably. With $\gamma = \beta/\sigma$ and $\theta = 1/\sigma$, the log-likelihood is

$$\ln L = \sum_{y_i > 0} -\frac{1}{2}[\ln(2\pi) - \ln \theta^2 + (\theta y_i - \mathbf{x}_i'\gamma)^2] + \sum_{y_i = 0} \ln[1 - \Phi(\mathbf{x}_i'\gamma)]. \qquad \textbf{(24-14)}$$

The results in this setting are now very similar to those for the truncated regression. The Hessian is always negative definite, so Newton's method is simple to use and usually converges quickly. After convergence, the original parameters can be recovered using $\sigma = 1/\theta$ and $\beta = \gamma/\theta$. The asymptotic covariance matrix for these estimates can be obtained from that for the estimates of $[\gamma, \theta]$ using the **delta method;** Est. Asy. Var$[\hat{\beta}, \hat{\sigma}] = \hat{\mathbf{J}}$ Asy. Var$[\hat{\gamma}, \hat{\theta}]\hat{\mathbf{J}}'$, where

$$\mathbf{J} = \begin{bmatrix} \partial\beta/\partial\gamma' & \partial\beta/\partial\theta \\ \partial\sigma/\partial\gamma' & \partial\sigma/\partial\theta \end{bmatrix} = \begin{bmatrix} (1/\theta)\mathbf{I} & (-1/\theta^2)\gamma \\ \mathbf{0}' & (-1/\theta^2) \end{bmatrix}.$$

Researchers often compute ordinary least squares estimates despite their inconsistency. Almost without exception, it is found that the OLS estimates are smaller in absolute value than the MLEs. A striking empirical regularity is that the maximum likelihood estimates can often be approximated by dividing the OLS estimates by the proportion of nonlimit observations in the sample.[12] The effect is illustrated in the last two columns of Table 24.1. Another strategy is to discard the limit observations, but we now see that just trades the censoring problem for the truncation problem.

### 24.3.4 SOME ISSUES IN SPECIFICATION

Two issues that commonly arise in microeconomic data, heteroscedasticity and nonnormality, have been analyzed at length in the tobit setting.[13]

#### 24.3.4.a Heteroscedasticity
Maddala and Nelson (1975), Hurd (1979), Arabmazar and Schmidt (1982a,b), and Brown and Moffitt (1982) all have varying degrees of pessimism regarding how inconsistent the maximum likelihood estimator will be when heteroscedasticity occurs. Not surprisingly, the degree of censoring is the primary determinant. Unfortunately, all the analyses have been carried out in the setting of very specific models—for example, involving only a single dummy variable or one with groupwise heteroscedasticity—so the primary lesson is the very general conclusion that heteroscedasticity emerges as an obviously serious problem.

---

[12]This concept is explored further in Greene (1980b), Goldberger (1981), and Chung and Goldberger (1984).

[13]Two symposia that contain numerous results on these subjects are Blundell (1987) and Duncan (1986b). An application that explores these two issues in detail is Melenberg and van Soest (1996).

**TABLE 24.2**   Estimates of a Tobit Model (standard errors in parentheses)

|  | Homoscedastic | Heteroscedastic | |
|---|---|---|---|
|  | $\beta$ | $\beta$ | $\alpha$ |
| Constant | −18.28 (5.10) | −4.11 (3.28) | −0.47 (0.60) |
| Beta | 10.97 (3.61) | 2.22 (2.00) | 1.20 (1.81) |
| Nonmarket | 0.65 (7.41) | 0.12 (1.90) | 0.08 (7.55) |
| Number | 0.75 (5.74) | 0.33 (4.50) | 0.15 (4.58) |
| Merger | 0.50 (5.90) | 0.24 (3.00) | 0.06 (4.17) |
| Option | 2.56 (1.51) | 2.96 (2.99) | 0.83 (1.70) |
| ln $L$ | −547.30 | −466.27 | |
| Sample size | 200 | 200 | |

One can approach the heteroscedasticity problem directly. Petersen and Waldman (1981) present the computations needed to estimate a tobit model with heteroscedasticity of several types. Replacing $\sigma$ with $\sigma_i$ in the log-likelihood function and including $\sigma_i^2$ in the summations produces the needed generality. Specification of a particular model for $\sigma_i$ provides the empirical model for estimation.

***Example 24.5   Multiplicative Heteroscedasticity in the Tobit Model***
Petersen and Waldman (1981) analyzed the volume of short interest in a cross section of common stocks. The regressors included a measure of the market component of heterogeneous expectations as measured by the firm's *BETA* coefficient; a company-specific measure of heterogeneous expectations, *NONMARKET*; the *NUMBER* of analysts making earnings forecasts for the company; the number of common shares to be issued for the acquisition of another firm, *MERGER*; and a dummy variable for the existence of *OPTION*s. They report the results listed in Table 24.2 for a model in which the variance is assumed to be of the form $\sigma_i^2 = \exp(\mathbf{x}_i'\alpha)$. The values in parentheses are the ratio of the coefficient to the estimated asymptotic standard error.
   The effect of heteroscedasticity on the estimates is extremely large. We do note, however, a common misconception in the literature. The change in the coefficients is often misleading. The marginal effects in the heteroscedasticity model will generally be very similar to those computed from the model which assumes homoscedasticity. (The calculation is pursued in the exercises.)
   A test of the hypothesis that $\alpha = \mathbf{0}$ (except for the constant term) can be based on the likelihood ratio statistic. For these results, the statistic is $-2[-547.3 - (-466.27)] = 162.06$. This statistic has a limiting chi-squared distribution with five degrees of freedom. The sample value exceeds the critical value in the table of 11.07, so the hypothesis can be rejected.

In the preceding example, we carried out a likelihood ratio test against the hypothesis of homoscedasticity. It would be desirable to be able to carry out the test without having to estimate the unrestricted model. A **Lagrange multiplier test** can be used for that purpose. Consider the heteroscedastic tobit model in which we specify that

$$\sigma_i^2 = \sigma^2[\exp(\mathbf{w}_i'\alpha)]^2. \tag{24-15}$$

This model is a fairly general specification that includes many familiar ones as special cases. The null hypothesis of homoscedasticity is $\alpha = \mathbf{0}$. (We used this specification in the probit model in Section 23.4.4.b and in the linear regression model in Section 16.9.2.a) Using the BHHH estimator of the Hessian as usual, we can produce a Lagrange multiplier statistic as follows: Let $z_i = 1$ if $y_i$ is positive and 0 otherwise,

$$a_i = z_i \left( \frac{\varepsilon_i}{\sigma^2} \right) \qquad + (1 - z_i) \left( \frac{(-1)\lambda_i}{\sigma} \right),$$

$$b_i = z_i \left( \frac{(\varepsilon_i^2/\sigma^2 - 1)}{2\sigma^2} \right) + (1 - z_i) \left( \frac{(\mathbf{x}_i'\boldsymbol{\beta})\lambda_i}{2\sigma^3} \right), \qquad \textbf{(24-16)}$$

$$\lambda_i = \frac{\phi(\mathbf{x}_i'\boldsymbol{\beta}/\sigma)}{1 - \Phi(\mathbf{x}_i'\boldsymbol{\beta}/\sigma)}.$$

The data vector is $\mathbf{g}_i = [a_i \mathbf{x}_i', b_i, b_i \mathbf{w}_i']'$. The sums are taken over all observations, and all functions involving unknown parameters $(\varepsilon_i, \phi_i, \Phi_i, \mathbf{x}_i'\boldsymbol{\beta}, \sigma, \lambda_i)$ are evaluated at the restricted (homoscedastic) maximum likelihood estimates. Then,

$$\text{LM} = \mathbf{i}'\mathbf{G}[\mathbf{G}'\mathbf{G}]^{-1}\mathbf{G}'\mathbf{i} = nR^2 \qquad \textbf{(24-17)}$$

in the regression of a column of ones on the $K + 1 + P$ derivatives of the log-likelihood function for the model with multiplicative heteroscedasticity, evaluated at the estimates from the restricted model. (If there were no limit observations, then it would reduce to the Breusch–Pagan statistic discussed in Section 8.5.2.) Given the maximum likelihood estimates of the tobit model coefficients, it is quite simple to compute. The statistic has a limiting chi-squared distribution with degrees of freedom equal to the number of variables in $\mathbf{w}_i$.

### 24.3.4.b    Misspecification of Prob[y* < 0]

In an early study in this literature, Cragg (1971) proposed a somewhat more general model in which the probability of a limit observation is independent of the regression model for the nonlimit data. One can imagine, for instance, the decision of whether or not to purchase a car as being different from the decision of how much to spend on the car, having decided to buy one. A related problem raised by Fin and Schmidt (1984) is that in the tobit model, a variable that increases the probability of an observation being a nonlimit observation also increases the mean of the variable. They cite as an example loss due to fire in buildings. Older buildings might be more likely to have fires, so that $\partial \text{Prob}[y_i > 0]/\partial \text{ age}_i > 0$, but, because of the greater value of newer buildings, older ones incur smaller losses when they do have fires, so that $\partial E[y_i \mid y_i > 0]/\partial \text{ age}_i < 0$. This fact would require the coefficient on age to have different signs in the two functions, which is impossible in the tobit model because they are the same coefficient.

A more general model that accommodates these objections is as follows:

1.  Decision equation:

$$\text{Prob}[y_i^* > 0] = \Phi(\mathbf{x}_i'\boldsymbol{\gamma}), \qquad z_i = 1 \text{ if } y_i^* > 0,$$
$$\text{Prob}[y_i^* \leq 0] = 1 - \Phi(\mathbf{x}_i'\boldsymbol{\gamma}), \qquad z_i = 0 \text{ if } y_i^* \leq 0. \qquad \textbf{(24-18)}$$

2.  Regression equation for nonlimit observations:

$$E[y_i \mid z_i = 1] = \mathbf{x}_i'\boldsymbol{\beta} + \sigma\lambda_i,$$

according to Theorem 24.2.

This model is a combination of the truncated regression model of Section 24.2 and the univariate probit model of Section 23.3, which suggests a method of analyzing it. The tobit model of this section arises if $\boldsymbol{\gamma} = \boldsymbol{\beta}/\sigma$. The parameters of the regression equation can be estimated independently using the truncated regression model of Section 24.2. A recent application is Melenberg and van Soest (1996).

Fin and Schmidt (1984) considered testing the restriction of the tobit model. Based only on the tobit model, they devised a Lagrange multiplier statistic that, although a bit cumbersome algebraically, can be computed without great difficulty. If one is able to estimate the truncated regression model, the tobit model, and the probit model separately, then there is a simpler way to test the hypothesis. The tobit log-likelihood is the sum of the log-likelihoods for the truncated regression and probit models. [To show this result, add and subtract $\sum_{y_i=1} \ln \Phi(\mathbf{x}_i'\boldsymbol{\beta}/\sigma)$ in (24-13). This produces the log-likelihood for the truncated regression model plus (23-20) for the probit model.][14] Therefore, a likelihood ratio statistic can be computed using

$$\lambda = -2[\ln L_T - (\ln L_P + \ln L_{TR})],$$

where

$L_T$ = likelihood for the tobit model in (24-13), with the same coefficients,

$L_P$ = likelihood for the probit model in (23-20), fit separately,

$L_{TR}$ = likelihood for the truncated regression model, fit separately.

### 24.3.4.c Corner Solutions

Many of the applications of the tobit model in the received literature are constructed not to accommodate censoring of the underlying data, but, rather, to model the appearance of a large cluster of zeros. The Cragg model of the previous section is clearly related to this phenomenon. Consider, for example, survey data on purchases of consumer durables, firm expenditure on research and development, or consumer savings. In each case, the observed data will consist of zero or some positive amount. Arguably, there are two decisions at work in these scenarios, first whether to engage in the activity or not, and second, given that the answer to the first question is yes, how intensively to engage in it—how much to spend, for example. This is precisely the motivation behind the model in the previous section. [This specification has been labeled a "corner solution model"; see Wooldridge (2002a, pp. 518–519).] An application appears in Section 25.5.2.

In practical terms, the difference between this and the tobit model should be evident in the data. Often overlooked in tobit analyses is that the model predicts not only a cluster of zeros (or limit observations), but also a grouping of observations *near zero* (or the limit point). For example, the tobit model is surely misspecified for the sort of (hypothetical) spending data shown in Figure 24.3 for a sample of 1,000 observations. Neglecting for the moment the earlier point about the underlying decision process, Figure 24.4 shows the characteristic appearance of a (substantively) censored variable.

The implication for the model builder is that, as in Section 24.3.4.b, an appropriate specification would consist of two equations, one for the "participation decision," and one for the distribution of the positive dependent variable. Formally, we might, continuing the development of Cragg's specification, model the first decision with a binary choice (e.g., probit or logit model) as in Sections 23.2–23.4. The second equation is a model for $y \mid y > 0$, for which the truncated regression model of Section 24.2.3 is a natural candidate. As we will see, this is essentially the model behind the sample selection treatment developed in Section 24.5.

---

[14]The likelihood function for the truncated regression model is considered in the exercises.

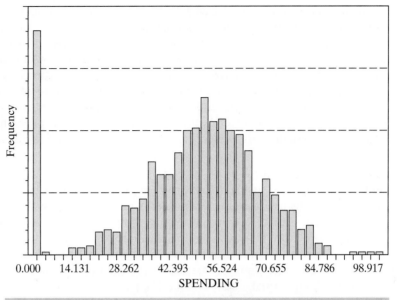

**FIGURE 24.3** Hypothetical Spending Data.

Two practical issues frequently intervene at this point. First, one might well have a model in mind for the intensity (regression) equation, but none for the participation equation. This is the usual backdrop for the uses of the tobit model, which produces the considerations in the previous section. The second issue concerns the appropriateness of the truncation or censoring model to data such as those in Figure 24.3. If we consider only

**FIGURE 24.4** Hypothetical Censored Data.

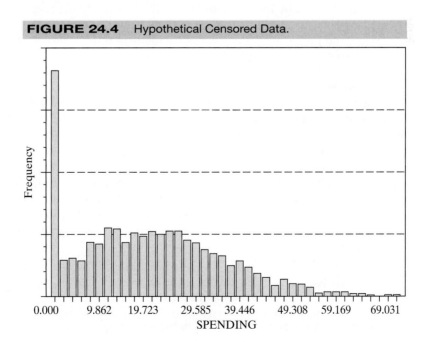

the nonlimit observations in Figure 24.3, the underlying distribution does not appear to be truncated at all. The truncated regression model in Section 24.2.3 fit to these data will not depart significantly from ordinary least squares [because the underlying probability in the denominator of (24-6) will equal one and the numerator will equal zero]. But, this is not the case of a tobit model forced on these same data. Forcing the model in (24-13) on data such as these will significantly distort the estimator—all else equal, it will significantly attenuate the coefficients, the more so the larger is the proportion of limit observations in the sample. Once again, this stands as a caveat for the model builder. The tobit model is manifestly misspecified for data such as those in Figure 24.3.

### 24.3.4.d  Nonnormality

Nonnormality is an especially difficult problem in this setting. It has been shown that if the underlying disturbances are not normally distributed, then the estimator based on (24-13) is inconsistent. Research is ongoing both on alternative estimators and on methods for testing for this type of misspecification.[15]

One approach to the estimation is to use an alternative distribution. Kalbfleisch and Prentice (2002) present a unifying treatment that includes several distributions such as the exponential, lognormal, and Weibull. (Their primary focus is on survival analysis in a medical statistics setting, which is an interesting convergence of the techniques in very different disciplines.) Of course, assuming some other specific distribution does not necessarily solve the problem and may make it worse. A preferable alternative would be to devise an estimator that is robust to changes in the distribution. Powell's (1981, 1984) least absolute deviations (LAD) estimator appears to offer some promise.[16] The main drawback to its use is its computational complexity. An extensive application of the LAD estimator is Melenberg and van Soest (1996). Although estimation in the nonnormal case is relatively difficult, testing for this failure of the model is worthwhile to assess the estimates obtained by the conventional methods. Among the tests that have been developed are Hausman tests, Lagrange multiplier tests [Bera and Jarque (1981, 1982), Bera, Jarque, and Lee (1982)], and **conditional moment tests** [Nelson (1981)]. The conditional moment tests are described in the next section.

To employ a Hausman test, we require an estimator that is consistent and efficient under the null hypothesis but inconsistent under the alternative—the tobit estimator with normality—and an estimator that is consistent under both hypotheses but inefficient under the null hypothesis. Thus, we will require a robust estimator of $\beta$, which restores the difficulties of the previous paragraph. Recent applications [e.g., Melenberg and van Soest (1996)] have used the Hausman test to compare the tobit/normal estimator with Powell's consistent, but inefficient (robust), LAD estimator. Another approach to testing is to embed the normal distribution in some other distribution and then use an LM test for the normal specification. Chesher and Irish (1987) have devised an LM test of normality in the tobit model based on **generalized residuals.** In many models, including the tobit model, the generalized residuals can be computed as the derivatives

---

[15]See Duncan (1983, 1986b), Goldberger (1983), Pagan and Vella (1989), Lee (1996), and Fernandez (1986). We will examine one of the tests more closely in the following section.

[16]See Duncan (1986a,b) for a symposium on the subject and Amemiya (1984). Additional references are Newey, Powell, and Walker (1990); Lee (1996); and Robinson (1988).

of the log-densities with respect to the constant term, so

$$e_i = \frac{1}{\sigma^2}[z_i(y_i - \mathbf{x}_i'\boldsymbol{\beta}) - (1 - z_i)\sigma\lambda_i],$$

where $z_i$ is defined in (24-18) and $\lambda_i$ is defined in (24-16). This residual is an estimate of $\varepsilon_i$ that accounts for the censoring in the distribution. By construction, $E[e_i \mid \mathbf{x}_i] = 0$, and if the model actually does contain a constant term, then $\sum_{i=1}^{n} e_i = 0$; this is the first of the necessary conditions for the MLE. The test is then carried out by regressing a column of ones on $\mathbf{d}_i$, where the elements of $\mathbf{d}_i$ are computed as follows:

$$a_i = (y_i - \mathbf{x}_i'\hat{\boldsymbol{\beta}})/\hat{\sigma},$$

$$\hat{\alpha}_i = -\mathbf{x}_i'\hat{\boldsymbol{\beta}}/\hat{\sigma}, \lambda_i = \phi(\hat{\alpha}_i)/\Phi(\hat{\alpha}_i),$$

$$e_{i1} = -(1 - z_i)\lambda_i \qquad + z_i a_i,$$

$$e_{i2} = -(1 - z_i)\hat{\alpha}_i\lambda_i \qquad + z_i\left(a_i^2 - 1\right),$$

$$e_{i3} = -(1 - z_i)\left(2 + \hat{\alpha}_i^2\right)\lambda_i \qquad + z_i a_i^3,$$

$$e_{i4} = -(1 - z_i)\left(3\hat{\alpha}_i + \hat{\alpha}_i^3\right)\lambda_i \quad + z_i\left(a_i^4 - 3\right),$$

$$\mathbf{d}_i' = [e_{i1}\mathbf{x}_i', e_{i2}, e_{i3}, e_{i4}].$$

Note that first $K + 1$ variables in $\mathbf{d}_i$ are the derivatives of the tobit log-likelihood. Let $\mathbf{D}$ be the $n \times (K + 3)$ matrix with $i$th row equal to $\mathbf{d}_i'$. Then, $\mathbf{D} = [\mathbf{G}, \mathbf{M}]$ where the $K + 1$ columns of $\mathbf{G}$ are the derivatives of the tobit log-likelihood and the two columns in $\mathbf{M}$ are the last two variables in $\mathbf{d}_i$. Then the chi-squared statistic is $nR^2$; that is,

$$\mathbf{LM} = \mathbf{i}'\mathbf{D}(\mathbf{D}'\mathbf{D})^{-1}\mathbf{D}'\mathbf{i}.$$

The necessary conditions that define the MLE are $\mathbf{i}'\mathbf{G} = \mathbf{0}$, so the first $K + 1$ elements of $\mathbf{i}'\mathbf{D}$ are zero. Using (A-74), then, the LM statistic becomes

$$\mathbf{LM} = \mathbf{i}'\mathbf{M}[\mathbf{M}'\mathbf{M} - \mathbf{M}'\mathbf{G}(\mathbf{G}'\mathbf{G})^{-1}\mathbf{G}'\mathbf{M}]^{-1}\mathbf{M}'\mathbf{i},$$

which is a chi-squared statistic with two degrees of freedom. Note the similarity to (24-17), where a test for homoscedasticity is carried out by the same method. As emerges so often in this framework, the test of the distribution actually focuses on the skewness and kurtosis of the residuals. Pagan and Vella (1989) and Ruud (1984) have developed similar tests for several specification errors.[17]

## 24.4 PANEL DATA APPLICATIONS

Extension of the familiar panel data results to the tobit model parallel the probit model, with the attendant problems. The random effects or random parameters models discussed in Chapter 23 can be adapted to the censored regression model using simulation or quadrature. The same reservations with respect to the orthogonality of the effects and the regressors will apply here, as will the applicability of the Mundlak (1978) correction to accommodate it.

---

[17]Developing specification tests for the tobit model has been a popular enterprise. A sampling of the received literature includes Nelson (1981); Bera, Jarque, and Lee (1982); Chesher and Irish (1987); Chesher, Lancaster, and Irish (1985); Gourieroux et al. (1984, 1987); Newey (1986); Rivers and Vuong (1988); Horowitz and Neumann (1989); and Pagan and Vella (1989). Newey (1985a, b) are useful references on the general subject of conditional moment testing. More general treatments of specification testing are Godfrey (1988) and Ruud (1984).

Most of the attention in the theoretical literature on panel data methods for the tobit model has been focused on fixed effects. The departure point would be the maximum likelihood estimator for the static fixed effects model,

$$y_{it}^* = \alpha_i + x_{it}'\beta + \varepsilon_{it}, \varepsilon_{it} \sim N[0, \sigma^2],$$

$$y_{it} = \text{Max}(0, y_{it}^*).$$

However, there are no firm theoretical results on the behavior of the MLE in this model. Intuition might suggest, based on the findings for the binary probit model, that the MLE would be biased in the same fashion, away from zero. Perhaps surprisingly, the results in Greene (2004) persistently found that not to be the case in a variety of model specifications. Rather, the incidental parameters, such as it is, manifests in a downward bias in the estimator of $\sigma$, not an upward (or downward) bias in the MLE of $\beta$. However, this is less surprising when the tobit estimator is juxtaposed with the MLE in the linear regression model with fixed effects. In that model, the MLE is the within-groups (LSDV) estimator which is unbiased and consistent. But, the ML estimator of the disturbance variance in the linear regression model is $\mathbf{e}_{\text{LSDV}}'\mathbf{e}_{\text{LSDV}}/(nT)$, which is biased downward by a factor of $(T-1)/T$. [This is the result found in the original source on the incidental parameters problem, Neyman and Scott (1948).] So, what evidence there is suggests that unconditional estimation of the tobit model behaves essentially like that for the linear regression model. That does not settle the problem, however; if the evidence is correct, then it implies that although consistent estimation of $\beta$ is possible, appropriate statistical inference is not. The bias in the estimation of $\sigma$ shows up in any estimator of the asymptotic covariance of the MLE of $\beta$.

Unfortunately, there is no conditional estimator of $\beta$ for the tobit (or truncated regression) model. First differencing or taking group mean deviations does not preserve the model. Because the latent variable is censored before observation, these transformations are not meaningful. Some progress has been made on theoretical, **semiparametric estimators** for this model. See, for example, Honorè and Kyriazidou (2000) for a survey. Much of the theoretical development has also been directed at dynamic models where the benign result of the previous paragraph (such as it is) is lost once again. Arellano (2001) contains some general results. Hahn and Kuersteiner (2004) have characterized the bias of the MLE, and suggested methods of reducing the bias of the estimators in dynamic binary choice and censored regression models.

## 24.5 SAMPLE SELECTION

The topic of sample selection, or **incidental truncation,** has been the subject of an enormous recent literature, both theoretical and applied.[18] This analysis combines both of the previous topics.

---

[18] A large proportion of the analysis in this framework has been in the area of labor economics. See, for example, Vella (1998), which is an extensive survey for practitioners. The results, however, have been applied in many other fields, including, for example, long series of stock market returns by financial economists ("survivorship bias") and medical treatment and response in long-term studies by clinical researchers ("attrition bias"). The four surveys noted in the introduction to this chapter provide fairly extensive, although far from exhaustive, lists of the studies. Some studies that comment on methodological issues are Heckman (1990), Manski (1989, 1990, 1992), and Newey, Powell, and Walker (1990).

***Example 24.6   Incidental Truncation***
In the high-income survey discussed in Example 24.2, respondents were also included in the survey if their net worth, not including their homes, was at least $500,000. Suppose that the survey of incomes was based *only* on people whose net worth was at least $500,000. This selection is a form of truncation, but not quite the same as in Section 24.2. This selection criterion does not necessarily exclude individuals whose incomes at the time might be quite low. Still, one would expect that, on average, individuals with a high net worth would have a high income as well. Thus, the average income in this subpopulation would in all likelihood also be misleading as an indication of the income of the typical American. The data in such a survey would be nonrandomly selected or incidentally truncated.

Econometric studies of nonrandom sampling have analyzed the deleterious effects of sample selection on the properties of conventional estimators such as least squares; have produced a variety of alternative estimation techniques; and, in the process, have yielded a rich crop of empirical models. In some cases, the analysis has led to a reinterpretation of earlier results.

### 24.5.1   INCIDENTAL TRUNCATION IN A BIVARIATE DISTRIBUTION

Suppose that $y$ and $z$ have a bivariate distribution with correlation $\rho$. We are interested in the distribution of $y$ given that $z$ exceeds a particular value. Intuition suggests that if $y$ and $z$ are positively correlated, then the truncation of $z$ should push the distribution of $y$ to the right. As before, we are interested in (1) the form of the incidentally truncated distribution and (2) the mean and variance of the incidentally truncated random variable. Because it has dominated the empirical literature, we will focus first on the bivariate normal distribution.[19]

The truncated *joint* density of $y$ and $z$ is

$$f(y, z \mid z > a) = \frac{f(y, z)}{\text{Prob}(z > a)}.$$

To obtain the incidentally truncated marginal density for $y$, we would then integrate $z$ out of this expression. The moments of the incidentally truncated normal distribution are given in Theorem 24.5.[20]

---

**THEOREM 24.5   Moments of the Incidentally Truncated Bivariate Normal Distribution**

*If $y$ and $z$ have a bivariate normal distribution with means $\mu_y$ and $\mu_z$, standard deviations $\sigma_y$ and $\sigma_z$, and correlation $\rho$, then*

$$E[y \mid z > a] = \mu_y + \rho\sigma_y\lambda(\alpha_z),$$
$$\text{Var}[y \mid z > a] = \sigma_y^2[1 - \rho^2\delta(\alpha_z)], \qquad \textbf{(24-19)}$$

*where*

$$\alpha_z = (a - \mu_z)/\sigma_z, \ \lambda(\alpha_z) = \phi(\alpha_z)/[1 - \Phi(\alpha_z)], \ and \ \delta(\alpha_z) = \lambda(\alpha_z)[\lambda(\alpha_z) - \alpha_z].$$

---

[19]We will reconsider the issue of the normality assumption in Section 24.5.5.

[20]Much more general forms of the result that apply to multivariate distributions are given in Johnson and Kotz (1974). See also Maddala (1983, pp. 266–267).

Note that the expressions involving $z$ are analogous to the moments of the truncated distribution of $x$ given in Theorem 24.2. If the truncation is $z < a$, then we make the replacement $\lambda(\alpha_z) = -\phi(\alpha_z)/\Phi(\alpha_z)$.

As expected, the truncated mean is pushed in the direction of the correlation if the truncation is from below and in the opposite direction if it is from above. In addition, the incidental truncation reduces the variance, because both $\delta(\alpha)$ and $\rho^2$ are between zero and one.

### 24.5.2 REGRESSION IN A MODEL OF SELECTION

To motivate a regression model that corresponds to the results in Theorem 24.5, we consider the following example.

#### Example 24.7 A Model of Labor Supply

A simple model of female labor supply that has been examined in many studies consists of two equations:[21]

1. *Wage equation*. The difference between a person's *market wage,* what she could command in the labor market, and her *reservation wage,* the wage rate necessary to make her choose to participate in the labor market, is a function of characteristics such as age and education as well as, for example, number of children and where a person lives.
2. *Hours equation*. The desired number of labor hours supplied depends on the wage, home characteristics such as whether there are small children present, marital status, and so on.

The problem of truncation surfaces when we consider that the second equation describes desired hours, but an actual figure is observed only if the individual is working. (In most such studies, only a *participation equation,* that is, whether hours are positive or zero, is observable.) We infer from this that the market wage exceeds the reservation wage. Thus, the hours variable in the second equation is incidentally truncated.

To put the preceding examples in a general framework, let the equation that determines the sample selection be

$$z_i^* = \mathbf{w}_i'\boldsymbol{\gamma} + u_i,$$

and let the equation of primary interest be

$$y_i = \mathbf{x}_i'\boldsymbol{\beta} + \varepsilon_i.$$

The sample rule is that $y_i$ is observed only when $z_i^*$ is greater than zero. Suppose as well that $\varepsilon_i$ and $u_i$ have a bivariate normal distribution with zero means and correlation $\rho$. Then we may insert these in Theorem 24.5 to obtain the model *that applies to the observations in our sample:*

$$
\begin{aligned}
E[y_i \mid y_i \text{ is observed}] &= E[y_i \mid z_i^* > 0] \\
&= E[y_i \mid u_i > -\mathbf{w}'\boldsymbol{\gamma}_i] \\
&= \mathbf{x}_i'\boldsymbol{\beta} + E[\varepsilon_i \mid u_i > -\mathbf{w}_i'\boldsymbol{\gamma}] \\
&= \mathbf{x}_i'\boldsymbol{\beta} + \rho\sigma_\varepsilon \lambda_i(\alpha_u) \\
&= \mathbf{x}_i'\boldsymbol{\beta} + \beta_\lambda \lambda_i(\alpha_u),
\end{aligned}
$$

---

[21] See, for example, Heckman (1976). This strand of literature begins with an exchange by Gronau (1974) and Lewis (1974).

where $\alpha_u = -\mathbf{w}_i' \boldsymbol{\gamma}/\sigma_u$ and $\lambda(\alpha_u) = \phi(\mathbf{w}_i'\boldsymbol{\gamma}/\sigma_u)/\Phi(\mathbf{w}_i'\boldsymbol{\gamma}/\sigma_u)$. So,

$$y_i \mid z_i^* > 0 = E[y_i \mid z_i^* > 0] + v_i$$
$$= \mathbf{x}_i'\boldsymbol{\beta} + \beta_\lambda \lambda_i(\alpha_u) + v_i.$$

Least squares regression using the observed data—for instance, OLS regression of hours on its determinants, using only data for women who are working—produces inconsistent estimates of $\boldsymbol{\beta}$. Once again, we can view the problem as an omitted variable. Least squares regression of $y$ on $\mathbf{x}$ *and* $\lambda$ would be a consistent estimator, but if $\lambda$ is omitted, then the **specification error** of an omitted variable is committed. Finally, note that the second part of Theorem 24.5 implies that even if $\lambda_i$ were observed, then least squares would be inefficient. The disturbance $v_i$ is heteroscedastic.

The marginal effect of the regressors on $y_i$ *in the observed sample* consists of two components. There is the direct effect on the mean of $y_i$, which is $\boldsymbol{\beta}$. In addition, for a particular independent variable, if it appears in the probability that $z_i^*$ is positive, then it will influence $y_i$ through its presence in $\lambda_i$. The full effect of changes in a regressor that appears in both $\mathbf{x}_i$ and $\mathbf{w}_i$ on $y$ is

$$\frac{\partial E[y_i \mid z_i^* > 0]}{\partial x_{ik}} = \beta_k - \gamma_k \left(\frac{\rho\sigma_\varepsilon}{\sigma_u}\right) \delta_i(\alpha_u),$$

where[22]

$$\delta_i = \lambda_i^2 - \alpha_i \lambda_i.$$

Suppose that $\rho$ is positive and $E[y_i]$ is greater when $z_i^*$ is positive than when it is negative. Because $0 < \delta_i < 1$, the additional term serves to reduce the marginal effect. The change in the probability affects the mean of $y_i$ in that the mean in the group $z_i^* > 0$ is higher. The second term in the derivative compensates for this effect, leaving only the marginal effect of a change *given that $z_i^* > 0$ to begin with*. Consider Example 24.9, and suppose that education affects both the probability of migration and the income in either state. If we suppose that the income of migrants is higher than that of otherwise identical people who do not migrate, then the marginal effect of education has two parts, one due to its influence in increasing the probability of the individual's entering a higher-income group and one due to its influence on income within the group. As such, the coefficient on education in the regression overstates the marginal effect of the education of migrants and understates it for nonmigrants. The sizes of the various parts depend on the setting. It is quite possible that the magnitude, sign, and statistical significance of the effect might all be different from those of the estimate of $\boldsymbol{\beta}$, a point that appears frequently to be overlooked in empirical studies.

In most cases, the selection variable $z^*$ is not observed. Rather, we observe only its sign. To consider our two examples, we typically observe only whether a woman is working or not working or whether an individual migrated or not. We can infer the sign of $z^*$, but not its magnitude, from such information. Because there is no information on the scale of $z^*$, the disturbance variance in the selection equation cannot be estimated. (We encountered this problem in Chapter 23 in connection with the probit model.)

---

[22]We have reversed the sign of $\alpha_u$ in (24-19) because $a = 0$, and $\alpha = \mathbf{w}'\boldsymbol{\gamma}/\sigma_M$ is somewhat more convenient. Also, as such, $\partial\lambda/\partial\alpha = -\delta$.

Thus, we reformulate the model as follows:

selection mechanism: $z_i^* = \mathbf{w}_i'\boldsymbol{\gamma} + u_i$, $z_i = 1$ if $z_i^* > 0$ and 0 otherwise;

$$\text{Prob}(z_i = 1 \mid \mathbf{w}_i) = \Phi(\mathbf{w}_i'\boldsymbol{\gamma}), \text{ and}$$

$$\text{Prob}(z_i = 0 \mid \mathbf{w}_i) = 1 - \Phi(\mathbf{w}_i'\boldsymbol{\gamma}). \tag{24-20}$$

regression model: $y_i = \mathbf{x}_i'\boldsymbol{\beta} + \varepsilon_i$ observed only if $z_i = 1$,

$$(u_i, \varepsilon_i) \sim \text{ bivariate normal } [0, 0, 1, \sigma_\varepsilon, \rho].$$

Suppose that, as in many of these studies, $z_i$ and $\mathbf{w}_i$ are observed for a random sample of individuals but $y_i$ is observed only when $z_i = 1$. This model is precisely the one we examined earlier, with

$$E[y_i \mid z_i = 1, \mathbf{x}_i, \mathbf{w}_i] = \mathbf{x}_i'\boldsymbol{\beta} + \rho\sigma_\varepsilon\lambda(\mathbf{w}_i'\boldsymbol{\gamma}).$$

### 24.5.3 ESTIMATION

The parameters of the sample selection model can be estimated by maximum likelihood.[23] However, Heckman's (1979) **two-step estimation** procedure is usually used instead. Heckman's method is as follows:[24]

1. Estimate the probit equation by maximum likelihood to obtain estimates of $\boldsymbol{\gamma}$. For each observation in the selected sample, compute $\hat{\lambda}_i = \phi(\mathbf{w}_i'\hat{\boldsymbol{\gamma}})/\Phi(\mathbf{w}_i'\hat{\boldsymbol{\gamma}})$ and $\hat{\delta}_i = \hat{\lambda}_i(\hat{\lambda}_i + \mathbf{w}_i'\hat{\boldsymbol{\gamma}})$.
2. Estimate $\boldsymbol{\beta}$ and $\beta_\lambda = \rho\sigma_\varepsilon$ by least squares regression of $y$ on $\mathbf{x}$ and $\hat{\lambda}$.

It is possible also to construct consistent estimators of the individual parameters $\rho$ and $\sigma_\varepsilon$. At each observation, the true conditional variance of the disturbance would be

$$\sigma_i^2 = \sigma_\varepsilon^2(1 - \rho^2\delta_i).$$

The average conditional variance for the sample would converge to

$$\text{plim } \frac{1}{n}\sum_{i=1}^{n}\sigma_i^2 = \sigma_\varepsilon^2(1 - \rho^2\bar{\delta}),$$

which is what is estimated by the least squares residual variance $\mathbf{e}'\mathbf{e}/n$. For the square of the coefficient on $\lambda$, we have

$$\text{plim } b_\lambda^2 = \rho^2\sigma_\varepsilon^2,$$

whereas based on the probit results we have

$$\text{plim } \frac{1}{n}\sum_{i=1}^{n}\hat{\delta}_i = \bar{\delta}.$$

We can then obtain a consistent estimator of $\sigma_\varepsilon^2$ using

$$\hat{\sigma}_\varepsilon^2 = \frac{1}{n}\mathbf{e}'\mathbf{e} + \hat{\bar{\delta}}b_\lambda^2.$$

---

[23] See Greene (1995a).

[24] Perhaps in a mimicry of the "tobit" estimator described earlier, this procedure has come to be known as the "Heckit" estimator.

Finally, an estimator of $\rho^2$ is

$$\hat{\rho}^2 = \frac{b_\lambda^2}{\hat{\sigma}_\varepsilon^2},$$

which provides a complete set of estimators of the model's parameters.[25]

To test hypotheses, an estimate of the asymptotic covariance matrix of $[\mathbf{b}', b_\lambda]$ is needed. We have two problems to contend with. First, we can see in Theorem 24.5 that the disturbance term in

$$(y_i \mid z_i = 1, \mathbf{x}_i, \mathbf{w}_i) = \mathbf{x}_i' \boldsymbol{\beta} + \rho\sigma_\varepsilon \lambda_i + v_i \tag{24-21}$$

is heteroscedastic;

$$\text{Var}[v_i \mid z_i = 1, \mathbf{x}_i, \mathbf{w}_i] = \sigma_\varepsilon^2(1 - \rho^2 \delta_i).$$

Second, there are unknown parameters in $\lambda_i$. Suppose that we assume for the moment that $\lambda_i$ and $\delta_i$ are known (i.e., we do not have to estimate $\boldsymbol{\gamma}$). For convenience, let $\mathbf{x}_i^* = [\mathbf{x}_i, \lambda_i]$, and let $\mathbf{b}^*$ be the least squares coefficient vector in the regression of $y$ on $\mathbf{x}^*$ in the selected data. Then, using the appropriate form of the variance of ordinary least squares in a heteroscedastic model from Chapter 8, we would have to estimate

$$\text{Var}[\mathbf{b}^*] = \sigma_\varepsilon^2[\mathbf{X}_*'\mathbf{X}_*]^{-1} \left[ \sum_{i=1}^n (1 - \rho^2 \delta_i) \mathbf{x}_i^* \mathbf{x}_i^{*'} \right] [\mathbf{X}_*'\mathbf{X}_*]^{-1}$$

$$= \sigma_\varepsilon^2[\mathbf{X}_*'\mathbf{X}_*]^{-1}[\mathbf{X}_*'(\mathbf{I} - \rho^2 \boldsymbol{\Delta})\mathbf{X}_*][\mathbf{X}_*'\mathbf{X}_*]^{-1},$$

where $\mathbf{I} - \rho^2 \boldsymbol{\Delta}$ is a diagonal matrix with $(1 - \rho^2 \delta_i)$ on the diagonal. Without any other complications, this result could be computed fairly easily using $\mathbf{X}$, the sample estimates of $\sigma_\varepsilon^2$ and $\rho^2$, and the assumed known values of $\lambda_i$ and $\delta_i$.

The parameters in $\boldsymbol{\gamma}$ do have to be estimated using the probit equation. Rewrite (24-21) as

$$(y_i \mid z_i = 1, \mathbf{x}_i, \mathbf{w}_i) = \mathbf{x}_i' \boldsymbol{\beta} + \beta_\lambda \hat{\lambda}_i + v_i - \beta_\lambda(\hat{\lambda}_i - \lambda_i).$$

In this form, we see that in the preceding expression we have ignored both an additional source of variation in the compound disturbance and correlation across observations; the same estimate of $\boldsymbol{\gamma}$ is used to compute $\hat{\lambda}_i$ for every observation. Heckman has shown that the earlier covariance matrix can be appropriately corrected by adding a term inside the brackets,

$$\mathbf{Q} = \hat{\rho}^2(\mathbf{X}_*'\hat{\boldsymbol{\Delta}}\mathbf{W})\text{Est. Asy. Var}[\hat{\boldsymbol{\gamma}}](\mathbf{W}'\hat{\boldsymbol{\Delta}}\mathbf{X}_*) = \hat{\rho}^2 \hat{\mathbf{F}}\hat{\mathbf{V}}\hat{\mathbf{F}}',$$

where $\hat{\mathbf{V}} = \text{Est. Asy. Var}[\hat{\boldsymbol{\gamma}}]$, the estimator of the asymptotic covariance of the probit coefficients. Any of the estimators in (23-22) to (23-24) may be used to compute $\hat{\mathbf{V}}$. The complete expression is[26]

$$\text{Est. Asy. Var}[\mathbf{b}, b_\lambda] = \hat{\sigma}_\varepsilon^2[\mathbf{X}_*'\mathbf{X}_*]^{-1}[\mathbf{X}_*'(\mathbf{I} - \hat{\rho}^2 \hat{\boldsymbol{\Delta}})\mathbf{X}_* + \mathbf{Q}][\mathbf{X}_*'\mathbf{X}_*]^{-1}.$$

---

[25]Note that $\hat{\rho}^2$ is not a sample correlation and, as such, is not limited to $[0, 1]$. See Greene (1981) for discussion.

[26]This matrix formulation is derived in Greene (1981). Note that the Murphy and Topel (1985) results for two-step estimators given in Theorem 11.3 would apply here as well. Asymptotically, this method would give the same answer. The Heckman formulation has become standard in the literature.

**TABLE 24.3** Estimated Selection Corrected Wage Equation

| | Two-Step | | Maximum Likelihood | | Least Squares | |
|---|---|---|---|---|---|---|
| | *Estimate* | *Std. Err.* | *Estimate* | *Std. Err.* | *Estimate* | *Std. Err.* |
| $\beta_1$ | −0.971 | (2.06) | −1.963 | (1.684) | −2.56 | (0.929) |
| $\beta_2$ | 0.021 | (0.0625) | 0.0279 | (0.0756) | 0.0325 | (0.0616) |
| $\beta_3$ | 0.000137 | (0.00188) | −0.0001 | (0.00234) | −0.000260 | (0.00184) |
| $\beta_4$ | 0.417 | (0.100) | 0.457 | (0.0964) | 0.481 | (0.0669) |
| $\beta_5$ | 0.444 | (0.316) | 0.447 | (0.427) | 0.318 | (0.449) |
| $(\rho\sigma)$ | −1.098 | (1.266) | | | | |
| $\rho$ | −0.343 | | −0.132 | (0.224) | 0.000 | |
| $\sigma$ | 3.200 | | 3.108 | (0.0837) | 3.111 | |

### Example 24.8  Female Labor Supply

Examples 23.1 and 23.5 proposed a labor force participation model for a sample of 753 married women in a sample analyzed by Mroz (1987). The data set contains wage and hours information for the 428 women who participated in the formal market (LFP = 1). Following Mroz, we suppose that for these 428 individuals, the offered wage exceeded the reservation wage and, moreover, the unobserved effects in the two wage equations are correlated. As such, a wage equation based on the market data should account for the sample selection problem. We specify a simple wage model:

$$Wage = \beta_1 + \beta_2\ Exper + \beta_3\ Exper^2 + \beta_4\ Education + \beta_5\ City + \varepsilon$$

where Exper is labor market experience and City is a dummy variable indicating that the individual lived in a large urban area. Maximum likelihood, Heckman two-step, and ordinary least squares estimates of the wage equation are shown in Table 24.3. The maximum likelihood estimates are FIML estimates—the labor force participation equation is reestimated at the same time. Only the parameters of the wage equation are shown below. Note as well that the two-step estimator estimates the single coefficient on $\lambda_i$ and the structural parameters $\sigma$ and $\rho$ are deduced by the method of moments. The maximum likelihood estimator computes estimates of these parameters directly. [Details on maximum likelihood estimation may be found in Maddala (1983).]

The differences between the two-step and maximum likelihood estimates in Table 24.3 are surprisingly large. The difference is even more striking in the marginal effects. The effect for education is estimated as $0.417 + 0.0641$ for the two step estimators and 0.149 in total for the maximum likelihood estimates. For the kids variable, the marginal effect is $-.293$ for the two-step estimates and only $-0.0113$ for the MLEs. Surprisingly, the direct test for a selection effect in the maximum likelihood estimates, a nonzero $\rho$, fails to reject the hypothesis that $\rho$ equals zero.

In some settings, the selection process is a nonrandom sorting of individuals into two or more groups. The mover-stayer model in the next example is a familiar case.

### Example 24.9  A Mover-Stayer Model for Migration

The model of migration analyzed by Nakosteen and Zimmer (1980) fits into the framework described in this section. The equations of the model are

$$\text{net benefit of moving:}\quad M_i^* = \mathbf{w}_i'\gamma + u_i,$$

$$\text{income if moves:}\quad I_{i1} = \mathbf{x}_{i1}'\boldsymbol{\beta}_1 + \varepsilon_{i1},$$

$$\text{income if stays:}\quad I_{i0} = \mathbf{x}_{i0}'\boldsymbol{\beta}_0 + \varepsilon_{i0}.$$

One component of the net benefit is the market wage individuals could achieve if they move, compared with what they could obtain if they stay. Therefore, among the determinants of

**TABLE 24.4** Estimated Earnings Equations

|  | *Migration* | *Migrant Earnings* | *Nonmigrant Earnings* |
|---|---|---|---|
| Constant | −1.509 | 9.041 | 8.593 |
| *SE* | −0.708 (−5.72) | −4.104 (−9.54) | −4.161 (−57.71) |
| $\Delta EMP$ | −1.488 (−2.60) | — | — |
| $\Delta PCI$ | 1.455 (3.14) | — | — |
| Age | −0.008 (−5.29) | — | — |
| Race | −0.065 (−1.17) | — | — |
| Sex | −0.082 (−2.14) | — | — |
| $\Delta SIC$ | 0.948 (24.15) | −0.790 (−2.24) | −0.927 (−9.35) |
| $\lambda$ | — | 0.212 (0.50) | 0.863 (2.84) |

the net benefit are factors that also affect the income received in either place. An analysis of income in a sample of migrants must account for the incidental truncation of the mover's income on a positive net benefit. Likewise, the income of the stayer is incidentally truncated on a nonpositive net benefit. The model implies an income after moving for all observations, but we observe it only for those who actually do move. Nakosteen and Zimmer (1980) applied the selectivity model to a sample of 9,223 individuals with data for 2 years (1971 and 1973) sampled from the Social Security Administration's Continuous Work History Sample. Over the period, 1,078 individuals migrated and the remaining 8,145 did not. The independent variables in the migration equation were as follows:

$$SE = \text{self-employment dummy variable; 1 if yes,}$$
$$\Delta EMP = \text{rate of growth of state employment,}$$
$$\Delta PCI = \text{growth of state per capita income,}$$
$$\mathbf{x} = \text{age, race (nonwhite} = 1\text{), sex (female} = 1\text{),}$$
$$\Delta SIC = \text{1 if individual changes industry.}$$

The earnings equations included $\Delta SIC$ and $SE$. The authors reported the results given in Table 24.4. The figures in parentheses are asymptotic $t$ ratios.

### 24.5.4 REGRESSION ANALYSIS OF TREATMENT EFFECTS

The basic model of selectivity outlined earlier has been extended in an impressive variety of directions.[27] An interesting application that has found wide use is the measurement of **treatment effects** and program effectiveness.[28]

An earnings equation that accounts for the value of a college education is

$$\text{earnings}_i = \mathbf{x}_i'\boldsymbol{\beta} + \delta C_i + \varepsilon_i,$$

where $C_i$ is a dummy variable indicating whether or not the individual attended college. The same format has been used in any number of other analyses of programs, experiments, and treatments. The question is: Does $\delta$ measure the value of a college education (assuming that the rest of the regression model is correctly specified)? The answer is

---

[27]For a survey, see Maddala (1983).

[28]This is one of the fundamental applications of this body of techniques, and is also the setting for the most longstanding and contentious debate on the subject. A *Journal of Business and Economic Statistics* symposium [Angrist (2001)] raised many of the important questions on whether and how it is possible to measure treatment effects.

no if the typical individual who chooses to go to college would have relatively high earnings whether or not he or she went to college. The problem is one of self-selection. If our observation is correct, then least squares estimates of $\delta$ will actually overestimate the treatment effect. The same observation applies to estimates of the treatment effects in other settings in which the individuals themselves decide whether or not they will receive the treatment.

To put this in a more familiar context, suppose that we model program participation (e.g., whether or not the individual goes to college) as

$$C_i^* = \mathbf{w}_i'\boldsymbol{\gamma} + u_i,$$

$$C_i = 1 \quad \text{if } C_i^* > 0, 0 \text{ otherwise.}$$

We also suppose that, consistent with our previous conjecture, $u_i$ and $\varepsilon_i$ are correlated. Coupled with our earnings equation, we find that

$$E[y_i \mid C_i = 1, \mathbf{x}_i, \mathbf{z}_i] = \mathbf{x}_i'\boldsymbol{\beta} + \delta + E[\varepsilon_i \mid C_i = 1, \mathbf{x}_i, \mathbf{z}_i]$$
$$= \mathbf{x}_i'\boldsymbol{\beta} + \delta + \rho\sigma_\varepsilon\lambda(-\mathbf{w}_i'\boldsymbol{\gamma}) \tag{24-22}$$

once again. [See (24-21).] Evidently, a viable strategy for estimating this model is to use the two-step estimator discussed earlier. The net result will be a different estimate of $\delta$ that will account for the self-selected nature of program participation. For nonparticipants, the counterpart to (24-22) is

$$E[y_i \mid C_i = 0, \mathbf{x}_i, \mathbf{z}_i] = \mathbf{x}_i'\boldsymbol{\beta} + \rho\sigma_\varepsilon\left[\frac{-\phi(\mathbf{w}_i'\boldsymbol{\gamma})}{1 - \Phi(\mathbf{w}_i'\boldsymbol{\gamma})}\right]. \tag{24-23}$$

The difference in expected earnings between participants and nonparticipants is, then,

$$E[y_i \mid C_i = 1, \mathbf{x}_i, \mathbf{z}_i] - E[y_i \mid C_i = 0, \mathbf{x}_i, \mathbf{z}_i] = \delta + \rho\sigma_\varepsilon\left[\frac{\phi_i}{\Phi_i(1 - \Phi_i)}\right]. \tag{24-24}$$

If the selectivity correction $\lambda_i$ is omitted from the least squares regression, then this difference is what is estimated by the least squares coefficient on the treatment dummy variable. But because (by assumption) all terms are positive, we see that least squares overestimates the treatment effect. Note, finally, that simply estimating separate equations for participants and nonparticipants does not solve the problem. In fact, doing so would be equivalent to estimating the two regressions of Example 24.9 by least squares, which, as we have seen, would lead to inconsistent estimates of both sets of parameters.

There are many variations of this model in the empirical literature. They have been applied to the analysis of education,[29] the Head Start program,[30] and a host of other settings.[31] This strand of literature is particularly important because the use of dummy variable models to analyze treatment effects and program participation has a long history in empirical economics. This analysis has called into question the interpretation of a number of received studies.

---

[29]Willis and Rosen (1979).

[30]Goldberger (1972).

[31]A useful summary of the issues is Barnow, Cain, and Goldberger (1981). See also Maddala (1983) for a long list of applications. A related application is the switching regression model. See, for example, Quandt (1982, 1988).

### 24.5.5 THE NORMALITY ASSUMPTION

Some research has cast some skepticism on the selection model based on the normal distribution. [See Goldberger (1983) for an early salvo in this literature.] Among the findings are that the parameter estimates are surprisingly sensitive to the distributional assumption that underlies the model. Of course, this fact in itself does not invalidate the normality assumption, but it does call its generality into question. On the other hand, the received evidence is convincing that sample selection, in the abstract, raises serious problems, distributional questions aside. The literature—for example, Duncan (1986b), Manski (1989, 1990), and Heckman (1990)—has suggested some promising approaches based on robust and nonparametric estimators. These approaches obviously have the virtue of greater generality. Unfortunately, the cost is that they generally are quite limited in the breadth of the models they can accommodate. That is, one might gain the robustness of a nonparametric estimator at the cost of being unable to make use of the rich set of accompanying variables usually present in the panels to which selectivity models are often applied. For example, the nonparametric bounds approach of Manski (1990) is defined for two regressors. Other methods [e.g., Duncan (1986b)] allow more elaborate specifications.

Recent research includes specific attempts to move away from the normality assumption.[32] An example is Martins (2001), building on Newey (1991), which takes the core specification as given in (24-20) as the platform, but constructs an alternative to the assumption of bivariate normality. Martins's specification modifies the Heckman model by employing an equation of the form

$$E[y_i \mid z_i = 1, \mathbf{x}_i, \mathbf{w}_i] = \mathbf{x}_i'\boldsymbol{\beta} + \mu(\mathbf{w}_i'\boldsymbol{\gamma})$$

where the latter, "selectivity correction" is not the inverse Mills ratio, but some other result from a different model. The correction term is estimated using the Klein and Spady model discussed in Section 23.6.1. This is labeled a "semiparametric" approach. Whether the conditional mean in the selected sample should even remain a linear index function remains to be settled. Not surprisingly, Martins's results, based on two-step least squares differ only slightly from the conventional results based on normality. This approach is arguably only a fairly small step away from the tight parameterization of the Heckman model. Other non- and semiparametric specifications, e.g., Honorè and Kyriazidou (1997, 2000) represent more substantial departures from the normal model, but are much less operational.[33] The upshot is that the issue remains unsettled. For better or worse, the empirical literature on the subject continues to be dominated by Heckman's original model built around the joint normal distribution.

### 24.5.6 ESTIMATING THE EFFECT OF TREATMENT ON THE TREATED

Consider a regression approach to analyzing treatment effects in a two-period setting,

$$y_{it} = \theta_t + \mathbf{x}_{it}'\boldsymbol{\beta} + \gamma C_i + u_i + \varepsilon_{it}, \quad t = 0, 1,$$

---

[32] Again, Angrist (2001) is an important contribution to this literature.

[33] This particular work considers selection in a "panel" (mainly two periods). But, the panel data setting for sample selection models is more involved than a cross-section analysis. In a panel data set, the "selection" is likely to be a decision at the beginning of Period 1 to be in the data set for all subsequent periods. As such, something more intricate than the model we have considered here is called for.

where $C_i$ is the treatment dummy variable and $u_i$ is the unobserved individual effect. The setting is the pre- and post-treatment analysis of the sort considered in this section, where we examine the impact of a job training program on post training earnings. Because there are two periods, a natural approach to the analysis is to examine the changes,

$$\Delta y_i = (\theta_1 - \theta_0) + \gamma \Delta C_i + (\Delta \mathbf{x}_{it})' \boldsymbol{\beta} + \Delta \varepsilon_{it}$$

where $\Delta C_i = 1$ for the treated and 0 for the nontreated individuals, and the first differences eliminate the unobserved individual effects. In the absence of controls (regressors, $\mathbf{x}_{it}$), or assuming that the controls are unchanged, the estimator of the effect of the treatment will be

$$\hat{\gamma} = \overline{\Delta y} \,|\, (\Delta C_i = 1) - \overline{\Delta y} \,|\, (C_i = 0),$$

which is the **difference in differences** estimator. This simplifies the problem considerably, but has several shortcomings. Most important, by using the simple differences, we have lost our ability to discern what induced the change, whether it was the program or something else, presumably in $\mathbf{x}_{it}$.

Even without the normality assumption, the preceding regression approach is more tightly structured than many are comfortable with. A considerable amount of research has focused on what assumptions are needed to reach that model and whether they are likely to be appropriate in a given setting.[34] The overall objective of the analysis of the preceding two sections is to evaluate the effect of a treatment, $C_i$ on the individual treated. The implicit counterfactual is an observation on what the "response" (dependent variable) of the treated individual would have been had they not been treated. But, of course, an individual will be in one state or the other, not both. Denote by $y_0$ the random variable that is the outcome variable in the absence of the treatment and by $y_1$ the outcome when the treatment has taken place. The **average treatment effect,** averaged over the entire population is

$$ATE = E[y_1 - y_0].$$

This is the impact of the treatment on an individual drawn at random from the entire population. However, the desired quantity is not necessarily the $ATE$, but the **average treatment effect on the treated,** which would be

$$ATE \,|\, T = E[y_1 - y_0 \,|\, C = 1].$$

The difficulty of measuring this is, once again, the counterfactual, $E[y_0 \,|\, C = 1]$. Whether these two measures will be the same is at the center of the much of the discussion on this subject. If treatment is completely randomly assigned, then $E[y_j \,|\, C = 1] = E[y_j \,|\, C = 0] = E[y_j \,|\, C = j], j = 0, 1$. This means that with completely random treatment assignment

$$ATE = E[y_1 \,|\, C = 1] - E[y_0 \,|\, C = 0].$$

To put this in our example, if college attendance were completely randomly distributed throughout the population, then the impact of college attendance on income (neglecting other covariates at this point), could be measured simply by averaging the incomes of

---

[34] A sampling of the more important parts of the literature on this issue includes Heckman (1992, 1997), Imbens and Angrist (1994), Manski (1996), and Wooldridge (2002a, Chapter 18).

college attendees and subtracting the average income of nonattendees. The preceding theory might work for the treatment "having brown eyes," but it is unlikely to work for college attendance. Not only is the college attendance treatment not randomly distributed, but the treatment "assignment" is surely related to expectations about $y_1$ versus $y_0$, and, at a minimum, $y_0$ itself. (College is expensive.) More generally, the researcher faces the difficulty in calculating treatment effects that assignment to the treatment might not be exogenous.

The **control function** approach that we used in (24-22)–(24-24) is used to account for the endogeneity of the treatment assignment in the regression context. The very specific assumptions of the bivariate normal distribution of the unobservables somewhat simplifies the estimation, because they make explicit what control function ($\lambda_i$) is appropriate to use in the regression. As Wooldridge (2002a, p. 622) points out, however, the binary variable in the treatment effects regression represents simply an endogenous variable in a linear equation, amenable to **instrumental variable estimation** (assuming suitable instruments are available). Barnow, Cain, and Goldberger (1981) proposed a two-stage least squares estimator, with instrumental variable equal to the predicted probability from the probit treatment assignment model. This is slightly less **parametric** than (22-24) because, in principle, its validity does not rely on joint normality of the disturbances. [Wooldridge (2002a, pp. 621–633) discusses the underlying assumptions.]

If the treatment assignment is "completely ignorable," then, as noted, estimation of the treatment effects is greatly simplified. Suppose, as well, that there are observable variables that influence both the outcome and the treatment assignment. Suppose it is possible to obtain pairs of individuals matched by a common $\mathbf{x}_i$, one with $C_i = 0$, the other with $C_i = 1$. If done with a sufficient number of pairs so as to average over the population of $\mathbf{x}_i$'s, then a **matching estimator,** the average value of $(y_i \mid C_i = 1) - (y_i \mid C_i = 0)$ would estimate $E[y_1 - y_0]$, which is what we seek. Of course, it is optimistic to hope to find a large sample of such matched pairs, both because the sample overall is finite and because there may be many regressors, and the "cells" in the distribution of $\mathbf{x}_i$ are likely to be thinly populated. This will be worse when the regressors are continuous, for example, with a "family income" variable. Rosenbaum and Rubin (1983) and others[35] suggested, instead, matching on the **propensity score,** $F(\mathbf{x}_i) = \text{Prob}(C_i = 1 \mid \mathbf{x}_i)$. Individuals with similar propensity scores are paired and the average treatment effect is then estimated by the differences in outcomes. Various strategies are suggested by the authors for obtaining the necessary subsamples and for verifying the conditions under which the procedures will be valid. [See, e.g., Becker and Ichino (2002) and Greene (2007c).]

### Example 24.10   Treatment Effects on Earnings

LaLonde (1986) analyzed the results of a labor market experiment, The National Supported Work Demonstration, in which a group of disadvantaged workers lacking basic job skills were given work experience and counseling in a sheltered environment. Qualified applicants were assigned to training positions randomly. The treatment group received the benefits of the program. Those in the control group "were left to fend for themselves." [The demonstration was run in numerous cities in the mid-1970s. See LaLonde (1986, pp. 605–609) for institutional

---

[35]Other important references in this literature are Becker and Ichino (1999), Dehejia and Wahba (1999), LaLonde (1986), Heckman, Ichimura, and Todd (1997, 1998), Heckman, Ichimura, Smith and Todd (1998), Heckman, LaLonde, and Smith (1999), Heckman, Tobias, and Vytlacil (2003), and Heckman and Vytlacil (2000).

details on the NSW experiments.] The training period was 1976–1977; the outcome of interest for the sample examined here was post-training 1978 earnings. LaLonde reports a large variety of estimates of the treatment effect, for different subgroups and using different estimation methods. Nonparametric estimates for the group in our sample are roughly $900 for the income increment in the post-training year. (See LaLonde, p. 609.) Similar results are reported from a two-step regression-based estimator similar to (24-22) to (24-24). (See LaLonde's footnote to Table 6, p. 616.)

LaLonde's data are fairly well traveled, having been used in replications and extensions in, e.g., Dehejia and Wahba (1999), Becker and Ichino (2002), and Greene (2007b, c). We have reestimated the matching estimates reported in Becker and Ichino. The data in the file used there (and here) contain 2,490 control observations and 185 treatment observations on the following variables:

$$t = \text{treatment dummy variable,}$$
$$age = \text{age in years,}$$
$$educ = \text{education in years,}$$
$$marr = \text{dummy variable for married,}$$
$$black = \text{dummy variable for black,}$$
$$hisp = \text{dummy variable for Hispanic,}$$
$$nodegree = \text{dummy for no degree (not used),}$$
$$re74 = \text{real earnings in 1974,}$$
$$re75 = \text{real earnings in 1975,}$$
$$re78 = \text{real earnings in 1978.}$$

Transformed variables added to the equation are

$$age2 = age \text{ squared,}$$
$$educ2 = educ \text{ squared,}$$
$$re742 = re74 \text{ squared,}$$
$$re752 = re75 \text{ squared,}$$
$$blacku74 = black \text{ times } 1(re74 = 0).$$

We also scaled all earnings variables by 10,000 before beginning the analysis. (See Appendix Table F24.2. The data are downloaded from the website http://www.nber.org/%7Erdehejia/nswdata.html. The two specific subsamples are in http://www.nber.org/%7Erdehejia//psid_controls.txt and http://www.nber.org/%7Erdehejia/nswre74_treated.txt.) (We note that Becker and Ichino report they were unable to replicate Dehejia and Wahba's results, although they could come reasonably close. We, in turn, were not able to replicate either set of results, though we, likewise, obtained quite similar results.)

The analysis proceeded as follows: A logit model in which the included variables were a *constant, age, age², education, education², marr, black, hisp, re74, re75, re742, re752,* and *black74* was computed for the treatment assignment. The fitted probabilities are used for the propensity scores. By means of an iterative search, the range of propensity scores was partitioned into 8 regions within which, by a simple $F$ test, the mean scores of the treatments and controls were not statistically different. The partitioning is shown in Table 24.5. The 1,347 observations are all the treated observations and the 1,162 control observations are those whose propensity scores fell within the range of the scores for the treated observations.

Within each interval, each treated observation is paired with a small number of the nearest control observations. We found the average difference between treated observation and control to equal $1,574.35. Becker and Ichino reported $1,537.94.

As an experiment, we refit the propensity score equation using a probit model, retaining the fitted probabilities. We then used the two-step estimator described earlier to fit (24-22)

| **TABLE 24.5** | Empirical Distribution of Propensity Scores | | | | | |
|---|---|---|---|---|---|---|
| *Percent* | *Lower* | *Upper* | | | | |
| 0–5 | 0.000591 | 0.000783 | | Sample size = 1,347 | | |
| 5–10 | 0.000787 | 0.001061 | | Average score = 0.137238 | | |
| 10–15 | 0.001065 | 0.001377 | | Std. Dev score = 0.274079 | | |
| 15–20 | 0.001378 | 0.001748 | | | | |
| 20–25 | 0.001760 | 0.002321 | | Lower | Upper | # obs |
| 25–30 | 0.002340 | 0.002956 | 1 | 0.000591 | 0.098016 | 1041 |
| 30–35 | 0.002974 | 0.004057 | 2 | 0.098016 | 0.195440 | 63 |
| 35–40 | 0.004059 | 0.005272 | 3 | 0.195440 | 0.390289 | 65 |
| 40–45 | 0.005278 | 0.007486 | 4 | 0.390289 | 0.585138 | 36 |
| 45–50 | 0.007557 | 0.010451 | 5 | 0.585138 | 0.779986 | 32 |
| 50–55 | 0.010563 | 0.014643 | 6 | 0.779986 | 0.877411 | 17 |
| 55–60 | 0.014686 | 0.022462 | 7 | 0.877411 | 0.926123 | 7 |
| 60–65 | 0.022621 | 0.035060 | 8 | 0.926123 | 0.974835 | 86 |
| 65–70 | 0.035075 | 0.051415 | | | | |
| 70–75 | 0.051415 | 0.076188 | | | | |
| 75–80 | 0.076376 | 0.134189 | | | | |
| 80–85 | 0.134238 | 0.320638 | | | | |
| 85–90 | 0.321233 | 0.616002 | | | | |
| 90–95 | 0.624407 | 0.949418 | | | | |
| 95–100 | 0.949418 | 0.974835 | | | | |

and (24-23) using the entire sample. The estimates of $\delta$, $\rho$, and $\sigma$ were $(-1.01437, 0.35519, 1.38426)$. Using the results from the probit model, we averaged the result in (24-24) for the entire sample, obtaining an estimated treatment effect of \$1,476.30.

## 24.5.7 SAMPLE SELECTION IN NONLINEAR MODELS

The preceding analysis has focused on an extension of the linear regression (or the estimation of simple averages of the data). The method of analysis changes in nonlinear models. To begin, it is not necessarily obvious what the impact of the sample selection is on the response variable, or how it can be accommodated in a model. Consider the model analyzed by Boyes, Hoffman, and Lowe (1989):

$$y_{i1} = 1 \text{ if individual } i \text{ defaults on a loan, 0 otherwise,}$$

$$y_{i2} = 1 \text{ if the individual is granted a loan, 0 otherwise.}$$

Wynand and van Praag (1981) also used this framework to analyze consumer insurance purchases in the first application of the selection methodology in a nonlinear model. Greene (1992) applied the same model to $y_1$ = default on credit card loans, in which $y_{i2}$ denotes whether an application for the card was accepted or not. [Mohanty (2002) also used this model to analyze teen employment in California.] For a given individual, $y_1$ is not observed unless $y_{i2} = 1$. Following the lead of the linear regression case in Section 24.5.3, a natural approach might seem to be to fit the second (selection) equation using a univariate probit model, compute the inverse Mills ratio, $\lambda_i$, and add it to the first equation as an additional "control" variable to accommodate the selection effect. [This is the approach used by Wynand and van Praag (1981).] The problems with this control function approach are, first, it is unclear what in the model is being "controlled" and, second, assuming the first model is correct, the appropriate model conditioned on the sample selection is unlikely to contain an inverse Mills ratio anywhere in it. That result is specific to the linear model, where it arises as $E[\varepsilon_i \,|\, \text{selection}]$. What would seem to be the apparent counterpart for this probit model,

$$\text{Prob}(y_{i1} = 1 \,|\, \text{selection on } y_{i2} = 1) = \Phi(\mathbf{x}'_{i1} \boldsymbol{\beta}_1 + \theta \lambda_i),$$

is not, in fact, the appropriate conditional mean, or probability. For this particular application, the appropriate conditional probability (extending the bivariate probit model of Section 23.8) would be

$$\text{Prob}[y_{i1} = 1 \,|\, y_{i2} = 1] = \frac{\Phi_2(\mathbf{x}'_{i1}\boldsymbol{\beta}_1, \mathbf{x}'_{i2}\boldsymbol{\beta}_2, \rho)}{\Phi(\mathbf{x}'_{i2}\boldsymbol{\beta}_2)}.$$

We would use this result to build up the likelihood function for the three observed outcomes, as follows: The three types of observations in the sample, with their unconditional probabilities, are

$$
\begin{aligned}
y_{i2} = 0: \text{Prob}(y_{i2} = 0 \quad &|\, \mathbf{x}_{i1}, \mathbf{x}_{i2}) = 1 - \Phi(\mathbf{x}'_{i2}\boldsymbol{\beta}_2), \\
y_{i1} = 0, y_{i2} = 1: \text{Prob}(y_{i1} = 0, y_{i2} = 1 \,|\, \mathbf{x}_{i1}, \mathbf{x}_{i2}) &= \Phi_2(-\mathbf{x}'_{i1}\boldsymbol{\beta}_1, \mathbf{x}'_{i2}\boldsymbol{\beta}_2, -\rho), \quad \textbf{(24-25)} \\
y_{i1} = 1, y_{i2} = 1: \text{Prob}(y_{i1} = 1, y_{i2} = 1 \,|\, \mathbf{x}_{i1}, \mathbf{x}_{i2}) &= \Phi_2(\mathbf{x}'_{i1}\boldsymbol{\beta}_1, \mathbf{x}'_{i2}\boldsymbol{\beta}_2, \rho).
\end{aligned}
$$

The log-likelihood function is based on these probabilities.[36]

### Example 24.11 Doctor Visits and Insurance

Continuing our analysis of the utilization of the German health care system, we observe that the data set (see Example 11.11) contains an indicator of whether the individual subscribes to the "Public" health insurance or not. Roughly 87 percent of the observations in the sample do. We might ask whether the selection on public insurance reveals any substantive difference in visits to the physician. We estimated a logit specification for this model in Example 23.4. Using (24-25) as the framework, we define $y_{i2}$ to be presence of insurance and $y_{i1}$ to be the binary variable defined to equal 1 if the individual makes at least one visit to the doctor in the survey year.

The estimation results are given in Table 24.6. Based on these results, there does appear to be a very strong relationship. The coefficients do change somewhat in the conditional model. A Wald test for the presence of the selection effect against the null hypothesis that $\rho$ equals zero produces a test statistic of $(-7.188)^2 = 51.667$, which is larger than the critical value of 3.84. Thus, the hypothesis is rejected. A likelihood ratio statistic is computed as the difference between the log-likelihood for the full model and the sum of the two separate log-likelihoods for the independent probit models when $\rho$ equals zero. The result is

$$\lambda_{\text{LR}} = 2[-23969.58 - (-15536.39 + (-8471.508)) = 77.796$$

The hypothesis is rejected once again. Partial effects were computed using the results in Section 23.8.3.

The large correlation coefficient can be misleading. The estimated $-0.9299$ does not state that the presence of insurance makes it much less likely to go to the doctor. This is the correlation among the unobserved factors in each equation. The factors that make it more likely to purchase insurance make it less likely to use a physician. To obtain a simple correlation between the two variables, we might use the tetrachoric correlation defined in Example 23.13. This would be computed by fitting a bivariate probit model for the two binary variables without any other variables. The estimated value is 0.120.

---

[36]Extensions of the bivariate probit model to other types of censoring are discussed in Poirier (1980) and Abowd and Farber (1982).

**TABLE 24.6** Estimated Probit Equations for Doctor Visits

| | Independent: No Selection | | | Sample Selection Model | | |
|---|---|---|---|---|---|---|
| Variable | Estimate | Standard Error | Partial Effect | Estimate | Standard Error | Partial Effect |
| Constant | 0.05588 | 0.06564 | | −9.4366 | 0.06760 | |
| Age | 0.01331 | 0.0008399 | 0.004971 | 0.01284 | 0.0008131 | 0.005042 |
| Income | −0.1034 | 0.05089 | −0.03860 | −0.1030 | 0.04582 | −0.04060 |
| Kids | −0.1349 | 0.01947 | −0.05059 | −0.1264 | 0.01790 | −0.04979 |
| Education | −0.01920 | 0.004254 | −0.007170 | 0.03660 | 0.004744 | 0.002703 |
| Married | 0.03586 | 0.02172 | 0.01343 | 0.03564 | 0.02016 | 0.01404 |
| ln L | −15536.39 | | | | | |
| Constant | 3.3585 | 0.06959 | | 3.2699 | 0.06916 | |
| Age | 0.0001868 | 0.0009744 | | −0.0002679 | 0.001036 | |
| Education | −0.1854 | 0.003941 | | −0.1807 | 0.003936 | |
| Female | 0.1150 | 0.02186 | 0.0000[a] | 0.2230 | 0.02101 | 0.01446[a] |
| ln L | −8471.508 | | | | | |
| ρ | 0.0000 | 0.0000 | | −0.9299 | 0.1294 | |
| ln L | −24007.90 | | | −23969.58 | | |

[a] Indirect effect from second equation.

More general cases are typically much less straightforward. Greene (1992, 2006) and Terza (1995, 1998) have developed sample selection models for nonlinear specifications based on the underlying logic of the Heckman model in Section 24.5.3, that the influence of the incidental truncation acts on the unobservable variables in the model. (That is the source of the "selection bias" in conventional estimators.) The modeling extension introduces the unobservables into the model in a natural fashion that parallels the regression model.

The generic model will take the form

1. Probit selection equation:

$$z_i^* = \mathbf{w}_i'\boldsymbol{\alpha} + u_i \text{ in which } u_i \sim N[0, 1], \qquad \text{(24-26)}$$
$$z_i = 1 \text{ if } z_i^* > 0, 0 \text{ otherwise.}$$

2. Nonlinear index function model with unobserved **heterogeneity** and sample selection:

$$\mu_i \mid \varepsilon_i = \mathbf{x}_i'\boldsymbol{\beta} + \sigma\varepsilon_i, \varepsilon_i \sim N[0, 1],$$
$$y_i \mid \mathbf{x}_i, \varepsilon_i \sim \text{density } g(y_i \mid \mathbf{x}_i, \varepsilon_i) = f(y_i \mid \mathbf{x}_i'\boldsymbol{\beta} + \sigma\varepsilon_i), \qquad \text{(24-27)}$$
$$y_i, \mathbf{x}_i \text{ are observed only when } z_i = 1,$$
$$[u_i, \varepsilon_i] \sim N[(0, 1), (1, \rho, 1)].$$

For example, in a Poisson regression model, the conditional mean function becomes $E(y_i \mid \mathbf{x}_i) = \lambda_i = \exp(\mathbf{x}_i'\boldsymbol{\beta} + \sigma\varepsilon_i) = \exp(\mu_i)$. (We will use this specification of the model in Chapter 25 to introduce random effects in the Poisson regression model for panel data.)

The log-likelihood function for the full model is the joint density for the observed data. When $z_i$ equals one, $(y_i, \mathbf{x}_i, z_i, \mathbf{w}_i)$ are all observed. To obtain the joint density

$p(y_i, z_i = 1 \mid \mathbf{x}_i, \mathbf{w}_i)$, we proceed as follows:

$$p(y_i, z_i = 1 \mid \mathbf{x}_i, \mathbf{w}_i) = \int_{-\infty}^{\infty} p(y_i, z_i = 1 \mid \mathbf{x}_i, \mathbf{w}_i, \varepsilon_i) f(\varepsilon_i) d\varepsilon_i.$$

Conditioned on $\varepsilon_i$, $z_i$ and $y_i$ are independent. Therefore, the joint density is the product,

$$p(y_i, z_i = 1 \mid \mathbf{x}_i, \mathbf{w}_i, \varepsilon_i) = f(y_i \mid \mathbf{x}_i'\boldsymbol{\beta} + \sigma\varepsilon_i)\text{Prob}(z_i = 1 \mid \mathbf{w}_i, \varepsilon_i).$$

The first part, $f(y_i \mid \mathbf{x}_i'\boldsymbol{\beta} + \sigma\varepsilon_i)$ is the conditional index function model in (24-27). By joint normality, $f(u_i \mid \varepsilon_i) = N[\rho\varepsilon_i, (1 - \rho^2)]$, so $u_i \mid \varepsilon_i = \rho\varepsilon_i + (u_i - \rho\varepsilon_i) = \rho\varepsilon_i + v_i$ where $E[v_i] = 0$ and $\text{Var}[v_i] = (1 - \rho^2)$. Therefore,

$$\text{Prob}(z_i = 1 \mid \mathbf{w}_i, \varepsilon_i) = \Phi\left(\frac{\mathbf{w}_i'\boldsymbol{\alpha} + \rho\varepsilon_i}{\sqrt{1 - \rho^2}}\right).$$

Combining terms and using the earlier approach, the unconditional joint density is

$$p(y_i, z_i = 1 \mid \mathbf{x}_i, \mathbf{w}_i) = \int_{-\infty}^{\infty} f(y_i \mid \mathbf{x}_i'\boldsymbol{\beta} + \sigma\varepsilon_i)\Phi\left(\frac{\mathbf{w}_i'\boldsymbol{\alpha} + \rho\varepsilon_i}{\sqrt{1 - \rho^2}}\right)\frac{\exp(-\varepsilon_i^2/2)}{\sqrt{2\pi}}d\varepsilon_i. \quad \textbf{(24-28)}$$

The other part of the likelihood function for the observations with $z_i = 0$ will be

$$\text{Prob}(z_i = 0 \mid \mathbf{w}_i) = \int_{-\infty}^{\infty} \text{Prob}(z_i = 0 \mid \mathbf{w}_i, \varepsilon_i) f(\varepsilon_i) d\varepsilon_i.$$

$$= \int_{-\infty}^{\infty} \left[1 - \Phi\left(\frac{\mathbf{w}_i'\boldsymbol{\alpha} + \rho\varepsilon_i}{\sqrt{1 - \rho^2}}\right)\right] f(\varepsilon_i) d\varepsilon_i \quad \textbf{(24-29)}$$

$$= \int_{-\infty}^{\infty} \Phi\left(\frac{-(\mathbf{w}_i'\boldsymbol{\alpha} + \rho\varepsilon_i)}{\sqrt{1 - \rho^2}}\right)\frac{\exp(-\varepsilon_i^2/2)}{\sqrt{2\pi}}d\varepsilon_i.$$

For convenience, we can use the invariance principle to reparameterize the likelihood function in terms of $\boldsymbol{\gamma} = \boldsymbol{\alpha}/\sqrt{1 - \rho^2}$ and $\tau = \rho/\sqrt{1 - \rho^2}$. Combining all the preceding terms, the log-likelihood function to be maximized is

$$\ln L = \sum_{i=1}^{n} \ln \int_{-\infty}^{\infty} [(1 - z_i) + z_i f(y_i \mid \mathbf{x}_i'\boldsymbol{\beta} + \sigma\varepsilon_i)]\Phi[(2z_i - 1)(\mathbf{w}_i'\boldsymbol{\gamma} + \tau\varepsilon_i)]\phi(\varepsilon_i)d\varepsilon_i. \quad \textbf{(24-30)}$$

This can be maximized with respect to $(\boldsymbol{\beta}, \sigma, \boldsymbol{\gamma}, \tau)$ using quadrature or simulation. When done, $\rho$ can be recovered from $\rho = \text{sign}(\tau) \times \tau/(1 + \tau^2)^{1/2}$ and $\boldsymbol{\alpha} = (1 - \rho^2)^{1/2}\boldsymbol{\gamma}$. All that differs from one model to another is the specification of $f(y_i \mid \mathbf{x}_i'\boldsymbol{\beta} + \sigma\varepsilon_i)$. This is the specification used in Greene (1992), Terza (1995), and Terza and Kenkel (2001). (In the latter two papers, the authors analyzed $E[y_i \mid z_i = 1]$ rather than the conditional density. Their estimator was based on nonlinear least squares, but as earlier, it is necessary to integrate the unobserved heterogeneity out of the conditional mean function.)

### 24.5.8 PANEL DATA APPLICATIONS OF SAMPLE SELECTION MODELS

The development of methods for extending sample selection models to panel data settings parallels the literature on cross-section methods. It begins with Hausman and Wise (1979) who devised a maximum likelihood estimator for a two-period model with attrition—the "selection equation" was a formal model for attrition from the sample.

Subsequent research has drawn the analogy between attrition and sample selection in a variety of applications, such as Keane et al. (1988) and Verbeek and Nijman (1992), and produced theoretical developments including Wooldridge (2002a, b).

The direct extension of panel data methods to sample selection brings several new issues for the modeler. An immediate question arises concerning the nature of the selection itself. Although much of the theoretical literature [e.g., Kyriazidou (1997, 2001)] treats the panel as if the selection mechanism is run anew in every period, in practice, the selection process often comes in two very different forms. First, selection may take the form of selection of the entire group of observations into the panel data set. Thus, the selection mechanism operates once, perhaps even before the observation window opens. Consider the entry (or not) of eligible candidates for a job training program. In this case, it is not appropriate to build the model to allow entry, exit, then reentry. Second, for most applications, selection comes in the form of attrition or retention. Once an observation is "deselected," it does not return. Leading examples would include "survivorship" in time-series–cross-section models of firm performance and attrition in medical trials and in panel data applications involving large national survey data bases, such as Contoyannis et al. (2004). Each of these cases suggests the utility of a more structured approach to the selection mechanism.

### 24.5.8.a   Common Effects in Sample Selection Models

A formal "effects" treatment for sample selection was first suggested in complete form by Verbeek (1990), who formulated a random effects model for the probit equation and a fixed effects approach for the main regression. Zabel (1992) criticized the specification for its asymmetry in the treatment of the effects in the two equations. He also argued that the likelihood function that neglected correlation between the effects and regressors in the probit model would render the FIML estimator inconsistent. His proposal involved fixed effects in both equations. Recognizing the difficulty of fitting such a model, he then proposed using the Mundlak correction. The full model is

$$y_{it}^* = \eta_i + \mathbf{x}_{it}'\boldsymbol{\beta} + \varepsilon_{it}, \quad \eta_i = \overline{\mathbf{x}}_i'\boldsymbol{\pi} + \tau w_i, w_i \sim N[0,1],$$

$$d_{it}^* = \theta_i + \mathbf{z}_{it}'\boldsymbol{\alpha} + u_{it}, \quad \theta_i = \overline{\mathbf{z}}_i'\boldsymbol{\delta} + \omega v_i, v_i \sim N[0,1], \tag{24-31}$$

$$(\varepsilon_{it}, u_{it}) \sim N_2[(0,0), (\sigma^2, 1, \rho\sigma)].$$

The "selectivity" in the model is carried through the correlation between $\varepsilon_{it}$ and $u_{it}$. The resulting log-likelihood is built up from the contribution of individual $i$,

$$L_i = \int_{-\infty}^{\infty} \prod_{d_{it}=0} \Phi[-\mathbf{z}_{it}'\boldsymbol{\alpha} - \overline{\mathbf{z}}_i'\boldsymbol{\delta} - \omega v_i]\phi(v_i)dv_i$$

$$\times \int_{-\infty}^{\infty}\int_{-\infty}^{\infty} \prod_{d_{it}=1} \Phi\left[\frac{\mathbf{z}_{it}'\boldsymbol{\alpha} + \overline{\mathbf{z}}_i'\boldsymbol{\delta} + \omega v_i + (\rho/\sigma)\varepsilon_{it}}{\sqrt{1-\rho^2}}\right]$$

$$\times \frac{1}{\sigma}\phi\left(\frac{\varepsilon_{it}}{\sigma}\right)\phi_2(v_i, w_i)dv_i dw_i, \tag{24-32}$$

$$\varepsilon_{it} = y_{it} - \mathbf{x}_{it}'\boldsymbol{\beta} - \overline{\mathbf{x}}_i'\boldsymbol{\pi} - \tau w_i.$$

The log-likelihood is then $\ln L = \Sigma_i \ln L_i$.

The log-likelihood requires integration in two dimensions for any selected observations. Vella (1998) suggested two-step procedures to avoid the integration. However, the bivariate normal integration is actually the product of two univariate normals, because in the preceding specification, $v_i$ and $w_i$ are assumed to be uncorrelated. As such, the likelihood function in (24-32) can be readily evaluated using familiar simulation or quadrature techniques. [See Sections 16.9.6.b and 17.5. Vella and Verbeek (1999) suggest this in a footnote, but do not pursue it.] To show this, note that the first line in the log-likelihood is of the form $E_v[\prod_{d=0} \Phi(\ldots)]$ and the second line is of the form $E_w[E_v[\Phi(\ldots)\phi(\ldots)/\sigma]]$. Either of these expectations can be satisfactorily approximated with the average of a sufficient number of draws from the standard normal populations that generate $w_i$ and $v_i$. The term in the simulated likelihood that follows this prescription is

$$
L_i^S = \frac{1}{R} \sum_{r=1}^{R} \prod_{d_{it}=0} \Phi[-\mathbf{z}_{it}'\boldsymbol{\alpha} - \overline{\mathbf{z}}_i'\boldsymbol{\delta} - \omega v_{i,r}]
$$

$$
\times \frac{1}{R} \sum_{r=1}^{R} \prod_{d_{it}=1} \Phi\left[ \frac{\mathbf{z}_{it}'\boldsymbol{\alpha} + \overline{\mathbf{z}}_i'\boldsymbol{\delta} + \omega v_{i,r} + (\rho/\sigma)\varepsilon_{it,r}}{\sqrt{1-\rho^2}} \right] \frac{1}{\sigma}\phi\left(\frac{\varepsilon_{it,r}}{\sigma}\right), \quad \textbf{(24-33)}
$$

$$
\varepsilon_{it,r} = y_{it} - \mathbf{x}_{it}'\boldsymbol{\beta} - \overline{\mathbf{x}}_i'\boldsymbol{\pi} - \tau w_{i,r}.
$$

Maximization of this log-likelihood with respect to $(\boldsymbol{\beta},\sigma,\rho,\boldsymbol{\alpha},\boldsymbol{\delta},\boldsymbol{\pi},\tau,\omega)$ by conventional gradient methods is quite feasible. Indeed, this formulation provides a means by which the likely correlation between $v_i$ and $w_i$ can be accommodated in the model. Suppose that $w_i$ and $v_i$ are bivariate standard normal with correlation $\rho_{vw}$. We can project $w_i$ on $v_i$ and write

$$
w_i = \rho_{vw} v_i + \left(1 - \rho_{vw}^2\right)^{1/2} h_i,
$$

where $h_i$ has a standard normal distribution. To allow the correlation, we now simply substitute this expression for $w_i$ in the simulated (or original) log-likelihood and add $\rho_{vw}$ to the list of parameters to be estimated. The simulation is still over independent normal variates, $v_i$ and $h_i$.

Notwithstanding the preceding derivation, much of the recent attention has focused on simpler two-step estimators. Building on Ridder and Wansbeek (1990) and Verbeek and Nijman (1992) [see Vella (1998) for numerous additional references], Vella and Verbeek (1999) purpose a two-step methodology that involves a random effects framework similar to the one in (24-31). As they note, there is some loss in efficiency by not using the FIML estimator. But, with the sample sizes typical in contemporary panel data sets, that efficiency loss may not be large. As they note, their two-step template encompasses a variety of models including the tobit model examined in the preceding sections and the mover-stayer model noted earlier.

The Vella and Verbeek model requires some fairly intricate maximum likelihood procedures. Wooldridge (1995) proposes an estimator that, with a few probably—but not necessarily—innocent assumptions, can be based on straightforward applications of conventional, everyday methods. We depart from a fixed effects specification,

$$
y_{it}^* = \eta_i + \mathbf{x}_{it}'\boldsymbol{\beta} + \varepsilon_{it},
$$

$$
d_{it}^* = \theta_i + \mathbf{z}_{it}'\boldsymbol{\alpha} + u_{it},
$$

$$
(\varepsilon_{it}, u_{it}) \sim N_2[(0,0), (\sigma^2, 1, \rho\sigma)].
$$

Under the **mean independence assumption** $E[\varepsilon_{it} \mid \eta_i, \theta_i, \mathbf{z}_{i1}, \ldots, \mathbf{z}_{iT}, v_{i1}, \ldots, v_{iT}, d_{i1}, \ldots, d_{iT}] = \rho u_{it}$, it will follow that

$$E[y_{it} \mid \mathbf{x}_{i1}, \ldots, \mathbf{x}_{iT}, \eta_i, \theta_i, \mathbf{z}_{i1}, \ldots, \mathbf{z}_{iT}, v_{i1}, \ldots, v_{iT}, d_{i1}, \ldots, d_{iT}] = \eta_i + \mathbf{x}'_{it}\boldsymbol{\beta} + \rho u_{it}.$$

This suggests an approach to estimating the model parameters; however, it requires computation of $u_{it}$. That would require estimation of $\theta_i$, which cannot be done, at least not consistently—and that precludes simple estimation of $u_{it}$. To escape the dilemma, Wooldridge (2002c) suggests Chamberlain's approach to the fixed effects model,

$$\theta_i = f_0 + \mathbf{z}'_{i1}\mathbf{f}_1 + \mathbf{z}'_{i2}\mathbf{f}_2 + \cdots + \mathbf{z}'_{iT}\mathbf{f}_T + h_i.$$

With this substitution,

$$
\begin{aligned}
d^*_{it} &= \mathbf{z}'_{it}\boldsymbol{\alpha} + f_0 + \mathbf{z}'_{i1}\mathbf{f}_1 + \mathbf{z}'_{i2}\mathbf{f}_2 + \cdots + \mathbf{z}'_{iT}\mathbf{f}_T + h_i + u_{it} \\
&= \mathbf{z}'_{it}\boldsymbol{\alpha} + f_0 + \mathbf{z}'_{i1}\mathbf{f}_1 + \mathbf{z}'_{i2}\mathbf{f}_2 + \cdots + \mathbf{z}'_{iT}\mathbf{f}_T + w_{it},
\end{aligned}
$$

where $w_{it}$ is independent of $\mathbf{z}_{it}, t = 1, \ldots, T$. This now implies that

$$E[y_{it} \mid \mathbf{x}_{i1}, \ldots, \mathbf{x}_{iT}, \eta_i, \theta_i, \mathbf{z}_{i1}, \ldots, \mathbf{z}_{iT}, v_{i1}, \ldots, v_{iT}, d_{i1}, \ldots, d_{iT}] = \eta_i + \mathbf{x}'_{it}\boldsymbol{\beta} + \rho(w_{it} - h_i)$$
$$= (\eta_i - \rho h_i) + \mathbf{x}'_{it}\boldsymbol{\beta} + \rho w_{it}.$$

To complete the estimation procedure, we now compute $T$ cross-sectional probit models (reestimating $f_0, \mathbf{f}_1, \ldots$ each time) and compute $\hat{\lambda}_{it}$ from each one. The resulting equation,

$$y_{it} = a_i + \mathbf{x}'_{it}\boldsymbol{\beta} + \rho\hat{\lambda}_{it} + v_{it},$$

now forms the basis for estimation of $\boldsymbol{\beta}$ and $\rho$ by using a conventional fixed effects linear regression with the observed data.

### 24.5.8.b  Attrition

The recent literature or sample selection contains numerous analyses of two-period models, such as Kyriazidou (1997, 2001). They generally focus on non- and semiparametric analyses. An early parametric contribution of Hausman and Wise (1979) is also a two-period model of attrition, which would seem to characterize many of the studies suggested in the current literature. The model formulation is a two-period random effects specification:

$$y_{i1} = \mathbf{x}'_{i1}\boldsymbol{\beta} + \varepsilon_{i1} + u_i \quad \text{(first period regression)},$$
$$y_{i2} = \mathbf{x}'_{i2}\boldsymbol{\beta} + \varepsilon_{i2} + u_i \quad \text{(second period regression)}.$$

Attrition is likely in the second period (to begin the study, the individual must have been observed in the first period). The authors suggest that the probability that an observation is made in the second period varies with the value of $y_{i2}$ as well as some other variables,

$$z^*_{i2} = \delta y_{i2} + \mathbf{x}'_{i2}\boldsymbol{\theta} + \mathbf{w}'_{i2}\boldsymbol{\alpha} + v_{i2}.$$

Attrition occurs if $z^*_{i2} \leq 0$, which produces a probit model,

$$z_{i2} = 1\left(z^*_{i2} > 0\right) \quad \text{(attrition indicator observed in period 2)}.$$

An observation is made in the second period if $z_{i2} = 1$, which makes this an early version of the familiar sample selection model. The reduced form of the observation equation is

$$
\begin{aligned}
z_{i2}^* &= \mathbf{x}_{i2}'(\delta\boldsymbol{\beta} + \boldsymbol{\theta}) + \mathbf{w}_{i2}'\boldsymbol{\alpha} + \delta\varepsilon_{i2} + v_{i2} \\
&= \mathbf{x}_{i2}'\boldsymbol{\pi} + \mathbf{w}_{i2}'\boldsymbol{\alpha} + h_{i2} \\
&= \mathbf{r}_{i2}'\boldsymbol{\gamma} + h_{i2}.
\end{aligned}
$$

The variables in the probit equation are all those in the second period regression plus any additional ones dictated by the application. The estimable parameters in this model are $\boldsymbol{\beta}, \boldsymbol{\gamma}, \sigma^2 = \text{Var}[\varepsilon_{it} + u_i]$, and two correlation coefficients,

$$
\rho_{12} = \text{Corr}[\varepsilon_{i1} + u_i, \varepsilon_{i2} + u_i] = \text{Var}[u_i]/\sigma^2,
$$

and

$$
\rho_{23} = \text{Corr}[h_{i2}, \varepsilon_{i2} + u_i].
$$

All disturbances are assumed to be normally distributed. (Readers are referred to the paper for motivation and details on this specification.)

The authors propose a full information maximum likelihood estimator. Estimation can be simplified somewhat by using two steps. The parameters of the probit model can be estimated first by maximum likelihood. Then the remaining parameters are estimated by maximum likelihood, conditionally on these first-step estimates. The Murphy and Topel adjustment is made after the second step. [See Greene (2007a).]

The Hausman and Wise model covers the case of two periods in which there is a formal mechanism in the model for retention in the second period. It is unclear how the procedure could be extended to a multiple period application such as that in Contoyannis et al. (2004), which involved a panel data set with eight waves. In addition, in that study, the variables in the main equations were counts of hospital visits and physican visits, which complicates the use of linear regression. A workable solution to the problem of attrition in a multiperiod panel is the **inverse probability weighted estimator** [Wooldridge (2002a, 2006b) and Rotnitzky and Robins (2005).] In the Contoyannis application, there are eight waves in the panel. Attrition is taken to be "ignorable" so that the unobservables in the attrition equation and in the main equation(s) of interest are uncorrelated. (Note that Hausman and Wise do not make this assumption.) This enables Contoyannis et al. to fit a "retention" probit equation for each observation present at wave 1, for waves 2–8, using characteristics observed at the entry to the panel. (This defines, then, "selection (retention) on observables.") Defining $d_{it}$ to be the indicator for presence ($d_{it} = 1$) or absence ($d_{it} = 0$) of observation $i$ in wave $t$, it will follow that the sequence of observations will begin at 1 and either stay at 1 or change to 0 for the remaining waves. Let $\hat{p}_{it}$ denote the predicted probability from the probit estimator at wave $t$. Then, their full log-likelihood is constructed as

$$
\ln L = \sum_{i=1}^{n} \sum_{t=1}^{T} \frac{d_{it}}{\hat{p}_{it}} \ln L_{it}.
$$

Wooldridge (2002b) presents the underlying theory for the properties of this weighted maximum likelihood estimator. [Further details on the use of the inverse probability weighted estimator in the Contoyannis et al. (2004) study appear in Jones, Koolman, and Rice (2006).]

## 24.6 SUMMARY AND CONCLUSIONS

This chapter has examined three settings in which, in principle, the linear regression model of Chapter 2 would apply, but the data generating mechanism produces a nonlinear form. In the truncated regression model, the range of the dependent variable is restricted substantively. Certainly all economic data are restricted in this way—aggregate income data cannot be negative, for example. But when data are truncated so that plausible values of the dependent variable are precluded, for example, when zero values for expenditure are discarded, the data that remain are analyzed with models that explicitly account for the truncation. When data are censored, values of the dependent variable that could in principle be observed are masked. Ranges of values of the true variable being studied are observed as a single value. The basic problem this presents for model building is that in such a case, we observe variation of the independent variables without the corresponding variation in the dependent variable that might be expected. Finally, the issue of sample selection arises when the observed data are not drawn randomly from the population of interest. Failure to account for this nonrandom sampling produces a model that describes only the nonrandom subsample, not the larger population. In each case, we examined the model specification and estimation techniques which are appropriate for these variations of the regression model. Maximum likelihood is usually the method of choice, but for the third case, a two-step estimator has become more common.

## Key Terms and Concepts

- Attrition
- Average treatment effect
- Average treatment effect on the treated
- Attenuation
- Censored regression model
- Censored variable
- Censoring
- Conditional moment test
- Control function
- Corner solution
- Degree of truncation
- Delta method
- Difference in differences
- Generalized residual
- Hazard function
- Heterogeneity
- Heteroscedasticity
- Incidental truncation
- Instrumetal variable estimation
- Inverse probability weighted estimator
- Inverse Mills ratio
- Lagrange multiplier test
- Marginal effects
- Matching estimator
- Mean independence assumption
- Olsen's reparameterization
- Parametric model
- Propensity score
- Sample selection
- Semiparametric estimator
- Specification error
- Tobit model
- Treatment effect
- Truncated bivariate normal distribution
- Truncated distribution
- Truncated mean
- Truncated normal distribution
- Truncated random variable
- Truncated standard normal distribution
- Truncated variance
- Two-step estimation

## Exercises

1. The following 20 observations are drawn from a censored normal distribution:

| | | | | | |
|---|---|---|---|---|---|
| 3.8396 | 7.2040 | 0.00000 | 0.00000 | 4.4132 | 8.0230 |
| 5.7971 | 7.0828 | 0.00000 | 0.80260 | 13.0670 | 4.3211 |
| 0.00000 | 8.6801 | 5.4571 | 0.00000 | 8.1021 | 0.00000 |
| 1.2526 | 5.6016 | | | | |

The applicable model is

$$y_i^* = \mu + \varepsilon_i,$$
$$y_i = y_i^* \quad \text{if } \mu + \varepsilon_i > 0, 0 \text{ otherwise,}$$
$$\varepsilon_i \sim N[0, \sigma^2].$$

Exercises 1 through 4 in this section are based on the preceding information. The OLS estimator of $\mu$ in the context of this tobit model is simply the sample mean. Compute the mean of all 20 observations. Would you expect this estimator to over- or underestimate $\mu$? If we consider only the nonzero observations, then the truncated regression model applies. The sample mean of the nonlimit observations is the least squares estimator in this context. Compute it and then comment on whether this sample mean should be an overestimate or an underestimate of the true mean.

2. We now consider the tobit model that applies to the full data set.
   a. Formulate the log-likelihood for this very simple tobit model.
   b. Reformulate the log-likelihood in terms of $\theta = 1/\sigma$ and $\gamma = \mu/\sigma$. Then derive the necessary conditions for maximizing the log-likelihood with respect to $\theta$ and $\gamma$.
   c. Discuss how you would obtain the values of $\theta$ and $\gamma$ to solve the problem in part b.
   d. Compute the maximum likelihood estimates of $\mu$ and $\sigma$.

3. Using only the nonlimit observations, repeat Exercise 2 in the context of the truncated regression model. Estimate $\mu$ and $\sigma$ by using the method of moments estimator outlined in Example 24.2. Compare your results with those in the previous exercises.

4. Continuing to use the data in Exercise 1, consider once again only the nonzero observations. Suppose that the sampling mechanism is as follows: $y^*$ and another normally distributed random variable $z$ have population correlation 0.7. The two variables, $y^*$ and $z$, are sampled jointly. When $z$ is greater than zero, $y$ is reported. When $z$ is less than zero, both $z$ and $y$ are discarded. Exactly 35 draws were required to obtain the preceding sample. Estimate $\mu$ and $\sigma$. (Hint: Use Theorem 24.5.)

5. Derive the marginal effects for the tobit model with heteroscedasticity that is described in Section 24.3.4.a.

6. Prove that the Hessian for the tobit model in (24-14) is negative definite after Olsen's transformation is applied to the parameters.

## Applications

1. In Section 25.5.2, we will examine Ray Fair's famous analysis of a *Psychology Today* survey on extramarital affairs. Although the dependent variable used in that study was a count, Fair used the tobit model as the platform for his study. Our analysis in Section 25.5.2 will examine the study, using a Poisson model for counts instead. Fair's original study also included but did not analyze a second data set that was a similar survey conducted by *Redbook* magazine. The data are reproduced in

Appendix Table F24.1. (Our thanks to Ray Fair for providing these data.) This sample contains observations on 6,366 women and the following variables:

$id$ = an identification number,

$C$ = constant, value = 1,

$yrb$ = a constructed measure of time spent in extramarital affairs,

$v1$ = a rating of the marriage, coded 1 to 4,

$v2$ = age, in years, aggregated,

$v3$ = number of years married,

$v4$ = number of children, top coded at 5,

$v5$ = religiosity, 1 to 4, 1 = not, 4 = very,

$v6$ = education, coded 9, 12, 14, 16, 17, 20,

$v7$ = occupation,

$v8$ = husband's occupation.

Three other variables were not used. Details on the variables in the model are given in Fair's (1978) *Journal of Political Economy* paper. Using these data, conduct a parallel study to the *Psychology Today* study that was done in Fair (1978) and replicated in Section 25.5.2. Are the results consistent? Report all results, including partial effects and relevant diagnostic statistics.

2. Continuing the analysis of the first application, note that these data conform precisely to the description of "corner solutions" in 24.3.4.c. The dependent variable is not censored in the fashion usually assumed for a tobit model. To investigate whether the dependent variable is determined by a two-part decision process (yes/no and, if yes, how much), specify and estimate a two-equation model in which the first equation analyzes the binary decision $A = 1$ if $y > 0$ and 0 otherwise and the second equation analyzes $y \mid y > 0$. What is the appropriate model? What do you find? Report all results. (Note, if you analyze the second dependent variable using the truncated regression, you should remove some extreme observations from your sample. The truncated regression estimator refuses to converge with the full data set, but works nicely for the example if you omit observations with $y > 5$.)

# 25

# MODELS FOR EVENT
# COUNTS AND DURATION

## 25.1 INTRODUCTION

This chapter is concerned with models of events. In some aspects, the regression-like models we have studied, such as the discrete choice models, are the appropriate tools. As in the previous two chapters, however, the models are nonlinear, and the familiar regression methods are not appropriate. Most of this analysis focuses on maximum likelihood estimators. In modeling duration, although an underlying regression model is in fact at work, it is not the conditional mean function that is of interest. More likely, as we will explore below, the objects of estimation are certain probabilities of events.

Consider the measurement of the interarrival time $t$ (i.e., the amount of time that passes between arrivals) of, say, customers at an ATM machine, messages in a telephone system, customers at a store, or patients at a hospital. A model that is often used for phenomena such as these is the **exponential model,**

$$f(t) = 1/\theta \exp(-t/\theta), \quad t \geq 0, \theta > 0.$$

The expected interarrival time in this distribution is $E[t] = 1/\theta$. With this in hand, then, consider the number of arrivals, $y$, that occur per unit of time. It can be shown that this discrete random variable has probability distribution

$$g(y) = \exp(-\lambda)\lambda^y/y!, \quad \lambda = 1/\theta > 0, y = 0, 1, \dots,$$

which is the Poisson distribution. The expected value of this random variable is $E[y] = 1/\theta$, which makes intuitive sense. If the average time between arrivals is 30 seconds (0.5 minutes), then we expect two arrivals per minute.

The modeling of *events* is concerned with these two clearly related phenomena. Different aspects will be of interest depending on the objectives of the study. In health economics, researchers are often interested in the number of occurrences of events. In several of our earlier applications we have examined models that describe utilization of the health system in terms of numbers of visits to the physician or to the hospital. In contrast, in a business application, one might be interested in the duration of events such as strikes or spells of unemployment, or of the amount of time that passes between events such as business failures. In medical statistics, much of the research is focused on duration between events, such as the length of survival of patients after treatment.

This chapter will describe modeling approaches for events.[1] As suggested, the two measures, counts of events and duration between events, are usually studied with different techniques, and for different purposes. Sections 25.2 to 25.5 will describe some of the econometric approaches to modeling event counts. The application of duration models to economic data is somewhat less frequent, but conversely, far more frequent in the other fields mentioned. The chapter, and this text, end in Section 25.6 with a discussion of models for duration.

## 25.2 MODELS FOR COUNTS OF EVENTS

Data on patents suggested in Section 23.2 are typical of **count data.** In principle, we could analyze these data using multiple linear regression. But the preponderance of zeros and the small values and clearly discrete nature of the dependent variable suggest that we can improve on least squares and the linear model with a specification that accounts for these characteristics. The **Poisson regression model** has been widely used to study such data.

The Poisson regression model specifies that each $y_i$ is drawn from a Poisson distribution with parameter $\lambda_i$, which is related to the regressors $\mathbf{x}_i$. The primary equation of the model is

$$\text{Prob}(Y = y_i \mid \mathbf{x}_i) = \frac{e^{-\lambda_i} \lambda_i^{y_i}}{y_i!}, \quad y_i = 0, 1, 2, \ldots. \qquad \textbf{(25-1)}$$

The most common formulation for $\lambda_i$ is the **loglinear model,**

$$\ln \lambda_i = \mathbf{x}_i' \boldsymbol{\beta}.$$

It is easily shown that the expected number of events *per period* is given by

$$E[y_i \mid \mathbf{x}_i] = \text{Var}[y_i \mid \mathbf{x}_i] = \lambda_i = e^{\mathbf{x}_i' \boldsymbol{\beta}},$$

so

$$\frac{\partial E[y_i \mid \mathbf{x}_i]}{\partial \mathbf{x}_i} = \lambda_i \boldsymbol{\beta}.$$

With the parameter estimates in hand, this vector can be computed using any data vector desired.

In principle, the Poisson model is simply a nonlinear regression.[2] But it is far easier to estimate the parameters with maximum likelihood techniques. The log-likelihood function is

$$\ln L = \sum_{i=1}^{n} [-\lambda_i + y_i \mathbf{x}_i' \boldsymbol{\beta} - \ln y_i!].$$

---

[1]Some particularly rich surveys of these topics (among dozens available) are Cameron and Trivedi (1986, 1998, 2005), Winkelmann (2003), and Kalbfleisch and Prentice (2002).

[2]We have estimated a Poisson regression model using two-step nonlinear least squares in Example 16.6.

The likelihood equations are

$$\frac{\partial \ln L}{\partial \boldsymbol{\beta}} = \sum_{i=1}^{n} (y_i - \lambda_i)\mathbf{x}_i = \mathbf{0}.$$

The Hessian is

$$\frac{\partial^2 \ln L}{\partial \boldsymbol{\beta} \partial \boldsymbol{\beta}'} = -\sum_{i=1}^{n} \lambda_i \mathbf{x}_i \mathbf{x}_i'.$$

The Hessian is negative definite for all $\mathbf{x}$ and $\boldsymbol{\beta}$. Newton's method is a simple algorithm for this model and will usually converge rapidly. At convergence, $[\sum_{i=1}^{n} \hat{\lambda}_i \mathbf{x}_i \mathbf{x}_i']^{-1}$ provides an estimator of the asymptotic covariance matrix for the parameter estimates. Given the estimates, the prediction for observation $i$ is $\hat{\lambda}_i = \exp(\mathbf{x}'\hat{\boldsymbol{\beta}})$. A standard error for the prediction interval can be formed by using a linear Taylor series approximation. The estimated variance of the prediction will be $\hat{\lambda}_i^2 \mathbf{x}_i' \mathbf{V} \mathbf{x}_i$, where $\mathbf{V}$ is the estimated asymptotic covariance matrix for $\hat{\boldsymbol{\beta}}$.

For testing hypotheses, the three standard tests are very convenient in this model. The Wald statistic is computed as usual. As in any discrete choice model, the likelihood ratio test has the intuitive form

$$\text{LR} = 2\sum_{i=1}^{n} \ln\left(\frac{\hat{P}_i}{\hat{P}_{\text{restricted},i}}\right),$$

where the probabilities in the denominator are computed with using the restricted model. Using the BHHH estimator for the asymptotic covariance matrix, the LM statistic is simply

$$\text{LM} = \left[\sum_{i=1}^{n} \mathbf{x}_i'(y_i - \hat{\lambda}_i)\right]'\left[\sum_{i=1}^{n} \mathbf{x}_i \mathbf{x}_i'(y_i - \hat{\lambda}_i)^2\right]^{-1}\left[\sum_{i=1}^{n} \mathbf{x}_i(y_i - \hat{\lambda}_i)\right] = \mathbf{i}'\mathbf{G}(\mathbf{G}'\mathbf{G})^{-1}\mathbf{G}'\mathbf{i},$$

$$(25\text{-}2)$$

where each row of $\mathbf{G}$ is simply the corresponding row of $\mathbf{X}$ multiplied by $e_i = (y_i - \hat{\lambda}_i)$, $\hat{\lambda}_i$ is computed using the restricted coefficient vector, and $\mathbf{i}$ is a column of ones.

### 25.2.1  MEASURING GOODNESS OF FIT

The Poisson model produces no natural counterpart to the $R^2$ in a linear regression model, as usual, because the conditional mean function is nonlinear and, moreover, because the regression is heteroscedastic. But many alternatives have been suggested.[3] A measure based on the standardized residuals is

$$R_p^2 = 1 - \frac{\sum_{i=1}^{n}\left[\frac{y_i - \hat{\lambda}_i}{\sqrt{\hat{\lambda}_i}}\right]^2}{\sum_{i=1}^{n}\left[\frac{y_i - \bar{y}}{\sqrt{\bar{y}}}\right]^2}.$$

---

[3]See the surveys by Cameron and Windmeijer (1993), Gurmu and Trivedi (1994), and Greene (1995b).

This measure has the virtue that it compares the fit of the model with that provided by a model with only a constant term. But it can be negative, and it can rise when a variable is dropped from the model. For an individual observation, the **deviance** is

$$d_i = 2[y_i \ln(y_i/\hat{\lambda}_i) - (y_i - \hat{\lambda}_i)] = 2[y_i \ln(y_i/\hat{\lambda}_i) - e_i],$$

where, by convention, $0\ln(0) = 0$. If the model contains a constant term, then $\sum_{i=1}^n e_i = 0$. The sum of the deviances,

$$G^2 = \sum_{i=1}^n d_i = 2 \sum_{i=1}^n y_i \ln(y_i/\hat{\lambda}_i),$$

is reported as an alternative fit measure by some computer programs. This statistic will equal 0.0 for a model that produces a perfect fit. (Note that because $y_i$ is an integer while the prediction is continuous, it could not happen.) Cameron and Windmeijer (1993) suggest that the fit measure based on the deviances,

$$R_d^2 = 1 - \frac{\sum_{i=1}^n \left[ y_i \log\left(\dfrac{y_i}{\hat{\lambda}_i}\right) - (y_i - \hat{\lambda}_i) \right]}{\sum_{i=1}^n \left[ y_i \log\left(\dfrac{y_i}{\bar{y}}\right) \right]},$$

has a number of desirable properties. First, denote the log-likelihood function for the model in which $\psi_i$ is used as the prediction (e.g., the mean) of $y_i$ as $\ell(\psi_i, y_i)$. The Poisson model fit by MLE is, then, $\ell(\hat{\lambda}_i, y_i)$, the model with only a constant term is $\ell(\bar{y}, y_i)$, and a model that achieves a perfect fit (by predicting $y_i$ with itself) is $l(y_i, y_i)$. Then

$$R_d^2 = \frac{\ell(\hat{\lambda}, y_i) - \ell(\bar{y}, y_i)}{\ell(y_i, y_i) - \ell(\bar{y}, y_i)}.$$

Both numerator and denominator measure the improvement of the model over one with only a constant term. The denominator measures the maximum improvement, since one cannot improve on a perfect fit. Hence, the measure is bounded by zero and one and increases as regressors are added to the model.[4] We note, finally, the passing resemblance of $R_d^2$ to the "pseudo-$R^2$," or "likelihood ratio index" reported by some statistical packages (e.g., Stata),

$$R_{\text{LRI}}^2 = 1 - \frac{\ell(\hat{\lambda}_i, y_i)}{\ell(\bar{y}, y_i)}.$$

Many modifications of the Poisson model have been analyzed by economists. In this and the next few sections, we briefly examine a few of them.

### 25.2.2   TESTING FOR OVERDISPERSION

The Poisson model has been criticized because of its implicit assumption that the variance of $y_i$ equals its mean. Many extensions of the Poisson model that relax this assumption have been proposed by Hausman, Hall, and Griliches (1984), McCullagh and Nelder (1983), and Cameron and Trivedi (1986), to name but a few.

---

[4]Note that multiplying both numerator and denominator by 2 produces the ratio of two likelihood ratio statistics, each of which is distributed as chi-squared.

The first step in this extended analysis is usually a test for overdispersion in the context of the simple model. A number of authors have devised tests for "overdispersion" within the context of the Poisson model. [See Cameron and Trivedi (1990), Gurmu (1991), and Lee (1986).] We will consider three of the common tests, one based on a regression approach, one a conditional moment test, and a third, a **Lagrange multiplier test,** based on an alternative model.

Cameron and Trivedi (1990) offer several different tests for overdispersion. A simple regression-based procedure used for testing the hypothesis

$$H_0: \text{Var}[y_i] = E[y_i],$$

$$H_1: \text{Var}[y_i] = E[y_i] + \alpha g(E[y_i]),$$

is carried out by regressing

$$z_i = \frac{(y_i - \hat{\lambda}_i)^2 - y_i}{\hat{\lambda}_i \sqrt{2}},$$

where $\hat{\lambda}_i$ is the predicted value from the regression, on either a constant term or $\hat{\lambda}_i$ without a constant term. A simple $t$ test of whether the coefficient is significantly different from zero tests $H_0$ versus $H_1$.

Cameron and Trivedi's regression based test for overdispersion is formulated around the alternative $\text{Var}[y_i] = E[y_i] + g(E[y_i])$. This is a very specific type of overdispersion. Consider the more general hypothesis that $\text{Var}[y_i]$ is completely given by $E[y_i]$. The alternative is that the variance is systematically related to the regressors in a way that is not completely accounted for by $E[y_i]$. Formally, we have $E[y_i] = \exp(\boldsymbol{\beta}'\mathbf{x}_i) = \lambda_i$. The null hypothesis is that $\text{Var}[y_i] = \lambda_i$ as well. We can test the hypothesis using a **conditional moment test.** The expected first derivatives and the moment restriction are

$$E[\mathbf{x}_i(y_i - \lambda_i)] = \mathbf{0} \quad \text{and} \quad E\{\mathbf{z}_i[(y_i - \lambda_i)^2 - \lambda_i]\} = \mathbf{0}.$$

To carry out the test, we do the following. Let $e_i = y_i - \hat{\lambda}_i$ and $\mathbf{z}_i = \mathbf{x}_i$ without the constant term.

1. Compute the Poisson regression by maximum likelihood.
2. Compute $\mathbf{r} = \sum_{i=1}^n \mathbf{z}_i[e_i^2 - \hat{\lambda}_i] = \sum_{i=1}^n \mathbf{z}_i v_i$ based on the maximum likelihood estimates.
3. Compute $\mathbf{M}'\mathbf{M} = \sum_{i=1}^n \mathbf{z}_i \mathbf{z}_i' v_i^2$, $\mathbf{D}'\mathbf{D} = \sum_{i=1}^n \mathbf{x}_i \mathbf{x}_i' e_i^2$, and $\mathbf{M}'\mathbf{D} = \sum_{i=1}^n \mathbf{z}_i \mathbf{x}_i' v_i e_i$.
4. Compute $\mathbf{S} = \mathbf{M}'\mathbf{M} - \mathbf{M}'\mathbf{D}(\mathbf{D}'\mathbf{D})^{-1}\mathbf{D}'\mathbf{M}$.
5. $C = \mathbf{r}'\mathbf{S}^{-1}\mathbf{r}$ is the chi-squared statistic. It has degrees of freedom equal to the number of variables in $\mathbf{z}_i$.

The next section presents the **negative binomial model.** This model relaxes the Poisson assumption that the mean equals the variance. The Poisson model is obtained as a parametric restriction on the negative binomial model, so a Lagrange multiplier test can be computed. In general, if an alternative distribution for which the Poisson model is obtained as a parametric restriction, such as the negative binomial model, can be specified, then a Lagrange multiplier statistic can be computed. [See Cameron and

Trivedi (1986, p. 41).] The LM statistic is

$$LM = \left[ \frac{\sum_{i=1}^n \hat{w}_i[(y_i - \hat{\lambda}_i)^2 - y_i]}{\sqrt{2 \sum_{i=1}^n \hat{w}_i \hat{\lambda}_i^2}} \right]^2. \tag{25-3}$$

The weight, $\hat{w}_i$, depends on the assumed alternative distribution. For the negative binomial model discussed later, $\hat{w}_i$ equals 1.0. Thus, under this alternative, the statistic is particularly simple to compute:

$$LM = \frac{(\mathbf{e}'\mathbf{e} - n\bar{y})^2}{2\hat{\lambda}'\hat{\lambda}}. \tag{25-4}$$

The main advantage of this test statistic is that one need only estimate the Poisson model to compute it. Under the hypothesis of the Poisson model, the limiting distribution of the LM statistic is chi-squared with one degree of freedom.

### 25.2.3   HETEROGENEITY AND THE NEGATIVE BINOMIAL REGRESSION MODEL

The assumed equality of the conditional mean and variance functions is typically taken to be the major shortcoming of the Poisson regression model. Many alternatives have been suggested [see Hausman, Hall, and Griliches (1984), Cameron and Trivedi (1986, 1998), Gurmu and Trivedi (1994), Johnson and Kotz (1993), and Winkelmann (2003) for discussion]. The most common is the negative binomial model, which arises from a natural formulation of cross-section heterogeneity. [See Hilbe (2007).] We generalize the Poisson model by introducing an individual, unobserved effect into the conditional mean,

$$\ln \mu_i = \mathbf{x}_i'\boldsymbol{\beta} + \varepsilon_i = \ln \lambda_i + \ln u_i,$$

where the disturbance $\varepsilon_i$ reflects either **specification error,** as in the classical regression model, or the kind of cross-sectional heterogeneity that normally characterizes micro-economic data. Then, the distribution of $y_i$ conditioned on $\mathbf{x}_i$ *and* $u_i$ (i.e., $\varepsilon_i$) remains Poisson with conditional mean and variance $\mu_i$:

$$f(y_i \mid \mathbf{x}_i, u_i) = \frac{e^{-\lambda_i u_i}(\lambda_i u_i)^{y_i}}{y_i!}.$$

The unconditional distribution $f(y_i \mid \mathbf{x}_i)$ is the expected value (over $u_i$) of $f(y_i \mid \mathbf{x}_i, u_i)$,

$$f(y_i \mid \mathbf{x}_i) = \int_0^\infty \frac{e^{-\lambda_i u_i}(\lambda_i u_i)^{y_i}}{y_i!} g(u_i)\, du_i.$$

The choice of a density for $u_i$ defines the unconditional distribution. For mathematical convenience, a gamma distribution is usually assumed for $u_i = \exp(\varepsilon_i)$.[5] As in other models of heterogeneity, the mean of the distribution is unidentified if the model contains a constant term (because the disturbance enters multiplicatively) so $E[\exp(\varepsilon_i)]$ is

---

[5] An alternative approach based on the normal distribution is suggested in Terza (1998), Greene (1995a, 1997a, 2007d), and Winkelmann (1997). The normal-Poisson mixture is also easily extended to the random effects model discussed in the next section. There is no closed form for the normal-Poisson mixture model, but it can be easily approximated by using Hermite quadrature or simulation. See Sections 16.9.6.b and 23.5.1.

assumed to be 1.0. With this normalization,

$$g(u_i) = \frac{\theta^\theta}{\Gamma(\theta)} e^{-\theta u_i} u_i^{\theta-1}.$$

The density for $y_i$ is then

$$f(y_i \mid \mathbf{x}_i) = \int_0^\infty \frac{e^{-\lambda_i u_i} (\lambda_i u_i)^{y_i}}{y_i!} \frac{\theta^\theta u_i^{\theta-1} e^{-\theta u_i}}{\Gamma(\theta)} du_i$$

$$= \frac{\theta^\theta \lambda_i^{y_i}}{\Gamma(y_i+1)\Gamma(\theta)} \int_0^\infty e^{-(\lambda_i+\theta)u_i} u_i^{\theta+y_i-1} du_i$$

$$= \frac{\theta^\theta \lambda_i^{y_i} \Gamma(\theta+y_i)}{\Gamma(y_i+1)\Gamma(\theta)(\lambda_i+\theta)^{\theta+y_i}}$$

$$= \frac{\Gamma(\theta+y_i)}{\Gamma(y_i+1)\Gamma(\theta)} r_i^{y_i} (1-r_i)^\theta, \quad \text{where } r_i = \frac{\lambda_i}{\lambda_i+\theta},$$

which is one form of the negative binomial distribution. The distribution has conditional mean $\lambda_i$ and conditional variance $\lambda_i(1 + (1/\theta)\lambda_i)$. [This model is Negbin 2 in Cameron and Trivedi's (1986) presentation.] The negative binomial model can be estimated by maximum likelihood without much difficulty. A test of the Poisson distribution is often carried out by testing the hypothesis $\alpha = 1/\theta = 0$ using the Wald or likelihood ratio test.

### 25.2.4 FUNCTIONAL FORMS FOR COUNT DATA MODELS

The equidispersion assumption of the Poisson regression model, $E[y_i \mid \mathbf{x}_i] = \text{Var}[y_i \mid \mathbf{x}_i]$, is a major shortcoming. Observed data rarely, if ever, display this feature. The very large amount of research activity on functional forms for count models is often focused on testing for equidispersion and building functional forms that relax this assumption. In practice, the Poisson model is typically only the departure point for an extended specification search.

One easily remedied minor issue concerns the units of measurement of the data. In the Poisson and negative binomial models, the parameter $\lambda_i$ is the expected number of events *per unit of time*. Thus, there is a presumption in the model formulation, for example, the Poisson, that the same amount of time is observed for each $i$. In a spatial context, such as measurements of the incidence of a disease per group of $N_i$ persons, or the number of bomb craters per square mile (London, 1940), the assumption would be that the same physical area or the same size of population applies to each observation. Where this differs by individual, it will introduce a type of heteroscedasticity in the model. The simple remedy is to modify the model to account for the **exposure, $T_i$,** of the observation as follows:

$$\text{Prob}(y_i = j \mid \mathbf{x}_i, T_i) = \frac{\exp(-T_i\phi_i)(T_i\phi_i)^j}{j!}, \quad \phi_i = \exp(\mathbf{x}_i'\boldsymbol{\beta}), \ j = 0, 1, \ldots.$$

The original model is returned if we write $\lambda_i = \exp(\mathbf{x}_i'\boldsymbol{\beta} + \ln T_i)$. Thus, when the exposure differs by observation, the appropriate accommodation is to include the log of exposure in the regression part of the model with a coefficient of 1.0. (For less than obvious reasons, the term "offset variable" is commonly associated with the exposure variable $T_i$.) Note that if $T_i$ is the same for all $i$, $\ln T_i$ will simply vanish into the constant term of the model (assuming one is included in $\mathbf{x}_i$).

The recent literature, mostly associating the result with Cameron and Trivedi's (1986, 1998) work, defines two familiar forms of the negative binomial model. The **Negbin 2** (NB2) **form** of the probability is

$$\text{Prob}(Y = y_i \mid \mathbf{x}_i) = \frac{\Gamma(\theta + y_i)}{\Gamma(y_i + 1)\Gamma(\theta)} r_i^{y_i} (1 - r_i)^{\theta},$$

$$\lambda_i = \exp(\mathbf{x}_i'\boldsymbol{\beta}), \tag{25-5}$$

$$r_i = \lambda_i / (\theta + \lambda_i).$$

This is the default form of the model in the received econometrics packages that provide an estimator for this model. The **Negbin 1** (NB1) **form** of the model results if $\theta$ in the preceding is replaced with $\theta_i = \theta\lambda_i$. Then, $r_i$ reduces to $r = 1/(1 + \theta)$, and the density becomes

$$\text{Prob}(Y = y_i \mid \mathbf{x}_i) = \frac{\Gamma(\theta\lambda_i + y_i)}{\Gamma(y_i + 1)\Gamma(\theta\lambda_i)} r^{y_i} (1 - r)^{\theta\lambda_i}. \tag{25-6}$$

This is not a simple reparameterization of the model. The results in Example 25.1 demonstrate that the log-likelihood functions are not equal at the maxima, and the parameters are not simple transformations in one model versus the other. We are not aware of a theory that justifies using one form or the other for the negative binomial model. Neither is a restricted version of the other, so we cannot carry out a likelihood ratio test of one versus the other. The more general **Negbin P** (NBP) family does nest both of them, so this may provide a more general, encompassing approach to finding the right specification. The Negbin $P$ model is obtained by replacing $\theta$ in the Negbin 2 form with $\theta\lambda_i^{2-P}$. We have examined the cases of $P = 1$ and $P = 2$ in (25-5) and (25-6). The full model is

$$\text{Prob}(Y = y_i \mid \mathbf{x}_i) = \frac{\Gamma(\theta\lambda_i^Q + y_i)}{\Gamma(y_i + 1)\Gamma(\theta\lambda_i^Q)} \left(\frac{\lambda_i}{\theta\lambda_i^Q + \lambda_i}\right)^{y_i} \left(\frac{\theta\lambda_i^Q}{\theta\lambda_i^Q + \lambda_i}\right)^{\theta\lambda_i^Q}, \quad Q = 2 - P.$$

The conditional mean function for the three cases considered is

$$E[y_i \mid \mathbf{x}_i] = \exp(\mathbf{x}_i'\boldsymbol{\beta}) = \lambda_i.$$

The parameter $P$ is picking up the scaling. A general result is that for all three variants of the model,

$$\text{Var}[y_i \mid \mathbf{x}_i] = \lambda_i\left(1 + \alpha\lambda_i^{P-1}\right), \quad \text{where } \alpha = 1/\theta.$$

Thus, the NB2 form has a variance function that is quadratic in the mean while the NB1 form's variance is a simple multiple of the mean. There have been many other functional forms proposed for count data models, including the generalized Poisson, gamma, and Polya-Aeppli forms described in Winkelmann (2003) and Greene (2007a, Chapter 24).

The heteroscedasticity in the count models is induced by the relationship between the variance and the mean. The single parameter $\theta$ picks up an implicit overall scaling, so it does not contribute to this aspect of the model. As in the linear model, microeconomic data are likely to induce heterogeneity in both the mean and variance of the response variable. A specification that allows independent variation of both will be of some virtue. The result

$$\text{Var}[y_i \mid \mathbf{x}_i] = \lambda_i \left(1 + (1/\theta)\lambda_i^{P-1}\right)$$

suggests that a natural platform for separately modeling heteroscedasticity will be the dispersion parameter, $\theta$, which we now parameterize as

$$\theta_i = \theta \exp(\mathbf{z}_i'\boldsymbol{\delta}).$$

Operationally, this is a relatively minor extension of the model. But, it is likely to introduce quite a substantial increase in the flexibility of the specification. Indeed, a heterogeneous Negbin P model is likely to be sufficiently parameterized to accommodate the behavior of most data sets. (Of course, the specialized models discussed in Section 25.4, for example, the zero inflation models, may yet be more appropriate for a given situation.)

### Example 25.1 Count Data Models for Doctor Visits

The study by Riphahn et al. (2003) that provided the data we have used in numerous earlier examples analyzed the two-count variables DocVis (visits to the doctor) and HospVis (visits to the hospital). The authors were interested in the joint determination of these two count variables. One of the issues considered in the study was whether the data contained evidence of moral hazard, that is, whether health care utilization as measured by these two outcomes was influenced by the subscription to health insurance. The data contain indicators of two levels of insurance coverage, PUBLIC, which is the main source of insurance, and ADDON, which is a secondary optional insurance. In the sample of 27,326 observations (family/years), 24,203 individuals held the public insurance. (There is quite a lot of within group variation in this. Individuals did not routinely obtain the insurance for all periods.) Of these 24,203, 23,689 had only public insurance and 514 had both types. (One could not have only the ADDON insurance.) To explore the issue, we have analyzed the DocVis variable with the count data models described in this section. The exogenous variables in our model are

$$\mathbf{x}_{it} = (1, Age, Education, Income, Kids, Public).$$

(Variables are described in Example 11.11.)

Table 25.1 presents the estimates of the several count models. In all specifications, the coefficient on PUBLIC is positive, large, and highly statistically significant, which is consistent with the results in the authors' study. The various test statistics strongly reject the hypothesis of equidispersion. Cameron and Trivedi's (1990) semiparametric tests from the Poisson model (see Section 25.2.2 have $t$ statistics of 22.147 for $g_i = \mu_i$ and 22.504 for $g_i = \mu_i^2$. Both of these are far larger than the critical value of 1.96. The LM statistic is 972,714.48, which is also larger than the (any) critical value. On these bases, we would reject the hypothesis of equidispersion. The Wald and likelihood ratio tests based on the negative binomial models produce the same conclusion. For comparing the different negative binomial models, note that Negbin 2 is the worst of the three by the likelihood function, although NB1 and NB2 are not directly comparable. On the other hand, note that in the NBP model, the estimate of $P$ is more than 10 standard errors from 1.0000 or 2.000, so both NB1 and NB2 are rejected in favor of the unrestricted NBP form of the model. The NBP and the heterogeneous NB2 model are not nested either, but comparing the log-likelihoods, it does appear that the heterogeneous model is substantially superior. We computed the Vuong statistic based on the individual contributions to the log-likelihoods, with $v_i = \ln L_i(\text{NBP}) = \ln L_i(\text{NB2-H})$. (See Section 7.3.4). The value of the statistic is $-3.27$. On this basis, we would reject NBP in favor of NB2-H. Finally, with regard to the original question, the coefficient on PUBLIC is larger than 10 times the estimated standard error in every specification. We would conclude that the results are consistent with the proposition that there is evidence of moral hazard.

**TABLE 25.1** Estimated Models for DOCVIS (standard errors in parentheses)

| Variable | Poisson | Negbin 2 | Negbin 2 Heterogeneous | Negbin 1 | Negbin P |
|---|---|---|---|---|---|
| Constant | 0.7162 | 0.7628 | 0.7928 | 0.6848 | 0.6517 |
| | (0.03287) | (0.07247) | (0.07459) | (0.06807) | (0.07759) |
| Age | 0.01844 | 0.01803 | 0.01704 | 0.01585 | 0.01907 |
| | (0.0003316) | (0.0007915) | (0.0008146) | (0.0007042) | (0.0008078) |
| Education | −0.03429 | −0.03839 | −0.03581 | −0.02381 | −0.03388 |
| | (0.001797) | (0.003965) | (0.004036) | (0.003702) | (0.004308) |
| Income | −0.4751 | −0.4206 | −0.4108 | −0.1892 | −0.3337 |
| | (0.02198) | (0.04700) | (0.04752) | (0.04452) | (0.05161) |
| Kids | −0.1582 | −0.1513 | −0.1568 | −0.1342 | −0.1622 |
| | (0.007956) | (0.01738) | (0.01773) | (0.01647) | (0.01856) |
| Public | 0.2364 | 0.2324 | 0.2411 | 0.1616 | 0.2195 |
| | (0.01328) | (0.02900) | (0.03006) | (0.02678) | (0.03155) |
| $P$ | 0.0000 | 2.0000 | 2.0000 | 1.0000 | 1.5473 |
| | (0.0000) | (0.0000) | (0.0000) | (0.0000) | (0.03444) |
| $\theta$ | 0.0000 | 1.9242 | 2.6060 | 6.1865 | 3.2470 |
| | (0.0000) | (0.02008) | (0.05954) | (0.06861) | (0.1346) |
| $\delta$ (Female) | 0.0000 | 0.0000 | −0.3838 | 0.0000 | 0.0000 |
| | (0.0000) | (0.0000) | (0.02046) | (0.0000) | (0.0000) |
| $\delta$ (Married) | 0.0000 | 0.0000 | −0.1359 | 0.0000 | 0.0000 |
| | (0.0000) | (0.0000) | (0.02307) | (0.0000) | (0.0000) |
| $\ln L$ | −104440.3 | −60265.49 | −60121.77 | −60260.68 | −60197.15 |

## 25.3 PANEL DATA MODELS

The familiar approaches to accommodating heterogeneity in panel data have fairly straightforward extensions in the count data setting. [Hausman, Hall, and Griliches (1984) give full details for these models.] We will examine them for the Poisson model. The authors [and Allison (2000)] also give results for the negative binomial model.

### 25.3.1 ROBUST COVARIANCE MATRICES

The standard asymptotic covariance matrix estimator for the Poisson model is

$$\text{Est. Asy. Var}[\hat{\boldsymbol{\beta}}] = \left[ -\frac{\partial^2 \ln L}{\partial \hat{\boldsymbol{\beta}} \partial \hat{\boldsymbol{\beta}}'} \right]^{-1} = \left[ \sum_{i=1}^{n} \hat{\lambda}_i \mathbf{x}_i \mathbf{x}_i' \right]^{-1} = [\mathbf{X}' \hat{\boldsymbol{\Lambda}} \mathbf{X}]^{-1},$$

where $\hat{\boldsymbol{\Lambda}}$ is a diagonal matrix of predicted values. The BHHH estimator is

$$\text{Est. Asy. Var}[\hat{\boldsymbol{\beta}}] = \left[ \sum_{i=1}^{n} \left( \frac{\partial \ln P_i}{\partial \hat{\boldsymbol{\beta}}} \right) \left( \frac{\partial \ln P_i}{\partial \hat{\boldsymbol{\beta}}} \right)' \right]^{-1}$$

$$= \left[ \sum_{i=1}^{n} \left( y_i - \hat{\lambda}_i' \right)^2 \mathbf{x}_i \mathbf{x}_i' \right]^{-1} = [\mathbf{X}' \hat{\mathbf{E}}^2 \mathbf{X}]^{-1},$$

where $\hat{\mathbf{E}}$ is a diagonal matrix of residuals. The Poisson model is one in which the MLE is robust to certain misspecifications of the model, such as the failure to incorporate latent heterogeneity in the mean (i.e., one fits the Poisson model when the negative binomial is appropriate). In this case, a robust covariance matrix is the "sandwich" estimator,

$$\text{Robust Est. Asy. Var}[\hat{\boldsymbol{\beta}}] = [\mathbf{X}'\hat{\boldsymbol{\Lambda}}\mathbf{X}]^{-1}[\mathbf{X}'\hat{\mathbf{E}}^2\mathbf{X}][\mathbf{X}'\hat{\boldsymbol{\Lambda}}\mathbf{X}]^{-1},$$

which is appropriate to accommodate this failure of the model. It has become common to employ this estimator with all specifications, including the negative binomial. One might question the virtue of this. Because the negative binomial model already accounts for the latent heterogeneity, it is unclear what *additional* failure of the assumptions of the model this estimator would be robust to. The questions raised in Section 16.8.3 and 16.8.4 about robust covariance matrices would be relevant here.

A related calculation is used when observations occur in groups that may be correlated. This would include a random effects setting in a panel in which observations have a common latent heterogeneity as well as more general, stratified, and clustered data sets. The parameter estimator is unchanged in this case (and an assumption is made that the estimator is still consistent), but an adjustment is made to the estimated asymptotic covariance matrix. The calculation is done as follows: Suppose the $n$ observations are assembled in $G$ clusters of observations, in which the number of observations in the $i$th cluster is $n_i$. Thus, $\sum_{i=1}^{G} n_i = n$. Denote by $\boldsymbol{\beta}$ the full set of model parameters in whatever variant of the model is being estimated. Let the observation-specific gradients and Hessians be $\mathbf{g}_{ij} = \partial \ln L_{ij}/\partial \boldsymbol{\beta} = (y_{ij} - \lambda_{ij})\mathbf{x}_{ij}$ and $\mathbf{H}_{ij} = \partial^2 \ln L_{ij}/\partial \boldsymbol{\beta}\partial \boldsymbol{\beta}' = -\lambda_{ij}\mathbf{x}_{ij}\mathbf{x}_{ij}'$. The uncorrected estimator of the asymptotic covariance matrix based on the Hessian is

$$\mathbf{V}_H = -\mathbf{H}^{-1} = \left(-\sum_{i=1}^{G}\sum_{j=1}^{n_i}\mathbf{H}_{ij}\right)^{-1}.$$

The corrected asymptotic covariance matrix is

$$\text{Est. Asy. Var}[\hat{\boldsymbol{\beta}}] = \mathbf{V}_H\left(\frac{G}{G-1}\right)\left[\sum_{i=1}^{G}\left(\sum_{j=1}^{n_i}\mathbf{g}_{ij}\right)\left(\sum_{j=1}^{n_i}\mathbf{g}_{ij}\right)'\right]\mathbf{V}_H.$$

Note that if there is exactly one observation per cluster, then this is $G/(G-1)$ times the sandwich (robust) estimator.

### 25.3.2 FIXED EFFECTS

Consider first a fixed effects approach. The Poisson distribution is assumed to have conditional mean

$$\log \lambda_{it} = \boldsymbol{\beta}'\mathbf{x}_{it} + \alpha_i, \tag{25-7}$$

where now, $\mathbf{x}_{it}$ has been redefined to exclude the constant term. The approach used in the linear model of transforming $y_{it}$ to group mean deviations does not remove the heterogeneity, nor does it leave a Poisson distribution for the transformed variable. However, the Poisson model with fixed effects can be fit using the methods described for the probit model in Section 23.5.2. The extension to the Poisson model requires only the minor modifications, $g_{it} = (y_{it} - \lambda_{it})$ and $h_{it} = -\lambda_{it}$. Everything else in that derivation applies with only a simple change in the notation. The first-order conditions for maximizing the log-likelihood function for the Poisson model will include

$$\frac{\partial \ln L}{\partial \alpha_i} = \sum_{t=1}^{T_i} (y_{it} - e^{\alpha_i} \mu_{it}) = 0 \quad \text{where } \mu_{it} = e^{x'_{it}\beta}.$$

This implies an explicit solution for $\alpha_i$ in terms of $\beta$ in this model,

$$\hat{\alpha}_i = \ln\left(\frac{(1/T_i)\sum_{t=1}^{T_i} y_{it}}{(1/T_i)\sum_{t=1}^{T_i} \hat{\mu}_{it}}\right) = \ln\left(\frac{\bar{y}_i}{\bar{\hat{\mu}}_i}\right). \tag{25-8}$$

Unlike the regression or the probit model, this does not require that there be within-group variation in $y_{it}$—all the values can be the same. It does require that at least one observation for individual $i$ be nonzero, however. The rest of the solution for the fixed effects estimator follows the same lines as that for the probit model. An alternative approach, albeit with little practical gain, would be to concentrate the log-likelihood function by inserting this solution for $\alpha_i$ back into the original log-likelihood, then maximizing the resulting function of $\beta$. While logically this makes sense, the approach suggested earlier for the probit model is simpler to implement.

An estimator that is not a function of the fixed effects is found by obtaining the joint distribution of $(y_{i1}, \ldots, y_{iT_i})$ conditional on their sum. For the Poisson model, a close cousin to the multinomial logit model discussed earlier is produced:

$$p\left(y_{i1}, y_{i2}, \ldots, y_{iT_i} \,\middle|\, \sum_{i=1}^{T_i} y_{it}\right) = \frac{\left(\sum_{t=1}^{T_i} y_{it}\right)!}{\left(\prod_{t=1}^{T_i} y_{it}!\right)} \prod_{t=1}^{T_i} p_{it}^{y_{it}}, \tag{25-9}$$

where

$$p_{it} = \frac{e^{x'_{it}\beta+\alpha_i}}{\sum_{t=1}^{T_i} e^{x'_{it}\beta+\alpha_i}} = \frac{e^{x'_{it}\beta}}{\sum_{t=1}^{T_i} e^{x'_{it}\beta}}. \tag{25-10}$$

The contribution of group $i$ to the conditional log-likelihood is

$$\ln L_i = \sum_{t=1}^{T_i} y_{it} \ln p_{it}.$$

Note, once again, that the contribution to $\ln L$ of a group in which $y_{it} = 0$ in every period is zero. Cameron and Trivedi (1998) have shown that these two approaches give identical results.

Hausman, Hall, and Griliches (1984) (HHG) report the following conditional density for the fixed effects negative binomial (FENB) model:

$$p\left(y_{i1}, y_{i2}, \ldots, y_{iT_i} \,\middle|\, \sum_{t=1}^{T_i} y_{it}\right) = \frac{\Gamma\left(1 + \sum_{t=1}^{T_i} y_{it}\right) \Gamma\left(\sum_{t=1}^{T_i} \lambda_{it}\right)}{\Gamma\left(\sum_{t=1}^{T_i} y_{it} + \sum_{t=1}^{T_i} \lambda_{it}\right)} \prod_{t=1}^{T_i} \frac{\Gamma(y_{it} + \lambda_{it})}{\Gamma(1 + y_{it})\Gamma(\lambda_{it})},$$

which is free of the fixed effects. This is the default FENB formulation used in popular software packages such as SAS, Stata, and LIMDEP. Researchers accustomed to the admonishments that fixed effects models cannot contain overall constants or time-invariant covariates are sometimes surprised to find (perhaps accidentally) that this fixed effects model allows both. [This issue is explored at length in Allison (2000) and Allison and Waterman (2002).] The resolution of this apparent contradiction is that the

HHG FENB model is not obtained by shifting the conditional mean function by the fixed effect, $\ln \lambda_{it} = \mathbf{x}'_{it}\boldsymbol{\beta} + \alpha_i$, as it is in the Poisson model. Rather, the HHG model is obtained by building the fixed effect into the model as an individual specific $\theta_i$ in the Negbin 1 form in (25-6). The conditional mean functions in the models are as follows (we have changed the notation slightly to conform to our earlier formulation):

$$\text{NB1(HHG): } E[y_{it} \mid \mathbf{x}_{it}] = \theta_i \phi_{it} = \theta_i \exp(\mathbf{x}'_{it}\boldsymbol{\beta}),$$

$$\text{NB2: } \qquad E[y_{it} \mid \mathbf{x}_{it}] = \exp(\alpha_i)\phi_{it} = \lambda_{it} = \exp(\mathbf{x}'_{it}\boldsymbol{\beta} + \alpha_i).$$

The conditional variances are

$$\text{NB1(HHG): } \text{Var}[y_{it} \mid \mathbf{x}_{it}] = \theta_i \phi_{it}[1 + \theta_i],$$

$$\text{NB2: } \qquad \text{Var}[y_{it} \mid \mathbf{x}_{it}] = \lambda_{it}[1 + \theta \lambda_{it}].$$

Letting $\mu_i = \ln \theta_i$, it appears that the HHG formulation does provide a fixed effect in the mean, as now, $E[y_{it} \mid \mathbf{x}_{it}] = \exp(\mathbf{x}'_{it}\boldsymbol{\beta} + \mu_i)$. Indeed, by this construction, it appears (as the authors suggest) that there are separate effects in both the mean and the variance. They make this explicit by writing $\theta_i = \exp(\mu_i)\gamma_i$ so that in their model,

$$\text{E}[y_{it} \mid \mathbf{x}_{it}] = \gamma_i \exp(\mathbf{x}'_{it}\boldsymbol{\beta} + \mu_i),$$

$$\text{Var}[y_{it} \mid \mathbf{x}_{it}] = \gamma_i \exp(\mathbf{x}'_{it}\boldsymbol{\beta} + \mu_i)/[1 + \gamma_i \exp(\mu_i)].$$

The contradiction arises because the authors assert that $\mu_i$ and $\gamma_i$ are separate parameters. In fact, they cannot vary separately, only $\theta_i$ can vary autonomously. The firm-specific effect in the HHG model is still isolated in the scaling parameter, which falls out of the conditional density. The mean is homogeneous, which explains why a separate constant, or a time invariant regressor (or another set of firm-specific effects) can reside there. [See Greene (2007d) and Allison and Waterman (2002) for further discussion.]

### 25.3.3 RANDOM EFFECTS

The fixed effects approach has the same flaws and virtues in this setting as in the probit case. It is not necessary to assume that the heterogeneity is uncorrelated with the included, exogenous variables. If the uncorrelatedness of the regressors and the heterogeneity can be maintained, then the random effects model is an attractive alternative model. Once again, the approach used in the linear regression model, partial deviations from the group means followed by generalized least squares (see Chapter 9), is not usable here. The approach used is to formulate the joint probability conditioned upon the heterogeneity, then integrate it out of the joint distribution. Thus, we form

$$p(y_{i1}, \ldots, y_{iT_i} \mid u_i) = \prod_{t=1}^{T_i} p(y_{it} \mid u_i).$$

Then the random effect is swept out by obtaining

$$p(y_{i1}, \ldots, y_{iT_i}) = \int_{u_i} p(y_{i1}, \ldots, y_{iT_i}, u_i) \, du_i$$

$$= \int_{u_i} p(y_{i1}, \ldots, y_{iT_i} \mid u_i) g(u_i) \, du_i$$

$$= E_{u_i}[p(y_{i1}, \ldots, y_{iT_i} \mid u_i)].$$

This is exactly the approach used earlier to condition the heterogeneity out of the Poisson model to produce the negative binomial model. If, as before, we take $p(y_{it} \mid u_i)$ to be Poisson with mean $\lambda_{it} = \exp(\mathbf{x}'_{it}\boldsymbol{\beta} + u_i)$ in which $\exp(u_i)$ is distributed as gamma with mean 1.0 and variance $1/\alpha$, then the preceding steps produce a negative binomial distribution,

$$p(y_{i1}, \ldots, y_{iT_i}) = \frac{\left[\prod_{t=1}^{T_i} \lambda_{it}^{y_{it}}\right] \Gamma\left(\theta + \sum_{t=1}^{T_i} y_{it}\right)}{\left[\Gamma(\theta) \prod_{t=1}^{T_i} y_{it}!\right]\left[\left(\sum_{t=1}^{T_i} \lambda_{it}\right)^{\sum_{t=1}^{T_i} y_{it}}\right]} Q_i^\theta (1 - Q_i)^{\sum_{t=1}^{T_i} y_{it}}, \quad \textbf{(25-11)}$$

where

$$Q_i = \frac{\theta}{\theta + \sum_{t=1}^{T_i} \lambda_{it}}.$$

For estimation purposes, we have a negative binomial distribution for $Y_i = \Sigma_t y_{it}$ with mean $\Lambda_i = \Sigma_t \lambda_{it}$.

Like the fixed effects model, introducing random effects into the negative binomial model adds some additional complexity. We do note, because the negative binomial model derives from the Poisson model by adding latent heterogeneity to the conditional mean, adding a random effect to the negative binomial model might well amount to introducing the heterogeneity a second time. However, one might prefer to interpret the negative binomial as the density for $y_{it}$ in its own right, and treat the common effects in the familiar fashion. Hausman et al.'s (1984) random effects negative binomial (RENB) model is a hierarchical model that is constructed as follows. The heterogeneity is assumed to enter $\lambda_{it}$ additively with a gamma distribution with mean 1, $\Gamma(\theta_i, \theta_i)$. Then, $\theta_i/(1+\theta_i)$ is assumed to have a beta distribution with parameters $a$ and $b$ [see Appendix B.4.6)]. The resulting unconditional density after the heterogeneity is integrated out is

$$p(y_{i1}, y_{i2}, \ldots, y_{iT_i}) = \frac{\Gamma(a+b)\Gamma\left(a + \sum_{t=1}^{T_i} \lambda_{it}\right)\Gamma\left(b + \sum_{t=1}^{T_i} y_{it}\right)}{\Gamma(a)\Gamma(b)\Gamma\left(a + \sum_{t=1}^{T_i} \lambda_{it} + b + \sum_{t=1}^{T_i} y_{it}\right)}.$$

As before, the relationship between the heterogeneity and the conditional mean function is unclear, because the random effect impacts the parameter of the scedastic function. An alternative approach that maintains the essential flavor of the Poisson model (and other random effects models) is to augment the NB2 form with the random effect,

$$\text{Prob}(Y = y_{it} \mid \mathbf{x}_{it}, \varepsilon_i) = \frac{\Gamma(\theta + y_{it})}{\Gamma(y_{it} + 1)\Gamma(\theta)} r_{it}^{y_{it}} (1 - r_{it})^\theta,$$

$$\lambda_{it} = \exp(\mathbf{x}'_{it}\boldsymbol{\beta} + \varepsilon_i),$$

$$r_{it} = \lambda_{it}/(\theta + \lambda_{it}).$$

We then estimate the parameters by forming the conditional (on $\varepsilon_i$) log-likelihood and integrating $\varepsilon_i$ out either by quadrature or simulation. The parameters are simpler to interpret by this construction. Estimates of the two forms of the random effects model are presented in Example 25.2 for a comparison.

There is a mild preference in the received literature for the fixed effects estimators over the random effects estimators. The virtue of dispensing with the assumption of uncorrelatedness of the regressors and the group specific effects is substantial. On the other hand, the assumption does come at a cost. To compute the probabilities or the marginal effects, it is necessary to estimate the constants, $\alpha_i$. The unscaled coefficients in these models are of limited usefulness because of the nonlinearity of the conditional mean functions.

Other approaches to the random effects model have been proposed. Greene (1994, 1995a), Riphahn et al. (2003) and Terza (1995) specify a normally distributed heterogeneity, on the assumption that this is a more natural distribution for the aggregate of small independent effects. Brannas and Johanssen (1994) have suggested a semiparametric approach based on the GMM estimator by superimposing a very general form of heterogeneity on the Poisson model. They assume that conditioned on a random effect $\varepsilon_{it}$, $y_{it}$ is distributed as Poisson with mean $\varepsilon_{it}\lambda_{it}$. The covariance structure of $\varepsilon_{it}$ is allowed to be fully general. For $t, s = 1, \ldots, T$, $\text{Var}[\varepsilon_{it}] = \sigma_i^2$, $\text{Cov}[\varepsilon_{it}, \varepsilon_{js}] = \gamma_{ij}(|t - s|)$. For long time series, this model is likely to have far too many parameters to be identified without some restrictions, such as first-order homogeneity ($\beta_i = \beta \, \forall i$), uncorrelatedness across groups, [$\gamma_{ij}(.) = 0$ for $i \neq j$], groupwise homoscedasticity ($\sigma_i^2 = \sigma^2 \, \forall i$), and nonautocorrelatedness [$\gamma(r) = 0 \, \forall r \neq 0$]. With these assumptions, the estimation procedure they propose is similar to the procedures suggested earlier. If the model imposes enough restrictions, then the parameters can be estimated by the method of moments. The authors discuss estimation of the model in its full generality. Finally, the latent class model discussed in Section 16.9.7 and the random parameters model in Section 17.5 extend naturally to the Poisson model. Indeed, most of the received applications of the latent class structure have been in the Poisson regression framework. [See Greene (2001) for a survey.]

---

### Example 25.2  Panel Data Models for Doctor Visits

The German health care panel data set contains 7,293 individuals with group sizes ranging from 1 to 7. Table 25.2 presents the fixed and random effects estimates of the equation for DocVis. The pooled estimates are also shown for comparison. Overall, the panel data treatments bring large changes in the estimates compared to the pooled estimates. There is also a considerable amount of variation across the specifications. With respect to the parameter of interest, *Public*, we find that the size of the coefficient falls substantially with all panel data treatments. Whether using the pooled, fixed, or random effects specifications, the test statistics (Wald, LR) all reject the Poisson model in favor of the negative binomial. Similarly, either common effects specification is preferred to the pooled estimator. There is no simple basis for choosing between the fixed and random effects models, and we have further blurred the distinction by suggesting two formulations of each of them. We do note that the two random effects estimators are producing similar results, which one might hope for. But, the two fixed effects estimators are producing very different estimates. The NB1 estimates include two coefficients, *Income* and *Education,* that are positive, but negative in every other case. Moreover, the coefficient on *Public*, which is large and significant throughout the table, has become small and less significant with the fixed effects estimators.

We also fit a three-class latent class model for these data. (See Section 16.9.7.) The three class probabilities were modeled as functions of *Married* and *Female,* which appear from the results to be significant determinants of the class sorting. The average prior probabilities for the three classes are 0.09212, 0.49361, and 0.41427. The coefficients on *Public* in the three classes, with associated t ratios are 0.3388 (11.541), 0.1907 (3.987), and 0.1084 (4.282). The qualitative result concerning evidence of moral hazard suggested at the outset of Example 25.1 appears to be supported in a variety of specifications (with FE-NB1 the sole exception).

**TABLE 25.2** Estimated Panel Data Models for Doctor Visits (standard errors in parentheses)

| | Poisson | | | Negative Binomial | | | | |
| | | | | | Fixed Effects | | Random Effects | |
| Variable | Pooled (Robust S.E.) | Fixed Effects | Random Effects | Pooled NB2 | FE-NB1 | FE-NB2 | HHG-Gamma | Normal |
|---|---|---|---|---|---|---|---|---|
| Constant | 0.7162 (0.1319) | 0.0000 | 0.4957 (0.05463) | 0.7628 (0.07247) | -1.2354 (0.1079) | 0.0000 | -0.6343 (0.07328) | 0.1169 (0.06612) |
| Age | 0.01844 (0.001336) | 0.03115 (0.001443) | 0.02329 (0.0004458) | 0.01803 (0.0007916) | 0.02389 (0.001188) | 0.04479 (0.002769) | 0.01899 (0.0007820) | 0.02231 (0.0006969) |
| Educ | -0.03429 (0.007255) | -0.03803 (0.01733) | -0.03427 (0.004352) | -0.03839 (0.003965) | 0.01652 (0.006501) | -0.04589 (0.02967) | -0.01779 (0.004056) | -0.03773 (0.003595) |
| Income | -0.4751 (.08212) | -0.3030 (0.04104) | -0.2646 (0.01520) | -0.4206 (0.04700) | 0.02373 (0.05530) | -0.1968 (0.07320) | -0.08126 (0.04565) | -0.1743 (0.04273) |
| Kids | -0.1582 (0.03115) | -0.001927 (0.01546) | -0.03854 (0.005272) | -0.1513 (0.01738) | -0.03381 (0.02116) | -0.001274 (0.02920) | -0.1103 (0.01675) | -0.1187 (0.01582) |
| Public | 0.2365 (0.04307) | 0.1015 (0.02980) | 0.1535 (0.01268) | 0.2324 (0.02900) | 0.05837 (0.03896) | 0.09700 (0.05334) | 0.1486 (0.02834) | 0.1940 (0.02574) |
| $\theta$ | 0.0000 | 0.0000 | 1.1646 (0.01940) | 1.9242 (0.02008) | 0.0000 | 1.9199 (0.02994) | 0.0000 | 1.0808 (0.01203) |
| $a$ | 0.0000 | 0.0000 | 0.0000 | 0.0000 | 0.0000 | 0.0000 | 2.1463 (0.05955) | 0.0000 |
| $b$ | 0.0000 | 0.0000 | 0.0000 | 0.0000 | 0.0000 | 0.0000 | 3.8011 (0.1145) | 0.0000 |
| $\sigma$ | 0.0000 | 0.0000 | 0.0000 | 0.0000 | 0.0000 | 0.0000 | 0.0000 | 0.9737 (0.008235) |
| ln L | -104440.3 | -60337.13 | -71763.13 | -60265.49 | -34016.16 | -49476.36 | -58182.52 | -58177.66 |

## 25.4 HURDLE AND ZERO-ALTERED POISSON MODELS

In some settings, the zero outcome of the data-generating process is qualitatively different from the positive ones. Mullahy (1986) argues that this fact constitutes a shortcoming of the Poisson (or negative binomial) model and suggests a **hurdle model** as an alternative.[6] In his formulation, a binary probability model determines whether a zero or a nonzero outcome occurs, then, in the latter case, a (truncated) Poisson distribution describes the positive outcomes. The model is

$$\text{Prob}(y_i = 0 \mid \mathbf{x}_i) = e^{-\theta}$$
$$\text{Prob}(y_i = j \mid \mathbf{x}_i) = \frac{(1 - e^{-\theta}) e^{-\lambda_i} \lambda_i^j}{j!(1 - e^{-\lambda_i})}, \quad j = 1, 2, \dots. \tag{25-12}$$

This formulation changes the probability of the zero outcome and scales the remaining probabilities so that the sum to one. It adds a new restriction that $\text{Prob}(y_i = 0 \mid \mathbf{x}_i)$ no longer depends on the covariates, however. Therefore, a natural next step is to parameterize this probability. Mullahy suggests some formulations and applies the model to a sample of observations on daily beverage consumption.

Mullahy (1986), Heilbron (1989), Lambert (1992), Johnson and Kotz (1993), and Greene (1994) have analyzed an extension of the hurdle model in which the zero outcome can arise from one of two regimes.[7] In one regime, the outcome is always zero. In the other, the usual Poisson process is at work, which can produce the zero outcome or some other. In Lambert's application, she analyzes the number of defective items produced by a manufacturing process in a given time interval. If the process is under control, then the outcome is always zero (by definition). If it is not under control, then the number of defective items is distributed as Poisson and may be zero or positive in any period. The model at work is therefore

$$\text{Prob}(y_i = 0 \mid \mathbf{x}_i) = \text{Prob}(\text{regime 1}) + \text{Prob}(y_i = 0 \mid \mathbf{x}_i, \text{ regime 2})\text{Prob}(\text{regime 2}),$$
$$\text{Prob}(y_i = j \mid \mathbf{x}_i) = \text{Prob}(y_i = j \mid \mathbf{x}_i, \text{ regime 2})\text{Prob}(\text{regime 2}), \quad j = 1, 2, \dots.$$

Let $z$ denote a binary indicator of regime 1 ($z = 0$) or regime 2 ($z = 1$), and let $y^*$ denote the outcome of the Poisson process in regime 2. Then the observed $y$ is $z \times y^*$. A natural extension of the splitting model is to allow $z$ to be determined by a set of covariates. These covariates need not be the same as those that determine the conditional probabilities in the Poisson process. Thus, the model is

$$\text{Prob}(z_i = 1 \mid \mathbf{w}_i) = F(\mathbf{w}_i, \gamma),$$

$$\text{Prob}(y_i = j \mid \mathbf{x}_i, z_i = 1) = \frac{e^{-\lambda_i} \lambda_i^j}{j!}.$$

---

[6]For a similar treatment in a continuous data application, see Cragg (1971).

[7]The model is variously labeled the "With Zeros," or WZ, model [Mullahy (1986)], the **Zero Inflated Poisson, or ZIP, model** [Lambert (1992)], and "Zero-Altered Poisson," or ZAP, model [Greene (1994)].

The mean in this distribution is

$$E[y_i \mid \mathbf{w}_i] = (1 - F) \times 0 + F \times E[y_i^* \mid \mathbf{x}_i, y_i^* > 0] = F \times \frac{\lambda_i}{1 - e^{-\lambda_i}}.$$

Lambert (1992) and Greene (1994) consider a number of alternative formulations, including logit and probit models discussed in Sections 23.3 and 23.4, for the probability of the two regimes.

Both of these modifications substantially alter the Poisson formulation. First, note that the equality of the mean and variance of the distribution no longer follows; both modifications induce overdispersion. On the other hand, the overdispersion does not arise from heterogeneity; it arises from the nature of the process generating the zeros. As such, an interesting identification problem arises in this model. If the data do appear to be characterized by overdispersion, then it seems less than obvious whether it should be attributed to heterogeneity or to the regime splitting mechanism. Mullahy (1986) argues the point more strongly. He demonstrates that overdispersion will always induce excess zeros. As such, in a splitting model, we are likely to misinterpret the excess zeros as due to the splitting process instead of the heterogeneity.

It might be of interest to test simply whether there is a regime splitting mechanism at work or not. Unfortunately, the basic model and the zero-inflated model are not nested. Setting the parameters of the splitting model to zero, for example, does not produce Prob$[z = 0] = 0$. In the probit case, this probability becomes 0.5, which maintains the regime split. The preceding tests for over- or underdispersion would be rather indirect. What is desired is a test of non-Poissonness. An alternative distribution may (but need not) produce a systematically different proportion of zeros than the Poisson. Testing for a different distribution, as opposed to a different set of parameters, is a difficult procedure. Because the hypotheses are necessarily nonnested, the power of any test is a function of the alternative hypothesis and may, under some, be small. Vuong (1989) has proposed a test statistic for **nonnested models** that is well suited for this setting when the alternative distribution can be specified. Let $f_j(y_i \mid \mathbf{x}_i)$ denote the predicted probability that the random variable $Y$ equals $y_i$ under the assumption that the distribution is $f_j(y_i \mid \mathbf{x}_i)$, for $j = 1, 2$, and let

$$m_i = \ln \left( \frac{f_1(y_i \mid \mathbf{x}_i)}{f_2(y_i \mid \mathbf{x}_i)} \right).$$

Then Vuong's statistic for testing the nonnested hypothesis of model 1 versus model 2 is

$$v = \frac{\sqrt{n} \left[ \frac{1}{n} \sum_{i=1}^{n} m_i \right]}{\sqrt{\frac{1}{n} \sum_{i=1}^{n} (m_i - \overline{m})^2}}.$$

This is the standard statistic for testing the hypothesis that $E[m_i]$ equals zero. Vuong shows that $v$ has a limiting standard normal distribution. As he notes, the statistic is bidirectional. If $|v|$ is less than two, then the test does not favor one model or the other. Otherwise, large values favor model 1 whereas small (negative) values favor model 2. Carrying out the test requires estimation of both models and computation of both sets of predicted probabilities.

In Greene (1994), it is shown that the Vuong test has some power to discern this phenomenon. The logic of the testing procedure is to allow for overdispersion by

**TABLE 25.3**   Estimates of a Split Population Model

| Variable | Poisson and Logit Models | | Split Population Model | |
|---|---|---|---|---|
| | Poisson for y | Logit for y > 0 | Poisson for y | Logit for y > 0 |
| Constant | −0.8196 | −2.2442 | 1.0010 | 2.1540 |
| | (0.1453) | (0.2515) | (0.1267) | (0.2900) |
| Age | 0.007181 | 0.02245 | −0.005073 | −0.02469 |
| | (0.003978) | (0.007313) | (0.003218) | (0.008451) |
| Income | 0.07790 | 0.06931 | 0.01332 | −0.1167 |
| | (0.02394) | (0.04198) | (0.02249) | (0.04941) |
| Expend | −0.004102 | | −0.002359 | |
| | (0.0003740) | | (0.0001948) | |
| Own/Rent | | −0.3766 | | 0.3865 |
| | | (0.1578) | | (0.1709) |
| ln L | −1396.719 | −645.5649 | −1093.0280 | |
| $n\hat{P}(0\,|\,\hat{\mathbf{x}})$ | 938.6 | | 1061.5 | |

specifying a negative binomial count data process, then examine whether, *even allowing for the overdispersion,* there still appear to be excess zeros. In his application, that appears to be the case.

**Example 25.3   A Split Population Model for Major Derogatory Reports**
Greene (1995c) estimated a model of consumer behavior in which the dependent variable of interest was the number of major derogatory reports recorded in the credit history for a sample of applicants for a type of credit card. The basic model predicts $y_i$, the number of major derogatory credit reports, as a function of $\mathbf{x}_i = [1, age, income, average\ expenditure]$. The data for the model appear in Appendix Table F25.1. There are 1,319 observations in the sample (10 percent of the original data set). Inspection of the data reveals a preponderance of zeros. Indeed, of 1,319 observations, 1060 have $y_i = 0$, whereas of the remaining 259, 137 have 1, 50 have 2, 24 have 3, 17 have 4, and 11 have 5—the remaining 20 range from 6 to 14. Thus, for a Poisson distribution, these data are actually a bit extreme. We propose to use Lambert's zero inflated Poisson model instead, with the Poisson distribution built around

$$\ln \lambda_i = \beta_1 + \beta_2\ age + \beta_3\ income + \beta_4\ expenditure.$$

For the splitting model, we use a logit model, with covariates $\mathbf{z} = [1, age, income, own/rent]$. The estimates are shown in Table 25.3. Vuong's diagnostic statistic appears to confirm intuition that the Poisson model does not adequately describe the data; the value is 6.9788. Using the model parameters to compute a prediction of the number of zeros, it is clear that the splitting model does perform better than the basic Poisson regression.

## 25.5   CENSORING AND TRUNCATION IN MODELS FOR COUNTS

Truncation and censoring are relatively common in applications of models for counts. Truncation often arises as a consequence of discarding what appear to be unusable data, such as the zero values in survey data on the number of uses of recreation facilities [Shaw (1988) and Bockstael et al. (1990)]. The zero values in this setting might represent a discrete decision not to visit the site, which is a qualitatively different decision from the positive number for someone who had decided to make at least one visit. In such a case, it might make sense to confine attention to the nonzero observations, thereby truncating the distribution. Censoring, in contrast, is often employed to make survey data more convenient to gather and analyze. For example, survey data on access to medical facilities might ask, "How many trips to the doctor did you make in the last year?" The responses might be 0, 1, 2, 3, or more.

### 25.5.1 CENSORING AND TRUNCATION IN THE POISSON MODEL

Models with these characteristics can be handled within the Poisson and negative binomial regression frameworks by using the laws of probability to modify the likelihood. For example, in the *censored* data case,

$$P_i(j) = \text{Prob}[y_i = j] = \frac{e^{-\lambda_i}\lambda_i^j}{j!}, \quad j = 0, 1, 2.$$

$$P_i(3) = \text{Prob}[y_i \geq 3] = 1 - [\text{Prob}(y_i = 0) + \text{Prob}(y_i = 1) + \text{Prob}(y_i = 2)].$$

The probabilities in the model with *truncation* above zero would be

$$P_i(j) = \text{Prob}[y_i = j] = \frac{e^{-\lambda_i}\lambda_i^j}{[1 - P_i(0)]j!} = \frac{e^{-\lambda_i}\lambda_i^j}{[1 - e^{-\lambda_i}]j!}, \quad j = 1, 2, \ldots. \quad \textbf{(25-13)}$$

These models are not appreciably more complicated to analyze than the basic Poisson or negative binomial models. [See Terza (1985b), Mullahy (1986), Shaw (1988), Grogger and Carson (1991), Greene (1998), Lambert (1992), and Winkelmann (1997).] They do, however, bring substantive changes to the familiar characteristics of the models. For example, the conditional means are no longer $\lambda_i$; in the censoring case,

$$E[y_i \mid \mathbf{x}_i] = \lambda_i - \sum_{j=3}^{\infty} (j - 3)P_i(j) < \lambda_i.$$

Marginal effects are changed as well. Recall that our earlier result for the count data models was $\partial E[y_i \mid \mathbf{x}_i]/\partial \mathbf{x}_i = \lambda_i \boldsymbol{\beta}$. With censoring or truncation, it is straightforward in general to show that $\partial E[y_i \mid \mathbf{x}_i]/\partial \mathbf{x}_i = \delta_i \boldsymbol{\beta}$, but the new scale factor need not be smaller than $\lambda_i$.

### 25.5.2 APPLICATION: CENSORING IN THE TOBIT AND POISSON REGRESSION MODELS

In 1969, the popular magazine *Psychology Today* published a 101-question survey on sex and asked its readers to mail in their answers. The results of the survey were discussed in the July 1970 issue. From the approximately 2,000 replies that were collected in electronic form (of about 20,000 received), Professor Ray Fair (1978) extracted a sample of 601 observations on men and women then currently married for the first time and analyzed their responses to a question about extramarital affairs. He used the tobit model as a platform. Fair's analysis in this frequently cited study suggests several interesting econometric questions. [In addition, his 1977 companion paper in *Econometrica* on estimation of the tobit model contributed to the development of the EM algorithm, which was published by and is usually associated with Dempster, Laird, and Rubin (1977).]

As noted, Fair used the tobit model as his estimation framework for this study. The nonexperimental nature of the data (which can be downloaded from the Internet at http://fairmodel.econ.yale.edu/rayfair/work.ss.htm) provides a fine laboratory case that we can use to examine the relationships among the tobit, truncated regression, and probit models. In addition, as we will explore later, although the tobit model seems to be a natural choice for the model for these data, a closer look suggests that the models for counts we have examined at several points earlier might be yet a better choice. Finally, the preponderance of zeros in the data that initially motivated the tobit model suggests that even the standard Poisson model, although an improvement, might still be inadequate. In this example, we will reestimate Fair's original model and then apply some of the specification tests and modified models for count data as alternatives.

The study was based on 601 observations on the following variables (full details on data coding are given in the data file and Appendix Table F25.2):

$y$ = number of affairs in the past year, 0, 1, 2, 3, 4–10 coded as 7, "monthly, weekly, or daily," coded as 12. Sample mean = 1.46. Frequencies = (451, 34, 17, 19, 42, 38).

$z_1$ = sex = 0 for female, 1 for male. Sample mean = 0.476.

$z_2$ = age. Sample mean = 32.5.

$z_3$ = number of years married. Sample mean = 8.18.

$z_4$ = children, 0 = no, 1 = yes. Sample mean = 0.715.

$z_5$ = religiousness, 1 = anti, . . . , 5 = very. Sample mean = 3.12.

$z_6$ = education, years, 9 = grade school, 12 = high school, . . . , 20 = Ph.D or other. Sample mean = 16.2.

$z_7$ = occupation, "Hollingshead scale," 1–7. Sample mean = 4.19.

$z_8$ = self-rating of marriage, 1 = very unhappy, . . . , 5 = very happy. Sample mean = 3.93.

The tobit model was fit to $y$ using a constant term and all eight variables. A restricted model was fit by excluding $z_1$, $z_4$, and $z_6$, none of which was individually statistically significant in the model. We are able to match exactly Fair's results for both equations. The log-likelihood functions for the full and restricted models are 2704.7311 and 2705.5762. The chi-squared statistic for testing the hypothesis that the three coefficients are zero is twice the difference, 1.6902. The critical value from the chi-squared distribution with three degrees of freedom is 7.81, so the hypothesis that the coefficients on these three variables are all zero is not rejected. The Wald and Lagrange multiplier statistics are likewise small, 6.59 and 1.681. Based on these results, we will continue the analysis using the restricted set of variables, $\mathbf{Z} = (\mathbf{1}, \mathbf{z}_2, \mathbf{z}_3, \mathbf{z}_5, \mathbf{z}_7, \mathbf{z}_8)$. Our interest is solely in the numerical results of different modeling approaches. Readers may draw their own conclusions and interpretations from the estimates.

Table 25.4 presents parameter estimates based on Fair's specification of the normal distribution. The inconsistent least squares estimates appear at the left as a basis for comparison. The maximum likelihood tobit estimates appear next. The sample is heavily dominated by observations with $y = 0$ (451 of 601, or 75 percent), so the **marginal effects** are very different from the coefficients, by a multiple of roughly 0.766. The scale factor

**TABLE 25.4**  Model Estimates Based on the Normal Distribution (standard errors in parentheses)

| | | Tobit | | | Probit | Truncated Regression | |
|---|---|---|---|---|---|---|---|
| Variable | Least Squares (1) | Estimate (2) | Marginal Effect (3) | Scaled by $1/\sigma$ (4) | Estimate (5) | Estimate (6) | Marginal Effect (7) |
| Constant | 5.61 | 8.17 | — | 0.991 | 0.977 | 8.32 | — |
| | (0.797) | (2.74) | — | (0.336) | (0.361) | (3.96) | — |
| $z_2$ | −0.0504 | −0.179 | −0.042 | −0.022 | −0.022 | −0.0841 | −0.0407 |
| | (0.0221) | (0.079) | (0.184) | (0.010) | (0.102) | (0.119) | (0.0578) |
| $z_3$ | 0.162 | 0.554 | 0.130 | 0.0672 | 0.0599 | 0.560 | 0.271 |
| | (0.0369) | (0.135) | (0.0312) | (0.0161) | (0.0171) | (0.219) | (0.106) |
| $z_5$ | −0.476 | −1.69 | −0.394 | −0.2004 | −0.184 | −1.502 | −0.728 |
| | (0.111) | (0.404) | (0.093) | (0.484) | (0.0515) | (0.617) | (0.299) |
| $z_7$ | 0.106 | 0.326 | 0.0762 | 0.0395 | 0.0375 | 0.189 | 0.0916 |
| | (0.0711) | (0.254) | (0.0595) | (0.0308) | (0.0328) | (0.377) | (0.182) |
| $z_8$ | −0.712 | −2.29 | −0.534 | −0.277 | −0.273 | −1.35 | −0.653 |
| | (0.118) | (0.408) | (0.0949) | (0.0483) | (0.0525) | (0.565) | (0.273) |
| $\sigma$ | 3.09 | 8.25 | | | | 5.53 | |
| ln $L$ | | −705.5762 | | | −307.2955 | −392.7103 | |

is computed using the results of Theorem 24.4 for left censoring at zero and the upper limit of $+\infty$, with all variables evaluated at the sample means and the parameters equal to the maximum likelihood estimates:

$$\text{scale} = \Phi\left[\frac{+\infty - \bar{\mathbf{x}}'\hat{\boldsymbol{\beta}}_{\text{ML}}}{\hat{\sigma}_{\text{ML}}}\right] - \Phi\left[\frac{0 - \bar{\mathbf{x}}'\hat{\boldsymbol{\beta}}_{\text{ML}}}{\hat{\sigma}_{\text{ML}}}\right] = 1 - \Phi\left[\frac{0 - \bar{\mathbf{x}}'\hat{\boldsymbol{\beta}}_{\text{ML}}}{\hat{\sigma}_{\text{ML}}}\right] = \Phi\left[\frac{\bar{\mathbf{x}}'\hat{\boldsymbol{\beta}}_{\text{ML}}}{\hat{\sigma}_{\text{ML}}}\right] = 0.234.$$

These estimates are shown in the third column. As expected, they resemble the least squares estimates, although not enough that one would be content to use OLS for estimation. The fifth column in Table 25.4 gives estimates of the probit model estimated for the dependent variable $q_i = 0$ if $y_i = 0$, $q_i = 1$ if $y_i > 0$. If the specification of the tobit model is correct, then the probit estimators should be consistent for $(1/\sigma)\boldsymbol{\beta}$ from the tobit model. These estimates, with standard errors computed using the **delta method,** are shown in column 4. The results are surprisingly close, especially given the results of the specification test considered later. Finally, columns 6 and 7 give the estimates for the truncated regression model that applies to the 150 nonlimit observations if the specification of the model is correct. Here the results seem a bit less consistent.

Several specification tests were suggested for this model. The Cragg/Greene test for appropriate specification of $\text{Prob}[y_i = 0]$ is given in Section 24.3.4.b. This test is easily carried out using the log-likelihood values in the table. The chi-squared statistic, which has seven degrees of freedom is $-2\{-705.5762 - [-307.2955 + (-392.7103)]\} = 11.141$, which is smaller than the critical value of 14.067. We conclude that the tobit model is correctly specified (the decision of whether or not is not different from the decision of how many, given "whether"). We now turn to the normality tests. We emphasize that these tests are nonconstructive tests of the skewness and kurtosis of the distribution of $\varepsilon$. A fortiori, if we do reject the hypothesis that these values are 0.0 and 3.0, respectively, then we can reject normality. But that does not suggest what to do next. We turn to that issue later. The Chesher–Irish and Pagan–Vella chi-squared statistics are 562.218 and 22.314, respectively. The critical value is 5.99, so on the basis of both of these values, the hypothesis of normality is rejected. Thus, both the probability model and the distributional framework are rejected by these tests.

Before leaving the tobit model, we consider one additional aspect of the original specification. The values above 4 in the observed data are not true observations on the response; 7 is an estimate of the mean of observations that fall in the range 4 to 10, whereas 12 was chosen more or less arbitrarily for observations that were greater than 10. These observations represent 80 of the 601 observations, or about 13 percent of the sample. To some extent, this coding scheme might be driving the results. [This point was not overlooked in the original study; "[a] linear specification was used for the estimated equation, and it did not seem reasonable in this case, given the range of explanatory variables, to have a dependent variable that ranged from, say, 0 to 365" [Fair (1978, p. 55)]. The tobit model allows for censoring in both tails of the distribution. Ignoring the results of the specification tests for the moment, we will examine a doubly censored regression by recoding all observations that take the values 7, or 12 as 4. The model is thus

$$y^* = \mathbf{x}'\boldsymbol{\beta} + \varepsilon,$$

$$y = 0 \quad \text{if } y^* \leq 0,$$

$$y = y^* \quad \text{if } 0 < y^* < 4,$$

$$y = 4 \quad \text{if } y^* \geq 4.$$

The log-likelihood is built up from three sets of terms:

$$\ln L = \sum_{y=0} \ln \Phi \left[ \frac{0 - \mathbf{x}'_i \boldsymbol{\beta}}{\sigma} \right] + \sum_{0 < y < 4} \ln \frac{1}{\sigma} \phi \left[ \frac{y_i - \mathbf{x}'_i \boldsymbol{\beta}}{\sigma} \right] + \sum_{y=4} \ln \left[ 1 - \Phi \left( \frac{4 - \mathbf{x}'_i \boldsymbol{\beta}}{\sigma} \right) \right].$$

Maximum likelihood estimates of the parameters of this model based on the doubly censored data appear in Table 25.5. The effect on the coefficient estimates is relatively minor, but the effect on the estimates of the marginal effects is very large; they are reduced by about 50 percent, which makes sense. With the original data, increases in the index were associated with increases in $y$ that could be from 3 to 7 or from 3 to 12. But with the data treated as censored, $y$ cannot increase past 4. Thus, the range of variation is greatly reduced. The numerical results are also suggestive. Recall that the scale factor

**TABLE 25.5** Estimates of a Doubly Censored Tobit Model

| Variable | Left Censored at 0 Only | | | Censored at Both 0 and 4 | | |
|---|---|---|---|---|---|---|
| | Estimate | Standard Error | Marginal Effect | Estimate | Standard Error | Marginal Effect |
| Constant | 8.17 | 2.74 | — | 7.90 | 2.804 | — |
| $z_2$ | −0.179 | 0.079 | −0.0420 | −0.178 | 0.080 | −0.0218 |
| $z_3$ | 0.554 | 0.135 | 0.130 | 0.532 | 0.141 | 0.0654 |
| $z_5$ | −1.69 | 0.404 | −0.394 | −1.62 | 0.424 | −0.199 |
| $z_7$ | 0.326 | 0.254 | 0.0762 | 0.324 | 0.254 | 0.0399 |
| $z_8$ | −2.29 | 0.408 | −0.534 | −2.21 | 0.459 | −0.271 |
| $\sigma$ | 8.25 Prob(nonlimit) $= 0.2338$ | | | 7.94 Prob(nonlimit) $= 0.1229$ | | |
| $E[y \mid \mathbf{x} = E[\mathbf{x}]]$ | 1.126 | | | 0.226 | | |

for the singly censored data was 0.2338. For the doubly **censored variable,** this factor is $\Phi[(4 - \boldsymbol{\beta}'\mathbf{x})/\sigma] - \Phi[(0 - \boldsymbol{\beta}'\mathbf{x})/\sigma] = 0.8930 - 0.7701 = 0.1229$. The regression model for $y^*$ has not changed much, but the effect now is to assign the upper tail area to the censored region, whereas before it was in the uncensored region. The effect, then, is to reduce the scale roughly by this 0.107, from 0.234 to about 0.123.

By construction, the tobit model should only be viewed as an approximation for these data. The dependent variable is a count, not a continuous measurement. (Thus, the testing results obtained earlier are not surprising.) The Poisson regression model, or perhaps one of the many variants of it, should be a preferable modeling framework. Table 25.6 presents estimates of the Poisson and negative binomial regression models. There is ample evidence of overdispersion in these data; the $t$ ratio on the estimated overdispersion parameter is $7.014/0.945 = 7.42$, which is strongly suggestive. The large absolute value of the coefficient is likewise suggestive.

Before proceeding to a model that specifically accounts for overdispersion, we can find a candidate for its source, at least to some degree. As discussed earlier, responses of 7 and 12 do not represent the actual counts. It is unclear what the effect of the first recoding would be, because it might well be the mean of the observations in this group. But the second is clearly a censored observation. To remove both of these effects, we have recoded both the values 7 and 12 as 4 and treated this observation (appropriately) as a censored observation, with 4 denoting "4 or more." As shown in the third and fourth sets of results in Table 25.6, the effect of this treatment of the data is greatly to reduce the measured effects, which is the same effect we observed for the tobit model. Although this step does remove a deficiency in the data, it does not remove the overdispersion; at this point, the negative binomial model is still the preferred specification.

**TABLE 25.6**  Model Estimates Based on the Poisson Distribution

| Variable | Poisson Regression | | | Negative Binomial Regression | | |
|---|---|---|---|---|---|---|
| | Estimate | Standard Error | Marginal Effect | Estimate | Standard Error | Marginal Effect |
| | **Based on Uncensored Poisson Distribution** | | | | | |
| Constant | 2.53 | 0.197 | — | 2.19 | 0.664 | — |
| $z_2$ | −0.0322 | 0.00585 | −0.0470 | −0.0262 | 0.0192 | −0.00393 |
| $z_3$ | 0.116 | 0.00991 | 0.168 | 0.0848 | 0.0350 | 0.127 |
| $z_5$ | −0.354 | 0.0309 | −0.515 | −0.422 | 0.111 | −0.632 |
| $z_7$ | 0.0798 | 0.0194 | 0.116 | 0.0604 | 0.0702 | 0.0906 |
| $z_8$ | −0.409 | 0.0274 | −0.0596 | −0.431 | 0.111 | −0.646 |
| $\alpha$ | | | | 7.01 | 0.786 | |
| ln $L$ | −1427.037 | | | −728.2441 | | |
| | **Based on Poisson Distribution Right Censored at $y=4$** | | | | | |
| Constant | 1.90 | 0.283 | — | 4.79 | 1.16 | — |
| $z_2$ | −0.0328 | 0.00838 | −0.0235 | −0.0166 | 0.0250 | −0.00428 |
| $z_3$ | 0.105 | 0.0140 | 0.0754 | 0.174 | 0.0568 | 0.045 |
| $z_5$ | −0.323 | 0.0437 | −0.232 | −0.723 | 0.198 | −0.186 |
| $z_7$ | 0.0798 | 0.0275 | 0.0521 | 0.0900 | 0.116 | 0.0232 |
| $z_8$ | −0.390 | 0.0391 | −0.279 | −0.854 | 0.216 | −0.220 |
| $\alpha$ | | | | 9.40 | 1.35 | |
| ln $L$ | −747.7541 | | | −482.0505 | | |

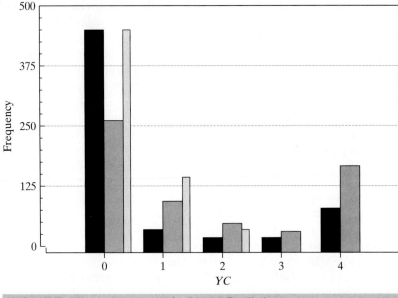

**FIGURE 25.1**    Histogram for Model Predictions.

The tobit model remains the standard approach to modeling a dependent variable that displays a large cluster of limit values, usually zeros. But in these data, it is clear that the zero value represents something other than a censoring; it is the outcome of a discrete decision. Thus, for this reason and based on the preceding results, it seems appropriate to turn to a different model for this dependent variable. The Poisson and negative binomial models look like an improvement, but there remains a noteworthy problem. Figure 25.1 shows a histogram of the actual values (solid dark bars) and predicted values from the negative binomial model estimated with the censored data (lighter bars). Predictions from the latter model are the integer values of $E[y \mid \mathbf{x}] = \exp(\boldsymbol{\beta}'\mathbf{x})$. As in the actual data, values larger than 4 are censored to 4. Evidently, the negative binomial model predicts the data fairly poorly. In fact, it is not hard to see why. The source of the overdispersion in the data is not the extreme values on the right of the distribution; it is the very large number of zeros on the left.

There are a large variety of models and permutations that one might turn to at this point. We will conclude with just one of these, Lambert's (1992) zero-inflated Poisson (ZIP) model with a logit "splitting" model discussed in Section 25.4 and Example 25.3. The doubly censored count is the dependent variable in this model. [Mullahy's (1986) hurdle model is an alternative that might be considered. The difference between these two is in the interpretation of the zero observations. In the ZIP formulation, the zero observations would be a mixture of "never" and "not in the last year," whereas the hurdle model assumes two distinct decisions, "whether or not" and "how many, given yes."] The estimates of the parameters of the ZIP model are shown in Table 25.7. The Vuong statistic of 21.64 strongly supports the ZIP model over the Poisson model. (An attempt to combine the ZIP model with the negative binomial was unsuccessful.

**TABLE 25.7** Estimates of a Zero-Inflated Poisson Model

| Variable | Poisson Regression | | Logit Splitting Model | | Marginal Effects | | |
|---|---|---|---|---|---|---|---|
| | 1.1 Estimate | Standard Error | Estimate | Standard Error | ZIP | Tobit (0) | Tobit (0, 4) |
| Constant | 1.27 | 0.439 | −1.85 | 0.664 | — | — | — |
| Age | −0.00422 | 0.0122 | 0.0397 | 0.0190 | −0.0216 | −0.0420 | −0.0218 |
| Years | 0.0331 | 0.0231 | −0.0981 | 0.0318 | 0.0702 | 0.130 | 0.0654 |
| Religion | −0.0909 | 0.0721 | 0.306 | 0.0951 | −0.210 | −0.394 | −0.199 |
| Occupation | 0.0205 | 0.0441 | 0.0677 | 0.0607 | 0.0467 | 0.0762 | 0.0399 |
| Happiness | −0.817 | 0.0666 | 0.458 | 0.0949 | −0.273 | −0.534 | −0.271 |

Because, as expected, the ancillary model for the zeros accounted for the overdispersion in the data, the negative binomial model degenerated to the Poisson form.) Finally, the marginal effects, $\delta = \partial E[y \mid \mathbf{x}]/\partial \mathbf{x}$, are shown in Table 25.7 for three models: the ZIP model, Fair's original tobit model, and the tobit model estimated with the doubly censored count. The estimates for the ZIP model are considerably lower than those for Fair's tobit model. When the tobit model is reestimated with the censoring on the right, however, the resulting marginal effects are reasonably close to those from the ZIP model, although uniformly smaller. (This result may be from not building the censoring into the ZIP model, a refinement that would be relatively straightforward.)

We conclude that the original tobit model provided only a fair approximation to the marginal effects produced by (we contend) the more appropriate specification of the Poisson model. But the approximation became much better when the data were recoded and treated as censored. Figure 25.1 also shows the predictions from the ZIP model (narrow bars). As might be expected, it provides a much better prediction of the dependent variable. (The integer values of the conditional mean function for the tobit model were roughly evenly split between zeros and ones, whereas the doubly censored model always predicted $y = 0$.) Surprisingly, the treatment of the highest observations does greatly affect the outcome. If the ZIP model is fit to the original uncensored data, then the vector of marginal effects is $\delta = [-0.0586, 0.2446, -0.692, 0.115, -0.787]$, which is extremely large. Thus, perhaps more analysis is called for—the ZIP model can be further improved, and one might reconsider the hurdle model—but we have tortured Fair's data enough. Further exploration is left for the reader.

## 25.6 MODELS FOR DURATION DATA[8]

Intuition might suggest that the longer a strike persists, the more likely it is that it will end within, say, the next week. Or is it? It seems equally plausible to suggest that the longer a strike has lasted, the more difficult must be the problems that led to it in the first place, and hence the *less* likely it is that it will end in the next short time interval.

---

[8]There are a large number of highly technical articles on this topic but relatively few accessible sources for the uninitiated. A particularly useful introductory survey is Kiefer (1988), upon which we have drawn heavily for this section. Other useful sources are Kalbfleisch and Prentice (2002), Heckman and Singer (1984a), Lancaster (1990), and Florens, Fougere, and Mouchart (1996).

A similar kind of reasoning could be applied to spells of unemployment or the interval between conceptions. In each of these cases, it is not only the duration of the event, per se, that is interesting, but also the likelihood that the event will end in "the next period" given that it has lasted as long as it has.

Analysis of the length of *time until failure* has interested engineers for decades. For example, the models discussed in this section were applied to the durability of electric and electronic components long before economists discovered their usefulness. Likewise, the analysis of *survival times*—for example, the length of survival after the onset of a disease or after an operation such as a heart transplant—has long been a staple of biomedical research. Social scientists have recently applied the same body of techniques to strike duration, length of unemployment spells, intervals between conception, time until business failure, length of time between arrests, length of time from purchase until a warranty claim is made, intervals between purchases, and so on.

This section will give a brief introduction to the econometric analysis of duration data. As usual, we will restrict our attention to a few straightforward, relatively uncomplicated techniques and applications, primarily to introduce terms and concepts. The reader can then wade into the literature to find the extensions and variations. We will concentrate primarily on what are known as **parametric models.** These apply familiar inference techniques and provide a convenient departure point. Alternative approaches are considered at the end of the discussion.

### 25.6.1 DURATION DATA

The variable of interest in the analysis of duration is the length of time that elapses from the beginning of some event either until its end or until the measurement is taken, which may precede termination. Observations will typically consist of a cross section of durations, $t_1, t_2, \ldots, t_n$. The process being observed may have begun at different points in calendar time for the different individuals in the sample. For example, the strike duration data examined in Example 25.4 are drawn from nine different years.

Censoring is a pervasive and usually unavoidable problem in the analysis of duration data. The common cause is that the measurement is made while the process is ongoing. An obvious example can be drawn from medical research. Consider analyzing the survival times of heart transplant patients. Although the beginning times may be known with precision, at the time of the measurement, observations on any individuals who are still alive are necessarily censored. Likewise, samples of spells of unemployment drawn from surveys will probably include some individuals who are still unemployed at the time the survey is taken. For these individuals, duration, or survival, is at least the observed $t_i$, but not equal to it. Estimation must account for the censored nature of the data for the same reasons as considered in Section 24.3. The consequences of ignoring censoring in duration data are similar to those that arise in regression analysis.

In a conventional regression model that characterizes the conditional mean and variance of a distribution, the regressors can be taken as fixed characteristics at the point in time or for the individual for which the measurement is taken. When measuring duration, the observation is implicitly on a process that has been under way for an interval of time from zero to $t$. If the analysis is conditioned on a set of covariates (the counterparts to regressors) $\mathbf{x}_t$, then the duration is implicitly a function of the entire time path of the variable $\mathbf{x}(t), t = (0, t)$, which may have changed during the interval. For example, the observed duration of employment in a job may be a function of the individual's rank in the firm. But their rank may have changed several times between the time they were hired and when the observation was made. As such, observed rank at the end of the job tenure is not necessarily a complete description of the individual's rank *while they were employed*. Likewise, marital status, family size, and amount of education are all variables that can change during the duration of unemployment and that one would like to account for in the duration model. The treatment of **time-varying covariates** is a considerable complication.[9]

## 25.6.2    A REGRESSION-LIKE APPROACH: PARAMETRIC MODELS OF DURATION

We will use the term *spell* as a catchall for the different duration variables we might measure. Spell length is represented by the random variable $T$. A simple approach to duration analysis would be to apply regression analysis to the sample of observed spells. By this device, we could characterize the expected duration, perhaps conditioned on a set of covariates whose values were measured at the end of the period. We could also assume that conditioned on an $\mathbf{x}$ that has remained fixed from $T=0$ to $T=t$, $t$ has a normal distribution, as we commonly do in regression. We could then characterize the probability distribution of observed duration times. But, normality turns out not to be particularly attractive in this setting for a number of reasons, not least of which is that duration is positive by construction, while a normally distributed variable can take negative values. (*Lognormality* turns out to be a palatable alternative, but it is only one among a long list of candidates.)

### 25.6.2.a    Theoretical Background

Suppose that the random variable $T$ has a continuous probability distribution $f(t)$, where $t$ is a realization of $T$. The cumulative probability is

$$F(t) = \int_0^t f(s) \, ds = \text{Prob}(T \le t).$$

We will usually be more interested in the probability that the spell is of length *at least* $t$, which is given by the **survival function,**

$$S(t) = 1 - F(t) = \text{Prob}(T \ge t).$$

Consider the question raised in the introduction: Given that the spell has lasted until time $t$, what is the probability that it will end in the next short interval of time, say, $\Delta t$? It is

$$l(t, \Delta t) = \text{Prob}(t \le T \le t + \Delta t \mid T \ge t).$$

A useful function for characterizing this aspect of the distribution is the **hazard rate,**

$$\lambda(t) = \lim_{\Delta t \to 0} \frac{\text{Prob}(t \le T \le t + \Delta t \mid T \ge t)}{\Delta t} = \lim_{\Delta t \to 0} \frac{F(t + \Delta t) - F(t)}{\Delta t \; S(t)} = \frac{f(t)}{S(t)}.$$

---

[9]See Petersen (1986) for one approach to this problem.

Roughly, the hazard rate is the rate at which spells are completed after duration $t$, given that they last at least until $t$. As such, the hazard function gives an answer to our original question.

The hazard function, the density, the CDF and the survival function are all related. The hazard function is

$$\lambda(t) = \frac{-d \ln S(t)}{dt},$$

so

$$f(t) = S(t)\lambda(t).$$

Another useful function is the **integrated hazard function**

$$\Lambda(t) = \int_0^t \lambda(s) \, ds,$$

for which

$$S(t) = e^{-\Lambda(t)},$$

so

$$\Lambda(t) = -\ln S(t).$$

The integrated hazard function is **generalized residual** in this setting. [See Chesher and Irish (1987) and Example 25.4.]

### 25.6.2.b    Models of the Hazard Function

For present purposes, the hazard function is more interesting than the survival rate or the density. Based on the previous results, one might consider modeling the hazard function itself, rather than, say, modeling the survival function then obtaining the density and the hazard. For example, the base case for many analyses is a hazard rate that does not vary over time. That is, $\lambda(t)$ is a constant $\lambda$. This is characteristic of a process that has no memory; the *conditional* probability of "failure" in a given short interval is the same regardless of when the observation is made. Thus,

$$\lambda(t) = \lambda.$$

From the earlier definition, we obtain the simple differential equation,

$$\frac{-d \ln S(t)}{dt} = \lambda.$$

The solution is

$$\ln S(t) = k - \lambda t,$$

or

$$S(t) = Ke^{-\lambda t},$$

where $K$ is the constant of integration. The terminal condition that $S(0) = 1$ implies that $K = 1$, and the solution is

$$S(t) = e^{-\lambda t}.$$

survival function $S(w) = \exp(-\exp(w))$.[11] Therefore, by using $\ln t$ instead of $t$, we greatly simplify the log-likelihood function. Details for these and several other distributions may be found in Kalbfleisch and Prentice (2002, pp. 68–70). The Weibull distribution is examined in detail in the next section.

### 25.6.2.d   Exogenous Variables

One limitation of the models given earlier is that external factors are not given a role in the survival distribution. The addition of "covariates" to duration models is fairly straightforward, although the interpretation of the coefficients in the model is less so. Consider, for example, the Weibull model. (The extension to other distributions will be similar.) Let

$$\lambda_i = e^{-\mathbf{x}_i'\boldsymbol{\beta}},$$

where $\mathbf{x}_i$ is a constant term and a set of variables that are assumed not to change from time $T = 0$ until the "failure time," $T = t_i$. Making $\lambda_i$ a function of a set of regressors is equivalent to changing the units of measurement on the time axis. For this reason, these models are sometimes called **accelerated failure time models.** Note as well that in all the models listed (and generally), the regressors do not bear on the question of duration dependence, which is a function of $p$.

Let $\sigma = 1/p$ and let $\delta_i = 1$ if the spell is completed and $\delta_i = 0$ if it is censored. As before, let

$$w_i = p\ln(\lambda_i t_i) = \frac{(\ln t_i - \mathbf{x}_i'\boldsymbol{\beta})}{\sigma},$$

and denote the density and survival functions $f(w_i)$ and $S(w_i)$. The observed random variable is

$$\ln t_i = \sigma w_i + \mathbf{x}_i'\boldsymbol{\beta}.$$

The Jacobian of the transformation from $w_i$ to $\ln t_i$ is $dw_i/d\ln t_i = 1/\sigma$, so the density and survival functions for $\ln t_i$ are

$$f(\ln t_i \mid \mathbf{x}_i, \boldsymbol{\beta}, \sigma) = \frac{1}{\sigma}f\left(\frac{\ln t_i - \mathbf{x}_i'\boldsymbol{\beta}}{\sigma}\right), \quad \text{and} \quad S(\ln t_i \mid \mathbf{x}_i, \boldsymbol{\beta}, \sigma) = S\left(\frac{\ln t_i - \mathbf{x}_i'\boldsymbol{\beta}}{\sigma}\right).$$

The log-likelihood for the observed data is

$$\ln L(\boldsymbol{\beta}, \sigma \mid \text{data}) = \sum_{i=1}^{n}[\delta_i \ln f(\ln t_i \mid \mathbf{x}_i, \boldsymbol{\beta}, \sigma) + (1 - \delta_i)\ln S(\ln t_i \mid \mathbf{x}_i, \boldsymbol{\beta}, \sigma)].$$

For the **Weibull model,** for example (see footnote 11)

$$f(w_i) = \exp(w_i - e^{w_i}),$$

and

$$S(w_i) = \exp(-e^{w_i}).$$

---

[11] The transformation is $\exp(w) = (\lambda t)^p$ so $t = (1/\lambda)[\exp(w)]^{1/p}$. The Jacobian of the transformation is $dt/dw = [\exp(w)]^{1/p}/(\lambda p)$. The density in Table 25.8 is $\lambda p[\exp(w)]^{-(1/p)-1}[\exp(-\exp(w))]$. Multiplying by the Jacobian produces the result, $f(w) = \exp[w - \exp(w)]$. The survival function is the antiderivative, $[\exp(-\exp(w))]$.

Making the transformation to $\ln t_i$ and collecting terms reduces the log-likelihood to

$$\ln L(\boldsymbol{\beta}, \sigma \mid \text{data}) = \sum_i \left[ \delta_i \left( \frac{\ln t_i - \mathbf{x}_i' \boldsymbol{\beta}}{\sigma} - \ln \sigma \right) - \exp \left( \frac{\ln t_i - \mathbf{x}_i' \boldsymbol{\beta}}{\sigma} \right) \right].$$

(Many other distributions, including the others in Table 25.8, simplify in the same way. The exponential model is obtained by setting $\sigma$ to one.) The derivatives can be equated to zero using the methods described in Section E.3. The individual terms can also be used to form the BHHH estimator of the asymptotic covariance matrix for the estimator.[12] The Hessian is also simple to derive, so Newton's method could be used instead.[13]

Note that the hazard function generally depends on $t$, $p$, and $\mathbf{x}$. The sign of an estimated coefficient suggests the direction of the effect of the variable on the hazard function when the hazard is monotonic. But in those cases, such as the loglogistic, in which the hazard is nonmonotonic, even this may be ambiguous. The magnitudes of the effects may also be difficult to interpret in terms of the hazard function. In a few cases, we do get a regression-like interpretation. In the Weibull and exponential models, $E[t \mid \mathbf{x}_i] = \exp(\mathbf{x}_i' \boldsymbol{\beta}) \Gamma[(1/p) + 1]$, whereas for the lognormal and loglogistic models, $E[\ln t \mid \mathbf{x}_i] = \mathbf{x}_i' \boldsymbol{\beta}$. In these cases, $\beta_k$ is the derivative (or a multiple of the derivative) of this conditional mean. For some other distributions, the conditional median of $t$ is easily obtained. Numerous cases are discussed by Kiefer (1988), Kalbfleisch and Prentice (2002), and Lancaster (1990).

### 25.6.2.e Heterogeneity

The problem of heterogeneity in duration models can be viewed essentially as the result of an incomplete specification. Individual specific covariates are intended to incorporate observation specific effects. But if the model specification is incomplete and if systematic individual differences in the distribution remain after the observed effects are accounted for, then inference based on the improperly specified model is likely to be problematic. We have already encountered several settings in which the possibility of heterogeneity mandated a change in the model specification; the fixed and random effects regression, logit, and probit models all incorporate observation-specific effects. Indeed, all the failures of the linear regression model discussed in the preceding chapters can be interpreted as a consequence of heterogeneity arising from an incomplete specification.

There are a number of ways of extending duration models to account for heterogeneity. The strictly nonparametric approach of the Kaplan–Meier estimator (see Section 25.6.3) is largely immune to the problem, but it is also rather limited in how much information can be culled from it. One direct approach is to model heterogeneity in the parametric model. Suppose that we posit a survival function conditioned on the individual specific effect $v_i$. We treat the survival function as $S(t_i \mid v_i)$. Then add to that a model for the unobserved heterogeneity $f(v_i)$. (Note that this is a counterpart to the incorporation of a disturbance in a regression model and follows the same procedures

---

[12] Note that the log-likelihood function has the same form as that for the tobit model in Section 24.3. By just reinterpreting the nonlimit observations in a tobit setting, we can, therefore, use this framework to apply a wide range of distributions to the tobit model. [See Greene (1995a) and references given therein.]

[13] See Kalbfleisch and Prentice (2002) for numerous other examples.

that we used in the Poisson model with random effects.) Then

$$S(t) = E_v[S(t \mid v)] = \int_v S(t \mid v) f(v) \, dv.$$

The gamma distribution is frequently used for this purpose.[14] Consider, for example, using this device to incorporate heterogeneity into the Weibull model we used earlier. As is typical, we assume that $v$ has a gamma distribution with mean 1 and variance $\theta = 1/k$. Then

$$f(v) = \frac{k^k}{\Gamma(k)} e^{-kv} v^{k-1},$$

and

$$S(t \mid v) = e^{-(v \lambda t)^p}.$$

After a bit of manipulation, we obtain the unconditional distribution,

$$S(t) = \int_0^\infty S(t \mid v) f(v) \, dv = [1 + \theta(\lambda t)^p]^{-1/\theta}.$$

The limiting value, with $\theta = 0$, is the **Weibull survival model,** so $\theta = 0$ corresponds to $\text{Var}[v] = 0$, or no heterogeneity.[15] The hazard function for this model is

$$\lambda(t) = \lambda p (\lambda t)^{p-1} [S(t)]^\theta,$$

which shows the relationship to the Weibull model.

  This approach is common in parametric modeling of heterogeneity. In an important paper on this subject, Heckman and Singer (1984b) argued that this approach tends to overparameterize the survival distribution and can lead to rather serious errors in inference. They gave some dramatic examples to make the point. They also expressed some concern that researchers tend to choose the distribution of heterogeneity more on the basis of mathematical convenience than on any sensible economic basis.

### 25.6.3  NONPARAMETRIC AND SEMIPARAMETRIC APPROACHES

The parametric models are attractive for their simplicity. But by imposing as much structure on the data as they do, the models may distort the estimated hazard rates. It may be that a more accurate representation can be obtained by imposing fewer restrictions.

  The Kaplan–Meier (1958) **product limit estimator** is a strictly empirical, nonparametric approach to survival and hazard function estimation. Assume that the observations on duration are sorted in ascending order so that $t_1 \leq t_2$ and so on and, for now, that no observations are censored. Suppose as well that there are $K$ distinct survival times in the data, denoted $T_k$; $K$ will equal $n$ unless there are ties. Let $n_k$ denote

---

[14]See, for example, Hausman, Hall, and Griliches (1984), who use it to incorporate heterogeneity in the Poisson regression model. The application is developed in Section 25.3.

[15]For the strike data analyzed in Figure 25.2, the maximum likelihood estimate of $\theta$ is 0.0004, which suggests that at least in the context of the Weibull model, latent heterogeneity does not appear to be a feature of these data.

the number of individuals whose observed duration is at least $T_k$. The set of individuals whose duration is at least $T_k$ is called the **risk set** at this duration. (We borrow, once again, from biostatistics, where the risk set is those individuals still "at risk" at time $T_k$). Thus, $n_k$ is the size of the risk set at time $T_k$. Let $h_k$ denote the number of observed spells completed at time $T_k$. A strictly empirical estimate of the survivor function would be

$$\hat{S}(T_k) = \prod_{i=1}^{k} \frac{n_i - h_i}{n_i} = \frac{n_i - h_i}{n_1}.$$

The estimator of the hazard rate is

$$\hat{\lambda}(T_k) = \frac{h_k}{n_k}. \tag{25-14}$$

Corrections are necessary for observations that are censored. Lawless (1982), Kalbfleisch and Prentice (2002), Kiefer (1988), and Greene (1995a) give details. Susin (2001) points out a fundamental ambiguity in this calculation (one which he argues appears in the 1958 source). The estimator in (25-14) is not a "rate" as such, as the width of the time window is undefined, and could be very different at different points in the chain of calculations. Because many intervals, particularly those late in the observation period, might have zeros, the failure to acknowledge these intervals should impart an upward bias to the estimator. His proposed alternative computes the counterpart to (25-14) over a mesh of defined intervals as follows:

$$\hat{\lambda}(I_a^b) = \frac{\sum_{j=a}^{b} h_j}{\sum_{j=a}^{b} n_j b_j},$$

where the interval is from $t = a$ to $t = b$, $h_j$ is the number of failures in each period in this interval, $n_j$ is the number of individuals at risk in that period and $b_j$ is the width of the period. Thus, an interval $(a, b)$ is likely to include several "periods."

Cox's (1972) approach to the **proportional hazard** model is another popular, **semiparametric** method of analyzing the effect of covariates on the hazard rate. The model specifies that

$$\lambda(t_i) = \exp(\mathbf{x}_i'\boldsymbol{\beta})\lambda_0(t_i)$$

The function $\lambda_0$ is the "baseline" hazard, which is the individual heterogeneity. In principle, this hazard is a parameter for each observation that must be estimated. Cox's **partial likelihood** estimator provides a method of estimating $\boldsymbol{\beta}$ without requiring estimation of $\lambda_0$. The estimator is somewhat similar to Chamberlain's estimator for the logit model with panel data in that a conditioning operation is used to remove the heterogeneity. (See Section 23.5.2.) Suppose that the sample contains $K$ distinct exit times, $T_1, \ldots, T_K$. For any time $T_k$, the risk set, denoted $R_k$, is all individuals whose exit time is at least $T_k$. The risk set is defined with respect to any moment in time $T$ as the set of individuals who have not yet exited just prior to that time. For every individual $i$ in risk set $R_k, t_i \geq T_k$. The probability that an individual exits at time $T_k$ given that *exactly one* *individual exits at this time* (which is the counterpart to the conditioning in the binary logit model in Chapter 23) is

$$\text{Prob}[t_i = T_k \mid \text{risk set}_k] = \frac{e^{x'_i \beta}}{\sum_{j \in R_k} e^{x'_j \beta}}.$$

Thus, the conditioning sweeps out the baseline hazard functions. For the simplest case in which exactly one individual exits at each distinct exit time and there are no censored observations, the partial log-likelihood is

$$\ln L = \sum_{k=1}^{K} \left[ x'_k \beta - \ln \sum_{j \in R_k} e^{x'_j \beta} \right].$$

If $m_k$ individuals exit at time $T_k$, then the contribution to the log-likelihood is the sum of the terms for each of these individuals.

The proportional hazard model is a common choice for modeling durations because it is a reasonable compromise between the Kaplan–Meier estimator and the possibly excessively structured parametric models. Hausman and Han (1990) and Meyer (1988), among others, have devised other, "semiparametric" specifications for hazard models.

### Example 25.4  Survival Models for Strike Duration

The strike duration data given in Kennan (1985, pp. 14–16) have become a familiar standard for the demonstration of hazard models. Appendix Table F25.3 lists the durations, in days, of 62 strikes that commenced in June of the years 1968 to 1976. Each involved at least 1,000 workers and began at the expiration or reopening of a contract. Kennan reported the actual duration. In his survey, Kiefer (1985), using the same observations, censored the data at 80 days to demonstrate the effects of censoring. We have kept the data in their original form; the interested reader is referred to Kiefer for further analysis of the censoring problem.[16]

Parameter estimates for the four duration models are given in Table 25.9. The estimate of the median of the survival distribution is obtained by solving the equation $S(t) = 0.5$. For example, for the Weibull model,

$$S(M) = 0.5 = \exp[-(\lambda M)^P],$$

or

$$M = [(\ln 2)^{1/P}]/\lambda.$$

For the exponential model, $p=1$. For the lognormal and loglogistic models, $M = 1/\lambda$. The delta method is then used to estimate the standard error of this function of the parameter estimates. (See Section 4.9.4.) All these distributions are skewed to the right. As such, $E[t]$ is

| TABLE 25.9 | Estimated Duration Models (estimated standard errors in parentheses) | | |
|---|---|---|---|
| | $\lambda$ | $p$ | *Median Duration* |
| Exponential | 0.02344 (0.00298) | 1.00000 (0.00000) | 29.571 (3.522) |
| Weibull | 0.02439 (0.00354) | 0.92083 (0.11086) | 27.543 (3.997) |
| Loglogistic | 0.04153 (0.00707) | 1.33148 (0.17201) | 24.079 (4.102) |
| Lognormal | 0.04514 (0.00806) | 0.77206 (0.08865) | 22.152 (3.954) |

---

[16]Our statistical results are nearly the same as Kiefer's despite the censoring.

greater than the median. For the exponential and Weibull models, $E[t] = [1/\lambda]\Gamma[(1/p) + 1]$; for the normal, $E[t] = (1/\lambda)[\exp(1/p^2)]^{1/2}$. The implied hazard functions are shown in Figure 25.2.

The variable $x$ reported with the strike duration data is a measure of unanticipated aggregate industrial production net of seasonal and trend components. It is computed as the residual in a regression of the log of industrial production in manufacturing on time, time squared, and monthly dummy variables. With the industrial production variable included as a covariate, the estimated Weibull model is

$$-\ln \lambda = 3.7772 - 9.3515\,x, \qquad p = 1.00288,$$
$$\qquad (0.1394) \quad (2.973) \qquad\qquad (0.1217),$$
$$\text{median strike length} = 27.35(3.667) \text{ days}, E[t] = 39.83 \text{ days.}$$

Note that the Weibull model is now almost identical to the exponential model ($p = 1$). Because the hazard conditioned on $x$ is approximately equal to $\lambda_i$, it follows that the hazard function is increasing in "unexpected" industrial production. A 1 percent increase in $x$ leads to a 9.35 percent increase in $\lambda$, which because $p \approx 1$ translates into a 9.35 percent decrease in the median strike length or about 2.6 days. (Note that $M = \ln 2/\lambda$.)

The proportional hazard model does not have a constant term. (The baseline hazard is an individual specific constant.) The estimate of $\beta$ is $-9.0726$, with an estimated standard error of 3.225. This is very similar to the estimate obtained for the Weibull model.

## 25.7 SUMMARY AND CONCLUSIONS

This chapter has surveyed models for events. We analyze these data in two forms. Models for "count data" are appropriate for describing numbers of events, such as hospital visits, arrivals of messages at a network node, and so on. The Poisson model is the central pillar of this area, although its limitations usually motivate researchers to consider alternative specifications. The count data models are essentially nonlinear regressions, but it is more fruitful to do the modeling in terms of the probabilities of events rather than as a model of a conditional mean. We considered basic cases, as well as extensions that accommodate features of data such as censoring, truncation, zero inflation, and unobserved heterogeneity. The second type of event history data that we considered are durations. It is useful to think of duration, or survival data, as the measurement of time between transitions or changes of state. We examined three modeling approaches that correspond to the description in Chapter 14, nonparametric (survival tables), semiparametric (the proportional hazard models), and parametric (various forms such as the Weibull model).

## Key Terms and Concepts

- Accelerated failure time model
- Censored variable
- Censoring
- Conditional moment test
- Count data
- Delta method
- Deviance
- Duration dependence
- Duration model
- Exponential model
- Exposure
- Generalized residual
- Hazard function
- Hazard rate
- Heterogeneity
- Hurdle model
- Integrated hazard function
- Lagrange multiplier test
- Loglinear model
- Marginal effects
- Negative binomial model
- Negative duration dependence
- Negbin 1 form
- Negbin 2 form
- Negbin $P$ model
- Nonnested models
- Overdispersion
- Parametric model
- Partial likelihood
- Poisson regression model

| | | |
|---|---|---|
| • Positive duration dependence | • Risk set | • Time-varying covariate |
| • Product limit estimator | • Semiparametric model | • Weibull survival model |
| • Proportional hazard | • Specification error | • Zero inflated Poisson model |
| | • Survival function | |

## Exercises

1.  For the zero-inflated Poisson (ZIP) model in Section 25.4, we derived the conditional mean function,

$$E[y_i \mid \mathbf{x}_i, \mathbf{w}_i] = \frac{F(\mathbf{w}_i'\boldsymbol{\gamma})\lambda_i}{1 - \exp(-\lambda_i)}, \quad \lambda_i = \exp(\mathbf{x}_i'\boldsymbol{\beta}).$$

a. For the same model, now obtain $Var[y_i \mid \mathbf{x}_i, \mathbf{w}_i]$. Then, obtain

$$\tau_i = \frac{Var[y_i \mid \mathbf{x}_i, \mathbf{w}_i]}{E[y_i \mid \mathbf{x}_i, \mathbf{w}_i]}.$$

Does the zero inflation produce overdispersion? (That is, is the ratio greater than one?)

b. Obtain the partial effect for a variable $z_i$ that appears in both $\mathbf{w}_i$ and $\mathbf{x}_i$.

2.  Consider estimation of a Poisson regression model for $y_i \mid x_i$. The data are truncated on the left—these are on-site observations at a recreation site, so zeros do not appear in the data set. The data are censored on the right—any response greater than 5 is recorded as a 5. Construct the log-likelihood for a data set drawn under this sampling scheme.

3.  The density for the Weibull survival model is $f(t) = \lambda p(\lambda t)^{p-1}\exp(-(\lambda t)^p)$. The survival function is $S(t) = \exp[-(\lambda t)^p]$. Obtain the hazard function. What is the median survival time (as a function of $\lambda$ and $p$)? Does this model exhibit duration dependence? If so, is it positive or negative?

## Applications

1.  Several applications in the preceding chapters using the German health care data have examined the variable DocVis, the reported number of visits to the doctor. The data are described in Appendix Table F11.1. A second count variable in that data set that we have not examined is HospVis, the number of visits to hospital. For this application, we will examine this variable. To begin, we treat the full sample (27,326) observations as a cross section.

a. Begin by fitting a Poisson regression model to this variable. The exogenous variables are listed in Example 11.11 and in the Appendix Table F11.1. Determine an appropriate specification for the right-hand side of your model. Report the regression results and the partial effects.

b. Estimate the model using ordinary least squares and compare your least squares results to the partial effects you computed in part a. What do you find?

c. Is there evidence of overdispersion in the data? Test for overdispersion. Now, reestimate the model using a negative binomial specification. What is the result? Do your results change? Use a likelihood ratio test to test the hypothesis of the negative binomial model against the Poisson.

2. The data are an unbalanced panel, with 7,293 groups. Continue your analysis in Application 1 by fitting the Poisson model with fixed and with random effects and compare your results. (Recall, like the linear model, the Poisson fixed effects model may not contain any time invariant variables.) How do the panel data results compare to the pooled results?

3. Appendix Table F25.4 contains data on ship accidents reported in McCullagh and Nelder (1983). The data set contains 40 observations on the number of incidents of wave damage for oceangoing ships. Regressors include "aggregate months of service," and three sets of dummy variables, Type (1, ..., 5), operation period (1960–1974 or 1975–1979), and construction period (1960–1964, 1965–1969, or 1970–1974). There are six missing values on the dependent variable, leaving 34 usable observations.

   a. Fit a Poisson model for these data, using the log of service months, four type dummy variables, two construction period variables, and one operation period dummy variable. Report your results.

   b. The authors note that the rate of accidents is supposed to be per period, but the exposure (aggregate months) differs by ship. Reestimate your model constraining the coefficient on log of service months to equal one.

   c. The authors take overdispersion as a given in these data. Do you find evidence of overdispersion? Show your results.

4. Data on $t$ = strike duration and $x$ = unanticipated industrial production for a number of strikes in each of 9 years are given in Appendix Table F25.3. Use the Poisson regression model discussed in this chapter to determine whether $x$ is a significant determinant of the *number of strikes* in a given year.

# MATRIX ALGEBRA

## A.1  TERMINOLOGY

A **matrix** is a rectangular array of numbers, denoted

$$
\mathbf{A} = [a_{ik}] = [\mathbf{A}]_{ik} =
\begin{bmatrix}
a_{11} & a_{12} & \cdots & a_{1K} \\
a_{21} & a_{22} & \cdots & a_{2K} \\
 & & \cdots & \\
a_{n1} & a_{n2} & \cdots & a_{nK}
\end{bmatrix}.
\tag{A-1}
$$

The typical element is used to denote the matrix. A subscripted element of a matrix is always read as $a_{\text{row,column}}$. An example is given in Table A.1. In these data, the rows are identified with years and the columns with particular variables.

A **vector** is an ordered set of numbers arranged either in a row or a column. In view of the preceding, a **row vector** is also a matrix with one row, whereas a **column vector** is a matrix with one column. Thus, in Table A.1, the five variables observed for 1972 (including the date) constitute a row vector, whereas the time series of nine values for consumption is a column vector.

A matrix can also be viewed as a set of column vectors or as a set of row vectors.[1] The **dimensions** of a matrix are the numbers of rows and columns it contains. "$\mathbf{A}$ is an $n \times K$ matrix" (read "$n$ by $K$") will always mean that $\mathbf{A}$ has $n$ rows and $K$ columns. If $n$ equals $K$, then $\mathbf{A}$ is a **square matrix.** Several particular types of square matrices occur frequently in econometrics.

- A **symmetric matrix** is one in which $a_{ik} = a_{ki}$ for all $i$ and $k$.
- A **diagonal matrix** is a square matrix whose only nonzero elements appear on the **main diagonal,** that is, moving from upper left to lower right.
- A **scalar matrix** is a diagonal matrix with the same value in all diagonal elements.
- An **identity matrix** is a scalar matrix with ones on the diagonal. This matrix is always denoted $\mathbf{I}$. A subscript is sometimes included to indicate its size, or **order.** For example, $\mathbf{I}_4$ indicates a $4 \times 4$ identity matrix.
- A **triangular matrix** is one that has only zeros either above or below the main diagonal. If the zeros are above the diagonal, the matrix is **lower triangular.**

## A.2  ALGEBRAIC MANIPULATION OF MATRICES

### A.2.1  EQUALITY OF MATRICES

Matrices (or vectors) $\mathbf{A}$ and $\mathbf{B}$ are equal if and only if they have the same dimensions and each element of $\mathbf{A}$ equals the corresponding element of $\mathbf{B}$. That is,

$$
\mathbf{A} = \mathbf{B} \quad \text{if and only if } a_{ik} = b_{ik} \quad \text{for all } i \text{ and } k.
\tag{A-2}
$$

---

[1] Henceforth, we shall denote a matrix by a boldfaced capital letter, as is $\mathbf{A}$ in (A-1), and a vector as a boldfaced lowercase letter, as in $\mathbf{a}$. Unless otherwise noted, a vector will always be assumed to be a *column vector*.

**TABLE A.1**   Matrix of Macroeconomic Data

| | | | Column | | |
|---|---|---|---|---|---|
| | | **2** | **3** | | **5** |
| | **1** | **Consumption** | **GNP** | **4** | **Discount Rate** |
| **Row** | **Year** | **(billions of dollars)** | **(billions of dollars)** | **GNP Deflator** | **(N.Y Fed., avg.)** |
| 1 | 1972 | 737.1 | 1185.9 | 1.0000 | 4.50 |
| 2 | 1973 | 812.0 | 1326.4 | 1.0575 | 6.44 |
| 3 | 1974 | 808.1 | 1434.2 | 1.1508 | 7.83 |
| 4 | 1975 | 976.4 | 1549.2 | 1.2579 | 6.25 |
| 5 | 1976 | 1084.3 | 1718.0 | 1.3234 | 5.50 |
| 6 | 1977 | 1204.4 | 1918.3 | 1.4005 | 5.46 |
| 7 | 1978 | 1346.5 | 2163.9 | 1.5042 | 7.46 |
| 8 | 1979 | 1507.2 | 2417.8 | 1.6342 | 10.28 |
| 9 | 1980 | 1667.2 | 2633.1 | 1.7864 | 11.77 |

*Source:* Data from the *Economic Report of the President* (Washington, D.C.: U.S. Government Printing Office, 1983).

## A.2.2   TRANSPOSITION

The **transpose** of a matrix $\mathbf{A}$, denoted $\mathbf{A}'$, is obtained by creating the matrix whose $k$th row is the $k$th column of the original matrix. Thus, if $\mathbf{B} = \mathbf{A}'$, then each column of $\mathbf{A}$ will appear as the corresponding row of $\mathbf{B}$. If $\mathbf{A}$ is $n \times K$, then $\mathbf{A}'$ is $K \times n$.

An equivalent definition of the transpose of a matrix is

$$\mathbf{B} = \mathbf{A}' \Leftrightarrow b_{ik} = a_{ki} \quad \text{for all } i \text{ and } k. \tag{A-3}$$

The definition of a symmetric matrix implies that

$$\text{if (and only if) } \mathbf{A} \text{ is symmetric, then } \mathbf{A} = \mathbf{A}'. \tag{A-4}$$

It also follows from the definition that for any $\mathbf{A}$,

$$(\mathbf{A}')' = \mathbf{A}. \tag{A-5}$$

Finally, the transpose of a column vector, $\mathbf{a}$, is a row vector:

$$\mathbf{a}' = [a_1 \quad a_2 \quad \cdots \quad a_n].$$

## A.2.3   MATRIX ADDITION

The operations of addition and subtraction are extended to matrices by defining

$$\mathbf{C} = \mathbf{A} + \mathbf{B} = [a_{ik} + b_{ik}]. \tag{A-6}$$

$$\mathbf{A} - \mathbf{B} = [a_{ik} - b_{ik}]. \tag{A-7}$$

Matrices cannot be added unless they have the same dimensions, in which case they are said to be **conformable for addition.** A **zero matrix** or **null matrix** is one whose elements are all zero. In the addition of matrices, the zero matrix plays the same role as the scalar 0 in scalar addition; that is,

$$\mathbf{A} + \mathbf{0} = \mathbf{A}. \tag{A-8}$$

It follows from (A-6) that matrix addition is commutative,

$$\mathbf{A} + \mathbf{B} = \mathbf{B} + \mathbf{A}. \tag{A-9}$$

and associative,

$$(\mathbf{A} + \mathbf{B}) + \mathbf{C} = \mathbf{A} + (\mathbf{B} + \mathbf{C}), \tag{A-10}$$

and that

$$(\mathbf{A} + \mathbf{B})' = \mathbf{A}' + \mathbf{B}'. \tag{A-11}$$

### A.2.4 VECTOR MULTIPLICATION

Matrices are multiplied by using the **inner product.** The inner product, or **dot product,** of two vectors, **a** and **b**, is a scalar and is written

$$\mathbf{a}'\mathbf{b} = a_1 b_1 + a_2 b_2 + \cdots + a_n b_n. \tag{A-12}$$

Note that the inner product is written as the transpose of vector **a** times vector **b**, a row vector times a column vector. In (A-12), each term $a_j b_j$ equals $b_j a_j$; hence

$$\mathbf{a}'\mathbf{b} = \mathbf{b}'\mathbf{a}. \tag{A-13}$$

### A.2.5 A NOTATION FOR ROWS AND COLUMNS OF A MATRIX

We need a notation for the $i$th row of a matrix. Throughout this book, an untransposed vector will always be a column vector. However, we will often require a notation for the column vector that is the transpose of a row of a matrix. This has the potential to create some ambiguity, but the following convention based on the subscripts will suffice for our work throughout this text:

- $\mathbf{a}_k$, or $\mathbf{a}_l$ or $\mathbf{a}_m$ will denote column $k, l$, or $m$ of the matrix **A**,
- $\mathbf{a}_i$, or $\mathbf{a}_j$ or $\mathbf{a}_t$ or $\mathbf{a}_s$ will denote the column vector formed by the transpose of row $i, j, t$, or $s$ of matrix **A**. Thus, $\mathbf{a}_i'$ is row $i$ of **A**. **(A-14)**

For example, from the data in Table A.1 it might be convenient to speak of $\mathbf{x}_i$, where $i = 1972$ as the $5 \times 1$ vector containing the five variables measured for the year 1972, that is, the transpose of the 1972 row of the matrix. In our applications, the common association of subscripts "$i$" and "$j$" with individual $i$ or $j$, and "$t$" and "$s$" with time periods $t$ and $s$ will be natural.

### A.2.6 MATRIX MULTIPLICATION AND SCALAR MULTIPLICATION

For an $n \times K$ matrix **A** and a $K \times M$ matrix **B**, the product matrix, $\mathbf{C} = \mathbf{AB}$, is an $n \times M$ matrix whose $ik$th element is the inner product of row $i$ of **A** and column $k$ of **B**. Thus, the product matrix **C** is

$$\mathbf{C} = \mathbf{AB} \Rightarrow c_{ik} = \mathbf{a}_i' \mathbf{b}_k. \tag{A-15}$$

[Note our use of (A-14) in (A-15).] To multiply two matrices, the number of columns in the first must be the same as the number of rows in the second, in which case they are **conformable for multiplication.**[2] Multiplication of matrices is generally not commutative. In some cases, **AB** may exist, but **BA** may be undefined or, if it does exist, may have different dimensions. In general, however, even if **AB** and **BA** do have the same dimensions, they will not be equal. In view of this, we define **premultiplication** and **postmultiplication** of matrices. In the product **AB**, **B** is *premultiplied* by **A**, whereas **A** is *postmultiplied* by **B**.

---

[2] A simple way to check the conformability of two matrices for multiplication is to write down the dimensions of the operation, for example, $(n \times K)$ times $(K \times M)$. The inner dimensions must be equal; the result has dimensions equal to the outer values.

**Scalar multiplication** of a matrix is the operation of multiplying every element of the matrix by a given scalar. For scalar $c$ and matrix $\mathbf{A}$,

$$c\mathbf{A} = [ca_{ik}]. \qquad \text{(A-16)}$$

The product of a matrix and a vector is written

$$\mathbf{c} = \mathbf{Ab}.$$

The number of elements in $\mathbf{b}$ must equal the number of columns in $\mathbf{A}$; the result is a vector with number of elements equal to the number of rows in $\mathbf{A}$. For example,

$$\begin{bmatrix} 5 \\ 4 \\ 1 \end{bmatrix} = \begin{bmatrix} 4 & 2 & 1 \\ 2 & 6 & 1 \\ 1 & 1 & 0 \end{bmatrix} \begin{bmatrix} a \\ b \\ c \end{bmatrix}.$$

We can interpret this in two ways. First, it is a compact way of writing the three equations

$$5 = 4a + 2b + 1c,$$
$$4 = 2a + 6b + 1c,$$
$$1 = 1a + 1b + 0c.$$

Second, by writing the set of equations as

$$\begin{bmatrix} 5 \\ 4 \\ 1 \end{bmatrix} = a \begin{bmatrix} 4 \\ 2 \\ 1 \end{bmatrix} + b \begin{bmatrix} 2 \\ 6 \\ 1 \end{bmatrix} + c \begin{bmatrix} 1 \\ 1 \\ 0 \end{bmatrix},$$

we see that the right-hand side is a **linear combination** of the columns of the matrix where the coefficients are the elements of the vector. For the general case,

$$\mathbf{c} = \mathbf{Ab} = b_1\mathbf{a}_1 + b_2\mathbf{a}_2 + \cdots + b_K\mathbf{a}_K. \qquad \text{(A-17)}$$

In the calculation of a matrix product $\mathbf{C} = \mathbf{AB}$, each column of $\mathbf{C}$ is a linear combination of the columns of $\mathbf{A}$, where the coefficients are the elements in the corresponding column of $\mathbf{B}$. That is,

$$\mathbf{C} = \mathbf{AB} \Leftrightarrow \mathbf{c}_k = \mathbf{Ab}_k. \qquad \text{(A-18)}$$

Let $\mathbf{e}_k$ be a column vector that has zeros everywhere except for a one in the $k$th position. Then $\mathbf{Ae}_k$ is a linear combination of the columns of $\mathbf{A}$ in which the coefficient on every column but the $k$th is zero, whereas that on the $k$th is one. The result is

$$\mathbf{a}_k = \mathbf{Ae}_k. \qquad \text{(A-19)}$$

Combining this result with (A-17) produces

$$(\mathbf{a}_1 \quad \mathbf{a}_2 \quad \cdots \quad \mathbf{a}_n) = \mathbf{A}(\mathbf{e}_1 \quad \mathbf{e}_2 \quad \cdots \quad \mathbf{e}_n) = \mathbf{AI} = \mathbf{A}. \qquad \text{(A-20)}$$

In matrix multiplication, the identity matrix is analogous to the scalar 1. For any matrix or vector $\mathbf{A}$, $\mathbf{AI} = \mathbf{A}$. In addition, $\mathbf{IA} = \mathbf{A}$, although if $\mathbf{A}$ is not a square matrix, the two identity matrices are of different orders.

A conformable matrix of zeros produces the expected result: $\mathbf{A0} = \mathbf{0}$.

Some general rules for matrix multiplication are as follows:

- **Associative law:** $(\mathbf{AB})\mathbf{C} = \mathbf{A}(\mathbf{BC})$. $\qquad \text{(A-21)}$
- **Distributive law:** $\mathbf{A}(\mathbf{B} + \mathbf{C}) = \mathbf{AB} + \mathbf{AC}$. $\qquad \text{(A-22)}$

- **Transpose of a product:** $(\mathbf{AB})' = \mathbf{B}'\mathbf{A}'$. (A-23)
- **Transpose of an extended product:** $(\mathbf{ABC})' = \mathbf{C}'\mathbf{B}'\mathbf{A}'$. (A-24)

## A.2.7   SUMS OF VALUES

Denote by $\mathbf{i}$ a vector that contains a column of ones. Then,

$$\sum_{i=1}^{n} x_i = x_1 + x_2 + \cdots + x_n = \mathbf{i}'\mathbf{x}. \tag{A-25}$$

If all elements in $\mathbf{x}$ are equal to the same constant $a$, then $\mathbf{x} = a\mathbf{i}$ and

$$\sum_{i=1}^{n} x_i = \mathbf{i}'(a\mathbf{i}) = a(\mathbf{i}'\mathbf{i}) = na. \tag{A-26}$$

For any constant $a$ and vector $\mathbf{x}$,

$$\sum_{i=1}^{n} ax_i = a \sum_{i=1}^{n} x_i = a\mathbf{i}'\mathbf{x}. \tag{A-27}$$

If $a = 1/n$, then we obtain the arithmetic mean,

$$\bar{x} = \frac{1}{n} \sum_{i=1}^{n} x_i = \frac{1}{n}\mathbf{i}'\mathbf{x}, \tag{A-28}$$

from which it follows that

$$\sum_{i=1}^{n} x_i = \mathbf{i}'\mathbf{x} = n\bar{x}.$$

The sum of squares of the elements in a vector $\mathbf{x}$ is

$$\sum_{i=1}^{n} x_i^2 = \mathbf{x}'\mathbf{x}; \tag{A-29}$$

while the sum of the products of the $n$ elements in vectors $\mathbf{x}$ and $\mathbf{y}$ is

$$\sum_{i=1}^{n} x_i y_i = \mathbf{x}'\mathbf{y}. \tag{A-30}$$

By the definition of matrix multiplication,

$$[\mathbf{X}'\mathbf{X}]_{kl} = [\mathbf{x}'_k \mathbf{x}_l] \tag{A-31}$$

is the inner product of the $k$th and $l$th columns of $\mathbf{X}$. For example, for the data set given in Table A.1, if we define $\mathbf{X}$ as the $9 \times 3$ matrix containing (year, consumption, GNP), then

$$[\mathbf{X}'\mathbf{X}]_{23} = \sum_{t=1972}^{1980} \text{consumption}_t \text{GNP}_t = 737.1(1185.9) + \cdots + 1667.2(2633.1)$$
$$= 19{,}743{,}711.34.$$

If $\mathbf{X}$ is $n \times K$, then [again using (A-14)]

$$\mathbf{X}'\mathbf{X} = \sum_{i=1}^{n} \mathbf{x}_i \mathbf{x}'_i.$$

This form shows that the $K \times K$ matrix $\mathbf{X}'\mathbf{X}$ is the sum of $n$ $K \times K$ matrices, each formed from a single row (year) of $\mathbf{X}$. For the example given earlier, this sum is of nine $3 \times 3$ matrices, each formed from one row (year) of the original data matrix.

### A.2.8   A USEFUL IDEMPOTENT MATRIX

A fundamental matrix in statistics is the one that is used to transform data to deviations from their mean. First,

$$\mathbf{i}\bar{x} = \mathbf{i}\frac{1}{n}\mathbf{i}'\mathbf{x} = \begin{bmatrix} \bar{x} \\ \bar{x} \\ \vdots \\ \bar{x} \end{bmatrix} = \frac{1}{n}\mathbf{i}\mathbf{i}'\mathbf{x}. \tag{A-32}$$

The matrix $(1/n)\mathbf{i}\mathbf{i}'$ is an $n \times n$ matrix with every element equal to $1/n$. The set of values in deviations form is

$$\begin{bmatrix} x_1 - \bar{x} \\ x_2 - \bar{x} \\ \cdots \\ x_n - \bar{x} \end{bmatrix} = [\mathbf{x} - \mathbf{i}\bar{x}] = \left[\mathbf{x} - \frac{1}{n}\mathbf{i}\mathbf{i}'\mathbf{x}\right]. \tag{A-33}$$

Because $\mathbf{x} = \mathbf{I}\mathbf{x}$,

$$\left[\mathbf{x} - \frac{1}{n}\mathbf{i}\mathbf{i}'\mathbf{x}\right] = \left[\mathbf{I}\mathbf{x} - \frac{1}{n}\mathbf{i}\mathbf{i}'\mathbf{x}\right] = \left[\mathbf{I} - \frac{1}{n}\mathbf{i}\mathbf{i}'\right]\mathbf{x} = \mathbf{M}^0\mathbf{x}. \tag{A-34}$$

Henceforth, the symbol $\mathbf{M}^0$ will be used only for this matrix. Its diagonal elements are all $(1 - 1/n)$, and its off-diagonal elements are $-1/n$. The matrix $\mathbf{M}^0$ is primarily useful in computing sums of squared deviations. Some computations are simplified by the result

$$\mathbf{M}^0\mathbf{i} = \left[\mathbf{I} - \frac{1}{n}\mathbf{i}\mathbf{i}'\right]\mathbf{i} = \mathbf{i} - \frac{1}{n}\mathbf{i}(\mathbf{i}'\mathbf{i}) = \mathbf{0},$$

which implies that $\mathbf{i}'\mathbf{M}^0 = \mathbf{0}'$. The sum of deviations about the mean is then

$$\sum_{i=1}^{n}(x_i - \bar{x}) = \mathbf{i}'[\mathbf{M}^0\mathbf{x}] = \mathbf{0}'\mathbf{x} = 0. \tag{A-35}$$

For a single variable $\mathbf{x}$, the sum of squared deviations about the mean is

$$\sum_{i=1}^{n}(x_i - \bar{x})^2 = \left(\sum_{i=1}^{n}x_i^2\right) - n\bar{x}^2. \tag{A-36}$$

In matrix terms,

$$\sum_{i=1}^{n}(x_i - \bar{x})^2 = (\mathbf{x} - \bar{x}\mathbf{i})'(\mathbf{x} - \bar{x}\mathbf{i}) = (\mathbf{M}^0\mathbf{x})'(\mathbf{M}^0\mathbf{x}) = \mathbf{x}'\mathbf{M}^{0'}\mathbf{M}^0\mathbf{x}.$$

Two properties of $\mathbf{M}^0$ are useful at this point. First, because all off-diagonal elements of $\mathbf{M}^0$ equal $-1/n$, $\mathbf{M}^0$ is symmetric. Second, as can easily be verified by multiplication, $\mathbf{M}^0$ is equal to its square; $\mathbf{M}^0\mathbf{M}^0 = \mathbf{M}^0$.

---

**DEFINITION A.1** Idempotent Matrix

*An **idempotent** matrix, $\mathbf{M}$, is one that is equal to its square, that is, $\mathbf{M}^2 = \mathbf{MM} = \mathbf{M}$. If $\mathbf{M}$ is a symmetric idempotent matrix (all of the idempotent matrices we shall encounter are symmetric), then $\mathbf{M'M} = \mathbf{M}$.*

---

Thus, $\mathbf{M}^0$ is a symmetric idempotent matrix. Combining results, we obtain

$$\sum_{i=1}^{n} (x_i - \overline{x})^2 = \mathbf{x}'\mathbf{M}^0\mathbf{x}. \tag{A-37}$$

Consider constructing a matrix of sums of squares and cross products in deviations from the column means. For two vectors $\mathbf{x}$ and $\mathbf{y}$,

$$\sum_{i=1}^{n} (x_i - \overline{x})(y_i - \overline{y}) = (\mathbf{M}^0\mathbf{x})'(\mathbf{M}^0\mathbf{y}), \tag{A-38}$$

so

$$\begin{bmatrix} \sum_{i=1}^{n} (x_i - \overline{x})^2 & \sum_{i=1}^{n} (x_i - \overline{x})(y_i - \overline{y}) \\ \sum_{i=1}^{n} (y_i - \overline{y})(x_i - \overline{x}) & \sum_{i=1}^{n} (y_i - \overline{y})^2 \end{bmatrix} = \begin{bmatrix} \mathbf{x}'\mathbf{M}^0\mathbf{x} & \mathbf{x}'\mathbf{M}^0\mathbf{y} \\ \mathbf{y}'\mathbf{M}^0\mathbf{x} & \mathbf{y}'\mathbf{M}^0\mathbf{y} \end{bmatrix}. \tag{A-39}$$

If we put the two column vectors $\mathbf{x}$ and $\mathbf{y}$ in an $n \times 2$ matrix $\mathbf{Z} = [\mathbf{x}, \mathbf{y}]$, then $\mathbf{M}^0\mathbf{Z}$ is the $n \times 2$ matrix in which the two columns of data are in mean deviation form. Then

$$(\mathbf{M}^0\mathbf{Z})'(\mathbf{M}^0\mathbf{Z}) = \mathbf{Z}'\mathbf{M}^0\mathbf{M}^0\mathbf{Z} = \mathbf{Z}'\mathbf{M}^0\mathbf{Z}.$$

## A.3 GEOMETRY OF MATRICES

### A.3.1 VECTOR SPACES

The $K$ elements of a column vector

$$\mathbf{a} = \begin{bmatrix} a_1 \\ a_2 \\ \cdots \\ a_K \end{bmatrix}$$

can be viewed as the coordinates of a point in a $K$-dimensional space, as shown in Figure A.1 for two dimensions, or as the definition of the line segment connecting the origin and the point defined by $\mathbf{a}$.

Two basic arithmetic operations are defined for vectors, **scalar multiplication** and **addition**. A scalar multiple of a vector, $\mathbf{a}$, is another vector, say $\mathbf{a}^*$, whose coordinates are the scalar multiple of $\mathbf{a}$'s coordinates. Thus, in Figure A.1,

$$\mathbf{a} = \begin{bmatrix} 1 \\ 2 \end{bmatrix}, \quad \mathbf{a}^* = 2\mathbf{a} = \begin{bmatrix} 2 \\ 4 \end{bmatrix}, \quad \mathbf{a}^{**} = -\frac{1}{2}\mathbf{a} = \begin{bmatrix} -\frac{1}{2} \\ -1 \end{bmatrix}.$$

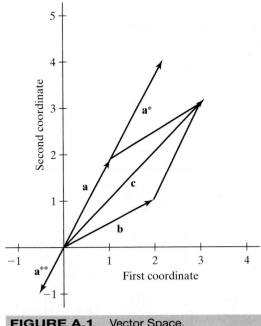

**FIGURE A.1**   Vector Space.

The set of all possible scalar multiples of **a** is the line through the origin, **0** and **a**. Any scalar multiple of **a** is a segment of this line. The sum of two vectors **a** and **b** is a third vector whose coordinates are the sums of the corresponding coordinates of **a** and **b**. For example,

$$\mathbf{c} = \mathbf{a} + \mathbf{b} = \begin{bmatrix} 1 \\ 2 \end{bmatrix} + \begin{bmatrix} 2 \\ 1 \end{bmatrix} = \begin{bmatrix} 3 \\ 3 \end{bmatrix}.$$

Geometrically, **c** is obtained by moving in the distance and direction defined by **b** from the tip of **a** or, because addition is commutative, from the tip of **b** in the distance and direction of **a**.

The two-dimensional plane is the set of all vectors with two real-valued coordinates. We label this set $\mathbb{R}^2$ ("R two," not "R squared"). It has two important properties.

- $\mathbb{R}^2$ *is closed under scalar multiplication;* every scalar multiple of a vector in $\mathbb{R}^2$ is also in $\mathbb{R}^2$.
- $\mathbb{R}^2$ *is closed under addition;* the sum of any two vectors in the plane is always a vector in $\mathbb{R}^2$.

---

**DEFINITION A.2**   **Vector Space**
*A **vector space** is any set of vectors that is closed under scalar multiplication and addition.*

---

Another example is the set of all real numbers, that is, $\mathbb{R}^1$, that is, the set of vectors with one real element. In general, that set of $K$-element vectors all of whose elements are real numbers is a $K$-dimensional vector space, denoted $\mathbb{R}^K$. The preceding examples are drawn in $\mathbb{R}^2$.

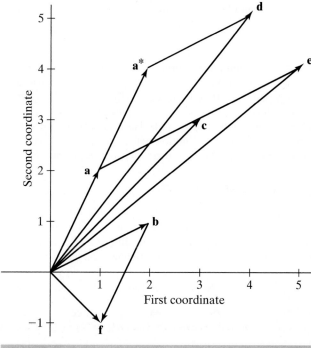

**FIGURE A.2** Linear Combinations of Vectors.

## A.3.2 LINEAR COMBINATIONS OF VECTORS AND BASIS VECTORS

In Figure A.2, $\mathbf{c} = \mathbf{a} + \mathbf{b}$ and $\mathbf{d} = \mathbf{a}^* + \mathbf{b}$. But since $\mathbf{a}^* = 2\mathbf{a}$, $\mathbf{d} = 2\mathbf{a} + \mathbf{b}$. Also, $\mathbf{e} = \mathbf{a} + 2\mathbf{b}$ and $\mathbf{f} = \mathbf{b} + (-\mathbf{a}) = \mathbf{b} - \mathbf{a}$. As this exercise suggests, any vector in $\mathbb{R}^2$ could be obtained as a **linear combination** of $\mathbf{a}$ and $\mathbf{b}$.

---

### DEFINITION A.3  Basis Vectors
*A set of vectors in a vector space is a **basis** for that vector space if any vector in the vector space can be written as a linear combination of that set of vectors.*

---

As is suggested by Figure A.2, any pair of two-element vectors, including $\mathbf{a}$ and $\mathbf{b}$, that point in different directions will form a basis for $\mathbb{R}^2$. Consider an arbitrary set of vectors in $\mathbb{R}^2$, $\mathbf{a}$, $\mathbf{b}$, and $\mathbf{c}$. If $\mathbf{a}$ and $\mathbf{b}$ are a basis, then we can find numbers $\alpha_1$ and $\alpha_2$ such that $\mathbf{c} = \alpha_1 \mathbf{a} + \alpha_2 \mathbf{b}$. Let

$$\mathbf{a} = \begin{bmatrix} a_1 \\ a_2 \end{bmatrix}, \quad \mathbf{b} = \begin{bmatrix} b_1 \\ b_2 \end{bmatrix}, \quad \mathbf{c} = \begin{bmatrix} c_1 \\ c_2 \end{bmatrix}.$$

Then

$$c_1 = \alpha_1 a_1 + \alpha_2 b_1,$$

$$c_2 = \alpha_1 a_2 + \alpha_2 b_2.$$

**(A-40)**

The solutions to this pair of equations are

$$\alpha_1 = \frac{b_2 c_1 - b_1 c_2}{a_1 b_2 - b_1 a_2}, \quad \alpha_2 = \frac{a_1 c_2 - a_2 c_1}{a_1 b_2 - b_1 a_2}. \tag{A-41}$$

This result gives a unique solution unless $(a_1 b_2 - b_1 a_2) = 0$. If $(a_1 b_2 - b_1 a_2) = 0$, then $a_1/a_2 = b_1/b_2$, which means that $\mathbf{b}$ is just a multiple of $\mathbf{a}$. This returns us to our original condition, that $\mathbf{a}$ and $\mathbf{b}$ must point in different directions. The implication is that if $\mathbf{a}$ and $\mathbf{b}$ are any pair of vectors for which the denominator in (A-41) is not zero, then any other vector $\mathbf{c}$ can be formed as a *unique* linear combination of $\mathbf{a}$ and $\mathbf{b}$. The basis of a vector space is not unique, since any set of vectors that satisfies the definition will do. But for any particular basis, only one linear combination of them will produce another particular vector in the vector space.

### A.3.3 LINEAR DEPENDENCE

As the preceding should suggest, $K$ vectors are required to form a basis for $\mathbb{R}^K$. Although the basis for a vector space is not unique, not every set of $K$ vectors will suffice. In Figure A.2, $\mathbf{a}$ and $\mathbf{b}$ form a basis for $\mathbb{R}^2$, but $\mathbf{a}$ and $\mathbf{a}^*$ do not. The difference between these two pairs is that $\mathbf{a}$ and $\mathbf{b}$ are linearly *independent*, whereas $\mathbf{a}$ and $\mathbf{a}^*$ are linearly *dependent*.

---

**DEFINITION A.4** **Linear Dependence**
*A set of vectors is **linearly dependent** if any one of the vectors in the set can be written as a linear combination of the others.*

---

Because $\mathbf{a}^*$ is a multiple of $\mathbf{a}$, $\mathbf{a}$ and $\mathbf{a}^*$ are linearly dependent. For another example, if

$$\mathbf{a} = \begin{bmatrix} 1 \\ 2 \end{bmatrix}, \quad \mathbf{b} = \begin{bmatrix} 3 \\ 3 \end{bmatrix}, \quad \text{and} \quad \mathbf{c} = \begin{bmatrix} 10 \\ 14 \end{bmatrix},$$

then

$$2\mathbf{a} + \mathbf{b} - \frac{1}{2}\mathbf{c} = \mathbf{0},$$

so $\mathbf{a}, \mathbf{b},$ and $\mathbf{c}$ are linearly dependent. Any of the three possible pairs of them, however, are linearly independent.

---

**DEFINITION A.5** **Linear Independence**
*A set of vectors is **linearly independent** if and only if the only solution to*

$$\alpha_1 \mathbf{a}_1 + \alpha_2 \mathbf{a}_2 + \cdots + \alpha_K \mathbf{a}_K = \mathbf{0}$$

*is*

$$\alpha_1 = \alpha_2 = \cdots = \alpha_K = 0.$$

---

The preceding implies the following equivalent definition of a basis.

> ## DEFINITION A.6    Basis for a Vector Space
> *A basis for a vector space of K dimensions is any set of K linearly independent vectors in that vector space.*

Because any $(K + 1)$st vector can be written as a linear combination of the $K$ basis vectors, it follows that any set of more than $K$ vectors in $\mathbb{R}^K$ must be linearly dependent.

## A.3.4    SUBSPACES

> ## DEFINITION A.7    Spanning Vectors
> *The set of all linear combinations of a set of vectors is the vector space that is **spanned** by those vectors.*

For example, by definition, the space spanned by a basis for $\mathbb{R}^K$ is $\mathbb{R}^K$. An implication of this is that if **a** and **b** are a basis for $\mathbb{R}^2$ and **c** is another vector in $\mathbb{R}^2$, the space spanned by [**a**, **b**, **c**] is, again, $\mathbb{R}^2$. Of course, **c** is superfluous. Nonetheless, any vector in $\mathbb{R}^2$ *can* be expressed as a linear combination of **a**, **b**, and **c**. (The linear combination will not be unique. Suppose, for example, that **a** and **c** are also a basis for $\mathbb{R}^2$.)

Consider the set of three coordinate vectors whose third element is zero. In particular,

$$\mathbf{a}' = [a_1 \quad a_2 \quad 0] \quad \text{and} \quad \mathbf{b}' = [b_1 \quad b_2 \quad 0].$$

Vectors **a** and **b** do not span the three-dimensional space $\mathbb{R}^3$. Every linear combination of **a** and **b** has a third coordinate equal to zero; thus, for instance, $\mathbf{c}' = [1 \ 2 \ 3]$ could not be written as a linear combination of **a** and **b**. If $(a_1 b_2 - a_2 b_1)$ is not equal to zero [see (A-41)], however, then *any vector whose third element is zero can be expressed as a linear combination of **a** and **b**.* So, although **a** and **b** do not span $\mathbb{R}^3$, they do span something, the set of vectors in $\mathbb{R}^3$ whose third element is zero. This area is a plane (the "floor" of the box in a three-dimensional figure). This plane in $\mathbb{R}^3$ is a **subspace,** in this instance, a two-dimensional subspace. Note that *it is not* $\mathbb{R}^2$; it is the set of vectors in $\mathbb{R}^3$ whose third coordinate is 0. Any plane in $\mathbb{R}^3$, regardless of how it is oriented, forms a two-dimensional subspace. Any two independent vectors that lie in that subspace will span it. But without a third vector that points in some other direction, we cannot span any more of $\mathbb{R}^3$ than this two-dimensional part of it. By the same logic, any line in $\mathbb{R}^3$ is a one-dimensional subspace, in this case, the set of all vectors in $\mathbb{R}^3$ whose coordinates are multiples of those of the vector that define the line. A subspace is a vector space in all the respects in which we have defined it. We emphasize that it is *not* a vector space of lower dimension. For example, $\mathbb{R}^2$ is not a subspace of $\mathbb{R}^3$. The essential difference is the number of dimensions in the vectors. The vectors in $\mathbb{R}^3$ that form a two-dimensional subspace are still three-element vectors; they all just happen to lie in the same plane.

The space spanned by a set of vectors in $\mathbb{R}^K$ has at most $K$ dimensions. If this space has fewer than $K$ dimensions, it is a subspace, or **hyperplane.** But the important point in the preceding discussion is that *every set of vectors spans some space;* it may be the entire space in which the vectors reside, or it may be some subspace of it.

### A.3.5 RANK OF A MATRIX

We view a matrix as a set of column vectors. The number of columns in the matrix equals the number of vectors in the set, and the number of rows equals the number of coordinates in each column vector.

---

**DEFINITION A.8** Column Space

*The* **column space** *of a matrix is the vector space that is spanned by its column vectors.*

---

If the matrix contains $K$ rows, its column space might have $K$ dimensions. But, as we have seen, it might have fewer dimensions; the column vectors might be linearly dependent, or there might be fewer than $K$ of them. Consider the matrix

$$\mathbf{A} = \begin{bmatrix} 1 & 5 & 6 \\ 2 & 6 & 8 \\ 7 & 1 & 8 \end{bmatrix}.$$

It contains three vectors from $\mathbb{R}^3$, but the third is the sum of the first two, so the column space of this matrix cannot have three dimensions. Nor does it have only one, because the three columns are not all scalar multiples of one another. Hence, it has two, and the column space of this matrix is a two-dimensional subspace of $\mathbb{R}^3$.

---

**DEFINITION A.9** Column Rank

*The* **column rank** *of a matrix is the dimension of the vector space that is spanned by its column vectors.*

---

It follows that the column rank of a matrix is equal to the largest number of linearly independent column vectors it contains. The column rank of $\mathbf{A}$ is 2. For another specific example, consider

$$\mathbf{B} = \begin{bmatrix} 1 & 2 & 3 \\ 5 & 1 & 5 \\ 6 & 4 & 5 \\ 3 & 1 & 4 \end{bmatrix}.$$

It can be shown (we shall see how later) that this matrix has a column rank equal to 3. Each column of $\mathbf{B}$ is a vector in $\mathbb{R}^4$, so the column space of $\mathbf{B}$ is a three-dimensional subspace of $\mathbb{R}^4$.

Consider, instead, the set of vectors obtained by using the *rows* of $\mathbf{B}$ instead of the columns. The new matrix would be

$$\mathbf{C} = \begin{bmatrix} 1 & 5 & 6 & 3 \\ 2 & 1 & 4 & 1 \\ 3 & 5 & 5 & 4 \end{bmatrix}.$$

This matrix is composed of four column vectors from $\mathbb{R}^3$. (Note that $\mathbf{C}$ is $\mathbf{B}'$.) The column space of $\mathbf{C}$ is at most $\mathbb{R}^3$, since four vectors in $\mathbb{R}^3$ must be linearly dependent. In fact, the column space of

**C** is $\mathbb{R}^3$. Although this is not the same as the column space of **B**, it does have the same dimension. Thus, the column rank of **C** and the column rank of **B** are the same. But the columns of **C** are the rows of **B**. Thus, the column rank of **C** equals the **row rank** of **B**. That the column and row ranks of **B** are the same is not a coincidence. The general results (which are equivalent) are as follows.

---

**THEOREM A.1   Equality of Row and Column Rank**
*The **column rank** and **row rank** of a matrix are equal. By the definition of row rank and its counterpart for column rank, we obtain the corollary,*

*the **row space** and **column space** of a matrix have the same dimension.*    **(A-42)**

---

Theorem A.1 holds regardless of the actual row and column rank. If the column rank of a matrix happens to equal the number of columns it contains, then the matrix is said to have **full column rank. Full row rank** is defined likewise. Because the row and column ranks of a matrix are always equal, we can speak unambiguously of the **rank of a matrix.** For either the row rank or the column rank (and, at this point, we shall drop the distinction),

$$\text{rank}(\mathbf{A}) = \text{rank}(\mathbf{A}') \leq \min(\text{number of rows, number of columns}).$$    **(A-43)**

In most contexts, we shall be interested in the columns of the matrices we manipulate. We shall use the term **full rank** to describe a matrix whose rank is equal to the number of columns it contains.

Of particular interest will be the distinction between **full rank** and **short rank matrices.** The distinction turns on the solutions to $\mathbf{Ax} = \mathbf{0}$. If a nonzero **x** for which $\mathbf{Ax} = \mathbf{0}$ exists, then **A** does not have full rank. Equivalently, if the nonzero **x** exists, then the columns of **A** are linearly dependent and at least one of them can be expressed as a linear combination of the others. For example, a nonzero set of solutions to

$$\begin{bmatrix} 1 & 3 & 10 \\ 2 & 3 & 14 \end{bmatrix} \begin{bmatrix} x_1 \\ x_2 \\ x_3 \end{bmatrix} = \begin{bmatrix} 0 \\ 0 \end{bmatrix}$$

is any multiple of $\mathbf{x}' = (2, 1, -\frac{1}{2})$.

In a product matrix $\mathbf{C} = \mathbf{AB}$, every column of **C** is a linear combination of the columns of **A**, so each column of **C** is in the column space of **A**. It is possible that the set of columns in **C** could span this space, but it is not possible for them to span a higher-dimensional space. At best, they could be a full set of linearly independent vectors in **A**'s column space. We conclude that the column rank of **C** could not be greater than that of **A**. Now, apply the same logic to the rows of **C**, which are all linear combinations of the rows of **B**. For the same reason that the column rank of **C** cannot exceed the column rank of **A**, the row rank of **C** cannot exceed the row rank of **B**. Row and column ranks are always equal, so we can conclude that

$$\text{rank}(\mathbf{AB}) \leq \min(\text{rank}(\mathbf{A}), \text{rank}(\mathbf{B})).$$    **(A-44)**

A useful corollary to (A-44) is:

If **A** is $M \times n$ and **B** is a square matrix of rank $n$, then $\text{rank}(\mathbf{AB}) = \text{rank}(\mathbf{A})$.    **(A-45)**

Another application that plays a central role in the development of regression analysis is, for any matrix $\mathbf{A}$,

$$\text{rank}(\mathbf{A}) = \text{rank}(\mathbf{A}'\mathbf{A}) = \text{rank}(\mathbf{A}\mathbf{A}'). \tag{A-46}$$

### A.3.6 DETERMINANT OF A MATRIX

The determinant of a square matrix—determinants are not defined for nonsquare matrices—is a function of the elements of the matrix. There are various definitions, most of which are not useful for our work. Determinants figure into our results in several ways, however, that we can enumerate before we need formally to define the computations.

> ## PROPOSITION
> *The determinant of a matrix is nonzero if and only if it has full rank.*

Full rank and short rank matrices can be distinguished by whether or not their determinants are nonzero. There are some settings in which the value of the determinant is also of interest, so we now consider some algebraic results.

It is most convenient to begin with a diagonal matrix

$$\mathbf{D} = \begin{bmatrix} d_1 & 0 & 0 & \cdots & 0 \\ 0 & d_2 & 0 & \cdots & 0 \\ & & & \cdots & \\ 0 & 0 & 0 & \cdots & d_K \end{bmatrix}.$$

The column vectors of $\mathbf{D}$ define a "box" in $\mathbb{R}^K$ whose sides are all at right angles to one another.[3] Its "volume," or determinant, is simply the product of the lengths of the sides, which we denote

$$|\mathbf{D}| = d_1 d_2 \ldots d_K = \prod_{k=1}^{K} d_k. \tag{A-47}$$

A special case is the identity matrix, which has, regardless of $K$, $|\mathbf{I}_K| = 1$. Multiplying $\mathbf{D}$ by a scalar $c$ is equivalent to multiplying the length of each side of the box by $c$, which would multiply its volume by $c^K$. Thus,

$$|c\mathbf{D}| = c^K |\mathbf{D}|. \tag{A-48}$$

Continuing with this admittedly special case, we suppose that only one column of $\mathbf{D}$ is multiplied by $c$. In two dimensions, this would make the box wider but not higher, or vice versa. Hence, the "volume" (area) would also be multiplied by $c$. Now, suppose that each side of the box were multiplied by a different $c$, the first by $c_1$, the second by $c_2$, and so on. The volume would, by an obvious extension, now be $c_1 c_2 \ldots c_K |\mathbf{D}|$. The matrix with columns defined by $[c_1 \mathbf{d}_1 \ c_2 \mathbf{d}_2 \ldots]$ is just $\mathbf{DC}$, where $\mathbf{C}$ is a diagonal matrix with $c_i$ as its $i$th diagonal element. The computation just described is, therefore,

$$|\mathbf{DC}| = |\mathbf{D}| \cdot |\mathbf{C}|. \tag{A-49}$$

(The determinant of $\mathbf{C}$ is the product of the $c_i$s since $\mathbf{C}$, like $\mathbf{D}$, is a diagonal matrix.) In particular, note what happens to the whole thing if one of the $c_i$s is zero.

---

[3]Each column vector defines a segment on one of the axes.

For $2 \times 2$ matrices, the computation of the determinant is

$$\begin{vmatrix} a & c \\ b & d \end{vmatrix} = ad - bc. \tag{A-50}$$

Notice that it is a function of all the elements of the matrix. This statement will be true, in general. For more than two dimensions, the determinant can be obtained by using an **expansion by cofactors.** Using *any* row, say, $i$, we obtain

$$|\mathbf{A}| = \sum_{k=1}^{K} a_{ik}(-1)^{i+k}|\mathbf{A}_{ik}|, \quad k = 1, \ldots, K, \tag{A-51}$$

where $\mathbf{A}_{ik}$ is the matrix obtained from $\mathbf{A}$ by deleting row $i$ and column $k$. The determinant of $\mathbf{A}_{ik}$ is called a **minor** of $\mathbf{A}$.[4] When the correct sign, $(-1)^{i+k}$, is added, it becomes a **cofactor.** This operation can be done using any column as well. For example, a $4 \times 4$ determinant becomes a sum of four $3 \times 3$s, whereas a $5 \times 5$ is a sum of five $4 \times 4$s, each of which is a sum of four $3 \times 3$s, and so on. Obviously, it is a good idea to base (A-51) on a row or column with many zeros in it, if possible. In practice, this rapidly becomes a heavy burden. It is unlikely, though, that you will ever calculate any determinants over $3 \times 3$ without a computer. A $3 \times 3$, however, might be computed on occasion; if so, the following shortcut will prove useful:

$$\begin{vmatrix} a_{11} & a_{12} & a_{13} \\ a_{21} & a_{22} & a_{23} \\ a_{31} & a_{32} & a_{33} \end{vmatrix} = a_{11}a_{22}a_{33} + a_{12}a_{23}a_{31} + a_{13}a_{32}a_{21} - a_{31}a_{22}a_{13} - a_{21}a_{12}a_{33} - a_{11}a_{23}a_{32}.$$

Although (A-48) and (A-49) were given for diagonal matrices, they hold for general matrices $\mathbf{C}$ and $\mathbf{D}$. One special case of (A-48) to note is that of $c = -1$. Multiplying a matrix by $-1$ does not necessarily change the sign of its determinant. It does so only if the order of the matrix is odd. By using the expansion by cofactors formula, an additional result can be shown:

$$|\mathbf{A}| = |\mathbf{A}'| \tag{A-52}$$

### A.3.7 A LEAST SQUARES PROBLEM

Given a vector $\mathbf{y}$ and a matrix $\mathbf{X}$, we are interested in expressing $\mathbf{y}$ as a linear combination of the columns of $\mathbf{X}$. There are two possibilities. If $\mathbf{y}$ lies in the column space of $\mathbf{X}$, then we shall be able to find a vector $\mathbf{b}$ such that

$$\mathbf{y} = \mathbf{Xb}. \tag{A-53}$$

Figure A.3 illustrates such a case for three dimensions in which the two columns of $\mathbf{X}$ both have a third coordinate equal to zero. Only $\mathbf{y}$s whose third coordinate is zero, such as $\mathbf{y}^0$ in the figure, can be expressed as $\mathbf{Xb}$ for some $\mathbf{b}$. For the general case, assuming that $\mathbf{y}$ is, indeed, in the column space of $\mathbf{X}$, we can find the coefficients $\mathbf{b}$ by solving the set of equations in (A-53). The solution is discussed in the next section.

Suppose, however, that $\mathbf{y}$ is not in the column space of $\mathbf{X}$. In the context of this example, suppose that $\mathbf{y}$'s third component is not zero. Then there is no $\mathbf{b}$ such that (A-53) holds. We can, however, write

$$\mathbf{y} = \mathbf{Xb} + \mathbf{e}, \tag{A-54}$$

where $\mathbf{e}$ is the difference between $\mathbf{y}$ and $\mathbf{Xb}$. By this construction, we find an $\mathbf{Xb}$ that is in the column space of $\mathbf{X}$, and $\mathbf{e}$ is the difference, or "residual." Figure A.3 shows two examples, $\mathbf{y}$ and

---

[4]If $i$ equals $k$, then the determinant is a **principal minor.**

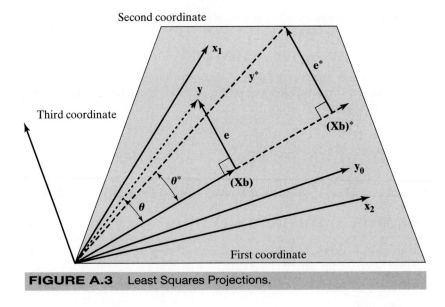

**FIGURE A.3** Least Squares Projections.

$\mathbf{y}^*$. For the present, we consider only $\mathbf{y}$. We are interested in finding the $\mathbf{b}$ such that $\mathbf{y}$ is as close as possible to $\mathbf{Xb}$ in the sense that $\mathbf{e}$ is as short as possible.

---

### DEFINITION A.10   Length of a Vector
*The length, or **norm,** of a vector $\mathbf{e}$ is*

$$\|\mathbf{e}\| = \sqrt{\mathbf{e}'\mathbf{e}}. \qquad \text{(A-55)}$$

---

The problem is to find the $\mathbf{b}$ for which

$$\|\mathbf{e}\| = \|\mathbf{y} - \mathbf{Xb}\|$$

is as small as possible. The solution is that $\mathbf{b}$ that makes $\mathbf{e}$ perpendicular, or *orthogonal,* to $\mathbf{Xb}$.

---

### DEFINITION A.11   Orthogonal Vectors
*Two nonzero vectors $\mathbf{a}$ and $\mathbf{b}$ are **orthogonal,** written $\mathbf{a} \perp \mathbf{b}$, if and only if*

$$\mathbf{a}'\mathbf{b} = \mathbf{b}'\mathbf{a} = 0.$$

---

Returning once again to our fitting problem, we find that the $\mathbf{b}$ we seek is that for which

$$\mathbf{e} \perp \mathbf{Xb}.$$

Expanding this set of equations gives the requirement

$$(\mathbf{Xb})'\mathbf{e} = \mathbf{0}$$
$$= \mathbf{b}'\mathbf{X}'\mathbf{y} - \mathbf{b}'\mathbf{X}'\mathbf{Xb}$$
$$= \mathbf{b}'[\mathbf{X}'\mathbf{y} - \mathbf{X}'\mathbf{Xb}],$$

or, assuming **b** is not **0**, the set of equations

$$\mathbf{X}'\mathbf{y} = \mathbf{X}'\mathbf{X}\mathbf{b}.$$

The means of solving such a set of equations is the subject of Section A.5.

In Figure A.3, the linear combination **Xb** is called the **projection** of **y** into the column space of **X**. The figure is drawn so that, although **y** and **y**\* are different, they are similar in that the projection of **y** lies on top of that of **y**\*. The question we wish to pursue here is, Which vector, **y** or **y**\*, is closer to its projection in the column space of **X**? Superficially, it would appear that **y** is closer, because **e** is shorter than **e**\*. Yet **y**\* is much more nearly parallel to its projection than **y**, so the only reason that its residual vector is longer is that **y**\* is longer compared with **y**. A measure of comparison that would be unaffected by the length of the vectors is the angle between the vector and its projection (assuming that angle is not zero). By this measure, $\theta^*$ is smaller than $\theta$, which would reverse the earlier conclusion.

---

**THEOREM A.2** **The Cosine Law**
*The angle $\theta$ between two vectors **a** and **b** satisfies*

$$\cos\theta = \frac{\mathbf{a}'\mathbf{b}}{\|\mathbf{a}\| \cdot \|\mathbf{b}\|}.$$

---

The two vectors in the calculation would be **y** or **y**\* and **Xb** or (**Xb**)\*. A zero cosine implies that the vectors are orthogonal. If the cosine is one, then the angle is zero, which means that the vectors are the same. (They would be if **y** were in the column space of **X**.) By dividing by the lengths, we automatically compensate for the length of **y**. By this measure, we find in Figure A.3 that **y**\* is closer to its projection, (**Xb**)\* than **y** is to its projection, **Xb**.

## A.4 SOLUTION OF A SYSTEM OF LINEAR EQUATIONS

Consider the set of $n$ linear equations

$$\mathbf{A}\mathbf{x} = \mathbf{b}, \tag{A-56}$$

in which the $K$ elements of **x** constitute the unknowns. **A** is a known matrix of coefficients, and **b** is a specified vector of values. We are interested in knowing whether a solution exists; if so, then how to obtain it; and finally, if it does exist, then whether it is unique.

### A.4.1 SYSTEMS OF LINEAR EQUATIONS

For most of our applications, we shall consider only square systems of equations, that is, those in which **A** is a square matrix. In what follows, therefore, we take $n$ to equal $K$. Because the number of rows in **A** is the number of equations, whereas the number of columns in **A** is the number of variables, this case is the familiar one of "$n$ equations in $n$ unknowns."

There are two types of systems of equations.

---

**DEFINITION A.12** **Homogeneous Equation System**
*A homogeneous system is of the form* $\mathbf{Ax} = \mathbf{0}$.

---

By definition, a nonzero solution to such a system will exist if and only if $\mathbf{A}$ does not have full rank. If so, then for at least one column of $\mathbf{A}$, we can write the preceding as

$$\mathbf{a}_k = -\sum_{m \neq k} \frac{x_m}{x_k} \mathbf{a}_m.$$

This means, as we know, that the columns of $\mathbf{A}$ are linearly dependent and that $|\mathbf{A}| = \mathbf{0}$.

---

**DEFINITION A.13** **Nonhomogeneous Equation System**
*A nonhomogeneous system of equations is of the form* $\mathbf{Ax} = \mathbf{b}$, *where* $\mathbf{b}$ *is a nonzero vector.*

---

The vector $\mathbf{b}$ is chosen arbitrarily and is to be expressed as a linear combination of the columns of $\mathbf{A}$. Because $\mathbf{b}$ has $K$ elements, this solution will exist only if the columns of $\mathbf{A}$ span the entire $K$-dimensional space, $\mathbb{R}^K$.[5] Equivalently, we shall require that the columns of $\mathbf{A}$ be linearly independent or that $|\mathbf{A}|$ not be equal to zero.

### A.4.2 INVERSE MATRICES

To solve the system $\mathbf{Ax} = \mathbf{b}$ for $\mathbf{x}$, something akin to division by a matrix is needed. Suppose that we could find a square matrix $\mathbf{B}$ such that $\mathbf{BA} = \mathbf{I}$. If the equation system is premultiplied by this $\mathbf{B}$, then the following would be obtained:

$$\mathbf{BAx} = \mathbf{Ix} = \mathbf{x} = \mathbf{Bb}. \tag{A-57}$$

If the matrix $\mathbf{B}$ exists, then it is the **inverse** of $\mathbf{A}$, denoted

$$\mathbf{B} = \mathbf{A}^{-1}.$$

From the definition,

$$\mathbf{A}^{-1}\mathbf{A} = \mathbf{I}.$$

In addition, by premultiplying by $\mathbf{A}$, postmultiplying by $\mathbf{A}^{-1}$, and then canceling terms, we find

$$\mathbf{AA}^{-1} = \mathbf{I}$$

as well.

If the inverse exists, then it must be unique. Suppose that it is not and that $\mathbf{C}$ is a different inverse of $\mathbf{A}$. Then $\mathbf{CAB} = \mathbf{CAB}$, but $(\mathbf{CA})\mathbf{B} = \mathbf{IB} = \mathbf{B}$ and $\mathbf{C}(\mathbf{AB}) = \mathbf{C}$, which would be a

---

[5]If $\mathbf{A}$ does not have full rank, then the nonhomogeneous system will have solutions for *some* vectors $\mathbf{b}$, namely, any $\mathbf{b}$ in the column space of $\mathbf{A}$. But we are interested in the case in which there are solutions for *all* nonzero vectors $\mathbf{b}$, which requires $\mathbf{A}$ to have full rank.

contradiction if **C** did not equal **B**. Because, by (A-57), the solution is $\mathbf{x} = \mathbf{A}^{-1}\mathbf{b}$, the solution to the equation system is unique as well.

We now consider the calculation of the inverse matrix. For a $2 \times 2$ matrix, $\mathbf{AB} = \mathbf{I}$ implies that

$$
\begin{bmatrix} a_{11} & a_{12} \\ a_{21} & a_{22} \end{bmatrix} \begin{bmatrix} b_{11} & b_{12} \\ b_{21} & b_{22} \end{bmatrix} = \begin{bmatrix} 1 & 0 \\ 0 & 1 \end{bmatrix} \quad \text{or} \quad \begin{bmatrix} a_{11}b_{11} + a_{12}b_{21} = 1 \\ a_{11}b_{12} + a_{12}b_{22} = 0 \\ a_{21}b_{11} + a_{22}b_{21} = 0 \\ a_{21}b_{12} + a_{22}b_{22} = 1 \end{bmatrix}.
$$

The solutions are

$$
\begin{bmatrix} b_{11} & b_{12} \\ b_{21} & b_{22} \end{bmatrix} = \frac{1}{a_{11}a_{22} - a_{12}a_{21}} \begin{bmatrix} a_{22} & -a_{12} \\ -a_{21} & a_{11} \end{bmatrix} = \frac{1}{|\mathbf{A}|} \begin{bmatrix} a_{22} & -a_{12} \\ -a_{21} & a_{11} \end{bmatrix}. \tag{A-58}
$$

Notice the presence of the reciprocal of $|\mathbf{A}|$ in $\mathbf{A}^{-1}$. This result is not specific to the $2 \times 2$ case. We infer from it that if the determinant is zero, then the inverse does not exist.

---

### DEFINITION A.14 Nonsingular Matrix
*A matrix is nonsingular if and only if its inverse exists.*

---

The simplest inverse matrix to compute is that of a diagonal matrix. If

$$
\mathbf{D} = \begin{bmatrix} d_1 & 0 & 0 & \cdots & 0 \\ 0 & d_2 & 0 & \cdots & 0 \\ & & \cdots & & \\ 0 & 0 & 0 & \cdots & d_K \end{bmatrix}, \quad \text{then} \quad \mathbf{D}^{-1} = \begin{bmatrix} 1/d_1 & 0 & 0 & \cdots & 0 \\ 0 & 1/d_2 & 0 & \cdots & 0 \\ & & \cdots & & \\ 0 & 0 & 0 & \cdots & 1/d_K \end{bmatrix},
$$

which shows, incidentally, that $\mathbf{I}^{-1} = \mathbf{I}$.

We shall use $a^{ik}$ to indicate the $ik$th element of $\mathbf{A}^{-1}$. The general formula for computing an inverse matrix is

$$
a^{ik} = \frac{|\mathbf{C}_{ki}|}{|\mathbf{A}|}, \tag{A-59}
$$

where $|\mathbf{C}_{ki}|$ is the $ki$th cofactor of $\mathbf{A}$. [See (A-51).] It follows, therefore, that for $\mathbf{A}$ to be nonsingular, $|\mathbf{A}|$ must be nonzero. Notice the reversal of the subscripts

Some computational results involving inverses are

$$
|\mathbf{A}^{-1}| = \frac{1}{|\mathbf{A}|}, \tag{A-60}
$$

$$
(\mathbf{A}^{-1})^{-1} = \mathbf{A}, \tag{A-61}
$$

$$
(\mathbf{A}^{-1})' = (\mathbf{A}')^{-1}. \tag{A-62}
$$

If $\mathbf{A}$ is symmetric, then $\mathbf{A}^{-1}$ is symmetric. $\qquad$ (A-63)

When both inverse matrices exist,

$$
(\mathbf{AB})^{-1} = \mathbf{B}^{-1}\mathbf{A}^{-1}. \tag{A-64}
$$

Note the condition preceding (A-64). It may be that **AB** is a square, nonsingular matrix when neither **A** nor **B** are even square. (Consider, e.g., **A′A**.) Extending (A-64), we have

$$(\mathbf{ABC})^{-1} = \mathbf{C}^{-1}(\mathbf{AB})^{-1} = \mathbf{C}^{-1}\mathbf{B}^{-1}\mathbf{A}^{-1}. \tag{A-65}$$

Recall that for a data matrix **X**, **X′X** is the sum of the *outer products* of the rows **X**. Suppose that we have already computed $\mathbf{S} = (\mathbf{X'X})^{-1}$ for a number of years of data, such as those given in Table A.1. The following result, which is called an **updating formula,** shows how to compute the new **S** that would result when a new row is added to **X**: For symmetric, nonsingular matrix **A**,

$$[\mathbf{A} \pm \mathbf{bb'}]^{-1} = \mathbf{A}^{-1} \mp \left[\frac{1}{1 \pm \mathbf{b'A}^{-1}\mathbf{b}}\right]\mathbf{A}^{-1}\mathbf{bb'A}^{-1}. \tag{A-66}$$

Note the reversal of the sign in the inverse. Two more general forms of (A-66) that are occasionally useful are

$$[\mathbf{A} \pm \mathbf{bc'}]^{-1} = \mathbf{A}^{-1} \mp \left[\frac{1}{1 \pm \mathbf{c'A}^{-1}\mathbf{b}}\right]\mathbf{A}^{-1}\mathbf{bc'A}^{-1}. \tag{A-66a}$$

$$[\mathbf{A} \pm \mathbf{BCB'}]^{-1} = \mathbf{A}^{-1} \mp \mathbf{A}^{-1}\mathbf{B}[\mathbf{C}^{-1} \pm \mathbf{B'A}^{-1}\mathbf{B}]^{-1}\mathbf{B'A}^{-1}. \tag{A-66b}$$

### A.4.3 NONHOMOGENEOUS SYSTEMS OF EQUATIONS

For the nonhomogeneous system

$$\mathbf{Ax} = \mathbf{b},$$

if **A** is nonsingular, then the unique solution is

$$\mathbf{x} = \mathbf{A}^{-1}\mathbf{b}.$$

### A.4.4 SOLVING THE LEAST SQUARES PROBLEM

We now have the tool needed to solve the least squares problem posed in Section A3.7. We found the solution vector, **b** to be the solution to the nonhomogenous system **X′y** = **X′Xb**. Let **a** equal the vector **X′y** and let **A** equal the square matrix **X′X**. The equation system is then

$$\mathbf{Ab} = \mathbf{a}.$$

By the preceding results, if **A** is nonsingular, then

$$\mathbf{b} = \mathbf{A}^{-1}\mathbf{a} = (\mathbf{X'X})^{-1}(\mathbf{X'y})$$

assuming that the matrix to be inverted is nonsingular. We have reached the irreducible minimum. If the columns of **X** are linearly independent, that is, if **X** has full rank, then this is the solution to the least squares problem. If the columns of **X** are linearly dependent, then this system has no unique solution.

## A.5 PARTITIONED MATRICES

In formulating the elements of a matrix—it is sometimes useful to group some of the elements in **submatrices.** Let

$$\mathbf{A} = \begin{bmatrix} 1 & 4 & 5 \\ 2 & 9 & 3 \\ 8 & 9 & 6 \end{bmatrix} = \begin{bmatrix} \mathbf{A}_{11} & \mathbf{A}_{12} \\ \mathbf{A}_{21} & \mathbf{A}_{22} \end{bmatrix}.$$

**A** is a **partitioned matrix.** The subscripts of the submatrices are defined in the same fashion as those for the elements of a matrix. A common special case is the **block-diagonal matrix:**

$$\mathbf{A} = \begin{bmatrix} \mathbf{A}_{11} & 0 \\ 0 & \mathbf{A}_{22} \end{bmatrix},$$

where $\mathbf{A}_{11}$ and $\mathbf{A}_{22}$ are square matrices.

### A.5.1 ADDITION AND MULTIPLICATION OF PARTITIONED MATRICES

For conformably partitioned matrices **A** and **B**,

$$\mathbf{A} + \mathbf{B} = \begin{bmatrix} \mathbf{A}_{11} + \mathbf{B}_{11} & \mathbf{A}_{12} + \mathbf{B}_{12} \\ \mathbf{A}_{21} + \mathbf{B}_{21} & \mathbf{A}_{22} + \mathbf{B}_{22} \end{bmatrix}, \tag{A-67}$$

and

$$\mathbf{AB} = \begin{bmatrix} \mathbf{A}_{11} & \mathbf{A}_{12} \\ \mathbf{A}_{21} & \mathbf{A}_{22} \end{bmatrix} \begin{bmatrix} \mathbf{B}_{11} & \mathbf{B}_{12} \\ \mathbf{B}_{21} & \mathbf{B}_{22} \end{bmatrix} = \begin{bmatrix} \mathbf{A}_{11}\mathbf{B}_{11} + \mathbf{A}_{12}\mathbf{B}_{21} & \mathbf{A}_{11}\mathbf{B}_{12} + \mathbf{A}_{12}\mathbf{B}_{22} \\ \mathbf{A}_{21}\mathbf{B}_{11} + \mathbf{A}_{22}\mathbf{B}_{21} & \mathbf{A}_{21}\mathbf{B}_{12} + \mathbf{A}_{22}\mathbf{B}_{22} \end{bmatrix}. \tag{A-68}$$

In all these, the matrices must be conformable for the operations involved. For addition, the dimensions of $\mathbf{A}_{ik}$ and $\mathbf{B}_{ik}$ must be the same. For multiplication, the number of columns in $\mathbf{A}_{ij}$ must equal the number of rows in $\mathbf{B}_{jl}$ for all pairs $i$ and $j$. That is, all the necessary matrix products of the submatrices must be defined. Two cases frequently encountered are of the form

$$\begin{bmatrix} \mathbf{A}_1 \\ \mathbf{A}_2 \end{bmatrix}' \begin{bmatrix} \mathbf{A}_1 \\ \mathbf{A}_2 \end{bmatrix} = [\mathbf{A}_1' \quad \mathbf{A}_2'] \begin{bmatrix} \mathbf{A}_1 \\ \mathbf{A}_2 \end{bmatrix} = [\mathbf{A}_1'\mathbf{A}_1 + \mathbf{A}_2'\mathbf{A}_2], \tag{A-69}$$

and

$$\begin{bmatrix} \mathbf{A}_{11} & 0 \\ 0 & \mathbf{A}_{22} \end{bmatrix}' \begin{bmatrix} \mathbf{A}_{11} & 0 \\ 0 & \mathbf{A}_{22} \end{bmatrix} = \begin{bmatrix} \mathbf{A}_{11}'\mathbf{A}_{11} & 0 \\ 0 & \mathbf{A}_{22}'\mathbf{A}_{22} \end{bmatrix}. \tag{A-70}$$

### A.5.2 DETERMINANTS OF PARTITIONED MATRICES

The determinant of a block-diagonal matrix is obtained analogously to that of a diagonal matrix:

$$\begin{vmatrix} \mathbf{A}_{11} & 0 \\ 0 & \mathbf{A}_{22} \end{vmatrix} = |\mathbf{A}_{11}| \cdot |\mathbf{A}_{22}|. \tag{A-71}$$

The determinant of a general $2 \times 2$ partitioned matrix is

$$\begin{vmatrix} \mathbf{A}_{11} & \mathbf{A}_{12} \\ \mathbf{A}_{21} & \mathbf{A}_{22} \end{vmatrix} = |\mathbf{A}_{22}| \cdot |\mathbf{A}_{11} - \mathbf{A}_{12}\mathbf{A}_{22}^{-1}\mathbf{A}_{21}| = |\mathbf{A}_{11}| \cdot |\mathbf{A}_{22} - \mathbf{A}_{21}\mathbf{A}_{11}^{-1}\mathbf{A}_{12}|. \tag{A-72}$$

### A.5.3 INVERSES OF PARTITIONED MATRICES

The inverse of a block-diagonal matrix is

$$\begin{bmatrix} \mathbf{A}_{11} & 0 \\ 0 & \mathbf{A}_{22} \end{bmatrix}^{-1} = \begin{bmatrix} \mathbf{A}_{11}^{-1} & 0 \\ 0 & \mathbf{A}_{22}^{-1} \end{bmatrix}, \tag{A-73}$$

which can be verified by direct multiplication.

For the general $2 \times 2$ partitioned matrix, one form of the **partitioned inverse** is

$$
\begin{bmatrix} \mathbf{A}_{11} & \mathbf{A}_{12} \\ \mathbf{A}_{21} & \mathbf{A}_{22} \end{bmatrix}^{-1} = \begin{bmatrix} \mathbf{A}_{11}^{-1}\left(\mathbf{I} + \mathbf{A}_{12}\mathbf{F}_2\mathbf{A}_{21}\mathbf{A}_{11}^{-1}\right) & -\mathbf{A}_{11}^{-1}\mathbf{A}_{12}\mathbf{F}_2 \\ -\mathbf{F}_2\mathbf{A}_{21}\mathbf{A}_{11}^{-1} & \mathbf{F}_2 \end{bmatrix}, \tag{A-74}
$$

where

$$
\mathbf{F}_2 = \left(\mathbf{A}_{22} - \mathbf{A}_{21}\mathbf{A}_{11}^{-1}\mathbf{A}_{12}\right)^{-1}.
$$

The upper left block could also be written as

$$
\mathbf{F}_1 = \left(\mathbf{A}_{11} - \mathbf{A}_{12}\mathbf{A}_{22}^{-1}\mathbf{A}_{21}\right)^{-1}.
$$

### A.5.4 DEVIATIONS FROM MEANS

Suppose that we begin with a column vector of $n$ values $\mathbf{x}$ and let

$$
\mathbf{A} = \begin{bmatrix} n & \sum_{i=1}^{n} x_i \\ \sum_{i=1}^{n} x_i & \sum_{i=1}^{n} x_i^2 \end{bmatrix} = \begin{bmatrix} \mathbf{i'i} & \mathbf{i'x} \\ \mathbf{x'i} & \mathbf{x'x} \end{bmatrix}.
$$

We are interested in the lower-right-hand element of $\mathbf{A}^{-1}$. Upon using the definition of $\mathbf{F}_2$ in (A-74), this is

$$
\mathbf{F}_2 = [\mathbf{x'x} - (\mathbf{x'i})(\mathbf{i'i})^{-1}(\mathbf{i'x})]^{-1} = \left\{\mathbf{x'}\left[\mathbf{Ix} - \mathbf{i}\left(\frac{1}{n}\right)\mathbf{i'x}\right]\right\}^{-1}
$$

$$
= \left\{\mathbf{x'}\left[\mathbf{I} - \left(\frac{1}{n}\right)\mathbf{ii'}\right]\mathbf{x}\right\}^{-1} = (\mathbf{x'M^0x})^{-1}.
$$

Therefore, the lower-right-hand value in the inverse matrix is

$$
(\mathbf{x'M^0x})^{-1} = \frac{1}{\sum_{i=1}^{n}(x_i - \overline{x})^2} = a^{22}.
$$

Now, suppose that we replace $\mathbf{x}$ with $\mathbf{X}$, a matrix with several columns. We seek the lower-right block of $(\mathbf{Z'Z})^{-1}$, where $\mathbf{Z} = [\mathbf{i}, \mathbf{X}]$. The analogous result is

$$
(\mathbf{Z'Z})^{22} = [\mathbf{X'X} - \mathbf{X'i}(\mathbf{i'i})^{-1}\mathbf{i'X}]^{-1} = (\mathbf{X'M^0X})^{-1},
$$

which implies that the $K \times K$ matrix in the lower-right corner of $(\mathbf{Z'Z})^{-1}$ is the inverse of the $K \times K$ matrix whose $jk$th element is $\sum_{i=1}^{n}(x_{ij} - \overline{x}_j)(x_{ik} - \overline{x}_k)$. Thus, when a data matrix contains a column of ones, the elements of the inverse of the matrix of sums of squares and cross products will be computed from the original data in the form of deviations from the respective column means.

### A.5.5 KRONECKER PRODUCTS

A calculation that helps to condense the notation when dealing with sets of regression models (see Chapters 10, 11 and 13) is the **Kronecker product**. For general matrices $\mathbf{A}$ and $\mathbf{B}$,

$$
\mathbf{A} \otimes \mathbf{B} = \begin{bmatrix} a_{11}\mathbf{B} & a_{12}\mathbf{B} & \cdots & a_{1K}\mathbf{B} \\ a_{21}\mathbf{B} & a_{22}\mathbf{B} & \cdots & a_{2K}\mathbf{B} \\ & & \cdots & \\ a_{n1}\mathbf{B} & a_{n2}\mathbf{B} & \cdots & a_{nK}\mathbf{B} \end{bmatrix}. \tag{A-75}
$$

Notice that there is no requirement for conformability in this operation. The Kronecker product can be computed for any pair of matrices. If $\mathbf{A}$ is $K \times L$ and $\mathbf{B}$ is $m \times n$, then $\mathbf{A} \otimes \mathbf{B}$ is $(Km) \times (Ln)$.

For the Kronecker product,

$$(\mathbf{A} \otimes \mathbf{B})^{-1} = (\mathbf{A}^{-1} \otimes \mathbf{B}^{-1}), \tag{A-76}$$

If $\mathbf{A}$ is $M \times M$ and $\mathbf{B}$ is $n \times n$, then

$$|\mathbf{A} \otimes \mathbf{B}| = |\mathbf{A}|^{n}|\mathbf{B}|^{M},$$

$$(\mathbf{A} \otimes \mathbf{B})' = \mathbf{A}' \otimes \mathbf{B}',$$

$$\text{trace}(\mathbf{A} \otimes \mathbf{B}) = \text{tr}(\mathbf{A})\text{tr}(\mathbf{B}).$$

For $\mathbf{A}, \mathbf{B}, \mathbf{C},$ and $\mathbf{D}$ such that the products are defined is

$$(\mathbf{A} \otimes \mathbf{B})(\mathbf{C} \otimes \mathbf{D}) = \mathbf{AC} \otimes \mathbf{BD}.$$

## A.6 CHARACTERISTIC ROOTS AND VECTORS

A useful set of results for analyzing a square matrix $\mathbf{A}$ arises from the solutions to the set of equations

$$\mathbf{Ac} = \lambda\mathbf{c}. \tag{A-77}$$

The pairs of solutions are the **characteristic vectors c** and **characteristic roots** $\lambda$. If $\mathbf{c}$ is any solution vector, then $k\mathbf{c}$ is also for any value of $k$. To remove the indeterminacy, $\mathbf{c}$ is **normalized** so that $\mathbf{c}'\mathbf{c} = 1$.

The solution then consists of $\lambda$ and the $n - 1$ unknown elements in $\mathbf{c}$.

### A.6.1 THE CHARACTERISTIC EQUATION

Solving (A-77) can, in principle, proceed as follows. First, (A-77) implies that

$$\mathbf{Ac} = \lambda\mathbf{Ic},$$

or that

$$(\mathbf{A} - \lambda\mathbf{I})\mathbf{c} = \mathbf{0}.$$

This equation is a homogeneous system that has a nonzero solution only if the matrix $(\mathbf{A} - \lambda\mathbf{I})$ is singular or has a zero determinant. Therefore, if $\lambda$ is a solution, then

$$|\mathbf{A} - \lambda\mathbf{I}| = 0. \tag{A-78}$$

This polynomial in $\lambda$ is the **characteristic equation** of $\mathbf{A}$. For example, if

$$\mathbf{A} = \begin{bmatrix} 5 & 1 \\ 2 & 4 \end{bmatrix},$$

then

$$|\mathbf{A} - \lambda\mathbf{I}| = \begin{vmatrix} 5 - \lambda & 1 \\ 2 & 4 - \lambda \end{vmatrix} = (5 - \lambda)(4 - \lambda) - 2(1) = \lambda^2 - 9\lambda + 18.$$

The two solutions are $\lambda = 6$ and $\lambda = 3$.

In solving the characteristic equation, there is no guarantee that the characteristic roots will be real. In the preceding example, if the 2 in the lower-left-hand corner of the matrix were $-2$ instead, then the solution would be a pair of complex values. The same result can emerge in the general $n \times n$ case. The characteristic roots of a symmetric matrix are real, however.[6] This result will be convenient because most of our applications will involve the characteristic roots and vectors of symmetric matrices.

For an $n \times n$ matrix, the characteristic equation is an $n$th-order polynomial in $\lambda$. Its solutions may be $n$ distinct values, as in the preceding example, or may contain repeated values of $\lambda$, and may contain some zeros as well.

### A.6.2 CHARACTERISTIC VECTORS

With $\lambda$ in hand, the characteristic vectors are derived from the original problem,

$$\mathbf{Ac} = \lambda \mathbf{c},$$

or

$$(\mathbf{A} - \lambda \mathbf{I})\mathbf{c} = \mathbf{0}. \tag{A-79}$$

Neither pair determines the values of $c_1$ and $c_2$. But this result was to be expected; it was the reason $\mathbf{c}'\mathbf{c} = 1$ was specified at the outset. The additional equation $\mathbf{c}'\mathbf{c} = 1$, however, produces complete solutions for the vectors.

### A.6.3 GENERAL RESULTS FOR CHARACTERISTIC ROOTS AND VECTORS

A $K \times K$ symmetric matrix has $K$ distinct characteristic vectors, $\mathbf{c}_1, \mathbf{c}_2, \ldots \mathbf{c}_K$. The corresponding characteristic roots, $\lambda_1, \lambda_2, \ldots, \lambda_K$, although real, need not be distinct. The characteristic vectors of a symmetric matrix are orthogonal,[7] which implies that for every $i \neq j$, $\mathbf{c}_i'\mathbf{c}_j = 0$.[8] It is convenient to collect the $K$-characteristic vectors in a $K \times K$ matrix whose $i$th column is the $\mathbf{c}_i$ corresponding to $\lambda_i$,

$$\mathbf{C} = [\mathbf{c}_1 \quad \mathbf{c}_2 \quad \cdots \quad \mathbf{c}_K],$$

and the $K$-characteristic roots in the same order, in a diagonal matrix,

$$\mathbf{\Lambda} = \begin{bmatrix} \lambda_1 & 0 & 0 & \cdots & 0 \\ 0 & \lambda_2 & 0 & \cdots & 0 \\ & & \cdots & & \\ 0 & 0 & 0 & \cdots & \lambda_K \end{bmatrix}.$$

Then, the full set of equations

$$\mathbf{Ac}_k = \lambda_k \mathbf{c}_k$$

is contained in

$$\mathbf{AC} = \mathbf{C\Lambda}. \tag{A-80}$$

---

[6] A proof may be found in Theil (1971).

[7] For proofs of these propositions, see Strang (1988).

[8] This statement is not true if the matrix is not symmetric. For instance, it does not hold for the characteristic vectors computed in the first example. For nonsymmetric matrices, there is also a distinction between "right" characteristic vectors, $\mathbf{Ac} = \lambda \mathbf{c}$, and "left" characteristic vectors, $\mathbf{d}'\mathbf{A} = \lambda \mathbf{d}'$, which may not be equal.

Because the vectors are orthogonal and $\mathbf{c}_i'\mathbf{c}_i = 1$, we have

$$\mathbf{C}'\mathbf{C} = \begin{bmatrix} \mathbf{c}_1'\mathbf{c}_1 & \mathbf{c}_1'\mathbf{c}_2 & \cdots & \mathbf{c}_1'\mathbf{c}_K \\ \mathbf{c}_2'\mathbf{c}_1 & \mathbf{c}_2'\mathbf{c}_2 & \cdots & \mathbf{c}_2'\mathbf{c}_K \\ & & \vdots & \\ \mathbf{c}_K'\mathbf{c}_1 & \mathbf{c}_K'\mathbf{c}_2 & \cdots & \mathbf{c}_K'\mathbf{c}_K \end{bmatrix} = \mathbf{I}. \qquad \text{(A-81)}$$

Result (A-81) implies that

$$\mathbf{C}' = \mathbf{C}^{-1}. \qquad \text{(A-82)}$$

Consequently,

$$\mathbf{C}\mathbf{C}' = \mathbf{C}\mathbf{C}^{-1} = \mathbf{I} \qquad \text{(A-83)}$$

as well, so the rows as well as the columns of C are orthogonal.

### A.6.4 DIAGONALIZATION AND SPECTRAL DECOMPOSITION OF A MATRIX

By premultiplying (A-80) by $\mathbf{C}'$ and using (A-81), we can extract the characteristic roots of **A**.

---

**DEFINITION A.15** Diagonalization of a Matrix
*The **diagonalization** of a matrix **A** is*

$$\mathbf{C}'\mathbf{A}\mathbf{C} = \mathbf{C}'\mathbf{C}\Lambda = \mathbf{I}\Lambda = \Lambda. \qquad \text{(A-84)}$$

---

Alternatively, by *post*multiplying (A-80) by $\mathbf{C}'$ and using (A-83), we obtain a useful representation of **A**.

---

**DEFINITION A.16** Spectral Decomposition of a Matrix
*The spectral decomposition of **A** is*

$$\mathbf{A} = \mathbf{C}\Lambda\mathbf{C}' = \sum_{k=1}^{K} \lambda_k \mathbf{c}_k \mathbf{c}_k'. \qquad \text{(A-85)}$$

---

In this representation, the $K \times K$ matrix **A** is written as a sum of $K$ rank one matrices. This sum is also called the **eigenvalue** (or, "own" value) decomposition of **A**. In this connection, the term *signature* of the matrix is sometimes used to describe the characteristic roots and vectors. Yet another pair of terms for the parts of this decomposition are the **latent roots** and **latent vectors** of **A**.

### A.6.5 RANK OF A MATRIX

The diagonalization result enables us to obtain the rank of a matrix very easily. To do so, we can use the following result.

---

**THEOREM A.3  Rank of a Product**

*For any matrix* **A** *and nonsingular matrices* **B** *and* **C**, *the rank of* **BAC** *is equal to the rank of* **A**. *The proof is simple. By (A-45),* rank(**BAC**) = rank[(**BA**)**C**] = rank(**BA**). *By (A-43),* rank(**BA**) = rank(**A′B′**), *and applying (A-45) again,* rank(**A′B′**) = rank(**A′**) *because* **B′** *is nonsingular if* **B** *is nonsingular (once again, by A-43). Finally, applying (A-43) again to obtain* rank(**A′**) = rank(**A**) *gives the result.*

---

Because **C** and **C′** are nonsingular, we can use them to apply this result to (A-84). By an obvious substitution,

$$\text{rank}(\mathbf{A}) = \text{rank}(\mathbf{\Lambda}). \qquad \text{(A-86)}$$

Finding the rank of $\mathbf{\Lambda}$ is trivial. Because $\mathbf{\Lambda}$ is a diagonal matrix, its rank is just the number of nonzero values on its diagonal. By extending this result, we can prove the following theorems. (Proofs are brief and are left for the reader.)

---

**THEOREM A.4  Rank of a Symmetric Matrix**

*The rank of a symmetric matrix is the number of nonzero characteristic roots it contains.*

---

Note how this result enters the spectral decomposition given earlier. If any of the characteristic roots are zero, then the number of rank one matrices in the sum is reduced correspondingly. It would appear that this simple rule will not be useful if **A** is not square. But recall that

$$\text{rank}(\mathbf{A}) = \text{rank}(\mathbf{A'A}). \qquad \text{(A-87)}$$

Because **A′A** is always square, we can use it instead of **A**. Indeed, we can use it even if **A** is square, which leads to a fully general result.

---

**THEOREM A.5  Rank of a Matrix**

*The rank of any matrix* **A** *equals the number of nonzero characteristic roots in* **A′A**.

---

The row rank and column rank of a matrix are equal, so we should be able to apply Theorem A.5 to **AA′** as well. This process, however, requires an additional result.

---

**THEOREM A.6  Roots of an Outer Product Matrix**

*The nonzero characteristic roots of* **AA′** *are the same as those of* **A′A**.

---

The proof is left as an exercise. A useful special case the reader can examine is the characteristic roots of $\mathbf{aa}'$ and $\mathbf{a}'\mathbf{a}$, where $\mathbf{a}$ is an $n \times 1$ vector.

If a characteristic root of a matrix is zero, then we have $\mathbf{Ac} = \mathbf{0}$. Thus, if the matrix has a zero root, it must be singular. Otherwise, no nonzero $\mathbf{c}$ would exist. In general, therefore, a matrix is singular; that is, it does not have full rank if and only if it has at least one zero root.

## A.6.6 CONDITION NUMBER OF A MATRIX

As the preceding might suggest, there is a discrete difference between full rank and short rank matrices. In analyzing data matrices such as the one in Section A.2, however, we shall often encounter cases in which a matrix is not quite short ranked, because it has all nonzero roots, but it is close. That is, by some measure, we can come very close to being able to write one column as a linear combination of the others. This case is important; we shall examine it at length in our discussion of multicollinearity in Section 4.8.1. Our definitions of rank and determinant will fail to indicate this possibility, but an alternative measure, the **condition number,** is designed for that purpose. Formally, the condition number for a square matrix $\mathbf{A}$ is

$$\gamma = \left[ \frac{\text{maximum root}}{\text{minimum root}} \right]^{1/2}. \tag{A-88}$$

For nonsquare matrices $\mathbf{X}$, such as the data matrix in the example, we use $\mathbf{A} = \mathbf{X}'\mathbf{X}$. As a further refinement, because the characteristic roots are affected by the scaling of the columns of $\mathbf{X}$, we scale the columns to have length 1 by dividing each column by its norm [see (A-55)]. For the $\mathbf{X}$ in Section A.2, the largest characteristic root of $\mathbf{A}$ is 4.9255 and the smallest is 0.0001543. Therefore, the condition number is 178.67, which is extremely large. (Values greater than 20 are large.) That the smallest root is close to zero compared with the largest means that this matrix is nearly singular. Matrices with large condition numbers are difficult to invert accurately.

## A.6.7 TRACE OF A MATRIX

The **trace** of a square $K \times K$ matrix is the sum of its diagonal elements:

$$\text{tr}(\mathbf{A}) = \sum_{k=1}^{K} a_{kk}.$$

Some easily proven results are

$$\text{tr}(c\mathbf{A}) = c(\text{tr}(\mathbf{A})), \tag{A-89}$$

$$\text{tr}(\mathbf{A}') = \text{tr}(\mathbf{A}), \tag{A-90}$$

$$\text{tr}(\mathbf{A} + \mathbf{B}) = \text{tr}(\mathbf{A}) + \text{tr}(\mathbf{B}), \tag{A-91}$$

$$\text{tr}(\mathbf{I}_K) = K. \tag{A-92}$$

$$\text{tr}(\mathbf{AB}) = \text{tr}(\mathbf{BA}). \tag{A-93}$$

$$\mathbf{a}'\mathbf{a} = \text{tr}(\mathbf{a}'\mathbf{a}) = \text{tr}(\mathbf{aa}')$$

$$\text{tr}(\mathbf{A}'\mathbf{A}) = \sum_{k=1}^{K} \mathbf{a}_k'\mathbf{a}_k = \sum_{i=1}^{K} \sum_{k=1}^{K} a_{ik}^2.$$

The permutation rule can be extended to any *cyclic* permutation in a product:

$$\text{tr}(\mathbf{ABCD}) = \text{tr}(\mathbf{BCDA}) = \text{tr}(\mathbf{CDAB}) = \text{tr}(\mathbf{DABC}). \tag{A-94}$$

By using (A-84), we obtain

$$\operatorname{tr}(\mathbf{C}'\mathbf{AC}) = \operatorname{tr}(\mathbf{ACC}') = \operatorname{tr}(\mathbf{AI}) = \operatorname{tr}(\mathbf{A}) = \operatorname{tr}(\mathbf{\Lambda}). \qquad \textbf{(A-95)}$$

Because $\mathbf{\Lambda}$ is diagonal with the roots of $\mathbf{A}$ on its diagonal, the general result is the following.

> **THEOREM A.7  Trace of a Matrix**
> *The trace of a matrix equals the sum of its characteristic roots.* $\qquad$ **(A-96)**

### A.6.8  DETERMINANT OF A MATRIX

Recalling how tedious the calculation of a determinant promised to be, we find that the following is particularly useful. Because

$$\mathbf{C}'\mathbf{AC} = \mathbf{\Lambda},$$
$$|\mathbf{C}'\mathbf{AC}| = |\mathbf{\Lambda}|. \qquad \textbf{(A-97)}$$

Using a number of earlier results, we have, for orthogonal matrix $\mathbf{C}$,

$$
\begin{aligned}
|\mathbf{C}'\mathbf{AC}| &= |\mathbf{C}'| \cdot |\mathbf{A}| \cdot |\mathbf{C}| = |\mathbf{C}'| \cdot |\mathbf{C}| \cdot |\mathbf{A}| = |\mathbf{C}'\mathbf{C}| \cdot |\mathbf{A}| = |\mathbf{I}| \cdot |\mathbf{A}| = 1 \cdot |\mathbf{A}| \\
&= |\mathbf{A}| \\
&= |\mathbf{\Lambda}|.
\end{aligned}
\qquad \textbf{(A-98)}
$$

Because $|\mathbf{\Lambda}|$ is just the product of its diagonal elements, the following is implied.

> **THEOREM A.8  Determinant of a Matrix**
> *The determinant of a matrix equals the product of its characteristic roots.*
> $\qquad$ **(A-99)**

Notice that we get the expected result if any of these roots is zero. The determinant is the product of the roots, so it follows that a matrix is singular if and only if its determinant is zero and, in turn, if and only if it has at least one zero characteristic root.

### A.6.9  POWERS OF A MATRIX

We often use expressions involving powers of matrices, such as $\mathbf{AA} = \mathbf{A}^2$. For positive integer powers, these expressions can be computed by repeated multiplication. But this does not show how to handle a problem such as finding a $\mathbf{B}$ such that $\mathbf{B}^2 = \mathbf{A}$, that is, the square root of a matrix. The characteristic roots and vectors provide a solution. Consider first

$$
\begin{aligned}
\mathbf{AA} = \mathbf{A}^2 &= (\mathbf{C}\mathbf{\Lambda}\mathbf{C}')(\mathbf{C}\mathbf{\Lambda}\mathbf{C}') = \mathbf{C}\mathbf{\Lambda}\mathbf{C}'\mathbf{C}\mathbf{\Lambda}\mathbf{C}' = \mathbf{C}\mathbf{\Lambda}\mathbf{I}\mathbf{\Lambda}\mathbf{C}' = \mathbf{C}\mathbf{\Lambda}\mathbf{\Lambda}\mathbf{C}' \\
&= \mathbf{C}\mathbf{\Lambda}^2\mathbf{C}'.
\end{aligned}
\qquad \textbf{(A-100)}
$$

Two results follow. Because $\mathbf{\Lambda}^2$ is a diagonal matrix whose nonzero elements are the squares of those in $\mathbf{\Lambda}$, the following is implied.

*For any symmetric matrix, the characteristic roots of $\mathbf{A}^2$ are the squares of those of $\mathbf{A}$, and the characteristic vectors are the same.* $\qquad$ **(A-101)**

The proof is obtained by observing that the second line in (A-100) is the spectral decomposition of the matrix $\mathbf{B} = \mathbf{AA}$. Because $\mathbf{A}^3 = \mathbf{AA}^2$ and so on, (A-101) extends to any positive integer. By convention, for any $\mathbf{A}$, $\mathbf{A}^0 = \mathbf{I}$. Thus, for any symmetric matrix $\mathbf{A}$, $\mathbf{A}^K = \mathbf{C}\mathbf{\Lambda}^K\mathbf{C}'$, $K = 0, 1, \ldots$. Hence, the characteristic roots of $\mathbf{A}^K$ are $\lambda^K$, whereas the characteristic vectors are the same as those of $\mathbf{A}$. If $\mathbf{A}$ is nonsingular, so that all its roots $\lambda_i$ are nonzero, then this proof can be extended to negative powers as well.

If $\mathbf{A}^{-1}$ exists, then

$$\mathbf{A}^{-1} = (\mathbf{C}\mathbf{\Lambda}\mathbf{C}')^{-1} = (\mathbf{C}')^{-1}\mathbf{\Lambda}^{-1}\mathbf{C}^{-1} = \mathbf{C}\mathbf{\Lambda}^{-1}\mathbf{C}', \qquad \text{(A-102)}$$

where we have used the earlier result, $\mathbf{C}' = \mathbf{C}^{-1}$. This gives an important result that is useful for analyzing inverse matrices.

---

**THEOREM A.9  Characteristic Roots of an Inverse Matrix**

*If $\mathbf{A}^{-1}$ exists, then the characteristic roots of $\mathbf{A}^{-1}$ are the reciprocals of those of $\mathbf{A}$, and the characteristic vectors are the same.*

---

By extending the notion of repeated multiplication, we now have a more general result.

---

**THEOREM A.10  Characteristic Roots of a Matrix Power**

*For any nonsingular symmetric matrix* $\mathbf{A} = \mathbf{C}\mathbf{\Lambda}\mathbf{C}'$, $\mathbf{A}^K = \mathbf{C}\mathbf{\Lambda}^K\mathbf{C}'$, $K = \ldots, -2, -1, 0, 1, 2, \ldots$.

---

We now turn to the general problem of how to compute the square root of a matrix. In the scalar case, the value would have to be nonnegative. The matrix analog to this requirement is that all the characteristic roots are nonnegative. Consider, then, the candidate

$$\mathbf{A}^{1/2} = \mathbf{C}\mathbf{\Lambda}^{1/2}\mathbf{C}' = \mathbf{C}\begin{bmatrix} \sqrt{\lambda_1} & 0 & \cdots & 0 \\ 0 & \sqrt{\lambda_2} & \cdots & 0 \\ & & \cdots & \\ 0 & 0 & \cdots & \sqrt{\lambda_n} \end{bmatrix}\mathbf{C}'. \qquad \text{(A-103)}$$

This equation satisfies the requirement for a square root, because

$$\mathbf{A}^{1/2}\mathbf{A}^{1/2} = \mathbf{C}\mathbf{\Lambda}^{1/2}\mathbf{C}'\mathbf{C}\mathbf{\Lambda}^{1/2}\mathbf{C}' = \mathbf{C}\mathbf{\Lambda}\mathbf{C}' = \mathbf{A}. \qquad \text{(A-104)}$$

If we continue in this fashion, we can define the powers of a matrix more generally, still assuming that all the characteristic roots are nonnegative. For example, $\mathbf{A}^{1/3} = \mathbf{C}\mathbf{\Lambda}^{1/3}\mathbf{C}'$. If all the roots are strictly positive, we can go one step further and extend the result to any real power. For reasons that will be made clear in the next section, we say that a matrix with positive characteristic roots is **positive definite.** It is the matrix analog to a positive number.

---

**DEFINITION A.17  Real Powers of a Positive Definite Matrix**

*For a **positive definite** matrix $\mathbf{A}$, $\mathbf{A}^r = \mathbf{C}\mathbf{\Lambda}^r\mathbf{C}'$, for any real number, r.* $\qquad \text{(A-105)}$

---

The characteristic roots of $\mathbf{A}^r$ are the $r$th power of those of $\mathbf{A}$, and the characteristic vectors are the same.

If $\mathbf{A}$ is only **nonnegative definite**—that is, has roots that are either zero or positive—then (A-105) holds only for nonnegative $r$.

### A.6.10 IDEMPOTENT MATRICES

Idempotent matrices are equal to their squares [see (A-37) to (A-39)]. In view of their importance in econometrics, we collect a few results related to idempotent matrices at this point. First, (A-101) implies that if $\lambda$ is a characteristic root of an idempotent matrix, then $\lambda = \lambda^K$ for all nonnegative integers $K$. As such, if $\mathbf{A}$ is a symmetric idempotent matrix, then all its roots are one or zero. Assume that all the roots of $\mathbf{A}$ are one. Then $\mathbf{\Lambda} = \mathbf{I}$, and $\mathbf{A} = \mathbf{C}\mathbf{\Lambda}\mathbf{C}' = \mathbf{C}\mathbf{I}\mathbf{C}' = \mathbf{C}\mathbf{C}' = \mathbf{I}$. If the roots are not all one, then one or more are zero. Consequently, we have the following results for symmetric idempotent matrices:[9]

- *The only full rank, symmetric idempotent matrix is the identity matrix* $\mathbf{I}$. **(A-106)**
- *All symmetric idempotent matrices except the identity matrix are singular.* **(A-107)**

The final result on idempotent matrices is obtained by observing that the count of the nonzero roots of $\mathbf{A}$ is also equal to their sum. By combining Theorems A.5 and A.7 with the result that for an idempotent matrix, the roots are all zero or one, we obtain this result:

- *The rank of a symmetric idempotent matrix is equal to its trace.* **(A-108)**

### A.6.11 FACTORING A MATRIX

In some applications, we shall require a matrix $\mathbf{P}$ such that

$$\mathbf{P}'\mathbf{P} = \mathbf{A}^{-1}.$$

One choice is

$$\mathbf{P} = \mathbf{\Lambda}^{-1/2}\mathbf{C}',$$

so that

$$\mathbf{P}'\mathbf{P} = (\mathbf{C}')'(\mathbf{\Lambda}^{-1/2})'\mathbf{\Lambda}^{-1/2}\mathbf{C}' = \mathbf{C}\mathbf{\Lambda}^{-1}\mathbf{C}',$$

as desired.[10] Thus, the **spectral decomposition** of $\mathbf{A}$, $\mathbf{A} = \mathbf{C}\mathbf{\Lambda}\mathbf{C}'$ is a useful result for this kind of computation.

The **Cholesky factorization** of a symmetric positive definite matrix is an alternative representation that is useful in regression analysis. Any symmetric positive definite matrix $\mathbf{A}$ may be written as the product of a **lower triangular matrix** $\mathbf{L}$ and its transpose (which is an **upper triangular matrix**) $\mathbf{L}' = \mathbf{U}$. Thus, $\mathbf{A} = \mathbf{L}\mathbf{U}$. This result is the Cholesky decomposition of $\mathbf{A}$. The square roots of the diagonal elements of $\mathbf{L}$, $d_i$, are the **Cholesky values** of $\mathbf{A}$. By arraying these in a diagonal matrix $\mathbf{D}$, we may also write $\mathbf{A} = \mathbf{L}\mathbf{D}^{-1}\mathbf{D}^2\mathbf{D}^{-1}\mathbf{U} = \mathbf{L}^*\mathbf{D}^2\mathbf{U}^*$, which is similar to the spectral decomposition in (A-85). The usefulness of this formulation arises when the inverse of $\mathbf{A}$ is required. Once $\mathbf{L}$ is

---

[9]Not all idempotent matrices are symmetric. We shall not encounter any asymmetric ones in our work, however.

[10]We say that this is "one" choice because if $\mathbf{A}$ is symmetric, as it will be in all our applications, there are other candidates. The reader can easily verify that $\mathbf{C}\mathbf{\Lambda}^{-1/2}\mathbf{C}' = \mathbf{A}^{-1/2}$ works as well.

computed, finding $\mathbf{A}^{-1} = \mathbf{U}^{-1}\mathbf{L}^{-1}$ is also straightforward as well as extremely fast and accurate. Most recently developed econometric software packages use this technique for inverting positive definite matrices.

A third type of decomposition of a matrix is useful for numerical analysis when the inverse is difficult to obtain because the columns of $\mathbf{A}$ are "nearly" collinear. Any $n \times K$ matrix $\mathbf{A}$ for which $n \geq K$ can be written in the form $\mathbf{A} = \mathbf{UWV}'$, where $\mathbf{U}$ is an orthogonal $n \times K$ matrix—that is, $\mathbf{U}'\mathbf{U} = \mathbf{I}_K$—$\mathbf{W}$ is a $K \times K$ diagonal matrix such that $w_i \geq 0$, and $\mathbf{V}$ is a $K \times K$ matrix such that $\mathbf{V}'\mathbf{V} = \mathbf{I}_K$. This result is called the **singular value decomposition** (SVD) of $\mathbf{A}$, and $w_i$ are the singular values of $\mathbf{A}$.[11] (Note that if $\mathbf{A}$ is square, then the spectral decomposition is a singular value decomposition.) As with the Cholesky decomposition, the usefulness of the SVD arises in inversion, in this case, of $\mathbf{A}'\mathbf{A}$. By multiplying it out, we obtain that $(\mathbf{A}'\mathbf{A})^{-1}$ is simply $\mathbf{VW}^{-2}\mathbf{V}'$. Once the SVD of $\mathbf{A}$ is computed, the inversion is trivial. The other advantage of this format is its numerical stability, which is discussed at length in Press et al. (1986).

Press et al. (1986) recommend the SVD approach as the method of choice for solving least squares problems because of its accuracy and numerical stability. A commonly used alternative method similar to the SVD approach is the QR decomposition. Any $n \times K$ matrix, $\mathbf{X}$, with $n \geq K$ can be written in the form $\mathbf{X} = \mathbf{QR}$ in which the columns of $\mathbf{Q}$ are orthonormal ($\mathbf{Q}'\mathbf{Q} = \mathbf{I}$) and $\mathbf{R}$ is an upper triangular matrix. Decomposing $\mathbf{X}$ in this fashion allows an extremely accurate solution to the least squares problem that does not involve inversion or direct solution of the normal equations. Press et al. suggest that this method may have problems with rounding errors in problems when $\mathbf{X}$ is nearly of short rank, but based on other published results, this concern seems relatively minor.[12]

### A.6.12   THE GENERALIZED INVERSE OF A MATRIX

Inverse matrices are fundamental in econometrics. Although we shall not require them much in our treatment in this book, there are more general forms of inverse matrices than we have considered thus far. A **generalized inverse** of a matrix $\mathbf{A}$ is another matrix $\mathbf{A}^+$ that satisfies the following requirements:

1. $\mathbf{AA}^+\mathbf{A} = \mathbf{A}$.
2. $\mathbf{A}^+\mathbf{AA}^+ = \mathbf{A}^+$.
3. $\mathbf{A}^+\mathbf{A}$ is symmetric.
4. $\mathbf{AA}^+$ is symmetric.

A unique $\mathbf{A}^+$ can be found for any matrix, whether $\mathbf{A}$ is singular or not, or even if $\mathbf{A}$ is not square.[13] The unique matrix that satisfies all four requirements is called the **Moore–Penrose inverse** or **pseudoinverse** of $\mathbf{A}$. If $\mathbf{A}$ happens to be square and nonsingular, then the generalized inverse will be the familiar ordinary inverse. But if $\mathbf{A}^{-1}$ does not exist, then $\mathbf{A}^+$ can still be computed.

An important special case is the overdetermined system of equations

$$\mathbf{Ab} = \mathbf{y},$$

---

[11] Discussion of the singular value decomposition (and listings of computer programs for the computations) may be found in Press et al. (1986).

[12] The National Institute of Standards and Technology (NIST) has published a suite of benchmark problems that test the accuracy of least squares computations (http://www.nist.gov/itl/div898/strd). Using these problems, which include some extremely difficult, ill-conditioned data sets, we found that the QR method would reproduce all the NIST certified solutions to 15 digits of accuracy, which suggests that the QR method should be satisfactory for all but the worst problems.

[13] A proof of uniqueness, with several other results, may be found in Theil (1983).

where $\mathbf{A}$ has $n$ rows, $K < n$ columns, and column rank equal to $R \leq K$. Suppose that $R$ equals $K$, so that $(\mathbf{A}'\mathbf{A})^{-1}$ exists. Then the Moore–Penrose inverse of $\mathbf{A}$ is

$$\mathbf{A}^+ = (\mathbf{A}'\mathbf{A})^{-1}\mathbf{A}',$$

which can be verified by multiplication. A "solution" to the system of equations can be written

$$\mathbf{b} = \mathbf{A}^+\mathbf{y}.$$

This is the vector that minimizes the length of $\mathbf{Ab} - \mathbf{y}$. Recall this was the solution to the least squares problem obtained in Section A.4.4. If $\mathbf{y}$ lies in the column space of $\mathbf{A}$, this vector will be zero, but otherwise, it will not.

Now suppose that $\mathbf{A}$ does not have full rank. The previous solution cannot be computed. An alternative solution can be obtained, however. We continue to use the matrix $\mathbf{A}'\mathbf{A}$. In the spectral decomposition of Section A.6.4, if $\mathbf{A}$ has rank $R$, then there are $R$ terms in the summation in (A-85). In (A-102), the spectral decomposition using the reciprocals of the characteristic roots is used to compute the inverse. To compute the Moore–Penrose inverse, we apply this calculation to $\mathbf{A}'\mathbf{A}$, using only the nonzero roots, then postmultiply the result by $\mathbf{A}'$. Let $\mathbf{C}_1$ be the $R$ characteristic vectors corresponding to the nonzero roots, which we array in the diagonal matrix, $\mathbf{\Lambda}_1$. Then the Moore–Penrose inverse is

$$\mathbf{A}^+ = \mathbf{C}_1\mathbf{\Lambda}_1^{-1}\mathbf{C}_1'\mathbf{A}',$$

which is very similar to the previous result.

If $\mathbf{A}$ is a symmetric matrix with rank $R \leq K$, the Moore–Penrose inverse is computed precisely as in the preceding equation without postmultiplying by $\mathbf{A}'$. Thus, for a symmetric matrix $\mathbf{A}$,

$$\mathbf{A}^+ = \mathbf{C}_1\mathbf{\Lambda}_1^{-1}\mathbf{C}_1',$$

where $\mathbf{\Lambda}_1^{-1}$ is a diagonal matrix containing the reciprocals of the *nonzero* roots of $\mathbf{A}$.

## A.7 QUADRATIC FORMS AND DEFINITE MATRICES

Many optimization problems involve double sums of the form

$$q = \sum_{i=1}^{n} \sum_{j=1}^{n} x_i x_j a_{ij}. \qquad \text{(A-109)}$$

This **quadratic form** can be written

$$q = \mathbf{x}'\mathbf{Ax},$$

where $\mathbf{A}$ is a symmetric matrix. In general, $q$ may be positive, negative, or zero; it depends on $\mathbf{A}$ and $\mathbf{x}$. There are some matrices, however, for which $q$ will be positive regardless of $\mathbf{x}$, and others for which $q$ will always be negative (or nonnegative or nonpositive). For a given matrix $\mathbf{A}$,

1. If $\mathbf{x}'\mathbf{Ax} > (<)\ 0$ for all nonzero $\mathbf{x}$, then $\mathbf{A}$ is **positive (negative) definite.**
2. If $\mathbf{x}'\mathbf{Ax} \geq (\leq)\ 0$ for all nonzero $\mathbf{x}$, then $\mathbf{A}$ is **nonnegative definite** or **positive semidefinite** (nonpositive definite).

It might seem that it would be impossible to check a matrix for definiteness, since $\mathbf{x}$ can be chosen arbitrarily. But we have already used the set of results necessary to do so. Recall that a symmetric matrix can be decomposed into

$$\mathbf{A} = \mathbf{C \Lambda C'}.$$

Therefore, the quadratic form can be written as

$$\mathbf{x' A x} = \mathbf{x' C \Lambda C' x}.$$

Let $\mathbf{y} = \mathbf{C'x}$. Then

$$\mathbf{x'Ax} = \mathbf{y'\Lambda y} = \sum_{i=1}^{n} \lambda_i y_i^2. \qquad \textbf{(A-110)}$$

If $\lambda_i$ is positive for all $i$, then regardless of $\mathbf{y}$—that is, regardless of $\mathbf{x}$—$q$ will be positive. This case was identified earlier as a positive definite matrix. Continuing this line of reasoning, we obtain the following theorem.

---

**THEOREM A.11** **Definite Matrices**
*Let **A** be a symmetric matrix. If all the characteristic roots of **A** are positive (negative), then **A** is* **positive definite** **(negative definite)**. *If some of the roots are zero, then **A** is* **nonnegative (nonpositive) definite** *if the remainder are positive (negative). If **A** has both negative and positive roots, then **A** is* **indefinite.**

---

The preceding statements give, in each case, the "if" parts of the theorem. To establish the "only if" parts, assume that the condition on the roots does not hold. This must lead to a contradiction. For example, if some $\lambda$ can be negative, then $\mathbf{y'\Lambda y}$ could be negative for some $\mathbf{y}$, so **A** cannot be positive definite.

## A.7.1   NONNEGATIVE DEFINITE MATRICES

A case of particular interest is that of nonnegative definite matrices. Theorem A.11 implies a number of related results.

- If **A** is nonnegative definite, then $|\mathbf{A}| \geq 0$. $\qquad$ **(A-111)**

   *Proof:* The determinant is the product of the roots, which are nonnegative.

   The converse, however, is not true. For example, a $2 \times 2$ matrix with two negative roots is clearly not positive definite, but it does have a positive determinant.

- If **A** is positive definite, so is $\mathbf{A}^{-1}$. $\qquad$ **(A-112)**

   *Proof:* The roots are the reciprocals of those of **A**, which are, therefore positive.

- The identity matrix **I** is positive definite. $\qquad$ **(A-113)**

   *Proof:* $\mathbf{x'Ix} = \mathbf{x'x} > 0$ if $\mathbf{x} \neq \mathbf{0}$.

A very important result for regression analysis is

- If **A** is $n \times K$ with full column rank and $n > K$, then $\mathbf{A'A}$ is positive definite and $\mathbf{AA'}$ is nonnegative definite. $\qquad$ **(A-114)**

   *Proof:* By assumption, $\mathbf{Ax} \neq \mathbf{0}$. So $\mathbf{x'A'Ax} = (\mathbf{Ax})'(\mathbf{Ax}) = \mathbf{y'y} = \sum_j y_j^2 > 0$.

A similar proof establishes the nonnegative definiteness of $\mathbf{AA}'$. The difference in the latter case is that because $\mathbf{A}$ has more rows than columns there is an $\mathbf{x}$ such that $\mathbf{A}'\mathbf{x} = \mathbf{0}$. Thus, in the proof, we only have $\mathbf{y}'\mathbf{y} \geq 0$. The case in which $\mathbf{A}$ does not have full column rank is the same as that of $\mathbf{AA}'$.

* If $\mathbf{A}$ is positive definite and $\mathbf{B}$ is a nonsingular matrix, then $\mathbf{B}'\mathbf{AB}$ is positive definite.

$$(\text{A-115})$$

  **Proof:** $\mathbf{x}'\mathbf{B}'\mathbf{ABx} = \mathbf{y}'\mathbf{Ay} > 0$, where $\mathbf{y} = \mathbf{Bx}$. But $\mathbf{y}$ cannot be $\mathbf{0}$ because $\mathbf{B}$ is nonsingular.

Finally, note that for $\mathbf{A}$ to be negative definite, all $\mathbf{A}$'s characteristic roots must be negative. But, in this case, $|\mathbf{A}|$ is positive if $\mathbf{A}$ is of even order and negative if $\mathbf{A}$ is of odd order.

### A.7.2 IDEMPOTENT QUADRATIC FORMS

Quadratic forms in idempotent matrices play an important role in the distributions of many test statistics. As such, we shall encounter them fairly often. Two central results are of interest.

* Every symmetric idempotent matrix is nonnegative definite. $\qquad$ (A-116)

  **Proof:** All roots are one or zero; hence, the matrix is nonnegative definite by definition.

Combining this with some earlier results yields a result used in determining the sampling distribution of most of the standard test statistics.

* If $\mathbf{A}$ is symmetric and idempotent, $n \times n$ with rank $J$, then every quadratic form in $\mathbf{A}$ can be written $\mathbf{x}'\mathbf{Ax} = \sum_{j=1}^{J} y_j^2$ $\qquad$ (A-117)

  **Proof:** This result is (A-110) with $\lambda =$ one or zero.

### A.7.3 COMPARING MATRICES

Derivations in econometrics often focus on whether one matrix is "larger" than another. We now consider how to make such a comparison. As a starting point, the two matrices must have the same dimensions. A useful comparison is based on

$$d = \mathbf{x}'\mathbf{Ax} - \mathbf{x}'\mathbf{Bx} = \mathbf{x}'(\mathbf{A} - \mathbf{B})\mathbf{x}.$$

If $d$ is always positive for any nonzero vector, $\mathbf{x}$, then by this criterion, we can say that $\mathbf{A}$ is larger than $\mathbf{B}$. The reverse would apply if $d$ is always negative. It follows from the definition that

$$\text{if } d > 0 \text{ for all nonzero } \mathbf{x}, \text{ then } \mathbf{A} - \mathbf{B} \text{ is positive definite.} \qquad (\text{A-118})$$

If $d$ is only greater than or equal to zero, then $\mathbf{A} - \mathbf{B}$ is nonnegative definite. The ordering is not complete. For some pairs of matrices, $d$ could have either sign, depending on $\mathbf{x}$. In this case, there is no simple comparison.

A particular case of the general result which we will encounter frequently is:

$$\text{If } \mathbf{A} \text{ is positive definite and } \mathbf{B} \text{ is nonnegative definite,}$$
$$\text{then } \mathbf{A} + \mathbf{B} \geq \mathbf{A}. \qquad (\text{A-119})$$

Consider, for example, the "updating formula" introduced in (A-66). This uses a matrix

$$\mathbf{A} = \mathbf{B}'\mathbf{B} + \mathbf{bb}' \geq \mathbf{B}'\mathbf{B}.$$

Finally, in comparing matrices, it may be more convenient to compare their inverses. The result analogous to a familiar result for scalars is:

$$\text{If } \mathbf{A} > \mathbf{B}, \text{ then } \mathbf{B}^{-1} > \mathbf{A}^{-1}. \qquad (\text{A-120})$$

To establish this intuitive result, we would make use of the following, which is proved in Goldberger (1964, Chapter 2):

---

**THEOREM A.12  Ordering for Positive Definite Matrices**

*If* **A** *and* **B** *are two positive definite matrices with the same dimensions and if every characteristic root of* **A** *is larger than (at least as large as) the corresponding characteristic root of* **B** *when both sets of roots are ordered from largest to smallest, then* **A** − **B** *is positive (nonnegative) definite.*

---

The roots of the inverse are the reciprocals of the roots of the original matrix, so the theorem can be applied to the inverse matrices.

## A.8  CALCULUS AND MATRIX ALGEBRA[14]

### A.8.1  DIFFERENTIATION AND THE TAYLOR SERIES

A variable $y$ is a function of another variable $x$ written

$$y = f(x), \quad y = g(x), \quad y = y(x),$$

and so on, if each value of $x$ is associated with a single value of $y$. In this relationship, $y$ and $x$ are sometimes labeled the **dependent variable** and the **independent variable,** respectively. Assuming that the function $f(x)$ is continuous and differentiable, we obtain the following derivatives:

$$f'(x) = \frac{dy}{dx}, \, f''(x) = \frac{d^2 y}{dx^2},$$

and so on.

A frequent use of the derivatives of $f(x)$ is in the **Taylor series approximation.** A Taylor series is a polynomial approximation to $f(x)$. Letting $x^0$ be an arbitrarily chosen expansion point

$$f(x) \approx f(x^0) + \sum_{i=1}^{P} \frac{1}{i!} \frac{d^i f(x^0)}{d(x^0)^i} (x - x^0)^i. \tag{A-121}$$

The choice of the number of terms is arbitrary; the more that are used, the more accurate the approximation will be. The approximation used most frequently in econometrics is the **linear approximation,**

$$f(x) \approx \alpha + \beta x, \tag{A-122}$$

where, by collecting terms in (A-121), $\alpha = [f(x^0) - f'(x^0)x^0]$ and $\beta = f'(x^0)$. The superscript "0" indicates that the function is evaluated at $x^0$. The **quadratic approximation** is

$$f(x) \approx \alpha + \beta x + \gamma x^2, \tag{A-123}$$

where $\alpha = [f^0 - f'^0 x^0 + \frac{1}{2}f''^0 (x^0)^2], \beta = [f'^0 - f''^0 x^0]$ and $\gamma = \frac{1}{2}f''^0$.

---

[14]For a complete exposition, see Magnus and Neudecker (1988).

We can regard a function $y = f(x_1, x_2, \ldots, x_n)$ as a **scalar-valued function** of a vector; that is, $y = f(\mathbf{x})$. The vector of partial derivatives, or **gradient vector,** or simply **gradient,** is

$$\frac{\partial f(\mathbf{x})}{\partial \mathbf{x}} = \begin{bmatrix} \partial y/\partial x_1 \\ \partial y/\partial x_2 \\ \cdots \\ \partial y/\partial x_n \end{bmatrix} = \begin{bmatrix} f_1 \\ f_2 \\ \cdots \\ f_n \end{bmatrix}. \tag{A-124}$$

The vector $\mathbf{g}(\mathbf{x})$ or $\mathbf{g}$ is used to represent the gradient. Notice that it is a column vector. The shape of the derivative is determined by the denominator of the derivative.

A **second derivatives matrix** or **Hessian** is computed as

$$\mathbf{H} = \begin{bmatrix} \partial^2 y/\partial x_1 \partial x_1 & \partial^2 y/\partial x_1 \partial x_2 & \cdots & \partial^2 y/\partial x_1 \partial x_n \\ \partial^2 y/\partial x_2 \partial x_1 & \partial^2 y/\partial x_2 \partial x_2 & \cdots & \partial^2 y/\partial x_2 \partial x_n \\ \cdots & \cdots & \cdots & \cdots \\ \partial^2 y/\partial x_n \partial x_1 & \partial^2 y/\partial x_n \partial x_2 & \cdots & \partial^2 y/\partial x_n \partial x_n \end{bmatrix} = [f_{ij}]. \tag{A-125}$$

In general, $\mathbf{H}$ is a square, symmetric matrix. (The symmetry is obtained for continuous and continuously differentiable functions from Young's theorem.) Each column of $\mathbf{H}$ is the derivative of $\mathbf{g}$ with respect to the corresponding variable in $\mathbf{x}'$. Therefore,

$$\mathbf{H} = \left[ \frac{\partial(\partial y/\partial \mathbf{x})}{\partial x_1} \frac{\partial(\partial y/\partial \mathbf{x})}{\partial x_2} \cdots \frac{\partial(\partial y/\partial \mathbf{x})}{\partial x_n} \right] = \frac{\partial(\partial y/\partial \mathbf{x})}{\partial(x_1 \ x_2 \ \cdots \ x_n)} = \frac{\partial(\partial y/\partial \mathbf{x})}{\partial \mathbf{x}'} = \frac{\partial^2 y}{\partial \mathbf{x} \partial \mathbf{x}'}.$$

The first-order, or linear Taylor series approximation is

$$y \approx f(\mathbf{x}^0) + \sum_{i=1}^{n} f_i(\mathbf{x}^0)\left(x_i - x_i^0\right). \tag{A-126}$$

The right-hand side is

$$f(\mathbf{x}^0) + \left[ \frac{\partial f(\mathbf{x}^0)}{\partial \mathbf{x}^0} \right]' (\mathbf{x} - \mathbf{x}^0) = [f(\mathbf{x}^0) - \mathbf{g}(\mathbf{x}^0)'\mathbf{x}^0] + \mathbf{g}(\mathbf{x}^0)'\mathbf{x} = [f^0 - \mathbf{g}^{0\prime}\mathbf{x}^0] + \mathbf{g}^{0\prime}\mathbf{x}.$$

This produces the linear approximation,

$$y \approx \alpha + \boldsymbol{\beta}'\mathbf{x}.$$

The second-order, or quadratic, approximation adds the second-order terms in the expansion,

$$\frac{1}{2}\sum_{i=1}^{n}\sum_{j=1}^{n} f_{ij}^0\left(x_i - x_i^0\right)\left(x_j - x_j^0\right) = \frac{1}{2}(\mathbf{x} - \mathbf{x}^0)'\mathbf{H}^0(\mathbf{x} - \mathbf{x}^0),$$

to the preceding one. Collecting terms in the same manner as in (A-126), we have

$$y \approx \alpha + \boldsymbol{\beta}'\mathbf{x} + \frac{1}{2}\mathbf{x}'\boldsymbol{\Gamma}\mathbf{x}, \tag{A-127}$$

where

$$\alpha = f^0 - \mathbf{g}^{0\prime}\mathbf{x}^0 + \frac{1}{2}\mathbf{x}^{0\prime}\mathbf{H}^0\mathbf{x}^0, \quad \boldsymbol{\beta} = \mathbf{g}^0 - \mathbf{H}^0\mathbf{x}^0 \quad \text{and} \quad \boldsymbol{\Gamma} = \mathbf{H}^0.$$

A linear function can be written

$$y = \mathbf{a}'\mathbf{x} = \mathbf{x}'\mathbf{a} = \sum_{i=1}^{n} a_i x_i,$$

so

$$\frac{\partial(\mathbf{a'x})}{\partial\mathbf{x}} = \mathbf{a}. \qquad\qquad \text{(A-128)}$$

Note, in particular, that $\partial(\mathbf{a'x})/\partial\mathbf{x} = \mathbf{a}$, not $\mathbf{a'}$. In a set of linear functions

$$\mathbf{y} = \mathbf{Ax},$$

each element $y_i$ of $\mathbf{y}$ is

$$y_i = \mathbf{a}_i'\mathbf{x},$$

where $\mathbf{a}_i'$ is the $i$th row of $\mathbf{A}$ [see (A-14)]. Therefore,

$$\frac{\partial y_i}{\partial\mathbf{x}} = \mathbf{a}_i = \text{transpose of } i\text{th row of } \mathbf{A},$$

and

$$\begin{bmatrix} \partial y_1/\partial\mathbf{x'} \\ \partial y_2/\partial\mathbf{x'} \\ \dots \\ \partial y_n/\partial\mathbf{x'} \end{bmatrix} = \begin{bmatrix} \mathbf{a}_1' \\ \mathbf{a}_2' \\ \dots \\ \mathbf{a}_n' \end{bmatrix}.$$

Collecting all terms, we find that $\partial\mathbf{Ax}/\partial\mathbf{x'} = \mathbf{A}$, whereas the more familiar form will be

$$\frac{\partial\mathbf{Ax}}{\partial\mathbf{x}} = \mathbf{A'}. \qquad\qquad \text{(A-129)}$$

A quadratic form is written

$$\mathbf{x'Ax} = \sum_{i=1}^{n}\sum_{j=1}^{n} x_i x_j a_{ij}. \qquad\qquad \text{(A-130)}$$

For example,

$$\mathbf{A} = \begin{bmatrix} 1 & 3 \\ 3 & 4 \end{bmatrix},$$

so that

$$\mathbf{x'Ax} = 1x_1^2 + 4x_2^2 + 6x_1 x_2.$$

Then

$$\frac{\partial\mathbf{x'Ax}}{\partial\mathbf{x}} = \begin{bmatrix} 2x_1 + 6x_2 \\ 6x_1 + 8x_2 \end{bmatrix} = \begin{bmatrix} 2 & 6 \\ 6 & 8 \end{bmatrix}\begin{bmatrix} x_1 \\ x_2 \end{bmatrix} = 2\mathbf{Ax}, \qquad\qquad \text{(A-131)}$$

which is the general result when $\mathbf{A}$ is a symmetric matrix. If $\mathbf{A}$ is not symmetric, then

$$\frac{\partial(\mathbf{x'Ax})}{\partial\mathbf{x}} = (\mathbf{A} + \mathbf{A'})\mathbf{x}. \qquad\qquad \text{(A-132)}$$

Referring to the preceding double summation, we find that for each term, the coefficient on $a_{ij}$ is $x_i x_j$. Therefore,

$$\frac{\partial(\mathbf{x'Ax})}{\partial a_{ij}} = x_i x_j.$$

The square matrix whose $ij$th element is $x_i x_j$ is $\mathbf{x}\mathbf{x}'$, so

$$\frac{\partial(\mathbf{x}'\mathbf{A}\mathbf{x})}{\partial\mathbf{A}} = \mathbf{x}\mathbf{x}'. \tag{A-133}$$

Derivatives involving determinants appear in maximum likelihood estimation. From the cofactor expansion in (A-51),

$$\frac{\partial|\mathbf{A}|}{\partial a_{ij}} = (-1)^{i+j}|\mathbf{A}_{ij}| = c_{ij}$$

where $|\mathbf{C}_{ji}|$ is the $ji$th cofactor in $\mathbf{A}$. The inverse of $\mathbf{A}$ can be computed using

$$\mathbf{A}_{ij}^{-1} = \frac{|\mathbf{C}_{ji}|}{|\mathbf{A}|}$$

(note the reversal of the subscripts), which implies that

$$\frac{\partial \ln|\mathbf{A}|}{\partial a_{ij}} = \frac{(-1)^{i+j}|\mathbf{C}_{ji}|}{|\mathbf{A}|},$$

or, collecting terms,

$$\frac{\partial \ln|\mathbf{A}|}{\partial \mathbf{A}} = \mathbf{A}^{-1'}.$$

Because the matrices for which we shall make use of this calculation will be symmetric in our applications, the transposition will be unnecessary.

## A.8.2 OPTIMIZATION

Consider finding the $x$ where $f(x)$ is maximized or minimized. Because $f'(x)$ is the slope of $f(x)$, either optimum must occur where $f'(x) = 0$. Otherwise, the function will be increasing or decreasing at $x$. This result implies the **first-order** or **necessary condition for an optimum** (maximum or minimum):

$$\frac{dy}{dx} = 0. \tag{A-134}$$

For a maximum, the function must be concave; for a minimum, it must be convex. The **sufficient condition for an optimum** is:

$$\text{For a maximum,} \frac{d^2 y}{dx^2} < 0;$$

$$\text{for a minimum,} \frac{d^2 y}{dx^2} > 0. \tag{A-135}$$

Some functions, such as the sine and cosine functions, have many **local optima,** that is, many minima and maxima. A function such as $(\cos x)/(1 + x^2)$, which is a damped cosine wave, does as well but differs in that although it has many local maxima, it has one, at $x = 0$, at which $f(x)$ is greater than it is at any other point. Thus, $x = 0$ is the **global maximum,** whereas the other maxima are only **local maxima.** Certain functions, such as a quadratic, have only a single optimum. These functions are **globally concave** if the optimum is a maximum and **globally convex** if it is a minimum.

For maximizing or minimizing a function of several variables, the first-order conditions are

$$\frac{\partial f(\mathbf{x})}{\partial \mathbf{x}} = \mathbf{0}. \tag{A-136}$$

This result is interpreted in the same manner as the necessary condition in the univariate case. At the optimum, it must be true that no small change in any variable leads to an improvement in the function value. In the single-variable case, $d^2y/dx^2$ must be positive for a minimum and negative for a maximum. The second-order condition for an optimum in the multivariate case is that, at the optimizing value,

$$\mathbf{H} = \frac{\partial^2 f(\mathbf{x})}{\partial \mathbf{x} \, \partial \mathbf{x}'} \tag{A-137}$$

must be positive definite for a minimum and negative definite for a maximum.

In a single-variable problem, the second-order condition can usually be verified by inspection. This situation will not generally be true in the multivariate case. As discussed earlier, checking the definiteness of a matrix is, in general, a difficult problem. For most of the problems encountered in econometrics, however, the second-order condition will be implied by the structure of the problem. That is, the matrix $\mathbf{H}$ will usually be of such a form that it is always definite.

For an example of the preceding, consider the problem

$$\text{maximize}_{\mathbf{x}} \, R = \mathbf{a}'\mathbf{x} - \mathbf{x}'\mathbf{A}\mathbf{x},$$

where

$$\mathbf{a}' = (5 \quad 4 \quad 2),$$

and

$$\mathbf{A} = \begin{bmatrix} 2 & 1 & 3 \\ 1 & 3 & 2 \\ 3 & 2 & 5 \end{bmatrix}.$$

Using some now familiar results, we obtain

$$\frac{\partial R}{\partial \mathbf{x}} = \mathbf{a} - 2\mathbf{A}\mathbf{x} = \begin{bmatrix} 5 \\ 4 \\ 2 \end{bmatrix} - \begin{bmatrix} 4 & 2 & 6 \\ 2 & 6 & 4 \\ 6 & 4 & 10 \end{bmatrix} \begin{bmatrix} x_1 \\ x_2 \\ x_3 \end{bmatrix} = \mathbf{0}. \tag{A-138}$$

The solutions are

$$\begin{bmatrix} x_1 \\ x_2 \\ x_3 \end{bmatrix} = \begin{bmatrix} 4 & 2 & 6 \\ 2 & 6 & 4 \\ 6 & 4 & 10 \end{bmatrix}^{-1} \begin{bmatrix} 5 \\ 4 \\ 2 \end{bmatrix} = \begin{bmatrix} 11.25 \\ 1.75 \\ -7.25 \end{bmatrix}.$$

The sufficient condition is that

$$\frac{\partial^2 R(\mathbf{x})}{\partial \mathbf{x} \, \partial \mathbf{x}'} = -2\mathbf{A} = \begin{bmatrix} -4 & -2 & -6 \\ -2 & -6 & -4 \\ -6 & -4 & -10 \end{bmatrix} \tag{A-139}$$

must be negative definite. The three characteristic roots of this matrix are $-15.746$, $-4$, and $-0.25403$. Because all three roots are negative, the matrix is negative definite, as required.

In the preceding, it was necessary to compute the characteristic roots of the Hessian to verify the sufficient condition. For a general matrix of order larger than 2, this will normally require a computer. Suppose, however, that $\mathbf{A}$ is of the form

$$\mathbf{A} = \mathbf{B}'\mathbf{B},$$

where $\mathbf{B}$ is some known matrix. Then, as shown earlier, we know that $\mathbf{A}$ will always be positive definite (assuming that $\mathbf{B}$ has full rank). In this case, it is not necessary to calculate the characteristic roots of $\mathbf{A}$ to verify the sufficient conditions.

### A.8.3 CONSTRAINED OPTIMIZATION

It is often necessary to solve an optimization problem subject to some constraints on the solution. One method is merely to "solve out" the constraints. For example, in the maximization problem considered earlier, suppose that the constraint $x_1 = x_2 - x_3$ is imposed on the solution. For a single constraint such as this one, it is possible merely to substitute the right-hand side of this equation for $x_1$ in the objective function and solve the resulting problem as a function of the remaining two variables. For more general constraints, however, or when there is more than one constraint, the method of Lagrange multipliers provides a more straightforward method of solving the problem. We

$$
\begin{aligned}
\text{maximize}_{\mathbf{x}} \, f(\mathbf{x}) \text{ subject to } c_1(\mathbf{x}) &= 0, \\
c_2(\mathbf{x}) &= 0, \\
&\cdots \\
c_J(\mathbf{x}) &= 0.
\end{aligned}
\tag{A-140}
$$

The Lagrangean approach to this problem is to find the stationary points—that is, the points at which the derivatives are zero—of

$$
L^*(\mathbf{x}, \boldsymbol{\lambda}) = f(\mathbf{x}) + \sum_{j=1}^{J} \lambda_j c_j(\mathbf{x}) = f(\mathbf{x}) + \boldsymbol{\lambda}' \mathbf{c}(\mathbf{x}).
\tag{A-141}
$$

The solutions satisfy the equations

$$
\begin{aligned}
\frac{\partial L^*}{\partial \mathbf{x}} &= \frac{\partial f(\mathbf{x})}{\partial \mathbf{x}} + \frac{\partial \boldsymbol{\lambda}' \mathbf{c}(\mathbf{x})}{\partial \mathbf{x}} = \mathbf{0} \, (n \times 1), \\
\frac{\partial L^*}{\partial \boldsymbol{\lambda}} &= \mathbf{c}(\mathbf{x}) = \mathbf{0} \, (J \times 1).
\end{aligned}
\tag{A-142}
$$

The second term in $\partial L^* / \partial \mathbf{x}$ is

$$
\frac{\partial \boldsymbol{\lambda}' \mathbf{c}(\mathbf{x})}{\partial \mathbf{x}} = \frac{\partial \mathbf{c}(\mathbf{x})' \boldsymbol{\lambda}}{\partial \mathbf{x}} = \left[ \frac{\partial \mathbf{c}(\mathbf{x})'}{\partial \mathbf{x}} \right] \boldsymbol{\lambda} = \mathbf{C}' \boldsymbol{\lambda},
\tag{A-143}
$$

where $\mathbf{C}$ is the matrix of derivatives of the constraints with respect to $\mathbf{x}$. The $j$th row of the $J \times n$ matrix $\mathbf{C}$ is the vector of derivatives of the $j$th constraint, $c_j(\mathbf{x})$, with respect to $\mathbf{x}'$. Upon collecting terms, the first-order conditions are

$$
\begin{aligned}
\frac{\partial L^*}{\partial \mathbf{x}} &= \frac{\partial f(\mathbf{x})}{\partial \mathbf{x}} + \mathbf{C}' \boldsymbol{\lambda} = \mathbf{0}, \\
\frac{\partial L^*}{\partial \boldsymbol{\lambda}} &= \mathbf{c}(\mathbf{x}) = \mathbf{0}.
\end{aligned}
\tag{A-144}
$$

There is one very important aspect of the constrained solution to consider. In the unconstrained solution, we have $\partial f(\mathbf{x}) / \partial \mathbf{x} = \mathbf{0}$. From (A-144), we obtain, for a constrained solution,

$$
\frac{\partial f(\mathbf{x})}{\partial \mathbf{x}} = -\mathbf{C}' \boldsymbol{\lambda},
\tag{A-145}
$$

which will not equal $\mathbf{0}$ unless $\boldsymbol{\lambda} = \mathbf{0}$. This result has two important implications:

- The constrained solution cannot be superior to the unconstrained solution. This is implied by the nonzero gradient at the constrained solution. (That is, unless $\mathbf{C} = \mathbf{0}$ which could happen if the constraints were nonlinear. But, even if so, the solution is still no better than the unconstrained optimum.)
- If the Lagrange multipliers are zero, then the constrained solution will equal the unconstrained solution.

To continue the example begun earlier, suppose that we add the following conditions:

$$x_1 - x_2 + x_3 = 0,$$

$$x_1 + x_2 + x_3 = 0.$$

To put this in the format of the general problem, write the constraints as $\mathbf{c}(\mathbf{x}) = \mathbf{Cx} = \mathbf{0}$, where

$$\mathbf{C} = \begin{bmatrix} 1 & -1 & 1 \\ 1 & 1 & 1 \end{bmatrix}.$$

The Lagrangean function is

$$R^*(\mathbf{x}, \lambda) = \mathbf{a'x} - \mathbf{x'Ax} + \lambda'\mathbf{Cx}.$$

Note the dimensions and arrangement of the various parts. In particular, $\mathbf{C}$ is a $2 \times 3$ matrix, with one row for each constraint and one column for each variable in the objective function. The vector of Lagrange multipliers thus has two elements, one for each constraint. The necessary conditions are

$$\mathbf{a} - 2\mathbf{Ax} + \mathbf{C'}\lambda = \mathbf{0} \quad \text{(three equations)}, \tag{A-146}$$

and

$$\mathbf{Cx} = \mathbf{0} \quad \text{(two equations)}.$$

These may be combined in the single equation

$$\begin{bmatrix} -2\mathbf{A} & \mathbf{C'} \\ \mathbf{C} & \mathbf{0} \end{bmatrix} \begin{bmatrix} \mathbf{x} \\ \lambda \end{bmatrix} = \begin{bmatrix} -\mathbf{a} \\ \mathbf{0} \end{bmatrix}.$$

Using the partitioned inverse of (A-74) produces the solutions

$$\lambda = -[\mathbf{CA}^{-1}\mathbf{C'}]^{-1}\mathbf{CA}^{-1}\mathbf{a} \tag{A-147}$$

and

$$\mathbf{x} = \frac{1}{2}\mathbf{A}^{-1}[\mathbf{I} - \mathbf{C'}(\mathbf{CA}^{-1}\mathbf{C'})^{-1}\mathbf{CA}^{-1}]\mathbf{a}. \tag{A-148}$$

The two results, (A-147) and (A-148), yield analytic solutions for $\lambda$ and $\mathbf{x}$. For the specific matrices and vectors of the example, these are $\lambda = [-0.5 \ -7.5]'$, and the constrained solution vector, $\mathbf{x}^* = [1.5 \ 0 \ -1.5]'$. Note that in computing the solution to this sort of problem, it is not necessary to use the rather cumbersome form of (A-148). Once $\lambda$ is obtained from (A-147), the solution can be inserted in (A-146) for a much simpler computation. The solution

$$\mathbf{x} = \frac{1}{2}\mathbf{A}^{-1}\mathbf{a} + \frac{1}{2}\mathbf{A}^{-1}\mathbf{C'}\lambda$$

suggests a useful result for the constrained optimum:

$$\text{constrained solution} = \text{unconstrained solution} + [2\mathbf{A}]^{-1}\mathbf{C'}\lambda. \tag{A-149}$$

Finally, by inserting the two solutions in the original function, we find that $R = 24.375$ and $R^* = 2.25$, which illustrates again that the constrained solution (in this *maximization* problem) is inferior to the unconstrained solution.

## A.8.4 TRANSFORMATIONS

If a function is strictly monotonic, then it is a **one-to-one function.** Each $y$ is associated with exactly one value of $x$, and vice versa. In this case, an **inverse function** exists, which expresses $x$ as a function of $y$, written

$$y = f(x)$$

and

$$x = f^{-1}(y).$$

An example is the inverse relationship between the log and the exponential functions.
    The slope of the inverse function,

$$J = \frac{dx}{dy} = \frac{df^{-1}(y)}{dy} = f^{-1\prime}(y),$$

is the **Jacobian** of the transformation from $y$ to $x$. For example, if

$$y = a + bx,$$

then

$$x = -\frac{a}{b} + \left[\frac{1}{b}\right] y$$

is the inverse transformation and

$$J = \frac{dx}{dy} = \frac{1}{b}.$$

Looking ahead to the statistical application of this concept, we observe that if $y = f(x)$ were *vertical,* then this would no longer be a functional relationship. The same $x$ would be associated with more than one value of $y$. In this case, at this value of $x$, we would find that $J = 0$, indicating a singularity in the function.
    If $\mathbf{y}$ is a column vector of functions, $\mathbf{y} = \mathbf{f}(\mathbf{x})$, then

$$\mathbf{J} = \frac{\partial \mathbf{x}}{\partial \mathbf{y}'} = \begin{bmatrix} \partial x_1/\partial y_1 & \partial x_1/\partial y_2 & \cdots & \partial x_1/\partial y_n \\ \partial x_2/\partial y_1 & \partial x_2/\partial y_2 & \cdots & \partial x_2/\partial y_n \\ & & \vdots & \\ \partial x_n/\partial y_1 & \partial x_n/\partial y_2 & \cdots & \partial x_n/\partial y_n \end{bmatrix}.$$

    Consider the set of linear functions $\mathbf{y} = \mathbf{Ax} = \mathbf{f}(\mathbf{x})$. The inverse transformation is $\mathbf{x} = \mathbf{f}^{-1}(\mathbf{y})$, which will be

$$\mathbf{x} = \mathbf{A}^{-1}\mathbf{y},$$

if $\mathbf{A}$ is nonsingular. If $\mathbf{A}$ is singular, then there is no inverse transformation. Let $\mathbf{J}$ be the matrix of partial derivatives of the inverse functions:

$$\mathbf{J} = \left[\frac{\partial x_i}{\partial y_j}\right].$$

The absolute value of the determinant of $\mathbf{J}$,

$$\text{abs}(|\mathbf{J}|) = \text{abs}\left(\det\left(\left[\frac{\partial \mathbf{x}}{\partial \mathbf{y}'}\right]\right)\right),$$

is the **Jacobian** determinant of the transformation from $\mathbf{y}$ to $\mathbf{x}$. In the nonsingular case,

$$\text{abs}(|\mathbf{J}|) = \text{abs}(|\mathbf{A}^{-1}|) = \frac{1}{\text{abs}(|\mathbf{A}|)}.$$

In the singular case, the matrix of partial derivatives will be singular and the determinant of the Jacobian will be zero. In this instance, the singular Jacobian implies that **A** is singular or, equivalently, that the transformations from **x** to **y** are functionally dependent. The singular case is analogous to the single-variable case.

Clearly, if the vector **x** is given, then **y** = **Ax** can be computed from **x**. Whether **x** can be deduced from **y** is another question. Evidently, it depends on the Jacobian. If the Jacobian is not zero, then the inverse transformations exist, and we can obtain **x**. If not, then we cannot obtain **x**.

# APPENDIX B

# PROBABILITY AND DISTRIBUTION THEORY

## B.1 INTRODUCTION

This appendix reviews the distribution theory used later in the book. A previous course in statistics is assumed, so most of the results will be stated without proof. The more advanced results in the later sections will be developed in greater detail.

## B.2 RANDOM VARIABLES

We view our observation on some aspect of the economy as the **outcome** of a random process that is almost never under our (the analyst's) control. In the current literature, the descriptive (and perspective laden) term **data-generating process,** or DGP is often used for this underlying mechanism. The observed (measured) outcomes of the process are assigned unique numeric values. The assignment is one to one; each outcome gets one value, and no two distinct outcomes receive the same value. This outcome variable, $X$, is a **random variable** because, until the data are actually observed, it is uncertain what value $X$ will take. Probabilities are associated with outcomes to quantify this uncertainty. We usually use capital letters for the "name" of a random variable and lowercase letters for the values it takes. Thus, the probability that $X$ takes a particular value $x$ might be denoted $\text{Prob}(X = x)$.

A random variable is **discrete** if the set of outcomes is either finite in number or countably infinite. The random variable is **continuous** if the set of outcomes is infinitely divisible and, hence, not countable. These definitions will correspond to the types of data we observe in practice. Counts of occurrences will provide observations on discrete random variables, whereas measurements such as time or income will give observations on continuous random variables.

### B.2.1 PROBABILITY DISTRIBUTIONS

A listing of the values $x$ taken by a random variable $X$ and their associated probabilities is a **probability distribution,** $f(x)$. For a discrete random variable,

$$f(x) = \text{Prob}(X = x). \tag{B-1}$$

The axioms of probability require that

1. $0 \leq \text{Prob}(X = x) \leq 1.$ **(B-2)**
2. $\sum_x f(x) = 1.$ **(B-3)**

For the continuous case, the probability associated with any particular point is zero, and we can only assign positive probabilities to intervals in the range of $x$. The **probability density function (pdf)** is defined so that $f(x) \geq 0$ and

1. $\text{Prob}(a \leq x \leq b) = \displaystyle\int_a^b f(x)\,dx \geq 0.$ **(B-4)**

This result is the area under $f(x)$ in the range from $a$ to $b$. For a continuous variable,

2. $\displaystyle\int_{-\infty}^{+\infty} f(x)\,dx = 1.$ **(B-5)**

If the range of $x$ is not infinite, then it is understood that $f(x) = 0$ anywhere outside the appropriate range. Because the probability associated with any individual point is 0,

$$\text{Prob}(a \leq x \leq b) = \text{Prob}(a \leq x < b)$$
$$= \text{Prob}(a < x \leq b)$$
$$= \text{Prob}(a < x < b).$$

### B.2.2 CUMULATIVE DISTRIBUTION FUNCTION

For any random variable $X$, the probability that $X$ is less than or equal to $a$ is denoted $F(a)$. $F(x)$ is the **cumulative distribution function (cdf)**. For a discrete random variable,

$$F(x) = \sum_{X \leq x} f(X) = \text{Prob}(X \leq x).$$ **(B-6)**

In view of the definition of $f(x)$,

$$f(x_i) = F(x_i) - F(x_{i-1}).$$ **(B-7)**

For a continuous random variable,

$$F(x) = \int_{-\infty}^x f(t)\,dt,$$ **(B-8)**

and

$$f(x) = \frac{dF(x)}{dx}.$$ **(B-9)**

In both the continuous and discrete cases, $F(x)$ must satisfy the following properties:

1. $0 \leq F(x) \leq 1.$
2. If $x > y$, then $F(x) \geq F(y).$
3. $F(+\infty) = 1.$
4. $F(-\infty) = 0.$

From the definition of the cdf,

$$\text{Prob}(a < x \leq b) = F(b) - F(a).$$ **(B-10)**

Any valid pdf will imply a valid cdf, so there is no need to verify these conditions separately.

## B.3 EXPECTATIONS OF A RANDOM VARIABLE

---

**DEFINITION B.1** Mean of a Random Variable

*The **mean**, or **expected value**, of a random variable is*

$$E[x] = \begin{cases} \sum_x x f(x) & \text{if } x \text{ is discrete,} \\ \int_x x f(x) \, dx & \text{if } x \text{ is continuous.} \end{cases}$$

(B-11)

---

The notation $\sum_x$ or $\int_x$, used henceforth, means the sum or integral over the entire range of values of $x$. The mean is usually denoted $\mu$. It is a weighted average of the values taken by $x$, where the weights are the respective probabilities. It is not necessarily a value actually taken by the random variable. For example, the expected number of heads in one toss of a fair coin is $\frac{1}{2}$.

Other **measures of central tendency** are the **median,** which is the value $m$ such that $\text{Prob}(X \leq m) \geq \frac{1}{2}$ and $\text{Prob}(X \geq m) \geq \frac{1}{2}$, and the **mode,** which is the value of $x$ at which $f(x)$ takes its maximum. The first of these measures is more frequently used than the second. Loosely speaking, the median corresponds more closely than the mean to the middle of a distribution. It is unaffected by extreme values. In the discrete case, the modal value of $x$ has the highest probability of occurring.

Let $g(x)$ be a function of $x$. The function that gives the expected value of $g(x)$ is denoted

$$E[g(x)] = \begin{cases} \sum_x g(x) \, \text{Prob}(X = x) & \text{if } X \text{ is discrete,} \\ \int_x g(x) f(x) \, dx & \text{if } X \text{ is continuous.} \end{cases}$$

(B-12)

If $g(x) = a + bx$ for constants $a$ and $b$, then

$$E[a + bx] = a + bE[x].$$

An important case is the expected value of a constant $a$, which is just $a$.

---

**DEFINITION B.2** Variance of a Random Variable

*The **variance** of a random variable is*

$$\text{Var}[x] = E[(x - \mu)^2]$$

$$= \begin{cases} \sum_x (x - \mu)^2 f(x) & \text{if } x \text{ is discrete,} \\ \int_x (x - \mu)^2 f(x) \, dx & \text{if } x \text{ is continuous.} \end{cases}$$

(B-13)

---

$\text{Var}[x]$, which must be positive, is usually denoted $\sigma^2$. This function is a measure of the dispersion of a distribution. Computation of the variance is simplified by using the following important result:

$$\mathrm{Var}[x] = E[x^2] - \mu^2. \tag{B-14}$$

A convenient corollary to (B-14) is

$$E[x^2] = \sigma^2 + \mu^2. \tag{B-15}$$

By inserting $y = a + bx$ in (B-13) and expanding, we find that

$$\mathrm{Var}[a + bx] = b^2 \, \mathrm{Var}[x], \tag{B-16}$$

which implies, for any constant $a$, that

$$\mathrm{Var}[a] = 0. \tag{B-17}$$

To describe a distribution, we usually use $\sigma$, the positive square root, which is the **standard deviation** of $x$. The standard deviation can be interpreted as having the same units of measurement as $x$ and $\mu$. For any random variable $x$ and any positive constant $k$, the **Chebychev inequality** states that

$$\mathrm{Prob}(\mu - k\sigma \leq x \leq \mu + k\sigma) \geq 1 - \frac{1}{k^2}. \tag{B-18}$$

Two other measures often used to describe a probability distribution are

$$\mathrm{skewness} = E[(x - \mu)^3],$$

and

$$\mathrm{kurtosis} = E[(x - \mu)^4].$$

Skewness is a measure of the asymmetry of a distribution. For symmetric distributions,

$$f(\mu - x) = f(\mu + x),$$

and

$$\mathrm{skewness} = 0.$$

For asymmetric distributions, the skewness will be positive if the "long tail" is in the positive direction. Kurtosis is a measure of the thickness of the tails of the distribution. A shorthand expression for other **central moments** is

$$\mu_r = E[(x - \mu)^r].$$

Because $\mu_r$ tends to explode as $r$ grows, the normalized measure, $\mu_r / \sigma^r$, is often used for description. Two common measures are

$$\mathrm{skewness\ coefficient} = \frac{\mu_3}{\sigma^3},$$

and

$$\mathrm{degree\ of\ excess} = \frac{\mu_4}{\sigma^4} - 3.$$

The second is based on the normal distribution, which has excess of zero.

For any two functions $g_1(x)$ and $g_2(x)$,

$$E[g_1(x) + g_2(x)] = E[g_1(x)] + E[g_2(x)]. \tag{B-19}$$

For the general case of a possibly nonlinear $g(x)$,

$$E[g(x)] = \int_x g(x) f(x) \, dx, \tag{B-20}$$

and

$$\text{Var}[g(x)] = \int_x \left(g(x) - E[g(x)]\right)^2 f(x)\, dx. \tag{B-21}$$

(For convenience, we shall omit the equivalent definitions for discrete variables in the following discussion and use the integral to mean either integration or summation, whichever is appropriate.)

A device used to approximate $E[g(x)]$ and $\text{Var}[g(x)]$ is the linear Taylor series approximation:

$$g(x) \approx [g(x^0) - g'(x^0)x^0] + g'(x^0)x = \beta_1 + \beta_2 x = g^*(x). \tag{B-22}$$

If the approximation is reasonably accurate, then the mean and variance of $g^*(x)$ will be approximately equal to the mean and variance of $g(x)$. A natural choice for the expansion point is $x^0 = \mu = E(x)$. Inserting this value in (B-22) gives

$$g(x) \approx [g(\mu) - g'(\mu)\mu] + g'(\mu)x, \tag{B-23}$$

so that

$$E[g(x)] \approx g(\mu), \tag{B-24}$$

and

$$\text{Var}[g(x)] \approx [g'(\mu)]^2 \text{Var}[x]. \tag{B-25}$$

A point to note in view of (B-22) to (B-24) is that $E[g(x)]$ will generally not equal $g(E[x])$. For the special case in which $g(x)$ is concave—that is, where $g''(x) < 0$—we know from **Jensen's inequality** that $E[g(x)] \le g(E[x])$. For example, $E[\log(x)] \le \log(E[x])$.

## B.4  SOME SPECIFIC PROBABILITY DISTRIBUTIONS

Certain experimental situations naturally give rise to specific probability distributions. In the majority of cases in economics, however, the distributions used are merely models of the observed phenomena. Although the normal distribution, which we shall discuss at length, is the mainstay of econometric research, economists have used a wide variety of other distributions. A few are discussed here.[1]

### B.4.1  THE NORMAL DISTRIBUTION

The general form of the normal distribution with mean $\mu$ and standard deviation $\sigma$ is

$$f(x \mid \mu, \sigma^2) = \frac{1}{\sigma\sqrt{2\pi}} e^{-1/2[(x-\mu)^2/\sigma^2]}. \tag{B-26}$$

This result is usually denoted $x \sim N[\mu, \sigma^2]$. The standard notation $x \sim f(x)$ is used to state that "$x$ has probability distribution $f(x)$." Among the most useful properties of the normal distribution

---

[1] A much more complete listing appears in Maddala (1977a, Chapters 3 and 18) and in most mathematical statistics textbooks. See also Poirier (1995) and Stuart and Ord (1989). Another useful reference is Evans, Hastings, and Peacock (1993). Johnson et al. (1974, 1993, 1994, 1995, 1997) is an encyclopedic reference on the subject of statistical distributions.

is its preservation under linear transformation.

$$\text{If } x \sim N[\mu, \sigma^2], \quad \text{then } (a + bx) \sim N[a + b\mu, b^2\sigma^2]. \tag{B-27}$$

One particularly convenient transformation is $a = -\mu/\sigma$ and $b = 1/\sigma$. The resulting variable $z = (x - \mu)/\sigma$ has the **standard normal distribution,** denoted $N[0, 1]$, with density

$$\phi(z) = \frac{1}{\sqrt{2\pi}} e^{-z^2/2}. \tag{B-28}$$

The specific notation $\phi(z)$ is often used for this distribution and $\Phi(z)$ for its cdf. It follows from the definitions above that if $x \sim N[\mu, \sigma^2]$, then

$$f(x) = \frac{1}{\sigma} \phi \left[ \frac{x - \mu}{\sigma} \right].$$

Figure B.1 shows the densities of the standard normal distribution and the normal distribution with mean 0.5, which shifts the distribution to the right, and standard deviation 1.3, which, it can be seen, scales the density so that it is shorter but wider. (The graph is a bit deceiving unless you look closely; both densities are symmetric.)

Tables of the standard normal cdf appear in most statistics and econometrics textbooks. Because the form of the distribution does not change under a linear transformation, it is not necessary to tabulate the distribution for other values of $\mu$ and $\sigma$. For any normally distributed variable,

$$\text{Prob}(a \leq x \leq b) = \text{Prob}\left( \frac{a - \mu}{\sigma} \leq \frac{x - \mu}{\sigma} \leq \frac{b - \mu}{\sigma} \right), \tag{B-29}$$

which can always be read from a table of the standard normal distribution. In addition, because the distribution is symmetric, $\Phi(-z) = 1 - \Phi(z)$. Hence, it is not necessary to tabulate both the negative and positive halves of the distribution.

**FIGURE B.1**    The Normal Distribution.

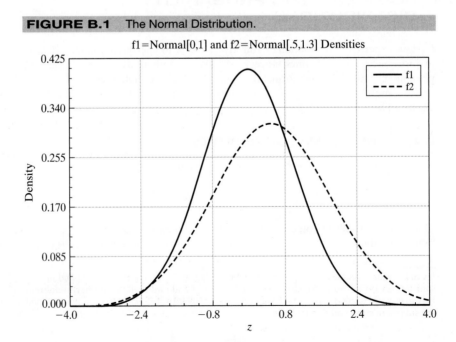

f1=Normal[0,1] and f2=Normal[.5,1.3] Densities

## B.4.2 THE CHI-SQUARED, $t$, AND $F$ DISTRIBUTIONS

The chi-squared, $t$, and $F$ distributions are derived from the normal distribution. They arise in econometrics as sums of $n$ or $n_1$ and $n_2$ other variables. These three distributions have associated with them one or two "degrees of freedom" parameters, which for our purposes will be the number of variables in the relevant sum.

The first of the essential results is

- If $z \sim N[0, 1]$, then $x = z^2 \sim$ chi-squared[1]—that is, **chi-squared** with one degree of freedom—denoted

$$z^2 \sim \chi^2[1].$$ (B-30)

This distribution is a skewed distribution with mean 1 and variance 2. The second result is

- If $x_1, \ldots, x_n$ are $n$ *independent* chi-squared[1] variables, then

$$\sum_{i=1}^{n} x_i \sim \text{chi-squared}[n].$$ (B-31)

The mean and variance of a chi-squared variable with $n$ degrees of freedom are $n$ and $2n$, respectively. A number of useful corollaries can be derived using (B-30) and (B-31).

- If $z_i, i = 1, \ldots, n$, are independent $N[0, 1]$ variables, then

$$\sum_{i=1}^{n} z_i^2 \sim \chi^2[n].$$ (B-32)

- If $z_i, i = 1, \ldots, n$, are independent $N[0, \sigma^2]$ variables, then

$$\sum_{i=1}^{n} (z_i/\sigma)^2 \sim \chi^2[n].$$ (B-33)

- If $x_1$ and $x_2$ are independent chi-squared variables with $n_1$ and $n_2$ degrees of freedom, respectively, then

$$x_1 + x_2 \sim \chi^2[n_1 + n_2].$$ (B-34)

This result can be generalized to the sum of an arbitrary number of independent chi-squared variables.

Figure B.2 shows the chi-squared density for three degrees of freedom. The amount of skewness declines as the number of degrees of freedom rises. Unlike the normal distribution, a separate table is required for the chi-squared distribution for each value of $n$. Typically, only a few percentage points of the distribution are tabulated for each $n$. Table G.3 in Appendix G of this book gives lower (left) tail areas for a number of values.

- If $x_1$ and $x_2$ are two *independent* chi-squared variables with degrees of freedom parameters $n_1$ and $n_2$, respectively, then the ratio

$$F[n_1, n_2] = \frac{x_1/n_1}{x_2/n_2}$$ (B-35)

has the **$F$ distribution** with $n_1$ and $n_2$ degrees of freedom.

The two degrees of freedom parameters $n_1$ and $n_2$ are the numerator and denominator degrees of freedom, respectively. Tables of the $F$ distribution must be computed for each pair of values of $(n_1, n_2)$. As such, only one or two specific values, such as the 95 percent and 99 percent upper tail values, are tabulated in most cases.

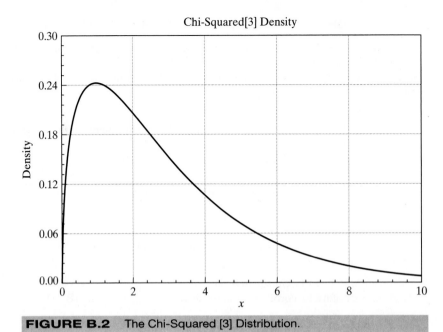

**FIGURE B.2** The Chi-Squared [3] Distribution.

● If $z$ is an $N[0, 1]$ variable and $x$ is $\chi^2[n]$ and is independent of $z$, then the ratio

$$t[n] = \frac{z}{\sqrt{x/n}} \qquad \text{(B-36)}$$

has the **$t$ distribution** with $n$ degrees of freedom.

The $t$ distribution has the same shape as the normal distribution but has thicker tails. Figure B.3 illustrates the $t$ distributions with three and 10 degrees of freedom with the standard normal distribution. Two effects that can be seen in the figure are how the distribution changes as the degrees of freedom increases, and, overall, the similarity of the $t$ distribution to the standard normal. This distribution is tabulated in the same manner as the chi-squared distribution, with several specific cutoff points corresponding to specified tail areas for various values of the degrees of freedom parameter.

Comparing (B-35) with $n_1 = 1$ and (B-36), we see the useful relationship between the $t$ and $F$ distributions:

● If $t \sim t[n]$, then $t^2 \sim F[1, n]$.

If the numerator in (B-36) has a nonzero mean, then the random variable in (B-36) has a noncentral $t$ distribution and its square has a noncentral $F$ distribution. These distributions arise in the $F$ tests of linear restrictions [see (5-6)] when the restrictions do not hold as follows:

1.  *Noncentral chi-squared distribution.* If $z$ has a normal distribution with mean $\mu$ and standard deviation 1, then the distribution of $z^2$ is *noncentral* chi-squared with parameters 1 and $\mu^2/2$.
    a.  If $\mathbf{z} \sim N[\boldsymbol{\mu}, \boldsymbol{\Sigma}]$ with $J$ elements, then $\mathbf{z}'\boldsymbol{\Sigma}^{-1}\mathbf{z}$ has a noncentral chi-squared distribution with $J$ degrees of freedom and noncentrality parameter $\boldsymbol{\mu}'\boldsymbol{\Sigma}^{-1}\boldsymbol{\mu}/2$, which we denote $\chi_*^2[J, \boldsymbol{\mu}'\boldsymbol{\Sigma}^{-1}\boldsymbol{\mu}/2]$.
    b.  If $\mathbf{z} \sim N[\boldsymbol{\mu}, \mathbf{I}]$ and $\mathbf{M}$ is an idempotent matrix with rank $J$, then $\mathbf{z}'\mathbf{M}\mathbf{z} \sim \chi_*^2[J, \boldsymbol{\mu}'\mathbf{M}\boldsymbol{\mu}/2]$.

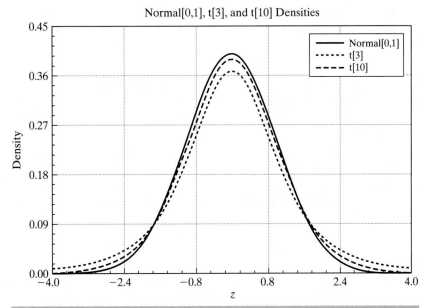

**FIGURE B.3**   The Standard Normal, $t[3]$, and $t[10]$ Distributions.

2.   *Noncentral F distribution.* If $X_1$ has a noncentral chi-squared distribution with noncentrality parameter $\lambda$ and degrees of freedom $n_1$ and $X_2$ has a central chi-squared distribution with degrees of freedom $n_2$ and is independent of $X_1$, then

$$F_* = \frac{X_1/n_1}{X_2/n_2}$$

has a noncentral $F$ distribution with parameters $n_1$, $n_2$, and $\lambda$.[2] Note that in each of these cases, the statistic and the distribution are the familiar ones, except that the effect of the nonzero mean, which induces the noncentrality, is to push the distribution to the right.

### B.4.3   DISTRIBUTIONS WITH LARGE DEGREES OF FREEDOM

The chi-squared, $t$, and $F$ distributions usually arise in connection with sums of sample observations. The degrees of freedom parameter in each case grows with the number of observations. We often deal with larger degrees of freedom than are shown in the tables. Thus, the standard tables are often inadequate. In all cases, however, there are **limiting distributions** that we can use when the degrees of freedom parameter grows large. The simplest case is the $t$ distribution. The $t$ distribution with infinite degrees of freedom is equivalent to the standard normal distribution. Beyond about 100 degrees of freedom, they are almost indistinguishable.

For degrees of freedom greater than 30, a reasonably good approximation for the distribution of the chi-squared variable $x$ is

$$z = (2x)^{1/2} - (2n - 1)^{1/2}, \qquad \textbf{(B-37)}$$

which is approximately standard normally distributed. Thus,

$$\text{Prob}(\chi^2[n] \le a) \approx \Phi[(2a)^{1/2} - (2n - 1)^{1/2}].$$

---

[2]The denominator chi-squared could also be noncentral, but we shall not use any statistics with doubly noncentral distributions.

As used in econometrics, the $F$ distribution with a large-denominator degrees of freedom is common. As $n_2$ becomes infinite, the denominator of $F$ converges identically to one, so we can treat the variable

$$x = n_1 F \tag{B-38}$$

as a chi-squared variable with $n_1$ degrees of freedom. The numerator degree of freedom will typically be small, so this approximation will suffice for the types of applications we are likely to encounter.[3] If not, then the approximation given earlier for the chi-squared distribution can be applied to $n_1 F$.

### B.4.4   SIZE DISTRIBUTIONS: THE LOGNORMAL DISTRIBUTION

In modeling size distributions, such as the distribution of firm sizes in an industry or the distribution of income in a country, the **lognormal distribution,** denoted $LN[\mu, \sigma^2]$, has been particularly useful.[4]

$$f(x) = \frac{1}{\sqrt{2\pi}\,\sigma x} e^{-1/2[(\ln x - \mu)/\sigma]^2}, \quad x > 0.$$

A lognormal variable $x$ has

$$E[x] = e^{\mu + \sigma^2/2},$$

and

$$\mathrm{Var}[x] = e^{2\mu + \sigma^2}\left(e^{\sigma^2} - 1\right).$$

The relation between the normal and lognormal distributions is

$$\text{If } y \sim LN[\mu, \sigma^2], \quad \ln y \sim N[\mu, \sigma^2].$$

A useful result for transformations is given as follows:

If $x$ has a lognormal distribution with mean $\theta$ and variance $\lambda^2$, then

$$\ln x \sim N(\mu, \sigma^2), \quad \text{where } \mu = \ln\theta^2 - \tfrac{1}{2}\ln(\theta^2 + \lambda^2) \quad \text{and} \quad \sigma^2 = \ln(1 + \lambda^2/\theta^2).$$

Because the normal distribution is preserved under linear transformation,

$$\text{if } y \sim LN[\mu, \sigma^2], \quad \text{then } \ln y^r \sim N[r\mu, r^2\sigma^2].$$

If $y_1$ and $y_2$ are independent lognormal variables with $y_1 \sim LN[\mu_1, \sigma_1^2]$ and $y_2 \sim LN[\mu_2, \sigma_2^2]$, then

$$y_1 y_2 \sim LN\left[\mu_1 + \mu_2, \sigma_1^2 + \sigma_2^2\right].$$

### B.4.5   THE GAMMA AND EXPONENTIAL DISTRIBUTIONS

The **gamma distribution** has been used in a variety of settings, including the study of income distribution[5] and production functions.[6] The general form of the distribution is

$$f(x) = \frac{\lambda^P}{\Gamma(P)} e^{-\lambda x} x^{P-1}, \quad x \geq 0, \lambda > 0, P > 0. \tag{B-39}$$

Many familiar distributions are special cases, including the **exponential distribution** ($P = 1$) and chi-squared ($\lambda = \frac{1}{2}$, $P = \frac{n}{2}$). The **Erlang distribution** results if $P$ is a positive integer. The mean is $P/\lambda$, and the variance is $P/\lambda^2$. The **inverse gamma distribution** is the distribution of $1/x$, where $x$

---

[3] See Johnson, Kotz, and Balakrishnan (1994) for other approximations.

[4] A study of applications of the lognormal distribution appears in Aitchison and Brown (1969).

[5] Salem and Mount (1974).

[6] Greene (1980a).

has the gamma distribution. Using the change of variable, $y = 1/x$, the Jacobian is $|dx/dy| = 1/y^2$. Making the substitution and the change of variable, we find

$$f(y) = \frac{\lambda^P}{\Gamma(P)} e^{-\lambda/y} y^{-(P+1)}, \ y \geq 0, \lambda > 0, P > 0.$$

The density is defined for positive $P$. However, the mean is $\lambda/(P-1)$ which is defined only if $P > 1$ and the variance is $\lambda^2/[(P-1)^2(P-2)]$ which is defined only for $P > 2$.

## B.4.6 THE BETA DISTRIBUTION

Distributions for models are often chosen on the basis of the range within which the random variable is constrained to vary. The lognormal distribution, for example, is sometimes used to model a variable that is always nonnegative. For a variable constrained between 0 and $c > 0$, the **beta distribution** has proved useful. Its density is

$$f(x) = \frac{\Gamma(\alpha + \beta)}{\Gamma(\alpha)\Gamma(\beta)} \left(\frac{x}{c}\right)^{\alpha-1} \left(1 - \frac{x}{c}\right)^{\beta-1} \frac{1}{c}. \tag{B-40}$$

This functional form is extremely flexible in the shapes it will accommodate. It is symmetric if $\alpha = \beta$, asymmetric otherwise, and can be hump-shaped or U-shaped. The mean is $c\alpha/(\alpha + \beta)$, and the variance is $c^2 \alpha\beta/[(\alpha + \beta + 1)(\alpha + \beta)^2]$. The beta distribution has been applied in the study of labor force participation rates.[7]

## B.4.7 THE LOGISTIC DISTRIBUTION

The normal distribution is ubiquitous in econometrics. But researchers have found that for some microeconomic applications, there does not appear to be enough mass in the tails of the normal distribution; observations that a model based on normality would classify as "unusual" seem not to be very unusual at all. One approach has been to use thicker-tailed symmetric distributions. The **logistic distribution** is one candidate; the cdf for a logistic random variable is denoted

$$F(x) = \Lambda(x) = \frac{1}{1 + e^{-x}}.$$

The density is $f(x) = \Lambda(x)[1 - \Lambda(x)]$. The mean and variance of this random variable are zero and $\pi^2/3$.

## B.4.8 THE WISHART DISTRIBUTION

The Wishart distribution describes the distribution of a random matrix obtained as

$$\mathbf{W} = \sum_{i=1}^{n} (\mathbf{x}_i - \boldsymbol{\mu})(\mathbf{x}_i - \boldsymbol{\mu}),$$

where $\mathbf{x}_i$ is the $i$th of $n$ $K$ element random vectors from the multivariate normal distribution with mean vector, $\boldsymbol{\mu}$, and covariance matrix, $\boldsymbol{\Sigma}$. This is a multivariate counterpart to the chi-squared distribution. The density of the Wishart random matrix is

$$f(\mathbf{W}) = \frac{\exp\left[-\frac{1}{2} trace\left(\boldsymbol{\Sigma}^{-1}\mathbf{W}\right)\right] |\mathbf{W}|^{-\frac{1}{2}(n-K-1)}}{2^{nK/2} |\boldsymbol{\Sigma}|^{K/2} \pi^{K(K-1)/4} \prod_{j=1}^{K} \Gamma\left(\frac{n+1-j}{2}\right)}.$$

The mean matrix is $n\boldsymbol{\Sigma}$. For the individual pairs of elements in $\mathbf{W}$,

$$\text{Cov}[w_{ij}, w_{rs}] = n(\sigma_{ir}\sigma_{js} + \sigma_{is}\sigma_{jr}).$$

---

[7]Heckman and Willis (1976).

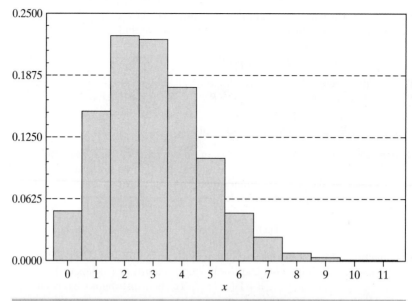

**FIGURE B.4**   The Poisson [3] Distribution.

### B.4.9   DISCRETE RANDOM VARIABLES

Modeling in economics frequently involves random variables that take integer values. In these cases, the distributions listed thus far only provide approximations that are sometimes quite inappropriate. We can build up a class of models for discrete random variables from the **Bernoulli distribution** for a single binomial outcome (trial)

$$\text{Prob}(x = 1) = \alpha,$$

$$\text{Prob}(x = 0) = 1 - \alpha,$$

where $0 \leq \alpha \leq 1$. The modeling aspect of this specification would be the assumptions that the success probability $\alpha$ is constant from one trial to the next and that successive trials are independent. If so, then the distribution for $x$ successes in $n$ trials is the **binomial distribution,**

$$\text{Prob}(X = x) = \binom{n}{x} \alpha^x (1 - \alpha)^{n-x}, \quad x = 0, 1, \dots, n.$$

The mean and variance of $x$ are $n\alpha$ and $n\alpha(1 - \alpha)$, respectively. If the number of trials becomes large at the same time that the success probability becomes small so that the mean $n\alpha$ is stable, then, the limiting form of the binomial distribution is the **Poisson distribution,**

$$\text{Prob}(X = x) = \frac{e^{-\lambda}\lambda^x}{x!}.$$

The Poisson distribution has seen wide use in econometrics in, for example, modeling patents, crime, recreation demand, and demand for health services. (See Chapter 25.) An example is shown in Figure B.4.

## B.5   THE DISTRIBUTION OF A FUNCTION OF A RANDOM VARIABLE

We considered finding the expected value of a function of a random variable. It is fairly common to analyze the random variable itself, which results when we compute a function of some random variable. There are three types of transformation to consider. One discrete random variable may be transformed into another, a continuous variable may be transformed into a discrete one, and one continuous variable may be transformed into another.

The simplest case is the first one. The probabilities associated with the new variable are computed according to the laws of probability. If $y$ is derived from $x$ and the function is one to one, then the probability that $Y = y(x)$ equals the probability that $X = x$. If several values of $x$ yield the same value of $y$, then Prob$(Y = y)$ is the sum of the corresponding probabilities for $x$.

The second type of transformation is illustrated by the way individual data on income are typically obtained in a survey. Income in the population can be expected to be distributed according to some skewed, continuous distribution such as the one shown in Figure B.5.

Data are often reported categorically, as shown in the lower part of the figure. Thus, the random variable corresponding to observed income is a discrete transformation of the actual underlying continuous random variable. Suppose, for example, that the transformed variable $y$ is the mean income in the respective interval. Then

$$\text{Prob}(Y = \mu_1) = P(-\infty < X \le a),$$

$$\text{Prob}(Y = \mu_2) = P(a < X \le b),$$

$$\text{Prob}(Y = \mu_3) = P(b < X \le c),$$

and so on, which illustrates the general procedure.

If $x$ is a continuous random variable with pdf $f_x(x)$ and if $y = g(x)$ is a continuous monotonic function of $x$, then the density of $y$ is obtained by using the change of variable technique to find

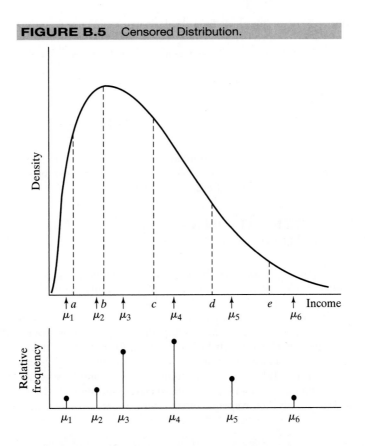

**FIGURE B.5**   Censored Distribution.

the cdf of $y$:

$$\text{Prob}(y \le b) = \int_{-\infty}^{b} f_x(g^{-1}(y))|g^{-1\prime}(y)|\, dy.$$

This equation can now be written as

$$\text{Prob}(y \le b) = \int_{-\infty}^{b} f_y(y)\, dy.$$

Hence,

$$f_y(y) = f_x(g^{-1}(y))|g^{-1\prime}(y)|. \tag{B-41}$$

To avoid the possibility of a negative pdf if $g(x)$ is decreasing, we use the absolute value of the derivative in the previous expression. The term $|g^{-1\prime}(y)|$ must be nonzero for the density of $y$ to be nonzero. In words, the probabilities associated with intervals in the range of $y$ must be associated with intervals in the range of $x$. If the derivative is zero, the correspondence $y = g(x)$ is vertical, and hence all values of $y$ in the given range are associated with the same value of $x$. This single point must have probability zero.

One of the most useful applications of the preceding result is the linear transformation of a normally distributed variable. If $x \sim N[\mu, \sigma^2]$, then the distribution of

$$y = \frac{x - \mu}{\sigma}$$

is found using the preceding result. First, the derivative is obtained from the inverse transformation

$$y = \frac{x}{\sigma} - \frac{\mu}{\sigma} \Rightarrow x = \sigma y + \mu \Rightarrow f^{-1\prime}(y) = \frac{dx}{dy} = \sigma.$$

Therefore,

$$f_y(y) = \frac{1}{\sqrt{2\pi}\sigma} e^{-[(\sigma y + \mu) - \mu]^2/(2\sigma^2)}|\sigma| = \frac{1}{\sqrt{2\pi}} e^{-y^2/2}.$$

This is the density of a normally distributed variable with mean zero and unit standard deviation one. This is the result which makes it unnecessary to have separate tables for the different normal distributions which result from different means and variances.

## B.6 REPRESENTATIONS OF A PROBABILITY DISTRIBUTION

The probability density function (pdf) is a natural and familiar way to formulate the distribution of a random variable. But, there are many other functions that are used to identify or characterize a random variable, depending on the setting. In each of these cases, we can identify some other function of the random variable that has a one to one relationship with the density. We have already used one of these quite heavily in the preceding discussion. For a random variable which has density function $f(x)$, the distribution function, $F(x)$, is an equally informative function that identifies the distribution; the relationship between $f(x)$ and $F(x)$ is defined in (B-6) for a discrete random variable and (B-8) for a continuous one. We now consider several other related functions.

For a continuous random variable, the **survival function** is $S(x) = 1 - F(x) = \text{Prob}[X \ge x]$. This function is widely used in epidemiology, where $x$ is time until some transition, such as recovery from a disease. The **hazard function** for a random variable is

$$h(x) = \frac{f(x)}{S(x)} = \frac{f(x)}{1 - F(x)}.$$

The hazard function is a conditional probability;

$$h(x) = \lim_{t \downarrow 0} \text{Prob}(X \le x \le X + t \mid X \ge x).$$

Hazard functions have been used in econometrics in studying the duration of spells, or conditions, such as unemployment, strikes, time until business failures, and so on. The connection between the hazard and the other functions is $h(x) = -d \ln S(x)/dx$. As an exercise, you might want to verify the interesting special case of $h(x) = 1/\lambda$, a constant—the only distribution which has this characteristic is the exponential distribution noted in Section B.4.5.

For the random variable $X$, with probability density function $f(x)$, if the function

$$M(t) = E[e^{tx}]$$

exists, then it is the **moment generating function.** Assuming the function exists, it can be shown that

$$d^r M(t)/dt^r \mid_{t=0} = E[x^r].$$

The moment generating function, like the survival and the hazard functions, is a unique characterization of a probability distribution. When it exists, the moment generating function (MGF) has a one-to-one correspondence with the distribution. Thus, for example, if we begin with some random variable and find that a transformation of it has a particular MGF, then we may infer that the function of the random variable has the distribution associated with that MGF. A convenient application of this result is the MGF for the normal distribution. The MGF for the standard normal distribution is $M_z(t) = e^{t^2/2}$.

A useful feature of MGFs is the following:

if $x$ and $y$ are independent, then the MGF of $x + y$ is $M_x(t) M_y(t)$.

This result has been used to establish the **contagion** property of some distributions, that is, the property that sums of random variables with a given distribution have that same distribution. The normal distribution is a familiar example. This is usually not the case. It is for Poisson and chi-squared random variables.

One qualification of all of the preceding is that in order for these results to hold, the MGF must exist. It will for the distributions that we will encounter in our work, but in at least one important case, we cannot be sure of this. When computing sums of random variables which may have different distributions and whose specific distributions need not be so well behaved, it is likely that the MGF of the sum does not exist. However, the characteristic function,

$$\phi(t) = E[e^{itx}], i^2 = -1,$$

will always exist, at least for relatively small $t$. The characteristic function is the device used to prove that certain sums of random variables converge to a normally distributed variable—that is, the characteristic function is a fundamental tool in proofs of the central limit theorem.

## B.7  JOINT DISTRIBUTIONS

The **joint density function** for two random variables $X$ and $Y$ denoted $f(x, y)$ is defined so that

$$\text{Prob}(a \le x \le b, c \le y \le d) = \begin{cases} \displaystyle\sum_{a \le x \le b}\sum_{c \le y \le d} f(x, y) & \text{if } x \text{ and } y \text{ are discrete,} \\ \displaystyle\int_a^b \int_c^d f(x, y)\, dy\, dx & \text{if } x \text{ and } y \text{ are continuous.} \end{cases} \tag{B-42}$$

The counterparts of the requirements for a univariate probability density are

$$f(x, y) \ge 0,$$

$$\sum_x \sum_y f(x, y) = 1 \qquad \text{if } x \text{ and } y \text{ are discrete,}$$

$$\int_x \int_y f(x, y)\, dy\, dx = 1 \quad \text{if } x \text{ and } y \text{ are continuous.} \tag{B-43}$$

The cumulative probability is likewise the probability of a joint event:

$$F(x, y) = \text{Prob}(X \le x, Y \le y)$$

$$= \begin{cases} \displaystyle\sum_{X \le x}\sum_{Y \le y} f(x, y) & \text{in the discrete case} \\ \displaystyle\int_{-\infty}^x \int_{-\infty}^y f(t, s)\, ds\, dt & \text{in the continuous case.} \end{cases} \tag{B-44}$$

### B.7.1  MARGINAL DISTRIBUTIONS

A **marginal probability density** or marginal probability distribution is defined with respect to an individual variable. To obtain the marginal distributions from the joint density, it is necessary to sum or integrate out the other variable:

$$f_x(x) = \begin{cases} \displaystyle\sum_y f(x, y) & \text{in the discrete case} \\ \displaystyle\int_y f(x, s)\, ds & \text{in the continuous case,} \end{cases} \tag{B-45}$$

and similarly for $f_y(y)$.

Two random variables are statistically independent if and only if their joint density is the product of the marginal densities:

$$f(x, y) = f_x(x) f_y(y) \Leftrightarrow x \text{ and } y \text{ are independent.} \tag{B-46}$$

If (and only if) $x$ and $y$ are independent, then the cdf factors as well as the pdf:

$$F(x, y) = F_x(x) F_y(y), \tag{B-47}$$

or

$$\text{Prob}(X \le x, Y \le y) = \text{Prob}(X \le x)\text{Prob}(Y \le y).$$

## B.7.2  EXPECTATIONS IN A JOINT DISTRIBUTION

The means, variances, and higher moments of the variables in a joint distribution are defined with respect to the marginal distributions. For the mean of $x$ in a discrete distribution,

$$
\begin{aligned}
E[x] &= \sum_x x f_x(x) \\
&= \sum_x x \left[ \sum_y f(x, y) \right] \\
&= \sum_x \sum_y x f(x, y).
\end{aligned}
\tag{B-48}
$$

The means of the variables in a continuous distribution are defined likewise, using integration instead of summation:

$$
\begin{aligned}
E[x] &= \int_x x f_x(x) \, dx \\
&= \int_x \int_y x f(x, y) \, dy \, dx.
\end{aligned}
\tag{B-49}
$$

Variances are computed in the same manner:

$$
\begin{aligned}
\mathrm{Var}[x] &= \sum_x \left( x - E[x] \right)^2 f_x(x) \\
&= \sum_x \sum_y \left( x - E[x] \right)^2 f(x, y).
\end{aligned}
\tag{B-50}
$$

## B.7.3  COVARIANCE AND CORRELATION

For any function $g(x, y)$,

$$
E[g(x, y)] =
\begin{cases}
\displaystyle\sum_x \sum_y g(x, y) f(x, y) & \text{in the discrete case} \\[2ex]
\displaystyle\int_x \int_y g(x, y) f(x, y) \, dy \, dx & \text{in the continuous case.}
\end{cases}
\tag{B-51}
$$

The covariance of $x$ and $y$ is a special case:

$$
\begin{aligned}
\mathrm{Cov}[x, y] &= E[(x - \mu_x)(y - \mu_y)] \\
&= E[xy] - \mu_x \mu_y \\
&= \sigma_{xy}.
\end{aligned}
\tag{B-52}
$$

If $x$ and $y$ are independent, then $f(x, y) = f_x(x) f_y(y)$ and

$$
\begin{aligned}
\sigma_{xy} &= \sum_x \sum_y f_x(x) f_y(y)(x - \mu_x)(y - \mu_y) \\
&= \sum_x (x - \mu_x) f_x(x) \sum_y (y - \mu_y) f_y(y) \\
&= E[x - \mu_x] E[y - \mu_y] \\
&= 0.
\end{aligned}
$$

The sign of the covariance will indicate the direction of covariation of $X$ and $Y$. Its magnitude depends on the scales of measurement, however. In view of this fact, a preferable measure is the correlation coefficient:

$$r[x, y] = \rho_{xy} = \frac{\sigma_{xy}}{\sigma_x \sigma_y}, \tag{B-53}$$

where $\sigma_x$ and $\sigma_y$ are the standard deviations of $x$ and $y$, respectively. The correlation coefficient has the same sign as the covariance but is always between $-1$ and $1$ and is thus unaffected by any scaling of the variables.

Variables that are uncorrelated are not necessarily independent. For example, in the discrete distribution $f(-1, 1) = f(0, 0) = f(1, 1) = \frac{1}{3}$, the correlation is zero, but $f(1, 1)$ does not equal $f_x(1) f_y(1) = (\frac{1}{3})(\frac{2}{3})$. An important exception is the joint normal distribution discussed subsequently, in which lack of correlation does imply independence.

Some general results regarding expectations in a joint distribution, which can be verified by applying the appropriate definitions, are

$$E[ax + by + c] = a E[x] + b E[y] + c, \tag{B-54}$$

$$\begin{aligned} \text{Var}[ax + by + c] &= a^2 \text{Var}[x] + b^2 \text{Var}[y] + 2ab \, \text{Cov}[x, y] \\ &= \text{Var}[ax + by], \end{aligned} \tag{B-55}$$

and

$$\text{Cov}[ax + by, cx + dy] = ac \, \text{Var}[x] + bd \, \text{Var}[y] + (ad + bc)\text{Cov}[x, y]. \tag{B-56}$$

If $X$ and $Y$ are uncorrelated, then

$$\begin{aligned} \text{Var}[x + y] &= \text{Var}[x - y] \\ &= \text{Var}[x] + \text{Var}[y]. \end{aligned} \tag{B-57}$$

For any two functions $g_1(x)$ and $g_2(y)$, if $x$ and $y$ are independent, then

$$E[g_1(x)g_2(y)] = E[g_1(x)]E[g_2(y)]. \tag{B-58}$$

### B.7.4 DISTRIBUTION OF A FUNCTION OF BIVARIATE RANDOM VARIABLES

The result for a function of a random variable in (B-41) must be modified for a joint distribution. Suppose that $x_1$ and $x_2$ have a joint distribution $f_x(x_1, x_2)$ and that $y_1$ and $y_2$ are two monotonic functions of $x_1$ and $x_2$:

$$y_1 = y_1(x_1, x_2),$$
$$y_2 = y_2(x_1, x_2).$$

Because the functions are monotonic, the inverse transformations,

$$x_1 = x_1(y_1, y_2),$$
$$x_2 = x_2(y_1, y_2),$$

exist. The Jacobian of the transformations is the matrix of partial derivatives,

$$J = \begin{bmatrix} \partial x_1/\partial y_1 & \partial x_1/\partial y_2 \\ \partial x_2/\partial y_1 & \partial x_2/\partial y_2 \end{bmatrix} = \begin{bmatrix} \dfrac{\partial \mathbf{x}}{\partial \mathbf{y}'} \end{bmatrix}.$$

The joint distribution of $y_1$ and $y_2$ is

$$f_y(y_1, y_2) = f_x[x_1(y_1, y_2), x_2(y_1, y_2)]\text{abs}(|J|).$$

The determinant of the Jacobian must be nonzero for the transformation to exist. A zero determinant implies that the two transformations are functionally dependent.

Certainly the most common application of the preceding in econometrics is the linear transformation of a set of random variables. Suppose that $x_1$ and $x_2$ are independently distributed $N[0, 1]$, and the transformations are

$$y_1 = \alpha_1 + \beta_{11}x_1 + \beta_{12}x_2,$$

$$y_2 = \alpha_2 + \beta_{21}x_1 + \beta_{22}x_2.$$

To obtain the joint distribution of $y_1$ and $y_2$, we first write the transformations as

$$\mathbf{y} = \mathbf{a} + \mathbf{Bx}.$$

The inverse transformation is

$$\mathbf{x} = \mathbf{B}^{-1}(\mathbf{y} - \mathbf{a}),$$

so the absolute value of the determinant of the Jacobian is

$$\text{abs}|J| = \text{abs}|\mathbf{B}^{-1}| = \frac{1}{\text{abs}|\mathbf{B}|}.$$

The joint distribution of $\mathbf{x}$ is the product of the marginal distributions since they are independent. Thus,

$$f_x(\mathbf{x}) = (2\pi)^{-1}e^{-(x_1^2+x_2^2)/2} = (2\pi)^{-1}e^{-\mathbf{x}'\mathbf{x}/2}.$$

Inserting the results for $\mathbf{x}(\mathbf{y})$ and $J$ into $f_y(y_1, y_2)$ gives

$$f_y(\mathbf{y}) = (2\pi)^{-1}\frac{1}{\text{abs}|\mathbf{B}|}e^{-(\mathbf{y}-\mathbf{a})'(\mathbf{BB}')^{-1}(\mathbf{y}-\mathbf{a})/2}.$$

This **bivariate normal distribution** is the subject of Section B.9. Note that by formulating it as we did earlier, we can generalize easily to the multivariate case, that is, with an arbitrary number of variables.

Perhaps the more common situation is that in which it is necessary to find the distribution of one function of two (or more) random variables. A strategy that often works in this case is to form the joint distribution of the transformed variable and one of the original variables, then integrate (or sum) the latter out of the joint distribution to obtain the marginal distribution. Thus, to find the distribution of $y_1(x_1, x_2)$, we might formulate

$$y_1 = y_1(x_1, x_2)$$

$$y_2 = x_2.$$

The absolute value of the determinant of the Jacobian would then be

$$J = \text{abs} \begin{vmatrix} \dfrac{\partial x_1}{\partial y_1} & \dfrac{\partial x_1}{\partial y_2} \\ 0 & 1 \end{vmatrix} = \text{abs} \left| \left( \dfrac{\partial x_1}{\partial y_1} \right) \right|.$$

The density of $y_1$ would then be

$$f_{y_1}(y_1) = \int_{y_2} f_x[x_1(y_1, y_2), y_2] \, \text{abs}|J| \, dy_2.$$

## B.8  CONDITIONING IN A BIVARIATE DISTRIBUTION

Conditioning and the use of conditional distributions play a pivotal role in econometric modeling. We consider some general results for a bivariate distribution. (All these results can be extended directly to the multivariate case.)

In a bivariate distribution, there is a **conditional distribution** over $y$ for each value of $x$. The conditional densities are

$$f(y \mid x) = \frac{f(x, y)}{f_x(x)}, \tag{B-59}$$

and

$$f(x \mid y) = \frac{f(x, y)}{f_y(y)}.$$

It follows from (B-46) that:

> If $x$ and $y$ are independent, then $f(y \mid x) = f_y(y)$ and $f(x \mid y) = f_x(x)$. **(B-60)**

The interpretation is that if the variables are independent, the probabilities of events relating to one variable are unrelated to the other. The definition of conditional densities implies the important result

$$f(x, y) = f(y \mid x) f_x(x)$$
$$= f(x \mid y) f_y(y). \tag{B-61}$$

### B.8.1  REGRESSION: THE CONDITIONAL MEAN

A **conditional mean** is the mean of the conditional distribution and is defined by

$$E[y \mid x] = \begin{cases} \displaystyle\int_y y f(y \mid x) \, dy & \text{if } y \text{ is continuous} \\[2ex] \displaystyle\sum_y y f(y \mid x) & \text{if } y \text{ is discrete.} \end{cases} \tag{B-62}$$

The conditional mean function $E[y \mid x]$ is called the **regression** of $y$ on $x$.

A random variable may always be written as

$$y = E[y \mid x] + \left( y - E[y \mid x] \right)$$
$$= E[y \mid x] + \varepsilon.$$

## B.8.2   CONDITIONAL VARIANCE

A conditional variance is the variance of the conditional distribution:

$$
\begin{aligned}
\mathrm{Var}[y \mid x] &= E\left[\left(y - E[y \mid x]\right)^2 \mid x\right] \\
&= \int_y \left(y - E[y \mid x]\right)^2 f(y \mid x)\, dy, \quad \text{if } y \text{ is continuous,}
\end{aligned}
$$

(B-63)

or

$$
\mathrm{Var}[y \mid x] = \sum_y \left(y - E[y \mid x]\right)^2 f(y \mid x), \quad \text{if } y \text{ is discrete.}
$$

(B-64)

The computation can be simplified by using

$$
\mathrm{Var}[y \mid x] = E[y^2 \mid x] - \left(E[y \mid x]\right)^2.
$$

(B-65)

The conditional variance is called the **scedastic function** and, like the regression, is generally a function of $x$. Unlike the conditional mean function, however, it is common for the conditional variance not to vary with $x$. We shall examine a particular case. This case does not imply, however, that $\mathrm{Var}[y \mid x]$ equals $\mathrm{Var}[y]$, which will usually not be true. It implies only that the conditional variance is a constant. The case in which the conditional variance does not vary with $x$ is called **homoscedasticity** (same variance).

## B.8.3   RELATIONSHIPS AMONG MARGINAL AND CONDITIONAL MOMENTS

Some useful results for the moments of a conditional distribution are given in the following theorems.

---

**THEOREM B.1**   **Law of Iterated Expectations**

$$
E[y] = E_x[E[y \mid x]].
$$

(B-66)

*The notation $E_x[.]$ indicates the expectation over the values of $x$. Note that $E[y \mid x]$ is a function of $x$.*

---

**THEOREM B.2**   **Covariance**

*In any bivariate distribution,*

$$
\mathrm{Cov}[x, y] = \mathrm{Cov}_x[x, E[y \mid x]] = \int_x \left(x - E[x]\right) E[y \mid x] f_x(x)\, dx.
$$

(B-67)

*(Note that this is the covariance of $x$ and a function of $x$.)*

The preceding results provide an additional, extremely useful result for the special case in which the conditional mean function is linear in $x$.

---

**THEOREM B.3    Moments in a Linear Regression**

*If $E[y \mid x] = \alpha + \beta x$, then*

$$\alpha = E[y] - \beta E[x]$$

*and*

$$\beta = \frac{\text{Cov}[x, y]}{\text{Var}[x]}. \qquad \text{(B-68)}$$

*The proof follows from (B-66).*

---

The preceding theorems relate to the conditional mean in a bivariate distribution. The following theorems, which also appear in various forms in regression analysis, describe the conditional variance.

---

**THEOREM B.4    Decomposition of Variance**

*In a joint distribution,*

$$\text{Var}[y] = \text{Var}_x[E[y \mid x]] + E_x[\text{Var}[y \mid x]]. \qquad \text{(B-69)}$$

---

The notation $\text{Var}_x[.]$ indicates the variance over the distribution of $x$. This equation states that in a bivariate distribution, the variance of $y$ decomposes into the variance of the conditional mean function plus the expected variance around the conditional mean.

---

**THEOREM B.5    Residual Variance in a Regression**

*In any bivariate distribution,*

$$E_x[\text{Var}[y \mid x]] = \text{Var}[y] - \text{Var}_x[E[y \mid x]]. \qquad \text{(B-70)}$$

---

On average, conditioning reduces the variance of the variable subject to the conditioning. For example, if $y$ is homoscedastic, then we have the unambiguous result that the variance of the conditional distribution(s) is less than or equal to the unconditional variance of $y$. Going a step further, we have the result that appears prominently in the bivariate normal distribution (Section B.9).

> **THEOREM B.6** **Linear Regression and Homoscedasticity**
> *In a bivariate distribution, if $E[y \mid x] = \alpha + \beta x$ and if $\mathrm{Var}[y \mid x]$ is a constant, then*
>
> $$\mathrm{Var}[y \mid x] = \mathrm{Var}[y]\left(1 - \mathrm{Corr}^2[y, x]\right) = \sigma_y^2 \left(1 - \rho_{xy}^2\right). \qquad \textbf{(B-71)}$$
>
> *The proof is straightforward using Theorems B.2 to B.4.*

### B.8.4  THE ANALYSIS OF VARIANCE

The variance decomposition result implies that in a bivariate distribution, variation in $y$ arises from two sources:

**1.**  Variation because $E[y \mid x]$ varies with $x$:

$$\textbf{regression variance} = \mathrm{Var}_x[E[y \mid x]]. \qquad \textbf{(B-72)}$$

**2.**  Variation because, in each conditional distribution, $y$ varies around the conditional mean:

$$\textbf{residual variance} = E_x[\mathrm{Var}[y \mid x]]. \qquad \textbf{(B-73)}$$

Thus,

$$\mathrm{Var}[y] = \text{regression variance} + \text{residual variance}. \qquad \textbf{(B-74)}$$

In analyzing a regression, we shall usually be interested in which of the two parts of the total variance, $\mathrm{Var}[y]$, is the larger one. A natural measure is the ratio

$$\textbf{coefficient of determination} = \frac{\text{regression variance}}{\text{total variance}}. \qquad \textbf{(B-75)}$$

In the setting of a linear regression, (B-75) arises from another relationship that emphasizes the interpretation of the correlation coefficient.

$$\text{If} \quad E[y \mid x] = \alpha + \beta x, \quad \text{then the coefficient of determination} = \text{COD} = \rho^2, \qquad \textbf{(B-76)}$$

where $\rho^2$ is the squared correlation between $x$ and $y$. We conclude that the correlation coefficient (squared) is a measure of the proportion of the variance of $y$ accounted for by variation in the mean of $y$ given $x$. It is in this sense that correlation can be interpreted as a **measure of linear association** between two variables.

## B.9  THE BIVARIATE NORMAL DISTRIBUTION

A bivariate distribution that embodies many of the features described earlier is the bivariate normal, which is the joint distribution of two normally distributed variables. The density is

$$f(x, y) = \frac{1}{2\pi\sigma_x\sigma_y\sqrt{1-\rho^2}} e^{-1/2[(\varepsilon_x^2 + \varepsilon_y^2 - 2\rho\varepsilon_x\varepsilon_y)/(1-\rho^2)]},$$

$$\varepsilon_x = \frac{x - \mu_x}{\sigma_x}, \quad \varepsilon_y = \frac{y - \mu_y}{\sigma_y}. \qquad \textbf{(B-77)}$$

The parameters $\mu_x, \sigma_x, \mu_y,$ and $\sigma_y$ are the means and standard deviations of the marginal distributions of $x$ and $y$, respectively. The additional parameter $\rho$ is the correlation between $x$ and $y$. The covariance is

$$\sigma_{xy} = \rho\sigma_x\sigma_y. \tag{B-78}$$

The density is defined only if $\rho$ is not 1 or $-1$, which in turn requires that the two variables not be linearly related. If $x$ and $y$ have a bivariate normal distribution, denoted

$$(x, y) \sim N_2\left[\mu_x, \mu_y, \sigma_x^2, \sigma_y^2, \rho\right],$$

then

- The marginal distributions are normal:

$$f_x(x) = N\left[\mu_x, \sigma_x^2\right],$$
$$f_y(y) = N\left[\mu_y, \sigma_y^2\right]. \tag{B-79}$$

- The conditional distributions are normal:

$$f(y\,|\,x) = N\left[\alpha + \beta x, \sigma_y^2(1 - \rho^2)\right],$$
$$\alpha = \mu_y - \beta\mu_x, \quad \beta = \frac{\sigma_{xy}}{\sigma_x^2}, \tag{B-80}$$

and likewise for $f(x\,|\,y)$.
- $x$ and $y$ are independent if and only if $\rho = 0$. The density factors into the product of the two marginal normal distributions if $\rho = 0$.

Two things to note about the conditional distributions beyond their normality are their linear regression functions and their constant conditional variances. The conditional variance is less than the unconditional variance, which is consistent with the results of the previous section.

## B.10 MULTIVARIATE DISTRIBUTIONS

The extension of the results for bivariate distributions to more than two variables is direct. It is made much more convenient by using matrices and vectors. The term **random vector** applies to a vector whose elements are random variables. The joint density is $f(\mathbf{x})$, whereas the cdf is

$$F(\mathbf{x}) = \int_{-\infty}^{x_n}\int_{-\infty}^{x_{n-1}}\cdots\int_{-\infty}^{x_1} f(\mathbf{t})\,dt_1\cdots dt_{n-1}\,dt_n. \tag{B-81}$$

Note that the cdf is an $n$-fold integral. The marginal distribution of any one (or more) of the $n$ variables is obtained by integrating or summing over the other variables.

### B.10.1 MOMENTS

The expected value of a vector or matrix is the vector or matrix of expected values. A mean vector is defined as

$$\mu = \begin{bmatrix} \mu_1 \\ \mu_2 \\ \vdots \\ \mu_n \end{bmatrix} = \begin{bmatrix} E[x_1] \\ E[x_2] \\ \vdots \\ E[x_n] \end{bmatrix} = E[\mathbf{x}]. \tag{B-82}$$

Define the matrix

$$(\mathbf{x} - \boldsymbol{\mu})(\mathbf{x} - \boldsymbol{\mu})' = \begin{bmatrix} (x_1 - \mu_1)(x_1 - \mu_1) & (x_1 - \mu_1)(x_2 - \mu_2) & \cdots & (x_1 - \mu_1)(x_n - \mu_n) \\ (x_2 - \mu_2)(x_1 - \mu_1) & (x_2 - \mu_2)(x_2 - \mu_2) & \cdots & (x_2 - \mu_2)(x_n - \mu_n) \\ \vdots & & & \vdots \\ (x_n - \mu_n)(x_1 - \mu_1) & (x_n - \mu_n)(x_2 - \mu_2) & \cdots & (x_n - \mu_n)(x_n - \mu_n) \end{bmatrix}.$$

The expected value of each element in the matrix is the covariance of the two variables in the product. (The covariance of a variable with itself is its variance.) Thus,

$$E[(\mathbf{x} - \boldsymbol{\mu})(\mathbf{x} - \boldsymbol{\mu})'] = \begin{bmatrix} \sigma_{11} & \sigma_{12} & \cdots & \sigma_{1n} \\ \sigma_{21} & \sigma_{22} & \cdots & \sigma_{2n} \\ \vdots & & \vdots & \\ \sigma_{n1} & \sigma_{n2} & \cdots & \sigma_{nn} \end{bmatrix} = E[\mathbf{x}\mathbf{x}'] - \boldsymbol{\mu}\boldsymbol{\mu}', \qquad \textbf{(B-83)}$$

which is the **covariance matrix** of the random vector $\mathbf{x}$. Henceforth, we shall denote the covariance matrix of a random vector in boldface, as in

$$\text{Var}[\mathbf{x}] = \boldsymbol{\Sigma}.$$

By dividing $\sigma_{ij}$ by $\sigma_i \sigma_j$, we obtain the **correlation matrix**:

$$\mathbf{R} = \begin{bmatrix} 1 & \rho_{12} & \rho_{13} & \cdots & \rho_{1n} \\ \rho_{21} & 1 & \rho_{23} & \cdots & \rho_{2n} \\ \vdots & \vdots & \vdots & & \vdots \\ \rho_{n1} & \rho_{n2} & \rho_{n3} & \cdots & 1 \end{bmatrix}.$$

## B.10.2   SETS OF LINEAR FUNCTIONS

Our earlier results for the mean and variance of a linear function can be extended to the multivariate case. For the mean,

$$\begin{aligned} E[a_1 x_1 + a_2 x_2 + \cdots + a_n x_n] &= E[\mathbf{a}'\mathbf{x}] \\ &= a_1 E[x_1] + a_2 E[x_2] + \cdots + a_n E[x_n] \\ &= a_1 \mu_1 + a_2 \mu_2 + \cdots + a_n \mu_n \\ &= \mathbf{a}'\boldsymbol{\mu}. \end{aligned} \qquad \textbf{(B-84)}$$

For the variance,

$$\begin{aligned} \text{Var}[\mathbf{a}'\mathbf{x}] &= E\left[\left(\mathbf{a}'\mathbf{x} - E[\mathbf{a}'\mathbf{x}]\right)^2\right] \\ &= E\left[\left\{\mathbf{a}'\left(\mathbf{x} - E[\mathbf{x}]\right)\right\}^2\right] \\ &= E[\mathbf{a}'(\mathbf{x} - \boldsymbol{\mu})(\mathbf{x} - \boldsymbol{\mu})'\mathbf{a}] \end{aligned}$$

as $E[\mathbf{x}] = \boldsymbol{\mu}$ and $\mathbf{a}'(\mathbf{x} - \boldsymbol{\mu}) = (\mathbf{x} - \boldsymbol{\mu})'\mathbf{a}$. Because $\mathbf{a}$ is a vector of constants,

$$\text{Var}[\mathbf{a}'\mathbf{x}] = \mathbf{a}' E[(\mathbf{x} - \boldsymbol{\mu})(\mathbf{x} - \boldsymbol{\mu})']\mathbf{a} = \mathbf{a}'\boldsymbol{\Sigma}\mathbf{a} = \sum_{i=1}^{n}\sum_{j=1}^{n} a_i a_j \sigma_{ij}. \qquad \textbf{(B-85)}$$

It is the expected value of a square, so we know that a variance cannot be negative. As such, the preceding quadratic form is nonnegative, and the symmetric matrix $\boldsymbol{\Sigma}$ must be nonnegative definite.

In the set of linear functions $\mathbf{y} = \mathbf{Ax}$, the $i$th element of $\mathbf{y}$ is $y_i = \mathbf{a}_i\mathbf{x}$, where $\mathbf{a}_i$ is the $i$th row of $\mathbf{A}$ [see result (A-14)]. Therefore,

$$E[y_i] = \mathbf{a}_i\boldsymbol{\mu}.$$

Collecting the results in a vector, we have

$$E[\mathbf{Ax}] = \mathbf{A}\boldsymbol{\mu}. \tag{B-86}$$

For two row vectors $\mathbf{a}_i$ and $\mathbf{a}_j$,

$$\text{Cov}[\mathbf{a}_i\mathbf{x}, \mathbf{a}_j\mathbf{x}] = \mathbf{a}_i\boldsymbol{\Sigma}\mathbf{a}_j'.$$

Because $\mathbf{a}_i\boldsymbol{\Sigma}\mathbf{a}_j'$ is the $ij$th element of $\mathbf{A}\boldsymbol{\Sigma}\mathbf{A}'$,

$$\text{Var}[\mathbf{Ax}] = \mathbf{A}\boldsymbol{\Sigma}\mathbf{A}'. \tag{B-87}$$

This matrix will be either nonnegative definite or positive definite, depending on the column rank of $\mathbf{A}$.

## B.10.3 NONLINEAR FUNCTIONS

Consider a set of possibly nonlinear functions of $\mathbf{x}$, $\mathbf{y} = \mathbf{g}(\mathbf{x})$. Each element of $\mathbf{y}$ can be approximated with a linear Taylor series. Let $\mathbf{j}^i$ be the row vector of partial derivatives of the $i$th function with respect to the $n$ elements of $\mathbf{x}$:

$$\mathbf{j}^i(\mathbf{x}) = \frac{\partial g_i(\mathbf{x})}{\partial \mathbf{x}'} = \frac{\partial y_i}{\partial \mathbf{x}'}. \tag{B-88}$$

Then, proceeding in the now familiar way, we use $\boldsymbol{\mu}$, the mean vector of $\mathbf{x}$, as the expansion point, so that $\mathbf{j}^i(\boldsymbol{\mu})$ is the row vector of partial derivatives evaluated at $\boldsymbol{\mu}$. Then

$$g_i(\mathbf{x}) \approx g_i(\boldsymbol{\mu}) + \mathbf{j}^i(\boldsymbol{\mu})(\mathbf{x} - \boldsymbol{\mu}). \tag{B-89}$$

From this we obtain

$$E[g_i(\mathbf{x})] \approx g_i(\boldsymbol{\mu}), \tag{B-90}$$

$$\text{Var}[g_i(\mathbf{x})] \approx \mathbf{j}^i(\boldsymbol{\mu})\boldsymbol{\Sigma}\mathbf{j}^i(\boldsymbol{\mu})', \tag{B-91}$$

and

$$\text{Cov}[g_i(\mathbf{x}), g_j(\mathbf{x})] \approx \mathbf{j}^i(\boldsymbol{\mu})\boldsymbol{\Sigma}\mathbf{j}^j(\boldsymbol{\mu})'. \tag{B-92}$$

These results can be collected in a convenient form by arranging the row vectors $\mathbf{j}^i(\boldsymbol{\mu})$ in a matrix $\mathbf{J}(\boldsymbol{\mu})$. Then, corresponding to the preceding equations, we have

$$E[\mathbf{g}(\mathbf{x})] \simeq \mathbf{g}(\boldsymbol{\mu}), \tag{B-93}$$

$$\text{Var}[\mathbf{g}(\mathbf{x})] \simeq \mathbf{J}(\boldsymbol{\mu})\boldsymbol{\Sigma}\mathbf{J}(\boldsymbol{\mu})'. \tag{B-94}$$

The matrix $\mathbf{J}(\boldsymbol{\mu})$ in the last preceding line is $\partial\mathbf{y}/\partial\mathbf{x}'$ evaluated at $\mathbf{x} = \boldsymbol{\mu}$.

## B.11 THE MULTIVARIATE NORMAL DISTRIBUTION

The foundation of most multivariate analysis in econometrics is the multivariate normal distribution. Let the vector $(x_1, x_2, \ldots, x_n)' = \mathbf{x}$ be the set of $n$ random variables, $\boldsymbol{\mu}$ their mean vector, and $\boldsymbol{\Sigma}$ their covariance matrix. The general form of the joint density is

$$f(\mathbf{x}) = (2\pi)^{-n/2} |\boldsymbol{\Sigma}|^{-1/2} e^{(-1/2)(\mathbf{x}-\boldsymbol{\mu})' \boldsymbol{\Sigma}^{-1}(\mathbf{x}-\boldsymbol{\mu})}. \tag{B-95}$$

If $\mathbf{R}$ is the correlation matrix of the variables and $\mathbf{R}_{ij} = \sigma_{ij}/(\sigma_i \sigma_j)$, then

$$f(\mathbf{x}) = (2\pi)^{-n/2} (\sigma_1 \sigma_2 \cdots \sigma_n)^{-1} |\mathbf{R}|^{-1/2} e^{(-1/2)\boldsymbol{\varepsilon} \mathbf{R}^{-1} \boldsymbol{\varepsilon}}, \tag{B-96}$$

where $\varepsilon_i = (x_i - \mu_i)/\sigma_i$.[8]

Two special cases are of interest. If all the variables are uncorrelated, then $\rho_{ij} = 0$ for $i \neq j$. Thus, $\mathbf{R} = \mathbf{I}$, and the density becomes

$$f(\mathbf{x}) = (2\pi)^{-n/2} (\sigma_1 \sigma_2 \cdots \sigma_n)^{-1} e^{-\boldsymbol{\varepsilon}' \boldsymbol{\varepsilon}/2}$$
$$= f(x_1) f(x_2) \cdots f(x_n) = \prod_{i=1}^{n} f(x_i). \tag{B-97}$$

As in the bivariate case, if normally distributed variables are uncorrelated, then they are independent. If $\sigma_i = \sigma$ and $\boldsymbol{\mu} = \mathbf{0}$, then $x_i \sim N[0, \sigma^2]$ and $\varepsilon_i = x_i/\sigma$, and the density becomes

$$f(\mathbf{x}) = (2\pi)^{-n/2} (\sigma^2)^{-n/2} e^{-\mathbf{x}'\mathbf{x}/(2\sigma^2)}. \tag{B-98}$$

Finally, if $\sigma = 1$,

$$f(\mathbf{x}) = (2\pi)^{-n/2} e^{-\mathbf{x}'\mathbf{x}/2}. \tag{B-99}$$

This distribution is the **multivariate standard normal,** or **spherical normal distribution.**

### B.11.1 MARGINAL AND CONDITIONAL NORMAL DISTRIBUTIONS

Let $\mathbf{x}_1$ be any subset of the variables, including a single variable, and let $\mathbf{x}_2$ be the remaining variables. Partition $\boldsymbol{\mu}$ and $\boldsymbol{\Sigma}$ likewise so that

$$\boldsymbol{\mu} = \begin{bmatrix} \boldsymbol{\mu}_1 \\ \boldsymbol{\mu}_2 \end{bmatrix} \quad \text{and} \quad \boldsymbol{\Sigma} = \begin{bmatrix} \boldsymbol{\Sigma}_{11} & \boldsymbol{\Sigma}_{12} \\ \boldsymbol{\Sigma}_{21} & \boldsymbol{\Sigma}_{22} \end{bmatrix}.$$

Then the marginal distributions are also normal. In particular, we have the following theorem.

---

**THEOREM B.7** **Marginal and Conditional Normal Distributions**
*If $[\mathbf{x}_1, \mathbf{x}_2]$ have a joint multivariate normal distribution, then the marginal distributions are*

$$\mathbf{x}_1 \sim N(\boldsymbol{\mu}_1, \boldsymbol{\Sigma}_{11}), \tag{B-100}$$

---

[8]This result is obtained by constructing $\boldsymbol{\Delta}$, the diagonal matrix with $\sigma_i$ as its $i$th diagonal element. Then, $\mathbf{R} = \boldsymbol{\Delta}^{-1} \boldsymbol{\Sigma} \boldsymbol{\Delta}^{-1}$, which implies that $\boldsymbol{\Sigma}^{-1} = \boldsymbol{\Delta}^{-1} \mathbf{R}^{-1} \boldsymbol{\Delta}^{-1}$. Inserting this in (B-95) yields (B-96). Note that the $i$th element of $\boldsymbol{\Delta}^{-1}(\mathbf{x} - \boldsymbol{\mu})$ is $(x_i - \mu_i)/\sigma_i$.

**THEOREM B.7** (Continued)
*and*

$$\mathbf{x}_2 \sim N(\boldsymbol{\mu}_2, \boldsymbol{\Sigma}_{22}). \tag{B-101}$$

*The conditional distribution of* $\mathbf{x}_1$ *given* $\mathbf{x}_2$ *is normal as well:*

$$\mathbf{x}_1 \mid \mathbf{x}_2 \sim N(\boldsymbol{\mu}_{1.2}, \boldsymbol{\Sigma}_{11.2}), \tag{B-102}$$

*where*

$$\boldsymbol{\mu}_{1.2} = \boldsymbol{\mu}_1 + \boldsymbol{\Sigma}_{12}\boldsymbol{\Sigma}_{22}^{-1}(\mathbf{x}_2 - \boldsymbol{\mu}_2), \tag{B-102a}$$

$$\boldsymbol{\Sigma}_{11.2} = \boldsymbol{\Sigma}_{11} - \boldsymbol{\Sigma}_{12}\boldsymbol{\Sigma}_{22}^{-1}\boldsymbol{\Sigma}_{21}. \tag{B-102b}$$

***Proof:*** *We partition* $\boldsymbol{\mu}$ *and* $\boldsymbol{\Sigma}$ *as shown earlier and insert the parts in (B-95). To construct the density, we use (A-72) to partition the determinant,*

$$|\boldsymbol{\Sigma}| = |\boldsymbol{\Sigma}_{22}| \left| \boldsymbol{\Sigma}_{11} - \boldsymbol{\Sigma}_{12}\boldsymbol{\Sigma}_{22}^{-1}\boldsymbol{\Sigma}_{21} \right|,$$

*and (A-74) to partition the inverse,*

$$\begin{bmatrix} \boldsymbol{\Sigma}_{11} & \boldsymbol{\Sigma}_{12} \\ \boldsymbol{\Sigma}_{21} & \boldsymbol{\Sigma}_{22} \end{bmatrix}^{-1} = \begin{bmatrix} \boldsymbol{\Sigma}_{11.2}^{-1} & -\boldsymbol{\Sigma}_{11.2}^{-1}\mathbf{B} \\ -\mathbf{B}'\boldsymbol{\Sigma}_{11.2}^{-1} & \boldsymbol{\Sigma}_{22}^{-1} + \mathbf{B}'\boldsymbol{\Sigma}_{11.2}^{-1}\mathbf{B} \end{bmatrix}.$$

*For simplicity, we let*

$$\mathbf{B} = \boldsymbol{\Sigma}_{12}\boldsymbol{\Sigma}_{22}^{-1}.$$

*Inserting these in (B-95) and collecting terms produces the joint density as a product of two terms:*

$$f(\mathbf{x}_1, \mathbf{x}_2) = f_{1.2}(\mathbf{x}_1 \mid \mathbf{x}_2) f_2(\mathbf{x}_2).$$

*The first of these is a normal distribution with mean* $\boldsymbol{\mu}_{1.2}$ *and variance* $\boldsymbol{\Sigma}_{11.2}$*, whereas the second is the marginal distribution of* $\mathbf{x}_2$.

The conditional mean vector in the multivariate normal distribution is a linear function of the unconditional mean and the conditioning variables, and the conditional covariance matrix is constant and is smaller (in the sense discussed in Section A.7.3) than the unconditional covariance matrix. Notice that the conditional covariance matrix is the inverse of the upper left block of $\boldsymbol{\Sigma}^{-1}$; that is, this matrix is of the form shown in (A-74) for the partitioned inverse of a matrix.

### B.11.2   THE CLASSICAL NORMAL LINEAR REGRESSION MODEL

An important special case of the preceding is that in which $\mathbf{x}_1$ is a single variable, $y$, and $\mathbf{x}_2$ is $K$ variables, $\mathbf{x}$. Then the conditional distribution is a multivariate version of that in (B-80) with $\boldsymbol{\beta} = \boldsymbol{\Sigma}_{\mathbf{xx}}^{-1}\sigma_{\mathbf{xy}}$, where $\sigma_{\mathbf{xy}}$ is the vector of covariances of $y$ with $\mathbf{x}_2$. Recall that any random variable, $y$, can be written as its mean plus the deviation from the mean. If we apply this tautology to the multivariate normal, we obtain

$$y = E[y \mid \mathbf{x}] + \big(y - E[y \mid \mathbf{x}]\big) = \alpha + \boldsymbol{\beta}'\mathbf{x} + \varepsilon,$$

where $\beta$ is given earlier, $\alpha = \mu_y - \beta'\mu_x$, and $\varepsilon$ has a normal distribution. We thus have, in this multivariate normal distribution, the **classical normal linear regression model.**

### B.11.3 LINEAR FUNCTIONS OF A NORMAL VECTOR

Any linear function of a vector of joint normally distributed variables is also normally distributed. The mean vector and covariance matrix of $\mathbf{Ax}$, where $\mathbf{x}$ is normally distributed, follow the general pattern given earlier. Thus,

$$\text{If } \mathbf{x} \sim N[\boldsymbol{\mu}, \boldsymbol{\Sigma}], \quad \text{then } \mathbf{Ax} + \mathbf{b} \sim N[\mathbf{A}\boldsymbol{\mu} + \mathbf{b}, \mathbf{A}\boldsymbol{\Sigma}\mathbf{A}']. \tag{B-103}$$

If $\mathbf{A}$ does not have full rank, then $\mathbf{A}\boldsymbol{\Sigma}\mathbf{A}'$ is singular and the density does not exist in the full dimensional space of $\mathbf{x}$ although it does exist in the subspace of dimension equal to the rank of $\boldsymbol{\Sigma}$. Nonetheless, the individual elements of $\mathbf{Ax} + \mathbf{b}$ will still be normally distributed, and the joint *distribution* of the full vector is still a multivariate normal.

### B.11.4 QUADRATIC FORMS IN A STANDARD NORMAL VECTOR

The earlier discussion of the chi-squared distribution gives the distribution of $\mathbf{x}'\mathbf{x}$ if $\mathbf{x}$ has a standard normal distribution. It follows from (A-36) that

$$\mathbf{x}'\mathbf{x} = \sum_{i=1}^{n} x_i^2 = \sum_{i=1}^{n}(x_i - \bar{x})^2 + n\bar{x}^2. \tag{B-104}$$

We know from (B-32) that $\mathbf{x}'\mathbf{x}$ has a chi-squared distribution. It seems natural, therefore, to invoke (B-34) for the two parts on the right-hand side of (B-104). It is not yet obvious, however, that either of the two terms has a chi-squared distribution or that the two terms are independent, as required. To show these conditions, it is necessary to derive the distributions of **idempotent quadratic forms** and to show when they are independent.

To begin, the second term is the square of $\sqrt{n}\,\bar{x}$, which can easily be shown to have a standard normal distribution. Thus, the second term is the square of a standard normal variable and has chi-squared distribution with one degree of freedom. But the first term is the sum of $n$ nonindependent variables, and it remains to be shown that the two terms are independent.

---

> **DEFINITION B.3** ✦ **Orthonormal Quadratic Form**
> *A particular case of (B-103) is the following:*
>
> *If* $\mathbf{x} \sim N[\mathbf{0}, \mathbf{I}]$ *and* $\mathbf{C}$ *is a square matrix such that* $\mathbf{C}'\mathbf{C} = \mathbf{I}$, *then* $\mathbf{C}'\mathbf{x} \sim N[\mathbf{0}, \mathbf{I}]$.

---

Consider, then, a quadratic form in a standard normal vector $\mathbf{x}$ with symmetric matrix $\mathbf{A}$:

$$q = \mathbf{x}'\mathbf{Ax}. \tag{B-105}$$

Let the characteristic roots and vectors of $\mathbf{A}$ be arranged in a diagonal matrix $\boldsymbol{\Lambda}$ and an orthogonal matrix $\mathbf{C}$, as in Section A.6.3. Then

$$q = \mathbf{x}'\mathbf{C}\boldsymbol{\Lambda}\mathbf{C}'\mathbf{x}. \tag{B-106}$$

By definition, $\mathbf{C}$ satisfies the requirement that $\mathbf{C'C} = \mathbf{I}$. Thus, the vector $\mathbf{y} = \mathbf{C'x}$ has a standard normal distribution. Consequently,

$$q = \mathbf{y'\Lambda y} = \sum_{i=1}^{n} \lambda_i y_i^2. \tag{B-107}$$

If $\lambda_i$ is always one or zero, then

$$q = \sum_{j=1}^{J} y_j^2, \tag{B-108}$$

which has a chi-squared distribution. The sum is taken over the $j = 1, \ldots, J$ elements associated with the roots that are equal to one. A matrix whose characteristic roots are all zero or one is idempotent. Therefore, we have proved the next theorem.

---

**THEOREM B.8  Distribution of an Idempotent Quadratic Form in a Standard Normal Vector**

*If $\mathbf{x} \sim N[\mathbf{0}, \mathbf{I}]$ and $\mathbf{A}$ is idempotent, then $\mathbf{x'Ax}$ has a chi-squared distribution with degrees of freedom equal to the number of unit roots of $\mathbf{A}$, which is equal to the rank of $\mathbf{A}$.*

---

The rank of a matrix is equal to the number of nonzero characteristic roots it has. Therefore, the degrees of freedom in the preceding chi-squared distribution equals $J$, the rank of $\mathbf{A}$.

We can apply this result to the earlier sum of squares. The first term is

$$\sum_{i=1}^{n} (x_i - \overline{x})^2 \doteq \mathbf{x'M^0x},$$

where $\mathbf{M^0}$ was defined in (A-34) as the matrix that transforms data to mean deviation form:

$$\mathbf{M^0} = \mathbf{I} - \frac{1}{n}\mathbf{ii'}.$$

Because $\mathbf{M^0}$ is idempotent, the sum of squared deviations from the mean has a chi-squared distribution. The degrees of freedom equals the rank $\mathbf{M^0}$, which is not obvious except for the useful result in (A-108), that

- The rank of an idempotent matrix is equal to its trace. (B-109)

Each diagonal element of $\mathbf{M^0}$ is $1 - (1/n)$; hence, the trace is $n[1 - (1/n)] = n - 1$. Therefore, we have an application of Theorem B.8.

- If $\mathbf{x} \sim N(\mathbf{0}, \mathbf{I})$, $\sum_{i=1}^{n}(x_i - \overline{x})^2 \sim \chi^2[n - 1]$. (B-110)

We have already shown that the second term in (B-104) has a chi-squared distribution with one degree of freedom. It is instructive to set this up as a quadratic form as well:

$$n\overline{x}^2 = \mathbf{x'}\left[\frac{1}{n}\mathbf{ii'}\right]\mathbf{x} = \mathbf{x'[jj']x}, \quad \text{where } \mathbf{j} = \left(\frac{1}{\sqrt{n}}\right)\mathbf{i}. \tag{B-111}$$

The matrix in brackets is the outer product of a nonzero vector, which always has rank one. You can verify that it is idempotent by multiplication. Thus, $\mathbf{x'x}$ is the sum of two chi-squared variables, one with $n - 1$ degrees of freedom and the other with one. It is now necessary to show that the two terms are independent. To do so, we will use the next theorem.

---

**THEOREM B.9** **Independence of Idempotent Quadratic Forms**
*If* $\mathbf{x} \sim N[\mathbf{0}, \mathbf{I}]$ *and* $\mathbf{x}'\mathbf{Ax}$ *and* $\mathbf{x}'\mathbf{Bx}$ *are two idempotent quadratic forms in* $\mathbf{x}$, *then* $\mathbf{x}'\mathbf{Ax}$ *and* $\mathbf{x}'\mathbf{Bx}$ *are independent if* $\mathbf{AB} = \mathbf{0}$. **(B-112)**

---

As before, we show the result for the general case and then specialize it for the example. Because both $\mathbf{A}$ and $\mathbf{B}$ are symmetric and idempotent, $\mathbf{A} = \mathbf{A}'\mathbf{A}$ and $\mathbf{B} = \mathbf{B}'\mathbf{B}$. The quadratic forms are therefore

$$\mathbf{x}'\mathbf{Ax} = \mathbf{x}'\mathbf{A}'\mathbf{Ax} = \mathbf{x}_1'\mathbf{x}_1, \quad \text{where } \mathbf{x}_1 = \mathbf{Ax}, \quad \text{and} \quad \mathbf{x}'\mathbf{Bx} = \mathbf{x}_2'\mathbf{x}_2, \quad \text{where } \mathbf{x}_2 = \mathbf{Bx}. \quad \textbf{(B-113)}$$

Both vectors have zero mean vectors, so the covariance matrix of $\mathbf{x}_1$ and $\mathbf{x}_2$ is

$$E(\mathbf{x}_1\mathbf{x}_2') = \mathbf{AIB}' = \mathbf{AB} = \mathbf{0}.$$

Because $\mathbf{Ax}$ and $\mathbf{Bx}$ are linear functions of a normally distributed random vector, they are, in turn, normally distributed. Their zero covariance matrix implies that they are statistically independent,[9] which establishes the independence of the two quadratic forms. For the case of $\mathbf{x}'\mathbf{x}$, the two matrices are $\mathbf{M}^0$ and $[\mathbf{I} - \mathbf{M}^0]$. You can show that $\mathbf{M}^0[\mathbf{I} - \mathbf{M}^0] = \mathbf{0}$ just by multiplying it out.

### B.11.5 THE $F$ DISTRIBUTION

The normal family of distributions (chi-squared, $F$, and $t$) can all be derived as functions of idempotent quadratic forms in a standard normal vector. The $F$ distribution is the ratio of two independent chi-squared variables, each divided by its respective degrees of freedom. Let $\mathbf{A}$ and $\mathbf{B}$ be two idempotent matrices with ranks $r_a$ and $r_b$, and let $\mathbf{AB} = \mathbf{0}$. Then

$$\frac{\mathbf{x}'\mathbf{Ax}/r_a}{\mathbf{x}'\mathbf{Bx}/r_b} \sim F[r_a, r_b]. \quad \textbf{(B-114)}$$

If $\text{Var}[\mathbf{x}] = \sigma^2\mathbf{I}$ instead, then this is modified to

$$\frac{(\mathbf{x}'\mathbf{Ax}/\sigma^2)/r_a}{(\mathbf{x}'\mathbf{Bx}/\sigma^2)/r_b} \sim F[r_a, r_b]. \quad \textbf{(B-115)}$$

### B.11.6 A FULL RANK QUADRATIC FORM

Finally, consider the general case,

$$\mathbf{x} \sim N[\boldsymbol{\mu}, \boldsymbol{\Sigma}].$$

We are interested in the distribution of

$$q = (\mathbf{x} - \boldsymbol{\mu})'\boldsymbol{\Sigma}^{-1}(\mathbf{x} - \boldsymbol{\mu}). \quad \textbf{(B-116)}$$

---

[9]Note that both $\mathbf{x}_1 = \mathbf{Ax}$ and $\mathbf{x}_2 = \mathbf{Bx}$ have singular covariance matrices. Nonetheless, every element of $\mathbf{x}_1$ is independent of every element $\mathbf{x}_2$, so the vectors are independent.

First, the vector can be written as $\mathbf{z} = \mathbf{x} - \boldsymbol{\mu}$, and $\boldsymbol{\Sigma}$ is the covariance matrix of $\mathbf{z}$ as well as of $\mathbf{x}$. Therefore, we seek the distribution of

$$q = \mathbf{z}'\boldsymbol{\Sigma}^{-1}\mathbf{z} = \mathbf{z}'\left(\text{Var}[\mathbf{z}]\right)^{-1}\mathbf{z}, \tag{B-117}$$

where $\mathbf{z}$ is normally distributed with mean $\mathbf{0}$. This equation is a quadratic form, but not necessarily in an idempotent matrix.[10] Because $\boldsymbol{\Sigma}$ is positive definite, it has a square root. Define the symmetric matrix $\boldsymbol{\Sigma}^{1/2}$ so that $\boldsymbol{\Sigma}^{1/2}\boldsymbol{\Sigma}^{1/2} = \boldsymbol{\Sigma}$. Then

$$\boldsymbol{\Sigma}^{-1} = \boldsymbol{\Sigma}^{-1/2}\boldsymbol{\Sigma}^{-1/2},$$

and

$$\begin{aligned}
\mathbf{z}'\boldsymbol{\Sigma}^{-1}\mathbf{z} &= \mathbf{z}'\boldsymbol{\Sigma}^{-1/2\prime}\boldsymbol{\Sigma}^{-1/2}\mathbf{z} \\
&= (\boldsymbol{\Sigma}^{-1/2}\mathbf{z})'(\boldsymbol{\Sigma}^{-1/2}\mathbf{z}) \\
&= \mathbf{w}'\mathbf{w}.
\end{aligned}$$

Now $\mathbf{w} = \mathbf{A}\mathbf{z}$, so

$$E(\mathbf{w}) = \mathbf{A}\,E[\mathbf{z}] = \mathbf{0},$$

and

$$\text{Var}[\mathbf{w}] = \mathbf{A}\boldsymbol{\Sigma}\mathbf{A}' = \boldsymbol{\Sigma}^{-1/2}\boldsymbol{\Sigma}\boldsymbol{\Sigma}^{-1/2} = \boldsymbol{\Sigma}^0 = \mathbf{I}.$$

This provides the following important result:

---

**THEOREM B.10** **Distribution of a Standardized Normal Vector**
*If* $\mathbf{x} \sim N[\boldsymbol{\mu}, \boldsymbol{\Sigma}]$, *then* $\boldsymbol{\Sigma}^{-1/2}(\mathbf{x} - \boldsymbol{\mu}) \sim N[\mathbf{0}, \mathbf{I}]$.

---

The simplest special case is that in which $\mathbf{x}$ has only one variable, so that the transformation is just $(x - \mu)/\sigma$. Combining this case with (B-32) concerning the sum of squares of standard normals, we have the following theorem.

---

**THEOREM B.11** **Distribution of $\mathbf{x}'\boldsymbol{\Sigma}^{-1}\mathbf{x}$ When $\mathbf{x}$ Is Normal**
*If* $\mathbf{x} \sim N[\boldsymbol{\mu}, \boldsymbol{\Sigma}]$, *then* $(\mathbf{x} - \boldsymbol{\mu})'\boldsymbol{\Sigma}^{-1}(\mathbf{x} - \boldsymbol{\mu}) \sim \chi^2[n]$.

---

### B.11.7 INDEPENDENCE OF A LINEAR AND A QUADRATIC FORM

The $t$ distribution is used in many forms of hypothesis tests. In some situations, it arises as the ratio of a linear to a quadratic form in a normal vector. To establish the distribution of these statistics, we use the following result.

---

[10]It will be idempotent only in the special case of $\boldsymbol{\Sigma} = \mathbf{I}$.

> **THEOREM B.12**  **Independence of a Linear and a Quadratic Form**
>
> *A linear function* **Lx** *and a symmetric idempotent quadratic form* **x′Ax** *in a standard normal vector are statistically independent if* **LA = 0.**

The proof follows the same logic as that for two quadratic forms. Write $\mathbf{x'Ax}$ as $\mathbf{x'A'Ax} = (\mathbf{Ax})'(\mathbf{Ax})$. The covariance matrix of the variables $\mathbf{Lx}$ and $\mathbf{Ax}$ is $\mathbf{LA} = \mathbf{0}$, which establishes the independence of these two random vectors. The independence of the linear function and the quadratic form follows because functions of independent random vectors are also independent.

The $t$ distribution is defined as the ratio of a standard normal variable to the square root of a chi-squared variable divided by its degrees of freedom:

$$t[J] = \frac{N[0,1]}{\left\{\chi^2[J]/J\right\}^{1/2}}.$$

A particular case is

$$t[n-1] = \frac{\sqrt{n}\,\bar{x}}{\left\{\frac{1}{n-1}\sum_{i=1}^{n}(x_i - \bar{x})^2\right\}^{1/2}} = \frac{\sqrt{n}\,\bar{x}}{s},$$

where $s$ is the standard deviation of the values of $\mathbf{x}$. The distribution of the two variables in $t[n-1]$ was shown earlier; we need only show that they are independent. But

$$\sqrt{n}\,\bar{x} = \frac{1}{\sqrt{n}}\mathbf{i'x} = \mathbf{j'x},$$

and

$$s^2 = \frac{\mathbf{x'M^0x}}{n-1}.$$

It suffices to show that $\mathbf{M^0 j} = \mathbf{0}$, which follows from

$$\mathbf{M^0 i} = [\mathbf{I} - \mathbf{i(i'i)^{-1}i'}]\mathbf{i} = \mathbf{i} - \mathbf{i(i'i)^{-1}(i'i)} = \mathbf{0}.$$

# APPENDIX C

═══◦◦◦═══

# ESTIMATION AND INFERENCE

## C.1 INTRODUCTION

The probability distributions discussed in Appendix B serve as models for the underlying data generating processes that produce our observed data. The goal of statistical inference in econometrics is to use the principles of mathematical statistics to combine these theoretical distributions and the observed data into an empirical model of the economy. This analysis takes place in one of two frameworks, classical or Bayesian. The overwhelming majority of empirical study in econometrics has been done in the classical framework. Our focus, therefore, will be on classical methods of inference. Bayesian methods are discussed in Chapter 18.[1]

## C.2 SAMPLES AND RANDOM SAMPLING

The classical theory of statistical inference centers on rules for using the sampled data effectively. These rules, in turn, are based on the properties of samples and sampling distributions.

A sample of $n$ observations on one or more variables, denoted $\mathbf{x}_1, \mathbf{x}_2, \ldots, \mathbf{x}_n$ is a **random sample** if the $n$ observations are drawn independently from the same population, or probability distribution, $f(\mathbf{x}_i, \boldsymbol{\theta})$. The sample may be univariate if $\mathbf{x}_i$ is a single random variable or multivariate if each observation contains several variables. A random sample of observations, denoted $[\mathbf{x}_1, \mathbf{x}_2, \ldots, \mathbf{x}_n]$ or $\{\mathbf{x}_i\}_{i=1,\ldots,n}$, is said to be **independent, identically distributed,** which we denote *i.i.d.* The vector $\boldsymbol{\theta}$ contains one or more unknown parameters. Data are generally drawn in one of two settings. A **cross section** is a sample of a number of observational units all drawn at the same point in time. A **time series** is a set of observations drawn on the same observational unit at a number of (usually evenly spaced) points in time. Many recent studies have been based on time-series cross sections, which generally consist of the same cross-sectional units observed at several points in time. Because the typical data set of this sort consists of a large number of cross-sectional units observed at a few points in time, the common term **panel data set** is usually more fitting for this sort of study.

## C.3 DESCRIPTIVE STATISTICS

Before attempting to estimate parameters of a population or fit models to data, we normally examine the data themselves. In raw form, the sample data are a disorganized mass of information, so we will need some organizing principles to distill the information into something meaningful. Consider, first, examining the data on a single variable. In most cases, and particularly if the number of observations in the sample is large, we shall use some summary **statistics** to describe the sample data. Of most interest are measures of **location**—that is, the center of the data—and **scale,** or the dispersion of the data. A few measures of central tendency are as follows:

$$\textbf{mean: } \overline{x} = \frac{1}{n}\sum_{i=1}^{n} x_i,$$

$$\textbf{median: } M = \text{middle ranked observation,} \tag{C-1}$$

$$\textbf{sample midrange: } \text{midrange} = \frac{\text{maximum} + \text{minimum}}{2}.$$

The dispersion of the sample observations is usually measured by the

$$\textbf{standard deviation: } s_x = \left[\frac{\sum_{i=1}^{n}(x_i - \overline{x})^2}{n-1}\right]^{1/2}. \tag{C-2}$$

Other measures, such as the average absolute deviation from the sample mean, are also used, although less frequently than the standard deviation. The shape of the distribution of values is often of interest as well. Samples of income or expenditure data, for example, tend to be highly

---

[1] An excellent reference is Leamer (1978). A summary of the results as they apply to econometrics is contained in Zellner (1971) and in Judge et al. (1985). See, as well, Poirier (1991, 1995). Recent textbooks on Bayesian econometrics include Koop (2003), Lancaster (2004) and Geweke (2005).

*Covariance:* $s_{IE} = \frac{1}{19}[20.5(12) + \cdots + 84.9(16) - 20(31.28)(14.6)] = 23.597$,

*Correlation:* $r_{IE} = \dfrac{23.597}{(22.376)(3.119)} = 0.3382$.

The positive correlation is consistent with our observation in the scatter diagram.

The statistics just described will provide the analyst with a more concise description of the data than a raw tabulation. However, we have not, as yet, suggested that these measures correspond to some underlying characteristic of the process that generated the data. We do assume that there is an underlying mechanism, the data-generating process, that produces the data in hand. Thus, these serve to do more than describe the data; they characterize that process, or population. Because we have assumed that there is an underlying probability distribution, it might be useful to produce a statistic that gives a broader view of the DGP. The **histogram** is a simple graphical device that produces this result—see Examples C.3 and C.4 for applications. For small samples or widely dispersed data, however, histograms tend to be rough and difficult to make informative. A burgeoning literature [see, e.g., Pagan and Ullah (1999) and Li and Racine (2007)] has demonstrated the usefulness of the **kernel density estimator** as a substitute for the histogram as a descriptive tool for the underlying distribution that produced a sample of data. The underlying theory of the kernel density estimator is fairly complicated, but the computations are surprisingly simple. The estimator is computed using

$$\hat{f}(x^*) = \frac{1}{nh} \sum_{i=1}^{n} K\left[\frac{x_i - x^*}{h}\right],$$

where $x_1, \ldots, x_n$ are the $n$ observations in the sample, $\hat{f}(x^*)$ denotes the estimated density function, $x^*$ is the value at which we wish to evaluate the density, and $h$ and $K[\cdot]$ are the "bandwidth" and "kernel function" that we now consider. The density estimator is rather like a histogram, in which the bandwidth is the width of the intervals. The kernel function is a weight function which is generally chosen so that it takes large values when $x^*$ is close to $x_i$ and tapers off to zero in as they diverge in either direction. The weighting function used in the example below is the logistic density discussed in Section B.4.7. The bandwidth is chosen to be a function of $1/n$ so that the intervals can become narrower as the sample becomes larger (and richer). The one used for Figure C.2 is $h = 0.9\text{Min}(s, \text{range}/3)/n^{.2}$. (We will revisit this method of estimation in Chapter 14.) Example C.2 illustrates the computation for the income data used in Example C.1.

### Example C.2  Kernel Density Estimator for the Income Data
Figure C.2 suggests the large skew in the income data that is also suggested by the box and whisker plot (and the scatter plot) in Example C.1.

## C.4  STATISTICS AS ESTIMATORS—SAMPLING DISTRIBUTIONS

The measures described in the preceding section summarize the data in a random sample. Each measure has a counterpart in the population, that is, the distribution from which the data were drawn. Sample quantities such as the means and the correlation coefficient correspond to population expectations, whereas the kernel density estimator and the values in Table C.1 parallel the population **pdf** and **cdf.** In the setting of a random sample, we expect these quantities to mimic

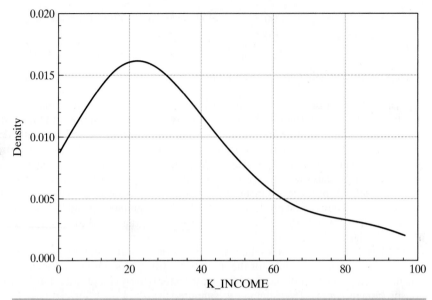

**FIGURE C.2**   Kernel Density Estimate for Income.

**TABLE C.1**   Income Distribution

| Range | Relative Frequency | Cumulative Frequency |
|---|---|---|
| <$10,000 | 0.15 | 0.15 |
| 10,000–25,000 | 0.30 | 0.45 |
| 25,000–50,000 | 0.40 | 0.85 |
| >50,000 | 0.15 | 1.00 |

the population, although not perfectly. The precise manner in which these quantities reflect the population values defines the sampling distribution of a sample statistic.

**DEFINITION C.1**   Statistic
*A statistic is any function computed from the data in a sample.*

If another sample were drawn under identical conditions, different values would be obtained for the observations, as each one is a random variable. Any statistic is a function of these random values, so it is also a random variable with a probability distribution called a **sampling distribution.** For example, the following shows an exact result for the sampling behavior of a widely used statistic.

---

**THEOREM C.1**  **Sampling Distribution of the Sample Mean**

*If $x_1, \ldots, x_n$ are a random sample from a population with mean $\mu$ and variance $\sigma^2$, then $\bar{x}$ is a random variable with mean $\mu$ and variance $\sigma^2/n$.*

**Proof:** $\bar{x} = (1/n)\Sigma_i x_i$. $E[\bar{x}] = (1/n)\Sigma_i \mu = \mu$. *The observations are independent, so* $\text{Var}[\bar{x}] = (1/n)^2 \text{Var}[\Sigma_i x_i] = (1/n^2)\Sigma_i \sigma^2 = \sigma^2/n$.

---

Example C.3 illustrates the behavior of the sample mean in samples of four observations drawn from a chi-squared population with one degree of freedom. The crucial concepts illustrated in this example are, first, the mean and variance results in Theorem C.1 and, second, the phenomenon of **sampling variability.**

Notice that the fundamental result in Theorem C.1 does not assume a distribution for $x_i$. Indeed, looking back at Section C.3, nothing we have done so far has required any assumption about a particular distribution.

### Example C.3   Sampling Distribution of a Sample Mean

Figure C.3 shows a frequency plot of the means of 1,000 random samples of four observations drawn from a chi-squared distribution with one degree of freedom, which has mean 1 and variance 2.

We are often interested in how a statistic behaves as the sample size increases. Example C.4 illustrates one such case. Figure C.4 shows two sampling distributions, one based on samples of three and a second, of the same statistic, but based on samples of six. The effect of increasing sample size in this figure is unmistakable. It is easy to visualize the behavior of this statistic if we extrapolate the experiment in Example C.4 to samples of, say, 100.

### Example C.4   Sampling Distribution of the Sample Minimum

If $x_1, \ldots, x_n$ are a random sample from an exponential distribution with $f(x) = \theta e^{-\theta x}$, then the sampling distribution of the sample minimum in a sample of $n$ observations, denoted $x_{(1)}$, is

$$f\left(x_{(1)}\right) = (n\theta)e^{-(n\theta)x_{(1)}}.$$

Because $E[x] = 1/\theta$ and $\text{Var}[x] = 1/\theta^2$, by analogy $E[x_{(1)}] = 1/(n\theta)$ and $\text{Var}[x_{(1)}] = 1/(n\theta)^2$. Thus, in increasingly larger samples, the minimum will be arbitrarily close to 0. [The Chebychev inequality in Theorem D.2 can be used to prove this intuitively appealing result.]

Figure C.4 shows the results of a simple sampling experiment you can do to demonstrate this effect. It requires software that will allow you to produce pseudorandom numbers uniformly distributed in the range zero to one and that will let you plot a histogram and control the axes. (We used *NLOGIT*. This can be done with *Stata, Excel,* or several other packages.) The experiment consists of drawing 1,000 sets of nine random values, $U_{ij}, i = 1, \ldots 1{,}000, j = 1, \ldots, 9$. To transform these uniform draws to exponential with parameter $\theta$—we used $\theta = 1.5$, use the inverse probability transform—see Section E.2.3. For an exponentially distributed variable, the transformation is $z_{ij} = -(1/\theta) \log(1 - U_{ij})$. We then created $z_{(1)} | 3$ from the first three draws and $z_{(1)} | 6$ from the other six. The two histograms show clearly the effect on the sampling distribution of increasing sample size from just 3 to 6.

Sampling distributions are used to make inferences about the population. To consider a perhaps obvious example, because the sampling distribution of the mean of a set of normally distributed observations has mean $\mu$, the sample mean is a natural candidate for an estimate of $\mu$. The observation that the sample "mimics" the population is a statement about the sampling

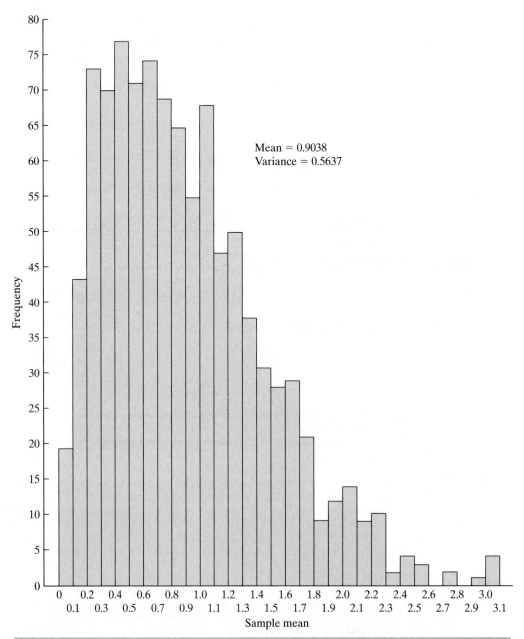

Mean = 0.9038
Variance = 0.5637

**FIGURE C.3**  Sampling Distribution of Means of 1,000 Samples of Size 4 from Chi-Squared [1].

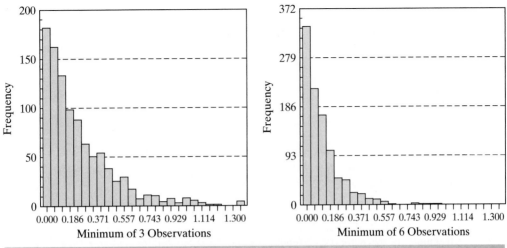

**FIGURE C.4**   Histograms of the Sample Minimum of 3 and 6 Observations.

distributions of the sample statistics. Consider, for example, the sample data collected in Figure C.3. The sample mean of four observations clearly has a sampling distribution, which appears to have a mean roughly equal to the population mean. Our theory of parameter estimation departs from this point.

## C.5   POINT ESTIMATION OF PARAMETERS

Our objective is to use the sample data to infer the value of a parameter or set of parameters, which we denote $\theta$. A **point estimate** is a statistic computed from a sample that gives a single value for $\theta$. The **standard error** of the estimate is the standard deviation of the sampling distribution of the statistic; the square of this quantity is the **sampling variance.** An **interval estimate** is a range of values that will contain the true parameter with a preassigned probability. There will be a connection between the two types of estimates; generally, if $\hat{\theta}$ is the point estimate, then the interval estimate will be $\hat{\theta}\pm$ a measure of sampling error.

   An **estimator** is a rule or strategy for using the data to estimate the parameter. It is defined before the data are drawn. Obviously, some estimators are better than others. To take a simple example, your intuition should convince you that the sample mean would be a better estimator of the population mean than the sample minimum; the minimum is almost certain to underestimate the mean. Nonetheless, the minimum is not entirely without virtue; it is easy to compute, which is occasionally a relevant criterion. The search for good estimators constitutes much of econometrics. Estimators are compared on the basis of a variety of attributes. **Finite sample properties** of estimators are those attributes that can be compared regardless of the sample size. Some estimation problems involve characteristics that are not known in finite samples. In these instances, estimators are compared on the basis on their large sample, or **asymptotic properties.** We consider these in turn.

### C.5.1   ESTIMATION IN A FINITE SAMPLE

The following are some finite sample estimation criteria for estimating a single parameter. The extensions to the multiparameter case are direct. We shall consider them in passing where necessary.

---

**DEFINITION C.2** **Unbiased Estimator**

*An estimator of a parameter θ is **unbiased** if the mean of its sampling distribution is θ.*
*Formally,*

$$E[\hat{\theta}] = \theta$$

*or*

$$E[\hat{\theta} - \theta] = \text{Bias}[\hat{\theta} \mid \theta] = 0$$

*implies that $\hat{\theta}$ is unbiased. Note that this implies that the expected sampling error is zero.*
*If $\boldsymbol{\theta}$ is a vector of parameters, then the estimator is unbiased if the expected value of every*
*element of $\hat{\boldsymbol{\theta}}$ equals the corresponding element of $\boldsymbol{\theta}$.*

---

If samples of size $n$ are drawn repeatedly and $\hat{\theta}$ is computed for each one, then the average value of these estimates will tend to equal $\theta$. For example, the average of the 1,000 sample means underlying Figure C.2 is 0.9038, which is reasonably close to the population mean of one. The sample minimum is clearly a biased estimator of the mean; it will almost always underestimate the mean, so it will do so on average as well.

Unbiasedness is a desirable attribute, but it is rarely used by itself as an estimation criterion. One reason is that there are many unbiased estimators that are poor uses of the data. For example, in a sample of size $n$, the first observation drawn is an unbiased estimator of the mean that clearly wastes a great deal of information. A second criterion used to choose among unbiased estimators is efficiency.

---

**DEFINITION C.3** **Efficient Unbiased Estimator**

*An unbiased estimator $\hat{\theta}_1$ is more **efficient** than another unbiased estimator $\hat{\theta}_2$ if the sam-*
*pling variance of $\hat{\theta}_1$ is less than that of $\hat{\theta}_2$. That is,*

$$\text{Var}[\hat{\theta}_1] < \text{Var}[\hat{\theta}_2].$$

*In the multiparameter case, the comparison is based on the covariance matrices of the two*
*estimators; $\hat{\boldsymbol{\theta}}_1$ is more efficient than $\hat{\boldsymbol{\theta}}_2$ if $\text{Var}[\hat{\boldsymbol{\theta}}_2] - \text{Var}[\hat{\boldsymbol{\theta}}_1]$ is a positive definite matrix.*

---

By this criterion, the sample mean is obviously to be preferred to the first observation as an estimator of the population mean. If $\sigma^2$ is the population variance, then

$$\text{Var}[x_1] = \sigma^2 > \text{Var}[\bar{x}] = \frac{\sigma^2}{n}.$$

In discussing efficiency, we have restricted the discussion to unbiased estimators. Clearly, there are biased estimators that have smaller variances than the unbiased ones we have considered. Any constant has a variance of zero. Of course, using a constant as an estimator is not likely to be an effective use of the sample data. Focusing on unbiasedness may still preclude a tolerably biased estimator with a much smaller variance, however. A criterion that recognizes this possible tradeoff is the mean squared error.

> ## DEFINITION C.4   Mean Squared Error
> *The mean squared error of an estimator is*
>
> $$\text{MSE}[\hat{\theta} \mid \theta] = E[(\hat{\theta} - \theta)^2]$$
>
> $$= \text{Var}[\hat{\theta}] + \left(\text{Bias}[\hat{\theta} \mid \theta]\right)^2 \qquad \text{if } \theta \text{ is a scalar,} \qquad \textbf{(C-9)}$$
>
> $$\text{MSE}[\hat{\boldsymbol{\theta}} \mid \boldsymbol{\theta}] = \text{Var}[\hat{\boldsymbol{\theta}}] + \text{Bias}[\hat{\boldsymbol{\theta}} \mid \boldsymbol{\theta}]\text{Bias}[\hat{\boldsymbol{\theta}} \mid \boldsymbol{\theta}]' \quad \text{if } \boldsymbol{\theta} \text{ is a vector.}$$

Figure C.5 illustrates the effect. In this example, on average, the biased estimator will be closer to the true parameter than will the unbiased estimator.

Which of these criteria should be used in a given situation depends on the particulars of that setting and our objectives in the study. Unfortunately, the MSE criterion is rarely operational; minimum mean squared error estimators, when they exist at all, usually depend on unknown parameters. Thus, we are usually less demanding. A commonly used criterion is **minimum variance unbiasedness.**

### Example C.5   Mean Squared Error of the Sample Variance
In sampling from a normal distribution, the most frequently used estimator for $\sigma^2$ is

$$s^2 = \frac{\sum_{i=1}^{n}(x_i - \bar{x})^2}{n - 1}.$$

It is straightforward to show that $s^2$ is unbiased, so

$$\text{Var}[s^2] = \frac{2\sigma^4}{n - 1} = \text{MSE}[s^2 \mid \sigma^2].$$

**FIGURE C.5**   Sampling Distributions.

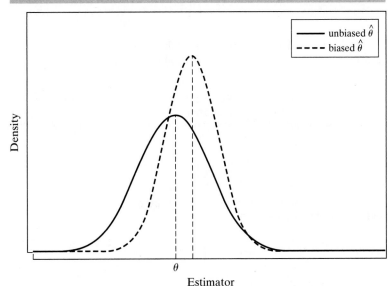

[A proof is based on the distribution of the idempotent quadratic form $(\mathbf{x} - \mathbf{i}\mu)'\mathbf{M}^0(\mathbf{x} - \mathbf{i}\mu)$, which we discussed in Section B11.4.] A less frequently used estimator is

$$\hat{\sigma}^2 = \frac{1}{n}\sum_{i=1}^{n}(x_i - \bar{x})^2 = [(n-1)/n]s^2.$$

This estimator is slightly biased downward:

$$E[\hat{\sigma}^2] = \frac{(n-1)E(s^2)}{n} = \frac{(n-1)\sigma^2}{n},$$

so its bias is

$$E[\hat{\sigma}^2 - \sigma^2] = \text{Bias}[\hat{\sigma}^2 \mid \sigma^2] = \frac{-1}{n}\sigma^2.$$

But it has a smaller variance than $s^2$:

$$\text{Var}[\hat{\sigma}^2] = \left[\frac{n-1}{n}\right]^2\left[\frac{2\sigma^4}{n-1}\right] < \text{Var}[s^2].$$

To compare the two estimators, we can use the difference in their mean squared errors:

$$\text{MSE}[\hat{\sigma}^2 \mid \sigma^2] - \text{MSE}[s^2 \mid \sigma^2] = \sigma^4\left[\frac{2n-1}{n^2} - \frac{2}{n-1}\right] < 0.$$

The biased estimator is a bit more precise. The difference will be negligible in a large sample, but, for example, it is about 1.2 percent in a sample of 16.

### C.5.2 EFFICIENT UNBIASED ESTIMATION

In a random sample of $n$ observations, the density of each observation is $f(x_i, \theta)$. Because the $n$ observations are independent, their joint density is

$$f(x_1, x_2, \ldots, x_n, \theta) = f(x_1, \theta)f(x_2, \theta)\cdots f(x_n, \theta)$$

$$= \prod_{i=1}^{n} f(x_i, \theta) = L(\theta \mid x_1, x_2, \ldots, x_n). \tag{C-10}$$

This function, denoted $L(\theta \mid \mathbf{X})$, is called the likelihood function for $\theta$ given the data $\mathbf{X}$. It is frequently abbreviated to $L(\theta)$. Where no ambiguity can arise, we shall abbreviate it further to $L$.

**Example C.6  Likelihood Functions for Exponential
and Normal Distributions**
If $x_1, \ldots, x_n$ are a sample of $n$ observations from an exponential distribution with parameter $\theta$, then

$$L(\theta) = \prod_{i=1}^{n} \theta e^{-\theta x_i} = \theta^n e^{-\theta \sum_{i=1}^{n} x_i}.$$

If $x_1, \ldots, x_n$ are a sample of $n$ observations from a normal distribution with mean $\mu$ and standard deviation $\sigma$, then

$$L(\mu, \sigma) = \prod_{i=1}^{n}(2\pi\sigma^2)^{-1/2}e^{-[1/(2\sigma^2)](x_i - \mu)^2}$$

$$= (2\pi\sigma^2)^{-n/2}e^{-[1/(2\sigma^2)]\Sigma_i(x_i - \mu)^2}. \tag{C-11}$$

The likelihood function is the cornerstone for most of our theory of parameter estimation. An important result for efficient estimation is the following.

---

### THEOREM C.2   Cramér–Rao Lower Bound

*Assuming that the density of x satisfies certain regularity conditions, the variance of an unbiased estimator of a parameter θ will always be at least as large as*

$$[I(\theta)]^{-1} = \left(-E\left[\frac{\partial^2 \ln L(\theta)}{\partial \theta^2}\right]\right)^{-1} = \left(E\left[\left(\frac{\partial \ln L(\theta)}{\partial \theta}\right)^2\right]\right)^{-1}. \qquad \text{(C-12)}$$

*The quantity I(θ) is the information number for the sample. We will prove the result that the negative of the expected second derivative equals the expected square of the first derivative in Chapter 16. Proof of the main result of the theorem is quite involved. See, for example, Stuart and Ord (1989).*

---

The regularity conditions are technical in nature. (See Section 16.4.1.) Loosely, they are conditions imposed on the density of the random variable that appears in the likelihood function; these conditions will ensure that the Lindeberg–Levy central limit theorem will apply to moments of the sample of observations on the random vector $\mathbf{y} = \partial \ln f(x_i \mid \theta)/\partial \theta, i = 1, \ldots, n$. Among the conditions are finite moments of $x$ up to order 3. An additional condition normally included in the set is that the range of the random variable be independent of the parameters.

In some cases, the second derivative of the log likelihood is a constant, so the Cramér–Rao bound is simple to obtain. For instance, in sampling from an exponential distribution, from Example C.6,

$$\ln L = n \ln \theta - \theta \sum_{i=1}^{n} x_i,$$

$$\frac{\partial \ln L}{\partial \theta} = \frac{n}{\theta} - \sum_{i=1}^{n} x_i,$$

so $\partial^2 \ln L/\partial \theta^2 = -n/\theta^2$ and the variance bound is $[I(\theta)]^{-1} = \theta^2/n$. In many situations, the second derivative is a random variable with a distribution of its own. The following examples show two such cases.

### Example C.7   Variance Bound for the Poisson Distribution

For the Poisson distribution,

$$f(x) = \frac{e^{-\theta}\theta^x}{x!},$$

$$\ln L = -n\theta + \left(\sum_{i=1}^{n} x_i\right) \ln \theta - \sum_{i=1}^{n} \ln(x_i!),$$

$$\frac{\partial \ln L}{\partial \theta} = -n + \frac{\sum_{i=1}^{n} x_i}{\theta},$$

$$\frac{\partial^2 \ln L}{\partial \theta^2} = \frac{-\sum_{i=1}^{n} x_i}{\theta^2}.$$

The sum of $n$ identical Poisson variables has a Poisson distribution with parameter equal to $n$ times the parameter of the individual variables. Therefore, the actual distribution of the first derivative will be that of a linear function of a Poisson distributed variable. Because $E[\sum_{i=1}^{n} x_i] = nE[x_i] = n\theta$, the variance bound for the Poisson distribution is $[I(\theta)]^{-1} = \theta/n$. (Note also that the same result implies that $E[\partial \ln L/\partial\theta] = 0$, which is a result we will use in Chapter 16. The same result holds for the exponential distribution.)

Consider, finally, a multivariate case. If $\theta$ is a vector of parameters, then $\mathbf{I}(\theta)$ is the **information matrix.** The Cramér–Rao theorem states that the difference between the covariance matrix of any unbiased estimator and the inverse of the information matrix,

$$[\mathbf{I}(\theta)]^{-1} = \left(-E\left[\frac{\partial^2 \ln L(\theta)}{\partial\theta\partial\theta'}\right]\right)^{-1} = \left\{E\left[\left(\frac{\partial \ln L(\theta)}{\partial\theta}\right)\left(\frac{\partial \ln L(\theta)}{\partial\theta'}\right)\right]\right\}^{-1}, \qquad \textbf{(C-13)}$$

will be a nonnegative definite matrix.

In many settings, numerous estimators are available for the parameters of a distribution. The usefulness of the Cramér–Rao bound is that if one of these is known to attain the variance bound, then there is no need to consider any other to seek a more efficient estimator. Regarding the use of the variance bound, we emphasize that if an unbiased estimator attains it, then that estimator is efficient. If a given estimator does not attain the variance bound, however, then we do not know, except in a few special cases, whether this estimator is efficient or not. It may be that no unbiased estimator can attain the Cramér–Rao bound, which can leave the question of whether a given unbiased estimator is efficient or not unanswered.

We note, finally, that in some cases we further restrict the set of estimators to linear functions of the data.

---

**DEFINITION C.5**   **Minimum Variance Linear Unbiased Estimator (MVLUE)**

*An estimator is the minimum variance linear unbiased estimator or **best linear unbiased estimator (BLUE)** if it is a linear function of the data and has minimum variance among linear unbiased estimators.*

---

In a few instances, such as the normal mean, there will be an efficient linear unbiased estimator; $\bar{x}$ is efficient among all unbiased estimators, both linear and nonlinear. In other cases, such as the normal variance, there is no linear unbiased estimator. This criterion is useful because we can sometimes find an MVLUE without having to specify the distribution at all. Thus, by limiting ourselves to a somewhat restricted class of estimators, we free ourselves from having to assume a particular distribution.

## C.6   INTERVAL ESTIMATION

Regardless of the properties of an estimator, the estimate obtained will vary from sample to sample, and there is some probability that it will be quite erroneous. A point estimate will not provide any information on the likely range of error. The logic behind an **interval estimate** is that we use the sample data to construct an interval, [lower $(\mathbf{X})$, upper $(\mathbf{X})$], such that we can expect this interval to contain the true parameter in some specified proportion of samples, or equivalently, with some desired level of confidence. Clearly, the wider the interval, the more confident we can be that it will, in any given sample, contain the parameter being estimated.

The theory of interval estimation is based on a **pivotal quantity,** which is a function of both the parameter and a point estimate that has a known distribution. Consider the following examples.

### Example C.8   Confidence Intervals for the Normal Mean

In sampling from a normal distribution with mean $\mu$ and standard deviation $\sigma$,

$$z = \frac{\sqrt{n}(\overline{x} - \mu)}{s} \sim t[n-1],$$

and

$$c = \frac{(n-1)s^2}{\sigma^2} \sim \chi^2[n-1].$$

Given the pivotal quantity, we can make probability statements about events involving the parameter and the estimate. Let $p(g, \theta)$ be the constructed random variable, for example, $z$ or $c$. Given a prespecified **confidence level,** $1 - \alpha$, we can state that

$$\text{Prob(lower} \le p(g, \theta) \le \text{upper)} = 1 - \alpha, \tag{C-14}$$

where lower and upper are obtained from the appropriate table. This statement is then manipulated to make equivalent statements about the endpoints of the intervals. For example, the following statements are equivalent:

$$\text{Prob}\left(-z \le \frac{\sqrt{n}(\overline{x} - \mu)}{s} \le z\right) = 1 - \alpha,$$

$$\text{Prob}\left(\overline{x} - \frac{zs}{\sqrt{n}} \le \mu \le \overline{x} + \frac{zs}{\sqrt{n}}\right) = 1 - \alpha.$$

The second of these is a statement about the interval, not the parameter; that is, it is the interval that is random, not the parameter. We attach a probability, or $100(1 - \alpha)$ percent confidence level, to the interval itself; in repeated sampling, an interval constructed in this fashion will contain the true parameter $100(1 - \alpha)$ percent of the time.

In general, the interval constructed by this method will be of the form

$$\text{lower}(\mathbf{X}) = \hat{\theta} - e_1,$$

$$\text{upper}(\mathbf{X}) = \hat{\theta} + e_2,$$

where $\mathbf{X}$ is the sample data, $e_1$ and $e_2$ are sampling errors, and $\hat{\theta}$ is a point estimate of $\theta$. It is clear from the preceding example that if the sampling distribution of the pivotal quantity is either $t$ or standard normal, which will be true in the vast majority of cases we encounter in practice, then the confidence interval will be

$$\hat{\theta} \pm C_{1-\alpha/2}[\text{se}(\hat{\theta})], \tag{C-15}$$

where se(.) is the (known or estimated) standard error of the parameter estimate and $C_{1-\alpha/2}$ is the value from the $t$ or standard normal distribution that is exceeded with probability $1 - \alpha/2$. The usual values for $\alpha$ are 0.10, 0.05, or 0.01. The theory does not prescribe exactly how to choose the endpoints for the confidence interval. An obvious criterion is to minimize the width of the interval. If the sampling distribution is symmetric, then the symmetric interval is the best one. If the sampling distribution is not symmetric, however, then this procedure will not be optimal.

### Example C.9 Estimated Confidence Intervals for a Normal Mean and Variance

In a sample of 25, $\bar{x} = 1.63$ and $s = 0.51$. Construct a 95 percent confidence interval for $\mu$. Assuming that the sample of 25 is from a normal distribution,

$$\text{Prob}\left(-2.064 \leq \frac{5(\bar{x} - \mu)}{s} \leq 2.064\right) = 0.95,$$

where 2.064 is the critical value from a $t$ distribution with 24 degrees of freedom. Thus, the confidence interval is $1.63 \pm [2.064(0.51)/5]$ or $[1.4195, 1.8405]$.

**Remark:** Had the parent distribution not been specified, it would have been natural to use the standard normal distribution instead, perhaps relying on the central limit theorem. But a sample size of 25 is small enough that the more conservative $t$ distribution might still be preferable.

The chi-squared distribution is used to construct a confidence interval for the variance of a normal distribution. Using the data from Example C.9, we find that the usual procedure would use

$$\text{Prob}\left(12.4 \leq \frac{24s^2}{\sigma^2} \leq 39.4\right) = 0.95,$$

where 12.4 and 39.4 are the 0.025 and 0.975 cutoff points from the chi-squared (24) distribution. This procedure leads to the 95 percent confidence interval $[0.1581, 0.5032]$. By making use of the asymmetry of the distribution, a narrower interval can be constructed. Allocating 4 percent to the left-hand tail and 1 percent to the right instead of 2.5 percent to each, the two cutoff points are 13.4 and 42.9, and the resulting 95 percent confidence interval is $[0.1455, 0.4659]$.

Finally, the confidence interval can be manipulated to obtain a confidence interval for a function of a parameter. For example, based on the preceding, a 95 percent confidence interval for $\sigma$ would be $[\sqrt{0.1581}, \sqrt{0.5032}] = [0.3976, 0.7094]$.

## C.7 HYPOTHESIS TESTING

The second major group of statistical inference procedures is hypothesis tests. The classical testing procedures are based on constructing a statistic from a random sample that will enable the analyst to decide, with reasonable confidence, whether or not the data in the sample would have been generated by a hypothesized population. The formal procedure involves a statement of the hypothesis, usually in terms of a "null" or maintained hypothesis and an "alternative," conventionally denoted $H_0$ and $H_1$, respectively. The procedure itself is a rule, stated in terms of the data, that dictates whether the null hypothesis should be rejected or not. For example, the hypothesis might state a parameter is equal to a specified value. The decision rule might state that the hypothesis should be rejected if a sample estimate of that parameter is too far away from that value (where "far" remains to be defined). The classical, or Neyman–Pearson, methodology involves partitioning the sample space into two regions. If the observed data (i.e., the test statistic) fall in the **rejection region** (sometimes called the **critical region**), then the null hypothesis is rejected; if they fall in the **acceptance region,** then it is not.

### C.7.1 CLASSICAL TESTING PROCEDURES

Since the sample is random, the test statistic, however defined, is also random. The same test procedure can lead to different conclusions in different samples. As such, there are two ways such a procedure can be in error:

1. **Type I error.** The procedure may lead to rejection of the null hypothesis when it is true.
2. **Type II error.** The procedure may fail to reject the null hypothesis when it is false.

To continue the previous example, there is some probability that the estimate of the parameter will be quite far from the hypothesized value, even if the hypothesis is true. This outcome might cause a type I error.

---

**DEFINITION C.6** **Size of a Test**
*The probability of a type I error is the size of the test. This is conventionally denoted α and is also called the significance level.*

---

The size of the test is under the control of the analyst. It can be changed just by changing the decision rule. Indeed, the type I error could be eliminated altogether just by making the rejection region very small, but this would come at a cost. By eliminating the probability of a type I error—that is, by making it unlikely that the hypothesis is rejected—we must increase the probability of a type II error. Ideally, we would like both probabilities to be as small as possible. It is clear, however, that there is a tradeoff between the two. The best we can hope for is that for a given probability of type I error, the procedure we choose will have as small a probability of type II error as possible.

---

**DEFINITION C.7** **Power of a Test**
*The power of a test is the probability that it will correctly lead to rejection of a false null hypothesis:*

$$\text{power} = 1 - \beta = 1 - \text{Prob(type II error)}. \qquad \textbf{(C-16)}$$

---

For a given significance level $\alpha$, we would like $\beta$ to be as small as possible. Because $\beta$ is defined in terms of the alternative hypothesis, it depends on the value of the parameter.

### Example C.10  Testing a Hypothesis About a Mean

For testing $H_0: \mu = \mu^0$ in a normal distribution with known variance $\sigma^2$, the decision rule is to reject the hypothesis if the absolute value of the z statistic, $\sqrt{n}(\overline{x} - \mu^0)/\sigma$, exceeds the predetermined critical value. For a test at the 5 percent significance level, we set the critical value at 1.96. The power of the test, therefore, is the probability that the absolute value of the test statistic will exceed 1.96 given that the true value of $\mu$ is, in fact, not $\mu^0$. This value depends on the alternative value of $\mu$, as shown in Figure C.6. Notice that for this test the power is equal to the size at the point where $\mu$ equals $\mu^0$. As might be expected, the test becomes more powerful the farther the true mean is from the hypothesized value.

Testing procedures, like estimators, can be compared using a number of criteria.

---

**DEFINITION C.8** **Most Powerful Test**
*A test is most powerful if it has greater power than any other test of the same size.*

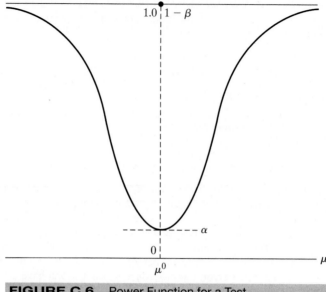

**FIGURE C.6**   Power Function for a Test.

This requirement is very strong. Because the power depends on the alternative hypothesis, we might require that the test be **uniformly most powerful (UMP),** that is, have greater power than any other test of the same size for all admissible values of the parameter. There are few situations in which a UMP test is available. We usually must be less stringent in our requirements. Nonetheless, the criteria for comparing hypothesis testing procedures are generally based on their respective power functions. A common and very modest requirement is that the test be unbiased.

---

**DEFINITION C.9**   **Unbiased Test**
*A test is **unbiased** if its power $(1 - \beta)$ is greater than or equal to its size $\alpha$ for all values of the parameter.*

---

If a test is **biased,** then, for some values of the parameter, we are more likely to accept the null hypothesis when it is false than when it is true.

The use of the term *unbiased* here is unrelated to the concept of an unbiased estimator. Fortunately, there is little chance of confusion. Tests and estimators are clearly connected, however. The following criterion derives, in general, from the corresponding attribute of a parameter estimate.

---

**DEFINITION C.10**   **Consistent Test**
*A test is **consistent** if its power goes to one as the sample size grows to infinity.*

---

**Example C.11   Consistent Test About a Mean**

A confidence interval for the mean of a normal distribution is $\bar{x} \pm t_{1-\alpha/2}(s/\sqrt{n})$, where $\bar{x}$ and $s$ are the usual consistent estimators for $\mu$ and $\sigma$ (see Section D.2.1), $n$ is the sample size, and $t_{1-\alpha/2}$ is the correct critical value from the $t$ distribution with $n-1$ degrees of freedom. For testing $H_0$: $\mu = \mu_0$ versus $H_1$: $\mu \neq \mu_0$, let the procedure be to reject $H_0$ if the confidence interval does not contain $\mu_0$. Because $\bar{x}$ is consistent for $\mu$, one can discern if $H_0$ is false as $n \to \infty$, with probability 1, because $\bar{x}$ will be arbitrarily close to the true $\mu$. Therefore, this test is consistent.

As a general rule, a test will be consistent if it is based on a consistent estimator of the parameter.

## C.7.2   TESTS BASED ON CONFIDENCE INTERVALS

There is an obvious link between interval estimation and the sorts of hypothesis tests we have been discussing here. The confidence interval gives a range of plausible values for the parameter. Therefore, it stands to reason that if a hypothesized value of the parameter does not fall in this range of plausible values, then the data are not consistent with the hypothesis, and it should be rejected. Consider, then, testing

$$H_0: \theta = \theta_0,$$

$$H_1: \theta \neq \theta_0.$$

We form a confidence interval based on $\hat{\theta}$ as described earlier:

$$\hat{\theta} - C_{1-\alpha/2}[se(\hat{\theta})] < \theta < \hat{\theta} + C_{1-\alpha/2}[se(\hat{\theta})].$$

$H_0$ is rejected if $\theta_0$ exceeds the upper limit or is less than the lower limit. Equivalently, $H_0$ is rejected if

$$\left| \frac{\hat{\theta} - \theta_0}{se(\hat{\theta})} \right| > C_{1-\alpha/2}.$$

In words, the hypothesis is rejected if the estimate is too far from $\theta_0$, where the distance is measured in standard error units. The critical value is taken from the $t$ or standard normal distribution, whichever is appropriate.

**Example C.12   Testing a Hypothesis About a Mean with**
**a Confidence Interval**

For the results in Example C.8, test $H_0$: $\mu = 1.98$ versus $H_1$: $\mu \neq 1.98$, assuming sampling from a normal distribution:

$$t = \left| \frac{\bar{x} - 1.98}{s/\sqrt{n}} \right| = \left| \frac{1.63 - 1.98}{0.102} \right| = 3.43.$$

The 95 percent critical value for $t(24)$ is 2.064. Therefore, reject $H_0$. If the critical value for the standard normal table of 1.96 is used instead, then the same result is obtained.

If the test is one-sided, as in

$$H_0: \theta \geq \theta_0,$$

$$H_1: \theta < \theta_0,$$

then the critical region must be adjusted. Thus, for this test, $H_0$ will be rejected if a point estimate of $\theta$ falls sufficiently below $\theta_0$. (Tests can usually be set up by departing from the decision criterion, "What sample results are inconsistent with the hypothesis?")

***Example C.13 One-Sided Test About a Mean***

A sample of 25 from a normal distribution yields $\bar{x} = 1.63$ and $s = 0.51$. Test

$$H_0: \mu \leq 1.5,$$
$$H_1: \mu > 1.5.$$

Clearly, no observed $\bar{x}$ less than or equal to 1.5 will lead to rejection of $H_0$. Using the borderline value of 1.5 for $\mu$, we obtain

$$\text{Prob}\left(\frac{\sqrt{n}(\bar{x} - 1.5)}{s} > \frac{5(1.63 - 1.5)}{0.51}\right) = \text{Prob}(t_{24} > 1.27).$$

This is approximately 0.11. This value is not unlikely by the usual standards. Hence, at a significant level of 0.11, we would not reject the hypothesis.

### C.7.3 SPECIFICATION TESTS

The hypothesis testing procedures just described are known as "classical" testing procedures. In each case, the null hypothesis tested came in the form of a restriction on the alternative. You can verify that in each application we examined, the parameter space assumed under the null hypothesis is a subspace of that described by the alternative. For that reason, the models implied are said to be "nested." The null hypothesis is contained within the alternative. This approach suffices for most of the testing situations encountered in practice, but there are common situations in which two competing models cannot be viewed in these terms. For example, consider a case in which there are two completely different, competing theories to explain the same observed data. Many models for censoring and truncation discussed in Chapter 24 rest upon a fragile assumption of normality, for example. Testing of this nature requires a different approach from the classical procedures discussed here. These are discussed at various points throughout the book, for example, in Chapter 24, where we study the difference between fixed and random effects models.

# APPENDIX D

# LARGE-SAMPLE DISTRIBUTION THEORY

## D.1 INTRODUCTION

Most of this book is about parameter estimation. In studying that subject, we will usually be interested in determining how best to use the observed data when choosing among competing estimators. That, in turn, requires us to examine the sampling behavior of estimators. In a few cases, such as those presented in Appendix C and the least squares estimator considered in Chapter 4, we can make broad statements about sampling distributions that will apply regardless of the size of the sample. But, in most situations, it will only be possible to make approximate statements about estimators, such as whether they improve as the sample size increases and what can be said about their sampling distributions in large samples as an approximation to the finite samples we actually observe. This appendix will collect most of the formal, fundamental theorems and results needed for this analysis. A few additional results will be developed in the discussion of time-series analysis later in the book.

## D.2 LARGE-SAMPLE DISTRIBUTION THEORY[1]

In most cases, whether an estimator is exactly unbiased or what its exact sampling variance is in samples of a given size will be unknown. But we may be able to obtain approximate results about the behavior of the distribution of an estimator as the sample becomes large. For example, it is well known that the distribution of the mean of a sample tends to approximate normality as the sample size grows, regardless of the distribution of the individual observations. Knowledge about the limiting behavior of the distribution of an estimator can be used to infer an approximate distribution for the estimator in a finite sample. To describe how this is done, it is necessary, first, to present some results on convergence of random variables.

### D.2.1 CONVERGENCE IN PROBABILITY

Limiting arguments in this discussion will be with respect to the sample size $n$. Let $x_n$ be a sequence random variable indexed by the sample size.

---

**DEFINITION D.1** **Convergence in Probability**
*The random variable $x_n$ **converges in probability** to a constant $c$ if $\lim_{n \to \infty} \text{Prob}(|x_n - c| > \varepsilon) = 0$ for any positive $\varepsilon$.*

---

Convergence in probability implies that the values that the variable may take that are not close to $c$ become increasingly unlikely as $n$ increases. To consider one example, suppose that the random variable $x_n$ takes two values, zero and $n$, with probabilities $1 - (1/n)$ and $(1/n)$, respectively. As $n$ increases, the second point will become ever more remote from any constant but, at the same time, will become increasingly less probable. In this example, $x_n$ converges in probability to zero. The crux of this form of convergence is that all the mass of the probability distribution becomes concentrated at points close to $c$. If $x_n$ converges in probability to $c$, then we write

$$\text{plim } x_n = c. \tag{D-1}$$

We will make frequent use of a special case of convergence in probability, **convergence in mean square** or **convergence in quadratic mean.**

---

**THEOREM D.1** **Convergence in Quadratic Mean**
*If $x_n$ has mean $\mu_n$ and variance $\sigma_n^2$ such that the ordinary limits of $\mu_n$ and $\sigma_n^2$ are $c$ and $0$, respectively, then $x_n$ converges in mean square to $c$, and*

$$\text{plim } x_n = c.$$

---

[1] A comprehensive summary of many results in large-sample theory appears in White (2001). The results discussed here will apply to samples of independent observations. Time series cases in which observations are correlated are analyzed in Chapters 19 through 22.

A proof of Theorem D.1 can be based on another useful theorem.

---

**THEOREM D.2** **Chebychev's Inequality**

*If $x_n$ is a random variable and $c$ and $\varepsilon$ are constants, then* $\text{Prob}(|x_n - c| > \varepsilon) \leq E[(x_n - c)^2]/\varepsilon^2$.

---

To establish the Chebychev inequality, we use another result [see Goldberger (1991, p. 31)].

---

**THEOREM D.3** **Markov's Inequality**

*If $y_n$ is a nonnegative random variable and $\delta$ is a positive constant, then* $\text{Prob}[y_n \geq \delta] \leq E[y_n]/\delta$.

*Proof:* $E[y_n] = \text{Prob}[y_n < \delta]E[y_n \mid y_n < \delta] + \text{Prob}[y_n \geq \delta]E[y_n \mid y_n \geq \delta]$. *Because $y_n$ is non-negative, both terms must be nonnegative, so* $E[y_n] \geq \text{Prob}[y_n \geq \delta]E[y_n \mid y_n \geq \delta]$. *Because $E[y_n \mid y_n \geq \delta]$ must be greater than or equal to $\delta$, $E[y_n] \geq \text{Prob}[y_n \geq \delta]\delta$, which is the result.*

---

Now, to prove Theorem D.1., let $y_n$ be $(x_n - c)^2$ and $\delta$ be $\varepsilon^2$ in Theorem D.3. Then, $(x_n - c)^2 > \delta$ implies that $|x_n - c| > \varepsilon$. Finally, we will use a special case of the Chebychev inequality, where $c = \mu_n$, so that we have

$$\text{Prob}(|x_n - \mu_n| > \varepsilon) \leq \sigma_n^2/\varepsilon^2. \tag{D-2}$$

Taking the limits of $\mu_n$ and $\sigma_n^2$ in (D-2), we see that if

$$\lim_{n \to \infty} E[x_n] = c, \quad \text{and} \quad \lim_{n \to \infty} \text{Var}[x_n] = 0, \tag{D-3}$$

then

$$\text{plim } x_n = c.$$

We have shown that convergence in mean square implies convergence in probability. Mean-square convergence implies that the distribution of $x_n$ collapses to a spike at plim $x_n$, as shown in Figure D.1.

### Example D.1 Mean Square Convergence of the Sample Minimum in Exponential Sampling

As noted in Example C.4, in sampling of $n$ observations from an exponential distribution, for the sample minimum $x_{(1)}$,

$$\lim_{n \to \infty} E\left[x_{(1)}\right] = \lim_{n \to \infty} \frac{1}{n\theta} = 0$$

and

$$\lim_{n \to \infty} \text{Var}\left[x_{(1)}\right] = \lim_{n \to \infty} \frac{1}{(n\theta)^2} = 0.$$

Therefore,

$$\text{plim } x_{(1)} = 0.$$

Note, in particular, that the variance is divided by $n^2$. Thus, this estimator converges very rapidly to 0.

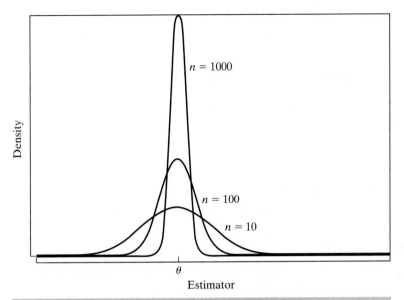

**FIGURE D.1**   Quadratic Convergence to a Constant, $\theta$.

Convergence in probability does not imply convergence in mean square. Consider the simple example given earlier in which $x_n$ equals either zero or $n$ with probabilities $1 - (1/n)$ and $(1/n)$. The exact expected value of $x_n$ is 1 for all $n$, which is not the probability limit. Indeed, if we let $\text{Prob}(x_n = n^2) = (1/n)$ instead, the mean of the distribution explodes, but the probability limit is still zero. Again, the point $x_n = n^2$ becomes ever more extreme but, at the same time, becomes ever less likely.

The conditions for convergence in mean square are usually easier to verify than those for the more general form. Fortunately, we shall rarely encounter circumstances in which it will be necessary to show convergence in probability in which we cannot rely upon convergence in mean square. Our most frequent use of this concept will be in formulating consistent estimators.

---

**DEFINITION D.2**   **Consistent Estimator**
*An estimator $\hat{\theta}_n$ of a parameter $\theta$ is a **consistent** estimator of $\theta$ if and only if*

$$\text{plim } \hat{\theta}_n = \theta. \tag{D-4}$$

---

**THEOREM D.4**   **Consistency of the Sample Mean**
*The mean of a random sample from any population with finite mean $\mu$ and finite variance $\sigma^2$ is a consistent estimator of $\mu$.*
***Proof:*** *$E[\bar{x}_n] = \mu$ and $\text{Var}[\bar{x}_n] = \sigma^2/n$. Therefore, $\bar{x}_n$ converges in mean square to $\mu$, or $\text{plim } \bar{x}_n = \mu$.*

Theorem D.4 is broader than it might appear at first.

---

**COROLLARY TO THEOREM D.4**  Consistency of a Mean of Functions

*In random sampling, for any function $g(x)$, if $E[g(x)]$ and $\text{Var}[g(x)]$ are finite constants, then*

$$\text{plim} \frac{1}{n} \sum_{i=1}^{n} g(x_i) = E[g(x)]. \qquad \text{(D-5)}$$

**Proof:** *Define $y_i = g(x_i)$ and use Theorem D.4.*

---

### Example D.2  Estimating a Function of the Mean
In sampling from a normal distribution with mean $\mu$ and variance 1, $E[e^x] = e^{\mu+1/2}$ and $\text{Var}[e^x] = e^{2\mu+2} - e^{2\mu+1}$. (See Section B.4.4 on the lognormal distribution.) Hence,

$$\text{plim} \frac{1}{n} \sum_{i=1}^{n} e^{x_i} = e^{\mu+1/2}.$$

### D.2.2  OTHER FORMS OF CONVERGENCE AND LAWS OF LARGE NUMBERS

Theorem D.4 and the corollary just given are particularly narrow forms of a set of results known as **laws of large numbers** that are fundamental to the theory of parameter estimation. Laws of large numbers come in two forms depending on the type of convergence considered. The simpler of these are "weak laws of large numbers" which rely on convergence in probability as we defined it above. "Strong laws" rely on a broader type of convergence called **almost sure convergence.** Overall, the law of large numbers is a statement about the behavior of an average of a large number of random variables.

---

**THEOREM D.5**  Khinchine's Weak Law of Large Numbers

*If $x_i, i = 1, \ldots, n$ is a random (i.i.d.) sample from a distribution with finite mean $E[x_i] = \mu$, then*

$$\text{plim} \, \bar{x}_n = \mu.$$

*Proofs of this and the theorem below are fairly intricate. Rao (1973) provides one.*

---

Notice that this is already broader than Theorem D.4, as it does not require that the variance of the distribution be finite. On the other hand, it is not broad enough, because most of the situations we encounter where we will need a result such as this will not involve i.i.d. random sampling. A broader result is

---

**THEOREM D.6  Chebychev's Weak Law of Large Numbers**

*If $x_i, i = 1, \ldots, n$ is a sample of observations such that $E[x_i] = \mu_i < \infty$ and $\text{Var}[x_i] = \sigma_i^2 < \infty$ such that $\overline{\sigma}_n^2/n = (1/n^2)\Sigma_i \sigma_i^2 \to 0$ as $n \to \infty$, then $\text{plim}(\overline{x}_n - \overline{\mu}_n) = 0$.*

---

There is a subtle distinction between these two theorems that you should notice. The Chebychev theorem does not state that $\overline{x}_n$ converges to $\overline{\mu}_n$, or even that it converges to a constant at all. That would require a precise statement about the behavior of $\overline{\mu}_n$. The theorem states that as $n$ increases without bound, these two quantities will be arbitrarily close to each other—that is, the difference between them converges to a constant, zero. This is an important notion that enters the derivation when we consider statistics that converge to random variables, instead of to constants. What we do have with these two theorems is extremely broad conditions under which a sample mean will converge in probability to its population counterpart. The more important difference between the Khinchine and Chebychev theorems is that the second allows for heterogeneity in the distributions of the random variables that enter the mean.

In analyzing time series data, the sequence of outcomes is itself viewed as a random event. Consider, then, the sample mean, $\overline{x}_n$. The preceding results concern the behavior of this statistic as $n \to \infty$ for a particular realization of the sequence $\overline{x}_1, \ldots, \overline{x}_n$. But, if the sequence, itself, is viewed as a random event, then limit to which $\overline{x}_n$ converges may be also. The stronger notion of almost sure convergence relates to this possibility.

---

**DEFINITION D.3  Almost Sure Convergence**

*The random variable $x_n$ converges almost surely to the constant c if and only if*

$$\text{Prob}\left( \lim_{n \to \infty} x_n = c \right) = 1.$$

---

This is denoted $x_n \xrightarrow{a.s.} c$. It states that the probability of observing a sequence that does not converge to $c$ ultimately vanishes. Intuitively, it states that once the sequence $x_n$ becomes close to $c$, it stays close to $c$.

Almost sure convergence is used in a stronger form of the law of large numbers:

---

**THEOREM D.7  Kolmogorov's Strong Law of Large Numbers**

*If $x_i, i = 1, \ldots, n$ is a sequence of independently distributed random variables such that $E[x_i] = \mu_i < \infty$ and $\text{Var}[x_i] = \sigma_i^2 < \infty$ such that $\sum_{i=1}^{\infty} \sigma_i^2/i^2 < \infty$ as $n \to \infty$ then $\overline{x}_n - \overline{\mu}_n \xrightarrow{a.s.} 0$.*

---

---

**THEOREM D.8** Markov's Strong Law of Large Numbers

*If $\{z_i\}$ is a sequence of independent random variables with $E[z_i] = \mu_i < \infty$ and if for some $\delta > 0$, $\sum_{i=1}^{\infty} E[|z_i - \mu_i|^{1+\delta}]/i^{1+\delta} < \infty$, then $\bar{z}_n - \bar{\mu}_n$ converges almost surely to 0, which we denote $\bar{z}_n - \bar{\mu}_n \xrightarrow{a.s.} 0$.*[2]

---

The variance condition is satisfied if every variance in the sequence is finite, but this is not strictly required; it only requires that the variances in the sequence increase at a slow enough rate that the sequence of variances as defined is bounded. The theorem allows for heterogeneity in the means and variances. If we return to the conditions of the Khinchine theorem, i.i.d. sampling, we have a corollary:

---

**COROLLARY TO THEOREM D.8** (Kolmogorov)

*If $x_i, i = 1, \ldots, n$ is a sequence of independent and identically distributed random variables such that $E[x_i] = \mu < \infty$ and $E[|x_i|] < \infty$ then $\bar{x}_n - \mu \xrightarrow{a.s.} 0$.*

---

Note that the corollary requires identically distributed observations while the theorem only requires independence. Finally, another form of convergence encountered in the analysis of time series data is convergence in $r$th mean:

---

**DEFINITION D.4** Convergence in $r$th Mean

*If $x_n$ is a sequence of random variables such that $E[|x_n|^r] < \infty$ and $\lim_{n\to\infty} E[|x_n - c|^r] = 0$, then $x_n$ converges in $r$th mean to c. This is denoted $x_n \xrightarrow{r.m.} c$.*

---

Surely the most common application is the one we met earlier, convergence in means square, which is convergence in the second mean. Some useful results follow from this definition:

---

**THEOREM D.9** Convergence in Lower Powers

*If $x_n$ converges in $r$th mean to c, then $x_n$ converges in $s$th mean to c for any $s < r$. The proof uses Jensen's Inequality, Theorem D.13. Write $E[|x_n - c|^s] = E[(|x_n - c|^r)^{s/r}] \leq \left\{E[(|x_n - c|^r)]\right\}^{s/r}$ and the inner term converges to zero so the full function must also.*

---

[2]The use of the expected absolute deviation differs a bit from the expected squared deviation that we have used heretofore to characterize the spread of a distribution. Consider two examples. If $z \sim N[0, \sigma^2]$, then $E[|z|] = \text{Prob}[z < 0]E[-z \mid z < 0] + \text{Prob}[z \geq 0]E[z \mid z \geq 0] = 0.7979\sigma$. (See Theorem 24.2.) So, finite expected absolute value is the same as finite second moment for the normal distribution. But if $z$ takes values $[0, n]$ with probabilities $[1 - 1/n, 1/n]$, then the variance of $z$ is $(n - 1)$, but $E[|z - \mu_z|]$ is $2 - 2/n$. For this case, finite expected absolute value occurs without finite expected second moment. These are different characterizations of the spread of the distribution.

---

**THEOREM D.10  Generalized Chebychev's Inequality**
*If $x_n$ is a random variable and $c$ is a constant such that with $E[|x_n - c|^r] < \infty$ and $\varepsilon$ is a positive constant, then $\text{Prob}(|x_n - c| > \varepsilon) \le E[|x_n - c|^r]/\varepsilon^r$.*

---

We have considered two cases of this result already, when $r = 1$ which is the Markov inequality, Theorem D.3, and when $r = 2$, which is the Chebychev inequality we looked at first in Theorem D.2.

---

**THEOREM D.11  Convergence in $r$th mean and Convergence in Probability**
*If $x_n \xrightarrow{r.m.} c$, for some $r > 0$, then $x_n \xrightarrow{p} c$. The proof relies on Theorem D.10. By assumption, $\lim_{n\to\infty} E[|x_n - c|^r] = 0$ so for some $n$ sufficiently large, $E[|x_n - c|^r] < \infty$. By Theorem D.10, then, $\text{Prob}(|x_n - c| > \varepsilon) \le E[|x_n - c|^r]/\varepsilon^r$ for any $\varepsilon > 0$. The denominator of the fraction is a fixed constant and the numerator converges to zero by our initial assumption, so $\lim_{n\to\infty} \text{Prob}(|x_n - c| > \varepsilon) = 0$, which completes the proof.*

---

One implication of Theorem D.11 is that although convergence in mean square is a convenient way to prove convergence in probability, it is actually stronger than necessary, as we get the same result for any positive $r$.

Finally, we note that we have now shown that both almost sure convergence and convergence in $r$th mean are stronger than convergence in probability; each implies the latter. But they, themselves, are different notions of convergence, and neither implies the other.

---

**DEFINITION D.5  Convergence of a Random Vector or Matrix**
*Let $\mathbf{x}_n$ denote a random vector and $\mathbf{X}_n$ a random matrix, and $\mathbf{c}$ and $\mathbf{C}$ denote a vector and matrix of constants with the same dimensions as $\mathbf{x}_n$ and $\mathbf{X}_n$, respectively. All of the preceding notions of convergence can be extended to $(\mathbf{x}_n, \mathbf{c})$ and $(\mathbf{X}_n, \mathbf{C})$ by applying the results to the respective corresponding elements.*

---

### D.2.3  CONVERGENCE OF FUNCTIONS

A particularly convenient result is the following.

---

**THEOREM D.12  Slutsky Theorem**
*For a continuous function $g(x_n)$ that is not a function of $n$,*

$$\text{plim } g(x_n) = g(\text{plim } x_n). \tag{D-6}$$

---

The generalization of Theorem D.12 to a function of several random variables is direct, as illustrated in the next example.

**Example D.3   Probability Limit of a Function of $\bar{x}$ and $s^2$**

In random sampling from a population with mean $\mu$ and variance $\sigma^2$, the exact expected value of $\bar{x}_n^2/s_n^2$ will be difficult, if not impossible, to derive. But, by the Slutsky theorem,

$$\text{plim} \frac{\bar{x}_n^2}{s_n^2} = \frac{\mu^2}{\sigma^2}.$$

An application that highlights the difference between expectation and probability is suggested by the following useful relationships.

---

**THEOREM D.13   Inequalities for Expectations**

*Jensen's Inequality. If $g(x_n)$ is a concave function of $x_n$, then $g\left(E[x_n]\right) \geq E[g(x_n)]$.*
*Cauchy–Schwarz Inequality. For two random variables,*

$$E[|xy|] \leq \left\{E[x^2]\right\}^{1/2} \left\{E[y^2]\right\}^{1/2}.$$

---

Although the expected value of a function of $x_n$ may not equal the function of the expected value—it exceeds it if the function is concave—the probability limit of the function *is* equal to the function of the probability limit.

The Slutsky theorem highlights a comparison between the expectation of a random variable and its probability limit. Theorem D.12 extends directly in two important directions. First, though stated in terms of convergence in probability, the same set of results applies to convergence in $r$th mean and almost sure convergence. Second, so long as the functions are continuous, the Slutsky theorem can be extended to vector or matrix valued functions of random scalars, vectors, or matrices. The following describe some specific applications. Some implications of the Slutsky theorem are now summarized.

---

**THEOREM D.14   Rules for Probability Limits**

*If $x_n$ and $y_n$ are random variables with $\text{plim} x_n = c$ and $\text{plim } y_n = d$, then*

$$\text{plim}(x_n + y_n) = c + d, \qquad \textbf{(sum rule)} \qquad \textbf{(D-7)}$$

$$\text{plim } x_n y_n = cd, \qquad \textbf{(product rule)} \qquad \textbf{(D-8)}$$

$$\text{plim } x_n/y_n = c/d \quad \text{if } d \neq 0. \quad \textbf{(ratio rule)} \qquad \textbf{(D-9)}$$

*If $\mathbf{W}_n$ is a matrix whose elements are random variables and if $\text{plim } \mathbf{W}_n = \mathbf{\Omega}$, then*

$$\text{plim } \mathbf{W}_n^{-1} = \mathbf{\Omega}^{-1}. \quad \textbf{(matrix inverse rule)} \qquad \textbf{(D-10)}$$

*If $\mathbf{X}_n$ and $\mathbf{Y}_n$ are random matrices with $\text{plim } \mathbf{X}_n = \mathbf{A}$ and $\text{plim } \mathbf{Y}_n = \mathbf{B}$, then*

$$\text{plim } \mathbf{X}_n \mathbf{Y}_n = \mathbf{AB}. \quad \textbf{(matrix product rule)} \qquad \textbf{(D-11)}$$

---

### D.2.4   CONVERGENCE TO A RANDOM VARIABLE

The preceding has dealt with conditions under which a random variable converges to a constant, for example, the way that a sample mean converges to the population mean. To develop a theory for the behavior of estimators, as a prelude to the discussion of limiting distributions, we now consider cases in which a random variable converges not to a constant, but to another random variable. These results will actually subsume those in the preceding section, as a constant may always be viewed as a degenerate random variable, that is one with zero variance.

---

### DEFINITION D.6   Convergence in Probability to a Random Variable

*The random variable $x_n$ **converges in probability** to the random variable $x$ if $\lim_{n\to\infty} \text{Prob}(|x_n - x| > \varepsilon) = 0$ for any positive $\varepsilon$.*

---

As before, we write plim $x_n = x$ to denote this case. The interpretation (at least the intuition) of this type of convergence is different when $x$ is a random variable. The notion of closeness defined here relates not to the concentration of the mass of the probability mechanism generating $x_n$ at a point $c$, but to the closeness of that probability mechanism to that of $x$. One can think of this as a convergence of the CDF of $x_n$ to that of $x$.

---

### DEFINITION D.7   Almost Sure Convergence to a Random Variable

*The random variable $x_n$ converges almost surely to the random variable $x$ if and only if $\lim_{n\to\infty} \text{Prob}(|x_i - x| > \varepsilon \text{ for all } i \geq n) = 0$ for all $\varepsilon > 0$.*

---

### DEFINITION D.8   Convergence in $r$th Mean to a Random Variable

*The random variable $x_n$ converges in $r$th mean to the random variable $x$ if and only if $\lim_{n\to\infty} E[|x_n - x|^r] = 0$. This is labeled $x_n \xrightarrow{r.m.} x$. As before, the case $r = 2$ is labeled convergence in mean square.*

---

Once again, we have to revise our understanding of convergence when convergence is to a random variable.

---

### THEOREM D.15   Convergence of Moments

*Suppose $x_n \xrightarrow{r.m.} x$ and $E[|x|^r]$ is finite. Then, $\lim_{n\to\infty} E[|x_n|^r] = E[|x|^r]$.*

---

Theorem D.15 raises an interesting question. Suppose we let $r$ grow, and suppose that $x_n \xrightarrow{r.m.} x$ and, in addition, all moments are finite. If this holds for any $r$, do we conclude that these random variables have the same distribution? The answer to this longstanding problem in probability theory—the problem of the sequence of moments—is no. The sequence of moments does not uniquely determine the distribution. Although convergence in $r$th mean and almost surely still both imply convergence in probability, it remains true, even with convergence to a random variable instead of a constant, that these are different forms of convergence.

### D.2.5 CONVERGENCE IN DISTRIBUTION: LIMITING DISTRIBUTIONS

A second form of convergence is **convergence in distribution.** Let $x_n$ be a sequence of random variables indexed by the sample size, and assume that $x_n$ has cdf $F_n(x_n)$.

---

**DEFINITION D.9** **Convergence in Distribution**
*$x_n$ converges in distribution to a random variable $x$ with cdf $F(x)$ if $\lim_{n\to\infty} |F_n(x_n) - F(x)| = 0$ at all continuity points of $F(x)$.*

---

This statement is about the probability distribution associated with $x_n$; it does not imply that $x_n$ converges at all. To take a trivial example, suppose that the exact distribution of the random variable $x_n$ is

$$\text{Prob}(x_n = 1) = \frac{1}{2} + \frac{1}{n+1}, \quad \text{Prob}(x_n = 2) = \frac{1}{2} - \frac{1}{n+1}.$$

As $n$ increases without bound, the two probabilities converge to $\frac{1}{2}$, but $x_n$ does not converge to a constant.

---

**DEFINITION D.10** **Limiting Distribution**
*If $x_n$ converges in distribution to $x$, where $F_n(x_n)$ is the cdf of $x_n$, then $F(x)$ is the **limiting distribution** of $x_n$. This is written*

$$x_n \xrightarrow{d} x.$$

---

The limiting distribution is often given in terms of the pdf, or simply the parametric family. For example, "the limiting distribution of $x_n$ is standard normal."

Convergence in distribution can be extended to random vectors and matrices, although not in the element by element manner that we extended the earlier convergence forms. The reason is that convergence in distribution is a property of the CDF of the random variable, not the variable itself. Thus, we can obtain a convergence result analogous to that in Definition D.9 for vectors or matrices by applying definition to the joint CDF for the elements of the vector or matrices. Thus, $\mathbf{x}_n \xrightarrow{d} \mathbf{x}$ if $\lim_{n\to\infty} |F_n(\mathbf{x}_n) - F(\mathbf{x})| = 0$ and likewise for a random matrix.

### Example D.4 Limiting Distribution of $t_{n-1}$
Consider a sample of size $n$ from a standard normal distribution. A familiar inference problem is the test of the hypothesis that the population mean is zero. The test statistic usually used is the $t$ statistic:

$$t_{n-1} = \frac{\bar{x}_n}{s_n/\sqrt{n}},$$

where

$$s_n^2 = \frac{\sum_{i=1}^{n}(x_i - \bar{x}_n)^2}{n-1}.$$

The exact distribution of the random variable $t_{n-1}$ is $t$ with $n-1$ degrees of freedom. The density is different for every $n$:

$$f(t_{n-1}) = \frac{\Gamma(n/2)}{\Gamma[(n-1)/2]} \, [(n-1)\pi]^{-1/2} \left[ 1 + \frac{t_{n-1}^2}{n-1} \right]^{-n/2}, \qquad \textbf{(D-12)}$$

as is the cdf, $F_{n-1}(t) = \int_{-\infty}^{t} f_{n-1}(x)\,dx$. This distribution has mean zero and variance $(n-1)/(n-3)$. As $n$ grows to infinity, $t_{n-1}$ converges to the standard normal, which is written

$$t_{n-1} \xrightarrow{d} N[0, 1].$$

---

**DEFINITION D.11**    **Limiting Mean and Variance**
*The **limiting mean** and **variance** of a random variable are the mean and variance of the limiting distribution, assuming that the limiting distribution and its moments exist.*

---

For the random variable with $t[n]$ distribution, the exact mean and variance are zero and $n/(n-2)$, whereas the limiting mean and variance are zero and one. The example might suggest that the limiting mean and variance are zero and one; that is, that the moments of the limiting distribution are the ordinary limits of the moments of the finite sample distributions. This situation is almost always true, but it need not be. It is possible to construct examples in which the exact moments do not even exist, even though the moments of the limiting distribution are well defined.[3] Even in such cases, we can usually derive the mean and variance of the limiting distribution.

Limiting distributions, like probability limits, can greatly simplify the analysis of a problem. Some results that combine the two concepts are as follows.[4]

---

**THEOREM D.16**    **Rules for Limiting Distributions**

**1.**   *If $x_n \xrightarrow{d} x$ and plim $y_n = c$, then*

$$x_n y_n \xrightarrow{d} cx, \qquad \textbf{(D-13)}$$

*which means that the limiting distribution of $x_n y_n$ is the distribution of $cx$. Also,*

$$x_n + y_n \xrightarrow{d} x + c, \qquad \textbf{(D-14)}$$

$$x_n/y_n \xrightarrow{d} x/c, \quad \text{if } c \neq 0. \qquad \textbf{(D-15)}$$

**2.**   *If $x_n \xrightarrow{d} x$ and $g(x_n)$ is a continuous function, then*

$$g(x_n) \xrightarrow{d} g(x). \qquad \textbf{(D-16)}$$

*This result is analogous to the Slutsky theorem for probability limits. For an example, consider the $t_n$ random variable discussed earlier. The exact distribution of $t_n^2$ is $F[1, n]$. But as $n \longrightarrow \infty$, $t_n$ converges to a standard normal variable. According to this result, the limiting distribution of $t_n^2$ will be that of the square of a standard normal, which is chi-squared with one*

---

[3]See, for example, Maddala (1977a, p. 150).
[4]For proofs and further discussion, see, for example, Greenberg and Webster (1983).

---

**THEOREM D.16** (Continued)

*degree of freedom. We conclude, therefore, that*

$$F[1, n] \xrightarrow{d} chi\text{-}squared[1]. \qquad \text{(D-17)}$$

*We encountered this result in our earlier discussion of limiting forms of the standard normal family of distributions.*

3. *If $y_n$ has a limiting distribution and plim $(x_n - y_n) = 0$, then $x_n$ has the same limiting distribution as $y_n$.*

---

The third result in Theorem D.16 combines convergence in distribution and in probability. The second result can be extended to vectors and matrices.

### Example D.5   The F Distribution

Suppose that $\mathbf{t}_{1,n}$ and $\mathbf{t}_{2,n}$ are a $K \times 1$ and an $M \times 1$ random vector of variables whose components are independent with each distributed as $t$ with $n$ degrees of freedom. Then, as we saw in the preceding, for any component in either random vector, the limiting distribution is standard normal, so for the entire vector, $\mathbf{t}_{j,n} \xrightarrow{d} \mathbf{z}_j$, a vector of independent standard normally distributed variables. The results so far show that $\dfrac{(\mathbf{t}'_{1,n}\mathbf{t}_{1,n})/K}{(\mathbf{t}'_{2,n}\mathbf{t}_{2,n})/M} \xrightarrow{d} F[K, M]$.

Finally, a specific case of result 2 in Theorem D.16 produces a tool known as the Cramér–Wold device.

---

**THEOREM D.17** Cramer–Wold Device

*If $\mathbf{x}_n \xrightarrow{d} \mathbf{x}$, then $\mathbf{c}'\mathbf{x}_n \xrightarrow{d} \mathbf{c}'\mathbf{x}$ for all conformable vectors $\mathbf{c}$ with real valued elements.*

---

By allowing $\mathbf{c}$ to be a vector with just a one in a particular position and zeros elsewhere, we see that convergence in distribution of a random vector $\mathbf{x}_n$ to $\mathbf{x}$ does imply that each component does likewise.

### D.2.6   CENTRAL LIMIT THEOREMS

We are ultimately interested in finding a way to describe the statistical properties of estimators when their exact distributions are unknown. The concepts of consistency and convergence in probability are important. But the theory of limiting distributions given earlier is not yet adequate. We rarely deal with estimators that are not consistent for something, though perhaps not always the parameter we are trying to estimate. As such,

$$\text{if plim } \hat{\theta}_n = \theta, \quad \text{then } \hat{\theta}_n \xrightarrow{d} \theta.$$

That is, the limiting distribution of $\hat{\theta}_n$ is a spike. This is not very informative, nor is it at all what we have in mind when we speak of the statistical properties of an estimator. (To endow our finite sample estimator $\hat{\theta}_n$ with the zero sampling variance of the spike at $\theta$ would be optimistic in the extreme.)

As an intermediate step, then, to a more reasonable description of the statistical properties of an estimator, we use a **stabilizing transformation** of the random variable to one that does have a well-defined limiting distribution. To jump to the most common application, whereas

$$\text{plim } \hat{\theta}_n = \theta,$$

we often find that

$$z_n = \sqrt{n}(\hat{\theta}_n - \theta) \xrightarrow{d} f(z),$$

where $f(z)$ is a well-defined distribution with a mean and a positive variance. An estimator which has this property is said to be **root-$n$ consistent.** The single most important theorem in econometrics provides an application of this proposition. A basic form of the theorem is as follows.

---

**THEOREM D.18   Lindeberg–Levy Central Limit Theorem (Univariate)**

*If $x_1, \ldots, x_n$ are a random sample from a probability distribution with finite mean $\mu$ and finite variance $\sigma^2$ and $\overline{x}_n = (1/n) \sum_{i=1}^{n} x_i$, then*

$$\sqrt{n}(\overline{x}_n - \mu) \xrightarrow{d} N[0, \sigma^2],$$

*A proof appears in Rao (1973, p. 127).*

---

The result is quite remarkable as it holds regardless of the form of the parent distribution. For a striking example, return to Figure C.2. The distribution from which the data were drawn in that figure does not even remotely resemble a normal distribution. In samples of only four observations the force of the central limit theorem is clearly visible in the sampling distribution of the means. The sampling experiment Example D.6 shows the effect in a systematic demonstration of the result.

The Lindeberg–Levy theorem is one of several forms of this extremely powerful result. For our purposes, an important extension allows us to relax the assumption of equal variances. The Lindeberg–Feller form of the central limit theorem is the centerpiece of most of our analysis in econometrics.

---

**THEOREM D.19   Lindeberg–Feller Central Limit Theorem (with Unequal Variances)**

*Suppose that $\{x_i\}, i = 1, \ldots, n$, is a sequence of independent random variables with finite means $\mu_i$ and finite positive variances $\sigma_i^2$. Let*

$$\overline{\mu}_n = \frac{1}{n}(\mu_1 + \mu_2 + \cdots + \mu_n), \quad \text{and} \quad \overline{\sigma}_n^2 = \frac{1}{n}(\sigma_1^2 + \sigma_2^2 + \cdots, \sigma_n^2).$$

*If no single term dominates this average variance, which we could state as $\lim_{n \to \infty} \max(\sigma_i)/(n\overline{\sigma}_n) = 0$, and if the average variance converges to a finite constant, $\overline{\sigma}^2 = \lim_{n \to \infty} \overline{\sigma}_n^2$, then*

$$\sqrt{n}(\overline{x}_n - \overline{\mu}_n) \xrightarrow{d} N[0, \overline{\sigma}^2].$$

---

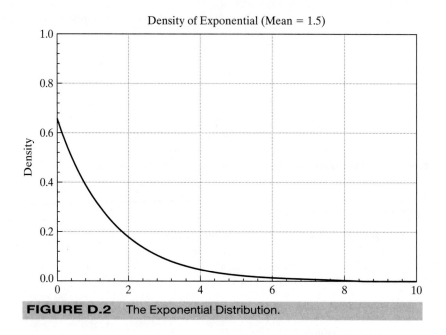

**FIGURE D.2** The Exponential Distribution.

In practical terms, the theorem states that sums of random variables, regardless of their form, will tend to be normally distributed. The result is yet more remarkable in that *it does not require the variables in the sum to come from the same underlying distribution. It requires, essentially, only that the mean be a mixture of many random variables, none of which is large compared with their sum.* Because nearly all the estimators we construct in econometrics fall under the purview of the central limit theorem, it is obviously an important result.

### Example D.6   The Lindeberg–Levy Central Limit Theorem

We'll use a sampling experiment to demonstrate the operation of the central limit theorem. Consider random sampling from the exponential distribution with mean 1.5 — this is the setting used in Example C.4. The density is shown in Figure D.2.

We've drawn 1,000 samples of 3, 6, and 20 observations from this population and computed the sample means for each. For each mean, we then computed $z_{in} = \sqrt{n}(\bar{x}_{in} - \mu)$, where $i = 1, \ldots, 1,000$ and $n$ is 3, 6 or 20. The three rows of figures in Figure D.3 show histograms of the observed samples of sample means and kernel density estimates of the underlying distributions for the three samples of transformed means.

Proof of the Lindeberg–Feller theorem requires some quite intricate mathematics [see, e.g., Loeve (1977)] that are well beyond the scope of our work here. We do note an important consideration in this theorem. The result rests on a condition known as the Lindeberg condition. The sample mean computed in the theorem is a mixture of random variables from possibly different distributions. The Lindeberg condition, in words, states that the contribution of the tail areas of these underlying distributions to the variance of the sum must be negligible in the limit. The condition formalizes the assumption in Theorem D.19 that the average variance be positive and not be dominated by any single term. [For an intuitively crafted mathematical discussion of this condition, see White (2001, pp. 117–118).] The condition is essentially impossible to verify in practice, so it is useful to have a simpler version of the theorem that encompasses it.

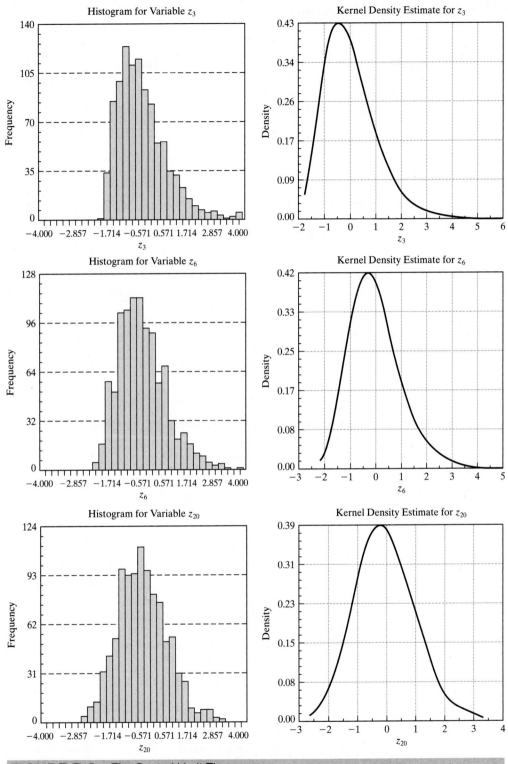

**FIGURE D.3**   The Central Limit Theorem.

---

**THEOREM D.20** **Liapounov Central Limit Theorem**

*Suppose that $\{x_i\}$, is a sequence of independent random variables with finite means $\mu_i$ and finite positive variances $\sigma_i^2$ such that $E[|x_i - \mu_i|^{2+\delta}]$ is finite for some $\delta > 0$. If $\bar{\sigma}_n$ is positive and finite for all $n$ sufficiently large, then*

$$\sqrt{n}(\bar{x}_n - \bar{\mu}_n)/\bar{\sigma}_n \xrightarrow{d} N[0, 1].$$

---

This version of the central limit theorem requires only that moments slightly larger than two be finite.

Note the distinction between the laws of large numbers in Theorems D.5 and D.6 and the central limit theorems. Neither assert that sample means tend to normality. Sample means (i.e., the distributions of them) converge to spikes at the true mean. It is the transformation of the mean, $\sqrt{n}(\bar{x}_n - \mu)/\sigma$, that converges to standard normality. To see this at work, if you have access to the necessary software, you might try reproducing Example D.6 using the raw means, $\bar{x}_{in}$. What do you expect to observe?

For later purposes, we will require multivariate versions of these theorems. Proofs of the following may be found, for example, in Greenberg and Webster (1983) or Rao (1973) and references cited there.

---

**THEOREM D.18A** **Multivariate Lindeberg–Levy Central Limit Theorem**

*If $\mathbf{x}_1, \ldots, \mathbf{x}_n$ are a random sample from a multivariate distribution with finite mean vector $\boldsymbol{\mu}$ and finite positive definite covariance matrix $\mathbf{Q}$, then*

$$\sqrt{n}(\bar{\mathbf{x}}_n - \boldsymbol{\mu}) \xrightarrow{d} N[\mathbf{0}, \mathbf{Q}],$$

*where*

$$\bar{\mathbf{x}}_n = \frac{1}{n} \sum_{i=1}^{n} \mathbf{x}_i.$$

*To get from D.18 to D.18A (and D.19 to D.19A) we need to add a step. Theorem D.18 applies to the individual elements of the vector. A vector has a multivariate normal distribution if the individual elements are normally distributed and if every linear combination is normally distributed. We can use Theorem D.18 (D.19) for the individual terms and Theorem D.17 to establish that linear combinations behave likewise. This establishes the extensions.*

---

The extension of the Lindeberg–Feller theorem to unequal covariance matrices requires some intricate mathematics. The following is an informal statement of the relevant conditions. Further discussion and references appear in Fomby, Hill, and Johnson (1984) and Greenberg and Webster (1983).

**THEOREM D.19A** **Multivariate Lindeberg–Feller Central Limit Theorem**

*Suppose that $\mathbf{x}_1, \ldots, \mathbf{x}_n$ are a sample of random vectors such that $E[\mathbf{x}_i] = \boldsymbol{\mu}_i$, $\mathrm{Var}[\mathbf{x}_i] = \mathbf{Q}_i$, and all mixed third moments of the multivariate distribution are finite. Let*

$$\overline{\boldsymbol{\mu}}_n = \frac{1}{n} \sum_{i=1}^{n} \boldsymbol{\mu}_i,$$

$$\overline{\mathbf{Q}}_n = \frac{1}{n} \sum_{i=1}^{n} \mathbf{Q}_i.$$

*We assume that*

$$\lim_{n \to \infty} \overline{\mathbf{Q}}_n = \mathbf{Q},$$

*where $\mathbf{Q}$ is a finite, positive definite matrix, and that for every $i$,*

$$\lim_{n \to \infty} (n\overline{\mathbf{Q}}_n)^{-1} \mathbf{Q}_i = \lim_{n \to \infty} \left( \sum_{i=1}^{n} \mathbf{Q}_i \right)^{-1} \mathbf{Q}_i = \mathbf{0}.$$

*We allow the means of the random vectors to differ, although in the cases that we will analyze, they will generally be identical. The second assumption states that individual components of the sum must be finite and diminish in significance. There is also an implicit assumption that the sum of matrices is nonsingular. Because the limiting matrix is nonsingular, the assumption must hold for large enough n, which is all that concerns us here. With these in place, the result is*

$$\sqrt{n}(\overline{\mathbf{x}}_n - \overline{\boldsymbol{\mu}}_n) \xrightarrow{d} N[\mathbf{0}, \mathbf{Q}].$$

## D.2.7 THE DELTA METHOD

At several points in Appendix C, we used a linear Taylor series approximation to analyze the distribution and moments of a random variable. We are now able to justify this usage. We complete the development of Theorem D.12 (probability limit of a function of a random variable), Theorem D.16 (2) (limiting distribution of a function of a random variable), and the central limit theorems, with a useful result that is known as the **delta method.** For a single random variable (sample mean or otherwise), we have the following theorem.

**THEOREM D.21** **Limiting Normal Distribution of a Function**

*If $\sqrt{n}(z_n - \mu) \xrightarrow{d} N[0, \sigma^2]$ and if $g(z_n)$ is a continuous function not involving n, then*

$$\sqrt{n}[g(z_n) - g(\mu)] \xrightarrow{d} N[0, \{g'(\mu)\}^2 \sigma^2]. \tag{D-18}$$

Notice that the mean and variance of the limiting distribution are the mean and variance of the linear Taylor series approximation:

$$g(z_n) \simeq g(\mu) + g'(\mu)(z_n - \mu).$$

The multivariate version of this theorem will be used at many points in the text.

---

**THEOREM D.21A  Limiting Normal Distribution of a Set of Functions**

*If $\mathbf{z}_n$ is a $K \times 1$ sequence of vector-valued random variables such that $\sqrt{n}(\mathbf{z}_n - \boldsymbol{\mu}) \overset{d}{\longrightarrow} N[\mathbf{0}, \boldsymbol{\Sigma}]$ and if $\mathbf{c}(\mathbf{z}_n)$ is a set of $J$ continuous functions of $\mathbf{z}_n$ not involving n, then*

$$\sqrt{n}[\mathbf{c}(\mathbf{z}_n) - \mathbf{c}(\boldsymbol{\mu})] \overset{d}{\longrightarrow} N[\mathbf{0}, \mathbf{C}(\boldsymbol{\mu})\boldsymbol{\Sigma}\mathbf{C}(\boldsymbol{\mu})'], \qquad \textbf{(D-19)}$$

*where $\mathbf{C}(\boldsymbol{\mu})$ is the $J \times K$ matrix $\partial\mathbf{c}(\boldsymbol{\mu})/\partial\boldsymbol{\mu}'$. The jth row of $\mathbf{C}(\boldsymbol{\mu})$ is the vector of partial derivatives of the jth function with respect to $\boldsymbol{\mu}'$.*

---

## D.3  ASYMPTOTIC DISTRIBUTIONS

The theory of limiting distributions is only a means to an end. We are interested in the behavior of the estimators themselves. The limiting distributions obtained through the central limit theorem all involve unknown parameters, generally the ones we are trying to estimate. Moreover, our samples are always finite. Thus, we depart from the limiting distributions to derive the asymptotic distributions of the estimators.

---

**DEFINITION D.12  Asymptotic Distribution**

*An asymptotic distribution is a distribution that is used to approximate the true finite sample distribution of a random variable.*[5]

---

By far the most common means of formulating an asymptotic distribution (at least by econometricians) is to construct it from the known limiting distribution of a function of the random variable. If

$$\sqrt{n}[(\overline{x}_n - \mu)/\sigma] \overset{d}{\longrightarrow} N[0, 1],$$

---

[5]We depart somewhat from some other treatments [e.g., White (2001), Hayashi (2000, p. 90)] at this point, because they make no distinction between an asymptotic distribution and the limiting distribution, although the treatments are largely along the lines discussed here. In the interest of maintaining consistency of the discussion, we prefer to retain the sharp distinction and derive the asymptotic distribution of an estimator, $\mathbf{t}$ by first obtaining the *limiting* distribution of $\sqrt{n}(\mathbf{t} - \boldsymbol{\theta})$. By our construction, the *limiting* distribution of $\mathbf{t}$ is degenerate, whereas the *asymptotic* distribution of $\sqrt{n}(\mathbf{t} - \boldsymbol{\theta})$ is not useful.

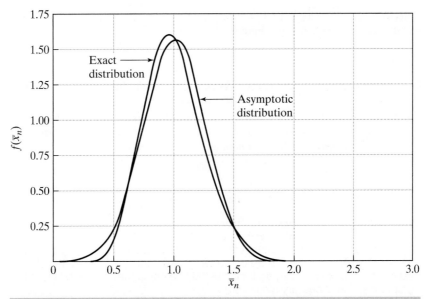

**FIGURE D.4** True Versus Asymptotic Distribution.

then approximately, or asymptotically, $\bar{x}_n \sim N[\mu, \sigma^2/n]$, which we write as

$$\bar{x} \overset{a}{\sim} N[\mu, \sigma^2/n].$$

The statement "$\bar{x}_n$ is asymptotically normally distributed with mean $\mu$ and variance $\sigma^2/n$" says only that this normal distribution provides an approximation to the true distribution, not that the true distribution is exactly normal.

### Example D.7 Asymptotic Distribution of the Mean of an Exponential Sample

In sampling from an exponential distribution with parameter $\theta$, the *exact* distribution of $\bar{x}_n$ is that of $\theta/(2n)$ times a chi-squared variable with $2n$ degrees of freedom. The *asymptotic* distribution is $N[\theta, \theta^2/n]$. The exact and asymptotic distributions are shown in Figure D.4 for the case of $\theta = 1$ and $n = 16$.

Extending the definition, suppose that $\hat{\boldsymbol{\theta}}_n$ is an estimator of the parameter vector $\boldsymbol{\theta}$. The asymptotic distribution of the vector $\hat{\boldsymbol{\theta}}_n$ is obtained from the limiting distribution:

$$\sqrt{n}(\hat{\boldsymbol{\theta}}_n - \boldsymbol{\theta}) \overset{d}{\longrightarrow} N[\mathbf{0}, \mathbf{V}] \qquad \textbf{(D-20)}$$

implies that

$$\hat{\boldsymbol{\theta}}_n \overset{a}{\sim} N\left[\boldsymbol{\theta}, \frac{1}{n}\mathbf{V}\right]. \qquad \textbf{(D-21)}$$

This notation is read "$\hat{\boldsymbol{\theta}}_n$ is asymptotically normally distributed, with mean vector $\boldsymbol{\theta}$ and covariance matrix $(1/n)\mathbf{V}$." The covariance matrix of the asymptotic distribution is the **asymptotic covariance matrix** and is denoted

$$\text{Asy. Var}[\hat{\boldsymbol{\theta}}_n] = \frac{1}{n}\mathbf{V}.$$

Note, once again, the logic used to reach the result; (D-20) holds exactly as $n \to \infty$. We assume that it holds approximately for finite $n$, which leads to (D-21).

---

**DEFINITION D.13** **Asymptotic Normality and Asymptotic Efficiency**

*An estimator $\hat{\theta}_n$ is asymptotically normal if (D-20) holds. The estimator is asymptotically efficient if the covariance matrix of any other consistent, asymptotically normally distributed estimator exceeds $(1/n)\mathbf{V}$ by a nonnegative definite matrix.*

---

For most estimation problems, these are the criteria used to choose an estimator.

**Example D.8** **Asymptotic Inefficiency of the Median in Normal Sampling**

In sampling from a normal distribution with mean $\mu$ and variance $\sigma^2$, both the mean $\bar{x}_n$ and the median $M_n$ of the sample are consistent estimators of $\mu$. The limiting distributions of both estimators are spikes at $\mu$, so they can only be compared on the basis of their asymptotic properties. The necessary results are

$$\bar{x}_n \overset{a}{\sim} N[\mu, \sigma^2/n], \quad \text{and} \quad M_n \overset{a}{\sim} N[\mu, (\pi/2)\sigma^2/n]. \tag{D-22}$$

Therefore, the mean is more efficient by a factor of $\pi/2$. (But, see Example 17.4 for a finite sample result.)

### D.3.1 ASYMPTOTIC DISTRIBUTION OF A NONLINEAR FUNCTION

Theorems D.12 and D.14 for functions of a random variable have counterparts in asymptotic distributions.

---

**THEOREM D.22** **Asymptotic Distribution of a Nonlinear Function**

*If $\sqrt{n}(\hat{\theta}_n - \theta) \overset{d}{\longrightarrow} N[0, \sigma^2]$ and if $g(\theta)$ is a continuous function not involving $n$, then $g(\hat{\theta}_n) \overset{a}{\sim} N[g(\theta), (1/n)\{g'(\theta)\}^2\sigma^2]$. If $\hat{\theta}_n$ is a vector of parameter estimators such that $\hat{\theta}_n \overset{a}{\sim} N[\theta, (1/n)\mathbf{V}]$ and if $\mathbf{c}(\theta)$ is a set of $J$ continuous functions not involving $n$, then $\mathbf{c}(\hat{\theta}_n) \overset{a}{\sim} N[\mathbf{c}(\theta), (1/n)\mathbf{C}(\theta)\mathbf{V}\mathbf{C}(\theta)']$, where $\mathbf{C}(\theta) = \partial\mathbf{c}(\theta)/\partial\theta'$.*

---

**Example D.9** **Asymptotic Distribution of a Function of Two Estimators**

Suppose that $b_n$ and $t_n$ are estimators of parameters $\beta$ and $\theta$ such that

$$\begin{bmatrix} b_n \\ t_n \end{bmatrix} \overset{a}{\sim} N \left[ \begin{pmatrix} \beta \\ \theta \end{pmatrix}, \begin{pmatrix} \sigma_{\beta\beta} & \sigma_{\beta\theta} \\ \sigma_{\theta\beta} & \sigma_{\theta\theta} \end{pmatrix} \right].$$

Find the asymptotic distribution of $c_n = b_n/(1 - t_n)$. Let $\gamma = \beta/(1 - \theta)$. By the Slutsky theorem, $c_n$ is consistent for $\gamma$. We shall require

$$\frac{\partial\gamma}{\partial\beta} = \frac{1}{1 - \theta} = \gamma_\beta, \quad \frac{\partial\gamma}{\partial\theta} = \frac{\beta}{(1 - \theta)^2} = \gamma_\theta.$$

Let $\Sigma$ be the $2 \times 2$ asymptotic covariance matrix given previously. Then the asymptotic variance of $c_n$ is

$$\text{Asy. Var}[c_n] = (\gamma_\beta \ \gamma_\theta) \, \Sigma \begin{pmatrix} \gamma_\beta \\ \gamma_\theta \end{pmatrix} = \gamma_\beta^2 \sigma_{\beta\beta} + \gamma_\theta^2 \sigma_{\theta\theta} + 2\gamma_\beta \, \gamma_\theta \sigma_{\beta\theta},$$

which is the variance of the linear Taylor series approximation:

$$\hat{\gamma}_n \simeq \gamma + \gamma_\beta(b_n - \beta) + \gamma_\theta(t_n - \theta).$$

### D.3.2 ASYMPTOTIC EXPECTATIONS

The asymptotic mean and variance of a random variable are usually the mean and variance of the asymptotic distribution. Thus, for an estimator with the limiting distribution defined in

$$\sqrt{n}(\hat{\theta}_n - \theta) \xrightarrow{d} N[\mathbf{0}, \mathbf{V}],$$

the asymptotic expectation is $\theta$ and the asymptotic variance is $(1/n)\mathbf{V}$. This statement implies, among other things, that the estimator is "asymptotically unbiased."

At the risk of clouding the issue a bit, it is necessary to reconsider one aspect of the previous description. We have deliberately avoided the use of consistency even though, in most instances, that is what we have in mind. The description thus far might suggest that consistency and asymptotic unbiasedness are the same. Unfortunately (because it is a source of some confusion), they are not. They are if the estimator is consistent and asymptotically normally distributed, or CAN. They may differ in other settings, however. There are at least three possible definitions of asymptotic unbiasedness:

1. The mean of the limiting distribution of $\sqrt{n}(\hat{\theta}_n - \theta)$ is 0.
2. $\lim_{n \to \infty} E[\hat{\theta}_n] = \theta$. **(D-23)**
3. $\text{plim } \theta_n = \theta$.

In most cases encountered in practice, the estimator in hand will have all three properties, so there is no ambiguity. It is not difficult to construct cases in which the left-hand sides of all three definitions are different, however.[6] There is no general agreement among authors as to the precise meaning of asymptotic unbiasedness, perhaps because the term is misleading at the outset; *asymptotic* refers to an approximation, whereas *unbiasedness* is an exact result.[7] Nonetheless, the majority view seems to be that (2) is the proper definition of asymptotic unbiasedness.[8] Note, though, that this definition relies on quantities that are generally unknown and that may not exist.

A similar problem arises in the definition of the asymptotic variance of an estimator. One common definition is[9]

$$\text{Asy. Var}[\hat{\theta}_n] = \frac{1}{n} \lim_{n \to \infty} E\left[\left\{\sqrt{n}\left(\hat{\theta}_n - \lim_{n \to \infty} E[\hat{\theta}_n]\right)\right\}^2\right]. \quad \textbf{(D-24)}$$

---

[6]See, for example, Maddala (1977a, p. 150).

[7]See, for example, Theil (1971, p. 377).

[8]Many studies of estimators analyze the "asymptotic bias" of, say, $\hat{\theta}_n$ as an estimator of a parameter $\theta$. In most cases, the quantity of interest is actually plim $[\hat{\theta}_n - \theta]$. See, for example, Greene (1980b) and another example in Johnston (1984, p. 312).

[9]Kmenta (1986, p.165).

This result is a **leading term approximation,** and it will be sufficient for nearly all applications. Note, however, that like definition 2 of asymptotic unbiasedness, it relies on unknown and possibly nonexistent quantities.

### Example D.10   Asymptotic Moments of the Sample Variance
The exact expected value and variance of the variance estimator

$$
m_2 = \frac{1}{n} \sum_{i=1}^{n} (x_i - \bar{x})^2 \tag{D-25}
$$

are

$$
E[m_2] = \frac{(n-1)\sigma^2}{n}, \tag{D-26}
$$

and

$$
\text{Var}[m_2] = \frac{\mu_4 - \sigma^4}{n} - \frac{2(\mu_4 - 2\sigma^4)}{n^2} + \frac{\mu_4 - 3\sigma^4}{n^3}, \tag{D-27}
$$

where $\mu_4 = E[(x - \mu)^4]$. [See Goldberger (1964, pp. 97–99).] The leading term approximation would be

$$
\text{Asy. Var}[m_2] = \frac{1}{n}(\mu_4 - \sigma^4).
$$

## D.4   SEQUENCES AND THE ORDER OF A SEQUENCE

This section has been concerned with sequences of constants, denoted, for example, $c_n$, and random variables, such as $x_n$, that are indexed by a sample size, $n$. An important characteristic of a sequence is the rate at which it converges (or diverges). For example, as we have seen, the mean of a random sample of $n$ observations from a distribution with finite mean, $\mu$, and finite variance, $\sigma^2$, is itself a random variable with variance $\gamma_n^2 = \sigma^2/n$. We see that as long as $\sigma^2$ is a finite constant, $\gamma_n^2$ is a sequence of constants that converges to zero. Another example is the random variable $x_{(1),n}$, the minimum value in a random sample of $n$ observations from the exponential distribution with mean $1/\theta$ defined in Example C.4. It turns out that $x_{(1),n}$ has variance $1/(n\theta)^2$. Clearly, this variance also converges to zero, but, intuition suggests, faster than $\sigma^2/n$ does. On the other hand, the sum of the integers from one to $n$, $S_n = n(n+1)/2$, obviously diverges as $n \to \infty$, albeit faster (one might expect) than the log of the likelihood function for the exponential distribution in Example C.6, which is $\ln L(\theta) = n(\ln \theta - \theta \bar{x}_n)$. As a final example, consider the downward bias of the maximum likelihood estimator of the variance of the normal distribution, $c_n = (n-1)/n$, which is a constant that converges to one. (See Example C.5.)

We will define the rate at which a sequence converges or diverges in terms of the order of the sequence.

---

**DEFINITION D.14**   Order $n^\delta$
*A sequence $c_n$ is of order $n^\delta$, denoted $O(n^\delta)$, if and only if $\text{plim}(1/n^\delta)c_n$ is a finite nonzero constant.*

---

> **DEFINITION D.15** Order less than $n^\delta$
>
> *A sequence $c_n$, is of order less than $n^\delta$, denoted $o(n^\delta)$, if and only if $\text{plim}(1/n^\delta)c_n$ equals zero.*

Thus, in our examples, $\gamma_n^2$ is $O(n^{-1})$, $\text{Var}[x_{(1),n}]$ is $O(n^{-2})$ and $o(n^{-1})$, $S_n$ is $O(n^2)(\delta$ equals $+2$ in this case), $\ln L(\theta)$ is $O(n)(\delta$ equals $+1)$, and $c_n$ is $O(1)(\delta = 0)$. Important particular cases that we will encounter repeatedly in our work are sequences for which $\delta = 1$ or $-1$.

The notion of order of a sequence is often of interest in econometrics in the context of the variance of an estimator. Thus, we see in Section D.3 that an important element of our strategy for forming an asymptotic distribution is that the variance of the limiting distribution of $\sqrt{n}(\bar{x}_n - \mu)/\sigma$ is $O(1)$. In Example D.10 the variance of $m_2$ is the sum of three terms that are $O(n^{-1})$, $O(n^{-2})$, and $O(n^{-3})$. The sum is $O(n^{-1})$, because $n\,\text{Var}[m_2]$ converges to $\mu_4 - \sigma^4$, the numerator of the first, or *leading term,* whereas the second and third terms converge to zero. This term is also the *dominant term* of the sequence. Finally, consider the two divergent examples in the preceding list. $S_n$ is simply a deterministic function of $n$ that explodes. However, $\ln L(\theta) = n\ln\theta - \theta\Sigma_i x_i$ is the sum of a constant that is $O(n)$ and a random variable with variance equal to $n/\theta$. The random variable "diverges" in the sense that its variance grows without bound as $n$ increases.

# APPENDIX E

# COMPUTATION AND OPTIMIZATION

## E.1 INTRODUCTION

The computation of empirical estimates by econometricians involves using digital computers and software written either by the researchers themselves or by others.[1] It is also a surprisingly balanced mix of art and science. It is important for software users to be aware of how results are obtained, not only to understand routine computations, but also to be able to explain the occasional strange and contradictory results that do arise. This appendix will describe some of the basic elements of computing and a number of tools that are used by econometricians.[2] Section E.2

---

[1]It is one of the interesting aspects of the development of econometric methodology that the adoption of certain classes of techniques has proceeded in discrete jumps with the development of software. Noteworthy examples include the appearance, both around 1970, of G. K. Joreskog's LISREL [Joreskog and Sorbom (1981)] program, which spawned a still-growing industry in linear structural modeling, and TSP [Hall (1982)], which was among the first computer programs to accept symbolic representations of econometric models and which provided a significant advance in econometric practice with its LSQ procedure for systems of equations. An extensive survey of the evolution of econometric software is given in Renfro (2007).

[2]This discussion is not intended to teach the reader how to write computer programs. For those who expect to do so, there are whole libraries of useful sources. Three very useful works are Kennedy and Gentle (1980), Abramovitz and Stegun (1971), and especially Press et al. (1986). The third of these provides a wealth of expertly written programs and a large amount of information about how to do computation efficiently and accurately. A recent survey of many areas of computation is Judd (1998).

then describes some techniques for computing certain integrals and derivatives that are recurrent in econometric applications. Section E.3 presents methods of optimization of functions. Some examples are given in Section E.4.

## E.2 COMPUTATION IN ECONOMETRICS

This section will discuss some methods of computing integrals that appear frequently in econometrics.

### E.2.1 COMPUTING INTEGRALS

One advantage of computers is their ability rapidly to compute approximations to complex functions such as logs and exponents. The basic functions, such as these, trigonometric functions, and so forth, are standard parts of the libraries of programs that accompany all scientific computing installations.[3] But one of the very common applications that often requires some high-level creativity by econometricians is the evaluation of integrals that do not have simple closed forms and that do not typically exist in "system libraries." We will consider several of these in this section. We will not go into detail on the nuts and bolts of how to compute integrals with a computer; rather, we will turn directly to the most common applications in econometrics.

### E.2.2 THE STANDARD NORMAL CUMULATIVE DISTRIBUTION FUNCTION

The standard normal cumulative distribution function (cdf) is ubiquitous in econometric models. Yet this most homely of applications must be computed by approximation. There are a number of ways to do so.[4] Recall that what we desire is

$$\Phi(x) = \int_{-\infty}^{x} \phi(t)\, dt, \quad \text{where } \phi(t) = \frac{1}{\sqrt{2\pi}} e^{-t^2/2}.$$

One way to proceed is to use a Taylor series:

$$\Phi(x) \approx \sum_{i=0}^{M} \frac{1}{i!} \frac{d^i \Phi(x_0)}{dx_0^i} (x - x_0)^i.$$

The normal cdf has some advantages for this approach. First, the derivatives are simple and not integrals. Second, the function is **analytic**; as $M \longrightarrow \infty$, the approximation converges to the true value. Third, the derivatives have a simple form; they are the **Hermite polynomials** and they can be computed by a simple recursion. The 0th term in the preceding expansion is $\Phi(x)$ evaluated at the expansion point. The first derivative of the cdf is the pdf, so the terms from 2 onward are the derivatives of $\phi(x)$, once again evaluated at $x_0$. The derivatives of the standard normal pdf obey the recursion

$$\phi^i/\phi(x) = -x\phi^{i-1}/\phi(x) - (i-1)\phi^{i-2}/\phi(x),$$

where $\phi^i$ is $d^i\phi(x)/dx^i$. The zero and one terms in the sequence are one and $-x$. The next term is $x^2 - 1$, followed by $3x - x^3$ and $x^4 - 6x^2 + 3$, and so on. The approximation can be made

---

[3]Of course, at some level, these must be programmed as approximations by someone.

[4]Many system libraries provide a related function, the *error function,* $\text{erf}(x) = (2/\sqrt{\pi}) \int_0^x e^{-t^2}\, dt$. If this is available, then the normal cdf can be obtained from $\Phi(x) = \frac{1}{2} + \frac{1}{2}\text{erf}(x/\sqrt{2})$, $x \geq 0$ and $\Phi(x) = 1 - \Phi(-x)$, $x \leq 0$.

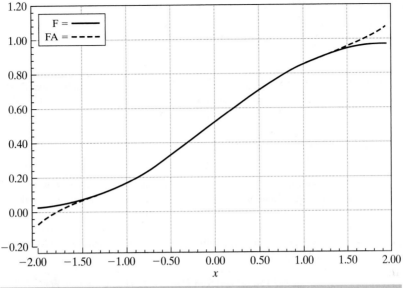

**FIGURE E.1** Approximation to Normal cdf.

more accurate by adding terms. Consider using a fifth-order Taylor series approximation around the point $x = 0$, where $\Phi(0) = 0.5$ and $\phi(0) = 0.3989423$. Evaluating the derivatives at zero and assembling the terms produces the approximation

$$\Phi(x) \approx \tfrac{1}{2} + 0.3989423[x - x^3/6 + x^5/40].$$

[Some of the terms (every other one, in fact) will conveniently drop out.] Figure E.1 shows the actual values ($F$) and approximate values ($FA$) over the range −2 to 2. The figure shows two important points. First, the approximation is remarkably good over most of the range. Second, as is usually true for Taylor series approximations, the quality of the approximation deteriorates as one gets far from the expansion point.

Unfortunately, it is the tail areas of the standard normal distribution that are usually of interest, so the preceding is likely to be problematic. An alternative approach that is used much more often is a polynomial approximation reported by Abramovitz and Stegun (1971, p. 932):

$$\Phi(-|x|) = \phi(x) \sum_{i=1}^{5} a_i t^i + \varepsilon(x), \quad \text{where } t = 1/[1 + a_0|x|].$$

(The complement is taken if $x$ is positive.) The error of approximation is less than $\pm 7.5 \times 10^{-8}$ for all $x$. (Note that the error exceeds the function value at $|x| > 5.7$, so this is the operational limit of this approximation.)

### E.2.3  THE GAMMA AND RELATED FUNCTIONS

The standard normal cdf is probably the most common application of numerical integration of a function in econometrics. Another very common application is the class of gamma functions. For positive constant $P$, the gamma function is

$$\Gamma(P) = \int_0^\infty t^{P-1}e^{-t}dt.$$

The gamma function obeys the recursion $\Gamma(P) = (P-1)\Gamma(P-1)$, so for integer values of $P$, $\Gamma(P) = (P-1)!$. This result suggests that the gamma function can be viewed as a generalization of the factorial function for noninteger values. Another convenient value is $\Gamma(\frac{1}{2}) = \sqrt{\pi}$. By making a change of variable, it can be shown that for positive constants $a$, $c$, and $P$,

$$\int_0^\infty t^{P-1}e^{-at^c}\,dt = \int_0^\infty t^{-(P+1)}e^{-a/t^c}\,dt = \left(\frac{1}{c}\right)a^{-P/c}\Gamma\left(\frac{P}{c}\right). \qquad \textbf{(E-1)}$$

As a generalization of the factorial function, the gamma function will usually overflow for the sorts of values of $P$ that normally appear in applications. The log of the function should normally be used instead. The function $\ln\Gamma(P)$ can be approximated remarkably accurately with only a handful of terms and is very easy to program. A number of approximations appear in the literature; they are generally modifications of **Sterling's approximation** to the factorial function $P! \approx (2\pi P)^{1/2}P^P e^{-P}$, so

$$\ln\Gamma(P) \approx (P-0.5)\ln P - P + 0.5\ln(2\pi) + C + \varepsilon(P),$$

where $C$ is the correction term [see, e.g., Abramovitz and Stegun (1971, p. 257), Press et al. (1986, p. 157), or Rao (1973, p. 59)] and $\varepsilon(P)$ is the approximation error.[5]

The derivatives of the gamma function are

$$\frac{d^r\Gamma(P)}{dP^r} = \int_0^\infty (\ln P)^r t^{P-1}e^{-t}\,dt.$$

The first two derivatives of $\ln\Gamma(P)$ are denoted $\Psi(P) = \Gamma'/\Gamma$ and $\Psi'(P) = (\Gamma\Gamma'' - \Gamma'^2)/\Gamma^2$ and are known as the **digamma** and **trigamma** functions.[6] The **beta function,** denoted $\beta(a, b)$,

$$\beta(a, b) = \int_0^1 t^{a-1}(1-t)^{b-1}\,dt = \frac{\Gamma(a)\Gamma(b)}{\Gamma(a+b)},$$

is related.

### E.2.4 APPROXIMATING INTEGRALS BY QUADRATURE

The digamma and trigamma functions, and the gamma function for noninteger values of $P$ and values that are not integers plus $\frac{1}{2}$, do not exist in closed form and must be approximated. Most other applications will also involve integrals for which no simple computing function exists. The simplest approach to approximating

$$F(x) = \int_{L(x)}^{U(x)} f(t)\,dt$$

---

[5]For example, one widely used formula is $C = z^{-1}/12 - z^{-3}/360 - z^{-5}/1260 + z^{-7}/1680 - q$, where $z = P$ and $q = 0$ if $P > 18$, or $z = P + J$ and $q = \ln[P(P+1)(P+2)\cdots(P+J-1)]$, where $J = 18 - \text{INT}(P)$, if not. Note, in the approximation, we write $\Gamma(P) = (P!)/P + $ a correction.

[6]Tables of specific values for the gamma, digamma, and trigamma functions appear in Abramovitz and Stegun (1971). Most contemporary econometric programs have built-in functions for these common integrals, so the tables are not generally needed.

is likely to be a variant of Simpson's rule, or the trapezoid rule. For example, one approximation [see Press et al. (1986, p. 108)] is

$$F(x) \approx \Delta \left[ \tfrac{1}{3} f_1 + \tfrac{4}{3} f_2 + \tfrac{2}{3} f_3 + \tfrac{4}{3} f_4 + \cdots + \tfrac{2}{3} f_{N-2} + \tfrac{4}{3} f_{N-1} + \tfrac{1}{3} f_N \right],$$

where $f_j$ is the function evaluated at $N$ equally spaced points in $[L, U]$ including the endpoints and $\Delta = (L - U)/(N - 1)$. There are a number of problems with this method, most notably that it is difficult to obtain satisfactory accuracy with a moderate number of points.

**Gaussian quadrature** is a popular method of computing integrals. The general approach is to use an approximation of the form

$$\int_L^U W(x) f(x) \, dx \approx \sum_{j=1}^M w_j f(a_j),$$

where $W(x)$ is viewed as a "weighting" function for integrating $f(x)$, $w_j$ is the **quadrature weight,** and $a_j$ is the **quadrature abscissa.** Different weights and abscissas have been derived for several weighting functions. Two weighting functions common in econometrics are

$$W(x) = x^c e^{-x}, \quad x \in [0, \infty),$$

for which the computation is called **Gauss–Laguerre quadrature,** and

$$W(x) = e^{-x^2}, \quad x \in (-\infty, \infty),$$

for which the computation is called **Gauss–Hermite quadrature.** The theory for deriving weights and abscissas is given in Press et al. (1986, pp. 121–125). Tables of weights and abscissas for many values of $M$ are given by Abramovitz and Stegun (1971). Applications of the technique appear in Section 16.9.6.b and Chapter 23.

## E.3 OPTIMIZATION

Nonlinear optimization (e.g., maximizing log-likelihood functions) is an intriguing practical problem. Theory provides few hard and fast rules, and there are relatively few cases in which it is obvious how to proceed. This section introduces some of the terminology and underlying theory of nonlinear optimization.[7] We begin with a general discussion on how to search for a solution to a nonlinear optimization problem and describe some specific commonly used methods. We then consider some practical problems that arise in optimization. An example is given in the final section.

Consider maximizing the quadratic function

$$F(\theta) = a + \mathbf{b}'\theta - \tfrac{1}{2}\theta'\mathbf{C}\theta,$$

where $\mathbf{C}$ is a positive definite matrix. The first-order condition for a maximum is

$$\frac{\partial F(\theta)}{\partial \theta} = \mathbf{b} - \mathbf{C}\theta = \mathbf{0}. \tag{E-2}$$

This set of *linear* equations has the unique solution

$$\theta = \mathbf{C}^{-1}\mathbf{b}. \tag{E-3}$$

---

[7]There are numerous excellent references that offer a more complete exposition. Among these are Quandt (1983), Bazaraa and Shetty (1979), Fletcher (1980), and Judd (1998).

This is a linear optimization problem. Note that it has a **closed-form solution;** for any $a$, **b**, and **C**, the solution can be computed directly.[8] In the more typical situation,

$$\frac{\partial F(\boldsymbol{\theta})}{\partial \boldsymbol{\theta}} = \mathbf{0} \tag{E-4}$$

is a set of nonlinear equations that cannot be solved explicitly for $\boldsymbol{\theta}$.[9] The techniques considered in this section provide systematic means of searching for a solution.

We now consider the general problem of maximizing a function of several variables:

$$\text{maximize}_\theta \, F(\boldsymbol{\theta}), \tag{E-5}$$

where $F(\boldsymbol{\theta})$ may be a log-likelihood or some other function. Minimization of $F(\boldsymbol{\theta})$ is handled by maximizing $-F(\boldsymbol{\theta})$. Two special cases are

$$F(\boldsymbol{\theta}) = \sum_{i=1}^{n} f_i(\boldsymbol{\theta}), \tag{E-6}$$

which is typical for maximum likelihood problems, and the **least squares problem,**[10]

$$f_i(\boldsymbol{\theta}) = -(y_i - f(\mathbf{x}_i, \boldsymbol{\theta}))^2. \tag{E-7}$$

We treated the nonlinear least squares problem in detail in Chapter 11. An obvious way to search for the $\boldsymbol{\theta}$ that maximizes $F(\boldsymbol{\theta})$ is by trial and error. If $\boldsymbol{\theta}$ has only a single element and it is known approximately where the optimum will be found, then a **grid search** will be a feasible strategy. An example is a common time-series problem in which a one-dimensional search for a correlation coefficient is made in the interval $(-1, 1)$. The grid search can proceed in the obvious fashion—that is, ..., $-0.1, 0, 0.1, 0.2, \ldots$, then $\hat{\theta}_{\max} - 0.1$ to $\hat{\theta}_{\max} + 0.1$ in increments of $0.01$, and so on—until the desired precision is achieved.[11] If $\boldsymbol{\theta}$ contains more than one parameter, then a grid search is likely to be extremely costly, particularly if little is known about the parameter vector at the outset. Nonetheless, relatively efficient methods have been devised. Quandt (1983) and Fletcher (1980) contain further details.

There are also systematic, derivative-free methods of searching for a function optimum that resemble in some respects the algorithms that we will examine in the next section. The **downhill simplex** (and other simplex) methods[12] have been found to be very fast and effective for some problems. A recent entry in the econometrics literature is the method of **simulated annealing.**[13] These derivative-free methods, particularly the latter, are often very effective in problems with many variables in the objective function, but they usually require far more function evaluations than the methods based on derivatives that are considered below. Because the problems typically analyzed in econometrics involve relatively few parameters but often quite complex functions involving large numbers of terms in a summation, on balance, the gradient methods are usually going to be preferable.[14]

---

[8]Notice that the constant $a$ is irrelevant to the solution. Many maximum likelihood problems are presented with the preface "neglecting an irrelevant constant." For example, the log-likelihood for the normal linear regression model contains a term—$(n/2)\ln(2\pi)$—that can be discarded.

[9]See, for example, the normal equations for the nonlinear least squares estimators of Chapter 11.

[10]Least squares is, of course, a minimization problem. The negative of the criterion is used to maintain consistency with the general formulation.

[11]There are more efficient methods of carrying out a one-dimensional search, for example, the **golden section** method. See Press et al. (1986, Chap. 10).

[12]See Nelder and Mead (1965) and Press et al. (1986).

[13]See Goffe, Ferrier, and Rodgers (1994) and Press et al. (1986, pp. 326–334).

[14]Goffe, Ferrier, and Rodgers (1994) did find that the method of simulated annealing was quite adept at finding the best among multiple solutions. This problem is common for derivative-based methods, because they usually have no method of distinguishing between a local optimum and a global one.

### E.3.1 ALGORITHMS

A more effective means of solving most nonlinear maximization problems is by an **iterative algorithm:**

> Beginning from initial value $\theta_0$, at entry to iteration $t$, if $\theta_t$ is not the optimal value for $\theta$, compute direction vector $\Delta_t$, step size $\lambda_t$, then

$$\theta_{t+1} = \theta_t + \lambda_t \Delta_t. \tag{E-8}$$

Figure E.2 illustrates the structure of an iteration for a hypothetical function of two variables. The direction vector $\Delta_t$ is shown in the figure with $\theta_t$. The dashed line is the set of points $\theta_t + \lambda_t \Delta_t$. Different values of $\lambda_t$ lead to different contours; for this $\theta_t$ and $\Delta_t$, the best value of $\lambda_t$ is about 0.5.

Notice in Figure E.2 that for a given direction vector $\Delta_t$ and current parameter vector $\theta_t$, a secondary optimization is required to find the best $\lambda_t$. Translating from Figure E.2, we obtain the form of this problem as shown in Figure E.3. This subsidiary search is called a **line search,** as we search along the line $\theta_t + \lambda_t \Delta_t$ for the optimal value of $F(.)$. The formal solution to the line search problem would be the $\lambda_t$ that satisfies

$$\frac{\partial F(\theta_t + \lambda_t \Delta_t)}{\partial \lambda_t} = \mathbf{g}(\theta_t + \lambda_t \Delta_t)' \Delta_t = 0, \tag{E-9}$$

**FIGURE E.2**  Iteration.

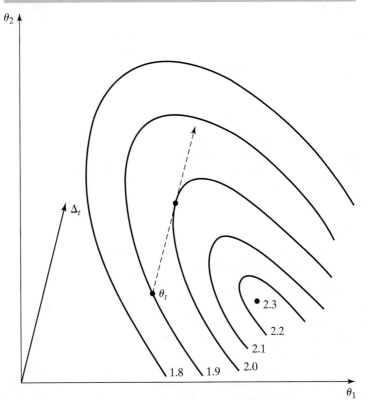

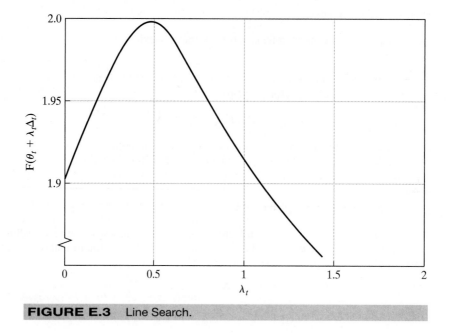

**FIGURE E.3**  Line Search.

where **g** is the vector of partial derivatives of $F(.)$ evaluated at $\boldsymbol{\theta}_t + \lambda_t \boldsymbol{\Delta}_t$. In general, this problem will also be a nonlinear one. In most cases, adding a formal search for $\lambda_t$ will be too expensive, as well as unnecessary. Some approximate or ad hoc method will usually be chosen. It is worth emphasizing that finding the $\lambda_t$ that maximizes $F(\boldsymbol{\theta}_t + \lambda_t \boldsymbol{\Delta}_t)$ at a given iteration does not generally lead to the overall solution in that iteration. This situation is clear in Figure E.3, where the optimal value of $\lambda_t$ leads to $F(.) = 2.0$, at which point we reenter the iteration.

### E.3.2  COMPUTING DERIVATIVES

For certain functions, the programming of derivatives may be quite difficult. Numeric approximations can be used, although it should be borne in mind that analytic derivatives obtained by formally differentiating the functions involved are to be preferred. First derivatives can be approximated by using

$$\frac{\partial F(\boldsymbol{\theta})}{\partial \theta_i} \approx \frac{F(\cdots \theta_i + \varepsilon \cdots) - F(\cdots \theta_i - \varepsilon \cdots)}{2\varepsilon}.$$

The choice of $\varepsilon$ is a remaining problem. Extensive discussion may be found in Quandt (1983).

There are three drawbacks to this means of computing derivatives compared with using the analytic derivatives. A possible major consideration is that it may substantially increase the amount of computation needed to obtain a function and its gradient. In particular, $K+1$ function evaluations (the criterion and $K$ derivatives) are replaced with $2K + 1$ functions. The latter may be more burdensome than the former, depending on the complexity of the partial derivatives compared with the function itself. The comparison will depend on the application. But in most settings, careful programming that avoids superfluous or redundant calculation can make the advantage of the analytic derivatives substantial. Second, the choice of $\varepsilon$ can be problematic. If it is chosen too large, then the approximation will be inaccurate. If it is chosen too small, then there may be insufficient variation in the function to produce a good estimate of the derivative.

A compromise that is likely to be effective is to compute $\varepsilon_i$ separately for each parameter, as in

$$\varepsilon_i = \text{Max}[\alpha|\theta_i|, \gamma]$$

[see Goldfeld and Quandt (1971)]. The values $\alpha$ and $\gamma$ should be relatively small, such as $10^{-5}$. Third, although numeric derivatives computed in this fashion are likely to be reasonably accurate, in a sum of a large number of terms, say, several thousand, enough approximation error can accumulate to cause the numerical derivatives to differ significantly from their analytic counterparts. Second derivatives can also be computed numerically. In addition to the preceding problems, however, it is generally not possible to ensure negative definiteness of a Hessian computed in this manner. Unless the choice of $\varepsilon$ is made extremely carefully, an indefinite matrix is a possibility. In general, the use of numeric derivatives should be avoided if the analytic derivatives are available.

### E.3.3   GRADIENT METHODS

The most commonly used algorithms are **gradient methods,** in which

$$\mathbf{\Delta}_t = \mathbf{W}_t \mathbf{g}_t, \tag{E-10}$$

where $\mathbf{W}_t$ is a positive definite matrix and $\mathbf{g}_t$ is the **gradient** of $F(\boldsymbol{\theta}_t)$:

$$\mathbf{g}_t = \mathbf{g}(\boldsymbol{\theta}_t) = \frac{\partial F(\boldsymbol{\theta}_t)}{\partial \boldsymbol{\theta}_t}. \tag{E-11}$$

These methods are motivated partly by the following. Consider a linear Taylor series approximation to $F(\boldsymbol{\theta}_t + \lambda_t \mathbf{\Delta}_t)$ around $\lambda_t = 0$:

$$F(\boldsymbol{\theta}_t + \lambda_t \mathbf{\Delta}_t) \simeq F(\boldsymbol{\theta}_t) + \lambda_t \mathbf{g}(\boldsymbol{\theta}_t)' \mathbf{\Delta}_t. \tag{E-12}$$

Let $F(\boldsymbol{\theta}_t + \lambda_t \mathbf{\Delta}_t)$ equal $F_{t+1}$. Then,

$$F_{t+1} - F_t \simeq \lambda_t \mathbf{g}_t' \mathbf{\Delta}_t.$$

If $\mathbf{\Delta}_t = \mathbf{W}_t \mathbf{g}_t$, then

$$F_{t+1} - F_t \simeq \lambda_t \mathbf{g}_t' \mathbf{W}_t \mathbf{g}_t.$$

If $\mathbf{g}_t$ is not $\mathbf{0}$ and $\lambda_t$ is small enough, then $F_{t+1} - F_t$ must be positive. Thus, if $F(\boldsymbol{\theta})$ is not already at its maximum, then we can always find a step size such that a gradient-type iteration will lead to an increase in the function. (Recall that $\mathbf{W}_t$ is assumed to be positive definite.)

In the following, we will omit the iteration index $t$, except where it is necessary to distinguish one vector from another. The following are some commonly used algorithms.[15]

**Steepest Ascent**   The simplest algorithm to employ is the **steepest ascent** method, which uses

$$\mathbf{W} = \mathbf{I} \text{ so that } \mathbf{\Delta} = \mathbf{g}. \tag{E-13}$$

As its name implies, the direction is the one of greatest increase of $F(.)$. Another virtue is that the line search has a straightforward solution; at least near the maximum, the optimal $\lambda$ is

$$\lambda = \frac{-\mathbf{g}'\mathbf{g}}{\mathbf{g}'\mathbf{H}\mathbf{g}}, \tag{E-14}$$

---

[15] A more extensive catalog may be found in Judge et al. (1985, Appendix B). Those mentioned here are some of the more commonly used ones and are chosen primarily because they illustrate many of the important aspects of nonlinear optimization.

where

$$\mathbf{H} = \frac{\partial^2 F(\boldsymbol{\theta})}{\partial \boldsymbol{\theta} \, \partial \boldsymbol{\theta}'}.$$

Therefore, the steepest ascent iteration is

$$\boldsymbol{\theta}_{t+1} = \boldsymbol{\theta}_t - \frac{\mathbf{g}_t' \mathbf{g}_t}{\mathbf{g}_t' \mathbf{H}_t \mathbf{g}_t} \mathbf{g}_t. \tag{E-15}$$

Computation of the second derivatives matrix may be extremely burdensome. Also, if $\mathbf{H}_t$ is not negative definite, which is likely if $\boldsymbol{\theta}_t$ is far from the maximum, the iteration may diverge. A systematic line search can bypass this problem. This algorithm usually converges very slowly, however, so other techniques are usually used.

**Newton's Method**    The template for most gradient methods in common use is Newton's method. The basis for **Newton's method** is a linear Taylor series approximation. Expanding the first-order conditions,

$$\frac{\partial F(\boldsymbol{\theta})}{\partial \boldsymbol{\theta}} = \mathbf{0},$$

equation by equation, in a linear Taylor series around an arbitrary $\boldsymbol{\theta}^0$ yields

$$\frac{\partial F(\boldsymbol{\theta})}{\partial \boldsymbol{\theta}} \simeq \mathbf{g}^0 + \mathbf{H}^0(\boldsymbol{\theta} - \boldsymbol{\theta}^0) = \mathbf{0}, \tag{E-16}$$

where the superscript indicates that the term is evaluated at $\boldsymbol{\theta}^0$. Solving for $\boldsymbol{\theta}$ and then equating $\boldsymbol{\theta}$ to $\boldsymbol{\theta}_{t+1}$ and $\boldsymbol{\theta}^0$ to $\boldsymbol{\theta}_t$, we obtain the iteration

$$\boldsymbol{\theta}_{t+1} = \boldsymbol{\theta}_t - \mathbf{H}_t^{-1} \mathbf{g}_t. \tag{E-17}$$

Thus, for Newton's method,

$$\mathbf{W} = -\mathbf{H}^{-1}, \qquad \boldsymbol{\Delta} = -\mathbf{H}^{-1}\mathbf{g}, \qquad \lambda = 1. \tag{E-18}$$

Newton's method will converge very rapidly in many problems. If the function is quadratic, then this method will reach the optimum in one iteration from any starting point. If the criterion function is globally concave, as it is in a number of problems that we shall examine in this text, then it is probably the best algorithm available. This method is very well suited to maximum likelihood estimation.

**Alternatives to Newton's Method**    Newton's method is very effective in some settings, but it can perform very poorly in others. If the function is not approximately quadratic or if the current estimate is very far from the maximum, then it can cause wide swings in the estimates and even fail to converge at all. A number of algorithms have been devised to improve upon Newton's method. An obvious one is to include a line search at each iteration rather than use $\lambda = 1$. Two problems remain, however. At points distant from the optimum, the second derivatives matrix may not be negative definite, and, in any event, the computational burden of computing $\mathbf{H}$ may be excessive.

The **quadratic hill-climbing method** proposed by Goldfeld, Quandt, and Trotter (1966) deals directly with the first of these problems. In any iteration, if $\mathbf{H}$ is not negative definite, then it is replaced with

$$\mathbf{H}_\alpha = \mathbf{H} - \alpha\mathbf{I}, \tag{E-19}$$

where $\alpha$ is a positive number chosen large enough to ensure the negative definiteness of $\mathbf{H}_\alpha$. Another suggestion is that of Greenstadt (1967), which uses, at every iteration,

$$\mathbf{H}_\pi = -\sum_{i=1}^{n} |\pi_i| \, \mathbf{c}_i \mathbf{c}_i', \tag{E-20}$$

where $\pi_i$ is the $i$th characteristic root of $\mathbf{H}$ and $\mathbf{c}_i$ is its associated characteristic vector. Other proposals have been made to ensure the negative definiteness of the required matrix at each iteration.[16]

**Quasi-Newton Methods: Davidon–Fletcher–Powell**   A very effective class of algorithms has been developed that eliminates second derivatives altogether and has excellent convergence properties, even for ill-behaved problems. These are the **quasi-Newton methods,** which form

$$\mathbf{W}_{t+1} = \mathbf{W}_t + \mathbf{E}_t,$$

where $\mathbf{E}_t$ is a positive definite matrix.[17] As long as $\mathbf{W}_0$ is positive definite—$\mathbf{I}$ is commonly used—$\mathbf{W}_t$ will be positive definite at every iteration. In the **Davidon–Fletcher–Powell (DFP) method,** after a sufficient number of iterations, $\mathbf{W}_{t+1}$ will be an approximation to $-\mathbf{H}^{-1}$. Let

$$\delta_t = \lambda_t \mathbf{\Delta}_t, \quad \text{and} \quad \gamma_t = \mathbf{g}(\theta_{t+1}) - \mathbf{g}(\theta_t). \tag{E-21}$$

The DFP **variable metric algorithm** uses

$$\mathbf{W}_{t+1} = \mathbf{W}_t + \frac{\delta_t \delta_t'}{\delta_t' \gamma_t} + \frac{\mathbf{W}_t \gamma_t \gamma_t' \mathbf{W}_t}{\gamma_t' \mathbf{W}_t \gamma_t}. \tag{E-22}$$

Notice that in the DFP algorithm, the change in the first derivative vector is used in $\mathbf{W}$; an estimate of the inverse of the second derivatives matrix is being accumulated.

The variable metric algorithms are those that update $\mathbf{W}$ at each iteration while preserving its definiteness. For the DFP method, the accumulation of $\mathbf{W}_{t+1}$ is of the form

$$\mathbf{W}_{t+1} = \mathbf{W}_t + \mathbf{a}\mathbf{a}' + \mathbf{b}\mathbf{b}' = \mathbf{W}_t + [\mathbf{a} \quad \mathbf{b}][\mathbf{a} \quad \mathbf{b}]'.$$

The two-column matrix $[\mathbf{a} \quad \mathbf{b}]$ will have rank two; hence, DFP is called a **rank two update** or **rank two correction.** The **Broyden–Fletcher–Goldfarb–Shanno (BFGS)** method is a rank three correction that subtracts $v\mathbf{d}\mathbf{d}'$ from the **DFP** update, where $v = (\gamma_t' \mathbf{W}_t \gamma_t)$ and

$$\mathbf{d}_t = \left(\frac{1}{\delta_t' \gamma_t}\right)\delta_t - \left(\frac{1}{\gamma_t' \mathbf{W}_t \gamma_t}\right)\mathbf{W}_t \gamma_t.$$

There is some evidence that this method is more efficient than DFP. Other methods, such as **Broyden's method,** involve a rank one correction instead. Any method that is of the form

$$\mathbf{W}_{t+1} = \mathbf{W}_t + \mathbf{Q}\mathbf{Q}'$$

will preserve the definiteness of $\mathbf{W}$, regardless of the number of columns in $\mathbf{Q}$.

The DFP and BFGS algorithms are extremely effective and are among the most widely used of the gradient methods. An important practical consideration to keep in mind is that although $\mathbf{W}_t$ accumulates an estimate of the negative inverse of the second derivatives matrix for both algorithms, in maximum likelihood problems it rarely converges to a very good estimate of the covariance matrix of the estimator and should generally not be used as one.

---

[16]See, for example, Goldfeld and Quandt (1971).

[17]See Fletcher (1980).

### E.3.4   ASPECTS OF MAXIMUM LIKELIHOOD ESTIMATION

Newton's method is often used for maximum likelihood problems. For solving a maximum likelihood problem, the **method of scoring** replaces $\mathbf{H}$ with

$$\overline{\mathbf{H}} = E[\mathbf{H}(\boldsymbol{\theta})], \tag{E-23}$$

which will be recognized as the asymptotic covariance of the maximum likelihood estimator. There is some evidence that where it can be used, this method performs better than Newton's method. The exact form of the expectation of the Hessian of the log likelihood is rarely known, however.[18] Newton's method, which uses actual instead of expected second derivatives, is generally used instead.

**One-Step Estimation**   A convenient variant of Newton's method is the **one-step maximum likelihood estimator.** It has been shown that if $\boldsymbol{\theta}^0$ is *any* consistent initial estimator of $\boldsymbol{\theta}$ and $\mathbf{H}^*$ is $\mathbf{H}, \overline{\mathbf{H}}$, or any other asymptotically equivalent estimator of $\text{Var}[\mathbf{g}(\hat{\boldsymbol{\theta}}_{\text{MLE}})]$, then

$$\boldsymbol{\theta}^1 = \boldsymbol{\theta}^0 - (\mathbf{H}^*)^{-1}\mathbf{g}^0 \tag{E-24}$$

is an estimator of $\boldsymbol{\theta}$ that has the same asymptotic properties as the maximum likelihood estimator.[19] (Note that it is *not* the maximum likelihood estimator. As such, for example, it should not be used as the basis for likelihood ratio tests.)

**Covariance Matrix Estimation**   In computing maximum likelihood estimators, a commonly used method of estimating $\mathbf{H}$ simultaneously simplifies the calculation of $\mathbf{W}$ and solves the occasional problem of indefiniteness of the Hessian. The method of Berndt et al. (1974) replaces $\mathbf{W}$ with

$$\hat{\mathbf{W}} = \left[\sum_{i=1}^{n} \mathbf{g}_i \mathbf{g}_i'\right]^{-1} = (\mathbf{G}'\mathbf{G})^{-1}, \tag{E-25}$$

where

$$\mathbf{g}_i = \frac{\partial \ln f(y_i \mid \mathbf{x}_i, \boldsymbol{\theta})}{\partial \boldsymbol{\theta}}. \tag{E-26}$$

Then, $\mathbf{G}$ is the $n \times K$ matrix with $i$th row equal to $\mathbf{g}_i'$. Although $\hat{\mathbf{W}}$ and other suggested estimators of $(-\mathbf{H})^{-1}$ are asymptotically equivalent, $\hat{\mathbf{W}}$ has the additional virtues that it is always nonnegative definite, and it is only necessary to differentiate the log-likelihood once to compute it.

**The Lagrange Multiplier Statistic**   The use of $\hat{\mathbf{W}}$ as an estimator of $(-\mathbf{H})^{-1}$ brings another intriguing convenience in maximum likelihood estimation. When testing restrictions on parameters estimated by maximum likelihood, one approach is to use the **Lagrange multiplier** statistic. We will examine this test at length at various points in this book, so we need only sketch it briefly here. The logic of the LM test is as follows. The gradient $\mathbf{g}(\boldsymbol{\theta})$ of the log-likelihood function equals $\mathbf{0}$ at the unrestricted maximum likelihood estimators (that is, at least to within the precision of the computer program in use). If $\hat{\boldsymbol{\theta}}_r$ is an MLE that is computed subject to some restrictions on $\boldsymbol{\theta}$, then we know that $\mathbf{g}(\hat{\boldsymbol{\theta}}_r) \neq \mathbf{0}$. The LM test is used to test whether, at $\hat{\boldsymbol{\theta}}_r$, $\mathbf{g}_r$ is *significantly* different from $\mathbf{0}$ or whether the deviation of $\mathbf{g}_r$ from $\mathbf{0}$ can be viewed as sampling variation. The covariance matrix of the gradient of the log-likelihood is $-\mathbf{H}$, so the Wald statistic for testing this hypothesis is $W = \mathbf{g}'(-\mathbf{H})^{-1}\mathbf{g}$. Now, suppose that we use $\hat{\mathbf{W}}$ to estimate $-\mathbf{H}^{-1}$. Let $\mathbf{G}$ be the $n \times K$ matrix with $i$th row equal to $\mathbf{g}_i'$, and let $\mathbf{i}$ denote an $n \times 1$ column of ones. Then the LM statistic can be

---

[18]Amemiya (1981) provides a number of examples.

[19]See, for example, Rao (1973).

computed as

$$LM = i'G(G'G)^{-1}G'i.$$

Because $i'i = n$,

$$LM = n[i'G(G'G)^{-1}G'i/n] = nR_i^2,$$

where $R_i^2$ is the *uncentered* $R^2$ in a regression of a column of ones on the derivatives of the log-likelihood function.

**The Concentrated Log-Likelihood**  Many problems in maximum likelihood estimation can be formulated in terms of a partitioning of the parameter vector $\theta = [\theta_1, \theta_2]$ such that at the solution to the optimization problem, $\theta_{2,ML}$, can be written as an explicit function of $\theta_{1,ML}$. When the solution to the likelihood equation for $\theta_2$ produces

$$\theta_{2,ML} = t(\theta_{1,ML}),$$

then, if it is convenient, we may "concentrate" the log-likelihood function by writing

$$F^*(\theta_1, \theta_2) = F[\theta_1, t(\theta_1)] = F_c(\theta_1).$$

The unrestricted solution to the problem $\text{Max}_{\theta_1} F_c(\theta_1)$ provides the full solution to the optimization problem. Once the optimizing value of $\theta_1$ is obtained, the optimizing value of $\theta_2$ is simply $t(\hat{\theta}_{1,ML})$. Note that $F^*(\theta_1, \theta_2)$ is a subset of the set of values of the log-likelihood function, namely those values at which the second parameter vector satisfies the first-order conditions.[20]

### E.3.5  OPTIMIZATION WITH CONSTRAINTS

Occasionally, some of or all the parameters of a model are constrained, for example, to be positive in the case of a variance or to be in a certain range, such as a correlation coefficient. Optimization subject to constraints is often yet another art form. The elaborate literature on the general problem provides some guidance—see, for example, Appendix B in Judge et al. (1985)—but applications still, as often as not, require some creativity on the part of the analyst. In this section, we will examine a few of the most common forms of constrained optimization as they arise in econometrics.

Parametric constraints typically come in two forms, which may occur simultaneously in a problem. Equality constraints can be written $c(\theta) = 0$, where $c_j(\theta)$ is a continuous and differentiable function. Typical applications include linear constraints on slope vectors, such as a requirement that a set of elasticities in a log-linear model add to one; exclusion restrictions, which are often cast in the form of interesting hypotheses about whether or not a variable should appear in a model (i.e., whether a coefficient is zero or not); and equality restrictions, such as the symmetry restrictions in a translog model, which require that parameters in two different equations be equal to each other. Inequality constraints, in general, will be of the form $a_j \le c_j(\theta) \le b_j$, where $a_j$ and $b_j$ are known constants (either of which may be infinite). Once again, the typical application in econometrics involves a restriction on a single parameter, such as $\sigma > 0$ for a variance parameter, $-1 \le \rho \le 1$ for a correlation coefficient, or $\beta_j \ge 0$ for a particular slope coefficient in a model. We will consider the two cases separately.

In the case of equality constraints, for practical purposes of optimization, there are usually two strategies available. One can use a Lagrangean multiplier approach. The new optimization problem is

$$\text{Max}_{\theta,\lambda} L(\theta, \lambda) = F(\theta) + \lambda'c(\theta).$$

---

[20]A formal proof that this is a valid way to proceed is given by Amemiya (1985, pp. 125–127).

The necessary conditions for an optimum are

$$\frac{\partial L(\boldsymbol{\theta}, \boldsymbol{\lambda})}{\partial \boldsymbol{\theta}} = \mathbf{g}(\boldsymbol{\theta}) + \mathbf{C}(\boldsymbol{\theta})'\boldsymbol{\lambda} = \mathbf{0},$$

$$\frac{\partial L(\boldsymbol{\theta}, \boldsymbol{\lambda})}{\partial \boldsymbol{\lambda}} = \mathbf{c}(\boldsymbol{\theta}) = \mathbf{0},$$

where $\mathbf{g}(\boldsymbol{\theta})$ is the familiar gradient of $F(\boldsymbol{\theta})$ and $\mathbf{C}(\boldsymbol{\theta})$ is a $J \times K$ matrix of derivatives with $j$th row equal to $\partial c_j / \partial \boldsymbol{\theta}'$. The joint solution will provide the constrained optimizer, as well as the Lagrange multipliers, which are often interesting in their own right. The disadvantage of this approach is that it increases the dimensionality of the optimization problem. An alternative strategy is to eliminate some of the parameters by either imposing the constraints directly on the function or by solving out the constraints. For exclusion restrictions, which are usually of the form $\theta_j = 0$, this step usually means dropping a variable from a model. Other restrictions can often be imposed just by building them into the model. For example, in a function of $\theta_1$, $\theta_2$, and $\theta_3$, if the restriction is of the form $\theta_3 = \theta_1\theta_2$, then $\theta_3$ can be eliminated from the model by a direct substitution.

Inequality constraints are more difficult. For the general case, one suggestion is to transform the constrained problem into an unconstrained one by imposing some sort of penalty function into the optimization criterion that will cause a parameter vector that violates the constraints, or nearly does so, to be an unattractive choice. For example, to force a parameter $\theta_j$ to be nonzero, one might maximize the augmented function $F(\boldsymbol{\theta}) - |1/\theta_j|$. This approach is feasible, but it has the disadvantage that because the penalty is a function of the parameters, different penalty functions will lead to different solutions of the optimization problem. For the most common problems in econometrics, a simpler approach will usually suffice. One can often reparameterize a function so that the new parameter is unconstrained. For example, the "method of squaring" is sometimes used to force a parameter to be positive. If we require $\theta_j$ to be positive, then we can define $\theta_j = \alpha^2$ and substitute $\alpha^2$ for $\theta_j$ wherever it appears in the model. Then an unconstrained solution for $\alpha$ is obtained. An alternative reparameterization for a parameter that must be positive that is often used is $\theta_j = \exp(\alpha)$. To force a parameter to be between zero and one, we can use the function $\theta_j = 1/[1 + \exp(\alpha)]$. The range of $\alpha$ is now unrestricted. Experience suggests that a third, less orthodox approach works very well for many problems. When the constrained optimization is begun, there is a starting value $\boldsymbol{\theta}^0$ that begins the iterations. Presumably, $\boldsymbol{\theta}^0$ obeys the restrictions. (If not, and none can be found, then the optimization process must be terminated immediately.) The next iterate, $\boldsymbol{\theta}^1$, is a step away from $\boldsymbol{\theta}^0$, by $\boldsymbol{\theta}^1 = \boldsymbol{\theta}^0 + \lambda_0\boldsymbol{\delta}^0$. Suppose that $\boldsymbol{\theta}^1$ violates the constraints. By construction, we know that there is some value $\boldsymbol{\theta}^1_*$ between $\boldsymbol{\theta}^0$ and $\boldsymbol{\theta}^1$ that does not violate the constraint, where "between" means only that a shorter step is taken. Therefore, the next value for the iteration can be $\boldsymbol{\theta}^1_*$. The logic is true at every iteration, so a way to proceed is to alter the iteration so that the step length is shortened when necessary when a parameter violates the constraints.

## E.3.6 SOME PRACTICAL CONSIDERATIONS

The reasons for the good performance of many algorithms, including DFP, are unknown. Moreover, different algorithms may perform differently in given settings. Indeed, for some problems, one algorithm may fail to converge whereas another will succeed in finding a solution without great difficulty. In view of this, computer programs such as GQOPT,[21] Gauss, and MatLab that offer a menu of different preprogrammed algorithms can be particularly useful. It is sometimes worth the effort to try more than one algorithm on a given problem.

---

[21]Goldfeld and Quandt (1972).

**Step Sizes** Except for the steepest ascent case, an optimal line search is likely to be infeasible or to require more effort than it is worth in view of the potentially large number of function evaluations required. In most cases, the choice of a step size is likely to be rather ad hoc. But within limits, the most widely used algorithms appear to be robust to inaccurate line searches. For example, one method employed by the widely used TSP computer program[22] is the method of *squeezing,* which tries $\lambda = 1, \frac{1}{2}, \frac{1}{4}$, and so on until an improvement in the function results. Although this approach is obviously a bit unorthodox, it appears to be quite effective when used with the Gauss–Newton method for nonlinear least squares problems. (See Chapter 11.) A somewhat more elaborate rule is suggested by Berndt et al. (1974). Choose an $\varepsilon$ between 0 and $\frac{1}{2}$, and then find a $\lambda$ such that

$$\varepsilon < \frac{F(\boldsymbol{\theta} + \lambda \boldsymbol{\Delta}) - F(\boldsymbol{\theta})}{\lambda \mathbf{g}' \boldsymbol{\Delta}} < 1 - \varepsilon. \tag{E-27}$$

Of course, which value of $\varepsilon$ to choose is still open, so the choice of $\lambda$ remains ad hoc. Moreover, in neither of these cases is there any optimality to the choice; we merely find a $\lambda$ that leads to a function improvement. Other authors have devised relatively efficient means of searching for a step size without doing the full optimization at each iteration.[23]

**Assessing Convergence** Ideally, the iterative procedure should terminate when the gradient is zero. In practice, this step will not be possible, primarily because of accumulated rounding error in the computation of the function and its derivatives. Therefore, a number of alternative convergence criteria are used. Most of them are based on the relative changes in the function or the parameters. There is considerable variation in those used in different computer programs, and there are some pitfalls that should be avoided. A critical absolute value for the elements of the gradient or its norm will be affected by any scaling of the function, such as normalizing it by the sample size. Similarly, stopping on the basis of small absolute changes in the parameters can lead to premature convergence when the parameter vector approaches the maximizer. It is probably best to use several criteria simultaneously, such as the proportional change in both the function and the parameters. Belsley (1980) discusses a number of possible stopping rules. One that has proved useful and is immune to the scaling problem is to base convergence on $\mathbf{g}'\mathbf{H}^{-1}\mathbf{g}$.

**Multiple Solutions** It is possible for a function to have several local extrema. It is difficult to know a priori whether this is true of the one at hand. But if the function is not globally concave, then it may be a good idea to attempt to maximize it from several starting points to ensure that the maximum obtained is the global one. Ideally, a starting value near the optimum can facilitate matters; in some settings, this can be obtained by using a consistent estimate of the parameter for the starting point. The method of moments, if available, is sometimes a convenient device for doing so.

**No Solution** Finally, it should be noted that in a nonlinear setting the iterative algorithm can break down, even in the absence of constraints, for at least two reasons. The first possibility is that the problem being solved may be so numerically complex as to defy solution. The second possibility, which is often neglected, is that the proposed model may simply be inappropriate for the data. In a linear setting, a low $R^2$ or some other diagnostic test may suggest that the model and data are mismatched, but as long as the full rank condition is met by the regressor matrix, a linear regression can *always* be computed. Nonlinear models are not so forgiving. The failure of an iterative algorithm to find a maximum of the criterion function may be a warning that the model is not appropriate for this body of data.

---

[22]Hall (1982, p. 147).

[23]See, for example, Joreskog and Gruvaeus (1970), Powell (1964), Quandt (1983), and Hall (1982).

## E.3.7 THE EM ALGORITHM

The latent class model can be characterized as a **missing data model.** Consider the mixture model we used for DocVis in Example 16.21, which we will now generalize to allow more than two classes:

$$f(y_{it} \mid \mathbf{x}_{it}, class_i = j) = \theta_{it,j}(1 - \theta_{it,j})^{y_{it}}, \theta_{it,j} = 1/(1 + \lambda_{it,j}), \lambda_{it,j} = \exp(\mathbf{x}'_{it}\boldsymbol{\beta}_j), y_{it} = 0, 1, \dots.$$

$$\text{Prob}(class_i = j \mid \mathbf{z}_i) = \frac{\exp(\mathbf{z}'_i\boldsymbol{\alpha}_j)}{\sum_{j=1}^{j} \exp(\mathbf{z}'_i\boldsymbol{\alpha}_j)}, j = 1, 2, \dots, J.$$

With all parts incorporated, the log-likelihood for this latent class model is

$$\ln L_M = \sum_{i=1}^{n} \ln L_{i,M}$$

$$= \sum_{i=1}^{n} \ln \left\{ \sum_{j=1}^{J} \frac{\exp(\mathbf{z}'_i\boldsymbol{\alpha}_j)}{\sum_{m=1}^{J} \exp(\mathbf{z}'_i\boldsymbol{\alpha}_m)} \prod_{t=1}^{T_i} \left( \frac{1}{1 + \exp(\mathbf{x}'_{it}\boldsymbol{\beta}_j)} \right) \left( \frac{\exp(\mathbf{x}'_{it}\boldsymbol{\beta}_j)}{1 + \exp(\mathbf{x}'_{it}\boldsymbol{\beta}_j)} \right)^{y_{it}} \right\}.$$

$$\text{(E-28)}$$

Suppose the actual class memberships were known (i.e., observed). Then, the class probabilities in $\ln L_M$ would be unnecessary. The appropriate **complete data log-likelihood** for this case would be

$$\ln L_C = \sum_{i=1}^{n} \ln L_{i,C}$$

$$= \sum_{i=1}^{n} \ln \left\{ \sum_{j=1}^{J} D_{ij} \prod_{t=1}^{T_i} \left( \frac{1}{1 + \exp(\mathbf{x}'_{it}\boldsymbol{\beta}_j)} \right) \left( \frac{\exp(\mathbf{x}'_{it}\boldsymbol{\beta}_j)}{1 + \exp(\mathbf{x}'_{it}\boldsymbol{\beta}_j)} \right)^{y_{it}} \right\}, \quad \text{(E-29)}$$

where $D_{ij}$ is an observed dummy variable that equals one if individual $i$ is from class $j$, and zero otherwise. With this specification, the log-likelihood breaks into $J$ separate log-likelihoods, one for each (now known) class. The maximum likelihood estimates of $\boldsymbol{\beta}_1, \dots, \boldsymbol{\beta}_J$ would be obtained simply by separating the sample into the respective subgroups and estimating the appropriate model for each group using maximum likelihood. The method we have used to estimate the parameters of the full model is to replace the $D_{ij}$ variables with their unconditional espectations, $\text{Prob}(class_i = j \mid \mathbf{z}_i)$, then maximize the resulting log-likelihood function. This is the essential logic of the **EM** (expectation–maximization) **algorithm** [Dempster et al. (1977)], however, the method uses the conditional (posterior) class probabilities instead of the unconditional probabilities. The iterative steps of the EM algorithm are

(E step)   Form the expectation of the missing data log-likelihood, conditional on the previous parameter estimates and the data in the sample;

(M step)   Maximize the expected log-likelihood function. Then either return to the E step or exit if the estimates have converged.

The EM algorithm can be used in a variety of settings. [See McLachlan and Krishnan (1997).] It has a particularly appealing form for estimating latent class models. The iterative steps for the latent class model are as follows:

(E step)   Form the conditional (posterior) class probabilities, $\pi_{ij} \mid \mathbf{z}_i$, based on the current estimates. These are based on the likelihood function.

(M step)    For each class, estimate the class-specific parameters by maximizing a weighted log-likelihood,

$$\ln L_{M\,step,j} = \sum_{i=1}^{n_c} \pi_{ij} \ln L_i \,|\, class = j.$$

The parameters of the class probability model are also reestimated, as shown later, when there are variables in $\mathbf{z}_i$ other than a constant term.

This amounts to a simple weighted estimation. For example, in the latent class linear regression model, the M step would amount to nothing more than weighted least squares. For nonlinear models such as the geometric model above, the M step involves maximizing a weighted log-likelihood function.

For the preceding geometric model, the precise steps are as follows: First, obtain starting values for $\boldsymbol{\beta}_1, \dots, \boldsymbol{\beta}_J, \boldsymbol{\alpha}_1, \dots, \boldsymbol{\alpha}_J$. Recall, $\boldsymbol{\alpha}_J = \mathbf{0}$. Then:

1.  Form the contributions to the likelihood function using (E-28),

$$L_i = \sum_{j=1}^{J} \pi_{ij} \prod_{t=1}^{T_i} f(y_{it} \,|\, \mathbf{x}_{it}, \boldsymbol{\beta}_j, class_i = j)$$

$$= \sum_{j=1}^{J} L_i \,|\, class = j. \tag{E-30}$$

2.  Form the conditional probabilities, $w_{ij} = \dfrac{L_i \,|\, class = j}{\sum_{m=1}^{J} L_i \,|\, class = m}. \tag{E-31}$

3.  For each $j$, now maximize the weighted log likelihood functions (one at a time),

$$\ln L_{j,M}(\boldsymbol{\beta}_j) = \sum_{i=1}^{n} w_{ij} \ln \prod_{t=1}^{T_i} \left( \frac{1}{1 + \exp(\mathbf{x}'_{it}\boldsymbol{\beta}_j)} \right) \left( \frac{\exp(\mathbf{x}'_{it}\boldsymbol{\beta}_j)}{1 + \exp(\mathbf{x}'_{it}\boldsymbol{\beta}_j)} \right)^{y_{it}} \tag{E-32}$$

4.  To update the $\boldsymbol{\alpha}_j$ parameters, maximize the following log-likelihood function

$$\ln L(\boldsymbol{\alpha}_1, \dots, \boldsymbol{\alpha}_J) = \sum_{i=1}^{n} \sum_{j=1}^{J} w_{ij} \ln \frac{\exp(\mathbf{z}'_i \boldsymbol{\alpha}_j)}{\sum_{j=1}^{J} \exp(\mathbf{z}'_i \boldsymbol{\alpha}_j)}, \quad \boldsymbol{\alpha}_J = \mathbf{0}. \tag{E-33}$$

Step 4 defines a multinomial logit model (with "grouped") data. If the class probability model does not contain any variables in $\mathbf{z}_i$, other than a constant, then the solutions to this optimization will be

$$\hat{\pi}_j = \frac{\sum_{i=1}^{n} w_{ij}}{\sum_{i=1}^{n} \sum_{j=1}^{J} w_{ij}}, \quad \text{then } \hat{\alpha}_j = \ln \frac{\hat{\pi}_j}{\hat{\pi}_J}. \tag{E-34}$$

(Note that this preserves the restriction $\hat{\alpha}_J = 0$.) With these in hand, we return to steps 1 and 2 to rebuild the weights, then perform steps 3 and 4. The process is iterated until the estimates of $\boldsymbol{\beta}_1, \dots, \boldsymbol{\beta}_J$ converge. Step 1 is constructed in a generic form. For a different model, it is necessary only to change the density that appears at the end of the expresssion in (E-32). For a cross section instead of a panel, the product term in step 1 becomes simply the log of the single term.

The EM algorithm has an intuitive appeal in this (and other) settings. In practical terms, it is often found to be a very slow algorithm. It can take many iterations to converge. (The estimates in Example 16.16 were computed using a gradient method, not the EM algorithm.) In its favor, the EM method is very stable. It has been shown [Dempster, Laird, and Rubin (1977)] that the algorithm always climbs uphill. The log-likelihood improves with each iteration. Applications differ widely in the methods used to estimate latent class models. Adding to the variety are the very many Bayesian applications, none of which use either of the methods discussed here.

## E.4 EXAMPLES

To illustrate the use of gradient methods, we consider some simple problems.

### E.4.1 FUNCTION OF ONE PARAMETER

First, consider maximizing a function of a single variable, $f(\theta) = \ln(\theta) - 0.1\theta^2$. The function is shown in Figure E.4. The first and second derivatives are

$$f'(\theta) = \frac{1}{\theta} - 0.2\theta,$$

$$f''(\theta) = \frac{-1}{\theta^2} - 0.2.$$

Equating $f'$ to zero yields the solution $\theta = \sqrt{5} = 2.236$. At the solution, $f'' = -0.4$, so this solution is indeed a maximum. To demonstrate the use of an iterative method, we solve this problem using Newton's method. Observe, first, that the second derivative is always negative for any admissible (positive) $\theta$.[24] Therefore, it should not matter where we start the iterations; we shall eventually find the maximum. For a single parameter, Newton's method is

$$\theta_{t+1} = \theta_t - [f'_t/f''_t].$$

**FIGURE E.4**    Function of One Variable Parameter.

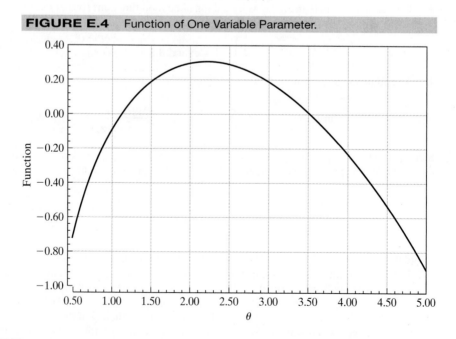

---

[24]In this problem, an inequality restriction, $\theta > 0$, is required. As is common, however, for our first attempt we shall neglect the constraint.

**TABLE E.1**  Iterations for Newton's Method

| Iteration | $\theta$ | $f$ | $f'$ | $f''$ |
|---|---|---|---|---|
| 0 | 5.00000 | −0.890562 | −0.800000 | −0.240000 |
| 1 | 1.66667 | 0.233048 | 0.266667 | −0.560000 |
| 2 | 2.14286 | 0.302956 | 0.030952 | −0.417778 |
| 3 | 2.23404 | 0.304718 | 0.000811 | −0.400363 |
| 4 | 2.23607 | 0.304719 | 0.0000004 | −0.400000 |

The sequence of values that results when 5 is used as the starting value is given in Table E.1. The path of the iterations is also shown in the table.

### E.4.2  FUNCTION OF TWO PARAMETERS: THE GAMMA DISTRIBUTION

For random sampling from the gamma distribution,

$$f(y_i, \beta, \rho) = \frac{\beta^\rho}{\Gamma(\rho)} e^{-\beta y_i} y_i^{\rho-1}.$$

The log-likelihood is $\ln L(\beta, \rho) = n\rho \ln \beta - n \ln \Gamma(\rho) - \beta \sum_{i=1}^{n} y_i + (\rho - 1) \sum_{i=1}^{n} \ln y_i$. (See Section 16.6.4 and Examples 15.5 and 15.7.) It is often convenient to scale the log-likelihood by the sample size. Suppose, as well, that we have a sample with $\bar{y} = 3$ and $\overline{\ln y} = 1$. Then the function to be maximized is $F(\beta, \rho) = \rho \ln \beta - \ln \Gamma(\rho) - 3\beta + \rho - 1$. The derivatives are

$$\frac{\partial F}{\partial \beta} = \frac{\rho}{\beta} - 3, \qquad \frac{\partial F}{\partial \rho} = \ln \beta - \frac{\Gamma'}{\Gamma} + 1 = \ln \beta - \Psi(\rho) + 1,$$

$$\frac{\partial^2 F}{\partial \beta^2} = \frac{-\rho}{\beta^2}, \qquad \frac{\partial^2 F}{\partial \rho^2} = \frac{-(\Gamma \Gamma'' - \Gamma'^2)}{\Gamma^2} = -\Psi'(\rho), \qquad \frac{\partial^2 F}{\partial \beta \, \partial \rho} = \frac{1}{\beta}.$$

Finding a good set of starting values is often a difficult problem. Here we choose three starting points somewhat arbitrarily: $(\rho^0, \beta^0) = (4, 1), (8, 3)$, and $(2, 7)$. The solution to the problem is $(5.233, 1.7438)$. We used Newton's method and DFP with a line search to maximize this function.[25] For Newton's method, $\lambda = 1$. The results are shown in Table E.2. The two methods were essentially the same when starting from a good starting point (trial 1), but they differed substantially when starting from a poorer one (trial 2). Note that DFP and Newton approached the solution from different directions in trial 2. The third starting point shows the value of a line search. At this

**TABLE E.2**  Iterative Solutions to Max$(\rho, \beta)\rho \ln \beta - \ln \Gamma(\rho) - 3\beta + \rho - 1$

| | Trial 1 | | | | Trial 2 | | | | Trial 3 | | | |
|---|---|---|---|---|---|---|---|---|---|---|---|---|
| | DFP | | Newton | | DFP | | Newton | | DFP | | Newton | |
| Iter. | $\rho$ | $\beta$ | $\rho$ | $\beta$ | $\rho$ | $\beta$ | $\rho$ | $\beta$ | $\rho$ | $\beta$ | $\rho$ | $\beta$ |
| 0 | 4.000 | 1.000 | 4.000 | 1.000 | 8.000 | 3.000 | 8.000 | 3.000 | 2.000 | 7.000 | 2.000 | 7.000 |
| 1 | 3.981 | 1.345 | 3.812 | 1.203 | 7.117 | 2.518 | 2.640 | 0.615 | 6.663 | 2.027 | −47.7 | −233. |
| 2 | 4.005 | 1.324 | 4.795 | 1.577 | 7.144 | 2.372 | 3.203 | 0.931 | 6.195 | 2.075 | — | — |
| 3 | 5.217 | 1.743 | 5.190 | 1.728 | 7.045 | 2.389 | 4.257 | 1.357 | 5.239 | 1.731 | — | — |
| 4 | 5.233 | 1.744 | 5.231 | 1.744 | 5.114 | 1.710 | 5.011 | 1.656 | 5.251 | 1.754 | — | — |
| 5 | — | — | — | — | 5.239 | 1.747 | 5.219 | 1.740 | 5.233 | 1.744 | — | — |
| 6 | — | — | — | — | 5.233 | 1.744 | 5.233 | 1.744 | — | — | — | — |

---

[25]The one used is described in Joreskog and Gruvaeus (1970).

starting value, the Hessian is extremely large, and the second value for the parameter vector with Newton's method is $(-47.671, -233.35)$, at which point $F$ cannot be computed and this method must be abandoned. Beginning with $\mathbf{H} = \mathbf{I}$ and using a line search, DFP reaches the point $(6.63, 2.03)$ at the first iteration, after which convergence occurs routinely in three more iterations. At the solution, the Hessian is $[(-1.72038, 0.191153)', (0.191153, -0.210579)']$. The diagonal elements of the Hessian are negative and its determinant is $0.32574$, so it is negative definite. (The two characteristic roots are $-1.7442$ and $-0.18675$). Therefore, this result is indeed the maximum of the function.

### E.4.3   A CONCENTRATED LOG-LIKELIHOOD FUNCTION

There is another way that the preceding problem might have been solved. The first of the necessary conditions implies that at the joint solution for $(\beta, \rho)$, $\beta$ will equal $\rho/3$. Suppose that we impose this requirement on the function we are maximizing. The **concentrated** (over $\beta$) **log-likelihood function** is then produced:

$$F_c(\rho) = \rho \ln(\rho/3) - \ln \Gamma(\rho) - 3(\rho/3) + \rho - 1$$

$$= \rho \ln(\rho/3) - \ln \Gamma(\rho) - 1.$$

This function could be maximized by an iterative search or by a simple one-dimensional grid search. Figure E.5 shows the behavior of the function. As expected, the maximum occurs at $\rho = 5.233$. The value of $\beta$ is found as $5.23/3 = 1.743$.

The concentrated log-likelihood is a useful device in many problems. (See Section 16.9.6.c for an application.) Note the interpretation of the function plotted in Figure E.5. The original function of $\rho$ and $\beta$ is a surface in three dimensions. The curve in Figure E.5 is a projection of that function; it is a plot of the function values above the line $\beta = \rho/3$. By virtue of the first-order condition, we know that one of these points will be the maximizer of the function. Therefore, we may restrict our search for the overall maximum of $F(\beta, \rho)$ to the points on this line.

**FIGURE E.5**   Concentrated Log-Likelihood.

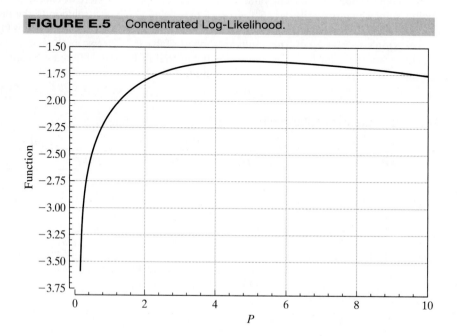

# APPENDIX F

# DATA SETS USED IN APPLICATIONS

The following tables list the variables in the data sets used in the examples and applications in the text. With the exception of the Bertschek and Lechner file, the data sets themselves can be downloaded either from the Web site for this text or from the URLs to the publicly accessible archives indicated below as "*Location*." The points in the text where the data are used for examples or suggested exercises are noted as "*Uses*."

## TABLE F1.1   Consumption and Income, 10 Yearly Observations, 1970–1979

$C =$ Consumption,
$Y =$ Disposable income.

*Source: Economic Report of the President,* 1987, Council of Economic Advisors
*Location:* http://pages.stern.nyu.edu/~wgreene/Text/econometricanalysis.htm
*Use:* Example 1.2.

## TABLE F2.1   Consumption and Income, 11 Yearly Observations, 1940–1950

$Year =$ Date,
$X \quad =$ Disposable income,
$C \quad =$ Consumption,
$W \quad =$ War years dummy variable, 1 in 1942–1945, 0 other years.

*Source: Economic Report of the President,* U.S. Government Printing Office, Washington, D.C., 1983.
*Location:* http://pages.stern.nyu.edu/~wgreene/Text/econometricanalysis.htm
*Uses:* Examples 2.1, 3.2.

## TABLE F2.2   The U.S. Gasoline Market, 36 Yearly Observations 1953–2004

Variables used in the examples are as follows:
$G \quad =$ Per capita U.S. gasoline consumption = expenditure/(population times price index),
$Pg \quad =$ Price index for gasoline,
$Y \quad =$ Per capita disposable income,
$Pnc =$ Price index for new cars,
$Puc =$ Price index for used cars,
$Pp_t =$ Price index for public transportation,
$Pd \quad =$ Aggregate price index for consumer durables,
$Pn \quad =$ Aggregate price index for consumer nondurables,
$Ps \quad =$ Aggregate price index for consumer services,
$Pop =$ U.S. total population in millions.

*Source:* The data were compiled by Professor Chris Bell, Department of Economics, University of North
    Carolina, Asheville. *Sources:* www.bea.gov and www.bls.gov.
*Location:* http://pages.stern.nyu.edu/~wgreene/Text/econometricanalysis.htm
*Uses:* Examples 2.3, 4.4, 4.7, 4.8, 6.7, 7.1, 19.2, 20.3, Sections 6.4, 19.9.3, Application 4.1.

| **TABLE F3.1** | Investment, 15 Yearly Observations, 1968–1982 |
|---|---|

*Year* = Date,
*GNP* = Nominal GNP,
*Invest* = Nominal investment,
*CPI* = Consumer price index,
*Interest* = Interest rate.

*Note:* CPI 1967 is 79.06. The interest rate is the average yearly discount rate at the New York Federal Reserve Bank

*Source: Economic Report of the President,* U.S. Government Printing Office, Washington, D.C., 1983.

*Location:* http://pages.stern.nyu.edu/~wgreene/Text/econometricanalysis.htm

*Uses:* Examples 3.1 and 3.3, Section 3.2.2, Exercise 3.12

| **TABLE F3.2** | Koop and Tobias Labor Market Experience, 17,919 Observations |
|---|---|

The data file is in two parts.
The first file contains the panel of 17,919 observations on 4 time-varying variables:
*Column 1 = Person id* (ranging from 1–2, 178),
*Column 2 = Education,*
*Column 3 = Log of hourly wage,*
*Column 4 = Potential experience,*
*Column 5 = Time trend.*

The second file contains time invariant variables for the 2,178 households.
*Column 1 = Ability,*
*Column 2 = Mother's education,*
*Column 3 = Father's education,*
*Column 4 = Dummy variable for residence in a broken home,*
*Column 5 = Number of siblings.*

*Source:* Koop and Tobias (2004).

*Location: Journal of Applied Econometrics* data archive.
       http://www.econ.queensu.ca/jae/2004-v19.7/koop-tobias/.

*Uses:* Example 9.17, Applications 3.1, 5.1, 6.1, 6.2.

| **TABLE F4.1** | Labor Supply Data from Mroz (1987), 753 Observations |
|---|---|

*LFP* = 1 if woman worked in 1975, else 0,
*WHRS* = Wife's hours of work in 1975,
*KL6* = Number of children less than 6 years old in household,
*K618* = Number of children between ages 6 and 18 in household,
*WA* = Wife's age,
*WE* = Wife's educational attainment, in years,
*WW* = Wife's average hourly earnings, in 1975 dollars,
*RPWG* = Wife's wage reported at the time of the 1976 interview (not = 1975 estimated wage),
*HHRS* = Husband's hours worked in 1975,
*HA* = Husband's age,
*HE* = Husband's educational attainment, in years,
*HW* = Husband's wage, in 1975 dollars,
*FAMINC* = Family income, in 1975 dollars,
*WMED* = Wife's mother's educational attainment, in years,
*WFED* = Wife's father's educational attainment, in years,
*UN* = Unemployment rate in county of residence, in percentage points,
*CIT* = Dummy variable = 1 if live in large city (SMSA), else 0,
*AX* = Actual years of wife's previous labor market experience.

*Source:* 1976 Panel Study of Income Dynamics, Mroz (1987)

*Location:* http://pages.stern.nyu.edu/~wgreene/Text/econometricanalysis.htm

*Uses:* Examples 4.3, 4.5, 6.1, 23.5, 23.13, 24.8.

**TABLE F4.2**   The Longley Data, 15 Yearly Observations, 1947–1962

*Employ* = Employment (1000s),
*Price*   = GNP deflator,
*GNP*    = Nominal GNP (millions),
*Armed*  = Armed forces,
*Year*   = Date.

*Source:* Longley (1967).
*Location:* http://pages.stern.nyu.edu/~wgreene/Text/econometricanalysis.htm
*Use:* Example 4.6.

**TABLE F4.3**   Cost Function, 158 1970 Cross-Section Firm Level Observations

*Id*   = Observation,
*Year* = 1970 for all observations,
*Cost* = Total cost,
*Q*    = Total output,
*Pl*   = Wage rate,
*Sl*   = Cost share for labor,
*Pk*   = Capital price index,
*Sk*   = Cost share for capital,
*Pf*   = Fuel price,
*Sf*   = Cost share for fuel.

*Note:* The file contains 158 observations. Christensen and Greene used the first 123. The extras are the holding companies. Use only the first 123 observations to replicate Christensen and Greene.
*Source:* Christensen and Greene (1976).
*Location:* http://pages.stern.nyu.edu/~wgreene/Text/econometricanalysis.htm
*Uses:* Examples 14.5, 14.8, Applications 4.2, 16.2.

**TABLE F5.1**   Macroeconomics Data Set, Quarterly, 1950I to 2000IV

*Year*    = Date,
*Qtr*     = Quarter,
*Realgdp* = Real GDP (billions),
*Realcons* = Real consumption expenditures,
*Realinvs* = Real investment by private sector,
*Realgovt* = Real government expenditures,
*Realdpi* = Real disposable personal income,
*CPI_U*   = Consumer price index,
*M1*      = Nominal money stock,
*Tbilrate* = Quarterly average of month end 90-day T-bill rate,
*Unemp*   = Unemployment rate,
*Pop*     = Population, mil. interpolate of year-end figures using constant growth rate per quarter,
*Infl*    = Rate of inflation (first observation is missing),
*Realint* = Ex post real interest rate = Tbilrate − Infl. (First observation missing).

*Source:* Department of Commerce, BEA website and *www.economagic.com*
*Location:* http://pages.stern.nyu.edu/~wgreene/Text/econometricanalysis.htm
*Uses:* Examples 5.1, 5.3, 5.4, 7.2, 7.3, 7.4, 11.5, 11.6, 11.8, 12.4, 12.6, 16.7, 19.1, 19.3, 19.4, 20.2, 20.4, 20.5, 20.6, 22.2, 22.3, 22,4, 22.7, Applications 7.1, 13.1, 19.3, Section 20.6.8.e.

| TABLE F5.2 | Production for SIC 33: Primary Metals, 27 Statewide Observations |
|---|---|

*Obs* = Observation number,
*Valueadd* = Value added,
*Labor* = Labor input,
*Capital* = Capital stock.

*Note:* Data are per establishment, labor is a measure of labor input, and capital is the gross value of plant and equipment. A scale factor used to normalize the capital figure in the original study has been omitted. Further details on construction of the data are given in Aigner et al. (1977).
*Source:* Hildebrand and Liu (1957).
*Location:* http://pages.stern.nyu.edu/~wgreene/Text/econometricanalysis.htm
*Use:* Example 5.2, Application 11.1.

| TABLE F6.1 | Costs for U.S. Airlines, 90 Total Observations on 6 Firms for 1970–1984 |
|---|---|

$I$ = Airline,
$T$ = Year,
$Q$ = Output, in revenue passenger miles, index number,
$C$ = Total cost, in $1000,
$PF$ = Fuel price,
$LF$ = Load factor, the average capacity utilization of the fleet.

*Note:* These data are a subset of a larger data set provided to the author by Professor Moshe Kim.
*Source:* Christensen Associates of Madison, Wisconsin.
*Location:* http://pages.stern.nyu.edu/~wgreene/Text/econometricanalysis.htm
*Uses:* Examples 6.2, 8.4, Applications 8.3, 9.2.

| TABLE F6.2 | World Health Organization Panel Data, 901 Total Observations |
|---|---|

*Primary variables:*
*COMP* = Composite measure of health care attainment,
*DALE* = Disability adjusted life expectancy (other measure),
*YEAR* = 1993, . . . , 1997,
*TIME* = 1, 2, 3, 4, 5, $T93$, $T94$, $T95$, $T96$, $T97$ = year dummy variables,
*HEXP* = Per capita health expenditure,
*HC3* = Educational attainment,
*SMALL* = Indicator for states, provinces, etc. (These are additional observations.)
       $SMALL > 0$ implies internal political unit, $= 0$ implies country observation,
*COUNTRY* = Number assigned to country,
*GROUPTI* = Number of observations when $SMALL = 0$. Usually 5, some = 1, one country = 4,
*OECD* = Dummy variable for OECD country (30 countries),
*GINI* = Gini coefficient for income inequality,
*GEFF* = World bank measure of government effectiveness,*
*VOICE* = World bank measure of democratization of the political process,*
*TROPICS* = Dummy variable for tropical location,
*POPDEN* = Population density,*
*PUBTHE* = Proportion of health expenditure paid by public authorities,
*GDPC* = Normalized per capita GDP.

**TABLE F6.2** *Continued*

*Constructed variables:*

| | |
|---|---|
| *LCOMP* | $= \ln COMP$, |
| *LDALE* | $= \ln DALE$, |
| *LGDPC* | $= \ln GDPC$, |
| *LGDPC2* | $= \ln^2 GDPC$, |
| *LHC* | $= \ln HC3$, |
| *LHC2* | $= \ln^2 HC3$, |
| *LHEXP* | $= \ln HEXP$, |
| *LHEXP2* | $= \ln^2 HEXP$, |
| *LHEXPHC* | $= \ln HEXP \times \ln HC3$. |

*Note:* Variables marked * were updated with more recent sources in Greene (2004a). Missing values for some of the variables in this data set are filled by using fitted values from a linear regression.

*Sources:* The World Health Organization [Evans et al. (2000) and www.who.int]

*Location:* http://pages.stern.nyu.edu/~wgreene/Text/econometricanalysis.htm

*Uses:* Examples 6.6, 9.3.

---

**TABLE F6.3** Solow's Technological Change Data, 41 Yearly Observations, 1909–1949

| | |
|---|---|
| *Year* | $=$ Date, |
| *Q* | $=$ Output, |
| *K* | $=$ Capital/labor ratio, |
| *A* | $=$ Index of technology. |

*Source:* Solow (1957, p. 314). Several variables are omitted.

*Location:* http://pages.stern.nyu.edu/~wgreene/Text/econometricanalysis.htm

*Uses:* Application 6.3.

---

**TABLE F8.1** Income and Expenditure Data. 100 Cross-Section Observations

| | |
|---|---|
| *MDR* | $=$ Number of derogatory reports, |
| *Acc* | $=$ Credit card application accepted (1 $=$ yes), |
| *Age* | $=$ Age in years $+$ 12ths of a year, |
| *Income* | $=$ Income, divided by 10,000, |
| *Avgexp* | $=$ Average monthly credit card expenditure, |
| *Ownrent* | $=$ Individual owns (1) or rents (0) home, |
| *Selfempl* | $=$ Self-employed (1 $=$ yes, 0 $=$ no). |

*Source:* Greene (1992)

*Location:* http://pages.stern.nyu.edu/~wgreene/Text/econometricanalysis.htm

*Uses:* Examples 8.1, 8.2, 8.3.

---

**TABLE F8.2** Baltagi and Griffin Gasoline Data, 18 OECD Countries, 19 Years

| | |
|---|---|
| *COUNTRY* | $=$ Name of country, |
| *YEAR* | $=$ Year, 1960–1978, |
| *LGASPCAR* | $=$ Log of consumption per car, |
| *LINCOMEP* | $=$ Log of per capita income, |
| *LRPMG* | $=$ Log of real price of gasoline, |
| *LCARPCAP* | $=$ Log of per capita number of cars. |

*Source:* See Baltagi and Griffin (1983) and Baltagi (2005).

*Location:* Website for Baltagi (2005) http://www.wiley.com/legacy/wileychi/baltagi/supp/Gasoline.dat

*Uses:* Example 8.5, Application 8.2.

---

**TABLE F9.1**     Cornwell and Rupert, Labor Market Data, 595 Individuals, 7 years

| | |
|---|---|
| *EXP* | = Work experience, |
| *WKS* | = Weeks worked, |
| *OCC* | = Occupation, 1 if blue collar, |
| *IND* | = 1 if manufacturing industry, |
| *SOUTH* | = 1 if resides in south, |
| *SMSA* | = 1 if resides in a city (SMSA), |
| *MS* | = 1 if married, |
| *FEM* | = 1 if female, |
| *UNION* | = 1 if wage set by union contract, |
| *ED* | = Years of education, |
| *BLK* | = 1 if individual is black, |
| *LWAGE* | = Log of wage. |

---

*Source:* See Cornwell and Rupert (1988).
*Location:* Website for Baltagi (2005) http://www.wiley.com/legacy/wileychi/baltagi/supp/WAGES.xls
*Location (ASCII form):* http://pages.stern.nyu.edu/~wgreene/Text/econometricanalysis.htm
*Uses:* Examples 9.1, 9.2, 9.4, 9.5, 9.6, 9.7, 9.8, 9.14, 12.3.

---

**TABLE F9.2**     Munnell Productivity Data, 48 Continental U.S. States, 17 years,1970–1986

| | |
|---|---|
| *STATE* | = State name, |
| *ST_ABB* | = State abbreviation, |
| *YR* | = Year, 1970, . . . ,1986, |
| *P_CAP* | = Public capital, |
| *HWY* | = Highway capital, |
| *WATER* | = Water utility capital, |
| *UTIL* | = Utility capital, |
| *PC* | = Private capital, |
| *GSP* | = Gross state product, |
| *EMP* | = Employment, |
| *UNEMP* | = Unemployment rate. |

---

*Source:* Munnell (1990), Baltagi (2005).
*Location:* Website for Baltagi (2005) http://www.wiley.com/legacy/wileychi/baltagi/supp/PRODUC.prn
*Uses:* Examples 9.9, 9.12, 9.13, 10.1, 10.2, 10.3, 10.4, 19.5.

---

**TABLE F9.3**     Grunfeld Investment Data, 100 Yearly Observations on 5 Firms for 1935–1954

*I* = Gross investment, from *Moody's Industrial Manual* and annual reports of corporations,
*F* = Value of the firm from *Bank and Quotation Record* and *Moody's Industrial Manual,*
*C* = Stock of plant and equipment, from *Survey of Current Business.*

---

*Source:* Grunfeld (1958), Boot and deWitt (1960).
*Location:* http://pages.stern.nyu.edu/~wgreene/Text/econometricanalysis.htm
*Uses:* Applications 9.1, 10.2.

**TABLE F10.1**   Cost Function, 145 U.S. Electricity Producers, Nerlove's 1955 Data

*Firm*   = Observation,
*Year*   = 1955 for all observations,
*Cost*   = Total cost,
*Output* = Total output,
*Pl*     = Wage rate,
*Sl*     = Cost share for labor,
*Pk*     = Capital price index,
*Sk*     = Cost share for capital,
*Pf*     = Fuel price,
*Sf*     = Cost share for fuel.

*Note:* The data file contains several extra observations that are aggregates of commonly owned firms. Use only the first 145 for analysis.
*Source:* Nerlove (1960) and Christensen and Greene (1976).
*Location:* http://pages.stern.nyu.edu/~wgreene/Text/econometricanalysis.htm
*Use:* Section 10.4.1.

**TABLE F10.2**   Manufacturing Costs, U.S. Economy, 25 Yearly Observations, 1947–1971

*Year* = Date,
*Cost* = Cost index,
*K*    = Capital cost share,
*L*    = Labor cost share,
*E*    = Energy cost share,
*M*    = Materials cost share,
*Pk*   = Capital price,
*Pl*   = Labor price,
*Pe*   = Energy price,
*Pm*   = Materials price.

*Source:* Berndt and Wood (1975).
*Location:* http://pages.stern.nyu.edu/~wgreene/Text/econometricanalysis.htm
*Use:* Example 10.8, Section 10.4.2.

**TABLE F11.1**   German Health Care Data, Unbalanced Panel, 7,293 Individuals, 27,326 Observations

*ID*        = Person - identification number,
*FEMALE*    = Female = 1; male = 0,
*YEAR*      = Calendar year of the observation,
*AGE*       = Age in years,
*HSAT*      = Health satisfaction, coded 0 (low)–10 (high),
*NEWHSAT*   = Health satisfaction, 0, . . . , 10; see note below,
*HANDDUM*   = Handicapped = 1; otherwise = 0,
*HANDPER*   = Degree of handicap in percent (0–100),
*HHNINC*    = Household nominal monthly net income in German marks/10,000,
*HHKIDS*    = Children under age 16 in the household = 1; otherwise = 0,
*EDUC*      = Years of schooling,
*MARRIED*   = Married = 1; otherwise = 0,
*HAUPTS*    = Highest schooling degree is Hauptschul degree = 1; otherwise = 0,
*REALS*     = Highest schooling degree is Realschul degree = 1; otherwise = 0,

**TABLE F11.1** *Continued*

*FACHHS* = Highest schooling degree is Polytechnical degree = 1; otherwise = 0,
*ABITUR* = Highest schooling degree is Abitur = 1; otherwise = 0,
*UNIV* = Highest schooling degree is university degree = 1; otherwise = 0,
*WORKING* = Employed = 1; otherwise = 0,
*BLUEC* = Blue-collar employee = 1; otherwise = 0,
*WHITEC* = White-collar employee = 1; otherwise = 0,
*SELF* = Self-employed = 1; otherwise = 0,
*BEAMT* = Civil servant = 1; otherwise = 0,
*DOCVIS* = Number of doctor visits in last three months,
*HOSPVIS* = Number of hospital visits in last calendar year,
*PUBLIC* = Insured in public health insurance = 1; otherwise = 0,
*ADDON* = Insured by add-on insurance = 1; otherwise = 0,

*Notes:* In the applications in the text, the following additional variables are used:
    *NUMOBS* = Number of observations for this person. Repeated in each row of data.
    *NEWHSAT* = *HSAT*; 40 observations on HSAT recorded between 6 and 7 were changed to 7.
    Frequencies are: 1 = 1525, 2 = 2158, 3 = 825, 4 = 926, 5 = 1051, 6 = 1000, 7 = 987.
*Source:* Riphahn et al. (2003).
*Location: Journal of Applied Econometrics* Data Archive
        http://qed.econ.queensu.ca/jae/2003-v18.4/riphahn-wambach-million/
*Uses:* Examples 11.10, 11.11, 16.16, 17.5, 18.6, 23.4, 23.8, 23.10, 23.11, 23.14, 23.15, 23.19, 24.11, 25.1, 25.2,
    Applications 16.1, 25.1, 25.2.

**TABLE F13.1** Klein's Model I, 22 Yearly Observations, 1920–1941

*Year* = Date,
*C* = Consumption,
*P* = Corporate profits,
*Wp* = Private wage bill,
*I* = Investment,
*K1* = previous year's capital stock,
*X* = GNP,
*Wg* = Government wage bill,
*G* = Government spending,
*T* = Taxes.

*Source:* Klein (1950).
*Location:* http://pages.stern.nyu.edu/~wgreene/Text/econometricanalysis.htm
*Uses:* Examples 13.6, 13.7, 13.8, Section 13.7.

**TABLE F14.1** Statewide Data on Transportation Equipment Manufacturing, 25 Observations

*State* = Observation,
*ValueAdd* = Output,
*Capita* = Capital input,
*Labor* = Labor input,
*Nfirm* = Number of firms.

*Note:* "Value added," "Capital," and "Labor" in millions of 1957 dollars. Data used in regression examples
    are per establishment. Totals are used for the stochastic frontier application in Chapter 16.
*Source:* A. Zellner and N. Revankar (1970, p. 249).
*Location:* http://pages.stern.nyu.edu/~wgreene/Text/econometricanalysis.htm
*Uses:* Examples 14.4, 16.9, Application 11.2.

**TABLE F15.1** Dahlberg and Johanssen Expenditure Data, 265 Municipalities, 9 Years

*ID* = Identification,
*Year* = Date,
*Expend* = Expenditure,
*Revenue* = Revenue from taxes and fees,
*Grants* = Grants from central government.

*Source:* Dahlberg and Johanssen (2000).
*Location: Journal of Applied Econometrics* data archive.
        http://qed.econ.queensu.ca/jae/2000-v15.4/dahlberg-johansson/dj-data.zip
*Uses:* Examples 15.10, 20.7.

**TABLE F16.1** Program Effectiveness, 32 Cross-Section Observations

*Obs* = Observation,
*TUCE* = Test score on economics test,
*PSI* = Participation in program,
*GRADE* = Grade increase (1) or decrease (0) indicator.

*Source:* Spector and Mazzeo (1980).
*Location:* http://pages.stern.nyu.edu/~wgreene/Text/econometricanalysis.htm
*Uses:* Examples 16.14, 16.15, 18.6, 23.3.

**TABLE F17.1** Bertschek and Lechner Binary Choice Data

$y_{it}$ = 1 if firm $i$ realized a product innovation in year $t$ and 0 if not,
$x_{it2}$ = Log of sales,
$x_{it3}$ = Relative size = ratio of employment in business unit to employment in the industry,
$x_{it4}$ = Ratio of industry imports to (industry sales + imports),
$x_{it5}$ = Ratio of industry foreign direct investment to (industry sales + imports),
$x_{it6}$ = Productivity = ratio of industry value added to industry employment,
$x_{it7}$ = Dummy variable indicating firm is in the raw materials sector,
$x_{it8}$ = Dummy variable indicating firm is in the investment goods sector.

*Source:* Bertcshek and Lechner (1998).
*Location:* These data are proprietary and may not be redistributed.
*Uses:* Examples 17.6, 23.16.

**TABLE F19.1** Bollerslev and Ghysels Exchange Rate Data, 1974 Daily Observations

$Y$ = Nominal return on mark/pound exchange rate, daily.

*Source:* Bollerslev (1986).
*Location:* http://pages.stern.nyu.edu/~wgreene/Text/econometricanalysis.htm
*Uses:* Examples 19.7, 19.8.

**TABLE F21.1** Bond Yield, Moody's Aaa Rated, Monthly, 60 Observations, 1990–1994

*Date* = Year.Month,
*Y* = Corporate bond rate in percent/year.

*Source: National Income and Product Accounts,* U.S. Department of Commerce, Bureau of Economic Analysis, *Survey of Current Business: Business Statistics.*
*Location:* http://pages.stern.nyu.edu/~wgreene/Text/econometricanalysis.htm
*Use:* Example 21.1.

**TABLE F21.2**   Money, Output, Price Deflator Data, 136 Quarterly Observations, 1950–1983

$Y$ = Nominal GNP,
$M1$ = M1 measure of money stock,
$P$ = Implicit price deflator for GNP.

*Source: National Income and Product Accounts,* U.S. Department of Commerce, Bureau of Economic
        *Analysis, Survey of Current Business: Business Statistics.*
*Location:* http://pages.stern.nyu.edu/~wgreene/Text/econometricanalysis.htm
*Uses:* Examples 21.3, 22.1, 22.5.

**TABLE F23.1**   Burnett Analysis of Liberal Arts College Gender Economics Courses, 132 Observations

$y_1$       = Presence of a gender economics course (0/1),
$y_2$       = Presence of a women's studies program on the campus (0/1),
$z_2$       = Academic reputation of the college, coded 1 (best), 2, . . . to 141,
$z_3$       = Size of the full time economics faculty, a count,
$z_4$       = Percentage of the economics faculty that are women, proportion (0 to 1),
$z_5$       = Religious affiliation of the college, 0 = no, 1 = yes,
$z_6$       = Percentage of the college faculty that are women, proportion (0 to 1),
$z_7 - z_{10}$ = Regional dummy variables, South, Midwest, Northeast, West.

*Source:* Burnett (1997). Data provided by the author.
*Location:* http://pages.stern.nyu.edu/~wgreene/Text/econometricanalysis.htm
*Use:* Section 23.8.4.

**TABLE F23.2**   Data Used to Study Travel Mode Choice, 840 Observations, on 4 Modes for 210 Individuals

$Mode$ = Choice: air, train, bus, or car,
$Ttme$  = Terminal waiting time, 0 for car,
$Invc$  = In-vehicle cost-cost component,
$Invt$  = Travel time, in vehicle,
$GC$   = Generalized cost measure,
$Hinc$  = Household income,
$Psize$ = Party size in mode chosen.

*Source:* Greene and Hensher (1997).
*Location:* http://pages.stern.nyu.edu/~wgreene/Text/econometricanalysis.htm
*Uses:* Section 23.11.7.

**TABLE F24.1**   Fair, *Redbook* Survey on Extramarital Affairs, 6,366 Observations

$id$  = Identification number,
$C$   = Constant, value = 1,
$yrb$ = Constructed measure of time spent in extramarital affairs,
$v1$  = Rating of the marriage, coded 1 to 4,
$v2$  = Age, in years, aggregated,
$v3$  = Number of years married,

## TABLE F24.1    Continued

$v4 =$ Number of children, top coded at 5,
$v5 =$ Religiosity, 1 to 4, 1 = not, 4 = very,
$v6 =$ Education, coded 9, 12, 14, 16, 17, 20,
$v7 =$ Occupation,
$v8 =$ Husband's occupation.

*Source:* Fair (1978), data provided by the author.
*Location:* http://pages.stern.nyu.edu/~wgreene/Text/econometricanalysis.htm
*Uses:* Applications 23.1, 23.2, 24.1.

## TABLE F24.2    LaLonde (1986) Earnings Data, 2,490 Control Observations and 185 Treatment Observations

| | |
|---|---|
| $t$ | $=$ Treatment dummy variable, |
| *age* | $=$ Age in years, |
| *educ* | $=$ Education in years, |
| *marr* | $=$ Dummy variable for married, |
| *black* | $=$ Dummy variable for black, |
| *hisp* | $=$ Dummy variable for Hispanic, |
| *nodegree* | $=$ Dummy for no degree (not used), |
| *re74* | $=$ Real earnings in 1974, |
| *re75* | $=$ Real earnings in 1975, |
| *re78* | $=$ Real earnings in 1978. |

Transformed variables added to the equation are
$age2 = Age^2,$
$educ2 = Educ^2,$
$re742 = Re74^2,$
$re752 = Re75^2,$
$blacku74 = Black$ times $\mathbf{1}(re74 = 0).$

*Note:* We also scaled all earnings variables by 10,000 before beginning the analysis.
*Source:* LaLonde (1986).
*Location:* http://www.nber.org/%7Erdehejia/nswdata.htm. The two specific subsamples are in
http://www.nber.org/%7Erdehejia//psid_controls.txt and
http://www.nber.org/%7Erdehejia/nswre74_treated.txt
*Use:* Example 24.10.

## TABLE F25.1    Expenditure and Default Data, 1,319 Observations

| | |
|---|---|
| *Cardhldr* | $=$ Dummy variable, 1 if application for credit card accepted, 0 if not, |
| *Majordrg* | $=$ Number of major derogatory reports, |
| *Age* | $=$ Age in years plus twelfths of a year, |
| *Income* | $=$ Yearly income (divided by 10,000), |
| *Exp_Inc* | $=$ Ratio of monthly credit card expenditure to yearly income, |
| *Avgexp* | $=$ Average monthly credit card expenditure, |
| *Ownrent* | $=$ 1 if owns their home, 0 if rent, |
| *Selfempl* | $=$ 1 if self employed, 0 if not, |
| *Depndt* | $=$ Number of dependents, |
| *Inc_per* | $=$ Income divided by (number of dependents +1), |
| *Cur_add* | $=$ Months living at current address, |
| *Major* | $=$ Number of major credit cards held, |
| *Active* | $=$ Number of active credit accounts. |

*Source:* Greene (1992).
*Location:* http://pages.stern.nyu.edu/~wgreene/Text/econometricanalysis.htm
*Use:* Example 25.3.

**TABLE F25.2** Fair's (1977) Extramarital Affairs Data, 601 Cross-Section Observations

$y$ = Number of affairs in the past year,
$z1$ = Sex,
$z2$ = Age,
$z3$ = Number of years married,
$z4$ = Children,
$z5$ = Religiousness,
$z6$ = Education,
$z7$ = Occupation,
$z8$ = Self-rating of marriage.

*Note:* Several variables not used are denoted $X1, \ldots, X5$.)
*Source:* Fair (1977).
*Location:* http://fairmodel.econ.yale.edu/rayfair/pdf/1978ADAT.ZIP
         http://pages.stern.nyu.edu/~wgreene/Text/econometricanalysis.htm
*Uses:* Section 25.5.2.


**TABLE F25.3** Strike Duration Data, 63 Observations in 9 Years, 1968–1976

$Year$ = Date,
$T$    = Strike duration in days,
$PROD$ = Unanticipated output.

*Source:* Kennan (1985).
*Location:* http://pages.stern.nyu.edu/~wgreene/Text/econometricanalysis.htm
*Uses:* Example 25.4, Application 25.4.


**TABLE F25.4** Ship Accidents, 40 Observations, 5 Types, 4 Vintages, and 2 Service Periods

$Type$     = Ship type,
           $TA, TB, TC, TD, TE$ = Type indicators,
$YearBuilt$ = Year, indicated by
           $Y6064, Y6569, Y7074, Y7579$ = Year constructed indicators,
$O6064, O7579$ = Years operated indicators,
$Months$   = Measure of service amount,
$Acc$      = Accidents.

*Source:* McCullagh and Nelder (1983).
*Location:* http://pages.stern.nyu.edu/~wgreene/Text/econometricanalysis.htm
*Use:* Applications 6.4, 25.3.


**TABLE FC.1** Observations on Income and Education, 20 Observations

$I$ = Observation,
$Y$ = Income.

*Source:* Data are artificial.
*Location:* http://pages.stern.nyu.edu/~wgreene/Text/econometricanalysis.htm
*Uses:* Examples 15.5, 15.7, 16.4, Section 16.6.4.

# APPENDIX G

# STATISTICAL TABLES

| **TABLE G.1** | Cumulative Normal Distribution. Table Entry Is $\Phi(z) = \text{Prob}[Z \le z]$ | | | | | | | | |
|---|---|---|---|---|---|---|---|---|---|
| z | .00 | .01 | .02 | .03 | .04 | .05 | .06 | .07 | .08 | .09 |
| .0 | .5000 | .5040 | .5080 | .5120 | .5160 | .5199 | .5239 | .5279 | .5319 | .5359 |
| .1 | .5398 | .5438 | .5478 | .5517 | .5557 | .5596 | .5636 | .5675 | .5714 | .5753 |
| .2 | .5793 | .5832 | .5871 | .5910 | .5948 | .5987 | .6026 | .6064 | .6103 | .6141 |
| .3 | .6179 | .6217 | .6255 | .6293 | .6331 | .6368 | .6406 | .6443 | .6480 | .6517 |
| .4 | .6554 | .6591 | .6628 | .6664 | .6700 | .6736 | .6772 | .6808 | .6844 | .6879 |
| .5 | .6915 | .6950 | .6985 | .7019 | .7054 | .7088 | .7123 | .7157 | .7190 | .7224 |
| .6 | .7257 | .7291 | .7324 | .7357 | .7389 | .7422 | .7454 | .7486 | .7517 | .7549 |
| .7 | .7580 | .7611 | .7642 | .7673 | .7704 | .7734 | .7764 | .7794 | .7823 | .7852 |
| .8 | .7881 | .7910 | .7939 | .7967 | .7995 | .8023 | .8051 | .8078 | .8106 | .8133 |
| .9 | .8159 | .8186 | .8212 | .8238 | .8264 | .8289 | .8315 | .8340 | .8365 | .8389 |
| 1.0 | .8413 | .8438 | .8461 | .8485 | .8508 | .8531 | .8554 | .8577 | .8599 | .8621 |
| 1.1 | .8643 | .8665 | .8686 | .8708 | .8729 | .8749 | .8770 | .8790 | .8810 | .8830 |
| 1.2 | .8849 | .8869 | .8888 | .8907 | .8925 | .8944 | .8962 | .8980 | .8997 | .9015 |
| 1.3 | .9032 | .9049 | .9066 | .9082 | .9099 | .9115 | .9131 | .9147 | .9162 | .9177 |
| 1.4 | .9192 | .9207 | .9222 | .9236 | .9251 | .9265 | .9279 | .9292 | .9306 | .9319 |
| 1.5 | .9332 | .9345 | .9357 | .9370 | .9382 | .9394 | .9406 | .9418 | .9429 | .9441 |
| 1.6 | .9452 | .9463 | .9474 | .9484 | .9495 | .9505 | .9515 | .9525 | .9535 | .9545 |
| 1.7 | .9554 | .9564 | .9573 | .9582 | .9591 | .9599 | .9608 | .9616 | .9625 | .9633 |
| 1.8 | .9641 | .9649 | .9656 | .9664 | .9671 | .9678 | .9686 | .9693 | .9699 | .9706 |
| 1.9 | .9713 | .9719 | .9726 | .9732 | .9738 | .9744 | .9750 | .9756 | .9761 | .9767 |
| 2.0 | .9772 | .9778 | .9783 | .9788 | .9793 | .9798 | .9803 | .9808 | .9812 | .9817 |
| 2.1 | .9821 | .9826 | .9830 | .9834 | .9838 | .9842 | .9846 | .9850 | .9854 | .9857 |
| 2.2 | .9861 | .9864 | .9868 | .9871 | .9875 | .9878 | .9881 | .9884 | .9887 | .9890 |
| 2.3 | .9893 | .9896 | .9898 | .9901 | .9904 | .9906 | .9909 | .9911 | .9913 | .9916 |
| 2.4 | .9918 | .9920 | .9922 | .9925 | .9927 | .9929 | .9931 | .9932 | .9934 | .9936 |
| 2.5 | .9938 | .9940 | .9941 | .9943 | .9945 | .9946 | .9948 | .9949 | .9951 | .9952 |
| 2.6 | .9953 | .9955 | .9956 | .9957 | .9959 | .9960 | .9961 | .9962 | .9963 | .9964 |
| 2.7 | .9965 | .9966 | .9967 | .9968 | .9969 | .9970 | .9971 | .9972 | .9973 | .9974 |
| 2.8 | .9974 | .9975 | .9976 | .9977 | .9977 | .9978 | .9979 | .9979 | .9980 | .9981 |
| 2.9 | .9981 | .9982 | .9982 | .9983 | .9984 | .9984 | .9985 | .9985 | .9986 | .9986 |
| 3.0 | .9987 | .9987 | .9987 | .9988 | .9988 | .9989 | .9989 | .9989 | .9990 | .9990 |
| 3.1 | .9990 | .9991 | .9991 | .9991 | .9992 | .9992 | .9992 | .9992 | .9993 | .9993 |
| 3.2 | .9993 | .9993 | .9994 | .9994 | .9994 | .9994 | .9994 | .9995 | .9995 | .9995 |
| 3.3 | .9995 | .9995 | .9995 | .9996 | .9996 | .9996 | .9996 | .9996 | .9996 | .9997 |
| 3.4 | .9997 | .9997 | .9997 | .9997 | .9997 | .9997 | .9997 | .9997 | .9997 | .9998 |

**TABLE G.2** Percentiles of the Student's $t$ Distribution. Table Entry Is $x$ Such that $\text{Prob}[t_n \leq x] = P$

| $n$ | .750 | .900 | .950 | .975 | .990 | .995 |
|------|------|------|------|------|------|------|
| 1 | 1.000 | 3.078 | 6.314 | 12.706 | 31.821 | 63.657 |
| 2 | .816 | 1.886 | 2.920 | 4.303 | 6.965 | 9.925 |
| 3 | .765 | 1.638 | 2.353 | 3.182 | 4.541 | 5.841 |
| 4 | .741 | 1.533 | 2.132 | 2.776 | 3.747 | 4.604 |
| 5 | .727 | 1.476 | 2.015 | 2.571 | 3.365 | 4.032 |
| 6 | .718 | 1.440 | 1.943 | 2.447 | 3.143 | 3.707 |
| 7 | .711 | 1.415 | 1.895 | 2.365 | 2.998 | 3.499 |
| 8 | .706 | 1.397 | 1.860 | 2.306 | 2.896 | 3.355 |
| 9 | .703 | 1.383 | 1.833 | 2.262 | 2.821 | 3.250 |
| 10 | .700 | 1.372 | 1.812 | 2.228 | 2.764 | 3.169 |
| 11 | .697 | 1.363 | 1.796 | 2.201 | 2.718 | 3.106 |
| 12 | .695 | 1.356 | 1.782 | 2.179 | 2.681 | 3.055 |
| 13 | .694 | 1.350 | 1.771 | 2.160 | 2.650 | 3.012 |
| 14 | .692 | 1.345 | 1.761 | 2.145 | 2.624 | 2.977 |
| 15 | .691 | 1.341 | 1.753 | 2.131 | 2.602 | 2.947 |
| 16 | .690 | 1.337 | 1.746 | 2.120 | 2.583 | 2.921 |
| 17 | .689 | 1.333 | 1.740 | 2.110 | 2.567 | 2.898 |
| 18 | .688 | 1.330 | 1.734 | 2.101 | 2.552 | 2.878 |
| 19 | .688 | 1.328 | 1.729 | 2.093 | 2.539 | 2.861 |
| 20 | .687 | 1.325 | 1.725 | 2.086 | 2.528 | 2.845 |
| 21 | .686 | 1.323 | 1.721 | 2.080 | 2.518 | 2.831 |
| 22 | .686 | 1.321 | 1.717 | 2.074 | 2.508 | 2.819 |
| 23 | .685 | 1.319 | 1.714 | 2.069 | 2.500 | 2.807 |
| 24 | .685 | 1.318 | 1.711 | 2.064 | 2.492 | 2.797 |
| 25 | .684 | 1.316 | 1.708 | 2.060 | 2.485 | 2.787 |
| 26 | .684 | 1.315 | 1.706 | 2.056 | 2.479 | 2.779 |
| 27 | .684 | 1.314 | 1.703 | 2.052 | 2.473 | 2.771 |
| 28 | .683 | 1.313 | 1.701 | 2.048 | 2.467 | 2.763 |
| 29 | .683 | 1.311 | 1.699 | 2.045 | 2.462 | 2.756 |
| 30 | .683 | 1.310 | 1.697 | 2.042 | 2.457 | 2.750 |
| 35 | .682 | 1.306 | 1.690 | 2.030 | 2.438 | 2.724 |
| 40 | .681 | 1.303 | 1.684 | 2.021 | 2.423 | 2.704 |
| 45 | .680 | 1.301 | 1.679 | 2.014 | 2.412 | 2.690 |
| 50 | .679 | 1.299 | 1.676 | 2.009 | 2.403 | 2.678 |
| 60 | .679 | 1.296 | 1.671 | 2.000 | 2.390 | 2.660 |
| 70 | .678 | 1.294 | 1.667 | 1.994 | 2.381 | 2.648 |
| 80 | .678 | 1.292 | 1.664 | 1.990 | 2.374 | 2.639 |
| 90 | .677 | 1.291 | 1.662 | 1.987 | 2.368 | 2.632 |
| 100 | .677 | 1.290 | 1.660 | 1.984 | 2.364 | 2.626 |
| ∞ | .674 | 1.282 | 1.645 | 1.960 | 2.326 | 2.576 |

**TABLE G.3**  Percentiles of the Chi-Squared Distribution. Table Entry Is $c$ such that $\text{Prob}[\chi_n^2 \leq c] = P$

| $n$ | .005 | .010 | .025 | .050 | .100 | .250 | .500 | .750 | .900 | .950 | .975 | .990 | .995 |
|---|---|---|---|---|---|---|---|---|---|---|---|---|---|
| 1 | .00004 | .0002 | .001 | .004 | .02 | .10 | .45 | 1.32 | 2.71 | 3.84 | 5.02 | 6.63 | 7.88 |
| 2 | .01 | .02 | .05 | .10 | .21 | .58 | 1.39 | 2.77 | 4.61 | 5.99 | 7.38 | 9.21 | 10.60 |
| 3 | .07 | .11 | .22 | .35 | .58 | 1.21 | 2.37 | 4.11 | 6.25 | 7.81 | 9.35 | 11.34 | 12.84 |
| 4 | .21 | .30 | .48 | .71 | 1.06 | 1.92 | 3.36 | 5.39 | 7.78 | 9.49 | 11.14 | 13.28 | 14.86 |
| 5 | .41 | .55 | .83 | 1.15 | 1.61 | 2.67 | 4.35 | 6.63 | 9.24 | 11.07 | 12.83 | 15.09 | 16.75 |
| 6 | .68 | .87 | 1.24 | 1.64 | 2.20 | 3.45 | 5.35 | 7.84 | 10.64 | 12.59 | 14.45 | 16.81 | 18.55 |
| 7 | .99 | 1.24 | 1.69 | 2.17 | 2.83 | 4.25 | 6.35 | 9.04 | 12.02 | 14.07 | 16.01 | 18.48 | 20.28 |
| 8 | 1.34 | 1.65 | 2.18 | 2.73 | 3.49 | 5.07 | 7.34 | 10.22 | 13.36 | 15.51 | 17.53 | 20.09 | 21.95 |
| 9 | 1.73 | 2.09 | 2.70 | 3.33 | 4.17 | 5.90 | 8.34 | 11.39 | 14.68 | 16.92 | 19.02 | 21.67 | 23.59 |
| 10 | 2.16 | 2.56 | 3.25 | 3.94 | 4.87 | 6.74 | 9.34 | 12.55 | 15.99 | 18.31 | 20.48 | 23.21 | 25.19 |
| 11 | 2.60 | 3.05 | 3.82 | 4.57 | 5.58 | 7.58 | 10.34 | 13.70 | 17.28 | 19.68 | 21.92 | 24.72 | 26.76 |
| 12 | 3.07 | 3.57 | 4.40 | 5.23 | 6.30 | 8.44 | 11.34 | 14.85 | 18.55 | 21.03 | 23.34 | 26.22 | 28.30 |
| 13 | 3.57 | 4.11 | 5.01 | 5.89 | 7.04 | 9.30 | 12.34 | 15.98 | 19.81 | 22.36 | 24.74 | 27.69 | 29.82 |
| 14 | 4.07 | 4.66 | 5.63 | 6.57 | 7.79 | 10.17 | 13.34 | 17.12 | 21.06 | 23.68 | 26.12 | 29.14 | 31.32 |
| 15 | 4.60 | 5.23 | 6.26 | 7.26 | 8.55 | 11.04 | 14.34 | 18.25 | 22.31 | 25.00 | 27.49 | 30.58 | 32.80 |
| 16 | 5.14 | 5.81 | 6.91 | 7.96 | 9.31 | 11.91 | 15.34 | 19.37 | 23.54 | 26.30 | 28.85 | 32.00 | 34.27 |
| 17 | 5.70 | 6.41 | 7.56 | 8.67 | 10.09 | 12.79 | 16.34 | 20.49 | 24.77 | 27.59 | 30.19 | 33.41 | 35.72 |
| 18 | 6.26 | 7.01 | 8.23 | 9.39 | 10.86 | 13.68 | 17.34 | 21.60 | 25.99 | 28.87 | 31.53 | 34.81 | 37.16 |
| 19 | 6.84 | 7.63 | 8.91 | 10.12 | 11.65 | 14.56 | 18.34 | 22.72 | 27.20 | 30.14 | 32.85 | 36.19 | 38.58 |
| 20 | 7.43 | 8.26 | 9.59 | 10.85 | 12.44 | 15.45 | 19.34 | 23.83 | 28.41 | 31.41 | 34.17 | 37.57 | 40.00 |
| 21 | 8.03 | 8.90 | 10.28 | 11.59 | 13.24 | 16.34 | 20.34 | 24.93 | 29.62 | 32.67 | 35.48 | 38.93 | 41.40 |
| 22 | 8.64 | 9.54 | 10.98 | 12.34 | 14.04 | 17.24 | 21.34 | 26.04 | 30.81 | 33.92 | 36.78 | 40.29 | 42.80 |
| 23 | 9.26 | 10.20 | 11.69 | 13.09 | 14.85 | 18.14 | 22.34 | 27.14 | 32.01 | 35.17 | 38.08 | 41.64 | 44.18 |
| 24 | 9.89 | 10.86 | 12.40 | 13.85 | 15.66 | 19.04 | 23.34 | 28.24 | 33.20 | 36.42 | 39.36 | 42.98 | 45.56 |
| 25 | 10.52 | 11.52 | 13.12 | 14.61 | 16.47 | 19.94 | 24.34 | 29.34 | 34.38 | 37.65 | 40.65 | 44.31 | 46.93 |
| 30 | 13.79 | 14.95 | 16.79 | 18.49 | 20.60 | 24.48 | 29.34 | 34.80 | 40.26 | 43.77 | 46.98 | 50.89 | 53.67 |
| 35 | 17.19 | 18.51 | 20.57 | 22.47 | 24.80 | 29.05 | 34.34 | 40.22 | 46.06 | 49.80 | 53.20 | 57.34 | 60.27 |
| 40 | 20.71 | 22.16 | 24.43 | 26.51 | 29.05 | 33.66 | 39.34 | 45.62 | 51.81 | 55.76 | 59.34 | 63.69 | 66.77 |
| 45 | 24.31 | 25.90 | 28.37 | 30.61 | 33.35 | 38.29 | 44.34 | 50.98 | 57.51 | 61.66 | 65.41 | 69.96 | 73.17 |
| 50 | 27.99 | 29.71 | 32.36 | 34.76 | 37.69 | 42.94 | 49.33 | 56.33 | 63.17 | 67.50 | 71.42 | 76.15 | 79.49 |

**TABLE G.4**   95th Percentiles of the *F* Distribution. Table Entry Is *f* Such that Prob$[F_{n1,n2} \leq f] = .95$

$n_1 = $ *Degrees of Freedom for the Numerator*

| $n_2$ | 1 | 2 | 3 | 4 | 5 | 6 | 7 | 8 | 9 |
|---|---|---|---|---|---|---|---|---|---|
| 1 | 161.45 | 199.50 | 215.71 | 224.58 | 230.16 | 233.99 | 236.77 | 238.88 | 240.54 |
| 2 | 18.51 | 19.00 | 19.16 | 19.25 | 19.30 | 19.33 | 19.35 | 19.37 | 19.38 |
| 3 | 10.13 | 9.55 | 9.28 | 9.12 | 9.01 | 8.94 | 8.89 | 8.85 | 8.81 |
| 4 | 7.71 | 6.94 | 6.59 | 6.39 | 6.26 | 6.16 | 6.09 | 6.04 | 6.00 |
| 5 | 6.61 | 5.79 | 5.41 | 5.19 | 5.05 | 4.95 | 4.88 | 4.82 | 4.77 |
| 6 | 5.99 | 5.14 | 4.76 | 4.53 | 4.39 | 4.28 | 4.21 | 4.15 | 4.10 |
| 7 | 5.59 | 4.74 | 4.35 | 4.12 | 3.97 | 3.87 | 3.79 | 3.73 | 3.68 |
| 8 | 5.32 | 4.46 | 4.07 | 3.84 | 3.69 | 3.58 | 3.50 | 3.44 | 3.39 |
| 9 | 5.12 | 4.26 | 3.86 | 3.63 | 3.48 | 3.37 | 3.29 | 3.23 | 3.18 |
| 10 | 4.96 | 4.10 | 3.71 | 3.48 | 3.33 | 3.22 | 3.14 | 3.07 | 3.02 |
| 15 | 4.54 | 3.68 | 3.29 | 3.06 | 2.90 | 2.79 | 2.71 | 2.64 | 2.59 |
| 20 | 4.35 | 3.49 | 3.10 | 2.87 | 2.71 | 2.60 | 2.51 | 2.45 | 2.39 |
| 25 | 4.24 | 3.39 | 2.99 | 2.76 | 2.60 | 2.49 | 2.40 | 2.34 | 2.28 |
| 30 | 4.17 | 3.32 | 2.92 | 2.69 | 2.53 | 2.42 | 2.33 | 2.27 | 2.21 |
| 40 | 4.08 | 3.23 | 2.84 | 2.61 | 2.45 | 2.34 | 2.25 | 2.18 | 2.12 |
| 50 | 4.03 | 3.18 | 2.79 | 2.56 | 2.40 | 2.29 | 2.20 | 2.13 | 2.07 |
| 70 | 3.98 | 3.13 | 2.74 | 2.50 | 2.35 | 2.23 | 2.14 | 2.07 | 2.02 |
| 100 | 3.94 | 3.09 | 2.70 | 2.46 | 2.31 | 2.19 | 2.10 | 2.03 | 1.97 |
| ∞ | 3.84 | 3.00 | 2.60 | 2.37 | 2.21 | 2.10 | 2.01 | 1.94 | 1.88 |

| $n_2$ | 10 | 12 | 15 | 20 | 30 | 40 | 50 | 60 | ∞ |
|---|---|---|---|---|---|---|---|---|---|
| 1 | 241.88 | 243.91 | 245.95 | 248.01 | 250.10 | 251.14 | 252.20 | 252.20 | 254.19 |
| 2 | 19.40 | 19.41 | 19.43 | 19.45 | 19.46 | 19.47 | 19.48 | 19.48 | 19.49 |
| 3 | 8.79 | 8.74 | 8.70 | 8.66 | 8.62 | 8.59 | 8.57 | 8.57 | 8.53 |
| 4 | 5.96 | 5.91 | 5.86 | 5.80 | 5.75 | 5.72 | 5.69 | 5.69 | 5.63 |
| 5 | 4.74 | 4.68 | 4.62 | 4.56 | 4.50 | 4.46 | 4.43 | 4.43 | 4.37 |
| 6 | 4.06 | 4.00 | 3.94 | 3.87 | 3.81 | 3.77 | 3.74 | 3.74 | 3.67 |
| 7 | 3.64 | 3.57 | 3.51 | 3.44 | 3.38 | 3.34 | 3.30 | 3.30 | 3.23 |
| 8 | 3.35 | 3.28 | 3.22 | 3.15 | 3.08 | 3.04 | 3.01 | 3.01 | 2.93 |
| 9 | 3.14 | 3.07 | 3.01 | 2.94 | 2.86 | 2.83 | 2.79 | 2.79 | 2.71 |
| 10 | 2.98 | 2.91 | 2.85 | 2.77 | 2.70 | 2.66 | 2.62 | 2.62 | 2.54 |
| 15 | 2.54 | 2.48 | 2.40 | 2.33 | 2.25 | 2.20 | 2.16 | 2.16 | 2.07 |
| 20 | 2.35 | 2.28 | 2.20 | 2.12 | 2.04 | 1.99 | 1.95 | 1.95 | 1.85 |
| 25 | 2.24 | 2.16 | 2.09 | 2.01 | 1.92 | 1.87 | 1.82 | 1.82 | 1.72 |
| 30 | 2.16 | 2.09 | 2.01 | 1.93 | 1.84 | 1.79 | 1.74 | 1.74 | 1.63 |
| 40 | 2.08 | 2.00 | 1.92 | 1.84 | 1.74 | 1.69 | 1.64 | 1.64 | 1.52 |
| 50 | 2.03 | 1.95 | 1.87 | 1.78 | 1.69 | 1.63 | 1.58 | 1.58 | 1.45 |
| 70 | 1.97 | 1.89 | 1.81 | 1.72 | 1.62 | 1.57 | 1.50 | 1.50 | 1.36 |
| 100 | 1.93 | 1.85 | 1.77 | 1.68 | 1.57 | 1.52 | 1.45 | 1.45 | 1.30 |
| ∞ | 1.83 | 1.75 | 1.67 | 1.57 | 1.46 | 1.39 | 1.34 | 1.31 | 1.30 |

**TABLE G.5**  99th Percentiles of the $F$ Distribution. Table Entry Is $f$ Such that $\text{Prob}[F_{n1,n2} \leq f] = .99$

### $n_1 = $ Degrees of Freedom for the Numerator

| $n_2$ | 1 | 2 | 3 | 4 | 5 | 6 | 7 | 8 | 9 |
|---|---|---|---|---|---|---|---|---|---|
| 1 | 4052.18 | 4999.50 | 5403.35 | 5624.58 | 5763.65 | 5858.99 | 5928.36 | 5981.07 | 6022.47 |
| 2 | 98.50 | 99.00 | 99.17 | 99.25 | 99.30 | 99.33 | 99.36 | 99.37 | 99.39 |
| 3 | 34.12 | 30.82 | 29.46 | 28.71 | 28.24 | 27.91 | 27.67 | 27.49 | 27.35 |
| 4 | 21.20 | 18.00 | 16.69 | 15.98 | 15.52 | 15.21 | 14.98 | 14.80 | 14.66 |
| 5 | 16.26 | 13.27 | 12.06 | 11.39 | 10.97 | 10.67 | 10.46 | 10.29 | 10.16 |
| 6 | 13.75 | 10.92 | 9.78 | 9.15 | 8.75 | 8.47 | 8.26 | 8.10 | 7.98 |
| 7 | 12.25 | 9.55 | 8.45 | 7.85 | 7.46 | 7.19 | 6.99 | 6.84 | 6.72 |
| 8 | 11.26 | 8.65 | 7.59 | 7.01 | 6.63 | 6.37 | 6.18 | 6.03 | 5.91 |
| 9 | 10.56 | 8.02 | 6.99 | 6.42 | 6.06 | 5.80 | 5.61 | 5.47 | 5.35 |
| 10 | 10.04 | 7.56 | 6.55 | 5.99 | 5.64 | 5.39 | 5.20 | 5.06 | 4.94 |
| 15 | 8.68 | 6.36 | 5.42 | 4.89 | 4.56 | 4.32 | 4.14 | 4.00 | 3.89 |
| 20 | 8.10 | 5.85 | 4.94 | 4.43 | 4.10 | 3.87 | 3.70 | 3.56 | 3.46 |
| 25 | 7.77 | 5.57 | 4.68 | 4.18 | 3.85 | 3.63 | 3.46 | 3.32 | 3.22 |
| 30 | 7.56 | 5.39 | 4.51 | 4.02 | 3.70 | 3.47 | 3.30 | 3.17 | 3.07 |
| 40 | 7.31 | 5.18 | 4.31 | 3.83 | 3.51 | 3.29 | 3.12 | 2.99 | 2.89 |
| 50 | 7.17 | 5.06 | 4.20 | 3.72 | 3.41 | 3.19 | 3.02 | 2.89 | 2.78 |
| 70 | 7.01 | 4.92 | 4.07 | 3.60 | 3.29 | 3.07 | 2.91 | 2.78 | 2.67 |
| 100 | 6.90 | 4.82 | 3.98 | 3.51 | 3.21 | 2.99 | 2.82 | 2.69 | 2.59 |
| ∞ | 6.66 | 4.63 | 3.80 | 3.34 | 3.04 | 2.82 | 2.66 | 2.53 | 2.43 |

| $n_2$ | 10 | 12 | 15 | 20 | 30 | 40 | 50 | 60 | ∞ |
|---|---|---|---|---|---|---|---|---|---|
| 1 | 6055.85 | 6106.32 | 6157.28 | 6208.73 | 6260.65 | 6286.78 | 6313.03 | 6313.03 | 6362.68 |
| 2 | 99.40 | 99.42 | 99.43 | 99.45 | 99.47 | 99.47 | 99.48 | 99.48 | 99.50 |
| 3 | 27.23 | 27.05 | 26.87 | 26.69 | 26.50 | 26.41 | 26.32 | 26.32 | 26.14 |
| 4 | 14.55 | 14.37 | 14.20 | 14.02 | 13.84 | 13.75 | 13.65 | 13.65 | 13.47 |
| 5 | 10.05 | 9.89 | 9.72 | 9.55 | 9.38 | 9.29 | 9.20 | 9.20 | 9.03 |
| 6 | 7.87 | 7.72 | 7.56 | 7.40 | 7.23 | 7.14 | 7.06 | 7.06 | 6.89 |
| 7 | 6.62 | 6.47 | 6.31 | 6.16 | 5.99 | 5.91 | 5.82 | 5.82 | 5.66 |
| 8 | 5.81 | 5.67 | 5.52 | 5.36 | 5.20 | 5.12 | 5.03 | 5.03 | 4.87 |
| 9 | 5.26 | 5.11 | 4.96 | 4.81 | 4.65 | 4.57 | 4.48 | 4.48 | 4.32 |
| 10 | 4.85 | 4.71 | 4.56 | 4.41 | 4.25 | 4.17 | 4.08 | 4.08 | 3.92 |
| 15 | 3.80 | 3.67 | 3.52 | 3.37 | 3.21 | 3.13 | 3.05 | 3.05 | 2.88 |
| 20 | 3.37 | 3.23 | 3.09 | 2.94 | 2.78 | 2.69 | 2.61 | 2.61 | 2.43 |
| 25 | 3.13 | 2.99 | 2.85 | 2.70 | 2.54 | 2.45 | 2.36 | 2.36 | 2.18 |
| 30 | 2.98 | 2.84 | 2.70 | 2.55 | 2.39 | 2.30 | 2.21 | 2.21 | 2.02 |
| 40 | 2.80 | 2.66 | 2.52 | 2.37 | 2.20 | 2.11 | 2.02 | 2.02 | 1.82 |
| 50 | 2.70 | 2.56 | 2.42 | 2.27 | 2.10 | 2.01 | 1.91 | 1.91 | 1.70 |
| 70 | 2.59 | 2.45 | 2.31 | 2.15 | 1.98 | 1.89 | 1.78 | 1.78 | 1.56 |
| 100 | 2.50 | 2.37 | 2.22 | 2.07 | 1.89 | 1.80 | 1.69 | 1.69 | 1.45 |
| ∞ | 2.34 | 2.20 | 2.06 | 1.90 | 1.72 | 1.61 | 1.50 | 1.50 | 1.16 |

**TABLE G.6** Durbin–Watson Statistic: 5 Percent Significance Points of dL and dU

| n | k = 1 dL | dU | k = 2 dL | dU | k = 3 dL | dU | k = 4 dL | dU | k = 5 dL | dU | k = 10 dL | dU | k = 15 dL | dU |
|---|---|---|---|---|---|---|---|---|---|---|---|---|---|---|
| 15 | 1.08 | 1.36 | .95 | 1.54 | .82 | 1.75 | .69 | 1.97 | .56 | 2.21 | | | | |
| 16 | 1.10 | 1.37 | .98 | 1.54 | .86 | 1.73 | .74 | 1.93 | .62 | 2.15 | .16 | 3.30 | | |
| 17 | 1.13 | 1.38 | 1.02 | 1.54 | .90 | 1.71 | .78 | 1.90 | .67 | 2.10 | .20 | 3.18 | | |
| 18 | 1.16 | 1.39 | 1.05 | 1.53 | .93 | 1.69 | .82 | 1.87 | .71 | 2.06 | .24 | 3.07 | | |
| 19 | 1.18 | 1.40 | 1.08 | 1.53 | .97 | 1.68 | .86 | 1.85 | .75 | 2.02 | .29 | 2.97 | | |
| 20 | 1.20 | 1.41 | 1.10 | 1.54 | 1.00 | 1.68 | .90 | 1.83 | .79 | 1.99 | .34 | 2.89 | .06 | 3.68 |
| 21 | 1.22 | 1.42 | 1.13 | 1.54 | 1.03 | 1.67 | .93 | 1.81 | .83 | 1.96 | .38 | 2.81 | .09 | 3.58 |
| 22 | 1.24 | 1.43 | 1.15 | 1.54 | 1.05 | 1.66 | .96 | 1.80 | .86 | 1.94 | .42 | 2.73 | .12 | 3.55 |
| 23 | 1.26 | 1.44 | 1.17 | 1.54 | 1.08 | 1.66 | .99 | 1.79 | .90 | 1.92 | .47 | 2.67 | .15 | 3.41 |
| 24 | 1.27 | 1.45 | 1.19 | 1.55 | 1.10 | 1.66 | 1.01 | 1.78 | .93 | 1.90 | .51 | 2.61 | .19 | 3.33 |
| 25 | 1.29 | 1.45 | 1.21 | 1.55 | 1.12 | 1.66 | 1.04 | 1.77 | .95 | 1.89 | .54 | 2.57 | .22 | 3.25 |
| 26 | 1.30 | 1.46 | 1.22 | 1.55 | 1.14 | 1.65 | 1.06 | 1.76 | .98 | 1.88 | .58 | 2.51 | .26 | 3.18 |
| 27 | 1.32 | 1.47 | 1.24 | 1.56 | 1.16 | 1.65 | 1.08 | 1.76 | 1.01 | 1.86 | .62 | 2.47 | .29 | 3.11 |
| 28 | 1.33 | 1.48 | 1.26 | 1.56 | 1.18 | 1.65 | 1.10 | 1.75 | 1.03 | 1.85 | .65 | 2.43 | .33 | 3.05 |
| 29 | 1.34 | 1.48 | 1.27 | 1.56 | 1.20 | 1.65 | 1.12 | 1.74 | 1.05 | 1.84 | .68 | 2.40 | .36 | 2.99 |
| 30 | 1.35 | 1.49 | 1.28 | 1.57 | 1.21 | 1.65 | 1.14 | 1.74 | 1.07 | 1.83 | .71 | 2.36 | .39 | 2.94 |
| 31 | 1.36 | 1.50 | 1.30 | 1.57 | 1.23 | 1.65 | 1.16 | 1.74 | 1.09 | 1.83 | .74 | 2.33 | .43 | 2.99 |
| 32 | 1.37 | 1.50 | 1.31 | 1.57 | 1.24 | 1.65 | 1.18 | 1.73 | 1.11 | 1.82 | .77 | 2.31 | .46 | 2.84 |
| 33 | 1.38 | 1.51 | 1.32 | 1.58 | 1.26 | 1.65 | 1.19 | 1.73 | 1.13 | 1.81 | .80 | 2.28 | .49 | 2.80 |
| 34 | 1.39 | 1.51 | 1.33 | 1.58 | 1.27 | 1.65 | 1.21 | 1.73 | 1.15 | 1.81 | .82 | 2.26 | .52 | 2.75 |
| 35 | 1.40 | 1.52 | 1.34 | 1.53 | 1.28 | 1.65 | 1.22 | 1.73 | 1.16 | 1.80 | .85 | 2.24 | .55 | 2.72 |
| 36 | 1.41 | 1.52 | 1.35 | 1.59 | 1.29 | 1.65 | 1.24 | 1.73 | 1.18 | 1.80 | .87 | 2.22 | .58 | 2.68 |
| 37 | 1.42 | 1.53 | 1.36 | 1.59 | 1.31 | 1.66 | 1.25 | 1.72 | 1.19 | 1.80 | .89 | 2.20 | .60 | 2.65 |
| 38 | 1.43 | 1.54 | 1.37 | 1.59 | 1.32 | 1.66 | 1.26 | 1.72 | 1.21 | 1.79 | .91 | 2.18 | .63 | 2.61 |
| 39 | 1.43 | 1.54 | 1.38 | 1.60 | 1.33 | 1.66 | 1.27 | 1.72 | 1.22 | 1.79 | .93 | 2.16 | .65 | 2.59 |
| 40 | 1.44 | 1.54 | 1.39 | 1.60 | 1.34 | 1.66 | 1.29 | 1.72 | 1.23 | 1.79 | .95 | 2.15 | .68 | 2.56 |
| 45 | 1.48 | 1.57 | 1.43 | 1.62 | 1.38 | 1.67 | 1.34 | 1.72 | 1.29 | 1.78 | 1.04 | 2.09 | .79 | 2.44 |
| 50 | 1.50 | 1.59 | 1.46 | 1.63 | 1.42 | 1.67 | 1.38 | 1.72 | 1.34 | 1.77 | 1.11 | 2.04 | .88 | 2.35 |
| 55 | 1.53 | 1.60 | 1.49 | 1.64 | 1.45 | 1.68 | 1.41 | 1.72 | 1.38 | 1.77 | 1.17 | 2.01 | .96 | 2.28 |
| 60 | 1.55 | 1.62 | 1.51 | 1.65 | 1.48 | 1.69 | 1.44 | 1.73 | 1.41 | 1.77 | 1.22 | 1.98 | 1.03 | 2.23 |
| 65 | 1.57 | 1.63 | 1.54 | 1.66 | 1.50 | 1.70 | 1.47 | 1.73 | 1.44 | 1.77 | 1.27 | 1.96 | 1.09 | 2.18 |
| 70 | 1.58 | 1.64 | 1.55 | 1.67 | 1.52 | 1.70 | 1.49 | 1.74 | 1.46 | 1.77 | 1.30 | 1.95 | 1.14 | 2.15 |
| 75 | 1.60 | 1.65 | 1.57 | 1.68 | 1.54 | 1.71 | 1.51 | 1.74 | 1.49 | 1.77 | 1.34 | 1.94 | 1.18 | 2.12 |
| 80 | 1.61 | 1.66 | 1.59 | 1.69 | 1.56 | 1.72 | 1.53 | 1.74 | 1.51 | 1.77 | 1.37 | 1.93 | 1.22 | 2.09 |
| 85 | 1.62 | 1.67 | 1.60 | 1.70 | 1.57 | 1.72 | 1.55 | 1.75 | 1.52 | 1.77 | 1.40 | 1.92 | 1.26 | 2.07 |
| 90 | 1.63 | 1.68 | 1.61 | 1.70 | 1.59 | 1.73 | 1.57 | 1.75 | 1.54 | 1.78 | 1.42 | 1.91 | 1.29 | 2.06 |
| 95 | 1.64 | 1.69 | 1.62 | 1.71 | 1.60 | 1.73 | 1.58 | 1.75 | 1.56 | 1.78 | 1.44 | 1.90 | 1.32 | 2.04 |
| 100 | 1.65 | 1.69 | 1.63 | 1.72 | 1.61 | 1.74 | 1.59 | 1.76 | 1.57 | 1.78 | 1.46 | 1.90 | 1.35 | 2.03 |

*Source:* Extracted from N.E. Savin and K.J. White, "The Dubin–Watson Test for Serial Correlation with Extreme Sample Sizes and Many Regressors," *Econometrica,* 45 (8), Nov. 1977, pp. 1992–1995.

*Note:* k is the number of regressors excluding the intercept.

# REFERENCES

Abowd, J., and H. Farber. "Job Queues and Union Status of Workers." *Industrial and Labor Relations Review,* 35, 1982, pp. 354–367.

Abramovitz, M., and I. Stegun. *Handbook of Mathematical Functions.* New York: Dover Press, 1971.

Abrevaya, J., "The Equivalence of Two Estimators of the Fixed Effects Logit Model." *Economics Letters,* 55, 1997, pp. 41–43.

Abrevaya, J. and J. Huang, "On the Bootstrap of the Maximum Score Estimator." *Econometrica,* 73, 4, 2005, pp. 1175–1204.

Achen, C., "Two-Step Hierarchical Estimation: Beyond Regression Analysis." *Political Analysis,* 13, 4, 2005 pp. 447–456.

Affleck-Graves, J., and B. McDonald. "Nonnormalities and Tests of Asset Pricing Theories." *Journal of Finance,* 44, 1989, pp. 889–908.

Afifi, T., and R. Elashoff. "Missing Observations in Multivariate Statistics." *Journal of the American Statistical Association,* 61, 1966, pp. 595–604.

Afifi, T., and R. Elashoff. "Missing Observations in Multivariate Statistics." *Journal of the American Statistical Association,* 62, 1967, pp. 10–29.

Ahn, S., and P. Schmidt. "Efficient Estimation of Models for Dynamic Panel Data." *Journal of Econometrics,* 68, 1, 1995, pp. 5–28.

Aigner, D. "MSE Dominance of Least Squares with Errors of Observation." *Journal of Econometrics,* 2, 1974, pp. 365–372.

Aigner, D., K. Lovell, and P. Schmidt. "Formulation and Estimation of Stochastic Frontier Production Models." *Journal of Econometrics,* 6, 1977, pp. 21–37.

Aitchison, J., and J. Brown. *The Lognormal Distribution with Special Reference to Its Uses in Economics.* New York: Cambridge University Press, 1969.

Aitken, A. C. "On Least Squares and Linear Combinations of Observations." *Proceedings of the Royal Statistical Society,* 55, 1935, pp. 42–48.

Akaike, H. "Information Theory and an Extension of the Maximum Likelihood Principle." In B. Petrov and F. Csake, eds., *Second International Symposium on Information Theory.* Budapest: Akademiai Kiado, 1973.

Akin, J., D. Guilkey, and R. Sickles, "A Random Coefficient Probit Model with an Application to a Study of Migration." *Journal of Econometrics,* 11, 1979, pp. 233–246.

Albert, J., and S. Chib. "Bayesian Analysis of Binary and Polytomous Response Data." *Journal of the American Statistical Association,* 88, 1993a, pp. 669–679.

Albert, J., and S. Chib. "Bayes Inference via Gibbs Sampling of Autoregressive Time Series Subject to Markov Mean and Variance Shifts." *Journal of Business and Economic Statistics,* 11, 1993b, pp. 1–15.

Aldrich, J., and F. Nelson. *Linear Probability, Logit, and Probit Models.* Beverly Hills: Sage Publications, 1984.

Ali, M., and C. Giaccotto. "A Study of Several New and Existing Tests for Heteroscedasticity in the General Linear Model." *Journal of Econometrics,* 26, 1984, pp. 355–374.

Allenby, G., and J. Ginter. "The Effects of In-Store Displays and Feature Advertising on Consideration Sets." *International*

*Journal of Research in Marketing,* 12, 1995, pp. 67–80.

Allison, P., "Problems with Fixed-Effects Negative Binomial Models." Manuscript, Department of Sociology, University of Pennsylvania, 2000.

Allison, P., and R. Waterman, "Fixed-Effects Negative Binomial Regression Models." *Sociological Methodology,* 32, 2002, pp. 247–256.

Allison, P., *Missing Data.* Beverly Hills: Sage Publications, 2002.

Almon, S. "The Distributed Lag Between Capital Appropriations and Expenditures." *Econometrica,* 33, 1965, pp. 178–196.

Altonji, J., and R. Matzkin, "Panel Data Estimators for Nonseparable Models with Endogenous Regressors." *NBER Working Paper t0267,* Cambridge, 2001.

Alvarez, R., G. Garrett, and P. Lange. "Government Partisanship, Labor Organization, and Macroeconomic Performance." *American Political Science Review,* 85, 1991, pp. 539–556.

Amemiya, T. "The Estimation of Variances in a Variance-Components Model." *International Economic Review,* 12, 1971, pp. 1–13.

Amemiya, T. "Regression Analysis When the Dependent Variable Is Truncated Normal." *Econometrica,* 41, 1973, pp. 997–1016.

Amemiya, T. "Some Theorems in the Linear Probability Model." *International Economic Review,* 18, 1977, pp. 645–650.

Amemiya, T. "Qualitative Response Models: A Survey." *Journal of Economic Literature,* 19, 4, 1981, pp. 481–536.

Amemiya, T. "Tobit Models: A Survey." *Journal of Econometrics,* 24, 1984, pp. 3–63.

Amemiya, T. *Advanced Econometrics.* Cambridge: Harvard University Press, 1985.

Amemiya, T., and T. MaCurdy, "Instrumental Variable Estimation of an Error Components Model." *Econometrica,* 54, 1986, pp. 869–881.

Andersen, D., "Asymptotic Properties of Conditional Maximum Likelihood Estimators." *Journal of the Royal Statistical Society,* Series B, 32, 1970, pp. 283–301.

Anderson, G., and R. Blundell, "Estimation and Hypothesis Testing in Dynamic Singular Equation Systems." *Econometrica,* 50, 1982, pp. 1559–1572.

Anderson, R., and J. Thursby. "Confidence Intervals for Elasticity Estimators in Translog Models." *Review of Economics and Statistics,* 68, 1986, pp. 647–657.

Anderson, T. *The Statistical Analysis of Time Series.* New York: John Wiley and Sons, 1971.

Anderson, T., and C. Hsiao. "Estimation of Dynamic Models with Error Components." *Journal of the American Statistical Association,* 76, 1981, pp. 598–606.

Anderson, T., and C. Hsiao. "Formulation and Estimation of Dynamic Models Using Panel Data." *Journal of Econometrics,* 18, 1982, pp. 67–82.

Anderson, T., and H. Rubin. "Estimation of the Parameters of a Single Equation in a Complete System of Stochastic Equations." *Annals of Mathematical Statistics,* 20, 1949, pp. 46–63.

Anderson, T., and H. Rubin. "The Asymptotic Properties of Estimators of the Parameters of a Single Equation in a Complete System of Stochastic Equations." *Annals of Mathematical Statistics,* 21, 1950, pp. 570–582.

Andrews, D. "A Robust Method for Multiple Linear Regression." *Technometrics,* 16, 1974, pp. 523–531.

Andrews, D. "Heteroskedasticity and Autocorrelation Consistent Covariance Matrix Estimation." *Econometrica,* 59, 1991, pp. 817–858.

Andrews, D. "Tests for Parameter Instability and Structural Change with Unknown Change Point." *Econometrica,* 61, 1993, pp. 821–856.

Andrews, D. "Hypothesis Tests with a Restricted Parameter Space." *Journal of Econometrics,* 84, 1998, pp. 155–199.

Andrews, D. "Estimation When a Parameter Is on a Boundary." *Econometrica,* 67, 1999, pp. 1341–1382.

Andrews, D. "Inconsistency of the Bootstrap When a Parameter Is on the Boundary of the Parameter Space." *Econometrica,* 68, 2000, pp. 399–405.

Andrews, D. "Testing When a Parameter is on a Boundary of the Maintained Hypothesis," *Econometrica,* 69, 2001, pp. 683–734.

Andrews, D. "GMM Estimation When a Parameter is on a Boundary." *Journal of Business and Economic Statistics,* 20, 2002, pp. 530–544.

Andrews, D., and R. Fair, "Inference in Nonlinear Econometric Models with Structural Change." *Review of Economic Studies,* 55, 1988, pp. 615–640.

Andrews, D., and W. Ploberger. "Optimal Tests When a Nuisance Parameter Is Present Only Under the Alternative." *Econometrica,* 62, 1994, pp. 1383–1414.

Andrews, D., and W. Ploberger. "Admissability of the LR Test When a Nuisance Parameter is Present Only Under the Alternative." *Annals of Statistics,* 23, 1995, pp. 1609–1629.

Angrist, J. "Estimation of Limited Dependent Variable Models with Dummy Endogenous Regressors: Simple Strategies for Empirical Practice." *Journal of Business and Economic Statistics,* 29, 1, 2001, pp. 2–15.

Aneuryn-Evans, G., and A. Deaton. "Testing Linear versus Logarithmic Regression Models." *Review of Economic Studies,* 47, 1980, pp. 275–291.

Anselin, L. *Spatial Econometrics:Methods and Models,* Dordrecht: Kluwer Academic Publishers, 1988.

Anselin, L. "Spatial Econometrics," in B. Baltagi, ed., *A Companion to Theoretical Econometrics,* Oxford: Blackwell Puplishers, 2001, pp. 310–330.

Anselin, L., and S. Hudak. "Spatial Econometrics in Practice: A Review of Software Options." *Regional Science and Urban Economics,* 22, 3, 1992, pp. 509–536.

Antweiler, W. "Nested Random Effects Estimation in Unbalanced Panel Data." *Journal of Econometrics,* 101, 2001, pp. 295–312.

Arabmazar, A., and P. Schmidt. "An Investigation into the Robustness of the Tobit Estimator to Nonnormality." *Econometrica,* 50, 1982a, pp. 1055–1063.

Arabmazar, A., and P. Schmidt. "Further Evidence on the Robustness of the Tobit Estimator to Heteroscedasticity." *Journal of Econometrics,* 17, 1982b, pp. 253–258.

Arellano, M. "Computing Robust Standard Errors for Within-Groups Estimators." *Oxford Bulletin of Economics and Statistics,* 49, 1987, pp. 431–434.

Arellano, M. "A Note on the Anderson-Hsiao Estimator for Panel Data." *Economics Letters,* 31, 1989, pp. 337– 341.

Arellano, M. "Discrete Choices with Panel Data." *Investigaciones Economica,* Lecture 25, 2000.

Arellano, M. "Panel Data: Some Recent Developments." In J. Heckman and E. Leamer, eds., *Handbook of Econometrics,* Vol. 5, North Holland, Amsterdam, 2001.

Arellano, M. *Panel Data Econometrics.* Oxford: Oxford University Press, 2003.

Arellano, M., and S. Bond. "Some Tests of Specification for Panel Data: Monte Carlo Evidence and an Application to Employment Equations." *Review of Economics Studies,* 58, 1991, pp. 277–297.

Arellano, M., and C. Borrego. "Symmetrically Normalized Instrumental Variable Estimation Using Panel Data." *Journal of Business and Economic Statistics,* 17, 1999, pp. 36–49.

Arellano, M., and O. Bover. "Another Look at the Instrumental Variables Estimation of Error Components Models." *Journal of Econometrics,* 68, 1, 1995, pp. 29–52.

Arrow, K., H. Chenery, B. Minhas, and R. Solow. "Capital-Labor Substitution and Economic Efficiency." *Review of Economics and Statistics,* 45, 1961, pp. 225–247.

Ashenfelter, O., and J. Heckman. "The Estimation of Income and Substitution Effects in a Model of Family Labor Supply." *Econometrica,* 42, 1974, pp. 73–85.

Ashenfelter, O., and A. Kreuger. "Estimates of the Economic Return to Schooling from a New Sample of Twins." *American Economic Review,* 84, 1994, pp. 1157–1173.

Attfield, C. "Bartlett Adjustments for Systems of Linear Equations with Linear Restrictions." *Economics Letters,* 60, 1998, pp. 277–283.

Avery, R. "Error Components and Seemingly Unrelated Regressions." Econometrica, 45, 1977, pp. 199–209.

Avery, R., L. Hansen, and J. Hotz. "Multiperiod Probit Models and Orthogonality Condition Estimation." *International Economic Review,* 24, 1983, pp. 21–35.

Bai, J. "Estimation of a Change Point in Multiple Regression Models." *Review of Economics and Statistics,* 79, 1997, pp. 551–563.

Bai, J. "Likelihood Ratio Tests for Multiple Structural Changes." *Journal of Econometrics,* 91, 1999, pp. 299–323.

Bai, J., R. Lumsdaine, and J. Stock. "Testing for and Dating Breaks in Integrated and Cointegrated Time Series." Mimeo, Department of Economics, MIT, 1991.

Bai, J., and P. Perron. "Estimating and Testing Linear Models with Multiple Structural Changes." *Econometrica,* 66, 1998a, pp. 47–78.

Bai, J., and P. Perron. "Testing for and Estimation of Multiple Structural Changes." *Econometrica,* 66, 1998b, pp. 817–858.

Baillie, R. "The Asymptotic Mean Squared Error of Multistep Prediction from the Regression Model with Autoregressive Errors." *Journal of the American Statistical Association,* 74, 1979, pp. 175–184.

Baillie, R. "Long Memory Processes and Fractional Integration in Econometrics." *Journal of Econometrics,* 73, 1, 1996, pp. 5–59.

Balestra, P., and M. Nerlove. "Pooling Cross Section and Time Series Data in the Estimation of a Dynamic Model: The Demand for Natural Gas." *Econometrica,* 34, 1966, pp. 585–612.

Baltagi, B. "Pooling Under Misspecification: Some Monte Carlo Evidence on the Kmenta and Error Components Techniques." *Econometric Theory,* 2, 1986, pp. 429–441.

Baltagi, B., "Applications of a Necessary and Sufficient Condition for OLS to be BLUE," *Statistics and Probability Letters,* 8, 1989, pp. 457–461.

Baltagi, B. *Econometric Analysis of Panel Data,* 2nd ed. New York: John Wiley and Sons, 2001.

Baltagi, B. *Econometric Analysis of Panel Data,* 3rd ed. New York: John Wiley and Sons, 2005.

Baltagi, G., S. Garvin, and S. Kerman. "Further Evidence on Seemingly Unrelated Regressions with Unequal Number of Observations." *Annales D'Economie et de Statistique,* 14, 1989, pp. 103–115.

Baltagi, B., and Griffin, J. "Gasoline Demand in the OECD: An Application of Pooling and Testing Procedures." *European Economic Review,* 22, 1983, pp. 117–137.

Baltagi, B., and W. Griffin. "A Generalized Error Component Model with Heteroscedastic Disturbances." *International Economic Review,* 29, 1988, pp. 745–753.

Baltagi, B., and C. Kao. "Nonstationary Panels, Cointegration in Panels and Dynamic Panels: A Survey." *Advances in Econometrics,* 15, pp. 7–51.

Baltagi, B., and Q. Li. "A Transformation That Will Circumvent the Problem of Autocorrelation in an Error Component Model." *Journal of Econometrics,* 48, 1991a, pp. 385–393.

Baltagi, B., and Q. Li. "A Joint Test for Serial Correlation and Random Individual Effects." *Statistics and Probability Letters,* 11, 1991b, pp. 277–280.

Baltagi. B., and Q. Li. "Double Length Artificial Regressions for Testing Spatial Dependence." *Econometric Reviews,* 20, 2001, pp. 31–40.

Baltagi, B., S. Song, and B. Jung. "The Unbalanced Nested Error Component Regression Model." *Journal of Econometrics,* 101, 2001, pp. 357–381.

Baltagi, B., S. Song, and W. Koh. "Testing Panel Data Regression Models with

Spatial Error Correlation." *Journal of Econometrics,* 117, 2003, pp. 123–150.

Bannerjee, A. "Panel Data Unit Roots and Cointegration: An Overview." *Oxford Bulletin of Economics and Statistics,* 61, 1999, pp. 607–629.

Barnow, B., G. Cain, and A. Goldberger. "Issues in the Analysis of Selectivity Bias." In E. Stromsdorfer and G. Farkas, eds. *Evaluation Studies Review Annual,* Vol. 5, Beverly Hills: Sage Publications, 1981.

Bartels, R., and D. Fiebig. "A Simple Characterization of Seemingly Unrelated Regressions Models in Which OLS is BLUE." *American Statistician,* 45, 1992, pp. 137–140.

Basmann, R. "A General Classical Method of Linear Estimation of Coefficients in a Structural Equation." *Econometrica,* 25, 1957, pp. 77–83.

Barten, A. "Maximum Likelihood Estimation of A Complete System of Demand Equations." *European Economic Review,* Fall, 1, 1969, pp. 7–73.

Bazaraa, M., and C. Shetty. *Nonlinear Programming: Theory and Algorithms.* New York: John Wiley and Sons, 1979.

Beach, C., and J. MacKinnon. "A Maximum Likelihood Procedure for Regression with Autocorrelated Errors." *Econometrica,* 46, 1978a, pp. 51–58.

Beach, C., and J. MacKinnon. "Full Maximum Likelihood Estimation of Second Order Autoregressive Error Models." *Journal of Econometrics,* 7, 1978b, pp. 187–198.

Beck, N., and J. Katz. "What to Do (and Not to Do) with Time-Series-Cross-Section Data in Comparative Politics." *American Political Science Review,* 89, 1995, pp. 634–647.

Beck, N., D. Epstein, and S. Jackman. "Estimating Dynamic Time Series Cross Section Models with a Binary Dependent Variable." Manuscript, Department of Political Science, University of California, San Diego, 2001.

Beck, N., D. Epstein, S. Jackman, and S. O'Halloran, "Alternative Models of Dynamics in Binary Time-Series Cross-Section Models: The Example of State Failure," Manuscript, Department of Political Science, University of California, San Diego, 2001.

Beck, N., J. Katz, R. Alvarez, G. Garrett, and P. Lange. "Government Partisanship, Labor Organization, and Macroeconomic Performance: A Corrigendum." *American Political Science Review,* 87, 4, 1993, pp. 945–948.

Becker, S. and A. Ichino, "Estimation of Average Treatment Effects Based on Propensity Scores," *The Stata Journal,* 2, 2002, pp. 358–377.

Beggs, S., S. Cardell, and J. Hausman. "Assessing the Potential Demand for Electric Cars." *Journal of Econometrics,* 17, 1981, pp. 19–20.

Behrman, J, and P. Taubman. "Is Schooling 'Mostly in the Genes'? Nature-Nurture Decomposition Using Data on Relatives." *Journal of Political Economy,* 97, 6, 1989, pp. 1425–1446

Bekker, P., and T. Wansbeek. "Identification in Parametric Models." In Baltagi, B. ed., *A Companion to Theoretical Econometrics,* Oxford: Blackwell, 2001.

Bell, K., and N. Bockstael. "Applying the Generalized Method of Moments Approach to Spatial Problems Involving Micro-Level Data." *Review of Economic and Statistics* 82, 1, 2000, pp. 72–82

Belsley, D. "On the Efficient Computation of the Nonlinear Full-Information Maximum Likelihood Estimator." Technical Report no. 5, Center for Computational Research in Economics and Management Science, Vol. II, Cambridge, MA, 1980.

Belsley, D., E. Kuh, and R. Welsh. *Regression Diagnostics: Identifying Influential Data and Sources of Collinearity.* New York: John Wiley and Sons, 1980.

Ben-Akiva, M., and S. Lerman. *Discrete Choice Analysis.* London: MIT Press, 1985.

Ben-Porath, Y. "Labor Force Participation Rates and Labor Supply." *Journal of Political Economy,* 81, 1973, pp. 697–704.

Bera, A., and C. Jarque. "Efficient Tests for Normality, Heteroscedasticity, and Serial Independence of Regression Residuals: Monte Carlo Evidence." *Economics Letters,* 7, 1981, pp. 313–318.

Bera, A., and C. Jarque. "Model Specification Tests: A Simultaneous Approach." *Journal of Econometrics,* 20, 1982, pp. 59–82.

Bera, A., C. Jarque, and L. Lee. "Testing for the Normality Assumption in Limited Dependent Variable Models." Mimeo, Department of Economics, University of Minnesota, 1982.

Bernard, J., and M. Veall. "The Probability Distribution of Future Demand." *Journal of Business and Economic Statistics,* 5, 1987, pp. 417–424.

Berndt, E. *The Practice of Econometrics.* Reading, MA: Addison-Wesley, 1990.

Berndt, E., and L. Christensen. "The Translog Function and the Substitution of Equipment, Structures, and Labor in U.S. Manufacturing, 1929–1968." *Journal of Econometrics,* 1, 1973, pp. 81–114.

Berndt, E., B. Hall, R. Hall, and J. Hausman. "Estimation and Inference in Nonlinear Structural Models." *Annals of Economic and Social Measurement,* 3/4, 1974, pp. 653–665.

Berndt, E., and E. Savin. "Conflict Among Criteria for Testing Hypotheses in the Multivariate Linear Regression Model." *Econometrica,* 45, 1977, pp. 1263–1277.

Berndt, E., and D. Wood. "Technology, Prices, and the Derived Demand for Energy." *Review of Economics and Statistics,* 57, 1975, pp. 376–384.

Beron, K., J. Murdoch, and M. Thayer. "Hierarchical Linear Models with Application to Air Pollution in the South Coast Air Basin." *American Journal of Agricultural Economics,* 81, 5, 1999, pp. 1123–1127.

Berry, S., J. Levinsohn, and A. Pakes. "Automobile Prices in Market Equilibrium." *Econometrica,* 63, 4, 1995, pp. 841–890.

Bertschek, I. "Product and Process Innovation as a Response to Increasing Imports and Foreign Direct Investment, *Journal of Industrial Economics.* 43, 4, 1995, pp. 341–357.

Bertschek, I., and M. Lechner. "Convenient Estimators for the Panel Probit Model." *Journal of Econometrics,* 87, 2, 1998, pp. 329–372.

Berzeg, K. "The Error Components Model: Conditions for the Existence of Maximum Likelihood Estimates." *Journal of Econometrics,* 10, 1979, pp. 99–102.

Beyer, A. "Modelling Money Demand in Germany." *Journal of Applied Econometrics,* 13, 1, 1998, pp. 57–76.

Bhargava, A., L. Franzini, and W. Narendranathan. "Serial Correlation and the Fixed Effects Model." *Review of Economic Studies,* 49, 1982, pp. 533–549.

Bhargava, A., and J. Sargan. "Estimating Dynamic Random Effects Models from Panel Data Covering Short Periods." *Econometrica,* 51, 1983, pp. 221–236.

Bhat, C. "A Heteroscedastic Extreme Value Model of Intercity Mode Choice." *Transportation Research,* 30, 1, 1995, pp. 16–29.

Bhat, C. "Accommodating Variations in Responsiveness to Level-of-Service Measures in Travel Mode Choice Modeling." Department of Civil Engineering, University of Massachusetts, Amherst, 1996.

Bhat, C. "Quasi-Random Maximum Simulated Likelihood Estimation of the Mixed Multinomial Logit Model." Manuscript, Department of Civil Engineering, University of Texas, Austin, 1999.

Bickel, P., and K. Doksum. *Mathematical Statistics.* San Francisco: Holden Day, 2000.

Billingsley, P. *Probability and Measure.* 3rd ed. New York: John Wiley and Sons, 1995.

Binkley, J. "The Effect of Variable Correlation on the Efficiency of Seemingly Unrelated Regression in a Two Equation Model." *Journal of the American Statistical Association,* 77, 1982, pp. 890–895.

Binkley, J., and C. Nelson. "A Note on the Efficiency of Seemingly Unrelated Regression." *American Statistician,* 42, 1988, pp. 137–139.

Birkes, D., and Y. Dodge. *Alternative Methods of Regression*. New York: John Wiley and Sons, 1993.

Black, F. "Capital Market Equilibrium with Restricted Borrowing." *Journal of Business*, 44, 1972, pp. 444–454.

Blanchard, O., and D. Quah. "The Dynamic Effects of Aggregate Demand and Supply Disturbances." *American Economic Review*, 79, 1989, pp. 655–673.

Blinder, A. "Wage Discrimination: Reduced Form and Structural Estimates." *Journal of Human Resources*, 8, 1973, pp. 436–455.

Blundell, R., ed. "Specification Testing in Limited and Discrete Dependent Variable Models." *Journal of Econometrics*, 34, 1/2, 1987, pp. 1–274.

Blundell, R., M. Browning, and I. Crawford. "Nonparametric Engel Curves and Revealed Preference." *Econometrica*, 71, 1, 2003, pp. 205–240.

Blundell, R., and S. Bond. "Initial Conditions and Moment Restrictions in Dynamic Panel Data Models." *Journal of Econometrics*, 87, 1998, pp. 115–143.

Blundell, R., F. Laisney, and M. Lechner. "Alternative Interpretations of Hours Information in an Econometric Model of Labour Supply." *Empirical Economics*, 18, 1993, pp. 393–415.

Bockstael, N., I. Strand, K. McConnell, and F. Arsanjani. "Sample Selection Bias in the Estimation of Recreation Demand Functions: An Application to Sport Fishing." *Land Economics*, 66, 1990, pp. 40–49.

Boes, S., and R. Winkelmann. "Ordered Response Models." Working Paper 0507, Socioeconomic Institute, University of Zurich, 2005.

Bollerslev, T. "Generalized Autoregressive Conditional Heteroscedasticity." *Journal of Econometrics*, 31, 1986, pp. 307–327.

Bollerslev, T., R. Chou, and K. Kroner. "ARCH Modeling in Finance." *Journal of Econometrics*, 52, 1992, pp. 5–59.

Bollerslev, T., and E. Ghysels. "Periodic Autoregressive Conditional Heteroscedasticity." *Journal of Business and Economic Statistics*, 14, 1996, pp. 139–151.

Bollerslev, T., and J. Wooldridge. "Quasi-Maximum Likelihood Estimation and Inference in Dynamic Models with Time-Varying Covariances." *Econometric Reviews*, 11, 1992, pp. 143–172.

Boot, J., and G. deWitt. "Investment Demand: An Empirical Contribution to the Aggregation Problem." *International Economic Review*, 1, 1960, pp. 3–30.

Borjas, G., and G. Sueyoshi. "A Two-Stage Estimator for Probit Models with Structural Group Effects." *Journal of Econometrics*, 64, 1/2, 1994, pp. 165–182.

Börsch-Supan, A., and V. Hajivassiliou. "Smooth Unbiased Multivariate Probability Simulators for Maximum Likelihood Estimation of Limited Dependent Variable Models." *Journal of Econometrics*, 58, 3, 1990, pp. 347–368.

Boskin, M. "A Conditional Logit Model of Occupational Choice." *Journal of Political Economy*, 82, 1974, pp. 389–398.

Bound, J., D. Jaeger, and R. Baker. "Problems with Instrumental Variables Estimation When the Correlation Between the Instruments and the Endogenous Explanatory Variables Is Weak." *Journal of the American Statistical Association*, 90, 1995, pp. 443–450.

Bourguignon, F., Ferriera, F., and P. Leite. "Beyond Oaxaca-Blinder: Accounting for Differences in Household Income Distributions Across Countries." Discussion Paper 452, Department of Economics, Pontifica University, Catolica do Rio de Janiero, 2002. http://www.econ.pucrio.rb/pdf/td452.pdf.

Bover, O., and M. Arellano. "Estimating Dynamic Limited Dependent Variable Models from Panel Data." *Investigaciones Economicas, Econometrics Special Issue*, 21, 1997, pp. 141–165.

Box, G., and D. Cox. "An Analysis of Transformations." *Journal of the Royal Statistical Society*, 1964, Series B, 1964, pp. 211–264.

Box, G., and G. Jenkins. *Time Series Analysis: Forecasting and Control*. 2nd ed. San Francisco: Holden Day, 1984.

Box, G., and M. Muller. "A Note on the Generation of Random Normal Deviates." *Annals of Mathematical Statistics,* 29, 1958, pp. 610–611.

Box, G., and D. Pierce. "Distribution of Residual Autocorrelations in Autoregressive Moving Average Time Series Models." *Journal of the American Statistical Association,* 65, 1970, pp. 1509–1526.

Boyes, W., D. Hoffman, and S. Low. "An Econometric Analysis of the Bank Credit Scoring Problem." *Journal of Econometrics,* 40, 1989, pp. 3–14.

Brannas, K. "Explanatory Variables in the AR(1) Count Data Model." Working Paper No. 381, Department of Economics, University of Umea, Sweden, 1995.

Brant, R. "Assessing Proportionality in the Proportional Odds Model for Ordered Logistic Regression." *Biometrics,* 46, 1990, pp. 1171–1178.

Brannas, K., and P. Johanssen. "Panel Data Regressions for Counts." Manuscript, Department of Economics, University of Umea, Sweden, 1994.

Breitung, J. "The Local Power of Some Unit Root Tests for Panel Data." *Advances in Econometrics,* 15, 2000, pp. 161–177.

Breslaw, J. "Evaluation of Multivariate Normal Probabilities Using a Low Variance Simulator." *Review of Economics and Statistics,* 76, 1994, pp. 673–682.

Breusch, T. "Testing for Autocorrelation in Dynamic Linear Models." *Australian Economic Papers,* 17, 1978, pp. 334–355.

Breusch, T., and A. Pagan. "A Simple Test for Heteroscedasticity and Random Coefficient Variation." *Econometrica,* 47, 1979, pp. 1287–1294.

Breusch, T., and A. Pagan. "The LM Test and Its Applications to Model Specification in Econometrics." *Review of Economic Studies,* 47, 1980, pp. 239–254.

Brock, W., and S. Durlauf. "Discrete Choice with Social Interactions." Working Paper #2007, Department of Economics, University of Wisconsin, Madison, 2000.

Brown, B., J. Durbin, and J. Evans. "Techniques for Testing the Constancy of Regression Relationships over Time." *Journal of the Royal Statistical Society, Series B,* 37, 1975, pp. 149–172.

Brown, P., A. Kleidon, and T. Marsh. "New Evidence on the Nature of Size Related Anomalies in Stock Prices." *Journal of Financial Economics,* 12, 1983, pp. 33–56.

Brown, B., and M. Walker. "Stochastic Specification in Random Production Models of Cost-Minimizing Firms." *Journal of Econometrics,* 66, 1995, pp. 175–205.

Brown, C., and R. Moffitt. "The Effect of Ignoring Heteroscedasticity on Estimates of the Tobit Model." Mimeo, University of Maryland, Department of Economics, June 1982.

Brundy, J., and D. Jorgenson. "Consistent and Efficient Estimation of Systems of Simultaneous Equations by Means of Instrumental Variables." *Review of Economics and Statistics,* 53, 1971, pp. 207–224.

Burnett, N. "Gender Economics Courses in Liberal Arts Colleges." *Journal of Economic Education,* 28, 4, 1997, pp. 369–377.

Burnside, C. and M. Eichenbaum. "Small-Sample Properties of GMM-Based Wald Tests." *Journal of Business and Economic Statistics,* 14, 3, 1996, pp. 294–308.

Buse, A. "Goodness of Fit in Generalized Least Squares Estimation." *American Statistician,* 27, 1973, pp. 106–108.

Buse, A. "The Likelihood Ratio, Wald, and Lagrange Multiplier Tests: An Expository Note." *American Statistician,* 36, 1982, pp. 153–157.

Butler, J., and R. Moffitt. "A Computationally Efficient Quadrature Procedure for the One Factor Multinomial Probit Model." *Econometrica,* 50, 1982, pp. 761–764.

Butler, J., and P. Chatterjee. "Pet Econometrics: Ownershop of Cats and Dogs." Working Paper 95-WP1, Department of Economics, Vanderbilt University, 1995.

Butler, J., and P. Chatterjee. "Tests of the Specification of Univariate and Bivariate Ordered Probit." *Review of Economics and Statistics,* 79, 1997, pp. 343–347.

Butler, J., T. Finegan, and J. Siegfried. "Does More Calculus Improve Student

Learning in Intermediate Micro and Macro Economic Theory?" *American Economic Review,* 84, 1994, pp. 206–210.

Butler, R., J. McDonald, R. Nelson, and S. White. "Robust and Partially Adaptive Estimation of Regression Models." *Review of Economics and Statistics,* 72, 1990, pp. 321–327.

Calhoun, C. "BIVOPROB: Computer Program for Maximum-Likelihood Estimation of Bivariate Ordered-Probit Models for Censored Data, Version 11.92." *Economic Journal,* 105, 1995, pp. 786–787.

Cameron, A., and P. Trivedi. "Econometric Models Based on Count Data: Comparisons and Applications of Some Estimators and Tests." *Journal of Applied Econometrics,* 1, 1986, pp. 29–54.

Cameron, A., and P. Trivedi. "Regression-Based Tests for Overdispersion in the Poisson Model." *Journal of Econometrics,* 46, 1990, pp. 347–364.

Cameron, C., and P. Trivedi. *Regression Analysis of Count Data.* New York: Cambridge University Press, 1998.

Cameron, C., and P. Trivedi. *Microeconometrics: Methods and Applications.* Cambridge: Cambridge University Press, 2005.

Cameron, C., T. Li, P. Trivedi, and D. Zimmer. "Modeling the Differences in Counted Outcomes Using Bivariate Copula Models: With Applications to Mismeasured Counts." *Econometrics Journal,* 7, 2004, pp. 566–584.

Cameron, C., and F. Windmeijer. "*R*-Squared Measures for Count Data Regression Models with Applications to Health Care Utilization." Working Paper No. 93–24, Department of Economics, University of California, Davis, 1993.

Campbell, J., A. Lo, and A. MacKinlay. *The Econometrics of Financial Markets.* Princeton: Princeton University Press, 1997.

Campbell, J., and G. Mankiw. "Consumption, Income, and Interest Rates: Reinterpreting the Time Series Evidence." Working Paper 2924, NBER, Cambridge, MA, 1989.

Campbell, J., and P. Perron. "Pitfalls and Opportunities: What Macroeconomists Should Know About Unit Roots." National Bureau of Economic Research, Macroeconomics Conference, Cambridge, MA, February 1991.

Cappellari, L., and S. Jenkins, "Calculation of Multivariate Normal Probabilities by Simulation, with Applications to Maximum Simulated Likelihood Estimation," Discussion Paper 2112, IZA, 2006.

Carey, K., "A Panel Data Design for Estimation of Hospital Cost Functions," *Review of Economics and Statistics,* 79, 3, 1997, pp. 443–453.

Carlin, B., and S. Chib. "Bayesian Model Choice via Markov Chain Monte Carlo." *Journal of the Royal Statistical Society, Series B,* 57, 1995, pp. 408–417.

Case, A. "Spatial Patterns in Household Demand." *Econometrica,* 59, No. 4, 1991, pp. 953–965.

Casella, G., and E. George. "Explaining the Gibbs Sampler." *American Statistician,* 46, 3, 1992, pp. 167–174.

Caudill, S. "An Advantage of the Linear Probability Model Over Probit or Logit." *Oxford Bulletin of Economics and Statistics,* 50, 1988, pp. 425–427.

Caves, D., L. Christensen, and M. Trethaway. "Flexible Cost Functions for Multiproduct Firms." *Review of Economics and Statistics,* 62, 1980, pp. 477–481.

Cecchetti, S. "The Frequency of Price Adjustment: A Study of the Newsstand Prices of Magazines." *Journal of Econometrics,* 31, 3, pp. 255–274.

Cecchetti, S.. "Comment." In G. Mankiw, ed., *Monetary Policy.* Chicago: University of Chicago Press, 1994.

Cecchetti, S., and R. Rich. "Structural Estimates of the U.S. Sacrifice Ratio. *Journal of Business and Economic Statistics,* 19, 4, 2001, pp. 416–427.

Chamberlain, G. "Omitted Variable Bias in Panel Data: Estimating the Returns to

Schooling." *Annales de L'Insee,* 30/31, 1978, pp. 49–82.

Chamberlain, G. "Analysis of Covariance with Qualitative Data." *Review of Economic Studies,* 47, 1980, pp. 225–238.

Chamberlain, G. "Multivariate Regression Models For Panel Data." *Journal of Econometrics,* 18, 1, 1982, pp. 5–46.

Chamberlain, G. "Panel Data." In Z. Griliches and M. Intriligator, eds., *Handbook of Econometrics.* Amsterdam: North Holland, 1984.

Chamberlain, G. "Heterogeneity, Omitted Variable Bias and Duration Dependence." in J. Heckman and B. Singer, eds., *Longitudinal Analysis of Labor Market Data.* Cambridge: Cambridge University Press, 1985.

Chamberlain, G. "Asymptotic Efficiency in Estimation with Conditional Moment Restrictions." *Journal of Econometrics,* 34, 1987, pp. 305–334.

Chamberlain, G., and E. Leamer. "Matrix Weighted Averages and Posterior Bounds." *Journal of the Royal Statistical Society, Series B,* 1976, pp. 73–84.

Chambers, R. *Applied Production Analysis: A Dual Approach.* New York: Cambridge University Press, 1988.

Charlier, E., B. Melenberg, and A. Van Soest. "A Smoothed Maximum Score Estimator for the Binary Choice Panel Data Model with an Application to Labor Force Participation." *Statistica Neerlander,* 49, 1995, pp. 324–343.

Chatfield, C. *The Analysis of Time Series: An Introduction,* 5th ed. London: Chapman and Hall, 1996.

Chavez, J., and K. Segerson. "Stochastic Specification and Estimation of Share Equation Systems." *Journal of Econometrics,* 35, 1987, pp. 337–358.

Chen, T. "Root N Consistent Estimation of a Panel Data Sample Selection Model." Manuscript, Hong Kong University of Science and Technology, 1998.

Chesher, A., and M. Irish. "Residual Analysis in the Grouped Data and Censored

Normal Linear Model." *Journal of Econometrics,* 34, 1987, pp. 33–62.

Chesher, A., T. Lancaster, and M. Irish. "On Detecting the Failure of Distributional Assumptions." *Annales de L'Insee,* 59/60, 1985, pp. 7–44.

Chung, C., and A. Goldberger. "Proportional Projections in Limited Dependent Variable Models." *Econometrica,* 52, 1984, pp. 531–534.

Cheung, Y. "Long Memory in Foreign-Exchange Rates." *Journal of Business and Economic Statistics,* 11, 1, 1993, pp. 93–102.

Chiappori, R. "Econometric Models of Insurance Under Asymmetric Information." Manuscript, Department of Economics, University of Chicago, 1998.

Chib, S. "Bayes Regression for the Tobit Censored Regression Model." *Journal of Econometrics,* 51, 1992, pp. 79–99.

Chou, R. "Volatility Persistence and Stock Valuations: Some Empirical Evidence Using GARCH." *Journal of Applied Econometrics,* 3, 1988, pp. 279–294.

Chib, S., and E. Greenberg. "Understanding the Metropolis-Hastings Alagorithm." *The American Statistician,* 49, 4, 1995, pp. 327–335.

Chib, S., and E. Greenberg. "Markov Chain Monte Carlo Simulation Methods in Econometrics." *Econometric Theory,* 12, 1996, pp. 409–431.

Chow, G. "Tests of Equality Between Sets of Coefficients in Two Linear Regressions." *Econometrica,* 28, 1960, pp. 591–605.

Chow, G. "Random and Changing Coefficient Models." In Griliches, Z. and M. Intriligator, eds., *Handbook of Econometrics,* Vol. 2, Amsterdam: North Holland, 1984.

Christensen, L., and W. Greene. "Economies of Scale in U.S. Electric Power Generation." *Journal of Political Economy,* 84, 1976, pp. 655–676.

Christensen, L., D. Jorgenson, and L. Lau. "Transcendental Logarithmic Utility Functions." *American Economic Review,* 65, 1975, pp. 367–383.

Christofides, L., T. Stengos, and R Swidinsky. "On the Calculation of Marginal Effects in the Bivariate Probit Model." *Economics Letters,* 54, 3, 1997, pp. 203–208.

Christofides, L., T. Hardin, and R. Stengos. "On the Calculation of Marginal Effects in the Bivariate Probit Model: Corrigendum." *Economics Letters,* 68, 2000, pp. 339–340.

Cleveland, W. "Robust Locally Weighted Regression and Smoothing Scatter Plots." *Journal of the American Statistical Association,* 74, 1979, pp. 829–836.

Coakley, J., F. Kulasi, and R. Smith. "Current Account Solvency and the Feldstein-Horioka Puzzle." *Economic Journal,* 106, 1996, pp. 620–627.

Cochrane, D., and G. Orcutt. "Application of Least Squares Regression to Relationships Containing Autocorrelated Error Terms." *Journal of the American Statistical Association,* 44, 1949, pp. 32–61.

Congdon, P. *Bayesian Models for Categorical Data.* New York: John Wiley and Sons, 2005.

Conniffe, D. "Estimating Regression Equations with Common Explanatory Variables but Unequal Numbers of Observations" *Journal of Econometrics,* 27, 1985, pp. 179–196.

Conniffe, D. "Covariance Analysis and Seemingly Unrelated Regression Equations." *American Statistician,* 36, 1982a, pp. 169–171.

Conniffe, D. "A Note on Seemingly Unrelated Regressions." *Econometrica,* 50, 1982b, pp. 229–233.

Conway, D., and H. Roberts. "Reverse Regression, Fairness and Employment Discrimination." *Journal of Business and Economic Statistics,* 1, 1, 1983, pp. 75–85.

Contoyannis, C., A. Jones, and N. Rice. "The Dynamics of Health in the British Household Panel Survey." *Journal of Applied Econometrics,* 19, 4, 2004, pp. 473–503.

Cooley, T., and S. LeRoy. "Atheoretical Macroeconomics: A Critique." *Journal of Monetary Economics,* 16, 1985, pp. 283–308.

Cornwell, C., and P. Rupert. "Efficient Estimation with Panel Data: An Empirical Comparison of Instrumental Variable Estimators." *Journal of Applied Econometrics,* 3, 1988, pp. 149–155.

Cornwell, C., and P. Schmidt. "Panel Data with Cross-Sectional Variation in Slopes as Well as in Intercept," Econometrics Workshop Paper No. 8404, Michigan State University, Department of Economics, 1984.

Coulson, N., and R. Robins. "Aggregate Economic Activity and the Variance of Inflation: Another Look." *Economics Letters,* 17, 1985, pp. 71–75.

Council of Economic Advisors. *Economic Report of the President.* Washington, D.C.: United States Government Printing Office, 1994.

Cox, D. "Tests of Separate Families of Hypotheses." *Proceedings of the Fourth Berkeley Symposium on Mathematical Statistics and Probability,* Vol. 1. Berkeley: University of California Press, 1961.

Cox, D. "Further Results on Tests of Separate Families of Hypotheses." *Journal of the Royal Statistical Society, Series B,* 24, 1962, pp. 406–424.

Cox, D. *Analysis of Binary Data.* London: Methuen, 1970.

Cox, D. "Regression Models and Life Tables." *Journal of the Royal Statistical Society, Series B,* 34, 1972, pp. 187–220.

Cox, D., and D. Oakes. *Analysis of Survival Data.* New York: Chapman and Hall, 1985.

Cragg, J. "On the Relative Small-Sample Properties of Several Structural-Equation Estimators." *Econometrica,* 35, 1967, pp. 89–110.

Cragg, J. "Some Statistical Models for Limited Dependent Variables with Application to the Demand for Durable Goods." *Econometrica,* 39, 1971, pp. 829–844.

Cragg, J. "Estimation and Testing in Testing in Time Series Regression Models with

Heteroscedastic Disturbances." *Journal of Econometrics*, 20, 1982, pp. 135–157.

Cragg, J. "More Efficient Estimation in the Presence of Heteroscedasticity of Unknown Form." *Econometrica*, 51, 1983, pp. 751–763.

Cragg., J., "Using Higher Moments to Estimate the Simple Errors in Variables Model," *Rand Journal of Economics*, 28, 0, 1997, pp. S71–S91.

Cragg, J., and R. Uhler. "The Demand for Automobiles." *Canadian Journal of Economics*, 3, 1970, pp. 386–406.

Cramèr, H. *Mathematical Methods of Statistics*. Princeton: Princeton University Press, 1948.

Cramer, J. "Predictive Performance of the Binary Logit Model in Unbalanced Samples." *Journal of the Royal Statistical Society, Series D (The Statistician)*, 48, 1999, pp. 85–94.

Culver, S. and D. Pappell. "Is There a Unit Root in the Inflation Rate? Evidence from Sequential Break and Panel Data Model." *Journal of Applied Econometrics*, 12, 1997, pp. 435–444.

Cumby, R., J. Huizinga, and M. Obstfeld. "Two-Step, Two-Stage Least Squares Estimation in Models with Rational Expectations." *Journal of Econometrics*, 21, 1983, pp. 333–355.

D'Addio, A., Eriksson, T., and P. Frijters. "An Analysis of the Determinants of Job Satisfaction when Individuals' Baseline Satisfaction Levels May Differ." Working Paper 2003-16, Center for Applied Microeconometrics, University of Copenhagen, 2003.

Dahlberg, M., and E. Johansson. "An Examination of the Dynamic Behaviour of Local Governments Using GMM Bootstrapping Methods."*Journal of Applied Econometrics*, 15, 2000, pp. 401–416.

Das, M., and A. van Soest. "A Panel Data Model for Subjective Information on Household Income Growth." *Journal of Economic Behavior and Organization* 40, 2000, 409–426.

Dastoor, N. "Some Aspects of Testing Nonnested Hypotheses." *Journal of Econometrics*, 21, 1983, pp. 213–228.

Davidson, A., and D. Hinkley. *Bootstrap Methods and Their Application*. Cambridge: Cambridge University Press, 1997.

Davidson, J. *Econometric Theory*. Oxford: Blackwell, 2000.

Davidson, R., and J. MacKinnon. "Several Tests for Model Specification in the Presence of Alternative Hypotheses." *Econometrica*, 49, 1981, pp. 781–793.

Davidson, R., and J. MacKinnon. "Convenient Specification Tests for Logit and Probit Models." *Journal of Econometrics*, 25, 1984, pp. 241–262.

Davidson, R., and J. MacKinnon. "Testing Linear and Loglinear Regressions Against Box–Cox Alternatives." *Canadian Journal of Economics*, 18, 1985, pp. 499–517.

Davidson, R. and J. MacKinnon. *Estimation and Inference in Econometrics*. New York: Oxford University Press, 1993.

Davidson, R., and J. MacKinnon. *Econometric Theory and Methods*. New York: Oxford University Press, 2004.

Davidson, R. and J. MacKinnon. "Bootstrap Methods in Econometrics." In T. Mills and K. Patterson, eds., *Palgrave Handbook of Econometrics, Volume 1: Econometric Theory*, Hampshire: Palgrave Macmillan, 2006.

Deaton, A. "Demand Analysis." In Z. Griliches and M. Intriligator, eds., *Handbook of Econometrics*, Vol. 2, pp. 1767–1839, Amsterdam: North Holland, 1986.

Deaton, A., and J. Muellbauer. *Economics and Consumer Behavior*. New York: Cambridge University Press, 1980.

Deaton, A. "Model Selection Procedures, or, Does the Consumption Function Exist?" In G. Chow and P. Corsi, eds., *Evaluating the Reliability of Macroeconomic Models*. New York: John Wiley and Sons, 1982.

Deb, P., and P. K. Trivedi. "The Structure of Demand for Health Care: Latent Class versus Two-part Models." *Journal of Health Economics*, 21, 2002, pp. 601–625.

Debreu, G. "The Coefficient of Resource Utilization." *Econometrica*, 19, 3, 1951, pp. 273–292.

DeMaris, A. *Regression with Social Data: Modeling Continuous and Limited Response Variables*. Hoboken, NJ: Wiley, 2004.

Dehejia, R., and S. Wahba. "Causal Effects in Non-Experimental Studies: Evaluating the Valuation of Training Programs." *Journal of the American Statistical Association*, 94, 1999, pp. 1053–1062.

Dempster, A., N. Laird, and D. Rubin. "Maximum Likelihood Estimation from Incomplete Data via the EM Algorithm." *Journal of the Royal Statistical Society, Series B*, 39, 1977, pp. 1–38.

Denton, F. "Single Equation Estimators and Aggregation Restrictions When Equations Have the Same Set of Regressors." *Journal of Econometrics*, 8, 1978, pp. 173–179.

DesChamps, P. "Full Maximum Likelihood Estimation of Dynamic Demand Models." *Journal of Econometrics*, 82, 1998, pp. 335–359.

Dezhbaksh, H. "The Inappropriate Use of Serial Correlation Tests in Dynamic Linear Models." *Review of Economics and Statistics*, 72, 1990, pp. 126–132.

Dhrymes, P. "Restricted and Unrestricted Reduced Forms." *Econometrica*, 41, 1973, pp. 119–134.

Dhrymes, P. *Distributed Lags: Problems of Estimation and Formulation*. San Francisco: Holden Day, 1971.

Dhrymes, P. "Limited Dependent Variables." In Z. Griliches and M. Intriligator, eds., *Handbook of Econometrics*, Vol. 2, Amsterdam: North Holland, 1984.

Dhrymes, P. "Specification Tests in Simultaneous Equation Systems." *Journal of Econometrics*, 64, 1994, pp. 45–76.

Dhrymes, P. *Time Series: Unit Roots and Cointegration*. New York: Academic Press, 1998.

Dickey, D., W. Bell, and R. Miller. "Unit Roots in Time Series Models: Tests and Implications." *American Statistician*, 40, 1, 1986, pp. 12–26.

Dickey, D., and W. Fuller. "Distribution of the Estimators for Autoregressive Time Series with a Unit Root." *Journal of the American Statistical Association*, 74, 1979, pp. 427–431.

Dickey, D., and W. Fuller. "Likelihood Ratio Tests for Autoregressive Time Series with a Unit Root." *Econometrica*, 49, 1981, pp. 1057–1072.

Dickey, D., D. Jansen, and D. Thornton. "A Primer on Cointegration with an Application to Money and Income." *Federal Reserve Bank of St. Louis, Review*, 73, 2, 1991, pp. 58–78.

Diebold, F. "The Past, Present, and Future of Macroeconomic Forecasting." *Journal of Economic Perspectives*, 12, 2, 1998, pp. 175–192.

Diebold, F. *Elements of Forecasting*, 2nd ed. Cincinnati: South-Western Publishing, 2003.

Diebold, F., and M. Nerlove. "Unit Roots in Economic Time Series: A Selective Survey." In T. Bewley, ed., *Advances in Econometrics*, Vol. 8. New York: JAI Press, 1990.

Dielman, T. *Pooled Cross-Sectional and Time Series Data Analysis*. New York: Marcel-Dekker, 1989.

Diewert, E. "Applications of Duality Theory." In M. Intriligator and D. Kendrick, *Frontiers in Quantitative Economics*. Amsterdam: North Holland, 1974.

Diggle, R., P. Liang, and S. Zeger. *Analysis of Longitudinal Data*. Oxford: Oxford University Press, 1994.

Ding, Z., C. Granger, and R. Engle. "A Long Memory Property of Stock Returns and a New Model." *Journal of Empirical Finance*, 1, 1993, pp. 83–106.

Domowitz, I., and C. Hakkio. "Conditional Variance and the Risk Premium in the Foreign Exchange Market." *Journal of International Economics*, 19, 1985, pp. 47–66.

Doan, T. *RATS 6.3, User's Manual*. Evanston, IL: Estima, 2007.

Doob, J., *Stochastic Process.* New York: John Wiley and Sons, 1953.

Doppelhofer, G., R. Miller, and S. Sala-i-Martin. "Determinants of Long-Term Growth: A Bayesian Averaging of Classical Estimates (BACE) Approach." NBER Working Paper Number 7750, June, 2000.

Dufour, J. "Some Impossibility Theorems in Econometrics with Applications to Structural and Dynamic Models." *Econometrica,* 65, 1997, pp. 1365–1389.

Dufour, J. "Identification, Weak Instruments and Statistical Inference in Econometrics." Scientific Series, Paper Number 2003s-49, CIRANO, University of Montreal, 2003.

Dufour, J. and J. Jasiak. "Finite Sample Limited Information Inference Methods for Structural Equations and Models with Generated Regressors." *International Economic Review,* 42, 2001, pp. 815–843.

Duncan, G. "Sample Selectivity as a Proxy Variable Problem: On the Use and Misuse of Gaussian Selectivity Corrections." *Research in Labor Economics,* Supplement 2, 1983, pp. 333–345.

Duncan, G. "A Semiparametric Censored Regression Estimator." *Journal of Econometrics,* 31, 1986a, pp. 5–34.

Duncan, G., ed. "Continuous/Discrete Econometric Models with Unspecified Error Distribution." *Journal of Econometrics,* 32, 1, 1986b, pp. 1–187.

Durbin, J. "Errors in Variables." *Review of the International Statistical Institute,* 22, 1954, pp. 23–32.

Durbin, J. "Testing for Serial Correlation in Least Squares Regression When Some of the Regressors Are Lagged Dependent Variables." *Econometrica,* 38, 1970, pp. 410–421.

Durbin, J., and G. Watson. "Testing for Serial Correlation in Least Squares Regression—I." *Biometrika,* 37, 1950, pp. 409–428.

Durbin, J., and G. Watson. "Testing for Serial Correlation in Least Squares Regression—II." *Biometrika,* 38, 1951, pp. 159–178.

Durbin, J., and G. Watson. "Testing for Serial Correlation in Least Squares Regression—III." *Biometrika,* 58, 1971, pp. 1–42.

Dwivedi, T., and K. Srivastava. "Optimality of Least Squares in the Seemingly Unrelated Regressions Model." *Journal of Econometrics,* 7, 1978, pp. 391–395.

Efron, B. "Regression and ANOVA with Zero-One Data: Measures of Residual Variation." *Journal of the American Statistical Association,* 73, 1978, pp. 113–212.

Efron, B. "Bootstrapping Methods: Another Look at the Jackknife." *Annals of Statistics,* 7, 1979, pp. 1–26.

Efron, B. and R. Tibshirani. *An Introduction to the Bootstrap.* New York: Chapman and Hall, 1994.

Eicker, F. "Limit Theorems for Regression with Unequal and Dependent Errors." In L. LeCam and J. Neyman, eds., *Proceedings of the Fifth Berkeley Symposium on Mathematical Statistics and Probability.* Berkeley: University of California Press, 1967, pp. 59–82.

Eisenberg, D., and B. Rowe. "The Effect of Serving in the Vietnam War on Smoking Behavior Later in Life." Manuscript, School of Public Health, University of Michigan, 2006.

Elliot, G., T. Rothenberg, and J. Stock. "Efficient Tests for an Autoregressive Unit Root." *Econometrica,* 64, 1996, pp. 813–836.

Enders, W. *Applied Econometric Time Series,* 2nd ed. New York: John Wiley and Sons, 2004.

Engle, R. "Autoregressive Conditional Heteroscedasticity with Estimates of the Variance of United Kingdom Inflations." *Econometrica,* 50, 1982, pp. 987–1008.

Engle, R. "Estimates of the Variance of U.S. Inflation Based on the ARCH Model." *Journal of Money, Credit, and Banking,* 15, 1983, pp. 286–301.

Engle, R. "Wald, Likelihood Ratio, and Lagrange Multiplier Tests in Econometrics."

In Z. Griliches and M. Intriligator, eds., *Handbook of Econometrics,* Vol. 2. Amsterdam: North Holland, 1984.

Engle, R., and C. Granger. "Co-integration and Error Correction: Representation, Estimation, and Testing." *Econometrica,* 35, 1987, pp. 251–276.

Engle, R., and D. Hendry. "Testing Super Exogeneity and Invariance." *Journal of Econometrics,* 56, 1993, pp. 119–139.

Engle, R., D. Hendry, and J. Richard. "Exogeneity." *Econometrica,* 51, 1983, pp. 277–304.

Engle, R., D. Hendry, and D. Trumble. "Small Sample Properties of ARCH Estimators and Tests." *Canadian Journal of Economics,* 18, 1985, pp. 66–93.

Engle, R., and D. Kraft. "Multiperiod Forecast Error Variances of Inflation Estimated from ARCH Models." In A. Zellner, ed., *Applied Time Series Analysis of Economic Data.* Washington D.C.: Bureau of the Census, 1983.

Engle, R., and D. McFadden, eds. *Handbook of Econometrics,* Vol. 4. Amsterdam: North Holland, 1994.

Engle, R., and M. Rothschild. "ARCH Models in Finance." *Journal of Econometrics,* 52, 1992, pp. 1–311.

Engle, R., D. Lilen, and R. Robins. "Estimating Time Varying Risk Premia in the Term Structure: The ARCH-M Model." *Econometrica,* 55, 1987, pp. 391–407.

Engel, R., and B. Yoo. "Forecasting and Testing in Cointegrated Systems." *Journal of Econometrics,* 35, 1987, pp. 143–159.

Estes, E., and B. Honorè. "Partially Linear Regression Using One Nearest Neighbor." Manuscript, Department of Economics, Princeton University, 1995.

Evans, D., A. Tandon, C. Murray, and J. Lauer. "The Comparative Efficiency of National Health Systems in Producing Health: An Analysis of 191 Countries." World Health Organization, GPE Discussion Paper, No. 29, EIP/GPE/EQC, 2000a.

Evans D., A. Tandon, C. Murray, and J. Lauer. "Measuring Overall Health System Performance for 191 Countries." World Health Organization GPE Discussion Paper, No. 30, EIP/GPE/EQC, 2000b.

Evans, G., and N. Savin. "Testing for Unit Roots: I." *Econometrica,* 49, 1981, pp. 753–779.

Evans, G., and N. Savin. "Testing for Unit Roots: II." *Econometrica,* 52, 1984, pp. 1241–1269.

Evans, M., N. Hastings, and B. Peacock. *Statistical Distributions,* 2nd ed. New York: John Wiley and Sons, 1993.

Fair, R. "A Note on Computation of the Tobit Estimator." *Econometrica,* 45, 1977, pp. 1723–1727.

Fair, R. "A Theory of Extramarital Affairs." *Journal of Political Economy,* 86, 1978, pp. 45–61.

Fair, R. *Specification and Analysis of Macroeconomic Models.* Cambridge: Harvard University Press, 1984.

Farrell, M. "The Measurement of Productive Efficiency." *Journal of the Royal Statistical Society, Series A, General,* 120, part 3, 1957, pp. 253–291.

Fiebig, D. "Seemingly Unrelated Regression." In B. Baltagi, ed., *A Companion to Theoretical Econometrics,* Oxford: Blackwell, 2001.

Fiebig, D., R. Bartels, and D. Aigner. "A Random Coefficient Approach to the Estimation of End Use Load Profiles." *Journal of Econometrics,* 50, 1991, pp. 297–328.

Feldstein, M. "The Error of Forecast in Econometric Models When the Forecast-Period Exogenous Variables Are Stochastic." *Econometrica,* 39, 1971, pp. 55–60.

Fernandez, A., and J. Rodriguez-Poo. "Estimation and Testing in Female Labor Participation Models: Parametric and Semiparametric Models." *Econometric Reviews,* 16, 1997, pp. 229–248.

Fernandez, L. "Nonparametric Maximum Likelihood Estimation of Censored Regression Models." *Journal of Econometrics,* 32, 1, 1986, pp. 35–38.

Ferrer-i-Carbonel, A., and P. Frijters. "The Effect of Methodology on the Determinants of Happiness." *Economic Journal,* 114, 2004, pp. 641–659.

Fin, T. and P. Schmidt. "A Test for the Tobit Specification versus an Alternative Suggested by Cragg." *Review of Economics and Statistics,* 66, 1984, pp. 174–177.

Finney, D. *Probit Analysis.* Cambridge: Cambridge University Press, 1971.

Fiorentini, G., G. Calzolari, and L. Panattoni. "Analytic Derivatives and the Computation of GARCH Estimates." *Journal of Applied Econometrics,* 11, 1996, pp. 399–417.

Fisher, F. "Tests of Equality Between Sets of Coefficients in Two Linear Regressions: An Expository Note." *Econometrica,* 28, 1970, pp. 361–366.

Fisher, G., and D. Nagin. "Random Versus Fixed Coefficients Coefficient Quantal Choice Models." In C. Manski and D. McFadden, eds., *Structural Analysis of Discrete Data with Econometric Applications.* Cambridge: MIT Press, 1981.

Fisher, R. "The Theory of Statistical Estimation" *Proceedings of the Cambridge Philosophical Society,* 22, 1925, pp. 700–725.

Fleissig, A., and J. Strauss. "Unit Root Tests on Real Wage Panel Data for the G7." *Economics Letters,* 54, 1997, pp. 149–155.

Fletcher, R. *Practical Methods of Optimization.* New York: John Wiley and Sons, 1980.

Florens, J., D. Fougere, and M. Mouchart. "Duration Models." In L. Matyas and P. Sevestre, *The Econometrics of Panel Data,* 2nd ed., Norwell, MA: Kluwer, 1996.

Fomby, T., C. Hill, and S. Johnson. *Advanced Econometric Methods.* Needham, MA: Springer-Verlag, 1984.

Frankel, J. and A. Rose. "A Panel Project on Purchasing Power Parity: Mean Reversion Within and Between Countries." *Journal of International Economics,* 40, 1996, pp. 209–224.

Freedman, D. "On the So-Called 'Huber Sandwich Estimator' and Robust Standard Errors." *The American Statistician,* 60, 4, 2006, pp. 299–302.

French, K., W. Schwert, and R. Stambaugh. "Expected Stock Returns and Volatility." *Journal of Financial Economics,* 19, 1987, pp. 3–30.

Fried, H., K. Lovell, and S. Schmidt. *The Measurement of Productive Efficiency and Productivity,* 2nd ed. Oxford, UK: Oxford University Press, 2007.

Friedman, M. *A Theory of the Consumption Function.* Princeton: Princeton University Press, 1957.

Frijters P., J. Haisken-DeNew, and M. Shields. "The Value of Reunification in Germany: An Analysis of Changes in Life Satisfaction." *Journal of Human Resources,* 39, 3, 2004, pp. 649–674.

Frisch, R. "Editorial." *Econometrica,* 1, 1933, pp. 1–4.

Frisch, R., and F. Waugh. "Partial Time Regressions as Compared with Individual Trends." *Econometrica,* 1, 1933, pp. 387–401.

Fry, J., T. Fry, and K. McLaren. "The Stochastic Specification of Demand Share Equations: Restricting Budget Shares to the Unit Simplex." *Journal of Econometrics,* 73, 1996, pp. 377–386.

Fuller, W. *Introduction to Statistical Time Series.* New York: John Wiley and Sons, 1976.

Fuller, W., and G. Battese. "Estimation of Linear Models with Crossed-Error Structure." *Journal of Econometrics,* 2, 1974, pp. 67–78.

Gabrielsen, A. "Consistency and Identifiability." *Journal of Econometrics,* 8, 1978, pp. 261–263.

Gali, J. "How Well Does the IS-LM Model Fit Postwar U.S. Data?" *Quarterly Journal of Economics,* 107, 1992, pp. 709–738.

Gallant, A. *Nonlinear Statistical Models.* New York: John Wiley and Sons, 1987.

Gallant, A., and A. Holly. "Statistical Inference in an Implicit Nonlinear Simultaneous Equation in the Context of Maximum Likelihood Estimation." *Econometrica,* 48, 1980, pp. 697–720.

Gallant, R., and H. White. *A Unified Theory of Estimation and Inference for*

*Nonlinear Dynamic Models.* Oxford: Basil Blackwell, 1988.

Garber, S., and S. Klepper. "Extending the Classical Normal Errors in Variables Model." *Econometrica,* 48, 1980, pp. 1541–1546.

Garber, S., and D. Poirier. "The Determinants of Aerospace Profit Rates." *Southern Economic Journal,* 41, 1974, pp. 228–238.

Gaver, K., and M. Geisel. "Discriminating Among Alternative Models: Bayesian and Non-Bayesian Methods." In P. Zarembka, ed., *Frontiers in Econometrics.* New York: Academic Press, 1974.

Gelfand, A., and A. Smith. "Sampling Based Approaches to Calculating Marginal Densities." *Journal of the American Statistical Association,* 85, 1990, pp. 398–409.

Gerfin, M. "Parametric and Semi-Parametric Estimation of the Binary Response Model." *Journal of Applied Econometrics,* 11, 1996, pp. 321–340.

Gelman, A., J. Carlin, H. Stern, and D. Rubin. *Bayesian Data Analysis,* 2nd ed. Suffolk: Chapman and Hall, 2004.

Gentle, J. *Elements of Computational Statistics.* New York: Springer-Verlag, 2002.

Gentle, J. *Random Number Generation and Monte Carlo Methods,* 2nd ed. New York: Springer-Verlag, 2003.

Geweke, J. "Inference and Causality in Econometric Time Series Models." In Z. Griliches and M. Intriligator, eds., *Handbook of Econometrics,* Vol. 2. Amsterdam: North Holland, 1984.

Geweke, J. "Exact Inference in the Inequality Constrained Normal Linear Regression Model." *Journal of Applied Econometrics,* 2, 1986, pp. 127–142.

Geweke, J. "Antithetic Acceleration of Monte Carlo Integration in Bayesian Inference." *Journal of Econometrics,* 38, 1988, pp. 73–90.

Geweke, J. "Bayesian Inference in Econometric Models Using Monte Carlo Integration." *Econometrica,* 57, 1989, pp. 1317–1340.

Geweke, J. *Contemporary Bayesian Econometrics and Statistics.* New York: John Wiley and Sons, 2005.

Geweke, J., M. Keane, and D. Runkle. "Alternative Computational Approaches to Inference in the Multinomial Probit Model." *Review of Economics and Statistics,* 76, 1994, pp. 609–632.

Geweke, J., and R. Meese. "Estimating Regression Models of Finite but Unknown Order." *International Economic Review,* 22, 1981, pp. 55–70.

Geweke, J., M. Keane, and D. Runkle. "Statistical Inference in the Multinomial Multiperiod Probit Model." *Journal of Econometrics,* 81, 1, 1997, pp. 125–166.

Geweke, J., R. Meese, and W. Dent. "Comparing Alternative Tests of Causality in Temporal Systems: Analytic Results and Experimental Evidence." *Journal of Econometrics,* 21, 1983, pp. 161–194.

Geweke, J., and S. Porter-Hudak. "The Estimation and Application of Long Memory Time Series Models." *Journal of Time Series Analysis,* 4, 1983, pp. 221–238.

Gill, J. *Bayesian Methods: A Social and Behavioral Sciences Approach.* Suffolk: Chapman and Hall, 2002.

Godfrey, L. "Testing Against General Autoregressive and Moving Average Error Models When the Regressors Include Lagged Dependent Variables." *Econometrica,* 46, 1978, pp. 1293–1302.

Godfrey, L. *Misspecification Tests in Econometrics.* Cambridge: Cambridge University Press, 1988.

Godfrey, L. "Instrument Relevance in Multivariate Linear Models." *Review of Economics and Statistics,* 81, 1999, pp. 550–552.

Godfrey, L. and H. Pesaran. "Tests of Nonnested Regression Models After Estimation by Instrumental Variables or Least Squares." *Journal of Econometrics,* 21, 1983, pp. 133–154.

Godfrey, L., and M. Wickens. "Tests of Misspecification Using Locally Equivalent Alternative Models." In G. Chow and P. Corsi, eds., *Evaluating the Reliability of Econometric Models*. New York: John Wiley and Sons, 1982, pp. 71–99.

Goffe, W., G. Ferrier, and J. Rodgers. "Global Optimization of Statistical Functions with Simulated Annealing." *Journal of Econometrics,* 60, 1/2, 1994, pp. 65–100.

Goldberger, A. "Best Linear Unbiased Prediction in the Generalized Regression Model." *Journal of the American Statistical Association,* 57, 1962, pp. 369–375.

Goldberger, A. *Econometric Theory*. New York: John Wiley and Sons, 1964.

Goldberger, A. "Estimation of a Regression Coefficient Matrix Containing a Block of Zeroes." University of Wisconsin, SSRI, EME, Number 7002, 1970.

Goldberger, A. "Selection Bias in Evaluating Treatment Effects: Some Formal Illustrations." Discussion Paper 123-72, Institute for Research on Poverty, University of Wisconsin, Madison, 1972.

Goldberger, A. "Dependency Rates and Savings Rates: Further Comment." *American Economic Review,* 63, 1, 1973, pp. 232–233.

Goldberger, A. "Linear Regression After Selection." *Journal of Econometrics,* 15, 1981, pp. 357–366.

Goldberger, A. "Abnormal Selection Bias." In S. Karlin, T. Amemiya, and L. Goodman, eds., *Studies in Econometrics, Time Series, and Multivariate Statistics*. New York: Academic Press, 1983.

Goldberger, A. *Functional Form and Utility: A Review of Consumer Demand Theory*. Boulder: Westview Press, 1987.

Goldberger, A. *A Course in Econometrics*. Cambridge: Harvard University Press, 1991.

Goldfeld, S. "The Demand for Money Revisited." *Brookings Papers on Economic Activity,* 3. Washington, D.C.: Brookings Institution, 1973.

Goldfeld, S., and R. Quandt. "Some Tests for Homoscedasticity." *Journal of the American Statistical Association,* 60, 1965, pp. 539–547.

Goldfeld, S., and R. Quandt. "Nonlinear Simultaneous Equations: Estimation and Prediction." *International Economic Review,* 9, 1968, pp. 113–136.

Goldfeld, S., and R. Quandt. *Nonlinear Methods in Econometrics*. Amsterdam: North Holland, 1971.

Goldfeld, S., and R. Quandt. "GQOPT: A Package for Numerical Optimization of Functions." Manuscript, Department of Economics, Princeton University, 1972.

Goldfeld, S., R. Quandt, and H. Trotter. "Maximization by Quadratic Hill Climbing." *Econometrica,* 1966, pp. 541–551.

Gonzaláz, P., and W. Maloney. "Logit Analysis in a Rotating Panel Context and an Application to Self Employment Decisions." Policy Research Working Paper Number 2069, Washington, D.C: World Bank, 1999.

Gordin, M. "The Central Limit Theorem for Stationary Processes." *Soviet Mathematical Dokl.,* 10, 1969, pp. 1174–1176.

Gourieroux, C., and A. Monfort. "Testing Non-Nested Hypotheses." In Z. Griliches and M. Intriligator, eds., *Handbook of Econometrics,* Vol. 4. Amsterdam: North Holland, 1994.

Gourieroux, C., and A. Monfort, "Testing, Encompassing, and Simulating Dynamic Econometric Models," *Econometric Theory,* 11, 1995, pp. 195–228.

Gourieroux, C., and A. Monfort. *Simulation-Based Methods Econometric Methods*. Oxford: Oxford University Press, 1996.

Gourieroux, C., A. Monfort, and A. Trognon. "Testing Nested or Nonnested Hypotheses." *Journal of Econometrics,* 21, 1983, pp. 83–115.

Gourieroux, C., A. Monfort, and A. Trognon. "Pseudo Maximum Likelihood Methods: Applications to Poisson Models." *Econometrica,* 52, 1984, pp. 701–720.

Gourieroux, C., A. Monfort, E. Renault, and A. Trognon. "Generalized Residuals." *Journal of Econometrics,* 34, 1987, pp. 5–32.

Granger, C. "Investigating Causal Relations by Econometric Models and Cross-Spectral Methods." *Econometrica,* 37, 1969, pp. 424–438.

Granger, C. "Some Properties of Time Series Data and Their Use in Econometric Model Specification." *Journal of Econometrics,* 16, 1981, pp. 121–130.

Granger, C., and Z. Ding. "Varieties of Long Memory Models." *Journal of Econometrics,* 73, 1996, pp. 61–78.

Granger, C., and P. Newbold. "Spurious Regressions in Econometrics." *Journal of Econometrics,* 2, 1974, pp. 111–120.

Granger, C., and P. Newbold. *Forecasting Economic Time Series,* 2nd ed. New York: Academic Press, 1996.

Granger, C., and M. Watson. "Time Series and Spectral Methods in Econometrics." In Z. Griliches and M. Intriligator, eds., *Handbook of Econometrics,* Vol. 2. Amsterdam: North Holland, 1984.

Granger, C., and R. Joyeux. "An Introduction to Long Memory Time Series Models and Fractional Differencing." *Journal of Time Series Analysis,* 1, 1980, pp. 15–39.

Granger, C., and M. Pesaran. "A Decision Theoretic Approach to Forecast Evaluation." In W. S. Chan, W. Li, and H. Tong, eds., *Statistics and Finance: An Interface.* London: Imperial College Press, 2000.

Gravelle H., R. Jacobs, A. Jones, and A. Street. "Comparing the Efficiency of National Health Systems: Econometric Analysis Should Be Handled with Care." Manuscript, University of York, Health Economics, UK, 2002a.

Gravelle H., R. Jacobs, A. Jones, and A. Street. "Comparing the Efficiency of National Health Systems: A Sensitivity Approach." Manuscript, University of York, Health Economics, UK, 2002b.

Greenberg, E., and C. Webster. *Advanced Econometrics: A Bridge to the Literature.* New York: John Wiley and Sons, 1983.

Greene, W. "Maximum Likelihood Estimation of Econometric Frontier Functions." *Journal of Econometrics,* 13, 1980a, pp. 27–56.

Greene, W. "On the Asymptotic Bias of the Ordinary Least Squares Estimator of the Tobit Model." *Econometrica,* 48, 1980b, pp. 505–514.

Greene, W. "Sample Selection Bias as a Specification Error: Comment." *Econometrica,* 49, 1981, pp. 795–798.

Greene, W. "Estimation of Limited Dependent Variable Models by Ordinary Least Squares and the Method of Moments." *Journal of Econometrics,* 21, 1983, pp. 195–212.

Greene, W. "A Gamma Distributed Stochastic Frontier Model." *Journal of Econometrics,* 46, 1990, pp. 141–163.

Greene, W. "A Statistical Model for Credit Scoring." Working Paper No. EC-92-29, Department of Economics, Stern School of Business, New York University, 1992.

Greene, W. *Econometric Analysis,* 2nd ed. Englewood Cliffs, NJ: Prentice Hall, 1993.

Greene, W. "Accounting for Excess Zeros and Sample Selection in Poisson and Negative Binomial Regression Models." Working Paper No. EC-94-10, Department of Economics, Stern School of Business, New York University, 1994.

Greene, W. "Count Data." Manuscript, Department of Economics, Stern School of Business, New York University, 1995a.

Greene, W. "Sample Selection in the Poisson Regression Model." Working Paper No. EC-95-6, Department of Economics, Stern School of Business, New York University, 1995b.

Greene, W. "Models for Count Data." Manuscript, Department of Economics, Stern School of Business, New York University, 1996a.

Greene, W. "Marginal Effects in the Bivariate Probit Model." Working Paper No. 96-11, Department of Economics, Stern School of Business, New York University, 1996b.

Greene, W. "FIML Estimation of Sample Selection Models for Count Data." Working Paper No. 97-02, Department of Economics, Stern School of Business, New York University, 1997a.

Greene, W. "Frontier Production Functions." In M. Pesaran and P. Schmidt, *Handbook of Applied Econometrics: Volume. II: Microeconomics.* London: Blackwell Publishers, 1997b.

Greene, W. "Gender Economics Courses in Liberal Arts Colleges: Further Results." *Journal of Economic Education,* 29, 4, 1998, pp. 291–300.

Greene W. "Marginal Effects in the Censored Regression Model." *Economics Letters,* 64, 1, 1999, pp. 43–50.

Greene, W. "Fixed and Random Effects in Nonlinear Models." Working Paper EC-01-01, Department of Economics, Stern School of Business, New York University, 2001.

Greene, W. "Simulated Maximum Likelihood Estimation of the Normal-Gamma Stochastic Frontier Model." *Journal of Productivity Analysis,* 19, 2003, pp. 179–190.

Greene, W. "Convenient Estimators for the Panel Probit Model." *Empirical Economics,* 29, 1, 2004a, pp. 21–47.

Greene, W. "Fixed Effects and Bias Due to the Incidental Parameters Problem in the Tobit Model." *Econometric Reviews,* 2004b, 23, 2, pp. 125–147.

Greene, W. "Distinguishing Between Heterogeneity and Inefficiency: Stochastic Frontier Analysis of the World Health Organization's Panel Data on National Health Care Systems." *Health Economics,* 13, 2004c, pp. 959–980.

Greene, W. "Censored Data and Truncated Distributions." In T. Mills and K. Patterson, eds., *Palgrave Handbook of Econometrics, Volume 1: Econometric Theory.* Hampshire: Palgrave, 2006.

Greene, W. "The Econometric Approach to Efficiency Analysis." In H. Fried, K. Lovell, and S. Schmidt, eds. *The Measurement of Productive Efficiency,* 2nd ed. Oxford: Oxford University Press, 2007a.

Greene, W. *LIMDEP 9.0 Reference Guide.* Plainview, NY: Econometric Software, Inc., 2007b.

Greene, W. "Matching the Matching Estimators." Manuscript, Department of Economics, Stern School of Business, New York University, 2007c.

Greene, W., "Functional Form and Heterogeneity and Models for Count Data," Working Paper EC-07-10, Department of Economics, Stern School of Business, New York University, 2007d.

Greene, W. "Discrete Choice Models." In T. Mills and K. Patterson, eds., *Palgrave Handbook of Econometrics, Volume 2: Applied Econometrics.* Hampshire: Palgrave, 2008, forthcoming.

Greene, W. and Hensher, D. "Specification and Estimation of Nested Logit Models." *Transportation Research,* B, 36, 1, pp. 1–18, 2002.

Greene, W., and D. Hensher. "Multinomial Logit and Discrete Choice Models." In W. Greene, *NLOGIT Version 4.0 User's Manual, Revised,* Plainview, NY: Econometric Software, Inc., 2007.

Greene, W., and D. Hensher. "Mixed Logit and Heteroscedastic Control for Random Coefficients and Error Components." *Transportation Research Part E: Logistics and Transportation,* 2007, forthcoming.

Greene, W., D. Hensher, and J. Rose. "Accounting for Heterogeneity in the Variance of the Unobserved Effects in Mixed Logit Models (NW Transport Study Data)." *Transportation Research Part B: Methodological,* 40, 1, 2006a, pp. 75–92.

Greene, W., and T. Seaks. "The Restricted Least Squares Estimator: A Pedagogical Note." *Review of Economics and Statistics,* 73, 1991, pp. 563–567.

Greenstadt, J. "On the Relative Efficiencies of Gradient Methods." *Mathematics of Computation,* 1967, pp. 360– 367.

Griffiths, W., C. Hill, and G. Judge. *Learning and Practicing Econometrics.* New York: John Wiley and Sons, 1993.

Griliches, Z. "Hedonic Price Indexes for Automobiles: An Econometric Analysis of Quality Change." In *Price Statistics of the Federal Government,* prepared by the Price Statistics Review Committee of the National Bureau of Economic Research. New York: National Bureau of Economic Research, 1961.

Griliches, Z. "Distributed Lags: A Survey." *Econometrica,* 35, 1967, pp. 16–49.

Griliches, Z. "Economic Data Issues." In Z. Griliches and M. Intriligator, eds., *Handbook of Econometrics,* Vol. 3. Amsterdam: North Holland, 1986.

Griliches, Z., and P. Rao. "Small Sample Properties of Several Two Stage Regression Methods in the Context of Autocorrelated Errors." *Journal of the American Statistical Association,* 64, 1969, pp. 253–272.

Grogger, J., and R. Carson. "Models for Truncated Counts." *Journal of Applied Econometrics,* 6, 1991, pp. 225–238.

Gronau, R. "Wage Comparisons: A Selectivity Bias." *Journal of Political Economy,* 82, 1974, pp. 1119–1149.

Groot, W., and H. Maassen van den Brink. "Match Specific Gains to Marriages: A Random Effects Ordered Response Model." *Quality and Quantity,* 37, 3, 2003, pp. 317–325.

Grunfeld, Y. "The Determinants of Corporate Investment." Unpublished Ph.D. thesis, Department of Economics, University of Chicago, 1958.

Grunfeld, Y., and Z. Griliches. "Is Aggregation Necessarily Bad?" *Review of Economics and Statistics,* 42, 1960, pp. 1–13.

Guilkey, D. "Alternative Tests for a First-Order Vector Autoregressive Error Specification." *Journal of Econometrics,* 2, 1974, pp. 95–104.

Guilkey, D., and P. Schmidt. "Estimation of Seemingly Unrelated Regressions with Vector Autoregressive Errors." *Journal of the American Statistical Association,* 1973, pp. 642–647.

Guilkey, D., K. Lovell, and R. Sickles. "A Comparison of the Performance of Three Flexible Functional Forms." *International Economic Review,* 24, 1983, pp. 591–616.

Gujarati, D. *Basic Econometrics,* 4th ed. New York: McGraw-Hill, 2002.

Gurmu, S. "Tests for Detecting Overdispersion in the Positive Poisson Regression Model." *Journal of Business and Economic Statistics,* 9, 1991, pp. 215–222.

Gurmu, S., P. Rilstone, and S. Stern. "Semiparametric Estimation of Count Regression Models." *Journal of Econometrics,* 88, 1, 1999, pp. 123–150.

Gurmu, S., and P. Trivedi. "Recent Developments in Models of Event Counts: A Survey." Manuscript, Department of Economics, Indiana University, 1994.

Haavelmo, T. "The Statistical Implications of a System of Simultaneous Equations." *Econometrica,* 11, 1943, pp. 1–12.

Hadri, K., "Testing for Heterogeneity in Heterogeneous Panel Data,"*Econometrics Journal,* 3, 2000, pp. 148–161.

Hahn, J., and J. Hausman. "A New Specification Test for the Validity of Instrumental Variables." *Econometrica,* 70, 2002, pp. 163–189.

Hahn, J., and J. Hausman. "Weak Instruments: Diagnosis and Cures in Empirical Economics." *American Economic Review,* 93, 2003, pp. 118–125.

Hahn, J., and G. Kuersteiner. "Bias Reduction for Dynamic Nonlinear Panel Mdels with Fixed Effects." Manuscript, Department of Economics, University of California, Los Angeles, 2004.

Haitovsky, Y. "Missing Data in Regression Analysis." *Journal of the Royal Statistical Society, Series B,* 1968, pp. 67–82.

Hajivassiliou, V. "Smooth Simulation Estimation of Panel Data LDV Models." Department of Economics, Yale University, 1990.

Hajivassiliou, A. "Some Practical Issues in Maximum Simulated Likelihood." In R. Mariano, T. Schuermann, and M. Weeks, eds., *Simulation Based Inference in Econometrics*. Cambridge: Cambridge University Press, 2000.

Hall, A., and A. Sen. "Structural Stability Testing in Models Estimated by Generalized Method of Moments." *Journal of Business and Economics and Statistics,* 17, 3, 1999, pp. 335–348.

Hall, B. *TSP Version 4.0 Reference Manual.* Palo Alto: TSP International, 1982.

Hall, B. "Software for the Computation of Tobit Model Estimates." *Journal of Econometrics,* 24, 1984, pp. 215–222.

Hall, R. "Stochastic Implications of the Life Cycle–Permanent Income Hypothesis: Theory and Evidence,"*Journal of Political Economy,* 86, 6, 1978, pp. 971–987.

Hamilton, J. *Time Series Analysis.* Princeton: Princeton University Press, 1994.

Hansen, B. "Testing for Parameter Instability in Linear Models." *Journal of Policy Modeling,* 14, 1992, pp. 517– 533.

Hansen, B. "Approximate Asymptotic P Values for Structural-Change Tests." *Journal of Business and Economic Statistics,* 15, 1, 1997, pp. 60–67.

Hansen, B. "Testing for Structural Change in Conditional Models." *Journal of Econometrics,* 97, 2000, pp. 93–115.

Hansen, B. "Challenges for Econometric Model Selection." *Econometric Theory,* 21, 2005, pp. 60–68.

Hansen, L., "Large Sample Properties of Generalized Method of Moments Estimators." *Econometrica,* 50, 1982, pp. 1029–1054.

Hansen, L., J. Heaton, and A. Yaron. "Finite Sample Properties of Some Alternative GMM Estimators." *Journal of Business and Economic Statistics,* 14, 3, 1996, pp. 262–280.

Hansen, L., and K. Singleton, "Generalized Instrumental Variable Estimation of Nonlinear Rational Expectations Models." *Econometrica,* 50, 1982, pp. 1269– 1286.

Hansen, L., and K. Singleton. "Efficient Estimation of Asset Pricing Models with Moving Average Errors." Manuscript, Department of Economics, Carnegie Mellon University, 1988.

Hanushek, E. "Efficient Estimators for Regressing Regression Coefficients." *The American Statistician,* 28(2), 1974, pp. 21–27.

Hanushek, E. "The Evidence on Class Size." In S. Mayer and P. Peterson, eds., *Earning and Learning: How Schools Matter.* Washington, D.C.: Brookings Institute Press, 1999.

Hardle, W. *Applied Nonparametric Regression.* New York: Cambridge University Press, 1990.

Hardle, W., and C. Manski, ed., "Nonparametric and Semiparametric Approaches to Discrete Response Analysis." *Journal of Econometrics,* 58, 1993, pp. 1–274.

Harris, M. N., and Zhao, X. "A Zero-Inflated Ordered Probit Model, with an Application to Modelling Tobacco Consumption." *Journal of Econometrics,* 2007, forthcoming.

Harvey, A. "Estimating Regression Models with Multiplicative Heteroscedasticity." *Econometrica,* 44, 1976, pp. 461– 465.

Harvey, A. *Forecasting, Structural Time Series Models and the Kalman Filter.* New York: Cambridge University Press, 1989.

Harvey, A. *The Econometric Analysis of Time Series,* 2nd ed. Cambridge: MIT Press, 1990.

Harvey, A., and G. Phillips. "A Comparison of the Power of Some Tests for Heteroscedasticity in the General Linear Model." *Journal of Econometrics,* 2, 1974, pp. 307–316.

Hashimoto, N., and K. Ohtani. "An Exact Test for Linear Restrictions in Seemingly Unrelated Regressions with the Same Regressors." *Economics Letters,* 32, 1990, pp. 243–246.

Hatanaka, M. "An Efficient Estimator for the Dynamic Adjustment Model with Autocorrelated Errors." *Journal of Econometrics,* 2, 1974, pp. 199–220.

Hatanaka, M. "Several Efficient Two-Step Estimators for the Dynamic Simultaneous Equations Model with Autoregressive Disturbances." *Journal of Econometrics,* 4, 1976, pp. 189–204.

Hatanaka, M. *Time-Series-Based Econometrics.* New York: Oxford University Press, 1996.

Hausman, J. "An Instrumental Variable Approach to Full-Information Estimators for Linear and Certain Nonlinear Models." *Econometrica,* 43, 1975, pp. 727–738.

Hausman, J. "Specification Tests in Econometrics." *Econometrica,* 46, 1978, pp. 1251–1271.

Hausman, J. "Specification and Estimation of Simultaneous Equations Models." In

Z. Griliches and M. Intriligator, eds., *Handbook of Econometrics*, Vol. 1, Amsterdam: North Holland, 1983.

Hausman, J., B. Hall, and Z. Griliches. "Economic Models for Count Data with an Application to the Patents—R&D Relationship." *Econometrica*, 52, 1984, pp. 909–938.

Hausman, J., and A. Han. "Flexible Parametric Estimation of Duration and Competing Risk Models." *Journal of Applied Econometrics*, 5, 1990, pp. 1–28.

Hausman, J., and D. McFadden. "A Specification Test for the Multinomial Logit Model." *Econometrica*, 52, 1984, pp. 1219–1240.

Hausman, J., and P. Ruud. "Specifying and Testing Econometric Models for Rank Ordered Data with an Application to the Demand for Mobile and Portable Telephones." Working Paper No. 8605, University of California, Berkeley, Department of Economics, 1986.

Hausman, J., J. Stock, and M. Yogo. "Asymptotic Properties of the Hahn-Hausman Test for Weak Instruments." *Economics Letters*, 89, 2005, pp. 333–342.

Hausman, J., and W. Taylor. "Panel Data and Unobservable Individual Effects." *Econometrica*, 49, 1981, pp. 1377–1398.

Hausman, J., and D. Wise. "Social Experimentation, Truncated Distributions, and Efficient Estimation." *Econometrica*, 45, 1977, pp. 919–938.

Hausman, J., and D. Wise. "A Conditional Probit Model for Qualitative Choice: Discrete Decisions Recognizing Interdependence and Heterogeneous Preferences." *Econometrica*, 46, 1978, pp. 403–426.

Hausman, J. and D. Wise. "Attrition Bias in Experimental and Panel Data: The Gary Income Maintenance Experiment." *Econometrica*, 47, 2, 1979, pp. 455–573.

Hayashi, F. *Econometrics*. Princeton: Princeton University Press, 2000.

Heckman, J. "The Common Structure of Statistical Models of Truncation, Sample Selection, and Limited Dependent Variables and a Simple Estimator for Such Models." *Annals of Economic and Social Measurement*, 5, 1976, pp. 475–492.

Heckman, J. "Simple Statistical Models for Discrete Panel Data Developed and Applied to the Hypothesis of True State Dependence Against the Hypothesis of Spurious State Dependence." *Annalse de l'INSEE*, 30, 1978, pp. 227–269.

Heckman, J. "Sample Selection Bias as a Specification Error." *Econometrica*, 47, 1979, pp. 153–161.

Heckman, J. "Statistical Models for Discrete Panel Data." In C. Manski and D. McFadden, eds., *Structural Analysis of Discrete Data with Econometric Applications*. Cambridge: MIT Press, 1981a.

Heckman, J. "Heterogeneity and State Dependence." In S. Rosen, ed., *Studies of Labor Markets*. NBER, Chicago: University of Chicago Press, 1981b.

Heckman, J. "Hetreogeneity and State Dependence." In S. Rosen, ed., *Studies in Labor Markets*. Chicago: University of Chicago Press, 1981c.

Heckman, J. "Varieties of Selection Bias." *American Economic Review*, 80, 1990, pp. 313–318.

Heckman, J. "Randomization and Social Program Evaluation." In C. Manski and I. Garfinkel, eds., *Evaluating Welfare and Training Programs*. Cambridge: Harvard University Press, 1992.

Heckman, J. "Instrumental Variables: A Study in Implicit Behavioral Assumptions Used in Making Program Evaluations." *Journal of Human Resources*, 32, 1997, pp. 441–462.

Heckman, J., and T. MaCurdy. "A Life Cycle Model of Female Labor Supply," *Review of Economic Studies*, 47, 1980, pp. 247–283.

Heckman, J. and T. MaCurdy. "A Simultaneous Equations Linear Probability Model. *Canadian Journal of Economics*, 18, 1985, pp. 28–37.

Heckman, J., H. Ichimura, J. Smith, and P. Todd. "Characterizing Selection Bias Using Experimental Data." *Econometrica*, 66, 5, 1998, pp. 1017–1098.

Heckman, J., H. Ichimura, and P. Todd. "Matching as an Econometric Evaluation Estimator: Evidence from Evaluating a Job Training Program." *Review of Economic Studies,* 64, 4, 1997 pp. 605–654.

Heckman, J., H. Ichimura, and P. Todd. "Matching as an Econometric Evaluation Estimator." *Review of Economic Studies,* 65, 2, 1998, pp. 261–294.

Heckman, J., R. LaLonde, and J. Smith. "The Economics and Econometrics of Active Labour Market Programmes." In O. Ashenfelter and D. Card, eds., *The Handbook of Labor Economics, Vol. 3.* Amsterdam: North Holland, 1999.

Heckman, J., J. Tobias, and E. Vytlacil. "Simple Estimators for Treatment Parameters in a Latent Variable Framework." *Review of Economics and Statistics,* 85, 3, 2003, pp. 748–755.

Heckman, J., and E. Vytlacil. "Instrumental Variables, Selection Models and Tight Bounds on the Average Treatment Effect." NBER Technical Working Paper 0259, 2000.

Heckman, J., and B. Singer. "Econometric Duration Analysis." *Journal of Econometrics,* 24, 1984a, pp. 63–132.

Heckman, J., and B. Singer. "A Method for Minimizing the Impact of Distributional Assumptions in Econometric Models for Duration Data." *Econometrica,* 52, 1984b, pp. 271–320.

Heckman, J., and R. Willis. "Estimation of a Stochastic Model of Reproduction: An Econometric Approach." In N. Terleckyj, ed., *Household Production and Consumption.* New York: National Bureau of Economic Research, 1976.

Heckman, J., and J. Snyder. "Linear Probability Models of the Demand for Attributes with an Empirical Application to Estimating the Preferences of Legislators." *Rand Journal of Economics,* 28, 0, 1997.

Heilbron, D. "Generalized Linear Models for Altered Zero Probabilities and Overdispersion in Count Data." Technical Report, Department of Epidemiology and Biostatistics, University of California, San Francisco, 1989.

Hendry, D. "Econometrics: Alchemy or Science?" *Economica,* 47, 1980, pp. 387–406.

Hendry, D. "Monte Carlo Experimentation in Econometrics." In Z. Griliches and M. Intriligator, eds., *Handbook of Econometrics,* Vol. 2. Amsterdam: North Holland, 1984.

Hendry, D. *Econometrics: Alchemy or Science?* Oxford: Blackwell Publishers, 1993.

Hendry, D. *Dynamic Econometrics.* Oxford: Oxford University Press, 1995.

Hendry, D., and N. Ericsson. "An Econometric Analysis of UK Money Demand." In M. Friedman and A. Schwartz, eds., *American Economic Review,* 81, 1991, pp. 8–38.

Hendry, D., and J. Doornik. *PC Give-8.* London: International Thomson Publishers, 1986.

Hendry, D., A. Pagan, and D. Sargan. "Dynamic Specification." In M. Intriligator and Griliches, Z., eds., *Handbook of Econometrics,* Vol. 2, Amsterdam: North Holland, 1984.

Hendry, D., and H. M. Krotzis. *Automatic Econometric Model Selection Using PCGetS.* London: Timberlake Consultants Press, 2001.

Hensher, D. "Sequential and Full Information Maximum Likelihood Estimation of a Nested Logit Model." *Review of Economics and Statistics,* 68, 4, 1986, pp. 657–667.

Hensher, D. "Efficient Estimation of Hierarchical Logit Mode Choice Models." *Journal of the Japanese Society of Civil Engineers,* 425/IV-14, 1991, pp. 117–128.

Hensher, D., ed. *Travel Behavior Research: The Leading Edge.* Amsterdam: Pergamon Press, 2001.

Hensher, D., and Greene, W. "The Mixed Logit Model: The State of Practice." *Transportation Research, B,* 30, 2003, pp. 133–176.

Hensher, D., and W. Greene. "Combining RP and SP Data: Biases in Using the Nested Logit 'Trick'—Constrasts with Flexible Mixed Logit Incorporating Panel and Scale Effects." Manuscript, Institute of Transport and Logistical Studies, Sydney University, 2006.

Hensher, D., Louviere, J., and J. Swait. *Stated Choice Methods: Analysis and Applications.* Cambridge: Cambridge University Press, 2000.

Hensher, D., J. Rose, and W. Greene. *Applied Choice Analysis.* Cambridge: Cambridge University Press, 2006.

Hildebrand, G., and T. Liu. *Manufacturing Production Functions in the United States.* Ithaca, NY: Cornell University Press, 1957.

Hildreth, C., and C. Houck. "Some Estimators for a Linear Model with Random Coefficients." *Journal of the American Statistical Association,* 63, 1968, pp. 584–595.

Hildreth, C., and J. Lu. "Demand Relations with Autocorrelated Disturbances." Technical Bulletin No. 276, Michigan State University Agricultural Experiment Station, 1960.

Hill, C., and L. Adkins. "Collinearity." In B. Baltagi, ed., *A Companion to Theoretical Econometrics.* Oxford: Blackwell, 2001.

Hilts, J. "Europeans Perform Highest in Ranking of World Health." *New York Times,* June 21, 2000.

Hite, S. *Women and Love.* New York: Alfred A. Knopf, 1987.

Hoeting, J., D. Madigan, A. Raftery, and C. Volinsky. "Bayesian Model Averaging: A Tutorial." *Statistical Science,* 14, 1999, pp. 382–417.

Hole, A. "A Comparison of Approaches to Estimating Confidence Intervals for Willingness to Pay Measures." Paper CHE 8, Center for Health Economics, University of York, 2006.

Hollingsworth, J., and B. Wildman. "The Efficiency of Health Production: Re-estimating the WHO Panel Data Using Parametric and Nonparametric Approaches to Provide Additional Information." *Health Economics* 11, 2002; 1–11.

Holt, M. "Autocorrelation Specification in Singular Equation Systems: A Further Look." *Economics Letters,* 58, 1998, pp. 135–141.

Holtz-Eakin, D. "Testing for Individual Effects in Autoregressive Models." *Journal of Econometrics,* 39, 1988, pp. 297–307.

Holtz-Eakin, D., W. Newey, and H. Rosen. "Estimating Vector Autoregressions with Panel Data." *Econometrica,* 56, 6, 1988, pp. 1371–1395.

Hong, H., B. Presting, and M. Shum. "Generalized Empirical Likelihood Based Model Selection Criteria for Moment Condition Models." *Econometric Theory,* 19, 2003, pp. 923–943.

Honorè, B., and E. Kyriazidou. "Estimation of a Panel Data Sample Selection Model," *Econometrica,* 65, 6, 1997, pp. 1335–1364.

Honorè, B., and E. Kyriazidou. "Panel Data Discrete Choice Models with Lagged Dependent Variables." *Econometrica,* 68, 4, 2000, pp. 839–874.

Honorè, B., and E. Kyriazidou. "Estimation of Tobit-Type Models with Individual Specific Effects." *Econometric Reviews,* 19, 3, 2000, pp. 341–367.

Horn, D., A. Horn, and G. Duncan. "Estimating Heteroscedastic Variances in Linear Models." *Journal of the American Statistical Association,* 70, 1975, pp. 380–385.

Horowitz, J. "A Smoothed Maximum Score Estimator for the Binary Response Model." *Econometrica,* 60, 1992, pp. 505–531.

Horowitz, J. "Semiparametric Estimation of a Work-Trip Mode Choice Model." *Journal of Econometrics,* 58, 1993, pp. 49–70.

Horowitz, J. "The Bootstrap." In J. Heckman and E. Leamer, eds. *Handbook of Econometrics,* Vol. 5. Amsterdam: North Holland, 2001, pp. 3159–3228.

Horowitz, J., and G. Neumann. "Specification Testing in Censored Regression Models." *Journal of Applied Econometrics,* 4(S), 1989, pp. S35–S60.

Hosking, J. "Fractional Differencing." *Biometrika,* 68, 1981, pp. 165–176.

Howrey, E., and H. Varian. "Estimating the Distributional Impact of Time-of-Day Pricing of Electricity." *Journal of Econometrics,* 26, 1984, pp. 65–82.

Hoxby, C. "Does Competition Among Public Schools Benefit Students and Taxpayers?" *American Economic Review,* 69, 5, 2000, pp. 1209–1238.

Hsiao, C. "Some Estimation Methods for a Random Coefficient Model." *Econometrica,* 43, 1975, pp. 305–325.

Hsiao, C. *Analysis of Panel Data.* Cambridge: Cambridge University Press, 1986.

Hsiao, C. *Analysis of Panel Data,* 2nd ed. New York: Cambridge University Press, 2003.

Hsiao, C. "Identification." In Z. Griliches and M. Intriligator, eds., *Handbook of Econometrics,* Vol. 1. Amsterdam: North Holland, 1983.

Hsiao, C. "Modeling Ontario Regional Electricity System Demand Using a Mixed Fixed and Random Coefficients Approach." *Regional Science and Urban Economics,* 19, 1989.

Hsiao, C. "Logit and Probit Models." In L. Matyas and P. Sevestre, eds., *The Econometrics of Panel Data: Handbook of Theory and Applications.* Dordrecht: Kluwer-Nijhoff, 1992.

Hsiao, C., K. Lahiri, L. Lee, and H. Pesaran. *Analysis of Panels and Limited Dependent Variable Models.* New York: Cambridge University Press, 1999.

Hsiao, C., M. Pesaran, and A. Tahmiscioglu. "A Panel Analysis of Liquidity Constraints and Firm Investment." In C. Hsiao, K. Lahiri, L. Lee, and M. Pesaran, eds., *Analysis of Panels and Limited Dependent Variable Models.* Cambridge: Cambridge University Press, 2002, pp. 268–296.

Huber, P. "The Behavior of Maximum Likelihood Estimates Under Nonstandard Conditions." In *Proceedings of the Fifth Berkeley Symposium in Mathematical Statistics,* Vol. 1. Berkeley: University of California Press, 1967.

Hurd, M. "Estimation in Truncated Samples When There Is Heteroscedasticity." *Journal of Econometrics,* 11, 1979, pp. 247–258.

Hurst, H. "Long Term Storage Capacity of Reservoirs." *Transactions of the American Society of Civil Engineers,* 116, 1951, pp. 519–543.

Hyslop, D. "State Dependence, Serial Correlation, and Heterogeneity in Labor Force Participation of Married Women." *Econometrica,* 67, 6, 1999, pp. 1255–1294.

Hwang, H. "Estimation of a Linear SUR Model with Unequal Numbers of Observations." *Review of Economics and Statistics,* 72, 1990, pp. 510–515.

Im, E. "Unequal Numbers of Observations and Partial Efficiency Gain." *Economics Letters,* 46, 1994, pp. 291–294.

Im, K., S. Ahn, P. Schmidt, and J. Wooldridge, "Efficient Estimation of Panel Data Models with Strictly Exogenous Explanatory Variables," *Journal of Econometrics,* 93, 1999, pp. 177–201.

Im, K., M. Pesaran, and Y. Shin. "Testing for Unit Roots in Heterogeneous Panels." *Journal of Econometrics,* 115, 2003, pp. 53–74.

Imbens, G., and J. Angrist. "Identification and Estimation of Local Average Treatment Effects." *Econometrica,* 62, 1994, pp. 467–476.

Imbens, G., and D. Hyslop. "Bias from Classical and Other Forms of Measurement Error." *Journal of Business and Economic Statistics,* 19, 2001, pp. 141–149.

Imhof, J. "Computing the Distribution of Quadratic Forms in Normal Variables." *Biometrika,* 48, 1980, pp. 419–426.

Inkmann, J. "Misspecified Heteroscedasticity in the Panel Probit Model: A Small Sample Comparison of GMM and SML Estimators." *Journal of Econometrics,* 97, 2, 2000, pp. 227–259.

Jain, D., N. Vilcassim, and P. Chintagunta. "A Random-Coefficients Logit Brand Choice Model Applied to Panel Data." *Journal of Business and Economic Statistics,* 12, 3, 1994, pp. 317–328.

Jarque, C. "An Application of LDV Models to Household Expenditure Analysis in Mexico." *Journal of Econometrics,* 36, 1987, pp. 31–54.

Jakubson, G. "The Sensitivity of Labor Supply Parameters to Unobserved Individual Effects: Fixed and Random Effects Estimates in a Nonlinear Model Using Panel Data." *Journal of Labor Economics,* 6, 1988, pp. 302–329.

Jayatissa, W. "Tests of Equality Between Sets of Coefficients in Two Linear Regressions When Disturbance Variances Are Unequal." *Econometrica,* 45, 1977, pp. 1291–1292.

Jennrich, R. I. "The Asymptotic Properties of Nonlinear Least Squares Estimators." *Annals of Statistics,* 2, 1969, pp. 633–643.

Jensen, M. "A Monte Carlo Study on Two Methods of Calculating the MLE's Covariance Matrix in a Seemingly Unrelated Nonlinear Regression." *Econometric Reviews,* 14, 1995, pp. 315–330.

Jobson, J., and W. Fuller. "Least Squares Estimation When the Covariance Matrix and Parameter Vector Are Functionally Related." *Journal of the American Statistical Association,* 75, 1980, pp. 176–181.

Johansen, S. "Estimation and Hypothesis Testing of Cointegrated Vectors in Gaussian VAR Models." *Econometrica,* 59, 6, 1991, pp. 1551–1580.

Johansen, S. "A Representation of Vector Autoregressive Processes of Order 2." *Econometric Theory,* 8, 1992, pp. 188–202.

Johansen, S. "Statistical Analysis of Cointegration Vectors." *Journal of Economic Dynamics and Control,* 12, 1988, pp. 231–254.

Johansen, S., and K. Juselius. "Maximum Likelihood Estimation and Inference on Cointegration, with Applications for the Demand for Money." *Oxford Bulletin of Economics and Statistics,* 52, 1990, pp. 169–210.

Johnson, N., and S. Kotz. *Distributions in Statistics—Continuous Multivariate Distributions.* New York: John Wiley and Sons, 1974.

Johnson, N., S. Kotz, and A. Kemp. *Distributions in Statistics—Univariate Discrete Distributions,* 2nd ed. New York: John Wiley and Sons, 1993.

Johnson, N., S. Kotz, and A. Balakrishnan. *Distributions in Statistics, Continuous Univariate Distributions— Vol. 1,* 2nd ed. New York: John Wiley and Sons, 1994.

Johnson, N., S. Kotz, and N. Balakrishnan. *Distributions in Statistics, Continuous Univariate Distributions—Vol. 2,* 2nd ed. New York: John Wiley and Sons, 1995.

Johnson, N., S. Kotz, and N. Balakrishnan. *Distributions in Statistics, Discrete Multivariate Distributions.* New York: John Wiley and Sons, 1997.

Johnson, R., and D. Wichern. *Applied Multivariate Statistical Analysis,* 5th ed. Englewood Cliffs, NJ: Prentice Hall, 2005.

Johnston, J. *Econometric Methods.* New York: McGraw-Hill, 1984.

Johnston, J., and J. DiNardo. *Econometric Methods,* 4th ed. New York: McGraw-Hill, 1997.

Jondrow, J., K. Lovell, I. Materov, and P. Schmidt. "On the Estimation of Technical Inefficiency in the Stochastic Frontier Production Function Model." *Journal of Econometrics,* 19, 1982, pp. 233–238.

Jones, A., X. Koolman, and N Rice. "Health-related Attrition in the BHPS and ECHP: Using Inverse Probability Weighted Estimators in Nonlinear Models." *Journal of the Royal Statistical Society Series A (Statistics in Society),* 169, 2006, pp. 543–569.

Jones, J., and J. Landwehr. "Removing Heterogeneity Bias from Logit Model Estimation." *Marketing Science,* 7, 1, 1988, pp. 41–59.

Joreskog, K. "A General Method for Estimating a Linear Structural Equation System." In A. Goldberger and O. Duncan, eds. *Structural Equation Models in the Social Sciences.* New York: Academic Press, 1973.

Joreskog, K., and G. Gruvaeus. "A Computer Program for Minimizing a Function of Several Variables." Educational Testing

Services, Research Bulletin No. 70-14, 1970.

Joreskog, K., and D. Sorbom. *LISREL V User's Guide*. Chicago: National Educational Resources, 1981.

Jorgenson, D. "Rational Distributed Lag Functions." *Econometrica, 34*, 1966, pp. 135–149.

Jorgenson, D. "Econometric Methods for Modeling Producer Behavior." In Z. Griliches and M. Intriligator, eds., *Handbook of Econometrics*, Vol. 3. Amsterdam: North Holland, 1983.

Judd, K. *Numerical Methods in Economics*. Cambridge: MIT Press, 1998.

Judge, G., W. Griffiths, C. Hill, and T. Lee. *The Theory and Practice of Econometrics*. New York: John Wiley and Sons, 1985.

Judge, G., C. Hill, W. Griffiths, T. Lee, and H. Lutkepol. *An Introduction to the Theory and Practice of Econometrics*. New York: John Wiley and Sons, 1982.

Jusko, K. "A Two-Step Binary Response Model for Cross-National Public Opinion Data: A Research Note." Presented at the Midwest Political Science Association National Conference, April 7–10, 2005, Chicago.

Kakwani, N., "The Unbiasedness of Zellner's Seemingly Unrelated Regression Equations Estimators." *Journal of the American Statistical Association, 62*, 1967, pp. 141–142.

Kalbfleisch, J., and R. Prentice. *The Statistical Analysis of Failure Time Data*, 2nd ed. New York: John Wiley and Sons, 2002.

Kamlich, R., and S. Polachek. "Discrimination: Fact or Fiction? An Examination Using an Alternative Approach." *Southern Economic Journal*, October 1982, pp. 450–461.

Kao, C. "Spurious Regression and Residual Based Tests for Cointegration in Panel Data." *Journal of Econometrics, 90*, 1999, pp. 1–44.

Kaplan, E. and P. Meier. "Nonparametric Estimation from Incomplete Observations." *Journal of the American Statistical Association, 53*, 1958, pp. 457–481.

Kay, R., and S. Little. "Assessing the Fit of the Logistic Model: A Case Study of Children with Haemolytic Uraemic Syndrome." *Applied Statistics, 35*, 1986, pp. 16–30.

Keane, M. "A Computationally Practical Simulation Estimator for Panel Data." *Econometrica, 62*, 1, 1994, pp. 95–116.

Keane, M. "Simulation Estimators for Panel Data Models with Limited Dependent Variables." In G. Maddala and C. Rao, eds., *Handbook of Statistics*, Volume 11, Chapter 20. Amsterdam: North Holland, 1993.

Keane, M., R. Moffitt, and D. Runkle. "Real Wages over the Business Cycle: Estimating the Impact of Heterogeneity with Micro-Data." *Journal of Political Economy, 96*, 6, 1988, pp. 1232–1265.

Kelejian, H. "Two-Stage Least Squares and Econometric Systems Linear in Parameters but Nonlinear in the Endogenous Variables." *Journal of the American Statistical Association, 66*, 1971, pp. 373–374.

Kaptery, A., and D. Fiebig. "When Are Two Stage and Three Stage Least Squares Identical?" *Economics Letters, 8*, 1981, pp. 53–57.

Kelejian, H., and I. Prucha. "A Generalized Moments Estimator for the Autoregressive Parameter in a Spatial Model." *International Economic Review, 40*, 1999, pp. 509–533.

Kelly, J. "Linear Cross Equation Constraints and the Identification Problem." *Econometrica, 43*, 1975, pp. 125–140.

Kennan, J. "The Duration of Contract Strikes in U.S. Manufacturing." *Journal of Econometrics, 28*, 1985, pp. 5–28.

Kennedy, W., and J. Gentle. *Statistical Computing*. New York: Marcel Dekker, 1980.

Keuzenkamp, H., and J. Magnus. "The Significance of Testing in Econometrics." *Journal of Econometrics, 67*, 1, 1995, pp. 1–257.

Keynes, J. *The General Theory of Employment, Interest, and Money*. New York: Harcourt, Brace, and Jovanovich, 1936.

Kiefer, N. "Testing for Independence in Multivariate Probit Models." *Biometrika, 69*, 1982, pp. 161–166.

Kiefer, N., ed. "Econometric Analysis of Duration Data." *Journal of Econometrics,* 28, 1, 1985, pp. 1–169.

Kiefer, N. "Economic Duration Data and Hazard Functions." *Journal of Economic Literature,* 26, 1988, pp. 646–679.

Kiefer, N., and Salmon, M. "Testing Normality in Econometric Models." *Economics Letters,* 11, 1983, pp. 123–127.

Killian, L. "Small-Sample Confidence Intervals for Impulse Response Functions." *The Review of Economics and Statistics,* 80, 2, 1998, pp. 218–230.

Kim, H., and J. Pollard. "Cube Root Asymptotics." *Annals of Statistics,* March 1990, pp. 191–219.

Kingdon, G., and R. Cassen. "Explaining Low Achievement at Age 16 in England." Mimeo, Department of Economics, University of Oxford, 2007.

Kiviet, J. "On Bias, Inconsistency, and Efficiency of Some Estimators in Dynamic Panel Data Models." *Journal of Econometrics,* 68, 1, 1995, pp. 63–78.

Kiviet, J., G. Phillips, and B. Schipp, "The Bias of OLS, GLS and ZEF Estimators in Dynamic SUR Models." *Journal of Econometrics,* 69, 1995, pp. 241–266.

Kleijn, R., and H. K. van Dijk. "Bayes Model Averaging of Cyclical Decompositions in Economic Time Series." *Journal of Applied Econometrics,* 21, 2, 2006, pp. 191–213.

Kleibergen, F. "Pivotal Statistics for Testing Structural Parameters in Instrumental Variables Regression." *Econometrica,* 70, 2002, pp. 1781–1803.

Klein, L. *Economic Fluctuations in the United States 1921–1941.* New York: John Wiley and Sons, 1950.

Klein, R., and R. Spady. "An Efficient Semiparametric Estimator for Discrete Choice Models." *Econometrica,* 61, 1993, pp. 387–421.

Klepper, S., and E. Leamer. "Consistent Sets of Estimates for Regressions with Errors in All Variables." *Econometrica,* 52, 1983, pp. 163–184.

Klugman, S., and R. Parsa. "Fitting Bivariate Loss Distributuins with Copulas." *Insurance: Mathematics and Economics,* 24, 2000, pp. 139–148.

Kmenta, J. "On Estimation of the CES Production Function." *International Economic Review,* 8, 1967, pp. 180–189.

Kmenta, J. *Elements of Econometrics.* New York: Macmillan, 1986.

Kmenta, J., and R. Gilbert. "Small Sample Properties of Alternative Estimators of Seemingly Unrelated Regressions." *Journal of the American Statistical Association,* 63, 1968, pp. 1180–1200.

Knapp, L., and T. Seaks. "An Analysis of the Probability of Default on Federally Guaranteed Student Loans." *Review of Economics and Statistics,* 74, 1992, pp. 404–411.

Knight, F. *The Economic Organization.* New York: Harper and Row, 1933.

Kobayashi, M. "A Bounds Test of Equality Between Sets of Coefficients in Two Linear Regressions When Disturbance Variances Are Unequal." *Journal of the American Statistical Association,* 81, 1986, pp. 510–514.

Koenker, R. "A Note on Studentizing a Test for Heteroscedasticity." *Journal of Econometrics,* 17, 1981, pp. 107–112.

Koenker, R., and G. Bassett. "Regression Quantiles." *Econometrica,* 46, 1978, pp. 107–112.

Koenker, R., and G. Bassett. "Robust Tests for Heteroscedasticity Based on Regression Quantiles." *Econometrica,* 50, 1982, pp. 43–61.

Koop, G. *Bayesian Econometrics.* New York: John Wiley and Sons, 2003.

Koop, G., and S. Potter. "Forecasting in Large Macroeconomic Panels Using Bayesian Model Averaging." *Econometrics Journal,* 7, 2, 2004, pp. 161–185.

Koop, G., and J. Tobias. "Learning About Heterogeneity in Returns to Schooling." *Journal of Applied Econometrics,* 19, 7, 2004, pp. 827–849.

Krailo, M., and M. Pike. "Conditional Multivariate Logistic Analysis of Stratified

Case-Control Studies." *Applied Statistics,* 44, 1, 1984, pp. 95–103.

Kreuger, A. "Economic Scene." *New York Times,* April 27, 2000, p. C2.

Kreuger, A., and S. Dale. "Estimating the Payoff to Attending a More Selective College." NBER, Cambridge, Working Paper 7322, 1999.

Krinsky, I., and L. Robb. "On Approximating the Statistical Properties of Elasticities." *Review of Economics and Statistics,* 68, 4, 1986, pp. 715–719.

Krinsky, I., and L. Robb. "On Approximating the Statisticl Properties of Elasticities: Correction." *Review of Economics and Statistics,* 72, 1, 1990, pp. 189–190.

Krinsky, I., and L. Robb. "Three Methods for Calculating Statistical Properties for Elasticities." *Empirical Economics,* 16, 1991, pp. 1–11.

Kumbhakar, S., and A. Heshmati. "Technical Change and Total Factor Productivity Growth in Swedish Manufacturing Industries." *Econometric Reviews,* 15, 1996, pp. 275–298.

Kumbhakar, S., and K. Lovell. *Stochastic Frontier Analysis.* New York: Cambridge University Press, 2000.

Kwiatkowski, D., P. Phillips, P. Schmidt, and Y. Shin. "Testing the Null Hypothesis of Stationarity Against the Alternative of a Unit Root." *Journal of Econometrics,* 54, 1992, pp. 159–178.

Kyriazidou, E. "Estimation of a Panel Data Sample Selection Model." *Econometrica,* 65, 1997, pp. 1335–1364.

Kyriazidou, E. "Estimation of Dynamic Panel Data Sample Selectioin Models." *Review of Economic Studies,* 68, 2001, pp. 543–572.

L'Ecuyer, P. "Good Parameters and Implementations for Combined Multiple Recursive Random Number Generators," Working Paper, Department of Information Science, University of Montreal, 1998.

LaLonde, R., "Evaluating the Econometric Evaluations of Training Programs with Experimental Data." *American Economic Review,* 76, 4, 1986, pp. 604–620.

Lambert, D. "Zero-Inflated Poisson Regression, with an Application to Defects in Manufacturing." *Technometrics,* 34, 1, 1992, pp. 1–14.

Lancaster, T. *The Analysis of Transition Data.* New York: Cambridge University Press, 1990.

Lancaster, T. "The Incidental Parameters Problem since 1948." *Journal of Econometrics,* 95, 2, 2000, pp. 391–414.

Lancaster, T. *An Introduction to Modern Bayesian Inference.* Oxford: Oxford University Press, 2004.

Landers, A. "Survey," *Chicago Tribune,* 1984, passim.

Lawless, J. *Statistical Models and Methods for Lifetime Data.* New York: John Wiley and Sons, 1982.

Leamer, E. *Specification Searches: Ad Hoc Inferences with Nonexperimental Data.* New York: John Wiley and Sons, 1978.

LeCam, L. "On Some Asymptotic Properties of Maximum Likelihood Estimators and Related Bayes Estimators." *University of California Publications in Statistics,* 1, 1953, pp. 277–330.

Lee, K., M. Pesaran, and R. Smith. "Growth and Convergence in a Multi-Country Empiridal Stochastic Solow Model." *Journal of Applied Econometrics,* 12, 1997, pp. 357–392.

Lee, L. "Estimation of Error Components Models with ARMA $(p, q)$ Time Component—An Exact GLS Approach." Number 78-104, University of Minnesota, Center for Economic Research, 1978.

Lee, L. "Generalized Econometric Models with Selectivity." *Econometrica,* 51, 1983, pp. 507–512.

Lee, L. "Specification Tests for Poisson Regression Models." *International Economic Review,* 27, 1986, pp. 689–706.

Lee, M. *Method of Moments and Semiparametric Econometrics for Limited Dependent Variables.* New York: Springer-Verlag, 1996.

Lee, M. *Limited Dependent Variable Models.* New York: Cambridge University Press, 1998.

Lee, M. *Method of Moments and Semi-parametric Econometrics for Limited Dependent Variable Models.* Heidelberg, Springer-Verlag, 1996.

Leff, N. "Dependency Rates and Savings Rates." *American Economic Review,* 59, 5, 1969, pp. 886–896.

Leff, N. "Dependency Rates and Savings Rates: Reply." *American Economic Review,* 63, 1, 1973, p. 234.

Lerman, R., and C. Manski. "On the Use of Simulated Frequencies to Approximate Choice Probabilities." In C. Manski and D. McFadden, eds., *Structural Analysis of Discrete Data with Econometric Applications.* Cambridge: MIT Press, 1981.

Levi, M. "Errors in the Variables in the Presence of Correctly Measured Variables." *Econometrica,* 41, 1973, pp. 985–986.

Levin, A., and C. Lin. "Unit Root Tests in Panel Data: Asymptotic and Finite Sample Properties." Discussion Paper 92-93, Department of Economics, University of California, San Diego, 1992.

Levin, A., C. Lin, and C. Chu. "Unit Root Test in Panel Data: Asumptotic and Finite Sample Properties." *Journal of Econometrics,* 108, 2002, pp. 1–25.

Lewbel, A. "Semiparametric Qualitative Response Model Estimation with Unknown Heteroscedasticity or Instrumental Variables." *Journal of Econometrics,* 97, 1, 2000, pp. 145–177.

Lewbel, A. "Semiparametric Estimation of Location and Other Discrete Choice Moments." *Econometric Theory,* 14, 1997, pp. 32–51.

Lewbel, A., and B. Honorè. "Semiparametric Binary Choice Panel Data Models without Strictly Exogenous Regressors." *Econometrica,* 70, 2002, pp. 2053–2063.

Lewis, H. "Comments on Selectivity Biases in Wage Comparisons." *Journal of Political Economy,* 82, 1974, pp. 1149–1155.

Li, M., and J. Tobias. "Calculus Attainment and Grades Received in Intermediate

Economic Theory." *Journal of Applied Economics,* 21, 9, 2006, pp. 893–896.

Li, Q., and J. Racine. *Nonparametric Econometrics.* Princeton: Princeton University Press, 2007.

Li, W., S. Ling, and M. McAleer. *A Survey of Recent Theoretical Results for Time Series Models with GARCH Errors.* Manuscript, Institute for Social and Economic Research, Osaka University, Osaka, 2001.

Liang, K. and S. Zeger. "Longitudinal Data Analysis Using Generalized Linear Models." *Biometrika,* 73, 1986, pp. 13–22.

Lillard, L., and R. Willis. "Dynamic Aspects of Earning Mobility." *Econometrica,* 46, 1978, pp. 985–1012.

Lintner, J. "Security Prices, Risk, and Maximal Gains from Diversification." *Journal of Finance,* 20, 1965, pp. 587–615.

Litterman, R. "Techniques of Forecasting Using Vector Autoregressions." Working Paper No. 15, Federal Reserve Bank of Minneapolis, 1979.

Litterman, R. "Forecasting with Bayesian Vector Autoregressions—Five Years of Experience." *Journal of Business and Economic Statistics,* 4, 1986, pp. 25–38.

Little, R., and D. Rubin. *Statistical Analysis with Missing Data.* New York: Wiley, 1987.

Liu, T. "Underidentification, Structural Estimation, and Forecasting." *Econometrica,* 28, 1960, pp. 855–865.

Ljung, G., and G. Box. "On a Measure of Lack of Fit in Time Series Models." *Biometrika,* 66, 1979, pp. 265–270.

Lo, A. "Long Term Memory in Stock Market Prices." *Econometrica,* 59, 1991, pp. 1297–1313.

Loeve, M., *Probability Theory.* New York: Springer-Verlag, 1977.

Long, S. *Regression Models for Categorical and Limited Dependent Variables.* Thousand Oaks, CA: Sage Publications, 1997.

Longley, J. "An Appraisal of Least Squares Programs from the Point of the User."

*Journal of the American Statistical Association,* 62, 1967, pp. 819–841.

Louviere, J., D. Hensher, and J. Swait. *Stated Choice Methods: Analysis and Applications.* Cambridge: Cambridge University Press, 2000.

Lovell, M. "Seasonal Adjustment of Economic Time Series and Multiple Regression Analysis." *Journal of the American Statistical Association,* 58, 1963, pp. 993–1010.

Lucas, R. "Econometric Policy Evaluation: A Critique." In K. Brunner and A. Meltzer, eds., *The Phillips Curve and the Labor Market.* Amsterdam: North Holland, 1976.

Lucas, R. *Money Demand in the United States: A Quantitative Review.* Carnegie-Rochester Conference Series on Public Policy, 29, 1988, pp. 137–168.

Lutkepohl, H. *Introduction to Multiple Time Series Analysis,* 2nd ed. New York: Marcel Dekker, 2005.

MacDonald, G. and H. White. "Some Large Sample Tests for Nonnormality in the Linear Regression Model." *Journal of the American Statistical Association,* 75, 1980, pp. 16–27.

MacKinnon, J., and H. White. "Some Heteroscedasticity Consistent Covariance Matrix Estimators with Improved Finite Sample Properties." *Journal of Econometrics,* 19, 1985, pp. 305–325.

MacKinnon, J., H. White, and R. Davidson. "Tests for Model Specification in the Presence of Alternative Hypotheses: Some Further Results." *Journal of Econometrics,* 21, 1983, pp. 53–70.

Maddala, G. "The Use of Variance Components Models in Pooling Cross Section and Time Series Data." *Econometrica,* 39, 1971, pp. 341–358.

Maddala, G. "Some Small Sample Evidence on Tests of Significance in Simultaneous Equations Models." *Econometrica,* 42, 1974, pp. 841–851.

Maddala, G. *Econometrics.* New York: McGraw-Hill, 1977a.

Maddala, G. "Limited Dependent Variable Models Using Panel Data." *Journal of Human Resources,* 22, 1977b, pp. 307–338.

Maddala, G. *Limited Dependent and Qualitative Variables in Econometrics.* New York: Cambridge University Press, 1983.

Maddala, G. "Disequilibrium, Self-Selection, and Switching Models." In Z. Griliches and M. Intriligator, eds., *Handbook of Econometrics,* Vol. 3. Amsterdam: North Holland, 1984.

Maddala, G. "Limited Dependent Variable Models Using Panel Data." *Journal of Human Resources,* 22, 1987, pp. 307–338.

Maddala, G. *Introduction to Econometrics,* 2nd ed. New York: Macmillan, 1992.

Maddala, G. *The Econometrics of Panel Data,* Vols. I and II. Brookfield, VT: E. E. Elgar, 1993.

Maddala, G. and A. Flores-Lagunes. "Qualitative Response Models." In B. Baltagi, ed., *A Companion to Theoretical Econometrics.* Oxford: Blackwell, 2001.

Maddala, G., and I. Kim. *Unit Roots, Cointegration and Structural Change.* Cambridge: Cambridge University Press, 1998.

Maddala, G., and T. Mount. "A Comparative Study of Alternative Estimators for Variance Components Models." *Journal of the American Statistical Association,* 68, 1973, pp. 324–328.

Maddala, G., and F. Nelson. "Specification Errors in Limited Dependent Variable Models." Working Paper 96, National Bureau of Economic Research, Cambridge, MA, 1975.

Maddala, G., and A. Rao. "Tests for Serial Correlation in Regression Models with Lagged Dependent Variables and Serially Correlated Errors." *Econometrica* 41, 1973, pp. 761–774.

Maddala, G., and S. Wu. "A Comparative Study of Unit Root Tests with Panel Data and a New Simple Test." *Oxford Bulletin of Economics and Statistics,* 61, 1999, pp. 631–652.

Maeshiro, A. "On the Retention of the First Observation in Serial Correlation Adjustment of Regression Models." *International Economic Review,* 20, 1979, pp. 259–265.

Magee, L., J. Burbidge, and L. Robb. "The Correlation Between Husband's and Wife's Education: Canada, 1971–1996." Social and Economic Dimensions of an Aging Population Research Papers, 24, McMaster University, 2000.

Magnac, T. "State Dependence and Heterogeneity in Youth Unemployment Histories." Working Paper, INRA and CREST, Paris, 1997.

Magnus, J. "Multivariate Error Components Analysis of Linear and Nonlinear Regression Models by Maximum Likelihood." *Journal of Econometrics,* 19, 1982, pp. 239–285.

Magnus, J., and H. Neudecker. *Matrix Differential Calculus with Applications in Statistics and Econometrics.* New York: John Wiley and Sons, 1988.

Malinvaud, E. *Statistical Methods of Econometrics.* Amsterdam: North Holland, 1970.

Mandy, D., and C. Martins-Filho. "Seemingly Unrelated Regressions Under Additive Heteroscedasticity: Theory and Share Equation Applications." *Journal of Econometrics,* 58, 1993, pp. 315–346.

Mann, H., and A. Wald. "On the Statistical Treatment of Linear Stochastic Difference Equations." *Econometrica,* 11, 1943, pp. 173–220.

Manski, C. "The Maximum Score Estimator of the Stochastic Utility Model of Choice." *Journal of Econometrics,* 3, 1975, pp. 205–228.

Manski, C. "Semiparametric Analysis of Discrete Response: Asymptotic Properties of the Maximum Score Estimator." *Journal of Econometrics,* 27, 1985, pp. 313–333.

Manski, C. "Operational Characteristics of the Maximum Score Estimator." *Journal of Econometrics,* 32, 1986, pp. 85–100.

Manski, C. "Semiparametric Analysis of the Random Effects Linear Model from Binary Response Data," *Econometrica,* 55, 1987, pp. 357–362.

Manski, C. "Learning About Treatment Effects from Experiments with Random Assignment of Treatments." *Journal of Human Resources,* 31, 1996, pp. 709–733.

Manski, C. "Anatomy of the Selection Problem." *Journal of Human Resources,* 24, 1989, pp. 343–360.

Manski, C. "Nonparametric Bounds on Treatment Effects." *American Economic Review,* 80, 1990, pp. 319–323.

Manski, C. *Analog Estimation Methods in Econometrics.* London: Chapman and Hall, 1992.

Manski, C. *Identification Problems in the Social Sciences.* Cambridge: Harvard University Press, 1995.

Manski, C., and S. Lerman. "The Estimation of Choice Probabilities from Choice Based Samples." *Econometrica,* 45, 1977, pp. 1977–1988.

Manski, C., and S. Thompson. "MSCORE: A Program for Maximum Score Estimation of Linear Quantile Regressions from Binary Response Data." Mimeo, University of Wisconsin, Madison, Department of Economics, 1986.

Mariano, R. "Analytical Small-Sample Distribution Theory in Econometrics: The Simultaneous Equations Case." *International Economic Review,* 23, 1982, pp. 503–534.

Marcus, A., and W. Greene. "The Determinants of Rating Assignment and Performance." Working Paper CRC528, Center for Naval Analyses, 1985.

Markowitz, H. *Portfolio Selection: Efficient Diversification of Investments.* New York: John Wiley and Sons, 1959.

Mariano, R. "Simultaneous Equation Model Estimators: Statistical Properties." In B. Baltagi, ed., *A Companion to Theoretical Econometrics.* Oxford: Blackwell, 2001.

Marsaglia, G. and T. Bray. "A Convenient Method of Generating Normal Variables." *SIAM Review,* 6, 1964, pp. 260–264.

Martins, M., "Parametric and Semiparametric Estimation of Sample Selection Models: An Empirical Application to the Female Labour Force in Portugal." *Journal of Applied Econometrics,* 16, 1, 2001, pp. 23–40.

Matyas, L. *Generalized Method of Moments Estimation.* Cambridge: Cambridge University Press, 1999.

Matyas, L., and P. Sevestre, eds. *The Econometrics of Panel Data: Handbook of Theory and Applications,* 2nd ed. Dordrecht: Kluwer-Nijhoff, 1996.

Matzkin, R. "Nonparametric Identification and Estimation of Polytomous Choice Models." *Journal of Econometrics,* 58, 1993, pp. 137–168.

Mazodier, P., and A. Trognon. "Heteroscedasticity and Stratification in Error Components Models." *Annales de l'Insee,* 30, 1978, pp. 451–482.

McAleer, M. "The Significance of Testing Empirical Non-Nested Models." *Journal of Econometrics,* 67, 1995, pp. 149–171.

McAleer, M., G. Fisher, and P. Volker. "Separate Misspecified Regressions and the U.S. Long-Run Demand for Money Function." *Review of Economics and Statistics,* 64, 1982, pp. 572–583.

McCallum, B. "Relative Asymptotic Bias from Errors of Omission and Measurement." *Econometrica,* 40, 1972, pp. 757–758.

McCallum, B., "A Note Concerning Covariance Expressions." *Econometrica,* 42, 1973, pp. 581—583.

McCoskey, S., and C. Kao. "Testing the Stability of a Production Function with Urbanization as a Shift Factor: An Application of Nonstationary Panel Data Techniques." *Oxford Bulletin of Economics and Statistics,* 61, 1999, pp. 671–690.

McCoskey, S., and T. Selden. "Health Care Expenditures and GDP: Panel Data Unit Root Test Results." *Journal of Health Economics,* 17, 1998, pp. 369–376.

McCullagh, P., and J. Nelder. *Generalized Linear Models.* New York: Chapman and Hall, 1983.

McCullough, B. "Consistent Forecast Intervals When the Forecast-Period Exogenous Variables Are Stochastic." *Journal of Forecasting,* 15, 1996, pp. 293–304.

McCullough, B. "Econometric Software Reliability: E-Views, LIMDEP, SHAZAM, and TSP." *Journal of Applied Econometrics,* 14, 2 1999, pp. 191–202.

McCullough, B., and C. Renfro. "Benchmarks and Software Standards: A Case Study of GARCH Procedures." *Journal of Economic and Social Measurement,* 25, 2, 1999, pp. 27–37.

McCullough, B., and H. Vinod. "The Numerical Reliability of Econometric Software." *Journal of Economic Literature,* 37, 2, 1999, pp. 633–665.

McDonald, J., and R. Moffitt. "The Uses of Tobit Analysis." *Review of Economics and Statistics,* 62, 1980, pp. 318–321.

McElroy, M. "Goodness of Fit for Seemingly Unrelated Regressions: Glahn's $R^2_{y,x}$ and Hooper's $\bar{r}^2$." *Journal of Econometrics,* 6, 1977, pp. 381–387.

McFadden, D. "Conditional Logit Analysis of Qualitative Choice Behavior." In P. Zarembka, ed., *Frontiers in Econometrics.* New York: Academic Press, 1974.

McFadden, D. "The Measurement of Urban Travel Demand." *Journal of Public Economics,* 3, 1974, pp. 303–328.

McFadden, D. "Econometric Analysis of Qualitative Response Models." In Z. Griliches and M. Intriligator, eds., *Handbook of Econometrics,* Vol. 2. Amsterdam: North Holland, 1984.

McFadden, D. "Regression Based Specification Tests for the Multinomial Logit Model." *Journal of Econometrics,* 34, 1987, pp. 63–82.

McFadden, D. "A Method of Simulated Moments for Estimation of Discrete Response Models without Numerical Integration." *Econometrica,* 57, 1989, pp. 995–1026.

McFadden, D., and K. Train. "Mixed Multinomial Logit Models for Discrete Response." *Journal of Applied Econometrics,* 15, 2000, pp. 447–470.

McFadden, D., and P. Ruud. "Estimation by Simulation." *Review of Economics and Statistics,* 76, 1994, pp. 591–608.

McGuire, T., J. Farley, R. Lucas, and R. Winston. "Estimation and Inference for Models in Which Subsets of the Dependent Variable Are Constrained." *Journal of the American Statistical Association,* 63, 1968, pp. 1201–1213.

McKenzie, C. "Microfit 4.0." *Journal of Applied Econometrics,* 13, 1998, pp. 77–90.

McKoskey, S., and C. Kao. "Testing the Stability of a Production Function with Urbanization as a Shift Factor: An Application of Nonstationary Panel Data Techniques." *Oxford Bulletin of Economics and Statistics,* 61, 1999, pp. 57–84.

McKoskey, S., and T. Selden. "Health Care Expenditures and GDP: Panel Data Unit Root Tests," *Journal of Health Economics,* 17, 1998, pp. 369–376.

McLachlan, G., and T. Krishnan. *The EM Algorithm and Extensions.* New York: John Wiley and Sons, 1997.

McLachlan, G., and D. Peel. *Finite Mixture Models.* New York: John Wiley and Sons, 2000.

McLaren, K. "Parsimonious Autocorrelation Corrections for Singular Demand Systems." *Economics Letters,* 53, 1996, pp. 115–121.

Melenberg, B., and A. van Soest. "Parametric and Semi-Parametric Modelling of Vacation Expenditures." *Journal of Applied Econometrics,* 11, 1, 1996, pp. 59–76.

Merton, R. "On Estimating the Expected Return on the Market." *Journal of Financial Economics,* 8, 1980, pp. 323–361.

Messer, K., and H. White. "A Note on Computing the Heteroscedasticity Consistent Covariance Matrix Using Instrumental Variable Techniques." *Oxford Bulletin of Economics and Statistics,* 46, 1984, pp. 181–184.

Meyer, B. "Semiparametric Estimation of Hazard Models." Northwestern University, Department of Economics, 1988.

Mills, T. *Time Series Techniques for Economists.* New York: Cambridge University Press, 1990.

Mills, T. *The Econometric Modelling of Financial Time Series.* New York: Cambridge University Press, 1993.

Min, C., and A. Zellner. "Bayesian and Non-Bayesian Methods for Combining Models and Forecasts with Applications to Forecasting International Growth Rates." *Journal of Econometrics,* 56, 1993, pp. 89–118.

Mittelhammer, R., G. Judge, and D. Miller. *Econometric Foundations.* Cambridge: Cambridge University Press, 2000.

Mizon, G. "A Note to Autocorrelation Correctors: Don't." *Journal of Econometrics,* 69, 1, 1995, pp. 267–288.

Mizon, G., and J. Richard. "The Encompassing Principle and its Application to Testing Nonnested Models." *Econometrica,* 54, 1986, pp. 657–678.

Moffitt, R. "Comment on Estimation of Limited Dependent Variable Models with Dummy Endogenous Regressors: Simple Strategies for Empirical Practice." *Journal of Business and Statistics,* 19, 1, 2001, pp. 26–27.

Moscone, F., M. Knapp, and E. Tosetti. "Mental Health Expenditures in England: A Spatial Panel Approach." *Journal of Health Economics,* forthcoming, 2007.

Mohanty, M. "A Bivariate Probit Approach to the Determination of Employment: A Study of Teen Employment Differentials in Los Angeles County," *Applied Economics,* 34, 2, 2002, pp. 143–156.

Moran, P. "Notes on Continuous Stochastic Phenomena." *Biometrika* 37, 1950, pp. 17–23.

Moshino, G., and D. Moro. "Autocorrelation Specification in Singular Equation Systems," *Economics Letters,* 46, 1994, pp. 303–309.

Mroz, T. "The Sensitivity of an Empirical Model of Married Women's Hours of Work to Economic and Statistical Assumptions." *Econometrica,* 55, 1987, pp. 765–799.

Mullahy, J. "Specification and Testing of Some Modified Count Data Models." *Journal of Econometrics,* 33, 1986, pp. 341–365.

Mullahy, J. "Weighted Least Squares Estimation of the Linear Probability Model, Revisited." *Economics Letters,* 32, 1990, pp. 35–41.

Mundlak, Y. "On the Pooling of Time Series and Cross Sectional Data." *Econometrica,* 56, 1978, pp. 69–86.

Munkin, M., and P. Trivedi. "Simulated Maximum Likelihood Estimation of Multivariate Mixed Poisson Regression Models with Application," *Econometric Journal,* 1, 1, 1999, pp. 1–21.

Munnell, A. "Why Has Productivity Declined? Productivity and Public Investment." *New England Economic Review,* 1990, pp. 3–22.

Murphy, K., and R. Topel. "Estimation and Inference in Two Step Econometric Models." *Journal of Business and Economic Statistics,* 3, 1985, pp. 370–379. Reprinted, 20, 2002, pp. 88–97.

Nagin, D., and K. Land. "Age, Criminal Careers, and Population Heterogeneity: Specification and Estimation of a Nonparametric Mixed Poisson Model." *Criminology,* 31, 3, 1993, pp. 327–362.

Nair-Reichert, U., and D. Weinhold. "Causality Tests for Cross Country Panels: A Look at FDI and Economic Growth in Less Developed Countries." *Oxford Bulletin of Economics and Statistics,* 63, 2, 2001, pp. 153–171.

Nakamura, A., and M. Nakamura. "On the Relationships Among Several Specification Error Tests Presented by Durbin, Wu, and Hausman." *Econometrica,* 49, 1981, pp. 1583–1588.

Nakamura, A., and M. Nakamura. "Part-Time and Full-Time Work Behavior of Married Women: A Model with a Doubly Truncated Dependent Variable." *Canadian Journal of Economics,* 1983, pp. 229–257.

Nakosteen, R., and M. Zimmer. "Migration and Income: The Question of Self-Selection." *Southern Economic Journal,* 46, 1980, pp. 840–851.

Nelder, J., and R. Mead. "A Simplex Method for Function Minimization." *Computer Journal,* 7, 1965, pp. 308–313.

Nelson, C., and H. Kang. "Pitfalls in the Use of Time as an Explanatory Variable in Regression." *Journal of Business and Economic Statistics,* 2, 1984, pp. 73–82.

Nelson, C., and C. Plosser. "Trends and Random Walks in Macroeconomic Time Series: Some Evidence and Implications." *Journal of Monetary Economics,* 10, 1982, pp. 139–162.

Nelson, F. "A Test for Misspecification in the Censored Normal Model." *Econometrica,* 49, 1981, pp. 1317–1329.

Nerlove, M. "Returns to Scale in Electricity Supply." In C. Christ, ed., *Measurement in Economics: Studies in Mathematical Economics and Econometrics in Memory of Yehuda Grunfeld.* Palo Alto: Stanford University Press, 1963.

Nerlove, M. "Further Evidence on the Estimation of Dynamic Relations from a Time Series of Cross Sections." *Econometrica,* 39, 1971a, pp. 359–382.

Nerlove, M. "A Note on Error Components Models." *Econometrica,* 39, 1971b, pp. 383–396.

Nerlove, M. "Lags in Economic Behavior." *Econometrica,* 40, 1972, pp. 221–251.

Nerlove, M. *Essays in Panel Data Econometrics.* Cambridge: Cambridge University Press, 2002.

Nerlove, M., and S. Press. "Univariate and Multivariate Log-Linear and Logistic Models." RAND—R1306-EDA/NIH, Santa Monica, 1973.

Nerlove, M., and K. Wallis. "Use of the Durbin–Watson Statistic in Inappropriate Situations." *Econometrica,* 34, 1966, pp. 235–238.

Newbold, P. "Testing Causality Using Efficiently Parameterized Vector ARMA Models." *Applied Mathematics and Computation,* 20, 1986, pp. 184–199.

Newbold, P. "Significance Levels of the Box–Pierce Portmanteau Statistic in Finite Samples." *Biometrika,* 64, 1977, pp. 67–71.

Newey, W. "A Method of Moments Interpretation of Sequential Estimators." *Economics Letters,* 14, 1984, pp. 201–206.

Newey, W. "Maximum Likelihood Specification Testing and Conditional Moment Tests." *Econometrica,* 53, 1985a, pp. 1047–1070.

Newey, W. "Generalized Method of Moments Specification Testing." *Journal of Econometrics,* 29, 1985b, pp. 229–256.

Newey, W. "Specification Tests for Distributional Assumptions in the Tobit Model." *Journal of Econometrics,* 34, 1986, pp. 125–146.

Newey, W. "Efficient Estimation of Limited Dependent Variable Models with Endogenous Explanatory Variables." *Journal of Econometrics,* 36, 1987, pp. 231–250.

Newey, W. "The Asymptotic Variance of Semiparametric Estimators," *Econometrica,* 62, 1994, pp. 1349–1382.

Newey, W., and D. McFadden. "Large Sample Estimation and Hypothesis Testing." In R. Engle and D. McFadden, eds., *Handbook of Econometrics,* Vol. IV, Chapter 36, 1994.

Newey, W., J. Powell, and J. Walker. "Semiparametric Estimation of Selection Models." *American Economic Review,* 80, 1990, pp. 324–328.

Newey, W. "Two Step Series Estimation of Sample Selection Models." Manuscript, Department of Economics, MIT, 1991.

Newey, W., and K. West. "A Simple Positive Semi-Definite, Heteroscedasticity and Autocorrelation Consistent Covariance Matrix." *Econometrica,* 55, 1987a, pp. 703–708.

Newey, W., and K. West. "Hypothesis Testing with Efficient Method of Moments Estimation." *International Economic Review,* 28, 1987b, pp. 777–787.

*New York Post.* "America's New Big Wheels of Fortune." May 22, 1987, p. 3.

Neyman, J., and E. Scott. "Consistent Estimates Based on Partially Consistent Observations." *Econometrica,* 16, 1948, pp. 1–32.

Nickell, S. "Biases in Dynamic Models with Fixed Effects." *Econometrica,* 49, 1981, pp. 1417–1426.

Oaxaca, R. "Male–Female Wage Differentials in Urban Labor Markets." *International Economic Review,* 14, 1973, pp. 693–708.

Oberhofer, W., and J. Kmenta. "A General Procedure for Obtaining Maximum Likelihood Estimates in Generalized Regression Models." *Econometrica,* 42, 1974, pp. 579–590.

Ohtani, K., and M. Kobayashi. "A Bounds Test for Equality Between Sets of Coefficients in Two Linear Regression Models Under Heteroscedasticity." *Econometric Theory,* 2, 1986, pp. 220–231.

Ohtani, K., and T. Toyoda. "Estimation of Regression Coefficients After a Preliminary Test for Homoscedasticity." *Journal of Econometrics,* 12, 1980, pp. 151–159.

Ohtani, K., and T. Toyoda. "Small Sample Properties of Tests of Equality Between Sets of Coefficients in Two Linear Regressions Under Heteroscedasticity." *International Economic Review,* 26, 1985, pp. 37–44.

Olsen, R. "A Note on the Uniqueness of the Maximum Likelihood Estimator in the Tobit Model." *Econometrica,* 46, 1978, pp. 1211–1215.

Orea, C., and S. Kumbhakar. "Efficiency Measurement Using a Latent Class Stochastic Frontier Model." *Empirical Economics,* 29, 2004, pp. 169–184.

Orcutt, G., S. Caldwell, and R. Wertheimer. *Policy Exploration through Microanalytic Simulation.* Washington, D.C.: Urban Institute, 1976.

Orme, C. "Nonnested Tests for Discrete Choice Models." Working Paper, Department of Economics, University of York, 1994.

Orme, C. "Double and Triple Length Regressions for the Information Matrix Test and Other Conditional Moment Tests." Mimeo, University of York, U.K., Department of Economics, 1990.

Osterwald-Lenum, M. "A Note on Quantiles of the Asymptotic Distribution of the

Maximum Likelihood Cointegration Rank Test Statistics." *Oxford Bulletin of Economics and Statistics,* 54, 1992, pp. 461–472.

Pagan, A., and A. Ullah. "The Econometric Analysis of Models with Risk Terms." *Journal of Applied Econometrics,* 3, 1988, pp. 87–105.

Pagan, A., and A. Ullah. *Nonparametric Econometrics.* Cambridge: Cambridge University Press, 1999.

Pagan, A., and F. Vella. "Diagnostic Tests for Models Based on Individual Data: A Survey." *Journal of Applied Econometrics,* 4, Supplement, 1989, pp. S29–S59.

Pagan, A., and M. Wickens. "A Survey of Some Recent Econometric Methods." *Economic Journal,* 99, 1989, pp. 962–1025.

Pagano, M., and M. Hartley. "On Fitting Distributed Lag Models Subject to Polynomial Restrictions." *Journal of Econometrics,* 16, 1981, pp. 171–198.

Pakes, A., and D. Pollard. "Simulation and the Asymptotics of Optimization Estimators." *Econometrica,* 57, 1989, pp. 1027–1058.

Park, R., R. Sickles, and L. Simar. "Semiparametric Efficient Estimation of Panel Data Models with AR(1) Errors." Manuscript, Demartment of Economics, Rice University, 2000.

Parks, R. "Efficient Estimation of a System of Regression Equations When Disturbances Are Both Serially and Contemporaneously Correlated." *Journal of the American Statistical Association,* 62, 1967, pp. 500–509.

Passmore, W. "The GSE Implicit Subsity and the Value of Government Ambiguity." *FEDS Working Paper No. 2005-05,* Board of Governors of the Federal Reserve—Household and Real Estate Finance Section, 2005.

Passmore, W., S. Sherlund, and G. Burgess. "The Effect of Housing Government Sponsored Enterprises on Mortgage Rates," *Real Estate Economics,* 33, 3, 2005, pp. 427–463.

Patterson, K. *An Introduction to Applied Econometrics.* New York: St. Martin's Press, 2000.

Pedroni, P., "Fully Modified OLS for Heterogeneous Cointegrated Panels," Advances in Econometrics, 15, 2000, pp. 93–130.

Pedroni, P. "Purchasing Power Parity Tests in Cointegrated Panels." *Review of Economics and Statistics,* 83, 2001, pp. 727–731.

Pedroni, P. "Panel Cointegration: Asymptotic and Finite Sample Properties of Pooled Time Series Tests with an Application to the PPP Hypothesis." *Econometric Theory,* 20, 2004, pp. 597–625.

Pesaran, H. "On the General Problem of Model Selection." *Review of Economic Studies,* 41, 1974, pp. 153–171.

Pesaran, M. *The Limits to Rational Expectations.* Oxford: Blackwell, 1987.

Pesaran, M., and A. Hall. "Tests of Non-Nested Linear Regression Models Subject to Linear Restrictions." *Economics Letters,* 27, 1988, pp. 341–348.

Pesaran, H., and A. Deaton. "Testing Non-Nested Nonlinear Regression Models." *Econometrica,* 46, 1978, pp. 677–694.

Pesaran, M., and B. Pesaran. "A Simulation Approach to the Problem of Computing Cox's Statistic for Testing Nonnested Models." *Journal of Econometrics,* 57, 1993, pp. 377–392.

Pesaran, M., and R. Smith. "Estimating Long Run Relationships from Dynamic Heterogeneous Panels." *Journal of Econometrics,* 68, 1995, pp. 79–113.

Pesaran, H., R. Smith, and K. Im. "Dynamic Linear Models for Heterogeneous Panels." In L. Matyas and P. Sevestre, eds., *The Econometrics of Panel Data: A Handbook of the Theory with Applications,* 2nd ed. Dordrecht: Kluwer Academic Publishers, 1996.

Pesaran, M., Y. Shin, and R. Smith. "Pooled Mean Group Estimation of Dynamic Heterogeneous Panels." *Journal of the American Statistical Association,* 94, 1999, pp. 621–634.

Pesaran, M., and P. Schmidt. *Handbook of Applied Econometrics: Volume II: Microeconomics*. London: Blackwell Publishers, 1997.

Pesaran, H., and M. Weeks. "Nonnested Hypothesis Testing: An Overview." In B. Baltagi ed., *A Companion to Theoretical Econometrics*, Blackwell, Oxford, 2001.

Petersen, D., and D. Waldman. "The Treatment of Heteroscedasticity in the Limited Dependent Variable Model." Mimeo, University of North Carolina, Chapel Hill, November 1981.

Petersen, T. "Fitting Parametric Survival Models with Time Dependent Covariates." *Journal of the Royal Statistical Society, Series C (Applied Statistics)*, 35, 1986, pp. 281–288.

Phillips, A. "Stabilization Policies and the Time Form of Lagged Responses." *Economic Journal*, 67, 1957, pp. 265–277.

Phillips, P. "Exact Small Sample Theory in the Simultaneous Equations Model." In Z. Griliches and M. Intriligator, eds., *Handbook of Econometrics*, Vol. 1. Amsterdam: North Holland, 1983.

Phillips, P. "Understanding Spurious Regressions." *Journal of Econometrics*, 33, 1986, pp. 311–340.

Phillips, P. "Time Series Regressions with a Unit Root." *Econometrica*, 55, 1987, pp. 277–301.

Phillips, P. and H. Moon, "Linear Regression Limit Theory for Nonstationary Panel Data," *Econometrica*, 67, 1999, pp. 1057–1111.

Phillips, P., and H. Moon. "Nonstationary Panel Data Analysis: An Overview of Some Recent Developments." *Econometric Reviews*, 19, 2000, pp. 263–286.

Phillips, P., and S. Ouliaris. "Asymptotic Properties of Residual Based Tests for Cointegration." *Econometrica*, 58, 1990, pp. 165–193.

Phillips, P., and P. Perron. "Testing for a Unit Root in Time Series Regression." *Biometrika*, 75, 1988, pp. 335–346.

Poirier, D. *The Econometrics of Structural Change*. Amsterdam: North Holland, 1974.

Poirier, D. "The Use of the Box–Cox Transformation in Limited Dependent Variable Models." *Journal of the American Statistical Association*, 73, 1978, pp. 284–287.

Poirier, D. "Partial Observability in Bivariate Probit Models." *Journal of Econometrics*, 12, 1980, pp. 209–217.

Poirier, D. "Frequentist and Subjectivist Perspectives on the Problems of Model Building in Economics." *Journal of Economic Perspectives*, 2, 1988, pp. 121–170.

Poirier, D., ed. "Bayesian Empirical Studies in Economics and Finance." *Journal of Econometrics*, 49, 1991, pp. 1–304.

Poirier, D. *Intermediate Statistics and Econometrics*. Cambridge: MIT Press, 1995, pp. 1–217.

Poirier, D., and A. Melino. "A Note on the Interpretation of Regression Coefficients Within a Class of Truncated Distributions." *Econometrica*, 46, 1978, pp. 1207–1209.

Poirier, D., and J. Tobias. "Bayesian Econometrics." In T. Mills and K. Patterson, eds., *Palgrave Handbook of Econometrics, Volume 1: Theoretical Econometrics*. London: Palgrave-Macmillan, 2006.

Powell, A. "Aitken Estimators as a Tool in Allocating Predetermined Aggregates." *Journal of the American Statistical Association*, 44, 1969, pp. 913–922.

Powell, J. "Least Absolute Deviations Estimation for Censored and Truncated Regression Models." Technical Report 356, Stanford University, IMSSS, 1981.

Powell, J. "Least Absolute Deviations Estimation for the Censored Regression Model." *Journal of Econometrics*, 25, 1984, pp. 303–325.

Powell, J. "Censored Regression Quantiles." *Journal of Econometrics*, 32, 1986a, pp. 143–155.

Powell, J. "Symmetrically Trimmed Least Squares Estimation for Tobit Models." *Econometrica*, 54, 1986b, pp. 1435–1460.

Powell, M. "An Efficient Method for Finding the Minimum of a Function of Several Variables without Calculating Derivatives." *Computer Journal,* 1964, pp. 165–172.

Prais, S., and H. Houthakker. *The Analysis of Family Budgets.* New York: Cambridge University Press, 1955.

Prais, S., and C. Winsten. "Trend Estimation and Serial Correlation." Cowles Commission Discussion Paper No. 383, Chicago, 1954.

Pratt, J. "Concavity of the Log Likelihood." *Journal of the American Statistical Association,* 76, pp. 103–106.

Prentice, R., and L. Gloeckler. "Regression Analysis of Grouped Survival Data with Application to Breast Cancer Data." *Biometrics,* 34, 1978, pp. 57–67.

Press, W., B. Flannery, S. Teukolsky, and W. Vetterling. *Numerical Recipes: The Art of Scientific Computing.* Cambridge: Cambridge University Press, 1986.

Pudney, S., and M. Shields. "Gender, Race, Pay and Promotion in the British Nursing Profession: Estimation of a Generalized Ordered Probit Model." *Journal of Applied Econometrics,* 15, 4, 2000, pp. 367–399.

Quandt, R. "Econometric Disequilibrium Models." *Econometric Reviews,* 1, 1982, pp. 1–63.

Quandt, R. "Computational Problems and Methods." In Z. Griliches and M. Intriligator, eds., *Handbook of Econometrics,* Vol. 1. Amsterdam: North Holland, 1983.

Quandt, R. *The Econometrics of Disequilibrium.* New York: Basil Blackwell, 1988.

Quandt, R., and J. Ramsey. "Estimating Mixtures of Normal Distributions and Switching Regressions." *Journal of the American Statistical Association,* 73, December 1978, pp. 730–738.

Quester, A., and W. Greene. "Divorce Risk and Wives' Labor Supply Behavior." *Social Science Quarterly,* 63, 1982, pp. 16–27.

Raftery, A., and S. Lewis. "How Many Iterations in the Gibbs Sampler?" In J. Bernardo et al., eds., *Proceedings of the Fourth Valencia International Conference on Bayesian Statistics.* New York: Oxford University Press, 1992, pp. 763–774.

Raj, B., and B. Baltagi, eds. *Panel Data Analysis.* Heidelberg: Physica-Verlag, 1992.

Rao, C. *Linear Statistical Inference and Its Applications.* New York: John Wiley and Sons, 1973.

Rao, C. "Information and Accuracy Attainable in Estimation of Statistical Parameters." *Bulletin of the Calcutta Mathematical Society,* 37, 1945, pp. 81–91.

Rasch, G. "Probabilistic Models for Some Intelligence and Attainment Tests." *Denmark Paedogiska,* Copenhagen, 1960.

Reichert, U., and D. Weinhold. "Causality Tests for Cross Country Panels: A New Look at FDI and Economic Growth in Developing Countries." Manuscript, Department of Economics, Georgia Institute of Technology, 2000.

Renfro, C. "Econometric Software," *Journal of Economic and Social Measurement,* forthcoming, 2007.

Revankar, N. "Some Finite Sample Results in the Context of Two Seemingly Unrelated Regression Equations." *Journal of the American Statistical Association,* 69, 1974, pp. 187–190.

Revankar, N. "Use of Restricted Residuals in SUR Systems: Some Finite Sample Results." *Journal of the American Statistical Association,* 71, 1976, pp. 183–188.

Revelt, D., and K. Train. "Incentives for Appliance Efficiency: Random-Parameters Logit Models of Households' Choices." Manuscript, Department of Economics, University of California, Berkeley, 1996.

Revelt, D., and K. Train. "Customer Specific Taste Parameters and Mixed Logit: Households' Choice of Electricity Supplier." Economics Working Paper, E00-274, Department of Economics, University of California at Berkeley, 2000.

Ridder, G., and T. Wansbeek. "Dynamic Models for Panel Data." In R. van der Ploeg, ed., *Advanced Lectures in Quantitative Economics.* New York: Academic Press, 1990, pp. 557–582.

Riersøl, O. "Identifiability of a Linear Relation Between Variables Which Are Subject to Error." *Econometrica,* 18, 1950, pp. 375–389.

Riphahn, R., A. Wambach, and A. Million. "Incentive Effects in the Demand for Health Care: A Bivariate Panel Count Data Estimation." *Journal of Applied Econometrics,* 18, 4, 2003, pp. 387–405.

Rivers, D., and Q. Vuong. "Limited Information Estimators and Exogeneity Tests for Simultaneous Probit Models." *Journal of Econometrics,* 39, 1988, pp. 347–366.

Roberts, G. "Convergence Diagnostics of the Gibbs Sampler." In J. Bernardo et al., eds., *Proceedings of the Fourth Valencia International Conference on Bayesian Statistics.* New York: Oxford University Press, 1992, pp. 775–782.

Robertson, D., and J. Symons. "Some Strange Properties of Panel Data Estimators." *Journal of Applied Econometrics,* 7, 1992, pp. 175–189.

Robinson, C., and N. Tomes. "Self Selection and Interprovincial Migration in Canada." *Canadian Journal of Economics,* 15, 1982, pp. 474–502.

Robinson, P. "Semiparametric Econometrics: A Survey." *Journal of Applied Econometrics,* 3, 1988, pp. 35–51.

Rogers, W. "Calculation of Quantile Regression Standard Errors." Stata Technical Bulletin No. 13, Stata Corporation, College Station, TX, 1993.

Rosenbaum, P., and D. Rubin. "The Central Role of the Propensity Score in Observational Studies for Causal Effects." *Biometrika,* 70, 1983, pp. 41–55.

Rosenblatt, D. "Remarks on Some Nonparametric Estimates of a Density Function." *Annals of Mathematical Statistics,* 27, 1956, pp. 832–841.

Rosett, R., and F. Nelson. "Estimation of the Two-Limit Probit Regression Model." *Econometrica,* 43, 1975, pp. 141–146.

Rossi, P., and G. Allenby. "Bayesian Statistics and Marketing." *Marketing Science,* 22, 2003, 304–328.

Rossi, P., and G. Allenby. "Marketing Models of Consumer Heterogeneity." *Journal of Econometrics,* 89, 1999, pp. 57–78.

Rossi, P., G. Allenby, and R. McCulloch. *Bayesian Statistics and Marketing.* New York: John Wiley and Sons, 2005.

Rothstein, J. "Does Competition Among Public Schools Benefit Students and Taxpayers? A Comment on Hoxby (2000)." Working Paper Number 10, Princeton University, Education Research Section, 2004.

Rotnitzky, A., and J. Robins. "Inverse Probability Weighted Estimation in Survival Analysis." In P. Armitage and T. Coulton, eds., *Encyclopedia of Biostatistics.* New York: Wiley, 2005.

Rubin, D. "Inference and Missing Data." *Biometrika,* 63, 1976, pp. 581–592.

Rubin, D. *Multiple Imputation for Nonresponse in Surveys.* New York: John Wiley and Sons, 1987.

Rubin, H. "Consistency of Maximum Likelihood Estimators in the Explosive Case." In T. Koopmans, ed., *Statistical Inference in Dynamic Economic Models.* New York: John Wiley and Sons, 1950.

Ruud, P. *An Introduction to Classical Econometric Theory.* Oxford: Oxford University Press, 2000.

Ruud, P. "A Score Test of Consistency." Manuscript, Department of Economics, University of California, Berkeley, 1982.

Ruud, P. "Tests of Specification in Econometrics." *Econometric Reviews,* 3, 1984, pp. 211–242.

Ruud, P. "Consistent Estimation of Limited Dependent Variable Models Despite Misspecification of the Distribution." *Journal of Econometrics,* 32, 1986, pp. 157–187.

Sala-i-Martin, X. "The Classical Approach to Convergence Analysis." *Economic Journal,* 106, 1996, pp. 1019–1036.

Sala-i-Martin, X. "I Just Ran Two Million Regressions." *American Economic Review,* 87, 1997, pp. 178–183.

Salem, D., and T. Mount. "A Convenient Descriptive Model of the Income

Distribution." *Econometrica,* 42, 6, 1974, pp. 1115–1128.

Saxonhouse, G. "Estimated Parameters as Dependent Variables." *American Economic Review,* 46, 1, 1976, pp. 178–183.

Savin, E., and K. White. "The Durbin–Watson Test for Serial Correlation with Extreme Sample Sizes or Many Regressors." *Econometrica,* 45(8), 1977, pp. 1989–1996.

Sawtooth Software. *The CBC/HB Module for Hierarchical Bayes Estimation.* 2006.

Saxonhouse, G. "Estimated Parameters as Dependent Variables." *American Economic Review,* 66, 1, 1976, pp. 178–183.

Schimek, M. (ed.). *Smoothing and Regression: Approaches, Computation, and Applications,* New York: John Wiley and Sons, 2000.

Schmidt, P. *Econometrics.* New York: Marcel Dekker, 1976.

Schmidt, P. "Estimation of Seemingly Unrelated Regressions with Unequal Numbers of Observations." *Journal of Econometrics,* 5, 1977, pp. 365–377.

Schmidt, P., and R. Sickles. "Some Further Evidence on the Use of the Chow Test Under Heteroscedasticity." *Econometrica,* 45, 1977, pp. 1293–1298.

Schmidt, P., and R. Sickles. "Production Frontiers and Panel Data." *Journal of Business and Economic Statistics,* 2, 1984, pp. 367–374.

Schmidt, P., and R. Strauss. "The Prediction of Occupation Using Multinomial Logit Models." *International Economic Review,* 16, 1975a, pp. 471–486.

Schmidt, P., and R. Strauss. "Estimation of Models with Jointly Dependent Qualitative Variables: A Simultaneous Logit Approach." *Econometrica,* 43, 1975b, pp. 745–755.

Schwert, W. "Tests for Unit Roots: A Monte Carlo Investigation." *Journal of Business and Economic Statistics,* 7, 1989, pp. 147–159.

Seaks, T., and K. Layson. "Box–Cox Estimation with Standard Econometric Problems." *Review of Economics and Statistics,* 65, 1983, pp. 160–164.

Sepanski, J. "On a Random Coefficients Probit Model." *Communications in Statistics—Theory and Methods,* 29, 2000, pp. 2493–2505.

Shapiro, M., and M. Watson. "Sources of Business Cycle Fluctuations." In O. Blanchard and S. Fischer, eds., NBER *Macroeconomics Annual,* Cambridge: MIT Press, 1988, pp. 111–148.

Sharpe, W. "Capital Asset Prices: A Theory of Market Equilibrium Under Conditions of Risk." *Journal of Finance,* 19, 1964, pp. 425–442.

Shaw, D. "On-Site Samples' Regression Problems of Nonnegative Integers, Truncation, and Endogenous Stratification." *Journal of Econometrics,* 37, 1988, pp. 211–223.

Shea, J. "Instrument Relevance in Multivariate Linear Models: A Simple Measure." *Review of Economics and Statistics,* 79, 1997, pp. 348–352.

Shephard, R. *The Theory of Cost and Production.* Princeton: Princeton University Press, 1970.

Shumway, R. *Applied Statistical Time Series.* Englewood Cliffs, NJ: Prentice Hall, 1988.

Sickles, R. "A Nonlinear Multivariate Error Components Analysis of Technology and Specific Factor Productivity Growth with an Application to U.S. Airlines." *Journal of Econometrics,* 27, 1985, pp. 61–78.

Sickles, R., B. Park, and L. Simar. "Semiparametric Efficient Estimation of Panel Models with AR(1) Errors." Manuscript, Department of Economics, Rice University, 2000.

Sickles, R., D. Good, and R. Johnson. "Allocative Distortions and the Regulatory Transition of the Airline Industry." *Journal of Econometrics,* 33, 1986, pp. 143–163.

Silk, J. "Systems Estimation: A Comparison of SAS, Shazam, and TSP." *Journal of Applied Econometrics,* 11, 1996, pp. 437–450.

Silva, J. "A Score Test for Non-Nested Hypotheses with Applications to Discrete Response Models." *Journal of Applied Econometrics,* 16, 5, 2001, pp. 577–598.

Silver, J. and M. Ali. "Testing Slutsky Symmetry in Systems of Linear Demand Equations." *Journal of Econometrics*, 41, 1989, pp. 251–266.

Sims, C. "Money, Income, and Causality." *American Economic Review*, 62, 1972, pp. 540–552.

Sims, C. "Exogeneity and Causal Ordering in Macroeconomic Models." In *New Methods in Business Cycle Research: Proceedings from a Conference*. Federal Reserve Bank of Minneapolis, 1977, pp. 23–43.

Sims, C. "Macroeconomics and Reality." *Econometrica*, 48, 1, 1980, pp. 1–48.

Sklar, A. "Random Variables, Joint Distributions and Copulas." *Kybernetica*, 9, 1973, pp. 449–460.

Smith, M. "Modeling Selectivity Using Archimedean Copulas." *Econometrics Journal*, 6, 2003, pp. 99–123.

Smith, M. "Using Copulas to Model Switching Regimes with an Application to Child Labour," *Economic Record*, 81, 2005, pp. S47-S57.

Smith, R. "Estimation and Inference with Nonstationary Panel Time Series Data." Manuscript, Department of Economics, Birkbeck College, 2000.

Smith, V. "Selection and Recreation Demand." *American Journal of Agricultural Economics*, 70, 1988, pp. 29–36.

Solow, R. "Technical Change and the Aggregate Production Function." *Review of Economics and Statistics*, 39, 1957, pp. 312–320.

Sowell, F. "Optimal Tests of Parameter Variation in the Generalized Method of Moments Framework." *Econometrica*, 64, 1996, pp. 1085–1108.

Spector, L., and M. Mazzeo. "Probit Analysis and Economic Education." *Journal of Economic Education*, 11, 1980, pp. 37–44.

Spencer, D., and K. Berk. "A Limited Information Specification Test." *Econometrica*, 49, 1981, pp. 1079–1085.

Srivistava, V., and T. Dwivedi. "Estimation of Seemingly Unrelated Regression Equations: A Brief Survey." *Journal of Econometrics*, 10, 1979, pp. 15–32.

Srivistava, V., and D. Giles. *Seemingly Unrelated Regression Models: Estimation and Inference*. New York: Marcel Dekker, 1987.

Staiger, D., J. Stock, and M. Watson. "How Precise Are Estimates of the Natural Rate of Unemployment?" NBER Working Paper Number 5477, Cambridge, 1996.

Staiger, D., and J. Stock. "Instrumental Variables Regression with Weak Instruments." *Econometrica*, 65, 1997, pp. 557–586.

Stata. *Stata User's Guide, Version 9*. College Station, TX: Stata Press, 2006.

Stern, S. "Two Dynamic Discrete Choice Estimation Problems and Simulation Method Solutions." *Review of Economics and Statistics*, 76, 1994, pp. 695–702.

Stewart, M. "Maximum Simulated Likelihood Estimation of Random Effects Dynamic Probit Models with Autocorrelated Errors." Manuscript, Department of Economics, University of Warwick, 2006, reprinted *Stata Journal*, 6, 2, 2006, pp. 256–272.

Stigler, S. *Statistics on the Table*. Cambridge, MA: Harvard University Press, 1999.

Stock, J. "Unit Roots, Structural Breaks, and Trends." In R. Engle and D. McFadden, eds., *Handbook of Econometrics*, Vol. 4. Amsterdam: North Holland, 1994.

Stock, J., and F. Trebbi. "Who Invented Instrumental Variable Regression?" *Journal of Economic Perspectives*, 17, 32, 2003, pp. 177–194.

Stock, J., and M. Watson. "Testing for Common Trends." *Journal of the American Statistical Association*, 83, 1988, pp. 1097–1107.

Stock, J., and M. Watson. "Forecasting Output and Inflation: The Role of Asset Prices." *NBER*, Working Paper #8180, Cambridge, MA, 2001.

Stock, J., and M. Watson. "Combination Forecases of Output Growth in a Seven-Country Data Set." *Journal of Forecasting*, 23, 6, 2004, pp. 405–430.

Stock, J., and M. Watson. *Introduction to Econometrics,* 2nd ed., 2007.

Stock, J., J. Wright, and M. Yogo. "A Survey of Weak Instruments and Weak Identification in Generalized Method of Moments." *Journal of Business and Economic Statistics,* 20, 2002, pp. 518–529.

Stock, J., and M. Yogo. "Testing for Weak Instruments in Linear IV Regression." In J. Stock and D. Andrews, eds. *Identification and Inference in Econometrics: A Festschrift in Honor of Thomas Rothenberg.* Cambridge: Cambridge University Press, 2005, pp. 80–108.

Stoker, T. "Consistent Estimation of Scaled Coefficients." *Econometrica,* 54, 1986, pp. 1461–1482.

Stone, R. *The Measurement of Consumers' Expenditure and Behaviour in the United Kingdom, 1920–1938.* Cambridge: Cambridge University Press, 1954a.

Stone, R. "Linear Expenditure Systems and Demand Analysis: An Application to the Pattern of British Demand." *Economic Journal,* 64, 1954b, pp. 511–527.

Strang, G. *Linear Algebra and Its Applications.* New York: Academic Press, 1988.

Strickland, A., and L. Weiss. "Advertising, Concentration, and Price Cost Margins." *Journal of Political Economy,* 84, 1976, pp. 1109–1121.

Stuart, A., and S. Ord. *Kendall's Advanced Theory of Statistics.* New York: Oxford University Press, 1989.

Srivastava, T., and Tiwari, R. "Efficiency of Two Stage and Three Stage Least Squares Estimators." *Econometrica,* 46, 1978, pp. 1495–1498.

Suits, D. "Dummy Variables: Mechanics vs. Interpretation." *Review of Economics and Statistics,* 66, 1984, pp. 177–180.

Susin, S. "Hazard Hazards: The Inconsistency of the "Kaplan-Meier Empirical Hazard," and Some Alternatives," Manuscript, U.S. Census Bureau, 2001.

Swamy, P. "Efficient Inference in a Random Coefficient Regression Model." *Econometrica,* 38, 1970, pp. 311–323.

Swamy, P. *Statistical Inference in Random Coefficient Regression Models.* New York: Springer-Verlag, 1971.

Swamy, P. "Linear Models with Random Coefficients." In P. Zarembka, ed., *Frontiers in Econometrics.* New York: Academic Press, 1974.

Swamy, P., and G. Tavlas. "Random Coefficients Models: Theory and Applications." *Journal of Economic Surveys,* 9, 1995, pp. 165–182.

Swamy, P., and G. Tavlas. "Random Coefficient Models." In B. Baltagi, ed., *A Companion to Theoretical Econometrics.* Oxford: Blackwell, 2001.

Tanner, M. *Tools for Statistical Inference,* 2nd ed. New York: Springer-Verlag, 1993.

Taqqu, M. "Weak Convergence to Fractional Brownian Motion and the Rosenblatt Process." *Zeitschrift fur Wahrscheinlichkeitstheorie und Verwandte Gebiete,* 31, 1975, pp. 287–302.

Tauchen, H. "Diagnostic Testing and Evaluation of Maximum Likelihood Models." *Journal of Econometrics,* 30, 1985, pp. 415–443.

Tauchen, H., A. Witte, and H. Griesinger. "Criminal Deterrence: Revisiting the Issue with a Birth Cohort." *Review of Economics and Statistics,* 3, 1994, pp. 399–412.

Taylor, L. "Estimation by Minimizing the Sum of Absolute Errors." In P. Zarembka, ed., *Frontiers in Econometrics.* New York: Academic Press, 1974.

Taylor, W. "Small Sample Properties of a Class of Two Stage Aitken Estimators." *Econometrica,* 45, 1977, pp. 497–508.

Telser, L. "Iterative Estimation of a Set of Linear Regression Equations." *Journal of the American Statistical Association,* 59, 1964, pp. 845–862.

Terza, J. "Ordinal Probit: A Generalization." *Communications in Statistics,* 14, 1985a, pp. 1–12.

Terza, J. "A Tobit Type Estimator for the Censored Poisson Regression Model." *Economics Letters,* 18, 1985b, pp. 361–365.

Terza, J. "Estimating Count Data Models with Endogenous Switching and Sample

Selection." Working Paper IPRE-95-14, Department of Economics, Pennsylvania State University, 1995.

Terza, J. "Estimating Count Data Models with Endogenous Switching: Sample Selection and Endogenous Treatment Effects." *Journal of Econometrics,* 84, 1, 1998, pp. 129–154.

Terza, J., and D. Kenkel. "The Effect of Physician Advice on Alcohol Consumption: Count Regression with an Endogenous Treatment Effect," *Journal of Applied Econometrics,* 16, 2, 2001, pp. 165–184.

Theil, H. "Repeated Least Squares Applied to Complete Equation Systems." Discussion Paper, Central Planning Bureau, The Hague, 1953.

Theil, H. *Economic Forecasts and Policy.* Amsterdam: North Holland, 1961.

Theil, H. *Principles of Econometrics.* New York: John Wiley and Sons, 1971.

Theil, H. "Linear Algebra and Matrix Methods in Econometrics." In Z. Griliches and M. Intriligator, eds., *Handbook of Econometrics,* Vol. 1. New York: North Holland, 1983.

Theil, H., and A. Goldberger. "On Pure and Mixed Estimation in Economics." *International Economic Review,* 2, 1961, pp. 65–78.

Thursby, J. "Misspecification, Heteroscedasticity, and the Chow and Goldfeld–Quandt Tests." *Review of Economics and Statistics,* 64, 1982, pp. 314–321.

Tobin, J. "Estimation of Relationships for Limited Dependent Variables." *Econometrica,* 26, 1958, pp. 24–36.

Toyoda, T., and K. Ohtani. "Testing Equality Between Sets of Coefficients After a Preliminary Test for Equality of Disturbance Variances in Two Linear Regressions." *Journal of Econometrics,* 31, 1986, pp. 67–80.

Train, K. *Discrete Choice Methods with Simulation.* Cambridge: Cambridge University Press, 2002.

Train, K. "Halton Sequences for Mixed Logit." Manuscript, Department of Economics, University of California, Berkeley, 1999.

Train, K. "A Comparison of Hierarchical Bayes and Maximum Simulated Likelihood for Mixed Logit." Manuscript, Department of Economics, University of California, Berkeley, 2001.

Train, K. *Discrete Choice Methods with Simulation.* Cambridge: Cambridge University Press, 2003.

Trivedi, P., and A. Pagan. "Polynomial Distributed Lags: A Unified Treatment." *Economic Studies Quarterly,* 30, 1979, pp. 37–49.

Trivedi, P., and D. Zimmer. "Copula Modeling: An Introduction for Practitioners." *Foundations and Trends in Econometrics,* forthcoming, 2007.

Tsay, R. *Analysis of Financial Time Series,* 2nd ed. New York: John Wiley and Sons, 2005.

Tunali, I. "A General Structure for Models of Double Selection and an Application to a Joint Migration/Earnings Process with Remigration." *Research in Labor Economics,* 8, 1986, pp. 235–282.

United States Department of Commerce. *Statistical Abstract of the United States.* Washington, D.C.: U.S. Government Printing Office, 1979.

United States Department of Commerce, Bureau of Economic Analysis. *National Income and Product Accounts, Survey of Current Business: Business Statistics,* 1984. Washington, D.C.: U.S. Government Printing Office, 1984.

Veall, M. "Bootstrapping the Probability Distribution of Peak Electricity Demand." *International Economic Review,* 28, 1987, pp. 203–212.

Veall, M. "Bootstrapping the Process of Model Selection: An Econometric Example." *Journal of Applied Econometrics,* 7, 1992, pp. 93–99.

Veall, M., and K. Zimmermann. "Pseudo-$R^2$ in the Ordinal Probit Model." *Journal of Mathematical Sociology,* 16, 1992, pp. 333–342.

Vella, F. "Estimating Models with Sample Selection Bias: A Survey." *Journal of Human Resources,* 33, 1998, pp. 439–454.

Vella, F., and M. Verbeek. "Whose Wages Do Unions Raise? A Dynamic Model of Unionism and Wage Rate Determination for Young Men." *Journal of Applied Econometrics,* 13, 2, 1998, pp. 163–184.

Vella, F., and M. Verbeek. "Two-Step Estimation of Panel Data Models with Censored Endogenous Variables and Selection Bias." *Journal of Econometrics,* 90, 1999, pp. 239–263.

Verbeek, M. "On the Estimation of a Fixed Effects Model with Selectivity Bias." *Economics Letters,* 34, 1990, pp. 267–270.

Verbeek, M., and T. Nijman. "Testing for Selectivity Bias in Panel Data Models." *International Economic Review,* 33, 3, 1992, pp. 681–703.

Verbon, H. "Testing for Heteroscedasticity in a Model of Seemingly Unrelated Regression Equations with Variance Components (SUREVC)." *Economics Letters,* 5, 1980, pp. 149–153.

Vinod, H. "Bootstrap, Jackknife, Resampling and Simulation: Applications in Econometrics." In G. Maddala, C. Rao, and H. Vinod, eds., *Handbook of Statistics: Econometrics, Vol II.,* Chapter 11. Amsterdam: North Holland, 1993.

Vinod, H., and B. Raj. "Economic Issues in Bell System Divestiture: A Bootstrap Application." *Applied Statistics (Journal of the Royal Statistical Society, Series C),* 37, 2, 1994, pp. 251–261.

Vuong, Q. "Likelihood Ratio Tests for Model Selection and Non-Nested Hypotheses." *Econometrica,* 57, 1989, pp. 307–334.

Vytlacil, E., A. Aakvik, and J. Heckman. "Treatment Effects for Discrete Outcomes When Responses to Treatments Vary Among Observationally Identical Persons: An Applicaton to Norwegian Vocational Rehabilitation Programs." *Journal of Econometrics,* 125, 1/2, 2005, pp. 15–51.

Waldman, D. "A Note on the Algebraic Equivalence of White's Test and a Variant of the Godfrey/Breusch-Pagan Test for Heteroscedasticity." *Economics Letters,* 13, 1983, pp. 197–200.

Wallace, T., and A. Hussain. "The Use of Error Components in Combining Cross Section with Time Series Data." *Econometrica,* 37, 1969, pp. 55–72.

Wan, G., W. Griffiths, and J. Anderson. "Using Panel Data to Estimate Risk Effects in Seemingly Unrelated Production Functions." *Empirical Economics,* 17, 1992, pp. 35–49.

Wang, P., I. Cockburn, and M. Puterman. "Analysis of Panel Data: A Mixed Poisson Regression Model Approach." *Journal of Business and Economic Statistics,* 16, 1, 1998, pp. 27–41.

Watson, M. "Vector Autoregressions and Cointegration." In R. Engle and D. McFadden, eds., *Handbook of Econometrics,* Vol. 4. Amsterdam: North Holland, 1994.

Weeks, M. "Testing the Binomial and Multinomial Choice Models Using Cox's Nonnested Test." *Journal of the American Statistical Association, Papers and Proceedings,* 1996, pp. 312–328.

Weiss, A. "Asymptotic Theory for ARCH Models: Stability, Estimation, and Testing." Discussion Paper 82-36, Department of Economics, University of California, San Diego, 1982.

Weiss, A. "Simultaneity and Sample Selection in Poisson Regression Models." Manuscript, Department of Economics, University of Southern California, 1995.

Wedel, M., W. DeSarbo, J. Bult, and V. Ramaswamy. "A Latent Class Poisson Regression Model for Heterogeneous Count Data." *Journal of Applied Econometrics,* 8, 1993, pp. 397–411.

Weinhold, D. "A Dynamic "Fixed Effects" Model for Heterogeneous Panel Data." Manuscript, Department of Economics, London School of Economics, 1999.

Weinhold, D. "Investment, Growth and Causality Testing in Panels" (in French). *Economie et Prevision,* 126-5, 1996, pp. 163–175.

West, K. "On Optimal Instrumental Variables Estimation of Stationary Time Series Models." *International Economic Review,* 42, 4, 2001, pp. 1043–1050.

White, H. "A Heteroscedasticity-Consistent Covariance Matrix Estimator and a Direct Test for Heteroscedasticity." *Econometrica*, 48, 1980, pp. 817–838.

White, H. "Maximum Likelihood Estimation of Misspecified Models." *Econometrica*, 53, 1982a, pp. 1–16.

White, H. "Instrumental Variables Regression with Independent Observations." *Econometrica*, 50, 2, 1982b, pp. 483–500.

White, H., ed. "Non-Nested Models." *Journal of Econometrics*, 21, 1, 1983, pp. 1–160.

White, H. *Asymptotic Theory for Econometricians, Revised*. New York: Academic Press, 2001.

Wickens, M. "A Note on the Use of Proxy Variables." *Econometrica*, 40, 1972, pp. 759–760.

Willis, J. "Magazine Prices Revisited." *Journal of Applied Econometrics*, 21, 3, 2006, pp. 337–344.

Willis, R., and S. Rosen. "Education and Self-Selection." *Journal of Political Economy*, 87, 1979, pp. S7–S36.

Windmeijer, F. "Goodness of Fit Measures in Binary Choice Models." *Econometric Reviews*, 14, 1995, pp. 101–116.

Winkelmann, R. *Econometric Analysis of Count Data*. 2nd ed., Heidelberg, Germany: Springer-Verlag, 1997.

Winkelmann, R. *Econometric Analysis of Count Data*, Springer-Verlag, Heidelberg, 2000.

Winkelmann, R. *Econometric Analysis of Count Data*, Springer-Verlag, Heidelberg, 4th ed. 2003.

Winkelmann, R. "Subjective Well-Being and the Family: Results from an Ordered Probit Model with Multiple Random Effects." Discussion Paper 1016, IZA/Bonn and University of Zurich.

Witte, A. "Estimating an Economic Model of Crime with Individual Data." *Quarterly Journal of Economics*, 94, 980, pp. 57–84.

Wong, W. "On the Consistency of Cross Validation in Kernel Nonparametric Regression." *Annals of Statistics*, 11, 1983, pp. 1136–1141.

Woolridge, J. "Specification Testing and Quasi-Maximum Likelihood Estimation." *Journal of Econometrics*, 48, 1/2, 1991, pp. 29–57.

Woolridge, J. "Selection Corrections for Panel Data Models Under Conditional Mean Assumptions." *Journal of Econometrics*, 68, 1995, pp. 115–132.

Wooldridge, J. "Asymptotic Properties of Weighted M Estimators for Variable Probability Samples." *Econometrica*, 67, 1999, pp. 1385–1406.

Wooldridge, J. *Econometric Analysis of Cross Section and Panel Data*. Cambridge: MIT Press, 2002a.

Wooldridge, J. "Inverse Probability Weighted M Estimators for Sample Selection, Attrition and Stratification," *Portuguese Economic Journal*, 1, 2002b, pp. 117–139.

Wooldridge, J., "Simple Solutions to the Initial Conditions Problem in Dynamic Nonlinear Panel Data Models with Unobserved Heterogeneity," CEMMAP Working Paper CWP18/02, Centre for Microdata and Practice, IFS and University College, London, 2002c.

Woolridge, J. *Introductory Econometrics: A Modern Approach*, 3rd ed. New York: Southwestern Publishers, 2006a.

Wooldridge, J. "Inverse Pobability Weighted Estimation for General Missing Data Problems." Manuscript, Department of Economics, Michigan State University, East Lansing, 2006b.

Working, E. "What Do Statistical Demand Curves Show?" *Quarterly Journal of Economics*, 41, 1926, pp. 212–235.

World Health Organization. *The World Health Report, 2000, Health Systems: Improving Performance*. Geneva. 2000.

Wright, J., "Forecasting U.S. Inflation by Bayesian Model Averaging," Board of Governors, Federal Reserve System, International Finance Discussion Papers Number 780, 2003.

Wu, D. "Alternative Tests of Independence Between Stochastic Regressors and Disturbances." *Econometrica*, 41, 1973, pp. 733–750.

Wu, J., "Mean Reversion of the Current Account: Evidence from the Panel Data Unit Root Test," *Economics Letters*, 66, 2000, pp. 215–222.

Wynand, P., and B. van Praag. "The Demand for Deductibles in Private Health Insurance: A Probit Model with Sample Selection." *Journal of Econometrics*, 17, 1981, pp. 229–252.

Yatchew, A., "Nonparametric Regression Techniques in Econometrics," *Journal of Econometric Literature*, 36, 1998, pp. 669–721.

Yatchew, A., "An Elementary Estimator of the Partial Linear Model," *Economics Letters*, 57, 1997, pp. 135–143.

Yatchew, A., "Scale Economies in Electricity Distribution," *Journal of Applied Econometrics*, 15, 2, 2000, pp. 187–210.

Yatchew, A., and Z. Griliches. "Specification Error in Probit Models." *Review of Economics and Statistics*, 66, 1984, pp. 134–139.

Zabel, J., "Estimating Fixed and Random Effects Models with Selectivity," *Economics Letters*, 40, 1992, pp. 269–272.

Zarembka, P. "Transformations of Variables in Econometrics." In P. Zarembka, ed., *Frontiers in Econometrics*. Boston: Academic Press, 1974.

Zavoina, R., and W. McKelvey. "A Statistical Model for the Analysis of Ordinal Level Dependent Variables." *Journal of Mathematical Sociology*, Summer, 1975, pp. 103–120.

Zellner, A. "An Efficient Method of Estimating Seemingly Unrelated Regressions and Tests of Aggregation Bias." *Journal of the American Statistical Association*, 57, 1962, pp. 500–509.

Zellner, A. "Estimators for Seemingly Unrelated Regression Equations: Some Exact Finite Sample Results." *Journal of the American Statistical Association*, 58, 1963, pp. 977–992.

Zellner, A. *Introduction to Bayesian Inference in Econometrics*. New York: John Wiley and Sons, 1971.

Zellner, A. "Statistical Analysis of Econometric Models." *Journal of the American Statistical Association*, 74, 1979, pp. 628–643.

Zellner, A. "Bayesian Econometrics." *Econometrica*, 53, 1985, pp. 253–269.

Zellner, A., and D. Huang. "Further Properties of Efficient Estimators for Seemingly Unrelated Regression Equations." *International Economic Review*, 3, 1962, pp. 300–313.

Zellner, A., J. Kmenta, and J. Dreze. "Specification and Estimation of Cobb-Douglas Production Functions." *Econometrica*, 34, 1966, pp. 784–795.

Zellner, A., and C. K. Min. "Gibbs Sampler Convergence Criteria." *Journal of the American Statistical Association*, 90, 1995, pp. 921–927.

Zellner, A., and N. Revankar. "Generalized Production Functions." *Review of Economic Studies*, 37, 1970, pp. 241–250.

Zellner, A., and A. Siow. "Posterior Odds Ratios for Selected Regression Hypotheses (with Discussion)." In J. Bernardo, M. DeGroot, D. Lindley, and A. Smith, eds., *Bayesian Statistics*, Valencia, Spain: University Press, 1980.

Zellner, A., and H. Theil. "Three Stage Least Squares: Simultaneous Estimation of Simultaneous Equations." *Econometrica*, 30, 1962, pp. 63–68.

# AUTHOR INDEX

## A

Aakyik, A, 557n29
Abowd, J., 896n36
Abramovitz, M., 436n2, 1061n2, 1063, 1064, 1065
Abrevaya, J., 587, 588, 801, 838
Achen, C., 231n30, 232n31
Adkins, L., 60n6
Afifi, T., 62n9
Ahn, S., 269n17, 342, 470n14, 472, 475, 476, 478
Aigner, D., 90n5, 263, 538
Aitchison, J., 996n4
Aitken, A.C., 154, 155
Akaike, H., 37, 143, 506, 677, 697
Akin, J., 795n22
Aldrich, J., 773n2, 774n3
Ali, M., 165n17, 273n20
Allenby, G., 841
Allison, P., 62, 915, 917
Altonji, J., 810n34
Amemiya, T., 37n5, 151n2, 152, 170n23, 170n25, 204n15, 285n1, 290, 333, 365n12, 380, 380n17, 406n2, 421, 422n8, 423, 425, 438, 445n8, 472, 490, 494n3, 512n12, 513, 635, 677n3, 770, 773n2, 779n9, 790n14, 791n15, 792n16, 809, 863n1, 869n9, 875, 880n16, 1072n18, 1073n20
*American Economic Review,* 41
Andersen, D., 587, 803
Anderson, G., 264n15
Anderson, R., 278n31
Anderson, T., 152, 208n19, 244, 246, 333, 341, 376n15, 378, 379, 387, 470n14, 537, 635
Andrews, D., 123n12, 236, 406b2, 709
Angrist. J., 5, 398, 773n2, 814n37, 817, 889n28, 891n32, 892n34
Anselin, L., 218, 219
Antwiler, 214, 215
Arabmazar, A., 875
Arellano, M., 181n2, 210n23, 211, 341, 342, 343, 346, 348, 455, 470, 470n14, 470n15, 471,

472, 478, 557n29, 794, 801, 804, 882
Arrow, K., 275
Ashenfelter, O., 5, 11, 330
Attfield, C., 534n23
Avery, R., 267, 796n23, 800, 814, 828

## B

Baillie, R., 658, 658n16
Baker, R., 350
Balakrishnan, N., 866n5, 996n3
Balestra, P., 205n16, 208, 208n19, 238, 470n14
Baltagi, B., 181n2, 184, 198, 207, 208n19, 208n21, 209, 212, 214, 215, 216, 216n25, 218, 219, 243n32, 244, 255n3, 257n6, 342, 343, 399n1, 547, 585, 653, 654, 768, 804
Bannerjee, A., 244
Barnow, B., 890n31, 893
Bartels, R., 257n6, 263
Barten, A., 274n23
Basmann, R., 378
Bassett, G., 166, 406n2, 407, 425
Battese, G., 204n15
Beach, C., 529, 649, 651
Beck, N., 794n21, 795n22
Becker, S., 893, 894
Beggs, S., 831n48, 842
Behrman, J., 331
Bekker, P., 365n12
Bell, C., 1081
Bell, W., 218, 219, 715n1
Belsley, D., 60, 1075
Ben-Akiva, M., 790n14, 791
Ben-Porath, Y., 181
Bera, A., 880, 881n17
Bernard, J., 689n6
Berndt, E., 14, 91n6, 264n15, 276n25, 276n26, 277n29, 278, 279n32, 279n33, 495, 506n10, 1072, 1087
Beron, K., 233
Berry, S., 589, 851
Bertschek, I., 593, 594, 800, 814, 828, 829, 1089
Berzeg, K., 207

Beyer, A., 764, 765
Bhargava, A., 207n18, 336, 470n14, 476n19
Bhat, C., 578, 591
Billingsley, P., 75n16, 637n6
Binkley, J., 257n9
Birkes, D., 406n2
Blanchard, O., 706n12
Blinder, A., 55
Blundell, R., 264n15, 348, 420, 474n17, 780, 787n12, 816
Bockstael, N., 218, 219, 924
Bollerslev, T., 658, 658n17, 660, 661, 661n21, 662, 662n22, 663n24, 665, 665n28, 666n29, 667n31, 1089
Bond, S., 342, 343, 346, 348, 352, 455, 470, 470n14, 474n17
Boot, J., 252, 283n34, 1086
Borjas, G., 231n30
Börsch-Supan, A., 583n7, 827n44
Bound, J., 350
Bourguignon, F., 55n4
Bover, O., 210n23, 211, 342, 348, 455, 470, 470n14, 478, 557n29
Box, G., 296n3, 575, 633n5, 645, 648n14, 650, 715n1, 726, 727, 729, 730, 731, 738, 768
Boyes, W., 792, 793, 895
Brannas, K., 920
Bray, T., 575
Breitung, J., 767
Breslaw, J., 583n6
Breusch, T., 166, 166n19, 178, 184, 205, 223n26, 236, 526, 534, 549, 644
Brock, W., 776n5
Brown, B., 272n19
Brown, J., 996n4
Brown, P., 267
Browning, M., 420
Brundy, J., 319
Burgess, G., 232
Burnett, N., 823, 824, 1090
Burnside, C., 454n10
Buse, A., 156, 498n5
Butler, J., 407n3, 592, 797, 798, 799, 802, 814, 827, 829, 835, 836, 838

## C

Cain, G., 890n31
Cain, G, 893
Caldwell, S., 874
Calhoun, C., 836
Calzolari, G., 660n20
Cameron, C., 63, 405, 517, 587,
    590n9, 597, 598, 601, 619,
    770, 907n1, 908n3, 909, 910,
    911, 912, 917
Campbell, J., 6, 715n1
Cappellari, L., 827
Cardell, S., 831n48, 842
Carey, K., 343, 437, 439
Carson, R., 925
Case, A., 218
Cassen, R., 557
Caudill, S., 773n2
Caves, D., 296
Cecchetti, S., 5, 695, 703, 704n11,
    706n12, 707, 748, 750,
    805, 806
Chamberlain, G., 207n18, 208n20,
    210n23, 230, 269, 269n17,
    270, 271, 439, 441n3, 556,
    557n28, 557n29, 608n9, 711,
    794, 795, 803, 805, 900
Chambers, R., 272n19
Chatfield, C., 731, 735
Chatterjee, P., 814, 836
Chavez, J., 272n19
Chen, T., 557n29
Chesher, A., 778n8, 880, 881n17,
    928, 934
Chiappori, R., 794
Chib, S., 399, 617, 623
Chintagunta, P., 851
Chou, R., 661
Chow, G., 120, 122, 123, 127,
    223n26, 284, 789
Christensen, L., 14, 79, 91n6, 104,
    116, 117, 273n20, 274,
    276n25, 276n26, 276n27,
    277n29, 278n30, 283, 286,
    296, 410, 411, 572, 1083, 1087
Christofides, L., 821n42
Chu, C., 767
Chung, C., 810, 868, 875n12
Cleveland, W., 418
Coakley, J., 243
Cochrane, D., 651
Congdon, P., 601n2
Conniffe, D., 255n3, 257n8
Contoyannis, C., 784, 841,
    899, 902
Conway, D., 129
Cooley, T., 355n2
Cornwell, C., 186, 194, 199, 231,
    549, 1086

Coulson, N., 658
Cox, D., 138, 142, 144, 296n3,
    935n10, 940
Cragg, J., 163n13, 327n5, 386,
    387n25, 467, 658, 790n14,
    877, 920, 927
Cramér, H., 490, 493, 519, 1031
Cramer, J., 790n14, 791, 792, 826
Crawford, I., 420
Culver, S., 243
Cumby, R., 441n3, 467

## D

D'Addio, A, 837
Dahlberg, M., 478, 695,
    712, 712n13
Dale, S., 5
Das, M., 837
Dastoor, N., 138n5
Davidson, A., 596n12
Davidson, J., 399n1, 447
Davidson, R., 139, 164, 257n7,
    285n1, 287, 290, 293, 312,
    324, 335, 358n6, 375, 377,
    421, 422, 425, 441n3, 467,
    488, 494, 522, 537, 598,
    636, 637, 638, 638n7, 641,
    664, 728n12, 740n2, 743n3,
    762, 787n12, 789
Deaton, A., 138n5, 272n19, 274n23,
    276n26
Debreu, G., 538
Dehejia, R., 893n35, 894
deMaris, A., 5, 863n1
Dempster, A., 925, 1076, 1078
Dent, W., 699n8
Denton, F., 273n20
DesChamps, P., 264n15
de Witt, G., 252, 283n34, 1086
Dezhbaksh, H., 646n13
Dhrymes, P., 75n16, 382n19, 384,
    387n26, 683n5, 770, 863n1
Dickey, D., 682, 708, 715n1, 745,
    748, 751, 752, 753, 754, 761,
    762, 764, 768
Diebold, F., 143, 670n1, 677n3,
    694n7, 703, 715n1
Dielman, T., 181n2
Diewert, E., 276n25, 276n27
Diggle, R., 796n23
DiNardo, J., 407
Doan, T., 707
Dodge, Y., 406n2
Domowitz, I., 658
Doob, J., 637n6
Doppelhofer, G., 145, 146
Dreze, J., 115
Dufour, J., 378, 379

Duncan, G., 163n11, 880n15,
    880n16, 891
Durbin, J., 116n6, 322, 387n26,
    645n12, 646, 646n13, 647,
    648, 650, 651, 655, 668,
    692, 1098
Durlauf, 776n5
Dwivedi, T., 253n2, 256

## E

*Econometrica*, 925
Efron, B., 596n12, 597, 790n14, 791,
    792, 826
Eichenbaum, M., 454n10
Eicker, F., 163n11
Eisenberg, D., 814n37, 823n43
Elashoff, R., 62n9
Elliot, G., 753
Enders, W., 670n1, 715n1,
    728, 739n1
Engle, R., 1, 357n5, 358, 658,
    658n17, 660, 660n20, 669,
    670n1, 698, 756n12, 761, 762,
    764, 765, 766, 787n12
Epstein, D., 794n21
Ericsson, N., 765
Estes, E., 409n5
Evans, D., 124
Evans, G., 744n8
Evans, M., 991n1

## F

Fair, R., 101n10, 123n12, 861, 869,
    904, 905, 925, 926, 1090, 1092
Farber, H., 896n36
Farrell, M., 538
Feldstein, M., 101
Fernandez, A., 780, 810, 880n15
Ferrer-i-Carbonel, A., 837
Fiebig, D., 253n2, 257n6,
    262n14, 263
Fin, T., 878
Fiorentini, G., 660n20, 664n25
Fisher, F., 122
Fisher, G., 140n7, 788n13
Fisher, R., 401, 428
Fletcher, R., 1071n17
Florens, J., 931n8
Flores-Lagunes, A., 770
Fomby, T., 170n25, 208n19, 297n6,
    773n2, 1054
Fougere, D., 931n8
Frankel, J., 243
Freedman, D., 551, 780
French, K., 660
Fried, H., 538n24
Friedman, M., 9

Frijters, P., 837
Frisch, R., 1, 28, 39, 40, 134
Fry, J., 272n19
Fry, T., 272n19
Fuller, W., 170n24, 204n15, 648n14, 682, 708, 731, 745, 748, 751, 752, 753, 754, 761, 762, 764, 768

## G

Gabrielsen, A., 365n12
Gali, J., 704n11, 709
Gallant, A., 358n6
Garber, S., 111n2, 327n5
Garvin, S., 255n3
Gelman, A., 601n2, 623
Gentle, J., 574, 1061n2
Gerfin, M., 810, 811, 811n36, 812
Geweke, J., 577n3, 581, 583n6, 583n7, 601, 601n2, 677, 699n8, 715n1, 796n23, 827n44
Ghysels, E., 658
Giaccotto, C., 165n17
Gilbert, R., 585n8
Giles, D., 253n2, 258n13
Gill, J., 601n2
Gloeckler, L., 557n28
Godfrey, L., 103, 178, 236, 351, 521, 526, 586, 644
Goldberger, A., 41, 257n8, 273n20, 363n10, 386, 393, 608n10, 658n15, 810, 868, 875n12, 880n15, 890n30, 890n31, 891, 893
Goldfeld, S., 285n1, 380, 558, 1069, 1070, 1071n16, 1074n21
Gonzaláz, P., 184
Good, D., 108
Gordin, M., 639n9, 640
Gourieroux, C., 137n3, 138n5, 512n12, 515, 583n6, 590n9, 591, 592, 666, 666n30, 809n31, 881n17
Granger, C., 1, 138n4, 357n5, 358, 670n1, 690, 699, 700, 712, 715n1, 727, 731, 741, 742, 743, 756n12, 761, 761n13, 762, 764, 765
Gravelle, H., 124, 193, 197
Greenberg, E., 399, 623, 1054
Greene, W., 72n14, 79, 88, 88n4, 104, 105, 108, 108n1, 116, 117, 193, 226, 274, 276n27, 278n30, 283, 304, 410, 411, 414, 538n24, 556, 557, 562, 565, 572, 574, 588, 589, 591, 594n11, 770, 774n3, 793,

794n21, 799, 801, 810, 810n33, 821n42, 824, 827, 827n45, 834, 836, 837n51, 838, 841, 842, 849, 851, 852, 852n59, 858, 859, 863n1, 869, 869n8, 872n10, 873, 875n12, 882, 887n26, 893, 894, 897, 898, 902, 908n3, 913, 918, 920, 922, 922n7, 923, 924, 925, 927, 938n12, 940, 996n6, 1059n8, 1083, 1085, 1087, 1090, 1091
Griesinger, H., 798
Griffin, J., 212
Griffiths, W., 422n8
Griliches, Z., 61, 62n9, 158, 240, 283n34, 327n5, 585n8, 649, 683n5, 787, 909, 915, 917, 939n14
Grogger, J., 925
Gronau, R., 884n21
Groot, W., 838
Grunfeld, Y., 252, 255, 283n34, 534, 1086
Gruvaeus, G., 1075n23, 1079n25
Guilkey, D., 264n15, 277n29, 795n22
Gurmu, S., 61, 903n3, 910, 911

## H

Haavelmo, T., 1, 354n1
Hadri, K., 767
Hahn, J., 350, 350n11, 351, 376n15, 377, 882
Haitovsky, Y., 62n9
Hajivassiliou, V., 583n7, 827n44
Hakkio, C., 658
Hall, R., 428, 429, 452, 909, 911, 915, 916, 939n14, 1061n1, 1075n22, 1075n23
Hamilton, J., 639, 641, 657, 670n1, 687, 689, 694, 699n9, 702n10, 703, 715n1, 728n12, 731, 745n9, 756n12, 760, 761n13
Han, A., 941
Hansen, L., 144, 145, 320n1, 429, 441n3, 444n7, 445, 445n8, 448, 452, 796n23, 800
Hanushek, E., 5, 231n30
Härdle, W., 406n2, 413n7, 420, 810n35
Hartley, M., 577n4
Harvey, A., 170, 523, 525, 526, 663, 670n1, 683n5, 687, 715n1, 740n2, 788
Hasimoto, N., 258n10
Hastings, N., 991n1
Hatanaka, M., 652, 731

Hausman, J., 208, 208n20, 209, 247, 322, 323, 324, 336, 339, 347, 350, 350n11, 351, 352, 363n10, 376n15, 377, 378, 384, 387, 387n26, 471, 472, 473, 788n13, 805, 831n48, 842, 853, 869n8, 880, 909, 911, 915, 916, 919, 939n14, 941
Hayashi, F., 399n1, 425, 441n3, 639n8, 639n9, 641, 643n10, 763, 1056
Heaton, J., 444n7
Heckman, J., 1, 2, 5, 557n29, 588, 589, 773n2, 779n10, 794, 795, 801, 806, 807, 868n7, 882n18, 884n21, 886, 887, 887n26, 891, 892n34, 893n35, 897, 931n8, 939, 997n7
Heilbron, D., 922
Hendry, D., 137, 357n5, 358, 585, 658, 670n1, 693, 698, 764, 765, 766
Hensher, D., 591, 841, 842, 846, 849, 849n58, 851, 852, 852n59, 858, 859, 1090
Heshmati, A., 263
Hildebrand, G., 90n5, 1084
Hildreth, C., 223n26, 242, 243
Hill, C., 60n6, 170n25, 208n19, 297n6, 422n8, 773n2, 1054
Hilts, J., 124
Hinkley, D., 596n12
Hite, S., 62n7
Hoeting, J., 145
Hoffman, D., 792, 793, 895
Hole, A., 71
Hollingsworth, J., 124
Holly, A., 358n6
Holt, M., 264n15
Holtz-Eakin, D., 475n18, 478, 711
Hong, H., 144
Honore, B., 409n5, 794, 795, 810n34, 882, 891
Horn, A., 163n11
Horn, D., 163n11
Horowitz, J., 597, 780, 788n13, 810, 811, 881n17
Hotz, J., 796n23, 800
Houck, C., 223n26, 242, 243
Houthakker, S., 158n8
Howrey, E., 267
Hoxby, C., 5, 320
Hsiao, C., 181n2, 207, 208n19, 212, 223n26, 224n28, 239, 242, 244, 246, 341, 352, 361n8, 470n14, 587, 588, 794n21, 801, 805, 838
Huang, D., 250, 258n11, 283n35

Huber, P., 512n12, 513
Hudak, S., 219
Huizinga, J., 441n3, 467
Hussain, A., 204n15
Hwang, H., 255n3
Hyslop, D., 795, 827n44
Hyslop, J., 325n2

**I**

Ichimura, H., 893n35
Ichino, A., 893, 894
Im, E., 255n3
Im, K., 243, 269n17
Imbens, G., 325n2
Inkmann, J., 800
Irish, M., 778n8, 880, 881n17, 928, 934

**J**

Jackman, S., 794n21
Jaeger, D., 350
Jain, D., 851
Jakubson, G., 795
Jansen, D., 715n1
Jarque, C., 869, 880, 881n17
Jayatissa, W., 124n13
Jenkins, G., 633n5, 648n14, 715n1, 726, 727, 738, 768
Jenkins, S., 827
Jennrich, R.I., 285n1
Jensen, M., 531n20
Jobson, J., 170n24
Johansen, S., 763, 765
Johanssen, P., 920
Johansson, E., 478, 695, 712, 712n13, 761, 763
Johnson, N., 108, 779n10, 866n5, 883n20, 911, 922, 991n1, 996n3, 1054
Johnson, R., 61, 265
Johnson, S., 170n25, 208n19, 297n6, 773n2
Johnston, J., 407, 1059n8
Jondrow, J., 541
Jones, A., 841, 902
Jones, J., 794
Joreskog, K., 533n21, 1061n1, 1075n23, 1079n25
Jorgenson, D., 104, 105, 273n20, 276n25, 276n26, 277n29, 286, 319
*Journal of Applied Econometrics,* 103, 307, 399, 412, 478, 1088
*Journal of Business and Economic Statistics, The,* 129, 303n11, 399, 889n28
*Journal of Econometrics,* 399
*Journal of Political Economy,* 905

Judd, K., 1061n2
Judge, G., 65n10, 135, 156, 202, 204n14, 208n19, 258n13, 262n14, 299n9, 399, 422n8, 603n3, 606n7, 608n9, 608n12, 657, 660n20, 677n3, 715n1, 773n2, 1020n1
Jung, B., 214
Juselius, K., 763
Jusko, K., 231n30

**K**

Kakwani, N., 258n12
Kalbfleisch, J., 587, 880, 907n1, 931n8, 935, 935n10, 937, 938, 938n13, 940
Kamlich, R., 129
Kang, H., 743n5
Kao, C., 243, 244, 768
Katz, J., 588
Kay, R., 790n14, 791
Keane, M., 583n6, 583n7, 795, 796n23, 827n44, 899
Kelejian, H., 380
Kelly, J., 370n13
Kenkel, D., 898
Kennan, J., 935
Kennedy, W., 1061n2
Kerman, S., 255n3
Keuzenkamp, H., 4n2
Keynes, J., 2, 3, 9–11, 694
Kiefer, N., 820n41, 931n8, 935, 938, 940, 941, 941n16
Killian, L., 702, 707
Kim, I., 753
Kingdon, G., 557
Kiviet, J., 246, 264n15, 341, 470n13, 470n15
Kleibergen, F., 350n11, 351, 378
Klein, L., 1, 369, 385, 388, 391, 392, 393, 396, 397, 537, 694, 810, 811, 891, 1088
Klein, R., 413
Klepper, S., 327n5
Klugman, S., 403
Kmenta, J., 115, 119, 173, 264n16, 277n29, 531, 533n22, 585n8, 1059n9
Knapp, M., 221, 788n13
Knight, F., 538
Kobayashi, M., 124, 124n13
Koenker, R., 166, 406n2, 407, 407n4, 425
Koh, W., 219
Koolman, X., 902
Koop, G., 41, 103, 130, 145, 235, 601, 601n2, 619, 621, 1082
Kotz, A., 779n10

Kotz, S., 863n20, 866n5, 911, 922, 996n3
Kraft, D., 662, 669
Krailo, M., 804
Kreuger, A., 5, 11, 330
Krinsky, I., 70, 71, 278n31
Kroner, K., 661
Kuersteiner, G., 882
Kuh, E., 60
Kumbhakar, S., 263, 538n24, 562
Kyriazidou, E., 794, 795, 882, 891, 899

**L**

Lahiri, K., 181n2
Laird, N., 925, 1078
Laisney, F., 780
LaLonde, R., 893n35, 894, 1091
Lambert, D., 922, 922n7, 923, 925, 930
Lancaster, T., 555, 557, 587, 601, 601n2, 778n8, 801, 881n17, 931n8, 935, 935n10, 938
Land, K., 594n11
Landers, A., 62n7
Landwehr, J., 794
Lau, L., 104, 273n20, 276n26, 277n29, 286
Lawless, J., 940
Layson, K., 296n5
Leamer, E., 145, 327n5, 601n2, 608n9, 1020n1
LeCam, L., 494n3
Lechner, M., 593, 594, 780, 814, 827, 828, 829, 1089
L'Ecuyer, P., 574
Lee, K., 239
Lee, L., 181n2, 403, 880, 880n15, 881n17, 910
Lee, M., 863n1
Leff, N., 41
Lerman, R., 582n5, 790n14, 791, 793
LeRoy, S., 355n2
Levi, M., 327n5
Levin, A., 243, 342, 767
Levinsohn, J., 589, 851
Lewbel, A., 411, 412, 794, 810n34
Lewis, H., 884n21
Li, M., 836
Li, Q., 413n7, 420, 653
Li, W., 218, 658n17
Liang, P., 796n23
Lin, C., 243, 767
Ling, S., 658n17
Litterman, R., 694, 702
Little, R., 61
Little, S., 790n14, 791
Liu, T., 90n5, 387, 1084

Ljung, G., 645, 650, 730, 731
Lo, A., 5
Loeve, M., 1052
Long, S., 5, 863n1
Longley, J., 60, 1083
Louviere, J., 842, 849n58
Lovell, K., 28, 39, 90n5, 277n29, 538, 538n24
Lowe, S., 792, 793, 895
Lucas, R., 764, 765
Lutkepohl, H., 670n1, 697, 698

**M**

Mackinlay, A., 5
MacKinnon, J., 139, 163n11, 163n14, 164, 257n7, 285n1, 287, 290, 293, 312, 324, 335, 358n6, 375, 377, 421, 422, 425, 441n3, 467, 488, 494, 522, 528, 529, 537, 598, 636, 637, 638, 638n7, 641, 649, 651, 664, 728n12, 740n2, 743n3, 762, 787n12, 789
MaCurdy, T., 472, 773n2, 795, 801
Maddala, G., 62n8, 181n2, 204n14, 204n15, 205n16, 207, 240, 243, 555, 603n3, 683n5, 744n7, 753, 768, 770, 774n3, 779n9, 790n14, 801, 823, 849, 863n1, 869n9, 875, 883n20, 888, 889n27, 991n1, 1059n6
Magee, L., 836
Magnac, T., 794
Magnus, J., 4n2, 267, 979n14
Malinvaud, E., 285n1, 438, 445n8
Maloney, W., 184
Mandy, D., 263
Mann, H., 75n16, 635, 745
Manski, C., 443, 582n5, 793, 794, 810, 810n35, 811, 882n18, 891, 892n34
Marcus, A., 834
Mariano, R., 377, 382
Marsagila, G., 575
Martins, M., 891
Martins-Filho, C., 263
Matyas, L., 181n2, 441n3
Matzkin, R., 810, 810n34
Mazodier, P., 212
Mazzeo, M., 781, 1089
McAleer, M., 137n3, 140n7, 658n17
McCallum, B., 67n13, 329
McCoskey, S., 243, 767, 768
McCullough, B., 101, 293, 313, 658n17, 660n20, 666n29, 667n31, 687, 689n6, 909, 944, 1092
McDonald, J., 407n3, 873

McFadden, D., 1, 2, 226, 421, 425, 441n3, 447, 454n10, 497, 506n10, 583, 583n6, 590, 670n1, 770, 790n14, 791n15, 826, 842, 847n57, 849, 858
McGuire, T., 274n23
McKelvey, W., 790n14, 791, 792, 831
McKenzie, C., 791
McLachlan, G., 562, 564, 565
McLaren, K., 264n15, 272n19
Meese, R., 677n3, 699m8
Melenberg, B., 407n3, 412, 869, 875n13, 878, 880
Merton, R., 660
Messer, K., 163n14
Miller, D., 399
Miller, R., 146, 715n1
Million, A., 307
Mills, T., 658n17, 670n1, 715n1, 728, 891, 895
Min, C., 145
Mittelhammer, R., 299n9, 399, 399n1, 447, 512n12, 603n3
Mizon, G., 138, 138n5, 629, 655, 693
Moffitt, R., 592, 773n2, 797, 798, 799, 802, 827, 829, 838, 873
Mohanty, M., 895
Monfort, A., 137n3, 512n12, 515, 583n6, 590n9, 591, 592, 666, 666n30
Moon, H., 244
Moro, D., 264n15
Moscone, F., 221
Moshino, G., 264n15
Mouchart, M., 931n8
Moulton, 216
Mount, T., 207, 996n5
Mroz, T., 53, 815, 816, 888
Muellbauer, J., 272n19, 276n26
Mullahy, J., 412, 773n2, 922, 923, 925, 930
Muller, M., 575
Mundlak, Y., 189, 200, 209, 210, 213, 230, 269, 881
Munkin, M., 403
Munnell, A., 216, 224, 252, 254, 653, 1086
Murdoch, J., 233
Murphy, K., 303n11, 887n26

**N**

Nagin, D., 594n11, 788n13
Nair-Reichert, U., 242, 253
Nakamura, A., 387n26, 872n10
Nakamura, M., 387n26, 872n10
Nakosteen, R., 776, 777
Nelder, J., 909, 944, 1092
Nelson, C., 257n9, 743n5, 744n6

Nelson, F., 773n2, 774n3, 872n10, 875, 881n17
Nerlove, M., 114, 115, 117, 181n2, 202, 205n16, 207, 208, 208n19, 238, 239, 274, 274n24, 276n27, 410, 470n14, 572, 646n13, 683n5, 715n1, 844n54, 1087
Neudecker, H., 979n14
Newbold, P., 670n1, 690, 715n1, 727, 731, 741, 742, 743
Newey, W., 190, 200, 421, 425, 441n3, 447, 453, 454, 454n10, 454n11, 465, 475n18, 478, 497, 557n29, 643, 667, 753, 880n16, 881n17, 882n18
*New York Post*, 866n6
Neyman, J., 138, 557, 587, 801, 882
Nickell, S., 207n17, 470n13
Nijman, T., 899, 900
Nuemann, G., 881n17

**O**

Oakes, D., 935n10
Oaxaca, R., 55
Oberhofer, W., 173, 264n16, 531, 533n22
Obstfeld, M., 441n3, 467
O'Halloran, S., 794n21
Ohtani, K., 123, 124, 165n16, 258n10
Orcutt, G., 651, 874
Ord, S., 137n2, 433n1, 487, 488, 490, 991n1
Orea, C., 562
Osterwald-Lenum, M., 763
Ouliaris, S., 762

**P**

Pagan, A., 166, 166n19, 178, 184, 205, 223n26, 236, 413n7, 416, 420, 441n3, 526, 534, 549, 661, 677n4, 715n1, 880n15, 881, 881n17, 928, 1023
Pagano, M., 677n4
Pakes, A., 589, 827n44, 851
Panattoni, L., 660n20
Papell, D., 243
Parsa, R., 403
Passmore, W., 232, 437, 439
Patterson, K., 399n1, 670n1, 715n1, 728
Pedroni, P., 243, 767, 768
Peel, D., 562, 564, 565
Perron, P., 715n1, 743n3, 752, 754
Pesaran, H., 137n3, 139, 181n2
Pesaran, M., 138n4, 239, 240, 241, 243, 253, 767

Petersen, D., 876, 933n9
Phillips, A., 627
Phillips, G., 264n15
Phillips, P., 244, 375, 668, 742, 743n3, 752, 754, 762
Pierce, D., 645, 729, 730, 731
Pike, M., 804
Ploberger, W., 236, 709
Plosser, C., 744n6
Poirier, D., 111n2, 399, 896n36, 897
Polachek, S., 129
Pollard, D., 827n44
Potter, S., 145
Powell, J., 274n23, 407n3, 412, 816, 880, 880n16, 882n18, 1075n23
Prais, S., 158n8, 527, 651, 668
Pratt, J., 838
Prentice, R., 557n28, 880, 907n1, 931n8, 935, 935n10, 937, 938, 938n13, 940
Press, W., 576, 738, 811n36, 844n54, 975n12, 1061n2
*Psychology Today,* 904, 905, 925
Pudney, S., 837n51

**Q**

Quah, D., 706n12
Quandt, R., 285n1, 380, 432, 444n6, 558, 890n31, 1068, 1069, 1070, 1071n16, 1074n21, 1075n23
Quester, A., 869, 873

**R**

Racine, J., 413n7, 420
Raj, B., 181n2, 597
Ramsey, J., 432, 444n6
Rao, P., 158, 240, 493, 519, 557n28, 585n8, 649, 1031, 1054, 1072n19
Rasch, G., 803
*Redbook,* 861, 862, 904
Renfro, C., 658n17, 660n20, 666n29, 667n31, 1061n1
Revankar, N., 257n8, 274n23, 541, 541n25, 1088
Revelt, D., 851, 858
*Review of Economics and Statistics,* 827n44
*Review of Economic Statistics,* 583n6
Rice, N., 841, 902
Rich, R., 5, 695, 703, 704n11, 706n12, 707, 748, 750
Richard, J., 138, 138n5, 357n5, 358, 698, 764, 766

Ridder, G., 470n13, 900
Rilstone, P., 61
Riphahn, R., 5, 181, 307, 837, 914, 1088
Rivers, D., 881n17
Robb, L., 70, 71, 278n31
Roberts, H., 129
Robertson, D., 239
Robins, J., 902
Robinson, C., 776n5, 880n16
Robons, R., 658
Rodriguez-Poo, J., 776n5, 780, 810
Rogers, W., 407
Rose, A., 243
Rose, J., 841, 842, 858
Rosen, H., 475n18, 478, 711
Rosen, S., 776n5, 890n29
Rosenblatt, D., 415
Rosett, R., 872n10
Rossi, P., 601n2, 841
Rothenberg, T., 753
Rothschild, M., 658n17
Rothstein, J., 320
Rotnitzky, A., 902
Rowe, B., 814n37, 823n43
Rubin, D., 61, 376n15, 378, 379, 387, 537, 745, 925, 1078
Runkle, D., 583n6, 796n23
Rupert, P., 186, 199, 231, 549, 1086
Ruud, P., 288, 399n1, 441n3, 583, 583n6, 809n31, 838n48, 881

**S**

Sala-i-Martin, S., 143, 146, 767
Salem, D., 996n5
Sargan, J., 207n18, 336, 470n14, 476n19, 715n1
Savin, E., 264n15, 506n10
Savin, N., 744n8
Saxonhouse, G., 231n30, 232n31
Schimek, M., 418
Schipp, B., 264n15
Schmidt, P., 90n5, 108, 123, 194, 255n3, 264n15, 269n17, 342, 374n14, 377n16, 383n20, 470n14, 472, 475, 476, 478, 841, 843, 875, 878
Schmidt, S., 538, 538n24
Schwartz, A., 143, 697
Schwert, W., 660, 752
Scott, E., 557, 587, 801, 882
Seaks, T., 88, 88n4, 108n1, 296n5, 788n13
Segerson, K., 272n19
Seldon, T., 767
Sepanski, J., 795n22
Sevestre, P., 181n2
Shapiro, M., 704n11, 709

Shaw, D., 864n4, 924
Shea, J., 351
Shephard, R., 276
Sherlund, S., 232
Shields, M., 837n51
Shin, Y., 239, 243, 767
Shum, M., 144
Shumway, R., 731
Sickles, R., 108, 123, 268, 277n29, 795n22
Silk, J., 384n21
Silva, J., 139n6
Silver. J., 273n20
Sims, C., 357n5, 694, 699, 699n8
Singer, B., 805, 806, 807, 931n8, 939
Singleton, K., 429, 452
Siow, A., 611n14
Sklar, A., 403
Smith, J., 893n35
Smith, M., 244, 403
Smith, R., 239, 240, 241, 242, 253, 768
Snyder, J., 773n2
Solow, R., 131, 181n2, 1085
Song, S., 214, 219
Sorbom, D., 1061n1
Spady, R., 413, 810, 811, 891
Spector, L., 781, 1089
Srivastava, T., 253n2, 256, 258n13
Staiger, D., 320n1, 350, 350n11, 377, 627
Stambuagh, R., 660
Stegun, I., 436n2, 1061n2, 1063, 1064, 1065
Stern, S., 61, 583n6
Stewart, M., 795
Stock, J., 145, 320n1, 350, 350n11, 377, 378, 694n7, 699n8, 715n1, 753, 760, 761, 763
Stoker, T., 810
Stone, R., 272
Strauss, R., 841, 843
Stuart, A., 137n2, 433n1, 487, 488, 490, 991n1
Sueyoshi, G., 231n30
Suits, D., 108n1, 197
Susin, S., 940
Swait, J., 842, 849n58
Swamy, P., 223n26, 223n27, 242, 243
Symons, J., 239

**T**

Tahmiscioglu, A., 239
Taubman, P., 331
Tauchen, H., 200, 798
Tavlas, G., 223n26, 223n27

Taylor, W., 158, 162, 208n20, 323, 336, 337, 339, 347, 351, 380, 406n2, 435, 471, 472, 473, 979
Telser, L., 256n5
Terza, J., 841, 897, 898, 920, 925
Thayer, M., 233
Theil, H., 101n10, 101n11, 258n13, 327n5, 375, 377n16, 378, 382, 608n10, 648, 968, 975n13, 1059n7
Thompson, S., 811
Thornton, D., 715n1
Thursby, J., 124n13, 166n18, 278n31
Tibshirani, R., 596n12
Tobias, J., 41, 103, 130, 235, 601n2, 836, 893n35, 1082
Tobin, J., 869, 871
Todd, P., 893n35
Tomes, N., 776n5
Topel, R., 303n11, 887n26
Tosetti, E., 221
Toyoda, T., 123, 165n16
Train, K., 226, 578, 590, 590n9, 600n1, 622, 622n19, 841, 842, 851, 858
Trebbi, F., 378
Trethaway, M., 296
Trivedi, P., 63, 402, 403, 404, 507, 517, 587, 590n9, 597, 598, 601, 619, 677n4, 770, 907n1, 908n3, 909, 910, 911, 912, 913
Trognon, A., 212, 512n12, 515, 666, 666n30
Trotter, H., 1070
Trumble, D., 658
Tsay, R., 670n1, 715n1, 739n1
Tunali, I., 776n5, 793

**U**

Uhler, R., 790n14
Ullah, A., 413n7, 416, 420, 661, 1023

**V**

van den Brink, H., 838
van Praag, B., 895
van Soest, A., 407n3, 412, 837, 869, 875n13, 878, 880

Varian, H., 267
Veall, M., 597, 689n6, 790n14, 791
Vella, F., 441n3, 794n21, 880n15, 881, 881n17, 882n18, 899, 900, 928
Verbeek, M., 794n21, 899, 900
Verbon, H., 267
Vilcassim, N., 851
Vinod, H., 293, 597
Volker, P., 140n7
Vuong, Q., 140, 140n8, 141, 142, 144, 546, 881n17, 923, 924, 930
Vytlacil, E., 557n29, 893n35

**W**

Wahba, S., 893n35, 894
Wald, A., 75n16, 249, 262, 284, 453, 454, 500, 501, 502, 503, 505, 520, 536, 635, 697, 700
Waldman, D., 876
Walker, M., 272n19, 880n16, 882n18
Wallace, T., 204n15
Wallis, K., 646n13
Wambach, A., 307
Wan, G., 268
Wang, P., 594n11
Wansbeek, T., 365n12, 470n13, 900
Waterman, R., 917, 918
Watson, G., 116n6, 645n12, 646, 647, 650, 651, 655, 668, 692
Watson, M., 145, 350, 694n7, 699n8, 704n11, 709, 715n1, 756n12, 760, 761, 1098
Waugh, F., 28, 39, 40, 134
Webster, C., 1054
Wedel, M., 562, 594n11
Weeks, M., 137n3, 139
Weinhold, D., 242, 253
Weiss, A., 666
Welsh, R., 60
Wertheimer, R., 874
West, K., 190, 453, 454, 454n11, 465, 472n16, 643, 667, 753
White, H., 65n11, 94, 137n3, 163n11, 163n12, 163n13, 163n14, 164, 312, 320n1,

358n6, 447, 463, 465, 512n12, 637, 637n6, 638n7, 639, 641, 666, 666n30, 1056
White, S., 407n3
Wichern, D., 61, 265
Wickens, M., 329, 441n3
Wildman, B., 124
Willis, R., 776n5, 805, 806, 890n29, 997n7
Windmeijer, F., 790n14, 908n3, 909
Winkelmann, R., 837, 840, 907n1, 911, 913, 925
Winsten, C., 527, 651, 668
Wise, D., 788n13, 869n8
Witte, A., 798, 869
Wood, D., 278, 279n32, 279n33, 1087
Wooldridge, J., 15, 100, 100n9, 210n23, 269n17, 319, 358n6, 380n17, 507, 665, 666n29, 667n31, 783, 797n24, 878, 892n34, 893, 900, 902
Working, E., 354n1, 362n9
Wright, J., 145, 350n11
Wu, S., 243, 322, 325, 387n26, 768
Wynand, P., 895

**Y**

Yaron, A, 444n7
Yatchew, A., 409, 410, 410n6, 787
Yogo, M., 350n11, 378

**Z**

Zabel, J., 899
Zarembka, P., 296n3
Zavoina, R., 790n14, 792, 831
Zeger, S., 796n23
Zellner, A., 115, 145, 250, 252, 255n4, 256, 256n5, 258n11, 283n35, 357n5, 382, 541, 541n25, 600, 601n2, 603n3, 604n4, 605n5, 605n6, 606n7, 608n12, 611n14, 612, 612n15, 619, 620, 1020n1, 1088
Zimmer, D., 402, 403, 404
Zimmer, M., 776, 777, 889
Zimmerman, K., 790n14, 791

# SUBJECT INDEX

## A

accelerated failure time models, 937
acceptance region, 1034
addition
  conformable for, 946
  matrices, 946–947
  partitioned matrices, 965
  variables, testing, 210
  vector spaces, 951
adjusted $R$-squared, 35–38, 142
adjustment
  equation, 239
  to equilibrium, 391–394
admissible theories, 365
age-earnings profile, 114
Aitken's theorem, 155
Akaike Information Criterion
  (AIC), 143
algebra
  calculus and matrix, 979–987
  characteristics of roots and
    vectors, 967–976
  least squares regression, 25
  matrices, 945
  matrices, geometry of,
    951–961
  matrices, manipulation of,
    945–951
  matrices, partitioned, 964–967
  quadratic forms, 976–979
  systems of linear equations,
    961–964
  terminology, 945
algorithms
  EM (expectation-maximization),
    1076–1078
  iterative, 1067
  Metropolis-Hastings, 622
  optimization, 1067–1068
  variable metric, 1071
almost sure convergence, 1043
alternative hypothesis, 83
analog estimation, 443
analysis
  *ceteris paribus*, 29
  of classical regression model,
    603–609
  cointegration, 765–766
  of covariance, 108–110
  of dynamic models, 689–693

of ordered choices, 831–841
panel data, 180, 182–183. *See also*
  panel data
parametric and semiparametric,
  412
policy, 703–710
of restrictions across equations,
  370n13
semiparametric, 809–813
specification, 692–693
spectral, 735
time-series, 6, 243, 629–632
of treatment effects, 11n2,
  889–890
of variances, 32–39
Vuong's test for nonnested
  models, 141
analysis of variance (ANOVA), 192
analytic functions, 1062
Anderson/Hsiao estimator, 340–348
application. *See also* panel data
  data sets in, 1081–1092
  of heteroscedasticity regression
    models, 170–175
  of likelihood-based tests, 504–506
  of maximum likelihood
    estimation (MLE), 517–567
  nonlinear regression models,
    294–297
  panel data, 267–272, 307–311
applied econometric methods, 6
approximation
  errors, 334
  integrals by quadrature,
    1064–1065
  leading term, 1060
  linear, 979
  to normal cdf, 1063
  quadratic, 979
  Sterling's, 1064
  Taylor series, 979
  to unknown functions, 13
AR(1), 632, 633–634, 648–649
ARCH-M model, 660–662
ARCH model, 658
ARCH(1) model, 659–660
ARCH($q$) model, 660–662
Arellano/Bond estimator,
  340–348
artificial nesting, 138

assessment, convergence, 1075
assignments, rating, 834
associative law, 948
assumptions
  of asymptotic properties, 421–424
  of the classical linear regression
    model, 44
  instrumental variables
    estimation, 315–316
  irrelevant alternatives, 847–850
  least squares estimator, 43
  mean independence, 189, 901
  of the nonlinear regression
    model, 286–287
  normality, 52–58, 100n9
  normality, sample selection, 891
  stationary, 631
asymptotically normally distributed
  (CAN), 150
asymptotic covariance
  matrices, 159, 317, 385n22, 446
  matrices, estimation, 163
  model, 531n20
  samples, 1057
asymptotic distribution, 44n1, 68,
    303, 317, 1056–1060
  of empirical moments, 449
  in generalized regression
    models, 153
  of GMM estimators, 450
  instrumental variables
    estimation, 333
  nonlinear instrumental variables
    estimation, 335
  of two-step MLE, 509
asymptotic efficiency, 71–75,
    487, 1058
  maximum likelihood estimation
    (MLE), 493–494
  properties, 420–421
asymptotic expectations, 1059–1060
asymptotic inefficiency, 1058
asymptotic moments, 1060
asymptotic negligibility of
  innovations, 639
asymptotic normality, 635, 1058
  of least squares estimator,
    65–67
  maximum likelihood estimation
    (MLE), 492–493

of nonlinear least squares
estimator, 292
proof, 152
properties, 420
asymptotic properties, 44, 64
assumptions of, 421–424
of estimators, 424–425
of least squares, 151
maximum likelihood estimate
(MLE), 486, 490
of method of moments, 434–436
asymptotic results, 635–640
asymptotics, small $T$, 196–197
asymptotic standard errors, 295
asymptotic uncorrelatedness, 639
asymptotic variance, 494–496
AT&T Corporation, 181n3
attenuation, 325–327, 868
attributes, 842
attrition, 61, 901–902
augmentation
Dickey-Fuller test, 751
unit roots, 754
augmentation, data, 616
autocorrelation, 17, 116n6,
256, 756n11
coefficient, 632
consistent covariance
estimator, 643
estimation, 649–651
forecasting, 656–658
and heteroscedasticity, 148–149
lagged variables, 682, 691–692
matrix, 632
maximum likelihood estimation
(MLE), 527–529
misspecification of the model, 626
negative, 627
negative, residuals, 629
Newey and West's estimator, 463
panel data, 185, 213, 652–655
partial, 723–726
regression equations, 263–264
spatial, 218–222
stationary stochastic process,
721–723
testing for, 644–647
autocovariance, 719
generating function, 732
matrix, 632
summability of, 639
autoregression, 716
autoregressive form, 633,
675, 718
conditional heteroscedasticity,
658–667
model, 675
moving-average processes,
716–718

processes, 632
univariate, 685
vector, 479
autoregressive distributed lag
(ARDL) models, 681–689
autoregressive integrated
moving-average (ARIMA)
model, 740
average partial effects, 780–785
averages
Bayesian model, 144–146
matrix weighted, 192
moving average (MA), 190
treatment effect on the
treated, 892

**B**

balanced panel data, 184, 269
bandwidth, 407, 416
basic statistical inference, 52–58
basis vectors, 953–954
Bayes factor, 611
Bayesian estimation, 192, 399,
600–601
analysis of classical regression
model, 603–609
Bayes theorem, 601–603
binomial probit model, 616–619
individual effects model, 619–621
inference, 609–613
posterior distributions, 613–616
random parameters model,
621–623
Bayesian Information Criterion
(BIC), 143
Bayesian model averaging, 144–146
Bayes theorem, 565, 601–603
behavior
of data, 423–424
of test statistics, 585
behavioral equations, 356
Behrens-Fisher problem, 123n11
Bernoulli distribution, 998
best linear unbiased (BLU), 150
beta distribution, 997
BHHH estimator, 495, 662
bias
caused by omission of variables,
133–134
omitted variables, 868
self-selection, 62n7
simultaneous equations, 355n3
binary choice, 571
choice-based sampling, 793–794
dynamic binary choice models,
794–796
endogenous right-hand-side
variables, 813–817

estimation, 777–796
estimators, 811
fit measures, 826
goodness of fit, measuring,
790–793
heteroscedasticity, 787, 788–790
inference, 777–796
maximum simulated likelihood
estimation, 593
models, 139, 411–412, 772–777
panel data, 796–809
testing, 785–787
binary variables, 106–112, 835
binomial distributions, 998
binomial probit model, 616–619
Gibbs sampler, 617
bivariate distribution, 578
conditioning in, 1006–1009
incidental truncation, 883–884
normal, 1005, 1009–1010
bivariate ordered probit models,
835–836
bivariate probit models, 817–826,
896n36
bivariate random variable
distribution, 1004–1006
bivariate regression, 23
block-diagonal matrix, 965
bootstrapping, 407, 596–598
Box and Pierce's test, 645
Box-Cox transformation, 296–297
Box-Jenkins methods, 726n11
Breusch-Pagan multiplier test, 166
Breusch-Pagan test, 167
British Household Panel Survey
(BHSP), 180, 841
Broyden-Fletcher-Goldfarb-
Shanno (BFGS)
method, 1071
Broyden's method, 1071
burn in, 614
Butler and Moffitt's method,
552, 798

**C**

calculus, 835, 979–987
canonical correlation, 763
case
exactly identified, 443, 459
overidentified, 439, 459
categorical variables, 110–111
categories of binary variables,
107–108
causality
Granger, 358
simultaneous equations model,
357–358
censored data, 869–881

censored distributions, 999
censored normal distribution, 869–871
censored random variables, 871
censored regression (tobit) model, 871–874
censoring, 896n36
  count data, 924–931
  Poisson model, 925–931
  tobit model, 925–931
  variables, 869
central limit theorem, 638–640, 1050–1055
central moments, 432, 990
central tendency, measure of, 1020
CES production function, 119, 285–286
*ceteris paribus* analysis, 29
Chamberlain's model, 230
characteristics
  equations, 684, 720
  of roots and vectors, 967–976
Chebychev's inequality, 990, 1040
Chebychev's Weak Law of Large Numbers, 1043
chi-squared distribution, 84, 993–995
choice based samples, 793–794, 852
Cholesky decomposition, 576n2
Cholesky factorization, 583, 974
Cholesky values, 974
Chow test, 120n8
classes, 564
classical estimates, Bayesian averaging and, 146
classical likelihood-based estimation, 400–402
classical model selection, 144
classical normal linear regression model, 1014–1015
classical regression model, 458, 603–609
classical testing procedures, 1034–1037
class membership, predicting, 561
closed-form solution, 1066
cluster estimator, 188, 515–517
clustering, 188
Cobb-Douglas cost function, 91, 116, 273, 276
Cobb-Douglas production function, 408
Cochrane and Orcutt estimator, 649
coefficients
  autocorrelation, 632
  change in a subset of, 122–123
  of determination, 34, 1009
  economies of scale, 116n7

estimated year dummy variables, 109
estimation, 440
hypothesis, testing, 52
linear combination of, 55–56
matrices, 393
partial autocorrelation, 724
partial correlation, 29–31
partial regression, 28
pretest estimators, 135
random model, 223–225, 851
regression, 28
scale factor, 100n9
structural, 369
vector, least squares regression, 21–22
cofactors, expansion by, 959
cohort effect, 11n2
cointegration, 181n2
  analysis, 765–766
  in consumption, 762
  nonstationary data, 756–767
  relationships, 764
  testing for, 761–763
cointegration rank, 759
collinearity, diagnosing, 60n6
columns
  notation, 947
  rank, 956
  spaces, 956
  vector, 945
common (base 10) logs, 115n3
common effects, 899–902
common factors, 655–656
common trends, 759–760
comparison
  of binary choice estimators, 811
  of matrices, 978–979
  of methods, 385
  of models, 38–39, 506–507
  of parametric and semiparametric analyses, 412
complete data log-likelihood, 1076
completeness condition, 360
complete system of equations, 355
components
  of equations, 367
  error model, 201
  heteroscedasticity, 212–213
  principal, 61
comprehensive model, 138
computation, 1061–1065
  derivatives, 1068–1069
  nonlinear least squares estimator, 292–293
concentrated log-likelihood function, 520, 1073, 1080
conditional density, 400, 433n1
conditional distribution, 1013–1014

conditional latent class model, 561–563
conditional likelihood function, 496–497, 803
conditional logit model, 842, 846–847, 852–858
conditional mean function, 417, 1006
conditional variance, 1007
conditions
  bivariate distributions, 1006–1009
  first-order, 982
  Grenander, 65
  identification, 119, 449, 457
  initial, 389, 631, 794
  numbers, 60
  numbers of matrices, 971
  Oberhofer-Kmenta, 533n22
  order, 449, 457
  orthogonality, 456
  orthogonality, estimation based on, 442–443
  rank, 449
  regularity, 487–488
confidence intervals, 295
  for parameters, 54–55
  testing, 505, 1037–1038
confidence level, 1033
conformable
  for addition, 946
  for multiplication, 947
conjugate prior, 607
consistency
  of estimation, 244–246, 429–436
  of estimators, 265, 318, 372, 1041
  of least squares estimator, 64–65
  of maximum likelihood estimation (MLE), 491–492
  of nonlinear least squares estimator, 291
  of ordinary least squares (OLS), 151
  of properties, 420
  of root-*n* consistent properties, 1051
  of sample mean, 1041
  testing, 1036
constants, 16n3
  elasticity, 13
  random, 857
constant term
  regression with a, 29
  R-squared and the, 37–38
constrained optimization, 984–985
constraints
  matrix, convergence, 151n1
  nonsingular matrix of, 435
  optimization with, 1073–1074
consumer price index (CPI), 22

consumption function, 314
  cointegration in, 757, 762
  fit of a, 34
  Hausman test for, 324–325
  instrumental variables
      estimation, 336
  *J* test for, 140
  life cycle, 428–429
  linear regression models, 9–11
  nonlinear function, 294–296
  relationship to income, 2–3
  Vuong's test for, 142
contagion property, 1001
contiguity, 218
contiguity matrix, W, 218
continuous distributions, 575
continuous random variables, 987
contrasts, effects, 198
control function, 816, 836
convergence
  almost sure, 1043
  assessment, 1075
  in distribution, 1048
  of empirical moments, 448
  in lower powers, 1044
  matrices, 151
  mean square, 68
  of moments, 1047
  nonsingular matrix of
      constraints, 435
  in probability, 1039–1042
  to random variables, 1046–1047
  of random vectors or
      matrices, 1045
  in *r*th mean, 1044, 1045
copula functions, 402–405
corner solutions, 878–880
corrections
  degrees of freedom, 519n14
  errors, 689, 756
  errors, nonstationary data,
      760–761
  errors, spatial, 221
  rank two, 1071
correlation
  autocorrelation. *See*
      autocorrelation
  canonical, 763
  cross-function, testing, 265
  joint distributions, 1003–1004
  matrices, 1011
  tetrachoric, 819
  zero, testing for, 820
correlogram, 728
Cosine Law, 961
count data, 542–547, 907
  censoring, 924–931
  fixed effects, 916–918
  function form, 912–915

Hurdle model, 920–924
  panel data, 915–920
  random effects, 918–920
  robust covariance matrices,
      915–916
  truncation, 924–931
  zero-altered Poisson model,
      920–924
covariance
  analysis of, 108–110
  asymptotic covariance matrix,
      385n22
  asymptotic matrices, 159, 317, 446
  asymptotic samples, 1057
  autocovariance. *See*
      autocovariance
  instrumental variables
      estimation, 333
  joint distributions, 1003–1004
  linear regression models, 17
  matrices, 1011
  matrices, ordinary least squares
      (OLS), 162–164
  restrictions, 355
  robust asymptotic matrices,
      511–517
  robust estimation, 210
  robust matrix, 307, 780
  stationary, 630
  structures model, 266
covariates, 8, 933
Cox test, 142
Cramér-Rao lower bound, 1031
Cramer-Wold device, 1050
credit scoring model, 304
criterion
  Akaike Information Criterion
      (AIC), 143
  Bayesian Information Criterion
      (BIC), 143
  focused information criterion
      (FIC), 144
  function, 421, 422, 437
  Kullback-Leibler Information
      Criterion (KLIC), 141
  mean-squared error, 135
  model selection, 142–143
  prediction criteria, 143
critical region, 1034
critical values, test statistics and, 388
cross-country growth
      regressions, 145
cross-function correlation,
      testing, 265
cross section of samples, 1020
cumulated effect, 673
cumulative distribution function
      (cdf), 988
cumulative multipliers, 390

Current Population Survey
      (CPS), 180

**D**

data analysis, 629–632
data augmentation, 616
data generating process (DGP),
      287, 436, 518n13, 743, 987
data generations, 11, 17–18
data imputation, 62
data sets in applications, 1081–1092
Davidon-Fletcher-Powell (DFP)
      method, 1071
decomposition, 33
  Oaxaca and Blinder's, 55
  singular value, 975
  of variance, 1008
definite matrices, 976–979
degrees of freedom
  correction, 204
  maximum likelihood estimation
      (MLE), 519n14
delta method, 69, 297, 927,
      1055–1056
demand
  equation, 69, 354
  relationship, 9n1
  system, 274
  systems of demand equations,
      272–280
  translog demand system, 286
density
  conditional, 433n1
  individual, 482
  informative prior, 606–609
  integration, 604n4
  inverted Wishart prior, 621
  kernel density estimator,
      811, 1023
  kernel estimator, 407, 414–416
  kernel methods, 411–413
  likelihood function, 482
  marginal probability, 1002
  model, 400
  posterior, 601–603
  probability density function
      (pdf), 1000
  regular, properties of, 488–490
  truncated random variables, 864
dependent observations, 635
dependent variables, 3, 8, 979
descriptive statistics, 1020–1023
determinants
  of matrices, 958–961
  of a matrix, 972
  of partitioned matrices, 965
determination, coefficients
      of, 1009

deterministic relationships, 3, 9
deviance, 909
diagonal elements of the inverse, 30
diagonalization of matrices, 969
diagonal matrix, 945
diagrams, scatter, 1021
Dickey-Fuller tests, 745–754
differences, 647
differencing, 739–741
digamma functions, 1064
dimensions of matrices, 945
discrepancies
   $F$ statistic, 83
   vectors, 84
discrete choice models, 770
discrete Fourier transform, 737
discrete random variables, 998
distance, minimum distance
     estimation (MDE), 233, 270,
   335, 428–429, 436–441
distributed lag
   form, 675
   model, 97
distribution
   assumptions of linear regression
     models, 44
   asymptotic, 44n1, 68, 303, 317,
     1056–1060
   asymptotic, in generalized
     regression models, 153
   asymptotic, of empirical
     moments, 449
   asymptotic, of GMM
     estimators, 450
   Bernoulli, 998
   beta, 997
   binomial, 998
   bivariate, 578
   bivariate, conditioning,
     1006–1009
   bivariate, incidental truncation,
     883–884
   bivariate normal, 1005,
     1009–1010
   bivariate random variables,
     1004–1006
   censored, 999
   censored normal, 869–871
   chi-squared, 84, 993–995
   conditional, 1013–1014
   continuous, 575
   convergence in, 1048
   Erlang, 996
   exponential, 996–997, 1052
   exponential, families of,
     433n1, 481
   $F$, 993–995, 1017–1018, 1050
   feasible generalized least squares
     (FGLS), 157

function of random variables,
   998–1000
gamma, 445, 996–997
gamma, example of, 1079–1080
gamma, parameters, 447
gamma prior, 605n6
instrumental variables
   estimation, 315, 333
inverse gamma, 996
inverse Gaussian, 431
inverted gamma, 604
joint, 402–405, 1002–1006
joint posterior, 605
Lagrange multiplier, 503
with large degrees of freedom,
   995–996
large-sample distribution theory,
   1038–1056
likelihood functions, 1030
likelihood ratio test, 500
limiting, 66, 95, 317, 995, 1048
logistic, 997
lognormal, 996
marginal, 1013–1014
marginal distributions of
   statistics, 57–58
moments of truncated, 864–867
multivariate, 1010–1012
multivariate normal, 1013–1019
multivariate $t$, 606
noncentral chi-squared, 501n8
nonlinear instrumental variables
   estimation, 335
normal, 11, 486, 864, 872n10,
   991–992, 1013–1014
normal, for sample moments, 458
normal, Gibbs sampler, 614
normal, limiting, 1055
normal, mixtures of, 432
normally distributed
   disturbances, 18
ordered probit models, 832n49
parameters, estimating, 430–434
Poisson, 485, 906, 998
Poisson, variance bound for, 1031
posterior, 613–616
prior, 604
probability, 987–988, 991–998
probability, representations of,
   1000–1001
sample minimum, 1025–1027
sampling, 44, 1023–1027
sampling, of least squares
   estimator, 47
size, 996
spherical normal, 1013
standard normal, 992
standard normal cumulative
   function, 1062–1063

survival, 935
$t$, 993–995
truncated normal, 576
truncated standard normal, 864
truncated uniform, 865
truncation, 863–864
of two-step MLE, 509
Wald test statistic, 501
Wishart, 997–998
distributive law, 948
disturbance, 9
   AR(1), 633–634, 648–649
   autocorrelation, 148
   feasible generalized least squares
     (FGLS), 203–205
   first order autoregressive, 527
   instrumental variables
     estimation, 333
   least squares regression, 20
   linearized regression model, 288
   linear regression models, 14
   maximum likelihood estimation
     (MLE), 538–542
   moving average (MA), 190
   Newey and West's estimator, 463
   nonnormal, 92–96
   nonspherical, 210–213
   normally distributed, 18
   processes, 632–634
   reduced-form, 360
   regression, 158–164
   restrictions, 355
   spherical, 16–17, 17n4, 149
   structural, 358
   SUR models, 264n16
   zero mean of the, 286
dominant root, 391
dot product, 947
double-length regression, 664
doubly censored tobit model, 928
downhill simplex, 1066
draws
   Halton, 578
   random, 577–580
dummy variables, 106, 122, 195
dummy variable trap, 108
duration, 906–907
   estimated duration models, 941
   exogenous variables, 937–938
   heterogeneity, 938–939
   log-likelihood function,
     938n12
   maximum likelihood estimation
     (MLE), 936–937
   models, 931–942
   nonparametric, 939–942
   parametric duration models,
     933–939
   semiparametric, 939–942

Durbin-Watson test, 116n6, 645–646
dynamic binary choice models, 794–796
dynamic equation, 684–686
dynamic labor study equation, 348
dynamic models, 356
    analysis of, 689–693
    properties of, 389–394
dynamic multipliers, 390
dynamic panel data models, 238–243, 314, 340–348, 469–479
    consistent estimation of, 244–246
dynamic regression models, 314, 670, 671–677
dynamic SUR models, 264n15

**E**

earnings equations, 10–11, 53–54
    dummy variable in, 106
econometric models, 355
    estimation of, 455–479
    maximum likelihood estimation (MLE), 496–497
econometrics
    computation in, 1062–1065
    modeling, 2–5
    practice of, 6
Econometric Society, 1
economic theory, 5
economies of scale, 116n7
education, 10–11
effects
    contrasts, 198
    fixed effect model, 193–200
    group, 197
    random, 200–210
    unobserved model, 209–210
efficiency
    asymptotic, 71–75, 487, 1058
    estimation by generalized least squares, 154–158
    feasible generalized least squares (FGLS), 158
    maximum likelihood estimation (MLE), 493–494
efficient estimation, 484–486, 647–648
efficient scale, 79
efficient score, 502
efficient two-step estimator, 664
efficient unbiased estimators, 1028
eigenvalue, 969
elasticities, 680
elasticity
    constant, 13
    estimation of, 279

income, confidence intervals for, 55
    long-run, 239
elements, $L$, 444
EM (expectation-maximization) algorithm, 1076–1078
empirical estimators, 596
empirical moments
    asymptotic distribution of, 449
    convergence of, 448
    equation, 442, 447, 456
empirical results, 707–710
empirical studies, 574n1
encompassing principle, 138
endogeneity, 357–358
endogenous right-hand-side variables, 813–817
endogenous variables, 355
environmental economics, 6
equality
    of column and row rank, 957
    information matrix, 488, 490
    of matrices, 945–946
equations
    adjustment, 239
    behavioral, 356
    characteristic, 684, 720, 967–968
    complete system of, 355
    components of, 367
    constant elasticity, 13
    demand, 354
    demand, regression for, 69
    dynamic labor study, 348
    earnings, 53–54, 106
    empirical moment, 442, 447
    empirical moment equation, 456
    estimated labor supply, 321
    estimated log wage, 340
    estimated rating assignment, 834
    estimated tobit, 873
    Euler, 428–429
    fixed effects, 199–200
    Gibbs sampler, 618
    illustrative systems of, 354–357
    intrinsic linearity, 117
    investment, 22–25
    $K$ moment, 431
    lags, 479
    least squares normal, 22
    likelihood, 490
    likelihood, binary choice models, 778
    linearized regression model, 288
    nonlinear systems of, 300–302
    normal, 27
    population moment, 456
    population regression, 8
    reduced form, 329
    regression, 252–254
    restricted investment, 86

semilog, 113
share, 278
simultaneous equations bias, 355n3
simultaneous equations models, 354, 466–469
single-equation linear models, 455–461
single-equation nonlinear models, 461–464
single-equation (pooled) estimators, 829n47
specification tests, 387
stability of a dynamic, 684–686
stacking, 301n10
structural, 355
supply, 354
systems of demand, 272–280
systems of linear, 961–964
wage, 186
Yule-Walker, 641, 722
equilibrium
    adjustment to, 391–394
    conditions, 354, 356
    errors, 689, 758
    market, 5
    multiplier, 674
    multipliers, 239, 390
    relationships, 689
ergodicity, 636, 728n12
Ergodic theorem, 448, 636–638
Erlang distribution, 996
errors
    approximation, 334
    asymptotic standard, 295
    components model, 201
    correction, 689, 756
    correction, nonstationary data, 760–761
    cost functions, 116
    equilibrium, 689, 758
    functions, 1062n4
    instrumental variables estimation, 327
    mean squared, 1029
    mean-squared error criterion, 135
    measurement, 63, 189, 314–315, 325–331
    root mean squared error, 101
    spatial error correction, 221
    specification, 885
    standard, 1027
    standard error of the estimator, 52
    standard error of the regression, 51
    type I, 1034
    type II, 1034
    weighted least squares, 168

estimated bivariate probit
    model, 822
estimated consumption
    functions, 295
estimated duration models, 941
estimated earnings equation,
    107, 889
estimated labor supply
    equation, 321
estimated labor supply model, 816
estimated latent class model, 595
estimated log wage equations, 340
estimated pooled probit model, 828
estimated production functions, 91
estimated random parameters
    model, 594
estimated rating assignment
    equation, 834
estimated selection corrected wage
    equation, 888
estimated SUR model, 259
estimated tobit equations, 873
estimated year-specific effects, 109
estimation, 1019–1020
    analog, 443
    of the ARDL model, 682–683
    asymptotic covariance
        matrix, 163
    autocorrelation, 649–651
    based on orthogonality
        conditions, 442–443
    Bayesian, 399, 600–601
    binary choice, 777–796
    classical, Bayesian
        averaging, 146
    classical likelihood-based,
        400–402
    coefficients, 393, 440
    with a conjugate prior, 607
    consistent, 244–246, 429–436
    of covariance matrix of b,
        160–162
    criterion, 400
    doubly censored tobit model, 928
    of econometric models, 455–479
    efficient, 484–486, 647–648
    of elasticity, 279
    feasible generalized least squares
        (FGLS), 203–205
    in finite samples, 1027–1030
    with first differences, 190–193
    frameworks, 398–400
    full information maximum
        likelihood (FIML), 508
    inconsistent, 201
    informative prior density,
        606–609
    instrumental variables,
        314–315, 893

by instrumental variables,
    372–373
intervals, 610, 1027, 1032–1034
with a lagged dependent variable,
    651–652
least absolute deviations (LAD),
    406–409
least squares, 149–154, 154–158,
    194–196
least squares, regression, 21n1
least squares, serial correlation,
    640–643
likelihood, random effects,
    214n14
limited information estimation
    methods 371-380
limited information maximum
    likelihood (LIML), 508
linear regression model, 401–402
lognormal mean, 578
maximum likelihood, bivariate
    probit models, 817–820
maximum likelihood estimation
    (MLE), 118, 482, 485
maximum simulated likelihood,
    228, 593
minimum distance, 428–429,
    436–441
minimum variance linear
    unbiased, 46–47
nonparametric, 398, 413–420
one-step, 1072
ordinary least squares (OLS),
    159–160
panel data, 229–233
parameters, 430–434, 471
parameters of univariate time
    series, 728–731
parametric, 398, 400–405
point, 609–610
point, of parameters, 1027–1032
Poisson model, 929
pretest, 134–135
pseudo-maximum likelihood,
    511–517, 666–667
random coefficients model, 225
random effects, 206, 207
robust, 153–154
robust, heteroscedasticity, 159
robust, using group means,
    188–190
robust covariance, 210
robust covariance matrix,
    185–188, 780
sample selection, 886–889
semiparametric, 398, 405–413,
    810–812
simulation-based, 226–229, 399,
    573, 589–596

simultaneous equations model,
    370–371
specification tests, 387–388
system methods of, 380–384
treatment effects, 891–895
truncation, 874–875
two-stage least squares, 356
two-step nonlinear least squares,
    302–307
unbiased, 46–47
variances, 51–52, 642–643
vector autoregression
    (VAR), 696
when $\Omega$ is unknown, 648–652
estimators, 1027. *See also*
    estimation
    Anderson/Hsiao, 340–348
    Arellano/Bond, 340–348
    asymptotic covariance
        matrices, 152
    asymptotic properties of, 424–425
    Bayesian, 192
    BHHH, 495
    binary choice, 811
    for binary choice models, 411–412
    cluster, 188, 515–517
    Cochrane and Orcutt, 649
    consistency of, 265, 318, 372, 1041
    efficient two-step, 664
    efficient unbiased, 1028
    empirical, 596
    extremum, 421
    extremum, assumptions for
        asymptotic properties,
        421–424
    feasible GLS, 258
    full information maximum
        likelihood (FIML), 383–384
    generalized method of moments
        (GMM), 441–451, 450
    generalized regression
        model, 156
    GMM, 288, 406
    Hausman and Taylor, 336, 337
    instrumental variables, 245,
        316–318, 334
    inverse probability weighted, 902
    kernel density, 407, 414–416,
        811, 1023
    least squares. *See* least squares
        estimator
    limited information, 371
    limited information maximum
        likelihood (LIML), 375,
        508, 570
    linear unbiased, 46
    M, 421
    matching, 893
    maximum likelihood, 72, 401, 428

maximum score, 792
maximum simulated
   likelihood, 227
method of moments, 431,
   434–436, 457
minimum distance, 233, 335
minimum distance estimator
   (MDE), 270, 437
minimum expected loss
   (MELO), 610
minimum variance linear
   unbiased estimator
   (MVLUE), 1032
Newey and West's, 463
Newey-West autocorrelation
   consistent covariance, 643
Newey-West robust
   covariance, 190
nonlinear instrumental
   variable, 462
nonlinear least squares, 290–292
nonparametric regression
   function, 812–813
ordinary least squares (OLS), 150
outer product of gradients
   (OPG), 495
partial likelihood, 940
Prais and Winsten, 649
pretest, 135
product limit, 939
properties of, 420–425
properties of generalized least
   squares, 155
quantile regression, 407
restricted least squares, 87–89
robust, 166
sampling theory, 610
sandwich, 514–515
single-equation (pooled),
   829n47
standard error of the, 52
statistics as, 1023–1027
straight-forward two-step
   GMM, 814
two-step, 169
unbiased, 1028
variables, comparing, 187
variance, for MLE, 496
White heteroscedasticity
   consistent, 162–164
within-groups, 191–193
Zellner's efficient, 258n11
Euler equations, 428–429
event counts, 906–915
events per unit of time, 912
evidence, 4
exact, finite-sample properties, 63
exactly identified case, 119, 436,
   443, 459

examples, 1078–1080
exclusions, 355, 367
   maximum likelihood estimation
      (MLE), 532–536
   restrictions, 90, 370
exogeneity
   assumptions of linear regression
      models, 44
   asymptotic properties, 72
   of independent variables, 11
   instrumental variables
      estimation, 315, 316
   specification tests, 387
   vector autoregression (VAR),
      698–699
exogenous variables duration,
   937–938
expansion by cofactors, 959
expectations, 670
   asymptotic, 1059–1060
   inequalities for, 1046
   in joint distributions, 1003
   of random variables, 989–991
expectations-augmented Phillips
   curve, 627, 679
explained variables, 8
explanatory variables, 8
exponential
   distributions, 996–997,
      1030, 1052
   families, 432, 433, 481
   model, 906
   model with fixed effects, 309
   ratios, 612n15
   regression model, 554
   samples, 1057
ex post forecasts, 101
exposure, 912
extensions
   bivariate probit model, 896n36
   panel data, 184
   random effects, 213–222
extremum estimators, 421–424

**F**

factoring matrices, 974–975
factorization, Cholesky, 583
families, exponential, 432, 433
$F$ distributions, 993–995,
   1017–1018, 1050
feasible generalized least squares
   (FGLS), 156–158, 337
   distribution, 157
   efficiency, 158
   estimators, 258
   GMM estimators, 464, 465
   groupwise heteroscedasticity, 173
   random effects, 203–205, 207

FGM (Farlie, Gumbel,
   Morgenstern) copula, 404
final form, 390
finite mixture models, 558, 559–560
finite moments, 435
finite sample properties, 44, 1027
   of b in generalized regression
      models, 150
   estimation in, 1027–1030
   exact, 63
   least squares estimator, 58–63
   of ordinary least squares
      (OLS), 150
first differences, 190–193
first-order autoregression. *See*
   AR(1)
first-order conditions, 288, 982
fit, competing model, 506–507
fit measures, 498–507, 826
fit of a consumption function, 34
fitted logs, 100n9
fitting criterion, 20, 32
fixed effects, 183
   count data, 916–918
   Hausman's specification test, 209
   linear regression model, 554n27
   maximum likelihood estimation
      (MLE), 554–558
   models, 193–200, 211–212,
      268–272, 797, 800–806
   panel data applications, 308–310
   probit models, 837–838
fixed panel, 184
fixed time and group effects,
   197–200
flexible cost function, 296
flexible functional form, 13,
   275–280
flexible functions, 276
focused information criterion
   (FIC), 144
forecasting, 99n8
   Bayesian model averaging, 145
   ex post forecasts, 101
   lagged variables, 686–689
   models, 358
   one-period-ahead forecast, 686
   serial correlation, 656–658
formulas, omitted variable, 134
fractionally integrated series, 740n2
fractional moments, 576
frameworks, estimation, 398–400
freedom correction, degrees of, 204
frequency domain, 731–738
Frish-Waugh-Lovell theorem, 28
$F$ statistic, 83, 298
$F$ table, 199–200
$F$ tests for firm and year effects, 109
full information, 371

full information maximum likelihood (FIML), 383–384, 508, 849
full MLE, 554–558
full rank, 11, 14, 15, 957
assumptions of linear regression models, 44
asymptotic properties, 72
instrumental variables estimation, 315
quadratic forms, 1017–1018
fully recursive model, 372
functional form, 4, 106, 112–114
flexible, 275–280
for nonlinear cost function, 114–117
nonlinear regression model, 286
function form, 912–915
function of random variables, 998–1000
fundamental probability transform, 403, 575

**G**

gamma distribution, 996–997
example of, 1079–1080
generalized method of moments (GMM) estimation, 445
parameters, 447
gamma functions, 1063–1064
gamma prior distribution, 605n6
gamma regression model, 72
GARCH model, 661–662
effects, 403
maximum likelihood estimation (MLE), 662–664
testing, 664–666
volatility, 665
Gauss-Hermite quadrature, 552, 1065
Gaussian quadrature, 1065
Gauss-Laguerre quadrature, 1065
Gauss-Markov theorem, 50
asymptotic efficiency, 71
least squares estimator, 48–49
multicollinearity, 59
general data generating processes, 72
generalized ARCH models, 660–662
generalized Chebychev's inequality, 1045
generalized inverse, 323, 975–976
generalized least squares, 154–156, 256–257
estimated covariance matrix of b, 160–162
random effects, 202

generalized linear regression model, 148
generalized method of moments (GMM), 399
asymptotic distribution of, 450
estimation of econometric models, 455–479
estimator, 288, 406, 441–451
identification condition, 457
maximum likelihood estimation (MLE), 496–497
properties, 447–451
serial correlation, 643–644
straight-forward two-step, 814
testing hypothesis in, 451–455
generalized regression model, 148–149, 256, 459
in asymptotic distribution, 153
consistency of ordinary least squares (OLS), 151
feasible generalized least squares (FGLS), 156–158
finite-sample properties of b in, 150
least squares estimation, 149–154
maximum likelihood estimation (MLE), 522–523
generalized residual, 778n8, 934
generalized sum of squares, 156, 522
general model building strategies, 136
general modeling framework, 182–183
General Theory of Employment, Interest, and Money, 2–3, 9–11
geometric regression model
maximum likelihood estimation (MLE), 542–547
panel data, 593
random effects, 592–593
geometry of matrices, 951–961
German Socioeconomic Panel (GSOEP), 180
GHK simulator, 582–583
Gibbs sampler
binomial probit model, 617
equations, 618
normal distribution, 614
globally concave, 982
globally convex, 982
global maximum, 982
goodness of fit, 32–39, 790–793, 908–909
Gordin's central limit theorem, 640
gradient methods, 1069–1071
Granger causality, 358, 699–701
Grenander conditions, 65
grid search, 1066

Gross National Product (GNP), 22
group effects
fixed time and, 197–200
testing, 197
groupings of dummy variables, 108–110
groups
means, robust estimation using, 188–190
within-groups estimator, 191–193
groupwise heteroscedasticity, 172
growth
cross-country growth regressions, 145
mixed fixed models, 242
surveys, 181n2
Grunfeld model, 255
Gumbel model, 774

**H**

Halton draws, 578
Halton sequences, 577–580
Hausman and Taylor estimator, 336, 337
Hausman and Taylor (HT) formulation, 470
Hausman test, 339
for consumption function, 324–325
instrumental variables estimation, 321–325
specification test, 208–209
hazard function, 866, 1001
hazard rate, 933
health care utilization, 307
health economics, 6
Heckman study, 588
Hermite polynomials, 1062
Hessian matrix, 981
heterogeneity, 182, 794
across units, 180
duration, 938–939
estimation with first differences, 190
measured and unmeasured, 560–561
modeling, 806–807
negative binomial regression model, 911–912
parameters, 222–244, 238–243, 807–809
heteroscedasticity, 16, 148–149, 158–164, 256
applications of, 170–175
autoregressive conditional, 658–667
binary choice, 787, 788–790

groupwise, 172
least squares estimation, 149–154
microeconomic data, 875–877
multiplicative, 170–172, 523–527
multiplicative, tobit model, 876
ordinary least squares (OLS)
    estimation, 159–160
random effects, 212–213
regression, 459
regression equations, 263
robust estimation, 159
robustness to unknown, 169
and serial correlation, 149
simultaneous equations models
    with, 466–469
testing, 165–167
weighted least squares, 168
White consistent estimator,
    162–164
heteroscedasticity extreme value
    (HEV) model, 856
heteroscedastic regression, 159
hierarchical linear model, 234
hierarchical model, 184, 230
highest posterior density (HPD)
    interval, 610
high-frequency time-series data,
    volatile, 148
histograms, 47, 414, 1023
homogeneity restriction, 262
homogeneous equation system,
    962, 964
homoscedasticity, 11, 16, 1007
    assumptions of linear regression
        models, 44
    asymptotic properties, 72
    instrumental variables
        estimation, 315
    nonlinear regression
        models, 286
hospital cost function, 439
H2SLS, 467
Hurdle model, 920–924
hybrid case, 842n53
hyperplane, 955
hypothesis
    binary choice, 785–787
    LM statistic, 454
    maximum likelihood estimation
        (MLE), 498–507
    nulls, restrictions of, 140
    restrictions, 115n4
    testing, 83–92, 259–263, 295,
        298–300
    testing, coefficients, 52
    testing, estimation, 425
    testing, inference, 1034–1038
    testing, nonnested, 138
    true size of the test, 585

**I**

idempotent matrices, 950–951, 974
idempotent quadratic forms,
    978, 1016
identical explanatory variables, 257
identical regressors, 257
identifiability
    maximum likelihood estimation
        (MLE), 497
    of model parameters, 286
    of parameters, 422
identification, 327
    of conditions, 14, 119, 292,
        449, 457
    instrumental variables
        estimation, 337
    of intrinsic linearity, 117–120
    of Klein's model, 369
    of nonlinearity, 114–117
    of parameters, 482–484
    problem of, 354, 356
    of rank and order conditions,
        354–370
    simultaneous equations model,
        361–370
    through nonsample
        information, 370
    of time series, 712
identify matrix, 945
identities, 355
ignorable case, 61
illustrative systems of equations,
    354–357
impact multiplier, 389, 673
importance
    function, 581
    sampling, 579–582
improper prior, 619–620
impulse response function, 394,
    701–702
incidental parameters problem,
    309, 557, 586–589, 797
incidental truncation, 882,
    883–884
inclusion of irrelevant variables, 136
income, 9n1, 11n2
    earnings and education, 10–11
    relationship to consumption,
        2–3
inconsistency
    estimates, 201
    least squares, 314–315
independence
    of b and s-squared, 53
    irrelevant alternatives
        assumptions, 847–850
    of linear forms, 1018–1019
    of quadratic forms, 1018–1019
independent variables, 3, 8, 979

asymptotic properties, 72
exogeneity of, 11
    instrumental variables
        estimation, 315
indicators, 329
indices
    index function models, 550, 775
    likelihood ratio index, 507
    qualification, 129
indirect least squares, 371
individual density, 482
individual effects model, 182,
    619–621
inefficiency
    asymptotic, 1058
    of least squares, 160
inequality
    Chebychev's, 990, 1040
    for expectations, 1046
    generalized Chebychev's, 1045
    Jensen's, 991
    likelihood, 491
    Markov's, 1040
inertia, 17
inference, 81, 400–405, 1019–1020
    Bayesian estimation, 609–613
    binary choice, 777–796
    hypothesis testing, 1034–1038
    vector autoregression
        (VAR), 707
infinite lag model, 677
infinite lag structures, 717n4
information matrix equality,
    488, 490
informative prior density, 606–609
initial conditions, 389, 631, 794
inner product, 947
innovations, 630
    asymptotic negligibility of, 639
    time-series models, 717
    vector autoregression
        (VAR), 702
instability
    models, testing, 766–767
    of vector autoregression
        (VAR), 712
instrumental variables estimation,
    245, 314–315, 327–331, 356,
    461, 893
    assumptions, 315–316
    dynamic panel data models,
        340–348
    empirical moment equation, 447
    generalized regression model,
        332–333
    Hausman test, 321–325
    measurement errors, 325–331
    models, 372–373
    nonlinear, 333–336

instrumental variables
        estimation (*continued*)
    nonlinear estimator, 462
    ordinary least squares (OLS), 316
    panel data, 336–349
    random effects, 336–339
    two-stage least squares, 318–321
    weak instruments, 350–352
    Wu test, 321–325
instruments
    streams as, 320
    weak, 350–352
    weak, testing, 377–380
insufficient observations, 121–122
integrals by quadrature,
        approximation, 1064–1065
integrated hazard function, 934
integrated order of one, 740
integrated processes, 739–741
integration
    density, 604n4
    Monte Carlo, 576–583
interaction terms, 113
interdependent systems, 355
intervals
    confidence, testing, 1037–1038
    estimation, 610, 1027, 1032–1034
    prediction, 99, 100
intrinsic linearity, 117–120
invariance
    lack of, 98
    maximum likelihood estimation
        (MLE), 494
invariants, 274, 278
inverse function, 986
inverse gamma distribution, 996
inverse Gaussian distribution, 431
inverse matrices, 465, 962–964
inverses
    Mills ratio, 866
    of partitioned matrices, 965–966
    probability weighted
        estimator, 902
inverted gamma distribution, 604
inverted Wishart prior density, 621
invertibility, time-series models,
        718–721
invertible polynomials, 676
investments
    equations, 22–25
    prediction for, 99–101
    restricted equations, 86
irrelevant alternatives assumptions,
        847–850
irrelevant variables, inclusion
        of, 136
*I* statistic, 219
iterations, 294
iterative algorithms, 1067

**J**
jackknife technique, 164
Jacobian, 298, 518
Jensen's inequality, 991
joint distributions, 402–405,
        1002–1006
jointly dependent variables, 355
joint posterior distribution, 605
*J* test, 139–140, 140

**K**
*k* class, 377
kernels
    density estimator, 407, 414–416,
        811, 1023
    density methods, 411–413
    method of, 812
Keyne's consumption function,
        2–3, 9–11
Khinchine's Weak Law of Large
        Numbers, 1042
Khinchine theorem, 67, 430
Klein's model, 355, 357, 369, 393
*K* moment equations, 431
Kolmogorov's Strong Law of Large
        Numbers, 1043
*K* parameters, 443n4
KPSS test of stationarity, 755–756
*K* regressors, 182
Krinsky and Robb method, 70
Kronecker products, 966–967
Kruskal's theorem, 176
Kullback-Leibler Information
        Criterion (KLIC), 141
kurtosis, 1021

**L**
labor economics, 882n18
labor supply model, 320, 324, 815
lack of invariance, 98
lagged dependent variable
    estimation with a, 651–652
    testing, 646
lagged variables
    analysis of dynamic models,
        689–693
    autocorrelation, 682, 691–692
    autoregressive distributed lag
        (ARDL) models, 681–689
    dynamic regression models,
        671–677
    forecasting, 686–689
    models with, 670–671
    simple distributed lag models,
        677–681
    vector autoregression (VAR),
        693–712

lag operator, 674, 717n3
Lagrange multiplier, 264
    autocorrelation, testing for,
        644–645
    binary choice, 786
    heteroscedasticity, 876
    maximum likelihood estimation
        (MLE), 502–504
    normal linear regression
        model, 520
    statistic, 454, 534
    testing, 96, 166, 205, 299–300, 505
lags
    dynamic models, 389
    equations, 479
    spatial, 221
    window, 735
large numbers, laws of, 1042–1045
large-sample distribution theory,
        1038–1056
large sample properties, 63–75,
        290–292
    maximum likelihood estimate
        (MLE), 486
    results, 613
    tests, 92–96
latent class models, 558
latent class regression model, 562
latent regression, 775–777
latent roots, 969
latent vectors, 969
Law of Iterated Expectations, 1007
laws of large numbers, 1042–1045
leading term approximation, 1060
least absolute deviations (LAD),
        406–409, 880
least squares, 43–44. *See also*
        nonlinear least squares
        estimator
    asymptotic normality of, 65–67
    asymptotic properties of, 151
    attenuation, 325–327
    basic statistical inference, 52–58
    coefficient vector, 21–22
    consistency of, 64–65
    dummy variable (LSDV), 195
    estimation, 149–154, 154–158,
        194–196
    estimation, serial correlation,
        640–643
    feasible generalized least squares
        (FGLS), 156–158
    finite-sample properties, 58–63
    *F* statistic, 83
    Gauss-Markov Theorem, 48–49
    generalized, 154–156, 256–257
    inconsistency, 314–315
    indirect, 371
    inefficiency of, 160

large sample properties of, 63–75
Lindeberg-Feller central limit theorem, 152
loss of fit from restricted, 89–92
maximum likelihood estimates, 118
motivating, 44–46
normal equations, 22
normality assumption, 52–58
ordinary least squares (OLS), 150, 159–160
problem, 1066
projections, 960
random effects, 202
regression, 20–26, 164
residuals, 541n25, 650
stochastic repressors, 49–50
three-stage (3SLS), 381–383, 537
two-stage (2SLS), 318–321, 356, 373–375
two-step nonlinear estimation, 302–307
unbiased estimation, 46–47
variances, 48–49
variances, estimating, 51–52
variances, estimation, 642–643
weighted, 167–169, 444
least variance ratio, 376
*L* elements, 444
length of vectors, 960
Liapounov central limit theorem, 1054
life cycle consumption, 428–429
life expectancy, 125
likelihood-based tests, application of, 504–506
likelihood equation, 490, 778
likelihood estimation, 214n14
likelihood function, 445n9, 482–484
exponential and normal distributions, 1030
prior density, 601
likelihood inequality, 491
likelihood ratio, 264
index, 507
statistic, 453, 534, 854
testing, 498–500, 505, 520, 786
Vuong's test of nonnested models, 140
limited information, 849
estimation methods 371-380
estimator, 371
limited information maximum likelihood (LIML) estimator, 375, 508, 570
limiting
distribution, 95, 317, 995, 1048
mean, 1049
normal distributions, 1055

probability, 67, 326, 430, 1046
variances, 1049
Lindeberg-Feller central limit theorem, 66, 152
Lindeberg-Levy central limit theorem, 435, 1051
linear approximation, 979
linear combination, 948
of coefficients, 55–56
of vectors, 953–954
linear dependence, 954–955
linear equations, 961–964
linear form, 1018–1019
linear functions
of normal vectors, 1015
sets of, 1011–1012
linear independence, 954
linearity, 11
assumptions of linear regression models, 44
asymptotic properties, 72
instrumental variables estimation, 315
of regression models, 12–19
linearized regression, 288–290
linear least squares regression, 4
linearly deterministic component, 726
linearly indeterministic component, 726
linear probability model, 772
linear random effects model, 547–550
linear regression model, 8–18, 304, 401–402
assumptions of, 44
generalized model, 148
homoscedasticity, 1009
moments, 1008
linear restrictions, 82, 85, 355
linear time trends, 16n3
linear unbiased estimator, 46
line search, 1067
Ljung-Box statistic, 729
Ljung's refinement, 645
LM. *See* Lagrange multiplier
local maxima, 982
local optima, 982
location, measures of, 1020
logistic distributions, 997
logit model, 774
for binary choice, 139
fixed effects, 805
log likelihood function, 485, 543
duration, 938n12
Kullback-Leibler Information Criterion (KLIC), 141
loglinear conditional mean function, 542

loglinear model, 13, 112, 305, 907
lognormal distributions, 996
lognormal mean estimation, 578
log-odds ratio, 844
log-quadratic cost function, 117
logs
common (base 10), 115n3
natural, 115n3
longitudinal data sets, 180
Longley data, multicollinearity in, 60
long-run elasticity, 239
long run multiplier, 239, 673
long run theoretical model, 765–766
loss function, 610
loss of fit, 89–92
lower powers, convergence in, 1044
lower triangular matrix, 945, 974

## M

macroeconomic models, 5, 356
maginal propensity to consume, 609
marginal distributions, 404, 1013–1014
marginal effects, 114, 775
binary choice, 780–785
binary variables, 835
bivariate probit models, 821–822
censored regression model, 872
marginal probability density, 1002
market equilibrium, 5
Markov Chain Monte Carlo (MCMC) methods, 573, 574, 600n1, 615
Markov's inequality, 1040
Markov's Strong Law of Large Numbers, 1044
Markov theorem, 67
Martingale difference central limit theorem, 638
Martingale difference sequence, 638
Martingale difference series, 449
Martingale sequence, 638
matching estimator, 893
mathematical statistics, 5
matrices
addition, 946–947
algebra, 945. *See also* algebra
asymptotic covariance, 153–154, 159, 317, 385n22, 446
autocorrelation, 632
autocovariance, 632
block-diagonal, 965
calculus, 979–987
coefficients, 393
comparing, 978–979
condition numbers of, 971

matrices (*continued*)
  convergence, 151
  correlation, 1011
  covariance, 1011
  covariance, ordinary least
    squares (OLS), 162–164
  definite, 976–979
  determinants of, 958–961, 972
  diagonalization of, 969
  equality of, 945–946
  estimation of covariance of b,
    160–162
  factoring, 974–975
  generalized inverse of, 975–976
  geometry of, 951–961
  Hessian, 981
  idempotent, 950–951, 974
  information matrix equality,
    488, 490
  inverse, 465, 962–964
  manipulation of, 945–951
  moments, 30
  multiplication, 947–950
  nonsingular, 963
  null, 946
  optimal weighting matrix, 438
  partitioned, 964–967
  powers of, 972–974
  precision, 612
  projection, 25
  rank, 956–958, 969–971
  residual maker, 25
  robust asymptotic covariance,
    511–517
  robust covariance, 307
  robust covariance, count data,
    915–916
  robust covariance estimation, 780
  second derivatives, 981
  short rank, 957
  singularity of the disturbance
    covariance, 278
  spectral decomposition of, 969
  symmetric, 974n9
  trace of, 971–972
  transformation, 473
  transposition, 946
  weighting, 439, 444n7, 459, 478
  weighting matrix, 438
  zeros, 946
matrix weighted average, 192
maximum likelihood estimation
    (MLE), 72, 118, 274, 401,
    428, 482, 485, 770
  applications of, 517–567
  asymptotic efficiency, 493–494
  asymptotic normality, 492–493
  asymptotic variance, 494–496
  autocorrelation, 527–529

bivariate probit models, 817–820
class membership, predicting, 561
cluster estimators, 515–517
conditional latent class model,
    561–563
consistency, 491–492
degrees of freedom, 519n14
duration, 936–937
exclusion restrictions, 532–536
finite mixture models, 558,
    559–560
fixed effects, 554–558
GARCH model, 662–664
generalized regression model,
    522–523
geometric regression model,
    542–547
heterogeneity, 560–561
invariance, 494
latent class models, 558
likelihood function, 482–484
linear random effects model,
    547–550
nonlinear regression models,
    537–538
nonnormal disturbances, 538–542
optimization, 1072–1073
panel data, 547, 564–567
pooled model, 530–531
principle of, 484–486
properties of, 486–496
quadrature, 550–554
residuals, 529
sandwich estimators, 514–515
seemingly unrelated regression
    (SUR) model, 529–530, 531
simultaneous equations model,
    536–537
stochastic frontier model,
    538–542
two-step, 507–511
maximum likelihood method, 399
maximum score estimator, 792
maximum simulated likelihood
    (MSL), 589, 595, 799
  estimates, 228
  estimation, 593
  estimator, 227
mean
  assumptions, 15
  asymptotic distributions, 1057
  conditional, 1006
  conditional mean function, 417
  deviations from, 966
  hypothesis testing, 1035
  independence, 182, 189
  independence, assumption, 901
  lag, 674
  limiting, 1049

lognormal, estimating, 578
  normal, confidence intervals
    for, 1033
  one-sided tests, 1038
  quadratic, convergence, 1–39
  of random variables, 989
  rth, convergence in, 1044, 1045
  sampling, 1025
  sampling, consistency of, 1041
  square convergence, 68
  squared error, 135, 1029
  truncated, 865
  value theorem, 450
measured heterogeneity, 560–561
measurement
  economies of scale, 116n7
  errors, 63, 189, 314–315, 325–331
  of a fit, 35–38
  goodness of fit, 790–793, 908–909
  of variables, 4
measure of central tendency, 1020
measure of linear association, 1009
measures of central tendency, 989
measures of location, 1020
median, 989
  asymptotic inefficiency, 1058
  lag, 674
  variance of, bootstrapping, 597
Medical Expenditure Panel Survey
    (MEPS), 180
medical research, 6
M estimators, 421
method of moments, 402, 406
  asymptotic properties of,
    434–436
  consistent estimation, 429–436
  estimator, 457
  estimators, 431
  generating functions, 432
methodology, 5, 6
methods
  bootstrap, 407
  Box-Jenkins, 726n11
  Broyden-Fletcher-Goldfarb-
    Shanno (BFGS), 1071
  Broyden's, 1071
  Butler and Moffitt's, 552, 798
  Davidon-Fletcher-Powell
    (DFP), 1071
  delta, 69, 927, 1055–1056
  gradient, 1069–1071
  of kernels, 812
  of kernels, density, 411–413
  Krinsky and Robb, 70
  Markov Chain Monte Carlo
    (MCMC), 573, 574
  Newton's, 524, 544, 1070, 1079
  QR, 975n12
  quadratic hill-climbing, 1070

quasi-Newton, 1071
rejection, 576
of scoring, 524, 779
of simulated moments, 590, 595–596
steepest ascent, 1069
Metropolis-Hastings algorithm, 622
Michigan Panel Study of Income Dynamics (PSID), 180
microeconomics
 models, 5
 vector autoregression (VAR) in, 711–712
minimal sufficient statistic, 803
minimization, 334
minimum distance estimation (MDE), 233, 270, 335, 428–429, 436–441, 437
 consistent estimation, 429–436
 generalized method of moments (GMM), 441–451
minimum expected loss (MELO) estimator, 610
minimum mean error predictor, 45–46
minimum simulated sum of squares function, 228
minimum variance linear unbiased estimation (MVLUE), 46–47, 1032
missing at random (MAR), 62
missing completely at random (MCAR), 61
missing data model, 1076
mixed fixed growth models, 242
mixed linear model, 235
mixed logit model, 851–852
mixed models, 233
mixtures of normal distributions, 432
mode, 989
models
 accelerated failure time, 937
 ARCH, 658
 ARCH(1), 659–660
 ARCH-M, 660–662
 ARCH($q$), 660–662
 autoregressive, 675
 autoregressive distributed lag (ARDL), 681–689
 autoregressive integrated moving-average (ARIMA), 740
 Bayesian estimation, 600–601
 Bayesian model averaging, 144–146
 binary choice, 139, 411–412, 772–777
 binomial probit, 616–619

bivariate ordered probit, 835–836
bivariate probit, 817–826, 896n36
building, 136–137
censored regression (tobit), 871–874
Chamberlain's, 230
classical normal linear regression, 1014–1015
Cobb-Douglas, 91
comparing, 38–39
comprehensive, 138
confirmation of, 4
constants, 16n3
covariance structures, 266
credit scoring, 304
density, 400
discrete choice, 770
distributed lag, 97
duration, 931–942
dynamic, 356
dynamic, binary choice, 794–796
dynamic, panel data, 238–243, 244–246, 340–348, 469–479
dynamic, properties of, 389–394
dynamic, regression, 670
econometric, 2–5, 355
econometric, estimation of, 455–479
error components, 201
estimated duration, 941
estimated latent class, 595
estimated random parameters, 594
estimated SUR, 259
event counts, 907–915
exponential, 906
exponential model with fixed effects, 309
exponential regression, 554
fit, computing, 506–507
fixed effects, 193–200, 211–212, 268–272, 797, 800–806
forecasting, 358
forms, 695
fully recursive, 372
GARCH, 661–662, 662–664
generalized ARCH, 660–662
generalized linear regression, 148
generalized regression, 148–149, 256
Grunfeld, 255
Gumbel, 774
heterogeneity, 806–807
heteroscedastistic extreme value (HEV), 856
hierarchical, 184, 230
hierarchical linear, 234
index function, 550, 775
individual effects, 619–621

infinite lag, 677
instability, testing, 766–767
joint distributions, 402–405
$J$ test, 139–140
Klein's, 357, 369
with lagged variables, 670–671
latent class regression, 562
linear probability, 772
linear regression, 8–18, 288–290, 304, 401–402, 554n27
linear regression, assumptions of, 44
logit, 774
logit, fixed effects, 805
loglinear, 13, 112, 305, 907
long-run theoretical, 765–766
macroeconomic, 356
mean-squared error criterion, 135
methodology, 5
missing data, 1076
mixed, 233
mixed fixed growth, 242
mixed linear, 235
$m$th, 145
multinomial probit, 850–851
multiple linear regression, 8
multivariate probit, 826–831
multivariate regression, 255
negative binomial, 910
negative binomial regression, heterogeneity, 911–912
nested, 81–83
nonlinear panel data regression, 308–310
nonlinear regression, 285–293
nonlinear regression, applications, 294–297
nonnested, 923
nonnested, selection of, 137–142
nonstationary data, 243–244
nonstructural, 355n2
nontested, 82
normal-Poisson mixture, 911n5
ordered choice, 842
ordered probit, 831–835
panel data, 180, 183–184
parametric duration, 933–939
partial adjustment, 679
partially linear, 409
piecewise loglinear, 116
pooled, 266–267
pooled regression, 185–193
population averaged, 185
probability, 400, 781
probit, 773, 776
qualitative response (QR), 770
random coefficient, 223–225, 225
random effects, 206, 268–272, 796, 797–800

models (*continued*)
random effects geometric regression, 553–554
random parameters, 621–623
random parameters logit (RPL), 851
random utility, 777
recursive, 359
recursive bivariate probit, 823–826
reduced form of, 355, 360
regression, analysis of classical, 603–609
regression, selection, 884–886
relational lag, 683
seemingly unrelated regression (SUR), 254–263, 464–466
selection, 143–146
selection criterion, 142–143
self-regressive, 716
semilog, 13
semiparametric regression, 52
simple distributed lag, 677–681
simultaneous equations, 354, 466–469
single-equation linear, 455–461
single-equation nonlinear, 461–464
spherical disturbances, 149
stochastic frontier, 402, 572
strongly exogenous, 358
structural, 328, 355n2
structural change, 120–128
time-series, 715
time-series, panel data, 181n1
time-space dynamic, 220
time-space simultaneous, 219
translog, 13–14
two-step estimation of panel data, 229–233
Two-Variable Regression, 48
uncorrelated linear regression, 304
underlying probability, 287
univariate time-series, 716, 726–728
unobserved effects, 209–210
unordered multiple choice, 841–859
vector moving average (VMA), 704
Weibull model, 937
Weibull survival, 939
zero-inflated Poisson (ZIP), 930
With Zeros (WZ), 922n7
modified zero-order regression, 62
moment-generating function, 1001
moments
asymptotic, 1060

of censored normal variables, 870
central, 432, 990
convergence of, 1047
diagonal elements of the inverse, 30
empirical, asymptotic distribution of, 449
empirical, convergence of, 448
empirical equation, 442, 447, 456
empirical moment equation, 456
finite, 435
fractional, 576
generalized method of, 399
of incidentally truncated bivariate normal distribution, 883
$K$ moment equations, 431
linear regression, 1008
method of, 402, 406
method of, asymptotic properties of, 434–436
method of, consistent estimation, 429–436
method of, estimators, 431
method of, generating functions, 432
method of simulated, 590, 595–596
multivariate distributions, 1010–1011
population equation, 456
relationships, 1007–1009
sample, normal distribution for, 458
of truncated distributions, 864–867
uncentered, 430
validity of moment restrictions, 452–455
money demand equation, 626
Monte Carlo integration, 576–583
Monte Carlo studies, 574n1, 584–589
Moore-Penrose inverse, 975
most powerful test, 1035
moving average (MA), 190
form, 633, 675, 718
processes, 633
MSCORE, 812
$m$th model, 145
multicollinearity, 59–61
dummy variables, 108
in nonlinear regression models, 296
multinomial logit model, 842, 843–845, 854
multinomial probit model, 850–851
multiple cointegration vectors, 759
multiple correlation, 37

multiple linear regression model, 8
multiple regression, 24
computation of, 22
frameworks, 328
multiple solutions, 1075
multiplication
conformable for, 947
matrices, 947–950
partitioned matrices, 965
scalars, 947–950, 951
vectors, 947
multiplicative heteroscedasticity, 170–172, 523–527, 876
multipliers
cumulative, 390
dynamic, 390
equilibrium, 239, 390, 674
impact, 389, 673
Lagrange, 264
Lagrange, binary choice, 786
long run, 239, 673
maximum likelihood estimation (MLE), 502–504
modes and, 389–390
multivariate distributions, 1010–1012
multivariate Lindeberg-Feller central limit theorem, 1055
multivariate Lindeberg-Levy central limit theorem, 1054
multivariate normal distribution, 1013–1019
multivariate normal population, 576
multivariate normal probabilities, 582–583
multivariate probit model, 826–831
multivariate regression model, 255
multivariate $t$ distribution, 606
Mundlak's approach, 209–210, 230

**N**

National Institute of Standards and Technology (NIST), 975n12
natural logs, 115n3
nearest neighbor concept, 417
necessary condition for an optimum, 982
negative autocorrelation, 627, 629
negative binomial model, 910
negative binomial regression model, 911–912
negative duration dependence, 935
Negbin 1 form, 913
Negbin 2 form, 913
Negbin $P$, 913
nested logit models, 847–850
nested models, 81–83
nested random effects, 214–217

net effect, 9
netting out, 28
Newey and West's estimator, 463
Newey-West autocorrelation consistent covariance estimator, 643
Newey-West robust covariance estimator, 190
Newton's method, 524, 544, 1070, 1079
Nobel prize in Economic Sciences, 1
noncausality, Granger, 699
noncentral chi-squared distribution, 501n8
nonconstructive, White test, 166
nonhomogeneous equation system, 962
noninformative prior, 604
nonlinear consumption function, 294–296
nonlinear cost function, 114–117
nonlinear functions, 1012
    asymptotic distribution, 1058
    of parameters, 69, 70
nonlinear instrumental variable estimator, 462
nonlinear instrumental variables estimation, 333–336
nonlinearity
    identification of, 114–117
    in variables, 112–120
nonlinear least squares
    estimator, computing, 292–293
    estimators, 290–292
    robust covariance matrix, 307
nonlinear models
    fixed effects, 554–558
    sample selection, 895–898
nonlinear models, sample selection, 895–898
nonlinear optimization, 228, 446, 462
nonlinear panel data regression model, 308–310
nonlinear regression model, 285–293
    applications, 294–297
    hypothesis testing, 300
    maximum likelihood estimation (MLE), 537–538
    multicollinearity in, 296
nonlinear restriction, 96–98, 120
nonlinear systems, 300–302, 358n6
nonnegative definite, 974, 976
nonnested hypothesis, testing, 138
nonnested models, 137–142, 923
nonnormal disturbances, 92–96, 538–542
nonnormality, 880–881

nonoautocorrelation, 11, 16
    assumptions of linear regression models, 44
    asymptotic properties, 72
    instrumental variables estimation, 315
    nonlinear regression models, 286
nonparametric average cost function, 418–419
nonparametric duration, 939–942
nonparametric estimation, 398, 413–420
nonparametric regression, 416–420, 812–813
nonrandom regressors, 18
nonsample information, 364, 370
nonsingular matrix, 435, 963
nonspherical disturbances, 210–213
nonstationary data, 243–244, 739
    cointegration, 756–767
    common trends, 759–760
    Dickey-Fuller tests, 745–754
    error correction, 760–761
    KPSS test of stationarity, 755–756
    panel data, 767–768
    processes, 739–756
nonstationary process, 740
nonstochastic data
    assumptions of linear regression models, 44
    instrumental variables estimation, 315
nonstochastic regressors, 17
nonstructural models, 355n2
nontested models, 82
normal distribution, 11, 486, 864, 872n10, 991–992, 1013–1014
    assumptions of linear regression models, 44
    censored, 869–871
    Gibbs sampler, 614
    instrumental variables estimation, 315
    likelihood functions, 1030
    limiting, 1055
    mixtures of, 432
    for sample moments, 458
normal equations, 27
normal-gamma prior, 608, 620
normality, 18–19
    assumptions of, 100n9
    asymptotic, 1058
    least squares estimator, 52–58
    sample selection, 891
normalization, 354, 359, 483
normal linear regression model, 518–522
normally distributed disturbances, 18

normal mean, 1033
normal-Poisson mixture model, 911n5
normal sampling, 1058
normal vectors, 1015
no solution, 1075
notation, 12, 947
not missing at random (NMAR), 62
null hypothesis, 83, 140
null matrix, 946
numbers
    large, laws of, 1042–1045
    pseudo-random numbers, generating, 574

**O**

Oaxaca and Blinder's decomposition, 55
Oberhofer-Kmenta conditions, 533n22
observationally equivalent theories, 361, 362–364
observations
    dependent, 635
    insufficient, 121–122
    linear regression models, 15–16
    missing, 61–63
    regression, 195
observed variables, 337
occupational choice, 843
odds ratio, 853
Olsen's reparameterization, 875
omission of relevant variables, 133
omitted variables
    bias, 868
    binary choice, 787
    formula, 134
one parameter, function of, 1078–1079
one-period-ahead forecast, 686
one-sided tests, mean, 1038
one-step estimation, 1072
one-to-one function, 986
optimal linear predictor, 45
optimal weighting matrix, 438
optimization, 982–983, 1065–1078
    algorithms, 1067–1068
    computation derivatives, 1068–1069
    constrained, 984–985
    with constraints, 1073–1074
    gradient methods, 1069–1071
    maximum likelihood estimation (MLE), 1072–1073
    nonlinear, 446, 462
order, 945
    of sequences, 1060–1061
order condition, 449, 457

ordered choice models,
831–841, 842
ordered probit model, 831–835
ordinary least squares (OLS)
asymptotic covariance
matrix, 516
consistency of, 151
covariance matrices, 162–164
estimation, 159–160
estimator, 150
groupwise heteroscedasticity, 173
instrumental variables
estimation, 316
panel data, 190
random effects, 207
residuals, 174
simultaneous equations model,
371–372
orthogonality condition, 287–288,
335, 442–443, 456
orthogonality population, 44–45
orthogonal partitioned
regression, 27
orthogonal regression, 24
orthogonal vectors, 960
orthonormal quadratic forms, 1015
outcome of random processes, 987
outer product of gradients (OPG)
estimator, 495
output, cointegration in, 757, 762
overdispersion, testing, 909–911
overidentified case, 439, 459
overidentified parameters, 120
overidentifying restrictions, 298,
388, 452

**P**

pair of event counts, joint modeling
of, 405
panel data, 73
analysis, 182–183
applications, 267–272, 307–311
autocorrelation, 213, 652–655
balanced and unbalanced, 184
Bayesian estimation, 619–621
binary choice, 796–809
consistent estimation of, 244–246
count data, 915–920
dynamic model, 238–243,
340–348, 469–479
estimation, 229–233
extensions, 184
generalized regression
model, 149
geometric regression, 593
group sizes, 235
instrumental variables
estimation, 336–349

maximum likelihood estimation
(MLE), 547, 564–567
models, 180, 183–184
nonstationary data, 243–244,
739n1, 767–768
ordinary least squares (OLS), 190
pooled regression model,
185–193
probit models, 837–841
sample selection, 898–899
sets, 1020
stated choice experiments,
858–859
tobit model, 881–882
within-groups estimator, 191–193
parameters
confidence intervals for, 54–55
estimation of, 430–434, 471
estimation of univariate time
series, 728–731
function of one, example,
1078–1079
gamma distribution, 447
heterogeneity, 222–244, 238–243,
807–809
identifiability of, 286, 422
identification of, 482–484
incidental parameters problem,
309, 557, 586–589, 797
instrumental variables
estimation, 327
$K$, 443n4
nested logit models, 849
nonlinear functions of, 69, 70
overidentified, 120
point estimation of, 1027–1032
precision, 494
random, 183, 226–229
random parameters logit (RPL)
model, 851
random parameters model,
621–623
space, 82, 400, 421–422, 497
unknown, 297
vectors, 121, 141n9
parametric duration models,
933–939
parametric estimation, 398, 400–405
parametric restrictions, 88n3,
298–300
partial adjustment model, 679
partial autocorrelation, 723–726
partial correlation
coefficients, 29–31
partial differences, 647
partial effects, 182
partialing out, 28
partial likelihood estimator, 940
partially linear model, 409

partially linear regression, 409–411
partially linear translog cost
function, 410
partial regression, 27–29, 28, 29–31
partitioned inverse, 966
partitioned matrices, 964–967
partitioned regression, 27–29
periodogram sample, 734
persistence, 794
Phillips curve, 627, 679
Phillips-Perron tests, 753
piecewise continuous, 112
piecewise loglinear model, 116
pivotal quantity, 1033
point estimation, 609–610,
1027–1032
Poisson distribution, 485, 906,
998, 1031
Poisson model
censoring, 925–931
censoring and truncation, 925
estimation, 929
regression, 542, 907
policy analysis, 703–710
political methodology, 6
polynomials
Hermite, 1062
invertible, 676
lag operators, 675
pooled model, 266–267, 530–531
pooled regression model, 183,
185–193
population
averaged model, 185
least squares regression, 21
moment equation, 456
multivariate normal, 576
quantity, 20
regression, equation, 8
regression, models, 20, 44–45
standard uniform, 575
positive duration dependence, 935
positive (negative) definite, 976
positive semidefinite, 976
posterior density, 601–603
posterior distributions, 613–616
postmultiplication, 947
power of tests, 585, 1035
powers
lower, convergence in, 1044
of a matrix, 972–974
Prais and Winsten estimator, 649
precision matrices, 612
precision parameter, 494
predetermined variables, 356, 358
prediction, 81, 99–102
Bayesian estimation, 609n13
class membership, 561
criteria, 37, 143

intervals, 99, 100
for investments, 99–101
probability, 834
probit models, 793
residuals, 117
variances, 99
predictive tests, 122, 127–128
predictors
minimum mean error, 45–46
optimal linear, 45
of variations, 32
preliminary tests for
heteroscedasticity, 165n16
premultiplication, 947
preponderance of evidence, 4
pretest estimation, 134–135
pretest estimator, 135
principal components, 61
principal minor, 959n4
principle of maximum likelihood,
484–486
prior beliefs, 602
prior distribution, 604
prior odds ratio, 611
prior probabilities, 611
probability
Bayesian estimation, 602
convergence in, 1039–1042
distributions, 987–988, 991–998
distributions, representations of,
1000–1001
finite moments, 435
fundamental transform, 403
inverse probability weighted
estimator, 902
limits, 326, 430, 1046
linear probability model, 772
marginal density, 1002
maximum likelihood estimation
(MLE), 565
models, 781
multivariate normal probabilities,
582–583
order probit models, 833
power of the test, 585
prediction, 834
prior probabilities, 611
simulating, 827n44
underlying probability
model, 287
of variances, 161
probability density function
(pdf), 1000
probability distribution function
(pdf), 988
probability limits, 67
probability model, 400
probit model, 773, 776
for binary choice, 139

bivariate, 817–826
bivariate, extensions, 896n36
bivariate, ordered, 835–836
fixed effects, 837–838
multinomial, 850–851
multivariate, 826–831
ordered, 831–835
panel data, 837–841
prediction, 793
random effects, 838–841
recursive bivariate, 823–826
problem of identification, 354, 356,
361–370
processes
autoregressive, 632
autoregressive moving-average,
716–718
data generating process (DGP),
436, 518n13, 743, 987
disturbances, 632–634
general data generating, 72
integrated, 739–741
moving-average, 633
nonstationary, 739–756, 740
outcome of random, 987
stationary, 671
stationary stochastic, 716–731
stationary stochastic,
autocorrelation, 721–723
time-series, 630
trend stationary, 743
production function, 90, 228
CES, 119, 285–286
Cobb-Douglas, 273
LAD estimation of a, 408
product limit estimator, 939
products
Kronecker, 966–967
transposition, 949
profiles
age-earnings, 114
time, 111
profit maximization, 5
projection, 25, 269
projects, 269n17
proof, asymptotic normality, 152
propensity score, 893
properties
asymptotic, 44, 64
asymptotic, assumptions of,
421–424
asymptotic, of estimators,
424–425
asymptotic, of least squares, 151,
640–642
asymptotic, of method of
moments, 434–436
contagion, 1001
of dynamic models, 389–394

of estimators, 420–425
exact, finite-sample, 63
finite sample, 44, 1027
finite sample, least squares
estimator, 58–63
finite sample, of b in generalized
regression models, 150
finite sample, of ordinary least
squares (OLS), 150
of generalized least squares
estimator, 155
of GMM estimators, 447–451
large sample, 290–292
large sample properties, 63–75
of maximum likelihood estimate
(MLE), 486–496
of regular densities, 488–490
root-$n$ consistent, 1051
sampling, 596
statistical, 43
proportional hazard, 940
proportions, 844n55
proxy variables, 328–331
pseudo-differences, 647
pseudoinverse, 975
pseudo-maximum likelihood
estimation, 511–517, 666–667
pseudo-random numbers,
generating, 574
pseudoregressors, 290
pseudotrue parameter vectors,
141n9
Pythagorean theorem, 26

**Q**

QR method, 975n12
quadratic approximation, 979
quadratic earnings equation, 113
quadratic form, 323
algebra, 976–979
full rank, 1017–1018
idempotent, 978, 1016
independence of, 1018–1019
orthonormal, 1015
standard normal vectors,
1015–1017
quadratic hill-climbing
method, 1070
quadratic mean, 1–39
quadratic term, 116
quadrature
Gauss-Hermite, 552, 1065
Gaussian, 1065
Gauss-Laguerre, 1065
maximum likelihood estimation
(MLE), 550–554
weight, 1065
qualification indices, 129

qualitative choices, 771
qualitative response (QR)
    models, 770
quantile regression estimator, 407
quantitative approach to
    economics, 1
quasi differences, 647
quasi-Newton methods, 1071

**R**
random coefficients model,
    223–225, 851
random constants, 857
random disturbance, 9
random draws, 577–580, 578
random effects, 183, 200–210
    count data, 918–920
    estimation, 207
    extensions, 213–222
    feasible generalized least squares
      (FGLS), 203–205, 207
    generalized least squares, 202
    geometric regression model,
      553–554, 592–593
    Hausman and Taylor (HT)
      formulation, 470
    Hausman's specification test,
      208–209
    heteroscedasticity, 212–213
    instrumental variables
      estimation, 336–339
    likelihood estimation, 214n14
    maximum likelihood estimation
      (MLE), 547–550
    models, 268–272, 796, 797–800
    nested, 214–217
    panel data applications,
      310–311
    probit models, 838–841
    SUR models, 267–268
    testing, 205–208
randomness of human
    behavior, 4
random number generation,
    573–576
random parameters logit (RPL)
    model, 851
random parameters model, 183,
    226–229, 621–623
random sampling, 429, 430, 1020
random terms, 234
random utility models, 777
random variables, 987–988
    bivariate, distribution, 1004–1006
    censored, 871
    continuous, 987
    convergence to, 1046–1047
    density of truncated, 864

    discrete, 998
    distributions, 998–1000
    expectations of, 989–991
random vector, 1010
random walks, 741–744
    Dickey-Fuller tests, 745
    with drift, 683, 739
rank
    cointegration, 759
    columns, 956
    condition, 449
    full, 957
    of matrices, 956–958, 969–971
    and order conditions, 354–370
rankings, 771
rank two
    correction, 1071
    update, 1071
rating assignments, 834
ratios
    exponential, 612n15
    inverse Mills, 866
    $J$ test, 139
    least variance, 376
    likelihood, 264
    likelihood ratio (LR), statistic,
      534, 854
    likelihood ratio (LR), test,
      498–500, 505, 786
    likelihood ratio (LR) test, 520
    likelihood statistics, 453
    log-odds, 844
    odds, 853
    prior odds, 611
    sacrifice, 704
    t, 53
real data, 573
recursive bivariate probit models,
    823–826
recursive models, 359
reduced form
    disturbances, 360
    equation, 329
    of models, 355, 360
regression, 15–16
    analysis of treatment effects,
      889–890
    approach, binary choice models,
      772–775
    binary variables, 106–112
    bivariate, 23
    classical, 458
    coefficients, 28
    conditional mean, 1006
    with a constant term, 29
    cross-country growth, 145
    demand equations, 55, 69
    disturbances, 158–164
    double-length, 664

    earnings equation, 54
    equations, 252–254
    generalized, 459
    generalized linear regression
      model, 148
    generalized model, 148–149, 256
    heteroscedasticity, 459
    intrinsic linear, 118
    latent, 775–777
    least squares, 164
    least squares estimator, 47
    linearized, 288–290
    linear least squares, 4
    in a model of selection, 884–886
    models. *See* regression models
    modified zero-order, 62
    multiple, 24
    multivariate regression
      model, 255
    nonparametric, 416–420
    nonparametric regression
      function, 812–813
    observations, 195
    orthogonal, 24
    partial, 29–31
    partially linear, 409–411
    Poisson model, censoring,
      925–931
    pooled, 183
    population, 20, 44–45
    quantile estimator, 407
    results for life expectancy, 125
    seemingly unrelated regressions
      (SUR), 254–263
    spline, 111–112
    spurious, 741–744
    standard error of the, 51
    testing, 56–57
    Two-Variable Regression
      model, 48
    variables, adding, 31
    vector autoregression, 479
regression models
    analysis of, 603–609
    censored, 871–874
    dynamic, 670
    dynamic, lagged variables,
      671–677
    gammas, 72
    heteroscedasticity, applications
      of, 170–175
    least squares regression, 20–26
    linear, 8–18
    linearity of, 12–19
    loglinear, 112
    multiple linear, 8
    nonlinear, 285–293
    Poisson, 907
    pooled, 185–193

seemingly unrelated, 464–466
semiparametric, 52
transformed, 168
truncation, 867–869
regressors, 8
  data generating processes for,
    17–18
  fixed time effects, 198n10
  identical, 257
  nonrandom, 18
  nonstochastic, 17
  subset of, 304
  transformation, 296n4
regular densities, 488–490
regularity conditions, 487–488
rejection
  method, 576
  region, 1034
relational lag model, 683
relationships
  cointegration, 764
  consumption to income, 2–3
  demand, 9n1
  deterministic, 3, 9
  between earnings and education,
    10–11
  equilibrium, 689
  moments, 1007–1009
  random disturbance, 9
relevance, 316
relevant variables, omission of, 133
residual, 20
residuals, 116n5
  consistent estimators, 163
  constrained generalized
    regression model, 156
  generalized, 778n8, 934
  least squares, 541n25, 650
  against load factor, 171
  maximum likelihood estimation
    (MLE), 529
  negative autocorrelation, 629
  ordinary least squares (OLS), 174
  panel data, 186
  of predicted cost, 117
  for production function, 408
  sum of squares, 680
  unstandardized, 628
  variance in a regression, 1008
  vectors, 25
response, treatment of, 107
restricted investment equation, 86
restricted least squares
  estimator, 87–89
  loss of fit from, 89–92
restrictions
  exclusion, 90
  exclusions, 370
  homogeneity, 262

linear, 82, 355
maximum likelihood estimation
    (MLE), 532–536
  and nested models, 81–83
  nonlinear, 120
  nonlinear, cost function, 115n4
  nonlinear, testing, 96–98
  of null hypothesis, 140
  overidentifying, 298, 452
  overidentifying, testing, 388
  parametric, 298–300
  testing, 85
  validity of moment, 452–455
results
  characteristic roots and vectors,
    968–969
  frequency domain, 732–734
  large sample, 613
  vector autoregression (VAR),
    707–710
revealed preference data, 858
revised beliefs, 602
risk set, 940
robust asymptotic covariance
    matrices, 511–517
robust covariance
  estimation, 210
  matrice, 915–916
  matrices, 185–188, 307, 780
robust estimation
  of asymptotic covariance
    matrices, 153–154
  heteroscedasticity, 159
  using group means, 188–190
robust estimators, 166
robustness to unknown
    heteroscedasticity, 169
root mean squared error, 101
root-$n$ consistent properties, 1051
roots
  characteristics of, 967–976
  dominant, 391
  latent, 969
rotating panel, 180, 184
rows
  notation, 947
  vectors, 945
$R$-squared, 35–38, 156
$r$th mean, convergence in,
    1044, 1045
rules
  for limiting distribution, 1049
  for probability limits, 1046

**S**

sacrifice ratio, 704
sample information, 400
sample mean, 1041

sample midrange, 1020
sample minimum, distributions,
    1025–1027
sample moments, 458
sample periodogram, 734
sample properties, 290–292
sample selection, 62, 863,
    882–902
  common effects, 899–902
  estimation, 886–889
  nonlinear models, 895–898
  normality assumption, 891
  panel data, 898–899
sample variance, 1060
sampling, 613n16
  asymptotic covariance
    samples, 1057
  choice based, 793–794, 852
  distributions, 44, 1023–1027
  Gibbs sampler, 613–616
  importance, 579–582
  large sample properties, 63–75
  large sample results, 613
  large sample tests, 92–96
  least squares estimator, 47
  mean, 1025
  method of moments, 429
  from multivariate normal
    population, 576
  normal, 1058
  properties, 596
  random, 430, 1020
  from standard uniform
    population, 575
  theory estimator, 610
  unbalanced samples, 792
  variances, 48, 1027
sandwich estimators, 514–515
*SAS*, 814n38
scalars
  matrix, 945
  multiplication, 947–950, 951
  scalar-valued function, 980
scale factor coefficients, 100n9
scaling, 88n3
scatter diagram, 1021
scedastic function, 1007
score, 502
  method of, 524, 779
  propensity, 893
  testing, 503
seasonal factors, correcting
    for, 107
second derivatives matrix, 981
second-order effects, 13
seed, 574
seemingly unrelated regression
    (SUR) model, 254–263,
    464–466, 529–530, 531

selection
    models, 142–143, 143–146
    regression in a model of, 884–886
    sample, 863, 882–902. *See also*
        sample selection
    sample, estimation, 886–889
self-regressive models, 716
self-selection bias, 62n7
semilog
    equation, 113
    models, 13
semiparametric, 287
    analysis, 809–813
    duration, 939–942
    estimation, 398, 405–413,
        411–412, 810–812
    models of heterogeneity, 806
    regression models, 52
sequences, 1060–1061
    Halton, 577–580
    Martingale, 638
    Martingale difference, 638
serial correlation, 626–629
    asymptotic results, 635–640
    autocorrelation, testing for
        644-647
    autoregressive conditional
        heteroscedasticity, 658–667
    central limit theorem, 638–640
    common factors, 655–656
    disturbance processes, 632–634
    efficient estimation, 647–648
    Ergodic theorem, 636–638
    forecasting, 656–658
    generalized method of moments
        (GMM), 643–644
    heteroscedasticity and, 149
    least squares estimation, 640–643
    panel data, 652–655
    time-series data analysis, 629–632
series
    fractionally integrated, 740n2
    Martingale difference, 449
    time. *See* time series
sets of linear functions, 1011–1012
several categories of binary
        variables, 107–108
several groupings of dummy
        variables, 108–110
share equations, 278
Shepard's lemma, 276
short rank, 14–15, 957
significance tests, 298
simple distributed lag models,
        677–681
simple model building
        strategies, 136
simple-to-general approach,
        136, 676

simulated annealing, 1066
simulated data, 573
simulated log likelihood, 227
simulation-based estimation,
        226–229, 399, 573, 589–596
    bootstrapping, 596–598
    continuous distributions, 575
    Monte Carlo integration, 576–583
    Monte Carlo studies, 584–589
    pseudo-random numbers,
        generating, 574
    random number generation,
        573–576
simulation results, 71
simultaneous equations model
    bias, 355n3
    causality, 357–358
    endogeneity, 357–358
    fundamental issues in, 354–261
    with heteroscedasticity, 466–469
    limited information estimation
        methods, 371–380
    maximum likelihood estimation
        (MLE), 536–537
    methods of estimation, 370–371
    ordinary least squares (OLS),
        371–372
    problem of identification,
        361–370
    specification tests, 387
    system methods of estimation,
        380–384
    two-stage least squares, 373–375
single-equation
    linear models, 455–461
    nonlinear models, 461–464
    pooled estimators, 829n47
singularity of the disturbance
        covariance matrix, 278
singular systems, 272–280
singular value decomposition, 975
size
    distributions, 996
    step, 1075
    of tests, 1035
skewness, 1021
Sklar's theorem, 403
slopes, 194
Slutsky theorem, 303, 445, 1045
small $T$ asymptotics, 196–197
smoothing functions, 418
sociology, 6
spaces
    columns, 956
    parameters, 497
    vectors, 951–954
spanning vectors, 954
spatial autocorrelation,
        218–222

spatial autoregression
    coefficient, 218
spatial error correction, 221
spatial lags, 221
special decomposition, 974
specification
    analysis, 133–137, 692–693
    binary choice, 787–790
    errors, 885
    Hausman's specification test,
        208–209
    Hausman test, 339
    instrumental variables
        estimation, 321–325
    maximum likelihood estimation
        (MLE), 498–507
    search for lag length, 676–677
    tests, 167, 387–388. *See also*
        testing
    tests, for SUR models, 264–266
    validity of moment restrictions,
        testing, 452–455
specificity, 585
spectral analysis, 735
spectral decomposition of
        matrices, 969
spectral density function, 732
spectrum, 732
spherical disturbances, 16–17,
        17n4, 149
spherical normal distribution, 1013
spline regression, 111–112
spurious regressions, 741–744
squares
    matrices, 945
    summable, 726
    sum of, 287–288, 292
stability, 389, 390–391, 684–686
stabilizing transformations, 1050
stacking equations, 301n10
standard definition of $x$, 990
standard deviation, 1020
standard errors, 1027
    of the estimator, 52
    of the regression, 51
standard normal cumulative
        distribution function,
        1062–1063
standard normal distribution, 992
standard normal vectors,
        1015–1017
standard uniform population, 575
starting values, 294
*Stata*, 814n38
stated choice
    data, 858
    experiments, 852n59
    panel data, 858–859
state dependence, 794

stationarity
  assumption, 632
  KPSS test of, 755–756
  time-series models, 718–721
stationary assumption, 631
stationary process, 671
stationary stochastic processes,
    716–731, 721–723
statistical properties, 43
statistics
  behavior of test, 585
  descriptive, 1020–1023
  as estimators, 1023–1027
  $F$, 83
  $I$, 219
  Lagrange multiplier,
    299–300, 534
  likelihood ratio, 453, 534, 854
  Ljung-Box, 729
  LM, 454
  marginal distributions of test,
    57–58
  minimal sufficient, 803
  properties of estimators, 420–421
  spatial autocorrelation, 221
  sufficient, 433
  summary, 1020
  tables, 1093–1098
  test and critical values, 388
  Theil $U$, 101
  Voung, 930
  Wald, 94, 262, 453, 520
steepest ascent method, 1069
step sizes, 1075
stepwise model building, 137
Sterling's approximation, 1064
stochastic data
  assumptions of linear regression
    models, 44
  instrumental variables
    estimation, 315
stochastic frontier model, 402,
    538–542, 572
stochastic regressors, 49–50
stochastic volatility, 658
Stone's expenditure system, 272
Stone's loglinear expenditure
    system, 273n20
straight-forward two-step GMM
    estimator, 814
stratification, 188
streams as instruments, 320
strong exogeneity, 699
strongly exogenous models, 358
strong stationarity, 636
structural breaks, 123–127
structural change, 106, 120–128
structural coefficients, 369
structural disturbances, 358

structural equations, 355
structural models, 328, 355n2
structural VARs, 702–703
structure and reduced form, 360
subequations, 367
submatrices, 964. *See also* matrices
subsets
  of coefficients, changes in,
    122–123
  of regressors, 304
subspace, 955
sufficient condition for an
    optimum, 982
sufficient statistics, 433
summability of
    autocovariances, 639
summary statistics, 1020
sum of squares, 287–288, 444n6
  changes in, 31
  generalized, 522
  minimizing, 292
  residuals, 680
superconsistent, 683, 762
supply equation, 354
surveys
  British Household Panel Survey
    (BHPS), 841
  estimation of commodity
    demands, 272n19
  growth, 181n2
  nontested models, 137
survival distributions, 935
survival function, 933, 1000
symmetric matrices, 945, 974n9
system methods of estimation,
    380–384
systems of demand equations,
    272–280
systems of linear equations, 961–964
systems of regression equations,
    252–254

**T**

tables, statistics, 1093–1098
Taylor series, 277, 979
$t$ distributions, 993–995
terminology, algebra, 945
testable implications, 81
testing
  augmented Dickey-Fuller
    test, 754
  for autocorrelation, 644–647
  Bayesian model averaging,
    144–146
  behavior of test statistics, 585
  binary choice, 785–787
  Breusch-Pagan, 166, 167
  Chow test, 120n8

classical testing procedures,
    1034–1037
cointegration, 761–763
common factors, 655–656
confidence intervals, 1037–1038
consistency, 1036
Cox test, 142
cross-function correlation, 265
Dickey-Fuller tests, 745–754
Durbin-Watson test, 116n6,
    645–646
$F$ tests for firm and year
    effects, 109
for GARCH effects, 664–666
group effects, 197
Hausman's specification test,
    208–209
Hausman test, 339
heteroscedasticity, 165–167
hypothesis, 83–92, 259–263, 295,
    298–300
hypothesis, about a coefficient, 52
hypothesis, estimation, 425
hypothesis, inference, 1034–1038
$J$ test, 139–140
KPSS test of stationarity,
    755–756
lagged dependent variable, 646
Lagrange multiplier, 96, 166, 205,
    299–300, 505
large sample tests, 92–96
likelihood-based tests,
    application of, 504–506
likelihood ratio, 498–500, 505, 786
linear restrictions, 85
LM statistic, 454
marginal distributions of
    statistics, 57–58
maximum likelihood estimation
    (MLE), 498–507
for model instability, 766–767
most powerful test, 1035
nonlinear restrictions, 96–98
nonnested hypothesis, 138
one-sided tests, 1038
overdispersion, 909–911
overidentifying restrictions, 388
Phillips-Perron tests, 753
power of tests, 1035
predictive, 122, 127–128
random effects, 205–208
regression, 56–57
significance, 298
size of tests, 1035
spatial autocorrelation, 221
specification, 167, 321–325,
    387–388
structural breaks, 123–127
structural change, 120–128

testing (*continued*)
SUR models, 264–266
unbiased tests, 1036
unit roots, 744–745
validity of moment restrictions, 452–455
variable addition, 210
vector autoregression (VAR), 696–698
Vuong's test, 140
Wald test, 124, 500–502, 505
weak instruments, 377–380
White test, 165, 167
for zero correlation, 820
test of economic literacy (TUCE), 560
tetrachoric correlation, 819
Theil $U$ statistic, 101
theorems
Aitken's, 155
Bayes, 565, 601–603
central limit, 638–640, 1050–1055
Ergodic, 448, 636–638
Gordin's central limit, 640
Khinchine, 430
Kruskal's, 176
Liapounov central limit, 1054
Lindeberg-Feller central limit, 152
Lindeberg-Levy Central Limit, 435
Lindeberg-Levy central limit, 1051
Martingale difference central limit, 638
mean value, 450
multivariate Lindeberg-Feller central limit, 1055
multivariate Lindeberg-Levy central limit, 1054
Sklar's, 403
Slutsky, 445, 1045
three-level random parameters, 234
three-stage least squares (3SLS), 381–383, 537
threshold effects, 110–111
time
accelerated failure time models, 937
events per unit of, 912
fixed and group effects, 197–200
linear trends, 16n3
until failure, 932
time-invariant, 187, 472
time profile, 111
time series, 715, 1020
analysis, 6, 243
autoregressive moving-average processes, 716–718

data, 6
data analysis, 629–632
frequency domain, 731–738
identification, 712
invertibility, 718–721
panel data, 181n1
partial autocorrelation, 723–726
processes, 630
stationarity, 718–721
stationary stochastic processes, 716–731
univariate time series modeling, 726–728
time-space
dynamic model, 220
simultaneous model, 219
time-varying covariates, 933
time window, 630
tobit model, 871–874
censoring, 925–931
multiplicative heteroscedasticity, 876
panel data, 881–882
tools for diagnosing collinearity, 60n6
total variation, 32
trace of a matrix, 971–972
transformations, 986–987
Box-Cox, 296–297
matrix, 473
regressors, 296n4
stabilizing, 1050
transformed regression model, 168
transformed regressors, 157
transforms, discrete Fourier, 737
translog cost function, 104, 275–280
translog demand system, 286
translog models, 13–14
transportation engineering, 6
transposition
matrices, 946
products, 949
t ratio, 53
treatment effects, 889
analysis of, 11n2, 889–890
estimation, 891–895
treatment of response, 107
trends, 741–744
linear time, 16n3
stationary process, 743
triangular matrix, 945
triangular systems, 359
trigamma function, 436n2, 1064
true size of the test, 585
truncated mean, 865
truncated normal distribution, 576
truncated standard normal distribution, 864
truncated uniform distribution, 865

truncated variances, 865
truncate random variable, 864
truncation, 863–869
count data, 924–931
distributions, 863–864
estimation, 874–875
incidental, 882
incidental, bivariate distribution, 883–884
moments of truncated distributions, 864–867
Poisson model, 925
regression models, 867–869
truth, 143
two-stage least squares estimation, 318–321, 356, 373–375
two-step estimation, 229–233, 886
two-step estimators, 169
two-step maximum likelihood approach, 849
estimation, 507–511
two-step nonlinear least squares estimation, 302–307
Two-Variable Regression model, 48
type I error, 1034
type II error, 1034

**U**
unbalanced panel data, 184
unbalanced samples, 792
unbiased estimation, 46–47
unbiased estimators, 1028
unbiasedness properties, 420
unbiased tests, 1036
uncentered moment, 430
uncorrelated linear regression models, 304
underlying probability model, 287
unequal variances, 123–127
unification, 1
uniform-inverse gamma prior, 619
uniformly most powerful (UMP), 1036
uniform prior, 619
uniqueness, 449
unit roots, 181n2, 739–756, 743
augmented Dickey-Fuller test, 754
KPSS test of stationarity, 755
testing, 744–745, 748–751
univariate autoregression, 685
univariate time series, 716
estimation of parameters, 728–731
modeling, 726–728
unknown heteroscedasticity, robustness to, 169
unknown parameter, 297

unmeasured heterogeneity, 560–561
unobserved effects model, 209–210
unordered choice models, 842
unordered multiple choice models,
    841–859
unstandardized residuals, 628
upper triangular matrix, 974
utility maximization, 5

## V

validity of moment restrictions,
    452–455
values
    Cholesky, 974
    heteroscedastistic extreme value
        (HEV) model, 856
    mean value theorem, 450
    singular value
        decomposition, 975
    starting, 294
    trigamma function, 436n2
variables, 3
    addition, testing, 210
    asymptotic properties, 72
    binary, 106–112
    binary, marginal effects, 835
    bivariate regression, 23
    categorical, 110–111
    censoring, 869
    constants, 16n3
    dependent, 8, 979
    dummy, 106, 122
    endogenous right-hand-side,
        813–817
    endogenus, 355
    estimators, comparing, 187
    exogenous, duration, 937–938
    explained, 8
    explanatory, 8
    Grunfeld model, 255
    identical explanatory, 257
    inclusion of irrelevant, 136
    independent, 8, 979
    independent, exogeneity of, 11
    instrumental, 245, 461
    instrumental, empirical moment
        equation, 447
    instrumental, estimation,
        314–315, 893
    jointly dependent, 355
    lagged. See lagged variables
    least squares dummy variable
        (LSDV), 195
    measurement of, 4
    metric algorithm, 1071
    nonlinear instrumental variable
        estimator, 462
    nonlinearity in, 112–120

omission of relevant, 133
omitted, 787
omitted, bias, 868
predetermined, 356, 358
pretest estimators, 135
proxy, 328–331
random, 987–988
random, censored, 871
random, continuous, 987
random, convergence to,
    1046–1047
random, density of truncated, 864
random, discrete, 998
random, distributions, 998–1000
random, expectations of, 989–991
regression, adding, 31
time-invariant, 472
Two-Variable Regression
    model, 48
variances
    analysis of variance (ANOVA),
        32–39, 192
    bound for Poisson
        distribution, 1031
    conditional, 1007
    decomposition of, 1008
    estimation, 51–52, 642–643
    feasible generalized least squares
        (FGLS), 203–205
    inflation factor, 60
    least ratio, 376
    least squares estimator, 48–49
    limiting, 1049
    linear regression models, 17
    maximum likelihood estimation
        (MLE), 494–496
    mean squared error of
        sample, 1029
    of the median, bootstrapping, 597
    minimum linear unbiased
        estimation, 46–47
    prediction, 99
    probability of, 161
    of random variables, 989
    sampling, 48, 1027
    sampling, asymptotic
        moments, 1060
    slopes, 194
    truncated, 865
    unequal, 123–127
vector autoregression (VAR), 685,
    693–712
    cointegration, 756n12
    empirical results, 707–710
    error correction and, 760–761
    instability of, 712
    in microeconomics, 711–712
    policy analysis, 703–710
    structural, 702–703

vector moving average (VMA)
    model, 704
vectors, 945
    autoregression, 479
    basis, 953–954
    characteristics of, 967–976
    coefficients, least squares
        regression, 21–22
    discrepancy, 84
    latent, 969
    least square residuals, 25
    length of, 960
    linear combination of, 953–954
    linear functions of normal, 1015
    multiple cointegration, 759
    multiplication, 947
    orthogonal, 960
    parameters, 121, 141n9
    random, 1010
    spaces, 951–954
    spanning, 954
    standard normal, quadratic
        forms, 1015–1017
volatility
    GARCH model, 665
    high-frequency time-series
        data, 148
    stochastic, 658
Voung statistic, 930
Vuong's test, 140

## W

$\Omega$, estimation when unknown,
    648–652
wage equation, 186
    fixed effects, 199–200
    random effects, 206
Wald statistic, 94, 262, 453, 520
    instrumental variables
        estimation, 322
    significance tests for, 298
Wald test, 124, 500–502, 505
weak instruments
    instrumental variables
        estimation, 350–352
    testing, 377–380
weakly exogenous, 358
weakly stationary, 630
weak stationarity, 636
Weibull model, 937
Weibull survival model, 939
weighted endogenous sampling
        maximum likelihood
        (WESML), 793
weighted least squares,
    167–169, 444
weighting matrix, 438, 439, 444n7,
    459, 478

weights
  lags, computation of, 683–684
  quadrature, 1065
  recomputing, 173
well-behaved data, 497
White estimator panel data, 186
White heteroscedasticity consistent
  estimator, 162–164
white noise, 632, 718
White test, 165, 167
Wishart distribution, 997–998
within-groups estimator, 192

With Zeros (WZ) model, 922n7
World Health Organization
  (WHO), 124
Wu test, 321–325

**X**

$x$, standard definition of, 990

**Y**

Yule-Walker equation, 641, 722

**Z**

Zellner's efficient estimator, 258n11
zero-altered Poisson model,
  920–924
zero-inflated Poisson (ZIP)
  model, 930
zero-order method, 62
zeros
  attenuation, 326
  correlation, testing for, 820
  matrices, 946
  mean of the disturbance, 286